MW01135543

Gale Environmental Sourcebook

Highlights

Citizens concerned with environmental issues can turn to the *Gale Environmental Sourcebook* for up-to-date information on organizations, agencies, programs, and publications concerned with the environment. This single convenient volume provides descriptive and contact information on approximately 9,000 resources that can offer the most current information available on all aspects of the environment, including:

- National and international organizations
- Foundations and funding sources
- Federal and state government organizations
- Independent agencies and commissions
- National forests, parks, and wildlife refuges
- Government and university research centers
- Research and development firms
- Educational programs
- Publishers
- Books
- Directories
- Magazines, newspapers, and newsletters
- Videos
- Databases
- Library collections
- Environmental corporate contacts
- Environmental products
- Scholarships and awards

Alphabetic and Subject Index Speeds Access to Information Resources

The *Gale Environmental Sourcebook* provides quick and easy access to the descriptive listings through the master Alphabetic and Subject Index. Citations to all of the organizations, agencies, and publications included are presented in a single alphabetic sequence. The citations are also grouped according to subject area, including topics such as:

- acid rain
- air pollution
- energy economics
- groundwater
- hazardous waste
- pesticides
- radon
- recycling
- sustainable agriculture
- wildlife protection

Glossary and Appendixes Add to Ready Reference Convenience

For quick reference, the *Gale Environmental Sourcebook* includes a glossary of over 250 current environmental terms and appendixes of information frequently requested by environmentally-concerned citizens and organizations. Included are:

- Government lists of the over 1,000 endangered plant and animal species. The lists, provided by the United States Department of the Interior, have been supplemented and enhanced by additional information on these rare species.

- The Environmental Protection Agency's Superfund clean-up sites, listed by state and by degree of toxicity for easy access.

ISSN 1059-0919

Gale Environmental Sourcebook

A Guide to Organizations, Agencies, and Publications

First Edition

Karen Hill and Annette Piccirelli, Editors

· DETROIT · LONDON

Editors: Karen Hill and Annette Piccirelli
Associate Editor: Joseph M. Palmisano
Assistant Editors: Charles A. Beaubien, Ned Burels, Anthony L. Gerring, Joyce Jakubiak, Evelyn L. Sullen
Contributing Editors: Donna Batten, Thomas J. Cichonski
Contributing Associate Editors: Camille Ann Killens, Christopher Kasic
Aided by: Cynthia Grayson

Research Manager: Victoria Cariappa
Research Supervisor: Jack Radike
Editorial Assistants: Brian Escamilla, Phil Naud, Delores S. Perelli, Phyllis Shepherd

Production Manager: Mary Beth Trimper
Production Assistant: Mary Winterhalter

Art Director: Arthur Chartow
Graphic Designer: Bernadette M. Gornie
Keyliner: C.J. Jonik
Photographer: Robert J. Huffman

Data Entry Supervisor: Benita Spight

Supervisor of Systems and Programming: Theresa A. Rocklin
Programmers: David Trotter, Susan Kemp
Programming Consultant: Donald G. Dillaman

∞™ This book is printed on acid-free paper that meets the minimum requirements of American National Standard for Information Sciences—Permanence Paper for Printed Library Materials, ANSI Z39.48-1984.

This book is printed on recycled paper that meets Environmental Protection Agency standards.

ISBN 0-8103-8403-5
ISSN 1059-0919

Published simultaneously in the United Kingdom
by Gale Research International Limited
(An affiliated company of Gale Research Inc.)

Contents

continues . . .

Acknowledgments

The editors would like to thank the following environmental information specialists for their advice and assistance in the preparation of this volume:

- Patricia Gayle Alston, Health Education Specialist, Agency for Toxic Substances and Disease Registry, Public Health Service, U.S. Department of Health and Human Services
- Kathy Deck, Technical Information Officer, Center for Environmental Health and Injury Control, Centers for Disease Control
- Laura Lang Huellmantel, Organic Chemist, Environmental Protection Agency
- Patricia Murray, Librarian, International Joint Commission, Great Lakes Regional Office
- Fred Stoss, Information and Communications Coordinator, Carbon Dioxide Information Analysis Center, Oak Ridge National Laboratory

A Word About Gale and the Environment

We at Gale would like to take this opportunity to publicly affirm our commitment to preserving the environment. Our commitment encompasses not only a zeal to publish information helpful to a variety of people pursuing environmental goals, but also a rededication to creating a safe and healthy workplace for our employees.

In our effort to make responsible use of natural resources, we are publishing all books in the Gale Environmental Library on recycled paper. Our Production Department is continually researching ways to use new environmentally safe inks and manufacturing technologies for all Gale books.

In our quest to become better environmental citizens, we've organized a task force representing all operating functions within Gale. With the complete backing of Gale senior management, the task force reviews our current practices and, using the Valdez Principles* as a starting point, makes recommendations that will help us to: reduce waste, make wise use of energy and sustainable use of natural resources, reduce health and safety risks to our employees, and finally, should we cause any damage or injury, take full responsibility.

We look forward to becoming the best environmental citizens we can be and hope that you, too, have joined in the cause of caring for our fragile planet.

The Employees of Gale Research Inc.

The Valdez Principles were set forth in 1989 by the Coalition for Environmentally Responsible Economies (CERES). The Principles serve as guidelines for companies concerned with improving their environmental behavior. For a copy of the Valdez Principles, write to CERES at 711 Atlantic Avenue, 5th Floor, Boston, MA 02111.

Introduction

The *Gale Environmental Sourcebook (GES)* is the most comprehensive single guide to the organizations, agencies, programs, publications and other resources that study, define, and report on the environment. It provides direct access to approximately 9,000 "live" and print sources of information on environmental topics of high current interest, including:

acid rain	erosion	radioactive hazards
aerosol	global warming	radon
air pollution	groundwater contamination	recycling
biomass	hazardous waste	soil conservation
chemical toxicology	industrial pollutants	strip mining
conservation	natural resources	sustainable agriculture
deep ecology	ozone depletion	toxic waste dumps
energy economics	pesticides	water quality
		wildlife protection

Students, information professionals, businesspeople, and concerned citizens conducting research on the environment can use *GES* to identify and contact authoritative resources with concrete answers to a broad spectrum of questions about environmental issues, activities, and topics.

Compiled With the Help of Environmental Experts

The information resources listed in the *Gale Environmental Sourcebook* were carefully selected for inclusion, based on their direct involvement with the environment. Prominent environmental information specialists helped to inform the selection process by providing advice and assistance on the scope, coverage, and information resources listed. Included are:

- Thousands of environmental organizations of national scope or interest, and selected key international organizations, involved in

  - advocacy and education
  - policy-making and enforcement
  - research and development
  - grant-making and awards
  - consumer issues and products

  Although much grassroots environmental activity is carried out through local organizations and programs, these are not listed in *GES* due to their often ephemeral nature. Users are advised to contact the national or regional headquarters of the organizations listed to learn about organizations currently active in their local areas.

- The Federal parks, lakeshores, seashores, forests, and wildlife refuges.

- Thousands of non-technical, general interest videos and publications, including books, magazines, newsletters, and directories.

Method of Compilation

The *Gale Environmental Sourcebook* was compiled from a wide variety of key information resources on the environment. Data was carefully selected from other Gale Research Inc. directory databases covering organizations, publications, and government agencies. Other information was provided by the Environmental Protection Agency, the Department of the Interior, and other units of the Federal government. And, thousands of entries compiled from important secondary sources and telephone research also have been included to provide the broadest possible spectrum of information resources.

Consult the User's Guide following this Introduction for detailed information on the sources used to compile each section of *GES*.

Convenient Arrangement and Thorough Indexing Provide Direct Access to Information Resources

The information resources in the *Gale Environmental Sourcebook* are arranged into 25 sections, which are followed by a master index.

- The Descriptive Listings sections include approximately 9,000 directory entries conveniently organized into six broad categories:
  - U.S. and International Organizations
  - Government Agencies and Programs
  - Research Facilities and Educational Programs
  - Publications and Information Services
  - Green Consumerism
  - Scholarships and Awards

These categories are subdivided into 25 sections by type of information resource, as outlined on the Contents pages. All entries include contact and, when appropriate, descriptive information.

- The unified Alphabetic and Subject Index provides quick and thorough access to all of the organizations, agencies, and publications included in the Descriptive Listings section, either by subject category or by name.

- The Glossary of Terms provides concise descriptions of over 250 current environmental terms and phrases.

- The Appendixes provide informative lists of hard to find data on high-interest subjects. Appendixes I and II list and describe all of the endangered and threatened animal and plant species included on the official U.S. Department of the Interior lists. Appendix III lists the Environmental Protection Agency's Superfund cleanup sites, over 1,000 to date, and arranges these toxic sites by state and by degree of toxicity.

For detailed information on the arrangement, content, and indexing of entries, consult the User's Guide immediately following this Introduction.

Comments Welcome

Every effort was made to provide the most accurate, up-to-date information possible. Comments and suggestions for improvements are welcome, including areas of additional coverage. Please contact:

Editor
Gale Environmental Sourcebook
Gale Research Inc.
835 Penobscot Bldg.
Detroit, MI 48226-4094
Phone: (313)961-2242
Fax: (313)961-6815
Toll-free: 800-347-GALE

User's Guide

Gale Environmental Sourcebook is divided into three parts:

Part 1: Descriptive Listings
Part 2: Alphabetic and Subject Index
Part 3: Glossary and Appendixes

Part 1: Descriptive Listings

Arrangement of entries within individual sections varies as appropriate to the material being presented. Entries may be arranged alphabetically or geographically. For sections that contain multinational as well as U.S. entries, the multinational entries will be listed at the beginning of the sections followed by the U.S. entries.

1. Associations

- **Content and Selection Criteria:** Includes the name, address, telephone number, contact name, date founded, membership, and description of nearly 600 multinational and U.S. national environmental associations.
- **Arrangement:** Alphabetical by organization name; multinational organizations are listed at the beginning of the section.
- **Sources:** *Encyclopedia of Associations* and *Encyclopedia of Associations International Organizations* (published by Gale Research Inc.); supplemented by original staff research.
- **Indexed By:** Organization name and subject terms.

2. Foundations and Funding Sources

- **Content and Selection Criteria:** Includes the name, address, telephone number, contact name, and description of nearly 200 multinational and U.S. national foundations and companies that support environmental causes.
- **Arrangement:** Alphabetical by organization name, with multinational organizations listed at the beginning of the section.
- **Sources:** *Charitable Organizations of the U.S.* (published by Gale Research Inc.); *Foundation Directory* and *Corporate Giving Directory* (published by the Taft Group); supplemented by additional staff research.
- **Indexed By:** Organization name and subject terms.

3. Federal Government Organizations

- **Content and Selection Criteria:** Provides the name, address, contact name, and phone number of over 350 U.S. federal government agencies and currently active advisory committees, boards, and commissions concerned with environmental issues. Coverage includes the Department of the Interior's Bureau of Land Management District Offices.
- **Arrangement:** Alphabetical by organization name.
- **Sources:** *Encyclopedia of Governmental Advisory Organizations* (published by Gale Research Inc.); supplemented by original research.
- **Indexed By:** Organization name and subject terms (if applicable).

4. State Government Organizations

- **Content and Selection Criteria:** Includes the name, address, contact name, and phone number of approximately 700 state government agencies and offices concerned with environmental issues.
- **Arrangement:** Alphabetical by state name, then alphabetical by agency name.
- **Sources:** *Government Research Directory* (published by Gale Research Inc.); supplemented by original research.
- **Indexed By:** Organization name and subject terms (if applicable).

5. **Independent Agencies and Commissions**

   - **Content and Selection Criteria:** Includes name, address, executive name, and telephone number of approximately 75 U.S. independent agencies and commissions concerned with environmental issues.
   - **Arrangement:** Alphabetical by agency name.
   - **Sources:** Original research.
   - **Indexed By:** Agency name and subject terms (if applicable).

6. **U.S. National Forests**

   - **Content and Selection Criteria:** Includes the name, address, superintendent name, and telephone number of the 145 U.S. national forests.
   - **Arrangement:** Alphabetical, first by state, then by forest name.
   - **Sources:** Lists provided by the USDA Forest Service.
   - **Indexed By:** Forest name.

7. **U.S. National Parks**

   - **Content and Selection Criteria:** Includes the name, address, superintendent name, and telephone number for 105 U.S. national parks, including national lakeshores, natural monuments, national recreational/nature areas, and national seashores.
   - **Arrangement:** Alphabetical by state, then by park name.
   - **Sources:** Lists provided by the National Park Service.
   - **Indexed By:** Park name.

8. **U.S. National Wildlife Refuges**

   - **Content and Selection Criteria:** Includes the name, address, superintendent name, and telephone number for the 272 U.S. national wildlife refuges.
   - **Arrangement:** Alphabetical by state, then by wildlife refuge name.
   - **Sources:** Lists provided by the U.S. Department of the Interior.
   - **Indexed By:** Wildlife refuge name.

9. **Commercial Research Centers**

   - **Content and Selection Criteria:** Includes the name, address, director name, telephone number, and research description for more than 300 U.S. companies that perform contract or fee-based research and development on environmental subjects.
   - **Arrangement:** Geographical by state, then alphabetical by center name.
   - **Sources:** *Research Services Directory* (published by Gale Research Inc.).
   - **Indexed By:** Company name and subject terms.

10. **Government Research Centers**

    - **Content and Selection Criteria:** Includes the name, address, contact name, telephone number, and description for more than 350 multinational and U.S. federal government research centers that conduct studies on environmental topics. Coverage does not include centers that focus their studies on small geographic areas.
    - **Arrangement:** Alphabetical by parent organization, then by intermediate office or agency and actual center name. Multinational centers are listed at the beginning of the section.
    - **Sources:** *Government Research Directory* and *International Research Centers Directory* (published by Gale Research Inc.); supplemented by original research.
    - **Indexed By:** Center name and subject terms.

11. **Nonprofit and University Research Centers**

    - **Content and Selection Criteria:** Includes name, address, contact name, telephone number, and description for nearly 800 U.S. nonprofit and university research centers conducting studies on environmental topics. Coverage does not include multidisciplinary centers.
    - **Arrangement:** Alphabetical by center name; multinational centers are listed at the beginning of the section.

- **Sources:** *Research Centers Directory* and *International Research Centers Directory* (published by Gale Research Inc.); supplemented by original research.
- **Indexed By:** Center name and subject terms.

12. Educational Programs

- **Content and Selection Criteria:** Includes name, address, contact name, telephone number, and program description for more than 700 U.S. educational programs, including recurring professional, academic, and community environmental studies programs, and nature study centers.
- **Arrangement:** Alphabetical within program category.
- **Sources:** Original research.
- **Indexed By:** Program name and subject terms (if applicable).

13. Publishers

- **Content and Selection Criteria:** Includes the name, address, telephone number, and description for more than 100 U.S. publishers who specialize in environmental books, directories, reports, newsletters, and other materials.
- **Arrangement:** Alphabetical by publisher name.
- **Sources:** *Publishers Directory* (published by Gale Research Inc.).
- **Indexed By:** Publisher name and subject terms.

14. Books

- **Content and Selection Criteria:** Includes book title, publisher name, address, telephone number, and description for more than 750 U.S.-distributed books published since 1988 that focus on conservation of natural resources, recycling, environmental protection, ecology, and other issues of environmental concern. Covers general-interest books; does not include technical publications.
- **Arrangement:** Alphabetical by publication title.
- **Sources:** Original research.
- **Indexed By:** Publication title and subject terms.

15. Directories

- **Content and Selection Criteria:** Includes publication title, publisher name, address, telephone number, and description for nearly 200 U.S. directories that list environmentally-oriented organizations and places of interest, such as associations, recycling facilities, and nature areas.
- **Arrangement:** Alphabetical by publication title.
- **Sources:** *Directories in Print* (published by Gale Research Inc.).
- **Indexed by:** Publication title and subject terms.

16. Magazines and Newspapers

- **Content and Selection Criteria:** Includes publication title, publisher name, address, telephone number, and description for more than 350 U.S. magazines and newspapers that focus on environmental issues. Does not include technical papers or publications.
- **Arrangement:** Alphabetical by publication title.
- **Sources:** *Gale Directory of Publications and Broadcast Media* (published by Gale Research Inc.).
- **Indexed by:** Publication title and subject terms.

17. Newsletters

- **Content and Selection Criteria:** Includes newsletter title, publisher name, address, telephone number, and description for more than 500 environmental newsletters published in the U.S.
- **Arrangement:** Alphabetical by publication name.
- **Sources:** *Newsletters in Print* (published by Gale Research, Inc.).
- **Indexed by:** Publication title and subject terms.

18. Videos

- **Content and Selection Criteria:** Includes video title, U.S. distributor, address, telephone number, and description for nearly 600 videos available in the U.S. and focusing on environmental concerns. Coverage does not include technical videos.
- **Arrangement:** Alphabetical by video title.
- **Sources:** *Video Sourcebook* (published by Gale Research, Inc.).
- **Indexed by:** Video title and subject terms.

19. Online Databases

- **Content and Selection Criteria:** Includes the database name, producer name, address, telephone number, and description for more than 100 online databases that can provide electronic access to environmental information.
- **Arrangement:** Alphabetical by database name.
- **Sources:** *Computer-Readable Databases* (published by Gale Research Inc.); supplemented by original research.
- **Indexed By:** Database name and subject terms.

20. Clearinghouses

- **Content and Selection Criteria:** Includes the clearinghouse name, address, telephone number, contact name, and description for more than 60 environmental clearinghouses and hotlines located in the U.S.
- **Arrangement:** Alphabetical by clearinghouse name.
- **Sources:** *The Clearinghouse Directory* (published by Gale Research Inc.).
- **Indexed By:** Clearinghouse name and subject terms.

21. Library Collections

- **Content and Selection Criteria:** Includes the library name, address, telephone number, librarian name, and description for nearly 500 environmental libraries and collections. Coverage includes major international libraries. Libraries closed to the public are not listed.
- **Arrangement:** Alphabetical by library name.
- **Sources:** *Directory of Special Libraries* (published by Gale Research Inc.).
- **Indexed By:** Library name and subject terms (if applicable).

22. Environmental Corporate Contacts

- **Content and Selection Criteria:** Provides the name, address, and telephone number of environmental contacts at more than 300 major U.S. industrial or manufacturing corporations. Companies included appear on well-known lists of top ranked companies such as those published by *Forbes* and *Fortune*.
- **Arrangement:** Alphabetical by company name.
- **Sources:** Original research.
- **Indexed By:** Company name.

23. Environmental Products

- **Content and Selection Criteria:** Includes the company name, address, telephone number, and description (when available) for more than 150 U.S. companies that manufacture or distribute products advertised as environmentally sound or pro-environment. Companies are listed within these product categories:
    - bags
    - composters
    - energy efficient products
    - environmental investing
    - games
    - household products
    - office products
    - organically grown foods
    - packing materials
    - personal products
    - recycled paper and plastic products
    - recycling bins
    - t-shirts and assorted apparel
- **Arrangement:** Alphabetical by product type, then alphabetical by company name.
- **Sources:** Original research.
- **Indexed By:** Company name.

24. Scholarships, Fellowships, and Loans

- **Content and Selection Criteria:** Includes the administering organization name, program name, address, contact name, telephone number, and description for more than 50 education-related financial aid programs supporting environmental study.
- **Arrangement:** Alphabetical by sponsor name.
- **Sources:** *Scholarships, Fellowships, and Loans* (published by Gale Research Inc.); supplemented by original research.
- **Indexed By:** Program name and subject terms (as applicable).

25. Awards, Honors, and Prizes

- **Content and Selection Criteria:** Includes the administering organization name, award name, address, contact name, telephone number, and description for more than 250 U.S. and international awards, honors, and prizes for achievement in environmental sciences.
- **Arrangement:** Alphabetical by administering organization name. International awards appear before those originating in the U.S.
- **Sources:** *Awards, Honors, and Prizes* (published by Gale Research Inc.).
- **Indexed By:** Award name and subject terms (as applicable).

Part 2: Alphabetic and Subject Index

The Alphabetic and Subject Index combines all listed organizations, agencies, publications, and information services into one comprehensive index. Index citations contain entry numbers rather than page numbers to provide the most specific access. All *GES* entries are indexed by name of organization or entity listed. In addition to this alphabetical arrangement of entries, citations may also appear under specific subject terms or keyword for quick access by environmental topic. If parent organizations are included in entry headings, then both the parent group and the unit name are included in the index citations for that entry. Sample entries that could appear in the index follow:

Conservation Outdoors Forum 333
Conservation Research Center—Univ. of Alabama 441
Hazardous Waste
- *Environmental Bibliography* 265
- *From the State Capitols: Waste Disposal and Pollution Control* 562
- *Hazardous Waste News* 927
- Hazardous Waste Research Center—Univ. of Connecticut 444
- Marine Pollution Institute 333
- NMPIS Database 1032
- *Oceanic Abstracts* 219

Renewable Energy Sources
- DOE Energy Data Base 507
- Reprotox 1197
- UAI Associates—Water Quality Education and Training Program 337

Part 3: Glossary and Appendixes

▸ The **Glossary** defines more than 250 current environmental terms and phrases, with particular emphasis on the terms used in the descriptive listings. Terms are cross-referenced and arranged alphabetically.

▸ The appendixes were compiled from official lists provided by the Federal government, including the Department of the Interior and the Environmental Protection Agency. These lists were supplemented by independent research to amplify, update, and enhance the original material:

Appendix I: Endangered and Threatened Wildlife. This appendix lists all of the mammals, reptiles, birds, and insects that appear on the endangered lists of the U.S. Department of the Interior, over 880 in all. Descriptive information supplements the alphabetical list of rare species.

Appendix II: Endangered and Threatened Plants. This appendix lists the more than 200 plants that appear on the endangered lists of the U.S. Department of the Interior. Descriptive information supplements the alphabetical list of rare species.

Appendix III: EPA National Priorities Lists. This appendix lists the Environmental Protection Agency's 1,189 identified toxic cleanup sites in the U.S. Civilian sites are presented by order of severity and by state. Federal facilities appear in a separate geographic list with codes indicating severity.

Geographic Abbreviations for U.S. States and Territories

AL	Alabama
AK	Alaska
AS	American Samoa
AZ	Arizona
AR	Arkansas
CA	California
CO	Colorado
CT	Connecticut
DE	Delaware
DC	District of Columbia
FL	Florida
GA	Georgia
GU	Guam
HI	Hawaii
ID	Idaho
IL	Illinois
IN	Indiana
IA	Iowa
KS	Kansas
KY	Kentucky
LA	Louisiana
ME	Maine
MD	Maryland
MA	Massachusetts
MI	Michigan
MN	Minnesota
MS	Mississippi
MO	Missouri
MT	Montana
NE	Nebraska
NV	Nevada
NH	New Hampshire
NJ	New Jersey
NM	New Mexico
NY	New York
NC	North Carolina
ND	North Dakota
OH	Ohio
OK	Oklahoma
OR	Oregon
PA	Pennsylvania
PR	Puerto Rico
RI	Rhode Island
SC	South Carolina
SD	South Dakota
TN	Tennessee
TX	Texas
UT	Utah
VT	Vermont
VI	Virgin Islands
VA	Virginia
WA	Washington
WV	West Virginia
WI	Wisconsin
WY	Wyoming

Gale Environmental Sourcebook

Associations

International

★ 1 ★ American Committee for International Conservation (ACIC)
Center for Marine Conservation
1725 DeSales St. NW, Ste. 500
Washington, DC 20036
Phone: (202)429-5609
Contact: Roger E. McManus, Pres.
Founded: 1930. ***Members:*** 25. Associations representing individuals in 40 countries. Promotes conservation and preservation of wildlife and other natural resources. Encourages and finances research on the status and ecology of threatened species. Maintains working relationship with the International Union for Conservation of Nature and Natural Resources and lends assistance to other organizations concerned with resource conservation. ***Former Name(s):*** American Committee for International Wild-Life Protection (1975).

★ 2 ★ Bat Conservation International (BCI)
PO Box 162603
Austin, TX 78716
Phone: (512)327-9721
Fax: (512)327-9724
Contact: Carol Brown, Adm. Dir.
Founded: 1982. ***Members:*** 8500. Individuals in 50 countries. Documents the value and conservation needs of bats. Seeks to: increase public awareness of the ecological importance of bats and promote bat conservation and management efforts. Publicizes conservation of the flying fox bat, found on Pacific islands.

★ 3 ★ Conservation International
1015 18th St. NW, Ste. 1000
Washington, DC 20036
Phone: (202)429-5660
Fax: (202)887-5188
Contact: Russel Mittermeier, Pres.
Founded: 1987. ***Members:*** 60,000. Corporations and individuals in 15 countries interested in environmental protection and conservation. Cooperates with governments and other organizations to help all nations develop the ability to sustain biological diversity and the ecosystems that support life on earth while addressing basic economic and social needs. Has sponsored an agreement whereby a portion of Bolivia's debt to United States banks was forgiven in exchange for Bolivia's promise to protect a part of the Amazon rainforest; other project sites include Costa Rica and Mexico. Promotes scientific understanding through research programs; encourages and facilitates ecosystem management and conservation-based development. Conducts public outreach programs; assists in formulation and implementation of policy. Maintains small library.

★ 4 ★ Convention on International Trade in Endangered Species of Wild Fauna and Flora
6, rue du Maupas
Case Postale 78
CH-1000 9 Lausanne, Switzerland
Phone: 21 200081
Fax: 21 200084
Telex: 454584 CTES CH
Contact: Eugene Lapointe, Sec.Gen.
Founded: 1973. ***Members:*** 105. Monitors and coordinates information on international trade of wild flora and fauna and quota programs. Collects scientific information on various species; initiates and formulates field projects for conservation studies and for the development of wildlife management methods. Conducts regional seminars on the enforcement of import regulations.

★ 5 ★ Environment Liaison Centre International (ELG1)
PO Box 72461
Nairobi, Kenya
Phone: 2 562015
Fax: 2 562175
Telex: 23240 ENVICENTE
Contact: S. Muntemba, Exec.Officer
Founded: 1974. ***Members:*** 280. Works to strengthen and build links among nongovernmental organizations working on environmental and related issues. Works to protect the earth's ecosystems for human health and well-being, and to promote sustainable utilization and equitable distribution of resources. Provides advice to Third World groups on project design and implementation and assists them with fundraising. ***Former Name(s):*** Environment Liaison Centre; NGO Liaison Board.

★ 6 ★ Fauna And Flora Preservation Society (FFPS)
79-83 N. St.
Brighton, E Sussex BN1 1ZA, England
Phone: 273 820445
Founded: 1903.
Members: 5200. Purpose is to prevent the extinction of species of wild animals and plants by promoting the conservation of wildlife, the establishment of new national parks, the enactment and enforcement of laws to protect wildlife, and the education of governments and individuals in the value of world wildlife as a non-renewable natural resource. Conducts research relating to endangered species. Bestons grants for projects and programs relating to endangered species of fauna and flora. Sponsors seminars. ***Former Name(s):*** Society for the Preservation of the Wild Fauna of the Empire (1950); Fauna Preservation Society (1980).

★ 7 ★ Inter-American Association of Sanitary Engineering and Environmental Sciences
18729 Considine Dr.
Brookville, MD 20833
Phone: (301)492-7686
Contact: Dr. Richard F. Cole, Sec.-Treas.
Founded: 1946. ***Members:*** 5000. Promotes study and solution of sanitary engineering and environmental problems as a necessary condition for economic and social development in the Americas and for advancing understanding; establihes uniform standards for permanent protection of health of all Western Hemisphere inhabitants. ***Former Name(s):*** Inter-American Association of Sanitary Engineers (1962); Inter-American of Association of Sanitary Engineering (1977); Inter-American Association of Sanitary Engineering and Environment (1980); Inter-American Association of Sanitary and Environmental Engineering (1987).

★ 8 ★ International Association for Bear Research and Management
c/o ADF & G
333 Raspberry Rd.
Anchorage, AK 99518-1599
Phone: (907)344-0541
Contact: Sterling D. Miller, Sec.-Treas.
Founded: 1968. ***Members:*** 360. Research biologists, animal and land managers, professionals, and laypersons in 22 countries. Fosters communication and cooperation in research, care, and management of bears and their habitat. Conducts regional bear workshops. ***Former Name(s):*** Bear Biology Association (1983).

★ 9 ★ International Association For Hydrogen Energy (IAHE)
PO Box 248266
Coral Gables, FL 33124
Phone: (305)284-4666
Fax: (305)284-4792
Contact: T. Nejat Veziroglu, Pres.
Founded: 1974. ***Members:*** 2000. Scientists and engineers professionally involved with the use of hydrogen. Promotes discussion and publication of ideas furthering realization of a clean, inexhaustible energy system based on hydrogen.

★10★ International Association for the Physical Sciences of the Ocean
PO Box 1161
Del Mar, CA 92014-1161
Phone: (619)481-0850
Contact: Dr. Robert E. Stevenson, Sec.Gen.
Founded: 1919. ***Members:*** 6000. Promotes the mathematical, physical, and chemical study of problems relating to the ocean and interactions taking place at its boundaries. ***Former Name(s):*** Section of Physical Oceanography of the International Union of Geodesy and Geophysics (1929); Association of Physical Oceanography (1948); International Association of Physical Oceanography (1976).

★11★ International Association of Theoretical and Applied Limnology
Univ. of Michigan
Dept. of Biology
Ann Arbor, MI 48109
Phone: (313)936-3193
Contact: Dr. Robert G. Wetzel, Gen.Sec.-Treas.
Founded: 1922. ***Members:*** 3000. Promotes the study of all aspects of limnology Encourages scientific discourse among those pursuing academic research and those concerned with practical fishery, pollution, and water-supply problems.

★12★ International Bird Rescue Research Center
699 Potter St.
Berkeley, CA 94710
Phone: (415)841-9086
Fax: (415)841-9089
Contact: Jay Holcomb, Dir.
Founded: 1971. Individuals, researchers, and associations wishing to contribute and receive information regarding the deleterious effects of man-made and natural phenomena on birds and on methods of bird rehabilitation. Concerned with developing methods for the rehabilitation of oiled water birds because of the great losses in bird population caused by oil slicks. Coordinates research in this field. Provides consulting services for governmental and industrial contingency planning; also offers consulting assistance in the event of an oil spill emergency.

★13★ International Board of Environmental Medicine (IBEM)
2114 Martingale Dr.
Norman, OK 73072
Phone: (405)329-8437
Contact: Clifton R. Brooks M.D., Exec.Dir.
Founded: 1988. An accrediting agency for physicians, osteopaths, and persons working in related environmental professions. Examines licensed practitioners, facilities, and relevant training programs. Offers programs to evaluate qualifications of healthcare professionals, training programs, and facilities offering special types of treatment. Plans and supervises accrediting examinations.

★14★ International Center for the Solution of Environmental Problems (ICSEP)
535 Lovett Blvd.
Houston, TX 77006
Phone: (713)527-8711
Contact: Joseph L. Goldman Ph.D., Tech.Dir.
Founded: 1976. Institutes, corporations, and individuals engaged in scientific, engineering, management, economic, and offshore environmental activities. Attempts to anticipate upcoming environmental problems and provide solutions for avoiding or reducing them. Involved in numerous civic activities related to the environment. Conducts research projects on: anticipating the effects of storms and reducing their causes and occurrences off- and onshore; effects of storms related to city design; changes in surface vegetation caused by spreading urbanization; flood control; reduction of land erosion; remote sensing applications; land subsidence and flooding by overpumping; decline in land value resulting from these changes; the effect of weather on soil and agriculture; the effect of herbicide sprays on users and groundwater.

★15★ International Committee on Consumers Unions
825 W. End Ave., Ste. 70
New York, NY 10025
Phone: (212)663-6378
Contact: Eileen Nic, Program Dir.
Founded: 1981. Consumer, environmental, women's health, and religious groups. Promotes the exchange of information on hazardous chemical products that are traded internationally; focus is on pesticides and pharmaceuticals that have been partially banned internationally, but are still legally used in some countries. Lobbies the United Nations, on issues relating to the trade of hazardous compounds. Acts as information clearinghouse on alternatives to hazardous pesticides and pharmaceuticals; provides referral service.

★16★ International Crane Foundation (ICF)
E-11376 Shady Ln. Rd.
Baraboo, WI 53913-9778
Phone: (608)356-9462
Fax: (608)356-9465
Telex: 297778 ICF UR
Contact: George W. Archibald Ph.D., Dir.
Founded: 1973. ***Members:*** 4000. Scientists and interested individuals in 20 countries committed to the preservation of the crane. Seeks to preserve and restock the crane population in its natural habitat and to increase captive propagation.

★17★ International Desalination Association (IDA)
PO Box 387
Topsfield, MA 01983
Phone: (508)356-2727
Fax: (508)356-9964
Telex: 2965002
Contact: Patricia A. Burke, Sec.Gen.
Founded: 1985. ***Members:*** 400. Users and suppliers of desalination equipment; water reuse and reclamation consultants. Seeks to develop and promote worldwide application of desalination and desalination technology in maintaining water suppliers, controlling water pollution, and purifying, treating, and reusing water. Disseminates information on desalination-related subjects and water reuse. Encourages the establishment of standards, specifications, procedures, and the efficient use of water for energy.

★18★ International Ecology Society (IES)
1471 Barclay St.
St. Paul, MN 55106-1405
Phone: (612)774-4971
Contact: R. J. F. Kramer, Pres.
Citizens working for the protection of wildlife, domestic animals, and the environment through legislation, litigation, public action, and education. Concerns include wetland protection, acid rain, hazardous and toxic wastes, national wildlife refuges, protection of endangered species, and humane treatment of all animals. Compiles statistics.

★19★ International Erosion Control Association (IECA)
Box 4904
Steamboat Springs, CO 80477
Phone: (303)879-3010
Fax: (303)879-8563
Contact: Ben Northcutt, Exec.Dir.
Founded: 1972. ***Members:*** 400. Landscape contractors, government officials, landscape architects, engineers, manufacturers and suppliers, and others in 12 countries. Encourages the exchange of information and ideas concerning effective and economical methods of erosion control. Recognizes the need for an organized discipline in soil erosion and sediment control so that laws, specifications, procedures, and restrictions concerning land disturbances may be written by qualified professionals.

★20★ International Joint Commission (IJC)
2001 S St. NW, 2nd Fl.
Washington, DC 20440
Phone: (202)673-6222
Contact: David A. LaRoche, Sec.
Founded: 1911. ***Members:*** 6. Joint U.S.-Canada quasi-judicial and advisory tribunal on boundary and transboundary water problems. Established from Boundary Waters Treaty of 1909 to prevent disputes on the use of boundary and transboundary waters and investigate questions arising from transboundary issues. Approves and disapproves applications from governments, companies, and individuals for obstructions, uses, and diversions of water that affect the natural level and flow of water on the other side of the international boundary; investigates particular questions, reports findings to the U.S. and Canadian governments, and offers recommendations; monitors compliance with IJC orders of approval. Maintains advisory boards of scientists, engineers, and other experts to supply IJC with technical studies and field work; answers student inquiries regarding the environmental quality of the Great Lakes. Conducts public hearings, workshops, and seminars.

★21★ International Mountain Society (IMS)
PO Box 1978
Davis, CA 95617-1978
Phone: (916)758-7618
Contact: Dr. Jack D. Ives, Pres.
Founded: 1980. ***Members:*** 1100. Individuals, libraries, and institutions concerned with the deterioration of mountain environments. Encourages collaboration for the protection of mountain lands and peoples. Promotes and participates in research concerning mountain regions; disseminates and applies information toward solving mountain-related problems. Provides assistance to governments and organizations concerned with mountain problems. Conducts seminars and workshops. Plans include establishment of a data bank for an information service center and compilation of a register of persons with professional, technical, and scientific skills pertaining to mountain environments and peoples.

★22★ International Ocean Pollution Symposium (IODS)
Dept. of Chemical & Environmental Engineering
Florida Inst. of Tech.
Melbourne, FL 32901
Phone: (407)768-8000
Contact: Dr. Iver W. Duedall, Organizing Comm.Chm.
Founded: 1978. Symposium held for the exchange of ideas and information among investigators researching problems associated

with waste disposal in the oceans. Drafts recommendations and guidelines for scientific studies of current and future ocean disposal practices. Organizes information resulting from symposia presentations into books prepared for worldwide distribution. Sponsors bibliographic seminars.

★23★ International Oceanographic Foundation (IOF)
4600 Rickenbacker Causeway
P.O. Box 499900
Miami, FL 33149-9900
Phone: (305)361-4888
Contact: Edward T. Foote, II, Pres.
Founded: 1953. ***Members:*** 30,000. Encourages the scientific study and exploration of oceans. Topics include: game and food fish; other creatures of sea and shore; ocean currents; geology, chemistry, and physics of the sea and sea floor; submarine detection; industrial applications of oceanography.

★24★ International Poplar Commission (IPC)
Food & Agriculture Orgn. of U. N.
Forest Resources Div.
Via delle Terme di Caracalla
I-00100 Rome, Italy
Phone: 6 57974047
Fax: 6 57973152/51446172
Contact: Jan Troensegaard, Sec.
Founded: 1947.
Members: 32. Studies the scientific, technical, social, and economic aspects of poplar and willow cultivation; promotes the exchange of ideas and material among research workers, producers, and users; arranges joint research programs; makes recommendations to the Conference of FAO and National Poplar Commissions.

★25★ International Rivers Network (IRN)
301 Broadway, Ste. B
San Francisco, CA 94133
Phone: (415)986-4694
Fax: (415)398-2732
Telex: 6502829302 MCI
Founded: 1985. ***Members:*** 1000. Environmental and human rights nongovernmental organizations and activists; water professionals. Primary purpose is to update and foster development of water policy worldwide by providing a means of communication between members. Publicizes problems with and alternatives to large water projects. Assists in local efforts to stop destructive dam projects, particularly in developing countries. Promotes research and disseminates information about solutions to social and environmental problems. Campaigns against World Bank funding of water projects that are destructive to the environment. Believes that action must be taken immediately in order to prevent further damage to the environment. Operates speakers' bureau. Maintains library on global water resources. ***Former Name(s):*** (1986) International Watershed Advocacy Project.

★26★ International Society of Tropical Foresters
c/o Society of American Foresters
5400 Grosvenor Ln.
Bethesda, MD 20814
Phone: (301)897-8720
Fax: (301)897-3690
Contact: Warren T. Doolittle, Pres.
Founded: 1961. ***Members:*** 2000. Transfers technology to natural resource managers and researchers in tropical forests.

★27★ International Water Resources Association
205 N. Mathews Ave.
Univ. of Illinois
Urbana, IL 61801
Phone: (217)333-0536
Fax: (217)333-8046
Contact: Glen E. Stout, Exec.Dir.
Founded: 1972. ***Members:*** 1400. Seeks to: advance the planning, development, management, education, and research of water resources; establish an international forum for those concerned with water resources; encourage international programs in the field; and cooperate with other organizations of common interest.

★28★ International Wildlife Coalition (IWC)
634 N. Falmouth Hwy.
PO Box 388
N. Falmouth, MA 02556
Phone: (508)564-9980
Fax: (508)563-2843
Contact: Daniel J. Morast, Pres.
Founded: 1982. Supporters: 130,000. Works to preserve wildlife and wildlife habitats. Publicizes the coalition's cause and activities; conducts research. ***Former Name(s):*** I KARE - Killing Animals for Recreational Enjoyment (1986).

★29★ Paris Commission
New Ct.
48 Carey St.
London WC2A 2JE, England
Phone: 71 2429927
Fax: 71 8317427
Telex: 21185 BOSPAR G
Contact: Ms. C. Nihoul, Sec.
Founded: 1974. ***Members:*** 12. Governments and international organizations working to uphold the Convention for the Prevention of Marine Pollution from Land-Based Sources. Sets regulations and standards; conducts research. Works in cooperation with the Oslo Commission.

★30★ Pesticides Action Network
c/o PAN Europe
115, rue Stevin
B-1040 Brussels, Belgium
Phone: 2 2300776
Telex: MA 40164
Contact: Marianne Wenning, Coord.
Founded: 1982. ***Members:*** 80. Conducts public awareness campaign stressing the dangers that accompany the use and proliferation of pesticides. Exposes what the network considers unethical practices in the marketing of pesticides; fosters the participation of nongovernmental organizations in international and national initiatives to halt what the network calls indiscriminate sale and use of hazardous pesticides; promotes alternatives to pesticide-dependent agriculture and pest control.

★31★ Planetary Association for Clean Energy
100 Bronson, No. 1001
Ottawa, Ontario, Canada K1R 6G8
Phone: (613)236-6265
Contact: Dr. A. Michrowski, Gen.Sec.
Founded: 1976. 3550 researchers, individuals, corporations, and instutitions in 60 countries seeking to facilitate research, development, demonstration, and evaluation of clean energy systems. The association defines clean energy systems as those which utilize natural sources, and are inexpensive, non-polluting, and universally applicable. Concerns include the bioeffects of low level electromagnetics, bioenergetics, and new energy technology. Tests and recommends products that facilitate the implementation of clean energy systems. Serves as a consultant to governments and other agencies.

★32★ Rainforest Information Centre
PO Box 368
Lismore NSW 2480, Australia
Phone: 66 218503
Contact: Ian Peter, Dir.
Founded: 1980. ***Members:*** 18,500. Environmental activists interested in the protection of dwindling rainforest resources. Generates public awareness of dangers to tropical forests through information campaigns.

★33★ Rural Advancement Fund International (RAFI)
PO Box 1029
Pittsboro, NC 27312
Phone: (919)542-5292
Contact: Cary Fowler, Program Dir.
Founded: 1983. Promotes international conservation of genetic agricultural resources. ***Former Name(s):*** International Genetic Resources Programme (1986).

★34★ Scientific Committee on Oceanic Research
Dept. of Oceanography
Dalhousie Univ.
Halifax, Nova Scotia, Canada B3H 4J1
Phone: (902)424-8865
Fax: (902)424-3877
Telex: 7401472 USA
Contact: Ms. E. Tidmarsh, Exec.Sec.
Founded: 1957. Promotes oceanic research. Establishes small working groups and committees to examine oceanographic problems that may be alleviated through international collaboration.

★35★ Scientific Committee on Problems of the Environment
51, boulevard de Montmorency
F-75016 Paris, France
Phone: 1 4525098
Fax: 1 42881466
Contact: F. di Castri, Pres.
Founded: 1969.
Members: 55. International scientific unions and national committees working to foster the influence of humans on their environment and the effect of environmental changes on people and their health and welfare. Serves as an interdisciplinary consultant to government and to intergovernmental and nongovernmental bodies with respect to environmental problems. Works on projects in the areas of: biogeochemical cycles; ecotoxicology and health effects; global change and ecosystem level studies; sustainable development.

★36★ Society for Underwater Technology
76 Mark Ln.
London EC3R 7JN, England
Phone: 71 4810750
Fax: 71 4814001
Contact: Cmdr. D.R. Wardle, Exec.Sec.
Founded: 1965. ***Members:*** 2000. Seeks to further understanding of the underwater environment by assisting in the exchange of practical information among workers in ocean science research, applied research and technology. Promotes proper economic and sociological use of the oceans for the benefit of humans.

★37★ Southern African Wildlife Management Association
PO Box 3051
Pietermaritzburg 3200, Republic of South Africa
Founded: 1970. ***Members:*** 503. Promotes wise management of wildlife resources of southern Africa and protects conservation efforts. Coordinates research in the field and fosters communication between members.

★38★ United Nations Environment Programme
PO Box 30552
Nairobi, Kenya
Phone: 2 333930
Fax: 2 520711
Telex: 22068 UNEPKE
Contact: Dr. Mostafa K. Tolba, Exec.Dir.
Founded: 1972. ***Members:*** 159. Advocates the protection of natural resources and encourages the integration of environmental considerations in development activites. Works in conjuntion with U.N. agencies. Monitors changes in the environment through Earthwatch, a worldwide surveillance system that collects data, offers information, studies threats to the environment such as chemical pollution, and warns against impending environmental crises. Works with national governments on such trans-boundary problems as ozone depletion, climatic change and global warming, desertification, species migration, oil spill management, acid rain and hazardous wastes, and biological diversity; sponsors Oceans and Coastal Areas Program for nations sharing common coastal waters.

★39★ World Aquaculture Society (WAS)
Louisiana State University
16 E. Fraternity
Baton Rouge, LA 70803
Phone: (504)388-3137
Fax: (504)388-3493
Contact: Juiette Massey, Mgr.
Founded: 1970. ***Members:*** 2300. Promotes exchange and cooperation between persons interested in aquaculture. Provides a forum for the exchange of information among scientists, fish farmers, businesspersons, bureaucrats, and others; promotes and evaluates the educational, scientific and technological development of aquaculture throughout the world. Advocates the training of aquaculture workers in accredited colleges and universities. Encourages private industry and government agencies to support aquaculture research, development, and educational activities. Disseminates information on the status, potential, and problems of aquaculture. ***Former Name(s):*** World Mariculture Society (1986).

★40★ World Commission on Environment and Development
Palais Wilson
52, rue de Paquis
CH-1201 Geneva, Switzerland
Founded: 1985. Promotes the concept of "sustainable growth" and encourages attention to environmental issues when addressing appropriate avenues toward development.

★41★ World Energy Council
34 St. James's St.
London SW1A 1HD, England
Phone: 71 9303966
Fax: 71 9250452
Telex: 264707 WECIHQ G
Contact: I.D. Lindsay, Sec.Gen.
Founded: 1924. ***Members:*** 89. Promotes the development and peaceful use of energy resources by considering: potential resources and all means of production, transportation, and utilization; energy consumption in its overall relationship to the growth of economic activity in the area; and the social and environmental aspects of energy supply and utilization. ***Former Name(s):*** World Power Conference (1986), World Energy Conference (1989).

★42★ World Environment And Resources Council (WERC)
13, avenue Lemaitre
B-1348 Louvain, Belgium
Phone: 16 418639
Telex: 59037 UCLB
Contact: Dr. P. Laconte, Pres.
Founded: 1972.
Members: 13. Seeks to improve utilization of the environment and resources with particular emphasis on the field of human settlements.

★43★ World Environment Center (WEC)
419 Park Ave., S.
Ste. 1404
New York, NY 10016
Phone: (212)683-4700
Fax: (212)683-5053
Telex: 261290 ENVIROCENT
Contact: Dr. Whitman Bassow, Pres.
Founded: 1974. Established with the support of the U.N. Environment Programme. Fosters cooperation in the fields of international environmental management and industrial safety. Provides information to public and the news media on the use of natural resource management for development; reports on environmental activities of governments, corporations, international organizations, and citizens' groups. Places pollution control experts in eligible developing countries. ***Former Name(s):*** Center for International Environment Information (1980).

★44★ World Information Service on Energy
Postbus 5627
NL-1007 Amsterdam, Netherlands
Phone: 20 853857
Contact: Egbert Dykstra, Contact
Founded: 1978.
Members: 500. Networking agent for anti-nuclear and safe energy groups worldwide. Disseminates information on subjects such as: nuclear power; nuclear weapons proliferation; acid rain; the greenhouse effect; energy costs and conservation; alternative energy sources; and energy development in developing countries.

★45★ World Pheasant Association
PO Box 5
Lower Basildon
Berks.
Reading RG8 9PF, England
Phone: 7357 5140
Contact: Jan Readman, Exec.Sec.
Founded: 1975. ***Members:*** 1340. Advocates the adoption of a coordinated policy for preservation and aviculture to save 48 species of pheasants. Seeks to increase public awareness, understanding, and appreciation of nature and, in particular, gallinaceous birds and their requirements for survival. Works to improve and ensure sound avicultural methods in countries of origin and elsewhere, especially where conservation of natural habitats is difficult and wild populations are threatened. Facilitates the establishment of reserve collections and buffer stocks of threatened or endangered species. Encourages habitat conservation and the support of national parks, reserves, and sanctuaries of importance of Galliformes.

★46★ World Rainforest Movement
c/o APPEN/TWN
87 Cantonment Rd.
10250 Penang, Malaysia
Phone: 4 373713
Telex: CAP PG MA 40989
Contact: Martin Khor Kok Peng, Coord.
Founded: 1986. ***Members:*** 50. Organizations interested in global environment and development issues. Is concerned with the destruction of rainforests worldwide and is attempting to reverse such destruction.

★47★ World Union of Stockholm Pioneers
46, rue Raffet
F-75016 Paris, France
Phone: 1 45277876
Contact: A. de Svid, Pres.
Founded: 1973.
Members: 407. Strives to increase awareness of nature and the holistic environment, including education, law, literature, and science. Conducts research on energy forms to preserve the environment.

★48★ Worldwide Fund for Nature
Avenue du Mont-Blanc
CH-1196 Gland, Switzerland
Phone: 22 649111
Fax: 22 644238
Telex: 419618WWF CH
Contact: Charles de Haes, Dir.Gen.
Founded: 1961.
Members: 1,500,000. Purpose is to promote the conservation of the natural environment and ecological processes essential to life on earth. Seeks to generate the strongest possible moral and financial support for the safeguarding of the living environment; encourages action based on scientific priorities. Seeks to heighten public awareness of threats to the environment. ***Former Name(s):*** World Wildlife Fund (1986).

United States

★49★ Abundant Life Seed Foundation
1029 Lawrence St.
Port Townsend, WA 98368
Phone: (206)385-5660
Contact: Forest Shomer, Dir.
Founded: 1975. ***Members:*** 8000. Home gardeners, small farmers, students, and marketing and consumer cooperatives. Purpose is to acquire, propagate, and preserve the plants and seeds of the North Pacific Rim, with particular emphasis on those species not commercially available, including rare and endangered species. Maintains permanent garden with propagation as its primary purpose. Plans to undertake the gathering of 2000 species native to the area. Offers one-day seminars on seeds and the self-sowing garden. Maintains small library.

★50★ The Acid Rain Foundation (TARF)
1410 Varsity Dr.
Raleigh, NC 27606
Phone: (919)828-9443
Contact: Dr. Harriett S. Stubbs, Exec.Dir.
Founded: 1981. ***Members:*** 600. Individuals, corporations, organizations, and students. Purpose is to develop and raise public awareness of the problems associated with acid rain, air pollutants, and global climate change.

Works to support research and supply educational resources and materials. Fosters long-range planning and informed decision-making to help bring about the resolution of acid deposition and air pollutants issues. Maintains library and speakers' bureau. Sponsors workshops.

★51★ Adirondack Council
Box D-2
Church St.
Elizabethtown, NY 12932
Phone: (518)873-2240
Contact: Gary Randorf, Exec.Dir.
Founded: 1975. ***Members:*** 18,000. Individuals and organizations concerned with preserving the Adirondack Park in northern New York. Fosters awareness of the values and resources of the Adirondack Park and promotes its preservation along with enhancement of its wild and scenic qualities. Seeks management of public lands in the park in a manner compatible with the park's needs and qualities. Opposes projects that threaten the wilderness area; assists in environmental education projects; presents positions before the New York State Legislature and at public hearings. Promotes interest in the problem of acid rain. Provides speakers; bestows awards.

★52★ Adopt-a-Stream Foundation
PO Box 5558
Everett, WA 98201
Phone: (206)388-3313
Promotes environmental education and stream enhancement.

★53★ African Wildlife Foundation (AWF)
1717 Massachusetts Ave. NW
Washington, DC 20036
Phone: (202)265-8393
Fax: (202)265-2361
Toll-Free: 800-344-TUSK
Contact: Paul T. Schindler, Pres.
Founded: 1961. Conducts training programs in wildlife management and ecology; offers technical assistance in park and reserve management. Has established schools of wildlife management in Tanzania and Cameroon. Offers continuing support and scholarships for these institutions. Provides vehicles, aircraft, tents, uniforms, radios, and training to antipoaching patrols; initiates and supports conservation education throughout Africa; supports management research; and works in conjunction with other conservation organizations. Maintains field office in Nairobi, Kenya to monitor and administer projects. ***Former Name(s):*** African Wildlife Leadership Foundation (1982).

★54★ Air and Waste Management Association (AWMA)
PO Box 2861
Pittsburgh, PA 15230
Phone: (412)232-3444
Fax: (412)232-3450
Contact: Martin Rivers, Exec.V.Pres.
Founded: 1907. ***Members:*** 11,000. Industrialists, researchers, equipment manufacturers, governmental control personnel, educators, meteorologists, and others dedicated to seeking economical answers to the problems of air pollution and hazardous waste management. Sponsors continuing education courses; maintains library; presents awards. ***Former Name(s):*** Smoke Prevention Association of America; Air Pollution Control Association (1987).

★55★ Air Resources Information Clearinghouse (ARIC)
46 Prince St.
Rochester, NY 14607-1016
Phone: (716)271-3550
Fax: (716)271-0606
Contact: Elizabeth Thorndike, Pres.
Founded: 1982. Individuals, organizations, educational institutions, government agencies, and corporate bodies. International project of a regional environmental group. Purpose is to gather, organize, and disseminate information on air resource issues such as acid rain, ozone depletion, indoor air pollution, and the greenhouse effect and global climatic change. Supports the belief that by removing communication barriers, individuals, public officials, businesses, and organizations will be motivated to work toward solutions to environmental problems. Does not take positions on issues. Maintains 7000 item reference library and archive; provides bibliographic services, including current awareness and retrospecific bibliographies, and online access to data bases. Organizes seminars, workshops, and conferences. Maintains speakers' bureau; provides children's services; compiles statistics. ***Former Name(s):*** Acid Rain Information Clearinghouse (1988).

★56★ Alaska Coalition (AC)
408 C St., NE
Washington, DC 20002
Phone: (202)547-1141
Fax: (202)547-6009
Contact: Mike Matz, Chm.
Founded: 1978. National, state, and local environmental and conservation organizations. Promotes education, research, and legislative pressure in an effort to preserve Alaska's wild heritage and natural resources. Currently working to preserve the Arctic National Wildlife Refuge and prevent its exploration and development by oil and gas industries. Worked for passage of the Alaska National Interest Lands Conservation Act, commonly known as the Alaska Lands Bill. Following passage of the bill in 1980, the coalition became inactive. The group reactivated in 1983 and succeeded in opposing proposed legislation that would have opened 12 million acres to sports hunting of the 24 million acres protected by the bill; this area is currently open only for subsistence hunting by rural Alaskans.

★57★ Alliance for Clean Energy (ACE)
1901 N. Fl. Myer Dr., 12th Fl.
Rosslyn, VA 22209
Phone: (703)841-0626
Contact: Nancy Prowitt, Asst.Dir.
Founded: 1983. Low-sulfur eastern and western coal producers, carriers, and consumers. Lobbies for federal acid rain legislation which allows utilities a choice in determining the most cost-efficient sulfur dioxide emission reduction strategy. Opposes a nationwide tax on coal producers.

★58★ Alliance for Environmental Education
10751 Ambassador Dr., No. 201
Manassas, VA 22110
Phone: (703)335-1025
Fax: (703)631-1651
Contact: Steven C. Kussmann, Chm.
Founded: 1972. ***Members:*** 150. Organizations, corporations, and government agencies that promote environmental education. Aims to advance all phases of formal and nonformal environmental education. Cooperates with state, federal, and international agencies and private organizations.

★59★ Alliance to Save Energy
1725 K St., NW
Washington, DC 20006
Phone: (202)857-0666
Conducts research and pilot projects to evaluate energy efficiency problems.

★60★ Aluminum Recycling Association (ARA)
1000 16th St. NW, Ste. 603
Washington, DC 20036
Phone: (202)785-0951
Contact: Richard M. Cooperman, Exec.Dir.
Founded: 1929. ***Members:*** 20. Producers of aluminum specification alloys from aluminum scrap. ***Former Name(s):*** Aluminum Research Institute; Aluminum Smelters Research Institute (1953); Aluminum Smelting and Recycling Institute (1971).

★61★ America the Beautiful Fund (ABF)
219 Shoreham Bldg., NW
Washington, DC 20005
Phone: (202)638-1649
Contact: Paul Bruce Dowling, Exec.Dir.
Founded: 1965. Offers recognition, technical support, and small seed grants to private citizens and community groups to initiate new local action projects that improve the quality of the environment. Projects affect environmental design, land preservation, green plantings, civic arts, and historical and cultural preservation, through citizens' volunteer services. Presents National Recognition Awards for superior projects in U.S.

★62★ American Academy of Environmental Medicine
PO Box 16106
Denver, CO 80216
Phone: (303)622-9755
Fax: (303)622-4224
Contact: R. R. Savely, Adm.Asst.
Founded: 1965. ***Members:*** 450. Physicians, engineers, and others interested in the clinical aspect of environmental medicine. Objectives are to promote a better understanding of ecologic illness and to stimulate methods of controlling ecologic illness. Conducts quarterly instructional meeting to educate physicians, nurses, and technicians in the basic techniques of clinical ecology and to keep members abreast of current advances in the field. Promotes research in the field. Provides educational aids such as tapes and audiovisual presentations. Bestows annual Jonathan Forman Award to an individual who has made an outstanding contribution to clinical ecology. ***Former Name(s):*** Society for Clinical Ecology (1984).

★63★ American Association in Support of Ecological Initiatives
c/o Brendan F. Sweeney
1906 Franwell Ave.
Silver Spring, MD 20902
Phone: (301)649-1123

★64★ American Board of Environmental Medicine (ABEM)
2114 Martingale Dr.
Norman, OK 73072
Phone: (405)329-8437
Contact: Clifton R. Brooks M.D., Exec.Dir.
Founded: 1988. An accrediting agency for medical doctors and osteopaths. Examines, evaluates, and certifies individuals in the field; evaluates training programs and hospital units, such as emergency care facilities, environmental control and biodetoxification units, and rehabilitation centers; makes recommendations to the medical and allied health science professions regarding standards

for establishing, improving, and maintaining the adequacy of care in the discipline. Maintains biographical archives; compiles statistics.

★65★ American Cave Conservation Association (ACCA)
131 Main & Cave Sts.
PO Box 409
Horse Cave, KY 42749
Phone: (502)786-1466
Contact: David G. Foster, Exec.Dir.
Founded: 1977. ***Members:*** 585. Individuals and organizations interested in the preservation and protection of caves, karstlands, and groundwater resources. Seeks to increase public awareness of the value of caves and the unique life-forms and resources associated with them. Serves as a support service offering: consulting on development and evaluation of cave management plans, land use activities, and educational programs; clearinghouse on cave management and conservation information; referral service for those involved in cave and karst management. Provides assistance to research programs and cave management projects including those that help better enforce state and federal environmental laws and policies. Sponsors educational development and training programs, primarily among elementary and secondary schoolchildren and professional land managers. Operates the American Cave and Karst Center and museum. Maintains library. Offers training seminars and courses; conducts periodic National Cave Management Training Seminar; offers $500 reward to those helping to deter vandalism of cave and karst resources.

★66★ American Cetacean Society
PO Box 2639
San Pedro, CA 90731
Phone: (213)548-6279
Protects whales and dolphins through research, conservation, and education. Projects have focused on the killing of dolphins by tuna fishermen, stopping whaling, ocean pollution, and gill net problems.

★67★ American Conservation Association, Inc.
30 Rockefeller Plaza, Rm. 5402
New York, NY 10112
Phone: (212)649-5600
Nonprofit organization concerned with the conservation of natural resources.

★68★ American Council for an Energy-Efficient Economy
1001 Connecticut Ave. NW, Ste. 535
Washington, DC 20036
Phone: (202)429-8873
Gathers, evaluates, and disseminates information to stilumate greater energy efficiency.

★69★ American Council on the Environment (ACE)
1301 20th St. NW, Ste. 113
Washington, DC 20036
Phone: (202)659-1900
Contact: John H. Gullett, Exec. Officer
Founded: 1972. ***Members:*** 470. Business and professional people, unions, and interested individuals united to enhance the environmental quality of the U.S. by means consistent with a balanced approach to the economic and social well-being of the nation. Conducts seminars.

★70★ American Forest Council
1250 Connecticut Ave. NW, Ste. 320
Washington, DC 20036
Phone: (202)463-2455
Educates and trains private forest land owners in forest management practices.

★71★ American Forestry Association (AFA)
1516 P St. NW
Washington, DC 20005
Phone: (202)667-3300
Fax: (202)667-7751
Toll-Free: 800-368-5748
Contact: R. Neil Sampson, Exec.V.Pres.
Founded: 1875. ***Members:*** 34,818. A citizens' conservation organization working to advance the intelligent management and use of forests, soil, water, wildlife, and all other natural resources. Promotes public appreciation of natural resources and the part they play in the social, recreational, and economic life of the U.S. Presents annual Distinguished Service Award, John Aston Warder Medal, William B. Greeley Award, biennial Fernow and Giono Awards. Sponsors Trees for People program which seeks to help meet national needs for forest products, enhance productivity of private nonindustrial forest resources, maximize benefits to private woodland owners, provide advice to forest owners, and make legislative recommendations at the federal level. Maintains 6000 volume library on forestry, conservation, and wildlife.

★72★ American Horse Protection Association (AHPA)
1000 29th St. NW, T100
Washington, DC 20007
Phone: (202)965-0500
Contact: Robin C. Lohnes, Exec.Dir.
Founded: 1966. ***Members:*** 15,000. Individuals interested in the protection and welfare of horses, both wild and domestic. Gained passage of both the Horse Protection Act of 1970, which makes illegal the showing of "sored" horses in interstate commerce, and the Wild Horse and Burro Protection Act of 1971.

★73★ American Humane Association
9725 E. Hampden Ave.
Denver, CO 80231
Phone: (303)695-0811
Protects animals and children from neglect, abuse, and explotation. Activities include training programs for animal care, humane education materials, and emergency relief for animal victims.

★74★ American Industrial Health Council
1330 Connecticut Ave., NW, Ste. 300
Washington, DC 20036
Phone: (202)659-0060
Organization focuses on issues related to the regulation of industrial chemicals.

★75★ American Institute of Biomedical Climatology
1023 Welsh Rd.
Philadelphia, PA 19115
Phone: (215)673-8368
Contact: Richmond Kent, Exec.Dir.
Founded: 1958. ***Members:*** 60. Meteorologists, biologists, epidemiologists, physicians, atmospheric physicists, engineers, architects, physiologists, climatologists, and other professionals interested in investigating the influence of the natural environment on the health and diseases of humans. Current areas of interest include: the greenhouse effect, acid rain, depletion of the ozone layer, indoor and outdoor air pollution, biological effects of electromagnetic fields and concentrated radon, and beneficial and detrimental effects of climate and weather on health. ***Former Name(s):*** American Institute of Medical Climatology (1988).

★76★ American Littoral Society
Sandy Hooks
Highland, NJ 07732
Phone: (201)291-0055
Nonprofit organization dedicated to conserving the littoral zone.

★77★ American Medical Fly Fishing Association
PO Box 768
Lock Haven, PA 17745
Phone: (717)769-7375
Contact: Veryl Frye M.D., Sec.-Treas.
Founded: 1969. ***Members:*** 220. Offers physicians interested in conservation and environmental and ecological problems an opportunity to work toward achieving a better environment.

★78★ American Nature Study Society
5881 Cold Brook Rd.
Homer, NY 13077
Phone: (607)749-3655
Founded: 1908. Promotes environmental education through workshops and field trips.

★79★ American Pheasant and Waterfowl Society
RR 1, Box 164-A
Granton, WI 54436
Phone: (715)238-7291
Contact: Lloyd Ure, Sec.-Treas.
Founded: 1936. ***Members:*** 2000. Hobbyists, aviculturists, and zoos. Works to perpetuate all varieties of upland game, ornamental birds, and waterfowl. Maintains speakers' bureau; compiles statistics; bestows awards. Operates film and tape library. ***Former Name(s):*** American Pheasant Society (1962).

★80★ American Resources Group (ARG)
374 Maple Ave. E., Ste. 204
Vienna, VA 22180
Phone: (703)255-2700

★81★ American Rivers
801 Pennsylvania Ave. SE, Ste. 303
Washington, DC 20003
Phone: (202)547-6900
Fax: (202)543-6142
Contact: W. Kent Olson, Pres.
Founded: 1973. ***Members:*** 12,000. A public interest group working for the preservation of free-flowing rivers and their adjacent landscapes in the U.S. Focuses on all types of river protection methods. ***Former Name(s):*** American Rivers Conservation Council (1986).

★82★ American Shore and Beach Preservation Association (ASBPA)
PO Box 279
Middletown, CA 95461
Phone: (707)987-2385
Contact: Orville T. Magoon, Pres.
Founded: 1926. ***Members:*** 1000. Federal, state, local, and foreign government agencies; private groups and individuals interested in conservation, development, and restoration of beaches and shorefronts of oceans, lakes, and rivers.

★83★ American Society for Environmental History
Center for Technical Studies
New Jersey Institute of Technology
Newark, NJ 07102
Phone: (201)596-3270
Contact: John Opie, Editor
Founded: 1976. ***Members:*** 500. Teachers and researchers in environmental studies, primarily in higher education, government, and business.

★84★ American Society for Surface Mining and Reclamation
21 Grandview Dr.
Princeton, WV 24740
Phone: (304)425-8332
Contact: William T. Plass, Exec.Dir.
Founded: 1973. ***Members:*** 450. Mining companies and corporations; representatives from federal agencies and state governments; individuals from the academic community. To encourage efforts to protect and enhance land disturbed by mining. Promotes, supports, and assists in research and demonstrations; fosters communication among research scientists, regulatory agencies, landowners, and the surface mining industry; identifies experts for organizations needing assistance; promotes and supports educational programs; disseminates scientific information. Maintains the Register of Reclamation Research and Demonstration Plots on Lands Surface Mined for Coal to collect and preserve information on such areas and to promote better reclamation through wider use of research and demonstration areas. Bestows awards. Technical Divisions: Forestry; International Tailing Reclamation; Landscape Architecture; Soil and Overburden; Ecology; Wethands. ***Former Name(s):*** Council for Surface Mining and Reclamation Research in Appalachia (1978); American Council for Reclamation Research (1982).

★85★ American Society for the Prevention of Cruelty to Animals
441 E. 92nd St.
New York, NY 10128
Phone: (212)876-7700
Focuses on the rights of companion animals, animals in research and testing, animals raised for food, wild animals, entertainment and work animals, and animals in education.

★86★ American Society for the Protection of Nature in Israel
330 7th Ave., 21st Fl.
New York, NY 10001
Phone: (212)947-2820
Fax: (212)629-0508
Contact: Tamar C. Podell, Exec.Dir.
Founded: 1986. ***Members:*** 3000. Persons interested in and concerned with conservation and environmental protection in Israel. Supports the work of the Society for the Protection of Nature in Israel. Educates the public about environmental issues; organizes annual trip to Israel and sends an environmental delegation to Isreal annually; facilitates information exchange and support between Israeli and American environmentalists.

★87★ American Wilderness Alliance
7600 E. Arapahoe, Ste. 114
Englewood, CO 80112
Phone: (303)771-0380
Wildlife, wetlands, watersheds, and fisheries management.

★88★ American Wildlands
7500 E. Arapahoe Rd., Ste. 355
Englewood, CO 80112
Phone: (303)771-0380
Fax: (303)694-9047
Contact: Clifton R. Merritt, Exec.Dir.
Founded: 1977. ***Members:*** 4000. Individuals dedicated to conserving the nation's wildland resources. Promotes the protection and proper management of wildland resources, including wilderness, watersheds, wetlands, free-flowing rivers, fisheries, and wildlife; works to identify and investigate wilderness areas, wild and scenic rivers, and other natural areas needing protection; conducts scientific and economic research of wildland resources, making findings available to the public. Sponsors programs, forums, and institutes on proper land and water management on publicly owned lands. Promotes proper use of earth, soil, water, plant, animal, and atmospheric resources; studies the interrelationship between man and wildland resources. Organizes citizen support to protect the wildlands and free-flowing rivers; assists citizens by preparing proposals to add areas to the National Wilderness System, National Wild and Scenic River System, and other land and water special management systems. Conducts educational and recreational wilderness and river trips. Sponsors American Wilderness Adventures, a program that offers over 80 wild country and river trips, ranging from Alaska to Hawaii, that include rafting, canoeing, sailing, horseback riding, photography, backpacking, and adventure study. Also sponsors Wildland Resource Conservation Program, which educates and coordinates citizens into action to help safeguard wildland resources by providing them with factual resource information. Maintains River Defense Fund, a program that is focused solely on protection of ri ver resources. Bestows conservation awards. ***Former Name(s):*** American Wilderness Alliance (1990).

★89★ Americans for the Environment
1400 16th St. NW
Washington, DC 20036
Phone: (202)797-6665
Educational organization concerned with electing environmentalists to public office.

★90★ Animal Protection Institute of America
2831 Fruitridge Rd.
Sacramento, CA 95822
Phone: (916)422-1921
Education for humane treatment of animals.

★91★ Animal Welfare Institute
PO Box 3650
Washington, DC 20007
Phone: (202)337-2332
Works to reduce pain inflicted on animals, including improving conditions of laboratory animals, food animals, and threatened species.

★92★ Antarctica Project
218 D St. SE
Washington, DC 20003
Phone: (202)544-2600
Monitors the region and lobbies at national and international levels, including research and policy analysis.

★93★ Arthur E. Howell Wildlife Educational Foundation, Inc. and Spruce Acres Refuge
HCR #61, Box 6
Lycette Rd.
Amity, MO 64465-9702
Phone: (207)532-6880
Promotes preservation and conservation of natural resources.

★94★ Asphalt Recycling and Reclaiming Association (ARRA)
3 Church Circle, Ste. 250
Annapolis, MD 21401
Phone: (301)267-0023
Contact: Michael R. Krissoff, Exec.Dir.
Founded: 1976. ***Members:*** 200. Contractors and engineers engaged in the reworking of asphalt; contractors employed in connection with the services of regular members and suppliers of material or equipment to members; governmental representatives, architects, and interested persons dealing with asphalt recycling; honorary members. Objective is to promote asphalt recycling. Maintains library of state asphalt specifications. Sponsors regional seminars; maintains speakers' bureau; bestows awards.

★95★ Association for Arid Lands Studies (AALS)
c/o International Center for Arid & Semiarid Land Studies
Texas Tech University
PO Box 4620
Lubbock, TX 79409-1036
Phone: (806)742-2218
Fax: (806)742-1900
Contact: Dr. Idris R. Traylor Jr., Exec.Dir.
Founded: 1977. ***Members:*** 250. Scientists, social scientists, and humanists interested in the study of arid lands. Encourages an increased awareness of the problems and potentials of arid and semiarid lands and man's impact on them. Seeks to stimulate interdisciplinary research and teaching. Sponsors professional programs and meetings.

★96★ Association for Conservation Information (ACI)
PO Box 10678
Reno, NV 89520
Phone: (702)688-1500
Fax: (702)688-1595
Contact: David K. Rice, Pres.
Founded: 1938. ***Members:*** 86. Professional society of information and education personnel of state, provincial, federal, and private conservation agencies. Sponsors annual awards program in conservation work. ***Former Name(s):*** American Association for Conservation Information.

★97★ Association for the Study of Man-Environment Relations
PO Box 57
Orangeburg, NY 10962
Phone: (914)634-8221
Contact: Aristide H. Esser M.D., Pres.
Founded: 1969. ***Members:*** 300. Behavioral scientists, design professionals, social scientists, and law and medical professionals. Purpose is to promote understanding of the nature of man-environment relationships through publications, workshops, and meetings in collaboration with other organizations. Maintains Ecology of Knowledge Network.

★98★ Association of Battery Recyclers (ABR)
Sanders Lead Co. Corp.
Sanders Rd.
PO Drawer 707
Troy, AL 36081
Phone: (205)566-1563
Contact: N. Kenneth Campbell, Exec.Sec.
Founded: 1976. ***Members:*** 45. Recyclers of lead, oxide manufacturers, industry equipment suppliers, and consulting companies. Objectives are: to provide information services relative to safety and environmental controls; to conduct continuing industry-wide studies. Offers safety and health program recommendations to eliminate hazards to the health and safety of employees. Conducts research in: engineering and administrative controls; respiratory protection; environmental and biological monitoring. Compiles statistics on industry-wide problems. ***Former Name(s):*** Secondary Lead Smelters Association (1990).

★99★ Association of Conservation Engineers (ACE)
Alabama Dept. of Conservation
64 N. Union St.
Montgomery, AL 36130
Phone: (205)261-3476
Contact: William P. Allinder, Sec.-Treas.
Founded: 1961. ***Members:*** 200. Persons employed by or retired from any state, federal, or provincial agency or allied discipline working to develop fisheries, wildlife forestry, or recreational facilities, either in an administrative, professional engineering, engineer-in-training, or general construction superintendent capacity. Encourages the educational, social, and economic interests of engineering practices which further the cause of fish, wildlife, and recreational developments. Presents Eugene Baker Conservation Engineering Award.

★100★ Association of Ecosystem Research Centers
Ecology Ctr.
Utah State University
Logan, UT 84322-5200
Phone: (801)750-2555
Fax: (801)750-3872
Contact: Frederic H. Wagner, Pres.
Founded: 1985. ***Members:*** 39. Ecosystem research centers and laboratories representing 800 individuals. Promotes ecosystem science as a specific branch of the field of ecology. Provides information to Congress, other federal agencies, and the public about ecosystem science and its application to policy issues. Monitors government agencies regarding their use of ecosystem science in determining policy. Assists in the establishment of new research centers. Sponsors workshops.

★101★ Association of Environmental and Resource Economists
1616 P St. NW
Washington, DC 20036
Phone: (202)328-5000
Fax: (202)265-8069
Contact: Paul R. Portney, Sec.
Members: 575. Professionals, economists, and individuals from universities and governmental agencies interested in resource and environmental issues. To address the problems and concerns in resource management. Is concerned with issues such as water and land resources and air pollution. Plans to conduct regional workshops.

★102★ Association of Environmental Engineering Professors
Univ. of Illinois
3221 Newmark CE Laboratory
208 N. Romine
Urbana, IL 61801
Phone: (217)333-6964
Contact: Bruce E. Rittmann, Pres.
Founded: 1963. ***Members:*** 400. College and university professors in the fields of environmental engineering, air, land, and water resources, pollution control, environmental health engineering, and related programs. Studies graduate curricula, entrance requirements, enrollment, and physical facilities at universities to establish criteria and improve education in environmental engineering. Bestows Outstanding Ph.D. Dissertation Award and Outstanding Publication Award annually. Sponsors annual distinguished lecturer series, with U.S. and foreign lecturers in alternate years. Holds seminars and workshops. Conducts annual enrollment survey of environmental engineering programs in North America. ***Former Name(s):*** American Association of Professors in Sanitary Engineering (1973).

★103★ Association of Ground Water Scientist and Engineers
6375 Riverside Dr.
Dublin, OH 43017
Phone: (614)761-1711
Provides technical assistance and information on groundwater protection.

★104★ Association of Local Air Pollution Control Officials (ALAPCO)
444 N. Capitol St. NW, Ste. 306
Washington, DC 20001
Phone: (202)624-7864
Fax: (202)624-7863
Contact: S. William Becker, Exec.Dir.
Founded: 1971. ***Members:*** 230. Directors of local air pollution control program agencies. Provides a means for members to share air quality related experiences and discuss solutions to problems; encourages communication and cooperation among federal, state, and local regulatory agencies; promotes air pollution control activities.

★105★ Association of Metropolitan Water Agencies (AMWA)
1717 K St. NW, Ste. 1006
Washington, DC 20036
Phone: (202)331-2820
Fax: (202)842-0621
Contact: Diane Van De Hei, Exec.Dir.
Founded: 1981. ***Members:*** 63. Municipal public water supply agencies. Represents members' interests before the Environmental Protection Agency and other federal bodies.

★106★ Association of New Jersey Environmental Commissions
PO Box 157, 300 Mendham Rd.
Mendham, NJ 07945
Phone: (201)539-7547
Contact: Sally Dudley
Statewide organization informs and assists volunteer municipal advisors and citizens about environmental protection.

★107★ Association of State and Interstate Water Pollution Control Administrators (ASIWPC)
444 N. Capitol St. NW, Ste. 330
Washington, DC 20001
Phone: (202)624-7782
Contact: Ms. Robbi J. Savage, Exec.Dir.
Founded: 1960. ***Members:*** 63. Administrators of state and interstate governmental agencies legally responsible for prevention, abatement, and control of water pollution. Promotes coordination among state agency programs and those of the Environmental Protection Agency, Congress, and other federal agencies. Conducts research; maintains speakers' bureau.

★108★ Association of State and Territorial Solid Waste Management Officials
444 N. Capitol St. NW, Ste. 388
Washington, DC 20001
Phone: (202)624-5828
Fax: (202)624-7875
Contact: Thomas J. Kennedy, Exec.Dir.
Founded: 1974. ***Members:*** 250. Represents state solid and hazardous waste directors and staff members. Works in close coordination with the Environmental Protection Agency to develop and advance positive programs in the management of all solid wastes by promoting uniform regulation and enforcement of pertinent laws and federal regulations at all levels of government. Disseminates information on technology and management techniques among and between states; conducts timely studies and analyses of critical issues; assists in the training of state employees in key areas of waste management. Conducts annual Solid Waste Forum and training workshops; compiles statistics.

★109★ Association of State Floodplain Managers
PO Box 2051
Madison, WI 53701-2051
Phone: (608)266-1926
Contact: Larry A. Larson, Exec.Dir.
Founded: 1977. ***Members:*** 1350. Corporations, agencies, and individuals interested in and responsible for floodplain management including coastal policies, flood insurance, floodplain regulations, mapping and engineering standards, mitigation issues, stormwater management, and information and education. Supports environmental protection for floodplain areas. Represents state and local flood hazard programs to national agencies; provides information for federal flood hazard management policies and programs. Encourages cooperation and the exchange of information on developments in the field; supports continuing education in floodplain management. Sponsors research. Maintains speakers' bureau and biographical archives; compiles statistics; sponsors competitions and symposial; bestows awards. Maintains a clearinghouse of information related to flood hazard management.

★110★ Association of State Wetland Managers
PO Box 2463
Berne, NY 12023
Phone: (518)872-1804
Contact: Jon Kusler, Exec.Dir.
Founded: 1984. ***Members:*** 460. Professionals and other interested individuals who are involved in wetland management. Seeks to: promote and improve protection and management of U.S. wetlands; fosters cooperation among government agencies and integration of public, private, and academic protection programs. Encourages the exchange and dissemination of information and ideas between members; identifies, coordinates, and conducts research concerning wetland protection needs and techniques. Works to improve public knowledge and awareness of the field. Sponsors lectures. Provides technical assistance in areas such as regulations, management, acquisition, assessment, mitigation, and land-use incentives.

★111★ Association of University Environmental Health/Sciences Centers
University of Cincinnati
Inst. Environmental Health
3223 Eden Ave.
Cincinnati, OH 45267-0056
Phone: (513)558-5701
Fax: (513)558-1756
Contact: Roy E. Albert M.D., Pres.
Founded: 1980. ***Members:*** 14. University-based environmental health science centers supported by the National Institute of Environmental Health Sciences. Serves as a forum for exchange of information, collaboration, and cooperation among the centers.

★112★ Association of University Fisheries and Wildlife Program Administrators
Texas & AM University
Department of Wildlife & Fisheries Sciences
College Station, TX 77843-2258
Phone: (409)845-1261
Fax: (409)845-3786
Contact: Dr. David J. Schmidly, Exec. Officer
Members: 75. Department heads of fishery and wildlife programs at U.S. and Canadian universities. Seeks to improve the quality of university research, teaching, and programs in the field. Communicates with the U.S. Congress, federal government agencies, and the public. Prepares reports.

★113★ Atlantic Center for the Environment
39 S. Main St.
Ipswich, MA 01938
Phone: (508)356-0038
Promotes environmental understanding and encourages public involvement in resolving natural resource issues in the Atlantic Ocean region.

★114★ Atlantic Waterfowl Council (AWC)
Department of Natural Resources
Game & Fish Division
205 Butler St.
Atlanta, GA 30334
Phone: (404)656-3523
Contact: Leon Kirkland, Chm.
Founded: 1952. ***Members:*** 23. Fish and game directors or fish and wildlife organizations of each of 17 Atlantic coastal states and six Canadian provinces. Coordinates waterfowl research and management in the Atlantic Flyway.

★115★ Audubon Naturalist Society of the Central Atlantic States
8940 Jones Mill Rd.
Chevy Chase, MD 20815
Phone: (301)652-9188
Contact: Ken Nicholls, Exec.Dir.
Founded: 1897. ***Members:*** 13,000. Persons interested in conservation of natural resources and ornithology. Seeks to further sound conservation practices, and to protect birds and other wildlife and the environment on which they depend. Conducts special program of natural history field studies jointly with the graduate school of the U.S. Department of Agriculture, an ecology program for inner-city schools in Washington, DC, and environmental education programs for children and adults. Operates Woodend, a 40-acre wildlife sanctuary and nature education center in Chevy Chase, MD. Sponsors series of illustrated lectures and field trips to varied habitats in the Central Atlantic Region; compiles statistics on local natural history; maintains museum. Operates speakers' bureau and library of 4000 volumes; bestows Paul Bartsch Award for distinguished contribution to natural history. Maintains Voice of Naturalist, a weekly recording of bird sightings. ***Former Name(s):*** Audubon Society of the District of Columbia (1960).

★116★ Automotive Dismantlers and Recyclers Association (ADRA)
10400 Eaton Pl., Ste. 203
Fairfax, VA 22030-2208
Phone: (703)385-1001
Fax: (703)385-1494
Contact: William P. Steinkuller, Exec.V.Pres.
Founded: 1943. ***Members:*** 5500. Firms selling used auto, truck, motorcycle, bus, and farm and construction equipment parts, retail and wholesale; operators of long line (telephone) circuits; firms selling equipment and services to the industry. Seeks to improve business practices and operating techniques through exchange of information via publications and meetings. Cooperates with public and private agencies in beautification efforts and developing solutions to the abandoned car and auto theft problems. Conducts seminars. Maintains speakers' bureau, college scholarship foundation for children of employees, and educational foundation; conducts annual beautification contest for members. Maintains 15 committees.

★117★ Balloon Alert Project
12 Pine Fork Dr.
Toms River, NJ 08755
Phone: (201)341-9506
Works to ban mass balloon releases and develops alternatives to such releases.

★118★ Barrier Islands Coalition
40 W. 20th St., 11th Fl.
New York, NY 10011
Phone: (212)727-2700
Contact: Lisa Speer, Exec. Officer
National and regional conservation groups seeking to preserve undeveloped coastal barrier islands, beaches, and associated aquatic ecosystems in the U.S. Conservationists hope that federal subsidies, which induce development and building on coastal barriers, will end for the remaining undeveloped barrier islands, and that key islands will be acquired by the federal government and added to its list of seashore parks and wilderness areas.

★119★ Basic Foundation
PO Box 47012
Saint Petersburg, FL 33743
Phone: (813)526-9562
Promotes efforts to balance population growth with natural resources and tropical rain forest preservation.

★120★ Beaver Defenders
Unexpected Wildlife Refuge
PO Box 765
Newfield, NJ 08344
Phone: (609)697-3541
Contact: Hope Sawyer Buyukmihci, Sec.
Founded: 1970. ***Members:*** 200. Persons interested in preserving and protecting wildlife, especially beavers. To educate the public and maintain a 450-acre wildlife refuge. Conducts research on beavers. Maintains 200 volume library.

★121★ Better World Society
1100 17th St., NW
Washington, DC 20036
Organization promotes public awareness of environmental issues worldwide.

★122★ Big Island Rainforest Action Group
PO Box 341
Kurtistown, HI 96760
Phone: (808)966-7622
Founded: 1989. Organizes and administers efforts to preserve the rainforests of the Hawaiian Islands, particularly those directed at stopping geothermal development in the Wao Kele O Puna forest on the Island of Hawaii. Programs have included testimony at public hearings, letter-writing campaigns, demonstrations and other forms of civil disobedience, and political action. Maintains speakers' bureau and library.

★123★ Big Thicket Association (BTA)
Box 198 - Hwy. 770
Saratoga, TX 77585
Phone: (409)274-5000
Founded: 1964. ***Members:*** 200. Conservationists and others interested in preserving the wilderness area of southeast Texas known as the "Big Thicket. " (A three million acre area containing a wide variety of both tropical and temperate vegetation, the Big Thicket is one of the major resting places along the Gulf Coast for migratory birds, and at least 300 species, many endangered, live there permanently. An 84,550 acre parcel of the Big Thicket was named a national preserve on Oct. 11, 1974.) Maintains a museum in Saratoga, TX, which attempts to interpret the area and serve as an information center for visitors and researchers. Sponsors environmental education programs, canoe trips, hiking tours, seminars, and nature retreats. Maintains nature trail in Lance Rosier Memorial Park. Holds Big Thicket Day Festival every spring.

★124★ Big Thicket Conservation Association (BTCA)
PO Box 12032
Beaumont, TX 77706
Phone: (214)324-3191
Contact: Billy Hallmon, Pres.
Founded: 1981. ***Members:*** 200. Conservationists and others concerned with the conservation, ecology, and preservation of wilderness areas. Purpose is to promote appreciation and preservation of the natural and cultural heritage of the Big Thicket region of southeastern Texas. Monitors the funding, development, and ecological welfare of the Big Thicket National Preserve, established in 1974 as the first biological preserve in the National Park System. The association drafts and submits plans of action to the National Park Service. Sponsors hikes throughout the Big Thicket area. Bestows awards.

★125★ Bio-Integral Center
PO Box 7414
Berkeley, CA 94707
Phone: (415)524-2567
Provides information on less-toxic pest control.

★126★ Bird Association of California
679 Prospect
Pasadena, CA 91103
Phone: (818)795-6621
Contact: Ferdinand R. Wagner, Exec.Mgr.
Founded: 153. ***Members:*** 100. National organization that seeks to develop, promote, and encourage the proper breeding, handling, and care of birds. Teaches proper care and feeding of different species; works with federal and local authorities and other organizations to prevent abuse and mishandling of birds. Compiles and disseminates information. Presents awards; conducts specialized education, children's services, and research

programs. Maintains biographical archives and small library.

★127★ Birds of Prey Rehabilitation Foundation
RR 2, Box 659
Broomfield, CA 80020
Phone: (303)460-0674
Contact: Sigrid Ueblacker, Exec. Officer
Founded: 1984. ***Members:*** 200. Concerned with the preservation and rehabilitation of birds of prey. Conducts educational programs focusing on raptors and their relation to the environment. Maintains library.

★128★ Bolton Institute for a Sustainable Future
4 Linden Sq.
Wellesley, MA 02181
Phone: (617)235-5320
Independent organization concerned with research and education on the ethics of limits-to-growth issues.

★129★ Boone and Crockett Club
241 S. Fraley Blvd.
Dumfries, VA 22026
Phone: (703)221-1888
Contact: William Harold Nesbitt, Exec.Dir.
Founded: 1887. Dedicated to the preservation of North American wildlife. Sponsors record keeping program on native North American big game trophies, and graduate-level research and workshops on wildlife species. Members were founders of the American Committee for International Conservation. Compiles statistics.

★130★ Bounty Information Service (BIS)
c/o Stephens Coll. Post Office
Columbia, MO 65215
Phone: (314)876-7186
Contact: H. Charles Laun, Dir.
Founded: 1965. ***Members:*** 2000. Individuals interested in the removal of wildlife bounties in the U.S. and Canada. Organizes bounty removal programs; publishes literature on the bounty system and methods for removal; compiles annual summary of bounties in North America; executes individual studies of areas. Maintains library.

★131★ Brooks Bird Club (BBC)
707 Warwood Ave.
Wheeling, WV 26003
Phone: (304)547-5253
Contact: Helen B. Conrad, Admin.
Founded: 1932. ***Members:*** 1000. Conducts bird population studies and surveys, winter bird and hawk counts, and field trips. Compiles migration records; sponsors backyard sanctuaries program and 2-week biotic study. Maintains library of 750 volumes on natural history; operates computerized information services.

★132★ California Marine Mammal Center
Golden Gate National Recreation Area
Sausalito, CA 94965
Phone: (415)331-7325
Rescues marine mammals.

★133★ Camp Fire Club of America (CFCA)
230 Camp Fire Rd.
Chappaqua, NY 10514
Phone: (914)941-0199
Contact: Thomas J. Fisher, Pres.
Founded: 1897. ***Members:*** 455. Sportsmen dedicated to the preservation of wildlife habitat and wise use of natural resources. Sponsors Camp Fire Conservation Fund. Sponsors competitions; bestows awards; maintains 2500 volume library on wildlife, hunting, fishing, and conservation, as well as books written by club members.

★134★ Camp Fire Conservation Fund (CFCF)
230 Camp Fire Rd.
Chappaqua, NY 10514
Phone: (914)941-0199
Contact: George R. Lamb, Pres.
Founded: 1977. ***Members:*** 300. Individuals concerned with the conservation of forests and wildlife. Seeks to: inform the public and governmental agencies on the use of natural resources; restore and publicize the role of the sportsman in conservation; organize and fund educational and public information projects. Coordinates activities of sportsmen's and conservation organizations. Supports wildlife conservation research.

★135★ Canada-United States Environmental Council (CUSEC)
c/o Defenders of Wildlife
1244 19th St. NW
Washington, DC 20036
Phone: (202)659-9510
Fax: (202)659-0680
Contact: James G. Deane, Co-Chm.
Founded: 1974. National and regional environmental and conservation groups. Works to facilitate interchange of information and cooperative action on current environmental issues such as acid precipitation, Great Lakes pollution, protection of Arctic wildlife habitat, and the future of the Antarctic and the oceans. Serves as a forum to discuss ideas, approve resolutions, and establish contacts.

★136★ Canvasback Society
PO Box 101
Gates Mills, OH 44040
Phone: (216)443-2340
Contact: Keith C. Russell, Chm.
Founded: 1975. ***Members:*** 250. Individuals and foundations concerned with the preservation of the canvasback species of duck in North America. Raises funds for research on the canvasback duck and for the creation, restoration, and preservation of duck habitat. Maintains small reference library.

★137★ Caribbean Conservation Corporation (CCC)
PO Box 2866
Gainesville, FL 32602
Phone: (904)373-6441
Fax: (904)375-2449
Toll-Free: 800-678-7853
Contact: David Carr, Exec.Dir.
Founded: 1959. ***Members:*** 400. Devoted to the study, preservation, and rehabilitation of marine turtles in the Caribbean and Atlantic. Sponsors the Joshua B. Powers Fellowship, which brings biology and fishery specialists to the Green Turtle Research Station at Tortuguero, Costa Rica.

★138★ Carrying Capacity Network
1325 G St. NW, Ste. 1003
Washington, DC 20005-3104
Phone: (202)879-3044
Contact: Stephen Mabley, Network Coord.
Founded: 1991. Focuses on carrying capacity of the earth, which is defined as the number of individuals that resources can support indefinitely without degradation of the physical, ecological, cultural, and social environments. Serves as forum for the development and exchange of information on relationships between issues such as population stabilization, environmental protection, growth control, resource conservation, and sustainable development. Facilitates cooperation between activist groups. Does not endorse particular policy positions. Operates speakers and writers bureau and fax network.

★139★ Cascade Holistic Economic Consultants (CHEC)
14417 SE Laurie Ave.
Oak Grove, OR 97207
Phone: (503)652-7049
Contact: Randal O'Toole, Exec. Officer
Founded: 1975. Nonprofit consulting firm supported by individuals, libraries, and corporations. Aids citizens in influencing public forest management. Proposes reforms of public forests that would save taxpayers money and resolve environmental controversies. Conducts research and educational programs. Maintains speakers' bureau.

★140★ CEIP Fund
68 Harrison Ave., 5th Fl.
Boston, MA 02111
Phone: (617)426-4375
Contact: Kevin Doyle, Gen.Mgr.
Founded: 1972. Participants are upper-level undergraduate, graduate, and doctoral students, or recent graduates seeking professional experience relevant to careers in environmental fields. Purpose is to foster professional development and the resolution of priority environmental issues in the public and private sectors. Offers paid, full-time assignments with private industry, government agencies, and nonprofit organizations requesting assistance for terms ranging from 12 to 52 weeks. Participants are employed by CEIP as research or field associates but are considered actual staff members of the sponsoring organization. Projects are in one of three divisions: Conservation Services; Public Policy and Community Development; Technical Services. Individual subject areas include administrative/legal assistance, communications, community development, education, energy, environmental assessments, hazardous substances, historic preservation, land use, natural resource management, pollution control, public/occupational health, recreation, transportation, and wildlife. Organizes regional activities designed to complement associates' work experience; facilitates exchange of information on environmental issues. Maintains Environmental Grant Program to subsidize quality projects offered by organizations with insufficient funds to support associates. Provides career counseling; maintains data base. ***Former Name(s):*** Center for Experiential Education (1979); Center for Environmental Intern Programs (1984).

★141★ Center for Alternative Mining Development Policy (CAMDP)
210 Avon St., Ste. 9
La Crosse, WI 54603
Phone: (608)784-4399
Contact: Al Gedicks, Exec.Dir.
Founded: 1977. ***Members:*** 300. Native Americans, farmers, and those living in urban areas concerned about threats to the environment of the Lake Superior region. Seeks to provide information and technical assistance to Indian tribes and rural communities affected by plans for mining development and radioactive waste disposal. Focuses on issues such as mining taxation, groundwater quality, hazards of uranium exploration, and the environmental impact of copper mining. Conducts TriState Anti Uranium Organizers Training Conference. Holds training workshops to inform citizens on how to involve themselves

in the environmental decision-making process. Operates speakers' bureau; maintains 1000 volume library of technical documents on mining and radioactive waste. Consults with similar international and national groups.

★142★ Center for Clean Air Policy (CCAP)
444 N. Capitol St., Ste. 526
Washington, DC 20001
Phone: (202)624-7709
Contact: Edward A. Helme, Exec.Dir.
Founded: 1985. Participants are U.S. state governors and corporate, academic, and public interest leaders. Develops and analyzes approaches to resolving air pollution issues. Seeks to inform decision makers and the public of the underlying environmental and economic implications of air pollution controls. Organizes and mediates discussions between all parties with an interest in air pollution control legislation. Conducts study projects to measure the impact of acid rain control strategies and policies, energy conservation efforts, and economic, environmental, and waste management control options. Is currently engaged in assessing the severity of western air quality problems. ***Former Name(s):*** Center for Acid Rain and Clean Air Policy Analyses.

★143★ Center for Coastal Studies (CCS)
59 Commercial St.
PO Box 1036
Provincetown, MA 02657
Phone: (508)487-3622
Contact: David L. DeKing, Exec.Dir.
Founded: 1976. ***Members:*** 1800. Individuals interested in environmental issues, especially as they pertain to the coastal environment. Fosters an interdisciplinary approach to education and research toward the understanding of processes and phenomena of the coastal environment; communicates research findings to managers and users of coastal zones. Offers educational and advisory services for coastal environment decision makers. Operates Cetacean Research Program, which conducts long-term habitat, demography, migration, social organization, and lineage research on fin, humpback, and right whales of the North Atlantic; collects and disseminates required governmental data to establish protection of critical whale habitats worldwide; promotes public awareness of the plight of the great whales. Sponsors Entanglement/ Stranding Support Team and summer Coastwatch Expeditions. Conducts lectures, seminars, slide presentations, and field trips; offers land-use advice and student internships. Maintains small library. ***Former Name(s):*** Provincetown Center for Coastal Studies (1985).

★144★ Center for Development and Environment
1709 New York Ave., NW
Washington, DC 20006
Organization advocates responsible use of world's natural resources; maintains offices in South America and Europe.

★145★ Center for Environment, Commerce, and Energy
733 6th St. SE, Ste. 1
Washington, DC 20003
Phone: (202)543-3939
Nonprofit organization which promotes conservation of natural resources and protects the environment.

★146★ Center for Hazardous Materials Research (CHMR)
320 William Pitt Way
University of Pittsburgh Applied Research Center
Pittsburgh, PA 15238
Phone: (412)826-5320
Fax: (412)826-5552
Contact: Edgar Berkey, Pres.
Founded: 1985. Seeks to develop practical solutions to the problems associated with hazardous and solid waste management. Conducts applied research programs on the use and disposal of hazardous materials and wastes. Develops and implements policy on the economic, environmental, institutional, public health, public policy, and technological issues presented by hazardous materials and wastes. Works in conjunction with industry and governmental agencies. Offers: technical assistance services to industry and government in the areas of pollution prevention, recycling, waste minimization and management, environmental compliance, and air dispersion analysis; independent third-party reviews, forensic investigations, and technical services to communities relating to hazardous waste site cleanup, transportation accidents, community right-to-know, and waste management; educational and training programs in health and safety, emergency response, hazardous materials handling, environmental regulations, pesticide application certification and registration, and pesticide fate studies; student internship program. Maintains speakers' bureau and 1400 volume library.

★147★ Center for Holistic Resource Management (CHRM)
PO Box 7128
Albuquerque, NM 87194
Phone: (505)242-9272
Fax: (505)247-1008
Toll-Free: (650)246-8554
Contact: Hal Norris, CEO
Founded: 1984. ***Members:*** 2000. Ranchers, farmers, foresters, environmentalists, conservationists, educators, business leaders, politicians, and interested persons. Seeks improvement of the human environment and quality of life through holistic management of land, water, human, wildlife, and financial resources. Objectives are to: produce stable environments with sound watersheds; restore profitability to agriculture; increase wildlife species and stability of populations; improve water resources of cities, industry, and agriculture; reestablish seriously damaged riparian (streamside) areas; prevent waste of financial resources by governments, international agencies, and private individuals due to poor resource management. Fosters citizen participation in sound resource management; works extensively on combatting the desertification process. Conducts seminars and courses for ranchers, farmers, and professional resource managers on holistic resource management. Collects and disseminates information; maintains speakers' bureau. Provides scientific and educational presentations and interviews. Operates consultation and advisory services particularly for persons and organizations in Third World countries.

★148★ Center for Investigative Reporting
530 Howard St., 2nd Fl.
San Francisco, CA 94105
Phone: (415)543-1200
Provides support for investigative journalism, including environmental stories.

★149★ Center for Marine Conservation (CMC)
1725 DeSales St. NW, Ste. 500
Washington, DC 20036
Phone: (202)429-5609
Fax: (202)872-0619
Contact: Roger E. McManus, Exec.Dir.
Founded: 1972. Dedicated to the conservation and protection of the oceans and their habitats, especially marine mammals such as whales and sea turtles. Promotes public awareness and education. Encourages and conducts science and policy research. Advocates correct management of marine resources and promotes conservation of endangered species and their habitats. Seeks to insure that human activities will not lead to the extinction of these species. CMC activities have included beach cleanups resulting in new state programs to reduce marine debris in the Gulf of Mexico and the establishment of a sanctuary for critically endangered humpback whales in the Caribbean. Also works to prevent accidental entanglement and drowning of marine animals in debris and fishing gear and has repeatedly thwarted efforts to increase international trade in sea turtle products. Sponsors scientific research; conducts international public information campaign. ***Former Name(s):*** Delta Organization (1974); Center for Environmental Education (1988).

★150★ Center for Plant Conservation (CPC)
125 Arborway
Jamaica Plain, MA 02130
Phone: (617)524-6988
Contact: Donald Falk, Exec.Dir.
Founded: 1984. Participants are individuals and organizations interested in rare plant conservation at botanical gardens and arboreta. Gathers and disseminates information regarding rare and endangered plants indigenous to the U.S. Saves seeds and cuttings of rare and endangered plants to preserve their genetic patterns. Presents educational slide show. Maintains speakers' bureau; bestows awards; compiles statistics.

★151★ Center for Resource Economics
1718 Connecticut Ave. NW, Ste. 300
Washington, DC 20009
Phone: (202)232-7933
Nonprofit organization which disseminates information on solving regional as well as global environmental problems.

★152★ Center for Science in the Public Interest
1875 Connecticut Ave. NW, Ste. 300
Washington, DC 20009
Phone: (202)265-4954
Consumer advocacy organization concerned with health, nutrition, and agriculture issues.

★153★ Center for Science Information
4252 20th St.
San Francisco, CA 94114
Phone: (415)553-8772
Educates decision makers on environmental issues concerning biotechnology.

★154★ Center for Short Lived Phenomena
PO Box 199, Harvard Sq. Sta.
Cambridge, MA 02238
Phone: (617)492-3310
Telex: (710)320-1628 WORLD
Contact: Richard Golob, Dir.
Founded: 1968. Established by the Smithsonian Institution; became a private, nonprofit organization in 1975. Specializes in the collection and dissemination of information

on oil spills worldwide. Provides users with comprehensive and authoritative reports on oil spill incidents and cleanups, related lawsuits, and the impact of oil spills on the environment. CSLP "has an international reputation for timeliness, objectivity, and accuracy in reporting information" on oil spill events. Compiles annual statistics on spill occurrence and volume. Undertakes information searches, compilations, and investigations on a contractual basis.

★155★ Center for the Study of Law and Politics
2962 Fillmore St.
San Francisco, CA 94123
Phone: (415)775-0791
Fax: (415)775-4159
Contact: Walter McGuire, Pres.
Founded: 1979. ***Members:*** 100. Serves as an environmental information service to cities and communities that maintain global cities projects. Studies public policy issues. Conducts annual workshop.

★156★ Cetacean Society International (CSI)
PO Box 290145
Wethersfield, CT 06109-0145
Phone: (203)563-6444
Contact: Dr. Robbins Barstow, Exec. Officer
Founded: 1974. ***Members:*** 350. Individuals in 25 countries interested in the preservation and conservation of cetaceans, including whales, dolphins, and porpoises. Promotes the elimination of outlaw whaling and trading in whale products; works to expose the actions of whalers. Supports strong legislation on driftnet fishing and legal protection for small cetaceans; works to establish whale sanctuaries and assists in rescuing stranded whales. Encourages effective international ocean pollution controls. Provides limited support for benign research projects. Sponsors whalewatching trips. Supports the conservation efforts of the International Whaling Commission ***Former Name(s):*** Connecticut Cetacean Society (1986).

★157★ Charles Darwin Foundation for the Galapagos Isles
National Zoological Park
Washington, DC 20008
Phone: (202)673-4705
Fax: (202)673-4607
Contact: Craig MacFarland, Pres.
Founded: 1959. Supports, organizes, and administers research work at a station authorized by the government of Ecuador, with primary emphasis on science and conservation. Provides for the protection of the wildlife of the Galapagos Islands; disseminates research findings; encourages and aids scientific education, particularly in Ecuador. Maintains museum with collection of Galapagos biological specimens. Awards scholarships to Ecuadorian science students for work at the Charles Darwin Research Station in the Galapagos. Conducts research and specialized education programs. Maintains library of scientific papers relating to the Galapagos and other topics.

★158★ Chihuahuan Desert Research Institute (CDRI)
Box 1334
Alpine, TX 79831
Phone: (915)837-8370
Contact: Dennis J. Miller, Exec.Dir.
Founded: 1974. ***Members:*** 600. Professionals and students of all disciplines. Seeks to promote an understanding and appreciation of the Chihuahuan Desert region of the U.S. and Mexico through scientific research and public education. (The region, which for the most part is sparsely populated, contains potentially valuable undeveloped resources.) Conducts its own research programs, expedites the research efforts of others, and serves as clearinghouse for information relating to the Chihuahuan Desert. Programs include: basic and applied research in the field and laboratories; monitoring the status of endangered wildlife and their habitat and evaluating the potential economic value of desert plants; development of a visitor complex; film production; adult and high school field seminars. Sponsors charitable programs and children's services. Bestows awards and scholarships; maintains museum and biographical archives; compiles statistics. Provides consulting services, teaching materials, and teacher training workshops.

★159★ Children of the Green Earth
PO Box 31550
Seattle, WA 98103
Phone: (206)781-0852
Contact: Michael Soule, Exec.Dir.
Founded: 1980. ***Members:*** 450. Individuals with an interest in promoting and organizing responsible children's tree planting projects and other educational activities. Seeks to "regreen the earth through the spiritual and practical act of planting trees" and by helping children care for trees, seeds, and seedlings in places where planting them will help to renew the land. Focuses on enhancing children's practical work with the earth, and on assisting children of other cultures who are doing similar work. Sponsors international project involving young people from various countries. Develops, collects, and distributes resources to help people begin efforts on a local level; maintains extensive library.

★160★ Citizen's Clearinghouse for Hazardous Wastes (CCHW)
PO Box 926
Arlington, VA 22216
Phone: (703)276-7070
Contact: Lois Marie Gibbs, Exec.Dir.
Founded: 1981. ***Members:*** 19,000. Individuals who live near hazardous waste dumps. Is concerned with the likelihood of adverse physical effects on adults and children from contact with toxic chemicals and other hazardous wastes. Established as a direct result of the problems encountered by the Love Canal Homeowners Association. Provides information and guidance in dealing with the problem; visits sites to determine the severity of the situation. Encourages members to pressure their lawmakers to take action. Conducts research on chemicals to determine dangerous levels of usage. Maintains speakers' bureau and library of 2000 volumes on waste management technology.

★161★ Citizens for a Better Environment (CBE)
407 S. Dearborn, Ste. 1775
Chicago, IL 60605
Phone: (312)939-1530
Contact: William Davis, Pres.
Founded: 1971. ***Members:*** 25,000. Citizens concerned with environmental protection. Works to reduce exposure to toxic substances in air, water, and land. Focuses on research, public information, and advocacy, including formal and informal interaction with policy-making bodies on a state, regional, and national level. A trained staff of scientists, research associates, and policy experts evaluate specific problems, testify at administrative hearings, and file suits in state and federal courts. Conducts public education program; provides technical assistance to local residents and community-based organizations, including minority and low-income urban dwellers. Maintains substantial library of books, reports, and articles on environmental pollution issues.

★162★ Citizens for Animals, Resources and Environment (CARE)
PO Box 18772
Milwaukee, WI 53218
Phone: (414)466-1250
Contact: Debi Zweifel, Dir.
Founded: 1989. Informational network for those interested in promoting humane treatment for all animals, wise use of the earth's resources, and environmental protection. Sponsors support groups; maintains speakers' bureau. Currently local, but plans to expand nationally.

★163★ Citizens for Sensible Control of Acid Rain (CSCAR)
1301 Connecticut Ave. NW, Ste. 700
Washington, DC 20036
Phone: (202)659-0330
Founded: 1983. ***Members:*** 135,000. Individuals organized and funded by electric, coal, and manufacturing companies. Purpose is to educate the public on clean air policy initiatives. Encourages individuals to write to Congress on clean air policy. Disseminates information on acid rain and clean coal technology issues.

★164★ Clean Air Working Group
818 Connecticut Ave. NW, Ste. 900
Washington, DC 20006
Phone: (202)857-0370
Contact: William D. Fay, Admin.
Founded: 1988. ***Members:*** 1950. Coalition of industries, large and small businesses, and trade associations. Works to ensure effective and responsible clean air policies in the U.S. Believes that concern for the environment should be balanced with a concern for the impact of regulation on the economy and employment, and that such regulations should not impose an undue burden on the economy. Operates speakers' bureau.

★165★ Clean Fuels Development Coalition (CFDC)
1129 20th St. NW, Ste. 500
Washington, DC 20036
Phone: (202)822-1715
Fax: (202)293-0147
Contact: Douglas A. Durante, Rep.
Founded: 1988. Advocates the development of a national energy policy that addresses environmental concerns and provides for increased production and use of nonpetroleum motor fuels. Has identified an environmental safe energy mix that included the use of ethanol, methanol, natural gas, ethers, electricity, and other natural resources. Provides support in areas such as education, promotion, and research; represents members' interests before Congress and federal agencies. Analyzes pertinent legislation and regulatory action; disseminates environmental, production, and usage information.

★166★ Clean Harbors Cooperative (CHC)
PO Box 1375
1200 State St.
Perth Amboy, NJ 08862
Phone: (201)738-2438
Contact: Edward M. Wirkowski, Mgr.
Founded: 1977. A joint venture of 10 petroleum companies including British Petroleum, Chevron, Citgo, Exxon, Mobil, Royal,

Shell Oil, Stolt Terminals, Sun Oil, and Texaco. Makes available oil spill clean-up equipment and trained equipment operators to member companies in the greater New York Harbor area who must then do the actual work of oil spill removal. Assists nonmember companies for a rental fee at the request of the U.S. Coast Guard.

★167★ Clean Ocean Action
PO Box 505
Sandy Hook, NJ 07732
Phone: (201)872-0111
Concerned about the ocean waters off the coasts of New Jersey and New York.

★168★ Clean Sites (CSI)
1199 N. Fairfax St.
Alexandria, VA 22314
Phone: (703)683-8522
Contact: Thomas Grumbly, Pres.
Founded: 1984. Representatives of environmental organizations and industries. To bring together parties responsible for abandoned hazardous waste sites, enabling them to negotiate a settlement and determine who will be financially responsible for the cleanup. Selects hazardous waste sites that need work and arranges for cleanup. Provides financial management services to collect, invest, and disburse responsible parties' funds for cleanup. Conducts seminars on alternative dispute resolution, research, and policy analysis of problems impeding the cleanup of hazardous waste.

★169★ Clean Water Action
1320 18th St. NW
Washington, DC 20003
Phone: (202)457-1286
Contact: David Zwick, Dir.
Founded: 1971. National citizen action organization established to work for strong pollution controls and safe drinking water. Active in toxic protection for communities and workplaces, preservation of nation's wetlands, and promotion of alternative treatment technologies that recycle wastes. CWA was influential in the 1986 Superfund for Toxic Cleanup. ***Former Name(s):*** Fishermen's Clean Water Action Project (1975); Clean Water Action Project (1989).

★170★ Clean Water Fund (CWF)
1320 18th St. NW, 3rd Fl.
Washington, DC 20036
Phone: (202)457-1286
Contact: David Zwick, Exec.Dir.
Founded: 1974. Research and educational organization promoting public interest and involvement in issues related to water, toxic materials, and natural resources. Participants include scientific and policy experts, writers of environmental legislation, politicians, and grass roots organizers. Works to improve the effectiveness of local environmental groups. Seeks to: protect marine habitats; secure safe water supplies for the future through groundwater conservation and restricted use of pesticides; stop environmental crime and prevent pollution; devise practical solutions to the U.S. solid waste disposal crisis. Encourages cooperation between business, labor, sportsmen, and conservationists in devising solutions to environmental problems. Provides research, scientific, and technical assistance to local environmental organizations whose programs emphasize: development of long-term solutions to environmental problems; close public scrutiny of government agencies, public officials, and corporations to ensure their compliance with environmental protection laws and regulations; coalition building and networking to strengthen the environmental movement nationwide. Compiles statistics.

★171★ Climate Institute
316 Pennsylvania Ave. SE, Ste. 403
Washington, DC 20003
Phone: (202)547-0104
Serves as a bridge between scientists and decision-makers on global warming and ozone depletion.

★172★ Coalition Against Pipeline Pollution (CAP)
PO Box 39A60
Los Angeles, CA 90039
Phone: (213)222-5951
Contact: Michelle Grumet, Exec. Officer
Founded: 1984. Petitions the legislature on environmental concerns, especially those that deal with crude oil and toxic waste.

★173★ Coalition for Environmentally Responsible Economics
711 Atlantic Ave.
Boston, MA 02111
Phone: (617)451-0927
Developed the Valdez Principles, a set of 10 corporate environmental responsibility principles to prevent environmental disasters and degradation.

★174★ Coalition for Responsible Waste Incineration (CRWI)
1330 Connecticut Ave. NW, Ste. 300
Washington, DC 20036
Phone: (202)659-0060
Contact: William S. Murray Ph.D., Exec.Dir.
Founded: 1987. ***Members:*** 17. Manufacturing companies; academic institutions; interested individuals and organizations. Promotes responsible incineration of industrial wastes as part of an overall waste management strategy. Serves as a forum for exchange of information among members and supplies members with technical, safety, health, and environmental information concerning waste incineration. Provides information on industrial incineration systems to the public, the media, and government officials at the local, state, and federal levels. Monitors and reports on the formulation of legislative and regulatory guidelines for industrial waste incineration. Encourages research in incineration.

★175★ Coalition for Scenic Beauty
216 7th St. SE
Washington, DC 20003
Phone: (202)546-1100
Protects scenic resources in the U.S.

★176★ Coalition on Resource Recovery and the Environment (CORRE)
U.S. Conf. of Mayors. Shaub
1620 I St. NW, Ste. 600
Washington, DC 20006
Phone: (202)293-7330
Fax: (202)293-2352
Contact: Dr. Walter M. Shaub, Technical Dir.
Founded: 1986. ***Members:*** 40. Local and regional governments and private companies. Seeks to provide information about resource recovery and related environmental issues. CORRE assumes no position concerning the appropriateness of one technology compared to others, but believes that successful waste management is an "integrated utilization of many technologies which, taken as a whole, are best selected by an informed public and informed public officials." Provides research reports on resource recovery. Operates speakers' bureau; maintains library of 1500 technical reports.

★177★ Coastal Conservation Association (CCA)
4801 Woodway, Ste. 220 W.
Houston, TX 77056
Phone: (713)626-4222
Fax: (713)951-3801
Contact: Walter W. Fondren III, Chm.
Founded: 1977. ***Members:*** 31,000. Organizations, corporations, and individuals interested in conserving the natural resources of U.S. saltwater coastal areas. Seeks to advance the protection and conservation of all marine life. Operates GCCA/John Wilson Hatchery near Corpus Christi, Texas, to bolster the redfish population in the Gulf of Mexico. Lobbies state governments to enact legislation favorable to conservation and sport fishing. Conducts seminars regarding current topics in marine conservation; bestows awards; maintains New Tide youth program. Contributes funds for marine ecological research. ***Former Name(s):*** Gulf Coast Conservation Association (1985).

★178★ Coastal Society
5410 Grosvenor Ln., Ste. 110
Bethesda, MD 20814
Phone: (301)897-8616
Promotes education on coastal environments.

★179★ Coastal States Organization
444 N. Capitol St. NW, Ste. 312
Washington, DC 20001
Phone: (202)628-9636
Represents coastal areas in ocean and coastal affairs.

★180★ Committee for Environmentally Effective Packaging (CEEP)
1000 Connecticut Ave., Ste. 304
Washington, DC 20036
Phone: (202)659-4805
Contact: James C. Benfield, Exec.Dir.
Founded: 1989. ***Members:*** 12. Corporations and trade associations. Educational and lobbying group that focuses on legislation at city, county, and state levels on the use of polystyrene (a transparent thermoplastic) in foodservice packaging.

★181★ Committee for the Preservation of the Tule Elk (CPTE)
PO Box 3696
San Diego, CA 92103
Phone: (619)485-0626
Contact: Jolene W. Steigerwalt, Sec.
Founded: 1960. ***Members:*** 2065. Individuals (2000) and organizations (65) interested in the preservation of wildlife, especially rare species, and in the aesthetic enjoyment of nature. Goal is to protect and preserve the Tule Elk. Conducts color slide lecture programs, exhibits, and field trips to disseminate information about the Tule Elk and its habitat and other wildlife. Maintains library of visual materials, slides, and brochures. Bestows awards; maintains speakers' bureau; conducts specialized education and children's services.

★182★ Community and Environmental Defense Association
PO Box 206
Maryland Line, MD 21105-0206
Phone: (301)329-8194
Shows citizens how to protect home and community from land development impacts and environmental threats.

★183★ Community Environmental Council (CEC)
930 Miramonte Dr.
Santa Barbara, CA 93109
Phone: (805)963-0583
Fax: (805)962-9080
Contact: Paul Relis, Dir.
Founded: 1970. ***Members:*** 600. Individuals and environmental organizations whose prime objective is environmental education, research, and consultation. Current focus is on waste management policy and technology, and land-use policy. Operates 4 recycling centers and 3 community gardens. Offers resident internships; conducts policy seminars.

★184★ Concern
1794 Columbia Rd. NW
Washington, DC 20009
Phone: (202)328-8160
Contact: Susan Boyd, Exec.Dir.
Founded: 1970. Provides environmental information to individuals and groups and encourages them to act in their communities. Funded by contributions from individuals, foundation grants, and proceeds from the sale of its publications.

★185★ Concerned Neighbors in Action (CNA)
PO Box 3847
Riverside, CA 92519
Contact: Penny Newman, Chwm.
Founded: 1979. ***Members:*** 2000. Families living near the Stringellow acid pits, a hazardous waste dump near Los Angeles, CA, who conduct advocacy activities for cleanup of the site. Though based in California, CNA disseminates information on hazardous waste nationwide. Compiles statistics; maintains speakers' bureau.

★186★ Connecticut River Watershed Council (CRWC)
125 Combs Rd.
Easthampton, MA 01027
Phone: (413)584-0057
Founded: 1952. ***Members:*** 2400. Individuals, corporations, businesses, and conservation organizations. Works for conservation and wise use of natural resources in the Connecticut River valley. Bestows annual conservation awards to individuals or groups for meritorius service to valley conservation. Maintains speakers' bureau; conducts public education programs; prepares reports; provides technical advisory service.

★187★ Conservation and Research Foundation (CRF)
240 Arapahoe E.
Lake Quivira, KS 66106
Phone: (913)268-0076
Contact: Dr. Richard H. Goodwin Sr., Pres.
Founded: 1953. Seeks to: encourage biological research; promote conservation of renewable natural resources; deepen the understanding of the relationship between humans and the environment. Offers conservation and research grants; conducts workshops; bestows Jeanette Siron Pelton Award for outstanding published contributions in experimental plant morphology.

★188★ Conservation Education Association (CEA)
Missouri Department of Conservation
Box 180
Jefferson City, MO 65536
Phone: (314)751-4115
Contact: Charles Jordan, Exec. Officer
Founded: 1947. ***Members:*** 400. Conservationists, scientists, educators, and others interested in improving conservation education in public schools, teacher training institutions, and organization programs. ***Former Name(s):*** National Committee on Policies in Conservation Education (1953).

★189★ Conservation Foundation
1250 24th St. NW, Ste. 400
Washington, DC 20037
Phone: (202)293-4800
Contact: Kathryn Fuller, Pres.
Founded: 1948. Encourages wise management of the earth's resources through research and communication. Conducts programs in land use (rural resources, urban conservation, public lands), water resources, environmental dispute resolution, environmental institutions and trends, and pollution and toxic substances control. Sponsors interdisciplinary research, education, and information programs to develop knowledge, improve techniques, and stimulate public and private awareness and action to improve the quality of the environment. Maintains 10,000 volume library.

★190★ Conservation Fund
1800 N. Kent St., Ste. 1120
Arlington, VA 22209
Phone: (703)525-6300
Fax: (703)525-4610
Contact: Patrick F. Noonan, Pres.
Established to work with public and private organizations and agencies to protect land, including parks, wildlife habitats, and historic sites. Aims to advance conservation through creative ideas and new resources. Projects include: American Greenways, helping establish public and private open space corridors to link natural, historic, and recreation areas; Civil War Battlefield Campaign, preserving historic battlefield lands; Conservation Leadership, increasing the effectiveness of nonprofit conservation organizations; Land Advisory Service, providing specialized skills in environmental land planning; Spring and Groundwater Institute, using new techniques to protect groundwater reserves.

★191★ Conservation Law Foundation of New England
3 Joy St.
Boston, MA 02108-1497
Phone: (617)742-2540
Promotes environmental law, resource management, and environmental protection. Lobbies in the Congress for strong environmental legislation.

★192★ Conservation Treaty Support Fund (CTSF)
3705 Cardiff Rd.
Chevy Chase, MD 20815
Phone: (301)654-3150
Fax: (301)652-6390
Contact: George A. Furness Jr., Pres.
Founded: 1986. Individuals supporting international treaties to conserve wild natural resources. Promotes public awareness and understanding of conservation treaties and their goals; works to enhance public support, compliance, and funding. Assists conservation treaties in obtaining funding from individuals, corporations, foundations, and government agencies. Maintains Conservation Treaty Support Forces and CITES Ambassadors Club, which provide financial assistance to international conservation efforts including the Convention on Wetlands of International Importance.

★193★ Consumer Pesticide Project
425 Mississippi St.
San Francisco, CA 94105
Phone: (415)826-6314
Works to eliminate dangerous pesticides from the environment.

★194★ Context Institute
PO Box 11470
Bainbridge Island, WA 98110
Phone: (206)842-0216
Promotes a humane society through "widespread, effective, direct participation."

★195★ Coolidge Center for Environmental Leadership (CCEL)
1675 Massachusetts Ave., Ste. 4
Cambridge, MA 02138
Phone: (617)864-5085
Fax: (617)864-6503
Contact: Robert Singer, Exec.Dir.
Founded: 1983. ***Members:*** 400. Seeks to increase awareness of the environment and sustainable development and to educate graduate students and mid-career professionals from developing nations on the environmental implications and responsibilities of their future decisions as leaders. Promotes leadership in all professions involving the environment. The center was created to honor and perpetuate the work of Harold J. Coolidge (1904-85), conservationist and author of scientific publications on international conservation. Conducts workshops and retreats on selected international environment/development topics; offers programs in conjunction with other institutions. Maintains a network of foreign graduate and nongovernmental organizations. Maintains resource center and 5000 volume library of books, transcripts, proceedings, and related materials. Conducts programs and provides materials for educators interested in teaching about international environmental issues and sustainable development.

★196★ Council on Economic Priorities
30 Irving Pl.
New York, NY 10003
Phone: (212)420-1133
Nonprofit research organization which analyzes public interest issues dealing with corporate social responsibility, the environment, and national security.

★197★ Council on Plastics and Packaging in the Environment (COPPE)
1275 K St. NW, Ste. 900
Washington, DC 20005
Phone: (202)789-1310
Fax: (202)289-1389
Contact: Edward J. Stana, Exec.Dir.
Founded: 1986. ***Members:*** 55. Plastic packaging manufacturers, resin suppliers, marketers of consumer packaging, recyclers, and related trade associations. Works to: increase awareness of solid waste management problems; develop and support solutions that promote a balanced combination of source reduction, recycling, waste-to-energy recovery, and landfilling. Provides a forum for the exchange of technical and scientific information between the industry, research institutions, environmental groups, government bodies, and the media. Serves as a resource for information about plastic and other packaging.

★198★ The Cousteau Society (TCS)
930 W. 21st St.
Norfolk, VA 23517
Phone: (804)627-1144
Fax: (804)627-7547

Contact: Jacques-Yves Cousteau, Pres.
Founded: 1973. ***Members:*** 300,000. Environmental education organization dedicated to the protection and improvement of the quality of life for present and future generations. Objectives are education, research, and evaluation of man-nature interrelationships. Organizes Project Ocean Search, two-week summer field trips designed to study marine ecosystems. Conducts research and lectures.

★199★ Cultural Survival
11 Divinity Ave.
Cambridge, MA 02138
Phone: (617)495-2562
Organization works to import sustainably managed rain forest products to the U.S.

★200★ Cycad Society
1161 Phyllis Ct.
Mountain View, CA 94040
Phone: (415)964-7898
Contact: David S. Mayo, Sec.-Treas.
Founded: 1977. ***Members:*** 400. International organization of individuals interested in conservation and propagation of endangered cycad species. Through the exchange of information about all phases of horticultural endeavor, ecology in habitat, and other scientific efforts, the society hopes to preserve and enjoy the species in nature. Conducts research on artificial propagation, pollen, and embryo culture; maintains seed bank.

★201★ Defenders of Wildlife
1244 19th St. NW
Washington, DC 20036
Phone: (202)659-9510
Fax: (202)833-3349
Contact: M. Rupert Cutler, Pres.
Founded: 1947. ***Members:*** 88,000. Persons interested in wildlife and conservation. Promotes the preservation and protection of wildlife and wildlife habitat through education, litigation, research, and advocacy. Programs focus on habitat preservation for biological diversity, prevention of wildlife mortality from pesticides and entanglement in plastic refuse, endangered species recovery, and wildlife on public lands such as wildlife refuges and marine sanctuaries. Maintains speakers' bureau; provides wildlife education and information; compiles statistics. ***Former Name(s):*** Defenders of Furbearers.

★202★ Desert Bighorn Council
1500 N. Decatur Blvd.
Las Vegas, NV 89108
Phone: (602)621-3845
Conservation and protection of bighorn sheep.

★203★ Desert Fishes Council (DFC)
PO Box 337
Bishop, CA 93514
Phone: (619)872-8751
Contact: E. P. Pister, Exec.Sec.
Founded: 1970. ***Members:*** 500. Scientists, resource specialists, members of conservation organizations, and individuals concerned with long-term environmental values. Originally concerned with native fish of the Death Valley region, the group's interest has spread to habitat integrity within all deserts of Mexico and the southwestern U.S. Promotes proper management of this resource; encourages research relative to desert ecosystems. Maintains informal library.

★204★ Desert Protective Council (DPC)
PO Box 4294
Palm Springs, CA 92263
Phone: (619)397-4264
Contact: Mary Swedelius, Exec.Dir.
Founded: 1954. ***Members:*** 400. Persons interested in safeguarding desert areas of unique, scenic, scientific, historical, spiritual, and recreational value. Seeks to educate children and adults to promote a better understanding of the desert. Works to bring about establishment of wildlife sanctuaries for protection of indigenous plants and animals. The Desert Protective Council Education Foundation, a subdivision of the council formed in 1960, handles educational activities and distributes desert and wildlife conservation articles. Bestows awards; has established Anza-Borrego Foundation and Coachella Valley Ecological Reserve Foundation.

★205★ Desert Tortoise Council (DTC)
PO Box 1738
Palm Desert, CA 92261-1738
Phone: (619)341-8449
Contact: Terrie Correll, Sec.
Founded: 1975. ***Members:*** 175. State and federal biologists, herpetologists, universities, museums, zoos, turtle and tortoise clubs, other conservation-oriented groups, and concerned individuals. Goal is to ensure the survival of viable populations of the desert tortoise (gopherus agassizii) throughout its existing range. Serves in a professional advisory capacity on matters involving management, conservation, and protection of desert tortoises. Stimulates and encourages studies on the status and phases of life history, biology, physiology, management, and protection of desert tortoises. Acts as information clearinghouse for agencies, organizations, and individuals engaged in work on desert tortoises. Bestows awards.

★206★ Desert Tortoise Preserve Committee (DTPC)
PO Box 453
Ridgecrest, CA 93556
Phone: (714)884-5906
Contact: Jean E. Jones, Corr.Sec. & Editor
Founded: 1974. ***Members:*** 600. Individuals, conservation organizations, wildlife groups, and scientists interested in the protection and preservation of the Desert Tortoise Natural Area and adjacent geographic range. (The Desert Tortoise Natural Area encompasses a 38 square mile area in the northwest Mojave Desert in Fremont Valley, CA, and is believed to have the finest known population of the desert tortoise, gopherus agassizii, the official California State Reptile.) To assure the continued survival of viable populations of the desert tortoise. Primary goal is to raise funds for purchasing privately owned parcels of land within the Desert Tortoise Natural Area. Cooperates with the Bureau of Land Management. Conducts conservation education programs and guided tours for schools, museums, and other groups. Bestows awards; maintains speakers' bureau.

★207★ Ducks Unlimited
One Waterfowl Way
Long Grove, IL 60047
Phone: (708)438-4300
Fax: (708)438-9236
Contact: Matthew B. Connolly Jr., Exec.V.Pres.
Founded: 1937. ***Members:*** 550,000. Conservationists in the U.S., Canada, Mexico, and New Zealand interested in migratory waterfowl and wildlife habitat conservation. Works to restore or build natural wetland areas for migratory waterfowl in the prairie provinces of Canada, which provide 70 percent of North America's wild geese and ducks, in prime nesting, staging, and wintering areas of the U.S., and in Mexico where millions of waterfowl spend winter. The American group raises funds for construction and rehabilitation work carried on by the field operating organizations. Maintains 16mm film library.

★208★ Earth Ecology Foundation
903 E. Fedora
Fresno, CA 93704
Phone: (209)222-2785
Contact: Erik Wunstell, Dir.
Founded: 1980. ***Members:*** 300. Individuals interested in earth science and human ecology. Purposes are: to study the interrelationships between humans, technology, and nature; to provide solutions to ecological problems; to examine technological culture and its effect on society and the environment; to promote the humane use of the earth. Conducts research and gathers information on earth ecology. Maintains 1000 volume library on ecology. Plans to open a research laboratory, science museum, nature center, film archive, and botanical garden.

★209★ Earth First!
PO Box 5871
Tucson, AZ 85703
Contact: John Davis, Editor
Founded: 1980. ***Members:*** 10,000. Environmentalists dedicated to the preservation of natural diversity. Promotes a biocentric world view. Conducts research and compiles statistics on remaining wildlands and preservation methods. Proposes a series of vast preserves for the U.S. Holds environmental rallies nationwide. Sponsors Earth First! Road Show.

★210★ Earth Island Institute
300 Broadway, Ste. 28
San Francisco, CA 94133
Phone: (415)788-3666
Fax: (415)788-7324
Telex: 650-2829302 MCI UW
Contact: David R. Brower, Chm.
Founded: 1985. ***Members:*** 33,000. Individuals working to coordinate environmental and wildlife protection projects. Seeks to prevent the destruction of the environment; promotes ecologically sound development in order to preserve the natural environment and diversity of wildlife. Sponsors Brower Fund to provide funding for environmental and peace projects; coordinates the Green Education and Development Fund, a network of groups addressing the future of environmental politics; administers International Marine Mammal Project, which works to protect whales and dolphins through the prevention of the slaughter of dolphins caught in tuna nets; sponsors Environmental Project on Central America. Compiles statistics; maintains speakers' bureau and 2000 volume library.

★211★ Earth Regeneration Society (ERS)
1442A Walnut St., No. 57
Berkeley, CA 94709
Phone: (415)525-7723
Contact: Alden Bryant, Pres.
Founded: 1983. ***Members:*** 500. Scientists and other individuals organized to study and develop practical and scientific solutions to environmental issues. Concerns include climate stabilization, reduction of atmospheric carbon dioxide through soil remineralization, reforestation, conservation, and the

development of alternative energy technology to abate the glaciation process. Maintains speakers' bureau; conducts research and educational programs.

★212★ Earth Society Foundation (ESF)
585 Fifth Ave.
New York, NY 10017
Phone: (212)935-9423
Fax: (718)366-7028
Contact: John McConnell, Chm.
Founded: 1970. Participants are individuals interested in environmental and sociological issues. Acts as an information clearinghouse; supports groups and persons concerned with individual rights, peace, and environmental care and protection of the earth. Fosters worldwide participation in Earth Day celebrations. Sponsors research programs; maintains archives. Operates speakers' bureau and charitable program; bestows awards.

★213★ Earthmind
PO Box 743
Mariposa, CA 95338
Contact: Michael A. Hackleman, Pres.
Founded: 1972. Individuals involved in research and education concerning alternative energy sources, organic gardening, and healthful and more self-reliant living. Conducts slide shows, lectures, and field trips; maintains library containing many rare works on wind, solar, and other energy forms.

★214★ EarthNet
PO Box 330072
Kahului, HI 96733
Phone: (808)872-6090
Online systems, database access network.

★215★ EarthSave
PO Box 949
Felton, CA 95018
Phone: (408)423-4069
Disseminates education materials on health and nutrition.

★216★ EarthVote International
777 U. N. Plaza, 12th Fl.
New York, NY 10017
Phone: (212)986-1882
Contact: Nicholas Dunlop, Exec. Officer
Founded: 1988. Promotes increased prominence for global survival issues, such as disarmament and environmental protection, in national election campaigns worldwide; efforts are currently concentrated in Brazil, Britain, Federal Republic of Germany, France, India, Japan, U.S., and USSR. Seeks to increase the United Nation's capacity to maintain peace, and promotes demilitarization of international relations. Encourages the formation of new international structures to protect the global environment. ***Former Name(s):*** Earthvote Network (1991).

★217★ EarthWise
P.O. Box 403
Ardmore, OK 73402
Sponsors "EarthFair" designed to introduce people to Earth issues.

★218★ Eastern Mineral Law Foundation (EMLF)
West Virginia University Law Center
PO Box 6130
Morgantown, WV 26506
Phone: (304)293-2470
Fax: (304)293-7654
Contact: Sharon J. Daniels, Exec.Dir.
Founded: 1979. ***Members:*** 360. Law firms, corporations, law schools, associations, and individuals interested in the development of natural resources. Established to stimulate research, discussion, and dissemination of information on the legal problems in the field. Sponsors institutes, educational programs, and legal writing competitions; offers law student scholarships and grants.

★219★ Ecological Society of America (ESA)
Arizona State University
Center for Environmental Studies
Tempe, AZ 85287
Phone: (602)965-3000
Contact: Duncan T. Patten, Business Mgr.
Founded: 1915. ***Members:*** 6100. Educators, professional ecologists, and scientists interested in the study of plants, animals, and humans in relation to their environment. Seeks to develop better understanding of biological processes and their contribution to agriculture, forestry, wildlife and range management, fisheries, industry, public health, and conservation. Bestows awards.

★220★ Ecology Center
2530 San Pablo Ave.
Berkeley, CA 94702
Phone: (415)548-2220

★221★ EcoNet
3228 Sacramento St.
San Francisco, CA 94114
Phone: (415)923-0900
Online systems, database access network.

★222★ Educational Communications, Inc.
PO Box 35473
Los Angeles, CA 90035
Phone: (213)559-9160
Promotes education on environmental conservation.

★223★ Elephant Interest Group (EIG)
106 E. Hickory Grove
Bloomfield Hills, MI 48013
Phone: (313)540-3947
Contact: Hezy Shoshani
Founded: 1977. ***Members:*** 500. University faculty and students, farmers, zoo keepers, circus animal trainers, and others interested in the study of elephants. Goals are to: promote interest in and increase public knowledge of elephants; work to protect elephant species; collect and disseminate information needed for education, and research on, and conservation of elephants. Maintains small library on elephants and related species. Works in cooperation with the American Society of Mammalogists, East African Wildlife Society, International Union for Conservation of Nature and Natural Resources, and World Wildlife Fund.

★224★ Eleventh Commandment Fellowship (ECF)
PO Box 14667
San Francisco, CA 94114
Phone: (415)626-6064
Contact: Frederick W. Krueger, Coordinator
Founded: 1979. ***Members:*** 3800. Individuals of all faiths who accept and practice the 11th Commandment as an environmental ethic. (Articulated by Roderick Nash and later expanded by Vincent Rossi and based on interpretive readings of Holy Scripture, the 11th Commandment states: "The earth is the Lord's and the fullness thereof; thou shall not despoil the earth nor destroy the life thereon.") To promote and urge the practice of the 11th Commandment as a benevolent and healing ethic of the environment, teach the commandment's implications, and address what the fellowship feels are the spiritual roots of environmental problems. Believes that environmental problems of pollution require a change in human attitudes based on a sense of the sacredness of nature and an acknowledgment of an urgent need to reintegrate human society into the earth's environment. Sponsors seminars on philosophy and practice of earth stewardship; conducts local ecology action, wilderness retreats, youth programs, and outings. Maintains 2000 volume library on Christian ecology.

★225★ Elmwood Institute
PO Box 5765
Berkeley, CA 94705-0765
Phone: (415)845-4595
Fax: (415)843-9398
Contact: Philippa Winkler, Exec.Dir.
Founded: 1983. ***Members:*** 1300. Acts as a forum for the formulation, discussion, and practical application of "Ecothinking," a philosophy which embodies awareness of global interdependence, ecological wisdom, peace and nonviolence, human rights, social and economic justice, personal and social responsibility, grassroots democracy, decentralization of economic and political power, cultural diversity, post-patriarchal consciousness, and ethical and spiritual values. Serves as an intellectual resource for the Green movement. Conducts symposia, workshops, seminars, and discussions on cultural paradigms and Ecothinking; maintains speakers' bureau.

★226★ Elsa Clubs of America (ELSA)
PO Box 4572
North Hollywood, CA 91617-0572
Phone: (818)761-8387
Contact: A. Peter Rasmussen Jr., Gen.Mgr.
Founded: 1969. ***Members:*** 3000. Sponsored by Elsa Wild Animal Appeal - U.S.A. Young people up to 18 years of age. Purpose is to educate young people about and involve them in their natural environment, especially wildlife. (Clubs are named after Elsa, the lioness, who was featured in the book and the movie Born Free). Develops in-class projects and wildlife teaching kits which include fact sheets, graphics, research questions, arts and crafts projects, and posters. Maintains library.

★227★ Elsa Wild Animal Appeal - U.S.A.
PO Box 4572
North Hollywood, CA 91617-0572
Phone: (818)761-8387
Contact: A. Peter Rasmussen Jr., Gen.Mgr.
Founded: 1969. ***Members:*** 10,000. Families and individuals interested in wildlife. Founded by Joy Adamson (1910-80), author of Born Free, and named after Elsa the lioness, subject of the book. Purposes are to: further the conservation of wildlife and wild places, particularly in America; educate children on the values and needs of wildlife and the environment; promote the establishment of protective wildlife reserves and viable wildlife conservation projects.

★228★ Endangered Species Act Reauthorization Coordinating Committee (ESARCC)
1725 DeSales St. NW, Ste. 500
Washington, DC 20036
Phone: (202)429-5609
Contact: Roger E. McManus, Pres.
Founded: 1981. ***Members:*** 23. Coalition of conservation groups working to extend the Endangered Species Act and to ensure its effective implementation. Objectives are to: provide protection for all endangered and threatened animals and plants; develop an

efficient means of listing endangered or threatened species based upon the best available scientific and commercial data; encourage international cooperation in the conservation of endangered and threatened species, and the implementation of conservation agreements. Seeks to secure a strong legal base for the effective conservation and recovery of plants and animals that are now, or may become, in danger of extinction; and to ensure that the Endangered Species Act furthers the purposes and policies that it now specifies. Encourages public participation through petitions for the listing of particular species and the initiation of citizens' lawsuits; promotes state development of effective complementary conservation programs. Conducts educational, grass roots, and direct lobbying activities; organizes meetings and letter-writing and telephone campaigns. Works with the electronic and print media, and with other groups concerned about the future of the nation's wildlife.

★229★ Entanglement Network Coalition (ENC)
Defenders of Wildlife
1244 19th St. NW
Washington, DC 20036
Phone: (202)659-9510
Fax: (202)833-3349
Contact: Dr. Albert Manville II, Chair
Founded: 1983. ***Members:*** 46. Coalition of national environmental, animal welfare, and marine wildlife conservation organizations. Purpose is to eliminate hazards to the marine and freshwater ecosystems resulting from the use and disposal of nondegradable materials (especially plastics) at sea. Reports that more than one million seabirds and 100,000 marine mammals die annually from becoming entangled in nets or from eating plastic debris. Assists the federal government in seeking appropriations and drafting legislation to eliminate hazardous materials. Conducts research and prepares studies on beach and sea debris. Operates speakers' bureau. Maintains a collection of videotapes, slides, scientific papers, and press clippings.

★230★ EnviroNet
Greenpeace Action
Bldg. E
Fort Mason, CA 94123
Phone: (415)474-6767
Online systems, database access network.

★231★ Environic Foundation International (EFI)
916 St. Vincent St.
South Bend, IN 46617
Phone: (219)233-3357
Contact: Leroy S. Troyer, Pres.
Founded: 1970. ***Members:*** 15 trustees. Individuals from Canada, England, Japan, and the United States. Promotes concepts of environic design beyond those of landscape and urban planning and architecture. Develops educational programs that examine numerous areas of environmental comprehension and design, conservation, architecture, and other forms of ecological structure. Conducts research and inspections. Organizes seminars, lectures, and demonstrations; contributes to conferences and exhibitions. Bestows Environic Foundation Fellowhips. Interests include: design of subterranean accommodation (geotecture) and by the design of littoral accommodation, above, on, or below water surfaces (thalatecture); protection and conservation of the exceptional landscapes and habitats, and the restoration of ravaged industrial areas for self-sustaining purposes (rehabilitation); the recycling of all materials of human use and their positive application toward the improvement of the environment (poietic encyclement); the particular dilemma of land-water margins (littoral design); the kinetics and aesthetics of highway design (visualization); the conflicting forces arising from transportation systems, their siting, environic penalties, and economic advantages (airport locations); the adaption of historic and other structures of quality to ensure their continuing cultural influence upon the community (enarmotecture). Encourages research in energies and measurement of the phenomenon of earth energies respecting historic sites and structures of sacred significance. Conducts seminars, lectures, and inspections. Maintains library of 12,000 volumes and numerous files. Bestows Environic Foundation Fellowships. Contributes to conferences and exhibitions.

★232★ Environmental Action
1525 New Hampshire Ave. NW
Washington, DC 20036
Phone: (202)745-4870
Organization lobbies Congress for passage of strong environmental laws such as Clean Air Act and Superfund. Works directly with citizen groups on recycling and toxic pollution.

★233★ Environmental Action Coalition (EAC)
625 Broadway, 2nd Fl.
New York, NY 10012
Phone: (212)677-1601
Fax: (212)941-8728
Contact: Nancy A. Wolf, Exec.Dir.
Founded: 1970. ***Members:*** 2000. Purposes are: to educate the public about the nature and scope of major environmental problems; to provide a resource center to help concerned citizens develop positive solutions to these problems; to motivate the public to become involved in these solutions. Current activities focus on the implementation of source-separation recycling projects, monitoring resource recovery installations, urban forestry programs, water supply and quality projects, and development of environmental education materials for both children and adults. Serves as a clearinghouse for environmental services in the New York City region and other urban areas nationwide. Advises and assists groups in organizing and operating recycling collection sites. Conducts research and drafts legislative proposals designed to penalize manufacturers of nonrecyclable products. Maintains environmental education program which develops curriculum units, produces films, and conducts teacher workshops. Operates water supply and conservation service and 2000 volume library of vertical files, books, reports, and periodicals. Conducts annual Arbor Day activities.

★234★ Environmental Action Foundation (EAF)
1525 New Hampshire Ave. NW
Washington, DC 20036
Phone: (202)745-4870
Contact: Ruth Caplan, Dir.
Founded: 1970. Environmental research and educational organization that serves as a resource for concerned citizens and organizations in the areas of energy policy, toxic substances, and solid waste reduction. Is currently concentrating on energy efficiency, utility deregulation, biological pesticides, plutonium production, solid waste management, and toxic substances. Promotes solar energy as a safe, economical alternative to nuclear power. Works for changes in utility pricing structures to promote energy efficiency and protect persons on low and fixed incomes. Advocates recycling, source reduction and control of hazardous waste, energy efficiency measures, and renewable energy sources. Operates Energy Project, which acts as resource and information clearinghouse. ***Former Name(s):*** Environmental Resource (1972).

★235★ Environmental and Energy Study Institute
122 C St. NW, Ste. 700
Washington, DC 20001
Phone: (202)628-1400
Public policy organization aimed at producing more informed congressional debate, credible analysis, and innovative polices for environmentally sustainable development.

★236★ Environmental Compliance Institute (ECI)
Aetna Bldg., Ste. 850
2350 Lakeside Blvd.
Richardson, TX 75082-4342
Phone: (214)644-8971
Fax: (214)234-6966
Contact: John P. Douglas, Exec. Officer
Founded: 1986. ***Members:*** 151. Corporations and attorneys with an interest in environmental law and federal regulations governing waste disposal and other matters related to environmental protection. Gathers and disseminates information on current Environmental Protection Agency regulations and litigation pursuant to them. Assists in negotiations arising from environmental compliance disputes; conducts research on providing environmental compliance training to industry. Compiles statistics. Plans to establish an environmental satellite television network. ***Former Name(s):*** American Hazardous Waste Association (1989).

★237★ Environmental Defense Fund (EDF)
257 Park Ave. S
New York, NY 10010
Phone: (212)505-2100
Fax: (212)505-2375
Contact: Frederic D. Krupp, Exec.Dir.
Founded: 1967. ***Members:*** 100,000. Public interest organization of lawyers, scientists, and economists dedicated to the protection and improvement of environmental quality and public health. Works toward responsible reform of public policy in the fields of toxic chemical regulation, toxicology, radiation, air quality, energy, water resources, agriculture, ozone depletion and the greenhouse effect, wildlife, and international environment. Initiates legal action and litigation in environment-related matters; conducts environmental public service and education campaigns. Promotes research, public education, and administrative and legislative action.

★238★ Environmental Hazards Management Institute
10 Newmarket Rd.
PO Box 932
Durham, NH 03824
Phone: (603)868-1496
Educates public and private sectors on hazardous waste.

★239★ Environmental Industry Council (EIC)
1825 K St. NW, Ste. 210
Washington, DC 20006
Phone: (202)331-7706

Contact: A. John Adams, Exec.Dir.
Founded: 1976. Manufacturers of pollution control equipment and systems; industry associations involved in pollution control. Promotes coordinated and consistent national environmental policies and serves as a liaison among federal policymakers and the environmental industry.

★240★ Environmental Law Institute (ELI)
1616 P St. NW, Ste. 200
Washington, DC 20036
Phone: (202)328-5150
Contact: J. William Futrell, Pres.
Founded: 1969. Launched by the Public Law Education Institute and the Conservation Foundation. Seeks to: conduct and sponsor research on environmental law and policy; maintain a clearinghouse for information regarding environmental law; engage in related educational activities, including conferences, seminar programs, and workshops. Has conducted environmental law courses with law schools, governmental agencies, and other nonprofit organizations. Cosponsors environmental law conferences with the American Bar Association, American Law Institute, and the Smithsonian Institution. Conducts summer and annual internship program for law students. Maintains library of 20,000 volumes of legal and environmental materials. Research Division includes projects on: Air and Water Pollution; Economics; State Environmental Law; Toxic Substances and Hazardous Waste. Holds roundtable discussions and seminars.

★241★ Environmental Policy Institute (EPI)
218 D St., SE
Washington, DC 20003
Phone: (202)544-2600
Fax: (202)543-4710
Contact: Michael S. Clark, Pres.
Founded: 1974. A division of Friends of the Earth. Public interest environmental organization engaged in research, education, and lobbying activities. Works for energy conservation, environmental protection, and the increased use of renewable sources of energy, both in the U.S. and abroad. Primary areas of interest include: protection of air, water, groundwater, land, and public health against toxic chemicals and pesticides; safe, clean use of oil, coal, and gas; reduction of U.S. dependency on foreign oil, nuclear power, and weaponry; safe disposal of nuclear wastes and transportation of hazardous substances. Acts as national information center on energy and environmental issues for governmental agencies, industries, the media, and individuals. Works to see that laws, once passed, are implemented by the Executive Branch. Comments on and influences the language of regulation, using its own research. Informs citizens of major developments in the executive branch and encourages public participation in the legislative process. Promotes maximum conservation of energy and water resources; attempts to minimize the adverse impact using these resources can have on the environment, on the economy, and on society as a whole.

★242★ Environmental Project on Central America (EPOCA)
Earth Island Institute
300 Broadway, Ste. 28
San Francisco, CA 94133
Phone: (415)788-3666
Fax: (415)788-7324
Telex: 650-2829302 MIC UW
Contact: Dave Henson, Co-Coordinator
Founded: 1985. ***Members:*** 3500. A project of the Earth Island Institute. Works to stop ecological devastation in Central America; monitors U.S. policy in Central America from an environmental perspective. Seeks to educate the public about the political, economic, and environmental issues in the area, including deforestation, soil erosion, and wildlife depletion caused by pesticide use, pollution, and U.S.-funded militarization. Fosters international understanding by uniting Central and North American environmentalists; sponsors annual Environmental Restoration Brigades in Nicaragua. Sponsors research programs; compiles statistics.

★243★ Environmental Safety
733 15th St. NW, Ste. 1120
Washington, DC 20005
Phone: (202)628-0370
Fax: (202)628-0376
Contact: William Drayton, Exec.Dir.
Founded: 1984. Advisory committee of former officials of the Environmental Protection Agency; lawyers, public health officials, and environmental specialists. Primary concerns are with ensuring that EPA and other federal agencies take active steps toward implementing their environmental protection responsibilities, particularly with respect to the dangers of toxic chemicals in the air, water, food, workplace, and waste streams. Collects and disseminates information on the EPA budget, budget trends, and funding of programs regarding specific environmental issues.

★244★ Environmental Studies Institute
800 Garden St., Ste. D
Santa Barbara, CA 93101
Phone: (805)965-5010
Encourages muldisciplinary research in the field of environmental studies.

★245★ Envirosouth
PO Box 11468
Montgomery, AL 36111
Phone: (205)277-7050
Disseminates information on recycling.

★246★ Epsilon Nu Eta
PO Box 22960 A
Dept. of Environmental Health
East Tennessee State University
Johnson City, TN 37614
Phone: (615)929-5250
Contact: Phillip R. Scheuerman, Advisor
Founded: 1978. ***Members:*** 130. Bestows annual award to an outstanding environmental health professional.

★247★ Federation of Environmental Technologists (FET)
PO Box 185
Milwaukee, WI 53201
Phone: (414)251-8163
Fax: (414)251-1669
Contact: David Scherzer, Bd.Chm.
Founded: 1983. ***Members:*** 800. Industries, educational groups, governmental agencies, and consultants professionally involved in pollution control and regulation. Seeks to control pollution and support economic growth. Bestows the Wisconsin Governor's Award for Excellence in Hazardous Waste Reduction; offers scholarships. Conducts educational seminars and professional training courses.

★248★ Federation of Western Outdoor Clubs (FWOC)
365 W. 29th St.
Eugene, OR 97405
Phone: (503)686-1365
Contact: Larry Cash, Pres.
Founded: 1932. ***Members:*** 45. Outdoor clubs in the western U.S. with combined membership of 350,000. Promotes conservation of forests, wildlife, and natural features.

★249★ Felicidades Wildlife Foundation (FWF)
PO Box 490
Waynesville, NC 28786
Phone: (704)926-0192
Contact: Rosemary K. Collett, Sec.-Treas.
Founded: 1970. Individuals and organizations interested in wildlife care and rehabilitation. Objectives are to: increase awareness of the natural interdependence of all living things; care for native wildlife; aid and restore ecological systems damaged by technological developments. (Felicidades is derived from the Spanish term, casa de felicidade, which means home of the happy.) Provides assistance to wildlife in distress through the development of foster parent groups; gives aid to animals, encourages community involvement, and offers advice on establishing wildlife care programs. Stresses belief that wild animals should not be kept as pets, but should be released as soon as they are well again. Trains interested laypersons and professionals in techniques of wildlife rehabilitation and on subjects such as capture and transport, housing, diet, treatment, hand-raising of infants, and preparation for successful release through workshops featuring slide lectures and live animals. Supports wildlife rehabilitation facility. Maintains 500 volume library.

★250★ FishAmerica Foundation (FAF)
c/o Sport Fishing Institute
1010 Massachusetts Ave. NW, Ste. 320
Washington, DC 20001
Phone: (202)898-0869
Fax: (202)371-2085
Contact: Andrew J. Loftus, Dir.
Founded: 1983. Provides funding for organizations and projects involved in action-oriented grass roots efforts that work toward the preservation and enhancement of water and fishery resources in the U.S. and Canada. Encourages anglers to demonstrate personal conservation measures; works to inform private and public sectors of opportunities to become involved with water conservation issues. Has funded over 208 projects in 39 states and 7 Canadian provinces involving fishery development and conservation measures, such as development of fish spawning beds and hatcheries, implementation of weed controls, fish egg plantings and fish stocking, and installation of water aeration systems; has also supported acid rain education campaigns and acidic water reclamation project. Bestows awards.

★251★ Florida Keys Wild Bird Rehabilitation Center
233 Coral Rd.
Islamorada, FL 33036
Phone: (305)852-4486
Founded: 1985. Offers emergency therapy, rehabilitation, medical, and convalescent services to sick or injured wild birds in the Florida Keys. Collects data in order to aid in the detection of potential environmental concerns in the Florida Keys. Plans to develop captive breeding program using permanently injured wading birds of special concern.

★252★ Forest Trust
PO Box 519
Santa Fe, NM 87504-0519
Phone: (505)983-8992
Contact: Henry H. Carey, Dir.
A sponsored project of the Tides Foundation dedicated to the protection of America's

forests. Works to improve the integrity, resilience, and productivity of forest and rangelands. Programs include: forestry development assistance for rural communities, through which traditional knowledge and values are used to create sustainable economic opportunity in forest and rangelands; planning and policy assistance for the U.S. Forest Service; land trusts, protecting forests and rangelands through land acquisition and easements; land management services for private landowners engaged in ranching or forestry on their property.

★253★ Fossil Fuels Policy Action Institute
PO Drawer 8558
Fredericksburg, VA 22404
Phone: (703)371-0222
Concerned with environmental conservation.

★254★ Fossil Rim Foundation
Rte. 1, Box 210
PO Box 329
Glen Rose, TX 76043
Phone: (817)897-3147
Concerned with preservation and conservation of rare and endangered species. Maintains 3,000 acre wildlife center.

★255★ Foundation for North American Wild Sheep
720 Allen Ave.
Cody, WY 82414-3402
Phone: (307)527-6261
Fax: (307)527-7117
Contact: Karen Werbelow, Office Mgr.
Founded: 1977. ***Members:*** 5500. Works to promote the management of and to safeguard against the extinction of all species of wild sheep native to the continent of North America. Provides funds for projects in areas including biological studies, buffer land acquisition, wild sheep transplants, re-establishment of wild sheep populations in historic habitats, wildlife habitat enhancement, prevention of poaching, and advancement of sportsmen's rights.

★256★ Foundation for the Preservation and Protection of the Przewalski Horse
380 Animal Sciences Bldg.
Virginia Tech
Blacksburg, VA 24061
Phone: (703)231-9162
Contact: Dr. Arden N. Huff, Educational Adviser
Founded: 1977. Founded for the preservation and protection of the Przewalski horse, believed to be the only wild horse still in existence. (The horse is named after a colonel who served in the Russian army in the mid-1800s and who first documented the sighting of this horse. Cave drawings exhibit evidence of its living in extensive areas of Europe and Asia in prehistoric times). Of the few remaining Przewalski horses in captivity today (approximately 300), an increasing number are dying young, the breeding rate is low, and average age is decreasing due to high inbreeding. Aims are: to save the Przewalski horse from extinction; to promote the possibility of the horses holding their own in health and in accordance with their nature, in conditions as natural as possible. Stimulates and conducts scientific research on wild horses; provides information on all Przewalski horses that have lived or are presently living in captivity; promotes justified breeding management for the Przewalski horse in captivity. Conducts lectures and exhibitions.

★257★ Freshwater Foundation
2500 Shadywood Rd., Box 90
Navarre, MN 55392
Phone: (612)471-8407
Research and education on potable water.

★258★ Friends of Africa in America (FAA)
330 S. Broadway
Tarrytown, NY 10591
Phone: (914)631-5168
Contact: Clement E. Merowit, Dir.
Founded: 1962. Promotes American involvement and interest in conservation in East Africa, especially of wildlife, and translates this into African-American cooperation.

★259★ Friends of Animals
PO Box 1244
Norwalk, CT 06856
Phone: (203)866-5223
Dedicated to the humane treatment of animals, including breeding control services. Maintains a wild animal orphanage and rehabilitation center in Liberia.

★260★ Friends of the Earth (FOE)
218 D St. SE
Washington, DC 20003
Phone: (202)544-2600
Fax: (202)543-4710
Contact: Michael S. Clark, Exec. Officer
Founded: 1969. ***Members:*** 14,000. Works to: generate a new responsibility to the environment; make important environmental issues the subject of public debate; deal legally with specific environmental problems. Lobbies before Congress and state governments; issues publications to further environmental goals.

★261★ Friends of the Earth Foundation (FEF)
218 D St. SE
Washington, DC 20003
Phone: (202)544-2600
Fax: (202)543-4710
Contact: Michael S. Clark, Exec. Officer
Founded: 1972. Dedicated to the preservation, restoration, and rational use of the earth's resources. Efforts are devoted to education, research, litigation, and publishing. Promotes public education on such issues as ozone depletion, tropical deforestation, misuse of pesticides, preservation of public lands, water quality and supply, soil conservation, acid rain, and toxic wastes. Has financed research on whales and the need to protect their habitats. Monitored the impact of coal-burning plants and nuclear waste dumps in the southwestern U.S.; prepared public service spot announcements on the hazards of nuclear power; supported a lawsuit against the EPA for its "non-enforcement of the Clean Air Act" and radiation standards. Monitored enforcement of the Endangered Species Act and called shortcomings to official attention.

★262★ Friends of the Everglades
202 Park St.
Miami Springs, FL 33166
Phone: (305)888-1230

★263★ Friends of the River (FOR)
Fl. Mason Center, Bldg. C
San Francisco, CA 94123
Phone: (415)771-0400
Fax: (415)771-0301
Contact: David Bolling, Exec.Dir.
Founded: 1973. ***Members:*** 10,000. Individuals and environmental groups united to preserve free flowing rivers and streams and promote water and energy policies that make maximum use of existing resources and do minimal harm to the environment. Major focus is California and the Far West. Projects include: winning federal Wild and Scenic River status for Tuolumne, Kings, Kern, and Merced rivers; efforts to defeat construction of Auburn Dam on North Fork American River; campaign to win Wild and Scenic River protection for more than 100 rivers and streams on National Forest Land in California; campaign to reform legislation which provides unfair incentives to hydropower developers intent on damming rivers for economic profit; development of a new water agenda to help guide future wa ter policy. Sponsors work-study and internship programs, research, political organizing, and fundraising projects. Maintains 100 volume libraries in Sacramento, CA and San Francisco, CA on water policy, water law, and river preservation. Projects funded through Friends of the River Foundation. Bestows awards; maintains speakers' bureau.

★264★ Friends of the Sea Lion Marine Mammal Center
20612 Laguna Canyon Rd.
Laguna Beach, CA 92651
Phone: (714)494-3050
Contact: W. H. Ford, Exec. Officer
Founded: 1971. ***Members:*** 2500. Individuals united to aid sick or injured marine animals and then return them to their natural habitats. Educates members and the public about marine wildlife and how to aid them when they are in trouble. Conducts citizen training for beached marine animals, basic research for treatment of beached animals, and lecture series. Maintains library. Bestows annual award to person most involved in treating beached animals.

★265★ Friends of the Sea Otter (FSO)
Box 221220
Carmel, CA 93922
Phone: (408)373-2747
Fax: (408)373-2749
Contact: Richard Magruder, Exec.Dir.
Founded: 1968. ***Members:*** 5000. Citizens organized to aid in the protection and maintenance of a healthy population of the southern sea otter and its marine habitat along the California coast. Works to educate the public. Monitors and alerts members to actions affecting the otter's welfare.

★266★ Game Conservation International (GAMECO)
PO Box 17444
San Antonio, TX 78217
Phone: (512)824-7509
Contact: Paula McGehee, Exec.Dir.
Founded: 1967. ***Members:*** 1000. Individuals interested in wildlife conservation.

★267★ GemNet
Global Education Motivators
Chestnut Hill College
Germantown & Northwestern Aves.
Chestnut Hill, MA 19118-2695
Phone: (215)248-1150
Online systems, database access network.

★268★ Get Oil Out (GOO!)
1114 State St., Ste. 301
Santa Barbara, CA 93102
Phone: (805)965-1519
Contact: Henry Feniger, Pres.
Founded: 1969. Monitors and seeks to limit offshore oil and gas operations in the Santa Barbara Channel. (The organization was founded after a blowout of the Union Oil Company's Platform A in the Santa Barbara Channel, dumping thousands of gallons of oil into the channel and subsequently onto the

beaches near the area.) Supports state and national legislation related to its objectives; helps groups in other states and countries to organize. Maintains the Get Oil Out Education and Legal Fund. Has become a national center for information and research on oil pollution and oil development, supplying universities, schools, organizations, and individuals with information, slides, and other visual aids. Maintains library.

★269★ Global Committee of Parliamentarians on Population and Development
304 E. 45th St., 12th Fl.
New York, NY 10017
Phone: (212)953-7947
Contact: Akio Matsumura
Serves as forum for ideas addressing the balance between resources and population.

★270★ Global Tomorrow Coalition
1325 G St. NW
Washington, DC 20005
Phone: (202)628-4016
Studies global trends in population growth, use of natural resources, and the environment.

★271★ Golden Lion Tamarin Management Committee
Dept. of Zoological Research
National Zoological Park
Washington, DC 20008
Phone: (202)673-4815
Fax: (202)673-4686
Contact: Dr. Devra Kleiman, Exec. Officer
Founded: 1980. ***Members:*** 90. Representatives from research and zoological institutions who participate in the Golden Lion Tamarin Conservation Program. Fosters conservation of the Golden Lion tamarin, a small marmoset indigenous to South America. Compiles statistics.

★272★ Governmental Refuse Collection and Disposal Association (GRCDA)
8750 Georgia Ave., Ste. 140
PO Box 7219
Silver Spring, MD 20910
Phone: (301)585-2898
Fax: (301)589-7068
Toll-Free: 800-586-4723
Contact: H. Lanier Hickman Jr., Exec.Dir.
Founded: 1961. ***Members:*** 5200. Public agency officials and private corporate officials, including employees, managers of public solid waste management agencies and their manufacturers, suppliers, consultants, and contractors. Goal is to improve solid waste management services to the public and industry via training, education, technical assistance, and technology transfer. Conducts 15 to 25 seminars annually. Sponsors training programs: Disposal Technologies and Practices; Hazardous Waste Technologies and Practices; Local Government and Hazardous Wastes; Manager of Landfill Operations; Principles of Landfill Operations; Resource Recovery Technologies and Practices; Safety Training for the Refuse Superintendent; Solid Waste Management Policies for Public Officials. Maintains library of 6000 documents on solid and hazardous waste management.

★273★ Graduation Pledge Alliance (GPA)
Box 4439
Arcata, CA 95521
Contact: Matt Nicodemus, Sec.
Founded: 1987. Participants include students, faculty members, school administrators, and other interested individuals. Promotes social and environmental responsibility by encouraging students to pledge upon graduation that they will investigate and consider the social and environmental consequences of any job opportunity they consider. Seeks to: develop a network of people interested in instituting a graduation pledge program at their respective schools; encourage employers to alter their policies and practices to reflect the social and environmental concerns of their employees; increase the role of school activities in developing an "informed, democratic" citizenry. Holds forums and workshops; sponsors essay contests; maintains speakers' bureau; offers consulting services.

★274★ Grand Canyon Trust
Rte. 4, Box 718
Flagstaff, AZ
Phone: (602)774-7488
Works to preserve, conserve, and manage the public lands, water, wildlife, and other natural resources of the Colorado Plateau.

★275★ Grass Roots Environmental Organization
Citizens Against Chemical Pollutants
PO Box 2018
Bloomfield, NJ 07003
Phone: (201)429-8965
Contact: Madelyn Hoffman
Provides organizing and technical assistance, and legal referral to citizens forming groups to fight chemical pollution.

★276★ Grass Roots the Organic Way
38 Llangollen Ln.
Newton Square, PA 19073
Phone: (215)353-2838
Provides information on harmful pesticides and safe alternatives.

★277★ Grassland Heritage Foundation (GHF)
PO Box 344
Shawnee Mission, KS 66201-0394
Contact: Phillip S. Brown, Pres.
Founded: 1976. ***Members:*** 1500. Purposes are: to foster appreciation for, create interest in, and promote a better understanding of the value of America's native grassland prairies; to purchase, lease, or acquire, for the public benefit, native tallgrass prairies in the U.S. for scientific, educational, and recreational purposes; to encourage the protection of natural prairie lands, including such lands now or at any subsequent time employed as grazing lands for domestic cattle, from forces alien to a natural prairie environment or a grazing economy. Manages 395 acres of prairie at Melvern Reservoir, KS to restore as a public interpretive area; owns the Prairie Center, a 300 acre site for environmental study, a nature center in metropolitan Kansas City, KS, and 160 acres near Topeka, KS. Maintains speakers' bureau; sponsors student naturalist sessions. ***Former Name(s):*** Tallgrass Prairie Foundation (1980).

★278★ Great Bear Foundation (GBF)
PO Box 2699
Missoula, MT 59806
Phone: (406)721-3009
Contact: Daniel Conner, Dir.
Founded: 1982. ***Members:*** 1200. Ranchers, loggers, biologists, environmentalists, and interested individuals. Aims to protect and conserve bears, particularly grizzly bears. Operates a program to reimburse Montana ranchers for livestock killed by grizzly bears. Monitors federal and state agencies and industries that affect bears and their habitat. Provides educational books and materials for people who live near bears.

★279★ Great Lakes Commission (GLC)
Argus II Bldg.
400 S. 4th St.
Ann Arbor, MI 48103
Phone: (313)665-9135
Fax: (313)665-4370
Contact: Dr. Michael J. Donahue, Exec.Dir.
Founded: 1955. ***Members:*** 36. Interstate Compact Commission. Designated or appointed officials (according to state statutes) in 8 states party to the Great Lakes Basin Compact. Serves as a research, coordinating, advisory, and advocacy agency on the development, use, and protection of the water and related land resources of the Great Lakes Basin. Compiles statistics and information on state, federal, and regional programs and projects. Maintains 4000 volume library and collection of reports, journals, and articles on Great Lakes environmental and economic development issues, programs, and projects.

★280★ Great Lakes United (GLU)
State University Coll. at Buffalo
Cassety Hall
1300 Elmwood Ave.
Buffalo, NY 14222
Phone: (716)886-0142
Fax: (716)886-0303
Contact: Philip E. Weller, Exec.Dir.
Founded: 1982. ***Members:*** 1100. International conservation coalition formed by representatives of environmental, sports, union, community, and business groups (200) that promote the conservation and enhancement of the Great Lakes ecosystem; interested individuals (900). Serves as an advisory organization and source of information exchange. Target issues include: water quality; hazardous and toxic substances; fish and wildlife management and habitat protection; energy development and distribution; land use. Holds workshops on Remedial Action Plans, wetlands, and attaining zero discharge of toxic chemicals. Maintains speakers' bureau; plans to produce educational programs.

★281★ Great Swamp Research Institute (GSRI)
Indiana University of Pennsylvania
College of Natural Sciences & Mathematics
Office of the Assoc. Dean
305 Weyandt Hall
Indiana, PA 15705
Phone: (412)357-2609
Contact: Harvey M. Katz, Co-Dir.
Founded: 1981. Goals are to: conduct basic and applied environmental conservation and ecological research concerning the relationship between urbanization and natural areas; provide results of research to the scientific community, government agencies, and the public; offer technical assistance to local, state, federal, and private organizations. Institute's name is derived from its founding location: New Jersey's Great Swamp, which embodies upland and wetland ecosystems. Sponsors community outreach programs where academic and professional groups and members of the public participate in workshops on environmental concerns and learn how to investigate environmental and biological phenomena in both field and laboratory. Also sponsors a technical assistance program. Offers ecological/environmental internships to students. Provides speakers. ***Former Name(s):*** Great Swamp Research (1983).

★282★ Greater Yellowstone Coalition (GYC)
13 S. Willson
PO Box 1874
Bozeman, MT 59715
Phone: (406)586-1593
Fax: (406)586-0851
Contact: Ed Lewis, Exec.Dir.
Founded: 1983. ***Members:*** 4200. Individuals and groups concerned with conservation, wildlife, and the environment. Purpose is to preserve and protect the Greater Yellowstone Ecosystem, the 14 million acre area including and surrounding Yellowstone National Park, WY and Grand Teton National Park, WY. Seeks to create a national awareness of issues and threats facing the GYE. Concerns include mining, drilling, logging, road construction and destruction of wildlife habitat, and human overuse of land in the region.

★283★ Greenhouse Crisis Foundation (GCF)
1130 17th St. NW, Ste. 630
Washington, DC 20036
Phone: (202)466-2823
Contact: Jeremy Rifkin, Pres.
Seeks to stimulate global awareness of the greenhouse effect and related environmental issues through education programs and litigation. Maintains the Greenhouse Crisis Education Campaign, a program to advise individuals about what they can do to address the crisis. Sponsors events to develop international communication on the greenhouse effect such as: International Local Government Network, which addressed how to implement changes in urban energy use, transportation, recycling, and urban reforestation; Global Greenhouse Network, comprised of environmental organizations, animal welfare/rights groups, health advocates, wilderness preservation groups, and individuals from the entertainment community offering recommendations to curb global warming. Initiated the Center for Sustainable Transportation.

★284★ Greenpeace U.S.A.
1436 U St., NW
Washington, DC 20009
Phone: (202)462-1177
Fax: (202)462-4507
Contact: Peter Bahouth, Exec.Dir.
Founded: 1979. *Supporters:* **1,500,000. Conservationists who believe that verbal protests against threats to environmental quality are not adequate. Initiates active, though nonviolent, measures to aid endangered species such as placing boats between harpoonists and whales and placing themselves bodily between hunters and seal pups. Monitors conditions of environmental concern including the greenhouse effect, radioactive and toxic waste dumping, and a comprehensive test ban for nuclear weapons.**

★285★ Greensward Foundation
104 Prospect Park W.
Brooklyn, NY 11215
Contact: Robert M. Makla, Dir.
Founded: 1964. ***Members:*** 2300. Works for the improvement of natural landscape urban parks, the proper understanding of these parks by the public, and the proper care of these parks by their custodians. Sponsors: Friends of Central Park, Friends of Prospect Park, Friends of Fort Greene Park, and Friends of Riverside Park in New York; Friends of Branch Brook Park, in Newark, NJ; Friends of Cadwalader Park, in Trenton, NJ; Friends of Druid Hill Park, in Baltimore, MD. Encourages the maintenance of urban parks to be made labor intensive by hiring and properly supervising unskilled and unemployed workers. Cautiously urges federalization of one or more urban parts, at least on an experimental basis. Sponsors Insomniacs Bicycle Tours, which begin around 2:30 a.m., and year-round walking tours. Raises funds to save historic, century-old trees in city parks, and to restore the Vale of Cashmere in Prospect Park and Bankrock Bay in Central Park.

★286★ Harvard Environmental Law Society
Harvard Law School
Austin 201
Cambridge, MA 02138
Phone: (617)495-3125
Contact: Trent Norris, Pres.
Founded: 1945. ***Members:*** 250. Harvard law students united to protect the environment through legal research and educational programs. Conducts research projects on nuclear power, toxic wastes, land-use planning, and wilderness preservation. Activities include advice, research, assistance in litigation, the drafting of legislation, promoting placement in environmental law, sponsoring speakers, symposia, lobbying, outings, and paper recycling. Maintains 300 volume library on environmental law. Sponsors moot court environmental law alternative. Operates placement services.

★287★ HASTI Friends of the Elephants
PO Box 477
Petaluma, CA 94953
Phone: (707)878-2369
Founded: 1984. Individuals working to save both Asian and African elephants. Seeks to find ways to stop the eventual extinction of elephants. Conducts research; offers education; maintains small library. (Hasti, the Sanskrit word for elephant, translates into English as "long arm." The group believes its purpose is to be "the long arm reaching out to help the elephants.")

★288★ Hawk Mountain Sanctuary Association (HMSA)
Rt. 2
Kempton, PA 19529
Phone: (215)756-6961
Contact: Cynthia Lenhart, Exec.Dir.
Founded: 1934. ***Members:*** 8000. Conserves and protects wildlife, especially birds of prey such as eagles, hawks, and falcons. Maintains 2200-acre wildlife sanctuary where more than 25,000 birds of prey migrate in fall. Sponsors annual lecture series and research programs; conducts college internship program. Provides specialized education programs. Monitors public policy issues related to birds of prey conservation. Maintains Natural History Interpretive Center and 1000 volume library. Compiles statistics.

★289★ Hazardous Materials Advisory Council
1110 Vermont Ave. NW, Ste. 250
Washington, DC 20005
Phone: (202)728-1460
Membership organization devoted to the safety of domestic and international transportation and handling of hazardous materials and wastes.

★290★ Hazardous Materials Control Research Institute
7237 Hanover Pkwy.
Greenbelt, MD 20770
Phone: (301)587-9390
Contact: Harold Bernard, Exec.Dir.
Founded: 1976. ***Members:*** 3500. Corporations, consultants, engineers, scientists, professors, government and corporate administrators, students, and others concerned with the safe management of hazardous materials and waste prevention, control, and cleanup. Purposes are to: disseminate information about technical advancements and institutional requirements in hazardous waste disposal; promote the use of risk assessment methods to achieve a tolerable balance between continuing industrial growth and a livable environment; encourage the minimization of hazardous materials released or discharged into the environment; conduct training programs on toxic and hazardous materials control and management; foster the development of reasonable standards, test procedures, and monitoring and reporting requirements; disseminate information to the public, industry, academia, and legislative and regulatory agencies about hazardous material control. Maintains a 500 volume library on environmental topics.

★291★ Hazardous Waste Federation (HWF)
c/o Department 3220
Div. 3314
PO Box 5800
Albuquerque, NM 87185
Phone: (505)845-8889
Contact: Gordon J. Smith, Chm.
Founded: 1986. Local and regional associations comprising individuals engaged in the management of hazardous wastes and materials. Seeks to increase public awareness and understanding of the problems related to hazardous waste management and to ensure protection of the environment. Promotes the study, evaluation, and control of environmental stresses resulting from the generation, transportation, storage, treatment, and disposal of hazardous wastes. Addresses issues concerning hazardous waste management, transportation, oil, tanks, radioactive materials, water and groundwater, and air pollution. Encourages interest and cooperation of private enterprise and governmental, industrial, educational, and research organizations concerning hazardous waste management. Proposes a comprehensive approach to the management of environmental pollutants and issues. Maintains speakers' bureau.

★292★ Hazardous Waste Treatment Council (HWTC)
1440 New York Ave. NW, Ste. 310
Washington, DC 20005
Phone: (202)783-0870
Telex: 89414
Contact: Richard C. Fortuna, Exec.Dir.
Founded: 1982. ***Members:*** 60. Firms dedicated to the use of high technology treatment in the management of hazardous wastes and to the restricted use of land disposal facilities in the interests of protecting human health and the environment. Advocates minimization of hazardous wastes and the use of alternative technologies in their treatment, including chemical and biological treatments, fixation, neutralization, reclamation, recycling, and thermal treatments such as incineration. Encourages land disposal prohibitions. Promotes reductions in the volume of hazardous waste generated annually and expansion of EPA hazardous waste list. Advocates use of treatment technology as a more cost-effective approach to Superfund site cleanups. Works with state, national, and international officials and firms to assist in

development of programs that utilize treatment and minimize land disposal. Provides technical and placement assistance to members; sponsors special studies, technical seminars, and workshops; participates in federal legislation, litigation, and regulatory development. Maintains library of materials on new technologies; operates speakers' bureau; compiles statistics and mailing list.

★293★ Holy Land Conservation Fund (HLCF)
969 Park Ave.
New York, NY 10028
Phone: (718)965-1057
Contact: Bertel Bruun, Pres.
Founded: 1972. Individuals with experience in the Middle East and/or conservation and environmental work. Supports conservation programs in Israel and neighboring countries. Has purchased rare and endangered species of animals, which populated the area in biblical times, for breeding on selected nature reserves in Israel. (The land for these reserves was contributed by the Israeli government and is administered by the Hai Bar Society, the HLCF's counterpart in Israel. Hai Bar means "wildlife" in Hebrew.) Sponsors adoption program whereby American "foster parents" provide funds to care for animals. Is currently formulating research and assistance programs to preserve and protect wetlands areas vital to indigenous and migratory bird populations. Cooperates with Egyptian and other officials in developing educational materials revelant to nature conservation in the region; has provided small grants to European and American ornithological groups to help finance field studies in the Sinai peninsula. Is developing a three-year campaign to protect and preserve the predatory animals of the Holy Land.

★294★ Household Hazardous Waste Project
901 S. National Ave., Box 108
Springfield, MO 65804
Phone: (417)836-5777
Educates public on household hazardous waste.

★295★ HOWL Wildlife Center
PO Box 1037
Lynnwood, WA 98046
Phone: (206)743-1884
Contact: Jeanne Wasserman
Seeks volunteers to rehabilitate injuried and orphaned wild animals.

★296★ Human Ecology Action League (HEAL)
PO Box 49126
Atlanta, GA 30359-1126
Phone: (404)248-1898
Contact: Ken Dominy, Pres.
Founded: 1976. ***Members:*** 5000. Individuals and organizations interested in the study of human ecology and ecological illness, specifically human health, as it is affected by synthetic and natural substances in the environment. Objectives are: to collect and disseminate information on human ecology and ecological illness to persons suffering from such illness, and to government agencies, scientists, and health care professionals; to work toward eliminating or reducing any conditions in the environment that are hazardous to human health.

★297★ Human Environment Center (HEC)
1001 Connecticut Ave. NW, Ste. 827
Washington, DC 20036
Phone: (202)331-8387
Contact: Margaret Rosenberry, Exec.Dir.
Founded: 1976. Fosters a common cause among advocates of greater opportunity for minorities and the disadvantaged and those committed to natural resource management and environmental protection. Supports the belief that sustained resource and environmental conservation cannot be achieved in the midst of substantial economic and social inequality. Encourages more equitable access to natural resources, increased minority participation in resource conservation management, and large-scale reform of the most degraded human environments. Seeks affirmative action solutions to the problems inherent in the traditional isolation of minority youth from role models and career paths in resource professions. The center is committed to the principles of environmentally sound employment, accomplished in part through conservation corps, urban corps, and youth service programs. Advocates cost-effective public and private conservation projects and the assurance that economic revitalization will afford full employment and environmental protection. Promotes and serves common aims and coordinates the efforts of environmental, human resources, minority, and urban organizations. Provides a forum for discussion and debate. Maintains minority careers program to aid educators and employers in increasing minority involvement in environmental and natural resource fields. Sponsors leadership conferences, research and monitoring projects, educational programs, and special studies. Coordinates minority internships and mentor-student projects. Supports environmental, minor ity, and urban leaders united to serve the needs of minority and other low-income individuals deprived of urban recreational opportunities.

★298★ Humane Society of the United States
2100 L St. NW
Washington, DC 20037
Phone: (202)452-1100
Educates public on such topics as animal control, cruelty investigation, and humane treatment of animals.

★299★ Industrial Gas Cleaning Institute (IGCI)
1707 L St. NW, Ste. 570
Washington, DC 20036
Phone: (202)457-0911
Fax: (202)331-1388
Contact: Jeffrey C. Smith, Exec.Dir.
Founded: 1960. ***Members:*** 40. Firms that manufacture industrial gas-cleaning (air pollution control) equipment; their general managers, research and development engineers, technicians, and sales engineers. Encourages general improvement of engineering and technical standards in the manufacture, installation, operation, and performance of equipment for stationary sources. Creates and improves methods of analyzing industrial gases. Disseminates information on air pollution, the effect of industrial gas cleaning on public health, and general economic, social, scientific, technical, and governmental matters affecting the industry. Compiles quarterly statistical reports of bookings in industry and other pertinent statistical reports. Monitors and seeks to influence congressional activities affecting industry. Acts as liaison and technical clearinghouse for architectural engineers and pollution control consultants. Presents President's and Outstanding Service awards annually. Operates joint technical committees with American Boiler Manufacturers Association.

★300★ Infact
256 Hanover
Boston, MA 02113
Phone: (617)742-4583
Focuses efforts on corporate accountability and responsibility.

★301★ Inform
381 Park Ave., S.
New York, NY 10016
Phone: (212)689-4040
Contact: Joanna Underwood, Exec.Dir.
Founded: 1973. Environmental research and education organization. Purpose is to report on practical actions for the protection and conservation of natural resources, clarify the extent of corporate social responsibility, and identify specific constructive options for change. Current topics of research include toxic waste reduction in the organic chemical industry, municipal solid waste management options, land development impact on Florida, agricultural and water conservation in California, and clean fuel alternatives for vehicles. Conducts seminars and educational briefings; provides speakers for conferences and meetings.

★302★ Institute for Conservation Leadership
1400 16th St. NW
Washington, DC 20036-2266
Phone: (202)797-6656
Concerned with cultivating volunteer conservation leaders.

★303★ Institute for Earth Education (IEE)
PO Box 288
Warrenville, IL 60555
Phone: (708)393-3096
Contact: David B. Wampler, Intl. Office Coord.
Founded: 1974. ***Members:*** 1500. International institute of environmental educators, naturalists, teachers, youth workers, camp counselors, park interpreters, nature center staff, and related organizations. Develops and implements environmental education programs. Conducts workshops, develops programs, and provides consulting services to help teachers and organizations design and implement earth education programs. ***Former Name(s):*** Acclimatization Experience Institute (1984).

★304★ Institute for Environmental Auditing
PO Box 23686
L'Enfant Plaza Station
Washington, DC 20026-3686
Phone: (703)818-1000
Develops guidelines for environmental audits and auditing programs.

★305★ Institute for Environmental Education (IEE)
32000 Chagrin Blvd.
Cleveland, OH 44124
Phone: (216)464-1775
Contact: Joseph H. Chadbourne, Pres.
Founded: 1971. Seeks to improve environmental education in schools. Provides information to businesses, government agencies, and educational institutions on an international basis. Sponsors Cleveland's Teacher Internship Program, which matches teachers with companies for 6 to 12-week summer internships revolving around business and industry and related needs. Teachers earn graduate credit through the program, experience the direct contact with community

problems which is often missed while teaching, and provide the companies with cost-effective consultants with fresh ideas and views. Students benefit in that their teachers return with current information. Internships concern all facets of business and industry.

★306★ Institute for Local Self-Reliance
2425 18th St., NW
Washington, DC 20009
Phone: (202)232-4108
Contact: Neil Seldman
Provides technical assistance, research, educational materials, and data about recycled materials and energy efficiency.

★307★ Institute for Resource Management (IRM)
262 S. 200 W.
Salt Lake City, UT 84101
Phone: (801)322-0530
Contact: Paul Parker, Exec. Officer
Founded: 1982. Promotes a balance between the preservation and use of America's natural resources. Educates businesspersons, environmental leaders, and the government on solving resource management problems. Offers conflict resolution mediation; encourages cooperation in the use and preservation of natural resources.

★308★ Institute for the Human Environment
c/o Institute International Educ.
41 Sutter, No. 510
San Francisco, CA 94104
Phone: (415)362-6520
Contact: Norman T. Gilroy, Pres.
Founded: 1972. International group whose objective is to improve the quality of decisions made involving the man-made, human environment. Organizes conferences, workshops, and seminars to facilitate problem-solving in a variety of human environment issues. Maintains library of 4000 volumes on architecture, health in the workplace, planning, interior design, handicapped accessibility, pipelines, and environmental issues.

★309★ Institute for Wildlife Research (IWR)
c/o Natl. Wildlife Fed.
1400 16th St. NW
Washington, DC 20036
Phone: (703)790-4267
Fax: (703)442-7332
Contact: Maurice N. LeFranc Jr., Dir.
Founded: 1976. Operated by the National Wildlife Federation. Federal and state agency biologists, university faculty, researchers, students, and other persons interested in birds of prey and other endangered species. Compiles statistics on wintering bald eagles in North America. Maintains 6000 volume library.

★310★ Institute of Noise Control Engineering
Box 3206, Arlington Branch
Poughkeepsie, NY 12603
Phone: (914)462-4006
Seeks to advance noise control technology, particularly engineering solutions to environmen tal noise problems.

★311★ Institute of Scrap Recycling Industries (ISRI)
1627 K St. NW, Ste. 700
Washington, DC 20006
Phone: (202)466-4050
Contact: Dr. Herschel Cutler, Exec.Dir.
Founded: 1987. ***Members:*** 1800. Processors, brokers, and consumers engaged in the recycling of ferrous, nonferrous, and nonmetallic scrap; related industry organizations. Conducts specialized education and research programs.

★312★ INTECOL - International Association for Ecology
c/o Institute of Ecology
University of Georgia
Athens, GA 30602
Phone: (404)542-2968
Contact: Frank B. Golley, Pres.
Founded: 1967. ***Members:*** 1300. Libraries and institutions; national and international ecological associations; and students and other individuals. Promotes and communicates the science of ecology and the application of ecological principles to global needs. Coordinates application of ecological principles and encourages public awareness of the economic and social importance of ecology. Collects and evaluates information; acts as clearinghouse and center for coordination and dissemination of information and materials related to ecology and the global environment; reports on programs and legislative events affecting the environment. Represents ecologists in international forums. Conducts a global census of ecologists; determines the status of environmental research in developing countries. Sponsors lectures series; fosters research; compiles statistics.

★313★ International Alliance for Sustainable Agriculture
Newman Center
University of Minnesota
1701 University Ave. SE, Rm. 202
Minneapolis, MN 55414
Phone: (612)331-1099
Promotes sustainable agriculture worldwide, focusing on three problems: 1) insufficient research; 2) lack of organizational support and networks; and 3) inadequate education and information dissemination.

★314★ International Association for the Advancement of Earth and Environmental Sciences (IAAEES)
Northeastern Illinois University
Geography & Environmental Studies Department
5500 N. St. Louis Ave.
Chicago, IL 60625
Phone: (312)794-2628
Contact: Dr. Musa Qutub, Pres.
Founded: 1972. Promotes the advancement of earth and environmental sciences. Stresses interdisciplinary cooperation and the relationship between science and social studies. Seeks to improve and encourage the study of science at elementary, secondary, and university levels. Initiates educational and research programs; conducts scientific meetings and symposia; develops model studies in various countries. Encourages interaction among private industry, the academic community, and society. Disseminates information on the status of earth resources.

★315★ International Association of Fish and Wildlife Agencies (IAFWA)
444 N Capitol St., NW, Ste. 534
Washington, DC 20001
Phone: (202)624-7890
Fax: (202)624-7891
Contact: R. Max Peterson, Exec.V.Pres.
Founded: 1902. ***Members:*** 450. State and provincial fish and wildlife agencies (68) and officials (382). Educates the public about the economic importance of conserving natural resources and managing wildlife property as a source of recreation and a food supply; supports better conservation legislation, administration, and enforcement. Presents annual Seth Gordon Award for distinguished service in wildlife conservation. ***Former Name(s):*** National Association of Game Commissioners and Wardens (1917); International Association of Game, Fish, and Conservation Commissioners (1976).

★316★ International Council for Bird Preservation, U.S. Section (ICBP)
c/o World Wildlife Fund
1250 24th St. NW
Washington, DC 20037
Phone: (202)778-9563
Fax: (202)293-9211
Contact: Christoph Imboden, Dir.
Founded: 1922. ***Members:*** 800. Organizations interested in conservation of birds; associate members are individuals providing financial support for conservation activities of the council. Promotes conservation and study of birds on an international basis; conducts research and educational activities; assists in establishing preserves. Aids studies of birds believed in danger of extirpation; awards research grants to help bring foreign ornithologists and conservationists to the U.S. to investigate conservation problems and methods. Informs members of U.S. state and federal legislation pertaining to conservation and environmental protection.

★317★ International Council for Outdoor Education
PO Box 17255
Pittsburgh, PA 15235
Phone: (412)372-5992
Concerned with education programs in conservation and outdoor recreation.

★318★ International Fund for Animal Welfare
PO Box 193
411 Main St.
Yarmouth Port, MA 02675
Phone: (508)362-4944
Protects wild and domestic animals, including harp and hood seals.

★319★ The International Osprey Foundation
PO Box 250
Sanibel, FL 33957
Phone: (813)472-5218
Contact: David Loveland, Pres.
Founded: 1981. ***Members:*** 300. Professional and amateur ornithologists. Promotes the study and preservation of the osprey and other birds of prey. Mediates the exchange of information; compiles statistics; maintains speakers' bureau and a program of public education on the ecology and status of ospreys. Monitors ospreys on Sanibel Island, Florida.

★320★ International Society for Environmental Toxicology and Cancer (ISETC)
PO Box 134
Park Forest, IL 60466
Phone: (708)748-0440
Fax: (312)755-2096
Contact: Dr. George Scherr, Exec. Officer
Founded: 1983. ***Members:*** 700. Clinicians and researchers working in the fields of environmental toxicology and oncology. Promotes research and information exchange. Maintains small library. Founded the World Institute of Ecology and Cancer jointly with the

European Institute of Ecology and Cancer and the Panafrican Institute of Ecology and Cancer.

★321★ International Society for the Protection of Mustangs and Burros (ISPMB)
c/o Helen A. Reilly
11790 Deodar Way
Reno, NV 89506
Phone: (702)972-1989
Contact: Helen A. Reilly, Exec.Dir.
Founded: 1960. ***Members:*** 19,000. Persons interested in the protection and preservation of wild horses and burros. Seeks to supervise wild horse and burro habitat where they will be protected by law against molestation or interference. Sponsors Foster Home Care Program for the placement and care of unadoptable wild horses and burros. ***Former Name(s):*** International Mustang Club (1985).

★322★ International Society of Arboriculture
303 W. University Ave.
Urbana, IL 61801
Phone: (217)328-2032
Promotes tree care and preservation, particularly in urban settings.

★323★ International Wild Waterfowl Association (IWWA)
Hidden Lake Waterfowl
5614 River Styx Rd.
Medina, OH 44256
Phone: (216)725-8782
Contact: Nancy Collins Jr., Sec.
Founded: 1958. ***Members:*** 500. Individuals in 15 countries concerned with conservation and the preservation of wild waterfowl. Works toward protection, conservation, and reproduction of any species considered in danger of eventual extinction; encourages the breeding of well-known and rare species in captivity. Bestows awards; maintains speakers' bureau. Established the Avicultural Hall of Fame.

★324★ International Wildlife Rehabilitation Council (IWRC)
4437 Central Place, Ste. B-4
Suisun, CA 94585
Phone: (707)864-1761

★325★ Interstate Conference on Water Policy (ICWP)
955 L'Enfant Plaza SW, 6th Fl.
Washington, DC 20024
Phone: (202)466-7287
Fax: (202)646-6210
Contact: James K. Coyne, Exec.Dir.
Founded: 1959. ***Members:*** 70. State, interstate, and intrastate officials with responsibility for all water quantity- and quality-related matters. Affiliate members are individuals, businesses, universities, and governmental agencies with primary interest in water. Facilitates interstate cooperation and exchange of information. Presents views to Congress and federal agencies. Researches water management, water for energy, and water technology.

★326★ Izaak Walton League of America (IWLA)
1401 Wilson Blvd., Level B
Arlington, VA 22209
Phone: (703)528-1818
Fax: (703)528-1836
Contact: Jack Lorenz, Exec.Dir.
Founded: 1922. ***Members:*** 50,000. Works to educate the public to conserve, maintain, protect, and restore the soil, forest, water, and other natural resources of the U.S.; promotes the enjoyment and wholesome utilization of these resources. Sponsors environmental programs including Wetlands Watch, Outdoor Ethics Information Center, Save Our Streams, Acid Rain Project, Chesapeake Bay Program, and a weekly television program, Make Peace With Nature. Conducts workshops.

★327★ Izaak Walton League of America Endowment
PO Box 824
Iowa City, IA 52244
Phone: (319)351-7073
Contact: Robert C. Russell, Exec.Sec.
Founded: 1943. ***Members:*** 50,000. Individuals, families, students, corporations, and members of Izaak Walton League of America (see separate entry) working towards saving America's natural resources. Dedicated to conservation goals through education, science, and the acquisition of endangered lands. Instrumental in purchasing strategic parcels of land without the burden of time-consuming decisions of government agencies. When funds become available, the areas are turned over to the U.S. Forest Service, National Park Service, or other public or private entities. Protects unique natural areas for the preservation, use, and enjoyment of future generations. Conserves, maintains, and restores soil, water, and wildlife in U.S. forests, marshes, grasslands, and prairies. Provides funding for youth conferences and educational activities.

★328★ J. N. "Ding" Darling Foundation
PO Box 657
Des Moines, IA 50303
Phone: (515)281-2371
Contact: Ralph Schlenker, Treas.
Founded: 1962. Trustees: 40. Purposes are to: coordinate programs, research, and education that will bring about conservation and sound management of water, woods, and soil; restore and preserve historical sites; create and assist in wildlife management plans; improve outdoor recreational opportunities for present and future generations. Provides financial assistance to national conservation groups. Supports tree planting programs, water resource studies, and educational conferences and workshops on water quality, conservation and proper land use. Awards educational grants at Iowa State University for wildlife management students; provides 12 additional educational grants at 7 other colleges. Named for the late J. N. "Ding" Darling, a professional cartoonist involved in conservation activities. ***Former Name(s):*** J. N. "Ding" Darling Foundation (1981); J. N. "Ding" Darling Conservation Foundation (1984).

★329★ Jane Goodall Institute for Wildlife Research, Education, and Conservation
PO Box 41720
Tucson, AZ 85717
Phone: (602)325-1211
Protects and conserves wild and captive chimpanzees.

★330★ John Muir Institute for Environmental Studies (JMI)
743 Wilson St.
Napa, CA 94559
Phone: (707)252-8333
Contact: Max Linn, Pres.
Founded: 1968. Research Associates: 100. Objectives are: to identify and study environmental problems the institute believes are not receiving adequate attention; to conduct research that will fill information gaps in natural resource management; to constructively appraise and advise institutions which have significant environmental impacts. Primary programs involve: water resources and management; environmental impacts of energy development in the West; air quality research with emphasis on problems of degraded visibility; long-term impacts of forestry practices; pesticides in urban areas; socioeconomic impacts of oil and gas exploration and shoreline ecology.

★331★ Kangaroo Protection Foundation (KPF)
1900 L St. NW, Ste. 500
Washington, DC 20036
Phone: (202)872-8840
Contact: Marian Newman, Program Dir.
Founded: 1982. Individuals interested in protecting Australia's kangaroos from becoming victims of cruelty and an endangered species. Objectives are to: promote the conservation and humane treatment of kangaroos, wallabies, and other land mammals; educate the public about the slaughter of kangaroos in Australia to satisfy the import demands of other nations; further scientific studies regarding habitat and behavior of wildlife and domestic animals. Disseminates materials regarding threats to endangered species. Urges the reinstatement of a governmental ban on imports of kangaroo hides and products.

★332★ Keep America Beautiful (KAB)
Mill River Plaza
9 W Broad St.
Stamford, CT 06902
Phone: (203)323-8987
Contact: Roger W. Powers, Pres.
Founded: 1953. ***Members:*** 125. Public service organization fostering cooperation among government, business, and the public to improve the physical quality of life. Sponsors Keep America Beautiful System, a comprehensive behavioral approach to improved waste handling by the entire community. Sponsors competitions, national awards programs, and Keep America Beautiful Month; prints posters and litter bags.

★333★ Kids for a Clean Environment
PO Box 158254
Nashville, TN 37215
Phone: (615)331-0708
Contact: Trish Poe
Children's environmental organization providing information and projects enabling children to make positive impacts on their environment.

★334★ Kids for Conservation — Today and Tomorrow
Illinois Dept. of Conservation
524 S. 2nd St.
Springfield, IL 62701
Phone: (217)524-4126
Contact: Glenda H. Burke
Family oriented club for children ages 3-15. Members receive free quarterly magazine and notices of upcoming conservation events.

★335★ Kids S.T.O.P.
PO Box 471
Forest Hills, NY 11375
Phone: (718)997-7387
Contact: Gayle Essary
Ecology club for elementary-aged children which teaches environmental goals.

★336★ Land Improvement Contractors of America (LICA)
PO Box 9
1300 Maybrook Dr.
Maywood, IL 60153
Phone: (708)344-0700
Contact: Henry Lamb, Exec.V.Pres.
Founded: 1951. ***Members:*** 5000. Federation of 37 state and two international associations of land improvement, excavation, and conservation contractors. Seeks to: protect the soil and foster efficient business principles on the basis of private and free enterprise in the field of soil saving and soil building; promote clean water. Conducts educational and research programs. Bestows awards and scholarships.

★337★ Land Trust Alliance (LTA)
900 17th St. NW, Ste. 410
Washington DC, 20006
Phone: (202)785-1410
Fax: (202)785-1408
Contact: Jean Hocker, Exec.Dir.
Founded: 1982. ***Members:*** 1100. Local, regional, and national land conservation organizations, often organized as land trusts; interested individuals. Works to advance the conservation of land resources; promotes the expansion of the land trust community. Fosters supportive public policies and seeks to increase public awareness of land trusts and their goals. Compiles statistics. ***Former Name(s):*** Land Trust Exchange (1990).

★338★ Last Chance Forever (LCF)
506 Ave. A
San Antonio, TX 78218
Phone: (512)655-6049
Contact: John Karger, Exec.Dir.
Founded: 1979. Purposes are to: shelter and rehabilitate birds of prey; conduct research and compile data; educate the public concerning birds of prey and their relation to the environment. Sponsors speaker and slide show exhibitions featuring birds for civic organizations and schools. Offers tours at summer festivals and environmental exhibits.

★339★ League for Ecological Democracy (LED)
PO Box 1858
San Pedro, CA 90733
Phone: (213)833-2633
Contact: Robert W. Long, Exec. Officer
Founded: 1969. Social ecologists working to reorganize global society on an egalitarian, decentralized, free, and ecologically sound basis in order to safeguard the planet from pollution and destruction. Maintains a network with environmental, political, and antinuclear groups. ***Former Name(s):*** League for Economic Democracy (1981).

★340★ League of Conservation Voters
320 4th St. NE
Washington, DC 20002
Phone: (202)785-8683
Works to elect pro-environmental candidates to Congress.

★341★ League to Save Lake Tahoe (LSLT)
Box 10110
South Lake Tahoe, CA 95731
Phone: (916)541-5388
Contact: Laurel W. Ames, Exec.Dir.
Founded: 1957. ***Members:*** 3500. Individuals and organizations that give financial support to the league. Purpose is to protect and preserve the natural beauty of the Lake Tahoe area of California and Nevada. Promotes the concept that all developments, improvements, and man-made changes which may be required to accommodate the growth of the area should place primary emphasis on preserving the natural beauty of the lake. The League to Save Lake Tahoe Charitable Trust funds the informational, educational, and legal activities of the league. ***Former Name(s):*** Tahoe Resource Conservation Society (1985).

★342★ Legacy International
346 Commerce St.
Alexandria, VA 22314
Phone: (703)549-3630
Fax: (703)549-0262
Telex: 510600 1584 LEGACY
Contact: Dr. Ira Kaufman, Exec.Dir.
Founded: 1979. ***Members:*** 150. Educational organization conducting research, development, and experiential activities in an effort to foster global understanding and environmental action. Sponsors International Summer Leadership Training Program, an education program for youth from 30 countries aged 11-18, providing guidance in intercultural relations, cross-cultural communication, leadership skills, and personal development. Offers undergraduate, graduate, and continuing education credits to staff for participation in its Training in Intercultural Relations Program. Provides human resources training and consulting on education, management, and international concerns. Sponsors Youths for Environment and Service (YES), an international organization which trains youths and young professionals in environmental protection and development; and Dialogue Program, which brings youth and adults together from countries and regions in conflict for cooperative interaction and training in cross-cultural understanding, conflict resolution, and leadership. Sponsors international exchanges and internships, youth tours, workshops, speakers' bureaus, and cooperative international work projects. Operates Middle East field office in Jerusalem, Israel.

★343★ Lighthawk
PO Box 8163
Santa Fe, NM 87504
Phone: (505)982-9656
Fax: (505)984-8381
Contact: Michael M. Stewartt, Exec.Dir.
Founded: 1980. ***Members:*** 5000. Provides professional and affordable light aircraft flight services to conservation efforts throughout the United States, Canada, and Central America. Promotes the advantages of flight to help correct environmental mismanagement. Seeks to enhance humankind's capacity to sustain biological diversity, intact ecosystems, and ecological processes that support life on earth. Recruits volunteer aircraft owner/pilots with at least 1,000 hours flight time. ***Former Name(s):*** Project Lighthawk (1989).

★344★ Living Lakes
1090 Vermont Ave., NW
Washington, DC 20005
Organization founded by energy industry to promote the restoration of acidic waters.

★345★ Louisiana Environmental Action Network
PO Box 66323
Baton Rouge, LA 70896
Phone: (504)928-1315
Contact: Marylee Orr
Supports revision of state laws and regulations. Holds workshops and skill training sessions.

★346★ Manufacturers of Emission Controls Association (MECA)
1707 L St. NW, Ste. 570
Washington, DC 20036
Phone: (202)296-4797
Contact: Bruce I. Bertelsen, Exec.Dir.
Founded: 1976. ***Members:*** 21. Manufacturers of automobile exhaust control devices and stationary source catalytic controls. Represents the emission controls industry before all levels of government; maintains close contact with policy planners and technical experts of governmental agencies worldwide concerned with environmental issues and regulations. Acts as a central source of information on emission technology and industry capabilities and views. Monitors and reports on congressional actions that affect industry; provides technical and industry information to congressional committees involved in environmental and related legislation. Consults with other industry organizations concerned with national environmental issues. Provides the media with background, corrective, and explanatory data. Undertakes special studies on issues of major importance to the industry.

★347★ Marine Mammal Stranding Center
PO Box 733
Brigantine, NJ 08203
Phone: (609)266-0538
Rescue and rehabilitation center for marine mammals and sea turtles.

★348★ Monitor Consortium
1506 19th St. NW
Washington, DC 20036
Phone: (202)234-6576
Contact: Craig VanNote, Exec.V.Pres.
Founded: 1971. ***Members:*** 35. Conservation, environmental, and animal welfare groups. Coordinates actions of and acts as information clearinghouse for members on issues pertaining to marine mammals, endangered species, and wildlife habitat. Monitors enforcement of treaties and federal wildlife laws including the Marine Mammal Protection Act, the Endangered Species Act, the International Whaling Convention, and the Convention of International Trade on Endangered Species of Wild Fauna and Flora. ***Former Name(s):*** Monitor (1979).

★349★ Mountain Gorilla Project (MGP)
1717 Massachusetts Ave. NW, Ste. 602
Washington, DC 20036
Phone: (202)265-8394
Fax: (202)265-2361
Contact: Diana McMeekin, V.Pres.
Founded: 1978. ***Members:*** 4. A project of the African Wildlife Foundation. Objectives are to: work with Rwandan authorities to establish a management plan for the Volcanoes National Park in Rwanda; provide technical assistance and advice; train, equip, and fund effective antipoaching forces; establish and support conservation education programs for Rwandans. The project works to safeguard the remaining gorillas and their habitat by addressing economic pressures facing Rwandans which have resulted in agricultural encroachment into the National Park. MGP also fosters controlled tourist development which provides revenue to fund the park and create local employment. ***Former Name(s):*** Project Survival.

★350★ NATICH
U.S. Environmental Protection Agency
Pollutant Assessment Branch, MD-12
Research Triangle Pk., NC 27711
Phone: (919)541-0850
Online systems, database access network.

★351★ National Accreditation Council for Environmental Health Curricula
Program Dir. of Environmental Health
Western Carolina University
Cullowhee, NC 28723
Phone: (704)227-7114
Contact: Joe Beck, Chm.
Founded: 1969. Purposes are: to establish a system for accreditation of environmental health curricula and related procedures; to accredit and carry out other responsibilities as may be essential to the accreditation of academic programs leading to associate degrees, baccalaureate degrees, and graduate degrees in environmental health. Assumes responsibility for all functions, related records, and correspondence pertaining to accreditation of environmental health curricula. Renders advice and counsel to institutions in the development of curricula and the conduct of educational programs in the environmental health sciences. Acts as clearinghouse for reports and information pertaining to the environmental health accreditation process and activities.

★352★ National Association for Plastic Container Recovery (NAPCOR)
4828 Pkwy. Plaza Blvd., Ste. 260
Charlotte, NC 28217
Phone: (704)357-3250
Fax: (704)357-3260
Toll-Free: 800-762-7267
Contact: Luke B. Schmidt, Pres.
Founded: 1988. ***Members:*** 15. Polyethylene terephthalate (PET) bottle and resin producers. Seeks to facilitate the economic recovery of plastic containers, particulary those used for beverages, through collection, reclamation, and development of end-use markets. Believes that educating the public about the recyclability of most waste, particularly plastic, is the first step toward solving the solid waste problem in the U.S. Provides technical, marketing, and promotional support for plastics recycling programs. Establishes projects with local organizations and communities to implement and enhance existing recycling programs. Seeks opportunities to promote plastics recycling by educating the public and supporting public efforts, as well as addressing waste managers, recycling professionals, and others within the plastics and packaging industry. Conducts research on the environmental impact of soft drink delivery systems.

★353★ National Association for State River Conservation Programs (NASRCP)
801 Pennsylvania Ave. SE, Ste. 302
Washington, DC 20003
Phone: (202)543-2682
Contact: Roger Fickes, Pres.
Founded: 1983. ***Members:*** 50. Managers of state river conservation programs. Works to: facilitate communication and cooperation among members to improve the efficiency and effectiveness of state river environmental preservation programs; educate the public on the importance of river conservation. Represents members' interests in formulation of national river conservation policy. ***Former Name(s):*** National Association of State River Program Managers (1987).

★354★ National Association of Conservation Districts (NACD)
509 Capitol Ct. NE
Washington, DC 20002
Phone: (202)547-6223
Fax: (202)547-6450
Contact: Ernest C. Shea, Exec.V.Pres.
Founded: 1947. ***Members:*** 3000. Soil and water conservation districts organized by the citizens of watersheds, counties, or communities under provisions of state laws. To direct and coordinate, through local self-government efforts, the conservation and development of soil, water, and related natural resources; districts include over 90% of the nation's privately-owned land. Presents awards; maintains library of approximately 1500 volumes. ***Former Name(s):*** National Association of Soil Conservation Districts; National Association of Soil and Water Conservation Districts (1970).

★355★ National Association of Environmental Professionals (NAEP)
PO Box 15210
Alexandria, VA 22309-0210
Phone: (703)660-2364
Contact: Joan A. Schroeder, Exec.Sec.
Founded: 1975. ***Members:*** 1600. Persons whose occupations are either directly or indirectly related to environmental management and assessment. Goal is to improve interdisciplinary communications and to advance the state-of-the-art environmental planning process. Has established Code of Ethical Practices. Conducts professional certification program; bestows awards.

★356★ National Association of Environmental Risk Auditors
4211 E. Third St.
Bloomington, IL 47401
Phone: (812)333-0077
Trains and certifies environmental professionals in the areas of environmental risk and audits.

★357★ National Association of Flood and Storm Water Management Agencies (NAFSMA)
1225 I St. NW, Ste. 300
Washington, DC 20005
Phone: (202)682-3761
Fax: (202)842-0621
Contact: Ron M. Linton, Pres.
Founded: 1977. ***Members:*** 44. State, county, and local governments concerned with management of water resources. Objectives are to reduce or eliminate flooding and provide for improved stormwater management and conservation of watersheds. ***Former Name(s):*** National Association of Flood and Storm Water Management (1988).

★358★ National Association of Solvent Recyclers (NASR)
1333 New Hampshire Ave., NW, Ste. 1100
Washington, DC 20036
Phone: (202)463-6956
Fax: (202)775-4163
Contact: Brenda Pulley, Dir.
Founded: 1980. ***Members:*** 70. Firms engaged in recycling and reclamation of used industrial solvents. Fosters energy conservation by using discarded materials for industrial fuels. Monitors and reports on regulatory and legislative action affecting solvent recycling. Compiles statistics.

★359★ National Association of State Land Reclamationists (NASLR)
459 B Carlisle Dr.
Herndon, VA 22070
Phone: (703)709-8654
Contact: A. J. Duplechin, Pres.
Founded: 1973. ***Members:*** 140. Individuals involved in administering state-sponsored land reclamation programs. Purposes are: to bring together state officials for discussion of problems of national interest; to keep abreast of the art of land reclamation; to promote cooperation between states, private mining groups, and the federal government; to discuss, encourage, endorse, or sponsor activities, programs, and legislation that will advance mined land reclamation.

★360★ National Association of Water Institute Directors
Montana Water Resources Research Center
Cobleigh Hall
Montana State University
Bozeman, MT 59717
Phone: (406)994-6690

★361★ National Audubon Society (NAS)
950 Third Ave.
New York, NY 10022
Phone: (212)832-3200

★362★ National Center for Environmental Health Strategies (NCEHS)
1100 Rural Ave.
Voorhees, NJ 08043
Phone: (609)429-5358
Contact: Mary Lamielle, Dir. & Pres.
Founded: 1986. ***Members:*** 1500. Persons with environmental illnesses, including those with chemical sensitivity disorders; medical, legal, and scientific professionals; government agencies; environmentalists; interested others. Promotes public awareness of health problems caused by chemical and environmental pollutants, focusing on chemical sensitivity disorders. Testifies before government agencies on behalf of persons with such health problems. Encourages the development and implementation of programs and policies aimed at assisting victims of pollutants and preventing future public health problems. Conducts educational programs and research. Gathers information and compiles statistics on indoor and outdoor pollutants, less-toxic products, pesticides, natural foods, and disability resources, including alternative employment, workplace accommodations, social security and workmen's compensation, and housing. Maintains library and speakers' bureau. Provides advocacy and technical, referral, and children's services. Acts as a clearinghouse. ***Former Name(s):*** Environmental Health Association of New Jersey (1989).

★363★ National Clean Air Coalition (NCAC)
1400 16th St., NW
Washington, DC 20036
Phone: (202)797-5436
Contact: Richard Ayres, Chm.
Founded: 1973. Network of state and local organizations and individuals concerned with environment, health, labor, parks, and other resources threatened by air pollutants. Lobbies for strong national clean air legislation and seeks to insure that legislation is effectively implemented through regulations and state and local air programs. Conducts workshops for the public on clean air issues.

★364★ National Coalition Against the Misuse of Pesticides
530 7th St. SE
Washington, DC 20003
Phone: (202)543-5450
Disseminates information on pesticides and their alternatives.

★365★ National Coalition for Marine Conservation (NCMC)
PO Box 23298
Savannah, GA 31403
Phone: (912)234-8062
Fax: (912)233-2909
Contact: Ken Hinman, Exec.Dir.
Founded: 1973. ***Members:*** 5000. Promotes conservation of marine resources and protection of the ocean environment; seeks legislative and administrative solutions to problems threatening marine resources.

★366★ National Coalition to Stop Food Irradiation
PO Box 59-0488
San Francisco, CA 94159
Phone: (415)626-2734
Works to prevent food irradiation.

★367★ National Council for Environmental Balance (NCEB)
4169 Westport Rd.
PO Box 7732
Louisville, KY 40207
Phone: (502)896-8731
Contact: I. W. Tucker Ph.D., Pres.
Founded: 1972. ***Members:*** 1320. Science professionals, students, educators, and others concerned about the environmental movement. Dedicated to a balanced approach to solving environmental and energy problems without destroying the economy "and people's right to a responsible life." Coordinates efforts of members of the scientific and academic communities who are willing to study, research, and speak on topics directly related to energy, economics, and environmental issues. Prepares and disseminates releases to the media; produces information sheets, studies, and other materials for the public, schools, and other organizations. ***Former Name(s):*** Council for Environmental Balance (1976).

★368★ National Elephant Collectors Society (NECS)
38 Medford St.
Somerville, MA 02145-3810
Phone: (617)625-4067
Contact: Richard W. Massiglia, Pres. & Founder
Founded: 1981. ***Members:*** 1000. Collectors of elephant memorabilia interested in contributing to and promoting the preservation of the elephant. Provides information on the origin, habitat, care, and folklore of the elephant. Aids members in expanding collections through correspondence with other collectors. Works with organizations to prevent the extinction of the elephant. Offers classes to school children in elephant collecting. Maintains small museum.

★369★ National Energy Foundation (NEF)
5160 Wiley Post Way, Ste. 200
Salt Lake City, UT 84116
Phone: (801)539-1406
Contact: Edward Dalton Ed.D., Pres.
Founded: 1976. Works to stimulate interest and increase knowledge of the current energy situation through nationwide educational programs for teachers and students. Focuses on usage, conservation, economics, renewable energy resources, new sources of energy, projected changes in lifestyle (economic, scientific, social, and political), and creation of dialogue among corporate and educational communities. Sponsors Student Exposition on Energy Resources (SEER), and teacher training programs.

★370★ National Environmental Development Association (NEDA)
1440 New York Ave. NW, Ste. 300
Washington, DC 20005
Phone: (202)638-1230
Contact: Steven B. Hellem, Exec.V.Pres.
Founded: 1972. ***Members:*** 305. Individuals from industry, business, labor, agriculture, and the academic community. Believes that both public and private interests would benefit from an environmental-economic interrelationship and that future ecological achievement will require concerted action by both, with a minimum of conflict, to avoid wasting either natural or financial resources. Works to achieve national progress and environmental advancement without destroying valuable economic resources. Seeks to assure continued development of industrial, agricultural, transportation, land, and water resources while solving environmental problems by: providing technical research, analyses, and other data for testimony before federal and state legislative bodies; supplying information to the media and to trade publications, scientific journals, and other private or government publications; conducting forums on environmental development; promoting exchanges of information between associations, foundations, institutions, and other groups.

★371★ National Environmental Health Association (NEHA)
720 S Colorado Blvd., Ste. 970
S. Tower
Denver, CO 80222
Phone: (303)756-9090
Fax: (303)691-9490
Contact: Nelson E. Fabian, Exec.Dir.
Founded: 1930. ***Members:*** 5500. Professional society of persons engaged in environmental health and protection for governmental agencies, public health and environmental protection agencies, industry, colleges, and universities. Conducts national professional registration program and continuing education programs. Provides self-paced learning modules for field professionals. Offers placement service; bestows awards; compiles statistics. Maintains speakers' bureau and 1000 volume library on environmental health and protection. Plans to offer an electronic bulletin board service. ***Former Name(s):*** California Association of Sanitarians (1937); National Association of Sanitarians (1970).

★372★ National Environmental Satellite, Data, and Information Service (NESDIS)
2069 Federal Bldg. 4
Washington, DC 20233
Phone: (301)763-7190
Fax: (301)763-4011
Contact: Russell Koffler, Deputy Asst.Admin.
Founded: 1965. A major line component of the National Oceanic and Atmospheric Administration, U.S. Department of Commerce. Responsible for acquiring, processing, archiving, recalling, and disseminating worldwide environmental data and environmental science information concerning the atmosphere, oceans, solid earth, and near space. Provides information on products for use by governmental agencies, the national and international scientific and engineering community, industry, commerce, agriculture, and the public. Products include assessments of the impact of environmental fluctuations on the national economy, national defense, energy development, global food supplies, natural resources, natural hazards, and human health. Maintains and services an archive of all data and information acquired by NOAA's operational geostationary and polar-orbiting satellites. Operates the National Climatic Data Center in Asheville, NC; the National Oceanographic Data Center and Assessment and Information Services Center in Washington, DC; and the National Geophysical Data Center in Boulder, CO. ***Former Name(s):*** Environmental Data Service (1980); Environmental Data and Information Service (1982).

★373★ National Environmental Training Association (NETA)
8687 Via De Ventura, Ste. 214
Scottsdale, AZ 85258
Phone: (602)951-1440
Fax: (602)483-0083
Contact: Charles L. Richardson, Exec.Dir.
Founded: 1977. ***Members:*** 1200. Professional society for environmental training professionals organized to promote better operation of pollution control facilities by means of personnel development. Organizes and delivers training in the fields of water supply, wastewater, air and noise pollution control, and solid and hazardous waste. Purposes are: to encourage communication among individual trainers, training institutions, and governmental agencies; to promote environmental personnel training and education; to set minimum standards for training and education programs and encourage reciprocity between states and training institutions on evaluation and acceptance of transfer credits. Sponsors research programs and seminars; bestows Environmental Education and Trainer of the Year awards. Operates information center. Conducts a national certification program for environmental trainers.

★374★ National Geographic Society
17th and M Sts. NW
Washington, DC 20036
Phone: (202)857-7000
Scientific educational nonprofit organization which supports environmental research.

★375★ National Institute for Urban Wildlife
10921 Trotting Ridge Way
Columbia, MD 21044-2831
Phone: (301)596-3311
Researches wildlife in urban and developing settings.

★376★ National Institute for Urban Wildlife (NIUW)
10921 Trotting Ridge Way
Columbia, MD 21044
Phone: (301)596-3311
Contact: Gomer E. Jones, Pres.
Founded: 1973. ***Members:*** 1000. Individuals, local and regional planning agencies, developers, environmental consultants, landscape architects, architects, land managers, wildlife biologists, government agencies, and national conservation organizations. Purpose is to conduct research on the relationship between man and wildlife under urban and urbanizing conditions. Develops and disseminates practical procedures for maintaining, enhancing, or controlling certain wildlife species in urban areas. Promotes appreciation for wildlife at the local level. Engages in environmental planning and management for new residential, commercial, and industrial developments.

Monitors human-wildlife relationships in existing urban or other developed areas. Develops reports and publications for planners, developers, and others concerned with creating a higher quality environment. Compiles statistics; prepares teaching manuals for professionals; conducts studies, seminars, lectures, and periodic symposium; maintains library. ***Former Name(s):*** Urban Wildlife Research Center (1983).

★377★ National Military Fish and Wildlife Association (NMFWA)
PO Box 128
Encinitas, CA 23509
Phone: (619)725-4540
Fax: (619)725-3528
Contact: Slader G. Buck, Pres.
Members: 430. Natural resource managers and professionals in related fields. Provides professional resource management for the Department of Defense's fish and wildlife resources. Conducts annual law enforcement course. Bestows awards.

★378★ National of Service and Conservation Corps
1001 Connecticut Ave. NW, Ste. 827
Washington, DC 20036
Phone: (202)331-9647
Promotes conservation and serves as an information network for members.

★379★ National Oil Recyclers Association
805 15th St. NW, Ste. 900
Washington, DC 20005
Phone: (202)962-3020
Represents the interests of used oil recyclers to the Environmental Protection Agency.

★380★ National Park Foundation
1101 17th St. NW, Ste. 1008
Washington, DC 20036
Phone: (202)785-4500
Seeks support for National Park System and educates public on conservation.

★381★ National Prairie Grouse Technical Council (NPGTC)
Western Energy Co.
Box 99
Colstrip, MT 59323
Phone: (406)748-2366
Contact: Bruce Waage, Chm.
Founded: 1952. ***Members:*** 120. Participants are technical personnel and administrators of state, provincial, and federal agencies, and individuals from private groups involved in preservation, research, and management of the prairie chicken and sharp-tailed grouse. Provides for the exchange of information on current research and management of these species, and reviews local and national legislation affecting the prairie grouse. Sponsors specialized education and research programs; compiles statistics. Maintains biographical archives. ***Former Name(s):*** National Committee on the Prairie Chicken (1956); Prairie Chicken Technical Committee (1961).

★382★ National Recycling Coalition (NRC)
1101 30th St. NW
Washington, DC 20007
Phone: (202)625-6406
Fax: (202)625-6409
Contact: David Loveland, Exec.Dir.
Founded: 1978. ***Members:*** 3000. Individuals and environmental, labor, and business organizations united to encourage the recovery, reuse, and conservation of materials and energy, and to make the benefits of recycling more widely known. Seeks to help change national policies on energy, waste management, taxes, and transportation that hinder recycling efforts. Believes consumers should be informed that recycled products are not inherently inferior to products made with virgin materials. Encourages manufacturers to invest in the equipment required to make recycled products, and to make more of such products available at reasonable prices. Acts as information network for persons interested in recycling. Answers requests for information; operates speakers' bureau; bestows awards. Maintains research library.

★383★ National Resource Recovery Association (NRRA)
1620 I St. NW
Washington, DC 20006
Phone: (202)293-7330
Contact: Ronald W. Musselwhite, Exec.Sec.
Founded: 1982. ***Members:*** 250. City, county, and state governmental units, and other public authorities and agencies involved in resource recovery (75); associate members are interested individuals and private sector organizations including systems contractors, equipment suppliers, and consultants (175). Objectives are to promote the development and successful operation of resource recovery facilities and of district heating and cooling systems. Encourages development of recycling programs and urban waste energy systems whereby municipal solid waste is: processed and burned; converted into steam or electricity; sold to utilities, industry, and private users. Promotes development of thermal distribution systems utilizing urban waste energy. Acts as forum for exchange of information; offers professional and technical services; conducts seminars; monitors related legislative activities.

★384★ National Solid Wastes Management Association (NSWMA)
1730 Rhode Island Ave. NW, Ste. 1000
Washington, DC 20036
Phone: (202)659-4613
Contact: Eugene J. Wingerter, Exec.Dir.
Founded: 1964. ***Members:*** 2500. Maintains speakers' bureau; compiles statistics; conducts research programs; sponsors competitions; presents awards.

★385★ National Toxics Campaign
37 Temple Pl., 4th Fl.
Boston, MA 02111
Phone: (617)482-1477
Works on Superfund-related activities, including citizen outreach and education programs.

★386★ National Tree Society
PO Box 10808
Bakersfield, CA 93389
Phone: (805)589-6912
Contact: Gregory W. Davis, Pres.
Founded: 1989. ***Members:*** 1000. Interested individuals organized to preserve the earth's biosphere by planting and caring for trees. Seeks to raise public understanding of the need for trees and the role they play in maintaining a healthy environment; works to acquire forest and other lands to ensure the continued growth of trees on such lands; establishes nurseries to supply the trees needed to "replace the millions destroyed annually and to offset Man's ever increasing use of combustion." Offers training in the planting and caring of trees; fosters research; is developing a specialized library focusing on the biosphere. Maintains and promotes the National Tree Fund, which provides financial support to plant and care for trees. Compiles statistics; maintains speakers' bureau.

★387★ National Water Center
PO Box 264
Eureka Springs, AR 72632
Phone: (501)253-9755
Disseminates information on water issues, emphasizing responsibility for human and hazardous waste.

★388★ National Water Resources Association
3800 N Fairfax Dr., #4
Arlington, VA 22203
Phone: (703)524-1544
Individuals and groups interested in water resource development projects.

★389★ National Waterfowl Council (NWC)
Minnesota Dept. of Natural Resources
500 Lafayette Rd.
Box 20
St. Paul, MN 55155
Phone: (612)297-1308
Contact: Roger Holmes, Chm.
Founded: 1952. ***Members:*** 50. States and federal and provincial governments of Canada. Coordinates waterfowl planning, research, and management. Provides data to and advises the U.S. Fish and Wildlife Service on management of migratory waterfowl and upland game birds.

★390★ National Watershed Congress (NWC)
c/o National Association of Conservation Districts
509 Capital Ct.
Washington, DC 20002
Phone: (202)547-6223
Fax: (202)547-6450
Contact: Ernest C. Shea, Exec. Officer
Founded: 1954. ***Members:*** 28. National conservation, farm, civic, and business organizations interested in fostering discussion and advancement of natural resources conservation and development through upstream watershed programs. The congress does not propagandize, adopt resolutions, promote projects, or take any action, but acts as a forum for discussion of methods to expedite and broaden local watershed programs. Though the first congresses were concerned primarily with water control and soil erosion, in recent years the NWC has dealt with river basin planning, land treatment, and national water policy in general. Bestows Oustanding Watershed Management Award to citizens and projects.

★391★ National Wetlands Technical Council (NWTC)
1616 P St. NW, 2nd Fl.
Washington, DC 20036
Phone: (202)328-5150
Contact: Nicole Veilleux, Exec.Sec.
Founded: 1977. ***Members:*** 14. Scientists in the field of wetlands ecology. Provides a forum for scientific and technical information exchange among members. Participates in the Wetlands Program of the Environmental Law Institute.

★392★ National Wild Turkey Federation (NWTF)
PO Box 530
Wild Turkey Bldg.
Edgefield, SC 29824
Phone: (803)637-3106
Fax: (803)637-0034
Contact: Rob Keck, Exec.V.Pres.
Founded: 1973. ***Members:*** 60,000. Wild turkey enthusiasts and biologists. Dedicated to

the wise conservation and management of the American wild turkey as a valuable natural resource. Assists state wildlife agencies, universities, and other state or local organizations in conducting research, management, and restoration programs. Maintains Wild Turkey Center and financial assistance programs for agencies, organizations, and individuals. Sponsors annual wild turkey stamp and print art program and turkey calling competition.

★393★ National Wildflower Research Center
2600 FM 973
Austin, TX 78725
Phone: (512)929-3600
Promotes the propagation and conservation of wildflowers.

★394★ National Wildlife Federation (NWF)
1400 16th St. NW
Washington, DC 20036-2266
Phone: (202)797-6800
Contact: Dr. Jay D. Hair, Pres.
Founded: 1936. ***Members:*** 6,200,000. Federation of state and territorial conservation organizations and associate members, including individual conservationist-contributors. Encourages the intelligent management of the life-sustaining resources of the earth and promotes greater appreciation of these resources, and their community relationship. Gives organizational and financial assistance to local conservation projects; annually awards fellowships for graduate study of conservation; publishes conservation-education teaching materials. Compiles and distributes annual survey of compensation in the fields of fish and wildlife management. Conducts guided nature trail tours, conservation summits, Ranger Rick's Wildlife Camp, CLASS (Conservation Learning Activities for Science and Social Studies) Program, Earth TREK for teens, and Institute for Wildlife Research. Sponsors National Wildlife Week, the Backyard Wildlife Habitat Program, and Ranger Rick's Nature Club (see separate entry). Produces Nature NewsBreak (daily radio program). Operates 8000 volume library; maintains Conservation Hall of Fame and Wildlife Gallery of Art; sponsors competitions.

★395★ National Wildlife Federation Corporate Conservation Council (NWFCCC)
1400 16th St. NW
Washington, DC 20036
Phone: (202)797-6870
Fax: (202)797-6871
Contact: Barbara Haas, Dir.
Founded: 1982. ***Members:*** 15. A program of the National Wildlife Federation. Corporations represented by senior officers responsible for compliance with environmental protection laws. Provides forum for discussion among members and for the creation and implementation of policy statements.

★396★ National Wildlife Refuge Association (NWRA)
10824 Fox Hunt Ln.
Potomac, MD 20854
Phone: (301)983-1238
Contact: Ginger Merchant Meese, Exec.V.Pres.
Founded: 1975. ***Members:*** 800. Conservation clubs, National Audubon Society chapters, birding groups, National Wildlife Refuge employees and retirees and interested individuals. Seeks to protect the integrity of the National Wildlife Refuge System and to increase public understanding and appreciation of it. Conducts education and information programs; stimulates public and private decision-making and action toward improvement of the quality of the refuge system. Sponsors special projects.

★397★ National Wildlife Rehabilitators Association (NWRA)
12805 St. Croix Trail
Hastin, MN 55033
Phone: (612)437-9194
Contact: Elaine M. Thrune, Pres.
Founded: 1982. ***Members:*** 830. Wildlife rehabilitators and other interested individuals including state and federal agency personnel, conservationists, educators, naturalists, researchers, veterinarians, and zoo and humane society staff. Supports the science and profession of wildlife rehabilitation and its pracitioners. Purposes are to: improve the profession through the development of high standards of practice, ethics, and conduct; disseminate and stimulate the growth of knowledge in the field; foster cooperation of professional and governmental agencies and other similar groups with the wildlife rehabilitation community. Has developed a National Standards and Accreditation Program, in conjunction with the International Wildlife Rehabilitation Council (see separate entry), to encourage the development of outstanding rehabilitation programs. Maintains unreleasable wildlife referral list to place permanently disabled animals with zoos, nature centers, breeding programs, research programs, and other institutions. Provides research grants; conducts networking; offers consulting services. Maintains slide collection. Bestows significant achievement and lifetime achievement awards. Operates speakers' bureau.

★398★ Native Seeds/SEARCH
2509 N. Campbell Ave., No. 325
Tucson, AZ 85719
Phone: (602)327-9123
Contact: Gary Nabhan, Pres.
Founded: 1982. ***Members:*** 2700. Works to conserve greater southwestern traditional crop seeds and related wild seeds. Coordinates networking and distribution of seeds; offers member discounts on seeds. Provides speakers; maintains demonstration and research garden. Sponsors workshops. ***Former Name(s):*** Meals for Millions; Southwest Traditional Crop Conservancy Garden and Seed Bank (1982).

★399★ Natural Area Council (NAC)
219 Shoreham Bldg. NW
Washington, DC 20005
Phone: (202)638-1649
Contact: Paul Bruce Dowling, Pres.
Founded: 1957. Persons concerned with the preservation of natural areas. Governed by ten-member board of leading conservationists.

★400★ Natural Areas Association (NAA)
320 S. 3rd St.
Rockford, IL 61104
Phone: (815)964-6666
Contact: Lydia S. Macauley, Sec.-Treas.
Founded: 1978. ***Members:*** 2200. Individuals promoting the preservation and effective management of natural areas and other elements of natural diversity. Goals are: to provide a channel for the exchange of information on natural area preservation and management; to promote preservation techniques consistent with sound biological and ecological principles to benefit society; to increase public awareness of natural areas; to support research. Formulates and adopts statements of policy.

★401★ Natural Resources Council of America (NRC)
801 Pennsylvania Ave. NW, No. 410
Washington, DC 20003
Phone: (202)547-7553
Contact: Andrea J. Yank, Exec.Dir.
Founded: 1946. ***Members:*** 50. Federation of national and regional conservation organizations and scientific societies interested in conservation of natural resources. Conducts studies and surveys. Sponsors occasional commemorative events. Bestows awards.

★402★ Natural Resources Defense Council (NRDC)
40 W. 20th St.
New York, NY 10011
Phone: (212)727-4412
Fax: (212)727-1773
Contact: John H. Adams, Exec.Dir.
Founded: 1970. ***Members:*** 150,000. Lawyers, scientists, public health specialists, and transportation, energy, land use, and economic planners. Dedicated to the wise management of natural resources through research, public education, and the development of public policies. Concerns include land use, coastal protection, air and water pollution, nuclear safety and energy production, toxic substances, and protection of wilderness and wildlife. Works to increase public understanding of the means by which law may be used to protect resources; engages in litigation that may set widely applicable precedents or preserve natural resources. Monitors federal departments and regulatory agencies concerned with the environment, to ensure that public interest is considered. Conducts several research projects. Sponsors the Nuclear Non-Proliferation Project.

★403★ Natural Resources Districts
1327 H St., Suite 102
Lincoln, NE 68508
Phone: (402)474-3383
Contact: Gordon Kissel
Regional national resources districts which address soil and water conservation issues.

★404★ The Nature Conservancy
1815 N. Lynn St.
Arlington, VA 22209
Phone: (703)841-5300
Contact: John C. Sawhill, Contact
Founded: 1917. ***Members:*** 550,000. Dedicated to the preservation of biological diversity through land protection of natural areas. Identifies ecologically significant lands and protects them through gift, purchase, or cooperative management agreements with government or private agencies, voluntary arrangements with private landowners, and cost-saving methods of protection. Provides long-term stewardship for 1600 conservancy-owned preserves and makes most conservancy lands available for nondestructive use on request by educational and scientific organizations. Bestows awards; compiles statistics. ***Former Name(s):*** Committee on Preservation of Natural Conditions, Ecological Society of America (1946); Ecologists Union (1950).

★405★ Negative Population Growth
PO Box 1206
210 The Plaza
Teaneck, NJ 07666
Phone: (201)837-3555

Contact: Donald Mann, President
Organization of individuals who believe a "drastic reduction in total population size represents the only viable option consistent with human survival."

★406★ New Alchemy Institute (NAI)
237 Hatchville Rd.
East Falmouth, MA 02536
Phone: (508)564-6301
Fax: (508)457-9680
Contact: Greg Watson, Exec.Dir.
Founded: 1969. ***Members:*** 2000. Works toward an "ecological future" for humanity through research and education. Conducts research and provides education for household and small farm economics on resource-efficient housing and landscape design, organic market gardening, solar greenhouse agriculture, integrated pest management, and lowering the use of toxins in the home and garden. Offers consulting services and internships; holds workshops for teachers and the community; conducts spring college semester program on sustainable design; developed the Green Classroom Program for schools.

★407★ New England WildFlower Society (NEWFS)
Hemenway Rd.
Framingham, MA 01701
Phone: (508)877-7630
Contact: Barbara Pryor, Exec. Officer
Founded: 1922. ***Members:*** 3500. Individuals, families, and horticultural and botanical organizations. Promotes conservation of North American flora through horticulture research and education. Acts as clearinghouse for plant projects (particularly research, education, and legislation) in New England. Activities include: classes for adults and children; field trips; international seed exchange; garden tours. Operates library of 3000 volumes and 20,000 slides. Bestows award for outstanding achievement in conservation. Displays landscaped collection of wildflowers in the Garden in the Woods, a 45-acre botanic garden of native plants. Maintains six other sanctuaries. ***Former Name(s):*** New England Wild Flower Preservation Society (1971).

★408★ New World Society (NWS)
5932 Rose Arbor Ave.
San Pablo, CA 94806
Phone: (415)237-7838
Contact: Guy W. Meyer, Exec. Officer
Founded: 1970. Individuals promoting human unity, peace, and the development of a healthy environment and ecological system. Encourages individuals to focus concern on human and ecological issues. Opposes nationalism, materialism, militarism, and what the group feels are other destructive and wasteful values and activities.

★409★ New York Turtle and Tortoise Society
163 Amsterdam Ave., Ste. 365
New York, NY 10023
Phone: (212)459-4803
Contact: Suzanne Dohm, Pres.
Founded: 1970. ***Members:*** 1000. Veterinarians, zookeepers, biologists, and pet owners nationwide. Purpose is the conservation, preservation, and propagation of turtles and tortoises. Advocates protective legislation for endangered species; encourages enforcement of humane laws. Disseminates information on the care and breeding of turtles and tortoises. Maintains the Turtle Rehab Program, dedicated to the care and rehabilitation of injured turtles found in the wild. Conducts annual seminar. Bestows awards; maintains speakers' bureau. Provides adoption program for unwanted animals; Sponsors field trips.

★410★ North American Association for Environmental Education (NAEE)
PO Box 400
Troy, OH 45373
Phone: (513)339-6835
Fax: (513)698-6493
Contact: Joan C. Heidelberg, Exec.V.Pres.
Founded: 1971. ***Members:*** 1000. Individuals associated with colleges, community colleges, public schools, and environmental organizations; associates include students in environmental education and environmental studies. Objectives are to: promote environmental education programs at all levels; coordinate environmental education activities among such programs and educational institutions; disseminate information about environmental education activities appropriate for such programs and institutions; assist educational institutions in beginning or developing programs of this kind and to serve as a resource to them; foster sharing of information about environmental education programs among institutions and individual members; promote communication about environmental education and the pooling of information, resources, and activities in connection with such programs; foster research and evaluation in connection with environmental education and other studies and investigations of such programs. Conducted a seminar to develop a curriculum in environmental education. Presents annual award to outstanding environmentalist or environmental educator and to deserving industry or individual. ***Former Name(s):*** National Association for Environmental Education (1983).

★411★ North American Benthological Society (NABS)
Savannah River Ecology Laboratory
Drawer E
Aiken, SC 29802
Phone: (803)725-7425
Fax: (803)725-7413
Contact: Cheryl R. Black, Exec. Officer
Founded: 1953. ***Members:*** 1500. Researchers in aquatic ecology. Promotes better understanding of the benthic biological community and its role in freshwater aquatic ecosystems. Conducts research into specific aquatic groups such as algae, vascular plants, zooplankton, phytoplankton, insects, crustaceans, mollusks, and fishes. Other areas of interest include: classification of aquatic biota; determination of pollution-tolerance ranges of aquatic species; the effect of water quality on distribution and abundance in the benthic community; hydrology; methods of sampling and measuring components of aquatic ecosystems. Disseminates information to the scientific community. Bestows awards. ***Former Name(s):*** Midwest Benthological Society.

★412★ North American Bluebird Society (NABS)
Box 6295
Silver Spring, MD 20916-6295
Phone: (301)384-2798
Contact: Mary D. Janetatos, Exec.Dir.
Founded: 1978. ***Members:*** 5500. Conservationists and other individuals and groups interested in bluebirds and other native cavity nesting birds of North America. To alert the public to the slow but definite disappearance of the bluebird due to lack of suitable nesting cavities and severe weather; to encourage establishment of bluebird trails of nesting boxes or individual nesting boxes; to keep scientific records of the bluebird's nesting habits and act as information clearinghouse. Presents slide shows; provides lecture demonstrations to schools and interested youth groups. Conducts research; provides research grants; compiles statistics; maintains speakers' bureau; bestows awards.

★413★ North American Lake Management Society
PO Box 217
Merrifield, VA 22116
Phone: (202)466-8550
Promotes a better understanding lakes, ponds, reservoirs, impoundments, and watersheds. Offers consulting to public and private agencies involved in lake management.

★414★ North American Loon Fund (NALF)
R.R. 4, Box 240C
Meredith, NH 03253
Phone: (603)279-6163
Toll-Free: 800-462-5666
Contact: Linda O'Bara, Operations Dir.
Founded: 1979. ***Members:*** 1800. Individuals, institutions, and other organizations interested in preservation of the common loon. Seeks to protect loons and their habitat by constructing artificial nesting sites, educating the public, and discouraging lakeshore development in areas frequented by loons. Provides educational programs in areas where loons and humans coexist. Conducts research on: loon biology and behavior; the impact of human activity and water pollution on loon reproduction; loon population levels in various regions. Bestows grants for research and management efforts.

★415★ North American Wildlife Foundation (NAWF)
102 Wilmot Rd., Ste. 410
Deerfield, IL 60015
Phone: (708)940-7776
Contact: Charles S. Potter Jr., Exec.V.Pres.
Founded: 1911. Trustees: 39. To ensure, through financial support, the continuity of effective, practical, and systematic research of management practices and techniques, locally, nationally, and internationally, in order to benefit wildlife and other natural resources in the public interest. The foundation works through cooperating agencies, organizations, and institutions and does not serve as an action group. Owns Delta Waterfowl Research Station in Manitoba, Canada. Maintains library of natural science subjects and wildlife restoration and management. ***Former Name(s):*** American Game Protective Association (1935); American Wildlife Institute (1946); American Wildlife Foundation (1951).

★416★ North American Wildlife Park Foundation (NAWPF)
Wolf Park
Battle Ground, IN 47920
Phone: (317)567-2265
Fax: (317)567-2084
Contact: Erich Klinghammer Ph.D., Pres.
Founded: 1972. ***Members:*** 1500. Conservationists and others interested in wolves and wildlife. Operates Wolf Park in Battle Ground, Indiana; conducts ongoing research into animal behavior; provides research opportunities to scientists and students; sponsors lectures, college internships, and teaching programs. Monitors legislation affecting predatory animals.

★417★ North American Wolf Society (NAWS)
PO Box 82950
Fairbanks, AK 99708
Phone: (907)474-6117
Contact: Anne K. Ruggles, Pres.
Founded: 1973. ***Members:*** 400. Professional biologists/zoologists, libraries, lay conservationists, state and federal agencies, and related organizations. Encourages a rational approach to the conservation of the wolf and other wild canids of North America. Seeks to provide accurate insight into the realities of wildlife and the wilderness today. Has conducted research of Potential of Wolf Transplant or Reintroduction Programs via State Wildlife Divisions; Survey of U.S. Zoos Regarding Number and Subspecies of Wolves in Captivity. Plans to conduct surveys of current university/agency/organizational research concerning wild canids, and of sources offering educational kits or services.

★418★ Ocean Alliance
Bldg. E, Ft. Mason Center
San Francisco, CA 94123
Phone: (415)441-5970
Protects water resources by fighting pollution and promoting ocean conservation and education.

★419★ Open Space Institute (OSI)
40 W. 20th St.
New York, NY 10011
Phone: (212)255-2605
Fax: (212)255-6369
Contact: Thomas Whyatt, Exec.Dir.
Founded: 1974. Assists groups in protecting open space and promoting environmental values through public education, litigation, and land conservation. Provides technical and administrative services to citizen environmental projects. ***Former Name(s):*** Open Space Action Committee.

★420★ Organization of Wildlife Planners (OWP)
DNR-Box 7921
Madison, WI 53707
Phone: (608)267-7591
Fax: (608)267-3579
Contact: Dennis A. Schenborn, Pres.
Founded: 1979. ***Members:*** 36. Directors and associate directors of wildlife planning programs; program directors of state and provincial natural resource agencies; university instructors of fish or wildlife management and policy. Dedicated to improving management in fish, wildlife, and natural resources agencies throughout North America. Promotes an organized, objective-oriented approach to the management of North America's wildlife resources. Facilitates the exchange of ideas among members; provides liaison with resource management agencies. Conducts seminars and on-site workshops. Bestows awards; maintains speakers' bureau.

★421★ Outdoor Ethics Guild (OEG)
General Delivery
Bucks Harbor, ME 04618
Contact: Bruce Bandurski, Pres.
Founded: 1967. Scientific/educational organization which promotes an individual's ethical behavior concerning the environment. Directs attention to applied sciences that foster self-sufficiency and self-government to the extent possible in an ecosphere. Is concerned with identification and consideration of all entities and relationships crucial to life-support systems for man and other organisms. Calls attention to exemplary instances of ecomanagement ethics.

★422★ Ozark Society
PO Box 2914
Little Rock, AR 72203
Phone: (501)847-3738
Contact: Stewart Noland, Pres.
Founded: 1962. ***Members:*** 1600. Individuals united for conservation, education, and recreation. Major emphasis is on preservation of scenic rivers and wilderness areas, particularly in the Ozark-Ouachita mountain region. Sponsors hiking and boating trips and clean-up campaigns.

★423★ Pacific Sea-bird Group (PSG)
University of California
Dept. of Avian Sciences
Davis, CA 95616
Phone: (916)752-1300
Contact: Dr. D. Michael Fry, Chm.
Founded: 1972. ***Members:*** 450. Persons interested in the study and conservation of Pacific seabirds which includes over 275 species of birds all related by their dependence on the ocean environment. Purpose is to increase the flow of information among seabird researchers, and to inform members and the public of conservation issues relating to seabirds and the marine environment.

★424★ Pacific Whale Foundation (PWF)
Kealia Beach Plaza, Ste. 25
101 N. Kihei Rd.
Kihei, HI 96753
Phone: (808)879-8811
Fax: (808)879-2615
Contact: Gregory D. Kaufman, Pres.
Founded: 1980. Scientists, conservationists, and volunteers united to prevent biological extinction of marine mammals. Goal is to scientifically identify adverse factors affecting the recovery of endangered marine mammals and work to eradicate those factors. Provides research, conservation, and educational programs involving whales, dolphins, porpoises, and other marine mammals. Believes that aside from philosophical, ethical, and emotional issues, whales, dolphins, and porpoises are biologically essential to the earth's ecosystem. Establishes primary and long-term contact with marine mammals in their natural environment allowing scientists to observe and analyze animal behavior and thus create and modify conservation programs to meet their needs. Conducts research programs throughout the Pacific, with recent whale studies in Hawaii, American and Western Samoa, Tonga, Fiji, Australia, and Alaska. Sponsors lectures for schools, community groups, and universities. Solicits funds through the Adopt-A-Whale Program, merchandise sales, whalewatching cruises, expeditions, and internships. Maintains speakers' bureau, and library of books and other publications on marine mammals and their habitat. Compiles statistics. Is currently studying the effects of increased human activity in the humpback whale's Hawaiian breeding grounds as a possible contributor to the whale's reduced biological fitness.

★425★ Paper Stock Institute (PSI)
c/o Institute of Scrap Recycling Industries
1627 K St. NW, Ste. 700
Washington, DC 20006
Phone: (202)466-4050
Fax: (202)775-9109
Contact: Herschel Cutler
A division of the Institute of Scrap Recycling Industries. Purpose is to recycle paper and paperboard. ***Former Name(s):*** Paper Stock Institute of America (1990).

★426★ Partners in Parks
1855 Quarley Pl.
Henderson, NV 89014
Phone: (702)454-5547
Assists individuals and organizations utilize gain access to national parks to work on projects.

★427★ Pelican Man's Bird Sanctuary
PO Box 2648
Sarasota, FL 34230
Phone: (813)955-2266
Contact: Dale Shields, Pres. & Founder
Founded: 1985. ***Members:*** 3000. Individuals and corporations interested in supporting environmental and wildlife preservation. Seeks to promote wildlife protection and rescue and operates a rehabilitation center for injured pelicans, blue herons, sea gulls, and other birds. Offers educational programs; maintains speakers' bureau. ***Former Name(s):*** Protect Our Pelican Society.

★428★ Pennsylvania Resources Council
25 W. 3rd St.
PO Box 88
Media, PA 19063
Phone: (215)565-9131
Sponsers recycling conference every spring.

★429★ People for the Ethical Treatment of Animals
PO Box 42516
Washington, DC 20015
Phone: (301)770-7444
Promotes the humane treatment of animals with special focus on laboratory test animals.

★430★ Peregrine Fund (PF)
World Center for Birds of Prey
5666 W. Flying Hawk Ln.
Boise, ID 83709
Phone: (208)362-3716
Fax: (208)362-2376
Contact: Dr. William Burnham, Pres.
Founded: 1970. Persons in the fields of biology, ecology, and natural resources concerned with the study and preservation of falcons and other birds of prey. Seeks to reestablish natural populations of the Peregrine falcon and other endangered raptors. Informs the public of the value of raptors and the need for their conservation. Operates World Center for Birds of Prey to serve as a research and education facility and to maintain and captively propagate rare birds of prey.

★431★ Plastics Recycling Foundation (PRF)
1275 K St. NW, Ste. 500
Washington, DC 20005
Phone: (202)371-5200
Contact: Wayne E. Pearson, Exec.Dir.
Founded: 1985. ***Members:*** 34. Suppliers, manufacturers, and users of plastics materials and products. Sponsors research in the recovery and reuse of plastics products (primarily plastic packaging material). Maintains speakers' bureau; offers research grants. Conducts technology transfer seminars.

★432★ Point Foundation (PF)
27 Gate Five Rd.
Sausalito, CA 94965
Phone: (415)332-1716

★433★ Population Council
1 Dag Hammarskjold Plaza
New York, NY 10017
Phone: (212)644-1300
Contact: George Zeidenstein, President
Conducts health and social science programs and research relevant to developing countries, including contraceptive technology, biomedicine, population policy, and reproductive health.

★434★ Population Crisis Committee
1120 19th St., NW, Ste. 550
Washington, DC 20036
Phone: (202)659-1833
Contact: J. Joseph Speidel, President
Private, nonprofit organization which encourages activities that promise the greatest impact on reducing world population growth.

★435★ Population-Environment Balance
1325 G St., NW, Ste. 1003
Washington, DC 20005
Phone: (202)879-3000
Contact: Rose Hanes, Executive Director
Concerned with the population growth of the U.S.

★436★ Population Institute
110 Maryland Ave., NE, Ste. 207
Washington, DC 20002
Phone: (202)544-3300
Contact: Werner Fornos, President
Seeks to marshall opinion on global overpopulation problems.

★437★ Population Resource Center
500 E. 62nd St.
New York, NY 10021
Phone: (212)888-2820
Contact: Jane S. De Lung, President
Prepares and conducts briefings, workshops, and policy discussions on population-related topics.

★438★ Porpoise Rescue Foundation (PRF)
2040 Harbor Island Dr., Ste. 202
San Diego, CA 92101
Phone: (619)574-1573
Contact: Jack Bowland, Pres.
Founded: 1977. Established by the U.S. Tuna Foundation. Works with tuna boat skippers to develop effective porpoise rescue methods for porpoises that are accidentally trapped and often killed in nets meant for tuna. Funds relevant studies.

★439★ Prairie Chicken Foundation (PCF)
1121 Timothy Ave.
Madison, WI 53716
Phone: (608)222-5631
Contact: Donald R. Hollatz, Pres.
Founded: 1958. Persons dedicated to the preservation of the prairie chicken in Wisconsin. Raises funds and acquires land to develop prairie chicken habitat in the state. Owns approximately 5000 acres; makes purchases cooperatively with the Society of Tympanuchus Cupido Pinnatus.

★440★ Programme for Belize
PO Box 1088
Vineyard Haven, MA 02568
Phone: (508)693-0856
Offers the protection of an acre of tropical rain forest for $50 contribution.

★441★ Public Citizen
2000 P St. NW
Washington, DC 20036
Phone: (202)293-9142
Conducts research, lobbying, and lawsuits on issues including stronger environmental programs.

★442★ Public Health Network (PHNET)
Public Health Foundation
1220 L St., NW, Ste. 350
Washington, DC 20005
Phone: (202)898-5600
Online systems, database access network.

★443★ Public Voice for Food and Health Policy
1001 Connecticut Ave. NW
Washington, DC 20036
Phone: (202)659-5930
Conducts research and education on issues related to health, nutrition, and food safety.

★444★ Purple Martin Conservation Association (PMCA)
Edinboro University of Pennsylvania
Edinboro, PA 16444
Phone: (814)734-4420
Contact: James R. Hill III, Exec. Officer
Founded: 1987. ***Members:*** 4600. Individuals interested in the purple martin. Gathers and disseminates information on techniques of attracting martins and managing nesting sites; conducts research on martin biology and breeding and migratory habits; cooperates with other organizations and government agencies to promote martin conservation. Operates Purple Martin Colony Registry Program, which seeks to locate and register every martin breeding site in North America. Conducts annual martin nesting survey; makes available martin husbandry supplies including bird houses, audiotaped martin calls for use in attracting birds, and house sparrow and starling traps. Maintains speakers' bureau; compiles statistics.

★445★ Quail Unlimited
PO Box 10041
Augusta, GA 30903
Phone: (803)637-5731
Fax: (803)637-0037
Contact: Joseph R. Evans, Exec.V.Pres.
Founded: 1981. ***Members:*** 45,000. Works for quail and upland bird conservation through its habitat management program and research. Conducts regional seminars; sponsors university research and scholarship programs; bestows awards. Operates Project Yield (Youth Involvement in Educational Land Development).

★446★ RACHEL
Environmental Awareness Foundation
PO Box 3541
Princeton, NJ 08543-3541
Phone: (609)683-0707
Online systems, database access network.

★447★ Radioactive Waste Campaign (RWC)
625 Broadway, 2nd Fl.
New York, NY 10012-2611
Phone: (212)473-7390
Contact: Patrick J. Malloy, Exec.Dir.
Founded: 1978. ***Members:*** 1000. Keeps concerned individuals informed of nuclear waste disposal problems, breakthroughs in waste technology, citizen battles against waste disposal in their areas, and tips on resources and organizing. Conducts research; provides speakers to community groups, churches, and educational forums. ***Former Name(s):*** Sierra Club Radioactive Waste Campaign (1986).

★448★ Rails-to-Trails Conservancy
1400 16th St. NW
Washington, DC 20036
Phone: (202)797-5400
Establishes trails on abandoned railroad tracks. Has established over 242 trails covering 3,200 miles across the U.S.

★449★ Rainforest Action Movement
430 E. University
Ann Arbor, MI 48109
Phone: (313)764-2147
Focuses on preservation, protection, and rational use of rain forests in Alaska, Oregon, Washington, Hawaii, and tropical areas.

★450★ Rainforest Action Network (RAN)
301 Broadway, Ste. A
San Francisco, CA 94133
Phone: (415)398-4404
Fax: (415)398-2732
Telex: Econet: RAINFOREST
Contact: Randall Hayes, Dir.
Founded: 1985. ***Members:*** 30,000. Seeks to preserve the world's rainforests through activism on issues including the logging and importation of tropical timber, cattle ranching in rainforests, the activities of international development banks, and the rights of indigenous rainforest peoples. Sponsors letter writing campaigns, boycotts, and demonstrations; conducts grass roots organizing in the U.S., builds coalitions, and collaborates with other environmental, scientific, and grass roots groups; facilitates communication among U.S. and Third World organizers. Works to educate the public about the effects of tropical hardwood logging; promotes ecologically sound plantations to restore degraded land. Conducts research; sponsors media outreach projects.

★451★ Rainforest Alliance
270 Lafayette St., Ste. 512
New York, NY 10012
Phone: (212)941-1900
Fax: (212)941-4986
Contact: Daniel Katz, Pres.
Founded: 1986. ***Members:*** 2500. Individuals concerned with the conservation of tropical forests. Seeks to expand awareness of the role the United States plays in the fate of tropical forests and to inform Americans about how their actions affect tropical forests. Works with financial and educational institutions, media, corporations, and the public to encourage policies and attitudes that will save rainforests. Maintains speakers' bureau and small library. Sponsors Periwinkle Project and Tropical Timber Project; operates Tropical Conservation Newsbureau in Costa Rica; offers Kleinhans Fellowship in Tropical Agroforestry. ***Former Name(s):*** New York Rainforest Alliance (1988).

★452★ Ranger Rick's Nature Club (RRNC)
8925 Leesburg Pike
Vienna, VA 22184
Phone: (703)790-4000
Contact: Gerald Bishop, Editor
Founded: 1967. ***Members:*** 900,000. Children's division of the National Wildlife Federation, purpose is to teach young children to know and respect all living things so that all may act to conserve and wisely use the natural resources of the world.

★453★ Raptor Research Foundation (RRF)
York College of Pennsylvania
Dept. of Biology
York, PA 17403-3426
Phone: (717)846-7788
Fax: (717)846-1274
Contact: Richard J. Clark, Pres.
Founded: 1966. ***Members:*** 1000. Individuals interested in birds of prey. Provides a forum for exchanging information concerning research in the biology and management of birds of prey. Promotes a better understanding and appreciation of the value of these birds. Offers small grants; conducts research and disseminates information.

★454★ RARE Center for Tropical Bird Conservation
19th & Parkway
Philadelphia, PA 19103
Phone: (215)299-1182
Contact: John Guarnaccia, Exec.Dir.
Founded: 1973. Generates and funds projects that will directly aid endangered tropical bird species of the Caribbean and Latin America. Conducts educational program for public information on endangered species. ***Former Name(s):*** Rare Animal Relief Effort (1987).

★455★ Rene Dubos Center for Human Environments
100 E. 85th St.
New York, NY 10028
Phone: (212)249-7745
Fax: (212)772-2033
Contact: Ruth A. Eblen, Exec.Dir.
Founded: 1969. ***Members:*** 500. Government and industry decision-makers, academicians, and environmentalists. Seeks, through research and education, to aid the public, businesses, and government in decision-making regarding environmental concerns. Promotes the creation of new environmental values. Named for scientist/humanist Rene Dubos (1901-82), who was noted for his concern for the environment. ***Former Name(s):*** Rene Dubos Forum (1975); Total Education in the Total Environment (1980).

★456★ Renew America
1400 16th St. NW, Ste. 710
Washington, DC 20036
Phone: (202)232-2252
Provides resources to individuals concerned with building a sustainable society.

★457★ Renewable Natural Resources Foundation (RNRF)
5430 Grosvenor Ln.
Bethesda, MD 20814
Phone: (301)493-9101
Fax: (301)493-6148
Contact: Robert D. Day, Exec.Dir.
Founded: 1972. ***Members:*** 17. Members are American Anthropological Association, American Congress on Surveying and Mapping, American Fisheries Society, American Geophysical Union, American Society of Landscape Architects, American Society for Photogrammetry and Remote Sensing, American Water Resources Association, Association of American Geographers, Association for Conservation Information, Coastal Society, Ecological Society of America, Humane Society of the United States, Nature Conservancy, Society for Range Management, Soil and Water Conservation Society, Wildlife Society, and Resources for the Future. Concerned with renewable natural resources subjects and public policy alternatives. Developed the Renewable Natural Resources Center, an office-park complex for natural resource organizations.

★458★ Resource Policy Institute (RPI)
1745 Selby, Ste. 11
Los Angeles, CA 90024
Phone: (213)475-1684
Contact: Dr. Arthur H. Purcell, Exec.Dir.
Founded: 1975. ***Members:*** 2000. Research, education, and consulting group concerned with environmental and resource policy issues dealing with water and minerals, resource conservation, energy and technology policy, and national waste issues. Specializes in domestic and international perspectives on how environmental changes influence humans and wildlife. Conducts Waste Resource Auditing Program; provides information on alternative energy, toxic substances, and the impact of federal legislation.

★459★ Resource Renewal Institute
Ft. Cronkhite, Bldg. 1055
Sausalito, CA 94965
Phone: (415)332-8082
Contact: Huey Johnson
Natural resources management model. Provides consultation to local, state, regional, and national governments worldwide.

★460★ Rocky Mountain Elk Foundation (RMEF)
PO Box 8249
Missoula, MT 59807
Phone: (406)721-0010
Fax: (406)549-4325
Contact: Robert W. Munson, Exec. Officer
Founded: 1984. ***Members:*** 50,000. Hunters and conservationists. Raises funds for conservation efforts aimed at the preservation of elk and other wildlife, and their habitats.

★461★ Rocky Mountain Institute
1739 Snowmass Creek Rd.
Old Snowmass, CO 81654
Phone: (303)927-3128
Promotes efficient and sustainable use of resources.

★462★ Roo Rat Society (RRS)
Whitman College
Walla Walla, WA 99362
Phone: (509)527-5229
Contact: James S. Todd, Scribe
Founded: 1963. ***Members:*** 256. Persons dedicated to the study and conservation of wildlife and natural resources on local, national, and international levels. Supports conservation projects by encouraging members to write to political leaders. Disseminates conservation news. Society derives its name from the kangaroo rat, a small rodent living in dry, sandy regions of North America.

★463★ Ruffed Grouse Society (RGS)
1400 Lee Dr.
Coraopolis, PA 15108
Phone: (412)262-4044
Contact: Dr. Samuel R. Pursglove Jr., Exec.Dir.
Founded: 1961. ***Members:*** 23,000. Conservationists dedicated to improving the environment for ruffed grouse, woodcock, and other forest wildlife. Encourages private, industrial, state, county, and federal landowners to manage their woodlands to benefit forest wildlife. Actively assists landholders by: publishing and distributing guides for habitat improvement; sponsoring symposia, conferences, training sessions, and on- and off-site consultations; directing and sponsoring habitat improvement demonstration areas. Also endows projects designed to obtain additional information on improving woodland habitat for wildlife. Conducts specialized education for children and adults. ***Former Name(s):*** Ruffed Grouse Society of America (1971); Ruffed Grouse Society of North America (1977).

★464★ Safari Club International (SCI)
4800 W. Gates Pass Rd.
Tucson, AZ 85745
Phone: (602)620-1220
Fax: (602)622-1205
Contact: Warren Parker, Pres.
Founded: 1971. ***Members:*** 20,000. Sportsmen united to encourage conservation of wildlife. Promotes hunting as a wildlife management tool; aims to preserve public hunting and protect hunters' rights. Fosters public education concerning conservation; sponsors research. Supports communication and good fellowship among members. Operates hall of fame; conducts seminars; bestows awards.

★465★ Saint Hubert Society of America (SHSA)
9 Dresser St.
Newport, RI 02840
Phone: (401)847-5697
Contact: Thomas C. Keister Jr., Pres.
Founded: 1958. ***Members:*** 100. Individuals interested in wildlife, conservation, hunting, and the lore of the outdoors. Promotes "conservation, hunting, fishing, and the preservation of the great American and European heritage of the outdoors and those traditions of sportsmanship and fair play which have become associated with the American way of life". Sponsors outings for members including shoots, hunts, and fishing expeditions. Acquaints underprivileged children in the greater New York and New England area with the natural beauty of wilderness areas and with various forms of American wildlife. Maintains Saint Hubert Society Conservation Fund. Named in honor of the patron saint of hunters who was born in Belgium in the middle of the seventh century. Parent societies have been in existence in Europe since the eighth century.

★466★ Save the Manatee Club (SMC)
500 N. Maitland Ave.
Maitland, FL 32751
Phone: (407)539-0990
Toll-Free: 800-432-JOIN
Contact: Judith Delaney Vallee, Exec.Dir.
Founded: 1981. ***Members:*** 24,000. Naturalists, students, businessmen, and other individuals. Purpose is to help save and protect the West Indian manatee, an endangered Florida marine mammal, and its habitat. Seeks to heighten public awareness and education regarding sanctuary areas, boating speed signs, and laws pertaining to protection of the manatees. Sponsors public service announcements that are distributed to television stations throughout the country, educational outreach programs for school classes and clubs, and manatee awareness workshops. Raises funds for research programs on manatee mortality reduction, population trends, and life history, and for the purchase of manatee warning signs to be posted in inland waterways. Conducts lobbying activities.

★467★ Save-the-Redwoods League (SRL)
114 Sansome St., Rm. 605
San Francisco, CA 94104
Phone: (415)362-2352
Contact: John B. Dewitt, Exec.Dir.
Founded: 1918. ***Members:*** 45,000. Persons interested in preserving representative stands

of Coast Redwoods and Giant Sequoias, as well as other trees, principally in California. Works with California State Parks Commission and the National Park Service to establish Redwood Parks. Purchases redwood groves through private subscription and supports reforestation and conservation of forest areas. Provides information about redwoods and the program to preserve them.

★468★ Save the Whales
PO Box 3650
Washington, DC 20007
Phone: (202)337-2332
Contact: Christine Stevens, Pres.
Founded: 1971. Contributors: 8000. Informs the public about the dilemma of great whales, seeks to save them from extinction, and works for whale regeneration. Opposes commercial whaling. Provides public service announcements on television and radio and places advertisements in newspapers and magazines. Sends representatives to the annual International Whaling Commission Conference. A project of the Animal Welfare Institute.

★469★ Scenic America (SA)
216 7th St. SE
Washington, DC 20003
Phone: (202)546-1100
Contact: Edward McMahon, Exec.Dir.
Founded: 1981. Coalition of individuals and organizations interested in preserving America's scenic beauty by controlling billboards and protecting landscapes; affilate organizations at the local and state level; planning and zoning commissions of local governments. Aims are to: promote sign control; provide legal advice and technical assistance on sign control and aesthetic regulation to municipalities and citizens' groups. Has established the Center for Sign Control in Washington, DC to provide advice to communities wishing to develop effective sign control strategies. Maintains speakers' bureau; compiles statistics; conducts seminars. ***Former Name(s):*** National Coalition to Preserve Scenic Beauty (1984); Coalition for Scenic Beauty (1989).

★470★ Sea Shepherd Conservation Society (SSCS)
PO Box 7000 S
Redondo Beach, CA 90277
Phone: (213)373-6979
Contact: Scott Trimingham, Exec. Officer
Founded: 1977. ***Members:*** 10,000. International activist conservation society concerned with the protection and conservation of marine mammals. Operates the research ship, Sea Shepherd. Opposes exploitation of all marine life and fights the problem through education, confrontation, and enforcement, although primary involvement is in confrontation and enforcement campaigns against illegal whaling and sealing activities. Has purchased land to create a wildlife sanctuary in the Orkney Islands. Sponsors art and educational projects. Conducts research on issues of conservation, national and international law, and environmental pollution. Maintains speakers' bureau and museum; bestows awards. Operates 300 volume library.

★471★ Seacoast Anti-Pollution League (SAPL)
5 Market St.
Portsmouth, NH 03801
Phone: (603)431-5089
Contact: Jean Lincoln, Field Dir.
Founded: 1969. ***Members:*** 850. Promotes the wise use of natural resources, especially in the seacoast region, and alerts and educates the community and relevant governmental agencies concerning threats to the quality of the environment. Seeks to prevent environmental, economic, and public health damage from the Seabrook nuclear reactor by means of legal intervention in the Seabrook licensing proceedings and intervention before the New Hampshire Public Utilities Commission and the U.S. bankruptcy courts. Conducts educational meetings and distributes leaflets.

★472★ Sierra Club
730 Polk St.
San Francisco, CA 94109
Phone: (415)776-2211
Contact: Michael Fischer, Exec.Dir.
Founded: 1892. ***Members:*** 565,000. Individuals concerned with nature and its interrelationship to man. Promotes protection and conservation of the natural resources of the U.S. and the world; educates others about the need to preserve and restore the quality of the environment and the integrity of those ecosystems. Works on urgent campaigns to save threatened areas; is concerned with problems of wilderness, forestry, clean air, coastal protection, energy conservation, and land use. Attempts to influence public policy at all governmental levels through legislative, administrative, legal, and electoral means. Schedules wilderness outings; presents awards; maintains biographical archives and library of 5000 volumes on mountaineering and environmental topics. Chapters and committees schedule outings, talks, films, exhibits, and conferences.

★473★ Sierra Club Legal Defense Fund
2044 Fillmore St.
San Francisco, CA 94115
Phone: (415)567-6100
Contact: Fredric P. Sutherland, Exec.Dir.
Founded: 1970. Purposes are to use existing legal remedies to protect the natural environment of the U.S. and develop a realistic and enforceable body of environmental law through the implementation of existing statutes, regulations, and common law principles. Maintains library.

★474★ Silent Running Society (SRS)
PO Box 529
Howell, NJ 07731
Contact: Steven Lance Hersh, Founder & Exec.Dir.
Founded: 1985. ***Members:*** 97. Businesses, industries, and individuals dedicated to the conservation of trees and reforestation. Attempts to save damaged trees; donates seedlings and trees for tree-planting events and large-scale reforestation on public and private property. Seeks legislation that will encourage the construction industry to protect trees and to replant where trees are destroyed. Believes that with careful planning new neighborhoods, highways, office parks, and shopping centers can be built without unnecessary destruction of trees. Sponsors competitions; bestows awards to individuals and organizations contributing to the preservation of trees. Compiles statistics; operates biographical archives; maintains speakers' bureau. The society's name is taken from the science fiction film Silent Running, which depicts the care taken by an astrobotanist to save last of the earth's forests, housed within a spaceship.

★475★ Society for Ecological Restoration (SER)
1207 Seminole Hwy.
Madison, WI 53711
Phone: (608)262-9547
Contact: William R. Jordan III, Supervisor of Admin.
Founded: 1988. ***Members:*** 1400. Scientists, researchers, educators, environmental consultants, and other interested individuals; government agencies. Promotes ecological restoration as a scientific and technical discipline that provides a strategy for environmental conservation, a technique for ecological research, and a means of developing a "mutually beneficial relationship" between humans and nature. ***Former Name(s):*** Society for Ecological Restoration and Management.

★476★ Society for Environmental Geochemistry and Health
University of Colorado, Denver
Center for Environmental Sciences
Campus Box 136
Denver, CO 80204
Phone: (303)556-3460
Fax: (303)556-4822
Contact: Willard R. Chappell, Sec.-Treas.
Founded: 1971. ***Members:*** 350. Organizations, scientists, and students committed to: furthering knowledge of the effects of the geochemical environment on the health and disease of plants and animals, including humans; promoting scientific communication and exchange of views among members and nonmembers.

★477★ Society for the Conservation of Bighorn Sheep (SCBS)
3113 Mesaloa Ln.
Pasadena, CA 91107
Phone: (818)797-1287
Contact: George Kerr, Pres.
Founded: 1963. ***Members:*** 25,000. Conservation groups organized to study, research, and monitor the preservation of bighorn sheep. Sponsors seminars, films, and slide shows; conducts lectures and field trips. Maintains small library of research data and biographical archives; compiles statistics. Bestows awards; conducts charitable programs; operates speakers' bureau.

★478★ Society for the Preservation of Birds of Prey (SPBP)
PO Box 66070
Los Angeles, CA 90066
Phone: (213)397-8216

★479★ Society of Tympanuchus Cupido Pinnatus
930 Elm Grove Rd.
Elm Grove, WI 53122
Phone: (414)782-6333
Contact: Bernard J. Westfahl, Pres.
Founded: 1960. Sportsmen dedicated to preserving the prairie chicken and other wildlife listed as endangered by Wisconsin Watch and "doing so with humor, excellent taste, and efficiency". Members' contributions are used to buy land for prairie chicken habitat, specifically to add acres to the Buena Vista Reservation in Portage County, WI.

★480★ Soil and Water Conservation Society (SCSA)
7515 NE Ankeny Rd.
Ankeny, IA 50021
Phone: (515)289-2331
Fax: (515)289-1227
Contact: Verlon C. Vrana, Exec.V.Pres.
Founded: 1945. ***Members:*** 13,000. Soil and water conservationists and others in fields

related to the use, conservation, and management of natural resources. Objective is to advance the science and art of good land and water use. Bestows awards; offers annual scholarships to qualified students. Maintains more than 25 committees including: College and University Relations; Conservation History; International Affairs; Student Services. ***Former Name(s):*** Soil Conservation Society of America (1987).

★481★ Southern Environmental Law Center
201 W. Main St., Ste. 14
Charlottesville, VA 22901
Phone: (804)977-4090
Offers legal assistance to citizens in the South.

★482★ Spill Control Association of America (SCAA)
400 Renaissance Center, Ste. 1900
Detroit, MI 48243
Phone: (313)567-0500
Fax: (313)259-8943
Contact: Marc K. Shaye, Gen. Counsel
Founded: 1973. ***Members:*** 120. Third party contractors; manufacturers or suppliers of pollution control and containment equipment; individuals in private or governmental capacities involved with spill clean-up and containment operations; associate companies. Provides information on the oil and hazardous material emergency response and remediation industry's practices, trends, and achievements; established a liaison with local, state, and federal government agencies responsible for laws and regulations regarding pollution caused by oil and hazardous materials; cooperates in the development of industry programs and efforts so that pollutants are properly controlled and removed from land and water. Provides certification for hazardous material technicians. Maintains Spill Control Institute, Technical Services Division; collects and disseminates educational and technical information; conducts seminars. Operates library and speakers' bureau; conducts research; bestows awards. Maintains placement service. ***Former Name(s):*** Oil Spill Control Association of America (1978).

★483★ State and Territorial Air Pollution Program Administrators (STAPPA)
444 N. Capitol St. NW, Ste. 306
Washington, DC 20001
Phone: (202)624-7864
Fax: (202)624-7863
Contact: S. William Becker, Exec.Dir.
Founded: 1968. ***Members:*** 53. State and territorial air pollution program administrators and members of their staffs. Provides an opportunity for state officials who are responsible for implementing air pollution control programs established under the Clean Air Act to share air quality-related experiences and to discuss problems. Encourages communication and cooperation among federal, state, and local regulatory agencies.

★484★ The Steamboaters
233 Howard Ave.
Eugene, OR 97404
Phone: (503)688-4980
Contact: Dick Bauer, Exec.Dir.
Founded: 1966. ***Members:*** 300. Fly fishermen who support the conservation of fishing waters and game fish.

★485★ Steel Can Recycling Institute (SCRI)
Foster Plaza X
680 Anderson Dr.
Pittsburgh, PA 15220
Phone: (412)922-2772
Fax: (412)922-3213
Toll-Free: 800-876-7274
Contact: Kurt Smalberg, Pres.
Founded: 1988. ***Members:*** 9. Steelmaking companies. Provides information and technical analyses to members and the public on methods of collection, preparation, and transportation of steel/bimetal can scrap. Aids in the research and development of new ideas and processes involved in recycling. Seeks to advance general knowledge of steel/bimetal can scrap uses. Sponsors competitions; bestows awards; maintains library and speakers' bureau; conducts research and educational programs; offers children's services; compiles statistics.

★486★ Stripers Unlimited
880 Washington St.
PO Box 3045
South Attleboro, MA 02703
Phone: (508)761-7983
Contact: Robert B. Pond, Exec.Dir.
Founded: 1965. ***Members:*** 600. Fishermen, conservationists, and fishing clubs united to promote, conserve, and protect the striped bass and its environment. Advocates an increase in the striped bass' areas of reproduction. Maintains research file and speakers' bureau; compiles statistics.

★487★ Student Conservation Association (SCA)
Box 550
Charlestown, NH 03603
Phone: (603)826-4301
Fax: (603)826-7755
Contact: Henry S. Francis Jr., Pres.
Founded: 1957. ***Members:*** 3500. Individuals, garden clubs, foundations, corporations, and groups who support the Student Conservation Program. The program, conducted in cooperation with the National Park Service, the U.S. Forest Service, and other federal, state, local, and private agencies which manage public lands, enlists the voluntary services of high school and college age persons to aid in preserving the natural beauty and resources of the national parks, forests, and resource areas. High school work group participants repair structures, maintain trails, and rehabilitate over-used areas. Older students assist the rangers and naturalists in interpretive and management projects, such as giving nature talks, cataloging materials, and trail patrol. Conducts educational and vocational programs providing job skill training, work experience, and exposure to career options in natural resource fields. Operates placement service.

★488★ Student Pugwash
1638 R St. NW
Washington, DC 20009
Phone: (202)328-6555
Sponsors educational programs for university students.

★489★ Teachers Response to Environmental Education
1112 Church Rd.
Wyncote, PA 19095
Contact: Tere Camarota

★490★ Thorne Ecological Institute
5398 Manhattan Circle
Boulder, CO 80303
Phone: (303)499-3647
Contact: Susan Q. Foster, Exec.Dir.
Founded: 1954. Dedicated to the application of ecological principles, stewardship of natural resources, and improvement of the human environment. Conducts seminars on ecology bringing together adults with diverse professions and interests. Offers environmental services to industry and government agencies on environmental assessments, wildlife management, and reclamation. ***Former Name(s):*** Thorne Ecological Foundation (1971).

★491★ Threshold, Inc.
International Center for Environmental Renewal
Drawer CU
Bisbee, AZ 85603
Phone: (602)432-7353
Educates the public about the environment and researches ecologically sound alternatives for practical application in society.

★492★ TRAFFIC USA
c/o World Wildlife Fund
1250 24th St. NW, Ste. 500
Washington, DC 20037
Phone: (202)293-4800
Fax: (202)293-9211
Contact: Ginette Hemley, Dir.
Founded: 1972. A program of the World Wildlife Fund. Conservation, government, university, press, foreign, and private groups. Scientific and statistical information-gathering program monitoring trade in wild plants and animals. (The acronym TRAFFIC stands for Trade Records Analysis of Flora and Fauna in Commerce.) ***Former Name(s):*** TRAFFIC - U.S.A. (1989).

★493★ TreePeople (TP)
12601 Mulholland Dr.
Beverly Hills, CA 90210
Phone: (818)753-4600
Fax: (818)753-4625
Toll-Free: (650)263-8793
Contact: Andy Lipkis, Exec.Dir.
Founded: 1970. ***Members:*** 19,500. Environmental problem solving organization, operating primarily in southern California, promoting community action, global awareness, and an active role in the planting and care of trees. Volunteers plant trees throughout Los Angeles and its surrounding mountain area. Conducted the Million Tree Campaign. Operates Environmental Leadership Program for elementary schoolchildren and Citizen's Forester Training Program for adults. Sponsors Africa Fruit Tree Project to assist in establishing nurseries for tree propagation in Ethiopia, Tanzania, Kenya, and Cameroun. Conducts educational programs, workshops, ECOtours (ecological tours) for school children, and lecture series. Maintains 45 acre Wilderness Park and conducts recycling education exhibits. Operates speakers' bureau. ***Former Name(s):*** California Conservation Project (1986).

★494★ Trees for Life
1103 Jefferson
Wichita, KS 67203
Phone: (316)263-7294
Provides funding and management to people in developing countries who want to plant food-bearing trees.

★495★ Trout Unlimited
501 Church St. NE
Vienna, VA 22180
Phone: (703)281-1100
Contact: Robert L. Herbst, Exec.Dir.
Founded: 1959. ***Members:*** 65,000. Purpose is to preserve and enhance the cold-water habitat of trout, salmon, and steelhead by influencing the activities and programs of governmental agencies, by keeping the public informed on water management problems, and by restoring and maintaining streams and lakes. Emphasizes the sport of fishing. Bestows annual Trout Conservation Award. Conducts research and education programs; compiles statistics; maintains speakers' bureau.

★496★ The Trumpeter Swan Society
3800 County Rd. 24
Maple Plain, MN 55359
Phone: (612)476-4663
Fax: (612)559-3287
Contact: David K. Weaver, Exec.Sec.-Treas.
Founded: 1968. ***Members:*** 500. Private waterfowl propagators, public zoos, park systems, federal, state, and county agencies, libraries, and interested individuals. Scientific and educational organization established to: promote research in ecology and management of the North American trumpeter swan; advance the science and art of trumpeter swan management, both in captivity and in the wild; assemble data and exchange information. Advocates restoration of trumpeter swans in their original range and makes funds available for research.

★497★ Trust for Public Land (TPL)
116 New Montgomery St., 4th Fl.
San Francisco, CA 94105
Phone: (415)495-5660
Fax: (415)495-0541
Contact: Martin J. Rosen, Pres.
Founded: 1972. Dedicated to acquiring and preserving land in urban and rural areas for public use. Provides urban and community groups with training and technical assistance in land acquisition. Assists ranchers, farmers, and rural communities in preserving agricultural land. Acquires recreational, historic, and scenic lands for conveyance to local, state, and federal agencies and nonprofit organizations for open space protection and public use.

★498★ Underground Injection Practices Council
525 Central Park Dr., Ste. 304
Oklahoma City, OK 73105
Phone: (405)525-6146
Contact: Michel Paque, Exec.Dir.
Founded: 1983. ***Members:*** 2000. Professionals and corporations involved in underground injection control. Conducts research in underground injection and hazardous materials problems. Provides training for mechanical integrity testing for machinery involved with underground injection. Serves as a liaison between industry and state and federal environmental groups. Represents states at congressional hearings. Sponsors symposia and workshops.

★499★ United Citizens Coastal Protection League (UCCPL)
PO Box 46
Cardiff By The Sea, CA 92007
Phone: (619)753-7477
Contact: Robert Bonde, Exec.Dir.
Founded: 1982. ***Members:*** 10,000. Organized to protest the California Bullet Train, a proposed train service that would have involved high-speed transportation along the West Coast between Los Angeles and San Diego; the proposal was defeated. Purpose is to represent citizens concerned with related environmental and social issues. Current activities include: promoting alternative transportation for commuters, such as improving the conditions of Amtrak; preserving lagoons in the California area; conducting research on water and transportation issues. Maintains speakers' bureau.

★500★ United New Conservationists (UNC)
PO Box 362
Campbell, CA 95009
Phone: (408)241-5769
Contact: Lilyann Brannon, Pres.
Founded: 1969. ***Members:*** 58. Environmentally concerned individuals and organizations, including senior citizen groups, and groups interested in transportation, population, historic preservation, and other issues. Primary objective is to strengthen conservation goals through education. Ongoing programs include protecting the Guadalupe River, providing community gardens, and conducting seminars on environmental subjects including backyard habitats, organic gardening, Med fly issues, pesticides and health, and hazardous wastes. Activities include urban and wilderness tree planting, urban river cleanups, historic preservation, hiking, and camping. Conducts seminars; maintains speakers' bureau, library, and clipping file. Bestows Environmentalist of the Year and Green Thumb awards. Maintains community garden.

★501★ United States Operating Committee of ETAD
1330 Connecticut Ave. NW, Ste. 300
Washington, DC 20036
Phone: (202)659-0060
Fax: (202)659-1699
Contact: C. Tucker Helmes Ph.D., Exec.Dir.
Founded: 1981. ***Members:*** 11. U.S. member companies of the Ecological and Toxicological Association of the Dyestuffs Manufacturing Industry. Works with government agencies in identifying and controlling potential health or environmental hazards from dyes.

★502★ United States Tourist Council (USTC)
Drawer 1875
Washington, DC 20013-1875
Phone: (301)565-5155
Contact: Dr. Stanford West, Exec.Dir.
Founded: 1969. ***Members:*** 18,700. Conservation-concerned individuals who travel; institutions and industries that supply goods and services to the traveler. Objectives are to achieve: historic and scenic preservation; wilderness and roadside development; ecology through sound planning and education; support of scientific studies of natural wilderness areas. Maintains library.

★503★ Upper Mississippi River Conservation Committee (UMRCC)
1830 2nd Ave.
Rock Island, IL 61201
Phone: (309)793-5800
Contact: Marion Conover, Chm.
Founded: 1943. ***Members:*** 133. Natural resources managers and biologists. Objectives are: to promote the preservation and wise use of the natural and recreational resources of the upper Mississippi River; to formulate policies, plans, and programs for conducting cooperative studies. Cooperative projects include creel census, commercial fishing statistics, waterfowl and wildlife censuses, hunter surveys, fish tagging, litter control, and collection of boating and other recreational use data. Helps to define land management for public properties such as state parks, public hunting grounds, wildlife refuges, flood plain reserves, and recreational lands. Functions as an advisory body on all technical aspects of fish, wildlife, and recreation. Makes recommendations on conservation laws, programs, and legislation to state and federal governments. Maintains a continuing evaluation of the effects of water control regulation and recreational resources. Sponsors research programs; maintains resource library. Technical Work Groups: Fisheries; Law Enforcement; Recreation and Water Use; Wildlife.

★504★ Urban Initiatives
530 W. 25th St.
New York, NY 10001
Phone: (212)620-9773
Contact: Gianni Longo, Pres.
Founded: 1973. Interdisciplinary organization of professionals committed to improving the quality of the built environment. Provides direct assistance in urban problem-solving and conducts research and communication on urban environmental issues. Assists federal, state, and city governments, corporations, businesses, community groups, academic and cultural institutions, architects, planners, and other environmental professionals. Has expertise in downtown and neighborhood development strategies; citizen participation programs; evaluation of plans for the design and use of urban open spaces; land-use control and zoning recommendations; planning and designing auto-restricted areas; institutional and financial mechanisms for urban improvements; historic preservation and inventories of historic structures; and life safety in the built environment. ***Former Name(s):*** Institute for Environmental Action (1985).

★505★ Walden Forever Wild (WFW)
PO Box 275
Concord, MA 01742
Phone: (203)429-2839
Contact: Mary P. Sherwood, Chm.
Founded: 1980. ***Members:*** 300. Organization composed of enthusiasts and scholars of Walden Pond, a retreat used by author Henry David Thoreau (1817-62). Objective is to persuade the Massachusetts state legislature to change Walden Pond Reservation from a recreational park to an educational, historical, and ecological sanctuary. Encourages procurement of a professional forester/ecology manager for the reservation; contributes toward the operation of an educational museum and visitor center and related activities. Has provided an electric water pump to restore eroded areas of the pond. Collects and maintains repository for letters, newspaper articles, and speeches endorsing the transformation of Walden Pond into an official sanctuary. Bestows awards; conducts specialized education program; compiles statistics. Maintains museum and biographical archives; operates small library. Sponsors Walden Guardians program for symbolic purchase of Walden parcels of land. ***Former Name(s):*** Walden Forever Wild Committee (1985).

★506★ Walden Pond Advisory Committee (WPAC)
Page Rd.
Lincoln, MA 01773
Phone: (617)259-9544

Contact: Kenneth E. Bassett, Chm.
Founded: 1974. ***Members:*** 7. Representatives of communities and organizations interested in the preservation and restoration of Walden Pond. The committee is concerned about destruction of the vegetation, damage to the woods, and littering which the group claims is caused by careless crowds. Reviews maintenance and management practices, long-term master plan objectives, and capital improvement programs at Walden Pond on an annual basis. ***Former Name(s):*** Walden Pond Restoration Committee (1974).

★507★ Waste Watch (WW)
PO Box 298
Livingston, KY 40445
Contact: Dr. A. J. Fritsch, Dir.
Founded: 1979. ***Members:*** 2000. A volunteer group of Technical Information Project. Citizens in private and government sectors concerned with national resource waste problems. Promotes constructive citizen action and participation in waste issues and policy-making; seeks to enhance public information flow and education on resource and environmental issues. Performs at-cost consulting work on waste management. Conducts seminars and workshops. Maintains library on energy conservation and waste.

★508★ Water Pollution Control Federation
601 Wythe St.
Alexandria, VA 22314-1994
Phone: (703)684-2400
Fax: (703)684-2492
Contact: Dr. Quincalee Brown, Exec.Dir.
Founded: 1928. ***Members:*** 36,000. Technical societies representing municipal engineers, consulting engineers, public health engineers, water pollution control works superintendents, chemists, operators, educational and research personnel, industrial wastewater engineers, municipal officials, equipment manufacturers, and university professors and students dedicated to the enhancement and preservation of water quality and resources. Seeks to advance fundamental and practical knowledge concerning the nature, collection, treatment, and disposal of domestic and industrial wastewaters, and the design, construction, operation, and management of facilities for these purposes. Disseminates technical information; promotes good public relations and regulations that improve water pollution control and the status of individuals working in this field. Maintains job bank for wastewater facility employees; conducts educational programs. Sponsors High School Science Fair National Award. Maintains library of 6000 volumes on water pollution and related topics. ***Former Name(s):*** Federation of Sewage Works Association (1949); Federation of Sewage and Industrial Wastes Association (1959).

★509★ Water Resources Congress
3800 N. Fairfax Dr., Ste. 5
Arlington, VA 22203
Phone: (703)525-4881
Group concerned with land and water use, conservation, and control.

★510★ Waterfowl U.S.A. (WUSA)
Box 50
Waterfowl Bldg.
Edgefield, SC 29824
Phone: (803)637-5767
Contact: Roger White, Exec. V. Pres.
Founded: 1983. ***Members:*** 15,000. Hunters, conservationists, and others dedicated to raising money for developing, preserving, restoring, and maintaining waterfowl habitats in the U.S. Seeks to: publicize the needs of waterfowl; develop state and local wetland projects; improve waterfowl resting areas, wood duck nest boxes, and planting areas that feed migrating and resident waterfowl; establish public shooting areas. Conducts wood duck research. Cooperates with other waterfowl groups. Maintains small library. ***Former Name(s):*** National Waterfowl Alliance, Waterfowl United States of America (1990).

★511★ Welder Wildlife Foundation
PO Box 1400
Sinton, TX 78387
Phone: (512)364-2643
Concerned with research, conservation, and education in wildlife ecology.

★512★ Wetlands for Wildlife
PO Box 344
West Bend, WI 53095
Phone: (414)334-0327
Acquires and preserves wetlands in the U.S.

★513★ The Whale Center
3933 Peidmont Ave., Ste. 2
Oakland, CA 94611
Phone: (415)654-6621
Nonprofit organization supporting whales. Operates Adopt-a-Grey-Whale program for $24.

★514★ Whitetails Unlimited
PO Box 422
Sturgeon Bay, WI 54235
Phone: (414)743-6777
Toll-Free: 800-274-5471
Contact: Peter J. Gerl, CEO
Founded: 1982. ***Members:*** 35,000. Dedicated to sound deer management. Supports research on the white-tailed deer; conducts seminars and workshops to educate the public about sound deer management. Sponsors fundraising events. Maintains library of films relating to the white-tailed deer (available to members only).

★515★ Whooping Crane Conservation Association (WCCA)
3000 Meadowlark Dr.
Sierra Vista, AZ 85635
Phone: (602)458-0971
Contact: Jerome J. Pratt, Sec.-Treas.
Founded: 1961. ***Members:*** 600. Naturalists, ornithologists, and aviculturists. Works to: prevent the extinction of the whooping crane; ensure that a proper management program is carried out for captive propagation to serve as a backup for the wild population; support the establishment of a second wild population to reinforce survival against disaster; promote harmony and unity among all organizations, institutions, and agencies involved in the preservation of endangered wildlife; collect and disseminate information to advocate and encourage public appreciation and understanding of the whooping crane's educational, scientific, aesthetic, and economic values. Conducts captive management studies for perpetuation of the species; distributes information and statistics on species to the press and interested individuals. Bestows award for contribution to North American wildlife. ***Former Name(s):*** Whooping Crane Conservation Group (1982).

★516★ Wild Canid Survival and Research Center - Wolf Sanctuary
PO Box 760
Eureka, MO 63025
Phone: (314)938-5900
Contact: Vicki O'Toole, Adm.Dir.
Founded: 1971. ***Members:*** 2800. Dedicated to the preservation of Red and Mexican wolves and their natural habitat through captive breeding and educational and informational programs. Has established captive breeding programs as a possible gene pool for endangered wolves. Maintains Friends of the Wolf Sanctuary which organizes and directs fundraising activities. Maintains educational staff to assist groups visiting the sanctuary and to provide schools and interested groups with tours, films, slides, and other material. Operates small library of material on wolves; maintains speakers' bureau. Issues educational packets on the Red Wolf and Mexican Wolf.

★517★ Wild Horse Organized Assistance (WHOA!)
PO Box 555
Reno, NV 89504
Phone: (702)851-4817
Contact: Dawn Y. Lappin, Chwm.
Founded: 1971. ***Members:*** 12,000. A foundation for the welfare and perpetuation of wild free-roaming horses and burros. WHOA! seeks to: provide surveillance patrols to assure the well-being of these animals; assist in the development and expansion of programs to provide for their care and protection; conduct research and field studies on wild horse and burro behavior patterns on the range; provide scholarships to encourage student research studies; maintain a national research center, library, and museum; maintain visitors' information centers at wild horse and burro ranges which may be designated and created by federal or state governments, or contributed by individuals.

★518★ Wild Horses of America Registry (WHAR)
6212 E. Sweetwater
Scottsdale, AZ 85254
Phone: (602)991-0273
Contact: Karen Sussman, Registrar
Founded: 1975. ***Members:*** 1033. Wild horse and burro registries organized to give recognition to America's wild horses removed from public lands. To establish a uniform program of management, protection, and control of wild horses and burros as called for under the Wild Horse and Burro Act of 1971. Unlike other equine registries, eligibility is not based on bloodlines or conformation to specific standards. Seeks to educate the public on the traits of wild horses and their suitability for show, for trail and endurance riding, and for use as children's horses. Conducts educational programs for schools and interested groups; supports research on wild horses and burros. Plans include annual horse show and trail rides.

★519★ Wilderness Education Association
20 Winona Ave., Box 89
Saranac Lake, NY 12983
Phone: (518)891-2915
Contact: Mark C. Wagstaff
Promotes outdoor leadership to improve and enhance the safety and quality of outdoor experiences. Dedicated to wilderness preservation through education.

★520★ The Wilderness Society (TWS)
900 17th St. NW
Washington, DC 20006-2596
Phone: (202)833-2300
Fax: (202)429-3958
Contact: George T. Frampton Jr., Pres.
Founded: 1935. ***Members:*** 390,000. Purposes are the establishment of the land ethic as a basic element of American culture and philosophy, and the education of a broader and more committed wilderness preservation and land protection constituency. Focuses on

federal, legislative, and administrative actions affecting public lands including national forests, national parks, wildlife refuges, and Bureau of Land Management lands. Encourages Congress to designate appropriate public lands as wilderness areas. Programs include grass roots organizing, lobbying, research, and public education. Presents annual awards; compiles statistics.

★521★ Wilderness Watch (WW)
PO Box 782
Sturgeon Bay, WI 54235
Phone: (414)743-1238
Contact: Jerome O. Gandt, Pres.
Founded: 1969. Scientists, attorneys, artists, writers, and other interested individuals. Advocates "sustained use of America's Sylvan lands and waters." Focuses on land use policies at the federal and state levels and seeks to halt environmental depredation. Conducts research and educational programs.

★522★ Wildlife Conservation Fund of America (WCFA)
50 W. Broad St., Ste. 1025
Columbus, OH 43215
Phone: (614)221-2684
Contact: James H. Glass, Pres.
Founded: 1978. Conservation organizations representing 1,000,000 members. To protect the heritage of the American sportsman to hunt, fish, and trap; and to protect scientific wildlife management practices. Provides litigation, legal research, and facts about wildlife conservation and management. Has developed a national education program concerning wildlife conservation. Operates Protect What's Right, which mobilizes sportsmen's organizations to enlighten the public concerning the status of wildlife in America and the role played by sportsmen in wildlife management. WCFA is the legal defense, information, public education, and research arm of the Wildlife Legislative Fund of America.

★523★ Wildlife Conservation International (WCI)
c/o New York Zoological Society
Bronx, NY 10460
Phone: (212)220-5155
Fax: (212)220-7114
Contact: John G. Robinson, Dir.
Founded: 1897. ***Members:*** 40,000. Supporters of international species survival strategies and habitat/ecosystem conservation projects. Objective is to save critical habitats, ecosystems, and indicator species. Conducts zoological field investigations, provides professional training of foreign field biologists, and prepares recommendations for parks and protected area management. Maintains an office in Nairobi, Kenya. ***Former Name(s):*** Animal Research and Conservation Center (1984).

★524★ Wildlife Disease Association (WDA)
PO Box 886
Ames, IA 50010
Phone: (515)233-1931
Contact: Dick Dale, Bus.Mgr.
Founded: 1951. ***Members:*** 1500. Professional workers in wildlife disease research, wildlife management, and public and veterinary health; others interested in the study of the factors that promote or prevent the successful propagation of wild animals as free living populations or as captives. Is concerned with diseases, nutritional requirements, physiological responses to population density, and relationship of population to environment. Maintains collection of audiovisual aids.

★525★ Wildlife Forever
12301 Whitewater Dr., Ste. 210
Minnetonka, MN 55343
Phone: (612)936-0605
Educates public about wildlife management and preservation.

★526★ Wildlife Habitat Enhancement Council (WHEC)
1010 Wayne Ave., Ste. 1240
Silver Spring, MD 20910
Phone: (301)588-8994
Contact: Joyce M. Kelly, Exec.Dir.
Founded: 1988. ***Members:*** 70. Corporations, conservation groups, and individuals interested in encouraging and supporting greater use of undeveloped corporate lands for increasing animal, fish, and plant life populations. Sponsors Corporate Wildlife Habitat Certification Program. Bestows awards.

★527★ Wildlife Information Center (WIC)
629 Green St.
Allentown, PA 18102
Phone: (215)434-1637
Contact: Donald S. Heintzelman, Pres.
Founded: 1986. Individuals who advocate wildlife protection. Objective is to promote nonkilling wildlife uses such as observation, photography, sound recording, drawing and painting, and wildlife tourism by: presenting expert testimony at governmental hearings; researching and preparing conservation and education reports; conducting public wildlife walks; teaching inservice, graduate level training courses for school teachers; conducting long-term hawk migration field studies; advocating preservation of wildlife areas. Maintains biographical archives and library; compiles statistics. Conducts seminars and workshops.

★528★ Wildlife Management Institute (WMI)
1101 14th St. NW, Ste. 725
Washington, DC 20005
Phone: (202)371-1808
Contact: Laurence R. Jahn, Pres.
Founded: 1911. Promotes better management and wise utilization of all renewable natural resources in the public interest. ***Former Name(s):*** American Wildlife Institute (1946).

★529★ Wildlife Preservation Trust International
34th St. & Girard Ave.
Philadelphia, PA 19104
Phone: (215)222-3636
Fax: (215)222-2191
Contact: William Konstant, Exec.Dir.
Founded: 1971. ***Members:*** 6000. Provides support for the captive breeding of endangered species to save them from extinction. Awards grants for breeding projects including those involving marmosets from South America, hutias from Jamaica, thick-billed parrots and black-toothed ferrets from the U.S., and bats and lemurs from Madagascar. Supports research in areas related to captive breeding of endangered species and the reintroduction to the wild of captive bred animals. Trains students in captive breeding techniques and operates public education programs. Maintains library on biology and wildlife; makes available films and slides for loan; operates speakers' bureau. ***Former Name(s):*** Save Animals From Extinction (1971).

★530★ The Wildlife Society (TWS)
5410 Grosvenor Ln.
Bethesda, MD 20814-2197
Phone: (301)897-9770
Fax: (301)530-2471
Contact: Harry E. Hodgdon, Exec.Dir.
Founded: 1937. ***Members:*** 8700. Professional society of wildlife biologists, research scientists, conservation law enforcement officers, resource managers, and others interested in resource conservation and wildlife management on a sound biological basis. Takes an active role in preventing human-induced environmental degradation; works to increase awareness and appreciation of wildlife values; seeks the highest standards in all activities of the wildlife profession. Believes wildlife, in its myriad forms, is a basic component of a high quality human culture. Bestows annual Aldo Leopold Award to an outstanding wildlife professional; also bestows awards annually for publications, group achievement, conservation education, and special recognition in the wildlife field. ***Former Name(s):*** Society of Wildlife Specialists (1936).

★531★ Windstar Foundation (WF)
2317 Snowmass Creek Rd.
Snowmass, CO 81654
Phone: (303)927-4777
Fax: (303)927-4779
Founded: 1976. Seeks to create opportunities for individuals to acquire the knowledge, skills, experiences, and commitment necessary to build a healthy and sustainable future for humanity; publicizes steps that individuals can take to improve environmental quality. Conducts educational programs in global resource management, food production technologies, and development of the human spirit; operates Land Education Program, which makes available apprenticeships in high-altitude gardening, small-scale farming, and land stewardship. Through Windstar Connection Groups, assists individuals and communities worldwide in creating effective environmental education programs. Maintains EarthPulse, which conducts research and disseminates information on environmental health. Has developed the Biodome, a geodesic structure designed to accomodate year-round cultivation of vegetables, fruit, and fish; provides instruction and other assistance to individuals and communities wishing to operate their own Biodome.

★532★ World Association of Soil and Water Conservation (WASWC)
7515 NE Ankeny Rd.
Ankeny, IA 50021
Phone: (515)289-2331
Fax: (515)289-1227
Contact: William C. Moldenhauer, Exec.Dir.
Founded: 1983. ***Members:*** 435. Soil and water conservationists, scientists, policy makers, and interested individuals. Serves as a forum for members to assess soil and water conservation needs worldwide.

★533★ World Forestry Center (WFC)
4033 SW Canyon Rd.
Portland, OR 97221
Phone: (503)228-1367
Fax: (503)228-3624
Contact: John Blackwell, Pres.
Founded: 1971. ***Members:*** 3000. Professional foresters; individuals concerned with forests and forest management. Educational organization promoting public awareness of the need for forest preservation and well-managed forest resources. Serves as an information clearinghouse. Conducts classes on subjects such as woodland management and woodworking. Sponsors exhibits. ***Former Name(s):*** Western Forestry Center (1986).

★534★ World Nature Association (WNA)
PO Box 673, Woodmoor Sta.
Silver Spring, MD 20901
Phone: (301)593-2522
Contact: Donald H. Messersmith Ph.D., Pres.
Founded: 1969. ***Members:*** 256. Professional and amateur naturalists interested in conservation and travel. Provides technical and financial assistance and equipment and educational materials to individuals and groups for small wildlife and habitat preservation projects worldwide. Projects include: a bird banding project in Cyprus; donation of equipment for the rescue of wildlife endangered by dam construction in Mexico; elementary school program in Sri Lanka; assistance with crane research and education in China. Offers annual scholarship to an American educator in the natural sciences; bestows grants to individuals for small research projects. Conducts tours. Maintains library of 2000 books and periodicals on conservation, nature study, and world travel.

★535★ World Pheasant Association of the U.S.A.
2412 Arrowmill St.
Los Angeles, CA 90023
Phone: (213)262-5143
Contact: Don C. Tucker, Pres.
Founded: 1982. ***Members:*** 130. U.S. branch of World Pheasant Association Conservationists. Purpose is to work for the conservation and preservation of gallinaceous birds. Sponsors research and education about galliformes. Participates in the development of a world conservation strategy for galliformes.

★536★ World Population Society
1333 H St., Ste. 760
Washington, DC 20005
Phone: (202)898-1303
Contact: Frank Oram, Executive Director
Supports research on population and its impact on the capacity to meet human needs.

★537★ World Research Foundation (WRF)
15300 Ventura Blvd., Ste. 405
Sherman Oaks, CA 91403
Phone: (818)907-5483
Contact: Steven A. Ross, Pres.
Founded: 1980. Informs the public of the latest developments in health and environmental issues. Provides health care professionals and the public with information on health tools and technologies currently available outside the U.S. but which have been overlooked or are unavailable in the U.S. Acts as a depository of public information. Maintains 20,000 volume library.

★538★ World Wildlife Fund (WWF)
1250 24th St., NW
Washington, DC 20037
Phone: (202)293-4800
Fax: (202)293-9211
Contact: Kathryn Fuller, Pres.
Founded: 1961. ***Members:*** 800,000. Supported by contributions from individuals, funds, corporations, and foundations. Seeks to protect the biological resources upon which human well-being depends. Emphasizes preservation of endangered and threatened species of wildlife and plants as well as habitats and natural areas anywhere in the world. Activities are scientifically based to produce immediate and long-term conservation benefits and provide models for natural management techniques and policies. Supports public and private conservation agencies and governments in carrying out projects and services. Maintains library of 8000 volumes; provides speakers' bureau. Administers J. Paul Getty Wildlife Conservation Prize. ***Former Name(s):*** (1986) World Wildlife Fund - U.S.

★539★ World Women in the Environment
1331 H St. NW, Ste. 903
Washington, DC 20005
Phone: (202)347-1514
Fax: (202)347-1524
Contact: Cynthia R. Helms, Chm.
Founded: 1982. ***Members:*** 1100. Women and men interested in environmental protection. Promotes strengthening the role of women in the development and implementation of environmental and natural resource policies. Educates and promotes communication among members and their families concerning the consequences of decisions affecting the environment, especially the contamination and destruction of ecological systems. Encourages members to include environmental and natural resource management activities in their lives; seeks to educate policymakers about problems of women and the environment and to foster increased inclusion of women and their perspectives in the development and implementation of policies and programs. Acts as a forum for women in developing countries to speak to other women in North America and Europe with regard to local development and environmental problems. Disseminates information on policies that are destroying the ability of natural biological systems to sustain and enhance life. Keeps members informed of environmental projects and women's activities in related areas. Conducts policy impact research programs to collect and document information on the impact of environmentally related policies on women. ***Former Name(s):*** World Women in Defense of the Environment (1987); World Women Dedicated to the Environment (1988).

★540★ WorldWIDE
1250 24th St. NW
Washington, DC 20037
Phone: (202)331-9863
Aims to mobilize women to maintain environmental quality and natural resource management.

★541★ Xerces Society
10 SW Ash St.
Portland, OR 97204
Phone: (503)222-2788
Contact: Melody Allen, Exec.Dir.
Founded: 1975. ***Members:*** 1930. Scientists working in conservation-related fields; interested individuals. Named for an extinct San Francisco butterfly, the Xerces Blue, the society is devoted to the preservation of invertebrates. Identifies and seeks to protect critical invertebrate habitats and their endangered ecosystems. Sponsors Monarch Project, which protects Monarch butterfly habitats in California. Sponsors annual international butterfly count on Independence Day. Compiles statistics.

★542★ Zero Population Growth
1400 16th St., NW, Ste. 320
Washington, DC 20036
Phone: (202)332-2200
Contact: Susan Weber, Executive Director
Supports population stabilization in U.S. and abroad.

Foundations and Funding Sources

International

★543★ Africa Institute of South Africa
PO Box 630
Cnr. Hamilton & Belvedere Sts.
Pretoria, Republic of South Africa
Phone: (12) 286970
Fax: (12) 323-8153
Contact: Dr. P. Smit, Chm.
Founded: 1960. Operates both nationally and internationally in many fields, including the conservation of natural resources.

★544★ Agromisa Foundation
PO Box 41
Gen. Foulkesweg 55
6700 AA Wageningen, Netherlands
Phone: (8370) 12-217
Founded: 1934.
Gives developing countries advice in the fields of nutrition, food processing, biogas, and water and soil management.

★545★ Alexander S. Onassis Foundation
18 Ploutarchou St.
106 76 Athens, Greece
Phone: (1) 7217724
Fax: (1) 7238918
Telex: (21) 9298
Contact: C.I. Georgakis, Pres.
Awards scholarships, research grants and three international prizes, including the Delphi Prize (Man and His Environment) for efforts to preserve the environment.

★546★ Asian Institute of Technology
PO Box 2754
Bangkok 10501, Thailand
Phone: (2) 529-0041
Fax: (2) 529-0374
Telex: 84276
Contact: Prof. Alastair M. North, Pres.
Founded: 1959. Provides research aimed towards the solution of technological problems relevant to Asia. Offers specialized information services such as the Environmental Sanitation Information Center and the Renewable Energy Resources Information Center.

★547★ Australian Academy of Science
PO Box 783
Canberra City, ACT 2601, Australia
Phone: (62) 47 5330
Fax: (62) 57 4620
Telex: 62406
Contact: P. Vallee, Exec. Sec.
Founded: 1954. Operates internationally in the fields of science and medicine and the conservation of natural resources for grants, fellowships and scholarships and through conferences, courses, publications and lectures.

★548★ Baring Foundation
8 Bishopsgate
London EC2N 4AE, England
Phone: (71) 280-1000
Telex: 883622
Contact: Hon. Sir John Baring, Chm.
Founded: 1969. Responds to national and international appeals in many fields, including conservation.

★549★ Charles Darwin Foundation for the Galapagos Islands
c/o Kobenhavns Universitet
Botanisk Have
Oster Farimagsgade 2B
1353 Copenhagen, Denmark
Contact: Dr. Craig MacFarland, Pres.
Founded: 1959. Operates internationally in the conservation of natural resources.

★550★ CONCAWE
Madouplein 1
1030 Brussels, Belgium
Phone: (2) 20-31-11
Fax: (2) 219-46-46
Telex: 20308
Contact: J.B. Berkley, Council Chm.
Founded: 1963. European organization for environmental and health protection related to the petroleum-refining industry.

★551★ Environmental Problems Foundation of Turkey
Kennnedy Caddesi 33/3
06660 Ankara, Turkey
Phone: (4) 255508
Fax: (4) 1185118
Contact: Prof. D. Necmi Sonmez, Pres.
Founded: 1978. Documentation center on the environmental problems of Turkey and other countries.

★552★ European Cultural Foundation
Jan van Goyenkade 5
1075 HN Amsterdam, Netherlands
Phone: (20) 76-02-22
Fax: (20) 75-22-31
Telex: 18710
Contact: Dr. R. Georis, Sec. - Gen.
Founded: 1954. Operates internationally in many fields, including the environment, through a grants program. Maintains the Institute for European Environmental Policy in Bonn, with branch offices in London, Paris, Brussels and Arnhem.

★553★ European Foundation for the Improvement of Living and Working Conditions
Loughlinstown House
Shankill
Dublin, Ireland
Phone: (1) 826888
Fax: (1) 826456
Contact: Dr. Clive Purkis, Director
Operates internationally in three main areas: man at work; time; and the environment, including urban environment and non-nuclear wastes.

★554★ Foundation for Ecological Development Alternatives
PO Box 151
2130 AD Hoofddorp, Netherlands
Phone: (2503) 32-305
Contact: Dr. R. Gerrits
Founded: 1972.
Aims to develop a global conservation strategy. Operates in the fields of aid to less developed countries, environmental conservation, international affairs, law, and human rights.

★555★ Foundation for Environmental Conservation
7 chemin Taverney
1218 Geneva, Switzerland
Phone: (22) 7982383
Fax: (22) 7982344
Contact: Prof. Dr. Nicholas Polunin, Pres.
Founded: 1975. Promotes studies of environmental change and ecosystems; organizes conferences (notably the International Conferences on Environmental Future); awards prizes for achievement in environmental conservation; supports such initiatives as the World Campaign for the Biosphere, in cooperation with the International Society for Environmental Education.

★556★ Foundation for Intermediate Technology
Eisenbahnstrasse 28-30
6750 Kaiserslautern, Germany
Phone: (631) 61776
Contact: K.W. Kieffer, Chm.
Founded: 1974.
Promotes the exchange of knowledge and experience in modern technologies involving the least possible environmental hazards.

★557★ Foundation for International Studies
Old University Bldg.
St. Paul St.
Valletta, Malta
Phone: 234121
Fax: 230551
Telex: 1673
Contact: Prof. Salvino Busuttil, Dir. - Gen.
Founded: 1986. Conducts environmental studies of the Mediterranean region; organizes international conferences.

★558★ Foundation for the Study of the Future
Saline de Chaux
25610 Arc-et-Senans, France
Phone: 81-54-45-00
Contact: Serge Antoine, Pres.
Founded: 1973.
Promotes study into the future at an international level in the areas of conservation, science, and technology.

★559★ FVS Foundation
Georgsplatz 10
2000 Hamburg 1, Germany
Phone: (40) 330400
Foreign Name: Stiftung FVS ***Founded:*** 1931. Operates nationally and in Europe to promote the conservation of natural resources.

★560★ Honda Foundation
6-20, Yaesu 2-chome
Chuo-ku
Tokyo 104, Japan
Contact: Takeso Shimoda, Pres.
Founded: 1977. Supports technological developments that do not harm or endanger the environment. Awards the Honda Prize annually.

★561★ Institute of Energy Economics
No. 10 Mori Bldg.
181 Toranomon 1-chome
Tokyo, Minato-ku, Japan
Phone: (3) 3501-7861
Fax: (3) 3508-8147
Telex: 2225427
Contact: Shuzo Inaba, Chm.
Foreign Name: Nihon Enerugi Keizai ***Founded:*** 1966. Operates nationally and internationally in the fields of economic affairs and the conservation of natural resources.

★562★ International Council for Bird Preservation
32 Cambridge Rd.
Cambridge, Girton CBE 0PJ, England
Phone: (223) 277318
Fax: (223) 277200
Telex: 818794
Contact: Dr. Christoph Imboden, Dir.-Gen.
Founded: 1922. Operates internationally in the field of conservation.

★563★ International Education Centre
Vestergade 45
5700 Svendborg, Denmark
Phone: 62-21-66-99
Fax: 62-21-68-92
Contact: Ingolf Knudsen, Director
Founded: 1986.
Encourages international understanding through education and exchange in the fields of conservation and the environment, economic affairs, international affairs and social welfare.

★564★ International Foundation for the Conservation of Game
15 rue de Teheran
75008 Paris, France
Phone: (1) 45-63-51-33
Fax: (1) 45-63-32-94
Telex: 250303
Contact: Bertrand des Clers, Director
Founded: 1977.
Promotes the conservation of wildlife and nature to encourage rational and reasonable harvesting of national and international game populations. Cooperates with the International Council for Game and Wildlife Conservation (CIC).

★565★ International Institute for Applied Systems Analysis
Schlossplatz 1
2361 Laxenburg, Austria
Phone: (2236) 71-5-21
Fax: (2236) 71-3-13
Telex: 079137
Contact: Dr. Peter de Janosi, Director
Founded: 1972. Focuses on global environment issues.

★566★ International Institute of Tropical Agriculture
Oyo Rd.
Street 2: PMB 5320
Ibadan, Nigeria
Phone: (22) 400300
Telex: 31417
Contact: L.B. Crouch, Chm.
Founded: 1967. Develops methods of land use and cropping systems that will enable efficient, economical and sustained production of food crops through the Resource and Crop Management Programme.

★567★ Japan Shipbuilding Industry Foundation
1-15-16 Toranomon
Tokyo 105, Minato-ku, Japan
Phone: (3) 3508-2377
Fax: (3) 3502-0041
Telex: 2222652
Contact: Ryoichi Sasakawa, Chm.
Founded: 1962.
Gives international humanitarian assistance for projects conducted by the United Nations Environment Programme.

★568★ Moorgate Trust Fund
1 S. Audley St.
London W1Y 5DQ, England
Contact: I.H.T. Garnett-Orme, Trustee
Founded: 1970. Provides financial assistance to organizations throughout the world operating in many areas, including the environment.

★569★ Netherlands Society for Industry and Trade
POB 205
2000 AE Haarlem, Netherlands
Phone: (23) 29-02-71
Fax: (23) 29-38-37
Contact: R.C. Kolff, Gen.- Sec.
Founded: 1777.
Operates nationally and internationally to promote the conservation of natural resources.

★570★ Peace and Co-operation
Calle Melendez Valdes 68
40 Izq.
28015 Madrid, Spain
Phone: (1) 2435282
Fax: (1) 2435282
Contact: Almudena Montes, Officer
Founded: 1982.
Operates internationally to promote disarmament, sustainable development in developing countries and human rights worldwide.

★571★ Porter Foundation
P.F.M.
22 Mt. Sion
Kent TN1 1UN, England
Contact: Sir Leslie Porter, Chm.
Founded: 1965. Operates nationally and internationally in the field of conservation.

★572★ Ripaille Foundation
Chateau de Ripaille
74200 Thonon-les-Bains, France
Phone: 50-26-64-44
Contact: Louis Necker, Exec. Pres.
Founded: 1977.
Focuses on ecology, human and physical geography, and the conscientious development of resources and the environment, particularly in underprivileged areas and countries. Organizes exchanges between institutions and associations at regional, national and international levels.

★573★ Royal Society
6 Carlton House Terr.
London SW1Y 5AG, England
Phone: (71) 839-5561
Fax: (71) 930-2170
Telex: 917876
Contact: Dr. P.T. Warren, Exec. Sec.
Founded: 1660. Operates both nationally and internationally in many fields including the conservation of natural resources.

★574★ Royal Society for the Encouragement of Arts, Manufactures and Commerce
John Adams St.
London, Adelphi WC2N 6EZ, England
Phone: (71) 930-5115
Fax: (71) 839-5805
Telex: 892351
Contact: Christopher Lucas, Secretary
Founded: 1754. Operates nationally and internationally in many fields, including education and the environment.

★575★ Ruralite-environnement-developpement (RED)
2 rue des Potiers
6702 Attert, Belgium
Phone: (63) 22-37-02
Contact: Georges Christophe, Pres.
Founded: 1980. Promotes rural development throughout the world in the fields of economic development, planning, environment, and appropriate technology.

★576★ Siam Society
131 Soi Asoke
Sukhumvit 21
PO Box 65
Bangkok 11, Thailand
Phone: (2) 258-3491
Contact: Dr. Piriya Krairiksh, Pres.
Founded: 1904. Operates internationally in many fields, including the conservation of natural resources.

★577★ Southern African Nature Foundation
PO Box 456
Stellenbosch 7600, Republic of South Africa
Phone: (2231) 72892
Fax: (2231) 79517
Telex: 555421
Contact: Dr. Anton Rupert, Pres.
Founded: 1968. Operates both nationally and internationally in the fields of education and conservation of natural resources, and also in aid to less-developed countries within the framework of its conservation activities.

Undertook the creation or development of 35 National Parks and game reserves, protection of 35 endangered species of bird and mammal, protection of many threatened plants and habitats and national environmental education programs.

★578★ Television Trust for the Environment
46 Charlotte St.
London W1P 1LX, England
Phone: (71) 637-4602
Fax: (71) 580-7780
Telex: 291721
Contact: Robert P. Lamb, Director
Founded: 1984. Aims to educate the public worldwide on the environment and natural resources using electronic communications.

★579★ Toyota Foundation
Shinjuku Mitsui Bldg. 37F
2-1-1 Nishi Shinjuku
Tokyo 163, Shinjuku-ku, Japan
Contact: Hideo Yamaguchi, Secretary
Founded: 1974. Operates nationally and internationally in many fields, including the environment.

★580★ Twenty-Seven Foundation
c/o Hays Allan
Southhampton House
317 High Holborn
London WC1V 7NL, England
Phone: (71) 831-6233
Contact: J.M. Carr, Trustee
Founded: 1962. Operates both nationally and internationally to promote the conservation of natural resources through grants to institutions.

★581★ World Conservation Union
Ave. du Mont-Blanc
1196 Gland, Switzerland
Phone: (22) 649114
Fax: (22) 642926
Telex: 419605
Contact: Dr. M.S. Swaminathan, Pres.
Founded: 1948.
Independent, international organization for the management and conservation of the world's living resources.

★582★ World Society for the Protection of Animals
1 Park Pl.
Lawn Ln.
London, Vauxhall SW8, England
Phone: (71) 793-0540
Contact: T.H. Scott, Exec. Dir.
Founded: 1981. Operates internationally in the field of protection of animals and conservation of their environment and in related areas of education, international relations and international law.

★583★ World University Service of Canada
PO Box 3000
Station C
Ottawa, Ontario, Canada K1Y 4M8
Phone: (613)232-0377
Fax: (613)725-1910
Telex: 053-3691
Contact: Dr. M. Gervais, Pres.
Founded: 1939.
Operates internationally in the fields of aid to less developed countries, conservation, education, medicine, and science and technology.

★584★ World Wide Fund for Nature-World Wildlife Fund (WWF)
Panda House
Weyside Park
Surrey, Godalming GU7 1XR, England
Phone: (483) 426444
Fax: (483) 426409
Telex: 859602
Contact: George Medley, Director
Founded: 1961. To promote the conservation of natural resources and the diversity of species and ecosystems worldwide.

★585★ Zaheer Science Foundation
Tower A, Flat 30
Zakir Bagh
Okhla Rd.
New Delhi 110025, India
Phone: (11) 633373
Contact: Prof. S. Nurul Hasan, Chm.
Operates both nationally and internationally in many fields, including the conservation of natural resources in so far as science and technology are concerned.

United States

★586★ The Acid Rain Foundation
1410 Varsity Dr.
Raleigh, NC 27606
Phone: (919)828-9443
Contact: Dr. Harriett S. Stubbs, Exec. Dir.
The Acid Rain Foundation was formed in 1981 to develop public awareness, information and educational materials, and research on acid deposition. Currently, the Foundation's scope has broadened to include other atmospheric problems such as air pollutants, air toxics, effects of air pollutants on forest ecosystems, global climate change, and overall air quality.

★587★ African Wildlife Foundation
1717 Massachusetts Ave., N. W.
Washington, DC 20036
Phone: (202)265-8393
Contact: Paul T. Schindler, Pres.
The African Wildlife Foundation is an international conservation organization in 1961. Focusing primarily on conservation education, the Foundation works closely with African governments and people to combat poaching and wildlife habitat destruction.

★588★ Amax Foundation
200 Park Ave.
New York, NY 10166
Phone: (212)856-4250
Contact: Sonja Michaud, Pres.
Recipients of recent grants and gifts include Conservation Foundation (Washington, DC) and Nature Conservancy (Arlington, VA).

★589★ American Electric Power
One Riverside Plaza
Columbus, OH 43215
Phone: (614)223-1000
Contact: Richard M. McMorrow, Asst. V. Pres., Community Relations
Recent years have seen an increased interest by the company in social service and civic and public affairs. In these categories, economic development and environmental affairs receive highest priority.

★590★ American Farmland Trust
1920 N St., N.W. Ste. 400
Washington, DC 20036
Phone: (202)659-5170
Contact: Ralph E. Grossi, Pres.
The American Farmland Trust is dedicated to protecting America's farmland from natural and manmade threats by promoting the conservation of agricultural land resources and educating the public about the importance of these resources.

★591★ American Rivers
801 Pennsylvania Ave., S.E. Ste. 303
Washington, DC 20003
Phone: (202)547-6900
Fax: (202)543-6142
Contact: Kevin J. Coyle, Pres.
Established in 1973, American Rivers is the nation's principal river-saving organization. By working with related government agencies, American Rivers has played a key role in the preservation of more than 12,000 river miles totaling more than 3.3 million steamside acres.

★592★ AMETEK Foundation
Station Sq. 2
Paoli, PA 19301
Phone: (215)647-2121
Contact: Robert W. Yannarell, Asst. Sec.
Recipients of recent grants and gifts include Natural Resources Defense Council (New York) and Alaska Conservation Foundation.

★593★ Amoco Foundation
200 E. Randolph Dr.
Chicago, IL 60601
Phone: (312)856-6306
Contact: Pamela J. Barbara, Exec. Dir.
Recipients of recent grants and gifts include Energy Projects for Nonprofits, Audubon Zoo (New Orleans, LA), and Nature Conservancy (Arlington, VA).

★594★ Andrew W. Mellon Foundation
140 E. 62nd St.
New York, NY 10021
Phone: (212)838-8400
Fax: (212)223-2778
Contact: T. Dennis Sullivan, Financial V. Pres.
Recipients of recent grants and gifts include Worldwatch Institute (Washington, DC) and Wilderness Society (Washington, DC).

★595★ ARCO Foundation
515 S. Flower St.
Los Angeles, CA 90071
Phone: (213)486-3342
Contact: Eugene R. Wilson, Pres.
Recipients of recent grants and gifts include International Institute for Environment and Development (Washington, DC). Between 5% and 10% of total contributions support environmental concerns. Supports organizations that focus on natural resource and land-use issues; environmental education programs; preservation of ecologically unique land for public access; wildlife conservation and protection of endangered species; and conflict resolution activities that expedite mediation of sensitive environmental issues.

★596★ Atherton Family Foundation
c/o Hawaii Community Foundation
222 Merchant St., 2nd Fl.
Honolulu, HI 96813
Phone: (808)537-6333
Fax: (808)521-6286
Contact: Ms. Jane R. Smith, Chief Exec. Officer
Recipients of recent grants and gifts include National Resource Defense Council (New York, NY) and Center for Plant Conservation (HI).

★597★ Audubon Naturalist Society of the Central Atlantic States
8940 Jones Mill Rd.
Chevy Chase, MD 20815
Phone: (301)652-9188
Contact: Kathy Rushing
The Audubon Naturalist Society of the Central Atlantic States, founded in 1897, is one of the oldest Audubon societies and a pioneer in the linking of natural history with conservation activities. From its inception, the Society has been motivated by a concern for the future of America's wild plants and animals and for the preservation of the natural environment, especially in the Potomac basin and Chesapeake Bay region.

★598★ Baltimore Gas & Electric Foundation
Gas & Electric Bldg.
PO Box 1475
Baltimore, MD 21203
Phone: (301)234-5311
Contact: Gary R. Fuhrman, Asst. Sec., Asst. Treas.
Recipients of recent grants and gifts include Baltimore Zoological Society (Maryland) and Chesapeake Bay Trust (Annapolis, Maryland).

★599★ Blandin Foundation
100 N. Pokegama Ave.
Grand Rapids, MN 55744
Phone: (218)326-0523
Fax: (218)327-1949
Contact: Mr. Paul M. Olson, Pres.
Recipients of recent grants and gifts include Mississippi Headwaters Board.

★600★ Boise Cascade Corp.
PO Box 50
Boise, ID 83728-0001
Phone: (208)384-7673
Contact: Connie E. Weaver, Contributions Admin.
Recipients of recent grants and gifts include Salmon and Trout Enhancement Program (Oregon) and Peregrine Fund (Yakima, Washington). Between 10% and 15% of total contributions are directed toward environmental concerns. Supports environmental and conservation organizations with multiple-use forest management policys. Also supports parks and zoos.

★601★ BP America Inc.
200 Public Square, 36-A
Cleveland, OH 44114
Phone: (216)586-8625
Contact: Lance C. Buhl, Dir., Corporate Contributions
Supports environmental groups concerned with waste minimization and energy conservation. Recipients of recent grants and gifts include Resources for the Future (Washington, DC).

★602★ California Department of Commerce
Hazardous Waste Reduction Loan Program
1121 L St., Ste. 501
Sacramento, CA 95821
Phone: (916)324-9325
Contact: Merrill Stevenson, Contact
Provides loans to help small businesses develop programs to reduce or eliminate hazardous waste. Provides up to $150,000 on a seven-year term at low interest.

★603★ Cargill Foundation
PO Box 9300
Minneapolis, MN 55440
Phone: (612)475-6213
Contact: James S. Hield, Sec., Cargill Contributions Committee
Supports groups involved with conservation and ecological concerns. Recipients of recent grants and gifts include Minnesota Landscape Arboretum (Minneapolis, Minnesota) and Nature Conservancy-Minnesota Chapter. Approximately 25% of total funding is directed toward environmental concerns.

★604★ Carolyn Foundation
1300 TCF Tower
Minneapolis, MN 55402
Phone: (612)339-7101
Contact: Ms. Carol Fetzer, Exec. Dir.
Recipients of recent grants and gifts include Wilderness Society (Washington, DC), Sierra Club Legal Defense Fund (San Francisco, CA), and Environmental Defense Fund (New York, NY).

★605★ Caterpillar Foundation
100 NE Adams St.
Peoria, IL 61629-1480
Phone: (309)675-4464
Contact: Edward W. Siebert, V. Pres. & Manager
Recipients of recent grants and gifts include Wildlife Prairie Park (Hanna City, Illinois).

★606★ Center for Environmental Information
99 Ct. St.
Rochester, NY 14604
Phone: (716)546-3796
Fax: (716)325-5131
Contact: Elizabeth Thorndike, Pres. & Exec. Dir.
The Center for Environmental Information was established in 1974 in Rochester, NY, as an answer to the growing need for timely, accurate, and comprehensive information on environmental issues. While maintaining a neutral position, the Center provides a current, multi-faceted program of publishing, education, and information services.

★607★ Center for Marine Conservation
1725 DeSales, N.W., Ste. 500
Washington, DC 20036
Phone: (202)429-5609
Contact: Roger E. McManus, Exec. Dir.
The Center for Marine Conservation, founded in 1972 and formerly known as the Center for Environmental Education, works toward the goals of conserving marine habitats, preventing marine pollution, managing fisheries for conservation, and protecting endangered marine species. To further these goals, the Center conducts policy-oriented research, promotes public education and citizen involvement, and supports domestic and international laws and programs for marine conservation.

★608★ Charles A. Lindbergh Fund
708 S. Third St., Ste. 110
Minneapolis, MN 55415
Phone: (612)338-1703
Incorporated in 1976, the Charles A. Lindbergh Fund aims to honor the Legacy of Charles Lindbergh and his vision of a balance between technological progress and the preservation of nature.

★609★ Charles Darwin Foundation for the Galapagos Isles
National Museum of Natural History
Tenth & Constitution Ave., N.W.
Washington, DC 20560
Phone: (202)357-2670
Contact: Craig McFarland, Pres.
The Charles Darwin Foundation for the Galapagos Isles, founded in 1959, provides for the protection of the wildlife of the Galapagos Islands; disseminates research findings; and encourages and aids scientific education, particularly in Ecuador.

★610★ Charles Engelhard Foundation
645 5th Ave., 7th Fl.
New York, NY 10022
Phone: (212)935-2430
Contact: Ms. Elaine Catterall, Sec.
Recipients of recent grants and gifts include Conservation International (Washington, DC), Craighead Wildlife-Wildlands Institute (Missoula, MT), and African Wildlife Foundation (Washington, DC).

★611★ Chase Manhattan Foundation
One Chase Plaza 29th, Fl.
New York, NY 10081
Phone: (212)552-8205
Contact: David S. Ford, V. Pres. & Dir. of Philanthropy
Recipients of recent grants and gifts include Central Park Conservancy (New York, New York), Shedd Aquarium (Chicago, Illinois), New York Botanical Garden, and Brooklyn Botanic Garden Fund (New York).

★612★ Chesapeake Bay Foundation
162 Prince George St.
Annapolis, MD 21401
Phone: (301)268-8816
Contact: William C. Baker, Pres.
Founded in 1966, the Chesapeake Bay Foundation is a conservation organization whose goal is to promote and contribute to the orderly management of the Chesapeake Bay with a special interest in maintaining a level of water quality that will support the bay's diverse aquatic species.

★613★ Chevron Corp.
575 Market St., 8th Fl.
San Francisco, CA 94105
Phone: (415)894-4193
Contact: Skip Rhodes, Manager, Corporate Contributions
Supports conservation programs and wildlife preservation, primarily in California. Includes grants to educational and research institutions with emphasis on environmental affairs. Administers the Chevron Conservation Awards Program in a variety of locations nationwide. Recipients of recent grants and gifts include Marine World Foundation (Vallejo, California) and Nature Conservancy (Baton Rouge, Louisiana).

★614★ Citizens Clearinghouse for Hazardous Wastes
Box 6806
Falls Church, VA 22040
Phone: (703)276-7070
Contact: Lois Marie Gibbs, Exec. Dir.
Citizens Clearinghouse for Hazardous Waste is concerned with the physical effects of contact with toxic chemicals and other hazardous wastes on adults and children. Established in 1981, the organization visits sites to determine the severity of toxic pollution and conducts research on chemicals to determine dangerous levels of usage.

★615★ Claiborne (Liz) Foundation
119 W 40th St., 4th Fl.
New York, NY 10018
Phone: (212)536-6424
Contact: Melanie Lyons, Dir.
Recipients of recent grants and gifts include The Nature Conservancy (Arlington, Virginia), New York Zoological Society, and Council on the Environment of NYC (New York, New York).

★616★ Clean Water Action Project Clean Water Fund
1320 18th ST., N.W.
Washington, DC 20003
Phone: (202)457-1286
Contact: Anita McCartin
Clean Water Action, founded in 1971, is a national citizen action organization established to work for strong pollution controls and safe drinking water. The organization conducts advocacy services in toxic protection for communities and workplaces, preserving the nation's wetlands, and promoting alternative treatment technologies that recycle wastes.

★617★ Collins Foundation
1618 SW 1st Ave., Ste. 305
Portland, OR 97201-5708
Phone: (503)227-7171
Contact: Mr. William C. Pine, Exec. V. Pres.
Recipients of recent grants and gifts include Trust for Public Land--Oregon (Portland), 1,000 Friends of Oregon (Portland), and Nature Conservancy (Portland, Oregon).

★618★ Compton Foundation
525 Middlefield Rd., Ste. 115
Menlo Park, CA 94025
Phone: (415)328-0101
Contact: Edith T. Eddy, Administrative Dir.
Recipients of recent grants and gifts include Environmental Defense Fund (CA), Nature Conservancy (HI), and Environmental Action Foundation (Washington, DC).

★619★ Conservation Foundation
1250 24th St., N.W.
Washington, DC 20037
Phone: (202)293-4800
Contact: William K. Reilly, Pres.
Founded in 1948 to counter current trends and impel responsible use of natural resources, the Conservation Foundation seeks to identify environmental challenges and devise workable solutions by promoting sound long-term use of natural resources and cooperative action among all interested parties.

★620★ Conservation International
1015 18th St., N.W., Ste. 1000
Washington, DC 20036
Phone: (202)429-5660
Fax: (202)887-5188
Contact: Russell A. Mittermeier, Pres.
Founded in 1987, Conservation International is dedicated to the conservation of diverse biological ecosystems by identifying critical areas and assisting countries in implementing effective conservation programs at the local level.

★621★ Cooper Industries Foundation
First City Tower, Ste. 4446
Houston, TX 77210
Phone: (713)739-5607
Contact: Thomas W. Campbell, Pres.
Recipients of recent grants and gifts include Central Houston Civic Improvement--Buffalo Bayou (Houston, Texas) and Friends of the Burnet Park Zoo (Syracuse, New York).

★622★ The Cousteau Society
930 W. 21st St.
Norfolk, VA 23517
Phone: (804)627-1144
Fax: (804)627-7547
Contact: Jacques-Yves Cousteau, Pres.
The Cousteau Society, founded in 1973, is an environmental education organization dedicated to the protection and improvement of the quality of life for present and future generations.

★623★ Defenders of Wildlife
1244 19th St., N.W.
Washington, DC 20036
Phone: (202)659-9510
Fax: (202)833-3349
Contact: M. Rupert Cutler, Pres.
Defenders of Wildlife has been working for more than four decades to protect wild animals. Founded in 1947 to combat the use of steel traps, the organization has grown into one of America's major national wildlife conservation organizations with a broad program of public education and action.

★624★ Digital Equipment Corp.
111 Powder Mill Rd.
MS01-1/B14
Maynard, MA 01754
Phone: (508)493-9210
Contact: Jane Hamel, Manager, Corporate Contributions Prog.
Energy conservation and environmental protection are concerns of the corporation.

★625★ Du Pont (E.I.) de Nemours & Co.
Du Pont Bldg., Rm 8065
1007 Market St.
Wilmington, DE 19898
Phone: (302)774-2036
Contact: Peter C. Morrow, Manager, Corporate Contributions
Between 10% and 15% of total contributions supports environmental organizations.

★626★ Earth Island Institute
300 Broadway, Ste. 28
San Francisco, CA 94133-3312
Phone: (415)788-3666
Fax: (415)788-7324
Telex: 6502829302 MCI UW
Contact: David R. Brower, Chm.
Earth Island Institute was founded in 1982 to develop innovative projects for conservation, preservation, and restoration of the global environment. The organization formulates critical analyses of contemporary problems, from traditionally environmental issues to ecologically-related concerns such as human rights, economic development in developing nations, economic conversion from militarization to peaceful production, and the impoverishment of inner city communities.

★627★ Educational Foundation of America
23161 Ventura Blvd., Ste. 201
Woodland Hills, CA 91364
Phone: (818)999-0921
Contact: Mr. Richard W. Hansen, Exec. Dir.
Recipients of recent grants and gifts include Conservation Law Foundation (Boston, MA), Land Institute (Salina, KS), and Ocean Arks International (Falmouth, MA).

★628★ Edward John Noble Foundation
32 E. 57th St.
New York, NY 10022
Phone: (212)759-4212
Contact: Mr. John F. Joline III, Exec. Dir.
Recipients of recent grants and gifts include Worldwatch Institute (Washington, DC), Natural Resources Defense Council (New York, NY), and Environmental Law Institute (Washington, DC).

★629★ Environmental Defense Fund
257 Park Ave., S.
New York, NY 10010
Phone: (212)505-2100
Contact: Frederic D. Krupp, Exec. Dir.
Founded in 1967, the Environmental Defense Fund has grown from a group of volunteer scientists into one of the largest environment action organizations, with six regional offices and over 125,000 members. The organization initiates legal action and litigation in environment-related matters; conducts environmental public service and education campaigns; and promotes research, public education, and administrative and legislative action.

★630★ Environmental Law Institute
1616 P St., N.W., Ste. 200
Washington, DC 20036
Phone: (202)328-5150
Contact: J. William Futrell, Pres.
The Environmental Law Institute is a national research and education institution with an interdisciplinary staff of lawyers, economists, scientists, and journalists. The Institute searches for solutions to environmental problems and works toward achieving national environmental goals. Founded in 1969, the organization maintains a leadership position on key policy research of air and water pollution, hazardous wasters and toxic substances, critical lands regulation, resource economics, and administrative law.

★631★ Environmental Policy Institute
218 D St., S.E.
Washington, DC 20003
Phone: (202)544-2600
Fax: (202)543-4710
Contact: Brent Blackwelder, V. Pres.
The Environmental Policy Institute (EPI), founded in 1974, is a public interest environmental organization engaged in research, education, and lobbying activities. It works for energy conservation, environmental protection, and the increased use of renewable sources of energy, both in the U.S. and abroad. EPI absorbed the Environmental Policy Center in 1983.

★632★ Exxon Education Foundation
225 E. John W. Carpenter Freeway, Rm, 1429
Irving, TX 75062-2298
Phone: (214)444-1000
Contact: Leonard Fleischer, Manager, Corporate Contributions
Recipients of recent grants and gifts include World Wildlife Fund and the Conservation Foundation (Washington, DC), Student Conservation Association (Charlestown, New Hampshire), Audubon Institute (New Orleans, Louisiana), and Nature Conservancy (Arlington, Virginia). Approximately 5% of total funding is directed toward environmental concerns. Areas of interest include botanical organizations, zoos, botanical gardens, wildlife preservation, and international environmental affairs.

★633★ First Hawaiian Foundation
165 S. King St.
Honolulu, HI 96813
Phone: (808)525-8144
Contact: Herbert E. Wolff, Sec.
Recipients of recent grants and gifts include Pacific Gamefish Research Foundation (Kailua-Kona, Hawaii) and Nature Conservancy of Hawaii (Honolulu, Hawaii). Approximately 5% of total contributions benefit environmental organizations.

★634★ First Interstate Bank of Nevada Foundation
PO Box 11007
Reno, NV 89520
Phone: (702)784-3844
Contact: Kevin Day, Pres.
Supports nature conservancy and other environmental and wildlife protection organizations. Recipients of recent grants and

gifts include Nature Conservancy (Arlington, VA) and Southern Nevada Clean Communities.

★635★ Florence and John Schumann Foundation
33 Park St.
Montclair, NJ 07042
Phone: (201)783-6660
Contact: Mr. Bill Moyers, Pres.
Recipients of recent grants and gifts include Renew America (Stanford, CA) and World Resources Institute (Washington, DC).

★636★ Ford Motor Co. Fund
American Road, Rm 960
PO Box 1899
Dearborn, MI 48121
Phone: (313)845-8711
Contact: Leo J. Brennan Jr., Exec. Dir.
Recipients of recent grants and gifts include National Park Foundation (Washington, DC) and Clean Sites (Alexandria, VA).

★637★ Friends of the Earth Foundation
218 D St., S.E.
Washington, DC 20003
Phone: (202)544-2600
Fax: (202)543-4710
Telex: 650-192-5483
Contact: Michael S. Clark, CEO
Friends of the Earth is dedicated to the preservation, restoration, and rational use of the earth's resources. FOE avocates environmental policies on the local, federal, and international levels.

★638★ Friends of the River Foundation
Fl. Mason Center, Bldg. C
San Francisco, CA 94123
Phone: (415)771-0400
Fax: (415)771-0301
Contact: David Bolling, Exec. Dir.
Friends of the River Foundation (FRF) supports research and public education on free flowing rivers, natural waterways, and water conservation, on behalf of the general public throughout California and the Colorado river basin.

★639★ Fund for Animals
200 W. 57th St.
New York, NY 10019
Phone: (212)246-2096
Works to help wild and domestic animals.

★640★ General Service Foundation
PO Box 4659
Boulder, CO 80306
Phone: (303)447-9541
Fax: (303)447-0595
Contact: Mr. Robert W. Musser, Pres.
Recipients of recent grants and gifts include Environmental Defense Fund (New York, NY), Rocky Mountain Institute (Old Snowmass, CO), and World Wildlife Fund (Washington, DC).

★641★ George B. Storer Foundation
PO Box 1270
Saratoga, WY 82331
Phone: (307)326-8308
Contact: Mr. Peter Storer, Pres.
Recipients of recent grants and gifts include Nature Conservancy of Florida, Conservation International (Washington, DC), and Florida Conservation Association (Winter Park).

★642★ Georgia-Pacific Foundation
133 Peachtree St. NE
Atlanta, GA 30303
Phone: (404)521-5228
Contact: Wayne Tamblyn, Pres.
Recipients of recent grants and gifts include Atlanta Botanical Garden, Atlanta Zoological Society, and World Forestry Center (Portland, OR). Between 5% and 10% of total contributions are directed towards environmental concerns, with many grants to environmental affairs organizations, zoological societies, and botanical gardens.

★643★ Geraldine R. Dodge Foundation
95 Madison Ave.
PO Box 1239
Morristown, NJ 07962-1239
Phone: (201)540-8442
Contact: Mr. Scott McVay, Exec. Dir.
Recipients of recent grants and gifts include Worldwatch Institute (Washington, DC), Environmental Defense Fund (New York, NY), and Natural Resources Defense Council (New York, NY).

★644★ German Marshall Fund of the United States
11 Dupont Circle, NW Ste. 750
Washington, DC 20036
Phone: (202)745-3950
Fax: (202)265-1662
Contact: Mr. Frank E. Loy, Pres.
Recipients of recent grants and gifts include World Wildlife Fund/Conservation Foundation (Washington, DC), Environmental Law Institute (Washington, DC), and Environmental Defense Fund (New York, NY).

★645★ Hawk Mountain Sanctuary Association
Rt. 2
Kempton, PA 19529
Phone: (215)756-6961
Contact: Stanley E. Senner, Exec. Dir.
The Hawk Mountain Sanctuary Association fosters the conservation of birds of prey and other wildlife and attempts to create better understanding of man's relationship to the environment through several educational activities.

★646★ Helen Clay Frick Foundation
PO Box 86190
Pittsburgh, PA 15221
Phone: (412)371-0600
Contact: Mr. DeCoursey E. McIntosh, Exec. Dir.
Recipients of recent grants and gifts include Westmoreland Sanctuary (New York, NY), Caribbean Conservation (Gainesville, FL), and North American Wildlife Foundation (Palatine, IL).

★647★ Hoffman-La Roche Foundation
PO Box 278
Nutley, NJ 07110
Phone: (201)235-3797
Contact: Rosemary Bruner, Administrative Dir.
Recipients of recent grants and gifts include New York Zoological Society and World Wildlife Fund (Washington, DC).

★648★ Inform
381 Park Ave., S.
New York, NY 10016
Phone: (212)689-4040
Fax: (212)447-0689
Contact: Joanna Underwood, Exec. Dir.
Studies the impact of U.S. corporations on the environment, employees, and consumers focusing on industrial waste reduction, municipal solid waste management, western water conservation, and urban air quality.

★649★ International Center for Development Policy
731 Eighth St., S.E.
Washington, DC 20003
Phone: (202)547-3800
Fax: (202)546-4784
Telex: 5106017738
Contact: Stuart N. Conway, Dir.
The New Forests Project is a people-to-people, direct action program established in 1982 to curb deforestation in developing countries. Since its inception, the Project has educated communities threatened by deforestation on the importance of forests and natural resource protection. It has helped families in more than 2,400 villages in 110 developing countries to begin tree-planting programs.

★650★ International Primate Protection League
PO Box 766
Summerville, SC 29484
Phone: (803)871-2280
Fax: (803)871-7988
Contact: Dr. Shirley McGreat, Chwm.
Founded with the purpose of conservation and protection of apes and monkeys. IPPL investigates illegal animal trade and works to protect primate habitats and captive primates. Maintains a gibbon sanctuary and provides grants for other projects and sanctuaries.

★651★ International Wildlife Coalition
634 N. Falmouth Hwy.
Box 388
N. Falmouth, MA 02556-0388
Phone: (508)564-9980
Fax: (508)563-2843
Contact: Daniel J. Morast, Pres.
The organization's goals include: 1) protecting wild animals and natural places; 2) preventing cruelty to wild animals and/or the destruction of natural places caused by unnecessary exploitation; 3) supporting and undertaking research relating to wild animals; and 4) gathering, publishing, and communicating educational information about wild creatures and their habitats.

★652★ J. Aron Charitable Foundation
126 E. 56th St., Ste. 2300
New York, NY 10022
Phone: (212)832-3405
Contact: Mr. Peter A. Aron, Exec. Dir.
Recipients of recent grants and gifts include Audubon Institute (New Orleans, LA), Nature Conservancy (Washington, DC), and Rhino Rescue U.S.A. (Washington, DC).

★653★ Jacob and Annita France Foundation
6301 N. Charles St., Ste. 7
Baltimore, MD 21212
Phone: (301)377-5251
Fax: (301)377-8770
Contact: Mr. Fredrick W. Lafferty, Exec. Dir.
Recipients of recent grants and gifts include Nature Conservancy (Chevy Chase, MD) and Baltimore Zoological Society (MD).

★654★ Jessie B. Cox Charitable Trust
c/o Grants Management Association
230 Congress St.
Boston, MA 02110
Phone: (617)426-7172
Contact: Mrs. Ala Reid, Admin.
Recipients of recent grants and gifts include Maine Audubon Society (Falmouth, ME), Vermont Natural Resources Council (Montpelier, VT), and Ocean Arks International.

★655★ J.M. Kaplan Fund
30 Rockefeller Plaza, Ste. 4250
New York, NY 10112
Phone: (212)767-0630
Contact: Ms. Suzanne Davis, Exec. Dir.
Recipients of recent grants and gifts include Natural Resources Defense Council (New York,

NY), Open Space Institute (New York, NY), and Nature Conservancy (Arlington, VA).

★656★ John D. and Catherine T. MacArthur Foundation
140 S. Dearborn St., Ste. 1100
Chicago, IL 60603
Phone: (312)726-8000
Fax: (312)917-0334
Contact: Ms. Adele S. Simmons, Pres.
Recipients of recent grants and gifts include Trust for Public Land (San Francisco, CA) and Nature Conservancy of Hawaii (Honolulu).

★657★ John Merck Fund
11 Beacon St., Ste. 600
Boston, MA 02108
Phone: (617)723-2932
Contact: Ms. Ruth Hennig, Admin.
Recipients of recent grants and gifts include Conservation Law Foundation of New England (Boston, MA), Vermont Natural Resources Council (Montpelier), and Conservation Law Foundation of New England (Boston, MA).

★658★ Johnson's Wax Fund
1525 Howe St.
Racine, WI 53403
Phone: (414)631-2267
Contact: Reva Holmes, V. Pres. & Sec.
Recipients of recent grants and gifts include Zoological Society of Milwaukee County (Wisconsin), Trees for Tomorrow (Eagle River, Wisconsin), and World Wildlife Fund (Washington, DC).

★659★ Joyce Foundation
135 S. LaSalle St., Ste. 4010
Chicago, IL 60603
Phone: (312)782-2464
Fax: (312)782-4160
Contact: Mr. Craig Kennedy, Pres.
Recipients of recent grants and gifts include Conservation Foundation (Washington, DC), Nature Conservancy of Canada (Toronto), and Natural Resources Defense Council (Washington, DC).

★660★ Jules and Doris Stein Foundation
PO Box 30
Beverly Hills, CA 90213
Phone: (213)276-2101
Alt. Phone: (213)276-0126
Contact: Mrs. Linda L. Valliant, Sec.
Recipients of recent grants and gifts include Trees for Life (Witchita, KS) and Nature Conservancy (St. Louis, MO).

★661★ Keep America Beautiful
Mill River Plaza
9 W. Broad St.
Stamford, CT 06902
Phone: (203)323-8987
Fax: (203)325-9199
Contact: Roger W. Powers, Pres.
Keep America Beautiful is a national educational organization dedicated to improving waste handling practices in American communities. The KAB network includes 441 communities in 40 states and 17 statewide affiliates. This network takes a systematic approach to changing personal attitudes about waste handling and devising local solutions to the disposal issue.

★662★ Kraft General Foods Foundation
Kraft Ct. 2W
Glenview, IL 60025
Phone: (708)998-7031
Contact: Pamela Hollie, Dir., Corporate Contributions
Recipients of recent grants and gifts include New York Botanical Garden, Chicago Horticultural, Society-Botanic Garden, and John G. Shedd Aquarium (Chicago, Illinois).

★663★ Kroger Co. Foundation
PO Box 1199
Cincinnati, OH 45201
Phone: (513)762-4443
Contact: Paul Bernish, V. Pres. & Sec.
Recipients of recent grants and gifts include Zoological Society of Greater Cincinnati, Greater Cincinnati Foundation City Gardens Project, and Toledo Zoo.

★664★ Louis and Anne Abrons Foundation
437 Madison Ave.
New York, NY 10017
Phone: (212)756-3376
Contact: Mr. Richard Abrons, Pres. and Dir.
Recipients of recent grants and gifts include Council on the Environment of New York City (NY), Environmental Defense Fund (New York, NY), and Central Park Conservancy (New York, NY).

★665★ Louisiana Land & Exploration Co. Foundation
PO Box 60350
New Orleans, LA 70160
Phone: (504)566-6500
Contact: Karen A. Overson, Contributions Coordinator
Recipients of recent grants and gifts include The Audubon Institute, Friends of City Park, Louisiana Nature Center, Inc., Audubon Park Institute, (all in New Orleans); and Louisiana Nature Conservancy (Baton Rouge).

★666★ Lyndhurst Foundation
Ste. 701, Tallan Bldg.
100 W. M.L. King Blvd.
Chattanooga, TN 37402-2561
Phone: (615)756-0767
Fax: (615)756-0770
Contact: Mr. Jack Murrah, Pres.
Recipients of recent grants and gifts include Tennessee Aquarium (Chattanooga) and Chattanooga Nature Center.

★667★ Mars Foundation
6885 Elm St.
McLean, VA 22101
Phone: (703)821-4900
Contact: Roger G. Best, Sec.
Recipients of recent grants and gifts include Chesapeake Bay Foundation (Annapolis, MD), World Wildlife Fund (Washington, DC), and Wildlife Preservation Trust (Philadelphia, PA).

★668★ Marshall & Ilsley Foundation
770 N. Water St.
Milwaukee, WI 53201
Phone: (414)765-7835
Contact: Diana L. Sebion, Sec.
Recipients of recent grants and gifts include Zoological Society of Milwaukee County (Wisconsin), Riveredge Nature Center (Newburg, Wisconsin), Trees for Tomorrow (Eagle River, Wisconsin), and Westside Conservation Corporation (Milwaukee, Wisconsin).

★669★ Mary Flagler Cary Charitable Trust
350 5th Ave., Rm. 6622
New York, NY 10118
Phone: (212)563-6860
Fax: (212)695-6538
Contact: Mr. Edward A. Ames, Trustee
Recipients of recent grants and gifts include New York Botanical Garden (Bronx), Trust for Public Land (San Francisco, CA), and Conservation Law Foundation (Boston, MA).

★670★ Mary Reynolds Babcock Foundation
102 Reynolda Village
Winston-Salem, NC 27106-5123
Phone: (919)748-9222
Contact: Mr. William L. Bondurant, Exec. Dir.
Recipients of recent grants and gifts include Environmental Defense Fund (New York, NY) and Southern Environmental Law Center (Charlottesville, VA).

★671★ Matlock Foundation
1201 Third Ave., Ste. 4900
Seattle, WA 98101-3009
Phone: (206)224-5196
Contact: Lin Smith, Public Affairs Asst.
Recipients of recent grants and gifts include Humboldt Area Foundation-Evergreen Lodge Project (Eureka, California), World Forestry Center (Portland, Oregon), and Sacramento River Preservation Project (Redding, California).

★672★ May Stores Foundation
611 Dr. St.
St. Louis, MO 63101
Phone: (314)342-6300
Contact: James Abrams, V. Pres., Corporate Communications
Recipients of recent grants and gifts include Rainforest Alliance.

★673★ McIntosh Foundation
215 5th St., Ste. 100
West Palm Beach, FL 33401
Phone: (407)832-8845
Contact: Michael A. McIntosh, Pres.
Recipients of recent grants and gifts include Alaska Conservation Foundation (Anchorage, AK) and National Parks and Conservation Association (Washington, DC).

★674★ MNC Financial Foundation
PO Box 987-MS251001
Baltimore, MD 21203
Phone: (301)547-4126
Contact: George B.P. Ward Jr., Sec. & Treas.
Recipients of recent grants and gifts include Balitmore Zoological Society (Maryland), Coalition/Preservation Oregon Ridge (Baltimore, Maryland), National Aquarium (Baltimore, Maryland), and Chesapeake Wildlife Heritage (Annapolis, Maryland).

★675★ National Arbor Day Foundation
100 Arbor Ave.
Nebraska City, NE 68410
Phone: (402)474-5655
Contact: John Rosenow, Exec. Dir.
The National Arbor Day Foundation comprises associations, corporations, communities, state government agencies, and individuals dedicated to tree planting and conservation. NADF promotes the observance of Arbor Day, creates an awareness and appreciation of the fundamental role trees play in day-to-day existence, supports and implements education programs that stimulate appreciation of trees, and initiates programs that encourge planting of trees.

★676★ National Audubon Society
950 Third Ave.
New York, NY 10022
Phone: (212)546-9100
Contact: Peter A.A. Berle, Pres.
The Society's purpose is to conserve native plants and animals and their habitats; to protect life from pollution, radiation, and toxic substances; to further the wise use of land and water; to seek solutions for global problems involving the interaction of population, resources, and the environment; and to

promote rational strategies for energy development and use, stressing conservation and renewable energy sources.

★677★ National Fish and Wildlife Foundation
1849 C St., NW
Washington, DC 20240
Phone: (202)208-3040
Contact: Charles H. Collins, Exec. Dir.

★678★ National Park and Conservation Association
1015 31st St., N.W.
Washington, DC 20007-4406
Phone: (202)944-8530
Contact: Paul C. Pritchard, Pres.
Founded in 1919 by Stephen Mather, the first director of the National Park Service, the National Parks and Conservation Association is a private, membership organization whose aim is to defend and expand the United States National Park System, and to educate the public on the significance of National Parks.

★679★ National Wildlife Federation
1400 Sixteenth St., N.W.
Washington, DC 20036-2266
Phone: (202)797-6800
Toll-Free: 800-432-6564
The National Wildlife Federation is the largest private conservation orgainization in the U.S. with 5.6 million members and supporters and 52 affiliate organizations. The Federation was created at the first North American Wildlife Conference in 1936. Today, its primary objective is to promote the wise use and proper management of natural resources.

★680★ Natural Resources Defense Council
40 W 20th St.
New York, NY 10168
Phone: (212)727-2700
Fax: (212)727-1773
Contact: John H. Adams, Exec. Dir.
The Natural Resources Defense Council, established in 1970, is dedicated to the wise management of natural resources through research, public education, and the development of public policies. Major concerns include land use, coastal protection, air and water pollution, nuclear safety and energy production, toxic substances, and protection of wilderness and wildlife.

★681★ The Nature Conservancy
1815 N. Lynn St.
Arlington, VA 22209
Phone: (703)841-5300
Contact: Frank D. Boren, Pres.
The Nature Conservancy is an international conservation organization committed to preserving natural diversity by finding and protecting lands and waters supporting the best examples of all elements of the natural world. This diversity includes tallgrass prairies, forests, wetlands, and the flora and fauna that depend on them. Founded in 1951, the Conservancy has protected nearly four million acres of ecologically important land and has 1100 preserves nationwide, making it the largest private system of nature sanctuaries in the world.

★682★ New York Times Co. Foundation
229 W. 43rd St.
New York, NY 10036
Phone: (212)556-1091
Contact: Arthur Gelb, Pres.
About 5% of total contributions support environmental organizations with emphasis on New York City. Matches employee gifts to environmental groups. Recipients of recent grants and gifts include Central Park Conservancy (New York, New York) and Council on the Environment.

★683★ North American Loon Fund
R.R. 4, Box 240C
Meredith, NH 03253
Phone: (603)279-6163
Toll-Free: 800-462-5666
Contact: Linda O'Bara, Exec. Dir.
Founded in 1979, the North American Loon Fund promotes the preservation of loons and their lake habitats through research, public education, and the involvement of people who share their lakes with loons. The organization sponsors programs throughout North America in an effort to check the population decline of the loon.

★684★ North American Wildlife Foundation
102 Wilmot Rd., Ste. 410
Deerfield, IL 60015
Phone: (708)940-7776
Contact: Charles S. Potter, Jr., Exec. V.Pres.
The North American Wildlife Foundation was established in 1911 by sportsmen and conservationists. Its mandate is to expand the knowledge of the interaction of agriculture, wildlife, and wetlands. The Foundation is discovering the critical links between the waterfowl resource and its diminishing habitats, and is dedicated to addressing the fundamental issues of sound land stewardship to ensure that a strong environmental heritage is passed on to future generations.

★685★ Northwest Area Foundation
W-975 First National Bank Bldg.
332 Minnesota St.
St. Paul, MN 55101-1373
Phone: (612)224-9635
Contact: Ms. Terry Tinson Saario, Pres.
Recipients of recent grants and gifts include Alternative Energy Resources Organization/ Montana State University (Helena, MT) and Oregon State University/Oregon Tilth (Corvallis, OR).

★686★ Overbrook Foundation
521 5th Ave., Rm. 1821
New York, NY 10175
Phone: (212)661-8710
Contact: Ms. Sheila McGoldrick, Corresponding Sec.
Recipients of recent grants and gifts include Conservation International (Washington, DC), Natural Resources Defense Fund (New York, NY), and World Resource Institute (Washington, DC).

★687★ Pacific Whale Foundation
Kealia Beach Plaza, Ste. 25
101 N. Kihei Rd.
Maui, HI 96753
Phone: (808)879-8811
Fax: (808)879-2615
Toll-Free: 800-941-5311
Contact: Gregory D. Kaufman, Pres.
The Pacific Whale Foundation is a marine mammal research and education organization dedicated to preserving marine life. The Foundation conducts research, conservation, and educational programs involving whales, dolphins, porpoises, and other marine mammals.

★688★ Patrick and Anna M. Cudahy Fund
PO Box 11978
Milwaukee, WI 53211
Phone: (708)866-0760
Contact: Sr. Judith Borchers, Admin.
Recipients of recent grants and gifts include Rails to Trails Conservancy (Washington, DC) and Wilderness Society (Washington, DC).

★689★ Peregrine Fund
World Center for Birds of Prey
5666 W. Flying Hawk Ln.
Boise, ID 83709
Phone: (208)362-3716
Fax: (208)362-2316
Contact: Dr. Burnham
The Peregrine Fund, founded in 1970, is concerned with the study and preservation of falcons and other birds of prey. The Fund seeks to reestablish natural populations of the Peregrine falcon and other endangered raptors. It operates the World Center for Birds of Prey to serve as a research and education facility and to maintain and captively propagate rare birds of prey.

★690★ Pew Charitable Trusts
Three Parkway, Ste. 501
Philadelphia, PA 19102
Phone: (215)587-4057
Alt. Phone: (215)587-4077
Contact: Ms. Deidra A. Lyngard, Communications Manager
Recipients of recent grants and gifts include Zoological Society of Philadelphia (PA) and American Council for an Energy Efficient Economy (Washington, DC).

★691★ Providence Journal Charitable Foundation
75 Fountain St.
Providence, RI 02902
Phone: (401)277-7514
Contact: Lincoln Pratt, Corporate Dir., Community Relations
Environment is a major area of concern with grants going to the Audubon Society and the Nature Conservancy. Recipients of recent grants and gifts include Mary Elizabeth Sharpe Street Tree Endowment and Audubon Society of Rhode Island.

★692★ Public Welfare Foundation
2600 Virginia Ave., NW, Ste. 505
Washington, DC 20037
Phone: (202)965-1800
Contact: Mr. Charles Glenn Ihrig, Pres. and Exec. Dir.
Recipients of recent grants and gifts include Environmental Defense Fund (New York, NY), Natural Resources Defense Council (New York, NY), and Sierra Club Legal Defense Fund (San Francisco, CA).

★693★ Puget Sound Power & Light Co.
Consumer Affairs Dept., OBC-09N
PO Box 97034
Bellevue, WA 98009
Phone: (206)462-3799
Contact: Beverley Dufort, Mgr., Corp. Contributions, Volunteerism
Focus of giving is on environmental education, air and water quality programs, wildlife enhancement, and preservation of ecologically unique land.

★694★ Rainforest Action Network
301 Broadway, Ste. A
San Francisco, CA 94133
Phone: (415)398-4404
Fax: (415)398-2732
Contact: Randall Hayes, Dir.
Since it was founded in 1985, the Rainforest Action Network has been working to protect rainforests and the human rights of those living in and around those forests. The Network plays

a key role in the worldwide rainforest conservation movement by supporting activists in tropical countries as well as organizing and mobilizing consumers and community action groups throughout the United States.

★695★ Rainforest Alliance
270 Lafayette St., Ste. 512
New York, NY 10012
Phone: (212)941-1900
Fax: (212)941-4986
Contact: Daniel R. Katz, Pres. & Exec. Dir.
The Rainforest Alliance was created in 1986 and is dedicated solely to conservation of the world's tropical forests and the development of a national, broad-based constituency acting on their behalf. To reach its goals, the Alliance educates the public and various professions about their interdependency with tropical forest, facilitates their active involvement in forest conservation, enhances cooperation among groups concerned with tropical forest, supports research leading to sustainable forest use, and channels resources to local organizations working in tropical countries to protect their forests.

★696★ RARE Center for Tropical Bird Conservation
19th & Parkway
Philadelphia, PA 19103
Phone: (215)299-1182
Contact: George S. Glenn, Jr., Exec. Dir.
The RARE Center for Tropical Bird Conservation, founded in 1973, seeks to protect endangered tropical bird species of the Caribbean and Latin America. The Center generates and funds projects that will directly aid endangered tropical birds in the Western Hemisphere. It also conducts educational programs for public information on endangered species.

★697★ Raytheon Co.
141 Spring St.
Lexington, MA 02173
Phone: (617)862-6600
Contact: Janet Taylor, Admin., Corporate Contributions
Supports efforts that work to improve or maintain water and air quality.

★698★ Richard King Mellon Foundation
PO Box 2930
Pittsburgh, PA 15230-2930
Phone: (412)392-2800
Contact: Mr. George H. Taber, V. Pres. and Dir.
Recipients of recent grants and gifts include Environmental Defense Fund (Washington, DC), Hornocker Wildlife Research Institute (Moscow, ID), and Pennsylvania Environmental Council (Philadelphia, PA).

★699★ Rockefeller Brothers Fund
1290 Ave. of the Americas, Rm. 3450
New York, NY 10104
Phone: (212)373-4200
Contact: Mr. Benjamin R. Shute Jr., Sec.
Recipients of recent grants and gifts include Worldwatch Institute (Washington, DC), Resources Development Foundation (Washington, DC), and Global Studies Center (Washington, DC).

★700★ Rockefeller Family Fund
1290 Ave. of the Americas, Rm. 3450
New York, NY 10104
Phone: (212)373-4252
Alt. Phone: (212)315-0996
Contact: Mr. Donald K. Ross, Dir. and Sec.
Recipients of recent grants and gifts include Conservation Law Foundation of New England (Boston, MA), Environmental Policy Institute (Washington, DC), and Non-Profit Resource Center (Albany, NY).

★701★ Safari Club International Conservation Fund
4800 W. Gates Pass Rd.
Tucson, AZ 85745
Phone: (602)620-1220
Fax: (602)622-1205
Contact: Warren Parker, Pres.
The Safari Club International, founded in 1971, consists of sportmen united to encourage the conservation of wildlife. The organization promotes hunting as a wildlife management tool and aims to preserve public hunting and protect hunter's rights. It also fosters public education concerning conservation, and sponsors research.

★702★ Save-the Redwoods League
114 Sansome St., Rm 605
San Francisco, CA 94104
Phone: (415)362-2352
Contact: John B. Dewitt, Exec. Dir.
The Save-the Redwoods League was founded in 1918 to purchase Redwood land for protection in public parks. League members have donated over $60 million to protect over 260,000 acres of Redwood land in public parks, including many ancient Redwood groves.

★703★ Scherman Foundation
315 W. 57th St., Ste. 2D
New York, NY 10019
Phone: (212)489-7143
Contact: Mr. David F. Freeman, Exec. Dir. and Treas.
Recipients of recent grants and gifts include Sierra Club Legal Defense Fund (San Francisco, CA), Southern Environmental Law Center (Charlottesville, VA), and Wilderness Society (Washington, DC).

★704★ Sequoia Foundation
820 A St., Ste. 545
Tacoma, WA 98402
Phone: (206)627-1634
Contact: Mr. Frank D. Underwood, Exec. Dir.
Recipients of recent grants and gifts include Conservation International Foundation (Washington, DC), Nature Conservancy International (Washington, DC), and World Wildlife Fund (Baltimore, MD).

★705★ Sierra Club Foundation
730 Polk St.
San Francisco, CA 94109
Phone: (415)923-5679
Contact: Stephen M. Stevick, Exec. Dir.
Founded in 1960, the Sierra Club Foundation is the sole source of tax deductible support to the Sierra Club for activities which include research, publication, and public education on environmental issues, presentation of testimony before administrative and regulatory agencies, environmental litigation, volunteer training, and on a limited scale, legislative lobbying.

★706★ Sierra Club Legal Defense Fund
2044 Fillmore St.
San Francisco, CA 94115
Phone: (415)567-1600
Contact: Fredric P. Sutherland, Exec. Dir.
Founded in 1971, the Sierra Club Legal Defense Fund is a public interest law firm providing legal representation for national, regional, and local groups and individuals committed to protecting the environment. It is involved in litigation to reduce acid rain and water pollution, to safeguard national forests, parks, wilderness areas, and seashores, to contain toxic materials, and to preserve wildlife habitat.

★707★ Texaco Foundation
2000 Westchester Ave.
White Plains, NY 10650
Phone: (914)253-4150
Contact: Maria Mike-Mayer, Sec.
Recipients of recent grants and gifts include Central Park Conservancy (New York, NY) and New York Botanical Garden (Bronx, NY). About 10% of all contributions support civic, public, and environmental interests.

★708★ Times Mirror Foundation
Times Mirror Sq.
Los Angeles, CA 90053
Phone: (213)237-3936
Contact: Cassandra Malry, Treas.
Recipients of recent grants and gifts include California Nature Conservancy.

★709★ Tinker Foundation
55 E. 59th St.
New York, NY 10022
Phone: (212)421-6858
Contact: Ms. Martha T. Muse, Chm. of the Board, Pres.
Recipients of recent grants and gifts include Center for Marine Conservation (Washington, DC), American Assembly (New York, NY), and World Environment Center (New York, NY).

★710★ TreePeople
12601 Mulholland Dr.
Beverly Hills, CA 90210
Phone: (213)273-8733
Contact: Andy Lipkis, Exec. Dir.
TreePeople, founded in 1970, is an environmental problem solving organization, operating primariy in southern California, promoting community action, global awareness, and an active role in planting and caring for trees.

★711★ Trout Unlimited
501 Church St., N.E.
Vienna, VA 22180
Phone: (703)281-1100
Fax: (703)281-1825
Contact: Robert L. Herbst, Exec. Dir.
Trout Unlimited was founded in 1959 by a group of Michigan anglers concerned about the future of wild trout populations in their state. Its mission is to conserve, restore, and enhance North America's trout, salmon, and steelhead and their watersheds. Trout Unlimited has more than 400 local chapters consisting of over 60,000 members in the United States, plus affiliations and cooperative agreements in Canada, Spain, France, Yugoslavia, New Zealand, China, and the Soviet Union.

★712★ Union of Concerned Scientists
26 Church St.
Cambridge, MA 02238
Phone: (617)547-5552
Fax: (617)864-9405
Contact: Howard C. Ris, Jr., Exec. Dir.
Formed in 1969, the Union of Concerned Scientists is an independent organization of scientists and other citizens concerned about the impact of advanced technology on society. Its programs focus on national energy policy, national security policy, and nuclear power safety.

★713★ U.S. Public Interest Research Group
215 Pennsylvania Ave., S.E.
Washington, DC 20003
Phone: (202)546-9707
Contact: Gene Karpinski, Exec. Dir.
The U.S. Public Interest Research Group was founded in 1983 as a group of individuals who contribute time, effort or funds for public interest research and advocacy. Current efforts include support for laws to protect consumers from unsafe products and unfair banking practices, laws to reduce the use of toxic chemicals, renewal of the Clean Air Act, efforts to reduce global warming and ozone depletion, energy conservation, and use of safe, renewable energy sources.

★714★ USF&G Foundation
100 Light St.
Baltimore, MD 21202
Phone: (301)547-3310
Contact: William Spliedt, Sec. & Treas.
Recipients of recent grants and gifts include Coalition to Preserve Oregon Ridge (Baltimore, Maryland) and Nature Conservancy (Chevy Chase, Maryland). Between 5% and 10% of all contributions are directed towards environmental organizations.

★715★ Victoria Foundation
40 S. Fullerton Ave.
Montclair, NJ 07042
Phone: (201)783-4450
Contact: Ms. Catherine M. McFarland, Exec. Officer
Recipients of recent grants and gifts include New Jersey Department of Environmental Protection (Trenton), Nature Conservancy (Pottersville, NJ), and New Jersey Conservation Foundation (Morristown).

★716★ W. Alton Jones Foundation
232 E. High St.
Charlottesville, VA 22901-5178
Phone: (804)295-2134
Contact: Dr. J.P. Myers, Dir.
Recipients of recent grants and gifts include Natural Resources Defense Council (New York, NY), Massachusetts Audubon Society (Lincoln, MA), and Wilderness Society (Washington, DC).

★717★ Waste Management
3003 Butterfield Rd.
Oak Brook, IL 60521
Phone: (708)572-8800
Contact: Paul Pyrcik, Dir. of Programs
Supports groups and programs committed to protecting the environment. Recipients include wildlife preservation organizations, litter prevention and cleanup projects, environmental study groups, recycling programs, and conservation funds.

★718★ White Lung Association
1601 St. Paul St.
Baltimore, MD 21202
Phone: (301)727-6029
Contact: James Fite, Exec. Dir.
The White Lung Association is a national asbestos victim's organization. Formed in 1979 to educate the public about asbestos hazards and how to avoid exposure, it also provides medical, legal, and technical information to asbestos victims and to persons exposed to asbestos. White Lung is a general term for asbestos-related disease.

★719★ The Wilderness Society
1400 Eye St., N. W.
Washington, DC 20005
Phone: (202)842-3400
Contact: George T. Frampton, Jr., Pres.
The Wilderness Society was founded in 1935 to protect America's forests, parks, rivers, deserts, wildlife refuges, and shorelands, and to foster an American land ethic. Focusing exclusively on U.S. federal public lands, the Society provides information and analyses on issues affecting these lands to the Department of the Interior, the U.S. Forest Service and other executive agencies, to Congress, and to the courts.

★720★ Wildlife Conservation Fund of America
801 Kingsmill Pkwy.
Columbus, OH 43229-1137
Phone: (614)883-4868
Contact: James H. Glass, Pres.
The Wildlife Conservation Fund of America was founded in 1978 to protect the heritage of the American sportsman to hunt, fish, and trap; and to protect scientific wildlife management practices. The Fund is the legal defense, information, public education, and research arm of the Wildlife Education Fund of America.

★721★ Wildlife Conservation International
c/o New Youk Zoological Society
Bronx, NY 10460
Phone: (212)220-5155
Contact: David Western, Dir.
Wildlife Conservation International is a division of the New York Zoological Society. The organization works to protect wildlife across the world from poachers and the influence of man on their habitat.

★722★ Wildlife Preservation Trust International
34th St. & Girard Ave.
Philadelphia, PA 19104
Phone: (215)222-3636
Contact: William Constant, Exec. Dir.
The Wildlife Preservation Trust International was founded in 1971 for the purpose of providing support for the captive breeding of endangered species to save them from extinction.

★723★ William and Flora Hewlett Foundation
525 Middlefield Rd., Ste. 200
Menlo Park, CA 94025
Phone: (415)329-1070
Contact: Mr. Roger W. Heyns, Pres.
Recipients of recent grants and gifts include American Energy Assurance Council (Denver, CO) and Conservation Foundation (Washington, DC).

★724★ William Bingham Foundation
1250 Leader Bldg.
Cleveland, OH 44114
Phone: (216)781-3275
Contact: Ms. Laura C. Hitchcox, Dir.
Recipients of recent grants and gifts include Environmental Defense Fund (New York, NY), Natural Resources Defense Council (New York, NY), Climate Research Institute (Washington, DC), and Wilderness Society (Washington, DC).

★725★ William H. Donner Foundation
500 5th Ave., Ste. 1230
New York, NY 10110
Phone: (212)719-9290
Fax: (212)302-8734
Contact: Mr. William T. Alpert, Senior Program Officer
Recipients of recent grants and gifts include African Wildlife Foundation (Washington, DC) and National Fish and Wildlife Foundation (Washington, DC).

★726★ William Penn Foundation
1630 Locust St.
Philadelphia, PA 19103
Phone: (215)732-5114
Contact: Mr. Bernard C. Watson, Pres. and Chief Exec. Officer
Recipients of recent grants and gifts include Natural Lands Trust (Philadelphia, PA) and Pennsylvania Horticultural Society (Philadelphia, PA).

★727★ Williams Cos. Foundation
PO Box 2400
Tulsa, OK 74102
Phone: (918)588-2106
Contact: Hannah Davis Robson, Manager
Recipients of recent grants and gifts include Nature Conservancy (Tulsa, Oklahoma), America's Clean Water Foundation (Washington, DC), and Tulsa Garden Center. Approximately 10% to 15% of total contributions supports environmental affairs.

★728★ Wisconsin Energy Corp. Foundation
231 W. Michigan St.
PO Box 2046
Milwaukee, WI 53201
Phone: (414)221-2105
Contact: Jerry G. Remmel, Treas.
Approximately 10% of annual contributions go toward environmental affairs. Recipients of recent grants and gifts include Zoological Society of Milwaukee County, Riveredge Nature Center (Newburg, Wisconsin), Tree For Tomorrow (Eagle River, Wisconsin), and Trees For Tomorrow (Eagle River, Wisconsin).

★729★ World Resources Institute
1709 New York Ave., N.W., 7th Floor, Ste. 700
Washington, DC 20006
Phone: (202)638-6300
Contact: James Gustave Speth, Pres.
The World Resources Institute, founded in 1982, addresses global resource and environmental issues. The Institute performs research and analysis on a broad range of environmental topics, and publishes the results in research reports and books.

★730★ World Wildlife Fund
1250 24th St., N.W.
Washington, DC 20037
Phone: (202)293-4800
Contact: Kathryn S. Fuller, Pres. and CEO
The World Wildlife Fund is the leading private organization working worldwide to protect endangered wildlife, establishing new protected areas, supporting scientific research, testing new approaches for environmentally sound rural development, promoting conservation education, and helping shape government policy.

★731★ Xerces Society
10 Ash St., S.W.
Portland, OR 97204
Phone: (503)222-2788
Contact: Melody Allen, Exec. Dir.
Founded in 1971 at a British ecology laboratory, the Xerces Socitey was based at Yale University for its first several years and focused on conservation of rare butterfly species. In 1985, however, as attention was drawn to diminishing biodiversity among insects and other invertebrates, the Society committed itself to gradually broadening its conservation concern to all invertebrates.

Federal Government Organizations

★732★ Acadia National Park Advisory Commission
Superintendent, Acadia National Park
PO Box 177
Bar Harbor, ME 04609
Commission consults with the Secretary of the Interior on matters relating to the management and development of Acadia National Park, including but not limited to the acquisition of lands and interests in lands (including conservation easements on islands), and termination of rights of use occupancy.

★733★ Acid Rain Advisory Committee
Acid Rain Division (ANR-445)
Environmental Protection Agency
401 M St. SW, Rm. M-3202
Washington, DC 20460
Phone: (202)475-9400
Contact: Paul Horwitz, Staff Contact
Committee provides informed advice and counsel to the Assistant Administrator, Office of Air and Radiation, Environmental Protection Agency, on policy and technical issues affecting the development and implementation of an acid rain regulatory program. Issues include the regulatory impact on industry, consumers, public health, and the environment; the structure and operations of the allowance trading and tracking systems and the permit program; integrating the acid rain control program with the Agency's ambient air program; and various conservation and innovative technology transfer options that can be used to comply with the regulatory requirements. A major focus of the Committee is on market-based initiatives to reduce sulfur dioxide and nitrogen oxide emissions.

★734★ Advisory Committee on Mining and Mineral Resources Research
Office of Mineral Institutes
Bureau of Mines
2401 E St. NW
Washington, DC 20241
Phone: (202)634-1328
Contact: Dr. Ronald A. Munson
Committee advises the Secretary of the Interior on all matters involving or relating to mining and mineral resources research, in particular with regard to the eligibility of universities to establish a Mineral Institute, the conduct of the Mineral Institute research program, and the making of grants under P.L. 98-409, the State Mining and Mineral Resources Research Institute Program Act of 1984.

★735★ Advisory Committee on Nuclear Facility Safety
Dept. of Energy
Forrestal Bldg., Rm. 8E 044
1000 Independence Ave. SW
Washington, DC 20585
Phone: (202)586-4400
Committee provides the Secretary of Energy with technical information, advice, and recommendations concerning the Department of Energy's nuclear facility safety.

★736★ Advisory Committee on Nuclear Waste
Nuclear Regulatory Commission
Washington, DC 20555
Phone: (301)492-4516
Contact: Raymond F. Fraley, Exec. Dir.
Committee provides advice and makes recommendations on aspects of nuclear waste management as directed by the Commission, including regulation of high-level waste. Committee's review addresses licensing and regulation of repositories handling, processing, transporting, storing, and safeguarding wastes, including spent fuel and other forms of nuclear wastes.

★737★ Advisory Committee on Reactor Safeguards
Nuclear Regulatory Commission
Washington, DC 20555
Phone: (301)492-7000
Fax: (301)492-7617
Contact: Raymond F. Fraley, Exec. Dir.
Committee reviews safety studies and facility license applications and makes reports thereon. Committee advises the Commission with regard to the hazards of proposed or existing reactor facilities and the adequacy of proposed reactor safety standards.

★738★ Advisory Committee on Renewable Energy and Energy Efficiency Joint Ventures
Asst. Secretary for Conservation & Renewable Energy
Dept. of Energy
Forrestal Building, 6C-016
1000 Independence Ave. SW
Washington, DC 20585
Committee advises the Secretary of Energy on the development of solicitation and evaluation criteria for joint ventures in research and development that further commercialization of renewable energy and energy efficiency technologies, particularly in the areas of photovoltaics, wind energy, solar-thermal energy, factory-made housing, and advanced district cooling. It also advises the Secretary on the implementation of the joint venture program.

★739★ Advisory Council on Hazardous Substances Research and Training
Office of Program Planning & Evaluation
National Institute of Environmental Health Sciences
PO Box 12233
Research Triangle Park, NC 27709
Phone: (919)541-3484
Contact: Daniel C. VanderMeer, Exec. Sec.
Council advises the Assistant Secretary for Health, the Director of the National Institutes of Health, and the Director of the National Institute of Environmental Health Sciences regarding the Hazardous Substances Research and Training Program, mandated and supported by the Secretary of Health and Human Services under P.L. 96-510, as amended by P.L. 99-499. Council assists in the coordination of the Program as well as other programs of research, demonstration, and training under the Act that are conducted or administered by the Environmental Protection Agency.

★740★ Advisory Panel for Ecology
Division of Biotic Systems & Resources
Directorate for Biological, Behavioral, & Social Sciences
National Science Foundation
1800 G St. NW
Washington, DC 20550
Phone: (202)357-9734
Contact: Dr. O.J. Reichman, Designated Foundation Official
Panel reviews and evaluates proposals requesting National Science Foundation support for research and research-related activities and provides oversight, general advice, and policy guidance to the National Science Foundation concerning ecology.

★741★ Advisory Panel for Ecosystem Studies
Division of Biotic Systems & Resources
Directorate for Biological, Behavioral, & Social Sciences
National Science Foundation
1800 G St. NW
Washington, DC 20550
Phone: (202)357-9596
Contact: Dr. James T. Callahan, Designated Foundation Official
Panel reviews and evaluates proposals requesting National Science Foundation support for research and research-related activities and provides oversight, general advice, and policy guidance to the National Science Foundation concerning ecosystem studies.

★742★ Advisory Panel for Population Biology and Physiological Ecology
Division of Biotic Systems & Resources
Directorate for Biological, Behavioral, & Social Sciences
National Science Foundation
1800 G St. NW
Washington, DC 20550
Phone: (202)357-9728
Contact: Dr. Mark W. Courtney, Designated Foundation Official
Panel reviews and evaluates proposals requesting National Science Foundation support for research and research-related activities and provides oversight, general advice, and policy guidance to the National Science Foundation concerning population biology and physiological ecology.

★743★ Air and Radiation Research Committee
Office of Air & Radiation
Office of Research & Development, R.D. 674
Environmental Protection Agency
401 M St. SW
Washington, DC 20460
Phone: (202)475-8934
Contact: Peter Principe, Staff Contact
Committee serves as a vehicle for communicating research needs, describing research programs to meet those needs, and advising the Assistant Administrator for the Office of Research and Development on matters regarding air and radiation.

★744★ Albuquerque District Advisory Council
Bureau of Land Management
Dept. of the Interior
435 Montano NE
Albuquerque, NM 87107
Phone: (505)761-4512
Contact: Alan Hoffmeister, Staff Contact
Council provides representative citizen counsel and advice to the Bureau of Land Management district manager regarding planning and management of the public lands resources within the Albuquerque district.

★745★ Appalachian States Low-Level Radioactive Waste Commission
Bureau of Radiation Protection
Pennsylvania Dept. of Environmental Resources
PO Box 2063
Harrisburg, PA 17120
Phone: (717)787-2480
Fax: (717)783-8965
Contact: Thomas Gerusky, Staff Contact
Commission was established to initiate proceedings or appear as an intervenor or party in interest before any court of law of any federal, state, or local agency, board, or commission that has jurisdiction over any matter arising under or relating to the terms of the provisions of the Appalachian States Low-Level Radioactive Waste Compact (authorized by P.L. 100-319); states authorized to enter the Compact are Pennsylvania, West Virginia, Delaware, and Maryland. The Compact provides for the efficient and economic management of low-level radioactive waste and for the protection of the health, safety, and welfare of the residents of the states party to the Compact. Marc Tenan, Executive Director.

★746★ Arizona Strip District Advisory Council
390 N. 3050 E.
St. George, UT 84770
Phone: (801)673-3545
Contact: G. William Lamb, Designated Federal Employee
Council provides representative citizen counsel and advice to the Bureau of Land Management district manager regarding planning and management of the public lands resources within the Arizona Strip district.

★747★ Army Coastal Engineering Research Board (CERB)
Waterways Experiment Sta.
3909 Halls Ferry Rd.
Vicksburg, MS 39180-6199
Phone: (601)634-2000
Contact: Col. Larry B. Fulton, Exec. Sec.
Board considers the coastal engineering research program of the Corps of Engineers; provides board policy guidance and review of plans and fund requirements for the conduct of research and development in the field; and recommends priorities of accomplishment of research projects in consonance with the needs of the coastal engineering field and the objectives of the Chief of Engineers.

★748★ Bakersfield District Advisory Council
Bureau of Land Management
800 Truxtun Ave., Rm. 311
Bakersfield, CA 93301
Phone: (805)861-4191
Contact: Nancy Cotner, Designated Federal Employee
Council provides representative citizen counsel and advice to the Bureau of Land Management's Bakersfield district manager regarding planning and management of the public lands resources within the Bakersfield district.

★749★ Basic Energy Sciences Advisory Committee (BESAC)
Office of Energy Research
Dept. of Energy
Washington, DC 20585
Phone: (301)353-3081
Contact: Dr. Louis Ianniello, Staff Contact
Committee provides advice to the Secretary of Energy, through the Director of Energy Research, on the Basic Energy Sciences (BES) Program. The BES Program was established as a means to pursue long-term research to build a base of scientific and engineering knowledge upon which the federal government and the private sector can develop new concepts, materials, and processes important for energy production, conversion, and use. Committee reviews elements of the Program and makes recommendations thereon. It advises on long-range plans, priorities, and strategies to address more effectively the basic energy issues in departmental policies and programs; on recommended levels of funding to develop those strategies and to help maintain balance between competing elements of the BES Program; and on any issues relating to the Program as requested by the Secretary or the Director.

★750★ Battle Mountain District Advisory Council
Bureau of Land Management
Dept. of the Interior
PO Box 1420
Battle Mountain, NV 89820
Phone: (702)635-5158
Contact: James D. Currivan, Designated Federal Employee
Council provides representative citizen counsel and advice to the Bureau of Land Management district manager regarding planning and management of the public lands resources within the Battle Mountain district.

★751★ Board of Directors, National Fish and Wildlife Foundation
Dept. of the Interior
18th & E Sts. NW, Rm. 2556
Washington, DC 20240
Phone: (202)208-3040
Contact: Charles H. Collins, Exec. Dir. and Sec.
Board governs the activities of the National Fish and Wildlife Foundation, which encourages, accepts, and administers gifts of property for benefit of, or in connection with, the activities and services of the U.S. Fish and Wildlife Service, Department of the Interior, and conducts other activities that will further conservation and management of fish, wildlife, and plant resources of the United States and its territories and possessions.

★752★ Board of Scientific Counselors, Agency for Toxic Substances and Disease Registry (ATSDR)
1600 Clifton Rd. NE
Atlanta, GA 30333
Phone: (404)488-4823
Contact: Charles Xintaras Sc.D., Exec. Sec.
Board provides advice and guidance to the Administrator, Agency for Toxic Substances and Disease Registry, on the Agency's programs to ensure scientific quality, timeliness, utility, and dissemination of results. Specifically, the Board advises on the adequacy of science in Agency-supported reports, emerging problems that require scientific investigation, accuracy and currency of the science in the Agency's reports, and program areas to emphasize or deemphasize.

★753★ Board of Scientific Counselors, Division of Biometry and Risk Assessment
National Institute of Environmental Health Sciences
PO Box 12233
Research Triangle Park, NC 27709
Contact: David G. Hoel Ph.D., Exec. Sec.
Board advises the Director and Deputy Director for Intramural Research, National Institutes of Health, and the Director, National Institute of Environmental Health Sciences, concerning the NIEHS's intramural research programs. It periodically visits research laboratories and branches to assess the research in progress and to evaluate the productivity and performance of staff scientists.

★754★ Board of Scientific Counselors, National Institute of Environmental Health Sciences (NIEHS)
National Institutes of Health
PO Box 12233
Research Triangle Park, NC 27709
Phone: (919)541-3201
Contact: Dr. John McLachlan, Designated Federal Employee
Board provides advice to the Secretary of Health and Human Services, the Assistant Secretary of Health, the Director of the National Institutes of Health, and the Director and Scientific Director of the National Institute of Environmental Health Sciences, on matters of the intramural scientific research program. It makes periodic visits to the NIEHS laboratories for assessment of the research in progress and evaluation of productivity and performance of staff scientists.

★755★ Boise District Advisory Council
Bureau of Land Management
Dept. of the Interior
3948 Development Ave.
Boise, ID 83705
Phone: (208)384-3304
Contact: J. David Brunner, Designated Federal Employee
Council provides representative citizen counsel and advice to the Bureau of Land Management district manager regarding planning and management of the public lands resources within the Boise district.

★756★ Burley District Advisory Council
Bureau of Land Management
Dept. of the Interior
Rte. 3, Box 1
Burley, ID 83318
Phone: (208)678-5514
Contact: Gerald L. Quinn, Designated Federal Employee
Council provides representative citizen counsel and advice to the Bureau of Land Management district manager regarding planning and management of the public lands resources within the Burley district.

★757★ Burns District Advisory Council
Bureau of Land Management
HC 74 12533 Hwy. 20 W.
Hines, OR 97738-9409
Phone: (503)573-5241
Contact: Mike Green, Designated Federal Employee
Council provides representative citizen counsel and advice to the Bureau of Land Management district manager regarding planning and management of the public lands resources within the Burns district.

★758★ Butte District Advisory Council
Bureau of Land Management
Department of the Interior
PO Box 3388
Butte, MT 59702
Phone: (406)494-5059
Contact: James R. Owings, Designated Federal Employee
Council provides representative citizen counsel and advice to the Bureau of Land Management district manager regarding planning and management of the public lands resources within the Butte district.

★759★ California Desert District Advisory Council
Bureau of Land Management
1695 Spruce St.
Riverside, CA 92507
Phone: (714)351-6383
Contact: Gerald E. Hillier, Designated Federal Employee
Council provides representative citizen counsel and advice to the Bureau of Land Management's California Desert district manager regarding planning and management of the public lands resources within the district. Council is also responsible for the implementation of the California Desert Plan for the California Desert Conservation Area.

★760★ Canadian River Commission
State Capital
Bataan Memorial Bldg.
407 Galisteo St.
Santa Fe, NM 87503
Phone: (505)827-8130
Contact: S.E. Reynolds, Sec.
Commission performs all functions required by the Canadian River Compact, which serves to promote interstate comity, to remove causes of controversy, to secure and protect developments within the states party to the Compact, and to provide for the construction of additional works for the conservation of the waters of the Canadian River, a tributary of the Arkansas River. Commission also establishes, maintains, and operates stream and evaporation stations as necessary for the administration of the Compact.

★761★ Canon City District Advisory Council
Bureau of Land Management
Department of the Interior
PO Box 2200
Canon City, CO 81215-2200
Phone: (719)275-0631
Contact: Donnie R. Sparks, Designated Federal Employee
Council provides representative citizen counsel and advice to the Bureau of Land Management district manager regarding planning and management of the public lands resources within the Canon City district.

★762★ Cape Cod National Seashore Advisory Commission
National Park Service
Dept. of Interior
18th & C Sts. NW
Washington, DC 20240
Commission advises the Secretary of the Interior on matters relating to the development of the Cape Cod National Seashore, with particular regard to the development of zoning standards and the acquisition of land within the Seashore.

★763★ Caribbean Fishery Management Council
Banco de Ponce Bldg., Ste. 1108
Hato Rey, PR 00918
Phone: (809)766-5926
Contact: Miguel A. Rolon, Staff Contact
Council develops and monitors fishery management plans for fisheries in the Caribbean Sea and Atlantic Ocean seaward of the Virgin Islands and the Commonwealth of Puerto Rico and amends the plans in accordance with the changing nature of marine resources. Council also prepares comments on foreign fishing applications and conducts public hearings and meetings eetings regarding fishery management planning and/or the development of such plans.

★764★ Carson City District Advisory Council
Bureau of Land Management
Dept. of the Interior
1535 Hot Springs Rd., Ste. 300
Carson City, NV 89706
Phone: (702)885-6000
Contact: James Elliott, Designated Federal Employee
Council provides representative citizen counsel and advice to the Bureau of Land Management district manager regarding planning and management of the public lands resources within the Carson City district.

★765★ Casper District Advisory Council
Bureau of Land Management
Dept. of the Interior
1701 E. E St.
Casper, WY 82601
Phone: (307)261-5101
Contact: James W. Monroe, Designated Federal Employee
Council provides representative citizen counsel and advice to the Bureau of Land Management district manager regarding planning and management of the public lands resources within the Casper district.

★766★ Cedar City District Advisory Council
Bureau of Land Management
Dept. of the Interior
176 E. D.L. Sargent Dr.
Cedar City, UT 84720
Phone: (801)586-2401
Contact: Gordon R. Staker, Designated Federal Employee
Council provides representative citizen counsel and advice to the Bureau of Land Management district manager regarding planning and management of the public lands resources within the Cedar City district.

★767★ Central Interstate Low-Level Radioactive Waste Commission
Office of Air Quality & Radiation Protection
Dept. of Environmental Quality
PO Box 14690
Baton Rouge, LA 70898
Phone: (504)925-4518
Commission was established to initiate proceedings or appear as an intervenor or party in interest before any court of law or any federal, state, or local agency, board, or commission that has jurisdiction over any matter arising under or relating to the terms of the provisions of the Central Interstate Low-Level Radioactive Waste Compact (authorized by P.L. 99-240; states in the Compact are Arkansas, Kansas, Louisiana, Nebraska, and Oklahoma). The Compact provides for the efficient and economic management of low-level radioactive waste and for the protection of the health, safety, and welfare of the residents of the states party to the Compact.

★768★ Central Midwest Interstate Low-Level Radioactive Waste Commission
Illinois Dept. of Nuclear Safety
1035 Outer Park Dr.
Springfield, IL 62704
Phone: (217)785-9937
Contact: Terry R. Lash, Sec. - Treas.
Commission was established to enter into agreement or contract with any person, state, or group of states for the right to use regional facilities for low-level radioactive waste generated outside the central midwest region of the United States and for the right to use facilities outside the region for waste generated within the region; to approve the disposal of low-level radioactive waste generated within the region at a facility other than a regional low-level radioactive waste facility; to appear as an intervenor or party in interest before any court of law or any federal, state, or local agency, board, or commission in any matter related to low-level radioactive waste management; to review the emergency enclosure of a regional facility, determine the appropriateness of the enclosure, and take necessary actions to ensure the interests of the central midwest region are protected; and to take any action necessary to carry out its duties and functions provided in the Central Midwest Interstate Low-Level Radioactive Waste Compact (states authorized to enter the Compact are Illinois and Kentucky). The Compact provides for sufficient facilities for the proper management of low-level radioactive waste generated in the region, the protection of the health and safety of residents of the region, a limitation of the number of facilities required to manage low-level radioactive waste generated in the region, the safeguard of ecological and economical management of low-level radioactive waste, and the promotion of above-ground facilities and

other disposal technologies for greater and safer confinement of low-level radioactive waste than shallow-land burial facilities.

★769★ CFC Advisory Committee
Office of the Deputy Asst. Secretary-Environment
Dept. of Defense
206 N. Washington St., Ste. 100
Alexandria, VA 22314
Phone: (703)325-2215
Fax: (703)325-2234
Contact: William D. Goins, Chm.
Committee advises the Secretary of Defense and the Under Secretary of Defense for Acquisition on Department of Defense requirements for chlorofluorocarbons (CFCs) and halons, which are increasingly cited as causes of stratospheric ozone depletion and global warming. Common uses for CFCs and halons, in both the military and civilian sectors, include refrigeration, solvent cleaning, and fire extinguishing. Military specific uses include CFCs for shipboard weapon and electronic systems cooling equipment, halons for fire suppression in aircraft engine nacelles, and critical electronics and optical surface cleaning applications. Issues considered by the Committee include the reduction of unnecessary releases of CFCs and halons through the application of existing technology, the potential for new technologies to obtain significant reductions in CFC and halon use, and the costs associated with adopting existing and new technologies to achieve use reductions.

★770★ Chattahoochee River National Recreation Area Advisory Commission
Department of the Interior
National Park Service
1978 Island Ford Pkwy.
Dunwood, GA 30350
Phone: (404)394-7912
Contact: Supt. Sybbald Smith, Staff Contact
Commission advises the Secretary of the Interior on the management and operation of the Chattahoochee River National Recreation Area, Georgia; on the protection of resources within the recreational area; and on the priority of lands to be acquired within the area.

★771★ Chief of Engineers Environmental Advisory Board
Army Corps of Engineers
20 Massachusetts Ave. NW
Washington, DC 20314-1000
Phone: (202)272-0166
Fax: (202)272-1163
Contact: Dr. William L. Klesch, Staff Contact
Board serves as environmental advisor to the Chief of Engineers to provide guidance for developing environmental policy and procedural matters for Corps programs. In performing this function, Board examines existing and proposed policies, programs, and activities from an environmental point of view to identify problems and weaknesses and to suggest how these can be remedied; advises on how the Corps can improve working relations with the conservation community and the general public; and advises on environmental problems or issues pertinent to specific plans or programs.

★772★ Clean Air Scientific Advisory Committee (CASAC)
Environmental Protection Agency (A-101F)
401 M St. SW
Washington, DC 20460
Phone: (202)382-2552
Contact: Randall C. Bond, Exec. Sec.
Committee was established to provide independent advice on the scientific and technical aspects of issues related to the criteria for air quality standards, research related to air quality, sources of air pollution, and the strategies to attain and maintain air quality standards and to prevent significant deterioration of air quality.

★773★ Coeur d'Alene District Advisory Council
Bureau of Land Management
Dept. of the Interior
1808 N. 3rd St.
Coeur d'Alene, ID 83814
Phone: (208)765-4678
Contact: Fritz Rennebaum, Designated Federal Employee
Council provides representative citizen counsel and advice to the Bureau of Land Management district manager regarding planning and management of the public lands resources within the Coeur d'Alene district.

★774★ Colorado River Basin Salinity Control Advisory Council
Colorado River Salinity Program Coordinator
U. S. Bureau of Reclamation
PO Box 25007, Code: D-5090
Denver, CO 80225
Phone: (801)292-4663
Contact: Stan Gappa, Designated Federal Employee
Council serves as liaison between the Secretary of the Interior, the Secretary of Agriculture, the Administrator of the Environmental Protection Agency, and the states of Arizona, California, Colorado, New Mexico, Nevada, Utah, and Wyoming in the development of programs for the enhancement and protection of the quality of water available in the Colorado River upstream of Imperial Dam. Council reviews reports from the Secretary of the Interior on the progress of the salinity control program and recommends appropriate studies of projects, techniques, and methods for furthering this program.

★775★ Committee of State Foresters
Forest Service
Dept. of Agriculture
2nd Fl., NW Wing
PO Box 96090
Washington, DC 20090
Phone: (202)382-9036
Contact: Pamgh Godsey, Designated Federal Employee
Committee advises the Secretary of Agriculture regarding the planning and implementation of federal programs affecting nonfederal forest lands for the advancement of forest resources management.

★776★ Committee on Earth and Environmental Sciences (CEES)
104 National Center
U. S. Geological Survey
Department of the Interior
Reston, VA 22092
Phone: (703)648-4450
Contact: Paul Dresler, Exec. Sec.
Committee was established to enhance the coordination of government research activities in the earth and environmental sciences. It addresses science and technology related to global, physical, chemical, and biological changes of the earth, including climate change, ozone depletion, and greenhouse warming. Specifically the Committee: Reviews federal R&D programs in earth and environmental sciences including both national and international programs; improves planning, coordination, and communication among federal agencies engaged in earth and environmental sciences R&D; identifies and defines earth and environmental sciences R&D needs; develops and updates long-range plans for the overall federal R&D effort in earth sciences; addresses specific programmatic and operational issues and problems which affect two or more federal agencies; provides reviews, analyses, advice and recommendations to the chairperson of FCCSET on federal policies and programs concerned with earth and environmental sciences R&D, particularly in assessing human impact on the global environment; and develops the Administration's response to the call in the NSF Authorization Act of 1987, concerning federal government action with respect to the establishment of an International Year of the Greenhouse Effect mandated in calendar year 1991.

★777★ Committee on Renewable Energy, Commerce, and Trade (CORECT)
Office of the Secretary
Dept. of Energy
1000 Independence Ave. SW
Washington, DC 20585
Phone: (202)586-1720
Contact: Ron Bowles, Staff Contact
Committee provides advice and makes recommendations to the Secretary of Energy on the use of renewable energy products and services. It also works to establish a government-industry plan to increase the market share of the United States in the trade of renewable energy technologies and products.

★778★ Committee on Scientific Advisors on Marine Mammals
Marine Mammal Commission
1825 Connecticut Ave. NW
Washington, DC 20009
Phone: (202)653-6237
Contact: Michael L. Gosliner, Designated Federal Employee
Committee provides scientific expertise on matters relating to the protection and conservation of marine mammals. Committee consults with the Marine Mammal Commission on all studies and recommendations made by the Commission, on research programs conducted under the Act, and on all applications for permits for scientific research submitted pursuant to the Act.

★779★ Committee to Coordinate Environmental and Related Programs
National Center for Toxicological Research
Food & Drug Administration
Parklawn Bldg., Rm. 14-101
5600 Fishers Ln.
Rockville, MD 20857
Phone: (301)496-3511
Contact: Ronald F. Coene, Designated Federal Employee
Committee provides a forum to ensure the exchange of information between agencies of the Public Health Service and other agencies of the federal government on environmental health, toxicology, and related programs; to coordinate these programs; to enhance the sharing of resources; and to provide advice to the Department.

★780★ Committee to Review the Outer Continental Shelf Environmental Studies Program
Board on Environmental Studies & Toxicology
Commission on Geosciences, Resources, & Environment
National Research Council
2101 Constitution Ave.
Washington, DC 20418
Phone: (202)334-2540
Contact: David Policansky, Project Dir.
Committee was established to assess the outer continental shelf (OCS) programs of the Environmental Studies Program, Minerals Management Service, Department of the Interior, and to make recommendations on future OCS programs. Its mission was later expanded to include a review of the adequacy of scientific and technical information pertaining to environmental concerns for the Georges Bank lease area in the north Atlantic; and, in response to a request by the President's Outer Continental Shelf Leasing and Development Task Force, a review of the adequacy of scientific and technical information pertaining to environmental concerns for lease areas in southwestern Florida, northern California, and southern California.

★781★ Connecticut River Atlantic Salmon Commission
One Migratory Way
PO Box 71
Turners Falls, MA 01376
Phone: (413)863-3555
Contact: Ted F. Meyers, Exec. Assistant
Commission makes inquiries into and ascertains such methods, practices, and circumstances in order to bring about the restoration of Atlantic salmon in the Connecticut River and its tributaries. It makes recommendations on and coordinates stocking programs, management procedures, and research projects, and promulgates regulations governing Atlantic salmon fishing in the mainstream of the Connecticut River.

★782★ Cooperative Forestry Research Advisory Council
Dept. of Agriculture
14th & Independence Ave. SW
Washington, DC 20250
Council oversees the management of the McIntire-Stennis forestry research program.

★783★ Coos Bay District Advisory Council
Bureau of Land Management
1300 Airport Ln.
North Bend, OR 97459-2023
Phone: (503)269-5880
Contact: Melvin Chase, Designated Federal Employee
Council provides representative citizen counsel and advice to the Bureau of Land Management district manager regarding planning and management of the public lands resources within the Coos Bay district.

★784★ Council on Environmental Quality (CEQ)
722 Jackson Pl. NW
Washington, DC 20503
Phone: (202)395-5750
Fax: (202)395-3744
Contact: Larry Flick, Designated Federal Employee
Council was established to analyze important environmental conditions and trends; review and appraise federal government programs having an impact upon the environment; recommend policies for protecting and improving the quality of the environment; prepare the President's annual report to Congress; and issue regulations for agencies to follow in meeting procedural requirements of the National Environmental Policy Act.

★785★ Craig District Advisory Council
Bureau of Land Management
Department of the Interior
455 Emerson St.
Craig, CO 81625
Phone: (303)824-8261
Contact: William Pulford, Designated Federal Employee
Council provides representative citizen counsel and advice to the Bureau of Land Management district manager regarding planning and management of the public lands resources within the Craig district.

★786★ Delaware River Basin Commission
Office of the Executive Director
25 State Police Dr.
PO Box 7360
West Trenton, NJ 08628
Phone: (609)883-9500
Contact: Gerald M. Hansler, Exec. Dir.
Commission is responsible for the development and maintenance of a comprehensive plan, and for programming, scheduling, and controlling projects and activities within the Delaware River Basin, which will provide regulation and development of ground and surface water supplies for municipal, industrial, and agricultural uses; abatement of stream pollution; flood damage reduction; promotion of forestry, soil conservation, and watershed projects; propagation of fish and wildlife; development of water-related recreational facilities; and development of hydroelectric power potential of the area.

★787★ Delaware Water Gap National Recreation Area Citizen Advisory Commission
PO Box 284
Bushkill, PA 18324
Phone: (717)588-2435
Contact: Richard G. Ring, Designated Federal Employee
Commission advises the Secretary of the Interior on matters pertaining to the management and operation of the Delaware Water Gap National Recreation Area, Bushkill, Pennsylvania, and on matters affecting the recreation area and its surrounding communities.

★788★ Delta Region Preservation Commission
2433 Lark St.
New Orleans, LA 70122
Phone: (504)589-3882
Contact: Dr. Fritz Wagner, Staff Contact
Commission advises the Secretary of the Interior in the selection of sites for inclusion in Jean Lafitte National Historical Park and Preserve, and in the development and implementation of a general management plan and a comprehensive interpretive program.

★789★ Department of Agriculture
Forest Service
Auditors Bldg., 201, 4th Fl., NW
14th St. SW
Washington, DC 20250
Phone: (202)447-6661
Contact: F. Dale Robertson, Chief

★790★ Department of Agriculture
Forest Service
Public Affairs Office
Auditors Bldg. 201, 2nd Fl., Central
14th St. SW
Washington, DC 20250
Phone: (202)447-3760
Contact: Susan B. Hess, Dir.

★791★ Department of Agriculture
Forest Service
Public Affairs Office
Land and Resources Information Division
Auditors Bldg., 201, 2nd Fl., Central
14th St. SW
Washington, DC 20250
Phone: (202)447-5006
Contact: Chris Holmes, Asst. Dir.

★792★ Department of Agriculture
National Forest System
Auditors Bldg., 201, 3rd Fl., NW
14th St. SW
Washington, DC 20250
Phone: (202)447-3523
Fax: (202)447-3610
Contact: James C. Overbay, Dep. Chief

★793★ Department of Agriculture
National Forest System
Lands Division
Auditors Bldg., 201, 4th Fl., S
14th St. SW
Washington, DC 20250
Phone: (202)453-8248
Contact: Gordon H. Small, Dir.

★794★ Department of Agriculture
National Forest System
Recreation, Cultural Resources, and Wilderness Management Division
Auditors Bldg., 201, 4th Fl., Central
14th St. SW
Washington, DC 20250
Phone: (202)447-3706
Contact: Elizabeth Estill, Dir.

★795★ Department of Agriculture
National Forest System
Recreation, Cultural Resources, and Wilderness Management Division
Wild and Scenic Rivers
Auditors Bldg., 201, 4th Fl., Central
14th St. SW
Washington, DC 20250
Phone: (202)382-9405
Contact: Deen Lundgren, Assistant

★796★ Department of Agriculture
National Forest System
Recreation, Cultural Resources, and Wilderness Management Division
Wilderness Program
Auditors Bldg., 201, 4th Fl., Central
14th St. SW
Washington, DC 20250
Phone: (202)447-2422
Contact: Anne Fege, Assistant

★797★ Department of Agriculture
National Forest System
Watershed and Air Management Division
Auditors Bldg., 201, 3rd Fl., S
14th St. SW
Washington, DC 20250
Phone: (202)453-9466
Contact: Kermit N. Larson, Dir.

★798★ Department of Agriculture
National Forest System
Watershed and Air Management Division
Air Resource Program
Auditors Bldg., 201, 3rd Fl., S.
14th St. SW
Washington, DC 20250
Phone: (202)453-9480
Contact: James G. Byrne, Manager

★799★ Department of Agriculture
National Forest System
Watershed and Air Management Division
Soil Resource Program
Auditors Bldg., 201, 3rd Fl., S.
14th St. SW
Washington, DC 20250
Phone: (202)453-9477
Contact: Peter E Avers, Manager

★800★ Department of Agriculture
National Forest System
Watershed and Air Management Division
Water Resource Program
Auditors Bldg., 201, 3rd Fl., S.
14th St. SW
Washington, DC 20250
Phone: (202)453-9475
Contact: Warren C. Harper, Manager

★801★ Department of Agriculture
National Forest System
Wildlife and Fisheries Management Division
Auditors Bldg., 201, 4th Fl., NW
14th St. SW
Washington, DC 20250
Phone: (202)453-8205
Contact: Robert D. Nelson, Dir.

★802★ Department of Agriculture
National Forest System
Wildlife and Fisheries Management Division
Fish Habitat Relationship Program
Wildlife & Fish Ecology Unit
Utah State University
Logan, UT 84322
Phone: (801)750-2500
Contact: Jeff Kershner, Coordinator

★803★ Department of Agriculture
National Forest System
Wildlife and Fisheries Management Division
Fisheries Program
Auditors Bldg., 201, 4th Fl., NW
14th St. SW
Washington, DC 20250
Phone: (202)453-9230
Contact: Jim Lloyd, Specialist

★804★ Department of Agriculture
National Forest System
Wildlife and Fisheries Management Division
Threatened and Endangered Species Program
Auditors Bldg., 201, 4th Fl., NW
14th St. SW
Washington, DC 20250
Phone: (202)453-8220
Contact: Kathy Johnson, Specialist

★805★ Department of Agriculture
National Forest System
Wildlife and Fisheries Management Division
Wildlife Habitat Relationship Program
Wildlife & Fish Ecology Unit
Utah State University
Logan, UT 84322
Phone: (801)750-2500
Contact: Wini Sidle, Coordinator

★806★ Department of Agriculture
National Forest System
Wildlife and Fisheries Management Division
Wildlife Program
Auditors Bldg., 201, 4th Fl., NW
14th St. SW
Washington, DC 20250
Phone: (202)453-9813
Contact: Tom Darden, Manager

★807★ Department of Agriculture
Natural Resources and Environment
14th St. & Independence Ave. SW, Rm. 217-E
Washington, DC 20250
Phone: (202)447-7173
Fax: (202)447-4732
Contact: James R. Moseley, Asst. Sec.

★808★ Department of Agriculture
Natural Resources and Environment
State and Private Forestry Division
Auditors Bldg., 201, 2nd Fl., NW
14th St. SW
Washington, DC 20250
Phone: (202)447-6657
Fax: (202)453-8272
Contact: Allan J. West, Dep. Chief

★809★ Department of Agriculture
Research Department
Forest Environment Research Division
Wildlife, Range & Fish Habitat Program
Auditors Bldg., 201, 1st Fl., Central
14th St. SW
Washington, DC 20250
Phone: (202)453-9524
Contact: Michael R. Lennart, Specialist

★810★ Department of Agriculture
Research Department
Forest Environment Research Staff
Auditors Bldg., 201, 1st Fl., Central
14th St. SW
Washington, DC 20250
Phone: (202)453-9524
Contact: Richard V. Smythe, Dir.

★811★ Department of Agriculture
Research Department
Forest Fire and Atmospheric Sciences Research Division
Fire Sciences Program
Auditors Bldg., 201, 1st Fl., Central
14th St. SW
Washington, DC 20250
Phone: (202)453-9561
Contact: Elvia E. Niebla, Specialist

★812★ Department of Agriculture
Research Department
Forest Fire and Atmospheric Sciences Research Staff
Auditors Bldg., 201, 1st Fl., Central
14th St. SW
Washington, DC 20250
Phone: (202)453-9561
Contact: William T. Sommers, Dir.

★813★ Department of Agriculture
Research Department
Forest Inventory, Economics, and Recreation Research Staff
Auditors Bldg., 201, 1st Fl., SW
14th St. SW
Washington, DC 20250
Phone: (202)447-2747
Contact: H. Fred Kaiser, Dir.

★814★ Department of Agriculture
Research Department
International Forestry Division
Auditors Bldg., 201, 1st Fl., SE
14th St. SW
Washington, DC 20250
Phone: (202)453-9575
Contact: David A. Harcharik, Dir.

★815★ Department of Agriculture
Research Department
International Forestry Division
Forestry Support Program
Auditors Bldg., 201, 1st Fl., SE
14th St. SW
Washington, DC 20250
Phone: (202)453-9589
Contact: Gary Wetterberg, Manager

★816★ Department of Agriculture
Research Department
International Forestry Division
Tropical Forestry Program
Auditors Bldg., 201, 1st Fl., SE
14th St. SW
Washington, DC 20250
Phone: (202)453-9577
Contact: Samuel H. Kunkle, Manager

★817★ Department of Agriculture
Soil Conservation Service
South Agriculture Bldg., Rm. 5105A
Independence Ave. SW
Washington, DC 20250
Phone: (202)447-4525
Contact: R. Mack Gray, Chief

★818★ Department of Agriculture
State and County Operations Division
Conservation and Environmental Protection Division
South Agriculture Bldg., Rm. 4714
Independence Ave., SW
Washington, DC 20250
Phone: (202)447-6221
Contact: James McMullen, Dir.

★819★ Department of Agriculture
State and Private Forestry Department
Cooperative Forestry Staff
Auditors Bldg., 201, 4th Fl., SE
14th St., SW
Washington, DC 20250
Phone: (202)453-9389
Contact: Tony Dorrell, Dir.

★820★ Department of Commerce
National Marine Fisheries Service
Metro One Bldg., Rm. 9334
1320 East-West Hwy.
Silver Spring, MD 20910
Phone: (301)427-2239
Contact: William W. Fox Jr., Asst. Adm.

★821★ Department of Commerce
National Marine Fisheries Service
Office of Fisheries Conservation and Management
Metro One Bldg., Rm. 8472
1335 East-West Hwy.
Silver Spring, MD 20910
Phone: (301)427-2334
Contact: Richard H. Schaefer, Dir.

★822★ Department of Commerce
National Marine Fisheries Service
Office of Protected Resources
Metro One Bldg., Rm. 8268
1335 East-West Hwy.
Silver Spring, MD 20910
Phone: (301)427-2333
Contact: Nancy M. Foster, Dir.

★823★ **Department of Commerce**
National Marine Fisheries Service
Office of Research and Environmental Information
One Metro Bldg., Rm. 6310
1335 East-West Hwy.
Silver Spring, MD 20910
Phone: (301)427-2367
Contact: John T. Everett, Dir.

★824★ **Department of Commerce**
National Ocean Service
Office of Ocean and Coastal Resource Management
Universal Bldg. South, Rm. 724
1825 Connecticut Ave. NW
Washington, DC 20235
Phone: (202)673-5158
Contact: James P. Burgess, Chief

★825★ **Department of Commerce**
National Ocean Service
Office of Ocean and Coastal Resource Management
Marine and Estuarine Management Division
Universal Bldg. South, Rm. 714
1825 Connecticut Ave. NW
Washington, DC 20235
Phone: (202)673-5122
Contact: Joseph A. Uravitch, Chief

★826★ **Department of Commerce**
National Ocean Service
Office of Ocean Services
Ocean Observations Division
Universal Bldg. S, Rm. 615
1825 Connecticut Ave. NW
Washington, DC 20235
Phone: (202)673-3957
Contact: William E. Woodward, Chief

★827★ **Department of Commerce**
National Ocean Service
Office of Oceanography and Marine Assessment
Washington Science Center, Bldg. 1, Rm. 212
6001 Executive Blvd.
Rockville, MD 20852
Phone: (301)443-8487
Contact: Charles N. Ehler, Dir.

★828★ **Department of Commerce**
National Ocean Service
Office of Oceanography and Marine Assessment
Ocean Assessment Division
Washington Science Center, Bldg. 1, Rm. 212
6001 Executive Blvd.
Rockville, MD 20852
Phone: (301)443-8933
Contact: Andrew Robertson, Chief

★829★ **Department of Commerce (NOAA)**
National Oceanic and Atmospheric Administration
Washington Science Center, Bldg. 5
6010 Executive Blvd.
Rockville, MD 20852
Phone: (202)377-8090
Fax: (202)377-8203
Contact: John A. Knauss, Under Secty. for Oceans & Atmosphere

★830★ **Department of Commerce**
National Oceanic and Atmospheric Administration
Atlantic Oceanographic and Meteorological Laboratory
4301 Rickenbacker Causeway
Virginia Key Miami, FL 33149
Phone: (305)361-4300
Contact: Hugo F. Bezdek, Director

★831★ **Department of Commerce**
National Oceanic and Atmospheric Administration
Environmental Research Laboratories
Research Lab 3
3100 Marine St.
Boulder, CO 80303
Phone: (303)497-6000
Contact: Joseph O. Fletcher, Dir.

★832★ **Department of Commerce**
National Oceanic and Atmospheric Administration
Environmental Research Laboratories
325 Broadway
Boulder, CO 80303
Phone: (303)497-6000
Contact: Joseph O. Fletcher, Director

★833★ **Department of Commerce**
National Oceanic and Atmospheric Administration
Great Lakes Environmental Research Laboratory
2205 Commonwealth Blvd.
Ann Arbor, MI 48105
Phone: (313)668-2335
Contact: Alfred M. Beeton, Dir.

★834★ **Department of Commerce**
National Oceanic and Atmospheric Administration
National Environmental Satellite, Data and Information Service
Federal Office Bldg. 4
Silver Hill & Suitland Rds.
Suitland, MD 20746
Phone: (301)763-7190
Contact: Thomas N. Pyke Jr., Assistant Administrator

★835★ **Department of Commerce**
National Oceanic and Atmospheric Administration
National Environmental Satellite, Data and Information Service
National Climatic Data Center
Federal Bldg.
Asheville, NC 28801
Phone: (704)259-0476
Contact: Kenneth D. Hadeen, Director

★836★ **Department of Commerce**
National Oceanic and Atmospheric Administration
National Environmental Satellite, Data and Information Service
National Geophysical Data Center
NOAA/NESDIS
325 Broadway.
Boulder, CO 80303
Phone: (303)497-6215
Contact: Michael A. Chimnery, Director

★837★ **Department of Commerce**
National Oceanic and Atmospheric Administration
National Environmental Satellite, Data and Information Service
National Oceanographic Data Center
Universal Bldg. South
1825 Connecticut Ave. NW
Washington, DC 20235
Phone: (202)673-5596
Contact: Gregory W. White, Director

★838★ **Department of Commerce**
National Oceanic and Atmospheric Administration
National Ocean Service
Universal Bldg. S, Rm. 611
1825 Connecticut Ave. NW
Washington, DC 20235
Phone: (202)673-5140
Fax: (202)673-3850
Contact: Virginia K. Tippie, Asst. Adm.

★839★ **Department of Commerce**
National Oceanic and Atmospheric Administration (NOAA)
National Marine Fisheries Service
Metro One Bldg.
1335 East-West Hwy.
Silver Spring, MD 20910
Phone: (301)427-2239
Contact: William W. Fox, Jr., Assistant Admin.

★840★ **Department of Commerce**
National Oceanic and Atmospheric Administration (NOAA)
National Weather Service
Silver Spring Metro Bldg. 2
1325 East West Hwy.
Silver Spring, MD 20910
Phone: (301)427-7689
Contact: Elbert W. Friday Jr., Assistant Administrator

★841★ **Department of Commerce**
National Oceanic and Atmospheric Administration
Sanctuaries and Reserves Divisions
Office of Ocean and Coastal Resource Management
1825 Connecticut Ave. NW
Washington, DC 20235
Phone: (202)673-5126

★842★ **Department of Commerce**
Oceanic and Atmospheric Research Department
Metro One Bldg., Rm. 4331
1335 East-West Hwy.
Silver Spring, MD 20910
Phone: (301)427-2458
Fax: (301)427-5167
Contact: Ned A. Ostenso, Asst. Adm.

★843★ **Department of Commerce**
Oceanic and Atmospheric Research Department
Office of Climatic and Atmospheric Research (Global Programs)
Metro One Bldg., Rm. 4210
1335 East-West Hwy.
Silver Spring, MD 20910
Phone: (301)427-2474
Contact: J. Michael Hall, Dir.

★844★ **Department of Commerce**
Oceanic and Atmospheric Research Department
Office of Oceanic Research Programs
Metro One Bldg., Rm. 5470
1335 East-West Hwy.
Silver Spring, MD 20910
Phone: (301)427-2448
Contact: Robert D. Wildman, Dir.

★845★ **Department of Commerce**
Pacific Marine Environmental Laboratory
7600 Sand Point Way NE
Bin No. C15700
Seattle, WA 98115
Phone: (206)526-6800
Contact: Eddie N. Bernard, Dir.

★846★ Department of Energy
Industrial Technologies Department
Office of Waste Reduction Technologies
Forrestal Bldg., Rm. 5G-030
1000 Independence Ave., SW
Washington, DC 20585
Phone: (202)586-9118

★847★ Department of Energy
Nuclear Energy Division
Office of Nuclear Safety Policy and Standards
Germantown Bldg., Rm. A-415
19901 Germantown Rd.
Germantown, MD 20545
Phone: (301)353-3660
Contact: Neal Goldenberg, Director

★848★ Department of Energy
Nuclear Energy Division
Office of Nuclear Safety Self Assessment
Forrestal Bldg., Rm. 5A-115
1000 Independence Ave., SW
Washington, DC 20585
Phone: (202)586-6450

★849★ Department of Energy
Office Alcohol Conservation and Renewable Energy Division
Office of Alcohol Fuels
Forrestal Bldg., Rm. 5G-086
1000 Independence Ave., S.W.
Washington, DC 20585
Phone: (202)586-9791
Contact: David M.L. Lindahl, Director

★850★ Department of Energy
Office of Civilian Radioactive Waste Management
Forrestal Bldg., Rm. 5A-085
1000 Independence Ave., SW
Washington, DC 20585
Phone: (202)586-6842
Contact: John W. Bartlett, Dir.

★851★ Department of Energy
Office of Energy Research
Forrestal Bldg., Rm. 7B-058
1000 Independence Ave., SW
Washington, DC 20585
Phone: (202)586-5430
Fax: (202)586-4120
Contact: James F. Decker, Dir.

★852★ Department of Energy
Office of Energy Research
Office of Health and Environmental Research
Germantown Bldg., Rm. F-208
19901 Germantown Rd.
Germantown, MD 20545
Phone: (301)353-3251
Contact: David J. Galas, Assoc. Dir.

★853★ Department of Energy
Office of Environmental Restoration and Waste Management
Forrestal Bldg., Rm. 7A-049
1000 Independence Ave., SW
Washington, DC 20585
Phone: (202)586-7710
Contact: Leo P. Duffy, Dir.

★854★ Department of Energy
Office of Environmental Restoration and Waste Management
Office of Environmental Quality Assurance and Quality Control
Forrestal Bldg., Rm. 1G-066
1000 Independence Ave., SW
Washington, DC 20585
Phone: (202)586-8754
Contact: Randall S. Scott, Assoc. Dir.

★855★ Department of Energy
Office of Environmental Restoration and Waste Management
Office of Environmental Restoration
Forrestal Bldg., Rm. 7A-049
1000 Independence Ave., SW
Washington, DC 20585
Phone: (202)586-7705
Contact: Roger P. Whitfield, Assoc. Dir.

★856★ Department of Energy
Office of Health and Environmental Research
Atmospheric and Climate Research Division
Germantown Bldg., Rm. E-209
19901 Germantown Rd.
Germantown, MD 20545
Phone: (301)353-4375
Contact: Aristides Patrinos, Dir.

★857★ Department of Energy
Office of Health and Environmental Research
Ecological Research Division
Germantown Bldg., Rm. E-233
19901 Germantown Rd.
Germantown, MD 20545
Phone: (301)353-4208
Contact: Helen McCammon, Dir.

★858★ Department of Energy
Office of Nuclear Safety
Forrestal Bldg., Rm. 7A-113
1000 Independence Ave., SW
Washington, DC 20585
Phone: (202)586-2407
Contact: Steven Blush, Dir.

★859★ Department of Energy
Office of Nuclear Safety
Nuclear Safety Enforcement Division
Forrestal Bldg., Rm. 8H-089
1000 Independence Ave., SW
Washington, DC 20585
Phone: (202)586-7594

★860★ Department of Energy
Office of Public Affairs
Forrestal Bldg., Rm. 7B-192
1000 Independence Ave., SW
Washington, DC 20585
Phone: (202)586-4940
Contact: Mary Joy Jameson, Dir.

★861★ Department of Energy
Office of the General Counsel
Environment, Conservation, and Legislation Division
Forrestal Bldg., Rm. 6A-141
1000 Independence Ave., SW
Washington, DC 20585
Phone: (202)586-6732
Contact: Mark C. Schroeder, Dep. Gen. Counsel

★862★ Department of Energy (DOE)
Office of the Secretary
Forrestal Bldg.
1000 Independence Ave., SW
Washington, DC 20585
Phone: (202)586-5575
Fax: (202)586-8134
Contact: Adm. James D. Watkins USN, Sec.

★863★ Department of Energy
Office of the Secretary
Conservation and Renewable Energy Division
Forrestal Bldg., Rm. 6C-016
1000 Independence Ave. SW
Washington, DC 20585
Phone: (202)586-9220
Contact: J. Michael Davis, Assistant Sec.

★864★ Department of Energy
Office of the Secretary
Environment, Safety and Health Division
Forrestal Bldg., Rm. 7A-097
1000 Independence Ave. SW
Washington, DC 20585
Phone: (202)586-6151
Contact: Paul L. Ziemer, Assistant Sec.

★865★ Department of Energy
Office of the Secretary
Office of Civilian Radioactive Waste Management
Forrestal Bldg., Rm. 5A-085
1000 Independence Ave. SW
Washington, DC 20585
Phone: (202)586-6842
Contact: John W. Bartlett, Dir.

★866★ Department of Energy
Transportation Technologies Department
Office of Alternate Fuels
Forrestal Bldg., Rm. 5G-046
1000 Independence Ave., SW
Washington, DC 20585
Phone: (202)586-8053
Contact: Jerry Allsup, Dir.

★867★ Department of Energy
Utility Technologies Department
Office of Renewable Energy Conversion
Forrestal Bldg., Rm. 5H-095
1000 Independence Ave., SW
Washington, DC 20585
Phone: (202)586-8084
Contact: Roland R. Kessler, Dir.

★868★ Department of Energy
Utility Technologies Department
Office of Solar Energy Conversion
Forrestal Bldg., Rm. 5F-081
1000 Independence Ave., S.W.
Washington, DC 20585
Phone: (202)586-1720
Contact: Robert H. Annan, Dir.

★869★ Dept. of Health and Human Services
Center for Environmental Health
4700 Buford Hwy.
Chamblee, GA 30341
Phone: (404)452-4111
Contact: Vernon Houk, Dir.

★870★ Dept. of Health and Human Services
National Institute of Environmental Health Sciences
Box 12233
Research Triangle Park, NC 27709
Phone: (919)541-3201
Contact: David G. Heol, Acting Dir.

★871★ Department of Health and Human Services
Public Health Service
Agency for Toxic Substances and Disease Registry
1600 Clifton Rd, NE
Atlanta, GA 30333
Phone: (404)639-3291
Contact: William L. Roper, Administrator

★872★ Department of Health and Human Services
Public Health Service
Centers for Disease Control
Center for Environmental Health and Injury Control
1600 Clifton Rd., NE
Atlanta, GA 30333
Phone: (404)488-4111

Contact: Vernon N. Houk, Director

★873★ Department of Health and Human Services
Public Health Service
National Institutes of Health
National Institute of Environmental Health Sciences
P.O. Box 12233
Research Triangle Park, NC 27709
Phone: (919)541-3201
Contact: David G. Hoel, Director

★874★ Department of Justice
Environment and Natural Resources Division
Environmental Crimes Section
10th St. & Constitution Ave. NW, Rm. 6101
Washington, DC 20530
Phone: (202)272-9877
Fax: (202)514-0557
Contact: Jerry G. Block, Chief

★875★ Department of Justice
Environment and Natural Resources Division
Environmental Enforcement
10th St. & Constitution Ave. NW, Rm. 1521
Washington, DC 20530
Phone: (202)514-5271
Fax: (202)514-0557
Contact: David T. Buente Jr., Chief

★876★ Department of Justice
Environment and Natural Resources Division
Wildlife and Marine Resources Section
10th & Constitution Ave. NW, Rm. 5000
Washington, DC 20530
Phone: (202)724-1010
Fax: (202)514-0557
Contact: James C. Kilbourne, Chief

★877★ Department of Justice
Environmental and Natural Resources Division
Tenth St. & Constitution Ave., NW, Rm. 2603
Washington, DC 20530
Phone: (202)514-2701
Fax: (202)514-0557
Contact: Richard B. Stewart, Asst. Attorney Gen.

★878★ Department of Justice
Environmental and Natural Resources Division
Environmental Defense Section
10th St. & Constitution Ave. NW, Rm. 7110
Washington, DC 20530
Phone: (202)514-2219
Fax: (202)514-0557
Contact: Margaret N. Strand, Chief

★879★ Department of State
Bureau of Economic and Business Affairs
Energy Resources and Food Policy Department
2201 C St., NW, Rm. 3336
Washington, DC 20520
Phone: (202)647-1498
Contact: William C. Ramsey, Dep. Asst. Secty.

★880★ Department of State
Bureau of Oceans and International Environmental and Scientific Affairs
2201 C St. NW, Rm. 7831
Washington, DC 20520
Phone: (202)647-1554
Fax: (202)647-0217
Contact: Curtis Bohlen, Asst. Secty.

★881★ Department of State
Bureau of Oceans and International Environmental and Scientific Affairs
Environment, Health, and Natural Resources Department
2201 C St., NW, Rm. 7825
Washington, DC 20520
Phone: (202)647-2232
Contact: Robert Reinstein, Dep. Asst. Secty.

★882★ Department of State
Bureau of Oceans and International Environmental and Scientific Affairs
Oceans and Fisheries Affairs Department
2201 C St., NW, Rm. 7829
Washington, DC 20520
Phone: (202)647-2396
Contact: David A. Colson, Dep. Asst. Secty.

★883★ Department of State
Energy Resources and Food Policy Department
Office of Global Energy
2201 C St., NW, Rm. 3329
Washington, DC 20520
Phone: (202)647-3019
Contact: David Brown, Dir.

★884★ Department of State
Environment, Health, and Natural Resources Department
Office of Ecology, Health, and Conservation
2201 C St., NW, Rm. 4325
Washington, DC 20520
Phone: (202)647-2418
Contact: Eleanor w. Savage, Dir.

★885★ Department of State
Environment, Health, and Natural Resources Department
Office of Environmental Protection
2201 C St., NW, Rm. 4325
Washington, DC 20520
Phone: (202)647-9266
Contact: Dwight Mason, Dir.

★886★ Department of State
Environment, Health, and Natural Resources Department
Office of Global Change
2201 C St., NW, Rm. 4329A
Washington, DC 20520
Phone: (202)647-2764
Contact: Daniel Reifsnyder, Dir.

★887★ Department of State
Oceans and Fisheries Affairs Department
Office of Fisheries Affairs
2201 C St., NW, Rm. 5806
Washington, DC 20520
Phone: (202)647-2335
Contact: Larry L. Snead, Dir.

★888★ Department of State
Oceans and Fisheries Affairs Department
Office of Oceans Affairs
2201 C St. NW, Rm. 5801
Washington, DC 20520
Phone: (202)647-3262
Contact: R. Tucker Scully, Director

★889★ Department of the Interior (DOI)
1849 C St., NW
Washington, DC 20240
Phone: (202)208-3171
Fax: (202)208-5048
Contact: Manuel Lujan Jr., Secretary

★890★ Department of the Interior
Bureau of Land Management
1849 C St., NW
Washington, DC 20240
Phone: (202)208-3801
Fax: (202)208-5902
Contact: Delos Cy Jamison, Dir.

★891★ Department of the Interior
Bureau of Land Management
Alaska State Office
Federal Bldg.
222 W 7th Ave.
Anchorage, AK 99513
Phone: (907)271-5076
Fax: (907)272-3430
Contact: Edward F. Spang, Dir.

★892★ Department of the Interior
Bureau of Land Management
Arizona State Office
3707 N 7th St.
PO Box 16563
Phoenix, AZ 85014
Phone: (602)640-5501
Fax: (602)640-5556
Contact: Lester K. Rosenkrance, Dir.

★893★ Department of the Interior
Bureau of Land Management
California State Office
Federal Bldg., Rm. E2853
2800 Cottage Way
Sacramento, CA 95825
Phone: (916)978-4743
Fax: (916)978-4715
Contact: Edward L. Hastey, Dir.

★894★ Department of the Interior
Bureau of Land Management
Colorado State Office
2850 Youngfield St.
Lakewood, CO 80215
Phone: (303)239-3700
Fax: (303)239-3933
Contact: H. Robert Moore, Dir.

★895★ Department of the Interior
Bureau of Land Management
Eastern State Office
350 S Pickett St.
Alexandria, VA 22304
Phone: (703)461-1400
Fax: (703)461-1376
Contact: Denise Meredith, Director
Serves the following states: Alabama, Arkansas, Connecticut, Delaware, District of Columbia, Florida, Georgia, Illinois, Iowa, Kentucky, Louisiana, Maine, Maryland, Massachusetts, Michigan, Minnesota, Mississippi, Missouri, New Hampshire, New Jersey, New York, North Carolina, Ohio, Pennsylvania, Rhode Island, South Carolina, Tennessee, Vermont, Virginia, West Virginia, and Wisconsin.

★896★ Department of the Interior
Bureau of Land Management
Idaho State Office
3380 Americana Terr.
Boise, ID 83706
Phone: (208)384-3001
Contact: Delmar Vail, Dir.

★897★ Department of the Interior
Bureau of Land Management
Land and Renewable Resources Department
1849 C St., NW, Rm. 5650
Washington, DC 20240
Phone: (202)208-4896
Contact: Michael J. Penfold, Asst. Dir.

★898★ Department of the Interior
Bureau of Land Management
Montana State Office
Granite Tower Bldg.
222 N 32nd St.
PO Box 36800
Billings, MT 59107
Phone: (406)255-2904
Fax: (406)255-2762
Also serves North Dakota and South Dakota.

★899★ Department of the Interior
Bureau of Land Management
Nevada State Office
850 Harvard Way
PO Box 12000
Reno, NV 89520-0006
Phone: (702)785-6590
Fax: (702)785-6411
Contact: Billy Templeton, Dir.

★900★ Department of the Interior
Bureau of Land Management
New Mexico State Office
Joseph M. Montaya Federal Bldg.
120 S Federal Pl.
PO Box 1449
Sante Fe, NM 87504-1449
Phone: (505)988-6030
Fax: (505)988-6530
Contact: Larry Woodward, Dir.
Also serves the states of Kansas, Oklahoma, and Texas.

★901★ Department of the Interior
Bureau of Land Management
Oregon State Office
1300 NE 44th Ave.
PO Box 2965
Portland, OR 97208
Phone: (503)280-7026
Fax: (503)280 7390
Contact: D. Dean Bibles, Dir.
Also serves Washington state.

★902★ Department of the Interior
Bureau of Land Management
Utah State Office
324 S State St., 4th Fl.
Salt Lake City, UT 84111
Phone: (801)539-4010
Fax: (801)539-4183
Contact: James Parker, Dir.
Mailing address: PO Box 45155, Salt Lake City, UT 84145.

★903★ Department of the Interior
Bureau of Land Management
Wyoming State Office
2515 Warren Ave.
PO Box 1828
Cheyenne, WY 82003
Phone: (307)775-6001
Fax: (307)775-6082
Contact: Ray Brubaker, Dir.
Also serves the state of Nebraska.

★904★ Department of the Interior
Fish and Wildlife and Parks Department
1849 C St. NW, Rm. 5100
Washington, DC 20240
Phone: (202)208-4416
Contact: Constance B. Harriman, Assistant Sec.

★905★ Department of the Interior
Land and Minerals Management Department
1849 C St. NW, Rm. 6608
Washington, DC 20240
Phone: (202)208-5676
Contact: David C. O'Neal, Assistant Sec.

★906★ Dept. of the Interior
Land and Minerals Mgmt. Office
Surface Mining Reclamation and Enforcement
1951 Constitution Ave., NW
Washington, DC 20240
Phone: (202)208-4006
Contact: Harry Snyder, Dir.

★907★ Department of the Interior
Land and Renewable Resources Department
Rangeland Resources Division
Premier Bldg., Rm. 909
1725 Eye St., NW
Washington, DC 20006
Phone: (202)653-9193
Contact: Billy R. Templeton, Chief

★908★ Department of the Interior
Land and Renewable Resources Department
Forestry Division
Premier Bldg., Rm. 901
1725 Eye St., NW
Washington, DC 20006
Phone: (202)653-8864
Contact: Mel Berg, Chief

★909★ Department of the Interior
Land and Renewable Resources Department
Lands and Realty Division
1849 C St., NW, Rm. 3643
Washington, DC 20240
Phone: (202)208-4200
Contact: Vincent J. Hecker, Chief

★910★ Department of the Interior
Land and Renewable Resources Department
Rangeland Resources Division
Range Management Branch
Bureau of Land Management
Washington, DC 20240
Phone: (202)653-9195
Contact: Marlowe E. Kinch, Chief

★911★ Department of the Interior
Land and Renewable Resources Department
Rangeland Resources Division
Soil, Water, and Air Branch
Bureau of Land Management
Washington, DC 20240
Phone: (202)653-9210
Contact: Donald D. Waite, Chief

★912★ Department of the Interior
Land and Renewable Resources Department
Recreation, Cultural, and Wilderness Resources Division
1849 C St., NW, Rm. 3360
Washington, DC 20240
Phone: (202)208-6064
Contact: Frank W. Snell, Chief

★913★ Department of the Interior
Land and Renewable Resources Department
Recreation, Cultural, and Wilderness Resources Division
Recreation and Cultural Resources Branch
1849 C St. NW, Rm. 3306
Washington, DC 20240
Phone: (202)208-3353
Contact: William T. Civish, Chief

★914★ Department of the Interior
Land and Renewable Resources Department
Recreation, Cultural, and Wilderness Resources Division
Wilderness Resources Branch
1849 C St. NW, Rm. 3360
Washington, DC 20240
Phone: (202)208-6064
Contact: Keith H. Corrigall, Chief

★915★ Department of the Interior
Land and Renewable Resources Department
Wild Horses and Burros Division
Premier Bldg., Rm. 901
1725 Eye St., NW
Washington, DC 20006
Phone: (202)653-9215
Contact: John S. Boyles, Chief

★916★ Department of the Interior
Land and Renewable Resources Department
Wildlife and Fisheries Division
Premier Bldg., Rm. 903
1725 Eye St. NW
Washington, DC 20006
Phone: (202)653-9202
Contact: J. David Almand, Chief

★917★ Department of the Interior
Land and Renewable Resources Department
Wildlife and Fisheries Division
Fisheries Program
Premier Bldg., Rm. 903
1725 Eye St. NW
Washington, DC 20006
Phone: (202)653-9205
Contact: Jack Williams, Manager

★918★ Department of the Interior
Land and Renewable Resources Department
Wildlife and Fisheries Division
Threatened and Endangered Species Program
Premier Bldg., Rm. 903
1725 Eye St. NW
Washington, DC 20006
Phone: (202)653-9202
Contact: William Radtkey, Manager

★919★ Department of the Interior
Land and Renewable Resources Department
Wildlife and Fisheries Division
Wildlife Program
Premier Bldg., Rm. 903
1725 Eye St. NW
Washington, DC 20006
Phone: (202)653-9202
Contact: Neal Middlebrook, Manager

★920★ Department of the Interior
Natinal Park Service
Appalachian Trail Project Office
Harpers Ferry, WV 25425
Phone: (304)535-2346 WRONG
Contact: John F. Byrne, Project Mgr.

★921★ Department of the Interior
National Park Foundation
1101 17th St., NW, Rm. 1008
Washington, DC 20036
Phone: (202)785-4500
Contact: Alan A. Rubin, Pres.

★922★ Department of the Interior
National Park Service
1849 C St., NW, Rm. 3104
Washington, DC 20240
Phone: (202)208-4621
Fax: (202)208-7520
Contact: James M. Ridenour, Dir.

★923★ Department of the Interior
National Park Service
Natural Resources Department
1849 C St., NW, Rm. 3127
Washington, DC 20240
Phone: (202)208-3884
Contact: F. Eugene Hester, Assoc. Dir.

★924★ Department of the Interior
National Park Service
Natural Resources Department
Air Quality Division
PO Box 25287
Denver, CO 80225
Phone: (303)969-2070
Contact: John Christiano, Chief

★925★ Department of the Interior
National Park Service
Natural Resources Department
Water Resources Division
Federal Bldg., Rm. 335
301 S. Howes St.
Ft. Collins, CO 80521
Phone: (303)221-5341
Contact: Stan Ponce, Chief

★926★ Department of the Interior
National Park Service
Natural Resources Department
Wildlife and Vegetation Division
1100 L St. NW, Rm. 3319
Washington, DC 20240
Phone: (202)343-8100
Contact: Michael Ruggiero, Chief

★927★ Dept. of the Interior
Office of Fish, Wildlife, and Parks
18th and C Sts., NW
Washington, DC 20240
Phone: (202)208-4684
Contact: Constance B. Harriman, Asst. Sec.

★928★ Department of the Interior
Office of Public Affairs
1849 C St., NW, Rm. 7214
Washington, DC 20240
Contact: I. Steven Goldstein, Dir.

★929★ Department of the Interior
Office of the Solicitor
Conservation and Wildlife Division
1849 C St., NW, Rm. 6560
Washington, DC 20240
Phone: (202)208-7957
Contact: Dave Watts, Assoc. Solicitor

★930★ Department of the Interior
Office of the Solicitor
Conservation and Wildlife Division
Fish and Wildlife Branch
1849 C St. NW, Rm. 6545
Washington, DC 20240
Phone: (202)208-6172
Contact: Charles P. Raynor, Assistant Solicitor

★931★ Department of the Interior
Office of the Solicitor
Conservation and Wildlife Division
National Capitol Parks Branch
1849 C St. NW , Rm. 6554
Washington, DC 20240
Phone: (202)208-4332
Contact: Richard G. Robbins, Assistant Solicitor

★932★ Department of the Interior
Office of the Solicitor
Conservation and Wildlife Division
Parks and Recreation Branch
1849 C St. NW, Rm. 6311
Washington, DC 20240
Phone: (202)208-7957
Contact: David A. Watts, Assistant Solicitor

★933★ Department of the Interior
Office of the Solicitor
Energy and Resources Division
1849 C St., NW, Rm. 6310
Washington, DC 20240
Phone: (202)208-5757
Contact: Michael A. Poling, Assoc. Solicitor

★934★ Department of the Interior
Patuxent Wildlife Research Center
Gabrielson Bldg.
Rte. 197
Laurel, MD 20708
Phone: (202)498-0300
Contact: Harold J. O'Connor, Dir.

★935★ Department of the Interior
Policy, Management, and Budget Division
Office of Environmental Affairs
1849 C St., NW
Washington, DC 20240
Phone: (202)208-3891
Contact: Jonathon P. Deason, Dir.

★936★ Department of the Interior
United States Fish and Wildlife Service
1849 C St., NW, Rm. 3256
Washington, DC 20240
Phone: (202)208-4717
Fax: (202)208-4473
Contact: John F. Turner, Dir.

★937★ Department of the Interior
United States Fish and Wildlife Service
Fish and Wildlife Enhancement Department
1849 C St., NW, Rm. 3024
Washington, DC 20240
Phone: (202)208-4646
Contact: Ralph O. Morgenweck, Asst. Dir.

★938★ Department of the Interior
United States Fish and Wildlife Service
Fish and Wildlife Enhancement Department
Endangered Species Division
Interior Bldg., Rm. 452
1849 C St. NW
Washington, DC 20240
Phone: (202)358-2171
Contact: Larry Shannon, Chief

★939★ Department of the Interior
United States Fish and Wildlife Service
Fish and Wildlife Enhancement Department
Environmental Contaminants Division
Interior Bldg., Rm. 330
1849 C St. NW
Washington, DC 20240
Phone: (202)358-2148
Contact: John A. Blackenship, Chief

★940★ Department of the Interior
United States Fish and Wildlife Service
Fish and Wildlife Enhancement Department
Habitat Conservation Division
Interior Bldg., Rm. 400
1849 C St. NW
Washington, DC 20240
Phone: (202)358-2161
Contact: William Knapp, Chief

★941★ Department of the Interior
United States Fish and Wildlife Service
Fisheries Department
1849 C St., NW, Rm. 3245
Washington, DC 20240
Phone: (202)208-6394
Contact: Gary B. Edwards, Asst. Dir.

★942★ Department of the Interior
United States Fish and Wildlife Service
Fisheries Department
Fish and Wildlife Management Division
Interior Bldg., Rm. 840
1849 C St. NW
Washington, DC 20240
Phone: (202)358-1718
Contact: John Bardwell, Chief

★943★ Department of the Interior
United States Fish and Wildlife Service
Fisheries Department
Fish Hatcheries Division
Interior Bldg., Rm. 833
1849 C St. NW
Washington, DC 20240
Phone: (202)358-1715
Contact: Joseph J. Webster, Chief

★944★ Department of the Interior
United States Fish and Wildlife Service
Refuges and Wildlife Department
1849 C St., NW, Rm. 3248
Washington, DC 20240
Phone: (202)208-5333
Contact: David L. Olsen, Asst. Dir.

★945★ Department of the Interior
United States Fish and Wildlife Service
Refuges and Wildlife Department
Refuges Division
Interior Bldg., Rm. 670
1849 C St. NW
Washington, DC 20240
Phone: (202)358-1744
Contact: Robert A. Karges, Chief

★946★ Department of the Interior
Water and Science Department
1849 C St., Rm. 6660
Washington, DC 20240
Phone: (202)208-3186
Contact: John M. Sayre, Assistant Sec.

★947★ Department of the Interior
Water and Science Division
Water Resources Division
1849 C St., NW, Rm. 5A402
Washington, DC 20240
Phone: (703)648-5215
Contact: Philip Cohen, Chief Hydrologist

★948★ Dept. of the Interior
Water and Science Office
Bureau of Reclamation (BuREC)
18th and C Sts., NW
Washington, DC 20240
Phone: (202)343-4157
Contact: Dennis Underwood, Commissioner

★949★ Department of Transportation
Research and Special Programs Administration
Office of Pipeline Safety
400 Seventh St., SW, Rm. 8417
Washington, DC 20590
Phone: (202)366-4595
Contact: George W. Tenley, Dir.

★950★ Department of Transportation
Research and Special Programs Administration
Office of Pipeline Safety
Alaska Natural Gas Pipeline Project
400 7th St. SW, Rm. 8417
Washington, DC 20590
Phone: (202)366-4556
Contact: Lloyd W. Ulrich, Dir.

★951★ Department of Transportation
United States Coast Guard
Office of Marine Safety, Security, and Environmental Protection
2100 Second St., SW, Rm. 2408
Washington, DC 20593
Phone: (202)267-2200
Fax: (202)426-1405
Contact: Rear Adm. Joel D. Sipes, Chief

★952★ Department of Transportation
United States Coast Guard
Office of Marine Safety, Security, and Environmental Protection
Marine Environmental Response Division
2100 Second St., SW, Rm. 2104
Washington, DC 20593
Phone: (202)267-0518
Contact: Capt. William F. Holt, Chief

★953★ Dickinson District Advisory Council
Bureau of Land Management
Department of the Interior
2933 3rd Ave., W.
Dickinson, ND 58601
Phone: (701)225-9148
Contact: Dan Mates, Designated Federal Officer
Council provides representative citizen counsel and advice to the Bureau of Land Management district manager regarding planning and management of the public lands resources within the Dickinson district.

★954★ Elko District Advisory Council
Bureau of Land Management
Department of the Interior
3900 E. Idaho St.
PO Box 831
Elko, NV 89801
Phone: (702)753-0200
Contact: Rodney Harris, Designated Federal Employee
Council provides representative citizen counsel and advice to the Bureau of Land Management district manager regarding planning and management of the public lands resources within the Elko district.

★955★ Ely District Advisory Council
Bureau of Land Management
Department of the Interior
702 N. Industrial Way, HC33
Box 150
Ely, NV 89301-9408
Phone: (702)289-4865
Contact: Kenneth G. Walker, Designated Federal Employee
Council provides representative citizen counsel and advice to the Bureau of Land Management district manager regarding planning and management of the public lands resources within the Ely district.

★956★ Endangered Species Committee
Department of the Interior
1849 C St., N.W., Rm. 4412
Washington, DC 20240
Phone: (202)208-4077
Contact: Jon H. Goldstein, Staff Dir.
Committee is authorized to grant exemptions from Section 7 of the Endangered Species Act to projects that threaten the survival or critical habitats of rare and endangered animals and plants, providing that no reasonable alternatives to the project are available and that the public benefits of the project clearly outweigh those of alternatives.

★957★ Energy Information Council
Office of Federal Statistical Policy & Standards
Department of Commerce
Washington, DC 20220
Council was established to advise the Director of Federal Statistical Policy and Standards and the Administrator of the Energy Information Administration on technical matters involving the collection, processing, analysis and dissemination of energy information and data files maintained by the federal government.

★958★ Environmental Health Sciences Review Committee
National Institute of Environmental Health Sciences
National Institutes of Health
PO Box 12233
Research Triangle Park, NC 27709
Phone: (919)541-0131
Contact: Dr. Thor Fjellstedt Ph.D., Designated Federal Employee
Committee reviews research grant applications for support of interdisciplinary programs where the major emphasis is on the effects of the environment on human health, and makes recommendations for approval of those programs that merit support. It also provides technical advice to the National Institute of Environmental Health Sciences in developing, monitoring, and evaluating special programs that include grant applications and, if appropriate, contract proposals.

★959★ Eugene District Advisory Council
Bureau of Land Management
Department of the Interior
1200 High St., Ste. No. 22
Eugene, OR 97401
Phone: (503)683-6415
Contact: Doug Huntington, Staff Contact
Council provides representative citizen counsel and advice to the Bureau of Land Management district manager regarding planning and management of the public lands resources within the Eugene district.

★960★ Farmington River Study Committee
Public Affairs Office
North Atlantic Regional Office
National Park Service
15 State St.
Boston, MA 02109
Phone: (617)223-5142
Contact: Philip Huffman, Project Manager
Committee advises the Secretary of the Interior in conducting a study on whether the West Branch of the Farmington River, which flows through Connecticut and Massachusetts, is eligible for inclusion in the National Wild and Scenic Rivers System of the National Park Service, Fish and Wildlife and Parks, Department of the Interior. It will also examine management alternatives for the River if it is to be included in the System.

★961★ Federal Asbestos Task Force
Asbestos Action Program, TS-794
Office of Pesticides & Toxic Substances
Environmental Protection Agency
401 M Street, S.W.
Washington, DC 20460
Phone: (202)382-3862
Contact: James K. Kwiat, Staff Contact
Task Force was established to coordinate programs administered by the federal government that control potential health hazards to the public from exposure to asbestos and other fibrous materials. It coordinates research, data gathering, and analyses; identifies areas for new research and analyzes the potential health hazards posed by exposure to asbestos and other fibrous materials. In addition, it develops recommendations concerning the identification of areas that should be of priority concern to the agencies represented on the Task Force, the need to consider revisions of existing health standards and regulations, the need to consider new regulatory actions, and the use of nonregulatory actions and educational materials.

★962★ Federal Insecticide, Fungicide, and Rodenticide Act Scientific Advisory Panel (FIFRA)
Office of Pesticide Programs (H7509C)
Environmental Protection Agency
401 M St., S.W.
Washington, DC 20460
Phone: (703)557-4369
Contact: Robert Bruce Jaeger, Staff Contact
Panel was established to comment on the impact on health and the environment of regulatory actions relating to pesticides. It comments on notices of intent to cancel or reclassify uses of specific pesticides, notices of intent to hold a hearing to determine whether or not to cancel or reclassify uses of pesticides, and regulations issued under the Act.

★963★ Federal-State Coal Advisory Board
Bureau of Land Management
Department of the Interior
1849 C St., N.W.
Washington, DC 20240
Phone: (202)208-4636
Contact: Dan Weddenburn, Staff Contact
Board advises the Secretary of the Interior and the Director, Bureau of Land Management, regarding the federal coal management program in accordance with the provisions of 43 CFR 3400.

★964★ Florida Keys National Marine Sanctuary Advisory Council
Office of the Secretary
Department of Commerce
14th St. & Constitution Ave. NW
Washington, DC 20230
Phone: (202)377-4951
Contact: Preston Moore, Staff Contact
Council advises the Secretary of Commerce on the development and implementation of a comprehensive management plan for the Florida Keys National Marine Sanctuary. The plan is required to: facilitate all public and private uses of the Sanctuary while ensuring protection of Sanctuary resources, which include seagrass meadows, mangrove islands, and extensive living coral reefs; consider temporal and geographical zoning for resource protection purposes; enforce any comprehensive water quality protection program that might be deemed necessary by federal and state officials; identify research needs and establish a long-term ecological monitoring program; ensure coordination and cooperation between federal, state, and local authorities with jurisdiction within or adjacent to the Sanctuary; promote the education of Sanctuary users with regard to coral reef conservation and navigational safety; incorporate the existing Looe Key and Key Largo National Marine Sanctuaries into the Florida Keys National Marine Sanctuary; and find alternative means to finance implementation of the plan.

★965★ **Garrison Diversion Unit Federal Advisory Council**
U. S. Fish & Wildlife Service
PO Box 25486
Denver Federal Center
Denver, CO 80225
Phone: (303)236-7920
Fax: (303)236-8295
Contact: Galen Buterbaugh, Designated Federal Employee
Council was established to ensure that the Garrison Diversion Unit (authorized by the U.S. Congress as a federally funded water development program for North Dakota) mitigation, enhancement, and other fish and wildlife programs proceed with broad oversight and coordination. Council will review implementation plans, budgetary requirements, and program results, and make annual recommendations for any needed revisions to the wildlife resource management programs for consideration by the Secretary of the Interior, the Governor of North Dakota, and other managing agencies.

★966★ **Gateway National Recreation Area Advisory Commission**
Headquarters, Bldg. 69
Floyd Bennett Field
Brooklyn, NY 11234
Phone: (718)338-3688
Contact: E.M. Strumpf, Designated Federal Employee
Commission consults with the Secretary of the Interior or the Secretary's designee with respect to matters relating to the development of the Gateway National Recreation Area, which is located in the New York Harbor area.

★967★ **Golden Gate National Recreation Area Advisory Commission (GGNRA)**
National Park Service
Fl. Mason, Bldg. 201
San Francisco, CA 94123
Phone: (415)556-4484
Contact: Michael Feinstein, Designated Federal Employee
Commission consults with the Secretary of the Interior, or his designee, on general policies and specific matters related to planning, administration, and development affecting the Golden Gate National Recreation Area and other units of the National Park System in Marin, San Mateo, and San Francisco Counties. Issues include the transfer of the Presidio from the Department of Defense to the National Park Service and the future management of the Presidio.

★968★ **Grand Junction District Advisory Council**
Bureau of Land Management
Department of the Interior
764 Horizon Dr.
Grand Junction, CO 81506
Phone: (303)243-6552
Contact: Joann Graham, Designated Federal Employee
Council provides representative citizen counsel and advice to the Bureau of Land Management district manager regarding planning and management of the public lands resources within the Grand Junction district.

★969★ **Great Lakes Fishery Commission**
1451 Green Rd.
Ann Arbor, MI 48105
Phone: (313)662-3209
Contact: Carlos M. Fetterolf Jr., Exec. Sec.
Commission's primary objective is to improve the quality, abundance, and productivity of the fishery resources of the Great Lakes for both sport and commercial use. Commission formulates and coordinates research programs, advises the governments of the United States and Canada on measures to improve fishery resources, and has implemented a program in four of the five Great Lakes to control the sea lamprey population.

★970★ **Gulf Islands National Seashore Advisory Commission**
Superintendent
1801 Gulf Breeze Pkwy.
Gulf Breeze, FL 32561
Phone: (904)934-2604
Contact: Suzanne Lewis, Staff Contact
Commission consults with the Secretary of the Interior with respect to matters relating to development of the Gulf Islands National Seashore.

★971★ **Gulf of Mexico Fishery Management Council**
5401 W. Kennedy Blvd., Ste. 881
Tampa, FL 33609
Phone: (813)228-2815
Contact: Wayne E. Swingle, Exec. Dir.
Council develops and monitors fishery management plans for fisheries in the Gulf of Mexico seaward of Texas, Louisiana, Mississippi, Alabama, and Florida and amends the plans in accordance with the changing nature of marine resources. Council also prepares comments on foreign fishing applications and conducts public hearings and meetings regarding fishery management planning and/or the development of such plans.

★972★ **Gulf of Mexico Regional Technical Working Group**
Gulf of Mexico OCS Region
Minerals Management Service
1201 Elmwood Park Blvd.
New Orleans, LA 70123-2394
Group advises the Secretary of the Interior on technical matters of regional concern regarding prelease sale activities, transportation-related study requirements, and transportation management plans for the Gulf of Mexico leasing region (Florida, Alabama, Mississippi, Louisiana, Texas).

★973★ **Health and Environmental Research Advisory Committee (HERAC)**
Office of Energy Research, ER-70
Department of Energy
Germantown, MD 70585
Phone: (301)353-2987
Contact: Jean Hummer, Staff Contact
Committee provides advice on a continuing basis to the Director of Energy Research on the programs of the Office of Health and Environmental Research (HER). This advice includes reviews of programs with recommendations for changes; advice on health and environmental concerns that bear on the Department's activities; advice on long-term plans, strategies, and priorities of HER to address energy-related health and environmental issues of departmental policies and programs; and advice on levels of funding appropriate to promote those strategies and to maintain balance between competing elements of the HER program.

★974★ **Idaho Falls District Advisory Council**
Bureau of Land Management
Department of the Interior
940 Lincoln Rd.
Idaho Falls, ID 83401
Phone: (208)529-1020
Contact: Lloyd H. Ferguson, Designated Federal Employee
Council provides representative citizen counsel and advice to the Bureau of Land Management district manager regarding planning and management of the public lands resources within the Idaho Falls district.

★975★ **Iditarod National Historic Trail Advisory Council**
Bureau of Land Management, Anchorage District
6881 Abbott Loop Rd.
Anchorage, AK 99507
Phone: (907)267-1225
Contact: Dean Littlepage, Staff Contact
Council gathers and analyzes information, hears public testimony, offers advice, and develops recommendations with regard to acquisition, management, development, and use of the Iditarod National Historic Trail, including the selection of rights-of-way, standards for the erection and maintenance of markers, and administration of the Trail.

★976★ **Innovative Control Technology Advisory Panel (ICTAP)**
Office of Environment, Safety & Health (EH-22)
Department of Energy, Rm. 4G 036
1000 Independence Avenue, S.W.
Washington, DC 20585
Phone: (202)586-2061
Contact: Edward R. Williams, Designated Federal Employee
Panel provides advice and recommendations to the Secretary of Energy concerning innovative control technologies that will broaden cost-effective and efficient options for controlling precursor emissions associated with acid deposition.

★977★ **Interagency Commission on Alternative Motor Fuels**
Office of the Deputy Secretary
Department of Energy
1000 Independence Ave., S.W.
Washington, DC 20585
Commission coordinates federal agency efforts to develop and implement a national alternative motor fuels policy. It ensures the development of a long-term plan for the commercialization of alcohols, natural gas, and other potential alternative motor fuels; ensures communication among representatives of all federal agencies involved in alternative fuels projects or have an interest in such; and provides for the exchange of information among persons working with or interested in the commercialization of alternative motor fuels.

★978★ **Interagency Task Force on Acid Precipitation**
National Acid Precipitation Assessment Program
722 Jackson Pl., N.W.
Washington, DC 20503
Phone: (202)395-5771
Contact: Dr. James R. Mahoney, Staff Contact
Task Force plans and manages the National Acid Precipitation Assessment Program (NAPAP), which was initially developed by the Acid Rain Coordination Committee. Task Force also maintains the inventory of all federally-sponsored acid deposition research projects; develops and updates the operating research plan of the NAPAP; ensures that research projects are technically sound and credible through peer reviews by the scientific community; and encourages production interaction between federal government, private sector, academic, state and local

government, and international acid precipitation research programs.

★979★ Interagency Testing Committee
TS-792
401 M St., S.W.
Washington, DC 20460
Phone: (202)382-3820
Fax: (202)382-3764
Contact: Dr. John D. Walker, Exec. Dir.
Committee selects and recommends chemicals and chemical groups for priority consideration for health effects, chemical fate, and ecological effects testing. It is concerned with chemicals or chemical groups that may: (1) present an unreasonable risk of injury to health or the environment, (2) reasonably be anticipated to enter the environment in substantial quantities, or (3) involve significant or substantial human exposure. At least every six months, the Committee furnishes the Administrator, EPA, with a revised Priority List of chemicals or chemical groups recommended for testing. In preparing the list, the Committee reviews unpublished studies and data submitted by chemical manufacturers, processors, and distributors. Committee promotes the exchange of information on chemicals and it assists in the coordination of chemical testing sponsored or required by the federal government.

★980★ Interagency Toxic Substances Data Committee (ITSDC)
Office of Program Integration & Information
Office of Toxic Substances
Environmental Protection Agency
401 M Street, S.W.
Washington, DC 20460
Contact: Sandra Lee, Exec. Sec.
Committee coordinates the planning and activities concerning chemical data and information projects of the major federal producers and users of chemical data so as to minimize the total burden of reporting which is placed upon the private sector. It also studies ways to facilitate the collection, analysis, and exchange of data among federal agencies and other user groups.

★981★ Interdisciplinary Research Committee
Office of Research & Development, R.D. 674
Environmental Protection Agency
401 M St., S. W., Rm. 308
North E. Mall
Washington, DC 20460
Phone: (202)382-7492
Contact: Charles Oakley, Staff Contact
Committee serves as a vehicle for communicating research needs, describing research programs to meet those needs, and advising the Assistant Administrator for the Office of Research and Development on matters regarding risk assessment, quality assurance management, exploratory research, technology transfer, and technical information.

★982★ Interstate Commission on the Potomac River Basin
6110 Executive Blvd., Ste. 300
Rockville, MD 20852
Phone: (301)984-1908
Contact: Barbara R. Barritt, Designated Federal Employee
Commission collects and analyzes technical data, conducts studies, and sponsors research on pollution and water problems of the Potomac Valley Conservancy District which comprises the areas in Maryland, Virginia, West Virginia, Pennsylvania, and the District of Columbia drained by the Potomac River and its tributaries. Commission disseminates information to the public and cooperates, assists, and provides liaison with public and nonpublic agencies and organizations on stream pollution problems and utilization, conservation, and development of the water and associated land resources of the Conservancy District. Commission also establishes physical, chemical, and bacteriological standards of water quality for various classifications of use for the district.

★983★ Klamath Fishery Management Council
U. S. Fish & Wildlife Service
PO Box 1006
Yreka, CA 96097-1006
Phone: (916)842-5763
Fax: (916)842-4517
Contact: Ronald A. Iverson, Staff Contact
Council will establish a comprehensive long-term plan and policy, consistent with the Klamath River Basin Conservation Area Restoration Program, for the management of the in-river and ocean harvesting that affects the Klamath and Trinity River Basin anadromous fish populations. Council also makes recommendations regarding harvest regulations to the California Fish and Game Commission, the Oregon Department of Fish and Wildlife, the Pacific Fisheries Management Council, the Bureau of Indian Affairs of the Department of the Interior, and the Hoopa Valley (California) Business Council; and coordinates its activities with those of the Klamath River Basin Fisheries Task Force.

★984★ Klamath River Basin Fisheries Task Force
U. S. Fish & Wildlife Service
PO Box 1006
Yreka, CA 96097
Phone: (916)842-5763
Fax: (916)842-4517
Contact: Ron Iverson, Staff Contact
Task Force assists the Secretary of the Interior in planning and implementing the Klamath River Basin Conservation Area Restoration Program, which will restore anadromous fish stocks in the Klamath River Basin. Task Force provides advice to and coordinates its activities with those of the Klamath Fishery Management Council.

★985★ Klamath River Compact Commission
280 Main St.
Klamath Falls, OR 97601
Phone: (503)882-4436
Contact: George Proctor, Exec. Dir.
Commission administers the Klamath River Basin Compact between the States of California and Oregon for the Klamath River Basin (the drainage area of the Klamath River and its tributaries within California and Oregon and all closed basins included in the Upper Klamath River Basin). The purpose of the Compact is to promote the development, use, and control of the use of water for domestic purposes; to develop lands by irrigation; to protect and enhance fish, wildlife, and recreational resources; and to facilitate and develop the use of water for industrial purposes and hydroelectric power production and the use and control of water for navigation and flood prevention.

★986★ Lakeview District Advisory Council
Bureau of Land Management
Department of the Interior
PO Box 151
Lakeview, OR 97630
Phone: (503)947-2177
Contact: Renee Snyder, Staff Contact
Council provides representative citizen counsel and advice to the Bureau of Land Management district manager regarding planning and management of the public lands resources within the Lakeview district.

★987★ Las Cruces District Advisory Council
Bureau of Land Management
Department of the Interior
1800 Marquess
Las Cruces, NM 80005
Phone: (505)525-8228
Contact: H. James Fox, Designated Federal Employee
Council provides representative citizen counsel and advice to the Bureau of Land Management district manager regarding planning and management of the public lands resources within the Las Cruces district.

★988★ Las Vegas District Advisory Council
Bureau of Land Management
Department of the Interior
4765 W. Vegas Dr.
PO Box 26569
Las Vegas, NV 89126
Phone: (702)647-5000
Contact: Ben F. Collins, Designated Federal Employee
Council provides representative citizen counsel and advice to the Bureau of Land Management district manager regarding planning and management of the public lands resources within the Las Vegas district.

★989★ Lewistown District Advisory Council
Bureau of Land Management
Department of the Interior
Drawer 1160
Aiport Rd.
Lewistown, MT 59457
Phone: (406)538-7461
Contact: Wayne Zinne, Designated Federal Employee
Council provides representative citizen counsel and advice to the Bureau of Land Management district manager regarding planning and management of the public lands resources within the Lewistown district.

★990★ Marine Mammal Commission
1825 Connecticut Ave., N.W., Rm. 512
Washington, DC 20009
Phone: (202)653-6237
Contact: John R. Twiss Jr., Exec. Dir.
Commission was established to undertake a review and study of activities of the United States pursuant to existing laws and international conventions relating to marine mammals; to conduct a continuing review of the condition of stocks of marine mammals, of methods for their protection and conservation, of humane means of taking them, of research programs to be conducted, and of all applications for permits to use marine mammals for public display and for scientific research; to recommend to the Secretary of the Interior revisions, as appropriate, to the Endangered Species List with regard to marine mammals; to recommend to the Secretary of State appropriate policies regarding existing or proposed international arrangements for the protection and conservation of marine mammals; and to undertake such other studies

and make such other recommendations as it deems necessary to further the protection and conservation of marine mammals.

★991★ Medford District Advisory Council
Bureau of Land Management
Department of the Interior
3040 Biddle Rd.
Medford, OR 97504
Phone: (503)776-4174
Contact: David A. Jones, District Manager
Council provides representative citizen counsel and advice to the Bureau of Land Management district manager regarding planning and management of the public lands resources within the Medford district.

★992★ Mid-Atlantic Fishery Management Council
Federal Bldg., Rm. 2115
300 S. New St.
Dover, DE 19901
Phone: (302)674-2331
Contact: John C. Bryson, Exec. Dir.
Council develops and monitors fishery management plans for fisheries in the Atlantic Ocean seaward of New Jersey, New York, Delaware, Pennsylvania, Maryland, and Virginia and amends the plans in accordance with the changing nature of marine resources. Council also prepares comments on foreign fishing applications and conducts public hearings and meetings regarding fishery management planning and/or the development of such plans.

★993★ Mid-Atlantic Regional Technical Working Group
Atlantic OCS Region
381 Elden St. Pkwy.
Atrium Bldg.
Herdon, VA 22070
Phone: (703)787-1113
Fax: (703)787-1104
Contact: Angie Graziano, Staff Contact
Group advises the Secretary of the Interior on technical matters of regional concern regarding prelease sale activities, transportation-related study requirements, and transportation management plans for the Mid-Atlantic leasing region (New York, New Jersey, Delaware, Pennsylvania, Maryland, Virginia, North Carolina).

★994★ Midwest Interstate Low-Level Radioactive Waste Commission
336 Robert St., N., No. 1303
St. Paul, MN 55101-1507
Phone: (612)293-0126
Contact: Gregg Larson, Exec. Dir.
Commission administers the Midwest Interstate Low-Level Radioactive Waste Compact which provides for sufficient facilities for the management of low-level radioactive waste generated in the region, the protection of the health and safety of residents of the region, a limitation of the number of facilities required to manage low-level radioactive waste generated in the region, the ensurance of ecological and economical management of low-level radioactive waste, and the promotion of above-ground facilities and other disposal technologies for greater and safer confinement of low-level radioactive waste than shallow-land burial facilities. Commission develops and implements a regional low-level radioactive waste management plan, identifies the number and types of new waste disposal sites needed for the region, identifies one or more of its member states (Indiana, Iowa, Michigan, Minnesota, Missouri, Ohio, Wisconsin) to serve as a "host" state(s) for the region's disposal facilities. In June 1987, Commission designated Michigan as the "host" state for the region's first disposal facility and is currently providing assistance to Michigan in facility development. It is anticipated that a regional disposal facility will be operational sometime in 1997.

★995★ Miles City District Advisory Council
Bureau of Land Management
Department of the Interior
PO Box 940
Miles City, MT 59301
Phone: (406)232-4331
Contact: Mat Millenbach, Designated Federal Employee
Council provides representative citizen counsel and advice to the Bureau of Land Management district manager regarding planning and management of the public lands resources within the Miles City district.

★996★ Mississippi River Corridor Study Commission
Office of the Director
National Park Service
Department of the Interior
1849 C St., N.W., 3104
Washington, DC 20240
Commission studies and makes recommendations regarding the feasibility of creating a Mississippi River National Heritage Corridor for the Mississippi River Corridor, and the preservation, protection, enhancement, enjoyment, and utilization of the historic, economic, natural, recreational, scenic, cultural, and scientific resources of the Corridor. Specifically, it is charged with providing a description of the Mississippi River Corridor and the proposed boundaries of a Mississippi River National Heritage Corridor (if so recommended); an inventory and assessment of the historic, economic, natural, recreational, scenic, cultural, and scientific resources of the Corridor; specific preservation and interpretation goals and a priority timetable for their achievement; proposals for alternative management strategies and for changes in federal, state, and local laws and regulations that are needed to further the goals of the Act; proposals to improve guidance and assistance provided to Mississippi River states, their political subdivisions, and other entities regarding their compliance with applicable provisions of the Clean Water Act, the Safe Drinking Water Act, and related laws; and recommendations with respect to public access to and interpretation of the natural and cultural resources of the river and related outdoor recreation opportunities.

★997★ Missouri National Recreational River Advisory Group
National Park Service
Midwest Regional Office
1709 Jackson St.
Omaha, NE 68102
Phone: (402)221-3481
Contact: Alan Hutchings, Designated Federal Employee
Group provides counsel to the Secretary of the Interior, through the Assistant Secretary for Fish and Wildlife and Parks, on the development of operational and administrative policies for the fifty-nine mile segment of the Missouri River from Gavins Point Dam, South Dakota, to Ponca State Park, Nebraska.

★998★ Moab District Advisory Council
Bureau of Land Management
Department of the Interior
82 E. Dogwood
PO Box 970
Moab, UT 84532
Phone: (801)259-6111
Contact: Gene Nodine, Designated Federal Employee
Council provides representative citizen counsel and advice to the Bureau of Land Management district manager regarding planning and management of the public lands resources within the Moab district.

★999★ Mono Basin National Forest Scenic Area Advisory Board
Forest Service
873 N. Main St.
Bishop, CA 93514
Phone: (619)873-5841
Contact: Dennis W. Martin, Staff Contact
Board advises and makes recommendations to the Secretary of Agriculture concerning the administration of the Mono Basin National Forest Scenic Area within and adjacent to the Inyo National Forest, California; the location of a visitor center to provide information through appropriate displays, printed material, and other interpretive programs about the natural and cultural resources of the scenic area; and the preparation and implementation of a comprehensive management plan, which includes an inventory of natural (including geologic) and cultural resources, general development plans for public use facilities, and measures for the preservation of the natural and cultural resources of the scenic area.

★1000★ Montrose District Advisory Council
Bureau of Land Management
Department of the Interior
2465 S. Townsend
Montrose, CO 81401
Phone: (303)249-7791
Contact: Alan Kesterke, Designated Federal Employee
Council provides representative citizen counsel and advice to the Bureau of Land Management district manager regarding planning and management of the public lands resources within the Montrose district.

★1001★ Mount St. Helens Scientific Advisory Board
Forest Service, Pacific NW Region
Box 3623
Portland, OR 97208
Phone: (503)326-3644
Fax: (503)326-3096
Contact: Joseph Higgins, Designated Federal Employee
Board gives advice and recommendations with respect to the measures needed to protect and manage the natural and scientific values of the Mount St. Helens National Volcanic Monument in the state of Washington which was established as national lands by this Act; the administration of the Monument, specifically policies, programs, and activities intended to retain the natural ecologic and geologic processes of the Monument; and to new research opportunities within the Monument designed to gain scientific information for future interpretation and enjoyment by visitors to the Monument.

★1002★ National Acid Precipitation Assessment Program (NAPAP)
722 Jackson Pl., N.W.
Washington, DC 20503
Phone: (202)395-5772
Contact: Dr. James R. Mahoney, Staff Contact
Program was initially developed by the Acid Rain Coordinating Committee and established under Title VII of P.L. 96-294, the Acid Precipitation Act of 1980. It is managed by the Interagency Task Force on Acid Precipitation, which functions under the Council on Environmental Quality. The goal of the Program is to increase public understanding of the cause and effects of acid precipitation. Its activities include research, monitoring, and assessments which emphasize a firmer scientific basis for decision making on issues concerning acid rain. Dr. James R. Mahoney, Director, NAPAP, serves as staff contact.

★1003★ National Advisory Council for Environmental Policy and Technology (NACEPT)
Environmental Protection Agency (A-101F6)
401 M St., S.W.
Washington, DC 20460
Phone: (202)475-9741
Contact: Robert L. Hardaker, Designated Federal Official
The Council provides independent advice and counsel to the Administrator on key international and domestic policy and technology issues and needs. It is focusing on identifying and reducing the barriers impeding international environmental technology transfer and training efforts; implementation of effective pollution prevention programs by business and governments; creating a positive institutional climate within EPA with respect to technology transfer and pollution prevention activities; promoting cooperative, mutually-supportive relationships increasing communication among all levels of government, the business community, and the academic community with the aim of increasing nonfederal resources and improving the effectiveness of Federal and nonfederal resources directed at solving environmental problems; developing and applying an appropriate array of delivery mechanisms for meeting technology transfer and training needs; implementing the Federal Technology Transfer Act of 1986 and Executive Order 12591, and other related legislation, executive orders and regulations to facilitate access to science and technology; and reviewing proposed EPA policies and reports. Council will analyze problems, present findings, make recommendations, conduct meetings and perform other activities necessary for the attainment of its objectives.

★1004★ National Advisory Environmental Health Sciences Council
National Institute of Environmental Health Sciences
National Institutes of Health
PO Box 12233
Research Triangle Park, NC 27709
Phone: (919)541-7723
Contact: Anne P. Sassman, Designated Federal Employee
Council reviews applications for grants-in-aid relating to research projects and for research and training activities in the environmental health sciences, and recommends to the Director of the National Institutes of Health approval of those projects which merit support. It consults with and advises the Secretary of Health and Human Services, the Assistant Secretary for Health, and the Directors of the National Institutes of Health and the National Institute of Environmental Health Sciences on matters relating to programs and activities in the area of environmental health sciences, such as toxicology, pharmacology, pathology, and biochemistry.

★1005★ National Air Pollution Control Techniques Advisory Committee
Emission Standards Division (MD-13)
Office of Air Quality Planning & Standards
Environmental Protection Agency
Research Triangle Park, NC 27711
Phone: (919)541-5571
Committee advises the Director, Office of Air Quality Planning and Standards, on latest available technology and economic feasibility of alternative methods to prevent and control air contamination to be published in air quality control techniques documents. Also, the Committee advises on informational documents regarding air pollution control techniques and testing and monitoring methodology for categories of new sources and air pollutants subject to the provisions of Sections 111 and 112 of the Clean Air Act, as amended in 1990.

★1006★ National Animal Damage Control Advisory Committee (NADCAC)
Office of Animal Damage Control
Animal & Plant Health Inspection Service
1624 S. Bldg.
Department of Agriculture
Washington, DC 20250
Phone: (202)447-2054
Contact: Bobby R. Acord, Exec. Sec.
Committee provides advice to the Secretary of Agriculture on policies and to protect America's program issues necessary to reduce animal damage, agricultural, industrial, and natural resources, and to safeguard public health and safety.

★1007★ National Coal Council (NCC)
2000 Fifteenth St.
North Ste. 500
Arlington, VA 22201
Phone: (703)527-1191
Contact: James McAvoy, Designated Federal Employee
Council provides advice and recommendations to the Secretary of Energy on general policy matters relating to coal, including: the federal policies that affect, directly or indirectly, the production, marketing, and use of coal; the plans, priorities, and strategies needed to more effectively address the technology, regulatory, and social impact issues relating to coal production and use; the appropriate balance between various elements of federal coal-related programs; the scientific and engineering aspects of coal technologies, including emerging coal conversion, utilization, or environmental control concepts; and the progress of coal research and development, pursuant to P.L. 86-599, the Office of Coal Research Act.

★1008★ National Conservation Review Group
Conservation Programs & Automation Branch
Conservation & Environmental Protection Div.
Agricultural Stabilization & Conservation Service
South Bldg., Rm. 4723
Washington, DC 20013
Phone: (202)447-7333
Contact: James R. McMullen
Group considers recommendations from the state and county reservation groups with respect to the operational features of the Agricultural Conservation Program (ACP), the Emergency Conservation Program (ECP), and the Forestry Incentives Program (FIP) of the Department of Agriculture. Group meets annually. It is an advisory group of the Agricultural Stabilization and Conservation Service, Department of Agriculture. Committee comprises twelve members and is chaired by Keith Bjerke of the Agricultural Stablilization and Conservation Service.

★1009★ National Drinking Water Advisory Council
Office of Drinking Water
Environmental Protection Agency
Washington, DC 20460
Phone: (202)382-2285
Contact: Charlene Shaw, Designated Foundation Official
Council provides practical and independent advice to the Environmental Protection Agency on matters and policies relating to drinking water quality and hygiene, and maintains an awareness of developing issues and problems relating to drinking water. It reviews and advises the Administrator on regulations and guidelines that are required by the Act; makes recommendations concerning necessary special studies and research; recommends policies with respect to the promulgation of drinking water standards; and assists in identifying emerging environmental or health problems related to potentially hazardous constituents in drinking water.

★1010★ National Ocean Pollution Policy Board
National Ocean Pollution Program Office
National Oceanic & Atmospheric Administration
15th & Constitution, N.W.
Washington, DC 20230
Phone: (202)673-5243
Contact: W. Lawrence Pugh, Staff Contact
Board is responsible for coordinated planning and progress review for the National Ocean Pollution Program, a comprehensive, coordinated, and effective ocean pollution research and development and monitoring program of the National Oceanic and Atmospheric Administration established under authority of P.L. 95-273, the National Ocean Pollution Planning Act of 1978. Board also reviews all department and agency budget requests submitted to it for carrying out federal pollution research and development and monitoring and consults with and seeks the advice of users and producers of ocean pollution data, information, and services.

★1011★ National Park Service Subsistence Resource Commission Aniakchak National Monument
National Park Service
2525 Gambell St.
Anchorage, AK 99503
Phone: (907)257-2548
Contact: Alan Eliason, Designated Federal Employee
Commission was established to devise and recommend to the Secretary of the Interior and the Governor of Alaska a program for subsistence hunting within Aniakchak National Monument.

★1012★ National Park Service Subsistence Resource Commission Cape Krusenstern National Monument
National Park Service
2525 Gambell St.
Anchorage, AK 99503
Phone: (907)257-2548

Contact: Ralph Tingey, Designated Federal Employee
Commission was established to devise and recommend to the Secretary of the Interior and the Governor of Alaska a program for subsistence hunting within the Cape-Krusenstern National Monument.

★1013★ National Park Service Subsistence Resource Commission Denali National Park
National Park Service
2525 Gambell St.
Anchorage, AK 99503
Phone: (907)257-2548
Contact: Russ Berry, Designated Federal Employee
Commission was established to recommend to the Secretary of the Interior and the Governor of Alaska a program for subsistence hunting within Denali National Park.

★1014★ National Park Service Subsistence Resource Commission Gates of the Arctic National Park
National Park Service
2525 Gambell St.
Anchorage, AK 99503
Phone: (907)257-2548
Contact: Roger Siglin, Designated Federal Employee
Commission was established to devise and recommend to the Secretary of the Interior and the Governor of Alaska a program for subsistence hunting within Gates of the Arctic National Park.

★1015★ National Park Service Subsistence Resource Commission Kobuk Valley National Park
National Park Service
2525 Gambell St.
Anchorage, AK 99503
Phone: (907)257-2548
Contact: Ralph Tingey, Designated Federal Employee
Commission was established to devise and recommend to the Secretary of the Interior and the Governor of Alaska a program for subsistence hunting within Kobuk Valley National Park.

★1016★ National Park Service Subsistence Resource Commission Lake Clark National Park
National Park Service
2525 Gambell St.
Anchorage, AK 99503
Phone: (907)257-2548
Contact: Andy Hutchison, Designated Federal Employee
Commission was established to devise and recommend to the Secretary of the Interior and the Governor of Alaska a program for subsistence hunting within Lake Clark National Park.

★1017★ National Park Service Subsistence Resource Commission Wrangell-St. Elias National Park
National Park Service
2525 Gambell St.
Anchorage, AK 99503
Phone: (907)257-2548
Contact: Karen Wade, Designated Federal Employee
Commission was established to devise and recommend to the Secretary of the Interior and the Governor of Alaska a program for subsistence hunting within Wrangell-St. Elias National Park.

★1018★ National Park System Advisory Board
National Park Service
Department of the Interior
1849 C St., N.W.
Washington, DC 20240
Phone: (202)343-4028
Contact: James M. Ridenour, Designated Federal Officer
Board was established to advise the Secretary of the Interior on matters relating to the National Park System and to the administration of the Historic Sites Act of 1935. It makes recommendations on the designation of national historic landmarks and natural landmarks. It also makes recommendations on the national historical significance of proposed national historic trails.

★1019★ National Petroleum Council (NPC)
1625 K St., N.W.
Washington, DC 20006
Phone: (202)393-6100
Council was established to advise, inform, and make recommendations to the Secretary of Energy or to the Assistant Secretary with respect to any matter relating to oil and gas or the oil and gas industries submitted to it by, or approved by, the Secretary of Energy. Matters considered by the Council include a wide range of technical and policy questions.

★1020★ National Public Lands Advisory Council
Bureau of Land Management, MS 5558
Department of the Interior
Washington, DC 20240
Phone: (202)208-5101
Contact: Nan Morrison, Staff Contact
Council advises the Secretary of the Interior, through the Director, Bureau of Land Management, on implementation of the Land Policy and Management Act of 1976 (P.L. 94-579), as well as on policies and programs of a national scope related to the resources and uses of public lands under the jurisdiction of the Bureau of Land Management.

★1021★ National Response Team for Oil and Hazardous Substances Incidents (NRT)
Assistant Administrator for Solid Waste & Emergency Respon
Environmental Protection Agency (05-120)
Washington, DC 20460
Phone: (202)475-8600
Fax: (202)252-0927
Contact: Jim Makris, Staff Contact
Team serves as the national body for intergovernmental coordination of response actions. It is responsible for planning and preparedness actions by federal agencies to protect the public health and the environment from the effects of oil and hazardous substances incidents and can be activated to assist regional forces during specific incidents.

★1022★ National Strategic Materials and Minerals Program Advisory Committee
Office of Water & Science
Department of the Interior
18th & C Sts., N.W.
Washington, DC 20240
Phone: (202)208-3136
Contact: Brenda Kay, Staff Contact
Committee was established to advise the Secretary of the Interior with respect to strategic and critical minerals and materials. Specifically, Committee evaluates the progress made in implementing the National Materials and Minerals Program Plan (in which the President called on the private sector to develop and supply materials essential to national defense), and identifies and recommends action to counter barriers that would hinder implementation of the Plan; identifies and develops recommendations on existing or potential deficiencies in the technological capability to process them, and reviews and recommends corrective action for completed and proposed stockpile transactions.

★1023★ Negotiated Rulemaking Advisory Committee for the Volatile Organic Chemical Equipment Leak Rule
Regulatory Negotiation Project
Environmental Protection Agency
401 M. St., S.W.
Washington, DC 20460
Phone: (202)887-1033
Contact: Philip Harter, Staff Contact
Committee assists in the development of a new regulatory approach to control fugitive emissions of toxic volatile organic compounds from chemical equipment leaks (valves, etc.). Such leaks contribute significantly to air quality problems. For example, some estimates indicate that fugitive emissions account for approximately one-third of all routine (nonaccidental) toxic air emissions.

★1024★ New England Fishery Management Council
5 Broadway (Route 1)
Saugus, MA 01906
Phone: (617)231-0422
Contact: Douglas G. Marshall, Exec. Dir.
Council develops and monitors fishery management plans for fisheries in the Atlantic Ocean seaward of Maine, New Hampshire, Massachusetts, Rhode Island, and Connecticut and amends the plans in accordance with the changing nature of marine resources. Council also prepares comments on foreign fishing applications and conducts public hearings and meetings regarding fishery management planning and/or the development of such plans.

★1025★ Nez Perce National Historic Trail Council
Forest Service
Department of Agriculture
PO Box 7669
Missoula, MT 59807
Phone: (406)329-3582
Contact: James M. Dolan, Staff Contact
Council secures advice from the private and public sectors on issues relating to the development and administration of the Nez Perce (Nee-Me-Poo) National Historic Trail, which passes through the States of Idaho, Montana, Oregon, and Wyoming. Council makes recommendations to the Secretary of Agriculture on policy, planning, and management with regard to the Trail.

★1026★ North American Wetlands Conservation Council
4401 N. Fairfax Dr.
Arlington, VA 22203
Phone: (703)358-1784
Contact: Dr. Robert Streeter, Coordinator
Council recommends wetlands conservation projects to the Migratory Bird Conservation Commission. Its recommendations are based on the following considerations: the extent to which any wetlands conservation project fulfills the purposes of the Wetlands Conservation Act and the North American Waterfowl Management Plan; the availability of sufficient nonfederal monies; the extent to which any project involves public-private partnership; the

consistency of any project in the United States with the National Wetlands Priority Conservation Plan developed under the Emergency Wetlands Resources Act; the extent to which any project would aid the conservation of migratory nongame birds and other fish and wildlife species, that are listed, or are candidates to be listed, as threatened or endangered under the Endangered Species Act; the recommendations of any public-private partnerships in Canada, Mexico, or the United States, which are actively participating in wetlands conservation projects; and the substantiality of the character and design of any project.

★1027★ North Atlantic Regional Technical Working Group
Atlantic OCS Region
381 Elden St. Pkwy.
Atrium Bldg.
Herdon, VA 22070
Phone: (703)787-1113
Fax: (703)787-1104
Contact: Angie Graziano, Staff Contact
Group advises the Secretary of the Interior on technical matters of regional concern regarding prelease sale activities, transportation-related study requirements, and transportation management plans for the North Atlantic leasing region (Maine, New Hampshire, Massachusetts, Rhode Island, Connecticut, New York, New Jersey).

★1028★ North Pacific Fishery Management Council
PO Box 103136
Anchorage, AK 99510
Phone: (907)271-2809
Fax: (907)271-2817
Contact: Clarence Pautzke, Exec. Dir.
Council develops and monitors fishery management plans for fisheries in the Arctic Ocean, Bering Sea, and Pacific Ocean seaward of Alaska and amends the plans in accordance with the changing nature of marine resources. Council also prepares comments on foreign fishing applications and conducts public hearings and meetings regarding fishery management planning and/or the development of such plans.

★1029★ Northeast Interstate Low-Level Radioactive Waste Commission
703 Hebron Ave.
Glastonbury, CT 06033
Phone: (203)633-2060
Fax: (203)633-2737
Contact: Ronald Gingerich, Exec. Dir.
Commission was established to develop, adopt, and maintain a regional management plan to ensure safe and effective management of low-level radioactive waste within the northeast region of the United States, pursuant to the Northeast Interstate Low-Level Radioactive Waste Management Compact (member states are Connecticut and New Jersey); to enter into agreements with any person, state, regional body, or group of states for the importation of low-level radioactive waste into the region and for the right of access to facilities outside the region for waste generated within the region; to grant an individual generator or group of generators in the region the right to export waste to a facility located outside the region; and to appear as an intervenor in party of interest before any court of law, federal, state, or local agency, board, or commission that has jurisdiction over the management of waste.

★1030★ Northern Alaska Advisory Council
Bureau of Land Management
Department of the Interior
1150 University Ave.
Fairbanks, AK 99709
Phone: (907)474-2231
Contact: William J. Robertson, Designated Federal Contact
Council provides representative citizen counsel and advice to the Bureau of Land Management district managers for the Arctic, Kobuk, and Steese-White Mountains districts, regarding multiple-use management of the public lands resources within northern Alaska.

★1031★ Northwest Interstate Low-Level Waste Compact Committee
Low-Level Radioactive Waste Program
Nuclear & Mixed Waste Management Program
Washington Department of Ecology
Mail Stop PV-11
Olympia, WA 98504-8711
Contact: Elaine Carlin, Exec. Dir.
Committee considers matters that arise under the Northwest Interstate Compact on Low-Level Radioactive Waste Management authorized by P.L. 99-240. The Compact provides the means for a cooperative effort among Alaska, Hawaii, Idaho, Montana, Oregon, Washington, and Utah so that the protection of citizens of the states and the maintenance of the viability of the states' economies will be enhanced while sharing the responsibilities of low-level radioactive waste management.

★1032★ Nuclear Safety Research Review Committee
Office of Nuclear Regulatory Research
U. S. Nuclear Regulatory Commission
Washington, DC 20555
Phone: (301)492-3700
Contact: Dr. Ralph O. Meyer, Designated Foundation Official
Committee advises the Director, Office of Nuclear Regulatory Research, on matters of overall management and direction of the Nuclear Safety Research Program. It will address the following questions: (1) Is the Program being planned, implemented, and managed in accordance with the Nuclear Regulatory Commission's philosophy of nuclear regulatory research? (2) Is the Program meeting the needs of the users of research? (3) Is there an appropriate long-range program, and is it going in the right direction? and (4) Is the Program free of bias and have the research products been given adequate, unbiased peer review?

★1033★ Nuclear Waste Technical Review Board (NWTRB)
1100 Wilson Blvd., Ste. 910
Arlington, VA 22201
Phone: (703)235-4473
Fax: (703)235-4495
Contact: William D. Barnard, Exec. Dir.
Board provides scientific and technical advice on the nation's spent nuclear and high-level waste disposal program. The Board's examination of the Department of Energy's program is to include a review of the Department's characterization of Yucca Mountain (located in southern Nevada) as a potential repository for long-term disposal of nuclear waste. Board also evaluates activities relating to the packaging and transportation of nuclear waste.

★1034★ Ohio River Valley Water Sanitation Commission
49 E. St., Ste. 300
Cincinnati, OH 45202
Phone: (513)421-1151
Contact: Alan H. Vicory Jr., Acting Exec. Dir.
Commission conducts a survey of the Ohio River Valley Water Sanitation District, the territory within the states that surrounds the Ohio River; studies pollution problems of the district; and reports on the prevention or reduction of stream pollution therein. Commission consults with any national or regional planning body and any department of the federal government authorized to deal with matters relating to pollution problems of the district. Commission also drafts and makes recommendations to the governors of the states involved concerning uniform legislation dealing with pollution of rivers, streams and waters, and other pollution problems within the district.

★1035★ Ouachita National Forest, LeFlore County, Oklahoma, Multiple Use Advisory Council
Ouachita National Forest
PO Box 1270
Hot Springs, AR 71902
Phone: (501)321-5281
Contact: Gary Pierson, Staff Contact
Council provides information and recommendations to the Secretary of Agriculture on conservation, timber, fish and wildlife, tourism and recreation, economic development, and any other matters having to do with the management and operation of the Ouachita National Forest in LeFlore County, Oklahoma.

★1036★ Outer Continental Shelf Advisory Board (OCS)
Minerals Management Service
Associate Director for Offshore Minerals Management
Department of the Interior, Rm. 4230
Washington, DC 20240
Phone: (202)343-3530
Contact: Thomas Gernhofer, Exec. Sec.
Board was established to advise the Secretary of the Interior, Director, Minerals Management Service, and other officers of the Department in the performance of discretionary functions under the Outer Continental Shelf Lands Act, including all aspects of leasing, exploration, development, and protection of outer continental shelf (OCS) resources. Concerns include resource evaluation, environmental assessment, rules and operations, and inspection and enforcement activities.

★1037★ Outer Continental Shelf Advisory Board Policy Committee (OCS)
Office of OCS Advisory Board Support
Minerals Management Service
Department of the Interior
18th & C Sts., N.W., Rm. 2070
Washington, DC 20240
Phone: (202)343-3530
Contact: Thomas Gernhofer, Exec. Sec.
Committee provides policy advice representing the collective viewpoint of coastal states, environmental interests, industry representatives, and other parties to the Secretary of the Interior, through the Director of the Minerals Management Service, and to other officers of the Department of the Interior in the performance of discretionary functions under the Outer Continental Shelf (OCS) Lands Act. This includes all aspects of leasing, exploration, development, assessment, leasing management, rules and operations, and inspection and enforcement activities.

★1038★ Outer Continental Shelf Advisory Board Scientific Committee (OCS)
Branch of Environmental Studies, MS4310
Environmental Policy & Programs Division
Minerals Managment Service
381 Elden St.
Herndon, VA 22070
Phone: (703)787-1716
Contact: Phyllis Treichel, Designated Federal Official
Committee advises the Director, Minerals Managment Service, on the feasibility, appropriateness, and scientific value of the Minerals Management Service's Outer Continental Shelf (OCS) Environmental Studies Program. Committee reviews the relevance of data produced by the program and recommends changes in its scope, direction, and emphasis.

★1039★ Pacific Fishery Management Council
Metro Center, Ste. 420
2000 S.W. First Ave.
Portland, OR 97201
Phone: (503)326-6352
Contact: Lawrence Six, Exec. Dir.
Council prepares and monitors fishery management plans for fisheries in the Pacific Ocean seaward of California, Oregon, Washington, and Idaho and amends the plans in accordance with the changing nature of marine resources. Council also prepares comments on foreign fishing applications and conducts public hearings and meetings regarding fishery management planning and/or the development of such plans.

★1040★ Pacific Northwest Electric Power and Conservation Planning Council
Suite 1100
851 S.W. Sixth Ave.
Portland, OR 97204
Phone: (503)222-5161
Contact: Edward Sheets, Exec. Dir.
Council was established to prepare and adopt a regional conservation and electric power plan and a program to protect, mitigate, and enhance fish and wildlife in the Columbia River Basin, and to effectively carry out the Council's responsibilities and functions under the Act, which is to assist the electrical consumers of the Pacific Northwest (Oregon, Washington, Idaho, and portions of Montana, Nevada, Utah, and Wyoming) through use of the Federal Columbia River Power System to achieve cost-effective energy conservation, encourage the development of renewable energy resources, assure the region of an efficient and adequate power supply, and restore fish and wildlife harmed by hydropower development and operations.

★1041★ Pacific Northwest Outer Continental Shelf Task Force
Minerals Management Service
Department of the Interior
18th & C Sts., N.W. Rm. 4211
Washington, DC 20241
Phone: (202)208-3500
Contact: Ed Cassidy, Designated Federal Employee
Task Force provides advice to the Secretary of the Interior and other officers of the Department of the Interior in the performance of discretionary functions of the Outer Continental Shelf Lands Act, as amended (43 USC 1331), including all aspects of shelf oil and gas leasing, exploration, development, and protection of the resources of the Outer Continental Shelf off Washington and Oregon.

★1042★ Pacific Regional Technical Working Group
Pacific OCS Region
Minerals Management Service
770 Paseo Camarillo
Camarillo, CA 93010
Phone: (805)389-7502
Fax: (805)389-7638
Contact: J. Lisle Reed, Designated Federal Officer
Group advises the Secretary of the Interior on technical matters of regional concern regarding prelease and postlease activities, transportation-related study requirements, and transportation management plans for the Pacific Outer Continental leasing region (California, Oregon, Washington).

★1043★ Pesticides/Toxics Research Committee
Office of Pesticides & Toxic Substances
Office of Research & Development, R.D. 674
Environmental Protection Agency
401 M St., S.W.
Washington, DC 20460
Phone: (202)382-5898
Contact: Hugh McKinnon, Staff Contact
Committee serves as a vehicle for communicating research needs, describing research programs to meet those needs, and advising the Assistant Administrator for the Office of Research and Development on matters regarding pesticides and toxic substances.

★1044★ Phoenix District Advisory Council
Bureau of Land Management
Department of the Interior
2015 W. Deer Valley Rd.
Phoenix, AZ 85027
Phone: (602)863-4464
Contact: Henri R. Bisson, Designated Federal Employee
Council provides representative citizen counsel and advice to the Bureau of Land Management district manager regarding planning and management of the public lands resources within the Phoenix district.

★1045★ Policy Review Board of the Gulf of Mexico Program
Gulf of Mexico Program
Bldg. 1103, Rm. 202
Stennis Space Center, MS 39529
Phone: (601)688-3726
Contact: Dr. Douglas A. Lipka, Staff Contact
Board guides and reviews activities of the Gulf of Mexico Program, established by EPA regions IV and VI and designed to develop and implement a comprehensive strategy to manage and protect the Gulf of Mexico. Board approves program goals and objectives and establishes priorities and direction for the Program.

★1046★ President's Commission on Environmental Quality
Council on Environmental Quality
722 Jackson Place, N.W.
Washington, DC 20503
Contact: Larry Flick, Contact
Commission advises the President, through the Chair, Council on Environmental Quality, on matters of national significance involving environmental quality.

★1047★ Prince William Sound Oil Spill Recovery Institute Advisory Board
Prince William Sound Center
PO Box 705
Cordova, AK 99574-0705
Phone: (907)424-5800
Contact: Gary L. Thomas Ph.D., Staff Contact
Board determines the policies of the Prince William Sound Oil Spill Recovery Institute which was established to (1) conduct research and carry out educational and demonstration projects designed to identify and develop the best available techniques, equipment, and materials for dealing with oil spills in arctic and subarctic marine environments; and (2) complement federal and state damage assessment efforts and determine, document, assess, and understand the long-range effects of the "Exxon Valdez" oil spill on the natural resources of Prince William Sound and its adjacent waters and environment, economy, and the lifestyle and well-being of the people who are dependent on them.

★1048★ Prineville District Advisory Council
Bureau of Land Management
Department of the Interior
PO Box 550
185 E. Fourth St.
Prineville, OR 97754
Phone: (503)447-4115
Contact: James Hancock, Designated Federal Employee
Council provides representative citizen counsel and advice to the Bureau of Land Management district manager regarding planning and management of the public lands within the Prineville district.

★1049★ Rawlins District Advisory Council
Bureau of Land Management
Department of the Interior
1300 N. Third St.
PO Box 670
Rawlins, WY 82301
Phone: (307)324-3872
Contact: Richard Bastin, Designated Federal Employee
Council provides representative citizen counsel and advice to the Bureau of Land Management district manager regarding planning and management of the public lands resources within the Rawlins district.

★1050★ Reclamation Reform Act Task Force
Office of the Assistant Secretary for Water & Science
Rm. 648
Department of the Interior Bureau of Reclamation
1849 C St., N.W., Mail Stop 7641
Washington, DC 20240
Phone: (202)208-4464
Contact: Wayne N. Marchant, Staff Contact
Task Force enforces irrigation rules and regulations set up by the Department of the Interior pursuant to the Reclamation Reform Act of 1982. It reviews, finalizes, and directs the implementation of acreage limitation auditing procedures which ensure that water subsidized by the Bureau of Reclamation, Department of the Interior, is provided only to qualified farms. In addition, Task Force directs enforcement actions, develops policy recommendations for preventing abuse of reclamation laws, and determines appropriate corrective and disciplinary actions.

★1051★ Richfield District Advisory Council
Bureau of Land Management
Department of the Interior
150 E. 900 N.
Richfield, UT 84701
Phone: (801)896-8221

Contact: Jerry W. Goodman, Designated Federal Employee
Council provides representative citizen counsel and advice to the Bureau of Land Management district manager regarding planning and management of the public lands resources within the Richfield district.

★1052★ Rock Springs District Advisory Council
Bureau of Land Management
Department of the Interior
PO Box 1869
Rock Springs, WY 82902
Phone: (307)382-5350
Contact: Mike Brown, Staff Contact
Council provides representative citizen counsel and advice to the Bureau of Land Management district manager regarding planning and management of the public lands resources within the Rock Springs district.

★1053★ Rocky Mountain Low-Level Radioactive Waste Board
1675 Broadway, Ste. 1400
Denver, CO 80202-4619
Phone: (303)825-1912
Contact: Leonard Slosky, Exec. Dir.
Board was established to assemble and make available to states party to the Rocky Mountain Low-Level Radioactive Waste Compact (states authorized to enter into the Compact are Arizona, Colorado, Nevada, New Mexico, Utah, and Wyoming) and to the public information concerning low-level waste management needs, technologies, and problems; to keep an inventory of all generators within the Rocky Mountain region of the United States and all regional low-level radioactive waste regional facilities; to ascertain the needs for regional facilities and capacity to manage each of the various classes for low-level waste; to develop a regional low-level waste management plan; and to make suggestions to the appropriate officials of the party states to ensure that adequate emergency response programs are available for dealing with an emergency that might arise with respect to low-level waste transportation or management.

★1054★ Roseburg District Advisory Council
Bureau of Land Management
Department of the Interior
777 N.W. Garden Valley Blvd.
Roseburg, OR 97470
Phone: (503)672-4491
Contact: Jim Moorhouse, Designated Federal Employee
Council provides representative citizen counsel and advice to the Bureau of Land Management district manager regarding planning and management of the public lands resources within the Roseburg district.

★1055★ Roswell District Advisory Council
Bureau of Land Management
Department of the Interior
1717 W. Second St.
PO Box 1397
Roswell, NM 88201
Phone: (505)622-9042
Contact: Francis Cherry, Designated Federal Employee
Council provides representative citizen counsel and advice to the Bureau of Land Management district manager regarding planning and management of the public lands resources within the Roswell district.

★1056★ Royalty Management Advisory Committee
Minerals Management Service
Staff Operations
Denver Federal Center, Bldg. 85
PO Box 25165
Denver, CO 80225
Phone: (303)231-3410
Fax: (303)231-3781
Contact: Deborah Gibbs, Staff Contact
Committee was established as part of a management action plan for improving the Department of the Interior's Royalty Management Program (RMP), which determines, collects, and distributes the bonuses, rents, and production royalties associated with leases for oil, gas, coal, and other minerals extracted from federal and Indian lands. Committee advises the Secretary of the Interior regarding policies and procedures which affect recipients of mineral leasing revenues; lessees, operators, and other royalty payors; and the users of the Minerals Management Service fiscal and production accounting systems.

★1057★ Safford District Advisory Council
Bureau of Land Management
Department of the Interior
425 E. Fourth St.
Safford, AZ 85546
Phone: (602)428-4400
Fax: (602)428-4040
Contact: Ray Brady, Staff Contact
Council provides representative citizen counsel and advice to the Bureau of Land Management district manager regarding planning and management of the public lands resources within the Safford district.

★1058★ Salem District Advisory Council
Bureau of Land Management
Department of the Interior
1717 Fabry Rd., S.E.
Salem, OR 97302
Phone: (503)375-5646
Contact: Van W. Manning, Designated Federal Employee
Council provides representative citizen counsel and advice to the Bureau of Land Management district manager regarding planning and management of the public lands resources within the Salem district.

★1059★ Salmon District Advisory Council
Bureau of Land Management
Department of the Interior
PO Box 430
Salmon, ID 83467
Phone: (208)756-5400
Contact: Ray Jackson, Designated Federal Employee
Council provides representative citizen counsel and advice to the Bureau of Land Management district manager regarding planning and management of the public lands resources within the Salmon district.

★1060★ Salt Lake District Multiple Use Advisory Council
Bureau of Land Management
Department of the Interior
Salt Lake District Office
2370 S. 2300 W.
Salt Lake City, UT 84119
Phone: (801)977-4300
Contact: Deane Zeller, Designated Federal Employee
Council provides representative citizen counsel and advice to the Bureau of Land Management district manager regarding planning and management of the public lands resources within the Salt Lake district.

★1061★ San Pedro Riparian National Conservation Area Advisory Committee
Bureau of Land Management, Safford District
San Pedro Project Office
R.R. No. 1, Box 9853
Huachuca City, AZ 85616
Phone: (602)457-2265
Fax: (602)428-4040
Contact: Greg Yuncevich, Staff Contact
Committee provides advice to the Safford District Manager, Bureau of Land Management, on management of public lands in the San Pedro Riparian National Conservation Area.

★1062★ Santa Fe National Historic Trail Advisory Council
National Park Service, SW Region
PO Box 728
Santa Fe, NM 87501
Phone: (505)988-6886
Contact: John E. Cook, Designated Federal Officer
Council advises the Secretary of the Interior regarding matters relating to the Santa Fe National Historic Trail, New Mexico, including selection of rights-of-way, standards for the erection and maintenance of markers along the Trail, and the administration of the Trail.

★1063★ Science Advisory Board
Room 1145, W. Tower
Environmental Protection Agency
401 M Street, S.W.
Washington, DC 20460
Phone: (202)382-4126
Contact: Dr. Donald G. Barnes, Staff Dir.
Board has overall responsibility for providing expert and independent advice to the Administrator of the Environmental Protection Agency on issues relating to the scientific and technical problems facing the Agency, the strategies devised to meet these problems, the technical programs to solve problems, and the priorities among these. This responsibility is discharged by coordinating the research and the activities of the scientific advisory committees (see below under Subsidiary Units) to see that they are fulfilling their responsibilities to make recommendations concerning needed research and development activities, assess the results of specific research efforts, and assist in identifying emerging environmental problems without overlapping with each other, and reviewing the scientific basis of Agency regulations, standards, criteria, and guidance. Board also provides advice to the Senate Committee on Environment and Public Works and the House Committees on Science and Technology, Energy and Commerce, and Public Works and Transportation.

★1064★ Scientific Advisory Panel (SAP)
Office of Pesticide Programs
Environmental Protection Agency
401 M St., S.W.
Washington, DC 20460
Phone: (703)557-2244
Fax: (703)557-2147
Contact: Robert Bruce Jaeger, Designated Foundation Official
Panel comments on the human and environmental effects of proposed regulations and regulatory actions affecting the use of pesticides.

★1065★ Shoshone District Advisory Council
Bureau of Land Management
Department of the Interior
400 W. F St.
PO Box 2B
Shoshone, ID 83352
Phone: (208)886-2206
Contact: K. Lynn Bennett, Designated Federal Employee
Council provides representative citizen counsel and advice to the Bureau of Land Management district manager regarding planning and management of the public lands resources within the Shoshone district.

★1066★ Sleeping Bear Dunes National Lakeshore Advisory Commission
PO Box 277
9922 Front St.
Empire, MI 49630
Phone: (616)326-5134
Contact: Ivan D. Miller, Designated Federal Employee
Commission consults with the Secretary of the Interior concerning matters relating to the development of the Lakeshore, and with respect to land acquisition and the construction and administration of scenic roads for the Lakeshore.

★1067★ South Atlantic Fishery Management Council
One Southpark Circle, Ste. 306
Charleston, SC 29407-4699
Phone: (803)571-4366
Contact: Robert Mahood, Exec. Dir.
Council develops and monitors fishery management plans for fisheries in the Atlantic Ocean seaward of North Carolina, South Carolina, Georgia, and Florida and amends the plans in accordance with the changing nature of marine resources. Council also prepares comments on foreign fishing applications and conducts public hearings and meetings regarding fishery management planning and/or the development of such plans. Advisory panels are created by the Council to provide guidance in the fishery management plan development and amendment process and the management of specific fish species.

★1068★ South Atlantic Regional Technical Working Group
Atlantic OCS Region
381 Elden St. Pkwy
Atrium Bldg.
Herdon, VA 22070
Phone: (703)787-1113
Fax: (703)787-1104
Contact: Angie Graziano, Staff Contact
Group advises the Secretary of the Interior on technical matters of regional concern regarding prelease sale activities, transportation-related study requirements, and transportation management plans for the South Atlantic leasing region (Virginia, North Carolina, South Carolina, Georgia, Florida).

★1069★ Southeast Interstate Low-Level Radioactive Waste Management Commission
3901 Barrett Dr., Ste. 100
Raleigh, NC 27609
Phone: (919)781-7152
Contact: Kathryn Visocki, Exec. Dir.
Commission was established to develop and use procedures for determining, consistent with consideration for public health and safety, the type and number of regional facilities necessary to manage low-level radioactive waste generated in the southeast region of the United States; to provide the states which are party to the Southeast Interstate Low-Level Radioactive Waste Management Compact (states authorized to enter the Compact are Alabama, Florida, Georgia, Mississippi, North Carolina, South Carolina, Tennessee, and Virginia) with reference guidelines for evaluating alternative locations for emergency or permanent regional facilities; to enter into agreements with any person, state, or similar regional body or group of states for the importation of low-level radioactive waste into the southeast region and for the right of access to facilities outside the region for waste generated within the region; and to act or appear on behalf of any state or states party to the Compact as an intervenor or party of interest before Congress, state legislatures, any court of law, or any federal, state, or local agency, board, or commission which has jurisdiction over the management of low-level radioactive waste.

★1070★ Southern Alaska Advisory Council
Bureau of Land Management
Anchorage Dist. Office
6881 Abbott Rd.
Anchorage, AK 99513
Phone: (907)267-1258
Fax: (907)272-3430
Contact: Danielle Allen, Staff Contact
Council provides representative citizen counsel and advice to the Bureau of Land Management district manager regarding planning and management of the public lands resources within the Anchorage and Glennallen districts.

★1071★ Spokane District Advisory Council
Bureau of Land Management
Department of the Interior
4217 E. Main Ave.
Spokane, WA 99202
Phone: (509)353-2570
Contact: Joseph K. Buefing, Designated Federal Employee
Council provides representative citizen counsel and advice to the Bureau of Land Management district manager regarding planning and management of the public lands resources within the Spokane district.

★1072★ State FIFRA Issues Research and Evaluation Group (SFIREG)
PO Box 1249
Hardwick, VA 05843
Phone: (802)472-6956
Contact: Philip H. Gray, Exec. Sec.
Group serves as a means of communication between state pesticide regulatory offices and the Environmental Protection Agency regarding the Federal Insecticide, Fungcide, and Rodenticide Act and the Environmental Protection Agency policies and procedures affecting the states.

★1073★ Steering Committee for the "Protecting Our National Parks" Symposium
Pacific NW Region
National Park Service
83 S. King St., Ste. 212
Seattle, WA 98104
Phone: (206)553-4653
Fax: (206)553-4896
Contact: William J. Briggle, Chair
Committee advises the Director, National Park Service, on specific matters pertaining to the "Protecting Our National Parks" Symposium, which will be held as part of the National Park Service's 75th anniversary observances. Its recommendations are guided by the findings of the working groups which it convenes.

★1074★ Susanville District Advisory Council
Bureau of Land Management
Department of the Interior
705 Hall St.
Susanville, CA 96130
Phone: (916)257-5381
Contact: Herrick E. Hanks, Designated Federal Employee
Council provides representative citizen counsel and advice to the Bureau of Land Management district manager regarding planning and management of the public lands resources within the Susanville district.

★1075★ Tahoe Regional Planning Agency Advisory Planning Commission
PO Box 1038
Zephyr Cove, NV 89448-1038
Phone: (702)588-4547
Contact: Jerry Wells, Deputy Dir.
Commission was established to advise the members of the Tahoe Regional Planning Agency on adopting and enforcing a regional plan of resource conservation and orderly development, exercising effective environmental controls and any other matters enumerated in the Act establishing the Agency.

★1076★ Take Pride in America Advisory Board
Department of the Interior, 5123-M1B
PO Box 1339-M
Jessup, MD 20794
Phone: (202)208-3726
Contact: Clifton White, Dir.
Board advises the Secretary of the Interior on the plans and procedures designed to further motivate participation in the Take Pride in America program. The program is designed to focus national attention on the problems of land abuse and misuse, and on the opportunities for promoting voluntary participation by individuals, organizations, and communities in caring for our natural and cultural resources.

★1077★ Trail of Tears National Historic Trail Advisory Council
Southeast Region
National Park Service
Department of the Interior
75 Spring St., S.W.
Atlanta, GA 30303
Phone: (404)331-5185
Contact: Robert Baker, Designated Federal Employee
Council consults with the Secretary of the Interior in regard to matters relating to the Trail of Tears National Historic Trail (The trail consists of water and overland routes travelled by the Cherokee Nation during its removal from ancestral lands in the east to Oklahoma during 1838-39, generally located within the corridor of Georgia, North Carolina, Alabama, Tennessee, Kentucky, Illinois, Missouri, Arkansas, and Oklahoma.). Council advises on the selection of rights-of-way, standards for the erection and maintenance of markers along the Trail, and the administration of the Trail.

★1078★ Trinity River Basin Fish and Wildlife Task Force
Mid-Pacific Region
Bureau of Reclamation
Department of the Interior
2800 Cottage Way
Sacramento, CA 95825
Phone: (916)978-5135
Contact: Lawrence F. Hancock, Staff Contact
Task Force assists the Secretary of the Interior in the formulation and implementation of the Trinity River Basin Fish and Wildlife

Management Program, which is designed to restore the fish and wildlife populations in the Trinity River Basin to the levels approximating those which existed immediately before the construction of the Central Valley project in California.

★1079★ Ukiah District Advisory Council
Bureau of Land Management
Department of the Interior
555 Leslie St.
Ukiah, CA 95482
Phone: (707)462-3873
Contact: Alfred W. Wright, Designated Federal Employee
Council provides representative citizen counsel and advice to the Bureau of Land Management district manager regarding planning and management of the public lands resources within the Ukiah district.

★1080★ United States Alternative Motor Fuels Council
Interagency Commission on Alternative Motor Fuels
Office of the Deputy Secretary
Department of Energy
1000 Independence Ave., S.W.
Washington, DC 20585
Council advises and reports to the Interagency Commission on Alternative Motor Fuels on matters related to alternative motor fuels.

★1081★ Upper Delaware Citizens Advisory Council
PO Box 84
Narrowsburg, NY 12764
Phone: (717)729-8251
Fax: (717)729-8565
Contact: John Hutzky, Designated Federal Employee
Council encourages maximum public involvement in the development and implementation of the plans and programs for the Upper Delaware River. Council reports to the Delaware River Basin Commission, the Secretary of the Interior, and the Governors of New York and Pennsylvania on the preparation of a management plan and on programs which relate to land and water use in the Upper Delaware region.

★1082★ Vale District Advisory Council
Bureau of Land Management
Department of the Interior
100 E. Oregon St.
Vale, OR 97918
Phone: (503)473-3144
Contact: William C. Calkins, Designated Federal Employee
Council provides representative citizen counsel and advice to the Bureau of Land Management district manager regarding planning and management of the public lands resources within the Vale district.

★1083★ Varroa Mite Negotiated Rulemaking Advisory Committee
Animal & Plant Health Inspection Service
Department of Agriculture
Federal Bldg., Rm. 816
6505 Belcrest Rd.
Hyattsville, MD 20782
Phone: (301)436-8247
Contact: Doug Ladner, Staff Contact
Committee was established to develop a recommended rulemaking proposal designed to prevent the interstate spread of Varroa mites (Varroa jacobsoni, Oudemans), a parasite of honeybees.

★1084★ Vernal District Advisory Council
Bureau of Land Management
Department of the Interior
170 S. 500 E.
Vernal, UT 84078
Phone: (801)789-1362
Contact: David E. Little, Designated Federal Employee
Council provides representative citizen counsel and advice to the Bureau of Land Management district manager regarding planning and management of the public lands resources within the Vernal district.

★1085★ Western Pacific Regional Fishery Management Council
1164 Bishop St. Ste. 1405
Honolulu, HI 96813
Phone: (808)523-1368
Fax: (803)526-0824
Contact: Kitty Simonds, Exec. Dir.
Council develops and monitors fishery management plans for fisheries in the Pacific Ocean seaward of Hawaii, American Samoa, Guam and the Commonwealth of the Northern Mariana Islands and amends the plans in accordance with the changing nature of marine resources. Council also prepares comments on foreign fishing applications and conducts public hearings and meetings regarding fishery management planning and/or the development of such plans.

★1086★ Winding Stair Tourism and Recreation Advisory Council
Ouachita National Forest
PO Box 1270
Hot Springs, AR 71902
Phone: (501)321-5317
Contact: Frank Yerby, Designated Federal Officer
Council was established to assist in the preparation of the tourism and recreation section of the Ouachita National Forest Land and Resource Management Plan, consistent with the purposes for which the wilderness areas, botanical areas, and National Scenic Area are designated.

★1087★ Winnemucca District Advisory Council
Bureau of Land Management
Department of the Interior
705 E. Fourth St.
Winnemucca, NV 89445
Phone: (702)623-3676
Contact: Ronald Wenker, Designated Federal Employee
Council provides representative citizen counsel and advice to the Bureau of Land Management district manager regarding planning and management of the public lands resources within the Winnemucca district.

★1088★ Worland District Multiple Use Advisory Council
Bureau of Land Management
Department of the Interior
101 S. 23rd St.
PO Box 119
Worland, WY 82401
Phone: (307)347-9871
Fax: (307)347-6195
Contact: Darrell Barnes, Designated Federal Employee
Council provides representative citizen counsel and advice to the Bureau of Land Management district manager regarding planning and management of the public lands resources within the Worland district.

★1089★ Yuma District Advisory Council
Bureau of Land Management
Department of the Interior
3150 Winsor Ave.
Yuma, AZ 85365
Phone: (602)726-6300
Contact: Herman Kast, Designated Federal Employee
Council provides representative citizen counsel and advice to the Bureau of Land Management district manager regarding planning and management of the public lands resources within the Yuma district.

State Government Organizations

Alabama

★1090★ Agriculture and Industries Department
Pesticide Laboratory
PO Box 370
Auburn, AL 36830
Phone: (205)844-4705
Contact: Danny Lecompte, Director

★1091★ Attorney General's Office
Environmental Protection Division
State House
Montgomery, AL 36130
Phone: (205)242-7395
Contact: R. Craig Kneisel, Director

★1092★ Conservation and Natural Resources Department
64 N. Union St., Rm. 702
Montgomery, AL 36130
Phone: (205)242-3486
Contact: Commissioner Jim Martin

★1093★ Conservation and Natural Resources Department
Game & Fish Division
64 N. Union St., Rm. 702
Montgomery, AL 36130
Phone: (205)242-3465
Contact: Charles D. Kelly, Director

★1094★ Conservation and Natural Resources Dept.
Lands Division
64 N. Union St., Rm. 702
Montgomery, AL 36130
Phone: (205)242-3484
Contact: James Griggs, Director

★1095★ Conservation and Natural Resources Department
Marine Resources Division
PO Box 189
Dauphin Island, AL 36528
Phone: (205)861-2882
Contact: Hugh A. Swingle, Director

★1096★ Conservation and Natural Resources Dept.
State Parks Division
64 N. Union St., Rm. 702
Montgomery, AL 36130
Phone: (205)242-3334
Contact: Gary Leach, Director

★1097★ Environmental Management Department
1751 Cong. W.L. Dickinson Dr.
Montgomery, AL 36130
Phone: (205)271-7706
Contact: Leigh Pegues, Director

★1098★ Environmental Management Department
Air Division
1751 Cong. W.L. Dickinson Dr.
Montgomery, AL 36130
Phone: (205)271-7861
Contact: Richard E. Grusnick, Chief

★1099★ Environmental Management Department
Land Division
1751 Cong. W.L. Dickinson Dr.
Montgomery, AL 36130
Phone: (205)271-7730
Contact: Sue Robertson, Chief

★1100★ Environmental Management Department
Public Affairs Office
1751 Cong. W.L. Dickinson Dr.
Montgomery, AL 36130
Phone: (205)271-7706
Contact: Catherine G. Lamar, Chief

★1101★ Environmental Management Department
Solid Waste Division
1751 Cong. W.L. Dickinson Dr.
Montgomery, AL 36130
Phone: (205)271-7823

★1102★ Environmental Management Department
Water Division
1751 Cong. W.L. Dickinson Dr.
Montgomery, AL 36130
Phone: (205)271-7823
Contact: Charles Horn, Chief

★1103★ Forestry Commission
513 Madison Ave.
Montgomery, AL 36130
Phone: (205)240-9304
Fax: (205)240-9390
Contact: C.W. Moody, State Forester

★1104★ Forestry Commission
Forest Resource Protection Division
513 Madison Ave.
Montgomery, AL 36130
Phone: (205)240-9335
Fax: (205)240-9390
Contact: David Frederick, Director

★1105★ Public Health Department
Management Services Office
Environmental and Health Service Standards Bureau
434 Monroe St.
Montgomery, AL 36130-1701
Phone: (205)242-5004
Fax: (205)242-5000
Contact: James W. Cooper, Director

★1106★ Public Health Department
Management Services Office
Environmental and Health Service Standards Bureau
Community Environmental Protection Division
434 Monroe St.
Montgomery, AL 36130-1701
Phone: (205)242-5007
Fax: (205)242-5000
Contact: Wade Pitchford, Director

★1107★ Public Health Department
Management Services Office
Environmental and Health Service Standards Bureau
Radiation Control Division
434 Monroe St.
Montgomery, AL 36130-1701
Phone: (205)242-5315
Fax: (205)242-5000
Contact: Aubrey V. Godwin, Director

★1108★ Soil and Water Conservation Committee
PO Box 3336
Montgomery, AL 36193
Phone: (205)242-2620
Fax: (205)240-3332
Contact: James Plaster, Exec. Sec.

Alaska

★1109★ Commerce and Economic Development Department
Oil and Gas Conservation Commission
3001 Porcupine Dr.
Anchorage, AK 99501
Phone: (907)279-1433
Fax: (907)276-7542
Contact: David W. Johnston, Chm. /Commissioner

★1110★ Enviromental Conservation Department
3220 Hospital Dr.
PO Box O
Juneau, AK 99811-1800
Phone: (907)465-2600
Fax: (907)586-1391
Contact: John A. Sander, Commissioner

★1111★ Environmental Conservation Department
Environmental Health Division
3220 Hospital Dr.
PO Box O
Juneau, AK 99811-1800
Phone: (907)465-2609
Fax: (907)586-1391
Contact: Douglas Donegan, Director

★1112★ Environmental Conservation Department
Environmental Quality Division
3320 Hospital Dr.
PO Box O
Juneau, AK 99811-1800
Phone: (907)465-2640
Fax: (907)586-1391
Contact: Keith Kelton, Director

★1113★ Fish and Game Department
Capital Office Park
PO Box 3-2000
Juneau, AK 99802-2000
Phone: (907)465-4100
Fax: (907)586-6595
Contact: Ron Somerville, Deputy Commissioner

★1114★ Fish and Game Department
Oil Spill Impact Assessment & Restoration Division
Capitol Office Park
PO Box 3-2000
Juneau, AK 99802-2000
Phone: (907)465-4120
Fax: (907)586-6595
Contact: Gregg Erickson, Director

★1115★ Fish and Game Department
Wildlife Conservation Division
333 Raspberry Rd.
Anchorage, AK 99502
Phone: (907)267-2231
Contact: W. Lewis Pamplin, Director

★1116★ Natural Resources Department
400 Willoughby Ave., 5th Fl.
Juneau, AK 99801
Phone: (907)465-2400
Fax: (907)586-2754
Contact: Harold C. Heinze, Commissioner

★1117★ Natural Resources Department
Forestry Division
3601 C St., Ste. 1058
PO Box 107005
Anchorage, AK 99510-7005
Phone: (907)762-2501
Fax: (907)762-2507
Contact: Bob Dick, State Forester

★1118★ Natural Resources Department
Land and Water Division
3601 C St.
PO Box 107005
Anchorage, AK 99510-7005
Phone: (907)762-2692
Fax: (970)762-2529
Contact: Gary Gustafson, Director

★1119★ Natural Resources Department
Parks and Outdoor Recreation Division
3601 C St.
PO Box 107001
Anchorage, AK 99510-7001
Phone: (907)762-2600
Fax: (907)762-2535
Contact: Neil Johannsen, Director

★1120★ Natural Resources Department
Public Affairs Information Office
3601 C St., Ste. 1210
PO Box 107005
Anchorage, AK 99510-7005
Phone: (907)762-2452
Contact: Carol D. Larsen, Public Affairs Information Officer

★1121★ Public Safety Department
Fish & Wildlife Protection Division
5700 E. Tudor Rd.
Anchorage, AK 99507
Phone: (907)259-5509
Contact: Col. Jack Jordan, Director

Arizona

★1122★ Arizona State Parks
800 W. Washington, Ste. 415
Phoenix, AZ 85007
Phone: (602)542-4174
Contact: Ken Travous, Exec. Dir.

★1123★ Environment Commission
1645 W. Jefferson, Rm. 416
Phoenix, AZ 85007
Phone: (602)542-2102
Fax: (602)542-2104
Contact: Marcia A. Dillman, Exec. Dir.

★1124★ Environmental Quality Department
2005 N. Central Ave.
Phoenix, AZ 85004
Phone: (602)257-6917
Fax: (602)257-6874
Contact: Randolph Wood, Director

★1125★ Environmental Quality Department
Air Quality Office
2005 N. Central Ave.
Phoenix, AZ 85004
Phone: (602)257-2308
Fax: (602)257-6874
Contact: Nancy Wrona, Director

★1126★ Environmental Quality Department
Waste Programs Office
2005 N. Central Ave.
Pheonix, AZ 85004
Phone: (602)257-2318
Fax: (602)257-6874
Contact: Norman Weiss, Director

★1127★ Environmental Quality Department
Water Quality Office
2005 N. Central Ave.
Phoenix, AZ 85004
Phone: (602)257-2305
Fax: (602)257-6874
Contact: Ron Miller, Director

★1128★ Game and Fish Department
2221 W. Greenway Rd.
Phoenix, AZ 85023-4399
Phone: (602)942-3000
Fax: (602)255-3475
Contact: Duane L. Shroufe, Director

★1129★ Game and Fish Department
Information Branch
2221 W. Greenway Rd.
Phoenix, AZ 85023-4399
Phone: (602)942-3000
Fax: (602)255-3475
Contact: Richard Beaudry, Supervisor

★1130★ Health Services Department
State Laboratory Services Division
Environmental and Analytical Chemistry Laboratory
1520 W. Adams
Phoenix, AZ 85007
Phone: (602)542-6108
Fax: (602)542-1169
Contact: Prabha Acharya, Supervisor

★1131★ Health Services Department
State Laboratory Services Division
Environmental and Clinical Microbiology Laboratory
1520 W. Adams
Phoenix, AZ 85007
Phone: (602)542-6128
Fax: (602)542-1169
Contact: Ron Cheshier, Supervisor

★1132★ Land Department
1616 W. Adams, Rm. 330
Phoenix, AZ 85007
Phone: (602)542-4621
Fax: (602)542-2590
Contact: M. Jean Hassell, Land Commissioner

★1133★ Land Department
Environmental Resources & Trespass Office
1616 W. Adams, Rm. 330
Phoenix, AZ 85007
Phone: (602)542-4454
Fax: (602)542-2590
Contact: William Dowdle, Director

★1134★ Land Department
Forestry Office
1616 W. Adams, Rm. 330
Phoenix, AZ 85007
Phone: (602)542-2515
Fax: (602)542-2590
Contact: Michael Hart, Director

★1135★ Land Department
Natural Resources Office
1616 W. Adams, Rm. 330
Phoenix, AZ 85007
Phone: (602)542-4625
Fax: (602)542-2590
Contact: Robert E. Yount, Director

★1136★ Oil and Gas Conservation Commission
5150 N. 16th St.
Ste. B-141
Phoenix, AZ 85016
Phone: (602)255-5161
Contact: Daniel J. Brennan, Exec. Dir.

★1137★ Water Resources Department
15 S. 15th Ave.
Phoenix, AZ 85007
Phone: (602)542-1540
Fax: (602)542-1553
Contact: N.W. Plummer, Director

Arkansas

★1138★ Arkansas Heritage Department
Natural and Scenic Rivers Commission
The Heritage Center
225 E. Markham St., Ste. 200
Little Rock, AR 72201
Phone: (501)324-9330
Fax: (501)324-9345
Contact: Jane Jones, Director

★1139★ Forestry Commission
PO Box 4523
Asher Sta.
Little Rock, AR 72214
Phone: (501)664-2531
Contact: Edwin E. Waddell, Director

★1140★ Game and Fish Commission
Wildlife Management Division
Two Natural Resource Dr.
Little Rock, AR 72205
Phone: (501)223-6359
Contact: Don Akers, Director

★1141★ Health Department
Environmental Health Services Bureau
4815 W. Markham
Little Rock, AR 72201
Phone: (501)661-2574
Fax: (501)661-2468
Contact: Jerry Hill, Director

★1142★ Health Department
Environmental Health Services Bureau
Radiation Control & Emergency Management Division
4815 W. Markham
Little Rock, AR 72201
Phone: (501)661-2301
Fax: (501)661-2468
Contact: Greta J. Dicus, Director

★1143★ Health Department
Environmental Health Services Bureau
Sanitarian Services Division
4815 W. Markham
Little Rock, AR 72201
Phone: (501)661-2171
Fax: (501)661-2468
Contact: Bill Teer, Director

★1144★ Health Department
Public Health Programs Bureau
Environmental & Health Maintenance Division
4815 W. Markham
Little Rock, AR 72201
Phone: (501)661-2199
Fax: (501)661-2468
Contact: Martha Hiett, Director

★1145★ Parks and Tourism Department
Great River Division
One Capital Mall
Little Rock, AR 72201
Phone: (501)682-1120
Contact: Judy Stough, Director

★1146★ Parks and Tourism Department
Parks Division
One Capital Mall
Little Rock, AR 72201
Phone: (501)682-7743
Contact: Greg Butts, Director

★1147★ Pollution Control and Ecology Department
8001 National Dr.
PO Box 9583
Little Rock, AR 72219
Phone: (501)562-7444
Fax: (501)562-4632
Contact: Randall Mathis, Director

★1148★ Pollution Control and Ecology Department
Air Division
8001 National Dr.
PO Box 9583
Little Rock, AR 72219
Phone: (501)562-7444
Fax: (501)562-4632
Contact: J.B. Jones, Chief

★1149★ Pollution Control and Ecology Department
Environmental Preservation Division
8001 National Dr.
PO Box 9583
Little Rock, AR 72219
Phone: (501)570-2121
Fax: (501)562-4632
Contact: John Giese, Chief

★1150★ Pollution Control and Ecology Department
Hazardous Waste Division
8001 National Dr.
PO Box 9583
Little Rock, AR 72219
Phone: (501)570-2872
Fax: (501)562-4632
Contact: Mike Bates, Chief

★1151★ Pollution Control and Ecology Department
Mining Division
8001 National Dr.
PO Box 9583
Little Rock, AR 72219
Phone: (501)570-2817
Fax: (501)562-4632
Contact: Floyd Durham, Chief

★1152★ Pollution Control and Ecology Department
Solid Waste Division
8001 National Dr.
PO Box 9583
Little Rock, AR 72219
Phone: (501)570-2858
Fax: (501)562-4632

★1153★ Pollution Control and Ecology Department
Water Division
8001 National Dr.
PO Box 9583
Little Rock, AR 72219
Phone: (501)570-2114
Fax: (501)562-4632
Contact: C.C. Bennett, Chief

★1154★ Soil and Water Conservation Commission
One Capitol Mall, Ste. 2D
Little Rock, AR 72201
Phone: (501)682-1611
Fax: (501)682-3991
Contact: J. Randy Young, Exec. Dir.

California

★1155★ Attorney General (Justice Department)
Environmental Law Asst. Atty. Gen. Office
3508 Wilshire Blvd., Rm. 800
Los Angeles, CA 90010
Phone: (213)736-2191
Contact: Theodora Berger, Environmental Law Asst. Atty. Gen.

★1156★ Attorney General (Justice Department)
Natural Resources Law Asst. Atty. Gen. Office
1515 K St., Ste. 511
PO Box 944255
Sacramento, CA 94244-2500
Phone: (916)324-5341
Contact: Robert H. Connett, Natural Resources Asst. Atty. Gen.

★1157★ Conservation Department
Recycling Division
1025 P St., Rm. 401
Sacramento, CA 95814
Phone: (916)323-3743

★1158★ Environmental Protection Office
1102 Q St.
PO Box 2815
Sacramento, CA 95812
Phone: (916)445-3846
Fax: (916)445-6401
Contact: James M. Strock, Secretary

★1159★ Environmental Protection Office
Air Resources Board
Air Quality Planning and Liaison Office
1102 Q St.
PO Box 2815
Sacramento, CA 95812
Phone: (916)322-3739
Fax: (916)322-6003
Contact: Catherine Witherspoon, Chief

★1160★ Environmental Protection Office
Air Resources Board
Stationary Source Division
Criteria Pollutants Branch
1102 Q St.
Sacramento, CA 95814
Phone: (916)322-6020
Fax: (916)327-7212
Contact: Dean Simeroth, Chief

★1161★ Environmental Protection Office
Air Resources Board
Stationary Source Division
Toxic Air Contaminant Control Branch
1102 Q St.
Sacramento, CA 95814
Phone: (916)322-8277
Fax: (916)327-7212
Contact: Susan Huscroft, Chief

★1162★ Environmental Protection Office
Air Resources Board
Stationary Source Division
Toxic Air Contaminant Identification Branch
1102 Q St.
Sacramento, CA 95814
Phone: (916)322-7072
Fax: (916)327-7212
Contact: Genevieve Shiroma, Chief

★1163★ Environmental Protection Office
California Integrated Waste Management Board
1020 9th St., Ste. 300
Sacramento, CA 95814
Phone: (916)322-3330
Fax: (916)323-3725
Contact: Michael Frost, Chm.

★1164★ Environmental Protection Office
California Integrated Waste Management Board
Resource Conservation Board
1020 9th St., Ste. 300
Sacramento, CA 95814
Phone: (916)327-9385
Fax: (916)323-3725
Contact: Carole Brow, Manager

★1165★ Environmental Protection Office
Hazardous Substance Cleanup Arbitrition Panel
1102 Q St.
PO Box 2815
Sacramento, CA 95812
Phone: (916)324-6881
Fax: (916)445-6401
Contact: Kirk C. Oliver, Administrator

★1166★ Environmental Protection Office
Water Resource Control Board
Clean Water Programs Division
2014 T St.
Sacramento, CA 95814
Phone: (916)739-4333
Contact: Harry M. Schueller, Chief

★1167★ Environmental Protection Office
Water Resource Control Board
Water Quality and Water Rights Division
901 P St.
PO Box 100
Sacramento, CA 95801
Phone: (916)445-9552
Fax: (916)322-2765
Contact: Jesse M. Diaz, Chief

★1168★ Environmental Protection Office
Water Resources Control Board
901 P St.
PO Box 100
Sacramento, CA 95801
Phone: (916)445-3993
Fax: (916)322-2765
Contact: W. Don Maughan, Chm.

★1169★ Lands Commission, California State
1807 13th St.
Sacramento, CA 95814
Phone: (916)322-4105
Fax: (916)322-3568
Contact: Charles Warren, Exec. Officer

★1170★ Lands Commission, California State
Environmental Planning and Management Division
1807 13th St.
Sacramento, CA 95814
Phone: (916)322-7827
Fax: (916)322-3658
Contact: Dwight E. Sanders, Chief

★1171★ Pollution Control Financing Authority
910 K St., Ste. 350
PO Box 942809
Sacramento, CA 94209-0001
Phone: (916)445-9597
Fax: (916)327-7584
Contact: Charles C. Harper, Exec. Dir.

★1172★ Resources Agency
California Coastal Commission
45 Fremont St., Ste. 2000
San Francisco, CA 94105-2219
Phone: (415)904-5200
Contact: Thomas W. Gwyn, Chm.

★1173★ Resources Agency
California Conservation Corps
1530 Capitol Ave.
Sacramento, CA 95814
Phone: (916)445-1469
Fax: (916)323-4989
Contact: Robert J. Sheble, Jr., Director

★1174★ Resources Agency
Conservation Department
1416 9th St., Rm. 1320
Sacramento, CA 95814
Phone: (916)322-1080
Contact: Howard A. Sarasohn, Deputy Director

★1175★ Resources Agency
Conservation Department
Governmental and Environmental Relations Office
1416 9th St., Rm. 1320
Sacramento, CA 95814
Phone: (916)445-8733
Fax: (916)324-0948
Contact: Luree Stetson, Assistant Director

★1176★ Resources Agency
Conservation Department
Oil and Gas Division
1416 9th St., Rm. 1320
Sacramento, CA 95814
Phone: (916)323-1777
Fax: (916)324-0948
Contact: M.G. Mefferd, Chief

★1177★ Resources Agency
Conservation Department
Recycling Division
1025 P St.
Sacramento, CA 95814
Phone: (916)323-3743
Contact: Ralph Chandler, Chief

★1178★ Resources Agency
Fish and Game Commission
1416 9th St.
Box 944209
Sacramento, CA 94244-2090
Phone: (916)445-5708
Fax: (916)324-8553
Contact: Robert Treanor, Exec. Sec.

★1179★ Resources Agency
Fish and Game Department
1416 9th St., 12th Fl.
Sacramento, CA 95814
Phone: (916)445-3535
Fax: (916)324-8553

★1180★ Resources Agency
Fish and Game Department
Environmental Services Division
1416 9th St., 12th Fl.
Sacramento, CA 95814
Phone: (916)445-1383
Fax: (916)324-8553
Contact: Don Lollock, Chief

★1181★ Resources Agency
Fish and Game Department
Wildlife Conservation Board
1416 9th St., 12th Fl.
Sacramento, CA 95814
Phone: (916)445-8448
Fax: (916)324-8553
Contact: W. John Schmidt, Exec. Dir.

★1182★ Resources Agency
Fish and Game Department
Wildlife Management Division
1416 9th St., 12th Fl.
Sacramento, CA 95814
Phone: (916)445-5561
Fax: (916)324-8553
Contact: Eldridge Hunt, Chief

★1183★ Resources Agency
Fish and Game Department
Wildlife Protection Division
1416 9th St., 12th Fl.
Sacramento, CA 95814
Phone: (916)324-7243
Fax: (916)324-8553
Contact: DeWayne Johnston, Chief

★1184★ Resources Agency
Forestry and Fire Protection Department
1416 9th St.
PO Box 944246
Sacramento, CA 94244-2460
Phone: (916)445-3976
Fax: (916)445-2655
Contact: Harold R. Walt, Director

★1185★ Resources Agency
Parks and Recreation Department
1416 9th St.
PO Box 942896
Sacramento, CA 95814
Phone: (916)324-9067
Fax: (916)322-6377
Contact: Henry R. Agonia, Director

★1186★ Resources Agency
Parks and Recreation Department
Resource Protection Division
1416 9th St.
PO Box 942896
Sacramento, CA 95814
Phone: (916)445-7067
Fax: (916)322-6377
Contact: Richard D. Rayburn, Chief

★1187★ Resources Agency
State Coastal Conservancy
1330 Broadway, Ste. 1100
Oakland, CA 94612-2530
Phone: (415)464-1015
Fax: (415)464-0470
Contact: Peter Grenell, Exec. Officer

★1188★ Resources Agency
Water Resources Department
1416 9th St.
PO Box 942836
Sacramento, CA 94236-0001
Phone: (916)445-6582
Fax: (916)445-0109
Contact: David N. Kennedy, Director

Colorado

★1189★ Energy Conservation Office
112 E. 14th Ave.
Denver, CO 80203
Phone: (303)866-2507

★1190★ Health Department
Air Pollution Control Division
4210 E. 11th Ave.
Denver, CO 80220
Phone: (303)331-8500

Fax: (303)322-9076
Contact: Bradley Beckham, Director

★1191★ Health Department
Hazardous Materials & Waste Management Division
4210 E. 11th Ave.
Denver, CO 80220
Phone: (303)331-4830
Fax: (303)322-9076
Contact: David Shelton, Director

★1192★ Health Department
Health & Environmental Protection
4210 E. 11th Ave.
Denver, CO 80220
Phone: (303)331-4513
Fax: (303)322-9076
Contact: Thomas Looby, Assistant Dir.

★1193★ Health Department
Radiation Control Division
4210 E. 11th Ave.
Denver, CO 80220
Phone: (303)331-8480
Fax: (303)322-9076
Contact: Robert Quillin, Director

★1194★ Health Department
Waste Management Division
4210 E. 11th Ave.
Denver, CO 80220
Phone: (303)331-4830

★1195★ Health Department
Water Quality Division
4210 E. 11th Ave.
Denver, CO 80220
Phone: (303)331-4534
Fax: (303)322-9076
Contact: Kenneth Mesch, Director

★1196★ Natural Resources Department
1313 Sherman St., Rm. 718
Denver, CO 80203
Phone: (303)866-3311
Fax: (303)866-2115
Contact: Hamlet J. Barry, Exec. Dir.

★1197★ Natural Resources Department
Mines Division
1313 Sherman St., Rm. 718
Denver, CO 80203
Phone: (303)866-3401
Contact: J.W. Nugent, Director

★1198★ Natural Resources Department
Oil & Gas Conservation Commission
1313 Sherman St., Rm. 718
Denver, CO 80203
Phone: (303)894-2100
Fax: (303)866-2115
Contact: Dennis Bicknell, Director

★1199★ Natural Resources Department
Parks & Outdoor Recreation Division
1313 Sherman St., Rm. 718
Denver, CO 80203
Phone: (303)866-3437
Fax: (303)866-2115
Contact: Ronald Holliday, Director

★1200★ Natural Resources Department
Soil Conservation Division
1313 Sherman St., Rm. 718
Denver, CO 80203
Phone: (303)866-3351
Fax: (303)866-2115
Contact: Dan Parker, Director

★1201★ Natural Resources Department
Water Conservation Division
1313 Sherman St., Rm 718
Denver, CO 80203
Phone: (303)866-3441
Fax: (303)866-2115
Contact: David Walker, Director

★1202★ Natural Resources Department
Water Resources Division
1313 Sherman St., Rm. 718
Denver, CO 80203
Phone: (303)866-3581
Fax: (303)866-2115
Contact: Jeris A. Danielson, State Engineer

★1203★ Natural Resources Department
Wildlife Division
6060 Broadway
Denver, CO 80216
Phone: (303)291-7208
Contact: Perry Olson, Director

★1204★ State Forest Service
Colorado State University
Fort Collins, CO 80523
Phone: (303)491-6303
Fax: (303)491-7736
Contact: James Hubbard, State Forester

★1205★ Water Resources and Power Development Authority
1580 Logan St., Ste. 620
Denver, CO 80203
Phone: (303)830-1550
Alt. Phone: (303)832-8205
Contact: Daniel L. Law, Exec. Dir.

Connecticut

★1206★ Agriculture Department
Aquaculture Division
Rogers Ave.
PO Box 97
Milford, CT 06460
Phone: (203)874-0696
Contact: John Volk, Director

★1207★ Attorney General's Office
Environment Division
55 Elm St.
Hartford, CT 06106
Phone: (203)566-2090
Fax: (203)566-1704
Contact: Joseph Rubin, Asst. Atty. Gen.

★1208★ Environmental Protection Department
165 Capitol Ave.
Hartford, CT 06106
Phone: (203)566-2110
Fax: (203)566-7932
Contact: Timothy R.E. Keeney, Commissioner

★1209★ Environmental Protection Department
Coastal Management Division
18-20 Trinity St.
Hartford, CT 06106
Phone: (203)566-7404
Contact: Art Rocque, Director

★1210★ Environmental Protection Department
Conservation and Preservation Branch
Fish and Wildlife Bureau
165 Capitol Ave.
Hartford, CT 06106
Phone: (203)566-2287
Contact: Robert A. Jones, Chief

★1211★ Environmental Protection Department
Conservation and Preservation Branch
Parks and Forests Bureau
165 Capitol Ave.
Hartford, CT 06106
Phone: (203)566-2304
Contact: Richard Clifford, Chief

★1212★ Environmental Protection Department
Environmental Quality Branch
Air Mamagement Bureau
165 Capitol Ave.
Hartford, CT 06106
Phone: (203)566-2506
Contact: Carl Pavetto, Chief

★1213★ Environmental Protection Department
Environmental Quality Branch
Waste Management Bureau
165 Capitol Ave.
Hartford, CT 06106
Phone: (203)566-8476
Contact: Richard Barlow, Chief

★1214★ Environmental Protection Department
Environmental Services Bureau
165 Capitol Ave.
Hartford, CT 06106
Phone: (203)566-5388
Fax: (203)566-7932
Contact: Hugo Thomas, Chief

★1215★ Environmental Protection Department
Solid Waste Division
122 Washington St.
Hartford, CT 06106
Phone: (203)566-5847

Delaware

★1216★ Agriculture Department
Forestry Office
2320 S. duPont Hwy.
Dover, DE 19901
Phone: (302)739-4811
Fax: (302)697-6287
Contact: Walter Gabel, Manager

★1217★ Agriculture Department
Pesticides Compliance Office
2320 S, duPont Hwy.
Dover, DE 19901
Phone: (302)739-4811
Fax: (302)697-6287
Contact: Grier Stayton, Supervisor

★1218★ Natural Resources and Environmental Control Department
89 Kings Hwy.
PO Box 1401
Dover, DE 19903
Phone: (302)739-4403
Fax: (302)739-6242
Contact: Edwin H. Clark, II, Sec.

★1219★ Natural Resources and Environmental Control Department
Air & Waste Management Division
89 Kings Hwy.
PO Box 1401
Dover, DE 19903
Phone: (302)739-4764
Fax: (302)739-6242
Contact: Phillip G. Retallick, Director

★1220★ Natural Resources and Environmental Control Department
Fish & Wildlife Division
89 Kings Hwy.
PO Box 1401
Dover, DE 19903
Phone: (302)739-5295
Fax: (302)739-6242
Contact: William C. Wagner, II, Director

★1221★ Natural Resources and Environmental Control Department
Parks & Recreation Division
89 Kings Hwy.
PO Box 1401
Dover, DE 19903
Phone: (302)739-4401
Fax: (302)739-6242
Contact: William J. Hopkins, Director

★1222★ Natural Resources and Environmental Control Department
Soil & Water Conservation Division
89 Kings Hwy.
PO Box 1401
Dover, DE 19903
Phone: (302)739-4411
Fax: (302)739-6242
Contact: John A. Hughes, Director

★1223★ Natural Resources and Environmental Control Department
Water Resources Division
89 Kings Hwy.
PO Box 1401
Dover, DE 19903
Phone: (302)739-4860
Fax: (302)739-6242
Contact: Gerard Esposito, Director

★1224★ River and Bay Authority
PO Box 71
New Castle, DE 19720
Phone: (302)577-6301
Contact: William J. Miller, Jr., Exec. Dir.

★1225★ Solid Waste Authority
PO Box 455
Dover, DE 19903-0455
Phone: (302)739-5361
Contact: N.C. Vasuki, Gen. Manager

District of Columbia

★1226★ Conservation Services Division
613 G St. NW
Washington, DC 20004
Phone: (202)727-4700

★1227★ Office of the Mayor
Energy Office
613 G St., N.W.
Washington, DC 20001
Phone: (202)727-1800
Fax: (202)727-9582
Contact: Charles Clinton, Director

Florida

★1228★ Agriculture and Consumer Services Department
Chemistry Division
Pesticide Laboratory Bureau
3125 Conner Blvd.
Tallahassee, FL 32399-1650
Phone: (904)488-9375
Fax: (904)488-0863
Contact: Marshall Gentry, Chief

★1229★ Agriculture and Consumer Services Department
Forestry Division
3125 Conner Blvd.
Tallahassee, FL 32399-1650
Phone: (904)488-4274
Fax: (904)488-0863
Contact: Harold K. Mikell, Director

★1230★ Environmental Regulation Department
2600 Blair Stone Rd.
Tallahassee, FL 32399-2400
Phone: (904)488-4805
Fax: (904)487-4938
Contact: Carol Browner, Secretary

★1231★ Environmental Regulation Department
Air Resources Management Division
2600 Blair Stone Rd.
Tallahassee, FL 32399-2400
Phone: (904)488-1344
Fax: (904)487-4938
Contact: Steve Smallwood, Director

★1232★ Environmental Regulation Department
Waste Management Division
2600 Blair Stone Rd.
Tallahassee, FL 32399-2400
Phone: (904)487-3299
Fax: (904)487-4938
Contact: Richard G. Wilkins, Director

★1233★ Environmental Regulation Department
Water Facilities Division
2600 Blair Stone Rd.
Tallahassee, FL 32399-2400
Phone: (904)487-1855
Fax: (904)487-4938
Contact: Howard Rhodes, Director

★1234★ Game and Fresh Water Fish Commission
620 S. Meridian St.
Tallahassee, FL 32399-1600
Phone: (904)488-2975
Fax: (904)488-6988
Contact: Col. Robert M. Brantly, Exec. Dir.

★1235★ Game and Fresh Water Fish Commission
Environmental Services
620 S. Meridian St.
Tallahassee, FL 32300-1600
Phone: (904)488-6661
Fax: (904)488-6988
Contact: Bradley J. Hartman, Director

★1236★ Game and Fresh Water Fish Commission
Fisheries Division
620 S. Meridian St.
Tallahassee, FL 32399-1600
Phone: (904)488-4066
Fax: (904)488-6988
Contact: Dennis E. Holcomb, Director

★1237★ Game and Fresh Water Fish Commission
Informational Services
620 S. Meridian St.
Tallahassee, FL 32399-1600
Phone: (904)488-4676
Fax: (904)488-6988
Contact: Dennis Hammond, Director

★1238★ Game and Fresh Water Fish Commission
Wildlife Division
620 S. Meridian St.
Tallahassee, FL 32399-1600
Phone: (904)488-3831
Fax: (904)488-6988
Contact: Frank Montalbano, Director

★1239★ Health and Rehabilitation Services Department
Environmental Health Division
Environmental Epidemiology Office
1317 Winewwod Blvd.
Tallahassee, FL 32399-0700
Phone: (904)488-3370
Contact: Tom Atkeson, Chief

★1240★ Health and Rehabilitation Services Department
Environmental Health Division
Environmental Health Office
1317 Winewood Blvd.
Tallahassee, FL 32399-0700
Phone: (904)488-4070
Contact: Ennix Poole, Chief

★1241★ Health and Rehabilitative Services Department
Environmental Health Division
1317 Winewood Blvd.
Tallahassee, FL 32399-0700
Phone: (904)488-4070
Contact: Richard Hunter, Asst. Health Officer

★1242★ Natural Resources Department
3900 Commonwealth Blvd.
Tallahassee, FL 32399-3000
Phone: (904)488-1554
Contact: Thomas E. Gardner, Exec. Dir.

★1243★ Natural Resources Department
Beaches & Shores Division
3900 Commonwealth Blvd.
Tallahassee, FL 32399-3000
Phone: (904)487-4469
Contact: Kirby Green, Director

★1244★ Natural Resources Department
Law Enforcement Division
3900 Commonwealth Blvd.
Tallahassee, FL 32399-3000
Phone: (904)488-5757
Contact: Don Ellingsen, Director

★1245★ Natural Resources Department
Marine Resources Division
3900 Commonwealth Blvd.
Tallahassee, FL 32399-3000
Phone: (904)488-6058
Contact: Pamela McVety, Director

★1246★ Natural Resources Department
Recreation & Parks Division
3900 Commonwealth Blvd.
Tallahassee, FL 32399-3000
Phone: (904)488-6131
Contact: Fran Mainella, Director

★1247★ Natural Resources Department
Resource Management Division
3900 Commonwealth Blvd.
Tallahassee, FL 32399-3000
Phone: (904)488-3177
Contact: Jeremy Craft, Director

★1248★ Natural Resources Department
State Lands Division
3900 Commonwealth Blvd.
Tallahassee, FL 32399-3000
Phone: (904)488-2725
Contact: Pete Mallison, Director

Georgia

★1249★ Attorney General's Office
Conservation Division
40 Capitol Sq.
Atlanta, GA 30334
Phone: (404)656-7273
Fax: (404)651-9148
Contact: Robert Bomar, Sr. Asst. Atty. Gen.

★1250★ Energy Resources Office
254 Washington St., SW
Ste. 401
Atlanta, GA 30334
Phone: (401)656-5176
Contact: Paul Burks, Director

★1251★ Forestry Commission
PO Box 819
Macon, GA 31298-4599
Phone: (912)744-3237
Fax: (912)744-3270
Contact: John W. Mixon, Director

★1252★ Forestry Commission
Forest Management Division
PO Box 819
Macon, GA 31298-4599
Phone: (912)744-3241
Fax: (912)744-3270
Contact: Lynn Hooven, Chief

★1253★ Forestry Commission
Forest Protection Division
PO Box 819
Macon, GA 31298-4599
Phone: (912)744-3251
Fax: (912)744-3270
Contact: Wesley Wells Jr., Chief

★1254★ Forestry Commission
Information and Education Division
PO Box 819
Macon, GA 31298-4599
Phone: (912)744-3364
Fax: (912)744-3270
Contact: Bob Lazenby, Chief

★1255★ Forestry Commission
Reforestation Division
PO Box 819
Macon, GA 31298-4599
Phone: (912)744-3354
Fax: (912)744-3270
Contact: Johnny R. Branan, Chief

★1256★ Hazardous Waste Authority
254 Washington St., SW
Rm. 624
Atlanta, GA 30334
Phone: (404)656-3819
Contact: Robert Kerr, Exec. Dir.

★1257★ Natural Resources Department
205 Butler St. SE
Ste. 1252
Atlanta, GA 30334
Phone: (404)656-3500
Fax: (404)656-2285
Contact: Joe D. Tanner, Commissioner

★1258★ Natural Resources Department
Coastal Resources Division
One Conservation Way
Brunswick, GA 31523-8600
Phone: (912)264-7218
Contact: Duane Harris, Director

★1259★ Natural Resources Department
Environmental Protection Division
205 Butler St. SE
Ste. 1252
Atlanta, GA 30334
Phone: (404)656-4713
Contact: Harold Reheis, Assistant Dir.

★1260★ Natural Resources Department
Environmental Protection Division
Air Protection Branch
205 Butler St. SE
Ste. 1252
Atlanta, GA
Phone: (404)656-6900
Contact: Bob Collom, Chief

★1261★ Natural Resources Department
Environmental Protection Division
Land Protection Branch
205 Butler St. SE
Ste. 1252
Atlanta, GA 30334
Phone: (404)656-2833
Contact: John Taylor, Chief

★1262★ Natural Resources Department
Environmental Protection Division
Water Protection Branch
205 Butler St. SE
Ste. 1252
Macon, GA 30334
Phone: (404)656-4708
Contact: David Word, Chief

★1263★ Natural Resources Department
Environmental Protection Division
Water Resources Management Branch
205 Butler St. SE
Ste. 1252
Atlanta, GA 30334
Phone: (404)656-4807
Contact: Nolton Johnson, Chief

★1264★ Natural Resources Department
Game and Fish Division
205 Butler St., SE
Ste. 1252
Atlanta, GA 30334
Phone: (404)656-3523
Contact: David Waller, Director

★1265★ Natural Resources Department
Parks and Historic Sites Division
205 Butler St., SE
Ste. 1252
Atlanta, GA 30334
Phone: (404)656-2753
Contact: Lonice Barrett, Director

Guam

★1266★ Energy Office
PO Box 2950
Agana, GU 96910
Phone: (671)734-4452
Fax: (671)734-6453
Contact: Jerry M. Rivera, Director

★1267★ Environmental Protection Agency
PO Box 2999
Agana, GU 96910
Phone: (671)646-8863
Fax: (671)646-9402
Contact: Fred Castro, Admin.

★1268★ Parks and Recreation Department
490 Naval Hospital Rd.
Agana Heights, GU 96910
Phone: (671)477-9620
Fax: (671)477-2822
Contact: Anthony C. Mariano, Director

Hawaii

★1269★ Hawaiian Home Lands Department
Land Development Division
PO Box 1879
Honolulu, HI 96805
Phone: (808)548-2686
Contact: Stewart Matsunaga, Admin.

★1270★ Health Department
Environmental Health Administration
Environmental Health Services Division
1250 Punchbowl St.
Honolulu, HI 96813
Phone: (808)548-6455
Fax: (808)548-3263
Contact: James Ikeda, Chief

★1271★ Health Department
Environmental Health Administration
Environmental Health Services Division
Noise & Radiation Branch
591 Ala Moana Blvd.
Honolulu, HI 96813
Phone: (808)548-4383
Contact: Thomas Anamizu, Chief

★1272★ Health Department
Environmental Health Administration
Environmental Management Division
Clean Air Branch
Five Waterfront Plaza
500 Ala Moana Blvd.
Ste. 250
Honolulu, HI 96813
Phone: (808)543-8200
Contact: Paul Aki, Chief

★1273★ Health Department
Environmental Health Administration
Environmental Management Division
Clean Water Branch
Five Waterfront Plaza
500 Ala Moana Blvd.
Ste. 250
Honolulu, HI 96813
Phone: (808)543-8311
Contact: Dennis Lau, Chief

★1274★ Health Department
Environmental Health Administration
Environmental Management Division
Safe Drinking Water Branch
Five Waterfront Plaza
500 Ala Moano Blvd.
Ste. 250
Honolulu, HI 96813
Phone: (808)543-8258
Contact: Thomas Arizumi, Chief

★1275★ Health Department
Environmental Health Administration
Environmental Management Division
Solid and Hazardous Waste Branch
Five Waterfront Plaza
500 Ala Moano Blvd.
Ste. 250
Honolulu, HI 96813
Phone: (808)543-8225
Contact: Arlene Kabei, Chief

★1276★ Health Department
Environmental Health Administration
Environmental Management Division
Wastewater Branch
Five Waterfront Plaza
500 Ala Moana Blvd.
Ste. 250
Honolulu, HI 96813
Phone: (808)543-8294
Contact: Dennis Tulang, Chief

★1277★ Health Department
Office of Environmental Quality Control
465 S. King St., Rm. 4
Honolulu, HI 96813
Phone: (808)548-6915
Contact: Brian Choy, Director

★1278★ Land and Natural Resources Department
Kalanimoku Bldg.
1151 Punchbowl St.
Honolulu, HI 96813
Phone: (808)548-6550
Fax: (808)548-6461
Contact: William W. Paty, Chm.

★1279★ Land and Natural Resources Department
Aquatic Resources Division
Kalanimoku Bldg.
1151 Punchbowl St.
Honolulu, HI 96813
Phone: (808)548-4001
Fax: (808)548-6461
Contact: Henry Sakuda, Head

★1280★ Land and Natural Resources Department
Conservation and Environmental Affairs Division
Kalanimoku Bldg.
1151 Punchbowl St.
Honolulu, HI 96813
Phone: (808)548-7837
Contact: Roger Evans, Administrator

★1281★ Land and Natural Resources Department
Forestry and Wildlife Division
Kalanimoku Bldg.
1151 Punchbowl St.
Honolulu, HI 96813
Phone: (808)548-8850
Fax: (808)548-6461
Contact: Michael Buck, Administrator

★1282★ Land and Natural Resources Department
Land Management Division
Kalanimoku Bldg.
1151 Punchbowl St.
Honolulu, HI 96813
Phone: (808)548-2574
Fax: (808)548-6461
Contact: W. Mason Young, Administrator

★1283★ Land and Natural Resources Department
Water Resources Commission
Kalanimoku Bldg.
1151 Punchbowl St.
Honolulu, HI 96813
Phone: (808)548-7533
Fax: (808)548-6461
Contact: Manabu Tagomori, Administrator

Idaho

★1284★ Agriculture Department
Plant Industries Division
Pesticides Bureau
2270 Old Penitentiary Rd.
Boise, ID 83712
Phone: (208)334-3243
Contact: Rodney A. Awe, Chief

★1285★ Attorney General's Office
Natural Resources Division
210 Statehouse
Boise, ID 83720-1000
Phone: (208)334-2400
Fax: (208)334-2530
Contact: Peter Anderson, Deputy Atty. Gen.

★1286★ Fish and Game Department
600 S. Walnut
PO Box 25
Boise, ID 83707
Phone: (208)334-5159
Fax: (208)334-2114
Contact: Jerry M. Conley, Director

★1287★ Fish and Game Department
Information and Education Division
600 S. Walnut
PO Box 25
Boise, ID 83707
Phone: (208)334-3746
Fax: (208)334-2114
Contact: Bill Goodnight, Chief

★1288★ Fish and Game Department
Wildlife Division
600 S. Walnut
PO Box 25
Boise, ID 83707
Phone: (208)334-2920
Fax: (208)334-2114
Contact: Tom Reinecker, Chief

★1289★ Health and Welfare Department
Legal Services Division
Environmental Quality Division
Towers Bldg.
450 W. State St.
Boise, ID 83720-9990
Phone: (208)334-0494
Contact: Curt A. Fransen, Sr. Dep. Atty. Gen.

★1290★ Lands Department
1215 W. State
Boise, ID 83720
Phone: (208)334-0200
Fax: (208)334-2339
Contact: Stanley F. Hamilton, Director

★1291★ Lands Department
Lands Bureau
1215 W. State
Boise, ID 83720
Phone: (208)334-0253
Fax: (208)334-2339
Contact: Jay G. Biladeau, Chief

★1292★ Lands Department
Minerals Bureau
1215 W. State
Boise, ID 83720
Phone: (208)334-0247
Fax: (208)334-2339
Contact: Thomas R. Markland, Chief

★1293★ Lands Department
Soil Conservation Commission
1215 W. State
Boise, ID 83720
Phone: (208)334-0214
Fax: (208)334-2339
Contact: Wayne R. Faude, Administrative Officer

★1294★ Parks and Recreation Department
2177 Warm Springs Ave.
Boise, ID 83720
Phone: (208)334-2154
Fax: (208)334-3812
Contact: Yvonne S. Ferrell, Director

★1295★ Water Resources Department
Statehouse
Boise, ID 83720
Phone: (208)327-7910
Fax: (208)327-7866
Contact: R. Keith Higginson, Director

★1296★ Water Resources Department
Energy Division
Statehouse
Boise, ID 83720
Phone: (208)327-7910
Fax: (208)327-7866
Contact: Robert W. Hopple, Director

Illinois

★1297★ Abandoned Mined Lands Reclamation Council
928 S. Spring St.
Springfield, IL 62704
Phone: (217)782-0588
Contact: Timothy J. Hickmann, Exec. Dir.

★1298★ Agriculture Department
Natural Resources Division
PO Box 19281
Springfield, IL 62794-9281
Phone: (217)782-6297
Fax: (217)524-5960
Contact: James Brim, Superintendent

★1299★ Attorney General's Office
Environmental Division
500 S. 2nd St.
Springfield, IL 62706
Phone: (217)782-1090
Contact: James Morgan, Chief

★1300★ **Conservation Department**
Land Management and Enforcement Office
Lincoln Tower Plaza
524 S. Second St.
Springfield, IL 62701-1787
Phone: (217)785-8285
Fax: (217)524-5612
Contact: Jay Johnson, Director

★1301★ **Conservation Department**
Resource Marketing and Education Office
Lincoln Tower Plaza
524 S. Second St.
Springfield, IL 62701-1787
Phone: (217)785-8955
Contact: Bob Winchester, Director

★1302★ **Conservation Department**
Resource Marketing and Education Office
Kids for Conservation Division
524 S. 2nd St.
Rm. 515
Springfield, IL 62701-1787
Phone: (217)524-4126
Contact: Glenda Burke, Chief

★1303★ **Conservation Department**
Resources Management Office
Lincoln Tower Plaza
524 S. Second St.
Springfield, IL 62701-1787
Phone: (217)785-8287
Fax: (217)785-8405
Contact: John Tranquilli, Director

★1304★ **Conservation Department**
Resources Management Office
Fisheries Division
Lincoln Tower Plaza
524 S. Second St.
Springfield, IL 62701-1787
Phone: (217)785-8287
Fax: (217)785-8405

★1305★ **Conservation Department**
Resources Management Office
Forestry Division
Lincoln Tower Plaza
524 S. Second St.
Springfield, IL 62701-1787
Phone: (217)782-2361
Fax: (217)785-8405
Contact: Al Mickelson, Manager

★1306★ **Conservation Department**
Resources Management Office
Wildlife Resources Division
Lincoln Tower Plaza
524 S. Second St.
Springfield, IL 62701-1787
Phone: (217)782-6384
Fax: (217)785-8405

★1307★ **Energy and Natural Resources Department**
325 W. Adams St.
Rm. 300
Springfield, IL 62704
Phone: (217)785-2800
Fax: (217)785-2618
Contact: John Moore, Director

★1308★ **Energy and Natural Resources Department**
Energy Conservation Division
325 W. Adams St.
Rm. 300
Springfield, IL 62704
Phone: (217)785-2800
Fax: (217)785-2616
Contact: Mitch Beaver, Director

★1309★ **Energy and Natural Resources Department**
Hazardous Waste Research and Information Center
1808 Woodfield Rd.
Savoy, IL 61874
Phone: (217)333-8941
Fax: (217)333-8944
Contact: David Thomas, Director

★1310★ **Energy and Natural Resources Department**
Research & Planning Division
325 W. Adams St.
Rm. 300
Springfield, IL 62704
Phone: (217)785-2800
Fax: (217)785-2618
Contact: Bob Lieberman, Director

★1311★ **Energy and Natural Resources Department**
Solid Waste & Renewable Resources Division
325 W. Adams St.
Rm. 300
Springfield, IL 62704
Phone: (217)785-2800
Fax: (217)785-2616
Contact: Tim Warren, Director

★1312★ **Energy and Natural Resources Department**
Water Survey
2204 Griffith Dr.
Champaign, IL 61820
Phone: (217)333-2210
Fax: (217)333-6540
Contact: Richard Semonin, Chief

★1313★ **Environmental Protection Agency**
PO Box 19276
Springfield, IL 62794
Phone: (217)782-3397
Contact: Mary Gade, Director

★1314★ **Environmental Protection Agency**
Air Pollution Control Division
PO Box 19276
Springfield, IL 62794
Phone: (217)785-4140
Contact: Bharat Mathur, Director

★1315★ **Environmental Protection Agency**
Land Pollution Control Division
PO Box 19276
Springfield, IL 62794
Phone: (217)782-2760
Contact: William Child, Director

★1316★ **Environmental Protection Agency**
Legal Counsel Division
PO Box 19276
Springfield, IL 62794
Phone: (217)782-5544
Contact: Joe Svoboda, Director

★1317★ **Environmental Protection Agency**
Water Pollution Control Division
PO Box 19276
Springfield, IL 62794
Phone: (217)782-1654
Contact: James Park, Director

★1318★ **Mines and Minerals Department**
300 W. Jefferson St., Ste. 300
PO Box 10137
Springfield, IL 62791-0137
Phone: (217)782-6791
Fax: (217)524-4819
Contact: Ronald E. Morse, Director

★1319★ **Mines and Minerals Department**
Land Reclamation Division
300 W. Jefferson St., Ste. 300
PO Box 10137
Springfield, IL 62791-0137
Phone: (217)782-4970
Fax: (217)524-4819
Contact: Paul Ehret, Director

★1320★ **Pollution Control Board**
100 W. Randolph St.
Ste. 11-500
Chicago, IL 60601-3286
Phone: (312)814-3620
Fax: (312)814-3669
Contact: John C. Marlin, Chairman

Indiana

★1321★ **Administration Department**
State Land Division
State Office Bldg.
Indianapolis, IN 46204
Phone: (317)232-3335
Contact: James Lewis, Director

★1322★ **Environmental Management Department**
105 S. Meridian St.
PO Box 6015
Indianapolis, IN 46206-6015
Phone: (317)232-8162
Fax: (317)232-5539
Contact: Kathy Prosser, Commissioner

★1323★ **Environmental Management Department**
Air Management Division
105 S. Meridian St.
PO Box 6015
Indianapolis, IN 46206-6015
Phone: (317)232-5586
Fax: (317)232-5539
Contact: Timothy Method, Asst. Commissioner

★1324★ **Environmental Management Department**
Environmental Response Division
105 S. Meridian St.
PO Box 6015
Indianapolis, IN 46206-6015
Phone: (317)232-8162
Fax: (317)232-5539
Contact: Corinne Wellish, Asst. Commissioner

★1325★ **Environmental Management Department**
Laboratories Division
105 S. Meridian St.
PO Box 6015
Indianapolis, IN 46206-6015
Phone: (317)232-8198
Fax: (317)232-5539
Contact: Monique Hinterberger, Director

★1326★ **Environmental Management Department**
Legal Division
105 S. Meridian St.
PO Box 6015
Indianapolis, IN 46206-6015
Phone: (317)232-8493
Fax: (317)232-5539
Contact: Harinder Kaur, Counsel

★1327★ Environmental Management Department
Solid and Hazardous Waste Management Division
105 S. Meridian St.
PO Box 6015
Indianapolis, IN 46206-6015
Phone: (317)232-3210
Fax: (317)232-5539
Contact: Marty Harmless, Asst. Commissioner

★1328★ Environmental Management Department
Water Management Division
105 S. Meridian St.
PO Box 6015
Indianapolis, IN 46206-6015
Phone: (317)232-8476
Fax: (317)232-5539
Contact: David Nelson, Asst. Commissioner

★1329★ Natural Resources Department
State Office Bldg.
Indianapolis, IN 46204
Phone: (317)232-4020
Contact: Patrick R. Ralston, Director

★1330★ Natural Resources Department
Land, Forest and Wildlife Resources Bureau
State Office Bldg.
Indianapolis, IN 46204
Phone: (317)232-4020
Contact: John T. Costello, Deputy Dir.

★1331★ Natural Resources Department
Land, Forest and Wildlife Resources Bureau
Entomology Division
State Office Bldg.
Indianapolis, IN 46204
Phone: (317)232-4120
Contact: Robert D. Waltz, Director

★1332★ Natural Resources Department
Land, Forest and Wildlife Resources Bureau
Fish & Wildlife Division
State Office Bldg.
Indianapolis, IN 46204
Phone: (317)232-4080
Contact: Ed Hansen, Director

★1333★ Natural Resources Department
Land, Forest and Wildlife Resources Bureau
Forestry Division
State Office Bldg.
Indianapolis, IN 46204
Phone: (317)232-4105
Contact: Burnell Fischer, Director

★1334★ Natural Resources Department
Land, Forest and Wildlife Resources Bureau
Nature Preserves Division
State Office Bldg.
Indianapolis, IN 46204
Phone: (317)232-4052
Contact: John Bacone, Director

★1335★ Natural Resources Department
Land, Forest and Wildlife Resources Bureau
Outdoor Recreation Division
State Office Bldg.
Indianapolis, IN 46204
Phone: (317)232-4070
Contact: Eric Myers, Director

★1336★ Natural Resources Department
Land, Forest and Wildlife Resources Bureau
State Parks Division
State Office Bldg.
Indianapolis, IN 46204
Phone: (317)232-4124
Contact: Gerald J. Pagac, Director

★1337★ Natural Resources Department
Water and Mineral Resources Bureau
State Office Bldg.
Indianapolis, IN 46204
Phone: (317)232-4022
Contact: Gary Doxtater, Deputy Dir.

★1338★ Natural Resources Department
Water and Mineral Resources Bureau
Reclamation Division
309 W. Washington St.
Rm. 201
Indianapolis, IN 46204
Phone: (317)232-1555
Contact: Johnny Reising, Director

★1339★ Natural Resources Department
Water and Mineral Resources Bureau
Soil Conservation Division
Purdue University
West Lafayette, IN 47906
Phone: (317)494-8383
Contact: Charles C. McKee, Exec. Dir.

★1340★ Natural Resources Department
Water and Mineral Resources Bureau
Water Division
2475 Directors Row
Indianapolis, IN 46241
Phone: (317)232-4160
Contact: John N. Simpson, Director

Iowa

★1341★ Agriculture and Land Stewardship Department
Soil Conservation Division
Wallace Bldg
Des Moines, IA 50319
Phone: (515)281-5851
Fax: (515)281-6236
Contact: James Gulliford, Director

★1342★ Agriculture and Land Stewardship Department
Soil Conservation Division
Mines and Minerals Bureau
Wallace Bldg.
Des Moines, IA 50319
Phone: (515)281-6147
Fax: (515)281-6236
Contact: Ken Tow, Chief

★1343★ Agriculture and Land Stewardship Department
Soil Conservation Division
Water Resources Bureau
Wallace Bldg.
Des Moines, IA 50319
Phone: (515)281-6143
Fax: (515)281-6236
Contact: Dan Lindquist, Chief

★1344★ Natural Resources Department
Wallace Bldg.
Des Moines, IA 50319-0034
Phone: (515)281-5385
Fax: (515)281-8895
Contact: Larry J. Wilson, Director

★1345★ Natural Resources Department
Coordination and Information Division
Wallace Bldg.
Des Moines, IA 50319-0034
Phone: (515)281-8857
Fax: (515)242-5967
Contact: James Combs, Admin.

★1346★ Natural Resources Department
Energy and Geological Resources Division
Wallace Bldg.
Des Moines, IA 50319-0034
Phone: (515)281-4308
Contact: Larry Bean, Admin.

★1347★ Natural Resources Department
Environmental Protection Department
Field Evaluation and Emergency Response Bureau
Wallace Bldg.
Des Moines, IA 50319-0034
Phone: (515)281-8934
Contact: Joe Obr, Chief

★1348★ Natural Resources Department
Environmental Protection Division
Wallace Bldg.
Des Moines, IA 50319-0034
Phone: (515)281-6284
Contact: Allan Stokes, Admin.

★1349★ Natural Resources Department
Environmental Protection Division
Air and Solid Waste Protection Bureau
Wallace Bldg.
Des Moines, IA 50319-0034
Phone: (515)281-8852
Contact: Pete Hamlin, Chief

★1350★ Natural Resources Department
Environmental Protection Division
Surface and Groundwater Project Bureau
Wallace Bldg.
Des Moines, IA 50319-0034
Phone: (515)281-8869
Contact: Darrell McAllister, Chief

★1351★ Natural Resources Department
Fish and Wildlife Division
Wallace Bldg.
Des Moines, IA 50319-0034
Phone: (515)281-5154
Contact: Allen Farris, Admin.

★1352★ Natural Resources Department
Forests and Forestry Division
Wallace Bldg.
Des Moines, IA 50319-0034
Phone: (515)281-8656
Contact: William Farris, Admin.

★1353★ Natural Resources Department
Parks, Recreation and Preservation Division
Wallace Bldg.
Des Moines, IA 50319-0034
Phone: (515)281-5207
Contact: Michael Carrier, Admin.

★1354★ Natural Resources Department
Waste Management Authority Division
Wallace Bldg.
Des Moines, IA 50319-0034
Phone: (515)281-8975
Contact: Teresa Hay, Admin.

Kansas

★1355★ Conservation Commission
109 SW 9th St.
Ste. 500
Topeka, KS 66612-1299
Phone: (913)296-3600
Contact: Kenneth F. Kern, Exec. Dir.

★1356★ Corporation Commission
Conservation Division
202 W. 1st St.
Wichita, KS 67202
Phone: (316)263-3238
Contact: Shari Feist Albrecht, Director

★1357★ Corporation Commission
Energy Division
1500 Arrowhead Rd.
Topeka, KS 66604
Phone: (913)271-3170
Fax: (913)271-3354
Contact: Emily Wellman, Director

★1358★ Health and Environment Department
Forbes Field, Bldg. 740
Topeka, KS 66620
Phone: (913)296-1522
Alt. Phone: (913)296-6247
Contact: Stanley C. Grant Ph.D., Secretary

★1359★ Health and Environment Department
Environment Division
Forbes Field, Bldg. 740
Topeka, KS 66620
Phone: (913)296-1535
Contact: James Power, Director

★1360★ Health and Environment Department
Environment Division
Air & Waste Management
Forbes Field, Bldg. 740
Topeka, KS 66620
Phone: (913)296-1593
Contact: John Irwin, Director

★1361★ Health and Environment Department
Environment Division
Environmental Quality
Forbes Field, Bldg. 740
Topeka, KS 66620
Phone: (913)296-0077
Contact: Ron Fox, Director

★1362★ Health and Environment Department
Environment Division
Environmental Remediation
Forbes Field, Bldg. 740
Topeka, KS 66620
Phone: (913)296-1660
Contact: Larry Knoche, Director

★1363★ Health and Environment Department
Environment Division
Water Office
Forbes Field, Bldg. 740
Topeka, KS 66620
Phone: (913)296-5500
Contact: Karl Mueldener, Director

★1364★ Health and Environment Department
Information Systems Division
Health & Environmental Education Office
Forbes Field, Bldg. 740
Topeka, KS 66620
Phone: (913)296-1226
Contact: Lesa Bray, Director

★1365★ Health and Environment Department
Information Systems Division
Public Information Services
Forbes Field, Bldg. 740
Topeka, KS 66620
Phone: (913)296-1529
Contact: Greg Crawford, Director

★1366★ Health and Environment Department
Kansas Health & Environmental Laboratories
Forbes Field, Bldg. 740
Topeka, KS 66620
Phone: (913)296-1620
Contact: Roger H. Carlson Ph.D., Manager

★1367★ Wildlife and Parks Department
502 Landon State Office Bldg.
900 SW Jackson St.
Topeka, KS 66612-1220
Phone: (913)296-2281
Fax: (913)296-6953
Contact: Jack Lacey, Secretary

Kentucky

★1368★ Attorney General's Office
Civil & Environmental Law Division
116 State Capitol
Frankfort, KY 40601
Phone: (502)564-7600
Fax: (502)564-2894
Contact: Ann Sheadel, Director

★1369★ Natural Resources and Environmental Protection Cabinet
Five Capital Plaza Tower
Frankfort, KY 40601
Phone: (502)564-3350
Fax: (502)564-2043
Contact: Carl H. Bradley, Secretary

★1370★ Natural Resources and Environmental Protection Cabinet
Administrative Division
Five Capital Plaza Tower
Frankfort, KY 40601
Phone: (502)564-7320
Fax: (502)564-2043
Contact: William Castle, Director

★1371★ Natural Resources and Environmental Protection Cabinet
Communications & Community Affairs Division
Five Capital Plaza Tower
Frankfort, KY 40601
Phone: (502)564-3350
Fax: (502)564-2043
Contact: Faun S. Fishback, Director

★1372★ Natural Resources and Environmental Protection Cabinet
Environmental Education Department
Five Capital Plaza Tower
Frankfort, KY 40601
Phone: (502)564-3350
Fax: (502)564-2043
Contact: Julie B. Smither, Coordinator

★1373★ Natural Resources and Environmental Protection Cabinet
Environmental Protection Department
Fort Boone Plaza
18 Reilly Rd.
Frankfort, KY 40601
Phone: (502)564-3035
Fax: (502)564-4245
Contact: William C. Eddins, Commissioner

★1374★ Natural Resources and Environmental Protection Cabinet
Environmental Protection Department
Air Quality Division
Fort Boone Plaza
18 Reilly Rd.
Frankfort, KY 40601
Phone: (502)564-3382
Fax: (502)564-4245
Contact: Hisham Saaid, Director

★1375★ Natural Resources and Environmental Protection Cabinet
Environmental Protection Department
Environmental Services Division
Fort Boone Plaza
18 Reilly Rd.
Frankfort, KY 40601
Phone: (502)564-2150
Fax: (502)564-4245
Contact: William Davis, Director

★1376★ Natural Resources and Environmental Protection Cabinet
Environmental Protection Department
Management Services Branch
Fort Boone Plaza
18 Reilly Rd.
Frankfort, KY 40601
Phone: (502)564-2150
Fax: (502)564-4245
Contact: Janet Goins, Manager

★1377★ Natural Resources and Environmental Protection Cabinet
Environmental Protection Department
Waste Management Division
Fort Boone Plaza
18 Reilly Rd.
Frankfort, KY 40601
Phone: (502)564-6716
Fax: (502)564-4245
Contact: Susan Bush, Director

★1378★ Natural Resources and Environmental Protection Cabinet
Environmental Protection Department
Water Division
Fort Boone Plaza
18 Reilly Rd.
Frankfort, KY 40601
Phone: (502)564-3410
Fax: (502)564-4245
Contact: Jack A. Wilson, Director

★1379★ Natural Resources and Environmental Protection Cabinet
Environmental Quality Commission
18 Reilly Rd.
Frankfort, KY 40601
Phone: (502)564-2150
Fax: (502)564-4245
Contact: William Horace Brown, Chm.

★1380★ Natural Resources and Environmental Protection Cabinet
Law Department
Five Capital Plaza Tower
Frankfort, KY 40601
Phone: (502)564-5576
Fax: (502)564-2043
Contact: Frank Dickerson, Commissioner

★1381★ Natural Resources and Environmental Protection Cabinet
Natural Resources Department
107 Mero St.
Frankfort, KY 40601
Phone: (502)564-2184

Alt. Phone: (502)564-6193
Contact: Robert F. Knarr, Commissioner

★1382★ Natural Resources and Environmental Protection Cabinet
Natural Resources Department
Conservation Division
691 Teton Trail
Frankfort, KY 40601
Phone: (502)564-3080
Contact: Stanley Head, Director

★1383★ Natural Resources and Environmental Protection Cabinet
Natural Resources Department
Energy Division
691 Teton Trail
Frankfort, KY 40601
Phone: (502)564-7192
Contact: Lana Rogers, Director

★1384★ Natural Resources and Environmental Protection Cabinet
Natural Resources Department
Forestry Division
627 Comanche Trail
Frankfort, KY 40601
Phone: (502)564-4496
Contact: Don Hamm, Director

★1385★ Natural Resources and Environmental Protection Cabinet
Natural Resources Department
Water Patrol Division
107 Mero St.
Frankfort, KY 40601
Phone: (502)564-3074
Fax: (502)564-6193
Contact: Charles Browning, Director

★1386★ Natural Resources and Environmental Protection Cabinet
Nature Preserves Commission
407 Broadway
Frankfort, KY 40601
Phone: (502)564-2886
Contact: Sally Lyons, Chm.

★1387★ Natural Resources and Environmental Protection Cabinet
Surface Mining Reclamation and Enforcement Department
Two Hudson Hollow
Frankfort, KY 40601
Phone: (502)564-6940
Fax: (502)564-5848
Contact: William J. Grable, Commissioner

★1388★ Public Protection and Regulation Cabinet
Mines and Minerals Department
PO Box 14080
Lexington, KY 40512-4080
Phone: (606)254-0367
Contact: Carl Ankrom, Commissioner

★1389★ Tourism Cabinet
Fish and Wildlife Resources Department
Arnold Mitchell Bldg.
One Game Farm Rd.
Frankfort, KY 40601
Phone: (502)564-3400
Fax: (502)564-6508
Contact: Don R. McCormick, Commissioner

★1390★ Tourism Cabinet
Fish and Wildlife Resources Department
Conservation Education Division
Arnold Mitchell Bldg.
One Game Farm Rd.
Frankfort, KY 40601
Phone: (502)564-4762
Fax: (502)564-6508
Contact: Lynn Garrison, Director

★1391★ Tourism Cabinet
Fish and Wildlife Resources Department
Fisheries Division
Arnold Mitchell Bldg.
One Game Farm Rd.
Frankfort, KY 40601
Phone: (502)564-3596
Fax: (502)564-6508
Contact: Peter Pfeiffer, Director

★1392★ Tourism Cabinet
Fish and Wildlife Resources Department
Wildlife Division
Arnold Mitchell Bldg.
One Game Farm Rd.
Frankfort, KY 40601
Phone: (502)564-4406
Fax: (502)564-6508
Contact: Lauren Schaff, Director

★1393★ Tourism Cabinet
Parks Department
10 Capital Plaza Tower
Frankfort, KY 40601
Phone: (502)564-2172
Fax: (502)564-6100
Contact: Rapier Smith, Commissioner

Louisiana

★1394★ Agriculture and Forestry Department
PO Box 94302
Baton Rouge, LA 70821-9302
Phone: (504)922-1234
Fax: (504)922-1253
Contact: Bob Odom, Commissioner

★1395★ Agriculture and Forestry Department
Agriculture and Environmental Sciences Office
PO Box 3596
Baton Rouge, LA 70821-3596
Phone: (504)925-3770
Fax: (504)922-1356
Contact: John Impson, Asst. Commissioner

★1396★ Agriculture and Forestry Department
Forestry Office
PO Box 1628
Baton Rouge, LA 70821-1628
Phone: (504)925-4500
Fax: (504)922-1356
Contact: Paul Frey, Asst. Commissioner

★1397★ Agriculture and Forestry Department
Forestry Office
Protection Division
PO Box 1628
Baton Rouge, LA 70821-1628
Phone: (504)925-4500
Fax: (504)922-1356
Contact: Cyril LeJeune, Director

★1398★ Agriculture and Forestry Department
Information & Education Division
PO Box 1628
Baton Rouge, LA 70821-1628
Phone: (504)925-4500
Fax: (504)922-1356
Contact: J.L. Culpepper, Director

★1399★ Agriculture and Forestry Department
Soil and Water Conservation Committee
PO Box 3554
Baton Rouge, LA 70821-3554
Phone: (504)922-1269
Contact: Bradley Spicer, Exec. Dir.

★1400★ Attorney General's Office (Justice Department)
Lands & Natural Resources Division
PO Box 94005
Baton Rouge, LA 70804-9005
Phone: (504)342-7900
Fax: (504)342-7335
Contact: Gary L. Keyser, Asst. Atty. Gen.

★1401★ Culture, Recreation and Tourism Department
State Parks Office
PO Box 44426
Baton Rouge, LA 70804-4426
Phone: (504)342-8111
Contact: Linton Ardoin, Asst. Secty.

★1402★ Environmental Quality Department
PO Box 44066
Baton Rouge, LA 70804
Phone: (504)765-0243
Contact: Tim Hardy, Asst. Secty.

★1403★ Environmental Quality Department
PO Box 44066
Baton Rouge, LA 70804
Phone: (504)765-0643
Contact: Maureen O'Neil, Asst. Secty.

★1404★ Environmental Quality Department
PO Box 44066
Baton Rouge, LA 70804
Phone: (504)765-0102
Contact: Mike McDaniel, Asst. Secty.

★1405★ Environmental Quality Department
PO Box 44066
Baton Rouge, LA 70804
Phone: (504)765-0370
Contact: Terry Rider, Asst. Secty.

★1406★ Environmental Quality Department
PO Box 44066
Baton Rouge, LA 70804
Phone: (504)765-0741
Contact: Paul Templet, Secretary

★1407★ Natural Resources Department
PO Box 94396
Baton Rouge, LA 70804-9396
Phone: (504)342-4500
Fax: (504)342-2707
Contact: Ron Gomez, Secretary

★1408★ Natural Resources Department
Coastal Management Office
PO Box 44124
Baton Rouge, LA 70804
Phone: (504)342-7591
Contact: Terry Howey, Director

★1409★ **Natural Resources Department**
Coastal Restoration Office
PO Box 94396
Baton Rouge, LA 70804-9396
Phone: (504)342-7308
Fax: (504)342-2707
Contact: Bill Good, Director

★1410★ **Natural Resources Department**
Conservation Office
PO Box 94275
Baton Rouge, LA 70804-9275
Phone: (504)342-5500
Contact: J. Patrick Batchelor, Commissioner

★1411★ **Natural Resources Department**
Conservation Office
Geological Oil & Gas Division
PO Box 94275
Baton Rouge, LA 70804-9275
Phone: (504)342-5510
Contact: Charles King, Director

★1412★ **Natural Resources Department**
Conservation Office
Injection & Mining Division
PO Box 94275
Baton Rouge, LA 70804-9275
Phone: (504)342-5515
Contact: James H. Welch, Director

★1413★ **Natural Resources Department**
Mineral Resources Office
PO Box 2827
Baton Rouge, LA 70821
Phone: (504)342-4615
Contact: Edward Rhorer, Dep. Asst. Secretary

★1414★ **Wildlife and Fisheries Department**
PO Box 15570
Baton Rouge, LA 70895
Phone: (504)765-2803
Contact: A. Kell McInnis, III, Secretary

Maine

★1415★ **Attorney General's Office**
Natural Resources Division
State House
Station B
Augusta, ME 04333
Phone: (207)289-3661
Fax: (207)289-3145
Contact: Jeff Pidot, Chief

★1416★ **Conservation Department**
State House
Station 22
Augusta, ME 04333
Phone: (207)289-4900
Fax: (207)289-2400
Contact: C. Edwin Meadows, Jr., Commissioner

★1417★ **Conservation Department**
Information & Education Division
State House
Station 22
Augusta, ME 04333
Phone: (207)289-4902
Fax: (207)289-2400
Contact: Marshall Wiebe, Director

★1418★ **Conservation Department**
Maine Conservation Corps & SERVE/Maine Division
State House
Station 22
Augusta, ME 04333
Phone: (207)289-2211
Fax: (207)289-2400
Contact: Kenneth Spalding, Director

★1419★ **Conservation Department**
Maine Forest Service
State House
Station 22
Augusta, ME 04333
Phone: (207)289-2793
Fax: (207)289-2791
Contact: John H. Cashwell, Director

★1420★ **Conservation Department**
Parks and Recreation Bureau
State House
Station 22
Augusta, ME 04333
Phone: (207)289-3821
Fax: (207)289-2400
Contact: Herbert Hartman, Director

★1421★ **Conservation Department**
Waste Reduction and Recycling Office
286 Water St.
State House Station 154
Augusta, ME 04333
Phone: (207)289-5300

★1422★ **Environmental Protection Department**
State House
Station 17
Augusta, ME 04333
Phone: (207)289-2812
Fax: (207)289-7826
Contact: Dean Marriott, Commissioner

★1423★ **Environmental Protection Department**
Air Quality Control Bureau
State House
Station 17
Augusta, ME 04333
Phone: (207)289-2437
Fax: (207)289-7826
Contact: Dennis Keschl, Director

★1424★ **Environmental Protection Department**
Land Quality Control Bureau
State House
Station 17
Augusta, ME 04333
Phone: (207)289-2111
Fax: (207)289-7826
Contact: Debrah Richard, Director

★1425★ **Environmental Protection Department**
Land Quality Control Bureau
Enforcement & Field Services Division
State House
Station 17
Augusta, ME 04333
Phone: (207)289-2111
Fax: (207)289-7826

★1426★ **Environmental Protection Department**
Land Quality Control Bureau
Natural Resources Division
State House
Station 17
Augusta, ME 04333
Phone: (207)289-2111
Fax: (207)289-7826
Contact: Don Witherill, Director

★1427★ **Environmental Protection Department**
Oil and Hazardous Materials Control Bureau
State House
Station 17
Augusta, ME 04333
Phone: (207)289-2651
Fax: (207)289-7826
Contact: Alan M. Prysunka, Director

★1428★ **Environmental Protection Department**
Oil and Hazardous Materials Control Bureau
Licensing & Enforcement Division
State House, Station 17
Augusta, ME 04333
Phone: (207)289-2651
Fax: (207)289-7826
Contact: Scott Whittier, Director

★1429★ **Environmental Protection Department**
Solid Waste Management Bureau
State House
Station 17
Augusta, ME 04333
Phone: (207)582-8740
Contact: Paula Clark, Director

★1430★ **Environmental Protection Department**
Water Quality Control Bureau
State House
Station 17
Augusta, ME 04333
Phone: (207)289-3901
Contact: Stephen W. Groves, Director

★1431★ **Environmental Protection Department**
Water Quality Control Bureau
Environmental & Evaluation Lake Studies Division
State House
Station 17
Augusta, ME 04333
Phone: (207)289-3901
Contact: David Courtemanch, Director

★1432★ **Inland Fisheries and Wildlife Department**
State House
Station 41
Augusta, ME 04333
Phone: (207)289-5202
Fax: (207)289-4471
Contact: William Vail, Commissioner

★1433★ **Inland Fisheries and Wildlife Department**
Public Information Division
State House
Station 41
Augusta, ME 04333
Phone: (207)289-2871
Fax: (207)289-4471
Contact: W. Thomas Shoener, Director

★1434★ **Inland Fisheries and Wildlife Department**
Resource Management Bureau
State House
Station 41
Augusta, ME 04333
Phone: (207)289-3651
Contact: Fred Hurley, Director

★1435★ Inland Fisheries and Wildlife Department
Resource Management Bureau
Fisheries & Hatcheries Division
State House
Station 41
Augusta, ME 04333
Phone: (207)289-5261
Contact: Peter Bourque, Director

★1436★ Inland Fisheries and Wildlife Department
Resource Management Bureau
Wildlife Division
State House
Station 41
August, ME 04333
Phone: (207)289-5252
Contact: Gary Donovan, Director

★1437★ Marine Resources Department
State House
Station 21
Augusta, ME 04333
Phone: (207)289-6550
Fax: (207)289-4474
Contact: William J. Brennan, Commissioner

★1438★ State Soil and Water Conservation Commission
Deering Bldg.
AHMI Complex, Station 28
Augusta, ME 04333
Phone: (207)289-2666

Maryland

★1439★ Agriculture Department
Land Preservation Foundation
50 Harry S Truman Pkwy.
Annapolis, MD 21401
Phone: (301)841-5860
Contact: Leonard Lowry, Chm.

★1440★ Agriculture Department
Resource Conservation Office
50 Harry S Truman Pkwy.
Annapolis, MD 21401
Phone: (301)841-5865
Contact: Rosemary Roswell, Asst. Secty.

★1441★ Agriculture Department
Resource Conservation Office
Conservation Grants Program
50 Harry S. Truman Pkwy.
Annapolis, MD 21401
Phone: (301)841-5864
Contact: Gould Charshee, Chief

★1442★ Agriculture Department
Soil Conservation Committee
50 Harry S Truman Pkwy.
Annapolis, MD 21401
Phone: (301)841-5863
Contact: George Godfrey, Chm.

★1443★ Natural Resources Department
Tawes State Office Bldg.
Annapolis, MD 21401
Phone: (301)974-3041
Fax: (301)974-5206
Contact: Torrey C. Brown M.D., Secretary

★1444★ Natural Resources Department
Forest, Park and Wildlife Division
Parks & Forests Office
Tawes State Office Bldg.
Annapolis, MD 21401
Phone: (301)974-3771
Fax: (301)974-5550
Contact: Rick Barton, Director

★1445★ Natural Resources Department
Forest, Park and Wildlife Division
Wildlife Office
Tawes State Office Bldg.
Annapolis, MD 21401
Phone: (301)974-3195
Fax: (301)974-5550
Contact: Gary Taylor, Director

★1446★ Natural Resources Department
Maryland Environmental Service
2020 Industrial Dr.
Annapolis, MD 21401
Phone: (301)974-7281
Fax: (301)974-7267
Contact: George Perdikakis, Director

★1447★ Natural Resources Department
Maryland Environmental Trust
275 W. Garrett Pl.
Annapolis, MD 21401
Phone: (301)974-5350
Fax: (301)974-5340
Contact: H. Grant Dehart, Exec. Dir.

★1448★ Natural Resources Department
Natural Resources Police Force
Tawes State Office Bldg.
Annapolis, MD 21401
Phone: (301)974-2240
Fax: (301)974-2740
Contact: Jack Taylor, Superintendent

★1449★ Natural Resources Department
Water Resources Administration
Tawes State Office Bldg.
Annapolis, MD 21401
Phone: (301)974-3846
Fax: (301)974-2618
Contact: Catherine Stevenson, Director

Massachusetts

★1450★ Attorney General's Office
Public Protection Bureau
Environmental Protection Division
One Ashburton Pl., 2010
Boston, MA 02108
Phone: (617)727-2200
Fax: (617)727-3251

★1451★ Consumer Affairs and Business Regulation Executive Office
Energy Resources Division
100 Cambridge St., Rm. 1500
Boston, MA 02202
Phone: (617)727-4731
Fax: (617)727-0030
Contact: Paul W. Gromer, Commissioner

★1452★ Environmental Affairs Executive Office
100 Cambridge St., Rm. 2000
Boston, MA 02202
Phone: (617)727-9800
Fax: (617)727-2754
Contact: Susan F. Tierney, Secretary

★1453★ Environmental Affairs Executive Office
Conservation Services Division
100 Cambridge St., Rm. 2000
Boston, MA 02202
Phone: (617)727-1552
Fax: (617)727-2754
Contact: Joel A. Lerner, Director

★1454★ Environmental Affairs Executive Office
Environmental Impact Review Division
100 Cambridge St., Rm. 2000
Boston, MA 02202
Phone: (617)727-5830
Fax: (617)727-2754
Contact: Janet McCabe, Director

★1455★ Environmental Affairs Executive Office
Environmental Management Department
100 Cambridge St.
Boston, MA 02202
Phone: (617)727-3163
Contact: Peter Webber, Commissioner

★1456★ Environmental Affairs Executive Office
Environmental Management Department
Forests & Parks Division
100 Cambridge St.
Boston, MA 02202
Phone: (617)727-3180
Contact: Charles Dane, Director

★1457★ Environmental Affairs Executive Office
Environmental Management Department
Insect Pest Control Division
100 Cambridge St.
Boston, MA 02202
Phone: (617)727-3184
Contact: Ernest DeRosa, Director

★1458★ Environmental Affairs Executive Office
Environmental Management Department
Safe Waste Management Division
100 Cambridge St.
Boston, MA 02202
Phone: (617)727-4293
Contact: Michael Brown, Director

★1459★ Environmental Affairs Executive Office
Environmental Management Department
Water Resources Division
100 Cambridge St.
Boston, MA 02202
Phone: (617)727-3267
Contact: Richard Thibeteau, Director

★1460★ Environmental Affairs Executive Office
Environmental Protection Department
One Winter St., 3rd Fl.
Boston, MA 02108
Phone: (617)292-5856
Contact: Daniel Greenbaum, Commissioner

★1461★ Environmental Affairs Executive Office
Environmental Protection Department
Air Quality Division
One Winter St., 3rd Fl.
Boston, MA 02108
Phone: (617)292-5575
Contact: Steve DeGabrielle, Asst. Deputy Commissioner

★1462★ **Environmental Affairs Executive Office**
Environmental Protection Department
Hazardous & Solid Waste Division
One Winter St., 3rd Fl.
Boston, MA 02108
Phone: (617)292-5589
Contact: William Cass, Director

★1463★ **Environmental Affairs Executive Office**
Environmental Protection Department
Water Supply Division
1 Winter St., 3rd Fl.
Boston, MA 02108
Phone: (617)292-5765
Contact: Patricia Deese, Director

★1464★ **Environmental Affairs Executive Office**
Fisheries, Wildlife and Environmental Law Enforcement Department
100 Cambridge St., Rm. 1901
Boston, MA 02202
Phone: (617)727-1614
Contact: Robert Austin, Asst. Commissioner

★1465★ **Environmental Affairs Executive Office**
Fisheries, Wildlife and Environmental Law Enforcement Department
Environmental Law Enforcement Division
100 Cambridge St., Rm. 1901
Boston, MA 02202
Phone: (617)727-3190
Contact: Allan McGroary, Director

★1466★ **Environmental Affairs Executive Office**
Fisheries, Wildlife and Environmental Law Enforcement Division
Fisheries & Wildlife Division
100 Cambridge St., Rm. 1901
Boston, MA 02202
Phone: (617)727-3151
Contact: Wayne MacCallum, Director

★1467★ **Environmental Affairs Executive Office**
Fisheries, Wildlife and Environmental Law Enforcement Division
Non-Game Endangered Species Division
100 Cambridge St., Rm. 1901
Boston, MA 02202
Phone: (617)727-3157
Contact: Thomas French, Director

★1468★ **Environmental Affairs Executive Office**
Hazardous Waste Facilities Site Safety Council
80 Boylston St., Ste. 955
Boston, MA 02116
Phone: (617)727-6629
Contact: Joan Gardner, Director

★1469★ **Environmental Affairs Executive Office**
Water Resource Commission
100 Cambridge St., Rm. 2000
Boston, MA 02202
Phone: (617)727-9800
Fax: (617)727-2754
Contact: Elizabeth Kline, Commissioner

★1470★ **Water Resources Authority**
Charlestown Navy Yard
100 First Ave.
Boston, MA 02129
Phone: (617)241-6000
Fax: (617)241-6070
Contact: John P. DeVillars, Chm.

Michigan

★1471★ **Attorney General's Office**
Environmental Protection Division
Law Bldg.
PO Box 30212
Lansing, MI 48909
Phone: (517)373-7780
Fax: (517)373-4916
Contact: A. Michael Leffler, Asst.-in-Charge

★1472★ **Attorney General's Office**
National Resources Division
Law Bldg.
PO Box 30212
Lansing, MI 48909
Phone: (517)373-7540
Fax: (517)373-4916
Contact: Thomas J. Emery, Asst.-in-Charge

★1473★ **Natural Resources Department**
PO Box 30028
Lansing, MI 48909
Phone: (517)373-2329
Fax: (517)373-1547
Contact: David F. Hales, Director

★1474★ **Natural Resources Department**
Environmental Protection
PO Box 30028
Lansing, MI 48909
Phone: (517)373-7917
Fax: (517)373-1547
Contact: Delbert Rector, Deputy Dir.

★1475★ **Natural Resources Department**
Environmental Protection
Air Quality Division
PO Box 30028
Lansing, MI 48909
Phone: (517)373-7023
Fax: (517)373-1547
Contact: Robert Miller, Chief

★1476★ **Natural Resources Department**
Environmental Protection
Environmental Response Division
PO Box 30028
Lansing, MI 48909
Phone: (517)373-9837
Fax: (517)373-1547
Contact: James Truchan, Chief

★1477★ **Natural Resources Department**
Environmental Protection
Surface Water Division
PO Box 30028
Lansing, MI 48909
Phone: (517)373-1949
Fax: (517)373-1547
Contact: Paul Zugger, Chief

★1478★ **Natural Resources Department**
Environmental Protection
Waste Management Division
PO Box 30028
Lansing, MI 48909
Phone: (517)373-2730
Fax: (517)373-1547
Contact: Alan Howard, Chief

★1479★ **Natural Resources Department**
Public Information Office
PO Box 30028
Lansing, MI 48909
Phone: (517)373-1214
Fax: (517)373-1547
Contact: Sue Henry, Chief

★1480★ **Natural Resources Department**
Resources Division
PO Box 30028
Lansing, MI 48909
Phone: (517)373-0046
Contact: Jack Bails, Deputy Dir.

★1481★ **Natural Resources Department**
Resources Division
Forest Management Division
PO Box 30028
Lansing, MI 48909
Phone: (517)373-1275

★1482★ **Natural Resources Department**
Resources Division
Land and Water Management Division
PO Box 30028
Lansing, MI 48909
Phone: (517)373-1170
Contact: Dennis Hall, Chief

★1483★ **Natural Resources Department**
Resources Division
Parks Division
PO Box 30028
Lansing, MI 48909
Phone: (517)373-1270
Contact: O.J. Scherschligt, Chief

★1484★ **Natural Resources Department**
Resources Division
Wildlife Division
PO Box 30028
Lansing, MI 48909
Phone: (517)373-1263
Contact: Karl Hosford, Chief

★1485★ **Water Resources Commission**
PO Box 30028
Lansing, MI 48909
Phone: (517)373-1949

Minnesota

★1486★ **Natural Resources Department**
500 Lafayette Rd.
St. Paul, MN 55155
Phone: (612)296-6157

★1487★ **Natural Resources Department**
500 Lafayette Rd.
St. Paul, MN 55155-4001
Phone: (612)296-2549
Fax: (612)296-3500
Contact: Rodney Sando, Commissioner

★1488★ **Natural Resources Department**
Operations Department
Enforcement Division
500 Lafayette Rd.
St. Paul, MN 55155-4001
Phone: (612)296-4828
Fax: (612)296-3500
Contact: Leo Haseman, Director

★1489★ **Natural Resources Department**
Operations Department
Forestry Division
500 Lafayette Rd.
St. Paul, MN 55155-4001
Phone: (612)296-4484
Fax: (612)296-3500
Contact: Gerald Rose, Director

★1490★ Natural Resources Department Operations Department Minerals Division
500 Lafayette Rd.
St. Paul, MN 55155-4001
Phone: (612)296-4807
Fax: (612)296-3500
Contact: Bill Brice, Director

★1491★ Natural Resources Department Operations Department Parks & Recreation Division
500 Lafayette Rd.
St. Paul, MN 55155-4001
Phone: (612)296-2270
Fax: (612)296-3500
Contact: Bill Morrissey, Director

★1492★ Natural Resources Department Operations Department Waters Division
500 Lafayette Rd.
St. Paul, MN 55155-4001
Phone: (612)296-4810
Fax: (612)296-3500
Contact: Kent Lokkesmoe, Director

★1493★ Natural Resources Department Operations Division
500 Lafayette Rd.
St. Paul, MN 55155-4001
Phone: (612)296-5229
Fax: (612)296-3500
Contact: Ray Hitchcock, Asst. Commissioner

★1494★ Natural Resources Department Operations Fish & Wildlife Division
500 Lafayette Rd.
St. Paul, MN 55155-4001
Phone: (612)297-1308
Contact: Roger Holmes, Director

★1495★ Pollution Control Agency
520 Lafayette Rd.
St. Paul, MN 55155
Phone: (612)296-7301
Fax: (612)297-1456
Contact: Charles Williams, Commissioner

★1496★ Pollution Control Agency Air Quality Division
520 Lafayette Rd.
St. Paul, MN 55155
Phone: (612)296-7331
Fax: (612)297-1456
Contact: Michael Valentine, Director

★1497★ Pollution Control Agency Environmental Analysis
520 Lafayette Rd.
St. Paul, MN 55155
Phone: (612)296-7799
Fax: (612)297-1456
Contact: Janet Cain, Director

★1498★ Pollution Control Agency Ground Water & Solid Waste Division
520 Lafayette Rd.
St. Paul, MN 55155
Phone: (612)296-7333
Fax: (612)297-1456
Contact: Rodney Massey, Director

★1499★ Pollution Control Agency Hazardous Waste Division
520 Lafayette Rd.
St. Paul, MN 55155
Phone: (612)643-3402
Fax: (612)297-1456
Contact: Richard Svanda, Director

★1500★ Waste Management Office
1350 Energy Ln.
St. Paul, MN 55108
Phone: (612)649-5403
Fax: (612)649-5749
Contact: Linda Bruemmer, Director

★1501★ Waste Management Office Hazardous and Special Wastes Division
1350 Energy Ln.
St. Paul, MN 55108
Phone: (612)649-5741
Fax: (612)649-5749
Contact: Brett Smith, Director

★1502★ Waste Management Office Solid Waste Program
1350 Energy Ln.
St. Paul, MN 55108
Phone: (612)649-5759
Fax: (612)649-5749
Contact: Cathy Berg Moeger, Supervisor

★1503★ Water and Soil Resources Board
155 S. Wabasha St.
Ste. 104
St. Paul, MN 55107
Phone: (612)296-0879
Fax: (612)297-5615
Contact: Donald Ogaard, Chm.

Mississippi

★1504★ Environmental Quality Department
PO Box 20305
Jackson, MS 39289-1305
Phone: (601)961-5000
Fax: (601)961-5025
Contact: James I. Palmer, Exec. Dir.

★1505★ Environmental Quality Department Land and Water Resources Office
PO Box 10631
Jackson, MS 39289-0631
Phone: (601)961-5202
Contact: Charles Branch, Director

★1506★ Environmental Quality Division Pollution Control Office
PO Box 10385
Jackson, MS 39289-0385
Phone: (601)961-5100
Fax: (601)961-5190
Contact: Charles Chisolm, Director

★1507★ Environmental Quality Division Pollution Control Office Air Quality Branch
PO Box 10385
Jackson, MS 39289-0385
Phone: (601)961-5104
Fax: (601)961-5190
Contact: Dwight Wylie, Chief

★1508★ Environmental Quality Division Pollution Control Office Groundwater Branch
PO Box 10385
Jackson, MS 39289-0385
Phone: (601)961-5171
Fax: (601)961-5190
Contact: Bill Barnett, Chief

★1509★ Environmental Quality Division Pollution Control Office Hazardous Waste Branch
PO Box 10385
Jackson, MS 39289-0385
Phone: (601)961-5171
Fax: (601)961-5190
Contact: Sam Mabry, Chief

★1510★ Environmental Quality Division Pollution Control Office Surface Water Branch
PO Box 10385
Jackson, MS 39289-0385
Phone: (601)961-5171
Fax: (601)961-5190
Contact: Barry Royals, Chief

★1511★ Forestry Commission
301 N. Lamar St.
Ste. 300
Jackson, MS 39201
Phone: (601)359-2800
Fax: (601)359-1349
Contact: Robert S. Moss, State Forester

★1512★ Land and Water Resources Bureau
Southport Mall
PO Box 10631
Jackson, MS 39209
Phone: (601)961-5200

★1513★ Natural Resource Department Pollution Control Bureau
PO Box 10385
Jackson, MS 39209
Phone: (601)961-5171
Contact: Charles H. Chisolm, Director

★1514★ Soil and Water Conservation Commission
PO Box 23005
Jackson, MS 39225
Phone: (601)359-1281
Fax: (601)359-6011

★1515★ Wildlife, Fisheries and Parks Department
PO Box 451
Jackson, MS 39205
Phone: (601)364-2000
Fax: (601)364-2125
Contact: Jack Herring, Exec. Dir.

★1516★ Wildlife, Fisheries and Parks Department Parks and Recreation Division
PO Box 451
Jackson, MS 39205
Phone: (601)364-2010
Fax: (601)364-2125
Contact: John King, Director

★1517★ Wildlife, Fisheries and Parks Department Wildlife and Fisheries Division
PO Box 451
Jackson, MS 39205
Phone: (601)364-2015
Fax: (601)364-2125
Contact: Ed Hackett, Director

★1518★ Wildlife, Fisheries and Parks Department Wildlife and Fisheries Division Environmental Education
PO Box 451
Jackson, MS 39205
Phone: (601)364-2182
Contact: John Burris, Director

★1519★ Wildlife, Fisheries and Parks Department
Wildlife and Fisheries Division
Marine Resources
2620 Beach Blvd
Biloxi, MS 39531
Phone: (601)385-5860
Contact: Joe Gill, Director

Missouri

★1520★ Conservation Department
2901 W. Truman Blvd.
PO Box 180
Jefferson City, MO 65102-0180
Phone: (314)751-4115
Fax: (314)751-4467
Contact: John Powell, Chm.

★1521★ Conservation Department
Fisheries Division
2901 W. Truman Blvd.
PO Box 180
Jefferson City, MO 65102-0180
Phone: (314)751-4115
Fax: (314)751-4467
Contact: James P. Fry, Chief

★1522★ Conservation Department
Protection Division
2901 W. Truman Blvd.
PO Box 180
Jefferson City, MO 65102-0180
Phone: (314)751-4115
Fax: (314)751-4467
Contact: Robert B. King, Chief

★1523★ Conservation Department
Public Information Division
2901 W. Truman Blvd.
PO Box 180
Jefferson City, MO 65102-0180
Phone: (314)751-4115
Fax: (314)751-4467
Contact: Shannon Cave, Chief

★1524★ Conservation Department
Wildlife Division
2901 W. Truman Blvd.
PO Box 180
Jefferson City, MO 65102-0180
Phone: (314)751-4115
Fax: (314)751-4467
Contact: Oliver A. Torgerson, Chief

★1525★ Natural Resources Department
PO Box 176
Jefferson City, MO 65102-0180
Phone: (314)751-4422
Fax: (314)751-9277
Contact: G. Tracy Mehan, III, Director

★1526★ Natural Resources Department
Energy Division
PO Box 176
Jefferson City, MO 65102
Phone: (314)751-2254
Fax: (314)751-9277
Contact: Robert Jackson, Director

★1527★ Natural Resources Department
Environmental Improvement Authority
PO Box 176
Jefferson City, MO 65102
Phone: (314)751-4919
Fax: (314)751-9277
Contact: Stephen Mahfood, Director

★1528★ Natural Resources Department
Environmental Quality Division
PO Box 176
Jefferson City, MO 65102
Phone: (314)751-4810
Fax: (314)751-9277
Contact: David Shorr, Director

★1529★ Natural Resources Department
Parks, Recreation & Historic Preservation Division
PO Box 176
Jefferson City, MO 65102
Phone: (314)751-2479
Fax: (314)751-9277
Contact: Wayne Gross, Director

Montana

★1530★ Agriculture Department
Environmental Management Division
Capitol Sta.
Agriculture & Livestock Bldg.
Helena, MT 59620-0201
Phone: (406)444-2944
Fax: (406)444-5409
Contact: Gary L. Gingery, Admin.

★1531★ Environmental Quality Council
State Capitol
Helena, MT 59620
Phone: (406)444-3742

★1532★ Fish, Wildlife and Parks Department
1420 E. Sixth Ave.
Helena, MT 59620
Phone: (406)444-3186
Fax: (406)444-4952
Contact: K.L. Cool, Director

★1533★ Fish, Wildlife and Parks Department
Conservation Education Division
1420 E. Sixth Ave.
Helena, MT 59620
Phone: (406)444-4041
Fax: (406)444-4952
Contact: Ron Aasheim, Administrator

★1534★ Fish, Wildlife and Parks Department
Field Services Division
1420 E. Sixth Ave.
Helena, MT 59620
Phone: (406)444-2602
Fax: (406)444-4952
Contact: Jerry Wells, Administrator

★1535★ Fish, Wildlife and Parks Department
Fisheries Division
1420 E. Sixth Ave.
Helena, MT 59620
Phone: (406)444-2449
Fax: (406)444-4952
Contact: Larry Peterman, Administrator

★1536★ Fish, Wildlife and Parks Department
Law Enforcement Division
1420 E. Sixth Ave.
Helena, MT 59620
Phone: (406)444-2452
Fax: (406)444-4952
Contact: Erwin J. Kent, Administrator

★1537★ Fish, Wildlife and Parks Department
Legal Division
1420 E. Sixth Ave.
Helena, MT 59620
Phone: (406)444-4594
Fax: (406)444-4952
Contact: Robert Lane, Administrator

★1538★ Fish, Wildlife and Parks Department
Parks Division
1420 E. Sixth Ave.
Helena, MT 59620
Phone: (406)444-3750
Fax: (406)444-4952
Contact: Arnold Olsen, Administrator

★1539★ Fish, Wildlife and Parks Department
Wildlife Division
1420 E. Sixth Ave.
Helena, MT 59620
Phone: (406)444-2612
Fax: (406)444-4952
Contact: Donald A. Childress, Administrator

★1540★ Health and Environmental Sciences Department
Environmental Sciences Division
Cogswell Bldg.
Helena, MT 69620
Phone: (406)444-3948
Fax: (406)444-2606
Contact: Steve Pilcher, Admin.

★1541★ Natural Resources and Conservation Department
1520 E. Sixth Ave.
Helena, MT 59620-2301
Phone: (406)444-6699
Fax: (406)444-6721
Contact: Karen Barclay, Director

★1542★ Natural Resources and Conservation Department
Conservation and Resource Development Division
1520 E. Sixth Ave.
Helena, MT 59620-2301
Phone: (406)444-6667
Fax: (406)444-6721
Contact: Ray Beck, Administrator

★1543★ Natural Resources and Conservation Department
Energy Division
1520 E. Sixth Ave.
Helena, MT 59620-2301
Phone: (406)444-6697
Fax: (406)444-6721
Contact: Van Jamison, Administrator

★1544★ Natural Resources and Conservation Department
Oil & Gas Conservation Division
2535 St. John's Ave.
Billings, MT 59620
Phone: (406)656-0040
Contact: Tom Richmond, Admin.

★1545★ Natural Resources and Conservation Department
Water Resources Division
1520 E. Sixth Ave.
Helena, MT 59620-2301
Phone: (406)444-6601
Fax: (406)444-6721
Contact: Gary Fritz, Administrator

Nebraska

★1546★ Environmental Control Department
State Office Bldg.
PO Box 98922
Lincoln, NE 68509-8922
Phone: (402)471-4231
Fax: (402)471-2909

★1547★ Environmental Control Department
Air Quality Division
State Office Bldg.
PO Box 98922
Lincoln, NE 68509-8922
Phone: (402)471-2189
Fax: (402)471-2909

★1548★ Environmental Control Department
Land Quality Division
State Office Bldg.
PO Box 98922
Lincoln, NE 68509-8922
Phone: (402)471-4210
Fax: (402)471-2909

★1549★ Environmental Control Department
Public Information Division
State Office Bldg.
PO Box 98922
Lincoln, NE 68509-8922
Phone: (402)471-4223
Fax: (402)471-2909

★1550★ Environmental Control Department
Water Quality Division
State Office Bldg.
PO Box 98922
Lincoln, NE 68509-8922
Phone: (402)471-4220
Fax: (402)471-2909

★1551★ Games and Parks Commission
2200 N. 33rd
PO Box 30370
Lincoln, NE 68503
Phone: (402)471-5539
Contact: Rex Amack, Director

★1552★ Games and Parks Commission
Fisheries Division
2200 N. 33rd
PO Box 30370
Lincoln, NE 68503
Phone: (402)471-5515
Contact: Wesley Sheets, Chief

★1553★ Games and Parks Commission
Information and Education Division
2200 N. 33rd
PO Box 30370
Lincoln, NE 68503
Phone: (402)471-5481
Contact: Paul Horton, Chief

★1554★ Games and Parks Commission
Resource Services Division
2200 N. 33rd
PO Box 30370
Lincoln, NE 68503
Phone: (402)471-5411
Contact: Harold Edwards, Chief

★1555★ Games and Parks Commission
Wildlife Division
2200 N. 33rd
PO Box 30370
Lincoln, NE 68503
Phone: (402)471-5435
Contact: Ken Johnson, Chief

★1556★ Natural Resources Commission
301 Centennial Mall S.
PO Box 94876
Lincoln, NE 68509
Phone: (402)471-2081
Fax: (402)471-3132
Contact: Dayle E. Williamson, Director

★1557★ Oil and Gas Conservation Commission
PO Box 399
Sidney, NE 69162
Phone: (308)254-4595
Fax: (308)254-7022
Contact: Paul H. Roberts, Director

★1558★ Water Resources Department
PO Box 94676
Lincoln, NE 68509-4676
Phone: (402)471-2363
Contact: J. Michael Jess, Director

Nevada

★1559★ Conservation and Natural Resources Department
123 W. Nye Ln.
Carson City, NV 89710
Phone: (702)687-4360
Fax: (702)687-6972
Contact: Peter G. Morros, Director

★1560★ Conservation and Natural Resources Department
Conservation Districts Division
123 W. Nye Ln.
Carson City, NV 89710
Phone: (702)687-4365
Fax: (702)687-6972
Contact: Pamela B. Wilcox, Admin.

★1561★ Conservation and Natural Resources Department
Environmental Protection Division
123 W. Nye Ln.
Carson City, NV 89710
Phone: (702)687-4670
Fax: (702)687-6972
Contact: Lewis Dodgon, Admin.

★1562★ Conservation and Natural Resources Department
Forestry Division
123 W. Nye Ln.
Carson City, NV 89710
Phone: (702)687-4350
Fax: (702)687-6972
Contact: Lowell V. Smith, State Forester

★1563★ Conservation and Natural Resources Department
Water Resources Division
123 W. Nye Ln.
Carson City, NV 89710
Phone: (702)687-4380
Fax: (702)687-6972
Contact: R. Michael Turnipseed, State Forester

★1564★ Wildlife Department
PO Box 10678
Reno, NV 89520
Phone: (702)688-1500
Fax: (702)688-1595
Contact: William Molini, Director

★1565★ Wildlife Department
Fisheries Division
PO Box 10678
Reno, NV 89520
Phone: (702)688-1500
Fax: (702)688-1595
Contact: Pat Coffin, Admin.

★1566★ Wildlife Department
Public Information Division
PO Box 10678
Reno, NV 89520
Phone: (702)688-1500
Fax: (702)688-1595
Contact: David Rice, Director

New Hampshire

★1567★ Agriculture Department
State Conservation Committee
Ca;ller Box 2042
Concord, NH 03302
Phone: (603)271-3576

★1568★ Attorney General's Office
Environmental Protection Bureau
208 State House Annex
Concord, NH 03301-6397
Phone: (603)271-3679
Fax: (603)271-2361
Contact: Steven M. Houran, Director

★1569★ Environmental Services Department
6 Hazen Dr.
Concord, NH 03301
Phone: (603)271-3503
Fax: (603)271-2867
Contact: Robert W. Varney, Commissioner

★1570★ Environmental Services Department
Air Resource Division
64 N. Main St.
Caller Box 2033
Concord, NH 03302-2033
Phone: (603)271-1370
Contact: Dennis R. Lunderville, Director

★1571★ Environmental Services Department
Waste Management Division
6 Hazen Dr.
Concord, NH 03301
Phone: (603)271-2905
Fax: (603)271-2867
Contact: Philip J. O'Brien Ph.D., Director

★1572★ Environmental Services Department
Water Resources Division
64 N. Main St.
PO Box 2008
Concord, NH 03301
Phone: (603)271-3406
Contact: Delbert F. Downing, Director

★1573★ Environmental Services Department
Water Supply & Pollution Control Division
6 Hazen Dr.
Concord, NH 03301
Phone: (603)271-3504
Fax: (603)271-2867
Contact: Edward J. Schmidt, Jr. Ph.D., Director

★1574★ Fish and Game Department
Wildlife Division
Two Hazen Dr.
Concord, NH 03301
Phone: (603)271-2462
Contact: Howard C. Nowell, Jr., Chief

★1575★ Resources and Development Council
State Planning Office
21 1/2 Baecon St.
Concord, NH 03301
Phone: (603)271-2155

New Jersey

★1576★ Environmental Protection Department
401 E. State St.
CN 402
Trenton, NJ 08625-0402
Phone: (609)292-2885
Fax: (609)984-3962
Contact: Judith A. Yaskin, Commissioner

★1577★ Environmental Protection Department
Environmental Management and Control
401 E. State St.
CN 402
Trenton, NJ 08625-0402
Phone: (609)292-8058
Fax: (609)633-1166
Contact: John S. Keith, Asst. Commissioner

★1578★ Environmental Protection Department
Environmental Management and Control
Environmental Quality Division
401 E. State St.
CN 402
Trenton, NJ 08625-0402
Phone: (609)292-5383
Fax: (609)633-1166
Contact: Anthony McMahon, Director

★1579★ Environmental Protection Department
Environmental Management and Control
Solid Waste Management Division
401 E. State St.
CN 402
Trenton, NJ 08625-0402
Phone: (609)530-8591
Fax: (609)633-1166
Contact: John V. Czapor, Director

★1580★ Environmental Protection Department
Environmental Management and Control
Water Resources Division
401 E. State St.
CN 402
Trenton, NJ 08625-0402
Phone: (609)292-1637
Fax: (609)633-1166
Contact: LeRoy T. Cattaneo, Codirector

★1581★ Environmental Protection Department
Hazardous Waste Management
401 E. State St.
CN 402
Trenton, NJ 08625-0402
Phone: (609)633-1408
Fax: (609)633-2360
Contact: Lance Miller, Asst. Commissioner

★1582★ Environmental Protection Department
Legal Affairs Office
401 E. State St.
CN 402
Trenton, NJ 08625-0402
Phone: (609)292-0716
Fax: (609)984-3962
Contact: Robert J. McManus, Director

★1583★ Environmental Protection Department
Pollution Prevention Office
401 E. State St.
CN 402
Trenton, NJ 08625-0402
Phone: (609)984-5339
Fax: (609)984-3962
Contact: Shelley Hearne, Director

New Mexico

★1584★ Attorney General's Office
Environmental Enforcement Division
PO Drawer 1508
Santa Fe, NM 87504-1508
Phone: (505)827-6020
Fax: (505)827-5826
Contact: Mike Dickman, Director

★1585★ Energy, Minerals and Natural Resources Department
2040 S. Pacheco
Santa Fe, NM 87505
Phone: (505)827-5950
Contact: Anita Lockwood, Secretary

★1586★ Energy, Minerals and Natural Resources Department
Energy Conservation Management Division
2040 S. Pacheco
Santa Fe, NM 87505
Phone: (505)827-5900
Contact: Dianne Caron, Director

★1587★ Energy, Minerals and Natural Resources Department
Forestry Division
2040 S. Pacheco
Santa Fe, NM 87505
Phone: (505)827-5830
Contact: Jim Norwick, Director

★1588★ Energy, Minerals and Natural Resources Department
Mining & Minerals Division
2040 S. Pacheco
Santa Fe, NM 87505
Phone: (505)827-5970
Contact: Carol Leach, Director

★1589★ Energy, Minerals and Natural Resources Department
Oil Conservation Division
2040 S. Pacheco
Santa Fe, NM 87505
Phone: (505)827-5802
Contact: William Lemay, Director

★1590★ Energy, Minerals and Natural Resources Department
Park & Recreation Division
2040 S. Pacheco
Santa Fe, NM 87505
Phone: (505)827-7465
Contact: Richard Cooper, Director

★1591★ Game and Fish Department
Villagra Bldg.
Santa Fe, NM 87503
Phone: (505)827-7899
Fax: (505)827-7915
Contact: Bill Montoya, Director

★1592★ Game and Fish Department
Fish Management Division
Villagra Bldg.
Santa Fe, NM 87503
Phone: (505)827-7905
Fax: (505)827-7915
Contact: Stephen Henry, Director

★1593★ Health and Environment Department
Environmental Improvement Division
1190 St. Francis Drive
PO Box 968
Sante Fe, NM 87504-0968
Phone: (505)827-0020
Contact: Michael Burkhart, Director

New York

★1594★ Attorney General's Office (Law Department)
Environmental Protection Bureau
State Capitol
Albany, NY 12224
Phone: (518)474-8096
Fax: (518)474-8995
Contact: James A. Sevinsky, Asst. Atty. Gen.

★1595★ Environmental Conservation Department
50 Wolf Rd.
Albany, NY 12233
Phone: (518)457-3446
Fax: (518)457-1088
Contact: Thomas C. Jorling, Commissioner

★1596★ Environmental Conservation Department
Environmental Quality Office
50 Wolf Rd.
Albany, NY 12233
Phone: (518)457-5768
Fax: (518)457-1088
Contact: R. Darryl Banks, Deputy Commissioner

★1597★ Environmental Conservation Department
Environmental Quality Office
Air Resources Division
50 Wolf Rd.
Albany, NY 12233
Phone: (518)457-7230
Fax: (518)457-1088
Contact: Thomas Allen, Director

★1598★ Environmental Conservation Department
Environmental Quality Office
Hazardous Substances Division
50 Wolf Rd.
Albany, NY 12233
Phone: (518)457-6943

Fax: (518)457-1088
Contact: N.G. Kaul, Director

★1599★ Environmental Conservation Department
Environmental Quality Office
Solid Waste Division
50 Wolf St.
Albany, NY 12233
Phone: (518)457-6603
Fax: (518)457-1088
Contact: Norman Nosenchuck, Director

★1600★ Environmental Conservation Department
Environmental Quality Office
Water Division
50 Wolf Rd.
Albany, NY 12233
Phone: (518)457-6674
Fax: (518)457-1088
Contact: Salvatore Pagano, Director

★1601★ Environmental Conservation Department
General Counsel's Office
Legal Affairs Division
50 Wolf Rd.
Albany, NY 12233
Phone: (518)457-3551
Fax: (518)457-1088
Contact: Anne Hill DeBarbieri, Director

★1602★ Environmental Conservation Department
Local Resource Reuse and Reovery Program
50 Wolf Rd.
Albany, NY 12233-4010
Phone: (518)457-6603
Contact: Norman Nosenchuck, Director

★1603★ Environmental Conservation Department
Natural Resources Office
50 Wolf Rd.
Albany, NY 12233
Phone: (518)457-0975
Fax: (518)457-1088
Contact: Robert L. Bendick, Jr., Deputy Commissioner

★1604★ Environmental Conservation Department
Natural Resources Office
Fish & Wildlife Division
50 Wolf Rd.
Albany, NY 12233
Phone: (518)457-5690
Fax: (518)457-1088
Contact: Kenneth Wich, Director

★1605★ Environmental Conservation Department
Natural Resources Office
Lands & Forests Division
50 Wolf Rd.
Albany, NY 12233
Phone: (518)457-2475
Fax: (518)457-1088
Contact: Robert Bathrick, Director

★1606★ Environmental Conservation Department
Natural Resources Office
Mineral Resources Division
50 Wolf Rd.
Albany, NY 12233
Phone: (518)457-9337
Fax: (518)457-1088
Contact: Gregory Sovas, Director

★1607★ Environmental Facilities Corporation
50 Wolf Rd.
Albany, NY 12205-2603
Phone: (518)457-4222
Fax: (518)485-8773
Contact: Terry Agriss, Pres.

★1608★ New York State Energy and Research Development Authority
Municipal Waste Materials Recycling Program
2 Rockefeller Plaza
Albany, NY 12223
Phone: (518)465-6251 ext. 243
Contact: Parker Mathusa, Director

★1609★ Parks, Recreation and Historic Preservation Office
Empire State Plaza
Building One
Albany, NY 12238
Phone: (518)474-0443
Fax: (518)474-4492
Contact: Orin Lehman, Commissioner

North Carolina

★1610★ Administration Department
Science and Technology Board
Administration Bldg.
116 W. Jones St.
Raleigh, NC 27603-8003
Phone: (919)733-6500
Contact: Earl Mac Cormac Ph.D., Director

★1611★ Environment, Health and Natural Resources Department
PO Box 27687
Raleigh, NC 27611
Phone: (919)733-4984
Fax: (919)733-0513
Contact: William W. Cobey, Jr., Secretary

★1612★ Environment, Health and Natural Resources Department
Environmental Protection Department
PO Box 27687
Raleigh, NC 27611
Phone: (919)733-4984
Fax: (919)733-0513
Contact: Edythe McKinney, Asst. Secty.

★1613★ Environment, Health and Natural Resources Department
Environmental Protection Department
Coastal Management Division
PO Box 27687
Raleigh, NC 27611
Phone: (919)733-2293
Fax: (919)733-0513
Contact: Roger Schector, Director

★1614★ Environment, Health and Natural Resources Department
Environmental Protection Department
Environmental Management Division
PO Box 27687
Raleigh, NC 27611
Phone: (919)733-7015
Fax: (919)733-0513
Contact: George Everett Ph.D., Director

★1615★ Environment, Health and Natural Resources Department
Environmental Protection Department
Land Resources Division
PO Box 27687
Raleigh, NC 27611
Phone: (919)733-3833
Fax: (919)733-0513
Contact: Charles Gardner, Director

★1616★ Environment, Health and Natural Resources Department
Environmental Protection Department
Marine Fisheries Division
PO Box 27687
Raleigh, NC 27611
Phone: (919)726-7021
Contact: William T. Hogarth, Director

★1617★ Environment, Health and Natural Resources Department
Environmental Protection Department
Radiation Protection Division
PO Box 27687
Raleigh, NC 27611
Phone: (919)733-4283
Fax: (919)733-0513
Contact: Dayne Brown, Director

★1618★ Environment, Health and Natural Resources Department
Environmental Protection Department
Solid Waste Management
PO Box 27687
Raleigh, NC 27611
Phone: (919)733-4996
Fax: (919)733-0513
Contact: Bill Meyer, Director

★1619★ Environment, Health and Natural Resources Department
Environmental Protection Department
Water Resources Division
PO Box 27687
Raleigh, NC 27611
Phone: (919)733-4064
Fax: (919)733-0513
Contact: John Morris, Director

★1620★ Environment, Health and Natural Resources Department
Natural Resources Department
PO Box 27687
Raleigh, NC 27611
Phone: (919)733-4984
Fax: (919)733-0513
Contact: Lynn Muchmore, Asst. Secty.

★1621★ Environment, Health and Natural Resources Department
Natural Resources Department
Forest Resources Division
PO Box 27687
Raleigh, NC 27611
Phone: (919)733-2162
Fax: (919)733-0513
Contact: Harry Layman, Director

★1622★ Environment, Health and Natural Resources Department
Natural Resources Department
Parks and Recreation Division
PO Box 27687
Raleigh, NC 27611
Phone: (919)733-4181
Fax: (919)733-0513
Contact: Phil McKnelly, Director

★1623★ **Environment, Health and Natural Resources Department**
Natural Resources Department
Soil & Water Conservation Division
PO Box 27687
Raleigh, NC 27611
Phone: (919)733-2302
Fax: (919)733-0513
Contact: David W. Sides, Director

★1624★ **Environment, Health and Natural Resources Department**
Pollution Prevention
PO Box 27687
Raleigh, NC 27611
Phone: (919)733-7015
Fax: (919)733-0513
Contact: Gary Hunt, Director

★1625★ **Environment, Health and Natural Resources Department**
Waste Management Board
325 N. Salisbury St.
Raleigh, NC 27611
Phone: (919)733-9020
Contact: Linda Little Ph.D., Exec. Dir.

★1626★ **Environment, Health and Natural Resources Department**
Wildlife Resources Commission
PO Box 27687
Raleigh, NC 27611
Phone: (919)733-3391
Fax: (919)733-0513
Contact: Charles Fullwood, Director

North Dakota

★1627★ **Atmospheric Resource Board**
1314 Basin Ave.
Box 1833
Bismarck, ND 58502
Phone: (701)224-2788
Fax: (701)224-4749
Contact: Bruce A. Boe, Director

★1628★ **Game and Fish Department**
100 N. Bismarck Expwy.
Bismarck, ND 58501
Phone: (701)221-6300
Contact: Lloyd A. Jones, Commissioner

★1629★ **Game and Fish Department**
Fisheries Division
100 N. Bismarck Expwy.
Bismarck, ND 58501
Phone: (701)221-6300
Contact: Terry Steinwand, Chief

★1630★ **Game and Fish Department**
Information and Education Division
100 N. Bismarck Expwy.
Bismarck, ND 58501
Phone: (701)221-6300
Contact: H Ted. Upgren, Chief

★1631★ **Game and Fish Department**
Natural Resources Division
100 N. Bismarck Expwy.
Bismarck, ND 58501
Phone: (701)221-6300
Contact: Mike McKenna, Chief

★1632★ **Game and Fish Department**
Wildlife Division
100 N. Bismarck Expwy.
Bismarck, ND 58501
Phone: (701)221-6300
Contact: Ron Stromstad, Chief

★1633★ **Health and Consolidated Laboratories Department**
Environmental Health Section
1200 Missouri Ave.
PO Box 5520
Bismarck, ND 58502-5520
Phone: (701)221-5150
Fax: (701)221-5200
Contact: Francis Schwindt, Chief

★1634★ **Health and Consolidated Laboratories Department**
Environmental Health Section
Waste Management Division
1200 Missouri Ave.
PO Box 5520
Bismarck, ND 58502-5520
Phone: (701)221-5188
Fax: (701)221-5200
Contact: Martin Schock, Director

★1635★ **Health and Consolidated Laboratories Department**
Environmental Health Section
Water Quality Division
1200 Missouri Ave.
PO Box 5520
Bismarck, ND 58502-5520
Phone: (701)221-5210
Fax: (701)221-5200
Contact: Dennis Fewless, Director

★1636★ **Parks and Recreation Department**
1424 W. Century Ave.
Ste. 202
Bismarck, ND 58501
Phone: (701)224-4887
Fax: (701)224-4878
Contact: Doug Eiken, Director

★1637★ **Soil Conservation Committee**
State Capitol
600 E. Blvd. Ave.
Bismarck, ND 58505-0790
Phone: (701)224-2651
Contact: Blake Vander Vorst, Exec. Sec.

★1638★ **Water Commission**
900 E. Blvd. Ave.
Bismarck, ND 58505-0187
Phone: (701)224-4940
Fax: (701)224-3696
Contact: Dave Sprynczynatyk, State Engineer and Sec.

Ohio

★1639★ **Air Quality Development Authority**
50 W. Broad St.
Ste. 1901
Columbus, OH 43215
Phone: (614)466-6825
Fax: (614)752-9188
Contact: Mark R. Shanahan Ph.D., Exec. Dir.

★1640★ **Attorney General's Office**
Environmental Enforcement Section
30 E. Broad St., 17th Fl.
Columbus, OH 43266-0410
Phone: (614)466-2766
Fax: (614)466-6135
Contact: Dennis Muchnicki, Section Chief

★1641★ **Environmental Protection Agency**
1800 Watermark
PO Box 1049
Columbus, OH 43266-0149
Phone: (614)644-2782
Fax: (614)644-2329
Contact: Richard L. Shank, Director

★1642★ **Environmental Protection Agency**
Air Pollution Control Division
1800 Watermark
PO Box 1049
Columbus, OH 43266-0149
Phone: (614)644-2270
Fax: (614)644-2329
Contact: Patricia Walling, Director

★1643★ **Environmental Protection Agency**
Groundwater Division
1800 Watermark
PO Box 1049
Columbus, OH 43266-0149
Phone: (614)644-2905
Fax: (614)644-2329
Contact: Carl Wilhelm, Director

★1644★ **Environmental Protection Agency**
Hazardous Waste Facility Board
1800 Watermark
PO Box 1049
Columbus, OH 43266-0149
Phone: (614)644-2742
Fax: (614)644-2329
Contact: Richard Sahli, Chm.

★1645★ **Environmental Protection Agency**
Solid and Hazardous Waste Management Division
1800 Watermark
PO Box 1049
Columbus, OH 43266-0149
Phone: (614)644-2917
Fax: (614)644-2329
Contact: Linda Welch, Director

★1646★ **Environmental Protection Agency**
Water Pollution Control Division
1800 Watermark
PO Box 1049
Columbus, OH 43266-0149
Phone: (614)644-2001
Fax: (614)644-2329
Contact: Andrew Turner, Director

★1647★ **Environmental Protection Agency**
Water Quality Planning and Assessment Division
1800 Watermark
PO Box 1049
Columbus, OH 43266-0149
Phone: (614)644-2856
Fax: (614)644-2329
Contact: Gary Martin, Director

★1648★ **Natural Resources Department**
Fountain Sq.
Columbus, OH 43224-1387
Phone: (614)265-6875
Fax: (614)262-2197
Contact: Frances Seiberling Buchholzer, Director

★1649★ **Natural Resources Department**
Forestry Division
Fountain Sq.
Columbus, OH 48224-1387
Phone: (614)265-6694
Contact: Ron Abraham, Chief

★1650★ Natural Resources Department Litter Prevention and Recycling Office
Fountain Sq.
Columbus, OH 43224-1387
Phone: (614)265-6333
Contact: Bruce McPherson, Chief

★1651★ Natural Resources Department Natural Areas and Preserves Division
Fountain Sq.
Columbus, OH 48224-1387
Phone: (614)265-6453
Contact: Richard E. Mosley, Chief

★1652★ Natural Resources Department Oil and Gas Division
Fountain Sq.
Columbus, OH 43224-1387
Phone: (614)265-6893
Contact: Scott Kell, Chief

★1653★ Natural Resources Department Parks and Recreation Division
Fountain Sq.
Columbus, OH 48224-1387
Phone: (614)265-6561
Contact: Stanley Spaulding, Chief

★1654★ Natural Resources Department Public Information and Education Office
Fountain Sq.
Columbus, OH 43224-1387
Phone: (614)265-6789
Contact: George Harris, Chief

★1655★ Natural Resources Department Reclamation Division
Fountain Sq.
Columbus, OH 43224-1387
Phone: (614)265-6675
Contact: Tim Dieringer, Chief

★1656★ Natural Resources Department Recreation Management Section
Fountain Sq.
Columbus, OH 48224-1387
Phone: (614)265-6888
Contact: Richard E. Moseley, Deputy Dir.

★1657★ Natural Resources Department Resource Management Section
Fountain Sq.
Columbus, OH 43224-1387
Phone: (614)265-6882
Contact: Anne M. Wickham, Deputy Dir.

★1658★ Natural Resources Department Resource Protection Section
Fountain Sq.
Columbus, OH 43224-1387
Phone: (614)265-6845
Contact: John Piehowicz, Deputy Dir.

★1659★ Natural Resources Department Soil and Water Conservation Division
Fountain Sq.
Columbus, OH 43224-1387
Phone: (614)265-6614
Contact: Larry Vance, Chief

★1660★ Natural Resources Department Water Division
Fountain Sq.
Columbus, OH 43224-1387
Phone: (614)265-6712
Contact: Bob Goettemoeller, Chief

★1661★ Natural Resources Department Wildlife Division
Fountain Sq.
Columbus, OH 48224-1387
Phone: (614)265-6305
Contact: Richard Pierce, Chief

★1662★ Water Development Authority
50 W. Broad St.
Ste. 1425
Columbus, OH 43215
Phone: (614)466-5822
Fax: (614)644-9964
Contact: Steven J. Grossman, Exec. Dir.

Oklahoma

★1663★ Conservation Commission
2800 N. Lincoln Blvd.
Rm. 160
Oklahoma City, OK 73105-4298
Phone: (405)521-2834
Contact: Edward Johnson, Chm.

★1664★ Conservation Commission Water Quality Division
2800 N. Lincoln Blvd.
Rm. 160
Oklahoma City, OK 73105-4298
Phone: (405)521-2384
Contact: John Hassell, Director

★1665★ Pollution Control Department
PO Box 53504
Oklahoma City, OK 73152
Phone: (405)271-4468
Contact: Lawrence R. Edmison, Director

★1666★ Water Resources Board
PO Box 150
Oklahoma City, OK 73101-0150
Phone: (405)231-2555
Fax: (405)231-2600

★1667★ Wildlife Conservation Department
PO Box 53465
Oklahoma City, OK 73152
Phone: (405)521-3851
Contact: Steven A. Lewis, Director

★1668★ Wildlife Conservation Department Fisheries Division
PO Box 53465
Oklahoma City, OK 73152
Phone: (405)521-3721
Contact: Kim Erickson, Director

★1669★ Wildlife Conservation Department Game Division
PO Box 53465
Oklahoma City, OK 73152
Phone: (405)521-2739
Contact: Greg Duffy, Director

★1670★ Wildlife Conservation Department Information and Education Division
PO Box 53465
Oklahoma City, OK 73152
Phone: (405)521-3855
Contact: Dean Graham, Director

Oregon

★1671★ Energy Department
625 Marion St., NE
Salem, OR 97310
Phone: (503)378-4128
Fax: (503)373-7806
Contact: David Yaden, Director

★1672★ Energy Department Conservation Services Division
625 Marion St., NE
Salem, OR 97310
Phone: (503)378-8607
Fax: (503)373-7806
Contact: Larry Gray, Admin.

★1673★ Energy Department Nuclear Safety & Energy Division
625 Marion St., NE
Salem, OR 97310
Phone: (503)378-6469
Fax: (503)373-7806
Contact: David Stewart, Admin.

★1674★ Energy Department Public Information Division
625 Marion St., NE
Salem, OR 97310
Phone: (503)378-4129
Fax: (503)373-7806
Contact: William Sanderson, Rep.

★1675★ Environmental Quality Department
811 SW Sixth Ave.
Portland, OR 97204-1390
Phone: (503)229-5300
Fax: (503)229-6124
Contact: Fred Hansen, Director

★1676★ Environmental Quality Department Air Quality Control Division
811 SW Sixth Ave.
Portland, OR 97204-1390
Phone: (503)229-5397
Fax: (503)229-6124
Contact:, Admin.

★1677★ Environmental Quality Department Environmental Cleanup Division
811 SW Sixth Ave.
Portland, OR 97204-1390
Phone: (503)229-5254
Fax: (503)229-6124
Contact: Michael J. Downs, Admin.

★1678★ Environmental Quality Department Hazardous & Solid Waste Division
811 SW Sixth Ave.
Portland, OR 97204-1390
Phone: (503)229-5356
Fax: (503)229-6124
Contact: Stephanie Hallock, Admin.

★1679★ Environmental Quality Department Laboratory & Applied Research Division
811 SW Sixth Ave.
Portland, OR 97204-1390
Phone: (503)229-5983
Fax: (503)229-6124
Contact: Alan Hose, Admin.

★1680★ Environmental Quality Department Water Quality Control Division
811 SW Sixth Ave.
Portland, OR 97204-1390
Phone: (503)229-5324
Fax: (503)229-6124
Contact: Lydia Taylor, Admin.

★1681★ **Fish and Wildlife Department**
PO Box 59
Portland, OR 97207
Phone: (503)976-6339
Fax: (503)229-5602
Contact: Randy Fisher, Director

★1682★ **Fish and Wildlife Department**
Fish Division
PO Box 59
Portland, OR 97207
Phone: (503)229-5400
Fax: (503)229-5602
Contact: Jim Martin, Chief

★1683★ **Fish and Wildlife Department**
Habitat Conservation & Planning Division
PO Box 59
Portland, OR 97207
Phone: (503)229-5400
Fax: (503)229-5602
Contact: Nancy MacHugh, Chief

★1684★ **Fish and Wildlife Department**
Wildlife Division
PO Box 59
Portland, OR 97207
Phone: (503)229-5400
Fax: (503)229-5602
Contact: Rod Ingram, Chief

★1685★ **Forestry Department**
2600 State St.
Salem, OR 97310
Phone: (503)378-2511
Fax: (503)363-0754
Contact: James E. Brown, State Forester

★1686★ **Land Conservation and Development Department**
1175 Ct. St., NE
Salem, OR 97310
Phone: (503)378-4928
Fax: (503)362-6705
Contact: Susan Brody, Director

★1687★ **Water Resources Department**
3850 Portland Rd., NE
Salem, OR 97310
Phone: (503)378-2982
Fax: (503)378-8130
Contact: William H. Young, Director

★1688★ **Water Resources Department**
Water Conservation Division
3850 Portland Rd., NE
Salem, OR 97310
Phone: (503)378-3671
Fax: (503)378-8130
Contact: Doug Parrow, Mgr.

★1689★ **Water Resources Department**
Water Resources Commission
3850 Portland Rd., NE
Salem, OR 97310
Phone: (503)378-7993
Fax: (503)378-8130
Contact: Jan Shaw

Pennsylvania

★1690★ **Environmental Resources Department**
PO Box 2063
Harrisburg, PA 17105
Phone: (717)787-2814
Fax: (717)783-8926
Contact: Arthur A. Davis, Secretary

★1691★ **Environmental Resources Department**
Environmental Protection Office
PO Box 2063
Harrisburg, PA 17105
Phone: (717)787-5208
Fax: (717)783-9186
Contact: Mark McClellan, Deputy Sec.

★1692★ **Environmental Resources Department**
Environmental Protection Office
Air Quality Control Bureau
PO Box 2063
Harrisburg, PA 17105
Phone: (717)787-9702
Fax: (717)783-9186
Contact: James K. Hambright, Director

★1693★ **Environmental Resources Department**
Environmental Protection Office
Community Environmental Control Bureau
PO Box 2063
Harrisburg, PA 17105
Phone: (717)787-9035
Fax: (717)783-9186
Contact: Glenn Maurer, Director

★1694★ **Environmental Resources Department**
Environmental Protection Office
Environmental Energy Management Office
PO Box 2063
Harrisburg, PA 17105
Phone: (717)787-4692
Fax: (717)783-9186
Contact: Karl Sheaffer, Director

★1695★ **Environmental Resources Department**
Environmental Protection Office
Environmental Management Office
PO Box 2063
Harrisburg, PA 17105
Phone: (717)787-5027
Fax: (717)783-9186
Contact: Richard Boardman, Director

★1696★ **Environmental Resources Department**
Environmental Protection Office
Environmental Management Office
Environmental Emergency Response Division
PO Box 2063
Harrisburg, PA 17105
Phone: (717)787-5027
Fax: (717)783-9186
Contact: Fred Osman, Coord.

★1697★ **Environmental Resources Department**
Environmental Protection Office
Laboratories Bureau
PO Box 2063
Harrisburg, PA 17105
Phone: (717)787-4669
Fax: (717)783-9186
Contact: Floyd Kefford, Director

★1698★ **Environmental Resources Department**
Environmental Protection Office
Mining and Reclamation Bureau
PO Box 2063
Harrisburg, PA 17105
Phone: (717)787-5103
Fax: (717)783-9186
Contact: Ernie Giovannitti, Director

★1699★ **Environmental Resources Department**
Environmental Protection Office
Oil and Gas Management Bureau
PO Box 2063
Harrisburg, PA 17105
Phone: (717)783-9645
Fax: (717)783-9186
Contact: James Erb, Director

★1700★ **Environmental Resources Department**
Environmental Protection Office
Radiation Protection Bureau
PO Box 2063
Harrisburg, PA 17105
Phone: (717)787-2480
Fax: (717)783-9186
Contact: Thomas Gerusky, Director

★1701★ **Environmental Resources Department**
Environmental Protection Office
Waste Management Bureau
PO Box 2063
Harrisburg, PA 17105
Phone: (717)787-9870
Fax: (717)783-9186
Contact: James Snyder, Director

★1702★ **Environmental Resources Department**
Environmental Protection Office
Water Quality Management Bureau
PO Box 2063
Harrisburg, PA 17105
Phone: (717)787-2666
Fax: (717)783-9186
Contact: Daniel Drawbaugh, Director

★1703★ **Environmental Resources Department**
Resources Management Office
PO Box 1467
Harrisburg, PA 17105
Phone: (717)787-2869
Fax: (717)783-8525
Contact: James Grace, Deputy Sec.

★1704★ **Environmental Resources Department**
Resources Management Office
Forestry Bureau
PO Box 1467
Harrisburg, PA 17105
Phone: (717)787-2703
Fax: (717)783-8525
Contact: James Nelson, Director

★1705★ **Environmental Resources Department**
Resources Management Office
Natural Resources Office
PO Box 1467
Harrisburg, PA 17105
Phone: (717)783-5338
Fax: (717)783-8525
Contact: Terry Fabian, Director

★1706★ **Environmental Resources Department**
Resources Management Office
Soil and Water Conservation Bureau
PO Box 1467
Harrisburg, PA 17105
Phone: (717)540-5080
Fax: (717)783-8525
Contact: Paul Swartz, Director

★1707★ Environmental Resources Department
Resources Management Office
State Parks Bureau
PO Box 1467
Harrisburg, PA 17105
Phone: (717)787-6640
Fax: (717)783-8525
Contact: William Forrey, Director

★1708★ Environmental Resources Department
Resources Management Office
Water Resources Management Bureau
PO Box 1467
Harrisburg, PA 17105
Phone: (717)541-7800
Fax: (717)783-8525
Contact: John McSparran, Director

★1709★ Fish Commission
PO Box 1673
Harrisburg, PA 17105-1673
Phone: (717)657-4515
Fax: (717)657-4549
Contact: Edward R. Miller, Exec. Dir.

★1710★ Fish Commission
Education and Information Bureau
PO Box 1673
Harrisburg, PA 17105-1673
Phone: (717)657-4518
Fax: (717)657-4549
Contact: Cheryl K. Riley, Director

★1711★ Game Commission
2001 Elmerton Ave.
Harrisburg, PA 17110-9797
Phone: (717)787-3633
Fax: (717)772-2411
Contact: Peter S. Duncan, Exec. Dir.

★1712★ Game Commission
Information and Education Bureau
2001 Elmerton Ave.
Harrisburg, PA 17110-9797
Phone: (717)787-6286
Fax: (717)772-2411
Contact: Lantz A. Hoffman, Director

★1713★ Governor's Office
Energy Office
116 Pine St.
Harrisburg, PA 17105
Phone: (717)783-9981
Contact: Jan Freeman, Exec. Dir.

★1714★ Governor's Office
Energy Office
Conservation and Renewable Energy Division
116 Pine St.
Harrisburg, PA 17105
Phone: (717)783-9981
Contact: Dan Desmond, Deputy Dir.

Puerto Rico

★1715★ Environmental Quality Board
PO Box 11488
Santurce, PR 00910
Phone: (809)767-8056
Fax: (809)767-2483
Contact: Santos Rohena Betancourt, Jr., Chm.

Rhode Island

★1716★ Environmental Management Department
9 Hayes St.
Providence, RI 02908
Phone: (401)277-2771
Fax: (401)274-7337
Contact: Louise C. Durfee, Director

★1717★ Environmental Management Department
Operations Section
Coastal Resources Division
22 Hayes St.
Providence, RI 02908
Phone: (401)277-3429
Contact: James Beattie, Chief

★1718★ Environmental Management Department
Operations Section
Fish and Wildlife Division
4808 Tower Hill Rd.
Wakefield, RI 02879
Phone: (401)277-3075
Contact: John Stolgitis, Chief

★1719★ Environmental Management Department
Operations Section
Forest Environment Division
1037 Hartford Pike, N.
Smithfield, RI 02857
Phone: (401)647-3367
Contact: Thomas Dupree, Chief

★1720★ Environmental Management Department
Operations Section
Parks and Recreation Division
2321 Hartford Ave.
Johnston, RI 02919
Phone: (401)277-2632
Contact: William Hawkins, Chief

★1721★ Environmental Management Department
Regulations Section
Groundwater & Freshwater Wetlands Division
291 Promenade St.
Providence, RI 02908
Phone: (401)277-3162
Fax: (401)521-4230
Contact: Stephen Morin, Chief

★1722★ Environmental Management Department
Regulations Section
Water Resources Division
291 Promenade St.
Providence, RI 02908
Phone: (401)277-3961
Fax: (401)521-4230
Contact: Edward Szymanski, Chief

★1723★ Health Department
Environmental Health Division
Drinking Water Quality Office
Three Capitol Hill
Providence, RI 02908
Phone: (401)277-6867
Contact: June Swallow, Chief

★1724★ Health Department
Environmental Health Division
Environmental Health Risk Assessment Office
Three Capitol Hill
Providence, RI 02908
Phone: (401)277-3424
Contact: Bela T. Matyas M.D., Chief

South Carolina

★1725★ Forestry Commission
PO Box 21707
Columbia, SC 29221
Phone: (803)737-8800
Fax: (803)798-8097
Contact: Robert J. Gould, State Forester

★1726★ Health and Environmental Control Department
Environmental Quality Control Division
Air Quality Control Bureau
2600 Bull St.
Columbia, SC 29201
Phone: (803)734-4750
Contact: Otto E. Pearson, Director

★1727★ Health and Environmental Control Department
Environmental Quality Control Division
Environmental Quality Control Laboratories
2600 Bull St.
Columbia, SC 29201
Phone: (803)737-7031
Contact: Noel M. Hurley, Director

★1728★ Health and Environmental Control Department
Environmental Quality Control Division
Radiological Health Bureau
2600 Bull St.
Columbia, SC 29201
Phone: (803)734-4700
Contact: Heyward Shealy, Director

★1729★ Health and Environmental Control Department
Environmental Quality Control Division
Solid and Hazardous Waste Management Bureau
2600 Bull St.
Columbia, SC 29201
Phone: (803)734-5200
Contact: Hartsill Truesdale, Director

★1730★ Health and Environmental Control Department
Environmental Quality Control Division
Water Pollution Control Bureau
2600 Bull St.
Columbia, SC 29201
Phone: (803)734-5300
Contact: James A. Joy, III, Director

★1731★ Health and Evironmental Control Department
Environmental Quality Control Division
Drinking Water Protection Bureau
2600 Bull St.
Columbia, SC 29201
Phone: (803)734-5310
Contact: Robert Malpass, Director

★1732★ Land Resources Conservation Commission
2221 Devine St.
Ste. 222
Columbia, SC 29205
Phone: (803)734-9200
Fax: (803)734-9100
Contact: John W. Parris, Exec. Dir.

★1733★ Land Resources Conservation Commission
Conservation Districts Division
2221 Devine St.
Ste. 222
Columbia, SC 29205
Phone: (803)734-9100
Fax: (803)734-9200
Contact: Von P. Snelgrove, Director

★1734★ Land Resources Conservation Commission
Conservation Programs Division
2221 Devine St.
Ste. 222
Columbia, SC 29205
Phone: (803)734-9100
Fax: (803)734-9200
Contact: Charles A. Logan, Deputy Dir.

★1735★ Land Resources Conservation Commission
Erosion Control and Stormwater Management
2221 Devine St.
Ste. 222
Columbia, SC 29205
Phone: (803)734-9100
Fax: (803)734-9200
Contact: K. Flint Holbrook, Chief

★1736★ Land Resources Conservation Commission
Land Resource Engineering Division
2221 Devine St.
Ste. 222
Columbia, SC 29205
Phone: (803)734-9100
Fax: (803)734-9200
Contact: William Spearman, Director

★1737★ Land Resources Conservation Commission
Mining & Reclamation Division
2221 Devine St.
Ste. 222
Columbia, SC 29205
Phone: (803)734-9100
Fax: (803)734-9200
Contact: Pat Walker, Director

★1738★ Land Resources Conservation Commission
Public Information Division
2221 Devine St.
Ste. 222
Columbia, SC 29205
Phone: (803)734-9100
Fax: (803)734-9200
Contact: Bonnie Schneider, Director

★1739★ Land Resources Conservation Commission
Soils & Resource Information Division
2221 Devine St.
Ste. 222
Columbia, SC 29205
Phone: (803)734-9100
Fax: (803)734-9200
Contact: Robert Somers, Director

★1740★ Parks, Recreation and Tourism Department
1205 Pendleton St.
Ste. 248
Columbia, SC 29201
Phone: (803)734-0166
Fax: (803)734-0671
Contact: Fred P. Brinkman, Exec. Dir.

★1741★ Parks, Recreation and Tourism Department
Parks Division
1205 Pendleton St.
Ste. 248
Columbia, SC 29201
Phone: (803)734-0159
Fax: (803)734-0671
Contact: Charles Harrison, Director

★1742★ Water Resources Commission
1201 Main St., Ste. 1100
Columbia, SC 29201
Phone: (803)737-0800
Fax: (803)765-9080
Contact: Alfred Vang, Exec. Dir.

South Dakota

★1743★ Attorney General's Office
Earth Resources
State Capitol
500 E. Capitol
Pierre, SD 57501-5070
Phone: (605)773-3215
Fax: (605)773-4106
Contact: John Guhin, Director

★1744★ Energy Policy, Governor's Office
217 W. Missouri
Ste. 200
Pierre, SD 57501-4516
Phone: (605)773-3603
Fax: (605)773-4802
Contact: Ron R. Reed, Commissioner

★1745★ Energy Policy, Governor's Office
Alternative Energy Program
217 W. Missouri
Ste. 200
Pierre, SD 57501-4516
Phone: (605)773-3603
Fax: (605)773-4802

★1746★ Energy Policy, Governor's Office
Energy Conservation Program
217 W. Missouri
Ste. 200
Pierre, SD 57501-4516
Phone: (605)773-3603
Fax: (605)773-4802
Contact: Mark McKillip, Director

★1747★ Energy Policy, Governor's Office
Institutional Conservation Program
217 W. Missouri
Ste. 200
Pierre, SD 57501-4516
Phone: (605)773-3603
Fax: (605)773-4802
Contact: Merrill Van Gerpen, Director

★1748★ Game, Fish, and Parks Department
523 E. Capitol
Pierre, SD 57501-3182
Phone: (605)773-3718
Contact: Richard Beringson, Secretary

★1749★ Game, Fish, and Parks Department
Wildlife Division
523 E. Capitol
Pierre, SD 57501-3182
Phone: (605)733-3381
Contact: Doug Hansen, Director

★1750★ Water and Natural Resources Department
Joe Foss Bldg.
523 E. Capitol
Pierre, SD 57501-3181
Phone: (605)773-3151
Fax: (605)773-6035
Contact: Robert E. Roberts, Secretary

★1751★ Water and Natural Resources Department
Water Resource Management Division
Joe Foss Bldg.
523 E. Capitol
Pierre, SD 57501-3181
Phone: (605)773-4216
Contact: Mark E. Steichen, Director

Tennessee

★1752★ Attorney General's Office
Environmental Protection Division
450 James Robertson Pkwy.
Nashville, TN 37243-0485
Phone: (615)741-5687
Contact: Michael Pearigen, Deputy Atty. Gen.

★1753★ Conservation Department
701 Broadway
Nashville, TN 37243-0345
Phone: (615)742-6747
Fax: (615)742-6594
Contact: Elbert T. Gill, Jr., Commissioner

★1754★ Conservation Department
Ecological Services Division
701 Broadway
Nashville, TN 37243-0345
Phone: (615)742-6553
Fax: (615)742-6594
Contact: Dan Eagar, Director

★1755★ Conservation Department
Forestry Division
701 Broadway
Nashville, TN 37243-0345
Phone: (615)742-6621
Fax: (615)742-6594
Contact: Roy Ashley, Director

★1756★ Conservation Department
Land Reclamation Division
701 Broadway
Nashville, TN 37243-0345
Phone: (516)594-6203
Fax: (516)742-6594
Contact: Tim Eagle, Director

★1757★ Health and Environment Department
344 Cordell Hull Bldg.
Nashville, TN 37247-0101
Phone: (615)741-3111
Fax: (615)741-2491
Contact: H. Russell White, Commissioner

★1758★ Health and Environment Department
Environmental Bureau
Terra Bldg.
150 Ninth Ave., N
Nashville, TN 37247-3001
Phone: (615)741-3657
Fax: (615)741-4608
Contact: Wayne K. Scharber, Director

★1759★ Health and Environment Department
Environmental Bureau
Air Pollution Control Division
Terra Bldg.
150 Ninth Ave., N
Nashville, TN 37247-3001
Phone: (615)741-3931
Fax: (615)741-4608
Contact: Harold E. Hodges, Director

★1760★ Health and Environment Department
Environmental Bureau
Water Quality Control Division
Terra Bldg.
150 Ninth St., N
Nashville, TN 37247-3001
Phone: (615)741-2275
Fax: (615)741-4608
Contact: Paul Davis, Director

★1761★ Wildlife Resources Agency
PO Box 40747
Nashville, TN 37204
Phone: (615)781-6552
Fax: (615)741-4606
Contact: Gary Myers, Exec. Dir.

★1762★ Wildlife Resources Agency
Fish Management Division
PO Box 40747
Nashville, TN 37204
Phone: (615)781-6575
Fax: (615)741-4606
Contact: Wayne Pollock, Chief

★1763★ Wildlife Resources Agency
Information Division
PO Box 40747
Nashville, TN 37204
Phone: (615)781-6502
Fax: (615)741-4606
Contact: Dave Woodward, Chief

★1764★ Wildlife Resources Agency
Wildlife Management Division
PO Box 40747
Nashville, TN 37204
Phone: (615)781-6610
Fax: (615)741-4606
Contact: Larry Marcum, Chief

Texas

★1765★ Air Control Board
6330 Hwy. 290 E
Austin, TX 78723
Phone: (512)451-5711
Fax: (512)371-0245
Contact: Steven N. Spaw, Exec. Dir.

★1766★ Attorney General's Office
Environmental Protection Division
Supreme Ct. Bldg.
PO Box 12548
Austin, TX 78711-2548
Phone: (512)463-2012
Fax: (512)463-2063
Contact: Nancy Lynch, Chief

★1767★ Parks and Wildlife Department
4200 Smith School Rd.
Austin, TX 78744
Phone: (512)389-4802
Contact: Andrew S. Sansom, Exec. Dir.

★1768★ Parks and Wildlife Department
Conservation Communication Division
4200 Smith School Rd.
Austin, TX 78744
Phone: (512)389-4800
Contact: Bill Rutledge, Director

★1769★ Parks and Wildlife Department
Fisheries and Wildlife Department
4200 Smith School Rd.
Austin, TX 78744
Phone: (512)389-4800
Contact: Rudolph Rosen, Director

★1770★ Parks and Wildlife Department
Legal Services Division
4200 Smith School Rd.
Austin, TX 78744
Phone: (512)389-4800
Contact: Paul Shinkawa, Director

★1771★ Parks and Wildlife Department
Resource Protection Division
4200 Smith School Rd.
Austin, TX 78744
Phone: (512)389-4864
Contact: Larry McKinney, Director

★1772★ Soil and Water Conservation Board
PO Box 658
Temple, TX 76503
Phone: (817)773-2250
Contact: Robert G. Buckley, Exec. Dir.

★1773★ Water Commission
PO Box 13087
Capitol Sta.
Austin, TX 78711
Phone: (512)463-7910
Fax: (512)463-8317
Contact: B.J. Wynne, III, Chm.

★1774★ Water Commission
Water Quality Division
PO Box 13087
Capitol Sta.
Austin, TX 78711
Phone: (512)463-8412
Fax: (512)463-8317
Contact: Clyde Bohmfalk, Director

★1775★ Water Development Board
PO Box 13231
Austin, TX 78711-3231
Phone: (512)463-7847
Fax: (512)475-2053
Contact: G.E. Kretzschmar, Exec. Admin.

Utah

★1776★ Health Department
Environmental Health
Drinking Water and Sanitation Division
288 N. 1460 West
Salt Lake City, UT 84116-0700
Phone: (801)538-6159
Fax: (801)538-6016
Contact: Gayle Smith, Director

★1777★ Health Department
Environmental Health Section
288 N. 1460 West
Salt Lake City, UT 84116-0700
Phone: (801)538-6121
Fax: (801)538-6016
Contact: Kenneth Alkema, Director

★1778★ Health Department
Environmental Health Section
Air Quality Division
288 N. 1460 West
Salt Lake City, UT 84116-0700
Phone: (801)538-6108
Fax: (801)538-6016
Contact: Burnell Cordner, Director

★1779★ Health Department
Environmental Health Section
Solid and Hazardous Waste Division
288 N. 1460 West
Salt Lake City, UT 84116-0700
Phone: (801)538-6170
Fax: (801)538-6016
Contact: Dennis Downs, Director

★1780★ Health Department
Environmental Health Section
Water Pollution Control Division
288 N. 1460 West
Salt Lake City, UT 84116-0700
Phone: (801)538-6146
Fax: (801)538-6016
Contact: Don Ostler, Director

★1781★ Natural Resources Department
1636 W. N. Temple
Rm. 316
Salt Lake City, UT 84116-3193
Phone: (801)538-7200
Fax: (801)538-7315
Contact: Dee C. Hansen, Exec. Dir.

★1782★ Natural Resources Department
Energy & Minerals Division
1636 W. N. Temple
Rm. 316
Salt Lake City, UT 84116-3193
Phone: (801)538-7200
Fax: (801)538-7315
Contact: Alton Frazier, Dir.

★1783★ Natural Resources Department
Energy Office
Three Triad Center
355 W. N. Temple
Ste. 450
Salt Lake City, UT 84180-1204
Phone: (801)538-5428
Fax: (801)521-0657
Contact: Richard Anderson, Director

★1784★ Natural Resources Department
Geological and Mineral Survey
606 Black Hawk Way
Salt Lake City, UT 84108-1280
Phone: (801)581-6831
Fax: (801)581-4450
Contact: M. Lee Allison, Director

★1785★ Natural Resources Department
Oil, Gas and Mining Section
Three Triad Center
355 W. N. Temple
Ste. 350
Salt Lake City, UT 84180-1203
Phone: (801)538-5340
Fax: (801)359-3940
Contact: Dianne Nielson, Director

★1786★ Natural Resources Department Parks and Recreation
1636 W. N. Temple
Rm. 316
Salt Lake City, UT 84116-3193
Phone: (801)538-7220
Fax: (801)538-7315
Contact: Jerry Miller, Director

★1787★ Natural Resources Department Resource Management Division
1636 W. N. Temple
Rm. 316
Salt Lake City, UT 84116-3193
Phone: (801)538-7200
Fax: (801)538-7315
Contact: Milo A. Barney, Dir.

★1788★ Natural Resources Department State Lands and Forestry Section
Three Triad Center
355 W. N. Temple
Ste. 400
Salt Lake City, UT 84180-1204
Phone: (801)538-5508
Fax: (801)521-0657
Contact: Richard J. Mitchell, Director

★1789★ Natural Resources Department Water Resources Section
1636 W. N. Temple
Rm. 316
Salt Lake City, UT 84116-3193
Phone: (801)538-7230
Fax: (801)538-7315
Contact: D. Larry Anderson, Director

★1790★ Natural Resources Department Wildlife Resources Section
1596 W. N. Temple
Salt Lake City, UT 84116-3154
Phone: (801)538-4700
Fax: (801)538-4709
Contact: Timothy H. Provan, Director

★1791★ Solid and Hazardous Waste Bureau
288 North 1460 West
Salt Lake City, UT 84116
Phone: (801)538-6170

Vermont

★1792★ Human Services Agency Health Department Environmental Health Division
PO Box 70
Burlington, VT 05402
Phone: (802)863-7220
Fax: (802)863-7425
Contact: Robert O'Grady, Director

★1793★ Natural Resources Agency
State Complex
103 S. Wissell
Waterbury, VT 05676
Phone: (602)244-7347
Fax: (602)244-1102
Contact: Jan Eastman, Secretary

★1794★ Natural Resources Agency Environmental Conservation Department
State Complex
103 S. Wissell
Waterbury, VT 05676
Phone: (802)244-8755
Fax: (802)244-5141
Contact: Timothy Burke, Commissioner

★1795★ Natural Resources Agency Environmental Conservation Department Air Pollution Control Division
State Complex
103 S. Wissell
Waterbury, VT 05676
Phone: (802)244-8731
Fax: (802)244-5141
Contact: Richard Valentinetti, Director

★1796★ Natural Resources Agency Environmental Conservation Department Hazardous Materials Management Division
State Complex
103 S. Wissell
Waterbury, VT 05676
Phone: (802)244-8702
Fax: (802)244-5141
Contact: William Ahearn, Director

★1797★ Natural Resources Agency Environmental Conservation Department Solid Waste Management Division
State Complex
103 S. Wissell
Waterbury, VT 05676
Phone: (802)244-7831
Fax: (802)244-5141
Contact: Ed Leonard, Director

★1798★ Natural Resources Agency Environmental Conservation Department Water Quality Division
State Complex
103 S. Wissell
Waterbury, VT 05676
Phone: (802)244-6951
Fax: (802)244-5141
Contact: David A. Clough, Director

★1799★ Natural Resources Agency Fish and Wildlife Department
State Complex
103 S. Wissell
Waterbury, VT 05676
Phone: (802)244-7331
Fax: (802)244-5141
Contact: Timothy VanZandt, Commissioner

★1800★ Natural Resources Agency Forests, Parks and Recreation Department
State Complex
103 S. Wissell
Waterbury, VT 05676
Phone: (802)244-8714
Contact: Paul Hannan, Commissioner

★1801★ Natural Resources Agency Forests, Parks and Recreation Department Forests Division
State Complex
103 S. Wissell
Waterbury, VT 05676
Phone: (802)244-8716
Contact: Conrad Motyka, Director

★1802★ Natural Resources Agency Forests, Parks and Recreation Department Parks Division
State Complex
103 S. Wissell
Waterbury, VT 05676
Phone: (802)244-8711
Contact: Edward Koenemann, Director

★1803★ Natural Resources Agency Natural Resources Conservation Council
State Complex
103 S. Wissell
Waterbury, VT 05676
Phone: (802)244-5164
Fax: (802)244-1102
Contact: Jon Anderson, Director

Virgin Islands

★1804★ Energy Office
21-22 Kongens Gade
St. Thomas, VI 00801
Phone: (809)772-2616
Fax: (809)772-0063
Contact: Claudettee Young-Hinds, Director

★1805★ Planning and Natural Resources Department
21-22 Kongens Gade
St. Thomas, VI 00801
Phone: (809)774-3320
Fax: (809)775-5706
Contact: Allan Smith, Commissioner

Virginia

★1806★ Economic Development Secretariat Forestry Department
PO Box 3758
Charlottesville, VA 22903
Phone: (804)977-6555
Contact: James W. Garner, Jr., State Forester

★1807★ Economic Development Secretariat Mines, Minerals and Energy Department
2201 W. Broad St.
Richmond, VA 23220
Phone: (804)367-0330
Contact: O. Gene Dishner, Director

★1808★ Economic Development Secretariat Mines, Minerals and Energy Department Energy Division
2201 W. Broad St.
Richmond, VA 23220
Phone: (804)367-6851
Contact: Ronald J. Des Roches, Director

★1809★ Economic Development Secretariat Mines, Minerals and Energy Department Gas and Oil Division
203 Charwood Dr.
Abingdon, VA 24210
Phone: (703)628-8115
Contact: B. Thomas Fulmer, Inspector

★1810★ Economic Development Secretariat Mines, Minerals and Energy Department Mine Land Reclamation Division
622 Powell Ave.
Big Stone Gap, VA 24219
Phone: (703)523-8152
Contact: Danny R. Brown, Commissioner

★1811★ Economic Development Secretariat Mines, Minerals and Energy Department Mineral Resources Division
Natural Resources Bldg.
McCormick Rd.
Charlottesville, VA 22903
Phone: (804)293-5121
Contact: Robert Milici, State Geologist

★1812★ Natural Resources Secretariat
733 Ninth St. Office Bldg.
Richmond, VA 23219
Phone: (804)786-0044
Fax: (804)371-8333
Contact: Elizabeth H. Haskell, Secretary

★1813★ Natural Resources Secretariat
Air Pollution Control Department
9th St. Office Bldg.
PO Box 10089
Richmond, VA 23240
Phone: (804)786-6035
Fax: (804)225-3933
Contact: Wallace N. Davis, Exec. Dir.

★1814★ Natural Resources Secretariat
Conservation and Recreation Department
203 Governor St., Ste. 302
Richmond, VA 23219
Phone: (804)786-6124
Fax: (804)786-6141
Contact: B.C. Leynes, Jr., Director

★1815★ Natural Resources Secretariat
Conservation and Recreation Department
Soil and Water Conservation Division
203 Governor St., Ste. 302
Richmond, VA 23219
Phone: (804)786-2064
Contact: Roland B. Geddes, Director

★1816★ Natural Resources Secretariat
Conservation and Recreation Department
State Parks Division
203 Governor St., Ste. 302
Richmond, VA 23219
Phone: (804)786-2132
Contact: Ronald D. Sutton, Commissioner

★1817★ Natural Resources Secretariat
Environment Council
202 N. Ninth St., Ste. 900
Richmond, VA 23219
Phone: (804)786-4500
Fax: (804)225-3933
Contact: Keith J. Buttleman, Admin.

★1818★ Natural Resources Secretariat
Game and Inland Fisheries Department
4010 W. Broad St.
Richmond, VA 23230
Phone: (804)367-1000
Fax: (804)367-9147
Contact: Bud Bristow, Director

★1819★ Natural Resources Secretariat
Game and Inland Fisheries Department
Fish Division
4010 W. Broad St.
Richmond, VA 23230
Phone: (804)367-1000
Fax: (804)367-9147
Contact: David Whitehurst, Chief

★1820★ Natural Resources Secretariat
Game and Inland Fisheries Department
Planning & Environmental Services Division
4010 W. Broad St.
Richmond, VA 23230
Phone: (804)367-1000
Fax: (804)367-9147
Contact: Jack Raybourne, Chief

★1821★ Natural Resources Secretariat
Game and Inland Fisheries Department
Wildlife Division
4010 W. Broad St.
Richmond, VA 23230
Phone: (804)367-1000
Fax: (804)367-9147
Contact: Robert W. Duncan, Chief

★1822★ Natural Resources Secretariat
Marine Resources Commission
2600 Washington Ave., 4th Fl.
PO Box 756
Newport News, VA 23607-0756
Phone: (804)247-2206
Fax: (804)247-2020
Contact: William A. Pruitt, Commissioner

★1823★ Natural Resources Secretariat
Marine Resources Commission
Fisheries Management Div.
2600 Washington Ave., 4th Fl.
PO Box 756
Newport News, VA 23607-0756
Phone: (804)247-2247
Fax: (804)247-2020
Contact: Jack G. Travelstead, Head

★1824★ Natural Resources Secretariat
Marine Resources Commission
Habitat Management Division
2600 Washington Ave., 4th Fl.
PO Box 756
Newport News, VA 23607-0756
Phone: (804)247-2250
Fax: (804)247-2020
Contact: Robert W. Grabb, Head

★1825★ Natural Resources Secretariat
State Water Control Board
2111 N. Hamilton St.
Box 11143
Richmond, VA 23230
Phone: (804)367-6384
Fax: (804)367-0122
Contact: Richard N. Burton, Exec. Dir.

★1826★ Natural Resources Secretariat
Waste Management Department
Administration Division
101 N. 14th St., 11th Fl.
Richmond, VA 23219
Phone: (804)225-2216
Fax: (804)225-3753
Contact: Chuck Harrigan, Director

★1827★ Natural Resources Secretariat
Waste Management Department
Litter Control and Recycling Division
101 N. 14th St., 11th Fl.
Richmond, VA 23219
Phone: (804)786-5764
Fax: (804)225-3753
Contact: Allan Lassiter, Director

Washington

★1828★ Conservation Commission
MS PV-11
Olympia, WA 98504-8711
Phone: (206)459-6227
Fax: (206)438-7753
Contact: Wayne Reid, Exec. Sec.

★1829★ Ecology Department
MS PV-11
Olympia, WA 98504-8711
Phone: (206)459-6168
Fax: (206)459-6007
Contact: Christine O. Gregoire, Director

★1830★ Ecology Department
Air Program
MS PV-11
Olympia, WA 98504-8711
Phone: (206)459-6255
Fax: (206)459-6007
Contact: Joseph Williams, Mgr.

★1831★ Ecology Department
Hazardous Waste Investigation & Cleanup Program
MS PV-11
Olympia, WA 98504-8711
Phone: (206)438-3007
Fax: (206)459-6007
Contact: Carol Fleskes, Mgr.

★1832★ Ecology Department
Nuclear & Mixed Waste Program
MS PV-11
Olympia, WA 98504-8711
Phone: (206)438-7020
Fax: (206)459-6007
Contact: Roger Stanley, Mgr.

★1833★ Ecology Department
Public Information and Eduation
MS PV-11
Olympia, WA 98504-8711
Phone: (206)459-6839
Fax: (206)459-6007
Contact: Melanie Luh, Asst. Dir.

★1834★ Ecology Department
Quality Control, Information Management & Comprehensive Planning Division
MS PV-11
Olympia, WA 98504-8711
Phone: (206)459-6690
Fax: (206)459-6007
Contact: Mike Reed, Asst. Dir.

★1835★ Ecology Department
Shorelands & Coastal Zone Management
MS PV-11
Olympia, WA 98504-8711
Phone: (206)459-6777
Fax: (206)459-6007
Contact: Rod Mack, Mgr.

★1836★ Ecology Department
Solid & Hazardous Waste Program
MS PV-11
Olympia, WA 98504-8711
Phone: (206)459-6316
Fax: (206)459-6007
Contact: Tom Eaton, Mgr.

★1837★ Ecology Department
Waste Management Division
MS PV-11
Olympia, WA 98504-8711
Phone: (206)459-6029
Fax: (206)459-6007
Contact: Terry Husseman, Asst. Dir.

★1838★ Ecology Department
Waste Reduction, Recycling & Litter Control Program
MS PV-11
Olympia, WA 98504-8711
Phone: (206)438-7145
Fax: (206)459-6007
Contact: Bill Alkire, Mgr.

★1839★ Ecology Department
Water and Shorelands Division
MS PV-11
Olympia, WA 98504-8711
Phone: (206)459-7494
Fax: (206)459-6007
Contact: Carol Jolly, Asst. Dir.

★1840★ Ecology Department
Water Quality Financial Assistance Program
MS PV-11
Olympia, WA 98504-8711
Phone: (206)459-6101
Fax: (206)459-6007
Contact: Cheryl Strange, Mgr.

★1841★ Ecology Department
Water Quality Program
MS PV-11
Olympia, WA 98504-8711
Phone: (206)438-7090
Fax: (206)459-6007
Contact: Mike Llewelyn, Mgr.

★1842★ Ecology Department
Water Resources Program
MS PV-11
Olympia, WA 98504-8711
Phone: (206)459-6056
Fax: (206)459-6007
Contact: Hedia Adelsman, Mgr.

★1843★ Energy Office
809 Legion Way, SE
MS FA-11
Olympia, WA 98504-1211
Phone: (206)956-2001
Fax: (206)753-2397
Contact: Richard Watson, Director

★1844★ Fisheries Department
115 General Administration Bldg.
Olympia, WA 98504
Phone: (206)753-6623
Fax: (206)586-2531
Contact: Joseph R. Blum, Director

★1845★ Natural Resources Department
Information Management Division
201 John A. Cherberg Bldg.
Olympia, WA 98504
Phone: (206)753-1308
Contact: Bob Edwards, Mgr.

★1846★ Natural Resources Department
Land & Water Conservation Division
201 John A. Cherberg Bldg.
Olympia, WA 98504
Phone: (206)753-2400
Contact: Arden Olsen, Mgr.

★1847★ Natural Resources Department
Lands & Minerals Division
201 John A. Cherberg Bldg.
Olympia, WA 98504
Phone: (206)753-2400
Contact: Bruce Mackey, Mgr.

★1848★ Natural Resources Department
Public Lands Division
201 John A. Cherberg Bldg.
Olympia, WA 98504
Phone: (206)753-5317
Contact: Brian Boyle, Commisioner

★1849★ State Parks and Recreation Commission
7150 Cleanwater Ln.
MS KY-11
Olympia, WA 98504
Phone: (206)753-5757
Fax: (206)753-1594
Contact: Jan Tveten, Director

★1850★ State Parks and Recreation Commission
Resources Development Division
7150 Cleanwater Ln.
MS KY-11
Olympia, WA 98504
Phone: (206)753-5767
Fax: (206)753-1594
Contact: Tom France, Asst. Dir.

★1851★ Wildlife Department
600 Capital Way N.
Olympia, WA 98501-1091
Phone: (206)753-5710
Fax: (206)586-0248
Contact: Curt Smitch, Director

★1852★ Wildlife Department
Fisheries Management
600 Capitol Way N.
Olympia, WA 98501-1091
Phone: (206)753-5713
Fax: (206)586-0248
Contact: Pat Doyle, Asst. Dir.

★1853★ Wildlife Department
Habitat Management
600 Capitol Way N.
Olympia, WA 98501-1091
Phone: (206)753-3318
Fax: (206)586-0248
Contact: Chris Drivdahl, Asst. Dir.

★1854★ Wildlife Department
Information and Education Division
600 Capital Way N.
Olympia, WA 98501-1091
Phone: (206)753-5707
Fax: (206)586-0248
Contact: Dave Workman, Officer

★1855★ Wildlife Department
Wildlife Management
600 Capitol Way N.
Olympia, WA 98501-1091
Phone: (206)753-5728
Fax: (206)586-0248
Contact: Tim Juelson, Asst. Dir.

West Virginia

★1856★ Attorney General's Office
Environmental and Energy Division
26-E State Capitol Bldg.
Charleston, WV 25305
Phone: (304)348-9160
Contact: Robert D. Pollitt, Deputy Atty. Gen.

★1857★ Commerce, Labor, and Environmental Resources Department
Air Pollution Control Commission
1558 Washington St., E.
Charleston, WV 25311-2599
Phone: (304)348-4022
Fax: (304)348-8887
Contact: G. Dale Farley, Director

★1858★ Commerce, Labor, and Environmental Resources Department
Energy Division
1615 Washington St., E.
Charleston, WV 25311
Phone: (304)348-3500
Contact: E.W. Wayland, Commissioner

★1859★ Commerce, Labor, and Environmental Resources Department
Natural Resources Division
State Capitol Complex
Bldg. 3, Rm. 669
Charleston, WV 25305
Phone: (304)348-2754
Fax: (304)348-2768
Contact: J. Edward Hamrick, III, Director

★1860★ Commerce, Labor, and Environmental Resources Department
Natural Resources Division
Environmental & Regulatory Affairs Division
State Capitol Complex
Bldg. 3, Rm. 669
Charleston, WV 25305
Phone: (304)348-2761
Fax: (304)348-2768
Contact: Frank Peluria, Admin.

★1861★ Commerce, Labor, and Environmental Resources Department
Natural Resources Division
Public Information Division
State Capitol Complex
Bldg. 3, Rm. 669
Charleston, WV 25305
Phone: (304)348-3381
Fax: (304)348-2768
Contact: Dianna Young, Officer

★1862★ Commerce, Labor, and Environmental Resources Department
Natural Resources Division
Waste Management Division
State Capitol Complex
Bldg. 3, Rm. 669
Charleston, WV 25305
Phone: (304)348-5929
Fax: (304)348-2768
Contact: Douglas Steele, Chief

★1863★ Commerce, Labor, and Environmental Resources Department
Natural Resources Division
Water Resources Division
State Capitol Complex
Bldg. 3, Rm. 669
Charleston, WV 25305
Phone: (304)348-2107
Fax: (304)348-2768
Contact: Laidley E. McCoy, Chief

★1864★ Commerce, Labor, and Environmental Resources Department
Natural Resources Division
Wildlife Resources Division
State Capitol Complex
Bldg. 3, Rm. 669
Charleston, WV 25305
Phone: (304)348-2771
Fax: (304)348-2768
Contact: Robert Miles, Chief

★1865★ Commerce, Labor, and Environmental Resources Department
Oil and Gas Conservation Commission
1615 Washington St., E.
Charleston, WV 25311
Phone: (304)348-3500
Contact: James A. Ray, Chm.

★1866★ Commerce, Labor, and Environmental Resources Department
Water Development Authority
1201 Dunbar Ave.
Dunbar, WV 25064
Phone: (304)348-3612
Fax: (304)348-0299
Contact: Daniel B. Yonkosky, Director

Wisconsin

★1867★ Natural Resources Department
PO Box 7921
Madison, WI 53707
Phone: (608)266-2121
Fax: (608)267-3579
Contact: Carroll D. Besadny, Secretary

★1868★ Natural Resources Department
Enforcement Division
Law Enforcement Bureau
PO Box 7921
Madison, WI 53707
Phone: (608)266-1115
Fax: (608)267-3579
Contact: Ralph E. Christensen, Director

★1869★ Natural Resources Department
Environmental Standards Division
PO Box 7921
Madison, WI 53707
Phone: (608)266-1099
Fax: (608)267-3579
Contact: Lyman Wible, Admin.

★1870★ Natural Resources Department
Environmental Standards Division
Air Management Bureau
PO Box 7921
Madison, WI 53707
Phone: (608)266-0603
Fax: (608)267-3579
Contact: Don Theiler, Director

★1871★ Natural Resources Department
Environmental Standards Division
Solid Waste Management Bureau
PO Box 7921
Madison, WI 53707
Phone: (608)266-1327
Fax: (608)267-3579
Contact: Paul Didier, Director

★1872★ Natural Resources Department
Environmental Standards Division
Waste Water Managment Bureau
PO Box 7921
Madison, WI 53707
Phone: (608)266-3910
Fax: (608)267-3579
Contact: Mary Jo Kopecky, Director

★1873★ Natural Resources Department
Environmental Standards Division
Water Resources Management Bureau
PO Box 7921
Madison, WI 53707
Phone: (608)266-8631
Fax: (608)267-3579
Contact: Bruce Baker, Director

★1874★ Natural Resources Department
Resources Management Division
PO Box 7921
Madison, WI 53707
Phone: (608)266-0837
Fax: (608)267-3579
Contact: James T. Addis, Admin.

★1875★ Natural Resources Department
Resources Management Division
Endangered Resources Bureau
PO Box 7921
Madison, WI 53707
Phone: (608)266-2625
Fax: (608)267-3579
Contact: Ronald F. Nicotera, Director

★1876★ Natural Resources Department
Resources Management Division
Fisheries Management Bureau
PO Box 7921
Madison, WI 53707
Phone: (608)266-7025
Fax: (608)267-3579
Contact: Lee Kernen, Director

★1877★ Natural Resources Department
Resources Management Division
Forestry Bureau
PO Box 7921
Madison, WI 53707
Phone: (608)266-0842
Fax: (608)267-3579
Contact: Charles Higgs, Director

★1878★ Natural Resources Department
Resources Management Division
Parks and Recreation Bureau
PO Box 7921
Madison, WI 53707
Phone: (608)266-2185
Fax: (608)267-3579
Contact: David L. Weizenicker, Director

★1879★ Natural Resources Department
Resources Management Division
Wildlife Management Bureau
PO Box 7921
Madison, WI 53707
Phone: (608)266-2193
Fax: (608)267-3579
Contact: Steve Miller, Director

Wyoming

★1880★ Environmental Quality Department
Herschler Bldg., 4th Fl.
122 W. 25th St.
Cheyenne, WY 82002
Phone: (307)777-7938
Fax: (307)634-0799
Contact: Dennis Hemmer, Director

★1881★ Water Development Commission
Herschler Bldg., 4th Fl.
122 W. 25th St.
Cheyenne, WY 82002
Phone: (307)777-7626
Contact: Michael K. Purcell, Admin.

Independent Agencies and Commissions

★1882★ Agency for International Development
Bureau of Science and Technology
Directorate for Energy and Natural Resources
Rosslyn Plaza Ctr., Rm. 509
1602 N Kent St.
Rossyln, VA 22209
Contact: Jack Vanderryn, Agency Dir.
Mailing address: State Dept. Bldg., 320 21st St., NW, Washington, DC 20523.

★1883★ Agency for International Development
Directorate for Energy and Natural Resources
Office of Forestry, Environment, and Natural Resources
Rossyln Plaza Ctr., Rm. 509
1601 N Kent St.
Rosslyn, VA 22209
Phone: (202)875-4106
Contact: Willard I. Johnson, Director
Mailing address: State Dept. Bldg., 320 21st St., NW, Washington, DC 20523.

★1884★ Arkansas River Compact Administration
PO Box 98
Meeker, CO 81641
Phone: (303)878-5065
Contact: Frank Cooley, Chairman
Includes Colorado and Kansas.

★1885★ Atlantic States Marine Fisheries Commission
1400 16th St., NW, Ste. 310
Washington, DC 20036
Phone: (202)387-5330
Contact: Robert A. Jones, Chairman
Includes Connecticut, Delaware, Florida, Georgia, Maine, Maryland, Massachusetts, New Hampshire, New Jersey, New York, and North Carolina.

★1886★ Bear River Commission
880 River Heights Blvd.
Logan, UT 84321
Phone: (801)752-6289
Contact: Wallace Jibson, Engineering Mgr.
Includes Idaho, Utah, and Wyoming.

★1887★ Canadian River Commission
HCR Star Rte.
PO Box 708
Texline, TX 79087
Phone: (806)362-4580
Contact: Joe Hershey, Chairman
Includes New Mexico, Oklahoma, and Texas.

★1888★ Central Interstate Low-Level Radioactive Waste Compact Commission
233 S. 13th St., Ste. 1200
Lincoln, NE 68508
Phone: (402)476-8247
Contact: Raymond Peery, Exec. Dir.
Includes Arizona, Iowa, Kansas, Louisiana, Minnesota, Missouri, Nebraska, and Oklahoma.

★1889★ Central Midwest Interstate Compact Commission on Low-Level Radioactive Waste
1035 Outer Park Dr.
Springfield, IL 62704
Phone: (217)785-9937
Contact: Clark W. Bullard, Chairman
Includes Illinois and Kentucky.

★1890★ Chesapeake Bay Commission
60 West St., Ste. 200
Annapolis, MD 21401
Phone: (301)263-3420
Contact: Ann Swanson, Exec. Dir.
Includes Maryland, Pennsylvania, and Virginia.

★1891★ Coastal States Organization
444 N. Capitol St., NW
Washington, DC 20001
Phone: (202)628-9636
Contact: R. Gary Magnuson, Dir.
Includes Alabama, Alaska, California, Connecticut, Delaware, Florida, Georgia, Hawaii, Illinois, Indiana, Louisiana, Maine, Maryland, Massachusetts, Michigan, Minnesota, Mississippi, New Hampshire, New Jersey, New York, North Carolina, Ohio, Oregon, Pennsylvania, Rhode Island, South Carolina, Texas, Virginia, Washington, and Wisconsin.

★1892★ Connecticut River Atlantic Salmon Commission
c/o U.S. Fish and Wildlife Service
463 West St.
Amherst, MA 01002
Phone: (413)548-9822
Contact: David F. Egan, Chairman
Includes Connecticut, Massachusetts, New Hampshire, and Vermont.

★1893★ Costilla Creek Compact Commission
c/o New Mexico State Engineer's Office
Bataan Memorial Bldg.
Santa Fe, NM 87503
Phone: (505)827-6175
Contact: Jeris A. Danielson, Colorado Commissioner
Includes Colorado and New Mexico.

★1894★ Council on Environmental Quality
722 Jackson Pl., NW , Rm. 154
Washington, DC 20503
Phone: (202)395-5080
Fax: (202)395-3744
Contact: Michael R. Deland, Chm.

★1895★ Council on Environmental Quality (NAPAP)
National Acid Precipitation Assessment Program
722 Jackson Pl., NW, Third Fl.
Washington, DC 20503
Phone: (202)395-5771
Contact: Patricia M. Irving, Assoc. Dir.

★1896★ Council on Environmental Quality
Natural Resources Program
722 Jackson Pl., NW
Washington, DC 20503
Phone: (202)395-5750
Contact: Robin O'Malley, Assoc. Dir.

★1897★ Council on Environmental Quality
Pollution Control and Prevention Program
722 Jackson Pl., NW
Washington, DC 20503
Phone: (202)395-5750
Contact: Scott Farrow, Assoc. Dir.

★1898★ Council on Environmental Quality
President's Commission of Environmental Quality
722 Jackson Pl., NW
Washington, DC 20503
Phone: (202)395-5750
Contact: Patricia Kearney, Sr. Advisor and Dir.

★1899★ Delaware River Basin Commission
1100 L St., NW, Rm. 5113
Washington, DC 20240
Phone: (202)343-5761
Contact: Irene B. Brooks, United States Commissioner
Mailing address: Department of the Interior, Washington, DC 20240.

★1900★ Environmental Protection Agency (EPA)
401 M St., SW
Washington, DC 20460
Phone: (202)260-2080
Fax: (202)260-7883
Contact: William K. Reilly, Admin.

★1901★ Environmental Protection Agency
Air and Radiation Department
Office of Air Quality Planning and Standards
Research Triangle Park, NC 27711
Phone: (919)541-5618
Fax: (919)541-5663

Contact: John S. Seitz, Director

★1902★ Environmental Protection Agency
Air and Radiation Department
Office of Atmospheric and Indoor Air Programs
West Tower of Waterside Mall, Rm. 735C
401 M St., SW
Washington, DC 20460
Phone: (202)260-7407
Contact: Eileen Claussen, Director

★1903★ Environmental Protection Agency
Air and Radiation Department
Office of Radiation Programs
Northeast Mall area of Waterside Mall, Rm. 201
401 M St., SW
Washington, DC 20460
Phone: (202)260-9600
Fax: (202)260-8347
Contact: Richard J. Guimond, Director

★1904★ Environmental Protection Agency
Enforcement Department
Office of Civil Enforcement
West Tower of Waterside Mall, Rm. 1039
401 M St., SW
Washington, DC 20460
Phone: (202)260-4540
Contact: Scott C. Fulton, Senior Enforcement Counsel

★1905★ Environmental Protection Agency
National Air and Radiation Environmental Laboratory
1504 Ave. A
Montgomery, AL 36115
Phone: (205)270-3400
Contact: Sam T. Windham, Director

★1906★ Environmental Protection Agency
Office of Air Quality Planning and Standards
Air Quality Management Division
Research Triangle Park, NC 27711
Phone: (919)541-5551
Contact: John Calcagni

★1907★ Environmental Protection Agency
Office of Air Quality Planning and Standards
Emissions Standards Division
Research Triangle Park, NC 27711
Phone: (919)541-5571
Fax: (919)541-5663
Contact: James Weingold

★1908★ Environmental Protection Agency
Office of Atmospheric and Indoor Air Programs
Acid Rain Division
Mall area of Waterside Mall, Rm. 3202
401 M St., SW
Washington, DC 20460
Phone: (202)260-9400
Contact: Brian J. McLean, Director

★1909★ Environmental Protection Agency
Office of Atmospheric and Indoor Air Programs
Global Change Division
West Tower of Waterside Mall, Rm. 739
401 M St., SW
Washington, DC 20460
Phone: (202)260-7750
Contact: John Hoffman, Director

★1910★ Environmental Protection Agency
Office of Atmospheric and Indoor Air Programs
Indoor Air Division
Crystal Sta. One, 8th Fl.
2800 Crystal Dr.
Arlington, VA 22202
Phone: (703)308-8470
Contact: Robert Axelrad, Director

★1911★ Environmental Protection Agency
Office of Civil Enforcement
Air Enforcement Division
Mall area of Waterside Mall, Rm. 3211
401 M St., SW
Washington, DC 20460
Phone: (202)260-2820
Contact: Michael S. Alushin, Assoc. Enforcement Counsel

★1912★ Environmental Protection Agency
Office of Civil Enforcement
Pesticides and Toxic Substances Enforcement Division
Northeast Mall area of Waterside Mall, Rm. 113
401 M St., SW
Washington, DC 20460
Phone: (202)260-8690
Contact: Michael J. Walker, Assoc. Enforcement Counsel

★1913★ Environmental Protection Agency (RCRA)
Office of Civil Enforcement
Resource Conservation and Recovery Act Division
Mall area of Waterside Mall, Rm. 3105
401 M St., SW
Washington, DC 20460
Phone: (202)260-2845
Contact: Kathy A. Stein, Assoc. Enforcement Counsel

★1914★ Environmental Protection Agency
Office of Civil Enforcement
Superfund Division
Mall area of Waterside Mall, Rm. 3105G
401 M St., SW
Washington, DC 20460
Phone: (202)260-3050
Contact: William White, Assoc. Enforcement Counsel

★1915★ Environmental Protection Agency
Office of Civil Enforcement
Water Enforcement Division
Mall area of Waterside Mall, Rm. 3109
401 M St., SW
Washington, DC 20460
Phone: (202)260-8180
Contact: Frederick F. Stiehl, Assoc. Enforcement Counsel

★1916★ Environmental Protection Agency
Office of Cooperative Environmental Management
Fairchild Bldg., Rm. 115
499 S. Capitol St., SW
Washington, DC 20032
Phone: (202)260-9741
Contact: R. Thomas Parker, Director

★1917★ Environmental Protection Agency
Office of Emergency and Remedial Response (Superfund)
Emergency Response Division
Mall area of Waterside Mall, Rm. 2710
401 M. St., SW
Washington, DC 20460
Phone: (202)260-8720
Contact: Steve Leftig, Director

★1918★ Environmental Protection Agency
Office of Emergency and Remedial Response (Superfund)
Hazardous Site Control Division
Crystal Sta. One, 6th Fl.
2800 Crystal Dr.
Arlington, VA 22202
Phone: (703)308-8313
Contact: Paul F. Nadeau, Director

★1919★ Environmental Protection Agency
Office of Emergency and Remedial Response (Superfund)
Hazardous Site Evaluation Division
Mall area of Waterside Mall, Rm. 2710
401 M St., SW
Washington, DC 20460
Phone: (202)260-8602
Contact: Larry Reed, Director

★1920★ Environmental Protection Agency
Office of Enforcement and Compliance Monitoring
National Enforcement Investigations Center
Bldg. 53
Box 25227
Denver, CO 80225
Phone: (303)236-5100
Contact: Frank Covington, Dir.

★1921★ Environmental Protection Agency
Office of Marine and Estuarine Protection
Marine Operations Division
Fairchild Bldg., Rm. 811
499 S. Capitol St., SW
Washington, DC 20032
Phone: (202)260-3952
Contact: Craig Vogt, Director

★1922★ Environmental Protection Agency
Office of Pesticide Programs
Environmental Fate and Effects Division
Crystal Mall Bldg. 2, Rm. 10th Fl.
1921 Jefferson Davis Hwy.
Arlington, VA 22202
Phone: (703)557-7695
Contact: Anne L. Barton, Director

★1923★ Environmental Protection Agency
Office of Pesticide Programs
Health Effects Division
Crystal Mall Bldg. 2, Rm. 821
1921 Jefferson Davis Hwy.
Arlington, VA 22202
Phone: (703)557-7351
Contact: Penelope A. Fenner-Crisp, Director

★1924★ Environmental Protection Agency
Office of Pollution Prevention
Pollution Prevention Division
Mall area of Waterside Mall, Rm. 3130
401 M St., SW
Washington, DC 20460
Phone: (202)260-3557
Contact: Gerald Kotas, Director

★1925★ Environmental Protection Agency
Office of Radiation Programs
Radon Division
Northeast Mall area of Waterside Mall, Rm. 200
401 M St., SW
Washington, DC 20460
Phone: (202)260-9622
Contact: Margo T. Oge, Director

★1926★ Environmental Protection Agency
Office of Research and Development
Center for Environmental Research Information
26 W. Martin Luther King Dr.
Cincinnati, OH 45268
Phone: (513)569-7562

Contact: Calvin Lawrence, Dir.

★1927★ Environmental Protection Agency
Office of Research and Development
Office of Environmental Processes and Effects Research
401 M St., SW, Rm. W609
Washington, DC 20460
Phone: (202)260-5950
Contact: Courtney Riordan, Dir.

★1928★ Environmental Protection Agency
Office of Research and Development
Office of Health and Environmental Assessment
401 M St., SW, Rm. M3700
Washington, DC 20460
Phone: (202)260-7317
Contact: William H. Farland, Dir.

★1929★ Environmental Protection Agency
Office of Solid Waste and Emergency Response
Chemical Emergency Preparedness and Prevention
401 M St., SW, Rm. M3103
Washington, DC 20460
Phone: (202)260-8600
Contact: James L. Makris, Dir.

★1930★ Environmental Protection Agency
Office of Solid Waste
Municipal and Industrial Solid Waste Programs Division
Mall area of Waterside Mall, Rm. 2105
401 M St., SW
Washington, DC 20460
Phone: (202)260-9872
Contact: Bruce R. Weddle, Director

★1931★ Environmental Protection Agency
Office of Solid Waste
Waste Management Division
Crystal Sta. One, 6th Fl.
2800 Crystal Dr.
Arlington, VA 22202
Phone: (703)308-8414
Contact: Russel Wyer, Director

★1932★ Environmental Protection Agency
Office of the Administrator
Science Advisory Board
401 M St., SW, Rm. W1145
Washington, DC 20460
Phone: (202)260-4126
Contact: Sam R. Rondberg, Chairman

★1933★ Environmental Protection Agency
Office of Toxic Substances
Environmental Assistance Division
East Tower of Waterside Mall, Rm. 543
401 M St., SW
Washington, DC 20460
Phone: (202)260-7024
Contact: Michael Stahl, Director

★1934★ Environmental Protection Agency
Office of Toxic Substances
Health and Environmental Review Division
East Tower of Waterside Mall, Rm. 617
401 M St., SW
Washington, DC 20460
Phone: (202)260-4241
Contact: Joseph A. Cotruvo, Director

★1935★ Environmental Protection Agency
Office of Waste Programs Enforcement
Comprehensive Environmental Response Compensation and Liability Act (CERCLA) Enforcement Division
Crystal Sta. One, 7th Fl.
2800 Crystal Dr.
Arlington, VA 22202
Phone: (703)308-8404
Contact: Sally S. Mansbach, Director

★1936★ Environmental Protection Agency
Office of Waste Programs Enforcement
Resource Conservation and Recovery Act (RCRA) Enforcement Division
Mall area of Waterside Mall, Rm. 2714
401 M St., SW
Washington, DC 20460
Phone: (202)260-4808
Contact: Susan Bromm, Director

★1937★ Environmental Protection Agency
Pesticides and Toxic Substances Department
Office of Pesticide Programs
Crystal Mall Bldg. 2, Rm. 1115
1921 Jefferson Davis Hwy.
Arlington, VA 22202
Phone: (703)557-7090
Contact: Douglas D. Campt, Director

★1938★ Environmental Protection Agency
Pesticides and Toxic Substances Department
Office of Toxic Substances
East Tower of Waterside Mall, Rm. 539
401 M St., SW
Washington, DC 20460
Phone: (202)260-3810
Contact: Mark A. Greenwood, Director

★1939★ Environmental Protection Agency
Policy, Planning, and Evaluation Department
Office of Pollution Prevention
West Tower of Waterside Mall, Rm. 1009
401 M St., SW
Washington, DC 20460
Phone: (202)260-4028
Contact: Stanley L. Liskowski, Director

★1940★ Environmental Protection Agency
Solid Waste and Emergency Response Department
Office of Emergency and Remedial Response (Superfund)
Southeast Mall area of Waterside Mall, Rm. 393
401 M St., SW
Washington, DC 20460
Phone: (202)260-2180
Fax: (202)260-2155
Contact: Henry L. Longest II, Director

★1941★ Environmental Protection Agency
Solid Waste and Emergency Response Department
Office of Solid Waste
Mall area of Waterside Mall, Rm. 2101
401 M St., SW
Washington, DC 20460
Phone: (202)260-4627
Contact: Sylvia K. Lowrance, Director

★1942★ Environmental Protection Agency
Solid Waste and Emergency Response Department
Office of Underground Storage Tanks
Mall area of Waterside Mall, Rm. 2107
401 M St., SW
Washington, DC 20460
Phone: (202)260-4756
Contact: Ronald Brand, Director

★1943★ Environmental Protection Agency
Solid Waste and Emergency Response Department
Office of Waste Programs Enforcement
Southeast Mall area of Waterside Mall, Rm. 364
401 M St., SW
Washington, DC 20460
Phone: (202)260-4814
Contact: Bruce M. Diamond, Director

★1944★ Environmental Protection Agency
Water Department
Office of Drinking Water
East Tower of Waterside Mall, Rm. 1011
401 M St., SW
Washington, DC 20460
Phone: (202)260-5543
Contact: Michael B. Cook, Director

★1945★ Environmental Protection Agency
Water Department
Office of GroundWater Protection
East Tower of Waterside Mall, Rm. 811
401 M St., SW
Washington, DC 20460
Phone: (202)260-7077
Contact: Marian Mlay, Director

★1946★ Environmental Protection Agency
Water Department
Office of Marine and Estuarine Protection
Fairchild Bldg., Rm. 811
499 S Capitol St., SW
Washington, DC 20032
Phone: (202)260-7166
Contact: Tudor Davies, Director

★1947★ Environmental Protection Agency
Water Department
Office of Municipal Pollution Control
East Tower of Waterside Mall, Rm. 1209D
401 M St., SW
Washington, DC 20460
Phone: (202)260-5850
Contact: Michael J. Quigley, Director

★1948★ Environmental Protection Agency
Water Department
Office of Water Regulations and Standards
East Tower of Waterside Mall, Rm. 837
401 M St., SW
Washington, DC 20460
Phone: (202)260-7040
Contact: Geoffrey Grubbs, Director

★1949★ Environmental Protection Agency
Water Department
Office of Wetlands Protection
Fairchild Bldg., Rm. 711
499 S Capitol St., SW
Washington, DC 20032
Phone: (202)260-7791
Fax: (202)260-2356
Contact: David G. Davis, Director

★1950★ Great Lakes Commission
Argus II Bldg.
400 S. 4th St.
Ann Arbor, MI 48103
Phone: (313)665-9135
Contact: Michael J. Donahue, Exec. Dir.

★1951★ Great Lakes Fishery Commission
1451 Green Rd.
Ann Arbor, MI 48105
Phone: (313)662-3209
Contact: Carlos M. Fetterolf Jr., Exec. Sec.

★1952★ Gulf States Marine Fisheries Commission
PO Box 726
Ocean Springs, MS 39564
Phone: (601)875-5912
Contact: Thomas Gollott, Chairman
Includes Alabama, Florida, Mississippi, and Texas.

★1953★ Interstate Commission on the Potomac River Basin
6110 Executive Blvd., Ste. 300
Rockville, MD 20852
Phone: (301)984-1908
Contact: L.E. Zeni, Exec. Dir.
Includes the District of Columbia, Maryland, Pennsylvania, Virginia, and West Virginia.

★1954★ Interstate Sanitation Commission
311 W. 43rd St., Rm. 201
New York, NY 10036
Phone: (212)582-0380
Contact: Alan Mytelka, Dir. and Chief Engineer
Includes Connecticut, New Jersey, and New York.

★1955★ Kansas-Nebraska Big Blue River Compact Commission
315 1st St.
Aurora, NE 68818
Phone: (402)694-2825
Contact: J. Michael Jess, Nebraska Chairman
Includes Kansas and Nebraska.

★1956★ Kansas-Oklahoma-Arkansas River Compact Commission
11435 E. Fifth St.
Tulsa, OK 74128
Phone: (918)437-1466
Contact: Paul Thornburgh, U.S. Chairman
Includes Kansas and Oklahoma.

★1957★ Klamath River Compact Commission
6600 Washburn Way
Klamath Falls, OR 97603
Phone: (503)882-4436
Contact: Nell Kuonen, Chairperson
Includes California and Oregon.

★1958★ La Plata River Compact Commission
Colorado Water Resources Div.
1313 Sherman, Rm. 818
Denver, CO 80203
Phone: (303)866-3581
Contact: Jeris Danielson, Colorado Commissioner
Includes Colorado and New Mexico.

★1959★ Marine Mammal Commission
1625 I St., NW
Washington, DC 20006
Phone: (202)653-6237
Contact: John Twiss Jr., Exec. Dir.

★1960★ Midwest Interstate Low-Level Radioactive Waste Commission
350 N. Robert St., Rm. 588
St. Paul, MN 55101
Phone: (612)293-0126
Contact: Gregg S. Larson, Exec. Dir.
Includes Indiana, Iowa, Michigan, Minnesota, Missouri, Ohio, and Wisconsin.

★1961★ National Academy of Sciences (NAS)
2101 Constitution Ave., NW
Washington, DC 20418
Phone: (202)334-2000
Contact: Frank Press, Pres.

★1962★ National Science Foundation
Biological and Critical Systems Division
Bioengineering and Environmental Systems Section
1800 G St., NW, Rm. 1132
Washington, DC 20550
Phone: (202)357-9545
Contact: Robert D. Hanson, Director

★1963★ National Science Foundation
Biological and Critical Systems Division
Hazard Mitigation Section
1800 G St., NW, Rm. 1132
Washington, DC 20550
Phone: (202)357-7737
Contact: William A. Anderson, Head

★1964★ National Science Foundation
Directorate for Biological, Behavioral, and Social Sciences
Biotic Systems and Resources Division
1800 G St., NW, Rm. 215
Washington, DC 20550
Phone: (202)357-7332
Contact: Patricia A. Werner, Director

★1965★ National Science Foundation
Directorate for Geosciences
1800 G St., NW, Rm. 510
Washington, DC 20550
Phone: (202)357-9715
Contact: Robert W. Corell, Asst. Dir.

★1966★ National Science Foundation
Directorate for Geosciences
Polar Programs Division
1800 G St., NW, Rm. 620
Washington, DC 20550
Phone: (202)357-7766
Contact: Peter E. Wilkniss, Director

★1967★ National Transportation Safety Board
Office of Aviation Safety
Hazardous Material Division
800 Independence Ave., SW, Rm. 834E
Washington, DC 20594
Phone: (202)382-6585
Contact: Robert J. Chipkevich, Chief

★1968★ National Transportation Safety Board
Office of Surface Transportation Safety
800 Independence Ave., SW, Rm. 800E
Washington, DC 20594
Phone: (202)382-6800
Contact: George L. Reagle, Director

★1969★ New England Interstate Water Pollution Control Commission
85 Merrimac St.
Boston, MA 02114
Phone: (617)367-8522
Contact: Ronald F. Poltak, Exec. Dir.
Includes Connecticut, Maine, Massachusetts, New Hampshire, New York, Rhode Island, and Vermont.

★1970★ Northeast Interstate Low-Level Radioactive Waste Commission
I-195 Nassau St.
Princeton, NJ 08540
Phone: (609)497-1447
Contact: Ron Gingerich, Exec. Dir.
Includes Connecticut, Delaware, Maryland, and New Jersey.

★1971★ Northeastern Forest Fire Protection Commission
10 Ladybug Ln.
Concord, NH 03301
Phone: (603)224-6966
Contact: Richard E. Mullavey, Exec. Dir.

★1972★ Northwest Interstate Compact on Low-Level Radioactive Waste Management
Washington Dept. of Ecology
Mailstop PV-11
Olympia, WA 98504
Phone: (206)459-6244
Fax: (206)459-6849
Contact: Elaine Carlin, Exec. Dir.
Includes Alaska, Hawaii, Idaho, Montana, Oregon, Utah, and Washington State.

★1973★ Nuclear Regulatory Commission
1 White Flint N. Bldg.
11555 Rockville Pike
Rockville, MD 20852
Phone: (301)492-0240
Fax: (301)492-0259
Contact: Ivan Selin, Chm. -Designate

★1974★ Nuclear Regulatory Commission
Advisory Committee on Nuclear Waste
Phillips Bldg., Rm. 434
7920 Norfolk Ave.
Bethesda, MD 20814
Phone: (301)492-4516
Contact: Dade W. Moeller, Chmn.

★1975★ Nuclear Regulatory Commission
Nuclear Materials, Safety, Safeguards, and Operations Support Dept.
1 White Flint N. Bldg.
11555 Rockville Pike
Rockville, MD 20852
Phone: (301)492-1713
Contact: Hugh L. Thompson Jr., Dep. Exec. Dir.

★1976★ Office of the Nuclear Waste Negotiator
3050 N. Lakeharbor Ln., Rm. 100
Boise, ID 83703
Phone: (208)334-9876
Fax: (208)334-9880
Contact: David H. Leroy, Negotiator

★1977★ Ohio River Valley Water Sanitation Commission (ORSANCO)
49 E. 4th St., Ste. 815
Cincinnati, OH 45202
Phone: (513)421-1151
Contact: Alan H. Vicory, Exec. Dir. & Chief Engineer
Includes Illinois, Indiana, Kentucky, New York, Ohio, Pennsylvania, and Virginia.

★1978★ Pacific Marine Fisheries Commission
2501 SW 1st Ave., Ste. 200
Portland, OR 97201
Phone: (503)326-7025
Contact: Guy N. Thornburgh, Exec. Dir.
Includes Alaska, California, Idaho, Oregon, and Washington.

★1979★ Pecos River Commission
PO Box 123
Carlsbad, NM 88220
Phone: (505)885-5939
Contact: Ronny McCracken, Dir.

★1980★ Republican River Compact Commission
Colorado Div. of Water Resources
1313 Sherman, Rm. 818
Denver, CO 80203
Phone: (303)866-3581
Contact: Jeris Danielson, Colorado Commissioner
Includes Colorado, Kansas, and Nebraska.

★1981★ **Rio Grande Compact Commission**
Federal Bldg., Rm. 115
Sante Fe, NM 87501
Phone: (505)988-6307
Contact: Arlene Ham, U.S. Chairperson
Includes Colorado, New Mexico, and Texas.

★1982★ **Rocky Mountain Low-Level Radioactive Waste Board**
1675 Broadway, Ste. 1400
Denver, CO 80202
Phone: (303)825-1912
Contact: Leonard C. Slosky, Exec. Dir.
Includes Arizona, Colorado, Nevada, New Mexico, Utah, and Wyoming.

★1983★ **Sabine River Compact Administration**
PO Box 66492
Baton Rouge, LA 70896
Phone: (504)389-0281
Contact: James B. Furth Jr., Chairman

★1984★ **Smithsonian Institution**
Research Dept.
Conservation and Research Ctr.
Front Royal, VA 22630
Phone: (703)635-4166
Contact: Christen M. Wemmer, Assoc. Dir.

★1985★ **Smithsonian Institution**
Research Dept.
Office of Environmental Awareness
S. Dillon Ripley Ctr., Rm. 3123
1100 Jefferson Dr., SW
Washington, DC 20560
Phone: (202)357-4797
Contact: Judith Gradwohl, Director

★1986★ **Smithsonian Institution**
Research Department
Smithsonian Environmental Research Center
PO Box 28
Edgewater, MD 21037
Phone: (301)798-4424
Fax: (301)261-7954
Contact: David L. Correll, Director

★1987★ **Smithsonian Institution**
Research Dept.
Smithsonian Tropical Research Institute
Arts & Industries Bldg., Rm. 2207
900 Jefferson Dr., SW
Washington, DC 20560
Phone: (202)786-2817
Contact: George Angehr, Liaison Officer
The Smithsonian Tropical Research Institute mailing address is APO Miami 34002-0011, Balboa, Panama. Ira Rubinoff acts as director of the Institute.

★1988★ **South Platte River Compact**
Colorado Water Resources Div.
1313 Sherman, Rm. 818
Denver, CO 80203
Phone: (303)866-3581
Contact: Jeris Danielson, Colorado Commissioner
Includes Colorado and Nebraska.

★1989★ **Southeast Compact Commission for Low-Level Radioactive Waste Management**
3901 Barrett Dr., Ste. 100
Raleigh, NC 27609
Phone: (919)781-7152
Contact: Kathryn Visocki, Exec. Dir.
Includes Alabama, Florida, Georgia, Mississippi, North Carolina, South Carolina, Tennessee, Virginia.

★1990★ **Susquehanna River Basin Commission**
1100 L St., NW
Washington, DC 20005
Contact: Sec. of the Interior Manuel Lujan Jr., Federal Member
Mailing address: Department of the Interior, Washington, DC 20240; (202) 208-7351.

★1991★ **Tennessee Valley Authority**
400 W. Summit Hill Dr.
Knoxville, TN 37902
Phone: (615)632-8000
Contact: Marvin T. Runyon, Chm.

★1992★ **Tennessee Valley Authority**
Clean Air Program
Missionary Ridge Pl.
1101 Market St.
Chattanooga, TN 37402
Phone: (615)751-6779
Contact: Jerry Golden, Mgr

★1993★ **Tennessee Valley Authority**
Resource Development Department
Office of Environmental Quality
Summer Pl. Bldg., Rm. 201
309 Walnut St.
Knoxville, TN 37902
Phone: (615)632-6578
Contact: M. Paul Schmierbach

★1994★ **Tennessee Valley Authority**
Resource Development Department
River Basin Operations Department
Old City Hall Bldg., Rm. 1E61E
601 W. Summit Hill Dr.
Knoxville, TN 37902
Phone: (615)632-6367

★1995★ **Tennessee Valley Authority**
River Basin Operations Department
Office of Land Resources
Forestry Bldg.
Ridgeway Rd.
Norris, TN 37828
Phone: (615)632-1802
Contact: Lawrence L. Calvert, Mgr

★1996★ **Tennessee Valley Authority**
River Basin Operations Department
Office of Water Resources
Evans Bldg., Rm. 1W141A
524 Union Ave.
Knoxville, TN 37902
Phone: (615)632-6770
Contact: Ralph H. Brooks, Mgr

★1997★ **U.S. International Development Cooperation Agency (AID)**
Agency for International Development
Department of State Bldg.
320 21st St., NW
Washington, DC 20523
Phone: (202)647-1850
Fax: (202)647-8518
Contact: Ronald W. Roskens, Adm.

★1998★ **Upper Colorado River Commission**
355 S. 400 East
Salt Lake City, UT 84111
Phone: (801)531-1150
Includes Arizona, Colorado, New Mexico, Utah, and Wyoming.

★1999★ **Yellowstone River Compact Commission**
821 E. Interstate Ave.
Bismarck, ND 58501
Phone: (701)250-4601
Contact: William Horak, U.S. Chairman
Includes Montana, North Dakota, and Wyoming.

U.S. National Forests

Alabama

★2000★ Conecuh National Forest
1765 Highland Ave.
Montgomery, AL 36107
Phone: (205)832-4470

★2001★ Talladega National Forest
1765 Highland Ave.
Montgomery, AL 36107
Phone: (205)832-4470

★2002★ Tuskegee National Forest
1765 Highland Ave.
Montgomery, AL 36107
Phone: (205)832-4470

★2003★ William B. Bankhead National Forest
1765 Highland Ave.
Montgomery, AL 36107
Phone: (205)832-4470

Alaska

★2004★ Chugach National Forest
201 E. Ninth Ave., Ste. 206
Anchorage, AK 99501
Phone: (907)271-2500

★2005★ Tongass National Forest: Chatham Area
204 Siginaka Way
Sitka, AK 99835
Phone: (907)747-6671

★2006★ Tongass National Forest: Ketchikan Area
Federal Bldg.
Ketchikan, AK 99901
Phone: (907)225-3101

★2007★ Tongass National Forest: Stikine Area
201 12th St.
PO Box 309
Petersburg, AK 99833
Phone: (907)772-3841

Arizona

★2008★ Apache-Sitgreaves National Forest
Federal Bldg.
309 S. Mountain Ave.
PO Box 640
Springerville, AZ 85938
Phone: (602)333-4301

★2009★ Coconino National Forest
2323 E. Greenlaw Ln.
Flagstaff, AZ 86004
Phone: (602)527-7400

★2010★ Coronado National Forest
300 W. Congress St., 6th Fl.
Tucson, AZ 85701
Phone: (602)629-6483

★2011★ Kaibab National Forest
800 S. Sixth St.
Williams, AZ 86046
Phone: (602)635-2681

★2012★ Prescott National Forest
344 S. Cortez
Prescott, AZ 86303
Phone: (602)445-1762

★2013★ Tonto National Forest
2324 E. McDowell Rd.
PO Box 5348
Phoenix, AZ 85010
Phone: (602)225-5200

Arkansas

★2014★ Ouachita National Forest
Federal Bldg.
100 Reserve St.
PO Box 1270
Hot Springs, AR 71902
Phone: (501)321-5202

★2015★ Ozark - St. Francis National Forest
605 W. Main St.
PO Box 1008
Russellville, AR 72801
Phone: (501)968-2354

California

★2016★ Angeles National Forest
701 N. Santa Anita Ave.
Arcadia, CA 91006
Phone: (818)574-1613

★2017★ Cleveland National Forest
880 Front St., Rm. 5-N-14
San Diego, CA 92188
Phone: (619)557-5050

★2018★ Eldorado National Forest
100 Forni Rd.
Placerville, CA 95667
Phone: (916)644-6048

★2019★ Inyo National Forest
873 N. Main St.
Bishop, CA 93514
Phone: (619)873-5841

★2020★ Klamath National Forest
1312 Fairlane Rd.
Yreka, CA 96097
Phone: (916)842-6131

★2021★ Lake Tahoe Basin Management Unit
870 Emerald Bay Rd.
PO Box 731002
South Lake Tahoe, CA 95731
Phone: (916)573-2600

★2022★ Lassen National Forest
55 S. Sacramento St.
Susanville, CA 96130
Phone: (916)257-2151

★2023★ Los Padres National Forest
6144 Calle Real
Goleta, CA 93117
Phone: (805)683-6711

★2024★ Mendocino National Forest
420 E. Laurel St.
Willows, CA 95988
Phone: (916)934-3316

★2025★ Modoc National Forest
441 N. Main St.
Alturas, CA 96101
Phone: (916)233-5811

★2026★ Plumas National Forest
159 Lawrence St.
PO Box 1500
Quincy, CA 95971
Phone: (916)283-2050

★2027★ San Bernardino National Forest
1824 S. Commercenter Circle
San Bernardino, CA 92408-3430
Phone: (714)383-5588

★2028★ Sequoia National Forest
900 W. Grand Ave.
Porterville, CA 93257
Phone: (209)784-1500

★2029★ Shasta-Trinity National Forests
2400 Washington Ave.
Redding, CA 96001
Phone: (916)246-5222

★2030★ Sierra National Forest
1130 O St., Rm. 3009
Fresno, CA 93721
Phone: (209)487-5155

★2031★ Six Rivers National Forest
507 F St.
Eureka, CA 95501
Phone: (707)442-1721

★2032★ Stanislaus National Forest
19777 Greenley Rd.
Sonora, CA 95370
Phone: (209)532-3671

★2033★ Tahoe National Forest
Highway 49 & Coyote St.
Nevada City, CA 95959
Phone: (916)265-4531

Colorado

★2034★ Arapaho National Forest
240 W. Prospect Rd.
Fort Collins, CO 80526
Phone: (303)498-1100

★2035★ Grand Mesa National Forest
2250 U. S. Hwy. 50
Delta, CO 81416
Phone: (303)874-7691

★2036★ Gunnison National Forest
2250 U. S. Hwy. 50
Delta, CO 81416
Phone: (303)874-7691

★2037★ Pike National Forest
1920 Valley Dr.
Pueblo, CO 81008
Phone: (719)545-8737

★2038★ Rio Grande National Forest
1803 W. U. S. Hwy. 160
Monte Vista, CO 81144
Phone: (719)852-5941

★2039★ Roosevelt National Forest
240 W. Prospect Rd.
Fort Collins, CO 80526
Phone: (303)498-1100

★2040★ Routt National Forest
29587 W. U. S. Hwy. 40, Ste. 20
Steamboat Springs, CO 80487
Phone: (303)879-1722

★2041★ San Isabel National Forest
1920 Valley Dr.
Pueblo, CO 81008
Phone: (719)545-8737

★2042★ San Juan National Forest
701 Camino Del Rio, Rm. 301
Durango, CO 81301
Phone: (303)247-4874

★2043★ Uncompahgre National Forest
2250 U. S. Hwy. 50
Delta, CO 81416
Phone: (303)874-7691

★2044★ White River National Forest
Old Federal Bldg.
Ninth St. & Grand Ave.
PO Box 948
Glenwood Springs, CO 81602
Phone: (303)945-2521

Florida

★2045★ Apalachicola National Forest
USDA Forest Service
227 N. Bronough St., Ste. 4061
Tallahassee, FL 32301
Phone: (904)681-7265

★2046★ Ocala National Forest
USDA Forest Service
227 N. Bronough St., Ste 4061
Tallahassee, FL 32301
Phone: (904)681-7265

★2047★ Osceola National Forest
USDA Forest Service
227 N. Bronough St., Ste 4061
Tallahassee, FL 32301
Phone: (904)681-7265

Georgia

★2048★ Chattahoochee-Oconee National Forest
508 Oak St., NW
Gainesville, GA 30501
Phone: (404)536-0541

Idaho

★2049★ Boise National Forest
1750 Front St.
Boise, ID 83702
Phone: (208)334-1516

★2050★ Caribou National Forest
Federal Bldg., Ste. 294
250 S. Fourth Ave.
Pocatello, ID 83201
Phone: (208)236-6700

★2051★ Challis National Forest
Forest Service Bldg.
U. S. Hwy. 93 N.
PO Box 404
Challis, ID 83226
Phone: (208)879-2285

★2052★ Clearwater National Forest
12730 Hwy. 12
Orofino, ID 83544
Phone: (208)476-4541

★2053★ Idaho Panhandle National Forests: Coeur d'Alene
1201 Ironwood Dr.
Coeur d'Alene, ID 83814
Phone: (208)765-7223

★2054★ Idaho Panhandle National Forests: Kaniksu
1201 Ironwood Dr.
Coeur d'Alene, ID 83814
Phone: (208)765-7223

★2055★ Idaho Panhandle National Forests: St. Joe
1201 Ironwood Dr.
Coeur d'Alene, ID 83814
Phone: (208)765-7223

★2056★ Nez Perce National Forest
East U. S. Hwy. 13
Rte. 2, PO Box 475
Grangeville, ID 83530
Phone: (208)983-1950

★2057★ Payette National Forest
106 W. Park St.
PO Box 1026
McCall, ID 83638
Phone: (208)634-8151

★2058★ Salmon National Forest
U. S. Hwy. 93 N.
PO Box 729
Salmon, ID 83467
Phone: (208)756-2215

★2059★ Sawtooth National Forest
2647 Kimberly Rd. E.
Twin Falls, ID 83301
Phone: (208)737-3200

★2060★ Targhee National Forest
420 N. Bridge St.
PO Box 208
St. Anthony, ID 83445
Phone: (208)624-3151

Illinois

★2061★ Shawnee National Forest
901 S. Commercial St.
Harrisburg, IL 62946
Phone: (618)253-7114

Indiana

★2062★ Wayne-Hoosier National Forests
811 Constitution Ave.
Bedford, IN 47421
Phone: (812)275-5987

Kentucky

★2063★ Daniel Boone National Forest
100 Vaught Rd.
Winchester, KY 40391
Phone: (606)745-3100

Louisiana

★2064★ Kisatchie National Forest
2500 Shreveport Hwy.
PO Box 5500
Pineville, LA 71360
Phone: (318)473-7160

Michigan

★2065★ Hiawatha National Forest
2727 N. Lincoln Rd.
Escanaba, MI 49829
Phone: (906)786-4062

★2066★ Huron-Manistee National Forests
421 S. Mitchell St.
Cadillac, MI 49601
Phone: (616)775-2421

★2067★ Ottawa National Forest
East U. S. Hwy. 2
Ironwood, MI 49938
Phone: (906)932-1330

Minnesota

★2068★ Chippewa National Forest
Rte. 3, PO Box 244
Cass Lake, MN 56633
Phone: (218)335-2226

★2069★ Superior National Forest
515 W. First St., PO Box 338
Duluth, MN 55801
Phone: (218)720-5324

Mississippi

★2070★ Bienville National Forest
100 W. Capitol St., Ste. 1141
Jackson, MS 39269
Phone: (601)965-4391

★2071★ Delta National Forest
100 W. Capitol St., Ste. 1141
Jackson, MS 39269
Phone: (601)965-4391

★2072★ DeSoto National Forest
100 W. Capitol St., Ste. 1141
Jackson, MS 39269
Phone: (601)965-4391

★2073★ Holly Springs National Forest
100 W. Capitol St., Ste. 1141
Jackson, MS 39269
Phone: (601)965-4391

★2074★ Homochitto National Forest
100 W. Capitol St., Ste. 1141
Jackson, MS 39269
Phone: (601)965-4391

★2075★ Tombigbee National Forest
100 W. Capitol St., Ste. 1141
Jackson, MS 39269
Phone: (601)965-4391

Missouri

★2076★ Mark Twain National Forest
401 Fairgrounds Rd.
Rolla, MO 65401
Phone: (314)364-4621

Montana

★2077★ Beaverhead National Forest
610 N. Montana St.
Dillon, MT 59725
Phone: (406)683-3900

★2078★ Bitterroot National Forest
316 N. Third St.
Hamilton, MT 59840
Phone: (406)363-3131

★2079★ Custer National Forest
2602 First Ave., N.
Billings, MT 59103
Phone: (406)657-6361

★2080★ Deerlodge National Forest
Federal Bldg.
Corner of Cooper & Main Sts.
PO Box 400
Butte, MT 59703
Phone: (406)496-3400

★2081★ Flathead National Forest
1935 Third Ave., E.
Kalispell, MT 59901
Phone: (406)755-5401

★2082★ Gallatin National Forest
Federal Bldg.
10 E. Babcock St.
PO Box 130
Bozeman, MT 59771
Phone: (406)587-6701

★2083★ Helena National Forest
Federal Bldg.
301 S. Park, Rm. 334
Drawer 10014
Helena, MT 59626
Phone: (406)449-5201

★2084★ Kootenai National Forest
506 U. S. Hwy. 2 W.
Libby, MT 59923
Phone: (406)293-6211

★2085★ Lewis and Clark National Forest
1101 15th St., N.
PO Box 871
Great Falls, MT 59403
Phone: (406)791-7700

★2086★ Lolo National Forest
Bldg. 24
Fort Missoula
Missoula, MT 59801
Phone: (406)329-3750

Nebraska

★2087★ Nebraska National Forest
270 Pine St.
Chadron, NE 69337
Phone: (308)432-3367

Nevada

★2088★ Humboldt National Forest
976 Mountain City Hwy.
Elko, NV 89801
Phone: (702)738-5171

★2089★ Toiyabe National Forest
1200 Franklin Way
Sparks, NV 89431
Phone: (702)355-5301

New Hampshire

★2090★ White Mountain National Forest
Federal Bldg.
719 N. Main St.
PO Box 638
Laconia, NH 03247
Phone: (603)524-6450

New Mexico

★2091★ Carson National Forest
Forest Service Bldg.
208 Cruz Alta Rd.
PO Box 558
Taos, NM 87571
Phone: (505)758-6200

★2092★ Cibola National Forest
10308 Candelaria NE
Albuquerque, NM 87112
Phone: (505)275-5207

★2093★ Gila National Forest
2610 N. Silver St.
Silver City, NM 88061
Phone: (505)388-8201

★2094★ Lincoln National Forest
Federal Bldg.
11th St. & New York Ave.
Alamogordo, NM 88310
Phone: (505)437-6030

★2095★ Santa Fe National Forest
Pinon Bldg.
1220 St. Francis Dr.
PO Box 1689
Santa Fe, NM 87504
Phone: (505)988-6940

North Carolina

★2096★ Croatan National Forest
100 Otis St.
PO Box 2750
Asheville, NC 28802
Phone: (704)257-4200

★2097★ Nantahala National Forest
100 Otis St.
P.O Box 2750
Asheville, NC 28802
Phone: (704)257-4200

★2098★ Pisgah National Forest
100 Otis St.
PO Box 2750
Asheville, NC 28802
Phone: (704)257-4200

★2099★ Uwharrie National Forest
100 Otis St.
PO Box 2750
Asheville, NC 28802
Phone: (704)257-4200

Oregon

★2100★ Columbia River Gorge National Scenic Area
Waucoma Ctr., Ste. 200
902 Wasco Ave.
Hood River, OR 97031
Phone: (503)386-2333

★2101★ Deschutes National Forest
1645 U. S. Hwy. 20 E.
Bend, OR 97701
Phone: (503)388-2715

★2102★ Fremont National Forest
524 N. G St.
Lakeview, OR 97630
Phone: (503)947-2151

★2103★ Malheur National Forest
139 NE Dayton St.
John Day, OR 97845
Phone: (503)575-1731

★2104★ Mount Hood National Forest
2955 NW Division St.
Gresham, OR 97030
Phone: (503)666-0700

★2105★ Ochoco National Forest
155 N. Ct. St.
PO Box 490
Prineville, OR 97754
Phone: (503)447-6247

★2106★ Rogue River National Forest
Federal Bldg
333 W. Eighth St.
PO Box 520
Medford, OR 97501
Phone: (503)776-3600

★2107★ Siskiyou National Forest
200 NE Greenfield Rd.
PO Box 440
Grants Pass, OR 97526
Phone: (503)479-5301

★2108★ Siuslaw National Forest
4077 Research Way
Corvallis, OR 97339
Phone: (503)757-4480

★2109★ Umatilla National Forest
2517 SW Hailey Ave.
Pendleton, OR 97801
Phone: (503)276-3811

★2110★ Umpqua National Forest
2900 NW Stewart Pkwy.
PO Box 1008
Roseburg, OR 97470
Phone: (503)672-6601

★2111★ Wallowa-Whitman National Forest
1550 Dewey Ave.
PO Box 907
Baker, OR 97814
Phone: (503)523-6391

★2112★ Willamette National Forest
211 E. Seventh Ave.
PO Box 10607
Eugene, OR 97440
Phone: (503)687-6521

★2113★ Winema National Forest
2819 Dahlia St.
Klamath Falls, OR 97601
Phone: (503)883-6714

Pennsylvania

★2114★ Allegheny National Forest
Spiridon Bldg.
222 Liberty St.
PO Box 847
Warren, PA 16365
Phone: (814)723-5150

Puerto Rico

★2115★ Caribbean National Forest
University of Puerto Rico
Agricultural Experiment Sta.
Call Box 2500
Rio Piedras, PR 00928
Phone: (809)763-3939

South Carolina

★2116★ Francis Marion-Sumter National Forests
1835 Assembly St.
PO Box 2227
Columbia, SC 29202
Phone: (803)765-5222

South Dakota

★2117★ Black Hills National Forest
Highway 385 N.
Rte. 2, PO Box 200
Custer, SD 57730
Phone: (605)673-2251

Tennessee

★2118★ Cherokee National Forest
2800 N. Ocoee St., NW
PO Box 2010
Cleveland, TN 37320
Phone: (615)476-9700

Texas

★2119★ Angelina National Forest
Homer Garrison Federal Bldg.
701 N. First St.
Lufkin, TX 75901
Phone: (409)639-8501

★2120★ Davy Crockett National Forest
Homer Garrison Federal Bldg.
701 N. First St.
Lufkin, TX 75901
Phone: (409)639-8501

★2121★ Sabine National Forest
Homer Garrison Federal Bldg.
701 N. First St.
Lufkin, TX 75901
Phone: (409)639-8501

★2122★ Sam Houston National Forest
Homer Garrison Federal Bldg.
701 N. First St.
Lufkin, TX 75901
Phone: (409)639-8501

Utah

★2123★ Ashley National Forest
355 N. Vernal Ave.
Vernal, UT 84078
Phone: (801)789-1181

★2124★ Dixie National Forest
82 N. 100 E.
PO Box 580
Cedar City, UT 84720
Phone: (801)586-2421

★2125★ Fishlake National Forest
115 E. 900 N.
Richfield, UT 84701
Phone: (801)896-4491

★2126★ Manti-LaSal National Forest
599 W. Price River Dr.
Price, UT 84501
Phone: (801)637-2817

★2127★ Uinta National Forest
88 W. 100 N.
Provo, UT 84601
Phone: (801)377-5780

★2128★ Wasatch-Cache National Forest
8230 Federal Bldg.
125 S. State St.
Salt Lake City, UT 84138
Phone: (801)524-5030

Vermont

★2129★ Green Mountain and Finger Lakes National Forests
Federal Bldg.
151 W. St.
PO Box 519
Rutland, VT 05701
Phone: (802)773-0300

Virginia

★2130★ George Washington National Forest
101 N. Main St.
PO Box 233
Harrison Plaza
Harrisonburg, VA 22801
Phone: (703)433-2491

★2131★ Jefferson National Forest
210 Franklin Rd, SW
Roanoke, VA 24001
Phone: (703)982-6270

Washington

★2132★ Colville National Forest
695 S. Main St.
Colville, WA 99114
Phone: (509)684-3711

★2133★ Gifford Pinchot National Forest
6926 E. Fourth Plain Blvd.
PO Box 8944
Vancouver, WA 98668
Phone: (206)696-7500

★2134★ Mount Baker-Snoqualmie National Forests
1022 First Ave.
Seattle, WA 98104
Phone: (206)442-5400

★2135★ Okanogan National Forest
1240 S. Second Ave.
PO Box 950
Okanogan, WA 98840
Phone: (509)422-2704

★2136★ Olympic National Forest
801 Capital Way
PO Box 2288
Olympia, WA 98507
Phone: (206)753-9534

★2137★ Wenatchee National Forest
301 Yakima St.
PO Box 811
Wenatchee, WA 98801
Phone: (509)662-4335

West Virginia

★2138★ Monongahela National Forest
USDA Bldg.
200 Sycamore St.
Elkins, WV 26241
Phone: (304)636-1800

Wisconsin

★2139★ Chequamegon National Forest
1170 Fourth Ave., S.
Park Falls, WI 54552
Phone: (715)762-2461

★2140★ Nicolet National Forest
Federal Bldg.
68 S. Stevens St.
Rhinelander, WI 54501
Phone: (715)362-3415

Wyoming

★2141★ Bighorn National Forest
1969 S. Sheridan Ave.
Sheridan, WY 82801
Phone: (307)672-0751

★2142★ Bridger-Teton National Forest
Forest Service Bldg.
340 N. Cache
PO Box 1888
Jackson, WY 83001
Phone: (307)733-2752

★2143★ Medicine Bow National Forest
605 Skyline Dr.
Laramie, WY 82070
Phone: (307)745-8971

★2144★ Shoshone National Forest
225 W. Yellowstone Ave.
PO Box 2140
Cody, WY 82414
Phone: (307)527-6241

U.S. National Parks

Alaska

★2145★ Aniakchak National Monument/ Preserve
PO Box 7
King Salmon, AK 99613
Phone: (907)246-3305
Contact: Alan Eliason, Supt.

★2146★ Bering Land Bridge National Preserve
PO Box 220
Nome, AK 99762
Phone: (907)443-2522
Contact: Ernest J. Suazo, Supt.

★2147★ Danali National Park and Preserve
PO Box 9
McKinley Park, AK 99755
Phone: (907)683-2294
Contact: Russell W. Berry, Supt.

★2148★ Gates of the Arctic National Park and Preserve
PO Box 74680
Fairbanks, AK 99707
Phone: (907)456-0281
Contact: Roger J. Siglin, Supt.

★2149★ Glacier Bay National Park and Preserve
PO Box 140
Gustavus, AK 99826
Phone: (907)697-2232
Contact: Marvin O. Jensen, Supt.

★2150★ Katmai National Park and Preserve
PO Box 7
King Salmon, AK 99613
Phone: (907)246-3305
Contact: Alan Eliason, Supt.

★2151★ Kenai Fjords National Park
PO Box 1727
Seward, AK 99664
Phone: (907)224-3874
Contact: Anne Castellina, Supt.

★2152★ Kobuk Valley National Park
PO Box 1029
Kotzebue, AK 99752
Phone: (907)442-3890
Contact: Ralph H. Tingey, Supt.

★2153★ Lake Clark National Park and Preserve
4230 University Dr., Ste. 311
Anchorage, AK 99508
Phone: (907)271-3751
Contact: Andrew H. Hutchison, Supt.

★2154★ Noatak National Preserve
PO Box 1029
Kotzebue, AK 99752
Phone: (907)442-3890
Contact: Ralph H. Tingey, Supt.

★2155★ Wrangell - St. Elias National Park and Preserve
PO Box 29
Glennallen, AK 99588
Phone: (907)882-5234
Contact: Karen Wade, Supt.

★2156★ Yukon-Charley Rivers National Preserve
PO Box 167
Eagle, AK 99738
Phone: (907)547-2233
Contact: Donald D. Chase, Supt.

Arizona

★2157★ Glen Canyon National Recreation Area
PO Box 1507
Page, AZ 86040
Phone: (602)645-2471
Contact: John Lancaster, Supt.

★2158★ Grand Canyon National Park
PO Box 129
Grand Canyon, AZ 86023
Phone: (602)638-7888
Contact: John H. David, Supt.

★2159★ Petrified Forest National Park
PO Box 217
Petrified Forest NP, AZ 86028
Phone: (602)524-6228

★2160★ Sunset Crater Volcano National Monument
Route 3, Box 149
Flagstaff, AZ 86004
Phone: (602)527-7042
Contact: Sam Henderson, Supt.

★2161★ Walnut Canyon National Park
Walnut Canyon Rd.
Flagstaff, AZ 86004-9705
Phone: (602)526-3367
Contact: Sam Henderson, Supt.

Arkansas

★2162★ Buffalo National River
PO Box 1173
Harrison, AR 72601
Phone: (501)741-5443
Contact: John Linahan, Supt.

★2163★ Hot Springs National Park
PO Box 1860
Hot Springs, AR 71902
Phone: (501)624-3383
Contact: Roger Giddings, Supt.

California

★2164★ Channel Islands National Park
1901 Spinnaker Dr.
Ventura, CA 93001
Phone: (805)644-8157

★2165★ Golden Gate National Recreation Area
Fort Mason, Bldg. 201
San Francisco, CA 94123

★2166★ Kings Canyon National Park
Three Rivers, CA 93271
Phone: (916)595-4444
Contact: Gilbert E. Blinn, Supt.

★2167★ Lassen Volcanic National Park
Mineral, CA 96063
Phone: (209)565-3341
Contact: Thomas Ritter, Supt.

★2168★ Pointe Reyes National Seashore
Point Reyes, CA 94956

★2169★ Redwood National Park
1111 2nd St.
Crescent City, CA 95531
Phone: (707)464-6101
Contact: William H. Ehorn, Supt.

★2170★ Santa Monica Mountains National Recreation Area
22900 Ventura Blvd. Ste. 140
Woodland Hills, CA 91364

★2171★ Sequoia National Park
Three Rivers, CA 93271
Phone: (209)565-3341
Contact: Thomas Ritter, Supt.

★2172★ Yosemite National Park
PO Box 577
Yosemite NP, CA 95389
Phone: (805)644-8157
Contact: B.J. Griffin, Supt.

Colorado

★2173★ Florissant Fossil Beds National Monument
PO Box 185
Florrissant, CO 80816
Phone: (719)748-3253
Contact: Dale Ditmanson, Supt.

★2174★ Great Sand Dunes National Monument
Mosca, CO 81146
Phone: (719)378-2312
Contact: Bill Wellman, Supt.

★2175★ Mesa Verde National Park
Hovenweep Natl. Monument
Mesa Verde National Park, CO 81330
Phone: (303)529-4465
Contact: Robert Heyder, Supt.
Contains the Hovenweep National Monument.

★2176★ Rocky Mountain National Park
Estes Park, CO 80517
Phone: (303)586-3565
Contact: Jim Thompson, Supt.

Florida

★2177★ Big Cypress National Preserve
Star Route, Box 110
Ochopee, FL 33943
Phone: (813)695-2000
Contact: Fred Fagergren

★2178★ Biscayne National Park
PO Box 1369
Homestead, FL 33030-1369
Phone: (305)247-2044
Contact: James A. Sanders, Supt.

★2179★ Canaveral National Seashore
2532 Garden St.
Titusville, FL 32796
Phone: (407)267-1110
Contact: Wendell Simpson, Supt.

★2180★ Everglades National Park
PO Box 279
Homestead, FL 33030
Phone: (305)247-6211
Alt. Phone: (305)247-7700
Contact: Robert Chandler, Supt.

★2181★ Gulf Islands National Seashore
1801 Gulf Breeze Pkwy.
Gulf Breeze, FL 32561
Phone: (904)934-2600
Contact: Jerry A. Eubanks, Supt.

★2182★ Timucuan Ecological and Historic Preserve
12713 Fl. Caroline Rd.
Jacksonville, FL 32225
Phone: (904)641-7155
Contact: Suzanne Lewis, Supt.

Georgia

★2183★ Chattahoochee River National Recreation Area
1978 Island Ford Pkwy.
Dunwoody, GA 30350
Phone: (404)394-7912
Contact: Sibbald Smith, Supt.

★2184★ Cumberland Island National Seashore
PO Box 806
St. Marys, GA 31558
Phone: (912)882-4338
Alt. Phone: (912)882-4336

Hawaii

★2185★ American Samoa National Park
c/o Pacific Area Region
PO Box 50165
Honolulu, HI 96850

★2186★ Haleakala National Park
PO Box 369, Makawao
Maui, HI 96768
Phone: (808)967-7311
Contact: Hugo H. Huntzinger, Supt.

★2187★ Hawaii Volcanoes National Park
Hawaii NP, HI 96718
Phone: (808)572-9177
Contact: Donald W. Reeser, Supt.

Indiana

★2188★ Indiana Dunes National Lakeshore
1100 N. Mineral Springs Rd.
Porter, IN 46304
Phone: (219)926-7561
Contact: Dale Engquist, Supt.

Kentucky

★2189★ Mammoth Cave National Park
Mammoth Cave, KY 42259
Phone: (502)758-2251
Alt. Phone: (502)758-2328
Contact: David A. Mihalic, Supt.

Louisiana

★2190★ Jean Lafitte National Historical Park and Preserve
419 Decatur St.
New Orleans, LA 70130
Phone: (504)589-3882
Contact: Robert Belous, Supt.

Maine

★2191★ Acadia National Park
PO Box 177
Bal Harbor, ME 04609
Phone: (207)288-3338
Fax: (207)288-5507
Contact: Bob Reynolds, Supt.

Maryland

★2192★ Assateague Island National Seashore
Route 2, Box 294
Berlin, MD 21811
Phone: (301)641-1443

Massachusetts

★2193★ Cape Cod National Seashore
South Wellfleet, MA 02663
Phone: (508)349-3785
Fax: (508)349-3785
Contact: Andrew Ringgold, Supt.

Michigan

★2194★ Isle Royale National Park
87 N. Ripley St.
Houghton, MI 49931
Phone: (906)482-0984
Contact: Bill Fink, Supt.

★2195★ Pictured Rocks National Lakeshore
PO Box 40
Munising, MI 49862
Phone: (906)387-2607
Contact: Grant Petersen, Supt.

★2196★ Sleeping Bear Dunes National Lakeshore
PO Box 277
9922 Front St.
Empire, MI 49630
Phone: (616)326-5134
Contact: Ivan Miller, Supt.

Minnesota

★2197★ Mississippi National River and Recreation Area
230 E. Fifth St.
St. Paul, MN 55101
Phone: (612)290-4160
Contact: Norm Reigle, Supt.

★2198★ Voyageurs National Park
PO Box 50
International Falls, MN 56649
Phone: (218)283-9821
Contact: Ben Clary, Supt.

Missouri

★2199★ Ozark National Scenic Riverways
PO Box 490
Van Buren, MO 63965
Phone: (314)323-4236
Contact: Art Sullivan, Supt.

Montana

★2200★ Glacier National Park
West Glacier, MT 59936
Phone: (406)888-5441
Contact: Gil Lusk, Supt.

Nebraska

★2201★ Agate Fossil Beds National Monument
PO Box 27
Gering, NE 69341-0027
Phone: (308)436-4340
Contact: John Rapier, Supt.

Nevada

★2202★ Great Basin National Park
Baker, NV 89311
Phone: (702)234-7331
Contact: Albert J. Hendricks, Supt.

New Mexico

★2203★ Capulin Volcano National Monument
PO Box 94
Capulin, NM 88414
Phone: (505)278-2201
Contact: Mary (Jeff) Karraker, Supt.

★2204★ Carlsbad Caverns National Park
3225 National Parks Hwy.
Carlsbad, NM 88220
Phone: (505)785-2251
Contact: Wallace Elms, Supt.

New York

★2205★ Fire Island National Seashore
120 Laurel St.
Patchogue (Long Island), NY 11772
Phone: (516)289-4810
Fax: (516)289-4898
Contact: Jack Hauptman, Supt.

★2206★ Gateway National Recreation Area
Floyd Bennett Field (Bldg. 69)
Brooklyn, NY 11234
Phone: (212)338-3687
Fax: (212)665-3876
Contact: Kevin Buckley, Supt.

★2207★ Upper Delaware Scenic and Recreational River
PO Box C
Narrowsburg, NY 12764
Phone: (717)729-7134

North Carolina

★2208★ Cape Hatteras National Seashore
Rte. 1, Box 675
Manteo, NC 27954
Phone: (919)473-2111
Contact: Thomas L. Hartman, Supt.

★2209★ Cape Lookout National Seashore
3601 Bridges St., Ste. F
Morehead City, NC 28557-2913
Phone: (919)240-1409
Contact: William A. Harris, Supt.

North Dakota

★2210★ Theodore Roosevelt National Park
PO Box 175
Stanton, ND 58571
Phone: (701)623-4466
Contact: Peter Hart, Supt.
Contains Knife River Indian Villages National Historic Site, and Fort Union Trading Post National Historic Site.

Oklahoma

★2211★ Chickasaw National Recreation Area
PO Box 201
Sulphur, OK 73086
Phone: (405)622-3161
Contact: Robert Peters, Supt.

Oregon

★2212★ Crater Lake National Park
PO Box 7
Crater Lake, OR 97604
Phone: (503)594-2111
Contact: Robert E. Benton, Supt.

Pennsylvania

★2213★ Delaware Water Gap National Recreation Area
Bushkill, PA 18324
Phone: (717)588-6637

South Dakota

★2214★ Badlands National Park
PO Box 6
Interior, SD 57750
Phone: (605)433-5361
Contact: Irvin L. Mortenson, Supt.

★2215★ Wind Cave National Park
R.R. 1, Box 190
Hot Springs, SD 57747-9430
Phone: (605)745-4600
Contact: Marty Ott, Supt.
Contains Jewel Cave National Monument.

Tennessee

★2216★ Big South Fork National River and Recreation Area
Rte. 3, Box 401
Oneida, TN 37841
Phone: (615)879-3625
Contact: William K. Dickinson, Supt.

★2217★ Great Smoky Mountains National Park
Gatlinburg, TN 37738
Phone: (615)436-1200
Contact: Randall R. Pope, Supt.

★2218★ Obed Wild and Scenic River
PO Box 429
Wartburg, TN 37887
Phone: (615)346-6294
Contact: William K. Dickinson, Supt.

Texas

★2219★ Alibates Flint Quarries National Monument
c/o Lake Meridith National Recreation Area
PO Box 1438
Fritch, TX 79036
Phone: (806)857-3151
Contact: Patrick McCrary, Supt.

★2220★ Amistad National Recreation Area
PO Box 420367
Del Rio, TX 78842-0367
Phone: (512)775-7491
Contact: Robert Reyes, Supt.

★2221★ Big Bend National Park
Big Bend National Park, TX 79834
Phone: (915)477-2251
Contact: Robert Arnberger, Supt.

★2222★ Big Thicket National Preserve
3785 Milam
Beaumont, TX 77701
Phone: (409)839-2689

Contact: Ronald Switzer, Supt.

★2223★ Guadalupe Mountains National Park
H.C. 60, Box 400
Salt Flat, TX 79847-9400
Phone: (915)828-3251
Contact: Larry Henderson, Supt.

★2224★ Lake Meredith National Recreation Area
PO Box 1438
Fritch, TX 79036
Phone: (806)857-3151
Contact: Patrick McCrary, Supt.

★2225★ Lyndon B. Johnson National Historical Park and Preserve
PO Box 329
Johnson City, TX 78636
Phone: (512)868-7128
Contact: Melody Webb, Supt.

★2226★ Padre Island National Seashore
9405 S. Padre Island Dr.
Corpus Christi, TX 78418-5597
Phone: (512)937-2621
Contact: Charles Farabee, Supt.

★2227★ Rio Grande Wild and Scenic River
c/o Big Bend National Park
Big Bend National Park, TX 79834
Phone: (915)477-2251
Contact: Robert Arnberger, Supt.

Utah

★2228★ Arches National Park
c/o Canyonlands National Park
446 S. Main St.
Moab, UT 84532
Phone: (801)259-8161
Contact: Paul D. Guraedy, Supt.

★2229★ Bryce Canyon National Park
Bryce Canyon, UT 84717
Phone: (801)834-5322
Contact: Robert W. Reynolds, Supt.

★2230★ Canyonlands National Park
446 S. Main St.
Moab, UT 84532
Phone: (801)259-7165
Contact: Harvey D. Wickware, Supt.

★2231★ Capitol Reef National Park
Torrey, UT 84775
Phone: (801)425-3871
Contact: Martin C. Ott, Supt.

★2232★ Timpanogos Cave National Monument
R.R. 2
American Fork, UT 84003
Phone: (801)756-5238
Contact: Sue McGill, Supt.

★2233★ Zion National Park
Springdale, UT 84767
Phone: (801)772-3256
Contact: Larry Weise, Supt.
Contains Pipe Spring National Monument.

Virgin Islands

★2234★ Virgin Islands National Park
6010 Estate Nazareth #10
St. Thomas, VI 00802-3406
Phone: (809)775-6238
Contact: Marc A. Koenings, Supt.

Virginia

★2235★ Shenandoah National Park
Route 4, Box 292
Luray, VA 22835
Phone: (703)999-2243

Washington

★2236★ Coulee Dam National Recreation Area
PO Box 37
Coulee Dam, WA 99116

★2237★ Lake Chelan National Recreation Area
800 State St.
Sedro Woolley, WA 98284

★2238★ Mount Rainier National Park
Tahoma Woods, Star Rte.
Ashford, WA 98304
Phone: (206)569-2211
Contact: Neal G. Guse, Supt.

★2239★ North Cascades National Park
800 State St.
Sedro Woolley, WA 98284
Phone: (206)855-1331
Contact: John J. Earnst, Supt.

★2240★ Olympic National Park
600 E. Park Ave.
Port Angeles, WA 98362
Phone: (206)452-4501
Contact: Robert S. Chandler, Supt.

★2241★ Ross Lake National Recreation Area
800 State St.
Sedro Woolley, WA 98284

West Virginia

★2242★ Bluestone National Scenic River
c/o New River Gorge National River
PO Box 1189
Oak Hill, WV 25901
Phone: (304)465-0508

★2243★ Gauley River National Recreation Area
c/o New River Gorge National River
PO Box 1189
Oak Hill, WV 25901
Phone: (304)465-0508

★2244★ New River Gorge National River
PO Box 1189
Oak Hill, WV 25901
Phone: (304)465-0508

Wisconsin

★2245★ Apostle Islands National Lakeshore
Rte. 1, Box 4
Bayfield, WI 54814
Phone: (715)779-3397
Contact: Jerry Banta, Supt.

★2246★ Ice Age National Scientific Reserve
700 Ray-O-Vac Dr.
Suite 100
Madison, WI 53711
Phone: (608)264-5610
Contact: Tom Gilbert, Supt.

★2247★ Saint Croix National Scenic Riverway
PO Box 708
St. Croix Falls, WI 54024
Phone: (715)483-3284
Contact: Tony Andersen, Supt.

Wyoming

★2248★ Grand Teton National Park
John D. Rockefeller Memorial Parkway
P.O. Drawer 170
Moose, WY 83012
Phone: (307)733-2880
Contact: Jack Stark, Supt.

★2249★ Yellowstone National Park
Yellowstone National Park, WY 82190
Phone: (307)344-7381
Contact: Bob Barbee, Supt.
Covers portions of Idaho and Montana.

U.S. National Wildlife Refuges

Alabama

★2250★ Bon Secour National Wildlife Refuge
PO Box 1650
Gulf Shores, AL 36542
Phone: (205)968-8623
Contact: Jerome T. Carroll, Mgr

★2251★ Choctaw National Wildlife Refuge
Box 808
2704 Westside College Ave.
Jackson, AL 36545
Phone: (205)246-3583
Contact: Douglas J. Baumgartner

★2252★ Eufaula National Wildlife Refuge
Route 2
Box 97-B
Eufaula, AL 36027
Phone: (205)687-4065

★2253★ Wheeler National Wildlife Refuge
Route 4
Box 250
Decatur, AL 35603
Phone: (205)353-7243
Contact: Harry T. Stone, Mgr
Includes Blowing Wind Cave, Fern Cave and Watercress Darter.

Alaska

★2254★ Alaska Maritime National Wildlife Refuge
202 W. Pioneer Ave.
Homer, AK 99603
Phone: (907)235-6546
Contact: John L. Martin, Mgr
Includes Alaska Peninsula Unit, Bering Sea Unit, Chukchi Sea Unit, and Gulf of Alaska Unit.

★2255★ Alaska Peninsula National Wildlife Refuge
PO Box 277
King Salmon, AK 99613
Phone: (907)246-3339
Contact: Ronald Hood, Mgr
Includes Becharof.

★2256★ Arctic National Wildlife Refuge
Box 20
101-12th Ave.
Fairbanks, AK 99701
Phone: (907)456-0250
Alt. Phone: (FTS)870-0250
Contact: Glenn Elison, Mgr

★2257★ Innoko National Wildlife Refuge
Box 69
McGrath, AK 99627
Phone: (907)524-3251
Contact: Phillip J. Feiger, Mgr

★2258★ Izembek National Wildlife Refuge
Box 127
Cold Bay, AK 99571
Phone: (907)532-2445
Contact: Robin West, Mgr

★2259★ Kanuti National Wildlife Refuge
Box 11
101-12th Ave.
Fairbanks, AK 99701
Phone: (907)456-0329
Alt. Phone: (FTS)870-0329
Contact: Tom Early, Mgr

★2260★ Kenai National Wildlife Refuge
2139 Ski Hill Rd.
Soldotna, AK 99669-2139
Phone: (907)262-7021
Contact: Daniel Doshier, Mgr

★2261★ Kodiak National Wildlife Refuge
1390 Buskin River Rd.
Kodiak, AK 99615
Phone: (907)487-2600
Contact: Jay Bellinger, Mgr

★2262★ Koyukuk/Nowitna National Wildlife Refuge
PO Box 287
Galena, AK 99741
Phone: (907)656-1231
Contact: Dave Stearns, Mgr

★2263★ Selawik National Wildlife Refuge
PO Box 270
Kotzebue, AK 99752
Phone: (907)442-3799

★2264★ Tetlin National Wildlife Refuge
PO Box 155
Tok, AK 99780
Phone: (907)883-5312
Contact: Steve Bresser, Mgr

★2265★ Togiak National Wildlife Refuge
PO Box 270
Dillingham, AK 99576
Phone: (907)842-1063

★2266★ Yukon Delta National Wildlife Refuge
PO Box 346
Bethel, AK 99559
Phone: (907)543-3151
Contact: Ron Perry, Mgr

★2267★ Yukon Flats National Wildlife Refuge
Box 14
101-12th Ave.
Fairbanks, AK 99701
Phone: (907)456-0440
Alt. Phone: (FTS)870-0440
Contact: Ted Huer, Mgr

Arizona

★2268★ Bill Williams Unit
Havasu Natl. Wildlife Refuge
PO Box 830
Parker, AZ 85344
Phone: (602)667-4144
Contact: Jay Banta, Mgr

★2269★ Buenos Aires National Wildlife Refuge
PO Box 109
Sasabe, AZ 85633
Phone: (602)823-4251
Contact: Wayne A. Shifflett, Mgr

★2270★ Cabeza Prieta National Wildlife Refuge
1611 N. Second Ave.
Ajo, AZ 85321
Phone: (602)387-6483
Contact: Robert W. Schumacher, Mgr

★2271★ Imperial National Wildlife Refuge
PO Box 72217
Martinez Lake, AZ 85365
Phone: (602)783-3371
Contact: Arnold W. Nidecker, Mgr

★2272★ Kofa National Wildlife Refuge
PO Box 6290
356 W. 1st
Yuma, AZ 85366-6290
Phone: (602)783-7861
Contact: Milton Haderlie, Mgr

★2273★ San Bernardino National Wildlife Refuge
1800 Estrella Ave.
Douglas, AZ 85607
Phone: (602)364-2104

Contact: Kevin S. Cobble, Mgr

Arkansas

★2274★ Big Lake
Northeast Arkansas Refuges
PO Box 67
Manila, AR 72442
Phone: (501)564-2429

★2275★ Cache River
Northeast Arkansas Refuges
PO Box 279
Turrell, AR 72384
Phone: (501)343-2595
Contact: Paul Gideon, Mgr

★2276★ Felsenthal National Wildlife Refuge
PO Box 1157
Crossett, AR 71635
Phone: (501)364-3167
Contact: Robert J. Bridges, Mgr
Includes Overflow area.

★2277★ Holla Bend National Wildlife Refuge
Box 1043
115 S. Denver St.
Russellville, AR 72801
Phone: (501)968-2800
Contact: Martin D. Perry, Mgr
Includes Logan Caves.

★2278★ Northeast Arkansas Refuges
PO Box 279
Turrell, AR 72384
Phone: (501)343-2595
Contact: Dennis Widner, Mgr

★2279★ Wapanocca
Northeast Arkansas Refuges
PO Box 279
Turrell, AR 72384
Phone: (501)343-2595
Contact: Glenn Miller, Mgr

★2280★ White River
Northeast Arkansas Refuges
Box 308
321 W. 7th St.
DeWitt, AR 72042
Phone: (501)946-1468
Contact: Marvin T. Hurdle, Mgr

California

★2281★ Cibola National Wildlife Refuge
PO Box AP
Blythe, CA 92226
Phone: (602)857-3253
Contact: Wesley V. Martin, Mgr

★2282★ Havasu National Wildlife Refuge
PO Box 3009
Needles, CA 92363
Phone: (619)326-3853
Contact: James R. Good, Mgr

★2283★ Humboldt Bay
San Francisco Bay Natl. Wildlife Refuge
Route 1
Box 76
Loleta, CA 95551
Phone: (707)733-5406
Contact: Kevin Foerster, Mgr

★2284★ Kern National Wildlife Refuge
PO Box 670
Delano, CA 93216-0219
Phone: (805)725-2767
Alt. Phone: (805)725-5284
Contact: Thomas J. Charmley, Mgr
Includes Bitter Creek, Blue Ridge, Hopper Mountain, Pixley, and Seal Beach.

★2285★ Klamath Basin Refuges
Route 1
Box 74
Tulelake, CA 96134
Phone: (916)667-2231
Contact: Roger D. Johnson, Mgr
Includes Bear Valley (OR), Clear Lake (OR), Lower Klamath (OR & CA), Tule Lake, and Upper Klamath (OR).

★2286★ Modoc National Wildlife Refuge
PO Box 1610
Alturas, CA 96101
Phone: (916)233-3572
Contact: Edward C. Bloom, Mgr

★2287★ Sacramento National Wildlife Refuge
Route 1
Box 311
Willows, CA 95988
Phone: (916)934-2801
Contact: Gary W. Kramer, Mgr
Includes Butte Sink Wildlife Management Area, Colusa, Delevan, Sacramento River, Sutter, and Willow Creek-Lurline Wildlife Management Area.

★2288★ Salton Sea National Wildlife Refuge
PO Box 120
Calipatria, CA 92233
Phone: (619)348-5278
Alt. Phone: (619)348-5310
Contact: Kenneth Voget, Mgr
Includes Coachella Valley.

★2289★ San Francisco Bay National Wildlife Refuge
PO Box 524
Newark, CA 94560
Phone: (415)792-0222
Contact: Richard A. Coleman, Mgr
Also includes Antioch Dunes, Castle Rock, Ellicott Slough, Farallon, Salinas River, and San Pablo Bay areas.

★2290★ San Luis National Wildlife Refuge
PO Box 2176
Los Banos, CA 93635
Phone: (209)826-3508
Contact: Gary R. Zahm, Mgr
Includes Grasslands Wildlife Management Area, Kesterson, Merced, and San Joaquin River.

★2291★ Tijuana Slough
Salton Sea Natl. Wildlife Refuge
PO Box 335
Imperial Beach, CA 92032
Phone: (619)575-1290
Contact: Marc M. Weitzel, Mgr
Includes Sweetwater Marsh.

Colorado

★2292★ Alamosa/Monte Vista National Wildlife Refuge
9383 El Rancho Ln.
Alamosa, CO 81101
Phone: (719)589-4021
Contact: Steve Berlinger, Mgr

★2293★ Arapaho National Wildlife Refuge
PO Box 457
Walden, CO 80480
Phone: (303)723-8202
Contact: Eugene C. Patten, Mgr
Includes Bamforth (WY), Hutton Lake (WY), and Pathfinder (WY) areas.

★2294★ Browns Park National Wildlife Refuge
1318 Hwy. 318
Maybell, CO 81640
Phone: (303)365-3613
Contact: Jerre L. Gamble, Mgr

Connecticut

★2295★ Stewart B. McKinney National Wildlife Refuge
Ninigret Natl. Wildlife Refuge
PO Box 123
Westbrook, CT 06498
Phone: (203)579-5617
Contact: Paul Casey, Mgr

Delaware

★2296★ Bombay Hook National Wildlife Refuge
Route 1
Box 147
Smyrna, DE 19977
Phone: (302)653-9345
Alt. Phone: (FTS)487-6237
Contact: Paul D. Daly, Mgr

★2297★ Prime Hook National Wildlife Refuge
Bombay Hook Natl. Wildlife Refuge
Route 3
Box 195
Milton, DE 19968
Phone: (302)684-8419
Contact: George F. O'Shea, Mgr

Florida

★2298★ Arthur R. Marshall Loxahatchee National Wildlife Refuge
Route 1
Box 278
Boynton Beach, FL 33437-9741
Phone: (407)732-3684
Contact: Burkett S. Neely, Jr., Mgr
Includes Hobe Sound.

★2299★ Chassahowitzka National Wildlife Refuge
7798 S. Suncoast Blvd.
Homosassa, FL 32646
Phone: (904)382-2201
Contact: Cameron Shaw, Mgr
Includes Crystal River, Egmont Key, Passage Key, and Pinellas areas.

★2300★ Florida Panther National Wildlife Refuge
2629 S. Horseshoe Dr.
Naples, FL 33942
Phone: (813)643-2636
Contact: Todd Logan, Mgr

★2301★ J.N. "Ding" Darling National Wildlife Refuge
One Wildlife Dr.
Sanibel, FL 33957
Phone: (813)472-1100
Contact: Louis Hinds, Mgr
Includes Caloosahatchee, Island Bay, Matlacha Pass, and Pine Island.

★2302★ Lake Woodruff National Wildlife Refuge
PO Box 488
DeLeon Springs, FL 32130
Phone: (904)985-4673
Contact: Leon I. Rhodes, Mgr

★2303★ Lower Suwannee National Wildlife Refuge
Route 1
Box 1193C
Chiefland, FL 32626
Phone: (904)493-0238
Contact: Jim C. Johnson, Mgr
Includes Cedar Keys.

★2304★ Merritt Island National Wildlife Refuge
PO Box 6504
Titusville, FL 32780
Phone: (407)867-0667
Alt. Phone: (FTS)823-0667
Contact: Albert R. Hight, Mgr
Includes Pelican Island and St. Johns.

★2305★ National Key Deer Refuge
PO Box 510
Big Pine Key, FL 33043
Phone: (305)872-2239
Contact: Deborah G. Holle, Mgr
Includes Crocodile Lake, Great White Heron, and Key West.

★2306★ St. Marks National Wildlife Refuge
PO Box 68
St. Marks, FL 32355
Phone: (904)925-6121
Contact: Joe D. White, Mgr

★2307★ St. Vincent National Wildlife Refuge
PO Box 447
Apalachicola, FL 32320
Phone: (904)653-8808
Contact: Don Kosin, Mgr

Georgia

★2308★ Okefenokee National Wildlife Refuge
Rt. 2
Box 338
Folkston, GA 31537
Phone: (912)496-7366
Contact: Don R. Perkuchin, Mgr
Includes Banks Lake.

★2309★ Piedmont National Wildlife Refuge
Rt. 1
Box 670
Round Oak, GA 31038
Phone: (912)986-5441
Contact: Ronnie L. Shell, Mgr
Includes Bond Swamp.

★2310★ Savannah Coastal Refuges
PO Box 8487
Savannah, GA 31412
Phone: (912)944-4415
Alt. Phone: (FTS)248-4415
Contact: John P. Davis, Mgr
Includes Blackbeard Island, Harris Neck, Pinckney Island (SC), Savannah (SC,GA), Tybee, Wassaw, and Wolf Island.

Hawaii

★2311★ Hakalau Forest National Wildlife Refuge
Hawaiian and Pacific Islands Complex
154 Waianuenue Ave.
Federal Bldg.
Room 219
Hilo, HI 96720
Phone: (808)969-9909
Contact: Richard C. Wass, Mgr

★2312★ Hawaiian and Pacific Islands Complex
PO Box 50167
300 Ala Moana Blvd.
Honolulu, HI 96850
Phone: (808)541-1201
Contact: Jerry F. Leinecke, Mgr

★2313★ James C. Campbell National Wildlife Refuge
Hawaiian and Pacific Islands Complex
PO Box 50167
300 Ala Moana Blvd.
Honolulu, HI 96850
Phone: (808)541-1201
Contact: James Glynn, Mgr
Includes Kakahaia and Pearl Harbor.

★2314★ Kilauea Point National Wildlife Refuge
Hawaiian and Pacific Islands Complex
PO Box 87
Kilauea
Kauai, HI 96754
Phone: (808)828-1413
Contact: Richard Voss, Mgr
Includes Hanalei and Huleia areas.

★2315★ Remote Island Refuges
Hawaiian and Pacific Islands Complex
PO Box 50167
300 Ala Moana Blvd.
Honolulu, HI 96850
Phone: (808)541-1201
Contact: Stewart Fefer, Mgr
Includes Baker Island, Hawaiian Islands, Howland Island, Johnston Atoll, Midway Atoll, and Rose Atoll.

Idaho

★2316★ Bear Lake National Wildlife Refuge
Southeast Idaho Refuge Complex
370 Webster
Box 9
Montpelier, ID 83254
Phone: (208)847-1757
Contact: Richard Sjostrom, Mgr

★2317★ Camas National Wildlife Refuge
Southeast Idaho Refuge Complex
2150 E. 2350 N.
Hamer, ID 83245
Phone: (208)662-5423
Contact: Jack L. Richardson, Mgr

★2318★ Deer Flat National Wildlife Refuge
13751 Upper Embankment Rd.
Nampa, ID 83686
Phone: (208)467-9278
Contact: Kevin Ryan, Mgr

★2319★ Grays Lake National Wildlife Refuge
Southeast Idaho Refuge Complex
74 Grays Lake Rd.
Wayan, ID 83285
Phone: (208)574-2755
Contact: Mike Fisher, Mgr

★2320★ Kootenai National Wildlife Refuge
HCR 60
Box 283
Bonners Ferry, ID 83805
Phone: (208)267-3888
Contact: Larry D. Napier, Mgr

★2321★ Minidoka National Wildlife Refuge
Southeast Idaho Refuge Complex
Route 4
PO Box 290
Rupert, ID 83350
Phone: (208)436-3589
Contact: Martha Collins, Mgr

★2322★ Southeast Idaho Refuge Complex
1246 Yellowstone Ave., A-4
Pocatello, ID 83201-4372
Phone: (208)237-6615
Contact: Charles S. Peck, Jr., Mgr

Illinois

★2323★ Brussels District
Mark Twain Natl. Wildlife Refuge
Star Rte.
Box 107
Brussels, IL 62013
Phone: (618)883-2524
Contact: Patti A. Meyers, Mgr

★2324★ Chautauqua National Wildlife Refuge
Rural Rte. 2
Havana, IL 62644
Phone: (309)535-2290
Alt. Phone: (FTS)380-9290

Contact: Andrew French, Mgr
Includes Meredosia area.

★2325★ Crab Orchard National Wildlife Refuge
PO Box J
Carterville, IL 62918
Phone: (618)997-3344
Contact: Norrel F. Wallace, Mgr

★2326★ Cypress Creek National Wildlife Refuge
Route 1
Box 53D
Ullin, IL 62992
Phone: (618)634-2231
Contact: Gerald Updike, Mgr

★2327★ Mark Twain National Wildlife Refuge
311 N. 5th St.
Suite 110
Quincy, IL 62301
Phone: (217)224-8580
Contact: Robert Stratton Jr., Mgr

★2328★ Savanna District
Upper Mississippi River Natl. Wildlife and Fish Refuge
Post Office Bldg.
Savanna, IL 61074
Phone: (815)273-2732
Contact: Larry A. Wargowsky, Mgr

Indiana

★2329★ Muscatatuck National Wildlife Refuge
Route 7
Box 189A
Seymour, IN 47274
Phone: (812)522-4352
Contact: Leland E. Herzberger, Mgr

★2330★ Patoka National Wildlife Refuge
PO Box 510
Winslow, IN 47598-0359
Phone: (812)789-2102
Contact: William McCoy, Mgr

Iowa

★2331★ DeSoto National Wildlife Refuge
Rural Rte. 1
Box 114
Missouri Valley, IA 51555
Phone: (712)642-4121
Contact: George E. Gage, Mgr

★2332★ McGregor District
Upper Mississippi River Natl. Wildlife and Fish Refuge
PO Box 460
McGregor, IA 52157
Phone: (319)873-3423
Contact: John R. Lyons, Mgr

★2333★ Union Slough National Wildlife Refuge
Route 1
Box 52
Titonka, IA 50480
Phone: (515)928-2523
Contact: Immanuel Johnson, Mgr

★2334★ Walnut Creek National Wildlife Refuge
PO Box 399
Prairie City, IA 50228
Phone: (515)994-2415
Contact: Richard Birger, Mgr

★2335★ Wapello District
Mark Twain Natl. Wildlife Refuge
Rural Rte. 1
Wapello, IA 52653
Phone: (319)523-6982
Contact: Thomas Bell, Mgr

Kansas

★2336★ Flint Hills National Wildlife Refuge
PO Box 128
Hartford, KS 66854
Phone: (316)392-5553
Contact: David Wiseman, Mgr

★2337★ Kirwin National Wildlife Refuge
Route 1
Box 103
Kirwin, KS 67644
Phone: (913)543-6673

★2338★ Quivira National Wildlife Refuge
Rt. 3
Box 48A
Stafford, KS 67578
Phone: (316)486-2393
Contact: David Hilley, Mgr

Louisiana

★2339★ Bogue Chitto National Wildlife Refuge
1010 Gause Blvd. Bldg., 936
Slidell, LA 70458
Phone: (504)646-7555
Alt. Phone: (FTS)680-7555
Contact: Howard E. Poitevint, Mgr
Includes Bayou Sauvage, Breton, and Delta areas.

★2340★ Cameron Prairie National Wildlife Refuge
Route 1
Box 643
Bell City, LA 70630
Phone: (318)598-2216
Contact: Paul Yakupzack, Mgr

★2341★ Catahoula National Wildlife Refuge
P.O. Drawer Z
Rhinehart, LA 71363-0201
Phone: (318)992-5261
Contact: Eric Sipco, Mgr

★2342★ D'Arbonne National Wildlife Refuge
PO Box 3065
Monroe, LA 71201
Phone: (318)325-1735
Alt. Phone: (FTS)493-6504
Contact: Lee R. Fulton, Mgr
Includes Upper Ouachita area.

★2343★ Lacassine National Wildlife Refuge
HCR 63
Box 186
Lake Arthur, LA 70549
Phone: (318)774-5923
Contact: Carrell Ryan, Mgr
Includes Atchafalaya, and Shells Keys.

★2344★ Lake Ophelia National Wildlife Refuge
PO Box 256
Marksville, LA 71351
Phone: (318)253-4238
Contact: Kenneth L. Merritt, Mgr
Includes Grand Cote area.

★2345★ Louisiana Wetland Management District
PO Box 1601
Monroe, LA 71210
Phone: (318)325-1735
Contact: Kelby Ouchley, Mgr

★2346★ Sabine National Wildlife Refuge
Hwy. 27
S. 3000 Main St.
Hackberry, LA 70645
Phone: (318)762-3816

★2347★ Tensas River National Wildlife Refuge
Route 2
Box 295
Tallulah, LA 71282
Phone: (318)574-2664
Contact: George Chandler, Mgr

Maine

★2348★ Moosehorn National Wildlife Refuge
PO Box 1077
Calais, ME 04619
Phone: (207)454-3521
Contact: Douglas M. Mullen, Mgr
Includes Cross Island, Franklin Island, and Seal Island.

★2349★ Petit Manan National Wildlife Refuge
Moosehorn Natl. Wildlife Refuge
PO Box 279
Milbridge, ME 04658
Phone: (207)546-2124

★2350★ Rachel Carson National Wildlife Refuge
Parker River Natl. Wildlife Refuge
Route 2
Box 751
Wells, ME 04090
Phone: (207)646-9226
Contact: Richard Steinbach, Mgr

★2351★ Sunkhaze Meadows National Wildlife Refuge
U. S. D.A. Bldg.
Room 221
Orono, ME 04469
Phone: (207)581-3670
Contact: Mark Sweeny, Mgr

Maryland

★2352★ Blackwater National Wildlife Refuge
2145 Key Wallace Dr.
Cambridge, MD 21613
Phone: (301)228-2692
Contact: Glenn A. Carowan Jr., Mgr
Includes Martin, and Susquehanna areas.

★2353★ Eastern Neck National Wildlife Refuge
Route 2
Box 225
Rock Hall, MD 21661
Phone: (301)639-7056
Contact: Thomas Goettel, Mgr

★2354★ Patuxent National Wildlife Refuge
Route 197
Laurel, MD 20708
Phone: (301)498-0300
Contact: Harold J. O'Connor, Mgr

Massachusetts

★2355★ Great Meadows National Wildlife Refuge
Weir Hill Rd.
Sudbury, MA 01776
Phone: (508)443-4661
Contact: Edward S. Moses, Mgr
Includes John Hay (NH), Massasoit, Monomoy, Nantucket, Oxbow, and Wapack (NH) areas.

★2356★ Parker River National Wildlife Refuge
Northern Blvd.
Plum Island
Newburyport, MA 01950
Phone: (508)465-5753
Contact: John L. Fillio, Mgr
Includes Pond Island (ME), and Thacher Island.

Michigan

★2357★ Seney National Wildlife Refuge
Seney, MI 49883
Phone: (906)586-9851
Contact: Michael Tansy, Mgr
Includes Harbor Island, and Huron.

★2358★ Shiawassee National Wildlife Refuge
6975 Mower Rd.
Rural Rte. 1
Saginaw, MI 48601
Phone: (517)777-5930
Alt. Phone: (FTS)378-4644
Includes Michigan Islands, and Wyandotte.

Minnesota

★2359★ Agassiz National Wildlife Refuge
Middle River, MN 56737
Phone: (218)449-4115
Alt. Phone: (FTS)751-4115
Contact: Joseph Kotok, Mgr

★2360★ Big Stone National Wildlife Refuge
25 NW 2nd St.
Ortonville, MN 56278
Phone: (612)839-3700
Contact: James Heinecke, Mgr

★2361★ Detroit Lakes Wetland Management District
Minnesota Waterfowl and Wetlands Management Complex
Route 3
Box 47D
Detroit Lakes, MN 56501
Phone: (218)847-4431
Contact: Howard J. Lipke, Mgr

★2362★ Fergus Falls Wetland Management District
Minnesota Waterfowl and Wetlands Management Complex
Route 1
Box 76
Fergus Falls, MN 56537
Phone: (218)739-2291
Alt. Phone: (FTS)783-5647
Contact: Kevin Brennan, Mgr

★2363★ Hamden Slough
Minnesota Waterfowl and Wetlands Management Complex
Route 3
Box 47D
Detroit Lakes, MN 56501
Phone: (218)847-4431
Contact: Mike Murphy, Mgr

★2364★ Litchfield Wetland Management District
Minnesota Waterfowl and Wetlands Management Complex
971 E. Frontage Rd.
Litchfield, MN 55355
Phone: (612)693-2849
Contact: Sammy J. Waldstein, Mgr

★2365★ Minnesota Valley National Wildlife Refuge
3815 E. 80th St.
Bloomington, MN 55425-1600
Phone: (612)854-5900
Alt. Phone: (FTS)725-3145
Contact: Thomas Larson, Mgr

★2366★ Minnesota Waterfowl and Wetlands Management Complex
Route 1
Box 76
Fergus Falls, MN 56537
Phone: (218)739-2291
Alt. Phone: (FTS)783-5647
Contact: Rollin Siegfried, Mgr

★2367★ Morris Wetland Management District
Minnesota Waterfowl and Wetlands Management Complex
Route 1
Box 877
Morris, MN 56267
Phone: (612)589-1001
Contact: Alfred Radtke, Mgr

★2368★ Rice Lake National Wildlife Refuge
Route 2
Box 67
McGregor, MN 55760
Phone: (218)768-2402
Alt. Phone: (FTS)380-9402
Contact: John Lindell, Mgr
Includes Mille Lacs, and Sandstone areas.

★2369★ Sherburne National Wildlife Refuge
Route 2
Zimmerman, MN 55398
Phone: (612)389-3323
Contact: Jay Hammernick, Mgr

★2370★ Tamarac National Wildlife Refuge
Rural Rte.
Rochert, MN 56578
Phone: (218)847-2641

★2371★ Upper Mississippi River Complex
51 E. 4th St.
Room 101
Winona, MN 55987
Phone: (507)452-4232
Contact: Richard Berry, Mgr

★2372★ Upper Mississippi River National Wildlife and Fish Refuge
51 E. 4th St., Rm. 101
Winona, MN 55987
Phone: (507)452-4232
Contact: James Lennartson, Mgr
Includes Iowa, Illinois, Minnesota and Wisconsin.

★2373★ Windom Wetland Management District
Minnesota Waterfowl and Wetlands Management Complex
Route 1
Box 273A
Windom, MN 56101
Phone: (507)831-2220
Contact: Steven Kallin, Mgr

★2374★ Winona District
Upper Mississippi River Natl. Wildlife and Fish Refuge
51 E. 4th St., Rm. 101
Winona, MN 55987
Phone: (507)454-7351
Contact: Robert L. Drieslein, Mgr

Mississippi

★2375★ Mississippi Sandhill Crane National Wildlife Refuge
7200 Crane Ln.
Gautier, MS 39553
Phone: (601)497-6322
Contact: Joe Hardy, Mgr
Includes Grand Bay.

★2376★ Mississippi Wetland Management District
PO Box 1070
Grenada, MS 38901
Phone: (601)226-8286
Contact: Steve Gard, Mgr
Includes Dahomey, and Tallahatchie areas.

★2377★ Noxubee National Wildlife Refuge
Route 1
Box 142
Brooksville, MS 39739
Phone: (601)323-5548
Contact: Jimmie L. Tisdale, Mgr

★2378★ St. Catherine Creek National Wildlife Refuge
PO Box 18639
Natchez, MS 39122
Phone: (601)442-6696
Contact: Tom Prusa, Mgr

★2379★ Yazoo National Wildlife Refuge
Route 1
Box 286
Hollandale, MS 38748
Phone: (601)839-2638
Contact: Tom Wilkins, Mgr
Includes Hillside, Mathews Brake, Morgan Brake, and Panther Swamp.

Missouri

★2380★ Annada District
Mark Twain Natl. Wildlife Refuge
PO Box 88
Annada, MO 63330
Phone: (314)847-2333
Alt. Phone: (FTS)751-0333
Contact: Ross Adams, Mgr
Includes Clarence Cannon area.

★2381★ Mingo National Wildlife Refuge
RR 1
Box 103
Puxico, MO 63960
Phone: (314)222-3589
Contact: Gerald L. Clawson, Mgr
Includes Pilot Knob.

★2382★ Squaw Creek National Wildlife Refuge
PO Box 101
Mound City, MO 64470
Phone: (816)442-3187
Contact: Ronald Bell, Mgr

★2383★ Swan Lake National Wildlife Refuge
RR 1
Box 29A
Sumner, MO 64681
Phone: (816)856-3323
Alt. Phone: (FTS)751-0187
Contact: John Guthrie, Mgr

Montana

★2384★ Benton Lake National Wildlife Refuge
PO Box 450
Black Eagle, MT 59414
Phone: (406)727-7400
Contact: Don Hultman, Mgr

★2385★ Bowdoin National Wildlife Refuge
PO Box J
Malta, MT 59538
Phone: (406)654-2863
Contact: Gene Sipe, Mgr
Includes Black Coulee, Creedman Coulee, Hewitt Lake, and Lake Thibadeau.

★2386★ Charles M. Russell National Wildlife Refuge
PO Box 110
Lewistown, MT 59457
Phone: (406)538-8706
Contact: John Foster, Mgr
Includes Hailstone, Halfbreed Lake, Lake Mason, UL Bend, and War Horse areas.

★2387★ Fort Peck Wildlife Station
Charles M. Russell Natl. Wildlife Refuge
PO Box 166
Fort Peck, MT 59223
Phone: (406)526-3464
Contact: James Alfonso, Mgr

★2388★ Jordan Wildlife Station
Charles M. Russell Natl. Wildlife Refuge
PO Box 63
Jordan, MT 59337
Phone: (406)557-6145
Contact: Bradley Knudsen, Mgr

★2389★ Lee Metcalf National Wildlife Refuge
PO Box 257
Stevensville, MT 59870
Phone: (406)777-5552
Contact: Margaret Anderson, Mgr

★2390★ Medicine Lake National Wildlife Refuge
HC 51
Box 2
Medicine Lake, MT 59247
Phone: (406)789-2305
Contact: James McCollum, Mgr
Includes Lamesteer area.

★2391★ National Bison Range
Moiese, MT 59824
Phone: (406)644-2211
Contact: Jon M. Malcolm, Mgr
Includes Nine-Pipe, and Pablo areas.

★2392★ Northwest Montana Wetland Management District
National Bison Range Natl. Wildlife Refuge
780 Creston Hatchery Rd.
Kalispell, MT 59901
Phone: (406)755-7870
Alt. Phone: (406)755-9311
Contact: Raymond L. Washtak, Mgr
Includes Swan River.

★2393★ Red Rock Lakes National Wildlife Refuge
Monida Star Rte.
Box 15
Lima, MT 59739
Phone: (406)276-3347
Contact: Daniel Gomez, Mgr

★2394★ Sand Creek Wildlife Station
Charles M. Russell Natl. Wildlife Refuge
PO Box 89
Roy, MT 59471
Phone: (406)464-5181
Contact: Gene Williams, Mgr

Nebraska

★2395★ Crescent Lake National Wildlife Refuge
HC 68
Box 21
Ellsworth, NE 69340
Phone: (308)762-4893
Contact: Royce Huber, Mgr

★2396★ Fort Niobrar/Valentine National Wildlife Refuge
Hidden Timber Rte.
HC 14
Box 67
Valentine, NE 69201
Phone: (402)376-3789
Contact: Robert M. Ellis, Mgr

★2397★ North Platte National Wildlife Refuge
Crescent Lake Natl. Wildlife Refuge
Box 125D
Minatare, NE 69356
Phone: (308)783-2477
Contact: Bradley McKinney, Mgr

★2398★ Rainwater Basin Wetland Management District
PO Box 1686
Kearney, NE 68847
Phone: (308)236-5015
Contact: Jon Kauffeld, Mgr

★2399★ Valentine National Wildlife Refuge
Fort Niobrar/Valentine Natl. Wildlife Refuge
Hidden Timber Route, HC 14
Box 67
Valentine, NE 69201
Phone: (402)376-3789
Contact: Leonard L. McDaniel, Mgr

Nevada

★2400★ Ash Meadows National Wildlife Refuge
Desert Refuge Complex
PO Box 2660
Pahrump, NV 89041
Phone: (702)372-5435
Contact: Larry Martin, Mgr

★2401★ Desert National Wildlife Range
Desert Refuge Complex
1500 N. Decatur Blvd.
Las Vegas, NV 89108
Phone: (702)646-3401
Contact: Bruce Zeller, Mgr

★2402★ Desert Refuge Complex
1500 N. Decatur Blvd.
Las Vegas, NV 89108
Phone: (702)646-3401
Alt. Phone: (FTS)598-6510
Contact: David J. Brown, Mgr
Includes Amargosa Pupfish Station, and Moapa Valley.

★2403★ Pahranagat National Wildlife Refuge
Desert Refuge Complex
Box 510
Alamo, NV 89001
Phone: (702)725-3417
Contact: Michael L. Goddard, Mgr

★2404★ Ruby Lake National Wildlife Refuge
Ruby Valley, NV 89833
Phone: (702)779-2237
Contact: Daniel L. Pennington, Mgr

★2405★ Stillwater National Wildlife Refuge
PO Box 1236
Fallon, NV 89406-1236
Phone: (702)423-5128
Contact: Ronald M. Anglin, Mgr
Includes Anaho Island, and Fallon.

New Jersey

★2406★ Barnegat Division
Edwin B. Forsythe Natl. Wildlife Refuge
70 Collinstown Rd.
PO Box 544
Barnegat, NJ 08005
Phone: (609)698-1387

★2407★ Cape May National Wildlife Refuge
Great Creek Rd.
Box 72
Oceanville, NJ 08231
Phone: (609)652-1665
Contact: Steven Atzert, Mgr

★2408★ Edwin B. Forsythe National Wildlife Refuge
Great Creek Rd.
Box 72
Oceanville, NJ 08231
Phone: (609)652-1665
Contact: David L. Beall, Mgr
Includes Brigantine Division.

★2409★ Great Swamp National Wildlife Refuge
Pleasant Plains Rd.
RD 1
Box 152
Basking Ridge, NJ 07920
Phone: (201)647-1222
Contact: William Koch, Mgr

★2410★ Supawna Meadows National Wildlife Refuge
Tinicum Natl. Environmental Center
RD. #3
Box 540
Salem, NJ 08079
Phone: (609)935-1487
Contact: Richard Guadagno, Mgr

New Mexico

★2411★ Bitter Lake National Wildlife Refuge
PO Box 7
Roswell, NM 88202-0007
Phone: (505)622-6755
Contact: LeMoyne B. Marlatt, Mgr

★2412★ Bosque del Apache National Wildlife Refuge
PO Box 1246
Socorro, NM 87801
Phone: (505)835-1828
Contact: Philip Norton, Mgr

★2413★ Las Vegas National Wildlife Refuge
Route 1
Box 399
Las Vegas, NM 87701
Phone: (505)425-3581
Contact: Joe B. Rodriguez, Mgr

★2414★ Maxwell National Wildlife Refuge
PO Box 276
Maxwell, NM 87728
Phone: (505)375-2331
Contact: Jerry D. French, Mgr

★2415★ San Andres National Wildlife Refuge
PO Box 756
Las Cruces, NM 88004
Phone: (505)382-5047

★2416★ Sevilleta National Wildlife Refuge
Bosque del Apache Natl. Wildlife Refuge
General Delivery
San Acacia, NM 87831
Phone: (505)864-4021
Contact: Theodore M. Stans, Mgr

New York

★2417★ Iroquois National Wildlife Refuge
PO Box 517
Casey Rd.
Alabama, NY 14003
Phone: (716)948-9154
Contact: Don V. Tiller, Mgr

★2418★ Montezuma National Wildlife Refuge
3395 Rte. 5/20 E.
Seneca Falls, NY 13148
Phone: (315)568-5987
Contact: Grady E. Hocutt, Mgr

★2419★ Seatuck National Wildlife Refuge
Wertheim Natl. Wildlife Refuge
PO Box 21
Shirley, NY 11967
Phone: (516)581-1538
Contact: Charles Stenvall, Mgr

★2420★ Target Rock National Wildlife Refuge
Wertheim Natl. Wildlife Refuge
PO Box 21
Shirley, NY 11967
Phone: (516)271-2409
Contact: Bill Kollinicki, Mgr

★2421★ Wertheim National Wildlife Refuge
PO Box 21
Shirley, NY 11967
Phone: (516)286-0485
Contact: Tom Stewart, Mgr
Includes Amagansett, Conscience Point, Elizabeth A. Morton, Lido Beach Wildlife Management Area, and Oyster Bay.

North Carolina

★2422★ Alligator River National Wildlife Refuge
PO Box 1969
Manteo, NC 27954
Phone: (919)473-1131
Includes Currituck, and Pea Island National Wildlife Refuge, (919) 987-2394.

★2423★ Mackay Island National Wildlife Refuge
PO Box 31
Knotts Island, NC 27950
Phone: (919)429-3100

★2424★ Mattamuskeet National Wildlife Refuge
Route 1
Box N-2
Swanquarter, NC 27885
Phone: (919)926-4021
Contact: Don Temple, Mgr
Includes Cedar Island, Pungo, and Swanquarter areas.

★2425★ Pee Dee National Wildlife Refuge
Box 92
Wadesboro, NC 28170
Phone: (704)694-4424
Contact: Mike Bryant, Mgr

★2426★ Pocosin Lakes National Wildlife Refuge
Route 1
Box 195-B
Creswell, NC 27928
Contact: Elton (Jim) Savery, Mgr

★2427★ Roanoke River National Wildlife Refuge
102 Dundee St.
Box 430
Windsor, NC 27983
Phone: (919)794-5326
Contact: Jerry Holloman, Mgr

North Dakota

★2428★ Arrowwood
Arrowwood Complex
Rural Rte. 1
Pingree, ND 58476
Phone: (701)285-3341
Contact: Paul Van Ningen, Mgr

★2429★ Arrowwood Complex
Rural Rte. 1
Pingree, ND 58476
Phone: (701)285-3341
Contact: Darold Walls, Mgr

★2430★ Arrowwood Wetland Management District
Arrowwood Complex
Rural Rte. 1
Pingree, ND 58476
Phone: (701)285-3341
Contact: Robert Johnson, Mgr

★2431★ Audubon Complex
Rural Rte. 1
Coleharbor, ND 58531
Phone: (701)442-5474
Contact: David G. Potter, Mgr

★2432★ Chase Lake Prairie Project
Arrowwood Complex
Rural Rte. 1
Box 144
Woodworth, ND 58496
Phone: (701)752-4218
Contact: Greg Seikaniec, Mgr

★2433★ Crosby Wetland Management District
Des Lacs Complex
PO Box 148
Crosby, ND 58730
Phone: (701)965-6488
Contact: Tim K. Kessler, Mgr

★2434★ Des Lacs Complex
PO Box 578
Kenmare, ND 58746
Phone: (701)385-4046
Contact: Delano Pierce, Mgr
Includes Lake Zahl.

★2435★ Des Lacs National Wildlife Refuge
Des Lacs Complex
PO Box 578
Kenmare, ND 58746
Phone: (701)385-4046
Contact: Peter Finley, Mgr

★2436★ Devils Lake Wetland Management District
PO Box 908
Devils Lake, ND 58301
Phone: (701)662-8611
Contact: Roger Hollevoet, Mgr
Includes Lake Alice.

★2437★ J. Clark Salyer Complex
Box 66
Upham, ND 58789
Phone: (701)768-2548
Contact: Robert Howard, Mgr

★2438★ Kulm Wetland Management District
PO Box E
Kulm, ND 58456
Phone: (701)647-2866
Contact: Robert VandenBerge, Mgr

★2439★ Lake Ilo National Wildlife Refuge
Audubon Complex
Dunn Center, ND 58626
Phone: (701)548-4407
Contact: Donald Bozovsky, Mgr

★2440★ Long Lake National Wildlife Refuge
Rural Rte. 1
Box 23
Moffit, ND 58560
Phone: (701)387-4397
Contact: Steve Knode, Mgr

★2441★ Lostwood National Wildlife Refuge
Des Lacs Complex
Rural Rte. 2
Box 98
Kenmare, ND 58746
Phone: (701)848-2722

★2442★ Lostwood Wetland Management District
Des Lacs Complex
Rural Rte. 2
Box 98
Kenmare, ND 58746
Phone: (701)848-2466
Contact: David Gillund, Mgr

★2443★ Sullys Hill National Game Preserve
Devils Lake Wetland Management District
PO Box 908
Devils Lake, ND 58301
Phone: (701)662-8611
Contact: Steven Kresl, Mgr

★2444★ Tewaukon Complex
Rural Rte. 1
Cayuga, ND 58013
Phone: (701)724-3598
Contact: Fred G. Giese, Mgr

★2445★ Upper Souris National Wildlife Refuge
Rural Rte. 1
Foxholm, ND 58738
Phone: (701)468-5467
Contact: Dean Knauer, Mgr

★2446★ Valley City Wetland Management District
Long Lake Natl. Wildlife Refuge
11515 River Rd.
Valley City, ND 58072-9619
Phone: (701)845-3466
Contact: Paulette Scherr, Mgr

Ohio

★2447★ Ottawa National Wildlife Refuge
14000 W. State Rte. 2
Oak Harbor, OH 43449
Phone: (419)898-0014
Contact: Charles Blair, Mgr
Includes Cedar Point, and West Sister Island.

Oklahoma

★2448★ Little River National Wildlife Refuge
PO Box 340
Broken Bow, OK 74728
Phone: (405)584-6211
Contact: Berlin A. Heck, Mgr
Includes Little Sandy area.

★2449★ Salt Plains National Wildlife Refuge
Route 1
Box 76
Jet, OK 73749
Phone: (405)626-4794
Contact: Rodney F. Krey, Mgr

★2450★ Sequoyah National Wildlife Refuge
Route 1
Box 18A
Vian, OK 74962
Phone: (918)773-5251
Contact: Ronald S. Sullivan, Mgr
Includes Oklahoma Bat Caves.

★2451★ Tishomingo National Wildlife Refuge
Route 1
Box 151
Tishomingo, OK 73460
Phone: (405)371-2402
Contact: David A. Stanbrough, Mgr

★2452★ Washita National Wildlife Refuge
Route 1
Box 68
Butler, OK 73625
Phone: (405)664-2205
Contact: Jon Brock, Mgr
Includes Optima area.

★2453★ Wichita Mountains National Wildlife Refuge
Route 1
Box 448
Indiahoma, OK 73552
Phone: (405)429-3221
Contact: James S. Smith, Mgr

Oregon

★2454★ Ankeny National Wildlife Refuge
Western Oregon Refuge Complex
2301 Wintel Rd.
Jefferson, OR 97352
Phone: (503)327-2444

★2455★ Baskett Slough
Western Oregon Refuge Complex
10995 Hwy. 22
Dallas, OR 97338
Phone: (503)623-2749
Contact: Ralph L. Lettenmaier, Mgr

★2456★ Hart Mountain
Sheldon/Hart Mountain Complex
PO Box 111
Room 308
U. S. Post Office Bldg.
Lakeview, OR 97630
Phone: (503)947-3315
Contact: Elizabeth Couch, Mgr

★2457★ Klamath Forest
Klamath Basin Refuges
HC 63
Box 303
Chiloquin, OR 97624
Contact: Ron Cole, Mgr

★2458★ Malheur National Wildlife Refuge
HC 72
Box 245
Princeton, OR 97721
Phone: (503)493-2612
Contact: Forrest Cameron, Mgr

★2459★ Sheldon
Sheldon/Hart Mountain Complex
PO Box 111
Room 308
U. S. Post Office Bldg.
Lakeview, OR 97630
Phone: (503)947-3315
Contact: Hugh Null, Mgr

★2460★ Sheldon/Hart Mountain Complex
PO Box 111
Room 308
U. S. Post Office Bldg.
Lakeview, OR 97630
Phone: (503)947-3315
Contact: Barry Reiswig, Mgr

★2461★ Umatilla National Wildlife Refuge
PO Box 239
Umatilla, OR 97882
Phone: (503)922-3232
Contact: Morris C. LeFever, Mgr
Includes Cold Springs, and McKay Creek.

★2462★ Western Oregon Refuge Complex
26208 Finley Refuge Rd.
Corvallis, OR 97333
Phone: (503)757-7236
Contact: Palmer Sekora, Mgr

★2463★ William L. Finley National Wildlife Refuge
Western Oregon Refuge Complex
26208 Finley Refuge Rd.
Corvallis, OR 97333
Phone: (503)757-7236
Includes Bandon Marsh, Cape Meares, Oregon Islands, and Three Arch Rocks.

Pennsylvania

★2464★ Erie National Wildlife Refuge
RD 1
Wood Duck Ln.
Guys Mills, PA 16327
Phone: (814)789-3585
Contact: Thomas Mountain, Mgr

★2465★ Tinicum National Environmental Center
Suite 104
Scott Plaza 2
Philadelphia, PA 19113
Phone: (215)521-0662
Contact: Richard F. Nugent, Mgr
Includes Killcohook (NJ) area.

Puerto Rico

★2466★ Caribbean Islands Refuges
Box 510
Boqueron, PR 00622
Phone: (809)851-7258
Contact: James Oland, Mgr
Includes Buck Island (Virgin Islands), Cabo Rojo, Culebra, Desecheo, Green Cay (Virgin Islands), Laguna Cartagena, and Sandy Point (Virgin Islands).

Rhode Island

★2467★ Ninigret National Wildlife Refuge
Shoreline Plaza
Route 1A
PO Box 307
Charlestown, RI 02813
Phone: (401)364-9124
Contact: Jim Kurth, Mgr
Includes Block Island, Pettaquamscutt Cove, Sachuest Point, Salt Meadow (CT), and Trustom Pond.

South Carolina

★2468★ Ace Basin National Wildlife Refuge
PO Box 1785
Mt. Pleasant, SC 29465
Phone: (803)762-1200
Contact: James (Donny) Browning, Mgr

★2469★ Cape Romain National Wildlife Refuge
390 Bulls Island Rd.
Awendaw, SC 29429
Phone: (803)928-3368
Contact: George R. Garris, Mgr

★2470★ Carolina Sandhills National Wildlife Refuge
Route 2
Box 330
McBee, SC 29101
Phone: (803)335-8401
Contact: Ronald C. Snider, Mgr

★2471★ Santee National Wildlife Refuge
Route 2
Box 66
Summerton, SC 29148
Phone: (803)478-2217
Contact: Glenn W. Bond Jr., Mgr

South Dakota

★2472★ Lacreek National Wildlife Refuge
HWC 3
Box 14
Martin, SD 57551
Phone: (605)685-6508
Contact: Rolf H. Kraft, Mgr

★2473★ Lake Andes National Wildlife Refuge
RR #1
Box 77
Lake Andes, SD 57356
Phone: (605)487-7603
Contact: William Wilson, Mgr
Includes Karl E. Mundt area.

★2474★ Madison Wetland Management District
PO Box 48
Madison, SD 57042
Phone: (605)256-2974
Contact: David L. Gilbert, Mgr

★2475★ Sand Lake National Wildlife Refuge
Rural Rte. 1
Box 25
Columba, SD 57433
Phone: (605)885-6320
Contact: John Koerner, Mgr
Includes Pocasse area.

★2476★ Waubay National Wildlife Refuge
Rural Rte. 1
Box 79
Waubay, SD 57273
Phone: (605)947-4521
Contact: Richard Gilbert, Mgr

Tennessee

★2477★ Cross Creeks National Wildlife Refuge
Route 1
Box 556
Dover, TN 37058
Phone: (615)232-7477
Contact: Vicki C. Grafe, Mgr

★2478★ Hatchie National Wildlife Refuge
PO Box 187
Brownsville, TN 38012
Phone: (901)772-0501
Contact: Marvin L. Nichols, Mgr
Includes Chickasaw, Lower Hatchie, and Sunk Lake.

★2479★ Reelfoot National Wildlife Refuge
Route 2
Hwy. 157
Union City, TN 38261
Phone: (901)538-2481
Contact: Randy Cook, Mgr
Includes Lake Isom.

★2480★ Tennessee National Wildlife Refuge
PO Box 849
Paris, TN 38242
Phone: (901)642-2091
Contact: John Taylor, Mgr

Texas

★2481★ Anahuac National Wildlife Refuge
PO Box 278
Anahuac, TX 77514
Phone: (409)267-3337
Alt. Phone: (FTS)527-2680
Contact: Domenick Ciccone, Mgr
Includes Moody area.

★2482★ Aransas National Wildlife Refuge
PO Box 100
Austwell, TX 77950
Phone: (512)286-3559
Contact: J. Brent Giezentanner, Mgr
Includes Matagorda area.

★2483★ Attwater Prairie Chicken National Wildlife Refuge
PO Box 519
Eagle Lake, TX 77434
Phone: (409)234-5940
Contact: Stephen Labuda Jr., Mgr

★2484★ Brazoria National Wildlife Refuge
PO Box 1088
Angleton, TX 77516-1088
Phone: (409)849-6062
Contact: Ronald G. Bisbee, Mgr
Includes Big Boggy area.

★2485★ Buffalo Lake National Wildlife Refuge
PO Box 228
Umbarger, TX 79091
Phone: (806)499-3382
Contact: Johnny H. Beall, Mgr
Includes Grulla (NM) area.

★2486★ Hagerman National Wildlife Refuge
Route 3
Box 123
Sherman, TX 75090-9564
Phone: (214)786-2826
Contact: James M. Williams, Mgr

★2487★ Laguna Atascosa National Wildlife Refuge
PO Box 450
Rio Hondo, TX 78583
Phone: (512)748-3607
Contact: Steven P. Thompson, Mgr

★2488★ Lower Rio Grande Valley
Lower Rio Grande Valley/Santa Ana Complex
Route 2
Box 202A
Alamo, TX 78516
Phone: (512)787-3079
Contact: Jonathan M. Andrew, Mgr

★2489★ Lower Rio Grande Valley/Santa Ana Complex
320 N. Main
Rm. A-103
McAllen, TX 78501
Phone: (512)630-4636
Contact: Larry R. Ditto, Mgr

★2490★ McFaddin/Texas Point National Wildlife Refuge
Anahuac Natl. Wildlife Refuge
PO Box 609
Sabine Pass, TX 77655
Phone: (409)971-2909
Contact: James Krakowski, Mgr

★2491★ Muleshoe National Wildlife Refuge
Buffalo Lake Natl. Wildlife Refuge
PO Box 549
Muleshoe, TX 79347
Phone: (806)946-3341
Contact: Donald Clapp, Mgr

★2492★ San Bernard National Wildlife Refuge
Brazoria Natl. Wildlife Refuge
PO Box 1088
Angleton, TX 77516-1088
Phone: (409)964-3639
Contact: Jack Crabtree, Mgr

★2493★ Santa Ana
Lower Rio Grande/Santa Ana Complex
Route 2
Box 202A
Alamo, TX 78516
Phone: (512)787-3079
Contact: Dennis E. Prichard, Mgr

Utah

★2494★ Bear R. Migratory Bird Refuge
866 S. Main
Brigham City, UT 84302
Phone: (801)723-5887
Contact: Alan K. Trout, Mgr

★2495★ Fish Springs National Wildlife Refuge
PO Box 568
Dugway, UT 84022
Phone: (801)831-5353

★2496★ Ouray National Wildlife Refuge
1680 W. Hwy. 40
Room 1220
Vernal, UT 84078
Phone: (801)789-0351
Contact: Gary Montoya, Mgr

Vermont

★2497★ Missisquoi National Wildlife Refuge
PO Box 163
Swanton, VT 05488
Phone: (802)868-4781
Contact: Robert A. Zelley, Mgr

Virginia

★2498★ Back Bay National Wildlife Refuge
4005 Sandpiper Rd.
PO Box 6286
Virginia Beach, VA 23456
Phone: (804)721-2412
Alt. Phone: (FTS)827-6635
Contact: Anthony Leger, Mgr
Includes Plum Tree Island.

★2499★ Chincoteague National Wildlife Refuge
Box 62
Chincoteague, VA 23336
Phone: (804)336-6122
Contact: John D. Schroer, Mgr
Includes Wallops Island.

★2500★ Eastern Shore of Virginia National Wildlife Refuge
RFD 1
Box 122B
Cape Charles, VA 23310
Phone: (804)331-2760
Contact: Sherman W. Stairs, Mgr
Includes Fisherman Island.

★2501★ Great Dismal Swamp National Wildlife Refuge
3100 Desert Rd.
PO Box 349
Suffolk, VA 23434
Phone: (804)986-3705
Contact: Lloyd Culp, Mgr
Includes Nansemond area.

★2502★ Mason Neck National Wildlife Refuge
14416 Jefferson Davis Hwy.
Suite 20A
Woodbridge, VA 22191
Phone: (703)690-1297
Contact: J. Frederick Milton, Mgr
Includes Featherstone, and Marumsco areas.

★2503★ Presquile National Wildlife Refuge
PO Box 620
Hopewell, VA 23860
Phone: (804)458-7541
Contact: Barry Brady, Mgr

Washington

★2504★ Aleutian Islands Unit
Alaska Maritime Natl. Wildlife Refuge
Box 5251
Naval Air Sta. Adak
FBO Seattle, WA 98791
Phone: (907)592-2406
Contact: Daniel Boone, Mgr

★2505★ Coastal Refuges Office
Nisqually Natl. Wildlife Refuge
PO Box 698
Sequim, WA 98382
Phone: (206)457-8792
Includes Dungeness, Protection Island, and Washington Islands.

★2506★ Columbia National Wildlife Refuge
735 E. Main St.
P.O. Drawer F
Othello, WA 99344
Phone: (509)488-2668
Contact: David E. Goeke, Mgr
Includes Saddle Mountain.

★2507★ Conboy Lake National Wildlife Refuge
Ridgefield Natl. Wildlife Refuge
100 Wildlife Refuge Rd.
Box 5
Glenwood, WA 98619
Phone: (509)364-3410
Contact: Harold E. Cole, Mgr

★2508★ Julia Butler Hansen National Wildlife Refuge for the Columbian White-tailed Deer
PO Box 566
Cathlamet, WA 98612
Phone: (206)795-3915
Contact: Anne Marocchini, Mgr
Contains Willapa National Wildlife Refuge.

★2509★ McNary National Wildlife Refuge
Umatilla Natl. Wildlife Refuge
PO Box 308
Burbank, WA 99323
Phone: (509)547-4942
Contact: David Linehan, Mgr

★2510★ Nisqually National Wildlife Refuge
100 Brown Farm Rd.
Olympia, WA 98506
Phone: (206)753-9467
Contact: Willard B. Hesselbart, Mgr
Includes San Juan Islands.

★2511★ Pierce National Wildlife Refuge
Ridgefield Natl. Wildlife Refuge
MP 36-06-R
SR 14
Stevenson, WA 98648
Phone: (509)427-5208
Contact: Jeff Holm, Mgr

★2512★ Ridgefield National Wildlife Refuge
301 N. Third St.
PO Box 457
Ridgefield, WA 98642
Phone: (206)887-4106
Contact: Bruce Wiseman, Mgr
Includes Steigerwald Lake.

★2513★ Toppenish National Wildlife Refuge
Umatilla Natl. Wildlife Refuge
Route 1
Box 1300
Toppenish, WA 98948
Phone: (509)865-2405
Contact: George J. Fenn, Mgr

★2514★ Turnbull National Wildlife Refuge
S. 26010 Smith Rd.
Cheney, WA 99004
Phone: (509)235-4723
Contact: Nancy Curry, Mgr

★2515★ Willapa National Wildlife Refuge
HC 01
Box 910
Ilwaco, WA 98624-9707
Phone: (206)484-3482
Contact: James A. Hidy, Mgr
Includes Lewis and Clark (OR) area.

Wisconsin

★2516★ Horicon National Wildlife Refuge
W. 4279 Headquarters Rd.
Mayville, WI 53050
Phone: (414)387-2658
Includes Fox River, Gravel Island, and Green Bay.

★2517★ La Crosse District
Upper Mississippi River Complex
Box 415
La Crosse, WI 54601-0415
Phone: (608)784-3910
Alt. Phone: (FTS)781-6307

Contact: James M. Nissen, Mgr

★2518★ Necedah National Wildlife Refuge
Star Rte. West
Box 386
Necedah, WI 54646
Phone: (608)565-2551
Contact: Thomas S. Sanford, Mgr

★2519★ Trempealeau National Wildlife Refuge
Route 1
Trempealeau, WI 54661
Phone: (608)539-2311
Contact: Richard Frietsche, Mgr

Wyoming

★2520★ National Elk Refuge
PO Box C
Jackson, WY 83001
Phone: (307)733-9212
Contact: Mike Hedrick, Mgr

★2521★ Seedskadee National Wildlife Refuge
PO Box 67
Green River, WY 82935
Phone: (307)875-2187
Contact: Francis Maiss, Mgr

Commercial Research Firms

Alabama

★2522★ Baldwin Testing Laboratory
PO Box 155
Highway 59
Summerdale, AL 36580
Phone: (205)989-6384
Contact: James Sellars, Owner
Conducts tests on textiles and apparel, plastics and paints, chemical compounds, pharmaceuticals, pesticides, air, water, wastewater, and soil. Provides atomic absorption analysis. Offers consultation regarding computers and electronics; Dwight Collier, Computer Consultant. Projects include an environmental study of intracoastal waterways.

★2523★ Harmon Engineering and Testing Company, Inc.
1550 Pumphrey Ave.
Auburn, AL 36830
Phone: (205)821-9250
Contact: Grady R. Harmon, Pres.
Founded: 1970. Environmental testing and control, hazardous solids and air pollution monitoring methods, chemistry and biology, and instrumentation development. Services include field monitoring, laboratory analysis, environmental impact assessments, economic feasibility studies, preliminary engineering, construction management, expert testimony, wastewater analysis, process evaluation, industrial hygiene analysis, explosion investigations, facility operation, research management, and personnel training design.

★2524★ P.E. LaMoreaux & Associates, Inc. (PELA)
PO Box 2310
Tuscaloosa, AL 35403
Phone: (205)752-5543
Telex: 466594 (PELA CI)
Contact: James W. LaMoreaux, Pres.
Founded: 1961. Hydrology, including water resource planning and management, geophysical prospecting, water quality testing and analysis, water and groundwater recharge systems design, water treatment, flood plain mapping, watershed management, construction inspection, well drilling planning and implementation, and permit application. Geologic studies focus on remote sensing, testing of soils and rocks, sanitary landfill engineering, mine stabilization, deep well disposal, mine drainage, rock mechanics, boring, land reclamation, foundation analysis, soil erosion abatement, and energy resource exploration, including oil and gas, lignite and coal, geothermal resources, and minerals. Environmental services include providing impact statements and maintaining an EPA quality control chemisty laboratory.

Alaska

★2525★ B & D Lab
Rt. 1, Box 795
Ketchikan, AK 99901
Phone: (907)247-2368
Contact: Dave Wieler, Microbiologist
Firm providing testing and analysis and product development services in the fields of water testing, paralytic shellfish poisoning, botulism, and acidic precipitation.

Arizona

★2526★ American Analytical Laboratories
3441 E. Milber
Tucson, AZ 85714
Phone: (602)889-5787
Contact: Dr. Athol L. Cline, Pres.
Founded: 1970. Data collection and analysis dealing with water, wastewater, and industrial processes.

★2527★ Arizona Testing Laboratories, Inc.
817 W. Madison St.
Phoenix, AZ 85007
Phone: (602)254-6181
Contact: Steven Hankins, Pres.
Founded: 1932. Testing of water, wastewater, hazardous wastes, and ores for inorganic and organic chemicals.

★2528★ Copper State Analytical Lab., Inc.
710 E. Evans Blvd.
Tucson, AZ 85713
Phone: (602)884-5811
Contact: D.A. Shah, Pres.
Founded: 1981. Geochemical testing and analysis, assays, analysis of lube oil, soil and stream sediments, plants, wastewater, and other environmental samples.

★2529★ Laboratory Consultants, Ltd.
9213 S. Hardy Dr.
Tempe, AZ 85284
Phone: (602)893-1788
Contact: Harry Owens, Dir.
Founded: 1977. Agricultural, horticultural, and environmental testing, including analysis of water, wastewater, and hazardous waste for inorganic and microbiological contaminants. Also provides soil, plant, irrigation water, feed and fertilizer, and aflatoxin testing; plant tissue analysis; water conservation studies; fertility management; and consultation on water reuse programs.

★2530★ Turner Laboratories
1895 W. Prince Rd.
PO Box 36385
Tucson, AZ 85705
Phone: (602)293-3406
Contact: W.W. Turner, Pres.
Founded: 1984. Firm providing analysis of water and wastewater and food and feeds.

Arkansas

★2531★ K.E. Sorrells Research Associates, Inc.
8002 Stanton Rd.
Little Rock, AR 72209
Phone: (501)562-8139
Contact: K.E. Sorrells, Pres.
Founded: 1976. Offers consultation in the areas of water technology and stream ecology, including environmental chemistry, water/wastewater analysis, and industrial pollution control. Conducts ecological and limnological studies. Provides project management and resource development assistance. Conducts pollution control and waste resource recovery equipment evaluations.

★2532★ Riverside Testing Laboratories
1005 Vulcan Rd.
Haskell, AR 72015
Phone: (501)776-1511
Contact: Ernest W. Kelly, Pres.
Founded: 1986. Analytical testing laboratory specializing in hazardous waste disposal and chemical reclamation.

California

★2533★ AeroVironment Inc.
825 Myrtle Ave.
Monrovia, CA 91016-3424
Phone: (818)357-9983
Fax: (818)359-9628
Telex: 467121 (AEROVIR-CI)

Contact: Dr. Paul MacCready, Pres.
Founded: 1971. Air pollution and hazardous waste measurements, modeling, and analysis; plume diffusion research; enviornmental impact studies; emission control strategy development; meteorology; wind energy assessments; wind tunnel testing, and quality assurance testing. Applied electronic, chemical, and engineering development includes emission control, atmospheric turbulence testing, and toxic waste clean-up. Areas of expertise include control technology, acoustic radar instrumentation and air data systems, specialized vehicle design (land, sea, air), alternative energy, and applied fluid mechanics in such areas as fuel conservation in vehicles and energy-efficient handling of fluid flows. Also offers expert witness testimony. Past projects include development of airfoils and aerodynamic and dynamic analysis of wind turbine systems.

★2534★ A.L. Burke Engineering, Inc.
1162 N. Kraemer Pl.
Anaheim, CA 92806
Phone: (714)666-1120
Telex: 272008 ALBEIUR
Contact: Annie Laurie Burke, Pres.
Founded: 1980. Hazardous waste management, industrial and municipal waste treatment, facilities management, pollution abatement systems engineering, gas treatment and handling facilities design, sewage gas treatment and utilization, cogeneration facilities design, resource and energy recovery systems engineering, and computer simulation. Field services include on-site organic vapor monitoring for subsurface investigations and leak detection monitoring for process piping. Also provides energy efficiency analysis, modeling of contaminant migration, and engineering services in gas and oil processing.

★2535★ Anametrix, Inc.
2754 Aiello Dr.
San Jose, CA 95111
Phone: (408)629-1132
Contact: Burt Sutherland, Pres.
Founded: 1985. Provides testing and analysis of hazardous wastes, groundwater and wastewater, and air samples.

★2536★ Anatec Laboratories, Inc.
435 Tesconi Circle
Santa Rosa, CA 95401
Phone: (707)526-7200
Contact: David Ball, Pres.
Laboratory offering biological, chemical, chromatographic, radiation, spectrographic, and environmental impact analysis in the areas of aquatic toxicology and hazardous wastes. Offers freshwater and marine bioassays.

★2537★ Anlab
1914 S St.
Sacramento, CA 95814
Phone: (916)447-2946
Contact: Tom Ikesaki, Dir.
Founded: 1978. Firm providing testing and analysis and product application of environmental and hazardous waste equipment, including studies of plastic pipe permeation.

★2538★ Arias Research Associates
9241 Cord Ave.
Downey, CA 90240
Phone: (213)862-4895
Contact: Jeffrey L. Arias, Pres.
Founded: 1974. Provides systems design and analysis, product development, and cost analysis of alternative energy systems. Conducts battery testing and development for military products and electrical vehicles, and vehicle road testing.

★2539★ Bendix Environmental Research, Inc.
1390 Market St.
Suite 902
San Francisco, CA 94102
Phone: (415)861-8484
Contact: Selina Bendix Ph.D., Pres.
Founded: 1980. Provides hazardous materials site evaluation and decontamination recommendations; evaluations of health and environmental effects involving biological, chemical, or radioactive agents; information and literature search and evaluation of environmental and medical effects of toxic substances; reports on chemical hazards encountered in industries; preparation, editing, and critique of environmental documents; expert testimony and litigation support; and consultation on chemical exposure problems, fire hazards, and emergency planning, with emphasis on hazardous material incident control. Areas of expertise include toxicology, hazardous materials management, combustion toxicology, and chemical carcinogenesis. Projects include studies of environmental effects of wastewater disposal programs and effects of port container facilities development.

★2540★ Brown and Caldwell Laboratories
1255 Powell St.
Emeryville, CA 94608
Phone: (415)428-2300
Provides radiochemistry, microbiology, and bioassay with applications in toxic and hazardous wastes, priority pollutants, odor characterization, water/wastewater characterization, flow monitoring, and process control.

★2541★ BTC Laboratories
2978 Seaborg Ave.
Ventura, CA 93003
Phone: (805)656-6074
Contact: Tom Williams, Dir.
Construction materials testing and inspection, including chemical, chromatographic, mechanical, nondestructive, spectrographic, and failure testing of concrete, masonry, steel, and aggregates. Also specializes in air pollution testing and hazardous materials analysis.

★2542★ Cal Recovery Systems, Inc.
160 Broadway, Ste. 200
Richmond, CA 94804
Phone: (415)232-3066
Telex: 172910 (CRS RCMD)
Contact: Dr. Luis F. Diaz, Pres.
Founded: 1975. Feedstock characterization, including biomass and solid, liquid, and hazardous wastes; waste processing, waste conversion via thermal, chemical, and biological means; system modeling and verification; and field testing of systems.

★2543★ Calvert Environmental
5191 Santa Fe St.
San Diego, CA 92109
Phone: (619)272-0050
Contact: Ronald G. Patterson, Pres.
Founded: 1970. Prototype product development, literature search, theoretical modeling, testing and evaluation of equipment, and consulting in the areas of particulate control, hot gas cleaning, and particulate measurement and dispersion. Research focuses on environmental control technology.
Former Name(s): Air Pollution Technology, Inc. (1988).

★2544★ Chemical Research Laboratories, Inc.
7440 Lincoln Way
Garden Grove, CA 92641
Phone: (714)898-6370
Fax: (714)891-5917
Toll-Free: 800-522-1275
Contact: Puri Romualdo, Exec. V. Pres.
Founded: 1979. Chemical and environmental testing, waste treatment, oilfield tracer studies, groundwater analysis, and soil analysis for underground leakage. Technical services in environmental technology include hazardous waste sampling, monitoring, and characterization; microbiology; toxicity bioassays; site investigations; pilot plant studies; drinking and wastewater analysis; ocean monitoring; sludge and wastewater treatment and analysis; oil and gas analysis; feedstock analysis; and corrosion testing. Other services include methods development, agricultural and food analysis, plating analysis, electronics testing, and other customized testing.

★2545★ C.L. Technology, Inc.
280 N. Smith
Corona, CA 91720
Phone: (714)734-9600
Contact: Sri Pfuntner, Gen. Manager
Specializes in environmental monitoring and chemical testing, including analysis of foods, fertilizer, water and wastewater, air, soils, hazardous wastes, residues, and spores. Additional services include pest management, product management, and methods development.

★2546★ Dellavalle Laboratory, Inc.
1910 W. McKinley
Suite 110
Fresno, CA 93728
Phone: (209)233-6129
Contact: Nat B. Dellavalle, Pres.
Founded: 1978. Testing, analysis, and consultation in soil, water, and environmental sciences, and studies in irrigation, agronomy, pomology, viticulture, nematology, and horticulture. Services include analysis of soils, plant tissue, water, fertilizers, and manure; pesticide residue testing; and consulting in the areas of crop feasibility, production evaluation, crop management and loss, soil reclamation, and irrigation management.

★2547★ Environmental Measurements, Inc.
PO Box 880124
San Francisco, CA 94188
Phone: (415)398-7664
Telex: 701777 (EMISFOUD)
Contact: Lee Langan, Pres.
Founded: 1968. Develops systems and instruments related to solving air pollution problems.

★2548★ ERYX Corporation
15898 Via Pinale
San Lorenzo, CA 94580
Phone: (415)351-5527
Contact: Eric A. Salo, Pres.
Founded: 1964. Provides new product development and analytical reports in the fields of energy and water conservation, energy auxiliaries, and hydrology. Long range projects include estuarine water conservation, jet propulsion for cargo vessels, and thermal power plant improvement.

★2549★ **GEOSERVICES**
1860 Obispo Ave.
Suite A
Long Beach, CA 90804
Phone: (213)597-3977
Fax: (213)579-0786
Toll-Free: 800-523-4786
Contact: Michael M. Mooradian, Pres.
Founded: 1984. Operating within the fields of chemistry, hydrology, geology, engineering, and industrial hygiene, firm's responsibilities include regulatory compliance testing, hazardous waste management, water resource assessment and development, water quality and geochemical investigation, environmental permitting and impact assessments, underground storage tank programs, landfill studies, and remedial action design and implementation. Programs include soil-gas testing, numerical modeling of groundwater and geochemical conditions, mobile laboratory services, and hazardous waste management database development.

★2550★ **Hydrocomp, Inc.**
201 San Antonio Circle
Mountain View, CA 94040
Phone: (415)948-3919
Contact: Dr. N. Crawford, Contact
Firm providing hydrologic analysis, including water quality and water resources planning. Specializes in development and application of computer models for water resources analysis.

★2551★ **Ike Yen Associates**
867 Marymount Ln.
Claremont, CA 91711
Phone: (714)621-2302
Contact: Ike Yen, Contact
Founded: 1983. Firm providing engineering and consulting services in the areas of environmental protection, hazardous materials, asbestos assessment, health and safety, environmental audits, risk analysis, chemical engineering, heat transfer, economic and feasibility studies, technical planning, project management, physics, and applied mathematics.

★2552★ **Montgomery Laboratories**
555 E. Walnut St.
Pasadena, CA 91101
Phone: (818)796-9141
Contact: Dr. Andrew Eaton, Laboratory Dir.
Analysis of environmental samples, including drinking water and hazardous wastes for priority pollutants. Conducts field sampling, viral testing, flow measurements, and composite sample collection, and provides data evaluation and validation.

★2553★ **Northrop Services, Inc.**
500 E. Orangethorpe Ave.
Anaheim, CA 92801
Phone: (714)441-3000
Contact: John Moore, V. Pres. & Gen. Manager
Founded: 1969. Air pollution programs, ambient air quality monitoring, health effects testing, source sampling and characterization, and quality control auditing. Areas of expertise include biological sciences, space biology applications, genetic and inhalation toxicology, and toxic substances research.

★2554★ **Ralph Stone and Company, Inc.**
10954 Santa Monica Blvd.
Los Angeles, CA 90025
Phone: (213)478-1501
Contact: Richard Kahle, Pres.
Founded: 1953. Waste management and pollution control, including development and testing of waste treatment processes and development of landfill methane gas recovery methods.

★2555★ **Ray W. Hawksley Company, Inc.**
220 Cutting Blvd.
Richmond, CA 94804
Phone: (415)235-5780
Founded: 1967. Provides laboratory services and consultation in the areas of water pollution and water treatment, including biologic examination of water, sludge, and bottom materials; corrosion deposit analysis; corrosivity testing of industrial water; and analytical and consulting services on sanitary and industrial wastes, boiler water, cooling water, irrigation water, and process water.

★2556★ **Reese-Chambers Systems Consultants, Inc.**
PO Box 8
Somis, CA 93066
Phone: (805)987-3209
Fax: (805)987-4008
Contact: Tim Chambers, Contact
Risk and system safety analysis in the areas of oil development, transportation, and processing, and contingency planning in the area of hazardous materials, including petroleum products and chemicals, and materials processing, storage, handling, and transportation.

★2557★ **SCS Engineers**
3711 Long Beach Blvd.
Long Beach, CA 90807
Phone: (213)426-9544
Telex: 2134270805
Contact: Jerome A. Young, Dir. of Business Development
Founded: 1970. Solid waste management, wastewater management, sludge and hazardous waste management, assessment of health impacts of contaminants in water supplies, energy conservation, landfill gas recovery and control, oil storage and oil spill control, systems engineering, environmental monitoring and impact assessment, and research on environmental protection measures. Conducts feasibility studies and designs environmental protection facilities.

★2558★ **Sequoia Analytical Laboratory, Inc.**
2549 Middlefield Rd.
Redwood City, CA 94063
Phone: (415)364-9222
Fax: (415)364-9233
Contact: Art Burton, Laboratory Dir.
Founded: 1978. Chemical and biochemical analysis of metals, organics (including PCBs, pesticides, and herbicides), inorganics, hydrocarbons, radiation, and asbestos. Also provides bioassays and microbiology services. ***Former Name(s):*** Cook Laboratory (1978).

★2559★ **Sidney R. Frank Group**
444 David Love Pl.
Goleta, CA 93117
Phone: (805)964-4477
Contact: S.R. Frank, Pres.
Founded: 1968. Conducts meteorological and environmental research, including remote sensing of atmospheric conditions, pollution damage analysis, mesometeorological studies, and forensics.

★2560★ **Systems Applications, Inc.**
101 Lucas Valley Rd.
San Rafael, CA 94903
Phone: (415)472-4011
Fax: (415)472-0907
Telex: 469287
Contact: Stanley M. Greenfield, Pres.
Founded: 1968. Provides analytic, engineering, and measurement services in the areas of chemical and biological air quality phenomena; air pollution control; multimedia transport; emissions inventory development; toxic and hazardous materials; source siting; risk assessment; land use planning; health effects assessment, economic and cost/benefit analyses, ambient air quality measurement, computer modeling, and environmental regulation compliance evaluation.

★2561★ **Tech-Art**
462 Douglass St.
San Francisco, CA 94114
Phone: (415)550-2435
Contact: Spring Kraeger, Contact
Firm providing toxic and hazardous waste site investigations, measurements of volatile organic vapors, and surface hydrology.

★2562★ **TMA/ARLI**
160 Taylor St.
Monrovia, CA 91016
Phone: (818)357-3247
Fax: (818)359-5036
Contact: John D. McCarthy, Business Development Manager
Founded: 1971. Data collection, including field sampling and analysis, design of sampling programs, and procedure development. Tests radioactive, organic, and inorganic materials and offers low-level radioactive waste analysis for utilities, decontamination of nuclear facilities, analysis of mixed waste samples, and industrial hygiene studies. Projects include studies of environmental radiation from hospitals, environmental impact of geothermal emissions, determination of breathing zone concentration of contaminants generated by diesel powered vehicles in underground mines, statistical evaluation of the procedure for counting asbestos fibers on membrane filters, and plutonium environmental studies. ***Former Name(s):*** LFE Environmental Analysis Laboratory (1980); EAL Corporation (1985).

★2563★ **TMA/Norcal**
2030 Wright Ave.
Richmond, CA 94804
Phone: (415)235-2633
Contact: B.E. Christensen, Marketing Dir.
Founded: 1948. Provides environmental impact investigations, treatability studies, and forensic research. ***Former Name(s):*** EAL Corporation (1987).

★2564★ **Toxscan, Inc.**
1234 Hwy. One
Watsonville, CA 95076
Phone: (408)724-5422
Contact: Philip D. Carpenter, Pres.
Founded: 1978. Provides biological and chemical analysis of marine and freshwaters, sediments, and tissues, including hazardous waste analysis, bioassays, and toxicity testing.

★2565★ **West Coast Analytical Service, Inc.**
9840 Alburtis Ave.
Santa Fe Springs, CA 90670
Phone: (213)948-2225
Contact: D.J. Northington Ph.D., Pres.
Provides environmental analysis of organic and inorganic trace elements, pesticides, wastewater, hazardous waste, drinking water, and air pollutants. Also provides industrial hygiene services, gas analysis, and contaminant and product analysis.

★2566★ Westec Services, Inc.
5510 Morehouse Dr.
San Diego, CA 92121
Phone: (619)294-9770
Contact: Michael W. Wright, Exec. V. Pres.
Founded: 1972. Conducts studies on air and water quality, hazardous waste, and fossil, nuclear, and geothermal energy systems. Services include communications systems.

Colorado

★2567★ Cenref Labs
PO Box 68
695 N. 7th
Brighton, CO 80215
Phone: (303)659-0497
Contact: Kevin Griffiths, Chemist
Founded: 1948. Provides analytical method development, testing and analysis, and product quality control of chemicals through gas chromatography, mass spectrometry, and on-site analysis in the areas of agrichemicals, air and water, crude oil, gycol, hazardous waste, metals and nonmetals, natural gas and liquids, pesticides, herbicides, refined products, engine exhaust, and polychlorinated biphenyl.

★2568★ Chematox Laboratory, Inc.
5401 Western Ave.
Boulder, CO 80301
Phone: (303)440-4500
Toll-Free: 800-334-1685
Contact: Dale C. Wingeleth Ph.D., Laboratory Dir.
Founded: 1977. Provides analysis of drugs and alcohol, pesticides, and organic chemicals for Environmental Protection Agency and Occupational Safety and Health Administration standards.

★2569★ DCM Science Laboratory, Inc.
12975 W. 24th Pl.
Golden, CO 80401
Phone: (303)237-1725
Contact: Cindy Mefford, V. Pres.
Founded: 1984. Provides asbestos and industrial mineral testing.

★2570★ Enseco-Rocky Mountain Analytical Laboratory
4955 Yarrow St.
Arvada, CO 80002
Phone: (303)421-6611
Contact: Steven H. Kramer, Sales Manager
Founded: 1980. Testing and analysis services specializing in toxic waste determinations in groundwater and biological hazard assessments to industry. ***Former Name(s):*** Rocky Mountain Analytical Laboratory (1987).

★2571★ Grand Junction Laboratories
435 North Ave.
Grand Junction, CO 81501
Phone: (303)242-7618
Contact: Brian Bauer, Dir.
Founded: 1956. Testing and analysis of water, minerals, soils, and agricultural products.

★2572★ Hach Company
Box 389
Loveland, CO 80539
Phone: (303)669-3050
Fax: (303)669-2932
Telex: 9109309038
Contact: Kathryn Hach, Pres.
Founded: 1938. Pollution control, aquatic ecology, and water and wastewater analysis. ***Former Name(s):*** Hach Chemical Company.

★2573★ JFT Agapito & Associates, Inc.
715 Horizon Dr.
Suite 340
Grand Junction, CO 81506
Phone: (303)242-4220
Fax: (303)245-9234
Contact: J.F.T. Agapito, Principal
Founded: 1978. Geology, geophysics, hydrology, and rock mechanics. Services include design and evaluation of mining methods, design of nuclear waste repositories, mine ventilation analysis, development of rock support systems and instrumentation, gas monitoring, geotechnical data management, technical assistance in preparation of environmental impact statements, and management of geotechnical programs.

★2574★ Western Environmental, Inc.
4320 Northpark Dr.
Colorado Springs, CO 80907
Phone: (303)528-6132
Contact: Dr. C.W. Gullikson, Pres.
Founded: 1974. Physics, analytical chemistry, and testing of air, water systems, industrial waste, commercial products, and groundwater contamination. Also offers mechanical and environmental testing and calibration services. ***Former Name(s):*** Western Environmental Testing Laboratory (1981).

Connecticut

★2575★ Energy Research Corporation
3 Great Pasture Rd.
Danbury, CT 06810
Phone: (203)792-1460
Contact: Dr. Bernard S. Baker, Pres.
Founded: 1969. Research and development in the fields of electrochemicals and energy conservation and storage, with special emphasis on fuel cells and batteries. Long-range projects include development of molten carbonate fuel cells, a fuel cell powered bus, and a nickle cadmium battery for submarines.

★2576★ Environmental Consulting Laboratory
240 Sargent Dr.
New Haven, CT 06511
Phone: (203)776-9624
Contact: David C. Barris, Pres.
Founded: 1985. Provides organic and inorganic testing of industrial wastewater, groundwater, hazardous wastes, sewage, sludge, sediment, and used oils. Also offers process control and development in the areas of environmental science, microbiology, and chemistry.

★2577★ Environmental Monitoring Laboratory, Inc.
Suite A
59 N. Plains Industrial Park
Wallingford, CT 06492
Phone: (203)284-0555
Contact: Lucille E. Dunn, V. Pres.
Laboratory providing environmental chemistry services, including analysis, bioassays, product efficacy, and research and development in the areas of water and wastewater, agricultural chemicals, protective coatings, petroleum products, metals, and chemicals and consumer products.

★2578★ Griswold and Fuss Environmental Lab
360 E. Center St.
Manchester, CT 06040
Phone: (203)646-5628
Contact: Patrick O. Vargo, Laboratory Dir.
Environmental laboratory providing biological, chemical, chromatographic, and environmental impact analysis of water, wastewater, and streams and lakes for priority pollutants, PCBs, herbicides, pesticides, and hazardous wastes.

★2579★ TRC Environmental Consultants, Inc.
800 Connecticut Blvd.
East Hartford, CT 06108
Phone: (203)289-8631
Contact: Vincent A. Rocco, Pres.
Founded: 1971. Air pollution control, acid rain research, and hazardous waste management. Services include consulting, applied research and development, and specialized analytical services to identify, define, and solve energy, environmental, and human health problems.

Delaware

★2580★ Artesian Laboratories, Inc.
630 Churchmans Rd.
Newark, DE 19702
Phone: (302)453-6920
Fax: (302)453-6957
Contact: Marlene O. Frey, V. Pres., Marketing
Founded: 1985. Provides testing and analysis for environmental research and monitoring, including drinking water quality and treatment, testing methods, and product quality control for third-party documentation. Projects include analysis of drinking water coolers for lead contamination and testing for residual solvents in printed material.

★2581★ ASTB/Crippen Laboratories, Inc.
4027 New Castle Ave.
New Castle, DE 19720
Phone: (302)571-8882
Contact: Dr. Raymond C. Crippen, Technical Dir.
Founded: 1975. Analysis of commercial and industrial chemical products and materials, environmental studies, research planning and organization, analysis of chemical processes, product and process development and testing, physical testing, information and literature research, identification and reduction of pollutants in chemical mixtures, aid in compliance with government regulations, and consultation on raw materials for chemical mixtures. Provides services in the fields of agricultural products, biochemicals, cleaners and industrial products, petroleum and energy sources, metals, paints and coatings, beverages, and water, wastewater, solid waste, and air pollutants. Long-range projects involve the development of products to relieve arthritis, kidney disorders, allergies, and cancer. ***Former Name(s):*** Crippen Laboratories; merged with American Standards Testing Bureau, Inc. (New York), in 1988.

★2582★ Batta Environmental Associates, Inc.
PO Box 9722
Newark, DE 19714
Phone: (302)737-3376
Provides asbestos sampling and testing, stack emission sampling, and other airborne contamination studies. Studies air pollution control equipment and evaluates coal and other fuels for contaminants and heat content. Also evaluates drinking water, industrial water, wastewater, solid wastes, groundwater, and soils.

★2583★ Envirocorp, Inc.
Church & Sewall Streets
PO Box D
Felton, DE 19943
Phone: (302)284-3004
Contact: H. Joseph Gannon Jr., Pres.
Founded: 1984. Provides testing and environmental monitoring related to compliance with the EPA's National Pollutant Discharge Elimination System and Resource Conservation and Recovery Act (1976). Provides groundwater monitoring, with emphasis on inorganic analysis through atomic absorption spectrophotometry.

★2584★ TetraTech Richardson, Inc.
910 S. Chapel St.
Box 675
Newark, DE 19711
Phone: (302)738-7551
Contact: Arkan Say P.E., Pres.
Founded: 1949. Engineering in the fields of environmental sciences, hazardous and toxic waste, transportation, landscape architecture, applied earth sciences, hydraulics, and energy. Services include site engineering, pollution control design, land use planning, and land development and design assistance. ***Former Name(s):*** Edward H. Richardson Associates, Inc. (1986).

★2585★ Wik Associates, Inc.
PO Box 287
New Castle, DE 19720
Phone: (302)322-8771
Contact: John D. Wik, Contact
Firm providing environmental auditing, environmental impact analysis, policy analysis, hazardous materials management, radioactive waste disposal, industrial process technology, technical writing, program management, and environmental testing.

District of Columbia

★2586★ RCG/Hagler, Bailly, Inc.
370 L'Enfant Promenade, S.W.
Suite 700
Washington, DC 20024-2518
Phone: (202)488-1500
Fax: (202)484-0702
Telex: 7108221150 HABACO WS
Contact: Dr. Michael Yokell, Pres.
Founded: 1980. Provides market and competitor analysis, management consulting, technology assessments, research and development planning, systems analysis, operations research, simulation modeling, and econometric studies in productivity, finance, environmental health and toxicology, fuel and mineral economics, federal resource procurement economics, environmental risk, hazardous waste, utilities, and energy conservation. ***Former Name(s):*** Hagler, Bailly & Company, Inc. (1988).

Florida

★2587★ Astro-Pure Water Purifiers
4900 NW 15th St.
No. 4478
Margate, FL 33063
Phone: (305)971-9680
Telex: 5109568680
Contact: R.L. Stefl, Pres.
Founded: 1971. Testing and analysis, systems design, and product development in the field of water treatment. ***Former Name(s):*** RLS Enterprises (1975).

★2588★ Enviropact, Inc.
4790 NW 157th St.
Miami, FL 33014
Phone: (305)620-1700
Contact: Robert Fletcher, Pres.
Founded: 1976. Provides analytical and field services, including analysis of hazardous wastes, petroleum products, soils, air, water, and wastewater. Conducts research and offers consultation on the prevention and correction of soil and groundwater contamination and the development of clean-up procedures. Studies and develops methods for removing hydrocarbons from ground water.

★2589★ Flowers Chemical Laboratories, Inc.
PO Box 597
481 Newburyport
Altamonte Springs, FL 32715-0597
Phone: (305)339-5984
Fax: (305)260-6110
Contact: Dr. Jefferson S. Flowers, Pres. /Technical Dir.
Founded: 1957. Provides environmental, industrial hygiene, and hazardous waste analytical services.

★2590★ Joyce Environmental Consultants, Inc.
5051 North Ln.
Orlando, FL 32808
Phone: (305)297-7980
Contact: Robert D. Blackburn, V. Pres.
Founded: 1972. Analysis of the effects of herbicides and pesticides on aquatic environments, including research on purification of stormwater runoff with wetland plants, methods of restoring wetlands, including removal of exotic species from native wetlands. Projects include design and monitoring of a stormwater purification system for a 2,400-acre development.

★2591★ Orlando Laboratories, Inc.
PO Box 19127
Orlando, FL 32814
Phone: (305)896-6645
Independent laboratory providing drinking water analysis, landfill and hazardous waste facility monitoring, forensic services, drug screening and confirmation, and laboratory training programs.

★2592★ Pioneer Laboratory, Inc.
11 E. Olive Rd.
Pensacola, FL 32514
Phone: (904)474-1001
Contact: W.F. Bowers, Pres. /Manager
Provides hazardous waste evaluation, water quality assurance, industrial waste surveys, industrial research, methods development, priority pollutant testing, environmental impact assessments, product quality testing, industrial hygiene services, field monitoring, corrosion studies, and fire and arson investigation.

★2593★ Water and Air Research, Inc.
Box 1121
Gainesville, FL 32602
Phone: (904)372-1500
Fax: (904)378-1500
Contact: William C. Zegel, Pres.
Founded: 1970. Data collection and analysis, systems design, and technological forecasting in the areas of environmental chemistry, including water chemistry and atmospheric chemistry, environmental engineering, hazardous waste disposal and detoxification, and applied ecology. Research projects include analysis of the water chemistry of new lakes, investigation into the dynamics of public hearings on environmental issues, a study of arctic plankton, an assessment of the environmental impact of the use of architectural lead products, and an evaluation of environmental and health effects of processes, products, and procedures.

Georgia

★2594★ Bowman Engineering, Inc.
400 B. Johnny Mercer Blvd.
Savannah, GA 31410
Phone: (912)897-7149
Contact: Donald R. Bowman, Pres.
Founded: 1981. Data collection and analysis, information and literature research, and design and evaluation of water and wastewater treatment plant and systems. Also conducts environmental studies.

★2595★ Engineering-Science, Inc.
57 Executive Park S.
Atlanta, GA 30329
Phone: (404)325-0770
Contact: T.N. Sargent, V. Pres.
Founded: 1946. Environmental impact studies and facilities design analysis in the areas of air pollution control, water treatment and solid waste management, industrial waste control, and inorganic chemistry.

★2596★ Hayden-Wegman
2200 Century Pkwy.
Suite 900
Atlanta, GA 30345
Phone: (404)325-5400
Contact: Deanna Ruffer, Dir. of Marketing
Data collection, information research, market research, system design, technological forecasting, and testing and analysis in the fields of environmental and transportation engineering. Services include waste-to-energy engineering, water pollution control, water supply studies, solid and hazardous waste engineering, site development, municipal services, and construction management. ***Former Name(s):*** Formed by a merger of Hayden, Harding & Buchanan and Wegman Engineers.

★2597★ Law and Company
1763 Montreal Circle
Tucker, GA 30084
Phone: (404)934-8200
Contact: R.E. Kieffer, Partner
Analytical laboratory specializing in water and wastewater, hazardous substances, air

monitoring, fuels specifications, concrete, metals, feeds, and vegetable oils. Also provides services in forest products, bituminous materials, soil and rock, chemicals, and lechates.

★2598★ MacMillan Research, Ltd.
Box 1305
Marietta, GA 30061
Phone: (404)427-3101
Contact: Dr. J.E. MacMillan, Pres.
Founded: 1956. Microbiological analysis (including evaluations of medical items and devices) and chemical analysis of foods, feeds, water, and wastewater. Laboratory services available for petroleum studies, metal analysis, corrosion evaluation, and air analysis. Provides consultation in manufacturing processes and control.

★2599★ S & ME, Inc.
300 Marjan Drive, N.E.
Atlanta, GA 30340
Phone: (404)451-5772
Contact: James Willmer, Laboratory Manager
Offers geotechnical, environmental, and construction materials testing, including asbestos analysis.

★2600★ Timber Products Inspection & Testing, Inc.
PO Box 919
884 S. Blacklawn Rd.
Conyers, GA 30207
Phone: (404)922-8000
Contact: Eugene Chiu, Laboratory Manager
Chemical and environmental testing of forestry products and wood treatments. Also provides testing of water, soil, hazardous substances, and leachates.

★2601★ Tribble & Richardson, Inc.
116 Pierce Ave.
PO Box 2445
Macon, GA 31203
Phone: (912)742-7395
Contact: Kathy Stege Bragg, Laboratory Dir.
Founded: 1956. Civil, environmental, and structural engineering specializing in environmental protection and monitoring, groundwater, surface water, and wastewater analysis, and landfill leachates. Provides land and topographical surveying. ***Former Name(s):*** Tribble & Associates, Inc. (1970).

Illinois

★2602★ Allied Laboratories, Ltd.
716 N. Iowa
Villa Park, IL 60181
Phone: (312)279-0390
Fax: (312)279-3114
Contact: Irving I. Domsky, Dir.
Founded: 1977. Water and wastewater sampling and analysis, industrial sludge and soil analysis, air pollution studies, and cosmetic and detergent formulations. Develops analytical methods. Provides expert testimony.

★2603★ Analytical Laboratory for Environmental Excellence, Inc. (ALEX)
485 S. Frontage Rd.
Suite 130
Burr Ridge, IL 60521
Phone: (312)789-6080
Contact: Erlo Roth M.D., Pres.
Founded: 1985. Testing and analysis and toxicology of hazardous substances, pollutants, and wastes, including asbestos survey and abatement.

★2604★ Aqualab, Inc.
850 W. Bartlett Rd.
Bartlett, IL 60103
Phone: (312)289-3100
Contact: Stan Zaworski, Pres.
Founded: 1972. Provides environmental disaster analysis, fuel analysis, nuclear generating station impact assessment, water purification studies, and quality assurance programs for public water supplies with emphasis on plants and tissues, trace elements, and liquid waste.

★2605★ ARDL, Inc.
1801 Forrest St.
PO Box 1566
Mount Vernon, IL 62864
Phone: (618)244-3235
Contact: L.V. Gibbons Ph.D., Pres.
Works toward solving problems in the chemical, environmental, and biomedical sciences. Provides chemical and physical property analysis of environmental samples, including liquid and solid wastes, stack gasses, workroom air, petroleum products, solvents, process streams, plating baths, ferrous and nonferrous metals, soils, and building materials.

★2606★ Arro Laboratories, Inc.
Caton Farm Rd.
PO Box 686
Joliet, IL 60434
Phone: (815)727-5436
Fax: (815)727-6523
Telex: 9106330599
Contact: Robert J. Rolih, Pres.
Founded: 1965. Trace metal analysis, microbiological studies, aqueous and oil matrix standards testing, environmental studies, water analysis, bacteriological surveys, pollution testing, stack sampling, ambient air testing, waste water testing and management, pesticides and polychlorinated biphenyl testing, compositional analysis, polymer characterization, and hazardous waste testing. Also provides analytical methods development, bench scale studies, process surveys, troubleshooting, quality control studies, and pilot plant tracking.

★2607★ Gabriel Laboratories, Ltd.
1421 N. Elston
Chicago, IL 60622
Phone: (312)486-2123
Contact: John Karrow, V. Pres.
Water, wastewater, and environmental testing, including analytical services, industrial hygiene evaluation, field monitoring, and consulting.

★2608★ Gulf Coast Laboratories, Inc.
2417 Bond St.
University Park, IL 60466
Phone: (312)534-5200
Specializes in the analysis of water, wastewater, and industrial waste. Also analyzes paper, metals, agricultural and food products, chemicals, pharmaceuticals, air samples, and soils and rocks.

★2609★ Moreco Energy, Technical Services
7601 W. 47th St.
McCook, IL 60525
Phone: (312)229-0673
Contact: Tom Corriveau, Dir. of Technical Services
Tests new and used petroleum lubricants, including environmental analysis of waste oils, through chemistry, chromatography, and spectroscopy. Assesses levels of sulfur and chlorine in oil, identifies PCBs in various matrices, and measures wear and additive levels in oil.

★2610★ Randolph & Associates, Inc.
8901 N. Industrial Rd.
Peoria, IL 61615
Phone: (309)692-4422
Contact: John Pivinski, Manager
Specializes in environmental monitoring, including analysis of water, wastewater, and hazardous wastes. Also tests and analyzes metals, cement and other construction materials, nonmetallic minerals, petroleum products, and chemical products.

★2611★ Suburban Laboratories, Inc.
4140 Litt Dr.
Hillside, IL 60162
Phone: (312)544-3260
Contact: S.I. Rosenberg, Pres.
Environmental laboratory providing chemical, chromatographic, and spectrographic analysis of biological materials, including water and groundwater, soil, and hazardous materials for priority pollutants, metals, and pesticide residues.

Indiana

★2612★ Environmental Consultants, Inc.
391 Newman Ave.
Clarksville, IN 47130
Phone: (812)282-8481
Contact: Robert E. Fuchs, Pres.
Founded: 1971. Conducts environmental monitoring and impact studies and offers methodologies development.

★2613★ Environmental Health Laboratories
430 N. Michigan
South Bend, IN 46601
Phone: (219)234-7212
Contact: James Larkin, Dir. of Marketing
Founded: 1986. Environmental analysis and product testing of analytical systems and water filtration devices. Provides environmental site assessments, underground storage tank monitoring, and organic chemical and pesticide analysis of water, soil, and food for EPA's National Pollutant Discharge Elimination System and Resource Conservation and Recovery Act.

★2614★ Gordon Consulting
PO Box 327
Cambridge City, IN 47327
Phone: (317)478-4801
Contact: Paul W. Gordon, Pres.
Founded: 1984. Research, testing, and analysis in the areas of soil, plant, and animal nutrition; industrial waste management and planning; and municipal sludge and wastewater management. Specific projects include reducing the magnesium level in east central Indiana soils to alleviate potassium availability problems. Laboratory services are provided through Brookside Farms Laboratory Association. ***Former Name(s):*** Paul W. Gordon Consulting (1986).

★2615★ Hoosier Microbiological Laboratory
912 W. McGalliard
Muncie, IN 47303
Phone: (317)288-1124

Contact: Donald A. Hendrickson, Owner
Provides microbiological analysis and environmental monitoring of food, water and wastewater, cosmetics, air, and animal and human tissue. Also provides nutritional labeling.

★2616★ National Laboratories, Inc.
Rivercity One
3210 Claremont Ave.
Evansville, IN 47712
Phone: (812)422-4119
Contact: Dr. Clifford G. Shultz, Pres.
Founded: 1969. Hazardous waste destruction and hazardous waste removal from soils and sludges. Offers data collection and analysis, testing, and product development.

★2617★ Northern Laboratories & Engineering, Inc.
2400 Cumberland Dr.
Valparaiso, IN 46304
Phone: (219)464-2389
Contact: Diane L. Harper, Manager
Provides industrial and municipal discharge analysis, including hazardous waste and groundwater monitoring. Provides on-site collection and process control services.

★2618★ Sherry Laboratories Inc.
2203 S. Madison St.
PO Box 2847
Muncie, IN 47307-0847
Phone: (317)747-9000
Contact: Patrick W. Berger, Marketing Manager
Metallurgical, chemical, and environmental testing and analysis, including studies in failure analysis; water, wastewater, and groundwater; and solid and hazardous wastes.

★2619★ Tenco Laboratories
1150 Junction Ave.
Schererville, IN 46375
Phone: (219)322-2560
Toll-Free: 800-428-3311
Contact: Robert W. Hoole, Marketing Dir.
Founded: 1968. Provides chemical analysis, identification, and quantification of organic components in environmental samples, including monitoring of drinking water, groundwater, surface water, wastewater, and air; assessment of potentially hazardous materials in spills, disposal, and cleanup operations; and evaluation of treatment processes for removal or reduction of organic compounds. Conducts inorganic chemical analysis, including testing of industrial and municipal effluents, natural and potable waters, and soils, vegetation, bottom sediments, and animal tissues. Also offers point source sampling, open stream and lake sampling, industrial source tracking, flow measurement, and flow proportional and time composited sampling.

Iowa

★2620★ Manchester Testing Laboratories, Ltd.
957 12th St.
Marion, IA 52302
Contact: Lawrence L. Stookey, Pres.
Founded: 1974. Chemical and environmental engineering, industrial air and water pollution control, wastewater treatment plant operation, industrial hygiene and meteorological monitoring, and analysis of water, wastewater, industrial materials, fertilizers, and pesticides. Conducts environmental impact studies in the fields of food processing, meat packing, milk processing, and surface mining. ***Former Name(s):*** Manchester Laboratories, Inc.

★2621★ Slater Environmental Analysis Laboratory (SEAL)
401 First Ave.
Slater, IA 50244
Phone: (515)685-3006
Contact: Colin D. Chriswell, Laboratory Dir.
Founded: 1985. Environmental testing and analysis. Services include analytical methods development, detergent formulation, on-site underground storage tank monitoring, and design of custom chromatographic equipment.

Kansas

★2622★ Butler Laboratories
J.C. Butler Associates, Inc.
2928 Arnold Ave.
Salina, KS 67401
Phone: (913)827-1682
Contact: Janis C. Butler, Laboratory Dir.
Provides analytical services in the field of environmental and biological materials, including hazardous waste detoxification and stabilization, treatability studies, and waste treatment process development.

★2623★ Langston Laboratories, Inc.
2005 W. 103 Terr.
Leawood, KS 66206
Phone: (913)341-7800
Contact: Dr. C. Walter Langston, Pres.
Founded: 1971. Microbiological testing and analysis of environmental conditions, foods, and related materials. Also provides services in water and wastewater analysis, air pollution abatement, solid waste disposal, nutritional labeling, industrial hygiene, and the analysis of antibiotics and pesticide residues.

★2624★ Purewater Corporation
PO Box 597
Shawnee Mission, KS 66201
Phone: (913)342-9436
Contact: Daniel Katz, Contact
Founded: 1984. Research, development, design, and operation of water treatment systems for variety of applications, including cooling towers, wastewater, drinking water, boilers, and swimming pools. Research areas include water treatment with ozone with applications in pre-treatment of municipal water to control trihalomethanes, point of use well water purification, and organic elimination prior to municipal water treatment.

Kentucky

★2625★ Mass Spec Services, Inc.
U. S. 127
PO Box 798
Frankfort, KY 40601
Phone: (502)223-0251
Contact: Steven Furnish, Pres.
Environmental testing laboratory specializing in studies of pollutants, including PCB. Provides failure analysis and conducts tests on water and hazardous wastes.

★2626★ Northern Kentucky Environmental Services
300 Doctors Bldg.
33 E. 7th St.
Covington, KY 41011
Phone: (606)431-6224
Contact: Dr. Kenneth P. Reed, Pres.
Analytical laboratory services include forensic studies, analysis of foods, and coliform bacteria quantification. Environmental studies concentrate on air sampling and analysis, isokinetic sampling, water and wastewater sampling and analysis, toxicity analysis, and challenge testing for classification and management of wastes. Industrial hygiene services focus on right-to-know law compliance, hazard recognition and labeling, industrial safety surveys, noise surveys, video display tube surveys, and radiation surveys. Other services include wastewater treatment plant operation, expert witness testimony, and sanitarian consulting services.

Louisiana

★2627★ Arch Consulting Services, Inc.
4425 Floynell
Baton Rouge, LA 70809
Phone: (504)928-1827
Contact: Arleen F. Goldberg, Pres.
Firm providing surface analysis, safety investigations, and consulting related to asbestos in bulk materials and air samples.

★2628★ Enviro-Med Laboratories, Inc.
414 W. California
Ruston, LA 71270
Phone: (318)255-0060
Toll-Free: 800-421-2933
Contact: Dr. Robert W. Flournoy, Pres.
Founded: 1974. Performs atomic absorption spectroscopy, raw product analysis, industrial surveys and sampling, toxicology studies, pesticide analysis, and drinking water analysis. Provides research and consultation in the environmental, chemical, instrumental, and industrial hygiene fields.

★2629★ Environmental Industrial Research Associates
161 Jame Dr. West
Suite 100
St. Rose, LA 70087
Phone: (504)467-2800
Contact: Peter Meehan, Pres.
Firm providing testing of hazardous wastes; analysis of soils, sludges, and waters; solidification of sludges; chemical fixation of hazardous and nonhazardous wastes; environmental consulting; and site assessments.

★2630★ Foundation Testing Lab Inc.
414 W. California Ave.
Ruston, LA 71270
Phone: (318)255-7256
Contact: R.W. Flournoy Ph.D., Contact
Founded: 1976. Data collection and analysis and testing in the areas of landfill reclamation, solid waste facility planning, and hazardous waste consulting and training.

★2631★ James Laboratories, Inc.
PO Box 9-2662
316 Mecca Dr.
Lafayette, LA 70509
Phone: (318)235-0483

Contact: F. Ben James III, Pres.
Founded: 1964. Chemical, physical, and bacteriological analysis of water, wastewater, soil, and sludge. Provides hazardous waste classification and drinking water monitoring services. Analyzes nonhazardous oilfield waste, ocean and fluvial sediments, drill cuttings and fluids, and overboard discharge water. Also conducts field sampling and analysis and monitors well samples.

★2632★ West-Paine Laboratories, Inc.
7979 GSRI Ave.
Baton Rouge, LA 70820
Phone: (504)769-4900
Contact: Jonny H. Vickers, Marketing Manager
Provides environmental and biological materials analysis, including industrial hygiene evaluations and tests of liquid and solid wastes, water, and air. Also provides expert witness testimony.

Maryland

★2633★ Aerosol Monitoring & Analysis, Inc.
PO Box 687
Hunt Valley, MD 21030
Phone: (301)666-5105
Contact: Michael Zinc, Contact
Laboratory, industrial hygiene, and architectural services related to asbestos identification and abatement, including microscopy, air monitoring, specifications, contract administration, and project management.

★2634★ Analyte Laboratories, Inc.
6630 Baltimore National Pike
Route 40 W.
Baltimore, MD 21228
Phone: (301)747-3844
Environmental, petroleum, and metallurgical analysis, including National Pollutant Discharge Elimination System tests, and analyses of corrosivity, reactivity, ignitability, waste characteristics, PCBs, pesticides, chemicals, paint, used oil, acids/bases, precious metals, antifreeze, fertilizers, and lubricants.

★2635★ Biospherics Incorporated
12051 Indian Creek Rd.
Beltsville, MD 20705
Phone: (301)369-3900
Telex: 898072 (WESTERN UNIO
Contact: Gilbert V. Levin Ph.D., Pres.
Founded: 1967. Provides analytical and environmental services, hazard assessments, information and telecommunications services, and biotechnology programs through its four main divisions. The Laboratory Division focuses on hazardous waste control, air and water quality, agricultural chemicals analysis, and environmental audits; the Information and Publications Division provides medical research support services and disseminates new research findings for government agencies and private organizations, with emphasis on health issues and disease prevention; the Industrial Hygiene Division specializes in indoor air quality control, asbestos assessment and control, and hazardous material audits; and the Biotech Programs division develops technologies, including a process for purifying wastewaters. Projects include studies of new AIDS drugs, development of low-calorie L sugars, and assessment agricultural pesticides leaching into groundwaters.

★2636★ E.A.I. Corporation
1308 Continental Dr.
Suite J
Abingdon, MD 21009
Phone: (301)676-1449
Contact: R.W. Mengel, Pres.
Founded: 1980. Provides research on toxic and hazardous materials.

★2637★ Fredericktowne Labs, Inc.
307 Main St.
PO Box 244
Myersville, MD 21773
Phone: (301)293-3340
Contact: Dr. Mary L. Miller, Lab Dir.
Founded: 1985. Stream water quality testing and analysis.

★2638★ Geomet Technologies, Inc.
20251 Century Blvd.
Germantown, MD 20874
Phone: (301)428-9898
Contact: C.I. Judkins Jr., Pres.
Founded: 1969. Provides program management and administrative support services to organizations concerned with environmental and human health problems, including air quality monitoring and hazardous waste management. Projects include monitoring of pollution sites and studies of toxin exposure tolerance.

★2639★ Hittman Ebasco Associates, Inc.
9151 Rumsey Rd.
Columbia, MD 21045
Phone: (301)730-8525
Contact: B. Chris Weathington, Marketing Manager
Provides environmental, chemical, and biological materials testing, including hazardous waste analysis, treatability studies, soil gas analysis, and organic and inorganic compound studies. Maintains mobile laboratory facilities.

★2640★ Mankind Research Unlimited, Inc.
1315 Apple Ave.
Silver Spring, MD 20910
Phone: (301)587-8686
Contact: Dr. Carl Schleicher, Pres.
Founded: 1972. Human systems design, alternate energy sources, research and development for innovative technology, and bionic, biocybernetics, biomedical, and high speed learning systems.

★2641★ Powell Labs Limited
705 S. Wolfe St.
Baltimore, MD 21231
Phone: (301)732-1606
Contact: Stephen E. Shelley, Laboratory Dir.
Analytical laboratory providing services related to water purity, including cooling waters, wastewater, and surface and groundwater. Metallographic studies and evaluations are performed in the areas of failure analysis and deposit densities for boiler and condenser tubes.

★2642★ Robert H. Wilder, Inc.
6706 Maxalea Rd.
Box 19108
Baltimore, MD 21204
Phone: (301)377-6533
Contact: Charles E. Sells, Pres.
Founded: 1969. Energy conservation and pollution control by means of incineration and development of economical methods of waste removal and handling, including shredding and compacting of trash.

★2643★ Soil and Land Use Technology, Inc. (SALUT)
Box 1153
Columbia, MD 21044
Phone: (301)596-5565
Telex: 892320 WU PUBTLX WSH
Contact: Dr. Arthur A. Theisen, Pres.
Founded: 1975. Data collection, experimental review, and information research regarding the environment, soils, and conservation. Conducts woody and herbaceous biomass evaluations, crop suitability studies, research into urban encroachment on agricultural land, and market feasibility studies on guayule and jojoba. Areas of specialization include agricultural chemicals, new crops, agricultural advancements in developing countries, wastewater treatment using aquatic plants, insect and disease control, and soil behavior with regard to plant growth, tillage, drainage, erosion, trafficability, wastes, and irrigation.

Massachusetts

★2644★ Atmospheric Science Associates
186 Peter Spring Rd.
Concord, MA 01742
Phone: (617)369-5191
Contact: Dr. Hillyer G. Norment, Proprietor
Founded: 1975. Specializes in atmospheric transport, mathematical and computer modeling of atmospheric processes, cloud microphysics, air pollution, aerosols, nuclear fallout, and aircraft icing.

★2645★ Biomarine Inc.
16 E. Main St.
Gloucester, MA 01930
Phone: (617)281-0222
Fax: (617)283-3374
Contact: John Louatt, Food Technologist
Founded: 1973. Conducts quality control testing of seafood products, including chemical, bacteriological, and physical analysis. Evaluates beach waters, well waters, harbor and stream waters, and wastewaters. Projects include research on the reconditioning of distressed seafood. ***Former Name(s):*** Biomarine Research Corporation (1987).

★2646★ Cambridge Analytical Associates
1106 Commonwealth Ave.
Boston, MA 02215
Phone: (617)232-2207
Analytical services include priority pollutant and hazardous waste analysis, groundwater testing and sampling, industrial effluent monitoring, petroleum hydrocarbon fingerprinting, and analysis of toxic organics in air. Provides bioremediation services, including biological treatment of hazardous materials and groundwater, research and development on microbial degradation, feasibility studies, and chemical fate studies and modeling. Also provides consulting services such as site assessments, litigation support and expert witness services, risk assessments, and chemical data interpretation. Maintains a mobile lab for on-site inspection.

★2647★ Certified Engineering & Testing Company
25 Mathewson Dr.
Weymouth, MA 02189
Phone: (617)337-7887
Fax: (617)337-8237

Contact: R. Wayne Crandlemere, Pres. /Technical Dir.
Founded: 1983. Industrial hygiene, environmental engineering, and groundwater contamination abatement, including asbestos services.

★2648★ ENG, Inc.
1430 Massachusetts Ave.
Harvard Sq.
Cambridge, MA 02138
Phone: (617)547-0360
Telex: 294116 (BOSTLX)
Contact: Dr. Trevor P. Castor, Pres.
Founded: 1980. Engineering design and development in energy, including cogeneration, solar, geothermal, and oil and gas technologies; environment, concentrating on waste, contamination, and biodegradation; and biotechnology. Projects include extraction of hydrothermal energy and brine sampling.

★2649★ ESA Laboratories, Inc.
43 Wiggins Ave.
Bedford, MA 01730
Phone: (617)275-0100
Contact: Reginald M. Griffin, V. Pres.
Analyzes water, wastewater, air, soil, biological samples, pollutants, and hazardous wastes.

★2650★ J.H. Clausen, Ph.D, Consulting Chemist
Box 400
Lexington, MA 02173
Phone: (617)862-9391
Contact: J.H. Clausen Ph.D., Consultant
Founded: 1969. Chemical hazards evaluation and control, management and monitoring of hazardous wastes, analysis of air quality effects on personnel and products, toxicology, product safety, process and product development and evaluation, instrument design and evaluation, personal protective equipment evaluation, technical management consulting, development of training and education programs, technical assistance to attorneys, development of computer applications, regulatory agency liaison, and auditing of occupational health, industrial hygiene, and environmental programs.

★2651★ Lycott Environmental Research, Inc.
600 Charlton St.
Southbridge, MA 01550
Phone: (617)765-0101
Contact: Lee D. Lyman, Pres.
Founded: 1971. Environmental studies, water analysis, and lake and pond management. Provides environmental impact assessments, land and water planning appraisals, land reclamation/landfill feasibility studies, and hazardous waste site evaluation. Manufactures aquatic weed harvesting equipment.

★2652★ New England Research, Inc.
15 Sagamore Rd.
Worcester, MA 01605
Phone: (617)752-0346
Contact: Dr. George Camougis, Pres.
Founded: 1970. Offers risk and hazard assessment applied to hazardous materials and wastes, risk management, legal support, consulting, testing, and training.

★2653★ Sigma Research Corporation
234 Littleton Rd.
Suite 2E
Westford, MA 01886
Phone: (508)692-0330
Contact: Dr. Steven Hanna, Contact
Firm providing research and development in the environmental sciences, emphasizing air quality meteorology, meteorological data analysis and modeling, statistical studies, and risk analysis for hazardous air pollutants.

★2654★ Tighe & Bond, Inc.
50 Payson Ave.
Easthampton, MA 01027
Phone: (413)527-5600
Contact: Peter A. Law, Laboratory Manager
Provides environmental analysis of water, wastewater, hazardous wastes, soil, and air. Performs both laboratory and field testing.

★2655★ Water Works Laboratories, Inc.
59 Main St.
Leamington, MA 01453
Phone: (617)534-1444
Toll-Free: 800-522-0081
Contact: Andrew J. Zichell, Pres.
Founded: 1984. Provides water, soil, and air analysis, including testing for metals, organics, and microbial organisms. Other services include well flow testing, site assessments, hazardous and toxic materials analysis, radon testing, and analysis for pesticides and PCBs.

★2656★ WCH Industries, Inc.
14 Felton St.
Waltham, MA 02154
Phone: (617)894-7022
Contact: Bill Clark Harrison, Pres.
Founded: 1978. Provides environmental planning and design, chemical and hazardous waste management services, and research in the areas of engineering control technologies, alternative fuels, and environmental control and assessment technology.

★2657★ Weather Services Corporation
131A Great Rd.
Bedford, MA 01730
Phone: (617)275-8860
Contact: J.E. Wallace, Pres.
Gauges weather/pollution interaction and provides environmental analysis.

★2658★ William W. Walker
1127 Lowell Rd.
Concord, MA 01742
Phone: (508)369-8061
Founded: 1978. Data collection and analysis, experimental review, information research, systems design, and technological forecasting with regard to development and application of water quality assessment methods for reservoirs, lakes, and rivers. Develops mathematical models, designs environmental databases, and applies microcomputers to environmental problems. Projects include research on sewer overflows into river basins, determining effects of algae on soil structure, evaluating impact of Federal Water Pollution Control Act on rivers and harbors, and modeling land and water interaction.

Michigan

★2659★ AAA & Associates, Inc.
1511 Michigan Mutual Bldg.
28 W. Adams
Detroit, MI 48226
Phone: (313)961-4122
Contact: Katherine Banicki, Pres.
Founded: 1980. Provides testing, engineering services, consultation, and inspection, to the construction industry, including environmental engineering, industrial hygiene and asbestos services, chemical product testing, groundwater contamination investigation, specification consultation, soil exploration, steel and metal testing, foundation testing, and caisson inspection. ***Former Name(s):*** AAA Drilling & Testing, Inc. (1987).

★2660★ Analytic & Biological Laboratories, Inc.
29079 Ford Rd.
Garden City, MI 48135
Phone: (313)422-7474
Telex: 234080
Contact: Francis B. McLaughlin, Dir.
Founded: 1956. Chemical, microbiological, mineral, and toxicological analysis; water quality, environmental, and lake and stream eutrophication studies; food and meat testing, fat core sampling, and nutritional labeling; industrial hygiene and in plant sanitation studies; drug screening determinations; animal irritation studies; quality assurance testing; and expert witness testimony.

★2661★ Asbestos Management, Incorporated
36700 S. Huron River Dr.
New Boston, MI 48164
Phone: (313)961-6135
Contact: Benjamin Calo, Gen. Manager
Founded: 1985. Provides surveying, sampling, analysis, abatement, and training programs in asbestos and environmental contamination management. Projects include development of a hazardous waste and chemical analysis laboratory.

★2662★ Brighton Analytical, Inc.
1576 Alloy Pkwy.
Highland, MI 48031
Phone: (313)887-6364
Contact: Gary Wagner, Laboratory Dir.
Environmental analysis, including tests of food and agricultural products, paints, forestry products, water and wastewater, soil, solid hazardous wastes, chemical compounds, fertilizers, and soaps and detergents. Specializes in studies of PCBs, volatile organics, and pesticides.

★2663★ Burmah Technical Services
408 Auburn Ave.
Pontiac, MI 48058
Phone: (313)334-4747
Contact: Douglas Schwartz, Pres.
Provides environmental testing for compliance requirements and research on water, wastewater, and solid waste treatments.

★2664★ Burmah Technical Services, Analytical Laboratories Division
408 Auburn Ave.
Pontiac, MI 48058
Phone: (313)334-4747
Fax: (313)334-1461
Contact: Linda Ercole, Manager
Founded: 1965. Data collection and analysis, field sample collection, and testing and analysis of water, wastewater, and solid waste. ***Former Name(s):*** Clow Corporation, Water Management Division (1986).

★2665★ Clayton Environmental Consultants, Inc.
22345 Roethel Dr.
Novi, MI 48050
Phone: (313)344-1770
Contact: Robert G. Uhler, Pres.
Founded: 1954. Provides consultation in the area of industrial hygiene, including assessment of physical stresses, program audits and surveys, determination of compliance, emergency response, expert testimony, noise

evaluation and control, ventilation system design, and recommendations for corrective action. Analytical laboratory services include biological analyses, hazardous waste characterization, method development and validation, particle and fiber identification, and asbestos, free silica, metals, and organic compounds analyses. Also offers consultative services in the field of hazardous waste management, including alternative treatment studies, environmental impairment liability studies, field sampling, groundwater monitoring and contaminant migration analyses, risk assessments, and hydrogeological and geophysical studies. Conducts environmental audits and air quality studies, including ambient air surveys, dispersion modeling, emission testing and compliance determination, meteorological studies, noncriteria pollutant evaluation and control, and pollution abatement feasibility studies.

★2666★ ENCOTEC
3985 Research Park Dr.
Ann Arbor, MI 48104
Phone: (313)761-1389
Fax: (313)761-1034
Contact: Peter F. Atkins Jr., Pres.
Founded: 1969. Environmental microbiology and chemical testing of air, water, sediment, and soil pollutants and basic research in analytical chemistry methods, hazardous waste disposal, and biological toxicity. Provides support services in wastewater treatment and solid waste management. Conducts ecological and water quality surveys, environmental assessments, mathematical modeling, and facilities evaluations. ***Former Name(s):*** Environmental Control Technology Corporation (1987).

★2667★ Kar Laboratories, Inc.
4425 Manchester Rd.
Kalamazoo, MI 49002-1834
Phone: (616)381-9666
Contact: John Karnemaat, Chief Operating Officer
Founded: 1956. Product development, waste material utilization, and solid waste research.

★2668★ Western Michigan Environmental Services, Inc.
245 E. Lakewood Blvd.
Holland, MI 49423
Phone: (616)396-1209
Contact: Leroy R. Dell, Pres.
Founded: 1976. Environmental analysis, including organic and inorganic testing and analysis of liquids and solids, air sampling, wastewater treatability studies, landfill studies, and soils studies.

Minnesota

★2669★ Aptus
PO Box 550
21750 Cedar Ave.
Lakeville, MN 55044
Phone: (612)469-3475
Fax: (612)469-5140
Contact: Thomas B. Johnson, Chief Exec. Officer
Founded: 1980. Offers testing and consultation on hazardous waste disposal and decontamination and chemical analysis. Research projects include chemical detoxification of polychlorinated biphenyl (PCB) fluids, incineration of RCRA and PCB wastes, and remediation of waste sites. ***Former Name(s):*** National Electric, Inc. (1987).

★2670★ A.W. Research Laboratories
711 Laurel St.
Brainerd, MN 56401
Phone: (218)829-7974
Contact: Alan W. Cibuzar, Chief Exec. Officer
Founded: 1972. Computer enhanced, low altitude remote sensing with applications to lake analysis and mapping, wetland mapping, and hazardous waste spill monitoring. Also provides water quality analysis, ground truth surveys, environmental consulting, land use planning, and water product consulting.

★2671★ BioTrol, Inc.
11 Peavey Rd.
Chaska, MN 55318
Phone: (612)448-2515
Fax: (612)448-6050
Contact: Dr. M. Boyd Burton, Pres. /C.E.O.
Founded: 1985. Provides on-site treatment for the remediation of toxic and hazardous contaminants in water and soil. Principal technology is based on microbiological degradation processes, paired with other compatible remediation approaches.

★2672★ Braun Engineering and Testing, Inc.
6800 S. County Rd. 18
PO Box 35108
Minneapolis, MN 55435-0108
Phone: (612)941-5600
Contact: J.S. Braun P.E., Pres.
Founded: 1957. Soils and foundation engineering, including site evaluations, exploratory drilling and coring, laboratory and field soil testing, specification preparation, expert testimony, site development and failure investigation. Materials testing concentrates on bituminous, concrete, steel, and roofing materials; also conducts speciality testing on windows, brick and mortar, wood and timber, fireproofing insulation, and plastics. Environmental services include environmental engineering, hydrogeologic studies, industrial hygiene testing, environmental chemistry, and hazardous waste analysis.

★2673★ Era Laboratories, Inc.
920 E. First St.
Duluth, MN 55805
Phone: (218)728-4473
Contact: Robert D. Magnuson, Pres., Lab Dir.
Analyzes water, wastes, raw materials, food products, soil, sediments, and air through chemical and microbiological methods.

★2674★ Minnesota Valley Testing Laboratories, Inc.
Center & German Streets
New Ulm, MN 56073
Phone: (507)354-8517
Toll-Free: 800-782-3557
Contact: Tom Berg, Laboratory Dir.
Founded: 1951. Bacteriological and chemical testing, including analysis of hazardous waste, leachates, sludge, priority pollutants, water and wastewater, irrigation runoff, soils, and groundwater. Agricultural testing services include soil studies and analysis of herbicides and pesticide residue, plant nutrients, manure and fertilizer, and feed grain and forages. Food and dairy product testing services include analytical testing of fats and oils, general chemicals, vitamins and minerals, milk, preservatives, and pesticides. Energy testing services include coal, fuel oil, and used oil analysis. Provides assistance for meeting requirements of public health services and other governmental regulatory organizations, including environmental monitoring and sanitary inspections.

★2675★ SERCO Laboratories
1931 W. County Rd. C-2
St. Paul, MN 55113
Phone: (612)636-7173
Contact: Carol Kuehn, Pres.
Founded: 1963. Provides laboratory testing, including analysis of groundwater, drinking water, wastewater, soil, sludge, hazardous wastes, and industrial hygiene samples for regulated and non-regulated compounds. Conducts industrial hygiene surveys and field surveys for pollution control systems and methods, monitors and measures water and wastewater, and chemically analyzes petroleum and coal products and asbestos. Also provides liaison assistance with regulatory agencies.

Mississippi

★2676★ Environmental Protection Systems
Box 20382
Jackson, MS 39209
Phone: (601)922-8242
Fax: (601)922-9163
Contact: Dr. E. Corbin McGriff Jr., Chief Operating Officer
Founded: 1973. Provides research, testing, and engineering services in the areas of environmental engineering, biology, ecology, toxicology, air and water pollution control, industrial hygiene, and hazardous wastes.

★2677★ Water Treatment Services
5760 Gallant Dr.
Jackson, MS 39206
Phone: (601)956-9393
Contact: W. Pat Freeman, Owner
Founded: 1972. Company providing water testing and analysis. ***Former Name(s):*** Analytical Laboratories (1987).

Missouri

★2678★ AZTEC Laboratories
PO Box 7953
6402 Stadium Dr.
Kansas City, MO 64129-1739
Phone: (816)921-3922
Contact: Merrill E. Nissen, Contact
Founded: 1974. Laboratory providing data collection and analysis, systems design, and product development in the areas of chemistry, biochemistry, waste management, and air and water quality.

★2679★ Chem-Staat Laboratories, Inc.
Industrial Park
Doniphan & Francis St.
PO Box 789
Neosho, MO 64850-1721
Phone: (417)451-5973
Contact: Garrett Staat Jr., Pres.
Founded: 1977. Testing and analysis of foods, animal feeds, water and wastewater, pesticides, feed premixes, and hazardous and toxic waste. Specializes in nutritional analysis of such products as soybean meal, cottonseed meal,

tallows, oils, greases, and meat meal. ***Former Name(s):*** Chem-Staat Company (1981).

★2680★ D.W. Ryckman and Associates, Inc.
2208 Welsh Industrial Ct.
Box 27310
St. Louis, MO 63141
Phone: (314)569-0991
Fax: (314)432-2845
Telex: 4312056
Contact: D.W. Ryckman, Pres.
Founded: 1975. Performs analysis, treatability studies, environmental impact assessments, bioassays, and employee health and safety investigations in the areas of sanitary and environmental health engineering, industrial hygiene, toxicology, and oil and hazardous substances control and handling, with emphasis on spill control planning and prevention.

★2681★ Envirodyne Engineers, Inc.
12161 Lackland Rd.
St. Louis, MO 63146
Phone: (314)434-6960
Contact: Paul R. Clifford, V. Pres.
Provides sampling and analysis of organic and inorganic materials, including studies for corrosivity, toxicity, and ignitability. Also provides research applied to environmental control and planning, pollution control and monitoring, hazardous and industrial waste control and monitoring, wastewater sampling, and process development.

★2682★ Environmental Analysis, Inc.
3278 N. Lindbergh Blvd.
Florissant, MO 63033
Phone: (314)921-4488
Laboratory services include sampling of water and wastewater, flow measurements, site surveys, solid and liquid waste analysis, sampling of waste drums and tanks, and contaminiation analysis of soils, lagoons, and wells.

★2683★ RMC Environmental & Analytical Laboratories, Inc.
214 W. Main Plaza
West Plains, MO 65775
Phone: (417)256-1101
Contact: R. Soundararajan, Dir.
Contract research laboratory providing priority pollutant analysis, toxicity characterization of leachates, hazardous waste solidification, incineration research and synthesis, and product quality control studies.

Nebraska

★2684★ Analytical Chemistry Laboratory, Inc.
1336 N. Saddle Creek Rd.
Omaha, NE 68132
Phone: (402)551-2433
Contact: Robert B. Soares, Pres.
Offers analytical services in petroleum, foods and feeds, hazardous substances, ambient air, and water and wastewater.

New Hampshire

★2685★ Advance Water & Filtration Systems
PO Box 102
Rt. 125, Barrington Mall
Barrington, NH 03825-0102
Phone: (603)749-3868
Contact: Lynn Davis-Woods, Business Manager
Founded: 1978. Water and wastewater analysis and radon screening. Also provides water conditioning, filtration, and purification equipment and water and sewage pumping systems. ***Former Name(s):*** Advance Water Systems, Inc. (1986).

★2686★ Enviro Systems, Inc.
PO Box 778
1 Lafayette Rd.
Hampton, NH 03842
Phone: (603)926-3345
Contact: Dr. Richard Sugatt, Senior Toxicologist
Founded: 1982. Environmental chemistry, including marine and freshwater toxicity testing for government regulatory compliance. Provides consultation in related areas.

★2687★ Normandeau Associates, Inc.
Nashua Rd.
Bedford, NH 03103
Phone: (603)472-5191
Contact: Pamela S. Hall, Pres.
Founded: 1970. Environmental compliance audits, environmental assessments and impact statements, hydropower environmental studies, air quality control, hydrographic and coastal surveys, aquatic and terrestrial ecological studies, and expert witness testimony.

New Jersey

★2688★ Alternative Ways, Inc.
1000 Essex Ave.
Bellmawr, NJ 08031
Phone: (609)933-3300
Contact: John R. Luxford, Exec. Dir.
Provides asbestos analysis, monitoring, and consulting.

★2689★ Bio/Dynamics Inc.
Box 2360
Mettlers Rd.
East Millstone, NJ 08875-2360
Phone: (201)873-2550
Fax: (201)873-3992
Telex: 844597
Contact: Dr. Geoffrey K. Hogan, Pres.
Founded: 1961. Toxicology and safety evaluation studies on materials produced or used by clients, including services in pharmacokinetics, metabolic and analytical chemistry, priority pollutants, histopathology, and facilities management.

★2690★ Century Laboratories
1501 Grandview Ave.
Box 248
Thorofare, NJ 08086
Phone: (609)848-3939
Contact: Craig McCaffrey, Marketing and Sales Manager
Founded: 1978. Environmental testing and analysis laboratory.

★2691★ Century Testing Laboratories, Inc.
PO Box 248
1501 Grandview Ave.
Thorofare, NJ 08086
Phone: (609)848-3939
Contact: John P. Johnson, V. Pres.
Hazardous waste testing, including ignitability, corrosivity, reactivity, and EP toxicity and water and wastewater analysis. Provides field sampling.

★2692★ Chyun Associates
267 Wall St.
Princeton, NJ 08540
Phone: (609)924-5151
Contact: Michael Wright, Dir.
Laboratory providing environmental sampling and analysis and industrial hygiene services in water, soils, air, waste, and chemical products.

★2693★ Environmental Testing Laboratories, Inc.
412 Rte. 9
Lanoka Harbor, NJ 08734
Phone: (609)693-3100
Contact: Walter Holm Jr., Lab Dir.
Founded: 1979. Environmental testing and analysis laboratory. ***Former Name(s):*** Central Jersey Water Testing (1979).

★2694★ E.W. Saybolt & Company, Inc.
400 Swenson Dr.
Kenilworth, NJ 07033
Phone: (201)245-3100
Contact: Joseph McCabe III, Pres.
Tests and analyzes petroleum products and petrochemicals, including jet fuels, gasoline, and crude, diesel, and fuel oils. Performs environmental monitoring of water and wastewaters and analyzes chemical compounds, fertilizers, feeds, and pesticides.

★2695★ J.R. Henderson Labs, Inc.
123 Seaman Ave.
Beachwood, NJ 08722
Phone: (201)341-1211
Contact: Margaret Ellis, Lab Manager
Founded: 1969. Analytical and research and development activities include compliance monitoring, Resource Conservation Recovery Act testing, groundwater sampling and monitoring, soil sampling and analysis, and chemical analysis of raw wastes. Provides field sampling.

★2696★ Laboratory Resources Inc.
363 Old Hook Rd.
Westwood, NJ 07675
Phone: (201)666-6644
Contact: Carol A. Price, Manager
Firm providing environmental sampling and analysis of drinking water, wastewater, sludge, and soils.

★2697★ Northeastern Analytical Corporation
234 Rte. 70
Medford, NJ 08055
Phone: (609)654-1441
Contact: William Dolan, Pres.
Sampling, analysis, and monitoring of asbestos, air samples, soil, volatile substances, dredge spoils, heavy metals, PCBs, pesticides, stack emissions, and hazardous wastes. ***Former Name(s):*** Rossnagle & Associates, Inc.

★2698★ Pool Ocean Company
PO Box 351
Cape May, NJ 08204
Phone: (609)884-8263
Contact: Joseph Poole, Pres.
Founded: 1986. Research and design innovation technology relating to envrionmental

conservation. Studies focus on air and water purification systems, oil spill control, solid waste management, recyclable material recovery systems, and toxic chemical disposal and storage systems. Long-range projects include research on coastal water purification, development of methods for compaction and recylcling of solid wastes, design of underground trash containers and trash vacuuming systems, and development of a glass-lined container for toxic chemicals.

★2699★ Princeton Testing Laboratory
PO Box 3108
Princeton, NJ 08543
Phone: (609)452-9050
Contact: William F. Pickup, Pres.
Industrial hygiene services include asbestos evaluation, hazardous site evaluation, building and plant surveys, and stationary source testing. Environmental analysis services concentrate on drinking water analysis, effluent characterization and monitoring, groundwater quality and monitoring, and analysis of hazardous waste, air, sludge, trace metals, pesticides and herbicides, PCBs, and priority pollutants. Microbiology services focus on evaluation of potable water, industrial waste, sewage, food products, cosmetics, pharmaceuticals, paper, beverages, and air; also sterility testing, environmental testing, shelf life studies, preservative efficacy, and antibiotic microbial assay. Through its Inorganic Chemistry and Precious Metal Analysis Division, provides analysis of precious metals, nonferrous alloys, steel ores, and minerals.

★2700★ Quality Control Laboratory, Inc.
243 White Horse Pike
Audubon, NJ 08106
Phone: (609)428-1303
Contact: Lee Greenwald, Pres. / Dir.
Provides environmental testing, including analysis of food, water, groundwater, and wastewater.

★2701★ Recon Systems, Inc.
Route 202 N.
PO Box 460
Three Bridges, NJ 08887
Phone: (201)782-5900
Contact: Dr. Norman J. Weinstein, Pres.
Founded: 1969. Offers field sampling, chemical analysis, and research services in the areas of hazardous wastes, contaminated site cleanup, waste oils, air pollution control, industrial water pollution control, and municipal solid wastes. Facilities include soil boring, well monitoring and installation, stack/air testing, and indoor air sampling equipment.

★2702★ Townley Research and Consulting, Inc.
1750 W. Front St.
Plainfield, NJ 07063
Phone: (201)757-1137
Contact: T.R. Komline, Pres.
Founded: 1961. Analytical chemistry and water pollution control, including testing on potable water, wastewater treatment, solid waste disposal, and industrial hygiene practices.

New Mexico

★2703★ Controls for Environmental Pollution, Inc.
1925 Rosina
Box 5351
Santa Fe, NM 87502
Phone: (505)982-9841
Fax: (505)982-9841EX
Toll-Free: 800-545-2188
Contact: James J. Mueller, Pres.
Founded: 1970. Identification and monitoring of possible pollution sources using radiochemical, radiobiological, microbiological, organic and inorganic chemistry, bioassay, and gamma spectral analysis. Provides sample collection, baseline studies, quality assurance services, and regulatory compliance testing, including determination of nuclides in water, air, vegetation, and milk; soil and overburden testing; hazardous waste analysis; sanitation analysis of drinking and wastewater; and aquatrace studies for uranium tailings.

★2704★ Kramer & Associates
121-C Eubank, N.E.
Albuquerque, NM 87123
Phone: (505)292-4084
Contact: Gary Kramer, Owner
Founded: 1973. Provides environmental research, systems design, and testing services, including analysis of air and water pollutants and hazardous wastes. Long-term projects focus on removal of nitrogen from heat packing wastewaters and removal of oils from washback wastewater. Maintains an air and water testing laboratory.

New York

★2705★ Beak Consultants, Inc.
12072 Main Rd.
Akron, NY 14001
Phone: (716)542-5544
Contact: Dr. James B. McClaren, Office Manager
Founded: 1968. Conducts site surveys, environmental impact assessments, industrial trouble-shooting for industrial plant problems related to the environment or plant-processing procedures, energy conservation research, data processing and management, and socioeconomic research and planning in the areas of energy and the environment, agriculture, physical and earth sciences, engineering and technology, and computer science.

★2706★ Beltran Associates, Inc.
1133 E. 35th St.
Brooklyn, NY 11210
Phone: (718)338-3311
Telex: 125031
Contact: E.V. Beltran, Pres.
Founded: 1946. Testing and analysis, data collection and analysis, experimental review and synthesis, systems design, and information/literature research in the areas of air pollution control and heat and material recovery.

★2707★ Buffalo Testing Laboratories, Inc.
902 Kenmore Ave.
Buffalo, NY 14216
Phone: (716)873-2302
Contact: Edward J. Kris, Pres.
Founded: 1927. Chemical analysis, concrete and soil testing, metallurgical analysis, physical testing, and biological and bacteriological analysis. Provides air and water pollution source sampling, asbestos testing, and lead-in-paint analysis. Conducts legal investigations and offers expert testimony.

★2708★ Earth Investigations, Ltd.
31 S. Grove St.
East Aurora, NY 14052
Phone: (716)655-1717
Contact: John Gratz, Pres.
Founded: 1987. Conducts environmental contaminant investigations, including soil surveys, lagoon sampling, wastewater treatment and testing, gasoline and petroleum site investigations, well sampling and monitoring, and remedial planning. ***Former Name(s):*** Earth Dimensions Engineers (1987).

★2709★ Ecology and Environment, Inc.
Buffalo Corporate Center
368 Pleasantview Dr.
Lancaster, NY 14068-1316
Phone: (716)684-8060
Fax: (716)632-4511
Telex: 6502696050
Contact: Gerhard Neumaier, Pres.
Founded: 1970. Offers research and consultation on air, water, groundwater, soil, and noise pollution control and hazardous materials and waste disposal management. Services include field investigations and remedial action engineering for hazardous waste sites, biological and chemical laboratory analysis, environmental impact assessments, bioassays, hazards and risks analysis, socioeconomic studies, hydrogeological evaluations, oil spill prevention and control surveys, spill emergency response, asbestos removal consultation and management, underground storage tank studies, and mixed nuclear and chemical waste management.

★2710★ EcoTest Laboratories, Inc.
377 Sheffield Ave.
North Babylon, NY 11703
Phone: (516)422-5777
Contact: Thomas Powell, V. Pres.
Founded: 1977. Provides environmental analysis, including wastewater and pollutant testing.

★2711★ Environment/One Corporation
PO Box 773
2773 Balltown Rd.
Schenectady, NY 12301
Phone: (518)346-6161
Telex: 382044 (EONE NY)
Contact: William R. Browne Ph.D., Consultant
Founded: 1968. Specializes in environmental analytical methods and development of instrumentation for detecting and counting submicron particles.

★2712★ Galson Technical Services, Inc.
6601 Kirkville Rd.
East Syracuse, NY 13057
Phone: (315)432-0506
Contact: Eva Galson, Dir.
Environmental analysis of air, water, and waste.

★2713★ H 2 M Labs, Inc.
575 Broad Hollow Rd.
Melville, NY 11747
Phone: (516)694-3040
Telex: 5166944122
Contact: Robert G. Holzmacher, Pres.
Founded: 1933. Provides chemical analysis of trace metals and organic and inorganic materials, including priority pollutants, drinking water, hazardous waste, dredge spoil, sewage and sludge, and leachates. Also provides

treatability studies, long-term monitoring programs, ambient and process air monitoring, protocol and methods development, and pilot plant studies. ***Former Name(s):*** H2M Corporation, Inc.

★2714★ Lawler, Matusky and Skelly Engineers
1 Blue Hill Plaza
Pearl River, NY 10965
Phone: (914)735-8300
Contact: Michael J. Skelly Ph.D., Partner
Founded: 1965. Data collection, experimentation, information research, systems design, and testing and analysis in the fields of environmental impact, industrial waste treatment and facilities, water supply, ecology, and hazardous waste. Services include facility siting studies, sewage treatment facilities design, model studies, groundwater investigations, and development of environmental decision-making tools for regulatory agencies. ***Former Name(s):*** Quirk, Lawler & Matusky Engineers.

★2715★ New York Testing Laboratories, Inc.
75 Urban Ave.
Westbury, NY 11590
Phone: (516)334-7770
Fax: (516)334-7720
Telex: 5102220283
Contact: Glenn Sherman, Quality Assurance Manager
Founded: 1919. Pollution control, including source testing and analysis, ambient air and toxic fume surveys and controls, asbestos health risk surveys, and bioassay and toxicity studies of industrial waste, municipal waste, and dredge materials. Provides nondestructive testing, environmental testing, materials evaluation, and consumer testing, including product evaluation and development and product liability assurance. Consulting engineering services include failure analysis, accident investigation, and expert court testimony.

★2716★ Nytest Environmental Inc.
60 Seaview Blvd.
Port Washington, NY 11050
Phone: (516)625-5500
Contact: John Gaspari, Pres.
Provides analysis and consultation relating to the identification, quantification, and safe management of hazardous wastes. Services include site evaluation and sampling, in compliance with Environmental Protection Agency standards, and energy conservation and development. Also involved with reclamation of energy products from waste materials.

★2717★ Parsons and Whittemore, Inc.
666 Third Ave.
New York, NY 10017
Phone: (212)972-2000
Contact: Arthur L. Schwartz, Chief Operating Officer
Reclamation of resources from waste materials, solid waste reprocessing, and recycling of metals.

★2718★ Pavlo Engineering Company, Inc.
500 8th Ave.
New York, NY 10018
Phone: (212)239-0250
Contact: Dr. E.L. Pavlo, Chief Engineer
Founded: 1954. Water and wastewater treatment, industrial waste treatment, drainage design, transportation planning, commercial and marine structure studies, construction management, on-site inspection, and road, highway, and bridge design.

★2719★ Volumetric Techniques Ltd.
317 Bernice Dr.
Bayport, NY 11708
Phone: (516)472-4848
Contact: Valerie Sternig, Gen. Manager
Environmental analysis and impact studies, including chemical, biological, spectrographic, and chromatographic investigations of petroleum products, metals and alloys, chemical products, pharmaceuticals, asbestos, air, water, soil, and hazardous wastes. Also provides site investigation, field monitoring, and formula development.

North Carolina

★2720★ Aquasystems, Inc.
PO Box 3795
Greenville, NC 27836
Phone: (919)757-3782
Contact: Richard Stephenson, Pres.
Founded: 1977. Provides environmental research and testing, including analysis of drinking water, groundwater, wastewater, soils, and sediments. Conducts geological, geographical, and microbiological research, focusing on atmosphere and climate, wind erosion and dunes, streams and estuaries, oceans, ponds and resevoirs, environmental impact, environmental health, and environmental quality. Environmental planning services include aesthetic and historical preservation studies, ecological planning, resource development and management evaluation, parking and traffic studies, leisure and cultural resource assessments, and growth management studies. Also offers technical support and environmental design services. Maintains certified analytical laboratories. ***Former Name(s):*** Stephenson Distributing Company (1978).

★2721★ EN-CAS Analytical Laboratories
2359 Farrington Point Dr.
Winston-Salem, NC 27107
Phone: (919)785-3252
Contact: Dr. Charles Ganz, Chief Operating Officer
Founded: 1975. Chemical testing and analysis, specializing in the environment and worker exposure. Conducts residue assays of pesticides, herbicides, fungicides, and related crop and soil treatment chemicals.

★2722★ Industrial & Environmental Analytst, Inc.
PO Box 12846
Research Triangle Park, NC 27709
Phone: (919)467-9919
Contact: Lisa S. Treadaway, Marketing Representative
Environmental and chemical monitoring, testing, research, and management, including regulatory compliance testing, groundwater monitoring, and analysis of water, wastewater, waste and hazardous substances, and pollutants.

★2723★ Research Triangle Laboratories, Inc.
1612 Carpenter Fletcher Rd.
Durham, NC 27713
Phone: (919)544-5775
Fax: (919)544-3770
Contact: Carol Ballard, Sec.
Founded: 1985. Environmental, water, and hazardous waste testing. Also provides drug screening.

★2724★ Roberts Environmental Services Inc.
Mako Building, Hwy. 24
PO Box 308
Swansboro, NC 28584
Phone: (919)393-6167
Contact: Dan Roberts, Pres.
Founded: 1986. Firm providing testing and analysis and information services on hazardous materials.

★2725★ Southern Testing and Research Laboratories, Inc.
607 Park Ave.
Box 1849
Wilson, NC 28793
Phone: (919)237-4175
Contact: Kenneth W. Boyer Ph.D., Pres.
Founded: 1961. Analytical chemistry and bacteriology with studies focusing on water, food, feed, fertilizer, soil, petroleum products, hazardous wastes, and pesticides. Performs sampling and analysis of environment for regulatory compliance of pollutants, environmental impact studies, and general plant process evaluations. Also provides nutritional labeling and shelf-life studies. ***Former Name(s):*** Agricultural Products Laboratory.

North Dakota

★2726★ Astro-Chem Services, Inc.
4102 Second Ave. W.
PO Box 972
Williston, ND 58802-0972
Phone: (701)572-7355
Contact: Charles H. McCauley, Pres.
Founded: 1971. Provides analysis of oil, water, gas, coal, soils, grain, and corrosion coupons and rings. Services include groundwater testing; fuel contamination testing; irrigation, livestock, and drinking water analysis; hay, silage, and feed testing; plant tissue analysis; fertilizer analysis; and metallurgical testing.

Ohio

★2727★ Alloway Testing
1325 N. Cole St.
Lima, OH 45801
Phone: (419)223-1362
Contact: John R. Hoffman, Pres.
Founded: 1982. Provides environmental testing and data collection, industrial quality control services, and methods development, including water and wastewater analysis, solid and hazardous waste characterization, flow monitoring, industrial and municipal pretreatment sampling and analysis, oxygen transfer testing, and river, lake, and stream monitoring. Also provides consulting services.

★2728★ Alpha Solarco, Inc.
11534 Gondola
Cincinnati, OH 45241
Phone: (513)771-8086

Contact: Edward Schmidt, Pres.
Founded: 1978. Basic and applied research in solar energy applications.

★2729★ Ameritech Inc.
Hines Hill Rd.
6855 Industrial Pkwy.
Hudson, OH 44236-1158
Phone: (216)656-5000
Contact: James P. Heffernan, Laboratory Manager
Founded: 1979. Performs testing and analysis and product development in the areas of oil reclamation, water purification, rust inhibiting fluids, oxidation resistance, thermal stability, heat exchange characteristics, and pyhsical property determinations as they apply to industrial fluids. Also provides feasibility studies of recycling used industrial lubricants and products. Projects include organics removal in aqueous systems, dewaxing of petroleum products, solvent extraction, and ultrafiltration.

★2730★ Aqua Tech Environmental Consultants, Inc.
181 S. Main
Marion, OH 43302
Phone: (614)382-5991
Contact: Jeffrey A. Smith, Laboratory Manager
Founded: 1975. Environmental testing laboratory. ***Former Name(s):*** Macola, Inc. (1981).

★2731★ Barnebey-Cheney Company
835 N. Cassady Ave.
Columbus, OH 43219
Phone: (614)258-9501
Contact: John Stagon, Application Engineer
Founded: 1919. Data collection and analysis and product testing and development in the area of air purification and air purification media.

★2732★ Bowser-Morner, Inc.
420 Davis Ave.
Box 51
Dayton, OH 45401
Phone: (513)253-8805
Fax: (513)253-2016
Contact: Steven M. Bowser, Chief Exec. Officer
Founded: 1911. Civil, geotechnical, geological, hydrological, environmental, mechanical, and mining engineering, including construction observation and testing, subsurface exploration, hazardous waste disposal and remedial actions, and facility and system design. Other areas of focus are analytical chemistry, biology, metallurgy, and mechanical and electro-mechanical technology, including environmental analysis and monitoring, corrosion studies, failure analysis, product evaluation, and litigation support. ***Former Name(s):*** Kurz Laboratories (1925); Bowser-Morner Testing Laboratories, Inc. (1985).

★2733★ Contract Laboratories Associates, Inc.
7142 Erie St.
Sylvania, OH 43560
Phone: (419)882-1643
Contact: K.F. Sporek, Pres.
Founded: 1969. Tests air and water samples for pollution. Techniques include chemical and elemental analysis, colorimetry, gas chromatography, and radiochemistry.

★2734★ Coshocton Environmental Testing Service, Inc.
PO Box 723
Coshocton, OH 43812
Phone: (614)622-3328
Contact: E. Christopher Broderick, V. Pres.
Chemical analysis and pretreatment of wastewater and solid waste and monitoring of groundwater.

★2735★ F.C. Broeman Company
830 Melbourne Ave.
Cincinnati, OH 45229
Phone: (513)751-1222
Founded: 1904. Environmental and industrial testing of water, wastewater, industrial effluents, priority pollutants, hazardous waste, petroleum products, coal and coke, and meat and foodstuffs. PCB analysis, microbiological testing, marine survey sampling, and bacterial analysis are among services offered.

★2736★ Jones & Henry Laboratories, Inc.
2567 Tracy Rd.
Northwood, OH 43619
Phone: (419)666-0411
Contact: Fred W. Doering, Pres.
Founded: 1971. Environmental sampling and testing laboratory specializing in water, wastewater, groundwater, industrial wastes, and PBCs.

★2737★ PEI Associates, Inc.
11499 Chester Rd.
Cincinnati, OH 45246
Phone: (513)782-4700
Contact: George Jutze, Pres.
Founded: 1965. Hazardous waste management, air monitoring, environmental studies, and field sampling and laboratory analysis. ***Former Name(s):*** Pedco Environmental, Inc. (1984).

★2738★ Pollution Control Science, Inc.
6015 Manning Rd.
Miamisburg, OH 45342
Phone: (513)866-5908
Contact: Phillip L. Hayden Ph.D., Pres.
Environmental and occupational health services, including drinking water analysis, groundwater monitoring, wastewater testing and process evaluation, industrial hygiene, air source sampling, solid and hazardous waste sampling and analysis, and pollution control certification.

★2739★ Stilson Laboratories, Inc.
170 N. High St.
Columbus, OH 43215
Phone: (614)228-4385
Contact: Wilson T. Walker, Pres.
Founded: 1972. Testing, analysis, and assessment of environmental problems, including evaluation of process and equipment performance, planning data for new designs, reports to regulatory agencies, source testing, abatement equipment testing, ambient air surveys, microbiological assessment, and sampling and analysis of stack and compressed gases, asbestos, formaldehyde, polychlorinated biphenyls, organohalides in drinking water, and pesticides.

★2740★ Systech Corporation
245 N. Valley Rd.
Xenia, OH 45385
Phone: (513)372-8077
Telex: 516724
Contact: Thomas Wittmann, Pres.
Founded: 1969. Air, water, solid, and hazardous waste testing and analysis, including waste audits, technology definition, feasibility studies, construction supervision, acceptance testing, personnel training, planning, waste to fuel research, and research on unconventional fuel combustion, small-scale resource recovery, and hazardous waste disposal. ***Former Name(s):*** Systems Technology Corporation (1980).

★2741★ Wadsworth/Alert Laboratories, Inc.
1600 Fourth Street, S.E. Box 208
Canton, OH 44701
Phone: (216)497-9396
Fax: (216)497-0772
Contact: Jack Custer, Pres.
Founded: 1938. Environmental sampling, testing, and consulting, including groundwater monitoring, priority pollutants analysis, hazardous waste site assessment, waste characterizations and product surveys, drinking water monitoring, polychlorinated biphenyls surveys, asbestos determination, industrial products and raw materials analysis, pretreatment program analysis, and compliance testing. Also provides mobile laboratory field services. ***Former Name(s):*** Wadsworth Testing Laboratories, Inc. (1986).

Oklahoma

★2742★ Engineering Enterprises, Inc.
1225 W. Main St.
Suite 215
Norman, OK 73069
Phone: (405)329-8300
Fax: (405)366-8722
Telex: 333668
Contact: John H. Marsh, Pres.
Founded: 1969. Water reuse and recycling, wastewater treatment and reuse, hydrocarbon recovery, ground water quality, and irrigated agriculture.

Oregon

★2743★ Bend Research, Inc.
64550 Research Rd.
Bend, OR 97701
Phone: (503)382-4100
Fax: (503)382-2713
Telex: 517787 BEND RESEARCH
Contact: Walter C. Babcock, Pres.
Founded: 1975. Specializes in membrane separations, controlled-release, and bioprocessing applications of membranes and thin films. Develops high-technology products based on synthetic membranes and thin films. Projects include development of reverse-osmosis systems for desalting water, purifying industrial wastes, and concentrating food; a coupled transport process for extracting and concentrating metals and other chemicals from solution; processes for the separation of various gasses; and techniques for separating and purifying products in biotechnology processes.

★2744★ Century West Engineering Corporation
PO Box 1174
Bend, OR 97709
Phone: (503)388-3500
Contact: J. Ned Dempsey, Pres.
Firm providing chemical analysis, environmental studies and engineering, hazardous waste management, priority pollutant analysis, hazardous substance list analysis, miscellaneous organic and inorganic analysis, and water quality analysis.

★2745★ Neilson Research Corporation
446 Highland Dr.
Medford, OR 97504
Phone: (503)770-5678
Contact: John W.T. Neilson, Chm.
Founded: 1980. Testing and analysis of waterborne bacteria, environmental study programs related to lakes and streams, and market research for advertising service-based companies. ***Former Name(s):*** Neilson Research Analytical Laboratory (1985).

★2746★ Soils Testing Lab, Inc.
130 W. Ninth St.
Medford, OR 97502
Phone: (503)779-2833
Contact: Robert Blanton P.E., Pres. and Gen. Manager
Founded: 1970. Conducts environmental assessment tests to determine the stability of sites, soils, and slopes for building construction. Provides environmental surveys, product development for building construction, analysis of building materials related to specifications, monitoring of water and wastewater, studies of characteristics of aqueous effluents, and studies of physical and biological parameters of land areas for environmental assessment.

★2747★ Water Analysis & Consulting, Inc.
304 Blair Blvd.
Eugene, OR 97402
Phone: (503)485-8404
Contact: Rory E. White, Senior Analyst
Founded: 1975. Water, wastewater, and other environmental, microbiological, and chemical analyses; systems design; and data collection and analysis.

Pennsylvania

★2748★ ASW Environmental Consultants, Inc.
847 N. Gilmore St.
Allentown, PA 18103
Phone: (215)434-1870
Contact: Michael C. Demyan, Manager
Founded: 1978. Provides environmental testing of air, water, waste, and noise. Industrial and commercial product testing includes studies of metal alloys, fuels and solvents, reagent chemicals, and construction materials, especially concrete, cement, lime, and aggregates. Also provides legal testing, consultation, and testimony.

★2749★ BCM Engineers
One Plymouth Meeting Mall
Plymouth Meeting, PA 19462
Phone: (215)825-3800
Fax: (215)834-8236
Contact: J.J. Jablonski, Pres. and Chm. of the Board
Founded: 1890. Environmental assessments, river basin studies, energy and solid waste tests, and air, water, and solid/hazardous waste management. ***Former Name(s):*** Betz-Converse-Murdoch, Inc.

★2750★ Bioscience Management, Inc.
BFTC, S. Mountain Dr.
Bethleham, PA 18015
Phone: (215)861-6911
Contact: R. Bleam, Laboratory Dir.
Provides biological, chemical, chromatographic, spectrographic, and environmental impact and simulation testing on chemical and biological samples, including remedial investigations of hazardous materials sites. Specializes in biological investigations and provides toxicity testing and biodegradation studies of slurries and sludges.

★2751★ C D S Laboratories, Inc.
Road 21, Box 234
Loganton, PA 17747
Phone: (717)725-3411
Contact: C.D. Sweeny, Manager
Founded: 1982. Tests, analyzes, and collects data on liquid and hazardous solid wastes.

★2752★ Conti Testing Laboratories
3190 Industrial Blvd.
Bethel Park, PA 15102
Phone: (412)854-3751
Contact: Patricia A. Otroba, Pres.
Founded: 1980. Provides consulting and analysis in the areas of coal, water, and alternative fuels; feasibility studies on coal reclamation projects; and research on new coal techniques.

★2753★ Environmental Laboratory for Chemical Studies
320 William Pitt Way
Pittsburgh, PA 15238
Phone: (412)826-5320
Contact: Samuel M. Creeger, Dir.
Laboratory providing biological, chemical, chromatographic, and spectrographic analysis geared toward environmental impact of pesticides.

★2754★ Free-Col Laboratories
PO Box 557
Cotton Rd.
Meadville, PA 16335-0557
Contact: Dr. J. Richard Wohler, Dir.
Provides testing and consultation in the areas of food science and environmental and occupational health. Services include aquatic bioassay, industrial hygiene surveys, smokestack emissions testing, asbestos determination, coal overburden evaluation, water quality analysis, and agricultural products testing.

★2755★ Hedenburg and Venable
6111 5 Ave.
Pittsburgh, PA 15232
Phone: (412)441-8045
Contact: Emerson Venable, Chief Operating Officer
Founded: 1951. Disaster and hazardous situation investigation, including fire prevention, air pollution, and hazardous waste analysis.

★2756★ JACA Corporation
550 Pinetown Rd.
Fort Washington, PA 19034
Phone: (215)643-5466
Contact: James A. Commins, Pres.
Founded: 1970. Provides research and consulting in the areas of environmental science and engineering, including water resource and land use planning and management, surface mine reclamation, air and water pollution control, solid waste disposal, and industrial health and safety. Performs economic, financial, and regulatory impact analysis.

★2757★ Lancy Environmental Services
PO Box 419
Pittsburgh, PA 15230
Phone: (412)772-0044
Contact: Linda Shingleton, Customer Service
Firm providing chemical, chromatographic, and spectrographic environmental analysis and sampling, including testing of water and groundwater, wastes, and soil for trace metals, PCBs, pesticides and herbicides, and other organic pollutants.

★2758★ Mateson Chemical Corporation
1025 E. Montgomery Ave.
Philadelphia, PA 19125
Phone: (215)423-3200
Contact: Jean F. Mateson, Chief Operating Officer
Performs evaluations of health effects of new building materials and construction on occupants, including evaluations of air quality and analysis of toxic fumes and irritant gases.

★2759★ Microbac Laboratories Inc.
4580 McKnight Rd.
Pittsburgh, PA 15237
Phone: (412)931-5851
Contact: A. Warne Boyce, Pres. and Chief Exec. Officer
Founded: 1958. Bacteriological testing of food and dairy products, pharmaceuticals, and aflatoxins; chemical analysis of trace metals, organic matter, petroleum, oil, and coal; asbestos determination; food chemistry; hazardous wastes analysis; priority pollutants analysis; testing, analysis, and treatment of waste, wastewater, and air; quality control; industrial hygiene and sanitation surveys; and combustion efficiency evaluation. ***Former Name(s):*** Seaway Industrial Laboratories, Inc. (1984).

★2760★ Nova Analytical Labs, Inc.
PO Box 888
Latrobe, PA 15650
Phone: (412)537-8686
Contact: Paul Baker, Lab Manager
Referee analysis of trace metals, metal assay, waste characterization, water analysis, and ceramic and glass analysis geared toward research and development, compliance, and quality control.

★2761★ Pennrun Corporation
150 William Pitt Way
Pittsburgh, PA 15238
Phone: (412)826-5300
Contact: Kathy Rygle Martin, Laboratory Dir.
Environmental analysis, including services in water, wastewater, and hazardous waste. Materials and products tested include paints and allied products, bituminous materials, nonmetallic ores, soil, petroleum products, chemicals, and biologics.

★2762★ Puricons, Inc.
101 Quaker Ave.
Malvern, PA 19355
Phone: (215)644-5488
Contact: Dr. Sallie A. Fisher, Pres.
Founded: 1968. Engineering of methods for water analysis and development of high-purity water treatment systems. Specialists in ion exchange.

★2763★ RMC-Environmental Services
R.D. 1 Fricks Lock Rd.
Pottstown, PA 19464
Phone: (215)326-9662
Contact: Paul L. Harmon, V. Pres.
Founded: 1977. Provides environmental impact studies with specialization in aquatic and terrestrial ecology, analytic chemistry, geology, water quality, and aquatic toxicology. Conducts environmental assessments, wetland studies, habitat evaluation, instream flow studies, fish and wildlife mitigation plans, bioassay toxicity testing, effluent characterization and monitoring, statistical

analysis and data management, expert testimony and litigation support, and groundwater sampling and analysis. Provides consultation for industrial facility siting, dredge and fill operations, hydroelectric development or relicensing, and highway, pipeline, and transmission line rights-of-way. Offers analysis of plant and animal communities including rare, endangered, or threatened species. Investigations focus on resource inventories, population studies and estimates, and land use surveys. ***Former Name(s):*** Radiation Management Corporation (1969).

★2764★ Roan Industries, Inc.
7278 Park Dr.
Bath, PA 18014
Phone: (215)837-7707
Contact: Charles E. Buchanon, V. Pres.
Founded: 1976. Grindability studies of portland cement, waste fuel burning, and environmental testing.

★2765★ Rogers, Golden and Halpern, Inc.
1216 Arch St.
Philadelphia, PA 19107
Phone: (215)563-4220
Contact: Fritts Golden, Pres.
Founded: 1975. Environmental impact analysis, land use analysis and planning, field testing, and waste management.

★2766★ Roy F. Weston, Inc.
Weston Way
West Chester, PA 19380
Phone: (215)692-3030
Telex: 835348
Contact: Roy F. Weston, Chief Exec. Officer
Founded: 1951. Environmental pollution control, process development, treatability research, industrial hygiene monitoring, regulations compliance reporting, quality control, and training in sample collection, analysis, and interpretation. Provides analytical testing of air, water, wastewater, solid and hazardous wastes, pesticides, toxic substances, soils, and fuels.

★2767★ Spotts, Stevens and McCoy, Inc.
30 Noble St.
PO Box 6527
Reading, PA 19611
Phone: (215)376-4595
Contact: L.J. McCoy P.E., Pres. and C.E.O.
Laboratory services include environmental testing of hazardous wastes, wastewater, solid waste, and priority pollutants. Industrial hygiene services focus on asbestos, organics, solvents, vapors, particulates, and metals. Conducts products testing relating to coatings, solvent residuals, corrosion, and methods development.

Puerto Rico

★2768★ Caribtec Laboratories, Inc.
G.PO Box 2242
San Juan, PR 00936
Phone: (809)754-7622
Telex: 3859397
Contact: Joseph G. Sandza Ph.D., Pres.
Chemical analysis of water, air, foods, soils, raw materials, and finished products. Environmental services include environmental impact statements, effluent monitoring, air monitoring, and bioassays. Consulting services for Puerto Rican plants include site selection, regulatory requirements, and agency contracts.

Rhode Island

★2769★ Environmental Science Services (ESS)
235 Promenade St.
Providence, RI 02908
Phone: (401)421-0398
Fax: (401)421-0396
Contact: Richard C. Hittinger, Pres.
Founded: 1979. Provides environmental monitoring of air, water, wastes, and soils; environmental impact studies; stack testing; groundwater modeling; and oceanographic, lake, and estuarine studies

★2770★ New England Testing Laboratory, Inc. (NETLAB)
1254 Douglas Ave.
North Providence, RI 02904
Phone: (401)353-3420
Contact: Robert T. Legere, V. Pres., Operations
Founded: 1957. Environmental testing, analysis, and consulting. Provides chemical analysis of wastewater, hazardous waste, priority pollutants, drinking water, plating solutions, metals, food, drugs, plastics, paint, ink, oils, solvents, and paper. Microbiology studies focus on water and foods, bioburden and pyrogen analysis, marine biology, and consumer liability. Performs physical testing of materials, specializing in tensile energy absorption, brightness, opacity, gloss, tear strength, emulsification, distillation, flashpoint, adhesion, construction analysis, load, and compression.

★2771★ R.I. Analytical Laboratories Inc.
231 Elm St.
Warwick, RI 02852
Phone: (401)467-2452
Contact: Robert L. Hoffman P.E., Operations Manager
Environmental laboratory offering analysis of water, waste, and hazardous waste for pesticides, PCBs, trace chemical residues, and metals.

South Carolina

★2772★ Environmental & Chemical Sciences
PO Box 1393
Aiken, SC 29801
Phone: (803)652-2206
Contact: Dr. James O'Hara, Contact
Founded: 1981. Provides research and testing in the areas of analytic chemistry and environmental chemistry, and environmental toxicology, with emphasis on aquatic, terrestrial, and marine ecosystems. Conducts fisheries studies, toxicity reduction identifications, wetlands assessments, and environmental assessments of thermal and chemical discharge on natural systems. Additional research focuses include hydroacoustics, endangered species, hazardous wastes, pesticides, and PCBs.

South Dakota

★2773★ ATC Environmental, Inc.
1515 E. 10th St.
Sioux Falls, SD 57103
Phone: (605)338-0555
Toll-Free: 800-522-9675
Contact: Donald Beck, Contact
Analytical laboratory providing asbestos testing, water testing, and environmental analysis. ***Former Name(s):*** Analytica Laboratories, Inc. (1988).

Tennessee

★2774★ AWARE Incorporated
227 French Landing Dr.
Nashville, TN 37228
Phone: (615)255-2288
Fax: (615)256-8332
Toll-Free: 800-251-2008
Contact: Perry W. Lankford, Chief Operating Officer/Controller
Founded: 1984. Bioassay studies, simulations, monitoring programs, treatability investigations, and testing and analysis of fertilizers, raw products, soil, drinking water, effluents, hazardous waste, heavy metal, pesticides, asphalt, and coal and petroleum products. ***Former Name(s):*** Associated Water and Air Resources Engineers, Inc.

★2775★ International Technology
5815 Middlebrook Pike
Knoxville, TN 37921
Phone: (615)588-6401
Contact: Murray Hutchinson, Pres.
Founded: 1968. Environmental and industrial hygiene, including analysis of trace metals, biocide residues, hazardous wastes, and metabolites in water, food, soil, and tissues; field surveys for sampling and identification; water and effluent characterization; and determination of metallic contaminants and additives in materials such as plastics, polymers, rubber, or textiles. ***Former Name(s):*** Stewart Laboratories, Inc.

★2776★ Oak Ridge Research Institute
113 Union Valley Rd.
Oak Ridge, TN 37830
Phone: (615)482-9604
Contact: Dr. Nathaniel W. Revis, Dir.
Founded: 1981. Testing of environmental or industrial pollutants, including monitoring of water, air, and soil for toxins; determination of pesticides, insecticides, and herbicides in food and drinking water samples; skin tumor bioassays; clinical biochemical testing; and risk assessment of environmental and industrial pollutants and new industrial products. Also supplies tumor-sensitive mice to research facilities around the country.

★2777★ Resource Consultants, Inc.
PO Box 1848
110 Westwood Pl.
Brentwood, TN 37220
Phone: (615)373-5040
Contact: Mary Louise Linn, Dir., Laboratory Services
Environmental sampling and analysis of water, wastewater, hazardous wastes, soils, oils, sludges, paints, and air.

★2778★ Tri-Tech Laboratories, Inc.
599 Waldron Rd.
LaVergne, TN 37086
Phone: (615)793-7547
Fax: (615)793-5050
Contact: Terry L. Robbins, Laboratory Dir. / V. Pres.
Founded: 1976. Physical, chemical, and biological treatability studies; bacteriology; trace metals and organics; water analysis; environmental engineering and training services; ambient and source air studies; and sludge, sediment, and solid waste research.

★2779★ Waste Water Engineers, Inc.
3200 Lebanon Rd.
Hermitage, TN 37076
Phone: (615)883-7100
Contact: Thomas H. Patton Jr., Pres. and Chief Research Dir.
Founded: 1973. Environmental science as applied to water and wastewater treatment systems and management. Also provides services in salt water systems.

Texas

★2780★ Agro-City, Inc.
7575 Wheatland Rd.
Dallas, TX 75249
Phone: (214)296-1955
Contact: Jeffrey Stafford, Dir.
Recycling of refuse and sewage for agricultural and energy applications. Projects include development of a two-phase system for production of methane by anaerobic digestion.

★2781★ Allied Analytical and Research Laboratories
PO Box 815006
Dallas, TX 75318-5006
Phone: (214)350-5841
Contact: Bobby Fletcher, Pres.
Founded: 1946. Industrial and municipal discharge analysis, including air, water, and solid wastes, fire debris analysis and investigation, microbiological analysis, food plant and warehouse inspections, and expert legal testimony.

★2782★ Ana-Lab Corporation
2600 Dudley Rd.
Kilgore, TX 75662
Phone: (214)984-0551
Contact: C.H. Whiteside, Pres.
Founded: 1965. Specializes in pollution monitoring and waste disposal analysis. Analyzes wastewater, groundwater, and solid waste for a full range of parameters, including heavy metals, pesticides, and polychlorinated biphenyls (PCBs). Tests solid waste for toxicity and petroleum and related materials for sulfur content, wear metal analysis, gasoline lead content, and fuel thermal content. Analyzes lignite and coal soils and tests feed, food, forage, and fertilizer for major nutrients and trace minerals. Conducts research on energy and aquatic plant utilization, including water hyacinths for possible uses in waste treatment, livestock feed, and renewable energy. Installs industrial and domestic waste disposal systems. Also provides waste discharge reporting and utility operating services.

★2783★ Applied Analogies
3909 Bosque
Plano, TX 75074
Phone: (214)423-5917
Contact: George Duke, Contact
Founded: 1985. Firm providing research, development, instruction, and application of technologies to advance the environmentally beneficial revitalization, biodegradation, or disposal by dissipation or deoxidation of nontoxic and toxic, nonradioactive waste. Also services storage sites for nonradioactive waste.

★2784★ Baker-Shiflett, Inc.
5450 E. Loop 820 S.
PO Box 15822
Fort Worth, TX 76119
Phone: (817)478-8254
Geotechnical services include foundation investigations, groundwater studies, and laboratory testing. Also provides environmental consulting, concrete batch design and testing, laboratory and field testing of soils, and plant and field inspections.

★2785★ Chemlab Service of Amarillo
1012 Melody Ln.
Amarillo, TX 79108
Phone: (806)383-5865
Contact: C.H. Scherer, Dir.
Founded: 1960. Water treatability studies and in-plant wastewater processing and control. Areas of focus include hazardous and industrial wastes.

★2786★ Coastal Ecosystems Management, Inc.
1031 N. Henderson St.
Fort Worth, TX 76107-1470
Phone: (817)870-1199
Contact: Dr. Robert H. Parker, Pres.
Founded: 1970. Data collection and analysis in the areas of geoscience, environmental science, wildlife management, mineral resource exploration and management, and plant and animal systematics and ecology. Projects include cultural and economic resource surveys and studies of barrier island development, strategic petroleum reserves, and pollution.

★2787★ EJS Consulting
816 Shady Creek Ct.
Cleburne, TX 76031-6162
Phone: (817)645-7410
Contact: Eric J. Schmitt, Contact
Environmental consulting service specializing in radiological monitoring and analysis, laboratory services, health physics services, radiation and hazardous waste analysis and monitoring, regulatory compliance, water treatment and monitoring, sewage treatment, and industrial waste outfall monitoring.

★2788★ Gymnurs Laboratories, Inc.
1601 N. Glenville Dr.
Suite 105
Richardson, TX 75081
Phone: (214)690-9431
Contact: Niranjan Shah, Laboratory Manager
Founded: 1982. Technical, economic, and scientific assessments related to solid and hazardous waste management, air pollution control, water quality and wastewater analysis, and industrial hygiene, including environmental sampling, residential health hazard assessment (formaldehyde, radon, odors, noise), organic and inorganic analytical services, elemental analysis, employee drug testing, and stack emission testing. Projects include the use of microorganisms to eliminate contamination in soil and groundwater.

★2789★ J.K. Research Associates, Inc.
3408 Bonnie Rd.
Austin, TX 78703
Phone: (512)476-4042
Contact: John E. Kelly, Pres.
Founded: 1983. Policy analysis regarding high- and low-level radioactive wastes, hazardous wastes, and biotechnology; market research on technological developments; and opinion research on contemporary issues. Specific projects include policy analysis for sub-seabed disposal of radioactive waste and for land-based repositories.

★2790★ L-H Laboratory Services
2410 1/2 Caplin
PO Box 21222
Houston, TX 77026
Phone: (713)694-4347
Contact: Uline Lovelady Hollins
Founded: 1982. Analytical laboratory specializing in water and wastewater testing.

★2791★ Martin Water Laboratories, Inc.
Box 1468
Monahans, TX 79759
Phone: (915)943-3234
Contact: Waylan C. Martin, Owner
Founded: 1953. Provides consultation services and analytical studies on water ecology, injection water systems, corrosion and scale problems, water origin, and other water problems involved in primary and secondary recovery of oil, agriculture, processing, and general plant usage.

★2792★ M.B.A. Labs
340 S. 66th St.
Houston, TX 77011
Phone: (713)928-2701
Contact: Herman J. Kresse, Contact
Founded: 1968. Provides analysis of chemicals, water, wastewaster, hazardous and nonhazardous wastes, marine cargos, petroleum products and chemicals, gases, foods, asbestos, and drugs, and body metabolites.

★2793★ NDRC Laboratories, Inc.
6284 Brookhill Dr.
Houston, TX 77087
Phone: (713)644-9437
Contact: Randall Evans, Pres.
Analysis, consulting, and engineering services related to drinking water, wastewater, soils, sludges, and hazardous wastes. Food services include nutritional studies, package integrity testing, and pesticide testing.

★2794★ Pattison's Laboratories Inc.
211 E. Monroe St.
PO Box 346
Harlingen, TX 78551-0346
Phone: (512)423-3196
Contact: Patricia A. Buttery, Pres.
Founded: 1936. Water and wastewater testing, fertilizer analysis, pesticide and residue analysis, and feed, soil, and plant tissue analysis.

★2795★ TRAC Laboratories, Inc.
PO Box 215
113 Cedar St.
Denton, TX 76201
Phone: (817)566-3359
Contact: Dr. Barney J. Venables, Pres.
Founded: 1980. Collects technical information for environmental regulatory compliance and insurance/litigation claims, focusing on analytical chemistry. Specialties include environmental science, pollution analysis, toxicity testing, hazardous waste analysis, and product development for mitigation of hazardous waste problems. Operates an aquatic toxicology laboratory.

★2796★ Water Quality Services
17459 Village Green Dr.
Houston, TX 77040
Phone: (713)466-0954
Contact: Lora Dunlap, Assistant Manager
Firm providing biological, chemical, chromatographic, and spectrographic analysis of chemicals in environmental materials and hazardous wastes.

Utah

★2797★ Bio/West, Inc.
1063 W. 1400 N.
Logan, UT 84321
Phone: (801)752-4202
Contact: Paul Holden, Principal
Founded: 1976. Provides environmental research and impact assessments, instream flow modeling, biological and geological studies, and soil and reclamation studies. Long-range projects include fisheries research in the Colorado River system, wildlife and rare game studies, and reservoir development studies.

★2798★ Ford Chemical Laboratory, Inc.
40 W. Louise Ave.
Salt Lake City, UT 84115
Phone: (801)466-8761
Contact: Lyle S. Ford, Pres.
Founded: 1960. Water and wastewater analysis and evaluation. Provides consulting services, research assistance, and water quality studies.

★2799★ H.E. Cramer Company, Inc.
136 W. Burton Ave.
PO Box 15581
Salt Lake City, UT 84115
Phone: (801)486-0121
Contact: Harry V. Geary Jr., Dir.
Founded: 1972. Offers technical consulting in the quantitative assessment of environmental air pollution problems. Conducts atmospheric dispersion modeling, meteorological and air quality measurements, baseline studies, and emission control evaluations. Provides development, implementation, and application of computer models for air quality impact and hazard assessments, and develops techniques for estimating the potential hazards of industrial pollutants, pesticides, rocket engine exhaust products, and chemical and biological agents.

★2800★ North American Weather Consultants
3761 S. 700 E.
Suite B
Salt Lake City, UT 84106
Phone: (801)263-3500
Telex: 820860 (NAWC UD)
Contact: Keith J. Brown, Pres.
Founded: 1950. Provides model development, verification and validation, new source siting, and environmental impact assessment in the areas of air quality, air pollution, weather modification, wind energy, and climatology.

Vermont

★2801★ New England Alternate Fuels, Inc.
67 Main St.
Box 921
Brattleboro, VT 05301
Phone: (802)257-0704
Contact: Louis G. Audette, Pres.
Founded: 1979. Conducts research on nontraditional fuels, including combustible waste and biomass. Projects includes extraction and utilization of landfill gas to generate electricity, converstion of waste paper and wood into heat and power, and development of cogeneration and district facilities. Manufactures waste-derived fuel pellets and develops and builds energy facilities, including project feasibilty, permitting, and determines materials handling, combustion, pollution control, and other technical particulars.

★2802★ Spectrum Research, Inc.
PO Box 122
Montpelier, VT 05602
Phone: (802)223-7088
Contact: Fred Kent, Pres.
Founded: 1978. Environmental monitoring, including quality tests of groundwater, drinking water, lakes, rivers, wastewater discharges, and landfills. Also tests air samples for formaldehyde.

Virginia

★2803★ American Resources Group
Bank of Vienna Bldg.
374 Maple Ave. East
Suite 210
Vienna, VA 22180
Phone: (703)255-2700
Contact: Dr. Keith A. Argow, Pres.
Founded: 1981. Environmental impact analysis and monitoring and environmental auditing of operations, especially in regard to heavy construction. Also provides technical assistance for private nonindustrial woodlot owners. Maintains specializations in forestry, small woodlot management, environmental impact, and wildlife. Operates the Land Conservation Fund of America, specializing in the acquisition of in-holdings within public lands from willing sellers, and the American Land Exchange, to expedite public land exchange procedures. National Forestry Network provides counsel to woodland owners for an annual subscription.

★2804★ Atlantic Research Corporation
5390 Cherokee Ave.
Alexandria, VA 22312
Phone: (703)642-4000
Contact: William H. Borten, Pres. and Chief Exec. Officer
Founded: 1949. Research and development of solid propellant rockets and gas generators, diagnosis and restoration of data communications networks, and research in pollution abatement and alternative energy sources.

★2805★ Biological Monitoring, Inc.
PO Box 184
Blacksburg, VA 24060
Phone: (703)953-2821
Contact: David Gruber Ph.D., Pres.
Firm providing aquatic toxicity testing and monitoring, including water quality, microbiological, and fish surveys.

★2806★ The Bionetics Corporation Analytical Laboratories
20 Research Dr.
Hampton, VA 23666-1396
Phone: (804)865-0880
Toll-Free: 800-423-9918
Contact: Joseph A. Stern, Pres.
Hazardous waste analysis of EPA priority pollutants, EP toxicity, and PCBs; chemical analysis of water, wastewater, and food; industrial discharge analysis; bacteriological analysis; and industrial hygiene analysis of solvents, metals, and asbestos.

★2807★ Central Virginia Laboratories and Consultants
2416 Langhorne Rd.
PO Box 10938
Lynchburg, VA 24506
Phone: (804)847-2852
Contact: Eddie D. Foster, Pres.
Founded: 1986. Provides groundwater monitoring and sampling, bacteriological analysis of water and food, air stack monitoring, bioassay analysis, and stream and lake sampling and analysis. Projects include the James River survey.

★2808★ Chem-Form, Inc.
660 Tower Ln.
PO Box 51
Floyd, VA 24091-0051
Phone: (703)745-3284
Contact: David G. Brown, Pres.
Founded: 1963. Refining of precious metals and recycling of thermoplastics, development of electroless and brush plating solutions, and literature and market research. Precious metal work includes recovery and refining of silver from secondary materials, such as photographic film.

★2809★ Clark Engineering
916 W. 25 St.
Norfolk, VA 23517
Phone: (804)625-1140
Contact: Stephen E. Clark, Pres.
Founded: 1979. Energy, specifically low temperature thermal energy conversion; environmental sciences, including pollution control device development and testing; engineering, economic, and marketing studies; computer simulation and analysis; patent evaluation; and prototype performance testing.
Former Name(s): Clark Power Systems, Inc. (1984).

★2810★ Commonwealth Laboratory, Inc.
Chemists Bldg.
2209 E. Broad St.
Richmond, VA 23223
Phone: (804)648-8358
Contact: Edwin Cox, Pres.
Founded: 1959. Chemical analysis and engineering in the areas of water and wastewater, pollutants, and pesticides. Performs source testing and ambient air monitoring.

★2811★ Decision Science Consortium, Inc.
1895 Preston White Dr.
Suite 300
Reston, VA 22091
Phone: (703)620-0660
Contact: Dr. James O. Chinnis Jr., Pres.
Founded: 1978. Offers consulting and research services in decision-making, cognitive

psychology, artificial intelligence, modeling, decision analysis, statistics, market research, personnel policy, strategic corporate management, decision support systems, new product decisions, resource allocation and capital budgeting, forecasting, manpower planning, facility location, military command and control, nuclear risks and safeguard, energy and environmental policy, and general business planning. Also provides quantitative decision analysis.

★2812★ Energy and Environmental Analysis, Inc.
1655 North Fl. Myer Dr.
Suite 600
Arlington, VA 22209
Phone: (703)528-1900
Fax: (703)528-0204
Contact: Dr. Michael O. Lerner, Pres.
Founded: 1974. Offers technical, analytical, and managerial services in the areas of energy engineering, air and water pollution, solid and hazardous wastes, energy and transportation policy, economics and finance, energy management systems and ventures, and coal production and use. Performs energy modeling and demand forecasting.

★2813★ Enseco/Cle Laboratory
PO Box 11106
2240 Dabney Rd.
Richmond, VA 23230
Phone: (804)359-1900
Contact: Bruce A. Petersen, Pres.
Provides environmental analysis of water, soil and rock, wastewater, and solid wastes. Tests chemical products and compounds, fertilizers, feeds and pesticides, and conducts bioanalytical assays on pharmaceuticals.

★2814★ James R. Reed & Associates, Inc.
813 Forrest Dr.
Newport News, VA 23606
Phone: (804)599-6750
Contact: Dr. James R. Reed Jr., Pres.
Founded: 1976. Aquatic toxicity testing, chemical pollution analysis, and environmental studies, including analysis of trace elements, water and sediments, groundwater, and leachates. Toxicology tests include effluent analysis, permitting studies, stream community assessments, and toxic reduction evaluations. Environemental studies include wetlands mitigation, ecological resource management and surveys, environmental impact studies, habitat mapping, benthic studies, and enumeration of rare, threatened, and endangered species.

★2815★ Olver Incorporated
1116 S. Main St.
Blacksburg, VA 24060
Phone: (703)552-5548
Contact: Dr. John W. Olver, Pres.
Founded: 1973. Civil and industrial engineering, with applications for the development and appraisal of water and wastewater treatment systems, and analytical chemistry. Studies recycling and solid waste treatment.

★2816★ Versar, Inc.
Box 1549
6850 Versar Center
Springfield, VA 22151
Phone: (703)750-3000
Contact: Dr. Michael Markels Jr., Pres.
Founded: 1969. Collects and analyzes data, conducts market research, performs testing, and provides systems design and technological forecasting with regard to advanced materials and environmental sciences and engineering. Services focus on environmental and energy studies development and manufacturing of specialty materials, hazardous waste destruction, process engineering, environmental investigations, toxic chemicals studies, analysis of emergency response services, and pollution control engineering, including air, water, and solid waste. Projects include lake acid rain studies, exposure risk assessments of toxic chemicals, underground storage tank studies, and environmental impairment assessments.

★2817★ V.J. Ciccone & Associates
14045 Jefferson Davis Hwy.
Woodbridge, VA 22191
Phone: (703)494-6503
Contact: Dr. Vincent J. Ciccone, Pres.
Founded: 1979. Conducts information review and evaluation to make conclusions and recommendations on environmental, engineering, and health safety issues, particularly in the fields of water and wastewater technologies, toxicology, pesticides, environmental fate, biochemistry, environmental exposure assessments, health effects of toxic substances, water contamination and treatment, and hazardous waste. Also develops hardware for pilot scale studies and prototype development.

★2818★ World Resources Company
1600 Anderson Rd.
McLean, VA 22102
Phone: (703)734-9800
Telex: 3792594 (WORLDCO)
Contact: Peter T. Halpin, Senior V. Pres.
Founded: 1976. Waste process engineering, metallurgy, process development, and environmental testing and analysis. Also provides market research, data collection, literature search, and systems design. Specializes in analyzing waste, developing recycling processes, and production of metals and minerals from waste.

Washington

★2819★ Analytical Resources, Inc.
333 Ninth Avenue, N.
Seattle, WA 98109-5187
Phone: (206)621-6490
Contact: Mark Weidner, Pres.
Founded: 1985. Environmental and ecological analysis, including toxic waste site evaluations.

★2820★ B & P Laboratories Inc.
5635 Delridge Way, S.W.
Seattle, WA 98106
Phone: (206)937-3644
Contact: Victor Broto, Pres.
Founded: 1972. Identification and description of hazardous wastes.

★2821★ Northwest Aquatic Analysis
7547 Henderson Blvd., 8
Olympia, WA 98503
Phone: (509)334-5323
Contact: Duane Hayman, Contact
Environmental science, including aquatic ecology, water quality, and fisheries. Services include ecosystem studies, biological inventory, habitat evaluation, subcontracting, and consultation.

★2822★ Nuclear Packaging, Inc.
1010 S. 336th St.
Federal Way, WA 98003
Phone: (206)874-2235
Fax: (206)874-2401
Telex: 152667 (PNSI UD)
Contact: P. Sherland, Contact
Design, development, and licensing of hazardous waste management systems. Focuses include waste containment, storage, transport, processing, and handling. Researches and develops concrete casks for spent-fuel storage. ***Former Name(s):*** BAME.

West Virginia

★2823★ Reliance Laboratories, Inc.
Benedum Airport Industrial Park
PO Box 625
Bridgeport, WV 26330
Phone: (304)842-5285
Contact: William F. Kirk Jr., Pres.
Provides environmental analysis of water, wastewater, air, soil, rock, coal, fuels, and oil. Special services include sampling, bioassays, benthic studies, and treatment planning.

Wisconsin

★2824★ Analytical Process Laboratories, Inc.
8222 W. Calumet
Milwaukee, WI 53223
Phone: (414)355-3909
Contact: Jitendra Shah, Pres.
Founded: 1976. Analysis of ferrous and nonferrous metals, chemicals, water and wastewater, sand, and toxic and hazardous wastes. Other services include consulting, material selection, quality control, physical and mechanical property evaluation, machining, failure investigation, and reporting. Sample pick up services provided within 50-mile radius.

★2825★ Aqua-Tech, Inc./Groce Laboratories
140 S. Park St.
Port Washington, WI 53074
Phone: (414)284-5746
Fax: (414)284-0243
Contact: Mark Wildhagen, National Sales Manager
Founded: 1969. Testing, analysis, treatment, and disposal of hazardous and laboratory chemical wastes. Also researches laboratory chemical disposal methods. Holds permits to handle hazardous materials, including explosives, reactives, oxidizers, aerosols, and cylinders.

★2826★ Badger Laboratories & Engineering Company, Inc.
1110 S. Oneida St.
Appleton, WI 54915
Phone: (414)739-9213
Toll-Free: 800-242-3556
Contact: Arthur B. Kaplan, Pres.
Founded: 1966. Water and wastewater analysis, hazardous waste testing, stack testing, ambient air quality monitoring, sludge analysis, fuel studies, soil analysis, pulp and paper chemistry, dairy product analysis, meat and food product analysis, and nondestructive testing. Projects include land disposal of

wastewater and effect of sanitary landfills on groundwater. Engineering services include design, installation, and sampling of water treatment systems; tracing industrial sewers and mapping; surveying; stream guaging; design of neutralization systems; landfill security; and contract operation of small sewage treatment plants. ***Former Name(s):*** Papertech Company.

★2827★ Donohue Analytical
4738 N. 40 St.
PO Box 1067
Sheboygan, WI 53083
Phone: (414)458-8711
Telex: 9102643888
Contact: Richard E. Fedler, V. Pres.
Founded: 1982. Tests and analyzes water, wastewater, and toxic and hazardous wastes. Services include investigative analysis of treatment and disposal methods for waste streams and products and analytical investigations of unknown waste materials.

★2828★ Enviro-Analysts, Inc.
949 Erie St.
Racine, WI 53402
Phone: (414)632-6169
Contact: John R. Ruetz, Pres.
Founded: 1976. Performs analytical laboratory services in the area of environmental chemistry. Offers field sampling and monitoring of wastewater, groundwater, waste, and flows. Conducts waste analysis, environmental audits, and technical feasibility studies. Provides consultation on related topics.

★2829★ George Banzhaf and Company
225 E. Michigan St.
Milwaukee, WI 53202
Phone: (414)276-2062
Contact: William H. Banzhaf, Pres.
Founded: 1939. Offers data collection and analysis, information and literature research, and market and opinion research in the areas of economic and financial management of forest resources, land use planning, environmental impact studies, and timber inventories. Services include development and application of computer simulation models and management of public sessions regarding natural resource issues.

★2830★ Kag Laboratories International, Inc.
2323 Jackson St.
Oshkosh, WI 54901
Phone: (414)426-2222
Contact: Dr. Akhtar Khwaja, Pres.
Founded: 1985. Tests and analyzes soil, plant tissue, water, and wastewater. Conducts soil fertility and fertilizer field trials for high value crops. ***Former Name(s):*** P & P Agricultural Lab (1985).

★2831★ Sommer-Frey Laboratories, Inc.
6125 W. National Ave.
PO Box 14513
Milwaukee, WI 53214
Phone: (414)475-6700
Contact: Edward Treick, Pres.
Tests and analyzes food, water, air, wastes, and asbestos.

★2832★ Zimpro/Passavant, Inc.
Rothschild, WI 54474
Phone: (715)359-7211
Contact: William Copa, Dir. of Research
Founded: 1942. Basic and applied research on wastewater. Projects include water and wastewater analysis, sewage and wastewater treatment, energy generation from low grade fuels, and chemical recovery. ***Former Name(s):*** Zimpro, Inc. (1986); merged with Passavant Corporation U.S.A.

Wyoming

★2833★ Inter-Mountain Laboratories, Inc.
1633 Terra Ave.
Sheridan, WY 82801
Phone: (307)672-8945
Contact: Roger Pasch, Pres.
Founded: 1979. Environmental testing and analysis laboratory specializing in groundwater contamination and soil overburden charaterization.

★2834★ Western Environmental Services and Testing, Inc.
6756 W. Uranium Rd.
Casper, WY 82604
Phone: (307)234-5511
Contact: James Meador, V. Pres.
Testing and analysis of air, water, and soil, including both in-house and field services. Conducts stack emissions tests in accordance with Environmental Protection Agency (EPA) specifications and provides inorganic and radiological analysis. Maintains and EPA certified water and soils laboratory for testing drinking water.

Government Research Centers

International

★2835★ International Atomic Energy Agency (IAEA)
UNESCO
Vienna International Center
Wagramer Strasse 5
Postfach 100
Vienna, Austria
Phone: (0222) 23600
Fax: (0222) 234564
Telex: 112645
Contact: H. Blix, Dir.-Gen.
Intergovernmental autonomous organization, administratively linked to the United Nations. ***Research Areas:*** Encourages research and development of the practical applications of atomic energy for peaceful uses; fosters the exchange of scientific and technical information between nations; establishes health and safety standards; and applies safeguards in accordance with the Treaty of the Non-Proliferation of Nuclear Weapons, the Treaty for the Prohibition of Nuclear Weapons in Latin America, and the South Pacific Nuclear Free Zone Treaty. IAEA also ensures that any assistance it gives is not used for military purposes.

★2836★ International Council for the Exploration of the Sea (ICES)
Palegade 2-4
DK-1261 Copenhagen K, Denmark
Phone: 33 15 42 25
Fax: 33 93 42 15
Telex: 22498
Contact: Dr. E.D. Anderson, Gen. Sec.
Intergovernmental organization, with membership for 18 countries. ***Research Areas:*** Promotes and encourages research and investigations of the sea, especially those studies related to the sea's living resources; and publishes and disseminates research results. Council is primarily concerned with studies of the Atlantic Ocean, particularly the North Atlantic, and its adjacent seas.

★2837★ International Hydrological Programme (IHP)
UNESCO
7, place de Fontenoy
75700 Paris, France
Phone: 45 68 40 02
Fax: 45 67 58 69
Telex: 204461
Contact: Dr. A. Szollosi-Nagy, Secretary
Long-term intergovernmental program under the auspices of UNESCO. ***Research Areas:*** Specific research includes: (1) hydrological research in a changing environment ; (2) management of water resources for sustainable development; and (3) education, training, the transfer of knowledge and public information.

★2838★ International Laboratory of Marine Radioactivity
International Atomic Energy Agency
19 ave. des Castellans
Monaco
Phone: (93) 50 44 88
Fax: (93) 25 73 46
Telex: 479378
Contact: Prof. Murdoch S. Baxter, Director
Operates under an agreement between the International Atomic Energy Agency and the Government of the Principality of Monaco. ***Research Areas:*** Conducts research on the occurrence and behavior of radioactive substances and other forms of pollution in the marine environment. Laboratory comprises three sections for marine radiogeochemistry, marine radioecology, and marine environmental studies of non-nuclear contaminants.

★2839★ Man and Biosphere Programme (MAB)
7, place de Fontenoy
75700 Paris, France
Phone: (1) 45 68 40 67
Contact: Dr. B. Von Droste, Director
Parent organization is UNESCO. International research and training program concerned with developing a scientific basis for the use and conservation of the biosphere's resources and with improving the relations between humans and the environment. ***Research Areas:*** Projects are aimed at solving practical problems of managing various ecosystems, biomes, or physiographic units throughout the world. Impact of human activities on the dynamics of ecosystems; ecological effects of human activities on the value and resources of lakes, marshes, rivers, deltas, estuaries, and coastal zones; conservation of natural areas and of the genetic material they contain; assessment of pest management and fertilizer use; effects of major engineering works on humans and the environment; ecological aspects of urban systems, with particular emphasis on energy utilization; perception of environmental quality; and environmental pollution and its effects on the biosphere.

★2840★ UNESCO Division of Marine Sciences
7, place de Fontenoy
75700 Paris, France
Phone: (1) 45 68 10 00
Contact: Dr. Dale C. Krause, Director
Research Areas: Marine science, including studies on the natural marine systems of coastal regions (i.e. the mangrove, coral reef, estuary, coastal lagoon, coastal erosion), and scientific tables and standards. Research is carried out for the Division under contract by universities, laboratories, and consultants. Sponsors the UNESCO Major Interregional Project on Research and Training leading to the Integrated Management of Coastal Systems (COMAR).

★2841★ World Meteorological Organization (WMO)
PO Box 5
41 ave. Giuseppe-Motta
CH-1211 Geneva, Switzerland
Phone: (022) 734 64 00
Fax: (022) 734 23 26
Telex: 23260
Contact: Prof. Dr. G.O.P. Obasi, Sec. Gen.
Specialized agency of the United Nations. ***Research Areas:*** WMO fosters international cooperation and data exchange concerning weather information and its applications. Principal areas of research interest include weather prediction, world climate, tropical meteorology, environmental pollution monitoring, and weather modification.

United States

★2842★ Agency for Toxic Substances and Disease Registry
1600 Clifton Rd., N.E.
Mail Stop E-28
Atlanta, GA 30333
Phone: (404)639-0700
Fax: (404)639-0744
Contact: Barry L. Johnson Ph.D.
Parent Agencies: Department of Health and Human Services, U.S. Public Health Service. ***Research Areas:*** Conducts and sponsors epidemiologic studies on human health effects related to hazardous substance exposure, emphasizing substance-specific research on priority hazardous substances. ***Databases:*** National Priority List, National Exposure Registry, and National Disease Registry.

★2843★ Air and Energy Engineering Research Laboratory
Environmental Protection Agency
Mail Drop 60
86 Alexander Dr.
Research Triangle Park, NC 27711
Phone: (919)541-2821
Fax: (919)541-2382

Contact: Frank Princiotta, Dir. ***Parent Agencies:*** Environmental Protection Agency, Office of Research and Development. ***Research Areas:*** Evaluates and develops cost effective control technologies, process modifications, and pollution prevention techniques for stationary sources of air pollution. Focuses on man-made sources of acid rain; indoor air pollution; and global air pollution problems such as stratospheric ozone depletion and global warming.

★2844★ Air Force Engineering and Services Laboratory
Environics Division
ATTN: HQ AFESC/ RD V
Tyndall Air Force Base, FL 32403-6001
Phone: (904)283-2097
Fax: (904)283-6499
Contact: Lt. Col. F. Thomas Lubozynski, Chief
Parent Agencies: As the Air Force's lead laboratory for environmental quality research and development, Division is the focal point for environmental research and development and coordinates this broad program with other Department of Defense and federal agencies. Research funds are applied to in-house projects and extramurally with universities, commercial research organizations, and other federal agencies. Research is conducted in atmospheric and groundwater chemistry, microbial degradation, and groundwater and industrial waste treatment.

★2845★ Air Resources Laboratory
1325 East-West Hwy.
Silver Spring, MD 20910
Phone: (301)427-7684
Fax: (301)427-8119
Contact: Bruce B. Hicks, Dir.
Parent Agencies: Department of Commerce, National Oceanic and Atmospheric Administration, Office of Oceanic and Atmospheric Research, Environmental Research Laboratories. ***Research Areas:*** The use of meteorology to understand and predict human influence on the environment. General areas of study include: turbulence and diffusion in the atmosphere, atmospheric trajectories from local to global scales, meteorology of air pollution, changing air chemistry and climate, and atmospheric deposition.

★2846★ Air Resources Laboratory
Climate Monitoring and Diagnostics Laboratory
Geophysical Monitoring for Climatic Change Division
325 Broadway
Boulder, CO 80303
Phone: (303)497-6650
Fax: (303)497-6290
Contact: Dr. James Peterson, Dir.
Parent Agencies: Department of Commerce, National Oceanic and Atmospheric Administration, Office of Oceanic and Atmospheric Research, Environmental Research Laboratories. ***Research Areas:*** Long-term studies on atmospheric greenhouse gases and long-range transport of aerosols in the atmosphere. The measurements, taken at NOAA's four geophysical monitoring for climatic change (GMCC) baseline observatories and other locations, are made to determine whether these gases and aerosols are changing with time and to identify natural and anthropogenic sources and sinks as well as temporal and hemispheric gradients and global budgets.

★2847★ Air Resources Laboratory
Meteorology Division
Environmental Research Center
Research Triangle Park, NC 27711
Parent Agencies: Department of Commerce, National Oceanic and Atmospheric Administration, Office of Oceanic and Atmospheric Research, Environmental Research Laboratories. ***Research Areas:*** Transport, diffusion, transformation, and deposition of air pollutants; air quality simulation models for inert and reactive pollutants on all temporal and spatial scales; effects of air pollutants on weather and climate; and relationships between air quality and meteorological parameters. Division also provides operational meteorological support to EPA abatement and compliance activities.

★2848★ Alabama Cooperative Fish and Wildlife Research Unit
331 Funchess Hall
Auburn University
Auburn, AL 36849
Phone: (205)826-4796
Fax: (205)844-9234
Contact: Nicholas R. Holler, Leader
Parent Agencies: Department of the Interior, U.S. Fish and Wildlife Service. ***Research Areas:*** Fishes, aquatic ecosystems, and wildlife management, including studies on fish taxonomy, fish cytogenetics, ecology of fish competition, gamefish and wildlife history, ecology of game and endangered species, habitat requirements, wildlife damage control, and captive propagation. Unit also provides training of graduate students in wildlife, fish, upland, and wetland ecosystems and fishery research.

★2849★ Alabama Water Resources Research Institute
202 Hargis Hall
Auburn University
Auburn, AL 36849-5124
Phone: (205)826-5075
Contact: Joseph F. Judkins Jr., Dir.
Parent Agencies: Department of the Interior, U.S. Geological Survey, Water Resources Division. ***Research Areas:*** Water resources.

★2850★ Alaska Cooperative Fishery Research Unit
University of Alaska
138 Arctic Health Research Bldg.
Fairbanks, AK 99775-0110
Phone: (907)474-7661
Fax: (907)474-6967
Contact: James B. Reynolds, Leader
Parent Agencies: Department of the Interior, U.S. Fish and Wildlife Service. ***Research Areas:*** Structure and function of aquatic ecosystems in interior and arctic Alaska. Projects focus on all aspects of a fishery (including organisms, habitat, and society) in pursuit of basic knowledge and management-oriented results. Activities emphasize graduate student research training and technical assistance to other agencies and individuals.

★2851★ Alaska Cooperative Wildlife Research Unit
University of Alaska
209 Irving Bldg.
Fairbanks, AK 99775-0990
Phone: (907)474-7673
Fax: (907)474-6967
Contact: David R. Klein, Leader
Parent Agencies: Department of the Interior, U.S. Fish and Wildlife Service. ***Research Areas:*** Wildlife ecology and management research, focusing on ungulate range relationships, carnivore ecology, wetlands, associated bird ecology, and impact of northern development on wildlife and habitats. Unit activities also include training of graduate students.

★2852★ Alaska Water Research Center
Institute of Northern Engineering
University of Alaska
Fairbanks, AK 99775-1760
Phone: (907)474-7775
Fax: (907)474-6087
Contact: Dr. Douglas Kane, Dir.
Parent Agencies: Department of the Interior, U.S. Geological Survey, Water Resources Division. ***Research Areas:*** Water resources.

★2853★ Argonne National Laboratory
9700 S. Cass Ave.
Argonne, IL 60439-4832
Phone: (312)972-3872
Contact: Alan Schriesheim Ph.D., Dir.
Parent Agencies: Department of Energy. ***Research Areas:*** Focuses on 1) engineering research, particularly for nuclear power and other advanced energy technologies; 2) basic science, particularly chemistry physics, materials science, and mathematics and computer science; and 3) biomedical and environmental science and technology. Environmental research concentrates on waste management, atmospheric physics, molecular physics and chemistry, instrumentation development, environmental remediation, and integrated assessments.

★2854★ Arizona Cooperative Fish and Wildlife Research Unit
University of Arizona
210 Biological Sciences Bldg. E.
Tucson, AZ 85721
Phone: (602)621-1959
Contact: Dr. O. Eugene Maughan, Leader
Parent Agencies: Department of the Interior, U.S. Fish and Wildlife Service. ***Research Areas:*** Unit conducts a program of field and laboratory research on fish and wildlife management and ecology. Activities also include graduate training and extension services in these fields.

★2855★ Arizona Water Resources Research Center
University of Arizona
Geology Bldg. 11
Tucson, AZ 85721
Phone: (602)621-7607
Fax: (602)621-1638
Contact: Dr. William B. Lord, Dir.
Parent Agencies: Department of the Interior, U.S. Geological Survey, Water Resources Division. ***Research Areas:*** Water resources, including technical and institutional aspects of conjunctive and integrated management, water conservation policies, effluent use, Indian water rights issues, and instream rights.

★2856★ Arkansas Water Resources Research Center
University of Arkansas
113 Ozark Hall
Fayetteville, AR 72701
Phone: (501)575-4403
Contact: Kenneth F. Steele, Dir.
Parent Agencies: Department of the Interior, U.S. Geological Survey, Water Resources Division. ***Research Areas:*** Water quality and quantity, including nonpoint agricultural pollution, septic and sewage treatment facilities, and water loss.

★2857★ Assistant Secretary for Conservation and Renewable Energy
Washington, DC 20585
Phone: (202)586-9220
Contact: J. Michael Davis, Assistant Sec.
Parent Agencies: Department of energy.
Research Areas: Responsible for programs that increase the efficiency of energy utilization and the amount of energy produced from renewable resources.

★2858★ Assistant Secretary for Fossil Energy
1000 Independence Ave., S.W., Rm. 4G084
Washington, DC 20585
Phone: (202)586-4695
Contact: Robert Gentile, Assistant Sec.
Parent Agencies: Department of Energy.
Research Areas: The primary mission of the fossil energy program is to support longer-term, high-risk research and development with high potential payoff that will help increase domestic production of oil and gas or that will permit the United States to shift from the use of oil and gas to more abundant coal and oil shale resources.

★2859★ Assistant Secretary for Nuclear Energy
US Dept. of Energy
1000 Independence Ave., SW
Washington, DC 20585
Phone: (202)586-6450
Fax: (202)586-8353
Contact: William H. Young, Asst. Sec.
Parent Agencies: Department of Energy.
Research Areas: Develops, interprets, and coordinates nuclear safety policy for all DOE reactors and nuclear facilities.

★2860★ Athens Environmental Research Laboratory
College Sta. Rd.
Athens, GA 30613
Phone: (404)546-3134
Fax: (404)546-2018
Contact: Rosemarie C. Russo, Dir.
Parent Agencies: Environmental Protection Agency, Office of Research and Development.
Research Areas: Conducts and manages fundamental and applied research to predict and assess the human and environmental exposures and risks associated with conventional and toxic pollutants in water, soil, and air. This includes programs to: 1) develop and refine mathematical models for exposure assessment, pollutant fate, and wasteload allocation; 2) identify and measure toxic pollutants and their transformation processes in industrial and municipal effluent, leachate, and groundwater; 3) develop mathematical expressions to quantify chemical and biological transformation processes; 4) develop and field test predictive models of pesticide migration through soil and runoff for exposure and risk assessments; and 5) develop ecological risk assessment methodologies for hazardous waste management of toxic organics and metals.

★2861★ Athens Environmental Research Laboratory
Biology Branch
College Sta. Rd.
Athens, GA 30613
Phone: (404)546-3103
Fax: (404)546-2018
Contact: Thomas E. Waddell, Acting Chief
Parent Agencies: Environmental Protection Agency, Office of Research and Development.
Research Areas: Conducts and manages intramural and extramural research to predict the rate, extent, and products of biological processes that control pollutant fate in soil and water ecosystems. This includes development and testing of methods for predicting relevant microbial kinetics in aerobic and anaerobic environments, equilibria, ecosystem behavior, and ecological risks posed by anthropogenic stress to natural systems.

★2862★ Athens Environmental Research Laboratory
Center for Exposure Assessment Modeling
College Sta. Rd.
Athens, GA 30613
Phone: (404)546-3130
Fax: (404)546-3340
Contact: Robert B. Ambrose Jr., Manager
Parent Agencies: Environmental Protection Agency, Office of Research and Development.
Research Areas: Provides exposure assessment technology and training for multimedia modeling of organic chemical and heavy metal pollutant fate, regional and local air contaminant modeling, source and site characterization monitoring and measurement, marine and estuarine pollutant fate modeling, and pollutant dose-response and ecological impact modeling.

★2863★ Athens Environmental Research Laboratory
Chemistry Branch
College Sta. Rd.
Athens, GA 30613
Phone: (404)546-3145
Contact: Arthur W. Garrison, Chief
Parent Agencies: Environmental Protection Agency, Office of Research and Development.
Research Areas: Conducts and manages intramural and extramural research to predict the rate, extent, and products of chemical/biochemical reactions that control metal and organic pollutants fate in soil and water ecosystems.

★2864★ Atmospheric Research and Exposure Assessment Laboratory
Mail Drop 75
Research Triangle Park, NC 27711
Phone: (919)541-2106
Contact: Gary J. Foley, Dir.
Parent Agencies: Environmental Protection Agency, Office of Research and Development.
Research Areas: Provides monitoring services, quality assurance techniques, and standardized analysis methods to those engaged in environmental research. It implements and maintains multipurpose pollutant monitoring stations and networks (including a 25-station National Air Surveillance network and a 55-station membrane filter network) to provide baseline data on air pollutants; and assists other laboratories and centers with the development and implementation of quality assurance programs.

★2865★ Battelle Northwest Laboratory
Battelle Blvd.
PO Box 999
Richland, WA 99352
Phone: (509)375-2201
Fax: (509)376-3876
Contact: Dr. William R. Wiley, Dir.
Parent Agencies: Department of Energy.
Research Areas: As the research and development laboratory for the Hanford site, BNL provides advanced technology and environmental surveillance to support Hanford operations. Emphasis is currently on solving environmental problems related to hazardous waste cleanup, radioactive waste management; air quality, and global changes. Evaluates human health hazards, identifies improved sources of energy and materials for energy efficiency, and works to modernize defense facilites and improve manufacturing processes.

★2866★ Battelle Northwest Laboratory
Hanford National Environmental Research Park
Battelle Blvd.
PO Box 999
Richland, WA 99352
Phone: (509)376-8256
Contact: Lee Rogers, Coordinator
Parent Agencies: Department of Energy
Research Areas: Established to provide protected land areas for research and education in the environmental sciences and to demonstrate the environmental compatibility of energy technology development and use. Research at this site is conducted in three areas: 1) habitats and populations; 2) toxic chemicals and mineral nutrients; and 3) landscape units or watersheds.

★2867★ Beltsville Agricultural Research Center
Natural Resources Institute
BARC-West
Bldg. 001, Rm. 231
Beltsville, MD 20705
Contact: Dr. P.C. Kearney, Dir.
Parent Agencies: Department of Agriculture, Agricultural Research Service, Beltsville Area.
Research Areas: Comprises seven laboratories: Environmental Chemistry, Hydrology, Model and Database Coordination, Pesticides Degradation, Plant Stress, Remote Sensing Research, and Soil-Microbial Systems.

★2868★ Brookhaven National Laboratory
Upton, NY 11973
Phone: (516)282-2123
Fax: (516)282-3000
Contact: Dr. Nicholas Samios, Dir.
Parent Agencies: Department of Energy.
Research Areas: High energy, nuclear and solid state physics, chemistry, biology, environmental science, medicine, and selected energy technologies. Investigates the physical, chemical, and biological effects of radiation and of chemical substances involved in the production and use of energy. Conducts applied research and development to solve problems of national interest in energy systems. Primary function of the Laboratory is to conceive, construct, and operate the research facilities used by Brookhaven and by the university and industrial communities.

★2869★ Brookhaven National Laboratory
Applied Science Department
Bldg. 179-A
Upton, NY 11973
Phone: (516)282-3037
Fax: (516)282-4130
Contact: L. Petrakis, Chm.
Parent Agencies: Department of Energy
Research Areas: Conducts research in energy sciences, energy technology, and environmental sciences. Energy science studies focus on the chemical, materials, and process sciences relevant to energy conversion, transmission, storage, and conservation. Areas of interest include artificial photosynthesis, superconductivity, the behavior of hydrogen in various metal and hydride systems, and combustion processes. Energy technology programs are directed at developing advanced energy systems and components; alternative fuel sources, such as solar power and hydrogen, are also studied. Environmental sciences studies focus on the effects of acid rain on lakes, crops, and forests; atmospheric

pollutants; air ventilation rates in homes and commercial buildings; and the behavior of coastal shelves and their ability to absorb the byproducts of energy-related activities along the shores.

★2870★ Brookhaven National Laboratory Safety and Environmental Protection Division
Bldg. 535
Upton, NY 11973
Phone: (516)282-4654
Contact: R. William Casey, Head
Parent Agencies: Department of Energy. ***Research Areas:*** Division serves in an advisory and review capacity regarding occupational and environmental health and safety to ensure that scientific programs and associated supporting efforts involving work with hazardous agents are conducted with minimum risk to people and the environment. Services are offered in the fields of health physics, industrial hygiene, occupational safety, and environmental protection. Division also conducts research in radiological physics, dosimetry, and methods of dose reduction, and conducts related cost-benefit evaluations at nuclear power plants. In addition, activities have involved analyzing bioassay data and providing health physics expertise and emergency action planning in a radiation safety program in the Marshall Islands.

★2871★ Bureau of Reclamation
18th & C Sts., N.W., Rm. 7654
Washington, DC 20240
Phone: (202)208-4157
Contact: C. Dale Duvall, Commissioner
Parent Agencies: Department of the Interior. ***Research Areas:*** Aims to stabilize and stimulate local and regional economies, enhance and protect the environment, and improve the quality of life through development of water, other renewable resources, and related land resources throughout the 17 contiguous Western states.

★2872★ California Cooperative Fishery Research Unit
Humboldt State University
Arcata, CA 95521
Phone: (707)826-3268
Contact: Roger A. Barnhart, Leader
Parent Agencies: Department of the Interior, U.S. Fish and Wildlife Service. ***Research Areas:*** Conducts programs of fishery research in response to local, state, regional, and national environmental problems affecting fishery-aquatic resources and to aid in the training of fishery students (primarily at the graduate level). Principal fields of study encompass anadromous and resident trout streams, reservoirs, and marine and estuarine habitats.

★2873★ California Water Resources Center
Rubidoux Hall
University of California
Riverside, CA 92521
Phone: (714)787-4327
Fax: (714)787-5295
Contact: Dr. Henry J. Vaux Jr., Dir.
Parent Agencies: Department of the Interior, U.S. Geological Survey, Water Resources Division. ***Research Areas:*** California surface and groundwater quality, water and land use, water resources management and development, and hydrology and climatology.

★2874★ Center for Environmental Health and Injury Control
Mail Stop F29
1600 Clifton Rd., N.E.
Atlanta, GA 30333
Phone: (404)488-4111
Contact: Dr. Vernon N. Houk, Dir.
Parent Agencies: Department of Health and Human Services, U.S. Public Health Service, Centers for Disease Control. ***Research Areas:*** Administers national programs that promote a healthy environment and prevent premature death and avoidable illness and disability caused by non-infectious, non-occupational, environmental, and related factors. The Center is organized in divisions on Birth Defects and Developmental Disabilities; Environmental Hazards and Health Effects; Environmental Health Laboratory Sciences; and Injury Epidemiology and Control.

★2875★ Center for Environmental Health and Injury Control
Environmental Hazards and Health Effects Division
1600 Clifton Rd., N.E.
Atlanta, GA 30333
Phone: (404)488-4772
Contact: Dr. Henry Falk, Dir.
Parent Agencies: Department of Health and Human Services, U.S. Public Health Service, Centers for Disease Control ***Research Areas:*** Conducts field investigations related to environmental public health problems and their prevention. Specific areas of interest include toxic chemicals, natural environmental hazards, environmentally-induced disease, international environmental health, and indoor air pollution.

★2876★ Center for Environmental Health and Injury Control
Environmental Hazards and Health Effects Division
Health Studies Branch
1600 Clifton Rd., N.E.
Atlanta, GA 30333
Phone: (404)488-4682
Contact: Ed Kilboune, Chief
Parent Agencies: Department of Health and Human Services, U.S. Public Health Service, Centers for Disease Control. ***Research Areas:*** Conducts epidemiologic studies on environmental exposure and health effects. This includes planning, implementing, and reporting epidemiologic research and providing technical assistance and assessment of risk from environmental hazards such as toxic chemicals, radiation, waste disposal, indoor air pollution, passive smoking, controlled substance analogs, and natural and man-made disasters.

★2877★ Central Great Plains Research Station
PO Box 400
Akron, CO 80720
Phone: (303)345-2259
Fax: (303)345-2088
Contact: Dr. Ardell D. Halvorson, Research Leader
Parent Agencies: Department of Agriculture, Agricultural Research Service, Northern Plains Area. ***Research Areas:*** Station conducts a program of field and laboratory research on soil and water resource conservation and management. Program is specifically related to problems associated with semi-arid croplands, rangelands, and irrigated lands, with secondary emphasis on crop breeding and testing programs.

★2878★ Coastal Engineering Information Analysis Center
U. S. Army Engineer Waterways Experiment Sta.
ATTN: CEIAC
3909 Halls Ferry Rd.
Vicksburg, MS 39180-6199
Phone: (601)634-2012
Contact: Dr. Fred E. Camfield, Dir.
Parent Agencies: Department of Defense, Defense Logistics Agency. ***Research Areas:*** Collects, evaluates, publishes, and disseminates data on coastal engineering. Specific areas of interest are: engineering, coastal regions, beaches, erosion, environments, oceanography, ocean waves, tides, estuaries, inlets, and hydrodynamics.

★2879★ Colorado Cooperative Fish and Wildlife Research Unit
Colorado State University
J.V.K. Wagar Bldg., Rm. 201
Fort Collins, CO 80523
Phone: (303)491-6942
Parent Agencies: Department of the Interior, U.S. Fish and Wildlife Service. ***Research Areas:*** Conducts research, trains fishery and wildlife personnel at the graduate level, provides technical services to conservation agencies, and promotes education in natural resources through demonstration, lecture, and publication. Unit's fishery studies are related to the assessment of environmental impacts of human activity, such as effects of nuclear and pumped storage power generation on streams and lakes; effects of forest management practices on water quality; effects of intensive visitor use on streams and lakes in national parks; and the impact of irrigation demand on lake productivity and limnology.

★2880★ Colorado Water Resources Research Institute
Colorado State University
410 University Service Center
Fort Collins, CO 80523
Phone: (303)491-6308
Fax: (303)491-2293
Contact: Dr. Neil S. Grigg, Dir.
Parent Agencies: Department of the Interior, U.S. Geological Survey, Water Resources Division. ***Research Areas:*** Water, including rights, management, groundwater, quality and quantity, and efficient use. Conducts studies on protecting high-quality instream water for fish, wildlife, recreation, and endangered species.

★2881★ Connecticut Institute of Water Resources
University of Connecticut
211A W. B. Young Bldg. U-18
Storrs, CT 06269-4018
Phone: (203)486-0335
Fax: (203)486-2840
Contact: David R. Miller, Dir.
Parent Agencies: Department of the Interior, U.S. Geological Survey, Water Resources Division. ***Research Areas:*** Water resources, water quality, industrial and commercial water utilization, and protection and management of lakes, rivers, and streams. Activities include investigating methods to remove gasoline and fuel oil contamination from soils, developing an improved septic tank system, evaluating methods to reduce water using ultraviolet light, and developing a low-cost system to reduce toxicity in metal plating waste waters.

★2882★ Consumer Product Safety Commission
Health Sciences Directorate
5401 Westbard Ave.
Bethesda, MD 20207
Phone: (301)492-6957
Contact: Dr. Andrew G. Ulsamer, Dir.
Research Areas: Conducts studies to determine exposure to hazardous chemicals from consumer products. This includes investigation of: 1) children's products; 2) pollutant emissions (both chemical and biological) from structural materials, consumer products, and indoor combustion sources and their impact on indoor air quality; 3) bioavailability and potential for consumer exposure to carcinogenic commercial substances; and 4) acute toxicity of various household products to determine proper precautionary and first aid labeling. Directorate is also responsible for implementation of the Poison Prevention Packaging Act with respect to hazardous household substances, including drugs; and processes requests seeking exemption from regulations under this Act.

★2883★ Cooperative Institute for Research in Environmental Sciences
University of Colorado
Campus Box 216
Boulder, CO 80309
Phone: (303)492-1143
Contact: Dr. Robert Sievers, Dir.
Parent Agencies: Department of Commerce, National Oceanic and Atmospheric Administration, Office of Oceanic and Atmospheric Research, Environmental Research Laboratories. ***Research Areas:*** Institute conducts research in: 1) environmental chemistry, including environmental measurements and analysis, reaction kinetics, biochemistry, surface science, and analytical instrumentation; 2) atmospheric and climate dynamics, including basic and applied research on atmosphere-ocean interaction, cryosphere-climate interaction, and the interaction of waves and turbulence with mean flows in order to develop a more coherent picture of the Earth's physical environment and its sensitivities to natural and anthropogenic change; and 3) solid earth geophysics, including theoretical and observational geodesy and geodynamics, laboratory studies of rock failure and rock properties under high stress, isotope geology, earthquake prediction and other observational seismology, theoretical studies of wave generation and propagation, engineering seismology, and global geology.

★2884★ Cooperative Whooping Crane Tracking
203 W. 2nd St.
Grand Island, NE 68801
Phone: (308)381-5571
Contact: Craig Faanes
Parent Agencies: Department of the Interior, U.S. Fish and Wildlife Service. ***Research Areas:*** Monitors and disseminates information on the migrational ecology of the endangered whooping crane. Confirmed sightings are monitored to provide protection from predators and human intrusion.

★2885★ Corvallis Environmental Research Laboratory
200 S.W. 35th St.
Corvallis, OR 97333-4901
Phone: (503)757-4601
Contact: Thomas A. Murphy, Dir.
Parent Agencies: Environmental Protection Agency, Office of Research and Development. ***Research Areas:*** Conducts research to determine the effects of pollution and other environmental stresses on terrestrial and freshwater ecosystems. This includes studies on air pollutant and acid rain effects on terrestrial and aquatic ecosystems; toxic effects of chemicals and biotechnology products on plants and animals in terrestrial ecosystems; restorative efforts for wetlands and lakes; the effects of loss and contamination of wetlands; and the ecological effects of climate change and increased ultraviolet radiation from stratospheric ozone depletion.

★2886★ Corvallis Environmental Research Laboratory
Terrestrial Branch
200 S.W. 35th St.
Corvallis, OR 97333-4901
Phone: (503)757-4634
Fax: (503)757-4799
Contact: Dr. Roger Blair, Acting Chief
Parent Agencies: Independent Agencies, Office of Research and Development. ***Research Areas:*** Effects of air pollution, global climate change, acid rain, hazard waste, air toxics, biotechnology, pesticide effects, biodiversity, and stratospheric ozone depletion.

★2887★ Council on Environmental Quality
722 Jackson Pl., N.W.
Washington, DC 20503
Phone: (202)395-5080
Contact: Michael R. Deland, Chm.
Research Areas: Conducts, supports, and coordinates studies on environmental issues. Serves as an executive branch interagency arbitrator of environmental issues and adminsters the National Environmental Policy Act. Develops initiatives for the President's environmental programs and prepares the President's annual report to Congress on the quality of the environment.

★2888★ Coweeta Hydrologic Laboratory
999 Coweeta Laboratory Rd.
Otto, NC 28763
Phone: (704)524-2128
Fax: (704)369-6768
Contact: Dr. Wayne T. Swank, Director's Rep.
Parent Agencies: Department of Agriculture, Forest Service, Southeastern Forest Experiment Station. ***Research Areas:*** Forests and water in the Southern Appalachian Mountains, focusing on soil and nutrient losses caused by forest disturbances and atmospheric deposition and climate change.

★2889★ Delaware Water Resources Center
University of Delaware
210 Hullihen Hall
Newark, DE 19716
Phone: (302)451-2136
Contact: Dr. Robert D. Varrin, Dir.
Parent Agencies: Department of the Interior, U.S. Geological Survey, Water Resources Division. ***Research Areas:*** Water resources, emphasizing groundwater contamination. Also studies eutrophication, sedimentation, acid precipitation, water supply, water resources planning and management, and the development of groundwater use.

★2890★ Denver Wildlife Research Center
Denver Federal Center, Bldg. 16
PO Box 25266
Denver, CO 80225-0266
Phone: (303)236-7820
Fax: (303)236-7863
Contact: Dr. Russell Reidinger Jr., Dir.
Parent Agencies: Department of Agriculture, Animal and Plant Health Inspection Service. ***Research Areas:*** Focuses on reducing the damage wildlife causes to agriculture, forests, industry, or other areas of human endeavor. Activities include damage assessment; laboratory and field studies of animal behavior and ecology; development and testing of methods for eliminating animal damage; and studies in predator-prey ecology. Studies involve wildlife biology and ecology, pharmacology, animal psychology, statistics, physiology, and analytical chemistry.

★2891★ District of Columbia Water Resources Research Center
University of the District of Columbia
4200 Connecticut Ave., N.W., MB 5004
Washington, DC 20008
Phone: (202)673-3442
Fax: (202)673-2085
Contact: Dr. Mamadou H. Watt, Dir.
Parent Agencies: Department of the Interior, U.S. Geological Survey, Water Resources Division. ***Research Areas:*** Water quantity and quality, particularly of the Anacostia River. Activities include studies of nonpoint source pollution, erosion of soil from land and streams, and urban runoff.

★2892★ Duluth Environmental Research Laboratory
6201 Congdon Blvd.
Duluth, MN 55804
Phone: (218)720-5550
Contact: Gilman D. Veith, Dir.
Parent Agencies: Environmental Protection Agency, Office of Research and Development. ***Research Areas:*** Develops national water quality criteria for the freshwater environment and has primary research responsibility for describing the fate and effects of pollutants in the Great Lakes. Located on Lake Superior, the Laboratory specializes in the toxicology of pesticides, industrial chemicals, and other pollutants in freshwater ecosystems.

★2893★ Duluth Environmental Research Laboratory
Large Lakes Research Station
9311 Groh Rd.
Grosse Ile, MI 48138
Phone: (313)675-2245
Fax: (313)675-7734
Contact: William L. Richardson, Station Chief
Parent Agencies: Environmental Protection Agency, Office of Research and Development. ***Research Areas:*** Collects data on the Great Lakes to determine the fate, transport, and effects of pollutants. Research activities include measurements and modeling of pollutant inputs and pollutant concentrations in the lakes and sediments and the effects of pollutants on the ecosystem and humans.

★2894★ Duluth Environmental Research Laboratory
Monticello Ecological Research Station
PO Box 500
Monticello, MN 55362
Phone: (612)295-5145
Contact: Steven F. Hedtke, Chief
Parent Agencies: Environmental Protection Agency, Office of Research and Development. ***Research Areas:*** Provides field assessment of laboratory data used to develop water quality criteria. Primary mission is to: 1) validate water quality criteria data produced in the laboratory through long-term research under field conditions; 2) identify significant responses by aquatic organisms to selected pollutants under field monitoring conditions; 3) provide information on methodology and interpretation of laboratory bioassays; and 4) combine studies

on fate and effect of pollutants. Principal fields of research are aquatic biology, toxicology, and ecology.

★2895★ Economic Research Service
Resources and Technology Division
1301 New York Ave., N.W., Ste. 524
Washington, DC 20005-4788
Phone: (202)786-1450
Contact: Dr. John A. Miranowski, Dir.
Parent Agencies: Department of Agriculture. ***Research Areas:*** Analyzes agricultural resources, technology, and inputs. Primary emphasis is on soil, water, land, manufactured inputs, and technology issues of regional and national importance. Division's research encompasses analyses, supply, demand, and prices of agricultural resources and inputs; agricultural resource conservation and environmental programs; agriculture's effects on resource use and the natural environment; and resource and input productivity, substitution possibilities, and response to technological change.

★2896★ Ecosystems Research Center
105 Wing Hall
Ithaca, NY 14853
Phone: (607)256-4617
Contact: Leonard Weinstein, Dir.
Parent Agencies: Environmental Protection Agency, Office of Research and Development. ***Research Areas:*** Established at Cornell University under a cooperative agreement with EPA, the Center conducts research related to ecosystems science. Primary goals are to identify fundamental principles and concepts of ecosystems and science and determine their importance in understanding and predicting the responses of ecosystems to stress; to describe the basic mechanisms that operate within ecosystems and the stability of ecosystems in the face of stress; and to evaluate the applicability of these theoretical concepts to problems of concern to EPA. The four principal components of the Center's program are: 1) in-depth studies of particular ecosystems; 2) across-systems comparisons of responses to stress; 3) the development of working collaborations with EPA program offices, task forces, and laboratories to test the applicability of ecosystem concepts to problems of concern to the Agency; and 4) the development of relations within the scientific community in order to identify the scientific issues relevant to EPA's needs and to attract basic scientists to the solution of these problems.

★2897★ Energy Information Administration
Office of Coal, Nuclear, Electric, and Alternate Fuels
Nuclear and Alternate Fuels Division
1707 H St., N.W., Rm. 701
Washington, DC 20585
Phone: (202)254-5500
Contact: Howard Walton, Dir.
Parent Agencies: Department of Energy. ***Research Areas:*** Manages the data information systems on all supply aspects of nuclear power and alternate fuels; prepares analyses and projections on the availability, production, cost, processing, transportation, and distribution of nuclear and alternate energy sources; and prepares projections about energy supply and production from alternate energy forms, including solar, wind, and wood.

★2898★ Energy Information Administration
Office of Oil and Gas
Reserves and Natural Gas Division
Mail Stop EI-44
1000 Independence Ave., S. W., Rm. BE064
Washington, DC 20585
Phone: (202)586-6090
Fax: (202)586-8134
Contact: Diane W. Lique, Dir.
Parent Agencies: Department of Energy. ***Research Areas:*** Designs, develops, and maintains statistical and projection information systems for domestic oil and gas reserves and production, and the natural gas industry. Performs data collection, processing, analysis, projections, and report preparation activities associated with oil, gas, and natural gas liquids reserves and production and natural gas supply and disposition.

★2899★ Environmental Measurements Laboratory
376 Hudson St.
New York, NY 10014
Phone: (212)620-3607
Contact: Dr. E. Gail de Planque, Dir.
Parent Agencies: Department of Energy. ***Research Areas:*** Studies pollutants and their effects on human health and the environment, including non-nuclear pollutants and natural and anthropogenic radionuclides. Activities emphasize analytical chemistry, radioanalytical procedures, specialized instrumentation, and quality assurance testing.

★2900★ Environmental Monitoring Systems Laboratory (Cincinnati, OH)
Environmental Protection Agency
26 W. Martin Luther King Dr.
Cincinnati, OH 45268
Phone: (513)569-7301
Fax: (513)569-7424
Contact: Thomas A. Clark, Acting Dir.
Parent Agencies: Environmental Protection Agency, Office of Research and Development. ***Research Areas:*** Aims to: 1) develop analytical test procedures to identify and measure major pollutants and quality characteristics in drinking water, ambient receiving waters, and municipal and industrial effluents; 2) develop monitoring techniques to identify and enumerate microorganisms of health significance in drinking water, ambient waters, and municipal wastes; 3) devise laboratory procedures to detect, identify, and measure viruses in water, municipal wastes, and sludges; and 4) devise field and laboratory procedures to determine the biological effects of waste discharges on receiving waters.

★2901★ Environmental Monitoring Systems Laboratory (Las Vegas, NV)
PO Box 93478
Las Vegas, NV 89193-3478
Phone: (702)798-2100
Contact: Robert N. Snelling, Acting Dir.
Parent Agencies: Environmental Protection Agency, Office of Research and Development. ***Research Areas:*** Aims to: 1) develop for EPA client offices multi-media monitoring technologies and approaches for assessing exposure of humans and the environment to pollutants; 2) demonstrate advanced monitoring systems and techniques by applying them to fulfill special monitoring needs of the Agency; 3) develop guidance on standardization and quality assurance aspects of radiation, hazardous waste, toxic substances, and pesticide measurements; and 4) provide monitoring and surveillance services around nuclear weapons testing sites and at sites with special environmental significance.

★2902★ Environmental Monitoring Systems Laboratory (Research Triangle Park, NC)
Mail Drop 75
Research Triangle Park, NC 27711
Phone: (919)541-2106
Contact: Gary Foley, Dir.
Parent Agencies: Independent Agencies, Environmental Protection Agency, Office of Research and Development, EPA Research Laboratories. ***Research Areas:*** Monitors pollutants in the environments; develops sampling strategies and techniques for monitoring hazardous waste leachates in soil and groundwater; develops remote sensing techniques; conducts human exposure monitoring and modeling studies covering several environmental media; evaluates analytical methods for the characterization and quantification of hazardous wastes; and provides quality assurance in support of the EPA's hazardous waste, Superfund, pesticides, ionizing radiation, and acid deposition programs.

★2903★ Environmental Mutagen Information Center
Bldg. 2001, Mail Stop 6050
PO Box 2008
Oak Ridge, TN 37831-6050
Phone: (615)574-7871
Fax: (615)574-9888
Contact: J.S. Wassom, Dir.
Parent Agencies: Department of Energy, Energy Data Centers. ***Research Areas:*** Collects, organizes, and disseminates information of relevance to the field of genetic toxicology.

★2904★ Environmental Protection Agency
Environmental Services Division
Ecological Support Branch
EPA Region IV
College Sta. Rd.
Athens, GA 30613
Phone: (404)546-3136
Contact: Delbert Hicks, Chief
Research Areas: Branch is responsible for coordinating and executing air, water, and terrestrial monitoring in support of regional and state implemented programs. This involves field testing and adapting newly developed methodology for routine field application.

★2905★ Environmental Protection Agency
Office of Pesticides and Toxic Substances
Economics and Technology Division
Mail Code TS-779
401 M St., S.W., Rm. E235
Washington, DC 20460
Phone: (202)260-3667
Contact: Susan Hazen, Acting Dir.
Research Areas: Provides technical support to the EPA's regulatory programs in the areas of applied environmental economics, occupational exposure, chemical emissions, industrial chemistry, and personal protective equipment.

★2906★ Environmental Protection Agency
Office of Research and Development
Office of Health and Environmental Assessment
Environmental Criteria and Assessment Office (Cincinnati, OH)
26 W. Martin Luther King Dr.
Cincinnati, OH 45268
Phone: (513)569-7531
Fax: (513)684-7276
Contact: Chris DeRosa, Acting Dir.
Research Areas: Preparing criteria and assessment documents for the protection of

human health from multimedia environmental pollutants and develops risk assessment methodology and guidelines. Serves as an ORD focal point to collect, evaluate, and assess literature generated by researchers (nationally and internationally) and to provide research information to those in EPA and in the Congress who are responsibile for regulatory and legislative decisions regarding environmental pollution control in the United States.

★2907★ Environmental Protection Agency
Office of Research and Development
Office of Health and Environmental Assessment
Environmental Criteria and Assessment Office (Research Triangle Park, NC)
Mail Drop 52
Research Triangle Park, NC 27711
Phone: (919)541-4173
Fax: (919)541-5078
Contact: Dr. Lester D. Grant, Dir.
Research Areas: Furnishes scientific information to those in EPA and in Congress who are responsible for making regulatory and legislative decisions regarding pollution control. Office does not generate research data, but collects and evaluates scientific literature produced by national and international researchers. Major objective is to comply with provisions in the Clean Air Act that deal with preparation and publication of criteria documents and to serve as the focal point for assessment of research results performed within the Agency. Basically, ECAO/RTP produces three types of documents: 1) revised or new criteria documents that serve as a basis for setting national ambient air quality standards for pollutants; 2) health assessment documents that deal with health effects of pollutants suspected of needing control; and 3) special reports required to meet a specific need or as dictated by legislation, usually involving risk assessment and/or health and welfare effects assessment. Also manages ORD's indoor air research program and development of inhalation reference dose methodology.

★2908★ Environmental Protection Agency
Office of Research and Development
Office of Health and Environmental Assessment
Exposure Assessment Group
Mail Code RD -689
401 M St., S.W.
Washington, DC 20460
Phone: (202)260-8909
Contact: Michael Callahan, Dir.
Research Areas: Group is responsible for developing exposure assessment guidance and reviewing and conducting exposure assessments. Principal research activity is the analysis of human exposure to toxic chemicals.

★2909★ Environmental Protection Agency
National Enforcement Investigations Center
Information Services Section
Denver Federal Center, Bldg. 53
PO Box 25227
Denver, CO 80225
Phone: (303)236-2378
Contact: Charlene Swibas, Chief
Parent Agencies: Environmental Protection Agency, Office of Enforcement and Compliance Monitoring. ***Research Areas:*** Distributes technical reports on site evaluations, field studies, and pollution abatement activities. Activities also involve collecting and analyzing data on enforcement and compliance of environmental laws and regulations.

★2910★ Environmental Protection Agency
National Enforcement Investigations Center
Laboratory Services Division
Denver Federal Center, Bldg. 53
PO Box 25227
Denver, CO 80225
Phone: (303)236-5132
Contact: Joe Lowry, Acting Dir.
Parent Agencies: Environmental Protection Agency, Office of Enforcement and Compliance Monitoring. ***Research Areas:*** Activities involve a broad range of analytical testing of air, water, soil, hazardous wastes, and other materials to obtain evidence for legal action against environmental polluters. Principal fields of research interest are environmental and analytical chemistry. Division comprises the Environmental Chemistry Branch and Pesticide and Toxic Substances Branch.

★2911★ Environmental Protection Agency
Office of Air Quality Planning and Standards
Monitoring and Data Analysis Division
Monitoring and Reports Branch
Mail Drop 14
Research Triangle Park, NC 27711
Phone: (919)541-5559
Fax: (919)541-5663
Contact: William F. Hunt Jr., Chief
Parent Agencies: Environmental Protection Agency, Office of Air and Radiation. ***Research Areas:*** Provides monitoring oversight of the national ambient air monitoring program; provides statistical analysis of ambient air quality and issues national and regional air quality trends analyses; and 3) develops emission factors for emission inventories and issues emission inventory guidance.

★2912★ Environmental Protection Agency
Eastern Environmental Radiation Facility
National Air and Radiation Environmental Laboratory
1504 Ave. A
Montgomery, AL 36115-2601
Phone: (205)270-3400
Fax: (205)270-3454
Contact: Charles R. Porter, Dir.
Parent Agencies: Environmental Protection Agency, Office of Air and Radiation. ***Research Areas:*** Assesses ambient radiation levels and levels resulting from nuclear accidents by operating the Environmental Radiation Ambient Monitoring System.

★2913★ Environmental Protection Agency
National Enforcement Investigations Center
Denver Federal Center, Bldg. 53
PO Box 25227
Denver, CO 80225
Phone: (303)236-5100
Contact: Frank Covington, Dir.
Parent Agencies: Environmental Protection Agency, Office of Enforcement and Compliance Monitoring. ***Research Areas:*** Provides legal expertise in civil and criminal cases and provides investigative support for national, regional, or state regulatory programs. Emphasis is on air, water, toxics, pesticides, radiation, and solid wastes pollution control. Activities involve providing scientific and technical evidence; providing quick response services in emergency situations; coordinating with the Office and regional offices' enforcement strategies; providing consultation and assistance in case preparation activities; providing management, training, and specialized assistance to regional offices on criminal investigations; and providing expert testimony in support of enforcement actions. In addition, Center coordinates the compilation and analysis of scientific and technical data; and provides support and training for federal, state, and local personnel and other agencies involved in civil and criminal cases.

★2914★ Environmental Protection Agency
Office of Research and Development
Office of Environmental Engineering and Technology Demonstration
Mail Code RD -681
401 M St., S.W.
Washington, DC 20460
Phone: (202)260-2600
Contact: John H. Skinner, Dir.
Research Areas: Develops and demonstrates methods to control environmental impacts associated with extracting, processing, converting, and transporting energy, minerals, and other resources and with industrial processing and manufacturing facilities; 2) develops and demonstrates methods to prevent or manage pollutant discharge or waste disposal into the environment from public sector activities (including wastewater and solid waste facilities); and 3) develops criteria to improve drinking water supply and system operations. Office's research program is implemented primarily by the Air and Energy Engineering Research Laboratory and the Risk Reduction Engineering Laboratory.

★2915★ Environmental Protection Agency
Office of Research and Development
Office of Environmental Processes and Effects Research
Mail Code RD -682
401 M St., S.W.
Washington, DC 20460
Phone: (202)260-5950
Contact: Courtney Riordan, Dir.
Research Areas: Develops the scientific and technological methods and data necessary to understand, predict, and manage the entry, movement, and fate of pollutants in the environment and the food chain and to determine the effects of pollutants upon nonhuman organisms and ecosystems.

★2916★ Environmental Protection Agency
Office of Research and Development
Office of Health and Environmental Assessment
Mail Code RD -689
401 M St., S.W.
Washington, DC 20460
Phone: (202)260-7317
Contact: Dr. William H. Farland, Dir.
Research Areas: Provides the EPA with a central capability for evaluating information on the potential health and environmental effects of toxic pollutants. Assessments are prepared on the risks to human health posed by the presence of toxic agents in water, air, and land. EPA uses this scientific and technical knowledge to implement its statutory responsibilities.

★2917★ Environmental Protection Agency
Office of Research and Development
Office of Health Research
Mail Code RD -683
401 M St., S.W.
Washington, DC 20460
Phone: (202)260-5900
Contact: Ken Sexton, Dir.
Research Areas: Develops and evaluates toxicity test methods and provides toxicity data to enable the Agency to accurately identify hazards and determine human risk from environmental exposure. Focuses on inhalation toxicology, genetic toxicology, neurotoxicology, developmental and reproductive toxicology, microbiology, epidemiology, and biometry.

★2918★ Environmental Protection Agency
Office of Research and Development
Office of Modeling, Monitoring Systems, and Quality Assurance
Mail Code RD -680
401 M St., S.W.
Washington, DC 20460
Phone: (202)260-5767
Fax: (202)260-0929
Contact: Rick A. Linthurst, Acting Dir.
Research Areas: Exposure modeling, exposure assessment, exposure classification, and monitoring and environmental characterization. Develops modeling, monitoring and quality assurance capabilities to assure the completion of precise, accurate exposure assessments. Focuses on the conduct of the Environmental Monitoring and Assessment Program (EMAP) designed to monitor indicators of the condition of our nations' ecological resources. Office is also responsible for coordinating the agency-wide Quality Assurance Program.

★2919★ Environmental Protection Agency
Office of Research and Development
RD -672
401 M St., S.W.
Washington, DC 20460
Phone: (202)260-7676
Fax: (202)260-0552
Contact: Erich Bretthauer, Assistant Admin.
Research Areas: Technological controls of all forms of pollution focusing on pollution prevention. Supervises the EPA's national laboratories and gives technical policy direction to those laboratories that support the program responsibilities of EPA's regional offices. General functions include management of selected demonstration programs; planning for Agency environmental quality monitoring programs; coordination of Agency monitoring efforts with those of other federal agencies, states, and other public bodies; and dissemination of Agency research, development, and demonstration results. EPA's research and development facilities are organized under six ORD offices: 1) the Office of Modeling, Monitoring Systems, and Quality Assurance; 2) Office of Environmental Engineering and Technology Demonstration; 3) Office of Environmental Processes and Effects Research; 4) Office of Exploratory Research; 5) Office of Health and Environmental Assessment; and 6) Office of Health Research.

★2920★ Environmental Protection Agency
Office of Air Quality Planning and Standards
Emission Standards Division
Pollutant Assessment Branch
Mail Drop 13
Research Triangle Park, NC 27711
Phone: (919)541-5645
Contact: Robert G. Kellam, Chief
Parent Agencies: Environmental Protection Agency, Office of Air and Radiation. ***Research Areas:*** Assessment of toxic air pollutants, particularly regarding exposure and risk analysis.

★2921★ Environmental Protection Agency
Office of Research and Development
Office of Exploratory Research
Research Centers Program
401 M St., S.W.
Washington, DC 20460
Phone: (202)260-5750
Fax: (202)260-0450
Contact: Karen Morehouse, Dir.
Research Areas: The Research Centers Program consists of two programs 1) the Hazardous Substance Research Center Program manages five university-based consortiums distributed throughout the U.S; conducts long and short term exploratory research on the manufacture, use, transport, disposal, treatment, and remediation of hazardous substances; maintains a training/technology transfer function; and 2) Exploratory Research Centers Program conducts multidisciplinary, long term research in epidemiology, advanced pollution control technology, groundwater, industrial waste elimination, intermedia transport, ecosystems, marine science, and hazardous wastes.

★2922★ Environmental Studies Center
University of Maine-Orono
11 Coburn Hall
Orono, ME 04469
Phone: (207)581-1490
Contact: Dr. Gregory K. White, Dir.
Parent Agencies: Department of the Interior, U.S. Geological Survey, Water Resources Division. ***Research Areas:*** Terrestrial and freshwater resources. Performs studies in the areas of radon levels in well water and household air, acid rain, groundwater protection, and land and stream protection.

★2923★ Federal Highway Administration
Office of Environmental Policy
Noise and Air Analysis Division
Mail Code HEV-30
400 Seventh St., S.W., Rm. 3240
Washington, DC 20590
Phone: (202)366-4836
Fax: (202)366-3409
Contact: James M. Shrouds, Chief
Parent Agencies: Department of Transportation. ***Research Areas:*** Division's activities include: 1) developing policies, regulations, and administrative procedures for the identification, measurement, evaluation, and mitigation of highway traffic noise and motor vehicular air pollution; 2) cooperating with the Transportation Research Board and offices of research and development to initiate, manage, and implement research; and 3) assisting federal, state, and local officials in the development of land near highways to assure that future development is compatible with expected traffic noise levels. Division also reviews and comments on proposed legislation and cooperates with other DOT and federal agencies to influence the development of noise and air quality legislations, policies, regulations, and administrative procedures; and maintains close relationships with offices of the FHWA to assure consideration of noise and air quality effects in all aspects of the highway program.

★2924★ Federal Interagency Sedimentation Project
St. Anthony Falls Hydraulic Laboratory
Third Avenue, S.E. & Hennepin Island
Minneapolis, MN 55414-2196
Phone: (612)370-2361
Contact: John V. Skinner, Project Chief
Parent Agencies: Department of the Interior, U.S. Geological Survey, Water Resources Division. ***Research Areas:*** Project functions as a research and development center for development of: 1) sediment sampling techniques and 2) field and laboratory equipment.

★2925★ Florida Cooperative Fish and Wildlife Research Unit
University of Florida
117 Newins-Ziegler Hall
Gainesville, FL 32611
Phone: (904)392-1861
Contact: Dr. Wiley M. Kitchens, Leader
Parent Agencies: Department of the Interior, U.S. Fish and Wildlife Service. ***Research Areas:*** Unit's program of wildlife research and management focuses primarily on the value of wetlands to fish and wildlife. Unit's functions also include graduate research training, university instruction, and extension services.

★2926★ Florida Water Resources Research Center
University of Florida
424 Black Hall
Gainesville, FL 32611
Phone: (904)392-0840
Contact: Dr. James P. Heaney, Dir.
Parent Agencies: Department of the Interior, U.S. Geological Survey, Water Resources Division. ***Research Areas:*** Water resources, including stormwater management, groundwater protection, pollutant transport through soil-water systems, and methods of quantifying the benefits of water projects. ***Databases:*** Florida lakes.

★2927★ Forest Service
South Bldg.
14th St. & Independence Ave., SW
PO Box 96090
Washington, DC 20090-6090
Phone: (202)447-3760
Parent Agencies: Department of Agriculture. ***Research Areas:*** Responsible for maintaining the national forest system. Areas of interest include forest fire protection, insects and disease, timber management, wood products and timber-harvesting methodology, wildlife habitat, recreation, and economics. Activities are administered at the Forest Products Laboratory in Madison, Wisconsin and at eight regional stations: Intermountain, North Central, Northeastern, Pacific Northwest, Pacific Southwest, Rocky Mountain, Southeastern, and Southern.

★2928★ Forest Service
Forest Environment Research Staff
U. S. Dept. of Agriculture
PO Box 96090
Washington, DC 20090-6090
Phone: (703)235-1071
Contact: Richard V. Smythe, Staff Dir.
Parent Agencies: Department of Agriculture. ***Research Areas:*** Coordinates the national Forest Service research program for forestry projects in range, wildlife, and fish research; recreation research; and watershed management and mineland rehabilitation research studies.

★2929★ Forest Service
Forest Fire and Atmospheric Sciences Research Center
PO Box 96090
Washington, DC 20090-6090
Phone: (703)235-8195
Contact: William T. Sommers, Dir.
Parent Agencies: Department of Agriculture. ***Research Areas:*** Coordinates the national Forest Service research program for forestry projects related to forest fires and atmospheric sciences. Principal fields of research involved are: 1) fire science; 2) atmospheric science; 3) forestry; 4) air pollution; and 5) acid rain.

★2930★ Forest Service
Timber Management Research Staff
PO Box 96090
Washington, DC 20090-6090
Phone: (202)453-9555
Contact: Dr. Stanley L. Krugman, Dir.
Parent Agencies: Department of Agriculture. ***Research Areas:*** Coordinates the national Forest Service research program for forestry projects in silviculture, ecology, forest genetics,

environmental forestry, special products, and biotechnology.

★2931★ Forestry Sciences Laboratory (Charleston, SC)
2730 Savannah Hwy.
Charleston, SC 29414
Phone: (803)556-4860
Contact: William R. Harms, Project Leader
Parent Agencies: Department of Agriculture, Forest Service, Southeastern Forest Experiment Station. ***Research Areas:*** Wetlands management and wildlife management.

★2932★ Forestry Sciences Laboratory (Corvallis, OR)
3200 S.W. Jefferson Way
Corvallis, OR 97331
Phone: (503)750-7250
Fax: (503)750-7329
Parent Agencies: Department of Agriculture, Forest Service, Pacific Northwest Research Station. ***Research Areas:*** Reforestation systems in the Pacific Northwest; genetic improvement of Pacific Northwest trees and studies to determine the ecological basis for management of Northwest coniferous forests; landscape ecology; coastal Oregon productivity enhancement; biological methods for managing western forest insect pests; symbiosis and disease in western ecosystems; and long-term site productivity. Fields of interest include forest ecology, genetics, entomology, and forest pathology; reforestation, forest watershed and soils management; diseases of forest trees; and anadromous fish habitats.

★2933★ Forestry Sciences Laboratory (Juneau, AL)
700 W. Ninth St.
PO Box 20909
Juneau, AK 99802
Phone: (907)586-8811
Fax: (907)586-7848
Contact: J.W. Henley, Project Co-Leader
Parent Agencies: Department of Agriculture, Forest Service, Pacific Northwest Research Station. ***Research Areas:*** Ecology of southeastern Alaska forests, including recommending improvements in silvicultural practices, investigating factors that influence forest diseases and insects, studying wildlife habitat and forest-management interactions, investigating relations between slope stability and soil mass movement, investigating forest hydrology, and identifying wildlife habitat in coastal wetlands; and anadromous fish habitat, including studies of the habitat requirements of salmonids, investigations of the effects of land-use activities on fish habitat, and recommendations on methods of rehabilitating and enhancing anadromous fish habitat.

★2934★ Forestry Sciences Laboratory (Olympia, WA)
3625 93rd Ave., S.W.
Olympia, WA 98502
Phone: (206)753-9470
Fax: (206)753-9597
Parent Agencies: Department of Agriculture, Forest Service, Pacific Northwest Research Station. ***Research Areas:*** Biology and silviculture of forests of the Douglas-fir region, including studies to measure growth and yield of intensively managed young Douglas-fir stands, determine the response of Pacific coast conifers to fertilization and nitrogen-fixing plants, develop silvicultural guidelines for upper-slope, mixed-conifer forests, and determine the effects of intensive culture on alder and poplar; and wildlife habitat relationships in western Washington and Oregon, including studies to describe patterns of wildlife abundance in Douglas-fir forests and identify species that depend on (or potentially depend on) late stages of forest development, describe the status and ecology of species that depend on or are closely associated with late successional forests, determine the effect of forest-habitat size, distribution, and management status on species abundance and distribution, and define ecological dependency and develop a paradigm for use in maintaining populations of late-successional wildlife species in managed forests.

★2935★ Forestry Sciences Laboratory (Wenatchee, WA)
1133 N. Western Ave.
Wenatchee, WA 98801
Phone: (509)662-4315
Contact: Richard L. Everett, Project Leader
Parent Agencies: Department of Agriculture, Forest Service, Pacific Northwest Research Station. ***Research Areas:*** Provides methods and guidelines for the maintenance of watershed stability, reforestation, and long-term productivity of upper slope forests of the interior Northwest. Principal fields of research include meteorology, plant ecology, forest tree physiology, soil productivity, and vegetation management.

★2936★ Fred Lawrence Whipple Observatory
Amado Rd.
PO Box 97
Amado, AZ 85645
Phone: (602)670-6741
Fax: (602)670-6779
Contact: Stephen J. Criswell, Program Manager
Parent Agencies: Smithsonian Institution. ***Research Areas:*** Spectroscopic observations of extragalactic, stellar, and planetary bodies, automatic photometry of variable stars, gamma-ray and cosmic-ray astronomy, and environmental studies.

★2937★ Georgia Cooperative Fish and Wildlife Research Unit
University of Georgia
School of Forest Resources
Athens, GA 30602
Phone: (404)542-5260
Contact: Dr. Michael J. Van Den Avyle, Leader
Parent Agencies: Department of the Interior, U.S. Fish and Wildlife Service. ***Research Areas:*** Management of fish and wildlife, with additional studies on environmental contaminants.

★2938★ Georgia Environmental Resources Center
Georgia Institute of Technology
205 Old Civil Engineering Bldg.
Atlanta, GA 30332
Phone: (404)894-3776
Contact: Dr. Bernd Kahn, Dir.
Parent Agencies: Department of the Interior, U.S. Geological Survey, Water Resources Division. ***Research Areas:*** Water resources, focusing on streamflow prediction, groundwater modeling, and industrial and wastewater treatment. Also studies social impacts of water programs, water use optimization in industry and agriculture, well location and yields, infrastructure financing, wetland management, and reservior designs. Develops computational models of surface and groundwater quantity for planning industrial and agricultural growth in the state.

★2939★ Goddard Space Flight Center Flight Projects Directorate Earth Observing System
(EOS) Study Project/Code 420
Grennbelt, MD 20771
Contact: J.J. Madden, Contact
Parent Agencies: National Aeronautics and Space Administration. ***Research Areas:*** Provides the long-term observations and the supporting information system necessary to develop a comprehensive understanding of the way Earth functions as a natural system, including the interactions of the atmosphere, oceans, cryopshere, biosphere and the solid earth, particularly as they are manifested in the flow of energy through the Earth system, the cycling of water and biochemicals, and the recycling of the Earth's crust driven by the energy of the interior of the Earth. The EOS Project is directed toward the gathering and dissemination of earth science data over a prolonged period (15 years) for use in systematic studies of the Earth's natural processes through the use of a series of polar orbiting observatories.

★2940★ Goddard Space Flight Center Earth Sciences Directorate
Mail Code 900
Greenbelt, MD 20771
Phone: (301)286-8601
Contact: Dr. Vincent Salomonson, Dir.
Parent Agencies: National Aeronautics and Space Administration. ***Research Areas:*** Conducts earth sciences research and development. Areas of interest include geophysics, geodynamics, hydrology, remote sensing of vegetation, computer sciences, global circulation and climate models.

★2941★ Goddard Space Flight Center Laboratory for Atmospheres
Mail Code 610
Greenbelt, MD 20771
Phone: (301)286-5002
Contact: Charles E. Cote, Associate Chief
Parent Agencies: National Aeronautics and Space Administration. ***Research Areas:*** Studies the Earth's atmosphere and the atmospheres of other planets in our solar system, with emphasis on the use of space techniques. Activities include data analysis, theory, and instrument development. Areas of interest are: solar radiation, global modeling, severe storms, climate, planetary aeronomy, mass spectrometry, atmospheric chemistry (stratosphere and troposphere), and laser techniques.

★2942★ Great Lakes Environmental Research Laboratory
2205 Commonwealth Blvd.
Ann Arbor, MI 48105-1593
Phone: (313)668-2235
Fax: (313)668-2055
Contact: Dr. Alfred M. Beeton, Dir.
Parent Agencies: Department of Commerce, National Oceanic and Atmospheric Administration, Office of Oceanic and Atmospheric Research, Environmental Research Laboratories. ***Research Areas:*** Conducts integrated, interdisciplinary environmental research in support of resource management and environmental services in coastal and estuarine waters, with special emphasis on the Great Lakes.

★2943★ Guam Water and Energy Research Institute of the Western Pacific
University of Guam
UOG Sta.
House #29, Dean's Circle
Mangilao, GU 96923
Phone: (671)734-3132
Fax: (671)734-3118
Contact: Dr. Shahram Khosrowpanah, Acting Dir.
Parent Agencies: Department of the Interior, U.S. Geological Survey, Water Resources Division. ***Research Areas:*** Water resources, focusing on groundwater, allocation of water resources, water supply and distribution, human health issues of water supply, including freshwater-saltwater lens systems, and waste disposal.

★2944★ Gulf Breeze Environmental Research Laboratory
Sabine Island
Gulf Breeze, FL 32561
Phone: (904)932-5311
Contact: Dr. Robert E. Menzer, Acting Dir.
Parent Agencies: Environmental Protection Agency, Office of Research and Development. ***Research Areas:*** Formulates standards, guidelines, and strategies for management of hazardous and biotechnological materials in aquatic environments. Develops and evaluates procedures and protocols for biological treatment of hazardous wastes and bioremediation of contaminated sites; mechanisms that affect biodegradation and bioaccumulation of toxicants in aquatic food webs; effects of carcinogens, mutagens, and teratogens on aquatic species, ecological risk assessments to predict effects of toxic chemicals, pesticides, and biotechnological products on aquatic organisms, and systems; diagnostic signs (bioindicators) of environmental stress in marine systems.

★2945★ Hawaii Cooperative Fishery Research Unit
University of Hawaii
2538 The Mall
Honolulu, HI 96822
Phone: (808)948-8350
Contact: Dr. James D. Parrish, Leader
Parent Agencies: Department of the Interior, U.S. Fish and Wildlife Service. ***Research Areas:*** Freshwater, estuarine, and inshore marine biology. Program includes studies on the life history of fishes; stream, estuarine, and marine ecosystems; trophic relationships; and aquatic communities.

★2946★ Hawaii Water Resources Research Center
University of Hawaii-Manoa
2540 Dole St., Holmes Hall 283
Honolulu, HI 96822
Phone: (808)948-7847
Fax: (808)948-5044
Contact: Dr. L. Stephen Lau, Dir.
Parent Agencies: Department of the Interior, U.S. Geological Survey, Water Resources Division. ***Research Areas:*** Water resources, including multidisciplinary studies in hydrology, geochemistry, microbiology/virology, sanitary engineering, public health, climatology, soil physics, agricultural engineering, agricultural economics, law, meteorology, zoology, and ocean engineering. Conducts research in Hawaii and the Pacific Basin area (American Samoa, Saipan, Bikini, Kwajalein, Majuro, Belau, and Pohnpei). ***Databases:*** Maintains databases on streamflow, rainfall, evapotranspiration, groundwater.

★2947★ Hazardous Materials Technical Center
PO Box 8168
Rockville, MD 20856-8168
Phone: 800-638-8958
Contact: Tom Bertell, Dir.
Parent Agencies: Department of Defense, Defense Logistics Agency, Defense Information Analysis Centers. ***Research Areas:*** Hazardous materials and waste management, from acquisition and handling to transport and disposal. Provides information on state-of-the-art technology and current regulations to persons involved with the safety, health, transportation, storage, handling, disposal, and environmental considerations of hazardous materials and wastes.

★2948★ Hazardous Waste Engineering Research Laboratory
Land Pollution Control Division
Releases Control Branch
U SE PA (MS-104)
2890 Woodbridge Ave., Bldg. 10
Edison, NJ 08837-3679
Phone: (201)321-6635
Contact: John Farlow, Branch Chief
Parent Agencies: Environmental Protection Agency, Office of Research and Development. ***Research Areas:*** Prevention, control, and abatement of multi-media pollution from releases of: oils and hazardous materials; leaking underground storage tanks; uncontrolled hazardous waste disposal sites; and stormwater run-off. Develops, tests, and evaluates personal protective clothing, breathing apparatus, and other safety equipment and procedures for those who must handle pesticides and other toxic substances (including those engaged in emergency response activities at chemical spills and hazardous waste sites).

★2949★ Health Effects Research Laboratory
Environmental Protection Agency
Research Triangle Park, NC 27711
Phone: (919)541-2281
Fax: (919)541-4324
Contact: Lawrence W. Reiter, Dir.
Parent Agencies: Environmental Protection Agency, Office of Research and Development. ***Research Areas:*** Formulates and implements a research program to investigate human health effects resulting from exposure to environmental pollutants. Also establishes cooperative research projects with academic and other scientific institutions which facilitate EPA effort in understanding health effects of environmental pollutants. This research program develops and applies biological assays, predictive models and extrapolation methods which serve as the basis for EPA's health risk assessments.

★2950★ Health Effects Research Laboratory
Genotoxic Toxicology Division
Biochemical and Molecular Toxicology Branch
Environmental Protection Agency
26 W. Martin Luther King Dr.
Cincinnati, OH 45268
Phone: (513)569-7401
Fax: (513)569-7609
Contact: F. Bernard Daniel Ph.D., Chief
Parent Agencies: Environmental Protection Agency, Office of Research and Development. ***Research Areas:*** Seeks to identify, characterize, and quantitate harmful effects of pollutants that may result from exposure to chemical, physical, or biological agents found in the environment. Attempts to predict as-yet-unsuspected future pollution problems for which an appropriate biochemical database can then be developed. Principal fields of research include the safe use of drinking water and other water exposures.

★2951★ Idaho Cooperative Fish and Wildlife Research Unit
University of Idaho
College of Forestry, Wildlife, & Range Sciences
Moscow, ID 83843
Phone: (208)885-6336
Fax: (208)885-6226
Contact: J. Michael Scott, Leader
Parent Agencies: Department of the Interior, U.S. Fish and Wildlife Service. ***Research Areas:*** Conducts a program of graduate student training and applied research in fish and wildlife ecology and management. Principal areas of research are: 1) biology and management of anadromous salmonid stocks; 2) effects of sediment and turbidity on fish and invertebrate populations; 3) effects of reduced stream discharge on fish and aquatic insect populations; 4) factors affecting survival and seaward migration of salmon; and 5) ecology of mammals and birds; 6) gap analysis of biodiversity protection; 7) preserve design for vertebrates and native vegetation; and 8) topics in conservation biology.

★2952★ Idaho National Engineering Laboratory
Idaho National Environmental Research Park
U. S. Department of Energy
785 DOE Pl.
Idaho Falls, ID 83402-4149
Phone: (208)526-2164
Fax: (208)526-2548
Contact: O.D. Markham, Coordinator
Parent Agencies: Department of Energy. ***Research Areas:*** Established to provide a controlled, protected outdoor laboratory for environmentally related research, particularly regarding the environmental impacts of energy research technologies and development. It is located on 572,000 acres of land in southeastern Idaho on a sagebrush step area that includes juniper-woodlands, grasslands, riparian habitat, plus limited seasonal and permanent surface water, rivers, ponds, river diversion spreading areas, and lost river sinks. Research conducted at this site involves: 1) characterization of vegetation, including succession, competition, water relationships, and responses to perturbations, 2) characterization of vertebrate and invertebrate fauna, including population dynamics, migration movements and activity patterns, and habitat requirements and use, and responses to perturbations, 3) development of ecological research techniques and equipment to identify and test ecological principles, pollutant behavior, and contaminant models, 4) characterization of transport vectors and pathways, radionuclide concentrations, and effects of energy related activities on biota, 5) migration and use of all, or particular parts (e.g. man-made ponds) of the Idaho Research Park by game and non-game wildlife species, 6) identification of effective bioindicators, 7) predator-prey relationships, predator behavior and ecology, prey cycles, and 8) assessment of abiotic and biotic intrusion mechanisms and the impacts on long-term waste disposal practices, 8) cooperative research on environmental changes with other research parks.

★2953★ Idaho Water Resources Research Institute
Morrill Hall, Rm. 106
University of Idaho
Moscow, ID 83843
Phone: (208)885-6429
Contact: Dr. Dale R. Ralston, Acting Dir.
Parent Agencies: Department of the Interior, U.S. Geological Survey, Water Resources Division. ***Research Areas:*** Water allocation and management and water quality, including studies on groundwater supply and management, pump station and surface diversion monitor systems for water and energy efficiency, fractured aquifer delineation using high resolution seismic methods in geothermal systems, nonpoint source pollution, and euthrophication thrends with shoreliine pheriphyton indices.

★2954★ Illinois Water Resources Center
University of Illinois
205 N. Mathews Ave.
Urbana, IL 61801
Phone: (217)333-0536
Fax: (217)333-8046
Contact: Dr. Glenn E. Stout, Dir.
Parent Agencies: Department of the Interior, U.S. Geological Survey, Water Resources Division. ***Research Areas:*** Groundwater quality, pollution from nonpoint sources, loss and degradation of water-based fish and wildlife habitat, water data management, and potential insufficiencies in water resources for urban, industrial, agricultural, and recreational uses. Activities include developing strategies for timing farm fertilizer applications to reduce nitrogen contamination of surface and ground waters. Administers research projects of the Illinois-Indiana Sea Grant Program.

★2955★ Indiana Water Resources Research Center
Purdue University
School of Civil Engineering
West Lafayette, IN 47907
Phone: (317)494-8041
Fax: (317)494-0395
Contact: Dr. Jeff R. Wright, Dir.
Parent Agencies: Department of the Interior, U.S. Geological Survey, Water Resources Division. ***Research Areas:*** Ground and surface water contamination and creation and deposition of acid rain, including studies on pesticides, fertilizers, and landfills.

★2956★ Institute of Northern Forestry
308 Tanana Dr.
Fairbanks, AK 99775-5500
Phone: (907)474-8163
Fax: (907)474-3350
Contact: Richard A. Werner, Project Leader
Parent Agencies: Department of Agriculture, Forest Service, Pacific Northwest Research Station. ***Research Areas:*** Ecology and management of taiga ecosystems in interior Alaska. Research involves: 1) long-term ecological research; 2) investigating the effects of fire on ecosystem components; 3) devising management strategies for regenerating and growing shrubs and trees; 4) investigating the interrelationships between forest insects, root decay, and host and site characteristics; 5) investigating relationships of hydrologic processes, sediment, and water quality in managed vegetation types; 6) characterizing habitat and forage relations for managing moose; and 7) effects of global climate change on boreal forests.

★2957★ Institute of Pacific Islands Forestry
1151 Punchbowl St., Rm. 323
Honolulu, HI 96813
Phone: (808)541-2628
Fax: 800-528-0556
Contact: C. Eugene Conrad, Institute Dir.
Parent Agencies: Department of Agriculture, Forest Service, Pacific Southwest Forest and Range Experiment Station. ***Research Areas:*** Research and development in: 1) timber and watershed management, including studies in nursery production and natural regeneration, tree improvement and productivity, stand management, and watershed improvement and protection; 2) American Pacific Islands forestry research, which involves analysis of the problems and potentials of forestry in Guam, the Federated States of Micronesia, Commonwealth of the Northern Mariana Islands, Republic of Palau, Republic of the Marshall Islands, and American Samoa, including development of data needed to determine tree species that would be successful in reforestation programs; and 3) Hawaii forest insect studies, which focus on identification and development of effective biological control of noxious weeds with insects. Institute's research programs include studies in plant ecology, hydrology, soils, forest management, and entomology.

★2958★ Institute of Tropical Forestry
Call Box 25000
Rio Piedras, PR 00928-2500
Phone: (809)766-5335
Fax: (809)250-6924
Contact: Dr. Ariel E. Lugo, Dir.
Parent Agencies: Department of Agriculture, Forest Service, Southern Forest Experiment Station. ***Research Areas:*** Serves as a source of information about tropical forests and forestry; generates new knowledge on this subject; and promotes application of forestry knowledge in the American tropics. ITF conducts both field and laboratory research and nursery and tropical forestry orientation and training; and collects and analyzes data. Additional areas of study include timber plantation culture; naturally regenerated forest ecosystems; conservation of forest wildlife, specifically the endangered Puerto Rican parrot; and watershed research.

★2959★ Iowa Cooperative Fish and Wildlife Research Unit
Iowa State University
Science Hall II
Ames, IA 50011
Phone: (515)294-3056
Contact: Dr. Paul A. Vohs, Leader
Parent Agencies: Department of the Interior, U.S. Fish and Wildlife Service. ***Research Areas:*** Biology, ecology, and management of fish and wildlife; wildlife-sociology interfaces; and pesticide-wildlife interactions. Other activities include technical and professional training in wildlife and fishery management.

★2960★ Iowa State Water Resources Research Institute
Iowa State University
355 Town Engineering Bldg.
Ames, IA 50011
Phone: (515)294-8921
Fax: (515)294-9273
Contact: Dr. T. Al Austin, Dir.
Parent Agencies: Department of the Interior, U.S. Geological Survey, Water Resources Division. ***Research Areas:*** Groundwater quality and management, treatment of drinking water, landfill alternatives, and recharge through glacial tills, including agricultural chemical fate and transport in groundwater, organic compounds in groundwater, nutrient recycling through subsurface irrigation and drainage, optimal pumping strategies, and radium removal from groundwater. Conducts demonstration projects on the control of stream degradation.

★2961★ Kansas Water Resources Research Institute
Kansas State University
144 Waters Hall
Manhattan, KS 66506
Phone: (913)532-5729
Contact: Dr. Hyde S. Jacobs, Dir.
Parent Agencies: Department of the Interior, U.S. Geological Survey, Water Resources Division. ***Research Areas:*** Water quality, environmental protection, and aquifer and river system analysis.

★2962★ Kentucky Water Resources Research Institute
University of Kentucky
219 Anderson Hall
Lexington, KY 40506-0046
Phone: (606)257-1832
Contact: Billy J. Barfield, Dir.
Parent Agencies: Department of the Interior, U.S. Geological Survey, Water Resources Division. ***Research Areas:*** Water quantity, including studies of acid mine drainage in the coal fields, groundwater pollution from nonpoint sources, illegal waste disposal pollution of surface and ground water, and sediment and stream turbidity caused by erosion, mines, and roads.

★2963★ Laboratory of Biomedical and Environmental Sciences
University of California-Los Angeles
900 Veteran Ave.
Los Angeles, CA 90024-1786
Phone: (213)825-9431
Fax: (213)825-9433
Contact: O.R. Lunt, Dir.
Parent Agencies: Department of Energy. ***Research Areas:*** Focuses on problems in energy-related medical, biomedical, and environmental fields. Research in environmental biology is concerned with the structure and function of arid region ecosystems, with emphasis on the physiological ecology of plants. The capability to predict the effects of perturbations due to energy activities or pollution is partially successful.

★2964★ Lawrence Berkeley Laboratory
1 Cyclotron Rd.
Berkeley, CA 94720
Phone: (415)486-4000
Fax: (415)486-5401
Contact: Dr. Charles V. Shank, Dir.
Parent Agencies: Department of Energy. ***Research Areas:*** Lawrence Berkeley Laboratory is a multi-program national laboratory that serves the nation and its scientific and educational communities. Its mission is to: perform multidisciplinary research in general sciences, energy sciences, and life sciences; develop and operate major national experimental facilities for use by qualified investigators; and provide educational and training opportunities for scientists and engineers. Its goal is to conduct research that is appropriate for an energy research laboratory, but not suited to the program goals or resources of a university or industrial laboratory. Programs encompass all the natural sciences as well as engineering, mathematics, and computer sciences. Conducts basic studies

of the nature of the atom and the cell, research on new treatments for cancer patients, and the development of advanced materials, instruments, facilities, and new energy sources. LBL comprises nine scientific divisions (Accelerator and Fusion Research, Applied Science, Cell and Molecular Biology, Chemical Biodynamics, Earth Sciences, Materials and Chemical Sciences, Nuclear Science, Physics, and Research Medicine and Radiation Biophysics) and a resources division that includes (Engineering, Information and Computing Sciences, and Occupational Health).

★2965★ Lawrence Berkeley Laboratory Earth Sciences Division
1 Cyclotron Rd.
Berkeley, CA 94720
Phone: (415)486-7347
Fax: (415)486-5686
Contact: T.V. McEvilly, Associate Dir.
Parent Agencies: Department of Energy. ***Research Areas:*** Geology and geochemistry, including aqueous geochemistry, petrology, and transport processes; geomechanics and geophysics, including electrical and electromagnetic research, seismology, and rock mechanics; and reservoir engineering and hydrogeology. Emphasizes aquifier and soil contamination, effective cleanup methods and instrumentation, geothermal research, advanced geophysical imaging, and multidisciplinary studies on underground storage of nuclear wastes.

★2966★ Lawrence Berkeley Laboratory Information and Computing Sciences Division
1 Cyclotron Rd.
Berkeley, CA 94720
Phone: (415)486-7474
Fax: (415)486-6363
Contact: Stewart C. Loken, Dir.
Parent Agencies: Department of Energy. ***Research Areas:*** Principal areas of research interest are: 1) advanced computer concepts, which involves research on problems concerning the effective use of distributed computer systems; 2) information analysis techniques, which involves research on innovative approaches to the management, manipulation, and display of large statistical and scientific databases that are not easily supported by existing commercial data management systems; and 3) the Populations at Risk to Environmental Pollution (PAREP) Project, which focuses on the collection, analysis, and interpretation of data pertaining to relationships between human health and environmental pollution.

★2967★ Lawrence Livermore National Laboratory
PO Box 808
Livermore, CA 94551
Phone: (415)422-1100
Contact: Dr. Roger E. Batzel, Dir.
Parent Agencies: Department of Energy. ***Research Areas:*** LLNL's mission is to conduct research, development, and educational activities related to the nuclear sciences and the use of energy. Much of the Laboratory's work is in nuclear weapons, including detailed designing of nuclear warheads, stockpile surveillance, non-proliferation analysis, treaty verification technology, and allied matters. Other LLNL activities involve research on energy and in biological and environmental science. Some research is conducted in energy conservation and resource recovery, with emphasis on in situ resource recovery (gas from coal, oil from shale); solar energy applications; and new approaches to old ideas (batteries and flywheels for automotive propulsion). Environmental programs include studies in aquatic and terrestrial ecology; pollutant transport processes; development of field instrumentation; and analyses of the implications of national energy policies. Also assists the Nuclear Regulatory Commission with technical problems related to reactor safety safeguards and waste management; engages in educational programs in coordination with University of California; and performs testing activities at the high explosives facility near Livermore and at the Nevada Test Site.

★2968★ Los Alamos National Laboratory Los Alamos National Environmental Research Park
PO Box 1663
Los Alamos, NM 87545
Phone: (505)677-3331
Fax: (505)665-3866
Contact: K.V. Bostick, Coordinator
Parent Agencies: Department of Energy. ***Research Areas:*** Established to provide protected land areas for research and education in the environmental sciences and to demonstrate the environmental compatibility of energy technology development and use. It is located at a 27,500-acre site on the Pajarito Plateau, which consists primarily of juniper-pinyon woodlands. Most of the research sponsored by the Los Alamos NERP has been in one of the following areas: plant habitat characterization; forest fire ecology; nutrient cycling; deer and elk habitat characterization and biotelemetry methods development; thermoregulation in poikilotherms; population dynamics; contaminant transport; hydrology and erosion; plant-soil-water relationships; endangered species; and computer databases involving plant species occurrence and rooting characteristics.

★2969★ Louisiana Cooperative Fish and Wildlife Research Unit
Louisiana State University
School of Forestry, Wildlife, & Fisheries
Baton Rouge, LA 70803-6202
Phone: (504)338-4184
Fax: (504)388-4227
Contact: C. Frederick Bryan, Leader
Parent Agencies: Department of the Interior, U.S. Fish and Wildlife Service. ***Research Areas:*** Wildlife ecology, conservation, management, and utilization. Recent projects have involved studies on the ecological factors affecting waterfowl foods; foods of cottontail and swamp rabbits; marsh plant ecology; deer nutrition; and endangered species biology and management.

★2970★ Louisiana Water Resources Research Institute
Louisiana State University
2401A CEBA Bldg.
Baton Rouge, LA 70803
Phone: (504)388-8508
Fax: (504)388-5990
Contact: Dr. W. David Constant, Dir.
Parent Agencies: Department of the Interior, U.S. Geological Survey, Water Resources Division. ***Research Areas:*** Urban flash flooding, coastal erosion, contamination resulting from oil and gas drilling, wastewater treatment, and aquifer restoration techniques. Investigates field methods to identify nonpoint sources of pollution and high-risk climatic conditions contributing to urban flash flooding.

★2971★ Maine Cooperative Fish and Wildlife Research Unit
University of Maine
240 Nutting Hall
Orono, ME 04469
Phone: (207)581-2870
Contact: Dr. William B. Krohn, Leader
Parent Agencies: Department of the Interior, U.S. Fish and Wildlife Service. ***Research Areas:*** Ecology of anadromous fish, migratory birds, furbearing predators, and large mammals. Other studies involve game and non-game species of Maine and adjacent areas, with emphasis on aquatic, riparian, forest, and coastal species. Unit's activities also include graduate research training and extension services.

★2972★ Marine Assessment Research Division
7600 Sand Point Way, N.E. Bldg. 3
Seattle, WA 98115-0070
Phone: (206)526-6209
Fax: (206)526-6744
Contact: Herbert C. Curl Jr., Research Leader
Parent Agencies: Department of Commerce, National Oceanic and Atmospheric Administration, Office of Oceanic and Atmospheric Research, Environmental Research Laboratories. ***Research Areas:*** Marine environmental assessment at PMEL emphasizes understanding the complex physical and geochemical processes that ultimately determine the health of marine systems and their ability to assimilate contaminants. Included are studies of the geochemistry of trace metals and organic compounds, distributions of hydrocarbons and synthetic organics, coastal and estuarine circulation, and modeling of transport processes. Although the geographic focus of these studies has been the Pacific Northwest and Alaskan coastal and estuarine waters, the scientific knowledge acquired and methodologies developed are applicable to other marine systems.

★2973★ Maryland Water Resources Research Center
University of Maryland
0313 Symons Hall
College Park, MD 20742-5595
Phone: (301)454-6406
Fax: (301)454-0317
Contact: Robert E. Menzer, Dir.
Parent Agencies: Department of the Interior, U.S. Geological Survey, Water Resources Division. ***Research Areas:*** Water resources and groundwater quality in Maryland, including effects of toxics and other chemical wastes on resources, effects of nutrients on waters, and causes and results of sedimentation in the Chesapeake Bay and its tributary rivers and streams.

★2974★ Massachusetts Cooperative Fish and Wildlife Research Unit
University of Massachusetts
Department of Forestry & Wildlife Management
College of Food & Natural Resources
Amherst, MA 01003
Phone: (413)545-0398
Fax: (413)545-1242
Contact: Dr. Rebecca Field, Unit Leader
Parent Agencies: Department of the Interior, U.S. Fish and Wildlife Service. ***Research Areas:*** Freshwater aquatic ecology, studies on coastal estuarine fisheries, wildlife populations and habitat, endangered species, and tropical biology in Latin America.

★2975★ Massachusetts Water Resources Research Center
University of Massachusetts
Blaisdell House
Amherst, MA 01003-0040
Phone: (413)545-2842
Fax: (413)545-2304
Contact: Dr. Paul J. Godfrey, Dir.
Parent Agencies: Department of the Interior, U.S. Geological Survey, Water Resources Division. ***Research Areas:*** Water resources, including floods, drought, surface and groundwater quality and quantity, river basin and watershed planning and management, water-related recreation, acid deposition, and technical, chemical, and hydrologic processes. Activities include implementing a computerized geographic information system, which maps local, commonwealth, and regional environmental data.

★2976★ Michigan Institute of Water Research
Michigan State University
334 Natural Resources Bldg.
East Lansing, MI 48824
Phone: (517)353-3742
Contact: Dr. Jon F. Bartholic, Dir.
Parent Agencies: Department of the Interior, U.S. Geological Survey, Water Resources Division. ***Research Areas:*** Water conservation, socioeconomic water planning, groundwater education, water quality, agriculture, fisheries, advanced waste utilization and treatment, and limnology.

★2977★ Minerals Management Service Pacific Outer Continental Shelf Region Environmental Studies Staff
1340 W. Sixth St.
Los Angeles, CA 90017
Phone: (213)894-7120
Contact: Dr. Fred Piltz, Chief
Parent Agencies: Department of the Interior, Minerals Management Service. ***Research Areas:*** Air quality, physical oceanography, meteorology, marine biology and ecology, marine mammal and seabird biology and ecology, long-term environmental monitoring, and social/economic impact studies.

★2978★ Minnesota Water Resources Research Center
University of Minnesota
866 Biological Sciences Center
1445 Gortner Ave.
St. Paul, MN 55108
Phone: (612)624-9282
Contact: Dr. Patrick L. Brezonik, Dir.
Parent Agencies: Department of the Interior, U.S. Geological Survey, Water Resources Division. ***Research Areas:*** Water resources, including groundwater contamination, lake water quality management, and treatment technology. Also studies the effects of climate change on water availability in the state.

★2979★ Mississippi Cooperative Fish and Wildlife Research Unit
Mississippi State University
Scales Bldg.
P.O. Drawer BX
Mississippi State, MS 39762
Phone: (601)325-2643
Contact: Edward P. Hill, Leader
Parent Agencies: Department of the Interior, U.S. Fish and Wildlife Service, U.S. Fish and Wildlife Service Cooperative Units. ***Research Areas:*** Unit's program of field research is concerned primarily with ecology of fish and wildlife. Activities also include graduate education at the University.

★2980★ Mississippi Water Resources Research Institute
Mississippi State University
P.O. Drawer AD
Mississippi State, MS 39762
Phone: (601)325-3620
Fax: (601)325-3621
Contact: Dr. Marvin T. Bond, Dir.
Parent Agencies: Department of the Interior, U.S. Geological Survey, Water Resources Division. ***Research Areas:*** Water quality. Activities focus on developing a water quality model for the Tennessee-Tombigbee Waterway, an agricultural sediment and transport model, and management strategies for drought or emergency conditions. Investigates the effect of water resources development on bottomland forested ecosystems and performs research for industry.

★2981★ Missouri Cooperative Fish and Wildlife Research Unit
University of Missouri
112 Stephens Hall
Columbia, MO 65211
Phone: (314)882-3524
Contact: Dr. Charles S. Rabeni, Leader
Parent Agencies: Department of the Interior, U.S. Fish and Wildlife Service, U.S. Fish and Wildlife Service Cooperative Units. ***Research Areas:*** Unit's fishery research and development program includes studies of: aquatic ecology, population dynamics, fishery management, limnology, water quality, and toxicology. Topics of wildlife ecology and management studies include: 1) population dynamics and social behavior in mourning doves; 2) wetland ecology and management and bioenergetics of wintering waterfowl; 3) effects of pesticides on mammalian reproduction; 4) effects of land-use practices on wild populations; and 5) responses of forest wildlife to small clearcuts. Activities also include education in fishery and wildlife research and management at the University, research training for graduate students, and extension services.

★2982★ Missouri Water Resources Research Center
University of Missouri-Columbia
0056 Engineering Complex
Columbia, MO 65211
Phone: (314)882-3132
Contact: Dr. Thomas E. Clevenger, Dir.
Parent Agencies: Department of the Interior, U.S. Geological Survey, Water Resources Division. ***Research Areas:*** Water quality and quantity, institutional relations, utilization and conservation of water, and ecological and environmental relationships in the Missouri River Basin Region.

★2983★ Montana Cooperative Fishery Research Unit
Montana State University
Biology Department
Bozeman, MT 59717
Phone: (406)994-3491
Fax: (406)994-2893
Contact: Dr. Robert G. White, Leader
Parent Agencies: Department of the Interior, U.S. Fish and Wildlife Service, U.S. Fish and Wildlife Service Cooperative Units. ***Research Areas:*** Unit's research projects are primarily management-oriented and deal largely with aquatic habitat-population relationships and the evaluation of fisheries. In recent years focus has been on habitat and population assessment, with data from Unit studies used to monitor influences of land use practices and, when necessary, to serve as a basis for mitigation. Examples include studies on the effects of supersaturation of dissolved gases on the trout fishery of the Bighorn River downstream of Yellowtail Afterbay Dam; winter habitat requirements of rainbow trout as impacted by small hydropower development; and impacts of angler wading on trout embryo survival. Unit has also been active in research related to the enhancement of fish habitat.

★2984★ Montana Cooperative Wildlife Research Unit
University of Montana
Natural Science 205
Missoula, MT 59812
Phone: (406)243-5372
Contact: Dr. Bart W. O'Gara, Leader
Parent Agencies: Department of the Interior, U.S. Fish and Wildlife Service, U.S. Fish and Wildlife Service Cooperative Units. ***Research Areas:*** Unit conducts a program of management-oriented wildlife research, with studies focused principally on predator-prey interactions, the impacts of human activities on wild ungulates, and waterfowl biology and management. Research is conducted primarily by graduate students as part of Unit's research training program.

★2985★ Montana Water Resources Research Center
Montana State University
412 Cobleigh Hall
Bozeman, MT 59717
Phone: (406)994-6690
Contact: Dr. Howard S. Peavy, Acting Dir.
Parent Agencies: Department of the Interior, U.S. Geological Survey, Water Resources Division. ***Research Areas:*** Water resources focusing on hydrology and quality interactions of groundwater in the coal mining areas of southeastern Montana and the causes and remedies of saline seep in small grain farming areas of the state. Other research includes nutrient assessment and waterborn metals.

★2986★ Narragansett Environmental Research Laboratory
27 Tarzwell Dr.
Narragansett, RI 02882
Phone: (401)782-3000
Contact: Norbert A. Jaworski, Dir.
Parent Agencies: Independent Agencies, Environmental Protection Agency, Office of Research and Development, EPA Research Laboratories. ***Research Areas:*** Laboratory conducts research on the effects of pollutants on marine ecosystems, including: 1) studies on the chemical and physical behavior of pollutants in marine systems; 2) investigation of significant responses of organisms to pollutant stress; 3) characterization of marine ecosystems and their responses to stress; 4) development of systems to quantitate response to specific pollutants; and 5) development of methods for determining the impact of specific pollution incidents.

★2987★ Narragansett Environmental Research Laboratory Pacific Ecosystems Branch
Hatfield Marine Science Center
2030 S. Marine Science Dr.
Newport, OR 97365
Phone: (503)867-4040
Fax: (503)867-4490
Contact: Harvey W. Holm, Chief
Parent Agencies: Independent Agencies, Environmental Protection Agency, Office of Research and Development, EPA Research Laboratories. ***Research Areas:*** Conducts research on benthic ecology, water and sediment quality criteria, bioaccumulation,

pollutant transport modeling, and stratospheric ozone impacts.

★2988★ National Appropriate Technology Assistance Service
PO Box 2525
Butte, MT 59702
Phone: 800-428-2525
Contact: Jeff Birkby, Project Manager
Parent Agencies: Department of Energy, Energy Data Centers. ***Research Areas:*** NATAS is an information and technical assistance service that answers questions about energy-related appropriate technologies (i.e., technologies that use the sun, wind, and water resources and energy conservation methods and devices). NATAS has two main objectives: to help people investigate or implement appropriate technologies and to help innovators solve problems they have on financing, licensing, and commercializing energy products and services.

★2989★ National Arboretum
3501 New York Ave., N.E.
Washington, DC 20002
Phone: (202)475-4815
Contact: Dr. Henry M. Cathey, Dir.
Parent Agencies: Department of Agriculture, Agricultural Research Service, Beltsville Area. ***Research Areas:*** The National Arboretum conducts research on trees, shrubs, and herbaceous plants and educates the public regarding these plants. It has a major herbarium of botanical specimens for research and plant collections. In addition, the Arboretum publishes botanical findings and provides technical information to the public. The Arboretum comprises five units: Administrative, Educational Services, Gardens and Collections, Maintenance, and Research.

★2990★ National Center for Atmospheric Research
PO Box 3000
Boulder, CO 80307
Phone: (303)497-1000
Contact: Dr. Robert Serafin, Dir.
Parent Agencies: Independent Agencies, National Science Foundation, Directorate for Geosciences, NSF-Supported Atmospheric Sciences Centers and Facilities. ***Research Areas:*** Currently, NCAR research programs are concerned with: 1) the dynamic and physical processes that govern the behavior and climatology of the oceans and atmosphere; 2) the chemical composition of the atmosphere on regional to global scales; 3) solar processes and solar terrestrial physics; 4) the physics of convection, thunderstorms, and precipitation formation; and 5) impact-assessment analyses to show the important links between atmospheric and societal activities. In addition to conducting its own programs, NCAR participates in national and international efforts conducted by government agencies, university scientists, and research groups.

★2991★ National Center for Ground Water Research
Oklahoma State University
003 Life Sciences E. Bldg.
Stillwater, OK 74078-0281
Phone: (405)744-9995
Fax: (405)744-7673
Contact: Norman N. Durham, Co- Dir.
Parent Agencies: Independent Agencies, Environmental Protection Agency, Office of Research and Development. ***Research Areas:*** NCGWR studies groundwater quality, and model simulation of point source pollution.

★2992★ National Center for Intermedia Transport Research
University of California-Los Angeles
Department of Chemical Engineering
7620E Math Sciences
Los Angeles, CA 90024
Phone: (213)825-9741
Fax: (213)206-4107
Contact: Dr. Yoram Cohen, Dir.
Parent Agencies: Independent Agencies, Environmental Protection Agency, Office of Research and Development. ***Research Areas:*** The primary objectives of the Center are to: 1) sponsor research on fundamental problems of pollutant exchange between media (for example, dry and wet deposition); 2) develop new methods of dealing with multimedia transport processes involving several interacting environmental compartments; 3) conduct studies for certain chemical compounds (many organic in nature) expected to be of special environmental importance in the future; and 4) sponsor seminars, conferences, and workshops related to these objectives. Research programs focus on atmospheric dry deposition processes; soil/ water processes; multimedia pollutant transport; wet removal processes; organic pollutants; atmospheric deposition and environmental assimilation of gases and aerosols in a desert ecosystem; and characterization of complex pollutant mixtures.

★2993★ National Climatic Data Center
Federal Bldg.
Asheville, NC 28801
Phone: (704)259-0682
Fax: (704)259-0876
Contact: Dr. Kenneth Hadeen, Dir.
Parent Agencies: Department of Commerce, National Oceanic and Atmospheric Administration, National Environmental Satellite, Data, and Information Service. ***Research Areas:*** NCDC is the national collection center and custodian of U.S. weather records. The Center obtains data generated by NOAA's National Weather Service, the weather services of the Air Force and the Navy, the Federal Aviation Administration, the U.S. Coast Guard, and other cooperative observers on land, at sea, and in the air. The Center also utilizes cloud photography and other data obtained from environmental satellites. NCDC provides centralized data services for the national community of users and some of the services for the international community. Center also administers World Data Center A for Meteorology, which provides for international data exchange. (World Data Centers A are operated under the auspices of the National Academy of Sciences and according to guidelines for data exchange of the International Council of Scientific Unions.) Principal areas of research interest are: climate, including temperature, pressure, precipitation, and wind; meteorology; solar radiation; and other atmospheric phenomena.

★2994★ National Coastal Resources Research and Development Institute
Hatfield Marine Science Center
2030 S. Marine Science Dr.
Newport, OR 97365-5296
Phone: (503)867-3300
Fax: (503)867-3301
Contact: Dr. Earle N. Buckley, Dir.
Parent Agencies: Department of Commerce, National Oceanic and Atmospheric Administration, Office of Oceanic and Atmospheric Research. ***Research Areas:*** Funds research, education, and demonstration projects aimed at improving the nation's coastal economy. Conducts two grants programs: 1) NCRI national program, which provides support for projects in the coastal United States; and 2) interstate coastal zone management program for the Northeast Pacific Ocean region (Alaska, Washington, Oregon, and California). Solicits proposals for both programs from individuals, educational institutions, state agencies, nonprofit groups, and commercial organizations on an annual basis.

★2995★ National Ecology Research Center
4512 McMurray Ave.
Fort Collins, CO 80525-3400
Phone: (303)226-9398
Fax: (303)226-9230
Contact: Dr. Rey C. Stendell, Acting Dir.
Parent Agencies: Department of the Interior, U.S. Fish and Wildlife Service, National Ecology Research Center. ***Research Areas:*** The National Ecology Research Center of the U.S. Fish and Wildlife Service plans and conducts field and laboratory research and development and transfers new methods and tools to better understand and manage fish and wildlife resources, habitats, and ecosystems. The Center also serves as a focal point for coordination with other federal and state agencies and with the fish and wildlife management programs conducted by fish and wildlife regions in the continental United States. Specific areas of research and development interest include: marine mammals (manatees, sea otters, dugongs, marine otters); stream, terrestrial, and aquatic habitat assessment and management; wetlands; effects of habitat management practices on wildlife, especially on Service lands; threatened and endangered species; effects of introduced or exotic plants or animals on native biota; systematics, distribution, ecology, and status of fishes, amphibians, reptiles, birds, and mammals; and curation of the National Collections of North American fishes, reptiles, birds, and mammals.

★2996★ National Ecology Research Center Biological Survey
National Museum of Natural History
Washington, DC 20560
Phone: (202)357-1930
Fax: (202)357-1932
Contact: Dr. Thomas H. Fritts, Chief
Parent Agencies: Department of the Interior, U.S. Fish and Wildlife Service, National Ecology Research Center. ***Research Areas:*** Research efforts of Survey personnel emphasize faunal surveys, systematic and life history studies, and related studies on the geographic and ecological distribution of mammals, birds, amphibians, and reptiles. Information resulting from such studies provides a basis upon which sound management decisions can be made by the U.S. Fish and Wildlife Service and other state and federal agencies. Survey personnel also cooperate with counterparts in similar agencies of foreign governments on research projects relating to biological survey, habitat and endangered species inventories, museum collections, and similar efforts.

★2997★ National Environmental Satellite, Data, and Information Service (NESDIS)
Washington, DC 20233
Phone: (301)763-7190
Fax: (301)763-4011
Contact: Thomas N. Pyke, Jr., Assistant Admin.
Parent Agencies: Department of Commerce, National Oceanic and Atmospheric Administration, National Environmental Satellite, Data, and Information Service. ***Research Areas:*** The National Environmental Satellite, Data, and Information Service

operates satellite systems that provide weather and flood forecasts, crop conditions, and ocean information to a wide variety of users. Areas of interest include climate and weather information vital to the food supply, the way homes are built, energy development, and human health. Principal components are: National Climatic Data Center, National Geophysical Data Center, National Oceanographic Data Center, Office of Research and Applications, Office of

★2998★ National Environmental Satellite, Data, and Information Service
Satellite Research Laboratory
Washington, DC 20233
Phone: (301)763-4248
Contact: George Ohring, Chief
Parent Agencies: Department of Commerce, National Oceanic and Atmospheric Administration, National Environmental Satellite, Data, and Information Service. ***Research Areas:*** Laboratory investigates the application of remotely sensed environmental data to solutions of problems in atmospheric, oceanic, and terrestrial sciences. Focus is on development and demonstration of the methodology for improved or expanded application of operational satellite data and for increased understanding of processes and phenomena in these fields. Principal components of the Laboratory are the Atmospheric Sciences Branch, Experimental Applications Branch, Land Sciences Branch, Oceanic Sciences Branch, and Physics Branch. Laboratory activities are coordinated with related efforts by other NOAA organizations and other government agencies and support is provided for research at universities and private research organizations.

★2999★ National Fisheries Contaminant Research Center
Rt. 1
Columbia, MO 65201
Phone: (314)875-5399
Contact: Dr. Richard A. Schoettger, Dir.
Parent Agencies: Department of the Interior, U.S. Fish and Wildlife Service, National Fisheries Contaminant Research Center. ***Research Areas:*** As part of the U.S. Fish and Wildlife Service's research and development function, Center research focuses on toxicology and analysis of chemical contaminants in aquatic organisms. Principal field components are research stations in Athens, GA; Columbus, OH; Dixon, CA; La Crosse, WI; Orono, ME; Yankton, SD; and Jackson, WY.; Corpus Christi, TX.

★3000★ National Fisheries Research Center (Gainesville)
7920 N.W. 71 St.
Gainesville, FL 32606
Phone: (904)378-8181
Contact: Dr. James A. McCann, Dir.
Parent Agencies: Department of the Interior, U.S. Fish and Wildlife Service, National Fisheries Research Center (Gainesville). ***Research Areas:*** The mission of this U.S. Fish and Wildlife Service center is to conduct and coordinate research programs on: 1) the beneficial and/or harmful effects of exotic fishes introduced or considered for introduction into U.S. waters; 2) the maintenance and/or restoration of anadromous fish populations in Southeastern rivers and coastal areas; 3) other fresh and estuarine species that are environmentally imperiled and/or depleted from overuse and inhabit transboundary and federally managed waters; 4) warmwater aquaculture; and 5) southeastern endangered fish species. Studies include life history, status, distribution, population dynamics, and fish husbandry.

★3001★ National Fisheries Research Center (Great Lakes)
1451 Green Rd.
Ann Arbor, MI 48105
Phone: (313)994-3331
Contact: Dr. Jon G. Stanley, Dir.
Parent Agencies: Department of the Interior, U.S. Fish and Wildlife Service, National Fisheries Research Center (Great Lakes). ***Research Areas:*** Headquartered in Ann Arbor, Michigan, the Great Lakes National Fisheries Research Center of the U.S. Fish and Wildlife Service has field stations with vessel bases at Ashland, WI, Oswego, NY, and Sandusky, OH; and vessel bases at Cheboygan and Saugatuck, MI. The mission of the Center is to develop the knowledge and technical basis for assessing, protecting, enhancing, and rehabilitating the valuable fish resources of the Great Lakes and their critical habitats. Research is conducted to determine: the distribution and abundancy of important recreational and commercial fishes; the effects of fishing, habitat alterations, and pollution of fish stocks; and the size and potential populations of forage fish such as the indigenous lake herring, chubs, shiners, and the exotic alewife and smelt on which important game and food fishes such as lake trout, Pacific salmon, walleyes, and yellow perch depend for food. Under the aegis of the International Great Lakes Fishery Commission and the International Joint Commission, Center scientists are involved in many interagency technical committees to assess the status of the fisheries resources and their habitats and recommend strategies to manage and protect them. Of particular importance is restoration of the lake trout resource, which suffered a catastrophic decline in the 1950s because of overfishing and sea lamprey predation. A major program of the U.S. Fish and Wildlife Service, along with state, provincial, and tribal resource agencies, involves control of the sea lamprey. Chemical eradication of larval lampreys in the spawning streams led to massive stocking of young, hatchery-reared lake trout in the lakes, and the Center is investigating the ability of these fish to survive and reproduce. Center also provides information on how contaminant burdens, habitat degradation, and climate change alters fish populations. Data are generated through the use of controlled laboratory experiments and efforts are made to verify results in the field. Particular emphasis is placed on the spawning requirements, survival of early life stages, forage requirements, and habitat requirements of important species such as lake trout.

★3002★ National Fisheries Research Center (La Crosse)
2630 Fanta Reed Rd.
PO Box 818
La Crosse, WI 54602-0818
Phone: (608)783-6451
Fax: (608)783-6066
Contact: Dr. Fred P. Meyer, Dir.
Parent Agencies: Department of the Interior, U.S. Fish and Wildlife Service, National Fisheries Research Center (La Crosse). ***Research Areas:*** This U.S. Fish and Wildlife Service research center has four main functions: 1) to coordinate and conduct research relating to registration of chemicals and drugs used in management of fishery resources and in fish culture; 2) to conduct research and develop tools for the management and control of populations of fish and nuisance aquatic organisms without adversely affecting the rest of the biota or contaminating the ecosystems; 3) to conduct environmental research on ecological problems (including the impact of human activity) of major river ecosystems; and 4) to develop methods for controlling sea lamprey in the Great Lakes. Primary areas of research include ecology, toxicology, and physiology of fish. Other studies involve fungal diseases of fish; endangered mollusks; and ecology of the Upper Mississippi River.

★3003★ National Fisheries Research Center (Leetown)
Rt. 3, Box 700
Kearneysville, WV 25430
Phone: (304)725-8461
Parent Agencies: Department of the Interior, U.S. Fish and Wildlife Service, National Fisheries Research Center (Leetown). ***Research Areas:*** Leetown Center of the U.S. Fish and Wildlife Service administers and interrelates various fish husbandry research, development, demonstration, information, and related activities of the U.S. Fish and Wildlife Service. Major objectives of the Center are to provide research and development information on methods of producing quality fish for management and aquaculture needs. Research activities are conducted at these Center components: 1) Fish Culture Research Laboratory, Leetown, WV; 2) National Fish Health Research Laboratory, Leetown, WV; 3) National Fishery Research and Development Laboratory, Wellsboro, PA; 4) Tunison Laboratory of Fish Nutrition, Cortland, NY, 5) Northeast Anadromous Fish Research Laboratory, Turners Falls, MA. and 6) its field station at Hagerman, ID. The National

★3004★ National Fisheries Research Center (Leetown)
Acid Precipitation Section
PO Box 700
Kearneysville, WV 25430
Phone: (304)725-2061
Contact: Dr. R. Kent Schreiber, Chief
Parent Agencies: Department of the Interior, U.S. Fish and Wildlife Service, National Fisheries Research Center (Leetown). ***Research Areas:*** Section's mission is to enhance the ability of the U.S. Fish and Wildlife Service to respond to potential impacts of increased energy-related development upon fish and wildlife and their habitats. This is accomplished by providing analysis and synthesis of existing information; development and assessment of new technologies and methodologies; and the transfer of information to Fish and Wildlife Service and other resource managers. Activities (including research) currently focus on the effects of acid precipitation.

★3005★ National Fisheries Research Center (Seattle)
Naval Station, Bldg. 204
Seattle, WA 98115
Phone: (206)526-6282
Fax: (206)526-6654
Contact: Dr. Alfred C. Fox, Dir.
Parent Agencies: Department of the Interior, U.S. Fish and Wildlife Service. ***Research Areas:*** Fish health, fish enhancement, and ecological and environmental requirements.

★3006★ National Fishery Research and Development Laboratory (Wellsboro)
RD 4, Box 63
Wellsboro, PA 16901
Phone: (717)724-3322
Fax: (717)724-2525
Contact: Dr. Garland B. Pardue, Dir.
Parent Agencies: Department of the Interior, U.S. Fish and Wildlife Service. ***Research Areas:***

Restoration of depleted, nationally significant fisheries resources, focusing on Atlantic salmon, lake trout, Amercian shad, and striped bass.

★3007★ National Geophysical Data Center Marine Geology/Geophysics Division
325 Broadway E/GC3
Boulder, CO 80303
Phone: (303)497-6487
Fax: (303)497-6315
Contact: Michael S. Loughridge, Chief
Parent Agencies: Department of Commerce, National Oceanic and Atmospheric Administration, National Environmental Satellite, Data, and Information Service. ***Research Areas:*** The Marine Geology/ Geophysics Division serves as the national repository for marine geological, marine geophysical, and related data; and operates the World Data Center A for Marine Geology and Geophysics. (World Data Centers A are operated under the auspices of the National Academy of Sciences and according to guidelines for data exchange of the International Council of Scientific Unions.) Division acquires, processes, archives, and disseminates data that result from international and national programs involving bathymetry, marine sediment and hard-rock descriptions, marine mineral resources, hazards to navigation, marine geophysics in support of outer continental shelf lease/sales, seismic profiles, and well logs.

★3008★ National Institute of Environmental Health Sciences
PO Box 12233
Research Triangle Park, NC 27709
Phone: (919)541-3345
Contact: Dr. David P. Rall, Dir.
Parent Agencies: Department of Health and Human Services, U.S. Public Health Service, National Institutes of Health, National Institute of Environmental Health Sciences. ***Research Areas:*** Institute conducts research in the environmental health sciences in the NIEHS laboratories at Research Triangle Park, NC, and supports research through its extramural programs. The Institute's Extramural Research and Training Division supports research within educational institutions, research institutes, and other public and private nonprofit organizations through individual grants, contracts, and Research Career Development Awards. Programs emphasize studies that provide information essential to an understanding of the way in which human health is adversely affected by environmental factors. Grant programs include support for Environmental Health Science Centers, Marine and Freshwater Biomedical Science Centers, and research manpower development programs, as well as the Superfund Basic Research Program, a university-based program of basic research supported by NIEHS as part of the 1986 Superfund Amendments and Reauthorization Act. This Program combines basic research in the fields of ecology, engineering, and hydrogeology into a core program of biomedical research to provide a broader and more detailed body of scientific information to be used in decision-making related to the management of hazardous substances. In addition to the extramural and intramural divisions, NIEHS also has Biometry and Risk Assessment as well as Toxicology Research and Testing divisions.

★3009★ National Marine Fisheries Service (NMFS)
1335 E. W. Hwy.
Silver Spring, MD 20910
Phone: (202)427-2239
Contact: William W. Fox Jr., Assistant Admin.
Parent Agencies: Department of Commerce, National Oceanic and Atmospheric Administration, National Marine Fisheries Service. ***Research Areas:*** Objectives of NMFS research activities are to discover, describe, develop, and support management actions to conserve the living resources of the sea within 200 miles of the U.S. coasts, especially as they affect the American economy and diet. The Service conducts biological research on economically important species, protected species, and critical habitat and analyzes the economic aspects of fisheries operations. It also studies recreational fishery resources and investigates the effects of thermal and chemical pollution. Principal research components of the Service are the Northeast Fisheries Center, the Northwest and Alaska Fisheries Center, the Southeast Fisheries Center, the Southwest Fisheries Center, and the National Seafood Inspection Laboratory.

★3010★ National Marine Fisheries Service Southeast Fisheries Center Beaufort Laboratory
Pivers Island
Beaufort, NC 28516
Phone: (919)728-3595
Fax: (919)728-8784
Contact: Dr. F.A. Cross, Dir.
Parent Agencies: Department of Commerce, National Oceanic and Atmospheric Administration, National Marine Fisheries Service. ***Research Areas:*** Laboratory's mission is to understand the biological productivity of estuaries and nearshore ecosystems, the dynamics of coastal fishery resources, and the effects of man on resource productivity in order to enhance recreational and commercial fishery resources along the southeastern and Gulf coasts of the United States. It currently has responsiblity for management of the Center's menhaden and fishery ecology programs. Research activities include development of a biological and fishery statistics database for monitoring and modeling Atlantic menhaden fishery and a full-scale simulation model to test management options; nearshore and estuarine research on fishery ecology; research on larval fish food webs; and trace metal research.

★3011★ National Marine Fisheries Service Southeast Fisheries Center Galveston Laboratory
4700 Ave. U
Galveston, TX 77550
Phone: (409)766-3500
Contact: Dr. Edward F. Klima, Dir.
Parent Agencies: Department of Commerce, National Oceanic and Atmospheric Administration, National Marine Fisheries Service. ***Research Areas:*** Manages shrimp and bottomfish program and Kemp's ridley sea turtle research and headstart program. Research activities include: 1) studies on growth, mortality, and migration including updated estimates of maximum sustained yield, estuarine habitat assessment, and predator-prey relationships of major shrimp and bottomfish species; 2) compilation of commercial statistics and economic information; 3) evaluation of affect of seasonal closure on offshore waters; 4) studies on sea turtle raising and head starting; 5) evaluation of catch rates of shrimp in TED-equipped trawls and in trawls without TEDs; and 6) evaluation of impact of oil rig removal operations on sea turtles, marine mammals, and fish.

★3012★ National Marine Fisheries Service Southwest Fisheries Center Honolulu Laboratory
2570 Dole St.
Honolulu, HI 96822-2396
Phone: (808)943-1221
Fax: (808)942-2062
Contact: Dr. George W. Bochlert, Dir.
Parent Agencies: Department of Commerce, National Oceanic and Atmospheric Administration, National Marine Fisheries Service. ***Research Areas:*** High-seas tropical, pelagic, and demersal fishery resources studied over an area of 13 million square miles. Supports fishery management needs of the Western Pacific Fishery Management Council; conducts studies on the skipjack and other tuna resources of the Pacific and Indian Oceans, including physiological and behavioral relationships of tuna; identifies and assesses the magnitude of commercially important fish and shellfish species in the waters of the Northwestern Hawaiian Islands and other central and western Pacific Islands; and conducts studies and recovery work on the threatened green turtle and the Hawaiian monk seal.

★3013★ National Marine Fisheries Service Southwest Fisheries Center La Jolla Laboratory
PO Box 271
La Jolla, CA 92038
Phone: (619)546-7000
Fax: (619)546-7003
Contact: Dr. Izadore Barrett, Dir.
Parent Agencies: Department of Commerce, National Oceanic and Atmospheric Administration. ***Research Areas:*** Research is centered at the La Jolla Laboratory, site of the headquarters of the Southwest Fisheries Center.

★3014★ National Marine Fisheries Service Northeast Fisheries Center Milford Laboratory
212 Rogers Ave.
Milford, CT 06460
Phone: (203)783-4200
Fax: (203)783-4217
Contact: Dr. Anthony Calabrese, Officer-in-Charge
Parent Agencies: Department of Commerce, National Oceanic and Atmospheric Administration, National Marine Fisheries Service. ***Research Areas:*** Contributes to the Northeast Fisheries Center's Fisheries

★3015★ National Marine Fisheries Service Northeast Fisheries Center Narragansett Laboratory
28 Tarzwell Dr.
Narragansett, RI 02882
Phone: (401)782-3200
Fax: (401)782-3201
Contact: Dr. Kenneth Sherman, Officer-in-Charge
Parent Agencies: Department of Commerce, National Oceanic and Atmospheric Administration, National Marine Fisheries Service. ***Research Areas:*** The Laboratory contributes to the Northeast Fisheries Center's Fishery Ecology and Environmental Processes divisions by conducting research on: 1) inter- and intra-specific associations affecting actual and potential production of the fish biomass of the Northwest Atlantic; 2) trophic exchange among benthos, plankton, and nekton and oceanographic dynamics (to provide estimates

of fish production and to forecast biomass levels); 3) marine species with recreational potential; 4) physiology, metabolism, and survival of larval, juvenile, and adult fishes; 5) plankton populations and growth mortality; 6) availability of principal fish stocks in the Northwest Atlantic; 7) archived oceanic and atmospheric data for climatological and monitoring studies; and 8) design and conduct of oceanographic studies, acquisition of environmental data, and interpretation of bioenvironmental relationships.

★3016★ National Marine Fisheries Service
Northwest and Alaska Fisheries Center
National Marine Mammal Laboratory
7600 Sand Point Way, N.E.
Seattle, WA 98115
Phone: (206)526-4047
Fax: (206)526-6615
Contact: Dr. Howard W. Braham, Dir.
Parent Agencies: Department of Commerce, National Oceanic and Atmospheric Administration, National Marine Fisheries Service. ***Research Areas:*** The National Marine Mammal Laboratory: 1) conducts research on numerous species of whales, porpoises, sea lions, and seals; 2) studies population dynamics, life history, behavior, and trophic relationships; 3) performs major investigations, including studies on the status of the decline of northern sea lions and the Western Arctic bowhead whale stock relative to the Eskimo subsistence hunt, determining the effect of management decisions relating to the Pribilof Islands fur seal herds and ascertaining the nature and extent of interactions between commercial fisheries and marine mammal populations; and 4) provides scientific support to U.S. delegations to the International Whaling Commission, Convention for the Conservation of Antarctic Marine Living Resources, International North Pacific Fisheries Commission, North Pacific Fisheries Management Council, and other commissions and councils.

★3017★ National Marine Fisheries Service
Northeast Fisheries Center
Water St.
Woods Hole, MA 02543
Phone: (508)548-5123
Fax: (508)548-5124
Contact: Allen E. Peterson Jr., Science & Research Dir.
Parent Agencies: Department of Commerce, National Oceanic and Atmospheric Administration, National Marine Fisheries Service. ***Research Areas:*** The Northeast Fisheries Center (NEFC) plans, develops, and manages multidisciplinary programs of basic and applied research designed to: better understand the living marine resources (including marine mammals) of the northwest Atlantic Ocean and the environmental quality essential for their existence and continued productivity; and describe and provide to management, industry, and the public options for the utilization and conservation of living marine resources and maintenance of environmental quality that are consistent with national and regional goals and needs and international commitments. To fulfill its mission the Center: 1) develops the scientific basis to determine and provide information on the status of stocks/populations of living marine resources, the status of fisheries for exploited species, the effects of pollution and human alterations on the habitats of the resources, the effects of environmental variability, the quality and safety of fishery products, and the enhancement of anadromous fishery resources; 2) collects, documents, and interprets scientific and economic data as technical support for management plans, international negotiations, and fishery development programs; 3) provides technical advice, review, and monitoring of fishery plans and grant programs; 4) pursues fundamental research on specified topics; and 5) maintains strong relations with the academic community and industry (through grants, contracts, and cooperative programs as appropriate) and with the users and the general public. Center cooperates with the other fisheries centers of the National Marine Fisheries Service in the sharing of expertise and in multi-Center programs consistent with national goals and needs and international commitments. The Center is organized into four research programs (Conservation and Utilization Division, Fishery Ecology Division, Environmental Processes Division, and National Systematics Laboratory) and three support programs (Research Planning and Coordination Staff, Program Support Staff, and Data Management Support Staff. Activities are carried out through NEFC's Gloucester Laboratory, Milford Laboratory, Narragansett Laboratory, National Systematics Laboratory, Oxford Laboratory, Sandy Hook Laboratory, and Woods Hole Laboratory.

★3018★ National Marine Fisheries Service
Northwest Fisheries Science Center
2725 Montlake Blvd., E.
Seattle, WA 98112
Phone: (206)442-1872
Fax: (206)442-4304
Contact: Dr. Richard J. Berry, Science and Research Dir.
Parent Agencies: Department of Commerce, National Oceanic and Atmospheric Administration, National Marine Fisheries Service. ***Research Areas:*** Mitigation studies of fishery habitat degradation in Northwest estuaries and the Columbia River drainage system; studies of contaminants in coastal waters and their effects on fishery stocks; and other studies to enhance the quality, value, and safety of fishery products from the West Coast.

★3019★ National Marine Fisheries Service
Northeast Fisheries Center
Oxford Laboratory
904 Morris
Oxford, MD 21654
Phone: (301)226-5193
Contact: Fred Kern, Chief
Parent Agencies: Department of Commerce, National Oceanic and Atmospheric Administration, National Marine Fisheries Service. ***Research Areas:*** The Laboratory contributes to the Northeast Fisheries Center's Fishery

★3020★ National Marine Fisheries Service
Southeast Fisheries Center
Panama City Laboratory
3500 Delwood Beach Rd.
Panama City, FL 32407-7499
Phone: (904)234-6541
Fax: (904)234-6543
Contact: Eugene L. Nakamura, Laboratory Dir.
Parent Agencies: Department of Commerce, National Oceanic and Atmospheric Administration, National Marine Fisheries Service. ***Research Areas:*** Primary mission of the Laboratory is to obtain fishery, biological, and ecological information that is useful for the conservation and management of marine species. Laboratory currently has responsibility for management of SEFC's coastal pelagics program. Research projects in progress include studies on: distribution and abundance, stock identification, age and growth, vital statistics, reproductive biology, migration and early life history and recruitment. Species under investigation include king mackerel, Spanish mackerel, bluefish, dolphin, cobia, snappers, groupers, and baitfishes. Special studies on the sportfishery for billfishes and on the biology and ecology of sea turtles are also in progress.

★3021★ National Marine Fisheries Service
Southeast Fisheries Center
75 Virginia Beach Dr.
Miami, FL 33149
Phone: (305)361-4284
Fax: (305)361-1219
Contact: Dr. Bradford E. Brown, Acting Science Dir.
Parent Agencies: Department of Commerce, National Oceanic and Atmospheric Administration, National Marine Fisheries Service. ***Research Areas:*** Aims to 1) provide scientific and technical information for decision-making in conserving, developing, and using marine fishery resources and in conserving and protecting the habitat, mammals, and endangered species of the marine environment; and 2) advance scientific understanding and research capabilities through the development of large-scale marine databases, new assessment technology, and new perceptions of biological, ecological, economic, and sociological principles. Scientific and technical information developed by the Center supports national and regional programs of the National Marine Fisheries Service and supports other fishery research, management, and development organizations (e.g., regional fisheries management councils) and user groups. Research programs include studies on: coastal pelagics, protected species, latent resources, menhaden, oceanic pelagics, reef resources, shrimp and bottomfish, molluscan shellfish, habitat, and product quality and safety. Activities encompass the living marine resources of the Gulf of Mexico, Caribbean Sea, and the Atlantic Ocean. Research is carried out at Center laboratories in Galveston, TX; Bay St. Louis and Pascagoula, MS; Panama City and Miami, FL; Charleston, SC; and Beaufort, NC.

★3022★ National Marine Fisheries Service
Southwest Fisheries Center
8604 La Jolla Shores Dr.
PO Box 271
La Jolla, CA 92038
Phone: (619)546-7000
Fax: (619)546-7003
Contact: Izadore Barrett, Dir.
Parent Agencies: Department of Commerce, National Oceanic and Atmospheric Administration. ***Research Areas:*** Fishery management and development, including 1) fishery biology; 2) population dynamics; 3) statistics; 4) marine mammalogy; 5) economics; 6) systems analysis; 7) computer analysis; 8) oceanography; 9) taxonomy; and 10) environmental research. Duties are performed by the SWFC divisions and laboratories, which include: Coastal Fisheries Resources Division, Pelagic Fisheries Resources Division, Fishery-Marine Mammal Interactions Division, and the U.S. Antarctic Marine Living Resources (AMLR) Program; located at the La Jolla Laboratory; Honolulu Laboratory; Tiburon Laboratory; and Pacific Fisheries Environmental Group (Monterey, CA).

★3023★ National Marine Fisheries Service
Northeast Fisheries Center
Woods Hole Laboratory
Water St.
Woods Hole, MA 02543
Phone: (617)548-5123
Contact: Marvin Grosslein, Officer-in-Charge
Parent Agencies: Department of Commerce, National Oceanic and Atmospheric Administration, National Marine Fisheries Service. ***Research Areas:*** The Laboratory contributes to the Northeast Fisheries Center's research program by conducting and coordinating resource assessment and marine ecosystems and environmental research programs. Activities involve: 1) determining the abundance, distribution, and surplus yields of selected finfish, shellfish, and crustaceans of Northeast waters; 2) developing and integrating fishery and bioeconomic data for the construction of fishery management decision models; 3) conducting ecosystem studies on the inter- and intra-specific associations affecting production of northeast marine species; 4) performing studies of food chains and trophic exchange among benthos, plankton, and nekton; and 5) conducting environmental studies in physical oceanography and on the effects of natural and man-induced variations on the productivity of marine species and ecosystems.

★3024★ National Museum of Natural History
Tenth St. & Constitution Ave., N.W.
Washington, DC 20560
Phone: (202)357-2664
Fax: (202)357-4779
Contact: Frank H. Talbot, Dir.
Parent Agencies: Independent Agencies, Smithsonian Institution. ***Research Areas:*** Maintains 19,000,000 natural science specimens and artifacts in the areas of anthropology, botany, entomology, invertebrate zoology, mineral sciences, paleobiology, and vertebrate zoology (see separate department entries). Activities include field observations such as an investigation of the Caribbean Coral Reef Ecosystems, biological diversity in tropical Latin America.

★3025★ National Ocean Service
1825 Connecticut Ave.
Washington, DC 20235
Phone: (202)673-5140
Fax: (202)673-3850
Contact: Virgina K. Tippie, Chief
Parent Agencies: Department of Commerce, National Oceanic and Atmospheric Administration, National Ocean Service. ***Research Areas:*** The National Ocean Service produces the nautical and aeronautical charts for travelers in the sea and air. It also utilizes research ships and aircraft to chart the nation's coastal waterways and collect environmental information needed to understand and use the marine environment; works with coastal states to manage the nation's coastal zone; and safeguards marine and estuarine sanctuaries and monitors ocean water quality.

★3026★ National Ocean Service
Office of Oceanography and Marine Assessments
Ocean Assessments Division
Alaska Office
222 W. 8th Ave., #56
Anchorage, AK 99513-7543
Phone: (907)271-3033
Fax: (907)271-3139
Contact: Dr. M.J. Hameedi, Manager
Parent Agencies: Department of Commerce, National Oceanic and Atmospheric Administration, National Ocean Service. ***Research Areas:*** Performs marine environmental research and assessment studies in the coastal and offshore waters of Alaska with emphasis on ocean circulation, coastal fisheries-oceanography, weathering of petroleum hydrocarbons, ecosystem analysis, and effects of oil pollution on biota.

★3027★ National Ocean Service
Office of Oceanography and Marine Assessments
Ocean Assessments Division
Hazardous Materials Response Branch
ATTN: N/OMA34
7600 Sand Point Way, N.E.
Seattle, WA 98115
Phone: (206)526-6317
Fax: (206)526-6329
Contact: John H. Robinson, Chief
Parent Agencies: Department of Commerce, National Oceanic and Atmospheric Administration, National Ocean Service. ***Research Areas:*** Provides scientific support, including contingency planning assistance and emergency response advice, to federal agencies dealing with hazardous materials spills and waste sites and their effects on marine resources in the coastal zone. Technical assistance provided by the Branch is closely coordinated with other federal, state, and local governments and industry. Areas of interest include oceanography, marine biology and geology, computer science, mathematics, and toxicology. Activities are carried out in the Branch's Chemical Assessment, Environmental Assessment, Information Management, Safety and Health, and Trajectory Modeling groups. The Chemical Assessment Group provides advice on the hazards caused by toxic chemicals and responds to questions about complex chemical reactions that are common during spill incidents. The Environmental Assessment Group recommends protection strategies based on shoreline types, wildlife sensitivity, and economic resources at risk during spills; and conducts scientific studies of hazardous waste impacts on coastal resources. The Information Management Group organizes data on spills into reports that are electronically transmitted to response groups; collects and verifies data received daily to establish a record of each incident; and provides central computer communications support for state and federal agencies during spill incidents. The Trajectory Modeling Group responds to questions regarding the movement and spread of pollutants in the environment. Computer models, that predict the path of the pollutant in a graphic formation, are used to: predict the course of oil and chemical spills in rivers, estuaries, and the ocean; model the trajectory of atmospheric pollutants; and aid in search and rescue operations. The Group also studies the physical processes that move and transform airborne and water pollutants. ***Databases:*** Response information for hazardous substances.

★3028★ National Oceanic and Atmospheric Administration (NOAA)
Washington, DC 20230
Phone: (202)377-2985
Parent Agencies: Department of Commerce, National Oceanic and Atmospheric Administration. ***Research Areas:*** The mission of NOAA is to: explore, map, and chart the global ocean and its living resources and manage, use, and conserve those resources; describe, monitor, and predict conditions in the atmosphere, ocean, sun, and space environment; issue warnings against impending destructive natural events; assess the consequences of inadvertent environmental modification over several scales of time; and manage and disseminate long-term environmental information. Major components of NOAA include: 1) the National Environmental Satellite, Data, and Information Service; 2) National Marine Fisheries Service; 3) National Ocean Service; 4) National Weather Service; and 5) Office of Oceanic and Atmospheric Research (see separate entries).

★3029★ National Oceanographic Data Center
1825 Connecticut Ave., N.W.
Washington, DC 20235
Phone: (202)673-5594
Fax: (202)673-5586
Contact: Gregory W. Withee, Dir.
Parent Agencies: Department of Commerce, National Oceanic and Atmospheric Administration, National Environmental Satellite, Data, and Information Service. ***Research Areas:*** NODC is the U.S. national service facility which acquires, processes, archives, and disseminates oceanographic data. The Center receives information for all oceans, seas, and estuaries from hundreds of domestic and foreign sources, including the national data centers of other countries. NODC also administers World Data Center A, Oceanography, a part of the World Data Center system that provides for international data exchange; and refers users to other marine data collections in the United States and to published marine science literature. NODC operations are carried out through the Office of the Director and four divisions: 1) Data Base Management; 2) Information Services; 3) ADP Support; and 4) Library and Information Services. Principal area of research interest is marine data ma nagement, including databases oriented toward the deep oceans and waters of the continental shelves. Recent activities have included: the development of NODC Ocean Science Inventory Exchange (NOSIE), an on-line interactive inventory and request service accessible via direct dial-up and via NASA's Space Physics Analysis Network (SPAN); Pacific Ocean Temperature and Salinity Profiles from 1900-1988 on CD-ROM NODC-01.

★3030★ National Oceanographic Data Center
National Environmental Data Referral Service
1825 Connecticut Ave., N.W.
Washington, DC 20235
Phone: (202)673-5548
Fax: (202)673-5586
Contact: Gerald S. Barton, Dir.
Parent Agencies: Department of Commerce, National Oceanic and Atmospheric Administration, National Environmental Satellite, Data, and Information Service. ***Research Areas:*** The NEDRES database is a catalog and index of non-bibliographic, publicly available, environmental data held by various public and private sources throughout the United States. NEDRES does not contain data, but refers users to the holder of the data. Types of data described in NEDRES include data files, data serial publications, atlases, manuals, catalogs, and data centers. Subjects covered include climatology and meteorology, ecology and pollution, geography, geophysics and geology, hydrology and limnology, oceanography, and data from remote sensing satellites. As of January 1989, NEDRES contains more than 22,200 data descriptions.

★3031★ National Oceanographic Data Center
Ocean Pollution Data and Information Network
1825 Connecticut Ave., N.W.
Washington, DC 20235
Phone: (202)673-5539
Contact: Rosalind E. Cohen, Contact
Parent Agencies: Department of Commerce, National Oceanic and Atmospheric Administration, National Environmental Satellite, Data, and Information Service.
Research Areas: The Ocean Pollution Data and Information Network (OPDIN) facilitates user access to the marine pollution data and information generated by 11 participating federal departments and agencies. It provides a wide range of products and services to researchers, managers, and others who need data and information on marine pollution. The Network was created in response to the National Ocean Pollution Planning Act of 1978 to ensure that the results and findings of federally conducted or sponsored marine pollution research, development, and monitoring programs are readily available to all users. (OPDIN is intended to supplement rather than replace existing federal data and information sources.)

★3032★ National Science Foundation
Directorate for Geosciences
Division of Ocean Sciences
Biological Oceanography Program
1800 G St., N.W., Rm. 609
Washington, DC 20550
Phone: (202)357-9600
Contact: Phillip R. Taylor, Program Dir.
Research Areas: Program supports study of the relationships among and variability of marine organisms; and the interactions of these organisms with geochemical and physical processes. A central focus is to understand ecosystems, ranging from ocean margins and continental shelves to central gyres and ocean basins, and ultimately to understand the role of organisms in global-scale processes. Biological oceanography involves research into primary production; microbial loop processes and the role of microorganisms as sources and sinks of materials and nutrients; higher trophic levels and food webs; and communities adapted to specialized extreme environments.

★3033★ National Science Foundation
Directorate for Geosciences
Division of Ocean Sciences
1800 G St., N.W.
Washington, DC 20550
Phone: (202)357-9639
Contact: M. Grant Gross, Dir.
Research Areas: The Ocean Sciences Division supports research to improve understanding of the sea and its relationship to human activities. Basic research programs support individual scientists and groups of scientists; research subjects include physical oceanography, marine chemistry, marine geology and geophysics, and biological oceanography. Program also supports acquisition and operation of oceanographic facilities needed to carry out these research programs, and ocean drilling activities.

★3034★ National Science Foundation
Directorate for Biological, Behavioral, and Social Sciences
Division of Biotic Systems and Resources
Ecology Program
1800 G St., N.W., Rm. 215
Washington, DC 20550
Phone: (202)357-9734
Fax: (202)357-7745
Contact: O.J. Reichman, Program Dir.
Research Areas: Program provides support for ecological research on relationships within and between communities of animals and plants in terrestrial and inland aquatic habitats. This includes studies of interspecific competition, predator-prey relationships, and symbiosis between species, as well as studies of species that comprise communities. The program funds research on the co-evolution of animals and plants, microbial ecology, and paleoecology, with emphasis on multi-species interactions at the community level and their responses to environmental change. Supports programs for women, minorities, handicapped and opportunities at primarily undergraduate institutions.

★3035★ National Science Foundation
Directorate for Biological, Behavioral, and Social Sciences
Division of Biotic Systems and Resources
Ecosystem Studies Program
1800 G St., N.W., Rm. 215
Washington, DC 20550
Phone: (202)357-9596
Contact: James E. Schindler, Program Dir.
Research Areas: Program supports multidisciplinary studies of the structure and function of complex biotic-abiotic associations. Processes, mechanisms, and system behavior comprise a major research focus, as in the study of energy and nutrient transfer through ecosystems. Landscape scale experiments leading to a better understanding of the spatial and temporal relations within and among ecosystems are supported. The development of new elements and synthesis of ecological theory is emphasized, and mathematical modeling of ecosystems for analysis and integration is encouraged. Both short-term and long-term research is supported, ranging from the behavior of individual processes to large ecosystem response to environmental changes.

★3036★ National Science Foundation
Directorate for Engineering
Division of Biological and Critical Systems
Environmental Engineering Program
1800 G St., N.W.
Washington, DC 20550
Phone: (202)357-7737
Contact: Edward H. Bryan, Program Dir.
Research Areas: Supports research to apply engineering principles to correct adverse effects on land, water and air resources which would otherwise impair the usefulness of those resources such as diffusion, dispersion and interactions of pollutants, innovative water and wastewater treatment processes and systems, and engineering approaches to manage or eliminate pollutants that adversely affect environmental quality.

★3037★ National Science Foundation
Directorate for Geosciences
Division of Earth Sciences
Geology and Paleontology Program
1800 G St., N.W.
Washington, DC 20550
Phone: (202)357-7866
Fax: (202)357-0364
Contact: John A. Maccini, Program Dir.
Research Areas: Support for geological studies includes research on physical and chemical processes occurring at or near the earth's surface. Projects include low-temperature geochemistry, geomorphology and quaternary geology, volcanology, study of surface and ground waters, glaciology, soil genesis and classification, fossil-fuel generation, and study of geologic hazards. Support for paleontology studies includes research on sedimentary rocks and fossils to determine past conditions and processes on the earth's surface. Projects include sedimentology, biostratigraphy, paleolimnology, micropaleontology, paleoecology, and vertebrate and invertebrate paleontology.

★3038★ National Science Foundation
Directorate for Engineering
Division of Biological and Critical Systems
Natural and Man-Made Hazard Mitigation Program
1800 G St., N.W.
Washington, DC 20550
Phone: (202)357-9780
Fax: (202)357-9803
Contact: J. Eleonora Sabadell, Program Dir.
Research Areas: The natural hazards of interest in this Program are geophysical in nature and are related to meteorologic, hydrologic, and geomorphic events that endanger, damage, or destroy lives, property, and resources. Research efforts are concerned with natural hazards such as hurricanes and tornadoes, floods and droughts, landslides and mudflows, snow drifts and ice-jams, ground subsidence and sinkholes, accelerated erosion and sedimentation, expansive soils, and other extreme events. Included also are hazards created by human activities that significantly alter the physical conditions of the environmental system (e.g., the uncontrolled deforestation in watersheds; the destabilization of slopes resulting from inappropriate land uses; and incorrectly built, designed, or placed buildings).

★3039★ National Science Foundation
Directorate for Geosciences
Division of Polar Programs
Polar Biology and Medicine Program
1800 G St., N. W.
Washington, DC 20550
Phone: (202)357-7894
Fax: (202)357-9422
Contact: Polly A. Penhale, Program Dir.
Research Areas: Program provides support for arctic and antarctic research in marine, freshwater, and terrestrial biology, ecology, ecosystem structure and processes, and the effects of human activities on the environment in order to promote an understanding of species, communities, and ecosystems. Program also supports process studies on nutrient cycling and land-atmosphere interactions, particularly in the context of regional and global changes.

★3040★ National Sedimentation Laboratory
PO Box 1157
Oxford, MS 38655
Phone: (601)232-2900
Contact: Dr. Calvin K. Mutchler, Dir.
Parent Agencies: Department of Agriculture, Agricultural Research Service, Mid South Area.
Research Areas: Soil erosion, sediment transport, river mechanics, watershed modeling, and related pollution problems.

★3041★ National Soil Dynamics Laboratory
PO Box 792
Auburn, AL 36831-0792
Phone: (205)887-8596
Contact: Jerrel B. Powell, Research Leader
Parent Agencies: Department of Agriculture, Agricultural Research Service, Mid South Area.
Research Areas: Soil-machinery relationships. Mission involves studies of soil dynamics, tillage

systems, root development in compact soils, and conservation of energy, soil, and water resources.

★3042★ National Toxicology Program
PO Box 12233
Research Triangle Park, NC 27709
Phone: (919)541-3991
Contact: Dr. David P. Rall, Dir.
Parent Agencies: Department of Health and Human Services, U.S. Public Health Service. ***Research Areas:*** Program's primary mission is to strengthen the science base in toxicology and coordinate research and testing activities on toxic chemicals. NTP's goals are to: 1) develop a reliable series of relatively inexpensive short-term tests and protocols useful for the public health regulation of toxic chemicals, including the development of test batteries to assess genetic, neurobehavioral, and immunological toxicities; 2) expand the toxicological profiles of chemicals tested; 3) increase the rate of testing of chemicals for such toxic effects as carcinogenicity, mutagenicity, and reproductive and developmental effects (NTP also examines the chemicals for neurobehavioral, immunological, and other toxic effects where appropriate within funding limits); and 4) disseminate results of NTP's testing and methods development programs to government research and regulatory agencies, industry, labor, and environmental groups, the scientific community, and the public. Chemicals chosen for testing are those that involve widespread or intense human exposure, or those for which existing data on toxic effects are inadequate. Some chemicals are selected for testing because study of them may tell more about how structurally related chemicals are likely to affect human health. Other criteria include: amount produced, significant physical and chemical properties, interest by regulatory and research agencies, and possible public health significance. The NTP testing strategy is to identify the major toxic effects of each chemical studied (genetic mutations; damage to critical organs such as the lungs, liver, and nervous system; birth defects; or cancer).

★3043★ National Wetlands Research Center
1010 Gause Blvd.
Slidell, LA 70458
Phone: (504)646-7564
Fax: (504)646-7288
Contact: Dr. Robert E. Stewart Jr., Dir.
Parent Agencies: Department of the Interior, U.S. Fish and Wildlife Service. ***Research Areas:*** As part of the U.S. Fish and Wildlife Service, the Center provides national leadership in research and development that addresses resource issues related to protecting, restoring, and managing wetlands, with an emphasis on wintering waterfowl. Studies focus on wetlands ecology, wintering waterfowl, and technology development. Disciplines include ecology, aquatic toxicology, hydrology, geography, oceanography, computer analysis, and wildlife, waterfowl, and fishery biology.

★3044★ National Wildlife Health Research Center
6006 Schroeder Rd.
Madison, WI 53711
Phone: (608)264-5411
Fax: (608)271-4640
Contact: Dr. Milton Friend, Dir.
Parent Agencies: Department of the Interior, U.S. Fish and Wildlife Service. ***Research Areas:*** Aims to determine the impact of disease on the wildlife resources under the stewardship of the U.S. Fish and Wildlife Service; identify the role of various pathogens in contributing to these losses; develop effective means for disease prevention; and significantly reduce wildlife losses when disease does occur.

★3045★ National Zoological Park Conservation and Research Center
Front Royal, VA 22630
Phone: (703)635-4166
Fax: (703)635-4166
Contact: Dr. Christen Wemmer, Curator-in-Charge
Parent Agencies: Smithsonian Institution. ***Research Areas:*** Center is a 3100-acre preserve managed by the National Zoological Park under the administration of the Smithsonian Institution. Its primary mission is to assure long-term successful management of rare and endangered species of mammals, birds, and terrestrial vertebrates through combined programs in captive propagation and research. The research goal is to sustain the gene pools of vanishing animals and to augment and convey knowledge about their biology and conservation.

★3046★ National Zoological Park Department of Zoological Research
Connecticut Ave., N.W.
Washington, DC 20008
Phone: (202)673-4825
Fax: (202)673-4686
Contact: Dr. Devra G. Kleiman, Assistant Dir. for Research
Parent Agencies: Smithsonian Institution. ***Research Areas:*** Studies in the Department of Zoological Research concentrate mainly on avian and mammalian behavior, physiology, nutrition, evolutionary biology, molecular and population genetics, and ecology. Close ties are maintained with the University of Maryland, and cooperative research with the University has permitted the development of graduate studies programs in the areas of behavior and ecology. In addition, active field research is being carried out in Sri Lanka, Brazil, and Venezuela as well as at the Conservation and Research Center in Front Royal and at several North American sites.

★3047★ Naval Civil Engineering Laboratory Energy and Environment Department
Port Hueneme, CA 93043
Phone: (805)982-1355
Fax: (805)982-1418
Contact: Stephen Ehret, Head
Parent Agencies: Department of the Navy, Chief of Naval Operations, Naval Facilities Engineering Command. ***Research Areas:*** The Energy and Environment Department is concerned with conservation of energy resources and development of solutions for environmental problems. Recent areas of interest have included technology for: hazardous waste minimization, hazardous waste disposal site clean-up, pollution abatement, energy conservation, energy systems, land use planning, geographic analysis, utility control and power systems, communication facilities and utilities survivability.

★3048★ Naval Energy and Environmental Support Activity
c/o Naval Civil Engineering Laboratory
Port Hueneme, CA 93043
Phone: (805)982-5952
Contact: Cdr. Morris, Commanding Officer
Parent Agencies: Department of the Navy, Chief of Naval Operations, Naval Facilities Engineering Command. ***Research Areas:*** Is concerned with conservation of energy resources and development of solutions for environmental problems. Recent areas of interest have included: reductions in fuel consumption; facility lighting management; very low frequency guyline insulators; wind generators; steam traps; biodegradation/biodetoxification of toxic substances; and hazardous waste sites.

★3049★ Naval Ocean Systems Center Marine Sciences and Technology Department Environmental Sciences Division
NOSC Code 52
271 Catalina Blvd.
San Diego, CA 92152-5000
Phone: (619)553-2760
Fax: (619)553-6305
Contact: Dr. Sachio Yamamoto, Head
Parent Agencies: Department of the Navy, Chief of Naval Operations, Space and Naval Warfare Systems Command. ***Research Areas:*** The Environmental Sciences Division conducts research and development in the areas of environmental chemistry and biology, chemical oceanography, biochemistry, bioluminescence, and radiation detection.

★3050★ Nebraska Water Center
University of Nebraska
103 Natural Resources Bldg.
Lincoln, NE 68583-0844
Phone: (402)472-3305
Fax: (402)472-3574
Contact: Dr. Dale H. Vanderholm, Interim Dir.
Parent Agencies: Department of the Interior, U.S. Geological Survey, Water Resources Division. ***Research Areas:*** Water management and quality, particularly irrigation water and nitrogen fertilizer management.

★3051★ Nevada Mineral Industry Waste Treatment and Recovery Generic Center
University of Nevada
Mackay School of Mines
Reno, NV 89557
Phone: (702)784-6115
Contact: Dr. James L. Hendrix, Dir.
Parent Agencies: Department of the Interior, Bureau of Mines, Mineral Technology Center. ***Research Areas:*** Center's program focuses on mineral industry waste treatment and disposal and the recovery of critical materials from waste products. Emphasis is on the physical chemical information needed to evaluate the technical and economic viability of these processes. Specific fields of research interest include: mineral processing, hydrometallurgy, pyrometallurgy, chemistry, mining hydrology, and hydrology. Activities are carried out at the Center and at several satellite facilities (see Remarks below). In addition, Center encourages participation from industry, the Bureau of Mines, and other mining and mineral resource research institutes and functions as a training center for graduate mineral industry students.

★3052★ Nevada Water Research Institute
University of Nevada System
Nevada Water Resources Center
PO Box 60220
Reno, NV 89506-0220
Phone: (702)673-7365
Contact: Jack W. Hess, Interim Dir.
Parent Agencies: Department of the Interior, U.S. Geological Survey, Water Resources Division. ***Research Areas:*** Groundwater recharge and transport processes and natural and artifical influences affecting groundwater quality.

★3053★ New Hampshire Water Resources Research Center
University of New Hampshire
218 Science/Engineering Research Bldg.
Durham, NH 03824-3525
Phone: (603)862-2144
Fax: (603)862-2030
Contact: Dr. Thomas Ballestero, Dir.
Parent Agencies: Department of the Interior, U.S. Geological Survey, Water Resources Division. ***Research Areas:*** Water resources. Activities focus on studies of groundwater, including radon occurrence, contaminant fate and transport, quality and decontamination of aquifers; and surface water, including lake eutrophication, control of aquatic plants, costs associated with small community systems, causes of contamination during the treatment process, flow characteristics, and response to contamination of water supply. Also studies acid rain.

★3054★ New Jersey Division of Water Resources
Rutgers University
Center for Coastal & Environmental Studies
Doolittle Hall, Busch Campus
New Brunswick, NJ 08903
Phone: (201)932-3596
Fax: (201)932-5811
Contact: Dr. Joan G. Ehrenfeld, Acting Dir.
Parent Agencies: Department of the Interior, U.S. Geological Survey, Water Resources Division. ***Research Areas:*** Water supply and quality. Supports research on the effects of stormflows on water quality, acid deposition in the northwestern section of the state, accumulation of heavy metals in freshwater tidelands, trace element accumulation by freshwater organisms, carcinogenic effects of volatile organic compounds in water, leaching from municipal land fills, fate of heavy metals in saltwater bays, and influence of septic tank waste water on pineland vegetation.

★3055★ New Mexico Water Resources Research Institute
New Mexico State University
PO Box 30001, Dept. 3167
Las Cruces, NM 88003-0001
Phone: (505)646-4337
Fax: (505)646-6418
Contact: Dr. Bobby J. Creel, Acting Dir.
Parent Agencies: Department of the Interior, U.S. Geological Survey, Water Resources Division. ***Research Areas:*** Water conservation, water quality, surface and ground water relationships, and saline water. Evaluates the efficiency of irrigation systems around the state.

★3056★ New York Cooperative Fish and Wildlife Research Unit
Cornell University
Fernow Hall
Ithaca, NY 14853-0188
Phone: (607)256-2014
Contact: Dr. Milo E. Richmond, Leader
Parent Agencies: Department of the Interior, U.S. Fish and Wildlife Service, U.S. Fish and Wildlife Service Cooperative Units. ***Research Areas:*** Unit's program of field and laboratory research on management and conservation of fish and wildlife species includes studies on: 1) habitat, productivity, growth, feeding, behavior, and movement of various birds, waterfowl, and animals; 2) reproduction among wild vertebrates; 3) pest management ecology; 4) the effects of acid precipitation and trace metals on fish populations; 5) mitigation strategies for acidification of surface waters; and 6) economic and biological effects of hydroelectric development on Atlantic salmon restoration. Unit's functions include instruction and graduate research training in fisheries and wildlife resources at the University.

★3057★ New York State Water Resources Institute
Center for Environmental Research
Cornell University
468 Hollister Hall
Ithaca, NY 14853-3501
Phone: (607)255-5941
Contact: Keith S. Porter, Dir.
Parent Agencies: Department of the Interior, U.S. Geological Survey, Water Resources Division. ***Research Areas:*** Water resources, especially groundwater contamination and management, including studies on the fate of chemicals in soil and groundwater. Develops computer software packages to diagnose groundwater problems.

★3058★ North Carolina Cooperative Fish and Wildlife Research Unit
North Carolina State University
Gardner Hall, Rm. 4105
PO Box 7617
Raleigh, NC 27695-7617
Phone: (919)737-2631
Contact: W. James Fleming, Leader
Parent Agencies: Department of the Interior, U.S. Fish and Wildlife Service, U.S. Fish and Wildlife Service Cooperative Units. ***Research Areas:*** Unit's program is focused on riverine and coastal wetlands, including species biology and ecology, toxicology, environmental contaminants, and man-made perturbations.

★3059★ North Carolina Water Resources Research Institute
North Carolina State University
219 Oberlin Road, Campus Box 7912
Raleigh, NC 27695-7912
Phone: (919)737-2815
Fax: (919)737-7802
Contact: Dr. David H. Moreau, Dir.
Parent Agencies: Department of the Interior, U.S. Geological Survey, Water Resources Division. ***Research Areas:*** Water management, including studies on workable water supply watershed protection programs, identifying and eliminating harmful substances in wastewater treatment plant effluent going into streams and rivers, methods to assist water treatment plants meet the Safe Drinking Water Act standards, urban stormwater management alternatives and financing mechanisms, management strategies for small water and wastewater systems, the effect of low stream flows on fish populations, the relationship between climate and regional and local water resources, leaking underground storage tanks and land fills, and land application of wastewater treatment plant sludge.

★3060★ North Dakota Water Resources Research Institute
North Dakota State University
Old Main, Box 5790
Fargo, ND 58105
Phone: (701)237-7033
Contact: Dr. R. Craig Schnell, Dir.
Parent Agencies: Department of the Interior, U.S. Geological Survey, Water Resources Division. ***Research Areas:*** Water quantity and quality. Activities focus on chemical evolution of water dissolved materials and on groundwater quality, contamination of groundwater by the migration of organic agents through the soil, and role of pesticides and fertilizers in polluting water quality.

★3061★ Northern Prairie Wildlife Research Center
PO Box 2096
Jamestown, ND 58402
Phone: (701)252-5363
Fax: (701)252-4217
Contact: Dr. Susan Haseltine, Dir.
Parent Agencies: Department of the Interior, U.S. Fish and Wildlife Service, Northern Prairie Wildlife Research Center. ***Research Areas:*** As part of the U.S. Fish and Wildlife Service, the Center's primary mission is to gather facts and information necessary for proper management and preservation of wildlife species in the midwestern and western United States. Emphasis is on waterfowl populations, including distribution and abundance, reproduction, and habitat requirements during breeding, migrating, and wintering periods. Specific areas of interest include: 1) waterfowl ecology, behavior, and population dynamics; 2) wetland ecology, classification, and management; 3) mammalian predator ecology, behavior, and management; 4) ecology and management of native and introduced grasslands; 5) invertebrate biology; 6) ecology and behavior of cranes, shorebirds, birds of prey, and other nonwaterfowl species; and 7) statistical and mathematical applications to wildlife ecology.

★3062★ Northwest Watershed Research Unit
270 S. Orchard St.
Boise, ID 83705
Phone: (208)334-1363
Fax: (208)334-1502
Contact: Wilbert H. Blackburn, Research Leader
Parent Agencies: Department of Agriculture, Agricultural Research Service, Pacific West Area. ***Research Areas:*** Unit's research mission is to quantitatively describe the hydrologic processes and interactive influences of climate, soils, vegetation, topography, and management on rangeland watersheds and to develop information, simulation models, and expert systems that can be used by action agencies and producers to assist in determining optimum management strategies. Research involves identifying and quantifying processes affecting climate, snow, evapotranspiration, saturated/unsaturated soil water, soil frost, runoff, and erosion. Watershed level research investigates the influence of hydrologic temporal and spatial variability on water supply and flood forecasting; the firm level effort is concerned with the development and validation of integrated watershed level models and expert systems.

★3063★ NRC/DRPS Reactor Safety Data Bank
Idaho National Engineering Laboratory
PO Box 1625/MS 2404
Idaho Falls, ID 83415
Phone: (208)526-9071
Fax: (208)526-9591
Contact: Mr. H.A. Hardy, Data Bank Admin.
Parent Agencies: Department of Energy. ***Research Areas:*** Data Bank is a computerized repository for nuclear reactor safety research experimental data. Data sources are worldwide and are stored in a common format with comprehensive data manipulation and display software. Service is available interactively to approved governmental agencies, educational institutions, and private industry conducting nuclear reactor research.

★3064★ Nuclear Regulatory Commission (NRC)
Washington, DC 20555
Phone: (301)492-0240
Contact: Kenneth M. Carr Jr., Chm.
Responsible for licensing and regulating nuclear facilities and materials and for conducting research in support of the licensing and regulatory process. These responsibilities include protecting public health safety, the environment, and materials and plants in the interest of national security; and assuring conformity with antitrust laws.

★3065★ Nuclear Regulatory Commission
Office of Nuclear Regulatory Research
Mail Stop NL-007
Washington, DC 20555
Phone: (301)492-3700
Contact: Eric S. Beckjord, Dir.
Research Areas: Office plans, recommends, and conducts an extensive safety research program relating to the industries and activities that the Nuclear Regulatory Commission regulates, including reactors, full cycle facilities, radioactive waste disposal, and licensed users of radioactive isotopes. Nuclear power reactor safety accounts for the greater part of research. Primary interests include primary system integrity; core damage prevention; reactor containment performance and public protection from radiation; safety of nuclear waste disposal; and resolution of generic safety issues. Activities are carried out in the Engineering Division, Reactor Accident Analysis Division, Reactor and Plant Systems Division, and Regulatory Applications Division.

★3066★ Oak Ridge National Laboratory (ORNL)
PO Box 2008
Oak Ridge, TN 37831-6255
Phone: (615)576-2900
Fax: (615)576-2912
Contact: Dr. Alvin W. Trivelpiece, Dir.
Parent Agencies: Department of Energy, Energy Laboratories. ***Research Areas:*** Conducts applied research and engineering development in support of DOE's programs in fusion, fission, fossil, renewables (biomass), and other energy technologies, such as conversion and conservation. Performs basic scientific research in selected areas of physical and life sciences. Applies resources to education, international competitiveness, hazardous waste research and development, and selected defense technologies. Research focuses on interaction of energy-related physical and chemical agents with the environment and with living organisms; work on expert systems, simulation, and decision research; high temperature materials, neutron scattering, surface physics, and aqueous, separations, analytical, and environmental chemistry; robotics; parallel computing; heavy-ion nuclear atomic physics; behavior aspects of emergency response plans, and studies on social impacts and causes of environmental changes.

★3067★ Oak Ridge National Laboratory
Biomedical and Environmental Information Analysis Section
PO Box 2008, MS-6050
Oak Ridge, TN 37831-6050
Phone: (615)574-7803
Fax: (615)574-9888
Contact: Dr. Po-Yung Lu, Head
Parent Agencies: Department of Energy, Energy Data Centers. ***Research Areas:*** BEIA analyzes scientific information and provides information services on energy, the environment, health effects, and toxicology. Activities also include development of new databases in these areas. The Section includes: 1) Human Genome and Toxicology; 2) Chemical Hazard Evaluation and Communication; and 3) Hazardous Materials and Environmental Information Groups.

★3068★ Oak Ridge National Laboratory
Biomedical and Environmental Sciences Directorate
Environmental Sciences Division
Ecosystem Studies Section
PO Box 2008
Oak Ridge, TN 37831-6038
Phone: (615)574-7398
Contact: Webster Van Winkle, Section Head
Parent Agencies: Department of Energy, Energy Laboratories. ***Research Areas:*** Section conducts research to understand quantitatively the ways in which terrestrial and aquatic ecosystems function and respond to the stresses of anthropogenic activities.

★3069★ Oak Ridge National Laboratory
Biomedical and Environmental Sciences Directorate
Environmental Sciences Division
Environmental Restoration Program
PO Box 2008
Oak Ridge, TN 37831-6036
Phone: (615)574-7726
Fax: (615)574-4946
Contact: D.D. Huff, Manager
Parent Agencies: Department of Energy, Energy Laboratories. ***Research Areas:*** Program conducts research, development, and demonstration projects in environmental restoration. Research activities include: development and application of models to describe surface and groundwater transport systems; basic research in the use of environmental tracers to study transport processes; support of remedial action programs through field characterization studies, waste disposal technology development and demonstration projects, and program management activities; field-scale studies of environmental engineering alternatives for waste disposal practices; and application of geostatistical methods to environmental characterization.

★3070★ Oak Ridge National Laboratory
Biomedical and Environmental Sciences Directorate
Environmental Sciences Division
Bldg. 1505, Mail Stop 6037
PO Box 2008
Oak Ridge, TN 37831-6037
Phone: (615)574-7374
Fax: (615)574-4946
Contact: R.I. Van Hook, Dir.
Parent Agencies: Department of Energy, Energy Laboratories. ***Research Areas:*** Conducts research on the environmental aspects of existing and emerging energy systems and applies this information to ensure that technology development and energy use are consistent with national environmental goals. Performs basic and applied research, environmental assessments, environmental engineering and demonstration projects, technology and operational support functions, and program management for the DOE, for other federal and state agencies, and for industry, working collaboratively with several federal agencies, universities, and the private sector. Consists of four disciplinary research sections (Ecological Studies, Environmental Analyses, Environmental Toxicology, and Geosciences); three national programs (Biomass Production, Carbon Dioxide Information Anaylsis and Research, and Environmental Waste); and one interdisciplinary center (Center for Global Environmental Studies).

★3071★ Oak Ridge National Laboratory
Biomedical and Environmental Sciences Directorate
Environmental Sciences Division
Geosciences Section
PO Box 2008
Oak Ridge, TN 37831-6038
Phone: (615)574-7830
Fax: (615)574-4946
Contact: S.H. Stow, Section Head
Parent Agencies: Department of Energy, Energy Laboratories. ***Research Areas:*** Section conducts basic and applied research on interdisciplinary problems related to the broad field of earth sciences, including studies in environmental chemistry, geochemistry, geology and geophysics, and soil science. Activities emphasize migration of radioactive and hazardous waste contaminants in natural systems.

★3072★ Oak Ridge National Laboratory
Oak Ridge National Environmental Research Park
Bldg. 1505 MS 6038
PO Box 2008
Oak Ridge, TN 37831-6038
Phone: (615)576-8123
Contact: Patricia Dreyer Parr, Manager
Parent Agencies: Department of Energy. ***Research Areas:*** Provides protected land areas (approximately 12,400 acres), for research and education in the environmental sciences and for demonstrating the compatability of energy technology facilities with a quality environment. Current research programs at Oak Ridge Research Park include a study of the effects of acid deposition on vegetation, a study of the effects of whole-tree harvesting on biomass production and soil nutrients, and studies on plant physiological processes and forest nutrient relationships as influenced by intensive silviculture. In addition, education in the environmental sciences is offered through the Ecological and Physical Sciences Study Center where students get "hands-on" experience in specific field activities.

★3073★ Oak Ridge National Laboratory
Biomedical and Environmental Information Analysis Section
Toxicology Information Response Group
Bldg. 2001
PO Box 2008
Mail Stop 6050
Oak Ridge, TN 37831-6050
Phone: (615)576-1743
Fax: (615)574-9888
Contact: Kimberly Slusher, Information Analyst
Parent Agencies: Department of Energy. ***Research Areas:*** Group serves as an international center for the collection, analysis, and dissemination of toxicology-related information. It provides information to the scientific and administrative communities and to the public on a variety of chemicals, including food additives, pharmaceuticals, industrial chemicals, environmental pollutants, heavy metals, and pesticides.

★3074★ Office of Civilian Radioactive Waste Management
Mail Stop RW-1
1000 Independence Ave., S.W.
Washington, DC 20585
Phone: (202)586-6842

Contact: Samuel Rousso, Acting Dir.
Parent Agencies: Department of Energy, Department of Energy Program Offices. ***Research Areas:*** Office is responsible for the Nuclear Waste Fund and for management of federal programs for: recommending, constructing, and operating repositories for disposal of high level radioactive waste and spent nuclear fuel; interim storage of spent nuclear fuel; monitored retrievable storage; and research, development, and demonstration regarding disposal of high-level radioactive waste and spent nuclear fuel.

★3075★ Office of Energy Research
1000 Independence Ave., SW
Washington, DC 20585
Phone: (202)586-5430
Contact: Robert Hunter Jr., Dir. -Designate
Parent Agencies: Department of Energy. ***Research Areas:*** Manages a research program aimed at determining the generic environmental, health, and safety aspects of energy technologies and programs.

★3076★ Office of Energy Utilization Research
U. S. Dept. of Energy (CE)
1000 Independence Ave., S.W.
Washington, DC 20585
Phone: (202)586-1477
Fax: (202)586-2707
Contact: John J. Brogan, Dir.
Parent Agencies: Department of Energy. ***Research Areas:*** The Office of Energy Utilization Research is the Department of Energy's headquarters program office for a long-range energy conservation research program in energy conversion and utilization (ECUT). The program focuses on development of advanced energy conversion and utilization technologies to improve energy efficiency, energy productivity, and fuel-switching capability for transportation, industry, residential/commercial, and utility sectors.

★3077★ Office of Environmental Restoration
U. S. Dept. of Energy
Mail Stop EM-40, GTN
Washington, DC 20545
Phone: (301)353-5006
Contact: William R. Voight, Dir.
Parent Agencies: Department of Energy, Department of Energy Program Offices, Nuclear Energy. ***Research Areas:*** Office provides direction for the planning, development, and execution of Department of Energy programs for civilian nuclear waste treatment, civilian low-level waste management, and decontamination and decommissioning of contaminated DOE and legislatively authorized non-government facilities and sites; and develops beneficial uses of nuclear waste byproducts.

★3078★ Office of Health and Environmental Research
Mail Stop ER-70, GTN
Washington, DC 20545
Phone: (301)353-3251
Fax: (301)353-5051
Contact: Dr. Robert Wood, Acting Associate Dir.
Parent Agencies: Department of Energy, Office of Energy Research. ***Research Areas:*** Office is the health and environmental research arm of the Department of Energy. Its mission is to achieve understanding of the health and environmental effects associated with energy technologies and to develop and sustain basic and applied research programs in the biomedical and environmental sciences in which the Department has responsibilities or unique capabilities. ons. Office is also responsible for technology transfer to the

★3079★ Office of Health and Environmental Research
Health Effects Research Division
Mail Stop ER, GTN
Washington, DC 20545
Phone: (301)353-5468
Fax: (301)353-5051
Contact: David A. Smith, Dir.
Parent Agencies: Department of Energy, Department of Energy Program Offices, Office of Energy Research. ***Research Areas:*** Division supports studies of animals, organs, tissues, cells, and subcellular systems in order to predict human health effects from exposure to energy pollutants in situations where human data are lacking. These studies involve: determining the toxicity of chemical and physical agents; characterizing adverse health effects; elucidating fundamental molecular and cellular mechanisms underlying toxicity; developing methods for early detection of health effects; obtaining quantitative data on dose-response relationships; and validating predictive estimates against available epidemiological and clinical data from studies on humans. Division also conducts a basic biological research program to support this mission-oriented function, with emphasis on selected areas of research in cell biology, biophysics, structural biology, molecular biology, and genetics. Aim is to elucidate the normal structure and function of key biological systems in order to provide a conceptual basis for better understanding and prediction of the health risks of energy activities.

★3080★ Office of Health and Environmental Research
Ecological Research Division
National Environmental Research Parks Program
Mail Stop ER-75, GTN
Washington, DC 20545
Phone: (301)353-4208
Contact: Dr. Clive Jorgensen, Program Manager
Parent Agencies: Department of Energy, Department of Energy Program Offices, Office of Energy Research. ***Research Areas:*** A National Environmental Research Park (NERP) is an outdoor laboratory where research is carried out to achieve agency and national environmental goals and to inform the public of the environmental and land-use options open to them. The basic operating premise of the NERP concept is to organize research on DOE lands to achieve agency-mandated environmental goals and aid in resolving environmental problems locally, regionally, nationally, and globally. NERPs represent large land areas located within major ecoregions of the United States and are available for research by individuals and organizations. Extensive and long term characterization data are also available from site coordinators.

★3081★ Office of Oceanic and Atmospheric Research
National Oceanic & Atmospheric Administration
6010 Executive Blvd.
Rockville, MD 20852
Phone: (301)443-8344
Fax: (301)443-5167
Contact: Dr. Alan R. Thomas, Acting Assistant Admin.
Parent Agencies: Department of Commerce, National Oceanic and Atmospheric Administration. ***Research Areas:*** Office administers research programs in the oceanic and atmospheric sciences conducted and/or supported by NOAA. This research includes: 1) studying and predicting tropical phenomena that cause short-term climate variations over North America and other economically important regions of the globe; 2) monitoring and analyzing the fates and effects of airborne pollutants (e.g., acid deposition) and the effects of radiatively and chemically important trace species on air quality and climate change (e.g., global greenhouse effect); 3) improving forecasts of weather systems ranging from localized storms to hurricanes by developing new remote observational systems, better data integration and display formats for forecasters, numerical models more capable of describing atmospheric behavior, and more thorough analyses of atmospheric processes; 4) developing and improving forecasts and warnings of solar activity and disturbances affecting the Earth and near-earth environments; 5) providing a sound scientific basis for the management, development, and use of coastal, esuarine, and Great Lakes waters by studying their physical and chemical processes and the impacts of both natural and human-induced changes; 6) studying the hydrothermal venting systems of the ocean floor, particularly their thermal and chemical effects on the ocean and their associated biological communities (potential sources of biologically and chemically important substances); 7) studying the environmental processes affecting the abundance of marine resources (e.g., fisheries recruitment) in order to improve the efficient use and management of these resources; 8) improving forecasts of hazardous winds, waves, and storm surges, lake levels, and ice growth, movement, and breakup; and 9) providing the facilities and tools necessary for conducting underwater, in situ marine research.

★3082★ Office of Oceanic and Atmospheric Research
Environmental Research Laboratories
National Oceanic and Atmospheric Administration
325 Broadway
Boulder, CO 80303
Phone: (303)497-6000
Contact: Joseph O. Fletcher, Dir.
Parent Agencies: Department of Commerce, National Oceanic and Atmospheric Administration. ***Research Areas:*** Major ERL laboratories and units include: Aeronomy Laboratory, Air Resources Laboratory, Atlantic Oceanographic and Meteorological Laboratory, Environmental Sciences Group, Geophysical Fluid Dynamics Laboratory, Great Lakes Environmental Research Laboratory, National Severe Storms Laboratory, Pacific Marine Environmental Laboratory, Space Environment Laboratory, and Wave Propagation Laboratory. Activities include: weather observation and prediction, cloud physics, air quality, climate research, solar-terrestrial studies, marine observation and prediction, marine assessment, and marine resources.

★3083★ Office of Oceanic and Atmospheric Research
National Sea Grant College Program
Silver Spring Metro Center No. 1
1335 East-West Hwy.
Silver Spring, MD 20910
Phone: (301)427-2448
Contact: Robert D. Wildman, Dir.
4***Parent Agencies:*** Department of Commerce, National Oceanic and Atmospheric

Administration. ***Research Areas:*** To increase understanding, assessment, development, utilization, and conservation of the nation's ocean and coastal resources by providing assistance to promote a strong educational base, research and training activities, and prompt dissemination of knowledge and techniques. Sea Grant colleges and institutions presently operate in 30 states through a network of more than 200 participating university and marine research institutions, which serve as the core of the Program. Projects are supported in a wide range of marine-related subjects through five Program divisions: 1)living resources (aquaculture, fisheries, seafood science and technology, and marine biotechnology); 2) non-living resources (coastal processes, energy, marine mineral resources, and diving physiology and safety); 3) technology and commercial development (marine transportation, ocean engineering, marine economics, marine recreation, and tourism); 4) environmental studies (environmental quality and estuarine studies); 5) and human resources (marine advisory services, education and training, marine policy and social sciences, ocean law, and communications).

★3084★ Office of Oceanic and Atmospheric Research
National Undersea Research Program
Silver Spring Metro Center No. 1
1335 East-West Hwy.
Silver Spring, MD 20910
Phone: (301)427-2427
Contact: David B. Duane, Dir.
Parent Agencies: Department of Commerce, National Oceanic and Atmospheric Administration, Office of Oceanic and Atmospheric Research. ***Research Areas:*** Manages and supports research programs in marine pollution, fisheries, ocean technology (including diving research and technology), and seafloor properties and processes. Current participants in the National Undersea Research Program are: University of Hawaii, University of North Carolina at Wilmington, University of Alaska Fairbanks, University of Connecticut, and Caribbean Marine Research Center (Lee Stocking Island, Bahamas).

★3085★ Office of Oceanic and Atmospheric Research
Office of Climatic and Atmospheric Research
National Oceanic & Atmospheric Administration
1335 E. W. Hwy., 4th Fl.
Silver Spring, MD 20910
Phone: (301)427-2474
Contact: Dr. J. Michael Hall, Dir.
Parent Agencies: Department of Commerce, National Oceanic and Atmospheric Administration. ***Research Areas:*** Office manages major national and international climatic and meteorological research programs which cross NOAA organizational lines and involve other federal agencies, foreign governments, and international organizations.

★3086★ Office of Renewable Energy Technologies
Mail Stop CE-34
1000 Independence Ave., S.W., Rm. 5H095
Washington, DC 20585
Phone: (202)586-8084
Contact: Ronald R. Loose, Dir.
Parent Agencies: Department of Energy, Department of Energy Program Offices, Conservation and Renewable Energy. ***Research Areas:*** The Office of Renewable Energy Technologies is responsible for the Department of Energy's programs in geothermal and hydropower technologies, biomass energy technology, and energy from municipal waste. Areas of research interest include: energy-related aspects of biomass (thermochemical and biochemical conversion, feedstock production, alcohol fuels, and municipal waste); geothermal technology (hardrock penetration, hot dry rock, reservoir technology); and hydropower technology (environmental and safety requirements). Principal components of the Office of Renewable Energy Technologies are: 1) Biofuels and Municipal Waste Technology Division; and 2) Geothermal Technology Division.

★3087★ Office of Renewable Energy Technologies
Biofuels and Municipal Waste Technology Division
Mail Stop CE-341
1000 Independence Ave., S.W., Rm. 5F072
Washington, DC 20585
Phone: (202)586-6750
Fax: (202)586-8134
Contact: Donald K. Walter, Dir.
Parent Agencies: Department of Energy, Department of Energy Program Offices, Conservation and Renewable Energy. ***Research Areas:*** Division develops and directs research and development aimed at increasing the supply of biomass feedstocks and developing conversion technologies that produce heat and gaseous/liquid fuels from a variety of biomass and municipal waste feedstocks. This includes studies of herbaceous and woody crops with potential to increase biomass yields, as well as thermochemical and biochemical conversion systems. Regional programs focus on technology transfer and matching of local feedstocks to conversion technologies. Emphasis is on the economics of biomass and the integration of biomass energy production and energy conversion. Research is also conducted on utilizing municipal waste as an energy source. This involves applied research and technology development projects in all aspects of the recovery of energy and materials from municipal waste.

★3088★ Office of Solar Electric Technologies
Mail Stop CE-35
1000 Independence Ave., S.W., Rm. 5F059
Washington, DC 20585
Phone: (202)586-5540
Contact: Robert Annan, Dir.
Parent Agencies: Department of Energy, Department of Energy Program Offices, Conservation and Renewable Energy. ***Research Areas:*** Office is responsible for research and development activities on wind energy systems, ocean energy systems, and photovoltaic energy systems. It serves as the solar energy program's focal point for electricity and interfaces with the electric utility industry. Principal components of the Office are the Photovoltaics Technology Division and the Wind/Ocean Technologies Division.

★3089★ Office of Technology Assessment
Science, Information, and Natural Resources Division
600 Pennsylvania Ave., S.E., 5th Fl.
Washington, DC 20510
Phone: (202)228-6750
Contact: John Andelin, Assistant Dir.
Parent Agencies: Legislative, Judicial, and Executive Offices. ***Research Areas:*** Principal areas of interest are: 1) communication and information technologies, including new communications technology and its implications for privacy and security, communications systems for an information age, and technology, public policy, and the changing nature of federal information dissemination; 2) oceans and environments, including air and water pollution and management of wastes, and global climate changes; and 3) science, education, and transportation, including sustaining the national technological base through education and employment of scientists and engineers and assessment of practice and potential involved in educational technology.

★3090★ Office of Transportation Systems
U. S. Dept. of Energy
Mail Stop CE-151
1000 Independence Ave., S.W.
Washington, DC 20585
Phone: (202)586-9118
Contact: Melvin H. Chiogioji, Dir.
Parent Agencies: Department of Energy, Department of Energy Program Offices, Conservation and Renewable Energy. ***Research Areas:*** The goal of the Office of Transportation Systems is to develop more energy-efficient vehicle propulsion system options; and to develop the ability to switch from petroleum to electricity and alternative fuels. Areas of special interest include the development of component and materials technologies; support for long-term, high risk technology research and development aimed at petroleum savings in the heavy duty transport sector; advancement of electric and hybrid vehicle technology; and development of means for using alternative fuels in vehicles. Office comprises the Electric and Hybrid Propulsion Division and the Heat Engine Propulsion Division.

★3091★ Ohio Cooperative Fish and Wildlife Research Unit
Ohio State University
1735 Neil Ave.
Columbus, OH 43210
Phone: (614)292-6112
Contact: Theodore A. Bookhout, Leader
Parent Agencies: Department of the Interior, U.S. Fish and Wildlife Service, U.S. Fish and Wildlife Service Cooperative Units. ***Research Areas:*** Unit activities include field and laboratory research and survey data collection on: wildlife ecology and the environment, including marsh ecosystems, surface mining reclamation, and environmental pollutants; and fish population ecology and behavioral ecology, including studies on Lake Erie fishes and evaluation of stocking piscivores in lakes.

★3092★ Ohio Water Resources Center
Ohio State University
1791 Neil Ave.
Columbus, OH 43210-1294
Phone: (614)292-2334
Contact: Dr. Robert C. Stiefel, Dir.
Parent Agencies: Department of the Interior, U.S. Geological Survey, Water Resources Division. ***Research Areas:*** Ground and surface water quality, including studies on pollution.

★3093★ Oklahoma Cooperative Fish and Wildlife Research Unit
Oklahoma State University
404 Life Sciences Bldg., W.
Stillwater, OK 74078
Phone: (405)744-6342
Fax: (405)744-7673
Contact: Dr. David M. Leslie Jr., Leader
Parent Agencies: Department of the Interior, U.S. Fish and Wildlife Service, U.S. Fish and Wildlife Service Cooperative Units. ***Research Areas:*** Unit conducts field research on fish and

wildlife species, non-game species; and upland species. Specific programs involve studies in animal damage control, biological services, interpretation and recreation, fish, mammals and non-migratory birds, and migratory birds.

★3094★ Oklahoma Water Resources Research Institute
Oklahoma State University
003 Life Sciences E. Bldg.
Stillwater, OK 74078-0281
Phone: (405)744-9994
Fax: (405)744-7673
Contact: Dr. Norman N. Durham, Dir.
Parent Agencies: Department of the Interior, U.S. Geological Survey, Water Resources Division. ***Research Areas:*** Water resources, including studies on surface and groundwater quality assessment, cleanup of existing contaminated water supplies, prevention of degradation of water supplies, and management of fixed water supplies such as exhaustible aquifers.

★3095★ Oregon Cooperative Fishery Research Unit
Oregon State University
Department of Fisheries & Wildlife
Corvallis, OR 97331-3808
Phone: (503)754-4531
Contact: Carl B. Schreck, Leader
Parent Agencies: Department of the Interior, U.S. Fish and Wildlife Service, U.S. Fish and Wildlife Service Cooperative Units. ***Research Areas:*** Unit conducts a program of field and laboratory research related to fish and aquatic systems. Principal areas of study include fish physiology, ecology, behavior, and genetics.

★3096★ Oregon Cooperative Wildlife Research Unit
Oregon State University
104 Nash Hall
Corvallis, OR 97331
Phone: (503)754-4531
Contact: Robert Anthony, Assistant Leader
Parent Agencies: Department of the Interior, U.S. Fish and Wildlife Service, U.S. Fish and Wildlife Service Cooperative Units. ***Research Areas:*** Unit's research program emphasizes forest wildlife management, particularly as related to old-growth associated wildlife and their habitat relationships.

★3097★ Oregon Water Resources Research Institute
Oregon State University
210 Strand Agric. Hall
Corvallis, OR 97331-2208
Phone: (503)737-4022
Fax: (503)737-3178
Contact: Dr. Benno P. Warkentin, Dir.
Parent Agencies: Department of the Interior, U.S. Geological Survey, Water Resources Division. ***Research Areas:*** Conducts multidisciplinary research on freshwater and estuarine resources in Oregon, including forest and agricultural watershed hydrology, effects of wastewater on fisheries and aquatic ecosystems, improved use of water for irrigation, river gravel management, estuarine resource evaluations, and the resource potential and effects of hydroelectric development. Projects include whitewater recreation uses of rivers and pollutant transport in aquifers.

★3098★ Pacific Marine Environmental Laboratory
ATTN: NOAA/PMEL/R/E/PM
Bin C15700
7600 Sand Point Way, N.E., Bldg. 3
Seattle, WA 98115-0070
Phone: (206)526-6800
Fax: (206)526-6815
Contact: Dr. Eddie N. Bernard, Dir.
Parent Agencies: Department of Commerce, National Oceanic and Atmospheric Administration, Office of Oceanic and Atmospheric Research, Environmental Research Laboratories. ***Research Areas:*** Conducts studies in physical, chemical, and geological oceanography, marine meteorology, and related disciplines to protect human health and safety from marine hazards and to ensure wise development of ocean resources. Participates in national and international programs that focus on global climate, marine services, marine environmental quality, and marine resources. Aims to improve understanding of coastal and open-ocean processes and, through observation and modeling, to develop a greater capability to monitor and predict marine environmental conditions. Focuses on the north and south Pacific Oceans, the Bering Sea, and adjacent coastal regions. Research emphasizes: 1) measurements and modeling of forcing mechanisms that drive ocean circulation and global climate; 2) understanding selected physical and geochemical processes that govern the extent and impact of human activity in the marine environment; 3) improvement of environmental forecasting capabilities and other services for marine commerce, fisheries, and recreation; and 4) investigations of physical and geochemical processes associated with formation and transformation of new marine resources at sea floor spreading centers.

★3099★ Patuxent Wildlife Research Center
Laurel, MD 20708
Phone: (301)498-0300
Fax: (301)498-0301
Contact: Harold J. O'Connor, Dir.
Parent Agencies: Department of the Interior, U.S. Fish and Wildlife Service, Patuxent Wildlife Research Center. ***Research Areas:*** Research at the U.S. Fish and Wildlife Service's Patuxent Wildlife Research Center and its 10 field stations focuses on three Fish and Wildlife programs: 1) Endangered Species Research Program; 2) Environmental Contaminant Research Program; and 3) Migratory Bird Research Program.

★3100★ Patuxent Wildlife Research Center Gulf Coast Research Group
Federal Bldg.
PO Box 2506
Victoria, TX 77902-2506
Phone: (512)573-3381
Contact: Dr. Thomas W. Custer, Leader
Parent Agencies: Department of the Interior, U.S. Fish and Wildlife Service, Patuxent Wildlife Research Center. ***Research Areas:*** Station's program of field research is concerned with effects of environmental pollutants on wildlife and their habitats. Principal subjects of study are marine and estuarine birds and terrestrial non-game birds.

★3101★ Patuxent Wildlife Research Center Hawaii Research Group
PO Box 44
Hawaii National Park, HI 96718
Phone: (808)967-7396
Contact: James D. Jacobi, Group Leader
Parent Agencies: Department of the Interior, U.S. Fish and Wildlife Service, Patuxent Wildlife Research Center. ***Research Areas:*** Station conducts research in avian and plant ecology and biology to: 1) determine the status and distribution of endangered plants and animals; and 2) identify ways in which their long-term survival can be assured. Specifically, research involves studies of limiting factors of endangered forest birds in Hawaii, including ecology, ethology, and demographics of these species; and studies on the distribution and abundance of endangered and rare plant species of the Hawaiian islands.

★3102★ Pennsylvania Cooperative Fish and Wildlife Research Unit
Pennsylvania State University
7 Ferguson Bldg.
University Park, PA 16802
Phone: (814)865-4511
Contact: Dr. Robert F. Carline, Leader
Parent Agencies: Department of the Interior, U.S. Fish and Wildlife Service, U.S. Fish and Wildlife Service Cooperative Units. ***Research Areas:*** Unit conducts a program of research involving game birds, fishes, and mammals. Principal areas of study are habitat manipulation, acid precipitation effects, other environmental impacts on fish and wildlife, and ecology.

★3103★ Pennsylvania Water Resources Research Center
Pennsylvania State University
Environmental Resources Research Institute
103 Land & Water Research Bldg.
University Park, PA 16802
Phone: (814)863-0291
Fax: (814)865-3378
Contact: Dr. Archie J. McDonnell, Institute Dir.
Parent Agencies: Department of the Interior, U.S. Geological Survey, Water Resources Division. ***Research Areas:*** Surface water and groundwater supply availability, floods and stormwater drainage damage, and water quality degradation from point and nonpoint source contaminants. Activities include developing and evaluating hydrologic models for drought and flood flow management, investigating ecological effects of acid precipitation, managing residual and hazardous wastes, studying environmental toxicology, and characterizing transport, fate, and effect of selected pollutants, including nutrients, erosion products, and toxins.

★3104★ Pesticides and Industrial Chemicals Research Center
1560 E. Jefferson Ave.
Detroit, MI 48207
Phone: (313)226-6260
Fax: (313)226-3076
Contact: Stephen M. Walters, Dir.
Parent Agencies: Department of Health and Human Services, U.S. Public Health Service, Food and Drug Administration, FDA Regional Research Centers. ***Research Areas:*** Center's mission is to develop methods for the analysis of pesticides and industrial chemicals as contaminants of foods, drugs, cosmetics, and related materials. Research areas focus on: 1) detection and measurements of pesticide and industrial chemical residues and the identification of metabolites; and 2) development of multiresidue screening procedures for surveillance analysis.

★3105★ Pine Bluff Cooperative Fishery Project
University of Arkansas-Pine Bluff
Department of Agriculture
PO Box 108
Pine Bluff, AR 71611
Phone: (501)541-6686
Fax: (501)541-0264
Contact: Dr. William Layher, Project Leader
Parent Agencies: Department of the Interior, U.S. Fish and Wildlife Service, U.S. Fish and Wildlife Service Cooperative Units. ***Research Areas:*** The Pine Bluff Cooperative Fishery Project involves research and educational programs on the environmental biology of fishes, pollution, and stream habitat modeling.

★3106★ Puerto Rico Water Resources Research Institute
University of Puerto Rico-Mayaguez
PO Box 5000
Mayaguez, PR 00709-5000
Phone: (809)833-4040
Fax: (809)832-0119
Contact: Dr. Rafael Munoz Candelario, Dir.
Parent Agencies: Department of the Interior, U.S. Geological Survey, Water Resources Division. ***Research Areas:*** Water resources, water quality and quanity, wastewater management and treatment, groundwater, and sludge management.

★3107★ Red Wolf Restoration Project
PO Box 1969
Manteo, NC 27954
Phone: (919)473-1131
Contact: Mike Phillips
Parent Agencies: Department of the Interior, U.S. Fish and Wildlife Service. ***Research Areas:*** Works to restore the red wolf, a species that is currently extinct in the wild. Aims to maintain 200 wolves in the wild and 300 in captivity.

★3108★ Remedial Action Program Information Center
Bldg. 2001
PO Box 2008
Oak Ridge, TN 37831-6050
Phone: (615)576-0568
Fax: (615)574-9888
Contact: Park T. Owen, Manager
Parent Agencies: Department of Energy, Energy Data Centers. ***Research Areas:*** RAPIC serves as a comprehensive, centralized source of information concerning the scientific, technological, regulatory, and socioeconomic aspects of radioactively contaminated facilities and site remedial actions. RAPIC scans both domestic and foreign reports, journals, conferences, books, theses, and patents for documents that are pertinent to remedial action work to be added to the database. RAPIC provides information services to a large number of DOE supported staff who are involved in remedial action and other related radioactive waste management activities. Services include: topical searches of RAPIC databases and other databases developed at ORNL; computerized literature searches of the commercially available databases; and assistance in locating hardcopies of documents referenced in the Center's bibliographies.

★3109★ Rhode Island Water Resources Center
University of Rhode Island
Bliss Hall, Rm. 204
Kingston, RI 02881
Phone: (401)792-2297
Contact: Dr. Calvin P.C. Poon, Dir.
Parent Agencies: Department of the Interior, U.S. Geological Survey, Water Resources Division.

★3110★ Risk Reduction Engineering Laboratory
Environmental Protection Agency
26 W. Martin Luther King Dr.
Cincinnati, OH 45219
Phone: (513)569-7418
Fax: (513)569-7276
Contact: E. Timothy Oppelt, Dir.
Parent Agencies: Independent Agencies, Environmental Protection Agency, Office of Research and Development, EPA Research Laboratories. ***Research Areas:*** RREL is responsible for research and development on hazardous waste treatment and disposal by thermal (e.g., incineration), biological, and chemical technologies. RREL also manages research for drinking water technologies, and research and development for Superfund activities, including the Superfund innovative technology evaluation program.

★3111★ Risk Reduction Engineering Laboratory
Superfund Technology Demonstration Division
Releases Control Branch
Bldg. 10, MS 104
2890 Woodbridge Ave.
Edison, NJ 08837-3679
Phone: (201)321-6635
Fax: (201)321-6640
Contact: John S. Farlow, Chief
Parent Agencies: Independent Agencies, Environmental Protection Agency, Office of Research and Development, EPA Research Laboratories. ***Research Areas:*** Conducts national programs of research, development, demonstration, test, and evaluation for the prevention, control, and abatement of multimedia pollution from releases of oils and hazardous materials, leaking underground storage tanks, and uncontrolled hazardous waste disposal sites. Develops techniques for the cleanup of damaged ecosystems and identifies environmentally sound methods for disposing contaminated wastes. Also tests, evaluates, and develops procedures and clothing to protect personnel who handle pesticides and other toxic substances. Research is conducted through in-house and extramural work.

★3112★ Robert S. Kerr Environmental Research Laboratory
PO Box 1198
Ada, OK 74820
Phone: (405)332-8800
Contact: Clinton Hall, Dir.
Parent Agencies: Independent Agencies, Environmental Protection Agency, Office of Research and Development, EPA Research Laboratories. ***Research Areas:*** Laboratory conducts research on the chemical, physical, and biological processes that affect contaminant transport and transformation in subsurface environments. The focus of the Laboratory's research is on both groundwater quality protection and utilization of the natural assimilative capacity of the subsurface as a waste disposal medium.

★3113★ Rocky Mountain Forest and Range Experiment Station
240 W. Prospect Rd.
Fort Collins, CO 80526
Phone: (303)498-1100
Fax: (303)498-1010
Contact: Hank M. Montrey, Station Dir.
Parent Agencies: Department of Agriculture, Forest Service, Rocky Mountain Forest and Range Experiment Station. ***Research Areas:*** Primary mission is to develop knowledge and techniques needed to balance economic and environmental demands on resources of forests and related rangelands. Principal fields of research interest include water yield and reclamation; range management; wildlife and fish habitat; trees and timber management; recreation management; resource and environmental protection; and multiresource inventory and evaluation. Forest Service Research Work Units at the Station are conducting projects in: 1) land and resource management planning techniques; 2) multiresource inventory techniques; 3) multiresource management of montane and subalpine zones in the Central Rocky Mountains; 4) effects of climate change on ecosystems; 5) forest meteorology and air quality; 6) tree diseases in the Rocky Mountains and Southwest; 7) evaluation of wildland resource benefits; and 8) impact of forest pests. In addition, the Station has forestry sciences laboratories located in Arizona, Nebraska, New Mexico, South Dakota, and Wyoming.

★3114★ Sandia National Laboratories
Albuquerque, NM 87185-5800
Phone: (505)844-8065
Contact: Albert Narath, Pres.
Parent Agencies: Department of Energy, Energy Laboratories. ***Research Areas:*** Sandia's primary mission involves research and development of weaponization of nuclear explosives: weapon safety, arming, fuzing, and firing systems; aerodynamics and structures, command, and control devices; and related testing and instrumentation. Other programs at Sandia are concerned with development of new or improved sources of energy. One of the largest programs, an outgrowth of the Laboratories' weapons studies of radiation effects, involves development of powerful particle beams for controlled thermonuclear fusion research. Other energy-related research includes studies in: 1) fossil energy (coal, oil, gas, and multisector); 2) solar energy; 3) geothermal energy; 4) magnetic fusion; 5) fission energy; 6) nuclear waste management; 7) environment; and 8) energy research (including research in combustion, geosciences, materials science, and heavy ion nuclear physics). Sandia also conducts research for the Nuclear Regulatory Commission to support safety assessment and licensing of nuclear facilities, standards development, nuclear material safety, and safeguards.

★3115★ Savannah River Ecology Laboratory
Drawer E
Aiken, SC 29801
Phone: (803)725-2472
Fax: (803)725-3309
Contact: Dr. Michael H. Smith, Dir.
Parent Agencies: Department of Energy, Energy Laboratories. ***Research Areas:*** SREL conducts extensive ecological studies on the Savannah River Site (SRS) to determine the effects of various energy technologies (including nuclear reactor operations) on the environment. Its mission is to expand the understanding of ecological principles through interdisciplinary, field-oriented research and to communicate results to the scientific community, government agencies, and the general public. Over the years, long-term

studies by SREL scientists on aquatic and terrestrial habitats of the SRS have assisted DOE in meeting environmental regulations and in anticipating and mitigating ecological problems. The Laboratory is structured in three research divisions: Biogeochemical Ecology, Wetlands Ecology, and Stress and Wildlife Ecology.

★3116★ Savannah River Ecology Laboratory
Savannah River National Environmental Research Park
Drawer E
Aiken, SC 29801
Phone: (803)725-2472
Fax: (803)725-3309
Contact: M.H. Smith, Coordinator
Parent Agencies: Department of Energy. ***Research Areas:*** The Savannah River National Environmental Research Park was established to provide protected land areas for research and education in the environmental sciences and to demonstrate the environmental compatibility of energy technology development and use. Located on a 192,000-acre site, the Research Park provides areas of cypress swamp, southeastern pine, and hardwood forests for research.

★3117★ Savannah River Ecology Laboratory
Stress and Wildlife Ecology Division
Drawer E
Aiken, SC 29802
Phone: (803)725-2472
Fax: (803)725-3309
Contact: J. Whitfield Gibbons, Head
Parent Agencies: Department of Energy, Energy Laboratories. ***Research Areas:*** Division's research programs focus on the study of natural populations and communities of animals, particularly in southeastern ecosystems, with special emphasis on determining the influence of human-caused disturbances. The primary objective is to understand the ecology and life history of wildlife populations, especially those native to the Savannah River Plant (SRP), and to assess the responses of wildlife species to natural stressors (e.g., drought) as well as man-made disturbances. Emphasis is on basic ecological studies that establish a solid foundation of information that can be applied to solving problems pertinent to Department of Energy (DOE) activities on the SRP.

★3118★ Smithsonian Environmental Research Center
PO Box 28
Edgewater, MD 21037-0028
Phone: (301)798-4424
Fax: (301)261-7954
Contact: David L. Correll, Dir.
Parent Agencies: Independent Agencies, Smithsonian Institution. ***Research Areas:*** Studies focus on the dynamics of an estuarine-watershed ecosystem. Current research programs of the Center emphasize studies of the landscape, ecosystem, and community levels of integration. SERC has compiled landscapes level time-series data for more than a decade.

★3119★ Smithsonian Marine Station at Link Port
5612 N. Old Dixie Hwy.
Fort Pierce, FL 34946
Phone: (407)465-6632
Fax: (407)461-8154
Contact: Mary E. Rice, Dir.
Parent Agencies: Independent Agencies, Smithsonian Institution. ***Research Areas:*** Station conducts marine biological research (along the coastline and adjacent ocean shelves), investigating systematics, ecology, and life histories of marine plants and animals.

★3120★ Smithsonian Oceanographic Sorting Center
Smithsonian Institution
Washington, DC 20560
Phone: (301)238-3548
Fax: (301)238-3667
Contact: Ernani G. Menez, Dir.
Parent Agencies: Independent Agencies, Smithsonian Institution. ***Research Areas:*** Center carries out basic classification of animal and plant materials collected in oceanographic expeditions sponsored by various organizations and federal agencies. These are distributed to scientists around the world who are concerned with marine pollution and the study of marine organisms. Requests by interested systematists for sorted marine biological specimens are evaluated by outside advisory committees.

★3121★ Solar Energy Research Institute
1617 Cole Blvd.
Golden, CO 80401
Phone: (303)231-1000
Contact: Dr. Gene G. Mannella, Managing Dir.
Parent Agencies: Department of Energy, Energy Laboratories. ***Research Areas:*** SERI is the nation's primary federal laboratory for solar energy research. It conducts long-term, high-risk research and development in such areas as photovoltaics, wind, ocean, biofuels, and solar thermal processes. It also coordinates similar work conducted by other organizations through granting and monitoring of subcontracts. Institute comprises three research divisions: Solar Electric, Solar Fuels, and Solar Heat.

★3122★ South Carolina Water Resources Research Institute
Clemson University
310 Lowry Hall
Clemson, SC 29634-2900
Phone: (803)656-3271
Contact: Dr. Paul B. Zielinski, Dir.
Parent Agencies: Department of the Interior, U.S. Geological Survey, Water Resources Division. ***Research Areas:*** Water quality and groundwater. Activities include a study of the occurrence and transport of polychlorinated biphenyl (PCB) from the sediments of the upper reservoir of Lake Hartwell. Supports research on locating high yield wells in the Piedmont region of the state, removing high levels of naturally occurring fluoride in groundwater, and removing toxic managanese compounds from the Russell Dam Impoundment.

★3123★ South Dakota Cooperative Fish and Wildlife Research Unit
South Dakota State University
PO Box 2077
Brookings, SD 57006-1696
Phone: (605)688-6121
Fax: (605)688-6065
Contact: Dr. Charles R. Berry Jr., Leader
Parent Agencies: Department of the Interior, U.S. Fish and Wildlife Service, U.S. Fish and Wildlife Service Cooperative Units. ***Research Areas:*** Unit conducts research on the value of wetlands in the prairie pothole region; fish and wildlife habitat; and recreational cool water fisheries.

★3124★ South Dakota Water Resources Institute
South Dakota State University
PO Box 2120
Brookings, SD 57007
Phone: (605)688-4910
Fax: (605)688-5878
Contact: Dr. Alan Bender, Acting Dir.
Parent Agencies: Department of the Interior, U.S. Geological Survey, Water Resources Division. ***Research Areas:*** Water quality and quantity, including studies on aquifer recharge and contamination, use of saline water for crop production, trade-offs between conserving irrigation water and energy consumption, natural sources of radioactivity, the relationship between plant water management and groundwater contamination, and the hydrology of glacial till.

★3125★ Southeastern Forest Experiment Station
PO Box 2680
Asheville, NC 28802
Phone: (704)257-4300
Fax: (704)251-5995
Contact: J. Lamar Beasley, Dir.
Parent Agencies: Department of Agriculture, Forest Service, Southeastern Forest Experiment Station. ***Research Areas:*** Primary mission is to acquire knowledge, develop technology, and disseminate research findings required to manage the Southeast's forest resources in ways that satisfy demands for goods and services while maintaining a quality environment. Principal fields of research include: 1) timber management and genetics; 2) forest insects and disease; 3) atmospheric and related sciences; 4) watershed management; 5) wildlife and fish habitat management; and 6) forest recreation and wilderness management. Research work units based in Asheville are conducting research aimed at: predicting hardwood development in coves and moist slopes and regenerating northern red oak on good sites; improving processing of low-grade hardwood trees and logs into short boards for furniture and other fine hardwood products; and conducting periodic surveys of renewable forest resources and measuring annual timber growth and removals from the forest. Other Station units are located in Virginia, South Carolina, Georgia, Florida, and at other North Carolina locations.

★3126★ Tennessee Cooperative Fishery Research Unit
Tennessee Technological University
Biology Department
PO Box 5114
Cookeville, TN 38505
Phone: (615)372-3094
Contact: R. Don Estes, Leader
Parent Agencies: Department of the Interior, U.S. Fish and Wildlife Service, U.S. Fish and Wildlife Service Cooperative Units. ***Research Areas:*** Unit's research program includes field research, research coordination, and data analysis. Principal fields of study involve: 1) computerized fish and wildlife databases (TADS and TABS) and use of computers in fish management; 2) stream ecology; 3) endangered species (fish and freshwater mussels) summaries and life history; and 4) genetics of selected fish species. Unit's activities include teaching at the University.

★3127★ Tennessee Valley Authority
River Basin Operations
Water Resources Division
Aquatic Biology Department
Haney Bldg., Rm. 2527OC
311 Broad St.
Chattanooga, TN 37402
Phone: (615)751-7324
Contact: Herbert C. Jones III, Manager
Parent Agencies: Independent Agencies, Tennessee Valley Authority. ***Research Areas:*** Activities include survey data collection and analysis and field research in aquatic resource protection. Subjects of research include medical entomology, aquatic macrophytes, fisheries, aquatic biology, and water quality control.

★3128★ Tennessee Valley Authority
River Basin Operations
Water Resources Division
Atmospheric Sciences Department
Chemical Engineering Bldg., Rm. 2W201A
Muscle Shoals Reservation
Muscle Shoals, AL 35660
Phone: (205)386-2555
Contact: John P. Blackwell, Manager
Parent Agencies: Independent Agencies, Tennessee Valley Authority. ***Research Areas:*** Performs laboratory and field research as well as data collection and analysis on: 1) atmospheric chemistry and long-range transport of air pollutants; and 2) effects of air pollutants on terrestrial ecosystems.

★3129★ Tennessee Valley Authority
Browns Ferry Aquatic Research Laboratory
PO Box 2000
Decatur, AL 35602
Phone: (205)729-3249
Contact: Dr. James R. Wright Jr., Manager
Parent Agencies: Independent Agencies, Tennessee Valley Authority. ***Research Areas:*** Laboratory functions as a research field station used to assess a wide range of issues relating to proper use, conservation, and development of water resources, as well as effects of substances and/or environmental conditions on freshwater aquatic life. Activities include: studies to support licensing and permitting of new and proposed Tennessee Valley Authority (TVA) facilities; evaluation of the environmental benefit of reaeration projects at TVA hydroelectric facilities; assessment of ecological consequences of contamination by toxic substances in TVA reservoirs and possible approaches for cleanup measures; and evaluation of innovative techniques for controlling aquatic vascular plants and undesirable algal growths. Research involves dissolved oxygen criteria studies (microcosm and mesocosm); fish, algal, and invertebrate bioassays on a variety of natural waters, compounds, and effluents; development of a computerized real-time biological monitoring system; evaluation of selected herbicides for control of aquatic weeds (cooperative project with the U.S. Army Corps of Engineers); uptake, fate, and effects studies with DDT; and dose response assays of pH and aluminum on early life stages of fish.

★3130★ Tennessee Valley Authority
National Fertilizer and Environmental Research Center
Chemical Research Department
National Fertilizer & Environmental Research Center, Rm. T
Muscle Shoals, AL 35660
Phone: (205)386-2371
Contact: Dr. Larry G. Kanipe, Manager
Parent Agencies: Independent Agencies, Tennessee Valley Authority. ***Research Areas:*** Department conducts basic and applied chemical investigations (frequently long-range) that produce new information needed for advances in waste management, environmental science, and fertilizer technology. Activities involve the evaluation of new products and processes and laboratory-scale studies of these new products or processes to guide decisions as to which should be evaluated at a larger scale. A comprehensive base of materials characterization and analytical instrumentation is used to solve problems in industrial processing, quality control, occupational health and safety, and waste management. Also provides analytical services to industry and other government agencies. Specific fields of research interest include inorganic, organic, physical, and analytical chemistry; materials science; chemical engineering; and minerals processing.

★3131★ Tennessee Valley Authority
Environmental Quality Staff
Summer Pl. Bldg.
Knoxville, TN 37902
Phone: (615)632-6578
Fax: (615)632-6855
Contact: M. Paul Schmierbach, Manager
Parent Agencies: Independent Agencies, Tennessee Valley Authority. ***Research Areas:*** Staff directs and coordinates environmental research activities for the agency; serves as a liaison with other federal agencies, states, universities, and other organizations in identifying collaborative environmental research opportunities; and provides technical advice in the design and implementation of environmental research projects. Principal areas of research are energy (particularly as related to control technology and environmental effects) and natural resources. Subjects of study include acid deposition, air emissions, groundwater, waste management, and surface water.

★3132★ Tennessee Valley Authority
Office of Power
Energy Demonstrations and Technology Division
Field Testing and Data Analysis Section
2S72B Missionary Ridge Pl.
1101 Market St.
Chattanooga, TN 37402-2801
Phone: (615)751-5323
Contact: James R. Crooks, Supervisor
Parent Agencies: Independent Agencies, Tennessee Valley Authority. ***Research Areas:*** Activities include pilot demonstrations, research and development testing, database management, statistical analysis and experimental design, and data communication system design. Principal areas of interest are fossil power and pollution control, fuel cells, electric vehicles, and electric vehicle battery systems.

★3133★ Tennessee Valley Authority
River Basin Operations
Land Between the Lakes
100 Van Morgan Dr.
Golden Pond, KY 42211-9001
Phone: (502)924-5602
Fax: (502)924-1123
Contact: Charles D. Buffington, Manager
Parent Agencies: Independent Agencies, Tennessee Valley Authority. ***Research Areas:*** Land Between the Lakes is a national research, test, and demonstration center for innovations in outdoor recreation, environmental education, and resource management. The 170,000-acre area is managed using multiple-use and integrated resource management principles to provide quality visitor activities. Research is primarily conducted through cooperative arrangements with colleges and universities, other governmental agencies, and, to a limited extent, private organizations.

★3134★ Tennessee Valley Authority
National Fertilizer and Environmental Research Center
2A214F NFDC-M
Muscle Shoals, AL 35660
Phone: (205)386-2708
Fax: (205)386-2284
Contact: C.H. Davis, V. Pres.
Parent Agencies: Independent Agencies, Tennessee Valley Authority. ***Research Areas:*** Conducts a full-scale fertilizer development program, as well as research in biomass, energy, waste managment, chemical processing, and agricultural resource development. Areas of study also include environmental pollution control or abatement; industrial quality control and problem solving; forensic sciences; determination of trace metals in phosphate rock, phosphate acid, and other matrices and environmental pollutants; and corrosion resistance and failure analysis on both metals and plastics.

★3135★ Tennessee Valley Authority
Office of Power
Research and Development Division
3N 78A Missionary Ridge Pl.
Chattanooga, TN 37402
Phone: (615)751-6140
Fax: (615)751-6403
Contact: E. David Daugherty, Manager
Parent Agencies: Independent Agencies, Tennessee Valley Authority. ***Research Areas:*** Division functions as a research and development center for studies in advanced energy and environmental technology. Division also demonstrates advanced technologies, such as fluidized-bed combustion.

★3136★ Tennessee Valley Authority
National Fertilizer and Environmental Research Center
Technology Development Program
NFDC 2A206E
Muscle Shoals Reservation
Muscle Shoals, AL 35660
Phone: (205)386-2583
Fax: (205)386-2284
Contact: Ron Kirkland, Manager
Parent Agencies: Independent Agencies, Tennessee Valley Authority. ***Research Areas:*** Center serves as the focus for development and demonstration of physical/chemical technologies and for the prevention, treatment, destruction, and/or recovery of waste materials through joint ventures and reimbursable projects in the waste management field. Activities support Tennessee Valley Authority programs for environmentally sound procedures for disposal and utilization of wastes, including waste-to-energy conversion. Develops and introduces environmental related fertilizer technology to reduce potential of water contamination.

★3137★ Tennessee Valley Authority
River Basin Operations
Water Resources Division
Evans Bldg., Rm. 1W 141A
524 Union Ave.
Knoxville, TN 37902
Phone: (615)632-6770
Fax: (615)632-6137
Contact: Ralph H. Brooks, Manager
Parent Agencies: Independent Agencies, Tennessee Valley Authority. ***Research Areas:***

Division conducts research in support of its responsibility for management of air and water resources in the Tennessee Valley. Research covers a wide range of water and air quality issues, fishery concerns, and proper uses of flood plains.

★3138★ Tennessee Water Resources Research Center
University of Tennessee
328 S. Stadium Hall
Knoxville, TN 37996-0710
Phone: (615)974-2151
Fax: (615)974-1838
Contact: Dr. E. William Colglazier, Dir.
Parent Agencies: Department of the Interior, U.S. Geological Survey, Water Resources Division. ***Research Areas:*** Water resources, including erosion control, wetland management, evapotranspiration, effects of tillage and herbicide practices on surface water quality, groundwater contamination from oil and gas wells, and pesticide migration. Develops criteria for siting hazardous waste management facilities and techniques to remove organic contaminants from groundwater. Models agricultural management practices. Activities include designing a statewide groundwater monitoring network.

★3139★ Texas Water Resources Institute
Texas & AM University
301 Scoates Hall
College Station, TX 77843-2118
Phone: (409)845-1851
Fax: (409)845-3932
Contact: Dr. Wayne R. Jordan, Dir.
Parent Agencies: Department of the Interior, U.S. Geological Survey, Water Resources Division. ***Research Areas:*** Water resources, especially water quality. Activities focus on studies of economics and water policy, groundwater and aquifer protection, surface water development, efficient use of water in agriculture, water conserving irrigation systems, drought-resistant crop species, water management systems that enhance rainfall utilization, rural water systems, surface water contamination, pollution potential of municipal landfills, and effects of the dairy industry on groundwater quality.

★3140★ U.S. Army Construction Engineering Research Laboratory
Environmental Division
Interstate Research Park
PO Box 4005
Champaign, IL 61824-4005
Phone: (217)352-6511
Fax: (217)373-7222
Contact: Louis R. Schaffer, Dir.
Parent Agencies: Department of the Army, U.S. Army Corps of Engineers, U.S. Army Construction Engineering Research Laboratory. ***Research Areas:*** Division activities are concerned with environmental systems and environmental effects, including development of systems for recycling and management of solid and hazardous wastes and the abatement of air, water, and noise pollution; management of land and other natural resources; and maintenance of a technology base to address unique Army needs.

★3141★ U.S. Army Corps of Engineers Water Resources Support Center
Hydrologic Engineering Center
609 Second St.
Davis, CA 95616
Phone: (916)756-1104
Contact: Darrell W. Davis, Dir.
Parent Agencies: Department of the Army, U.S. Army Corps of Engineers. ***Research Areas:*** The goal of the Hydrologic Engineering Center (HEC) is to support the nation in its water resources management responsibilities by increasing the Corps technical capability in hydrologic engineering and water resources planning and management; and provide leadership in improving the state-of-the-art in hydrologic engineering and water resources planning. Programs involve research, training, planning analysis, and technical assistance. HEC conducts applied research on the properties, distribution, and circulation of water on the surface of the land, in the soil and underlying rocks, and in the atmosphere in relation to river basins. Principal fields of research include hydrologic engineering and water resources planning through computer simulation of flood control, water supply, hydropower, and navigation projects. Activities also include preparation of technical manuals for international use.

★3142★ U.S. Army Corps of Engineers Water Resources Support Center
Institute for Water Resources
Casey Bldg.
Fort Belvoir, VA 22060
Phone: (202)355-2016
Parent Agencies: Department of the Army, U.S. Army Corps of Engineers. ***Research Areas:*** IWR was established to develop methodologies, techniques, and guidance for the Corps in planning development of the nation's water resources; and to analyze water resources policy issues. Research studies focus on the water resources planning activities of the Corps and include efforts to improve methods for analyzing the social, economic, and environmental impacts of water resources projects and for predicting the impacts of and risks associated with potential projects. Studies that evaluate existing policies, assess modifications, examine alternative policy options, and investigate issuance of new policy guidance are conducted by IWR at the request of the Director of Civil Works.

★3143★ U.S. Army Corps of Engineers Water Resources Support Center
Army Institute for Water Resources
Research Division
Casey Bldg.
Fort Belvoir, VA 22060
Phone: (202)355-2217
Fax: (202)355-3171
Contact: Kenneth H. Murdock, Dir.
Parent Agencies: Department of the Army, U.S. Army Corps of Engineers. ***Research Areas:*** Activities of the Research Division involve economic and demographic forecasting risk management and studies on the evaluation of water resources projects. Recent projects have included research on a model for dredge material disposal evaluation; and development of a water demand forecasting model for use in water supply and conservation studies, a contingent valuation methodology for receation assessment, and deep draft evaluation procedures.

★3144★ U.S. Army Engineer Waterways Experiment Station
Environmental Laboratory
Analytical Laboratory Group
3909 Halls Ferry Rd.
Vicksburg, MS 39180-6199
Phone: (601)634-2726
Fax: (601)634-3833
Contact: Ann B. Strong, Chief
Parent Agencies: Department of the Army, U.S. Army Corps of Engineers, U.S. Army Engineer Waterways Experiment Station. ***Research Areas:*** The Analytical Laboratory Group (ALG) serves as the primary WES chemical testing facility for water and wastewater analysis for the Corps Lower Mississippi Valley Division. ALG performs chemical analyses needed to support controlled laboratory research or field studies of environmental pollutants in water, sediment, plant tissue, animal tissue, and waste material. A wide range of chemical parameters encountered in environmental investigations such as dredged and fill material projects, reservoirs evaluation, construction projects, wetlands investigation, and hazardous waste sites are routinely assayed. In addition, quality assurance/quality control procedures comprise approximately 20 percent of ALG's total analytical effort. This involves using a system of duplicates, spikes, standard reference materials, and collaborative testing to validate the quality control of the analysis process; and conducting laboratory inspections of contractor, Corps district, and division laboratories as part of the overall Corps quality control activities.

★3145★ U.S. Army Engineer Waterways Experiment Station
Environmental Laboratory
PO Box 631
Vicksburg, MS 39180
Phone: (601)634-3227
Contact: Dr. John Harrison, Chief
Parent Agencies: Department of the Army, U.S. Army Corps of Engineers, U.S. Army Engineer Waterways Experiment Station. ***Research Areas:*** Laboratory investigates the effects of man's activities on the environment as well as the effects of environment on military operations in order to develop methods to minimize or mitigate adverse effects. Laboratory is structured to perform three major functions of environmental research: 1) inventory and assess the environment; 2) simulate and model the ecosystem; and 3) engineer (modify) the environment. Laboratory also pursues environmentally related studies involving water resources systems, environmental management, and applied remote sensing. In addition, Laboratory administers major Corps of Engineers research programs in Aquatic Plant Control, Environmental Impact, Water Quality, Environmental Effects of Dredging (Dredging Operations Technical Support, Field Verification, and Long-Term Effects of Dredging Operations), Natural Resources, Wetlands, and Aquaculture in Dredged Material Containment Areas. The Laboratory also conducts military research in the fields of minefield detection and simulation, sensor systems, camouflage, military hydrology, and water supply.

★3146★ U.S. Coast Guard (COIL)
Oil Identification Laboratory
Avery Point
Groton, CT 06340-6096
Phone: (203)441-2645
Fax: (203)441-2641
Contact: Commander L.H. Gibson, Commanding Officer
Parent Agencies: Department of Transportation, U.S. Coast Guard. ***Research Areas:*** COIL was established as the operating facility to implement the Coast Guard's Oil Identification System (OIS) for determining the unique, intrinsic properties that allow the matching of a spilled oil with its correct source. (The process is also known as oil fingerprinting.) OIS is based on five analytical methods: thin-layer chromatography, high performance liquid chromatography, fluorescence spectroscopy, infrared

spectroscopy, and gas chromatography. Each method measures different chemical properties of an oil and has been shown to produce results independent of others. (The multi-method approach was chosen because no single technique gives unequivocal results in all cases.)

★3147★ U.S. Fish and Wildlife Service
C St. between 18th & 19th Sts., N.W.
Washington, DC 20240
Phone: (202)343-4717
Contact: John Turner, Dir.
Parent Agencies: Department of the Interior, U.S. Fish and Wildlife Service. ***Research Areas:*** The mission of the United States Fish and Wildlife Service is to conserve, protect, and enhance fish and wildlife and their habitats. Within this framework, the Service assists in the development of environmental standards; works with the States to improve the conservation and management of the nation's fish and wildlife resources; and administers a national program providing opportunities to the American public to understand, appreciate, and use these resources. The Service is responsible for improving and maintaining fish and wildlife resources by proper management of migratory birds and other wildlife. It also assists in fulfilling public demands for recreational fishing while maintaining the nation's fisheries to ensure their continued survival. Activities in resource management include: biological monitoring through scientific research; surveillance of pesticides, heavy metals, and thermal pollution; studies of fish and wildlife populations; ecological studies; environmental impact assessment.

★3148★ U.S. Fish and Wildlife Service-Region 8 (Research and Development) Cooperative Fish and Wildlife Research Units Center
18th & C Sts., N.W.
Arlington Sq. Bldg.
MS-725
Washington, DC 20240
Phone: (703)358-1709
Fax: (703)358-2202
Contact: Edward T. LaRoe, Dir.
Parent Agencies: Department of the Interior, U.S. Fish and Wildlife Service. ***Research Areas:*** Fish and Wildlife Service Cooperative Units are jointly supported by the U.S. Fish and Wildlife Service, the Wildlife Management Institute, and the state game and fish agency and land grant university in the state where each Unit is located. The Units' activities include fish and wildlife research, training at the graduate level, and technical assistance. Unit direction is provided by a Coordinating Committee composed of representatives from each cooperating agency. The Committee provides counsel and plans the long-term program to serve the mutual needs of the cooperators. Day-to-day operation is the responsibility of the Unit Leaders and the Assistant Unit Leaders, who are employees of the U.S. Fish and Wildlife Service. Units are headquartered on campuses of cooperating universities, which provide expertise in related scientific fields; office, laboratory, and storage space; secretarial services; and utilities. All cooperators contribute funds and equipment to the Units, and additional research funds are obtained from various sources as grants and contracts. The Leaders and Assistant Leaders are granted full faculty status by the cooperating universities and thus they are qualified to advise and direct graduate students and to teach formal courses.

★3149★ U.S. Geological Survey
National Center
12201 Sunrise Valley Dr.
Reston, VA 22092
Phone: (703)648-6892
Contact: Dallas L. Peck, Dir.
Parent Agencies: Department of the Interior, U.S. Geological Survey. ***Research Areas:*** The Geological Survey is one of the federal government's major earth science research and fact-finding agencies. The broad objectives of the Survey are to: 1) conduct research in geology, hydrology, mapping, geography, and related sciences; 2) analyze water, energy, and mineral resources of the United States; and 3) publish reports and maps, establish and maintain earth-science databases, and disseminate information. The Survey is organized in three main program divisions (Geologic, Water Resources, and National Mapping) and two support divisions (Administrative and Information Systems). Headquarters for all is at the National Center in Reston, VA. In addition, the Survey's field organization includes regional offices around the country. ***Databases:*** Water Data Storage and Retrieval System, National Digital Cartographic Data Base, and National Coal Resoruces Data System.

★3150★ U.S. Geological Survey Geologic Division
National Center
12201 Sunrise Valley Dr.
Reston, VA 22092
Phone: (703)648-6600
Contact: Benjamin A. Morgan, Chief Geologist
Parent Agencies: Department of the Interior, U.S. Geological Survey, Geologic Divisions. ***Research Areas:*** The Geologic Division conducts programs to assess energy and mineral resources, identify and predict geologic hazards, and investigate the effects of climate. In recent years Division programs have been concerned particularly with assessing the nation's resources in the areas of energy (oil and gas, coal, geothermal, and uranium). Activities have involved: 1) mineral assessments of areas designated by Congress as Wilderness Areas; 2) studies to evaluate the energy-resource potential of offshore areas and environmental hazards related to development of that energy; 3) a program for earthquake hazard mitigation and prediction; and 4) investigation of geologic hazards related to nuclear reactor siting. Division programs are supported by extensive, on-going basic research on geologic processes and events.

★3151★ U.S. Geological Survey National Mapping Division
516 National Center
12201 Sunrise Valley Dr.
Reston, VA 22092
Phone: (703)648-5747
Contact: Lowell E. Starr, Chief
Parent Agencies: Department of the Interior, U.S. Geological Survey, National Mapping Division. ***Research Areas:*** Compiles cartographic data from aerial photographs, other remotely sensed images, historical records, legal documents, and direct field observations and surveys and comply with standards of content, geometric accuracy, and presentation. Research is also conducted in the mapping sciences, geography, geographic information systems, and spatial data analysis.

★3152★ U.S. Geological Survey National Mapping Division Office of Geographic and Cartographic Research
National Center, Mail Stop 521
12201 Sunrise Valley Dr.
Reston, VA 22092
Phone: (703)648-4505
Contact: James R. Jancaitis, Chief
Parent Agencies: Department of the Interior, U.S. Geological Survey, National Mapping Division. ***Research Areas:*** Conducts research in the fields of global change, environmental and land use/cover modeling and mapping, geographic information systems (GIS) hardware/software and applications, computer-based thematic mapping, digital image processing, side-looking airborne radar, and a standardized, digital geographic names data base for the U.S. The Office provides leadership and direction in the sciences of geography and cartography to facilitate and augment the research and mapping programs of the U.S. Geological Survey (USGS) and its National Mapping Division. Employing the techniques and methods of geographic and cartographic analyses, the Office studies the problems presented in obtaining information on man's use of land and changes in these uses and participates in a variety of multidisciplinary studies in order to provide needed resource and environmental data to decision-makers. The Office serves as the focal point within the federal government for interagency coordination in the development of a national digital cartographic database; and coordinates the development of geographic information systems and spatial data handling techniques.

★3153★ U.S. Geological Survey Water Resources Division
409 National Center
12201 Sunrise Valley Dr.
Reston, VA 22092
Phone: (703)648-5215
Contact: Philip Cohen, Chief Hydrologist
Parent Agencies: Department of the Interior, U.S. Geological Survey, Water Resources Division. ***Research Areas:*** Mission of the Water Resources Division is to provide the hydrologic information and understanding needed for the best use and management of the nation's water resources. To accomplish this mission, Division: 1) collects data needed to determine and evaluate the quantity, quality, and use of water resources; 2) conducts analytical and interpretive water-resource appraisals to describe the occurrence, availability, and physical, chemical, and biological characteristics of surface and groundwater; 3) conducts supportive basic and problem-oriented research in hydraulics, hydrology, and related fields of science and engineering; and 4) disseminates water data and results of investigations and research. Division operates in cooperation with other federal agencies and with state and local governments, coordinating the activities of federal agencies in acquiring water data for streams, lakes, reservoirs, estuaries, and groundwater and providing scientific and technical assistance in hydrologic fields to other federal, state, and local agencies.

★3154★ U.S. Water Conservation Laboratory
4331 E. Broadway Rd.
Phoenix, AZ 85040
Phone: (602)261-4356
Contact: Dr. Herman Bouwer, Dir.
Parent Agencies: Department of Agriculture, Agricultural Research Service, Pacific West Area. ***Research Areas:*** Laboratory was

established to conduct research on conserving water and water quality in systems involving soils, plants, the atmosphere, and aquifers. Laboratory comprises four units: Arid Zone Crop Production Group; Groundwater Quality Group; Irrigation and Hydraulics Group; and Soil-Plant-Atmosphere Systems Group.

★3155★ USDA Aridland Watershed Management Research Unit
2000 E. Allen Rd.
Tucson, AZ 85719
Phone: (602)670-6381
Fax: (602)670-6493
Contact: Dr. David A. Woolhiser, Research Leader
Parent Agencies: Department of Agriculture, Agricultural Research Service, Pacific West Area. ***Research Areas:*** Unit conducts a research program in hydrology and rangeland conservation and improvement. Primary mission is to study the hydrology of rangeland watersheds and the effects of changing land use and practices on the hydrologic cycle. The work also includes establishment of improved plant species. Activities involve studies of rainfall, which is natural input to the watersheds; quality and movement of water on and below the surface; erosion from watersheds and channels within the watersheds; sedimentation within the channels and reservoirs; and the present and potential uses of available water. Active experimental watersheds operated by the Unit include: the Walnut Gulch

★3156★ USDA Big Spring Field Station
PO Box 909
Big Spring, TX 79720
Phone: (915)263-0293
Contact: Donald W. Fryrear, Research Leader
Parent Agencies: Department of Agriculture, Agricultural Research Service, Southern Plains Area. ***Research Areas:*** Unit conducts field research on wind erosion and moisture conservation on dryland sandy soils, including studies of wind erosion of soils and plant damage, dryland cropping systems, and development of moisture conservation technology.

★3157★ USDA Coastal Plains Soil and Water Conservation Research Center
Darlington Hwy.
PO Box 3039
Florence, SC 29502-3039
Phone: (803)669-5203
Contact: Dr. Patrick G. Hunt, Research Leader
Parent Agencies: Department of Agriculture, Agricultural Research Service, South Atlantic Area. ***Research Areas:*** Center conducts basic and applied research to improve soil and water conservation practices in the southeastern coastal plains. Emphasis is on aspects of total soil and water management to overcome problems of water excess and deficiency as well as problems of soil physical properties, low soil fertility, and erosive conditions. Crops investigated include high value horticultural crops, soybeans, corn, and cotton. Specific areas of research involve: 1) development of engineering criteria for controlled and reversible drainage systems; 2) determination of soil-water criteria for enhanced nitrogen fixation and increased yield of soybeans; 3) development of soil and water management criteria for high value horticultural crops for small farm units; 4) improvement of irrigation system operation and design criteria to minimize energy and maintain or increase crop production; 5) establishment of crop residue requirements for efficient soil water use and erosion control; 6) development of reduced tillage-multiple cropping systems in compacted soils; and 7) determination of soil, water, and nutrient management criteria to improve soybean yield.

★3158★ USDA Grassland, Soil, and Water Research Laboratory
808 E. Blackland Rd.
Temple, TX 76502
Phone: (817)770-6500
Fax: (817)770-6561
Contact: Dr. Clarence Richardson, Dir.
Parent Agencies: Department of Agriculture, Agricultural Research Service, Southern Plains Area. ***Research Areas:*** Laboratory's mission is to develop technology to: 1) maximize forage and crop production; 2) revegetate brush-infested watersheds; 3) control noneconomic brush and weeds; 4) breed forages with increased quality and yield potential; and 5) solve problems relating to soil and water management, soil fertility, erosion, hydrology, and water quality. Principal fields of research include soil and water management; plant breeding; weed control; hydrology; erosion control; conservation tillage; and crop physiology. Laboratory comprises: Forage Improvement Research Unit, Grassland Protection Research Unit, and Natural Resources Systems Research Unit.

★3159★ USDA Hydro-Ecosystem Research Unit
301 S. Howes St., Rm. 247
PO Box E
Fort Collins, CO 80522
Phone: (303)221-0578
Fax: (303)493-4347
Contact: Dr. Donn G. DeCoursey, Research Leader
Parent Agencies: Department of Agriculture, Agricultural Research Service, Northern Plains Area. ***Research Areas:*** Conducts field, laboratory, and modeling research on the effects of agricultural practices on runoff and water quality. Principal areas of research include hydrology, hydraulics, nutrient dynamics, erosion, and nonpoint pollution.

★3160★ USDA Land Management and Water Conservation Research Unit
Washington State University
215 Johnson Hall
Pullman, WA 99164-6216
Phone: (509)335-1552
Fax: (509)335-7648
Contact: Dr. Robert I. Papendick, Research Leader
Parent Agencies: Department of Agriculture, Agricultural Research Service, Pacific West Area. ***Research Areas:*** Mission is to: 1) evaluate the individual and combined effects of soil, topography, climate, and land treatment on water infiltration, evaporation, soil moisture, runoff, and soil erosion phenomena on Northwest croplands; and 2) develop management systems that optimize agricultural use of water for crop production and control erosion through combined use of improved tillage, residue management, weed control, and fertilizer application methods.

★3161★ USDA Northern Regional Research Center
Oil Chemical Research Unit
1815 N. University St.
Peoria, IL 61604
Phone: (309)685-4011
Fax: (309)671-7814
Contact: Marvin O. Bagby, Research Leader
Parent Agencies: Department of Agriculture, Agricultural Research Service, Mid West Area. ***Research Areas:*** Identifying and developing new concepts in utilizing soybean oil as an alternative chemical; identifying and evaluating formulations containing vegetable oils for diesel fuel. Research emphasis is on obtaining new knowledge from basic physicochemical properties of soybean oil, other vegetable oils, and various derivatives. Activities involve: 1) preparing new products by biochemical as well as chemical means and correlating their properties with potential industrial product applications; 2) conducting basic investigations on the physical and colloidal properties of transparent and aqueous systems referred to as microemulsions; 3) developing and applying fundamental knowledge for the evaluation of vegetable oils as diesel fuel; 4) developing new technologies for soybean oil printing inks; and 5) carrying out collaborative programs with scientists and engineers to evaluate fuels and new ink formulations and soybean oil derived vehicles for ink.

★3162★ USDA Salinity Laboratory
4500 Glenwood Dr.
Riverside, CA 92501
Phone: (714)369-4815
Fax: (714)369-4818
Contact: Dr. J.D. Rhoades, Dir.
Parent Agencies: Department of Agriculture, Agricultural Research Service, Pacific West Area. ***Research Areas:*** Laboratory conducts basic research into problems of salt-affected soils, the use of saline waters for irrigation, and the response of plants to saline environments. Its mission is to: 1) enhance understanding and management of water, solute, and gas transport through soil-plant systems; 2) model soil-water-salinity systems; 3) elaborate agronomic, biochemical, physiological, and genetic factors that affect production of crops on salt-affected soils; 4) describe the chemical reactions between salt-affected soils and irrigation waters, the dynamics of absorption and ion exchange in soils, and the kinetics of mineral dissolution/precipitation reactions, all in relation to plant growth; and 5) develop management practices and assessment methodology for salt-affected soils and waters and develop methods for evaluating, predicting, and reducing pollution of soil and water by salts, pesticides, and related organic chemicals. Research involves the fields of engineering, physics, plant science, and chemistry. Activities are carried out in three units: Plant Sciences Research, Soil Physics Research, and Soil and Water Chemistry Research.

★3163★ USDA Soil and Water Management Research Unit
University of Minnesota
439 Borlaug Hall
1991 Upper Buford Circle
St. Paul, MN 55108
Phone: (612)625-9270
Contact: Robert H. Dowdy, Research Leader
Parent Agencies: Department of Agriculture, Agricultural Research Service, Mid West Area. ***Research Areas:*** The Soil and Water Management Research Unit conducts research on conservation tillage/water quality.

★3164★ USDA Subtropical Agricultural Research Laboratory
Remote Sensing Research Unit
USDA-ARS-RSRU
2413 E. Hwy. 83
Weslaco, TX 78596-8344
Phone: (512)968-5533
Fax: (512)565-6133
Contact: James Everitt, Research Leader
Parent Agencies: Department of Agriculture, Agricultural Research Service, Southern Plains

Area. ***Research Areas:*** Major research objectives are to: obtain spectral reflectance and other information from crop and rangeland areas; relate information to crop condition assessment and early warning of problems; and contribute to remote sensing technology used in the management of natural resources. Research activities involve developing: 1) remote sensing technology for use by government and others in discriminating among plant species and assessing the condition of vegetation (including stress effects) using satellite and aircraft data; and 2) crop growth and yield models that use remotely sensed information as input.

★3165★ USDA Water Management Research Laboratory
2021 S. Peach Ave.
Fresno, CA 93727
Phone: (209)453-3100
Fax: (209)453-3011
Contact: Dr. C.J. Phene, Research Leader
Parent Agencies: Department of Agriculture, Agricultural Research Service, Pacific West Area. ***Research Areas:*** WMRL conducts both field and laboratory research associated with soil, plant, water, and atmosphere in arid and semi-arid regions. Its mission is to: 1) develop advanced water management practices, methods, equipment, and systems to utilize soil, water, and energy resources efficiently and increase agricultural productivity in irrigated agriculture; 2) evaluate and predict consequences of water management practices on the quantity and quality of surface- and groundwater; 3) reduce pollution of soil, water, and air by agricultural chemicals through improved water management; and 4) develop improved procedures for conserving and a ugmenting irrigation water supplies. The research program is concerned primarily with irrigation and drainage of agricultural land; other interests include infiltration and water quality of surface- and groundwater.

★3166★ Utah Center for Water Resources Research
Utah State University
Logan, UT 84332-8200
Phone: (801)750-3168
Fax: (801)750-3663
Contact: Dr. L. Douglas James, Dir.
Parent Agencies: Department of the Interior, U.S. Geological Survey, Water Resources Division. ***Research Areas:*** Water management. Performs applied research for applications in surface water hydrology, groundwater hydrology, protection of natural and potable water qualities from hazardous wastes and other pollutants, water resources planning and systems operations, hydraulics and fluid mechanics, and cloud processes that can be modified for snowfall augmentation.

★3167★ Utah Cooperative Fish and Wildlife Research Unit
Utah State University
Department of Fisheries & Wildlife
UMC-5210
Logan, UT 84322-5210
Phone: (801)750-2509
Contact: Dr. John A. Bissonette, Leader
Parent Agencies: Department of the Interior, U.S. Fish and Wildlife Service, U.S. Fish and Wildlife Service Cooperative Units. ***Research Areas:*** Unit's wildlife research focuses on habitat related studies of terrestrial and avian vertebrates with emphasis on sensitive species. Geographic Information System (GIS) and remote sensing methodology is used. Fishery research emphasizes the effect of habitat alteration on fish populations; genetics, strain evaluation, and endangered species; and training and extension services.

★3168★ Vermont Water Resources Research Center
University of Vermont
321 George D. Aiken Center
Burlington, VT 05405
Phone: (802)656-4057
Contact: Dr. Alan W. McIntosh, Acting Dir.
Parent Agencies: Department of the Interior, U.S. Geological Survey, Water Resources Division. ***Research Areas:*** Water quality, including studies on effects of acid deposition on the environment, lake eutrophication, toxic wastes, agricultural nonpoint source pollution, groundwater management, and hazardous materials.

★3169★ Virgin Islands Water Resources Research Center
University of the Virgin Islands
Caribbean Research Institute
St. Thomas, VI 00802
Phone: (809)776-9484
Contact: Dr. J. Hari Krishna, Dir.
Parent Agencies: Department of the Interior, U.S. Geological Survey, Water Resources Division. ***Research Areas:*** Cistern water quality and domestic water conservation practices, including developing computer models to predict rainfall variability.

★3170★ Virginia Cooperative Fish and Wildlife Research Unit
Virginia Polytechnic Institute & State University
106 Cheatham Hall
Blacksburg, VA 24061
Phone: (703)231-5927
Contact: Dr. Richard J. Neves, Leader
Parent Agencies: Department of the Interior, U.S. Fish and Wildlife Service, U.S. Fish and Wildlife Service Cooperative Units. ***Research Areas:*** Unit's fisheries research program is concerned primarily with stream fishes and endangered species. Other research interests include fishery management practices and stream ecology. Unit's wildlife research program emphasizes forest wildlife. Specific subjects of research include: 1) animal ecology; 2) habitat evaluation; 3) physiology; 4) nutrition; 5) behavior; and 6) population dynamics. Activities also include graduate research training and conservation instruction at the University.

★3171★ Virginia Water Resources Research Center
Virginia Polytechnic Institute & State University
617 N. Main St.
Blacksburg, VA 24060-3397
Phone: (703)961-5624
Fax: (703)231-6673
Contact: Dr. William R. Walker, Dir.
Parent Agencies: Department of the Interior, U.S. Geological Survey, Water Resources Division. ***Research Areas:*** Water resources planning, land-use effects on water resources, land application of sewage sludge, and water-related health concerns. ***Databases:*** Streamflow, weather information, and current water-related research in the commonwealth.

★3172★ Washington Cooperative Fishery Research Unit
University of Washington
College of Fisheries, WH-10
Seattle, WA 98195
Phone: (206)543-6475
Contact: Christian E. Grue, Leader
Parent Agencies: Department of the Interior, U.S. Fish and Wildlife Service, U.S. Fish and Wildlife Service Cooperative Units. ***Research Areas:*** Unit's program of research is related to recreational fisheries and is concerned primarily with lake, marine and estuarine, and disease studies. Lake studies projects involve research on: 1) effects of lake restoration on fish populations; 2) effects of water chemistry on benthic biota; 3) interactions between smallmouth and largemouth bass; 4) hydroacoustic analysis of fish populations in lakes and rivers; and 5) river studies involving salmon biology and behavior. Disease studies focus on the feasibility of immunizing rainbow trout. Unit's activities also include training of fishery biologists.

★3173★ Washington Water Research Center
Washington State University
Pullman, WA 99164-3002
Phone: (509)335-5531
Fax: (509)335-7632
Contact: Dr. William H. Funk, Dir.
Parent Agencies: Department of the Interior, U.S. Geological Survey, Water Resources Division. ***Research Areas:*** Center conducts and coordinates research on all aspects of water and related resources contributing to the welfare of the state, including interdisciplinary basic and applied studies in water resource economics, political institutions, water law and rights, water quality, hydrogeology, hydrology, hydraulics, fisheries, forestry, irrigated agriculture, related land-use, and environmental effects.

★3174★ West Virginia Cooperative Fish and Wildlife Research Unit
PO Box 6125
Morgantown, WV 26506-6125
Phone: (304)293-3794
Fax: (304)293-2441
Contact: F. Joseph Margraf, Unit Leader
Parent Agencies: Department of the Interior, U.S. Fish and Wildlife Service, U.S. Fish and Wildlife Service Cooperative Units. ***Research Areas:*** Unit is primarily concerned with natural resources research, including algae, invertebrate, and fish aquatic community studies; aquatic habitat and water quality assessment; and wetlands, waterfowl, upland bird, and riparian bird community studies.

★3175★ West Virginia Water Research Institute
West Virginia University
258 Stewart St.
Morgantown, WV 26506
Phone: (304)293-2757
Fax: (304)293-3749
Contact: Prof. Charles R. Jenkins, Dir.
Parent Agencies: Department of the Interior, U.S. Geological Survey, Water Resources Division. ***Research Areas:*** Flooding, acid mine drainage, water quality, and wastewater treatment.

★3176★ Wildlife Habitat and Silviculture Laboratory
506 Hayter St.
PO Box 7600, SF Sta. A
Nacogdoches, TX 75962
Phone: (409)569-7981
Contact: Dr. Ronald E. Thill, Project Leader
Parent Agencies: Department of Agriculture, Forest Service, Southern Forest Experiment Station. ***Research Areas:*** Laboratory conducts research on the integration of wildlife habitat into forest management. Its mission is to define ecological relationships of wildlife and forest habitat and provide information for the incorporation of wildlife into forest

management. Activities involve assessing wildlife responses to streamside management zones and the effects of alternative silviculture practices on habitat and wildlife habitat communities. Lab also develops information on the specific habitat requirements of cavity nesting wildlife and management practices for sensitive wetlands such as hillside bogs.

★3177★ Winchester Engineering and Analytical Center
109 Holton St.
Winchester, MA 01890
Phone: (617)729-5700
Contact: James W. Fitzgerald, Dir.
Parent Agencies: Department of Health and Human Services, U.S. Public Health Service, Food and Drug Administration, FDA Regional Research Centers. ***Research Areas:*** Center is a multipurpose facility that supports FDA's mission to protect consumer health and safety by: 1) monitoring radiation emitted by electronic products such as microwave ovens and television sets; 2) testing medical devices; 3) conducting performance verifications of medical products such as hearing aids, diagnostic X-ray, and ultrasound therapy equipment; 4) analyzing foods for pesticide residues, filth, extraneous materials, and food additives such as colors; 5) analyzing fish and seafood for decomposition, heavy metals, and marine toxins; 6) analyzing food contact products such as ceramic-ware for leachable lead and cadmium; and 7) examining food, drugs, and cosmetics for microbiological contamination.

★3178★ Wisconsin Cooperative Fishery Research Unit
University of Wisconsin
College of Natural Resources
Stevens Point, WI 54481
Phone: (715)346-2178
Contact: Dr. Daniel W. Coble, Leader
Parent Agencies: Department of the Interior, U.S. Fish and Wildlife Service, U.S. Fish and Wildlife Service Cooperative Units. ***Research Areas:*** Objectives include research and training of students at the graduate level in aquatic sciences. Areas of study that have been emphasized are: 1) management; 2) fishery biology; 3) genetics; 4) physiology; 5) systematics; and 6) limnology.

★3179★ Wisconsin Cooperative Wildlife Research Unit
University of Wisconsin
211 Russell Laboratories
1630 Lyndon Dr.
Madison, WI 53706
Phone: (608)263-6882
Contact: Dr. Donald Rusch, Dir.
Parent Agencies: Department of the Interior, U.S. Fish and Wildlife Service, U.S. Fish and Wildlife Service Cooperative Units. ***Research Areas:*** Unit identifies, quantifies, and evaluates pressures on wildlife species and habitats from recreational, agricultural, and forestry uses. Principal emphasis is on population dynamics of migratory birds and of upland game birds.

★3180★ Wisconsin Water Resources Center
University of Wisconsin
1975 Willow Dr.
Madison, WI 53706
Phone: (608)262-3838
Fax: (608)262-0591
Contact: Dr. Gordon Chesters, Dir.
Parent Agencies: Department of the Interior, U.S. Geological Survey, Water Resources Division. ***Research Areas:*** Ground and surface water quality. Activities focus on investigating the incursion of nutrients, pesticides, toxic metals, and volatile organic compounds into water systems and assessing the importance to public health; defining institutional arrangements to establish a cost-effective, implementable program of nonpoint pollution control; developing an inventory on a regional basis (Wisconsin, Minnesota, and Illinois) for the resources of the Upper Mississippi River to evaluate the need for a new lock and dam at Alton Illinois; evaluating performance and applicability of the Wisconsin Mound Septic System; examining the environmental effects of coal-fired power plants; and assessing air pollution effects on humans.

★3181★ Wyoming Cooperative Fish and Wildlife Research Unit
University of Wyoming
PO Box 3166, University Sta.
Laramie, WY 82071
Phone: (307)766-5415
Contact: Dr. Stanley H. Anderson, Leader
Parent Agencies: Department of the Interior, U.S. Fish and Wildlife Service, U.S. Fish and Wildlife Service Cooperative Units. ***Research Areas:*** Unit coordinates research on fish and wildlife populations and habitat in the region. Primary area of research is habitat selection of wildlife and fish. Current projects include studies of the habitat needs of big game (mule deer, elk, antelope) and of endangered species (such as black-footed ferret). Unit also is working on developing a better understanding of the habitat associations and population dynamics of large carnivores like the mountain lion and of raptors like the bald eagle and prairie falcon. Aquatic projects include development of fish habitat assessment methods for streams and lakes as well as evaluations of sport fisheries across Wyoming. Management needs of state and federal agencies are directly assessed through studies on oil and gas development, timber harvesting, and urbanization impacts in Wyoming. Additional ongoing research deals with riparian communities, reservoir management, non-game bird communities, and aquatic stock assessment.

★3182★ Wyoming Water Research Center
University of Wyoming
PO Box 3067, University Sta.
Laramie, WY 82071-3067
Phone: (307)766-2143
Fax: (307)766-3718
Contact: Dr. Steven P. Gloss, Dir.
Parent Agencies: Department of the Interior, U.S. Geological Survey, Water Resources Division. ***Research Areas:*** Multidisciplinary studies of water resources encompassing the areas of water planning, hydrology, hydraulics, water quality, water treatment, limnology, microbiology, fisheries, geology, geohydrology, geochemistry, water law, resource economics, recreation, agricultural engineering, range management, statistics, toxicology, plant science, soils, mathematical modeling, atmospheric science and climatology. ***Databases:*** Maintains Water Resources Data System, information on hydrologic and climatologic conditions in the state and Wyoming Water Bibliography, 12,000 citations on the state's water resources.

Nonprofit and University Research Centers

International

★3183★ Institute for Groundwater Research
University of Waterloo
Waterloo, Ontario, Canada 2NL 3G1
Phone: (519)885-1211
Fax: (519)888-4654
Research Areas: Groundwater. Special Resources: Environmental isotope, groundwater quality, aqueous geochemistry, organic geochemistry, microbiological, and physical properties laboratories; radioactive tracers facility. Computers: Network of microcomputers; VAX 3500 mini-computer with VAX 2000 graphics workstation; high speed drum plotter.

★3184★ International Agency for Research on Cancer (IARC)
18th World Health Assembly
150, cours Albert-Thomas
69372 Lyon 8, France
Phone: 72 73 84 85
Fax: 72 73 85 75
Telex: 380023
Contact: Dr. Lorenzo Tomatis, Director
Autonomous cancer research arm of the World Health Organization. ***Research Areas:*** Focuses on the etiology and prevention of human cancer, with emphasis on the total environment, including surveillance of environmental factors and evaluation of screening methods for the early detection of cancer.

★3185★ International Association for Hydraulic Research
Rotterdamseweg 185
Postbus 177
2600 MH Delft, Netherlands
Phone: 569353
Fax: 619674
Telex: 38176
Contact: J.E. Prins, Sec. Gen.
Research Areas: Promotes basic and applied research in hydraulic engineering aimed at solving the world's water problems.

★3186★ International Association on Water Pollution Research and Control
1 Queen Anne's Gate
London SW1H 9BT, England
Phone: (071) 222-3848
Fax: (071) 233-1197
Telex: 918518 WASSOC G
Contact: A. Milburn, Exec. Dir.
Nongovernmental, nonprofit membership organization with national, associate, and individual members in more than 85 countries. ***Research Areas:*** promotes research on water pollution abatement and control; exchange of information on water pollution research and water quality protection; practical application of research in engineering design, construction, operation, control of wastewater collection systems, of purification and reclamation of plants, and of water quality management problems; and promotion of liaison among scientists, engineers, and administrators in the area of water pollution control.

★3187★ International Institute for Environment and Development
3 Endsleigh St.
London WC1H ODD, England
Phone: (071) 388-2117
Fax: (071) 388-2826
Telex: 261681
Contact: Richard Sandbrook, Exec. Dir.
Research Areas: Conducts policy research and provides consultancy services in the areas of: forestry, land use, energy, human settlements, marine resources, sustainable agriculture, dryland farming, and economics.

★3188★ International Juridical Organization for Environment and Development
Via Barberini 3
00187 Rome, Italy
Phone: (6) 474 2117
Fax: (6) 474 5779
Telex: 614046
Contact: Mario Guttieres, Pres.
Nongovernmental, nonprofit institute. ***Research Areas:*** Promotes the study of the various legal aspects of transnational problems, including environmental protection.

★3189★ International Society for the Prevention of Water Pollution
Little Orchard
Bentworth
Alton, Hampshire GU34 5RB, England
Phone: 0252-624837
Contact: R. Maitland Earl, Chm.
Research Areas: Charitable organization concerned with the causes of water pollution in seas, lakes, rivers, and streams. Governments, local authorities, municipalities, and water authorities worldwide are alerted to water pollution problems in their areas and offered solutions.

★3190★ International Union for Conservation of Nature and Natural Resources
World Conservation Union
Ave. du Mont-Blanc
CH-1196 Gland, Switzerland
Phone: (022) 64 91 14
Fax: (022) 64 29 26
Telex: 419605
Contact: Dr. Martin W. Holdgate, Dir. - Gen.
Research Areas: Overall goal of IUCN is to promote the use and conservation of natural resources. Specific objectives are: to ensure that development is sustainable so that the potential of renewable natural resources is maintained; to ensure that areas of land or sea which do not have special protection are managed so that natural resources are conserved and the many species and varieties of plants and animals can survive in adequate numbers; to protect areas of land, and fresh and sea waters, which contain representative or exceptional communities of plant and animals; and to devise special measures to ensure that species of fauna and flora do not become endangered or extinct. In support of its goals, IUCN carries out the following activities; (1) monitoring events in the field of conservation and bringing conservation requirements to the attention of the appropriate organizations; (2) planning conservation action at the strategic, program, and project levels; (3) Promoting conservation action by through the effective dissemination of information; and (4) providing assisstance and advice related to conservation action. In addition, IUCN undertakes projects of its own and helps design and manage projects for the World Wide Fund for Nature.

★3191★ International Waterfowl and Wetlands Research Bureau
Slimbridge, Gloucester GL2 7BX, England
Phone: (0453) 890624
Fax: (0453) 890827
Telex: 437145 WWFG
Contact: Dr. M. Moser, Director
Nongovernmental organization and registered charity. ***Research Areas:*** Coordinates international activities to promote the conservation of waterfowl and their wetland habitats. Research activities are carried out by professionals working at institutes worldwide and by a group of several thousand voluntary amateur ornithologists. Principal subjects of study include waterfowl (ducks, geese, flamingos, swans, and coots), and wetlands and wetland-management.

★3192★ Ispra Establishment
Joint Research Center
21020 Ispra, Italy
Phone: (332) 78 91 11
Telex: 380042
Contact: G.R. Bishop, Dir.-Gen.
Established as nuclear research center, with emphasis on nuclear safety. ***Research Areas:*** Alternative energy sources and conservation, protection of the environment, remote sensing for marine pollution and land use, and industrial risk.

★3193★ Monitoring and Assessment Research Centre (MARC)
The Old Coach House
Campden Hill
London W8 7AD, England
Phone: (071) 376-1577
Fax: (071) 937-5396
Telex: 915407 MARC G
Contact: Prof. P.J. Peterson, Director
Cosponsored by: the University of London, the United Nations Environment Programme, and the World Health Organization. ***Research Areas:*** Program in environmental pollution is divided into three principal areas: exposure assessment, effects evaluations, and monitoring.

★3194★ OECD International Energy Agency (IEA)
2, rue Andre Pascal
75016 Paris, France
Phone: (1) 45 24 82 00
Fax: (1) 45 24 99 88
Telex: 630190
Contact: Helga Steeg, Exec. Dir.
Autonomous organization within the framework of the Organization for Economic Cooperation and Development (OECD). ***Research Areas:*** Coordinates a program of international energy research among 21 of OECD's 24 member countries. IEA research projects are carried out in two main areas: conventional energy systems, including energy conservation technology, coal technology, and enhanced oil recovery; and non-conventional energy systems, including geothermal energy, solar energy, heating and cooling, electric power generation, biomass conversion, ocean energy systems, wind power, fusion power, and hydrogen production.

★3195★ OECD Nuclear Energy Agency (NEA)
OECD
38, blvd. Suchet
75016 Paris, France
Phone: (1) 45 24 82 00
Fax: (1) 45 24 96 24
Telex: 630668
Contact: Kunihiko Uematsu, Dir.-Gen.
Parent organization is the Organization for Economic Cooperation and Development (OECD). ***Research Areas:*** Promotes the development of peaceful uses of nuclear energy and encourages cooperation on the safety and regulatory aspects of nuclear development (including the safety of nuclear installations, protection against ionizing radiation and preservation of the environment, radioactive waste management, and nuclear third party liability and insurance).

★3196★ St. Lawrence National Institute of Ecotoxicology
310 ave. des Ursulines
Rimouski, Quebec, Canada G5L 3A1
Phone: (418)724-1746
Contact: Dr. Pierre Beland, Pres.
Research Areas: Beluga whale population, distribution, and life cycle, including behavior, social life, habitat, group dynamics, state of health, and toxicology. Additional studies trace the flow of contaminants and their effects on organisms and the structure of food webs in the St. Lawrence basin, focusing on fish, birds, and mammals. Special Resources: Le BLEUVET, a research boat.

United States

★3197★ 49th Parallel Institute
Montana State Univ.
1-156 Wilson Hall
Bozeman, MT 59717
Phone: (406)994-6691
Contact: Dr. Lauren McKinsey, Dir.
Research Areas: Western U.S.-Canada relations on the state-provincial governmental level, including transboundary pollution, comparative water policy and other economic matters such as trade and investment. Activities include Borderlands, a study of transborder attributes focusing on five adjacent regions of the borderlands (the Atlantic, the St. Lawrence, the Great Lakes, the Prairies, and the Pacific/Rockies); the study explores regional geography and environment, patterns of historical settlement, and comparative landscape analysis.

★3198★ Academy of Natural Sciences of Philadelphia, Division of Environmental Research
19th St. & the Pkwy.
Philadelphia, PA 19103
Phone: (215)299-1081
Contact: Dr. Louis E. Sage, V. Pres.
Research Areas: Studies in freshwater and estuarine biology and ecology, including environmental impact studies, water quality assessments, and resource management. Examines the environmental impact of bacterial growths, physical alterations such as highway construction, dredging, and flow modification, and discharges of such substances as heavy metals, nutrients, oil, pesticides, radioactivity, and sewage. Assesses the chemical, thermal, radiological, and biological properties of water quality. Develops resource management programs, including fisheries management, watershed planning, control of nuisance organisms, lake restoration, and wildlife enhancement. Research methodology incorporates biomonitoring, bioassay/toxicological studies, chemical analysis, primary productivity studies, population monitoring, hydrographic/effluent plume surveys, and statistical modeling. Special Resources: Maintains identified reference collections of freshwater and marine fishes, mollusks, crustaceans, lower invertebrates, aquatic insects, diatoms, and algae.

★3199★ Adirondack Ecological Center
SUNY Coll. of Environmental Science and Forestry
Huntington Forest
Newcomb, NY 12852
Phone: (518)582-4551
Contact: Dr. William F. Porter, Dir.
Research Areas: Biology, ecology, and forest resource management studies, including studies of field ecology problems of animal life in forest environments, silviculture, wildlife, recreation, ecosystem dynamics, vertebrate population ecology, plant-animal interaction, renewable resource management, and environmental problems of the Adirondack region.

★3200★ Adirondack Lakes Survey Corporation
New York State Dept. of Environmental Conservation
Ray Brook, NY 12977
Phone: (518)891-2758
Contact: Walter Kretser, Project Dir.
Research Areas: Fish populations, water chemistry, and physical characteristics of lake and pond waters in New York's Adirondack and southern and eastern regions, especially to learn the extent and effects of man-induced acidification processes.

★3201★ Advanced Environmental Control Technology Research Center
University of Illinois
3230 Newmark C. E. Lab.
205 N. Mathews Ave.
Urbana, IL 61801
Phone: (217)333-3822
Fax: (217)333-9464
Contact: Dr. R.S. Engelbrecht, Dir.
Research Areas: Problem-oriented fundamental research addressing technology of environmental quality control, specifically separation technology and detoxification and destruction of toxic and hazardous contaminants, as applied to control of water and air pollution. Representative projects include studies on thermodynamic behavior and application of the supercritical fluid extraction process; simultaneous collection of sulfur dioxide, nitrogen oxides, and hydrochloric acid; thermal regeneration of activated carbon; rates of genetic transfer in biological treatment processes; humic substances removal by coagulation and ultrafiltration; and removal of sulfure dioxide and nitrogen oxides from flue gas by combined plasma photolysis.

★3202★ Advanced Sciences Research and Development Corporation
PO Box 127
Lakemont, GA 30552
Phone: (404)782-2092
Contact: Dr. Sarah Heronymus, Pres. /Research Dir.
Research Areas: Agricultural and environmental health research, including chemical pollution of farm lands; limnological studies of lakes, rivers, and streams; acid rain and sugar maple forest devastation; insects and plant and orchard diseases; and animal diseases and remedies, particularly those of hogs, cattle, and fowl.

★3203★ AESOP Institute
PO Box 880
Sebastopol, CA 95473
Phone: (707)829-7754
Fax: (707)829-1002
Contact: Mark Goldes, Chief Exec. Officer
Research Areas: Sponsors research in alternative energy systems based on electricity and magnetics, including electric cars, solid state generators, solid state high efficiency refrigeration, ambient temperature superconductivity, advanced energy and propulsion systems. The Institute also studies economic alternatives.

★3204★ Agricultural Engineering Research Center
Texas A&M Univ.
College Station, TX 77843
Phone: (409)845-3931
Fax: (409)845-3932

Contact: Prof. Donald L. Reddell, Head
Research Areas: Engineering problems and systems for controlling and managing the production, processing, and distribution of food and fiber, including studies on quality control in food and fiber products, biosystems modeling, management and control systems in water control and use, water and air quality control, forest engineering, biochemical engineering, energy utilization and efficiency, microelectronic applications, alternate energy systems, bioprocessing, and bioremediation.

★3205★ Agricultural Experiment Station
University of District of Columbia
4200 Connecticut Ave., NW
Washington, DC 20008
Phone: (202)282-3675
Contact: James R. Allen, Dir.
Research Areas: Urban gardening, sewage waste water quality, Dutch elm disease, and biotechnology. Special Resources: Maintains an environmental pollution laboratory and a 143-acre farm.

★3206★ Agricultural Research and Development Center
University of Nebraska-Lincoln
PO Box 163
Mead, NE 68041
Phone: (402)624-2275
Contact: Dr. Warren W. Sahs, Superintendent
Research Areas: Agriculture, alternative farming systems, conservation tillage, energy efficient engineering, conservation of natural resources, agronomy, animal science, horticulture, entomology, agricultural engineering, agricultural meteorology, veterinary science, plant pathology, forestry, fisheries, and wildlife, especially increased crop yields, weed and insect control, efficient livestock production, efficient irrigation practices, conservation of energy in agriculture and cultural practices, evapotranspiration, windbreak utilization, and more efficient use of forage residues and pastures in beef production. Located on 9,400 acres, the Center uses 464 buildings for either educational or research purposes. Serves primarily as field research facility for staff of Nebraska Agricultural Experiment Station headquartered on campus in Lincoln. Special Resources: 165-acre lateral move irrigation system; rhizotron for turf research.

★3207★ Agromedicine Program
Medical Univ. of S. Carolina
171 Ashley Ave.
Charleston, SC 29425
Phone: (803)792-2281
Contact: Dr. Stanley Schuman, Dir.
Research Areas: Health effects of pesticides on humans, including epidemiology, residues in tissues and plasma, health of agricultural workers, acute poisonings, biochemistry of the exposed, environmental monitoring, and metabolism. Also studies occupational medicine applied to agriculture: prevention of heat stress illness, skin cancer, hearing loss, dermatitis, and pesticide safety.

★3208★ Air Pollution Health Effects Laboratory
University of California, Irvine
Dept. of Community & Environmental Medicine
Irvine, CA 92717
Phone: (714)856-5860
Fax: (714)856-4763
Contact: Dr. Robert F. Phalen, Dir.
Research Areas: Lung defenses, particle deposition in the lungs, chronic inhalation exposure to acidic aerosol mixtures, inhalation exposure methodology, and environmental and occupational inhalation toxicology, emphasizing particle plus gas mixtures. Also develops and validates mathematical models of inhaled particle deposition.

★3209★ Air Pollution Research Laboratory
University of Florida
408 Black Hall
Gainsville, FL 32611
Phone: (904)392-0845
Fax: (904)392-3076
Contact: Dr. Dale Lundgren, Dir.
Research Areas: Causes, effects, evaluation, and control of air pollution, and problems of occupational health, specializing in atmospheric and air pollution chemistry, photochemistry, chemical kinetics, and atmospheric aerosol mechanics and dynamics.

★3210★ Air Pollution Research Laboratory
New Jersey Inst. of Technology
323 Martin Luther King Blvd.
Newark, NJ 07102
Phone: (201)596-3587
Fax: (201)643-3934
Contact: Dr. J. Bozzelli, Codirector
Research Areas: Organic, analytic, and physical chemistry, including electrochemical detection, atmospheric chemistry, destruction of chloro-organics, and development of analyses for major mutagens on airborne particulate and for volatile organics.

★3211★ Air Quality Group
University of California, Davis
Crocker Nuclear Laboratories
Davis, CA 95616
Phone: (916)752-1124
Contact: Thomas A. Cahill, Group Dir.
Research Areas: Air quality, including chemical size-analysis and source identification of air pollutants, particulate monitoring, and development of sampling equipment.

★3212★ Air Resources Research Consortium
North Carolina State Univ.
1509 Varsity Dr.
Raleigh, NC 27606
Phone: (919)737-3311
Contact: Dr. Walter W. Hick, Dir.
Research Areas: Effects of air pollution on ecosystems.

★3213★ Alabama Solar Energy Center
University of Alabama in Huntsville
Johnson Research Center
Huntsville, AL 35899
Phone: (205)895-6707
Contact: Dr. Gerald Guinn, Dir.
Research Areas: Commercial solar systems testing, solar thermal energy studies for domestic hot water and space heating applications, testing of photovoltaic cells and power conditioning equipment for photovoltaic cells, biomass fuel evaluation, cogeneration feasibility studies, and heating, ventilation, and air conditioning systems analysis.

★3214★ Alabama Waste Exchange (AWE)
University of Alabama
Box 870203
Tuscaloosa, AL 35487-0203
Phone: (205)348-5889
Fax: (205)348-8573
Contact: William J. Herz, Dir.
Research Areas: Identifies and develops uses for industrial waste and helps businesses minimize production of waste materials.

★3215★ Alaska Fisheries Science Center
7600 Sand Point Way NE
BIN C15700
Seattle, WA 98115
Phone: (206)526-4000
Fax: (206)526-4004
Contact: Dr. William Aron, Science and Research Dir.
Research Areas: Marine fish and shellfish, marine mammals, and international fisheries issues in the northeastern Pacific Ocean, particularly in the Bering Sea, the Gulf of Alaska, and the U.S. west coast. Studies include resource surveys monitoring variations in abundance and distribution of fish, shellfish, and marine mammals; the biology, ecology, and utilization of marine resources to assist in the development and management of U.S. and foreign fisheries; habitat investigations; entanglement studies; and the effects of environmental contaminants on the life processes of marine fish, shellfish, and mammals. Projects are carried out through four divisions: Auke Bay Laboratory, National Marine Mammal Laboratory, Resource Assessment and Conservation Enginering Division, and the Resource and Ecology and Fisheries Management Division.

★3216★ Alaska Sea Grant College Program
University of Alaska Fairbanks
138 Irving II
Fairbanks, AK 99775-5040
Phone: (907)474-7086
Contact: Ronald K. Dearborn, Dir.
Research Areas: Renewable marine resources, aquaculture, and ecosystems.

★3217★ Albrook Hydraulics Laboratory
Washington State Univ.
Pullman, WA 99164-3001
Phone: (509)335-4546
Fax: (509)335-7632
Contact: Prof. Howard D. Copp, Dir.
Research Areas: Hydraulic engineering, fluid mechanics, water resources, and fisheries engineering. Hydraulic engineering studies focus on hydraulic structures, conduits, transients in open and closed conduits, turbines and pumps, trashracks, surge tanks, outlet control structures, high velocity flow analysis, groundwater hydraulics and contamination transport, and cavitation. Fluid mechanics research focuses on analysis of basic flow equations, boundary layers, turbulence, diffusion, drag, lift, thermal effects, and numerical modeling. Water resources investigations concentrate on systems planning and management, allocation among competing uses, surface and groundwater hydrology, geomorphology, river engineering, sediment transport, floods and flood plain management, hydrologic modeling, basin/stream systems analysis, natural channel hydraulic geometry, stochastic hydrology, and ungaged streamflow models. Fisheries engineering studies are applied to fishways, habitat improvement structures, downstream migration bypass facilities at dams, analysis of barriers to upstream migration, stream habitat restoration, and methods for estimating spawning and rearing habitat.

★3218★ Alternative Energy Institute
West Texas State Univ.
PO Box 248, WT Sta.
Canyon, TX 79016
Phone: (806)656-2295
Contact: Dr. Vaughn Nelson, Dir.
Research Areas: Alternative sources of energy, with primary emphasis on wind energy systems

for agricultural applications that will also apply directly to homes and industries. Project areas include wind characteristics, evaluation and design of wind energy conversion systems, feasibility studies, and ongoing measurement program to determine the wind resource base. Databases: Windspeeds at different heights in northwest Texas and New Mexico. Special Resources: 28-acre Wind Test Center, equipped with five wind turbines.

★3219★ American Council for an Energy-Efficient Economy
1001 Connecticut Ave., NW, Ste. 535
Washington, DC 20036
Phone: (202)429-8873
Contact: Howard Geller, Associate Dir.
Research Areas: Gathers, evaluates, and disseminates information to stimulate greater energy efficiency. Areas of research include buildings, appliances, indoor air quality, conservation in developing countries, and conservation in the industrial and transportation sectors. Provides independent assessments of energy technologies and policies. Examines the linkages between energy efficiency and broader societal issues such as acid rain and other forms of environmental pollution, economic well-being, and global security.

★3220★ American Institute for Pollution Prevention
University of Cincinnati
741 Rhodes Hall
Mail Location 71
Cincinnati, OH 45221
Phone: (513)556-3693
Contact: Prof. Thomas Hauser, Exec. Dir.
Research Areas: Pollution prevention concepts. AIPP is organized into four councils: Economics, Education, Implementation, and Technology. Economics Council emphasizes the value of pollution prevention, identifies demonstration projects, examines effectiveness of economic models, determines efficacy of state programs in pollution prevention, and promotes case history projects demonstrating pollution prevention. Education Council fosters the pollution prevention ethic in private and public sectors, develops educational materials and curricula, and promotes specialty conferences on pollution prevention. Implementation Council assists industry and governments in developing and implementing pollution prevention programs, surveys government agencies and associations, defines regulatory and legislative barriers to pollution prevention, and identifies industry incentives. Technology Council studies technology with the potential for significant pollution rrevention, reviews EPA technical documents, supports technology-based demonstration projects, and cooperates with small businesses in pollution prevention projects.

★3221★ American Iron and Steel Institute (AISI)
1133 15th St., NW
Washington, DC 20005-2701
Phone: (202)452-7265
Contact: William E. Dennis, V. Pres.
Research Areas: Construction, engineering, fire protection, and air and water quality, as well as basic research in areas such as direct steelmaking process development, conventional iron making, steelmaking, product processing and properties. Collaborative research programs include projects in recycling and resource recovery, projects in process control sensing, including rapid in-process analysis of molten metal and internal temperature measurement of hot blooms, billets, and slabs.

★3222★ American Petroleum Institute
1220 L St., NW
Washington, DC 20005
Phone: (202)682-8000
Fax: (202)682-8030
Contact: Charles J. DiBona, Pres.
Research Areas: Petroleum economics, refining, products, and production, energy supply issues, petroleum measurement, prevention and control of pollution by oil and hazardous substances, oil spills, fate and effects of oil in marine environments, management of solid wastes, occupational health, toxicology, environmental biology, standards for production equipment, offshore structures and refinery equipment, and utilization of petroleum products.

★3223★ American Planning Association
1313 E. 60th St.
Chicago, IL 60637
Phone: (312)955-9100
Contact: Frank So, Deputy Exec. Dir.
Research Areas: Analyzes the critical issues of urban growth and change, including studies of environmental and social balance, and land use.

★3224★ Ames Laboratory
Iowa State Univ.
109 Office & Laboratory Bldg.
Ames, IA 50011
Phone: (515)294-2770
Fax: (515)294-4456
Contact: Dr. Thomas Barton, Dir.
Research Areas: Basic research to increase the understanding of physical, chemical, and materials sciences to improve energy-related technologies. Activities are carried out in the following program areas: experimental nuclear physics, fossil energy, fundamental interactions, high energy physics, materials chemistry, metallurgy and ceramics, processes and techniques, safeguards and security, geosciences, applied mathematical sciences, and solid-state physics.

★3225★ Anadromous Fish and Aquatic Invertebrate Research Facility
University of New Hampshire
Marine Institute
Durham, NH 03824
Phone: (603)862-2103
Contact: Dr. Stacia A. Sower, Dir.
Research Areas: Aquaculture of anadromous fish, including Pacific and Atlantic salmon and lamprey and stream invertebrates, including studies on the endocrinology and physiology of fishes, fishery management, the effects of acid rain on the distribution of aquatic organisms in streams, and the effects of acid rain on the eggs of brook trout. Special Resources: Flow-thru fresh water system and artificial streams.

★3226★ Analytical Lab
University of Maine
Dept. of Plant, Soil, & Environmental Science
s
Orono, ME 04469
Phone: (207)581-2997
Contact: Dr. Susan Erich, Dir.
Research Areas: Elemental analysis of plant tissue, soils, farm manures, animal feeds, fertilizers, municipal sludges and sludge composts, water, and wastewater samples for commercial and campus-wide research customers.

★3227★ Applied Energy Research Laboratory
North Carolina State Univ.
Campus Box 7910
Dept. of Mechanical & Aerospace Engineering
Raleigh, NC 27695-7910
Phone: (919)737-2365
Contact: Dr. John A. Edwards, Dir.
Research Areas: Energy conversion, combustion, direct contact heat transfer, statistical property determination, and earth-coupled heat pumps.

★3228★ Applied Marine Research Laboratory
Old Dominion Univ.
Norfolk, VA 23529-0456
Phone: (804)683-4195
Contact: Raymond W. Alden III, Dir.
Research Areas: Marine biology and biological oceanography, including ichthyology, benthic ecology, zooplankton ecology, phytoplankton ecology, mycology, biofouling, microbiology, wetlands ecology, larval ecology, fisheries modeling, mariculture, and toxicity testing with a variety of lethal and sublethal bioassays and microcosms. Geological and physical oceanography studies include sedimentology, sediment transport, hydrography, geomorphology, geological history (micropaleontology), optical and acoustic properties of sea water, wind-driven currents, mesoscale circulation patterns, hydraulic models, and pollutant mixing/spreading models. Speciality areas of research in environmental chemistry include studies in biogeochemistry, priority pollutant analysis in sea water sediments and biological tissue, analysis of toxins and carcinogens in wastewater and drinking water, the biochemistry of hormones and pheromones, and effects of open ocean disposal of wastes. The Laboratory also has research expertise in computer science, systems analysis, multivariate statistics, coastal zone planning, and marine resources management. Databases: Benthic, biological, sediment toxicants, and body burden of New York Bight. Also maintains database of the lower Chesapeake Bay and coastal waters. Special Resources: Maintains two research vessels.

★3229★ Aquatic Station
Southwest Texas State Univ.
H.M. Freeman Aquatic Biology Bldg.
San Marcos, TX 78666-4616
Phone: (512)245-2284
Contact: Bobby Whiteside, Dir.
Research Areas: Aquatic invertebrate ecology, limnology, fisheries biology, aquatic parasitology, pollution biology, aquatic toxicology, aquatic plant ecology, stream ecology, groundwater ecology, and aquatic mycology.

★3230★ Aquatics Research Lab
Lake Superior State Univ.
Sault St. Marie, MI 49783
Phone: (906)635-1949
Contact: Prof. David Behmer, Dir.
Research Areas: Salmonid aquaculture, including phosphorus pollution of fish rearing and movement and harvest of Atlantic salmon in upper Great Lakes.

★3231★ Architecture and Planning Research Laboratory
University of Michigan
Art & Architecture Bldg., Rm. 1248
2000 Bonisteel Blvd.
Ann Arbor, MI 48109-2069
Phone: (313)764-1340

Fax: (313)763-2322
Contact: Colin W. Clipson, Dir.
Research Areas: Building technology developments (especially in energy conservation and lighting and daylighting), new possibilities in building design and community planning created by scientific and industrial advances, techniques and applications of simulation in various design processes, urban design, international development, and economic planning for better hospitals, schools, court facilities, and housing. Serves as a center for special research projects conducted by graduate students in architecture and urban planning and design. Special Resources: Full-scale simulation laboratory.

★3232★ Architecture Research Laboratory
University of Arizona
College of Architecture
Tucson, AZ 85721
Phone: (602)621-6751
Contact: Prof. Fred S. Matter, Dir.
Research Areas: Desert architecture and community design, energy analysis of buildings, historic preservation of buildings, residential design for water conservation, and research on architectural modeling and simulation techniques.

★3233★ Argonne National Laboratory (ANL)
9700 S. Cass Ave.
Argonne, IL 60439-4832
Phone: (708)972-3872
Contact: Alan Schriesheim, Dir.
Research Areas: Primary focus on energy related issues. Programs in the physical sciences include high energy physics, nuclear physics, chemical sciences, materials sciences and engineering, and geosciences. Engineering research programs focus on integral fast reactor technology, including fuel performance demonstration, pyroprocessing development, safety analyses, reactor core design, fuel cycle demonstration in the Hot Cell and liquid-metal reactor technology research and development. Other engineering programs include new production reactors, advanced reactor research, fusion energy, nuclear fuel cycle, nuclear waste repositories, remedial action programs and waste management (commercial and defense). Biological and environmental research includes studies in biochemistry of metals, biostatistics, carcinogenesis studies, cellular biology, environmental health, epidemiology, gene expression, low-level radiation effects, molecular biology mutagenesis (heritable and somatic), neurobehavioral chronobiology, nuclear medicine, photobiology, energy conservation, fossil energy, renewable energy, advanced energy systems programs, atmospheric chemistry, atmospheric physics, environmental effects, environmental geoscience and engineering, environmental impacts, fundamental molecular physics and chemistry, integrated assessments, instrumentation development and site characterization and remedial action. Special Resources: User facilities at Argonne available to qualified researchers from industry and academia include the Advanced Computing Research Facility, Argonne Fusion Electromagnetic Induction Experiment, Argonne Superconductivity Heavy-Ion Linac, Biological Materials Growth Facility, Electrochemical Energy Storage Analysis and Diagnostics Laboratory, Facility for High-Resolution Atomic Spectroscop y, Facility for High-Sensitivity Magnetization Measurements, Fossil Energy Users Laboratory, Heat Exchanger Test Facility, High-Voltage Electron Microscope-Tandem Facility, Hot Cell Facilities, Intense Pulsed Neutron Source, Janus Reactor, Midwest Area Detector Facility, Pulsed Electron Linac, Salt Gradient Solar Pond, Tandem Accelerator Facility, 3-MeV Van de Graaff Accellerator, 4-MV Dynamitron Facility, 60-inch Cyclotron, and Advanced Photon Source.

★3234★ Arizona Cooperative Fish and Wildlife Research Unit
University of Arizona
210 Biological Sciences Bldg.
Tucson, AZ 85721
Phone: (602)621-1959
Fax: (602)621-8801
Contact: Dr. O. Eugene Maughan, Unit Leader
Research Areas: Fish and wildlife history, ecology, conservation, and management.

★3235★ Arkansas Water Resources Research Center
University of Arkansas
113 Ozark Hall
Fayetteville, AR 72701
Phone: (501)575-4403
Fax: (501)575-3846
Contact: Kenneth F. Steele, Dir.
Research Areas: Water and other resources relating to water, including studies on improved irrigation systems, design of septic systems, pesticide contamination of water, land use effects on groundwater quality, and stream and river water quality and ecology. Established under the Water Resources Research Act of 1964 to encourage statewide water research, to train scientists in the field, and to disseminate information.

★3236★ Art and Craft Materials Institute, Inc.
715 Boylston St.
Boston, MA 02116
Phone: (617)266-6800
Contact: Deborah M. Fanning, Exec. V. Pres.
Research Areas: Reviews and tests the toxicity and quality of art materials. Conducts a certification program to ensure that art and craft materials are non-toxic, meet voluntary standards of quality and performance, and are affixed with health warning labels where appropriate. Products that have earned the Institute's CP (Certified Product) or AP (Approved Product) seal include crayons, water colors, tempera colors, finger paints, chalks, modeling materials, block printing inks and media, screen printing inks and media, school pastes and adhesives, acrylic and oil paints and media, marking crayons, and other art materials.

★3237★ Atmospheric Radioactivity Laboratory
New Mexico Inst. of Mining and Technology
Socorro, NM 87801
Phone: (505)835-5341
Fax: (505)835-5895
Contact: Dr. Stephen Schery, Dir.
Research Areas: Radon and thoron and their daughter products in indoor and underground environments; effects of radon on atmospheric electric parameters; importance of thoron and thoron daughters as contributors to indoor radiation dose; radon and daughter product ion-aerosol interactions; indoor-outdoor radon levels and their relation to air exchange processes; diffusion and flow of radon in homogeneous and fractured media; radon levels and their use for measuring air exchange in caves; sorption of radon on porous materials; atmospheric aerosols and dry deposition.

★3238★ Atmospheric Sciences Program
Ohio State Univ.
103 Bricker Hall
190 N. Oval Mall
Columbus, OH 43210
Phone: (614)422-2514
Contact: John Rayner, Dir.
Research Areas: Meteorology, geophysical fluid dynamics, microclimatology, radiation solar-terrestrial relations, air-sea interactions, boundary layer theory, energy, and climate change. Administrates research and teaching in the atmospheric sciences, coordinates activities, and promotes multidisciplinary and interdisciplinary studies in various affiliated departments and schools of the University and in Center for Lake Erie Area Research, Byrd Polar Research Institute, and Water Resources Center.

★3239★ BCR National Laboratory
500 William Pitt Way
Pittsburgh, PA 15238
Phone: (412)826-3030
Fax: (412)826-3094
Contact: Dr. John A. DeMarchis, V. Pres.
Research Areas: Activities are conducted in three broad areas of research: mining, environmental control, and coal utilization. Mining research includes instrumentation, mine monitoring and communications, dust control, and illumination. Environmental control research includes air and water quality and solid waste disposal. Utilization research includes combustion, coal conversion, and beneficiation studies. Developmental research is conducted on chemical, physical, and petrographic properties of coal.

★3240★ Beef Improvement Center
Colorado State Univ.
Star Rte. Box 18
Saratoga, CO 82331
Phone: (307)327-5339
Fax: (307)327-5363
Contact: Jack Moon, Manager
Research Areas: Fertilizer studies on irrigated mountain meadows, including long-term nitrogen fertilizer requirements for meadow-mountain hay production, effectiveness of ammonium nitrate and urea fertilizer, effectiveness of phosphorus and potassium fertilizer on soils low in these nutrients, and long-term effects of fertilizers on hay quality and yield. Also studies annual and long-term economics of nitrogen, phosphorus, potassium, and sulphur fertilization on mountain meadows.

★3241★ Belle W. Baruch Institute for Marine Biology and Coastal Research
University of South Carolina at Columbia
Columbia, SC 29208
Phone: (803)777-5288
Contact: Dr. F. John Vernberg, Dir.
Research Areas: Interaction of geological, physical, chemical, and biotic processes in estuaries and coastal waters, including biological studies of molecular, organismic microorganisms, and ecosystem analyses of mechanisms of adaptation to stress of environmental factors, and geological processes, including sedimentation, beach erosion, and mineral cycling. Databases: Biotic and abiotic factors in southeastern estuary.

★3242★ Benedict Estuarine Research Laboratory
Academy of Natural Sciences
Benedict Ave.
Benedict, MD 20612
Phone: (301)274-3134
Fax: (215)299-1199

Contact: Dr. James G. Sanders, Dir.
Research Areas: Aquatic toxicology, plankton communities, benthic communities, fish, and commercially important invertebrates. Evaluates the trophic interactions in aquatic environments, studies changes in primary productivity in perturbed environments, examines the transport and toxicity of trace metals in aquatic systems, and investigates the effects of competition among individuals in aquatic communities. Special Resources: Flow-through seawater microcosms and a 42-foot fiberglass research vessel, the Joseph Leidy. Databases: Water quality and biota of the Middle Chesapeake Bay and Patuxent River.

★3243★ Bigelow Laboratory for Ocean Sciences
McKown Point
West Boothbay Harbor, ME 04575
Phone: (207)633-2173
Fax: (207)633-6584
Contact: Dennis L. Taylor, Dir.
Research Areas: Physical, chemical, and biological processes in the sea, including physical and chemical oceanography, remote sensing operations, phytoplankton physiology and ecology, microbial metabolism, benthic flora and fauna, and red tide organism, a toxic substance that attacks shellfish. Studies the bacteria that perform a vital role in recycling the nutrients required by plants and the large attached algae or seaweed found in coastal regions.

★3244★ BioIntegral Resource Center
PO Box 7414
Berkeley, CA 94707
Phone: (415)524-2567
Fax: (415)524-1758
Contact: Dr. William Olkowski, Dir.
Research Areas: Integrated pest management (IPM) and least-toxic methods of pest control. Components of IPM include: monitoring, determining injury levels, spot treatment, selecting least disruptive treatment for non-target organisms, and evaluating results.

★3245★ Biological Investigation of Marine Antarctic Systems and Stocks Program (BIOMASS)
Texas A&M Univ.
Dept. of Oceanography
College Station, TX 77843
Phone: (409)845-2134
Contact: Dr. Sayed Z. El-Sayed, Chm.
Research Areas: Conservation of the living marine resources of Antarctica, including krill, whales, seals, fishes, squids, spiny lobsters, and seaweed. Databases: FIBEX and SIBEX (first and second international BIOMASS experiments).

★3246★ Bioresources Research Facility
University of Arizona
250 E. Valencia Rd.
Tucson, AZ 85706
Phone: (602)741-1691
Fax: (602)741-1468
Contact: Dr. Joseph J. Hoffmann, Dir.
Research Areas: Development of renewable sources of energy-yielding biomass such as terrestrial plants that can be processed into specialty products, chemicals, petroleum-replacement products, proteins, pharmaceuticals, agrichemicals, and liquid, solid, and gaseous fuels. Specific topics studied include industrial cash crops for arid lands, development of biotechnology and bioenergy infrastructure, selection of economic botany criteria, agronomic feasibility, product and economic analysis, and process development and demonstration, including fermentation, microbial conversion, solvent extraction, and pyrolysis.

★3247★ Biotechnology Center
Utah State Univ.
Logan, UT 84322-4430
Phone: (801)750-2730
Fax: (801)750-2755
Contact: Steven D. Aust, Dir.
Research Areas: Biodegradation and bioremediation of environmental pollutants, including degradation and mineralization by white rot fungi of polyaromatic hydrocarbons, polychlorinated hydrocarbons, pesticides, and TNT; and iron toxicity, including the role of iron metabolism in diseases and toxicities, and methods to regulate iron metabolism. Supports biotechnology research projects throughout the University, including studies of plant response genes to physical and microbial stress, hydrogenase uptake gene transfer, vaccine development for ram epididymitis, somatic embryogenesis in wheat, molecular biology of bluetongue virus, analytical techniques to identify and verify plant hybrids, and development of improved bacterial starter cultures. Maintains three service laboratories: Macromolecular Synthesis and Analysis Laboratory, for DNA and RNA synthesis and peptide synthesis and sequencing; Monoclonal Antibody Laboratory, for production of monoclonal antibodies and ascities fluid, mammalian cell line repository, and immunoassays; and Fermentation Laboratory, for growth of cells.

★3248★ Bodega Marine Laboratory
University of California
PO Box 247
Bodega Bay, CA 94923
Phone: (707)875-2010
Contact: Prof. James S. Clegg, Dir.
Research Areas: Marine sciences, including marine ecology of Bodega Head area, systematics of marine plants and animals, physiology, biological oceanography, biology of shorebirds, comparative biochemistry and physiology, endocrinology, seawater chemistry, aquaculture and fisheries, and biology of pollution. Databases: Water quality, meteorology, and waves. Special Resources: Maintains a 42-foot research vessel, high volume seawater and freshwater systems with temperature controls, and automated meteorological and oceanographic monitoring system.

★3249★ Brookhaven National Laboratory
Upton, Long Island, NY 11973
Phone: (516)282-2123
Fax: (516)282-3000
Contact: N.P. Samios, Dir.
Research Areas: High-energy physics, basic energy sciences, nuclear energy, nuclear and medium energy physics and chemistry, and basic life sciences, including biology and medical use and effects of radiation, radioisotopes, and other nuclear tools. Environmental and energy research emphasizes energy transfer mechanisms at the edge of the continental shelf, effects of energy pollution on air quality, new energy technologies and energy conservation, and reactor safety analyses and safeguards. Encourages use of its facilities by qualified scientists from universities, other laboratories, and industrial research groups. Special Resources: Operates the 33 GeV Alternating Gradient Synchrotron, the National Synchrotron Light Source, the High Flux Beam Reactor, an emperor tandem Van de Graaff accelerator, several small cyclotrons, a 2.5 A resolution Scanning Transmission Electron Microscope (STEM), a medical research center, a computing facility, biology greenhouses, and controlled environment laboratories.

★3250★ Brush Control Research Center
Texas Tech Univ.
Goddard Range & Wildlife Bldg.
Lubbock, TX 79409
Phone: (806)742-2841
Contact: Dr. Sam E. Curl, Dir.
Research Areas: Research areas encompass plant ecology and physiology, fire ecology and prescribed burning, range seeding, livestock and pasture management, fisheries, waterfowl and wetlands, and upland and big game. Range science studies cover physiological, ecological, and economic phenomena associated with biological, herbicidal, mechanical, and fire control of mesquite, yucca, snakeweed, common broomweed, and other undesirable and noxious plants. Objectives include the development and evaluation of brush and weed control techniques (including prescribed burning in redberry juniper), evaluation of the impact of various brush control procedures on range watersheds, development of expert systems for prescribed burning, determination of the nutritive value of range plants, the study of range improvement, development of helitorch techniques to burn brush, and study of supplemental feeding of livestock on ranges in winter, spring, and summer. Wildlife studies concentrate on habitat relationships of game and nongame species and the impact of brush control on populations, improved pasture effects on Texas wildlife, ecology of mountain lions in Big Bend National Park, water quality and management of playa lakes, pond management for fish, winter conditions of mallards in Texas, lead residues in blue-winged teal, characteristics of Texas waterfowl hunters, effects of grazing on bobwhites, ring-necked pheasant ecology and habitat requirements, genetics, morphology, and parasites of sandhill cranes, response of mourning doves to habitat management, physiological ecology of the collared peccary in south Texas, and competition between cattle, mule deer, and elk. Special Resources: Experimental ranch of 2,100 acres with three sets of livestock pens.

★3251★ Buffalo Organization for Social and Technological Innovation
1479 Hertel Ave.
Buffalo, NY 14216
Phone: (716)837-7120
Contact: Mike Brill, Pres.
Research Areas: Architectural and environmental design, including effects of office design on worker productivity.

★3252★ Building Technology Center
Stevens Inst. of Technology
Castle Point Sta.
Hoboken, NJ 07030
Phone: (201)420-5360
Fax: (201)420-5593
Contact: Thomas P. Konen, Dir.
Research Areas: Water supply and drainage systems for buildings, residential water conservation, product development for the plumbing industry, heat transfer through windows and other fenestrations, piping system analysis, product analysis and testing for protection of the potable water supply system, and passive solar systems.

★3253★ Bureau of Mines
Capstone Dr.
PO Box L
Univ. of Alabama
Tuscaloosa, AL 35486-9777
Phone: (205)759-9421
Fax: (205)759-9440
Contact: Dr. David R. Flinn, Research Dir.
Research Areas: Environmental technology and mineral and material sciences. Specific areas of research include the following: the use of modeling and expert systems for optimization of mineral processing, strategic minerals and metals, hydrodynamics of flotation, acid/alcohol leaching of phosphate ores, dielectric heating properties of minerals, advanced ceramic composites for severe service conditions, controlled microstructure of ceramic materials, and chemical and physical mechanisms of solid-liquid separation techniques.

★3254★ Bureau of Water and Environmental Resources Research
University of Oklahoma
PO Box 2850
Norman, OK 73070
Phone: (405)325-2960
Contact: Ralph C. Martin, Dir.
Research Areas: Environmental studies and sanitary engineering and economics, including interdisciplinary studies of water resources of the state, nation, and southwest U.S., and appropriate technology for developing countries.

★3255★ Bushy Run Research Center
Carnegie Mellon Univ.
RD #4, Mellon Rd.
Export, PA 15632
Phone: (412)733-5200
Contact: Dr. Fred R. Frank, Dir.
Research Areas: Acute and chronic mammalian toxicity of synthetic organic chemicals by all portals of entry, including studies in analytical chemistry, radioactive isotopic analysis, biochemistry, pharmacology, histopathology, biostatistics, carcinogenicity, sensitization, teratology, reproduction, and air and water pollution as related to chemical contaminants.

★3256★ Business and Government Center
Harvard Univ.
79 John F. Kennedy St.
Cambridge, MA 02138
Phone: (617)495-1446
Fax: (617)495-9118
Contact: Richard Cavanaugh, Dir.
Research Areas: Governmental regulations, focusing on energy and environmental industries.

★3257★ Byrd Polar Research Center
Ohio State Univ.
125 S. Oval Mall
Columbus, OH 43210
Phone: (614)292-6531
Fax: (614)292-4697
Contact: Dr. Kenneth C. Jezek, Dir.
Research Areas: Anthropology, archeology, geochemistry, glaciology, geophysics, bedrock geology, glacial geology, climatology, meteorology, history of polar exploration, lichenology, limnology, paleobotany, paleontology, palynology, phycology, soil studies, permafrost, agronomy, and plant ecology, mainly of Antarctica, Arctic North America, Tibetan Plateau, Andes, and Greenland.

★3258★ Caesar Kleberg Wildlife Research Institute
Texas A&I Univ.
College of Agriculture & Home Economics
Campus Box 218
Kingsville, TX 78363
Phone: (512)595-3922
Contact: Dr. Sam L. Beasom, Dir.
Research Areas: Native plants, commercial utilization of wildlife, and basic ecology of native plant and animal species. Animal research deals primarily with deer, nilgai antelope, javelina, feral swine, quail, and nongame birds and mammals. The Institute's subsidiary unit conducts research on the region's flora.

★3259★ California Institute of Public Affairs
517 19th St.
PO Box 189040
Sacramento, Canada 95818
Phone: (916)442-2472
Fax: (916)442-2478
Contact: Thaddeus C. Trzyna, Pres.
Research Areas: California public affairs, emphasizing environmental and natural resources policy, government and politics, and environmental policy in the U.S. and abroad. Edits directories, bibliographies, and information services on California current affairs and international environmental problems.

★3260★ California Public Health Foundation
2001 Addison St.
Ste. 210
Berkeley, CA 94704-1103
Phone: (415)644-8200
Fax: (415)644-9319
Contact: Joseph M. Hafey, Exec. Dir.
Research Areas: Conducts research on a broad range of public health issues, including epidemiology, occupational health, toxic chemicals, viruses, genetics, air and industrial hygiene, diet and nutrition, and cancer prevention.

★3261★ California Sea Grant College Program
University of California
9500 Gilman Dr.
La Jolla, CA 92093-0232
Phone: (619)534-4440
Fax: (619)534-2231
Contact: James J. Sullivan, Dir.
Research Areas: Development and use of oceanic resources, including coastal research, aquaculture research (plants and animals), fisheries research and development, ocean technology, economic and institutional analysis of marine affairs, education, and management. Seeks to solve scientific and engineering questions and social and legal problems through its advisory programs and cooperation with other institutions and agencies.

★3262★ California Water Resources Center
University of California
Riverside, CA 92521
Phone: (714)787-4327
Fax: (714)787-5295
Contact: Dr. Henry J. Vaux Jr., Dir.
Research Areas: Developing, coordinating, and funding of water research programs conducted throughout the University. Research objectives emphasize issues involving energy, land, people, and the environment, including environmental protection, agriculture, human and institutional factors, water systems, economic and financial considerations, water quality, and saline conversion.

★3263★ Carbon Dioxide Information Analysis Center
MS-6335, Bldg. 1000
Oak Ridge National Laboratory
PO Box 2008
Oak Ridge, TN 37831-6335
Phone: (615)574-0390
Fax: (615)574-2232
Contact: Dr. Paul Kanciruk, Dir.
Research Areas: Elevated atmospheric carbon dioxide, potential climate change, and evaluates complex environmental issues related to elevated carbon dioxide.

★3264★ Cedar Creek Natural History Area
University of Minnesota
2660 Fawn Lake Dr. NE
Bethel, MN 55005
Phone: (612)434-5131
Contact: Dr. John R. Tester, Dir.
Research Areas: Plant and animal ecology and various other aspects of field biology, including studies on botanical, zoological, geological, and outer space problems, properties of the ionosphere, responses of animals to environmental changes by use of radio telemetry, behavior of waterfowl, fossil plant pigments, productivity of aquatic environments, and solar radiation in differing habitats. Special Resources: Insect and botanical collection; tract of 5,400 acres.

★3265★ Center for Advanced Research and Engineering
Texas Tech Research Foundation
MS 3105
Lubbock, TX 79409-4200
Phone: (806)742-3489
Fax: (806)742-1900
Contact: Dr. Ernst W. Kiesling P.E., Dir.
Research Areas: Contracts with industry and government to conduct applied research, development, and design projects in a broad range of fields, including electrical, chemical, civil, agricultural, mechanical, industrial, and petroleum engineering, computer science and technology, and physics and chemistry. Major thrusts have included hazardous waste treatment and control, protective structures, and magnetic energy storage.

★3266★ Center for Advanced Study of International Development (CASID)
Michigan State Univ.
306 Berkey Hall
East Lansing, MI 48824-1111
Phone: (517)353-5925
Fax: (517)355-1912
Contact: Prof. Tom W. Carroll, Dir.
Research Areas: International social, economic, and technological change from a social science and humanities perspective with respect to key development issues such as health, energy, rural development, human and resource development, ecosystems, migration, and industry. Projects in other countries include basic research and implementation in developing educational systems, comprehensive resource inventory evaluation systems, edible bean/cowpeas collaborative research support, employment and enterprises policy analysis, food security in Africa, Senegal agricultural research and planning and training, small enterprises approaches to employment, and University of Zimbabwe faculty expansion.

★3267★ Center for Agricultural Impacts on Water Quality
University of Minnesota
S501 Soil Science
St. Paul, MN 55108
Phone: (612)625-8209
Fax: (612)625-2208
Contact: Jim Anderson, Dir.
Research Areas: Effects of agricultural management practices on water quality, including studies on chemical and nutrient behavior in the environment, chemical management practices, groundwater and soil contamination by agricultural chemicals, and social and economic impacts of management practices.

★3268★ Center for Air Pollution Impact and Trend Analysis (CAPITA)
Washington Univ.
Campus Box 1124
319 Urbauer
St. Louis, MO 63130
Phone: (314)889-6099
Fax: (314)726-4434
Contact: Dr. Rudolf B. Husar, Dir.
Research Areas: Global, continental haziness. Conducts studies on origins, spatial/temporal distribution, properties, and effect of haze on atmospheric radiation. Also studies the distribution of man-made sulfur, nitrogen, and hydrogen pollutants. Develops computer sofware for data analysis.

★3269★ Center for Applied Energy Research
University of Kentucky
3572 Iron Works Pike
Lexington, KY 40511
Phone: (606)257-0305
Fax: (606)257-0220
Contact: Frank Derbyshire, Dir.
Research Areas: Technical, economic, and environmental problems related to the use of coal and oil shale for energy. Other areas of study include synthetic fuels, alcohol fuels, and alternative energies such as biomass and solid waste conversion. Conducts joint research projects with coal companies, utilities, high technology industries, and government agencies to help bring new developments into practical application.

★3270★ Center for Applied Research and Technology
University of Minnesota, Duluth
3151 Miller Trunk Hwy.
Duluth, MN 55811
Phone: (218)720-4294
Contact: Dr. Robert Naiman, Dir.
Research Areas: Activities are carried out through the BioProducts Division and the Minerals Division. The BioProducts Division operates programs in peat, short rotation forestry, solid wood manufacturing, resource assessment, underutilized species, and specialty crops; programs focus on economic utilization of forestry resources and forest products. The Minerals Division operates programs on taconite, nonferrous minerals, industrial minerals, and hazardous waste.

★3271★ Center for Aquatic Research and Resource Management
Florida State Univ.
136-B/Conradi Bldg.
Tallahassee, FL 32306
Phone: (904)644-4887
Contact: Dr. Robert J. Livingston, Dir.
Research Areas: Validation of freshwater bioassays with field data at toxic waste sites along three rivers in the southeastern U.S.; development of validation criteria for bioassays of multi-species marine microcosms in both seagrass and soft-sediment communities; identification of key features of oyster population dynamics in Apalachicola Bay; analysis of long-term spatial and temporal dynamics of freshwater, estuarine, and marine communities; impact assessment of pulp mill effluents, storm water runoff, toxic substances, and dredging/spoiling activities; systems modeling, including interactions of climate, habitat characteristics, primary production, inter- and intra-specific relationships, and food web structure; and ecosystem study of Choctawhatchee Bay with a view toward predicting environmental response to development alternatives. Databases: Information from 12 years of monthly trawl collections in Apalachicola Bay, nine years of monthly benthos collections in Apalachicola Bay, eight years of monthly trawl collections in Apalachee Bay, three years of weekly trawl and benthos collecions near the University marine laboratory, freshwater macroinvertebrate collections from seven rivers in the southeastern U.S., field validation of laboratory microcosm and bioassay studies (fresh and salt water), and numerous studies on zooplankton, fish larvae, plant productivity microand macrodetritus, and trophic (stomach content) analysis. Special Resources: Experimental greenhouse with static and flow-through bioassay systems and microcosms.

★3272★ Center for Atmospheric and Space Sciences (CASS)
Utah State Univ.
Logan, UT 84322-4405
Phone: (801)750-2961
Fax: (801)750-2992
Contact: Robert W. Schunk, Dir.
Research Areas: Aeronomy and space science, including interdisciplinary aurora, airglow, ionosphere, and air pollution studies. Coordinates research efforts of related units at the University and exchange of interdisciplinary ideas among them.

★3273★ Center for Atmospheric Chemistry Studies
University of Rhode Island
Narragansett, RI 02882
Phone: (401)792-6222
Fax: (401)792-6160
Contact: Prof. Robert A. Duce, Dir.
Research Areas: Global atmospheric cycles of trace substances, air/sea exchange chemistry, tracers of long-range atmospheric transport of natural and pollution substances, numerical models of atmospheric transport, and acidic precipitation. Special Resources: Maintains counting equipment for gamma-ray spectroscopy. Databases: Maintains atmospheric concentrations and meteorological data from the Atmospheric/Ocean Chemistry Experiments (AEROCE) Program.

★3274★ Center for Atomic Radiation Studies (CARS)
94 Pleasant St.
Arlington, MA 02174
Phone: (617)497-2277
Contact: Donnell W. Boardman M.D., Pres.
Research Areas: Discovery and dissemination of information on health effects of exposure to radioactive materials; physical, psychosocial, and family aspects of people affected by radiation; legal aspects of exposure; and the compilation of related data. Special projects include case studies of radiation recipients with emphasis on radiation effects and atypical symptoms, and first and second generational effects of occupational exposures to ionizing radiation.

★3275★ Center for Biochemical Engineering Research
New Mexico State Univ.
Dept. of Chemical Engineering
Box 30001, Dept. 3805
Las Cruces, NM 88003-0001
Phone: (505)646-1214
Fax: (505)646-3549
Contact: Dr. Ron Bhada, Dir.
Research Areas: Laboratory and pilot plant experimental studies on the industrial production of primary and secondary metabolites, including the design and construction of new prototypes of industrial fermenters which eliminate foaming and decrease adverse shear effects. Also studies applications of newly developed fermenters in photosynthesis and industrial waste treatment. Special Resources: Bench fermenters, bioreactors, culture collection of industrially important microorganisms, and prototype of centrifugal film fermenter.

★3276★ Center for Biomass Energy Systems
University of Florida
Bldg. 803, Rm. 11
Gainesville, FL 32611-0342
Phone: (904)392-1511
Fax: (904)392-9033
Contact: Dr. Wayne H. Smith, Dir.
Research Areas: Coordinates biomass research activities throughout the University, including studies on biomass feedstock development, handling, and conversion to energy using conventional and new scientific approaches. Serves as a focal point for assessing the needs, planning, and development of programs that involve biomass for energy in Florida.

★3277★ Center for Biomedical Toxicological Research and Hazardous Waste Management
Florida State Univ.
Bellamy Bldg.
Tallahassee, FL 32306
Phone: (904)644-5524
Fax: (906)574-6704
Contact: Dr. Roy C. Herndon, Dir.
Research Areas: Provides an administrative and resource base from which faculty within the University can conduct research in the areas of biomedicine, environmental toxicology, health effects assessment, environmental assessment, risk analysis, and hazardous waste management. Other areas include occupational health concerns, ecological effects of aquatic pollutants, effects of toxic organic substances in the environment, and the effects of heavy metals and other inorganic pollutants on aquatic organisms.

★3278★ Center for Biotic Systems
University of Wisconsin-Madison
1042 WARF Office Bldg.
610 Walnut St.
Madison, WI 53705
Phone: (608)262-9937
Fax: (608)262-0014
Contact: Prof. Michael Adams, Dir.
Research Areas: Scientific study of ecosystems and biological aspects of environment, including investigation of steps to alleviate water quality problems due to nutrient loading in a future reservoir impoundment and assessment of groundwater flow, nutrient runoff, aquatic plant production, and fish growth in a lake ecosystem and its surrounding

urban watershed. Other research interests include adaptation of submersed aquatic plants to low nutrient environments, phytoplankton, and productivity in oligotrophic lakes. Predicts urban impact on land-water systems through computer simulations based on mathematical models developed for describing hydrologic, biologic, and nutrient cycles in a man-modified lake basin. Assists research development in Indonesia.

★3279★ Center for Cave and Karst Studies
Western Kentucky Univ.
Dept. of Geography & Geology
Bowling Green, OH 42101
Phone: (502)745-5989
Contact: Dr. Nicholas Crawford, Dir.
Research Areas: Groundwater flow in karst regions and the problems of pollution, water supply, sinkhole flooding, sinkhole collapse, radon, and construction of highways, pipelines, and buildings on karst terrain.

★3280★ Center for Coastal and Environmental Studies
Rutgers Univ.
104 Doolittle Bldg.
Busch Campus
New Brunswick, NJ 08903
Phone: (201)932-3738
Fax: (201)932-5811
Contact: Dr. Norbert P. Psuty, Dir.
Research Areas: Marine sciences and coastal environmental inquiry, including studies on beach processes, sediments, barrier island processes, aquaculture, marshland productivity, recreational use of coastal zone, effects of thermal enrichment, sea level change, coastal zone management, food web analysis and benthic community studies, nonpoint source pollutants, urban runoff, and fate and effects of toxic contaminants in surface waters. Also studies upland ecology with special reference to the outer coastal plain, including nutrient cycling, ground and surface water, plant and animal ecology, and land use management. Works closely with state and community environmental agencies and distributes research results through its reports and publications. Assists in development of natural resource educational programs and contributes to graduate training in a wide variety of studies at the University. Special Resources: Four research vessels, a coastal research laboratory in New Brunswick, the Little Egg Inlet Marine Field Station near Tuckerton, and Pineland Field Research Station at Pemberton.

★3281★ Center for Coastal and Environmental Studies, Division of Water Resources
Rutgers Univ.
Doolittle Hall
New Brunswick, NJ 08903
Phone: (201)932-3609
Fax: (201)932-5811
Contact: Joan G. Ehrenfeld, Dir.
Research Areas: Water and other resources that affect water, including studies on urbanization and its effect upon water resources, urban runoff, non-point pollution sources, and fate and effects of toxic substances in water. Coordinates research and trains scientists in these fields and coordinates research on water resources within the state.

★3282★ Center for Computational Hydroscience and Engineering
University of Mississippi
University, MS 38677
Phone: (601)232-7788
Fax: (601)232-7796
Contact: Dr. Sam S.Y. Wang, Dir.
Research Areas: Basic and applied research in the areas of computational modeling and simulation of hydroscience and hydroengineering systems, including hydrodynamics, hydrology, hydraulics, sedimentation, water resources, environmental engineering, and computational methodologies. Develops computational simulation models of water flows and sediment transport on farms, in streams, rivers, reservoirs, and lakes, and along coastal regions. Conducts studies and engineering projects for governmental and private organizations. Special Resources: Supercomputers Cray XMP and Cyber 205; computer graphics display and animation equipment; and a database on hydrological and geomorphological data.

★3283★ Center for Conservation Biology
Stanford Univ.
Dept. of Biological Sciences
Stanford, CA 94305-5020
Phone: (415)723-5924
Fax: (415)723-5920
Contact: Prof. Paul R. Ehrlich, Pres.
Research Areas: Conservation biology, including studies in the areas of species, populations, habitat and ecosystem resources, restoration ecology, and endangered species management.

★3284★ Center for Crops Utilization Research
Iowa State Univ.
Dairy Industries Bldg.
Ames, IA 50011
Phone: (515)294-4365
Contact: Dr. Lawrence A. Johnson, Professor-In-Charge
Research Areas: Develops products and processes that will add value to and enhance the utilization of crops grown in the Midwest. Interests include replacing petrochemical-derived products with those derived from renewable agricultural products and channeling the application of biotechnology into the utilization of agricultural products. Conducts scale-up research, economic marketing and policy studies, and technology transfer to industry. Special Resources: Pilot plant facilities for wet processing, dry processing, fermentation, and biomaterials.

★3285★ Center for Design Research
University of California, Davis
Dept. of Environmental Design
Davis, CA 95616
Phone: (916)752-6223
Fax: (916)752-6363
Contact: Mark Francis, Dir.
Research Areas: Ecologically appropriate design (environmental design that aims at resource and nature conservation), socially responsible design (environmental design that emphasizes user needs and participation), and personal expression through design.

★3286★ Center for Dredging Studies
Texas A&M Univ.
Texas Engineering Experiment Sta.
College Station, TX 77843-3136
Phone: (409)845-4517
Contact: Dr. John B. Herbich, Dir.
Research Areas: Ocean engineering, including dredging technology, dredging equipment, cutterhead dredge design elements, open water disposal sites, effects of dredging on the environment (particularly generation of turbidity by cutterhead dredges), and evaluation of navigable depth concept. Special Resources: Dredge pump and slurry pipelines test loops.

★3287★ Center for Earth and Environmental Science
State Univ. Coll. at Plattsburgh
Plattsburgh, NY 12901
Phone: (518)564-2028
Fax: (518)564-7827
Contact: Dr. Malcolm Fairweather, Dir.
Research Areas: Earth and environmental science, especially environmental problems relating to northern New York and its Lake Champlain region, including studies in mapping science, acid rain, soil science, hydrology/water resources, geology, geography, remote sensing, applied sedimentology, mineral resources, petrology, resource management, land planning, and forest and systems ecology. Special Resources: Operates a satellite campus at William H. Miner Agricultural Research Institute devoted to regional environmental research problems and undergraduate education.

★3288★ Center for Electrochemical Systems and Hydrogen Research
Texas A&M Univ.
238 Wisenbaker, ERC
Texas Engineering Experiment Sta.
College Station, TX 77843-3577
Phone: (409)845-8281
Fax: (409)845-9287
Contact: Dr. John Appleby, Dir.
Research Areas: Hydrogen technologies and electrochemical energy storage and conversion studies. Activities include research on fuel cells, battery systems, co-production of electricity and hydrogen from coal, and oceanic disposal of waste carbon dioxide.

★3289★ Center for Energy and Environmental Studies
Princeton Univ.
Engineering Quadrangle
Princeton, NJ 08544
Phone: (609)258-5445
Fax: (609)258-3661
Contact: Prof. Robert H. Socolow, Dir.
Research Areas: Local, regional, national, and global studies of energy and environmental problems, including energy generation, conservation and utilization, nuclear policy alternatives, resource depletion, and arms control. Utilizes various multidisciplinary teams in research projects.

★3290★ Center for Energy and Environmental Studies
Carnegie Mellon Univ.
Schenley Park
Pittsburgh, PA 15213
Phone: (412)268-5897
Contact: Dr. Edward S. Rubin, Dir.
Research Areas: Fuel and energy conversion technology, environmental science and technology, and environmental systems and policy, including research and educational activities covering a broad range of interdisciplinary activities with emphasis on science, engineering, technology, and public policy interactions.

★3291★ Center for Energy and Environmental Studies (CEES)
Boston Univ.
675 Commonwealth Ave.
Boston, MA 02215
Phone: (617)353-3083
Fax: (617)353-5986
Contact: Dr. T.R. Lakshmanan, Dir.
Research Areas: Economic-energy interactions, modeling and policy analysis,

environmental effects of energy development, energy transport models, facility locations analysis, energy development in developing nations, models of sustainable development assessment in developing nations, global modeling of carbon emissions, hazardous waste disposal, environmental analysis, urban modeling, air quality studies, environmental health, risk assessment and management, remote sensing, water resources planning, impact of technical change, and regional economic analysis.

★3292★ Center for Energy and the Environment
University of Pennsylvania
127 Meyerson Hall
Philadelphia, pa 19104-6311
Phone: (215)898-7185
Contact: Dr. Mark Bernstein, Dir.
Research Areas: Multidisciplinary studies on technological, social, and managerial aspects of energy management, energy allocation, solar heating and cooling of buildings, photovoltaics, bioconversion, electrochemical energy conversion, fuel cells, thermal energy storage, power distribution networks, energy system modeling strategies for load management, implementation of energy conservation, analysis of passive solar systems, conversion of ocean thermal energy, and analysis of energy-environment policy.

★3293★ Center for Energy and Urban Policy Research
University of Delaware
College of Urban Affairs & Public Policy
Newark, NJ 19716
Phone: (302)451-8405
Fax: (302)292-3587
Contact: Dr. John M. Byrne, Dir.
Research Areas: Energy, environmental and urban policy issues, focusing on social, political, and economic dimensions of technology, resources, and use. Of particular interest are analyses of social choices that shape systems of energy production and use, technology and energy choice, utility regulatory policy, energy and environment, conservation and solar policies, energy implications of developing nations, and energy planning.

★3294★ Center for Energy Policy and Research
New York Inst. of Technology
Old Westbury, NY 11568
Phone: (516)686-7578
Fax: (516)626-2627
Contact: Gale Tenen Spak, Dir.
Research Areas: Energy conservation information, research, and dissemination, to assist public and private organizations in the practical utilizations of current knowledge in the energy field in order to help develop viable energy policies and alternative energy systems.

★3295★ Center for Energy Policy Research
Massachusetts Inst. of Technology
E40-437
Cambridge, MA 02139
Phone: (617)253-3551
Fax: (617)253-8013
Contact: David O. Wood, Dir.
Research Areas: Energy regulation, energy and the environment, energy and economic growth, domestic and international energy markets, energy investment, contracts, and financing.

★3296★ Center for Energy, Public Lands and Environmental Law
University of Utah
College of Law
Salt Lake City, UT 84112
Phone: (801)581-5880
Contact: Prof. Robert L. Schmid, Dir.
Research Areas: Energy, natural resource, and environmental law. Specialities of the staff include administrative law, public lands law, antitrust law, regulated industries, constitutional law, state and local government law, legal history, wildlife law, litigation on natural resources and environmental issues, property law, water law, and occupation health aspects of energy development.

★3297★ Center for Energy Research
Texas Tech Univ.
PO Box 4200
MS 3103
Lubbock, TX 79409
Phone: (806)742-3451
Fax: (806)742-1900
Contact: Ernst W. Kiesling, Dir.
Research Areas: Sponsors energy related research with the purpose of expanding its research base and serving the needs of energy users.

★3298★ Center for Energy Studies (CES)
Louisiana State Univ.
E. Fraternity Circle
Baton Rouge, LA 70803-0301
Phone: (504)388-4400
Fax: (504)388-4556
Contact: Robert H. Baumann, Exec. Dir.
Research Areas: Coordinates research in energy and environment, including enhanced gas recovery, enhanced oil recovery, combustion, surface sciences/catalysis, solar/photovoltaics, biomass conversion processes, polymers, conservation, and policy issues. Databases: Maintains monthly and annual Louisiana energy statistical databases, which include energy production, consumption, employment, prices, and related state revenues; CES Drilling Cost Database, which includes information on number of wells, total footage, and costs for wells by completion type, geographical area, and depth; the Oil and Gas Field Database, which includes a file of 22,000 records of geologic and engineering information on 3,500 oil and gas fields in the U.S. and a second file of 1,500 records of field production and drilling histories; and the Louisiana Energy Researchers Database, which identifies energy researchers in Louisiana.

★3299★ Center for Energy Studies
San Diego State Univ.
Dept. of Physics
San Diego, CA 92182
Phone: (619)594-6240
Fax: (619)594-5485
Contact: Dr. Alan Sweedler, Dir.
Research Areas: Energy modeling for local regions, economic analysis for energy systems, photovoltaic system design and installation, load management, and geothermal energy programs with Mexico and Brazil.

★3300★ Center for Engineering Geosciences
Texas A&M Univ.
College Station, TX 77843
Phone: (409)845-3224
Fax: (409)845-6162
Contact: Christopher C. Mathewson, Dir.
Research Areas: Engineering geology, engineering geophysics, site characterization, remote sensing, groundwater resources, groundwater contamination, seismic risk analyses, lignite mining and reclamation, environmental impact and assessment, urban planning, mineral exploration, and mine planning and design. Research is related to graduate teaching in the Departments of Geology, Geophysics, Geography, Meteorology, and Oceanography.

★3301★ Center for Environmental and Human Toxicology
University of Florida
Progress Center
One Progress Blvd., Box 17
Alachua, FL 32615
Phone: (904)462-3281
Contact: Dr. Raymond D. Harbison, Dir.
Research Areas: Environmental and human toxicology, including studies on the effects of polychlorinated biphenyls on human health.

★3302★ Center for Environmental Biotechnology
University of Tennessee at Knoxville
10515 Research Dr.
Ste. 200
Knoxville, TN 37932
Phone: (615)675-9450
Fax: (615)675-9456
Contact: Gary S. Sayler, Dir.
Research Areas: Hazardous materials management, biotechnology applications, biocorrosion, environmental biosensors, microbial biodegradation, systems analysis, and gene probe technology.

★3303★ Center for Environmental Education
Oklahoma State Univ.
206 Gunderson Hall
Stillwater, OK 74078
Phone: (405)744-7125
Fax: (405)744-7713
Contact: Dr. Ted J. Mills, Dir.
Research Areas: Develops programs and curriculum material in natural resource and environmental concepts and attitudes, particularly concerning water resources. Develops teacher environmental science education training models and environmental education curriculum materials for schools. Special Resources: Multiuser interactive computerized water resource management simulator; database on environmental education curricula.

★3304★ Center for Environmental, Energy and Science Education
Memphis State Univ.
Dept. of Curriculum & Instruction
College of Education
Rm. 415
Memphis, TN 38152
Phone: (901)678-2545
Fax: (901)678-4478
Contact: Ron Cleminson, Dir.
Research Areas: Environmental issues, including groundwater standards, energy conservation, and environmental quality.

★3305★ Center for Environmental Epidemiology
University of Pittsburgh
Graduate School of Public Health
Pittsburgh, PA 15261
Phone: (412)624-1559
Fax: (412)624-3013
Contact: Bruce W. Case M.D., Dir.
Research Areas: Multidisciplinary studies of environmental epidemiology, incorporating biological exposure assessment, disease registries, biostatistics, microbiology, and

occupational and environmental hygiene and health sciences.

★3306★ Center for Environmental Health Sciences
Massachusetts Inst. of Technology
Rm. E18-666
77 Massachusetts Ave.
Cambridge, MA 02139
Phone: (617)253-6220
Fax: (617)258-5424
Contact: William G. Thilly Sc.D., Dir.
Research Areas: Mutagens and carcinogens in fuel combustion, cooking processes, fungal contamination, and losses from hazardous waste sites. Studies include direct measurement of chemical and genetic change in humans. Develops ways to assess the importance of individual chemicals in causing human cancer or genetic defects and to identify alternative methods and utilization strategies that could mitigate health hazards. Special Resources: Maintains three core laboratories.

★3307★ Center for Environmental Management
Tufts Univ.
Curtis Hall
474 Boston Ave.
Medford, MA 02155
Phone: (617)381-3486
Fax: (617)381-3084
Contact: Dr. William R. Moomaw, Dir.
Research Areas: Problems of hazardous and solid wastes and toxic substances. Research organized into three areas: 1) health effects, including evaluation of biological markers as indicators of absorbed toxicant dose and related human health risk, strategies to decrease the bioavailability of toxicants and measure and reduce body burden in exposed individuals, and evaluation of biological sentinels as indicators of toxicants; 2) risk assessment and management, including investigating methods of assessing, managing, and reducing environmental risks by concentrating on the roles of risk communication, public participation in policymaking, and private sector environmental management; 3) pollution prevention, including preventing the generation of pollutants by developing technologies, strategies, and policies to minimize or eliminate the production of toxic and solid wastes.

★3308★ Center for Environmental Research
Cornell Univ.
470 Hollister Hall
Ithaca, NY 14853-3501
Phone: (607)255-7535
Fax: (607)255-5945
Contact: Gilbert Levine, Dir.
Research Areas: Composed of seven independently-governed environmental programs: Biological Resources Program, focusing on wetland conservation and management, habitat protection, and sustainable development; Cornell Laboratory for Environmental Applications of Remote Sensing (CLEARS), focusing on remote sensing, geographic information systems, and resource inventory; Cornell Waste Management Institute, focusing on waste reduction, recycling, risk management and public policy, waste treatment and disposal through incineration, digestion, and landfilling; Ecosystem Research Center, focusing on ecosystem modeling, effects of air pollutants on forests and lakes, effects of drilling on coastal plant communities, and wetlands assessment; Environmental Policy Program, focusing on ocean incineration, hazardous waste management, and risk assessment; Global Environment Program, focusing on changes in the global environment from human activities; and national and regional effects of environmental stresses such as ozone depletion and the greenhouse effect; and the NYS Water Resources Institute, focusing on agricultural chemicals and groundwater, non-agricultural contaminant sources, mathematical models for evaluating the mobility and persistence of contaminants, water supplies, surface waters and runoff, and watershed management.

★3309★ Center for Environmental Research
IIT Research Institute
10 W. 35th St.
Chicago, IL 60616
Phone: (312)567-4250
Fax: (312)567-4577
Contact: Dr. Demetrios Moschandreas, Dir.
Research Areas: Performs basic, applied, and policy research on hazardous waste management. Specific study areas include: 1) development of treatment and management techniques, 2) toxic and odorous air emissions, 3) development and use of analytical methods, 4) toxicology, 5) ground water, 6) evaluation of innovative technologies, 7) environmental assessment, 8) asbestos abatement, and 9) risk assessment and management. Special Resources: Maintains the Toxic Materials Laboratories. Databases: Maintains a hazardous waste management computer bulletin board (see above).

★3310★ Center for Environmental Research
c/o Water Utility
PO Box 1088
Austin, TX 78767
Phone: (512)322-2779
Contact: Andrew P. Covar, Dir.
Research Areas: Environmental problems affecting municipalities, including studies of innovative and alternative approaches to wastewater treatment, solid waste management, water conservation, treated wastewater reuse, noise pollution, soil pollution, air pollution, and nonpoint source pollution. Special Resources: Maintains a research laboratory.

★3311★ Center for Environmental Research Education (CERE)
State Univ. Coll. at Buffalo
Upton Hall, Rm. 314
1300 Elmwood Ave.
Buffalo, NY 14222-1095
Phone: (716)878-6018
Contact: Dr. Charles Beasley, Contact
Research Areas: Biology, hydrology, chemistry, and environmental education, including: zebra mussel infestation and remediation; Buffalo River contamination; fish behavior, physiology, and ecology; water levels and flows; and environmental carcinogens. Special Resources: Maintains an aquatic field station, and a 42-foot research vessel to facilitate water and sediment sampling, fish tagging, and the study of toxic accumulations in lake fish.

★3312★ Center for Environmental Sciences (CES)
University of Colorado-Denver
1200 Larimer St.
Denver, CO 80204
Phone: (303)556-4277
Fax: (303)556-4822
Contact: Dr. Herman Sievering, Dir.
Research Areas: Effects of energy production on health and the environment, including studies on the relationship between coal burning and air and water pollution. Also studies biophysicochemical cycles, especially the exchange of pollutants at air/land and air/water interfaces.

★3313★ Center for Environmental Studies
Arizona State Univ.
Tempe, 85287-1201
Phone: (602)965-2975
Fax: (602)965-8087
Contact: Dr. Duncan T. Patten, Dir.
Research Areas: Ecology, land use, resources, and environmental studies, including fish, wildlife, and ecological research on lower Colorado basin, ecological impacts of man on desert systems, reclamation, hazard and risk management, policy and social behavioral research, water quality, and energy. Coordinates environmental research and instructional programs throughout the University. Special Resources: Operates Sierra Ancha Research Station with room and board accommodations for groups of 40 to 50 people.

★3314★ Center for Environmental Studies
Williams Coll.
Kellogg House
Williamstown, MA 01267
Phone: (413)597-2346
Fax: (413)458-2158
Contact: Dr. Benjamin W. Labaree, Dir.
Research Areas: Problems of resource planning, historical land use, and local land development issues in economics, transportation planning, ecological studies, pollution issues in both urban and rural regions of the nation, and forest, stream, and wetlands ecology. Research emphasizes a local county and regional orientation. Special Resources: Utilizes 2,500 acres of land in Hopkins Forest for research and educational use.

★3315★ Center for Environmental Studies
University of Akron
302 Buchtel Ave.
Akron, OH 44325
Phone: (216)375-7991
Contact: Dr. Jim L. Jackson, Dir.
Research Areas: Waste disposal and environmental problems, including brine contamination of groundwater, environmental geology, fluvial systems, mass movement, and soils. Studies include gas chromatography/mass spectrometry, atomic absorption analyses of water from/near Superfund sites, water contamination studies, and biological indicators of water quality.

★3316★ Center for Environmental Studies
California State University, Bakersfield
9001 Stockdale Hwy.
Bakersfield, CA 93311-1099
Phone: (805)664-3167
Contact: Dr. Ted D. Murphy, Dir.
Research Areas: Environmental biology, ecology, air pollution, meteorology, and soil science, primarily related to educational program of the College in those areas. Special Resources: 40-acre Environmental Study Area on campus. Operates Facility for Animal Care and Treatment (FACT), a program dedicated to the conservation of wildlife through educational activities and through the rehabilitation of non-game species of native animals.

★3317★ Center for Environmental Studies
Brown Univ.
Box 1943
Providence, RI 02912
Phone: (401)863-3449

Fax: (401)863-3503
Contact: Dr. Harold Ward, Dir.
Research Areas: Environmental studies, with special focus on Narragansett Bay, solid waste management in Rhode Island, hazardous waste reduction, and energy conservation and recycling at the University.

★3318★ Center for Environmental Studies
Bemidji State Univ.
Bemidji, MN 56601
Phone: (218)755-2910
Fax: (218)755-4048
Contact: Steven A. Spigarelli, Dir.
Research Areas: Conducts laboratory and field exploratory research on environmental matters, including technology for small-scale chemical utilization of peat, environmental impact assessment, microbial degradation of oil spills, and environmental toxicology.

★3319★ Center for Environmental Study
Grand Rapids Junior Coll.
143 Bostwick NE
Grand Rapids, MI 49503
Phone: (616)771-3935
Fax: (616)771-3907
Contact: Kay T. Dodge Ph.D., Exec. Dir.
Research Areas: Environment preservation, focusing on education, communication, and research. Operates a conservation program called Tree Amigos.

★3320★ Center for Environmental Toxicology
Michigan State Univ.
C231 Holden Hall
East Lansing, MI 48824
Phone: (517)353-6469
Fax: (517)335-4603
Contact: Lawrence J. Fischer Ph.D., Dir.
Research Areas: Analytical toxicology, behavioral toxicology, biochemical toxicology, botany and plant pathology, carcinogenesis, ecotoxicology, environmental law, fate of chemicals in the environment, food toxicology, genetic toxicology, human epidemiology, risk/benefit assessment and regulatory decision making, terrestrial toxicology, and hazardous waste management.

★3321★ Center for Exploration of Geoscience Computing
Colorado School of Mines
Dept. of Geology & Geological Engineering
1500 Illinois
Golden, CO 80523
Phone: (303)273-3978
Contact: Dr. Samuel Adams, Dir.
Research Areas: Develops new methods to explore oil and natural gas deposits, map geological hazards, and reduce national waste disposal using computer technology. Activities include subsurface imaging of the earth and developing neural networks and sedimentary basin fluid flow prediction models to aid resource exploration. Computers: Network of 31 RISC System/6000s.

★3322★ Center for Field Biology
Austin Peay State Univ.
PO Box 4718
Clarksville, TN 37044
Phone: (615)648-7019
Contact: Dr. Benjamin Stone, Dir.
Research Areas: Nonpoint source water pollution, including agricultural and logging industry runoff, water pollutant monitoring, and new monitoring strategies.

★3323★ Center for Global Change
University of Maryland
Executive Bldg., Ste. 401
7100 Baltimore Ave.
College Park, MD 20740
Phone: (301)403-4165
Fax: (301)454-0954
Contact: Alan Miller, Exec. Dir.
Research Areas: Identifies and implements solutions for changes in the earth's atmosphere, especially ozone depletion and global warming. Develops technologies and policy strategies to reduce pollution and support other societal goals, particularly economic growth. Conducts studies on legal and institutional issues, economic policy, and science policy. Performs international assessments of sea level rise.

★3324★ Center for Global Change Science
Massachusetts Inst. of Technology
Room 54-1312
Cambridge, MA 02139
Phone: (617)253-4902
Fax: (617)253-0354
Contact: Dr. Ronald G. Prinn, Dir.
Research Areas: Mechanisms controlling the environmental global change. Specific studies within this framework include: convection and cloud formation, oceanic circulation and ocean-atmosphere coupling, land surface hydrology and hydology-vegetation coupling, biogeochemistry of greenhouse gases, and upper atmosphere chemistry and circulation. Seeks to accurately predict environmental changes over the next century and develop general circulation climate prediction models.

★3325★ Center for Global Change Science
Massachusetts Institute of Tecchnology
Center for Meteorology and Physical Oceanography
Cambridge, MA 02139
Contact: Peter H. Stone, Director

★3326★ Center for Global Environmental Studies
Bldg. 1000, PO Box 2008,
Mail Stop 6335
Oak Ridge, TN 37831
Phone: (615)574-0390
Contact: Robert I. Van Hook, Dir.
Research Areas: Center's goals are: 1) to improve understanding of global-scale workings of environments in air, land, and water; 2) to develop capabilities to anticipate long-term, large-scale consequences of human actions on biosphere; and 3) to identify appropiate options for technological and societal responses. Topics of study include climate change, ozone depletion, globally distributed contaminants, erosion and desertification, water, resource depletion, biodiversity, and deforestation.

★3327★ Center for Global Environmental Technologies
University of New Mexico
Albuquerque, NM 87131-1376
Phone: (505)272-7252
Fax: (505)272-7203
Contact: Robert E. Tapscott Ph.D., Dir.
Research Areas: Interdisciplinary research in environmental problems, including stratospheric ozone depletion, global warming, acid rain, and protection of the global commons. Specific projects include assessment of the impact of international environmental treaties, development of new engineering approaches to reduce reliance on halons, recycling/recovery of chemicals restricted by international relations, assessment of alternative cleaning technologies, and development of alternatives to ozone-depleting technologies. Databases: Alternative technologies to address global problems.

★3328★ Center for Ground Water Management
Wright State Univ.
056 Library
Dayton, OH 45435
Phone: (513)873-3648
Fax: (513)873-4106
Contact: Prof. Ronald Schmidt, Dir.
Research Areas: Availability, protection, and management of groundwater.

★3329★ Center for Hazardous Materials Research
Univ. of Pittsburgh Applied Research Center
320 William Pitt Way
Pittsburgh, PA 15238
Phone: (412)826-5320
Fax: (412)826-5552
Contact: Edgar Berkey Ph.D., Pres.
Research Areas: Use and disposition of hazardous materials and waste, including treatment, processing, and disposal, health and environmental effects, and health and safety training for hazardous waste workers and emergency response personnel.

★3330★ Center for Hazardous Substance Research
Kansas State Univ.
Durland Hall 112
Manhattan, KS 66506
Phone: (913)532-5584
Fax: (913)532-7810
Contact: Dr. Larry E. Erickson, Dir.
Research Areas: Administers and stimulates interdisciplinary research in removing, processing, and storing hazardous materials and waste. Studies focus on container-materials for the storage of toxic and nuclear wastes, methods for utilizing the ash and particulates from coal-fired power plants, processes for degrading toxic chemicals, and systems for utilizing or processing sewage/plant residue. Identifies combustion methods to reduce the potential for acid rain. Activities emphasize preserving the quality of ground and drinking water.

★3331★ Center for Hazardous Waste Remediation Research
University of Idaho
Food Research Center 202
Moscow, ID 83843
Phone: (208)885-6580
Fax: (208)885-5741
Contact: Dr. Ronald L. Crawford, Codirector
Research Areas: Application of biotechnology and chemical technology to solving the problems of soils and waters contaminated by hazardous chemicals. Research is organized into three areas. Biological Remediation research includes uses of aerobic or anaerobic microbial consortia for in situ remediation of chemical contamination of soils and waters, fate and effects of genetically engineered microorganisms in the environment, uses of immobilized and/or stabilized bacteria for remediation of chemical contaminants, deep groundwater microbiology, bioreactor design, and applications of recombinant DNA technology to bioremediation problems. Geochemical Remediation research concerns technology to remove metals and other substances from water, mining wastes, and contaminated ground. The research includes metal extraction directly from rock, both in situ

and after mining, transport processes, and related geochemistry. Emphasis is placed on contaminant interactions with earth materials and groundwater. Characterization of Hazardous Waste Sites research includes microbial ecology of waste sites, Hydrogeology of aquifers, groundwater flow and water infiltration processes, groundwater hydraulics, geochemistry investigations, soil chemistry and physics, and development of instrumentation.

★3332★ Center for Human Systems
University of Wisconsin-Madison
1042 WARF Bldg.
610 Walnut St.
Madison, WI 53705
Phone: (608)262-9937
Fax: (608)262-0014
Contact: Prof. Marty S. Kanarek, Dir.
Research Areas: Human interactions with environment, focusing on pollution and health, global sustainability, and risk assessment and management.

★3333★ Center for Indoor Air Research
1099 Winterson Rd., Ste. 280
Linthicum, MD 21090
Phone: (301)684-3777
Fax: (301)684-3729
Contact: Max Eisenberg Ph.D., Exec. Dir.
Research Areas: Sponsors, supports, and monitors individual investigators' research on the chemistry, physics, health consequences, or psychosocial factors of environmental tobacco smoke (ETS), chemical contaminants from organic and inorganic sources, and biological agents, including aeroallegens and aeropathogens. ETS research focuses on characterizing the distribution of various components between vapor and particulate phases of ETS, studying the chemistry of ETS components during aging, investigating the effects of air cleaning systems on ETS, and developing animal and in vitro models to study the effects of ETS on cardiovascular function, morphometry of the lung, pulmonary function, immune and respiratory defense systems, and pre-natal and perinatal development. Research on organic and inorganic chemical contaminants emphasize investigating the effects of long-term steady exposures to low levels of oxidants (such as ozone) to determine overall adverse health effects, and evaluating methods to elucidate interactions of low-level complex exposures. Research on biological agents focuses on human diseases in the form of immunological disorders or respiratory infections. Activities emphasize standardizing indoor air sampling methods of moisture levels and environmental temperatures provided by heating and air conditioning systems and humidifiers to accurately study aeropathogens that induce allergenic responses, including bacteria, viruses, fungal spores, algae, arthropod fragments and dropping, and dander from animals and humans. Multidisciplinary studies focus on the role of individual, perceptual, occupational, and psychosocial factors in mediating the effects of indoor air quality on health and developing improved self-reporting measures and interview techniques to assess health problems and contributing factors affecting building occupants. Also develops experimental protocols for measuring emission rates of improved indoor sources such as presswood, carpet, and combustion sources.

★3334★ Center for Infrastructure Research
University of Nebraska-Lincoln
Omaha, NE 68182-0461
Phone: (402)554-2980
Contact: Maher K. Tadros Ph.D., Interim Dir.
Research Areas: Transportation, water supply, wastewater collection and treatment, solid and hazardous waste management, and construction technologies, procedures, policies, and systems. Areas of emphasis include risk assessment applied to hazardous waste sites.

★3335★ Center for Integrative Studies
State Univ. of New York at Buffalo
School of Architecture & Planning
333 Hayes Hall
Buffalo, NY 14214
Phone: (716)831-3727
Contact: Prof. Magda Cordell McHale, Dir.
Research Areas: Future international consequences for the human environment of social, cultural, and technological trends and changes. Typical project topics have dealt with children in world terms, women in world terms, future of the past, information communication, and new perspectives on changing relationships for Canada, Mexico, and U.S.

★3336★ Center for International Development Research
Duke Univ.
Institute of Policy Studies
4875 Duke Sta.
Durham, NC 27706
Phone: (919)684-6360
Fax: (919)684-2861
Contact: Dr. William Ascher, Codirector
Research Areas: Public policy of the environment, natural resource management, and sustainable economic development in Central America. Databases: State oil and mining enterprises.

★3337★ Center for International Food and Agricultural Policy
University of Minnesota
332 Classroom Office Bldg.
1994 Buford Ave.
St. Paul, MN 55108
Phone: (612)625-9208
Fax: (612)625-6245
Contact: Carlisle Ford Runge, Dir.
Research Areas: Food, agricultural, and resources issues and policies of developed and developing countries, including: economics of agricultural research and science and technology policies relating to food, agriculture, and forestry; and natural resource and environmental policies on topics including irrigation and water management, farming systems and biological nitrogen fixation, soil erosion, watershed management, deforestation and the environmental effects of export-oriented crop production, forestry for sustainable development, and management of international common-property resources.

★3338★ Center for International Studies
Massachusetts Inst. of Technology
E38-648
Cambridge, MA 02139
Phone: (617)253-8093
Contact: Dr. Myron Weiner, Dir.
Research Areas: International policy questions on technology, including studies on arms control and defense policy, energy, U.S.-Japanese and U.S.-Chinese relations in regard to trade and technology, international environment issues, risk assessment, toxic chemicals, Soviet science and technology, development issues, human migration, and international business and economy. Special Resources: Maintains a collection of Russian language materials on Soviet defense.

★3339★ Center for Lake Erie Area Research (CLEAR)
Ohio State Univ.
1541 Research Center
1314 Kinnear Rd.
Columbus, OH 43212-1194
Phone: (614)292-8949
Fax: (614)292-4315
Contact: Dr. Jeffrey M. Reutter, Dir.
Research Areas: Scientific, technological, and socioeconomic problems associated with Lake Erie, including interdisciplinary studies of nuclear power plants, fish parasites, estuaries and related mineral resources, mercury contamination, beach erosion, instrumentation, water quality improvement, and environmental systems modeling. Coordinates and expands programs of interdisciplinary research and technical services on these problems.

★3340★ Center for Land Information Studies
University of Wisconsin-Madison
1042 WARF Office Bldg.
610 Walnut St.
Madison, WI 53705
Phone: (608)262-9937
Contact: Prof. James C. Clapp, Dir.
Research Areas: Mechanisms for storing, retrieving, and exchanging geographic information for the development of land information system for uses ranging from real-estate and tax records to maps of land use and land cover. Also analyzes environmental problems related to geographic aspects of man-environment systems, especially land and water interactions, including studies of economic, climatological, and eutrophic assessments of Great Lakes water quality or quantity, the relationships between climatic variation topography and geology in influencing sediment storage and delivery of streams, and the development of multipurpose land information and cadastral systems.

★3341★ Center for Marine Conservation
1725 DeSales NW, Ste. 500
Washington, DC 20036
Phone: (202)429-5609
Contact: Roger E. McManus, Pres.
Research Areas: Conducts and supports policy oriented research focused primarily on conservation of whales, seals, sea turtles, seabirds, marine habitat, and other endangered species, including commercial utilization of seal and whale populations, and utilization and biology of sea turtles.

★3342★ Center for Marine Science
University of Southern Mississippi
John C. Stennis Space Center
Stennis Space Center, MS 39529
Phone: (601)688-3177
Fax: (601)688-1121
Contact: Dr. George A. Knauer, Dir.
Research Areas: Global geochemical cycling of major elements and particulate organic matter in the ocean, biological and chemical variability around ocean fronts, cycling of trace metals in the marine environment, and the production and fate of marine snow. Special Resources: Maintains instrumentation for analysis of trace metal concentrations, plant pigments, particulate organic carbon and nitrogen, primary production, and marine snow concentration and particle size spectra.

★3343★ Center for Natural Resource Policy and Management
University of Minnesota
110 Green Hall
1530 N. Cleveland Ave.
St. Paul, MN 55108
Phone: (612)624-9796
Fax: (612)625-5212
Contact: Dr. James Perry, Dir.
Research Areas: Watershed management, forestry, forest water quality, and policy and economic analysis of natural resource management decisions. Evaluates management alternatives, studies technical and sociocultural management schemes, and investigates methods of quantitative decision analyses, including database management and development of expert systems.

★3344★ Center for Natural Resources
University of Florida
1066 McCarty Hall
Gainesville, FL 32611
Phone: (904)392-7622
Fax: (904)392-3462
Contact: Dr. Joseph C. Joyce, Dir.
Research Areas: Waste management, biological and systems technology for integrated pest management, ecological chemistry (including non-point source pollution, pesticide movement, atmospheric pollution, toxicants and animal/plant health), resource inventory and assessment, water conservation, ecology and natural ecosystems, energy conservation and production, disturbed land reclamation/pollution abatement, groundwater and surface water quality, water management, water policy, agricultural/urban interface and effects on water and other natural resources. Activities also emphasize assessing and enhancing Florida's natural resources. Administers and coordinates state and federal grant programs and conducts energy programs within the Institute of Food and Agricultural Sciences ((IFAS) at the University of Florida and Florida Cooperative Extension Service. Coordinates all water-related research and extension programs within IFAS.

★3345★ Center for Neighborhood Technology
2125 W. N. Ave.
Chicago, IL 60647
Phone: (312)278-4800
Contact: Scott Bernstein, Pres.
Research Areas: Manages and supports programs in energy efficiency and least-cost planning; the environment, including solid waste recycling and industrial pre-treatment and source reduction; housing, including cooperative forms of ownership and land trust mechanisms; economics, including job retention and job creation through environmental improvement; and socially responsible investment by foundations and corporations. Mission is to identify, demonstrate, and promote affordable and sustainable strategies for city residents to meet needs for food, housing, energy, jobs, and a healthy environment.

★3346★ Center for Northern Studies
Wolcott, VT 05680
Phone: (802)888-4331
Contact: Dr. Steven B. Young, Dir.
Research Areas: Composition, interaction, and history of polar ecosystems (with special reference to the Bering land bridge), Canadian high arctic archeology, ethnohistory and historical demography of north Baffin Island, management of marine resources (especially commercial fisheries), alternative structures of property rights, northern resource conflicts, legal statutes of arctic sea ice, response of plants to snowcover and extreme cold, impact of human use on high altitude vegetation, and population trends and kinship structures in Inuit communities of the eastern Canadian arctic. Other research projects include a study of the impact of the antisealing movement on the economic viability and cultural integrity of Inuit communities in arctic Canada, disturbance ecology in subarctic muskeg, Quaternary studies in the North Atlantic, contribution of wildlife harvest products to rural Vermont household economies, and compilation of an Arctic field guide. Special Resources: Maintains an herbarium with approximately 10,000 specimens and manages 300 acres of land, which provides field resources for research and study.

★3347★ Center for Plant Conservation
125 Arborway
Jamaica Plain, MA 02130-3520
Phone: (617)524-6988
Contact: Donald A. Falk, Exec. Dir.
Research Areas: Coordinates efforts of member organizations to protect, cultivate, and study the more than 3,000 rare and endangered plants native to the U.S, only ten percent of which are protected by law. The Center's primary task is development of the National Collection of Endangered Plants, a network of live plant collections facilitating research, seed collection, and plant propagation and reintroduction. Special Resources: Operates a seed storage bank in cooperation with the Agricultural Research Service of the USDA. Databases: 17 major datafiles, the largest of which contains 366 fields of information on over 7,000 kinds of plants.

★3348★ Center for Plastics Recycling Research
Rutgers Univ.
Bldg. 3529, Busch Campus
PO Box 1179
Piscataway, NJ 08855-1179
Phone: (908)932-3683
Fax: (908)932-5636
Contact: Jack Wenzel, Dir.
Research Areas: Collection, reclamation, and reprocessing of plastic materials. Studies focus on process design and operating parameters, including process improvements, product purity, and economics in plastics recycling pilot plants; process simplification, such as washing technology; quality assurance for plastics recycling; reclamation, reprocessing, and reutilization of plastics, alone and in combination with other plastic and nonplastic materials; selective separation of polyvinyl chloride from polyethylene in a bottle recycle stream; recycling of high density polyethylene milk bottles; environmental impact disposal of plastics in municipal solid waste; and field trials of both electrostatic and electromagnetic separation methods for removing aluminum from reclaimed plastics.

★3349★ Center for Public Health Studies
Portland State Univ.
PO Box 751
Portland, OR 97207
Phone: (503)725-3473
Fax: (503)725-4882
Contact: Dr. David A. Dunnette, Dir.
Research Areas: Public health, including studies of environmental and occupational disease, with emphasis on hazard assessment and control. Cancer prevention research specializing in strategies for disseminating screening modalities.

★3350★ Center for Public Interest Research
One Savoy Ct.
Lansing, MI 48933
Phone: (517)487-6001
Contact: Donald J. Rounds, Exec. Dir.
Research Areas: Studies groundwater contamination, community development and organization, and airborne pollutants.

★3351★ Center for Quantitative Science in Forestry, Fisheries and Wildlife
University of Washington
3737 15th Ave. NE, HR-20
Seattle, WA 98195
Phone: (206)543-1191
Fax: (206)534-6263
Contact: E. David Ford, Dir.
Research Areas: Model building in ecology and resource management problems, including development of mathematical models for description and management of terrestrial and aquatic ecosystems, risk assessment, contaminant effects, aquaculture, population dynamics, community ecology, systems ecology, and physiological ecology.

★3352★ Center for Research and Technology Development
1825 K St., NW
Washington, DC 20006-1202
Phone: (202)785-3756
Contact: Dr. Howard Clark, Dir.
Research Areas: Determines the technical, environmental, managerial, and economic feasibility of vitrifying residue from different sources, including fly-ash or a combination of fly-ash and grate. Test samples of residue from municipal waste combustion facilities.

★3353★ Center for Research in Water Resources
University of Texas at Austin
Balcones Research Center, Bldg. 119
Austin, TX 78712
Phone: (512)471-3131
Fax: (512)471-0072
Contact: Dr. Randall J. Charbeneau, Dir.
Research Areas: Stimulates and coordinates interdisciplinary research and training at the University in water resources, including water quality, water resources planning and management, policy issues, water law, financing alternatives, safe reuse of water, water and economics, waste disposal, groundwater management, coastal zone needs, and water conservation. Special Resources: Indoor model river.

★3354★ Center for Research on Energy Alternatives
Florida Inst. of Technology
150 W. Univ. Blvd.
Melbourne, FL 32901
Phone: (407)768-8000
Fax: (407)984-8461
Contact: Dr. Ronald G. Barile, Dir.
Research Areas: Computer simulation of energy systems, groundwater-coupled energy systems, photochemical production of hydrogen, energy storage in hydrides, biomass-derived fuel extenders, and enthalpy storage and moisture handling in buildings in warm, moist climates. Seepage and solid waste degradation.

★3355★ Center for Resource and Environmental Policy
Vanderbilt Univ.
1208 18th Ave. S.
Nashville, TN 37212
Phone: (615)322-8505
Fax: (615)322-8081
Contact: Clifford S. Russell, Dir.
Research Areas: Issues related to pollution control, especially pollution monitoring and law enforcement and the management of hazardous wastes.

★3356★ Center for Resource Policy Studies
University of Wisconsin-Madison
240 Agricultural Hall
Madison, WI 53706
Phone: (608)262-6968
Contact: Thomas A. Heberlein, Dir.
Research Areas: Natural resources and economic aspects of policy, primarily social science and economic studies on a variety of natural resource topics.

★3357★ Center for Restoration Ecology
University of Wisconsin-Madison
Arboretum
1207 Seminole Hwy.
Madison, WI 53711
Phone: (608)263-7889
Contact: Evelyn Howell, Dir.
Research Areas: Restoration of disturbed ecological communities and restoration as a technique for basic ecological research. Projects include the restoration of aboriginal communities of the Caribbean and Bahama islands and restoration of forest, prairie, and wetland communities of the upper midwest. Utilizes the University's Arboretum.

★3358★ Center for Risk Management
Resources for the future
1616 P St., NW
Washington, DC 20036
Phone: (202)328-5000
Fax: (202)265-8069
Research Areas: Health and environmental risk management in modern society, focusing on environmental threats related to air and water pollutants, pesticides, toxic substances, hazardous wastes, and climate modification. Studies include uncertainties in environmental health risk assessments, level of food-chain contamination caused by incinerator-released chemicals, public acceptance of regulatory programs, sheltering during chemical release emergencies, and use of information resulting from ambient environmental monitors.

★3359★ Center for River Studies
Memphis State Univ.
104 Engineering Science Bldg.
Memphis, TN 38152
Phone: (901)678-3275
Fax: (901)678-4180
Contact: Marvin L. Jacobs P.E., Dir.
Research Areas: Rivers and alluvial valleys, including studies of streams and nonpoint source agricultural pollution.

★3360★ Center for Short-Lived Phenomena
PO Box 199
Harvard Sq. Sta.
Cambridge, MA 02238
Phone: (617)492-3310
Fax: (617)492-3312
Contact: Richard Golob, Dir.
Research Areas: Environmental sciences, pollution control, marine pollution, hazardous waste management, and natural disasters.

★3361★ Center for Statistical Ecology and Environmental Statistics
Pennsylvania State Univ.
Dept. of Statistics
303 Pond Laboratory
University Park, PA 16802
Phone: (814)865-9442
Contact: Ganapati P. Patil Ph.D., Dir.
Research Areas: Statistical ecology, environmental statistics, and quantitative risk analysis. Emphasis is on mathematical statistics, statistical methodology, and data interpretation for future use. Focus is on improving the quantification and communication of man's impact on the environment with special attention to renewable resources and their habitats as well as statistical investigations of the impact of the environment on man. Specific interests include hazardous waste site characterization and remediation statistics, spatial statistics, composite sampling, encountered data analysis, and ecotoxicological statistics.

★3362★ Center for Study of Marine Policy
University of Delaware
Newark, DE 19711
Phone: (302)451-8086
Contact: Prof. Biliana Cicin-Sain, Codirector
Research Areas: U.S. national security, American merchant marine, living resources of the sea, mineral and energy resources of seabed, and means of improving marine environment.

★3363★ Center for Sustainable Agriculture
University of Minnesota
411 Borlaug Hall
1991 Buford Circle
St. Paul, MN 55108
Phone: (612)625-0220
Fax: (612)625-1268
Contact: Dr. Kent Crookston, Dir.
Research Areas: Sustainable agriculture.

★3364★ Center for Sustainable Agriculture
PO Box 1300
Colfax, CA 95713
Phone: (916)346-2777
Contact: David Katz, Dir.
Research Areas: Small farm technology, including studies of land, food, and water pollution. Special Resources: Maintains an 80-acre research site.

★3365★ Center for Technology, Environment, and Development (CENTED)
Clark Univ.
16 Claremont St.
Worcester, MA 01610
Phone: (508)751-4606
Fax: (508)751-4600
Contact: Samuel Ratick, Dir.
Research Areas: Risk analysis, global environmental change, environment and development, and technological hazards. Databases: Cover radioactive waste, global change, and government hearings.

★3366★ Center for the Biology of Natural Systems
Queens Coll. of City Univ. of New York
Flushing, NY 11367
Phone: (718)670-4180
Contact: Dr. Barry Commoner, Dir.
Research Areas: Interdisciplinary investigations into problems generated by development of modern production technologies, environmental degradation, and intensified use of energy and other resources, including problems of environmental health and health-related problems of the environment, studies on nitrogen cycle, transport of nutrients and pesticides from croplands to surface waters, refinement of a new methodology to permit detection of carcinogenic chemicals in environmental samples, resource-conserving agricultural production methods, problems related to municipal solid waste disposal and development of alternative methods of disposal, and an analysis of economic and resource impact of readjusting production in petrochemical industry.

★3367★ Center for the Environment
Cornell Univ.
Hollister Hall
Ithaca, NY 14853
Phone: (607)255-7535
Contact: Dr. Robert Barker, Dir.
Climate modeling, indoor air pollution, acid rain, solid waste, environmental law, environmental policy, and environmental decision-making by consumers.

★3368★ Center for the Study of Earth from Space
University of Colorado-Boulder
CB 449
Boulder, CO 80309-0449
Phone: (303)492-5086
Contact: Dr. Alexander Goetz, Dir.
Research Areas: Global geosciences, especially use of satellite observations to investigate global change. Projects emphasize land and land-atmosphere interactions and include studies of the atmosphere, vegetation, mineralogical mapping, soils, and geological and ecological applications of imaging spectrometry. Activities include collaborating with the Environmental Protection Agency to use imaging spectrometry to measure the stress that trees are subjected to due to ozone in air pollution and developing a high-resolution imaging spectrometer (HIRIS) for deployment on NASA's Polar-Orbiting Space Platform in 1998.

★3369★ Center for Theoretical Studies
University of Miami
PO Box 249055
Coral Gables, FL 33124-5510
Phone: (305)284-4455
Fax: (305)284-4456
Contact: Prof. Behram N. Kursunoglu, Dir.
Research Areas: Theoretical natural sciences and history and philosophy of science, including studies on the global problem of energy. Provides research facilities and training for postdoctoral fellows.

★3370★ Center for Tropical Agriculture
University of Florida
3028 McCarty Hall
Gainesville, FL 32611
Phone: (904)392-1965
Fax: (904)392-7127
Contact: Dr. Hugh L. Popenoe, Dir.
Research Areas: Coordinates international research activities of Institute staff in the areas of integrated pest management, animal health and nutrition, biological nitrogen fixation, tropical soils, farming systems research and extension, agroforestry, sustainable agricultural systems, agricultural research and extension management, and biosphere reserve development and management.

★3371★ Center for Urban and Regional Studies
University of North Carolina at Chapel Hill
Campus Box 3410
Hickerson House
Chapel Hill, NC 27599-3410
Phone: (919)962-3074
Fax: (919)962-2518
Contact: Jonathan B. Howes, Dir.
Research Areas: City and regional planning, including studies on management of natural and man-made hazards, land use management in reservoir and water supply watershed areas, coastal zone management, and relationships of urban planning and development control systems with environmental quality goals.

★3372★ Center for Values and Social Policy
University of Colorado-Boulder
CB 232
Boulder, CO 80309-0232
Phone: (303)492-6364
Fax: (303)492-5105
Contact: Dr. Dale Jamieson, Dir.
Research Areas: Values and social policy, particularly environmental policy and science and technology policy. Promotes interaction among philosophers, academics, and decision makers in business and government.

★3373★ Center for Waste Minimization and Management
Dept. of Chem. Eng.
North Carolina State Univ.
PO Box 7905
Raleigh, NC 27695-7905
Phone: (919)737-2325
Fax: (919)737-3465
Contact: Michael R. Overcash, Dir.
Research Areas: Waste minimization and management, including pollution prevention, process improvement, material substitution, theoretical base for waste reduction, recycling and reuse, and manufactured product quality. Maintains research divisions for chemical engineering, wood and paper science, hazardous waste, and environmental studies.

★3374★ Center for Waste Reduction Technologies
American Institute of Chemical Engineers
345 E. 47th St.
New York, NY 10017
Phone: (212)705-7407
Contact: Dr. Larry Ross, Dir.
Research Areas: Waste reduction.

★3375★ Center for Water and the Environment
University of Minnesota, Duluth
Natural Resources Research Institute
5013 Miller Trunk Hwy.
Duluth, MN 55811
Phone: (218)720-4270
Fax: (218)720-4219
Contact: Dr. Gerald J. Niemi, Dir.
Research Areas: Examines the state's resources for economic and environmental decisions. Operates programs in environmental chemistry and ecosystem studies. Special Resources: Facilities for analytical chemistry and geographical information systems.

★3376★ Center for Wetlands
University of Florida
Phelps Laboratory
Gainesville, FL 32611
Phone: (904)392-2424
Fax: (904)392-3624
Contact: Dr. G. Ronnie Best, Associate Dir.
Research Areas: Wetlands and their role in partnership of man and nature, including studies on wetlands ecosystem dynamics, wetlands reclamation, use of wetlands for advance treatment of wastewater, and various studies of freshwater and coastal wetlands ecosystems. Conducts environmental impact analyses and energy analyses at local, regional, and national levels. Acts as a campus catalyst for matters dealing with issues of man and nature.

★3377★ Center for World Environment and Sustainable Development
North Carolina State University
Box 7619
Raleigh, NC 27695-7619
Phone: (919)737-5300
Contact: Isabel Valencia, Exec. Officer
Research Areas: Studies problems in tropical conservation and development. Conducts projects addressing global climate change and environmental degradation in industrializing countries, especially in Eastern Europe.

★3378★ Center Hill Solid and Hazardous Waste Research Laboratory
5995 Center Hill Rd.
Cincinnati, OH 45224
Phone: (513)569-7885
Contact: P.E. Gerard Roberto, Project Manager
Research Areas: Solid and hazardous wastes. Provides geotechnical, geochemical, and geoscientific technical support services to EPA for various SUPERFUND and RCRA (Resource Conservation and Recovery Act) projects. Special Resources: Laboratories to support research on soil/chemical/hydrological interactions focusing on chemical stabilization of contaminated soils and contaminant control systems to protect the groundwater regime.

★3379★ Center of Excellence for Reservoir Research
Murray State Univ.
College of Science
Murray, KY 42071
Phone: (502)762-2886
Contact: Gary Boggess Ph.D., Dean
Research Areas: Conducts reservoir studies and analyzes environmental problems associated with ecosystems in the region.

★3380★ Chemical Industry Institute of Toxicology
6 Davis Dr.
PO Box 12137
Research Triangle Park, NC 27709
Phone: (919)541-2070
Fax: (919)541-9015
Contact: Roger O. McClellan D.V.M., Pres.
Research Areas: Toxicity data obtained at various levels of biological organization in order to assess exposure-related human health risks. Specific research includes chemical carcinogenesis with investigations in DNA-reactive, mitogenic, cytotoxic, and receptor-mediated agents; risk assessment methodology and extrapolation modeling; respiratory/fiber toxicology; genetic toxicology; neurotoxicology; and reproductive/developmental toxicology.

★3381★ Chesapeake Research Consortium, Inc.
PO Box 1280
Solomons, MD 20688
Phone: (301)326-6700
Fax: (301)326-6771
Contact: Dr. Joseph Mihursky, Dir.
Research Areas: Multidisciplinary facility specializing in the problems affecting Chesapeake Bay. Coordinates staff and facilities from the four affiliated institutions to achieve a broad-based approach to management of the Chesapeake estuary, specifically estuarine science, pollution problems, and fisheries management.

★3382★ Clean Energy Research Institute
University of Miami
218 McArthur Bldg.
Coral Gables, FL 33124
Phone: (305)284-4666
Fax: (305)284-4792
Contact: Dr. T. Nejat Veziroglu, Dir.
Research Areas: Energy- and environment-related problems, including multidisciplinary studies on solar cooling and heating, synthetic fuels, hydrogen energy, ocean thermal energy conversion, remote sensing, air and thermal pollution control, two-phase flow, heat transfer, photovoltaics, solar collectors, acid rain, greenhouse effect, and biosphere.

★3383★ Clemson Hydraulics Laboratory
Clemson Univ.
Lowry Hall
Clemson, SC 29634-0911
Phone: (803)656-3325
Fax: (803)656-2670
Contact: Dr. Earl J. Hayter, Dir.
Research Areas: Conducts laboratory, field, and numerical studies relating to coastal processes, wind engineering, turbulent mixing, cohesionless and cohesive sediment transport, and physical hydraulic models, including an experimental program directed at such natural hazards as erosion, water consumption (evaporation), groundwater pollutant migration, and wind and wave effects. Special Resources: Maintains a 50x70-foot modeling basin equipped with a 30-foot wave generator and a 30x40-foot basin with a 10-foot wave generator. Operates flumes (one 100-foot, one 30-foot tilting, and smaller units), two wind tunnels, and three boats.

★3384★ Coastal Ocean Action Strategies Institute
State Univ. of New York at Stony Brook
Stony Brook, NY 11794
Phone: (516)632-8700
Contact: Dr. J.R. Schubel, Dean and Dir.
Research Areas: Major rivers and their estuaries, effects of population growth on the coastal ocean, marine plant and animal habitat destruction, excess fertilization of coastal waters, and plastics and other litter.

★3385★ Coastal Research Center
Woods Hole Oceanographic Institution
Woods Hole, MA 02543
Phone: (508)548-1400
Fax: (508)457-2172
Contact: Dr. David G. Aubrey, Dir.
Research Areas: Physics, chemistry, biology, geology, and engineering of the coastal ocean, including studies on waste disposal effects. Specific concerns include the identification and quantification of processes responsible for the transport, mixing, diffusion, and resuspension of particulate matter; the chemical fate of contaminants; pollution effects on marine organisms and ecosystems; and regional coastal ecosystems such as Georges Bank, Massachusetts-Cape Cod Bay, Buzzards Bay, and international systems such as the Gulf of Maine and the Black Sea. Special focus is on the changing sea level worldwide and its consequences, including coastal erosion. Special Resources: Maintains seawater experimentation facilities in the Laboratory, seawater flumes, field instrument fabrication and test facilities, and a fleet of small boats.

★3386★ Coastal Zone Laboratory
Texas A&M Univ. at Galveston
PO Box 1675
Galveston, TX 77553
Phone: (409)740-4465
Contact: Dr. C.S. Giam, Dir.
Research Areas: Biology, chemistry, geology, geography, physics, zoology, and botany, including baseline studies of microbiology, fishes, benthic organisms, chemistry of waters and sediments of continental shelf of Gulf of Mexico, estuarine ecology, man/land relationships in coastal zone, nearshore sediment processes, and industrial siting in coastal zone.

★3387★ Collaborative Radiological Health Laboratory
Colorado State Univ.
Fort Collins, CO 80521
Phone: (303)491-8522
Contact: Dr. Stephen A. Benjamin, Dir.
Research Areas: Hazards associated with prenatal and early postnatal exposure to ionizing radiation or environmental toxic agents, including problems involved in growth and development, reproductive capacity, immune development, and cancer and aging. Studies the effects of low level radiation and toxic agents on beagle dogs, emphasizing the role of age as a factor modifying sensitivity to toxic substances, to provide information on health effects in human beings. Databases: Beagle dog diseases and neoplasms.

★3388★ Colorado Center for Public Policy Research
University of Colorado-Boulder
Campus Box 330
125 Ketchum Bldg.
Boulder, CO 80309
Phone: (303)492-8586
Fax: (303)492-5105
Contact: Susan E. Clarke, Dir.
Research Areas: Energy policy, space policy, growth management policy, policy information systems, and political analysis methods.

★3389★ Colorado Institute for Fuels and High-Altitude Engine Research (CIFER)
Colorado School of Mines
311 Alderson Hall
Golden, CO 80401
Phone: (303)273-3246
Fax: (303)273-3730
Research Areas: Identifies the fuels and engine components that help mitigate the atmospheric contamination attributable to tailpipe emissions from trucks and buses at high altitudes. Focuses on alternative fuels, catalyst systems, combustion processes, materials, and engine design.

★3390★ Colorado Water Resources Research Institute
410 Univ. Services Center
Colorado State Univ.
Fort Collins, CO 80523
Phone: (303)491-6308
Fax: (303)491-2293
Contact: Dr. Neil S. Grigg, Dir.
Research Areas: Conducts and coordinates research on water, water-related disciplines, and other natural resources at the universities and within the state, including studies on hydraulics, environmental problems, river mechanics, bridge pier scour, erosion and sedimentation, open channel flow, mathematical and physical modeling, irrigation, fluvial geometronics, fluid dynamics, wind engineering, industrial aerodynamics, turbulent boundary and diffusion, statistical and stochastic methods in hydrology, and water quality. Special Resources: Maintains a hydraulic experimental laboratory. Also operates a solar energy applications laboratory composed of three separate solar houses and a solar greenhouse located adjacent to Engineering Research Center.

★3391★ Combustion & Environmental Systems Research Institute
University of North Dakota
Box 8213, Univ. Sta.
Grand Forks, ND 58202
Phone: (701)777-5152
Fax: (701)777-5181
Contact: Michael L. Jones, Dir.
Research Areas: Fuel combustion and its effects on environmental systems with emphasis on low-rank coals. Interests include 1) combustion science, focusing on ash and slag chemistry, mineral matter transformations and deposition, advanced analytical techniques, coal combustion chemistry, and corrosion and erosion; 2) combustion systems, focusing on fuels evaluation, fluidized-bed combustion, coal-fired gas turbines, coal-fired diesels, and slurry combustion; and 3) environmental systems, focusing on hot gas cleanup, clean coal technologies, and sulfur dioxide, nitrogen oxide, and particulate control.

★3392★ Community Research Service (CRS)
Kentucky State Univ.
Atwood Research Facility
Frankfort, KY 40601
Phone: (502)227-6356
Fax: (502)227-5933
Contact: Harold R. Benson, Research Dir.
Research Areas: Aquaculture and plant and soil science, focusing on warm and cold water fish farming, insect pest management, plant tissues culture, and water quality. Also studies rural development and human nutrition, focusing on the elderly population.

★3393★ Complex Systems Research Center
University of New Hampshire
Science & Engineering Research Bldg.
Durham, NH 03824
Phone: (603)862-1792
Fax: (603)862-1915
Contact: Dr. John Aber, Dir.
Research Areas: Measurement and modelling of global scale biogeochemical processes. Fields include global carbon cycle, nitrogen cycling in forest ecosystems and estuarine/riverine systems, measurement of atmospheric chemistry, pollution effects on ecosystems, remote sensing, role of models in policy process, effects of resource supplies on economic systems, and management of georeferenced databases at local to global scales. Databases: Global vegetation, soils, climate, rivers, economics, and energy.

★3394★ Computational Engineering Research Institute (CERI)
PO Box 14
University, MS 38677-0014
Phone: (601)234-7841
Contact: Dr. Sam S.Y. Wang, Pres.
Research Areas: Application of computational modeling methodologies to engineering problems in the areas of structural mechanics geotech problems, hydrodynamics, ocean and coastal engineering, groundwater flows, and pollutant transport studies.

★3395★ Conservation and Survey Division
University of Nebraska-Lincoln
113-E Nebraska Hall
901 N. 17th St.
Lincoln, NE 68588
Phone: (402)472-3471
Fax: (402)472-2410
Contact: Perry B. Wigley, Dir.
Research Areas: Groundwater and water resources, mineral resources, soils, remote sensing, geographic information systems, and natural resource systems, including broad framework studies and interpretation of basic data. Conducts state geological survey.

★3396★ Conservation of Soil, Water, Energy and Biological Resources Program
Cornell University
6126 Comstock Hall
Ithaca, NY 14853
Phone: (607)255-2212
Contact: David Pimentel, Director
Conservation of soil, water, energy, and biological resources for a sustainable agriculture. The ideas and approaches developed have been highly successful in helping set up ecologically sound agricultural programs.

★3397★ Consortium for International Development
6367 E. Tanque Verde Rd., #200
Tucson, AZ 85715-3832
Phone: (602)885-0055
Fax: (602)886-3244
Contact: Dr. Earl D. Kellogg, Exec. Dir.
Research Areas: Provides technical assistance, training, and management services to developing countries in the following areas: irrigation and water resources, agriculture and rural development, education, environment and natural resources, and human health and nutrition.

★3398★ Cooling Tower Institute
530 Wells Fargo Dr., Ste. 113
Houston, tx 77273
Phone: (713)583-4087
Fax: (713)537-1721
Contact: Dorothy Garrison, Exec. Dir.
Research Areas: Investigates ways to improve technology, design, performance, and maintenance of water cooling towers. Works to reduce water and air pollution.

★3399★ Cooperative Institute for Applied Remote Sensing
University of Oklahoma
100 E. Boyd, Rm. F132
Norman, OK 73019-0628
Phone: (405)325-6526
Contact: Dr. Lee Williams, Dir.
Research Areas: Remote sensing. Projects include developing a environmental impact assessment model for oil spills from pipelines and head wells, surveying the oil industry for applications of remote sensing, investigating offshore satellite applications in the Gulf of Mexico; and conducting a feasibility study for distributed image processing services on computer networks.

★3400★ Cooperative Institute for Research in Environmental Sciences
University of Colorado-Boulder
Campus Box 216
Boulder, CO 80309-0216
Phone: (303)492-1143
Fax: (303)492-1149
Contact: Dr. Robert Sievers, Dir.
Research Areas: Theoretical studies, laboratory experiments, and field investigations

in atmospheric chemistry and physics, air pollution, climate dynamics, environmental biochemistry, geochemistry, environmental biology, and solid earth geophysics. Research has included studies in kinetics of reactions in the stratosphere and troposphere, gas and liquid chromatography, mass spectrometry, analytical chemistry, measurement of constituents and reactions in the atmosphere, microcomputer interfaced instrumentation, remote sensing, surface science, separation science, metal complex chemistry, aerosol chemistry, laser chemistry, rare earth super conductors, contemporary and paleoclimatology, air-sea interactions, ocean dynamics, ice nucleation, cryosphere studies, ice sheet modeling, earthquake physics, plate tectonics, seismic wave propagation, nuclear test discrimination, rock deformation and fracture, numerical hydrodynamics, dynamics of the atmospheric boundary layer, strains and tilts associated with earthtides and secular deformation, geodesy, geophysical inverse studies, and normal modes of vibration of the earth. The Institute serves as a center for collaboration of research workers from the University of Colorado-Boulder and other institutions.

★3401★ Cooperative Institute for the Remote Sensing of Biogeophysical Processes
University of New Hampshire
Complex Systems Research Center
Durham, NH 03824
Phone: (603)862-1792
Fax: (603)862-1915
Contact: Dr. Barrett N. Rock, Codirector
Research Areas: Global climate changes. Applies remotely sensed data to global and regional studies, including the global carbon cycle, the greenhouse effect, and conifer forest decline in the U.S. and Europe. Satellite datasets from NOAA are used to assess vegetation damage in forests and coastal wetlands as well as studying land use changes such as deforestation in the tropics. Land satellite data are used for detecting, mapping, and monitoring a variety of land resources.

★3402★ Cooperative National Park Resources Studies Unit
University of California, Davis
Institute of Ecology
Davis, CA 95616
Phone: (916)752-7119
Fax: (916)752-3350
Contact: Stephen D. Veirs Jr., Unit Leader
Research Areas: Develops and facilitates ecological, environmental, and sociological programs on the use, conservation, and management of natural areas and other components of the National Park system in California.

★3403★ Cooperative National Park Resources Studies Unit (Honolulu)
Univ. of Hawaii at Manoa
3190 Maile Way, #409
Honolulu, HI 96822
Phone: (808)956-8218
Contact: Dr. Clifford W. Smith, Dir.
Research Areas: Endangered species research, species inventory, vegetation mapping, population biology of feral mammals, vegetation analysis, biological and herbicidal control of weeds, archeological base mapping, fire ecology, and resource management problems in Hawaiian national parks. Databases: Birds, flowering plants, and ferns for all Pacific area National Parks. Special Resources: Insect quarantine facility for screening potential biological control agents.

★3404★ Cooperative Park Studies Unit
University of Idaho
College of Forestry, Wildlife & Range Sciences
Moscow, ID 83843
Phone: (208)885-7990
Fax: (208)885-6226
Contact: Dr. R. Gerald Wright, Coproject Leader
Research Areas: Conducts social and biological research in relation to the management of parks, preserves, and recreation areas. Past projects have dealt with tourism, human interactions with wildlife, ungulate habitat use, mountain goat population dynamics, and natural resource data-based management, including geographic information systems.

★3405★ Cooperative Wildlife Research Laboratory
Southern Illinois Univ. at Carbondale
Carbondale, IL 62901-6504
Phone: (618)536-7766
Contact: Dr. Alan Woolf, Dir.
Research Areas: Basic and applied wildlife ecology of terrestrial vertebrates and rare and endangered species. Vertebrate natural history, distribution, population dynamics, environmental toxicology, wildlife diseases, and impact of surface and subsurface mining on land use are also studied. Special Resources: Specimen collection.

★3406★ Council on Economic Priorities
30 Irving Pl.
New York, NY 10003
Phone: (212)420-1133
Fax: (212)420-0988
Contact: Alice Tepper Marlin, Exec. Dir.
Research Areas: Pollution control, ethnical investment, socially responsible shopping, occupational safety and health, corporate social responsibillity awards program, and energy.

★3407★ Craighead Environmental Research Institute
PO Box 156
Moose, WY 83012
Phone: (307)733-3387
Contact: Dr. Frank Craighead, Pres.
Research Areas: Working association of scientists conducting field research in the areas of wildlife ecology and conservation biology. Specific projects include the following: satellite systems for tracking wildlife and mapping and inventorying vegetation; plant and animal phenology; threatened species, including environmental changes, environmental contaminants, population dynamics, behavior, and relationships with man; and wilderness management problems with special reference to human impacts on wildlife habitat.

★3408★ C.S. Mott Center for Human Growth and Development
Wayne State Univ.
275 E. Hancock St.
Detroit, MI 48201
Phone: (313)577-1068
Contact: Dr. Ernest L. Abel, Dir.
Research Areas: Human growth and development, including causative factors, identification, prevention, and remedy of birth defects. Uses mechanical, chemical, and hormonal devices as well as acceptable social, psychological, ethical, and moral approaches. Identifies environmental pollutants, drugs, infections, and other teratogens responsible for increasing incidence of birth defects and studies the relationships between environmental deterioration, dwindling natural resources, population density, and quality of human existence. Develops and implements population controls.

★3409★ DC Water Resources Research Center
University of District of Columbia
4200 Connecticut Ave., NW MB5004
Washington, DC 20008
Phone: (202)673-3442
Fax: (202)637-2085
Contact: Dr. M.H. Watt, Dir.
Research Areas: Water and resources which affect water, including studies of water quality and quantity, groundwater, basic scientific water-related problems, water planning and policy, social, economic, and institutional aspects, conservation, computer modeling, water information system, and technology transfer. Established under the Water Resources Act of 1964, Public Law 88-379, to conduct and coordinate research on water resources at the University and at other universities in the District of Columbia. Special Resources: Sedimentation, water quality, demonstration laboratories, and information center.

★3410★ Degradable Plastics Laboratory
University of Illinois
1304 W. Green St.
Urbana, IL 61801
Phone: (217)333-1441
Contact: Dr. Richard Wool, Dir.
Research Areas: Degradable plastics. Develops disposal products using cornstarch and plastics.

★3411★ Department of Civil and Environmental Engineering, Sanitary Engineering Division
University of Wisconsin-Madison
Madison, WI 53706
Phone: (608)262-1776
Contact: Dr. William C. Boyle, Head
Research Areas: Environmental protection, water chemistry, toxic chemicals, industrial pollution control, hazardous waste treatment and management, water pollution control, treatment process design optimization, on-site small-scale treatment, solid waste disposal, drinking water supply, hydraulics of water distribution networks and sewer systems, natural environmental systems, environmental data analysis, and treatment plant control. Special Resources: Laboratory for chemical analysis.

★3412★ Department of Environmental Health
University of Cincinnati
3223 Eden Ave.
Cincinnati, OH 45267-0056
Phone: (513)558-5701
Fax: (513)558-1756
Contact: Dr. Roy E. Albert, Dir.
Research Areas: Environmental health sciences, including research in areas related to heavy metals, water quality, behavioral toxicology, health aspects of fossil fuel sources, environmental carcinogenesis, mutagenesis, pulmonary metabolism and toxicology, metabolism and toxicology of environmental chemicals and drugs, epidemiology and biostatistics, and cutaneous problems of environmental origin. Conducts clinical studies on problems encountered in industry and the community; environmental hygiene and pollution studies; field surveys; and bibliographic studies.

★3413★ Department of Environmental Health Sciences
Case Western Reserve Univ.
School of Medicine
2119 Abington Rd.
Cleveland, OH 44106
Phone: (216)368-5963
Fax: (216)368-3194
Contact: Prof. G. David McCoy, Acting Chm.
Research Areas: Conducts cancer research, risk assessments, and environmental etiology of disease investigations. Analyzes the potential of environmental agents to cause cancer. Special Resources: Operates biohazard and tissue culture facilities.

★3414★ Department of Forest Resources
University of Arkansas at Monticello
Monticello, AR 71655
Phone: (501)460-1052
Contact: R. Scott Beasley, Head
Research Areas: Forest management, forest biometrics, forest economics, forest regeneration, forest protection, forest hydrology, wildlife management, and silviculture.

★3415★ Department of Medicinal Chemistry, Bionucleonics Division
Purdue Univ.
Civil Engineering Bldg.
West Lafayette, IN 47907
Phone: (317)494-1419
Contact: Dr. Paul L. Ziemer, Research Coordinator
Research Areas: Research is conducted in three primary areas: (1) bionucleonics and nuclear pharmacy, including radioisotope tracer methodology, analytical applications of radionuclides, instrumental methods of analysis, development of radiopharmaceuticals, and nuclear medicine imaging; (2) radiological health sciences, including health physics, solid-state methods of radiation dosimetry, radioactive waste management, biological effects of radiation, evaluation of environmental radiation hazards, and radiation risk assessment; and (3) environmental health sciences, including environmental toxicology, inhalation toxicology, occupational health, and industrial hygiene.

★3416★ Department of Toxicology
North Carolina State Univ.
Box 7633
Raleigh, NC 27695
Phone: (919)737-2274
Fax: (919)737-7169
Contact: Dr. Ernest Hodgson, Head
Research Areas: Biochemical and general aspects of environmental health sciences, including studies on enzyme kinetics, enzyme purification, environmental contaminants, synthesis and metabolism of pesticides, genetic effects of pesticides, induction of oxidative enzyme, localization of pesticides, mode of action of pesticides and structure-activity relationship, clarification of mode of action, genetic effects of pesticides sought, enzyme pathways, absorption and distribution, pesticide residues, and behavioral effects, with special emphasis on tools and methods of molecular biology.

★3417★ Department of Wildlife and Fisheries Sciences
Texas A&M Univ.
College Station, TX 77843
Phone: (409)845-5777
Fax: (409)845-3786
Contact: Dr. David J. Schmidly, Head
Research Areas: Genetics, physiology, behavior, ecology, biodiversity, management, and production studies revelant to aquatic and terrestrial wildlife systems, emphasizing biotechnical and artifical intelligence applications to wildlife and fisheries management, aquaculture, and bioconservation in American subtemperate, subtropical, and tropical zones. Conducts intensive ecological research in Texas, the southwestern U.S., Mexico, Central America, and South America. Special Resources: Maintains the Texas Cooperative Wildlife Collections of over 1,000,000 vertebrate specimens. Operates the Aquacultural Research Center to conduct research and educational activities related to warmwater aquaculture; the Small Ungulate Research Facility to study behavior and physiology of small wild ungulates and to maintain a breeding colony of collared peccaries; the Wildlife Habitat Analysis Laboratory to conduct comparative studies of animal nutrition and bioenergetics, determine the chemical qualities of range forage plants and their influence on digestive processes, and compare the morphological and physiological adaptations of wildlife to terrestrial environments; the Ecological Systems Laboratory to develop systems approaches to the solution of ecological problems, including simulation models of wildlife behavior, wildlife/habitat interactions, and wildlife management needs; the Wildlife Genetics Laboratory to investigate the genetics of natural populations of terrestrial wildlife species, especially population genetics, systematics, genetic toxicology, and the application of genetics to wildlife management; and the Fish Genetics Laboratory to provide facilities for studies in the population, chromosomal, and molecular genetics of freshwater and marine fishes.

★3418★ Desert Research Institute
University of Nevada-Reno
PO Box 60220
Reno, NV 89506
Phone: (702)673-7300
Fax: (702)673-7372
Contact: Dr. James V. Taranik, Pres.
Research Areas: DRI is organized into five research centers: the Atmospheric Sciences Center, which performs meteorological and atomospheric science research; the Biological Sciences Center, which studies the effects of the desert environment upon biological processes; the Energy and Environmental Engineering Center, which specializes in air resources research; the Quaternary Sciences Center, which researches archeological and paleoecological science applications in arid regions; and the Water Resources Center, which studies hydrology and its applications. Special Resources: Maintains an isotope laboratory, a pollen paleoecology laboratory, a cloud chamber and ice laboratory, a great basin environmental research laboratory, and equipment for mass spectrometry, atomic absorption, spectrophotometry, chromatography, remote sensing, microwave radiometry, and microprobe analysis.

★3419★ Desert Research Institute, Atmospheric Chemistry Laboratory
University of Nevada-Reno
P.O Box 60220
Reno, NV 89506
Phone: (702)673-7300
Contact: Prof. David Miller, Dir.
Research Areas: Chemical reactions in the atmosphere, fates of pollutants, wet and dry deposition, and air-quality measurements. Studies include in-cloud reactions such as oxidation of nitric oxide and sulfur dioxide to acids and gas-to-particle conversion such as the photochemical reactions of gases in plumes from electricity generating power plants. Special Resources: Utilizes a cloud chamber which provides a controlled environment for humid air studies.

★3420★ Desert Research Institute, Biological Sciences Center
University of Nevada-Reno
PO Box 60220
Reno, NV 89506
Phone: (702)673-7321
Fax: (702)673-7397
Contact: Dr. Carl A. Fox, Exec. Dir.
Research Areas: Basic and applied research focused on the assessment, environmental interaction, and management of biological resources from a local, regional, and global perspective. Areas include microbiology, plant physiology, plant ecology, biogeochemistry, and remote sensing. Special Resources: Image processing laboratory, field research station, and research greenhouse (a phytotron is under development).

★3421★ Desert Research Institute, Energy and Environmental Engineering Center
University of Nevada-Reno
P.O Box 60220
Reno, NV 89506
Phone: (702)677-3107
Fax: (702)677-3157
Contact: William R. Pierson, Exec. Dir.
Research Areas: Design, installation, and operation of air quality networks in the Great Basin and California, including studies on air quality and visibility in the southwestern U.S.; development and application of novel measurement methods for aerosols, visibility, and acid deposition; and development and application of models apportioning ambient pollutant concentrations to their emission sources.

★3422★ Desert Research Institute, Quaternary Sciences Center
University of Nevada-Reno
PO Box 60220
Reno, NV 89506
Phone: (702)673-7303
Fax: (702)673-7397
Contact: Dr. Dale F. Ritter, Dir.
Research Areas: Interdisciplinary studies on western region of North America involving anthropology, archeology, history, ethnobotany, geomorphology, paleoenvironment, palynology, faunal analysis, and packrat midden analysis. Research focuses on paleoclimate, climate change, and arid lands archeology, with active projects in the Great Basin, the Southwest, and Near East.

★3423★ Desert Research Institute, Water Resources Center
University of Nevada-Reno
PO Box 60220
Reno, NV 89506-0220
Phone: (702)673-7365
Fax: (702)673-7397
Contact: Dr. John Hess, Exec. Dir.
Research Areas: Water and other resources which affect water, including studies on chemical and physical aspects of water resources, water quality, limnology, groundwater flow systems, water table mapping, radionuclide migration in groundwater, application of simulation theory to water resources planning and management, effect of water management on quality of groundwater and surface recharge, rainfall and runoff relationships and water quality regimes of river systems, floodplain management,

geothermal resources evaluation, determination of water resources available for energy production in the arid West, and analysis and statistical studies of precipitation data and water usage in Nevada. Trains scientists in hydrology and hydrogeology.

★3424★ Division of Industrial Technology and Energy Management
Univ. City Science Center
3624 Market St.
Philadelphia, PA 19104
Phone: (215)387-2255
Fax: (215)382-0056
Contact: F. William Kirsch Ph.D., V. Pres.
Research Areas: Industrial energy use and conservation, industrial hazardous waste reduction, database and information system design, and technology assessment and application. Studies include cogeneration of electric power and steam and assessment of technology applications in the food industry, including supercritical fluid extraction. Manages the Energy Analysis and Diagnostic Center program sponsored by the U.S. Department of Energy. The EADC provides energy audits to small- and medium-sized manufacturers throughout the country. Also operates the Waste Minimization Assessment Center (WMAC) project for the U.S. Environmental Protection Agency. Special Resources: EADC Database/Information System.

★3425★ Division of Occupational and Environmental Medicine
University of California, Davis
Davis, CA 95616
Phone: (916)752-4256
Contact: Dr. Marc B. Schenker, Division Chief
Research Areas: Epidemiology of occupational and environmental health problems, focusing on agricultural health problems, occupational cancer, reproductive hazards, and respiratory disease. Collaborates on studies of biologic markers of exposure.

★3426★ Drinking Water Research Center
Florida Intl. Univ.
College of Engineering & Applied Sciences
Univ. Park
Miami, FL 33199
Phone: (305)348-2826
Fax: (305)348-3894
Contact: William J. Cooper, Dir.
Research Areas: Chemistry, microbiology, and engineering considerations of drinking water and water resources. Conducts research on trace contaminants, microbiological changes, and chlorine chemistry. Serves Florida agencies in water problems.

★3427★ Dry Lands Research Institute
University of California, Riverside
PO Box 112
Riverside, CA 92521
Phone: (714)787-5797
Contact: Wesley M. Jarrell, Dir.
Research Areas: Problems and potentials of arid and semi-arid regions, including occupancy, development, utilization, and conservation of these regions and their resources. Research fields include agricultural development, regional economic and social development, ecosystem analysis, agroforestry, landscape, alternative building materials, ethnobotany, revegetation, environmental management and land use, environmental economics, and water resources.

★3428★ Eagle Lake Field Station
Dept. of Biological Sciences
California State Univ., Chico
Chico, CA 95929-0515
Phone: (916)898-4490
Contact: Raymond J. Bogiatto, Dir.
Research Areas: Ecology in the Eagle Lake area, including studies on garter snakes, nesting behaviors, bird breeding, lake nutrients, plankton populations, California rainbow trout, juniper berries, and Great Basin evening-primroses.

★3429★ Earthmind
PO Box 743
Mariposa, CA 95338
Contact: Michael Hackleman, Pres.
Research Areas: Alternative energy sources, including wind energy, restoration of wind machines, and electric vehicles.

★3430★ Earthwatch
680 Mt. Auburn St.
Box 403
Watertown, MA 02172
Phone: (617)926-8200
Fax: (617)926-8532
Contact: Brian Rosborough, Pres.
Research Areas: Field research in the earth, marine, and life sciences and the humanities, including animal behavior, anthropology, applied ecology, archeology, art history, herpetology, marine archeology, marine ecology, nutrition, ornithology, paleontology, primatology, and volcanology. Earthwatch is a national volunteer organization offering its members the opportunity to join research expeditions to help university and museum faculty accomplish their field work. Approximately 100 scholars receive research support each year.

★3431★ East-West Environment and Policy Institute (EAPI)
East-West Center
1777 East-West Rd.
Honolulu, HI 96848
Phone: (808)944-7266
Fax: (808)947-7970
Contact: Dr. John E. Bardach, Interim Dir.
Research Areas: Involved in four research programs: risk, resources, and development, which helps policy and decision makers with risk assessment and economic analysis of development based on natural systems; habitat and society, which uses a comprehensive conceptual framework to study social responses to environmental change; land, air, and water management, which focuses on problems of resource use on a sustained basis; and oceans-related research, which is directed toward management of marine resources, nternational relations stemming from extended mariti me jurisdictions, and coastal zone management.

★3432★ Ecology Center
Utah State Univ.
Logan, UT 84322-5200
Phone: (801)750-2555
Contact: Frederic H. Wagner, Dir.
Research Areas: Ecology and related environmental sciences, including interdisciplinary studies on terrestrial and aquatic ecology, population ecology, systems ecology, water quality, nutrient cycling, animal behavior, physiological ecology, and man's usage. Conducts research in desert, alpine, grassland, and other areas. Provides professional ecological advice at state, national, and international levels. Special Resources: Maintains laboratories and a variety of logistic equipment at Bear Lake Biological Laboratory, Green Canyon Ecology Compound, and other research stations in the state.

★3433★ Ecology Research Center
Miami Univ.
Oxford, OH 45056
Phone: (513)529-6187
Fax: (513)529-5634
Contact: Dr. Gary W. Barrett, Codirector
Research Areas: Stress effects on natural ecosystems, integrated pest management, acid rain, solar energy, and behavioral, agricultural, community, and population ecology. Databases: Precipitation chemistry. Special Resources: 16 quarter-acre animal enclosures in addition to aviaries.

★3434★ Economic Development Laboratory
Georgia Inst. of Technology
Georgia Tech Research Institute
Atlanta, GA 30332
Phone: (404)894-3841
Fax: (404)853-9172
Contact: Dr. David S. Clifton Jr., Dir.
Research Areas: Agricultural technology, industrial energy conservation, hazardous waste management, safety engineering, industrial hygiene, asbestos abatement, market planning and research, target industry analysis, cost-benefit analysis, energy modelling, technology transfer, industrial training, productivity improvement, small business assistance, analytical chemistry, and indoor air pollution. Supports 12 regional offices throughout Georgia to assist local industries.

★3435★ Ecosystems Center
Marine Biological Laboratory
Water St.
Woods Hole, MA 02543
Phone: (508)548-3705
Fax: (508)540-6902
Contact: Dr. Jerry M. Melillo, Codirector
Research Areas: Global carbon cycle, sulfur in estuaries, nitrogen cycles in terrestrial systems, trace gases in forests, nitrogen cycles in forests, arctic freshwaters, and nutrients in arctic landscapes. Special Resources: Stable isotope mass spectrometer and chemical laboratory.

★3436★ Ecosystems Research Center (ERC)
Cornell Univ.
125 Boyce Thompson Institute
Tower Rd.
Ithaca, NY 14853
Phone: (607)255-3972
Fax: (607)255-8088
Contact: Dr. Leonard H. Weinstein, Dir.
Research Areas: Ecosystems science, including ecotoxicology, biotechnology, forest decline, wetlands, air pollution, case studies of the Hudson River, cumulative impact assessments, and cross-system comparison of responses to stress. Identifies fundamental principles and concepts of ecosystems science to determine their importance in understanding and predicting the responses of ecosystems to stress and evaluates the applicability of these theoretical concepts to problems of concern to the EPA.

★3437★ Edith Angel Environmental Research Center
Clemson Univ.
Institute of Wildlife & Environmental Toxicology
Rt. 2, Box 106A
Chariton, IA 50049
Phone: (515)774-5116

Fax: (515)774-2365
Contact: Karen Craft, Coordinator
Research Areas: Field studies of pesticide influences on agroecosystems; effects of soil erosion, sedimentation, and differing agricultural practices on soil and water ecology as it relates to the exposure of wildlife to pesticides and other environmental contaminants; and laboratory analyses and technique development in toxic exposure assessments.

★3438★ Empire State Electric Energy Research Corporation
1155 Ave. of the Americas
New York, NY 10036
Phone: (212)302-1212
Contact: James A. Carrigg, Pres.
Research Areas: Environmental issues, including studies of acid rain and wintertime chemistry of the atmosphere, aquatic resources in the Adirondack region of New York State, right-of-way management of transmission lines, and causes of earthquakes in New York State; fossil fuel and advanced generation, focusing on cleaning of coal, coal gasification, power plant life extension, and development of an on-line carbon monitor for measurement of carbon content in fly ash; electrical systems and equipment, covering high-phase order transmission and development of more energy efficient distribution and power transformers, particularly amorphous steel core transformers; nuclear research, including the development of annular fuel pellets to increase the energy output of fuel assemblies and the improvement of moisture separator reheaters. Special Resources: Maintains a 100 megawatt cool water integrated gasification/combined cycle (IGCC) demonstration plant.

★3439★ Empire State Paper Research Institute
SUNY Coll. of Environmental Science and Forestry
Syracuse, NY 13210
Phone: (315)470-6502
Contact: Dr. Leland R. Schroeder, Dir.
Research Areas: Research basic to the production of pulp and paper, including conservation of raw materials and studies aimed at improving environmental conditions, paper-making process, and paper and board properties.

★3440★ Energy & Environmental Research Center
University of North Dakota
Box 8213, Univ. Sta.
Grand Forks, ND 58202
Phone: (701)777-5000
Fax: (701)777-5181
Contact: Dr. Gerald H. Groenewold, Dir.
Research Areas: Projects fall within three research institutes: Fuels & Process Chemistry Research Institute, including high-pressure/high-temperature process development, synthetic fuels, coal/water fuels, and critical fluid environmental analyses; Combustion & Environmental Systems Research Institute, including pilot-plant and fundamental combustion, sulfur and nitrogen oxides and particulate control, fuel evaluation, combustion test service, ash and slag characterization, and inorganic chemistry; and North Dakota Mining & Mineral Resources Research Institute, including groundwater studies, energy and mineral resource characterization, mined land reclamation, underground coal gasification, water and wastewater characterization and treatment, and waste management and disposal. Special Resources: Tubing bombs, batch autoclaves, and continuous process units for evaluating high-pressure/high-temperature processes for chemical and synthetic fuel production (flow rates to 7.5 tons per day); laboratory and pilot-plant coal combustors (up to 1.4 million Btu per hour); units for evaluation of wastewater treatment and reuse systems, fuel preparation and beneficiation, structure and properties of coal and coal mineral matter, and other fuel properties and chemical processes; and a coal analysis laboratory and instruments for organic, inorganic, surface, mineralogic, thermal, and microbiological analysis. Also maintains Western Fly Ash Research, Development, and Data Center.

★3441★ Energy and Water Research Center
West Virginia Univ.
PO Box 6064
617 N. Spruce St.
Morgantown, WV 26506-6064
Phone: (304)293-2867
Fax: (304)293-3749
Contact: Dr. John D. Holmgren, Interim Dir.
Research Areas: Energy research program, designed to benefit and assist economic and industrial development in West Virginia, focuses on exploration and recovery of eastern oil and natural gas and on all aspects of coal, including studies of coal mining and processing, coal conversion and utilization, energy policy, economics and social issues in mining, land reclamation, alternative energy sources and conservation, energy transportation and transmission, and energy-related health research. Water research program addresses environmental and municipal water problems, including acid mine drainage, underground water supplies, rural waste treatment, flooding, and fate of pesticides and fertilizers in the environment.

★3442★ Energy, Environment and Resources Center
University of Tennessee at Knoxville
327 S. Stadium Hall
Knoxville, TN 37996
Phone: (615)974-4251
Contact: Dr. William Colglazier, Dir.
Research Areas: Critical issues in energy, environment, natural resources, science and technology policy, and economic development. Coordinates research by subsidiary centers in water resources and solid waste reduction, recycling, and disposal. Conducts data systems and decision systems research.

★3443★ Energy Laboratory
Massachusetts Inst. of Technology
Rm. E40-455
Cambridge, MA 02139
Phone: (617)253-3400
Contact: Dr. Jefferson W. Tester, Dir.
Research Areas: Technological problems involved in supply, conversion, and consumption of energy, including interdisciplinary studies on combustion and related reactions, health effects, transportation propulsion, fuel conversion and substitution, electric power systems, environmental research, resource recovery, building systems, conservation and energy efficiency in industrial processes, and energy/environmental management, economics, and policy.

★3444★ Energy Laboratory
University of Houston
4800 Calhoun
Houston, TX 77204-5505
Phone: (713)749-4861
Fax: (713)749-3272
Contact: Dr. Alvin F. Hildebrandt, Dir.
Research Areas: Sponsors 20-30 small faculty research programs each year and supports these faculty members in obtaining major funding from outside sources for research in bioconversion, built environment, coal, conservation, energy materials, energy storage, energy transmission, improved oil recovery, geothermal energy, policy and economics, and solar thermal power systems.

★3445★ Energy Research Center
Lehigh Univ.
Packard Laboratory #19
Bethlehem, PA 18015
Phone: (215)758-4090
Contact: Prof. Edward K. Levy, Dir.
Research Areas: Supply and use of energy, including fuels and energy resources, energy conversion systems, energy conservation, and environmental problems, involving faculty and students from engineering, business and economics, life sciences, and physical and social sciences.

★3446★ Energy Resources Center
University of Illinois at Chicago
Box 4348
Chicago, IL 60680
Phone: (312)996-4490
Fax: (312)996-5620
Contact: Dr. James P. Hartnett, Dir.
Research Areas: Interdisciplinary public service organization conducting studies in the field of energy, including passive solar energy conservation, energy conservation in buildings, heat transfer and rheology, and community energy management and planning. Supports special studies such as a campus energy conservation program, energy audits of municipal bus garages, weatherization of mobile homes, high efficiency residential heating and cooling systems, site selection and evaluation process for urban industrial cogeneration, and heat transfer with viscoelastic fluids.

★3447★ Energy Systems & Policy Research Program
University of Wisconsin-Madison
4th Fl., Rm. 405
1402 Univ. Ave.
Madison, WI 53706
Phone: (608)263-5597
Contact: Dr. Wesley K. Foell, Dir.
Research Areas: Policy analysis and design of energy/environment planning and management strategies, emphasizing energy expertise in developing countries; energy usage, trends, and attitudes in Wisconsin industries; and evaluation of design and implementation of government energy programs. International projects include the University of Philippines Graduate Energy Program, in cooperation with University of Philippines, USAID, and government of Philippines. Develops computerized models and databases.

★3448★ Enersol Associates, Inc.
One Summer St.
Somerville, MA 02143
Phone: (617)628-3550
Contact: Richard D. Hansen, Dir.
Research Areas: Photovoltaics in developing nations, including solar-based rural electrification in Latin America. Studies include comparative energy economics and market research on energy technologies.

★3449★ Engineering Energy Laboratory
Oklahoma State Univ.
Rm. 216 Engineering S.
Stillwater, OK 74078
Phone: (405)744-5157
Fax: (405)744-6187
Contact: Dr. Rama Ramakumar, Dir.
Research Areas: Renewable energy sources, including integrated renewable energy systems (IRES) and electric utility problems with unconventional power generation, energy storage, and power electronics.

★3450★ Engineering Experiment Station
South Dakota State Univ.
Box 2220
Brookings, SD 57007
Phone: (605)688-4184
Contact: LaDell R. Swiden P.E., Dir.
Research Areas: Image processing, engineering sciences, including development and control of land, water, and energy resources, industrial development, biological and ecological problems, water supply, waste disposal, pollution control, environmental protection, microelectronics, communication, materials, structures, neutron activation analysis, low-level radioactivity, and remote sensing.

★3451★ Engineering Research and Development Center
University of Nevada-Reno
Dean's Office
College of Engineering
Reno, NV 89557
Phone: (702)784-6925
Contact: Dr. Jon A. Epps, Dean and Dir.
Research Areas: Water resources, solar energy, and environmental engineering.

★3452★ Engineering Research Center
University of Alaska Fairbanks
Fairbanks, AK 99775-1760
Phone: (907)474-7775
Contact: Dr. John P. Zarling, Dir.
Research Areas: Practical engineering problems associated with northern environments, including heat transfer and building performance, structural and roadbed engineering in permafrost and frozen ground, electrical power distribution in rural arctic environments, telecommunications engineering, waste disposal in the northern environment, and environmental and transportation engineering in the arctic and subarctic.

★3453★ Engineering Research Center
Colorado State Univ.
Foothills Campus
Fort Collins, CO 80523
Phone: (303)491-8657
Fax: (303)491-8671
Contact: Dr. Fred W. Smith, Associate Dean for Research
Research Areas: Broad research programs in civil, mechanical, agricultural, chemical, and electrical engineering, atmospheric science, and water resources with emphasis on multidisciplinary and environmental aspects.

★3454★ Engineering Research Center for Hazardous Substances Control
University of California, Los Angeles
6722 Boelter Hall
Los Angeles, CA 90024
Phone: (213)206-3071
Fax: (213)206-3906
Contact: Prof. Sheldon K. Friedlander, Dir.
Research Areas: Interdisciplinary science and engineering systems approach to hazardous substances control, emphasizing pollution prevention and toxics use reduction. Research thrusts are waste minimization, hazardous wastewater treatment, and thermal treatment.

★3455★ Environmental Action Foundation
1525 New Hampshire Ave., NW
Washington, DC 20036
Phone: (202)745-4870
Contact: Ruth Caplan, Exec. Dir.
Research Areas: Electric utility structure and economics, hazardous waste reduction, energy efficiency, biological alternatives to pesticides, and solid waste recycling. Databases: Solid waste policies.

★3456★ Environmental and Energy Study Institute
122 C St. NW, #700
Washington, DC 20001
Phone: (202)628-1400
Contact: Kenneth Murphy, Exec. Dir.
Research Areas: Acts as a forum for public policy analysis and a catalyst for innovative policy initiatives. Areas of emphasis include groundwater quality, hazardous and solid waste, alternative energy and energy efficiency, acid rain, climate change, water conservation, and natural resource management and development in developing nations. Provides policy recommendations.

★3457★ Environmental and Energy Study Institute
122 C St., NW, Ste. 700
Washington, DC 20001
Phone: (202)628-1400
Contact: Ken Murphy, Exec. Dir.
Research Areas: Study of timely issues, including groundwater protection, agriculture, waste management, environmental concerns, energy, acid rain, global climate change, water efficiency, and sustainable development.

★3458★ Environmental & Ground Water Institute
University of Oklahoma
200 Felgar St., Rm. 127
Norman, OK 73019-0470
Phone: (405)325-5202
Fax: (405)325-7596
Contact: Dr. Larry W. Canter, Dir.
Research Areas: Groundwater pollution control, pollutant transport and fate, groundwater quality management, groundwater reclamation, and techniques for predicting environmental impact assessment and alternative comparisons.

★3459★ Environmental and Natural Resources Program
Harvard Univ.
79 John F. Kennedy St.
Cambridge, MA 02138
Phone: (617)495-1122
Fax: (617)495-9118
Contact: William Clark, Assistant Dir.
Research Areas: Environmental and energy issues and policies.

★3460★ Environmental and Water Resources Engineering Area
Texas A&M Univ.
Civil Engineering Dept.
College Station, TX 77843
Phone: (409)845-3011
Contact: Bill Batchelor, Area Leader
Research Areas: Municipal water supply, water quality, air pollution, marine pollution, wastewater treatment and reuse, and mathematical modeling, including studies on water resources, water quality criteria, advanced waste treatment, remote sensing, air quality control, gas and particulate dynamics, aquatic microbiology, chemical oceanography, solid and hazardous waste disposal, optimal reservoir operation, watershed modeling, aquatic systems analysis, fate and transport of toxic substances in natural waters, contaminant transport in groundwater. Special Resources: Maintains environmental engineering laboratories, in-house computer facility, a portable drilling rig, a mobile laboratory/field research vehicle, diving and air supply equipment for submarine studies, and extensive visual documentation equipment.

★3461★ Environmental Awareness Center
B 105 Steenbock Library
Univ. of Wisconsin
Madison, WI 53706
Phone: (608)263-2808
Contact: Prof. Philip H. Lewis Jr., Dir.
Research Areas: Environmental problems, including interdisciplinary team projects applying regional design to environmental situations and opportunities in wilderness and wilderness fringe areas; rural communities; and urban, urban fringe, and inner city areas throughout upper midwest. Works with state agencies, community groups, and corporations in identifying and developing creative options involving physical changes protecting human and environmental rights.

★3462★ Environmental Center
University of Hawaii at Manoa
2550 Campus Rd.
Honolulu, HI 96822
Phone: (808)956-7361
Fax: (808)956-2535
Contact: Dr. John T. Harrison, Environmental Coordinator
Research Areas: Hawaiian environmental problems, including studies on ecological relationships, natural resources, environmental quality, and natural hazards as they relate to human needs and social institutions. Reviews environmental impact statements and proposed environmental legislation and regulation.

★3463★ Environmental Communication Research Program
Rutgers Univ.
Cook College
PO Box 231
New Brunswick, NJ 08903-0231
Phone: (201)932-8795
Fax: (201)932-7815
Contact: Peter M. Sandman, Dir.
Research Areas: Public opinion about naturally occurring radon, mass media coverage of envirnmental-risk issues, and what industry, governmental agencies, and advocacy groups think the public should know about environmental risk.

★3464★ Environmental Defense Fund (EDF)
257 Park Ave. S.
New York, NY 10010
Phone: (212)505-2100
Fax: (212)505-2375
Contact: Frederic D. Krupp, Exec. Dir.
Research Areas: The environment, including studies on toxic chemicals and hazardous waste management, recycling, land and water resources, air quality, wildlife, energy, and global issues such as rainforest destruction, endangered species, and the greenhouse effect. Activities have included participation in the writing of the acid rain title of the 1989 Clean Air Act amendments.

★3465★ Environmental Engineering and Sciences Group
Virginia Polytechnic Inst. and State Univ.
330 Norris Hall
Dept. of Civil Engineering
Blacksburg, VA 24061
Phone: (703)961-6635
Contact: Clifford W. Randall, Program Chm.
Research Areas: Wastewater treatment technology, odor control technology, groundwater pollution control, industrial waste management, toxic substance control, sludge processing, biological nutrient removal processes, landfill leachate management, trace substance removal from drinking water, watershed monitoring and eutrophication control, public health engineering for developing countries, and onsite, rural, waste disposal systems. Evaluates acid precipitation and constructs models for water quality and wastewater treatment analyses.

★3466★ Environmental Engineering Center for Water and Waste Management
Michigan Technological Univ.
Houghton, MI 49931
Phone: (906)487-2758
Contact: Dr. C. Robert Baillod, Dir.
Research Areas: Environmental engineering, waste management, percolation processes, ground water modeling, carbon adsorption, fate and transformation of toxicants, advanced oxidation processes, and air foundry waste reduction and reuse. Research is directed toward developing and refining advanced waste management and resource recovery technology.

★3467★ Environmental Engineering Laboratory
Pennsylvania State Univ.
212 Sackett Bldg.
University Park, PA 16802
Phone: (814)863-4385
Fax: (814)863-7304
Contact: Prof. Brian A. Dempsey, Contact
Research Areas: Environmental engineering, aquatic chemistry of trace pollutants, municipal and industrial water, wastewater treatment, hazardous and toxic waste treatment, solid waste disposal, ground water contamination, and stream and estuarine analyses, including sponsored and unsponsored projects conducted principally by graduate students under direction of professional staff members.

★3468★ Environmental Engineering Laboratory
University of Arizona
Civil Engineering Dept.
Rm. 206
Tucson, AZ 85721
Phone: (602)621-6586
Contact: Dr. Raymond Sierka, Contact
Research Areas: Environmental engineering, including studies on water quality, pollution, reuse, and reclamation.

★3469★ Environmental Engineering Research Center
University of Florida
College of Engineering
217 Black Hall
Gainesville, FL 32611
Phone: (904)392-0841
Fax: (904)392-3076
Contact: Dr. Joseph J. Delfino, Chm.
Research Areas: Air pollution control, systems ecology, environmental biology and microbiology, radiological health, sewage treatment, solid and hazardous wastes, water supply and treatment, stream sanitation, water resources management, atmospheric chemistry, evaluation of acid rain impacts, environmental surveillance for radioactivity, lake eutrophication studies, water chemistry, and the fate and transport of chemicals in the environment.

★3470★ Environmental Engineering Research Laboratory
Washington State Univ.
141 Sloan
Pullman, WA 99164-2910
Phone: (509)335-2576
Contact: Dr. David R. Yonge, Dir.
Research Areas: Fundamental and applied research on fate and transport of hazardous compounds, water quality, and environmental toxicology. The Laboratory is composed of ten facilities used for teaching and research, equipment storage, chemical analysis, sample preparation, and bioassay procedures. The Unit Operation Laboratory evaluates various unit operations and processes used for the treatment of municipal and industrial wastewaters. Microbiology Laboratory functions involve the fate and role of bacteria and viruses in subsurface and aquatic environments. Limnology Laboratory is associated with the water quality evaluations of lakes and streams. Water Chemistry Laboratory investigates the chemical aspects of water quality. Instrumentation Laboratory houses equipment used in the determination of the concentrations of organic and inorganic toxic and nontoxic compounds in air, water, wastewater, sludges, and plant and fish tissue. Analytical Laboratory is used for wet chemical analysis of water and wastewater samples. Research Laboratory is assigned to special research needs in the area of environmental engineering. Radiochemistry Laboratory is used for preparing samples involving the use of radionuclides. Bioassay and Aquaculture Laboratory is equipped for bioassay using algae, bacteria, microinvertebrates, macroinvertebrates, and fish. Computers: IBM mainframe, Prime minicomputer.

★3471★ Environmental Engineering Research Laboratory
State Univ. of New York at Buffalo
202 Jarvis Hall
Buffalo, NY 14260
Phone: (716)636-2783
Fax: (716)636-3667
Contact: A. Scott Weber, Dir.
Research Areas: Development, analysis, and pilot plant testing of biochemical and physicochemical processes for environmental management; modeling the fate and transport of contaminates in natural and engineered environmental systems; and development of advanced techniques for pollutant analysis. Current projects include the study of combined physicochemical/biological processes for enhanced organic pollutant degradation, application of non-indigenous bacteria populations for xenobiotic compound biodegradation, the use of UV/ozone treatment for chemical constituents, process development for hazardous waste site remediation, and fate and transport modeling in the Great Lakes and subsurface systems.

★3472★ Environmental Exposure Laboratory
University of California, Los Angeles
1000 Veterans Ave.
Rehabilitation Center, Rm A 163
Los Angeles, CA 90024
Phone: (213)825-2739
Contact: Dr. Henry Gong Jr., Dir.
Research Areas: Air pollution, including effects of ozone on healthy subjects and patients with mild asthma, and physiological and cellular responses to acute exposures to ozone and sulfur dioxide. Special Resources: Smog chamber, and gas generating and monitoring equipment.

★3473★ Environmental Hazards Management Institute
10 Newmarket Rd.
PO Box 932
Durham, NH 03824
Phone: (603)868-1496
Fax: (603)868-1547
Contact: Alan J. Borner, Exec. Dir.
Research Areas: International hazardous waste management, including education in remedial response, technology, toxic waste reduction (both in volume and toxicity), and ultimate disposal/destruction.

★3474★ Environmental Health Program
Dept. of Civil Engineering
Learned Hall
Univ. of Kansas
Lawrence, KS 66045
Phone: (913)864-3731
Contact: Dr. Ross E. McKinney, Dir.
Research Areas: Environmental studies, including biological wastewater treatment, trace organics in surface water and groundwater, water treatment chemistry, and air pollution sampling, particularly toxic pollutant analysis. Research conducted by staff-supervised graduate students.

★3475★ Environmental Health Sciences Center
Oregon State Univ.
317 Weniger Hall
Corvallis, OR 97331-6504
Phone: (503)737-3608
Fax: (503)737-0481
Contact: Dr. Donald J. Reed, Dir.
Research Areas: Provides and stimulates coordinated multidisciplinary research to assess the impact of environmental chemicals on human health and to predict associated short- and long-term effects. Specific research draws upon capabilities of faculty, staff, and graduate students in chemistry, biochemistry, agricultural chemistry, biology, food science, fisheries and wildlife, veterinary medicine, pharmacology, toxicology, immunology, and statistics. Focal areas include toxicology of environmental chemicals and naturally occurring toxins, cellular and biochemical toxicology, carcinogenesis of environmental chemicals, mechanisms of toxicity, genetic toxicology, immunotoxicology, mass spectrometry, statistical studies, and analysis of enumerative data related to environmental health research.

★3476★ Environmental Health Sciences Research Laboratory
Tulane Univ.
F. Edward Hebert Research Center
Belle Chasse, LA 70037
Phone: (504)394-2233
Contact: Jamal Y. Shamas, Lab Supervisor/ Research Coordinator
Research Areas: Air and water pollution abatement, water quality evaluation and control, environmental health management, bacterial and mammalian cell mutagenesis, vector control, toxicology, and occupational safety and health, including interdisciplinary studies of toxic effects of pesticides on the environment, biological and physical-chemical

treatment of industrial waste, fumigation with air contaminants, environmental toxicology, industrial hygiene, and heavy metal, hazardous waste management, and related studies.

★3477★ Environmental Institute for Waste Management Studies
University of Alabama
PO Box 870203
Tuscaloosa, AL 35487
Phone: (205)348-8401
Fax: (205)348-8573
Contact: Dr. Robert A. Griffin, Dir.
Research Areas: Safe management of wastes, especially hazardous wastes, including criteria for the exclusion of certain hazardous wastes from land disposal, criteria for selection of alternative treatment and disposal technologies, ground- and surface-water contamination mechanisms, reliability of groundwater monitoring and modeling techniques, soil attenuation, toxicological impacts of contaminate migration, and environmental remedial action techniques. Projects include a study of public understanding and acceptance of risk assessment and a review of the continued use of injection wells for disposal of liquid hazardous wastes.

★3478★ Environmental Law Institute (ELI)
1616 P St., NW
Ste. 200
Washington, DC 20036
Phone: (202)328-5150
Fax: (202)328-5002
Contact: J. William Futrell, Pres.
Research Areas: Legal, administrative, economic, scientific, and technical aspects of environmental policy in such areas as enforcement, air and water pollution, toxic substances, hazardous wastes, surface mining, wetlands, and environment management. Research projects include studies on regulatory enforcement and reform, Superfund implementation, economics, international control strategies and training for professionals, and land use.

★3479★ Environmental Liability Law Program
University of Houston
Law Center
4800 Calhoun
Houston, TX 77204-6381
Phone: (713)749-1393
Fax: (713)749-2567
Contact: Prof. Sanford E. Gaines, Dir.
Research Areas: Environmental liability law, focusing on contamination of the natural (air, water, and soil) environment by human action, including personal injury or property damage arising from environmental contamination and the international dimensions of environmental liability. Seeks to improve the legal system's response to health and natural resource damage from pollution.

★3480★ Environmental Policy Institute
218 D St., SE
Washington, DC 20003
Phone: (202)544-2600
Contact: Michael Clark, Pres.
Research Areas: Energy conservation, water, coal, oil, gas, nuclear energy, synthetic fuels, oceans and coasts, and agricultural resources, including studies on surface mining, biotechnology, rural land, groundwater protection, synthetic fuels assessment, water conservation, Chesapeake Bay preservation, protection of natural resources internationally, nuclear and hazardous waste transportation, nuclear waste storage, nuclear industry insurance, radiation and health, and nuclear weapons testing and production. Serves as a national information center.

★3481★ Environmental Quality Laboratory
California Inst. of Technology
105-96
Pasadena, Canada 91125
Phone: (818)356-4400
Contact: Prof. Norman H. Brooks, Dir.
Research Areas: Policy-oriented studies of problems of environmental quality and natural resources, including research on air pollution, energy economics and conservation, water resources, water quality (surface and ground waters), ocean disposal of wastewater and sludge, residuals management, and hazardous substances. Research conducted by engineers, natural scientists, and social scientists, most of whom are faculty members and graduate students in various departments of the Institute.

★3482★ Environmental Remote Sensing Center
University of Wisconsin-Madison
1225 W. Dayton St.
Madison, WI 53706
Phone: (608)263-3251
Contact: Prof. Thomas M. Lillesand, Dir.
Research Areas: Develops research expertise and training opportunities in the application of remote sensing and geographic information systems (GIS) to environmental problems, including problems in water resources, agriculture, forestry, and land use planning.

★3483★ Environmental Research Center
Washington State Univ.
305 Troy Hall
Pullman, WA 99164-4430
Phone: (509)335-8536
Fax: (509)335-7636
Research Areas: Environmental concerns, including nuclear and hazardous wastes, risk assessment, environmental planning, land use, energy, environmental impacts of technology, ecosystem studies, and modeling of environmental systems.

★3484★ Environmental Research Center
University of the Virgin Islands
St. Thomas, VI 00802
Phone: (809)776-9200
Contact: Dr. MaryLou Coulston, Coordinator
Research Areas: Environmental research, including studies on recreation, water quality, water management, ecosystem analysis and management, natural resources identification and development, tropical biology, seagrass, and coral reef monitoring.

★3485★ Environmental Research Center
University of Notre Dame
Dept. of Biological Sciences
Notre Dame, IN 46556
Phone: (219)239-7186
Fax: (219)239-7413
Contact: Ronald A Hellenthal, Assoc. Prof. and Gillen Dir.
Research Areas: Land/water interface and materials cycling in abiotic and biotic systems. Conducts sampling and experimental work throughout the year in winterized laboratory facilities and performs large-scale manipulation of aquatic ecosystems using 30 ponds and lakes of various sizes. Conducts whole ecosystem experiments and studies on aquatic food webs and productivity, limnology, littoral zone predator-prey interactions, and reproductive physiology of fishes. Databases: Solar radiation, physical/chemical limnology, phytoplankton, and zooplankton for three area lakes.

★3486★ Environmental Research Center
University of Nevada-Las Vegas
4505 S. Maryland Pkwy.
Las Vegas, NV 89154-4009
Phone: (702)739-3382
Fax: (702)739-3094
Contact: Dr. Delbert S. Barth, Dir.
Research Areas: Conducts environmental monitoring, exposure assessments, hazardous waste analyses, sampling and analytical quality assurance, statistical analyses and modeling, cultural resource inventories, geothermal potential assessments, and monitoring methods development, including radiation, noise, toxic and hazardous waste, integrated exposure and risk assessments, terrestrial and aquatic community structure, remote sensing, toxicity testing, and surface and fluid geochemistry.

★3487★ Environmental Research Center
University of Missouri-Rolla
Rolla, MO 65401
Phone: (314)341-4485
Contact: Dr. Ju-Chang Huang, Dir.
Research Areas: Engineering and science, including interdisciplinary studies on health effects of altered geochemistry associated with mine drainage from western interior coals, effects of natural organic materials on the mobilization and removal of toxic organics during coagulation, reduction of toxic metal concentrations from municipal waste treatment sludges, effect of heavy metal toxicities on fish, adsorption and desorption of volatile organic compounds in groundwater environment, growths and activities of fixed film in waste treatment, use of pure oxygen in rotating biological contactors, complete treatment of water and wastewater by alternative innovative technologies, sludge digestion by anaerobic fluidized beds and submerged rotating biological contactors, and polishing of lagoon effluent by land treatment. Provides graduate training in water and wastewater engineering, air pollution control, and solid waste management fields, utilizing Center's laboratories and research facilities of cooperating academic departments.

★3488★ Environmental Research Foundation
PO Box 3541
Princeton, NJ 08543-3541
Phone: (609)683-0707
Contact: Peter Montague Ph.D., Contact
Research Areas: Toxic, hazardous, and solid waste problems, including management, incineration, and landfills. Databases: RACHEL (Remote Access Chemical Hazards Electronic Library) holds documents on a range of problems associated with hazardous materials, including acid rain biotechnology, and drinking water quality.

★3489★ Environmental Research Institute for Hazardous Materials and Wastes
University of Connecticut
191 Auditorium Rd.
Box U210
Storrs, CT 06268
Phone: (203)486-4015
Contact: Dr. George Hoag, Dir.
Research Areas: Hazardous wastes and materials management, including contamination of groundwater, surface waters, soils, sediments, and the atmosphere; hazardous material and waste generation and

control technologies; and potential public health and environmental problems caused by new and emerging industries.

★3490★ Environmental Research Laboratory
University of Arizona
Tucson International Airport
2601 E. Airport Dr.
Tucson, AZ 85706
Phone: (602)741-1990
Fax: (602)573-0852
Contact: Carl N. Hodges, Dir.
Research Areas: Controlled-environment agriculture and controlled-environment aquaculture, primarily for coastal desert areas, and solar energy.

★3491★ Environmental Resource Center
San Jose State Univ.
One Washington Sq.
San Jose, CA 95192-0116
Phone: (408)924-5467
Contact: Stephen Shunk, Dir.
Research Areas: Alternative energy and renewable resources, wildlife, conservation, general ecology, and environmental education. Undertakes research consistent with interests and experience of faculty members of the University and develops research projects to be undertaken jointly by academic departments of the University. With assistance of area environmental industry, the Center serves as an environmental resource through which research on area environmental quality may be channeled and guided.

★3492★ Environmental Resources Research Institute
Pennsylvania State Univ.
100 Land & Water Resource Bldg.
University Park, PA 16802
Phone: (814)863-0291
Fax: (814)865-3378
Contact: Dr. Archie J. McDonnell, Dir.
Research Areas: Air, land, and water resources, including land recycling of wastes, remote sensing of Earth resources, environmental toxicology, hazardous and toxic waste management, acid precipitation, air pollution control techniques, water quality management, technical assessment and information transfer, water supply management, alternative waste disposal systems, resource policy and economic forecasting, resource conservation and supply protection, energy production and the environment, resource management for economic growth, impact assessment of public programs, resource valuation and taxation, water resource planning and modeling, and resource use. Special Resources: Maintains field research sites statewide for acid rain monitoring and watershed studies. Also operates laboratories for remote sensing, water quality testing, soil and environmental chemistry, and forest hydrology.

★3493★ Environmental Science and Engineering Program
Clarkson Univ.
Rowley Laboratories
Potsdam, NY 13676
Phone: (315)268-3853
Contact: Dr. Thomas L. Theis, Professor
Research Areas: Engineering studies in aquatic environmental quality and pollution control, including studies on water supplies and drinking water, toxic and nutrient pollutants in natural waters, hazardous wastes, wastewater renovation, acid precipitation and acidified aquatic systems, and groundwater systems. Special Resources: Equipment for physical, chemical, and biological experimentation and engineering testing of processes on a pilot-plant scale.

★3494★ Environmental Science Laboratory
Texas Tech Univ.
Dept. of Civil Engineering
PO Box 4089
Lubbock, TX 79409-1023
Phone: (806)742-0161
Fax: (806)742-3488
Contact: Dr. Tony Mollhagen, Dir.
Research Areas: Protecting natural surface waters and groundwater through basic and applied science and technology.

★3495★ Environmental Studies Center
University of Maine
Coburn Hall #11
Orono, ME 04469
Phone: (207)581-1490
Fax: (207)581-1426
Contact: Gregory K. White, Dir.
Research Areas: Stimulates and coordinates research, educational activities, and public service in physical, biological, and social aspects of the environment, especially water resources and closely related disciplines. Specific studies include landspreading of municipal and pulp and paper sludges, fish and food processing waste, and bioash.

★3496★ Environmental Studies Center
Lehigh Univ.
Chandler-Ullman Bldg. #17
Bethlehem, PA 18015
Phone: (215)758-3670
Contact: Dr. Gerard P. Lennon, Acting Dir.
Research Areas: Environmental engineering, coastal and wetlands processes and engineering, water and waste treatment, solids and hazardous waste control, environmental economics, groundwater and surface water hydrology, and marine sciences, including biology, geology, chemistry, and interdisciplinary applications to environmental studies.

★3497★ Environmental Studies Institute
Drexel Univ.
Philadelphia, PA 19104
Phone: (215)895-2265
Contact: Dr. Bernard Hamel, Dir.
Research Areas: Water and wastewater treatment, environmental chemistry, environmental toxicology, environmental planning and management, air resources, environmental health, hazardous wastes, food toxicology and safety, and environmental assessment. Special Resources: Instrumental capabilities include a total organic carbon analyzer, ultraviolet spectrophotometer, atomic absorption spectrophotometer, ion chromatograph, automated chemical analyzer, high speed centrifuge, liquid scintillation counter, polarography, research pH meters, four high performance liquid chromatographs, eight gas chromatographs, and specialized water and wastewater analysis equipment.

★3498★ Environmental Systems Application Center (ESAC)
Indiana Univ.
School of Public & Environmental Affairs
Bloomington, IN 47405
Phone: (812)885-4556
Contact: William W. Jones, Dir.
Research Areas: Conducts sponsored research and educational activities in collaboration with local, state, federal, and private groups in science and policy aspects of energy development, environmental impact analysis, water quality, lake management, terrestrial and wetlands ecology, groundwater modeling, and solid and hazardous waste management. Seeks to solve crucial environmental problems facing municipalities, state of Indiana, and nation through study of ecological systems and environmental policies.

★3499★ Environmental Systems Engineering Institute
University of Central Florida
Dept. of Civil Engineering & Environmental Science
PO Box 25000
Orlando, FL 32816
Phone: (305)275-2785
Contact: Dr. James S. Taylor Ph.D., Dir.
Research Areas: Environmental systems engineering. Areas of concern are water resources, potable water, wastewater, land, noise, air, solid waste, and chemical analysis. The Institute serves as an environmental information center in cooperation with other environmental information centers in the state of Florida. Special Resources: Operates the Priority Pollutants Laboratory (PPL), a chemical laboratory offering chemical analysis for environmental applications.

★3500★ Environmental Testing Laboratory
Arizona State Univ.
School of Architecture
Tempe, AZ 85287-1605
Phone: (602)965-2764
Fax: (602)965-1594
Contact: Mr. M. Underhill, Head
Research Areas: Testing of solar energy devices, especially passive and hybrid solar cooling and solar water heaters. Specific projects include daylighting, sensory perception, variable environmental conditions, human factor studies, cooling strategies for hot and arid climates, and solar and earth-integrated architecture. Conducts building materials testing. Special Resources: Environmental testing chamber, sky simulator, environmental simulation laboratory, and IBM 3081 computer.

★3501★ Environmental Toxicology Center
University of Wisconsin-Madison
309 Infirmary
Madison, WI 53706
Phone: (608)263-4580
Contact: Prof. Colin R. Jefcoate, Dir.
Research Areas: Toxicology and problems related to presence of potentially hazardous synthetic and naturally occurring chemicals in the environment, e.g. heavy metals, chlorinated hydrocarbons, pesticides, mycotoxins, and food-borne toxins, including identification, quantification, and toxicologic studies of such chemicals.

★3502★ Environmental Trace Substances Research Center
University of Missouri
5450 S. Sinclair Rd.
Columbia, MO 65203
Phone: (314)882-2151
Fax: (314)882-3031
Contact: Dr. Armon F. Yanders, Dir.
Research Areas: Trace substances in the environment, including studies in organic and inorganic chemistry and direct and indirect studies on environmental problems associated with pollution and pollution abatement. Provides analytical chemistry services to University personnel, governmental agencies, and industry.

★3503★ E.P.A. National Small Flows Clearinghouse
West Virginia Univ.
617 Spruce St.
PO Box 6064
Morgantown, WV 26506-6064
Phone: 800-624-8301
Fax: (304)293-3947
Contact: John L. Mori, Operations Dir.
Research Areas: Small community wastewater collection, treatment, and management systems. Designs and manages alternative wastewater technologies. Databases: Small community wastewater technology literature, innovative and alternative wastewater systems constructed by the E.P.A., state regulations, key persons in state government agencies, newsletters for professionals and for officials of small communities, training programs for engineers and regulatory officials. Also maintains a toll-free computer bulletin board.

★3504★ ERIC Clearinghouse for Science, Mathematics and Environmental Education (ERIC/SMEAC)
Ohio State Univ.
1200 Chambers Rd., Rm. 310
Columbus, OH 43212
Phone: (614)292-6717
Contact: Dr. Robert W. Howe, Dir.
Research Areas: Science, mathematics, and environmental education-kindergarten through college, including postsecondary and nonformal education. Conducts surveys, compilations of abstracts, annual reviews of research, research synthesis, meta-analysis, and policy reviews.

★3505★ Experimental Cities, Inc.
PO Box 731
Pacific Palisades, Canada 90272-0731
Phone: (213)276-0686
Fax: (213)274-7401
Contact: Dr. Genevieve Marcus, Co- Pres.
Research Areas: Endeavors to discover and create innovative approaches to social and environmental problems. Conducts design research on Earthlab, a research center in the form of an experimental, semiautonomous community of 20,000 to 50,000 inhabitants. Also studies electronically-based relationships and group conflict resolution. Administers the Equal Relationships Institute, which studies and implements cooperation and equal relationships between individuals and groups. Special Resources: Computer-based World Citizens Network; XLNET; and International News Network.

★3506★ Federal Interagency Sedimentation Project
St. Anthony Falls Hydraulic Lab.
Hennepin Island & 3rd Ave., SE
Minneapolis, MN 55414
Phone: (612)370-2362
Fax: (612)627-4609
Contact: John V. Skinner, Project Leader
Research Areas: Improvement and standardization of methods for measuring quantity and character of sediment transported in natural streams. Develops automatic equipment for sampling and in situ measurement of sediment concentration.

★3507★ Feed and Fertilizer Laboratory
Louisiana State Univ.
Baton Rouge, LA 70893
Phone: (504)388-2755
Contact: Prof. Hershel F. Morris Jr., Dir.
Research Areas: Feeds, fertilizers, agricultural lime, pesticides, and pesticide residues, including work on analytical methods development.

★3508★ Fitch Natural History Reservation
University of Kansas
Lawrence, KS 66044
Phone: (913)843-3612
Contact: Prof. Henry S. Fitch, Superintendent
Research Areas: Systematics and ecology, including entomology and botany. The Reservation is 590 acres of land preserved in its natural state for research on ecological processes in natural communities, primarily oak-hickory deciduous forest. Utilizes live traps for mammals and reptiles. Special Resources: Maintains weather records since 1950.

★3509★ Florida Institute of Oceanography
830 First St. S.
St. Petersburg, FL 33701
Phone: (813)893-9100
Contact: Dr. John C. Ogden, Dir.
Research Areas: Develops and manages statewide oceanographic research programs requiring multidisciplinary expertise and/or facilities not available at one university or agency, including programs in environmental assessment, ocean resource development, coastal zone management, ocean currents, endangered species, beach erosion, fisheries conservation and management, red tide, water quality, tourism, shipping, oil and gas, and coastal and port construction. Operates the Keys Regional Marine Laboratory joint with the Florida Department of Natural Resources. Special Resources: Two oceanographic research vessels (71-foot R/V Bellows and 110-foot R/V Suncoaster) and an associated pool of oceanographic equipment.

★3510★ Florida Museum of Natural History
University of Florida
Museum Dr.
Gainesville, FL 32611
Phone: (904)392-1721
Fax: (904)392-8783
Contact: Dr. Thomas Peter Bennett, Dir.
Research Areas: Natural history, including zoology, botany, paleobotany, systematics, ecology, zooarchaeology, history, ethnology, archeology, and physical anthropology, including cultural prehistory of southeastern U.S. and Caribbean areas and forensic anthropology. Special Resources: Maintains research collections of birds, mammals, fish, reptiles, amphibians, molluscs, vertebrate, invertebrate and plant fossils, plants, human osteology and cultural artifacts, also a bioacoustic archive, an animal behavior laboratory, and research facilities for postdoctoral fellows and visiting scientists. Administratively controls the 9,000-acre Ordway Preserve, the adjunct Comparative Behavior Laboratory, the Florida State Herbarium, and the Allyn Museum of Entomology in Sarasota, Florida.

★3511★ Florida Resources and Environmental Analysis Center
Florida State Univ.
361 Bellamy Bldg.
Tallahassee, FL 32306
Phone: (904)644-2007
Contact: Edward A. Fernald, Dir.
Research Areas: Land use, resource management, and environmental problems, including water resources management, hazardous waste, and geographic information systems. Multidisciplinary projects utilize teams of physical and social scientists, specialists in environmental science, biology, geography, oceanography, urban and regional planning, economics, business, education, population, and law.

★3512★ Florida Solar Energy Center
300 State Rd. 401
Cape Canaveral, FL 32920
Phone: (407)783-0300
Fax: (407)783-2571
Contact: Dr. David L. Block, Dir.
Research Areas: Photovoltaics, energy building design, innovative air conditioning systems, hydrogen, hot water systems, and other solar energy activities for the state of Florida. Program objectives include research and development, testing, certification, establishment of standards, educational services, and information dissemination. Responsible for mandatory certification of all solar energy systems manufactured and sold in Florida.

★3513★ Florida State University Center for Study of Population
653 Bellamy Social Science Bldg.
Tallahassee, FL 32306
Phone: (904)644-1762
Fax: (904)644-8818
Contact: Dr. William J. Serow, Director
Research Areas: Environmental quality and population change.

★3514★ Fluid Dynamics and Diffusion Laboratory
Colorado State Univ.
College of Engineering
Foothills Campus
Fort Collins, CO 80523
Phone: (303)491-8574
Fax: (303)491-8671
Contact: Dr. Robert N. Meroney, Dir.
Research Areas: Wind engineering, including air pollution control, behavior of smoke plumes from power plant stacks, hazard analysis of liquid natural gas storage, industrial aerodynamics, environmental design for urban centers, wind power, heat transfer from buildings, and wind forces on buildings and bridges; electrohydrodynamics, including effects of turbulence on the performance of particle precipitators; and instrumentation, including aerosol and tracer gas concentration sensors and hot wire anemometry. Special Resources: Meteorological wind tunnel, industrial aerodynamics wind tunnel, environmental wind tunnel, gust wind tunnel, wind tunnel-flume facility, thermal stratification wind tunnel, transpiration wind tunnel, separation wind tunnel, aerosol test facility with remote sensing laser-powered particle spectrometer.

★3515★ Forest, Wildlife and Range Experiment Station
University of Idaho
Moscow, ID 83843
Phone: (208)885-6441
Fax: (208)885-6226
Contact: John C. Hendee, Dir.
Research Areas: Forestry science, including forest management, economics, nursery management, entomology, genetics, pathology, soils, and policy analysis. Other programs concentrate on wildlife, fisheries, range ecology and management, forest products, resource recreation management, and tourism.

★3516★ Forestry Experiment Stations and Arboretum
University of Tennessee at Knoxville
901 Kerr Hollow Rd.
Oak Ridge, TN 37830
Phone: (615)483-3571
Contact: Richard M. Evans, Superintendent
Research Areas: Forest tree breeding, stripmine reclamation, Christmas trees, forest

fertilization, timber stand improvement, species adaptation, soil-site-production relations, urban forestry, forest wildlife, tree genetics and improvement, and tree irrigation.

★3517★ Formaldehyde Institute, Inc.
1330 Connecticut Ave., NW, Ste. 300
Washington, DC 20036
Phone: (202)659-0060
Fax: (202)659-1699
Contact: John F. Murray, Pres.
Research Areas: Health and toxicity studies on formaldehyde, including technical research on decay rates and methods of analysis. Seeks to ascertain the health effects of exposure to formaldehyde and formaldehyde-containing products.

★3518★ Gannett Energy Laboratory
Florida Inst. of Technology
150 W. Univ. Blvd.
Melbourne, FL 32901
Phone: (407)768-8000
Contact: Robert A. Merrill, Contact
Research Areas: Solar energy, thermal energy and storage, ocean thermal energy conversion, and solar, fluid, and thermal simulation. Special Resources: Solar test platform, two-phase flow loop, VAX-11/780 computer.

★3519★ Genetics Laboratory
University of Vermont
Vermont Regional Cancer Center
32 N. Prospect St.
Burlington, VT 05401
Phone: (802)863-5716
Fax: (802)656-8429
Contact: Dr. Richard Albertini, Dir.
Research Areas: Genetic toxicology, including investigations of the mechanisms of mutation, development of tests for detecting the consequences of exposure to environmental toxicants which damage genes (genotoxicants), definition of human populations which are unusually susceptible to certain mutations, and correlation of the presence of indicators of genotoxicant exposure and/or genetic damage with subsequent health outcomes of monitored human populations.

★3520★ Geo-Heat Center
Oregon Inst. of Technology
3201 Campus Dr.
Klamath Falls, OR 97601
Phone: (503)885-1750
Contact: Paul Lienau, Dir.
Research Areas: Low temperature, geothermal direct heat systems for use in space heating and cooling, greenhouse heating, aquaculture, industrial processes, and geothermal heat pumps. Projects include determining the location of geothermal resources, prioritizing exploration needs, designing injection wells, monitoring network systems for environmental impacts, determining the effects of geothermal fluids on braced-plate heat exchangers, and evaluating the effects of vertical pump thermal oil on groundwater quality.

★3521★ Geological Survey of Alabama
420 Hackberry Ln.
PO Box O
Tuscaloosa, AL 35486-9780
Phone: (205)349-2852
Contact: Dr. E.A. Mancini, State Geologist and Dir.
Research Areas: Assessments of mineral, coastal, energy, and water resources of the state to determine quality, character, and capacity for development. The Survey provides information and evaluations to the State Oil and Gas Board of Alabama and other state agencies to assist with the acquisition of baseline data needed for regulatory decisions. Research activities are conducted to benefit the citizens of Alabama. Special Resources: Geochemistry laboratory.

★3522★ Geothermally-Heated Greenhouse Research Facility
New Mexico State Univ.
Box 30001
Las Cruces, NM 88003
Phone: (505)646-1846
Contact: Dr. Rudi Schoenmachers, Dir.
Research Areas: Geothermal energy-based horticulture. Special Resources: Two 6,000 square foot free-standing greenhouses.

★3523★ Glacier Research Group
University of New Hampshire
Durham, 03824
Phone: (603)862-3146
Contact: Dr. Paul A. Mayewski, Dir.
Research Areas: Glaciology, climate change, atmospheric chemistry, global distribution of pollution, glaciochemistry, and glacial geomorphology. Programs concentrate on high alpine and polar ice masses in the Himalaya Mountains, Antarctica, and Greenland.

★3524★ Global Change and Environmental Quality Program
University of Colorado-Boulder
Campus Box 334
Boulder, CO 80309
Phone: (303)492-6378
Contact: Dr. William Lewis, Dir.
Research Areas: Global change and environmental quality research, including global climate change, local and regional environmental quality, and sustainable development.

★3525★ Global Foundation, Inc.
PO Box 248103
Coral Gables, FL 33124-8103
Phone: (305)284-4457
Contact: Dr. Behram N. Kursunoglu, Chm.
Research Areas: Global issues and frontier problems in science including international environment issues such as climate control, greenhouse effect, and ocean pollution; and interdependence of developing and industrialized nations, including interdependence on fuel. Also conducts theoretical studies on elementary particles and the nature of the universe, origin of the solar system, evolution of the genetic code, physics and chemistry of memory and neural membranes, and new forms of matter.

★3526★ Graduate Program in Community and Regional Planning
University of Texas at Austin
Austin, TX 78712
Phone: (512)471-8135
Contact: Terry D. Kahn, Ph.D.
Research Areas: Community and regional planning, including growth management, land use and development planning, environmental resource planning, housing, transportation planning, public service planning, and economic development planning.

★3527★ Great Lakes Area Resource Studies Unit
Michigan Technological Univ.
Dept. of Biological Sciences
Houghton, MI 49931
Phone: (906)487-2478
Fax: (906)487-2398
Contact: Dr. J. Robert Stottlemeyer, Head
Research Areas: Structure and functioning of boreal and northern hardwood ecosystems, nutrient release following natural fire in Rocky Mountain and Alaskan systems, effect of atmospheric pollutants on watershed/lake ecosystems, and research on biosphere reserve ecosystems.

★3528★ Great Lakes Coastal Research Laboratory
Purdue Univ.
c/o School of Civil Engineering
West Lafayette, IN 47907
Phone: (317)494-3713
Contact: Dr. William L. Wood, Dir.
Research Areas: Coastal erosion, coastal change modeling, lake level variation, flow and sediment transport in submarine canyons, wave climatology, storm effects, fate and transport of contaminated sediments, and water circulation. Studies are concerned with the Great Lakes Basin, especially Lake Michigan and Lake Huron. Prepares environmental impact statements. Collaborates with the civil engineering hydromechanics laboratory on many of its research projects. Special Resources: Wind tunnel, towing tank, circulation flumes. Computers: VAX-11/750; IBM 3090; CRAY.

★3529★ Great Lakes Laboratory
State Univ. Coll. at Buffalo
1300 Elmwood Ave.
Buffalo, NY 14222
Phone: (716)878-5422
Contact: Dr. Harish C. Sikka, Dir.
Research Areas: Environmental problems of the Great Lakes region with particular emphasis on the environmental toxicology and chemistry of pollutants and their socioeconomic impact. Also studies shoreline utilization and waterfront planning, and develops and evaluates pollution abatement technology. Special Resources: Maintains an all-weather field station at confluence of Lake Erie and Niagara River, a 66-foot research vessel, and supporting craft.

★3530★ Great Lakes Research Consortium
214 Baker Laboratory
SUNY College of Environmental Science & Forestry
Syracuse, NY 13210
Phone: (315)470-6894
Contact: Richard Smardon Ph.D., Codirector
Research Areas: Facilitates research and scholarly activity at member campuses on issues affecting the Great Lakes, especially Lakes Erie and Ontario, the Niagara and St. Lawrence Rivers, and the Great Lakes Basin ecosystem. Interests include water quantity, recreation, aquaculture, maintenance of habitat and species, socio-economic impact of management strategies, information systems and mathematical modeling, and public attitudes on utilization and protection of resources in the Great Lakes system.

★3531★ Great Lakes Tomorrow
PO Box 41248
Brecksville, OH 44141
Phone: (216)838-4176
Contact: James W. Cowden, Dir.
Research Areas: Policy research as it relates to Great Lakes issues, including the ecosystem management, water quantity/quality relationships, energy, coastal planning and erosion and flooding, wastewater management, toxic and hazardous materials, Great Lakes impact assessments, institutional issues in Great Lakes management, and remedial action programs in Ohio.

★3532★ Great Swamp Research Institute
Office of the Associate Dean
Natural Sciences & Math, 305 Weyandt Hall
Indiana Univ. of Pennsylvania
Indiana, PA 15705
Phone: (412)357-5700
Contact: Anne Harris Katz, Codirector
Research Areas: Ecology, wetlands, and effects of urbanization on natural ecosystems. Conducts basic research into effects of land planning decisions on natural ecosystems, reviews existing environmental impact statements, and investigates the degree of influence that regulations exert on protecting natural systems. Databases: Water quality, plants, invertebrates, fish, amphibians, reptiles, and mammals of northern New Jersey.

★3533★ Greenley Memorial Research Center
University of Missouri-Columbia
RR -1 Box 228
Novelty, MO 63460
Phone: (816)739-4410
Contact: Randy Smoot, Supervisor
Research Areas: Monitoring and developing ways to conserve energy, particularly fossil energy, in growing and harvesting farm products, including irrigation, double-cropping, machinery management, erosion control, crop breeding, soil fertility, weed and disease control, variety testing, beef cattle backgrounding, and pest management. Located on a 700-acre tract of land in Knox County.

★3534★ Groundwater Research Center
University of Cincinnati
College of Engineering
Mail Location 18
Cincinnati, OH 45221-0018
Phone: (513)475-2933
Contact: Dr. Constantine Papadakis, Dir.
Research Areas: Development of techniques for testing, calibration, and validation of software for modeling the transport and fate of groundwater contaminants; development of a knowledge base expert system for selection and application of appropriate models for predicting the fate of groundwater pollutants and analyzing remedial action alternatives; use of subsurface monitoring and mathematical modeling to study the processes of dispersion and absorption of solutes; study of physical processes governing the migration of contaminants in the saturated, unsaturated, and partially-saturated soil zones; quantitative and qualitative health risk characterization involving biomedical and biomathematical analysis; exposure assessment of toxic substances involving source characterization transport, chemical transformations, and human intake; and analysis of the shifting chemical composition, toxicity, and migration patterns of complex mixtures. The Center is organized into a Groundwater Management Group, concerned with the migration and remediation of chemicals in groundwater, and a Groundwater Health Risk Assessment Group, concerned with the health risks of groundwater contaminated with hazardous wastes. Special Resources: Available facilities include an inductively coupled plasma/atomic emission spectrophotometer, a high-resolution gas chromatography/mass spectroscopy facility, various lysimeters, and pilot plant.

★3535★ Growth Management Studies
University of Florida
College of Law
Holland Hall, Rm. 319
Gainesville, FL 32611
Phone: (904)392-6642
Fax: (904)392-8727
Contact: Prof. Julian Conrad Juergensmeyer, Codirector
Research Areas: Legal and policy issues dealing with growth management planning and law, emphasizing land use planning and environment planning.

★3536★ Gulf Coast Hazardous Substance Research Center
Lamar University
PO Box 10613
Beaumont, TX 77710
Phone: (409)880-8768
Contact: William A. Cawley, Dir.
Research Areas: Alternative solutions to hazardous waste management, including waste minimization, alternate treatment technology development, andbioremediation.

★3537★ Hawaii Cooperative Fishery Research Unit
University of Hawaii at Manoa
2538 The Mall
Honolulu, HI 96822
Phone: (808)965-8350
Fax: (808)956-6751
Contact: Dr. James D. Parrish, Unit Leader
Research Areas: Freshwater, estuarine, and inshore marine ecology, including studies in life history of fishes and invertebrates, analysis of marine, stream, and estuarine ecosystems, trophic systems, and aquatic communities.

★3538★ Hawaii Undersea Research Laboratory
University of Hawaii at Manoa
1000 Pope Rd., MSB 303
Honolulu, HI 96822
Phone: (808)956-6335
Fax: (808)956-2136
Contact: Dr. Alexander Malahoff, Dir.
Research Areas: Fisheries, pollution, sea floor properties and processes, and ocean technology and services, including studies of ecosystems and trophic dynamics; habitat degradation and enhancement; harvesting impact; animal behavior; gear development for fisheries; physical effects of waste disposal at sea; behavioral, biochemical, and physiological responses of marine organisms to pollutants; geological, geochemical, and geophysical aspects of the sea floor; marine sanctuary monitoring; submersible development; engineering and equipment testing and recovery; medical and diving physiology; and marine archeology. Special Resources: Maintains an operations center 15 miles east of Honolulu at Makapuu Point, a two-man submersible (Makali'i), a three-man submersible (PISCES V) with 2,000-meter depth capability, two submersible launch, recovery, and transport vehicles (LRT), and remotely operated vehicles.

★3539★ Hazardous Materials Control Research Institute
9300 Columbia Blvd.
Silver Spring, MD 20910
Phone: (301)587-9390
Fax: (301)589-0182
Contact: Hal Bernard, Dir.
Research Areas: Hazardous materials, hazardous materials control, toxic materials, risk assessment, spills, and uncontrolled hazardous waste sites.

★3540★ Hazardous Materials Management and Resource Recovery (HAMMARR)
University of Alabama
Dept. of Chemical Engineering
PO Box 870203
Tuscaloosa, AL 35487-0203
Phone: (205)348-8401
Contact: John E. Moeller, Dir.
Research Areas: Conducts basic and applied research in waste minimization. Interests include groundwater contamination, development of low and/or non-pollution technology, reduction of volume and toxicity of landfill wastes, and heat recovery and air pollution control for municipal waste incineration. Special Resources: Maintains a municipal waste incinerator with spray dryer and bag house.

★3541★ Hazardous Substances Research Center for U.S. EPA Regions 7 and 8
Dept. of Chemical Engineering
Durland Hall
Manhattan, KS 66506-5102
Phone: (913)532-5584
Fax: (913)532-7810
Contact: Dr. Larry Erickson, Dir.
Research Areas: Identification, treatment and reduction of hazardous waste substances resulting from agriculture, forestry, mining, and mineral processing. Specific research has been undertaken in the following areas: 1) soil and water contamination by heavy metals; 2) soil and groundwater contamination from a variety of sources; 3) development of incineration, biodegradation, and immobilization technology; 4) development of simplified and inexpensive methods for analyzing contaminated soil; 5) hazardous waste minimization; and 6) determination of the safe concentration levels of hazardous substances in soils and in water. In addition, the Center has assigned the highest priority to research on soil and processes to clean up contaminate

★3542★ Hazardous Waste and Toxic Substance Research and Management Center
Clarkson Univ.
Rowley Laboratories
Potsdam, NY 13699
Phone: (315)268-6400
Contact: Thomas L. Theis Ph.D., Dir.
Research Areas: Hazardous waste management, including assessments of exposure, the environment, technology, and policy. Also studies toxicology, microbiology, biology, organic and inorganic chemistry, ecosystems, aquatic chemistry, groundwater and seepage, environmental health, transportation of waste, and air pollution.

★3543★ Hazardous Waste Research and Information Center
One E. Hazelwood Dr.
Champaign, IL 61820
Phone: (217)333-8940
Fax: (217)333-8944
Contact: Dr. David L. Thomas, Dir.
Research Areas: Integrates research, industrial and technical assistance, database management, laboratory services, and information resources in a program to manage and help solve Illinois' hazardous waste problems. Topics include: characterization and assessment; environmental process and effects; prevention and source reduction; treatment, disposal, and remediation; risk assessment; and policy analysis. Collects, analyzes, synthesizes, and disseminates information on hazaradous waste management.

Databases: Maintains research and regulatory data on hazardous wastes in Illinois.

★3544★ Hazardous Waste Research Center
Louisiana State Univ.
3418 CEBA Bldg.
Baton Rouge, LA 70803
Phone: (504)388-6770
Fax: (504)388-5990
Contact: Prof. L.J. Thibodeaux, Dir.
Research Areas: Hazardous waste, including incineration, alternate methods of treatment/destruction, and chemical/materials interaction and stabilization.

★3545★ Health and Energy Institute
PO Box 5357
Takoma Park, MD 20913
Phone: (301)585-5541
Contact: Kathleen M. Tucker, Dir.
Research Areas: Effects of radiation on health, environmental hazards and their effects on children, food irradiation, nuclear waste sites, and weapons production and health.

★3546★ Health Effects Institute
141 Portland St., Ste. 7300
Cambridge, MA 02139
Phone: (617)621-0266
Fax: (617)621-0267
Contact: Andrew Sivak Ph.D., Pres.
Research Areas: Conducts, supports, and evaluates research and testing related to the health effects of emissions from motor vehicles. Specific research activities focus on the following program areas: health effects of diesel emissions; effects of nitrogen dioxide on susceptibility to infection and on lung development; effects of nitrogen oxides, ozone, and diesel exhausts on susceptible populations; identification of early markers of lung disease related to mobile source emissions; dose to target tissues; health effects of carbon monoxide; health effects of methanol and aldehydes; and mechanisms of oxidant injury in the lung. HEI's Health Research Committee defines objectives, directs activities, selects studies from an international competition, and administers research programs. The Health Review Committee, a committee of scientists, evaluates reports of sponsored studies to assess their validity and significance in resolving scientific questions of regulatory importance.

★3547★ Health Research, Inc.
1683 Empire State Plaza Tower Bldg.
Albany, NY 12237
Phone: (518)474-1689
Contact: David Axelrod M.D., Pres.
Research Areas: Public health and cancer, including basic and clinical research in cause and treatment of cancer and related malignancies and environmental studies to determine long-range health hazards of pesticides, industrial discharge, and radioactive and sewage wastes. Also studies rehabilitation biology, chemistry, toxicology, and environment.

★3548★ High Altitude Balloon Research Group
University of Wyoming
Physics & Astronomy Dept., Box 3905
Laramie, WY 82071
Phone: (307)766-4323
Contact: Dr. David J. Hofmann, Codirector
Research Areas: High altitude balloon studies focusing on seasonal depletion of Antarctica's ozone layer.

★3549★ Highlands Biological Station
P.O. Drawer 580
Highlands, NC 28741
Phone: (704)526-2602
Contact: Richard C. Bruce, Exec. Dir.
Research Areas: The biota of the southern Appalachians through independent and cooperative research, including the effects of timber harvest on vegetational succession and accompanying changes in the composition of animal communities and an experimental study of disturbance effects on species interactions and on the effects of size of forest openings on ecosystem structure and function. Special Resources: The Station is situated on a 19-acre tract of land bordering a lake and contains laboratories, conference rooms, an herbarium, a nature center, a library, and a botanical garden.

★3550★ Holcomb Research Institute
Butler Univ.
4600 Sunset Ave.
Indianapolis, IN 46208
Phone: (317)283-9421
Fax: (317)283-9519
Contact: Paul K.M. van der Heijde, Dean
Research Areas: Conducts research in water science and modeling through the Water Science Program and the IGWMC; the Biotic Resource Program, which focuses on global carbon modeling, forest growth and nutrient cycling, air pollution impacts on lakes and forests, and dynamics of threatened species; the Economic and Policy Program, which focuses on implications of resource use and risk of degradation; and Institute Projects, which fosters interdisciplinary studies on impacts of global climate change, risk assessment of toxic materials, and environmental pharmaceutics. Serves as an Environmental Protection Agency groundwater modeling clearinghouse (Groundwater Research Data Center). Databases: Groundwater Modeling Abstracts (MARS).

★3551★ Houston Advanced Research Center, Center for Growth Studies
4800 Research Forest Dr.
The Woodlands, TX 77381
Phone: (713)363-7913
Fax: (713)363-7914
Contact: Dr. Jurgen Schmandt, Dir.
Research Areas: Policies for managing global change, including international and regional environmental issues, ways to reconcile environmental protection and economic development, and the social and policy implications of science and technology. Specific areas include effects of global climate change on regions around the world, energy-transportation-environment linkages, alternative vehicle fuels, U.S./Mexico relations, and environment and natural resource issues in Texas.

★3552★ Hudsonia Ltd.
Bard College Field Sta.
Annandale, NY 12504
Phone: (914)758-1881
Contact: Erik Kiviat, Exec. Dir.
Research Areas: Distribution and conservation of rare plants and animals; stream, lake, estuarine, and wetland ecology; ecological relationships of human populations; environmental archeology; and recycling technology. Special Resources: Regional biological specimen collections.

★3553★ Hydraulic Laboratories
University of California, Berkeley
412 O'Brien Hall
Berkeley, CA 94720
Phone: (415)642-6777
Contact: Prof. R.J. Sobey, Dir.
Research Areas: Hydraulic engineering, including studies of dispersion of pollutants, stratified flow processes in lakes and rivers, sediment transport in rivers and along beaches, coastal engineering, open channel flow, and groundwater and surface water hydrology.

★3554★ Hydraulics and Hydromachinery Research Laboratories
Colorado State Univ.
Engineering Research Center
Fort Collins, CO 80523
Phone: (303)491-8404
Fax: (303)491-8671
Contact: J.F. Ruff Ph.D, Contact
Research Areas: Undertakes research related to solving hydraulic, geomorphic, hydrologic, water resources, and environmental problems. Major areas of concentration include river mechanics; bridge, pier, and culvert scour; erosion and sedimentation; diffusion and turbulence in closed- and open-channel flow; porous media flow and groundwater problems; transport of solids through pipelines and viscous drag reduction; design and performance of hydraulic structures; design and operation of water conveyance systems; energy development and conservation; cavitation, noise, and vibration problems; physical and mathematical modeling of hydraulic structures, rivers, and river systems; hydromachinery; hydraulic testing of valves, pumps, pump intakes, turbines, and other hydromachinery devices; and calibration and development of flow measurement instrumentation. Databases: Colorado Water Database, Colorado Climate Database. Special Resources: Hydraulics Laboratory, equipped with a variety of sediment, erosion, and river mechanics flumes, including a power-tilting recirculating sediment flume with a discharge capacity of 120 cubic feet per second (cfs); Hydromachinery Laboratory, equipped with pipelines up to 36 inches capable of discharges up to 100 cfs at heads of 250 feet (water source for the Laboratories is the U.S. Bureau of Reclamation's Horsetooth Reservoir).

★3555★ Hydrosystems Laboratory
University of Illinois
Dept. of Civil Engineering
Urbana, IL 61801
Phone: (217)333-0107
Contact: Dr. W. Hall C. Maxwell, Dir.
Research Areas: Development of criteria and methodology for planning and design of water resources systems, development and application of physical and mathematical theories in hydrologic systems, and application of basic fluid mechanics to solution of problems in hydraulic engineering. Specific areas include groundwater hydrology and contamination, surface water hydrology, density currents, sediment transport and river mechanics, water supply and drought management, methodtogies for flow prediction in urban storm drainage systems, stochastic analysis of hydrologic systems, environmental hydraulics, risk analysis, and design and management of storm water systems.

★3556★ Idaho Cooperative Fish and Wildlife Research Unit
University of Idaho
College of Forestry, Wildlife & Range Sciences
Moscow, ID 83843
Phone: (208)885-6336
Contact: Dr. J. Michael Scott, Unit Leader
Research Areas: Fish and wildlife ecology and management. Principal areas of research include biology and management of anadromous salmonid stocks; effects of sediment and turbidity on fish and invertebrate populations; effects of reduced stream discharge on fish and aquatic insect populations; factors affecting survival and seaward migration of salmon; biology and management of vertebrate populations; limiting factors for endangered species; factors affecting distribution and abundance of animals; development of new methods to estimate animal numbers; and protecting biological diversity through optimum preserve design.

★3557★ Idaho Water Resources Research Institute
University of Idaho
Morrill Hall, 106
Moscow, ID 83843
Phone: (208)885-6429
Fax: (208)885-6431
Contact: Roy Mink, Dir.
Research Areas: Water, energy, and related resources of the state, including studies on irrigation and drainage problems, sprinkler and surface irrigation, groundwater reserves, wild and scenic rivers, watershed management, and economic, sociological, and legal problems of water resource use, allocation, and conservation.

★3558★ IES Center for Human Systems
University of Wisconsin-Madison
1042 WARF Bldg.
Madison, WI 53705
Phone: (608)262-9937
Contact: Marty S. Kanarek, Dir.
Research Areas: Probes the social, cultural, and behavioral aspects of people's interaction with the environment. Recent analyses have centered around the effects of air pollution, including indoor air pollution, the effects of nitrogen dioxide, and how radon, formaldehyde, particulates, and other air pollutant levels are affected by insulation in homes. Water quality and health studies focus on the potential health effects of low-level chemical contamination in groundwater and whether chloroform and other volatile organic chemicals in drinking water are related to cancer. Future research will explore population ecology, agricultural systems, the economics of development, environmental policies and institutions, and risk-assessment policies and techniques.

★3559★ Illinois Mining and Mineral Resources Research Institute
Southern Illinois Univ. at Carbondale
Coal Extraction & Utilization Research Center
Carbondale, IL 62901
Phone: (618)536-6637
Fax: (618)453-7455
Contact: Dr. Y. Paul Chugh, Dir.
Research Areas: Conducts research on all aspects of mining, including mineral science, health and safety issues, waste disposal and mine-land reclamation. Institute is currently developing more efficient coal mining techniques, flourspar processing techniques, and subsidence prediction models.

★3560★ Illinois State Water Survey
2204 Griffith Dr.
Champaign, IL 61820-7495
Phone: (217)333-2210
Fax: (217)333-6540
Contact: Richard G. Semonin, Chief
Research Areas: Engineering, hydraulics, physical chemistry, precipitation physics, and meteorology, as applied to water resources. Studies concentrate on surface and groundwater; nature, extent, and quality of water resources of the state; water treatment, usage, conservation and water supply development and management; reservoir sedimentation; hydraulic design for water storage; and meteorologic factors related to water resources, climate change, and weather modifications. Special Resources: In addition to main research laboratories, maintains research laboratories at Peoria, Illinois and field facilities in special study areas around the state. Databases: Hydrology, climate, and water quality and resources.

★3561★ Indian River Marine Science Research Center
Florida Inst. of Technology
805 46th Pl. E.
Vero Beach, FL 32963
Phone: (407)234-4096
Fax: (407)984-8461
Contact: Dr. Walter G. Nelson, Dir.
Research Areas: Ecology of open coast sand beach systems, evaluation of environmental impact of artificial reef construction with stabilized oil-ash blocks, atmospheric and immersion studies of material coatings to prevent marine corrosion, and aquaculture. Special Resources: Maintains running seawater and laboratories for studies in sand beach ecology, sea grass ecosystems, reef fish, aquaculture, corrosion testing, and wave data aquisition.

★3562★ Industrial Waste Elimination Research Center
Illinois Inst. of Technology
3200 S. State St.
Chicago, IL 60616
Phone: (312)567-3535
Fax: (312)567-3548
Contact: Kenneth E. Noll, Dir.
Research Areas: In-plant reduction or elimination of industrial air and water pollutants and solid wastes. Research priorities are 1) methods of recycling, recovery, and reuse of by-products of industrial processes; 2) modifications of manufacturing processes to avoid or reduce waste generation; and 3) development of clean manufacturing technologies that minimize or eliminate the generation of pollutants. Projects include heavy metals speciation, separation, and recovery from wastewaters; kinetic analysis of the solution-precipitate interface for particle size control; evaluation of the dynamics of multicomponent sorption/desorption; development of oxides of iron as sorbates for the control, separation, and recovery of inorganics contained in industrial process and waste streams; and conversion of wastes containing chlorinated hydrocarbons into useful products.

★3563★ INFORM
381 Park Ave. S.
New York, NY 10016
Phone: (212)689-4040
Contact: Joanna Underwood, Exec. Dir.
Research Areas: Impact of U.S. industry on the environment and public health, including studies on municipal solid waste management, toxic waste reduction in the chemical industry, western agricultural water conservation, and urban air quality.

★3564★ Inland Lakes Research and Study Center
Michigan State Univ.
334 Natural Resources Bldg.
East Lansing, MI 48824
Phone: (517)353-3742
Fax: (517)353-1812
Contact: Dr. Jon Bartholic, Dir.
Research Areas: Basic aquatic research in lake management, fish aquaculture, water quality, and aquatic fertility. Specific topics include nutrient uptake in marsh plants, biomanipulation, nonpoint pollution sources, atmospheric deposition, mechanics of eutrophication, and the ecological and hydrological mechanisms that influence wetlands. Special Resources: Field site consisting of four lakes totaling 40 acres and three one-acre marshes.

★3565★ Institute for Alternative Agriculture
9200 Edmonston Rd., Ste. 117
Greenbelt, MD 20770
Phone: (301)441-8777
Contact: Dr. I. Garth Youngberg, Exec. Dir.
Research Areas: Promotes research and education on low-cost, resource conserving, environmentally safe farming methods. Acts as a national information clearinghouse on alternative agriculture.

★3566★ Institute for Applied Research
840 La Goleta Way
Sacramento, Canada 95825
Phone: (916)482-3120
Contact: Daniel B. Syrek, Dir.
Research Areas: Applied environmental studies in resource, energy, and recreation management. Conducts litter, opinion, and traffic volume surveys, vehicle speed measurements, and acoustical noise measurements. Databases: 1,600,000 items on litter acquired from 4,794 sampling locations in seventeen states and three Canadian provinces; over 340 observed incidents of littering, containing information as to the age, sex, vehicle, locale, time, and item littered.

★3567★ Institute for Biopsychological Studies of Color, Light, Radiation, Health
San Jose State Univ.
Dept. of Psychology
San Jose, CA 95192
Phone: (408)277-2786
Contact: Dr. Robert J. Pellegrini, Dir.
Research Areas: Organismic effects of electromagnetic energy, particularly studies of physical health and behavior as affected by environmental color and lighting in institutional settings and toxic radiation exposure.

★3568★ Institute for Comparative and Environmental Toxicology
Cornell Univ.
16 Fernow Hall
Ithaca, NY 14853-3001
Phone: (607)255-8008
Fax: (607)255-2812
Contact: James W. Gillett, Dir.
Research Areas: Focuses and coordinates toxicology interests and research activities at Cornell University, including individual faculty research in organismic and biochemical toxicology, nutritional toxicology, ecotoxicology and environmental chemistry, and risk

assessment, communication, management and public policy development.

★3569★ Institute for Crustal Studies
University of California, Santa Barbara
Santa Barbara, Canada 93105
Phone: (805)961-8231
Fax: (805)961-8649
Contact: Prof. Bruce Luyendyk, Dir.
Research Areas: Crustal structure and tectonics, crustal materials, earthquakes, and hazardous waste disposal. Special Resources: Database of earthquake statistics.

★3570★ Institute for Development Anthropology (IDA)
99 Collier St.
PO Box 2207
Binghamton, NY 13902
Phone: (607)772-6244
Fax: (607)773-8993
Contact: Dr. Muneera Salem-Murdock, Exec. Officer
Research Areas: Applies social and environmental sciences to achieve socioeconomic growth in developing countries. Projects include studies on integrated rural development, pastoralism in east and west Africa, provision of potable water in central Tunisia, settlement of west African areas previously controlled for the onchocerciasis vector, the relationship between economic underdevelopment and environmental destruction in Bolivia, long-term demographic and socioeconomic change in southern Zambia, pastoral and agrarian change in Kenya, and the effects of large-scale involuntary relocation in China.

★3571★ Institute for Ecological Studies
University of North Dakota
Box 8278, Univ. Sta.
Grand Forks, ND 58202
Phone: (701)777-2851
Contact: Dr. Rodney D. Sayler, Dir.
Research Areas: Ecology and ecosystem studies in upper midwestern U.S., including specialized studies in areas of wildlife biology, wetland ecology, land use planning, remote sensing, socioeconomics, and natural areas preservation and environmental education. Special Resources: Environmental resources center.

★3572★ Institute for Energy and Environmental Analysis
Oak Ridge Associated Universities
PO Box 117
Oak Ridge, TN 37831
Phone: (615)576-3171
Fax: (202)477-0547
Contact: John C. Maheu, Dir.
Research Areas: Analyzes alternative energy supply and demand strategies with respect to their economic, social, and environmental implications. Focus is primarily on U.S. energy policy, but is also concerned with regional and international energy questions and their solution, including nuclear waste management, carbon dioxide, electricity, natural gas, nuclear power, energy and the economy, and biological risks.

★3573★ Institute for Energy Research
Syracuse Univ.
103 College Pl.
Syracuse, NY 13244-4010
Phone: (315)423-3353
Contact: Dr. Walter Meyer, Dir.
Research Areas: Application of advanced industrial processes, forecasting of technological trends, planning and evaluation of research and technology transfer programs, technology assessment of direct coal liquifaction, low-level radioactive waste disposal, development of corrosion-resistant thin films to reduce radiation build-up in nuclear reactors, development of pattern recognition artificial intelligence-based electric and gas load forecasting systems, nondestructive analysis for hydrogen in steel and other materials, and energy-related computer-based information systems. Databases: Utility rate payer, New York manufacturers, national R&D laboratories.

★3574★ Institute for Engineering Research
Memphis State Univ.
Memphis, TN 38152
Phone: (901)678-2171
Fax: (901)678-4180
Contact: Dr. John D. Ray, Dean and Dir.
Research Areas: Wastewater treatment, water quality, transportation planning, traffic engineering, highway safety, environmental impact studies, energy studies, biomedical engineering, lasers and electrooptics, and hydrological studies.

★3575★ Institute for Environmental Design
California State Polytechnic Univ.
3801 W. Temple Ave.
Pomona, CA 91768
Phone: (714)869-2674
Fax: (714)869-4355
Contact: Prof. Denise L. Lawrence Ph.D., Dir.
Research Areas: Environmental design, primarily architecture, urban and regional planning, and landscape architecture. Activities include investigation and application of environment-behavior research to facility design, and research on energy conservation, water conservation, regenerative technologies, and urban and rural preservation.

★3576★ Institute for Environmental Education
32000 Chagrin Blvd.
Cleveland, OH 44124
Phone: (216)464-1775
Contact: Joseph H. Chadbourne, Pres.
Research Areas: Training, curriculum development, and consulting on solid waste minimization, environmental impairment assessment, water quality, land management investigations, and environmental systems for government agencies, corporations, and individuals. Databases: Serves to match candidates of intern program with needs of corporations.

★3577★ Institute for Environmental Negotiation
University of Virginia
Campbell Hall
Charlottesville, VA 22903
Phone: (804)924-1970
Fax: (804)924-0231
Contact: Dr. Richard C. Collins, Dir.
Research Areas: Resolution of land use and environmental policy disputes through mediation, negotiation, and consensus building as a way to supplement litigation and other decision making processes. Issues of disputes considered include groundwater, surface waters, wetlands, toxic and hazardous wastes, nuclear waste, historic preservation, annexation, zoning and development, resource management plans, and state and local regulations.

★3578★ Institute for Environmental Policy and Planning
SUNY Coll. of Environmental Science and Forestry
Bray Hall, Rm. 320
Syracuse, NY 13210
Phone: (315)470-6636
Contact: Richard C. Smardon Ph.D., Dir.
Research Areas: Cultural environmental values, environmental communication, land information systems, water resources, waste management, and urban environmental systems.

★3579★ Institute for Environmental Quality
Hope Coll.
Dept. of Chemistry
Holland, MI 49423
Phone: (616)392-3213
Contact: Dr. Donald H. Williams, Professor of Chemistry
Research Areas: Environmental and ecological concerns, including studies of water quality parameters as they relate to the Great Lakes, nutrient balance in marshes, and heavy metal transport and sedimentation problems in the Great Lakes and adjacent harbor waters. Also concerned with public education in scientific matters and nuclear power issues.

★3580★ Institute for Environmental Research
Kansas State Univ.
Manhattan, KS 66506
Phone: (913)532-5620
Fax: (913)532-7810
Contact: Dr. Byron W. Jones, Dir.
Research Areas: Human response to the environment, including studies on environmental design, human thermal comfort, physiology, heat stress, protective clothing and outer wear, temperature-related product design and testing, and human engineering for children and the elderly. Special Resources: Five environmental chambers, two electrically heated thermal mannequins, a sweating hotplate, an infrared thermal imaging system, and thermal environmental instrumentation.

★3581★ Institute for Environmental Science
University of Texas at Dallas
PO Box 830688
Richardson, TX 75083-0688
Phone: (214)690-2571
Contact: Dr. John Ward, Dir.
Research Areas: Environmental issues, including simulation modeling and reliability analysis, systems ecology, surface and groundwater hydrology, and scientific, social, and economic concept integration.

★3582★ Institute for Environmental Studies
University of North Carolina at Chapel Hill
CB# 7410
315 Pittsboro St.
Chapel Hill, NC 27599-7410
Phone: (919)966-2358
Fax: (919)966-7141
Contact: Dr. Richard N.L. Andrews, Dir.
Research Areas: Environmental policy options and impacts, with specific research conducted in management of solid and hazardous wastes, comparative evaluation of environmental policy instruments, environmental applications of biotechnology, interplay of values and science in environmental standards and regulations, and utilization of scientific and technical information by government agencies.

★3583★ Institute for Environmental Studies
University of Illinois
1101 W. Peabody Dr.
Urbana, IL 61801
Phone: (217)333-4178
Fax: (217)333-8046
Contact: Dr. Roger A. Minear, Dir.
Research Areas: Identifies and investigates current environmental problems and develops methods of long-range planning for future environmental quality. Specific studies include interdisciplinary and multidisciplinary research in water resources, air pollution, environmental toxicology, environmental chemistry, environmental and resource economics, ecology, biostatistics and epidemiology, environmental psychology, and social impact assessment. Also conducts research on the environmental management approach to the study of mutagens/carcinogens, including detection, characterization, environmental transport, and risk assessment for human health.

★3584★ Institute for Environmental Studies
University of Washington
Engineering Annex FM-12
Seattle, WA 98195
Phone: (206)543-1812
Fax: (206)543-9285
Contact: Gordon H. Orians, Dir.
Research Areas: Environmental studies, including human habitat preferences, seabird ecology and seabirds as indicators of environmental conditions, value of genetic resources, liver excretion of poisonous substances, biological indicators,cadmium pollution, influence of atmospheric particles on optical properties of the atmosphere, acid rain and long-term effects of atmospheric particles on climate, transport of ozone and trace gases in the stratosphere, restoration of runs of anadromous fishes, radioactive waste management policy, tropical forest dynamics, structure of the Hoh rain forest, adaptive management, and environmental politics.

★3585★ Institute for Environmental Studies
Louisiana State Univ.
Atkinson Hall, Rm. 42
Baton Rouge, LA 70803
Phone: (504)388-5821
Fax: (504)388-4286
Contact: Dr. Edward Overton, Dir.
Research Areas: Studies man's impact on the environment and seeks to solve environmental quality problems. Promotes, conducts, and coordinates programs in environmental studies within the University community and disseminates knowledge to the public with the goal of increasing awareness toward conserving environmental quality.

★3586★ Institute for Land Rehabilitation
Utah State Univ.
College of Natural Resources
Logan, UT 84322-5230
Phone: (801)750-2547
Contact: J.B. Dobrowolski, Codirector
Research Areas: Land rehabilitation, including seeding, reclamation, rehabilitation, restoration, and improvement of range lands and other altered landscapes. Specific studies include range plant structure and physiology, plant introduction, hydrology, soil chemistry and engineering, waste disposal and treatment, watershed management, water quality, plant science, biology, economics, ecology, forestry, range management, and wildlife. Emphasizes ecological studies of plants adapted to harsh sites, develops new or adapts existing methods for plant establishment, and formulates revegetation strategies that can be applied on a wide variety of sites. Data analysis techniques include pattern recognition and mathematical modeling.

★3587★ Institute for Molecular and Agricultural Genetic Engineering (IMAGE)
University of Idaho
Food Research Center 202
Moscow, ID 83843
Phone: (208)885-6580
Fax: (208)885-5741
Contact: Dr. R.L. Crawford, Dir.
Research Areas: Bioconversion, hazardous waste management, crop improvement and protection, molecular diagnosis, and molecular genetics of plants/animals/microbes. Bioconversion studies focus on the production of chemicals, minerals, liquids, biomass, and single cell protein. Hazardous waste studies include bioremediation of toxic chemical problems in soils and natural waters (includes in situ work). Crop improvement and protection studies concentrate on biological insect and weed control, plant protoplasts, and genetic engineering. Special Resources: Maintains equipment for molecular biology, recombinant DNA technology, and continuous fermentation.

★3588★ Institute for Recyclable Materials
Louisiana State Univ.
3304 CEBA
Baton Rouge, LA 70803-6401
Phone: (504)388-8650
Fax: (504)388-5990
Contact: Roger K. Seals Ph.D., Dir.
Research Areas: Recycling and utilization of municipal and industrial solid wastes. Emphasis is on the development of technology for high volume use of industrial solid wastes and by-products, especially the use of phosphogypsum in road base materials.

★3589★ Institute for Regenerative Studies
California State Polytechnic Univ.
Bldg. 1, Rm. 319
3801 W. Temple Ave.
Pomona, CA 91768
Phone: (714)869-4449
Contact: Dr. Edwin A. Barnes, Dir.
Research Areas: Regenerative technologies, including integrated agriculture/aquaculture systems, agroforestry, passive solar heating and cooling, waste water recycling, and small scale intensive agriculture.

★3590★ Institute for Regional and Community Studies
Western Illinois Univ.
Macomb, IL 61455
Phone: (309)298-1566
Contact: Dr. Donald W. Griffin, Dir.
Research Areas: Problems of rural America, including studies on land use suitability, land use policy, and solid waste management.

★3591★ Institute for Resource Management
262 S. 200 W.
Salt Lake City, UT 84101
Phone: (801)322-0530
Fax: (801)328-3457
Contact: Terrell Minger, Pres. and CEO
Research Areas: Development, use, and conservation of the world's natural resources, including areas concerned with Indian lands, public lands, energy, atmosphere and climate, and the environment.

★3592★ Institute of Agricultural Medicine and Occupational Health
University of Iowa
Preventive Medicine & Environmental Health Dept.
AMRF, Oakdale Campus
Iowa City, IA 52242
Phone: (319)335-4415
Contact: James A. Merchant M.D., Dir.
Research Areas: Occupational injury and disease research and prevention and environmental health among farmers, those living in rural areas, and general industry. Conducts multidisciplinary studies of health effects due to modern agricultural and industrial practices, particularly in the areas of agricultural medicine, occupational medicine, industrial hygiene, environmental health, and environmental chemistry.

★3593★ Institute of Analytical and Environmental Chemistry
University of New Haven
300 Orange Ave.
West Haven, CT 06516
Phone: (203)932-7171
Contact: Prof. George Wheeler, Dir.
Research Areas: Soil and water testing and analysis for environmental pollutants such as lead, trace metals, pesticides, herbicides, and polychlorinated biphenyl (PCB).

★3594★ Institute of Applied Sciences
University of North Texas
PO Box 13078
Denton, TX 76203
Phone: (817)565-2694
Fax: (817)565-4297
Contact: Dr. Kenneth L. Dickson, Dir.
Research Areas: Seeks solutions to issues and problems related to the development of natural and human resources. Water research occupies a priority position among the Institute's activities and has included studies on the use of remote sensing and geographic information systems for watershed studies, development of computer-based decision support systems for aquatic weed control, assessment of water quality associated with paper mill sites and industrially derived municipal waste waters, non-point pollution problems in Texas, and analysis of biodegradation and biotransformation of priority pollutants and pesticides. Land-oriented studies include development of techniques for ecological management practices, assessment of siting methodologies for hazardous waste facilities, collection of site-specific and regional data pursuant to environmental impact statements, and investigations of paleoenvironments in Texas, Oklahoma, and New Mexico. Energy projects have included investigation of applicability of biomass conversion, development of solar-powered desalination techniques, assessment of the fate of sediment-sorbed petrochemicals, and preparation of guidelines for revegetation of surface-mined lands for wildlife. Archaeological projects include assessment of cultural resources preceding land or reservoir development, exploration and historical background for the French Fort Saint Leon near New Orleans and Spanish missions in Texas. Special Resources: Operates Aquatic Toxicology Laboratory, Water Resources Field Station, and Center for Remote Sensing and Land Use Analysis. Maintains special collections of comparative osteological materials and historic glass and ceramics.

★3595★ Institute of Chemical Biology
University of San Francisco
Ignarian Heights
Rm. H342
San Francisco, CA 94117-1080
Phone: (415)666-6415
Fax: (415)386-1074
Contact: Dr. R. James Brown, Dir.
Research Areas: Environmental toxicology, including techniques for analysis of heavy metals in mammalian tissues and water and soil pollution field studies on the accumulation of heavy metals in the biota such as nickel, cadmium, mercury, and arsenic.

★3596★ Institute of Chemical Toxicology
Wayne State Univ.
2727 Second Ave.
Detroit, MI 48201
Phone: (313)577-0100
Contact: Dr. Raymond F. Novak, Dir.
Research Areas: Chemical hazards of the environment and industrial workplace, including toxicology of air pollutants, solvents, and heavy metals. Also studies carcinogenesis, metabolic, and hematologic effects resulting from exposure to toxic agents.

★3597★ Institute of Community and Area Development
University of Georgia
Treanor House
1234 S. Lumpkin St.
Athens, GA 30602
Phone: (404)542-3350
Fax: (404)542-6189
Contact: Dr. Joseph W. Whorton, Dir.
Research Areas: Development of quality growth patterns in communities and areas, including studies in environmental quality, and land use decision making.

★3598★ Institute of Ecology
University of California, Davis
Davis, CA 95616
Phone: (916)752-3026
Contact: Dr. Charles R. Goldman, Dir.
Research Areas: Ecological and environmental problems, including basic and applied interdisciplinary studies on ecosystem management, man's impact on his environment, resource policy analysis, limnology, and relationships of a single species to its environment. Special Resources: Provides facilities for research in these fields by faculty members and advanced students from Davis and other campuses of the University. Maintains a 10,000-square foot laboratory building, ponds, and limnological research vessels.

★3599★ Institute of Energy Conversion
University of Delaware
Newark, DE 19716
Phone: (302)451-6200
Fax: (302)451-6226
Contact: Dr. T.W. Fraser Russell, Dir.
Research Areas: Thin-film photovoltaic solar cells.

★3600★ Institute of Environmental and Industrial Health
University of Michigan
School of Public Health
Ann Arbor, MI 48109
Phone: (313)764-3188
Fax: (313)763-5455
Contact: Robert Gray, Dir.
Research Areas: Environmental and industrial health and safety, including studies on water and air pollution; radiation protection; risk assessment; environmental toxicology and epidemiology; environmental monitoring and modeling; toxic contamination of the environment; molecular mechanisms of the effects of chemicals on biological systems; biomechanics; ergonomics; law and policy; ventilation control; occupational and preventive medicine; hazardous materials evaluation, control, and environmental impacts; and measurement, evaluation, and control of radiation in the workplace.

★3601★ Institute of Environmental Medicine
New York Univ.
550 First Ave.
New York, NY 10016
Phone: (212)340-5280
Contact: Dr. Arthur Upton, Dir.
Research Areas: Toxicology, chemical carcinogenesis, radiation carcinogenesis and dosimetry, respiratory disease and aerosol physiology, environmental pollution and ecology, epidemiology, and biostatistics and biomathematics, including studies on skin, bladder, and lung cancer from environmental sources, environmental hazards to which industrial and community populations are exposed, industrial and environmental health hazards and means for their control, and sources of human exposures to radiation.

★3602★ Institute of Environmental Studies
Baylor Univ.
PO Box 97266
Waco, TX 76798-7266
Phone: (817)755-3406
Contact: Dr. W. Merle Alexander, Dir.
Research Areas: All phases of environmental analysis, including collection and analysis of environmental, structural, and pollution data with an emphasis on integration of energy and agriculture. Special Resources: Uses a plane to conduct atmospheric research, including measurement of solar radiation, ozone, carbon dioxide, nitric oxide, and particles.

★3603★ Institute of Environmental Toxicology and Chemistry
Western Washington Univ.
Huxley College
Environmental Studies Center
Mail Stop 9079
Bellingham, WA 98225
Phone: (206)647-6136
Fax: (206)647-7284
Contact: Dr. Wayne Landis, Dir.
Research Areas: Effects of toxic substances on terrestrial and aquatic organisms.

★3604★ Institute of Forest Resources
University of Washington
102 Anderson Hall
College of Forest Resources
Seattle, WA 98195
Phone: (206)685-1928
Fax: (206)685-0790
Contact: David B. Thorud, Dir. and Dean
Research Areas: Forest products research, including forest ecosystem analysis, quantitative resource management, silviculture and forest protection, social sciences, wildlife science, forest economics, urban horticulture, forest engineering, forest hydrology, and pulp and paper science performed by faculty members in forestry, botany, civil engineering, fisheries, economics, and mathematics.

★3605★ Institute of Gas Technology
3424 S. State St.
Chicago, IL 60616
Phone: (312)567-3650
Fax: (312)567-5209
Contact: Dr. B.S. Lee, Pres.
Research Areas: Energy technology in the areas of utilization, supply, environmental quality, energy systems analysis, and education and information services. Studies emphasize production of synthetic fuels such as coal, oil shale, tar sands, peat, biomass, and other renewable resources; biological gasification processes; the development of improved combustion and incineration processes; the application of biotechnology to solve environmental problems; recovery of natural gas from unconventional sources such as geopressured aquifers, western tight sands, coal seams, and methane hydrates; residential and commercial energy conservation, including studies on heat pumps and furnace efficiency; development of advanced designs for heat-recuperating furnaces and water heaters; second generation molten-carbonate fuel cells; natural gas vehicle storage systems; advanced gas distribution systems; flue-gas pressurization; fluidized-bed heat transfer; and energy storage.

★3606★ Institute of Hydraulic Research
University of Iowa
Iowa City, IA 52242
Phone: (319)335-5236
Fax: (319)335-5238
Contact: Dr. John F. Kennedy
Hydrology and hydrodynamics, including basic and applied studies on boundary layers, cavitation, turbulence, irration flow, visccus and stratified flow, biological flows, computer solution on nonuniform unsteady flow, dispersion and diffusion, sedimentation, ice processes, management of waste heat from power generation, water resource systems, hydrometerorology, computer simulation and optimization systems, and development of electronic measurement instrumentation.

★3607★ Institute of Marine and Atmospheric Sciences
City Coll. of City Univ. of New York
Science Bldg.
138th St. & Convent Ave.
New York, NY 10031
Phone: (212)650-7000
Contact: Dr. Dennis Weiss, Dir.
Research Areas: Urban oceanography and atmospheric sciences, including studies on air-sea interaction, salt marsh ecology, dynamics of coastal zones, and pollution studies of Hudson River Basin and New York estuaries. Special Resources: 90-foot estuarine research vessel.

★3608★ Institute of Marine and Coastal Sciences
Rutgers Univ.
Old Blakeman Hall
PO Box 231
New Brunswick, NJ 08903-0231
Phone: (908)932-6555
Contact: Dr. Frederick Grassle, Dir.
Research Areas: Applied genetics and evolution, aquaculture, biogeochemistry, bottom boundary layer studies, coastal processes, community ecology, ecosystem level studies, habitat fragmentation, histopathology, larval transport and recruitment, marine genetics, nutrient cycling, population biology, remote sensing, shellfish and fish biology, and wetland ecology. Current studies includes predictive ocean models for coastal New Jersey, beach erosion, juvenile populations of commercially important fish, oil pollution, effects of offshore sludge disposal, pollutant toxicity, effects of sea-level rise, maintenance of clam beds, oyster disease, hydrothermal vents,

and genetics of marine population. Special Resources: Sea-water laboratory.

★3609★ Institute of Marine and Coastal Studies
Nova Univ.
8000 N. Ocean Dr.
Dania, FL 33004
Phone: (305)920-1909
Fax: (305)947-8559
Contact: Dr. Richard Dodge, Dir.
Research Areas: Marine physics, biology, chemistry, and geology, coastal zone management, coral reef assessment, and lacustrine pollution.

★3610★ Institute of Natural Resources
University of Georgia
Rm. 13, Ecology Bldg.
Athens, ga 30602
Phone: (404)542-1555
Contact: Dr. Ronald M. North, Dir.
Research Areas: Development, law, economics, policy, and management of natural resources, including studies on water resources, climatology, wildlife management, and energy economics. Basic scientific findings used to develop policy and management alternatives.

★3611★ Institute of Political Economy
Utah State Univ.
Main 342F/UMC 0725
Logan, UT 84322-0725
Phone: (801)750-2064
Fax: (801)750-3751
Contact: Dr. Randy T. Simmons, Dir.
Research Areas: The environment, private and public management, and political theory.

★3612★ Institute of State and Regional Affairs
Pennsylvania State Univ.
Middletown, PA 17057
Phone: (717)948-6178
Fax: (717)948-6306
Contact: Prof. Irving Hand, Dir.
Research Areas: Public policy and planning for the private sector as well as state and local government organizations, including ennvironmental planning, energy resource and conservation, water quality management, hazardous and solid waste, stormwater management, and geographic information systems.

★3613★ Institute of Sustainability
PO Box 40442
Berkeley, CA 94704
Contact: David V. Walker, Codirector
Research Areas: Traditional systems of sustainable agricultural/ecological practices in developing countries. Research emphasis is on ecology, agro-ecology, biology, sociology, forestry, developmental policy, and international agricultural development. Special Resources: 15-acre research facility in Sri Lanka.

★3614★ Institute of Toxicology and Environmental Health
University of California, Davis
Davis, CA 95616
Phone: (916)752-1340
Fax: (916)752-5300
Contact: Dr. James W. Overstreet, Dir.
Research Areas: Coordinates interdisciplinary research on biomedical and toxicological problems related to exposure to chemical, physical, and biological toxic agents or to ionizing radiation. Seeks to determine basic mechanisms of toxic effects and to predict human health hazards from continual exposure to realistic levels of toxic substances in the environment or in the workplace. Special Resources: Maintains animal holding facilities for studies on toxic, radioactive, and carcinogenic compounds. Also operates laboratories for studies in analytical chemistry, radiochemistry, cell biology, inhalation toxicology, and human epidemiology.

★3615★ Institute of Water Research
Michigan State Univ.
334 Natural Resources Bldg.
East Lansing, MI 48824
Phone: (517)353-3742
Fax: (517)353-1812
Contact: Dr. Jon F. Bartholic, Dir.
Research Areas: Water resources, including studies on problems of water pollution, water rights, water management, groundwater protection, limnology, and usage of water for industry, health, agriculture, transportation, fisheries, recreation, and tourism. Serves the state of Michigan as coordinating agency for water studies.

★3616★ Institute of Water Resources
University of Connecticut
U-18
Storrs, CT 06269-4018
Phone: (203)486-0335
Fax: (203)486-2840
Contact: Dr. David Miller, Dir.
Research Areas: Water and resources which affect water, including basic and applied studies on biological, engineering, economic, legal, physical, recreational, and social aspects of water resources use and development. Established under Water Resources Research Act of 1964, Public Law 88-379, and reauthorized under the Water Resources Research Act of 1984, Public Law 98-242, to conduct and coordinate interdisciplinary research and training of scientists in these fields.

★3617★ Institute of Wildlife and Environmental Toxicology
Clemson Univ.
1 Tiwet Dr.
PO Box 709
Pendleton, SC 29670
Phone: (803)646-7265
Fax: (803)646-9377
Contact: Dr. Ronald J. Kendall, Dir.
Research Areas: Toxic substances and environmental contamination effects on fisheries, wildlife, and other environmental resources, focusing on the effects of toxic substances on avian reproduction, wildlife exposure and impacts at hazardous waste sites, age-related sensitivity to organophosphates in passerine species, impacts of waste incinerator systems, pesticide effects in tropical ecosystems, wildlife utilization and golf courses, pesticide transport into farm ponds, organophosphate movement in agricultural ecosystems, herbicide and agricultural insecticide effects on wildlife, and computer modeling of pesticide effects in the environment. Special Resources: Maintains field stations in South Carolina, Iowa, and Washington.

★3618★ Interdisciplinary Center for Aeronomy and Other Atmospheric Sciences
University of Florida
311 Space Sciences Research Bldg.
Gainesville, FL 32611
Phone: (904)392-2001
Contact: Prof. Alex E.S. Green, Dir.
Research Areas: Pure and applied research in atmospheric sciences. Aeronomical programs deal with physical, chemical, and electrical processes in the upper atmosphere, including tropospheric and micrometeorological studies as well as biological, ecological, and technological research related to air quality. Interdisciplinary programs deal with the scientific, technical, socioeconomic, and legal aspects of ultraviolet radiation levels, ozone perturbations from supersonic transport effluents and chlorofluorocarbons, community noise levels, environmental impact of Florida electric generating plants, acid deposition in Florida, coal-slurry gas assist combustion, coal/natural gas displacement of power plant oil usage, and interplay of energy production needs relative to air quality standards. Special Resources: Converted steam boiler.

★3619★ International Association for Advancement of Earth and Environmental Sciences
Northeastern Illinois Univ.
Dept. of Geography & Environmental Studies
5500 N. St. Louis Ave.
Chicago, IL 60625
Phone: (312)794-2628
Contact: Dr. Musa Qutub, Pres.
Research Areas: Encourages research in earth and environmental sciences, including studies on energy, mineral, water, and natural resources; pollution; planetary, physical, and biological sciences; medicine and public health, social systems, and education. Initiates educational programs, develops model studies among countries, encourages science learning at elementary, secondary, and university levels, and promotes the individual's role in better management of earth resources. Operates a speakers bureau.

★3620★ International Center for Marine Resource Development (ICMRD)
University of Rhode Island
126 Woodward Hall
Kingston, RI 02881
Phone: (401)792-2479
Fax: (401)789-3342
Contact: Dr. Spiros Constantinides, Deputy Dir.
Research Areas: Development of programs to aid small-scale, capture fisheries in developing countries. Activities focus on fisheries stock assessment, coastal resources management, marine policy, marketing of fisheries products, socioeconomic and sociocultural aspects of fisheries development, role of women in fisheries development, post harvest fishery product technology, and fishery resource development and enhancement. Databases: Small scale fisheries development.

★3621★ International Center for the Solution of Environmental Problems
535 Lovett Blvd.
Houston, TX 77006
Phone: (713)527-8711
Contact: Dr. Joseph L. Goldman, Technical Dir.
Research Areas: Environmental modeling of atmospheric pollution, chemical movement through soils, and human responses to chemical treatments in agriculture. Other studies concentrate on climatic change due to construction of tall buildings, world freshwater supply, air/soil interaction, mathematical modeling and computer development, remote sensing implementation and analyses, satellite image processing, and world consumption of oil and refined products. The Center is also working on the development of a museum of science and technology in Houston.

licensing; and high technology in plant operations.

★3622★ International Ground Water Modeling Center
Butler Univ.
Holcomb Research Institute
Indianapolis, IN 46208
Phone: (317)283-9458
Fax: (317)293-9519
Contact: Paul K.M. van der Heijde, International Coordinator
Research Areas: Applied research and development in groundwater modeling to study fundamental aspects of transport and fate of contaminants. Current projects include model screening and testing, evaluation of model use and model needs, software development and improvement, and development of new approaches to teaching and training in groundwater modeling. Monitors new developments in modeling and related fields such as computer hardware, software for data handling, and graphics. Databases: Various model information and research data.

★3623★ International Institute for Food, Agriculture and Development
Cornell Univ.
Ithaca, NY 14853
Phone: (607)255-3037
Contact: Prof. Daniel Sisler, Contact
Research Areas: Rural proverty, malnutrition, population change, and environmental degradation in developing countries in Africa, Asia, and Latin America. Activities focus on agricultural technology and productivity, human nutritional needs, conservation of natural resources, environmental protection, international trade, viability of families and the role of women in development, and policy improvement and implementation.

★3624★ International Plant Protection Center
Oregon State Univ.
Corvallis, OR 97331-3904
Phone: (503)737-3541
Fax: (503)737-3080
Contact: Dr. Frank Conklin, Interim Dir.
Research Areas: Weed management and pesticide safety in developing countries, including socioeconomic evaluation and technical assistance with an emphasis on training. Special Resources: Maintains a worldwide communication network of weed control researchers, with language capabilities in English, Spanish, Portuguese, and French.

★3625★ International Union of Operating Engineers, Department of Research
1125 17th St., NW
Washington, DC 20036
Phone: (202)429-9100
Contact: James VanDyke, Dir.
Research Areas: Collective bargaining contract analysis; market analysis; work rules, job site safety, and health conditions; health and welfare plans; employment in the construction industry, including equipment repair shops, material yards, stone quarries, gravel pits, field engineers, survey teams, surface mining, dredging, and drilling; and employment in stationary industry, including boiler plants, power plants, high-vacuum systems, plant maintenance, wastewater plants, water filtration plants, refrigeration, cryogenic systems, pumping stations, and nondestructive testing. Also conducts studies of planning, operations, and administration of trends in fiber optics; multinational corporations; international trade; international labor affairs; construction, design, and operation of nuclear power plants; nuclear wastes and toxic chemicals; industrial standards; stationary and operating engineer licensing; and high technology in plant operations.

★3626★ Investor Responsibility Research Center
1755 Massachusetts Ave., NW
Washington, DC 20036
Phone: (202)939-6500

★3627★ Iowa Cooperative Fish and Wildlife Research Unit
Iowa State Univ.
Ames, IA 50011
Phone: (515)294-3056
Fax: (515)294-5468
Contact: Dr. Paul A. Vohs, Leader
Research Areas: Biology, ecology, and management of fish and wildlife, wildlife/sociology interfaces, pesticide/wildlife interactions, fish culture, habitat associations with fish and wildlife species, and agroecology.

★3628★ Iowa Test and Evaluation Facility
Iowa State Univ.
Engineering Research Institute
111A Coover Hall
Ames, IA 50011
Phone: (515)294-4072
Contact: Clayton L. Christensen, Program Coordinator
Research Areas: Effects of high-voltage transmission lines (69, 161, and 345 kV lines) on the surrounding environment, especially farm crops and farm animals. Seeks to document any long-range biological effects due to the electric and magnetic fields which may exist in the vicinity of such transmission lines. The facility is used to generate new information on the effects of high-voltage power lines, to simulate alleged problem conditions, and to develop predictive measures for safe handling and design of high-voltage and ultra high-voltage power transmission systems. Serves as a laboratory and training center for students from the University and engineers from participating utilities. Special Resources: Maintains equipment for measuring harmonics in power systems and electric field strengths.

★3629★ Jasper Ridge-Herrin Labs
Stanford Univ.
Rm. 223
Stanford, CA 94305
Phone: (415)723-1589
Contact: Alan Grundmann, Administrative Dir.
Research Areas: Functions as an outdoor laboratory in which field scientists can pursue long-range investigations. Reseach efforts concentrate on population biology and physiological ecology, but span a broad range, including geology and anthropology. The preserve is one of the last naturally vegetated open spaces in the area and is available to qualified researchers from any institution. Special Resources: Equipment for climate monitoring of several vegetation types.

★3630★ John B. Pierce Laboratory, Inc.
290 Congress Ave.
New Haven, CT 06519
Phone: (203)562-9901
Fax: (203)624-4950
Contact: Dr. Ethan R. Nadel, Dir.
Research Areas: Heating, sanitation, and ventilation as they affect man's habitation and human comfort, including studies on physiology of temperature regulation; effects of heat and cold on man; physiology of respiratory systems; effects of airborne particulates and noxious gases; systems analysis of physiological functions; and psychological responses of man to heat, cold, noise, light, and other environmental factors.

★3631★ John D. MacArthur AgroEcology Research Center
550 Buck Island Ranch Rd.
Lake Placid, FL 33852
Phone: (813)669-0242
Contact: Dr. John W. Fitzpatrick, Exec. Dir.
Research Areas: Ecology of wildlife systems on cattle ranches and citrus groves, water quality in relation to agricultural practices, and plant ecology. Special Resources: 10,000-acre cattle ranch, 180-acre citrus grove, and residential housing for visiting scientists. Databases: Climate data, pasture treatments, and bird populations.

★3632★ Joint Center for Energy Management (JCEM)
Univ. of Colorado-Boulder
Campus Box 428
Boulder, CO 80309-0428
Phone: (303)492-3915
Fax: (303)492-5105
Contact: Dr. Jan F. Kreider, Dir.
Research Areas: Energy efficiency in buildings and renewable energy applications, including microcomputer software development for design, control, and diagnosis of building system design, HVAC systems, building performance, building-to-ground heat transfer, photovoltaic systems, solar design methods, and non-imaging optics. Special Resources: HVAC systems and controls laboratory; energy teaching and training laboratory.

★3633★ Joint Center for Environmental and Urban Problems
220 SE 2nd Ave., Rm. 709
Fort Lauderdale, FL 33301
Phone: (305)355-5255
Fax: (305)760-5666
Contact: Dr. John DeGrove, Dir.
Research Areas: Land use and growth management, including government structure and finance; local, regional, state, national, and international planning issues; natural resources protection; and health and human resources.

★3634★ Joint Facility for Regional Ecosystem Analysis
University of Colorado-Boulder
Boulder, CO 80309
Contact: Dr. Donald Walker, Contact
Research Areas: Animal and plant ecology, including ecosystem response to natural and man-made change.

★3635★ Joseph M. Long Marine Laboratory
University of California, Santa Cruz
100 Shaffer
Santa Cruz, CA 95060
Phone: (408)459-2883
Fax: (408)459-3383
Contact: Dr. William T. Doyle, Dir.
Research Areas: Marine biology and coastal zone problems. Specific areas of research include the following: human impact on coastal resources (urbanization, waste disposal, mineral and petroleum extraction, recreation, and fishing), marine chemistry, diseases of fish, coral genetics, larval culture, phytoculture, marine aquaculture, photobiology, environmental toxicology, and marine mammal behavior, cognition, and physiology. Special Resources: Maintains a variety of marine research laboratories, aquaria, and tanks (including three 25-foot diameter and 6-foot deep marine mammal tanks and a 40-foot by

50-foot by 9-foot deep community tank for marine mammal and seabird studies).

★3636★ Kansas Rural Center
PO Box 133
304 Pratt St.
Whiting, KS 66552
Phone: (913)873-3431
Contact: Vic Studer, Exec. Dir.
Research Areas: Agriculture, natural resource, and rural community issues, including energy conservation, sustainable agriculture, water resources, farm credit, rural leadership development, and corporate farming policies. Conducts public policy analysis and advocacy on agricultural and natural resource concerns.

★3637★ Kansas Water Resources Research Institute
144 Waters Hall
Kansas State Univ.
Manhattan, KS 66506
Phone: (913)532-5729
Fax: (913)532-6563
Contact: Dr. Hyde S. Jacobs, Dir.
Research Areas: Water and other resources that affect water, including studies on water quality, evapotranspiration, scientific and engineering hydrology, hydraulics and fluid dynamics, stream and lake regimen, socioeconomic and legal problems, climatology and agriculture, municipal, industrial, and recreational water management, economic impact of water resources, engineering and hydraulic aspects of water resources, and ecological relationships to impounded surface waters. Established under Water Resources Research Act of 1964, Public Law 88-379, to conduct and coordinate research on water resources at both universities and other institutions in the state and training of scientists in this field.

★3638★ Kemper Research Foundation
122 Main St.
Milford, OH 45150
Phone: (513)249-2200
Contact: Richard Kemper, Dir.
Research Areas: Building related illnesses, focusing on the effects of microorganisms on man and the environment, including heating, ventilating, and air conditioning equipment.

★3639★ Kenneth E. Johnson Research Center
University of Alabama in Huntsville
Huntsville, Albania
Phone: (205)895-6361
Contact: Dr. Bernard J. Schroer, Dir.
Research Areas: Solar energy, alcohol fuels, electric vehicles, motor vehicle inspections, air pollution, water pollution, operation of liquid and air solar test facility, solar radiation, advanced manufacturing systems, and biomass conversion.

★3640★ Kentucky Water Resources Research Institute
University of Kentucky
219 Anderson Hall
Lexington, KY 40506-0046
Phone: (606)257-1832
Contact: Dr. Ralph R. Huffsey, Dir.
Research Areas: Water and other resources which affect water, including studies on economics, hydrology, climatology, water quantity management, water quality control, and strip mine polluted water. Presently interested in economic effects of major water resources projects, recreational benefits of water resource development, coal slurry pipelines, impact of surface mining, bacterial contamination of ground water, and wetlands research. Established under Water Resources Research Act of 1984, Public Law 98-242, to conduct and coordinate research at the University and at other universities within the state in relation to water and water related resources and to train scientists and engineers in this field.

★3641★ Keystone Center
PO Box 606
Keystone, CO 80435
Phone: (303)468-5822
Contact: Robert W. Craig, Pres.
Research Areas: Facilitates the development of effective policy and the resolution of environmental and natural resource disputes by providing a forum, the Science and Public Policy Program, for information exchange between individuals in the private sector, environmental community, academia, and government. Activities focus on negotiations for policies in the fields of energy, environment, and science/technology, including future energy, the role of oceans in hazardous waste management, ocean incineration, product liability, biotechnology regulation, toxic waste, public utilities, and drug safety.

★3642★ Kresge Center for Environmental Health
Harvard Univ.
665 Huntington Ave.
Boston, MA 02115
Phone: (617)732-1272
Contact: John B. Little M.D., Dir.
Research Areas: Environmental health, including interdisciplinary studies on effects and control of air pollutants, occupational health and medicine, safeguards for nuclear power reactors, environmental and respiratory physiology, radiation biology, toxicology and air sampling, monitoring, and personnel protection. Serves as a focus for environmental health activities within the School.

★3643★ Laboratory for Atmospheric Research
Washington State Univ.
Dept. of Civil & Environmental Engineering
College of Engineering & Architecture
Pullman, 99164
Phone: (509)335-8546
Fax: (509)335-7632
Contact: Prof. Brian Lamb, Contact
Research Areas: Pollutant dispersion over complex terrain, atmospheric mixing and transport processes, measurement of short-lived oxidizing species in the atmosphere, the fate of natural hydrocarbons in the atmosphere, and determination of methane emission rates from natural gas systems and from livestock. Field measurement programs are conducted in China, Antarctica, Caribbean Sea, Pacific Ocean, and the U.S. Databases: Biogenic sulfur and hydrocarbon emission inventories; ambient halocarbon concentration data for remote sites; case studies of atmospheric diffusion. Special Resources: Mobile field laboratories and airborne sampling facilities.

★3644★ Laboratory for Pest Control Application Technology
Ohio State Univ.
Ohio Agricultural Research & Development Center
Wooster, OH 44691
Phone: (216)263-3726
Fax: (216)263-3713
Contact: Dr. Franklin R. Hall, Head
Research Areas: Pest control agents, pest control application technology, and the basic processes and biological responses of the pesticide delivery system. Insecticides (conventional, biological, and hormonal), fungicides, plant growth regulators, nematicides, and herbicides are all studied in relation to various cropping systems used in growing corn, soybeans, fruit, vegetables, and turf. Research objectives are aimed at reducing involuntary pesticide exposure to humans, nontarget plants, or other organisms and developing improved procedures for pesticide waste management. Develops pesticide risk/benefit computer models to assist regulatory decision making.

★3645★ Laboratory for Wetland Soils and Sediments
Louisiana State Univ.
105 Wetland Soils Bldg.
Baton Rouge, LA 70803
Phone: (504)388-8806
Fax: (504)388-6423
Contact: William H. Patrick Jr., Dir.
Research Areas: Sediment chemistry/plant relations in natural wetland ecosystems (salt marshes, fresh and brackish marshes and swamps, and floodplains) and the chemical and biological behavior of plant nutrients and toxic substances in wetland ecosystems. Studies concentrate on the environmental impact of pesticides, toxic heavy metals, hydrocarbons, and plant nutrients in wetlands.

★3646★ Laboratory of Architecture and Planning (LAP)
Massachusetts Inst. of Technology
77 Massachusetts Ave., 7-231
Cambridge, MA 02139
Phone: (617)253-1354
Contact: Michael L. Joroff, Dir.
Research Areas: Energy and buildings, environmental management, architecture, urban design, community analysis, and policy analysis. Conducts East Asian Program, special education programs, and field-linked education.

★3647★ Laboratory of Climatology
Arizona State Univ.
Tempe, AZ 85287-1508
Phone: (602)965-6265
Fax: (602)965-8313
Contact: Dr. Robert C. Balling Jr., Dir.
Research Areas: Solar energy, climatic change, urban and building climatology, and water resources, including monitoring of atmospheric conditions, analysis of air pollution data, operation of state climatology program, compilation of weather reports, inventory and analysis of precipitation and solar radiation data, and preparation of climatic maps of Arizona.

★3648★ Laboratory of Microbial Ecology
New York Univ.
752 Brown Bldg.
New York, NY 10003
Phone: (212)998-8268
Fax: (212)995-4015
Contact: Dr. Guenther Stotzky, Dir.
Research Areas: Microbial ecology, soil and water microbiology, medical microbiology, environmental virology, clay mineralogy, immunology, and pollution, including studies on survival of genetically engineered microbes in natural environments and acid rain, heavy metals, and other pollutants.

★3649★ Laboratory of Populations
Rockefeller Univ.
1230 York Ave.
New York, NY 10021-6399
Phone: (212)570-8884

Fax: (212)570-7974
Contact: Joel E. Cohen, Head
Research Areas: Conducts mathematical studies, statistical analysis, and computations in the field of populations, including studies of food webs, ecology and evolution, demography of age-structured populations, and malarial epidemiology.

★3650★ Laboratory of Radiation Ecology
University of Washington
Fisheries Research Center
College of Fisheries
Seattle, WA 98195
Phone: (206)543-4259
Contact: Prof. Nevissi, Dir.
Research Areas: Undertakes research programs related to contaminants in marine and freshwater environments, including man-produced radionuclides, naturally occurring radionuclides, and heavy metals. Special Resources: Equipment and facilities for the measurement and identification of alpha-, beta-, and gamma-emitting radionuclides and heavy metals in animal, plant, soil, sediment, water, and air samples.

★3651★ Laboratory of Renewable Resources Engineering
Purdue Univ.
Potter Bldg.
West Lafayette, IN 47907
Phone: (317)494-7022
Contact: Dr. George T. Tsao, Dir.
Research Areas: Efficient use and conversion of renewable natural resources to liquid fuels, chemical feedstocks, and food sources. Conducts studies on fermentation engineering, enzyme technology, molecular genetics, conversion of cellulose and other polysaccharides, and processors for producing chemicals, fuels, hydrocarbons, and food from renewable resources.

★3652★ Lacawac Sanctuary Foundation
RD #1, Box 518
Lake Ariel, PA 18436
Phone: (717)689-9494
Contact: Sally J. Jones, Curator
Research Areas: Scientific investigations of acid rain and lake ecology and chemistry. The Sanctuary is a 500-acre wilderness area serving colleges, schools, universities, and the local community Special Resources: 52-acre Lake Lacawac, extensive bog and marsh areas, virgin forest, second-growth woods, and an open field and old orchard.

★3653★ Land Information and Computer Graphics Facility
University of Wisconsin-Madison
College of Agriculture & Life Sciences
School of Natural Resources
Landscape Architecture Dept., 25 Agriculture Hall
Madison, WI 53706
Phone: (608)263-5534
Contact: Dr. Bernard J. Niemann Jr., Principal Investigator
Research Areas: Uses geographic information system technology, including ARC/INFO, ODYSSEY, and System 9 software, to investigate the modernization and integration of land records, including zoning, land cover, land use, ownership, wetlands, floodplains, and soil survey records. Studies modern geopositioning technologies and surveying equipment to accurately determine coordinates for public land survey corners. Develops software and methods for linking geographic information systems with analytical nonpoint water quality models. Special Resources: Maintains digitizers, graphics terminals, and plotters.

★3654★ The Land Institute
2440 E. Water Well Rd.
Salina, KS 67401
Phone: (913)823-5376
Contact: Dana Jackson, Codirector
Research Areas: Sustainable agriculture, including agroecology, plant breeding and genetics, and plant population biology. Research focuses on the development of perennial grain crops grown in mixtures. Special Resources: 98 acres of never-plowed native prairie.

★3655★ Land Reclamation Research Center
North Dakota State Univ.
NDSU-Reclamation, PO Box 459
Mandan, ND 58554
Phone: (701)663-6445
Fax: (701)667-1811
Contact: Dr. Eugene C. Doll, Superintendent
Research Areas: Reclamation of land disturbed by coal strip-mining or degraded due to oil drilling and exploration. Projects concern differential subsidence of leveled strip-mined lands, root zone hydrology as related to reestablishment of moisture regimes, salt movement in reclaimed soils and in soil contaminated with salt, reestablishment of crop productivity, and soil development in reclaimed soils.

★3656★ Land Use Analysis Laboratory
Iowa State Univ.
Agronomy Dept.
Ames, IA 50011
Phone: (515)294-2411
Fax: (515)294-3163
Contact: Dr. T.E. Fenton, Dir.
Research Areas: Encodes and processes natural resource information, primarily detailed soil survey for land ownership tract, to aid county assessors in valuation of agricultural land. Activities include the digitizing of all published soil survey maps for the state of Iowa.

★3657★ LANDLAB
California State Polytechnic Univ.
3801 W. Temple Ave.
Pomona, CA 91768
Phone: (714)869-4449
Fax: (714)869-2292
Contact: Dr. Edwin A. Barnes III, Dir.
Research Areas: Landfill effects on the environment, recycling, composting, and resource utilization. Special Resources: Active class III non-hazardous landfill used for research and education.

★3658★ Large Experimental Aquifer Program (LEAP)
Oregon Graduate Center
19600 NW Von Neumann Dr.
Beaverton, OR 97006
Phone: (503)690-1193
Contact: Prof. Richard Johnson, Dir.
Research Areas: Tests remediation technologies on gasoline spills and develops solutions for local spills. Activities include studies on the conditions under which vapors containing dense volatile organic compounds sink faster than air, and research on how degradation of contaminants takes place at the interface between groundwater and oxygenated zones. Special Resources: Maintains a 70-foot long, 30-foot wide, and 15-foot deep artificial aquifer.

★3659★ Law of the Sea Institute
Richardson School of Law
2515 Dole St., Rm. 208
Honolulu, HI 96822
Phone: (808)956-6750
Fax: (808)956-6402
Contact: Dr. John P. Craven, Dir.
Research Areas: Legal and jurisdictional problems in ocean resource exploitation, marine law and policy, national and international organizations dealing with marine problems, and marine economics. Compiles research from annual conferences and workshops.

★3660★ Lawrence Berkeley Laboratory, Applied Science Division
1 Cyclotron Rd.
Berkeley, CA 94720
Phone: (415)486-5001
Fax: (415)486-5172
Contact: Elton J. Cairns, Dir.
Research Areas: Energy conversion and storage, environmental research, building sciences, and policy analysis, including studies on advanced batteries, solar and fossil fuel conversion, biotechnology, materials for energy applications, atmospheric and biospheric effects of technology, combustion processes, techniques in analytical chemistry, membrane bioenergetics, advanced electrical lighting, windows, daylighting, thermally driven heat pumps, building energy use measurement, computer simulation and prediction, building data compilation and analysis, indoor air quality, energy conservation by utilities, international energy demand, natural resource market mechanisms, and appliance efficiency standards. Special Resources: Artificial skydome, mobile window thermal test unit, environmental chamber for contaminant measurements, cloud chamber, and building energy use database.

★3661★ Lawrence Berkeley Laboratory, Chemical Biodynamics Division
One Cyclotron Rd.
Berkeley, CA 94720
Phone: (415)486-4311
Contact: Dr. Sung-Hou Kim, Dir.
Research Areas: Energy sciences and structural biology, including chemistry and physics, solar technology, biological energy conversion, biochemistry and biophysics, environmental biology, and general life sciences. Emphasizes photon conversion, genetics and molecular mechanisms of photosynthesis, and effects of environmental pollutants on plant and animal cells.

★3662★ Lawrence Livermore National Laboratory
P.O Box 808
Livermore, CA 94550
Phone: (415)422-1100
Contact: John H. Nuckolls, Dir.
Research Areas: Programs range through a wide spectrum of scientific and engineering disciplines, approximately 70% the effort devoted to national security research and the other 30% concerned with energy and other research. Principal projects include studies on laser fusion, laser isotope separartion, magnetic fusion, biomedical and environmental research, in situ gasification of coal, in situ oil shale retorting, gas stimulation, nuclear waste disposal, and atmospheric and climatic modeling.

★3663★ Lenox Institute of Water Technology
101 Yokun Ave.
PO Box 1639
Lenox, MA 01240
Phone: (413)637-3025
Fax: (413)637-0768
Contact: S. Malumphy, Administrative Manager
Research Areas: Development of technology in water and wastewater treatment, with specific emphasis on flotation technology for solids-liquid separation, including studies on drinking water supply, municipal/industrial wastewater treatment, water quality analysis, analytical chemistry, groundwater contamination, solid waste management, and water, air, and land pollution control (acid rain, odor, hazardous wastes, asbestos, and toxic organics). Special Resources: Maintains and demonstrates water/ wastewater treatment pilot plants.

★3664★ Leopold Center for Sustainable Agriculture
Iowa State Univ.
126 Soil Tilth Bldg.
Ames, IA 50011
Phone: (515)294-3711
Fax: (515)294-9696
Contact: Prof. Dennis R. Keeney, Dir.
Research Areas: Identification and reduction of negative environmental and socioeconomic impacts of agricultural practices and development of alternative practices consistent with sustainable agriculture.

★3665★ Life Sciences and Public Policy Program
Rockefeller Univ.
1230 York Ave.
New York, NY 10021
Phone: (212)570-8679
Contact: Dr. William W. Lowrance, Dir.
Research Areas: Legal, social, and ethical problems in science and technology. Subjects of research include toxic wastes, risk assessment and management, ethics in health care, chemical pollution, and the U.S. chemical industry after the Bhopal, India, accident (Indian national disaster caused by the leak of a toxic gas used in pesticide production).

★3666★ Limnological Research Unit
Gannon Univ.
Univ. Sq.
Erie, PA 16541
Phone: (814)871-7641
Contact: Prof. Stanley J. Zagorski, Dir.
Research Areas: Chemical, physical, and biological analysis of benthic, limnetic, and littoral areas of Lake Erie. Conducts fall, spring, and summer samplings of Lake Erie bay.

★3667★ Living Marine Resources Institute
State Univ. of New York at Stony Brook
Stony Brook, NY 11794-5000
Phone: (516)632-8656
Contact: Dr. Bill Wise, Dir.
Research Areas: Commercial fisheries, sport fisheries, and aquaculture. Activities focus on shellfish biology, population dynamics, finfish biology, algal blooms (commonly known as brown tides), seaweed physiology and mariculture, and bay scallop population dynamics. Conducts studies on the economic structure of living marine resource industries and the effects of development on fisheries habitat. Collaborates with the Waste Management Institute in examining the relationship between sewage sludge dumping and the incidence of crustacean shell burn disease.

★3668★ Lobund Laboratory
University of Notre Dame
Notre Dame, IN 46556
Phone: (219)239-7564
Fax: (219)239-7595
Contact: Dr. Morris Pollard, Dir.
Research Areas: Germfree technology, microbiology, immunology, gerontology, biochemistry, radiation biology, micro-ecology, physiology, pathology, and experimental surgery, including studies on carcinogenesis; environmental pollution; radiation effects; cardiovascular diseases; cancer, particularly prostate cancer and benign prostate hyperplasia model systems; nutrition, particularly diet restriction and longevity; histopathology; electron microscopy; host-parasite relationships; genetic diseases; bone marrow transplantation; and environmental stress, with emphasis on use of germfree animals as experimental tools and model systems. Special Resources: Germfree facility.

★3669★ Long-Term Ecological Research Project (CULTER)
University of Colorado-Boulder
INSTAAR
CB 450
Boulder, CO 80309
Phone: (303)492-6198
Contact: Dr. Nelson Caine, Dir.
Research Areas: High altitude ecology in the Front Range of the Rocky Mountains, including studies in climatology, hydrology, paleoecology, geochemistry, and geomorphology, and focusing on ecosystem models, decomposition and nutrient cycling, vertebrate and aquatic invertebrate populations, disturbance and recovery of plant communities, and soil water and movement. Special Resources: Water chemistry laboratory, 8 meteorological stations, Alpine Tundra Biosphere Reserve, herbarium, geographic information system, and a database of meteorological records covering the past 38 years.

★3670★ Los Alamos National Laboratory
PO Box 1663
Los Alamos, NM 87545
Phone: (505)667-5061
Fax: (505)667-1754
Contact: Siegfried S. Hecker, Dir.
Research Areas: Nuclear, high-energy, plasma, low temperature, and cryogenic physics, earth and space sciences, engineering and environmental sciences, life sciences, inorganic chemistry, metallurgy, molecular biology, mesons, mathematics, biomedicine, and energy, including research and development programs relating to use of nuclear energy for production of power, energy lasers, controlled release of thermonuclear energy, and thermionic conversion.

★3671★ Lovelace Inhalation Toxicology Research Institute
PO Box 5890
Albuquerque, NM 87185
Phone: (505)844-6835
Fax: (505)846-1900
Contact: Dr. Joe L. Mauderly, Pres. and Dir.
Research Areas: Inhalation toxicology of airborne particles, fibers, vapors, and gases that may be encountered in the general environment or in occupational settings. Studies focus on the chemical and radioactive properties of materials. Research program includes 5 basic and applied studies of aerosol generation and characterization, deposition and retention of inhaled materials, pathogenesis of respiratory diseases, treatment for accidental inhalation of radionuclides, and toxicokinetics of inhaled materials. Activities emphasize mechanisms of lung cancer and noncancerous lung disease.

★3672★ Maine Cooperative Fish and Wildlife Research Unit
U. S. Fish & Wildlife Service
240 Nutting Hall
Univ. of Maine
Orono, ME 04469
Phone: (207)581-2870
Fax: (207)581-2858
Contact: Dr. William B. Krohn, Leader
Research Areas: Ecology and management of migratory and resident game species. Research emphasizes habitat evaluation and ecology of migratory birds, anadromous fish, and impacts of forest management on fish and wildlife in northern New England, including studies on impacts of acid precipitation and aquaculture of fishes and shellfish.

★3673★ Maine Medical Center Research Department
22 Bramhall St.
Portland, ME 04102
Phone: (207)871-2163
Contact: Peter W. Rand M.D., Associate V. Pres.
Research Areas: Environmental health research and laboratory-based clinical research. Provides instruction, consultation, and research development and support for medical staff of the 565-bed Medical Center.

★3674★ Marine Biomedical Center
Duke Univ.
Duke Univ. Marine Laboratory
Beaufort, NC 28516
Phone: (919)728-2111
Fax: (919)728-2514
Contact: Dr. Joseph Bonaventura, Dir.
Research Areas: Marine organisms and marine systems as they relate to human health and the health of the environment. Research conducted in the fields of oceanography, chemistry, biochemistry, developmental and behavioral biology, and physiology has led to specific studies on the continental shelf, trace metals in marine and estuarine ecosystems, photosynthetic physiology of marine plants, maritime and pelagic birds, and behavioral toxicology. Special Resources: Utilizes facilities from the Duke University Marine Laboratory, including an analytical chemistry facility and a facility for growing and maintaining marine organisms.

★3675★ Marine Ecosystems Research Laboratory
University of Rhode Island
Graduate School of Oceanography
Narragansett, RI 02882
Phone: (401)792-6104
Fax: (401)792-6160
Contact: Prof. Michael E.Q. Pilson, Dir.
Research Areas: Ecological studies of coastal marine ecosystems and comparative studies on adjacent coastal waters, including studies on the fates and effects of anthropogenic and natural substances. Experiments are carried out in mesocosms, which maintain ecosystems that behave similarly to those in coastal waters.

★3676★ Marine/Freshwater Biomedical Center
Oregon State Univ.
Wiegand Hall
Corvallis, OR 97339
Phone: (503)737-3164
Contact: Dr. George S. Bailey, Dir.
Research Areas: Chemical carcinogenesis in trout and other fish. Projects include

histopathology, histochemistry, and ultrastructure of neoplasia in fish.

★3677★ Marine Laboratory
Duke Univ.
Beaufort, NC 28516
Phone: (919)728-2111
Fax: (919)726-2514
Contact: Dr. Joseph S. Ramus, Dir.
Research Areas: Biological oceanography, marine chemistry and ecology, physiological ecology, geological oceanography, chemical ecology, stress physiology, membrane physiology and osmoregulation, and algal ecological physiology. Staff research concentrates on primary production, molecular controls of hemoglobin function, structure/function relationships in protein molecules, effects of insecticides on development of mud- and blue-crabs, endocrine mechanisms in marine invertebrate larvae, photobiology of marine animals and dinoflagellates, evolutionary processes in marine microzooplankton, mechanisms and functions of ion transport across cell membranes, effect of temperature on development of fouling communities, water quality ramifications on estuaries of converting bordering forests to agricultural uses, competition and predation in benthic marine communities, distribution and physical state of hydrocarbons in an oceanic water column, ability of colloidal material to transport hydrophobic compounds in aquatic ecosystems, fish behavior, marsh ecology, and seaweed systematics. Special Resources: Reference collection of 2,000 species of animals and macroalgae from estuaries and the continental shelf of North Carolina. Also maintains a 131-foot R/V Cape Hatteras for oceanographic studies, operated by Duke University/University of North Carolina Oceanographic Consortium; a 50-foot boat for trawling and dredging in sounds and estuaries; and small craft for individual and class use.

★3678★ Marine Science Center
Northeastern Univ.
E. Point
Nahant, MA 01908
Phone: (617)581-7370
Fax: (617)581-6076
Contact: Dr. Kenneth P. Sebens, Dir.
Research Areas: Marine ecology, neurobiology of marine animals, interstitial invertebrates, functional morphology of bivalve mollusks, effects of pollutants on invertebrates, coastal geology, invertebrate development, and fish biology. Special Resources: 50-foot research vessel (Mysis); several 10- to 18-foot boats for scientific investigations in coastal waters; direct-flow seawater system; transmission electron microscope.

★3679★ Marine Sciences Research Center
State Univ. of New York at Stony Brook
Stony Brook, NY 11794-5000
Phone: (516)632-8700
Fax: (516)632-8820
Contact: Dr. J.R. Schubel, Dean and Dir.
Research Areas: Coastal marine sciences, including coastal oceanography, coastal zone management and planning, pollution in coastal waters, waste disposal in the sea, and ocean policy. The Center conducts a comprehensive research program that delves into the biology, chemistry, geology, and physics of the coastal ocean and the effects that society has had on the coastal ocean. Conducts programs in coastal environments throughout the world. Special Resources: Maintains a fleet of coastal research vessels and Flax Pond Laboratory (Setauket, New York).

★3680★ Marine Station
Bowdoin Coll.
Brunswick, ME 04011
Phone: (207)725-3166
Contact: Dr. Edward S. Gilfillan, Dir.
Research Areas: Secondary productivity and biological/chemical aspects of air pollution, including follow-up studies of accidental oil spills in temperate and tropical environments. Available as collecting site for local and visiting biologists, especially during the summer.

★3681★ Marine Studies Center
University of Wisconsin-Madison
1269 Engineering Bldg.
1415 Johnson Dr.
Madison, WI 53706
Phone: (608)262-3883
Fax: (608)262-6707
Contact: Dr. Erhard F. Joeres, Acting Dir.
Research Areas: Multidisciplinary research on the oceans and Great Lakes aimed at solving marine resource problems and studying marine resource policy. Topics include the reestablishment of self-sustaining stocks of lake trout in Lake Michigan, effects of high lake levels on erosion and coastal installations, and economic consequences of diversions of Great Lakes water.

★3682★ Maryland Agricultural Experiment Station
University of Maryland
College Park, MD 20742
Phone: (301)405-1210
Fax: (301)314-9089
Contact: Dr. Robert A. Kennedy, Dir.
Research Areas: Natural resources and forestry, plants, crops, animals and poultry, economics and rural life, robotics, aquaculture, biotechnology, and general resource technology, including integrated pest management and sustainable agriculture. Develops methods to optimize agricultural production through new varieties and more efficient management systems for crops, livestock, and poultry. Special Resources: WYE Angus herd, Crane Aquaculture Facility.

★3683★ Massachusetts Cooperative Fish and Wildlife Unit
University of Massachusetts
Holdsworth Hall
Amherst, MA 01003
Phone: (413)545-0398
Contact: Dr. Rebecca Field, Unit Leader
Research Areas: Ecology of various species of animals, environment, and fish and wildlife habitat, relating to management needs.

★3684★ Massachusetts Public Interest Research Group (MassPIRG)
29 Temple Pl.
Boston, MA 02111
Phone: (617)292-4800
Fax: (617)292-8057
Contact: Janet S. Domenitz, Dir.
Research Areas: Public interest issues on the state level, including environmental preservation, corporate and governmental accountability, and energy policy. Areas of interest include hazardous chemical use reduction and cleanup, nuclear power and safe energy alternatives, and water and air pollution. Organizes student and citizen groups, designs issue campaigns, and develops legislative lobbying strategies.

★3685★ Massachusetts Water Resources Research Center
University of Massachusetts
Blaisdell House
Amherst, MA 01003
Phone: (413)545-2842
Fax: (413)545-2304
Contact: Dr. Paul J. Godfrey, Dir.
Research Areas: Water and water-related resources, including basic and applied studies on acid deposition in soil and water, supply and demand problems, quality of water, drinking water treatment, and management and development of water resources for all uses. Research projects on lakes, streams, groundwater, and estuaries involve problems of engineering, resource planning and management, economics, geohydrology, archeology, ecology, and social sciences. Specific studies include a state and regional geographic information systems project. Reports acidity of each precipitation event to state and federal agencies and to over 20 radio and television stations and newspapers in Massachusetts. Established under Water Resources Research Act of 1964, Public Law 88-379, to conduct and coordinate research on water and water-related resources at the University and within the state and to provide training of scientists and graduate students through research investigations and experiments. Databases: Long-term acid rain monitoring, including information on 4,500 Massachusetts water bodies.

★3686★ Mesoamerican Ecology Institute
Tulane Univ.
Center for Latin American Studies
New Orleans, LA 70118
Phone: (504)865-5164
Contact: Dr. Arthur Welden, Program Dir.
Research Areas: Man-land relationships and general ecology of Mexico, Central America, and the Caribbean. Coordinates Mesoamerican research and teaching activities of the University's natural and social scientists, including individual and group ecology field research and a semester-long course on the natural history and archaeology of Mesoamerica.

★3687★ Michigan Atmospheric Deposition Laboratory
University of Michigan
2126 Space Research Bldg.
Ann Arbor, MI 48109-2143
Phone: (313)763-6213
Contact: Prof. Perry J. Samson, Dir.
Research Areas: Development and application of air and precipitation quality simulation models, including ongoing analyses of existing air pollution dispersion models and development of new models to assess transport of pollutants over a variety of distances. Deploys instrumentation for meteorological and air pollution studies.

★3688★ Michigan Biotechnology Institute
3900 Collins Rd.
PO Box 27609
Lansing, MI 48909
Phone: (517)337-3181
Fax: (517)337-2122
Contact: Dr. J. Gregory Zeikus, Pres.
Research Areas: Appied research and development of applications of industrial and environmental biotechnology. Research areas include commodity oxychemicals; specialty materials and products, including fibers, enzymes, and biodegradable plastics; and biological waste treatment and bioremediation. Develops new technology for the commercial

sector. Special Resources: Pilot plant with industrial scale-up capabilities.

★3689★ Michigan Sea Grant College Program
Univ. of Michigan
2200 Bonisteel Blvd.
Ann Arbor, MI 48109
Phone: (313)763-1437
Fax: (313)747-0036
Contact: Dr. Michael Parsons, Dir.
Research Areas: Great Lakes and marine transportation and engineering, limnology and water quality, education, diving safety, toxic substances, Great Lakes fishery rehabilitation, recreational use of the Great Lakes, waterfront development, shore erosion control, and Great Lakes policy research.

★3690★ Midwest Research Institute (MRI)
425 Volker Blvd.
Kansas City, MO 64110-2299
Phone: (816)753-7600
Fax: (816)753-8420
Contact: John C. McKelvey, Pres. and CEO
Research Areas: Conducts research and development activities in the major areas of health, chemistry, the environment, and engineering and technology. Specific interests in the area of health include the following: pharmaceutical analysis; toxicology and metabolism; product chemistry; systems and services, including laboratory automation and robotics, hazardous materials handling, microencapsulation, repository operations, and photochemical analysis; behavioral sciences, including psychophysiology, smoking cessation, electromagnetic field effects, behavioral medicine, and human performance/ productivity; and chemistry support for toxicology. In the field of chemistry, MRI focuses on analytical chemistry methods, including method development, improvement, validation, and application; and analytical and environmental chemistry, including exposure assessment, human monitoring, physiological fluid analysis, consumer products/packaging exposure, development and evaluation of dosimeters and other instrumentation, fate and transport studies, field sampling and onsite analysis, and field screening method development for site remediation. Environmental studies include the following: environmental regulatory support; environmental management and assessment, including risk assessments for all environmental media, subsurface/ hydrogeologic investigations, water/ wastewater treatment, and hazardous waste planning and assessment; waste combustion; and underground storage tanks. Specific interests in engineering and technology include hazardous materials transportation, accident analysis, and environmental management support.

★3691★ Mililani Technology Park
300 Kahelu Ave. #35
Mililani, HI 96789
Phone: (808)548-8996
Contact: William M. Bass, Exec. Dir.
Research Areas: Facilitates cooperative research and development activities between Park tenants and University community, particularly in the areas of marine microbiology, oceanography, and alternative energy production and other forms of ocean-related high technology. Special Resources: Operates a pumping system capable of delivering approximately 13,300 gallons per minute of nutrient rich, pathogen-free, cold seawater from 2,100 feet below the ocean surface.

★3692★ Millar Wilson Laboratory for Chemical Research
Jacksonville Univ.
Jacksonville, FL 32211
Phone: (904)744-3950
Contact: Dr. R. Del Delumyea, Dir.
Research Areas: Development of methods for sampling, analysis and interpretation of atmospheric gases and particulates; determination of anthropogenic emissions in urban atmospheres; indoor air pollution; and studies of sediment chemistry using chemically-reactive probes designed and developed in the laboratory.

★3693★ Mining and Mineral Resources Research Center
Michigan Technological Univ.
Dept. of Metallurgical & Materials Engineering
1400 Townsend Dr.
Houghton, MI 49931
Phone: (906)487-2630
Contact: Dr. Carl C. Nesbitt, Dir.
Research Areas: Mining and mineral resources, including studies on industrial waste treatment and recovery, environmentally safe column flotation techniques, and reagents which aid in wastewater treatment and mineral recovery.

★3694★ Minnesota Sea Grant College Program
University of Minnesota
Ste. 302
1518 Cleveland Ave. N.
St. Paul, MN 55108
Phone: (612)625-9288
Fax: (612)625-0263
Contact: Donald C. McNaught, Dir.
Research Areas: Studies related to Lake Superior and the Great Lakes, including fisheries and aquaculture, coastal environmental processes, applied economics, tourism and recreation, port studies, biotechnology, and water policies.

★3695★ Minnesota Transgenic Fish Group
University of Minnesota
Dept. of Animal Science
1988 Fitch Ave.
St. Paul, MN 55108
Phone: (612)624-4277
Fax: (612)625-2743
Contact: Dr. Kevin S. Guise, Dir.
Research Areas: Fish molecular genetics and gene transfer, with emphasis on gene analysis, cloning techniques, and creation of transfer vectors.

★3696★ Mississippi Law Research Institute
University of Mississippi
Law Center, Rm. 518
University, MS 38677
Phone: (601)232-7775
Contact: Dr. William Hooper Jr., Dir.
Research Areas: General statutory reform, mining and mineral law, and coastal, wetlands, and ocean law. The Institute was established by the Board of Trustees of the State Institutions of Higher Learning and the Mississippi Legislature to provide in-depth law research to the state legislature and agencies on questions requiring extensive research. Special Resources: Houses law research computer facilities.

★3697★ Mississippi State Chemical Laboratory
Mississippi State Univ.
PO Box CR
Mississippi State, MS 39762
Phone: (601)325-3324
Contact: Dr. James P. Minyard, State Chemist
Research Areas: Chemistry, toxicology of pesticides, natural toxins, industrial chemicals and exposure of humans in work environments, and priority pollutants, including analytical studies on fertilizers, foods, animal feeds, paints, oils, varnishes, gasoline, and environmental distribution and degradation of pesticides. Special Resources: Maintains chemical analysis and petroleum products laboratories.

★3698★ Missouri Water Resources Research Center
University of Missouri-Columbia
0056 Engineering Complex
Columbia, MO 65211
Phone: (314)882-3132
Fax: (314)882-4784
Contact: Dr. Thomas E. Clevenger, Dir.
Research Areas: Water and other resources which affect water, including administrative coordination of multidisciplinary studies on availability, distribution, quantity and quality of water, water yields to be expected from different land areas in the state, a systems approach to river basin development, water quality alteration through acid and heat pollution, biochemical capabilities of surface film and benthic bacteria in a refinery waste lagoon, geochemistry and origin of sulfo-saline groundwater, and availability of subsurface water for consumptive use by plants.

★3699★ MIT-Remergence Laboratory
Massachusetts Inst. of Technology
Dept. of Civil Engineering
Cambridge, MA 02139
Phone: (617)253-3598
Fax: (617)253-6044
Contact: Prof. H.H. Einstein, Head
Research Areas: Resource extraction, environmental engineering, geotechnical engineering, structural engineering, and construction.

★3700★ MIT Sea Grant College Program
Massachusetts Inst. of Technology
292 Main St.
Cambridge, MA 02139
Phone: (617)253-7041
Fax: (617)253-8000
Contact: Chryssostomos Chryssostomidis, Dir.
Research Areas: Marine and coastal sciences, engineering, technology, and policy. Seeks to solve critical technological, economic, ecological, social, and political problems in marine resources utilization and coastal zone development caused by increasing and conflicting uses of the sea. Programs include creation of new and improved technologies for using oceans and their resources, search for opportunities and solutions to problems in extracting the sea's mineral resources, application of technology to expanding and improving the harvesting and utilization of living marine resources, and creation of technology and policy perspectives needed for proper coastal zone development. Cooperative studies of Institute faculty members are conducted in coastal engineering and mathematical modeling of hydrodynamics and biochemistry of coastal waters; fisheries engineering, health benefits of seafood, and use of underutilized species; marine biotechnology, including industrial use of chitin and its derivatives, angiogenesis inhibitors from shark cartilage, and marine polymer use in controlled release of drugs; environmental and economic effects of offshore oil mining; and offshore structures, particularly risers, cables, moorings, open-ended piles, wave forces, and

the development of remotely operated, unmanned, underwater work vehicles.

★3701★ Montana Forest and Conservation Experiment Station
University of Montana
Missoula, MT 59812
Phone: (406)243-5521
Fax: (406)243-4510
Contact: Dr. Sidney S. Frissell, Dir.
Research Areas: Forest biology, management, economics, and administration, including wildlife biology and conservation, range biology and conservation, outdoor recreation, soils, hydrology, watershed management, and geographic information systems. Special Resources: Maintains the 30,000-acre Lubrecht Experimental Forest and a 3,400-acre operating ranch.

★3702★ Montana University System Water Resources Center
208 Cobleigh Hall
Bozeman, MT 59717
Phone: (406)994-6690
Contact: Dr. Howard S. Peavy, Acting Dir.
Research Areas: Water and other resources related to water, including studies on hydrology, economic and legal water problems, groundwater, water-soil-plant relations, water quality, instrumentation, and development of water resource data for planning and action in the state.

★3703★ Mote Marine Laboratory
1600 City Island Park
Sarasota, FL 34236
Phone: (813)388-4441
Fax: (813)388-4312
Contact: Dr. Selvakumaran Mahadevan, Exec. Dir.
Research Areas: Wetland and estuarine ecology, habitat restoration, toxic organic chemistry, physical chemistry, biochemistry, analytical chemistry, marine chemistry, fisheries, aquaculture, fish stock enhancement, benthic fauna, phytoplankton, meroplankton, ichthyoplankton, marine mammals and turtles, sediments, red tide, neurobiology, absence of cancer in sharks, echolocation in saltwater catfish, bioassays, toxicology, bioactive substances, aerosols, development of skate as a standardized laboratory animal, and reproductive patterns of sharks, skates, and rays. Special Resources: Marine biological and chemical research laboratories with ichthyoplankton and benthic invertebrate reference collections, marine animal holding and culture facilities with flow-through seawater, Technicon autoanalyzer, sedimentology laboratory, complete environmental sampling and processing facilities, and a 135,000 gallon large animal aquarium.

★3704★ Museum of Zoology
University of Massachusetts
Dept. of Zoology
Amherst, MA 01003
Phone: (413)545-0457
Contact: Dr. D.J. Klingener, Dir.
Research Areas: Ecology of invertebrates, fish, birds, mammals, amphibians, and reptiles, including evolutionary relationships above the species level. Other studies concentrate on ecological problems, watersheds, and water quality in New England.

★3705★ National Center for Appropriate Technology
3040 Continental Dr., Box 3838
Butte, MT 59702
Contact: George Purman, Pres.
Research Areas: Energy, agriculture, rehabilitation technologies, building technologies, and companion areas of ventilation and indoor air quality. Conducts field studies and performs energy end use load monitoring and research for utilities in several states.

★3706★ National Center for Food and Agricultural Policy
Resources for the Future
1616 P St., NW
Washington, DC 20036
Phone: (202)328-5082
Fax: (202)265-8069
Contact: George E. Rossmiller, Dir.
Research Areas: Examines interrelated public policy issues involving agriculture, food safety and health, natural resources, and the environment internationally.

★3707★ National Center for Ground Water Research
Univ. of Oklahoma
200 Telgar St.
Rm. 127
Norman, OK 73019-0470
Phone: (405)325-5202
Contact: Dr. Larry Canter, Dir.
Research Areas: Transport and fate of pollutants, including development and evaluation of physical models of soil and subsoil profiles; subsurface characterization, including establishment and evaluation of standardized methods for characterizing and classifying soils and subsurface materials based on parameters influencing pollutant behavior, characterization of subsurface microbial activity in relation to its biodegradation potential, and examination of the relationship between geochemistry and groundwater contamination; and methods for groundwater quality assessment and protection, including development and evaluation of drilling and coring technology and equipment that produce uncontaminated samples and evaluation of methodologies for detecting and tracing plumes of groundwater contamination.

★3708★ National Center for Intermedia Transport Research
University of California, Los Angeles
5531 Boelter Hall
Dept. of Chemical Engineering
Los Angeles, CA 90024-1592
Phone: (213)825-9741
Fax: (213)206-4107
Contact: Prof. Yoram Cohen, Dir.
Research Areas: Pollutant exchange between media (air, water, and soil), multimedia transport processes involving several interacting environmental compartments, and the application of these processes to chemical compounds expected to be of special environmental importance. Specific studies include atmospheric dry deposition processes and the calculation of deposition velocity in soil, gravel, grass, and water; soil/water processes and the development of models for predicting the movement of contaminants in the unsaturated soil zone; mathematical models of pollutant transport; determination of the distribution of organic substances in rain, fog, and mist and the basic mechanisms determining distribution; atmospheric deposition and environmental assimilation of gases and aerosols in a desert ecosystem; and development of methods for characterizing pollutant mixtures. Special Resources: Air Quality/Aerosol Technology Laboratory, Soil Transport Processes Laboratory.

★3709★ National Center for Toxicological Research Associated Universities, Inc. (NCTR-AU)
4301 W. Markham
UAMS 522-7
Little Rock, AR 72205
Phone: (501)686-6501
Fax: (501)686-8315
Contact: Robert P. Cullen, Exec. Dir.
Research Areas: Toxicology and pharmacology. Promotes interaction between universities, government, and industry in these areas of research.

★3710★ National Center for Vehicle Emissions Control and Safety
Colorado State Univ.
Dept. of Industrial Sciences
Old Industrial Sciences Bldg.
Fort Collins, CO 80523
Phone: (303)491-7240
Fax: (303)491-7801
Contact: Dr. Birgit Wolff, Dir.
Research Areas: Vehicle emission technology. Projects include an annual tampering and fuel-switching survey involving 500 cars nationwide, experiments on computer linkages and vehicle emissions, an opinion survey of diesel vehicle owners, and studies on diesel opacity, oxygenated fuels, after-market equipment, and high altitude emission. Maintains laboratory facilities with FTP capabilities.

★3711★ National Council of the Paper Industry for Air and Stream Improvement, Inc.
260 Madison Ave.
New York, NY 10016
Phone: (212)532-9000
Fax: (212)779-2849
Contact: Dr. Isaiah Gellman, Pres.
Research Areas: Environmental quality protection problems and concerns of forest products industry (pulp, paper, paperboard, wood products, and industrial forestry), including studies on air and water pollution, solid waste management, forest health and wildlife management, and factory workplace air quality. Performs control technology studies, environmental impact assessments of manufacturing operations and industrial forestry, pollutant measurements, and potential air quality impact evaluations on forest health and productivity. Databases: Discharge and emission levels, control technology, and performance capability for pulp and paper mills.

★3712★ National Institute for Global Environmental Change, Midwest Regional Center
Indiana Univ.
School of Public & Environmental Affairs
SPEA Rm. 441
Bloomington, IN 47405
Phone: (812)855-2457
Fax: (812)855-7802
Contact: Prof. J.C. Randolph, Dir.
Research Areas: Past climates and factors that regulate climate change, the natural cycling of greenhouse gases such as carbon dioxide through systems such as oceans and forests, the impact of global warming on natural ecosystems, climate modeling, energy policies, fuel consumption, and how specific regions might respond to global environmental change.

Operates Supermerit Program, which supports multi-region and multidisciplinary projects.

★3713★ National Institute for Global Environmental Change, Northeast Regional Center
Harvard Univ.
327 Lyman Laboratory
9 Rear Oxford
Cambridge, MA 02138
Phone: (617)495-3387
Fax: (617)495-0416
Contact: Prof. Richard Wilson, Dir.
Research Areas: Past climates and factors that regulate climate change, the natural cycling of greenhouse gases such as carbon dioxide through systems such as oceans and forests, the impact of global warming on natural ecosystems, climate modeling, energy policies, fuel consumption, and how specific regions might respond to global environmental change. Operates Supermerit Program, which supports multi-region and multidisciplinary projects.

★3714★ National Institute for Global Environmental Change, Southern Regional Center
Tulane Univ.
605 Lindy Boggs Center
New Orleans, LA 70118-5674
Phone: (504)865-5775
Fax: (504)865-5345
Contact: Robert G. Watts, Dir.
Research Areas: Causes, impacts, and appropriate responses to global change related to energy use. Studies include past climates and factors that regulate climate change, the natural cycling of greenhouse gases such as carbon dioxide through systems such as oceans and forests, the impact of global warming on natural ecosystems, climate modeling, energy policies, fuel consumption, and how specific regions might respond to global environmental change. Operates Supermerit Program, which supports multi-region and multidisciplinary projects.

★3715★ National Institute for Global Environmental Change, Western Regional Center
University of California, Davis
1477 Drew Ave., Ste. 104
Davis, CA 95616-8756
Phone: (916)757-3403
Fax: (916)756-6499
Contact: Prof. Marvin Goldman, Codirector
Research Areas: Agricultural, hydrological, and ecological effects of global environmental change, including atmospheric and oceanographic modeling, the role of trace gases in climate change, environmental risk assessments, and policies and educational programs focusing on global environmental change. Operates Supermerit Program, which supports multi-region and multidisciplinary projects.

★3716★ National Institute for Petroleum and Energy Research
PO Box 2128
220 NW Virginia Ave.
Bartlesville, OK 74005
Phone: (918)336-2400
Fax: (918)337-4365
Contact: James M. Deterding, Dir.
Research Areas: All fields of petroleum and unconventional hydrocarbon technology, from extraction through processing to utilization. Extraction research emphasizes enhanced oil recovery (EOR) and includes projects on the interaction of reservoir rock and EOR fluids, reservoir screening and recovery predictions, environmental compatibility of microbial EOR, basic studies of EOR chemicals, and gas displacement methods. Processing research includes studies on thermodynamics, stability and processing, and characterization of heavy oils and synthetic fluid mixtures. Utilization research examines the effect of alternative feedstocks on emissions, efficiency of transportation fuels, particulates from the exhaust of diesel engines, and alternative fuels and re-formulated gasolines. Databases: Crude Oil Analysis Data Bank.

★3717★ National Institute for Urban Wildlife
10921 Trotting Ridge Way
Columbia, MD 21044
Phone: (301)596-3311
Contact: Gomer E. Jones, Pres.
Research Areas: Conservation problems involving effects of man's activities on wildlife and wildlife habitat, including environmental and wildlife planning and management for new and existing developments and construction of reports useful to planners, developers, and others concerned with planning and maintaining higher quality urban environments.

★3718★ National Mine Land Reclamation Center, Eastern Region
108 Land & Water Resource Bldg.
University Park, PA 16802
Phone: (814)863-0291
Contact: Paul F. Ziemkiewicz, Dir.
Research Areas: Improved methods and equipment related to cost effective and environmentally acceptable reclamation of lands disturbed by surface and underground mining. Research activities include acid mine drainage, use of fly ash and sludge to revegetate surface mined areas and abandoned coal refuse banks, finite element analysis, proton adsorption and desorption by pyrite surfaces, and inverse solution techniques for parameter identification in steady and unsteady groundwater systems.

★3719★ National Mine Land Reclamation Center, Midwestern Region
Southern Illinois Univ. at Carbondale
Plant & Soil Sciences
Carbondale, IL 62901
Phone: (618)453-2496
Contact: Donald Stucky, Dir.
Research Areas: Improved scientific methods and equipment related to cost effective and environmentally acceptable reclamation of lands disturbed by surface and underground mining. Research activities include: restoration and preservation of agricultural land and water resources; soil decompacting techniques which increase plant-useable soil volume, pore size, aeration, and infiltration; and revegetation of mining sites using corn plants and trees.

★3720★ National Mine Land Reclamation Center, Western Region
Mandan, ND 58554
Phone: (701)663-6445
Contact: K.C. Vining, Dir.
Research Areas: Reclamation of lands disturbed by surface and underground mining. Research activities include: groundwater movement and subsidence; spoil geochemistry; subsurface water chemical evolution in abandoned mine land sites, currently mined areas, and adjacent unmined settings; technology for filling and stabilizing abandoned underground mines using fly ash; and leaching properties of fly ash fill material.

★3721★ National Park Service Cooperative Park Studies Unit
Univ. of Washington
College of Forest Resources AR-10
Seattle, WA 98195
Phone: (206)543-1587
Fax: (206)543-3254
Contact: David L. Peterson, Co-leader
Research Areas: The Unit is comprised of a biology and sociology program, both of which emphasize research applicable to park management and related extension activities, such as environmental change, forest restoration, geographic information systems, role of forest fires and fire management, ecology and management of natural systems, National Park Service employee survey, study of backcountry users in Alaskan parks, and interpretation of the behavior of park visitors.

★3722★ National Park Service Cooperative Unit (Athens)
Institute of Ecology
Univ. of Georgia
Athens, GA 30602
Phone: (404)542-8301
Contact: Dr. Susan Power Bratton, Research Biologist
Research Areas: National Park management, ecology, water quality, fire management, protection and study of rare and endangered species, and coastal ecosystems. The research program concentrates on resources management information needs in U.S. National Park Service areas, particularly Cumberland Island National Seashore, Cape Hatteras National Seashore, Canaveral National Seashore, and Blue Ridge Parkway.

★3723★ National Undersea Research Center
University of Hawaii at Manoa
1000 Pope Rd., MSB 303
Honolulu, HI 96822
Phone: (808)956-6802
Contact: Alexander Malahoff, Dir.
Research Areas: Ecosystems and mineral resources of the Pacific Ocean centered around the Hawaiian Archipelago, including the effect of humans on the Pacific, colonization and carbonate production rates of benthic organisms, Sand Island sewer outfall, deep benthic shrimp behavior and metabolic studies of habitat, deepsea echinoderm reproductive ecology, deepsea gorgonian beds, marine pharmaceuticals, recolonization rates of pink coral, fish and invertebrate development in artificial reefs, chemical and mineralogical studies of cobalt-rich ferromanganese crusts, environmental damage caused by ocean mining, drowned coral reefs, and the geology, geochemistry, and microbiology of an active submarine volcanoe. Special Resources: Remotely operated vehicles, atowed camera sled, and the submersible Pisces V.

★3724★ Natural Energy Laboratory of Hawaii Authority
PO Box 1749/Keahole Point
Kailua-Kona, HI 96745
Phone: (808)329-7341
Fax: (808)326-3262
Contact: Thomas H. Daniel Ph.D., Scientific/ Technical Manager
Research Areas: Ocean thermal energy conversion, particularly biofouling, corrosion, countermeasures, water quality, open cycle heat and mass transfer, seawater gas content, and cold water aquaculture (trout, salmon, nori, abalone, and lobster). Also conducts aquaculture feasibility research in larval hatching and growout development. Leases

land for commercial development of research projects, including abalone, microalgae, nori seaweed, and Maine lobster. Databases: Water quality; trace organic and inorganic materials; air and water temperatures; wind, rain, and insolation; and heat transfer changes due to biofouling. Special Resources: Research facilities include a continuous flow of cold seawater at 20,000 gallons per minute from 600-meter depth, a system pumping surface seawater at 10,000 gallons per minute, and a water quality facility. Manages the 3 MW geothermal plant at Pohoiki and the associated Puna Geothermal Research Facility.

★3725★ Natural Resource Ecology Laboratory
Colorado State Univ.
Fort Collins, CO 80523
Phone: (303)491-1982
Fax: (303)491-1965
Contact: Dr. James E. Ellis, Acting Dir.
Research Areas: Ecosystem analysis, especially grasslands and man's activities affecting these ecosystems. Activities include studies of acid rain through the National Atmospheric Deposition Program, below ground ecosystems, plant-animal interactions, biogeochemistry, subsistence pastoralism, and semiarid agricultural ecosystems. Special Resources: NSF Long Term Ecological Research Program database, National Atmospheric Deposition Program database, and wet and dry deposition chemistry database; also maintains automated nutrient analysis equipment and simulation modeling, geographic information system, and image processing facilities.

★3726★ Natural Resources Center
University of Alabama
PO Box 870268
Tuscaloosa, AL 35487-0268
Phone: (205)348-7007
Contact: Dr. Stanley Jones, Dir.
Research Areas: Water, water-related energy, solar energy, biomass, residential energy conservation, environmental management, thermal storage in aquifers, alternative energy, liquified natural gas as a substitute fuel for diesel engines, natural heritage inventory, and coal bed methane development.

★3727★ Natural Resources Defense Council
40 W. 20th St.
Ste. 300
New York, NY 10011
Phone: (212)727-2700
Fax: (212)727-1773
Contact: John H. Adams, Exec. Dir.
Research Areas: Use of the judicial system to enforce environmental protection laws and environmental policy studies, including studies related to public health and the environment, public lands and the coast, nuclear energy and weapons, energy conservation, and the global environment. Specific concerns include air quality, acid rain, airborne toxic pollutants, metropolitan air pollution, stratospheric ozone loss, solid waste disposal, water pollution, sewage treatment, industrial pollution, hazardous waste disposal, drinking water, pesticide policy, antibiotics in animal feed, biotechnology policy, national forest management, agricultural resource conservation, public lands protection, irrigation policy, endangered species conservation, offshore oil leasing, shoreline protection, sea level rise, Nuclear Test Ban verification, nuclear weapons, environmental effects of nuclear production, nuclear winter, energy conservation, energy efficiency of appliances, energy efficient buildings, habitat protection, desertification, deforestation, famine, wetlands conservation, and international wildlife trade.

★3728★ Natural Resources Research Institute (NRRI)
University of Minnesota, Duluth
5013 Miller Trunk Hwy.
Duluth, MN 55811
Phone: (218)720-4294
Fax: (218)720-4219
Contact: Dr. Michael J. Lalich, Dir.
Research Areas: Economic development of the state's natural resources in an environmentally sound manner, including applied research on the technological and economic factors that impede the establishment or expansion of many resource-based industries. NRRI research activities are carried out through three centers: 1) Center for Applied Research and Technolgy Development, comprised of two divisions, BioProducts Division, studying economic utilization of peat, forestry resources, and value added forest products and the Minerals Division, emphasizing programs on taconite, non-ferrous minerals, industrial minerals, and hazardous waste; 2) Center for Water and the Environment, which examines the state's resources to develop sound economic development and enviornmental decisions; 3) Center for Economic Development, jointly administered with the University School of Business and Economics, providing business development support.

★3729★ Nebraska Statewide Arboretum
112 Forestry Sciences Laboratory
Lincoln, NE 68583-0823
Phone: (402)472-2971
Fax: (402)472-8095
Contact: L. Finke, Educational Dir.
Research Areas: Discovery, collection, evaluation, and distribution of useful plants for Nebraska landscapes. Maintains a tract for growing trees, shrubs, vines, and prairie and woodland plants; participates in seed and plant exchanges; cultivates endangered, threatened, and rare plants in conjunction with the National Center for Plant Conservation.

★3730★ New Alchemy Institute
237 Hatchville Rd.
East Falmouth, MA 02536
Phone: (508)564-6301
Fax: (508)457-9680
Contact: Dave Simser, Research Dir.
Research Areas: Sustainable agriculture, greenhouse agriculture, energy-efficient design, and biological, physical, and cultural pest control. Conducts economic analyses of vegetable production; designs, builds, and tests composting systems and enclosed compost/greenhouse systems; and studies cover crops, weed control, and soil and crop nitrogen relations.

★3731★ New Products Group
University of Missouri
210 Agricultural Engineering Bldg.
Columbia, MO 65211
Phone: (314)882-7044
Contact: Dr. Gene Ianotti, Dir.
Research Areas: Cornstarch-based degradable plastics research, including studies on anaerobic and aerobic degradation processes.

★3732★ New York Cooperative Fish and Wildlife Research Unit
Cornell Univ.
Dept. of Natural Resources
Fernow Hall
Ithaca, NY 14853
Phone: (607)255-2151
Contact: Dr. Milo Richmond, Unit Leader
Research Areas: Fish and wildlife research and management, including ecotoxicology, habitat, productivity, growth, feeding, behavior, and movement studies of various birds, waterfowl, mammals, and fish. Also conducts reproductive studies of wild vertebrates and pest management ecology studies.

★3733★ New York Sea Grant Institute
Dutchess Hall
State Univ. of New York
Stony Brook, NY 11794-5001
Phone: (516)632-6905
Fax: (516)632-6917
Contact: Dr. Robert Malouf, Dir.
Research Areas: Provides funds to university faculty for research on issues affecting New York coastal areas, including coastal law, aquaculture, sport fisheries, commercial fisheries, coastal structures and processes, recreation, waste management, seafood science, energy from the sea, offshore mining, erosion control, coastal tourism, and marine education. Research needs are assessed by Extension Program offices and made known to the Institute; research results are in turn disseminated by the offices to local groups, industry, and governments.

★3734★ New York State Center for Hazardous Waste Management
State Univ. of New York at Buffalo
Jarvis Hall 207
Buffalo, NY 14260
Phone: (716)636-3446
Contact: Ralph R. Rumer Sc.D., Exec. Dir.
Research Areas: Fosters collaborative research in hazardous waste management, including elimination of toxic residuals associated with industrial production or manufacturing processes; recovery, recycling, or neutralization of toxic substances and hazardous wastes stored or introduced into the environment; and treatment, storage, or disposal technologies. Promotes and funds university/industry/government partnerships and interuniversity research and development programs.

★3735★ New York State Water Resources Institute
468 Hollister Hall
Cornell Univ.
Ithaca, NY 14853
Phone: (607)255-7535
Contact: Keith S. Porter, Dir.
Research Areas: Water resources, including agricultural chemicals and water use, nonagricultural contaminant sources, environmental fate and effect of contaminants, risk management, public health, groundwater management, water supply management, and emergency planning and crisis response capacity. Databases: Statewide Water Management.

★3736★ North Carolina Alternative Energy Corporation
PO Box 12699
Research Triangle Park, NC 27709
Phone: (919)361-8000
Fax: (919)544-6149
Contact: Dr. Robert Koger, Pres.
Research Areas: Chartered to moderate the rate of growth in electric power demand and to

defer the need to build new electricity generating facilities through use of renewable energy sources, load management techniques, and energy conservation. Conducts research in agriculture, community, industry, residential, commercial, and utility sectors. Identifies potentially attractive energy-efficient systems for the state, field tests the techniques and technologies to demonstrate cost- and performance-effectiveness, and promotes end user investment in new technologies.

★3737★ North Carolina Water Resources Research Institute
North Carolina State Univ.
Box 7912
Raleigh, NC 27695-7912
Phone: (919)737-2815
Contact: Dr. David H. Moreau, Dir.
Research Areas: Water and other resources which affect water, including multidisciplinary studies on water resource planning, water quantity, water quality management, and water problems of North Carolina. Established to conduct and coordinate research activities to improve ability of the state and region to conserve and manage their total water resources. Provides opportunities for interdisciplinary graduate training.

★3738★ North Dakota Water Resources Research Institute
North Dakota State Univ.
Old Main 201
Fargo, ND 58105
Phone: (701)237-7033
Fax: (701)237-7050
Contact: R. Craig Schnell Ph.D., Dir.
Research Areas: Water and water resources, including evaluations of water quality with respect to dissolved chemicals, movement of herbicides and insecticides into groundwater, and development of wetland policies.

★3739★ Northeast Watershed Research Center
111 Research Bldg. A
Pennsylvania State Univ.
University Park, PA 16802
Phone: (814)865-2048
Contact: Dr. Harry B. Pionke, Research Leader
Research Areas: Laboratory and field research in agricultural and urban hydrology, water and soil chemistry, water and nutrient transport in unsaturated and saturated soil and geologic systems, erosion and sediment transport, soil science, and development of hydrologic and water quality simulation for land use planning. Utilizes Mahantango Creek watershed near Klingerstown, Pennsylvania, as an outdoor laboratory for testing and developing more general hydrological and water quality relationships that can be applied or subsequently tested on problem sites elsewhere. Databases: Hydrologic, chemical, and climatic databases for the Mahantango Creek watershed.

★3740★ Northern Lights Institute
210 N. Higgins, #227
Missoula, MT 59802
Phone: (406)721-7415
Contact: Donald Snow, Program Dir.
Research Areas: Natural resources, including the allocation of water from the Missouri River, a study of the Clark Fork of the Columbia River, and resource management policies throughout the Rocky Mountain region. Conducts studies in community and economic development as related to the history and culture of northern Rocky Mountains and in environmental and natural resource management problem solving.

★3741★ Northwest Fisheries Science Center
2725 Montlake Blvd. E.
Seattle, WA 98112
Phone: (206)442-1872
Fax: (206)442-4304
Contact: Dr. Richard J. Berry, Science & Research Dir.
Research Areas: Mitigation of fishery habitat degradation in Northwest estuaries and the Columbia River drainage system, monitoring of contaminants U.S. coastal waters and their effects on fishery stocks, and enhancement of the quality, value and safety of fishery products from the West Coast. Mitigations studies focus on survival of salmonids passing dams during migration, ecological effects of the removal and disposal of dredge spoils, and research on the physiology and diseases of hatchery fish. Coastal pollution studies document trends in major estuaries and determine the effects of chemical contaminants on the reproductive capabilities of fish and marine invertebrates. Fishery products studies concentrate on removing impediments to the full use of available fishery resources and upgrading the value of underutilized species. Activities emphasize controlling bacterial contaminations, production of surmi, exploring the potentials of fish oils in human nutrition, and developing economic uses for fish wastes.

★3742★ Nuclear Center
Louisiana Tech Univ.
PO Box 3015
Ruston, LA 71272
Phone: (318)257-2603
Contact: Dr. R.H. Thompson, Dir.
Research Areas: Environmental measurement, industrial and agricultural uses of radioisotopes, and radiation effects of materials. Develops new separation techniques and studies radioactivity of lignite and neutron activity of trace elements. Currently conducting baseline radioactivity measurements and studying transport of radionuclides in groundwater.

★3743★ Nuclear Fuel Cycle Research Program
University of Arizona
Dept. of Nuclear & Energy Engineering
Tucson, AZ 85721
Phone: (602)626-4985
Contact: Dr. James G. McCray, Acting Dir.
Research Areas: Nuclear fuel cycle, with emphasis on research associated with high- and low-level nuclear waste management and disposal.

★3744★ Oak Creek Laboratory of Biology
Oregon State Univ.
Dept. of Fisheries & Wildlife
104 Nash Hall
Corvallis, OR 97331
Phone: (503)737-3503
Fax: (503)737-3590
Contact: Dr. Larry Curtis, Project Leader
Research Areas: Aquatic biology, including problems relating to the biological effects and control of water pollution. Also conducts experimental studies on the physiology, toxicology, and ecology of freshwater fish and other aquatic organisms, their environmental requirements, and their responses to water quality changes.

★3745★ Oak Ridge Associated Universities (ORAU)
PO Box 117
Oak Ridge, TN 37831-0117
Phone: (615)576-3146
Fax: (615)576-3643
Contact: Dr. Jon M. Veigel, Pres.
Research Areas: Research and development in the areas of education, training, health, and energy and the environment. The association is composed of four research units: the Institute for Energy/Environment Analysis, the Medical Sciences Division, the University Isotope Separator at Oak Ridge, and the Marmoset Research Center at Oak Ridge, a consortium of pharmaceutical laboratories, university and college medical schools, and research hospitals. Institute for Energy/Environment Analysis develops, analyzes, and evaluates policies and regulations affecting energy and environmental issues. Medical Sciences Division conducts biomedical research and training in studies of respiratory and gastrointestinal diseases and cancers related to occupational exposures to chemical toxicants and ionizing radiation involved in energy production. Research disciplines within the Division include immunobiology, biological chemistry, cell biology, radiopharmaceutical chemistry, nuclear medicine, experimental pathology, cytogenetics, microbiology, epidemiology, and human reliability. The University Isotope Separator at Oak Ridge (UNISOR) is a consortium studying rare, extremely unstable nuclei. Maintains a helium dilution refrigerator and recoil mass spectrometer. Marmoset Research Center at Oak Ridge explores the relationships between colon cancer and possible causes or contributing factors, such as hereditary and immune system deficiencies. Other programs of the association are concerned with education, training, and academic outreach and include the Science/Engineering Education Division, the Training and Management Systems Division, and the Energy/Environment Systems Division.

★3746★ Oak Ridge National Laboratory (ORNL)
PO Box 2008
Oak Ridge, TN 37831-6255
Phone: (615)576-2900
Fax: (615)576-2912
Contact: Dr. Alvin W. Trivelpiece, Dir.
Research Areas: Nuclear energy development, biomedical and environmental problems, basic physical sciences, and magnetic fusion energy, involving a broad research, development, and demonstration program in support of the Department's mission to provide efficient and environmentally and socially acceptable energy options. Conducts studies on fossil, nuclear, and geothermal fuel cycles, nuclear waste management, high-temperature and resistant materials, reactor physics, reactor safety, somatic, carcinogenic, and genetic effects of energy effluents, environmental fate of energy effluents, energy conservation and utilization, synthetic fuels (e.g., coal-conversion), properties of materials, radiation effects, heavy-ion physics, catalysis, actinide chemistry, plasma physics, neutral-beam injection, superconducting-magnet development, and fusion/reactor technology. Special Resources: Maintains Atomic Physics EN Tandem Accelerator, Bioprocessing Research Facility, Health Physics Research Reactor, High Temperature Materials Laboratory, Holifield Heavy Ion Research Facility, Low Temperature Neutron Irradiation Facility, National Center for Small-Angle Scattering Research, Neutron Scattering Facility, Oak Ridge Electron Linear Accelerator Oak Ridge National Environmental Research Park, Roof Test Facility Shared Research Equipment Collaborative Research Program and Surface Modification and Characterization Collaborative Research

Center, Dosimetry Applications Research Facility, computers, information centers, an ecological preserve, stable isotope separation, radioisotope production capabilities, and user facilities for use by universities and industries.

★3747★ Occupational Lung Disease Center
Tulane Univ.
School of Medicine
1700 Perdido St.
New Orleans, LA 70112
Phone: (504)588-5265
Fax: (504)588-5035
Contact: Dr. Hans Weill, Dir.
Research Areas: Occupational lung diseases, including epidemiologic studies of fibrotic, immunologic, and neoplastic diseases caused by occupational inhalants. Research focuses on studies of employed populations and includes industries whose workers may have been exposed to any of three categories of airborne contaminants: minerals (asbestos, silica, fibrous glass), organic dusts (cotton, coffee, proteolytic detergent enzymes), and chemicals (isocyanates, chlorine). Assesses the respiratory health of workers and takes detailed environmental measurements to determine potential relationships between exposure dose and biologic response.

★3748★ Ocean and Coastal Law Center
University of Oregon
Law School
Eugene, OR 97403-1221
Phone: (503)346-3845
Fax: (503)346-3985
Contact: Jon L. Jacobson, Codirector
Research Areas: Ocean and coastal law, international law of the sea, and legal regime for the exclusive economic zone. Studies include U.S. federal fisheries management, offshore oil and gas development, seabed minerals mining, and state ocean management.

★3749★ Ocean and Coastal Policy Center
University of California, Santa Barbara
Woolley-5134
Santa Barbara, CA 93106
Phone: (805)893-8393
Contact: Dr. James Lima, Contact
Research Areas: Coastal and ocean policy issues, including conservation and management of resources. Topics include socioeconomic impacts of offshore oil development and the use of California shipwreck resources. Concentrates on development, dissemination, and application of policy information.

★3750★ Oceanic Institute
2000 L St., NW
Ste. 200
Washington, DC 20036
Phone: (202)785-8505
Contact: Bill Hougart, Dir.
Research Areas: Technology and the seas, focusing on the technological gap between theory and technical practice in the seas.

★3751★ Oceanic Society
218 D St., SE
Washington, DC 20003
Phone: (202)544-2600
Fax: (202)543-4710
Contact: Eric Corens, Policy Associate
Research Areas: Identifies critical areas of ocean policy, especially relating to ocean pollution, and sponsors analytical research and policy assessments, including studies of oceanic law, coastal environments, and international cooperation. Dedicated to protecting the oceans for the people and wildlife that depend on them for life, livelihood, and enjoyment.

★3752★ Office of Applied Energy Studies
Washington State Univ.
305 Troy Hall
Pullman, WA 99164-4430
Phone: (509)335-8688
Fax: (509)335-7636
Contact: Dr. George W. Hinman, Dir.
Research Areas: Energy, including supply, demand, policy, and conservation.

★3753★ Office of Arid Lands Studies
University of Arizona
845 N. Park Ave.
Tucson, AZ 85719
Phone: (602)621-1955
Fax: (602)621-3816
Contact: Dr. Kennith Foster, Dir.
Research Areas: Arid and semiarid lands investigations, including land productivity in arid and semiarid environments, opposing land-use issues, farming systems research, applied remote sensing, water use and conservation, and bioenergy studies. Conducts interdisciplinary research using information from the fields of agriculture, archeology, biology, climatology, geochronology, geography, hydrogeology, and sociology. Integrates research activities at the University of Arizona aimed toward solution of problems of arid lands, analyzes economic arid lands plants, provides economic development assistance, offers international technology transfer, prepares environmental impact assessments, provides information management services, and maintains a computerized system of information storage, retrieval, and dissemination. Distributes HALOPH: A Data Base of Salt Tolerant Plants of the World, a computerized reference listing of over 1,560 species focusing on economic uses of these plants.

★3754★ Office of Building Research
Louisiana State Univ.
School of Architecture
Baton Rouge, LA 70803
Phone: (504)388-6885
Contact: Dr. Jason C. Shih, Dir.
Research Areas: Passive solar and solar energy, energy conservation, daylighting, radiant barriers, building standards, historic preservation, community environmental design, facility management, and structural form and system.

★3755★ Office of Environmental Science, Technology and Policy
Georgia Inst. of Technology
Atlanta, GA 30341
Phone: (404)894-3883
Fax: (404)853-0232
Contact: Dr. C.S. Kiang, Dir.
Research Areas: Environmental sciences, including hazardous and solid waste management, industrial process development, environmental policy, atmospheric chemistry and global warming, geophyics, geochemistry, remote sensing, water resources, solar energy, health systems, and forest products.

★3756★ Office of Hazardous and Toxic Waste Management
Pennsylvania State Univ.
Land & Water Resources Research Bldg.
University Park, PA 16802
Phone: (814)863-0291
Fax: (814)865-3378
Contact: Raymond W. Regan, Dir.
Research Areas: Provides small industries in Pennsylvania with technical assistance and research in the management of hazardous and toxic wastes.

★3757★ Oklahoma Biological Survey
University of Oklahoma
Sutton Hall, Rm. 303
625 Elm Ave.
Norman, OK 73019
Phone: (405)325-4034
Fax: (405)325-7504
Contact: Dr. Gary D. Schnell, Dir.
Research Areas: Biology of the nation, state, and region, including the relationship of plants and animals to their environment in Oklahoma and the surrounding region. Emphasizes biological inventory, environmental effects, ecological land use planning, and applications of multivariate and computer techniques to biological problems. Analyzes rare and endangered species. Databases: Oklahoma's life resources. Special Resources: Maintains data files and maps of Oklahoma Natural Heritage Inventory.

★3758★ Oklahoma Water Resources Research Institute
Oklahoma State Univ.
Univ. Center for Water Research
003 Life Sciences E.
Stillwater, OK 74078
Phone: (405)744-9994
Fax: (405)744-7673
Contact: Carol Engle, Coordinator
Research Areas: Water resources, including studies of biofilms, water resources facilities, pesticide transport, groundwater and stream water quality, and hydrologic modeling.

★3759★ Oregon Cooperative Park Studies Unit
College of Forestry
Oregon State Univ.
Corvallis, OR 97331
Phone: (503)737-2056
Contact: Dr. Edward E. Starkey, Codirector
Research Areas: Ecological and environmental resource management issues and recreational use of parklands in National Parks System in state of Oregon and other similar areas, with emphasis on aquatic ecology, ungulate ecology, and human ecology. Conducts and facilitates natural and social science research and instruction at the University relating to parks, wild land, and management of our national and cultural resources.

★3760★ Pacific Basin Consortium for Hazardous Waste Research
c/o East-West Center
Environmental & Policy Institute
1777 East-West Rd.
Honolulu, HI 96848
Phone: (808)944-7555
Fax: (808)944-7970
Contact: Richard R. Cirillo, Exec. Sec.
Research Areas: Hazardous waste in the Pacific Basin, including waste reduction, treatment, and handling. Seeks to promote technology and information exchange and to develop network of experts on hazardous waste.

★3761★ Pacific Estuarine Research Laboratory
San Diego State Univ.
San Diego, CA 92182-0057
Phone: (619)594-5809
Fax: (619)594-5676

Contact: Joy Zedler, Dir.
Research Areas: Estuarine ecosystems, wetland restoration, wastewater wetlands, and long-term dynamics of coastal wetland communities (salt marshs and tidal channels). Also monitors water quality. Special Resources: Maintains long-term data sets and data on regional biodiversity.

★3762★ Pacific International Center for High Technology Research
711 Kapiolani Blvd., Ste. 200
Honolulu, HI 96813
Phone: (808)533-7500
Fax: (808)538-0677
Contact: Ronald J. Hays, Pres. and Chief Exec. Officer
Research Areas: Four areas of emphasis are 1) energy and resources, including research and development toward the commercialization of a broad range of alternative energy technology, with emphasis on ocean thermal energy conversion (OTEC), geothermal, wind, solar thermal, hydrogen, biomass gasification, seabed minerals processing, energy storage, and desalination; and 2) biotechnology, including genetic engineering and immunology in agriculture and aquaculture.

★3763★ Pacific Northwest Research Foundation
720 Broadway
Seattle, WA 98122
Phone: (206)726-1210
Fax: (206)726-1217
Contact: William B. Hutchinson M.D., Dir.
Research Areas: Medical sciences, including environmental biochemistry, histocompatability, virus behavior in feline leukemia, biochemical oncology, aquatic toxicology, effects of radiation exposure, and natural products and acupuncture.

★3764★ Pennsylvania Cooperative Fish and Wildlife Research Unit
Pennsylvania State Univ.
Ferguson Bldg.
University Park, PA 16802
Phone: (814)865-6592
Contact: Dr. Robert F. Carline, Leader
Research Areas: Fish and wildlife, including habitat improvements to maintain and/or increase production and diversity of aquatic and terrestrial fauna in the deciduous forest biome and associated waters and effects of man-made disturbances on aquatic and terrestrial environments and fauna. Specific activities include studies on the effects of clear-cutting on ruffed grouse and cottontail rabbits, habitat quality and the abundance of male American woodcock on breeding grounds in the Commonwealth, factors affecting abundance of earthworms in woodcock habitat, accumulation of heavy metals in small mammals inhabiting reclaimed strip-mined lands, habitat use and abundance of black and turkey vultures at Gettysburg (Pennsylvania), life history studies of stream invertebrates, effects of acid precipitation on aquatic organisms in central Pennsylvania, vulnerability of lakes and streams in the middle Atlantic states to acid precipitation, and assessment and management of predators in fish hatcheries. Research and demonstration have been conducted in the areas of habitat manipulations such as channel modification, clear cutting, and acid neutralization.

★3765★ Pennsylvania Environmental Council
1211 Chestnut St., Ste. 900
Philadelphia, PA 19107
Phone: (215)563-0250
Fax: (215)563-0528
Contact: Joanne R. Denworth, Pres.
Research Areas: Growth management, land use, water resource allocation, groundwater, wetlands, open space, and hazardous and solid waste treatment, management, and disposal.

★3766★ People, Food and Land Foundation
Sun Mountain Center
35751 Oak Springs Dr.
Tollhouse, CA 93667
Phone: (209)855-3710
Contact: George Ballis, Coordinator
Research Areas: Native edible and medicinal plants, sustainable farming and gardening, low technology energy, and conservation. Conducts tests of plant material for culinary uses and of interplanting for yield increase and pest and weed control. Special Resources: Maintains a 40-acre agricultural land trust, botanical gardens, and a 5,000-square-foot passive solar house powered by photovoltaic cells demonstrating grey water recycling, a composting toilet system, and passive cooling and heating.

★3767★ Pest Control and Application Systems Technology Unit
Texas & AM Univ.
Rm. 231 Agricultural Engineering Bldg.
College Station, TX 77843
Phone: (409)260-9364
Fax: (409)845-3932
Contact: Dr. L.F. Bouse, Research Leader
Research Areas: Agricultural engineering, weed science, and entomology, including development of equipment and methods for control of pests, aerial application of pest control materials, aerial application of seeds and fertilizers, integrated pest management, and use of herbicides to control weed and brush on rangeland while maintaining groundwater quality.

★3768★ Pesticide Laboratory
University of Puerto Rico
Puerto Rico Agricultural Experiment Sta.
PO Box 21360
Rio Piedras, PR 00928
Phone: (809)767-9705
Fax: (809)758-5158
Contact: Nilsa M. Acin-Diaz, Dir.
Research Areas: Behavior of pesticides in soils, fate of pesticides in the environment, and development of methodology for determination of pesticide residues. Conducts pesticide analyses of soils, water samples, and plant tissues for Experiment Station personnel and agricultural agencies of the state.

★3769★ Pesticide Research Center
Michigan State Univ.
East Lansing, MI 48824-1311
Phone: (517)353-9430
Contact: Robert M. Hollingworth, Dir.
Research Areas: All aspects of pesticide science, including toxicology, environmental effects, resistance, biotechnology, field applications, integrated pest management, and alternatives to pesticides. Focuses on water quality and food safety. The Center's work is a coordinated effort involving several departments of the University. Special Resources: Equipment and laboratories for trace organic analysis and electron microscopy.

★3770★ Pesticide Research Laboratory
University of Florida
Gainesville, FL 32611
Phone: (904)392-1978
Fax: (904)392-1988
Contact: Prof. A. Moye
Research Areas: Pesticide residues in food, water, and soil, new analytical methodology, and metabolism and binding of pesticides in plants and soils. Utilizes techniques and instrumentation such as thin layer chromatography, gas chromatography, high performance liquid chromatography, spectrophotofluorometry, emission spectroscopy, radio tracer techniques, photolysis, and mass spectrometry.

★3771★ Pesticide Research Laboratory and Graduate Study Center
Pennsylvania State Univ.
Dept. of Entomology
University Park, PA 16802
Phone: (814)863-0844
Fax: (814)865-3048
Contact: James L. Frazier, Dir.
Research Areas: Insects and the environment. Studies the environmental fate of pesticides and the toxicology and physiology of insects.

★3772★ Pesticide Residue Research Laboratory
North Carolina State Univ.
3709 Hillsborough St.
Raleigh, NC 27607
Phone: (919)737-3391
Contact: Dr. T.J. Sheets, Dir.
Research Areas: Pesticide residues on food and feed crops and losses of pesticide residues from tobacco and their incorporation into tobacco products. Also studies behavior and fate of pesticides in soils, air, and water.

★3773★ Pesticide Residue, Toxic Waste and Basic Research Analytical Laboratory
University of Miami
Bldg. B
12500 SW 152 St.
Miami, FL 33177-1411
Phone: (305)232-8202
Fax: (305)232-7461
Contact: Jon B. Mann, Lab Manager
Research Areas: Pesticides, air pollutants, carcinogens, and chemicals, with emphasis on biological samples. Special Resources: Gas chromatography, gas chromatography/mass spectrometry/data systems (GC/MS/DS), high-pressure liquid chromatography (HPLC) equipment, and facilities for ultraviolet and infrared spectrophotometry, and atomic absorption.

★3774★ Phycology Laboratory
University of Wisconsin-Madison
Dept. of Botany
132 Birge Hall
Madison, WI 53706
Phone: (608)262-1057
Contact: Prof. Linda E. Graham, Dir.
Research Areas: Ecology, physiological ecology, cell structure, and evolution of algae. Studies evolution of plants from green algae. Identifies nuisance algae and evaluates nuisance algal problems and possible solutions.

★3775★ PIXE Laboratory
Florida State Univ.
Nuclear Research Bldg.
Tallahasee, FL 32306
Phone: (904)644-6250
Fax: (904)644-9848
Contact: Dr. J. William Nelson, Dir.
Research Areas: Conducts proton-induced X-ray emission (PIXE) analysis of substances.

Samples examined include city air to determine the impact and location of pollution, shark meat for levels of lead and other heavy metals in their flesh, hair and nail clippings as indicators of body mineral content, and trace metals in clay pottery to determine the migrating and social habits of Indians 6,000 years ago. Special Resources: Maintains a 4 MEV proton accelerator, an air-monitoring system, and automatic air particulate samplers.

★3776★ Planning Institute
University of Southern California
School of Urban & Regional Planning
351 VKC
Los Angeles, CA 90089-0042
Phone: (213)743-7125
Contact: Peter Gordon, Dir. of Research
Research Areas: Regional planning, including social and economic impacts of air cleanup programs in southern California.

★3777★ Plastics Waste Recycling Program
Rensselaer Polytechnic Inst.
110 Eight St.
Troy, NY 12180-3590
Phone: (518)276-6000
Contact: Robert W. Messler Jr., Codirector
Research Areas: Recycling plastics, including chemical processes and possible uses of by-products.

★3778★ Pollution Prevention Research Center
North Carolina State Univ.
Dept. of Chemical Engineering
Box 7905
Raleigh, NC 27695-7905
Phone: (919)737-2325
Contact: Dr. Michael Overcash, Dir.
Research Areas: Methods of reducing toxic chlorinated byproducts in pulp and paper production.

★3779★ Practical Farmers of Iowa
Rte. 2
Box 132
Boone, IA 50036
Phone: (515)432-1560
Contact: Richard L. Thompson, Research Dir. Contract Officer
Research Areas: Conducts on-farm research and demonstration projects that show profitable and environmentally safe farming practices. Special interests include ridge till without herbicides, low-cost weed control, reduced usage of nitrogen fertilizer, band placement of P and K fertilizers, and fall cover crops. Study crops are planted and harvested by machine and arranged in randomized, six-replication side-by-side narrow strips.

★3780★ Program on Participation and Labor-Managed Systems
Cornell Univ.
Uris Hall 490
Ithaca, NY 14853
Phone: (607)255-4867
Fax: (607)255-2818
Contact: Prof. Jaroslav Vanek, Dir.
Research Areas: International study of theory, practice, and implementation of self-management, including development of low cost solar energy technology for less developed countries with worker cooperatives and measurement of economic performance of participating and employee-owned firms. Also studies problems of economic reform in eastern Europe.

★3781★ Project in Conservation Science
University of California, San Diego
Dept. of Biology C-016
La Jolla, CA 92093
Phone: (619)534-2375
Fax: (619)534-7108
Contact: David S. Woodruff, Coordinator
Research Areas: Wildlife conservation, including population vulnerability analysis, characterizing evolutionarily significant units for conservation management, biomedical technology and captive propagation, community management in the global environment, and conservation and sustainable development.

★3782★ Project ROSE
University of Alabama
PO Box 870203
Tuscaloosa, AL 35487-0203
Phone: (205)348-4878
Fax: (205)348-8573
Contact: Janet Graham, Coordinator
Research Areas: Identifies and provides collection network for used oil; documents energy savings due to recycling; and monitors EPA alternative regulatory options for used oil. Studies include statistical surveys of used oil dumping in Alabama. Databases: Waste Exchange.

★3783★ Puerto Rico Water Resources Research Institute
College of Engineering
Univ. of Puerto Rico
PO Box 5000
Mayaguez, PR 00709-5000
Phone: (809)834-4040
Fax: (809)832-0119
Contact: Dr. Rafael Munoz Candelario, Dir.
Research Areas: Water and resources related to water, including studies on hydrology, economic and legal water and wastewater problems, groundwater, water-soil-plant relations, water quality and pollution, and instrumentation. Also develops water resources data for planning and action in the commonwealth. Established under Water Resources Research Act 1964, Public Law 88-379 to coordinate research, train scientists, and disseminate information on water and water-related problems.

★3784★ Quaternary Research Center
University of Washington
AK-60
Seattle, WA 98195
Phone: (206)543-1166
Fax: (206)543-3836
Contact: Dr. Stephen C. Porter, Dir.
Research Areas: Interdisciplinary study of global environmental changes of the last two million years, the Quaternary Period, with emphasis on biological and physical influences and interactions, including studies in archeology, paleobotany, climatology and paleoclimatology, paleoecology, forestry, geomorphology, glacial geology, glaciology, limnology, meteorology, oceanography, paleontology, pedology, periglacial research, photointerpretation and photogrammetry, radiometric dating, sedimentology, soil mechanics, stratigraphy, zoology, isotope studies, and tephrochronology. Special Resources: Mass spectrometer to calibrate climatic change by measuring carbon-14 levels and a cold room for studying freezing and thawing soils.

★3785★ Ralph M. Parsons Laboratory
Massachusetts Inst. of Technology
Rm. 48-311
15 Vassar St.
Cambridge, MA 02139
Phone: (617)253-2117
Fax: (617)258-8850
Contact: Dr. Rafael L. Bras, Dir.
Research Areas: Hydrodynamics, coastal engineering, hydrology, hydroclimatology, water resource systems, water quality control, aquatic environment, and environmental engineering. Opportunities for graduate study and research include both departmental and interdisciplinary programs in the analytical and managerial aspects of water resources.

★3786★ Reclamation Research Unit
Montana State Univ.
Animal & Range Science Dept.
Bozeman, MT 59717
Phone: (406)994-4821
Fax: (406)994-6579
Contact: Dr. Frank F. Munshower, Dir.
Research Areas: Disturbed land rehabilitation, including mined sites, energy-related disturbances, and inorganic Superfund sites.

★3787★ Red Butte Gardens and Arboretum
University of Utah
Arboretum Center
Salt Lake City, UT 84112
Phone: (801)581-5322
Contact: W. Richard Hildreth, Dir.
Research Areas: Oak hybridization, urban tree development and evaluation, plant propagation techniques, cultivar selection and evaluation of native Utah plants, and rare and endangered species multiplication and culture. Special Resources: Over 47 artificial hybrids among various species and between subgenera of the genus Quercus.

★3788★ Red Buttes Environmental Biology Laboratory
University of Wyoming
Box 3166, Univ. Sta.
Laramie, WY 82071
Phone: (307)745-8504
Contact: Dr. Harold Bergman, Dir.
Research Areas: Aquatic toxicology, fish physiology, and physiological ecology of large and small mammals and birds. Specific projects include studies on acid deposition effects on fish, acclimation of fish to organic and metal pollutants, stress in bighorn sheep, and energetics of pronghorn antelope. Special Resources: Maintains an analytical chemistry laboratory and outdoor pen facilities for maintenance of medium- to large-sized mammals such as bobcats, coyotes, badgers, and wild ungulates and for the maintenance and propagation of native fish and other aquatic fauna.

★3789★ Regional Resources Development Institute
Clemson Univ.
265B Lehotsky Hall
Clemson, SC 29631-1007
Phone: (803)656-2194
Contact: Dr. Robert H. Becker
Research Areas: Natural resource allocation policy, environmental and social impact assessment, and rural development activities. Also conducts contract research, including a rural enterprise market program intended to improve rural business opportunities and increase business skills among certain segments of the rural population.

★3790★ Remote Sensing Center
Rutgers Univ.
Dept. of Environmental Resources
Cook College
PO Box 231
New Brunswick, NJ 08903
Phone: (201)932-9631
Contact: Dr. Teuvo Ariola, Dir.
Research Areas: Environmental remote sensing.

★3791★ Remote Sensing Laboratory (ISURSL)
Indiana State Univ.
Dept. of Geography & Geology
Terre Haute, IN 47809
Phone: (812)237-2264
Contact: Dr. Robert C. Howe, Acting Dir.
Research Areas: Remote sensing, utilizing land satellite (LANDSAT), geostationary operation environmental satellite (GOES), radar, advanced very-high-resolution radiometer (AVHRR), SPOT, videography, and thematic mapper data for analysis of weather, pollution, biomass resources, mineral resources, and land use features. ISURSL is organized into distinctive units for specialized and collaborative multidisciplinary research and applications for ecological, energy, mineral, geographic, geologic, and geomorphologic resource management and planning and urban planning purposes. Databases: Maintains a geographic database and spatial information systems. Special Resources: Maintains imaging processing systems, a cartography laboratory, and other facilities necessary for remote sensing and GIS applications.

★3792★ Renew America
1400 16th St., NW, Ste. 710
Washington, DC 20036
Phone: (202)232-2252
Contact: Tina Hobson, Exec. Dir.
Research Areas: Serves as a public information and networking forum dedicated to the efficient use of natural resources. Specific topics include air pollution, soil conservation, solid waste, hazardous waste, groundwater protection, renewable energy, energy and pollution, indoor pollution, land use planning, pesticides, surface water, transportation, food safety, solid waste and recycling, forestry, growth management, drinking water, and global warming.

★3793★ Rensselaer Fresh Water Institute
Rensselaer Polytechnic Inst.
MRC 203
Troy, NY 12181-3590
Phone: (518)276-6757
Fax: (518)276-8554
Contact: Dr. Charles W. Boylen, Dir.
Research Areas: Freshwater ecology, limnology, and oceanography. Investigates water use and related problems, including studies of waterborne diseases, Legionnaire's disease, biofouling and biological corrosion, acidic precipitation, and aquatic plants. Special Resources: Aquatic plant herbarium, database on lake water quality.

★3794★ Research Center
State Univ. Coll. at Oswego
King Hall
Oswego, NY 13126
Phone: (315)341-3639
Fax: (315)341-5346
Contact: Dr. R.J. Scrudato, Dir.
Research Areas: Solid and hazardous waste, environmental and ecological research, including the following: fisheries ecology and limnology of small lakes and Lake Ontario; toxic contamination of groundwater, lake watersheds, and Lake Ontario; and environmental communication to enhance public awareness and environmental management. Projects include studies in analytical chemistry, geochemistry (trace metals, chlorinated hydrocarbons), thermal effluent studies, bioassays, shore erosion, sublethal effects of microcontaminants on fish and mammals, water quality, zooplankton of Lake Ontario, hazardous wastes, and acid precipitation and aquatic toxicology.

★3795★ Research Center
Mississippi State Univ.
John C. Stennis Space Center
Stennis Space Center, MS 39529-6000
Phone: (601)688-3227
Fax: (601)688-3673
Contact: Roy A. Crochet Ph.D., Dir.
Research Areas: Engineering and environmental studies, including acid rain, forest hydrology, solid waste propellant, environmental impact analysis, ecological monitoring, remote sensing, computer imaging, and oceanography.

★3796★ Research Center for Biotechnology
Georgia Inst. of Technology
Atlanta, GA 30332
Phone: (404)853-9404
Fax: (404)894-7466
Contact: Dr. Thomas Tornabene, Dir.
Research Areas: Biotechnology, including development and application of analytical instrumentation, bioconversion of waste with designed microbial consortia, bioreactor design for steady state fermentation and whole cell immobilization, structure and function of biological macromolecules with emphasis on DNA and proteins, environmental toxicology, and enzyme catalysis and its control. Studies various aspects of industrial microbiology, medicinal chemistry, metabolic regulation, molecular genetics, natural products, and product recovery.

★3797★ Research Triangle Institute
PO Box 12194
3040 Cornwallis Rd.
Research Triangle Park, NC 27709-2194
Phone: (919)541-6000
Fax: (919)541-5985
Contact: F. Thomas Wooten, Pres.
Research Areas: Chemical analysis, chemical synthesis, polymer science, life sciences and toxicology, environmental sciences and engineering, physics and aerosol technology, earth sciences, policy analysis and public sector management, public health research, health effects, environmental protection, social issues, public services, digital systems and computer architecture, semiconductors, energy, and industrial processes. Specific interests include aerospace technology, clean rooms, environmental measurements and quality assurance, risk assessment, and hazardous materials.

★3798★ Resources for the Future, Inc.
1616 P St. NW
Washington, DC 20036
Phone: (202)328-5000
Contact: Robert W. Fri, Pres.
Research Areas: Social science aspects of problems associated with the development, conservation, and efficient use of natural resources, including fundamental and applied studies on basic resources of land, water, minerals, and air, goods and services derived from them, environmental quality, and energy policy. Research activities are carried out through four units: Energy and Natural Resources Division, Quality of the Environment Division, Center for Risk Management, and National Center for Food and Agricultural Policy.

★3799★ Resources for the Future, Inc., Energy and Natural Resources Division
1616 P St., NW
Washington, DC 20036
Phone: (202)328-5000
Fax: (202)265-8069
Contact: Kenneth Frederick, Senior Fellow
Research Areas: Impacts of current and alternative management practices on the resource base and the effects of alternative policies on the long-term benefits to society derived from its energy, land, water, and atmospheric resources. The Division's Forest Economics and Policy Program analyzes long-term timber supply, multiple use management of public forest land, and the economics of below-cost timber sales. The Climate Resources Program examines effective use of climate information for national management of renewable resources, impact of climate change on the management of renewable resources in the future, and how management policies and practices can best facilitate adjustment to climatic change. Other areas of research conducted by the Division include the off-farm effects of cropland erosion, nonstructural alternatives for meeting long-term water needs, and compilation of county-based nationwide pesticide usage and water quality data inventories.

★3800★ Resources for the Future, Inc., Quality of the Environment Division
1616 P St., NW
Washington, DC 20036
Phone: (202)328-5000
Fax: (202)265-8069
Contact: Raymond J. Kopp, Dir.
Research Areas: Management of air, water, and land pollution and the conservation of natural and environmental resources. Focuses on the environmental consequences of human activity and how public decisions affecting the environment are made. Past research projects include an estimate of the recreation benefits accruing from water pollution control, the health benefits from reducing drinking water contamination, the crop damages avoided by reducing ground-level ozone concentrations, the relationship between air pollution and lung infection, the economics of controlling groundwater pollution, development of an improved methodology for determining the costs of regulation, design of studies for development of fish and wildlife mitigation policies, and development of alternatives for reducing generation of hazardous wastes, and assessment of natural resource damage from oil spills and releases of hazardous substances.

★3801★ Rhode Island Agricultural Experiment Station
University of Rhode Island
Kingston, RI 02881
Phone: (401)792-2474
Fax: (401)789-3342
Contact: Dr. Robert H. Miller, Dir.
Research Areas: Agriculture and resource development as influenced by the state's high human population density and extensive coastline. Studies land use planning, environmental quality, water development and management, pollution control, coastal zone management, offshore fisheries management, agricultural commodities, rural development, turfgrass and ornamentals management, food

technology, biodegradation, economics of alternative land and coastal use, closed system aquaculture technology, economics of extended coastal jurisdiction, mechanisms of plant disease resistance, integrated pest management, social aspects of human nutrition, biotechnology, genetic engineering, and hydroponics. Special Resources: Environmental Data Center, Marine Pathology Laboratory, International Center for Marine Resource Development, and 53-foot research vessel.

★3802★ Risk and Systems Analysis for the Control of Toxics Program (RSACT)
University of California, Los Angeles
Dept. of Mechanical, Aerospace, & Nuclear Eng.
48-121 Engineering IV
Los Angeles, CA 90024
Phone: (213)825-2045
Fax: (213)825-0761
Contact: Dr. William Kastenberg, Dir.
Research Areas: Control of hazardous substances from source to human exposure, including studies on risk analysis, behavior and treatment of contaminated soil sites, exposure assessment, and waste minimization. Also develops risk assessment methods relating to toxic substance control.

★3803★ Risk Science Research Center
2801 S. Univ. Ave.
Little Rock, AR 72204-1085
Phone: (501)371-1980
Contact: Joyce Wroten, Dir.
Research Areas: Methods for assessing and verifying the risk of chemical agents to human health, including studies on reproductive and developmental problems. Also investigates chemical contamination of food.

★3804★ River Studies Center
University of Wisconsin-La Crosse
4032 Cowley Hall
La Crosse, WI 54601
Phone: (608)785-8238
Contact: Ron Rada, Codirector
Research Areas: Eutrophication, microbiology of sediments, fish habitats, effects of humans on the Mississippi River, simulation model of a navigation pool of the upper Mississippi River, heavy metal contaminants in the upper Mississippi and Wisconsin Rivers and north-central Wisconsin lakes, microbial transformation of metals, and aquatic toxicology. Special Resources: Maintains a 60-foot research vessel, a fleet of smaller boats, and related equipment for use in river studies.

★3805★ Robert J. Bernard Biological Field Station
Claremont McKenna Colleges
Claremont, CA 91711
Phone: (714)621-5425
Contact: Clyde H. Eriksen, Dir.
Research Areas: Aquaculture, focusing on tilapia; birds of prey, emphasizing biology and relocation of the burrowing owl; urban wildlife, focusing on coyotes; and vernal pools, concentrating on biology, distribution, and status of fairy shrimp.

★3806★ Rocky Mountain Center for Occupational and Environmental Health
University of Utah
Bldg. 512
Salt Lake City, UT 84112
Phone: (801)581-8719
Fax: (801)581-7224
Contact: Royce Moser Jr., M, Dir.
Research Areas: Occupational and environmental health and safety with emphasis on neurobehavioral effects of toxic exposures, asbestos-related health problems, computer-assisted interactive education in occupational and environmental health, musculoskeletal and other injury evaluation and prevention, and ergonomic aspects of the work environment.

★3807★ Rocky Mountain Mineral Law Foundation
Porter Administration Bldg., 3rd Fl.
7039 E. 18th Ave.
Denver, CO 80220
Phone: (303)321-8100
Fax: (303)321-7657
Contact: David P. Phillips, Exec. Dir.
Research Areas: Mineral law, with aim to foster and encourage industry and participating law schools toward a scholarly and practical study of natural resources law, including mining, oil and gas, water, public land, and environmental law. Foundation functions as a centralized collection, compilation, and dissemination point for scholarly legal research, selected federal and state laws and regulations, published and unpublished decisions and memoranda, and other related materials in the field of natural resources law.

★3808★ Rodale Research Center
Box 323
R.D. #1
Kutztown, PA 19530
Phone: (215)683-6383
Fax: (215)683-8548
Contact: Bob Hart, Dir.
Research Areas: Gardening, farming systems, and new crops. Specific areas of interest include vegetables, herbs, flowers, apples, small fruits, composting, cover crops, soil fertility, regenerative agriculture, interseeding, overseeding, weed control, nitrogen cycling, tillage systems, perennial grains, and grain amaranth.

★3809★ Romberg Tiburon Centers
San Francisco State Univ.
PO Box 855
3150 Paradise Dr.
Tiburon, CA 94920
Phone: (415)435-1717
Contact: Dr. James Hollibaugh, Dir.
Research Areas: San Francisco Bay and other estuarine and coastal areas, including studies of freshwater diversions, benthic and pelagic ecosystems, freshwater and salt marshes, the effects of pollution, restoration of marshes, and systematics of birds and fishes.

★3810★ Roosevelt Wildlife Institute
SUNY Coll. of Environmental Science and Forestry
Syracuse, NY 13210
Phone: (315)470-6741
Contact: Dr. Robert L. Burgess, Acting Dir.
Research Areas: Forestry and wildlife management and ecology, limnology, environmental assessments, and animal behavior, including studies of effects of forest management and various forest uses on animal constituent of forest community. Special Resources: Maintains vertebrate laboratories and collections.

★3811★ St. Anthony Falls Hydraulic Laboratory
University of Minnesota
Mississippi River at 3rd Ave. SE
Minneapolis, MN 55414-2196
Phone: (612)627-4010
Fax: (612)627-4609
Contact: Dr. Roger E.A. Arndt, Dir.
Research Areas: Hydraulics, hydrology, water resources systems, fluid mechanics, and hydrodynamics, including studies on underwater ballistics, underwater acoustics, sedimentation and sediment transport, surface and internal waves, hydrofoils, flows of stratified fluids, air entrainment and flow of air/water mixtures, flow through permeable media, cavitation and supercavitation, ship model towing, water tunnel and experimental design of hydraulic structures such as spillways for dams, intakes and diffusers for condenser cooling water, ship locks, and river control structures, numerical modeling of above phenomena, and systems analysis. Special Resources: Equipment and facilities include a large boundary-layer wind tunnel; a Turbine Test Facility capable of testing model hydraulic machines and pumps up to 100 horsepower; a multipurpose tank 270 feet long by nine feet wide by six feet deep, equipped with a wave maker and a towing carriage, through which the Mississippi River may be diverted for experimental purposes; several open channels, (some for sediment transport studies); a free jet water tunnel; a water tunnel especially designed for research on free surface effects in water control structures and devices; and a low turbulence buoyant body facility for basic studies of transition and noise on axisymmetric bodies.

★3812★ Salt Institute
700 N. Fairfax St., Ste. 600
Alexandria, VA 22314
Phone: (703)549-4648
Contact: Richard Hannemann, Pres.
Research Areas: Engineering and chemical research, field studies, and laboratory investigations on all uses of salt, including winter road maintenance, road base construction, manufacturing and industry, water conditioning, human nutrition, and agricultural feeding.

★3813★ San Francisco Bay-Delta Aquatic Habitat Institute
180 Richmond Field Sta.
1301 S. 46th St.
Richmond, CA 94804
Phone: (415)231-9539
Fax: (415)231-9520
Contact: Margaret R. Johnston, Exec. Dir.
Research Areas: Coordinates research and monitoring programs relative to the impacts of pollution on the beneficial uses of the San Francisco Bay and Delta. Major activities include development of monitoring and research framework for the Estuary and development and management of databases. Databases: Estuarine Data Index (summaries of 70 ecological research and monitoring programs), Bay-Delta Hearing Testimony and Exhibits Database, San Francisco Bay-Delta Bibliography, San Francisco Estuary Effluent Monitoring Database, and Public Education Display.

★3814★ Sanitary Engineering and Environmental Health Research Laboratory (SEEHRL)
University of California, Berkeley
Bldg. 112
1301 S. 46th
Richmond, CA 94804
Phone: (415)231-9449
Fax: (415)231-9500
Contact: Prof. Robert C. Cooper, Dir.
Research Areas: Sanitary engineering, wastewater treatment, algology, limnology, reclamation and reuse, drinking water quality, occupational health, microbiology and chemistry of water and wastewater, and impact and abatement of hazardous waste such as

organic solvents in groundwater. Special Resources: Maintains a 70,000 GPD secondary wastewater treatment plant, and an estuarine water system.

★3815★ Savannah River Ecology Laboratory
University of Georgia
P.O. Drawer E
Aiken, SC 29801
Phone: (803)725-2472
Contact: Dr. Michael Smith, Dir.
Research Areas: Activities are divided between three divisions: 1) Biogeochemical Cycling, which studies environmental chemistry, physiological ecology, radionuclide cycling, radioecology of actinide elements, and modelling of the transport and fate of heavy metals and radionuclides; 2) Wetlands Ecology, which studies structure and dynamics of southeastern wetland ecosystems, industrial impact on productivity and nutrient cycling in manmade ponds and lakes and in natural swamps and creeks, and water quality; and 3) Stress and Wildlife Ecology, which studies effects of reactor effluents on aquatic organisms, alternative habitats for displaced populations, basic ecology of endangered species and response to perturbation, and game and non-game species such as deer, waterfowl, turtles, and fish. Special Resources: Maintains a radioisotope laboratory, analytical chemistry laboratory, elemental analysis laboratory, controlled environment chambers, cold room, aquatic ecology laboratory, telemetry laboratory and radiotelemetry tracking system, electrophoresis laboratory, animal holding facilities, experimental ponds, aviaries, greenhouse with a controlled atmosphere room for the study of low level radionuclide activity, sample preparation and transfer rooms, a variety of field facilities, an herbarium of local plants, and a collection of local invertebrates and vertebrates.

★3816★ School for Field Studies
16 Broadway, Box S
Beverly, MA 01915
Phone: (508)927-7777
Fax: (508)927-5127
Contact: James L. Elder, Pres.
Research Areas: Environmental problems and issues in unusual ecosystems around the world, wildlife studies, animal behavior, marine biology, botany, environmental geology, paleoecology, and resource management and policy. Students and faculty leaders live and work in the field during the research and expedition course. Academic credit is available through Northeastern University.

★3817★ School of Marine Affairs
University of Washington
College of Ocean & Fishery Sciences
3707 Brooklyn Ave., NE
Seattle, WA 98195
Phone: (206)543-7004
Fax: (206)543-1417
Contact: Dr. Edward L. Miles, Dir.
Research Areas: Ocean environment, ocean and coastal uses, the economics of ocean and coastal resources, and policy sciences, including studies on international law of the sea, the implications of extended coastal state jurisdiction for the management of world fisheries, oil spill damage assessment and liability, international regulation to control global climate change, design and economic analysis of limited entry alternative for Pacific fisheries, use and management of harbors, estuaries and urban waterfronts, organization of marine work and occupations, recreation and tourism, and management of ocean waste disposal.

★3818★ School of Natural Resources, Research Division
University of Michigan
430 E. Univ.
Ann Arbor, MI 48109
Phone: (313)764-6823
Fax: (313)936-2195
Contact: E. Wayne Say, Research Development Coordinator
Research Areas: Seeks to define and analyze natural resource and environmental problems, develop an understanding of the biophysical and socio-behavioral components of such problems, and develop and evaluate strategies for their mitigation. Organizes research according to six major themes: ecosystems, aquatic resources and management, terrestrial resources and management, landscape resource planning and management, natural resources and environmental policy, and human impacts and change processes. Specific projects include acid rain effects in forest ecosystems, interdisciplinary forest pest management and technology transfer, development and refinement of remote sensing techniques for forestry applications, ecological studies of foraging strategies of large herbivores (especially moose), fate and effects of toxic materials in Great Lakes sediment, landscape perception and environmental changes congruent with ecological and human requirements, conflict management studies and methods to resolve issues having multiple claims on a single resource, computer-based methods for evaluating multi-objective water resource management plans, bioenergetics in aquatic systems, principles and methods of wildland management, and development of selection criteria for parkland aquisition based on theories of perception, ecological requirements, and site characteristics. Special Resources: Maintains a number of natural habitats that afford opportunities for field studies in various natural resources areas. Also maintains wet laboratories, climate-controlled chambers, plant pathology laboratories, inorganic chemistry laboratories, remote sensing laboratories, and wildlife specimen collections.

★3819★ Science and Public Policy Program
University of Oklahoma
601 Elm Ave., Rm. 431
Norman, OK 73019
Phone: (405)325-2554
Fax: (405)325-7695
Contact: Dr. Thomas E. James, Dir.
Research Areas: Interdisciplinary applied policy research on technology transfer and innovation, environmental policy, energy technology development, natural resource management, and energy policy.

★3820★ Science for Citizens Center
Western Michigan Univ.
238 Moore Hall
Kalamazoo, MI 49008
Phone: (616)387-2715
Contact: Dr. Donald J. Brown, Dir.
Research Areas: Applied scientific and technical research, including studies on water quality, groundwater management, solid and hazardous wastes, lake reclamation, public health, agricultural chemicals, open space-urban development and land use, science education, nutrition education, nuclear weapons, and forest management.

★3821★ Sea Grant College
University of Maryland
1224 H.J. Patterson Hall
College Park, MD 20742
Phone: (301)405-6371
Fax: (301)314-9581
Contact: Dr. Christopher D'Elia, Dir.
Research Areas: Marine science, marine policy, and marine economics, including studies on fisheries dynamics, aquaculture, seafood processing and technology, environmental quality, marine and estuarine ecosystem processes, marine microbiology, marine biotechnology, trophic dynamics, resource economics, public policy, marine law, and finfish and shellfish nutrition; growth, and reproduction.

★3822★ Sea Grant College Program
Texas A&M Univ.
College Station, TX 77843
Phone: (409)845-3854
Contact: Thomas J. Bright, Dir.
Research Areas: Aquaculture, marine fisheries, coastal and ocean processes, marine environmental quality, water safety, and marine law, policy, and economics.

★3823★ Sea Grant Program
University of Southern California
Univ. Park
Los Angeles, CA 90089-1231
Phone: (213)740-1961
Fax: (213)748-9047
Contact: James A. Fawcett Ph.D., Associate Dir.
Research Areas: Management and planning of ports and other coastal zone resources in the southern California region, including studies of water pollution, marine water quality, marine recreation, marine transportation, and conflict resolution.

★3824★ Separation and Ingredient Sciences Laboratory
Texas A&M Univ.
Food Protein Research & Development Center
College Station, TX 77843-2476
Phone: (409)845-2741
Fax: (409)845-2744
Contact: Dr. Edmund W. Lusas, Dir.
Research Areas: Conducts research on processing and utilization of biological materials and renewable resources; mechanical and solvent extractions and membrane separations; and detoxification fermentations of biomaterials and foodstuffs.

★3825★ Shannon Point Marine Center
Western Washington Univ.
1900 Shannon Point Rd.
Anacortes, WA 98221
Phone: (206)293-2188
Fax: (206)293-1083
Contact: Prof. Stephen D. Sulkin, Dir.
Research Areas: Watershed ecology, estuarine dynamics, productivity and nutrient dynamics, crustacean larval ecology, and environmental effects of petroleum spills. Special Resources: Sundquist Marine Laboratory, research vessel fleet, diode-array spectrophotometry equipment, running seawater system, and databases containing local species lists and water quality and nutrient parameters.

★3826★ Skidaway Institute of Oceanography
PO Box 13687
McWhorter Dr., Skidaway Island
Savannah, GA 31416
Phone: (912)356-2453
Fax: (912)356-2751

Contact: Dr. David W. Menzel, Dir.
Research Areas: Studies of physical, chemical, and geological processes affecting the seafloor and biological communities of nearshore and continental shelf, experimental and field studies of the energetics and population dynamics of marine food chains, and marine biogeochemistry, including atmospheric transport and cycling of trace elements in oceanic systems, marine biochemistry, chemical ecology, and organic pollutants. Provides support for graduate student research in marine and estuarine science, oceanography, coastal geology, and marsh ecology. Databases: Hydrographic database for the southeast continental shelf. Special Resources: Temperature-controlled seawater systems, 72-foot R/V Blue Fin coastal vessel, and several smaller boats.

★3827★ Sludge and Residuals Utilization Research Foundation
University of Maine
11 Coburn Hall
Orono, ME 04469
Phone: (207)581-1490
Fax: (207)581-1426
Contact: Dr. Gregory K. White, Dir.
Research Areas: Sludge and residual materials, including nutrients, heavy metals, bacteria, contaminants, methods to reduce calcium saturation, and physical change during storage. Also studies chemical and physical properties, and treatment processes such as reed beds and composting. Specific studies include determining the chemical nature of Maine's soil amended with wood ash and investigating the impact of wood ash on groundwater and soil-water.

★3828★ Social Research and Applications
PO Box 7833
Missoula, MT 59807
Phone: (406)543-8023
Contact: Dr. Raymond L. Gold, Dir.
Research Areas: Social impact and community change studies related to natural resource development in the rural west, with an emphasis on how development affects schools and other social institutions, the elderly, individual residents, local decision making processes, and the community's established way of life. Helps industry conduct natural resource development projects more cost effectively to avoid and minimize problems of rapid growth and change associated with such ventures.

★3829★ Societal Institute of the Mathematical Sciences (SIMS)
97 Parish Rd. S.
New Canaan, CT 06840
Phone: (203)966-1008
Fax: (203)972-6069
Contact: Donald L. Thomsen Jr., Pres.
Research Areas: Conducts and coordinates studies relating to the application of mathematics and statistics to societal problems. Projects include development of statistical methods for monitoring air pollution, emphasizing acid rain deposits and their effects on human health, and determination of surface and subsurface toxic pollutants. Also develops and evaluates statistical methods for drug use and AIDS research.

★3830★ Society for the Application of Free Energy
PO Box 8276
Silver Spring, MD 20910
Phone: (301)587-8686
Contact: Dr. Carl Schleicher, Pres.
Research Areas: Solar energy and other alternate energy programs, including research and development activities using photovoltaic cells, coal gasification, and desulfurization systems.

★3831★ Soil and Environmental Chemistry Lab
Pennsylvania State Univ.
104 Research Unit A
University Park, PA 16802
Phone: (814)865-1221
Fax: (814)865-3378
Contact: Dr. Dale E. Baker, Dir.
Research Areas: Soil analysis related to capacities for loading and sorbing trace metals. Also involved with analysis of sludge for inorganics, land application of wastes, and soil/water monitoring for nitrates and phosphates from land to the Chesapeake Bay. Applies the Baker Soil Test to monitor spoils and coal ashes for reclamation of surface-mined lands and coal refuse piles.

★3832★ Soil and Water Research
Louisiana State Univ.
PO Box 25071, Univ. Sta.
Baton Rouge, LA 70894-5071
Phone: (504)387-2783
Contact: Dr. Guye H. Willis, Research Leader
Research Areas: Subsurface drainage, subsurface irrigation, and water management for agriculture. Also studies persistence, degradation, and movement of pesticides in agricultural ecosystems. Conducts experiments to determine ways of overcoming water barriers that limit crop production while maintaining water quality. Special Resources: Soil moisture measuring equipment, water level recorders, soil and water laboratory, subsurface drained field plots, and pesticide analytical laboratory.

★3833★ Soil-Plant Analysis Laboratory
Northeast Louisiana Univ.
Rm. 117, Chemistry & Natural Sciences Bldg.
Monroe, LA 71209-0505
Phone: (318)342-1948
Fax: (318)342-3000
Contact: Debbie Moore, Dir.
Research Areas: Conducts soil fertility, lignite, water, pesticide and herbicide, and heavy metal analyses. Also studies residues in soils, plant, and animal tissues and analyzes water and wastewater.

★3834★ Solar and Energy Research Facility (SERF)
University of Arizona
College of Engineering & Mines
Tucson, AZ 85721
Phone: (602)621-7496
Contact: Donald E. Osborn, Sr. Research Specialist
Research Areas: Wide range of interdisciplinary research and development programs in solar energy and energy management. Representative projects include the following: development of devices that separate incoming concentrated sunlight into distinct spectral windows, improving the performance of hybrid solar quantum and thermal systems; solar application of advanced composite materials used in aerospace technology; development of bi-desiccant staged and ejector-compression cycle solar cooling systems for residential and commercial use; investigation of the application of cogenerative technologies to improve energy conversion efficiency in the state of Arizona; performance monitoring and analysis of four passive solar homes in Phoenix, Tucson, Cave Creek, and Payson; application of the Tessellated Optical Reflector (TOR) telescope, a gamma ray telescope on Mount Hopkins, as an ultra-high flux solar furnace; monitoring and analysis of the Coolidge Solar Irrigation Project, a 150-kilowatt solar-thermal power plant with electric utility system intertie; and an analysis of the potential of active solar cooling systems in the state. Special Resources: 2,500-square-foot solar testing and monitoring facility located on the roof of the Civil Engineering Building; ten separate testing pads; solar furnace with a 1.5m mirror and a 500-sun concentration ratio; TOR telescope with a 10m mirror and a concentration ratio of 5,000-8,000 suns; azimuth-tracking floating carousel collector; 3kW photovoltaic test facility; and a wide range of data collection and analysis instrumentation, including pyranometers, digital multimeters, digital thermometers, recorders, and computerized data acquisition systems.

★3835★ Solar Energy and Energy Conversion Laboratory
University of Florida
Dept. of Mechanical Engineering
Gainesville, FL 32611
Phone: (904)392-0812
Fax: (904)392-1071
Contact: Dr. D. Yogi Goswami, Dir.
Research Areas: Solar energy, alternative energy technology, and energy conservation. Also conducts studies in alternate forms of energy conversion and space research, particularly zero gravity environment. Seeks to apply solar energy technology to water heating, swimming pool heating, house heating, baking, distillation, refrigeration and air conditioning, energy concentration, power plants, cooking, pumps, turbines, solar-gravity motor, solar reciprocating engines, sewage treatment, hazardous waste detoxifications and transportation. Special Resources: Maintains a solar calorimeter to measure solar properties of materials, three solar instrumented homes, a solar steam generating station, a weather station, windmills, gasifiers, a training center machine shop, an indoor solar simulator, and a solar air-conditioning system.

★3836★ Solar Energy Applications Laboratory (SEAL)
Colorado State Univ.
College of Engineering
Fort Collins, CO 80523
Phone: (303)491-8617
Fax: (303)491-8544
Contact: Dr. Douglas C. Hittle, Dir.
Research Areas: Research, development, and demonstration center for practical applications of passive and active solar heating and cooling systems. Studies building energy analysis software, load management, control of heating and air conditioning, and artificial intelligence for HVAC design. Special Resources: The Solar Village, including three solar houses, a greenhouse/residence building, and a passive solar heating test facility.

★3837★ Solar Energy Center
University of Oregon
Dept.s of Architecture & Physics
Eugene, OR 97403
Phone: (503)686-3696
Contact: Prof. John S. Reynolds, Dir.
Research Areas: Solar radiation monitoring and analysis of climate in terms of architectural response.

★3838★ Solar Energy Group
University of Chicago
5640 S. Ellis Ave.
Chicago, IL 60637
Phone: (312)702-7756

Contact: Prof. Roland Winston, Head
Research Areas: Design and development of solar energy concentrators using the principles of nonimaging optics. Projects include studies of stationary solar collectors for high temperature, photovoltaic concentrators with nonimaging second stage, and point focus thermal concentrators with second stage. Special Resources: Maintains a solar test station and an Apollo Domain work station.

★3839★ South Central Research & Extension Center
University of Nebraska-Lincoln
Box 66
Clay Center, NE 68933
Phone: (402)762-3535
Fax: (402)762-4422
Contact: Dr. Charles L. Stonecipher, District Dir.
Research Areas: Irrigated crops production systems, agronomics, irrigation, plant pathology, and entomology, including studies on soil fertility, irrigation systems design, irrigation water management, ground water quality, pesticide leaching, nitrate leaching and soil movement, wheat breeding experiments and wheat, corn, sorghum, and soybean variety testing. Special Resources: 480 acres for irrigated crop production.

★3840★ Southeast Research & Extension Center
University of Nebraska-Lincoln
211 Mussehl Hall
E. Campus
Lincoln, NE 68583
Phone: (402)472-3674
Fax: (402)472-3858
Contact: Dr. Loyd L. Young, Dir.
Research Areas: Agriculture and natural resources, agronomy, farm management, horticulture, community resource development, family living, 4-H and youth development, and urban community forestry.

★3841★ Southeast Waste Exchange
University of North Carolina at Charlotte
Charlotte, NC 28223
Phone: (704)547-2307
Contact: Maxie L. May, Dir.
Research Areas: Hazardous and nonhazardous waste management and industrial recyclying. Databases: Maintains a bulletin board service.

★3842★ Southeast Watershed Research Laboratory
PO Box 946
Tifton, GA 31793
Phone: (912)386-3462
Fax: (912)382-8092
Contact: Dr. Adrian Thomas, Dir.
Research Areas: Watershed systems, including optimum use of soil and water resources of the Southeast considering short- and long-term productivity requirements, ecosystem stability and water quality standards. Also investigates pesticides and nutrients in surface and groundwater, riparian systems analysis, water quality modeling, and hydrologic modeling. Special Resources: Pesticide and nutrient labs, and hydrologic gaging stations. Databases: Hydrologic Records (precipitation, stream flow, and water quality).

★3843★ Southeastern Clinical Occupational Medicine/Environmental Health Evaluation Center
Emory Univ.
c/o Emory Dept. of Community Health
American Cancer Society, 4th Fl.
1599 Clifton St.
Atlanta, GA 30329
Phone: (404)727-8743
Contact: Thomas Sellers Jr., M, Acting Dir.
Research Areas: Occupational medicine and environmental health.

★3844★ Southwest Consortium on Plant Genetics and Water Resources
New Mexico State Univ.
Box 3GL
Las Cruces, NM 88003
Phone: (505)646-5453
Contact: Dr. John D. Kemp, Chm., Steering Committee
Research Areas: Addresses the agricultural problems and needs of the arid southwest, including water resources, including underground water reserves and their contamination, plant salinity tolerance, heavy metal tolerant plants (such as the jimson weed and monkeyflower) and the use of such plants to control industrial contamination, and improved water supply and distribution through alternative irrigation methods and decreased emphasis on high productivity.

★3845★ Southwest Research and Information Center
PO Box 4524
Albuquerque, NM 87106
Phone: (505)262-1862
Fax: (505)262-1864
Contact: Don Hancock, Information Coordinator
Research Areas: The Center maintains ongoing projects that seek to protect the environment, improve the quality of life, and empower citizens and communities through research, public advocacy and consulting, and dissemination of information. Secondary and applied research in resource development, water quality, toxic chemicals, and nuclear waste handling, including studies of health effects of uranium, radioactive waste disposal, medical uses of radiation, coal development, in-state electricity demand and rates, coal supply and demand, mine reclamation, water impacts, and relocation of native Americans from mining areas.

★3846★ Southwest Research Institute (SwRI)
6220 Culebra Rd.
P.O. Drawer 28510
San Antonio, TX 78228-0510
Phone: (512)684-5111
Fax: (512)522-3559
Contact: Martin Goland, Pres.
Environmental sciences and engineering, bioengineering, radiolocation sciences and development, communications, electromagnetic compatibility, electronic systems, geophysical instrumentation, nondestructive evaluation and research, nuclear reactor engineering, nuclear waste regulatory analysis, fluid dynamics and hydraulics, offshore systems, structural analysis and testing, engine emissions analysis and control, alternate energy systems, alternate fuels, mining systems engineering, vehicle and highway safety, and fire research. Computers: IBM Model 4341-2 and DEC VAX 8800.

★3847★ Southwest Technology Development Institute
Box 3 SOL
New Mexico State Univ.
Las Cruces, NM 88003
Phone: (505)646-1846
Contact: Dr. Rudi Schoenmackers, Dir.
Research Areas: Solar analysis and design, photovoltaic research and design, geothermal exploration and applications, bioenergy, and greenhouse technology.

★3848★ Space Technology Center
University of Kansas
Raymond Nichols Hall
Lawrence, KS 66045
Phone: (913)864-4775
Contact: Prof. B.G. Barr, Dir.
Research Areas: Supports development of new knowledge, concepts, and technology for surveying earth resources and evaluating environmental quality, including remote sensing, technology transfer, flight research, economic and business research, microprocessor control, computer integrated manufacturing, mineral resource surveys, geochronology, and energy research. Staff also works with industry and government in applying newly developed technology. The Center facilitates the activities of the Augmented Telerobotic Laboratory, Computer Aided Systems Engineering Laboratory, Flight Research Laboratory, Isotope Geochemistry Laboratory, Kansas Applied Remote Sensing Program, Kansas Biological Survey, Radiation Physics Laboratory, Radar Systems and Remote Sensing Laboratory, and Telecommunications and Information Systems Laboratory. Special Resources: Houses a congressional exhibit on the nation's space program from 1960.

★3849★ Spangler Geotechnical Laboratory
Iowa State Univ.
College of Engineering
Ames, IA 50011
Phone: (515)294-7690
Fax: (515)294-7689
Contact: Dr. R.L. Handy, Professor-in-Charge
Research Areas: Geotechnical engineering, including studies on utilization of fly ash, groundwater hydrology, hazardous wastes, development of new laboratory and field in situ test methods, and engineering and hydrologic properties of soils. Special Resources: Maintains X-ray diffractometer, fluorescent analyzer, highway load test truck, drilling machines, and in situ soil and rock testing devices.

★3850★ Spirit of the Future-Creative Institute
Studio #7
20 Beaver St.
San Francisco, CA 94114
Phone: (415)861-3968
Contact: Mark Futuri, Public Relations
Research Areas: Provides advisory services, future planning, and applied research in the following areas: renewable energy, recycling and conservation, survival and self-reliance, natural health and fitness, and food farming.

★3851★ Stable Isotope Laboratory
Arizona State Univ.
Dept. of Geology
Tempe, AZ 85287-1404
Phone: (602)965-3731
Contact: L. Paul Knauth Ph.D., Dir.
Research Areas: High-level nuclear waste disposal, especially stable isotope characterization of brines, rocks, and gases at

the Texas Salt Site, nominated by the U.S. Department of Energy as a National Nuclear Waste Repository. Other projects include techniques for oxygen isotope analysis for rocks and minerals, isotope studies relevant to oil production and exploration in offshore California, origin of deep basin brines, and climatic history of the Earth. Special Resources: Double-focusing analytical mass spectrometer and custom, high-vacuum extraction lines.

★3852★ State of Washington Water Research Center
Washington State Univ.
Pullman, WA 99164-3002
Phone: (509)335-5531
Fax: (509)335-1590
Contact: Dr. William H. Funk, Dir.
Research Areas: Political, economic, social, scientific, engineering, and legal aspects of water resource management, including interdisciplinary studies in water resource economics, political institutions, water law and water rights, water quality, hydrogeology, hydrology, hydraulics, fisheries, forestry, irrigated agriculture and related land-use, lake restoration, and wetlands. Authorized to disseminate water resource information under the Water Resources Research Act of 1984, Public Law 98-242. Acts as focal point for the University of Washington and Washington State University for water research matters and as a coordinating agency for faculty members interested in water resources research, assisting in preparation of proposals and location of funds.

★3853★ Statewide Air Pollution Research Center
University of California, Riverside
Riverside, CA 92521
Phone: (714)787-5124
Fax: (714)787-5004
Contact: J. Brian Mudd, Dir.
Research Areas: Studies atmospheric chemistry and the effects of pollutants on plant systems, conducts ambient air monitoring, and models photochemical smog formation to yield information relevant to the development of rational and cost-effective air pollution control strategies. Research program includes studies of chemical and physical transformations of pollutants in the atmosphere, chemical composition and related mutagenicity of gaseous and particulate organic pollutants, spectroscopic identification and measurement of atmospheric constituents, effects of pollutants on agricultural crops, native forest species and ornamentals, estimation of associated economic losses, definition of tolerance levels for specified plant species and description of symptom expression of plants, modeling atmospheric transformations of pollutants, and translation of research results into models suitable for direct application to control strategies by state and federal agencies and public officials. Special Resources: Smog chamber laboratory consisting of an all-Teflon smog chamber, a second evacuable smog chamber, and a 25-KW solar simulator with associated analytical and data acquisition systems; a rapid-scanning differential optica l absorption spectrometer operable at pathlengths up to 17 kilometers with corresponding detection limits for many inorganic and organic species of approximately 0.1 ppb; a mutagen testing facility for performance of mutagenicity bioassays of ambient particulate organic matter; specialized plant fumigation chambers for plant studies; two specially constructed facilities consisting of open-top and closed-top greenhouses; and a linear gradient fumigation for the study of plant injury caused by air pollutants.

★3854★ Stelle Group, Office of Technology
127 Sun St.
Stelle, IL 60919
Phone: (815)256-2200
Contact: Timothy J. Wilhelm, Dir.
Research Areas: Studies and develops self-sufficiency systems and machinery that are ecologically safe. Recent activities include design, construction, and monitoring of ethanol plant for the conversion of corn to alcohol and design, construction, operation, and monitoring of a commercial size solar greenhouse using liquid foam as insulation.

★3855★ Stroud Water Research Center
512 Spencer Rd.
Avondale, PA 19311
Phone: (215)268-2153
Contact: B.W. Sweeney, Laboratory Dir.
Research Areas: Limnology and ecology with emphasis on streams and rivers and the surrounding environment.

★3856★ Sustainable Agriculture Program
University of California, Davis
Dept. of Agronomy & Range Science
Davis, CA 95616
Phone: (916)752-7645
Contact: Mark Van Horn, Program Coordinator
Research Areas: Sustainable agriculture technologies, including studies in biological control, composting, fertility, solarization, and organic and biological gardening and farming. Investigates farming methods that are ecologically sound and economically viable, studies appropriate technologies for small farmers, and conducts marketing research, research in agriculture policy, and surveys to assess farmers needs. Also promotes international agriculture development by researching technologies applicable to developing nations and by creating opportunities for foreign students to conduct research relevant to their own agricultural systems. Special Resources: Maintains and administers the 25-acre Student Experimental Farm.

★3857★ Sustainable Agriculture Research and Education Program
University of California, Davis
395 Oser Ave.
Davis, CA 95616
Phone: (916)752-2379
Contact: William C. Liebhardt, Director
A university-based program which promotes sustainable agriculture through the administration of competitive grants, the development and distribution of information, and the establishment of long-term farmland research.

★3858★ Syracuse Research Corporation
Merrill Ln.
Syracuse, NY 13210
Phone: (315)425-5100
Fax: (315)425-1339
Contact: Kenneth A. Kun, Pres.
Research Areas: Operates the Life and Environmental Sciences Division, which conducts food protection testing, chemical analysis, aquatic toxicology, and industrial hygiene studies; Chemical Hazard and Risk Assessment Division, which assesses chemical hazards; and the Science Technology Policy Center, which provides policy analysis related to national, state, and local problems.

★3859★ Systematics Museums
University of Kansas
Dyche Hall
Lawrence, KS 66045
Phone: (913)864-4541
Fax: (913)864-5335
Contact: Dr. Philip S. Humphrey, Chm.
Research Areas: Ecology, systematics, population ecology, human ecology, and related natural and social sciences. Special Resources: Houses part of the University library system's vertebrate collection of 15,000 volumes.

★3860★ Tall Timbers Research Station
R.R. 1
Box 678
Tallahassee, FL 32312
Phone: (904)893-4153
Fax: (904)668-7981
Contact: Larry Landers, Dir.
Research Areas: Wildlife management, especially in regard to fire ecology and habitat needs of game and nongame wildlife and plants.

★3861★ Tellus Institute
89 Broad St.
Boston, MA 02110
Phone: (617)426-5844
Fax: (617)426-7692
Contact: Paul D. Raskin, Pres.
Research Areas: Resource management and environmental issues, emphasizing rational and equitable strategies for the public good. Also conducts policy research regarding economic development, social equity, and environmental sustainability. Institute includes the Energy Systems Research Group (ESRG), which conducts energy planning and regulatory programs; the Solid Waste Group, which undertakes planning, technical, economic, and regulatory studies of solid waste management; the Risk Analysis Group, which evaluates the environmental, health and safety, and financial risks of projects, and provides policy, regulatory, and technical analysis; and the Stockholm Environment Institute-Boston Center, which performs research, policy evaluations, and field applications concerned with environmentally sound development.

★3862★ Texas Water Resources Institute
Texas A&M Univ.
College Station, TX 77843-2118
Phone: (409)845-1851
Fax: (409)845-3932
Contact: Dr. Wayne R. Jordan, Dir.
Research Areas: Water and other resources that affect water, including bay and estuary studies, furrow diking, the effects of demographic and social factors on water use in Texas cities (WATFORE Model), development of portable flow meters, land application of wastewater, optimizing reservoir operations in Texas, irrigation, irrigation water management guidelines, and the water analysis, technical evaluation, and retrieval system (WATERS). Program expanded under Water Resources Research Act of 1964 to coordinate research on water resources at Texas universities and training of scientists in the field.

★3863★ Throckmorton-Purdue Agricultural Center
Purdue Univ.
Agricultural Administration Bldg., Rm. 120
West Lafayette, IN 47905
Phone: (317)494-8370
Contact: John Trott, Farm Dir.
Research Areas: Forage (biomass) production management systems and alternative agricultural systems.

★3864★ Tintic Experimental Area
Utah State Univ.
UMC 52
Range Science
Logan, UT 84322
Phone: (801)750-2471
Contact: Dr. J.C. Malechek
Research Areas: Range management, livestock grazing effects, watershed studies, and ecological studies.

★3865★ Touch of Nature Environmental Center
Southern Illinois Univ. at Carbondale
Carbondale, IL 62901-6623
Phone: (618)453-1121
Contact: Phillip Lindberg, Dir.
Research Areas: Acts as a model facilty for experiential education, recreation, and research in the areas of environmental education, ecology, forestry, special education, rehabilitation, botany, plant and soil science, and youth at risk. Three major programs include camping and therapeutic recreation for the handicapped, ecological/ environmentaleducation, and experiential education. Other activities include The Wilderness Program (concentrating on initiative, wilderness survival skills, and group processes). The Center is a 3,100-acre field campus conference/retreat center adjacent to the Shawnee National Forest and Crab Orchard National Wildlife Refuge, seven miles southeast from the main campus.

★3866★ Toxic Chemicals Laboratory
Cornell Univ.
New York State College of Agriculture
Tower Rd.
Ithaca, NY 14853-7401
Phone: (607)255-4538
Contact: Dr. Donald J. Lisk, Dir.
Research Areas: Toxic materials in the environment, with emphasis on sewage sludge and coal and incinerator fly ash studies and trace heavy metal analysis. Conducts pesticide and toxic chemical metabolite studies of soils, fruits, vegetables, plants, animals, fish, and other farm products, as well as on forage crops and resultant products, meat, milk, and eggs. Collaborates with similar research program at New York State Agricultural Experiment Station at Geneva for study of fruits and vegetables used largely for processing and their resulting processed foods.

★3867★ Toxics Use Reduction Institute (TURI)
University of Lowell
One Univ. Ave.
Lowell, MA 01854-9985
Phone: (508)934-3250
Fax: (508)452-5711
Contact: Ken Geiser, Dir.
Research Areas: Toxic chemical use reduction technologies, including chemical input substitution, production processes redesign, and product reformulation. Studies on toxics use reduction methods include toxics use reduction audits, safe substitute analyses, life cycle impact models, full cost accounting procedures, technology transfer programs, technical education and diffusion practice, occupational and environmental health effects assessments, and social and economic impact analyses. Investigates toxic chemical restriction policies for Massachusetts.

★3868★ Tri-State Bird and Research Inc.
110 Possum Hollow Rd.
Newark, DE 19711
Phone: (302)737-9543
Contact: Lynne Frink, Director
A multidisciplined group of biologists, veterinarians, government agents, chemists, statisticians, and concerned citizens studying the effects of oil on birds. Serves as a full-time wild bird research and rehabilitation center.

★3869★ Tri-State Bird Rescue and Research, Inc.
110 Possum Hollow Rd.
Wilmington, DE 19711
Phone: (302)737-9543
Contact: Lynne Frink, Dir.
Research Areas: Medical and biological ornithology geared to wildlife rehabilitation and strengthening the health of wildlife populations. Projects include studies on effects of toxins such as oil and organophosphates on individuals and populations of animals, wildlife diets and nutrition, and medical care.

★3870★ Tropical Resources Institute (TRI)
Yale Univ.
Yale School of Forestry & Environmental Studies
205 Prospect St.
New Haven, CT 06511
Phone: (203)432-5116
Fax: (203)432-5942
Contact: Dr. William R. Bentley, Dir.
Research Areas: Tropical resources; natural secondary forest management; wildland protection management; bioenergy systems; agroforestry, social forestry, wildlife management and biodiversity; policy planning; economics of rural and urban development; and curriculum development for professional and scientific education.

★3871★ Turfgrass Field Research Lab
Cornell Univ.
Dept. of Floriculture
Plant Science Bldg., Rm. 20
Ithaca, NY 14853
Phone: (607)255-1796
Fax: (607)255-9998
Contact: Dr. Martin Petrovic
Research Areas: Conducts studies into the environmental fate of pesticides on turfgrass, water use management of grasses, fertilizer performances, new and experimental testing of grasses, and integrated pest management relating to turf grass.

★3872★ Turnbull Laboratory of Ecological Studies
Eastern Washington Univ.
MS 72
Cheney, WA 99004
Phone: (509)359-2498
Fax: (509)359-6927
Contact: Dr. Allan Scholz, Dir.
Research Areas: All areas of ecological studies, including causal factors determining eutrophication rate of refuge lakes, marsh rehabilitation and its relation to waterfowl use, vegetational changes related to timber harvest, tree-thinning and controlled burns, ecology and succession of primary noxious weeds, disease and parasite loads of waterfowl, quantitative wetland habitat survey, coyote predation and its significance on waterfowl, and public attitude on the types of public use allowed on wildlife refuges. The Laboratory encourages and supports field research activities and is available for use by other universities, as well as federal or private groups where appropriate. Special Resources: Aquatics lab, microscopy lab, dry preparation lab, analytical lab, and environmental chamber rooms.

★3873★ Tyson Research Center
Washington Univ.
PO Box 258
Eureka, MO 63025
Phone: (314)938-5346
Contact: Dr. Richard W. Coles, Dir.
Research Areas: Multi- and interdisciplinary academic research. Specific study areas include: raptor rehabilitation and propagation; endangered species rehabilitation and propagation; care to orphaned or injured wildlife; medical research on animals, seismology, weather monitoring, physics, ecology and field biology (including bird populations, social behavior of insects, oak fruit production, and studies on salamanders, herbaceous plants, bats, and endangered plants), and energy conservation (wind turbine research, solar energy, and demonstration of a self-sufficient, autonomous dwelling capsule for one person). The Center's facilities are available to universities, colleges, and visiting investigators. Databases: Meteorology, salamander population, and oak-hickory fruit production. Special Resources: 2,000-acre fenced tract of second growth oak-hickory forest and fields; 75 buildings, including 52 subterranean munitions storage bunkers; a wolf sanctuary; a seismic study site.

★3874★ UNC Sea Grant College Program
Box 8605
North Carolina State Univ.
Raleigh, NC 27695-8605
Phone: (919)737-2454
Fax: (919)737-7095
Contact: Dr. B.J. Copeland, Dir.
Research Areas: Biological, physical, chemical, geological, social, economic, and developmental aspects of coastal and marine resources, particularly as related to North Carolina, through a combination of research, extension, and educational activities focused on solving marine and coastal resources problems.

★3875★ Underground Space Center
University of Minnesota
790 Civil & Mineral Engineering Bldg.
500 Pillsbury Dr. SE
Minneapolis, MN 55455
Phone: (612)624-0066
Fax: (612)624-0293
Contact: Dr. Raymond L. Sterling, Dir.
Research Areas: Use and design of underground/earth-sheltered facilities for residential and nonresidential purposes, including research in energy use, planning, security, environment, building design, construction techniques, discrete mechanics, frost heave effects on buildings, landscaping, building codes, financing, and psychological considerations. Participates in the Stirling engine loss mechanism understanding program funded by the NASA-Lewis Research Center. Develops technical guidelines for construction of earth-sheltered houses, monitors energy performance of underground buildings, writes books on design and construction, prepares technical resource guides for city subsurface space use, and studies passive cooling heat transfer process. Special Resources: Instrumentation for thermal studies of buildings; test-site for underground grain storage; foundation test facility for gathering performance data and validating heat transfer simulation models; and database on energy performance of five earth-sheltered houses and one highly insulated conventional house.

★3876★ U.S. EPA Test and Evaluation Facility
1600 Gest St.
Cincinnati, OH 45204
Phone: (513)684-2621
Fax: (513)684-2628
Contact: Francis L. Evans III, Manager
Research Areas: Bench and pilot-plant studies on wastewater and sludge, control of air pollution, toxic substances, industrial-municipal pollution, solid wastes management, health and ecological effects of pollution control technology, and energy conservation. Conducts tests of treatment concepts and estimates the limits of process capabilities and scale-up factors for full-scale design. Special Resources: 24,000-square-foot, two-story, high-bay experimental area with wastewater water streams piped into 16 stations; two five-ton bridge cranes; greenhouse for agricultural studies of soil pollution.

★3877★ U.S. Forest Service, Aquatic Ecosystem Analysis Laboratory
105 Page
Brigham Young Univ.
Provo, UT 84602
Phone: (801)378-4928
Contact: Dr. Fred A. Mangum, Dir.
Research Areas: Water quality, aquatic ecology, environmental assessment, and fish and wildlife habitat. Past projects have included development of a water quality management model for the western U.S. based upon environmental ranges and tolerances of aquatic macroinvertebrates; the health and condition of the macroinvertebrate community are measured against the biological potential for that habitat given the existing physical and chemical environment. Databases: Biotic Condition Index (BCI), a taxonomic, density, and biomass database of over 20,000 aquatic macroinvertebrate stream samples from 1970 to the present.

★3878★ U.S. Forest Service, Forest Engineering Research Project
George W. Andrews Forestry Sciences Laboratory
Devall St.
Auburn University, AL 36849
Phone: (205)826-8700
Fax: (205)821-0037
Contact: Donald L. Sirois, Project Leader
Research Areas: Development of mechanized systems for intensive forest management, including systems for thinning forest stands, biomass harvesting, and final harvest of forest. Emphasis is on new technology for felling trees, ground-based primary extraction, in-woods processing and transport systems, and ergonomic, environmental, and forest regeneration studies. Mission is to provide new engineering knowledge for economical harvesting and regeneration systems for southern U.S. timberland that is silviculturally sound and to reduce adverse environmental impacts. Special Resources: Engineering shop, instrumentation laboratory, and database of production rates of timber harvesting machines.

★3879★ U.S. Forest Service, Forest Hydrology Laboratory (Oxford, MS)
Southern Forest Experiment Sta.
PO Box 947
Oxford, MS 38655
Phone: (601)234-2744
Fax: (601)237-8318
Contact: Jack B. Waide, Project Leader
Research Areas: Watershed management and fish habitat research in hilly upland sections of the mid-south coastal plain and in the Ozark-Ouachita highlands. Mission is to evaluate effects of forest management practices and other human activities on streamflow amount and distribution, water quality, long-term site productivity, and fish habitat; and to develop environmentally acceptable management practices which maintain or enhance production of multiple watershed resources. Also conducts research on atmospheric deposition; geomorphic controls over stream channel morphology, sediment transport, and terrestrial-aquatic linkages in riparian zones; and nutrient cycling processes in forest and stream ecosystems. Conducts both in-house investigations and cooperative studies with other federal and state agencies, universities, and the forest industry in the mid-south region. Special Resources: Maintains databases on stormflow volumes, time stage readings, sediment and nutrient concentrations and yields by storm event, precipitation amounts and nutrient concentrations by storm event, select climatic variables, and other select watershed components.

★3880★ U.S. Forest Service, Forestry Sciences Laboratory (Logan)
860 N. 1200 E.
Logan, UT 84321
Phone: (801)752-1311
Contact: Dr. Roy Sidle, Project Leader
Research Areas: Reclamation of disturbed lands in the Intermountain West, including erosion, plant ecology, and stress physiology studies.

★3881★ U.S. Forest Service, Forestry Sciences Laboratory (Tempe)
Arizona State Univ.
Tempe, AZ 85287
Phone: (602)261-4365
Contact: Dr. Leonard F. Debano, Dir. Representative
Research Areas: Watersheds and range, wildlife, and fish habitat management in the southwest U.S. Specific concerns include water quantity and quality related to vegetation management; the relationship between flood peaks, vegetation management, and soil erosion; rates and productivity relations; interrelationships among livestock and wildlife; nutrient and energy dynamics in southwestern U.S. ecosystems; and habitat requirements of selected threatened, endangered, and/or sensitive species in southwestern U.S.

★3882★ U.S. Forest Service, North Central Forest Experiment Station (East Lansing)
1407 S. Harrison Rd., Ste. 220
East Lansing, MI 48823
Phone: (517)355-7740
Contact: Dr. J. Michael Vasievich, Dir. Representative
Research Areas: Forest entomology, including field and laboratory work to determine the role of insects in natural and planted forest ecosystems, concentrating on mechanisms of insect/host resistance, tree stress physiology relative to insect impact, and diseases of forest insects; wildland fires, including methodologies for quantifying the effectiveness of fire prevention programs and the effects of weather and climate on fire activity; and forest economics, including economic returns from alternative management options for northern forests, assessment of economic risks in forest production, and development of methods for economic forest management decisions.

★3883★ U.S. Forest Service, Redwood Sciences Laboratory
1700 Bayview Dr.
Arcata, CA 95521
Phone: (707)822-3691
Fax: (707)822-5628
Contact: Dr. Robert R. Ziemer, Project Leader
Research Areas: Effects of forest management on hillslope processes, fishery resources, and stream environments. Investigates timber management and wildlife interactions, focusing on threatened and endangered species including the spotted owl, marbled murrelet, and rare breeds of amphibians. Special Resources: Caspar Creek Experimental Watersheds; Yukon Experimental Forest.

★3884★ U.S. Forest Service, Rocky Mountain Forest and Range Experiment Station
240 W. Prospect Rd.
Fort Collins, CO 80526-2098
Phone: (303)498-1126
Fax: (303)498-1010
Contact: H.M. Montrey, Dir.
Research Areas: Management, protection, and utilization of forests and related ranges in central and southern Rocky Mountains, including studies on forest diseases and insects, watersheds management, resource inventory and assessment, wildlife habitat, atmospheric deposition and mountain meteorology, climate change, land use planning and timber management. Maintains seven research centers located within the ten-state area served.

★3885★ U.S. Forest Service, Wildlife Habitat and Silviculture Laboratory
Box 7600 S. F.A. Sta.
Nacogdoches, TX 75962
Phone: (409)569-7981
Contact: Ronald E. Thill, Project Leader
Research Areas: Wildlife habitat and timber resources management, including effects of streamside management zones (SMZs) on wildlife habitats; effects of alternative silvicultural practices using uneven-age management techniques; and management of wetland and relict communities. Special Resources: Stephen F. Austin Experimental Forest (part of Angelina National Forest).

★3886★ Universities Associated for Research and Education in Pathology, Inc.
9650 Rockville Pike
Bethesda, MD 20814
Phone: (301)571-1880
Fax: (301)571-1879
Contact: Frances A. Pitlick Ph.D., Exec. Officer
Research Areas: Administers and coordinates educational and research activities in human pathology, including studies on environmental factors in human diseases, environmental pathology, safety of food additives, health effects attributed to unregulated toxic waste disposal sites, accident and forensic pathology, and environmental health policies. Provides core material for pathology instruction to medical students and residents. Operates the Registry of Comparative Pathology.

★3887★ University Center for Environmental and Hazardous Materials Studies
Virginia Polytechnic Inst. and State Univ.
1020 Derring Hall
Blacksburg, VA 24061-0415
Phone: (703)951-5538
Contact: Dr. John Cairns Jr., Dir.
Research Areas: Environmental problems, including studies on aquatic ecology and water

quality, environmental effects of genetically engineered microorganisms, hazard evaluation of toxic chemicals, recovery and restoration of damaged ecosystems, and steam/electric power plants. Conducts interdisciplinary investigations and cooperative projects with other research units at the University. Also responsible for stimulating, encouraging, and coordinating faculty research and instruction related to quality of human environment.

★3888★ University Center for Water Research
Oklahoma State Univ.
003 Life Sciences E.
Stillwater, OK 74078
Phone: (405)744-9995
Fax: (405)744-7673
Contact: Dr. Norman N. Durham, Dir.
Research Areas: Administers research programs of Oklahoma Water Resources Research Institute, the National Center for Ground Water Research, and the state's Water Research Center, including studies in aquatic ecology, limnology, reservoir circulation and recreation, environmental engineering, wastewater treatment, ecological effects of contaminants, evapotranspiration, efficiency of irrigation, water economics, water-based recreation, properties of water, rural water districts, institutional aspects of water management, subsurface characterization, modeling of groundwater systems, modeling plumes, transporting pollutants, acid water and rain, water management education, aquifer recharge, and biomass assessment.

★3889★ University Forest
West Virginia Univ.
Morgantown, WV 26506
Phone: (304)293-2941
Fax: (304)293-2441
Contact: Dr. Jack E. Coster, Dir.
Research Areas: Forest regeneration and management, forest genetics and tree improvement, diseases, forest hydrology, wildlife management, strip mine reclamation, and wood utilization. Provides facilities for field research of Experiment Station staff. Serves as the permanent weather station site for the Department of Commerce.

★3890★ University Forest
University of Missouri-Columbia
1-30 Agriculture Bldg.
Columbia, MO 65211
Phone: (314)222-8373
Contact: Albert R. Vogt, Dir.
Research Areas: Forest management, including silviculture, watershed and fire management, and ecology.

★3891★ University Hygienic Laboratory
University of Iowa
Oakdale Campus
Iowa City, IA 52242
Phone: (319)335-4500
Fax: (319)335-4555
Contact: Dr. W.J. Hausler Jr., Dir.
Research Areas: Virology, limnology, industrial hygiene, neonatal metabolic and prenatal diseases detection, microbiology, health physics, and organic, inorganic, and radiation chemistry. Conducts research and service in all areas relating to public and environmental health, including rapid diagnosis of disease agents by fluorescent microscopy and enzyme immunoassay. Studies the epidemiology of brucellosis, listeriosis, food quality control, surface water/groundwater contaminants, radioisotopes in groundwaters, and airborne infections, including legionellosis. The Laboratory's Des Moines branch is primarily concerned with complete inorganic chemical analyses of water, stream pollution problems, and neonatal metabolic screening.

★3892★ University of Georgia Center for Global Policy Studies
303 Baldwin Hall
Athens, GA 30602
Phone: (404)542-5747
Contact: Dr. Martin Hillenbrand, Director
Research Areas: Population growth and its pressure upon limited resources.

★3893★ Universitywide Energy Research Group (UERG)
University of California
Bldg. T-9, Rm. 216
Berkeley, CA 94720
Phone: (415)642-9588
Fax: (415)643-5180
Contact: Prof. Richard J. Gilbert, Dir.
Research Areas: UERG funds two research programs. The California Energy Studies Program fosters and supports faculty research on critical energy problems and issues facing California, including studies in the following areas: energy use and conservation, energy resources and supply systems, environmental issues in energy supply and use, and economics, politics, and regulation of energy systems. The Energy Science and Technology Research Program, emphasizes basic science and engineering research related to development of energy technologies and understanding of energy systems, including studies in health and environmental research, conservation and renewable energy, and conventional energy sources. Special Resources: UERG maintains an energy research catalog, which describes and lists the energy-related research projects on the nine campuses of the University of California system.

★3894★ Upper Cumberland Biological Station at Tech Aqua
Tennessee Technological Univ.
Box 5063
Cookeville, TN 38505
Phone: (615)372-3129
Contact: Dr. Henri Willard, Dir.
Research Areas: Aquatic and terrestrial studies.

★3895★ Urban Environmental Laboratory
Brown Univ.
Box 1943
Providence, RI 02912
Phone: (401)863-2715
Fax: (401)863-3503
Contact: Harold Ward, Dir.
Research Areas: Urban environment, including, solar collectors, heat storage, composting and recycling, energy comsumption, home food production, and water conservation. Special Resources: Operates a solar greenhouse to provide organic produce and the Community Garden to demonstrate pesticide-free gardening and self-reliance.

★3896★ Urban Harbors Institute
University of Massachusetts at Boston
Harbor Campus
Boston, MA 02125
Phone: (617)287-5570
Fax: (617)265-7173
Contact: Dr. Richard F. Delaney, Dir.
Research Areas: Urban harbors and coastlines, especially water quality, toxicology, fish and shellfish biology, harbor ecosystems, public policy, management, economics and law, and recreational use. Specific research areas include the following: microbial physiology and ecology, organic geochemistry and oceanography, environmental policy and management, environmental law, benthic ecology, polychaete biology, succession in biological systems, predator-prey relationships, physical oceanography, biological oceanography, aquatic toxicology, aquatic and atmospheric chemistry, environmental economics, viruses in aquatic systems, public health microbiology, and phytoplankton ecology. Special Resources: Maintains an electron microscopy unit, a benthic ecology unit, a physical oceanography unit, cold rooms, and various small boats.

★3897★ Urban Initiatives, Inc.
530 W. 25th St.
New York, NY 10001
Phone: (212)620-9773
Contact: Gianni Longo, Pres.
Research Areas: Built environment, livability of cities, urban marketing, and citizen participation.

★3898★ Urban Land Institute
1090 Vermont Ave NW
Washington, DC 20005
Phone: (202)289-8500
Contact: Jill Devlin, Senior Marketing Associate
Research Areas: Land planning and development of urban areas, including studies on central city problems, industrial development, new community development, residential developments of all types, taxation, shopping center development and economics, metropolitan and urbanized area growth and development, mixed use development, and environmental factors affecting development.

★3899★ Urban Vegetation Laboratory
Morton Arboretum
Rte. 53
Lisle, IL 60532
Phone: (708)968-0074
Contact: Dr. George Ware, Research Admin.
Research Areas: Seeks to minimize the environmental impact of modern highways through research on the adversities confronting trees and other plants in urban environments, including studies on remnant natural forests and prairies, preservation and management of wetlands, and landscape aesthetics. Develops and manages coping plants (plants that tolerate airborne deicing compounds and other pollutants) and plants that tolerate inhospitable urban soil (excavated clay and fill material from disposal of urban rubble).

★3900★ USDA Grassland, Soil and Water Research Laboratory
808 E. Blackland Rd.
Temple, TX 76502
Phone: (817)770-6500
Fax: (817)770-6561
Contact: Dr. Clarence W. Richardson, Dir.
Research Areas: Develops technology to maximize forage and crop production, revegetate depleted, brush-infested watersheds, control noneconomic brush and weeds, and breed forages for increased quality and yield potential. Seeks to solve problems related to efficient use of soil and water, crop production, soil fertility, erosion, hydrology, and water quality. Activities are carried out through three units: the Natural Resources Systems Research Unit, the Grassland Protection Research Unit, and the Forage Improvement Research Unit.

★3901★ USDA Great Plains Systems Research Unit
Crops Research Laboratory
Colorado State Univ.
1701 Center Ave.
Fort Collins, CO 80523
Phone: (303)484-8777
Contact: Dr. James Welsh, Research Leader
Research Areas: Ecology and management of shortgrass rangelands and semiarid croplands for improvements in cattle grazing and crop production, including studies in autecology, soil science, range science, physiology, genetics, agronomy, and systems science. Special Resources: The Unit operates the U.S. Central Great Plains Experimental Range, a 16,000-acre shortgrass plains field station in northeastern Weld County, Colorado, with living quarters for three technicians. The Range represents the shortgrass steppe in the NSF-sponsored Long-Term Ecological Research Network (LTER).

★3902★ USDA Horticultural Insects Research Lab
Ohio Agricultural R & D Center
Ohio State Univ.
Wooster, OH 44691
Phone: (216)263-3897
Contact: Dr. Thyril L. Ladd Jr., Research Leader
Research Areas: Develops management procedures for insect pests of horticultural crops, including studies of pheromones, insecticides, cultural controls, parasites, and pathogens.

★3903★ USDA National Sedimentation Laboratory
PO Box 1157
Oxford, MS 38655
Phone: (601)232-2900
Fax: (601)232-2915
Contact: Dr. C.K. Mutchler, Dir.
Research Areas: Critical sedimentation and water quality problems in southern loess hills area of Mississippi and soil and water conservation, including coordinated field and laboratory studies of erosion and sedimentation processes, detachment, entrainment, transportation, deposition of soil materials, and factors affecting stream channel equilibrium. Provides knowledge for assessing sedimentation and channel problems and for designing corrective measures in programs for watershed development and protection. Special Resources: Maintains sediment analysis facility for processing sediment and soil samples and hydraulic laboratory for flume and model experiments on sediment transport. Also maintains chemistry and water quality laboratories, outdoor research facilities, topographical analysis facility, and database on Goodwin Creek Research Watershed.

★3904★ USDA Northern Great Plains Research Center
Box 459
Mandan, ND 58554
Phone: (701)663-6445
Contact: Alfred L. Black, Dir.
Research Areas: Agricultural production in northern Great Plains, including basic and applied studies on irrigation and dryland agricultural water use, erosion and soil productivity, conservation tillage and no-till cropping systems, crop residue and nitrogen fertilizer management to reduce potential groundwater pollution, grazing systems and range management, improved forage plants through breeding, and shelter belt breeding and management.

★3905★ USDA Northern Plains Soil and Water Research Center
Montana State Univ.
PO Box 1109
Sidney, MT 59270
Phone: (406)482-2020
Contact: Dr. J. Kristian Aase, Location Coordinator
Research Areas: Development of sound soil and water conservation practices for northern Great Plains agricultural lands, primarily in Montana but extending into North Dakota, South Dakota, and Wyoming, including studies on soil and water management, soil fertility, moisture conservation, stubble mulch processes, wind and water erosion control practices, and remote sensing. Aims to develop systems sensing methodology to measure phytomass production and crop yields; quantify microclimatic and soil factors that affect evapotranspiration and plant growth; design management systems which beneficially alter the plant environment on cultivated drylands; determine nutrient requirements of cultivated crops in order to optimize plant yield, plant quality, and use of soil and water resources; develop methods of controlling wind and water erosion on cultivated lands that are physically and economically compatible with farm operations; and develop weed control practices on intensively cropped drylands and biological control practices for noxious weeds such as leafy spurge.

★3906★ USDA Palouse Conservation Field Station
215 Johnson Hall
Washington State Univ.
Pullman, WA 99164
Phone: (509)335-1552
Contact: Dr. R.I. Papendick
Research Areas: Soil, water, and crop management, including soil erosion, thermal and hydraulic properties of soils and soil chemistry, and fertility studies.

★3907★ USDA Soil and Water Management Research Unit
Rte. 1, 3793 N., 3600 E.
Kimberly, ID 83341
Phone: (208)423-5582
Contact: Dr. David L. Carter, Location Coordinator
Research Areas: Soil and water management, including studies of irrigation water management, basic factors causing cohesion in soils, efficient use of water on nonirrigated and crop land, forage quality, plant nutrition, soil chemistry, erosion control, nitrate leasing control and the effects of erosion on crop production. Conducts a field and laboratory program involving irrigation system investigations, extensive irrigation and plant nutrition experiments, micrometeorological studies, and erosion and infiltration control investigations. Special Resources: Greenhouses, hydraulics laboratory, irrigated and dryland field research sites.

★3908★ USDA Water Conservation Laboratory
4331 E. Broadway
Phoenix, AZ 85040
Phone: (602)379-4356
Fax: (602)379-4355
Contact: Allen R. Dedrick, Dir.
Research Areas: Water conservation in systems involving groundwater, soils, plants, and the atmosphere. Projects include development of more efficient irrigation systems, irrigation scheduling, water management in irrigation districts, remote sensing of evapotranspiration, protection of groundwater quality in irrigated areas, introduction of new crops, effect of increasing carbon dioxide concentrations in the atmosphere on crop yields and crop water requirements, artificial recharge of groundwater, and reuse of wastewater.

★3909★ Utah Cooperative Fish and Wildlife Research Unit
Utah State Univ.
Logan, UT 84322-5210
Phone: (801)750-2509
Fax: (801)750-3798
Contact: Dr. John A. Bissonette, Leader
Research Areas: Fish habitat requirements, reservoir ecology, endangered fish, forage fish management, strain evaluation, fish physiology, stream ecology, avian ecology, terrestrial vertebrate ecology, and wetland habitat evaluation. Acts as consultant to federal and state wildlife and fishery biologists in area.

★3910★ Utah Water Research Laboratory
Utah State Univ.
Logan, UT 84322-8200
Phone: (801)750-3168
Fax: (801)750-3663
Contact: Dr. L. Douglas James, Dir.
Research Areas: Atmospheric water resources, water and waste treatment, natural systems engineering, risk-benefit assessment, hydraulics and fluid mechanics, hydroclimatic measurements, hydrologic systems analysis, water and energy, water resources planning and management, environmental quality modeling, surface and groundwater resources, irrigation engineering, scientific hydrology, hazardous waste management, water history, risk analysis in engineering design, and studies related to fish. Serves as the research arm to many agencies that encounter water problems affecting agricultural, municipal, industrial, and recreational users of water and hazardous waste management for public health and environmental protection. Special Resources: Environmental water quality laboratory (with gas, liquid, and integrated chromatographs, a GC-mass spectrophotometer, and AA, ICP, microscopy, bioassay, and Ames test and treatability study capabilities); a hydraulics laboratory (housing flumes, channels, pumps, and pipelines); and computer and data acquisition facilities.

★3911★ Vermont Institute of Natural Science
Church Hill
Woodstock, VT 05091
Phone: (802)457-2779
Contact: Sarah B. Laughlin, Dir.
Research Areas: Ornithology, focusing on endangered and threatened species. Conducts ongoing population monitoring and management programs for the common loon, peregrine falcon, bald eagle, and common tern. Activities include long-term bird banding operation, studies of passerine breeding and molt ecology, and long-term study of forest bird populations in Vermont. Operates the Vermont Raptor Center.

★3912★ Vertebrate Museum
Shippensburg Univ.
Franklin Science Center
Shippensburg, PA 17257
Phone: (717)532-1407
Fax: (717)532-1273
Contact: Dr. Gordon L. Kirkland Jr., Dir.
Research Areas: Ecology, zoogeography, and systematics of small mammals, with emphasis on responses of small mammals to ecosystem

disturbances (such as clearcutting and surface mining). Conducts both field and museum-based research. Coordinates research projects with Department of Biology courses and emphasizes graduate and undergraduate student research participation. Databases: Cover individual research projects. Special Resources: Houses approximately 42,000 vertebrate research specimens, including 20,000 fish, 2,000 reptiles and amphibians, 2,200 birds, and 18,000 mammals.

★3913★ Vineyard Environmental Research Institute (VERI)
RFD 862
Martha's Vineyard Airport
Tisbury, MA 02568
Phone: (508)693-4632
Contact: William E. Marks, Exec. V. Pres.
Research Areas: Environmental studies, including acid rain, groundwater, metal mobilization, estuaries, wetlands, ponds, forestry, and erosion control. The Institute is a state-certified laboratory for water testing. Special Resources: Maintains three lighthouses.

★3914★ Virginia Center for Coal and Energy Research
Virginia Polytechnic Inst. and State Univ.
617 N. Main St.
Blacksburgh, VA 24060-0411
Phone: (703)231-5038
Contact: Dr. John Randolph, Dir.
Research Areas: Virginia energy policy and economy, including coal cleaning, conversion, and combustion; mined land reclamation; mine safety; mining techniques; coal transport and marketing; coal field economy; electrical power; energy consumption and efficiency; environmental issues relating to energy production and use; oil and natural gas; renewable energy (including wind and solar); and nuclear energy. Databases: Virginia Coal and Energy Data System; Virginia Coal Mine License Directory.

★3915★ Virginia Cooperative Fish and Wildlife Research Unit
Virginia Polytechnic Inst. and State Univ.
106 Cheatham Hall
Blacksburg, VA 24061-0321
Phone: (703)231-5927
Fax: (703)231-3330
Contact: Dr. Richard Neves, Unit Leader
Research Areas: Mussel biology, fisheries ecology, wildlife management, population dynamics, behavior, limnology, and pollution biology, emphasizing stream ecology, wildlife ecology, and endangered species. Special Resources: Maintains wet laboratory and behavior laboratory facilities.

★3916★ Virginia Institute of Marine Science-School of Marine Science
College of William and Mary
Gloucester Point, VA 23062
Phone: (804)642-7000
Fax: (804)642-7097
Contact: Dr. Frank O. Perkins, Dean and Dir.
Research Areas: Fundamental and applied marine science emphasizing research on Chesapeake Bay, including mathematical modelling, geology, physical and biological oceanography, fisheries biology, marine geology of estuarine and inshore oceanic waters, invertebrate ecology, aquatic toxicology, wetlands ecology, environmental engineering, marine resources management, coastal resources management, and ocean and coastal law. Areas also include environmental toxicology, ichthyology, malacology, crustaceology, microbiology, pathology, parasitology, physiology, chemical oceanography, benthic ecology, planktology, pollution, and sedimentation. Special Resources: Side scan sonar, REMOTS camera system, Del Norte Trisponder, AMR scanning electron microscope, Zeiss transmission electron microscope, and a DeHaviland U-6 aircraft. Databases: Hydrological and environmental parameters of historical fisheries.

★3917★ Vitreous State Laboratory
Catholic Univ. of America
620 Michigan Ave., NE
Washington, DC 20064
Phone: (202)319-5327
Fax: (202)319-4469
Contact: Dr. P.B. Macedo, Codirector
Research Areas: Structure and dynamics of glassy and liquid states, vitrification of nuclear wastes, and treatment processes for mixed and radioactive wastes. Uses ICPMS, DCP, IC, electron microscopy, small angle X-ray ultrasonic, and laser light scattering techniques to characterize materials and probe kinetics of microstructure growth and mechanisms of transport in liquids.

★3918★ Waste Management Education and Research Consortium (WERC)
New Mexico State University
Box 30001
Dept. 3805
Las Cruces, NM 88003-0001
Phone: (505)646-2038
Fax: (505)646-4149
Contact: Ron Bhada, Dir.
Research Areas: Waste management, including studies of hazardous, radioactive, and solid waste management.

★3919★ Waste Management Institute
State Univ. of New York at Stony Brook
Stony Brook, NY 11794-5000
Phone: (703)771-6800
Contact: Dr. Bill Wise
Research Areas: Regional waste management problems of New York and their effect on surrounding states, including waste disposal and recycling. WMI investigates the economic effect of flotable waterborne waste materials and debris on tourism and marine recreational industries; studies degradable plastics, including a cornstarch-based degradable polyethylene plastic and the rate of degradation in soils, landfills and compost sites, and marine environments; evaluates toxicants in the food web; researches the biogeochemical processes affecting organic compounds, primarily hydrophobic pollutant compounds, in coastal, estuarine, and groundwater environments; examines the physical and chemical characteristics of ash from incinerators; studies the development of blocks from incinerator ash to build reefs; and investigates the use of incinerator ash in the production of asphalt for paving highway roads. Also collaborates on a shell disease research project with the Living Marine Resources Institute.

★3920★ Waste Management Research and Education Institute
University of Tennessee at Knoxville
327 S. Stadium Hall
Knoxville, TN 37996-0710
Phone: (615)974-4251
Contact: Dr. E. William Colglazier, Dir.
Research Areas: Chemical, radioactive, solid and mixed waste issues. Institute examines the interface between corporate, regulatory and public interests. Also conducts research on biotechnological use of microorganisms to solve environmental problems.

★3921★ Waste Management Research and Education Institute
University of Tennessee at Knoxville
327 S. Stadium Hall
Knoxville, TN 37996-0710
Phone: (615)974-4251
Contact: Dr. E. William Colglazier, Dir.
Research Areas: Chemical, nuclear, and solid waste management, especially waste policy and environmental biotechnology studies. Three main areas of waste policy research are 1) issues of hazardous waste management, including trends in waste generation, the need for new treatment, storage, and disposal (TSD) facilities, siting criteria for waste management facilities, alternative siting processes, and means to encourage waste reduction; 2) issues of public acceptance in management of both hazardous and radioactive wastes, including understanding public risk perceptions, use of risk assessment and risk management as tools in setting environmental regulations, strategies for public involvement, and ways of compensating communities which accept waste treatment or disposal facilities; and 3) radioactive and mixed waste policy issues, emphasizing policy conflicts, technical controversies, institutional obstacles, and siting disputes in both highand low-level waste management. Areas of interests in environmental biotechnology include isolation and microbial strain improvement for developing microorganisms with greater capacity for destruction of hazardous wastes and environmental contaminants, evaluation of microbial degradation processes contributing to overall contaminant fate predictions in a given system, systems analysis to determine dynamic stability and enhance knowledge of community structure and critical processes, and biological destruction of hazardous wastes and environmental contaminants.

★3922★ Waste Systems Institute of Michigan, Inc.
400 Ann NW , Ste. 204
Grand Rapids, MI 49504-2054
Phone: (616)363-3262
Contact: Jeffrey L. Dauphin, Exec. Dir.
Research Areas: Provides information research services on topics related to solid and hazardous waste management, hazardous waste reduction stategies, toxic substances, and pollution control in Michigan and internationally. Conducts research on markets for solid and hazardous waste materials and uses thereof in association with Great Lakes/ Atlantic Waste Exchange (initiated by the Institute in 1982) and Pacific Materials Exchange (Spokane, WA). Also studies small business environmental management and compliance problems. Recently investigated management systems for small quantities of hazardous wastes and the development of waste management assistance centers. Special Resources: Maintains indexing and management systems for the Michigan Hazardous Waste Management Act and for Small Quantity Hazardous Waste Generators. Works with several companies to supply and maintain Envirox, a multiuser, mainframe-supported database on waste exchange, environmental management, and legislative tracking. Other databases include Michigan Waste Types & Volumes, International Waste Exchange, and a ten-year data/information base for waste management activities in Michigan.

★3923★ Water and Energy Research Institute of the Western Pacific (WERI)
University of Guam
UOG Station, GU 96923
Phone: (671)734-3132
Fax: (671)734-3118
Contact: Dr. Shahram Khosrowpanah, Acting Dir.
Research Areas: Fresh water and alternate energy resources, including hydroelectric technology, engineering hydrology and hydraulic, wastewater disposal, groundwater resources, water quality, coastal engineering, affluent dispersal and movement, erosion control, and cultural impact of water and energy development projects. Special Resources: Operates a laboratory for water quality analysis. Maintains a collection of reports on water topics relevant to the area.

★3924★ Water Center
University of Nebraska-Lincoln
103 Natural Resources Hall
Lincoln, NE 68583-0844
Phone: (402)472-3305
Fax: (402)472-3574
Contact: Dale Vanderholm, Interim Dir.
Research Areas: Water quantity management, water use efficiency and conservation (supply and demand management), water quality, and legal, institutional, economic, and social aspects of water resources. Coordinates and administers water-related activities within existing units of Nebraska's post-secondary education system. Research results applied to water problems of Nebraska, the surrounding region, and the nation.

★3925★ Water Chemistry Program
University of Wisconsin-Madison
660 N. Park St.
Madison, WI 53706
Phone: (608)262-2470
Contact: D.E. Armstrong, Head
Research Areas: Chemistry of hazardous organic compounds in lakes, atmospheric input of chemicals into lakes, trace metal chemistry in lakes, adsorption reactions at particle surfaces in aqueous systems, photochemical reactions on oxide surfaces, and ceramic membrane studies.

★3926★ Water Pollution Control Federation Research Foundation
601 Wythe St.
Alexandria, VA 22314-1994
Phone: (703)684-2400
Contact: Glenn Reinhardt, Dir.
Research Areas: Water pollution control, including groundwater, toxic substances, hazardous wastes, and the nature, collection, treatment, and disposal of domestic and industrial wastewater. Addresses water quality issues with the goal of finding publically acceptable, cost-effective, environmentally sound solutions for water pollution prevention and abatement.

★3927★ Water Quality Laboratory
Western Illinois Univ.
Dept. of Chemistry
Macomb, IL 61455
Phone: (309)298-1356
Contact: Dr. Robert E. Neas, Dir.
Research Areas: Analysis of environmental samples, primarily water samples, including potable waters and natural waters.

★3928★ Water Quality Laboratory
Western Wyoming Coll.
PO Box 428
Rock Springs, WY 82901
Phone: (307)382-2121
Contact: Craig Thompson, Dir.
Research Areas: Water quality, including trace metal analysis of glacier core samples, studies on phosphorous and nitrogen, research on total salt loading in the Green River Basin, studies on nutrient dynamics in ephemeral streams in arid regions, and monitoring of ground and stream waters for drainage impact of development.

★3929★ Water Quality Laboratory
Heidelberg Coll.
Tiffin, OH 44883
Phone: (419)448-2201
Contact: Dr. David Baker, Dir.
Research Areas: Conducts research and monitoring activities in support of water quality management programs in the Great Lakes region. Operates a long-term, large-scale agricultural ecosystem study in the agricultural river basins emptying into Lake Erie. Specializes in quantification of effects of land use activities on surface and groundwater quality, including measurements of sediments, nutrients and pesticides. Long-term goals include evaluation of the effects of changing agricultural technology, especially the adoption of conservation tillage, on regional water quality. Other studies include wetland processing of pollutants, pesticide removal at water treatment plants, and rainfall deposition of pesticides. Special Resources: Maintains an automated analytical laboratory for nutrients, sediments, and current generation pesticides. Also maintains a database on nutrient, sediment, and pesticide concentrations in selected Lake Erie tributaries and on nitrate contamination in private rural wells throughout Ohio.

★3930★ Water Quality Research Laboratory
Oklahoma State Univ.
Stillwater, OK 74074
Phone: (405)744-5551
Contact: Dr. Sterling L. Burks, Dir.
Research Areas: Biological aspects of water pollution, including transport, fate, and effect of water pollutants, ecotoxicology, analysis of pollutants with chromatography-mass spectrometry, atomic absorption, and bioassays with aquatic organisms. Also sponsors theses research on doctoral level.

★3931★ Water Research Center
University of Alaska Fairbanks
Fairbanks, AK 99775-1760
Phone: (907)474-7350
Fax: (907)474-6087
Contact: Dr. Douglas L. Kane, Dir.
Research Areas: Water and other resources related to water, with emphasis on water resource environment of Alaska. Studies include water quality management, biological effects of pollution, water resource economics, hydrodynamics, physical, chemical, and biological waste treatment in cold climates, hydrology of arctic regions with special emphasis on techniques that are useful in sparse data regions, effects of thermal discharges into arctic streams, environmental planning in developing recreational areas, effects of urbanization on watersheds, pathways of pollutants in natural water systems, environmental effects of development on lakes and streams, hydrogeochemistry, biotechnology, environmental microbiology, alternative (especially solar) energy, acid mine drainage, environmental effects of oil development on estuaries and estuarine ecology, and water law.

★3932★ Water Research Institute
West Virginia Univ.
Morgantown, WV 26506
Phone: (304)293-2757
Contact: Charles R. Jenkins, Dir.
Research Areas: Water resources problems of the state with emphasis on biological and geochemical aspects of water quality, acid mine drainage control, groundwater contamination, wastewater treatment, and public policy.

★3933★ Water Resources Center
University of Wisconsin-Madison
1975 Willow Dr.
Madison, WI 53706
Phone: (608)262-3577
Fax: (608)262-0591
Contact: Prof. Gordon Chesters, Dir.
Research Areas: Water and other resources that affect water, including interdisciplinary studies on methods for management of water quality, criteria for such regulation, problems of administration and enforcement, eutrophication, and economics of water quality, management, and control. Coordinates research on water resources at the University, at other colleges and universities in Wisconsin, and at state agencies.

★3934★ Water Resources Center
University of Rhode Island
202 Bliss Hall
Kingston, RI 02881
Phone: (401)792-2297
Fax: (401)782-1066
Contact: Dr. Calvin P.G. Poon, Dir.
Research Areas: Water pricing structure and water policy in Rhode Island; water quality and trophic state of Rhode Island lakes and the Scituate Reservoir; impact of composted organic wastes on turf and groundwater quality; use of composted material for landfill cover; leachate studies of simulated incinerator ash landfill; electroflotation process for metal and cyanide removal; and technology transfer. Conducts and coordinates research on water resources at the University and within the state and trains scientists and engineers.

★3935★ Water Resources Center
University of Illinois
2535 Hydrosystems Laboratory
205 N. Mathews Ave.
Urbana, IL 61801
Phone: (217)333-0536
Fax: (217)333-8046
Contact: Dr. Glenn E. Stout, Dir.
Research Areas: Water and other resources which affect water, including studies in agricultural, civil, and environmental engineering, hydraulics, theoretical and applied mechanics, geology, hydrogeology, agricultural and natural resource economics, forestry, agronomy, climatology, life sciences, and law. Supports and coordinates research on all areas of water resources conducted in academic departments of the University and associated state scientific survey organizations, as well as other universities in Illinois.

★3936★ Water Resources Center
University of Delaware
210 Hullihen Hall
Newark, DE 19716
Phone: (302)451-2191
Fax: (302)451-2828
Contact: Dr. Robert D. Varrin, Dir.
Research Areas: Water and other resources which affect water, including basic and practical

studies on supply, use, conservation, and reuse of water. Also studies wastewater reclamation, economic, governmental, and other social aspects of water resource development, groundwater flow, and water use efficiency in agriculture. Established under Water Resources Research Act of 1964, Public Law 88-379; authorized currently under Water Research Act of 1984, Public Law 98-242, to conduct and coordinate research activities to assure the state and surrounding region of a supply of water sufficient in quantity and quality to meet requirements of its expanding population and economy. Assists in training of scientists for research on water resources problems.

★3937★ Water Resources Center
Texas Tech Univ.
Box 4630
Lubbock, TX 79409
Phone: (806)742-3597
Contact: Dr. Lloyd V. Urban, Dir.
Research Areas: Water quality, hydrology, in situ groundwater quality restoration, artificial recharge, municipal water conservation, and management, use, and conservation of water resources, including studies in several areas of agriculture, engineering, and basic sciences.

★3938★ Water Resources Center
Ohio State Univ.
262 Agriculture Bldg.
590 Woody Hayes Dr.
Columbus, OH 43210
Phone: (614)292-2334
Fax: (614)292-9448
Contact: Dr. Robert C. Stiefel, Dir.
Research Areas: Administers and coordinates research in the University and within the state on water and water-related problems, including water quality, hydrology, water and wastewater treatment, industrial waste treatment, and water resource economics. Trains scientists and technicians in water management.

★3939★ Water Resources Institute
University of Kansas
Lawrence, KS 66045
Phone: (913)864-3807
Contact: Dr. Ernest E. Angino, Dir.
Research Areas: Water and other resources which affect water, including studies on water quality, scientific and engineering hydrology, stream and lake regimen, fluid dynamics, and water management. Coordinates research on water and water-related resources by investigators in various departments at the University of Kansas and with Kansas Water Resources Research Institute at Kansas State University. Established under Water Resources Research Act of 1964, Public Law 88-379, to conduct and coordinate research on water resources at the University and other institutions in the state and to train scientists in this field.

★3940★ Water Resources Institute
South Dakota State Univ.
Brookings, SD 57007
Phone: (605)688-4910
Fax: (605)688-6065
Contact: Mylo Hellickson, Acting Dir.
Research Areas: Conducts and coordinates University research in water and related resources, especially those concerned with the agricultural effect on lakes, streams, and groundwater, including the plant, soil, and groundwater continuum. Specific concerns include irrigation technology, water management, water supply (hydrologic quantity and quality), water use, non-point source pollution, lake management, watershed studies, and water treatment. Databases: Water quality, soil chemical, and land use. Special Resources: Operates hydraulics lab, water quality lab (for drinking water certification), and pesticide lab.

★3941★ Water Resources Institute
Grand Valley State Univ.
Allendale, MI 49401
Phone: (616)895-3749
Fax: (616)895-3864
Contact: Dr. Ronald W. Ward, Dir.
Research Areas: Water resources, focusing on groundwater, fisheries, the Great Lakes, and Michigan watersheds (including the Grand River watershed). Other areas of interest include science education and information systems research. Special Resources: Maintains a research vessel, the D.J. Angus, for operation on Lake Michigan and its tributaries.

★3942★ Water Resources Research Center
University of New Hampshire
218 Science & Engineering Research Bldg.
Durham, NH 03824
Phone: (603)862-2144
Fax: (603)862-2364
Contact: Thomas P. Ballestero, Dir.
Research Areas: Water and other resources which affect water, including interdisciplinary studies on water quality, pollution, supply, and demand, and on the socioeconomics of water resources. Established to conduct and coordinate research at the University on water resources and to train scientists in this field.

★3943★ Water Resources Research Center
University of Minnesota
Ste. 302
1518 Cleveland Ave.
St. Paul, MN 55108
Phone: (612)624-9282
Fax: (612)625-1263
Contact: Prof. Patrick L. Brezonik, Dir.
Research Areas: Water and other resources which affect water, including modeling and prediction of water and pollutant transport in Minnesota aquifers, on-site biodegradation of organic pollutants in contaminated soils and groundwater, tracking agricultural and industrial pollutants through karst hydrologic systems, effects of climatic change on Minnesota's water resources, development of loading-response relationships for acid-sensitive lakes, groundwater pollution by human and animal enteric viruses, development of new methods to assess nutrient limitation and trophic status of lakes, mercury sources and cycling in wilderness lakes, innovative physico-chemical methods to treat toxic and hazardous wastes, and effects of wetlands on downstream water quality. Coordinates University research with water resources programs throughout the state and assists in training of additional scientists for work in this field.

★3944★ Water Resources Research Center
University of Hawaii at Manoa
2540 Dole St.
Honolulu, HI 96822
Phone: (808)948-7847
Fax: (808)956-5044
Contact: Dr. L. Stephen Law
Research Areas: Water resources (terrestrial/coastal), including multidisciplinary studies in hydrology, hydraulic engineering, economics, geohydrology, geochemistry, microbiology, sanitary engineering, public health, climatology, soil physics, agricultural engineering, agricultural economics, law, meteorology, zoology, and ocean engineering. Conducts water resource activities in Hawaii and the Pacific Basin area. Databases: Streamflow, rainfall, evapotranspiration, and solar radiation. Special Resources: Maintains two deep research wells, one stream gauge station, rain gauges, evaporimeters, global pyranometers, environmental virology, water quality, water bacteriology, and soil-hydrology laboratories.

★3945★ Water Resources Research Center
University of Florida
424 Black Hall
Gainesville, FL 32611
Phone: (904)392-0840
Fax: (904)392-3076
Contact: Dr. J.P. Heaney, Dir.
Research Areas: Agricultural, biological, chemical, economic, engineering, geological, hydrological, legal, and sociological aspects of water and water-related resources. Established under Water Resources Research Act of 1964, Public Law 88-379, to conduct and coordinate research in Florida universities in relation to water resources and to train scientists in that field. Databases: Florida lakes.

★3946★ Water Resources Research Center
University of Arizona
350 N. Campbell
Tucson, AZ 85721
Phone: (602)621-7607
Fax: (602)621-8518
Contact: Prof. Hanna J. Cortner, Dir.
Research Areas: Works with government agencies and concerned public and private organizations to identify and address critical water problems in the state of Arizona and the southwest U.S. Areas of study include water conservation, urban hydrology, artificial and natural groundwater recharge, water quality, supply enhancement and augmentation, policy, and water resource management. Databases: Water-related numerical information; directory of water investigators at the Universities.

★3947★ Water Resources Research Center
Purdue Univ.
School of Civil Engineering
West Lafayette, IN 47907
Phone: (317)494-8041
Fax: (317)494-0395
Contact: Jeff R. Wright, Dir.
Research Areas: Water and resources that affect water. Established under Water Resource Research Act of 1964, Public Law 88-379; authorized currently under Water Resources Research Act of 1984, Public Law 98-242, to conduct and coordinate research on water resources at Indiana universities and within the state. Trains scientists in water resource management and collaborates with various departments of the University concerned with water resources.

★3948★ Water Resources Research Center
University of Tennessee at Knoxville
Knoxville, TN 37996
Phone: (615)974-2151
Fax: (615)974-1838
Contact: Dr. E. William Colglaizer, Dir.
Research Areas: Water and other resources that affect water, including studies on agricultural runoff and water use, biological and ecological effects of altering the aquatic environment, water and wastewater treatment processes, occurrence of natural and

introduced pollutants, modeling of water quality and hydrology, fish farming and aquaculture, dam safety, remote sensing, aquatic weed control, economics and law of water management, water research management, and social, political, and institutional interactions of water management. Conducts and coordinates research on water resources at the University of Tennessee at Knoxville and other academic institutions of the state and supports information and technology transfer.

★3949★ Water Resources Research Center
University of the Virgin Islands
St. Thomas, VI 00802
Phone: (809)776-9200
Contact: Dr. J. Hari Krishna, Dir.
Research Areas: Water quality and quantity in the Virgin Islands. Specific research involves cistern water quality and domestic water conservation development. Uses computer models to predict rainfall variability.

★3950★ Water Resources Research Institute
Kent State Univ.
McGilvery Hall
Kent, OH 44242-0001
Phone: (216)672-2529
Contact: Dr. Donald F. Palmer, Dir.
Research Areas: Water-related issues and resources, including limnology, lake and reservoir management, lake biogeochemistry, aquatic entomology, phycology, microbial ecology, heavy metal and organic material interaction, water policy, meteorology, climatology, land-use planning, ground water exploration, water quantity and quality evaluation, surface drainage, flooding, erosion, acid mine drainage, water chemistry, environmental chambers and experimental systems, and computer modeling and analysis.

★3951★ Water Resources Research Institute
Oregon State Univ.
210 Strand Agriculture Hall
Corvallis, OR 97331-2208
Phone: (503)737-4022
Fax: (503)737-3178
Contact: Benno P. Warkentin, Dir.
Research Areas: Biological, economic, legal, and physical aspects of water resources, including studies on water supply and quality, planning and management, systems analysis, water uses and use impact, watershed management, water and soil relations, irrigation and drainage, water pollution, stream ecology, water bacteriology, waste treatment, hydrology, and hydraulics.

★3952★ Water Resources Research Institute
Mississippi State Univ.
P.O. Drawer AD
Mississippi State, MS 39762
Phone: (601)325-3620
Contact: Dr. Marvin T. Bond, Dir.
Research Areas: Water and resources that affect water, including both basic and applied studies in agricultural engineering, business and economics, civil engineering, forestry, geology, microbiology, social science, and wildlife management in connection with the development, use, and conservation of water resources. Specific topics include control of pollutants in surface water, water quality in aquaculture, water management, sediment transport, and industrial and municipal conservation.

★3953★ Water Resources Research Institute
Clemson Univ.
223 Strom Thurmond Bldg.
Clemson, SC 29634-2900
Phone: (803)656-3271
Fax: (803)656-4780
Contact: Dr. Paul B. Zielinski, Dir.
Research Areas: Water and water resources, including studies on hydrology, soil and water relationships, sedimentation, water quality, water supply, drainage, irrigation, water policy, industrial use of water, taxes and subsidies, water recreation, estuary quality, thermal loading, thermal stress, siting powerplants, planning techniques, and water resources modeling. Continued under Water Resources Research Act of 1984, Public Law 98-242, to conduct and coordinate research on water and resources that affect water.

★3954★ Water Resources Research Institute (WRRI)
Auburn Univ.
202 Hargis Hall
Auburn University, AL 36849-5124
Phone: (205)844-5080
Contact: Dr. Joseph F. Judkins Jr., Dir.
Research Areas: Water and resources which affect water, including studies on aquatic weed control, protecting the quality of groundwater, water resource planning and economics, fisheries biology and management, geochemistry, geophysics, hydrology, hydraulics, management of run-off water, movement of water through soil, pollution control, impact of water on farming and industry, waste treatment, privatization of public wastewater facilities, and water economics and law.

★3955★ Wayne State University C.S. Mott Center for Human Growth and Development
275 E. Hancock St.
Detroit, MI 48201
Phone: (313)577-1068
Contact: Dr. Ernest L. Abel, Director
Research Areas: Studies the relationships between environmental deterioration, dwindling natural resources, population density, and quality of human existence. Develops and implements population controls.

★3956★ Weather Analysis
University of Michigan
Atmospheric, Oceanic, & Space Dept.
2455 Hayward
Ann Arbor, MI 48109-2143
Phone: (313)764-3335
Contact: Prof. Steve Mullen, Dir.
Research Areas: Atmospheric science, including design of wind- and turbulence-sensing instruments, theoretical studies of atmospheric energetics and predictability, empirical studies of scavenging of pollutants by precipitation, assessment and prediction of the environmental impact of power plant cooling methods, and the immediate and climatological effects of large rockets and high-flying aircraft. Special Resources: Laboratories include special facilities for cloud physics and air quality research, meteorological instrumentation and electronics laboratories, a wind tunnel, a climatological station, and airways teletype for weather information. Off-campus facilities include instrumentation towers for micrometeorological research and a network of surface recording stations for mesometeorological research.

★3957★ Wells National Estuarine Research Reserve
Laudholm Trust
PO Box 1007
Wells, ME 04090
Phone: (207)646-4521
Contact: Morton Mather, Director
A 250-acre coastal research and educational facility. Supports hundreds of species of wildlife. Offers public tours, exhibits, and hands-on educational tools.

★3958★ West Virginia Agricultural and Forestry Experiment Station
West Virginia Univ.
College of Agriculture & Forestry
Evansdale Campus
PO Box 6108
Morgantown, WV 26506
Phone: (304)293-2395
Contact: Dr. Robert Maxwell, Dir.
Research Areas: Agricultural biochemistry and nutrition, agricultural engineering, environmental protection, land reclamation, bacteriology, dairy science, entomology, forestry, wood science, wildlife, recreation and parks, horticulture, plant pathlogy, soil and land use, poultry science, and veterinary science.

★3959★ Western Research Center
Rural Rte.
Castana, IA 51010
Phone: (712)885-2802
Contact: Bob Burcham, Superintendent
Research Areas: Soil and water loss, soil fertility, and soil management, including studies on tillage methods, fertilizers, crop varieties, herbicides, insecticides, improved pasture management, livestock feeding trials, pasture farrowing swine, horticulture, and sustainable agriculture.

★3960★ Weston Institute
Weston Way
West Chester, PA 19380
Phone: (215)430-3100
Fax: (215)692-6503
Contact: William Gaither, Dir.
Research Areas: Environmental and health problems.

★3961★ Wetland Center
Duke Univ.
School of Forestry & Environmental Studies
Durham, NC 27706
Phone: (919)684-2619
Fax: (919)684-8741
Contact: Dr. Curtis J. Richardson, Dir.
Research Areas: Researches wetlands, including cattail invasions of and phosphorus cycling in the everglades.

★3962★ Wetlands Research Area
Unity Coll.
Unity, ME 04988
Phone: (207)948-3131
Fax: (207)948-5626
Contact: Joel Dickinson, Academic Dean
Research Areas: Wetlands ecology, focusing on wood duck nesting, feeding habits of wintering bald eagles, burr oak floodplains ecology, and fishery studies. Special Resources: Small working collection of local vertebrates.

★3963★ Whole-Body Counter
Colorado State Univ.
Dept. of Radiation Biology
Fort Collins, CO 80523
Phone: (303)491-5380
Contact: Dr. James E. Johnson, Dir.
Research Areas: Natural and man-made radioactivity transport in the environment.

Measures radioactivity in food chains and models results. Conducts high resolution gamma ray spectrometry analyses.

★3964★ Wilderness Institute
University of Montana
Forestry Bldg., Rm. 207
Missoula, MT 59812
Phone: (406)243-5361
Contact: Dr. Alan McQuilan, Exec. Dir.
Research Areas: Management of wilderness resources. Field studies have involved natural resource inventories, geographic information systems, wilderness inventories, recreational use studies, and documentation of potential boundaries for proposed wilderness legislation. Databases: All 470 units of the National Wilderness Preservation System.

★3965★ Wilderness Research Center
University of Idaho
Moscow, ID 83843
Phone: (208)885-7911
Contact: Ed Krumpe, Dir.
Research Areas: Wilderness, including studies on dynamic process of natural ecosystems, proper use and management of wilderness, human values and benefits of wilderness, and wildlife. Conducts comparative experimentation on man-altered environments versus natural, unaltered ecosystems.

★3966★ Wildland Management Center
University of Michigan
School of Natural Resources
430 E. Univ.
Ann Arbor, MI 48109-1115
Phone: (313)763-1312
Contact: Paul Nowak, Dir.
Research Areas: Management of wildland systems-land and water systems in which natural processes retain sufficient integrity to maintain and restore regime characteristics. Promotes the management of the Earth's wild species and natural ecosystems to enable human needs to be met on a sustainable basis. Encourages research that is likely to have practical consequences. Participates in the Eastern Caribbean Natural Areas Management Program, a collaborative effort to enhance the ability of several Caribbean nations to effectively manage natural resources.

★3967★ Wildland Resources Center
University of California
145 Mulford Hall
Berkeley, CA 94720
Phone: (415)642-0263
Fax: (415)643-5438
Contact: Don C. Erman, Dir.
Research Areas: Wildland problems, including biological, social, and economic aspects of the protection, management, and use of wildland soils and vegetation. Also studies forestry, range, watershed, and wildlife management in California in relation to the use of wildlands for commodity production and recreational, wilderness, and protective services. Coordinates research and extension activities in these areas at the Agricultural Experiment Station and various departments of the University of California. Serves as a liaison between 840 University faculty and staff on eight campuses and 34 county offices.

★3968★ Wisconsin Applied Water Pollution Research Consortium
Univ. of Wisconsin-Madison
3204 Engineering Bldg.
1415 Johnson Dr.
Madison, WI 53706
Phone: (608)262-7248
Contact: Prof. P. Mac Berthouex, Dir.
Research Areas: Pollution control technology and policy, toxic and hazardous waste treatment and management, groundwater protection and cleanup, geotechnical investigations, risk assessment, systems operation, and process design and optimization. Special Resources: Laboratory and fermenters and reactors for treatability studies.

★3969★ Wisconsin Rural Development Center
1406 Bus. Hwy. 18-151 E.
Mount Horeb, WI 53572
Phone: (608)437-5971
Contact: Denny Caneff, Exec. Dir.
Research Areas: Sustainable agriculture, emphasizing no-chemical weed control in row crops, alternative fertilizers for dairy farms, rotational grazing for sheep and dairy, and soil microbial life in organic farming systems. Investigates and promotes rural economic development strategies, including heritage tourism and self-employment education in rural high schools.

★3970★ W.M. Keck Laboratory of Hydraulics and Water Resources
California Inst. of Technology
138-78
Pasadena, CA 91125
Phone: (818)356-4404
Fax: (818)356-2940
Contact: Dr. Norman H. Brooks
Research Areas: Water resources, hydraulics and hydraulic structures, coastal engineering, water pollution control, thermal pollution, sediment transportation, materials science, applied physics, air pollution, and water chemistry.

★3971★ Woods Hole Oceanographic Institution
Woods Hole, MA 02543
Phone: (508)457-2000
Fax: (508)457-2190
Contact: Dr. Craig E. Dorman, Dir.
Research Areas: All aspects of oceanography and related problems in five interrelated departments: biology, including microbiology, biochemistry, physiology, ecology, planktonology, ichthyology, benthic biology, marine pollution, marine mammal acoustics, and animal behavior; chemistry, including studies in organic and inorganic chemistry, biochemistry, geochemistry, radiochemistry, and sea water chemistry; geology and geophysics, which examines the structure and evolution of the earth beneath the sea floor through studies in seismic reflection and refraction, magnetism, gravity, heat flow, ocean acoustics, sea floor bathymetry, and micropaleontology; physical oceanography, including studies on physical characteristics of the sea (its temperature, salinity, currents, and other motions) and studies on the interaction of the sea with its boundaries, the atmosphere above, the sea floor below, and the shoreline; and ocean engineering, which studies acoustics and microstructure, supplies engineering and analytical services for conducting research and development in ocean-related subjects, and develops and studies instruments in acoustics, deep submergence engineering and operations, information processing, instrumentation, and ocean structures, moorings, and materials. Also operates three interdepartmental programs, the Coastal Research Center, the Marine Policy and Ocean Management Center, which conducts research on the social, economic, and political aspects of problems generated by man's use of the sea, and the Center for Marine Exploration. Special Resources: Maintains a fleet of five research vessels, including two which are more than 200 feet in length with ranges of 8,000 to 10,000 miles, and the 25-foot submersible, Alvin, which can dive to more than 13,000 feet.

★3972★ World Resources Institute
1709 New York Ave., NW, Ste. 700
Washington, DC 20006
Phone: (202)638-6300
Fax: (202)638-0036
Contact: James Gustave Speth, Pres.
Research Areas: Policy research and analysis addressed to global resource and environmental issues, including freshwater resources, agricultural lands and desertification, genetic diversity and species conservation, tropical deforestation, fisheries and ocean resources, inadvertent climate modification (including build up of carbon dioxide in the atmosphere), ozone depletion, energy resources and nonfuel minerals, multipollutants in the atmosphere, resource management needs of Africa, role of economic incentives and subsidies in shaping resource management in less developed countries, impact of the debt crisis on resource management programs in less developed nations, technology transfer, and loss of plant and animal habitat. Databases: World Resources Report (containing environment data).

★3973★ World Wildlife Fund and the Conservation Foundation, Inc.
1250 24th St., NW
Washington, DC 20037
Phone: (202)293-4800
Fax: (202)293-9211
Contact: Kathryn S. Fuller, Pres.
Research Areas: International field activities in the areas of environmental trends and institutions, environmental dispute resolution, land use (land conservation and international development, rural resources, public lands management, and urban conservation), biodiversity, habitat protection, sustainable development, water resources, and air pollution and toxic substances control.

★3974★ Worldwatch Institute
1776 Massachusetts Ave., NW
Washington, DC 20036
Phone: (202)452-1999
Fax: (202)296-7365
Contact: Lester R. Brown, Pres.
Research Areas: Global trends in the availability and management of both human and natural resources, including research in energy, food policy, population, development, technology, the environment, economics, toxics, and recycling.

★3975★ Worldwatch Institute
1776 Massachusetts Ave., NW
Washington, DC 20036
Phone: (202)452-1999
Fax: (202)296-7365
Contact: Lester R. Brown, President
Research Areas: Global trends in the availability and management of both human and natural resources, including reserch in energy, food policy, population, development, technology, the environment, economics, toxics, and recycling.

★3976★ Wye Research and Education Center
University of Maryland
Box 169
Queenstown, MD 21658
Phone: (301)827-6202
Fax: (301)827-9039
Contact: Russell B. Brinsfield, Center Head
Research Areas: Agricultural research in the following areas: Integrated pest management, including pest population dynamics, plant diseases, and control tactics and monitoring techniques based on economics; energy development, use, and conservation, including alternative crops for energy sources, new technologies and management strategies, and advances in no-tillage and minimum tillage systems of crop management; quality of life, including impact of broad changes in agriculture on rural America and the physical, social, and community surroundings that add aesthetically to the environment; and interaction of land and water on agriculture and aquaculture, including nutrient, sediment, and pesticide movement through agricultural watersheds, designs for vegetated buffers to control nutrient loss, impact of acid rain on ecosystems, and models of pond aquaculture production. Databases: Wye Angus herd history.

★3977★ Wyoming Cooperative Fishery and Wildlife Research Unit
Univ. of Wyoming
Box 3166, Univ. Sta.
Laramie, WY 82071
Phone: (307)766-5415
Fax: (307)766-5630
Contact: Dr. Stanley H. Anderson, Unit Leader
Research Areas: Fishery and wildlife habitats in northern Rocky Mountain ecosystems and endangered species.

★3978★ Yale Institute of Biospheric Studies
Yale Univ.
Osborne Memorial Laboratory
165 Prospect St.
New Haven, CT 06511
Phone: (203)432-3691
Contact: Dr. Leo Buss, Dir.
Research Areas: Biospheric and global environmental studies.

Educational Programs

This section lists education programs operating in the United States. Programs are arranged by area of emphasis, including academic, nature, professional, and youth programs.

Academic Programs

★3980★ Advanced Sciences Research and Development Corporation
Institute of Advanced Science
PO Box 127
Lakemont, GA 30552
Phone: (404)782-2092
Contact: Dr. Sarah Heronymus, Pres. /Research Dir.
A home study course.

★3981★ Alabama Photovoltaics Education Project
University of Alabama
Huntsville, AL 35899
Phone: (205)895-6361
Contact: Bernard M. Levine
Provides classroom demonstration kit and instruction manual.

★3982★ Alaska Cooperative Wildlife Research Unit
Univ. of Alaska Fairbanks
Fairbanks, AK 99775
Phone: (907)474-7673
Fax: (907)474-6967
Contact: Dr. David R. Klein, Unit Leader
Provides graduate training and seminars in population ecology.

★3983★ Alaska Cooperative Wildlife Research Unit
Conservation and Resource Management
Univ. of Alaska Fairbanks
Fairbanks, AK 99775
Phone: (907)474-7673
Fax: (907)474-6967
Contact: Dr. David R. Klein, Unit Leader
A short course offered biennially in February.

★3984★ Antioch New England Graduate School
103 Roxbury St.
Keene, NH 03431
Phone: (603)357-3122
Offers M.S. degrees in Environmental Studies; Resource Management and Administration. Subjects studied include environmental communications, education, and biology.

★3985★ Arizona State University
Center for Environmental Studies
Hazardous Waste Workshop
Tempe, AZ 85287-1201
Phone: (602)965-2975
Fax: (602)965-8087
Contact: Dr. Duncan T. Patten, Dir.
Sponsored bimonthly.

★3986★ Arizona State University
Center for Environmental Studies
Wildlife and Fisheries Management Programs
Tempe, AZ 85287
Phone: (602)965-3585
Offers undergraduate degree program.

★3987★ Arizona State University
Stable Isotope Laboratory
Geochemistry Graduate Program
Dept. of Geology
Tempe, AZ 85287-1404
Phone: (602)965-3731
Contact: L. Paul Knauth Ph.D., Dir.
Offers master's and doctoral degrees.

★3988★ Arizona State University
Stable Isotope Laboratory
Geology Graduate Program
Dept. of Geology
Tempe, AZ 85287-1404
Phone: (602)965-3731
Contact: L. Paul Knauth Ph.D., Dir.
Offers master's and doctoral degrees.

★3989★ Arizona State Unversity
Environmental Testing Laboratory
Building Design Program
School of Architecture
Tempe, AZ 85287-1605
Phone: (602)965-2764
Fax: (602)965-1594
Contact: M. Underhill, Head
Offers master's degrees.

★3990★ Arkansas State University
Wildlife Management Degree Program
State University, AR 72467
Phone: (501)972-3082
Offers undergraduate degree program.

★3991★ Auburn University
School of Forestry
108 M. White Smith Hall
Auburn, AL 36849
Phone: (205)844-1007
Offers university courses in forestry.

★3992★ Bard College
Graduate School of Environmental Studies
Annandale Rd.
Annandale, NY 12504
Phone: (914)758-6822
Offers M.S. degree in Environmental Studies. Fields of study include education, business, government, and public planning.

★3993★ Baylor University
Institute of Environmental Studies
Environmental Studies Graduate Degree Program
PO Box 97266
Waco, TX 76798-7266
Phone: (817)755-3406
Contact: Dr. W. Merle Alexander, Dir.

★3994★ Beloit College
Department of Biology
700 College Ave.
Beloit, WI 53511
Phone: (608)363-2287
Offers degree in environmental biology.

★3995★ Bemidji State University
Center for Environmental Studies
Peat and Regional Environmental Affairs Conference
Bemidji, MN 56601
Phone: (218)755-2910
Fax: (218)755-4048
Contact: Steven A. Spigarelli, Dir.

★3996★ Bio-Integral Resource Center
Integrated Pest Management Training Center
PO Box 7414
Berkeley, CA 94707
Phone: (415)524-2567
Fax: (415)524-1758
Contact: Dr. William Olkowski, Dir.

★3997★ Boston University
Center for Energy and Environmental Studies
Energy and Environmental Studies Degree Program
675 Commonwealth Ave.
Boston, MA 02215
Phone: (617)353-3083
Fax: (617)353-5986
Contact: Dr. T.R. Lakshmanan, Dir.

★3998★ Boston University
Center for Energy and Environmental Studies
International Relations and Resource and Environmental Management Degree Program
675 Commonwealth Ave.
Boston, MA 02215
Phone: (617)353-3083
Fax: (617)353-5986
Contact: Dr. T.R. Lakshmanan, Dir.
Offers a joint master's degree.

★3999★ Bowling Green State University
Center for Environmental Programs
Bowling Green, OH 43403
Phone: (419)372-8207

★4000★ Brown University
Urban Environmental Laboratory Soup Seminar
Box 1943
Providence, RI 02912
Phone: (401)863-2715
Fax: (401)863-3503
Contact: Harold Ward, Dir.
Held weekly.

★4001★ Butler University
Holcomb Research Institute
Groundwater Hydrology Short Course
4600 Sunset Ave.
Indianapolis, IN 46208
Phone: (317)283-9421
Fax: (317)283-9519
Contact: Paul K.M. van der Heijde, Dean
Held annually, March through July.

★4002★ Butler University
Holcomb Research Institute
Groundwater Modeling Short Course
4600 Sunset Ave.
Indianapolis, IN 46208
Phone: (317)283-9421
Fax: (317)283-9519
Contact: Paul K.M. van der Heijde, Dean
Held annually, March through July.

★4003★ California Institute of Technology
W.M. Keck Laboratory of Hydraulics and Water Resources Graduate Program
138-78
Pasadena, CA 91125
Phone: (818)356-4404
Fax: (818)356-2940
Contact: Dr. Norman H. Brooks
Offers master's and doctoral degrees in environmental engineering and hydraulics. Sponsors weekly seminars.

★4004★ California Polytechnic State University
Natural Resources Management and Soil Science and Conservation Degree Programs
San Luis Obispo, CA 93407
Phone: (805)546-0111
Contact: Dr. Norman H. Pillsbury, Head

★4005★ California State Polytechnic University
LANDLAB
Regenerative Studies Course
3801 W. Temple Ave.
Pomona, CA 91768
Phone: (714)869-4449
Fax: (714)869-2292
Contact: Dr. Edwin A. Barnes III, Dir.

★4006★ California State University at Hayward
Department of Teacher Education
Hayward, CA 94542
Phone: (415)881-3016
Program in environmental studies and leadership training.

★4007★ California State University
Biological Conservation Degree Program
Sacramento, CA 95819
Phone: (916)454-6752
Contact: Dr. David C. Vanicek, Director

★4008★ Center for Alaskan Coastal Studies
PO Box 2225
Homer, AK 99603
Phone: (907)235-6667
Conducts outdoor education focusing on northwest coast rainforest, forest ecology, and intertidal studies.

★4009★ Center for Environmental Research
IIT Research Institute
10 W. 35th St.
Chicago, IL 60616
Phone: (312)567-4250
Fax: (312)567-4577
Contact: Dr. Demetrios Moschandreas, Dir.
Offers bachelor's, master's, and doctoral degrees in science and engineering disciplines related to hazardous wastes and an environmental law program through Chicago-Kent College of Law. Also offers National Institute of Health Laboratory safety courses. Sponsors short courses for industrial and governmental hazardous materials managers. Holds seminars on advanced wastewater techniques and conferences on environmental aspects of real estate transfers.

★4010★ Center for Northern Studies
Circumpolar North
Wolcott, VT 05680
Phone: (802)888-4331
Contact: Dr. Steven B. Young, Dir.
In cooperation with Middlebury College, the Center offers a one-year course of study.

★4011★ Center for Northern Studies
Northern Studies Lecture Series
Wolcott, VT 05680
Phone: (802)888-4331
Contact: Dr. Steven B. Young, Dir.
Held weekly during the fall and spring semesters.

★4012★ City College of City University of New York
Institute of Marine and Atmospheric Sciences
Meteorology and Oceanography Graduate Research Training Program
Science Bldg.
138th St. & Convent Ave.
New York, NY 10031
Phone: (212)650-7000
Contact: Dr. Dennis Weiss, Dir.

★4013★ Claremont McKenna Colleges
Robert J. Bernard Biological Field Station Degree Program
Claremont, CA 91711
Phone: (714)621-5425
Contact: Clyde H. Ericksen, Dir.
Offers a bachelor of arts degree program.

★4014★ Clarkson University
Environmental Science and Engineering Program
Environmental Engineering Graduate Degree Programs
Rowley Laboratories
Potsdam, NY 13676
Phone: (315)268-3853
Contact: Dr. Thomas L. Theis, Professor
Grants master of science and doctoral degrees.

★4015★ Clarkson University
Environmental Science and Engineering Seminar Program
Rowley Laboratories
Potsdam, NY 13676
Phone: (315)268-3853
Contact: Dr. Thomas L. Theis, Professor
Sponsored for faculty, graduate students, and outside speakers.

★4016★ Clarkson University
Hazardous Waste and Toxic Substance Research and Management Center
Waste Management Degree Program
Rowley Laboratories
Potsdam, NY 13699
Phone: (315)268-6400
Contact: Thomas L. Theis Ph.D., Dir.

★4017★ Clemson University
Edith Angel Environmental Research Center
Environmental Toxicology Graduate Research Training Program
Institute of Wildlife and Environmental Toxicology
Rte. 2, Box 106A
Chariton, IA 50049
Phone: (515)774-5116
Fax: (515)774-2365
Contact: Karen Craft, Coordinator

★4018★ Clemson University
Institute of Wildlife and Environmental Toxicology
Environmental Toxicology Educational Program
1 Tiwet Dr.
PO Box 709
Pendleton, SC 29670
Phone: (803)646-7265
Fax: (803)646-9377
Contact: Dr. Ronald J. Kendall, Dir.
Offers undergraduate coursework and graduate degrees.

★4019★ College of the Atlantic
Environmental Sciences Programs
105 Eden St.
Bar Harbor, ME 04609
Phone: (207)288-5015
Offers degrees in marine biology, environmental studies and ecology, and environmental design.

★4020★ Colorado Mountain College
PO Box 10001BW
Glenwood Springs, CO 81602
Phone: (303)945-8691
Conducts outdoor education, degree program, and other programs in recreation management; outdoor leadership; avalanche awareness; rock climbing; nordic and alpine skiing; and mountain, desert, snow, and canyon orientation.

★4021★ Colorado State University
Environmental Studies Programs
Fort Collins, CO 80523
Phone: (303)491-1101
Contact: Dr. Jay M. Hughes, Dean
Offers undergraduate and graduate degrees in forestry and natural resources, fishery and

wildlife, forest and wood sciences, and earth resources.

★4022★ Colorado State University
Fluid Dynamics and Diffusion Laboratory
Fluid Mechanics, Hydraulics, and Wind Engineering Program Seminar Series
College of Engineering
Foothills Campus
Fort Collins, CO 80523
Phone: (303)491-8574
Fax: (303)491-8671
Contact: Dr. Robert N. Meroney, Dir.
Held weekly during the academic year.

★4023★ Cornell University
Center for the Environment
Environmental Management Master's Degree Program
Hollister Hall
Ithaca, NY 14853
Phone: (607)255-7535

★4024★ Cornell University
Cornell Laboratory of Ornithology
159 Sapsucker Woods Rd.
Ithaca, NY 14850
Phone: (607)254-2473
International center for study, appreciation, and conservation of birds. Develops, applies, and shares tools for understanding and protecting birds.

★4025★ Cornell University
Institute for Comparative and Environmental Toxicology
Environmental Toxicology Graduate Program
16 Fernow Hall
Ithaca, NY 14853-3001
Phone: (607)255-8008
Fax: (607)255-2812
Contact: James W. Gillett, Dir.

★4026★ Cornell University
International Institute for Food, Agriculture and Development International Training Program
Ithaca, NY 14853
Phone: (607)255-3037
Contact: Prof. Daniel Sisler
Offers academic training to graduate students in developing countries.

★4027★ Cornell University
New York Cooperative Fish and Wildlife Research Unit
Fish and Wildlife Conservation and Management Graduate Research Training Program
Dept. of Natural Resources
Fernow Hall
Ithaca, NY 14853
Phone: (607)255-2151
Contact: Dr. Milo Richmond, Unit Leader

★4028★ De Anza College
Environmental Studies/Biology
1250 Stevens Creek Blvd.
Cupertino, CA 95014
Phone: (408)864-8525
Promotes environmental education and awareness.

★4029★ Defenders of Wildlife
1244 19th St. NW
Washington, DC 20036
Phone: (202)659-9510
Provides factsheets and information on wildlife to students and educators upon request.

★4030★ Delaware Dept. of Natural Resources and Environmental Control
Water Quality Program
89 Kings Hwy.
PO Box 1401
Dover, DE 19903
Phone: (302)739-5731
Contact: Pearl Burbage
Water quality curriculum in state schools.

★4031★ Drexel University
Environmental Studies Institute
Philadelphia, PA 19104
Phone: (215)895-2000
Contact: Herbert E. Allen, Dir.

★4032★ Duke University
School of Forestry and Environmental Studies Graduate Program
Durham, NC 27706
Phone: (919)684-2136
Contact: Dr. George F. Dutrow, Dean

★4033★ Eagle Lake Field Station Summer Field Courses
California State Univ., Chico
Dept. of Biological Sciences
Chico, CA 95929-0515
Phone: (916)898-4490
Contact: Raymond J. Bogiatto, Dir.
Holds annual summer courses in field biology, field ichthyyology, zooarcheology, and field ecology.

★4034★ Eastern Kentucky University
Department of Environmental Health Science
Rowlett 145
Richmond, KY 40475-3130
Phone: (606)622-1939
Offers B.S. in Environmental Health Science.

★4035★ Eastern Kentucky University
Wildlife Management and Environmental Resources Degree Programs
Moore 235
Richmond, KY 40475
Phone: (606)622-1531
Contact: Dr. M. Pete Thompson, Dir.

★4036★ Eastern Michigan University
Kresge Environemntal Education Center
Ypsilanti, MI 48197
Phone: (313)487-1849
Contact: Ben Czinski, Res. Mgr.

★4037★ Environmental Health Program
Environmental Health Engineering Graduate Program
Univ. of Kansas
Dept. of Civil Engineering
Learned Hall
Lawrence, KS 66045
Phone: (913)864-3731
Contact: Dr. Ross E. McKinney, Dir.
Offers master's and doctoral degrees.

★4038★ Environmental Health Program
Environmental Health Science Graduate Program
Univ. of Kansas
Dept. of Civil Engineering
Learned Hall
Lawrence, KS 66045
Phone: (913)864-3731
Contact: Dr. Ross E. McKinney, Dir.
Offers master's and doctoral degrees.

★4039★ Florida Institute of Technology
Indian River Marine Sciences Research Center Educational Program
805 46th Pl. E.
Vero Beach, FL 32963
Phone: (407)234-4096
Fax: (407)984-8461
Contact: Dr. Walter G. Nelson, Dir.
Offers graduate research opportunities in marine biology, geology, and physics as well as graduate and undergraduate instruction.

★4040★ Florida State University
Geophysical Fluid Dynamics Institute Colloquium Series
18 Keen Bldg.
Tallahassee, FL 32306
Phone: (904)644-5594
Contact: Prof. Richard L. Pfeffer, Dir.
Sponsors colloquium series for faculty members and graduate students in geophysical fluid dynamics, meteorology, oceanography, and applied mathematics (weekly).

★4041★ Foundation for Glacier and Environmental Research, Inc.
Institute of Geological and Arctic Sciences
514 E. 1st St.
Moscow, ID 83843
Contact: Dr. Maynard M. Miller, Exec. Dir.
Cosponsered with the University of Idaho to serve undergraduate and eligible high school students, including National Science Foundation participants.

★4042★ Garrett Community College
Environmental Studies Programs
Mosser Rd.
McHenry, MD 21541
Phone: (301)387-6666
Toll-Free: 800-533-1000
Offers educational programs in wildlife management, soil and water conservation, fisheries management, water quality monitoring, and other natural resource areas.

★4043★ Glassboro State College
Pinelands Institute for Natural and Environmental Studies
120-13 Whitesbog Rd.
Browns Mills, NJ 08015
Phone: (609)893-1765
Contact: Gary Patterson, Dir.

★4044★ Hillsborough Community College
Institute of Florida Studies
1206 N. Park Rd.
Plant City, FL 33566
Phone: (813)757-2104
Contact: Frederick J. Webb
Natural history center sponsors educational programs.

★4045★ Houston Advanced Research Center, Center for Growth Studies
Woodlands Conference Series
4800 Research Forest Dr.
The Woodlands, TX 77381
Phone: (713)363-7913
Fax: (713)363-7914
Contact: Dr. Jurgen Schmandt, Dir.

★4046★ Hudsonia Ltd.
Bard College Field Sta.
Annandale, NY 12504
Phone: (914)758-1881
Contact: Erik Kiviat, Exec. Dir.
Offers seminars and advanced natural history courses in spring and summer.

★4047★ Humboldt State University College of Natural Resources
Arcata, CA 95521
Phone: (707)826-3561
Contact: Dr. Richard L. Ridenhour, Dean
Offers undergraduate and graduate degrees in the areas of fisheries, forestry, natural resources planning and interpretation, wildlife, oceanography, range management, watershed management, and cooperative fishery research. Also operates the Native American Career Education in Natural Resources Program.

★4048★ Huxley College of Environmental Studies
Western Washington University
Bellingham, WA 98225
Phone: (206)676-3520
Contact: Dr. John C. Miles, Dean
A two-year upper division and master's of science degree program of Western Washington University.

★4049★ Illinois State University Department of Health
103 Moulton Hall
Normal, IL 61761
Phone: (309)438-8329
Offers B.S. degrees in Environmental Health and Health Education.

★4050★ Indiana State University Conservation Degree Program
Terre Haute, IN 47809
Phone: (317)237-2261
Contact: Dr. William Brooks, Dir.
Offers undergraduate and graduate degrees in conservation, ecology, and wildlife management.

★4051★ Indiana University Environmental Systems Application Center Environmental Studies Seminar
School of Public & Environmental Affairs
Bloomington, IN 47405
Phone: (812)885-4556
Contact: William W. Jones, Dir.
Held weekly.

★4052★ Indiana University School of Public and Environmental Affairs
Bloomington, IN 47405
Phone: (812)335-9485
Contact: A. James Barnes, Dean

★4053★ International Center for the Solution of Environmental Problems Engineering and Environmental Science Work/Study Program
535 Lovett Blvd.
Houston, TX 77006
Phone: (713)527-8711
Contact: Dr. Joseph L. Goldman, Technical Dir.
Offered in conjunction with Rice University.

★4054★ Iowa State University Environmental Studies Program
201 Bessey Hall
Ames, IA 50011
Phone: (515)294-4787
Alt. Phone: (515)294-4911
Offers multidisciplinary environmental courses.

★4055★ John B. Peirce Laboratory, Inc. Environmental Physiology Educational Program
290 Congress Ave.
New Haven, CT 06519
Phone: (203)562-9901
Fax: (203)624-4950
Contact: Dr. Ethan R. Nadel, Dir.
Open to doctoral candidates.

★4056★ Joint Center for Energy Management Degree Program
Univ. od Colorado—Boulder
CB 428
Boulder, CO 80309-0428
Phone: (303)492-3915
Fax: (303)492-5105
Contact: Dr. Jan F. Kreider, Dir.
Confers undergraduate and graduate degrees.

★4057★ Jordan College Energy Institute
155 Seven Mile Rd. NW
Comstock Park, MI 49321
Phone: (616)784-7595
Offers degree programs in renewable energies, applied environmental technology, energy management, and solar retrofit technology.

★4058★ Kansas State University Environmental Sciences Program
Manhattan, KS 66506
Phone: (913)532-6011
Contact: Dr. Robert J. Robel, Dir.
Offers undergraduate and graduate degrees in wildlife, soil, and weter conservation.

★4059★ Lake Superior State University Aquatics Research Lab
Lake Superior State Univ.
Sault St. Marie, MI 49783
Phone: (906)635-1949
Contact: Prof. David Behmer, Director
Offers B.S. degrees. Degree Programs in Fisheries and Wildlife Management

★4060★ Lake Superior State University Aquatics Research Lab Environmental Science Degree Program
Sault Ste. Marie, MI 40783
Phone: (906)635-1949
Contact: Prof. David Behmer, Dir.
Offers B.S. degree.

★4061★ Lake Superior State University Aquatics Research Lab Fisheries and Wildlife Management Degree Program
Sault Ste. Marie, MI 49783
Phone: (906)635-1949
Contact: Prof. David Behmer, Dir.
Offers B.S. degree.

★4062★ Laredo Demonstration Farm
Center for Maximum Potential Building Systems
8604 F.M. 969
Austin, TX 78724
Phone: (512)928-4786
Contact: Plinky Fisk III
Demonstration farm emphasizing renewable energy sources.

★4063★ Louisiana Tech University Nuclear Center
PO Box 3015
Ruston, LA 71272
Phone: (318)257-2603
Contact: Dr. R.H. Thompson, Dir.
Offers introductory courses in nuclear engineering and chemistry.

★4064★ Lovelace Inhalation Toxicology Research Institute
PO Box 5890
Albuquerque, NM 87185
Phone: (505)844-6835
Fax: (505)846-1900
Contact: Dr. Joe L. Mauderly, Pres. and Dir.
Offers summer undergraduate and science teacher research programs, a doctoral program in inhalation toxicology, and postdoctoral and sabbatical research programs. Holds periodic seminars, professional meetings, and conferences.

★4065★ Maine Cooperative Fish and Wildlife Research Unit
U. S. Fish & Wildlife Service
Univ. of Maine
240 Nutting Hall
Orono, ME 04469
Phone: (207)581-2870
Fax: (207)581-2858
Contact: Dr. William B. Krohn, Leader
Provides graduate training in wildlife management and ecology at the University of Maine.

★4066★ Manomet Bird Observatory
PO Box 936
Manomet, MA 02345
Phone: (508)224-6521
Contact: Janis Burton, Director
Environmental research and education focusing on wildlife populations and natural systems and emphasizing conservation.

★4067★ Massachusetts Institute of Technology Center for Global Change Science Educational Program
Rm. 54-1312
Cambridge, MA 02139
Phone: (617)253-4902
Fax: (617)253-0354
Contact: Dr. Ronald G. Prinn, Dir.
Sponsors educational program to coordinate existing undergraduate and graduate courses in meteorology, oceanography, and hydrology.

★4068★ Massachusetts Institute of Technology Ralph M. Parsons Laboratory Environmental Engineering Science Undergraduate Degree Program
Rm. 48-311
15 Vassar St.
Cambridge, MA 02139
Phone: (617)253-2117
Fax: (617)258-8850
Contact: Dr. Rafael L. Bras, Dir.

★4069★ McNeese State University Department of Biological and Environmental Sciences
PO Box 92000-0655
Lake Charles, LA 70609-2000
Phone: (318)475-5674
Graduate programs in air and water quality studies.

★4070★ Memphis State University Center for River Studies Graduate Program
104 Engineering Science Bldg.
Memphis, TN 38152
Phone: (901)678-3275
Fax: (901)678-4180
Contact: Marvin L. Jacobs P.E., Dir.

★4071★ Miami University Ecology Research Center Field Ecology Courses
Oxford, OH 45056
Phone: (513)529-6187
Fax: (513)529-5634
Contact: Dr. Gary W. Barret, Codirector

★4072★ Miami University Institute of Environmental Sciences Environmental Sciences Master's Degree Program
Oxford, OH 45056
Phone: (513)529-5811
Fax: (513)529-5814

Contact: Gene E. Willeke, Dir.

★4073★ Michigan State University
Center for Environmental Toxicology
Environmental Toxicology Training Program
C231 Holden Hall
East Lansing, MI 48824
Phone: (517)353-6469
Fax: (517)335-4603
Contact: Lawrence J. Fischer Ph.D., Dir.
Offered to doctoral and postdoctoral students.

★4074★ Michigan State University
Institute of Water Research
Groundwater Education in Michigan Program (GEM)
334 Natural Resources
E. Lansing, MI 48824
Phone: (517)353-3742
Contact: Carol Misseldine
Promotes statewide groundwater protection and educational network.

★4075★ Michigan Technological University
Environmental Engineering Center for Water and Waste Management
Houghton, MI 49931
Phone: (906)487-2758
Provides undergraduate and graduate education in environmental engineering and waste management. Holds biweekly seminars.

★4076★ National Audubon Expedition Institute
PO Box 67
Mt. Vernon, ME 04325
Phone: (207)685-3111
A nonprofit traveling education program which offers year and semester expeditions for students.

★4077★ National Center for Toxicological Research Associated Universities, Inc.
UAMS 522-7
4301 W. Markham
Little Rock, AR 72205
Phone: (501)686-6501
Fax: (501)686-8315
Contact: Robert P. Cullen, Exec. Dir.
Sponsors a one-week course in basic environmental toxicology and cosponsors workshops for professional scientists on related topics.

★4078★ National Oceanic and Atmospheric Administration
Marine and Estuarine Management Division
National Estuarine Research Reserves
1825 Connecticut Ave., NW
Washington, DC 20235
Phone: (202)673-5126
National Estuarine Research Reserves, comprised of twenty reserves located throughout the U.S., operates student and teacher activities in cooperation with NOAA. Programs include outdoor study and focus on the function, management, and protection of estuaries in the U.S.

★4079★ National Pollution Prevention Center
Univ. of Michigan
School of Natural Resources
430 E. University
Ann Arbor, MI 48109-1115
Phone: (313)764-1412
Contact: Jonathan W. Buckley, Dir.
Collaborates with faculty from the College of Engineering and the Schools of Business Administration and Art (Industrial Design Program) to develop educational materials, including lecture materials, case study examples, open-ended problems, group problem-solving exercises, and videos. Seeks to incorporate pollution prevention and resource conservation principles into engineering and business education. Activities focus on integrating pollution prevention into the early stages of product design and development. Provides internships for students at business and industrial facilities and offers continuing education courses and seminars.

★4080★ New Mexico State University
Fishery and Wildlife Sciences Program
Box 30003
Dept. 4901
Las Cruces, NM 88003-0003
Phone: (505)646-1544

★4081★ New York Institute of Technology
Center for Energy Policy and Research
Energy Management Graduate Program
Old Westbury, NY 11568
Phone: (516)686-7578
Fax: (516)626-2627
Contact: Gale Tenan Pak, Dir.
Offers a master's of science degree through the New York Institute of Technology's School of Management.

★4082★ New York University
Environmental Conservation Education Graduate Program
737 E. Bldg., 239 Greene St.
Washington Sq.
New York, NY 10003
Phone: (212)998-5637
Alt. Phone: (212)998-5495
Offers nonscience interdisciplinary M.A. based on core courses in social, philosophical, and organizational aspects of the environment.

★4083★ Newfound Harbor Marine Institute at Seacamp
Rte. 3, Box 170
Big Pine Key, FL 33043
Phone: (305)872-2331
Offers marine environmental courses to increase understanding of the ocean and natural ecosystems, including coral reef, shallow bay, mangrove, and coastal ecosystems.

★4084★ North American Association for Environmental Education
PO Box 400
Troy, OH 45373
Phone: (513)339-6835
Develops educational materials and programs.

★4085★ North Carolina State University
Program in Conservation
Box 7103
Raleigh, NC 27695-7103
Phone: (919)737-2437
Contact: Dr. H. Joseph Kleiss, Teaching Coord.

★4086★ Northern Arizona University
School of Forestry
Box 4098
Flagstaff, AZ 86011
Phone: (602)523-3031
Offers graduate and undergraduate degree programs.

★4087★ Northern Michigan University
Department of Geography, Earth Science, Conservation, and Planning
Marquette, MI 49855
Phone: (906)227-2500
Contact: D. Alfred N. Joyal III, Head

★4088★ Northern State University
Center for Understanding Environments, Science and Technology
Box 740
Aberdeen, SD 57401
Phone: (605)622-2627
Environmental resource center for teachers that offers educational workshops, pre-service and in-service teacher training, and other activities.

★4089★ Nova University
Institute of Marine and Coastal Studies Degree Program
8000 N. Ocean Dr.
Dania, FL 33004
Phone: (305)920-1909
Fax: (305)947-8559
Contact: Dr. Richard Dodge, Dir.
Offers master of science degrees in marine biology and coastal zone management.

★4090★ Oberlin College
Environmental Studies Program
Rice Hall
Oberlin, OH 44074
Offers A.B. degree in Environmental Studies.

★4091★ Ohio State University
Byrd Polar Research Center
Polar Seminar
125 S. Oval Mall
Columbus, OH 43210
Phone: (614)292-6531
Fax: (614)292-4697
Contact: Dr. Kenneth C. Jezek, Dir.
Open to graduate students each spring quarter.

★4092★ Ohio State University
School of Natural Resources
Joint Education Initiative (JEdI Program)
2021 Coffey Rd.
Columbus, OH 43210
Phone: (614)292-2265
Contact: Dr. Rosanne Fortner, Director
Environmental education program.

★4093★ Oklahoma State University
Summer Academy for Environmental Science
Oklahoma State University
302 Gunderson
Stillwater, OK 74078
Phone: (405)744-7125
Contact: Ted Mills
University-sponsored high school summer academy.

★4094★ Opportunities in Science, Inc.
PO Box 1176
Bemidji, MN 56601
Phone: (218)751-1110
Computer-based, in-service training for science teachers. Computerized curriculum aid includes modules on extinction, wildlife management, citizen action, and population ecology.

★4095★ Oregon State University
Oak Creek Laboratory of Biology
Aquatic Biology Training Program
Dept. of Fisheries & Wildlife
104 Nash Hall
Corvallis, OR 97331
Phone: (503)737-3503
Fax: (503)737-3590
Contact: Dr. Larry Curtis, Project Leader
Conducts training program for graduate students in aqutic biology, with special emphasis on fisheries, water pollution biology, toxicology, stream ecology, and watershed classification.

★4096★ Pennsylvania State University Center for Statistical Ecology and Environmental Statistics
Dept. of Statistics
303 Pond Laboratory
University Park, PA 16802
Phone: (814)865-9442
Contact: Ganapati P. Patil Ph.D., Dir.
Offers graduate research assistantships that lead to completion of master's and doctoral degrees for students enrolled in statistics and ecology degree programs. Also sponsors miniseminars on individual collaborative research between interested university faculty and visiting agency scientists.

★4097★ Prescott College
Environmental Studies Programs
220 Grove Ave.
Prescott, AZ 86301
Phone: (602)778-2090
Liberal arts college with emphasis on environmental studies, human development, outdoor leadership.

★4098★ Purdue University
Department of Forestry and Natural Resources
West Lafayette, IN 47907
Phone: (317)494-3590
Contact: Dr. Dennis C. Le Master, Head

★4099★ Purdue University
Environmental Engineering Department
1284 Civil Engineering
W. Lafayette, IN 47907-1284
Phone: (317)494-2194
Areas of study include industrial waste treatment, drinking water, air toxics/noise, municipal/hazardous waste, environmental chemistry, and groundwater remediation.

★4100★ Ramapo College of New Jersey
Environmental Sciences Programs
505 Ramapo Valley Rd.
Mahwah, NJ 07430-1680
Phone: (201)529-7743
Degree programs in environmental science and environmental studies.

★4101★ Resources for the Future, Inc.
1616 P St., NW
Washington, DC 20036
Phone: (202)328-5000
Contact: Robert W. Fri, Pres.
Holds periodic symposia and seminars on current research.

★4102★ Rutgers University
Institute of Marine and Coastal Sciences Education Programs
Old Blakeman Hall
PO Box 231
New Brunswick, NJ 08903-0231
Phone: (908)932-6555
Contact: Dr. Frederick Grassle, Dir.
Offers graduate programs in biology, ecology, environmental sciences, geography, geological sciences, metereorology, physiology, plant biology, and toxicology.

★4103★ San Diego State University
Dept. of Psychology EOP-EA
Therapy for a Dying Planet
San Diego, CA 92182
Phone: (619)594-5717
Contact: Kathryn Wullner
A two-year program, including zoo laboratory internship. Offered in cooperation with the Zoological Society of San Diego.

★4104★ San Francisco State University
Wildlands Studies Program
Mosswood Cir.
Cazadero, CA 95421
Phone: (707)632-5665
Contact: Crandall Bay, Dir.
Offers a year round series of field study program in North American and international wilderness location. Participants collaborate with research teams on wildlife population and wildland habitat issues.

★4105★ San Jose State University
Environmental Studies Program
San Jose, CA 95192
Phone: (408)277-2000
Contact: Dr. Donald Aitken, Coord.
Offers undergraduate degrees in wildlife management and environemntal studies.

★4106★ Sonoma State University
Department of Environmental Studies and Planning
1801 E. Cotati Ave.
Rohnert Park, CA 94928
Phone: (707)664-2306
Offers B.S. degree program in Environmental Education. Areas of study include energy management, hazardous materials management, natural resources, and water quality.

★4107★ Southern Vermont College
Environmental Sciences Programs
Monument Ave. Ext.
Bennington, VT 05201
Phone: (802)442-5427
Offers 2-year Associate and 4-year Bachelor degrees in Environmental Studies.

★4108★ State University College at Buffalo
Great Lakes Laboratory
Aquatic and Terrestrial Environment Studies Program
1300 Elmwood Ave.
Buffalo, NY 14222
Phone: (716)878-5422
Contact: Dr. Harish C. Sikka, Dir.
Provides graduate and undergraduate instruction.

★4109★ State University College at Plattsburgh
Center for Earth and Environmental Science
Plattsburgh, NY 12901
Phone: (518)564-2028
Fax: (518)564-7827
Contact: Dr. Malcolm Fairweather, Dir.
Conducts undergraduate programs in environmental science, geography, and geology.

★4110★ State University of New York at Stony Brook
Marine Sciences Research Center
Stony Brook, NY 11794-5000
Phone: (516)632-8700
Fax: (516)632-8820
Contact: Dr. J.R. Schubel, Dean and Dir.
Conducts master of science and doctoral programs, undergraduate courses, and adult education courses. Sponsors workshops (by invitation).

★4111★ State University of New York College at Cortland
Environmental Education Program
PO Box 2000
Park Center
Cortland, NY 13045
Phone: (607)753-4941
Undergraduate and graduate degrees in environmental education.

★4112★ State University of New York
Division of Natural Science
Project River Watch - Environmental Science
Purchase, NY 10577-1400
Phone: (914)251-6641
Contact: Barbara L. Dexter
Environmental education and research in freshwater and coastal marine environments.

★4113★ Tennessee Technological University
Upper Cumberland Biological Station at Tech Aqua
Wildlife and Fisheries Science Program
Box 5063
Cookeville, TN 38505
Phone: (615)372-3129
Contact: Dr. Henri Willard, Dir.
Conducts a ten-week, two-station summer school.

★4114★ Texas A&M University
Department of Wildlife and Fisheries Science
Fisheries and Wildlife Management Degree Program
College Station, TX 77843
Phone: (409)845-5777
Fax: (409)845-3786
Contact: Dr. David J. Schmidly, Head

★4115★ Thiel College
Environmental Sciences Program
75 College Ave.
Greenville, PA 16125
Phone: (412)589-2068
B.A. in environmental science with emphasis on land analysis.

★4116★ Troy State University
Center for Environmental Research and Service
Troy, AL 36082
Phone: (205)670-3624
Contact: Michael W. Mullen
Public service program.

★4117★ Trumbull Area Multi-Purpose Environmental Education
347 N. Park Ave.
Warren, OH 44481
Phone: (216)394-5247
Contact: Norm Downing
Outdoor environmental learning for middle school students.

★4118★ Tufts University
Center for Environmental Management Educational Program
Curtis Hall
474 Boston Ave.
Medford, MA 02155
Phone: (617)381-3486
Fax: (617)381-3084
Contact: Dr. William R. Moomaw, Dir.
Provides a master's degree in hazardous materials management, and training courses on asbestos, lead-based paint abatement, and local management of chemical risks.

★4119★ **Tulane University**
Mesoamerican Ecology Institute
Natural History and Archeology of the Yucatan Pennisula Summer Field Colloquium
Center for Latin American Studies
New Orleans, LA 70118
Phone: (504)865-5164
Contact: Dr. Arthur Weldon, Program Dir.

★4120★ **UNC Sea Grant College Program**
Coastal and Estuarine Studies on Seawater Program
North Carolina State Univ.
Box 8605
Raleigh, NC 27695-8605
Phone: (919)737-2454
Fax: (919)737-7095
Contact: Dr. B.J. Copeland, Dir.
Affiliated with Duke, North Carolina State, East Carolina, North Carolina Agricultural and Technical State, and North Carolina Central Universities, and University of North Carolina at Chapel Hill and Wilmington.

★4121★ **UNC Sea Grant College Program**
Coastal Geology and Ecology Program
North Carolina State Univ.
Box 8605
Raleigh, NC 27695-8605
Phone: (919)737-2454
Fax: (919)737-7095
Contact: Dr. B.J. Copeland, Dir.
Affiliated with Duke, North Carolina State, East Carolina, North Carolina Agricultural and Technical State, and North Carolina Central Universities, and University of North Carolina at Chapel Hill and Wilmington.

★4122★ **University of Akron**
Center for Environmental Studies Educational Programs
302 Buchtel Ave.
Akron, OH 44325
Phone: (216)375-7991
Contact: Dr. Jim L. Jackson, Dir.
Sponsors lecture courses, independent study, field work, meetings, and regular seminars.

★4123★ **University of Akron**
Center for Environmental Studies
Evaluation of Environmental Data
302 Buchtel Ave.
Akron, OH 44325
Phone: (216)375-7991
Contact: Dr. Jim L. Jackson, Dir.
Held late spring.

★4124★ **University of Alaska, Fairbanks**
Agriculture and Land Resource Management
Fairbanks, AK 99775-0990
Phone: (907)474-7083
Offers M.S. and Ph.D. programs.

★4125★ **University of Arizona**
School of Natural Resources
Watershed Management Degree Program
Tucson, AZ 85721
Phone: (602)621-7255
Undergraduate and graduate degree programs.

★4126★ **University of Arizona**
School of Renewable Natural Resources
Range Management Program
Tucson, AZ 85721
Phone: (602)621-7255
Offers graduate and undergraduate degrees.

★4127★ **University of Arizona**
School of Renewable Natural Resources
Renewable Natural Resources Studies Program
Tucson, AZ 85721
Phone: (602)621-7255
Offers graduate and undergraduate degrees.

★4128★ **University of Arizona**
School of Renewable Natural Resources
Wildlife, Fisheries, and Recreation Degree Program
Tucson, AZ 85721
Phone: (602)621-7255
Offers graduate and undergraduate degree programs.

★4129★ **University of Arkansas at Little Rock**
Department of Biology
Environmental Health Science Program
Rm. NS406C
2801 S. University Ave.
Little Rock, CA 72204
Phone: (501)569-3501
Contact: Dr. Carl R. Stapleton, Director

★4130★ **University of California, Berkeley**
Environmental Studies Program
Berkeley, CA 94720
Phone: (415)642-0376
Contact: John A. Helms, Chair
Offers undergraduate and graduate degrees in the areas of forestry and resource management, range management, wildlife, and natural resources.

★4131★ **University of California, Davis**
Environmental Studies Programs
Davis, CA 95616
Phone: (916)752-6586
Contact: Daniel W. Anderson, Chair
Offers undergraduate degrees in the areas of wildlife and fisheries biology and range and wildland science. Oversees the Graduate Group in Ecology.

★4132★ **University of California, Davis**
Sustainable Agriculture Program
Introduction to Sustainable Agricultural Systems
Dept. of Agronomy & Range Science
Davis, CA 95616
Phone: (916)752-7645
Contact: Mark Van Horn, Program Coordinator
A summer program.

★4133★ **University of California, Los Angeles**
Environmental Science and Engineering Programs
Los Angeles, CA 90024
Phone: (213)825-4321
Contact: Dr. William Glaze, Director

★4134★ **University of California, Riverside**
Statewide Air Pollution Research Center
Riverside, CA 92521
Phone: (714)787-5124
Fax: (714)787-5004
Contact: J. Brian Mudd, Dir.
Provides undergraduate and graduate instruction through academic departments on campus. Sponsors conferences and workshops on current topics in air pollution research, also seminars and technical briefings for legislative and state administrative officials, members and staff of control agencies, and the general public.

★4135★ **University of Cincinnati**
Department of Environmental Health
Environmental Health Sciences Education Program
3223 Eden Ave.
Cincinnati, OH 45267-0056
Phone: (513)558-5701
Fax: (513)558-1756
Contact: Dr. Roy E. Albert, Dir.

★4136★ **University of Cincinnati**
Groundwater Research Center
College of Engineering
Mail Location 18
Cincinnati, OH 45221-0018
Phone: (513)475-2933
Contact: Dr. Constantine Papadakis, Dir.
Holds monthly seminars with invited speakers on groundwater.

★4137★ **University of Connecticut**
Department of Natural Resources Management and Engineering Degree Programs
Box U-87
1376 Storrs Rd.
WBY, Rm. 308
Storrs, CT 06269-4087
Phone: (203)486-2840
Contact: David B. Schroeder, Head

★4138★ **University of Delaware**
Center for Study of Marine Policy
Marine Policy Annual Conference
Newark, DE 19711
Phone: (302)451-8086
Contact: Prof. Biliana Cicin-Sain, Codirector

★4139★ **University of District of Columbia**
Agricultural Experiment Station Degree Program
4200 Connecticut Ave. NW
Washington, DC 20008
Phone: (202)282-3675
Contact: James R. Allen, Dir.
Offers B.S. programs in environmental science and ornamental horticulture.

★4140★ **University of District of Columbia**
DC Water Resources Research Center
Water Resources Technology and Management Policy
4200 Connecticut Ave. NW, MB5004
Washington, DC 20008
Phone: (202)673-3442
Fax: (202)637-2085
Contact: Dr. M.H. Watt, Dir.
Monthly seminar series.

★4141★ **University of Florida**
Air Pollution Research Laboratory
Air Pollution Training Institute
408 Black Hall
Gainesville, FL 32611
Phone: (904)392-0845
Fax: (904)392-3076
Contact: Dr. Dale Lundgren, Dir.

★4142★ **University of Florida**
School of Forest Resources and Conservation
Gainesville, FL 32611
Phone: (904)392-1791

★4143★ **University of Florida**
Solar Energy and Energy Conversion Laboratory
Caribbean Universities Seminar Series
Dept. of Mechanical Engineering
Gainesville, FL 32611
Phone: (904)392-0812
Fax: (904)392-1071

Contact: Dr. D. Yogi Goswami, Dir.

★4144★ University of Florida
Solar Energy and Energy Conversion Laboratory
International Training Center
Dept. of Mechanical Engineering
Gainseville, FL 32611
Phone: (904)392-0812
Fax: (904)392-1071
Contact: Dr. D. Yogi Goswami, Dir.
Sponsors guest lectures, field trips, classroom and laboratory exercises, and special projects that encourage participants to design, build, and evaluate a device or system applicable to their countries' needs.

★4145★ University of Georgia
Institute of Ecology
Athens, GA 30602
Phone: (404)542-2968
Contact: L.A. Hargreaves Jr., Dean
Offers degrees in forestry, wildlife sciences, and fisheries management.

★4146★ University of Georgia
Savannah River Ecology Laboratory Research Participation Program
PO Drawer E
Aiken, SC 29801
Phone: (803)725-2472
Contact: Dr. Michael Smith, Dir.
A 200,000-acre ecological research facility located on the grounds of the Savannah River Site and operated by the University of Georgia under contract with the Department of Energy. Program is open to undergraduates, graduates, and faculty members.

★4147★ University of Idaho
Forest, Wildlife and Range Experiment Station Degree Program
Moscow, ID 83843
Phone: (208)885-6441
Fax: (208)885-6226
Contact: John C. Hendee, Dir.
Offers bachelor's, master's and doctoral degrees in forestry, forest products, fisheries, wildlife, wildland recreation management, and tourism.

★4148★ University of Iowa
Institute of Agricultural Medicine and Occupational Health
Occupational Health and Safety Training Programs
Preventative Medicine & Environmental Health Dept.
AMRF, Oakdale Campus
Iowa City, IA 52242
Phone: (319)335-4415
Contact: James A. Merchant M.D., Dir.
Open to graduate students.

★4149★ University of Iowa
Institute of Agricultural Medicine and Occupational Health
Preventive Medicine Graduate Degree Program
Preventive Medicine & Environmental Health Dept.
AMRF, Oakdale Campus
Iowa City, IA 52242
Phone: (319)335-4415
Contact: James A. Merchant M.D., Dir.
Offers M.S. and Ph.D. degrees with an emphasis in occupational and environmental health.

★4150★ University of Kansas
Environemntal Studies Undegraduate Degree Program
Lawrence, KS 66045
Phone: (913)864-4301
Contact: Hans-Peter Schultze, Chair

★4151★ University of Maryland
Maryland Agricultural Experiment Station Field Day
College Park, MD 20742
Phone: (301)405-1210
Fax: (301)314-9089
Contact: Dr. Robert A. Kennedy, Dir.
Sponsors annual research field days.

★4152★ University of Massachusetts at Boston
Urban Harbors Institute
Annual Symposium on Science and Policy of Boston Harbor and Massachusetts Bay
Harbor Campus
Boston, MA 02125
Phone: (617)287-5570
Fax: (617)265-7173
Contact: Dr. Richard F. Delaney, Dir.

★4153★ University of Massachusetts at Boston
Urban Harbors Institute Educational Programs
Harbor Campus
Boston, MA 02125
Phone: (617)287-5570
Fax: (617)265-7173
Contact: Dr. Richard F. Delaney, Dir.
Holds continuing education programs for government officials concerned with environmental issues. Offers doctoral and postdoctoral programs.

★4154★ University of Miami
Center for Theoretical Studies
PO Box 249055
Coral Gables, FL 33124-5510
Phone: (305)284-4455
Fax: (305)284-4456
Contact: Prof. Behram N. Kursunoglu, Dir.
Sponsors formal and informal lectures at the graduate and undergraduate levels.

★4155★ University of Miami
Pesticide Residue, Toxic Waste and Basic Research Analytical Laboratory
Pesticide Residue Training Course
12500 SW 152nd St., Bldg. B
Miami, FL 33177-1411
Phone: (305)232-8202
Fax: (305)232-7461
Contact: Jon B. Mann, Lab Manager
A semiannual three-month course.

★4156★ University of Miami
Rosenstiel School of Marine and Atmoshperic Science
4600 Rickenbacker Causeway
Miami, FL 33149
Phone: (305)361-4000
Contact: Dr. Bruce R. Rosendahl
Offers degrees in marine biology and fisheries, marine and atmospheric chemistry, marine geology and geophysics, meteorology and physical oceanography, and marine sciences.

★4157★ University of Michigan
School of Natural Resources
Global River Environmental Education Network
Dana Bldg., Rm. 3004
430 E. University
Ann Arbor, MI 48109-1115
Phone: (313)763-8155
A school outreach program to teach water quality monitoring.

★4158★ University of Minnesota, Duluth
Natural Resources Research Institute Seminar Series
5013 Miller Trunk Hwy.
Duluth, MN 55811
Phone: (218)720-4294
Fax: (218)720-4219
Contact: Dr. Michael J. Lalich, Dir.
Sponsors weekly seminar on ecology, geology, and natural resources, open to the public, free of charge.

★4159★ University of Minnesota
St. Anthony Falls Hydraulics Laboratory
Hydromechanics Colloquia
Mississippi River at 3rd Ave SE
Minneapolis, MN 55414-2196
Phone: (612)627-4010
Fax: (612)627-4609
Contact: Dr. Roger E.A. Arndt, Dir.
Held annually.

★4160★ University of Minnesota
Underground Space Center
Underground Space Use and Development Course
790 Civil & Mineral Engineering Bldg.
500 Pillsbury Dr., SE
Minneapolis, MN 55455
Phone: (612)624-0066
Fax: (612)624-0293
Contact: Dr. Raymond L. Sterling, Dir.

★4161★ University of Minnesota
Water Resources Research Center
Water Resources Research Conference
1518 Cleveland Ave., Ste. 302
St. Paul, MN 55108
Phone: (612)624-9282
Fax: (612)625-1263
Contact: Prof. Patrick L. Brezonik, Dir.
Held biennially.

★4162★ University of Missouri
Environmental Trace Substances Research Center
Trace Substances in Environmental Health Conference
5450 S. Sinclair Rd.
Columbia, MO 65203
Phone: (314)882-2151
Fax: (314)882-3031
Contact: Dr. Armon F. Yanders, Dir.
Held annually.

★4163★ University of Montana
Wilderness Institute
Wilderness and Civilization
Forestry Bldg., Rm. 207
Missoula, MT 59812
Phone: (406)243-5361
Contact: Dr. Alan McQuilan, Exec. Dir.
An intensive 18-credit hour interdisciplinary program.

★4164★ **University of North Carolina at Chapel Hill**
Institute for Environmental Studies
Carolina Environmental Lecture Series
CB 7410
315 Pittsboro St.
Chapel Hill, NC 27599-7410
Phone: (919)966-2358
Fax: (919)966-7141
Contact: Dr. Richard N.L. Andrews, Dir.
Held annually.

★4165★ **University of North Dakota**
Institute for Ecological Studies
Environmental Sciences Regional Center for Advanced Studies
Box 8278, Univ. Sta.
Grand Forks, ND 58202
Phone: (701)777-2851
Contact: Dr. Rodney D. Sayler, Dir.

★4166★ **University of North Dakota**
Institute for Ecological Studies
Environmental Sciences Research Training Program
Box 8278, Univ. Sta.
Grand Forks, ND 58202
Phone: (701)777-2851
Contact: Dr. Rodney D. Sayler, Dir.
Offered to pre- and postdoctoral students.

★4167★ **University of Notre Dame**
Lobund Laboratory
Notre Dame, IN 46556
Phone: (219)239-7564
Fax: (219)239-7595
Holds periodic seminars, short courses, an informal training program, and conferences on germfree technology and on research using germfree animals.

★4168★ **University of Oklahoma**
Environmental & Ground Water Institute
200 Felgar St., Rm. 127
Norman, OK 73019-0470
Phone: (405)325-5202
Fax: (405)325-7596
Contact: Dr. Larry W. Canter, Dir.
Conducts graduate and continuing education program in groundwater and environmental assessments.

★4169★ **University of Oregon**
Ocean and Coastal Law Center
Ocean and Coastal Law Training Program
Law School
Eugene, OR 97403-1221
Phone: (503)346-3845
Fax: (503)346-3985
Contact: Jon L. Jacobson, Codirector
Open to law students.

★4170★ **University of Oregon**
Solar Energy Center
Solar Seminars
Depts. of Architecture & Physics
Eugene, OR 97403
Phone: (503)686-3696
Contact: Prof. John S. Reynolds, Dir.
Topics are associated with energy resources and architectural applications.

★4171★ **University of Pennsylvania**
Center for Energy and the Environment Educational Programs
127 Meyerson Hall
Philadelphia, PA 19104-6311
Phone: (215)898-7185
Contact: Dr. Mark Bernstein, Dir.
Offers M.S. and Ph.D. degree programs and a joint degree program in collaboration with the French Institute of Petroleum. Holds weekly seminars for graduate students during the academic year.

★4172★ **University of Pennsylvania**
Morris Arboretum Adult Education Program
9414 Meadowbrook Ave.
Philadelphia, PA 19118
Phone: (215)247-5777
Contact: Dr. William M. Klein, Dir.
Offers adult education courses in horticulture and botany on a 166-acre tract with a living collection of 5,500 specimens.

★4173★ **University of Pennsylvania**
Morris Arboretum Graduate Program
9414 Meadowbrook Ave.
Philadelphia, PA 19118
Phone: (215)247-5777
Contact: Dr. William M. Klein, Dir.
Offers opportunities for graduate research in taxonomy, phytopathology, and landscape architecture on a 166-acre tract with a living collection of 5,500 specimens.

★4174★ **University of Pennsylvania**
Morris Arboretum Internship Program
9414 Meadowbrook Ave.
Philadelphia, PA 19118
Phone: (215)247-5777
Contact: Dr. William M. Klein, Dir.

★4175★ **University of Rhode Island**
International Center for Marine Resource Development
International Artemia Study Group
126 Woodward Hall
Kingston, RI 02881
Phone: (401)792-2479
Fax: (401)789-3342
Contact: Dr. Spiros Constantinides, Deputy Dir.

★4176★ **University of Rhode Island**
International Center for Marine Resource Development
International Workshop on Post Harvest Fishery Project Technology
126 Woodward Hall
Kingston, RI 02881
Phone: (401)792-2479
Fax: (401)789-3342
Contact: Dr. Spiros Constantinides, Deputy Dir.

★4177★ **University of South Carolina at Columbia**
Belle W. Baruch Institute for Marine Biology and Coastal Research
Marine Sciences Training Program
Columbia, SC 29208
Phone: (803)777-5288
Contact: Dr. F. John Vernberg, Dir.

★4178★ **University of Southern California, Los Angeles**
Environmental Engineering Programs
Los Angeles, CA 90089-9231
Phone: (213)743-7517
Contact: Mihran S. Agbabian, Director

★4179★ **University of Southern Mississippi**
Center for Marine Science
Marine Science Graduate Program
John C. Stennis Space Center
Stennis Space Center, MS 39529
Phone: (601)688-3177
Fax: (601)688-1121
Contact: Dr. George A. Knauer, Dir.
Offers M.S. and Ph.D. programs.

★4180★ **University of Tennessee at Knoxville**
Waste Management Research and Education Institute Internship Program
327 S. Stadium Hall
Knoxville, TN 37996-0710
Phone: (615)974-4251
Contact: Dr. E. William Colglazier, Dir.
Provides M.S. and undergraduate students with work experience in fields related to waste management, including chemical and environmental engineering, environmental science and ecology, hydrology and geology, biology, and public health.

★4181★ **University of Utah**
Center for Energy, Public Lands and Environmental Law
Energy Law Degree Program
College of Law
Salt Lake City, UT 84112
Phone: (801)581-5880
Contact: Prof. Robert L. Schmidt, Dir.

★4182★ **University of Utah**
Rocky Mountain Center for Occupational and Environmental Health Continuing Education Program
Bldg. 512
Salt Lake City, UT 84112
Phone: (801)581-8719
Fax: (801)581-7224
Contact: Royce Moser Jr.
Offers programs in industrial hygiene, occupational medicine, occupational health nursing, and occupational safety and ergonomics (over 1,000 attendees per year).

★4183★ **University of Utah**
Rocky Mountain Center for Occupational and Environmental Health Graduate Programs
Bldg. 512
Salt Lake City, UT 84112
Phone: (801)581-8719
Fax: (801)581-7224
Contact: Royce Moser Jr.
Conducts master's level programs in industrial hygiene, occupational medicine, and occupational health nursing. Offers master's and doctoral training in occupational safety and ergonomics and residency programs in occupational medicine.

★4184★ **University of Vermont**
School of Natural Resources
Burlington, VT 05405
Phone: (802)656-4280
Contact: Dr. Lawrence K. Forcier, Dean

★4185★ **University of Washington**
Center for Quantitative Science in Forestry, Fishing, and Wildlife
Biomathematics Program
3737 15th Ave. NE, HR-20
Seattle, WA 98195
Phone: (206)543-1191
Fax: (206)543-6263
Contact: E. David Ford, Dir.
A graduate program in quantitative ecology and resource management.

★4186★ **University of Washington**
Institute for Environmental Studies
FM-12
Seattle, WA 98195
Phone: (206)543-1812
Contact: Prof. Gordon H. Orians, Dir.
Develops undergraduate and graduate environmental curricula, encourages interdisciplinary reseach, and develops public service and continuing education programs.

★4187★ University of Washington
Quaternary Research Center
Quaternary Environments Graduate Seminar
AK-60
Seattle, WA 98195
Phone: (206)543-1166
Fax: (206)543-3836
Contact: Dr. Stephen C. Porter, Dir.
Held for ten weeks.

★4188★ University of Washington
School of Marine Affairs
Fisheries Management Program
College of Ocean & Fishery Sciences
3707 Brooklyn Ave. NE
Seattle, WA 98195
Phone: (206)543-7004
Fax: (206)543-1417
Contact: Dr. Edward L. Miles, Dir.
Maintains jointly with the School of Fisheries.

★4189★ University of Washington
School of Marine Affairs
Marine Affairs Degree Program
College of Ocean & Fishery Sciences
3707 Brooklyn Ave. NE
Seattle, WA 98195
Phone: (206)543-7004
Fax: (206)543-1417
Contact: Dr. Edward L. Miles, Dir.
Offered as a master's degree.

★4190★ University of West Florida
Department of Biology
Coastal Zone Studies
Pensacola, FL 32514-5751
Phone: (904)474-2746

★4191★ University of Wisconsin—Madison
Environmental Toxicology Center
Environmental Toxicology Training Program
309 Infirmary
Madison, WI 53706
Phone: (608)263-4580
Contact: Prof. Colin R. Jefcoate, Dir.
Sponsors pre- and postdoctoral students.

★4192★ University of Wisconsin—Madison
School of Natural Resources
Environmental Awarness Center
Madison, WI 53706
Phone: (608)262-1234
Contact: Philip H. Lewis Jr., Dir.

★4193★ University of Wisconsin—Madison
School of Natural Resources
Envrionmental Toxicology Center
Madison, WI 53706
Phone: (608)262-1234
Contact: Colin R. Jefcoate, Dir.

★4194★ University of Wisconsin—Madison
School of Natural Resources
Institute for Environmental Studies
Madison, WI 53706
Phone: (608)262-1234
Contact: Daniel Bromley, Act.Dir.
Offers a master's of science in water resources.

★4195★ Utah State University
Biotechnology Center
Biotechnology Seminar
Logan, UT 84322-4430
Phone: (801)750-2730
Fax: (801)750-2755
Contact: Steven D. Aust, Dir.
Biweekly series.

★4196★ Utah State University
Ecology Center Lecture Series
Logan, UT 84322-5200
Phone: (801)750-2555
Contact: Frederick H. Wagner, Dir.

★4197★ Utah State University
Institute for Land Rehabilitation
Land Rehabilitation Graduate Co-op Research Program
College of Natural Resources
Logan, UT 84322-5230
Phone: (801)750-2547
Contact: J.B. Dobrowolski, Codirector
Graduate program for companies with reclamation/rehabilitation problems.

★4198★ Utah State University
Utah Water Research Laboratory
Irrigation Short Courses
Logan, UT 84322-8200
Phone: (801)750-3168
Fax: (801)750-3663
Contact: Dr. L. Douglas James, Dir.
Cosponsors approximately five four-week courses annually with the International Irrigation Center.

★4199★ Vermont Law School
Environmental Law Center
South Royalton, VT 05068
Phone: (802)763-8303
Contact: Douglas M. Costle, Dean

★4200★ Washington State University
Albrook Hydraulics Laboratory Graduate Degree Program
Pullman, WA 99164-3001
Phone: (509)335-4546
Fax: (509)335-7632
Contact: Prof. Howard D. Copp, Dir.
Graduate programs offered in hydraulic engineering, fluid mechanics, water resources, and fisheries engineering.

★4201★ Western Kentucky University
Center for Cave and Karst Studies Degree Program
Dept. of Geography & Geology
Bowling Green, KY 42101
Phone: (502)745-5989
Contact: Dr. Nicholas Crawford, Dir.
Offers undergraduate and graduate coursework. Also offers an M.S. degree with an emphasis on karst hydrology through the Department of Geography and Geology.

★4202★ Western Kentucky University
Center for Cave and Karst Studies
Karst Field Studies Program at Mammoth Cave
Dept. of Geography & Geology
Bowling Green, KY 42101
Phone: (502)745-5989
Contact: Dr. Nicholas Crawford, Dir.
Six or seven one week field courses/workshops offered each summer.

★4203★ Western Kentucky University
Center for Cave and Karst Studies
Karst Groundwater Pollution Workshop
Dept. of Geography & Geology
Bowling Green, KY 42101
Phone: (502)745-5989
Contact: Dr. Nicholas Crawford, Dir.

★4204★ Western Washington University
Shannon Point Marine Center Education Program
1900 Shannon Point Rd.
Anacortes, WA 98221
Phone: (206)293-2188
Fax: (206)293-1083
Contact: Prof. Stephen D. Sulkin, Dir.
Offers a master's degree in marine and estuarine sciences. Conducts ad-hoc special workshops, an undergraduate quarter-in-residence program, and a visiting scholars program (including sabbatical leave support and summer research awards).

★4205★ Western Wyoming College
Water Quality Laboratory
Flaming Gorge Reservoir Conference
PO Box 428
Rock Springs, WY 82901
Phone: (307)382-2121
Contact: Craig Thompson, Dir.

★4206★ Williams College
Center for Environmental Studies
Kellogg House
PO Box 622
Williamstown, MA 01267
Phone: (413)597-2346
Offers undergraduate degree with concentration in environmental studies.

★4207★ Williams College
Center for Environmental Studies
Environmental Lecture
Kellogg House
Williamstown, MA 01267
Phone: (413)597-2346
Fax: (413)458-2158
Contact: Dr. Benjamin W. Labaree, Dir.
Held weekly.

★4208★ Wisconsin Environmental Education Initiatives
PO Box 7841
Madison, WI 53707
Phone: (608)267-9226
Alt. Phone: (608)267-9266
Contact: David C. Engleson
Statewude education coordination, including training and curriculum planning.

★4209★ Woods Hole Oceanographic Institution Degree Program
Woods Hole, MA 02543
Phone: (508)457-2000
Fax: (508)457-2190
Contact: Dr. Craig E. Dorman, Dir.
Offers programs of study and research leading to a master's or doctoral degree in oceanography or ocean engineering.

★4210★ Wyoming Outdoor Council Education Program
201 Main St.
Lander, WY 82520
Phone: (307)332-7031
Contact: Don Kesselheim
Curriculum, classroom, and field studies focusing on conservation issues.

★4211★ Yale University
School of Forestry Studies Program
205 Prospect St.
New Haven, CT 06511
Phone: (203)432-5100
Contact: John C. Gordon, Dean

★4212★ Yale University
Tropical Resources Institute Graduate Degree Program
Yale School of Forestry & Environmental Studies
205 Prospect St.
New Haven, CT 06511
Phone: (203)432-5116
Fax: (203)432-5942
Contact: Dr. William R. Bentley, Dir.
Offers master's and Ph.D. degrees in forestry, forest science, and environmental studies specializing in tropical resources. Sponsors

meetings, lecture series, and international symposia.

Community Programs

★4213★ Acid Rain Foundation, Inc.
1410 Varsity Dr.
Raleigh, NC 27606
Phone: (919)828-9443
Information, curriculum, and education services in the areas of acid rain, air quality, global changes, air pollution, and forests.

★4214★ Adopt-A-Stream Foundation
Environmental Education and Stream Restoration Program
Box 5558
Everett, WA 98206
Phone: (206)388-3313
Contact: Thomas Murdoch
Environmental education and training focusing on stream restoration.

★4215★ Alaska Department of Environmental Conservation
Remote Area Maintenance Worker Program
PO Box 0
Juneau, AK 99811
Phone: (907)465-2610
Contact: Gary L. Hayden
Provides sanitation educational and technical assistance to rural communities.

★4216★ American Forest Council
The American Tree Farm System
1250 Connecticut Ave., NW
Washington, DC 20036
Phone: (202)463-2455
Contact: Lester A. Decoster
Teaches private landowners forest care. Backyard Tree Farming program teaches urban residents proper tree care.

★4217★ Andorra Natural Area
Northwestern Ave.
Philadelphia, PA 19118
Phone: (215)685-9285
Offers interpretive programs centering on natural and woodland stream areas of urban Fairmount Park.

★4218★ Association of Forest Service Employees for Environmental Ethics
National Forests Protection Program
PO Box 11615
Eugene, OR 97440
Phone: (503)484-2692
Contact: Jeff DeBonis
Education of Forest Service employees and the general public. Provides support of activism of Forest Service and other land management employees.

★4219★ Audubon Naturalist Society of the Central Atlantic States
8940 Jones Mill Rd.
Chevy Chase, MD 20815
Phone: (301)652-5964
Conducts environmental education classes and field studies for all ages.

★4220★ Bok Tower Gardens
PO Box 3810
Lake Wales, FL 33859
Phone: (813)676-1408
Conducts adult education program, special class for fourth graders, lectures, and workshops on horticulture, Florida history, and natural history.

★4221★ Brown University
Center for Environmental Studies
Indoor Air Pollution Workshops
Box 1943
Providence, RI 02912
Phone: (401)863-3449
Fax: (401)863-3503
Contact: Dr. Harold Ward, Dir.

★4222★ Brown University
Center for Environmental Studies
Organic Gardening Workshop
Box 1943
Providence, RI 02912
Phone: (401)863-3449
Fax: (401)863-3503
Contact: Dr. Harold Ward, Dir.

★4223★ Brown University
Center for Environmental Studies
Recycling Workshops
Box 1943
Providence, RI 02912
Phone: (401)863-3449
Fax: (401)863-3503
Contact: Dr. Harold Ward, Dir.

★4224★ Brown University
Center for Environmental Studies
Solar Energy Systems Workshop
Box 1943
Providence, RI 02912
Phone: (401)863-3449
Fax: (401)863-3503
Contact: Dr. Harold Ward, Dir.

★4225★ Butte Environmental Council
708 Cherry St.
Chico, CA 95928
Phone: (916)891-6424
Contact: Kelly Meagher
Area environmental information and referral service.

★4226★ Cabrillo Marine Museum
3720 Stephen White Dr.
San Pedro, CA 90731
Phone: (213)548-7563
Conducts one-day workshops and week-long morning day camps which focus on California marine life, including tidepools, mudflats, and sandy beaches.

★4227★ Cal Wood Environmental Education Resource Center
PO Box 347
Jamestown, CO 80455
Phone: (303)449-0603
Conducts programs for schools and organizations on outdoor education, natural science, and natural resources.

★4228★ California State University, San Bernardino
Inland Empire Environmental EXPO
Network for Environmental Science Training
5500 University Pkwy.
San Bernardino, CA 92407
Phone: (714)880-5640
Contact: Darleen Stoner
Annual environmental fair for the general public.

★4229★ Cape Cod Museum of Natural History
PO Box 1710
Rte. 6A
Brewster, MA 02631
Phone: (508)896-3867
Environmental education and research science center focusing on the natural environment of Cape Cod. Seeks to promote a better understanding and appreciation of the environment and the means to sustain it.

★4230★ Capital Coalition for Safe Food
Safe Food Education and Outreach Program
11 Devon Rd.
Silver Springs, MD 20910
Phone: (301)434-6313
Contact: Barbara Francisco
Promotes safe food.

★4231★ Carrie Murray Outdoor Education Campus
1901 Ridgetop Rd.
Baltimore, MD 21207
Phone: (301)396-0808
Operates year-round education program for children and adults.

★4232★ Center for Atomic Radiation Studies
94 Pleasant St.
Arlington, MA 02174
Phone: (617)497-2277
Contact: Donnell W. Boardman M.D., Pres.
Offers public education on human and environmental effects of ionizing radiation exposure.

★4233★ Center for Holistic Resource Management
800 Rio Grande, NW
Albuquerque, NM 87107
Toll-Free: 800-654-3619
Contact: Shannon A. Horst
Focuses on holistic teaching in conserving Earth's Resources.

★4234★ Center for Indoor Air Research
1099 Winterson Rd., Ste. 280
Linthicum, MD 21090
Phone: (301)684-3777
Fax: (301)684-3729
Contact: Max Eiesenberg Ph.D., Exec. Dir.
Sponsors workshops and seminars on indoor air related issues as needed.

★4235★ Citizens for Alternatives to Chemical Contamination
Backyard Eco-Conference
9496 School St.
Lake, MI 48632
Phone: (517)544-3318
Contact: Ann Hunt
Annual conference of grass roots citizens.

★4236★ City of Boulder Adventure Program
PO Box 791
Boulder, CO 80306
Phone: (303)443-5173
Conducts outdoor education and natural science/history program in mountaineering, including rock climbing, canoeing, mountain biking, and kayaking.

★4237★ Claremont McKenna College
Robert J. Bernard Biological Field Station
Environmental Education Course
Claremont, CA 91711
Phone: (714)621-5425
Contact: Clyde H. Ericksen, Dir.
Open to the public.

★4238★ Clay Pit Ponds State Park Reserve
83 Nielsen Ave.
Staten Island, NY 10309
Phone: (718)967-1976
Offers year-round nature programs. The 250-acre park, once the site of a clay mine, contains

wetlands, sandy barrens, fields, and other habitats.

★4239★ Clemson University
Water Resources Research Institute
Water Resources Conference
223 Strom Thurmond Bldg.
Clemson, SC 29634-2900
Phone: (803)656-3271
Fax: (803)656-4780
Contact: Dr. Paul B. Zielinski, Dir.
Open to interested persons.

★4240★ Colorado University Environmental Center
Campus Box 207
Boulder, CO 80309
Phone: (303)492-8308
Contact: Roz McClellan, Dir.
Educates students and the community on environmental issues through conferences, programs, and a resource files. Operates a campus recycling program.

★4241★ Cornell University
Center for Environmental Research
Master Gardner Program
Hollister Hall
Ithaca, NY 14853
Phone: (607)255-7535
Contact: Dr. Robert Barker, Dir.
Teaches homeowners how to achieve an attractive lawn without polluting groundwater.

★4242★ Cornell University
Institute for Comparative and Environmental Toxicology
Toxicology and Risk Management Educational Program
16 Fernow Hall
Ithaca, NY 14853-3001
Phone: (607)255-8008
Fax: (607)255-2812
Contact: James W. Gillett, Dir.
Open to the public.

★4243★ Cornell University
Institute for Comparitive and Environmental Toxicology Community Program
16 Fernow Hall
Ithaca, NY 14853-3001
Phone: (607)255-8008
Fax: (607)255-2812
Contact: James W. Gillett, Dir.
Conducts an extension/outreach program of symposia, bulletins, press releases, policy analyses, and workshops.

★4244★ Customized Guided Excursions
PO Box 964
Hershey, PA 17033-0964
Phone: (717)944-2724
Conducts individual and small group programs in outdoor education, including such topics as the natural world, local and national geology, natural resources, and respect for the environment.

★4245★ Delaware Nature Society
PO Box 700
Hockessin, DE 19707
Phone: (302)239-2334
Contact: Michael E. Riska
Programs for students, teachers, graduates, senior citizens, and people with disabilities.

★4246★ Earthtrends
Earthtrends Expo
2650 N. Military Tr., Ste. 243
Boca Raton, FL 33431
Toll-Free: 800-226-6700
Consumer-oriented exhibition of environmentally progressive products and services, including automotive, baby care, beauty, energy, garden, recycling, household supplies, and toy products.

★4247★ Environmental Education Initiatives
2 N. Ninth St.
Allentown, PA 18101
Phone: (215)774-5950
Contact: John Seager
Environmental education programs for teachers, schools, businesses, industries and the general public that reach thousands of people a year.

★4248★ Environmental Health Program
Annual Environmental Engineering Conference
Univ. of Kansas
Dept. of Civil Engineering
Learned Hall
Lawrence, KS 66045
Phone: (913)864-3731
Contact: Dr. Ross E. McKinney, Dir.
Held in February, open to the public.

★4249★ Environmental Law Institute
Environmental Law Course
1616 P St. NW, Ste. 200
Washington, DC 20036
Phone: (202)328-5150
Fax: (202)328-5002
Contact: J. William Futrell, Pres.
Held annually in February.

★4250★ Environmental Law Institute
Hazardous Wastes, Superfund, and Toxic Substances Course
1616 P St. NW, Ste. 200
Washington, DC 20036
Phone: (202)328-5150
Fax: (202)328-5002
Contact: J. William Futrell, Pres.
Cosponsored by the American Law Institute-American Bar Association, open to the public (scholarships for course available to qualified professionals and students).

★4251★ Florida Power and Light Wildlife Awareness Program
PO Box 078768
West Palm Beach, FL 33407-0768
Phone: (407)697-6980
Contact: J.R. Wilcox
Community program focusing on endangered species in Florida.

★4252★ Florida Solar Energy Center
Solar Energy Short Course
300 State Rd., 401
Cape Canaveral, FL 32920
Phone: (407)783-0300
Fax: (407)783-2571
Contact: Dr. David L. Block, Dir.

★4253★ Great Smokey Mountains Institute at Tremont
Rte. 1, Box 81
Townsend, TN 37882
Phone: (615)448-6709
Conducts school programs, adult workshops, teacher training, camps, and elder hostels in cultural and natural resources of Great Smokey Mountains National Park.

★4254★ Hazardous Waste Research and Information Center
Community-Based Outreach Assistance
1 E. Hazelwood Dr.
Champaign, IL 61820
Phone: (217)333-8940
Fax: (217)333-8944
Contact: Dr. David L. Thomas, Dir.
Conducts programs on community waste minimization and pollution prevention.

★4255★ Household Hazardous Waste Project
901 S. National
Box 108
Springfield, MO 65804
Phone: (417)836-5777
Conducts community education program to reduce household hazardous waste.

★4256★ Inspirada Americana
Man and Mother Earth Concert
Box 111, Railroad Ave.
Ringling, MT 59642
Phone: (406)547-2272
Contact: Connie Bellet
Live multimedia concert promotes environmental awareness.

★4257★ Interfaith Coalition on Energy
PO Box 26577
Philadelphia, PA 19141
Phone: (215)635-1122
Contact: Andrew Rudin
Offers workshops, booklets, newsletters and videotapes on conservation of electrical and fuel for congregations and their buildings.

★4258★ International Learning and Livestock Center
Heifer Project International Small Farm Education
Rt. 2 Box 33
Perryville, AR 72126
Phone: (501)376-6836
Contact: Jennifer Shumaker
Working farm employing sustainable agriculture practices.

★4259★ Iowa Department of Natural Resources
Groundwater Protection Education Program
Wallace Bldg.
Des Moines, IA 50319-0034
Phone: (515)281-5135
Contact: Gail George
Education and training program for teachers, public schools.

★4260★ Iowa State University
Leopold Center for Sustainable Agriculture
126 Soil Tilth Bldg.
Ames, IA 50011
Phone: (515)294-3711
Fax: (515)294-9696
Contact: Prof. Dennis R. Keeney, Dir.
Research and education on sustainable agriculture.

★4261★ Isaac W. Bernheim Foundation
Research Institute for Education and the Environment
Bernheim Forest Arboretum
Clermont, KY 40110
Phone: (502)543-2451
Environmental outdoor education.

★4262★ Island Institute
4004 58th Pl. SW
Seattle, WA 98116
Phone: (206)938-0345
Offers marine science immersion experiences and whale watching.

★4263★ Izaak Walton League of America, Charles County Chapter
Southern Maryland Outdoor Education Center
PO Box 248
Hughesville, MD 20637
Phone: (301)344-2720
Contact: Steve Berberich
140-acre working farm.

★4264★ Keystone Center
Science Education Program
PO Box 606
Keystone, CO 80435
Phone: (303)468-5822
Contact: Robert W. Craig, Pres.
Offers outdoor educational opportunities to the public.

★4265★ Lac Lawrann Conservancy
724 Elm St.
West Bend, WI 53095
Phone: (414)335-5080
Conducts environmental education programs for the general public.

★4266★ Lacawac Sanctuary Foundation
RD 1, Box 518
Lake Ariel, PA 18436
Phone: (717)689-9494
Contact: Sally J. Jones, Curator
Sponsors ecology seminars and youth conservation camps (annually), a cultural program, and regularly scheduled interpretive nature walks (each Saturday, June through August, and at other times by apointment).

★4267★ The Land Institute
Prairie Festival
2440 E. Water Well Rd.
Salina, KS 67401
Phone: (913)823-5376
Contact: Dana Jackson, Coordinator
Held annually.

★4268★ Law of the Sea Institute
Law of the Sea Conference
Richardson School of Law
2515 Dole St., Rm. 208
Honolulu, HI 96822
Phone: (808)956-6750
Fax: (808)956-6402
Contact: Dr. John P. Craven, Dir.
Held annually, open to the public.

★4269★ Lower Colorado River Authority
Water Resource Management Simulator
PO Box 220
Austin, TX 78767
Toll-Free: 800-776-5272
Contact: Don Chovanec
Computer model for water resources education.

★4270★ Maine Conservation School
PO Box 188
Bryant Pond, ME 04219
Phone: (207)665-2068
Nature study and conservation education through residential program of issues-oriented topics.

★4271★ Maine Offices of Energy Resources
Weatherize Homes in Maine Program
Maine Offices of Energy Resources
State House Sta. No. 53
Augusta, ME 04333
Phone: (207)289-6025
Contact: Peter Thibeault
A workshop which provides educational and cash incentives to participants with the purchase of weatherization materials from local stores.

★4272★ Michigan State University Cooperative Extension Service
Water Quality Protection Program
311-A Natural Resources Bldg.
Resource Development Dept.
E. Lansing, MI 48824
Phone: (517)355-9578
Contact: Cynthia Fridgen
Statewide educational and assistance program for farmers, home-owners and small business owners in the management of hazardous products and waste.

★4273★ Michigan State University
Inland Lakes Research and Study Center
Lake Management Conference
334 Natural Resources Bldg.
East Lansing, MI 48824
Phone: (517)353-3742
Fax: (517)353-1812
Contact: Dr. Jon Bartholic, Dir.
Held during the summer with demonstrations at lake sites.

★4274★ Michigan State University
Inland Lakes Research and Study Center
Water Quality Nontechnical Conference
334 Natural Resources Bldg.
East Lansing, MI 48824
Phone: (517)353-3742
Fax: (517)353-1812
Contact: Dr. Jon Bartholic, Dir.
Held for property owners, environmental groups, consultants, and public officials regarding problems and possible alternatives.

★4275★ Midcoast Audubon Society Environmental Education
PO Box 862
Rockland, ME 04841
Phone: (207)563-3578
Contact: Joe Gray
Education courses for elementary through college students.

★4276★ Midwest Research Institute
Science Pioneers
425 Volker Blvd.
Kansas City, MO 64110-2299
Phone: (816)753-7600
Fax: (816)753-8420
Contact: John C. McKelvey, Pres. and CEO
Provides science-related activities, written materials, and other services for students and teachers in the 36 school districts of Greater Kansas City.

★4277★ Minnesota Pollution Control Agency
Agricultural Nonpoint Source Pollution Model
520 Lafayette Rd.
St. Paul, MN 55155
Phone: (612)296-7323
Contact: Wayne P. Anderson
A computer model to assist management agencies and farmers. The model has been distributed around the world.

★4278★ Minnesota Valley National Wildlife Refuge
3815 E. 80th St.
Bloomington, MN 55425
Phone: (612)854-5900
Offers environmental education for public and training for teachers in the areas of wildlife and natural resources.

★4279★ Mohican School in the Out-of-Doors, Inc.
3296 T.R. 629
Rt. 2
Coudonville, OH 44842
Phone: (419)994-3201
Curriculum emphasizes outdoor/ environmental education, including resident programs and field trips for grades 4-7.

★4280★ National Institute for Urban Wildlife
Urban Wildlife Seminar
10921 Trotting Ridge Way
Columbia, MD 21044
Phone: (301)596-3311
Contact: Gomer E. Jones, Pres.
Held occasionally, open to the public.

★4281★ National Marine Sanctuary Program
1825 Connecticut Ave. NW
Ste. 714
Washington, DC 20235
Phone: (202)673-5126
Long-term protection, research, and education in environmental issues.

★4282★ Natural Organic Farmers Association of Connecticut
Organic Landscaping Initiative
Box 386
Northford, CT 06427
Phone: (203)888-9280
Contact: Bill Duesing
Helps professionals and homeowners reduce and recycle landscaping materials.

★4283★ Nature Science Center
Museum Dr.
Winston Salem, NC 27105
Phone: (919)767-6730
Programs address issues of environmental awareness and protection.

★4284★ Nebraska Groundwater Foundation
10015 S. 9th Ct.
Omaha, NE 68123
Phone: (402)294-4061
Alt. Phone: (402)294-5303
Contact: Wanda Schroeder
Educational center devoted solely to groundwater.

★4285★ Nebraska Statewide Arboretum
Trees for Nebraska Symposium
112 Forestry Sciences Laboratory
Lincoln, NE 68583-0823
Phone: (402)472-2971
Fax: (402)472-8095
Contact: L. Finke, Educational Dir.
Held annually, open to the public.

★4286★ New Mexico Health and Environment Department
EID Groundwater
New Mexico Water Fair Program
Runnels Bldg.
Santa Fe, NM 87503
Phone: (505)827-2912
Contact: Dennis McQuillan
Environmental education for users of private wells.

★4287★ New York Rural Water Association Water and Wastewater Technical Assistance and Training Program
546 Columbia St.
Hudson, NY 12534
Phone: (518)828-5040
Public information and assistance program focusing on water and wastewater problems.

★4288★ New York State Energy Office
Bureau of Industry, Commission & Transportation
2 Rockfeller Plaza, 20th Fl.
Albany, NY 12223
Phone: (518)474-7657
Contact: Brain M. Henderson
Provides energy surveys to help industrial and commercial companies identify and implement energy conservation opportunities. Offers seminars and technical assistance.

★4289★ North Carolina State University North Carolina Solar Center Solar Communities Program
Box 7401
Raleigh, NC 27695
Phone: (919)737-3480
Contact: Mary Owens Fitzerald
Educational programs designed to demonstrate and inform the community on ways to increase energy efficiency and the use of renewable resources.

★4290★ North Dakota State University Central Grasslands Research Center Grass-n-Beef
Box 21
Streeter, ND 58483
Phone: (701)424-3606
Fax: (701)424-3616
Contact: Paul E. Nyren, Superintendent
Research roundup in January, open to the public.

★4291★ North Park Village Nature Center
5801 N. Pulaski
Chicago, IL 60646
Phone: (312)583-3714
Offers nature discovery school field trip program, teacher workshops, bird walks, and wildflower identification classes.

★4292★ Olympic Renewable Resources Association Energy Outreach Center
503 W. 4th
Olympia, WA 98501
Phone: (206)943-4595
Contact: Lyle S. Tribwell
Provides information on and promotes renewable energy with emphasis on solar energy use, recycling, shared transportation and water conservation through special projects and contests.

★4293★ Oregon Natural Resources Council Ancient Forests Campaign
522 SW 5th, Ste. 1050
Portland, OR 97204
Phone: (503)223-0991
Contact: Andy Kerr
Coordinates grass roots action and public education.

★4294★ Pacific Whale Foundation Ocean Outreach Program
101 N. Kihei Rd.
Kihei, HI 96753
Phone: (808)879-8860
Toll-Free: 800-879-4253
Contact: Paul H. Forestell
Program focuses on conservation of oceans and marine mammals.

★4295★ Pennsylvania State University Environmental Resources Research Institute Low-Level Radioactive Waste Disposal Seminar
100 Land and Water Resource Bldg.
University Park, PA 16802
Phone: (814)863-0291
Fax: (814)865-3378
Contact: Dr. Archie J. McDonnell, Dir.

★4296★ Piedmont Environmental Council Piedmont Environmental Education
PO Box 460
Warrenton, VA 22186
Phone: (703)347-2334
Contact: Cynthia DeCanio
Sponsors teacher workshops, day-camps, and community programs.

★4297★ Piedmont Environmental Council Virginia Growth Management Forum
PO Box 460
Warrenton, VA 22186
Phone: (703)347-2334
Contact: Josephine DeGive
State conference on growth management. Focuses on sustaining the economy, environment and quality of life.

★4298★ Potomac Overlook Regional Park and Nature Center
2845 Marcey Rd.
Arlington, VA 22207
Phone: (703)528-5406
Outdoor education and canoe trips.

★4299★ Practical Farmers of Iowa On-Farm Research: Design and Demonstration
Iowa State University
2104 Agronomy Hall
Ames, IA 50011
Phone: (515)294-1923
Provides farmers information on sustainable agriculture.

★4300★ The Pure Sound Society
PO Box 526
Vashon Island, WA 98070
Phone: (206)463-5607
Contact: Brad Wetmore
Conducts marine research, shoreline conservation and educational boat trips around the sound.

★4301★ Rocky Mountain National Park Rocky Mountain Seminars
Estes Park, CO 80517
Phone: (303)586-2371
Uses natural resources of Rocky Mountain National Park as an educational tool.

★4302★ Safari Club International
4800 W. Gates Pass Rd.
Tucson, AZ 85745
Phone: (602)620-1220
Ten-day workshops provide outdoor education in wildlife ecology, management, and conservation.

★4303★ Safe Environments
2512 9th St., No. 17
Berkeley, CA 94710
Phone: (415)843-6042
Holds public indoor pollution workshop and 4-day program on indoor environmental consulting.

★4304★ Seattle Aquarium State of the Sound Educational Programs
Pier 39, Waterfront Park
Seattle, WA 98101
Phone: (206)386-4333
Hands-on exhibits focusing on clean water issues.

★4305★ Seattle Tilth Community Compost Education Program
4649 Sunnyside Ave., N.
Seattle, WA 98103
Phone: (206)633-0224
Contact: Howard Stenn
A national information resource for home composting education. Trains volunteers for community outreach.

★4306★ Slide Ranch
2025 Shoreline Hwy.
Muir Beach, CA 94965
Phone: (415)381-6155
Programs focus on earth resources that provide food, clothing, shelter, and energy.

★4307★ Smithsonian Institution Travelling Exhibition Service
Washington, DC 20560
Phone: (202)786-2235
Contact: Elizabeth C. Hennings
Environmental exhibition programs. Exhibited nationwide.

★4308★ Society for the Protection of New Hampshire Forests
54 Portsmouth St.
Concord, NH 03301
Phone: (603)224-9945
Contact: Sandra Zicus
Volunteer training program.

★4309★ Somerset County Park Commission Environmental Education Center
190 Lord Stirling Rd.
Basking Ridge, NJ 07920
Phone: (908)766-2489
Conducts environmental education programs for schools and the general public.

★4310★ Sonoran Arthropod Studies, Inc.
PO Box 5624
Tucson, AZ 85703
Phone: (602)883-3945
Environmental science and education focusing on insects and other anthropods. Offers a large variety of programs, from lectures to expeditions.

★4311★ Southface Energy Institute ECOS - An Environmental Education House
PO Box 5506
Atlanta, GA 30307
Phone: (404)525-7657
Contact: Dennis Creech
A traveling environmental education expo focusing on residential conservation.

★4312★ SUNY College of Environmental Science and Forestry
Adirondack Ecological Center
Huntington Lecture Series
Huntington Forest
Newcomb, NY 12852
Phone: (518)582-4551
Contact: Dr. William F. Forest, Dir.
Topics focus on ecology and history of Adirondack region, open to the public, held in July and August.

★4313★ Texas A&I University
Caesar Kleberg Wildlife Research Institute Symposium
College of Agriculture & Home Economics
218 Campus Box
Kingsville, TX 78363
Phone: (512)595-3922
Contact: Dr. Sam L. Beamsom, Dir.
Sponsors a symposium series in October on wildlife topics, open to all.

★4314★ Tree Hill, Jacksonville Nature Center
7152 Lone Star Rd.
Jacksonville, FL 32211
Phone: (904)724-4646
Environmental education focusing on forest ecology. Programs include grade school through elderly education and science day camp.

★4315★ Trees for Tomorrow
611 Sheridan Rd.
PO Box 609
Eagle River, WI 54521
Phone: (715)479-6456
Program focuses on management of natural resources.

★4316★ United States Botanic Garden
245 1st St., SW
Washington, DC 20024
Phone: (202)226-4082
Garden contains plants from around the world, including many rare and endangered plants. Offers classes in horticulture.

★4317★ U.S. EPA Radon Program
401 M St., SW
Washington, DC 20460
Phone: (202)475-9622
Contact: Margo T. Oge
After developing monitoring and prevention technologies that addressed the nations' problem of indoor radon gas, the program now seeks to educate the public.

★4318★ University of Alabama
Environmental Institute for Waste Management Studies
Waste Management Seminar
PO Box 870203
Tuscaloosa, AL 35487
Phone: (205)348-8401
Fax: (205)348-8573
Contact: Dr. Robert A. Griffin, Dir.
Held for industry, government, and the public.

★4319★ University of California, Riverside
Dry Lands Research Institute
Dry Lands Management Symposia
PO Box 112
Riverside, CA 92521
Phone: (714)787-5797
Contact: Wesley M. Jarrell, Dir.

★4320★ University of Delaware Sea Grant College Program
Graduate College of Marine Studies
Coast Day
University of Newark
Robinson Hall
Newark, DE 19716
Phone: (302)451-8083
Contact: Tracey Bryant
Annual open house and tour emphasizing University's marine research program.

★4321★ University of Florida
Center for Tropical Agriculture
International Livestock and Poultry Conference
3028 McCarty Hall
Gainesville, FL 32611
Phone: (904)392-1965
Fax: (904)392-7127
Contact: Dr. Hugh L. Popenoe, Dir.
Held annually in May, open to anyone interested; conference offered with Spanish translation.

★4322★ University of Florida
Center for Wetlands
Wetland Seminar
Phelps Laboratory
Gainesville, FL 32611
Phone: (904)392-2424
Fax: (904)392-3624
Contact: Dr. G. Ronnie Best, Associate Dir.
Held weekly on Wednesdays, open to the public.

★4323★ University of Idaho
Idaho Water Resources Research Institute
Morrill Hall, 106
Moscow, ID 83843
Phone: (208)885-6429
Fax: (208)885-6431
Contact: Roy Mink, Dir.
Sponsors state water conferences, weekly water resources seminars, open to the public.

★4324★ University of Idaho
Idaho Water Resources Research Institute
Irrigation Research Workshop
Morrill Hall, 106
Moscow, ID 83843
Phone: (208)885-6429
Fax: (208)885-6431
Contact: Roy Mink, Dir.
Open to the public.

★4325★ University of Illinois at Chicago
Energy Resources Center
Illinois Energy Conference
Box 4348
Chicago, IL 60680
Phone: (312)996-4490
Fax: (312)996-5620
Contact: Dr. James P. Hartnett, Dir.
Held fall, open to all.

★4326★ University of Nebraska—Lincoln
Agricultural Research and Development Center
Ag Expo
PO Box 163
Mead, NE 68041
Phone: (402)624-2275
Contact: Dr. Warren W. Sahs, Superintendent
Open to the public.

★4327★ University of Pennsylvania
Morris Arboretum High School Community Service Program
9414 Meadowbrook Ave.
Philadelphia, PA 19118
Phone: (215)247-5777
Contact: Dr. Willam M. Klein, Dir.

★4328★ University of Tennessee at Knoxville
Forestry Experiment Stations and Arboretum
Arboretum Fall Walk
901 Kerr Hollow Rd.
Oak Ridge, TN 37830
Phone: (615)483-3571
Contact: Richard M. Evans, Superintendent
Held annually.

★4329★ University of Tennessee at Knoxville
Forestry Experiment Stations and Arboretum
Forestry Field Days
901 Kerr Hollow Rd.
Oak Ridge, TN 37830
Phone: (615)483-3571
Contact: Richard M. Evans, Superintendent
Held annually.

★4330★ Urban Options
135 Linden St.
East Lansing, MI 48823
Phone: (517)337-0422
Provides educational programs, including an environmental information service, library, and weatherization and tool lending programs.

★4331★ USDA Soil Conservation Service
Alternative Crop Technology Program
Room 5404 Federal Bldg.
700 W. Capitol
Little Rock, AR 72201
Phone: (501)378-5445
Contact: Ronnie Murphy
Holds demonstration field days showcasing soil and water conservation practices. Strengthens farm profits and provides incentives for youths to stay on family farms.

★4332★ USDA Soil Conservation Service
Conservation Reserve Program
PO Box 2890
Washington, DC 20013
Phone: (202)382-1869
Contact: Donald Butz
Provides technical and financial aid to farmers that remove cropland from production.

★4333★ USDA Sustainable Agriculture Research and Education
Rm. 342, Aerospace Bldg.
14th & Independence Ave.
Washington, DC 20250-2200
Phone: (202)447-3640
Contact: Neill Schaller
Serves as an information source on low-input/ sustainable agriculture.

★4334★ Vermont Institute of Natural Science
Vermont Birds Conference
Church Hill
Woodstock, VT 05091
Phone: (802)457-2779
Contact: Sarah B. Laughlin, Dir.
Held annually in June, open to the general public.

★4335★ Vineyard Environmental Research Institute
Martha's Vineyard Airport
RFD 862
Tisbury, MA 02568
Phone: (508)693-4632
Contact: William E. Marks, Exec. V. Pres.
Sponsors occasional speakers and periodic pond walks for the public and local schools.

★4336★ Waste Management Education and Research Consortium Educational Programs
New Mexico State University
Box 30001
Dept. 3805
Las Cruces, NM 88003-0001
Phone: (505)646-2038
Fax: (505)646-4149
Contact: Ron Bhada, Dir.
Conducts education programs designed to increase awareness of environmental issues.

★4337★ Water Pollution Control Federation Research Foundation
Water Pollution Control Annual Conference and Exposition
601 Wythe St.
Alexandria, VA 22314-1994
Phone: (703)684-2400
Contact: Glenn Reinhardt, Dir.
Held in October, open to the public.

★4338★ Whole Foods Market Consumer Alert Campaign
2524 Wallingwood Dr., Ste. 1400
Austin, TX 78746
Phone: (512)328-7541
Contact: Patti Lang
Educates consumers on environmental and food safety issues, including food additives, water quality, and the trapping of dolphins in tuna nets.

★4339★ Wild Basin Wilderness Preservation
PO Box 13455
Austin, TX 78711
Phone: (512)327-7622
Offers education in all aspects of the environment at its 227-acre preserve.

★4340★ Wisconsin Department of Agriculture
Trade and Consumer Protection Div.
Wisconsin Sustainable Agriculture Program
4702 University Ave.
PO Box 7883
Madison, WI 53707-7883
Phone: (608)267-3319
Contact: Kenneth C. Rineer
Facilitates alternative farming systems, including research and education.

★4341★ Wisconsin Rural Development Center
Summer On-Farm Field Days
1406 Bus. Hwy. 18-151 E.
Mount Horeb, WI 53572
Phone: (608)437-5971
Contact: Denny Caneff, Exec. Dir.

★4342★ Wisconsin Rural Development Center
Sustainable Agriculture Workshop
1406 Bus. Hwy. 18-151 E.
Mount Horeb, WI 53572
Phone: (608)437-5971
Contact: Denny Caneff, Exec. Dir.

★4343★ YMCA of the Rockies—Estes Park Center
Tunnel Rd.
Estes Park, CO 80511
Phone: (303)586-3341
Provides outdoor education in curriculum, hands-on instruction, and exploration of the natural world.

Nature Programs

★4344★ Adirondack Outdoor Education Center
Pilot Knob, NY 12844
Phone: (518)656-9462
Outdoor education on Lake George that includes lake and wetland study.

★4345★ Alley Pond Environmental Center
22806 Northern Blvd.
Douglaston, NY 11363
Phone: (718)757-8376
School programs set in a natural environment; includes lectures and nature hikes.

★4346★ Anita Purves Nature Center
1505 N. Broadway
Urbana, IL 61801
Phone: (217)384-4062
Provides natural resource for individuals, families, and school. Exhibits include animals, birds, and natural phenomena.

★4347★ Appalachian Mountain Club
Pinkham Notch Camp
Gorham, NH 03581
Phone: (603)466-2721
Offers guide hikes, field seminars, workshops, residential school programs, mountain leadership school, and program for inner city youth on a variety of of environmental and conservation programs.

★4348★ Bear Mountain Outdoor School, Inc.
Rt. 250
Hightown, VA 24444
Phone: (703)468-2700
Offers mountain ecology and outdoor education for teachers and schools.

★4349★ Citizens United to Protect the Maurice River
Box 476
Millville, NJ 08332
Phone: (609)327-1161
Contact: Jane Morton Galetto
Educates public through river trips and hands-on activities.

★4350★ Four Corners School of Outdoor Education
East Rte.
Monticello, UT 84535
Toll-Free: 800-525-4456
Conducts educational field programs, focusing on archeology, geology, ethnography, backpacking, and river rafting.

★4351★ Hawaii Nature Center
2131 Makiki Heights Dr.
Honolulu, HI 96822
Phone: (808)973-0100
Contact: Tamar Chotzen
Environmental field programs for elementary school children.

★4352★ Izaak Walton League, Minneapolis Chapter
Environmental Education Nature Center
6601 Auto Club Rd.
Bloomington, MN 55438
Phone: (612)722-8152
Contact: Alida Quinn
Sponsors field trips, nature trails, and other activities.

★4353★ Little Sewickley Creek Nature Trail
504 Beaver Rd.
Sewickley, PA 15143
Phone: (412)741-5767
Contact: Mary Lee Parrington
Elementary school programs.

★4354★ Marine Mammal Stranding Center
PO Box 773
Brigantine, NJ 08203
Phone: (609)266-0538
Rescues, rehabilitates, and releases marine mammals and turtles in New Jersey.

★4355★ Nature Center GEM Program
Kalamazoo Nature Center
7000 N. Westnedge
Kalamazoo, MI 49007
Phone: (616)381-1584
Contact: Beth Carpenter
Integrates groundwater education into state's nature centers. Hands-on activities in natural surroundings to teach dynamics of groundwater.

★4356★ Olgebay Institute
Oglebay Park
Wheeling, WV 26003
Phone: (304)242-6855
Explores habitats of birds, reptiles, and amphibians; studies wildflowers, wild mushrooms, geology, and astronomy. Conducts mountain nature camp for adults.

★4357★ Protect Our Woods
PO Box 352
Paoli, IN 47454
Phone: (812)723-2430
Contact: Andy Mahler
Educational program to protect public forests and to encourage sound, private forest timber management.

★4358★ Rogers State College
Conservation Education Reserve
Will Rogers & College Hill
Claremore, OK 74017
Phone: (918)341-7510
Contact: Dianna McGuire
120-acre wilderness used as an environmental study area; open to students, kindergarten through college, and to general public.

★4359★ San Francisco Bay Bird Observatory
PO Box 247
Alviso, CA 95002
Phone: (408)946-6548
Research and education focuses on marshes, sloughs, and salt ponds of South San Francisco Bay.

★4360★ Thorne Ecological Institute
Institute of River Ecology
5398 Manhattan Circle
Boulder, CO 80303
Phone: (303)499-3647
Contact: Susan Foster
Provides five-day field study program on the Upper Platte River.

★4361★ U.S. Fish and Wildlife Service
National Bison Range Education Program
132 Bison Range Rd.
Moiese, MT 59824
Phone: (406)644-2211
Contact: Marcy Bishop
Teacher workshops, outdoor study, summer day camps, and a resource lending library.

★4362★ Virginia 4-H Outback
Madison & Rappahannock Cooperative Extension Services
PO Box 10
Madison, VA 22727
Phone: (703)948-6881
Contact: Brad Jarvis
Outdoor education program.

★4363★ West Michigan Environmental Action Council
Grand River Expedition
1432 Wealthy St.
Grand Rapids, MI 49506
Phone: (616)451-3051
Contact: Shari Schaftlin
Annual 13-day canoe expedition on Michigan's Grand River.

★4364★ Wilderness Southeast
711 Sandtown Rd.
Savannah, GA 31410
Phone: (912)897-5108
Conducts 3-4 day expeditions to study ecosystems.

★4365★ Yosemite Association
PO Box 230
El Portal, CA 95318
Phone: (209)379-2646
Offers outdoor natural history and science seminars, including geology and botany.

★4366★ Yosemite National Institutes
Golden Gate National Recreation Area
Bldg. 1033
Sausalito, CA 94965
Phone: (415)332-5771
Offers environmental learning experiences for teachers, students, and the general public.

Professional Programs

★4367★ Advanced Sciences Research and Development Corporation
Energy Seminar
PO Box 127
Lakemont, GA 30552
Phone: (404)782-2092
Contact: Dr. Sarah Heronymus, Pres. /Research Dir.

★4368★ Alaska Craftsman Home Program, Inc.
PO Box 876130
Wasilla, AK 99687
Phone: (907)373-2247
Contact: William Harvey Bowers
Educates Alaskan builders, owners and purchasers about the benefits of energy efficiency. Has developed efficiency guidelines.

★4369★ American Council for an Energy-Efficient Economy
Energy Efficiency in Building Conference
1001 Connecticut Ave., Ste. 535
Washington, DC 20036
Phone: (202)429-8873
Contact: Howard Geller, Associate Dir.
Held biennially.

★4370★ American Ecology Services
OSHA Emergency Response Courses
127 E. 59th St.
New York, NY 10022
Phone: (212)371-1620
Contact: Dick Miller
OSHA training courses. Attendees earn certificate upon course completion.

★4371★ American Iron and Steel Institute
1133 15th St. NW
Washington, DC 20005-2701
Phone: (202)452-7265
Contact: William E. Dennis, Pres.
Holds technical symposia for the membership on such subjects as innovative hot strip mill technology, recovery of alloys from specialty steel waste, ladle metallurgy, EAF dust disposal, steel can recycling, and statistical process control for steelmaking refractories.

★4372★ American Petroleum Institute
Oil Spills Conference
1220 L St. NW
Washington, DC 20005
Phone: (202)682-8000
Fax: (202)682-8030
Contact: Charles J. DiBona, Pres.

★4373★ American Petroleum Institute
Pipelines, Marketing, Production, Refining, and Technology Conference
1220 L St. NW
Washington, DC 20005
Phone: (202)682-8000
Fax: (202)682-8030
Contact: Charles J. DiBona, Pres.
Held annually.

★4374★ Appropriate Technology Associates
Solar Energy Training Program
PO Box 1115
Carbondale, CO 81623
Phone: (303)963-0715
Contact: Ken Olson
Teaches practical engineering and hands-on skills in photovoltaics, solar thermal applications and energy efficiency in buildings.

★4375★ Argonne National Laboratory
Nuclear Engineering Education Conference
9700 S. Cass Ave.
Argonne, IL 60439-4832
Phone: (708)972-3872
Contact: Alan Schriesheim, Dir.
Held annually, affiliated with the University of Chicago.

★4376★ Auburn University
Water Resources Research Institute
Water Resource Seminar
202 Hargis Hall
Auburn University, AL 36849-5124
Phone: (205)844-5080
Contact: Dr. Joseph F. Judkins Jr., Dir.
Held periodically.

★4377★ Austin Peay State University
Center for Field Biology Training Seminar
PO Box 4718
Clarksville, TN 37044
Phone: (615)648-7019
Contact: Dr. Benjamin Stone, Dir.
Sponsors technical training seminars for field biologists and other technical staff.

★4378★ BioCycle National Conference
Biocycle
Box 351
Emmaus, PA 18049
Phone: (215)967-4135
Annual conference on composting and recycling, including meetings on research findings, international projects, operator training, and private sector opportunities.

★4379★ B.O.C.E.S./Outdoor Environmental Education
PO Box 604
Smithtown, NY 11787
Phone: (516)360-3652
Conducts in-service teacher training for integrating environmental education into tradition curricula and focuses on hands-on learning.

★4380★ Boston University
Center for Energy and Environmental Studies Lecture Series
675 Commonwealth Ave.
Boston, MA 02215
Phone: (617)353-3083
Fax: (617)353-5986
Contact: Dr. T.R. Lakshmanan, Dir.
Sponsors a series of 14 lectures in spring.

★4381★ Brookhaven National Laboratory
Annual Biology Symposium
Upton Long Island, MA 11973
Phone: (516)282-2123
Fax: (516)282-3000
Contact: N.P. Samios, Dir.

★4382★ Brookyhaven National Laboratory
Upton Long Island, NY 11973
Phone: (516)282-2123
Fax: (516)282-3000
Contact: N.P. Samios, Dir.
Provides research training in science and technology for Ph.D. recipients, visiting scientists, and engineers. Holds weekly seminars and colloquia.

★4383★ California State Polytechnic University
LANDLAB
Recycling Coordinators Certification Program
3801 W. Temple Ave.
Pomona, CA 91768
Phone: (714)869-4449
Fax: (714)869-2292
Contact: Dr. Edwin A. Barnes III, Dir.

★4384★ Casper College
Environmental Training and Resource Center
125 College Dr.
Casper, WY 82601
Phone: (307)268-2670
Contact: William Mixer
Outreach training and quality techical assistance to operators of wastewater treatment plants statewide.

★4385★ Center for Environmental Research
Biological Wastewater Treatment Seminar
c/o Water Utility
PO Box 1088
Austin, TX 78767
Phone: (512)322-2779
Contact: Andrew P. Covar, Dir.

★4386★ Center for Environmental Research
EPA Air Pollution Training Courses
IIT Research Institute
10 W. 35th St.
Chicago, IL 60616
Phone: (312)567-4250
Fax: (312)567-4577
Contact: Dr. Demetrios Moschandreas, Dir.

★4387★ Center for Environmental Research
Metal Speciation, Separation, and Recovery Conference.
IIT Research Institute
10 W. 35th St.
Chicago, IL 60616
Phone: (312)567-4250
Fax: (312)567-4577
Contact: Dr. Demetrios Moschandreas, Dir.

★4388★ Center for Environmental Research
Wastewater Operator Certification Training Program.
c/o Water Utility
PO Box 1088
Austin, TX 78767
Phone: (512)322-2779
Contact: Andrew P. Covar, Dir.

★4389★ Center for Hazardous Materials Research
Hazardous Materials Training Program
Univ. of Pittsburgh Applied Research Center
320 William Pitt Way
Pittsburgh, PA 15238
Phone: (412)826-5320
Fax: (412)826-5552
Contact: Edgar Berkey Ph.D., Pres.

★4390★ Center for Hazardous Materials Research
Health and Safety Training Program
Univ. of Pittsburgh Applied Research Center
320 William Pitt Way
Pittsburgh, PA 15238
Phone: (412)826-5320
Fax: (412)826-5552
Contact: Edgar Berkey, Ph.D., Pres.

★4391★ Center for Hazardous Materials Research
Pesticide Certification Training Program
Univ. of Pittsburgh Applied Research Center
320 William Pitt Way
Pittsburgh, PA 15238
Phone: (412)826-5320
Fax: (412)826-5552
Contact: Edgar Berkey Ph.D., Pres.

★4392★ Center for War/Peace Studies
Global Decision Making Conference
218 E. 18th St.
New York, NY 10003
Phone: (212)475-1077
Fax: (212)260-6384
Contact: Richard Hudson, Exec. Dir.

★4393★ Center Hill Solid and Hazardous Waste Research Laboratory
Land Disposal, Remedial Action, and Treatment of Hazardous Wastes Annual Symposium
5995 Center Hill Rd.
Cincinnati, OH 45224
Phone: (513)569-7885
Contact: P.E. Gerard Roberto, Project Manager

★4394★ Chemical Industry Institute of Toxicology Annual Meeting
6 Davis Dr.
PO Box 12137
Research Triangle Park, NC 27709
Phone: (919)541-2070
Fax: (919)541-9015
Contact: Roger O. McClellan D.V.M., Pres.

★4395★ Colorado State University
National Center for Vehicle Emissions Control and Safety
Mobile Sources/Clean Air Conference
Dept. of Industrial Sciences
Old Industrial Sciences Bldg.
Fort Collins, CO 80523
Phone: (303)491-7240
Fax: (303)491-7801
Contact: Dr. Birgit Wolff, Dir.
Held annually in September.

★4396★ Colorado State University
National Center for Vehicle Emissions Control and Safety Workshops Series
Dept. of Industrial Sciences
Old Industrial Sciences Bldg.
Fort Collins, CO 80523
Phone: (303)491-7240
Fax: (303)491-7801
Contact: Dr. Birgit Wolff, Dir.
Develops instructional curricula and courses for clean air program managers, automotive instructors, and automotive service technicians. Offers courses and workshops on air-tampering, vehicle emissions, fixing inspection/mainenance failures on computer-cotrolled cars, and alternative fuels and the catalytic converter function.

★4397★ Colorado State University
Whole-Body Counter
Occupational and Environmental Radiation Protection Training Program
Dept. of Radiation Biology
Fort Collins, CO 80523
Phone: (303)491-5380
Contact: Dr. James E. Johnson, Dir.

★4398★ Creative Media and Environmental Education
9730 Manitou Pl.
Bainbridge Island, WA 98110
Phone: (206)842-2229
Offers environmental education program and workshops for educators on wetlands, recycling, and water quality.

★4399★ Duke University
Center for International Development Research Professional Training Program
Institute of Policy Studies
4875 Duke Sta.
Durham, NC 27706
Phone: (919)684-6360
Fax: (919)684-2861
Contact: Dr. William Ascher, Codirector
Offers academic year and short-term training for mid-career professionals from developing countries. Also offers degree program in International Development Policy.

★4400★ Duke University
Center for International Development Research
Rethinking Development Policy Workshop
Institute of Policy Studies
4875 Duke Sta.
Durham, NC 27706
Phone: (919)684-6360
Fax: (919)684-2861
Contact: Dr. William Ascher, Codirector
Held during the academic year.

★4401★ Edudex Associates, Kettle Moraine Division
604 2nd Ave.
West Bend, WI 53095
Phone: (414)334-4978
Natural and human resources organization designs, delivers, and evaluates outdoor, conservation, and environmental experiential programs internationally.

★4402★ Electric Power Research Institute
Air Pollution Control Program
3412 Hillview Ave.
Palo Alto, CA 94303
Phone: (415)855-2422
Contact: Ian Torrens
Develops cost-effective air pollution control technologies for power plants and utilities. Informational guides and computer software available from program.

★4403★ Emergency Response National Conference
c/o Tower Conference Management Co.
800 Roosevelt Rd., Bldg. E, Ste. 408
Glen Ellyn, IL 60137-5835
Phone: (708)469-3373
Fax: (708)469-7477
Annual conference and exhibition for environmental emergency response specialists, sponsored by Roosevelt University, National Spill Control School, National Fire Protection Association, National Coordinating Council on Emergency Management, International Hazards Materials Association, *911 Magazine*, among others.

★4404★ Environmental Hazards Management Institute
First 12 Hours: A Hazardous Materials Seminar & Simulation
10 New Market Rd.
PO Box 932
Durham, NH 03824
Phone: (603)868-1496
Fax: (603)868-1547
Contact: Alan J. Borner, Exec. Dir.
Held quarterly.

★4405★ Environmental Hazards Management Institute
Hazmat
10 Newmarket Rd.
PO Box 932
Durham, NH 03824
Phone: (603)868-1496
Fax: (603)868-1547
Contact: Alan J. Borner, Exec. Dir.
A series of conferences on hazardous waste, open to the industry, regulatory personnel, and citizens.

★4406★ Environmental Media
PO Box 1016
Chapel Hill, NC 27514
Phone: (919)933-3003
Manages design, production, and distribution of media to support environmental education, concentrating on television programs and guides.

★4407★ Environmental Resource Center
3679 Rosehill Rd.
Fayetteville, NC 28311-6634
Offers hazardous waste management seminars for environmental professionals.

★4408★ Federal Interagency Sedimentation Project
Sedimentation Lecture Series
St. Anthony Falls Hydraulic Laboratory
Hennepin Island & 3rd Ave. SE
Minneapolis, MN 55414
Phone: (612)370-2362
Fax: (612)627-4609
Contact: John V. Skinner, Project Leader

★4409★ **Federal Publications**
Environmental Law Seminars
1120 20th St., NW
Washington, DC 20036
Phone: (202)337-7000
Courses on environmental law.

★4410★ **Florida Defenders of the Environment**
Environmental Networking Program
2606 NW 6th St.
Gainesville, FL 32609
Phone: (904)372-6965
Contact: Dr. Marjorie Abrams
Education and information network for county and regional environmental issues.

★4411★ **Florida Governor's Energy Office**
Home Builder Design and Education
The Capitol
Tallahassee, FL 32399-0001
Phone: (904)488-2475
Contact: Daryl O'Conner
A State program designed to improve housing and development planning; to conserve energy, land and water resources. Offers conferences, workshops and seminars for developers and planners.

★4412★ **Foundation for Glacier and Environmental Research, Inc.**
514 E. 1st St.
Moscow, ID 83848
Contact: Dr. Maynard M. Miller, Exec. Dir.
Holds conferences and seminars on glaciology, glacier climatology, Pleistocene stratigraphy, and arctic and mountain environmental sciences.

★4413★ **Foundation for Glacier and Environmental Research, Inc.**
Polar and Alpine Geoscience Training Project
514 E. 1st St.
Moscow, ID 83848
Contact: Dr. Maynard M. Miller, Exec. Dir.
Cosponsored with the International Training Section of the U.S. Geological Survey, for scientists from less developed countries.

★4414★ **Georgia Institute of Technology**
Economic Development Laboratory Continuing Education Office
Georgia Tech Researtch Institute
Atlanta, GA 30332
Phone: (404)894-3841
Fax: (404)853-9172
Contact: Dr. David S. Clifton Jr., Dir.
Conducts courses, conferences, and workshops for professionals on topics such as economic development, asbestos, industrial safety and hygeine, industrial toxicology, formaldehyde, hazardous waste, and industrial technology.

★4415★ **Global Foundation, Inc.**
PO Box 248103
Coral Gables, FL 33124-8103
Phone: (305)284-4457
Contact: Dr. Behrem N. Kursunoglu, Chm.
Organizes university courses on nuclear war and nuclear peace; also offers teacher workshops on the nuclear era.

★4416★ **Global Foundation, Inc.**
International Scientific Forum on Energy
PO Box 248103
Coral Gables, FL 33124-8103
Phone: (305)284-4457
Contact: Dr. Behrem N. Kursunoglu, Chm.
Held annually.

★4417★ **Harvard University**
Kresge Center for Environmental Health
Air Cleaning Conference
665 Huntington Ave.
Harvard, MA 02115
Phone: (617)732-1272
Contact: John B. Little M.D., Dir.
Held biennially in August for air cleaning experts from colleges, industry, and government research orginizations. Also offers 15 courses for mid-career personnel as part of the Center's Continuing Education Program.

★4418★ **Hazardous Materials Control Research Institute**
Annual Superfund Conference
9300 Columbia Blvd.
Silver Springs, MD 20910
Phone: (301)587-9390
Fax: (301)589-0182
Contact: Hal Bernard, Dir.

★4419★ **Hazardous Materials Management Conference and Exhibition**
c/o Tower Conference Management Co.
800 Roosevelt Rd., Bldg. E408
Glen Ellyn, IL 60137-5835
Phone: (708)469-3373
Annual conference and exhibition focusing on hazardous waste management.

★4420★ **Hazardous Substances Research Center for U.S. EPA Regions 7 & 8 AnnualConference**
University of Kansas
Dept. of Chemical Engineering
Durland Hall
Manhattan, KS 66506-5102
Phone: (913)532-5584
Fax: (913)532-7810
Contact: Dr. Larry Erickson, Dir.

★4421★ **Hazardous Waste Research and Information Center**
Hazardous Waste Research Seminar
1 E. Hazelwood Dr.
Champaign, IL 61820
Phone: (217)333-8940
Fax: (217)333-8944
Contact: Dr. David L. Thomas, Dir.
Held periodically.

★4422★ **Hazardous Waste Research and Information Center**
Pollution Prevention Conference
1 E. Hazelwood Dr.
Champaign, IL 61820
Phone: (217)333-8940
Fax: (217)333-8944
Contact: Dr. David L. Thomas, Dir.
Held annually.

★4423★ **Health and Energy Institute**
Annual Radiation Victims Roundtable
PO Box 5357
Tacoma Park, MD 20913
Phone: (301)585-5541
Contact: Kathleen M. Tucker, Dir.

★4424★ **Health Effects Institute**
HEI Annual Conference
141 Portland St., Ste. 7300
Cambridge, MA 02139
Phone: (617)621-0266
Fax: (617)621-0267
Contact: Andrew Sivak Ph.D., Pres.

★4425★ **Heidelberg College**
Water Quality Laboratory
Nonpoint-Source Pollution Research Workshop
Tiffin, OH 44883
Phone: (419)448-2201
Contact: Dr. David Baker, Dir.
Held annually.

★4426★ **Illinois Department of Energy and Natural Resources**
Sustainable Agriculture Program
325 W. Adams
Springfield, IL 62704
Phone: (217)785-8582
Contact: Deborah Cavanaugh-Grant
Tests and teaches sustainable agriculture practices to farmers.

★4427★ **Illinois Institute of Technology**
Industrial Waste Elimination Research Center
3200 S. State St.
Chicago, IL 60616
Phone: (312)567-3535
Fax: (312)567-3548
Contact: Kenneth E. Noll, Dir.
Holds semiannual review meetings with industry and scientific advisory committees and scientists and engineers of the U.S. Environmental Protection Agency.

★4428★ **Illinois Institute of Technology**
Industrial Waste Elimination Research Center
Metals Speciation, Separation, and Recovery International Symposium
3200 S. State St.
Chicago, IL 60616
Phone: (312)567-3535
Fax: (312)567-3548
Contact: Kenneth E. Noll, Dir.
Held biennially.

★4429★ **Illinois State Water Survey**
2204 Griffith Dr.
Champaign, IL 61820-7495
Phone: (217)333-2210
Fax: (217)333-6540
Contact: Richard G. Semonin, Chief
Holds annual conferences for institutional powerplant engineers, short courses in groundwater engineering, and periodic seminars and lectures.

★4430★ **Indiana University**
National Institute for Global Environmental Change Annual Conference
School of Public & Environmental Affairs
SPEA, Rm. 441
Bloomington, IN 47405
Phone: (812)855-2457
Fax: (812)855-7802
Contact: Prof. J.C. Randolph, Dir.

★4431★ **Institute for Earth Education**
Box 288
Warrenville, IL 60555
Phone: (708)393-3096
Program development and support for education professionals.

★4432★ **Institute for Environmental Education**
Cleveland Teacher's Internship Program
32000 Chagrin Blvd.
Cleveland, OH 44124
Phone: (216)464-1775
Contact: Joseph H. Chadbourne, Pres.
A professional advancement course series for area K-12 teachers and college and university faculty; the Program allows teachers to learn

on-the-job applications of their instructional fields through interning with 60 corporations.

★4433★ Institute for Resource Management Symposia Series
262 S. 200 W.
Salt Lake City, UT 84101
Phone: (801)322-0530
Fax: (801)328-3457
Contact: Terrell Minger, Pres. and CEO
Holds conferences and symposia on solid waste management, global climate change, nuclear power, and other environmental concerns.

★4434★ Iowa State University
Leopold Center for Sustainable Agriculture
Cropping and Livestock Management Practices Annual Conference
126 Soil Tilth Bldg.
Ames, IA 50011
Phone: (515)294-3711
Fax: (515)294-9696
Contact: Prof. Dennis R. Keeney, Dir.

★4435★ Land Trust Alliance
1017 Duke St.
Chicago, IL 22314
Phone: (703)683-7778
Provides education materials to land conservation professionals.

★4436★ Lenox Institute of Water Technology
Environmental and Flotation Technology Program
101 Yokun Ave.
PO Box 1639
Lenox, MA 01240
Phone: (413)637-3025
Fax: (413)637-0768
Contact: S. Malumphy, Administrative Manager

★4437★ Lenox Institute of Water Technology
Flotation Technology Continuing Education Program
101 Yokun Ave.
PO Box 1639
Lenox, MA 01240
Phone: (413)637-3025
Fax: (413)637-0768
Contact: S. Malumphy, Administrative Manager

★4438★ Lenox Institute of Water Technology
Symposia on Environmental Technology and Management
101 Yokun Ave.
PO Box 1639
Lenox, MA 01240
Phone: (413)637-3025
Fax: (413)637-0768
Contact: S. Malumphy, Administrative Manager
Holds one to five per year.

★4439★ Lighting Design Laboratory
NRDC/Northwest Conservation Act Coalition/ City of Seattle
400 E. Pine St.
Seattle, WA 98104
Phone: (206)325-9695
Contact: Diana Campbell
Provides technical assistance and education to architects, developers and lighting designers on energy-efficient lighting technology and design in buildings.

★4440★ Louisiana State University
Hazardous Waste Research Center Annual Meeting
3418 CEBA Bldg.
Baton Rouge, LA 70803
Phone: (504)388-6770
Fax: (504)388-5990
Contact: Prof. L.J. Thibodeaux, Dir.
Sponsors annual meeting in October to evaluate on-going hazardous waste research.

★4441★ Mark Trail/Ed Dodd Foundation
PO Box 2807
Gainesville, GA 30503
Phone: (404)532-4274

★4442★ Massachusetts Institute of Technology
MIT Sea Grant College Program
MIT Marine Industry Collegium Workshop
292 Main St.
Cambridge, MA 02139
Phone: (617)253-7041
Fax: (617)253-8000
Contact: Chryssostomos Chryssostomidis, Dir.
Held four times per year, open members only.

★4443★ Michigan State University
Pesticide Research Center
Environmental Toxicology Annual Conference
East Lansing, MI 48824-1311
Phone: (517)353-9430

★4444★ Michigan State University
Pesticide Research Center
Integrated Pest Management Training
East Lansing, MI 48824-1311
Phone: (517)353-9430
Contact: Robert M. Hollingsworth, Dir.

★4445★ Michigan State University
Pesticide Research Center
Pesticide Applicator Certification Training
East Lansing, MI 48824-1311
Phone: (517)353-9430
Contact: Robert M. Hollingsworth, Dir.

★4446★ Midwest Research Institute
Annual Economic Outlook Conference
425 Volker Blvd.
Kansas City, MO 64110-2299
Phone: (816)753-7600
Fax: (816)753-8420
Contact: John C. McKelvey, Pres. and CEO

★4447★ Midwest Research Institute
Midcontinent Perspectives
425 Volker Blvd.
Kansas City, MO 64110-2299
Phone: (816)753-7600
Fax: (816)753-8420
Contact: John C. McKelvey, Pres. and CEO
Bimonthly lecture series.

★4448★ Minnesota Pollution Control Agency
Hazardous Waste Generators Program
520 Lafayette Road N.
St. Paul, MN 55155
Phone: (612)643-3496
Contact: Ed Meyer
Focuses on safe management of hazardous waste.

★4449★ Montana State University
Reclamation Research Unit
Billings Symposium on Surface Mining on the Great Plains
Animal & Range Science Dept.
Bozeman, MT 59717
Phone: (406)994-4821
Fax: (406)994-6579
Contact: Dr. Frank F. Munshower, Dir.
Held on a 2-3 year rotation, in March.

★4450★ MPC Environmental Services
MPC Training Center
PO Box 610
Calverton, NY 11193
Phone: (516)369-4900
Provides professional training in emergency response and environmental cleanup, including oil spill response. Programs are available for corporate executives, consultants, site workers, and cleanup crews.

★4451★ National Association of Water Institute Directors
Water Resources Institute Program
c/o Montana Water Resources Research Center
Cobleigh Hall
Montana State Univ.
Bozeman, MT 59717
Phone: (406)994-6690
Professional training through a network of 45 university-sponsored water research institutes.

★4452★ National Center for Food and Agricultural Policy
Leadership Development in Food and Ag Policy
Resources for the Future
1616 P St. NW
Washington, DC 20036
Phone: (202)328-5082
Fax: (202)265-8069
Contact: George E. Rossmiller, Dir.
Held annually in February and March, open to individuals with bachelor's degrees and five years experience.

★4453★ National Energy Management Institute
601 N. Fairfax St., Ste. 160
Alexandria, VA 22314
Phone: (703)739-7100
Contact: Donald L. Lahr
Trains contractors and technicians in energy management and conservation techniques.

★4454★ National Environmental Training Association
Certified Environmental Trainer Program
8687 E. Via de Ventura, Ste. 214
Scottsdale, AZ 85258
Phone: (602)951-1440
Fax: (602)483-0083
National voluntary credentialing system providing certification in areas such as asbestos abatement, hazard communication, hazardous waste operation and emergency response, occupational health and safety, transporation of hazardous substances, wastewater and water treatment.

★4455★ National Oceanic and Atmospheric Administration
NOAA Educational Affairs Division
Rm. 105, Rockwall Bldg.
11400 Rockville Pike
Rockville, MD 20852
Phone: (202)673-5381
Educational division of NOAA works with major universities and nonprofit organizations to support the design of curriculum materials. Provides tours of facilities, internships, and supports educational projects.

★4456★ National Wildlife Federation Educators' Summit
1400 16th St. NW
Washington, DC 20036-2266
Toll-Free: 800-432-6564
Provides professional educators with training in environmental education, including creative lesson planning, hands-on activities, field trips, and teaching strategies and techniques.

★4457★ National Wildlife Federation Nature Quest
1400 16th St. NW
Washington, DC 20036-2266
Toll-Free: 800-432-6564
Certified training center for camp directors, nature and science councelors, naturalists, and outdoor educators. Participants design hands-on nature programs for their individual sites and needs.

★4458★ National Wildlife Federation Nature Scope Workshops
1400 16th St. NW
Washington, DC 20036-2266
Phone: (703)790-4359
Hands-on program for K-8 educators to learn how to integrate environmental education into the curriculum.

★4459★ Natural Organic Farmers Association of Vermont
Organic Farm Certification and Education
15 Barre St.
Montpelier, VT 05602
Phone: (802)223-7222
Contact: Enid Wonnacott
Certification program for commercial organic producers.

★4460★ New Mexico State University
Center for Biochemical Engineering Research
Joint Symposium on Biosynthesis
Dept. of Chemical Engineering
Box 30001, Dept. 3805
Las Cruces, NM 88003-0001
Phone: (505)646-1214
Fax: (505)646-3549
Contact: Dr. Ron Bhada, Dir.
Held biennially in September.

★4461★ North Carolina Alternative Energy Corp.
North Carolina Heat Pump Skills Center
PO Box 12699
Research Triangle, NC 27709
Phone: (919)361-8018
Contact: C. Leon Neal
A training and certification program that teaches energy conservation ethics and techniques to central air conditioner and heat pump service technicians on a voluntary basis.

★4462★ North Dakota State University
Land Reclamation Research Center
NDSU-Reclamation
PO Box 459
Mandan, ND 58554
Phone: (701)663-6445
Fax: (701)667-1811
Contact: Dr. Eugene C. Doll, Superintendent
Holds periodic research review workshops.

★4463★ Oklahoma State University
Center for Environmental Education
Environmental Education Workshops
206 Gunderson Hall
Stillwater, OK 74078
Phone: (405)744-7125
Fax: (405)744-7713
Contact: Dr. Ted J. Mills, Dir.
Held annually in October, March, April, and June.

★4464★ Oklahoma State University
Center for Environmental Education
Environmental Science Graduate Education Program
206 Gunderson Hall
Stillwater, OK 74078
Phone: (405)744-7125
Fax: (405)744-7713
Contact: Dr. Ted J. Mills, Dir.

★4465★ Oklahoma State University
Engineering Energy Laboratory Annual Meeting
Rm. 216 Engineering S.
Stillwater, OK 74078
Phone: (405)744-5157
Fax: (405)744-6187
Contact: Dr. Rama Ramakumar, Dir.
Sponsors annual meeting of utility companies.

★4466★ Oklahoma State University
Engineering Energy Laboratory
Frontiers of Power Conference
Rm. 216 Engineering S.
Stillwater, OK 74078
Phone: (405)744-5157
Fax: (405)744-6187
Contact: Dr. Rama Ramakumar, Dir.
Held annually.

★4467★ Outdoor Leadership Training Seminars/Breaking Through Adventures
PO Box 200281
Denver, CO 80200
Phone: (303)333-7831
Alt. Phone: (303)320-0372
Trains outdoor leaders in outdoor skills with emphasis on deep ecology.

★4468★ Project WILD
National Office, PO Box 18060
Dept. B
Boulder, CO 80308-8060
Phone: (303)444-2390
Workshops for K-12 educators on environmental and conservation issues. Available in all 50 states.

★4469★ Rocky Mountain Law Foundation
Rocky Mountain Mineral Law Institute
Porter Administration Bldg., 3rd Fl.
7039 E. 18th Ave.
Denver, CO 80220
Phone: (303)321-8100
Fax: (303)321-7657
Contact: David P. Phillips, Exec. Dir.
Held annually for three days.

★4470★ Rocky Mountain Mineral Law Foundation
Mineral Law
Porter Administration Bldg., 3rd Fl.
7039 E. 18th Ave.
Denver, CO 80220
Phone: (303)321-8100
Fax: (303)321-7657
Contact: David P. Phillips, Exec. Dir.
A week-long course.

★4471★ Roger Tory Peterson Institute
110 Marvin Pkwy.
Jamestown, NY 14701
Phone: (716)665-2473
Nature in education programs for teachers and nature education professionals.

★4472★ Salt Institute Seminars
700 N. Fairfax St., Ste. 600
Alexandria, VA 22314
Phone: (703)549-4648
Contact: Richard Hanneman, Pres.
Holds salting seminars for highway maintenance personnel.

★4473★ San Diego State University
Center for Energy Studies
U.S./Mexico Energy Seminar
Dept. of Physics
San Diego, CA 92182
Phone: (619)594-6240
Fax: (619)594-5485
Contact: Dr. Alan Sweedler, Dir.

★4474★ Southern Illinois University at Carbondale
Touch of Nature Environmental Center
Wilderness Workshops for Professionals
Carbondale, IL 62901-6623
Phone: (618)453-1121
Contact: Phillip Lindberg, Dir.
Sponsored three times per year; spring, summer, and fall.

★4475★ Southwest Environmental Hazards Conference and Expo
c/o Tower Conference Management Co.
800 Roosevelt Rd., Bldg. E408
Glen Ellyn, IL 60137-5835
Phone: (708)469-3373
Alt. Phone: (708)469-7477
Annual conference focusing on hazardous waste management.

★4476★ State University of New York at Stony Brook
Living Marine Resources Institute Conference
Stony Brook, NY 11794-5000
Phone: (516)632-8656
Contact: Dr. Bill Wise, Dir.
Sponsors periodic conferences and symposia on issues related to fisheries and their effects on the environment.

★4477★ State University of New York at Stony Brook
Waste Management Institute Symposia
Stony Brook, NY 11794-5000
Phone: (703)771-6800
Contact: Dr. Bill Wise
Sponsors periodic workshops and symposia on solid waste disposal, recycling, and other waste management issues.

★4478★ Syracuse University
Institute for Energy Research
Knowledged-Based Systems Seminar
103 College Pl.
Syracuse, NY 13244-4010
Phone: (315)423-3353
Contact: Dr. Walter Meyer, Dir.
Offered to EPRI-member utility employees.

★4479★ Teaching Environmental Awareness
Pennsylvania Power & Light
Two N. Ninth St.
Allentown, PA 18101
Phone: (215)774-6914
One-day, in-service training session sponsored by utility provides teachers with materials and background information needed to enhance students environmental awareness.

★4480★ Tennessee Valley Authority
Forest Resource Development
Norris, TN 37828
Phone: (615)494-9800

Contact: Rick Toennisson
Conducts technical assistance and educational programs.

★4481★ Texas A&M University
Center for Dredging Studies
Dredging Engineering Short Course
Texas Engineering Experiment Sta.
College Station, TX 77843-3136
Phone: (409)845-4517
Contact: Dr. John B. Herbich, Dir.
Held annually in January.

★4482★ Texas A&M University
Center for Dredging Studies
Dredging Seminar
Texas Engineering Experiment Sta.
College Station, TX 77843-3136
Phone: (409)845-4517
Contact: Dr. John B. Herbich, Dir.
Held annually, September-November.

★4483★ Texas A&M University
Environmnental and Water Resources Engineering Area
Water Distribution Short Course
Civil Engineering Dept.
College Station, TX 77843
Phone: (409)845-3011
Contact: Bill Batchelor, Area Leader

★4484★ Texas A&M University
Environmental and Water Resources Area
Flood and Flood Rain Analysis Short Course
Civil Engineering Dept.
College Station, TX 77843
Phone: (409)845-3011
Contact: Bill Batchelor, Area Leader

★4485★ Texas A&M University
Environmental and Water Resources Engineering Area
Steam Hydrology and Hydraulics Short Course
Civil Engineering Dept.
College Station, TX 77843
Phone: (409)845-3011
Contact: Bill Batchelor, Area Leader

★4486★ Texas A&M University
Environmental and Water Resources Engineering Area
System Analysis Short Course
Civil Engineering Dept.
College Station, TX 77843
Phone: (409)845-3011
Contact: Bill Batchelor, Area Leader

★4487★ Texas A&M University
Environmental and Water Resources Engineering Area
Two-Dimensional River Modeling Short Course
Civil Engineering Dept.
College Station, TX 77843
Phone: (409)845-3011
Contact: Bill Batchelor, Area Leader

★4488★ Texas A&M University
Sea Grant College Program
Marine Industry Management Seminars
College Station, TX 77843
Phone: (409)845-3854
Contact: Thomas J. Bright, Dir.
Holds two or three annually.

★4489★ Thames Science Center
Gallows Ln.
New London, CT 06320
Phone: (203)442-0391
Conducts lab and field experiments on local watersheds, open to classroom teachers.

★4490★ Tufts University
Center for Environmental Management
Environmental Management Institute
Curtis Hall
474 Boston Ave.
Medford, MA 02155
Phone: (617)381-3486
Fax: (617)381-3084
Contact: Dr. William R. Moomaw, Dir.
A three-week summer program.

★4491★ Tulane University
Environmental Health Sciences Research Laboratory
International Water Quality Seminar
Edward Hebert Research Center
Belle Chasse, LA 70037
Phone: (504)394-2233
Contact: Jamal Y. Shamas, Lab Supervisor/ Research Coordinator
Held periodically.

★4492★ Tulune University
Environmental Health Sciences Research Laboratory Training Program
F. Edward Hebert Research Center
Belle Chasse, LA 70037
Phone: (504)394-2233
Contact: Jamal Y. Shamas, Lab Supervisor/ Research Coordinator
Provides master's and doctoral research training.

★4493★ University and Forest Service Cooperative Forest-Fire Fighter Training Program
Ozark National Forest/Arkansas Technical University
PO Box 1008
Russellville, AR 72801
Phone: (501)968-2354
Contact: Jack Kriesel
Provides field training and academic credit in forest firefighting.

★4494★ University of Alabama
Alabama Waste Exchange Workshop
Box 870203
Tuscaloosa, AL 35487-0203
Phone: (205)348-5889
Fax: (205)348-8573
Contact: William J. Herz, Dir.
Sponsors workshop series for small quantity generators of individual waste.

★4495★ University of Arizona
Natural Resources Conservation Workshops
RNR/B SE 325
Tucson, AZ 85704
Phone: (602)621-7269
Natural resources conservation workshop for educators.

★4496★ University of Arizona
Solar and Energy Research Facility
National Conference on Microcomputer Applications for Conservation and Renewable Energy
College of Engineering & Mines
Tuscon, AZ 85721
Phone: (602)621-7496
Contact: Donald E. Osborn, Sr. Research Specialist

★4497★ University of Arizona
Solar and Energy Research Facility
SOLERAS Student Short Course on Monitoring, Data Acquisition and Performance Evaluation of Solar Energy Projects
College of Engineering & Mines
Tucson, AZ 85721
Phone: (602)621-7496
Contact: Donald E. Osborn, Sr. Research Specialist

★4498★ University of California
California Water Resources Center
Ground Water Conference
Riverside, CA 92521
Phone: (714)787-4327
Fax: (714)787-5295
Contact: Dr. Henry J. Vaux, Dir.
Held biennially.

★4499★ University of California, Davis
Center for Design Research
Environmental Design Symposia
Dept. of Environmental Design
Davis, CA 95616
Phone: (916)752-6223
Fax: (916)752-6363
Contact: Mark Francis, Dir.

★4500★ University of California, Davis
Division of Occupational and Environmental Medicine
Northern California Occupational Health Symposium
Davis, CA 95616
Phone: (916)752-4256
Contact: Dr. Marc B. Schenker, Division Chief
Held annually, open to occupational medicine practioners, interns, and representatives from industry.

★4501★ University of California, Davis
Sustainable Agriculture Program
Women in Agriculture Conference
Dept. of Agronomy & Range Science
Davis, CA 95616
Phone: (916)752-7645
Contact: Mark Van Horn, Program Coordinator
Held annually in February.

★4502★ University of California, Irvine
Air Pollution Health Effects Laboratory Scientific Seminar
Dept. of Community & Enviromental Medicine
Irvine, CA 92717
Phone: (714)856-5860
Fax: (714)856-4763
Contact: Dr. Robert F. Phalen, Dir.
Sponsors scientific seminars for visiting and staff scientists (approximately monthly).

★4503★ University of California, Santa Cruz
Agroecology Program
Santa Cruz, CA 95064
Phone: (408)459-4540
Contact: Jackelyn Lundy
Educational and research program.

★4504★ University of Delaware
Center for Energy and Urban Policy Research
Annual Energy Policy Research Colloquium Series
College of Urban Affairs & Public Policy
Newark, DE 19716
Phone: (302)451-8405
Fax: (302)292-3587
Contact: Dr. John M. Byrne, Dir.

★4505★ University of Delaware
Center for Energy and Urban Policy Research
International Symposium on Energy and the Environment
College of Urban Affairs & Public Policy
Newark, DE 19716
Phone: (302)451-8405
Fax: (302)292-3587
Contact: Dr. John M. Byrne, Dir.

★4506★ University of Findlay
Emergency Response Training Center
Findlay, OH 45840
Phone: (419)424-4647
Toll-Free: 800-521-1292
Offers approximately 30 seminars and training programs on emergency response, OSHA safety, RCRA regulations regarding waste disposal, environment/property issues, groundwater problems, and specialized courses as needed.

★4507★ University of Hawaii at Manoa
Hawaii Cooperative Fishery Research Unit
Fishery Biologists Training Program
2538 The Mall
Honolulu, HI 96822
Phone: (808)965-8350
Fax: (808)956-6731
Contact: Dr. James D. Parrish, Unit Leader

★4508★ University of Kentucky
Kentucky Water Resources Research Institute
Urban Hydrology Symposia
219 Anderson Hall
Lexington, KY 40506-0046
Phone: (606)257-1832
Contact: Dr. Ralph R. Huffsey, Dir.

★4509★ University of Kentucky
Kentucky Water Resources Research Institute
Water Resources Research in Kentucky Symposia
219 Anderson Hall
Lexington, KY 40506-0046
Phone: (606)257-1832
Contact: Dr. Ralph R. Huffsey, Dir.

★4510★ University of Lowell
Toxics Use Reduction Institute
1 University Ave.
Lowell, MA 01854-9985
Phone: (508)934-3250
Fax: (508)452-5711
Contact: Ken Geiser, Dir.
Conducts workshops on toxics use reduction.

★4511★ University of Massachusetts
Massachusetts Cooperative Fish and Wildlife Unit
Fishery Biologists Research Training Program
Holdsworth Hall
Amherst, MA 01003
Phone: (413)545-0398
Contact: Dr. Rebecca Field, Unit Leader

★4512★ University of Miami
Center for Theoretical Studies
International Scientific Forums on Energy
PP Box 249055
Coral Gables, FL 33124-5510
Phone: (305)284-4455
Fax: (305)284-4456
Contact: Prof. Behram N. Kursunoglu, Dir.
Held annually in November.

★4513★ University of Miami
Center for Theoretical Studies
Orbis Scientiae
PO Box 249055
Coral Gables, FL 33124-5510
Phone: (305)284-4455
Fax: (305)284-4456
Contact: Prof. Behram N. Kursunoglu, Dir.
Held annually in January.

★4514★ University of Miami
Clean Energy Research Institute
Energy and Environment Seminar
218 Arthur Bldg.
Coral Gables, FL 33124
Phone: (305)284-4666
Fax: (305)284-4792
Contact: Dr. T. Nejat Veziroglu, Dir.

★4515★ University of Miami
Clean Energy Research Institute
Miami International Conference on Alternative Energy Sources
218 McArthur Bldg.
Coral Gables, FL 33124
Phone: (305)284-4666
Fax: (305)284-4792
Contact: Dr. T. Nejat Veziroglu, Dir.
Held annually.

★4516★ University of Michigan
Institute of Environmental and Industrial Health
Environmental Health Sciences Discussional
School of Public Health
Ann Arbor, MI 48109
Phone: (313)764-3188
Fax: (313)763-5455
Contact: Robert Gray, Dir.
Held annually, attendance by invitation to environmentalists in state and local governments and industry.

★4517★ University of Michigan
Institute of Environmental and Industrial Health
Industrial Hygiene Discussional
School of Public Health
Ann Arbor, MI 48109
Phone: (313)764-3188
Fax: (313)763-5455
Contact: Robert Gray, Dir.
Held annually, attendance by invitation to industrial hygienists in U.S. and Canada.

★4518★ University of Michigan
Institute of Environmental and Industrial Health
Selby Discussional
School of Public Health
Ann Arbor, MI 48109
Phone: (313)764-3188
Fax: (313)763-5455
Contact: Robert Gray, Dir.
Held annually, on mutual problems and new proceedings in occupational health, attendance by invitation to medical directors in U.S. and Canada.

★4519★ University of Minnesota
Center for International Food and Agricultural Policy
U.S. Italy Conference on Agricultural Policy and the Environment
332 Classroom Office Bldg.
1994 Buford Ave.
St. Paul, MN 55108
Phone: (612)625-9208
Fax: (612)625-6245
Contact: Carlisle Ford Runge, Dir.
Annually each summer.

★4520★ University of Minnesota
St. Anthony Falls Hydraulic Laboratory
Small-Scale Hydropower Short Course
Mississippi River at 3rd Ave., SE
Minneapolis, MN 55414-2196
Phone: (612)627-4010
Fax: (612)627-4609
Contact: Dr. Roger E.A. Arndt, Dir.
Held annually.

★4521★ University of Mississippi
Center for Computational Hydroscience and Engineering
Computational Hydrosciences and Sedimentation Research International Symposia
University, MS 38677
Phone: (601)232-7788
Fax: (601)232-7796
Contact: Dr. Sam S.Y. Wang, Dir.

★4522★ University of Montana
Wilderness Institute
Forestry Bldg., Rm. 207
Missoula, MT 59812
Phone: (406)243-5361
Contact: Dr. Alan McQuilan, Exec. Dir.
Offers professional continuing education opportunities and provides educational services to local elementary schools. Sponsors Wilderness Lecture Series (nine times per year).

★4523★ University of Nevada—Las Vegas
Environment Research Center Seminar Series
4505 S. Maryland Pkwy.
Las Vegas, NV 89154-4009
Phone: (702)739-3382
Fax: (702)739-3094
Contact: Dr. Delbert S. Barth, Dir.
Sponsors national and international seminars in geophysical methods, geostatistical techniques, exposure assessment, multimedia monitoring, active remote sensing, sampling design, chemical/physical methods development, and quality assurance.

★4524★ University of New Hampshire
Cooperative Institute for the Remote Sensing of Biogeophysical Processes
Geographic Information Systems Training Workshops
Complex Systems Research Center
Durham, NH 03824
Phone: (603)862-1792
Fax: (603)862-1915
Contact: Dr. Barret N. Rock, Codirector

★4525★ University of New Hampshire
Cooperative Institute for the Remote Sensing of Biogeophysical Processes
Image Processing Training Workshop
Complex Systems Research Center
Durham, NH 03824
Phone: (603)862-1792
Fax: (603)862-1915
Contact: Dr. Barret N. Rock, Codirector

★4526★ University of North Carolina at Charlotte
Southeast Waste Exchange
Small Quantity Generator Workshops
Charlotte, NC 28223
Phone: (704)547-2307
Contact: Maxie L. May, Dir.
Held each spring and fall for industry representatives with some agency and environmental group representatives in attendance.

★4527★ University of North Carolina at Charlotte
Southeast Waste Exchange
Waste Minimization: Success Through Waste Exchange Workshops
Charlotte, NC 28223
Phone: (704)547-2307
Contact: Maxie L. May, Dir.
Held each spring and fall for industry representatives with some agency and environmental group representatives in attendance.

★4528★ University of North Dakota
Energy & Environmental Research Center
Asphalt Paving Conference
Box 8213, Univ. Sta.
Grand Forks, ND 58202
Phone: (701)777-5000
Fax: (701)777-5181
Contact: Dr. Gerald H. Groenewold, Dir.
Held annually.

★4529★ University of North Dakota
Energy & Environmental Research Center
Biennial Low-Rank Fuels Symposium
Box 8213, Univ. Sta.
Grand Forks, ND 58202
Phone: (701)777-5000
Fax: (701)777-5181
Contact: Dr. Gerald H. Groenewold, Dir.
Held in May of odd-numbered years.

★4530★ University of North Dakota
Energy & Environmental Research Center
Opportunities in SynFuels Industry Conference
Box 8213, Univ. Sta.
Grand Forks, ND 58202
Phone: (701)777-5000
Fax: (701)777-5181
Contact: Dr. Gerald H. Groenewold, Dir.
Held in even-numbered years.

★4531★ University of North Dakota
Energy & Environmental Research Center
Utilization of Ash Workshop
Box 8213, Univ. Sta.
Grand Forks, ND 58202
Phone: (701)777-5000
Fax: (701)777-5181
Contact: Dr. Gerald H. Groenewold, Dir.
Held annually.

★4532★ University of North Texas
Institute of Applied Sciences
Hazard Assesment of Industrial Wastes Workshops
PO Box 13078
Denton, TX 76203
Phone: (817)565-2694
Fax: (817)565-4297
Contact: Dr. Kenneth L. Dickson, Dir.
Offered to governmental and industrial personnel.

★4533★ University of North Texas
Institute of Applied Sciences
Microbiology Certification Workshops
PO Box 13078
Denton, TX 76203
Phone: (817)565-2694
Fax: (817)565-4297
Contact: Dr. Kenneth L. Dickson, Dir.
Offered to meat inspectors.

★4534★ University of North Texas
Institute of Applied Sciences
Toxicity Testing Workshop
PO Box 13078
Denton, TX 76203
Phone: (817)565-2694
Fax: (817)565-4297
Contact: Dr. Kenneth L. Dickson, Dir.
Offered to governmental and industrial personnel.

★4535★ University of Pennsylvania
Morris Arboretum
Arborist Professional Development Course
9414 Meadowbrook Ave.
Philadelphia, PA 19118
Phone: (215)247-5777
Contact: Dr. William M. Klein, Dir.

★4536★ University of Rhode Island
Center for Atmospheric Chemistry Studies
AEROCE Program Annual Meeting
Narragansett, RI 02882
Phone: (401)792-6222
Fax: (401)792-6160
Contact: Prof. Robert A. Duce, Dir.
Held for invited guests.

★4537★ University of Southern California
Sea Grant Program
Port Management Research Confernce
Univ. Park
Los Angeles, CA 90089-1231
Phone: (213)740-1961
Fax: (213)748-9047
Contact: James A. Fawcett Ph.D., Associate Dir.
Sponsors about one per year.

★4538★ University of Tennessee at Knoxville
Center for Environmental Biotechnology
International Symposia on Environmental Biotechnology
10515 Research Dr., Ste. 200
Knoxville, TN 37932
Phone: (615)675-9450
Fax: (615)675-9456
Contact: Gary S. Sayler, Dir.

★4539★ University of Washington
School of Marine Affairs
Economic Zones Management Training Program
College of Ocean & Fishery Sciences
3707 Brooklyn Ave. NE
Seattle, WA 98195
Phone: (206)543-7004
Fax: (206)543-1417
Contact: Dr. Edward L. Miles, Dir.

★4540★ University of Wisconsin—Madison
Water Resources Center
AWRA-Wisconsin Section Annual Meeting
1975 Willow Dr.
Madison, WI 53706
Phone: (608)262-3577
Fax: (608)262-0591
Contact: Prof. Gordon Chesters, Dir.

★4541★ USDA Soil and Water Management Research Unit
Cablegation Workshop
3793 N. 3600 E.
Rte. 1
Kimberly, ID 83341
Phone: (208)423-5582
Contact: Dr. David L. Carter, Location Coordinator
Held annually in January, open to users, manufacturers, and installers.

★4542★ Vermont Institute of Natural Science
Avian Medicine Conference
Church Hill
Woodstock, VT 05091
Phone: (802)457-2779
Contact: Sarah B. Laughlin, Dir.
Held annually in the fall, open to veterinarians and individuals involved in raptor rehabilitation.

★4543★ Virginia Polytechnic Institute and State University
Virginia Cooperative Fish and Wildlife Research Unit
Fish and Wildlife Graduate Professional Training Program
106 Cheatham Hall
Blacksburg, VA 24061-0321
Phone: (703)231-5927
Fax: (703)231-3330
Contact: Dr. Richard Neves, Unit Leader

★4544★ Wayne State University
Institute of Chemical Toxicology
Toxicology and Hazardous Waste Seminar
2727 2nd Ave.
Detroit, MI 48201
Phone: (313)577-0100
Contact: Dr. Raymond F. Novak, Dir.

★4545★ West Texs State University
Alternative Energy Institute
Wind and Solar Energy Seminar
PO Box 248, WT Sta.
Canyon, TX 79016
Phone: (806)656-2295
Contact: Dr. Vaughan Nelson, Dir.
Offered to public and industrial personnel.

★4546★ Wisconsin Electric Power Co.
Bringing Imagination to Science
Wisconsin Eletric Power Co.
33 W. Everett St., A413
Milwaukee, WI 53201
Phone: (414)221-2895
Contact: Arthur L. Flowers
Teacher training program.

★4547★ Zero Population Growth, Inc.
1400 16th St. NW, Ste. 320
Washington, DC 20036-2266
Phone: (202)332-2200
Workshops for training teachers in hands-on activities for population education in K-12.

Youth Programs

★4548★ Antioch University
Glen Helen Outdoor Education Center
Antioch University
1075 Rte. 343
Yellow Springs, OH 45387
Phone: (513)767-7648
Contact: Joan Horn
Residential environmental education program for school children; internships for college students, including stipends for room and board and college credit.

★4549★ Betsy-Jeff Penn 4-H Educational Center
Rte. 9, Box 249X
Reidsville, NC 27320
Phone: (919)349-9445
Interdisciplinary approach to exploring the environment. Programs include environmental education for grades 2-8; global awareness seminars for high school students; and teaching in a living classroom for teachers.

★4550★ Cape Outdoor Discovery
47 Old County Rd.
East Sandwich, MA 02537
Phone: (508)888-4741
Offers outdoor education, natural science/ history, and natural resources to students in marine environments and ecology. Programs include group challenges, whale watching, and local history.

★4551★ Chewonki Foundation, Inc.
Rte. 2, Box 1200
Wiscasset, ME 04578
Phone: (207)882-7323
Environmental education programs for school groups, including summer camps and wilderness expeditions.

★4552★ Children's Beach House, Inc.
1800 Bay Ave.
Lewes, DE 19958
Phone: (302)645-9184
Contact: Mary V. Sprague
Student education program focusing on coastal conservation. Activities include overnight trips for students and children with disabilities.

★4553★ City of Aurora, Utilities Department
1470 S. Havanna, Ste. 400
Aurora, CO 80012
Phone: (303)695-7381
Conducts K-12 education program in water conservation.

★4554★ Colorado Outdoor Education Center, Sandborn Western Camps
2000 Old Stage Rd.
Florissant, CO 80816
Phone: (719)748-3341
Operates 5-week summer camp outdoor education programs for boys and girls.

★4555★ Convent of the Sacred Heart School
4 Lauer Rd.
Poughkeepsie, NY 12603
Phone: (914)485-8438
Contact: Suzanne Rogers
Working organic farm serves as an environmental study center.

★4556★ Cornell Waste Management Institute
468 Hollister Hall
Ithaca, NY 14853-3501
Phone: (607)255-8444
Solid waste, recycling, and composting education for K-12. Resources include audio visual equipment, games, workbooks, posters, videos, and computer disks.

★4557★ The Dawes Arboretum
7770 Jacksontown Rd. SE
Newark, OH 43055
Phone: (614)323-2355
Contact: Lori A. Totman
Elementary student field trip program on evironmental awareness.

★4558★ Denver Audubon Society's Urban Education
3000 S. Clayton, No. 207
Denver, CO 80210
Phone: (303)757-8376
Contact: Peggy Lehmann
An outdoor biology education program for inner-city youths.

★4559★ Department of Natural Resources Wisconsin Recycling Education Program
Wisconsin Department of Natural Resources
101 S. Webster St., Box 7921
Madison, WI 53707
Phone: (608)266-2711
Contact: Joel Stone
Encourages and teaches youth to recycle and reduce solid waste.

★4560★ Ebersole Environmental Education and Conference Center
3400 2nd St.
Wayland, MI 49348
Phone: (616)792-6294
Environmental education programs with an emphasis on discovery-oriented curriculum for school-age children. Site includes fen, lake, climax hardwood forest, and prairie.

★4561★ Educational Development Specialists
5505 E. Carson St.
Ste. 250
Lakewood, CA 90713
Phone: (213)420-6814
Developes natural resource and energy education programs for K-12.

★4562★ Edwards Camp and Conference Center
1275 Army Lake Rd.
PO Box 16
East Troy, WI 53120
Phone: (414)642-7466
Operates 15-day environmental education camp which stresses diversity of ecosystems, lessons and curriculum, and recreation in the areas of wildlife, aquatics, environmental awareness, weather, and astronomy.

★4563★ Expedition Yellowstone!
National Park Service
PO Box 168
Yellowstone National Park, WY 82190
Phone: (307)344-7381
Environmental education focusing on geology, history, and wildlife for grades 4-6. Conducts expeditions to the park in spring and autumn.

★4564★ Florida Governor's Energy Office Florida Energy and Environment Program for Children
214 S. Bronough St.
Tallahassee, FL 32301
Phone: (904)488-2475
Contact: Paula Donaldson
Statewide conservation curriculum for kindergarten and first grade students.

★4565★ Greenkill Outdoor Environmental Education Center
YMCA Greenkill
Huguenot, NY 12746
Phone: (914)856-4382
Environmental education resident experience for elementary through high school students, focusing on environmental science, outdoor skills, and history.

★4566★ Guided Discoveries, Inc.
PO Box 1360
Claremont, CA 91711
Phone: (714)949-0678
Conducts education programs in marine biology, island ecology, physical science, and astronomy.

★4567★ HDR Engineering, Inc. Preschool Recycling Education Initiative
709 Westchester Ave.
White Plains, NY 10604-3103
Phone: (914)328-8505
Contact: John F. Williams
Recycling education program for preschoolers; video features Mr. Rogers.

★4568★ Horn Point Environmental Lab
PO Box 775
Cambridge, MD 21613
Phone: (301)228-8200
Contact: Cathy Baptist
Outdoor youth programs. Sponsors beach activities, including cleanup and erosion control.

★4569★ Izaak Walton League of America, White Oak Chapter Environmental Education Program
219 Bouge Sound Dr.
Cape Cartaret
Swansboro, NC 28584
Phone: (919)393-8004
Contact: Frank Osborne
Elementary school program on conservation.

★4570★ Jackson Community College Dahlem Environmental Education Center
2111 Emmons Rd.
Jackson, MI 49201
Phone: (517)782-3453
Comprehensive field study for grades P-6. Internships offered to college students and graduates in wildlife biology and research.

★4571★ Joan and Hy Rosner Environmental Education Fund
4300 Sunningdale Rd., NE
Albuquerque, NM 87110
Phone: (505)265-6346
Contact: Hy Rosner
Provides environmental resource books for teachers and companion readers for children.

★4572★ Joy Outdoor Education Center
Box 157
Clarksville, OH 45113
Phone: (513)289-2031
Conducts environmental education for elementary and high schools, and summer camp for disadvantaged children.

★4573★ Kaleidoscope Environmental Education Program
Sierra Club/Hoy Nature Club/River Bend Nature Center
810 Sycamore
Racine, WI 53406
Phone: (414)637-3141
Contact: Donna Peterson
Wildlife presentations at theaters and schools.

★4574★ Keewaydin Environmental Education Center
Lake Dunmore
Salisbury, VT 05766
Phone: (802)352-4247
Conducts outdoor education on natural communities, human impact, and responsibility.

★4575★ Kiwanis Camp Wyman
600 Kiwanis Dr.
Eureka, MO 63025
Phone: (314)938-5245
Conducts environmental education. Resources include summer camp, day camp, and retreat facilities.

★4576★ Lake Erie Nature and Science Center
28728 Wolf Rd.
Bay Village, OH 44140
Phone: (216)871-2900
Provides nature experiences and stimulates environmental action through education.

★4577★ Lower Colorado River Authority
Water Education Program
PO Box 220
Austin, TX 78767
Toll-Free: 800-776-5272
Contact: Wanda McMurray
Elementary school student program in water resources management.

★4578★ Minnesota Zoo
Minnesota Zoological Gardens
Apple Valley, MN 55124
Phone: (612)431-9234
Contact: Pamela O'Brien
Sponsors teacher conservation education workshops at zoo and throughout the state.

★4579★ Mote Marine Laboratory
JASON Project
1600 City Island Park
Sarasota, FL 34236
Phone: (813)388-4441
Fax: (813)388-4312
Contact: Dr. Selvakumaran Mahadevan, Exec. Dir.
Marine education for grades 4-12.

★4580★ National Environmental Education Development
PO Box 896
Truro, MA 02666
Phone: (508)349-3475
Program conducts outdoor education for elementary students in pond study, dune ecology, saltmarsh exploration, astronomy, and field trips to national seashore.

★4581★ National Wildlife Federation Leadership Training
1400 16th St. NW
Washington, DC 20036-2266
Toll-Free: 800-432-6564
Program teaches leadership skills to ages 14-17. Trainees assist with crafts, recreation activities, evening programs, and daily camp activities.

★4582★ National Wildlife Federation Teen Adventure
1400 16th St. NW
Washington, DC 20036-2266
Toll-Free: 800-432-6564
Program teaches teenagers about the environment through hiking and backpacking in wilderness areas.

★4583★ National Wildlife Federation Wildlife Camp
1400 16th St. NW
Washington, DC 20036-2266
Toll-Free: 800-432-6564
Fosters an understanding of nature in children ages 9-13 and covers such areas as plant ecology, lakes and streams, birds, and wilderness survival.

★4584★ Nebraska Groundwater Foundation
Groundwater Festival
Nebraska Groundwater Foundation
PO Box 2558
Lincoln, NE 68502-0558
Phone: (402)423-7155
Alt. Phone: (402)472-1446
Contact: Wanda Schroeder
Student event focusing on groundwater awareness.

★4585★ New Jersey Public Service Electric & Gas Co.
Living Tidal Marsh Program
80 Park Plaza, T-10C
Newark, NJ 07101
Phone: (201)430-5861
Contact: Jo Ann Dow
Videotape tidal marsh education series with corresponding teacher's guides.

★4586★ North American Wildlife Park Foundation
Wolf Park
Battle Ground, IN 47920
Phone: (317)567-2265
Sponsors education programs for children.

★4587★ North Carolina Alternative Energy Program
PO Box 12699
Research Triangle, NC 27709
Phone: (919)361-8002
Contact: Diana Woolley
Statewide public school education/ presentation program.

★4588★ Ocean Alliance
Bldg. E
Fort Mason, CA 94123
Phone: (415)441-9570
Marine education and conservation programs for children.

★4589★ Orange County Outdoor Science School
1829 Mentone Blvd.
Mentone, CA 92359
Phone: (714)794-1988
Natural science program for grades 5-6.

★4590★ Pocono Environmental Education Center
RD 2 Box 1010
Dingmans Ferry, PA 18328
Phone: (717)828-2319
Contact: John J. Padalino
Offers program focusing on outdoor education for urban youth.

★4591★ Point Bonita YMCA Outdoor Education Conference Center
Bldg. 981, Fl. Barry
Sausalito, CA 94965
Phone: (415)331-9622
Outdoor environmental education program, including hands-on learning experiences about coastal ecology, environment, and habitat.

★4592★ Project Learning Tree
American Forest Foundation & Western Regional Env. Education Council
1250 Connecticut Ave., NW
Washington, DC 20036
Phone: (202)463-2468
Contact: Kathy McGlauflin
K-12 curriculum concerning forestry and related environmental topics coordinated by state.

★4593★ Resource Center For Environmental Education
PO Box 3243
Flagstaff, AZ 86003
Phone: (602)779-1745
Contact: Susan M. Lowry
Outreach services for students in grades K-12.

★4594★ Riverbend Environment Education Center
Camp Green Heron
PO Box 2
Gladwyne, PA 19035
Phone: (215)527-5234
Summer day camp for ages 2-11 focusing on environmental themes.

★4595★ Seacamp
Rte. 3, Box 170
Big Pine Key, FL 33043
Phone: (305)872-2331
Marine science program includes SCUBA, snorkling, and other hands-on, field-oriented activities.

★4596★ Solid Waste Environmental Education Program
PO Box 666
Whitmore, MI 48198
Phone: (313)971-7490
Contact: Stephine Glysson
Elementary school program, includes "Rad Ric Recycle" coloring books.

★4597★ Thorne Ecological Institute
Natural Science School
5398 Manhattan Circle
Boulder, CO 80303
Phone: (303)499-3647
Contact: Deborah J. Long
Natural history courses primarily during summer months.

★4598★ Trailside Discovery Programs
519 W. 8th, Ste. 201
Anchorage, AK 99501
Phone: (907)274-5437
Nature camps and outdoor education programs for ages 4-18. Subjects studied include marine science, ornithology, and alpine ecology.

★4599★ Trout Unlimited-Rapidan
Kids' Day
7503 Cedar Knolls Dr.
Warrenton, VA 22186
Phone: (703)347-3531
Contact: Frank Raiter
Fishing conservation and environmental education outing for children.

★4600★ University of Arizona
School of Renewable Resources
The Green Scene
School of Renewable Resources
Tucson, AZ 85731
Curriculum for grades 4-8 on forest ecology and wilderness. Program operates in cooperation with USDA Forest Service and the Wilderness Society.

★4601★ University of Georgia
Environmental Education Program
350 Rock Eagle Rd. NE
Rock Eagle 4-H Center
Eatonton, GA 31024
Phone: (404)485-2831
Environmental education for grades 3-8. College students can apply for internships.

★4602★ University of North Texas
Institute of Applied Sciences
Zooarcheology, Prehistory, and Ecology Workshop
PO Box 13078
Denton, TX 76203
Phone: (817)565-2694
Fax: (817)565-4297
Contact: Dr. Kenneth L. Dickson, Dir.
Offers presentations to public school children.

★4603★ Valley Forge Audubon Society
234 E. Third St.
Media, PA 19063
Phone: (215)565-4028
Contact: Vivian Williams
Student environmental education program focusing on schoolyard nature studies.

★4604★ Vermont Institute of Natural Science
PO Box 86
Woodstock, VT 05091
Phone: (802)457-2779
Contact: Margaret Baker, Prog. Dir.
Developed WASTE AWAY, a nationwide teaching manual, through its Environmental Learning for the Future (ELF) program. Offers teacher workshops and operates the Vermont Raptor Center, an educational display.

★4605★ Wisconsin Department of Natural Resources
Groundwater Study Guide (Environmental Education Program)
IE/4, GEF 2
PO Box 7921
Madison, WI 53707
Phone: (608)267-7529
Contact: Cathy Cliff
Program for grades 5-12. Available through mail or by participating in a workshop.

★4606★ YMCA of Albuquerque
Elementary School Science Camp
7201 Paseo del Norte, NE
Albuquerque, NM 87113
Phone: (505)822-9922
Contact: Lynn Rosnar
Three-day science camp for elementary public school children.

Publishers

International

★4607★ Friends of the Earth
251 Laurier Ave. W, Ste. 701
Ottawa, Ontario, Canada KIP 5J6
Phone: (613)230-3352
Publishes on environmental improvement in Canada, through research, advocacy, and public education campaigns. Offers two periodicals, Earthwords and Atmosphers. Distributes for World Wildlife Fund. Reaches market through direct mail. Formerly known as Info Earth and Infoetox. ***Selected Titles:*** How to Get Your Lawn and Garden Off Drugs by Carole Rubin; Healing the Sky by Kai Millyard, Andrea Prazmowski, and Julia Langer; A Living Legend by T. Wright and J. Fraser; Pesticide Policy: The Environmental Perspective edited by Friends of the Earth; The Heat Trap by Karas and Kelly.

United States

★4608★ Acid Rain Foundation Inc.
1410 Varsity Dr.
Raleigh, NC 27606
Phone: (919)828-9443
A tax-exempt organization whose main objective is to support research into global atmospheric issues. Publishes a newsletter, curriculum materials, posters, slides, and reviews. Reaches market trough direct mail exhibits and journals. ***Selected Titles:*** Acid Rain Curriculum: Grades 4-9; The Acid Rain Reader, both by Harriet S. Stubbs, Mary Lou Klinkhammer, and Marsha Knitting; The Air Around Us by Jon R. Luoma; Air Pollutants: Effects on Forest Ecosystems; Acid Rain in Minnesota, both by Minnesota Dept. of Education et al.; and Acid Rain Resource Directory.

★4609★ Adirondack Mountain Club, Inc.
RR 3, Box 3055
Luzerne Rd.
Lake George, NY 12845
Phone: (518)668-4447
A nonprofit organization dedicated to conservation, recreation, and education. Publishes books, guides, educational brochures, maps, calendars, and a magazine. Distributes for Adirondack Conservancy. Reaches market through direct mail and trade sales.

★4610★ American Land Resource Association
1516 P Street, NW
Washington, DC 20005
Phone: (202)265-5000
Nonprofit interdisciplinary organization working to promote an understanding of the American land and establish an ethic for its use and protection. Publishes the bimonthly journal, The New American Land, and the bimonthly newsletter, ALRA Bulletin. ***Subjects:*** Land use, planning, geography.

★4611★ Association for Rational Environmental Alternatives (AREA)
PO Box 771885
Houston, TX 77215
Phone: (713)977-5644
National organization which seeks out and investigates voluntary and non-governmental solutions to urban and environmental problems. Publishes on land use regulations and aesthetic controls. Also publishes Environmental Alternatives, a quarterly journal. Reports and documents are copyrighted and available direct from AREA.

★4612★ Association of Boards of Certification
426 1/2 5th St.
PO Box 786
Ames, IA 50010-0786
Phone: (515)232-3623
Fax: (515)232-3778
Publishes on water treatment and wastewater management for educational services associated with water and air pollution control boards. Also publishes a newsletter, The Certifier. Reaches market through direct mail.

★4613★ Association of New Jersey Environmental Commissions
300 Mendham Rd.
Box 157
Mendham, NJ 07945
Phone: (201)539-7547
Fax: (201)539-7713
Provides information needed for effective action by local environmental commissions and private citizens. Also offers a quarterly newsletter, ANJEC Report. Accepts manuscripts relating to environmental concerns. Reaches market through reviews. ***Subjects:*** Environmental planning/management, natural resource preservation, recycling.

★4614★ Association of State and Interstate Water Pollution Control Administrators (ASIWPCA)
444 N Capitol St., NW, Ste. 330N
Washington, DC 20001-1512
Phone: (202)624-7782
A nonprofit professional association whose members are state administrators of the water program. Membership consists of representatives of the fifty states, District of Columbia, interstate agencies, and territories. ***Selected Titles:*** 1987 Water Quality Act Highlights of Legislative History; Comprehensive Data Management Project Report to the Administrator; and The States' Conference on Groundwater Management: ASIWPCA Conference Proceedings.

★4615★ Aylmer Press
PO Box 2735
Madison, WI 53701
Phone: (608)251-2506
Selected Titles: Money Saving Conservation Products and Projects by Stephen Kokette.

★4616★ Banyan Tree Books
1963 El Dorado Ave.
Berkeley, CA 94707
Phone: (415)524-2690
Distributed by BookPeople. ***Subjects:*** Ecology, futurism, politics. ***Selected Titles:*** Ecotopia, Ecotopia Emerging, both by Ernest Callenbach; Citizen Legislature by Ernest Callenbach and Michael Phillips.

★4617★ Beech Leaf Press
7000 N Westnedge Ave.
Kalamazoo, MI 49007
Phone: (616)381-1574
Subjects: Natural history, environmental education, ecological research.

★4618★ Blake Publishing
2222 Beebee St.
San Luis Obisop, CA 93401
Phone: (805)543-7314
Publishes a line of full-color photobooks on wildlife, habitats and some regional travel titles. Also offers postcards. Reaches market through direct mail, commission representatives, telephone sales, and trade sales.

★4619★ Boxwood Press
183 Ocean View Blvd.
Pacific Grove, CA 93950
Phone: (408)375-9110
Fax: (408)375-0430
Offers newsletters and journals. Accepts unsolicited manuscripts. Reaches market through direct mail. ***Subjects:*** Natural history, invertebrates, ecology, psychiatry. ***Selected***

Titles: Basic Ecology by Ralph and Mildred Buchsbaum; Environmental Ethics by K. Shrader-Frechette.

★4620★ Business Publishers, Inc.
951 Pershing Dr.
Silver Spring, MO 20910-4464
Phone: (301)587-6300
Publishes directories and over sixty newsletters in a variety of fields including energy and the environment. ***Selected Titles:*** World Environmental Directory, edited by Jane Via.

★4621★ Center for Analysis of Public Issues
16 Vandeventer Ave.
Princeton, NJ 08540
Phone: (609)924-9750
Promotes understanding of public affairs in New Jersey through study, research, and analysis conducted on a non-partisn and objective basis. Publishes New Jersey Reporter, a journal of public issues. Accepts unsolicited manuscripts for magazine. Reaches market through direct mail.

★4622★ Center for Environmental Information, Inc. (CEI)
46 Prince St.
Rochester, NY 14607-1016
Phone: (716)271-3550
Alt. Phone: (716)271-0606
A nonprofit clearinghouse for local environmental information, especially on acid rain and global warming. Publishes Acid Precipitaion Digest and Global Climate Change Digest. Accepts unsolicited manuscripts on Upstate New York environment. Reaches market through direct mail. ***Subjects:*** Acid precipitation, land use, energy, global climate change, hazardous wastes. ***Selected Titles:*** Self-Study Guide for Commercial Pesticide Applicators; The Directory of Environmental Agencies and Organizations (annual); Establishing an Environmental Information Center; Liming Acidic Waters: Environmental and Policy Concerns; Acid Rain: A New York State Agenda; Annual Report.

★4623★ Center for the Great Lakes
435 N Michigan Ave.
Chicago, IL 60611
Phone: (312)645-0901
Publishes economic and environmental reports about the Great Lakes. Offers The Great Lakes Reporter six times a year.

★4624★ Chelsea Green Publishing Co.
Rte. 113
PO Box 130
Post Mills, VT 05058
Phone: (802)333-9073
Fax: (802)333-9092
Offers books and audio cassettes. Accepts unsolicited manuscripts; query first with outline. Distributes for Nature Sound Studio, Scarecrow Enterprises, and Nimbus. Reaches market through commission representatives, direct mail, and telephone sales. ***Subjects:*** Environment, travel, natural history, New England, how-to. ***Selected Titles:*** The Man Who Planted Trees by Jean Giono; The New Organic Grower by Eliot Coleman; Backtracking: The Way of a Naturalist by Ted Levin; Voyage to the Whales by Hal Whitehead; Dangerous River by R.M. Patterson.

★4625★ Clean Yield Publications
Box 1880
Greensboro Bend, VT 05842
Phone: (802)533-7178

★4626★ Commission on the Arizona Environment
1645 W Jefferson, Ste. 416
Phoenix, AZ 85007
Phone: (602)255-2102
Publishes quarterly reports on selected environmental issues. Also produces a natural resource organizational directory, an annual report, and a number of environmental fact sheets for educational use. Reaches market through direct mail. ***Selected Titles:*** 1988 Arizona Environmental and Resource Conservation Directory; Environment Learning Opportunities; Indoor Air Contaminants; Arizona's Environmental Priorities for 1989; CAE Annual Report.

★4627★ Community Environmental Council
Gildea Resource Center
930 Miramonte Dr.
Santa Barbara, CA 93109
Phone: (805)963-0835
Fax: (805)962-9080
Nonprofit environmental education organization. Publishes booklets and articles on recycling, hazardous waste collection, and land use policy as educational supplements to projects it sponsors. Also publishes a biannual newsletter, The Gildea Review. Reaches market through direct mail. ***Selected Titles:*** The Next Frontier: Solid Waste Source Reduction by Hurst; Beyond the Crisis: Integrated Waste Management by Relis and Dominski; Waste Futures: IWM Systems by Dominski, Schatzki, and Melcher; Waste Paper Markets by Halapatz and Kessler; Recycling Markets--California and the Pacific Rim by Gitlitz; Siting a Hazardous Waste Collection Facility for Small Quantity Generators by Feeney.

★4628★ Concern, Inc.
1794 Columbia Rd. NW
Washington, DC 20009
Phone: (202)328-8160
Fax: (202)387-3378
Publishes community action guides and booklets about the environment. Reaches market through direct mail and reviews. ***Selected Titles:*** Groundwater: A Community Action Guide, edited by Susan Boyd; Drinking Water: A Community Action Guide, edited by Susan Boyd, Cynthia Bumstead, and Adelyn Jones; Waste: Choices for Communities, Household and Waste: Issues and Opportunities, both edited by Andy Knaus.

★4629★ Conservation Foundation
1250 24th Street, NW
Washington, DC 20037
Phone: (202)338-6951
Fax: (202)338-6998
Publishes on the quality of environment and state of Earth's resources. Reaches market through direct mail, trade sales, and wholesalers. ***Subjects:*** Water and coastal resources, agriculture and forestry, environmental trends, pollution control. ***Selected Titles:*** International Wildlife Trade: Whose Business Is It? by Sarah Fitzgerald; Integrated Pollution Control: Dealing with Cross Media Problems by Nigel Haigh and Francis H. Irwin; Ecotourism: The Potentials and Pitfalls by Elizabeth Boo; and Negotiating Hazardous Waste Facility: Siting and Permitting Agreements edited by Gail Bingham and Timothy J. Mealey.

★4630★ Cove Press
PO Box 325
Severna Park, MD 21146
Phone: (301)757-0134
Specializes in management, organization, and technologies, especially in environment and conservation.

★4631★ Eagle Foundation, Inc.
209 N Main St.
Galena, IL 61036
Phone: (815)777-3500
Publishes results of bald eagle research and symposia. Also publishes a newsletter and magazine. Reaches market through direct mail and reviews. Formerly Eagle Valley Environmentalists, Inc.

★4632★ Eco Images
PO Box 61413
Virginia Beach, VA 23462
Phone: (804)421-3929
Publishes environmental educational materials and nature publications. Also offers note cards, slide sets, posters, games, and art prints. Reaches market through direct mail and telephone sales. ***Selected Titles:*** A Coastal Ecology Coloring Book, A Naturalist's Field Guide to Coastal Communities, Coastal Plant Communities, Nature Exploration Activity Guide, all by Vickie Shufer.

★4633★ Ecology Center
2530 San Pablo Ave.
Berkeley, CA 94702
Phone: (415)548-2220
Information center on environmental issues and ecological alternatives. Publishes a monthly newsletter; distributes its own and other publishers' materials. ***Selected Titles:*** Backyard Composting by Helga Olkowski; The Home Vegetable Garden by H. Butterfield.

★4634★ Educational Communications
PO Box 35473
Los Angeles, CA 90035
Phone: (213)559-9160
Publishes environmental information for the public. Offers a bimonthly newsletter, Compendium. Also offers audio and video cassettes. Produces a nationwide radio and television series. Accepts unsolicited manuscripts. Reaches market through direct mail, trade sales, and wholesalers. Formerly Ecology Center of Southern California. ***Selected Titles:*** Directory of Environmental Organizations edited by Nancy Pearlman; Elonews; Environmental Directions.

★4635★ Envirographics
PO Box 334
Hiram, OH 44234
Phone: (216)527-5207
Publishes informative and self-help books on environmental pollution problems and how they relate to the general public. Offers stationery and note cards. Reaches market through direct mail and reviews. ***Selected Titles:*** Drinking Water Hazards by John Cary Stewart.

★4636★ Environment Books, Inc.
4905 Smith Rd.
Plano, TX 75094-9556
Phone: (214)881-1331
Publishes on environmental affairs and on environmental compliance with government requirements for corporations. Offers typesetting, printing, and publishing. Accepts unsolicited manuscripts. Reaches market through direct mail, trade sales, and other advertising.

★4637★ **Environmental Action Coalition**
625 Broadway
New York, NY 10012
Phone: (212)677-1601
Publishes on waste management and ecology. Offers a quarterly newsletter, Cycle. Produces environmental education material and a film, Something for the Trees, Something for the City. Reaches market through direct mail, environmental groups, and teachers. ***Selected Titles:*** City Trees, Country Trees; Green Spaces in City Places; Plant a Tree for Arbor Day; Don't Waste Waste; Less Power for the People; Woods and Water; Plastics: America's Packaging Dilemma.

★4638★ **Environmental Action Foundation**
1525 New Hampshire Avenue, NW
Washington, DC 20036
Phone: (202)745-4870
Subjects: Environment, waste and toxic substances, utility and energy issues.

★4639★ **Environmental Defense Fund**
257 Park Ave. S
New York, NY 10010
Phone: (212)505-2100
Fax: (212)505-2375
Publishes a citizen's guide and scientific reports on environmental subjects. Offers a quarterly newsletter, calendars, prints, and decals. Reaches market through direct mail. ***Selected Titles:*** Ominous Future: Under the Ozone Hole by Mary Voytek; Protecting the Ozone Layer: What You Can Do by S. L. Clark; Radon: The Citizen's Guide by R. E. Yuhnke and J. Caswell.

★4640★ **Environmental Information Center**
1251-B Miller Ave.
Winter Park, FL 32789
Phone: (407)644-5377
Publishes on environmental subjects in terms the general public can understand and can use; emphasis is on Florida. Offers a quarterly newsletter and a calendar. Reaches market through direct mail. ***Subjects:*** Environment, energy, nature.

★4641★ **Environmental Information Ltd.**
4801 W 81st St., No. 119
Minneapolis, MN 55437-1111
Phone: (618)831-2473
Publishes environmental data and a comprehensive directory on treatment, storage, disposal, transportation, and other aspects of industrial and hazardous waste. Offers El Digest, a monthly report on industrial and hazardous waste management. Reaches market through direct mail and telephone sales. ***Selected Titles:*** Environmental Services Directory: EPA Regions I, II, and III; EPA Region IV; EPA Regions V; EPA Regions VI, VII, and VIII; EPA Regions IX and X.

★4642★ **Environmental Law Institute**
1616 P St. NW, Ste. 200
Washington, DC 20036
Phone: (202)328-5150
Nonpartisan, nonprofit national center for research on environmental law and policy. Also publishes National Wetlands Newsletter. Reaches market through direct mail. ***Selected Titles:*** Clean Water Deskbook: California Hazardous Waste Enforcement; Community Right-to-Know Deskbook; Environmental Law Deskbook; NEPA Deskbook.

★4643★ **Environmental Publications Associates Ltd.**
17 Jefryn Blvd., W
Deer Park, NY 11729
Phone: (516)667-8896
Selected Titles: An Introduction to Environmental Science: The Ecology of Long Island by Jeffrey Wenig.

★4644★ **Eureka Publications**
PO Box 372
Mantua, NJ 08051
Phone: (609)468-4145
Provides publishing service for doctoral students, researchers, scientists, environmentalists, statespersons, and the layperson. ***Subjects:*** Environment, cancer, pollution medicine. ***Selected Titles:*** New Jersey: Environment and Cancer, Syndromes for the Layperson, both by Eustace A. Dixon; Air Pollution and Mortality by Frederick W. Lipfert.

★4645★ **Fairmont Press, Inc.**
700 Indian Trail
Lilburn, GA 30247
Phone: (404)925-9388
Publishes reference, professional, and how-to books. ***Subjects:*** Noise control, safety, energy, environment.

★4646★ **Finn Hill Arts**
PO Box 542
Silverton, CO 81433
Phone: (303)387-5729
Subjects: Environment and nature study.

★4647★ **Frederick Clare**
7870 SE 21st St.
Portland, OR 97202
Phone: (503)236-4465
Self-publisher of a book on nuclear weapons testing around the world and its impact on the weather. Reaches market through direct mail.

★4648★ **Free Enterprise Press**
12500 NE 10th Pl.
Bellevue, WA 98005
Phone: (206)455-5038
Publishes books on free enterprise issues and government policy. Reaches market through direct mail, trade sales, and wholesalers. ***Selected Titles:*** Stealing the National Parks by Don Hummel; Ecology Wars by Ron Arnold.

★4649★ **Government Institutes, Inc.**
966 Hungerford Dr., Ste. 24
Rockville, MD 20850
Phone: (301)251-9250
Subjects: Environment and energy. ***Selected Titles:*** Hazardous Wastes Handbook, 8th ed. by Crowell and Moring; Environmental Audits, 6th ed. by Lawrence B. Cahill and Raymond W. Kane; Environmental Law Handbook, 11th ed.; Environmental Statutes; State Environmental Law Compliance Center; Directory of Environmental Information Sources, 3rd ed.

★4650★ **Green Earth Foundation**
PO Box 327
El Verano, CA 95433
Phone: (707)935-7257
Publishes on the relationship between humanity and nature. Offers a newsletter, The Green Earth Observer, and audio cassettes. Formerly known as Four Trees Publications. Distributes for Northpoint Press, New Society Publishers, Earthworks Press, and others. Reaches market through direct mail, trade sales, and wholesalers. ***Selected Titles:*** Through the Gateway of the Heart by Sophia Adamson; Gaia Consciousness: The Re-Emergent Goddess and the Living Earth edited by Ralph Metzner.

★4651★ **Hamaker-Weaver Publishers**
PO Box 1961
Burlingame, CA 94010
Reaches market through direct mail. ***Subjects:*** Climate change, economics. ***Selected Titles:*** The Survival of Civilizations by Hamaker and Weaver.

★4652★ **Hazardous Materials Control Research Institute**
7237 Hanover Pkwy.
Greenbelt, MD 20770-3602
Phone: (301)982-9500
Publishes proceedings of conferences in the environmental, hazardous materials, and energy fields. Also offers a periodical, Hazardous Materials Control, and a newsletter, FOCUS. Offers resume services for members. Accepts unsolicited manuscripts. Reaches market through direct mail and conferences. Formerly known as Information Transfer, Inc. ***Selected Titles:*** Site Cleanup by Incineration by Calvin Brunner; The Soil Chemistry of Hazardous Materials by James Dragun; Management of Uncontrolled Hazardous Waste Sites; Risk and Decision Analysis for Hazardous Waste Disposal; Hazardous Wastes and Hazardous Materials 1991; Superfund '90.

★4653★ **Illinois State Water Survey**
2204 Griffith Dr.
Champaign, IL 61820
Phone: (217)333-2210
Publishes reports on Illinois water and atmospheric resources. Reports are listed with NTIS.

★4654★ **INFORM, Inc.**
381 Park Ave. S
New York, NY 10016
Phone: (212)689-4040
A nonprofit environmental research organization whose purpose is to identify and report on practical actions for the conservation and preservation of natural resources. Offers a quarterly newsletter, Inform Reports, and research publications. Reaches market through direct mail and wholesalers, including Baker & Taylor and Brookfield Publishing. ***Selected Titles:*** Garbage Management in Japan: Leading the Way by Hershkowitz and Salerni; Garbage Burning Lessons from Europe by Hershkowitz; Cutting Chemical Wastes by Sarokin et al.; A Citizen's Guide to Promoting Toxic Waste Reduction by Kenworthy and Schaefer; Drive for Clean Air by Cannon; Business Recycling Manual.

★4655★ **Institute for Earth Education**
PO Box 288
Warrenville, IL 60555
Phone: (708)393-3085
Alt. Phone: (509)395-2299
Develops and disseminates educational programs that will help people build an understanding of, appreciation for, and harmony with the Earth and its life. Offers a seasonal journal, conferences, consulting, an annual catalog, and program development, and publishes books and program materials. Distributes for American Camping Association. Reachs market through commission representatives, direct mail, BookPeople, Pacific Pipeline, and The Distributors. ***Selected Titles:*** Acclimatization, Acclimatizing, Sunship Earth, EarthKeepers, Earth Education...A New Beginning, all by Steve Van Matre; The Earth Speaks by Steve Van Matre and Bill Weiler.

★4656★ Institute for Local Self-Reliance
2425 18th St. NW
Washington, DC 20009
Phone: (202)232-4108
Fax: (202)332-0463
Publishers technical reports on urban economic development. ***Selected Titles:*** Self-Reliant Cities; Proven Profits from Pollution Prevention; Be Your Own Power Company; Resource Recovery State-of-the Arts; Garbage Disposal Economics: A Statistical Snapshot; An Environmental Review of Incineration Technologies.

★4657★ Institute for Resource and Security Studies
27 Ellsworth Ave.
Cambridge, MA 02139
Phone: (617)491-5177
Fax: (617)491-6904
Publishes on energy, environment, and international security. Offers research for public education. Reaches market through direct mail. ***Selected Titles:*** Sustainable Cities by Rosalie Anders; Regulatory Responses to the Potential for Reactor Accidents by Gordon Thompson.

★4658★ Institute of Environmental Sciences
940 E NW Hwy.
Mount Prospect, IL 60056
Phone: (708)255-1561
Publishes proceedings of annual technical meeting and seminars. Reaches market through direct mail and reviews. ***Subjects:*** Environmental technology, engineering, science, contamination control, areospace testing.

★4659★ International Academy at Santa Barbara
800 Garden St., Ste. D
Santa Barbara, CA 93101-1552
Phone: (805)965-5010
Fax: (805)965-6071
Sponsors and promotes research in social sciences, international relations, and environmental and energy issues. Publications are available online and on CD-ROM. Reaches market through direct mail. ***Selected Titles:*** Environmental Periodicals Bibliography edited by Miriam Flacks and Paula Meza; Environmental Bibliography Search Guide edited by Cathy McNamara.

★4660★ International Institute of Technology, Inc.
830 Wall St.
Joplin, MO 64801
Phone: (417)782-4514
Publishes on chemical engineering, environment, energy, and current events. Offers writing and training services and consulting in engineering. Reaches market through direct mail. ***Selected Titles:*** Energy/ Pollution Illustrated Glossary, Environmental Pollution Awareness and Control, by Esber I. Saheen.

★4661★ International Ozone Association/ Pan American Committee
83 Oakwood Ave.
Norwalk, CT 06850
Phone: (203)847-8169
Nonprofit organization that publishes books about the ozone layer. Offers a newsletter, Ozone News, and a technical quarterly, Ozone Science and Engineering.

★4662★ Island Press
1718 Connecticut Ave. NW, Ste. 300
Washington, DC 20009
Phone: (202)232-7933
Fax: (707)983-6414
Toll-Free: 800-828-1302
Publishes information on the environment and conservation. Accepts unsolicited manuscripts. Reaches market through direct mail and trade sales. ***Selected Titles:*** The Global Citizen by Donella Meadows; Crossroads: Environmental Priorities for the Future by Peter Borrelli; Saving the Tropical Forests by Judith Gradwohl; War on Waste: Can America Win Its Battle with Garbage? by Louis Blumberg; Complete Guide to Environmental Careers by CEIP Fund; Green Index by Institute for Southern Studies.

★4663★ Joan and Hy Rosner Environmental Education Fund
202 Park St.
Miami Springs, FL 33166
Phone: (305)888-1230
Aim is to produce environmental resource books on individual cities or counties nationwide that will teach people about every aspect (i.e. the total ecosystem of their environment) of the places where they live. Offers databases, video cassettes, newsletters, brochures, and art prints. Reaches market through direct mail.

★4664★ Land Educational Associates Foundation, Inc. (LEAF)
3368 Oak Ave.
Stevens Point, WI 54481
Phone: (715)344-6158
Subjects: Nuclear energy, conservation, radiation, alternative power, nuclear weapons.

★4665★ League for Ecological Democracy
PO Box 1858
San Pedro, CA 90733
Phone: (213)833-2633
Publishes on social ecology and bioregionalism. Publications include Green Synthesis, a quarterly journal.

★4666★ League of Women Voters of the Tri-State Metropolitan Region
817 Broadway
New York, NY 10003
Phone: (212)677-5050
Publishes reports on waste, water quality, and the environment. Offers audios, videos, and National Voter: Report from the Hill. Reaches market through direct mail and McGraw-Hill.

★4667★ Lewis Publishers, Inc.
121 S Main St.
Chelsea, MI 48118
Phone: (313)475-8619
Publishes reference and college textbooks on environmental pollution control and health topics, concentrating on engineering, chemistry, waste, hazardous and toxic materials, and occupational health. Considers unsolicited manuscripts. Reaches market through direct mail, telephone sales, trade sales, wholesalers, trade shows, and conventions.

★4668★ Life's Resources, Inc.
114 E Main St.
Addison, MI 49220
Phone: (517)547-7494
Publishes books on the environment and how it affects health and welfare. Offers a newsletter. Accepts unsolicited manuscripts. Reaches market through direct mail. ***Selected Titles:*** Residential and Institutional Hygiene, Residential Health and Hygiene Guide, Your Hidden Risks, all by Fannin.

★4669★ M Jay Publishing Co.
1111 Archwood Dr.
Olympia, WA 98502
Phone: (206)754-4890
Publishes on environmental science. Reaches market through direct mail.

★4670★ Magic Unicorn Publications
PO Box 793
Yucca Valley, CA 92286
Phone: (619)365-0401
Fax: (619)369-3701
Subjects: Environment. ***Selected Titles:*** Alana and the Dolphins by Wendy Mateja.

★4671★ Massachusetts Audubon Society
South Great Rd.
Lincoln, MA 01773
Phone: (617)259-9500
Publishes to promote the Society's goals. Also publishes Sanctuary magazine and cards. Distributes for Prentice Hall, Curious Naturalist, Energy Saver's Handbook, Rodale, and Godine. Reaches market through direct mail and reviews. ***Subjects:*** Birds, environment, conservation, natural history, energy and water resources, teaching resources. ***Selected Titles:*** Schoolground Science: Activities for Elementary School by Cervoni and Roth; Sensible Pest Control by Rachel Freed; The Wilds of Cape Ann by Eleanor Popr; Whale Watchers Guide to the North Atlantic; Watershed Decisions; Vineyard Birds.

★4672★ McCoy and Associates, Inc.
13701 W Jewell Ave., Ste. 202
Lakewood, CA 80228
Phone: (303)987-0333
Fax: (303)989-7917
Provides reference information on hazardous waste regulations. Offers seminars and a bimonthly journal, The Hazardous Waste Consultant. Reaches market through direct mail. ***Selected Titles:*** RCRA Regulations and Keyword Index, 1991 ed.; RCRA Land Disposal Restrictions: A Guide to Compliance, 1991 ed.; Regulatory Analysis Service; The Hazardous Waste Consultant; McCoy's Hazardous Waste Regulatory Update Service; The Clean Air Amendments of 1990: Statutory Requirements and Keyword Index.

★4673★ McIlvaine Co.
2970 Maria Ave.
Northbrook, IL 60062
Phone: (312)272-0010
Publishes books, newsletters, abstracts, and reports on air pollution equipment and legislation. Reaches market through direct mail and reviews.

★4674★ Mountain Agricultural Institute
Seabeck, WA 98380-0370
Phone: (206)830-4758
Subjects: Natural resources, environment, industry.

★4675★ National Council for Environmental Balance, Inc.
4169 Westport Rd.
PO Box 7732
Louisville, KY 40207-0732
Phone: (502)896-8731
Purpose is "to work for the development and preservation of the most wholesome and productive environment possible through the intelligent application of scientific knowledge." Publishes Energy and Environment Alert, a bimonthly newsletter. Reaches market through

direct mail. ***Selected Titles:*** Acid Rain: The Whole Story to Date by John J. McKetta; The Positive Side of Pesticides by Keith C. Barrons; Worried about Pesticides in Food and Water? Here Are the Facts by J. Gordon Edwards; Environmental Policy Guidelines by I. W. Tucker; Science, Economics, and the Spontaneous Order by Bruce Ames; U.S. Energy Today and In The Nineties by John J. McKetta.

★4676★ National Environmental Training Association
8687 Via de Ventura, Ste. 214
Scottsdale, AZ 85258
Phone: (602)483-0083
Publishes training materials and resources for vocational education instructors in the pollution control and environmental fields. Accepts unsolicited manuscripts. Reaches market through direct mail and trade sales.

★4677★ National Institute for Urban Wildlife
10921 Trotting Ridge Way
Columbia, MD 21044
Phone: (301)596-3311
National scientific and educational organization dedicated to the conservation of wildlife and habitat for the benefit of people in cities, suburbs, and developing areas. Publishes Urban Wildlife News, a quarterly newsletter, and research reports. Formerly known as Urban Wildlife Research Center, Inc.

★4678★ National Water Well Association
6375 Riverside Dr.
Dublin, OH 43017
Publishes on water conservation, hydrology, and management. Also publishes newsletters, journals, and a magazine. Also offers slide presentations, films, and videotapes. Sponsors educational seminars, expositions, and conventions. ***Selected Titles:*** Domestic Water Treatment; A Ground Water Quality Atlas of the United States.

★4679★ National Wildlife Federation
1400 16th St., NW
Washington, DC 40036
Phone: (703)790-4000
Entertains and educates readers about wildlife so that their increased interest and appreciation for wildlife may motivate them to support conservation measures, especially the protection of wildlife habitat. Reaches market through direct mail and Sewall Co. ***Selected Titles:*** Conservation Directory 1991.

★4680★ Ned Ludd Books
2721 Calle Carapan
Tucson, AZ 85745
Phone: (602)628-9610
Publishes books on the environment. Reaches market through direct mail, and BookPeople. ***Selected Titles:*** Ecodefense, The Big Outside, both by Dave Foreman; Li'L Green Songbook by Johnny Sagebrush.

★4681★ Noble Press
213 W Institute Pl., Ste. 508
Chicago, IL 60610
Phone: (312)642-1168
Fax: (312)642-7682
Publishes on social and environmental issues. Accepts unsolicited manuscripts; query first. Reaches market through commission representatives, direct mail, and telephone and trade sales. ***Selected Titles:*** Embracing the Earth: Choices for Environmentally Sound Living by Mark Harris; Understanding the Radical Environmental Movement by Rik Scarce.

★4682★ North American Water Office
PO Box 174
3394 Lake Elmo Ave.
Lake Elmo, MN 55042
Phone: (612)770-3861
Assesses and makes available point source pollution information to be used as a basis for private/public action to move the electrical utilities toward sustainable resource management. Focuses on air and water pollution indices as measures of the magnitude of the problem. Reaches market through direct mail.

★4683★ Ohio River Valley Sanitation Commission
49 E 4th St., Ste. 815
Cincinnati, OH 45202
Phone: (513)421-1151
A pollution control agency that publishes about water pollution control on the Ohio River. Reaches market through direct mail.

★4684★ Outdoor Education Association
143 Fox Hill Rd.
Denville, NJ 07834
Phone: (201)627-7214
Promotes outdoor education, including school camping, environmental education, and nature study. Works with colleges, elementary and secondary schools, and private agencies.

★4685★ Ozark Society Books
PO Box 3503
Little Rock, AR 72203
Phone: (501)847-3738
A nonprofit foundation; publishes books relating to conservation and enjoyment of the natrual heritage of the Ozark-Ouachita mountain region of Arkansas, Missouri, and Oklahoma. Reaches market through direct mail. ***Subjects:*** Natural history, travel, outdoor recreation, conservation.

★4686★ Pacific Northwest and Range Experiment Station
PO Box 3890
Portland, OR 97208
Phone: (503)234-3361
Publishes on the environment, forestry management, forestry research, biology, and science. Publishes a quarterly list of recent publications.

★4687★ Passaic River Coalition
246 Madisonville Rd.
Basking Ridge, NJ 07920
Phone: (908)766-7550
Fax: (908)766-7550
Nonprofit watershed association advising government, citizens, and industry on topics of water and land resource management. Reports cover regional topics. Also publishes quarterly and semi-annual periodicals.

★4688★ Pathfinder Publishing
458 Dorothy Ave.
Ventura, CA 93003
Phone: (805)642-9278
Fax: (805)650-3656
Publishes books and audio cassettes on historical events, analysis of natural resources, environmental and economic issues concerning the public, and profiles of pathfinders in various fields. Reaches market through direct mail, trade sales, Baker & Taylor, Quality Books, Inc., Ingram Book Co., and Pacific Pipeline.

★4689★ Peerless Publishing Co.
2745 Lafitte Ave.
New Orleans, LA 70119
Phone: (504)486-6222
Subjects: Environment. ***Selected Titles:*** Sanitarian's Handbook by Ben Freedman.

★4690★ Pennsylvania Academy of Science
Lafayette College
13 Kunkle Hall
Easton, PA 18042
Phone: (215)250-5464
Fax: (215)250-6557
Publishes books on waste, endangered species, and industrial concerns. Also publishes a journal. Accepts unsolicited manuscripts. Reaches market through direct mail.

★4691★ Permanent Press
RD 2, Noyac Rd.
Sag Harbor, NY 11963
Phone: (516)725-1101
Specializes in fiction, political, and environmental books. Accepts unsolicited manuscripts. Reaches market through Baker & Taylor.

★4692★ Perry-Wagner Publishing Co., Inc.
3524 S. Wakefield St., No. A1
Arlington, VA 22206-1729
Phone: (703)820-5083
Publishes technical books on hazardous waste and materials. ***Selected Titles:*** The Complete Handbook of Hazardous Waste Regulation by Travis Wagner.

★4693★ Pesticide Action Network North America Regional Center
965 Mission St., No. 514
San Francisco, CA 94103
Phone: (415)514-9140
Fax: (415)541-9253
Publishes on pesticides' effect on the environment. Offers posters and a newsletter, Global Pesticide Campaigner. ***Selected Titles:*** Problem Pesticides, Pesticide Problems and The Pesticide Code Monitor, both by Gretta Goldenman and Sarojini Rengam; Monitoring the International Code of Conduct on the Distribution and Use of Pesticides in North America by Marian Moses; Escape from the Pesticide Treadmill: Alternatives to Pesticides in Developing Countries by Michael Hasen; Breaking the Pesticide Habit: Alternatives to 12 Hazardous Pesticides by Terry Gips.

★4694★ Pill Enterprises
N 22790 Hwy. 101
Shelton, WA 98584
Phone: (206)877-5825
Publishes how-to and educational nature books. Distributes for Naturegraph, Happy Camp, Stan Jones, and Olympic Publishing, Inc. Reaches market through commission representatives, direct mail, telephone sales, Pacific Pipeline, Doug McDonald, and Robert Hale and Co.

★4695★ Planning and Conservation League
909 12th St., Ste. 203
Sacramento, CA 95814
Phone: (916)444-8726
Publishes occasional national reports and analyses on the environment of California. Also publishes California Today, a bimonthly newsletter. Reaches market through press and reporting service. ***Selected Titles:*** Dollars and Sense: The Economic Context of the California Coastal Plan; The California Land: Planning for People; Land and the Environment: Planning in Approach; Environmental Budget Analysis;

Citizens Guide to California Environmental Quality Act.

★4696★ Premier Press
PO Box 4428
Berkeley, CA 94704
Phone: (415)841-2091
Subjects: Water resources. ***Selected Titles:*** Waste Disposal Effects on Ground Water edited by Miller; Water Well Specifications by National Water Well Association; Subsurface Wastewater Injection by Don L. Warner and Jay H. Lehr.

★4697★ Radioactive Waste Campaign
625 Broadway, 2nd Fl.
New York, NY 10012
Phone: (212)473-7390
Publishes fact sheets and books on radioactive waste issues, including the transport, impact on groundwater sources, health effects, and storage issues. Offers slide shows, a newsletter, a map of transport routes, and a planned map of American groundwater sources. Reaches market through direct mail. ***Selected Titles:*** Deadly Defense: Living without Landfills by Resnikoff.

★4698★ Resources for the Future, Inc.
1616 P St., NW
Washington, DC 20036
Phone: (202)328-5086
An independent nonprofit organization for research and education in the development, conservation, and use of natural resources, including the quality of the environment. Distributed by Johns Hopkins University Press. Reaches market through commission representatives, direct mail, and telephone sales.

★4699★ Society for Occupational and Environmental Health
6728 Old McLean Village Dr.
McLean, VA 22101
Phone: (202)737-5045
A nonprofit organization that publishes the proceedings of its conferences.

★4700★ Society for the Protection of New Hampshire Forests
54 Portsmouth St.
Concord, NH 03301
Phone: (603)224-9945
Subjects: Conservation.

★4701★ Soil and Water Conservation Society
7515 NE Ankeny Rd.
Ankeny, IA 50021
Phone: (515)289-2331
To advance the science and art of good land and water use. Offers a journal and educational material. Reaches market through direct mail.

★4702★ Solo Publications
214 Wilkes Circle
Santa Cruz, CA 95060
Phone: (408)425-6559
Publishes literature with an environmental theme. Reaches market through commission representatives, direct mail, and BookLink Distributors.

★4703★ Southwest Research and Information Center
PO Box 4524
Alburquerque, NM 87106
Phone: (505)262-1862
Provides legal and technical information to the public and citizen organizations on various public interest issues. Publishes a periodical, The Workbook, and a newsletter, Nuclear Waste News.

★4704★ Specialty Books, International
PO Box 1785
Ann Arbor, MI 48106
Phone: (517)456-4764
Publishes books on careers, family living, and environment for schools, libraries, and parents. Reaches market through direct mail and reviews. ***Selected Titles:*** All People and Waste, All People and Water, both by H. E. Fraumann.

★4705★ Stanford Environmental Law Society
Stanford Law School
Stanford, CA 94305
Phone: (415)723-4421
Publishes articles on legal issues of environmental concern and handbooks for practitioners in environmental law. Reaches market through direct mail and wholesalers. ***Selected Titles:*** The Endangered Species Act: A Guide to Its Protections and Implementations by Daniel Rohlf; Who Runs the Rivers? by B. Andrews and M. Sansone; Hazardous Wastes and Superfund; Agriculture and the Environment: Land Use Regulation; Private Initiatives in Environmental Law.

★4706★ Technical Information Project, Inc.
1745 Kelly Ave., No. 11
Los Angeles, CA 90024
Phone: (202)466-2954
Subjects: Waste, materials policy, energy, nuclear power, food. ***Selected Titles:*** Toxic Substances: Decisions and Values; Tin Cans and Trash Recovery: Saving Energy through Utilizing Municipal Ferrous Waste; Defederalization of Energy, Environment, and Resource Programs: Obstacles and Impacts; The Water Paper: An Analysis of Issues and Obstacles in National Water Policy, II Review of Groups Active in Water Issues.

★4707★ Treepeople
12601 Mulholland Dr.
Beverly Hills, CA 90210
Phone: (818)753-4625
A private, nonprofit organization working to help Southern Californians by education, example, and by assistance in caring for and improving the environment. Provides educational materials, pamphlets, and a newsletter. ***Subjects:*** Environment, urban forestry.

★4708★ U.S. Environmental Directories, Inc.
PO Box 65156
St. Paul, MN 55165
Publishes a directory which lists addresses and descriptions of over 375 non-governmental environmental and conservation organizations in alphabetical order. Reaches market through direct mail. ***Selected Titles:*** The Directory of National Environmental Organizations, 3rd ed. edited by John C. Brainard and Roger N. McGrath.

★4709★ University of Georgia, Athens Institute of Ecology
Athens, GA 30602
Phone: (404)542-2968
Selected Titles: Institute of Ecology Annual Report edited by Janice Sand.

★4710★ Water Information Center, Inc.
125 E Bethpage Rd.
Plainview, NY 11803
Phone: (516)249-7634
Publishes references and textbooks in the water field. Also publishes Groundwater Newsletter, Water Newsletter/Research & Development News, and International Water Report. Also offers several software programs.

★4711★ Water Pollution Control Federation
601 Wythe St.
Alexandria, VA 22314-9990
Phone: (703)684-2400
Fax: (703)684-2492
Nonprofit technical education organization devoted to the collection and dissemination of information concerning the nature, collection, treatment, and disposal of domestic and industrial wastewater. Also offers eight periodicals, video cassettes, and training materials. Reaches market through direct mail.

★4712★ Western Michigan University New Issues Press
Kalamazoo, MI 49008
Phone: (616)383-3983
Subjects: Environmental concerns, politics, social science, humanities. ***Selected Titles:*** Environmental Concerns: A Bibliography of U.S. Government Publications by Burk and Hayes.

★4713★ Wide Skies Press
Rte. 1, Box 7
Polk, NE 68654
Phone: (402)765-7212
Encourages conservation of natural resources. ***Selected Titles:*** Grassland by James and Alice Wilson, with Steven C. Wilson photography.

★4714★ Wildlife Management Institute
1101 14th St., NW, Ste. 725
Washington, DC 20005
Phone: (202)347-1774
Co-publishes books on selected species of wildlife for both professionals and interested laypersons. Offers the monthly Outdoor News Bulletin. ***Subjects:*** Wildlife conservation and management.

★4715★ Wildlife Society Inc.
5410 Grosvenor Ln.
Bethesda, MD 20814-2197
Phone: (301)897-9770
Subjects: Scientific wildlife management and conservation of wildlife resources. ***Selected Titles:*** Readings in Wildlife Conservation edited by J. A. Bailey et al.; Wildlife Conservation Principles and Practices edited by R. D. Teague and E. Decker; Wildlife Management Techniques Manual edited by S. D. Schemnitz.

★4716★ William T. Lorenz & Co.
85 Warren St.
Concord, NH 03301
Phone: (603)228-3373
Publishes market research studies in the environmental field. Also offers management and marketing consulting. Reaches market through direct mail. ***Selected Titles:*** 1986 Updates: Air Pollution Control Industry Outlook by W.T. Lorenz and T.B. Whiton; 1990 Update: Water Pollution Control Industry Outlook by A.L. Ropes and W.T. Lorenz; 1990 Update: Hazardous Waste Control Industry Outlook by W.T. Lorenz, J.M. Immel, and J.C. Lorenz; 1991 Update: Solid Waste Control Industry Outlook by William T. Lorenz.

★4717★ World Environment Center
419 Park Ave. S, Ste. 1403
New York, NY 10016
Phone: (212)683-4700
An international network for environmental management. Publishes books for environmental professionals involved in international natural resource management, environmental policy, and training. Reaches market through direct mail and reviews. ***Selected Titles:*** Pollution Prevention Pays.

★4718★ World Resources Institute
1709 New York Ave., NW
Washington, DC 20006
Phone: (202)638-6300
Fax: (202)638-0036
Publishes on global resources and environmental conditions, analysis of emerging issues, and creative policy responses. Reaches market through direct mail, trade sales, Baker & Taylor, and other wholesalers. ***Selected Titles:*** Ill Winds: Airborne Pollution's Toll on Trees and Crops by James J. MacKenzie and Mohamed T. El-Ashry; The Forest for the Trees? Government Policies and the Misuse of Forest Resources by Robert Repetto; Energy for a Sustainable World by Jose Goldemberg et al.; Breathing Easier: Taking Action on Climate Change, Air Pollution, and Energy Insecurity by James J. MacKenzie; Wasting Assets by Robert Repetto; World Resources 1990-91.

★4719★ Yankee Permaculture
7781 Lenox Ave.
Jacksonville, FL 32221
"Permaculture is the design process of bringing our lives back into participation with the process of the earth." Offers courses, workshops, lectures, and design consulting. Also offers a journal, International Permaculture Solutions Journal, and a newsletter, Robin. Distributes for Tagari and Island Press. Reaches market through direct mail.

Books

★4720★ **30 Simple Energy Things You Can Do to Save the Earth**
Pacific Gas & Electric Co. and the Earthworks Group
77 Beale St., Rm. 1764
San Francisco, CA 94106
Phone: (415)973-5860
Describes energy conservation techniques for consumers. Alison Silverstein, author.

★4721★ **50 Simple Things Kids Can Do to Save the Earth**
Andrews and McMeel
4900 Main St.
Kansas City, MO 64112
Phone: (816)932-6700
Fax: (816)932-6706
Editor(s): The Earth Works Group. ***Frequency:*** 1990. Explains how specific things in a child's environment are connected to the rest of the world, how using them affects the planet, and how the individual can develop habits and projects that are environmentally sound.

★4722★ **365 Ways For You and Your Children to Save the Earth One Day at a Time**
Warner Books, Inc.
666 Fifth Ave.
New York, NY 10103
Phone: (212)484-2900
Editor(s): Michael Viner with Pat Hilton. ***Frequency:*** 1991.

★4723★ **1990 Safety Catalog**
Coastal Video Communications Corp.
3083 Brickhouse Ct.
Virginia Beach, VA 23452
Phone: (804)498-9014
Lists more than 40 video training programs on safety, industrial hygiene, and environmental training.

★4724★ **1991-1992 Green Index**
Island Press
Box 7
Covelo, CA 95428
A state-by-state guide to the nation's environmental health. Hall, Bob and Kerr, Mary Lee. 1991. ***Price:*** $29.95 hardbound, $18.95 paperback. 168 pp.

★4725★ **Acceptable Risk?: Making Decisions in a Toxic Environment**
University of California Press
2120 Berkeley Way
Berkeley, CA 94720
Phone: (415)642-4247
Editor(s): Lee Clarke. ***Frequency:*** 1989.

★4726★ **Access EPA: Clearinghouses and Hotlines**
National Technical Information Service
5285 Port Royal Rd.
Springfield, VA 22161
Phone: (703)487-4650
From Information Managment and Services Division of the U.S. Environmental Protection Agency. August 1990. ***Price:*** $15/paper, $8/microfiche.

★4727★ **Access EPA: Library and Information Services**
National Technical Information Service
5285 Port Royal Rd
Springfield, VA 22161
Phone: (703)487-4650
From Information Management and Services Division, U.S. Environmental Protection Agency. July 1990. ***Price:*** $23/paper, $8/microfiche.

★4728★ **Acid Rain**
Chelsea House Publishers
1974 Sprout Rd., Ste. 400
Broomall, PA 19008
Phone: (215)353-5166
Fax: (215)359-1439
Editor(s): Peter Tyson. ***Frequency:*** 1992. Discusses the problem of acid rain, its causes, how it spreads, and its devastating effects on the environment. Also examines possible solutions to the problem.

★4729★ **Acid Rain: Earth Alert Series**
Maxwell Macmillan International Publishing Group
Export Div.
28100 US Hwy. 19 N., Ste. 200
Clearwater, FL 34621
Turck, Mary. 1990. Crestwood House. ***Price:*** $10.95. 47 pp.

★4730★ **The Acid Rain Foundation Conference Proceedings**
The Acid Rain Found.
1410 Varsity Dr.
Raleigh, NC 27606
Phone: (919)828-9443
Frequency: Annual.

★4731★ **Acid Rain: Suggested Background Readings**
Air Resources Information Clearinghouse
46 Prince St.
Rochester, NY 14607-1016
Phone: (716)271-3550
Fax: (716)271-0606

★4732★ **Active and Passive Smoking Hazards in the Workplace**
Van Nostrand Reinhold Co.
Mail Order Dept.
PO Box 668
Florence, KY 41042-0668
Phone: (606)525-6600
Editor(s): Douville, Judith A. 1990. ***Price:*** $29.95.

★4733★ **Advances in Technology Provide—Environmental Solutions: A User-Friendly Guide to the Latest Technology**
Kendall/Hunt Publishing Co.
2460 Kerper Blvd.
Dubuque, IA 52001
Phone: (319)588-1451
Editor(s): Daniel Burrus and Patti Thomsen. ***Frequency:*** 1990.

★4734★ **Adventures in Conservation with Franklin D. Roosevelt**
Northland Publishing Co.
PO Box N
Flagstaff, AZ 86002
Phone: (602)774-5251
Fax: (602)774-0592
Editor(s): Irving Brant. ***Frequency:*** 1989.

★4735★ **Agatha's Feather Bed: Not Just Another Wild Goose Story**
Peachtree Publishers, Ltd.
494 Armour Circle, NE
Atlanta, GA 30324
Phone: (404)876-8761
Editor(s): Carmen Agra Deedy. ***Frequency:*** 1991. When Agatha buys a new feather bed and six angry naked geese show up to get their feathers back, the incident reminds her to think about where things come from.

★4736★ **Ages of Gaia: Biography of Our Living Earth**
W.W. Norton & Co.
500 5th Ave.
New York, NY 10110
Phone: (212)354-5500
Toll-Free: 800-223-2584
James Lovelock, author. 1988. ***Price:*** $16.95.

★4737★ **Air and Waste Management Association Directory and Resource Book**
Air and Waste Management Assn.
PO Box 2861
Pittsburgh, PA 15230
Phone: (412)232-3444
Fax: (412)232-3450
Frequency: Annual.

★4738★ Air Pollution, Acid Rain, and the Environment
Elsevier Science Publishing Co.
52 Vanderbilt Ave.
New York, NY 10017
Phone: (212)370-5520
Editor(s): Kenneth Mellanby. ***Frequency:*** 1988.

★4739★ Air Pollution Control and the German Experience: Lessons for the United States
Center for Clean Air Policy
444 N. Capitol St., Ste. 526
Washington, DC 20001
Phone: (202)624-7709

★4740★ Air Risk Information Support Center: Assistance for State and Local Agencies
Environmental Protection Agency
Public Information Center
401 M St., SW PM-211B
Washington, DC 20460
Phone: (202)475-7751
Brochure. 1988. ***Price:*** Contact the Air Risk Hotline: (919)541-0888.

★4741★ Alliance for Environmental Education Annual Report
Alliance for Environmental Education
10751 Ambassador Dr., No. 201
Manassas, VA 22110
Phone: (703)335-1025
Fax: (703)631-1651

★4742★ Alluvial Fans, Mudflows, and Mud Floods
Association of State Floodplain Managers
PO Box 2051
Madison, WI 53701-2051
Phone: (608)266-1926

★4743★ Alternative Energy Sourcebook
Real Goods
966 Mazzoni St.
Ukiah, CA 95482
Toll-Free: 800-762-7325
Price: $14. 400 pp.

★4744★ Alternatives to Deforestation: Steps Toward Sustainable Use of the Amazon Rain Forest
Columbia University Press
Marketing Dept.
562 W. 113th St.
New York, NY 10025
Anderson, Anthony B. ***Frequency:*** 1990. ***Price:*** $65.00.

★4745★ America in the 21st Century: Environmental Concerns
Population Reference Bureau, Inc.
1875 Connecticut Ave.
Washington, DC 20009-5728

★4746★ American Coal Ash Association Annual Report
Amer. Coal Ash Assn.
1913 I St NW, 6th Fl.
Washington, DC 20001
Phone: (202)659-2303
Fax: (202)223-4984

★4747★ American Environmental History
Merrill Publishing Co.
PO Box 508
Columbus, OH 43216
Phone: (614)890-1111
Editor(s): Joseph M. Pettula. ***Frequency:*** 1988.

★4748★ American Environmentalism: Readings in Conservation History
Alfred A. Knopf, Inc.
201 E. 50th St.
New York, NY 10022
Phone: (201)751-2600
Editor(s): Roderick Frazier Nash. ***Frequency:*** 1990.

★4749★ The American West as Living Space
University of Michigan Press
839 Green St.
PO Box 1104
Ann Arbor, MI 48106
Phone: (313)764-4394
Editor(s): Wallace Stegner. ***Frequency:*** 1987.

★4750★ American Wilderness Adventures
Amer. Wildlands
7500 E. Arapahoe Rd., Ste. 355
Englewood, CO 80112
Phone: (303)771-0380
Fax: (303)694-9047
Guide to wilderness adventure trips sponsored by the alliance. ***Frequency:*** Annual. ***Price:*** Free.

★4751★ America's Waste: Managing for Risk Reduction
Conservation Found.
1250 24th St., NW
Washington, DC 20037
Phone: (202)293-4800
Fax: (202)293-9211
Frequency: 1987. A report issued by the Conservation Foundation.

★4752★ And Then There Was One: The Mysteries of Extinction
Little, Brown and Co.
Children's Books/Sales
34 Beacon St.
Boston, MA 02108-1493
Facklam, Margery. 1990. Children's book. ***Price:*** $14.95. 56 pp.

★4753★ Annotated Bibliography of the Desert Tortoise
Desert Tortoise Coun.
PO Box 1738
Palm Desert, CA 92261-1738
Phone: (619)341-8449
Frequency: Transactions of meetings, and papers.

★4754★ Anthony Anthony's Boring Day
Doubleday & Co., Inc.
666 Fifth Ave.
New York, NY 10103
Phone: (212)984-7561
Editor(s): Dennis Reader. ***Frequency:*** 1992. Acting on his grandfather's advice, Anthony combats his boredom by taking on such environmental projects as saving the rain forests and mending the hole in the ozone layer.

★4755★ The Antinuclear Movement: Revised Edition
G.K. Hall & Co.
Marketing Dept.
70 Lincoln St.
Boston, MA 02111
Price, Jerome. 1990. ***Price:*** $12.95. 212 pp.

★4756★ Appraising Easements: Guidelines for the Valuation of Historic Preservation and Land Conservation Easements
Land Trust Alliance
900 17th St. NW, Ste. 410
Washington DC, 20006
Phone: (202)785-1410
Fax: (202)785-1408

★4757★ Arctic Environmental Problems
Tampere Peace Research Inst.
Tampere, Finland
Editor(s): Lassi Heininen. ***Frequency:*** 1990.

★4758★ The Art & Science of Composting
BioCycle
419 State Ave.
Emmaus, PA 18049
Phone: (215)967-4135
Guide to composting of municipal, industrial, and agricultural wastes. Covers composting principles, processes, management, materials, and markets. ***Price:*** $55.

★4759★ Association of State and Interstate Water Pollution Control Administrators Position Statements
Association of State and Interstate Water Pollution Control Administrators
444 N. Capitol St. NW, Ste. 330
Washington, DC 20001
Phone: (202)624-7782
Frequency: Annual.

★4760★ Association of State Wetland Managers Symposium Proceedings
Association of State Wetland Managers
PO Box 2463
Berne, NY 12023
Phone: (518)872-1804
Frequency: 1-3/year.

★4761★ At Odds with Progress: Americans and Conservation
University of Arizona Press
1230 N. Park Ave.
Ste. 102
Tuscon, AZ 85719
Phone: (602)621-1441
Editor(s): Bret Wallach. ***Frequency:*** 1991.

★4762★ The Atlas of Endangered Species
Macmillan Publishing Co.
366 Third Ave.
New York, NY 10022
Phone: (212)702-2000
Editor(s): John A. Burton. ***Frequency:*** 1991. Describes the various animals and plants throughout the world whose survival is being threatened and the steps being taken to save them from extinction.

★4763★ Atlas of Environmental Issues
Facts On File, Inc.
460 Park Ave.
New York, NY 10016
Phone: (212)683-2244
Editor(s): Nick Middleton. ***Frequency:*** 1989. Describes and explains major environmental issues of the world today including soil erosion, deforestation, mechanized agriculture, oil pollution of the oceans, acid rain, overfishing, and nuclear power.

★4764★ Atlas of the Environment
Prentice Hall Press
1 Gulf and Western Plaza
New York, NY 10023
Lean, Geoffrey et al. ***Price:*** $19.95.

★4765★ Atlas of United States Environmental Issues
MacMillan Publishing Corp.
Front and Brown St.
Riverside, NJ 08075
Mason, Robert and Mattson, Mark. 1990. ***Price:*** $80. 252 pp.

★4766★ Audubon Perspectives: Fight for Survival: A Companion to the Audubon Television Specials
John Wiley & Sons, Inc.
605 Third Ave.
New York, NY 10158
Phone: (212)850-6000
Editor(s): Roger L. DiSilvestro. ***Frequency:*** 1990.

★4767★ Aunt Ippy's Museum of Junk
HarperCollins Inc.
10 E. 53rd St.
New York, NY 10022
Phone: (212)207-7000
Editor(s): Rodney Alan Greenblat. ***Frequency:*** 1991. A brother and sister visit their ecology-minded Aunt Ippy and her world famous Museum of Junk.

★4768★ Balancing on the Brink of Extinction
Island Press
Box 7
Covelo, CA 95428
Discussion on the ramifications of the Endangered Species Act. ***Editor(s):*** Kohm, Kathryn A. 1990. ***Price:*** $34.95. 316 pp.

★4769★ Barriers to a Better Environment: What Stops Us Solving Environmental Problems?
Belhaven Press
London, England
Editor(s): Stephen Trudgill. ***Frequency:*** 1990.

★4770★ Bears: Their Biology and Management
International Assn. for Bear Research and Management
c/o ADF & G
333 Raspberry Rd.
Anchorage, AK 99518-1599
Phone: (907)344-0541
Conference proceedings. ***Frequency:*** Triennial.

★4771★ Beauty, Health, and Permanence: Environmental Politics in the United States, 1955-1985
Cambridge Univ. Press
40 W. 20th St.
New York, NY 10011
Phone: (212)924-3900
Fax: (212)691-3239
Editor(s): Samuel P. Hays in collaboration with Barbara D. Hays.

★4772★ Beneficial Use of Waste Solids
Water Pollution Control Fed.
601 Wythe St.
Alexandria, VA 22314-9990
Phone: (703)684-2400
Prepared by Task Force on Beneficial Use of Waste Solids under the direction of the Technical Practice Committee. ***Frequency:*** 1989.

★4773★ The Berenstain Bears Don't Pollute (Anymore)
Random House, Inc.
201 E. 50th St.
New York, NY 10022
Phone: (212)751-2600
Editor(s): Stan and Jan Berenstain. ***Frequency:*** 1991. The bears in Bear Country grow concerned about how pollution and waste of natural resources are damaging the world around them, so they form The Earthsavers Club.

★4774★ Beyond 25 Percent: Materials Recovery Comes of Age
Institute for Local Self-Reliance
2425 18th St., NW
Washington, DC 20009
Phone: (202)232-4108
Editor(s): Theresa Allan, Brenda Platt, and David Morris. ***Frequency:*** 1989.

★4775★ Beyond 40 Percent: Record-Setting Recycling and Composting Programs
Institute for Local Self-Reliance
2425 18th St., NW
Washington, DC 20009
Phone: (202)232-4108
Editor(s): Brenda Platt. ***Frequency:*** 1990.

★4776★ Beyond Black Bear Lake
W.W. Norton & Co., Inc.
500 Fifth Ave.
New York, NY 10110
Phone: (212)354-5500
Fax: (212)869-0856
Editor(s): Anne LaBastille. ***Frequency:*** 1987.

★4777★ Beyond Spaceship Earth: Environmental Ethics and the Solar System
Sierra Club Books/Random House
201 E. 50th St.
New York, NY 10022
Phone: (212)751-2600
Toll-Free: 800-726-0600
1986. ***Editor(s):*** Eugene C. Hargrove. ***Price:*** $25.

★4778★ Beyond the Mythic West
Peregrine Smith Books
Salt Lake City, UT
Editor(s): Stewart L. Udall. ***Frequency:*** 1990.

★4779★ The Bhopal Syndrome: The World's Worst Industrial Accident
Sierra Club Books
Maryland
Business
San Francisco, CA 94104
Weir, David. 1987. ***Price:*** $8.95. 210 pp.

★4780★ Biodiversity
National Academy Press
Maryland
2101 Constitution Ave., N.W.
Washington, DC 20418
Wilson, E.O. 1988. ***Price:*** $23.50. 538 pp.

★4781★ Biologic: Environmental Protection By Design
Johnson Books
1880 S 57th Ct.
Boulder, CO 80301
Phone: (303)443-1576
Editor(s): David Wann. ***Frequency:*** 1990.

★4782★ Biologic Markers of Air-Pollution Stress and Damage in Forests
National Academy Press
Maryland
2101 Constitution Ave., N.W.
Washington, DC 20418
National Research Council. 1989. ***Price:*** $42. 380 pp.

★4783★ Bioremediation for Marine Oil Spills
US Congress - Office of Technology Assessment
Washington, DC
Frequency: 1990.

★4784★ Biosphere 2: The Human Experiment
Penguin USA
Academic Marketing
375 Hudson St.
New York, NY 10014
Allen, John. 1991. ***Price:*** $16.95. 156 pp.

★4785★ Bird Conservation
International Coun. for Bird Preservation, U.S. Sect.
c/o World Wildlife Fund
1250 24th St. NW
Washington, DC 20037
Phone: (202)778-9563
Fax: (202)293-9211
Frequency: Annual.

★4786★ Bluebird Bibliography
North Amer. Bluebird Soc.
Box 6295
Silver Spring, MD 20916-6295
Phone: (301)384-2798

★4787★ Blueprint for a Green Planet: Your Practical Guide to Restoring the World's Environment
Prentice Hall Press
1 Gulf & Western Plaza
New York, NY 10023
Phone: (212)373-8500
Editor(s): John Seymour and Herbert Girardet. ***Frequency:*** 1987.

★4788★ Blueprint for the Environment: A Plan for Action
Howe Brothers Publishers
PO Box 6394
Salt Lake City, UT 84106
Phone: (801)485-7409
Toll-Free: 800-426-5387
1989. ***Editor(s):*** T. Allan Comp. ***Price:*** $13.95.

★4789★ Borrowed Earth, Borrowed Time: Healing America's Chemical Wounds
Plenum Publishing Corp.
233 Spring St.
New York, NY 10013
Phone: (212)620-8000
Editor(s): Glenn E. Schweitzer. ***Frequency:*** 1991.

★4790★ Breaking New Ground
Island Press
1718 Connecticut Ave., NW
Ste. 300
Washington, DC 20009
Phone: (202)232-7933
Fax: (202)234-1328
Editor(s): Gifford Pinchot. ***Frequency:*** 1987.

★4791★ Breathing Easier: Taking Action on Climate Change, Air Pollution, and Energy Insecurity
State University of New York Press
Maryland
State University Plaza
Albany, NY 12246
Mackenzie, James J. 1989. ***Price:*** $10.00. 23 pp.

★4792★ Brother Eagle, Sister Sky!: The Words of Chief Seattle
Dial Books for Young Readers
2 Park Ave.
New York, NY 10016
Phone: (212)725-1818
Editor(s): Chief Seattle. ***Frequency:*** 1991. A Suquamish Indian chief describes his people's respect and love for the earth, and concern for its destruction.

★4793★ Bureaucratic Politics and Regulatory Reform: The EPA and Emissions Trading
Greenwood Press, Inc.
88 Post Rd., W
PO Box 5007
Westport, CT 06881
Phone: (203)226-3571
Editor(s): Brian J. Cook. ***Frequency:*** 1988.

★4794★ A Call for Action: Airborne Toxic Pollution in the Great Lakes Basin
Great Lakes United
State University Coll. at Buffalo
Cassety Hall
1300 Elmwood Ave.
Buffalo, NY 14222
Phone: (716)886-0142

★4795★ Call to Action Handbook for Ecology, Peace, and Justice
Sierra Club Books
Maryland
100 Bush St., 13th Fl.
San Francisco, CA 94104
Erickson, Brad. 1989. ***Price:*** $14.95. 250 pp.

★4796★ Can the Whales Be Saved?: Questions About the Natural World and the Threats to its Survival Answered by the Natural History Museum
Viking Kestrel
40 W 23rd St.
New York, NY 10010
Phone: (212)337-5200
Editor(s): Philip Whitfield. ***Frequency:*** 1989.

★4797★ The Care Bears and the Big Cleanup
Random House, Inc.
201 E. 50th St.
New York, NY 10022
Phone: (212)751-2600
Editor(s): Bobbi Katz. ***Frequency:*** 1991. When Lisa and Simon move to the country and discover that litter is ruining the woods, the join forces with the Care Bears to motivate the community into organizing the Big Clean-up.

★4798★ Caring for Our Air
Enslow Publishers
Bloy St. & Ramsey Ave.
PO Box 777
Hillside, NJ 07205
Phone: (201)964-4116
Editor(s): Carol Greene. ***Frequency:*** 1991. Simple text and illustrations describe the ecological issue of air pollution and ways children can help to control the problem.

★4799★ Caring for Our Land
Enslow Publishers
Bloy St. & Ramsey Ave.
PO Box 777
Hillside, NJ 07205
Phone: (201)964-4116
Editor(s): Carol Greene. ***Frequency:*** 1991. Simple text and illustrations describe the ecological issues related to land use, such as pollution and overdevelopment, and ways children can help.

★4800★ Caring for Our People
Enslow Publishers
Bloy St. & Ramsey Ave.
PO Box 777
Hillside, NJ 07205
Phone: (201)964-4116
Editor(s): Carol Greene. ***Frequency:*** 1991. Explains, in simple terms, why people are important, how pollutants and deforestation threaten human existence, and what children can do to take care of the earth.

★4801★ Caring for Our Water
Enslow Publishers
Bloy St. & Ramsey Ave.
PO Box 777
Hillside, NJ 07205
Phone: (201)964-4116
Editor(s): Carol Greene. ***Frequency:*** 1991. Simple text and illustrations describe different ecological problems relating to water, and suggest ways to preserve this resource.

★4802★ Caring for Planet Earth: The World Around Us
Lion Publishing Corp.
1705 Hubbard Ave.
Batavia, IL 60510
Phone: (708)879-0707
Fax: (708)879-0843
Editor(s): Barbara Holland and Hazel Lucas. ***Frequency:*** 1990. Describes different environments around the world, the interdependence of plants, animals, and people, the depletion of natural resources and wildlife species, and efforts to protect the earth's natural environment.

★4803★ Cartons, Cans, and Orange Peels—Where Does Your Garbage Go?
Clarion Books
215 Park Ave., S.
New York, NY 10003
Phone: (212)420-5800
Fax: (212)420-5850
Editor(s): Joanna Foster. ***Frequency:*** 1991. Outlines the composition of gargage and trash and discusses the various methods of disposing of it with and emphasis on recycling.

★4804★ A Case of Poison
Crestwood House, Inc.
c/o Macmillan Publishing Co.
866 Third Ave.
New York, NY 10022
Phone: (212)702-9632
Editor(s): Dana Brenford, created and edited by Marion Dane Bauer. ***Frequency:*** 1988. A chemical smell in the swamp and suspicious behavior on their neighbors' property alert twelve-year-old sibling investigators Peter, Jason, and Kim to the possibility of a threat to the environment.

★4805★ CEIP Fund Annual Report
CEIP Fund
68 Harrison Ave., 5th Fl.
Boston, MA 02111
Phone: (617)426-4375

★4806★ Center for Marine Conservation Annual Report
Center for Marine Conservation
1725 DeSales St. NW, Ste. 500
Washington, DC 20036
Phone: (202)429-5609
Fax: (202)872-0619

★4807★ The Challenge of Global Warming
Island Press
Sales Dept.
PO Box 7
Covelo, CA 95428
Abrahamson, Dean Edwin. 1989. ***Price:*** $19.95. 355 pp.

★4808★ The Changing Atmosphere: A Global Challenge
Yale University Press
Exhibits Dept.
92 A Yale Sta.
New Haven, CT 06520
Firor, John. 1990. ***Price:*** $19.95. 145 pp.

★4809★ Charles Darwin Foundation for the Galapagos Isles Annual Report
Charles Darwin Found. for the Galapagos Isles
c/o Craig MacFarland
National Zoological Park
Washington, DC 20008
Phone: (202)673-4705
Fax: (202)673-4607

★4810★ Chemical Sensitivity and Public Health Policy: The Clinical Ecology Debate
Foundation for Advancements in Science and Education
Park Mile Plaza, Ste. 215
4801 Wilshire Blvd.
Los Angeles, CA 90010
FASE, 1989.

★4811★ The Chemo Kid: A Novel
HarperCollins Inc.
10 E. 53rd St.
New York, NY 10022
Phone: (212)207-7000
Editor(s): Robert Lipsyte. ***Frequency:*** 1992. When the drugs that he takes as part of his chemotherapy suddenly transform him from wimp into superhero, sixteen-year-old Fred and his friends plot to rid the town of its most lethal environmental hazard, toxic waste in the water supply.

★4812★ Children's Atlas of the Environment
Rand McNally & Co.
8255 N. Central Park Ave.
Skokie, IL 60076-2970
Phone: (312)673-9100
Frequency: 1991. Maps and text portray the world's ecosystems, environmental concerns, and positive suggestions of what can be done to help the planet.

★4813★ A Child's Organic Garden
Earth Foods Associates
11221 Markwood Dr.
Wheaton, MD 20902
Phone: (301)649-6212
Organic, sustainable agriculture for children and adults. Co-authored by a child and an environmentalist.

★4814★ A Citizens Guide: 101 Ways to Help Heal the Earth
Greenhouse Crisis Found.
1130 17th St. NW, Ste. 630
Washington, DC 20036
Phone: (202)466-2823

★4815★ Citizen's Guide to Clean Water
Izaak Walton League of America
1401 Wilson Blvd., Level B
Arlington, VA 22209
Phone: (703)528-1818
Fax: (703)528-1836

★4816★ A Citizen's Guide to Plastics in the Ocean
Center for Marine Conservation
1725 DeSales St., NW
Washington, DC 20036
Phone: (202)429-5609
Editor(s): Kathryn J. O'Hara and Suzanne Iudicello. ***Frequency:*** 1988. ***Price:*** $2 postpaid.

★4817★ A Citizen's Guide to Promoting Toxic Waste Reduction
INFORM
Publications Dept.
381 Park Ave. S.
New York, NY 10016
Kenworthy, Lauren and Schaeffer, Eric. 1989. ***Price:*** $15. 128 pp.

★4818★ Citizens Guide to the Great Lakes Water Quality Agreement
Great Lakes United
State University Coll. at Buffalo
Cassety Hall
1300 Elmwood Ave.
Buffalo, NY 14222
Phone: (716)886-0142

★4819★ Clean Air
Chelsea House Publishers
1974 Sprout Rd., Ste. 400
Broomall, PA 19008
Phone: (215)353-5166
Fax: (215)359-1439
Editor(s): Ed Edelson. ***Frequency:*** 1992. Discusses the devastating effects of population growth and industry on air quality; the different types of pollutants that can be found in the atmosphere; the health and economical effects of pollution; and ways to clean up the air.

★4820★ Clean Air Act: A Primer and Glossary
Clean Air Working Group
818 Connecticut Ave. NW, Ste. 900
Washington, DC 20006
Phone: (202)857-0370

★4821★ Clean Sites, Inc. Annual Report
Clean Sites, Inc.
1199 N. Fairfax St.
Alexandria, VA 22314
Phone: (703)683-8522

★4822★ Cleaning Up
Julian Messner
Englewood Cliffs, NJ
Editor(s): Eve and Albert Stwertka. ***Frequency:*** 1992. Discusses the problem of trash and what can be done with it, including the partial solution of recycling.

★4823★ Cleaning Up: U.S. Waste Management Technology and Third World Development
State University of New York Press
Maryland
State University Plaza
Albany, NY 12246
Elkington, John and Shopley, Jonathan. 1989. ***Price:*** $12.50. 80 pp.

★4824★ Clearer, Cleaner, Safer, Greener: A Blueprint for Detoxifying Your Environment
Random House Inc.
International
201 E. 50th St.
New York, NY 10022
Null, Gary. 1990. ***Price:*** $18.95. 293 pp.

★4825★ Climate Change: The IPCC Response Strategies
Island Press
Sales Dept.
PO Box 7
Covelo, CA 95428
Intergovernmental Panel on Climate Change. 1991. ***Price:*** $34.95. 328 pp.

★4826★ Coalition for Responsible Waste Incineration Seminar Proceedings
Coalition for Responsible Waste Incineration
1330 Connecticut Ave. NW, Ste. 300
Washington, DC 20036
Phone: (202)659-0060
Frequency: Annual.

★4827★ Coastal Alert
Island Press
Box 7
Covelo, CA 95428
Holing, Dwight. Natural Resources Defense Council. 1990. ***Price:*** $10.95. 120 pp.

★4828★ Coming Full Circle: Successful Recycling Today
Environmental Defense Fund
EDF
257 Park Ave. S
New York, NY 10010
Phone: (212)505-2100
Environmental Defense Fund. 1988. ***Price:*** $20.00.

★4829★ Common Property Resources: Ecology and Community-based Sustainable Development
Belhaven Press

Editor(s): Fikret Berkes. ***Frequency:*** 1989. Includes papers presented at the Conference on Conservation and Development: Implementing the World Conservation Strategy, held June, 1986, Ottawa, Canada, and the Fourth Internation Congress of Ecology, held August, 1986, Syracuse, NY.

★4830★ The Complete Guide to Environmental Careers
Island Press
1718 Connecticut Ave., NW
Ste. 300
Washington, DC 20009
Phone: (202)232-7933
Fax: (202)234-1328
Editor(s): Distributed by the CEIP Fund. ***Frequency:*** 1989.

★4831★ The Complete Guide to Recycling at Home: How to Take the Responsibility, Save Money, and Protect the Environment
Betterway Publications, Inc.
White Hall, VA 22987
Phone: (804)823-5661
Editor(s): Gary D. Branson. ***Frequency:*** 1991.

★4832★ Complete Trash: The Best Way to Get Rid of Practically Everything Around the House
M. Evans & Co., Inc.
216 E. 49th St.
New York, NY 10017
Phone: (212)688-2810
Editor(s): Norm Crampton. ***Frequency:*** 1989.

★4833★ Concern's Community Action Guides on Environmental Topics
Concern, Inc.
Publications Dept.
1794 Columbia Rd. NW
Washington, DC 20009
Frequency: 1991.

★4834★ Confronting Climate Change: Strategies for Energy Research and Development
National Academy Press
Maryland
2101 Constitution Ave., N.W.
Washington, DC 20418
National Research Council. 1990. ***Price:*** $21.75. 143 pp.

★4835★ Connecting With Nature: Creating Moments that Let Earth Teach
World Peace University
Box 10869
Eugene, OR 97440
Michael J. Cohen, author. 88 pp. ***Price:*** $10.95.

★4836★ Connections: Linking Population and the Environment Teaching Kit
Population Reference Bureau, Inc.
1875 Connecticut Ave.
Washington, DC 20009-5728

★4837★ Conservation and Practical Morality: Challenges to Education and Reform
Macmillan Publishing Co.
366 Third Ave.
New York, NY 10022
Phone: (212)702-2000
Editor(s): Les Brown. ***Frequency:*** 1987.

★4838★ Conservation and Research Foundation Five Year Report
Conservation and Research Found.
240 Arapahoe E.
Lake Quivira, KS 66106
Phone: (913)268-0076

★4839★ The Conservation Atlas of Tropical Forests: Asia and the Pacific
Simon & Schuster, Inc.
Simon & Schuster Bldg.
1230 Ave. of the Americas
New York, NY 10020
Phone: (212)698-7000
Editor(s): N. Mark Collins, Jeffrey A. Sayer, and Timothy C. Whitmore. ***Frequency:*** 1991.

★4840★ The Conservation Easement Handbook
Trust for Public Land
116 New Montgomery St., 4th Fl.
San Francisco, CA 94105
Phone: (415)495-5660
Fax: (415)495-0541

★4841★ The Conservation Easement Handbook: Managing Land Conservation and Historic Preservation Easement Programs
Land Trust Alliance
900 17th St. NW, Ste 410
Washington, DC 20006
Phone: (202)785-1410
Fax: (202)785-1408

★4842★ Conservation Engineering Handbook
Association of Conservation Engineers
c/o William P. Allinder
Alabama Department of Conservation
64 N. Union St.
Montgomery, AL 36130
Phone: (205)261-3476
Frequency: Periodic.

★4843★ Conservation in Africa: People, Policies, and Practice
Cambridge Univ. Press
40 W. 20th St.
New York, NY 10011
Phone: (212)924-3900
Fax: (212)692-3239
Editor(s): David Anderson and Richard Grove. ***Frequency:*** 1987.

★4844★ Conservation of Natural Resources
Prentice Hall
Rte. 9W
Englewood Cliffs, NJ 07632
Phone: (201)592-2000
Editor(s): Gary A. Klee. ***Frequency:*** 1991.

★4845★ Conservators of Hope: The Horace M. Albright Conservation Lectures
University of Idaho Press
Moscow, ID 83843
Phone: (208)885-6245
Editor(s): Horace M. Albright. Foreword by Michael Frome; preface by Horace M. Albright; introduction by Dennis E. Teeguarden. ***Frequency:*** 1988.

★4846★ Conserving the Polar Regions
Steck-Vaughn Co.
PO Box 26015
Austin, TX 78755
Phone: (512)343-8227
Barbara James. ***Frequency:*** 1990. Focuses on the two polar regions, the Arctic and the Antarctic, and discusses their uniqueness, their relation to world climate, their development and conservation, and the threat of pollution.

★4847★ Conserving the World's Biological Diversity
World Wildlife Fund
The Conservation Foundation
Publications Dept.
1250 Twenty-Fourth St., NW
Washington, DC 20037
McNeeley, Jeffrey A., Miller, Kenton R., and Reid, W.V. 1990. ***Price:*** $14.95. 193 pp.

★4848★ Contaminated Communities: The Social and Psychological Impacts of Residential Toxic Exposure
Island Press
1718 Connecticut Ave., NW
Ste. 300
Washington, DC 20036
Phone: (202)232-7933
Michael R. Edelstein. ***Frequency:*** 1988. ***Price:*** $29.95.

★4849★ The Control of Nature
Farrar, Straus & Giroux, Inc.
19 Union Sq. W.
New York, NY 10003
Phone: (212)741-6900
Fax: (212)633-9385
Editor(s): John McPhee. ***Frequency:*** 1989.

★4850★ Controlling the Greenhouse Effect: Five Global Regimes Compared
Brookings Institution
Publications Dept.
1775 Massachusetts Ave., NW
Washington, DC
Epstein, Joshua M. and Gupta, Raj. ***Frequency:*** 1990. ***Price:*** $4.95.

★4851★ Cool Energy: The Renewable Solution to Global Warming
State University of New York Press
Maryland
State University Plaza
Albany, NY 12246

★4852★ Coping With an Oiled Sea: An Analysis of Oil Spill Response Technologies
US Congress, Office of Technology Assessment
Washington, DC
Frequency: 1990.

★4853★ Coral Reefs of Florida
Pineapple Press
Maryland
P.O. Drawer 16008
Sarasota, FL 34239
Voss, Gilbert L. 1988. ***Price:*** $14.95. 80 pp.

★4854★ Council on Economic Priorities Studies
Council on Economic Priorities
30 Irving Pl.
New York, NY 10003
Phone: (212)420-1133
Fax: (212)420-0988
Frequency: Semiannual.

★4855★ Cradled in Human Hands: A Textbook on Environmental Responsibility
Sheed & Ward
PO Box 419492
Kansas City, MO 64141
Phone: (816)531-0538
Fax: (816)931-5082
Editor(s): Eileen P. Flynn. ***Frequency:*** 1991.

★4856★ Creating a Health World: 101 Practical Tips for Home and Work: Everyday Chemicals
Windstar Found.
Snowmass, CO
Editor(s): Beth Richman and Susan Hassol. ***Frequency:*** 1989.

★4857★ Creating Successful Communities
Island Press
Box 7
Covelo, CA 95428
Guide to growth management strategies. 1989. ***Price:*** $39.95. 230 pp.

★4858★ Crossroads: Environmental Priorities for the Future
Island Press
1718 Connecticut Ave., NW
Ste. 300
Washington, DC 20009
Phone: (202)232-7933
Fax: (202)234-1328
Editor(s): Peter Borrelli. ***Frequency:*** 1988.

★4859★ The Crucial Decade: The 1990s and the Global Environmental Challenge
World Resources Institute
1750 New York Ave., NW
Washington, DC 20006
Phone: (202)393-4055
1989. ***Price:*** $5.

★4860★ Dead Heat: The Race Against the Greenhouse Effect
Basic Books, Inc.
10 E. 53rd St.
New York, NY 10022
Phone: (212)207-7057
Editor(s): Michael Oppenheimer and Robert H. Boyle. ***Frequency:*** 1990.

★4861★ The Decade of Destruction: The Crusade to Save the Amazon Rain Forest
Henry Holt and Company Inc.
Sales and Marketing Dept.
115 W. 18th St.
New York, NY 10011
Cowell, Adrian. 1990. ***Price:*** $19.95. 215 pp.

★4862★ Deep Ecology
Gibbs Smith, Publisher/Peregrine Smith Books
PO Box 667
Layton, UT 84041
Phone: (801)544-9800
Toll-Free: 800-421-8714
Bill Devall and George Sessions, authors. 1987. ***Price:*** $11.95.

★4863★ Deer Special
Safari Club Intl.
4800 W. Gates Pass Rd.
Tucson, AZ 85745
Phone: (602)620-1220
Fax: (602)622-1205

★4864★ Demanding Clean Food and Water: The Fight for a Basic Human Right
Plenum Publishing Corp.
233 Spring St.
New York, NY 10013
Phone: (212)620-8000
Editor(s): Joan Goldstein. ***Frequency:*** 1990.

★4865★ Demands on Rural Lands: Planning for Resource Use
Westview Press, Inc.
5500 Central Ave.
Boulder, CO 80301
Phone: (303)444-3541
Fax: (303)449-3356
Editor(s): Chris Cocklin, Barry Smit, and Tom Johnston. ***Frequency:*** 1987.

★4866★ Deserts on the March
Island Press
1718 Conecticut Ave., NW
Ste. 300
Washington, DC 20009
Phone: (202)232-7933
Fax: (202)234-1328
Editor(s): Paul B. Sears. ***Frequency:*** 1988.

★4867★ Design for a Livable Planet: How You Can Help Clean Up the Environment
Perennial Library
New York, NY
Editor(s): Jon Naar. ***Frequency:*** 1990.

★4868★ Dictionary of Environmental Science and Technology
Open Univ. Press
c/o Taylor & Francis Group
1900 Frost Rd., Ste. 101
Bristol, PA 19007
Phone: (215)785-5800
Fax: (215)785-5515
Editor(s): Andrew Porteous. ***Frequency:*** 1991.

★4869★ Dinosaurs to the Rescue!: A Guide to Protecting Our Planet
Little, Brown & Co., Inc.
34 Beacon St.
Boston, MA 02108
Phone: (617)227-0730
Editor(s): Laurie Krasny Brown and Marc Brown. ***Frequency:*** 1992. Text and illustrations of dinosaur characters introduce the earth's major environmental problems and suggest ways children can help.

★4870★ Directory of Environmental Information Sources
Government Institutes, Inc.
966 Hungerford Dr., Ste. 24
Rockville, MD 20850
Phone: (301)251-9250
Editor(s): Thomas F.P. Sullivan. ***Frequency:*** 1990.

★4871★ Discordant Harmonies: A New Ecology for the Twenty-first Century
Oxford Univ. Press, Inc.
200 Madison Ave.
New York, NY 10016
Phone: (212)679-7300
Editor(s): Daniel B. Botkin. ***Frequency:*** 1990.

★4872★ Down to Earth: Speeches and Writings of His Royal Highness Prince Philip, Duke of Edinburgh, on the Relationship of Man with His Environment
Stephen Greene Press/Pelham Books
15 Muzzey St.
Lexington, MA 02173
Phone: (617)861-0170
Frequency: 1989.

★4873★ The Dream of the Earth
Sierra Club Books
Maryland
100 Bush St., 13th Fl.
San Francisco, CA 94104
Berry, Thomas. 1988. ***Price:*** $9.95. 247 pp.

★4874★ Drinking Water: A Community Action Guide
Concern, Inc.
1794 Columbia Rd. NW
Washington, DC 20009
Phone: (202)328-8160

★4875★ Drinking Water Treatment Technologies: Comparative Health Effects Assessment
Government Institutes, Inc.
Publications Dept.
966 Hungerford Rd.
Rockville, MD 20850-1714
Government Institutes Inc., 1988. ***Price:*** $49. 206 pp.

★4876★ Drive for Clean Air: Natural Gas and Methanol
INFORM
Publications Dept.
381 Park Ave. S.
New York, NY 10016
Cannon, James S. 1989. ***Price:*** $65. 248 pp.

★4877★ Driving Forces: Motor Vehicle Trends and their Implications for Global Warming, Energy Strategies and Transportation Planning
State University of New York Press
Maryland
State University Plaza
Albany, NY 12246
Mackenzie, James J. and Walsh, Michael P. 1990. ***Price:*** $12.50. 49 pp.

★4878★ Ducks Unlimited Annual Report
Ducks Unlimited
One Waterfowl Way
Long Grove, IL 60047
Phone: (708)438-4300
Fax: (708)438-9236

★4879★ The Ducks Unlimited Story
Ducks Unlimited
One Waterfowl Way
Long Grove, IL 60047
Phone: (708)438-4300
Fax: (708)438-9236

★4880★ Dying Oceans
Gareth Stevens, Inc.
7317 W. Green Tree Rd.
Milwaukee, WI 53223
Phone: (414)466-7550
Fax: (414)466-2951
Editor(s): Paula Hogan. ***Frequency:*** 1991. Discusses the ecological balance of life in the world's oceans and how it is endangered by ocean pollution.

★4881★ The Eagle Bird: Searching for an Ethic of Place
Pantheon Books, Inc.
201 E. 50th St.
New York, NY 10022
Phone: (212)751-2600
Editor(s): Charles F. Wilkinson. ***Frequency:*** 1992.

★4882★ Eagles: Sierra Club Wildlife Library
Little, Brown and Co.
Children's Books/Sales
34 Beacon St.
Boston, MA 02108-1493
Lang, Aubrey. 1990. ***Price:*** $14.95. 62 pp.

★4883★ Earth, Air, and Water: Resources and Environment in the Late 20th Century
Edward Arnold
29 W. 35th St.
New York, NY 10001-2291
Phone: (212)244-3336
Editor(s): Ian Gordon Simmons. ***Frequency:*** 1991.

★4884★ Earth and Other Ethics
Prentice Hall
Prentice Hall Bldg.
Sylvan Ave.
Englewood Cliffs, NJ 07632
Phone: (201)592-2000
1987. ***Price:*** $7.95.

★4885★ Earth Book for Kids: Activities to Help Heal the Environment
Linda Schwartz, author. 184 pp. ***Price:*** $9.95.

★4886★ The Earth Care Annual 1991
Rodale Press Inc.
Maryland
33 E. Minor St.
Emmaus, PA 18098
Wild, Russell. 1991. ***Price:*** $17.95. 235 pp.

★4887★ Earth Conference One: Sharing a Vision for Our Planet
Random House, Inc.
201 E. 50th St.
New York, NY 10022
Phone: (212)751-2600
Editor(s): Anuradha Vittachi. ***Frequency:*** 1989.

★4888★ Earth Day
Carolrhoda Books, Inc.
241 First Ave., N.
Minneapolis, MN 55401
Toll-Free: 800-328-4929
Editor(s): Linda Lowery. ***Frequency:*** 1991. Tells the story of Earth Day 1970 and 1990 in the United States and the special activities planned to call global attention to the problems of pollution, environmental destruction, and waste of natural resources.

★4889★ Earth Day Every Day
Abdo & Daughters
Edina, MN
Editor(s): Jill C. Wheeler. ***Frequency:*** 1991. Suggests various ways in which all of us can help save the environment and preserve the Earth.

★4890★ Earth Education Sourcebook
Institute for Earth Education
PO Box 288
Warrenville, IL 60555
Phone: (708)393-3096
Contact: David B. Wampler, Intl. Office Coord.
Frequency: Annual.

★4891★ The Earth First! Reader: Ten Years of Radical Environmentalism
Peregrine Smith Books
Salt Lake City, UT
Editor(s): John Davis. ***Frequency:*** 1991.

★4892★ Earth Keeping
Zondervan Publishing House
1415 Lake Dr., SE
Grand Rapids, MI 49506
Phone: (616)698-6900
Editor(s): Sydney Donahoe. ***Frequency:*** 1991.

★4893★ Earth Observations and Global Change Decision: Making Vol. 1: A National Partnership
Robert E. Krieger Publishing Co.
Int'l Sales
PO Box 9542
Melbourne, FL 32902
Ginsberg, Irving R. and Angelo, Jr., Joseph A. 1990. ***Price:*** $64.50. 376 pp.

★4894★ The Earth Report: The Essential Guide to Global Ecological Issues
Price Stern Sloan, Inc.
360 N. La Cienega Blvd.
Los Angeles, CA 90048
Phone: (213)657-6100
Fax: (213)855-8993
Editor(s): Edward Goldsmith and Nicholas Hildyard. ***Frequency:*** 1988.

★4895★ Earth Rising: Ecological Belief in an Age of Science
Oregon State University Press
Waldo Hall 101
Corvallis, OR 97331
Oates, David. 1989. ***Price:*** $14.95. 255 pp.

★4896★ Earthborn: In Celebration of Wild Places
Sierra Club Books
Maryland
100 Bush St., 13th Fl.
San Francisco, CA 94104
Beatty, John. 1988. ***Price:*** $15.95. 110 pp.

★4897★ EarthPulse Handbook Series
Windstar Found.
2317 Snowmass Creek Rd.
Snowmass, CO 81654
Phone: (303)927-4777
Fax: (303)927-4779

★4898★ Earthright
Prima Publishing & Communications
4970 Topaz Ave.
PO Box 1260
Rocklin, CA 95677
Phone: (916)624-5718
Editor(s): H. Patricia Hynes. ***Frequency:*** 1990.

★4899★ Earth's Energy and Fuel
Gareth Stevens, Inc.
7317 W. Green Tree Rd.
Milwaukee, WI 53223
Phone: (414)466-7550
Fax: (414)466-2951
Editor(s): Julie and Robert Brown. ***Frequency:*** 1991. Provides a simple introduction to the kinds of fuels, both fossil fuels and alternative energy sources, used throughout the world, and discusses the problems of fuel shortages and environmental safety.

★4900★ The Earth's Fragile Systems: Perspectives on Global Change
Westview Press, Inc.
5500 Central Ave.
Boulder, CO 80301
Phone: (303)444-3541
Fax: (303)449-3356
Editor(s): Thorkil Kristensen and Johan Peter Paludan. ***Frequency:*** 1988.

★4901★ Earthwatching III: An Environmental Reader with Teacher's Guide
University of Wisconsin Press
Institute for Environmental Studies
114 N. Murray
Madison, WI 53715
Phone: (608)262-4928
Fax: (608)262-7560
Frequency: 1990. A collection of scripts from "Earthwatch", a radio program exploring environmental trends and concerns.

★4902★ Eco-Justice: Church and Society-While the Earth Remains
Eco-Justice Project and Network
Cornell University
Anabel Taylor Hall
Ithaca, NY 14850
Frequency: 1990. 109 pp.

★4903★ Eco-Justice: Keeping and Healing the Creation
Eco-Justice Project and Network
Cornell University
Anabel Taylor Hall
Ithaca, NY 14850
Frequency: 1990. ***Price:*** $4.00. 114 pp.

★4904★ Ecological Communication
University of Chicago Press
5801 Ellis Ave.
Chicago, IL 60637
Phone: (312)702-7700
Foreign Name: Okologische Kommunik
Editor(s): Niklas Luhmann; translated by John Bedharz, Jr. ***Frequency:*** 1989.

★4905★ Ecological Risks: Perspectives from Poland and the United States
National Academy Press
Maryland
2101 Constitution Ave. NW
Washington, DC 20418
Cowling, E.B. et al. 1990. ***Price:*** $42. 428 pp.

★4906★ Ecological Society of America Directory
Ecological Soc. of America
Arizona State University
Center for Environmental Studies
Tempe, AZ 85287
Phone: (602)965-3000
Frequency: Biennial.

★4907★ Ecologue: The Environmental Catalogue and Consumer's Guide for a Safe Earth
Prentice Hall Press
1 Gulf & Western Plz.
New York, NY 10023
Phone: (212)373-8500
Editor(s): Bruce N. Anderson. ***Frequency:*** 1990.

★4908★ Ecology and Conservation
Gareth Stevens, Inc.
7317 W. Green Tree Rd.
Milwaukee, WI 53223
Phone: (414)466-7550
Fax: (414)466-2951
Editor(s): Steven Seidenberg. ***Frequency:*** 1990. Surveys pressing issues of conservation and pollution as they affect the earth.

★4909★ Ecology: Our Living Planet
Gareth Stevens, Inc.
7317 W. Green Tree Rd.
Milwaukee, WI 53223
Phone: (414)466-7550
Fax: (414)466-2951
Editor(s): P. Hogan. ***Frequency:*** 1990. Presents for the primary level a survey of pressing issues of conservation as they affect the earth. Adapted from Steven Seidenberg's Ecology and Conservation.

★4910★ Economic Development and Environmental Protection in Latin America
L. Rienner Publishers, Inc.
1800 30th St., No. 314
Boulder, CO 80301
Phone: (303)444-6684
Editor(s): Joseph S. Tulchin with Andrew I. Rudman. ***Frequency:*** 1991.

★4911★ Economic Instruments for Environmental Protection
Organization for Economic Cooperation and Development
2001 L St., NW, Ste. 700
Washington, DC 20036
Phone: (202)785-6323
Frequency: 1989.

★4912★ Economics As If the Earth Really Mattered
New Society Publishers
PO Box 582
Santa Cruz, CA 90061
Phone: (408)458-1191
Editor(s): Susan Meeker-Lowry. ***Frequency:*** 1988. ***Price:*** $9.95.

★4913★ Economics of Protected Areas
Island Press
Box 7
Covelo, CA 95428
Dixon, John A. and Sherman, Paul B. 1990. ***Price:*** $34.95. 234 pp.

★4914★ Ecophilosophy: A Field Guide to the Literature
R. & E. Miles Publishers
Int'l Sales
PO Box 1916
San Pedro, CA 90733
Davis, Donald Edward. 1989. ***Price:*** $8.95. 137 pp.

★4915★ Elephant Memories: Thirteen Years in the Life of an Elephant Family
Fawcett
201 E. 50th St.
New York, NY 10022
Phone: (212)751-2600
Toll-Free: 800-726-0600
Cynthia Moss, author. 1989. ***Price:*** $10.95.

★4916★ Eli's Songs
Macmillan Publishing Co.
366 Third Ave.
New York, NY 10022
Phone: (212)702-2000
Editor(s): Monte Killingsworth. ***Frequency:*** 1991. Shipped off to relatives in Oregon while his father is touring with his rock band, twelve-year-old Eli comes to love the magnificent trees of a nearby forest and tries to prevent their imminent destruction.

★4917★ Embracing the Earth: Choice for Environmentally Sound Living
Noble Press
Chicago, IL
Editor(s): D. Mark Harris. ***Frequency:*** 1990.

★4918★ The Encyclopedia of Environmental Issues
Facts On File, Inc.
460 Park Ave., S.
New York, NY 10016
Phone: (212)683-2244
Editor(s): William Ashworth. ***Frequency:*** 1991.

★4919★ The End of Nature
Random House, Inc.
201 E. 50th St.
New York, NY 10022
Phone: (212)751-2600
Editor(s): Bill McKibben. ***Frequency:*** 1989.

★4920★ The Endangered Kingdom: The Struggle to Save America's Wildlife
John Wiley & Sons
605 Third Ave
New York, NY 10158
Phone: (212)850-6222
Roger L. DiSilvestro, author. 1989. ***Price:*** $19.95.

★4921★ Endangered Species
Lucent Books
PO Box 289011
San Diego, CA 92128
Phone: (619)485-7424
Editor(s): Sunni Bloyd. ***Frequency:*** 1989. Describes how and why various species of animals and the tropical rain forests are threatened with extinction and discusses the importance of ensuring their survival.

★4922★ Energy & Environmental Strategies for the 1990's
Fairmont Press Inc.
Int'l Sales
700 Indian Tr.
Lilburn, GA 30247
Wiher, Mary Jo and Jackson, Marilyn. 1991. ***Price:*** $62. 636 pp.

★4923★ Energy Digest
Social Issues Resources Series Inc.
PO Box 2348
Boca Raton, FL 33427-2348

★4924★ Energy, Food, Environment: Realities, Myths, Options
Oxford Univ. Press, Inc.
200 Madison Ave.
New York, NY 10016
Phone: (212)679-7300
Editor(s): Vaclav Smil. ***Frequency:*** 1987.

★4925★ Energy, Land, and Public Policy: Energy Policy Studies Volume 5
State University of New York Press
Maryland
State University Plaza
Albany, NY 12246
Cullingworth, J. Barry. 1989. ***Price:*** $18.95. 250 pp.

★4926★ Energy on the Road: Transportation and the Environment
State University of New York Press
Maryland
State University Plaza
Albany, NY 12246

★4927★ Entering Adulthood. Creating a Healthy Environment: A Curriculum for Grades 9-12
Network Publications
PO Box 1830
Santa Cruz, CA 95061-1830
Phone: (408)438-4060
Fax: (408)438-4284
Editor(s): Donna Lloyd-Kolkin. ***Frequency:*** 1990.

★4928★ Entropy: Into the Greenhouse World
Bantam Books
666 Fifth Ave.
New York, NY 10103
Phone: (212)765-6500
Toll-Free: 800-223-6834
Editor(s): Jeremy Rifkin with Ted Howard. ***Frequency:*** 1989. ***Price:*** $9.95.

★4929★ The Environment
Rourke Publishing Group
PO Box 3328
Vero Beach, FL 32964
Phone: (305)465-4575
Editor(s): Adam Markham. ***Frequency:*** 1988. Examines how various ecosystems are being destroyed by human activities, efforts to stop the destruction, and the cost of implementing environmental policies.

★4930★ The Environment
Facts On File, Inc.
460 Park Ave., S.
New York, NY 10016
Phone: (212)683-2244
Editor(s): Gerald Leinwand. ***Frequency:*** 1990. Surveys environmental problems in the United States, examines legal and social aspects of environmentalism, and discusses political plans in place to deal with the environmental decline.

★4931★ Environment and the Poor: Development Strategies for a Common Agenda
State University of New York Press
Maryland
State University Plaza
Albany, NY 12246
Leonard, H. Jeffrey and Contributors. 1989. ***Price:*** $15.95. 192 pp.

★4932★ The Environment at Risk: Responding to Growing Dangers
Kendall/Hunt Publishing Co.
2460 Kerper Blvd.
Dubuque, IA 52001
Phone: (319)588-1451
Frequency: 1989.

★4933★ Environment in Peril
Smithsonian Institution Press
470 L'Enfant Plz.
No. 7100
Washington, DC 20560
Phone: (202)287-3738
Editor(s): Anthony B. Wolbarst. ***Frequency:*** 1991.

★4934★ The Environment: Issues and Choices for Society
Jones and Bartlett Publishers, Inc.
20 Park Plz.
Boston, MA 02116
Phone: (617)482-5243
Editor(s): Penelope ReVelle and Charles ReVelle. ***Frequency:*** 1988.

★4935★ The Environmental Address Book: How to Reach the Environment's Greatest Champions and Worst Offenders
Perigee Books
New York, NY
Editor(s): Michael Levine. ***Frequency:*** 1991. Contains over 2,000 names and addresses of organizations, agencies, celebrities, political figures, and businesses (local, state, national, and international level) concerned with the state of the world's environment.

★4936★ Environmental America: The North Central States
Millbrook Press
Brookfield, CT
Editor(s): D.J. Herda. ***Frequency:*** 1991. Focuses on environmental issues and concerns in the Middle West and steps being taken to counteract the damage.

★4937★ Environmental America: The Northeastern States
Millbrook Press
Brookfield, CT
Editor(s): D.J. Herda. ***Frequency:*** 1991. Focuses on environmental issues and concerns in the Northeastern States and steps being taken to counteract the damage.

★4938★ Environmental America: The Northwestern States
Millbrook Press
Brookfield, CT
Editor(s): D.J. Herda. ***Frequency:*** 1991. Focuses on environmental issues and concerns in the Pacific Northwest and steps being taken to counteract the damage.

★4939★ Environmental America: The South Central States
Millbrook Press
Brookfield, CT
Editor(s): D.J. Herda. ***Frequency:*** 1991. Focuses on environmental issues and concerns in the South Central States and steps being taken to counteract the damage.

★4940★ Environmental America. The Southeastern States
Millbrook Press
Brookfield, CT
Editor(s): D.J. Herda. ***Frequency:*** 1991. Focuses on environmental issues and concerns in the South Atlantic States and steps being taken to counteract the damage.

★4941★ Environmental America. The Southwestern States
Millbrook Press
Brookfield, CT
Editor(s): D.J. Herda. ***Frequency:*** 1991. Focuses on environmental issues and concerns in the Southwestern States and steps being taken to counteract the damage.

★4942★ Environmental Audits, 6th ed.
Government Institutes, Inc.
Publications Dept.
966 Hungerford Rd.
Rockville, MD 20850-1714
Cahill, Lawrence B. and Kane, Raymond W. 1989. ***Price:*** $75. 592 pp.

★4943★ Environmental Awareness—Solid Waste
Bancroft-Sage Publishing
533 Eighth St., S.
Naples, FL 33939
Phone: (813)642-5600
Editor(s): Mary Ellen Snodgrass and Majorie L. Oelerich. ***Frequency:*** 1991. Focuses on the ever-growing problem of managing the many types of solid waste and the hazards they pose to people and the environment. Readers learn how they can help in waste reduction efforts.

★4944★ Environmental Awareness—Water Pollution
Bancroft-Sage Publishing
533 Eighth St., S.
Naples, FL 33939
Phone: (813)642-5600
Editor(s): Mary Ellen Snodgrass and Marjorie L. Oelerich. ***Frequency:*** 1991. Discusses the importance of a clean water supply and how water pollution threatens the lives and health of people, animals, and plants. Readers learn how to contribute to anti-pollution and conservation efforts.

★4945★ Environmental Career Guide: Job Opportunities with the Earth in Mind
J. Wiley & Sons, Inc.
605 Third Ave.
New York, NY 10158
Phone: (212)850-6000
Editor(s): Nicholas Basta. ***Frequency:*** 1991.

★4946★ The Environmental Challenge: The New International Agenda
Australian Natl. Univ.
Research School of Pacific Studies
Canberra, Australia
Editor(s): Stuart Harris. ***Frequency:*** 1990.

★4947★ Environmental Communication and Public Relations Handbook
Government Institutes, Inc.
966 Hungerford Dr., Ste. 24
Rockville, MD 20850
Phone: (301)251-9250
Editor(s): E. Bruce Harrison. ***Frequency:*** 1988.

★4948★ Environmental Concern in Florida and the Nation
University of Florida Press
210 Library
Gainesville, FL 32600
Phone: (904)392-0342
Editor(s): Lance deHaven-Smith. ***Frequency:*** 1991.

★4949★ The Environmental Crisis—Opposing Viewpoints
Greenhaven Press, Inc.
PO Box 289009
San Diego, CA 92128-9009
Phone: (619)485-9549
Editor(s): Neal Bernards. ***Frequency:*** 1991. Presents opposing views on questions of environmental protection and damage resulting from air and water pollution, toxic wastes, pesticides, and the ever-growing tide of refuse.

★4950★ Environmental Decision Making: A Multidisciplinary Perspective
Van Nostrand Reinhold Co., Inc.
115 Fifth Ave.
New York, NY 10003
Phone: (212)254-3232
Editor(s): Richard A. Chechile and Susan Carlisle. ***Frequency:*** 1991.

★4951★ Environmental Defense Fund Annual Report
Environmental Defense Fund
257 Park Ave. S
New York, NY 10010
Phone: (212)505-2100
Fax: (212)505-2375

★4952★ The Environmental Detective
HarperCollins Inc.
10 E. 53rd St.
New York, NY 10022
Phone: (212)207-7000
Editor(s): Douglas Herridge and Susan Hughes. ***Frequency:*** 1991. Explains how to be an environmental detective by observing clues that reveal information about backyard ecosystems. Includes activities and space to write in observations.

★4953★ The Environmental Dictionary
Executive Enterprises Publications Co., Inc.
22 W. 21st St.
New York, NY 10010-6904
Phone: (212)645-7880
Fax: (212)675-4883
Editor(s): James J. King. ***Frequency:*** 1989.

★4954★ Environmental Disputes: Community Involvement in Conflict Resolution
Island Press
P.O. Box 7
Covelo, CA 95428
Crowfoot, James E. and Wondolleck, Julia M. 1990. ***Price:*** $22.95. 275 pp.

★4955★ Environmental Ethics
Temple University Press
1601 N. Broad St.
USB 306
Philadelphia, PA 19122
Phone: (215)787-8787
Holmes Tolston, author. 1988. ***Price:*** $16.95 paper, $39.95 cloth.

★4956★ Environmental Guidelines for Overland Coal Transportation
Editor(s): Herbert H. Webber. ***Frequency:*** 1987.

★4957★ Environmental Hazards and Bioresource Management in the United States-Mexico Borderlands
University of California, Los Angeles
Latin Amer. Center Publications
405 Hilgard Ave.
Los Angeles, CA 90024-1147
Phone: (213)825-6634
Fax: (213)206-3555
Editor(s): Paul Ganster and Hartmut Walter. ***Frequency:*** 1990.

★4958★ Environmental Investments: The Cost of a Clean Environment
Island Press
1718 Connecticut Ave., NW
Ste. 300
Washington, DC 20009
Phone: (202)232-7933
Fax: (202)234-1328
A report of the Administrator of the Environment Protection Agency to the Congress of the United States. ***Frequency:*** 1991.

★4959★ Environmental Monitoring, Assessment, and Management: The Agenda for Long-term Research and Development
Editor(s): Sidney Draggan, John J. Cohrssen, and Richard E. Morrison. ***Frequency:*** 1987. Findings and recommendations of the Expert Panel Meeting on Monitoring, Assessment, and Environmental Management held May, 1984, in Washington, DC, presented to the Council on Long-term Environmental Quality, and the Interagency Subcabinet Committee on Long-term Environmental Research.

★4960★ Environmental Policy in the 1990's
Congressional Quarterly Press
Publications Dept.
1414 22nd St., NW
Washington, DC 20037
Vig, Norman J. and Kraft, Michael E. ***Frequency:*** 1990. ***Price:*** $18.95.

★4961★ Environmental Policy Institute Annual Report
Environmental Policy Inst.
218 D St., SE
Washington, DC 20003
Phone: (202)544-2600
Fax: (202)543-4710

★4962★ Environmental Politics and Policy
Congressional Quarterly Press
Publications Dept.
1414 22nd St. NW
Washington, DC 20037
Rosenbaum, Walter A. ***Price:*** $16.95.

★4963★ Environmental Problems and Solutions: Greenhouse Effect, Acid Rain, Pollution
Hemisphere Publishing Corp.
79 Madison Ave., Ste. 1110
New York, NY 10016
Phone: (212)725-1999
Editor(s): T. Nejat Veziroglu. ***Frequency:*** 1990.

★4964★ The Environmental Program for the Mediterranean; Preserving a Shared Heritage and Managing a Common Resource
World Bank Publications
1818 H St., NW
Washington, DC 20433
Phone: (202)473-2943
Fax: (202)417-0482
Frequency: 1990.

★4965★ Environmental Progress and Challenges: EPA's Update
Environmental Protection Agency
Office of Planning and Evaluation
Waterside Mall
401 M St., SW
Washington, DC 20460
Frequency: 1988.

★4966★ Environmental Protection: A Strategic Issue for the 1990s—A Report Prepared for Chubu Electric Power Company
The Associates
20 University Rd.
Cambridge, MA 02138
Editor(s): Cambridge Energy Research Associates. ***Frequency:*** 1990.

★4967★ The Environmental Protection Agency
Chelsea House Publishers
1974 Sprout Rd., Ste. 400
Broomall, PA 19008
Phone: (215)353-5166
Fax: (215)359-1439
Editor(s): Kevin J. Law. ***Frequency:*** 1988.

★4968★ The Environmental Protection Agency: Asking the Wrong Questions
Oxford Univ. Press, Inc.
200 Madison Ave.
New York, NY 10016
Phone: (212)679-7300
Editor(s): Marc K. Landy, Marc J. Roberts, and Stephen R. Thomas. ***Frequency:*** 1990.

★4969★ Environmental Protection in the United States Industry, Agencies, Environmentalists
San Francisco Study Center

Editor(s): Joseph M. Petulla. ***Frequency:*** 1987.

★4970★ Environmental Quality Index
National Wildlife Fed.
1400 16th St. NW
Washington, DC 20036-2266
Phone: (202)797-6800
Frequency: Annual.

★4971★ Environmental Quality: The Twentieth Annual Report of the Council on Environmental Quality
Council on Environmental Quality
Exec. Office of the Pres.
722 Jackson Pl., NW
Washington, DC 20503
Frequency: 1990. ***Price:*** $17.95.

★4972★ Environmental Restoration: Science and Strategies for Restoring the Earth
Island Press
P.O. Box 7
Covelo, CA 95428
Berger, John J., editor. 1989. ***Price:*** $19.95. 398 pp.

★4973★ Environmental Science
W.B. Saunders Co.
W. Washington Sq.
Philadelphia, PA 19105
Phone: (215)238-7800
Editor(s): Johnathan Turk and Amos Turk. ***Frequency:*** 1988.

★4974★ Environmental Science
Merrill Publishing Co.
PO Box 508
Columbus, OH 43216
Phone: (614)890-1111
Editor(s): Stanley H. Anderson, Ronald E. Beiswenger, and P. Walton Purdom. ***Frequency:*** 1987.

★4975★ Environmental Science: A Global Concern
Wm. C. Brown Group
2460 Kerper Blvd.
Dubuque, IA 52001
Phone: (319)588-1451
Fax: (319)589-2955
Editor(s): William P. Cunningham and Barbara Woodworth Saigo. ***Frequency:*** 1990.

★4976★ Environmental Science: Action for a Sustainable Future
Benjamin-Cummings Publishing Co.
390 Bridge Pkwy.
Redwood City, CA 94065
Phone: (415)594-4400
Editor(s): Daniel D. Chiras. ***Frequency:*** 1991.

★4977★ Environmental Science and Engineering
Prentice Hall
Rte. 9W
Englewood Cliffs, NJ 07632
Phone: (201)592-2000
Editor(s): J. Glynn Henry and Gary W. Heinke. ***Frequency:*** 1989.

★4978★ Environmental Studies: Earth as a Living Planet
Merrill Publishing Co.
PO Box 508
Columbus, OH 43216
Phone: (614)890-1111
Editor(s): Daniel B. Botkin and Edward A. Keller. ***Frequency:*** 1987.

★4979★ Envisioning a Sustainable Society
State University of New York Press
Maryland
State University Plaza
Albany, NY 12246
Milbrath, Lester W. 1989. ***Price:*** $18.95. 403 pp.

★4980★ Essays in Environment Management
Springer-Verlag New York, Inc.
175 Fifth Ave., 19th Fl.
New York, NY 10010
Phone: (212)460-1500
Editor(s): Ralf Buckley. ***Frequency:*** 1991.

★4981★ Ethics and the Environmental Responsibility
Avebury

Editor(s): N. Dower. ***Frequency:*** 1989.

★4982★ The Everglades River of Grass
Pineapple Press
Maryland
P.O. Drawer 16008
Sarasota, FL 34239
Douglas, Marjory Stoneman. 1988. ***Price:*** $17.95. 448 pp.

★4983★ The Expendable Future: U.S. Politics and the Protection of Biological Diversity
Duke University Press
6697 College Station
Durham, NC 27708
Tobin, Richard. ***Price:*** $17.95. 304 pp.

★4984★ Experiments that Explore: Recycling
Millbrook Press
Brookfield, CT
Editor(s): Martin J. Gutnik. ***Frequency:*** 1992. Uses experiments to demonstrate the effects of dumping solid waste into our environment and explores what can be done about it.

★4985★ Exploitation, Conservation, Preservation: A Geographic Perspective on Natural Resource Use
J. Wiley & Sons, Inc.
605 Third Ave.
New York, NY 10158
Phone: (212)850-6000
Editor(s): Susan L. Cutter, Hilary Lambert Renwick, and William H. Renwick. ***Frequency:*** 1991.

★4986★ Factory Farming: The Experiment that Failed
Animal Welfare Institute
PO Box 3650
Washington, DC 20007
Smith, David Luck. ***Frequency:*** 1987.

★4987★ The Facts On File Dictionary of Environmental Science
Facts On File, Inc.
460 Park Ave., S
New York, NY 10016
Phone: (212)683-2244
Editor(s): L. Harold Stevenson and Bruce C. Wyman. ***Frequency:*** 1990.

★4988★ Farming in Nature's Image
Island Press
Box 7
Covelo, CA 95428
Soule, Judith D. and Piper, John K. 1992. ***Price:*** $34.95. 290 pp.

★4989★ Federal Tax Law of Conservation Easements
Land Trust Alliance
900 17th St. NW, Ste. 410
Washington, DC 20006
Phone: (202)785-1410
Fax: (202)785-1408

★4990★ Fifty Simple Things You Can Do to Save the Earth
G.K. Hall & Co., Inc.
70 Lincoln St.
Boston, MA 02111
Phone: (617)423-3990
Editor(s): The Earth Works Group. ***Frequency:*** 1989.

★4991★ Fight Global Warming: 29 Things You Can Do
Environmental Defense Fund
257 Park Ave., S.
New York, NY 10010
Phone: (212)505-2100
Fax: (212)505-2375
Editor(s): Sarah Clark. ***Frequency:*** 1991.

★4992★ Fighting Toxics
Island Press
Box 7
Covelo, CA 95428
Editor(s): Cohen, Gary and O'Connor John. 1990. ***Price:*** $31.95. 346 pp.

★4993★ Fire & Ice: The Greenhouse Effect, Ozone Depletion & Nuclear Winter
HarperCollins Publishers
Corporate Exhibits
10 E. 53rd St.
New York, NY 10022
Fisher, David E. 1990. ***Price:*** $19.95. 232 pp.

★4994★ For the Common Good—Preserving Private Lands with Conservation
Land Trust Alliance
900 17th St. NW, Ste. 410
Washington, DC 20006
Phone: (202)785-1410
Fax: (202)785-1408

★4995★ The Forest and The Trees
Island Press
Box 7
Covelo, CA 95428
Robinson, Gordon. 1988. ***Price:*** $34.95. 272 pp.

★4996★ The Forest for the Trees? Government Policies and the Misuse of Forest Resources
State University of New York Press
Maryland
State University Plaza
Albany, NY 12246
Repetto, Robert. 1988. ***Price:*** $10. 105 pp.

★4997★ A Forest Journey: The Role of Wood in the Development of Civilization
Harvard University Press
Marketing Dept.
79 Garden St.
Cambridge, MA 02138-9983
Perlin, John. 1989. ***Price:*** $14.95. 445 pp.

★4998★ Forest Primeval: The Natural History of an Ancient Forest
Sierra Club Books
Random House
201 E. 50th St.
New York, NY 10022
Phone: (212)751-2600
Toll-Free: 800-726-0600
Maser, Chris. 1989. ***Price:*** $25.00.

★4999★ Forest Trust Two-Year Report
Forest Trust
PO Box 519
Santa Fe, NM 87504-0519
Phone: (505)983-8992

★5000★ The Forgotten Forest
Sierra Club Books
730 Polk St.
San Francisco, CA 60610
Phone: (415)776-2211
Editor(s): Laurence Anholt. ***Frequency:*** 1992. The vast forests of a country are all cut down to make room for development, until finally only one small wooded area remains like an island in the endless noisy sea of the city.

★5001★ Fourth Grade Loser
Troll Associates
100 Corporate Dr.
Mahwah, NJ 07430
Phone: (201)529-4000
Editor(s): Ellen Kahaner. ***Frequency:*** 1992. Rich kid Mike Russell's campaign to make friends in the fourth grade brings him in conflict with his father, a real estate developer, when the class decides to oppose the development of forest land near the school.

★5002★ The Fragile Environment: The Darwin College Lectures
Cambridge Univ. Press
40 W. 20th St.
New York, NY 10011
Phone: (212)924-3900
Fax: (212)691-3239
Editor(s): Laurie Friday and Ronald Laskey. ***Frequency:*** 1989.

★5003★ Fragile Majesty: The Battle for North America's Last Great Forest
Mountaineers Books
Maryland
306 2nd Ave. W.
Seattle, WA 98119
Ervin, Keith. 1989. ***Price:*** $14.95. 272 pp.

★5004★ Fragile Mountains
Gareth Stevens, Inc.
7317 W. Green Tree Rd.
Milwaukee, WI 53223
Phone: (414)466-7550
Fax: (414)466-2951
Editor(s): Paula Hogan. ***Frequency:*** 1991. Examines mountain ecology and habitats in various parts of the world, discusses how they can be damaged environmentally, and suggests solutions.

★5005★ Friends of the Earth Foundation Annual Report
Friends of the Earth Found.
218 D St. SE
Washington, DC 20003
Phone: (202)544-2600
Fax: (202)543-4710

★5006★ Friends of the River Citizens' Manual
Friends of the River
Ft. Mason Center, Bldg. C
San Francisco, CA 94123
Phone: (415)771-0400
Fax: (415)771-0301

★5007★ From Walden Pond to Muir Woods: Alternative Ways Across America
Appalachia—Science in the Public Interest
Livingston, KY
Editor(s): Mary Dymond Davis. ***Frequency:*** 1990.

★5008★ Fundamentals of Negotiation: A Guide for Environmental Professionals
Environmental Law Institute
Publications Dept.
1616 P St., NW
Washington, DC 20036
Miller, Jeffery G. and Colosi, Thomas R. ***Frequency:*** 1989. 76 pp.

★5009★ The Future of the Environment: The Social Dimensions of Conservation and Ecological Alternatives
Routledge, Champman and Hall, Inc.
29 W. 35th St.
New York, NY 10001-2291
Phone: (212)244-3336
Fax: (212)563-2269
Editor(s): D.C. Pitt. ***Frequency:*** 1988.

★5010★ The Future of Urbanization: Facing the Ecological and Economic Constraints
Worldwatch Inst.
1776 Massachusetts Ave., NW
Washington, DC 20036
Phone: (202)452-1999
Editor(s): Lester R. Brown and Jodi L. Jacobson. ***Frequency:*** 1987.

★5011★ Garbage and Recycling
Gareth Stevens, Inc.
7317 W. Green Tree Rd.
Milwaukee, WI 53223
Phone: (414)466-7550
Fax: (414)466-2951
Editor(s): Judith Woodburn. ***Frequency:*** 1991. Discusses the solid waste crisis, the causes of landfill crowding, and solutions in recycling various substances.

★5012★ Garbage and Recycling
Enslow Publishers
Bloy St. & Ramsey Ave.
PO Box 777
Hillside, NJ 07205
Phone: (201)964-4116
Editor(s): Kathlyn Gay. ***Frequency:*** 1991. Examines the problem of garbage accumulation in America and different recycling solutions which may prevent the situation from getting worse in the future.

★5013★ Garbage: Understanding Words in Context
Greenhaven Press, Inc.
PO Box 289009
San Diego, CA 92128-9009
Phone: (619)485-7424
Fax: (619)485-9549
Editor(s): Robert Anderson and JoAnne Buggey. ***Frequency:*** 1991. Opposing viewpoints debate the seriousness of the gargage crisis; whether incineration or recycling is the answer; and if using cloth diapers will reduce the garbage problem. Vocabulary exercises teach critical thinking and reading skills.

★5014★ Global Change and Our Common Future: Papers From a Forum
National Academy Press
Maryland
2101 Constitution Ave., N.W.
Washington, DC 20418
Defries, Ruth S. and Malone, Thomas F. 1989. ***Price:*** $29. 244 pp.

★5015★ Global Change: Geographical Approaches
University of Arizona Press
1230 N. Park Ave.
Ste. 102
Tuscon, AZ 85719
Phone: (602)621-1441
Editor(s): John R. Mather and Galina V. Sdasyuk. ***Frequency:*** 1991.

★5016★ The Global Citizen
Island Press
Box 7
Covelo, CA 95428
Meadows, Donella H. 1991. ***Price:*** $24.95. 300 pp.

★5017★ Global Climate Change: Human and Natural Influences
Paragon House
Maryland
90 Fifth Ave.
New York, NY 10011
Singer, S. Fred. 1989. ***Price:*** $34.95. 424 pp.

★5018★ The Global Commons: Policy for the Planet
Aspen Institute
Communications Office
Box 222
Queenstown, MD 21658
Cleveland, Harlan. ***Frequency:*** 1990. ***Price:*** $13.75.

★5019★ Global Dumping Ground: The International Traffic in Hazardous Waste
Seven Locks Press
Maryland
PO Box 27
Cabin John, MD 20818
Moyers, Bill and the Center for Investigative Reporting. 1990. ***Price:*** $11.95. 152 pp.

★5020★ The Global Ecology Handbook: What You Can Do About the Environmental Crisis
Beacon Press
25 Beacon St.
Boston, MA 02108
Phone: (617)742-2110
Fax: (617)723-3097
Editor(s): Walter H. Corson. ***Frequency:*** 1990.

★5021★ Global Environment Protection Strategy Through Thermal Engineering: Countermeasures
Hemisphere Publishing Corp.
79 Madison Ave., Ste. 1110
New York, NY 10016
Phone: (212)725-1999
Editor(s): Keizo Hatta and Yasuo Mori. ***Frequency:*** 1992. Papers from the final report of the research subcommittee in the thermal engineering division of the Japan Society of Mechanical Engineers.

★5022★ Global Environmental Change
Springer-Verlag New York, Inc.
175 Fifth Ave.
19th Fl.
New York, NY 10010
Phone: (212)460-1500
Editor(s): Robert W. Corell and Patricia A. Anderson. ***Frequency:*** 1991. Proceedings of the NATO Advanced Research Workshop on the Science of Global Environmental Change, held and Il Ciocco, Lucca, Italy, May 31 - June 2, 1990.

★5023★ Global Resources: Opposing Viewpoints
Greenhaven Press, Inc.
PO Box 289009
San Diego, CA 92128-9009
Phone: (619)485-7424
Fax: (619)485-9549
Editor(s): Matthew Polesetsky. ***Frequency:*** 1991. Sets out differing views on the nature and extent of depletion of the Earth's resources and whether development has caused environmental and population crises.

★5024★ Global Science: Energy, Resources, Environment
Kendall/Hunt Publishing Co.
2460 Kerper Blvd.
Dubuque, IA 52001
Phone: (319)588-1451
Editor(s): John W. Christensen. ***Frequency:*** 1991.

★5025★ Global Warming
Gloucester Press
New York, NY
Editor(s): Alexander Peckham. ***Frequency:*** 1991. Discusses the issue of the greenhouse effect and possible solutions to the global warming trend.

★5026★ Global Warming
Facts On File, Inc.
460 Park Ave., S.
New York, NY 10016
Phone: (212)683-2244
Editor(s): Jenny E. Tesar. ***Frequency:*** 1991. Discusses the gradual warming of our planet, its possible causes and effects, and some solutions.

★5027★ Global Warming: Are We Entering the Greenhouse Century?
Sierra Club Books
Maryland
Business
San Francisco, CA 94104
Schneider, Stephen H. 1989. ***Price:*** $18.95. 317 pp.

★5028★ The Global Warming Debate: Answers to Controversial Questions
State University of New York Press
Maryland
State University Plaza
Albany, NY 12246

★5029★ Going Green: A Kid's Handbook to Saving the Planet
Puffin Books
New York, NY
Editor(s): John Elkington. ***Frequency:*** 1990. A guide to saving the environment, including explanations of ecological issues and projects.

★5030★ Going Off the Beaten Path: An Untraditional Travel Guide
Noble Press
Chicago, IL
Editor(s): Mary Dymond Davis. ***Frequency:*** 1991.

★5031★ The Great Kapok Tree: A Tale of the Amazon Rain Forest
Harcourt Brace Jovanovich, Inc.
6277 Sea Harbor Dr.
Orlando, FL 32821
Phone: (407)345-2000
Editor(s): Lynne Cherry. ***Frequency:*** 1990. The many different animals that live in a great kapok tree in the Brazilian rainforest try to convince a man with an ax of the importance of not cutting down their home.

★5032★ Great Lakes, Great Legacy?
Conservation Found.
1250 24th St., NW
Washington, DC 20037
Phone: (202)293-4800
Fax: (202)293-9211
Editor(s): Theodora E. Colborn. ***Frequency:*** 1990.

★5033★ The Great Shalom
Herald Press
616 Walnut Ave.
Scottdale, PA 15683
Phone: (412)887-8500
Editor(s): Peter J. Dyck. ***Frequency:*** 1990. Safe and happy in the forest, the animals and birds try to find a way to stop the farmer from cutting down trees and destroying their home.

★5034★ The Great Trash Bash
Holiday House, Inc.
18 E. 53rd St.
New York, NY 10022
Phone: (212)688-0085
Editor(s): Loreen Leedy. ***Frequency:*** 1991. The animal citizens of Beaston discover better ways to recycle and control their trash.

★5035★ The Great Yellowstone Fire
Little, Brown and Co.
Chilren's Books/Sales
34 Beacon St.
Boston, MA 02108-1493
Vogel, Carole G. and Goldner, Kathryn A. 1990 ***Price:*** $14.95. 30 pp.

★5036★ The Green Activity Book
Lion Publishing Corp.
1705 Hubbard Ave.
Batavia, IL 60510
Phone: (708)879-0707
Fax: (708)879-0843
Editor(s): Meryl Doney. ***Frequency:*** 1991. Presents facts about current environmental problems and includes relevant activities and projects.

★5037★ The Green Alternative: Creating an Ecological Future
R. & E. Miles Publishers
Int'l Sales
PO Box 1916
San Pedro, CA 90733
Tokar, Brian. 1987. ***Price:*** $8.95. 174 pp.

★5038★ Green Business Made Black and White: CEP Environmental Research Report
Council on Economic Priorities
Publications Dept.
30 Irving Pl.
New York, NY 10003

★5039★ The Green Consumer
Penguin USA
1633 Broadway
New York, NY 10019
Phone: (212)397-8000
Editor(s): John Elkington, Julia Hailes, and Joel Makower. ***Frequency:*** 1990.

★5040★ Green Earth Resource Guide: A Comprehensive Guide About Environmentally-Friendly
Blue Bird Publishing
1713 E. Broadway
No. 306
Tempe, AZ 85282
Phone: (602)968-4088
Editor(s): Cheryl Gorder. ***Frequency:*** 1990.

★5041★ The Green Economy: Environment, Sustainable Development, and the Politics of the Future
Pluto Press
Concord, MA
Editor(s): Michael Jacobs. ***Frequency:*** 1991.

★5042★ The Green Entepreneur: Business Opportunities that Can Save the Earth and Make You Money
Liberty Hall Press
Blue Ridge Summit, PA
Editor(s): Gustav Berle. ***Frequency:*** 1991.

★5043★ The Green Lifestyle Handbook
Henry Holt & Co.
115 W. 18th St.
New York, NY 10011
Phone: (212)886-9200
Editor(s): Jeremy Rifkin. ***Frequency:*** 1990.

★5044★ The Green Machine and the Frog Crusade
Delacorte Press
666 Fifth Ave.
New York, NY 10103
Phone: (212)605-3000
Editor(s): Stephen Tchudi. ***Frequency:*** 1987. Sixteen-year-old David chooses to fight his father, other area businessmen, and a powerful developer when a planned shopping mall threatens to destroy wildlife in nearby marshland.

★5045★ The Green Magician Puzzle
Simon & Schuster, Inc.
Simon & Schuster Bldg.
1230 Ave. of the Americas
New York, NY 10020
Phone: (212)698-7000
Editor(s): Susan Pearson. ***Frequency:*** 1991. Ernie and the other Martian club members hope to win the school contest by solving clues about the environment, which will allow them to appear as Green Magicians in the class play.

★5046★ The Green Pages: Your Everyday Shopping Guide to Environmentally Safe Products
Random House, Inc.
201 E. 50th St.
New York, NY 10022
Phone: (212)751-2600
Editor(s): The Bennett Information Group. ***Frequency:*** 1990.

★5047★ Green Rage: Radical Environmentalism and the Unmaking of Civilization
Little, Brown & Co., Inc.
34 Beacon St.
Boston, MA 02108
Phone: (617)227-0730
Editor(s): Christopher Manes. ***Frequency:*** 1990.

★5048★ The Greenhouse Effect
State University of New York Press
Maryland
State University Plaza
Albany, NY 12246

★5049★ The Greenhouse Effect: Earth Alert Series
Maxwell Macmillan International Publishing Group
Export Div.
28100 US Hwy. 19 N., Ste. 200
Clearwater, FL 34621
Harris, Jack C. 1990. Crestwood House. ***Price:*** $10.95. 48 pp.

★5050★ The Greenhouse Trap: What We're Doing to the Atmosphere and How We Can Slow Global Warming
Beacon Press
Int'l Sales
25 Beacon St.
Boston, MA 02108
Lyman, Francesca. ***Frequency:*** 1990. ***Price:*** $9.95.

★5051★ The Greenie
Wolgemuth & Hyatt, Publishers, Inc.
5110 Maryland Way, Ste. 200
Brentwood, TN 37027
Phone: (615)371-1210
Fax: (615)370-0150
Editor(s): Mary Pride. ***Frequency:*** 1990. The Greenie has some good ideas about animal rights, pollution, and environmental protection, but he is so extreme his ideas become unreasonable.

★5052★ The Greenpeace Book of the Nuclear Age: The Hidden History, The Human Cost
Random House Inc.
International
201 E. 50th St.
New York, NY 10022
May, John. 1989. ***Price:*** $14.95. 378 pp.

★5053★ Grover's 10 Terrific Ways to Help Our World
Random House, Inc.
201 E. 50th St.
New York, NY 10022
Phone: (212)751-2600
Editor(s): Anna Ross. ***Frequency:*** 1992. Grover describes ten ways to help the world, from planting trees to recycling trash. Published in conjunction with the Children's Television Network.

★5054★ The Guide to Conservation Action
Izaak Walton League of America
1401 Wilson Blvd., Level B
Arlington, VA 22209
Phone: (703)528-1818
Fax: (703)528-1836

★5055★ A Guide to Environmental Law in Washington, DC
Environmental Law Institute
Publications Dept.
1616 P St., NW
Washington, DC 20036
Openchowski, Charles. ***Frequency:*** 1990. 236 pp.

★5056★ Guide to Urban Wildlife Management
National Inst. for Urban Wildlife
10921 Trotting Ridge Way
Columbia, MD 21044
Phone: (301)596-3311

★5057★ The Gumby Book of Forest Animals
Doubleday & Co., Inc.
666 5th Ave.
New York, NY 10103
Phone: (212)984-7361
Editor(s): Jane Hyman. ***Frequency:*** 1990. After their search for treasure in the forest disturbs the animals living there, Gumby and Pokey hear a story from Mr. Owl that changes their thinking about the land and animals around them.

★5058★ Habitat Destruction
Gloucester Press
New York, NY
Editor(s): Tony Hare. ***Frequency:*** 1991. Examines factors threatening various animal and plant habitats, such as pollution and depletion of our natural resources, explaining what we can do to conserve and preserve our planet instead.

★5059★ Handbook for Survival, 1990
Futures Found.
Castle Park, MN
Editor(s): Harold L. Ericson. ***Frequency:*** 1989.

★5060★ Hands-On Ecology
Children's Press
5440 N. Cumberland Ave.
Chicago, IL 60656
Phone: (312)693-0800
Fax: (312)693-0574
Editor(s): Ovid K. Wong. ***Frequency:*** 1991. Presents activities to explore and emphasize ecology and to demonstrate practical ways of conserving the environment.

★5061★ Hawk Mountain Sanctuary Association Annual Report
Hawk Mountain Sanctuary Assn.
Rt. 2
Kempton, PA 19529
Phone: (215)756-6961

★5062★ The Hazard Communications Standard
Fairmont Press, Inc.
Int'l Sales
700 Indian Tr.
Lilburn, GA 30247
Wells, John W., 1989. ***Price:*** $85.00. 149 pp.

★5063★ Hazardous Waste Treatment Council Conference Proceedings
Hazardous Waste Treatment Coun.
1440 New York Ave. NW, Ste. 310
Washington, DC 20005
Phone: (202)783-0870
Frequency: Annual.

★5064★ Healing Gaia: Practical Medicine for the Planet
Harmony Books
225 Park Ave., S.
New York, NY 10003
Phone: (212)254-1600
Editor(s): James E. Lovelock. ***Frequency:*** 1991.

★5065★ Healing the Environment Part One: State Options for Addressing Global Warming
Center for Clean Air Policy
444 N. Capitol St., Ste 526
Washington, DC 20001
Phone: (202)624-7709

★5066★ Healing the Planet: Strategies for Resolving the Environmental Crisis
Addison-Wesley Publishing Co., Inc.
Rte. 128
Reading, MA 01867
Phone: (617)944-3700
Editor(s): Paul R. Ehrlich and Anne H Ehrlich. ***Frequency:*** 1991.

★5067★ Health, Safety, and Environmental Control
Van Nostrand Reinhold Co., Inc.
115 Fifth Ave.
New York, NY 10003
Phone: (212)254-3232
Editor(s): Reynold L. Hoover. ***Frequency:*** 1989.

★5068★ Healthy Homes, Healthy Kids: Protecting Your Children from Everyday Environmental Hazards
Island Press
Box 7
Covelo, CA 95428
Schoemaker, Joyce M. and Vitale, Charity Y. 1991. ***Price:*** $19.95. 220 pp.

★5069★ Heloise, Hints for a Healthy Planet
Perigee Books
New York, NY
Frequency: 1990.

★5070★ The History of the Sierra Club
Sierra Club Books
Maryland
100 Bush St., 13th Fl.
San Francisco, CA 94104
Cohen, Michael P. 1988. ***Price:*** $29.95. 550 pp.

★5071★ Home Ecology: Simple and Practical Ways to Green Your Home
Fulcrum, Inc.
350 Indiana St., Ste. 510
Golden, CO 80401
Phone: (303)277-1623
Fax: (303)279-7111
Editor(s): Karen Christensen. ***Frequency:*** 1989.

★5072★ How Green Are You?
Clarkson N. Potter, Inc.
225 Park Ave., S.
New York, NY 10003
Phone: (212)254-1600
Editor(s): David Bellamy. ***Frequency:*** 1991. Provides information and projects about ecology and environmental concerns that teach children and their families how to conserve energy, protect wildlife, and reduce pollution.

★5073★ How On Earth Do We Recycle Glass?
Millbrook Press
Brookfield, CT
Editor(s): Joanna Randolph Rott and Seli Groves. ***Frequency:*** 1992. Describes the making of glass and the problems caused by glass waste. Also gives suggestion for ways of using discarded glass.

★5074★ How on Earth Do We Recycle Metal?
Millbrook Press
Brookfield, CT
Editor(s): Rudy Kouhoupt with Don Marti. ***Frequency:*** 1992. Examines the problems associated with the disposal of metal waste and describes how it can be recycled by creating objects such as jewelry, weathervanes, and Christmas ornaments.

★5075★ How On Earth Do We Recycle Paper?
Millbrook Press
Brookfield, CT
Editor(s): Helen Jill Fletcher and Seli Groves. ***Frequency:*** 1992. Discusses how paper is produced and how it is recycled. Presents crafts projects using paper discards.

★5076★ How On Earth Do We Recycle Plastic?
Millbrook Press
Brookfield, CT
Editor(s): Janet D'Amato with Laura S. Carter. ***Frequency:*** 1992. Discusses the environmental problems caused by the manufacture and disposal of plastic and describes how it can be recycled.

★5077★ How to Make the World a Better Place: A Beginner's Guide
William Morrow and Co.
105 Madison Ave.
New York, NY 10016
Phone: (212)889-3050
Toll-Free: 800-843-9389
Jeffrey Hollender. ***Frequency:*** 1990. ***Price:*** $9.95 paper.

★5078★ How You Can Fight Global Warming: An Action Guide
State University of New York Press
Maryland
State University Plaza
Albany, NY 12246

★5079★ Ice Time: Climate, Science, and Life on Earth
HarperCollins Publishers
Corporate Exhibits
10 E. 53rd St.
New York, NY 10022
Levenson, Thomas. 1989. ***Price:*** $9.95. 242 pp.

★5080★ Ill Winds: Airborne Pollution's Toll on Trees and Crops
State University of New York Press
Maryland
State University Plaza
Albany, NY 12246
Mackenie, James J. and El Ashry, Mohamed T. 1988. ***Price:*** $410.00. 74 pp.

★5081★ Imperiled Planet, Restoring our Endangered Ecosystems
MIT Press
55 Hayward St.
Cambridge, MA 02142
Goldsmith, Edward, et al. 1990.

★5082★ In Defense of the Land Ethic: Essays in Environmental Philosophy
State Univ. of New York Press
State University Plz.
Albany, NY 12246
Phone: (518)472-5000
Editor(s): J. Baird Callicott. ***Frequency:*** 1989.

★5083★ In Praise of Nature
Island Press
1718 Connecticut Ave., NW
Ste. 300
Washington, DC 20009
Phone: (202)232-7933
Fax: (202)234-1328
Editor(s): Stephanie Mills and Jeanne Carstensen. ***Frequency:*** 1990.

★5084★ In Search of Environmental Excellence: Moving Beyond Blame
Simon & Schuster, Inc.
1230 Ave. of the Americas
Simon & Schuster Bldg.
New York, NY 10020
Phone: (212)698-7000
Editor(s): Bruce Piasecki

★5085★ In the U.S. Interest: Resources, Growth, and Security in the Developing World
State University of New York Press
Maryland
State University Plaza
Albany, NY 12246
Brown, Janet Welsh. 1990. ***Price:*** $19.95. 228 pp.

★5086★ In the Wake of the Exxon Valdez: The Devastating Impact of the Alaska Oil Spill
Sierra Club Books
Maryland
100 Bush St., 13th Fl.
San Francisco, CA 94104
Davidson, Art. 1990. ***Price:*** $19.95. 333 pp.

★5087★ Indoor Air Quality-Design Guide Book
Fairmont Press, Inc.
Int'l Sales
700 Indian Tr.
Lilburn, GA 30247
Meckler, Milton. ***Frequency:*** 1991. ***Price:*** $62.00. 283 pp.

★5088★ Industry, the Environment, and Corporate Social Responsibility: A Selected and Annotated Bibliography
Council of Planning Librarians
Chicago, IL
Editor(s): Sonia Labatt. ***Frequency:*** 1990.

★5089★ Inside the Environmental Movement: Meeting the Leadership Challenge
Island Press
1718 Connecticut Ave., NW
Ste. 300
Washington, DC 20009
Phone: (202)232-7933
Fax: (202)234-1328
Editor(s): Donald Snow. ***Frequency:*** 1991.

★5090★ Institute for Resource Management Symposium Proceedings
Institute for Resource Management
262 S. 200 W.
Salt Lake City, UT 84101
Phone: (801)322-0530
Frequency: 2-3/year.

★5091★ Integrated Pollution Control in Europe and North America
World Wildlife Fund
The Conservation Foundation
Publications Dept.
1250 Twenty-Fourth St., NW
Washington, DC 20037
Haigh, Nigel, Irwin, Frances. 1990. ***Price:*** $20. 242 pp.

★5092★ International Environmental Diplomacy
Cambridge University Press
32 E. 57th St.
New York, NY 10022
Carroll, John E., editor. 1988. ***Price:*** $54.50. 291 pp.

★5093★ International Environmental Policy: Emergence and Dimensions
Duke Univ. Press
College Sta.
Box 6697
Durham, NC 27708
Phone: (919)684-2173
Editor(s): Lynton Keith Caldwell. ***Frequency:*** 1990.

★5094★ International Joint Commission Report
International Joint Commn.
2001 S St. NW, 2nd Fl.
Washington, DC 20440
Phone: (202)673-6222
Contains information on water quality in the Great Lakes system. ***Frequency:*** Biennial.

★5095★ International Wildlife Rehabilitation Council Conference Proceedings
International Wildlife Rehabilitation Coun.
4437 Central Place, Ste. B-4
Suisun, CA 94585
Phone: (707)864-1761

★5096★ International Wildlife Trade: Whose Business Is It?
World Wildlife Fund
The Conservation Foundation
Publications Dept.
1250 Twenty-Fourth St., NW
Washington, DC 20037
Fitzgerald, Sarah. 1989. ***Price:*** $25. 459 pp.

★5097★ Interstate Conference on Water Policy Annual Report
Interstate Conference on Water Policy
955 L'Enfant Plaza SW, 6th Fl.
Washington, DC 20024
Phone: (202)466-7287
Fax: (202)646-6210

★5098★ Interstate Conference on Water Policy Statement
Interstate Conference on Water Policy
955 L'Enfant Plaza SW, 6th Fl.
Washington, DC 20024
Phone: (202)466-7287
Fax: (202)646-6210
Frequency: Annual.

★5099★ Into Adolescence. Caring for Our Planet and Our Health: A Curriculum for Grades 5-8
Network Publications
PO Box 1830
Santa Cruz, CA 95061-1830
Phone: (408)438-4060
Fax: (408)438-4284
Editor(s): Lisa K. Hunter. ***Frequency:*** 1991.

★5100★ Introduction to Environmental Engineering and Science
Prentice Hall
Rte. 9W
Englewood Cliffs, NJ 07632
Phone: (201)592-2000
Editor(s): Gilbert M. Masters. ***Frequency:*** 1991.

★5101★ Introduction to Wildlife Rehabilitation
National Wildlife Rehabilitators Assn.
12805 St. Croix Trail
Hastin, MN 55033
Phone: (612)437-9194

★5102★ Irrigation-Induced Water Quality Problems
National Academy Press
Maryland
2101 Constitution Ave. N.W.
Washington, DC 20418
National Research Council. 1989. ***Price:*** $30. 178 pp.

★5103★ It's My Earth, Too: How I Can Help the Earth Stay Alive
Doubleday & Co., Inc.
666 Fifth Ave.
New York, NY 10103
Phone: (212)984-7561
Editor(s): Kathleen Krull. ***Frequency:*** 1992. Text and illustrations pay homage to the earth and its resources. Includes suggestions that children can follow to help preserve the environment.

★5104★ Izaak Walton League of America Annual Report
Izaak Walton League of America
1401 Wilson Blvd., Level B
Arlington, VA 22209
Phone: (703)528-1818
Fax: (703)528-1836

★5105★ Jacques Cousteau's Amazon Journey
Harry N. Abrams Publishers
100 Fifth Ave.
New York, NY 10011
Phone: (212)206-7715
Toll-Free: 800-345-1359
Jacques-Yves Cousteau and Mose Richards. ***Price:*** $39.95.

★5106★ John McPhee Reader
Farrar, Straus and Giroux
19 Union Sq. W.
New York, NY 10003
Phone: (212)741-6900
Toll-Free: 800-242-7737
Howarth, William L. ***Price:*** $9.95.

★5107★ The Jungle Is My Home
Viking Penguin, Inc.
40 W 23rd St.
New York, NY 10010
Phone: (212)337-5200
Editor(s): Laura Fischetto. ***Frequency:*** 1991. Describes the jungle and how man's destructive behavior threatens to ruin it as a unique home to a multitude of animals.

★5108★ Just a Dream
Houghton Mifflin Co.
1 Beacon St.
Boston, MA 02108
Phone: (617)725-5000
Editor(s): Chris Van Allsburg. ***Frequency:*** 1990. When he has a dream about a future Earth devastated by pollution, Walter begins to understand the importance of taking care of the environment.

★5109★ Keep America Beautiful—Annual Review
Keep America Beautiful
Mill River Plaza
9 W. Broad St.
Stamford, CT 06902
Phone: (203)323-8987
Price: Free.

★5110★ Keeping Options Alive: The Scientific Basis for Conserving Biodiversity
State University of New York Press
Maryland
State University Plaza
Albany, NY 12246
Reid, Walter V. amd Miller, Kenton R. 1989. ***Price:*** $10. 128 pp.

★5111★ The Kids' Earth Handbook
Atheneum Publishers
866 Third Ave.
New York, NY 10022
Phone: (212)702-2000
Editor(s): Sandra Markle. ***Frequency:*** 1991. Presents activities and experiments which demonstrate how living things interact with each other and the environment. Includes instructions for making miniature ecosystems.

★5112★ The Kid's Environment Book: What's Awry and Why
John Muir Publications, Inc.
PO Box 613
Santa Fe, NM 87504
Phone: (505)982-4078
Editor(s): Anne Pedersen. ***Frequency:*** 1991. Examines how our environmental problems, humankind's historic relationship with the earth and its living species, how industrialization has dramatically changed our planet, and what must be done to repair the damage.

★5113★ The Kingdom Wildlife in North America
Sierra Club Books
Maryland
Business
San Francisco, CA 94104
Wolfe, Art and Chadwick, Douglas. 1990. ***Price:*** $45. 197 pp.

★5114★ Lady Bird Johnson and the Environment
University Press of Kansas
329 Carruth
Lawrence, KS 66045
Phone: (913)864-4154
Editor(s): Lewis L. Gould. ***Frequency:*** 1988.

★5115★ Land Improvement Contractors of America Official Handbook
Land Improvement Contractors of America
PO Box 9
1300 Maybrook Dr.
Maywood, IL 60153
Phone: (708)344-0700

★5116★ The Land of Gray Wolf
Dial Books for Young Readers
2 Park Ave.
New York, NY 10016
Phone: (212)725-1818
Editor(s): Thomas Locker. ***Frequency:*** 1991. Running Deer and his fellow tribesmen take special care of their land until they lose it to invading white settlers, who wear it out and leave it to recover on its own.

★5117★ Land Planner's Environmental Issues
Noyes Publications
120 Mill Rd.
Park Ridge, NJ 07656
Phone: (201)391-8484
Fax: (201)391-6833
Editor(s): William B. Honachefsky. ***Frequency:*** 1991.

★5118★ Landscape Linkages and Biodiversity
Island Press
Box 7
Covelo, CA 95428
Editor(s): Hudson, Wendy E. Defenders of Wildlife. 1991. ***Price:*** $34.95. 214 pp.

★5119★ The Last Extinction
MIT Press
55 Hayward St.
Cambridge, MA 02138
Phone: (617)253-5646
Kaufman, Les and Malloy, Kenneth. ***Price:*** $16.95.

★5120★ Law of Environmental Protection
Environmental Law Inst.
1616 P St. NW, Ste. 200
Washington, DC 20036
Phone: (202)328-5150
Frequency: Annual.

★5121★ A Lawyer's Primer—Wildlife Conservation Fund of America
Wildlife Conservation Fund of America
50 W. Broad St., Ste. 1025
Columbus, OH 43215
Phone: (614)221-2684

★5122★ Learning to Listen to the Land
Island Press
1718 Connecticut Ave., NW
Ste. 300
Washington, DC 20009
Phone: (202)232-7933
Fax: (202)234-1328
Editor(s): Bill Willers. ***Frequency:*** 1991.

★5123★ Legacy International Occasional Papers
Legacy Intl.
346 Commerce St.
Alexandria, VA 22314
Phone: (703)549-3630
Fax: (703)549-0262
Frequency: 1-2/year.

★5124★ Legal Handbook on Sign Control
Scenic America
216 7th St. SE
Washington, DC 20003
Phone: (202)546-1100

★5125★ Lessons Learned in Global Environmental Governance
Island Press
Sales Dept.
PO Box 7
Covelo, CA 95428
Sand, Peter H. 1990. ***Price:*** $10. 60 pp.

★5126★ Lessons of the Rain Forest
Sierra Club Books
Maryland
Business
San Francisco, CA 94104
Head, Suzanne and Heinzman, Robert. 1990. ***Price:*** $14.95. 275 pp.

★5127★ Let's Talk Trash: The Kids' Book About Recycling
Waterfront Books
98 Brookes Ave.
Burlington, VT 05401
Phone: (802)658-7477
Editor(s): Kelly McQueen and David Fassler with the Environmental Law Foundation. ***Frequency:*** 1991. Discusses trash and the different ways in which it can be handled, with an emphasis on recycling. Incorporates the thoughts, questions, and drawings of children.

★5128★ Life Above the Jungle Floor
Fireside Press
Simon & Schuster
Simon & Schuster Bldg.
1230 Ave. of the Americas
New York, NY 10020
Phone: (212)698-7000
Toll-Free: 800-223-2348
Perry, Donald. 1988. ***Price:*** $39.50.

★5129★ Life in the Balance
National Audobon Society
950 Third Ave.
New York, NY 10022
Phone: (212)832-3200
Wallace, David R. 1987. ***Price:*** $29.95.

★5130★ Literature Review—Water Pollution Control Federation
Water Pollution Control Fed.
601 Wythe St.
Alexandria, VA 22314-1994
Phone: (703)684-2400
Fax: (703)684-2492
Frequency: Annual.

★5131★ The Living Ocean
Island Press
Box 7
Covelo, CA 95428
Understanding and protecting marine biodiversity. Thorne-Miller, Boyce and Catena, John G. 1990. ***Price:*** $10.95. 185 pp.

★5132★ The Long Shadowed Forest
W.W. Norton and Co.
500 Fifth Ave.
New York, NY 10110
Phone: (212)354-5500
Toll-Free: 800-223-2584
Hoover, Helene. ***Price:*** $4.95.

★5133★ The Magic Circle: Recycling in America
Atheneum Publishers
866 Third Ave.
New York, NY 10022
Phone: (212)702-2000
Editor(s): Gordon Bishop. ***Frequency:*** 1991. Discusses recycling and technologies that don't "waste" as a means of controlling the threat of global pollution.

★5134★ Making Peace with the Planet
Pantheon Books, Inc.
201 E. 50th St.
New York, NY 10022
Phone: (212)751-2600
Editor(s): Barry Commoner. ***Frequency:*** 1990.

★5135★ Man and Environment Curriculum Guides
North Amer. Assn. for Environmental Education
PO Box 400
Troy, OH 45373
Phone: (513)339-6835
Fax: (513)698-6493

★5136★ Managing Coastal Erosion
National Academy Press
Maryland
2101 Constitution Ave., N.W.
Washington, DC 20418
National Research Council. 1990. ***Price:*** $29.50. 204 pp.

★5137★ Managing Indoor Air Quality
Fairmont Press, Inc.
Int'l Sales
700 Indian Tr.
Lilburn, GA 30247
Hansen, Shirley J., Ph.D. ***Frequency:*** 1991. ***Price:*** $62.00. 317 pp.

★5138★ Managing National Park System Resources: A Handbook on Legal Duties, Opportunities and Tools
Conservation Found.
1250 24th St., NW
Washington, DC 20037
Phone: (202)293-4800
Fax: (202)293-9211
Editor(s): Michael A. Mantell. ***Frequency:*** 1990.

★5139★ Managing Our Natural Resources
Delmar Publishers, Inc.
2 Computer Dr., W
PO Box 15015
Albany, NY 12212
Phone: (518)459-1150
Fax: (518)459-3552
Editor(s): William G. Camp and Thomas B. Daugherty. ***Frequency:*** 1988. Examines the nature, history, and management of natural resources ranging from soil and water to forests, wildlife, and marine resources. Includes suggested activities and discussion of occupations in the field.

★5140★ Managing Planet Earth: Perspectives on Population, Ecology, and the Law
Bergin & Garvey Publishers, Inc.
670 Amherst Rd.
Granby, MA 01033
Phone: (413)467-3113
Editor(s): Miguel A. Santos. ***Frequency:*** 1990.

★5141★ Managing the Environmental Crisis: Incorporating Competing Values in Natural Resource Administration
Duke Univ. Press
College Sta.
Box 6697
Durham, NC 27708
Phone: (919)684-2173
Editor(s): Daniel H. Henning and William R. Mangun. ***Frequency:*** 1989.

★5142★ Managing Troubled Water: The Role of Marine Environmental Monitoring
National Academy Press
Maryland
2101 Constitution Ave., N.W.
Washington, DC 20418
National Research Council. 1990. ***Price:*** $29.50. 140 pp.

★5143★ Mandatory Deposit Legislation and Alternatives for Managing Solid Waste: A Review of the Evidence
University of Maryland, Coll. Park
Institute for Governmental Service
College Park, MD 20742
Editor(s): Joan Rohlfs. ***Frequency:*** 1988.

★5144★ Manual of Wildlife Medicine
National Wildlife Rehabilitators Assn.
12805 St. Croix Trail
Hastin, MN 55033
Phone: (612)437-9194

★5145★ Manuals of Practice
Water Pollution Control Fed.
601 Wythe St.
Alexandria, VA 22314-1994
Phone: (703)684-2400
Fax: (703)684-2492
Frequency: Public education brochures, and a water quality curriculum for schoolchildren.

★5146★ Media and the Environment
Island Press
1718 Connecticut Ave., NW
Ste. 300
Washington, DC 20009
Phone: (202)232-7933
Fax: (202)234-1328
Editor(s): Craig L. LaMay and Everette E. Dennis. ***Frequency:*** 1992.

★5147★ Media Guide to Environmental Resources
National Wildlife Fed.
1400 16th St. NW
Washington, DC 20036-2266
Phone: (202)797-6800
Frequency: Annual.

★5148★ Meeting the Environmental Challenge: EPA Review of Progress and New Directions in Environmental Protection
Environmental Protection Agency
Department of Public Affairs
401 M St., SW
Washington, DC 20460

★5149★ Mending the Earth: A World for Our Grandchildren
North Atlantic Books
2800 Woolsey St.
Berkeley, CA 94705
Phone: (415)652-5309
Editor(s): Paul Rothkrug and Robert L. Olson. ***Frequency:*** 1991.

★5150★ Minding the Carbon Store: Weighing U.S. Forestry Strategies to Slow Global Warming
Island Press
Sales Dept.
PO Box 7
Covelo, CA 95428
Trexler, Mark C. 1991. ***Price:*** $12.50. 81 pp.

★5151★ Mining Urban Wastes: The Potential for Recycling
Worldwatch Inst.
1776 Massachusetts Ave., NW
Washington, DC 20036
Phone: (202)452-1999
Editor(s): Cynthia Pollock. ***Frequency:*** 1987.

★5152★ Money to Burn? The High Costs of Energy Subsidies
State University of New York Press
Maryland
State University Plaza
Albany, NY 12246
Kosmo, Mark. 1987. ***Price:*** $10.00. 68 pp.

★5153★ Mother Earth
Atheneum Publishers
866 Third Ave.
New York, NY 10022
Phone: (212)702-2000
Editor(s): Nancy Luenn. ***Frequency:*** 1992. Describes the gifts that the earth gives to us and the gifts that we can give back to her.

★5154★ The Mother Earth Handbook: What You Need to Know and Do—At Home, in Your Community, and Through Your Church—To Help Heal Our Planet Now
Continuum Publishing Corp.
370 Lexington Ave.
New York, NY 10017
Phone: (212)532-3650
Editor(s): Judith S. Scherff. ***Frequency:*** 1991.

★5155★ Mountains
Marshall Cavendish Corp.
2415 Jerusalem Ave.
Billmore, NY 11710
Phone: (516)546-4200
Editor(s): Lawrence Williams. ***Frequency:*** 1990. Explores the question of how mountains are made, how they are changed by weather, wildlife, and the efforts of humanity, and how their resources may be protected.

★5156★ Mousekin's Lost Woodland
Simon & Schuster, Inc.
Simon & Schuster Bldg.
1230 Ave. of the Americas
New York, NY 10020
Phone: (212)698-7000
Editor(s): Edna Miller. ***Frequency:*** 1992. A white-footed mouse finds himself all alone as the woodland he lives in is destroyed.

★5157★ Moving Mountains: Coping With Change in Mountain Communities
Appalachian Mountain Club Books
5 Joy St.
Boston, MA 02108
Phone: (617)523-0722
Fax: (617)523-0722
Editor(s): Sara Neustadtl. ***Frequency:*** 1987.

★5158★ Mr. Pumpkin
Harcourt Brace Jovanovich, Inc.
6277 Sea Harbor Dr.
Orlando, FL 32821
Phone: (407)345-2000
Editor(s): Mary Lyn Ray. ***Frequency:*** 1992. A man harvests and sells a bountiful crop of pumpkins so that he will be able to preserve the field from developers.

★5159★ Mr. Rumples Recycles
Hyacinth House Publishing
P.O. Box 14603
Baton Rouge, LA 70898
Coltharpe, Barbara Anne. Illustrated children's book. ***Price:*** $6.50. 30 pp.

★5160★ Municipal Waste Disposal
Chilton Book Co.
Chilton Way
Radnor, PA 19089
Phone: (215)964-4000
Editor(s): Bela Liptak. ***Frequency:*** 1991.

★5161★ My First Green Book
Alfred A. Knopf, Inc.
201 E. 50th St.
New York, NY 10022
Phone: (201)751-2600
Editor(s): Angela Wilkes. ***Frequency:*** 1991. Features environmental activities and projects in such areas as water pollution, recycling, acid rain, and wildlife gardens.

★5162★ National Wildlife Rehabilitators Association Annual Report
National Wildlife Rehabilitators Assn.
12805 St. Croix Trail
Hastin, MN 55033
Phone: (612)437-9194

★5163★ Natural Endowments: Financing Resource Conservation for Development
Island Press
Sales Dept.
PO Box 7
Covelo, CA 95428
1989. ***Price:*** $12.50. 33 pp.

★5164★ Natural Gas Applications for Air Pollution Control
Fairmont Press, Inc.
Int'l Sales
700 Indian Tr.
Lilburn, GA 30247
Hay, Nelson E. ***Frequency:*** 1987. ***Price:*** $43.00. 360 pp.

★5165★ Natural Resource Conservation: An Ecological Approach
Macmillan Publishing Co.
366 Third Ave.
New York, NY 10022
Phone: (212)702-2000
Editor(s): Oliver S. Owen and Daniel D. Chiras. ***Frequency:*** 1990.

★5166★ Natural Resources for the 21st Century
Island Press
P.O. Box 7
Covelo, CA 95428
Sampson, Neil and Hair, Dwight, editors. 1989. ***Price:*** $19.95. 349 pp.

★5167★ Nature and the American: Three Centuries of Changing Attitudes
University of Nebraska Press
901 N. 17th St.
Lincoln, NE 68588
Phone: (402)472-3581
Editor(s): Hans Huth. ***Frequency:*** 1991.

★5168★ The Nature Directory: A Guide to Environmental Organizations
Walker & Co.
720 Fifth Ave.
New York, NY 10019
Phone: (212)265-3632
Editor(s): Susan D. Lanier-Graham. ***Frequency:*** 1991.

★5169★ Nature in Danger
Troll Associates
100 Corporate Dr.
Mahwah, NJ 07430
Phone: (201)529-4000
Editor(s): Mary O'Neill. ***Frequency:*** 1991. Discusses how the natural resources of the Earth and the living things on it are all linked together and how the natural order of things is being continually threatened by our modern way of life.

★5170★ Nature's End: The Consequences of the Twentieth Century
Warner Books
666 Fifth Ave.
New York, NY
Phone: (212)484-2900
Streiber, Whitley and Kunetka, James. 1987. ***Price:*** $4.95.

★5171★ Nature's Last Strongholds
Oxford Univ. Press, Inc.
200 Madison Ave.
New York, NY 10016
Phone: (212)679-7300
Editor(s): Robert Burton. ***Frequency:*** 1991.

★5172★ New England Wildflower Society Annual Report
New England Wildflower Soc.
c/o Barbara Pryor
Hemenway Rd.
Framingham, MA 01701
Phone: (508)877-7630

★5173★ The New Environmental Age
Cambridge Univ. Press
40 W. 20th St.
New York, NY 10011
Phone: (212)924-3900
Fax: (212)691-3239
Editor(s): Max Nicholson. ***Frequency:*** 1987.

★5174★ New Ideas in Environmental Education
Routledge, Chapman and Hall, Inc.
29 W. 35th St.
New York, NY 10001-2291
Phone: (212)244-3336
Fax: (212)563-2269
Editor(s): Salvano Briceno and David C. Pitt. ***Frequency:*** 1988.

★5175★ New World, New Mind

★5176★ New York Zoological Society Annual Report
Wildlife Conservation Intl.
c/o New York Zoological Society
Bronx, NY 10460
Phone: (212)220-5155
Fax: (212)220-7114

★5177★ The North Sea: Perspectives on Regional Environmental Co-operation
Graham & Trotman Martinus Nijhoff
Boston, MA
Editor(s): David Freestone and Ton Ijlstra. ***Frequency:*** 1990.

★5178★ The Northwest Greenbook: A Regional Guide to Protecting and Preserving Our Environment
Sesquatch Books
Seattle, WA
Editor(s): Jonathan King. ***Frequency:*** 1991.

★5179★ Not Far Afield; U.S. Interests and the Global Environment
State University of New York Press
Maryland
State University Plaza
Albany, NY 12246
Meyers, Norman. 1987. ***Price:*** $10.00. 71 pp.

★5180★ Nuclear Power: Past and Future
State University of New York
Maryland
State University Plaza
Albany, NY 12246

★5181★ Nuclear Reactor Containments: Sieve or Shield?
State University of New York
Maryland
State University Plaza
Albany, NY 12246

★5182★ The Ocean in Human Affairs
Paragon House
Maryland
90 Fifth Ave.
New York, NY 10011
Slinger, S. Fred. 1990. ***Price:*** $34.95. 374 pp.

★5183★ One Earth
Collins Publishers/A Day in the Life
50 Osgood Pl.
San Francisco, CA 94133
Brower, Kenneth. ***Frequency:*** 1990. ***Price:*** $24.95.

★5184★ One Earth, One Future: Our Changing Global Environment
National Academy Press
Maryland
2101 Constitution Ave., N.W.
Washington, DC 20418
Silver, Cheryl Simon and Defries, Ruth S. 1990. ***Price:*** $18. 208 pp.

★5185★ Operations Forum
Water Pollution Control Fed.
601 Wythe St.
Alexandria, VA 22314-1994
Phone: (703)684-2400
Fax: (703)684-2492
Frequency: Monthly.

★5186★ Opportunities in Environmental Careers
VGM Career Horizons
4255 W. Touhy Ave.
Lincolnwood, IL 60646
Phone: (312)679-5500
Editor(s): Odom Fanning. ***Frequency:*** 1991.

★5187★ Options for Conservation: The Different Roles of Nongovernmental Conservation Organizations
Conservation Found.
1250 24th St., NW
Washington, DC 20037
Phone: (202)293-4800
Fax: (202)293-9211
Editor(s): Sarah Fitzgerald. ***Frequency:*** 1990.

★5188★ Ordinance Information Packet
Scenic America
216 7th St. SE
Washington, DC 20003
Phone: (202)546-1100

★5189★ Organic Waste Recycling
John Wiley & Sons, Inc.
605 Third Ave.
New York, NY 10158
Phone: (212)850-6000
Editor(s): Chongrak Polprasert. ***Frequency:*** 1989.

★5190★ Our Angry Earth: A Ticking Time Bomb
Tor Books
49 W. 24th St.
9th Fl.
New York, NY 10010
Phone: (212)741-3100
Fax: (212)627-2941
Editor(s): Isaac Asimov and Frederik Pohl. ***Frequency:*** 1991.

★5191★ Our Common Lands: Defending the National Parks
Island Press
1718 Connecticut Ave., NW
Ste. 300
Washington, DC 20009
Phone: (202)232-7933
Fax: (202)234-1328
Editor(s): David J. Simon. ***Frequency:*** 1988.

★5192★ Our Earth, Ourselves: The Action-Oriented Guide to Help You Protect and Preserve Our Planet
Bantam Books
666 Fifth Ave.
New York, NY 10103
Phone: (212)765-6500
Editor(s): Ruth Caplan and the staff of Environmental Action. ***Frequency:*** 1990.

★5193★ Our Endangered Earth: The Fragile Environment and What We Can Do to Save It
Little, Brown & Co., Inc.
34 Beacon St.
Boston, MA 02108
Phone: (617)227-0730
Editor(s): John Lagone. ***Frequency:*** 1992. Discusses the environmental crisis, focusing on such problems as overpopulation, the pollution of water, air and land, ozone depletion, global warming, and disappearing wildlife. Suggests ways to improve life in the twenty-first century.

★5194★ Our National Parks
Little, Brown and Co.
Children's Books/Sales
34 Beacon St.
Boston, MA 02108-1493
Young, Donald. 1990. ***Price:*** $14.95. 64 pp.

★5195★ Our Natural Resources and Their Conservation
Interstate Printers and Publishers, Inc.
19 N Jackson St.
PO Box 50
Danville, IL 61834-0050
Phone: (217)446-0500
Editor(s): Harry B. Kircher, Donald L. Wallace, and Dorothy J. Gore. ***Frequency:*** 1988.

★5196★ Our Poisoned Planet: Can We Save It?
Facts On File, Inc.
460 Park Avenue, S.
New York, NY 10016
Phone: (212)683-2244
Editor(s): Oliver Trager. ***Frequency:*** 1989. Examines environmental issues through the words and images of the nation's leading editorial writers and cartoonists.

★5197★ Our Two Gardens
Oliver-Nelson Books
Nelson Pl. at Elm Hill Pike
Nashville, TN 37214
Phone: (615)889-9000
Fax: (615)391-5225
Editor(s): Margaret Hebblethwaite. ***Frequency:*** 1991. Describes the world as a garden, planted by God; discusses the pollution of land, air, and water; and suggests ways of cleaning up the environment.

★5198★ Outdoor Survival Handbook for Kids
Harbinger House
Marketing Department
2802 N. Alvernon Way
Tuscon, AZ 80712
Whitefeathers, Willy. 1990. ***Price:*** $6.95. 96 pp.

★5199★ Outposts of Eden: A Curmudgeon at Large in the American West
Sierra Club Books
730 Polk St.
San Francisco, CA 94109
Phone: (415)776-2211
Editor(s): Page Stegner. ***Frequency:*** 1989.

★5200★ Over California
Collins Publishers/A Day in the Life
50 Osgood Pl.
San Francisco, CA 94133
Starr, Kevin. ***Frequency:*** 1990. ***Price:*** $45.00.

★5201★ Over New England
Collins Publishers/A Day in the Life
50 Osgood Pl.
San Francisco, CA 94133
Peirce, Neal R. ***Frequency:*** 1990. ***Price:*** $45.00.

★5202★ Overtapped Oasis
Island Press
Box 7
Covelo, CA 95428
1989.
Discussion of the water supply problems in the Western United States. ***Price:*** $31.95. 200 pp.

★5203★ Ozone Crisis: The 15-Year Evolution of a Sudden Global Emergency
John Wiley & Sons
605 Third Ave.
New York, NY 10158
Phone: (212)850-6000
Editor(s): Sharon Roan. ***Frequency:*** 1989. ***Price:*** $18.95.

★5204★ Ozone Depletion, Greenhouse Gases, and Climate Change
National Academy Press
Maryland
2101 Constitution Ave, N.W.
Washington, DC 20418
National Research Council. 1989. ***Price:*** $24. 136 pp.

★5205★ Ozone Diplomacy: New Directions in Safeguarding the Planet
Harvard University Press
Marketing Departent
79 Garden St.
Cambridge, MA 02138-9983
Benedick, Richard Elliot. 1991. ***Price:*** $10.95. 300 pp.

★5206★ The Ozone Layer
Chelsea House Publishers
1974 Sproul Road, Ste. 400
Broomall, PA 19008
Phone: (215)353-5166
Fax: (215)353-1439
Editor(s): Marshall John Fisher. ***Frequency:*** 1992. The ozone layer protects life on earth from harmful ultraviolet radiation but this protective shield is being damaged by the chlorofluorocarbons and other pollutants that are now being generated on the earth.

★5207★ The Ozone Layer: Earth Alert Series
Maxwell Macmillan International Publishing Group
Export Division
28100 US Hwy. 19 N., Ste. 200
Clearwater, FL 34621
Duden, Jane. 1990. Crestwood House. ***Price:*** $10.95. 48 pp.

★5208★ A Path Where No Man Thought: Nuclear Winter and the End of the Arms Race
Random House Inc.
International
201 E. 50th St.
New York, NY 10022
Sagan, Carl and Turco, Richard. 1990. ***Price:*** $27.95. 499 pp.

★5209★ People of the Tropical Rain Forest
University of California Press
Island Press
1718 Connecticut Ave. NW, Ste. 300
Washington, DC 20036
Phone: (202)232-7933
Denslow, Julie Sloan and Padoch, Christine. 1988. ***Price:*** $19.95 paper, $39.50 cloth.

★5210★ Peregrine Fund Annual Report
Peregrine Fund
World Center for Birds of Prey
5666 W. Flying Hawk Ln.
Boise, ID 83709
Phone: (208)362-3716
Fax: (208)362-2376

★5211★ Perspectives in Wildlife Management: A How-to for Corporate Lands
Wildlife Habitat Enhancement Coun.
1010 Wayne Ave., Ste. 1240
Silver Spring, MD 20910
Phone: (301)588-8994

★5212★ Perspectives on Ecosystem: Management for the Great Lakes
State University of New York Press
P.O. Box 6525
Ithaca, NY 14850
Caldwell, Lynton K., editor. 1988. ***Price:*** $16.95. 365 pp.

★5213★ Pesticide Alert: A Guide to Pesticides in Fruits and Vegetables
Sierra Club Books
Maryland
Business
San Francisco, CA 94104
Mott, Lawrie and Snyder, Karen. 1987. ***Price:*** $6.95. 179 pp.

★5214★ Picture Pocket: Our Planet
Simon & Schuster, Inc.
Simon & Schuster Bldg.
1230 Ave. of the Americas
New York, NY 10020-'
Phone: (212)698-7000
Editor(s): Lionel Bender. ***Frequency:*** 1992. Discusses the many aspects of our amazing planet, including its atmosphere, oceans, interior, life, and constantly changing nature.

★5215★ Planet in Peril: A View from the Campus; An Environmental Opinion Survey; Detailed Findings
National Wildlife Fed.
1400 16th St., NW
Washington, DC 20036
Phone: (703)790-4000
Frequency: 1989.

★5216★ A Planter's Guide to the Urban Forest
TreePeople
12601 Mulholland Dr.
Beverly Hills, CA 90210
Phone: (818)753-4600
Fax: (818)753-4625
Toll-Free: (650)263-8793

★5217★ Plastics: America's Packaging Dilemma
Island Press
Box 7
Dept. 4H1
Covelo, CA 95428
Wolf, Nancy and Feldman, Ellen. ***Price:*** $12.95. 128 pp.

★5218★ Plastics Recycling Foundation Annual Report
Plastics Recycling Found.
1275 K St. NW, Ste. 500
Washington, DC 20005
Phone: (202)371-5200

★5219★ Poetry from the Amicus Journal
Tioga Publishing Co.
150 Coquito Way
Portola Valley, CA 94025
Phone: (415)854-2445
Editor(s): Brian Swann and Peter Borrelli. ***Frequency:*** 1990.

★5220★ Polar Lands
Marshall Cavendish Corp.
2415 Jerusalem Ave.
Billmore, NY 11710
Phone: (516)546-4200
Editor(s): Lawrence Williams. ***Frequency:*** 1990. Explores the possibility of living and working in the polar regions without destroying the environment.

★5221★ Policy Options for Stabilizing Global Climate
Hemisphere Publishing Corp.
79 Madison Ave., Ste. 1110
New York, NY 10016
Phone: (212)725-1999
Editor(s): Daniel A. Lashof and Dennis A. Tirpak. ***Frequency:*** 1990.

★5222★ The Political Limits of Environmental Regulation: Tracking the Unicorn
Quorum Books
New York, NY
Editor(s): Bruce Yandle. ***Frequency:*** 1989.

★5223★ Pollution and Conservation
Silver Burdett Press
Englewood Cliffs, NJ
Editor(s): Malcolm Penny. ***Frequency:*** 1989. Describes the various kinds of pollution and what is being done to protect the natural environment.

★5224★ Pollution Digest: Habitat
Social Issues Resources Series Inc.
PO Box 2348
Boca Raton, FL 33427-2348
Latest issue: Volume 3.

★5225★ Pollution Knows No Frontiers
Paragon House of Publishers
90 Fifth Ave.
New York, NY 10011
Phone: (212)620-2820
Editor(s): Klaus Schleicher. ***Frequency:*** 1991.

★5226★ Population Matters: People, Resources, Environmental Immigration
State University of New York Press
Maryland
State University Plaza
Albany, NY 12246
Simon, Julian L. 1989. ***Price:*** $34.95. 425 pp.

★5227★ Population: Resources, Environment and Sustainable Development
Global Tomorrow Coalition
Publications Dept.
1325 G St., NW, Ste. 915
Washington, DC 20005-3104

★5228★ Position Paper on the Clean Air Act
State and Territorial Air Pollution Program Administrators
444 N. Capitol St. NW, Ste. 306
Washington, DC 20001
Phone: (202)624-7864
Fax: (202)624-7863

★5229★ Practical Guide to Environmental Management
Environmental Law Inst.
1616 P St., NW
Ste. 200
Washington, DC 20036
Phone: (202)328-5150
Editor(s): Frank B. Friedman. ***Frequency:*** 1988.

★5230★ Preserving the World Ecology
H.W. Wilson Co.
950 University Ave.
Bronx, NY 10452
Phone: (212)588-8400
Editor(s): Steven Anzovin. ***Frequency:*** 1990. A compilation of essays dealing with world ecological-environmental issues and their political and possible preservational dimensions.

★5231★ Prevention of Toxic Substances in Large Lakes: Managing a Large Ecosystem for Sustainable Development
Lewis Publishers, Inc.
121 S. Main St.
PO Drawer 519
Chelsea, MI 48118
Phone: (313)475-8619
Editor(s): Norbert W. Schmidtke. ***Frequency:*** 1988. Proceedings of a technical session of the World Conference on Large Lakes, held May 18-21, 1986, Mackinac Island, MI.

★5232★ Principles of Environmental Science and Technology
Elsevier Science Publishing Co.
52 Vanderbilt Ave.
New York, NY 10017
Phone: (212)370-5520
Editor(s): S.E. Jorgensen and I. Johnsen. ***Frequency:*** 1989.

★5233★ Proceedings of the Organization of Wildlife Planners Conference
Organization of Wildlife Planners
DNR-Box 7921
Madison, WI 53707
Phone: (608)267-7591
Fax: (608)267-3579
Includes membership list. ***Frequency:*** Annual.

★5234★ The Professional Practice of Environmental Management
Springer-Verlag New York, Inc.
175 Fifth Ave.
19th Fl.
New York, NY 10010
Phone: (212)460-1500
Editor(s): Robert S. Dorney and Lindsay C. Dorney. ***Frequency:*** 1989.

★5235★ Promoting Environmentally Sound Economic Progress: What the North Can Do
State University of New York Press
Maryland
State University Plaza
Albany, NY 12246
Repetto, Robert. ***Price:*** $10. 21 pp.

★5236★ Promoting Source Reduction and Recyclability in the Marketplace
EPA, RCRA Docket
401 M St., SW
Washington, DC 20460
Phone: (202)475-9327
Frequency: 1989. ***Price:*** Free.

★5237★ Prospect Park Handbook
Greensward Found.
104 Prospect Park W.
Brooklyn, NY 11215

★5238★ Prosperity and Poverty: The Compassionate Use of Resources in a World of Scarcity
Crossway Books
Westchester, IL
Editor(s): E. Calvin Beisner. ***Frequency:*** 1988.

★5239★ Prosperity Without Pollution: The Prevention Strategy for Industry and Consumers
Van Nostrand Reinhold Co., Inc.
115 Fifth Ave.
New York, NY 10003
Phone: (212)254-3232
Editor(s): Joel S. Hirschhorn and Kirsten U. Oldenburg. ***Frequency:*** 1991.

★5240★ Protect and Enhance: "Juridical Democracy" and the Prevention of Significant Deterioration of Air Quality.
Garland Publishing, Inc.
136 Madison Ave.
New York, NY 10016
Phone: (212)686-7492
Editor(s): A. Stanley Meiburg. ***Frequency:*** 1991.

★5241★ Protecting Nature
Franklin Watts, Inc.
387 Park Ave., S.
New York, NY 10016
Phone: (212)686-7070
Editor(s): Donna Bailey. ***Frequency:*** 1992. Focuses on dangers posed to nature and ways of protecting nature.

★5242★ Protecting the Environment: Old Rhetoric, New Imperatives
Capital Research Center
1612 K St., NW
Ste. 704
Washington, DC 20006
Editor(s): Jo Kwong Echard. ***Frequency:*** 1990.

★5243★ Protecting the Ozone Layer
Environmental Defense Fund
257 Park Ave., S.
New York, NY 10010
Phone: (212)505-2100
Frequency: 1988. ***Price:*** $2.

★5244★ Protection of River Basins, Lakes, and Estuaries: Fifteen Years of Cooperation Toward Solving Environmental Problems in the USSR and USA
Amer. Fisheries Soc.
5410 Grosvenor Ln.
Bethesda, MD 20814
Phone: (301)897-8616
Fax: (301)897-8096
Editor(s): Robert C. Ryans. ***Frequency:*** 1988.

★5245★ Proven Profits from Pollution Prevention: Case Studies in Resource Conservation and Waste Reduction
Institute for Local Self-Reliance
2425 18th St., NW
Washington, DC 20009
Phone: (202)232-4108
Editor(s): Donald Huisingh. ***Frequency:*** 1989.

★5246★ The Quiet Crisis and the Next Generation
Peregrine Smith Books
Salt Lake City, UT
Editor(s): Stewart L. Udall. ***Frequency:*** 1988.

★5247★ Quill's Adventures in Grozzieland
John Muir Publications, Inc.
PO Box 613
Santa Fe, NM 87504
Phone: (505)982-4078
Editor(s): John Waddington-Feather. ***Frequency:*** 1991. Quill Hedgehog and his friends from the Great Beyond try to thwart the plan to blot out the sun and moon that alley cat Mungo Brown has devised with the help of the underground Grozzies in order to take over the world.

★5248★ Quill's Adventures in the Great Beyond
John Muir Publications, Inc.
PO Box 613
Santa Fe, NM 87504
Phone: (505)982-4078
Editor(s): John Waddington-Feather. ***Frequency:*** 1991. Quill Hedgehog and his friends from the Great Beyond battle the villainous alley cat Mungo Brown and the Wasteland rats who threaten to destroy the countryside.

★5249★ Quill's Adventures in Wasteland
John Muir Publications, Inc.
PO Box 613
Santa Fe, NM 87504
Phone: (505)982-4078
Editor(s): John Waddington-Feather. ***Frequency:*** 1991. Quill Hedgehog and the Great Beyonders try to thwart a treacherous alley cat's plan to exploit the land around Black Wood.

★5250★ Race to Save the Tropics: Ecology and Economics for a Sustainable Future
Island Press
Sales Dept.
PO Box 7
Covelo, CA 95428
Goodland, Robert. 1990. ***Price:*** $24.95. 219 pp.

★5251★ RARE Center for Tropical Bird Conservation Annual Report
RARE Center for Tropical Bird Conservation
19th & Parkway
Philadelphia, PA 19103
Phone: (215)299-1182

★5252★ RARE Center for Tropical Bird Conservation Special Report
RARE Center for Tropical Bird Conservation
19th & Parkway
Philadelphia, PA 19103
Phone: (215)299-1182
Frequency: Periodic.

★5253★ Record Book of Trophy Animals
Safari Club Intl.
4800 W. Gates Pass Rd.
Tucson, AZ 85745
Phone: (602)620-1220
Fax: (602)622-1205

★5254★ Recoverable Materials and Energy from Industrial Waste Streams
Amer. Water Works Assn.
666 W. Quincy Ave.
Denver, CO 80235
Phone: (303)794-7711
Fax: (303)794-7310
Editor(s): Fran V. Kremer and Larry Fradkin. ***Frequency:*** 1987.

★5255★ Recycle!: A Handbook for Kids
Little, Brown, & Co., Inc.
34 Beacon St.
Boston, MA 02108
Phone: (617)227-0730
Editor(s): Gail Gibbons. ***Frequency:*** 1992. Explains the process of recycling from start to finish an discusses what happens to paper, glass, aluminum cans, and plastic when they are recycled into new products.

★5256★ The Recycler's Handbook: Simple Things You Can Do
Earth-Works Press
1400 Shattuck Ave. #25
Berkeley, CA 94709
Frequency: 1990. ***Price:*** $4.95.

★5257★ Recycling
Children's Press
5440 N. Cumberland Ave.
Chicago, IL 60656
Phone: (312)693-0800
Fax: (312)693-0574
Editor(s): Joan Kalbacken and Emilie U. Lepthien. ***Frequency:*** 1991. Shows how the ever-growing tide of refuse threatens the environment and wastes resources, and how recycling helps in conservation efforts.

★5258★ Recycling
Children's Press
5440 N. Cumberland Ave.
Chicago, IL 60656
Phone: (312)693-0800
Fax: (312)693-0574
Editor(s): Jean F. Blashfield and Wallace B. Black. ***Frequency:*** 1991. Discusses the advantages of recycling and how we can help protect the environment from further damage.

★5259★ Recycling
Gloucester Press
New York, NY
Editor(s): Tony Hare. ***Frequency:*** 1991. Discusses methods of recycling metal, plastic, paper, and glass, and why such conservation efforts are important.

★5260★ Recycling
Chelsea House Publishers
1974 Sproul Rd., Ste. 400
Broomall, PA 19008
Phone: (215)353-5166
Fax: (215)359-1439
Editor(s): Rebecca Stefoff. ***Frequency:*** 1991. Examines the evolution of recycling as a concept, its role in controlling the world's trash problems, and possible future developments.

★5261★ Recycling
Council on Plastics and Packaging in the Environment
1275 K St. NW, Ste. 900
Washington, DC 20005
Phone: (202)789-1310
Fax: (202)289-1389

★5262★ Recycling and Incineration: Evaluating the Choices
Island Press
1718 Connecticut Ave., NW
Ste. 300
Washington, DC 20009
Phone: (202)232-7933
Fax: (202)234-1328
Editor(s): Richard A. Denison and John Ruston (Environmental Defense Fund). ***Frequency:*** 1990.

★5263★ Recycling Garbage
Franklin Watts, Inc.
387 Park Ave., S.
New York, NY 10016
Phone: (212)686-7070
Editor(s): Donna Bailey. ***Frequency:*** 1991. Discusses how various waste materials are recycled and proposes ways for children to act more responsibly toward the environment.

★5264★ Recycling Glass
Franklin Watts, Inc.
387 Park Ave., S.
New York, NY 10016
Phone: (212)686-7070
Editor(s): Judith Condon. ***Frequency:*** 1991. Discusses the problems caused by the manufacture and disposal of glass products, and proposes methods for recycling them to reduce such threats.

★5265★ Recycling in the States: Update 1989
National Solid Wastes Management Assn.
1730 Rhode Island Ave., NW
Ste. 1000
Washington, DC 20036
Frequency: 1989.

★5266★ Recycling: Meeting the Challenge of the Trash Crisis
G.P. Putnam
200 Madison Ave.
New York, NY 10016
Phone: (212)576-8900
Editor(s): Alvin, Virginia, and Robert Silverstein. ***Frequency:*** 1991. Discusses different methods of recycling waste, associated advantages and problems, and the possible future.

★5267★ Recycling Metal
Franklin Watts, Inc.
387 Park Ave., S.
New York, NY 10016
Phone: (212)686-7070
Editor(s): Joy Palmer. ***Frequency:*** 1991. Explains the environmental problems that result from the manufacture and disposal of everyday items made of metal and shows how the recycling of these objects can reduce these threats.

★5268★ Recycling Opportunities
Leading Edge Reports
Cleveland Heights, OH
Editor(s): John J. Breckling, Margaret L. Mullally, and Monica P. Muniak. ***Frequency:*** 1990.

★5269★ Recycling Paper: From Fiber to Finished Product
TAPPI Press
Technology Park/Atlanta
PO Box 105113
Atlanta, GA 30348
Phone: (404)394-6130
Editor(s): Matthew J. Coleman. ***Frequency:*** 1990.

★5270★ Recycling PET: A Guidebook for Community Programs
National Assn. for Plastic Container Recovery
4828 Pkwy. Plaza Blvd., Ste. 260
Charlotte, NC 28217
Phone: (704)357-3250
Fax: (704)357-3260
Toll-Free: 800-NAP-CORP

★5271★ Recycling Plastic
Franklin Watts, Inc.
387 Park Avenue, S.
New York, NY 10016
Phone: (212)686-7070
Editor(s): Joy Palmer. ***Frequency:*** 1990. Discusses the environmental problems caused by the manufacture and disposal of plastic products and shows how the recycling of these products can reduce these threats.

★5272★ Recycling: Recent Publications
Vance Bibliographies
112 N. Charter St.
Monticello, IL 61856
Phone: (217)762-3831
Editor(s): Mary Vance. ***Frequency:*** 1990.

★5273★ The Redesigned Forest
R. & E. Miles Publishers
Int'l Sales
PO Box 1916
San Pedro, CA 90733
Maser, Chris. 1988. ***Price:*** $12.95. 234 pp.

★5274★ Renewable Energy and Developing Countries
State University of New York Press
Maryland
State University Plaza
Albany, NY 12246

★5275★ Replenish the Earth
Humane Society of the United States
Publications Dept.
2100 L St., NW
Washington, DC 20037
Regenstein, Lewis G. 1991. ***Price:*** $14.95. 304 pp.

★5276★ Research Strategies for the U.S. Global Change Research Program
National Academy Press
Maryland
2101 Constitution Ave., N.W.
Washington, DC 20418
National Research Council. 1990. ***Price:*** $33.75. 303 pp.

★5277★ Resource Conservation and Management
Wadsworth Publishing Co.
10 Davis Dr.
Belmont, CA 94002
Phone: (415)595-2350
Editor(s): G. Tyler Miller, Jr. ***Frequency:*** 1989.

★5278★ Resources on Energy and the Environment: A Listing and Description of UCS Publications
State University of New York Press
Maryland
State University Plaza
Albany, NY 12246

★5279★ Restoring Our Earth
Enslow Publishers
Bloy St. & Ramsey Ave.
PO Box 777
Hillside, NJ 07205
Phone: (201)964-4116
Editor(s): Laurence Pringle. ***Frequency:*** 1987.

★5280★ Restoring the Earth: How Americans are Working to Renew Our Damaged Environment
Anchor Publishing
PO Box 30
Homer, AK 99603
Phone: (907)235-6188
Editor(s): John J. Berger. ***Frequency:*** 1987.

★5281★ Rivers at Risk: The Concerned Citizen's Guide to Hydropower
Island Press
Box 7
Covelo, CA
Echeverria, John D., Barrow, Pope and Roos-Collins, Richard. 1989. ***Price:*** $29.95. 220 pp.

★5282★ Rivers, Ponds, and Lakes
Dillon Press, Inc.
242 Portland Ave., S.
Minneapolis, MN 55415
Phone: (612)333-2691
Editor(s): Anita Ganeri. ***Frequency:*** 1992. Describes how modern life is affecting ponds, rivers, and lakes globally and discusses possible ways of saving the endangered species in these waterways.

★5283★ Robert O. Anderson: Oilman/Environmentalist and His Leading Role in the International Environmentalist Movement
Aspen Inst. for Humanistic Studies Publications Office
PO Box 222
Queenstown, MD 21658
Phone: (301)827-7168
Fax: (301)827-9174
Editor(s): Jack Raymond. ***Frequency:*** 1988.

★5284★ Ronald Reagan and the Public Lands: America's Conservation Debate, 1979-1984
Texas A & M Univ. Press
Lewis St.
Drawer C
College Station, TX 77843
Phone: (409)845-1436
Editor(s): C. Brant Short. ***Frequency:*** 1989.

★5285★ Rural Environmental Planning for Sustainable Communities
Island Press
Box 7
Covelo, CA 95428
Sargent, Frederic O. et al. 1991. ***Price:*** $39.95. 260 pp.

★5286★ Rush to Burn: Solving America's Garbage Crisis
Island Press
Box 7
Covelo, CA 95428
Newsday. 1989. ***Price:*** $22.95. 269 pp.

★5287★ Sacred Mountain of the World
Sierra Club Books
Maryland
100 Bush St., 13th Fl.
San Francisco, CA 94104
Bernbaum, Edwin. 1990. ***Price:*** $50. 291 pp.

★5288★ Salvaging the Future: Waste-Based Production
Institute for Local Self-Reliance
2425 18th St., NW
Washington, DC 20009
Phone: (202)232-4108
Editor(s): Caroline Rennie and Alair MacLean. ***Frequency:*** 1989.

★5289★ Save Our Planet: 750 Everyday Ways You Can Help Clean Up the Earth
Dell Publishing Co.
666 Fifth Ave.
New York, NY 10103
Phone: (212)765-6500
Editor(s): Diane MacEachern. ***Frequency:*** 1990.

★5290★ Save the Earth: An Action Handbook for Kids
Alfred A. Knopf, Inc.
201 E. 50th Ave.
New York, NY 10022
Phone: (201)751-2600
Editor(s): Betty Miles. ***Frequency:*** 1991. An overview of the environmental problems of land, atmosphere, water, energy, plants, animals, and people. Includes projects and a section on becoming an environmental activist.

★5291★ Save-the-Redwoods League Brochure
Save-the-Redwoods League
114 Sansome St., Rm. 605
San Francisco, CA 94104
Phone: (415)362-2352
Frequency: Annual.

★5292★ Saving America's Countryside: A Guide to Rural Conservation
Johns Hopkins Univ. Press
701 W. 40th St., Ste. 275
Baltimore, MD 21211
Phone: (301)338-6900
Fax: (301)338-6998
Editor(s): Samuel N. Stokes and Elizabeth Watson. ***Frequency:*** 1989.

★5293★ Saving Our Wetlands and Their Wildlife
Franklin Watts, Inc.
387 Park Ave., S.
New York, NY 10016
Phone: (212)686-7070
Editor(s): Karen Liptak. ***Frequency:*** 1991. Describes different types of wetlands and their wildlife, including endangered plants and animals, explaining the environmental threats to the wetlands themselves.

★5294★ Saving the Earth: A Citizen's Guide to Environmental Action
Alfred A. Knopf, Inc.
201 E. 50th St.
New York, NY 10022
Phone: (201)751-2600
Editor(s): Will Steger and Jon Bowermaster. ***Frequency:*** 1990.

★5295★ Saving the Forests: A Rabbit's Story
Children's Press
5440 N. Cumberland Ave.
Chicago, IL 60656
Phone: (312)693-0800

Fax: (312)693-0574
Editor(s): Janet Riehecky. *Frequency:* 1990. Sniffles the rabbit is angry when people carelessly destroy his beautiful forest home.

★5296★ Saving the Tropical Forests
Island Press
Box 7
Covelo, CA 95428
Gradwohl, Judith and Greenberg, Russell. Smithsonian Institution. 1988. *Price:* $24.95. 207 pp.

★5297★ Seed Listing
Native Seeds/SEARCH
2509 N. Campbell Ave., No. 325
Tucson, AZ 85719
Phone: (602)327-9123
Frequency: Annual.

★5298★ Seeds of Change
Bradbury Press
866 Third Ave.
New York, NY 10022
Phone: (212)702-2000
Editor(s): Sarah Sargent. *Frequency:* 1989. Rachel discovers the beauties and dangers of a swamp when she travels to Georgia with her father who plans to convert the swamp into a theme park.

★5299★ Setting National Priorities: Policy for the Nineties
Brookings Institution
Publications Dept.
1775 Massachusetts Ave., N.W.
Washington, DC 20036-2188
Aaron, Henry J. *Frequency:* 1990. *Price:* $11.95.

★5300★ Shading Our Cities
Island Press
Box 7
Covelo, CA 95428
Editor(s): Moll, Gary and Ebenreck, Sara. 1989. *Price:* $34.95. 330 pp.

★5301★ The Shaping of Environmentalism in America
University of Washington Press
PO Box 50096
Seattle, WA 98145-5096
Phone: (206)543-4050
Editor(s): Victor B. Scheffer. *Frequency:* 1991.

★5302★ Shopping for a Better Environment: A Brand Name Guide to Environmentally Responsible Shopping
Meadowbrook Press, Inc.
18318 Minnetonka Blvd.
Deephaven, MN 55391
Phone: (612)473-5400
Editor(s): Laurence Tasaday. *Frequency:* 1991.

★5303★ Shopping for a Better World
Council on Economic Priorities
30 Irving Pl.
New York, NY 10003
Phone: (212)420-1133
Fax: (212)420-0988
Guide to socially responsible supermarket shopping. *Frequency:* Annual.

★5304★ The Shrinking Planet-U.S. Information Technology and Sustainable Development
State University of New York Press
Maryland
State University Plaza
Albany, NY 12246
Elkington, John and Shopley, Jonathan. 1988. *Price:* $12.50. 78 pp.

★5305★ Sierra Club Legal Defense Fund Annual Report
Sierra Club Legal Defense Fund
2044 Fillmore St.
San Francisco, CA 94115
Phone: (415)567-6100

★5306★ Simple in Means, Rich in Ends: Practicing Deep Ecology
Peregrine Smith Books
Salt Lake City, UT
Editor(s): Bill Devall. *Frequency:* 1988.

★5307★ Social Science in Natural Resource Management Systems
Westview Press, Inc.
5500 Central Ave.
Boulder, CO 80301
Phone: (303)444-3541
Fax: (303)449-3356
Editor(s): Marc L. Miller, Richard P. Gale, and Perry J. Brown. *Frequency:* 1987. Social behavior and natural resources series.

★5308★ Solar Hydrogen: Moving Beyond Fossil Fuels
State University of New York Press
Maryland
State University Plaza
Albany, NY 12246
Ogden, Joan M. Williams, Robert H. *Price:* $10.00. 123 pp.

★5309★ Solar Power: Energy for Today & Tomorrow
State University of New York Press
Maryland
State University Plaza
Albany, NY 12246

★5310★ Solid Waste Disposal and Reuse in the United States
CRC Press, Inc.
2000 Corporate Blvd., NW
Boca Raton, FL 33431
Phone: (407)994-0555
Editor(s): Ishwar P. Murarka. *Frequency:* 1987.

★5311★ Solid Waste Education Recycling Directory
Lewis Publishers, Inc.
121 S. Main St.
PO Drawer 519
Chelsea, MI 48118
Phone: (313)475-8619
Editor(s): Teresa Jones. *Frequency:* 1990.

★5312★ Solid Waste Recycling: The Complete Resource Guide
Bureau of Natl. Affairs
Washington, DC
Frequency: 1990.

★5313★ The Solution to Pollution: 101 Things You Can Do to Clean Up Your Environment
MasterMedia Ltd.
215 Park Ave., S.
Ste. 1601
New York, NY 10003
Phone: (212)260-5600
Fax: (212)489-6944
Editor(s): Laurence Sombke. *Frequency:* 1990.

★5314★ The Solution to Pollution: Your Personal Environmental Handbook to Recycling and Cleaning Up Your Home
MasterMedia Ltd.
215 Park Ave., S.
Ste. 1601
New York, NY 10003
Phone: (212)260-5600
Fax: (212)489-6944
Editor(s): Laurence Sombke. *Frequency:* 1990.

★5315★ Southern Exposure: Deciding Antarctica's Future
State University of New York Press
Maryland
State University Plaza
Albany, NY 12246
Kimball, Lee A. 1990. *Price:* $10.00. 39 pp.

★5316★ Starting a Land Trust
Land Trust Alliance
900 17th St. NW, Ste. 410
Washington, DC 20006
Phone: (202)785-1410
Fax: (202)785-1408

★5317★ The State of the Environment
United Nations Environment Programme

Prepared by Essam El-Hinnawi and Manzur H. Hashmi. *Frequency:* 1987.

★5318★ State of the Environment: A View Toward the Nineties
Conservation Found.
1250 24th St., NW
Washington, DC 20037
Phone: (202)293-4800
Fax: (202)293-9211
Frequency: 1987. A report from the Conservation Foundation sponsored by the Charles Stewart Mott Foundation.

★5319★ State of the World-1991
Worldwatch Institute
Publications Dept.
1776 Massachusetts Ave., NW
Washington, DC 20036
Brown, Lester R. 1991. *Frequency:* Annually. *Price:* $10.95. 254 pp.

★5320★ Statement of Policy and Practices for Conservation of Soil
National Wildlife Fed. Corporate Conservation Coun.
1400 16th St. NW
Washington, DC 20036
Phone: (202)797-6870
Fax: (202)797-6871

★5321★ Statement of Policy and Practices for Protection of Wetlands
National Wildlife Fed. Corporate Conservation Coun.
1400 16th St. NW
Washington, DC 20036
Phone: (202)797-6870
Fax: (202)797-6871

★5322★ Steering a New Course Transportation, Energy, and the Environment
State University of New York Press
Maryland
State University Plaza
Albany, NY 12246
Gordon, Deborah. 1991. ***Price:*** $9.50. 230 pp.

★5323★ Student Conservation Association Evaluation Report
Student Conservation Assn.
Box 550
Charlestown, NH 03603
Phone: (603)826-4301
Fax: (603)826-7755
Frequency: Annual.

★5324★ Student Conservation Association Listing of Available Positions
Student Conservation Assn.
Box 550
Charlestown, NH 03603
Phone: (603)826-4301
Fax: (603)826-7755
Frequency: Annual.

★5325★ Summary of Government Affairs Seminar
Air and Waste Management Assn.
PO Box 2861
Pittsburgh, PA 15230
Phone: (412)232-3444
Fax: (412)232-3450
Frequency: Annual.

★5326★ Superfund Update: A Comprehensive Guide to EPA Settlement Policies and Title III Reporting
Aspen Publishers, Inc.
1600 Research Blvd.
Rockville, MD 20850
Phone: (301)251-5000
Frequency: 1987.

★5327★ A Survey of U.S. Based Efforts to Research and Conserve Biological Diversity in Developing Country
State University of New York Press
Maryland
State University Plaza
Albany, NY 12246
Abramovitz, Janet N. 1989. ***Price:*** $10.00. 71 pp.

★5328★ Sustainable Development: A Guide to Our Common Future
Global Tomorrow Coalition
Publications Dept.
1325 G St., NW, Ste. 915
Washington, DC 20005-3104
Lebel, Gregory G., and Kane, Hal. Report of the World Commission on Environment and Development. 1989. ***Price:*** $7.00. 77 pp.

★5329★ Sustainable Development: A New Path for Progress
Global Tomorrow Coalition
Publications Dept.
1325 G St., NW, Ste. 915
Washington, DC 20005-3104
Lesh, Donald R. and Lowrie, Diane G. 1990. ***Price:*** $15. 160 pp.

★5330★ Sustaining Earth: Response to the Environmental Threat
St. Martin's Press, Inc.
175 Fifth Ave.
New York, NY 10010
Phone: (212)674-5151
Editor(s): D.J.R. Angell, J.D. Comer, and M.L.N. Wilkinson. ***Frequency:*** 1991.

★5331★ Sustaining the Earth
Harvard Univ. Press
79 Garden St.
Cambridge, MA 02138
Phone: (617)495-2600
Editor(s): John Young. ***Frequency:*** 1990.

★5332★ Take a Hike: The Sierra Club Kids Guide to Hiking and Backpacking
Little, Brown and Co.
Children's Books/Sales
34 Beacon St.
Boston, MA 02108-1493
Foster, Lynne. 1991. ***Price:*** $8.95. 176 pp.

★5333★ Taking a Stand Against Environmental Pollution
Franklin Watts, Inc.
387 Park Ave., S.
New York, NY 10016
Phone: (212)686-7070
Editor(s): David E. Newton. ***Frequency:*** 1990. Examines current environmental issues and suggests ways to become involved in solving problems with pollution.

★5334★ Taking Sides: Clashing Views on Controversial Environmental Issues
Dushkin Publishing Group, Inc.
Sluice Dock
Guilford, CT 06437
Phone: (203)453-4351
Editor(s): Theodore D. Goldfarb. ***Frequency:*** 1987.

★5335★ Taking Stock: The Tropical Forestry Action Plan After Five Years
Island Press
Sales Dept.
PO Box 7
Covelo, CA 95428
Winterbottom, Robert. 1990. ***Price:*** $12.50. 59 pp.

★5336★ Tallgrass Prairie Alliance
Tallgrass Prairie Alliance
4101 W. 54th Terrance
Shawnee Mission, KS 66205
Frequency: Annual.

★5337★ Technology and Environment
National Acad. Press
2101 Constitution Ave., NW
Washington, DC 20418
Phone: (202)334-3318
Editor(s): Jesse H. Ausubel and Hedy E. Sladovich. ***Frequency:*** 1989.

★5338★ Technology Transfer: EPA Office of Research and Development, Technology Transfer and Regulatory Support
Environmental Protection Agency
Department of Public Affairs
401 M St., SW
Washington, DC 20460

★5339★ Teenage Mutant Ninja Turtles ABC's for a Better Planet
Random House, Inc.
201 E. 50th St.
New York, NY 10022
Phone: (212)751-2600
Editor(s): J.K. Rosser. ***Frequency:*** 1991. The renowned warrior turtles use the alphabet to inform readers of the problems of pollution and environmental degradation, and what children can do to help protect the environment and the Earth's resources. Based on the Teenage Mutant Ninja Turtles characters and comic books created by Kevin Eastman and Peter Laird.

★5340★ Think About the Environment
Walker & Co.
720 Fifth Ave.
New York, NY 10019
Phone: (212)265-3632
Editor(s): Cathryn Jakobson. ***Frequency:*** 1991. Describes the history of the environmental movement, its successes and failures, and the problems which continue to fall on us all.

★5341★ This Planet is Mine: Teaching Environmental Awareness and Appreciation to Children
Simon & Schuster, Inc.
Simon & Schuster Bldg.
1230 Ave. of the Americas
New York, NY 10020
Phone: (212)698-7000
Editor(s): Mary Metzger and Cinthya P. Whittaker. ***Frequency:*** 1991.

★5342★ To Breathe Free: Eastern Europe's Environmental Crisis
Wilson Center Press
Washington, DC
Editor(s): Joan DeBardeleben. ***Frequency:*** 1991.

★5343★ Top Guns and Toxic Whales: Our Security, Our Environment
Chelsea Green Publishing Co.
Rte. 113
PO Box 130
Post Mills, VT 05058
Phone: (802)333-9073
Fax: (802)333-9092
Editor(s): Gwyn Prins and Robbie Stamp. ***Frequency:*** 1991.

★5344★ Toxic Waste
Gloucester Press
New York, NY
Editor(s): Tony Hare. ***Frequency:*** 1991. Examines the origins of toxic waste, both in industry and the home, and explains what we can do to avoid some of its dangers.

★5345★ Toxic Waste: Earth Alert Series
Maxwell Macmillan International Publishing Group
Export Div.
28100 US Hwy. 19 N., Ste. 200
Clearwater, FL 34621
Gold, Susan Dudley. 1990. Crestwood House. ***Price:*** $10.95. 47 pp.

★5346★ Tracking Hazardous Substances at Industrial Facilities: Engineering Mass Balance Versus Materials
National Academy Press
Maryland
2101 Constitution Ave., N.W.
Washington, DC 20418
National Research Council. 1990. ***Price:*** $18. 100 pp.

★5347★ Transactions of Annual North American Wildlife and Natural Resources Conference
Wildlife Management Inst.
1101 14th St. NW, Ste. 725
Washington, DC 20005
Phone: (202)371-1808

★5348★ Trash!
Carolrhoda Books, Inc.
241 First Ave., N.
Minneapolis, MN 55401
Toll-Free: 800-328-4929
Editor(s): Charlotte Wilcox. ***Frequency:*** 1988. Examines various methods of garbage disposal,

with an emphasis on sanitary landfills, mass burn and recycling.

★5349★ Trashing the Planet: How Science Can Help Us Deal With Acid Rain, Depletion of the Ozone, and Nuclear Waste (Among Other Things)
Regnery Gateway, Inc.
1130 17th St., NW
Washington, DC 20036
Phone: (202)457-0978
Fax: (202)457-0774
Editor(s): Dix Lee Ray and Lou Guzzo. ***Frequency:*** 1990.

★5350★ Tree Crops: A Permanent Agriculture
Island Press
Box 7
Covelo, CA 95428
Smith, J. Russell. Conservation Classics Series. 1987. ***Price:*** $19.95. 428 pp.

★5351★ Trees, Why Do You Wait?
Island Press
Box 7
Covelo, CA 95428
Critchfield, Richard. 1991. ***Price:*** $29.95. 270 pp.

★5352★ The Tropical Rain Forest: A First Encounter
Springer-Verlag
Island Press
1718 Connecticut Ave. NW, Ste 300
Washington, DC 20036
Phone: (202)232-7933
Jacobs, Marius and Oldeman, R.A.A. 1988. ***Price:*** $39.95.

★5353★ Trout Magazine
Trout Unlimited
501 Church St. NE
Vienna, VA 22180
Phone: (703)281-1100
Frequency: Quarterly.

★5354★ Trout Unlimited Chapter and Council Handbook
Trout Unlimited
501 Church St. NE
Vienna, VA 22180
Phone: (703)281-1100
Frequency: Annual.

★5355★ The Trumpeter Swan Society Conference Proceedings and Papers
The Trumpeter Swan Soc.
3800 County Rd. 24
Maple Plain, MN 55359
Phone: (612)476-4663
Fax: (612)559-3287
Frequency: Biennial.

★5356★ Trust for Public Land Annual Report
Trust for Public Land
116 New Montgomery St., 4th Fl.
San Francisco, CA 94105
Phone: (415)495-5660
Fax: (415)495-0541

★5357★ Turning the Tide: Saving the Chesapeake Bay
Island Press
Box 7
Covelo, CA 95428
Horton, Tom and Eichbaum, William M. The Chesapeake Bay Foundation. 1991. ***Price:*** $22.95. 327 pp.

★5358★ Underground Injection Practices Council Proceedings
Underground Injection Practices Coun.
525 Central Park Dr., Ste. 304
Oklahoma City, OK 73105
Phone: (405)525-6146
Frequency: Semiannual.

★5359★ Understanding Environmental Administration and Law
Island Press
Box 7
Covelo, CA 95428
Buck, Susan J. 1991. ***Price:*** $34.95. 224 pp.

★5360★ Unfulfilled Promises: A Citizen Review of the International Water Quality Agreement
Great Lakes United
State University Coll. at Buffalo
Cassety Hall
1300 Elmwood Ave.
Buffalo, NY 14222
Phone: (716)886-0142

★5361★ United Citizens Coastal Protection League Technical Report
United Citizens Coastal Protection League
PO Box 46
Cardiff By The Sea, CA 92007
Phone: (619)753-7477
Frequency: Periodic.

★5362★ The U.S. Global Change Research Program: An Assessment of the FY 1991 Plans
National Academy Press
Maryland
2101 Constitution Ave., N.W.
Washington, DC 20418
National Research Council. 1990. ***Price:*** $18. 128 pp.

★5363★ The Untold Story: The Silver Lining for West Virginia in Acid Rain Control
Center for Clean Air Policy
444 N. Capitol St., Ste. 526
Washington, DC 20001
Phone: (202)624-7709

★5364★ Urban Wildlife Manager's Notebook
National Inst. for Urban Wildlife
10921 Trotting Ridge Way
Columbia, MD 21044
Phone: (301)596-3311
Series of informational leaflets published as a supplement to Urban Wildlife News. ***Frequency:*** Quarterly.

★5365★ US Energy Today and in the Nineties
National Coun. for Environmental Balance
4169 Westport Rd.
PO Box 7732
Louisville, KY 40207
Phone: (502)896-8731
Frequency: Annual.

★5366★ Using Geographic Information Systems for Environmental Decision Making
Georgia Dept. of Natural Resources
Environmental Protection Div.
Georgia Geologic Survey

Editor(s): William H. McLemore and S. Jack Alhadeff. ***Frequency:*** 1988.

★5367★ Valuing Health Risks, Costs, and Benefits for Environmental Decision Making: Report of a Conference
National Academy Press
Maryland
2101 Constitution Ave., N.W.
Washington, DC 20418
Hammond, P. Brett and Coppock, Rob. 1990. ***Price:*** $24. 244 pp.

★5368★ Vanishing Arctic: Alaska's National Wildlife Refuge
State University of New York Press
Maryland
State University Plaza
Albany, NY 12246
Wilderness Society. 1988. 43 pp.

★5369★ Vanishing Habitats
Gloucester Press
New York, NY
Editor(s): Tony Hare. ***Frequency:*** 1991. Examines the life-threatening changes in the natural habitat of a variety of animals and explores ways in which these endangered species can be preserved and protected.

★5370★ Voices for the Land: An Environmental Reader
Allyn and Bacon, Inc.
7 Wells Ave.
Newton, MA 01890
Phone: (617)455-1200
Editor(s): Sarah Morgan and Dennis Okerstrom. ***Frequency:*** 1992.

★5371★ War on Waste: Can America Win Its Battle With Garbage?
Island Press
Box 7
Dept. 4H1
Covelo, CA 95428
Blumberg, Louis and Gottlieb, Robert. ***Price:*** $19.95. 325 pp.

★5372★ Washington's Wild Rivers: The Unfinished Work
Mountaineers Books
Maryland
306 2nd Ave. W
Seattle, WA 98119
McNulty, Tim and OHara, Pat. 1990. ***Price:*** $35. 144 pp.

★5373★ Waste
Steck-Vaughn Co.
PO Box 26015
Austin, TX
Phone: (512)343-8227
Editor(s): Kay Davies and Wendy Oldfield. ***Frequency:*** 1992. Examines various aspects of waste and pollution, including water waste, water pollution, oil spills, air pollution, rust, and recycling.

★5374★ Waste and Recycling
Steck-Vaughn Co.
PO Box 26015
Austin, TX 78755
Phone: (512)343-8227
Editor(s): Barbara James. ***Frequency:*** 1989. Discusses types of waste, including domestic, industrial, agricultural, and radioactive, and how it can be handled and controlled.

★5375★ Waste Disposal and Recycling
Gloucester Press
New York, NY
Editor(s): Sue Becklake. ***Frequency:*** 1991. A look at such waste disposal problems as overflowing landfills and hazardous waste and possible solutions for them, primarily recycling.

★5376★ Waste Not, Want Not: State and Federal Roles in Source Reduction and Recycling of Solid Waste
Northeast-Midwest Inst.
218 D St., SE
Washington, DC 20003
Editor(s): Carol Andress. ***Frequency:*** 1989.

★5377★ Wasting Assets: Natural Resources in the National Income Accounts
State University of New York Press
Maryland
State University Plaza
Albany, NY 12246
Repetto, Robert, Magrath, William, and Wells, Michael. ***Price:*** $10. 68 pp.

★5378★ Wasting Water
Franklin Watts, Inc.
387 Park Ave., S.
New York, NY 10016
Phone: (212)686-7070
Editor(s): Donna Bailey. ***Frequency:*** 1991. Discusses how water is wasted and how it can be conserved and used more effectively.

★5379★ The Water Planet
Crown Publishers/Random House
201 E. 50th St.
New York, NY 10022
Phone: (212)751-2600
Toll-Free: 800-726-0600
Editor(s): Lyall Watson. ***Frequency:*** 1988. ***Price:*** $30.

★5380★ Waterman's Boy
Bradbury Press
866 Third Ave.
New York, NY 10022
Phone: (212)702-2000
Editor(s): Susan Sharpe. ***Frequency:*** 1990. Two Boys from a small town on the Chesapeake Bay help a scientist interested in cleaning up the water for the benefit of animals, plants, and people, while risking parental disapproval of people with too much education and of outsiders' interference in their means of earning a living.

★5381★ Were You a Wild Duck, Where Would You Go?
Stewart, Tabori & Chang, Publishers
740 Broadway
New York, NY 10003
Phone: (212)460-5000
Fax: (212)995-0582
Editor(s): George Mendoza. ***Frequency:*** 1990. A wild duck narrator looks at the past when the environment was bountiful, serarches through today's polluted environment for a home, and encourages saving and restoring the environment for the future.

★5382★ Wetland Creation and Restoration
Island Press
Box 7
Covelo, CA 95428
Editor(s): Kusler, Jon A. and Kentula, Mary E. 1990. ***Price:*** $60. 594 pp.

★5383★ The Whale War
Sierra Club Books
Maryland
100 Bush St., 13th Fl.
San Francisco, CA 94014
Day, David. 1987. ***Price:*** $9.95. 168 pp.

★5384★ What a Load of Trash!
Millbrook Press
Brookfield, CT
Editor(s): Steve Skidmore. ***Frequency:*** 1990. Humorous illustrations accompany a discussion of the problems of waste disposal and of recycling as one possible solution.

★5385★ Whatever Happened to Ecology?
Sierra Club Books
730 Polk St.
San Francisco, CA 94109
Phone: (415)776-2211
Editor(s): Stephanie Mills. ***Frequency:*** 1989.

★5386★ Where Does Garbage Go?
Gareth Stevens, Inc.
7317 W. Green Tree Rd.
Milwaukee, WI 53223
Phone: (414)466-7550
Fax: (414)466-2951
Editor(s): Isaac Asimov. ***Frequency:*** 1991. Briefly examines how we get rid of the things we throw away, describing some of the problems and solutions of waste disposal.

★5387★ Who Really Killed Cock Robin?: An Ecological Mystery
HarperCollins Inc.
10 E. 53rd St.
New York, NY 10022
Phone: (212)207-7000
Editor(s): Jean Craighead George. ***Frequency:*** 1991. Eighth-grader Tony Isidoro follows a trail of environmental clues to try and figure out what ecological imbalances might have caused the death of the town's best-known robin.

★5388★ Whole Earth Ecology: The Best of Environmental Tools and Ideas
Harmony Books
225 Park Ave., S.
New York, NY 10003
Phone: (212)254-1600
Editor(s): J. Baldwin. ***Frequency:*** 1990.

★5389★ Why Waste a Second Chance?: A Small Town Guide to Recycling
National Assn. of Towns and Townships
1522 K St., NW, Ste. 730
Washington, DC 20005
Phone: (202)737-5200
Editor(s): National Center for Small Communities. ***Frequency:*** 1989.

★5390★ Wild by Law: The Sierra Club Legal Defense Fund and the Places It Has Saved
Sierra Club Books
Maryland
100 Bush St., 13th Fl.
San Francisco, CA 94104
Clifton, Carr, and Turner, Tom. 1990. ***Price:*** $50. 154 pp.

★5391★ The Wilderness Society Annual Report
The Wilderness Soc.
900 17th St. NW
Washington, DC 20006-2596
Phone: (202)833-2300
Fax: (202)429-3958

★5392★ Wildlands: Their Protection and Management in Economic Development
World Bank Publications
1818 H St., NW
Washington, DC 20433
Phone: (202)473-2943
Fax: (202)417-0482
Editor(s): George Ledec and Robert Goodland. ***Frequency:*** 1988.

★5393★ Wildlife and Habitats in Managed Landscapes
Island Press
P.O. Box 7
Covelo, CA 95428
Rodiek, Jon, editor. 1990. ***Price:*** $24.95. 250 pp.

★5394★ Wildlife Preservation Trust International Annual Report
Wildlife Preservation Trust Intl.
34th St. & Girard Ave.
Philadelphia, PA 19104
Phone: (215)222-3636
Fax: (215)222-2191

★5395★ Wildlife Rehabilitation
National Wildlife Rehabilitators Assn.
12805 St. Croix Trail
Hastin, MN 55033
Phone: (612)437-9194
Conference proceedings. ***Frequency:*** Annual.

★5396★ Winning with Water: Soil Moisture Monitoring for Efficient Irrigation
INFORM
Publications Dept.
381 Park Ave. S.
New York, NY 10016
Richardson, Gail and Mueller-Beilschmidt, Peter. 1988. ***Price:*** $24.95. 192 pp.

★5397★ World Directory of Environmental Organizations: A Handbook of National and International Organizations and Programs—Governmental and Non-governmental —Concerned With Protecting the Earth's Resources
California Inst. of Public Affairs
PO Box 189040
Sacramento, CA 95818
Phone: (916)442-2472
Fax: (916)442-2478
Editor(s): Thaddeus C. Trzyna. ***Frequency:*** 1989.

★5398★ World on Fire: Saving an Endangered Earth
Scribner Educational Publishers
866 Third Ave.
New York, NY 10022
Phone: (212)702-2000
Editor(s): George J. Mitchell. ***Frequency:*** 1991.

★5399★ World Pheasant Association of the U.S.A. Annual Journal
World Pheasant Assn. of the U.S.A.
2412 Arrowmill St.
Los Angeles, CA 90023
Phone: (213)262-5143

★5400★ World Research Foundation Proceedings
World Research Found.
15300 Ventura Blvd., Ste. 405
Sherman Oaks, CA 91403
Phone: (818)907-5483
Frequency: Annual.

★5401★ World Resources 1990-1991: A Guide to the Global Environment
Oxford University Press
200 Madison Ave.
New York, NY 10016
World Resources Institute. 1990. ***Price:*** $17.95. 384 pp.

★5402★ A World to Make: Development in Perspective
State University of New York Press
Maryland
State University Plaza
Albany, NY 12246
Sutton, Francis X. 1989.*Price:* $18.95. 255 pp.

★5403★ World Wildlife Fund Annual Report
World Wildlife Fund
1250 24th St., NW
Washington, DC 20037
Phone: (202)293-4800
Fax: (202)293-9211

★5404★ World, World, What Can I Do?
Morehouse Publishing Co.
78 Danbury Rd.
Wilton, CT 06897
Phone: (203)762-0721
Fax: (203)762-0727
Editor(s): Barbara Shook Hazen. *Frequency:* 1991. A young child discovers, in a rhymed question and answer dialogue, what he can do to help his environment.

★5405★ Worldwatch Paper 75: Reassessing Nuclear Power: The Fallout from Chernobyl
Worldwatch Institute
Publications Dept.
1776 Massachusetts Ave., NW
Washington, DC 20036
Flavin, Christopher. 1987. *Price:* $4. 48 pp.

★5406★ Worldwatch Paper 78: On the Brink of Extinction: Conserving the Diversity of Life
Worldwatch Institute
Publications Dept.
Massachusetts
Washington, DC 20036
Wolf, Edward C. 1987. *Price:* $4. 28 pp.

★5407★ Worldwatch Paper 79: Defusing the Toxics Threat: Controlling Pesticides and Industrial Waste
Worldwatch Institute
Publications Dept.
Massachusetts
Washington, DC 20036
Postel, Sandra. 1987. *Price:* $4. 36 pp.

★5408★ Worldwatch Paper 81: Renewable Energy: Today's Contribution Tomorrow's Promise
Worldwatch Institute
Publications Dept.
Massachusetts
Washington, DC 20036
Shea, Cynthia Pollock. 1988. *Price:* $4. 24 pp.

★5409★ Worldwatch Paper 82: Building on Success: The Age of Energy Efficiency
Worldwatch Institute
Publications Dept.
Massachusetts
Washington, DC 20036
Flavin, Christopher and Durning, Alan B. 1988. *Price:* $4. 38 pp.

★5410★ Worldwatch Paper 83: Reforesting the Earth
Worldwatch Institute
Publications Dept.
Massachusetts
Washington, DC 20036
Postel, Sandra and Heise, Lori. 1988. *Price:* $4. 34 pp.

★5411★ Worldwatch Paper 84: Rethinking the Role of the Automobile
Worldwatch Institute
Publications Dept.
Massachusetts
Washington, DC 20036
Renner, Michael. 1988. *Price:* $4. 36 pp.

★5412★ Worldwatch Paper 87: Protecting Life on Earth: Steps to Save the Ozone Layer
Worldwatch Institute
Publications Dept.
Massachusetts
Washington, DC 20036
Shea, Cynthia Pollock. 1988. *Price:* $4. 24 pp.

★5413★ Worldwatch Paper 89: National Security: The Economic and Environmental Dimensions
Worldwatch Institute
Publications Dept.
Massachusetts
Washington, DC 20036
Renner, Michael. 1989. *Price:* $4. 40 pp.

★5414★ Worldwatch Paper 91: Slowing Global Warming: A World Wide Strategy
Worldwatch Institute
Publications Dept.
Massachusetts
Washington, DC 20036
Flavin, Christopher. 1989. *Price:* $4. 47 pp.

★5415★ Worldwatch Paper 93: Water for Agriculture: Facing the Limits
Worldwatch Institute
Publications Dept.
Massachusetts
Washington, DC 20036
Postel, Sandra. 1989. *Price:* $4. 28 pp.

★5416★ Worldwatch Paper 94: Clearing the Air: A Global Agenda
Worldwatch Institute
Publications Dept.
Massachusetts
Washington, DC 20036
French, Hilary F. 1990. *Price:* $4. 28 pp.

★5417★ Worldwatch Paper 99: Green Revolutions: Environmental Reconstructions in Eastern Europe and the Soviet Union
Worldwatch Institute
Publications Dept.
Massachusetts
Washington, DC 20036
French, Hilary F. 1990. *Price:* $4. 32 pp.

★5418★ Worldwatch Paper 100: Beyond the Petroleum Age: Designing a Solar Economy
Worldwatch Institute
Publications Dept.
Massachusetts
Washington, DC 20036
Flavin, Christopher and Lenssen, Nicholas. 1990. *Price:* $4. 34 pp.

★5419★ Worldwatch Paper 101: Discarding the Throwaway Society
Worldwatch Institute
Publications Dept.
Massachusetts
Washington, DC 20036
Young, John E. 1991. *Price:* $4. 24 pp.

★5420★ Worldwide Hunting Annual
Safari Club Intl.
4800 W. Gates Pass Rd.
Tucson, AZ 85745
Phone: (602)620-1220
Fax: (602)622-1205

★5421★ Worried About Pesticides in Your Water? Here Are the Facts
National Coun. for Environmental Balance
4169 Westport Rd.
PO Box 7732
Louisville, KY 40207
Phone: (502)896-8731
Contact: I. W. Tucker Ph.D., Pres.

★5422★ The Yosemite
Sierra Club Books
San Francisco, CA 94104
Muir, John and Rowell, Galen. 1989. *Price:* $40. 218 pp.

★5423★ Zilya's Secret Plan
Lion Publishing Corp.
1705 Hubbard Ave.
Batavia, IL 60510
Phone: (708)879-0707
Fax: (708)879-0843
Foreign Name: Siljas geheimer Plan *Editor(s):* Ulrich Schaffer. *Frequency:* 1991. A young girl convinces her fellow townspeople to conserve the natural resources of their beautiful valley.

Directories

★5424★ Access America: An Atlas and Guide to the National Parks for Visitors with Disabilities
Northern Cartographic
Box 133
Burlington, VT 05402
Phone: (802)860-2886
About 40 national parks with facilities for visitors with mobility impairments, hearing, visual, or developmental disabilities. ***Editor(s):*** Peter Shea. ***Frequency:*** Irregular; latest edition 1988; next edition expected 1992. ***Price:*** $89.95.

★5425★ The Acid Rain Foundation Resources Directory
The Acid Rain Found.
1410 Varsity Dr.
Raleigh, NC 27606
Phone: (919)828-9443
Guide to informational material on acid rain available from governmental and nongovernmental organizations in the United States, Canada, and abroad, and other sources. ***Frequency:*** Every 18-24 months. ***Price:*** $12/copy.

★5426★ Acid Rain Foundation Speakers Bureau
Acid Rain Foundation, Inc.
1410 Varsity Dr.
Raleigh, NC 27606
Phone: (919)828-9443
Fax: (919)737-3593
More than 400 scientists, educators, economists, naturalists, policy experts, and others available to speak on acid rain (natural precipitation carrying chemical pollutants). ***Editor(s):*** Dr. Harriett Stubbs, Executive Director. ***Frequency:*** Irregular; latest edition August 1984; new edition expected, date not set. ***Price:*** $8.00.

★5427★ Acid Rain Resources Directory
Acid Rain Foundation, Inc.
1410 Varsity Dr.
Raleigh, NC 27606
Phone: (919)737-3311
Fax: (919)737-3593
About 950 agencies and organizations engaged in legislation, education, public information, or some other form of action regarding acid rain (natural precipitation carrying chemical pollutants); international coverage. ***Editor(s):*** Dr. Harriett Stubbs, Executive Director. ***Frequency:*** Irregular; latest edition 1988. ***Price:*** $10.00, plus $3.50 shipping.

★5428★ Air and Waste Management Association Government Agencies Directory
Air and Waste Management Assn.
Box 2861
Pittsburgh, PA 15230
Phone: (412)232-3444
United States and Canadian air pollution control and hazardous waste management agencies and personnel at federal, state or provincial, regional, and county levels, and the national sections of the International Joint Commission. ***Editor(s):*** Harold M. Englund. ***Frequency:*** Annual, April. ***Price:*** $8.00.

★5429★ Air Pollution Control Directory
Amer. Business Directories, Inc.
American Business Information, Inc.
5711 S. 86th Circle
Omaha, NE 68127
Phone: (402)593-4600
Fax: (402)331-1505
Listing of 1,032 air pollution control organizations. ***Frequency:*** Annual. ***Price:*** $85.00, payment with order. Significant discounts offered for standing orders.

★5430★ All State Motor Club Park Guide
Simon & Schuster, Inc.
200 Old Tappan Rd.
Old Tappan, NJ 07675
Phone: (201)767-5937
Toll-Free: 800-223-2348
All national parks, plus about 300 other areas in the National Park Service system; also includes nearby accommodations. ***Editor(s):*** Nelda Pake. ***Frequency:*** Annual, January. ***Price:*** $14.95.

★5431★ Alliance for Environmental Education Center Directory
Alliance for Environmental Education
10751 Ambassador Dr., No. 201
Manassas, VA 22110
Phone: (703)335-1025
Fax: (703)631-1651
Frequency: Periodic.

★5432★ American Academy of Environmental Medicine Directory
Amer. Acad. of Environmental Medicine
PO Box 16106
Denver, CO 80216
Phone: (303)622-9755
Fax: (303)622-4224
Frequency: Annual.

★5433★ American Consulting Engineering Council Engineering Services Directory for Waste Management
Amer. Consulting Engineering Coun. Research & Management Found.
1015 15th St., NW, Ste. 802
Washington, DC 20005
Phone: (202)347-7474
Fax: (202)898-0068
Over 400 engineering companies specializing in waste management. ***Editor(s):*** Brian Land, Analyst. ***Frequency:*** Irregular; previous edition 1979; latest edition May 1986. ***Price:*** $15.00.

★5434★ American Minor Breeds Conservancy—Breeders Directory Livestock
Amer. Minor Breeds Conservancy
PO Box 477
Pittsboro, NC 27312
Phone: (919)542-5704
About 100 member breeders of endangered and uncommon livestock varieties. ***Frequency:*** Annual, spring. ***Price:*** Available to members only.

★5435★ American Oil and Gas Reporter—The American Directory of State Regulatory Agencies Issue
Domestic Petroleum Publishers, Inc.
Box 343
Derby, KS 67037
Phone: (316)681-3560
State oil and natural gas regulatory agencies. ***Editor(s):*** Bill Campbell. ***Frequency:*** Annual, March. ***Price:*** $25.00.

★5436★ American Recycling Market Directory/Reference Manual
Recoup Publishing Ltd.
PO Box 577
Ogdensburg, NY 13669
Phone: (315)471-0707
Fax: (613)448-2268
Toll-Free: 800-267-0707
About 20,000 recycling companies, centers, state and federal government agencies responsible for recycling, and industry associations; limited international coverage. ***Editor(s):*** Robert E. Boulanger, Publisher. ***Frequency:*** Annual, January. ***Price:*** $125.00 (ISSN 0885-2537).

★5437★ Audubon Society Field Guide to the Natural Places of the Mid-Atlantic States
National Audubon Soc.
950 Third Ave.
New York, NY 10022
Phone: (212)832-3200
More than 100 private nature preserves; federal, state, and local parks; Nature

Conservancy lands; and other sites of interest to naturalists. Volume 1 covers coastal areas; volume 2 covers inland areas. ***Editor(s):*** Susannah Lawrence and Barbara Gross. ***Frequency:*** Published 1984. ***Price:*** $11.95 per volume.

★5438★ Audubon Society Field Guide to the Natural Places of the Northeast
Alfred A. Knopf, Inc.
201 E. 50th St.
14th Fl.
New York, NY 10022
Phone: (212)832-3200
More than 100 private nature preserves; federal, state, and local parks; and other sites of interest to naturalists. Volume 1 covers coastal areas; volume 2 covers inland areas. ***Editor(s):*** Steven Kulik et al. ***Frequency:*** Published 1984. ***Price:*** $11.95 per volume.

★5439★ Best's Safety Directory
A.M. Best Company
Ambest Rd.
Oldwick, NJ 08858
Phone: (201)439-2200
Fax: (201)439-3363
More than 2,300 manufacturers and distributors of safety, industrial hygiene, security, and pollution control products and services. ***Editor(s):*** Kathleen M. Guindon. ***Frequency:*** Annual, November. ***Price:*** $30.00, plus $4.25 shipping (current edition); $30.00, plus $5.00 shipping (1992 edition).

★5440★ Biomass Directory
Stockton Press
15 E. 26th St., Rm. 1503
New York, NY 10010
Phone: (212)481-1342
Fax: (212)779-9479
Toll-Free: 800-221-2123
Over 2,000 publishers, companies, and organizations involved in the field of biomass conversion of natural wastes into usable energy forms; international coverage. ***Editor(s):*** James Coombs. ***Frequency:*** Published February 1987. ***Price:*** $120.00.

★5441★ Chemicals Directory 1991
Cahners Publishing Company
275 Washington St.
Newton, MA 02158
Phone: (617)964-3030
Fax: (617)558-4327
Manufacturers and suppliers of 7,500 chemicals and raw materials; manufacturers and suppliers of containers and packaging; transportation services and storage facilities; environmental services companies. ***Editor(s):*** Kevin R. Fitzgerald. ***Frequency:*** Annual, September. ***Price:*** $40.00.

★5442★ Chesapeake Bay Education Resources Directory
Mid Atlantic Marine Education Assn.
Virginia Institute of Marine Science Sea Grant Program
Gloucester Point, VA 23062
Phone: (804)642-7172
More than 20 organizations involved with educational or promotional programs about the natural environment in the Chesapeake Bay area, as well as a list of approximately 50 publishers and distributors of educational materials relating to the Chesapeake Bay. ***Editor(s):*** Mary Sparrow. ***Frequency:*** Latest edition July 1985; out of print. ***Price:*** $4.00 (current edition); $3.50 (tentative, 1990 edition).

★5443★ Chesapeake Citizen Directory: A Guide to Agencies and Organizations
Alliance for Chesapeake Bay
6600 York Rd.
Baltimore, MD 21212
Phone: (301)377-6270
Fax: (301)377-7144
Toll-Free: 800-662-CRIS
Over 400 agencies and organizations in Pennsylvania, Maryland, Virginia, and the District of Columbia which are involved in the management of Chesapeake Bay, including the removal of waste and toxins. ***Editor(s):*** Frances Flanigan, Director. ***Frequency:*** Biennial, summer of even years. ***Price:*** $15.00.

★5444★ Citizen's Directory for Water Quality Abuses
Izaak Walton League of America
1401 Wilson Dr., Level B
Arlington, VA 22209
Phone: (703)528-1818
About 150 environmental agencies, including about 500 state and regional offices interested in providing quality control by eliminating pollution and dumping of wastes into water resources; includes hotlines. ***Editor(s):*** Karen Firehock. ***Frequency:*** Annual, September. ***Price:*** $2.00 (for all states); $1.00 (one state only).

★5445★ City Currents—Resource Recovery Activities Issue
HCI Publications
410 Archibald St.
Kansas City, MO 64111
Over 100 operating or proposed resource recovery plants in the United States and Canada. ***Editor(s):*** Ronald W. Musselwhite. ***Frequency:*** Annual, October. ***Price:*** $25.00.

★5446★ Co-Op America's Business and Organizational Member Directory
Co-Op America
2100 M St. NW, No. 403
Washington, DC 20063
Phone: (202)872-5307
Toll-Free: 800-424-2667
500 small businesses, co-operatives, and nonprofit organizations in the U.S. that produce environmentally benign products such as non-toxic household products, plant based paints, organic foods, and energy saving devices. ***Editor(s):*** Jyotsna Screenivasan and Cindy Mitlo. ***Frequency:*** Annual, fall. ***Price:*** $2.00 (ISSN 0885-9930).

★5447★ Committee for Sustainable Agriculture—Ecological Farming Conference Participants Directory
Committee for Sustainable Agriculture
Box 1300
Colfax, CA 95713
Phone: (916)346-2777
Fax: (916)346-6884
About 800 organic farmers, farm suppliers and consultants, produce handlers, researchers, extension agents, students, organization representatives, and others who attended the annual Ecological Farming Conference. Attendees are primarily from California. ***Editor(s):*** Otis Wollan. ***Frequency:*** Annual, February. ***Price:*** $5.00, postpaid.

★5448★ Complete Guide to America's National Parks: The Official Visitor's Guide of the National Park Foundation
National Park Found.
1101 17th St., NW, Ste. 1008
Washington, DC 20036
Phone: (202)785-4500
Fax: (202)785-3539
Approximately 370 areas administered by the National Park Service. ***Frequency:*** Biennial, January of even years. ***Price:*** $11.95.

★5449★ Congressional Directory: Environment
Grupenhoff Communications
6410 Rockledge Dr., Ste. 203
Bethesda, MD 20817
Phone: (301)571-9793
Fax: (301)530-8910
Members of the U.S. Congress; also includes congressional committees dealing with the environment. ***Editor(s):*** John T. Grupenhoff and Betty Farley. ***Frequency:*** Biennial, April of odd years. ***Price:*** $87.50.

★5450★ Conservation and Service Corps Profiles
Human Environment Center
1001 Connecticut Ave. NW, Ste. 827
Washington, DC 20036
Phone: (202)331-8387
Frequency: Semiannual.

★5451★ Conservation Directory
National Wildlife Fed.
1400 16th St., NW
Washington, DC 20036
Phone: (703)790-4402
Fax: (703)442-7332
Toll-Free: 800-432-6564
About 90 federal agencies, 467 national and international organizations, 1,000 state government agencies and citizens groups, and 113 Canadian agencies and groups concerned with conservation of natural resources and preservation of the environment; colleges and universities with environmental education programs. ***Editor(s):*** Rue E. Gordon. ***Frequency:*** Annual, January. ***Price:*** $18.00, plus $3.95 shipping; payment must accompany orders from individuals.

★5452★ Contemporary World Issues Series
ABC-CLIO
PO Box 1911
Santa Barbara, CA 93116-1911
Phone: (805)963-4221
Toll-Free: 800-422-2546
Series of reference handbooks with the following individual titles: "Environmental Hazards: Radioactive Materials and Wastes: A Reference Handbook," and "Nuclear Energy Policy: A Reference Handbook." Each publication includes a directory section of organizations involved in work on that topic. ***Editor(s):*** E. Willard Miller and Ruby M. Miller (Environmental), Lucille Whalen (Rights), Earl R. Kruschke and Byron M. Jackson (Nuclear), Marie Costa (Literacy), Mary Ellen Hombs (Homelessness). ***Frequency:*** Published between 1988 and 1990. ***Price:*** $39.00 each.

★5453★ Coordination Directory of State and Federal Agency Water Resources Officials Missouri Basin
Missouri Basin States Assn.
c/o J. Michael Jess
Box 94676
Lincoln, NE 68509
Phone: (402)471-2363
More than 300 state and federal government officials with responsibilities in water resources in the 10-state Missouri River Basin area. ***Editor(s):*** Dave Peterson et al. ***Frequency:*** Irregular; previous edition 1984; latest edition spring 1987. ***Price:*** $5.00.

★5454★ Criteria Pollutant Point Source Directory
North Amer. Water Office
Box 174
Lake Elmo, MN 55042
Phone: (612)770-3861
Over 1,600 utilities, smelters, refineries, and other facilities that emit more than 1,000 tons of particulates, sulfur oxides, nitrogen oxides, volatile organic compounds, or carbon monoxide. ***Editor(s):*** George Crocker, Director. ***Frequency:*** Biennial, January of even years. ***Price:*** $33.00.

★5455★ Current Federal Aid Research Report: Wildlife
U.S. Div. of Federal Aid
Fish & Wildlife Service
Department of the Interior
18th & C Sts., NW
Washington, DC 20240
Phone: (703)235-1526
Wildlife research projects funded by the Pittman-Robertson grant program. ***Editor(s):*** Claude Stephens, Writer-Editor. ***Frequency:*** Annual, spring. ***Price:*** Free.

★5456★ Directory of Aquaculture Information Resources
National Agricultural Library
U. S. Department of Agriculture
10301 Baltimore Blvd.
Aquaculture Information Center, Rm. 304
Beltsville, MD 20705
Phone: (301)344-3704
Over 60 libraries, government agencies, and other organizations with special collections in aquaculture which offer information service without undue restriction. ***Frequency:*** Irregular; latest edition December 1982. ***Price:*** $11.95, plus $3.00 shipping (PB83-169474).

★5457★ Directory of Biomass Installations in 13 Southeastern States
Southeastern Regional Biomass Energy Program
Tennessee Valley Authority
CEB 1C
Muscle Shoals, AL 35660
Phone: (205)386-3086
Fax: (205)386-2815
About 1,020 biomass energy and alcohol and methane production facilities in Alabama, Arkansas, Florida, Georgia, Kentucky, Louisiana, Missouri, Mississippi, North Carolina, South Carolina, Tennessee, Virginia, and West Virginia. ***Editor(s):*** Phillip C. Badger, Program Manager. ***Frequency:*** Irregular; latest edition December 1986. ***Price:*** Free.

★5458★ Directory of Commercial Hazardous Waste Treatment and Recycling Facilities
Office of Solid Waste
Environmental Protection Agency
Washington, DC 20460
Phone: (202)475-8710
About 500 commercial facilities that accept hazardous waste for treatment and/or recycling. ***Frequency:*** Irregular; previous edition December 1986; latest edition August 1987. ***Price:*** $23.00, plus shipping (PB88178431).

★5459★ Directory of Environmental Groups in New England
Office of Public Affairs
Region 1
Environmental Protection Agency
John F. Kennedy Federal Building, Rm. 2203
Boston, MA 02203
Phone: (617)565-3187
About 350 nonprofit organizations concerned with the protection of the environment; listings include health planning agencies, land conservation and acquisition associations and firms, state and federal government agencies, nature centers and clubs, zoos, etc. ***Editor(s):*** Evelyn Sullivan. ***Frequency:*** Irregular; previous edition 1988; latest edition May 1990. ***Price:*** Free.

★5460★ Directory of Environmental Information Sources
Government Institutes, Inc.
966 Hungerford Dr., No. 24
Rockville, MD 20850
Phone: (301)251-0638
Fax: (301)251-0638
More than 1,400 federal and state government agencies, professional and scientific organizations, trade associations, periodical, database and other organizations that provide information on the environment. ***Editor(s):*** Thomas F. Sullivan. ***Frequency:*** Irregular; latest edition September 1990. ***Price:*** $65.00, plus $3.00 shipping.

★5461★ Directory of Environmental Investing
Environmental Economics
1026 Irving St.
Philadelphia, PA 19107
Phone: (215)925-7168
Fax: (301)587-1081
Approximately 80 publicly-traded companies, plus Fortune 500 firms involved in environmental services such as air pollution control, asbestos abatement, hazardous waste management, waste testing and analysis, nuclear waste handling, recycling, solid waste disposal, waste-related infrastructure work, waste-to-energy systems, and water treatment. ***Editor(s):*** Michael Silverstein. ***Frequency:*** Annual, July. ***Price:*** $60.00.

★5462★ Directory of Environmental Investing
Environmental Economics
1026 Irving St.
Philadelphia, PA 19017
Phone: (215)925-7168

★5463★ Directory of Federal Contacts on Environmental Protection
Naval Energy and Environmental Support Activity
Department of Navy
Code 112
Port Hueneme, CA 93043
Phone: (805)982-5667
Over 50 federal government agencies engaged in some aspect of environmental protection, including the Navy Department, the Marine Corps, the Transportation Department, and the Environmental Protection Agency. ***Editor(s):*** Patricia Murray. ***Frequency:*** Biennial, even years. ***Price:*** Free.

★5464★ Directory of Field Biologists and Law Enforcement Officers Along the Upper Mississippi River
Upper Mississippi River Conservation Comm.
1830 Second Ave.
Rock Island, IL 61201
Phone: (309)793-5800
Wildlife biologists, fishery biologists, and conservation officers responsible for activities in counties along the Mississippi River in Minnesota, Wisconsin, Iowa, Illinois, and Missouri. ***Editor(s):*** Gail Carmody, Coordinator. ***Frequency:*** Annual, May. ***Price:*** Free.

★5465★ Directory of Forest Tree Nurseries in the United States
Forest Service
Department of Agriculture
Box 96090
Washington, DC 20090
Phone: (202)475-3750
Fax: (202)453-8271
About 360 commercial and governmental nurseries producing forest tree seedlings. ***Frequency:*** Irregular; previous edition 1981; latest edition December 1987. ***Price:*** Free.

★5466★ The Directory of National Environmental Organizations
U.S. Environmental Directories
Box 65156
St. Paul, MN 55165
Over 350 organizations outside of government concerned with the environment and conservation. ***Editor(s):*** John C. Brainard and Roger N. McGrath. ***Frequency:*** Irregular; previous edition July 1988; latest edition spring 1991. ***Price:*** $50.00, postpaid; payment must accompany order.

★5467★ Directory of North American Fisheries and Aquatic Scientists
Amer. Fisheries Soc.
5410 Grosvenor Lane, Ste. 110
Bethesda, MD 20814
Phone: (301)897-8616
Fax: (301)897-8096
Over 10,000 individuals engaged in all aspects of fisheries and related aquatic sciences. ***Editor(s):*** Beth D. McAleer. ***Frequency:*** Irregular; latest edition December 1987; new edition expected 1990. ***Price:*** $25.00, payment with order; $28.50, billed.

★5468★ Directory of Public High Technology Corporations
Amer. Investor, Inc.
311 Bainbridge St.
Philadelphia, PA 19147
Phone: (215)925-2761
2,000 high-technology publicly held corporations in all aspects of computer technology, electronics, aerospace, telecommunications, medical devices and services, biotechnology, artificial intelligence, pharmaceuticals, optics and electro-optics, lasers, chemicals, materials, environmental control, robotics, scientific instruments, and technical services. ***Editor(s):*** Ronald P. Smolin. ***Frequency:*** Annual. ***Price:*** Base edition, $195.00 (ISSN 0738-7369).

★5469★ Directory of Published Proceedings Meetings
InterDok Corp.
173 Halstead Ave.
PO Box 326
Harrison, NY 10528
Phone: (914)835-3506
Fax: (914)835-6757
Approximately 3,000 published proceedings of congresses, conferences, summer schools,

symposia, meetings, and seminars from 1964 to present; separate listing of publishers. "Series SEMT" covers science, engineering, medicine, and technology proceedings; "Series SSH" covers social sciences and humanities proceedings; "Series PCE" covers pollution control and ecology proceedings. ***Frequency:*** "Series SEMT" published ten times yearly with cumulated index supplement published three times yearly; "Series SSH" published quarterly; "Series PCE" published annually. ***Price:*** "Series SEMT," $495.00 per year (ISSN 0012-3293).

★5470★ Directory of Resource Recovery Projects and Services
Institute of Resource Recovery
National Solid Wastes Management Association
1730 Rhode Island Ave., NW, Ste. 1000
Washington, DC 20036
Phone: (202)659-4613
Fax: (202)775-5917
Member firms in the United States active in recovering energy from solid waste materials. ***Editor(s):*** Julie C. Grady. ***Frequency:*** Annual, February. ***Price:*** Free.

★5471★ Directory of Socially Responsible Investments
Funding Exchange
666 Broadway, 5th Fl.
New York, NY 10012
Phone: (212)529-5300

★5472★ Directory of Solar Rating and Certification Corporation Certified Collectors and Solar Water Heating Systems Ratings
Solar Rating & Certification Corp.
777 N. Capital St., NE, Ste. 805
Washington, DC 20002
Phone: (202)408-0660
Nearly 30 manufacturers of solar collectors and water heaters certified by the organization. ***Editor(s):*** Linda Ladas, Administrative Manager. ***Frequency:*** Irregular; previous edition April 1988; latest edition July 1991. ***Price:*** $23.00, plus $2.50 shipping.

★5473★ Directory of Solar Rating and Certification Corporation Certified Solar Collector and System Ratings
Solar Rating & Certification Corp.
777 N. Capitol St., NE, Ste. 865
Washington, DC 20002
Phone: (202)408-0660
About 35 manufacturers of solar collectors and systems certified by the organization. ***Editor(s):*** Linda Ladas, Administrative Manager. ***Frequency:*** Annual, October. ***Price:*** $20.00, plus $3.50 shipping.

★5474★ Directory of Solar-Terrestrial Physics Monitoring Stations
Air Force Geophysics Laboratory
c/o M. A. Shea
Department of Defense
Hanscom Air Force Base, MA 01731
Phone: (617)377-3977
Fax: (617)377-4498
Over 1,000 ground-based observing stations, worldwide, engaged in the monitoring of the solar-terrestrial environment. These stations are part of the MONSEE (Monitoring Sun-Earth Environment) network. ***Editor(s):*** M. A. Shea et al. ***Frequency:*** Irregular; latest edition August 1984; new edition possible 1989 or 1990. ***Price:*** Free.

★5475★ Directory of State Certification Officers for Drinking Water Laboratories
Association of State Drinking Water Administrators
1911 N. Fl. Myer Dr.
Arlington, VA 22209
Phone: (703)524-2428
Fax: (703)524-1453
53 certification officials for drinking water laboratories for each U.S. state and territory. ***Frequency:*** Semiannual. ***Price:*** $17.00.

★5476★ Directory of State Environmental Agencies
Environmental Law Inst.
1616 P St., NW, No. 200
Washington, DC 20036
Phone: (202)328-5150
State and territorial government agencies responsible for environmental supervision, issues, and programs. ***Editor(s):*** Kathryn Hubler and Timothy Henderson. ***Frequency:*** Latest edition September 1985; suspended indefinitely. ***Price:*** $22.50, plus $2.50 shipping (ISSN 0733-6128).

★5477★ Directory of State Waste Management Program Officials
Association of State & Territorial Solid Waste Management Officials (ASTSWMO)
444 N. Capitol St., Ste. 388
Washington, DC 20001
Phone: (202)624-5828
Fax: (202)624-7875
Approximately 60 state and territorial government agencies that regulate solid waste, recycling, site remediation, hazardous waste, and Superfund activities. ***Editor(s):*** Barbara Simcoe, Deputy Director. ***Frequency:*** Annual, October. ***Price:*** $36.00; payment must accompany order.

★5478★ Directory of U.S. and Canadian Scrap Plastics Processors and Buyers
Resource Recycling
Box 10540
Portland, OR 97210
Phone: (503)227-1319
Fax: (503)227-6135
Toll-Free: 800-227-1424
Approximately 200 recycled plastics processors and end users; coverage includes Canada. ***Editor(s):*** Jerry Powell. ***Frequency:*** Annual, spring. ***Price:*** $40.00.

★5479★ Directory of Waste Utilization Technologies in Europe and the United States
Institute for Local Self-Reliance
2425 18th St., NW
Washington, DC 20009
Phone: (202)232-4108
Fax: (202)332-0463
About 80 waste utilization companies offering plastics recycling, mixed waste processing, anaerobic digestion, composting, collection equipment, and pyrolysis technologies in the United States and Europe. ***Editor(s):*** Diana Douglas White. ***Frequency:*** First edition March 1989. ***Price:*** $50.00, plus $2.50 shipping; $25.00 for local community organizations.

★5480★ Directory of Water Resources Expertise
California Water Resources Center
Rubidoux Hall
University of California
Riverside, CA 92521
Phone: (714)787-4327
Over 375 University of California faculty and staff active in water resource research. ***Editor(s):*** Rex J. Woods, Assistant Director. ***Frequency:*** Biennial, summer of odd years. ***Price:*** Free (ISSN 0575-4968).

★5481★ Directory of Water Resources Organizations
National Water Data Exchange
Water Resources Division
U. S. Geological Survey
Department of the Interior
421 National Center
Reston, VA 22092
Phone: (703)860-6031
Nearly 2,000 organizations worldwide that are sources of water data and water-related data, or that provide information about water resources activities. ***Editor(s):*** Cassandra D. Blackwell. ***Frequency:*** Irregular; latest edition 1983.

★5482★ Emergency Response Directory for Hazardous Materials Accidents
Odin Press
Box 536
New York, NY 10021
Phone: (212)744-2538
Over 1,000 federal, state, and local governmental agencies, chemical manufacturers and transporters, hotlines and strike teams, burn care centers, civil defense and disaster centers, and other organizations concerned with the containment and cleanup of chemical spills and other hazardous materials accidents. ***Editor(s):*** Pamela Lawrence. ***Frequency:*** Biennial; odd years. ***Price:*** $34.00.

★5483★ Encyclopedia of Public Affairs Information Sources
Gale Research Inc.
835 Penobscot Bldg.
Detroit, MI 48226-4094
Phone: (313)961-2242
Fax: (313)961-6083
Toll-Free: 800-877-GALE
Telex: 810 221 7086
About 8,000 associations, publications, and databases providing information on 300 public affairs topics such as the environment, public welfare, capital punishment, birth control, housing, poverty, smoking, etc. ***Editor(s):*** James R. Kelly, Desider L. Vikor, and Paul Wasserman. ***Frequency:*** First edition published 1988. ***Price:*** $145.00.

★5484★ Energy and Education Directory of Energy Education Materials Issue
National Science Teachers Assn.
5112 Berwyn Rd., 3rd Fl.
College Park, MD 20740
Phone: (202)328-5800
List of nearly 100 publishers of educational information on energy, including classroom activities, books, videos, software, games, workshops. ***Editor(s):*** Jane M. Ponton. ***Frequency:*** Annual, April. ***Price:*** $3.00.

★5485★ Energy Conservation Products Retail Directory
Amer. Business Directories, Inc.
American Business Information, Inc.
5711 S. 86th Circle
Omaha, NE 68127
Phone: (402)593-4600
Fax: (402)331-1505
Geographical list of 1,371 energy conservation product retailers. ***Frequency:*** Annual. ***Price:*** $85.00, payment with order. Significant discounts offered for standing orders.

★5486★ Energy Education Guide
Amer. Forum for Global Education
45 John St., Ste. 1200
New York, NY 10038
Phone: (212)732-8606
List of groups that provide educational material on energy conservation and alternative forms of energy. ***Editor(s):*** David C. King. ***Price:*** $2.50.

★5487★ Energy Information Centers Directory
U.S. Coun. for Energy Awareness
1776 I St., N.W., Ste. 400
Washington, DC 20006-2495
Phone: (202)293-0770
Fax: (202)785-4019
More than 90 energy information centers located at electric generating plants, research facilities, and other energy-related installations in the United States and Canada. ***Editor(s):*** Patricia Bryant, Director, Industry Communications. ***Frequency:*** Irregular; previous edition 1988; latest edition 1990. ***Price:*** Free.

★5488★ Energy Micro Software Directory
Government Institutes, Inc.
966 Hungerford Dr., No. 24
Rockville, MD 20850
Phone: (301)251-9250
Fax: (301)251-0638
List of about 170 suppliers of computer software designed to save energy. ***Editor(s):*** Dr. Richard F. Hill. ***Frequency:*** Irregular; latest edition July 1985; suspended indefinitely. ***Price:*** $68.00.

★5489★ Energy Research Institute Directory of Energy Alternatives
Energy Research Inst.
6850 Rattlesnake Hammock Rd.
Naples, FL 33962
Phone: (813)793-1922
About 2,200 individuals and companies interested in development of alternative energy sources, particularly alcohol but including wind, methane, solar, biomass, waste, and hydrogen; some international coverage. ***Editor(s):*** J. C. Caruthers, Executive Director. ***Frequency:*** Semi-monthly. ***Price:*** $5.00 per issue; $24.00 per year.

★5490★ EnergyWare: The World Directory of Energy Conservations and Renewable Energy Software for Microcomputers
Wind Books
Box 4008
St. Johnsbury, VT 05819-4008
Phone: (802)748-3360
Fax: (802)748-1327
Toll-Free: 800-522-4485
More than 300 software programs that provide technical and economic analysis of energy problems, projects, and applications for energy conservation. ***Editor(s):*** F. S. Seiler. ***Frequency:*** Biennial, January. ***Price:*** $79.50.

★5491★ The Environment: Books by Small Presses
Small Press Center
20 W. 44th St.
New York, NY 10036
Phone: (212)764-7021
Over 200 small presses that publish books on the environment/natural history. ***Editor(s):*** Paula Matta. ***Frequency:*** Published April 1990. ***Price:*** $6.50, postpaid.

★5492★ Environmental Conservation/ Ecological Organizations Directory
Amer. Business Directories, Inc.
American Business Information, Inc.
5711 S. 86th Circle
Omaha, NE 68127
Phone: (402)593-4600
Fax: (402)331-1505
Geographical list of 1,611 ecology and conservation organizations. ***Frequency:*** Annual. ***Price:*** $105.00, payment with order. Significant discounts offered for standing orders.

★5493★ Environmental Hazards Air Pollution: A Reference Handbook
ABC-CLIO
PO Box 1911
Santa Barbara, CA 93116-1911
Phone: (805)963-4221
Fax: (805)685-6349
Toll-Free: 800-422-2546
Listing of organizations and authorities in field of air pollution. ***Editor(s):*** E. Willard Miller and Ruby Miller. ***Price:*** $39.50.

★5494★ Environmental Information—Environmental Services Directory
Environmental Information Ltd.
4801 W. 81st St., Ste. 119
Bloomington, MN 55437
Phone: (612)831-2473
Over 400 waste-handling facilities, 700 transportation firms, 375 spill response firms, 1,700 consultants, 470 laboratories, 420 soil boring/well drilling firms; also includes incineration services, polychlorinated biphenyl (PCB) detoxification and mobile solvent-recovery services, asbestos services and underground tank services, summaries of states' regulatory programs. ***Editor(s):*** Cary L. Perket. ***Frequency:*** Annual, December. ***Price:*** $275.00, postpaid; payment must accompany order.

★5495★ Environmental Telephone Directory
Government Institutes, Inc.
966 Hungerford Dr., No. 24
Rockville, MD 20850
Phone: (301)251-9250
Over 1,000 federal, regional, and state environmental agencies and officials; United States senators and representatives and their environmental aides; United States Senate and House Committees and Subcommittees dealing with environmental issues. ***Frequency:*** Every 18 months; latest edition December 1989. ***Price:*** $55.00, plus $3.00 shipping.

★5496★ EPA Information Resources Directory
National Technical Information Service
5285 Port Royal Rd.
Springfield, VA 22161
Phone: (703)487-4600
Contacts for environmental information, federal agencies, and commissions; local, national, and international environmental interest groups, including scientific, professional, and advocacy groups; manufacturing and trade associations. ***Frequency:*** Published 1989.

★5497★ Essential Whole Earth Catalog
Point
27 Gate Five Rd.
Sausalito, CA 94965
Phone: (415)332-1716
Includes sections on recyling and land use. ***Editor(s):*** J. Baldwin. ***Frequency:*** Irregular; latest edition 1986. ***Price:*** $18.95.

★5498★ Fibre Market News—Directory of Paper Stock Dealers Issue
GIE Publishing Company
4012 Bridge Ave.
Cleveland, OH 44113
Phone: (216)961-4130
Fax: (216)961-0364
Toll-Free: 800-456-0707
List of approximately 1,500 dealers, brokers, packers, and graders of paper stock in the United States and Canada. Also includes paper mills and end users of recycled paper stock and paperboard. ***Editor(s):*** Dan Sandoval. ***Frequency:*** Annual, January. ***Price:*** $29.00, plus $3.00 shipping; $21.75, plus $3.00 shipping; payment must accompany order.

★5499★ Florida Environet Directory
Friends of the Everglades
202 Park St.
Miami Springs, FL 33166
Phone: (305)888-1230

★5500★ Forest Service Volunteer
Forest Service
Department of Agriculture
Box 96090
Washington, DC 20013
Phone: (202)475-3750
National forests, experiment stations, and state and private forestry directors. Local addresses are provided by another untitled publication which is sent with "Forest Service Volunteer." ***Frequency:*** Irregular; previous edition 1982; latest edition 1984. ***Price:*** Free.

★5501★ Fusion Facilities Directory
Fusion Power Associates
2 Professional Dr., Ste. 248
Gaithersburg, MD 20879
Phone: (301)258-0545
Fax: (301)975-9869
About 40 government and private institutions and laboratories involved in atomic fusion research. ***Editor(s):*** Ruth A. Watkins, Secretary-Treasurer. ***Frequency:*** Biennial. ***Price:*** $20.00.

★5502★ Geothermal World Directory
Sun Words
861 Central Pkwy.
Schenectady, NY 12309
Phone: (518)372-1799
Lists of about 9,000 national and international manufacturers, utilities, governmental agencies, universities, exploration companies, and individuals working in research on, and exploration and development of, geothermal energy. ***Frequency:*** latest editon 1988, suspended indefinitely. ***Price:*** $55.00.

★5503★ Grant Seekers Guide
Moyer Bell Ltd.
RFD 1, Colonial Hill
Mt. Kisco, NY 10549
Phone: (914)666-0084
Fax: (914)666-9384
Toll-Free: 800-759-4100
About 450 funding sources for nonprofit organizations involved in social change, the environment, civil liberties, women's issues, gay issues, AIDS and other causes. ***Editor(s):*** Jill R. Shellow and Nancy C. Stella. ***Frequency:*** Irregular; previous edition 1985; latest edition 1989. ***Price:*** $34.95, cloth; $24.95, paper.

★5504★ Great Lakes Directory of Natural Resource Agencies and Organizations
Center for the Great Lakes
435 N. Michigan Ave., Ste. 1408
Chicago, IL 60611
Phone: (312)645-0901
Over 725 agencies and organizations in the United States and Canada concerned with Great

Lakes natural resource issues. ***Editor(s):*** Paula Ripley. ***Frequency:*** Irregular; latest edition November 1984. ***Price:*** $8.00.

★5505★ Great Lakes Region Biomass Energy Facilities Directory
Council of Great Lakes Governors
310 S. Michigan, 10th Fl.
Chicago, IL 60604
Phone: (312)427-0092
Fax: (312)427-8540
List of approximately 780 biomass energy, alcohol and methane production, crop residue and wood combustion, and waste-to-energy facilities in Illinois, Indiana, Iowa, Michigan, Minnesota, Ohio, and Wisconsin. ***Frequency:*** Irregular; previous edition 1985; latest edition September 1988. ***Price:*** Free.

★5506★ Guide to Experts in Forestry and Natural Resources
Northeastern Forest Experiment Station
Forest Service
United States Department of Agriculture
5 Radnor Corporate Center, Ste. 200
100 Matsonford Rd.
Radnor, PA 19087
Phone: (215)975-4229
Approximately 70 consulting scientists and researchers trained in forestry, biology, economics, plant pathology, entomology, meteorology, genetic engineering, sociology, hydrology, wildlife biology, and other fields pertaining to natural resource conservation. ***Editor(s):*** Jane Gamal-Eldin, Technology Transfer Specialist. ***Frequency:*** Irregular; latest edition fall 1987. ***Price:*** Free.

★5507★ Guide to State Environmental Programs
BNA Books
Bureau of National Affairs (BNA)
1231 25th St., NW
Washington, DC 20037
Phone: (202)452-4531
Fax: (202)452-9186
State regulated programs relating to air pollution, waste management, water quality and use, mining, industrial site selection, utilities, and other environmental concerns; regional offices and laboratories of the Environmental Protection Agency and the Army Corps of Engineers; state economic development agencies; county and regional environmental offices. ***Editor(s):*** Deborah Hitchcock Jessup. ***Frequency:*** Irregular; previous edition 1988; latest edition 1990. ***Price:*** $48.00.

★5508★ Guide to the National Park Areas: Eastern States
Globe Pequot Press
138 W. Main St.
Chester, CT 06412
Phone: (203)526-9571
Fax: (203)526-5748
Toll-Free: 800-243-0495
About 200 national parks in 26 states east of the Mississippi River. ***Editor(s):*** David and Kay Scott. ***Frequency:*** Irregular. ***Price:*** $11.95.

★5509★ Guide to the National Park Areas: Western States
Globe Pequot Press
138 W. Main St.
Chester, CT 06412
Phone: (203)526-9571
Fax: (203)526-5748
Toll-Free: 800-243-0495
About 170 national parks in 25 states west of the Mississippi River. ***Editor(s):*** David and Kay Scott. ***Frequency:*** Irregular. ***Price:*** $12.95.

★5510★ Hazardous Materials Control Directory
Hazardous Materials Control Research Inst.
7237 Hanover Pkwy.
Greenbelt, MD 20770
Phone: (301)587-9390
Frequency: Biennial.

★5511★ Hazardous Waste Consultant Directory of Commercial Hazardous Waste Management Facilities Issue
McCoy and Associates, Inc.
13701 W. Jewell Ave., Ste. 202
Lakewood, CO 80228
Phone: (303)987-0333
List of nearly 130 licensed commerical facilities that process, store, and dispose of hazardous waste material. ***Editor(s):*** Lark H. McCoy. ***Frequency:*** Annual, March/ April. ***Price:*** $90.00.

★5512★ Hazardous Waste Practitioners Directory
Hazardous Waste Action Coalition
c/o American Consulting Engineers Council
1015 15th St., NW, No. 802
Washington, DC 20005
Phone: (202)347-7474
Fax: (202)898-0068
HWAC's 100 member engineering firms responsible for designing cleanup solutions for hazardous waste sites. ***Frequency:*** Annual, November. ***Price:*** $50.00.

★5513★ Hazardous Waste Services Directory
J.J. Keller & Associates, Inc.
145 W. Wisconsin Ave.
Neenah, WI 54957
Phone: (414)722-2848
Fax: (414)727-7516
Toll-Free: 800-558-5011
Over 1,000 firms that provide services related to the handling of dangerous materials, including haulers, processors, disposal sites, operators, laboratories, and consultants. ***Editor(s):*** George McDowell. ***Frequency:*** Base edition supplied upon subscription; semiannual updates. ***Price:*** $95.00.

★5514★ Hazardous Waste Sites: Descriptions of Sites on Current National Priorities List
Office of Emergency and Remedial Response
Environmental Protection Agency
401 M St. SW
Washington, DC 20460
Phone: (202)382-2080
Almost 540 hazardous waste sites currently on the National Priorities List and eligible for federal assistance for cleanup through Superfund. ***Frequency:*** Irregular; latest edition February 1991; periodic updates. ***Price:*** Free (PB85-224756).

★5515★ Health Detective's Handbook: A Guide to the Investigation of Environmental Health Hazards by Nonprofessionals
Johns Hopkins Univ. Press
701 W. 40th St., Ste. 275
Baltimore, MD 21211
Phone: (301)338-6956
List of organizations that are of assistance to individuals who want to identify and investigate environment health hazards. ***Editor(s):*** Marvin S. Legator et al. ***Frequency:*** Published June 1985. ***Price:*** $12.95 paperback.

★5516★ Helping Out in the Outdoors: A Directory of Volunteer Opportunities on Public Lands
Amer. Hiking Soc.
1015 31st St. NW
Washington, DC 20007
Phone: (703)385-3252
Approximately 500 volunteer or low-pay jobs available with agencies in county, state, and national parks and forests in 50 states. ***Editor(s):*** Eric Seaborg. ***Frequency:*** Annual. ***Price:*** $5.00 per issue; $15.00 for three year subscription.

★5517★ Hospitality Directory
Human Ecology Action League
PO Box 49126
Atlanta, GA 30359-1126
Phone: (404)248-1898
Lists environmentally safe lodgings in the United States for allergic and chemical-sensitive travelers; arranged by state. ***Frequency:*** Periodic. ***Price:*** $3.

★5518★ How-To: 1,400 Best Books on Doing Almost Everything
R.R. Bowker Company
245 W. 17th St.
New York, NY 10011
Phone: (212)645-9700
About 1,400 publishers of how-to books including such subjects as traveling, handicrafts, raising dogs and cats, photography, home energy conservations, using microcomputers, and car maintenance. ***Editor(s):*** Bill Katz and Linda Katz. ***Frequency:*** Irregular; latest edition 1984. ***Price:*** $39.95.

★5519★ Human Ecology Action League Directory
Human Ecology Action League
PO Box 49126
Atlanta, GA 30359-1126
Phone: (404)248-1898
Lists physicians practicing clinical ecology. ***Frequency:*** Periodic.

★5520★ In Business
The JG Press
PO Box 323
Emmaus, PA 18049
Phone: (215)967-4135
Companies and persons manufacturing environmentally responsible products. ***Editor(s):*** Jerome Goldstein, Publisher. ***Price:*** $3.95.

★5521★ INFOTERRA—World Directory of Environmental Expertise
United States Natl. Focal Point for UNEP/ INFOTERRA
Environmental Protection Agency
401 M St., SW, Rm. 2903
Washington, DC 20460
Phone: (202)382-5917
Fax: (202)382-7886
Environmental organizations, government agencies, universities, research centers, and environmental libraries that are sources of environmental information; INFOTERRA national focal point offices. ***Frequency:*** Annual. ***Price:*** $200.00.

★5522★ International Directory for Sources of Environmental Information
United States Natl. Focal Point for UNEP/ INFOTERRA
Environmental Protection Agency
401 M St., SW, Rm. 2903
Washington, DC 20460
Phone: (202)382-5917

Fax: (202)382-3923
Lists environmental organizations, government agencies, universities, research centers, and other sources of environmental information worldwide. ***Frequency:*** Base edition, triennial; inderedition supplements. ***Price:*** $200.00.

★5523★ International Directory of Acid Deposition Researchers, World Edition
Acid Rain Foundation, Inc.
1410 Varsity Dr.
Raleigh, NC 27606
Phone: (919)828-9443
Fax: (919)737-3593
More than 1,700 scientists involved in some aspect of acid precipitation research in North America and Europe. ***Editor(s):*** Steven F. Vozzo. ***Frequency:*** Irregular; latest edition August 1986. ***Price:*** $10.00, plus $3.50 shipping.

★5524★ International Green Front Report
Friends of the Trees
PO Box 1064
Tonasket, WA 98855
Phone: (509)486-4726
Fax: (509)486-4726
Organizations and periodicals dealing with sustainable forestry and agriculture and related fields. ***Editor(s):*** Michael Pilarski. ***Frequency:*** Irregular; previous edition 1988; new edition expected 1991. ***Price:*** $7.00, plus $1.05 shipping.

★5525★ International Wildlife Rehabilitation Council Directory
International Wildlife Rehabilitation Coun.
4437 Central Place, Ste. B-4
Suisun, CA 94585
Phone: (707)864-1761

★5526★ Interstate Oil Compact Commission and State Oil and Gas Agencies Directory
Interstate Oil Compact Commn.
Box 53127
Oklahoma City, OK 73152
Phone: (405)525-3556
Fax: (405)525-3592
Toll-Free: 800-822-4015
About 600 state representatives to the commission from 29 oil and gas producing states and six associate states, and committee members from related industries and government agencies. ***Editor(s):*** W. Timothy Dowd, Executive Director. ***Frequency:*** Annual. ***Price:*** Free.

★5527★ Inventory of Lake Michigan Research Projects
Illinois State Geological Survey Div.
Illinois Department of Energy & Natural Resources
615 E. Peabody Dr.
Champaign, IL 61820
Phone: (217)333-4747
Approximately 330 ecological and limnological research projects on Lake Michigan. ***Editor(s):*** Nancy Peterson Holm, Assistant Limnologist. ***Frequency:*** Published December 1987. ***Price:*** $5.00.

★5528★ Izaak Walton League of America National Directory
Izaak Walton League of America
1401 Wilson Blvd., Level B
Arlington, VA 22209
Phone: (703)528-1818
Fax: (703)528-1836
Frequency: Annual.

★5529★ Life Sciences Organizations and Agencies Directory
Gale Research Inc.
835 Penobscot Bldg.
Detroit, MI 48226-4094
Phone: (313)961-2242
Fax: (313)961-6083
Toll-Free: 800-877-GALE
Telex: 810 221 7086
About 7,500 associations, government agencies, research centers, educational institutions, libraries and information centers, museums, consultants, electronic information services, and other organizations and agencies active in agriculture, biology, ecology, forestry, marine science, nutrition, wildlife and animal sciences, and other natural and life sciences. ***Editor(s):*** Brigitte T. Darnay and Margaret Labash Young. ***Frequency:*** First edition 1988. ***Price:*** $175.00.

★5530★ Lions and Tigers and Bears: A Guide to Zoological Parks, Visitor Farms, Nature Centers and Marine Life Displays...
Garland Publishing, Inc.
136 Madison Ave.
New York, NY 10016
Phone: (212)686-7492
Fax: (212)889-9399
Toll-Free: 800-627-6273
Over 850 public zoos, aquariums, aviaries, demonstration and game farms, wildlife research facilities, reptile exhibits, nature centers, and museums for children. ***Editor(s):*** Jefferson G. Ulmer. ***Frequency:*** Published 1984. ***Price:*** $24.00.

★5531★ List of PET Recyclers in the United States and Canada
National Assn. for Plastic Container Recovery
4828 Pkwy. Plaza Blvd., Ste. 260
Charlotte, NC 28217
Phone: (704)357-3250
Fax: (704)357-3260
Frequency: Monthly.

★5532★ List of Water Pollution Control Administrators
Association of State and Interstate Water Pollution Control Administrators
444 N. Capitol St., NW, Ste. 330N
Washington, DC 20001
Phone: (202)624-7782
About 60 member administrators. ***Editor(s):*** Robbi Savage, Executive Director. ***Frequency:*** Annual, August. ***Price:*** $4.00.

★5533★ Macrocosm U.S.A.
Macrocosm U.S.A.
Box 969
Cambria, CA 93428-0969
Phone: (805)927-8030
Fax: (805)927-1987
Covers over 4,000 organizations, businesses, publishers, and publications concerned with various global and humaritarian issues relevant to the progressive movement, including peace, developing countries, ecology, energy, ethical and spiritual concerns, human rights, feminism, labor, and the arts. ***Editor(s):*** Sandra L. Brockway and Carl W. Moodispaugh. ***Frequency:*** Annual. ***Price:*** $45.95 for students; $65.95 for others.

★5534★ Methane Recovery from Landfill Yearbook
Government Advisory Associates
177 E. 87th St., Ste. 404
New York, NY 10128
Phone: (212)410-4165
Fax: (212)410-6607
Approximately 155 methane recovery facilities or projects. ***Editor(s):*** Robert N. Gould, Senior Associate. ***Frequency:*** Biennial. ***Price:*** $225.00 for individuals; $175.00 for government or non-profit agencies.

★5535★ Mineral and Energy Information Sources
Mineral Information Inst.
1125 17th St., Ste. 1800
Denver, CO 80202
Phone: (303)297-3226
List of associations, government agencies, businesses, and special interest groups in North America that are sources of free and low-cost filmstrips, films, videotapes, and publications on energy and mineral related subjects. ***Editor(s):*** Jacqueline R. Evanger, Deputy Director. ***Frequency:*** Irregular; new edition expected fall 1991. ***Price:*** $15.00.

★5536★ National Association of Conservation Districts Directory
National Assn. of Conservation Districts
509 Capitol Ct. NE
Washington, DC 20002
Phone: (202)547-6223
Fax: (202)547-6450
Frequency: Annual.

★5537★ National Directory of Certified Personnel
Water Quality Assn.
4151 Naperville Rd.
Lisle, IL 60532
Phone: (708)505-0160
Fax: (708)505-9637
About 1,900 distributors and assemblers of water treatment equipment and supplies for home and industrial use, and individuals with professional certification from the Water Quality Association. ***Editor(s):*** Elizabeth Kanak, Manager of Educational Services. ***Frequency:*** Annual, August. ***Price:*** $6.00.

★5538★ National Directory of Conservation Land Trusts
The Land Trust Alliance
900 17th St., NW, Ste. 410
Washington, DC 20006-2501
Phone: (202)785-1410
Fax: (202)785-1408
Approximately 740 nonprofit land conservation organizations at the local and regional levels. ***Frequency:*** Biennial, odd years, latest edition. ***Price:*** $16.00, plus $3.00 shipping.

★5539★ National Directory of Safe Energy Organizations
Public Citizen's Critical Mass Energy Project
215 Pennsylvania Ave., SE
Washington, DC 20003
Phone: (202)546-4996
Fax: (202)547-7392
Over 700 consumer and environmental organizations opposed to nuclear reactor construction that promote safer energy alternatives in the United States. ***Editor(s):*** Ken Bossong. ***Frequency:*** Semiannual. ***Price:*** $5.00 per issue.

★5540★ National Listing of Fisheries Offices
U.S. Fish and Wildlife Service
U. S. Department of the Interior
MS 820 ARSLQ
18th & C Sts., N.W.
Washington, DC 20240
Phone: (703)358-1861
Approximately 140 national fish hatcheries and substations, headquarters and regional offices, Fishery Assistance Stations, fish technology centers, fish health centers, and other offices.

Editor(s): George L. Podpaly. ***Frequency:*** Annual, January. ***Price:*** Free.

★5541★ National Parks: Index
National Park Service
Department of the Interior
Box 37127
Washington, DC 20013
Phone: (202)208-6985
Over 350 areas administered by the National Park Service, including parks, shores, historic sites, 80 national trails, and wild and scenic rivers. ***Frequency:*** Biennial, odd years. ***Price:*** $3.00, payment must accompany order (S/N 024-005-01024-6).

★5542★ National Parks: Lesser-Known Areas
National Park Service
Department of the Interior
Box 37127
Washington, DC 20013
Phone: (202)208-6985
Over 175 areas of the National Park System chosen by park service regional officials as "lesser-used." ***Frequency:*** Irregular; latest edition 1985; new edition possible. ***Price:*** $1.50, payment must accompany order (S/N 024-005-00911-6).

★5543★ National Parks—National Park Campgrounds Issue
National Parks & Conservation Assn.
1051 31st St. NW
Washington, DC 20007
Phone: (202)944-8530
List of National Park System campgrounds. ***Editor(s):*** Michele Strutin. ***Frequency:*** Annual, spring. ***Price:*** $3.00.

★5544★ National Pesticide Information Retrieval System Database
National Pesticide Information Retrieval System
Purdue University
Entomology Hall, Rm. 1158
West Lafayette, IN 47907
Phone: (317)494-6616
Information on 45,000 pesticides registered with the Environmental Protection Agency. ***Editor(s):*** Jim White, User Services Manager.

★5545★ National Registry of Laboratories Certified to Test for Drinking Water Parameters
Association of State Drinking Water Administrators
1911 N. Fl. Myer Dr.
Arlington, VA 22209
Phone: (703)524-2428
Fax: (703)534-1453
About 3,500 laboratories that are certified to test drinking water and state certification officers. ***Frequency:*** Annual, February; first edition 1990. ***Price:*** $250.00 per issue, $450.00 per year.

★5546★ National Seashores: The Complete Guide to America's Scenic Coastal Parks
Woodbine House
5615 Fishers Ln.
Rockville, MD 20852
Phone: (301)468-8800
Fax: (301)468-5784
Toll-Free: 800-843-7323
Information bureaus, sites and attractions, and nearby accommodations for 10 coastal areas designated as national parks. ***Editor(s):*** Ruthe Wolverton and Walt Wolverton. ***Frequency:*** Irregular; latest edition 1988. ***Price:*** $9.95.

★5547★ National Utility Contractors Association Directory and Information Guide
National Utility Contractors Assn.
1235 Jefferson Davis Hwy., Ste. 606
Arlington, VA 22202
Phone: (703)486-2100
Fax: (703)979-8628
Approximately 2,500 member utility contractors; state water pollution control agencies, regional Environmental Protection Agency and Occupational Safety and Health Administration offices, and one-call systems. ***Editor(s):*** Joy Goodwin, Advertising Sales Representative. ***Frequency:*** Annual, August. ***Price:*** $50.00.

★5548★ National Wildlife Refuges: A Visitor's Guide
U.S. Fish and Wildlife Service
Department of the Interior
1849 C. St., NW, Rm. 670-ARLSQ
Washington, DC 20240
Phone: (703)358-2043
About 330 national wildlife refuges. ***Editor(s):*** Nancy Marx, Public Use Specialist. ***Frequency:*** Irregular; previous edition 1985; latest edition 1988. ***Price:*** $1.00 (S/N 024-010-00660-9).

★5549★ Nonprofit Sample and Core Repositories Open to the Public in the United States
Branch of Sedimentary Processes
U. S. Geological Survey
Department of the Interior
Box 25046
Denver Federal Center, MS975
Denver, CO 80225-0046
Phone: (303)236-1930
Nearly 100 repositories that hold well samples, cores, and other data for wells drilled for water, mining, oil, gas, and waste disposal; Army Corps of Engineers district offices. ***Editor(s):*** J.W. Schmoker, T.C. Michalski, and P.B. Worl. ***Frequency:*** Irregular; latest edition 1984. ***Price:*** Free.

★5550★ Northeast Industrial Waste Exchange Listings Catalog
Northeast Industrial Waste Exchange, Inc.
90 Presidential Plaza, Ste. 122
Syracuse, NY 13202
Phone: (315)422-6572
Fax: (315)422-9051
250-300 manufacturers and others in the northeastern United States that have wastes for sale or that wish to purchase wastes for reuse or resource recovery. ***Editor(s):*** Nancy Groenhof, Research Associate. ***Frequency:*** Quarterly; February, May, August, and November. ***Price:*** Free.

★5551★ Notes on Sedimentation Activities
Water Resources Div.
U. S. Geological Survey
417 National Center
Reston, VA 22092
Phone: (703)648-5019
Geographical list of National Water Data Exchange assistance centers. ***Frequency:*** Annual, summer.

★5552★ Nuclear Power Plant Construction Activity
Energy Information Administration
Department of Energy
1000 Independence Ave., SW, EI 231
Washington, DC 20585
Phone: (202)586-8800
Nuclear power plants; includes operating and completed but inoperative plants, plants under construction, and canceled projects. ***Frequency:*** Irregular; previous edition 1988; latest edition June 1989. ***Price:*** $3.25 (S/N 061-003-00406-7; DOE/EIA 0473).

★5553★ Nuclear Regulatory Commission Public Document Room Directory
Local Public Document Room Program
Nuclear Regulatory Commission
1717 H St., NW
Washington, DC 20555
Phone: (301)492-7536
Toll-Free: 800-638-8081
About 90 university and public libraries that are depositories for documents on commercial nuclear power reactors, fuel cycle facilities, and radioactive waste disposal sites. Depositories are located near one of these facilities or sites. ***Editor(s):*** Teresa D. Linton, Information Services Librarian. ***Frequency:*** Irregular; latest edition February 1989. ***Price:*** Free.

★5554★ Oil Spill Data Base
Center for Short-Lived Phenomena
Box 199, Harvard Sq. Sta.
Cambridge, MA 02238
Phone: (617)492-3310
Fax: (617)492-3312
Covers oil spills that have taken place around the world since 1967. Provides extensive details on each occurrence, including site and source of spill, date, substance involved, amount cause, details of clean-up and damages, information on vessel involved, etc. ***Editor(s):*** Richard Golob.

★5555★ The Organic Network
Eden Acres, Inc.
12100 Lima Center Rd.
Clinton, MI 49236
Phone: (517)456-4288
Nearly 1,500 organic growers, organizations concerned with organic farming, and suppliers of natural fibers and other natural materials, medical supplies for individuals allergic to chemical, plastic, and other manmade materials, and hypoallergenic chemicals and other products; international coverage. ***Frequency:*** Latest edition August 1984. ***Price:*** Base edition, $15.00, postpaid.

★5556★ Park Areas and Employment Opportunities for Summer
National Park Service
Department of the Interior
Box 37127
Washington, DC 20013
Phone: (202)208-6985
Seasonal job openings in three job categories anticipated in the National Park Service; regional offices are listed. ***Editor(s):*** Ella Williams. ***Frequency:*** Annual, August. ***Price:*** Free.

★5557★ Pesticide Directory: A Guide to Producers & Products, Regulators, Researchers & Associations in the United States
Thomson Publications
Box 9335
Fresno, CA 93791
Phone: (209)435-2163
Fax: (209)435-8319
Pesticide manufacturers and formulators, universities, research centers, government regulatory offices, and national organizations interested in pesticides. ***Editor(s):*** W.T. Thomson and Lori Thomson Harvey. ***Frequency:*** Annual, April. ***Price:*** $75.00.

★5558★ Professional Workers in State Agricultural Experiment Stations and Other Cooperating State Institutions
Cooperative State Research Service
Department of Agriculture
Aerospace Bldg., Rm. 348
901 D St., SW
Washington, DC 20250
Academic and research personnel in all agricultural, forestry, aquacultural, home economics, and animal husbandry fields at experiment stations and academic institutions with agricultural programs. ***Frequency:*** Biennial, even years; supplement in odd years. ***Price:*** $15.00 (S/N 001-000-04567-9).

★5559★ Program Activities: Department of Energy State and Local Assistance Programs
Office of State and Local Assistance Programs
Conservation & Renewable Energy
Department of Energy
1000 Independence Ave., S.W.
Washington, DC 20585
Phone: (202)586-2311
List of state and territorial energy offices throughout the United States. ***Editor(s):*** Estelle S. Wiser, Conservation Specialist. ***Frequency:*** Formerly Annual; latest edition 1988. ***Price:*** Free.

★5560★ Promoting Recycling to the Public
National Soft Drink Assn.
1101 16th St. NW
Washington, DC 20036
Phone: (202)463-6770
Fax: (202)463-6731
Waste recycling and anti-litter programs. ***Frequency:*** Irregular; latest edition 1988. ***Price:*** $15.00.

★5561★ Public Interest Group Directory—Pacific Northwest
Environmental Protection Agency
Region 10
1200 6th Ave., Mail Stop MD-107
Attn: Region 10-Public Information Center
Seattle, WA 98101
Phone: (206)553-4973
Regional voluntary organizations, EPA regional offices, and state, local, and provincial environmental and pollution control agencies in Alaska, Idaho, Oregon, and Washington. ***Editor(s):*** Mary M. Neilson, Constituency Coordinator. ***Frequency:*** Irregular; latest edition 1989. ***Price:*** Free.

★5562★ Raise the Stakes—North "America" Plus Issue Bioregionalism
Planet Drum Found.
Box 31251
San Francisco, CA 94131
Phone: (415)285-6556
List of over 150 groups in North America and 20 in Australia, Europe, the Pacific Islands, and South America concerned with bioregionalism, an ecological and cultural concept of living-in-place and urban sustainability. ***Editor(s):*** Marie Dolcini. ***Frequency:*** Semiannual, spring and fall. ***Price:*** $5.00, postpaid (ISSN 0278-7016).

★5563★ Recreation Information Management System (RIM) National Forest Database
Forest Service
Department of Agriculture
Box 96090
Washington, DC 20090
Phone: (202)382-9409
Fax: (202)447-4145
Database of about 9,000 facilities and areas within the National Forrest System, including site name, location, state and county, geographical coordinates; general description, types of recreation available; information on use, facility conditions; services available, distance to nearest post office, etc; ranger district office phone. ***Editor(s):*** TAh Yang.

★5564★ Recreation Sites in Southwestern National Forests
Southwestern Region
Forest Service
Department of Agriculture
517 Gold Ave., S.W.
Albuquerque, NM 87102
Phone: (505)842-3292
Recreation sites, including campgrounds, public access sites, etc., in the national forests of Arizona and New Mexico. ***Editor(s):*** Sandra Roberts, Printing Specialist. ***Frequency:*** Approximately annual; previous edition February 1987; latest edition September 1989. ***Price:*** Free.

★5565★ Recycling Centers Directory
Amer. Business Directories, Inc.
American Business Information, Inc.
5711 S. 86th Circle
Omaha, NE 68127
Phone: (402)593-4600
Fax: (402)331-1505
Contains a listing of 5,569 recycling centers. ***Frequency:*** Annual. ***Price:*** $215.00, payment with order. Significant discounts offered for standing orders.

★5566★ Reel Change: A Guide to Social Issue Films
New York Zoetrope
838 Broadway
New York, NY 10003
Phone: (212)420-0590
Fax: (212)529-3330
Toll-Free: 800-CHAPLIN
List of over 300 distributors of 16mm films on social issues, including disarmament, nuclear freeze, environmental concerns, racial and sexual justice, and occupational health and safety; publishers of film-related books and periodicals. ***Frequency:*** Irregular; previous edition 1979; latest edition 1987. ***Price:*** $6.95.

★5567★ Regional Regenerative Farming Groups
Regenerative Agriculture Assn.
222 Main St.
Emmaus, PA 18049
Phone: (215)967-5171
About 40 regional associations of organic growers; coverage includes Canada. ***Editor(s):*** George DeVault. ***Frequency:*** Latest editon fall 1985; suspended indefinitely. ***Price:*** $1.00.

★5568★ Register of Environmental Engineering Graduate Programs
Association of Environmental Engineering Professors
c/o Desmond Lawler
Department of Civil Engineering (ECJ 8.b)
University of Texas
Austin, TX 78712
Phone: (512)471-4595
100 college programs. ***Editor(s):*** William R. Knocke and Gary L. Amy. ***Frequency:*** Every three to five years; latest edition 1989. ***Price:*** $50.00.

★5569★ Register of the American Board of Environmental Medicine
Amer. Bd. of Environmental Medicine
2114 Martingale Dr.
Norman, OK 73072
Phone: (405)329-8437
Frequency: Annual.

★5570★ Rene Dubos Center for Human Environments Conference Proceedings
Rene Dubos Center for Human Environments
100 E. 85th St.
New York, NY 10028
Phone: (212)249-7745
Directory of about 500 environmentalists, including college and university professors, representatives of industrial firms, and government officials; international coverage. ***Frequency:*** Annual.

★5571★ Resource Efficient Housing: An Annotated Bibliography
Rocky Mountain Inst.
1739 Snowmass Creek Rd.
Snowmass, CO 81654
Phone: (303)927-3851
Fax: (303)927-4178
List of over 125 agencies that provide information on home resource efficiency. ***Frequency:*** Biennial. ***Price:*** $15.00.

★5572★ Resource Recovery Yearbook: A Directory and Guide
Governmental Advisory Associates, Inc.
177 E. 87th St., Ste. 404
New York, NY 10128
Phone: (212)410-4165
Fax: (212)410-6607
Approximately 415 existing, proposed, and cancelled resource recovery facilities. ***Editor(s):*** Robert Gould. ***Frequency:*** Biennial. ***Price:*** $395.00 to government and nonprofit organizations; $525.00 to others; postpaid.

★5573★ Resources for Organic Pest Control
Rodale's Organic Gardening
Rodale Press, Inc.
33 E. Minor St.
Emmaus, PA 18098
Phone: (215)967-5171
Fax: (215)965-5670
Over 40 manufacturers and suppliers of natural pesticides and beneficial organisms; associations and other organizations providing information on non-natural pesticides. ***Frequency:*** Biennial, January of odd years. ***Price:*** Send self-addressed, stamped, business-size envelope.

★5574★ River Conservation Directory
National Assn. for State River Conservation Programs
801 Pennsylvania Ave. SE, Ste. 302
Washington, DC 20003
Phone: (202)543-2682
Lists over 1,000 organizations involved with river conservation education on federal, state, and local levels. ***Frequency:*** Biennial. ***Price:*** $6/issue.

★5575★ SATIVA Opportunities Directory
Society for Agricultural Training through Integrated Voluntary Activities (SATIVA)
Route 2
Viola, WI 54664
Phone: (608)625-2217
Training programs and work opportunities in organic farming and homesteading in the mid Atlantic and midwestern United States. ***Frequency:*** Annual, fall. ***Price:*** $5.00.

★5576★ Sierra Club Guide to the Natural Areas...
Sierra Club Books
The Sierra Club Bookstore
730 Polk St.
San Francisco, CA 94107
Phone: (415)923-5604
State parks, national forests, wildlife refuges, and private lands over 10,000 acres that are open to public recreational use. Separate editions in the series cover New Mexico, Arizona, and Nevada; Oregon and Washington; Idaho, Montana, and Wyoming; California; Colorado and Utah; New England. ***Editor(s):*** John Perry and Jane Greverus Perry. ***Price:*** $9.95-$12.95.

★5577★ Solar Collector Manufacturing Activity and Applications in the Residential Sector
Solar Energy Research Inst.
Energy Research & Development Administration
1617 Cole Blvd.
Golden, CO 80401
Phone: (303)231-1000
Nearly 265 solar collector manufacturers and importers, 20 photovoltaic module manufacturers, and 30 wind energy system manufacturers, importers, and distributors. ***Frequency:*** Reported as biennial; latest edition 1986. ***Price:*** $3.50 (S/N 061-003-00243-9; DE82-00928).

★5578★ Solar Energy Directory
Grey House Publishing, Inc.
Pocket Knife Sq.
Lakeville, CT 06039
Phone: (203)435-0868
Fax: (203)435-0867
Over 2,000 professional, industry, and trade organizations with solar interests; government agencies with solar responsibilities; utilities; manufacturers; colleges and universities and other educational institutions; architects, homebuilders, and engineers involved in solar construction and design; publishers of related periodicals and books. ***Editor(s):*** Richard Gottlieb. ***Frequency:*** Irregular; latest edition 1984. ***Price:*** $50.00.

★5579★ Solar Energy Equipment Directory
Amer. Business Directories, Inc.
American Business Information, Inc.
5711 S. 86th Circle
Omaha, NE 68127
Phone: (402)593-4600
Fax: (402)331-1505
Frequency: Annual. ***Price:*** $95.00, payment with order. Significant discounts offered for standing orders.

★5580★ Solar Industry Journal
Solar Energy Industries Assn.
777 N. Capitol St., NE, Ste. 805
Washington, DC 20002
Phone: (703)524-6100
Fax: (703)527-2833
About 120 manufacturers of solar energy systems and components; distributors, contractors, and engineers. ***Editor(s):*** Scott Sklar. ***Frequency:*** Quarterly. ***Price:*** $25.00, annual subscription.

★5581★ State Solar Directory
Interstate Solar Coordination Coun.
900 American Center Bldg.
St. Paul, MN 55101
Phone: (612)296-4737
State energy offices, consumer protection agencies; education contacts; administering agencies for equipment certification and contractor licensing, grants and loans; utility incentives; delegate to the Interstate Solar Coordination Council; also includes national energy information sources. ***Editor(s):*** Judy Carroll, Publications Coordinator. ***Frequency:*** Annual, summer. ***Price:*** $25.00, postpaid.

★5582★ Summaries of DOE Hydrogen Programs
Hydrogen Energy Coordinating Comm.
Office of Conservation & Renewable Energy
Department of Energy
1000 Independence Ave., SW
Washington, DC 20585
Phone: (202)586-2826
Research projects (about 45 in most recent year) funded by the Department of Energy on hydrogen production, storage, and transport. ***Frequency:*** Annual, January. ***Price:*** $12.95 (DE82-020494).

★5583★ Summary of Federal Programs and Projects
National Marine Pollution Program Office
National Oceanic & Atmospheric Administration
Department of Commerce
Universal Bldg., Rm. 625
1825 Connecticut Ave. NW
Washington, DC 20235
Phone: (202)673-5243
Fax: (202)387-8945
Over 550 marine pollution research, monitoring, and resource development projects organized in 65 programs funded by federal government agencies participating in the National Marine Pollution Program. ***Frequency:*** Annual, Fall. ***Price:*** Free.

★5584★ Systems Sciences
Elmwood Inst.
PO Box 5765
Berkeley, CA 94705-0765
Phone: (415)845-4595
Fax: (415)843-9398
Lists of schools and institutions worldwide promoting systems thinking. ***Frequency:*** Periodic.

★5585★ Tensleep's National Forest Campground Guide
Tensleep Publications
Box 925
Aberdeen, SD 57401
Phone: (605)226-0488
Over 4,000 primitive to developed campgrounds in national forests; state government agencies with responsibilities related to parks, game and fish conservation, etc. ***Editor(s):*** Ken Melius. ***Frequency:*** Irregular; latest edition January 1983. ***Price:*** $9.95.

★5586★ Three Mile Island Sourcebook: Annotations of a Disaster
Garland Publishing, Inc.
136 Madison Ave.
New York, NY 10016
Phone: (212)686-7492
List of nuclear energy organizations and libraries with information on nuclear energy. Principal content is annotations of newspaper and magazine articles, federal and state documents, and professional papers about Three Mile Island covering its first day of construction on November 18, 1986, to the second anniversary of the nuclear accident, March 29, 1981. ***Editor(s):*** Philip Starr and William A. Pearman. ***Frequency:*** Published 1981. ***Price:*** $115.00.

★5587★ Turtle Help Network
New York Turtle and Tortoise Soc.
c/o Suzanne Dohm
163 Amsterdam Ave., Ste. 365
New York, NY 10023
Phone: (212)459-4803
Lists of volunteers and their areas of interest and expertise. ***Frequency:*** Periodic.

★5588★ Visiting Our Western National Parks
Perkins Publications
Box 129
Mineral, CA 96063
Phone: (916)544-2100
25 national parks in the western region of the United States. ***Frequency:*** Published 1987. ***Price:*** $12.95.

★5589★ Waste Age: Resource Recovery Activities Update Issue
National Solid Wastes Management Assn.
1730 Rhode Island Ave., N.W., Ste. 1000
Washington, DC 20036
Phone: (202)659-4613
List of about 90 cities, countries, cooperatives, etc., which operate materials and energy recovery facilities using solid waste; products include steam, hot water, refuse-derived fuel, ferrous and non-ferrous metals, glass, humus, methane, carborn dioxide, etc.; includes list of cities which are planning such facilities. ***Editor(s):*** Joseph Salimando. ***Frequency:*** Annual, November. ***Price:*** $10.00.

★5590★ Waste Paper Directory
Amer. Business Directories, Inc.
American Business Information, Inc.
5711 S. 86th Circle
Omaha, NE 68127
Phone: (402)593-4600
Fax: (402)331-1505
Geographical list of 1,283 waste paper organizations. ***Frequency:*** Annual. ***Price:*** $85.00, payment with order. Significant discounts offered for standing orders.

★5591★ Waste Reduction/Disposal/ Recycle Service Industries Directory
Amer. Business Directories, Inc.
American Business Information, Inc.
5711 S. 86th Circle
Omaha, NE 68127
Phone: (402)593-4600
Fax: (402)331-1505
Geographical list of 2,176 industries involved in recycling, disposal, and waste reduction. ***Frequency:*** Annual. ***Price:*** $105.00, payment with order. Significant discounts offered for standing orders.

★5592★ Wastes and their Treatment Information Sources
United States Natl. Focal Point for UNEP/ INFOTERRA
Environmental Protection Agency
410 M St., SW, Rm. 2903
Washington, DC 20460
Phone: (202)382-5917
Fax: (202)382-7886
Several hundred institutions that are sources of information on wastes and waste treatment; international coverage. ***Frequency:*** Published 1986. ***Price:*** $30.00.

★5593★ Wastes to Resources: Appropriate Technologies for Sewage Treatment and Conversion
National Center for Appropriate Technology
Box 3838
Butte, MT 59702
Phone: (406)494-4572
Each chapter contains a list of agencies or individuals concerned with aspects of sewage treatment and management. The appendix contains a list of about 15 selected sewage treatment projects from the Department of Energy Appropriate Technology Small Grants Program. ***Editor(s):*** S.G. Thomas and D.M. Smith. ***Frequency:*** Published July 1983. ***Price:*** $5.00, plus $1.00 shipping.

★5594★ Water and Water-Related Sources Directory
National Water Data Exchange (NAWDEX)
Water Resources Division
U. S. Geological Survey
Department of the Interior
421 National Center
Reston, VA 22092
Phone: (703)860-6031
Combines two other publications described separately under the titles, "Water Data Sources Directory" and "Water-Related Data Sources Directory". ***Frequency:*** Irregular. ***Price:*** $34.00, including binder; $30.00, without binder.

★5595★ Water Data Sources Directory
National Water Data Exchange
Water Resources Division
U. S. Geological Survey
Department of the Interior
421 National Center
Reston, VA 22092
Phone: (703)648-5672
More than 2,000 organizations that are sources of water data; worldwide coverage. ***Frequency:*** Irregular; previous edition 1983; latest edition May 1991.

★5596★ Water-Related Data Sources Directory
National Water Data Exchange
Water Resources Division
U. S. Geological Survey
Department of the Interior
421 National Center
Reston, VA 22092
Phone: (703)860-6031
Organizations that are sources of water-related data or that provide services or information products pertinent to water-related data, such as meteorological, soils, water use, and other types. ***Frequency:*** Irregular. ***Price:*** $9.50, including binder; $7.00, without binder; payment must accompany order.

★5597★ Western Mining Directory
Howell Publishing Company
PO Box 37510
Denver, CO 80237
Phone: (303)770-6794
Fax: (303)770-6796
About 700 mining firms and organizations in the mining industry of the western United States, including active hardrock and coal mines, uranium and vanadium mines, mining firms, active oil shale projects; consultants, contractors-developers, suppliers of equipment and services, exploration and drilling companies; educational institutions; mining associations; related government agencies; and mining exhibitions and conferences. ***Editor(s):*** Don E. Howell, Publisher. ***Frequency:*** Annual, winter. ***Price:*** $46.00, plus $3.00 shipping.

★5598★ Whalewatching Guide
Pacific Whale Found.
Kealia Beach Plaza, Ste. 25
101 N. Kihei Rd.
Kihei, HI 96753
Phone: (808)879-8811
Fax: (808)879-2615

★5599★ Who's Who in Energy Recovery from Waste
Biofuels and Municipal Waste Technology Div.
Office of Renewable Energy Technologies
Office of Conservation & Renewable Energy
Department of Energy
Washington, DC 20585
Phone: (202)586-6750
Over 675 individuals, government agencies, institutes and universities, associations, publishers of trade journals and books, public interest groups, manufacturers and distributors of equipment and systems, investment bankers and counselors, and consultants involved in energy recovery from municipal wastes. ***Editor(s):*** Dick Richards. ***Frequency:*** Irregular; previous edition October 1985; latest edition February 1989. ***Price:*** $13.95 (DE 89007702).

★5600★ Wildlife Rehabilitation Minimum Standards and Accreditation Program
National Wildlife Rehabilitators Assn.
12805 St. Croix Trail
Hastin, MN 55033
Phone: (612)437-9194
Contact: Elaine M. Thrune, Pres.

★5601★ World Directory of Environmental Organizations
California Inst. of Public Affairs
PO Box 189040
Sacramento, CA 95818
Phone: (916)442-2472
Fax: (916)442-2478
Over 2,100 governmental and non-governmental environmental protection organizations in 218 countries; 165 intergovernmental agencies; 300 international nongovernmental groups. ***Editor(s):*** Thaddeus C. Trzyna. ***Frequency:*** Irregular; latest edition June 1989; new edition possible 1991. ***Price:*** $35.00 (ISSN 0092-0908).

★5602★ World Environmental Directory
WED Div.
Business Publishers, Inc.
951 Pershing Dr.
Silver Spring, MD 20910
Phone: (301)587-6300
Agencies, organizations, manufacturers, and professionals in the United States and Canada that emphasize environmental interests. ***Frequency:*** Irregular; latest edition 1991. ***Price:*** $225.00, plus $7.50 shipping.

★5603★ Your Resource Guide to Environmental Organizations
Smiling Dolphins Press
4 Segura
Irvine, CA 92715
Describes 150 nonprofit environmental organizations, both national and international. ***Editor(s):*** John Seredich. 1991. ***Price:*** $15.95.

Magazines and Newspapers

★5604★ Acid Precipitation
U.S. Dept. of Energy, OSTI
PO Box 62
Oak Ridge, TN 37831
Phone: (615)576-1223
Fax: (615)576-2865
Journal containing abstracts on the effects of acid precipitation and possible control measures. ***Frequency:*** Monthly. ***Price:*** $90; $180 other countries.

★5605★ Acid Rain: Road to a Middleground Solution
Center for Clean Air Policy
444 N. Capitol St., Ste. 526
Washington, DC 20001
Phone: (202)624-7709

★5606★ Acid Rain: Science Projects
The Acid Rain Found.
1410 Varsity Dr.
Raleigh, NC 27606
Phone: (919)828-9443

★5607★ Action Line Newspaper
Trout Unlimited
501 Church St. NE
Vienna, VA 22180
Phone: (703)281-1100
Frequency: Quarterly.

★5608★ Adirondac
Adirondack Mountain Club, Inc.
RR 3 Box 3055
Lake George, NY 12845
Phone: (518)668-4447
Fax: (518)668-3746
Magazine focusing on outdoor activities and environmental issues. ***Frequency:*** Monthly (Feb./March and Oct./Nov. are combined). ***Price:*** $20; $4.25 single issue.

★5609★ African Special
Safari Club Intl.
4800 W. Gates Pass Rd.
Tucson, AZ 85745
Phone: (602)620-1220
Fax: (602)622-1205
Contact: Warren Parker, Pres.

★5610★ The African Women's Assembly: Women and Sustainable Development
World Women in the Environment
1331 H St. NW, Ste. 903
Washington, DC 20005
Phone: (202)347-1514
Fax: (202)347-1524

★5611★ Aftercare of Oil Covered Birds
National Wildlife Health Found.
c/o James L. Naviaux
606 El Pintado Rd.
Danville, CA 94526
Phone: (415)939-3456

★5612★ Air and Waste Management Association Proceedings Digests
Air and Waste Management Assn.
PO Box 2861
Pittsburgh, PA 15230
Phone: (412)232-3444
Fax: (412)232-3450
Frequency: Annual.

★5613★ The Air Around Us
The Acid Rain Found.
1410 Varsity Dr.
Raleigh, NC 27606
Phone: (919)828-9443

★5614★ Alabama Conservation
Alabama Dept. of Conservation and Natural Resources
64 N. Union St.
Montgomery, AL 36130-1901
Phone: (205)242-3151
Fax: (205)240-3009
State Department of Conservation magazine covering wildlife, state parks, marine resources, and water safety. ***Frequency:*** 6x/yr. ***Price:*** $8.

★5615★ Alabama Forests
Alabama Forestry Assn.
555 Alabama St.
Montgomery, AL 36104
Phone: (205)265-8733
Fax: (205)262-1258
Magazine devoted to forest management and wood products. ***Frequency:*** 6x/yr. ***Price:*** $24.

★5616★ Allocation of Superfund Site Costs Through Mediation
Clean Sites, Inc.
1199 N. Fairfax St.
Alexandria, VA 22314
Phone: (703)683-8522

★5617★ American Birds
National Audubon Soc.
950 Third Ave.
New York, NY 10022
Phone: (212)832-3200

★5618★ American Caves
Amer. Cave Conservation Assn.
131 Main & Cave Sts.
PO Box 409
Horse Cave, KY 42749
Phone: (502)786-1466
Magazine includes information on national and local cave issues and calendar of events. ***Frequency:*** Periodic. ***Price:*** Included in membership dues; $3/copy for nonmembers.

★5619★ American Federation of Aviculture Watchbird
Amer. Fed. of Aviculture
3118 W. Thomas Rd., No. 713
PO Box 56218
Phoenix, AZ 85079-6218
Phone: (602)484-0931
Fax: (602)484-0109
Magazine on bird conservation. ***Frequency:*** 6x/yr. ***Price:*** $20.

★5620★ American Forests: The Magazine of Trees & Forests
Amer. Forestry Assn.
PO Box 2000
Washington, DC 20013-2000
Phone: (202)667-3300
Fax: (202)667-7751
Forest conservation magazine. ***Frequency:*** 6x/yr. ***Price:*** $24.

★5621★ American Midland Naturalist
University of Notre Dame
Notre Dame, IN 46556
Phone: (219)239-7481
Primary journal covering basic research in biology; including animal and plant ecology, systematics and physiology, entomology, mammalogy, ichthyology, parasitology, invertebrate zoology, and limnology. ***Frequency:*** Quarterly. ***Price:*** $60.

★5622★ America's Neighborhood Bats
Bat Conservation Intl.
PO Box 162603
Austin, TX 78716
Phone: (512)327-9721
Fax: (512)327-9724

★5623★ The Amicus Journal
Natural Resources Defense Coun.
40 W. 20 St.
New York, NY 10011
Phone: (212)727-2700
Fax: (212)727-1773
Journal covering national and international environmental affairs. ***Frequency:*** Quarterly. ***Price:*** $10 with membership; $8 libraries.

★5624★ Appalachia Bulletin
Appalachian Mountain Club
5 Joy St.
Boston, MA 02108
Phone: (617)523-0636
Fax: (617)523-0722
Outdoor recreation and conservation magazine. ***Frequency:*** 10x/yr. ***Price:*** $15.50; $2.50 single issue.

★5625★ Appalachian Trailway News
Appalachian Trail Conference
PO Box 807
Harpers Ferry, WV 25425
Phone: (304)535-6331
Fax: (304)535-2667
Magazine on hiking, Appalachian Trail protection, and general conservation issues. ***Frequency:*** 5x/yr. ***Price:*** $18.

★5626★ Archives of Clinical Ecology
Amer. Acad. of Environmental Medicine
PO Box 16106
Denver, CO 80216
Phone: (303)622-9755
Fax: (303)622-4224
Journal. ***Frequency:*** Quarterly.

★5627★ Archives of Environmental Contamination and Toxicology
Springer-Verlag New York, Inc.
175 5th Ave.
New York, NY 10010
Phone: (212)460-1500
Fax: (212)473-6272
Professional journal focusing on environmental contaminants. ***Frequency:*** 6x/yr. ***Price:*** $342.

★5628★ Archives of Environmental Health: An International Journal
Heldref Publications
(Helen Dwight Reid Educational Foundation)
4000 Albermarle St. NW
Washington, DC 20016-1851
Bimonthly journal. ***Price:*** $85/year.

★5629★ Arid Soil Research and Rehabilitation
Taylor & Francis
1900 Frost Rd., Ste. 101
Bristol, PA 19007
Phone: (215)785-5800
Fax: (215)785-5515
Journal publishing scientific studies on desert, arid, and semi-arid soil research and recovery. ***Editor(s):*** J. Skujins. ***Frequency:*** Quarterly. ***Price:*** $50; $90 institutions.

★5630★ Arid West Floodplain Management Issues
Association of State Floodplain Managers
PO Box 2051
Madison, WI 53701-2051
Phone: (608)266-1926

★5631★ Association of Metropolitan Water Agencies Monthly Report
Association of Metropolitan Water Agencies
1717 K St. NW, Ste. 1006
Washington, DC 20036
Phone: (202)331-2820
Fax: (202)842-0621

★5632★ ATALA: The Journal of Invertebrate Conservation
Xerces Soc.
c/o Melody Allen
10 SW Ash St.
Portland, OR 97204
Phone: (503)222-2788
Includes book reviews and abstracts of papers presented at annual meeting. ***Frequency:*** Periodic. ***Price:*** Included in membership dues.

★5633★ Atlantic Naturalist
Audubon Naturalist Soc. of the Central Atlantic States
8940 Jones Mill Rd.
Chevy Chase, MD 20815
Phone: (301)652-9188
Frequency: Annual.

★5634★ Atmosphere Crises
Social Issues Resources Series, Inc.
PO Box 2348
Baton Rouge, LA 33427-2348

★5635★ Atmospheric Environment, Parts A and B
Pergamon Press, Inc.
Maxwell House
Fairview Park
Elmsford, NY 10523
Phone: (914)592-7700
Fax: (914)592-3625
Journal publishing papers on all aspects of man's interactions with his environment including the administrative, economic, and political aspects of these interactions. ***Frequency:*** 15x/yr. ***Price:*** $1,320 institutions

★5636★ Audubon
National Audubon Soc.
950 3rd Ave.
New York, NY 10022
Phone: (212)832-3200
Fax: (212)755-3752
Nature and conservation magazine. ***Frequency:*** 6x/yr. ***Price:*** $20; $4 single issue.

★5637★ Balance
National Environmental Development Assn.
1440 New York Ave. NW, Ste. 300
Washington, DC 20005
Phone: (202)638-1230
Frequency: Monthly.

★5638★ Balancing the Scales
Kentuckians for the Commonwealth
PO Box 864
Prestonburg, KY 41653
Phone: (606)886-0043
Covers environmental affairs in Kentucky. ***Editor(s):*** Jerry Hardt. ***Frequency:*** Monthly.

★5639★ Basic Wildlife Rehabilitation
International Wildlife Rehabilitation Coun.
4437 Central Place, Ste. B-4
Suisun, CA 94585
Phone: (707)864-1761

★5640★ Bats, Pesticides and Politics
Bat Conservation Internationnal
PO Box 162603
Austin, TX 78716
Phone: (512)327-9721
Fax: (512)327-9724
Contact: Toni Turner, Contact

★5641★ Bear News
Great Bear Found.
PO Box 2699
Missoula, MT 59806
Phone: (406)721-3009
Frequency: Periodic.

★5642★ Becoming an Environmental Professional
CEIP Fund
68 Harrison Ave., 5th Fl.
Boston, MA 02111
Phone: (617)426-4375

★5643★ Big Island Rainforest Action Group Rag
Big Island Rainforest Action Group
PO Box 341
Kurtistown, HI 96760
Phone: (808)966-7622
Journal includes calendar of events. ***Frequency:*** Periodic.

★5644★ BioCycle: Journal of Waste Recycling
PO Box 351
Emmaus, PA 18049
Phone: (215)967-4135
Magazine focusing on management of city and industrial wastes. ***Frequency:*** Monthly. ***Price:*** $55.

★5645★ Biodynamics
Biodynamic Farming & Gardening Assn.
PO Box 550
Kimberton, PA 19442-0550
Phone: (215)935-7797
Magazine on soil conservation, organic agriculture, and goethean science. ***Frequency:*** Quarterly. ***Price:*** $30.

★5646★ Biofouling
Harwood Academic Publishers
PO Box 786, Cooper Sta.
New York, NY 10276
Phone: (212)206-8900
Fax: (212)645-2459
Science journal. ***Frequency:*** Quarterly.

★5647★ The Black Bear in Modern North America
Boone and Crockett Club
241 S. Fraley Blvd.
Dumfries, VA 22026
Phone: (703)221-1888

★5648★ BNA's National Environmental Watch
Bureau of National Affairs
1231 25th St., NW
Washington, DC 20037
Phone: (202)452-4200
Fax: (202)822-8092
Toll-Free: 800-452-7773
Telex: 28-5656 BNAI WSH
Aimed at corporate managers. Provides news, technological reviews, and regulatory information regarding industry's impact on the environment. ***Frequency:*** Weekly.

★5649★ Boom
Society of Tympanuchus Cupido Pinnatus
c/o Bernard J. Westfahl
930 Elm Grove Rd.
Elm Grove, WI 53122
Phone: (414)782-6333
Frequency: Quarterly.

★5650★ Both Sides Now
Free People Press
Rte. 6
Box 28
Tyler, TX 75704
Phone: (903)592-4263
Magazine identifying with the Green movement's concerns with ecology, nonviolence, grassroots democracy, and social awareness. ***Frequency:*** Irregular. ***Price:*** $6 ten issues; $4 six issues; $.75 single issue.

★5651★ BUGLE Magazine
Rocky Mountain Elk Found.
PO Box 8249
Missoula, MT 59807
Phone: (406)721-0010
Fax: (406)549-4325
Frequency: Quarterly.

★5652★ Building Sustainable Communities
Center for the Study of Law and Politics
2962 Fillmore St.
San Francisco, CA 94123
Phone: (415)775-0791
Fax: (415)775-4159
Frequency: Periodic.

★5653★ The Bulletin of the California Water Pollution Control Association
California Water Pollution Control Assn.
PO Box 575
Lafayette, CA 94549-0575
Phone: (415)284-1240
Water pollution control magazine. ***Frequency:*** Quarterly. ***Price:*** $20.

★5654★ Buzzworm: The Environmental Journal
Buzzworm, Inc.
2305 Canyon Blvd., No. 206
Boulder, CO 80302-5655
Phone: (303)442-1969
Fax: (303)442-4875
Environmental magazine for general audiences. ***Frequency:*** 6x/yr. ***Price:*** $18.

★5655★ California Environment Reporter
The Bur. of Natl. Affairs, Inc.
1231 25th St. NW
Washington, DC 20037
Phone: (202)452-4200
Fax: (202)822-8092
A notification service covering state, local and pertinent federal legislative, regulatory, legal and enforcement developments across all environmental areas. ***Frequency:*** Every other week. ***Price:*** $495.

★5656★ Calypso Log
The Cousteau Soc.
8440 Santa Monica Blvd.
Los Angeles, CA 90069
Phone: (213)656-4422
Fax: (213)656-4891
Magazine containing articles on environmental issues, ecology, and the ocean. ***Frequency:*** 6x/yr. ***Price:*** $28 membership.

★5657★ Canadian Environmental Protection
Baum Publications Ltd.
831 Helmcken St.
Vancouver, British Columbia, Canada V6Z 1B1
Phone: (604)689-2804
Fax: (604)682-8347
Founded: 1989. Magazine for the pollution, sewage, and waste management industries. ***Frequency:*** 6x/yr.

★5658★ Carrying Capacity Network—Focus
Carrying Capacity Network
1325 G St. NW, Ste. 1003
Washington, DC 20005-3104
Phone: (202)879-3044
Contact: Stephen Mabley, Network Coord.
Frequency: Periodic.

★5659★ Case Update
Eastern Mineral Law Found.
West Virginia University Law Center
PO Box 6130
Morgantown, WV 26506
Phone: (304)293-2470
Fax: (304)293-7654
Frequency: 3-4/year.

★5660★ Center for the Study of Law and Politics Newsletter
Center for the Study of Law and Politics
2962 Fillmore St.
San Francisco, CA 94123
Phone: (415)775-0791
Fax: (415)775-4159
Frequency: Quarterly.

★5661★ Chemosphere
Pergamon Press, Inc.
Maxwell House
Fairview Park
Elmsford, NY 10523
Phone: (914)592-7700
Fax: (914)592-3625
Journal presenting articles from a variety of scientific disciplines concerned with the security and preservation of mankind and of the biosphere. ***Frequency:*** Bimonthly. ***Price:*** $875.

★5662★ CITES Junior Patrol
Conservation Treaty Support Fund
3705 Cardiff Rd.
Chevy Chase, MD 20815
Phone: (301)654-3150
Fax: (301)652-6390

★5663★ Clean Air Act Report
National Environmental Development Assn.
1440 New York Ave. NW, Ste. 300
Washington, DC 20005
Phone: (202)638-1230
Frequency: Quarterly.

★5664★ Clearing Magazine
Environmental Education Project
19600 S. Molalla Ave.
Oregon City, OR 97045
Phone: (503)656-0155
Provides resource materials, teaching ideas, and information for those interested in providing environmental education. ***Frequency:*** 5x/yr. ***Price:*** $10.

★5665★ Clearwaters
New York Water Pollution Control Assn., Inc.
90 Presidential Plaza, Ste. 122
Syracuse, NY 13202
Phone: (315)422-7811
Magazine for planners, engineers, scientists, municipal officials, government agencies and environmental groups concerned with water quality management in New York State. ***Frequency:*** Quarterly. ***Price:*** $6.

★5666★ Climatic Data for the World
National Environmental Satellite, Data, and Information Service
2069 Federal Bldg. 4
Washington, DC 20233
Phone: (301)763-7190
Fax: (301)763-4011
Frequency: Monthly.

★5667★ Coalition for Responsible Waste Incineration Information Kit
Coalition for Responsible Waste Incineration
1330 Connecticut Ave. NW, Ste. 300
Washington, DC 20036
Phone: (202)659-0060
Membership brochure. ***Frequency:*** Periodic.

★5668★ Coalition on Resource Recovery and the Environment Bulletin
Coalition on Resource Recovery and the Environment
c/o Dr. Walter M. Shaub
U. S. Conf. of Mayors
1620 I St. NW, Ste. 600
Washington, DC 20006
Phone: (202)293-7330
Fax: (202)293-2352
Frequency: Periodic.

★5669★ Coalition on Resource Recovery and the Environment Technotes
Coalition on Resource Recovery and the Environment
c/o Dr. Walter M. Shaub
U. S. Conf. of Mayors
1620 I St. NW, Ste. 600
Washington, DC 20006
Phone: (202)293-7330
Fax: (202)293-2352
Frequency: Periodic.

★5670★ Comprehensive Planning for Wildlife Resources
Organization of Wildlife Planners
DNR-Box 7921
Madison, WI 53707
Phone: (608)267-7591
Fax: (608)267-3579

★5671★ Conservation Bits and Bytes
National Assn. of Conservation Districts
509 Capitol Ct. NE
Washington, DC 20002
Phone: (202)547-6223
Fax: (202)547-6450
Frequency: Quarterly.

★5672★ The Conservationist
New York State Dept. of Environmental Conservation
50 Wolf Rd., Rm. 516
Albany, NY 12233-4502
Phone: (518)457-5547
Fax: (518)457-1088
Magazine covering conservation issues. ***Frequency:*** 6x/yr. ***Price:*** $5; $9 two years.

★5673★ Conservogram
Soil and Water Conservation Soc.
7515 NE Ankeny Rd.
Ankeny, IA 50021
Phone: (515)289-2331
Fax: (515)289-1227
Frequency: Bimonthly.

★5674★ Coolidge Calendar
Coolidge Center for Environmental Leadership
1675 Massachusetts Ave., Ste. 4
Cambridge, MA 02138
Phone: (617)864-5085
Fax: (617)864-6503
Frequency: 7/year.

★5675★ Council on Plastics and Packaging in the Environment Quarterly
Council on Plastics and Packaging in the Environment
1275 K St. NW, Ste. 900
Washington, DC 20005
Phone: (202)789-1310
Fax: (202)289-1389

★5676★ Council on Plastics and Packaging in the Environment Update
Council on Plastics and Packaging in the Environment
1275 K St. NW, Ste. 900
Washington, DC 20005
Phone: (202)789-1310

Fax: (202)289-1389
Contains legislative, research, and recycling information and calendar of events. ***Frequency:*** Monthly. ***Price:*** Available to members only.

★5677★ Cranes, Cranes, Cranes
International Crane Found.
E-11376 Shady Ln. Rd.
Baraboo, WI 53913-9778
Phone: (608)356-9462
Fax: (608)356-9465

★5678★ Cross Currents
Friends of the River
Fl. Mason Center, Bldg. C
San Francisco, CA 94123
Phone: (415)771-0400
Fax: (415)771-0301

★5679★ The Dade County Environmental Story
Friends of the Everglades
202 Park St.
Miami Springs, FL 33166
Phone: (305)888-1230

★5680★ Dangerous Properties of Industrial Materials Report
Van Nostrand Reinhold
115 5th Ave.
New York, NY 10003
Phone: (212)254-3232
Fax: (212)673-1239
Chemical and environmental review of hazardous industrial materials. ***Frequency:*** 6x/yr. ***Price:*** $195; $235 other countries.

★5681★ Deadly Defense—Military Radioactive Landfills
Radioactive Waste Campaign
625 Broadway, 2nd Fl.
New York, NY 10012-2611
Phone: (212)473-7390

★5682★ The Debt for Nature Exchange
Conservation Intl.
1015 18th St. NW, Ste. 1000
Washington, DC 20036
Phone: (202)429-5660
Fax: (202)887-5188

★5683★ Deer Unlimited
Deer Unlimited of America
PO Box 1129
Abbeville, SC 29620
Phone: (803)391-2300
Frequency: Bimonthly.

★5684★ Deer Unlimited of America Periodical
Deer Unlimited of America
PO Box 1129
Abbeville, SC 29620
Phone: (803)391-2300
Frequency: Periodic.

★5685★ Defenders
Defenders of Wildlife
1244 19th St. NW
Washington, DC 20036
Phone: (202)659-9510
Fax: (202)659-0680
Wildlife and conservation magazine. ***Frequency:*** 6x/yr. ***Price:*** $20 (included with membership).

★5686★ Degradability Incineration
Council on Plastics and Packaging in the Environment
1275 K St. NW, Ste. 900
Washington, DC 20005
Phone: (202)789-1310
Fax: (202)289-1389

★5687★ Desert Tortoise Council Proceedings of Symposium
Desert Tortoise Coun.
PO Box 1738
Palm Desert, CA 92261-1738
Phone: (619)341-8449
Frequency: Annual.

★5688★ Directory of Speakers and Referral Service
The Acid Rain Found.
1410 Varsity Dr.
Raleigh, NC 27606
Phone: (919)828-9443
Frequency: Periodic.

★5689★ Dolphin Log
The Cousteau Soc.
930 W. 21st St.
Norfolk, VA 23517
Phone: (804)627-1144
Fax: (804)627-7547
Educational journal for children ages seven to 15 covering all areas of science, history, and arts related to the world's water system. ***Frequency:*** Bimonthly. ***Price:*** Included in family membership dues.

★5690★ Ducks Unlimited Magazine
Ducks Unlimited
1 Waterfowl Way
Long Grove, IL 60047
Phone: (708)438-4300
Fax: (708)438-9236
Magazine on waterfowl, wildlife conservation. ***Frequency:*** 6x/yr. ***Price:*** $1.50 single issue.

★5691★ E Magazine: The Environmental Magazine
Earth Action Network
PO Box 5098
Westport, CT 06881
Phone: (203)854-5559
Fax: (203)866-0602
Frequency: 6x/yr. ***Price:*** $20; $36 two years; $3.50 single issue.

★5692★ Earth Echo
Earth Ecology Found.
903 E. Fedora
Fresno, CA 93704
Phone: (209)222-2785

★5693★ Earth Island Journal: An International Environmental News Magazine
Earth Island Inst.
300 Broadway, Ste. 28
San Francisco, CA 94133-3312
Phone: (415)788-3666
Fax: (415)788-7324
Magazine publishing environmental success stories and problems from around the world. ***Frequency:*** Quarterly. Price: Free to Earth Island Institute members; $25 nonmembers.

★5694★ Earth Work
Student Conservation Assoc., Inc.
Circulation Office
P.O. Box 550
Charlestown, NH 03603-0550
Phone: (603)826-4301
Fax: (603)826-7755
Deals with conservation/environmental career issues, targeting those individuals who seek employment in the environmental field. ***Frequency:*** Monthly.

★5695★ Earthwalks and Conceptual Encounters
Institute for Earth Education
PO Box 288
Warrenville, IL 60555
Phone: (708)393-3096

★5696★ East West: The Journal of Natural Health and Living
PO Box 1200
Brookline Village, MA 02147
Phone: (617)232-1000
Fax: (617)232-1572
Frequency: Bimonthly. ***Price:*** $18.50; $3.50 single issue.

★5697★ Eco-Justice: Restoring Creation for Ecology and Justice
Eco-Justice Project and Network
Cornell University
Anabel Taylor Hall
Ithaca, NY 14850
Frequency: Bimonthly. 111 pp.

★5698★ EcoAction
Greater Yellowstone Coalition
13 S. Willson
PO Box 1874
Bozeman, MT 59715
Phone: (406)586-1593
Fax: (406)586-0851
Frequency: Periodic.

★5699★ Ecolog
Point Found.
27 Gate Five Rd.
Sausalito, CA 94965
Phone: (415)332-1716

★5700★ Ecological Monographs
Ecological Soc. of America
Arizona State University
Center for Environmental Studies
Tempe, AZ 85287-1201
Phone: (602)965-3000
Journal promoting ecological research and the development of the utilities which may be served by ecological principles. ***Frequency:*** Quarterly. ***Price:*** $30; $45 institutions.

★5701★ Ecology
Ecological Soc. of America
Center for Environmental Studies
Arizona State University
Tempe, AZ 85287-1201
Phone: (602)965-3000
Scientific journal promoting ecological research and the development of utilities that may be served by ecological principles. ***Frequency:*** 6x/yr. ***Price:*** $80; $150 institutions.

★5702★ Ecology Abstracts
Cambridge Scientific Abstracts
7200 Wisconsin Ave.
Bethesda, MD 20814
Phone: (301)961-6750
Fax: (301)961-6720
Scientific journal. ***Frequency:*** Monthly. ***Price:*** $685; $790 other countries.

★5703★ Ecology International
INTECOL - Intl. Assn. for Ecology
c/o Institute of Ecology
University of Georgia
Athens, GA 30602
Phone: (404)542-2968
Frequency: Semiannual.

★5704★ Ecotoxicology and Environmental Safety
Academic Press, Inc.
1250 6th Ave.
San Diego, CA 92101
Phone: (619)699-6825
Fax: (619)699-6800
Journal reporting research of the biologic and toxic effects of natural or synthetic chemical pollutants on animal, plant, or microbial ecosystems. ***Frequency:*** 6x/yr. ***Price:*** $200 U.S. and Canada; $251 other countries.

★5705★ Educational Hawkwatcher
Wildlife Information Center
629 Green St.
Allentown, PA 18102
Phone: (215)434-1637
Frequency: Periodic.

★5706★ An Efficient Approach to Reducing Acid Rain: The Environmental Benefits of Energy Conservation
Center for Clean Air Policy
444 N. Capitol St., Ste. 526
Washington, DC 20001
Phone: (202)624-7709

★5707★ The Egg-An Eco-Justice Quarterly
Eco-Justice Project and Network
Cornell University
Anabel Taylor Hall
Ithaca, NY 14850
Frequency: Quarterly.

★5708★ EHMI Re:Source
Environmental Hazards Management Institute
10 Newmarket Rd.
PO Box 932
Durham, NH 03824
Subscription information available from EHMI.

★5709★ Elephant
Elephant Interest Group
106 E. Hickory Grove
Bloomfield Hills, MI 48013
Phone: (313)540-3947
Contact: Hezy Shoshani, Contact
Journal; includes membership roster. ***Frequency:*** Periodic.

★5710★ The Eleventh Commandment: Toward an Ethic of Ecology
Eleventh Commandment Fellowship
PO Box 14667
San Francisco, CA 94114
Phone: (415)626-6064
Frequency: Semiannual.

★5711★ Endangered Species Act Reauthorization Coordinating Committee Bulletin
Endangered Species Act Reauthorization Coordinating Comm.
1725 DeSales St. NW, Ste. 500
Washington, DC 20036
Phone: (202)429-5609
Frequency: Periodic.

★5712★ Endangered Species Report
Defenders of Wildlife
1244 19th St. NW
Washington, DC 20036
Phone: (202)659-9510
Fax: (202)833-3349
Frequency: Annual.

★5713★ Energy from Biomass and Municipal Waste
U.S. Dept. of Energy, OSTI
PO Box 62
Oak Ridge, TN 37831
Phone: (615)576-1168
Fax: (615)576-2865
Journal containing abstracts on biomass and municipal waste production, conversion, and use for energy. ***Frequency:*** Monthly. ***Price:*** $90; $180 other countries.

★5714★ Environet
Friends of the Everglades
202 Park St.
Miami Springs, FL 33166
Phone: (305)888-1230

★5715★ Environment
Heldref Publications
Helen Dwight Reid Educational Foundation
4000 Albemarle St. NW
Washington, DC 20016
Phone: (202)362-6445
Fax: (202)537-0287
Trade magazine covering environmental problems and solutions. ***Frequency:*** 10x/yr. ***Price:*** $24; $38 institutions.

★5716★ Environment Today
Enterprise Communications Inc.
1483 Chain Bridge Rd., Ste. 202
McLean, VA 22101-4599
Phone: (703)448-0322
Fax: (703)827-8214
Magazine for environmental professionals, including corporate waste generators, municipal utilities managers, and governmental decision makers. Focuses on trend-spotting and problem-solving. ***Frequency:*** 9x/yr. ***Price:*** $36; $56 other countries; $5 single issue.

★5717★ Environment West: Natural History of Western North America
San Diego Soc. of Natural History
PO Box 1390
San Diego, CA 92112
Phone: (619)232-3821
Fax: (619)232-0248
Frequency: Quarterly. ***Price:*** $10.

★5718★ Environmental Action Magazine
Environmental Action, Inc.
1525 New Hampshire Ave. NW
Washington, DC 20036
Phone: (202)745-4870
Fax: (202)745-4880
Magazine. ***Frequency:*** 6x/yr. ***Price:*** $20; $30 for-profit institutions.

★5719★ Environmental Auditor: Compliance-Risk Assessment-Resource Management
Springer-Verlag
175 5th Ave.
New York, NY 10010
Phone: (212)460-1500
Fax: (212)473-6272
Journal. ***Frequency:*** Quarterly. PRC $169.

★5720★ The Environmental Communicator
North Amer. Assn. for Environmental Education
PO Box 400
Troy, OH 45373
Phone: (513)339-6835
Fax: (513)698-6493
Frequency: Bimonthly. ***Price:*** Included in membership dues.

★5721★ Environmental Education Guide Series
Institute for Environmental Education
32000 Chagrin Blvd.
Cleveland, OH 44124
Phone: (216)464-1775

★5722★ Environmental Entomology
Entomological Soc. of America
9301 Annapolis Rd., Ste. 300
Lanham, MD 20706
Phone: (301)731-4535
Fax: (301)731-4538
Entomology journal focusing on environmental issues. ***Frequency:*** 6x/yr. ***Price:*** $25; $65 nonmembers; $110 institutions.

★5723★ Environmental Ethics
Environmental Philosophy, Inc.
Athens, GA 30602
Quarterly. ***Price:*** $36/yr.

★5724★ Environmental Geochemistry and Health
Society for Environmental Geochemistry and Health
c/o Willard R. Chappell
University of Colorado, Denver
Center for Environmental Sciences
Campus Box 136
Denver, CO 80204
Phone: (303)556-3460
Fax: (303)556-4822
Frequency: Quarterly.

★5725★ Environmental History Review
American Society for Environmental History
New Jersey Institute for Technology
Clifton, NJ 07012
Frequency: Quarterly. 95 pp.

★5726★ Environmental Impact Assessment Review
Elsevier Science Publishing Co., Inc.
655 Ave. of the Americas
New York, NY 10010
Phone: (212)989-5800
Fax: (212)633-3990
Environmental journal. ***Frequency:*** Quarterly. ***Price:*** $138 institutions; $159 other countries.

★5727★ Environmental Impact of Soft Drink Delivery Systems
National Assn. for Plastic Container Recovery
4828 Pkwy. Plaza Blvd., Ste. 260
Charlotte, NC 28217
Phone: (704)357-3250
Fax: (704)357-3260
Toll-Free: 800-NAP-CORP

★5728★ Environmental Lab
Mediacom, Inc.
760 Whalers Way, Ste. 100
Bldg. A
Fort Collins, CO 80525
Phone: (303)229-0029
Fax: (303)229-0028
Magazine for environmental professionals. ***Frequency:*** Monthly.

★5729★ Environmental Law Forum
Environmental Law Inst.
1616 P St. NW, Ste. 200
Washington, DC 20036
Phone: (202)328-5150
Frequency: Bimonthly.

★5730★ Environmental Law Reporter
Environmental Law Inst.
1616 P St. NW, Ste. 200
Washington, DC 20036
Phone: (202)328-5150
Frequency: Monthly.

★5731★ Environmental Management
Springer-Verlag New York, Inc.
175 5th Ave.
New York, NY 10010
Phone: (212)460-1500
Fax: (212)473-6272
Journal committed to the principle of stewardship, the obligation to seek knowledge that helps protect and sustain the planet and all its life. ***Frequency:*** 6x/yr. ***Price:*** $122.50; $221.50 institutions.

★5732★ Environmental Management: Journal of Industrial Sanitation and Facilities Management
Environmental Management Assn.
255 Detroit St., Ste. 200
Denver, CO 80206
Phone: (303)320-7855
Fax: (303)393-0770
Frequency: Quarterly. ***Price:*** Free to qualified subscribers; $40; $10 single issue.

★5733★ The Environmental Manager's Compliance Advisor
Environmental Hazards Management Institute
10 Newmarket Rd.
PO Box 932
Durham, NH 03824
Subscription information available from EHMI.

★5734★ Environmental Periodicals Bibliography
International Acad. at Santa Barbara
800 Garden St., Ste. D
Santa Barbara, CA 93101-1552
Phone: (805)965-5010
Fax: (805)965-6071
Publication containing index of articles from more than 380 international environmental periodicals. Provides reproductions of tables of contents, subject, and author indexes. ***Frequency:*** 6x/yr.

★5735★ Environmental Policy Institute Quarterly Report
Environmental Policy Inst.
218 D St., SE
Washington, DC 20003
Phone: (202)544-2600
Fax: (202)543-4710
Price: $5/copy.

★5736★ Environmental Review
Citizens for a Better Environment
407 S. Dearborn, Ste. 1775
Chicago, IL 60605
Phone: (312)939-1530
Journal on the public health effects of pollution and measures aided at reducing pollution of toxic substances; includes updates of the organization's activities and research reports. ***Frequency:*** Quarterly. ***Price:*** Included in membership dues; $25/year for nonmembers.

★5737★ Environmental Review
Amer. Soc. for Environmental History
c/o John Opie
Center for Technical Studies
New Jersey Institute of Technology
Newark, NJ 07102
Phone: (201)596-3270
Contact: John Opie, Editor
Frequency: Quarterly.

★5738★ Environmental Science and Engineering
Davcom Communications Inc.
10 Petch Circle
Aurora, Ontario, Canada L4G 5N7
Phone: (416)727-4666
Fax: (416)841-7271
Trade magazine dealing with water, sewage, and pollution control. ***Frequency:*** 6x/yr. ***Price:*** $45.

★5739★ Environmental Wheels from EHMI: Household Hazardous Waste
Environmental Hazards Management Institute
10 Newmarket Rd.
PO Box 932
Durham, NH 03824
Subscription information available from EHMI.

★5740★ The Environmentalist
Environmental Technology Seminar
PO Box 391
Bethpage, NY 11714
Phone: (516)931-3200
Frequency: Periodic.

★5741★ EPA Journal
U. S. Environmental Protection Agency
401 M. St. SW, A-107
Washington, DC 20460
Phone: (202)382-4359
Fax: (202)252-0231
Journal on regulations and the environment. ***Frequency:*** Monthly. (Jan./Feb. and Jul./Aug. combined issues.) ***Price:*** $11; $13.75 other countries.

★5742★ EPA's Real Needs
Environmental Safety
733 15th St. NW, Ste. 1120
Washington, DC 20005
Phone: (202)628-0370
Fax: (202)628-0376
Position papers, and informational material on specific environmental issues.

★5743★ Everglades Reporter
Friends of the Everglades
202 Park St.
Miami Springs, FL 33166
Phone: (305)888-1230

★5744★ Everyone's Backyard
Citizen's Clearinghouse for Hazardous Wastes
PO Box 926
Arlington, VA 22216
Phone: (703)276-7070
Frequency: 6/year.

★5745★ Exchange
Land Trust Alliance
900 17th St. NW, Ste. 410
Washington DC, 20006
Phone: (202)785-1410
Fax: (202)785-1408
Frequency: Quarterly. ***Price:*** $30/year.

★5746★ Explorer
The Cleveland Museum of Natural History
University Circle
1 Wade Oval Dr.
Cleveland, OH 44106
Phone: (216)231-4600
Fax: (216)231-5919
Magazine featuring articles on natural history and science. ***Frequency:*** Quarterly. ***Price:*** $35; $10 libraries and educational institutions.

★5747★ Farmland: A Community Issue
Concern, Inc.
1794 Columbia Rd. NW
Washington, DC 20009
Phone: (202)328-8160

★5748★ Fin and Fluke Report
Pacific Whale Found.
Kealia Beach Plaza, Ste. 25
101 N. Kihei Rd.
Kihei, HI 96753
Phone: (808)879-8811
Fax: (808)879-2615
Frequency: Quarterly.

★5749★ First Breedings of Wild Waterfowl
International Wild Waterfowl Assn.
c/o Nancy Collins
Hidden Lake Waterfowl
5614 River Styx Rd.
Medina, OH 44256
Phone: (216)725-8782
Frequency: Periodic.

★5750★ FishAmerica Forum
FishAmerica Found.
c/o Sport Fishing Institute
1010 Massachusetts Ave. NW, Ste. 320
Washington, DC 20001
Phone: (202)898-0869
Fax: (202)371-2085
Frequency: 3/year.

★5751★ Flood Planning Assistance to Small Towns
Association of State Floodplain Managers
PO Box 2051
Madison, WI 53701-2051
Phone: (608)266-1926

★5752★ Florida Environments: Florida's Number One Environmental New Source
Florida Environments Publishing, Inc.
215 N. Main St.
PO Box 1617
High Springs, FL 32643-1617
Phone: (904)454-2007
Fax: (904)454-3113
Frequency: Monthly. ***Price:*** $14.95.

★5753★ The Florida Naturalist
Florida Audubon Soc.
1101 Audubon Way
Maitland, FL 32751
Phone: (407)647-2615
Fax: (407)647-6020
Magazine on Florida's natural history. ***Frequency:*** Quarterly. ***Price:*** $15; $12 libraries.

★5754★ Florida Specifier: Practical Information for Environmental Professionals
National Technical Communications Company, Inc.
385 W. Fairbanks Ave.
Winter Park, FL 32789
Phone: (407)740-7950
Fax: (407)740-7957
Magazine covering water, wastewater, hazardous waste, soup waste, and air quality. ***Frequency:*** Monthly. ***Price:*** Free to qualified subscribers; $24.95; $5 single issue.

★5755★ Florida Water Resources Journal
PO Box 1702-518
Gainesville, FL 32602-1702
Phone: (904)374-4946
Fax: (904)372-6229
Water, wastewater, and environmental magazine. ***Frequency:*** Monthly. ***Price:*** $24.

★5756★ Food Additives and Contaminants
Taylor & Francis
1900 Frost Rd., Ste. 101
Bristol, PA 19007
Phone: (215)785—580
Fax: (215)785-5515
Publishing original research papers and reviews covering natural and man-made additives and contaminants in the food chain. ***Frequency:*** 6x/yr. ***Price:*** $250 institutions.

★5757★ Forest and Conservation History
Forest History Soc.
701 Vickers Ave.
Durham, NC 27701
Phone: (919)682-9319
Journal on the history of forest use and conservation. ***Frequency:*** Quarterly. ***Price:*** $25; $35 institutions.

★5758★ Forest Notes
Society for the Protection of New Hampshire Forests
54 Portsmouth St.
Concord, NH 03301-5400
Phone: (603)224-9945
Journal on forestry and conservation. ***Frequency:*** Quarterly. ***Price:*** $26.

★5759★ Forest Science
Society of Amer. Foresters
5400 Grosvenor Ln.
Bethesda, MD 20814-2198
Phone: (301)897-8720
Fax: (301)897-3690
Magazine publishing research results covering silviculture, soils, biometry, diseases, recreation, photosynthesis, tree physiology, management, harvesting, and policy analysis. ***Frequency:*** Quarterly. ***Price:*** $30; $90 institutions.

★5760★ Forest Watch: The Citizen's Forestry Magazine
Cascade Holistic Economic Consultants
14417 SE Laurie Ave.
Oak Grove, OR 97207
Phone: (503)652-7049
Journal promoting public forest management. ***Frequency:*** 11/year. ***Price:*** $21.

★5761★ Forest World
World Forestry Center
4033 SW Canyon Rd.
Portland, OR 97221
Phone: (503)228-1367
Fax: (503)228-3624
Magazine covering forest and natural resource issues. ***Frequency:*** Quarterly. ***Price:*** $20; $25 families; $15 students and instructors; $2.50 single issue.

★5762★ Forests and People
Louisiana Forestry Assn.
PO Drawer 5067
Alexandria, LA 71307-5067
Phone: (318)443-2558
Magazine for forest products industries, foresters, and forest landowners. ***Frequency:*** Quarterly. ***Price:*** $10.

★5763★ Game Coin
Game Conservation Intl.
PO Box 17444
San Antonio, TX 78217
Phone: (512)824-7509
Frequency: Quarterly.

★5764★ Garbage: The Practical Journal for the Environment
Old House Journal Corp.
435 9th St.
Brooklyn, NY 11215
Phone: (718)788-1700
Fax: (718)788-9051
Magazine exploring environmental issues. ***Frequency:*** 6x/yr. ***Price:*** $21; $3.95 single issue.

★5765★ Global Climate Change Digest: A Guide to Current Information on Greenhouse Gases and Ozone Depletion
Elsevier Science Publishing Co., Inc.
655 Ave. of the Americas
New York, NY 10010
Phone: (212)989-5800
Fax: (212)633-3990
Frequency: Monthly. ***Price:*** $295 institutions; $335 other countries.

★5766★ Grazing and Riparian Ecosystems
Trout Unlimited
501 Church St. NE
Vienna, VA 22180
Phone: (703)281-1100

★5767★ Great Lakes Commission Special Publications
Great Lakes Commn.
Argus II Bldg.
400 S. 4th St.
Ann Arbor, MI 48103
Phone: (313)665-9135
Fax: (313)665-4370
Frequency: Periodic.

★5768★ Great Lakes Research Checklist
Great Lakes Commn.
Argus II Bldg.
400 S. 4th St.
Ann Arbor, MI 48103
Phone: (313)665-9135
Fax: (313)665-4370
Frequency: Semiannual.

★5769★ Great Lakes United Bulletin
Great Lakes United
State University Coll. at Buffalo
Cassety Hall
1300 Elmwood Ave.
Buffalo, NY 14222
Phone: (716)886-0142
Frequency: Monthly.

★5770★ Green Alternative Information for Action
Earth Island Inst.
300 Broadway, Ste. 28
San Francisco, CA 94133
Phone: (415)788-3666
Fax: (415)788-7324
Calendar of events. ***Frequency:*** Monthly.

★5771★ Green Library Journal
University of Idaho Library
Moscow, ID 83843
Phone: (208)885-6817
Fax: (208)885-6817
Covers conservation, ecologically-balanced regional development, environmental protection, and natural resource management. ***Editor(s):*** Maria A. Jankowska, Ph.D., M.L.I.S. ***Frequency:*** 3x/yr. ***Price:*** $20 individuals; $40 libraries and institutions; $45 institutions outside the U.S.

★5772★ Greenpeace
Greenpeace U.S.A.
1436 U St., NW
Washington, DC 20009
Phone: (202)462-1177
Fax: (202)462-4507
Frequency: Bimonthly.

★5773★ Greenpeace Magazine
Greenpeace U.S.A.
1436 U St. NW
Washington, DC 20009
Phone: (202)462-1177
Fax: (202)462-4507
Magazine covering environmental issues and the activities of Greenpeace. ***Frequency:*** 6x/yr. ***Price:*** $1.50 single issue.

★5774★ Groundwater: A Community Action Guide
Concern, Inc.
1794 Columbia Rd. NW
Washington, DC 20009
Phone: (202)328-8160

★5775★ Grus Americana
Whooping Crane Conservation Assn.
c/o Jerome J. Pratt
3000 Meadowlark Dr.
Sierra Vista, AZ 85635
Phone: (602)458-0971
Frequency: Quarterly.

★5776★ Guide for the Removal of Bounties
Bounty Information Service
c/o Stephens Coll. Post Office
Columbia, MO 65215
Phone: (314)876-7186

★5777★ Hazard Monthly
Research Alternatives, Inc.
966 Hungerford Dr., Ste. 1
Rockville, MD 20850
Phone: (301)424-2803
Fax: (301)738-1026
Tabloid covering natural and man-made disaster management. ***Frequency:*** Monthly. ***Price:*** $29; $39 institutions and libraries.

★5778★ Hazardous Waste and Hazardous Materials
Mary Ann Liebert, Inc.
1651 3rd Ave.
New York, NY 10128
Phone: (212)289-2300
Fax: (212)289-4697
Journal on industrial waste technology. ***Frequency:*** Quarterly. ***Price:*** $136.

★5779★ Hazardous Waste Litigation Reporter
Andrews Publications
Box 1000
Westtown, PA 19395
Phone: (215)399-6600
Fax: (215)399-6610
Journal for attorneys handling hazardous waste litigation involving Superfund and other environmental statutes. ***Frequency:*** 2x/mo. ***Price:*** $850.

★5780★ Hazmat World
Environmental Hazards Management Institute
10 Newmarket Rd.
PO Box 932
Durham, NH 03824
Subscription information available from EHMI.

★5781★ Headwaters
Friends of the River
Ft. Mason Center, Bldg. C
San Francisco, CA 94123
Phone: (415)771-0400
Fax: (415)771-0301
Frequency: Bimonthly. ***Price:*** Included in membership dues; $25/year for nonmembers.

★5782★ History of the California Tule Elk
Committee for the Preservation of the Tule Elk
PO Box 3696
San Diego, CA 92103
Phone: (619)485-0626

★5783★ The Holocene: An Interdisciplinary Journal Focusing on Recent Environmental Change
Edward Arnold
c/o Cambridge University Press
40 W. 20th St.
New York, NY 10011-4211
Phone: (212)924-3900
Fax: (212)691-3239
Frequency: 3x/yr. ***Price:*** $57; $145 institutions.

★5784★ Hot Topics from the Tropics
Rainforest Alliance
270 Lafayette St., Ste. 512
New York, NY 10012
Phone: (212)941-1900
Fax: (212)941-4986
Frequency: Bimonthly bulletin.

★5785★ Household Wastes: Issues and Opportunities
Concern, Inc.
1794 Columbia Rd. NW
Washington, DC 20009
Phone: (202)328-8160

★5786★ Humpback Whales of the Southern Gulf of Maine
Center for Coastal Studies
59 Commercial St.
PO Box 1036
Provincetown, MA 02657
Phone: (508)487-3622

★5787★ Idaho Wildlife
Idaho Dept. of Fish and Game
600 S. Walnut St.
Box 25
Boise, ID 83707
Phone: (208)334-3748
Fax: (208)334-2114
Magazine on conservation and natural history. ***Frequency:*** 6x/yr. ***Price:*** $10.

★5788★ Illinois Natural History Survey Bulletin
Illinois Natural History Survey
607 E. Peabody Dr.
Champaign, IL 61820
Phone: (217)333-6882
Fax: (217)333-4949
Bulletin presenting research results on and descriptions of the natural resources of Illinois. ***Frequency:*** Irregular. ***Price:*** $3 single issue.

★5789★ Illinois Parks and Recreation Magazine
Illinois Assn. of Park Districts
211 E. Monroe, Ste. 101
Springfield, IL 62701
Phone: (217)523-4554
Fax: (217)523-4273
Publication for park conservation, recreation, and forest preservation agencies. ***Frequency:*** 6x/yr. ***Price:*** $20.

★5790★ Illinois Wildlife
Illinois Wildlife Fed.
123 S. Chicago
Rossville, IL 60963
Phone: (217)748-6365
Tabloid focusing on conservation. ***Frequency:*** 6x/yr. ***Price:*** $10.

★5791★ Impact of Science on Society
Taylor & Francis
1900 Frost Rd., Ste. 101
Bristol, PA 19007
Phone: (215)785-5800
Fax: (215)785-5515
Forum for discusssion on issues concerning the interaction between science/technology and society. Written for a non-specialist readership. ***Frequency:*** Quarterly. ***Price:*** $56 institutions.

★5792★ Information Packets
International Wildlife Coalition
634 N. Falmouth Hwy.
PO Box 388
N. Falmouth, MA 02556
Phone: (508)564-9980
Fax: (508)563-2843
Frequency: Every 6 weeks.

★5793★ Institute Proceedings
Eastern Mineral Law Found.
West Virginia University Law Center
PO Box 6130
Morgantown, WV 26506
Phone: (304)293-2470
Fax: (304)293-7654
Frequency: Annual.

★5794★ Integrating Man and Nature in the Metropolitan Environment
National Inst. for Urban Wildlife
10921 Trotting Ridge Way
Columbia, MD 21044
Phone: (301)596-3311

★5795★ International Council for Bird Preservation, U.S. Section Bulletin
International Coun. for Bird Preservation, U.S. Sect.
c/o World Wildlife Fund
1250 24th St. NW
Washington, DC 20037
Phone: (202)778-9563
Fax: (202)293-9211
Frequency: Periodic.

★5796★ International Environmental Affairs: A Journal for Research and Policy
University Press of New England
17 1/2 Lebanon St.
Hanover, NH 03755
Phone: (603)646-1472
Fax: (603)643-1540
Journal promoting international environmental management. ***Frequency:*** Quarterly. ***Price:*** $45; $65 institutions; $55 other countries.

★5797★ International Journal of Environmental Studies: Sections A & B
Gordon and Breach Science Publishers
PO Box 786, Cooper Sta.
New York, NY 10276
Phone: (212)206-8900
Fax: (212)645-2459
Science journal. ***Frequency:*** Quarterly.

★5798★ International Waterfowl Symposium Transactions
Ducks Unlimited
One Waterfowl Way
Long Grove, IL 60047
Phone: (708)438-4300
Fax: (708)438-9236
Frequency: Periodic.

★5799★ International Wildlife
National Wildlife Fed.
8925 Leesburg Pike
Vienna, VA 22184
Phone: (703)790-4510
Fax: (703)442-7332
Magazine featuring nature and wildlife from around the world. ***Frequency:*** 6x/yr. ***Price:*** $16.

★5800★ Involvement Packets
Elsa Clubs of America
PO Box 4572
North Hollywood, CA 91617-0572
Phone: (818)761-8387
Frequency: Periodic.

★5801★ Iowa Conservationist
Iowa Dept. of Natural Resources
Wallace State Office Bldg.
Des Moines, IA 50319-0034
Phone: (515)281-5145
Fax: (515)281-8895
Magazine discussing conservation and environmental issues. ***Frequency:*** Monthly. ***Price:*** $6; $12 for three years.

★5802★ Journal of Environmental Economics and Management
Academic Press, Inc.
1250 6th Ave.
San Diego, CA 92101
Phone: (619)699-6825
Fax: (619)699-6800
Journal publishing theoretical and empirical papers on the relation between economic systems and environmental and natural resources systems. ***Frequency:*** 6x/yr. ***Price:*** $168 U.S. and Canada; $208 other countries.

★5803★ Journal of Environmental Education
Heldref Publications
Helen Dwight Reid Educational Foundation
4000 Albemarle St. NW Ste. 500
Washington, DC 20016
Phone: (202)362-6445
Fax: (202)537-0287
Environmental education journal. ***Frequency:*** Quarterly. ***Price:*** $47; $11.75 single issue.

★5804★ Journal of Environmental Pathology, Toxicology and Oncology
International Soc. for Environmental Toxicology and Cancer
PO Box 134
Park Forest, IL 60466
Phone: (708)748-0440
Fax: (312)755-2096
Frequency: Bimonthly.

★5805★ Journal of Environmental Quality
Amer. Soc. of Agronomy
677 S. Segoe Rd.
Madison, WI 53711
Phone: (608)273-8080
Fax: (608)273-2021
Journal on environmental control. ***Frequency:*** Quarterly. ***Price:*** $30.

★5806★ Journal of Environmental Science and Health, Part C: Environmental Carcinogenesis Reviews
Marcel Dekker, Inc.
270 Madison Ave.
New York, NY 10016
Phone: (212)696-9000

Fax: (212)685-4540
Science and medical journal. ***Editor(s):*** Joseph C. Arcos. ***Frequency:*** 2x/yr. ***Price:*** $82.50; $165 institutions.

★5807★ Journal of Forestry
Society of Amer. Foresters
5400 Grosvenor Ln.
Bethesda, MD 20814-2198
Phone: (301)897-8720
Fax: (301)897-3690
Journal covering measurement, protection, management, and use of forests for wildlife, recreation, water, wilderness, and graying, as well as the growing and harvesting for timber and energy. ***Frequency:*** Monthly. ***Price:*** $20; $90 institutions.

★5808★ Journal of Natural History
Taylor & Francis
1900 Frost Rd., Ste. 101
Bristol, PA 19007
Phone: (215)785-5800
Fax: (215)785-5515
Journal for environmental scientists and others. ***Frequency:*** 6x/yr. ***Price:*** $500 institutions.

★5809★ Journal of Natural History: An International Journal of Systematics, Interactive Biology, and Biodiversity
Taylor & Francis
1900 Frost Rd., Ste. 101
Bristol, PA 19007
Phone: (215)785-5800
Fax: (215)785-5515
Journal for ecologists, entomologists, evolutionary biologists, and environmental scientists. ***Frequency:*** 6x/yr. ***Price:*** $560 institutions.

★5810★ Journal of Range Management
Society for Range Management
1839 York St.
Denver, CO 80206-1213
Phone: (303)355-7070
Fax: (303)355-5059
Journal focusing on the rangeland ecosystem. ***Frequency:*** 6x/yr. ***Price:*** $56.

★5811★ Journal of Soil and Water Conservation
Soil and Water Conservation Soc.
7515 NE Ankeny Rd.
Ankeny, IA 50021-9764
Phone: (515)289-2331
Fax: (515)289-1227
Magazine featuring land and water conservation news; including general interest features, applied research reports, viewpoints, commentary, book reviews, and current events. ***Frequency:*** 6x/yr. ***Price:*** $30; $35 other countries; $6 single issue.

★5812★ Journal of the Air and Waste Management Association
Air and Waste Management Assn.
PO Box 2861
Pittsburgh, PA 15230
Phone: (412)232-3444
Fax: (412)232-3450
Environmental science engineering journal. ***Editor(s):*** Harold M. Englund. ***Frequency:*** Monthly. ***Price:*** $175.

★5813★ Journal of the Institute of Environmental Sciences
Institute of Environmental Sciences
940 E. NW Hwy.
Mount Prospect, IL 60056
Phone: (708)255-1561
Fax: (708)255-1699
Journal of the Institute of Environmental Sciences. ***Frequency:*** 6x/yr. ***Price:*** $25.

★5814★ Journal of the North American Benthological Society
North Amer. Benthological Soc.
c/o Cheryl R. Black
Savannah River Ecology Laboratory
Drawer E
Aiken, SC 29802
Phone: (803)725-7425
Fax: (803)725-7413
Frequency: Periodic. ***Price:*** $25/year for members; $50/year for nonmembers.

★5815★ Journal of Toxicology and Environmental Health
Hemisphere Publishing Corp.
1101 Vermont Ave. NW, No. 200
Washington, DC 20005
Phone: (202)289-2174
Fax: (202)289-3665
Medical research journal publishing refereed papers on environmental factors affecting health. ***Frequency:*** Monthly. ***Price:*** $172; $598 institutions.

★5816★ Journal of Wildlife Management
The Wildlife Soc.
5410 Grosvenor Ln.
Bethesda, MD 20814-2197
Phone: (301)897-9770
Fax: (301)530-2471
Covers research in all aspects of wildlife science and management. ***Frequency:*** Quarterly. ***Price:*** $44/year for members; $65/year for nonmembers.

★5817★ Journal on Hazardous Waste and Hazardous Materials
Hazardous Materials Control Research Inst.
7237 Hanover Pkwy.
Greenbelt, MD 20770
Phone: (301)587-9390
Frequency: Quarterly. ***Price:*** $99/year.

★5818★ KIND News: Kids in Nature's Defense Club
National Assn. for Humane and Environmental Education
67 Salem Rd.
East Haddam, CT 06423-0362
Phone: (203)434-8666
In-classroom newsprint magazine for children. ***Frequency:*** 9x/yr. ***Price:*** $25 (includes 32 copies per issue).

★5819★ Land and People
Trust for Public Land
116 New Montgomery St., 4th Fl.
San Francisco, CA 94105
Phone: (415)495-5660
Fax: (415)495-0541
Frequency: 3/year. ***Price:*** Included in membership dues.

★5820★ Land and Water
Rte. 3, PO Box 1197
Fort Dodge, IA 50501
Phone: (515)576-3191
Fax: (515)576-5675
Magazine on erosion control and water management. ***Frequency:*** 8x/yr. ***Price:*** $12.

★5821★ LAND GRAB: The Corporate Theft of Wisconsin's Mineral Resources
Center for Alternative Mining Development Policy
210 Avon St., Ste. 9
La Crosse, WI 54603
Phone: (608)784-4399

★5822★ Lander's Herald
720 Morrow Ave.
Clayton, NJ 08312
Phone: (609)881-0319
Ecology magazine. ***Frequency:*** 6x/yr. ***Price:*** $7.95.

★5823★ Learning from the U.S. Series
Urban Initiatives
530 W. 25th St.
New York, NY 10001
Phone: (212)620-9773
Frequency: Periodic.

★5824★ Local Climatological Data
National Environmental Satellite, Data, and Information Service
2069 Federal Bldg. 4
Washington, DC 20233
Phone: (301)763-7190
Fax: (301)763-4011
Frequency: Monthly.

★5825★ Lykos
North Amer. Wolf Soc.
PO Box 82950
Fairbanks, AK 99708
Phone: (907)474-6117
Conservation report. ***Frequency:*** 4/year.

★5826★ Magnet
Steel Can Recycling Inst.
Foster Plaza X
680 Anderson Dr.
Pittsburgh, PA 15220
Phone: (412)922-2772
Fax: (412)922-3213
Toll-Free: (00))76-7274.
Frequency: Quarterly. ***Price:*** Free.

★5827★ Maine Fish and Wildlife
Maine Dept. of Inland Fisheries and Wildlife
284 State St., No. 41
Augusta, ME 04333
Phone: (207)289-2871
Fax: (207)289-6395
Fish and wildlife conservation periodical. ***Frequency:*** Quarterly. ***Price:*** $5.95.

★5828★ Making a Difference
Institute for the Human Environment
c/o Institute International Educ.
41 Sutter, No. 510
San Francisco, CA 94104
Phone: (415)362-6520
Frequency: 3-4/year.

★5829★ Making Plant Extinction a Rare Thing
Center for Plant Conservation
125 Arborway
Jamaica Plain, MA 02130
Phone: (617)524-6988

★5830★ Man-Environment Relations Focus Series
Association for the Study of Man-Environment Relations
PO Box 57
Orangeburg, NY 10962
Phone: (914)634-8221
Frequency: Periodic.

★5831★ Man-Environment Systems
Association for the Study of Man-Environment Relations
PO Box 57
Orangeburg, NY 10962
Phone: (914)634-8221
Frequency: Bimonthly.

★5832★ Management of World Wastes
Communication Channels, Inc.
6255 Barfield Rd.
Atlanta, GA 30328
Phone: (404)256-9800
Fax: (404)256-3116
Wastes, removal, and disposal magazine. ***Frequency:*** Monthly. ***Price:*** $35.

★5833★ Marine Mammals of the World
Elsa Clubs of America
PO Box 4572
North Hollywood, CA 91617-0572
Phone: (818)761-8387

★5834★ Marine Policy Reports
Taylor & Francis
1900 Frost Rd., Ste. 101
Bristol, PA 19007
Phone: (215)785-5800
Fax: (215)785-5515
Journal on naval policies, shipping, fisheries management, and protection of the marine environment. ***Editor(s):*** Gerard J. Mangone. ***Frequency:*** Quarterly. ***Price:*** $35; $59 institutions.

★5835★ Marine Pollution Bulletin
Pergamon Press, Inc.
Maxwell House
Fairview Park
Elmsford, NY 10523
Phone: (914)592-7700
Fax: (914)592-3625
Journal on marine environment and research. ***Frequency:*** Bimonthly. ***Price:*** $270.

★5836★ Mariners Weather Log
National Environmental Satellite, Data, and Information Service
2069 Federal Bldg. 4
Washington, DC 20233
Phone: (301)763-7190
Fax: (301)763-4011
Frequency: Bimonthly.

★5837★ Material Aid Bulletin
Environmental Project on Central America
Earth Island Institute
300 Broadway, Ste. 28
San Francisco, CA 94133
Phone: (415)788-3666
Fax: (415)788-7324
Frequency: Periodic.

★5838★ Methods of Air Sampling and Analyses
Intersociety Comm. on Methods for Air Sampling and Analysis
c/o Dr. Richard J. Thompson
12113 Shropshire Blvd.
Austin, TX 78753
Phone: (512)835-5118

★5839★ Midwest Coal by Wire: Addressing Regional Acid Rain and Energy Problems
Center for Clean Air Policy
444 N. Capitol St., Ste. 526
Washington, DC 20001
Phone: (202)624-7709

★5840★ Mountain Ecosystems: Stability and Instability
International Mountain Soc.
PO Box 1978
Davis, CA 95617-1978
Phone: (916)758-7618

★5841★ Mountain Research and Development
International Mountain Soc.
PO Box 1978
Davis, CA 95617-1978
Phone: (916)758-7618
Frequency: Quarterly.

★5842★ NAACOG Certification Corporation News
NAACOG Certification Corp.
645 N. Michigan Ave., Ste. 1058
Chicago, IL 60611
Phone: (312)951-0207
Frequency: Periodic.

★5843★ National Geographic
National Geographic Soc.
17th & M Sts. NW
Washington, DC 20036
Phone: (202)857-7000
Fax: (202)828-5658
Magazine featuring articles on geography, culture, natural history, and the environment. ***Frequency:*** Monthly. ***Price:*** $21; $2.25 single issue.

★5844★ National Leaders of American Conservation
Natural Resources Coun. of America
801 Pennsylvania Ave. NW, No. 410
Washington, DC 20003
Phone: (202)547-7553

★5845★ National Wildlife
National Wildlife Fed.
8925 Leesburg Pike
Vienna, VA 22180
Phone: (703)790-4000
Magazine focusing on nature and wildlife. ***Frequency:*** 6x/yr. ***Price:*** $16.

★5846★ Natural Areas Journal
Natural Areas Assn.
320 S. 3rd St.
Rockford, IL 61104
Phone: (815)964-6666
Covers rare species management and land preservation techniques; includes book reviews. ***Frequency:*** Quarterly. ***Price:*** Included in membership dues; $25/year for nonmembers; $50/year for libraries; $100/year for institutional sponsors.

★5847★ Natural History
Amer. Museum of Natural History
Central Park W. at 79th St.
New York, NY 10024
Phone: (212)769-5500
Fax: (212)769-5511
Magazine on natural science, anthropology, archeology, and zoology. ***Frequency:*** Monthly. ***Price:*** $20; $2.50 single issue.

★5848★ Natural Resources Journal
1117 Stanford Dr. NE
Albuquerque, NM 87131
Phone: (505)277-4910
Fax: (505)277-0068
Journal of resource economics and law. ***Frequency:*** Quarterly. ***Price:*** $25.

★5849★ The Nature Conservancy Magazine
The Nature Conservancy
1815 N. Lynn St.
Arlington, VA 22209
Phone: (703)841-5300
Fax: (703)841-1283
Magazine reporting on the global preservation of natural diversity. ***Frequency:*** 6x/yr. ***Price:*** $15, included with membership.

★5850★ Nature Study: Journal of Environmental Education and Interpretation
Amer. Nature Study Soc.
44 College Dr.
Jersey City, NJ 07305
Phone: (201)432-1053
Journal for the members of American Nature Study Society. ***Frequency:*** Quarterly. ***Price:*** $15; $10 students; $18 institutions; $4 single issue.

★5851★ NatureScope
Ranger Rick's Nature Club
8925 Leesburg Pike
Vienna, VA 22184
Phone: (703)790-4000
Publication for teachers. ***Frequency:*** Periodic.

★5852★ New Alchemy Institute Catalogue: Books and Products for Ecological Living
New Alchemy Inst.
237 Hatchville Rd.
East Falmouth, MA 02536
Phone: (508)564-6301
Fax: (508)457-9680
Frequency: Periodic.

★5853★ The New Crucible: A Magazine about Man and His Environment
De Young Press
PO Box 7252
Spencer, IA 51301
Environmental magazine covering political, sociological, and legal issues. ***Frequency:*** Monthly. ***Price:*** $24; $5 single issue.

★5854★ News & Analysis
Environmental Law Institute
Publications Dept.
1616 P St., NW
Washington, DC 20036
Periodical.

★5855★ North American Predators
Elsa Clubs of America
PO Box 4572
North Hollywood, CA 91617-0572
Phone: (818)761-8387

★5856★ North American Wolf Society Journal
North Amer. Wolf Soc.
PO Box 82950
Fairbanks, AK 99708
Phone: (907)474-6117
Frequency: 3/year.

★5857★ North Dakota Outdoors
North Dakota Game and Fish Dept.
100 N. Bismarck Expy.
Bismarck, ND 58501-5095
Phone: (701)221-6300
Natural resources magazine. ***Frequency:*** 10x/yr. ***Price:*** $7.

★5858★ North of the 48
Safari Club Intl.
4800 W. Gates Pass Rd.
Tucson, AZ 85745
Phone: (602)620-1220
Fax: (602)622-1205

★5859★ The North Woods Call
Rte. 1, 00955 Turkey Run Rd.
Charlevoix, MI 49720
Phone: (616)547-9797
Tabloid on natural resources, nature, and the outdoors. Editor: Glen L. Sheppard. ***Frequency:*** 2x/mo. ***Price:*** $20; $36 two years.

★5860★ Not Man Apart
Friends of the Earth
218 D St. SE
Washington, DC 20003
Phone: (202)544-2600
Fax: (202)543-4710
Frequency: Bimonthly.

★5861★ Noticias de Galapagos
Charles Darwin Found. for the Galapagos Isles
c/o Craig MacFarland
National Zoological Park
Washington, DC 20008
Phone: (202)673-4705
Fax: (202)673-4607
Frequency: Semiannual.

★5862★ Nursery Sources: Native Plants and Wild Flowers
New England WildFlower Soc.
c/o Barbara Pryor
Hemenway Rd.
Framingham, MA 01701
Phone: (508)877-7630
Calendar of courses, booklets on the propagation and cultivation of native plants.

★5863★ Ocean View
National Coalition for Marine Conservation
PO Box 23298
Savannah, GA 31403
Phone: (912)234-8062
Fax: (912)233-2909
Features position papers on subjects such as licensing, fisheries research, and gear problems. ***Frequency:*** Periodic. ***Price:*** Included in membership dues.

★5864★ Ohio Woodlands: Conservation in Action
The Ohio Forestry Assn., Inc.
1301 Worthington Woods Blvd.
Worthington, OH 43085
Phone: (614)846-9456
Fax: (614)846-9457
Magazine promoting public understanding of the role of forestry. ***Frequency:*** Quarterly. ***Price:*** $8.

★5865★ Orion Nature Quarterly
Conservation Intl.
1015 18th St. NW, Ste. 1000
Washington, DC 20036
Phone: (202)429-5660
Fax: (202)887-5188

★5866★ The Otter Raft
Friends of the Sea Otter
Box 221220
Carmel, CA 93922
Phone: (408)373-2747
Fax: (408)373-2749
Frequency: Semiannual.

★5867★ Our Land
Our Land Soc.
530 Park Ave.
Idaho Falls, ID 83402
Phone: (208)523-5000
Fax: (208)522-5241
Nature and ecology magazine covering the use of natural resources. ***Frequency:*** Quarterly.

★5868★ Outdoor America
Izaak Walton League of America
1401 Wilson Blvd., Level B
Arlington, VA 22209
Phone: (703)528-1818
Fax: (703)528-1836
Association magazine on outdoor recreation and the conservation of America's natural resources. ***Frequency:*** Quarterly. ***Price:*** $20.

★5869★ Outdoor Oklahoma
Dept. of Wildlife Conservation
1801 N. Lincoln Blvd.
Oklahoma City, OK 73105
Phone: (405)521-3855
Fax: (405)521-6535
Magazine on wildlife conservation. ***Frequency:*** 6x/yr. ***Price:*** $8; $2.50 single issue.

★5870★ Owens Valley, Home of the Tule Elk
Committee for the Preservation of the Tule Elk
PO Box 3696
San Diego, CA 92103
Phone: (619)485-0626

★5871★ Ozark Society Journal
Ozark Soc.
PO Box 2914
Little Rock, AR 72203
Phone: (501)847-3738
Frequency: Periodic.

★5872★ Pacific Discovery: Magazine about Nature and Culture in the Western U.S.
California Acad. of Sciences
Golden Gate Park
San Francisco, CA 94118
Phone: (415)750-7116
Fax: (415)750-7106
Frequency: Quarterly. ***Price:*** $13; $17 other countries; $11 agencies.

★5873★ Pacific Seabird Group Bulletin
Pacific Seabird Group
c/o Dr. D. Michael Fry
University of California
Department of Avian Sciences
Davis, CA 95616
Phone: (916)752-1300
Frequency: Semiannual. ***Price:*** Available to members only.

★5874★ Partnerships: Effective Flood Hazard Management
Association of State Floodplain Managers
PO Box 2051
Madison, WI 53701-2051
Phone: (608)266-1926

★5875★ Pennsylvania Forests
Pennsylvania Forestry Assn.
410 E. Main St.
Mechanicsburg, PA 17055
Phone: (717)766-5371
Magazine on natural resources conservation, primarily forest-related. ***Frequency:*** Quarterly. ***Price:*** $20.

★5876★ The Phoenix
Institute of Scrap Recycling Industries
1627 K St. NW, Ste. 700
Washington, DC 20006
Phone: (202)466-4050
Frequency: Quarterly.

★5877★ Planet Three - The Earth-Based Magazine for Kids
P3 Foundation
PO Box 52
Montgomery, VT 05470
Phone: (802)326-4002
Educates children 6-12 years old on environmental affairs and ecologically safe practices. ***Editor(s):*** Randi Hacker.

★5878★ Plastic Packaging and the Environment
Council on Plastics and Packaging in the Environment
1275 K St. NW, Ste. 900
Washington, DC 20005
Phone: (202)789-1310
Fax: (202)289-1389

★5879★ Plastics Recycling: A Strategic Vision
Plastics Recycling Found.
1275 K St. NW, Ste. 500
Washington, DC 20005
Phone: (202)371-5200

★5880★ Plastron Papers
New York Turtle and Tortoise Soc.
c/o Suzanne Dohm
163 Amsterdam Ave., Ste. 365
New York, NY 10023
Phone: (212)459-4803
Journal includes information on turtle behavior, husbandry, diet, medical care, habitat, conservation, legislation, and turtle lore. ***Frequency:*** Bimonthly.

★5881★ Policy Statement on Hazardous Waste Reduction from Industry
National Wildlife Fed. Corporate Conservation Coun.
1400 16th St. NW
Washington, DC 20036
Phone: (202)797-6870
Fax: (202)797-6871

★5882★ Pollution
Social Issues Resource Series Inc.
PO Box 2348
Boca Raton, FL 33427-2348
Latest edition, Vol 4.

★5883★ Pollution Abstracts
Cambridge Scientific Abstracts
7200 Wisconsin Ave.
Bethesda, MD 20814
Phone: (301)961-6750
Fax: (301)961-6720
Journal covering environmental pollution. ***Frequency:*** 6x/yr. plus annual index. ***Price:*** $745; $875 other countries.

★5884★ Power Energy Ecology
Taylor & Francis
1900 Frost Rd., Ste. 101
Bristol, PA 19007
Phone: (215)785-5800
Fax: (215)785-5515
Journal on energy conservation, power efficiency, renewable energy development, and global environment protection. ***Frequency:*** Quarterly. ***Price:*** $225 institutions.

★5885★ Power Energy Ecology
Taylor & Francis
1900 Frost Rd., Ste. 101
Bristol, PA 19007
Phone: (215)785-5800
Fax: (215)785-5515
Journal on energy conservation, power efficiency, renewable energy development and global environment protection. ***Editor(s):*** O.G. Martynenko. ***Frequency:*** Quarterly. ***Price:*** $225 institutions.

★5886★ Power Line
Environmental Action Found.
1525 New Hampshire Ave. NW
Washington, DC 20036
Phone: (202)745-4870
Energy news journal focusing on energy efficiency, nuclear and utility accountability,

and federal and state legislation. ***Frequency:*** Bimonthly. ***Price:*** $10/year for low-income and senior citizens; $15/year for individuals and grassroots groups; $25/year for governmental and institutional groups; $50/year for business institutions.

★5887★ Prairie Grouse
Society of Tympanuchus Cupido Pinnatus
c/o Bernard J. Westfahl
930 Elm Grove Rd.
Elm Grove, WI 53122
Phone: (414)782-6333

★5888★ Prairie Naturalist
North Dakota Natural Science Soc.
University Sta.
Box 8238
Grand Forks, ND 58202-8238
Phone: (701)777-2199
Fax: (701)777-3650
Natural history journal. ***Frequency:*** Quarterly. ***Price:*** $20; $25 other countries.

★5889★ Proceedings of The Desert Fish Council
Desert Fishes Coun.
PO Box 337
Bishop, CA 93514
Phone: (619)872-8751
Frequency: Annual.

★5890★ Progress in Physical Geography
Cambridge Univ. Press
40 W. 20th St.
New York, NY 10011
Phone: (914)937-9600
Forum for studies on animate and inanimate aspects of the earth, ocean, and atmosphere with interest in man-environment interaction. ***Frequency:*** Quarterly. ***Price:*** $69.50; $108 institutions; $35 single issue.

★5891★ Purple Martin Update
Purple Martin Conservation Assn.
Edinboro University of Pennsylvania
Edinboro, PA 16444
Phone: (814)734-4420
Magazine includes reports from Brazil, the wintering ground of the purple martin. ***Frequency:*** Quarterly. ***Price:*** Included in membership dues.

★5892★ Quail Unlimited
Quail Unlimited
PO Box 10041
Augusta, GA 30903
Phone: (803)637-5731
Fax: (803)637-0037
Frequency: Bimonthly.

★5893★ Ranger Rick
National Wildlife Federation
1400 16th St., NW
Washington, DC 20036-2266
Toll-Free: 800-432-6564
Environmental/natural history magazine for children ages 6-12. ***Price:*** $15.

★5894★ The Raptor Report
Society for the Preservation of Birds of Prey
PO Box 66070
Los Angeles, CA 90066
Phone: (213)397-8216

★5895★ Raptor Research
Raptor Research Found.
c/o Richard J. Clark
York College of Pennsylvania
Department of Biology
York, PA 17403-3426
Phone: (717)846-7788
Fax: (717)846-1274
Frequency: Quarterly.

★5896★ Raptor Research Foundation Reports
Raptor Research Found.
c/o Richard J. Clark
York College of Pennsylvania
Department of Biology
York, PA 17403-3426
Phone: (717)846-7788
Fax: (717)846-1274
Frequency: Periodic.

★5897★ Records of North American Big Game
Boone and Crockett Club
241 S. Fraley Blvd.
Dumfries, VA 22026
Phone: (703)221-1888

★5898★ Records of North American Whitetail Deer
Boone and Crockett Club
241 S. Fraley Blvd.
Dumfries, VA 22026
Phone: (703)221-1888

★5899★ Recycling Plastic Containers
National Assn. for Plastic Container Recovery
4828 Pkwy. Plaza Blvd., Ste. 260
Charlotte, NC 28217
Phone: (704)357-3250
Fax: (704)357-3260
Toll-Free: 800-NAPCORP

★5900★ Recycling Times: The Newspaper of Recycling Markets
NSWMA
1730 Rhode Island Ave. NW, Ste. 1000
Washington, DC 20036
Phone: (202)861-0708
Fax: (202)659-0925
Newspaper (tabloid) covering industrial and commercial waste recycling. ***Frequency:*** Every other week. ***Price:*** $95.

★5901★ Recycling Today
G.I.E., Inc.
4012 Bridge Ave.
Cleveland, OH 44113
Phone: (216)961-4130
Fax: (216)961-0364
Magazine covering recycling of secondary raw materials and solid waste management. ***Frequency:*** Monthly. ***Price:*** $28; $39 Canada; $98 other countries; $105 other countries airmail.

★5902★ Remedial Action Plan Revival: Recommendations of Great Lakes Citizens
Great Lakes United
State University Coll. at Buffalo
Cassety Hall
1300 Elmwood Ave.
Buffalo, NY 14222
Phone: (716)886-0142

★5903★ Renewable Resources Journal
Renewable Natural Resources Found.
5430 Grosvenor Ln.
Bethesda, MD 20814
Phone: (301)493-9101
Fax: (301)493-6148
Frequency: Quarterly.

★5904★ Report of the Legal Documents Concerning Walden and Walden Abuse
Walden Forever Wild
PO Box 275
Concord, MA 01742
Phone: (203)429-2839

★5905★ Research Journal Water Pollution Control Federation
Water Pollution Control Fed.
601 Wythe St.
Alexandria, VA 22314-1994
Phone: (703)684-2400
Fax: (703)684-2492
Frequency: Bimonthly.

★5906★ Resource Policy Institute Reports
Resource Policy Inst.
c/o Dr. Arthur H. Purcell
1745 Selby, Ste. 11
Los Angeles, CA 90024
Phone: (213)475-1684
Frequency: Periodic.

★5907★ Resource Recycling: North America's Recycling Journal
Resource Recycling Inc.
PO Box 10540
Portland, OR 97210
Phone: (503)227-1319
Fax: (503)227-6135
Journal reporting on the recycling of solid waste. ***Frequency:*** Monthly. ***Price:*** $42. $4 single issue.

★5908★ Resources, Conservation and Recycling
Pergamon Press, Inc.
Maxwell House
Fairview Park
Elmsford, NY 10523
Phone: (914)592-7700
Fax: (914)592-3625
Journal on engineering, science, and electronics. ***Frequency:*** Quarterly.

★5909★ The Return of the Tule Elk
Committee for the Preservation of the Tule Elk
PO Box 3696
San Diego, CA 92103
Phone: (619)485-0626

★5910★ Returnable Times
Environmental Action Found.
1525 New Hampshire Ave. NW
Washington, DC 20036
Phone: (202)745-4870
Frequency: Quarterly.

★5911★ Safari Magazine
Safari Club Intl.
4800 W. Gates Pass Rd.
Tucson, AZ 85745
Phone: (602)620-1220
Fax: (602)622-1205
Frequency: Periodic.

★5912★ Sanctuaries for the Protection of Rare Species
Committee for the Preservation of the Tule Elk
PO Box 3696
San Diego, CA 92103
Phone: (619)485-0626

★5913★ Save-the-Redwoods League Bulletin
Save-the-Redwoods League
114 Sansome St., Rm. 605
San Francisco, CA 94104
Phone: (415)362-2352
Frequency: Semiannual.

★5914★ **Saving Oiled Seabirds**
International Bird Rescue Research Center
699 Potter St.
Berkeley, CA 94710
Phone: (415)841-9086
Fax: (415)841-9089

★5915★ **Science and Ethics**
Elmwood Inst.
PO Box 5765
Berkeley, CA 94705-0765
Phone: (415)845-4595
Fax: (415)843-9398

★5916★ **Scrap Processing and Recycling Magazine**
Institute of Scrap Recycling Industries
1627 K St. NW, Ste. 700
Washington, DC 20006
Phone: (202)466-4050
Contact: Dr. Herschel Cutler, Exec.Dir.
Frequency: Periodic.

★5917★ **Sea Shepherd**
Sea Shepherd Conservation Soc.
PO Box 7000 S
Redondo Beach, CA 90277
Phone: (213)373-6979

★5918★ **Sea Shepherd Log**
Sea Shepherd Conservation Soc.
PO Box 7000 S
Redondo Beach, CA 90277
Phone: (213)373-6979
Frequency: Quarterly.

★5919★ **Sheep Special**
Safari Club Intl.
4800 W. Gates Pass Rd.
Tucson, AZ 85745
Phone: (602)620-1220
Fax: (602)622-1205

★5920★ **Sheepherder**
Society for the Conservation of Bighorn Sheep
3113 Mesaloa Ln.
Pasadena, CA 91107
Phone: (818)797-1287
Frequency: Quarterly.

★5921★ **Sialia**
North Amer. Bluebird Soc.
Box 6295
Silver Spring, MD 20916-6295
Phone: (301)384-2798
Frequency: Quarterly. ***Price:*** Available to members only.

★5922★ **Sierra**
Sierra Club
730 Polk St.
San Francisco, CA 94109
Phone: (415)776-2211
Provides essays on the wilderness, reports on environmental politics, conservation movement, and outdoor adventure; includes color photography, book reviews, new equipment news, young readers' section, and profiles of leaders in the conservation movement. ***Frequency:*** Bimonthly. ***Price:*** Included in membership dues; $15/year for nonmembers.

★5923★ **Sierra: The Natural Resource**
The Sierra Club
730 Polk
San Francisco, CA 94109
Phone: (415)776-2211
Fax: (415)776-0350
Magazine on conservation and the environment. ***Frequency:*** 6x/yr. ***Price:*** $35 members; $2.95 single issue.

★5924★ **Society and Natural Resources: An International Journal**
Taylor & Francis
1900 Frost Rd., Ste. 101
Bristol, PA 19007
Phone: (215)785-5800
Fax: (215)785-5515
Publication on social science research and the environment. ***Frequency:*** Quarterly. ***Price:*** $90 institutions.

★5925★ **Society for the Preservation of Birds of Prey Leaflets Series**
Society for the Preservation of Birds of Prey
PO Box 66070
Los Angeles, CA 90066
Phone: (213)397-8216

★5926★ **Solar Energy: Official Journal of the International Solar Energy Society**
Pergamon Press, Inc.
Maxwell House
Fairview Park
Elmsford, NY 10523
Phone: (914)592-7700
Fax: (914)592-3625
Journal on the science and technology of solar energy applications. ***Frequency:*** Monthly. ***Price:*** $510.

★5927★ **Solar Geophysical Data**
National Environmental Satellite, Data, and Information Service
2069 Federal Bldg. 4
Washington, DC 20233
Phone: (301)763-7190
Fax: (301)763-4011
Frequency: Monthly.

★5928★ **Solid Waste and Power: The Waste-To-Energy Magazine**
HCI Publications
410 Archibald St., Ste. 100
Kansas City, MO 64111
Phone: (816)931-1311
Fax: (816)931-2015
Magazine reporting on waste-to-energy field. Includes information on environmental considerations and proven approaches for dealing with such concerns and requirements. ***Frequency:*** 6x/yr. ***Price:*** $49; $60 other countries; $9 single issue.

★5929★ **South Carolina Wildlife**
South Carolina Wildlife & Marine Resources Dept.
1000 Assembly St.
PO Box 167
Columbia, SC 29202-0167
Phone: (803)734-3944
Magazine promoting resource management, wildlife, and a better understanding of South Carolina's environment. ***Frequency:*** 6x/yr. ***Price:*** $10.

★5930★ **State Watch**
Minnesota Public Interest Research Group
2512 Delaware St. SE
Minneapolis, MN 55414-3432
Phone: (612)627-4035
Magazine featuring news and opinions for the consumer on environmental protection, peace, and social justice. ***Frequency:*** Quarterly. ***Price:*** $30.

★5931★ **A Statement of Policy and Practices for Protection of Groundwater**
National Wildlife Fed. Corporate Conservation Coun.
1400 16th St. NW
Washington, DC 20036
Phone: (202)797-6870
Fax: (202)797-6871

★5932★ **Storm Data**
National Environmental Satellite, Data, and Information Service
2069 Federal Bldg. 4
Washington, DC 20233
Phone: (301)763-7190
Fax: (301)763-4011
Frequency: Monthly.

★5933★ **Summit: The Mountain Journal**
Summit Publications, Inc.
111 Schweitz Rd.
Fleetwood, PA 19522
Phone: (215)682-1701
Fax: (215)682-1708
Magazine promoting mountains, culture, environment, and adventure. ***Frequency:*** Quarterly. ***Price:*** $20.

★5934★ **Sunrise**
International Ecology Soc.
1471 Barclay St.
St. Paul, MN 55106-1405
Phone: (612)774-4971
Frequency: Monthly.

★5935★ **Surplus Lists of Waterfowl**
International Wild Waterfowl Assn.
c/o Nancy Collins
Hidden Lake Waterfowl
5614 River Styx Rd.
Medina, OH 44256
Phone: (216)725-8782
Frequency: Semiannual.

★5936★ **Sustainable Development: A Call to Action**
Legacy Intl.
346 Commerce St.
Alexandria, VA 22314
Phone: (703)549-3630
Fax: (703)549-0262
Toll-Free: (510)600 1584 LEGACY

★5937★ **Take the First Step**
National Assn. for Plastic Container Recovery
4828 Pkwy. Plaza Blvd., Ste. 260
Charlotte, NC 28217
Phone: (704)357-3250
Fax: (704)357-3260
Toll-Free: 800-NAP-CORP

★5938★ **Talking Leaves**
Institute for Earth Education
PO Box 288
Warrenville, IL 60555
Phone: (708)393-3096
Contact: David B. Wampler, Intl. Office Coord.
Journal covering programs and events dealing with earth and ecology education. ***Frequency:*** Quarterly. ***Price:*** Included in membership dues.

★5939★ **Terra**
Natural History Museum, Los Angeles County
900 Exposition Blvd.
Los Angeles, CA 90007
Phone: (213)744-3330
Fax: (213)742-0730
Natural history magazine. ***Frequency:*** Quarterly. ***Price:*** $12 (included in membership).

★5940★ **Texas Environmental News**
AES Marketing, Inc.
760 Whalers Way, Ste. 100-A
Fort Collins, CO 80525
Monthly. ***Price:*** $18/yr.

★5941★ Thorne Ecological Institute Update
Thorne Ecological Inst.
5398 Manhattan Circle
Boulder, CO 80303
Phone: (303)499-3647
Frequency: Quarterly.

★5942★ Tide
Coastal Conservation Assn.
4801 Woodway, Ste. 220 W.
Houston, TX 77056
Phone: (713)626-4222
Fax: (713)951-3801
Frequency: Bimonthly.

★5943★ Toxic Substances Journal
Hemisphere Publishing Corp.
1900 Frost Rd., Ste. 101
Bristol, PA 19007
Phone: (215)785-5800
Fax: (215)785-5515
Magazine covering legislation, testing, and guidelines relating to toxic substances. ***Frequency:*** Quarterly. ***Price:*** $60; $120 institutions.

★5944★ Toxic Substances Report
Friends of the Everglades
202 Park St.
Miami Springs, FL 33166
Phone: (305)888-1230

★5945★ Toxicological and Environmental Chemistry
Gordon and Breach Science Publishers
PO Box 786, Cooper Sta.
New York, NY 10276
Phone: (212)206-8900
Fax: (212)645-2459
Life sciences journal. ***Frequency:*** Quarterly.

★5946★ Turkey Call
National Wild Turkey Fed.
PO Box 530
Wild Turkey Bldg.
Edgefield, SC 29824
Phone: (803)637-3106
Fax: (803)637-0034
Frequency: Bimonthly.

★5947★ Underground Injection Practices Council Journal
Underground Injection Practices Coun.
525 Central Park Dr., Ste. 304
Oklahoma City, OK 73105
Phone: (405)525-6146
Frequency: Periodic.

★5948★ U.S. Birdwatch
International Coun. for Bird Preservation, U.S. Sect.
c/o World Wildlife Fund
1250 24th St. NW
Washington, DC 20037
Phone: (202)778-9563
Fax: (202)293-9211
Frequency: 3/year.

★5949★ Upper Missippi River Recreation Facility Guide
Upper Mississippi River Conservation Comm.
1830 2nd Ave.
Rock Island, IL 61201
Phone: (309)793-5800
Frequency: Periodic.

★5950★ Virginia Forests
Virginia Forestry Assn.
1205 E. Main St.
Richmond, VA 23219
Phone: (804)644-8462
Fax: (804)643-4110
Magazine on forests and related resources. ***Frequency:*** Quarterly. ***Price:*** $30; $2.50 single issue.

★5951★ Walden Loon
Walden Forever Wild
PO Box 275
Concord, MA 01742
Phone: (203)429-2839

★5952★ Washington Report
Interstate Conference on Water Policy
955 L'Enfant Plaza SW, 6th Fl.
Washington, DC 20024
Phone: (202)466-7287
Fax: (202)646-6210
Frequency: Bimonthly.

★5953★ Waste Age: The Authoritative Voice of Waste Systems and Technology
Natl. Solid Wastes Management Assn.
1730 Rhode Island Ave. NW, Ste. 1000
Washington, DC 20036
Phone: (202)861-0708
Fax: (202)659-0925
Magazine containing news on solid and hazardous wastes, recycling, and pollution control. ***Frequency:*** Monthly. ***Price:*** Free; $45 (mail).

★5954★ Waste: Choices for Communities
Concern, Inc.
1794 Columbia Rd. NW
Washington, DC 20009
Phone: (202)328-8160

★5955★ Waste Management: Nuclear, Chemical, Biological, and Municipal
Pergamon Press, Inc.
Maxwell House
Fairview Park
Elmsford, NY 10523
Phone: (914)592-7700
Fax: (914)592-3625
International journal presenting information encompassing the entire field of hazardous waste, including high-space and low-level radioactive waste, chemical waste, and transuranic waste. ***Frequency:*** Quarterly. ***Price:*** $210.

★5956★ Waste Paper
Environmental Action Coalition
625 Broadway, 2nd Fl.
New York, NY 10012
Phone: (212)677-1601
Fax: (212)941-8728

★5957★ Waste Tech News: The Newspaper for the Waste and Pollution Control Industries
Schouweiler Communications Group
131 Madison St.
Denver, CO 80206-5427
Phone: (303)394-2905
Fax: (303)394-3011
Frequency: Every other week. ***Price:*** Free to qualified subscribers; $25.

★5958★ Waste Watchers
Waste Watch
PO Box 298
Livingston, KY 40445

★5959★ Watch It
Wilderness Watch
PO Box 782
Sturgeon Bay, WI 54235
Phone: (414)743-1238
Frequency: Periodic.

★5960★ Water and Wastes Digest
Scranton Gillette Communications, Inc.
380 NW Hwy.
Des Plaines, IL 60016
Phone: (312)298-6622
Fax: (312)390-0408
Magazine (tabloid) featuring product news for decision makers in the municipal and industrial water and water pollution control industries. ***Frequency:*** 6x/yr. ***Price:*** $10; $13 other countries; $2 single issue.

★5961★ Water Conditioning and Purification
Publicom Inc.
4651 N. 1st Ave., Ste. 101
Tucson, AZ 85718
Phone: (602)293-5446
Fax: (602)887-2383
Domestic and commercial water conditioning and purification magazine. ***Frequency:*** Monthly. ***Price:*** Free to qualified subscribers; $34.

★5962★ Water, Environment, and Technology
Water Pollution Control Fed.
601 Wythe St.
Alexandria, VA 22314-1994
Phone: (703)684-2400
Fax: (703)684-2492
Frequency: Monthly.

★5963★ Water Research: The Journal of the International Association on Water Pollution Research and Control
Pergamon Press, Inc.
Maxwell House
Fairview Park
Elmsford, NY 10523
Phone: (914)592-7700
Fax: (914)592-3625
Journal covering research in water pollution. ***Frequency:*** Monthly. ***Price:*** $895.

★5964★ Water Technology
National Trade Publications, Inc.
13 Century Hill Dr.
Latham, NY 12110
Phone: (518)783-1281
Fax: (518)783-1386
Magazine focusing on water treatment. ***Frequency:*** Monthly. ***Price:*** $31.

★5965★ Water Ways
North River Communications
PO Box 11
Croton-on-Hudson, NY 10520
Phone: (914)271-6041
Periodical covering news, legislation, the environment, conservation, development, pollution, preservation, architecture, education, travel, history, recreation, and events of various New York state waterways. ***Frequency:*** 6x/yr. ***Price:*** $18.50; $15 schools and libraries.

★5966★ Waterfowl Magazine
Waterfowl U.S.A.
Box 50
Waterfowl Bldg.
Edgefield, SC 29824
Phone: (803)637-5767
Frequency: Bimonthly.

★5967★ Whales vs. Whalers
Save the Whales
PO Box 3650
Washington, DC 20007
Phone: (202)337-2332

★5968★ Whalewatch
International Wildlife Coalition
634 N. Falmouth Hwy.
PO Box 388
N. Falmouth, MA 02556
Phone: (508)564-9980
Fax: (508)563-2843
Frequency: Quarterly.

★5969★ The Whole Earth Catalog
Point Found.
27 Gate Five Rd.
Sausalito, CA 94965
Phone: (415)332-1716

★5970★ Whole Earth Review: Access to Tools and Ideas
Point Found.
27 Gate Five Rd.
Sausalito, CA 94965
Phone: (415)332-1716

★5971★ Why Save Bats
Bat Conservation Intl.
PO Box 162603
Austin, TX 78716
Phone: (512)327-9721
Fax: (512)327-9724
Contact: Toni Turner, Contact

★5972★ Wild America Magazine
Amer. Wildlands
7500 E. Arapahoe Rd., Ste. 355
Englewood, CO 80112
Phone: (303)771-0380
Fax: (303)694-9047
Frequency: Annual.

★5973★ Wild Horse and Burro Diary
International Soc. for the Protection of Mustangs and Burros
c/o Helen A. Reilly
11790 Deodar Way
Reno, NV 89506
Phone: (702)972-1989
Frequency: Quarterly.

★5974★ Wild Sheep
Foundation for North Amer. Wild Sheep
720 Allen Ave.
Cody, WY 82414-3402
Phone: (307)527-6261
Fax: (307)527-7117
Frequency: Periodic.

★5975★ Wild Sheep in Modern North America
Boone and Crockett Club
241 S. Fraley Blvd.
Dumfries, VA 22026
Phone: (703)221-1888

★5976★ Wilderness
The Wilderness Soc.
900 17th St. NW
Washington, DC 20006
Phone: (202)833-2300
Fax: (202)429-3958
Conservation magazine featuring articles devoted to preserving wilderness and wildlife, protecting America's prime forests, parks, rivers, shorelands, and fostering an American land ethic. ***Frequency:*** Quarterly. ***Price:*** $14.95.

★5977★ Wildland Resource Economic Report
Amer. Wildlands
7500 E. Arapahoe Rd., Ste. 355
Englewood, CO 80112
Phone: (303)771-0380
Fax: (303)694-9047

★5978★ Wildlife Activist
Wildlife Information Center
629 Green St.
Allentown, PA 18102
Phone: (215)434-1637
Frequency: Quarterly.

★5979★ Wildlife Book Review
Wildlife Information Center
629 Green St.
Allentown, PA 18102
Phone: (215)434-1637
Frequency: Periodic.

★5980★ Wildlife Conservation
Wildlife Conservation Intl.
c/o New York Zoological Society
Bronx, NY 10460
Phone: (212)220-5155
Fax: (212)220-7114
Magazine includes WCI Members Bulletin. ***Frequency:*** Bimonthly.

★5981★ Wildlife Conservation Report
Wildlife Information Center
629 Green St.
Allentown, PA 18102
Phone: (215)434-1637
Frequency: Periodic.

★5982★ Wildlife Disease Association Journal
Wildlife Disease Assn.
PO Box 886
Ames, IA 50010
Phone: (515)233-1931
Frequency: Quarterly.

★5983★ Wildlife Journal
International Wildlife Rehabilitation Coun.
4437 Central Place, Ste. B-4
Suisun, CA 94585
Phone: (707)864-1761

★5984★ Wildlife Monographs
The Wildlife Soc.
5410 Grosvenor Ln.
Bethesda, MD 20814-2197
Phone: (301)897-9770
Fax: (301)530-2471
Frequency: Periodic.

★5985★ Wildlife Reserves and Corridors in the Urban Environment
National Inst. for Urban Wildlife
10921 Trotting Ridge Way
Columbia, MD 21044
Phone: (301)596-3311

★5986★ Wildlife Society Bulletin
The Wildlife Soc.
5410 Grosvenor Ln.
Bethesda, MD 20814-2197
Phone: (301)897-9770
Fax: (301)530-2471
Journal covering administration, contemporary problems, economics, education, law enforcement, management, and philosophy related to wildlife. ***Frequency:*** Quarterly. ***Price:*** $36/year for members; $40/year for nonmembers.

★5987★ Windstar Journal
Windstar Found.
2317 Snowmass Creek Rd.
Snowmass, CO 81654
Phone: (303)927-4777
Fax: (303)927-4779
Frequency: Quarterly.

★5988★ Wings: Essays on Invertebrate Conservation
Xerces Soc.
c/o Melody Allen
10 SW Ash St.
Portland, OR 97204
Phone: (503)222-2788
Journal; includes essays by scientists and conservationists. ***Frequency:*** 3/year. ***Price:*** Included in membership dues.

★5989★ Women Outdoors
Women Outdoors, Inc.
55 Talbot Ave.
Medford, MA 02155
Magazine with outdoor and environmental focus sent to Women Outdoors members. ***Frequency:*** Quarterly. ***Price:*** $20.

★5990★ World Rainforest Report
Rainforest Action Network
301 Broadway, Ste. A
San Francisco, CA 94133
Phone: (415)398-4404
Fax: (415)398-2732
Contains progress reports of RAN programs, list of educational materials, and calendar of events. ***Frequency:*** Quarterly (in conjunction with Friends of the Earth, Malaysia and Rainforest Information Centre). ***Price:*** Included in membership dues.

★5991★ World Research Foundation Journal
World Research Found.
15300 Ventura Blvd., Ste. 405
Sherman Oaks, CA 91403
Phone: (818)907-5483
Frequency: Quarterly.

★5992★ World Rivers Review
International Rivers Network
301 Broadway, Ste. B
San Francisco, CA 94133
Phone: (415)986-4694
Fax: (415)398-2732
Frequency: Bimonthly.

★5993★ Worldwatch: A Magazine of the Worldwide Institute
Worldwatch Inst.
1776 Massachusetts Ave. NW
Washington, DC 20036
Phone: (202)452-1999
Fax: (202)296-7365
Magazine reporting on economic and ecological development worldwide. ***Frequency:*** 6x/yr. ***Price:*** $15.

★5994★ Your Big Backyard
National Wildlife Federation
1400 16th St., NW
Washington, DC 20036-2266
Toll-Free: 800-432-6564
Environmental/natural history magazine for children ages 3-5. ***Price:*** $12.00.

Newsletters

★5995★ Abundant Life Seed Foundation Newsletter
Abundant Life Seed Found.
1029 Lawrence St.
Port Townsend, WA 98368
Phone: (206)385-5660
Contact: Forest Shomer, Dir.
Frequency: Quarterly.

★5996★ Access to Energy
Dr. Petr Beckmann
PO Box 2298
Boulder, CO 80306
Phone: (303)444-0841
Characterized as a pro-science, pro-technology, pro-free enterprise publication, aimed to report technological advances in lay language. Focuses on the economic and political background of energy problems, and on what is economically profitable as well as scientifically feasible in this realm. ***Editor(s):*** Dr. Petr Beckmann. ***Frequency:*** Monthly. ***Price:*** $25/yr., U.S.; $27 Canada; $30 elsewhere.

★5997★ Acid Precipitation Digest: A Summary of Current News, Research and Events
Air Resources Information Clearinghouse
46 Prince St.
Rochester, NY 14607-1016
Phone: (716)271-3550
Fax: (716)271-0606
Lists and describes information sources on acid rain; lists professional publications, technical reports, books, proceedings, and miscellaneous educational material. ***Frequency:*** Monthly. ***Price:*** $190/year.

★5998★ The Acid Rain Foundation—Update
The Acid Rain Found.
1410 Varsity Dr.
Raleigh, NC 27606
Phone: (919)828-9443
Newsletter concerned with acid rain and air pollution. ***Frequency:*** Quarterly. ***Price:*** Included in membership dues.

★5999★ Action Alert
Rainforest Action Network
301 Broadway, Ste. A
San Francisco, CA 94133
Phone: (415)398-4404
Fax: (415)398-2732
Bulletin on issues requiring immediate public action. ***Frequency:*** Monthly. ***Price:*** Included in membership dues.

★6000★ Activist Newsletter
Defenders of Wildlife
1244 19th St. NW
Washington, DC 20036
Phone: (202)659-9510
Fax: (202)833-3349
Frequency: Quarterly.

★6001★ Adirondack Council Newsletter
Adirondack Coun.
Box D-2
Church St.
Elizabethtown, NY 12932
Phone: (518)873-2240
Frequency: Quarterly.

★6002★ Advanced Fossil Energy Technologies
National Technical Information Service
U.S. Dept. of Commerce
5285 Port Royal Rd.
Springfield, VA 22161
Phone: (703)487-4630
Abstracts all Department of Energy-sponsored reports in the field of fossil energy technology. ***Frequency:*** Semimonthly. ***Price:*** $130/yr., U.S., Canada, and Mexico; $260 elsewhere.

★6003★ Advanced Oil and Gas Recovery Technologies
National Technical Information Service
U.S. Dept. of Commerce
5285 Port Royal Rd.
Springfield, VA 22161
Phone: (703)487-4630
Abstracts worldwide information on enhanced and unconventional recovery of petroleum and natural gas. Includes oil shales and tar sands, natural gas production from coal mines, gas hydrates, and geopressured systems. ***Frequency:*** Monthly. ***Price:*** $100/yr., U.S., Canada, and Mexico; $200 elsewhere.

★6004★ Air and Water Pollution Control Newsletter
Bureau of Natl. Affairs, Inc.
1231 25th St., N.W.
Washington, DC 20037
Phone: (202)452-4200
Fax: (202)822-8092
Toll-Free: 800-372-1033
Telex: 285656 BNAI WSH
Reviews developments in pollution laws, regulations, and trends in the government and industry. ***Editor(s):*** Eileen Z. Joseph. ***Frequency:*** Biweekly. ***Price:*** $236/yr.

★6005★ Air Pollution Control
Bureau of Natl. Affairs, Inc.
1231 25th St., N.W.
Washington, DC 20037
Phone: (202)452-4200
Deals with complex air pollution rules and regulations of the Environmental Protection Agency. Covers ambient air quality standards, permits and licenses, control technologies, and enforcement. Also provides information on state and federal policies concerning the reporting, monitoring, and managing of regulated substances; court rulings and Agency actions; and assistance programs. ***Editor(s):*** Eileen Z. Joseph. ***Frequency:*** Biweekly. ***Price:*** $416/yr.

★6006★ Air Pollution Titles
Center for Air Environment Studies of the Environmental Resources Research Inst.
Pennsylvania State Univ.
226 Fenske Laboratory
University Park, PA 16802
Phone: (814)865-1415
Provides the title and place of publication for articles on air pollution research, including air pollution control, automobile and industrial emissions, airborne gases, aerosol research, gas cleaning and purification, and health and ecological effects, including agricultural studies and toxicology. ***Editor(s):*** Elizabeth J. Carroll. ***Frequency:*** Bimonthly, with annual cumulative issue on microfiche. ***Price:*** $110/yr., U.S. and Canada; $120 elsewhere.

★6007★ Air Toxics Report
Business Publishers, Inc.
951 Pershing Dr.
Silver Spring, MD 20910
Phone: (301)587-1081
Fax: (301)587-1081
Report on changes in federal legislation and actions involving toxic air pollutants. ***Frequency:*** Monthly. ***Price:*** $210/yr.

★6008★ Air/Water Pollution Report
Business Publishers, Inc.
951 Pershing Dr.
Silver Spring, MD 20910
Phone: (301)587-6300
Fax: (301)587-1081
Reports on law, technology, and markets affecting the environmental pollution control area. Covers national policy, regulations, enforcement and litigation, state and local news, and grants and contracts. ***Editor(s):*** Donna Engelgau. ***Frequency:*** 50/yr. ***Price:*** $406/yr., U.S. and Canada; $442 elsewhere.

★6009★ Alerts
Alaska Coalition
408 C St., NE
Washington, DC 20002
Phone: (202)547-1141
Fax: (202)547-6009
Frequency: Periodic.

★6010★ Alliance Exchange
Alliance for Environmental Education, Inc.
3421 M St., N.W.
Box 1040
Washington, DC 20007
Phone: (202)797-4530
Promotes the philosophy and objectives of the Alliance, which aims to advance all phases of formal and nonformal environmental education. Articles provide general interest news and reports in curricula, conferences, changes in personnel, activities of organizations, and discussion of policy, philosopy, and controversy surrounding resource management, sustainable economic practices, development and protection of natural resources, energy use and conservation, and geography. ***Editor(s):*** Dixie Ann Pemberton. ***Frequency:*** Quarterly. ***Price:*** Included in membership; $5 for nonmembers.

★6011★ Alliance for Clean Energy Newsletter
Alliance for Clean Energy
1901 N. Fl. Myer Dr., 12th Fl.
Rosslyn, VA 22209
Phone: (703)841-0626
Frequency: Weekly.

★6012★ Alternate Energy Transportation
Campbell Publishing
EV Consultants, Inc.
PO Box 20041
New York, NY 10025
Phone: (212)222-0160
Provides news and articles relating to vehicles powered by natural gas, methanol, hydrogen, direct energy from the sun, or any other source except petroleum. ***Editor(s):*** Edward A. Campbell. ***Frequency:*** Monthly. ***Price:*** $100/yr., U.S.; $115 elsewhere.

★6013★ Alternative Energy
AE Publications
205 S. Beverly Dr., Ste. 208
Beverly Hills, CA 90212
Phone: (213)273-3486
Publishes information concerning advances and trends in the field of alternative energy technology. Covers a range of energy sources, including biomass, solar photovoltaic, solar thermal, hydrogen fuel, nuclear fusion, battery systems, congeneration, and various conservation techniques. ***Editor(s):*** Irwin Stambler. ***Frequency:*** Monthly. ***Price:*** $85/yr., U.S.; $87, Canada; $101 elsewhere.

★6014★ Alternative Energy Resources Organization Sun-Times
Alternative Energy Resources Organization
44 N. Last Chance Gulch
Helena, MT 59601
Phone: (406)443-7272
Publishes information concerning solar energy, energy conservation, sustainable agriculture, and economic development. Reports AERO activities; national, regional, and state news; and legislative action affecting renewable energies. ***Frequency:*** Quarterly. ***Price:*** $15/yr; $2.50 per issue.

★6015★ American Academy of Environmental Medicine Newsletter
Amer. Acad. of Environmental Medicine
PO Box 16106
Denver, CO 80216
Phone: (303)622-9755
Fax: (303)622-4224
Frequency: Quarterly.

★6016★ American Cave Conservation Association Newsletter
Amer. Cave Conservation Assn.
131 Main & Cave Sts.
PO Box 409
Horse Cave, KY 42749
Phone: (502)786-1466
Includes association and regional news, legislative information, and calendar of events. ***Frequency:*** Periodic.

★6017★ American Council on the Environment Newsletter
Amer. Coun. on the Environment
1301 20th St. NW, Ste. 113
Washington, DC 20036
Phone: (202)659-1900
Frequency: Periodic.

★6018★ An American Crusade for Wildlife
Boone and Crockett Club
241 S. Fraley Blvd.
Dumfries, VA 22026
Phone: (703)221-1888

★6019★ American Horse Protection Association Newsletter
Amer. Horse Protection Assn.
1000 29th St. NW, T100
Washington, DC 20007
Phone: (202)965-0500

★6020★ American Rivers
Amer. Rivers
801 Pennsylvania Ave., S.E., Ste. 303
Washington, DC 20003
Phone: (202)547-6900
Fax: (202)543-6142
Concerned with the preservation and protection of natural rivers. Covers local, state, and federal action on river issues. ***Editor(s):*** Randy Showstack. ***Frequency:*** Quarterly. ***Price:*** Included in membership.

★6021★ American Shore and Beach Preservation Association Newsletter
Amer. Shore and Beach Preservation Assn.
412 O'Brien Hall
Univ. of California, Berkeley
Berkeley, CA 94720
Phone: (415)642-2666
Discusses coastal management projects, association news, conservation issues, and relevant government policies. Announces new publications, seminars, conferences, and symposia. ***Editor(s):*** Gerald J. Giefer. ***Frequency:*** Quarterly. ***Price:*** Included in membership.

★6022★ American Water Works Association Washington Report
Amer. Water Works Assn.
1010 Vermont Ave., N.W., Ste. 810
Washington, DC 20005
Phone: (202)628-8303
Relates news of political and legislative developments affecting the water supply industry. Focuses on such topics as water resources, pollution, programs for waste disposal, research, and environmental issues. ***Editor(s):*** Jacqueline Block. ***Frequency:*** Monthly. ***Price:*** Included in membership.

★6023★ Americans for Energy Independence Newsletter
Amer. s for Energy Independence
1629 K St., N.W.
Washington, DC 20006
Phone: (202)466-2105
Fax: (202)466-2108
Monitors developments in the energy field and in energy policy. Outlines the organization's legislative, educational, and media strategies to promote reliance on domestic energy resources. ***Editor(s):*** Tom Stern and Melissa Grace. ***Frequency:*** Quarterly. ***Price:*** Free.

★6024★ America's Endangered Wildlife
Elsa Clubs of America
PO Box 4572
North Hollywood, CA 91617-0572
Phone: (818)761-8387

★6025★ America's Rivers: An Assessment of State River Conservation Programs
Amer. Rivers
801 Pennsylvania Ave. SE, Ste. 303
Washington, DC 20003
Phone: (202)547-6900
Fax: (202)543-6142

★6026★ Andrews School Asbestos Alert
Andrews Publications, Inc.
PO Box 200
Edgemont, PA 19028
Phone: (215)353-2565
Toll-Free: 800-345-1101
Alerts school districts to current legal proceedings, construction, and medical problems relating to exposure to asbestos in schools. Also monitors Environmental Protection Agency and state government regulations. ***Frequency:*** Monthly. ***Price:*** $180/yr.

★6027★ Animals International
World Soc. for the Protection of Animals
29 Perkins St.
PO Box 190
Boston, MA 02130
Phone: (617)522-7000
Reports on international programs and issues related to animal protection and wildlife conservation. Promotes citizen action and examines disasters affecting animals. ***Editor(s):*** Jonathan Pearce. ***Price:*** Included in membership; $20/yr. for nonmembers.

★6028★ Asbestos Abatement Report
Buraff Publications, Inc.
Bureau of Natl. Affairs, Inc.
1350 Connecticut Ave., N.W., Ste. 1000
Washington, DC 20036
Phone: (202)452-7889
Fax: (202)862-0999
Examines issues related to the removal or containment of asbestos. Studies issues related to legislation, regulation and enforcement activities, litigation, liability insurance, and cost of abatement. ***Editor(s):*** Ken Doyle. ***Frequency:*** Biweekly. ***Price:*** $327/yr., U.S. and Canada; $349 elsewhere.

★6029★ Asbestos Control Report
Business Publishers, Inc.
951 Pershing Dr.
Silver Spring, MD 20910-4464
Phone: (301)587-6300
Fax: (301)587-1081
Aimed at asbestos industry professionals, covering such topics as control techniques, government regulations, waste disposal, and insurance. ***Frequency:*** Biweekly. ***Price:*** $355.50.

★6030★ **Association for Arid Lands Studies Newsletter**
Association for Arid Lands Studies
c/o International Center for Arid & Semiarid Land Studies
Texas Tech University
PO Box 4620
Lubbock, TX 79409-1036
Phone: (806)742-2218
Fax: (806)742-1900
Includes associate research update. ***Frequency:*** Annual. ***Price:*** Available to members only.

★6031★ **Association for the Preservation of Cape Cod Shore Lines**
Association for the Preservation of Cape Cod
PO Box 636
Orleans, MA 02653
Phone: (617)255-4142
Covers policies and programs that promote the preservation of natural resources on Cape Cod. Reports on earthkeeping efforts, local environmental issues, and legislation having an impact on Cape Cod and the Massachusetts environment. ***Editor(s):*** Susan L. Nickerson. ***Frequency:*** 4-5/yr. ***Price:*** Included in membership.

★6032★ **Association of Battery Recyclers Newsletter**
Association of Battery Recyclers
Sanders Lead Co. Corp.
Sanders Rd.
PO Drawer 707
Troy, AL 36081
Phone: (205)566-1563
Frequency: Bimonthly.

★6033★ **Association of Conservation Engineers Newsletter**
Association of Conservation Engineers
c/o William P. Allinder
Alabama Department of Conservation
64 N. Union St.
Montgomery, AL 36130
Phone: (205)261-3476
Frequency: Semiannual.

★6034★ **Association of Ecosystem Research Centers News**
Association of Ecosystem Research Centers
Utah State University
Ecology Ctr.
Logan, UT 84322-5200
Phone: (801)750-2555
Fax: (801)750-3872
Contact: Frederic H. Wagner, Pres.
Newsletter. ***Frequency:*** Semiannual.

★6035★ **Association of Environmental and Resource Economists Newsletter**
Association of Environmental and Resource Economists
1616 P St. NW
Washington, DC 20036
Phone: (202)328-5000
Fax: (202)265-8069
Frequency: Semiannual. ***Price:*** Free to members.

★6036★ **Association of Environmental Engineering Professors Newsletter**
Association of Environmental Engineering Professors
c/o Prof. Bruce Rittmann
Univ. of Illinois
3221 Newmark CE Laboratory
208 N. Romine
Urbana, IL 61801
Phone: (217)333-6964
Frequency: 3/year.

★6037★ **Association of Local Air Pollution Control Officials Washington Update**
Association of Local Air Pollution Control Officials
444 N. Capitol St. NW, Ste. 306
Washington, DC 20001
Phone: (202)624-7864
Fax: (202)624-7863
Covers congressional and Environmental Protection Agency activities, and current issues related to air pollution. ***Frequency:*** Monthly. ***Price:*** Included in membership dues.

★6038★ **Association of Midwest Fish and Wildlife Agencies Proceedings**
Association of Midwest Fish and Wildlife Agencies
c/o John Urbain
Michigan Department of Natural Resources
Box 30028
Lansing, MI 48909
Phone: (517)373-1263
Frequency: Annual.

★6039★ **Association of State and Territorial Solid Waste Management Officials Washington Update**
Association of State and Territorial Solid Waste Management Officials
444 N. Capitol St. NW, Ste. 388
Washington, DC 20001
Phone: (202)624-5828
Fax: (202)624-7875
Frequency: 10/year.

★6040★ **Association of the New Jersey Environmental Commissions Report**
Association of the New Jersey Environmental Commissions
PO Box 157
Mendham, NJ 07945
Phone: (201)539-7547
Fax: (201)539-7713
Deals with environmental issues and environmental management in New Jersey. Features articles on such topics as land-use planning, hazardous waste, water quality protection, soil surveys, and state and federal environmental regulations. ***Editor(s):*** Susan Hanna. ***Frequency:*** Quarterly. ***Price:*** Included in membership.

★6041★ **Atmospheres**
Friends of the Earth Found.
218 D St. SE
Washington, DC 20003
Phone: (202)544-2600
Fax: (202)543-4710
Reports on ozone depletion. ***Frequency:*** Quarterly.

★6042★ **Atomic Energy Clearing House**
Congressional Information Bureau, Inc.
1325 G St., N.W., Ste. 1005
Washington, DC 20005
Phone: (202)347-2275
Fax: (202)347-2278
Carries news of activities in the domestic, peaceful uses of nuclear energy. Reports on licensing, inspection, and legislation affecting commercial nuclear power plants, nuclear waste legislation, medical uses of radioactive isotopes, and new plant construction. ***Editor(s):*** Elyse F. Sternberg. ***Frequency:*** Weekly. ***Price:*** $525/yr.

★6043★ **Audubon Activist**
National Audubon Soc.
950 Third Ave.
New York, NY 10022
Phone: (212)832-3200

★6044★ **Audubon Adventures**
National Audubon Soc.
950 Third Ave.
New York, NY 10022
Phone: (212)832-3200

★6045★ **Audubon Naturalist News**
Audubon Naturalist Soc. of the Central Atlantic States
8940 Jones Mill Rd.
Chevy Chase, MD 20815
Phone: (301)652-9188
Frequency: Monthly.

★6046★ **Audubon Society of Rhode Island Report**
Audubon Soc. of Rhode Island
12 Sanderson Rd.
Smithfield, RI 02917
Phone: (401)521-1670
Concerned with the natural history of Rhode Island and with environmental issues and legislation. ***Editor(s):*** Eugenia S. Marks. ***Frequency:*** 6/yr. ***Price:*** $5/yr.

★6047★ **Backlog**
Camp Fire Club of America
230 Camp Fire Rd.
Chappaqua, NY 10514
Phone: (914)941-0199
Frequency: Semiannual.

★6048★ **Balance Report**
Population-Environment Balance, Inc.
1325 G St., N.W., Ste. 1003
Washington, DC 20005
Phone: (202)879-3000
Covers a variety of U.S. population issues such as birth control, environmental carrying capacity, and immigration policy. ***Editor(s):*** Dayna Petete. ***Frequency:*** Quarterly. ***Price:*** Included in membership.

★6049★ **The Balance Wheel**
Association for Conservation Information
c/o David K. Rice
PO Box 10678
Reno, NV 89520
Phone: (702)688-1500
Fax: (702)688-1595
Frequency: Quarterly.

★6050★ **B&C Associates Newsletter**
Boone and Crockett Club
241 S. Fraley Blvd.
Dumfries, VA 22026
Phone: (703)221-1888
Frequency: Quarterly.

★6051★ **Barrier Islands Newsletter**
National Wildlife Fed.
1412 16th St., N.W.
Washington, DC 20036-2266
Phone: (202)637-3731
Discusses developments, programs, and setbacks in the movement to protect and conserve the undeveloped barrier islands and beaches along the Atlantic, Great Lakes, Pacific, and Gulf coasts. ***Editor(s):*** Elise Jones. ***Frequency:*** Periodic. ***Price:*** Free.

★6052★ **Bats**
Bat Conservation International, Inc.
PO Box 162603
Austin, TX 78716
Phone: (512)327-9721
Promotes the conservation and preservation of bats through research and conservation efforts. Seeks to educate the public as to the value and importance of bats. ***Editor(s):*** Mari Murphy. ***Frequency:*** Quarterly. ***Price:*** Included in membership.

★6053★ The Beaver Defenders
Unexpected Wildlife Refuge
PO Box 765
Newfield, NJ 08344
Phone: (609)697-3541
Provides humane education concerning the beaver and other wildlife, through news reporting, feature articles, editorials, poetry, photos, and pen sketches. ***Editor(s):*** Hope Sawyer Buyukmihci. ***Frequency:*** Quarterly. ***Price:*** $10/yr.

★6054★ The Bench Sheet
Water Pollution Control Fed.
601 Wythe St.
Alexandria, VA 22314-1994
Phone: (703)684-2400
Fax: (703)684-2492
Frequency: Bimonthly.

★6055★ Berkshire Museum Aquarium Quarterly
Berkshire Museum
39 S. St.
U. S. Rte. 7
Pittsfield, MA 01201
Phone: (413)443-7171
Alt. Phone: (413)443-7172
Aims to educate about the world ecosystems and value of the oceans, especially along the Massachusetts shore. ***Frequency:*** Quarterly.

★6056★ Better Times
America the Beautiful Fund
219 Shoreham Bldg.
Washington, DC 20005
Phone: (202)638-1649
Reports on local volunteer environmental action projects initiated by community groups or private citizens involving environmental design, land preservation, green plantings, civic arts, and historical and cultural preservation. Profiles the projects and volunteers, and includes environmental updates. ***Frequency:*** Semiannual. ***Price:*** $10/yr. for members.

★6057★ Big Bend Bulletin
Sea Grant Extension Program
615 Paul Russell Rd.
Tallahassee, FL 32301
Phone: (904)487-3007
Publishes news used to inform the public of current issues regarding fisheries, coastal processes, and marine education. ***Editor(s):*** Scott Andree. ***Frequency:*** Quarterly. ***Price:*** Free.

★6058★ Big Thicket Conservationist
Big Thicket Conservation Assn.
PO Box 12032
Beaumont, TX 77706
Phone: (214)324-3191
Frequency: Quarterly.

★6059★ The Biosphere
International Soc. for Environmental Education
Ohio State Univ.
210 Kottman Hall
2021 Coffey Rd.
Columbus, OH 43210
Phone: (614)292-2265
Fax: (614)292-7162
Provides articles concerning international environmental education. ***Editor(s):*** Rosanne W. Fortner. ***Frequency:*** 3/yr. ***Price:*** $10/yr.

★6060★ Blue Goose Flyer
National Wildlife Refuge Assn.
PO Box 124
Winona, MN 55987
Phone: (409)252-3346
Covers preservation and perpetuation of the National Wildlife Refuge System, including legislation, budgetary problems, management, and advocacy for national wildlife refuges and game ranges in the U.S. Also reports news and announcements of the ***Editor(s):*** Russel W. Clapper. ***Frequency:*** Quarterly. ***Price:*** Included in membership.

★6061★ Born Free News
Elsa Wild Animal Appeal, U.S.A.
PO Box 4572
North Hollywood, CA 91607
Phone: (818)761-8387
Serves the purposes of the Elsa Wild Animal Appeal, which are to: further the conservation of wildlife and wild places, particularly in America; educate people on the values and needs of natural environment, especially wildlife; promote the establishment of protective wildlife reserves and viable wildlife conservation projects. Includes news of conservation and educational activities and develops wildlife education materials for children. ***Editor(s):*** A. Peter Rasmussen, Jr. ***Frequency:*** Triannually. ***Price:*** Included in membership.

★6062★ Bounty Information Service News
Bounty Information Service
c/o Stephens Coll. Post Office
Columbia, MO 65215
Phone: (314)876-7186
Frequency: 1-3/year.

★6063★ Bounty News
Bounty Information Service
Stephens College Post Office
Columbia, MO 65215
Phone: (314)876-7186
Reports on wildlife bounties in North America and methods for removing bounties. ***Editor(s):*** Charles Laun. ***Frequency:*** 1-2/yr. ***Price:*** Free (include postage stamp with request).

★6064★ Branching Out
World Forestry Center
4033 SW Canyon Rd.
Portland, OR 97221
Phone: (503)228-1367
Fax: (503)228-3624
Frequency: Monthly.

★6065★ Briar Patch Observer
Thornton W. Burgess Soc.
6 Discovery Hill Rd.
East Sandwich, MA 02537
Phone: (508)888-6870
Discusses aspects of natural history; updates Burgess Society members on organizational programs and activities. ***Editor(s):*** Joan DiPersio. ***Frequency:*** 3-4/yr. ***Price:*** Included in membership.

★6066★ Buildings Energy Technology
National Technical Information Service
U.S. Dept. of Commerce
5285 Port Royal Rd.
Springfield, VA 22161
Phone: (703)487-4630
Abstracts worldwide information on the technology required for economic energy conservation in buildings and communities. Covers energy conservation for general buildings, residential buildings, office buildings, schools, municipal and ther public buildings, an commercial and industrial buildings. ***Frequency:*** Monthly. ***Price:*** $100/yr., U.S., Canada, and Mexico; $200 elsewhere.

★6067★ Bulletin of the North American Benthological Society
North Amer. Benthological Soc.
c/o Cheryl R. Black
Savannah River Ecology Laboratory
Drawer E
Aiken, SC 29802
Phone: (803)725-7425
Fax: (803)725-7413
Frequency: Periodic.

★6068★ Business and the Environment
Cutter Information Corp.
Box 713
Rte. 2
Harpers Ferry, WV 25425
Phone: (304)725-6542
Provides global news and analysis on environmental regulatory and policy trends, along with business opportunities, market developments and company actions related to "green innovations" and regulatory actions. ***Frequency:*** 24x/yr.

★6069★ Buzzards Bay Project Newsletter
Buzzards Bay Project
c/o Massachusetts C2M
2 Spring St.
Marion, MA 02738
Phone: (508)748-3600
Reports on the goals of the Project which researches and monitors water quality in Buzzards Bay for resource management purposes. ***Editor(s):*** Elizabeth Sego. ***Frequency:*** 4/yr. ***Price:*** Free.

★6070★ The Canopy
Rainforest Alliance
270 Lafayette St., Ste. 512
New York, NY 10012
Phone: (212)941-1900
Fax: (212)941-4986
Frequency: Quarterly. ***Price:*** Included in membership dues.

★6071★ Canvasbacker
Canvasback Soc.
2100 Society Bldg.
Cleveland, OH 44114
Phone: (216)443-2340
Concerned with the preservation of the canvasback species of duck in North America. Reports on preservation efforts and offers information on canvasback habitat areas. ***Frequency:*** Seminannual. ***Price:*** Included in membership.

★6072★ Carrying Capacity News
Carrying Capacity Network
1325 G St. NW, Ste. 1003
Washington, DC 20005-3104
Phone: (202)879-3044
Short collection of articles and reviews on links between environmental, population, resource, social, and related economic issues. ***Frequency:*** Periodic. ***Price:*** $25.

★6073★ The CERCular
U.S. Army Engineer Waterways Experiment Station
c/o CEWES-CV-I
3909 Hulls Ferry Rd.
Vicksburg, MS 39180
Phone: (601)634-2012
Covers CERC, the U.S. Army Coastal Engineering Research Center and its work on shore and beach erosion; flood and storm protection; navigation improvements; and the design, construction, operation, and maintenance of coastal structures. ***Editor(s):*** Dr. Fred E. Camfield; Bettye Stephens. ***Frequency:*** Quarterly. ***Price:*** Free.

★6074★ ChemEcology
Chemical Manufacturers Assn.
2501 M St., N.W.
Washington, DC 20037
Phone: (202)887-1204
Covers environmental and health and safety issues of concern to both the chemical industry and the public. Summarizes federal and state regulatory actions, research, industry developments, emerging technologies, and advances in pollution control. Features member companies and quotes from speeches by industry leaders. ***Editor(s):*** Laurie L. Hayes. ***Frequency:*** 10/yr. ***Price:*** Free.

★6075★ Chihuahuan Desert Discovery
Chihuahuan Desert Research Inst.
Box 1334
Alpine, TX 79831
Phone: (915)837-8370
Frequency: Semiannual. ***Price:*** Included in membership dues.

★6076★ Chihuahuan Newsbrief
Chihuahuan Desert Research Inst.
Box 1334
Alpine, TX 79831
Phone: (915)837-8370
Frequency: Semiannual.

★6077★ Children of the Green Earth Newsletter
Children of the Green Earth
PO Box 31550
Seattle, WA 98103
Phone: (206)781-0852
Frequency: Quarterly.

★6078★ Children's Environments Quarterly
Lawrence Erlbaum Associates
365 Broadway
Hillsdale, NJ 07642
Phone: (212)790-4550
Focuses on children's and adolescents' environments, specifically research, research applications, and policy. Concentrates each issue on a single theme such as children's museums, playgrounds, cognition, and children and water. Feautures an annual "Collected Papers" issue. ***Editor(s):*** Roger A. Hart and Cindi R. Katz. ***Frequency:*** Quarterly. ***Price:*** $30/yr. for individuals, $70 for institutions, U.S. and Canada; $50 for individuals, $90 for institutions, elsewhere.

★6079★ Citizens Against Throwaways Tracks
Citizens Against Throwaways
Florida Conservation Foundation, Inc.
1251-B Miller Ave.
Winter Park, FL 32789
Phone: (305)644-5377
Carries news about the association's campaign for mandatory beverage container deposit laws and other recycling projects in Florida and throughout the U.S. ***Editor(s):*** Robert Stamps.

★6080★ Citizens for a Better Environment—Environmental Review, Midwest Edition
Citizens for a Better Environment
33 E. Congress St., Ste. 523
Chicago, IL 60605
Phone: (312)939-1530
Reflects the organization's commitment to clean air and water and a healthy environment. Features articles on toxic pollution and environmental health issues in the Midwest. ***Editor(s):*** Sharon McGowan. ***Frequency:*** Quarterly. ***Price:*** $25/yr.

★6081★ Citizens for a Better Environment—Environmental Review, Western Edition
Citizens for a Better Environment
942 Market St., Ste. 505
San Francisco, CA 94102
Phone: (415)788-0690
Fax: (415)788-0423
Publishes news of the Citizens for a Better Environment, an organization concerned with protecting the public and the environment from toxic pollution. Contains articles on such topics as toxics in the home, pesticides, and air and water pollution. ***Editor(s):*** Hannah Creighton. ***Frequency:*** Quarterly. ***Price:*** Included in membership.

★6082★ Clean Coal Technologies
National Technical Information Service
U.S. Dept. of Commerce
5285 Port Royal Rd.
Springfield, VA 22161
Phone: (703)487-4630
Abstracts worldwide information on clean coal, including mechanical coal cleaning, desulfurization, coal gasification and liquefaction, flue gas cleanup, and advanced coal combustion. ***Frequency:*** Monthly. ***Price:*** $100/yr., U.S., Canada, and Mexico; $200 elsewhere.

★6083★ Clean Sites Forum Newsletter
Clean Sites, Inc.
1199 N. Fairfax St.
Alexandria, VA 22314
Phone: (703)683-8522
Frequency: Quarterly.

★6084★ Clean Water Report
Business Publishers, Inc.
951 Pershing Dr.
Silver Spring, MD 20910
Phone: (301)587-6300
Fax: (301)587-1081
Provides information on water pollution control, drinking water supply and safety, and water resources issues. Covers national policy, legislation, regulations, enforcement and litigation, and state and local news. ***Editor(s):*** Elaine Eiserer. ***Frequency:*** Biweekly. ***Price:*** $195.72/yr., U.S. and Canada; $214 elsewhere.

★6085★ Clearing House Newsletter
National Inst. on Park and Grounds Management
PO Box 1936
Appleton, WI 54913
Phone: (414)733-2301
Disseminates information and serves as an idea exchange to help improve grounds management. Focuses on the management of large outdoor areas such as parks, campuses, and industrial areas; discusses grounds management problems unique to such areas. ***Frequency:*** Bimonthly. ***Price:*** Included in membership.

★6086★ Coalition on Resource Recovery and the Environment Newsletter
Coalition on Resource Recovery and the Environment
c/o Dr. Walter M. Shaub
U. S. Conf. of Mayors
1620 I St. NW, Ste. 600
Washington, DC 20006
Phone: (202)293-7330
Fax: (202)293-2352
Frequency: Monthly.

★6087★ Coastal Research
Geology Dept.
Florida State Univ.
Tallahassee, FL 32306-3026
Phone: (904)644-3208
Reports on developments and findings relating to coastal studies. Considers relevant scientific issues such as sea level, meteorology, coastal and near shore environments, coastal geology, sedimentary research, coastal engineering, and pollution. ***Editor(s):*** Dr. W.F. Tanner. ***Frequency:*** 3/yr. ***Price:*** $5/yr., U.S. and Canada; $6 elsewhere.

★6088★ Coastlines
New York State Sea Grant Inst.
Dutchess Hall
SUNY at Stony Brook
Stony Brook, NY 11794-5001
Phone: (516)632-6905
Covers marine and Great Lakes activities of New York Sea Grant Institute's research and extension programs. ***Editor(s):*** Diana Puglisi. ***Frequency:*** Quarterly. ***Price:*** Free.

★6089★ Coastlines
Executive Office of Environmental Affairs
Massachusetts Coastal Zone Management Office
Saltonstall State Off. Bldg., Rm. 2006
100 Cambridge St.
Boston, MA 02202
Phone: (617)727-9530
Fax: (617)727-2754
Aims to implement Massachusetts Coastal Zone Management Program, which concentrates on coastal land and water management, port and harbor development, water quality, recreation, public access, and coastal development. ***Editor(s):*** Anne L. Smrcina. ***Frequency:*** 9/yr. ***Price:*** Free.

★6090★ Coastlines
League for Coastal Protection
PO Box 421698
San Francisco, CA 94142-1698
Increases public awareness of actions taken by the California Coastal Commission, as well as of legislation and planning issues affecting the California coastline. Urges citizen involvement in coastal protection activities. Contains informational articles on wetlands, off-shore oil drilling, and the Coastal Act. ***Editor(s):*** Jon Stewart. ***Frequency:*** Bimonthly. ***Price:*** Included in membership; $20/yr. for nonmembers.

★6091★ Coastwatch
Sea Grant Coll. Program
Univ. of North Carolina
PO Box 8605
Raleigh, NC 27695-8605
Phone: (919)737-2454
Covers activities of Sea Grant, a program promoting use and development of the North Carolina coast through research, extension, and education. Each issue offers two or three articles on a single topic of coastal concern, such as shellfish contamination, beach erosion, and hurricanes. ***Editor(s):*** Kathy Hart. ***Frequency:*** Monthly, except July and December. ***Price:*** Free.

★6092★ Coastwatch
Center for Coastal Studies
59 Commercial St.
PO Box 1036
Provincetown, MA 02657
Phone: (508)487-3622
Covers research updates on projects in coastal ecology and biology, whale research, and conservation issues. ***Editor(s):*** Karen Steuer.

Frequency: Bimonthly. *Price:* Included in membership.

★6093★ Common Sense Pest Control Quarterly
Bio-Integral Resource Center
PO Box 7414
Berkeley, CA 94707
Phone: (415)524-2567
Presents information regarding least-toxic pest management in layperson's terms. Evaluates alternative strategies for many pest problems treated exclusively with pesticides. Discusses such concerns as least-toxic management of pests on indoor plants, pests that damage paper, controlling fleas and ticks on pets, and garden pests. *Editor(s):* Sheila Daar, Helga Olkowski, and William Olkowski. *Frequency:* 4/yr. *Price:* $30/yr. for individuals, $50 for institutions, U.S. and Canada; $40 for individuals, $60 for institutions elsewhere.

★6094★ Communities at Risk: Environmental Dangers in Rural America
Renew America
Publications Dept.
1400 Sixteenth St., NW
Washington, DC 20036

★6095★ The Compendium Newsletter
Educational Communications
PO Box 35473
Los Angeles, CA 90035
Phone: (213)559-9160
Concerned with ecological issues, including wildlife preservation, overpopulation, toxics and chemicals, air quality, urban blight, water quality, resource management, transportation, acid rain, solid waste, noise, nuclear power, food and hunger, and alternative technology. *Editor(s):* Nancy Pearlman. *Frequency:* Bimonthly. *Price:* $20/yr.

★6096★ Concensus Newsletter
The Keystone Center
PO Box 606
Keystone, CO 80435
Phone: (303)468-5822
Fax: (303)262-0152
Reports on the activities of the Center, which provides mediation and facilitation services to resolve disputes concerning science, technology, energy, health, and the environment; and focuses on environmental quality and health, biotechnology and genetic resources, and natural resources. *Editor(s):* Cindy Fisk. *Frequency:* 3/yr. *Price:* Free.

★6097★ Concerned Neighbors in Action Newsletter
Concerned Neighbors in Action
PO Box 3847
Riverside, CA 92519
Frequency: Quarterly.

★6098★ Connecticut Whale
Cetacean Soc. Intl.
PO Box 290145
Wethersfield, CT 06109-0145
Phone: (203)563-6444
Frequency: Bimonthly.

★6099★ Connections: The CEIP Fund Newsletter
CEIP Fund
68 Harrison Ave., 5th Fl.
Boston, MA 02111
Phone: (617)426-4375
Describes current activities and programs of organizations and projects. *Frequency:* Quarterly. *Price:* Free.

★6100★ Conservation 87
National Wildlife Fed.
1412 16th St., N.W.
Washington, DC 20036-2266
Phone: (202)737-2024
Publishes news and informational items on a variety of current conservation issues. Discusses legislative and regulatory developments with regard to environmental quality and directs individual support. Reports on conservation-related rallies, meetings, and educational opportunities of interest. *Editor(s):* Dena Leibman. *Frequency:* Every 3 weeks. *Price:* Free to members of the NWF's Resource Conservation Alliance.

★6101★ Conservation Education Association Newsletter
Conservation Education Assn.
College of Natural Resources
Humboldt State Univ.
Arcata, CA 95521
Phone: (707)826-4291
Provides information concerning trends in environmental and conservation education and curriculum materials in conservation and ecology. *Editor(s):* John G. Hewston. *Frequency:* 4/yr. *Price:* Included in membership.

★6102★ Conservation Education Association Newsletter
Conservation Education Assn.
c/o Charles Jordan
Missouri Department of Conservation
Box 180
Jefferson City, MO 65536
Phone: (314)751-4115
Frequency: Quarterly.

★6103★ The Conservation Exchange
National Wildlife Fed. Corporate Conservation Coun.
1400 16th St. NW
Washington, DC 20036
Phone: (202)797-6870
Fax: (202)797-6871
Frequency: Quarterly.

★6104★ Conservation Foundation Letter
The Conservation Foundation, Inc.
1250 24th St., N.W.
Washington, DC 20037
Phone: (202)293-4800
Fax: (202)293-9211
Covers a variety of resource and environmental concerns, including solar energy, pesticides, appropriate technology, barrier islands, and coastal zone management. Examines a single topic in each issue. *Editor(s):* Jonathan Adams. *Frequency:* Bimonthly. *Price:* Free.

★6105★ Conservation Law Foundation of New England Newsletter
Conservation Law Found. of New England
3 Joy St.
Boston, MA 02108
Phone: (617)742-2540
Describes activities of the Foundation. Contains articles covering various environmental topics; occasionally a special theme per issue (such as the environmental hazards of the automobile). *Editor(s):* Daniel Grossman. *Frequency:* Quarterly. *Price:* Included in membership.

★6106★ Conservation News Digest
Amer. Resources Group
374 Maple Ave., E., Ste. 204
Vienna, VA 22180
Phone: (703)255-2700
Covers non-industrial private forestry and conservation issues nationwide. Publishes news of the monitoring, educational, and research activities engaged in by the Group. Reports on issues, current events, and legislative developments affecting the use of U.S. natural resources. *Editor(s):* Keith A. Argow. *Frequency:* Bimonthly. *Price:* Included in membership.

★6107★ Coolidge Center Letter
Coolidge Center for Environmental Leadership
1675 Massachusetts Ave.
Cambridge, MA 02138-1836
Phone: (617)864-5085
Offers information on Coolidge Center programs and sustainable development of the environment. Contains reprints of publications of Third World nongovernmental organizations and successful strategies of grassroot examples to block environmental degradation. Treats issues such as deforestation, large dams, toxic waste, and alternative energy. *Editor(s):* Catherine Crumbley. *Frequency:* Quarterly. *Price:* Included in membership.

★6108★ Corporate Examiner
Interfaith Center on Corporate Responsibility
475 Riverside Dr., Rm. 566
New York, NY 10115
Phone: (212)870-2293
Includes opinions of corporate responsibility leaders and publication reviews. *Frequency:* 10/year. *Price:* $35/year.

★6109★ Corporate Public Affairs Council Newsmemo
Public Affairs Coun.
1019 19th St. NW, Ste. 200
Washington, DC 20036
Phone: (202)872-1790
Fax: (202)835-8343
Frequency: Periodic. *Price:* Available only to members and administrators of corporate political action committees.

★6110★ Council on Economic Priorities Newsletter
Council on Economic Priorities
30 Irving Pl.
New York, NY 10003
Phone: (212)420-1133
Fax: (212)420-0988
Frequency: Monthly.

★6111★ Council on Economic Priorities Reports
Council on Economic Priorities
30 Irving Pl.
New York, NY 10003
Phone: (212)420-1133
Fax: (212)420-0988
Frequency: 3/year.

★6112★ Critical Mass Energy Bulletin
Public Citizen Critical Mass Energy Project
215 Pennsylvania Ave., S.E.
Washington, DC 20003
Phone: (202)546-4996
Provides news updates and articles on nuclear power, nuclear waste, nuclear weapons facilities, renewable energy, solar technologies, energy conservation and energy efficiency, and global warming. *Editor(s):* Ken Bossong. *Frequency:* Bimonthly. *Price:* $18/yr., individual and libraries; $48 for others.

★6113★ Current & Eddies
Connecticut River Watershed Coun.
125 Combs Rd.
Easthampton, MA 01027
Phone: (413)584-0057
Frequency: Bimonthly.

★6114★ Currents
National Coalition for Marine Conservation
PO Box 23298
Savannah, GA 31403
Phone: (912)234-8062
Fax: (912)233-2909
Summarizes coalition news and activities. ***Frequency:*** Bimonthly. ***Price:*** Included in membership dues.

★6115★ Cycle/The Waste Paper
Environmental Action Coalition, Inc.
625 Broadway
New York, NY 10012
Phone: (212)677-1601
Provides information on the disposal of solid waste materials, such as paper, used containers, metal, and garbage. Carries news of the activities of the Coalition, which is dedicated to environmental protection and education. ***Editor(s):*** Jennie Tichenor. ***Frequency:*** Periodic. ***Price:*** Free.

★6116★ The Deer Trail
Whitetails Unlimited
PO Box 422
Sturgeon Bay, WI 54235
Phone: (414)743-6777
Reflects the organization's commitment to sound deer management. Reports on research being conducted on the white-tailed deer and discusses developments and legislation affecting the control of animal populations. ***Editor(s):*** Dale G. Deckman. ***Frequency:*** Quarterly. ***Price:*** Included in membership.

★6117★ Defense Cleanup
Pasha Publications, Inc.
1401 Wilson Blvd., Ste. 909
Arlington, VA 22209
Phone: (703)528-1244
Reports on projects to analyze, recycle, treat, transport, and dispose of defense wastes at weapons plants and military facilities, both active and inactive. ***Frequency:*** Biweekly.

★6118★ The Delicate Balance
National Center for Environmental Health Strategies
c/o Mary Lamielle
1100 Rural Ave.
Voorhees, NJ 08043
Phone: (609)429-5358
Newsletter on environmental illnesses and issues. ***Frequency:*** Quarterly. ***Price:*** Included in membership dues; $20/year for nonmembers.

★6119★ Department of Natural Resources—Focus
Dept. of Natural Resources
607 State Office Bldg.
Indianapolis, IN 46204
Phone: (317)232-4080
Reports on the Department's activities in Indiana. ***Editor(s):*** Hannah Kirchner. ***Frequency:*** Monthly. ***Price:*** Free.

★6120★ Design Research News
Environmental Design Research Assn.
PO Box 24083
Oklahoma City, OK 73124
Phone: (405)232-2655
Fax: (405)232-3152
Covers environmental policy, planning, design, and education. Examines current research on human behavior and its implications for environmental designing. Provides information on employment, educational, and funding opportunities. ***Editor(s):*** Sherry Ahrentzen. ***Frequency:*** Quarterly. ***Price:*** Included in membership.

★6121★ Dodo Dispatch
Wildlife Preservation Trust Intl.
34th St. & Girard Ave.
Philadelphia, PA 19104
Phone: (215)222-3636
Fax: (215)222-2191
Newsletter for children. ***Frequency:*** 3/year.

★6122★ Drinking Water & Backflow Prevention
Elizabeth Gold
PO Box 33209
Northglenn, CO 80233
Phone: (303)451-0980
Fax: (303)452-9776
Presents articles directed toward individuals, companies, organizations, agencies, and municipalities with an interest in drinking water protection and backflow prevention. Contains information on safety standards, water system protection, training programs, cross-connection control, and all issues related to preventing the contamination of potable drinking water supplies with backflow prevention devices. ***Editor(s):*** Elizabeth Gold. ***Frequency:*** Monthly. ***Price:*** $32.50/yr., U.S.; $46.50, Canada; $50.50 elsewhere.

★6123★ Ducks Unlimited News
Ducks Unlimited
1 Waterfowl Way
Long Grove, IL 60047
Phone: (708)438-4300
Fax: (708)438-9236
Reports on the activities of the Association which aims to restore or build natural wetland areas for migratory waterfowl in North America and New Zealand. ***Frequency:*** 2/yr. ***Price:*** Included in membership.

★6124★ e-Lab
Energy Laboratory
Massachusetts Institute of Technology
Room E40-495
Cambridge, MA 02139
Phone: (617)253-3405
Fax: (617)253-8013
Contains three or four articles describing the results of research at the Energy Lab. Provides lists of recent publications and projects that have received funding during the period covered. ***Editor(s):*** Nancy W. Stauffer. ***Frequency:*** Quarterly. ***Price:*** Free.

★6125★ Earth First! Journal in Defense of Wilderness and Biodiversity
Earth First!
PO Box 5871
Tucson, AZ 85703
Editor(s): John Davis. ***Frequency:*** 8/year. ***Price:*** $20/year.

★6126★ Earth Regeneration Society Newsletter
Earth Regeneration Soc.
1442A Walnut St., No. 57
Berkeley, CA 94709
Phone: (415)525-7723
Frequency: Periodic.

★6127★ Earthcare Appeals
c/o Michael McCloskey
408 C St., NE
Washington, DC 20002
Phone: (202)547-1141
Publishes research updates concerning global environmental protection and public environmental policy. Reports on the Network's efforts to modify policies regarding coastal ecosystems management, the ozone, hazardous substances, and other environmental problems. ***Frequency:*** Quarterly. ***Price:*** Included in membership.

★6128★ Earthmind Newsletter
Earthmind
PO Box 743
Mariposa, CA 95338
Frequency: Periodic.

★6129★ Eastern Mineral Law Foundation Newsletter
Eastern Mineral Law Found.
West Virginia University Law Center
PO Box 6130
Morgantown, WV 26506
Phone: (304)293-2470
Fax: (304)293-7654
Frequency: 3-4/year.

★6130★ Eco-Humane Letter
International Ecology Soc.
1471 Barclay St.
St. Paul, MN 55106-1405
Phone: (612)774-4971
Focuses on environmental protection, wild and domestic animal protection, and habitat preservation. Covers related news, events, decisions, and politics. ***Editor(s):*** Stephanie O'Brien. ***Frequency:*** Periodic. ***Price:*** Included in membership; $10/yr. for nonmembers.

★6131★ Eco-News: An Environmental Newsletter for Children
Environmental Action Coalition
625 Broadway, 2nd Fl.
New York, NY 10012
Phone: (212)677-1601
Fax: (212)941-8728
Frequency: Periodic.

★6132★ Eco Newsletter
Antarctica Project
218 D St., S.E.
Washington, DC 20003
Phone: (202)544-2600
Fax: (202)543-4710
Monitors activities that affect the Antarctic environment. Disseminates information on the future of the Antarctic with the purpose of preserving the region and its wildlife. ***Editor(s):*** James Barnes. ***Frequency:*** Irregular. ***Price:*** Included in membership.

★6133★ EcoDemocracy
Fossil Fuels Policy Action Inst.
PO Box 8558
Fredericksburg, VA 22404
Phone: (703)371-0222
Fax: (703)371-0646
Promotes the efforts of the coalition EcoDemocracy, which seeks to effect change in the ecology. ***Editor(s):*** Bill Van Doren. ***Price:*** Included in membership.

★6134★ Ecological Society of America Bulletin
Ecological Soc. of America
Arizona State University
Center for Environmental Studies
Tempe, AZ 85287
Phone: (602)965-3000
Frequency: Quarterly.

★6135★ Ecology Center Newsletter
Ecology Center
2530 San Pablo Ave.
Berkeley, CA 94702
Phone: (415)548-2220

★6136★ Ecology USA
Business Publishers, Inc.
951 Pershing Dr.
Silver Spring, MD 20910-4464
Phone: (301)587-6300
Fax: (301)587-1081
Publishes information on ecology ranging from wildlife conservation to environmental cancer and offshore drilling. ***Editor(s):*** Elaine Eiserer. ***Frequency:*** Biweekly. ***Price:*** $82.72/yr.

★6137★ ECOSPHERE Magazine/ Newsletter
International Ecosystems Univ.
310 Oakvue Rd.
Pleasant Hill, CA 94523
Phone: (415)946-1500
Examines the medical, chemical, and cultural aspects of ecology, the environment, and ecodevelopment, and their effect on tourism. ***Editor(s):*** Dr. Nicolas D. Hetzer. ***Frequency:*** Quarterly. ***Price:*** $8/yr.

★6138★ EIS Newsletter
Friends of the Everglades
202 Park St.
Miami Springs, FL 33166
Phone: (305)888-1230
Newsletter on the conservation of the everglades area and issues such as water and land management, overpopulation, waste and pollution, and destruction of natural resources. ***Frequency:*** Periodic.

★6139★ El Paisano
Desert Protective Council, Inc.
PO Box 4294
Palm Springs, CA 92263
Phone: (619)670-7127
Focuses on environmental study of the desert, including the areas of ecology, archeology, natural history, biology, and geography. Includes news of the activities of the Council. ***Editor(s):*** Harriet Allen. ***Frequency:*** Quarterly. ***Price:*** Included in membership.

★6140★ Electric Energy Systems
National Technical Information Service
U.S. Dept. of Commerce
5285 Port Royal Rd.
Springfield, VA 22161
Phone: (703)487-4630
Abstracts worldwide information on electric power, including fossil and hydroelectric power generation, transmission, environmental control technology, and policy. ***Frequency:*** Monthly. ***Price:*** $100/yr., U.S., Canada, and Mexico; $200 elsewhere.

★6141★ Electrical Women's Round Table National Newsletter
The Electrical Women's Round Table, Inc.
PO Box 292793
Nashville, TN 37229-2793
Phone: (615)254-4479
Updates on energy affairs, ideas and information exchanges, and other timely topics and promotes the efficient use of electricity. ***Frequency:*** Quarterly. ***Price:*** Included in membership.

★6142★ Eleventh Commandment Fellowship Chapter News
Eleventh Commandment Fellowship
PO Box 14667
San Francisco, CA 94114
Phone: (415)626-6064
Frequency: Periodic.

★6143★ The Elmwood Newsletter
Elmwood Inst.
PO Box 5765
Berkeley, CA 94705-0765
Phone: (415)845-4595
Fax: (415)843-9398
Contains articles on systemic thinking; includes book summaries and members' forum. ***Frequency:*** Quarterly. ***Price:*** $2/copy.

★6144★ Energy: An Abstract Newsletter
National Technical Information Service
U.S. Dept. of Commerce
5285 Port Royal Rd.
Springfield, VA 22161
Phone: (703)487-4630
Reports on energy use, supply, and demand; power and heat generation; energy conservation, transmission, and storage; fuel conversion processes; energy policies, regulations, and studies; and engines and fuels. ***Frequency:*** Weekly. ***Price:*** $135/yr., U.S., Canada, and Mexico; $185 elsewhere.

★6145★ Energy and Environment Alert
National Coun. for Environmental Balance, Inc.
4169 Westport Rd.
PO Box 7732
Louisville, KY 40257-0732
Phone: (502)896-8731
Fax: (502)339-1745
Covers development and preservation of the environment through the application of scientific knowledge. Focuses on energy, agriculture, chemistry, entomology, and mineral resources; deals with technical information in lay persons' language. ***Editor(s):*** I.W. Tucker, Ph.D. ***Frequency:*** Quarterly. ***Price:*** $20/yr. U.S. and Canada; $25 for individuals, $35/yr. for organizations and elsewhere.

★6146★ Energy and Environment Alert: Brief Notes About National Council for Environmental Balance and NCEB Associates
National Coun. for Environmental Balance
4169 Westport Rd.
PO Box 7732
Louisville, KY 40207
Phone: (502)896-8731
Covers environmental issues. ***Frequency:*** Bimonthly. ***Price:*** Included in membership dues; $20/year for nonmember individuals; $25/year for groups.

★6147★ Energy and Housing Report
Business Publishers, Inc.
951 Pershing Dr.
Silver Spring, MD 20910
Phone: (301)587-6300
Fax: (301)587-1081
Concerned with residential energy conservation problems. Reports on new laws, regulations, technology, and programs; developments in the home energy industry; and on potential hazards in energy products. ***Editor(s):*** Allan L. Frank. ***Frequency:*** Monthly. ***Price:*** $108/yr.

★6148★ Energy Conservation Digest
Editorial Resources, Inc.
PO Box 21133
Washington, DC 20009
Phone: (202)332-2267
Focuses on economic implications of current commercial, residential, and industrial energy conservation issues. Also monitors legislative and policy developments, including least-cost planning. ***Editor(s):*** David L. Howell. ***Frequency:*** Semimonthly. ***Price:*** $155/yr., U.S.; $170, Canada; $185 elsewhere.

★6149★ The Energy Daily
King Publishing, Inc.
627 National Press Bldg.
Washington, DC 20045
Phone: (202)662-9725
Fax: (202)662-9744
Covers the field of energy as it relates to government, policy, and industry. Discusses all forms of energy: nuclear, geothermal, coal, solar, oil, natural gas, wind, shale oil, and wave power. Includes analysis, editorial comment, and hard reporting. ***Editor(s):*** John McCaughey. ***Frequency:*** Daily, Monday-Friday. ***Price:*** $995/yr.

★6150★ Energy from Biomass and Municipal Wastes
National Technical Information Service
U.S. Dept. of Commerce
5285 Port Royal Rd.
Springfield, VA 22161
Phone: (703)487-4630
Abstracts worldwide information on biomass production, conversion, and utilization for energy. Includes topics on selection, growth, and harvesting of terrestial and aquatic plants. ***Frequency:*** Monthly. ***Price:*** $100/yr., U.S., Canada, and Mexico; $200 elsewhere.

★6151★ Energy Modeling Forum Update
Energy Modeling Forum
406 Terman Engineering Center
Stanford University
Stanford, CA 94305
Phone: (415)723-0645
Presents news of the Forum, which fosters communication between the analysts and users of analysis in energy planning and policy analysis. Covers such topics as energy and the economy, electric load forecasting, and macroeconomic impacts of energy shocks. ***Editor(s):*** Dorothy Sheffield. ***Frequency:*** Semiannual. ***Price:*** Free.

★6152★ Energy News Exchange
Kentucky Utilities Company
One Quality St.
Lexington, KY 40507
Phone: (606)255-1461
Provides news and information on energy. ***Editor(s):*** Joyce C. Barr. ***Frequency:*** 6/yr.

★6153★ The Energy Report
Pasha Publications, Inc.
1401 Wilson Blvd., Ste. 900
Arlington, VA 22209-9970
Phone: (703)528-1244
Covers all aspects of energy policy, reporting on government decisions, technological innovations, cogeneration, and fuel conservation. Also carries energy statistics and forecasts. ***Editor(s):*** Tom Choman. ***Frequency:*** 50/yr. ***Price:*** $535/yr., U.S. and Canada; $609 elsewhere.

★6154★ Energy Scout
Virginia Center for Coal and Energy Research
Virginia Polytechnic Inst. and State Univ.
617 N. Main St.
Blackburg, VA 24060
Phone: (703)231-5038
Presents information on a wide range of energy-related issues of current and future interest. Carries guest editorials on organizations of interest. ***Editor(s):*** Ted Clutter. ***Frequency:*** Bimonthly. ***Price:*** Free in Virginia; $5.00/yr. elsewhere.

★6155★ Energy Storage Systems
National Technical Information Service
U.S. Dept. of Commerce
5285 Port Royal Rd.
Springfield, VA 22161
Phone: (703)487-4630
Abstracts current worldwide information on energy storage. ***Frequency:*** Bimonthly. ***Price:*** $100/yr., U.S., Canada, and Mexico; $200 elsewhere.

★6156★ Energy Studies
Center for Energy Studies
University of Texas at Austin
10100 Burnet Rd.
Austin, TX 78758
Phone: (512)471-7792
Focuses on energy research at the Center and the university. ***Editor(s):*** Jennifer Evans. ***Frequency:*** 6/yr. ***Price:*** Free in U.S., Canada, and Mexico.

★6157★ Energy Today
Trends Publishing, Inc.
1079 National Press Bldg.
Washington, DC 20045
Phone: (202)393-0031
Fax: (202)393-1732
Examines energy programs, policy, regulation, and conservation. Discusses fossil, solar, and nuclear energy and other power sources. Includes a section titled Energy Trends, which reports in brief on upcoming conferences, papers and studies, energy education, new multimedia items, and international energy news. ***Editor(s):*** A. Kranish. ***Frequency:*** Monthly. ***Price:*** $695/yr.

★6158★ ENFO
Environmental Information Center
Florida Conservation Foundation, Inc.
1251-B Miller Ave.
Winter Park, FL 32789
Phone: (305)644-5377
Reports on and analyzes a wide variety of environmental subjects such as land use, water quality, energy conservation, population, wildlife, and toxic industrial wastes, particularly as they affect the state of Florida. Contains information on state and federal environmental rules and regulations, EPA guidelines, and various pollution standards. ***Editor(s):*** Gerald Grow. ***Frequency:*** Bimonthly. ***Price:*** Included in membership.

★6159★ The Entanglement Network Newsletter
Entanglement Network Coalition
c/o Dr. Albert Manville II
Defenders of Wildlife
1244 19th St. NW
Washington, DC 20036
Phone: (202)659-9510
Fax: (202)833-3349
Frequency: Periodic.

★6160★ Environment Report
Trends Publishing, Inc.
1079 National Press Bldg.
Washington, DC 20045
Phone: (202)393-0031
Fax: (202)393-1732
Covers environmental pollution problems such as acid rain, water and air quality, industrial waste disposal, carcinogens, rural water loans, irrigation reforms, and water reclamation. Monitors environmental research, recently released congressional environment documents, pertinent books, journal articles, and conferences. ***Editor(s):*** A. Kranish. ***Frequency:*** Semimonthly. ***Price:*** $480/yr.

★6161★ Environment Reporter
Bureau of Natl. Affairs, Inc.
1231 25th St., N.W.
Washington, DC 20037
Phone: (202)452-4200
Fax: (202)822-8092
Toll-Free: 800-372-1033
Telex: 285656 BNAI WSH
Offers a notification and reference service covering legislative, administrative, judicial, industrial, and technological developments in pollution control and environmental protection. ***Editor(s):*** Wallis E. McClain, Jr. ***Frequency:*** Weekly. ***Price:*** $1,899/yr.

★6162★ Environment Week
King Communications Group, Inc.
627 National Press Bldg.
Washington, DC 20045
Phone: (202)662-9720
Covers aspects and issues of environmental problems, potential solutions, federal and state regulatory actions; addresses hydrocarbon contamination, acid rain, "greenhouse effect," and toxic and hazardous waste. ***Frequency:*** Weekly.

★6163★ Environmental Chronicle
Great Swamp Research Inst.
Indiana University of Pennsylvania
College of Natural Sciences & Mathematics
Office of the Assoc. Dean
305 Weyandt Hall
Indiana, PA 15705
Phone: (412)357-2609
Journal covering institute activities and environmental issues. ***Frequency:*** Quarterly. ***Price:*** Available to members only.

★6164★ Environmental Conservation Library News
Environmental Conservation Library
Minneapolis Public Library & Information Center
300 Nicollet Mall
Minneapolis, MN 55401
Phone: (612)372-6570
Contains articles and bibliographies on environmental and energy topics and informs readers of available resources in the library. Addresses a broad spectrum of environmental concerns with emphasis on Minnesota. ***Editor(s):*** William Johnston. ***Frequency:*** Semiannual. ***Price:*** Free.

★6165★ Environmental Control Report
Graphic Arts Technical Found.
4615 Forbes Ave.
Pittsburgh, PA 15213
Phone: (412)621-6941
Discusses the effects of environmental control regulation and legislation on the printing industry. Covers such topics as air and water pollution, control of toxic substances, solid hazardous waste, energy, and conservation of resources. Also concerned with occupational safety and health in the printing industry. ***Editor(s):*** Gary A. Jones. ***Frequency:*** 3-4/yr. ***Price:*** Included in membership; $7.50/copy for nonmembers.

★6166★ Environmental Defense Fund Letter
Environmental Defense Fund
257 Park Ave., S., 16th Fl.
New York, NY 10010-7304
Phone: (212)505-2100
Reports on EDF actions concerning a range of national and global environmental problems in the areas of air quality, energy and resource concervation, wildlife protection, water resource management, and toxic chemical use and regulation. ***Editor(s):*** Norma H. Watson. ***Frequency:*** Bimonthly. ***Price:*** Included in membership; $20/yr. for nonmembers.

★6167★ Environmental Effects of Dredging
U.S. Army Engineer Waterways Experiment Station
3909 Halls Ferry Rd.
Vicksburg, MS 39180-6199
Phone: (601)634-3616
Acts as an information exchange covering Dredging Operations Technical Support Program activities, which include determining the effects of dredging and dredged material disposal operations and the development of technically, environmentally, and economically feasible dredging and disposal alternatives. ***Editor(s):*** Robert Baylot, Jr. ***Frequency:*** Quarterly. ***Price:*** Free.

★6168★ Environmental Engineering News
School of Civil Engineering
Purdue Univ.
c/o Prof. John M. Bell
Civil Engineering Bldg.
Purdue University
West Lafayette, IN 47907
Phone: (317)494-2194
Fax: (317)494-0395
Carries unusual environmental facts and statistics from around the world. ***Editor(s):*** Prof. John M. Bell. ***Frequency:*** Monthly. ***Price:*** Free.

★6169★ Environmental Hazards
Law and Business, Inc.
Prentice-Hall, Inc.
910 Sylvan Ave.
Englewood Cliffs, NJ 07632
Phone: (201)894-8538
Reports on hazardous waste and toxic tort issues. ***Frequency:*** Monthly. ***Price:*** $245/yr.

★6170★ Environmental Health and Safety News
Department of Environmental Health
Univ. of Washington
School of Public Health
Seattle, WA 98195
Phone: (206)543-4252
Covers pollution, safety, and health in occupations. ***Editor(s):*** Peter A. Breysse. ***Frequency:*** Irregular. ***Price:*** Free.

★6171★ Environmental Health Letter
Business Publishers, Inc.
951 Pershing Dr.
Silver Spring, MD 20910-4464
Phone: (301)587-6300
Fax: (301)587-1081
News on environmental issues from a health perspective. ***Frequency:*** Biweekly. ***Price:*** $231.50.

★6172★ Environmental Health News
School of Public Health
Dept. of Environmental Health
Univ. of Washington
461 Health Science Bldg.
Seattle, WA 98195
Phone: (206)543-6955
Fax: (206)543-8123
Concentrates on industrial hygiene, environmental problems, and safety issues. ***Editor(s):*** David Kalman, Ph.D. ***Frequency:*** 3/yr. ***Price:*** Free.

★6173★ Environmental Health Trends Report
National Environmental Health Assn.
720 S. Colorado Blvd., Ste. 970, S. Tower
Denver, CO 80222
Phone: (303)756-9090
Fax: (303)691-9490
Frequency: Quarterly. ***Price:*** $10/year.

★6174★ Environmental Legislative Bulletin
Environmental Lobby of Massachusetts
3 Joy St.
Boston, MA 02108
Phone: (617)742-2553
Promotes environmental legislation. ***Frequency:*** 6/yr. ***Price:*** Included in membership.

★6175★ Environmental Liability Monitor
Business Publishers, Inc.
951 Pershing Dr.
Silver Spring, MD 20910-4464
Phone: (301)587-6300
Fax: (301)587-1081
Reports on new laws, rules, and court cases involving real estate and the environment. ***Frequency:*** Monthly. ***Price:*** $383.

★6176★ Environmental Litigation News
Environmental Compliance Inst.
Aetna Bldg., Ste. 850
2350 Lakeside Blvd.
Richardson, TX 75082-4342
Phone: (214)644-8971
Fax: (214)234-6966
Analyzes trends in environmental compliance legislation. ***Frequency:*** Monthly. ***Price:*** $485/year.

★6177★ Environmental Manager
Executive Enterprises Publications Company, Inc.
22 W. 21st St.
New York, NY 10010-6904
Phone: 800-332-1105
Fax: (212)645-8689
Toll-Free: 800-332-8804
Provides regulatory and legislative news, environmental case studies, interviews, reports on key court decisions, recycling updates, news on cleanup and waste control technology, and coverage of health and safety issues. ***Frequency:*** Monthly. ***Price:*** $120/yr.

★6178★ Environmental OUTLOOK
Massachusetts Executive Off. of Environmental Affairs
100 Cambridge St.
Boston, MA 02202
Phone: (617)727-9800
Covers legislative matters involved in protecting the Massachusetts environment. ***Editor(s):*** Marjorie Molloy. ***Frequency:*** Monthly. ***Price:*** Free.

★6179★ Environmental Pollution and Control: An Abstract Newsletter
National Technical Information Service
U.S. Dept. of Commerce
5285 Port Royal Rd.
Springfield, VA 22161
Phone: (703)487-4630
Provides succinct summaries of reports published by NTIS and other agencies on air, noise, solid waste, water, and pesticide pollution and control; radiation; and environmental health and safety. Also summarizes environmental impact statements. Includes complete bibliographic information for each report, price, and an indication of the form(s) in which it is available (i.e., paper copy, microform, and/or magnetic tape). ***Frequency:*** Weekly. ***Price:*** $135/yr., U.S., Canada, and Mexico; $185 elsewhere.

★6180★ Environmental Professional
National Assn. of Environmental Professionals
PO Box 15210
Alexandria, VA 22309-0210
Phone: (703)660-2364
Frequency: Quarterly. ***Price:*** Included in membership dues; $95/year for nonmembers.

★6181★ Environmental Profile
Massachusetts State Dept. of Environmental Quality Engineering
Public Information Off.
1 Winter St., 10th Fl.
Boston, MA 02108
Phone: (617)292-5515
Informs readers on issues, laws, and events pertinent to the environment. ***Editor(s):*** Tom Higgins. ***Frequency:*** Quarterly. ***Price:*** Free.

★6182★ Environmental Resources Research Institute Newsletter
Environmental Resources Research Inst.
Pennsylvania State Univ.
Land & Water Research Bldg.
University Park, PA 16802
Phone: (814)863-0291
Focuses on Institute research projects and activities. Contains articles on current research in environmental resources. ***Editor(s):*** Lonnie Balaban. ***Frequency:*** Quarterly. ***Price:*** Free.

★6183★ Environmental Sabbath Newsletter
United Nations Environment Programme
DC2-803, United Nations
New York, NY 10017
Phone: (212)963-8093
Fax: (212)963-4116
Contains information on perserving the earth and its life, with a spiritual view. ***Editor(s):*** Libby Bassett. ***Frequency:*** 4/yr.

★6184★ Environmental Spectrum
Cooperative Extension Service
Cook Coll.
Rutgers Univ.
PO Box 231
New Brunswick, NJ 08903
Phone: (201)932-9443
Contains pertinent information on air and noise pollution and other environmental topics. Includes a listing of current publications of interest. ***Editor(s):*** Joseph J. Soporowski, Ed.D. ***Frequency:*** Bimonthly. ***Price:*** Free in Continental U.S.

★6185★ ENVIRONOTES
Federation of Environmental Technologists
PO Box 185
Milwaukee, WI 53201
Phone: (414)251-8163
Fax: (414)251-1669
Contains regulatory updates, employment opportunities, and calendar of events. ***Frequency:*** Monthly. ***Price:*** Included in membership dues.

★6186★ Environs
Marine Biomedical Center
Marine Laboratory
Duke Univ.
Beaufort, NC 28516
Phone: (919)728-2111
Focuses on issues related to environmental biomedicine, with particular emphasis on toxicology and pollution. Reports on seminars, conferences, and feasibility studies in progress. ***Editor(s):*** Shirley Tesh. ***Frequency:*** 6/yr. ***Price:*** Free.

★6187★ EPA Environmental News
Public Affairs Off.
U.S. Environmental Protection Agency
JFK Federal Bldg.
Boston, MA 02203
Phone: (617)565-3424
Discusses the federal government's programs in air pollution, water pollution, waste management, drinking water, toxic substances, and pesticide control. ***Editor(s):*** Brooke Chamberlain-Cook and Curt Spaulding.

★6188★ ERConnection
Environmental Research Center
Univ. of Nevada-Las Vegas
4505 S. Maryland Pkwy.
Las Vegas, NV 89154-4009
Phone: (702)739-3382
Fax: (702)739-3094
Contains articles on environmental research. Updates reports, publications, seminars, and events of interest to environmental research scientists. ***Editor(s):*** Shirley Burns. ***Frequency:*** Quarterly.

★6189★ The Eyas
Institute for Wildlife Research
National Wildlife Fed.
1412 16th St., N.W.
Washington, DC 20036-2266
Phone: (703)790-4543
Notifies readers of research, education, and management programs about birds of prey in the United States, Canada, and Latin America. Also describes the Institute's technical activities on the behalf of birds of prey. ***Editor(s):*** Beth Giron Pendleton. ***Frequency:*** 2/yr. ***Price:*** $5/yr.

★6190★ Farmland
Amer. Farmland Trust
1920 N St., N. W., Ste. 400
Washington, DC 20036
Phone: (202)659-5170
Fax: (202)659-8339
Disseminates information on establishing voluntary land protection programs to protect American farmland from conversion pressures, soil erosion, and other environmental impacts. ***Editor(s):*** Patricia Obester. ***Frequency:*** Quarterly. ***Price:*** Included in membership.

★6191★ FAVA News
Aprovecho Inst.
80574 Hazelton Rd.
Cottage Grove, OR 97424
Phone: (503)942-9434
Provides information on research of the fava bean, which replenishes the soil with nitrogen and other necessary nutrients. ***Frequency:*** Irregular. ***Price:*** Donation requested.

★6192★ FAWN - Fish and Wildlife News
National Military Fish and Wildlife Assn.
c/o Slader G. Buck
PO Box 128
Encinitas, CA 23509
Phone: (619)725-4540
Fax: (619)725-3528
Membership activities newsletter. ***Frequency:*** 3/year. ***Price:*** Included in membership.

★6193★ FDA Surveillance Index for Pesticides
National Technical Information Service
U.S. Dept. of Commerce
5285 Port Royal Rd.
Springfield, VA 22161
Phone: (703)487-4630
Alerts readers to potential health risks of individual pesticides from a dietary exposure standpoint. Provides an evaluation that

includes FDA monitoring results, chemical, biological, and toxicological data, and usage estimates. ***Frequency:*** Monthly. ***Price:*** $50/ copy.

★6194★ Feather in the Wind
Last Chance Forever
506 Ave. A
San Antonio, TX 78218
Phone: (512)655-6049
Frequency: Semiannual.

★6195★ Federal Parks and Recreation
Resources Publishing Co.
1010 Vermont Ave., N.W., Ste. 708
Washington, DC 20005
Phone: (202)638-7529
Tracks policy changes in Washington, D.C., affecting national parks and federal, state, and local park and recreation areas. Covers such issues as annual appropriations, protection of park resources, and user fees. ***Editor(s):*** James B. Coffin. ***Frequency:*** Biweekly. ***Price:*** $157/yr.

★6196★ Felicidades Wildlife Foundation Newsletter
Felicidades Wildlife Found.
PO Box 490
Waynesville, NC 28786
Phone: (704)926-0192
Frequency: Periodic.

★6197★ Flashpoint
National Assn. of Solvent Recyclers
1333 New Hampshire Ave., NW, Ste. 1100
Washington, DC 20036
Phone: (202)463-6956
Fax: (202)775-4163
Frequency: Periodic.

★6198★ The Flyway
Detroit Audubon Soc.
121 S. Main St.
Royal Oak, MI 48067
Phone: (313)545-2929
Discusses issues affecting environmental and wildlife protection. Reports on activities of the Society and provides information on wildlife preserves and parks in the U.S. open to vistors. ***Editor(s):*** Gary and Karen Schiltz. ***Frequency:*** 10/yr. ***Price:*** Included in membership.

★6199★ Focus on International Joint Commission Activities
Great Lakes Regional Off.
International Joint Commn.
PO Box 32869
Detroit, MI 48232
Phone: (313)226-2170
Fax: (519)256-7791
Concerned with the cleanup of the Great Lakes area through the Great Lakes Water Quality Agreement between the United States and Canada. Reports on a wide variety of environmental issues and organizations. Reviews relevant federal, state, and provincial governmental decisions. ***Editor(s):*** Sally Cole-Misch. ***Frequency:*** 3/yr. ***Price:*** Free.

★6200★ Forestry, Conservation Communications Association News and Views
Forestry, Conservation Communications Assn.
c/o Donald W. Pfohl
PO Box 1466
Mesa, AZ 85211-1466
Phone: (602)644-3166
Fax: (602)644-3173
Frequency: Quarterly.

★6201★ Fossil Fuels Action Update
Fossil Fuels Policy Action Institute
PO Box 8558
Fredericksburg, VA 22404
Phone: (703)371-0222
Fax: (703)371-0646
Serves the aims of the coalition EcoDemocracy, which seeks to effect change in ecological concerns. ***Editor(s):*** Bill Van Doren and Jan Lundberg. ***Frequency:*** Monthly. ***Price:*** $30/yr.

★6202★ Friends of Legacy
Legacy Intl.
346 Commerce St.
Alexandria, VA 22314
Phone: (703)549-3630
Fax: (703)549-0262
Newsletter containing organizational information. ***Frequency:*** Quarterly. ***Price:*** Included in membership dues.

★6203★ Friends of the Earth Newsletter
Friends of the Earth
218 D St., S.E.
Washington, DC 20003
Phone: (202)544-2600
Fax: (203)543-4710
Covers environmental issues, emphasing congressional and international situations. ***Editor(s):*** Dave Malakoff. ***Frequency:*** 10/yr. ***Price:*** Included in membership.

★6204★ From the State Capitals: Parks and Recreation Trends
Wakeman/Walworth, Inc.
300 N. Washington St., Ste. 204
Alexandria, VA 22314
Phone: (703)549-8606
Fax: (703)549-1372
Provides updates on what states and municipalities are doing in conservation, land management and development, and financial assistance to parks and recreational programs. Also carries information on wildlife preserves, state fisheries, river management, poaching and game restrictions, and systems of licensing and fees. ***Editor(s):*** Keyes Walworth. ***Frequency:*** Monthly. ***Price:*** $79/yr.

★6205★ From the State Capitals: Waste Disposal and Pollution Control
Wakeman/Walworth, Inc.
300 N. Washington St., Ste. 204
Alexandria, VA 22314
Phone: (703)549-8606
Fax: (703)549-1372
Covers state and municipal environmental laws and regulations. Reports on developments in the pollution control industry and news affecting the transportation, storage, and clean-up of hazardous wastes. Also monitors pesticide policies, insurance protection, resource recovery, and air and water pollution controls ranging from acid rain to sewage disposal. ***Editor(s):*** Keyes Walworth. ***Frequency:*** Monthly. ***Price:*** $118/yr.

★6206★ Fusion Power Report
Business Publishers, Inc.
951 Pershing Dr.
Silver Spring, MD 20910
Phone: (301)587-6300
Fax: (301)587-1081
Focuses on scientific, engineering, economic, and political developments in the field of fusion energy. Provides concise coverage of significant fusion energy activities and achievements in the U.S. and internationally. ***Editor(s):*** Thecla R. Fabian. ***Frequency:*** Monthly. ***Price:*** $418/yr., U.S. and Canada; $429 elsewhere.

★6207★ Geothermal Energy
National Technical Information Service
U.S. Dept. of Commerce
5285 Port Royal Rd.
Springfield, VA 22161
Phone: (703)487-4630
Abstracts worldwide information on the technology required for economic recovery of geothermal energy and its eventual use, either directly or for electric power production. ***Frequency:*** Bimonthly. ***Price:*** $100/yr., U.S., Canada, and Mexico; $200 elsewhere.

★6208★ Gildea Review
Community Environmental Coun.
930 Miramonte Dr.
Santa Barbara, CA 93109
Phone: (805)963-0583
Fax: (805)962-9080
Reviews the work of the Council at the Gildea Resource Center, including practical projects in recycling, industrial and hazardous waste management, toxic-free gardening, and land-use decision making. ***Editor(s):*** Michael Colin. ***Frequency:*** Semiannual. ***Price:*** Included in membership.; $5.00 for nonmembers.

★6209★ Global Environmental Change Report
Cutter Information Corp.
Box 713
Rte. 2
Harpers Ferry, WV 25425
Phone: (304)725-6542
Covers worldwide developments in policy, industry and science pertaining to global environmental change with a focus on global warming, ozone depletion, deforestation, and acid rain. ***Frequency:*** Biweekly.

★6210★ Global File Monitor
Elmwood Inst.
PO Box 5765
Berkeley, CA 94705-0765
Phone: (415)845-4595
Fax: (415)843-9398
Contains report summaries. ***Frequency:*** Periodic.

★6211★ Global Tomorrow Coalition—Interaction
Global Tomorrow Coalition
1325 G St., N.W., Ste. 915
Washington, DC 20005-3104
Phone: (202)628-4016
Seeks to educate and broaden public awareness in the U.S. about worldwide problems in population growth, resource consumption, environmental deterioration, and economic development affecting the future of the U.S. and the world. ***Editor(s):*** Don Lesh. ***Frequency:*** Semiannual. ***Price:*** Included in membership.

★6212★ Governmental Refuse Collection and Disposal Newsletter
Governmental Refuse Collection and Disposal Association, Inc.
8750 Georgia Ave., Ste. 140
PO Box 7219
Silver Spring, MD 20910
Phone: (301)585-2898
Concerned with solid waste management. Publishes news of technological advances, pertinent developments in the U.S. federal government and Canadian provincial governments, and activities of the Association. ***Editor(s):*** H. Lanier Hickman, Jr. ***Frequency:*** Monthly. ***Price:*** Included in membership; $60/ yr. for nonmembers.

★6213★ Grassroots
Div. of Soil and Water Conservation
Virginia State Dept. of Conservation and Historic Resources
203 Governor St., Ste. 206
Richmond, VA 23219-2094
Phone: (804)786-3334
Aims to help farmers, soil and water conservation district directors, and environmentalists establish conservation programs and practices. Acts as a forum for the exchange of information and ideas among resource management professionals. ***Editor(s):*** Steven R. Hawks. ***Frequency:*** Quarterly. ***Price:*** Free.

★6214★ Great Lakes Commission—Advisor
Great Lakes Commn.
The Argus II Bldg.
400 S. Fourth St.
Ann Arbor, MI 48103-4816
Phone: (313)665-9135
Fax: (313)665-4370
Communicates information and views from throughout the binational Great Lakes Basin to environmental, economic, political, and policy workers. ***Editor(s):*** Carol Ratza. ***Frequency:*** Monthly. ***Price:*** Free.

★6215★ Great Lakes Troller
District Extension Sea Grant Agent
333 Clinton
Grand Haven, MI 49417
Phone: (616)846-8250
Fax: (616)846-0655
Reports on issues concerning Great Lakes fisheries. ***Editor(s):*** Charles Pistis. ***Frequency:*** Quarterly. ***Price:*** Free.

★6216★ Great Lakes United
Great Lakes United
State University Coll. at Buffalo
Cassety Hall
1300 Elmwood Ave.
Buffalo, NY 14222
Phone: (716)886-0142
Fax: (716)886-030
Frequency: Quarterly. ***Price:*** $20/year for individuals; $100/year for organizations.

★6217★ Greater Yellowstone Report Newsletter
Greater Yellowstone Coalition
PO Box 1874
Bozeman, MT 59771-1874
Phone: (406)586-1593
Fax: (406)586-0851
Explores environmental issues in the Greater Yellowstone ecosystem. Also includes federal land management planning, wilderness, mineral development, watershed protection, wildlife and biodiversity, and private lands protection. ***Editor(s):*** Mary Carr. ***Frequency:*** Quarterly. ***Price:*** Included in membership.

★6218★ Green Marketing Report
Business Publishers, Inc.
951 Pershing Dr.
Silver Spring, MD 20910-4464
Phone: (301)587-6300
Fax: (301)587-1081
Covers the steps taken by product manufacturers and advertisers to address consumers' environmental concerns - as well as government explanation of some companies' environmental claims. ***Frequency:*** Monthly. ***Price:*** $330.

★6219★ Green Mountain Post Films Bulletin
Green Mountain Post, Inc.
PO Box 229
Turners Falls, MA 01376
Phone: (413)863-4754
Provides descriptions of documentary films and videos on environmental, energy, and related topics for rent or for sale by Green Mountain Post Films. ***Editor(s):*** Charles Light and Daniel Keller. ***Frequency:*** Periodic. ***Price:*** $11.

★6220★ Green Perspectives
Box 111
Vermont, VT 05402
Provides news and information on the Green Program Project. ***Frequency:*** Monthly. ***Price:*** $10/yr.

★6221★ Green Sheet
Camp Fire Club of America
230 Camp Fire Rd.
Chappaqua, NY 10514
Phone: (914)941-0199
Frequency: Monthly.

★6222★ Green Synthesis
League for Ecological Democracy
PO Box 1858
San Pedro, CA 90733
Phone: (213)833-2633
Concerned with social ecology, deep ecology, bioregionalism, ecofeminism, and the green movement; ideas and activities, and networking ecological democracy towards an autonomous ecological global society. ***Frequency:*** Quarterly. ***Price:*** $10/8 issues.

★6223★ Greenhouse Effect Report
Business Publishers, Inc.
951 Pershing Dr.
Silver Spring, MD 20910
Phone: (301)587-6300
Fax: (301)587-1081
Covers legislation, regulation, and news of the Environmental Protection Agency regarding the greenhouse effect. ***Editor(s):*** Bryan Lee. ***Frequency:*** Monthly. ***Price:*** $378/yr.

★6224★ Greenpeace Newsletter
Greenpeace, New England
Greenpeace U.S.A.
1436 J St., N.W.
Washington, DC 20009
Reports on the goals of the organization which aims to protect the natural environment worldwide, taking an ecosystems approach. ***Editor(s):*** Andre Carlothers. ***Frequency:*** 4/yr.

★6225★ Ground Water Monitor
Business Publishers, Inc.
951 Pershing Dr.
Silver Spring, MD 20910
Phone: (301)587-6300
Fax: (301)587-1081
Highlights legislation, regulations, litigation, technology, and funding for the protection of U.S. ground water supply. Carries ***Editor(s):*** Kathleen Hart. ***Frequency:*** Biweekly. ***Price:*** $227/yr., U.S. and Canada.

★6226★ Ground Water Monitor
Business Publishers, Inc.
951 Pershing Dr.
Silver Spring, MD 20910-4464
Phone: (301)587-6300
Coverage of ground water policy decisions at a federal, state, and local level. Examines new technological developments in ground water monitoring, sampling, and analysis. ***Frequency:*** Biweekly.

★6227★ Groundswell
Nuclear Information and Resource Service, Inc.
1424 16th St., N.W., No. 601
Washington, DC 20036
Phone: (202)328-0002
Focuses on the energy problem, particularly the hazards of nuclear energy and safe alternative sources. Contains news briefs on legislative and regulatory trends, policies of utility corporations, and funding. ***Editor(s):*** Michael Mariotte. ***Frequency:*** Quarterly. ***Price:*** $20/yr. for individuals; $25 for "safe energy" organizations; $50 for others.

★6228★ The Groundwater Newsletter
Water Information Center, Inc.
125 E. Bethpage Rd.
Plainview, NY 11803
Phone: (516)249-7634
Concerned with groundwater contamination and with other water-related topics: management, development, exploration, recharge, and underground waste disposal. Carries groundwater news from the individual states. ***Editor(s):*** Fred L. Troise and Judith Schoeck. ***Frequency:*** Semimonthly. ***Price:*** $197/yr., U.S. and Canada; $227 eleswhere.

★6229★ Groundwater Pollution News
Buraff Publications, Inc.
Bureau of Natl. Affairs, Inc.
1350 Connecticut Ave., N.W., Ste. 1000
Washington, DC 20036
Phone: (202)862-0900
Fax: (202)862-0999
Telex: 285656 BNAI WSH
Covers legislation, regulation, and litigation concerning groundwater pollution. ***Editor(s):*** Richard Hagan. ***Frequency:*** Biweekly. ***Price:*** $467/yr.

★6230★ Habitat Institute for the Environment Newsletter
Habitat Inst. for the Environment, Inc.
10 Juniper Rd.
PO Box 136
Belmont, MA 02178
Phone: (617)489-5050
Provides educational articles for adults and children on natural history and environmental issues. ***Frequency:*** 4/yr.

★6231★ HASTI Newsletter
HASTI Friends of the Elephants
PO Box 477
Petaluma, CA 94953
Phone: (707)878-2369
Frequency: Quarterly. ***Price:*** $10/year.

★6232★ Hawk Mountain News
Hawk Mountain Sanctuary Assn.
R.D. 2
Kempton, PA 19529
Phone: (215)756-6961
Presents news from the Sanctuary and the Association on the conservation of birds of prey and other wildlife and understanding the natural environment. Carries articles on birds and natural history, and raptor conservation and migration. ***Editor(s):*** Michael Harwood. ***Frequency:*** Semiannual. ***Price:*** Included in membership; $15 for nonmembers.

★6233★ Hazardous Materials Control Research Institute—FOCUS
Hazardous Materials Control Research Inst.
7237 Hanover Pkwy.
Greenbelt, MD 20770
Phone: (301)587-9390
Frequency: Monthly.

★6235★ Hazardous Waste News
Business Publishers, Inc.
951 Pershing Dr.
Silver Spring, MD 20910-4464
Phone: (301)587-6300
Reports on changing regulations imposed by the EPA on hazardous waste from generation and source reduction to ultimate disposal and recycling. ***Frequency:*** Weekly.

★6236★ Hazardous Waste Report
Aspen Publishers, Inc.
1600 Research Blvd.
Rockville, MD 20850
Phone: (301)251-5341
Fax: (301)251-5784
Toll-Free: 800-638-8437
Covers environmental issues, including Environmental Protection Agency policies, the Resource Conservation and Recovery Act, Superfund, state requirements, environmental litigation and enforcement, and congressional activity. ***Editor(s):*** Patricia Papa. ***Frequency:*** Biweekly. ***Price:*** $420/yr.

★6237★ HazTECH News
Business Publishers, Inc.
951 Pershing Dr.
Silver Spring, MD 20910-4464
Phone: (301)587-6300
Fax: (301)587-1081
Provides information on hazardous waste management technology as it applies to storage, treatment, and disposal requirements. ***Frequency:*** Biweekly. ***Price:*** $333.

★6238★ HazTech Transfer
Hazardous Substance Research Center
Kansas State Univ.
EPA Regions 7 & 8
133 Ward Hall
Manhattan, KS 66506
Phone: (913)532-6026
Fax: (913)532-6952
Targets research on hazardous substances and Center activities. ***Editor(s):*** Mike Dorcey and Steven Galitzer. ***Frequency:*** Quarterly. ***Price:*** Free.

★6239★ Heal Prints
HEAL of Louisiana
8618 GSRI Ave.
Baton Rouge, LA 70808
Phone: (504)383-2028
Focuses on human ecology and other related information of interest. ***Editor(s):*** Diane Hamilton. ***Frequency:*** Quarterly. ***Price:*** $15/yr.

★6240★ Health Facilities Energy Report
Health Resources Publishing
Brinley Professional Plaza, 3100 Hwy. 138
PO Box 1442
Wall Township, NJ 07719-1442
Phone: (201)681-1133
Reports on important developments in energy conservation in health facilities, especially hospitals. Provides facts on federal and state energy regulations, government policies, laws, industry developments and trends, and on what hospitals are doing to conserve energy. ***Editor(s):*** Phillip Sharkey. ***Frequency:*** Monthly. ***Price:*** $137/yr., U.S. and Canada.

★6241★ The HELM
Illinois-Indiana Sea Grant Program
Univ. of Illinois
65 Mumford Hall
1301 W. Gregory Dr.
Champaign, IL 61820
Phone: (217)333-9448
Fax: (217)333-1952
Provides information to the public and private sectors on various coastal issues and events in the southern area of Lake Michigan. ***Editor(s):*** Robin Goettel and Kimberly Meenen. ***Frequency:*** Quarterly. ***Price:*** Free.

★6242★ Holistic Resource Management Newsletter
Center for Holistic Resource Management
800 Rio Grande Blvd., N. W., Ste. 10
Albuquerque, NM 87104
Phone: (505)242-9272
Fax: (505)247-1008
Reflects the Center's aim to improve the human environment and quality of life through dissemination of information on the holistic management of land, water, human, wildlife, and financial resources. ***Editor(s):*** Jody Butterfield. ***Frequency:*** Quarterly. ***Price:*** Included in membership.

★6243★ Home, Yard and Garden Pest Newsletter
Agriculture Newsletter Service
Univ. of Illinois
116 Mumford Hall
1301 W. Gregory Dr.
Urbana, IL 61801
Covers current pest controls, application equipment and methods, and storage and disposal of pesticides for the yard and garden. ***Frequency:*** 20/yr. ***Price:*** $15/yr.

★6244★ Human Environment Center Newsletter
Human Environment Center
1001 Connecticut Ave. NW, Ste. 827
Washington, DC 20036
Phone: (202)331-8387
Frequency: Quarterly.

★6245★ Idaho Clean Water
Div. of Environment
Idaho State Dept. of Health and Welfare
450 W. State St.
Boise, ID 83720
Phone: (208)334-5855
Concerned with water quality and water pollution control in Idaho. Monitors the activities of state and national environmental organizations, and profiles prominent environmentalists in Idaho. ***Editor(s):*** Tom Aucutt. ***Frequency:*** Quarterly. ***Price:*** Free.

★6246★ Illinois Energy Newsletter
Energy Resources Center
Univ. of Illinois, Chicago
PO Box 4348
Chicago, IL 60680
Phone: (312)996-4490
Focuses on energy news, programs, and research in Illinois. Contains news of new and ongoing energy research projects. Reports new state-level energy appointments and Illinois energy meetings. Discusses funding for research and utility rates for consumers. ***Editor(s):*** James J. Wiet. ***Frequency:*** Bimonthly. ***Price:*** Free.

★6247★ The Impossible Human Newsletter
Pyramid Research Center
PO Box 5271
Ft. Lauderdale, FL 33310
Provides information about anticipated projects supported by the Center. Discusses accelerated learning techniques, unusual agricultural advances, and non-conventional energy. ***Editor(s):*** M.D. Saunders. ***Frequency:*** 4/yr. ***Price:*** $12/yr., U.S. and Canada; $18 elsewhere.

★6248★ Imprint
Bell Museum of Natural History
University of Minnesota
17th & University Ave. S.E.
Minneapolis, MN 55455
Phone: (612)624-4112
Explores trends in natural history and environmental issues. Provides information on activities. ***Editor(s):*** Janet Pelley and Kevin Williams. ***Frequency:*** Quarterly. ***Price:*** Free.

★6249★ Indoor Pollution Law Report
Leader Publications
New York Law Publishing Co.
111 Eighth Ave.
New York, NY 10011
Phone: (212)463-5709
Seeks to prepare attorneys for the expected surge in radon litigation cases, as well as those involving asbestos and formaldehyde. Discusses "preventative measures, the cutting edge of technology, what the government's up to, and the alternatives to litigation." ***Editor(s):*** Laurence S. Kirsch. ***Frequency:*** Monthly. ***Price:*** $155/yr.

★6250★ Infectious Wastes News
Richard H. Freeman
Washington Sq.
PO Box 65686
Washington, DC 20035-5686
Phone: (202)861-0708
Furnishes reports on the handling and disposal of infectious wastes. Informs readers of up-to-date industry developments on such topics as new methods and technologies, sterilization and incineration of waste, and environmental standards. ***Editor(s):*** Thomas Naber. ***Frequency:*** Biweekly. ***Price:*** $320/yr., U.S. and Canada; $450 elsewhere.

★6251★ INFORM Reports
INFORM, Inc.
381 Park Ave. S.
New York, NY 10016
Phone: (212)689-4040
Publishes news of INFORM and identifies ways to protect natural resources and public health. Concerned with research in the areas of chemical hazards prevention (includes industrial toxic wastes and hazardous materials in household and building products), municipal solid waste management, urban air quality (focuses on reducing vehicular pollution), and agricultural water conservation. ***Editor(s):*** Sibyl R. Golden. ***Frequency:*** Quarterly. ***Price:*** $35/yr.

★6252★ Inside Energy/With Federal Lands
McGraw-Hill, Inc.
1221 Ave. of the Americas
New York, NY 10020
Phone: (212)512-4375
Covers latest developments in government energy policy. Ranges over entire field of energy resources. ***Editor(s):*** William E. Loveless. ***Frequency:*** Weekly. ***Price:*** $740/yr., U.S. and Canada; $790 elsewhere.

★6253★ Inside EPA
Inside Washington Publishers
PO Box 7167, Ben Franklin Sta.
Washington, DC 20044
Phone: (703)892-8500
Fax: (703)685-2606
Toll-Free: 800-424-9068
Covers the development of environmental policy, regulation, and legislation within the Environmental Protection Agency, Capitol Hill, and courts. ***Editor(s):*** Julie Edelson. ***Frequency:*** Weekly. ***Price:*** $730/yr.

★6254★ Institute for Energy and Environmental Analysis Newsletter
Institute for Energy and Environmental Analysis
Oak Ridge Associated Universities
PO Box 117
Oak Ridge, TN 37831
Phone: (615)576-3292
Fax: (615)576-9384
Tracks the activities of the Institute and provides information and news of interest on energy and environmental analysis. ***Editor(s):*** Harry T. Burn. ***Frequency:*** Irregular. ***Price:*** Free.

★6255★ Institute of Ecosystem Studies Newsletter
Institute of Ecosystem Studies
Box AB
Millbrook, NY 12545-0129
Phone: (914)677-5343
Fax: (914)677-5976
Features articles concerning ecology, natural history, and environmental issues. Provides updates on Institute research and education programs. ***Editor(s):*** Jill Cadwallader. ***Frequency:*** Bimonthly. ***Price:*** Included in membership.

★6256★ Institute of Scrap Recycling Industries Report
Institute of Scrap Recycling Industries, Inc.
1627 K St., N.W.
Washington, DC 20006
Phone: (202)466-4050
Covers news of the scrap processing and conservation industries, including metals (ferrous and nonferrous), paper, textiles, and plastics. Reports on governmental and legislative actions. ***Editor(s):*** Gerry Romano. ***Frequency:*** Biweekly. ***Price:*** Included in membership.

★6257★ Integrated Risk Information System
National Technical Information Service
U.S. Dept. of Commerce
5285 Port Royal Rd.
Springfield, VA 22161
Phone: (703)487-4630
Provides information regarding the effects of chemicals on human health and includes information on reference doses and carcinogen assessments. ***Frequency:*** Quarterly. ***Price:*** $130/yr. for an IBM PC/AT; $230 for an IBM PC (available on datafile-diskette only).

★6258★ International Association for Bear Research and Management Newsletter
International Assn. for Bear Research and Management
Alaska Dept. of Fish & Game
333 Raspberyy Rd.
Anchorage, AK 99518-1599
Phone: (907)334-0541
Carries news of events and research pertaining to the study, care, and management of bears and their habitat. Offers research biologists, animal and land managers, professionals, and lay persons in the field a forum for discussing current issues. ***Frequency:*** 2-4/yr. ***Price:*** Included in membership.

★6259★ International Association for Ecology Newsletter
International Assn. for Ecology
Inst. of Ecology
Univ. of Georgia
Athens, GA 30606
Phone: (404)542-2968
Fax: (404)542-6040
Reflects the aims of the Association, which promotes, develops, and communicates the science of ecology and applies ecological principles to global needs through international cooperation. ***Editor(s):*** David C. Duffy. ***Frequency:*** Bimonthly. ***Price:*** Included in membership.

★6260★ International Association of Fish and Wildlife Agencies Newsletter
International Assn. of Fish and Wildlife Agencies
444 N. Capitol St., N.W., Ste. 534
Washington, DC 20001
Phone: (202)624-7890
Promotes the economic importance of conserving natural resources and managing wildlife property as sources of recreation and food supply. Provides information on conservation legislation, administration, and enforcement. ***Editor(s):*** Mark J. Reeff. ***Frequency:*** Bimonthly. ***Price:*** $25/yr.; U.S. and Canada.

★6261★ The International Crane Foundation Bugle
International Crane Found.
E-11376, Shady Ln. Rd.
Baraboo, WI 53913
Phone: (608)356-9462
Fax: (608)356-9465
Carries articles on conservation, biology, and preservation of endangered birds worldwide, particularly cranes. Sample issue included stories on captive management and breeding, sex determination in chicks, migration, crane hunting in Pakistan, and prairie restoration in Wisconsin. Also covers news of the Foundation, which is committed to research, habitat preservation, captive propagation, and restocking of the crane. ***Editor(s):*** David Thompson. ***Frequency:*** Quarterly. ***Price:*** Included in membership.

★6262★ International Environment Reporter
Bureau of Natl. Affairs, Inc.
1231 25th St., N.W.
Washington, DC 20037
Phone: (202)452-4200
Fax: (202)822-8092
Toll-Free: 800-372-1033
Telex: 285656 BNAI WSH
Covers international environmental law and developing policy in major industrial nations. ***Editor(s):*** Marlon Allen. ***Frequency:*** Monthly. ***Price:*** $1,286/yr.

★6263★ International Erosion Control Association Newsletter
International Erosion Control Assn.
Box 4904
Steamboat Springs, CO 80477
Phone: (303)879-3010
Fax: (303)879-8563
Frequency: Bimonthly.

★6264★ The International Osprey Foundation Newsletter
The Intl. Osprey Found.
PO Box 250
Sanibel, FL 33957
Phone: (813)472-5218
Promotes the study and preservation of the osprey and other birds of prey. ***Frequency:*** Annual.

★6265★ International Solar Energy Intelligence Report
Business Publishers, Inc.
951 Pershing Dr.
Silver Spring, MD 20910
Phone: (301)587-6300
Fax: (301)587-1081
Covers federal, state, and local government decision-making that affects solar power development. Reports on legislation, financial support, research and development, and emerging technologies in the fields of solar heating and cooling, bioconversion, and wind energy systems. ***Editor(s):*** Allan Frank. ***Frequency:*** Weekly. ***Price:*** $271/yr., U.S. and Canada; $307 elsewhere.

★6266★ International Wild Waterfowl Association Newsletter
International Wild Waterfowl Assn.
c/o Nancy Collins
Hidden Lake Waterfowl
5614 River Styx Rd.
Medina, OH 44256
Phone: (216)725-8782
Frequency: Bimonthly.

★6267★ Investor's Environmental Report
Investor Responsibility Research Center
1755 Massachusetts Ave., NW, Ste. 600
Washington, DC 20036
Phone: (202)234-7500
Fax: (202)332-8570
Focuses on environmental topics of particular relevance to the investment and corporate communities. ***Frequency:*** Quarterly. ***Price:*** $100 annually.

★6268★ It's Time to Go Wild
Amer. Wilderness Alliance
7600 E. Arapahoe Rd., Ste. 114
Englewood, CO 80112
Phone: (303)771-0380
Supports the Alliance's efforts to promote the protection and proper use of wilderness lands and areas, and develop awareness of the Alliance's wilderness adventure program. Covers the Alliance's work in identifying wilderness areas, wild and scenic rivers, and other natural areas and to study the interrelationship between man and wilderness areas. ***Editor(s):*** Sally Ranney. ***Frequency:*** Quarterly. ***Price:*** Included in membership.

★6269★ Jumbo Jargon
National Elephant Collectors Soc.
c/o Richard W. Massiglia
38 Medford St.
Somerville, MA 02145-3810
Phone: (617)625-4067
Frequency: Quarterly. ***Price:*** Included in membership dues.

★6270★ Keep America Beautiful—Network
Keep America Beautiful
Mill River Plaza
Nine W. Broad St.
Stamford, CT 06902
Phone: (203)323-8987
Concerned with litter reduction and community improvement. Covers KAB meetings, training institutes, available literature, ideas and

activities from different KAB System programs, and news of research. ***Editor(s):*** Kit Tobin and Teresa Creech. ***Frequency:*** Monthly. ***Price:*** Free to KAB System coordinators.

★6271★ Keep America Beautiful Vision
Keep America Beautiful
Mill River Plaza
9 W. Broad St.
Stamford, CT 06902
Phone: (203)323-8987
Promotes the work of the organization, which encourages Americans to "assume more responsibility for improving the physical quality of life in their own communities." Reports news of KAB activities, including its primary program, Keep America Beautiful System. ***Editor(s):*** John Kazzi. ***Frequency:*** Quarterly. ***Price:*** Free.

★6272★ Keep Tahoe Blue
League to Save Lake Tahoe
PO Box 10110
South Lake Tahoe, CA 95731
Phone: (916)541-5388
Committed to preserving the natural beauty and grandeur of the Lake Tahoe area of California and Nevada. Reviews conservation developments and activities in the region. ***Frequency:*** Quarterly. ***Price:*** Included in membership.

★6273★ Lake Line
North Amer. Lake Management Soc.
1000 Connecticut Ave., N.W., Ste. 300
Washington, DC 20036
Phone: (202)466-8550
Fax: (202)466-8554
Provides a medium of exchange and communication concerning lake management. Includes articles on developments in limnology and lake maangement. ***Editor(s):*** Judith Taggert. ***Frequency:*** Bimonthly. ***Price:*** Included in membership.

★6274★ Lake Superior News
Save Lake Superior Assn.
PO Box 101
Two Harbors, MN 55616
Reflects the Association's concern for the quality of Lake Superior's waters and environment. Keeps members informed of the ways in which acid rain, industrial discharges, PCBs (polychlorinated biphenyls), vessal wastes, and other pollutants affect Lake Superior and reports on corresponding action taken by the ***Editor(s):*** Alden Lind. ***Frequency:*** Quarterly. ***Price:*** Included in membership.

★6275★ Land Letter
The Conservation Fund
1800 N. Kent St., Ste. 1120
Arlington, VA 22209
Phone: (703)522-8008
Fax: (703)525-4610
Covers national land use and conservation policy. Reports on significant legislative, regulatory, legal, and general developments that affect the conservation, management, and use of private and public lands. ***Editor(s):*** Jim Howe. ***Frequency:*** 34/yr. ***Price:*** $165/yr.

★6276★ Land Use Planning Report
Business Publishers, Inc.
951 Pershing Dr.
Silver Spring, MD 20910-4464
Phone: (301)587-6300
Fax: (301)587-1081
Aimed at land use professionals, and covers planning issues affecting urban, suburban, agricultural, and natural resource land jurisdictions, with an eye toward environmental protection and endangered species. ***Frequency:*** Biweekly. ***Price:*** $215.50.

★6277★ The Leader
National Wildlife Fed.
1400 16th St. NW
Washington, DC 20036-2266
Phone: (202)797-6800
Frequency: Monthly.

★6278★ League Leader
Izaak Walton League of America
1401 Wilson Blvd., Level B
Arlington, VA 22209
Phone: (703)528-1818
Fax: (703)528-1836
Works to educate the public to conserve, maintain, protect, and restore the soil, forest, water, and other natural resources of the U.S. Reports on a variety of environmental programs sponsored by the League aimed at conserving and protecting the environment. ***Editor(s):*** Laury Marshall-Forbes. ***Frequency:*** Bimonthly. ***Price:*** Included in membership.

★6279★ Leisure Lines
California Park & Recreation Society, Inc.
PO Box 161118
Sacramento, CA 95816-1118
Phone: (916)446-2777
Discusses parks and recreation news of interest. ***Editor(s):*** Norma Minas. ***Frequency:*** Monthly. ***Price:*** $2/yr.

★6280★ Lighthawk Newsletter: The Wings of Conservation
Lighthawk
PO Box 8163
Santa Fe, NM 87504
Phone: (505)982-9656
Fax: (505)984-8381
Includes column on charitable giving strategies. ***Frequency:*** Quarterly. ***Price:*** Included in membership dues.

★6281★ Lines to Leaders
Trout Unlimited
501 Church St., N.E.
Vienna, VA 22180
Phone: (703)281-1100
Reflects the organization's commitment to preserving the coldwater habitat of trout, salmon, and steelhead. Discusses water management problems and reviews governmental actions in the area. ***Frequency:*** Monthly. ***Price:*** Included in membership.

★6282★ Little News
Greensward Found.
104 Prospect Park W.
Brooklyn, NY 11215
Bulletin on the improvement of natural landscape urban parks, the proper understanding of these parks by the public, and the proper care of these parks by their custodians. ***Frequency:*** Quarterly.

★6283★ Littoral Drift
Sea Grant Institute
Univ. of Wisconsin
1800 University Ave.
Madison, WI 53705
Phone: (608)263-3259
Fax: (608)263-2063
Reports on research and activities of the Wisconsin Sea Grant Program, which focuses on the Great Lakes, their problems and opportunities through marine research, education, and public service activities with support from the state and federal governments. ***Editor(s):*** Stephen Wittman. ***Frequency:*** 10/yr. ***Price:*** Free.

★6284★ Living Without Landfills: Confronting the "Low-Level" Radioactive Waste Crisis
Radioactive Waste Campaign
625 Broadway, 2nd Fl.
New York, NY 10012-2611
Phone: (212)473-7390

★6285★ The Log
Silent Running Soc.
PO Box 529
Howell, NJ 07731
Newsletter for businesses, industries, and individuals dedicated to reforestation and the conservation of trees. ***Frequency:*** Annual.

★6286★ The Loon Call
North Amer. Loon Fund
R.R. 4, Box 240C
Meredith, NH 03253
Phone: (603)279-6163
Contains reports on research and management projects, photographs, and publication notices. ***Frequency:*** Quarterly. ***Price:*** Included in membership dues.

★6287★ Mail Bag
Brooks Bird Club
707 Warwood Ave.
Wheeling, WV 26003
Phone: (304)547-5253
Frequency: Quarterly.

★6288★ Manomet Bird Observatory Research Report
Manomet Bird Observatory
PO Box 936
Manomet, MA 02345
Phone: (508)224-6521
Fax: (508)224-9220
Provides research information on conservation and wildlife problems with emphasis on birds as indicators of environmental change. ***Frequency:*** 4/year. ***Price:*** Included in membership.

★6289★ Marine Bulletin
National Coalition for Marine Conservation, Inc.
PO Box 23298
Savannah, GA 31403
Phone: (912)234-8062
Fax: (912)233-2909
Covers conserving marine resources and protecting the ocean environment. Carries articles on marine fisheries, biological research, marine environmental pollution, and the prevention of the over-exploitation of ocean fish. ***Editor(s):*** Ken Hinman. ***Frequency:*** Monthly. ***Price:*** Included in membership.; $10/yr for nonprofit institutions.

★6290★ Marine Conservation News
Center for Marine Conservation
1725 DeSales St. NW, Ste. 500
Washington, DC 20036
Phone: (202)429-5609
Fax: (202)872-0619
Covers developments in the conservation of marine species and their habitats, including CMC projects and legislative activities. ***Frequency:*** Quarterly. ***Price:*** Included in membership dues; available to nonmembers for a nominal fee.

★6291★ Marine Debris Newsletter
Center for Marine Conservation
1725 DeSales St. NW, Ste. 500
Washington, DC 20036
Phone: (202)429-5609
Fax: (202)872-0619
Describes efforts aimed at reducing plastic debris and other nondegradable trash in oceans and waterways. ***Frequency:*** Quarterly.

★6292★ Marine Pollution Bulletin
International Ocean Pollution Symposium
c/o Dr. Iver W. Duedall
Department of Chemical & Environmental Engineering
Florida Inst. of Tech.
Melbourne, FL 32901
Phone: (407)768-8000

★6293★ Marine Sanctuaries News
Center for Marine Conservation
1725 DeSales St. NW, Ste. 500
Washington, DC 20036
Phone: (202)429-5609
Fax: (202)872-0619
Updates current issues regarding marine sanctuaries. ***Frequency:*** Quarterly.

★6294★ Massachusetts Inshore Draggerman's Association Newsletter
Massachusetts Inshore Draggermen's Assn.
460 Main St.
Marshfield, MA 02050
Phone: (617)837-5159
Promotes the goals of the Association which establishes cooperation among various segments of the industry, works for favored legislation, encourages good conservation measures and to improve conditions of the fisheries. ***Frequency:*** 8/yr.

★6295★ Massachusetts Wildlife
Division of Fisheries and Wildlife
Massachusetts Dept. of Fisheries, Wildlife and Environmental Law Enforcement
Field Headquarters
Westboro, MA 01581
Phone: (617)366-4479
Aims to conserve and manage fish and wildlife resources. Highlights information on freshwater and anadromous sport fisheries, wildlife research and management and coastal species, and restoration of endangered species. ***Frequency:*** Quarterly. ***Price:*** $6/yr.

★6296★ Measuring and Scoring North American Big Game Trophies
Boone and Crockett Club
241 S. Fraley Blvd.
Dumfires, VA 22026
Phone: (703)221-1888

★6297★ Medical Waste News
Business Publishers, Inc.
951 Pershing Dr.
Silver Spring, MD 20910
Phone: (301)587-6300
Fax: (301)587-1081
Covers regulation, legislation, and technology related to medical waste. Reports on businesses involved in in waste management and Environmental Protection Agency efforts to control waste levels. ***Frequency:*** Biweekly. ***Price:*** $283.50/yr.

★6298★ The Minimizer
Center for Hazardous Materials Research
University of Pittsburgh Applied Research Center
320 William Pitt Way
Pittsburgh, PA 15238
Phone: (412)826-5320
Fax: (412)826-5552
Toll-Free: 800-334-2467
Provides environmental and regulatory information regarding solid and hazardous waste. ***Editor(s):*** Robin A. Day. ***Frequency:*** Quarterly. ***Price:*** Free.

★6299★ Minnesota Energy Alternatives
Minnesota Energy Div.
Minnesota State Dept. of Public Service
900 American Center Bldg.
150 E. Kellogg Blvd.
St. Paul, MN 55101
Phone: (612)296-9097
Provides an update of public and government sponsored projects in the area of energy conservation and alternative energies. Focuses on the continued growth of alternative energy technologies, which are dependent on Minnesota's economic future. ***Editor(s):*** Rick Korinek. ***Frequency:*** Quarterly. ***Price:*** Free.

★6300★ Modesto Peace/Life Center Newsletter
Modesto Peace/Life Center
PO Box 134
Modesto, CA 95353
Phone: (209)529-5750
Contains announcements and reviews of Center activities. Features articles on social change issues, energy policy, sustainable agriculture, growth environment, housing, health care, quality of life concerns, and community policies. ***Editor(s):*** Fred Herman. ***Frequency:*** Monthly. ***Price:*** Included in membership.

★6301★ Mono Lake Committee Newsletter
Mono Lake Committee, Inc.
PO Box 29
Lee Vining, CA 93541
Phone: (619)647-6595
Discusses developments affecting Mono Lake. Includes articles on natural and human history at Mono Lake and the Great Basin Lakes. ***Editor(s):*** Lauren Davis. ***Frequency:*** Quarterly. ***Price:*** $20/yr.

★6302★ Multinational Environmental Outlook
Business Publishers, Inc.
951 Pershing Dr.
Silver Spring, MD 20910
Phone: (301)587-6300
Fax: (301)587-1081
Reports on environmental problems, solutions, and policies in other countries, and analyzes their effects on U.S. government policies and the operations of U.S. companies. Covers environmental protection, energy and natural resources development, air and water pollution control, and waste management and toxic substances. ***Editor(s):*** Hiram Reisner. ***Frequency:*** Biweekly. ***Price:*** $295/yr.

★6303★ Multinational Environmental Outlook
Business Publishers, Inc.
951 Pershing Dr.
Silver Spring, MD 20910-4464
Phone: (301)587-6300
Reports on international environmental problems and issues and what various countries are doing to solve problems related to air, water, toxic substances, nuclear waste management and disposal, and the potential effect on operations and plans of multinational corporations. ***Frequency:*** Biweekly.

★6304★ The Mustang
National Mustang Association, Inc.
PO Box 42
New Castle, UT 84756
Phone: (801)439-5440
Reports general information on wild horses to promote their continuing existence in their natural habitat. Also includes news of Association membership activities. ***Price:*** Included in membership.

★6305★ My Orphans of the World: Rescue and Home Care of Native Wildlife
Felicidades Wildlife Found.
PO Box 490
Waynesville, NC 28786
Phone: (704)926-0192

★6306★ National Association of Environmental Professionals Newsletter
National Assn. of Environmental Professionals
PO Box 15210
Alexandria, VA 22309-0210
Phone: (703)660-2364
Frequency: Quarterly.

★6307★ National Association of Flood and Storm Water Management Agencies Newsletter
National Assn. of Flood and Storm Water Management Agencies
1225 I St. NW, Ste. 300
Washington, DC 20005
Phone: (202)682-3761
Fax: (202)842-0621
Frequency: Monthly.

★6308★ National Association of State Land Reclamationists Newsletter
National Assn. of State Land Reclamationists
459 B Carlisle Dr.
Herndon, VA 22070
Phone: (703)709-8654
Frequency: Quarterly.

★6309★ National Coalition Against the Misuse of Pesticides Technical Report
National Coalition Against the Misuse of Pesticides
530 Seventh St., S.E.
Washington, DC 20003
Phone: (202)543-5450
Tracks congressional rulings and legislative action taken on pesticides. Also covers court settlements and pesticide poisonings. ***Editor(s):*** Catherine Karr. ***Frequency:*** Monthly.

★6310★ National Energy Foundation News Update
National Energy Found.
5160 Wiley Post Way, Ste. 200
Salt Lake City, UT 84116
Phone: (801)539-1406
Frequency: Quarterly.

★6311★ National Environmental Development Association Update
National Environmental Development Assn.
1440 New York Ave. NW, Ste. 300
Washington, DC 20005
Phone: (202)638-1230
Frequency: Monthly.

★6312★ National Environmental Enforcement Journal
National Assn. of Attorneys General
444 N. Capitol St., Ste. 403
Washington, DC 20001
Phone: (202)628-0447
Reports recent developments in environmental enforcement from the U.S. Environmental Protection Agency, U.S. Department of Justice, State Attorneys General, State Regulatory Agencies, and District Attorneys Offices. ***Editor(s):*** Judith E. McKee. ***Frequency:*** Monthly. ***Price:*** $195/yr. for nonprofit organizations.

★6313★ National Environmental Health Association Newsletter
National Environmental Health Assn.
720 S. Colorado Blvd., Ste. 970, S. Tower
Denver, CO 80222
Phone: (303)756-9090
Fax: (303)691-9490
Reports on state environmental issues. ***Frequency:*** Quarterly. ***Price:*** Included in membership dues.

★6314★ National Food and Energy Council News & Notes
National Food & Energy Council, Inc.
409 Vandiver W., Ste. 202
Columbia, MO 65202
Phone: (314)875-7155
Focuses on the interdependence of food and energy. Discusses factors relating to electric energy suppliers and their planning, including the management and substitution of electric energy for dwindling fossil fuels and conservation. Emphasizes efficient use and management of electricity on farms and assurance of continuing energy for the food system. ***Editor(s):*** Kenneth L. McFate. ***Frequency:*** Bimonthly. ***Price:*** Included in membership.

★6315★ National Recycling Coalition Newsletter
National Recycling Coalition
1101 30th St. NW
Washington, DC 20007
Phone: (202)625-6406
Fax: (202)625-6409
Frequency: Quarterly.

★6316★ National Registry of Champion Big Trees and Famous Historical Trees
Amer. Forestry Assn.
1516 P St. NW
Washington, DC 20005
Phone: (202)667-3300
Fax: (202)667-7751

★6317★ National Tree Society Newsletter
National Tree Soc.
PO Box 10808
Bakersfield, CA 93389
Phone: (805)589-6912
Frequency: Periodic.

★6318★ National Wetlands Newsletter
Environmental Law Institute
1616 P St., N.W., Ste. 200
Washington, DC 20036
Phone: (202)328-5150
Fax: (202)328-5002
Monitors federal, state, and local laws, policies, and programs concerning wetlands, floodplains, and coastal water resources. Reports on private wetlands protection efforts. ***Editor(s):*** Hazel Groman. ***Frequency:*** Bimonthly. ***Price:*** $48/yr.

★6319★ National Wildlife Health Foundation Newsletter
National Wildlife Health Found.
c/o James L. Naviaux
606 El Pintado Rd.
Danville, CA 94526
Phone: (415)939-3456
Frequency: Annual.

★6320★ National Wildlife Rehabilitators Association Newsletter
National Wildlife Rehabilitators Assn.
12805 St. Croix Trail
Hastin, MN 55033
Phone: (612)437-9194
Frequency: 3-4/year. ***Price:*** Included in membership dues.

★6321★ Natural Resource Recovery Association Reporter
National Resource Recovery Assn.
1620 I St. NW
Washington, DC 20006
Phone: (202)293-7330
Frequency: Periodic.

★6322★ Natural Resources and Earth Sciences: An Abstract Newsletter
National Technical Information Service
U.S. Dept. of Commerce
5285 Port Royal Rd.
Springfield, VA 22161
Phone: (703)487-4630
Carries abstracts and bibliographic citations in the fields of mineral industries, natural resources management and surveys, soil sciences, geology and geophysics, and hydrology and limnology. ***Frequency:*** Weekly. ***Price:*** $115/yr., U.S., Canada, and Mexico; $155 elsewhere.

★6323★ Natural Resources Council of America News
Natural Resources Coun. of America
801 Pennsylvania Ave. NW, No. 410
Washington, DC 20003
Phone: (202)547-7553
Frequency: Monthly.

★6324★ Natural Resources Defense Council Newsline
Natural Resources Defense Coun.
40 W. 20th St.
New York, NY 10011-4211
Phone: (212)949-0049
Fax: (212)727-1773
Reports activities and interests of the Council and describes work of staff attorneys and scientists. ***Editor(s):*** Catherine A. Dold. ***Frequency:*** 5/yr. ***Price:*** Included in membership.

★6325★ Natural Resources Research Institute Now Newsletter
Natural Resources Research Inst.
Univ. of Minnesota, Duluth
5013 Miller Trunk Hwy.
Duluth, MN 55811
Phone: (218)720-4294
Fax: (218)720-4219
Toll-Free: 800-234-0054
Provides information on the programs and projects of the Institute. ***Editor(s):*** Patricia E. Miller. ***Frequency:*** Quarterly. ***Price:*** Free.

★6326★ Naturalist Review of Books
Audubon Naturalist Soc. of the Central Atlantic States
8940 Jones Mill Rd.
Chevy Chase, MD 20815
Phone: (301)652-9188
Frequency: Quarterly.

★6327★ NetaNews
National Environmental Training Assn.
8687 Via De Ventura, Ste. 214
Scottsdale, AZ 85258
Phone: (602)951-1440
Fax: (602)483-0083
Covers association activities and efforts to inform Congress and the Environmental Protection Agency of environmental training issues. ***Frequency:*** Bimonthly. ***Price:*** Included in membership dues; $12/year for nonmembers.

★6328★ Network Exchange
Alliance for Environmental Education
10751 Ambassador Dr., No. 201
Manassas, VA 22110
Phone: (703)335-1025
Fax: (703)631-1651
Frequency: Bimonthly. ***Price:*** $20.

★6329★ The New Alchemy Quarterly
New Alchemy Inst., Inc.
237 Hatchville Rd.
East Falmouth, MA 02536
Phone: (617)564-6301
Fax: (508)457-9680
Promotes the goals of the NAI, which develops sustainable technologies for providing food, energy, shelter and landscape design. Concerned with aquaculture, bioshelters, education, energy and finances. ***Editor(s):*** Bill O'Neill. ***Frequency:*** Quarterly. ***Price:*** Included in membership.

★6330★ The New Bird Association of California
Bird Assn. of California
c/o Ferdinand R. Wagner
679 Prospect
Pasadena, CA 91103
Phone: (818)795-6621
Frequency: Bimonthly.

★6331★ New England Environmental Network News
Lincoln Filene Center for Citizenship and Public Affairs
Tufts Univ.
Medford, MA 02155
Phone: (617)381-3451
Fax: (617)666-1008
Offers articles by experts covering a wide range of environmental issues, particularly those concerning the New England states. ***Editor(s):*** Nancy W. Anderson. ***Frequency:*** Quarterly. ***Price:*** $10/yr.

★6332★ New England Sierran
New England Chapter
3 Joy St., Rm. 12
Boston, MA 02108
Phone: (617)227-5339
Provides news and information on protecting marine and coastal environments, including technical, legal, human health, and environmental information. ***Editor(s):*** Wanda Goldbaum and Priscilla Chapman. ***Price:*** $29/yr.

★6333★ New England WildFlower Society Newsletter
New England WildFlower Soc.
c/o Barbara Pryor
Hemenway Rd.
Framingham, MA 01701
Phone: (508)877-7630
Frequency: Semiannual.

★6334★ New York Turtle and Tortoise Society NewsNotes
New York Turtle and Tortoise Soc.
c/o Suzanne Dohm
163 Amsterdam Ave., Ste. 365
New York, NY 10023
Phone: (212)459-4803
Membership activities newsletter. ***Frequency:*** Periodic.

★6335★ News and Views of Boston Harbor
Save Our Shores, Inc.
PO Box 103
North Quincy, MA 02171
Phone: (508)888-4694
Reports on the goals of the Organization which aims to establish a National Recreation Area and Historic Site in Boston Harbor and encourages the protection or promotion of the marine resources of Massachusetts Bay and its natural, scenic, historic and recreation areas. ***Frequency:*** 4/yr. ***Price:*** Free.

★6336★ News From Environmental Coalition on Nuclear Power
Environmental Coalition on Nuclear Power
433 Orlando Ave.
State College, PA 16803
Phone: (814)237-3900
Addresses nuclear power and energy policy issues. Contains information on radioactive waste and its affect on health, the nuclear fuel cycle, nuclear weapons, alternative energy sources, and electric utility rates and operational issues. Also monitors nuclear energy litigation and pending legislation. ***Editor(s):*** J.H. Johnsrud. ***Frequency:*** Periodic. ***Price:*** $10/yr. for individuals; $25 for public interest organizations; $50 for industry.

★6337★ NGO Networker
World Resources Inst.
1709 New York Ave., N.W.
Washington, DC 20006
Phone: (202)638-6300
Covers non-governmental organizations (NGOs) with emphasis on international environmental and developmental issues and the juncture between them. Informs Third World NGOs of actions and inititatives taken on their behalf by NGOs in the North with World Bank and other multilateral and bilateral development aid agencies. ***Editor(s):*** Bill Nagle. ***Frequency:*** Quarterly. ***Price:*** Free.

★6338★ Noise Regulation Report
Business Publishers, Inc.
951 Pershing Dr.
Silver Spring, MD 20910-4464
Phone: (301)587-6300
Fax: (301)587-1081
Covers developments in the noise abatement and control field. ***Frequency:*** Biweekly. ***Price:*** $345.50.

★6339★ North American Association for Environmental Education Newsletter
North Amer. Assn. for Environmental Education
PO Box 400
Troy, OH 45373
Phone: (513)339-6835
Fax: (513)698-6493
Frequency: Bimonthly.

★6340★ The Nuclear Advocate
Amer. s for Nuclear Energy, Inc.
2525 Wilson Blvd.
Arlington, VA 22201
Phone: (703)528-4430
Serves as "a guide for the pro-energy citizens movement with a decidedly pro-nuclear stance." Discusses energy and Washington legislative developments. ***Editor(s):*** Douglas O. Lee. ***Frequency:*** Bimonthly. ***Price:*** $15/yr.

★6341★ The Nuclear Monitor
Nuclear Information and Resource Service, Inc.
1424 16th St., N.W., No. 601
Washington, DC 20036
Phone: (202)328-0002
Tracks the records of nuclear utilities in both operation and construction of nuclear power plants. Reviews new reports on nuclear safety and economics. ***Editor(s):*** Michael Mariotte. ***Frequency:*** Biweekly. ***Price:*** $250/yr. for individuals; $150 for public and university libraries.

★6342★ Nuclear Waste News
Business Publishers, Inc.
951 Pershing Dr.
Silver Spring, MD 20910-4464
Phone: (301)587-6300
Fax: (301)587-1081
Provides information on radioactive wastes, from generation through disposal for a variety of nuclear wastes including defense program waste and mixed waste. ***Frequency:*** Weekly. ***Price:*** $531.50.

★6343★ Nuclear Waste News
Business Publishers, Inc.
951 Pershing Dr.
Silver Spring, MD 20910-4464
Phone: (301)587-6300
Reports on requirements and regulations affecting nuclear waste activities. Provides facts relating to all aspects of radioactive wastes including generation and disposal, for all types of wastes including spent fuel and defense program waste. ***Frequency:*** Weekly.

★6344★ Nucleus
Union of Concerned Scientists
26 Church St.
Cambridge, MA 02238
Phone: (617)547-5552
Concerns the impact of advanced technology on society and covers arms control and energy-policy issues such as global warming, renewable energy, energy efficiency, nuclear reactor safety, and radioactive waste disposal. ***Editor(s):*** Steven Krauss. ***Frequency:*** Quarterly. ***Price:*** Included in membership.

★6345★ Ocean Wave and Tidal Energy Systems
National Technical Information Service
U.S. Dept. of Commerce
5285 Port Royal Rd.
Springfield, VA 22161
Phone: (703)487-4630
Abstracts information on all aspects of ocean thermal energy conversion systems based on exploitation of the temperature difference between the surface water and ocean depth, salinity gradient power systems based on extracting energy from mixing fresh water with seawater, and information on wave and tidal power. ***Frequency:*** Bimonthly. ***Price:*** $100/yr., U.S., Canada, and Mexico; $200 elsewhere.

★6346★ Oil Spill Intelligence Report
Cutter Information Corp.
1100 Massachusetts Ave.
Arlington, MA 02174-4328
Phone: (617)648-8700
Fax: (617)648-8707
Telex: 650 100 9891 MCIUW
Provides international coverage of oil spills and related events, offering detailed accounts of all major spills. ***Editor(s):*** Amy M. Stolls. ***Frequency:*** Weekly. ***Price:*** $477/yr.; $390 for academic institutions in the U.S. and Canada; $597 elsewhere.

★6347★ On the Edge
Wildlife Preservation Trust Intl.
34th St. & Girard Ave.
Philadelphia, PA 19104
Phone: (215)222-3636
Focuses on developments concerning the captive breeding of endangered species and the reintroduction to the wild of captive bred animals. Reports on breeding projects and research being conducted in the area. ***Frequency:*** Semiannual. ***Price:*** Included in membership.

★6348★ On the Wild Side Bulletin
Amer. Wildlands
7500 E. Arapahoe Rd., Ste. 355
Englewood, CO 80112
Phone: (303)771-0380
Fax: (303)694-9047
Frequency: Quarterly.

★6349★ Organization for Tropical Studies Newsletter
Organization for Tropical Studies
Box DM, Duke Sta.
Durham, NC 27706
Phone: (919)684-5774
Fax: (919)684-5412
Covers OTS research efforts and graduate training programs and courses in Costa Rica, with emphasis on tropical ecology and conservation. ***Editor(s):*** Jonathan Giles. ***Frequency:*** Quarterly. ***Price:*** $30/yr.

★6350★ Outdoor Ethics
Izaak Walton League of America
1401 Wilson Blvd., Level B
Arlington, VA 22209
Phone: (703)528-1818
Fax: (703)528-1836
Works to educate the public on responsible outdoor behavior. Features hunting and angling ethics, responsible use of recreational vehicles, and low-impact camping and wilderness-use techniques. ***Editor(s):*** Laury Marshall-Forbes. ***Frequency:*** Quarterly. ***Price:*** Free.

★6351★ Outdoor Highlights
Illinois State Dept. of Conservation
524 S. 2nd St.
Springfield, IL 62706
Phone: (217)782-7454
Focuses on news of environmental, conservation, and recreational issues concerning natural resources in Illinois. ***Editor(s):*** Gary Thomas. ***Frequency:*** Biweekly. ***Price:*** $8/yr.

★6352★ Outdoor News Bulletin
Wildlife Management Inst.
1101 14th St., N.W., Ste. 725
Washington, DC 20005
Phone: (202)371-1808
Concerned with better management and wise utilization of all renewable natural resources. Reviews legislative actions, conservation programs, and other developments of interest. ***Frequency:*** Biweekly. ***Price:*** Included in membership.

★6353★ Outdoors Unlimited: News Notes
Outdoors Unlimited, Inc.
PO Box 373
Kaysville, UT 84037
Phone: (801)544-0960
Provides news and information on public land use issues. Supports development of public land for multiple uses, including recreation, lumber and mining, energy exploration, grazing, and agriculture. Covers state and national legislation affecting public land use. ***Editor(s):*** Patricia Hirschi. ***Frequency:*** Monthly. ***Price:*** Included in membership.

★6354★ Outdoors West
Federation of Western Outdoor Clubs
365 W. 29th St.
Eugene, OR 97405
Phone: (503)686-1365
Frequency: Semiannual. ***Price:*** $2.

★6355★ **Pack and Paddle**
Ozark Soc.
PO Box 2914
Little Rock, AR 72203
Phone: (501)847-3738
Frequency: Periodic.

★6356★ **Passaic River Restoration Newsletter**
Passaic River Coalition
246 Madisonville Rd.
Basking Ridge, NJ 07920
Phone: (201)766-7550
Provides news and information relating to waterfront environment projects in the Passaic River Watershed. Discusses the problems of an urban river system, including such topics as explosive population growth, water pollution, water shortages, flood control, sewage and garbage disposal, and urban decay. Reports on research on land use, water quality and supply, wildlife and vegetation, flood control, and historic preservation. ***Editor(s):*** Ella F. Fillippone, M.D. ***Frequency:*** Quarterly. ***Price:*** Included in membership.

★6357★ **Pelican Man's Bird Sanctuary Newsletter**
Pelican Man's Bird Sanctuary
PO Box 2648
Sarasota, FL 34230
Phone: (813)955-2266
Frequency: 3-4/year.

★6358★ **Peregrine Fund Newsletter**
Peregrine Fund, Inc.
5666 W. Flying Hawk Ln.
Boise, IN 83709
Phone: (208)362-3716
Reports year-by-year progress in research and efforts towards the reestablishment of the peregrine falcon. Includes information on endangered birds of prey the Fund is working with internationally. ***Editor(s):*** Tom J. Cade and William A. Burnham. ***Frequency:*** Semiannual. ***Price:*** Included in membership.

★6359★ **Pest Management and Crop Development Bulletin**
Agriculture Newsletter Service
Univ. of Illinois
116 Mumford Hall
1301 W. Gregory Dr.
Urbana, IL 61801
Reports on the current agricultural insect and plant disease situation, giving advice on control methods and covering new developments in pesticide application techniques. ***Frequency:*** Weekly, April through August, plus five additonal issues (25/yr. total). ***Price:*** $20/yr.

★6360★ **Pesticide and Toxic Chemical News**
Food Chemical News, Inc.
1101 Pennsylvania Ave., SE
Washington, DC 20003
Phone: (202)544-1980
Provides news and analysis of chemical regulatory and legislative activities covering the full spectrum of pesticides, hazardous wastes and toxic substances. ***Frequency:*** Weekly.

★6361★ **Pesticides and You**
National Coalition Against the Misuse of Pesticides
530 7th St., S.E.
Washington, DC 20003
Phone: (202)543-5450
Concerned with pesticide hazards and safety. Aims to advance awareness of public health, environmental, and economic problems caused by pesticide abuse and promotes alternatives to pesticide use. Also monitors relevant government and congressional activities. ***Frequency:*** 5/yr. ***Price:*** Included in membership.

★6362★ **PET Projects**
National Assn. for Plastic Container Recovery
4828 Pkwy. Plaza Blvd., Ste. 260
Charlotte, NC 28217
Phone: (704)357-3250
Fax: (704)357-3260
Frequency: Quarterly.

★6363★ **Petals, Pine, and Print**
Big Thicket Assn.
Box 198 - Hwy. 770
Saratoga, TX 77585
Phone: (409)274-5000
Frequency: Bimonthly.

★6364★ **P.G. News**
National Prairie Grouse Technical Coun.
Western Energy Co.
Box 99
Colstrip, MT 59323
Phone: (406)748-2366
Frequency: Semiannual.

★6365★ **Planet Walker**
Planet Walk, Inc.
PO Box 701
Inverness, CA 94937
Follows the progress of John Francis's eighteen-year pilgrimage around the world on foot to promote earth stewardship and world peace. Provides commentary on environmental and peace issues, and reports on walks by other people and organizations. ***Editor(s):*** John Francis. ***Frequency:*** Quarterly. ***Price:*** $20/yr., U.S. and Canada; $27 elsewhere.

★6366★ **Plant Conservation**
Center for Plant Conservation
125 Arborway
Jamaica Plain, MA 02130
Phone: (617)524-6988
Reports on center activites. ***Frequency:*** Quarterly.

★6367★ **The Plastic Bottle Reporter**
Plastic Bottle Information Bur.
1275 K St., N.W., Ste. 400
Washington, DC 20005
Phone: (202)371-5244
Covers recycling activities and technology, new plastic bottle applications, and environmental issues concerning plastic bottles. Alerts readers to new literature available from the Bureau and the Society of the Plastics Industry, Inc. ***Editor(s):*** Deanne H. Dillingham. ***Frequency:*** Quarterly. ***Price:*** Free.

★6368★ **Plastic Waste Strategies**
Washington Business Information, Inc.
1117 N. 19th St., Ste. 200
Arlington, VA 22209-1798
Phone: (703)247-3422
Fax: (703)247-3421
Focus on recycling, degradability, incineration, and alternative methods of handling solid and plastic waste. Covers legislative, technological, and competitive issues. ***Editor(s):*** John Sisson. ***Frequency:*** Monthly. ***Price:*** $407, U.S. and Canada, and Mexico; $432 elsewhere.

★6369★ **Plastics Recycling Report**
Plastics Recycling Inst.
Rutgers Univ.
PO Box 909
Piscataway, NJ 08854
Phone: (201)932-4420
Provides an overview of current plastics recycling technology.

★6370★ **Pollution Prevention News**
U.S. Environmental Protection Agency
Pollution Prevention News
401 M St., SW, PM-219
Washington, DC 20460
Phone: (202)382-4023
Pollution prevention and source reduction. ***Editor(s):*** Priscilla Flattery. ***Frequency:*** Monthly. ***Price:*** Free.

★6371★ **Population Report**
International Population Program
Sierra Club
DC Legislative Off.
408 C St., N.E.
Washington, DC 20002
Phone: (202)547-1141
Fax: (202)547-6009
Examines problems related to human population and the environment. Discusses international family planning, local growth, and land use controversies from an environmental point of view, emphasizing stabilization, sustainable development, and carrying capacity. Covers national and state legislation on matters related to U.S. population policy, U.S. funding of family planning in developing countries, and population programs of the World Bank and other multilateral development institutions. ***Editor(s):*** Nancy Wallace. ***Frequency:*** 6/yr. ***Price:*** Free.

★6372★ **Portable Sanitation Association in Action**
Portable Sanitation Assn. Intl.
7800 Metro Pkwy., Ste. 104
Bloomington, MN 55425
Phone: (612)854-8300
Fax: (612)854-7560
Frequency: Monthly.

★6373★ **Potomac Appalachian**
Potomac Appalachian Trail Club
1718 N St., N.W.
Washington, DC 20036
Phone: (202)638-5307
Carries articles on matters concerning the Appalachian Trail, especially the area from the Susquehanna River to the Shenandoah National Park. ***Editor(s):*** Janice Lloyd. ***Frequency:*** Monthly. ***Price:*** $6/yr.

★6374★ **The Prairie Dog's Companion**
Grassland Heritage Found.
5450 Buena Vista
Shawnee Mission, KS 66205
Phone: (913)677-3326
Serves as a forum of communication for the Foundation, which fosters appreciation for, creative interest in, and better understanding of the value of America's native grassland prairies. Discusses the development of the Foundation's 300 acre Prairie Center near Olathe, Kansas. ***Frequency:*** 3/yr. ***Price:*** Included in membership.

★6375★ **Protect What's Right**
Wildlife Conservation Fund of America
50 W. Broad St., Ste. 1025
Columbus, OH 43215
Phone: (614)221-2684
Frequency: Quarterly.

★6376★ Public Affairs Council—Impact
Public Affairs Coun.
1019 19th St. NW, Ste. 200
Washington, DC 20036
Phone: (202)872-1790
Fax: (202)835-8343
Frequency: Monthly. ***Price:*** Included in membership dues.

★6377★ Public Land News
Resources Publishing Co.
1010 Vermont Ave., N.W., Ste. 708
Washington, DC 20005
Phone: (202)638-7529
Tracks public land issues and environmentalists' struggle for control with business and industry. Covers government regulation, energy leasing, wilderness designation for parks use, and timber harvesting. ***Editor(s):*** James B. Coffin. ***Frequency:*** 24/yr. ***Price:*** $177/yr.

★6378★ Rachel's Hazardous Waste News
Environmental Research Found.
PO Box 3541
Princeton, NJ 08543-3541
Phone: (609)683-0707
Focuses on hazardous waste management issues such as landfills, regulations, toxins, incinerators, health and environment, grassroots lobbying, toxins, and community energy conservation. ***Editor(s):*** Peter Montaque, Ph.D. ***Frequency:*** Weekly. ***Price:*** $25/yr, individuals; $8, students and senior citizens; $50, government agencies; $250, businesses, U.S.; $29, Canada and Mexico; $36 elsewhere.

★6379★ Radioactive Waste Campaign Report
Radioactive Waste Campaign
625 Broadway, 2nd Fl.
New York, NY 10012-2611
Phone: (212)473-7390
Contains articles on the environmental and social impact of the generation, transportation, storage, and management of radioactive waste. ***Frequency:*** Quarterly. ***Price:*** Included in membership dues; $15/year for nonmembers; $25/year for institutions.

★6380★ Radioactive Waste Management
National Technical Information Service
U.S. Dept. of Commerce
5285 Port Royal Rd.
Springfield, VA 22161
Phone: (703)487-4630
Abstracts worldwide information on the critical topics of spent-fuel transport and storage, radioactive effluents from nuclear facilities, and techniques of processing wastes, their storage, and ultimate disposal. Includes information on remedial actions and other environmental aspects. ***Frequency:*** Monthly. ***Price:*** $100/yr., U.S., Canada, and Mexico; $200 elsewhere.

★6381★ RARE Center News
RARE Center for Tropical Bird Conservation
19th & Parkway
Philadelphia, PA 19103
Phone: (215)299-1182
Frequency: Periodic.

★6382★ Recreation Executive Report
Leisure Industry/Recreation News
PO Box 43563
Washington, DC 20010
Phone: (202)232-7107
Carries articles on issues and trends in park and recreation area management. Interprets governmental actions and reports on current legislation. Covers local, state, and national parks. ***Editor(s):*** Marj Jensen. ***Frequency:*** Monthly. ***Price:*** $85/yr., U.S. and Canada; $105 elswhere.

★6383★ Recycling Update
Update Publicare Co.
Prosperity & Profits Unl.
PO Box 570213
Houston, TX 77257-0213
Focuses on various aspects of recycling. ***Editor(s):*** A.C. Doyle. ***Frequency:*** Semiannual. ***Price:*** $4/yr.

★6384★ Redstart
Brooks Bird Club
707 Warwood Ave.
Wheeling, WV 26003
Phone: (304)547-5253
Includes field and banding notes. ***Frequency:*** Quarterly. ***Price:*** Included in membership dues; $14/year for nonmembers.

★6385★ Reducing the Rate of Global Warming
Renew America
Publications Dept.
1400 Sixteenth St., NW
Washington, DC 20036
Pamphlet.

★6386★ Rene Dubos Center for Human Environments Newsletter
Rene Dubos Center for Human Environments
100 E. 85th St.
New York, NY 10028
Phone: (212)249-7745
Fax: (212)772-2033
Frequency: Periodic.

★6387★ Renewable Energy News Digest
Sun Words
861 Central Pkwy.
Schenectady, NY 12309
Phone: (518)372-1799
Focuses on news on renewable energy, including solar, photovoltaic, wind, wave action, hydro, thermal conversion, and biomass. ***Editor(s):*** Sandra Oddo. ***Frequency:*** Monthly. ***Price:*** $50/yr.

★6388★ Renewable Resources in Hawaii
Hawaii Natural Energy Inst.
Univ. of Hawaii at Manoa
2540 Dole St., Holmes 246
Honolulu, HI 96822
Phone: (808)956-2332
Fax: (808)956-2336
Reports on renewable energy (geothermal, wind, solar, and ocean thermal) and ocean resource technology. ***Frequency:*** Quarterly. ***Price:*** Free.

★6389★ Report on Defense Plant Wastes
Business Publishers, Inc.
951 Pershing Dr.
Silver Spring, MD 20910-4464
Phone: (301)587-6300
Fax: (301)587-1081
Reports on environmental laws, regulations, cleanups, contracting and court action affecting U.S. defense, weapons production and other government facilities. ***Frequency:*** Biweekly. ***Price:*** $405.50.

★6390★ Report on Defense Plant Wastes
Business Publishers, Inc.
951 Pershing Dr.
Silver Spring, MD 20910-4464
Phone: (301)587-6300
Covers issues concerning waste from defense industry plants, including cleanup of contamination, funding, Congressional actions, legal actions, and actions to protect health and environment. ***Frequency:*** Biweekly.

★6391★ Report to the Consumer
Honor Publications
1275 Carson Woods Rd.
Fortuna, CA 95540
Phone: (707)725-4995
Explores the effects of mental, physical, and environmental pollutants such as herbicides, drugs, food additives, and others. ***Editor(s):*** Ida Honorof. ***Frequency:*** Semiannual. ***Price:*** $8/yr.

★6392★ Resolve
Conservation Found.
1250 24th St. NW, Ste. 400
Washington, DC 20037
Phone: (202)293-4800
Details dispute resolution. ***Frequency:*** Periodic.

★6393★ Resource Hotline
Amer. Forestry Assn.
1516 P St. NW
Washington, DC 20005
Phone: (202)667-3300
Fax: (202)667-7751
Frequency: Biweekly. ***Price:*** $14.

★6394★ Resource Recovery Report
Frank McManus
5313 38th St., N.W.
Washington, DC 20015
Phone: (202)362-3034
Fax: (202)362-6632
Covers all aspects of energy and material recovery from waste, with more than 100 news items on recycling and other successful projects. Monitors federal, state, and local activities concerning resource recovery, including relevant business developments and international news. ***Editor(s):*** Frank McManus. ***Frequency:*** Monthly. ***Price:*** $187/yr., U.S. and Canada; $199 elsewhere.

★6395★ Resources for the Future, Inc.—Resources
Resources for the Future, Inc.
1616 P St., N.W.
Washington, DC 20036
Phone: (202)328-5113
Fax: (202)265-8069
Features natural resources and enviromental articles on renewable resources, food and agriculture policy, energy, climate, the quality of the environment, and risk assessment and management. ***Editor(s):*** Samuel Allen. ***Frequency:*** Quarterly. ***Price:*** Free.

★6396★ Restoration and Management Notes
Univ. of Wisconsin Press, Journals Div.
114 N. Murray St.
Madison, WI 53715
Phone: (608)262-4952
Fax: (608)262-7560
Concerned with the science and art of ecosystem restoration and management. Addresses the problems and questions bearing on restoration and management of a variety of ecosystems native to North America. Discusses propagation and introduction of native species and control of exotic species. ***Editor(s):*** William R. Jordan, III. ***Frequency:*** Semiannually. ***Price:*** $15/yr.

★6397★ Reuse/Recycle
Technomic Publishing Co. Inc.
851 New Holland Ave.
PO Box 3535
Lancaster, PA 17604-3535
Phone: (717)291-5609

Toll-Free: 800-233-9936
Contains information on new processes, machinery, and uses for both industrial and municipal recycling. Publishes news of energy recovery, recycling, and other energy-related events. Provides updates on energy-related legislation, energy industry changes and personnel, and pollution/recycling problems facing scientists and industry. ***Editor(s):*** Jack Milgrom. ***Frequency:*** Monthly. ***Price:*** $125/yr.

★6398★ Rising Tide
Coastal Conservation Assn.
4801 Woodway, Ste. 220 W.
Houston, TX 77056
Phone: (713)626-4222
Fax: (713)951-3801
Newsletter for New Tide members. ***Frequency:*** Bimonthly.

★6399★ Safety and Health Bulletin
Water Pollution Control Fed.
601 Wythe St.
Alexandria, VA 22314-1994
Phone: (703)684-2400
Fax: (703)684-2492
Frequency: Quarterly.

★6400★ Salt Ponds
Rhode Island Sea Grant Program
Univ. of Rhode Island
Coastal Resources Center
Bay Campus
Narragansett, RI 02882
Phone: (401)792-6224
Updates events and management issues in the salt pond region, including barrier beaches, coastal lagoons, and costal zones of southern Rhode Island; provides articles on fisheries, water quality, and history of the region; and describes results of pond watcher volunteer environmental monitoring. ***Editor(s):*** Virginia Lee. ***Frequency:*** Quarterly. ***Price:*** Free.

★6401★ Sanctuary
Massachusetts Audubon Soc.
S. Great Rd.
Lincoln, MA 01773
Phone: (617)259-9500
Provides educational and research information on water resources, ecosystem conservation, and energy transition. ***Frequency:*** 10/yr. ***Price:*** Included in membership.

★6402★ Save the Dunes Council Newsletter
Save the Dunes Council, Inc.
PO Box 114
Beverly Shores, IN 46301
Phone: (219)879-3937
Describes activities, events, and actions affecting the preservation and protection of Indiana Dunes National Lakeshore and other national, state, and local dunes parks in northwestern Indiana. ***Editor(s):*** Anne Bayless and Charlotte J. Read. ***Frequency:*** Bimonthly. ***Price:*** $15/yr. to individuals; $25/yr. to institutions.

★6403★ Save the Harbor, Save the Bay Newsletter
Save the Harbor, Save the Bay
25 W. St., 4th Fl.
Boston, MA 02111
Phone: (617)451-2860
Promotes and monitors the cleanup of Boston Harbor and Massachusetts Bay. ***Editor(s):*** Bud Erland and Beth Nicholson. ***Frequency:*** 6/yr. ***Price:*** Free.

★6404★ Save the Manatee Club Newsletter
Save the Manatee Club
500 N. Maitland Ave.
Maitland, FL 32751
Phone: (407)539-0990
Frequency: 5/year.

★6405★ Savory Letter
Center for Holistic Resource Management
PO Box 7128
Albuquerque, NM 87194
Phone: (505)242-9272
Fax: (505)247-1008
Frequency: Quarterly.

★6406★ Sea Shepherd News
Sea Shepherd Conservation Soc.
PO Box 7000 S
Redondo Beach, CA 90277
Phone: (213)373-6979
Frequency: Monthly.

★6407★ The Seedhead News
Native Seeds/SEARCH
2509 N. Campbell Ave., No. 325
Tucson, AZ 85719
Phone: (602)327-9123
Concerned with the conservation of native crops and their wild relatives in the Southwestern United States. Discusses seed searching and the native crop seedstocks available through the organization. ***Editor(s):*** Kevin Dahl. ***Frequency:*** Quarterly. ***Price:*** Included in membership.

★6408★ Seedling News
TreePeople
12601 Mulholland Dr.
Beverly Hills, CA 90210
Phone: (818)753-4600
Fax: (818)753-4625
Frequency: Bimonthly.

★6409★ Shore and Beach
Amer. Shore and Beach Preservation Assn.
PO Box 279
Middletown, CA 95461
Phone: (707)987-2385
Frequency: Quarterly.

★6410★ Shoreline
Shorelines
Massachusetts Audubon Society: North Shore
159 Main St.
Gloucester, MA 01930
Phone: (617)283-0598
Aims to provide education and technical assistance regarding protection of the coastal environment. Focuses on coastal water quality, wastewater treatment, shellfish management, salt marsh mosquito control, dune restoration and protection, open space mangement, and coastal water quality monitoring. ***Frequency:*** Quarterly. ***Price:*** Free.

★6411★ Sierra Club Legal Defense Fund—In Brief
Sierra Club Legal Defense Fund
2044 Fillmore St.
San Francisco, CA 94115
Phone: (415)567-6100
Provides news of the Fund's litigation activities. ***Editor(s):*** Tom Turner. ***Frequency:*** Quarterly. ***Price:*** $10/yr., U.S., $15, Canada; $20 elsewhere.

★6412★ Sierra Club National News Report
Sierra Club
730 Polk St.
San Francisco, CA 94109
Phone: (415)776-2211
Supplies news of legislative and administrative developments at the national and regional level on environmental issues, emphasizing the Club's involvement. ***Editor(s):*** Pam Goddard and Sharon Symington. ***Frequency:*** 27/yr. ***Price:*** $18/yr., U.S. and Canada; $30 elsewhere.

★6413★ Sign Control News
Scenic America
216 7th St. SE
Washington, DC 20003
Phone: (202)546-1100
Frequency: Bimonthly.

★6414★ Sinai Newsletter
Holy Land Conservation Fund
969 Park Ave.
New York, NY 10028
Phone: (212)249-8591
Reports on the organization and its programs of wildlife conservation in the Middle East. Reviews the status of endangered species in the region and reports on the implementation of nature reserves in Israel. Contains news of research and field study updates concerning wildlife in the region. ***Frequency:*** Periodic. ***Price:*** Included in membership.

★6415★ Skipping Stones
Aprovecho Institute
80574 Hazelton Rd.
Cottage Grove, OR 97424
Phone: (503)942-9434
Focuses on environmental and cultural enrichment. ***Frequency:*** Quarterly. ***Price:*** $15/yr., U.S.; $20 elsewhere.

★6416★ Sludge
Business Publishers, Inc.
951 Pershing Dr.
Silver Spring, MD 20910-4464
Phone: (301)587-6300
Fax: (301)587-1081
Monitors developments in the area of municipal and industrial residuals management, by-products of air and water pollution control. Covers the four basic problems of sludge: generation, treatment, utilization, and disposal. Reports on related legislation, business and technology news, publications, personalities, and meetings. ***Editor(s):*** Sue Darcey. ***Frequency:*** Biweekly. ***Price:*** $194.72/yr., U.S. and Canada; $214 elsewhere.

★6417★ Society for Ecological Restoration News
Society for Ecological Restoration
1207 Seminole Hwy.
Madison, WI 53711
Phone: (608)262-9547
Frequency: Quarterly.

★6418★ Society for Environmental Geochemistry and Health—Interface
Society for Environmental Geochemistry and Health
c/o Willard R. Chappell
University of Colorado, Denver
Center for Environmental Sciences
Campus Box 136
Denver, CO 80204
Phone: (303)556-3460
Fax: (303)556-4822
Frequency: Quarterly.

★6419★ Soil and Water Conservation News
Soil Conservation Service
PO Box 2890
Washington, DC 20013
Phone: (202)447-4543
Communicates Agency policies and technical and practical information concerning natural resource conservation. ***Editor(s):*** Leslie J. Wilder. ***Frequency:*** Bimonthly. ***Price:*** $8.50/yr., U.S.; $10.65 elsewhere.

★6420★ Soil Conservation Service Current Developments
Soil Conservation Service
U.S. Dept. of Agriculture
Massachusetts State Office
451 W. St.
Amherst, MA 01002
Phone: (413)256-0441
Fax: (413)256-8861
Provides news and information on the Service and discusses soil conservation and related issues. ***Editor(s):*** Suzanne C. Schenkel. ***Frequency:*** 4/yr. ***Price:*** Free.

★6421★ Solar Buildings Technology
National Technical Information Service
U.S. Dept. of Commerce
5285 Port Royal Rd.
Springfield, VA 22161
Phone: (703)487-4630
Abstracts worldwide information on solar energy use in buildings, including desulfurization, photovoltaic systems, solar thermal, solar collectors, and heat storage. ***Frequency:*** Bimonthly. ***Price:*** $100/yr., U.S., Canada, and Mexico; $200 elsewhere.

★6422★ The Solar Collector
Florida Solar Energy Center
300 State Rd., 401
Cape Canaveral, FL 32920-4099
Phone: (407)783-0300
Provides information on solar and renewable energy research and center activities and programs. Focuses on research and development, education and information, and technology transfer. ***Editor(s):*** Carolyn King Burns. ***Frequency:*** Quarterly. ***Price:*** Free.

★6423★ Solar Life
Solar Energy Inst. of North America
221 L St., N.W., Ste. 250
Washington, DC 20036
Phone: (202)289-4411
Fosters the development and use of economical solar energy systems. Covers developments in the field. Encourages the cooperation of professionals in different areas to implement full-scale production programs. ***Frequency:*** Monthly. ***Price:*** Included in membership.

★6424★ Solar Thermal Energy Technology
National Technical Information Service
U.S. Dept. of Commerce
5285 Port Royal Rd.
Springfield, VA 22161
Phone: (703)487-4630
Abstracts worldwide research and development information that would expand the technology base required for the advancement of solar thermal systems as a significant energy source, including advanced concepts in materials research, concentrator and receiver technology, and salinity-gradient solar pond technology. ***Frequency:*** Bimonthly. ***Price:*** $100/yr., U.S., Canada, and Mexico; $200 elsewhere.

★6425★ Solid Waste Report
Business Publishers, Inc.
951 Pershing Dr.
Silver Spring, MD 20910
Phone: (301)587-6300
Fax: (301)587-1081
Concerned with solid waste collection, processing, disposal, resource recovery, and recycling. Covers legislation, regulations, enforcement and litigation, state and local news, and business and technology news. ***Editor(s):*** Sue Darcey. ***Frequency:*** Weekly. ***Price:*** $368/yr., U.S. and Canada; $415 elsewhere.

★6426★ Soundings
Pacific Whale Found.
Kealia Beach Plaza
101 N. Kihei Rd., Ste. 25
Kihei, HI 96753
Phone: (808)879-8860
Fax: (808)879-2615
Toll-Free: 800-942-5311
Provides information concerning humpback whales and updates on sightings by Foundation researchers. ***Editor(s):*** Sue Kelley. ***Frequency:*** Semiannual. ***Price:*** Included in membership.

★6427★ Spill Briefs
Spill Control Assn. of America
400 Renaissance Center, Ste. 1900
Detroit, MI 48243
Phone: (313)567-0500
Fax: (313)259-8943
Current information, issues, and regulation regarding hazardous materials, oil spill cleanup, and the response industry. ***Frequency:*** Monthly. ***Price:*** Free, for members only.

★6428★ Spill Control Association of America Newsletter
Spill Control Assn. of America
400 Renaissance Center, Ste. 1900
Detroit, MI 48243-1509
Phone: (313)567-0500
Fax: (313)259-8943
Contains material relevant to oil and hazardous substance spill control technology. Includes Association news. ***Editor(s):*** Marc K. Shaye and Clayton W. Evans. ***Frequency:*** Biweekly. ***Price:*** Included in membership.

★6429★ Splash
Izaak Walton League of America
1401 Wilson Blvd., Level B
Arlington, VA 22209
Phone: (703)528-1818
Fax: (703)528-1836
Provides updates on national stream monitoring programs, tips on how to be an effective activist, and descriptions of the affects of major industry on water quality. ***Editor(s):*** Karen Firehock. ***Frequency:*** Quarterly. ***Price:*** Free.

★6430★ SPOOF Newsletter
Society for the Protection of Old Fishes, Inc. (SPOOF)
School of Fisheries WH-10
University of Washington
Seattle, WA 98195
Phone: (206)778-7397
Concerned with protecting sea life from overexploitation, especially the coelacanth, once thought to be extinct. Refers to articles on oceanography and rare fish that were originally published in newspapers and professional journals. ***Editor(s):*** Susan Brown. ***Frequency:*** Periodic. ***Price:*** Included in membership.

★6431★ Sports Fishing Institute Bulletin
Sport Fishing Inst.
1010 Massachusetts Ave., N.W., Ste. 100
Washington, DC 20001
Phone: (202)898-0770
Serves as an educational tool regarding the Institute's efforts in fish conservation. Covers fisheries science and management, habitat protection, aquatic ecology and ecosystems management, water pollution control and abatement, and recreational fisheries development. ***Editor(s):*** Gilbert C. Radonski. ***Frequency:*** 10/yr. ***Price:*** $10/yr.

★6432★ State Environment Report
Business Publishers, Inc.
951 Pershing Dr.
Silver Spring, MD 20910-4464
Phone: (301)587-6300
Fax: (301)587-1081
Focuses on state regulation of toxic chemicals in the workplace, the marketplace, and the environment at large. Covers legislation and regulations that affect toxic substances control, hazardous waste management, pesticide certification and enforcement, hazardous materials transportation, and consumer, occupational, and environmental health. ***Editor(s):*** Phil Zahodiakin. ***Frequency:*** Weekly. ***Price:*** $263.50/yr.

★6433★ State Environmental Report
Business Publishers, Inc.
951 Pershing Dr.
Silver Spring, MD 20910-4464
Phone: (301)587-6300
Provides information on state legislation regarding toxic substances and hazardous wastes. Covers issues such as insurance problems, environmental liability, and waste minimization. ***Frequency:*** Biweekly.

★6434★ State of the Adirondack Park
Adirondack Coun.
Box D-2
Church St.
Elizabethtown, NY 12932
Phone: (518)873-2240
Frequency: Annual.

★6435★ The State of the States-Fund for Renewable Energy and the Environment
Renew America
Publications Dept.
1400 Sixteenth St., NW
Washington, DC 20036

★6436★ The State of the States-Searching for Common Ground
Renew America
Publications Dept.
1400 Sixteenth St. NW
Washington, DC 20036

★6437★ State Regulation Report
Business Publishers, Inc.
951 Pershing Dr.
Silver Spring, MD 20910
Phone: (301)587-6300
Fax: (301)587-1081
Focuses on information concerning toxins and hazardous wastes. Reports on legislation, insurance issues, environmental activities, disposal sites, and minimizing waste. ***Frequency:*** Biweekly.

★6438★ **Steamboat Whistle**
The Steamboaters
c/o Dick Bauer
233 Howard Ave.
Eugene, OR 97404
Phone: (503)688-4980
Frequency: Quarterly.

★6439★ **Student Conservation Association Newsletter**
Student Conservation Assn.
Box 550
Charlestown, NH 03603
Phone: (603)826-4301
Fax: (603)826-7755
Frequency: Semiannual.

★6440★ **Superfund**
Pasha Publications, Inc.
1401 Wilson Blvd., Ste. 909
Arlington, VA 22209
Phone: (703)528-1244
Covers developments in the cleanup of hazardous wastes required under the federal and various state Superfund laws, including inside information on cleanup programs and allocation of cleanup liability. ***Frequency:*** Biweekly.

★6441★ **Sustainable Energy**
Renew America
Publications Dept.
1400 Sixteenth St., NW
Washington, DC 20036
Pamphlet.

★6442★ **TBHA Newsletter**
Boston Harbor Assn.
51 Sleeper St.
Boston, MA 02210
Phone: (617)330-1134
Provides news on Boston Harbor. Also provides information on Harbor clean-up, its development, ferry transportation, port issues, and public access. ***Editor(s):*** Pat Wells. ***Frequency:*** Semimonthly. ***Price:*** Included in membership.

★6443★ **Texas Energy**
Center for Energy and Mineral Resources
Texas A&M Univ.
College Station, TX 77843-1243
Phone: (409)845-8025
Reports on energy and energy-related topics, including energy research, resources, technology, and conservation. Focuses in particular on subjects affecting Texas and its residents. ***Editor(s):*** Rhonda Snider. ***Frequency:*** Bimonthly. ***Price:*** Free.

★6444★ **Texas Shoreline**
Marine Information Service
Sea Grant Coll. Program
Texas A&M Univ.
PO Box 1675
Galveston, TX 77553
Phone: (409)740-4460
Covers events and issues related to Texas marine environment and programs and research activities of the Texas Marine Advisory Service. ***Editor(s):*** Laura Murray. ***Frequency:*** Quarterly. ***Price:*** Free.

★6445★ **Tiger Tales**
Conus MI Group
Ft. George G. Meade, MD 20755-5930
Phone: (301)677-6254
Provides news and information on education, environment, ecology, science, sports, travel, health, and outdoor activities. ***Editor(s):*** Sgt. John A. Bergeron. ***Frequency:*** Monthly.

★6446★ **Tomorrow's Management**
Organization of Wildlife Planners
DNR-Box 7921
Madison, WI 53707
Phone: (608)267-7591
Fax: (608)267-3579
Frequency: Quarterly. ***Price:*** Free.

★6447★ **Tortoise Tracks**
Desert Tortoise Preserve Comm.
PO Box 453
Ridgecrest, CA 93556
Phone: (714)884-5906
Editor(s): Jean E. Jones. ***Frequency:*** Quarterly.

★6448★ **Toxic Materials News**
Business Publishers, Inc.
951 Pershing Dr.
Silver Spring, MD 20910-4464
Phone: (301)587-6300
Fax: (301)587-1081
Monitors developments in toxic substance control that affect business practices and occupational health standards. Reports legislation and agency regulations concerning such issues as manufacturing, handling, disposal, transportation, and distribution of toxic materials. ***Editor(s):*** Charles Knebl. ***Frequency:*** Weekly. ***Price:*** $407.50/yr., U.S. and Canada; $442 elsewhere.

★6449★ **Toxic Materials Transport**
Business Publishers, Inc.
951 Pershing Dr.
Silver Spring, MD 20910
Phone: (301)587-6300
Fax: (301)587-1081
Covers current news and trends relating to hazardous materials shipments by rail, truck, barge, air, and pipeline. Monitors federal legislation and federal, state, and local regulations affecting the routing of hazardous and radioactive materials. Also reports on new hazardous materials, transportation technology, compliance efforts, and transportation costs. ***Editor(s):*** Melanie Scott. ***Frequency:*** Weekly. ***Price:*** $259/yr., U.S. and Canada; $262 elsewhere.

★6450★ **TRAFFIC (USA)**
World Wildlife Fund
1250 24th St., N.W.
Washington, DC 20037
Phone: (202)293-4800
Fax: (202)293-9211
Studies international trade in wild plants and animals, with emphasis on endangered and threatened species and on trade involving the United States. Provides data analysis and information on CITES (Convention on International Trade in Endangered Species). ***Editor(s):*** Andrea L. Gaski. ***Frequency:*** Quarterly. ***Price:*** 10/yr.; free to conservationists working in wildlife trade.

★6451★ **Transportation Energy Research**
National Technical Information Service
U.S. Dept. of Commerce
5285 Port Royal Rd.
Springfield, VA 22161
Phone: (703)487-4630
Summarizes worldwide information on engineering and design of energy-efficient advanced automotive propulsion systems and other aspects of energy conservation measures involving transportation. ***Frequency:*** Monthly. ***Price:*** $100/yr., U.S., Canada, and Mexico; $200 elsewhere.

★6452★ **Tropicus**
Conservation Intl.
1015 18th St. NW, Ste. 1000
Washington, DC 20036
Phone: (202)429-5660
Fax: (202)887-5188
Frequency: Quarterly. ***Price:*** Available to members only.

★6453★ **Truly Loving Care: For Our Kids and for Our Planet**
Natural Resources Defense Coun.
40 W. 20th St.
New York, NY 10011
Phone: (212)727-4412
Fax: (212)727-1773
Frequency: Quarterly. ***Price:*** $10/year for members; $15/year for nonmembers.

★6454★ **The Trumpeter Swan Society Newsletter**
The Trumpeter Swan Soc.
3800 County Rd. 24
Maple Plain, MN 55359
Phone: (612)476-4663
Fax: (612)559-3287
Frequency: Quarterly.

★6455★ **The Trustees of Reservations Newsletter**
Trustees of Reservations
572 Essex St.
Beverly, MA 01915
Phone: (508)921-1944
Fax: (508)921-1948
Presents short features on land conservation programs, ecology programs, events on reservation properties, volunteer activities, and volunteers deserving of special mention. ***Editor(s):*** Eloise W. Hodges. ***Frequency:*** Quarterly. ***Price:*** Included in membership.

★6456★ **Tuesday Letter**
National Assn. of Conservation Districts
PO Box 855
League City, TX 77573
Phone: (713)332-3402
Reports on legislation dealing with conservation issues along with district self-government activities and development. Monitors the progress of legislative proposals and congressional priorities and actions. ***Editor(s):*** Ronald Francis. ***Frequency:*** Monthly. ***Price:*** $35/yr.

★6457★ **Twine Line**
Ohio Sea Grant Coll. Program
Ohio State Univ.
c/o Research Center
1541 Kinnear Rd.
Columbus, OH 43212-1194
Phone: (614)292-8949
Reflects the Program's goals, which are to promote the development, utilization, and conservation of the oceans, Great Lakes, and coastal resources, specifically Lake Erie, through research, education, and advisory services. ***Editor(s):*** Maran Brainard. ***Frequency:*** Bimonthly. ***Price:*** $4.50/yr.

★6458★ **UNCommon Ground**
United New Conservationists
PO Box 362
Campbell, CA 95009
Phone: (408)241-5769
Frequency: 10/year.

★6459★ Underground Injection Practices Council Newsletter
Underground Injection Practices Coun.
525 Central Park Dr., Ste. 304
Oklahoma City, OK 73105
Phone: (405)525-6146
Frequency: Quarterly.

★6460★ United Citizens Coastal Protection League Newsletter
United Citizens Coastal Protection League
PO Box 46
Cardiff By The Sea, CA 92007
Phone: (619)753-7477
Frequency: Periodic.

★6461★ United Nations Environment Programme North American News
United Nations Environment Programme
DC2-803, United Nations
New York, NY 10017
Phone: (202)963-8093
Fax: (212)963-4116
Addresses news of interest to North Americans on the Program and its work on global environmental issues and solutions. ***Editor(s):*** Libby Bassett. ***Frequency:*** Bimonthly. ***Price:*** Free.

★6462★ U.S. Government Books
U.S. Government Printing Off.
Boston Bookstore
JFK Federal Bldg., Rm. G25
Sudbury St.
Boston, MA 02203
Phone: (617)223-6071
Provides a listing of books on commercial fisheries, marine and coastal recreation, environments, safety and standards, natural history, marine industries, boating, and sports. ***Frequency:*** 4/yr. ***Price:*** Free.

★6463★ United States Tourist Council Bulletin
United States Tourist Coun.
Drawer 1875
Washington, DC 20013-1875
Phone: (301)565-5155
Frequency: Periodic.

★6464★ Upper Mississippi River Conservation Committee Fisheries Compendium
Upper Mississippi River Conservation Comm.
1830 2nd Ave.
Rock Island, IL 61201
Phone: (309)793-5800
Frequency: Bimonthly.

★6465★ The Upper Mississippi River Conservation Committee Newsletter
Upper Mississippi River Conservation Comm.
1830 Second Ave.
Rock Island, IL 61201
Phone: (309)793-5800
Provides conservationist and recreational information on the Upper Mississippi River in connection with the goals of the Committee, to promote the utilization of natural and recreational resources. ***Frequency:*** Bimonthly. ***Price:*** Free.

★6466★ Upwellings
Michigan Sea Grant Coll. Program
2200 Bonisteel Blvd.
Ann Arbor, MI 48109
Phone: (313)764-1138
Covers research, extension, environmental education, and other services of Sea Grant programs in the Great Lakes states, especially in Michigan. Focuses on commercial and sport fishing, ecology, shipping, recreation, pollution, and water safety. ***Editor(s):*** Carol Ann Smith. ***Frequency:*** Quarterly. ***Price:*** Free.

★6467★ Urban Wildlife News
National Institute for Urban Wildlife
10921 Trotting Ridge Way
Columbia, MD 21044
Phone: (301)596-3311
Covers current urban wildlife research and management activities. Coordinates information and comments on relevant legislation. Summarizes the work of the National Institute for Urban Wildlife. ***Editor(s):*** Louise E. Dove. ***Frequency:*** Quarterly. ***Price:*** Included in membership.

★6468★ Utility Reporter-Fuels Energy and Power
Merton Allen Assoc.
2307 Dean St.
Schenectady, NY 12309
Phone: (518)393-1933
Covers current activities in energy conservation, alternative energy devices and systems, and other subjects encompassing the entire energy arena. ***Frequency:*** Monthly.

★6469★ Valley Newsletter
Connecticut River Watershed Coun.
125 Combs Rd.
Easthampton, MA 01027
Phone: (413)584-0057
Frequency: Quarterly.

★6470★ Velador
Caribbean Conservation Corp.
PO Box 2866
Gainesville, FL 32602
Phone: (904)373-6441
Fax: (904)375-2449
Frequency: Quarterly.

★6471★ The Voice of Walden
Walden Forever Wild
PO Box 275
Concord, MA 01742
Phone: (203)429-2839
Frequency: Quarterly.

★6472★ WAPITI Newsletter
Rocky Mountain Elk Found.
PO Box 8249
Missoula, MT 59807
Phone: (406)721-0010
Fax: (406)549-4325
Frequency: Quarterly.

★6473★ Washington Bulletin
Water Pollution Control Fed.
601 Wythe St.
Alexandria, VA 22314-1994
Phone: (703)684-2400
Fax: (703)684-2492
Frequency: Monthly.

★6474★ Washington Environmental Protection Report
Callahan Publications
PO Box 3751
Washington, DC 20007
Phone: (703)356-1925
Fax: (703)356-9614
Provides information on environmental issues, including legislation, research on new developments, and contracting opportunities with the Environmental Protection Agency and other federal agencies. ***Editor(s):*** Vincent F. Callahan, Jr. ***Frequency:*** Semimonthly. ***Price:*** $175/yr.

★6475★ Waste Information Digests
International Academy at Santa Barbara
800 Garden St., Ste. D
Santa Barbara, CA 93101
Phone: (805)965-5010
Provides information about waste collection, management, recycling, and disposal. ***Frequency:*** 8x/yr.

★6476★ Waste Management Research and Education Institute Newsletter
Waste Management Research and Education Inst.
Univ. of Tennessee at Knoxville
327 S. Stadium Hall
Knoxville, TN 37996-0710
Phone: (615)974-4251
Discusses policy analysis and environmental biotechnology research of the Institute. ***Editor(s):*** Jean H. Peretz. ***Frequency:*** Quarterly. ***Price:*** Free.

★6477★ Waste Recovery Report
ICON, Inc.
211 S. 45th St.
Philadelphia, PA 19104
Phone: (215)349-6500
Contains news of the recycling, waste-to-energy, and other resource recovery fields. Supplies news on legislative and regulatory changes, new facilities and technologies, and environmental concerns. ***Editor(s):*** Alan Krigman. ***Frequency:*** Monthly. ***Price:*** $50/yr., U.S. and Canada; $75 elsewhere.

★6478★ Waste Treatment Technology News
Business Communications Company, Inc.
25 Van Zant St.
Norwalk, CT 06855
Phone: (203)325-2208
Provides information on technologies and developments in clean-up, control, recycling, and disposal necessary for effective management of industrial waste generated in the processing of energy, chemical, and minerals. Covers acid rain, water, and hazardous wastes. ***Frequency:*** Monthly.

★6479★ Waste Watch
Div. of Solid Waste Management
Dept. of Environmental Quality Engineering
1 Winter St., 4th Fl.
Boston, MA 02108
Phone: (617)292-5989
Reports solid waste management programs implemented in Massachusetts. Includes news on landfill cleanup, solid waste regulations, recycling programs, and compost projects. ***Editor(s):*** Natalie U. Roy. ***Frequency:*** Quarterly.

★6480★ Water and Energy Research Institute of the Western Pacific Newsletter
Water and Energy Research Inst. of the Western Pacific
Univ. of Guam
UOG Station, GU 96923
Phone: (671)734-3132
Reports on research and other activities regarding water and energy research. ***Editor(s):*** Paulette M. Coulter. ***Frequency:*** 2-3/yr. ***Price:*** Free.

★6481★ Water Connection
New England Interstate Water Pollution Control Commn.
85 Merrimac St.
Boston, MA 02114
Phone: (617)437-1524
Discusses regional water quality, air quality, and hazardous waste management issues. Reports on state and federal legislation and program

developments, and Commission activities. ***Editor(s):*** Ellen Frye. ***Frequency:*** Quarterly. ***Price:*** Free.

★6482★ Water Impacts
Inst. of Water Research
Michigan State Univ.
334 Natural Resources Bldg.
East Lansing, MI 48824
Phone: (517)353-3742
Fax: (517)353-1812
Concerned with water quality in Michigan and the Great Lakes region. Reports on scientific research and examines problems such as groundwater contamination and the competition for water use through irrigation or diversion of the Great Lakes. Also monitors the status of federal and state legislation affecting water quality and resources. ***Editor(s):*** Lois Wolfson. ***Frequency:*** Monthly. ***Price:*** Free.

★6483★ Water Pollution Control Federation Highlights
Water Pollution Control Fed.
601 Wythe St.
Alexandria, VA 22314
Phone: (703)684-2400
Carries news of the Federation, its members, committees, and member associations. ***Editor(s):*** Nancy Blatt. ***Frequency:*** Monthly. ***Price:*** Included in membership.

★6484★ Waterfront World
Waterfront Center
1536 44th St., N.W.
Washington, DC 20007
Phone: (202)337-0356
Covers issues and case examples of changes on urban waterfronts, principally in North America. Includes conservation and preservation interests, civic art, public access, commercial installations and other reuse of ignored waterfront territory. ***Editor(s):*** Ann Breen and Dick Rigby. ***Frequency:*** 6/yr. ***Price:*** $35/yr. for individuals, $55 for groups, U.S.; $34 for individuals, $60 for groups, Canada; $36 for individuals, $62 for groups elsewhere.

★6485★ Wellfleet Bay Wildlife Sanctuary Newsletter
Massachusetts Audubon Soc.
PO Box 236
South Wellfleet, MA 02663
Phone: (508)349-2615
Contains news and announcements of programs offered by the Sanctuary. ***Frequency:*** 4/yr. ***Price:*** Included in membership; free to Sanctuary visitors.

★6486★ Wetland News
Association of State Wetland Managers
PO Box 2463
Berne, NY 12023
Phone: (518)872-1804
Frequency: 4/year.

★6487★ Whale Adoption Project Newsletter
Whale Adoption Project
International Wildlife Coalition
634 N. Falmouth Hwy.
Box 388
North Falmouth, MA 02556
Phone: (508)564-9980
Fax: (508)563-2843
Informs members as to the progress of the Coalition's whale adoption project. ***Frequency:*** Quarterly. ***Price:*** $15/yr.

★6488★ Whale One Dispatch
Pacific Whale Found.
Kealia Beach Plaza, Ste. 25
101 N. Kihei Rd.
Kihei, HI 96753
Phone: (808)879-8811
Fax: (808)879-2615
Internship newsletter. ***Frequency:*** Periodic.

★6489★ Whitetails Unlimited Insider
Whitetails Unlimited
PO Box 422
Sturgeon Bay, WI 54235
Phone: (414)743-6777
Frequency: Periodic.

★6490★ Wild Canid Survival and Research Center—Wolf Sanctuary Bulletin
Wild Canid Survival and Research Center—Wolf Sanctuary
PO Box 760
Eureka, MO 63025
Phone: (314)938-5900
Frequency: Quarterly.

★6491★ Wild Flower Notes
New England WildFlower Soc.
c/o Barbara Pryor
Hemenway Rd.
Framingham, MA 01701
Phone: (508)877-7630
Frequency: Annual.

★6492★ Wildlands News
Plymouth County Wildlands Trust
PO Box 1732
Plymouth, MA 02360
Phone: (617)934-9018
Discusses topics related to preserving natural areas in southeastern Massachusetts. ***Editor(s):*** Leo MacNeil. ***Frequency:*** Quarterly. ***Price:*** Free.

★6493★ Wildlife Conservation International News
Wildlife Conservation Intl.
New York Zoological Society
Bronx, NY 10460
Phone: (212)220-5090
Provides news and updates from the various projects sponsored by Wildlife Conservation International. Investigates the status of endangered species, habitats, and ecosystems in developing countries, primarily in Africa, Latin America, and Asia. ***Editor(s):*** Geoffrey Mellor. ***Frequency:*** Quarterly. ***Price:*** $23/yr. minimum donation requested.

★6494★ Wildlife in the News
Wildlife Habitat Enhancement Coun.
1010 Wayne Ave., Ste. 1240
Silver Spring, MD 20910
Phone: (301)588-8994
Includes symposia announcements and agenda. ***Frequency:*** Quarterly. ***Price:*** $20/year.

★6495★ Wildlife Issues and News
Wildlife Information Center
629 Green St.
Allentown, PA 18102
Phone: (215)434-1637
Frequency: Periodic.

★6496★ Wildlife News
African Wildlife Found.
1717 Massachusetts Ave., N.W.
Washington, DC 20036
Phone: (202)265-8393
Reports on the Foundation's work training and supporting Africans in wildlife protection, ecology, and park and reserve management. Carries news of the Foundation's field offices in Kenya and Rwanda, its schools of wildlife management in Tanzania and Cameroon, and its conservation clubs throughout Africa. ***Editor(s):*** Diana McMeekin. ***Frequency:*** Quarterly. ***Price:*** Included in membership.

★6497★ Wildlife Report
National Audubon Soc.
950 Third Ave.
New York, NY 10022
Phone: (212)832-3200

★6498★ Wildlife Resource Notes
Environmental Laboratory
USAE Waterways Experiment Station
c/o CEWES-ER-R/C.O. Martin
3909 Halls Ferry Rd.
Vicksburg, MS 39180-6199
Phone: (601)634-3958
Contains articles on wildlife and natural resource activities and management applicable to civil works projects. Serves as a technology transfer medium for providing natural resource information to district and project offices. ***Editor(s):*** Chester O. Martin. ***Frequency:*** Quarterly. ***Price:*** Free.

★6499★ The Wildlifer
Wildlife Soc.
5410 Grosvenor Ln.
Bethesda, MD 20814
Phone: (301)897-9770
Serves as the Society's official publication of record. Contains items on section and chapter activities, meetings of interest, career notes, job opportunities, and timely articles on significant developments in conservation issues. ***Editor(s):*** Harry E. Hodgdon. ***Frequency:*** Bimonthly. ***Price:*** $21/yr.; $11 for students.

★6500★ Wind Energy Technology
National Technical Information Service
U.S. Dept. of Commerce
5285 Port Royal Rd.
Springfield, VA 22161
Phone: (703)487-4630
Abstracts worldwide information on all aspects of energy from the wind. ***Frequency:*** Bimonthly. ***Price:*** $100/yr., U.S., Canada, and Mexico; $200 elsewhere.

★6501★ The Windwalker
Birds of Prey Rehabilitation Found.
RR 2, Box 659
Broomfield, CA 80020
Phone: (303)460-0674
Frequency: Annual.

★6502★ Wisconsin Energy News
Wisconsin Energy Bur.
PO Box 7868
Madison, WI 53707
Phone: (608)266-8871
Fax: (608)266-2164
Covers programs, policies, and research in energy conservation, renewable energy technology, and other energy resources in Wisconsin and the Upper Midwest. Monitors state, regional, and national issues and events. ***Editor(s):*** Barbara Samuel. ***Frequency:*** Bimonthly. ***Price:*** Free.

★6503★ Wolf Park News
North Amer. Wildlife Park Foundation, Inc.
Wolf Park
Battle Ground, IN 47920
Phone: (317)567-2265
Fax: (317)567-2084
Profiles individual wolves at the Park and the progress of fundraising. Disseminates news about animal issues and related legislation.

Editor(s): Barbara Fischler. ***Frequency:*** Quarterly. ***Price:*** Included in membership.

★6504★ Woodland Report
National Woodland Owners Assn.
374 Maple Ave., E., Ste. 204
Vienna, VA 22180
Phone: (703)255-2700
Covers view of private landowners on forestry, wildlife, and resource conservation issues. Reports legislative and association news from Washington, D.C. and state capitals. ***Editor(s):*** Keith A. Argow. ***Frequency:*** 8/yr. ***Price:*** Included in membership.

★6505★ Words on Wilderness
Badger Chapter/Glacier-Two
Medicine Alliance
Box 8374
Missoula, MT 59807
Phone: (406)243-5361
Addresses the status of and threats to the wildlife and wildlands in U.S. Forest Service Lands on the Rocky Mountain front of Montana. ***Editor(s):*** Susan VanRooy. ***Frequency:*** 1-2/quarter. ***Price:*** Free.

★6506★ World Association of Soil and Water Conservation Newsletter
World Assn. of Soil and Water Conservation
7515 NE Ankeny Rd.
Ankeny, IA 50021
Phone: (515)289-2331
Fax: (515)289-1227
Frequency: Quarterly.

★6507★ World Birdwatch
International Coun. for Bird Preservation, U.S. Sect.
c/o World Wildlife Fund
1250 24th St. NW
Washington, DC 20037
Phone: (202)778-9563
Fax: (202)293-9211
Frequency: Bimonthly.

★6508★ World Environment Center Newsletter
World Environment Center
419 Park Ave., S., Ste. 1404
New York, NY 10016
Phone: (212)683-4700
Fax: (212)683-5053
Frequency: Periodic.

★6509★ World Nature News
World Nature Association, Inc.
708 Valley Rd.
Upper Montclair, NJ 07043
Phone: (201)744-6070
Provides news on federal legislation concerning conservation. ***Editor(s):*** Martha Belote. ***Frequency:*** Biennial. ***Price:*** Included in membership.

★6510★ World Peace One Newsletter
World Peace One
c/o Linda Muelkin
7114 Idlewild
St. Louis, MO 63136
Phone: (314)385-8510
Features information on current economic and environmental issues and reports on the actions and experiences of those living out peace pacts; includes calendar of events. ***Frequency:*** Bimonthly.

★6511★ World Pheasant Association of the U.S.A. Newsletter
World Pheasant Assn. of the U.S.A.
2412 Arrowmill St.
Los Angeles, CA 90023
Phone: (213)262-5143
Frequency: Quarterly.

★6512★ World Research News
World Research Found.
15300 Ventura Blvd., Ste. 405
Sherman Oaks, CA 91403
Phone: (818)907-5483
Frequency: Monthly.

★6513★ World Wildlife Fund & Conservation Foundation Letter
The Conservation Foundation, Inc.
1250 24th St., N.W.
Washington, DC 20037
Phone: (202)293-4800
Fax: (202)923-9211
Presents an in-depth analysis of a specific environmental issue. Reports on activities within the Foundation. ***Editor(s):*** Jonathan Adams. ***Frequency:*** Bimonthly. ***Price:*** Free.

★6514★ World Wildlife Fund—Focus
The Conservation Foundation, Inc.
1250 24th St., N.W., 500
Washington, DC 20037
Phone: (202)293-4800
Fax: (202)293-9211
Covers the World Wildlife Fund-U.S., concerns endangered wildlife and habitats around the world, and protecting biological resources. Discusses issues such as acid rain, migratory birds, development of national parks, illegal trade in wildlife, and the Lacey Act. ***Editor(s):*** Pamela S. Cubberly. ***Frequency:*** Bimonthly. ***Price:*** Included in membership.

★6515★ Worldwide Energy
Worldwide Videotex
Babson Park
P.O. Box 138
Boston, MA 02157
Phone: (617)449-1603
Provides news and information on types of energy sources and applications including oil, gas, coal, nuclear, and the latest energy alternatives. Covers exploration and operation of various energy sources. ***Frequency:*** Monthly.

★6516★ WorldWIDE News
World Women in the Environment
1331 H St. NW, Ste. 903
Washington, DC 20005
Phone: (202)347-1514
Fax: (202)347-1524
Frequency: Bimonthly.

★6517★ YES Newsletter
Legacy Intl.
346 Commerce St.
Alexandria, VA 22314
Phone: (703)549-3630
Fax: (703)549-0262
Frequency: 3/year.

Videos

★6518★ The 29th Day
Pennsylvania State Univ. AV Services
University Division of Media & Learning Resources
Special Services Bldg.
Pennsylvania State University
University Park, PA 16802
Phone: (814)865-6314
1978. 29 mins. From the "Finite Earth Series." A program of examples that explain the mathematical concept of exponential growth in terms of the consumption of our finite natural resources.

★6519★ 500 Miles to Earth
New York State Education Dept.
Center for Learning Technologies
Media Distribution Network
Room C-7, Concourse Level
Albany, NY 12230
Phone: (518)474-1265
1975. 30 mins. This program shows how Earth Resource Monitoring from satellites can detect various forms of pollution.

★6520★ Acadia National Park and Cape Cod National Seashore
Finley-Holiday Film Corp.
PO Box 619
Whittier, CA 90608
Phone: (213)945-3325
1980. 30 mins. Two short films look respectively at the two national tourist sites.

★6521★ Acid Precipitation: Particles and Rain
Film Fair Communications
10900 Ventura Blvd.
PO Box 1728
Studio City, CA 91604
Phone: (818)985-0244
1984. 16 mins. This tape examines the problem of acid rain.

★6522★ Acid Rain
Film Fair Communications
10900 Ventura Blvd.
PO Box 1728
Studio City, CA 91604
Phone: (818)985-0244
1984. 17 mins. A comprehensive and basic view of the causes and disastrous effects of acid rain on the environment; for students.

★6523★ Acid Rain
Time-Life Video
1271 Ave. of the Americas
New York, NY 10020
Phone: (212)484-5940
1984. 57 mins. An in-depth look at this phenomenal environmental problem, first aired as an episode of NOVA.

★6524★ Acid Rain
Films for the Humanities
743 Alexander Rd.
Princeton, NJ 08540
Phone: (609)452-1128
1989. 20 mins. Gives history and explanation of acid rain, including chemical definitions, geological and meteorological interactions, and traces the sources of acid precipitation. Ecological concepts and possible solutions are demonstrated.

★6525★ Acid Rain: A North American Challenge
National Film Bd. of Canada
16th Fl.
1251 Ave. of the Americas
New York, NY 10020-1173
Phone: (212)586-5131
1988. 16 mins. A shortened version of the film "Trouble in the Forest," the film summarizes what we know about the scourge of acid rain.

★6526★ Acid Rain: Requiem or Recovery
Direct Cinema Limited, Inc.
Box 69799
Los Angeles, CA 90069
Phone: (213)652-8000
1983. 27 mins. Documentary footage, graphs and animation help to provide a basic understanding of what acid rain is and where it originates.

★6527★ Acid Rain: The Choice Is Ours
TV Sports Scene, Inc.
5804 Ayrshire Blvd.
Minneapolis, MN 55436
Phone: (612)925-9661
1982. 20 mins. A study of the environmental killer: acid rain. Acid precipitation, attributed to increased fossil fuel consumption in industrial regions of Europe and North America, is examined for its negative effects on life.

★6528★ Acid Rainbows
PBS Video
1320 Braddock Pl.
Alexandria, VA 22314-1698
Phone: (703)739-5380
1988. 30 mins. Acid rain and its effects are just beginning to poison the once pristine air of the Rockies and the southwest.

★6529★ The Adirondacks
Direct Cinema Limited, Inc.
Box 69799
Los Angeles, CA 90069
Phone: (213)652-8000
1987. 30 mins. A visually striking portrait of the Adirondack Park of New York State, the largest wilderness area in the Eastern United States.

★6530★ After the Whale
Time-Life Video
1271 Ave. of the Americas
New York, NY 10020
Phone: (212)484-5940
1971. 30 mins. Studies the behavior of the whale, a marvelous creature on the verge of extinction. From the "Life Around Us" series.

★6531★ The Aging of Lakes
Britannica Films
310 S. Michigan Ave.
Chicago, IL 60604
Phone: (312)347-7958
1971. 14 mins. Introduces geological and ecological factors of normal aging of lakes and shows how man is speeding up this natural process by indiscriminate disposal of sewage, fertilizers, and industrial waste.

★6532★ AIMS MEDIA, Inc.—Resources
AIMS Media, Inc.
6901 Woodley Ave.
Van Nuys, CA 91406-4878
Phone: (818)785-4111
1981. 9 mins. For kids, this tape is a look at conservation alternatives regarding mineral, agricultural and other natural resources.

★6533★ Air Is Life
International Film Bureau, Inc.
332 S. Michigan Ave.
Chicago, IL 60604-4382
Phone: (312)427-4545
1978. 16 mins. Discusses the threat of air pollution, gives a global perspective of the problem, and suggests possible solutions.

★6534★ Air Pollution: A First Film
Phoenix/BFA Films
468 Park Ave. South
New York, NY 10016
Phone: (212)684-5910
1985. 12 mins. This revised program updates the subject of air pollution, and offers suggestions on how to keep this problem under control.

★6535★ Air Pollution and Solid Wastes
University of Wisconsin Extension
Department of Engineering & Applied Science
432 N. Lake St.
Madison, WI 53706
Phone: (608)262-2061
1977. 30 mins. The basic chemistry and problems of air pollution control both in work places and the community as a whole are covered in this module course. The problems of solid waste recovery and recycling are examined. Programs below are also available individually. Part of the "Environmental Engineering" series.

★6536★ Air Pollution: Outdoor
Films for the Humanities
743 Alexander Rd.
Princeton, NJ 08540
Phone: (609)452-1128
1989. 26 mins. A tape that explores the burning of fuels, methods to burn fuel more efficiently with less hazardous by-products, the filtering out of pollutants, safe recycling and disposal of by-products, and the state of research on new and cleaner fuels and combustion methods.

★6537★ Air Pollution: Sweetening the Air
Cinema Guild
1697 Broadway
Room 802
New York, NY 10019
Phone: (212)246-5522
20 mins. This film explains the laws of entropy and demonstrates that through effort and invention, desire and legislative action, even the harmful pollutants of modern man can be changed into useful forms.

★6538★ Altered Environments: An Inquiry into the American Wildlands
Phoenix/BFA Films
468 Park Ave. South
New York, NY 10016
Phone: (212)684-5910
1970. 10 mins. This program raises questions about the values to be found in remaining wildlands and involves students in decisions about future use of our wild areas.

★6539★ Amazing Grace
National AudioVisual Center
National Archives & Records Administration
Customer Services Section PZ
8700 Edgeworth Dr.
Capitol Heights, MD 20743-3701
Phone: (301)763-1896
1979. 10 mins. Filmed in the Sequoia National Park in California, this program gives an enchanting look at the giant Sequoia in all seasons.

★6540★ The Amazon: A Vanishing Rainforest
Cinema Guild
1697 Broadway
Room 802
New York, NY 10019
Phone: (212)246-5522
1988. 29 mins. The destruction of the Amazon tropical rainforest is documented. Examines clear cutting of the forest to raise beef cattle, the planned construction of a hydroelectric dam, and the effects these and other man-made developments are having on the whole ecosystem.

★6541★ The American Island
National AudioVisual Center
National Archives & Records Administration
Customer Services Section PZ
8700 Edgeworth Dr.
Capitol Heights, MD 20743-3701
Phone: (301)763-1896
1970. 29 mins. A discussion of one of America's last unspoiled resources; her islands. Shows how intelligent planning for use provides a variety of recreational activities and protects the environment for future generations.

★6542★ America's Environment
Dallas County Community Coll. District
Center for Telecommunications
4343 North Hwy. 67
Mesquite, TX 75150-2095
Phone: (214)324-7988
1980. 28 mins. This program examines how America has treated and used its lands from a historical perspective.

★6543★ America's National Parks
Visual Horizons
180 Metro Park
Rochester, NY 14623-2666
Phone: (716)424-5300
1988. 30 mins. See Mount Rushmore, the redwood forests and many more of the nation's wildlife reserves.

★6544★ America's Wetlands
Media Design Associates, Inc.
PO Box 3189
Boulder, CO 80307-3189
Phone: (303)443-2800
1988. 28 mins. The benefits of swamps and marshes are discussed.

★6545★ And God Created Whales
Filmakers Library, Inc.
133 E. 58th St.
New York, NY 10022
Phone: (212)355-6545
1979. 28 mins. This program provides detailed information on the habits of the killer whale.

★6546★ Antarctica
Films for the Humanities
743 Alexander Rd.
Princeton, NJ 08540
Phone: (609)452-1128
1989. 26 mins. This tape explores Antarctica and the use of this continent as a garbage dump and details the geography of Antarctica and the discovery of the depletion of the ozone layer in that region.

★6547★ Arches
Eastman Kodak Company
c/o Wood Knapp
Knapp Press
5900 Wilshire Blvd.
Los Angeles, CA 90036
Phone: (213)937-5486
1989. 30 mins. The wind, sand and water process that created the famous rock formations in this Utah park are shown.

★6548★ At the Crossroads
Marty Stouffer Productions, Ltd.
300 S. Spring St.
Aspen, CO 81611
Phone: (303)925-5536
1975. 26 mins. This exploration of wildlife's struggle for survival presents many endangered mammals, birds, and fishes that have never been filmed before.

★6549★ The Atom and the Environment
Handel Film Corp.
8730 Sunset Blvd.
West Hollywood, CA 90069
Phone: (213)657-8990
1971. 22 mins. A look at how nuclear energy relates to our ecology.

★6550★ The Bald Eagle in New Jersey
New Jersey Network
1573 Parkside Ave.
Trenton, NJ 08625
Phone: (609)292-5252
1985. 30 mins. This film follows the efforts of conservationists to prevent the bald eagle's impending extinction.

★6551★ Banking on Disaster
Bullfrog Films, Inc.
PO Box 149
Oley, PA 19547
Phone: (215)779-8226
1988. 78 mins. A unique and vitally important documentary about this century's worst environmental disaster - the destruction of the Amazon rain forest.

★6552★ Before the Mountain Was Moved
CRM/McGraw-Hill Films
674 Via de la Valle
PO Box 641
Del Mar, CA 92014
Phone: (619)453-5000
1971. 58 mins. This program is the story of how a miner and his people fought to save the mountains of Raleigh County, West Virginia from being strip mined. Along with this, they succeed in obtaining strong state legislation concerning environmental conservation. The program is available as a whole or in two parts.

★6553★ Big Bend Encounter
National AudioVisual Center
National Archives & Records Administration
Customer Services Section PZ
8700 Edgeworth Dr.
Capitol Heights, MD 20743-3701
Phone: (301)763-1896
1986. 12 mins. This is a film of the wildlife in Big Bend National Park in Texas, as shown in that park to visitors, and newly available outside of Texas.

★6554★ Big Bend National Park, Texas
Finley-Holiday Film Corp.
PO Box 619
Whittier, CA 90608
Phone: (213)945-3325
1986. 30 mins. The river and its surrounding scenery are surveyed for the armchair tourist.

★6555★ The Bitter Rain
Journal Films, Inc.
930 Pitner Ave.
Evanston, IL 60202
Phone: (312)328-6700
22 mins. The long and short term effects and solutions to the acid rain problem in Scandinavia and Canada are documented.

★6556★ Bryce, Zion and Grand Canyon's North Rim
Finley-Holiday Film Corp.
PO Box 619
Whittier, CA 90608
Phone: (213)945-3325
1983. 25 mins. A visual tour through the three national parks.

★6557★ Bryce/Zion National Parks
Videocassette Marketing Corp.
137 Eucalyptus St.
El Segundo, CA 90245
Phone: (213)322-1140
1985. 60 mins. A video travelogue of the famous Utah parks.

★6558★ The Burial Ground
Commonwealth Films, Inc.
223 Commonwealth Ave.
Boston, MA 02116
Phone: (617)262-5634
1988. 30 mins. A story of industrial waste and environmental laws.

★6559★ The California Forum: Hazardous Wastes
University of California at Berkeley Educational TV Office
9 Dwinelle Hall
Berkeley, CA 94720
Phone: (415)642-2535
1983. 59 mins. Six expert panelists discuss the issues of hazardous waste in California, moderated by Ira Michael Heyman.

★6560★ Career Profiles: Environmental Series
Cambridge Career Products
One Players Club Dr.
Charleston, WV 25311
Phone: (304)344-8550
1989. 15 mins. Environmental careers of all sorts are examined.

★6561★ Caring About Our Community Series
AIMS Media, Inc.
6901 Woodley Ave.
Van Nuys, CA 91406-4878
Phone: (818)785-4111
1973. 49 mins. Films about individual responsibility and the environment. Programs available individually.

★6562★ Century III—Man and His Environment
National AudioVisual Center
National Archives & Records Administration
Customer Services Section PZ
8700 Edgeworth Dr.
Capitol Heights, MD 20743-3701
Phone: (301)763-1896
1978. 28 mins. This program speaks of man's efforts to stabilize the delicate balances of his environment through architecture, industrial and urban conservation, solar energy, and working models of small-scale rural self-sufficiency.

★6563★ Chain of Life
Indiana Univ. Audio-Visual Center
Bloomington, IN 47405-5901
Phone: (812)335-8087
1970. 30 mins. This program examines dangers to the environment, from pesticides used for crops to industrial chemical waste.

★6564★ The Challenge of Survival Series
Walt Disney Educational Media Company
500 S. Buena Vista St.
Burbank, CA 91521
Phone: 800-423-2555
1987. 11 mins. This series illustrates our current uses of land, water and chemicals, to create an awareness of the need for proper management of our resources.

★6565★ Challenge of Yellowstone
Harpers Ferry Historical Assn.
PO Box 197
Harpers Ferry, WV 25425
Phone: (304)535-6881
1980. 25 mins. This program traces the history of the national park idea from its origins at Yellowstone National Park to the conservation ethics of today's park system.

★6566★ The Chosen Place
New York State Education Dept.
Center for Learning Technologies
Media Distribution Network
Room C-7, Concourse Level
Albany, NY 12230
Phone: (518)474-1265
1986. 28 mins. A look at how biologists are creating projects that would help endangered animals survive environmental changes caused by industry.

★6567★ Cinema Guild—Water
Cinema Guild
1697 Broadway
Room 802
New York, NY 10019
Phone: (212)246-5522
1970. 20 mins. This film examines the availability of water and the pollution control measures necessary to keep it pure.

★6568★ Clean Water: What's in it for You
New York State Education Dept.
Center for Learning Technologies
Media Distribution Network
Room C-7, Concourse Level
Albany, NY 12230
Phone: (518)474-1265
19 mins. Sewage disposal remains a constant threat to the environment's clean water bodies, and this program discusses measures and actions being taken to resolve this crisis.

★6569★ Common Ground: Changing Values and the National Forests
Bullfrog Films, Inc.
PO Box 149
Oley, PA 19547
Phone: (215)779-8226
1978. 29 mins. A study of current forest policies in regard to conservation.

★6570★ Conserving Our Environment: The Pollution Crisis
Coronet/MTI Film & Video
108 Wilmot Rd.
Deerfield, IL 60015-9990
Phone: (312)940-1260
1972. 15 mins. An examination of the ways we are polluting our land, sea, and air, and various solutions for protecting our environment.

★6571★ Cooperation Across Boundaries: The Acid Rain Dilemma
Umbrella Films
60 Blake Rd.
Brookline, MA 02146
Phone: (617)277-6639
1988. 32 mins. The political dilemma of an environmental problem that crosses national borders, and possible solutions are discussed.

★6572★ Crops Protected: Water Threatened
Cornell Univ.
Media Services Distribution Center
7-8 Research Park
Ithaca, NY 14850
Phone: (607)255-2091
1982. 20 mins. The danger pesticides pose to water supplies is examined.

★6573★ The Cry of the Beluga
Icarus Films
200 Park Ave. South
Suite 1319
New York, NY 10003
Phone: (212)674-3375
1989. 51 mins. Depicts the struggle of conservationists to save the beluga whales, dying from pollution, in the St. Lawrence estuary.

★6574★ Cry of the Marsh
AIMS Media, Inc.
6901 Woodley Ave.
Van Nuys, CA 91406-4878
Phone: (818)785-4111
1972. 12 mins. Man's destruction of environment for farmland, urban development, and garbage dumps.

★6575★ Dammed Forever
TV Sports Scene, Inc.
5804 Ayrshire Blvd.
Minneapolis, MN 55436
Phone: (612)925-9661
1975. 28 mins. This program investigates man's construction of dams and the devastation of the Great Northwest Territory, and the effects on the salmon and other game fish that once abounded in the rivers of this territory.

★6576★ Death Valley
Finley-Holiday Film Corp.
PO Box 619
Whittier, CA 90608
Phone: (213)945-3325
1984. 26 mins. For tourists, a survey of the famed hot spot.

★6577★ Denali National Park, Alaska
International Video Network (IVN)
2242 Camino Ramon
San Ramon, CA 94583
Phone: (415)866-1121
1986. 45 mins. The park which houses Mt. McKinley, bears, and moose is seen in both winter and spring.

★6578★ Denali Wilderness
Finley-Holiday Film Corp.
PO Box 619
Whittier, CA 90608
Phone: (213)945-3325
1979. 30 mins. Alaska's Denali National Park is the backdrop for a year-round struggle for survival. Wolves, grizzlies, moose and caribou are depicted in dramatic life-and-death sequences in this snowy, desolate environment.

★6579★ Designing the Environment
NETCHE (Nebraska ETV Coun. for Higher Education)
Box 83111
Lincoln, NE 68501
Phone: (402)472-3611
1971. 30 mins. This three lesson series is designed to assist the student in becoming more familiar with the problems, causes, and long-term results of man-induced environmental changes.

★6580★ Deterioration of Water
Learning Corp. of America
108 Wilmot Rd.
Deerfield, IL 60015-9990
Phone: (312)940-1260
1972. 20 mins. Describes the cyclical nature of water, illustrates sources and hazards of water pollution, and discusses prevention methods such as better sewage treatment, recycling of garbage, and wise consumerism.

★6581★ Disappearance of the Great Rainforest
Arthur Mokin Productions, Inc.
PO Box 1866
Santa Rosa, CA 95402-1866
Phone: (707)542-4868
1983. 12 mins. An investigation into the studies that scientists have done on the effects of deforestation in the Amazon.

★6582★ Do No Harm
Michigan Media
University of Michigan
400 Fourth St.
Ann Arbor, MI 48109
Phone: (313)764-8228
1976. 29 mins. An introduction to the concept of technology assessment and what judgments this assessment entitles us to make. Part of "On to Tomorrow" series.

★6583★ Do We Really Need the Rockies?
Time-Life Video
1271 Ave. of the Americas
New York, NY 10020
Phone: (212)484-5940
1981. 57 mins. This entry in the "Nova" series investigates the pros and cons of shale oil production in the western Rocky Mountains. Although full of oil, every attempt to extract the fuel thus far has proved too costly and environmentally unsound.

★6584★ Dr. Seuss: Lorax
Playhouse Video
1211 Ave. of the Americas
New York, NY 10036
Phone: (212)819-3238
1971. 48 mins. An environmentally concerned tale about a creature trying to preserve his world against over-development.

★6585★ Dolly Sods
Maryland Center for Public Broadcasting
11767 Bonita Ave.
Owings Mills, MD 21117
Phone: (301)356-5600
30 mins. As part of the Monongahela National Forest, Dolly Sods contains arctic vegetation, moss and cranberry bogs, and beaver ponds.

★6586★ Dolphin
Media Guild
11722 Sorrento Valley Rd.
Suite E
San Diego, CA 92121
Phone: (619)755-9191
1978. 22 mins. Takes us to aquariums where dolphins are trained and where their intelligence is being studied. Part of the "Animals, Animals, Animals" series.

★6587★ Dolphins
National Geographic Soc.
17th & M Streets NW
Washington, DC 20036
Phone: (202)857-7378
1983. 15 mins. This program introduces young students to dolphins, explains that they are mammals, and gives demonstrations of their intelligence.

★6588★ Dolphins in the Zoo
Britannica Films
310 S. Michigan Ave.
Chicago, IL 60604
Phone: (312)347-7958
1979. 12 mins. Explains how zoos try to keep the dolphins' environment as close to the natural state as possible, and shows how their abilities and personalities are brought out through training.

★6589★ Double Life of the Whooping Crane, The
Beacon Films
930 Pinter Ave.
Evanston, IL 60202
Phone: (312)328-6700
1983. 15 mins. This program from the "North American Species" series studies the remaining wild flock of the rare whooping crane.

★6590★ Down in the Dumps
Films for the Humanities
743 Alexander Rd.
Princeton, NJ 08540
Phone: (609)452-1128
1989. 26 mins. Technological approaches to garbage disposal are explained, including composting, resource recovery, and high-tech incinerators, and public reaction to the development of new waste treatment facilities.

★6591★ Down the Drain
VCA Teletronics
50 Leyland Dr.
Leonia, NJ 17605
Toll-Free: 800-822-1105
Produced by 3-2-1 Contact Extras and Children's Television Workshop, this 30-minute program deals with the subject of water. For children ages 8-12 and their families. ***Price:*** $14.95.

★6592★ Down to Earth
Journal Films, Inc.
930 Pitner Ave.
Evanston, IL 60202
Phone: (312)328-6700
1984. 28 mins. This program documents three applications where satellites have been used to improve the quality of life.

★6593★ Down to the Last Drop
Films for the Humanities
743 Alexander Rd.
Princeton, NJ 08540
Phone: (609)452-1128
1989. 26 mins. Examines water management techniques in Israel and the U.S. where conservation and resource management are emphasized. Also examines the management strategy of a groundwater planning project in Manasquan, New Jersey.

★6594★ Down Wind/Down Stream
Bullfrog Films, Inc.
PO Box 149
Oley, PA 19547
Phone: (215)779-8226
1987. 58 mins. A documentary on environmental issues in the Southwest.

★6595★ Draggerman's Haul
Film Fair Communications
10900 Ventura Blvd.
PO Box 1728
Studio City, CA 91604
Phone: (818)985-0244
1971. 12 mins. Shows how pollution and conservation policies are a threat to natural resources. Follows a fleet of fishermen fishing by a modern factory and tells of the dangers involved.

★6596★ The Drowning Bay
Phoenix/BFA Films
468 Park Ave. South
New York, NY 10016
Phone: (212)684-5910
1970. 9 mins. "The Drowning Bay" vividly illustrates the ecological plight of a city which has allowed pollution to destroy a major part of a famous and scenic natural resource.

★6597★ Durrell in Russia
Crocus Entertainment, Inc.
762 Twelve Oaks Center
15500 Wayzata Blvd.
Wayzata, MN 55391
Phone: (612)473-9002
1990. 30 mins. The noted naturalists Gerald and Lee Durrell explore the people, places and wildlife of the Soviet Union, including many locations never before seen by western eyes.

★6598★ The Eagleman
Centre Productions, Inc.
1800 30th St.
Suite 207
Boulder, CO 80301
Phone: (303)444-1166
1988. 20 mins. This program features generous portions of footage of the endangered golden eagle populations in this country.

★6599★ The Earth Day Special
Warner Home Video, Inc.
4000 Warner Blvd.
Burbank, CA 91522
Phone: (818)954-6000
1990. 95 mins. The episodic conservationist TV special, featuring a myriad of stars acting out environmentally-aware vignettes.

★6600★ Earth Education Slide Show
Institute for Earth Education
P.O. Box 288
Warrenville, IL 60555
Phone: (509)395-2299
This slide/tape show presents an introduction to the appreciation and understanding upon which Earth education is based. Lasting twenty minutes, over 120 slides are presented. ***Price:*** $100.00.

★6601★ Earth First: The Struggle for the Australian Rainforest
Educational Film & Video Project
5332 College Ave.
Suite 101
Oakland, CA 94618
Phone: (415)655-9050
1986. 58 mins. This remarkable film documents the plight of Australia's once mighty rainforest and the people trying to save the remaining acreage of the continents primeval past.

★6602★ The Earth: Its Atmosphere
Coronet/MTI Film & Video
108 Wilmot Rd.
Deerfield, IL 60015-9990
Phone: (312)940-1260
1982. 9 mins. The structure, characteristics, and importance of the earth's atmosphere are shown. One of a series on the earth.

★6603★ Earth: No Vacancy
Cinema Guild
1697 Broadway
Room 802
New York, NY 10019
Phone: (212)246-5522
19 mins. This film reviews the evidence suggesting our planet faces chaos by the year 2040 if nothing is done to stunt the population growth and increase discovery of natural resources. It describes the efforts proponents of zero population growth have undertaken to stabilize population growth.

★6604★ Earth People
Phoenix/BFA Films
468 Park Ave. South
New York, NY 10016
Phone: (212)684-5910
1975. 54 mins. This program documents the efforts to make companies polluting the Monongahela River accountable for their damage. It is also available as three shorter programs: "Save the Water," "Save the Air," and "Recycle and Earth Day."

★6605★ Earth Science: Water vs. Land
Indiana Univ. Audio-Visual Center
Bloomington, IN 47405-5901
Phone: (812)335-8087
1974. 16 mins. A look at how water is continually leveling the land through weathering, erosion, and depositing of wastes.

★6606★ Earth's Physical Resources
Media Guild
11722 Sorrento Valley Rd.
Suite E
San Diego, CA 92121
Phone: (619)755-9191
1985. 50 mins. This video, part of the Energy Education Series, examines the finite resources of the earth that humans have come to depend on. Includes information on water, building stone, metals, and fossil fuels.

★6607★ Ebb Tide at Mono Lake
California Dept. of Water Resources
PO Box 388
Sacramento, CA 95802
Phone: (916)445-8569
1981. 11 mins. This program discusses solutions to the problem of Mono Lake's drop in elevation which is detrimental to the ecology.

★6608★ Echo in the Island
Centre Productions, Inc.
1800 30th St.
Suite 207
Boulder, CO 80301
Phone: (303)444-1166
1988. 18 mins. This thought-provoking documentary presents arguments for and against off-shore oil exploration and drilling on the California coast.

★6609★ Echoes of Denali
International Video Network
2242 Camino Ramon
San Ramon, CA 94583
Phone: (415)866-1121
1986. 30 mins. The viewer is taken up the slopes of Mt. McKinley.

★6610★ Ecology: Barry Commoner's Viewpoint
Britannica Films
310 S. Michigan Ave.
Chicago, IL 60604
Phone: (312)347-7958
1977. 19 mins. An introduction to ecology by one of America's most outspoken biologists. Dr. Barry Commoner explains the threat of technology to the environment by describing four principles of ecology.

★6611★ Ecology Primer
Amer. Educational Films
3807 Dickerson Rd.
Nashville, TN 37207
Phone: 800-822-5678
1973. 20 mins. A discussion of man's place and responsibilities in preserving "spaceship Earth."

★6612★ Ecology: The Silent Bomb
Cinema Guild
1697 Broadway
Room 802
New York, NY 10019
Phone: (212)246-5522
20 mins. The use of computers and technology in solving our environmental problems, our future energy requirements and using the thermo-nuclear reaction for peaceful purposes is discussed.

★6613★ Ecology...Wanted Alive?
AIMS Media, Inc.
6901 Woodley Ave.
Van Nuys, CA 91406-4878
Phone: (818)785-4111
1972. 10 mins. A view of the endangered species of animals and birds that have become extinct through man's destruction of their natural environment.

★6614★ E.F. Schumacher...As if People Mattered
Bullfrog Films, Inc.
PO Box 149
Oley, PA 19547
Phone: (215)779-8226
1978. 16 mins. This program was made in Montana, a resource-rich western state experiencing the full effects of America's energy addiction. Schumacher describes what he terms "internal colonization" as being the development of parts of countries, not for their own sake but to serve the needs of large commercial and industrial centers. The result of this behavior is a top-heavy economy set for collapse once the resource is spent and a diminishing rural population resentful of the destruction of the landscape.

★6615★ The Effluents of Affluence
Michigan Media
University of Michigan
400 Fourth St.
Ann Arbor, MI 48109
Phone: (313)764-8228
1978. 29 mins. A look at current waste disposal methods - land fills and metal reclamation - and a survey of the requirements and potential of resource recovery. Part of the "Future without Shock" series.

★6616★ Endangered Species of New Jersey
New Jersey Network
1573 Parkside Ave.
Trenton, NJ 08625
Phone: (609)292-5252
1975. 20 mins. A visual study of the fifteen endangered species inhabiting New Jersey and how environmentalists are fighting to keep these creatures in the balance of nature.

★6617★ Energy Alternatives
Dallas County Community Coll. District
Center for Telecommunications
4343 North Hwy. 67
Mesquite, TX 75150-2095
Phone: (214)324-7988
1977. 29 mins. This program presents topics such as hydroelectric, tidal, and nuclear power as alternatives to oil.

★6618★ Energy Alternatives
National Aeronautics and Space Administration
Lewis Audiovisual Library
6100 Columbus Ave.
Sandusky, OH 44870
Phone: (419)626-2594
1979. 15 mins. An examination into the research being done on alternate sources of energy.

★6619★ Energy Alternatives II
Bergwall Productions
106 Charles Lindbergh Blvd.
Uniondale, NY 11553-3695
Phone: (516)222-1111
1983. 42 mins. On 3 tapes, a look at renewable energy, energy conservation and an energy overview.

★6620★ Energy Alternatives: Solar
Films for the Humanities
743 Alexander Rd.
Princeton, NJ 08540
Phone: (609)452-1128
1989. 26 mins. An examination of the research of developing solar energy as an economical energy source and why the cost is prohibitive in the present market.

★6621★ Energy Conservation for the Home
University of Arizona VideoCampus
Harvill Bldg. #76
Box 4
Tucson, AZ 85721
Phone: (602)621-1735
1983. 60 mins. This series primarily covers those people, with homes in the desert southwest that were built between the 1950's and 1970's, who are concerned with energy conservation.

★6622★ Energy Crunch: The Best Way Out
Carousel Film & Video
260 Fifth Ave.
New York, NY 10016
Phone: (212)683-1660
1979. 51 mins. This documentary outlines practical and specific ways to conserve energy at home, in the community, and in industry. The potential of alternative energy sources is also explored.

★6623★ Energy-Efficient Living
Rodale Press, Inc.
33 E. Minor St.
Emmaus, PA 18049
Phone: (215)967-5171
1980. 55 mins. Amory and Hunter Lovins demonstrate their "soft path" approach to energy conservation in the first program on this cassette, "Lovins' on the Soft Path." The second program, "Living Lightly," documents the energy-efficient lifestyle of a 76-year-old rural mountain woman.

★6624★ Energy from the Day Star
Modern Talking Picture Service
5000 Park Street N.
St. Petersburg, FL 33709
Phone: (813)541-7571
1984. 27 mins. Builders, architects, and homeowners show how the sun can provide energy in light of dwindling fossil fuel sources.

★6625★ Energy from the Sun
Britannica Films
310 S. Michigan Ave.
Chicago, IL 60604
Phone: (312)347-7958
1980. 18 mins. The program shows the various ways modern technology is used to capture and

store the sun's energy. The sun is said to be an alternative to fossil fuel and a key to developing domestic energy sources for the future.

★6626★ Energy in the '80's
Amer. Inst. of Physics
Public Information Division
335 E. 45th St.
New York, NY 10017
Phone: (212)661-9404
1987. 10 mins. A short series of reports on progress in energy management, including looks at fusion energy, solar power, and recycling fuel.

★6627★ Energy Problems
Dallas County Community Coll. District
Center for Telecommunications
4343 North Hwy. 67
Mesquite, TX 75150-2095
Phone: (214)324-7988
1977. 29 mins. This program discusses the effects of the oil shortage on energy consumption.

★6628★ Energy: The Alternatives
Media Guild
11722 Sorrento Valley Rd.
Suite E
San Diego, CA 92121
Phone: (619)755-9191
1985. 24 mins. As the world continues to use up finite energy resources, new sources of energy must be found. This film explores alternative and renewable energy forms, including geothermal power, windmills, tidal flow, and alcohol fuels.

★6629★ The Environment
Amer. Inst. of Physics
Public Information Division
335 E. 45th St.
New York, NY 10017
Phone: (212)661-9404
1987. 10 mins. Short professional reports on various environmental issues, including airport noise pollution, waste dumps, carbon dioxide pollution and more.

★6630★ The Environment: Everything Around Us
Britannica Films
310 S. Michigan Ave.
Chicago, IL 60604
Phone: (312)347-7958
1972. 13 mins. Studies a variety of environments and observes man-made changes in each. Notes the harmful effects of pollutants on the environment.

★6631★ Environmental Engineering Series
University of Wisconsin Extension
Department of Engineering & Applied Science
432 N. Lake St.
Madison, WI 53706
Phone: (608)262-2061
1977. 30 mins. This course contains health aspects and the evolution of environmental concerns. Topics include water and wastewater treatment, air quality and pollution control, solid waste recovery and recycling, energy pollution of the environment, and noise and radiation concerns. The programs in this series are available individually, as four separate module courses, or as a whole.

★6632★ Environmental Geology
Dallas County Community Coll. District
Center for Telecommunications
4343 North Hwy. 67
Mesquite, TX 75150-2095
Phone: (214)324-7988
1979. 29 mins. This program emphasizes the importance of considering geological factors in the environment.

★6633★ Environmental Sciences Series
Learning Corp. of America
108 Wilmot Rd.
Deerfield, IL 60015-9990
Phone: (312)940-1260
1972. 17 mins. A series which studies the problems that face our environment due to air, water, land, and noise pollution. Possible solutions are discussed.

★6634★ Environmental Suicide Part I
University of Arizona
Biomedical Communications
Arizona Health Sciences Center
The University of Arizona
Tucson, AZ 85724
Phone: (602)626-7343
1973. 58 mins. Dr. Arthur Grollman discusses "Man and His Environment" and "Polluted Waters." Part one of a series of two.

★6635★ Environmental Suicide Part II
University of Arizona
Biomedical Communications
Arizona Health Sciences Center
The University of Arizona
Tucson, AZ 85724
Phone: (602)626-7343
1973. 53 mins. Dr. James T. Weston discusses "The Pathological Effects of Pollutants" and the "Psychiatric Aspects of Environmental Deterioration." Part of a series of two.

★6636★ The Everglades
AIMS Media, Inc.
6901 Woodley Ave.
Van Nuys, CA 91406-4878
Phone: (818)785-4111
1978. 7 mins. A conservationist's visual survey of the Everglades National Park.

★6637★ Fantastic Yellowstone
National AudioVisual Center
National Archives & Records Administration
Customer Services Section PZ
8700 Edgeworth Dr.
Capitol Heights, MD 20743-3701
Phone: (301)763-1896
1979. 25 mins. In 1872, Congress made Yellowstone the first national park. This visual account of the park includes the U.S. Army's operation in the early years.

★6638★ The Fence at Red Rim
University of California at Berkeley Extension Media Center
2176 Shattuck Ave.
Berkeley, CA 94704
Phone: (415)642-0460
1987. 30 mins. Environmentalists battle developers over what is to be done with a section of land in Wyoming.

★6639★ The Finite Earth Series
Pennsylvania State Univ. AV Services
University Division of Media & Learning Resources
Special Services Bldg.
Pennsylvania State University
University Park, PA 16802
Phone: (814)865-6314
1978. 29 mins. This series examines the limits of the earth's materials and energy resources, and the interrelationship of the consumption of materials, energy, food, and society.

★6640★ Food from the Rainforest
Media Guild
11722 Sorrento Valley Rd.
Suite E
San Diego, CA 92121
Phone: (619)755-9191
1987. 24 mins. The great diversity of life in tropical rainforests is being threatened by modern agriculture practices. This film examines slash and burn farming, the raising of crops which destroy already sensitive soils, and cattle ranching.

★6641★ For Earth's Sake: The Life and Times of David Brower
Bullfrog Films, Inc.
PO Box 149
Oley, PA 19547
Phone: (215)779-8226
1989. 58 mins. A profile of the historic battles which David Brower led to save many irreplacable natural wonders, revealing the gifts for lobbying, public persuasion, and moving others to action that he now brings to international conservation issues.

★6642★ Forever Wild
Agency for Instructional Technology
Box A
Bloomington, IN 47402
Phone: (812)339-2203
1987. 15 mins. A tape which emphasizes the responsible use of land.

★6643★ The Four Corners: A National Sacrifice Area
Bullfrog Films, Inc.
PO Box 149
Oley, PA 19547
Phone: (215)779-8226
1983. 58 mins. This documentary examines the cultural and environmental impact of energy development on the Colorado Plateau.

★6644★ From the Face of the Earth
Phoenix/BFA Films
468 Park Ave. South
New York, NY 10016
Phone: (212)684-5910
1970. 16 mins. Set in the year 2020, this program vividly underscores the value of our fragile natural resources and the awesome potential repercussions of our actions today.

★6645★ Gambling With Our Lives
Barr Films
3490 E. Foothill Blvd.
PO Box 5667
Pasadena, CA 91107
Phone: (213)681-2165
1978. 21 mins. A discussion of potential health hazards in the environment caused by substances that modern technology produces.

★6646★ The Garbage Explosion
Britannica Films
310 S. Michigan Ave.
Chicago, IL 60604
Phone: (312)347-7958
1970. 16 mins. Investigates the nature, volume, and composition of solid wastes, presents advantages and disadvantages of current disposal methods, and shows possible long-range solutions.

★6647★ Gentle on the Land
Ohio Univ. Telecommunications Center
9 S. College St.
Athens, OH 45701
Phone: (614)594-5244
1984. 30 mins. This program shows how environmentalists and architects worked together to bring the Raven Rocks project in Beallsville, Ohio to life.

★6648★ Glacier National Park
Norman Beerger Productions
3217 S. Arville St.
Las Vegas, NV 89102-7612
Phone: (702)876-2328
1989. 57 mins. General survey of the sights of America's northernmost national park. Recommended by the National Park Service.

★6649★ The Grand Canyon
RMI Media Productions, Inc.
2807 W. 47th St.
Shawnee Mission, KS 66205
Phone: (913)262-3974
1984. 120 mins. All the beauty and grandeur of the Grand Canyon is captured in this film.

★6650★ Grand Canyon: Amphitheater of the Gods
Norman Beerger Productions
3217 S. Arville St.
Las Vegas, NV 89102-7612
Phone: (702)876-2328
1988. 55 mins. Another video tour of the spectacular Grand Canyon.

★6651★ Grand Canyon National Park
Norman Beerger Productions
3217 S. Arville St.
Las Vegas, NV 89102-7612
Phone: (702)876-2328
1988. 55 mins. A panoramic look at the national treasure.

★6652★ Grand Canyon National Park
Videocassette Marketing Corp.
137 Eucalyptus St.
El Segundo, CA 90245
Phone: (213)322-1140
1985. 60 mins. A travelogue look at the famous American tourist site.

★6653★ The Grand Canyon of the Colorado
Rainbow Educational Video, Inc.
170 Keyland Ct.
Bohemia, NY 11716
Phone: (516)589-6643
1988. 18 mins. The history and geology of the Grand Canyon are the main topics of this tape.

★6654★ Grand Teton National Park
Finley-Holiday Film Corp.
PO Box 619
Whittier, CA 90608
Phone: (213)945-3325
1988. 30 mins. The amazing landscapes and wildlife of Wyoming are shown in this video.

★6655★ The Great Clean-Up
National AudioVisual Center
National Archives & Records Administration
Customer Services Section PZ
8700 Edgeworth Dr.
Capitol Heights, MD 20743-3701
Phone: (301)763-1896
1976. 53 mins. What remains to be done to stop the incredible pollution of the Great Lakes and what has been done are presented in this program.

★6656★ The Great Lakes: A Matter of Survival
Phoenix/BFA Films
468 Park Ave. South
New York, NY 10016
Phone: (212)684-5910
1972. 11 mins. This show is about what can be and is being done to save the Great Lakes.

★6657★ The Great Lakes: No Free Lunch
Michigan Media
University of Michigan
400 Fourth St.
Ann Arbor, MI 48109
Phone: (313)764-8228
1981. 30 mins. A graphic description of unforeseen costs associated with our use of the lakes, examining a number of problem areas including toxics, wetlands, erosion, dredging, winter navigation, and eutrophication.

★6658★ Great Lakes: Troubled Waters
Umbrella Films
60 Blake Rd.
Brookline, MA 02146
Phone: (617)277-6639
1988. 48 mins. The huge fresh water supply shared by America and Canada is now facing a growing threat from pollution.

★6659★ Great National Parks
International Video Network
2242 Camino Ramon
San Ramon, CA 94583
Phone: (415)866-1121
1988. 60 mins. A travel series on United States national parks, prepared through the auspices of Reader's Digest, featuring spectacular views of the natural wonders on display.

★6660★ Green Energy
Films for the Humanities
743 Alexander Rd.
Princeton, NJ 08540
Phone: (609)452-1128
1989. 26 mins. Renewable alternatives to petroleum products are examined; also details the usage of biological and organic products such as wood chips, corn, and garbage for energy.

★6661★ Greenpeace Voyages to Save the Whales
Pyramid Film & Video
Box 1048
Santa Monica, CA 90406
Phone: (213)828-7577
1978. 27 mins. An expedition to protest the needless slaughter of the whaling industry is conducted by a concerned organization of environmentalists.

★6662★ Greenpeace's Greatest Hits
J2 Communications
10850 Wilshire Blvd.
Suite 1000
Los Angeles, CA 90024
Phone: (213)474-5252
1988. 60 mins. A celebratory video about the conservationist group's most successful nature-preserving exploits, including their campaigns to preserve Antarctica, stop the slaughtering of baby seals and protect the grey whale from extinction. Features its own theme, "We Are the People," written by Peter Kater and performed by John Mellencamp.

★6663★ Growing Concerns
National Aeronautics & Space Administration
Lewis Audiovisual Library
6100 Columbus Ave.
Sandusky, OH 44870
Phone: (419)626-2594
1976. 14 mins. An introduction to the Landsat satellite and its role as monitor of the Earth's environment.

★6664★ Gulf Islands
National AudioVisual Center
National Archives & Records Administration
Customer Services Section PZ
8700 Edgeworth Dr.
Capitol Heights, MD 20743-3701
Phone: (301)763-1896
1979. 13 mins. Recreational activities and historical features are highlighted in this look at the Gulf Islands National Seashore Park on the Gulf of Mexico.

★6665★ Hazardous Chemicals: Handle With Care
Educational Images
PO Box 3456, W. Side
Elmira, NY 14905
Phone: (607)732-1090
1984. 60 mins. An unbiased exploration shows the importance of hazardous chemicals in our lives as well as the environmental problems caused by their use and disposal.

★6666★ Hazardous Waste
Direct Cinema Limited, Inc.
Box 69799
Los Angeles, CA 90069
Phone: (213)652-8000
1984. 35 mins. Documents how a group of concerned citizens organized themselves to clean up some of the 17,000 toxic chemical dumps which have littered the countryside.

★6667★ The Hole in the Sky
New Dimension Media, Inc.
85895 Lorane Hwy.
Eugene, OR 97405
Phone: 800-288-4456
1989. 15 mins. The depletion of our ozone layer and the dangers it poses to our planet are outlined.

★6668★ How Man Adapts to His Physical Environment
CRM/McGraw-Hill Films
674 Via de la Valle
PO Box 641
Del Mar, CA 92014
Phone: (619)453-5000
1970. 20 mins. This program from the "History of Man" series illustrates how man abuses his environment and suggests that we have to use our technology to protect our environment if we want to survive.

★6669★ Humboldt Bay (Qual A Wa Loo)
University of California at Berkeley Extension Media Center
2176 Shattuck Ave.
Berkeley, CA 94704
Phone: (415)642-0460
1980. 22 mins. A study of the ecology of an estuarian environment, using California's Humboldt Bay, one of the few Pacific estuaries that is relatively undisturbed by human tampering, as an example.

★6670★ If You Can See a Shadow
Bullfrog Films, Inc.
PO Box 149
Oley, PA 19547
Phone: (215)779-8226
1980. 28 mins. A clear and comprehensive account of passive solar techniques, stressing simplicity. Energy conservation techniques which go along with passive design are covered.

★6671★ Images of Life
National Aeronautics and Space Administration
Lewis Audiovisual Library
6100 Columbus Ave.
Sandusky, OH 44870
Phone: (419)626-2594
1976. 25 mins. This video explains the uses of the Landsat satellite in providing new information on agriculture, mineral deposits, oceanography, geology, and the environment. Contains Landsat data.

★6672★ The Impact of Environmental Regulations on Business Transactions
Practicing Law Inst.
810 7th Ave.
New York, NY 10019
Phone: (212)765-5700
1988. 250 mins. A look at how environmental standards affect business dealings.

★6673★ In Celebration of America's Wildlife
Cornell Univ.
Media Services Distribution Center
7-8 Research Park
Ithaca, NY 14850
Phone: (607)255-2091
1988. 57 mins. The story of several species which have rebounded from the brink of extinction.

★6674★ In Memory of the Land and People
Green Mountain Post Films, Inc.
PO Box 229
Turners Falls, MA 01376
Phone: (413)863-4754
1979. 50 mins. A lyrical look at the massive, irreparable damage done by strip mining to our nation's coal belt.

★6675★ In Our Own Backyards: Uranium Mining in the U.S.
Bullfrog Films, Inc.
PO Box 149
Oley, PA 19547
Phone: (215)779-8226
1982. 29 mins. This film deals with uranium mining in the United States.

★6676★ In Our Water
New Day Films
853 Broadway
Suite 1210
New York, NY 10003
Phone: (212)477-4304
1981. 58 mins. This program chronicles the discovery of toxic drinking water in South Brunswick, New Jersey in 1975. The toxicity was caused by a nearby hazardous waste dump site.

★6677★ In Partnership With Earth
Versar Inc.
6850 Versar Center
Springfield, VA 22151
Phone: (703)750-3000
One-hour videotape designed to educate the public about pollution prevention and reduction efforts. Shows steps companies, states, and citizens are taking to prevent pollution.

★6678★ In Search of the Bowhead Whale
National Film Bd. of Canada
16th Fl.
1251 Ave. of the Americas
New York, NY 10020-1173
Phone: (212)586-5131
1974. 49 mins. A nine-man expedition sets out in search of the mammal near extinction: the bowhead whale. The Alaskan wilderness, environment, and people of the Arctic region are presented.

★6679★ In the Kingdom of the Dolphins
Home Vision
5547 N. Ravenswood Ave.
Chicago, IL 60640-1199
Phone: (312)878-2600
1986. 50 mins. This video features copious footage of dolphins at work and play. Underwater photography by Howard Hall.

★6680★ In the Land of the Polar Bear
Time-Life Video
1271 Ave. of the Americas
New York, NY 10020
Phone: (212)484-5940
1985. 57 mins. An episode from the "Nova" series about Soviet naturalist Yuri Lendin's expedition to Wrangel Island to learn about animal life there.

★6681★ In Your Own Backyard: The First Love Canal
Bullfrog Films, Inc.
PO Box 149
Oley, PA 19547
Phone: (215)779-8226
1982. 59 mins. This program documents the nation's first encounter with toxic waste. A complete account of the way the people involved, both in government and in the community, responded to a frightening situation.

★6682★ Incident at Brown's Ferry
Time-Life Video
1271 Ave. of the Americas
New York, NY 10020
Phone: (212)484-5940
1982. 58 mins. An exploration of the 1975 blaze at Brown's Ferry, Alabama, the world's largest nuclear power plant, which set into motion the debate on power plant hazards and protection. Part of "Nova" series.

★6683★ The Incredible Wilderness
National AudioVisual Center
National Archives & Records Administration
Customer Services Section PZ
8700 Edgeworth Dr.
Capitol Heights, MD 20743-3701
Phone: (301)763-1896
1973. 10 mins. Colorful views are featured in this rich panorama of the back country of Olympic National Park.

★6684★ The Indiana Dunes
International Film Bureau, Inc.
332 S. Michigan Ave.
Chicago, IL 60604-4382
Phone: (312)427-4545
1981. 14 mins. This program examines the Indiana Dunes, a rich storehouse of natural beauty and ecological information on Lake Michigan.

★6685★ Industry: Outdoor Partner
New Jersey Network
1573 Parkside Ave.
Trenton, NJ 08625
Phone: (609)292-5252
1985. 30 mins. A survey of New Jersey industry and how it variously affects, positively or not, the surrounding environment.

★6686★ Inside The Golden Gate
Time-Life Video
1271 Ave. of the Americas
New York, NY 10020
Phone: (212)484-5940
1976. 76 mins. San Francisco Bay has an abundance of plant and animal life, but its food chain has been seriously disrupted. This program from the "Nova" series explores the problem and what is being done to solve it.

★6687★ International Film Foundation, Inc.—Water
International Film Foundation, Inc.
155 W. 72nd St.
New York, NY 10023
Phone: (212)580-1111
8 mins. This film shows how people need water, from a woman carrying water from the well in a jar on her head, to a sophisticated hydroelectric plant.

★6688★ The Invisible Flame
Time-Life Video
1271 Ave. of the Americas
New York, NY 10020
Phone: (212)484-5940
1979. 57 mins. This program explores the possibility of another source of energy that is generally overlooked in these days of the energy crisis - hydrogen. (Part of public television's "Nova" series.)

★6689★ Is Nuclear Power Safe? A
Amer. Enterprise Inst. for Public Policy Research
1150 17th St. NW
Washington, DC 20036
Phone: (202)862-5800
60 mins. An expert panel debates whether there are social, environmental, and security risks that make futher development of nuclear power unwise.

★6690★ Is Nuclear Power Safe? B
Amer. Enterprise Inst. for Public Policy Research
1150 17th St. NW
Washington, DC 20036
Phone: (202)862-5800
60 mins. An expert panel debates whether there are social, environmental, and security risks that make further development of nuclear power unwise. A continuation of "Is Nuclear Power Safe? A."

★6691★ Island at the Edge
Films, Inc.
5547 N. Ravenswood Ave.
Chicago, IL 60640-1199
Phone: (312)878-2600
1979. 26 mins. Documents the dolphin crisis on the Iki Island in Japan, where fishermen are slaughtering dolphins because they are consuming the fish on which the islanders depend for food. Industrial pollution has destroyed the dolphins' normal feeding grounds.

★6692★ It Can't Happen Here
Commonwealth Films, Inc.
223 Commonwealth Ave.
Boston, MA 02116
Phone: (617)262-5634
1987. 39 mins. This docu-drama based on actual case records, illustrates eight basic operational requirements for an effective waste management program. It is designed to train industrial supervisors and personnel to meet those requirements and comply with environmental laws.

★6693★ Ivory Hunters
Turner Home Entertainment Company
5 Penn Plaza
19th Fl.
New York, NY 10001
Phone: (404)827-1264
1990. 94 mins. An unlikely trio of conservationists band together in an attempt to end the massacre of elephants for their tusks.

★6694★ Joe Albert's Fox Hunt
Education Development Center
39 Chapel St.
Newton, MA 02160
Phone: (617)969-7100
1981. 60 mins. A series of vignettes about the inhabitants, the conservationists, and the developers involved in the conflict over the future of "The Pine Barrens" of New Jersey, the last remaining wilderness in the Boston to Washington corridor.

★6695★ Jojoba
University of California at Berkeley Extension Media Center
2176 Shattuck Ave.
Berkeley, CA 94704
Phone: (415)642-0460
1980. 23 mins. A look at the world's most promising renewable resource, the jojoba tree, whose nut oil is the purest and most versatile known.

★6696★ Journal Films, Inc.—Water
Journal Films, Inc.
930 Pitner Ave.
Evanston, IL 60202
Phone: (312)328-6700
1977. 14 mins. This program examines the world's need for water from the point of view of doctors, meteorologists, agronomists, hydrologists, and engineers.

★6697★ Journey for Survival
Barr Films
3490 E. Foothill Blvd.
PO Box 5667
Pasadena, CA 91107
Phone: (213)681-2165
1987. 15 mins. Water shortages around the world and possible solutions are discussed.

★6698★ Journey of the Kings
Amer. Educational Films
3807 Dickerson Rd.
Nashville, TN 37207
Phone: 800-822-5678
1984. 20 mins. A study of the efforts of conservationists to restore fish runs and natural habitats in the Columbia River Basin.

★6699★ Journey to the High Arctic
National Geographic Soc.
17th & M Streets NW
Washington, DC 20036
Phone: (202)857-7378
1971. 52 mins. A look at the seldom-seen animals of the Canadian Arctic, such as the caribou, narwhal, musk ox, and arctic wolf.

★6700★ Jungle
University of California at Berkeley Extension Media Center
2176 Shattuck Ave.
Berkeley, CA 94704
Phone: (415)642-0460
1984. 55 mins. Anthropologist David Attenborough explores the plants and creatures that make up the tropical rain forests.

★6701★ Jungles: The Green Oceans
Britannica Films
310 S. Michigan Ave.
Chicago, IL 60604
Phone: (312)347-7958
1980. 23 mins. The program shows viewers how jungles have survived as successful and self-contained ecosystems through the delicately balanced interaction of plants, animals, and climate.

★6702★ Junk Ecology
Troll Associates
320 Rte. 17
Mahwah, NJ 07430
Phone: (201)529-4000
1988. 72 mins. A series that teaches kids about the environment and how to clean it up.

★6703★ Junkdump
AIMS Media, Inc.
6901 Woodley Ave.
Van Nuys, CA 91406-4878
Phone: (818)785-4111
1972. 16 mins. Problems in solid waste disposal.

★6704★ Kangaroo Island
Lucerne Media
37 Ground Pine Rd.
Morris Plains, NJ 07950
Phone: (201)538-1401
1978. 17 mins. A non-narrative look at a wildlife sanctuary on an Australian island, and the opossum, pelicans, seals, emus, kangaroos, black swans, koalas, and other inhabitants.

★6705★ Kaniapiskau
Phoenix/BFA Films
468 Park Ave. South
New York, NY 10016
Phone: (212)684-5910
1979. 19 mins. The Kaniapiskau River in Northern Quebec has long been a favorite of canoers for its challenging rapids and majestic beauty. It is being dammed and diverted to build a large hydroelectric project.

★6706★ Keepers of the Forest
Umbrella Films
60 Blake Rd.
Brookline, MA 02146
Phone: (617)277-6639
1988. 28 mins. The problems resulting from the destruction of the tropical rainforest are seen, as well as suggested solutions.

★6707★ Keepers of Wildlife
National Film Bd. of Canada
16th Fl.
1251 Ave. of the Americas
New York, NY 10020-1173
Phone: (212)586-5131
1974. 21 mins. Studies the conservation of wildlife.

★6708★ Keith County Journal
NETCHE (Nebraska ETV Coun. for Higher Education)
Box 83111
Lincoln, NE 68501
Phone: (402)472-3611
1986. 90 mins. The naturalist Janovy explains why people are more a part of the environment than they might think.

★6709★ The Killing Ground
MTI Teleprograms, Inc.
108 Wilmot Rd.
Deerfield, IL 60015-9990
Phone: (312)940-1260
48 mins. A close-up look at the problem of chemical wastes. Corporate executives, EPA officials, and medical experts consider how chemical waste disposal can be controlled fairly and effectively. The program examines corporate liability, and questions the ability of government agencies to handle the problem.

★6710★ Kilowatts from Cowpies
Bullfrog Films, Inc.
PO Box 149
Oley, PA 19547
Phone: (215)779-8226
1981. 25 mins. An important energy resource, biogas, can be produced by almost any organic material, including crop and forestry residues, animal wastes, human sewage, and food processing wastes.

★6711★ Know the Land and the People
Maryland Center for Public Broadcasting
11767 Bonita Ave.
Owings Mills, MD 21117
Phone: (301)356-5600
1983. 30 mins. This series looks at the relationship between people and environment.

★6712★ Lake Powell and Canyon Country
Norman Beerger Productions
3217 S. Arville St.
Las Vegas, NV 89102-7612
Phone: (702)876-2328
1988. 60 mins. Spectacular views of these natural locations are featured.

★6713★ Lake Tahoe: The Politics of Ecology
Video Free America
442 Shotwell
San Francisco, CA 94110
Phone: (415)648-9040
1978. 60 mins. Examines the endangered wilderness area of Lake Tahoe through interviews with politicians, local residents, and casino owners.

★6714★ Lakes: Aging and Pollution
Centron Films
108 Wilmot Rd.
Deerfield, IL 60015-9990
Phone: (312)940-1260
1971. 15 mins. The aging process of lakes and the various plant and animal life found in different lake habitats are investigated along with changing water quality.

★6715★ Land for Man, Land for Bears
National Aeronautics & Space Administration (NASA)
Lewis Audiovisual Library
6100 Columbus Ave.
Sandusky, OH 44870
Phone: (419)626-2594
1976. 14 mins. An exploration of the Landsat satellite's revolutionary ability in providing high resolution photographs taken from outer space for map making and environmental studies.

Much of the imagery has been useful in monitoring land development and helping to relocate endangered animals into areas that are not threatened by human encroachment.

★6716★ Land Pollution: A First Film
Phoenix/BFA Films
468 Park Ave. South
New York, NY 10016
Phone: (212)684-5910
1985. 12 mins. The program explores the answers to many questions that must be considered in deciding how best to use our land resources.

★6717★ Land Use and Misuse
Learning Corp. of America
108 Wilmot Rd.
Deerfield, IL 60015-9990
Phone: (312)940-1260
1975. 13 mins. Explains why careful use of our land surface is vital to man's very existence.

★6718★ Land: With Love and Respect
Cornell Univ.
Media Services Distribution Center
7-8 Research Park
Ithaca, NY 14850
Phone: (607)255-2091
1980. 26 mins. The social and economic conflicts and the consequences related to land-use decisions are explored. Traditional values of rural charm, green space, and agriculture are stressed.

★6719★ Landsat: Satellite for All Seasons
Agency for Instructional Technology
Box A
Bloomington, IN 47402
Phone: (812)339-2203
1977. 15 mins. This series examines the various ways scientists and researchers use satellites to help solve environmental problems and gather data about world resources.

★6720★ The Last Chance
Bullfrog Films, Inc.
PO Box 149
Oley, PA 19547
Phone: (215)779-8226
1980. 28 mins. Endangered species such as the Pere David deer, scimitar-horned oryx, and lesser panda are seen in this program, which shows an attitude of respect and inquiry toward these animals.

★6721★ The Last Epidemic
Educational Film & Video Project
5332 College Ave.
Suite 101
Oakland, CA 94618
Phone: (415)655-9050
1981. 29 mins. This film graphically illustrates the effects of a nuclear detonation over a civilian population and the long term effects it would have on the environment and the planet.

★6722★ Last Stronghold of the Eagles
Learning Corp. of America
108 Wilmot Rd.
Deerfield, IL 60015-9990
Phone: (312)940-1260
1981. 30 mins. This program explores the habitat and entire life cycle of the American bald eagle.

★6723★ Last Tree
Phoenix/BFA Films
468 Park Ave. South
New York, NY 10016
Phone: (212)684-5910
1975. 10 mins. An ecological parable which traces the evolution of matter from the first amorphous blob right up to the emergence of man, when the balance of nature became threatened.

★6724★ The Law of Nature: Park Rangers in Yosemite Valley
Umbrella Films
60 Blake Rd.
Brookline, MA 02146
Phone: (617)277-6639
1988. 28 mins. The real-life problems in our national parks caused by increased use and decreased budgets are dramatized.

★6725★ Learning About Solar Energy
AIMS Media, Inc.
6901 Woodley Ave.
Van Nuys, CA 91406-4878
Phone: (818)785-4111
1975. 12 mins. The Sun's power to heat water, homes, etc.

★6726★ Less Is More
AIMS Media, Inc.
6901 Woodley Ave.
Van Nuys, CA 91406-4878
Phone: (818)785-4111
1977. 14 mins. By looking at the simple battery, the efficent uses of natural resources to yield the maximum amount of energy are explored.

★6727★ Let Me Say This...
Cinema Guild
1697 Broadway
Room 802
New York, NY 10019
Phone: (212)246-5522
1984. 30 mins. The efforts of individuals and groups working to prevent nuclear disaster are examined.

★6728★ Let No Man Regret
Alfred Higgins Productions, Inc.
6350 Laurel Canyon Blvd.
North Hollywood, CA 91606
Phone: (818)762-3300
1973. 11 mins. This video production reminds us of our responsibility to preserve the beauty of our recreational areas.

★6729★ Let's Help Recycle
AIMS Media, Inc.
6901 Woodley Ave.
Van Nuys, CA 91406-4878
Phone: (818)785-4111
1978. 11 mins. For children, several methods of conservation and community maintainance, such as recycling cans and papers, are demonstrated.

★6730★ Libra
World Research, Inc.
Campus Studies Institute Division
Box 9359
San Diego, CA 92109-0100
Phone: (619)566-3456
1978. 39 mins. The story of a theoretical, new, energy-abundant society in which giant solar power satellites beam low cost microwave energy to a desperate Earth ravaged by fuel shortages.

★6731★ The Life and Death of an African Pan
Centre Productions, Inc.
1800 30th St.
Suite 207
Boulder, CO 80301
Phone: (303)444-1166
1983. 11 mins. This film studies the processes of the natural creation and destruction of the shallow water-filled pans on the fringe of the Kalahari desert in Africa.

★6732★ The Linn Cove Viaduct...A Bridge In Harmony With Nature
National AudioVisual Center
National Archives & Records Administration
Customer Services Section PZ
8700 Edgeworth Dr.
Capitol Heights, MD 20743-3701
Phone: (301)763-1896
1985. 20 mins. This video shows engineers how the Linn Cove Viaduct was built top-down to avoid disturbing the landscape, and encourages them to create projects that are similarly environmentally friendly.

★6733★ The Living Environment
Dallas County Community Coll. District
Center for Telecommunications
4343 North Hwy. 67
Mesquite, TX 75150-2095
Phone: (214)324-7988
1979. 30 mins. This series of twenty-two half-hour programs, is a college credit course in various aspects of environmental studies.

★6734★ Magnificence in Trust
National AudioVisual Center
National Archives & Records Administration
Customer Services Section PZ
8700 Edgeworth Dr.
Capitol Heights, MD 20743-3701
Phone: (301)763-1896
1975. 28 mins. Wildlife and natural wonders are featured in this look at three national parks: the icebergs of Glacier Bay National Monument; leaping salmon, brown bears and volcanoes of Katmai National Monument; grizzly bears, caribou, and moose of Mount McKinley.

★6735★ Mammoth Cave National Park, Kentucky
Finley-Holiday Film Corp.
PO Box 619
Whittier, CA 90608
Phone: (213)945-3325
1988. 30 mins. Take a tour through the world's longest cave, exploring both the unusual rock formations and its plant life.

★6736★ Man Builds—Man Destroys
Great Plains Natl. Instructional Television Library (GPN)
University of Nebraska at Lincoln
PO Box 80669
Lincoln, NE 68501-0669
Phone: (402)472-2007
1975. 30 mins. This series on environmental education points out that we can manage our destiny, live in harmony with our surroundings and ourselves. Presents environmental problems, solutions, and evaluations. Programs are available individually.

★6737★ Man in His Environment
University of California at Berkeley Extension Media Center
2176 Shattuck Ave.
Berkeley, CA 94704
Phone: (415)642-0460
1976. 29 mins. An essay on the checks and balances of the natural cycle, showing how the processes that regulate other forms of life ultimately regulate humanity as well.

★6738★ Man Makes a Desert
Phoenix/BFA Films
468 Park Ave. South
New York, NY 10016
Phone: (212)684-5910
1985. 10 mins. This show depicts the changes that can occur when man upsets the delicate

balance between the plants and animals that inhabit an area. In this case, grassland was turned into desert.

★6739★ Managing the Old Growth Forest
Centre Productions, Inc.
1800 30th St.
Suite 207
Boulder, CO 80301
Phone: (303)444-1166
1987. 20 mins. This documentary explains the debate now raging over "old growth" forests in the American Northwest.

★6740★ Man's Effect on the Environment
Phoenix/BFA Films
468 Park Ave. South
New York, NY 10016
Phone: (212)684-5910
1970. 14 mins. This program shows some of the effects of man's exploitation of natural resources. It raises questions as to the quality of life that such environmental changes might cause.

★6741★ Men at Bay
Phoenix/BFA Films
468 Park Ave. South
New York, NY 10016
Phone: (212)684-5910
1970. 26 mins. This program compels the viewer to face the disastrous results of ecological unconcern.

★6742★ Mount Rainier
Finley-Holiday Film Corp.
PO Box 619
Whittier, CA 90608
Phone: (213)945-3325
1980. 28 mins. A tourist's look at the famous Washington mountain.

★6743★ Mt. Rushmore and the Black Hills of South Dakota
Finley-Holiday Film Corp.
PO Box 619
Whittier, CA 90608
Phone: (213)945-3325
1985. 30 mins. A tourist's look at the national monument and its surrounding countryside.

★6744★ The Mountain in the City
New York State Education Dept.
Center for Learning Technologies
Media Distribution Network
Room C-7, Concourse Level
Albany, NY 12230
Phone: (518)474-1265
1986. 52 mins. This tape analyzes the problem of urban waste disposal.

★6745★ National Parks I
Dallas County Community Coll. District
Center for Telecommunications
4343 North Hwy. 67
Mesquite, TX 75150-2095
Phone: (214)324-7988
1977. 29 mins. This program studies the history of the national park system through footage of Yellowstone National Park and the Petrified Forest Park.

★6746★ National Parks II
Dallas County Community Coll. District
Center for Telecommunications
4343 North Hwy. 67
Mesquite, TX 75150-2095
Phone: (214)324-7988
1977. 29 mins. National park rangers help examine three major national parks: Mesa Verde, Platt, and Big Bend.

★6747★ National Parks: Playground or Paradise
National Geographic Soc.
17th & M Streets NW
Washington, DC 20036
Phone: (202)857-7378
1981. 59 mins. Visits to Yellowstone, Yosemite, and the Grand Canyon point out the dilemma of trying to both use and preserve our parks. A look at Alaska's wilderness reserve and urban parks is included.

★6748★ National Parks: Promise and Challenge
National Geographic Soc.
17th & M Streets NW
Washington, DC 20036
Phone: (202)857-7378
1981. 23 mins. This is a visit to Yosemite, Yellowstone, Mount McKinley, and the Grand Canyon and a discussion of whether our parks are a playground for everyone's use or a paradise to be preserved.

★6749★ The Natural History of Our World: The Time of Man
Phoenix/BFA Films
468 Park Ave. South
New York, NY 10016
Phone: (212)684-5910
1970. 50 mins. The program conveys the message that if man is to survive, he must maintain the environment that sustains him.

★6750★ New Alchemy: A Rediscovery of Promise
Bullfrog Films, Inc.
PO Box 149
Oley, PA 19547
Phone: (215)779-8226
1984. 29 mins. This is a film about the New Alchemy Institute, which was founded to develop ecological approaches to food, energy and shelter. This film is also available in an expanded 58-minute version.

★6751★ New Directions in Superfund and RCRA
Amer. Law Inst.
American Bar Association Committee on Continuing Education
4025 Chestnut St.
Philadelphia, PA 19104
Phone: (215)243-1650
1985. 210 mins. A distinguished faculty, including the Environmental Protection Agency Administrator, discusses the implications of the Superfund Act and the amendments to the Resource Conservation and Recovery Act.

★6752★ No Way to Treat a River
Plexus Communications Corp.
15760 Ventura Blvd.
Suite 532
Encino, CA 91436
Phone: (818)995-1947
30 mins. An investigative report into the effects of water pollution and the community's health.

★6753★ Noise: Polluting the Environment
Britannica Films
310 S. Michigan Ave.
Chicago, IL 60604
Phone: (312)347-7958
1971. 16 mins. The need for concern over our greatly increased noise level and the complexities of controlling noise are explored in detail.

★6754★ The Ocean: Resource for the World
Handel Film Corp.
8730 Sunset Blvd.
West Hollywood, CA 90069
Phone: (213)657-8990
1980. 15 mins. The nature and diversity of the ocean's resources (fish and plant life, oil and minerals, transportation and recreation) are examined, and the need for conservation is stressed.

★6755★ Odyssey: A Quest for Energy
New York State Education Dept.
Center for Learning Technologies
Media Distribution Network
Room C-7, Concourse Level
Albany, NY 12230
Phone: (518)474-1265
1984. 30 mins. Domestic energy supplies must be increased - in harmony with the environment. This program addresses the following energy resources and presents the pros and cons of each: coal, solar, synthetics, geothermal and nuclear.

★6756★ Offshore
Modern Talking Picture Service
5000 Park Street N.
St. Petersburg, FL 33709
Phone: (813)541-7571
18 mins. Examines the painstaking effort to preserve the ocean while drilling oil.

★6757★ Offshore Oil A
Amer. Enterprise Inst. for Public Policy Research
1150 17th St. NW
Washington, DC 20036
Phone: (202)862-5800
60 mins. A panel discusses the substantial petroleum reserves that lie within America's continental shelves and the prices we must pay to tap them.

★6758★ Offshore Oil: Are We Ready?
National Film Bd. of Canada
16th Fl.
1251 Ave. of the Americas
New York, NY 10020-1173
Phone: (212)586-5131
1981. 38 mins. A cautionary film that explores in depth the impact that offshore oil discoveries can have on local industries, particularly fisheries.

★6759★ Offshore Oil B
Amer. Enterprise Inst. for Public Policy Research
1150 17th St. NW
Washington, DC 20036
Phone: (202)862-5800
60 mins. A panel discusses the substantial petroleum reserves that lie within America's continental shelves and the prices we must pay to tap them. A continuation of "Offshore Oil A."

★6760★ Ohio River: Industry and Transportation
Phoenix/BFA Films
468 Park Ave. South
New York, NY 10016
Phone: (212)684-5910
1970. 16 mins. Industries use the navigable Ohio River as a means of transport. But problems have evolved - pollution of the water and the air.

★6761★ Oil
PBS Video
1320 Braddock Pl.
Alexandria, VA 22314-1698
Phone: (703)739-5380
1987. 60 mins. This series examines the history of oil - its discovery, the first use in internal combustion engines, the modern petrochemical industry, and the economic and political power held by those sitting on top of the oil.

★6762★ The Oil Invasion
Pacific Coast Community Video
635 Chapala St.
Santa Barbara, CA 93101
Phone: (805)965-5051
1976. 25 mins. This program discusses the 1969 oil spill with comments on the topic by reporters who were present at the time and Paul Newman, Joanne Woodward, and Jack Lemmon.

★6763★ Oil on Washington Waters
University of Washington Instructional Media Services
Kane Hall, DG-10
Seattle, WA 98195
Phone: (206)543-9909
1975. 60 mins. A film documentary, "Oil and Water: Will They Mix?" is followed by a studio discussion addressing the question of oil transfer and the potential dangers to the environment and economy.

★6764★ Oil Pollution Prevention Regulations
University of Texas at Austin
Petroleum Extension Service
10100 Burnet Rd.
Austin, TX 78758
Phone: (512)835-3154
1975. 18 mins. This program is an orientation to the Federal Water Pollution Control Act of 1972 and the Spill Prevention Control and Countermeasure (SPCC) plans required to comply with the act.

★6765★ Oil Spills
University of Toronto
Media Centre
University of Toronto
121 St. George St.
Toronto, Ontario, Canada M5S 1A1
Phone: (416)978-6049
1977. 7 mins. A description about the research being conducted on oil properties that are located under arctic conditions. Part of the "Discovery" series.

★6766★ Oklahoma Oasis
National AudioVisual Center
National Archives & Records Administration
Customer Services Section PZ
8700 Edgeworth Dr.
Capitol Heights, MD 20743-3701
Phone: (301)763-1896
1974. 15 mins. Chief Dan George comments on the natural beauty and colorful history of Platt National Park.

★6767★ The Old Quabbin Valley: Politics and Conflict in Water Distribution
Direct Cinema Limited, Inc.
Box 69799
Los Angeles, CA 90069
Phone: (213)652-8000
1983. 28 mins. The history of Boston's water supply, the construction of the Quabbin Reservoir, and the nationwide debate over urban use of rural water supplies are explored in this film.

★6768★ Olympic Range
Eastman Kodak Company
c/o Wood Knapp
Knapp Press
5900 Wilshire Blvd.
Los Angeles, CA 90036
Phone: (213)937-5486
1989. 30 mins. Washington state's famous rain forest is explored in this program, from peaceful streams to snow-covered mountains.

★6769★ On American Soil
Bullfrog Films, Inc.
PO Box 149
Oley, PA 19547
Phone: (215)779-8226
1983. 28 mins. A study of the problem of modern-day soil erosion.

★6770★ On the Edge of Extinction: Panthers and Cheetahs
Vestron Video
c/o LIVE Home Video
15400 Sherman Way
Suite 500
Van Nuys, CA 91410-0124
Phone: (203)978-5400
1988. 60 mins. An Audubon documentary about African cheetahs and panthers, and how they must be preserved.

★6771★ On the Edge of the Forest
Bullfrog Films, Inc.
PO Box 149
Oley, PA 19547
Phone: (215)779-8226
1979. 32 mins. This program is a revelation of the special importance of trees and forests, from which we can learn about healthy survival in our biosphere. Walking through a virgin forest in Western Australia, E.F. Schumacher makes a powerful appeal to preserve rather than exploit our resources in the name of economics, growth, and progress.

★6772★ On to Tomorrow Series
Michigan Media
University of Michigan
400 Fourth St.
Ann Arbor, MI 48109
Phone: (313)764-8228
1976. 29 mins. This series examines a new procedure called technology assessment - the systematic analysis of the social, economic, environmental, and societal impacts of new technology. All programs available individually.

★6773★ Once There Were Bluebirds
Film Fair Communications
10900 Ventura Blvd.
PO Box 1728
Studio City, CA 91604
Phone: (818)985-0244
1971. 5 mins. Animated scenes of bluebirds, butterflies, meadows, and seashore. Introduces air planes, insecticides, and freeway traffic as a major cause of eliminating and destroying them.

★6774★ One Man's Alaska
National AudioVisual Center
National Archives & Records Administration
Customer Services Section PZ
8700 Edgeworth Dr.
Capitol Heights, MD 20743-3701
Phone: (301)763-1896
1977. 27 mins. A profile of conservationist Dick Proenneke at his home in the Lake Clark area of Alaska. Proenneke's rapport with his environment and the wildlife he photographs is demonstrated in picture and commentary.

★6775★ Onshore Planning for Offshore Oil: Voices of Scotland
Bullfrog Films, Inc.
PO Box 149
Oley, PA 19547
Phone: (215)779-8226
1976. 21 mins. The ecological and social effects of oil-based industrialization on the Scotland shores are discussed.

★6776★ Opening Your Home to Solar Energy
Bullfrog Films, Inc.
PO Box 149
Oley, PA 19547
Phone: (215)779-8226
1980. 27 mins. This exploration of retrofitting your home with passive solar structures includes interviews with solar engineers, builders, and homeowners. Part of the "Mastering Self-Sufficiency" series.

★6777★ Organic Farming
Cinema Guild
1697 Broadway
Room 802
New York, NY 10019
Phone: (212)246-5522
1976. 20 mins. An investigation of organic farming as an alternative to traditional methods of farming using herbicides, pesticides, and fertilizers.

★6778★ Organic Gardening: Composting
Bullfrog Films, Inc.
PO Box 149
Oley, PA 19547
Phone: (215)779-8226
1972. 11 mins. A program demonstrating how to turn everyday leftovers into sweet-smelling humus or topsoil, alleviating the need to use expensive and destructive chemicals. Such items include garbage, grass clippings, wood ash, sawdust, and hair trimmings. From live action and animated sequences one can learn to build a compost heap; what ingredients to use; in what amounts; how to layer the heap to ensure proper decomposition; and what types of containers to use.

★6779★ The Osprey
New Jersey Network
1573 Parkside Ave.
Trenton, NJ 08625
Phone: (609)292-5252
1975. 23 mins. How biologists restored the osprey through egg transplants from Maryland back into New Jersey's wildlife population.

★6780★ Osprey's Domain
Learning Corp. of America
108 Wilmot Rd.
Deerfield, IL 60015-9990
Phone: (312)940-1260
1981. 15 mins. The osprey and its fascinating fish-catching technique is shown. Also shown is how pesticides and habitat destruction have placed the bird on the endangered list. Part of the "Animals and Plants of North America" series.

★6781★ Our Precious Environment
Educational Images
PO Box 3456, W. Side
Elmira, NY 14905
Phone: (607)732-1090
1987. 60 mins. This program describes various threats to the environment and some solutions in which students may take part.

★6782★ Our Round Earth: How It Changes
Coronet/MTI Film & Video
108 Wilmot Rd.
Deerfield, IL 60015-9990
Phone: (312)940-1260
1971. 10 mins. Water, wind, gravity and temperature changes are shown as factors of continual geological change. One of a series on earth studies.

★6783★ Our Round Earth: Its Atmosphere
Coronet/MTI Film & Video
108 Wilmot Rd.
Deerfield, IL 60015-9990
Phone: (312)940-1260
1971. 10 mins. Clouds, mist, smoke, and dust help to survey the invisible atmosphere that protects the planet. One of a series on earth studies.

★6784★ Our Round Earth: Its Land
Coronet/MTI Film & Video
108 Wilmot Rd.
Deerfield, IL 60015-9990
Phone: (312)940-1260
1971. 10 mins. A survey of the earth's land forms and a discussion of the importance of soil and conservation. One of a series on earth studies.

★6785★ Our Round Earth: Its Waters
Coronet/MTI Film & Video
108 Wilmot Rd.
Deerfield, IL 60015-9990
Phone: (312)940-1260
1971. 11 mins. Views of the oceans from miles above to thousands of feet below help survey the earth's water cycle. One of a series on earth studies.

★6786★ Our Vanishing Lands
CRM/McGraw-Hill Films
674 Via de la Valle
PO Box 641
Del Mar, CA 92014
Phone: (619)453-5000
1967. 24 mins. This program produced for the Smithsonian Institute contributes to the conservation of America's resources.

★6787★ Our Water, Our Lives
Barr Films
3490 E. Foothill Blvd.
PO Box 5667
Pasadena, CA 91107
Phone: (213)681-2165
1988. 30 mins. A chronicle of water sanitation efforts in various parts of the world.

★6788★ Perspectives in Science
National Film Bd. of Canada
16th Fl.
1251 Ave. of the Americas
New York, NY 10020-1173
Phone: (212)586-5131
1985. 59 mins. These programs explore the implications of man's scientific knowledge and manipulation of nature, and are aimed at a secondary school audience.

★6789★ Pest, Pesticides and Safety
Great Plains Natl. Instructional Television Library (GPN)
University of Nebraska at Lincoln
PO Box 80669
Lincoln, NE 68501-0669
Phone: (402)472-2007
30 mins. A series of 5 untitled programs on the need for pesticides and their impact on the environment. Presents the broad range of pesticides now on the market and their chemical properties.

★6790★ Pesticides and the Environment
NETCHE (Nebraska ETV Coun. for Higher Education)
Box 83111
Lincoln, NE 68501
Phone: (402)472-3611
1975. 30 mins. This three lesson series details some of the research and research methods which have altered our understanding of pesticides and their effects.

★6791★ Pesticides: The Hidden Assassins
Video Out
1102 Homer St.
Vancouver, British Columbia, Canada V68 2X6
Phone: (604)688-4336
1979. 29 mins. This program examines the use of pesticide spraying in British Columbia, Canada.

★6792★ PET Recycling: A Model Solution
National Assn. for Plastic Container Recovery
4828 Pkwy. Plaza Blvd., Ste. 260
Charlotte, NC 28217
Phone: (704)357-3250
Fax: (704)357-3260
Toll-Free: 800-NAP-CORP

★6793★ Phenomenal World Series
Britannica Films
310 S. Michigan Ave.
Chicago, IL 60604
Phone: (312)347-7958
1988. 21 mins. Some of the wonders of nature are displayed in this series.

★6794★ Philosophy, Policy and Problems in Environmental Engineering
University of Wisconsin Extension
Department of Engineering & Applied Science
432 N. Lake St.
Madison, WI 53706
Phone: (608)262-2061
1977. 30 mins. This module course is an introduction to the general problems of the environment and environmental control. It is intended for administrators, managers, and policymakers concerned with environmental engineering. Programs below are also available individually. Part of the "Environmental Engineering" series.

★6795★ A Plague on Our Children
Time-Life Video
1271 Ave. of the Americas
New York, NY 10020
Phone: (212)484-5940
1980. 57 mins. This two-part program looks at the consequences of the use of products such as Dioxins and PCBs. These toxic chemicals are blamed for gross birth defects, miscarriages, cancer, and other illness. They have not yet been banned because of the chemical industry's lobbyists and lawyers. The programs are available individually.

★6796★ Planet Earth
Annenberg/CPB Collection
1111 16 St. NW
Washington, DC 20036
Phone: (202)955-5100
1986. 60 mins. Nobel Prize-winning scientists discuss new and startling information about planet Earth.

★6797★ Plankton: The Breathing Sea
New Dimension Media, Inc.
85895 Lorane Hwy.
Eugene, OR 97405
Phone: 800-288-4456
1986. 26 mins. An up-to-date survey of the workings of the seminal lifeform and its relationship with the environment.

★6798★ Planning the Land
AIMS Media, Inc.
6901 Woodley Ave.
Van Nuys, CA 91406-4878
Phone: (818)785-4111
1975. 24 mins. Legal methods for preserving open space are featured on this video.

★6799★ Plants and Animals Share Space and Food
Coronet/MTI Film & Video
108 Wilmot Rd.
Deerfield, IL 60015-9990
Phone: (312)940-1260
1976. 10 mins. A study of how living things share non-living things, such as sunlight, water, and soil.

★6800★ Pointless Pollution: America's Water Crisis
Bullfrog Films, Inc.
PO Box 149
Oley, PA 19547
Phone: (215)779-8226
1990. 28 mins. Nonpoint source pollution, the dirtying of waters from many places rather than only one source, is explained.

★6801★ Poison and the Pentagon
PBS Video
1320 Braddock Pl.
Alexandria, VA 22314-1698
Phone: (703)739-5380
1988. 58 mins. A "Frontline" investigation into the U.S. government's negligence in cleaning up toxic waste.

★6802★ The Poisoning of Michigan
Media Guild
11722 Sorrento Valley Rd.
Suite E
San Diego, CA 92121
Phone: (619)755-9191
1977. 65 mins. This tape examines the effects of the chemical PBB on the environment of Michigan.

★6803★ Pollution Below
National Aeronautics and Space Administration
Lewis Audiovisual Library
6100 Columbus Ave.
Sandusky, OH 44870
Phone: (419)626-2594
1975. 15 mins. This presentation follows three ordinary men and their hazardous encounters with pollution. Jacob Heath is in a pollution caused snowstorm; Jimmy Howard catches fish in a lake polluted by acid; and Tom McEwen is kayaking in Congress' idea of a clean river, the Potomac. Video is highlighted with satellite images of badly polluted areas.

★6804★ Pollution Control—The Hard Decisions
BNA Communications, Inc.
9439 Key West Ave.
Rockville, MD 20850
Phone: (301)948-0540
28 mins. This program from the "Managing Discontinuity" series discusses the impact of environmental problems on the individual company.

★6805★ Pollution of the Upper and Lower Atmosphere
Learning Corp. of America
108 Wilmot Rd.
Deerfield, IL 60015-9990
Phone: (312)940-1260
1975. 17 mins. Analyzes the effects of such fixtures in the world as the internal combustion engine and jet aircraft.

★6806★ Pollution Solution
National Aeronautics and Space Administration
Lewis Audiovisual Library
6100 Columbus Ave.
Sandusky, OH 44870
Phone: (419)626-2594
1976. 14 mins. The ability of Landsat to monitor the environment is examined in this film. The satellite has the capability of tracking airborne pollutants and monitoring industrial activity.

★6807★ Population and Pollution
International Film Bureau, Inc.
332 S. Michigan Ave.
Chicago, IL 60604-4382
Phone: (312)427-4545
1971. 17 mins. Portrays the present environmental crisis in North America caused both by misuse of the environment and by the great demands of a constantly growing population. Worldwide distribution rights.

★6808★ Potential for Contamination of Groundwater by Abandoned Landfills: The Use of Airphotos as an Assessment Tool
Cornell Univ.
Media Services Distribution Center
7-8 Research Park
Ithaca, NY 14850
Phone: (607)255-2091
1988. 19 mins. Learn how to use aerial pictures to see whether or not abandoned dumps are polluting local groundwater.

★6809★ The Power Switch
Maryland Center for Public Broadcasting
11767 Bonita Ave.
Owings Mills, MD 21117
Phone: (301)356-5600
1983. 30 mins. This is a series of programs that examines a variety of the newest tools and gadgets that can help save energy and money.

★6810★ Power Without End
Center for Humanities, Inc.
Communications Park
Box 1000
Mount Kisco, NY 10549
Phone: (914)666-4100
1975. 16 mins. A look at inexhaustable sources of power - the sun, the wind, the tides, geothermal heat, and water.

★6811★ Prairie Killers
Indiana Univ. Audio-Visual Center
Bloomington, IN 47405-5901
Phone: (812)335-8087
1970. 30 mins. A look at the problem keeping the prairie ecologically balanced. Ranchers are killing coyotes and prairie dogs, which are ecologically important.

★6812★ Prairie: Our Natural Heritage
NETCHE (Nebraska ETV Coun. for Higher Education)
Box 83111
Lincoln, NE 68501
Phone: (402)472-3611
1983. 30 mins. This two-part series on the grasslands of Central North America focuses on the wonderfully complex and unique ecological system.

★6813★ The Prairie That Was
AIMS Media, Inc.
6901 Woodley Ave.
Van Nuys, CA 91406-4878
Phone: (818)785-4111
1975. 19 mins. A visit to wildlife refuges shows prairie life as it was before the domination of man.

★6814★ Pre-Manufacture Notification Rule (EPA, May 1983)—A Series
National AudioVisual Center
National Archives & Records Administration
Customer Services Section PZ
8700 Edgeworth Dr.
Capitol Heights, MD 20743-3701
Phone: (301)763-1896
1983. 26 mins. Everything you need to know about notifing the Environmental Protection Agency that you are going to manufacture something dangerous is on these three tapes.

★6815★ Predator Control: "Kill That Coyote"
Centre Productions, Inc.
1800 30th St.
Suite 207
Boulder, CO 80301
Phone: (303)444-1166
1987. 20 mins. This program focuses on the poison control used by ranchers to keep coyotes off lands used to raise sheep and lambs.

★6816★ The Predators
Marty Stouffer Productions, Ltd.
300 S. Spring St.
Aspen, CO 81611
Phone: (303)925-5536
1977. 50 mins. North America's wild predators are shown, not as fearsome enemies of humans, but as vital parts of a wilderness ecosystem (Also available in a 26 minute version).

★6817★ Prehistoric Mammals
Phoenix/BFA Films
468 Park Ave. South
New York, NY 10016
Phone: (212)684-5910
1981. 16 mins. The question of survival for many of today's threatened species is answered.

★6818★ Primitives to Present
Michigan Media
University of Michigan
400 Fourth St.
Ann Arbor, MI 48109
Phone: (313)764-8228
1970. 29 mins. An examination of how primitive man practiced land conservation and what effect an increasing separation from nature has had on modern man. Part of the "Ecology: Man and the Environment" series.

★6819★ The Probable Passing of Elk Creek
Cinema Guild
1697 Broadway
Room 802
New York, NY 10019
Phone: (212)246-5522
1983. 60 mins. This video explores the conflict between a proposed dam, the white community it may flood, and the Indian tribal homeland it will destroy.

★6820★ Problems of Conservation: Air
Britannica Films
310 S. Michigan Ave.
Chicago, IL 60604
Phone: (312)347-7958
1988. 15 mins. The effects of man-made pollution are studied, as well as action being taken to correct the problem.

★6821★ Problems of Conservation: Minerals
Britannica Films
310 S. Michigan Ave.
Chicago, IL 60604
Phone: (312)347-7958
1988. 17 mins. Increasing dependency on nonrenewable minerals is presenting a new problem: the sources are finite.

★6822★ Problems of Conservation: Our Natural Resources
Britannica Films
310 S. Michigan Ave.
Chicago, IL 60604
Phone: (312)347-7958
1970. 11 mins. A broad overview of developing crises in natural resources; establishes man's reliance on them; his misuse of many of them; and current efforts in conservation.

★6823★ Problems of Conservation: Wildlife
Britannica Films
310 S. Michigan Ave.
Chicago, IL 60604
Phone: (312)347-7958
1970. 13 mins. Identifies endangered species; examines current efforts to conserve wildlife; and emphasizes the importance of every species to the biosphere.

★6824★ Productivity of the Sea
NETCHE (Nebraska ETV Coun. for Higher Education)
Box 83111
Lincoln, NE 68501
Phone: (402)472-3611
1970. 30 mins. Dr. John M. Teal explains some of the factors which influence plant life in the sea and offers a projection of the future of sea farming.

★6825★ Project Puffin
Learning Corp. of America
108 Wilmot Rd.
Deerfield, IL 60015-9990
Phone: (312)940-1260
1982. 13 mins. The Atlantic Puffin lives only on the open ocean, coming to remote offshore islands to breed. Though not endangered, the puffin population has declined due to pollution and decreased food supplies.

★6826★ Projections for the Future Series
Crystal Productions
1812 Johns Dr.
Post Office 2159
Glenview, IL 60025
Phone: (708)657-8144
1983. 18 mins. Each program in this series is divided into three parts: an introduction, an interview portion where futurists present their views and a scenario showing what life might be like if ideas presented in the first sections became a reality.

★6827★ Protecting the Global Environment
Cinema Guild
1697 Broadway
Room 802
New York, NY 10019
Phone: (212)246-5522
1989. 60 mins. This documentary series focuses on the ecological problems facing the world today, and looks at methods to help preserve the Earth's ecosystem.

★6828★ Protecting the Web
Pyramid Film & Video
Box 1048
Santa Monica, CA 90406
Phone: (213)828-7577
1989. 14 mins. A spider's web is used to show that all parts of nature are useful and necessary to the environment.

★6829★ Prudhoe Bay—or Bust
Indiana Univ. Audio-Visual Center
Bloomington, IN 47405-5901
Phone: (812)335-8087
1970. 30 mins. An examination of how 800 miles of pipeline will affect the wildlife of Alaska and the natural environment.

★6830★ Putting Aside Pesticides
Films for the Humanities
743 Alexander Rd.
Princeton, NJ 08540
Phone: (609)452-1128
1989. 26 mins. This tape explores pest-control alternatives, including biological pesticdes, insects destroyed by genetically-engineered microbes, predators of natural insects, and cross-breeding and genetical engineered plant strains with built in anti-pest toxins.

★6831★ A Question of Quality
National AudioVisual Center
National Archives & Records Administration
Customer Services Section PZ
8700 Edgeworth Dr.
Capitol Heights, MD 20743-3701
Phone: (301)763-1896
1977. 29 mins. We are only just beginning to protect our forests and wilderness areas against damage while allowing visitors to enjoy them at the same time. The quality of the wilderness experience, of the earth's resources, and of our own lives is important.

★6832★ The Quiet Crisis
Indiana Univ. Audio-Visual Center
Bloomington, IN 47405-5901
Phone: (812)335-8087
1980. 55 mins. This program examines water's vital role in transportation, industry, recreation, energy, and food production.

★6833★ Radiation and Its Effects
Educational Images
PO Box 3456, W. Side
Elmira, NY 14905
Phone: (607)732-1090
1987. 15 mins. This series examines ionizing radiation, its usages, and its dangers.

★6834★ Radiation and Your Environment
Educational Materials & Equipment Company
PO Box 17
Pelham, NY 10803
Phone: 800-848-2050
1982. 25 mins. An introduction to radioactive emissions, where they come from, their characteristics, uses and dangers.

★6835★ Radium City
Praeses Productions
28 Greene St.
New York, NY 10013
Phone: (212)925-1599
1987. 89 mins. A disturbing documentary about Ottawa, Illinois, where large chunks of the population have died of radiation-produced cancer, due to the large employment of a clock-making factory that required its mostly-female staff to use, with no protection, radium-based paint. The film also emphasizes the bureaucratic snares confronted by the populace when it looked for retribution.

★6836★ Rain Forest
Vestron Video
c/o LIVE Home Video
15400 Sherman Way
Suite 500
Van Nuys, CA 91410-0124
Phone: (203)978-5400
1983. 59 mins. This documentary looks at the paradoxical ecosystem of the Costa Rican tropical rain forests.

★6837★ The Rainbow Warrior Affair
Wombat Productions, Inc.
Division of Cortech, Inc.
250 W. 57th St.
Suite 916
New York, NY 10019
Phone: (212)315-2502
1989. 48 mins. A docudrama about violence and the Greenpeace organization in New Zealand.

★6838★ Rainy Days
Journal Films, Inc.
930 Pitner Ave.
Evanston, IL 60202
Phone: (312)328-6700
1988. 15 mins. The effects that rain can have on the environment are studied.

★6839★ Rampaging Carbons
Stanfield House
PO Box 3208
Santa Monica, CA 90403
Phone: (213)820-4568
1984. 27 mins. A documentary about the research that the National Environment Research Council is doing on carbon release and carbon absorption into the atmosphere.

★6840★ The Ravaged Land
Media Guild
11722 Sorrento Valley Rd.
Suite E
San Diego, CA 92121
Phone: (619)755-9191
1973. 14 mins. Focuses on the problems of surface mining in America. From the "Ecology" series.

★6841★ Reach for the Sun
KCET
4401 Sunset Blvd.
Los Angeles, CA 90027
Phone: (213)667-9237
1981. 30 mins. Science fiction, humor, special effects, and instructional highlights are used to teach children the wise use of energy resources.

★6842★ Recycled Reflections
Film Fair Communications
10900 Ventura Blvd.
PO Box 1728
Studio City, CA 91604
Phone: (818)985-0244
1973. 12 mins. Emphasizes the waste in automobile bumpers. Follows the process of transforming the damaged bumpers into new ones. Shows the recycling process.

★6843★ Recycling in Action
Film Fair Communications
10900 Ventura Blvd.
PO Box 1728
Studio City, CA 91604
Phone: (818)985-0244
1973. 14 mins. The need to recycle solid waste products: bottles, paper, plastic, etc.

★6844★ Recycling Our Resources
AIMS Media, Inc.
6901 Woodley Ave.
Van Nuys, CA 91406-4878
Phone: (818)785-4111
1973. 10 mins. Conservation and recycling of resources.

★6845★ Recycling Waste
Journal Films, Inc.
930 Pitner Ave.
Evanston, IL 60202
Phone: (312)328-6700
1972. 12 mins. This program shows how raw materials can be conserved and pollution curbed by turning waste material into useful products.

★6846★ Recycling: Waste into Wealth
Bullfrog Films, Inc.
PO Box 149
Oley, PA 19547
Phone: (215)779-8226
1985. 29 mins. This film outlines the benefits and actual process of mass recycling.

★6847★ The Redox Story
National Aeronautics and Space Administration
Lewis Audiovisual Library
6100 Columbus Ave.
Sandusky, OH 44870
Phone: (419)626-2594
1979. 4 mins. An examination of future petroleum storage methods that could save three-quarters of a billion barrels of oil a year.

★6848★ Reducing the Risk of PCBs
National AudioVisual Center
National Archives & Records Administration
Customer Services Section PZ
8700 Edgeworth Dr.
Capitol Heights, MD 20743-3701
Phone: (301)763-1896
1986. 12 mins. This video explains Environmental Protection Agency statutes on PCBs, and is of special interest to those in the utilities industries.

★6849★ Remote Possibilities
National Aeronautics and Space Administration
Lewis Audiovisual Library
6100 Columbus Ave.
Sandusky, OH 44870
Phone: (419)626-2594
1976. 14 mins. This film explores the role of Landsat and its mission of providing visual imagery so humans can better manage the planet's dwindling natural resources. The program also explains remote sensing.

★6850★ Renewable Energy Resources
Center for Humanities, Inc.
Communications Park
Box 1000
Mount Kisco, NY 10549
Phone: (914)666-4100
1980. 45 mins. This program offers an overview of the many promising alternative solutions to the energy problem.

★6851★ Replanting the Tree of Life
Bullfrog Films, Inc.
PO Box 149
Oley, PA 19547
Phone: (215)779-8226
1987. 12 mins. This program covers both the practical and spiritual value of trees, from explaining how they purify the air we breathe and process the water we depend on to pointing out the central place trees and tree symbols have played in different cultures.

★6852★ Resource Recovery
King Features Entertainment
235 E. 45th St.
New York, NY 10017
Phone: (212)682-5600
1983. 14 mins. This program studies the various ways raw materials and garbage can be turned into energy.

★6853★ Resources and World Trade
Phoenix/BFA Films
468 Park Ave. South
New York, NY 10016
Phone: (212)684-5910
1978. 14 mins. This show takes viewers around the world to see how resources such as minerals, energy, food, and trees are used to produce goods for home needs and for trade.

★6854★ Restoring the Environment
Films for the Humanities
743 Alexander Rd.
Princeton, NJ 08540
Phone: (609)452-1128
1989. 26 mins. Examines the technology used to correct environmental problems created through technological advances, focusing the EPA's Oils and Hazardous Materials Spills branch which developed a mobile incinerator to destroy PCBs and a private electroplating business which developed a pollution control system.

★6855★ Rethinking America
Michigan Media
University of Michigan
400 Fourth St.
Ann Arbor, MI 48109
Phone: (313)764-8228
1979. 29 mins. Several ways of rethinking our attitudes about our energy uses and wastes are discussed. Programs are available individually.

★6856★ Return of the Desert Bighorn
Centre Productions, Inc.
1800 30th St.
Suite 207
Boulder, CO 80301
Phone: (303)444-1166
1986. 28 mins. This is a program about America's extraordinary Desert Bighorn Sheep, and the efforts of wildlife agencies and conservationists to return them to their historic range.

★6857★ Return of the Great Whale
Home Vision
5547 N. Ravenswood Ave.
Chicago, IL 60640-1199
Phone: (312)878-2600
1985. 50 mins. This is a chronicle of the resurgence in numbers of the humpback and blue whales in the North Pacific.

★6858★ Return of the Peregrine Falcon
New Jersey Network
1573 Parkside Ave.
Trenton, NJ 08625
Phone: (609)292-5252
1979. 20 mins. A documentary about the efforts of the Cornell Ornithology Laboratories and the New Jersey Division of Fish, Game and Shell Fisheries to restore the endangered Peregrine Falcon to its natural habitat.

★6859★ Return of the Sea Otter
Filmakers Library, Inc.
133 E. 58th St.
New York, NY 10022
Phone: (212)355-6545
1987. 28 mins. The sea otter, once near extinction, made a remarkable comeback because of the efforts of scientists and conservationists. This film documents the transplanting of colonies into secure areas, and the lifestyle and behavior of the otter.

★6860★ Return to Michigan
Media Guild
11722 Sorrento Valley Rd.
Suite E
San Diego, CA 92121
Phone: (619)755-9191
1978. 28 mins. This tape looks at the 1976 shipping error that caused the poisoning of cattle and people in Michigan.

★6861★ Rhino Rescue
Phoenix/BFA Films
468 Park Ave. South
New York, NY 10016
Phone: (212)684-5910
1974. 22 mins. The rhinocerous is hunted in Africa merely for the price of its horn. Rhodesian game wardens have taken on the task of capturing, tagging, crating, and transporting the rhinos to a safer area.

★6862★ The Rhino War
Vestron Video
c/o LIVE Home Video
15400 Sherman Way
Suite 500
Van Nuys, CA 91410-0124
Phone: (203)978-5400
1987. 60 mins. A National Geographic special about the conservationist fight to save the rhinoceros from extinction.

★6863★ Riches from the Earth
National Geographic Soc.
17th & M Streets NW
Washington, DC 20036
Phone: (202)857-7378
1982. 23 mins. The discovery, depletion, and conservation of ores and other valuable minerals is examined.

★6864★ Right-To-Know Training Video
Marcom Group Ltd
#4 Denny Rd.
Wilmington, DE 19809
Phone: (302)764-3400
Seven-part videotape education and training series introduces employees to "right-to-know" regulations and provides training on all groups of chemicals found in the workplace. Available in English and Spanish.

★6865★ The Right Whale: An Endangered Species
National Geographic Soc.
17th & M Streets NW
Washington, DC 20036
Phone: (202)857-7378
1976. 23 mins. A look at this rare type of whale, explained by a zoologist.

★6866★ Riparian Vegetation
California Dept. of Water Resources
PO Box 388
Sacramento, CA 95802
Phone: (916)445-8569
1981. 14 mins. Natural plant growth along California's rivers must be managed to strike a balance between competing interests of farming and flood control. This program examines the problem.

★6867★ River (Planet Earth)
CRM/McGraw-Hill Films
674 Via de la Valle
PO Box 641
Del Mar, CA 92014
Phone: (619)453-5000
1978. 27 mins. A young student writes a paper on Canadian river systems, pointing out the problems of pollution. His teacher cannot understand the depredations that man is inflicting on his natural resources.

★6868★ The River That Came Back
AIMS Media, Inc.
6901 Woodley Ave.
Van Nuys, CA 91406-4878
Phone: (818)785-4111
1978. 10 mins. A record of the conservation efforts exercised to preserve the Au Sable River in lower Michigan.

★6869★ The River That Harms
Educational Film & Video Project
5332 College Ave.
Suite 101
Oakland, CA 94618
Phone: (415)655-9050
1987. 45 mins. This program examines the radioactive waste spill from the United Nuclear Corporation in 1979. 94 million gallons of uranium contaminated water spilled into the Puerco River in New Mexico after the UNC storage dam broke. While animals died and Navajo Indians became ill, the American media paid little attention.

★6870★ River Town
Bullfrog Films, Inc.
PO Box 149
Oley, PA 19547
Phone: (215)779-8226
1984. 28 mins. This is a fascinating film that examines the rebuilding of a flood devastated town that would run essentially on free solar energy.

★6871★ Rock, Ice and Oil
National Film Bd. of Canada
16th Fl.
1251 Ave. of the Americas
New York, NY 10020-1173
Phone: (212)586-5131
1987. 58 mins. This film focuses on research in the far north as part of the Polar Continental Shelf Project.

★6872★ The Rocky Mountains: The Last Stand
Journal Films, Inc.
930 Pitner Ave.
Evanston, IL 60202
Phone: (312)328-6700
30 mins. This program looks at a growing controversy in the National Parks between naturalists, tourists, and industry. The question "Whose land is it?" is posed.

★6873★ The Role of Coal
Indiana Univ. Audio-Visual Center
Bloomington, IN 47405-5901
Phone: (812)335-8087
1979. 17 mins. Coal as an energy source, a raw material in chemical and industrial products, and a natural resource is the subject of this program.

★6874★ The Role of Research
Media Design Associates, Inc.
PO Box 3189
Boulder, CO 80307-3189
Phone: (303)443-2800
1988. 15 mins. The impact that modern technology has on the environment is examined.

★6875★ A Room Full of Energy
National Film Bd. of Canada
16th Fl.
1251 Ave. of the Americas
New York, NY 10020-1173
Phone: (212)586-5131
1987. 10 mins. This film was designed to teach children about energy conservation.

★6876★ The Rotten Truth
VCA Teletronics
50 Leyland Dr.
Leonia, NJ 17606
Phone: 800-822-1105
Produced by 3-2-1 Contact Extras and Children's Television Workshop, this 30-minute program examines the topic of garbage. For children ages 8-12 and their families. ***Price:*** $14.95.

★6877★ Rubbish to Riches
AIMS Media, Inc.
6901 Woodley Ave.
Van Nuys, CA 91406-4878
Phone: (818)785-4111
1979. 11 mins. A look at some of the ways waste products can be converted into fuel, and trash can be recycled into usable products.

★6878★ Running on Empty—The Fuel Economy
National AudioVisual Center
National Archives & Records Administration
Customer Services Section PZ
8700 Edgeworth Dr.
Capitol Heights, MD 20743-3701
Phone: (301)763-1896
1978. 27 mins. This program shows how average drivers, driving average cars, can practice ways to achieve gasoline savings while travelling city and country roads and major highways.

★6879★ Saddleback
Journal Films, Inc.
930 Pitner Ave.
Evanston, IL 60202
Phone: (312)328-6700
1979. 24 mins. This program is designed as a primer in conservation, an account of exactly how to go about saving a species that is on the edge of extinction.

★6880★ Safe and Effective Pest Management
California Dept. of Water Resources
PO Box 388
Sacramento, CA 95802
Phone: (916)445-8569
1982. 19 mins. This program explains the California Department of Water Resources' program to protect the environment from plant and animal pests.

★6881★ St. Barbe of the Trees
Filmakers Library, Inc.
133 E. 58th St.
New York, NY 10022
Phone: (212)355-6545
1984. 16 mins. International conservationist Richard St. Barbe Baker discusses the environmental benefits of maintaining our forests.

★6882★ The Salt Marsh: A Question of Values
Britannica Films
310 S. Michigan Ave.
Chicago, IL 60604
Phone: (312)347-7958
1975. 22 mins. Documents the value of the biological communities that exist between sea and land - irreplaceable systems that man has been exploiting.

★6883★ Salt Marshes: A Special Resource
Educational Images
PO Box 3456, W. Side
Elmira, NY 14905
Phone: (607)732-1090
1987. 30 mins. This video provides a scientific examination of the importance of salt marshes to the environment.

★6884★ Sam
Direct Cinema Limited, Inc.
Box 69799
Los Angeles, CA 90069
Phone: (213)652-8000
1986. 22 mins. A sensitive portrait of a New York State farmer who strongly believes in balance and harmony between nature and humanity.

★6885★ Sanctuary: The Great Smoky Mountains
National AudioVisual Center
National Archives & Records Administration
Customer Services Section PZ
8700 Edgeworth Dr.
Capitol Heights, MD 20743-3701
Phone: (301)763-1896
1979. 10 mins. Glimpses of the Great Smoky Mountains in all seasons show the diversity of geography and wilderness in the national park.

★6886★ Sand and Gravel Is for the Birds: A Mining
Centre Productions, Inc.
1800 30th St.
Suite 207
Boulder, CO 80301
Phone: (303)444-1166
1987. 8 mins. This film shows how mining and environmental awareness can work together to produce increased environmental diversity while still removing needed rocks and minerals.

★6887★ Sand Dune Erosion Project
Cornell Univ.
Media Services Distribution Center
7-8 Research Park
Ithaca, NY 14850
Phone: (607)255-2091
1983. 14 mins. The program looks at the raising of beach grass in order to control sand dune erosion.

★6888★ Santa Barbara—Everybody's Mistake
Indiana Univ. Audio-Visual Center
Bloomington, IN 47405-5901
Phone: (812)335-8087
1970. 30 mins. An examination of the 1969 California offshore oil leak, and the question of endangering life because of our society's need for oil.

★6889★ Santa Cruz, Sanctuary of the Sea
New York State Education Dept.
Center for Learning Technologies
Media Distribution Network
Room C-7, Concourse Level
Albany, NY 12230
Phone: (518)474-1265
30 mins. The history of Santa Cruz, California is depicted, showing how the residents have kept the island pristine and beautiful.

★6890★ A Sauk County Almanac
Centre Productions, Inc.
1800 30th St.
Suite 207
Boulder, CO 80301
Phone: (303)444-1166
1990. 29 mins. The environmental writings of Aldo Leopold are reviewed.

★6891★ Save the Panda
Vestron Video
c/o LIVE Home Video
15400 Sherman Way
Suite 500
Van Nuys, CA 91410-0124
Phone: (203)978-5400
1983. 59 mins. This program travels to the People's Republic of China to study the giant panda, of which there may be no more than 1000 left in the world.

★6892★ Save the Planet
Green Mountain Post Films, Inc.
PO Box 229
Turners Falls, MA 01376
Phone: (413)863-4754
1979. 18 mins. A fast-paced documentary following the history of the atomic age and the debate over nuclear power.

★6893★ Save the Wetlands
Centre Productions, Inc.
1800 30th St.
Suite 207
Boulder, CO 80301
Phone: (303)444-1166
1986. 11 mins. This film provides information on the music, culture and scenery of New Orleans, Louisiana.

★6894★ Save Water
California Dept. of Water Resources
PO Box 388
Sacramento, CA 95802
Phone: (916)445-8569
1978. 5 mins. Features an animated character telling everyone that California doesn't have enough water to waste, especially during their long hot summers. Shows the responses of children when asked how they waste water. From the "What Do You Know About H20?" series.

★6895★ Saving the Gorilla
National Geographic Soc.
17th & M Streets NW
Washington, DC 20036
Phone: (202)857-7378
1982. 23 mins. Dr. Dian Fossey works with the endangered mountain gorilla in Rwanda, Africa; at several zoos, scientists attempt to breed the lowland gorilla to preserve it.

★6896★ Science in the Seventies
National AudioVisual Center
National Archives & Records Administration
Customer Services Section PZ
8700 Edgeworth Dr.
Capitol Heights, MD 20743-3701
Phone: (301)763-1896
1974. 52 mins. Four topics: man and society; the world and its resources; industry and

technology; and the relevance of the sciences to contemporary problems, are covered in this program.

★6897★ Science—New Frontiers: No Easy Answers
Phoenix/BFA Films
468 Park Ave. South
New York, NY 10016
Phone: (212)684-5910
1974. 14 mins. Scientific progress creates incredible opportunity and frightening risks.

★6898★ Scrap and Rubbish Control
General Motors Corp.
Management & Organization Development Department
1700 W. Third Ave.
Flint, MI 48502
Phone: (313)762-9867
25 mins. Emphasizes the need for effective screening of by-products of scrap material. Describes the three points of control in the flow of scrap; demonstrates methods of effectively but simply mutilating scrap to prevent use in the market. Suggests proper plant conditions and the methods a security officer uses to maintain them.

★6899★ Sea Turtles' Last Dance
PBS Video
1320 Braddock Pl.
Alexandria, VA 22314-1698
Phone: (703)739-5380
1988. 30 mins. This program provides footage of certain sea turtles, which have been around since the age of the dinosaur, and are now on the verge of becoming extinct.

★6900★ Sealion Summer
Wombat Productions, Inc.
Division of Cortech, Inc.
250 W. 57th St.
Suite 916
New York, NY 10019
Phone: (212)315-2502
1989. 24 mins. A rare breed of animal - Hookers Sealion breeds on Enderby Island during the brief sub-Arctic summer.

★6901★ Seals
Media Guild
11722 Sorrento Valley Rd.
Suite E
San Diego, CA 92121
Phone: (619)755-9191
1987. 25 mins. This film examines the major increase of grey seals along Great Britain's coast and the possible ecological damage this increase may cause.

★6902★ Seals: The Salmon Eaters
Centre Productions, Inc.
1800 30th St.
Suite 207
Boulder, CO 80301
Phone: (303)444-1166
1987. 20 mins. This film examines the debate between those who seek to protect seals against indiscriminate killing and fishermen who find that seals damage a large percentage of their salmon catch.

★6903★ Search for Survival
United Home Video
4111 S. Darlington St.
Suite 600
Tulsa, OK 74135
Phone: (918)622-6460
90 mins. This tape offers a view of wildlife in Australia, Africa and North America and how it relates to local food and water supplies.

★6904★ Second Chance: Sea
Pyramid Film & Video
Box 1048
Santa Monica, CA 90406
Phone: (213)828-7577
1976. 11 mins. A refreshing animated serenade to the sea, celebrating its glories while moving us to care about the ocean crises.

★6905★ A Second Change
New York State Education Dept.
Center for Learning Technologies
Media Distribution Network
Room C-7, Concourse Level
Albany, NY 12230
Phone: (518)474-1265
1986. 27 mins. A look at the encroachment on wildlife by industry, and how the latter can coexist and incorporate environmental concerns into its design.

★6906★ Secret Agent
Icarus Films
200 Park Ave. South
Suite 1319
New York, NY 10003
Phone: (212)674-3375
1983. 57 mins. This film explores the Sahel region of North Africa, and the ecological balance there which is in mortal danger.

★6907★ Secrets of Limestone Groundwater
Indiana Univ. Audio-Visual Center
Bloomington, IN 47405-5901
Phone: (812)335-8087
1980. 14 mins. Septic systems, garbage landfills, barnyard waste, and dumping in sink holes may be polluting groundwater in springs, wells, and underground rivers.

★6908★ Seeds of Survival
Film Fair Communications
10900 Ventura Blvd.
PO Box 1728
Studio City, CA 91604
Phone: (818)985-0244
1983. 28 mins. This program looks at the problem of chemically tainted farm soil.

★6909★ A Sense of Humus
Bullfrog Films, Inc.
PO Box 149
Oley, PA 19547
Phone: (215)779-8226
1977. 28 mins. Documents organic farming, the practice of growing food commercially without chemical fertilizers, pesticides, or herbicides to preserve the topsoil for future generations. In one instance, land unfit for agriculture yielded nearly twice the national average of wheat.

★6910★ A Sense of Value
New Jersey Network
1573 Parkside Ave.
Trenton, NJ 08625
Phone: (609)292-5252
1981. 30 mins. An overview that features all the unique park and recreation sites New Jersey has to offer.

★6911★ Sentenced to Success
Green Mountain Post Films, Inc.
PO Box 229
Turners Falls, MA 01376
Phone: (413)863-4754
1978. 60 mins. A "solution" to the nuclear waste problem is suggested.

★6912★ Shaping Education for the 70's
NETCHE (Nebraska ETV Coun. for Higher Education)
Box 83111
Lincoln, NE 68501
Phone: (402)472-3611
1971. 30 mins. America faces simple survival issues in the 1970's, including environmental deterioration, disillusionment of youth, and decay in the cities. This lesson shows how educational institutions have prepared to cope with these issues.

★6913★ Shenandoah—The Gift
Finley-Holiday Film Corp.
PO Box 619
Whittier, CA 90608
Phone: (213)945-3325
1982. 20 mins. This is a tourist's look at the Virginia national park.

★6914★ Shield of Plenty
Films, Inc.
5547 N. Ravenswood Ave.
Chicago, IL 60640-1199
Phone: (312)878-2600
1976. 29 mins. The earth's four billion-year-old Precambrian mountain remnants are explored. The formation of ancient mountains and their subsequent erosion are illustrated.

★6915★ Shipping: The Tankard Hazard
Journal Films, Inc.
930 Pitner Ave.
Evanston, IL 60202
Phone: (312)328-6700
12 mins. The increased threat of oil spills and wrecks due to trafficking of super tankers in the seas is discussed. New methods to alleviate the problems are documented.

★6916★ Short Rotation Forestry
Bullfrog Films, Inc.
PO Box 149
Oley, PA 19547
Phone: (215)779-8226
1987. 29 mins. A look at an old technique that saves money for reforestation, prevents erosion, and provides surprisingly high yields.

★6917★ Sidewalks of Shade
Cornell Univ.
Media Services Distribution Center
7-8 Research Park
Ithaca, NY 14850
Phone: (607)255-2091
1981. 25 mins. This tape looks at neighborhood and community tree-planting programs around the Northeast.

★6918★ Silent Forest
Barr Films
3490 E. Foothill Blvd.
PO Box 5667
Pasadena, CA 91107
Phone: (213)681-2165
1978. 23 mins. Examines the underwater forest of giant kelp that supports a unique community of marine life and is being destroyed by pollution.

★6919★ Silver Wires and Golden Wings
New York State Education Dept.
Center for Learning Technologies
Media Distribution Network
Room C-7, Concourse Level
Albany, NY 12230
Phone: (518)474-1265
1986. 26 mins. An ecological look at the life of the endangered Golden Eagle in relation to the high-voltage wires it alights on and gets electrocuted by.

★6920★ The Sky's the Limit
Univ. of California at Berkeley Extension Media Center
2176 Shattuck Ave.
Berkeley, CA 94704
Phone: (415)642-0460
1980. 23 mins. An investigation of the causes and consequences of urban air pollution, using the San Francisco Bay Area as a case study. Contributing factors such as industry, refineries, and automobiles are examined.

★6921★ Smoky Mountain Magic
International Video Projects, Inc.
250 Bird Rd.
Suite 307
Coral Gables, FL 33146
Phone: (305)442-8910
1989. 45 mins. The beauty of the national park in all four seasons is captured.

★6922★ The Solar Horizon
AIMS Media, Inc.
6901 Woodley Ave.
Van Nuys, CA 91406-4878
Phone: (818)785-4111
1981. 10 mins. A look at what experiments are being done in harnessing solar power, and how use of the sun for energy can replace our dwindling supply of fossil fuels.

★6923★ Solutions and Projections
Dallas County Community Coll. District
Center for Telecommunications
4343 North Hwy. 67
Mesquite, TX 75150-2095
Phone: (214)324-7988
1977. 29 mins. This program explores the ecological future of mankind.

★6924★ Sound of the Lake Country
Centre Productions, Inc.
1800 30th St.
Suite 207
Boulder, CO 80301
Phone: (303)444-1166
1986. 11 mins. This video documents the hazards to the loon's survival and the efforts conservationists are making to save this endangered species.

★6925★ Space Research and Your Home and Environment
National Aeronautics and Space Administration
Lewis Audiovisual Library
6100 Columbus Ave.
Sandusky, OH 44870
Phone: (419)626-2594
1981. 15 mins. This video explains how homes and the environment can be protected by using the research gathered by the space program. Includes information on energy-saving household appliances, new sewage treatment technologies, and protection of natural resources.

★6926★ Stopping the Coming Ice Age
Educational Film & Video Project
5332 College Ave.
Suite 101
Oakland, CA 94618
Phone: (415)655-9050
1988. 40 mins. This film provides evidence that human industrial activity on the planet is causing global climatic changes, warming some areas, cooling others.

★6927★ Strip Mining: Energy, Environment and Economics
Appalshop Films
306 Madison St.
Box 743A
Whitesburg, KY 41858
Phone: (606)633-0108
1980. 50 mins. A look at the long-term environmental effects of strip mining, the need for jobs created by strip mining, and the increased demand for coal.

★6928★ Strip Mining in Appalachia
Appalshop Films
306 Madison St.
Box 743A
Whitesburg, KY 41858
Phone: (606)633-0108
1973. 29 mins. A view of the destruction left in the wake of strip mining.

★6929★ Survival
Journal Films, Inc.
930 Pitner Ave.
Evanston, IL 60202
Phone: (312)328-6700
28 mins. Pollution, population growth and the depletion of non-renewable resources are discussed along with solutions to these contemporary problems.

★6930★ Technology and Values: The Energy Connection
Barr Films
3490 E. Foothill Blvd.
PO Box 5667
Pasadena, CA 91107
Phone: (213)681-2165
1979. 19 mins. We have been using the earth's energy resources for millions of years. This program develops an understanding for the need to alter our daily lives to conserve this diminishing resource, via alternative answers, to preserve our environment.

★6931★ The Technology of Trash
New York State Education Dept.
Center for Learning Technologies
Media Distribution Network
Room C-7, Concourse Level
Albany, NY 12230
Phone: (518)474-1265
1984. 22 mins. This program shows how environmentally safe and economical answers to our waste problems lie in innovative sanitary landfill procedures.

★6932★ Terra: Our World
Agency for Instructional Technology
Box A
Bloomington, IN 47402
Phone: (812)339-2203
1980. 20 mins. This series is designed to make the viewer aware of environmental issues such as food, energy and pollution. At the beginning of each program, television newswoman Connie Chung introduces an environmental issue. Interviews, explanations, and on-site visits follow, all of which provide information and raise questions about the scientific, aesthetic, social, and economic implications of the problem and its possible solutions. The programs are available individually.

★6933★ Teton Country
Finley-Holiday Film Corp.
PO Box 619
Whittier, CA 90608
Phone: (213)945-3325
1986. 30 mins. A nature film examining the wonders of the famous Wyoming national park.

★6934★ Thin Edge of the Bay
University of California at Berkeley Extension Media Center
2176 Shattuck Ave.
Berkeley, CA 94704
Phone: (415)642-0460
1980. 22 mins. Using San Francisco Bay as a focus, this program studies the economic and political conflicts over shrinking environmental resources in urban areas.

★6935★ The Tides of Time
Films for the Humanities
743 Alexander Rd.
Princeton, NJ 08540
Phone: (609)452-1128
1989. 26 mins. Explores the short-term fight to save endangered coastlines and the long-term implications of the "greenhouse" effect.

★6936★ The Time Will Be
S-L Film Productions
PO Box 41108
Los Angeles, CA 90041
Phone: (213)254-8528
1978. 3 mins. A look at the possible outcome of our auto-polluted world.

★6937★ To Defeat the Doomsday Doctrine: The World Isn't Running out of Everything Quite Yet
Cinema Guild
1697 Broadway
Room 802
New York, NY 10019
Phone: (212)246-5522
1984. 20 mins. A roundtable discussion of current ecological issues with John Maddox, author of "The Doomsday Syndrome," Dennis Meadows, author of "Limits to Growth" and Paul Ehrlich.

★6938★ To Save Our Environment: Conservation
Journal Films, Inc.
930 Pitner Ave.
Evanston, IL 60202
Phone: (312)328-6700
1971. 13 mins. This program discusses man's use of natural resources, differentiating between renewable and non-renewable resources.

★6939★ To Save the Amazon's Green Hell
Cinema Guild
1697 Broadway
Room 802
New York, NY 10019
Phone: (212)246-5522
20 mins. The imposing Amazon River and the tropical rain forest it permeates support the most complex ecosystem in the world, but as this film points out, the rain forest is shrinking, fishing along the river bank is slowing, and thousands of wildlife species have shrunk in population. Time is running out.

★6940★ Touring America's National Parks
Norman Beerger Productions
3217 S. Arville St.
Las Vegas, NV 89102-7612
Phone: (702)876-2328
1988. 60 mins. All the great national wildlife areas, such as Yosemite, the Everglades, and Acadia, are shown.

★6941★ A Town That Washes Its Water
King Features Entertainment
235 E. 45th St.
New York, NY 10017
Phone: (212)682-5600
1983. 13 mins. This program takes a look at the town of Santee, California that converts

sewage water into usage for irrigation and recreation purposes.

★6942★ The Toxic Goldrush
Films for the Humanities
743 Alexander Rd.
Princeton, NJ 08540
Phone: (609)452-1128
1989. 26 mins. Examines the hazardous waste disposal industry, focusing on the safety of plans and plants currently being discussed, the possible need for additional disposal sites, and other issues of toxic waste disposal.

★6943★ Toxic Waste: Information is the Best Defense
Bullfrog Films, Inc.
PO Box 149
Oley, PA 19547
Phone: (215)779-8226
1986. 26 mins. In two parts this program shows how community groups can organize protests and ordinances to fight toxic dumping.

★6944★ Travel Florida, State and National Parks
International Video Projects, Inc.
250 Bird Rd.
Suite 307
Coral Gables, FL 33146
Phone: (305)442-8910
1990. 30 mins. The parks of Florida are visited in this program.

★6945★ Troubled Waters
University of California at Berkeley Extension Media Center
2176 Shattuck Ave.
Berkeley, CA 94704
Phone: (415)642-0460
1985. 28 mins. This documentary examines how oil exploration is threatening California's coastal wildlife.

★6946★ Turn Off Pollution
Britannica Films
310 S. Michigan Ave.
Chicago, IL 60604
Phone: (312)347-7958
1971. 11 mins. Shows how elementary school-age children learn to identify major sources of pollution and take active steps to eliminate pollution from their community.

★6947★ Turning the Tide
Bullfrog Films, Inc.
PO Box 149
Oley, PA 19547
Phone: (215)779-8226
1990. 26 mins. Bellamy talks about some of the different problems that our Earth's environment faces.

★6948★ Uncle Smiley Goes Recycling
Learning Corp. of America
108 Wilmot Rd.
Deerfield, IL 60015-9990
Phone: (312)940-1260
1972. 13 mins. A visit to a recycling station shows children how cans, bottles, and paper can be reused. It also starts them on their own neighborhood collection project.

★6949★ Uncle Smiley Goes Up the River
Learning Corp. of America
108 Wilmot Rd.
Deerfield, IL 60015-9990
Phone: (312)940-1260
1972. 11 mins. Uncle and his friends learn what people can do to prevent pollution, as they join a community-action program to clean up a river.

★6950★ Unwasted Stories
Intermedia Arts of Minnesota, Inc.
425 Ontario St. SE
Minneapolis, MN 55414
Phone: (612)627-4444
1988. 75 mins. A challenging documentary about the use and misuse of society's waste. The question of what we can do to protect our environment is raised.

★6951★ Urban Wildlife
Centre Productions, Inc.
1800 30th St.
Suite 207
Boulder, CO 80301
Phone: (303)444-1166
1987. 20 mins. This program shows the numerous problems which erupt when human beings and wild animals encounter each other in urban areas.

★6952★ Use it, Use it Up
University of California at Berkeley Extension Media Center
2176 Shattuck Ave.
Berkeley, CA 94704
Phone: (415)642-0460
1975. 26 mins. This program examines how simple changes in domestic and commercial habits can have profound social and environmental effects.

★6953★ Using Solar Energy
Rodale Press, Inc.
33 E. Minor St.
Emmaus, PA 18049
Phone: (215)967-5171
1980. 55 mins. Two programs which describe how to use solar energy to help heat your home and how to build a solar-powered greenhouse are contained on this cassette: "Opening Your Home to Solar Energy" and "The Attached Solar Greenhouse."

★6954★ The Valley Green
Umbrella Films
60 Blake Rd.
Brookline, MA 02146
Phone: (617)277-6639
1988. 28 mins. The effects of civilization are seen destroying the natural areas of Wissahickon Creek outside of Philadelphia.

★6955★ The Vanishing Earth
Cornell Univ.
Media Services Distribution Center
7-8 Research Park
Ithaca, NY 14850
Phone: (607)255-2091
1985. 30 mins. A video documentary on the environmental concerns of the T'boli people, who live in the hills of Mindanao in the Philippines.

★6956★ Vanishing Wilderness
Media Home Entertainment, Inc.
5730 Buckingham Pkwy.
Culver City, CA 90230
Phone: (213)216-7900
1973. 90 mins. This documentary looks at the wild animals roaming across North America.

★6957★ Video Film Series: Nature Episodes
Educational Images
PO Box 3456, W. Side
Elmira, NY 14905
Phone: (607)732-1090
1987. 20 mins. This series of programs examines specific aspects of the natural world.

★6958★ A Visit with Amory and Hunter Lovins
Bullfrog Films, Inc.
PO Box 149
Oley, PA 19547
Phone: (215)779-8226
1985. 14 mins. A tour of the Lovin house, where the energy experts prove how to live comfortably and simultaneously be environmentally responsible.

★6959★ A Visit With J.I. Rodale
Bullfrog Films, Inc.
PO Box 149
Oley, PA 19547
Phone: (215)779-8226
1972. 15 mins. This program is about J.I. Rodale, who foresaw our current environmental crisis over thirty years ago and pioneered the organic movement in America.

★6960★ A Voice in the Wilderness
Focus On Animals
PO Box 150
Trumbull, CT 06611
Phone: (203)377-1116
1989. 50 mins. One man who has fought against legalized hunting for fifteen years tells some of the indecencies involved in the activity.

★6961★ A Voice in the Wilderness
Nature Preservation Network
PO Box 801
Trumbull, CT 06611
Phone: (203)576-4585
1986. 27 mins. A look at the work of conservationist Luke A. Dommer, president of the Committee to Abolish Sport Hunting, the effects of sport hunting on the environment and the lies which hunting lobbies use to foster the American public's belief that hunting is beneficial and necessary.

★6962★ Voyage of the San Carlos
California Dept. of Water Resources
PO Box 388
Sacramento, CA 95802
Phone: (916)445-8569
1978. 18 mins. This program takes the viewer on a tour of the Sacramento-San Joaquin Delta on the water quality monitoring ship "San Carlos." Tells how the California Department of Water Resources goes to great lengths to monitor the water quality of the Delta in attempts to preserve this estuary.

★6963★ Voyages to Save the Whale
Focus On Animals
PO Box 150
Trumbull, CT 06611
Phone: (203)377-1116
1989. 27 mins. A documentary about Greenpeace's early efforts to save the whales.

★6964★ A Walk in the Woods
Coronet/MTI Film & Video
108 Wilmot Rd.
Deerfield, IL 60015-9990
Phone: (312)940-1260
1972. 6 mins. A boy, exploring woods near his home, becomes aware of litter and decides to do something about it.

★6965★ Walter Cronkite's Universe: Disappearance of the Great Rainforest
Arthur Mokin Productions, Inc.
PO Box 1866
Santa Rosa, CA 95402-1866
Phone: (707)542-4868
1983. 12 mins. This program looks at the work of concerned scientists who have been studying the effects of deforestation in the Amazon.

★6966★ Warming Warning
Media Guild
11722 Sorrento Valley Rd.
Suite E
San Diego, CA 92121
Phone: (619)755-9191
1988. 52 mins. This Nova program warns of the impending global warming crisis.

★6967★ Warning: Breathing May Be Hazardous To Your Health
Trainex Corp.
PO Box 116
Garden Grove, CA 92642
Phone: 800-854-2485
25 mins. An interview with Dr. Joseph Boyle, specialist in internal medicine and diseases of the chest and lungs, tells of how bad pollution is and what a threat it is to mankind.

★6968★ Waste
Bullfrog Films, Inc.
PO Box 149
Oley, PA 19547
Phone: (215)779-8226
1985. 29 mins. The problems of waste disposal in our society are made plain, along with alternate solutions.

★6969★ Waste
Cinema Guild
1697 Broadway
Room 802
New York, NY 10019
Phone: (212)246-5522
1976. 20 mins. Recycling techniques are examined as an answer to the problem of waste disposal.

★6970★ Waste Not
Umbrella Films
60 Blake Rd.
Brookline, MA 02146
Phone: (617)277-6639
1988. 35 mins. Despite government regulation, there is still a problem with a build-up of hazardous waste products. This film looks at ways to reduce the amount of waste created.

★6971★ Waste: Recycling the World
Cinema Guild
1697 Broadway
Room 802
New York, NY 10019
Phone: (212)246-5522
This film addresses the problem of excessive waste materials accumulating in some cities and measures undertaken or planned that will stem the flow of garbage.

★6972★ Waste—The Penalty of Affluence
International Film Bureau, Inc.
332 S. Michigan Ave.
Chicago, IL 60604-4382
Phone: (312)427-4545
1972. 18 mins. This program outlines the environmental hazards of improper disposal of household, commercial, and industrial waste, and demonstrates three basic methods of disposal: sanitary landfill, composting, and incineration.

★6973★ Wastewater Management—Options for Unsewered Areas
National AudioVisual Center
National Archives & Records Administration
Customer Services Section PZ
8700 Edgeworth Dr.
Capitol Heights, MD 20743-3701
Phone: (301)763-1896
1982. 25 mins. This video demonstrates alternatives to the traditional septic tank system of wastewater disposal in use across the country in smaller towns that cannot afford an extensive sewer system.

★6974★ Water: A Clear and Present Danger
MTI Teleprograms, Inc.
108 Wilmot Rd.
Deerfield, IL 60015-9990
Phone: (312)940-1260
1983. 26 mins. A look at the problem of ground water contamination and what's being done about it.

★6975★ Water: A Precious Resource
National Geographic Soc.
17th & M Streets NW
Washington, DC 20036
Phone: (202)857-7378
1979. 23 mins. A number of topics about water are examined, such as where it comes from and how to protect it.

★6976★ Water: A Treasure in Trouble
Pyramid Film & Video
Box 1048
Santa Monica, CA 90406
Phone: (213)828-7577
1989. 14 mins. Water, although it is essential to life in many ways, is becoming scarce.

★6977★ Water and Life: A Delicate Balance
Films for the Humanities
743 Alexander Rd.
Princeton, NJ 08540
Phone: (609)452-1128
1989. 13 mins. Examines the role of water in the human body, cycles of water, industrial water consumption and pollution, methods to increase water supply, and the misconception of water as a renewable resource.

★6978★ Water and Wastewater Treatments
University of Wisconsin Extension
Department of Engineering & Applied Science
432 N. Lake St.
Madison, WI 53706
Phone: (608)262-2061
1977. 30 mins. This module course is designed as an introduction for those specifically concerned with the chemistry and methods of water supply and treatment and wastewater treatment and disposal. Programs below are also available individually. Part of the "Environmental Engineering" series.

★6979★ Water California Style
California Dept. of Water Resources
PO Box 388
Sacramento, CA 95802
Phone: (916)445-8569
1976. 16 mins. This program traces California's water development for the past 200 years via original paintings, historic photographs, and live-action scenes. Also illustrates current water management policies, emphasizing water conservation and water reclamation practices.

★6980★ Water Crisis?
Self Reliance Found.
Box 1
Las Trampas, NM 87576
Phone: (505)689-2250
1982. 45 mins. This program examines water conservation techniques for small farmers.

★6981★ The Water Crisis
Time-Life Video
1271 Ave. of the Americas
New York, NY 10020
Phone: (212)484-5940
1981. 57 mins. This entry in the "Nova" series shows that water scarcity could become the next natural issue. Water problems, from the Adirondack mountains in New York, to the Mississippi River, to the West Coast, are discussed.

★6982★ The Water Film
Barr Films
3490 E. Foothill Blvd.
PO Box 5667
Pasadena, CA 91107
Phone: (213)681-2165
1977. 9 mins. A young rabbit learns about the different forms water takes and realizes the importance of protecting it from pollution.

★6983★ Water: Fluid for Life
Coronet/MTI Film & Video
108 Wilmot Rd.
Deerfield, IL 60015-9990
Phone: (312)940-1260
1978. 16 mins. A photographic documentary that reveals the decisive role water has played and still plays in the emergence and survival of life on earth.

★6984★ Water for Farming
California Dept. of Water Resources
PO Box 388
Sacramento, CA 95802
Phone: (916)445-8569
1978. 5 mins. An animated character tells the story that agriculture is the largest consumer of water in California. Children learn where farmers get their water and how they get it to crops during the long hot summer. Various methods of irrigation are illustrated. From the "What Do You Know About H2O?" series.

★6985★ Water for Industry
California Dept. of Water Resources
PO Box 388
Sacramento, CA 95802
Phone: (916)445-8569
1978. 5 mins. A cartoon character tells the story that industry uses water to process many food products. The cleaning and recycling of industrial water is shown as an important way to use water more efficiently. From the "What Do You Know About H2O?" series.

★6986★ Water for the City
Phoenix/BFA Films
468 Park Ave. South
New York, NY 10016
Phone: (212)684-5910
11 mins. Whatever the source, water must be purified and piped into our homes.

★6987★ Water: It's What We Make It
PBS Video
1320 Braddock Pl.
Alexandria, VA 22314-1698
Phone: (703)739-5380
1986. 18 mins. A documentary about the earth's water supply, man's pollution of it over the years, and the recent efforts to preserve it.

★6988★ Water Means Life
Great Plains Natl. Instructional Television Library
University of Nebraska at Lincoln
PO Box 80669
Lincoln, NE 68501-0669
Phone: (402)472-2007
1979. 20 mins. The need for more sophisticated water systems and related

problems in countries such as Tanzania, Guatemala, and Mexico are focused on.

★6989★ Water, More Precious Than Oil
PBS Video
1320 Braddock Pl.
Alexandria, VA 22314-1698
Phone: (703)739-5380
1982. 60 mins. This program examines the quality of current water supplies, water-related diseases, pollution, and the uneven distribution of water throughout the world.

★6990★ Water Pollution
Journal Films, Inc.
930 Pitner Ave.
Evanston, IL 60202
Phone: (312)328-6700
1970. 12 mins. This program points out that man uses water for many purposes, and that is part of the reason for water pollution. It also presents information concerning the sources of water pollution and suggests what individuals can do about the problem.

★6991★ Water Pollution: A First Film
Phoenix/BFA Films
468 Park Ave. South
New York, NY 10016
Phone: (212)684-5910
1985. 12 mins. This updated program is designed to help viewers understand water pollution, with information on aquifiers to aid in the learning process.

★6992★ Water Purification
AIMS Media, Inc.
6901 Woodley Ave.
Van Nuys, CA 91406-4878
Phone: (818)785-4111
1970. 9 mins. Study of water and the process of purifying it for our use.

★6993★ Water Resources
Dallas County Community Coll. District
Center for Telecommunications
4343 North Hwy. 67
Mesquite, TX 75150-2095
Phone: (214)324-7988
1977. 29 mins. This program details the importance of water in the ecosystem.

★6994★ Water Resources Videos
Educational Images
PO Box 3456, W. Side
Elmira, NY 14905
Phone: (607)732-1090
1987. 28 mins. This series of programs examines water usage and quality in California.

★6995★ Water Roundup
California Dept. of Water Resources
PO Box 388
Sacramento, CA 95802
Phone: (916)445-8569
1982. 15 mins. This program explains how California's State Water Project works, the facilities they use and how the Project benefits the state.

★6996★ Water Supply and Sanitation in Development
Indiana Univ. Audio-Visual Center
Bloomington, IN 47405-5901
Phone: (812)335-8087
1985. 30 mins. These videos focus on effective water management and sewage treatment systems in developing nations, including Nepal, Malawi, and Burma.

★6997★ Water: The Effluent Society
Cinema Guild
1697 Broadway
Room 802
New York, NY 10019
Phone: (212)246-5522
20 mins. This film examines the availability of water and the pollution control measures necessary to maintain a constantly fresh supply.

★6998★ Water Wars: The Battle of Mono Lake
University of California at Berkeley Extension Media Center
2176 Shattuck Ave.
Berkeley, CA 94704
Phone: (415)642-0460
1984. 39 mins. The controversy surrounding the diversion of fresh water from California's Mono Lake to the city of Los Angeles is examined.

★6999★ We Are of the Soil
International Film Bureau, Inc.
332 S. Michigan Ave.
Chicago, IL 60604-4382
Phone: (312)427-4545
1983. 23 mins. A discussion of the problem of soil erosion and how it affects everyone.

★7000★ We Call Them Killers
National Film Bd. of Canada
16th Fl.
1251 Ave. of the Americas
New York, NY 10020-1173
Phone: (212)586-5131
1972. 16 mins. A rare view of two killer whales, filmed at the Victoria (British Columbia) Sealand of the Pacific aquarium.

★7001★ We Have Met the Enemy and He Is Us?
Communications Group West
1640 Fifth St. #202
Santa Monica, CA 90401
Phone: (213)451-2525
1974. 13 mins. Looks at attiudes and problems of pollution in our environment.

★7002★ We Will Freeze in the Dark
CRM/McGraw-Hill Films
674 Via de la Valle
PO Box 641
Del Mar, CA 92014
Phone: (619)453-5000
1977. 42 mins. A dramatization of what might happen if the United States continues using fuel at the present rate without instituting a good national energy policy.

★7003★ The Wet Look
National Aeronautics & Space Administration (NASA)
Lewis Audiovisual Library
6100 Columbus Ave.
Sandusky, OH 44870
Phone: (419)626-2594
1976. 14 mins. The ability of Landsat to help solve water resource problems is illustrated. Includes the monitoring of floods and the mapping of snow packs.

★7004★ Wetlands: Development, Progress, and Environmental Protection under the Changing Law
Amer. Law Inst.
American Bar Association Committee on Continuing Education
4025 Chestnut St.
Philadelphia, PA 19104
Phone: (215)243-1650
1987. 210 mins. This program examines the legal issues of wetlands protection.

★7005★ Whale Hunters of San Miguel
Journal Films, Inc.
930 Pitner Ave.
Evanston, IL 60202
Phone: (312)328-6700
15 mins. The whaling industry and the pros and cons of hunting whales as a source of income are discussed.

★7006★ Whales
Brighton Video
250 W. 57th St.
Suite 2421
New York, NY 10019
Phone: (212)315-2502
1988. 50 mins. Whale footage is combined with interviews of people who kill them for a living.

★7007★ Whales and the Threat of Nets
Focus On Animals
PO Box 150
Trumbull, CT 06611
Phone: (203)377-1116
1988. 30 mins. The danger that fishing nets pose to whales is graphically depicted in this program, part of which shows a whale rescue operation.

★7008★ Whales: Can They Be Saved?
Britannica Films
310 S. Michigan Ave.
Chicago, IL 60604
Phone: (312)347-7958
1976. 24 mins. Examines the behavior of many types of whales and explains the steps people must take to save this nearly extinct species.

★7009★ Whales, Dolphins, and Men
Films, Inc.
5547 N. Ravenswood Ave.
Chicago, IL 60640-1199
Phone: (312)878-2600
1973. 50 mins. The film explains that the dolphin is not only an entertainer in water shows, but actually is very intelligent. The whale has a common ancestor, but is a victim of commercialization and is in danger of extinction.

★7010★ What About Tomorrow?
Indiana Univ. Audio-Visual Center
Bloomington, IN 47405-5901
Phone: (812)335-8087
1978. 19 mins. A look at basic scientific research focusing on scientists working in four areas: physics, agriculture, chemistry and environmental studies.

★7011★ What Ecologists Do
Centron Films
108 Wilmot Rd.
Deerfield, IL 60015-9990
Phone: (312)940-1260
1971. 16 mins. The ecologist studies interrelationships between living things and their surroundings. In this program the ecologist works with bald eagles, water supply, and animal tracking.

★7012★ What Energy Means
National Geographic Soc.
17th & M Streets NW
Washington, DC 20036
Phone: (202)857-7378
1982. 15 mins. Sources of energy such as coal, natural gas, petroleum, and the sun are examined.

★7013★ What Is Ecology?
Britannica Films
310 S. Michigan Ave.
Chicago, IL 60604
Phone: (312)347-7958
1977. 21 mins. An introduction to ecology. Defines and shows examples of ecosystems, stressing plant-animal-environment relationships. Shows how human activity presents a constant danger to ecological balance.

★7014★ What's a Natural Resource?
Alfred Higgins Productions, Inc.
6350 Laurel Canyon Blvd.
North Hollywood, CA 91606
Phone: (818)762-3300
1985. 16 mins. A vignette wherein a park ranger explains what natural resources are to kids, dealing with water, wood and oil.

★7015★ Wheat Today, What Tomorrow?
Bullfrog Films, Inc.
PO Box 149
Oley, PA 19547
Phone: (215)779-8226
1988. 32 mins. Filmed in Western Australia, this program offers a look at a new environmental ethic and mass planting of trees, both to protect the soil for wheat crops and to harvest as productive food and fodder plants.

★7016★ When the Rivers Run Dry
University of California at Berkeley Extension Media Center
2176 Shattuck Ave.
Berkeley, CA 94704
Phone: (415)642-0460
1980. 29 mins. A cultural history of water use in the semiarid Southwest, a region marked by alternating problems of drought and flood.

★7017★ When There Are No More Fish in the Sea
Japan Society, Inc.
333 E. 47th St.
New York, NY 10017
Phone: (212)832-1155
33 mins. A TV-docudrama which employs a symphony orchestra, experimental video and Japanese singers and dancers to conceptualize man's disregard for nature.

★7018★ Which Is My World?
Phoenix/BFA Films
468 Park Ave. South
New York, NY 10016
Phone: (212)684-5910
1971. 10 mins. Our demand for new things leads us to discard still usable items. We must decide what changes in life style are necessary for our safe and pleasant survival. No narration.

★7019★ Who Speaks for Earth
Films, Inc.
5547 N. Ravenswood Ave.
Chicago, IL 60640-1199
Phone: (312)878-2600
1980. 60 mins. Dr. Carl Sagan reviews the first twelve episodes of the "Cosmos" series in this final chapter. The ideas of cosmic evolution, the scientific approach, and history as an exemplary teacher are woven together with cautionary warnings about the types of futures we face as a species and a planet.

★7020★ Who's Killing Calvert City?
PBS Video
1320 Braddock Pl.
Alexandria, VA 22314-1698
Phone: (703)739-5380
1989. 60 mins. This town in Kentucky was nicknamed "cancer city" because of the toxic waste from several large chemical plants. The struggle between concerned environmentalists and chemical manufacturers is examined in this FRONTLINE special.

★7021★ Why We Conserve Energy: The Witch of the Great Black Pool
Learning Corp. of America
108 Wilmot Rd.
Deerfield, IL 60015-9990
Phone: (312)940-1260
1978. 12 mins. A story for children that teaches them to conserve energy.

★7022★ Wild in the City
National Film Bd. of Canada
16th Fl.
1251 Ave. of the Americas
New York, NY 10020-1173
Phone: (212)586-5131
1987. 16 mins. This film focuses on wild animals that have adapted to an urban environment.

★7023★ Wild River
National Geographic Soc.
17th & M Streets NW
Washington, DC 20036
Phone: (202)857-7378
1970. 52 mins. Two families challenge the white-water rivers of Idaho. Also looks at pollution problems in the Hudson and Potomac Rivers.

★7024★ Wilderness—An American Ideal
West Wind Productions, Inc.
PO Box 3532
Boulder, CO 80307
Phone: (303)443-2800
1975. 15 mins. The value of wilderness past and present are considered, quoting from people who have expressed strong feelings about the wilderness.

★7025★ Wilderness Quest
TV Sports Scene, Inc.
5804 Ayrshire Blvd.
Minneapolis, MN 55436
Phone: (612)925-9661
1981. 24 mins. Different wilderness regions of the U.S. are explored, and methods of conservation of these diminishing areas are discussed.

★7026★ Wilderness Series
Phoenix/BFA Films
468 Park Ave. South
New York, NY 10016
Phone: (212)684-5910
8 mins. The many aspects of the wilderness are covered in these films intended to motivate the audience. Programs are available as a series and/or individually.

★7027★ Wildlife—An American Heritage
West Wind Productions, Inc.
PO Box 3532
Boulder, CO 80307
Phone: (303)443-2800
1975. 14 mins. Historic facts and basic concepts of wildlife management are presented as a starting point for considering the value and conservation of America's wildlife.

★7028★ Wildlife Management
Dallas County Community Coll. District
Center for Telecommunications
4343 North Hwy. 67
Mesquite, TX 75150-2095
Phone: (214)324-7988
1977. 29 mins. This program discusses man's attempts to manage wildlife in his environment, and such topics as extinction of species.

★7029★ Will the Gator Glades Survive
Indiana Univ. Audio-Visual Center
Bloomington, IN 47405-5901
Phone: (812)335-8087
1970. 30 mins. A look at wildlife inhabiting the Florida Everglades, which is in danger because man is interfering with the natural water supply.

★7030★ Will They Survive
Centre Productions, Inc.
1800 30th St.
Suite 207
Boulder, CO 80301
Phone: (303)444-1166
1983. 12 mins. This program deals with the status of a variety of North America's endangered species.

★7031★ Wind: An Energy Alternative
National AudioVisual Center
National Archives & Records Administration
Customer Services Section PZ
8700 Edgeworth Dr.
Capitol Heights, MD 20743-3701
Phone: (301)763-1896
1980. 12 mins. This program looks at the history and uses of wind power, used for centuries by humans to move boats, pump water and grind grain, including discussions on efficiency, problems in the urban environment, experimental systems and windmill use across the United States.

★7032★ Wind and Water Energy
Time-Life Video
1271 Ave. of the Americas
New York, NY 10020
Phone: (212)484-5940
1977. 25 mins. Examines ways to harness the powers of the sun through wind and water energy.

★7033★ Wind Energy
NETCHE (Nebraska ETV Coun. for Higher Education)
Box 83111
Lincoln, NE 68501
Phone: (402)472-3611
1976. 30 mins. Dwindling hydrocarbon fuels and the energy crisis in general have forced us to take a look at windmills as energy generators. Dr William L. Hughes explains the nuances of this method of energy generation.

★7034★ Wind Power: Living with Tomorrow
Willow Mixed Media, Inc.
PO Box 194
Glenford, NY 12433
Phone: (914)657-2914
1981. 12 mins. A visit with a Massachusetts couple who have a working wind generator producing about 25% of their current energy needs.

★7035★ Windows in Time: Research Today for Energy Tomorrow
Modern Talking Picture Service
5000 Park Street N.
St. Petersburg, FL 33709
Phone: (813)541-7571
1985. 29 mins. This film captures the joys and frustrations of five scientists working in energy research.

★7036★ Windsong
Centre Productions, Inc.
1800 30th St.
Suite 207
Boulder, CO 80301
Phone: (303)444-1166
1984. 19 mins. This film provides an informative and poetic introduction to the history and uses of wind energy.

★7037★ Winter Range
Centre Productions, Inc.
1800 30th St.
Suite 207
Boulder, CO 80301
Phone: (303)444-1166
1987. 19 mins. This beautifully shot documentary examines the environmental problems created by civilization's continued expansion into winter range lands used by animals such as elk.

★7038★ Wolves and Coyotes of the Rockies
Beacon Films
930 Pinter Ave.
Evanston, IL 60202
Phone: (312)328-6700
1983. 15 mins. Part of the "North American Species" series, this is a documentary about the remaining wolves and coyotes that live in the Rocky Mountain wilderness.

★7039★ Wolves and the Wolf Men
Films, Inc.
5547 N. Ravenswood Ave.
Chicago, IL 60640-1199
Phone: (312)878-2600
1972. 52 mins. Only about 5000 wolves exist in the U.S. today and they are in danger of extinction. A handful of people known as wolf men are dedicated to saving the species from hunters.

★7040★ The Wonder of Dolphins
Centron Films
108 Wilmot Rd.
Deerfield, IL 60015-9990
Phone: (312)940-1260
1980. 11 mins. A look at the behavior, habitat, and communication system of the dolphin.

★7041★ Wood Heat
Bullfrog Films, Inc.
PO Box 149
Oley, PA 19547
Phone: (215)779-8226
1980. 27 mins. Interviews with a wood supplier, a wood stove dealer, and a forester reveal the advantages and disadvantages of heating homes with wood. Part of the "Home Energy Conservation" series.

★7042★ Wood Is Too Good to Burn
PBS Video
1320 Braddock Pl.
Alexandria, VA 22314-1698
Phone: (703)739-5380
1980. 29 mins. This program examines the new uses for wood that scientists are discovering in research laboratories. It has been found that wood may be a source for synthetic fibers, plastics, and medicine, among other things.

★7043★ The World in 1984
New York State Education Dept.
Center for Learning Technologies
Media Distribution Network
Room C-7, Concourse Level
Albany, NY 12230
Phone: (518)474-1265
30 mins. Nigel Calder, editor of "New Scientist" discusses the future based upon present conditions and known possibilities.

★7044★ The World Is a Bank
Phoenix/BFA Films
468 Park Ave. South
New York, NY 10016
Phone: (212)684-5910
1972. 10 mins. This show explores some of the ways we can safeguard our wealth of natural resources.

★7045★ World of the Future
Cinema Guild
1697 Broadway
Room 802
New York, NY 10019
Phone: (212)246-5522
19 mins. An interview with Alvin Toffler, author of "Future Shock," is featured in this film addressing the exploding changes that have and will take place in modern society.

★7046★ Year of the Eagle
Centre Productions, Inc.
1800 30th St.
Suite 207
Boulder, CO 80301
Phone: (303)444-1166
1985. 27 mins. This video shows how pesticides, population expansion into wilderness areas, and even killing for profit have all contributed to the drastic reduction of the eagle population in America.

★7047★ Yellow Creek, Kentucky Part I
Appalshop Films
306 Madison St.
Box 743A
Whitesburg, KY 41858
Phone: (606)633-0108
1984. 28 mins. A study of the Yellow Creek Concerned Citizens' efforts to stop a local tannery from dumping toxic wastes.

★7048★ Yellowstone
Eastman Kodak Company
c/o Wood Knapp
Knapp Press
5900 Wilshire Blvd.
Los Angeles, CA 90036
Phone: (213)937-5486
1989. 30 mins. A visit to Yellowstone National Park's thermal basin. Visual highlights include rock formations, geysers and rare plant life.

★7049★ Yellowstone and Grand Teton
Finley-Holiday Film Corp.
PO Box 619
Whittier, CA 90608
Phone: (213)945-3325
1985. 42 mins. A visual tour through the renowned national parks.

★7050★ Yellowstone in Winter
Britannica Films
310 S. Michigan Ave.
Chicago, IL 60604
Phone: (312)347-7958
1982. 27 mins. A look at Yellowstone National Park in winter.

★7051★ Yellowstone National Park (1983)
Wilderness Video
PO Box 2175
Redondo Beach, CA 90278
Phone: (213)542-5813
1983. 60 mins. This tape includes many scenic shots of Yellowstone National Park, including: Old Faithful; Yellowstone Falls; Tower Falls; animal wildlife; Mammoth Hot Springs; Fountain Geyser; Yellowstone Lake; Lewis Canyon; and much more

★7052★ Yellowstone National Park (1988)
Rainbow Educational Video, Inc.
170 Keyland Ct.
Bohemia, NY 11716
Phone: (516)589-6643
1988. 19 mins. The many areas of natural beauty highlight this tape about America's famous national park.

★7053★ Yellowstone: The First National Park
Norman Beerger Productions
3217 S. Arville St.
Las Vegas, NV 89102-7612
Phone: (702)876-2328
1988. 55 mins. A Reader's Digest presentation of the breathtaking sights to be found in Yellowstone.

★7054★ Yellowstone—The Living Sculpture
National AudioVisual Center
National Archives & Records Administration
Customer Services Section PZ
8700 Edgeworth Dr.
Capitol Heights, MD 20743-3701
Phone: (301)763-1896
1972. 9 mins. The natural cycles of geysers, bubbling mud pots, and hot springs at Yellowstone Park are described.

★7055★ Yellowstone Under Fire
PBS Video
1320 Braddock Pl.
Alexandria, VA 22314-1698
Phone: (703)739-5380
1989. 60 mins. The impact of accelerated development of minerals, timber and tourism on America's most famous wilderness is examined in this video.

★7056★ Yellowstone's Burning Question
Vestron Video
c/o LIVE Home Video
15400 Sherman Way
Suite 500
Van Nuys, CA 91410-0124
Phone: (203)978-5400
1989. 60 mins. From Public Broadcasting's "Nova" series. Dr. Sagan discusses the decision by forest management officials to let Yellowstone's fires burn when naturally started, regardless of the size of the fire.

★7057★ Yes We Can
Pyramid Film & Video
Box 1048
Santa Monica, CA 90406
Phone: (213)828-7577
1988. 10 mins. This mystical vision of life and the universe employs poetry, music, and dazzling animated visuals to relate the struggles of Mother Earth as she witnesses the plunder of Earth's resources.

★7058★ Yosemite
Rainbow Educational Video, Inc.
170 Keyland Ct.
Bohemia, NY 11716
Phone: (516)589-6643
1988. 24 mins. The highlights of the famous national park, equal in size to Rhode Island, have been photographed.

★7059★ Yosemite: A Gift of Creation
Norman Beerger Productions
3217 S. Arville St.
Las Vegas, NV 89102-7612
Phone: (702)876-2328
1988. 55 mins. See all the best parts of Yosemite, such as Yosemite Falls, Bridalveil Falls and Half Dome.

★7060★ Yosemite National Park
Wilderness Video
PO Box 2175
Redondo Beach, CA 90278
Phone: (213)542-5813
1983. 60 mins. This program explores Yosemite National Park and includes scenic shots of: Yosemite Falls; Bridal Veil Falls; the lower valley area; animal wildlife; Vernal Falls; Glacier Point; and much more.

★7061★ Yosemite—Seasons and Splendor
Finley-Holiday Film Corp.
PO Box 619
Whittier, CA 90608
Phone: (213)945-3325
1985. 40 mins. A year-round tourist's look at the renowned national park.

★7062★ You Can't Grow Home Again
VCA Teletronics
50 Leyland Dr.
Leonia, NJ 17605
Toll-Free: 800-822-1105
Produced by 3-2-1 Contact Extras and Children's Television Workshop, this 60-minute program deals with the subject of rainforests. For children ages 8-12 and their families. ***Price:*** $19.95.

★7063★ You Can't Grow Potatoes Up There!
Kinetic Film Enterprises, Ltd.
255 Delaware Ave.
Suite 340
Buffalo, NY 14202
Phone: (716)856-7631
1981. 27 mins. This program illustrates the importance of seal hunting in the traditional life of the Arctic Inuit Eskimos.

Online Databases

★7064★ ACIDOC
Quebec-New York State Clearinghouse on Acid Rain
New York State Dept. of Environmental Conservation
Division of Air Resources
50 Wolf Rd.
Albany, NY 12233
Phone: (518)457-2823
Covers all Canadian, American and European documentation relating to acid precipitation. It contains articles from scientific, technical and general interest periodicals, as well as monographs, reports, studies, conference proceedings and official publications published since 1975. A bilingual database (French and English), it covers all aspects of acid precipitation from its source to its control, including air and atmospheric process, environmental effects, political and socioeconomic factors, and technological control. Contact the Quebec-New York State Clearinghouse on Acid Rain.

★7065★ Aerometric Information Retrieval System (AIRS)
Environmental Protection Agency
Office of Air Quality Planning and Standards
National Air Data Branch
MD-14
Research Triangle Park, NC 27711
Phone: (919)541-5583
Contact: John Fink, Chief, Requests & Info. Sect.
Contains data reported by more than 5000 air monitoring stations located throughout the United States. Producer offers search services.

★7066★ AGRICOLA
U.S. National Agricultural Library
10301 Baltimore Blvd.
Beltsville, MD 20705
Phone: (301)344-3813
Fax: (301)344-3675
Contact: Gary K. McCone, Head of Database Admin. Branch
Contains complete bibliographic and cataloging information for all monographs and serials received at the National Agricultural Library and indexing records for articles from agricultural literature. Covers forestry, pesticides, and pollution. Available online through BRS Information Technologies.

★7067★ Air Pollution Technical Information Center File (APTIC)
Environmental Protection Agency
Library Services Office
Air Information Center (MD-35)
Research Triangle Park, NC 27711
Phone: (919)541-2777
Fax: (919)541-3636
Contact: Rosemary Thorn, Lib.
Provides citations and abstracts of the world's literature on air quality and air pollution prevention and control. Available online through DIALOG Information Services, Inc.

★7068★ Air/Water Pollution Report
Business Publishers, Inc.
951 Pershing Dr.
Silver Spring, MD 20910-4464
Phone: (301)587-6300
Fax: (301)587-1081
Toll-Free: 800-274-0122
Contact: Kimberlee Brown, Prod./Mktg.Mgr.
Provides coverage of environmental legislation, regulation, and litigation. Available online through NewsNet, Inc.

★7069★ Alaskan Marine Contaminants Database
U.S. National Oceanic and Atmospheric Administration (NOAA)
National Ocean Service
222 W. 8th Ave., Box 56
Anchorage, AK 99513
Phone: (907)271-3033
Fax: (907)271-3139
Contains data sets on the occurrence of contaminants in faunal tissue and sediments in Alaskan marine waters. Covers quality of study, species and sediment agency, and area of study. Available on CD-ROM through the producer.

★7070★ APILIT
American Petroleum Institute
Central Abstracting and Indexing Service
275 Seventh Ave., 9th Floor
New York, NY 10001
Phone: (212)366-4040
Fax: (212)366-4298
Telex: 4938591 API UI
Contact: Monica Pronin, Mgr.
Provides worldwide coverage of the significant technical literature of petroleum refining, the petrochemical industry, and synthetic fuels. Indexes articles and publications covered in the weekly API Abstracts/Literature, which is issued in four sections: Petroleum Refining and Petrochemicals, Health and Environment, Transportation and Storage, and Petroleum Substitutes (issued monthly). Available online through DIALOG Information Services, Inc.

★7071★ Aqualine
Water Research Center
Medmenham Laboratory
Marlow
Buckinghamshire SL7 2HD, England
Covers the world's literature on water and wastewater technology and environmental protection. Scans over 600 primary journals, technical reports, monographs, conference papers theses and other printed materials. ***Subjects:*** Water resources and supplies; water quality and treatment; monitoring and analysis of water and wastes; low-cost technology; underground services and water use; sewage; industrial effluents; and effects on pollution. Available online through ORBIT Search Service.

★7072★ Aquatic Information Retrieval (AQUIRE)
Chemical Information Systems, Inc. (CIS)
7215 York Rd.
Baltimore, MD 21212
Phone: (301)321-8440
Fax: (301)296-0712
Toll-Free: 800-CIS-USER
Telex: 910 380 1738
Provides information on the toxic effects of more than 5000 chemicals on 2400 freshwater and saltwater organisms, with the exclusion of bacteria, birds, and aquatic mammals. Available online through Chemical Information Systems, Inc.

★7073★ Asbestos Control Report
Business Publishers, Inc. (BPI)
951 Pershing Dr.
Silver Spring, MD 20910-4464
Phone: (301)587-6300
Fax: (301)587-1081
Toll-Free: 800-274-0122
Contact: Kimberlee Brown, Prod./Mktg. Mgr.
Reports news and developments of interest to asbestos industry professionals. Covers industry ramifications of the Asbestos Hazard Emergency Response Act of 1986, with technical information on control techniques, worksite health and safety, U.S. federal standards, state and local regulations, waste disposal, insurance requirements, and contracts available and awarded. Available online through NewsNet, Inc.

★7074★ Asbestos Information System (AIS)
Environmental Protection Agency
Office of Pesticides and Toxic Substances
PM-218B
401 M St., SW
Washington, DC 20460
Phone: (202)883-8844
Contains various types of information on asbestos, including chemical use, exposure, manufacturing, the human population, and environmental releases. Available online through the producer.

★7075★ Battery & EV Technology
Business Communications Company (BCC)
25 Van Zant St.
Norwalk, CT 06855
Phone: (203)853-4266
Covers advances and applications in the battery and electric vehicle industries. Reports on current legislation, corporate developments, industry personnel news, and electric vehicle use in the United States and Europe. Available online through NewsNet, Inc.

★7076★ Bioprocessing Technology
Technical Insights, Inc.
P.O. Box 1304
Fort Lee, NJ 07024-9967
Phone: (201)568-4744
Fax: (201)568-8247
Telex: 425900 SWIFT UI
Contact: Annette Latrorre, Mktg.Dir.
Covers new patents, technical papers, meetings, and industry news related to new technical opportunities in the conversion of biomaterials. Available online through NewsNet, Inc.

★7077★ BNA Daily News
The Bureau of National Affairs, Inc. (BNA)
BNA ONLINE
1231 25th St., N.W.
Washington, DC 20037
Phone: (202)452-4132
Fax: (202)822-8092
Toll-Free: 800-862-4636
Contains the complete text of 15 BNA publications that provide coverage of news on national and international government and private sector activities in the areas of environment, hazardous materials, pollutions control, recycling, solid waste, Superfund, and toxics litigation. Available online through DIALOG Information Services, Inc.

★7078★ Bowker's Acid Rain Database
Bowker A & I Publishing
245 W. 17th St.
New York, NY 10011
Phone: (212)337-6989
Contains citations and abstracts of the world's published literature relating to acid rain research, development, policy, causes, and effects worldwide. Available online through ESA/IRS. For more information contact Marcia Wells, Asst. Product Mgr., Scientific, Technical, & Medical Publishing at (212)463-6871 or toll-free at 1-800-323-3288.

★7079★ Business and the Environment
Cutter Information Corp.
37 Broadway
Arlington, MA 02174-5539
Phone: (617)648-8700
Telex: 650 100 9891 MCIUW
Contact: Jay McLaughlin, Editor
Reports on the trend of environmentally concerned businesses, including new packaging policies, product labeling, plant pollution, deforestation, and type and quantity of energy used. Available online through NewsNet, Inc.

★7080★ CERCLIS
Chemical Information Systems, Inc.
7215 York Rd.
Baltimore, MD 21212
Phone: (301)321-8440
Contains information on hazardous waste disposal sites that have either been listed by the EPA on the National Priority List (NPL) or nominated for consideration for the NPL. For each entry in the database, information generally includes: one or more names for the site; a variety of geographic locators; a variety of codes classifying the site, and a series of tables indicating actions taken or proposed to be taken with regard to the site under the Superfund program. Available online through Chemical Information Systems, Inc.

★7081★ CHEM-BANK
SilverPlatter Information, Inc.
37 Walnut St.
Wellesley Hills, MA 02181
Phone: (617)239-0306
Fax: (617)235-1715
Toll-Free: 800-343-0064
Telex: 4900002329
Contact: Elizabeth Morley, Communications Mgr.
Contains information relating to potentially hazardous chemicals. Comprises the following four databases: Registry of Toxic Effects of Chemical Substances; Oil and Hazardous Materials Technical Assistance Data System; Chemical Hazard Response Information System; and the Toxic Substances Control Act (TOSCA) Initial Inventory. Available on CD-ROM through SilverPlatter Information, Inc.

★7082★ Chemical Carcinogenesis Research Information System (CCRIS)
National Library of Medicine
8600 Rockville Pike
Bethesda, MD 20894
Phone: 800-638-8480
Individual assay results and test conditions for 1,451 chemicals in the areas of carcinogenicity, mutagenicity, tumor promotion, and cocarcinogenicity. Generally speaking, studies were obtained from selected literature reviews, surveys of chemicals present in the environment, and NIH-sponsored activities. Bibliographic information for each study. Available on CIS and NLM's TOXNET System, part of its Toxicology Information Program.

★7083★ Chemical Collection System/Request Tracking (CCS/RTS)
U.S. Environmental Protection Agency
Office of Pesticides and Toxic Substances
TS-793
401 M St., NW
Washington, DC 20460
Phone: (202)382-3619
Information on various properties of a number of chemicals, including environmental effects, test and analysis methods, and health effects. Available online through the producer.

★7084★ Chemical Evaluation Search and Retrieval System (CESARS)
Michigan State Department of Natural Resources
Surface Water Quality Division
Great Lakes and Environmental Assessment Section
Knapp's Office Centre
P.O. Box 30028
Lansing, MI 48909
Phone: (517)373-2190
Contact: Gary Hurlburt, Unit Chief
Contains toxicology information on compounds of environmental concern, providing acute and chronic toxicity data for aquatic and terrestrial life as well as information on carcinogenicity, mutagenicity, and reproductive and developmental effects, bioconcentration, and environmental fate. Available online through CCINFOline.

★7085★ Chemical Exposure
Dialog Information Services, Inc.
Marketing Dept.
3460 Hillview Ave.
Palo Alto, CA 94304
Phone: (415)858-3810
Toll-Free: 800-334-2564
Chemicals that have been identified in both human tissues and body fluids and in feral and food animals. Includes information on chemical properties, formulas, tissues measured, analytical method used, demographics and more. Available online through DIALOG Information Services, Inc.

★7086★ Chemical Hazard Response Information System (CHRIS)
U.S.Coast Guard
Office of Research and Development
Rm. 5410 C
2100 Second St., NW
Washington, DC 20593
Phone: (202)267-1042
Contains information needed to respond to emergencies that occur during the transport of hazardous chemicals.

★7087★ Chemical Regulations and Guidelines System
Network Management Inc./CRC Systems, Inc.
11242 Waples Mill Rd.
Fairfax, VA 22030
Phone: (703)359-9400
Fax: (703)273-2719
Contact: Michael Weaver, Tech. Info. Spec.
Indexes U.S. federal regulatory material relating to the control of chemical substances. Follows the regulatory cycle, providing a reference to each document. Covers federal statutes, promulgated regulations and available federal guidelines, standards, and support documents. Available online through DIALOG Information Services, Inc.

★7088★ CHEMTOX Database
Resource Consultants, Inc. (RCI)
7121 CrossRoads Blvd.
P.O. Box 1848
Brentwood, TN 37024-1848
Phone: (615)373-5040
Fax: (615)370-4339
Toll-Free: 800-338-2815
Contact: Richard P. Pohanish, V.Pres.
Covers chemicals regulated by government agencies. Provides information on more than 6000 chemical substances that are hazardous and that are common to the environment and the workplace due to their economic importance. Available on diskette through the producer.

★7089★ COMPENDEX
Engineering Information, Inc.
345 E. 47th St.
New York, NY 10017
Phone: (212)705-7600
Fax: (212)832-1857
Toll-Free: 800-221-1044
Telex: 4990438
Contact: Ruth A. Miller, Acct. Dev. Head
Contains citations and abstracts of journal and other literature encompassing all fields of engineering, including marine, ocean, petroleum, pollution, sanitary, water, and waterworks engineering. Available online through BRS Information Technologies.

★7090★ Computer-Aided Environmental Legislative Data System (CELDS)
U.S. Army Corps of Engineers
Planning Information Program
Department of Urban and Regional Planning
University of Illinois
1003 West Nevada
Urbana, IL 61801
Phone: (217)333-1369
Collection of abracted federal and state environmental regulations and standards.

★7091★ Concentrations of Indoor Pollutants (CIP)
CIP Database Coordinator
Bldg. 90, Rm 3058
Lawrence Berkeley Laboratory
1 Cyclotron Rd.
Berkeley, CA 94720
Phone: (415)486-6591
Contains field data from studies monitoring indoor air quality in occupied buildings in the U.S. and Canada.

★7092★ CRIS/USDA
Cooperative State Research Service
Current Research Information System (CRIS)
U. S. Department of Agriculture (USDA)
National Agricultural Library Bldg., 5th Fl.
Beltsville, MD 20705
Phone: (301)344-3846
Fax: (301)344-2272
Database of about 35,000 ongoing and recently completed agricultral, food and nutrition, and forestry research projects sponsored by the U.S. Department of Agriculture, Land-grant universities and colleges, forestry and veterinary medicine schools, state agricultural experiment stations, and other cooperating institutions. Database includes the HNRIMS (Human Nutrition Research and Information Management System) subfile of project information on human nutrition research of the USDA, the National Institutes of Health,and other federal agencies. ***Contact:*** Philip L. Dopkowski, Database Manager. ***Databases:*** DIALOG Information on Services.

★7093★ Dermal Absorption
Environmental Protection Agency
Office of Pesticides and Toxic Substances
401 M St., S.W., MS-TS799
Washington, DC 20460
Phone: (202)554-1404
Provides data on toxic effects, absorption, distribution, metabolism, and excretion relating to the dermal absorption of 655 chemicals. Includes data on the effects of other exposure, such as oral or inhalation, if such information is included in the article with the dermal data. Available online through Chemical Information Systems, Inc. For more information contact CIS at (301)821-5980 or toll-free at 1-800-CIS-USER.

★7094★ Digests of Environmental Impact Statements
Cambridge Scientific Abstracts (CSA)
7200 Wisconsin Ave.
Bethesda, MD 20814
Phone: (301)961-6750
Fax: (301)961-6720
Toll-Free: 800-843-7751
Telex: 910 250 7547 CAMB MD
Contact: Deb Wiley, Database Svcs.
Provides abstracts and indexes of approximately 500 environmental impact studies issued by the United States government each year. Available on magnetic tape through the producer.

★7095★ Directory of Used Oil Collectors Handlers and Recyclers Serving the Southeast
Project ROSE
Box 870203
University of Alabama
Tuscaloosa, AL 35487-0203
Phone: (205)348-4878
Toll-Free: 800-452-5901 and (800)39
Database of about 40 used oil collectors, handlers, and recyclers operating in Alabama, Florida, Georgia, Kentucky, Mississippi, North Carolina, South Carolina, and Tennessee.

★7096★ DOE Energy Data Base
U.S. Department of Energy
Office of Scientific and Technical Information
P.O. Box 62
Oak Ridge, TN 37831
Phone: (615)576-1188
Contact: Charles E. Spath, Asst.Mgr. for Info.Mgmt.
Contains citations and abstracts of energy-related scientific and technical literature generated by the U.S. Department of Energy, other U.S. government agencies, and selected outside sources. Provides information on the environment, fossil and synthetic fuels, renewable energy resources, and energy conservation, storage, and conversion. Available online through Integrated Technical Information Systems.

★7097★ Ecology Abstracts
Cambridge Scientific Abstracts (CSA)
7200 Wisconsin Ave.
Bethesda, MD 20814
Phone: (301)961-6750
Fax: (301)961-6720
Toll-Free: 800-843-7751
Telex: 910 250 7547 CAMB MD
Contact: Deb Wiley, Database Svcs.
Contains citations and abstracts of international periodical and other literature covering ecology, including terrestrial and aquatic ecosystems, soil studies, human ecology, human impact and environmental degradation, and pollution. Available online and on CD-ROM through the producer.

★7098★ Ei Energy/Environment Disc
Engineering Information, Inc. (Ei)
345 E. 47th St.
New York, NY 10017
Phone: (212)705-7600
Fax: (212)832-1857
Toll-Free: 800-221-1044
Telex: 4990438
Contact: Ruth A. Miller, Acct. Dev. Head
Contains citations and abstracts of journal articles, conference papers, and other literature dealing with energy and environmental issues, including coal and petroleum, environmental protection, ecosystems, energy conservation, heating, air and water pollution, hazardous materials, meteorological phenomenon, and land reclamation. Available on CD-ROM through DIALOG OnDisc.

★7099★ Electronic Information Exchange System (EIES)
Office of Research and Development
U.S. Environmental Protection Agency
RD-618
401 M St.
Washington, DC 20460
Phone: (703)506-1025
Includes two databases: Legislative Tracking System, which tracks the status of both state and federal legislation pertaining to source reduction and recycling; and National Waste Exchange, which provides a national online catalog of wastes available and wastes needed for exchange throughout the U.S.

★7100★ Energy Conservation News
Business Communications Company (BCC)
25 Van Zant St.
Norwalk, CT 06855
Phone: (203)853-4266
Reports news and developments on issues relating to the technology and economics of energy conservation at industrial, commercial, and institutional facilities. Available online through NewsNet, Inc.

★7101★ Energy Design Update
Cutter Information Corp.
37 Broadway
Arlington, MA 02174-5539
Phone: (617)648-8700
Fax: (617)648-8707
Telex: 650 100 9891 MCIUW
Contact: J.D. Nisson, Editor
Reports developments in energy-efficient design and construction, including insulation, passive solar heating, pressurization, testing, and indoor air quality. Covers regulatory trends, standards, and legal decisions. Features profiles of energy-conserving homes in North America, a calendar of national and international events, an annual special report on superinsulation, news of research, reviews of related computer software, new product and materials reviews, and construction tips. Available online through NewsNet, Inc.

★7102★ Energyline
Bowker A & I Publishing
245 W. 17th St.
New York, NY 10011
Phone: (212)337-6989
Fax: (212)645-0475
Toll-Free: 800-323-3288
Telex: 12 7703
Contact: Marcia Wells, Asst.Prod.Mgr.
Contains references and abstracts of the world's periodical and other published and unpublished literature dealing with the technical and policy-oriented aspects of energy. Available online through DIALOG Information Services, Inc.

★7103★ ENFLEX INFO
ERM Computer Services, Inc.
855 Springdale Dr.
Exton, PA 19341
Phone: (215)524-3600
Toll-Free: 800-544-3118
Contact: George Esry, Natl. Sales Mgr.
Provides the complete text of all U.S. federal and state environmental regulations, including those covering hazardous materials, the transportation of hazardous materials, and health and safety. Available on CD-ROM through the producer.

★7104★ Enviro/Energyline Abstracts Plus
Bowker A & I Publishing
245 W. 17th St.
New York, NY 10011
Phone: (212)337-6989
Provides citations and abstracts of the world's periodical and other published and unpublished literature dealing with environmental and energy-related topics. Comprises three files: Acid Rain; Energyline; Enviroline. Available on CD-ROM through Bowker Electronic Publishing. For more information contact Marcia Wells, Asst. Product Mgr., Scientific, Technical, & Medical Publishing, at (212)463-6871 or toll-free at 1-800-323-3288.

★7105★ Enviroline
Bowker A & I Publishing
245 W. 17th St.
New York, NY 10011
Phone: (212)337-6989
Provides citations and abstracts of the world's periodical and other published and unpublished literature dealing with technical and policy-oriented environmental topics. Available online through DIALOG Information Services, Inc. For more information, contact Marcia Wells, Asst. Product Mgr., Scientific, Technical, & Medical Publishing, at (212)463-6871 or toll-free at 1-800-323-3288.

★7106★ Environment Library
OCLC Online Computer Library Center, Inc.
6565 Frantz Rd.
Dublin, OH 43017
Phone: (614)764-6000
Fax: (614)764-6096
Toll-Free: 800-848-5878
Telex: 810 339 2026
Contains full bibliographic and cataloging information for English- and foreign-language materials published in all formats on the topic of environmental issues, selected from the OCLC Online Union Catalog (OLUC) by a combination of Library of Congress and Dewey Decimal classification numbers. Available on CD-ROM through the producer.

★7107★ Environmental Bibliography
International Academy at Santa Barbara
Environmental Studies Institute
800 Garden St., Suite D
Santa Barbara, CA 93101-1553
Phone: (805)965-5010
Contact: Joanne St. John, V.Pres.
Contains citations to current international periodical literature dealing with environmental topics such as air pollution, water treatment, energy conservation, noise abatement, soil mechanics, wildlife preservation, and chemical wastes. Available online through DIALOG Information Services, Inc.

★7108★ Environmental Fate (ENVIROFATE)
Environmental Protection Agency
Office of Pesticides and Toxic Substances
401 M St., S.W., MS-TS799
Washington, DC 20460
Phone: (202)554-1404
Provides information on the environmental fate or behavior of 800 chemicals which are released into the environment. Available online through Chemical Information Systems, Inc. For more information contact CIS at (301)821-5980 or toll-free at 1-800-CIS-USER.

★7109★ Environmental Fate Database (ENVIROFATE)
Chemical Information Systems, Inc.
72115 York Rd.
Baltimore, MD 21212
Phone: (301)321-8440
Contains information on the environmental fate of approximately 450 chemicals in more than 8,000 records. Available online through Chemical Information Systems, Inc.

★7110★ Environmental Fate Database
Technical Database Services, Inc.
10 Columbus Circle
New York, NY 10019
Phone: (212)245-0044
Contains over 100,000 records of bibliographic and numeric information for 15,000 chemicals.

★7111★ Environmental Health News
Occupational Health Services, Inc.
450 7th Ave., Suite 2407
New York, NY 10123
Phone: (212)967-1100
Fax: (212)268-9276
Toll-Free: 800-445-MSDS
Provides news alerts on late-breaking events, court decisions, regulatory changes, and medical and scientific news related to hazardous substances. Available online through Human Resource Information Network.

★7112★ Environmental Information Connection (EIC)
Planning Information Program
Dept. of Urban and Regional Planning
University of Illinois
1003 West Nevada
Urbana, IL 61801
Phone: (217)333-1369
EIC acts as an information clearinghouse for any type of environmental topic, having access to the University of Illinois Library, to over 300 databases through DIALOG, MEDLARS (of the National Library of Medicine), and to several other databases.

★7113★ Environmental Law Reporter
Environmental Law Institute
1616 P St., N.W., Suite 200
Washington, DC 20036
Phone: (202)328-5150
Toll-Free: 800-WESTLAW
Provides news, analysis, commentary, primary documents, and other materials dealing with environmental law, including statutes and regulations, pending litigation, and Superfund cases. Available online through WESTLAW.

★7114★ Environmental Mutagen Information Center (EMIC)
U.S. Department of Energy
Oak Ridge National Laboratory
Environmental Mutagen Information Center
Bldg. 9224, PO Box Y
Oak Ridge, TN 37830
Phone: (615)574-7871
Provides information on chemical, biological and physical agents tested for mutagenicity.

★7115★ Environmental Organization Computer Readable Directory Database
Environmental Research Information, Inc.
575 8th Ave.
New York, NY 10018-3011
Phone: (212)465-1060
Database of federal, state, and local agencies, legislative committees, public and private organizations, and individuals concerned with environmental issues. ***Frequency:*** Annual; semiannual updates. ***Price:*** $495.00, plus $30.00 shipping.

★7116★ Environmental Technical Information System (ETIS)
U.S. Army Corps of Engineers
Construction Engineering Research Laboratory
ETIS Support Program
1003 W. Nevada St.
Urbana, IL 61801
Phone: (217)333-1369
Toll-Free: 800-USA-CERL
Contact: Clyde W. Forrest, Community Planner
Contains information used to analyze and assess the environmental effects of U.S. Department of Defense activities and other major governmental programs. Available online through the producer (through the University of Illinois Department of Urban and Regional Planning Research).

★7117★ Farmer's Own Network for Education (FONE)
Rodale Institute
222 Main St.
Emmaus, PA 18098
Phone: (215)967-5171
Contact: Mike Bruske
Summarizes efforts/results of farmers who have cut chemical use, diversified their farms, and adopted other regenerative agricultural techniques.

★7118★ Federal Register Search System
Chemical Information Systems, Inc.
7215 York Rd.
Baltimore, MD 21212
Phone: (301)321-8440
Fax: (301)296-0712
Toll-Free: 800-CIS-USER
Telex: 910 380 1738
Provides citations and abstracts of items appearing in the Federal Register covering regulations, rules, standards, and guidelines involving chemical substances. Includes cross-referencing to other citations on related substances. Available online through Chemical Information Systems, Inc.

★7119★ Fish and Wildlife Reference Service Database
U.S. Fish and Wildlife Service
The Maxima Corporation
5430 Grosvenor Lane, Suite 110
Bethesda, MD 20814
Phone: (301)492-6403
Toll-Free: 800-582-3421
Contact: Mary J. Nickum, Proj.Mgr.
Contains citations to selected state fish and game agency technical reports covering American fish and wildlife. Producer offers search services.

★7120★ From the State Capitals: Waste Disposal and Pollution Control
Wakeman/Walworth, Inc.
300 N. Washington St., Suite 204
Alexandria, VA 22314
Phone: (703)549-8606
Fax: (703)549-1372
Contact: Keyes Walworth, Editor
Covers state and municipal environmental laws and regulations. Reports developments concerning the transportation, storage, and clean-up of hazardous wastes as well as monitoring pesticide policies, insurance protection, resource recovery, and pollution controls. Available online through WESTLAW.

★7121★ Genetic Toxicity (GENETOX)
Environmental Protection Agency
Office of Pesticides and Toxic Substances
401 M St., S.W., MS-TS799
Washington, DC 20460
Phone: (202)554-1404
Provides mutagenicity information on more than 2600 chemicals tested on 38 biological systems. Available online through Chemical Information Systems, Inc. For more information contact CIS at (301)821-5980 or toll-free at 1-800-CIS-USER.

★7122★ Global Environmental Change Report
Cutter Information Corp.
37 Broadway
Arlington, MA 02174-5539
Phone: (617)648-8700
Fax: (617)648-8707
Telex: 650 100 9891 MCIUW
Contact: Brad Hurley, Editor
Reports on environmental issues worldwide, including global warming, ozone depletion,

deforestation, and acid rain. Focuses on scientific findings, significant domestic and foreign policy trends, and industry involvement. Available online through NewsNet, Inc.

★7123★ Global Indexing System
U.S. Environmental Protection Agency
TS-793
401 M St., SW
Washington, DC 20460
Phone: (202)382-3625
Collection of databases offering international information on various qualities of chemicals. Available online through the producer.

★7124★ Great Lakes Water Quality Data Base
Environmental Protection Agency
Office of Research and Development
Large Lakes Research Station
9311 Groh Rd.
Grosse Ile, MI 48138
Phone: (313)675-2245
Contains water data related to the Great Lakes (Michigan, Superior, Ontario, Erie, and Huron) and related tributaries and watersheds. Includes data on water quality, fish, and sediment. Available online as part of STORET.

★7125★ Greenhouse Effect Report
Business Publishers, Inc. (BPI)
951 Pershing Dr.
Silver Spring, MD 20910-4464
Phone: (301)587-6300
Fax: (301)587-1081
Toll-Free: 800-274-0122
Contact: Kimberlee Brown, Prod./Mktg. Mgr.
Covers U.S. regulatory, legislative, business, and technological news and developments as well as international actions relating to global warming and the greenhouse effect. Reports on relevant activities of the U.S. Congress, U.S. Environmental Protection Agency (EPA), U.S. National Aeronautics and Space Administration (NASA), and U.S. National Oceanic and Atmospheric Administration (NOAA). Available online through NewsNet, Inc.

★7126★ Ground Water On-Line
National Water Well Association
National Ground Water Information Center
6375 Riverside Dr.
Dublin, OH 43017
Phone: (614)761-1711
Fax: (614)761-1711
Telex: 241302
Contact: Janet Bix, Chief Lib.
Contains references to technical literature covering all aspects of groundwater and well technology. Available online through Electronic Knowledge Services.

★7127★ HAZARDLINE
Occupational Health Services, Inc.
Four 57th Ave., Ste. 2407
New York, NY 10123
Phone: (212)967-1100
Contains full-text information on more than 3,600 dangerous materials. Components include physical and chemical descriptions, standards and regulations, and safety precautions for handling.

★7128★ Hazardous Materials Intelligence Report
World Information Systems
P.O. Box 535
Cambridge, MA 02238
Phone: (617)491-5100
Fax: (617)492-3312
Reviews federal, state, and local legislation, regulations, and programs related to hazardous waste and hazardous material management and includes research news, book reviews, listings of contract opportunities, and calendar of events. Available online through NewsNet, Inc.

★7129★ Hazardous Waste Database (HAZARD)
Environmental Protection Agency
Office of Administration and Resources Management
OS-312
401 M St., SW
Washington, DC 20460
Phone: (202)475-8710
Hazardous waste directives, treatment and disposal of hazardous waste, and its storage.

★7130★ Hazardous Waste News
Business Publishers, Inc.
951 Pershing Dr.
Silver Spring, MD 20910-4464
Phone: (301)587-6300
Fax: (301)587-1081
Toll-Free: 800-274-0122
Contact: Kimberlee Brown, Prod./Mktg.Mgr.
Covers legislative, regulatory, and judicial decisions at the federal and state levels relating to the field of hazardous waste management. Available online through NewsNet, Inc.

★7131★ Hazardous Waste Site Data Base
U.S. Environmental Protection Agency
Environmental Monitoring Systems Lab
P.O. Box 93478
Las Vegas, NV 89193-3478
Phone: (702)798-2525
Identifies a total of 944 chemical constituents for more than 5000 wells at over 350 hazardous waste sites nationwide.

★7132★ Information System for Hazardous Organics in Water (ISHOW)
Environmental Protection Agency
Office of Pesticides and Toxic Substances
401 M St., S.W., MS-TS799
Washington, DC 20460
Phone: (202)554-1404
Provides information on more than 5000 hazardous chemical substances found in water. Available online through Chemical Information Systems, Inc. For more information contact CIS at (301)821-5980 or toll-free at 1-800-CIS-USER.

★7133★ Instructional Resources Information System (IRIS)
Ohio State University
Environmental Quality Instructional Resources Center
1200 Chambers Rd., Room 310
Columbus, OH 43212
Phone: (614)292-6717
Contact: Dr. Robert W. Howe, Director
Provides citations and abstracts of training materials in the area of water resources, water quality, solid wastes, hazardous wastes, and toxic materials. Includes ordering information. Producer offers search services.

★7134★ Integrated Risk Information System (IRIS)
Environmental Protection Agency
Office of Research and Development
Research Triangle Park, NC 27711
Phone: (202)382-5949
Contains information on how levels of exposure to some 400 chemicals effect human health.

★7135★ International Air Data Base (WHO-WMO)
U.S. Environmental Protection Agency
Office of Monitoring Systems and Quality Assurance
401 M St., SW
Washington, DC 20460
Phone: (919)541-3887
An international database containing ambient air data from the World Health Organization and precipitation data from the World Meteorological Organization.

★7136★ Managed Area Basic Record
The Nature Conservancy
1815 N. Lynn St.
Arlington, VA 22209
Phone: (703)841-5300
Database of about 3,100 nature preserves, preserved by or with the assistance of The Nature Conservancy; includes about 800 that have been transferred to national, state, or local governments or to private organization s; preserves located in United States, Latin America, Canada, and the Caribbean. ***Contact:*** John Prince, Site Information Management Specialist. ***Databases:*** Producer.

★7137★ Master Water Data Index
U.S. Geological Survey
Water Resources Division
National Water Data Exchange (NAWDEX)
421 National Center
Reston, VA 22092
Phone: (703)648-6848
Fax: (703)648-5295
Contact: James S. Burton, Program Mgr.
Holds information on more than 450,000 water data collection sites. Available online through NAWDEX.

★7138★ Medical Waste News
Business Publishers, Inc. (BPI)
951 Pershing Dr.
Silver Spring, MD 20910-4464
Phone: (301)587-6300
Fax: (301)587-1081
Toll-Free: 800-274-0122
Contact: Kimberlee Brown, Prod./Mktg. Mgr.
Covers U.S. regulation, legislation, and technological news and developments related to medical waste management and disposal. Reports on businesses involved in medical waste management as well as U.S. Environmental Protection Agency (EPA) efforts to control waste levels. Available online through NewsNet, Inc.

★7139★ Multinational Environmental Outlook (MEO)
Business Publishers, Inc.
951 Pershing Dr.
Silver Spring, MD 20910-4464
Phone: (301)587-6300
Fax: (301)587-1081
Toll-Free: 800-274-0122
Contact: Kimberlee Brown, Prod./Mktg.Mgr.
Reports environmental problems and solutions in countries outside the United States and their impact on the United States. Available online through NewsNet, Inc.

★7140★ Multispectral Scanner and Photographic Imagery (IMAGERY)
U.S. Environmental Protection Agency
Office of Modeling and Monitoring Systems and Quality Assurance
RD-680
401 M St., SW
Washington, DC 20460
Phone: (702)798-2260
An index for various data tapes containing multispectral imagery from aircraft and

satellite. Concerned with identified sources of pollution and effects of pollution.

★7141★ National Emissions Data System (NEDS)
Environmental Protection Agency
Office of Air Quality Planning and Standards
National Air Data Branch
MD-14
Research Triangle Park, NC 27711
Phone: (919)541-5583
Contact: John Fink, Chief, Requests & Info. Sect.
Contains data on pollutant emissions and 10,000 sources in 3300 areas across the United States and its territories. Producer offers search services.

★7142★ National Environmental Data Referral Service (NEDRES) Database
U.S. National Environmental Satellite, Data, and Information Service (NESDIS)
Assessment and Information Services Center (AISC)
National Environmental Data Referral Service (NEDRES)
1825 Connecticut Ave., N.W.
Washington, DC 20235
Phone: (202)673-5548
Contact: Gerald S. Barton, Chief, NEDRES Program Office
Catalogs and indexes publicly available environmental data held by public and private organizations worldwide. Contains descriptions of data files, published data sources, documentation references, and organizations that make environmental data available. Available online through BRS Information Technologies.

★7143★ National Environmental Data Referral Service (NEDS) Database
National Environmental Data Referral Service (NEDRES)
National Oceanic & Atmospheric Administration
Department of Commerce
1825 Connecticut Ave. N.W.
Washington, DC 20235
Phone: (202)673-5548
More than 22,200 data resources that have available data on climatology and meteorology, ecology and pollution, geography, geophysics and geology, hydrology and limnology, oceangraphy, and transmissions from remote sensing satellites. Also cited as "NEDRES Database."

★7144★ National Eutrophication Study Data Base
Environmental Protection Agency
Environmental Monitoring Systems Laboratory, Las Vegas
P.O. Box 15027
Las Vegas, NV 89104
Phone: (702)798-2000
Contact: Victor W. Lambou, Aquatic Biologist
Holds water quality data collected over a one-year period for each of some 800 lakes and their tributaries in 48 states. Available online as part of STORET.

★7145★ National Pesticide Information Retrieval System
Entomology Hall
Purdue University
West Lafayette, IN 47907
Phone: (317)494-6616
Fax: (317)494-0535
Contact: Ed Ramsey, NPIRS User Svcs. Mgr.
Provides information on pesticide products registered with the Environmental Protection Agency, as well as similar information from 36 states. Available online through the producer.

★7146★ National Stream Quality Accounting Network (NASQAN)
National Water Data Exchange
U.S. Geological Survey
421 National Center
Reston, VA 22092
Phone: (703)648-4000
Contains more than 150 hydrologic measurements collected at daily, monthly and quarterly intervals from more than 500 monitoring stations in the U.S.

★7147★ National Waste Exchange Data Base
Northeast Industrial Waste Exchange
90 Presidential Plaza, Ste. 122
Syracuse, NY 13202
Phone: (315)422-6572
Computerized catalog of waste materials listed with the Northeast Industrial Exchange.

★7148★ National Water Data Exchange
National Water Exchange
U.S. Geological Survey
421 National Center
Reston, VA 22092
Phone: (703)648-4000
Information on the identification, location, and acquisition of water data.

★7149★ National Water Data Storage and Retrieval System (WATSTORE)
U.S. Geological Survey
Water Resources Division
440 National Center
Reston, VA 22092
Phone: (703)648-5687
Contact: Arthur L. Putnam, Hydrologist
Provides data covering all aspects of surface and underground water resources of the United States.

★7150★ Natural Resources Metabase
National Information Services Corporation (NISC)
Suite 6, Wyman Towers
3100 St. Paul St.
Baltimore, MD 21218
Phone: (301)243-0797
Fax: (301)243-0982
Contact: Fred Durr, Pres.
Provides the complete text of published and unpublished reports and other materials dealing with natural resources and environmental issues released by U.S. and Canadian government agencies and organizations. Comprises some 45 files organized in the following six clusters: geographic families; habitat families; wildlife management families; land management families; research families; administrative files. Available on CD-ROM through NISC.

★7151★ NMPIS Database
U.S. National Environmental Satellite, Data, and Information Service (NESDIS)
National Oceanographic Data Center (NODC)
1825 Connecticut Ave., N.W., Suite 406
Washington, DC 20235
Phone: (202)673-5594
Telex: DIB 7678
Contains descriptions of marine pollution research, development, or monitoring projects conducted or funded by federal agencies. Available online through the producer.

★7152★ NODC Data Inventory Data Base
U.S. National Environmental Satellite, Data, and Information Service (NESDIS)
National Oceanographic Data Center (NODC)
1825 Connecticut Ave., N.W., Suite 406
Washington, DC 20235
Phone: (202)673-5594
Telex: DIB 7678
Provides information on National Oceanographic Data Center holdings. Available online through the producer.

★7153★ NPIRS Pesticide and Hazardous Chemical Databases
National Pesticide Information Retrieval System (NPIRS)
Purdue University
Entomology Hall, Rm. 1158
West Lafayette, IN 47907
Phone: (317)494-6616
"Product Datebase" covering more than 60,000 pesticides registered with the Environmental Protection Agency (EPA) and with state government agencies. ***Editor(s):*** Ed Ramsey, User Services Manager. ***Databases:*** Producer, Telenet.

★7154★ Nuclear Facility Decommissioning and Site Remedial Actions
Oak Ridge National Laboratory
Remedial Action Program Information Center
P.O. Box 2008, Bldg. 2001
Oak Ridge, TN 37831-6050
Phone: (615)576-0568
Telex: 854511 ORNL IRA-HML
Contact: Park T. Owen, Director
Contains references to U.S. and international literature relating to radioactively contaminated facilities and site remedial actions. Producer offers search services.

★7155★ Nuclear Waste News
Business Publishers, Inc. (BPI)
951 Pershing Dr.
Silver Spring, MD 20910-4464
Phone: (301)587-6300
Fax: (301)587-1081
Toll-Free: 800-274-0122
Contact: Kimberlee Brown, Prod./Mktg. Mgr.
Covers U.S. federal and legislation regulation and research and development activities concerning the generation, packaging, transportation, processing, and disposal of nuclear wastes. Includes technical reports. Available online through NewsNet, Inc.

★7156★ Occupational Safety and Health (NIOSH)
National Institute of Occupational Safety and Health
Standards Development and Technology Transfer Division
4676 Columbia Pkwy.
Cincinnati, OH 45226
Phone: (513)684-8326
Covers aspects of occupational safety and health, including such topics as hazardous agents and waste, unsafe workplace environment, toxicology, chemistry, and control technology, as they pertain to occupational health and safety.

★7157★ Oceanic Abstracts
Cambridge Scientific Abstracts (CSA)
7200 Wisconsin Ave.
Bethesda, MD 20814
Phone: (301)961-6750
Fax: (301)961-6720
Toll-Free: 800-843-7751
Telex: 910 250 7547 CAMB MD
Contact: Deb Wiley, Database Svcs.
Indexes the world's technical literature dealing with oceanic research and related engineering

studies, including marine pollution, pollution detection, pollutant control and prevention, and conservation of oceanic resources. Available online through DIALOG Information Services, Inc.

★7158★ Oceanographic Literature Review
Woods Hole Data Base, Inc.
P.O. Box 712
Woods Hole, MA 02574
Phone: (508)548-2743
Provides citations and abstracts of international periodical literature dealing with oceanography and related disciplines, including ocean waste disposal and pollution. Available online through ORBIT Search Service.

★7159★ Oil and Hazardous Materials Technical Assistance Data System (OHM-TADS)
Environmental Protection Agency
Office of Solid Waste and Emergency Response
Emergency Response Division
OS210
401 M St., S.W.
Washington, DC 20460
Phone: (202)382-2190
Fax: (202)755-2155
Telex: 892758 EPA WSH
Contact: John Cunningham, Env. Engineer/Project Officer
Provides numerical data and interpretive comments relating to approximately 1400 oil and hazardous substances and their deleterious effects on water quality and other environmental media. Intended primarily to serve emergency spill response personnel with immediate information for the identification of substances from their physical, chemical, and toxological properties, and for formulation of correct reactions. Available online through Chemical Information Systems, Inc.

★7160★ Oil Spill Intelligence Report
Cutter Information Corp.
37 Broadway
Arlington, MA 02174-5539
Phone: (617)648-8700
Fax: (617)648-8707
Telex: 650 100 9891 MCIUW
Contact: Amy M. Stolls, Editor
Reports on the occurrences of oil spills and related events worldwide. Covers cleanup efforts, contingency planning and response, legislative and regulatory developments, new spill cleanup technologies, and research findings. Includes a database of every significant oil spill (more than 10,000 gallons) worldwide since 1978. Available online through NewsNet, Inc.

★7161★ Olsen's Biomass Energy Report (OLBIEN)
G.V. Olsen Associates
170 Broadway, Room 201
New York, NY 10038
Phone: (212)866-5034
Telex: 233405 RCA API UR
Contact: Gustav Olsen, Pres.
Provides citations and abstracts of published literature relating to biodegradable renewable energy sources and uses. Producer offers search services.

★7162★ OPTS Regulation Tracking System (OPTS/RTS)
U.S. Environmental Protection Agency
Office of Pesticides and Toxic Substances
TS-793
401 M St., SW
Washington, DC 20460
Phone: (202)382-3619
Provides information on the histories of various regulations, as well as compliance with them.

★7163★ Outdoors Forum
CompuServe Information Service
5000 Arlington Centre Blvd.
P.O. Box 20212
Columbus, OH 43220
Phone: (614)457-8600
Provides a bulletin board where outdoor enthusiasts can share information with other outdoor enthusiasts. Contains information on outdoor sports, hobbies, and entertainment. Includes search and rescue, nature, wildlife, equipment, and park and campground information. Enables users to contact members of such groups as: Outdoor Writers Association of America, National Audubon Society, National Wildlife Federation, Sierra Club, Trout Unlimited, Federation of Fly Fishers, Earth First!, Sport Fishing Institute, Ducks Unlimited, and the U.S. Fish and Wildlife Service. Available online through the producer.

★7164★ Petroleum Abstracts
University of Tulsa
600 S. College
Tulsa, OK 74104
Phone: (918)631-2296
Fax: (918)599-9361
Toll-Free: 800-247-8678
Telex: 49 7543 INFOSVCTUTUL
Contact: Pat Mitcho, Mktg.Mgr.
Contains references and abstracts of technical literature and patents worldwide relating to petroleum exploration and production, including pollution and alternative fuels and energy sources. Available online through DIALOG Information Services, Inc.

★7165★ Pollution Abstracts
Cambridge Scientific Abstracts (CSA)
7200 Wisconsin Ave.
Bethesda, MD 20814
Phone: (301)961-6750
Fax: (301)961-6720
Toll-Free: 800-843-7751
Telex: 910 250 7547 CAMB MD
Contact: Deb Wiley, Database Svcs.
Contains references and abstracts of international technical literature dealing with environmental pollution research and related engineering studies. Available online through Data-Star.

★7166★ Pollution/Toxicology CD-ROM (PolTox)
Cambridge Scientific Abstracts (CSA)
Compact Cambridge
7200 Wisconsin Ave.
Bethesda, MD 20814
Phone: (301)961-6750
Fax: (301)961-6720
Toll-Free: 800-843-7751
Telex: 910 250 7547 CAMB MD
Contact: Deb Wiley, Database Svcs.
Contains citations and abstracts of international periodical and other literature covering pollution and toxicology. Comprises the following seven databases: Aquatic Sciences and Fisheries Abstracts, Part 3: Aquatic Pollution and Environmental Quality; Ecology Abstracts; Food and Science Technology Abstracts; Health and Science Safety Abstracts; Pollution Abstracts; Toxicology Abstracts; and TOXLINE. Available on CD-ROM through Compact Cambridge.

★7167★ POWER
U.S. Department of Energy
Energy Library
MA-232.2
Washington, DC 20585
Phone: (202)586-9534
Contact: Denise B. Diggin, Lib.
Provides full bibliographic descriptions of monographs, proceedings, and other materials related to the energy field, including energy conservation and environmental aspects of energy production and use. Available online through ORBIT Search Service.

★7168★ PressNet Environmental Reports (PER)
Chemical Information Systems, Inc.
7215 York Rd.
Baltimore, MD 21212
Phone: (301)321-8440
A collection of summaries of articles on environmental issues published in newspapers around the U.S.

★7169★ Registry of Toxic Effects of Chemical Substances (RTECS)
National Institute for Occupational Safety and Health
U.S. Public Health Service
Standards Development and Technology Transfer Div.
4676 Columbia Pkwy.
Cincinnati, OH 45226
Phone: (513)684-8326
Results of tests on more than 101,458 chemical substances. Data is in four categories: Substance Identification; Toxicity/Biomedical Effects; Toxicology and Carcinogenicity Review; and Exposure Standards and Regulations.

★7170★ Report on Defense Plant Wastes
Business Publishers, Inc. (BPI)
951 Pershing Dr.
Silver Spring, MD 20910-4464
Phone: (301)587-6300
Fax: (301)587-1081
Toll-Free: 800-274-0122
Contact: Kimberlee Brown, Prod./Mktg. Mgr.
Reports on U.S. environmental laws, regulations, cleanup actions, contracts, and court actions affecting U.S. defense, weapons production, government hospitals and laboratories, and other government institutions. Available online through NewsNet, Inc.

★7171★ REPRORISK System
Micromedex, Inc.
600 Grant St.
Denver, CO 80203
Phone: (303)831-1400
Toll-Free: 800-525-9083
Database contains several modules covering the reproductive risks to females and males of drugs, chemicals, and physical and environmental agents.

★7172★ REPROTOX
Columbia Hospital for Women
Reproductive Toxicology Center (RTC)
2440 M St., N.W., Suite 217
Washington, DC 20037-1404
Phone: (202)293-5137
Contact: Anthony R. Scialli M.D., Director
Provides up-to-date information and summaries of relevant articles dealing with industrial and environmental chemicals and their effects on human fertility, pregnancy, and

fetal development. Available online through the producer.

★7173★ Selected Water Resources Abstracts
U.S. Geological Survey
Water Resources Scientific Information Center (WRSIC)
425 National Center
Reston, VA 22092
Phone: (703)648-6820
Contact: Raymond A. Jensen, WRSIC Chief
Provides citations and abstracts of international scientific and technical literature dealing with water resources management and research. Available online through DIALOG Information Services, Inc.

★7174★ SIRS Science CD-ROM
Social Issues Resources Series, Inc.
P.O. Box 2348
Boca Raton, FL 33427-2348
Phone: (407)994-0079
Fax: (407)994-4704
Toll-Free: 800-232-SIRS
Contains the complete text of articles providing current information on climatology, ecology, and oceanography. Available on CD-ROM through the producer.

★7175★ SIRS Social Issues and Critical Issues CD-ROM
Social Issues Resources Series, Inc.
P.O. Box 2348
Boca Raton, FL 33427-2348
Phone: (407)994-0079
Fax: (407)994-4704
Toll-Free: 800-232-SIRS
Contains the complete text of articles providing current information on the latest issues affecting the general citizenry, including pollution, population, and the atmosphere. Available on CD-ROM through the producer.

★7176★ Sludge
Business Publishers, Inc. (BPI)
951 Pershing Dr.
Silver Spring, MD 20910-4464
Phone: (301)587-6300
Fax: (301)587-1081
Toll-Free: 800-274-0122
Contact: Kimberlee Brown, Prod./Mktg. Mgr.
Provides coverage of management of sludge residuals and byproducts generated by industrial and municipal air and water pollution control measures. Available online as part of the PTS Newsletter Database.

★7177★ SPI/ERS Plastics Data Base
Ernst & Young
1225 Connecticut Ave., N.W.
Washington, DC 20036
Phone: (202)862-6042
Contact: Mona Hall, Mgr., Association Svcs. Group
Provides monthly, quarterly, and annual time series on the production and sales of plastic resins in the United States. Available online through the producer.

★7178★ State Regulation Report: Toxics
NewsNet, Inc.
945 Haverford Rd.
Bryn Mawr, PA 19010
Phone: (215)527-8030
Toll-Free: 800-345-1301
Covers toxic substances control and hazardous waste management at the state program level, with particular interest given to programs relating to indusry.

★7179★ STORET
Environmental Protection Agency
Office of Information Resources Management
PM-218B
401 M St., S.W.
Washington, DC 20460
Phone: (703)833-8861
Fax: (703)556-1174
Toll-Free: 800-424-9067
Contact: Joseph A. Sierra, Chief, Client Svcs. Branch
Contains water pollution measurement data collected from more than 700,000 observation stations across the United States. Available online and on magnetic tape through the producer.

★7180★ Suspect Chemicals Sourcebook
Roytech Publications, Inc.
840 Hinckley Rd., Suite 147
Burlingame, CA 94010
Phone: (415)697-0541
Fax: (415)697-6255
Contact: Kenneth B. Clansky, Pres.
Contains references to U.S. federal regulations and precautionary data pertaining to the manufacture, sale, storage, use, and transportation of more than 5000 industrial chemical substances. Covers more than 50 federal regulatory and advisory programs, as well as selected state, national, and international regulations. Includes information on toxic chemicals, health and safety regulations, hazardous substances, dioxins/furans, air and water quality criteria and hazardous pollutants, and carcinogens. Available online through Chemical Information Systems, Inc.

★7181★ Toxic Chemical Release Inventory (TRI)
Office of Research and Development
U.S. Environmental Protection Agency
RD-689
401 M St., SW
Washington, DC 20460
Phone: (202)382-3596
Contains information on the annual estimated releases of toxic chemicals to the environment. Data includes names and addresses of the facilities and the amount of certain toxic chemicals they release to the air, water, or land.

★7182★ Toxic Chemical Release Inventory (TRI)
U.S. Natl. Library of Medicine (NLM)
Toxicology Information Program (TIP)
8600 Rockville Pike
Bethesda, MD 20894
Phone: (301)496-1131
Database of 320 toxic chemicals used by industrial firms and released into the air, water, and land. ***Databases:*** MEDLARS.

★7183★ Toxic Materials News
Business Publishers, Inc.
951 Pershing Dr.
Silver Spring, MD 20910-4464
Phone: (301)587-6300
Fax: (301)587-1081
Toll-Free: 800-274-0122
Contact: Kimberlee Brown, Prod./Mktg.Mgr.
Monitors developments in legislation, regulations, and litigation concerning toxic substances. Available online through NewsNet, Inc.

★7184★ Toxic Substances Control Act Test Submissions (TSCATS)
Chemical Information Systems, Inc.
7215 York Rd.
Baltimore, MD 21212
Phone: (301)321-8440
An index of unpublished health and safety studies submitted to the U.S. Environmental Protection Agency under the Toxic Substances Control Act.

★7185★ Toxic Substances Control Act (TSCA) Chemical Substances Inventory
Environmental Protection Agency
Office of Pesticides and Toxic Substances
401 M St., S.W., MS-TS799
Washington, DC 20460
Phone: (202)554-1404
Telex: 892758
Lists chemical substances manufactured, imported, or processed in the United States for commercial purposes. Available online through DIALOG Information Services, Inc.

★7186★ TOXLINE
U.S. National Library of Medicine
Toxicology Information Program
8600 Rockville Pike
Bethesda, MD 20894
Phone: (301)496-1131
Fax: (301)480-3537
Contact: Jeanne C. Goshorn, Chief of Bio. Info. Svcs. Sect.
Provides citations to published sources of information on the pharmacological, biochemical, physiological, and toxicological effects of drugs and other chemicals. Comprises the following four files: TOXLINE, covering the period 1981 to the present; TOXLINE65, covering the period 1965 through 1980; TOXLIT (Toxicology Literature from Special Sources); TOXLIT65, covering the period 1965 through 1980. Available online through BRS Information Technologies.

★7187★ Transportation Legislative Data Base
Battelle Memorial Institute
Office of Transportation Systems and Planning (OTSP)
505 King Ave.
Columbus, OH 43201-2693
Phone: (614)424-5606
Contact: Jo Ellen Balon, Transportation Policy Analyst
Holds references to legislative actions concerning the shipment of radioactive materials which have been introduced, enacted, or denied at U.S. federal, state, or local levels of government. Includes references to selected federal and state administrative regulations. Producer offers search services.

★7188★ TSCA Plant and Production Data (TSCAPP)
Chemical Information Systems, Inc.
7215 York Rd.
Baltimore, MD 21212
Phone: (301)321-8440
Fax: (301)296-0712
Toll-Free: 800-CIS-USER
Telex: 910 380 1738
Contains 127,000 production citations for some 53,000 unique substances, representing the non-confidential portion of reports received by the Environmental Protection Agency as a result of the U.S. Toxic Substances Control Act (TSCA). Available online through the producer.

★7189★ Waste Treatment Technology News
Business Communications Company (BCC)
25 Van Zant St.
Norwalk, CT 06855
Phone: (203)853-4266
Covers the handling and management of all types of hazardous waste. Reports news and developments in the areas of clean-up, control, recycling, and disposal of industrial wastes generated in the processing of energy, chemicals, and minerals. Available online through NewsNet, Inc.

★7190★ WasteInfo
Waste Management Information Bureau
Harwell Laboratory
ORBIT Search Service
Maxwell Online, Inc.
8000 West Park Dr.
McLean, VA 22102
Phone: (703)442-0900
Toll-Free: 800-421-7229
Contains bibliographic references on all aspects of non-radioactive waste management, compiled in over 56,000 records. Provides extensive coverage in the areas of waste disposal and treatment, waste recycling, and waste management policy.

★7191★ Water Data Sources Directory
U.S. Geological Survey
Water Resources Division
National Water Data Exchange (NAWDEX)
421 National Center
Reston, VA 22092
Phone: (703)648-6848
Fax: (703)648-5295
Contact: James S. Burton, Program Mgr.
Identifies more than 2000 domestic and foreign organizations that are sources of water data, particularly on the quantity and quality of surface and groundwater. Available online through NAWDEX.

★7192★ WATERNET
American Water Works Association (AWWA)
Technical Library
6666 W. Quincy Ave.
Denver, CO 80235
Phone: (303)794-7711
Fax: (303)794-7310
Telex: 45 0895 AWWADVR
Contact: Kurt Keeley, Dir. of Info. Svcs.
Provides references and abstracts to international published literature and other materials dealing with water and wastewater. Available online through DIALOG Information Services, Inc.

★7193★ WESTLAW Environmental Law Library
West Publishing Company
50 W. Kellogg Blvd.
P.O. Box 64526
St. Paul, MN 55164-0526
Phone: (612)228-2500
Toll-Free: 800-WESTLAW.
Contains the complete text of U.S. federal court decisions, statutes and regulations, administrative law publications, specialized files, and texts and periodicals dealing with environmental law. Includes relevant decisions made by the U.S. Supreme Court (1790 to the present), U.S. Courts of Appeals (1891 to the present), and U.S. District Courts (1789 to the present); related statutes and regulations from the U.S. Code (current), the Federal Register (1980 to the present), and the Code of Federal Regulations (current); Environmental Protection Agency General Counsel Memoranda (1979 to the present); Ocean Resources and Wildlife Reporter (1971 to the present); Administrative Environmental Law decisions for all available states; and such specialized files as BNA Environment Daily, BNA Toxics Law Daily, BNA Environment Database (comprising the Chemical Regulation Reporter and the Environment Reporter), Environmental Law Reporter, From the State Capitals: Waste Disposal and Pollution Control (October 1988 to the present); and the Gower Federal Service (1971 to the present). Available online through WESTLAW.

★7194★ Wildlife Data Base
Julie Moore & Associates
9956 N. Highway 85
Los Cruces, NM 88005
Contact: Julie Lee Moore, Bibliographer
Indexes the scientific literature on wildlife, including North American waterfowl, shore and marsh birds, upland game birds, birds of prey, rodents and lagomorphs, carnivores, and ungulates; international oceanic birds, marine mammals including whales, and bats. Available on diskette through the producer.

Clearinghouses

★7195★ Acid Rain Information Clearinghouse
33 S. Washington St.
Rochester, NY 14608
Phone: (716)546-3796
Provides comprehensive reference and referral and educational services to professionals, academics, and public interest groups.

★7196★ Air Resources Information Clearinghouse (ARIC)
Center for Environmental Information, Inc.
99 Ct. St.
Rochester, NY 14604-1824
Phone: (716)546-3796
Fax: (716)325-5131
Contact: Elizabeth Thorndike, President
Originally established as the Acid Rain Information Clearinghouse (ARIC); name changed in 1988. It is a nonprofit organization sponsored by the Center for Environmental Information, Inc. (CEI) and addresses the topics of acid rain, global warming, ozone depletion, air toxics, and indoor air pollution. ***Founded:*** 1983. ***Staff:*** 16. ***Databases:*** ARIC is open to the public and maintains the ACIDOC, a bilingual database on acidic deposition, under a contract with the New York State Department of Environmental Conservation and in cooperation with the Documentation Center for Acid Rain, Ministry of the Environment, Quebec, Canada. Holdings: 6,060.

★7197★ Air Risk Hotline
Phone: (919)541-0888
Operated by the Air Risk Information Support Center to answer technical questions on health, exposure, and risk assessment to toxic air pollutants, including asbestos.

★7198★ Alternative Treatment Technology Information Center (ATTIC)
U. S. Environmental Protection Agency
401 M. St., S.W.
Washington, DC 20460
Phone: (202)475-7161
Toll-Free: 800-424-9346
Contact: Myles Morse, Exec. Officer
Founded: 1988. The Center is sponsored by the Office of Environmental Engineering and Technology Demonstration, U.S. Environmental Agency to serve the needs of the EPA staff with information on hazardous waste technologies for Superfund cleanup activities. ***Databases:*** ATTIC is a computer-based information retrieval system that collects data from the Superfund Innovative Technology Evaluation (SITE) Program, California Summary of Treatment Technology Demonstration Projects, Summary of Treatment Technology Effectiveness for Contaminated Soil program, NATO and other international organizations, Innovative Technologies Program, Removal Sites Technologies Data program, Resource Conservation and Recovery Act delisting actions, United States Army Toxic and Hazardous Materials Agency installation restoration and hazardous waste control technologies, records of decisions since 1988, and treatability studies. Additionally, ATTIC contains the RREL Water Treatability Database, Robert S. Kerr Environmental Research Laboratory Soil Transport and Fate Database, EPA Library Hazardous Waste Collection, ORD Technical Assistance Directory, Cost of Remedial Action Model, Geophysics Advisor Expert System, and online access to the Computerized Online Information System, Office of Solid Waste and Emergency Response Bulletin Board, Dialcom, National Technical Information Service, and Records of Decisions Database. Abstracts from the Database contain date last reviewed, title, EPA contact and organization, developer contact, organization, source, hazardous constituents, media, location, history, technology, reported concentrations, action level, reported percentage reduction, and summary paragraph. The Center also maintains the Hazardous Waste Remediation Technologies Database.

★7199★ Asbestos Ombudsman Clearinghouse
401 M. St., S.W.
A-149 C
Washington, DC 20460
Phone: (703)557-1938
Contact: Karen Brown, Ombudsman
Founded: 1986. The Clearinghouse is sponsored by the Office of Small and Disadvantaged Business Utilization, U.S. Environmental Protection Agency to provide information on handling and abatement of asbestos in schools, the workplace, and the home. Focuses on asbestos-in-schools requirements and handles questions and complaints. In addition, interpretation of the asbestos-in-school requirements and publications are provided to explain recent legislation.

★7200★ BACT/LAER Clearinghouse
U. S. EPA, Control Technology Center, OAQPS
MD-13
Research Triangle Park, NC 27711
Phone: (919)541-5432
Contact: Bob Blaszczak, EO
The Clearinghouse is sponsored by the Emission Standards and Engineering Division, U.S. Environmental Protection Agency. It was established to assist state and local air pollution control agencies in selecting the best control technology (BACT) and the lowest achievable emission rate (LAER) controls for new or modified sources in a nationally consistent manner. Goals of the Clearinghouse include providing current information on case-by-case technology nationally and promoting communication, cooperation, and sharing of control technology information among agencies. ***Databases:*** The BACT/LAER Information System (BLIS), a database accessible with a personal computer, communicationsoftware, a modem, and an account number for the IBM mainframe computer with "TSO" command language, is operated by the Clearinghouse.

★7201★ Bureau of Explosives Hotline
Phone: (202)639-2222
A 24-hour emergency number operated by the Association of American Railroads for assistance in hazardous materials incidents involving railroads.

★7202★ Cancer Information Service Hotline
Toll-Free: 800-422-6237
Operated by the National Institutes of Health to provide cancer information.

★7203★ Carbon Dioxide Information Analysis Center (CDIC)
Environmental Sciences Division, Bldg. 1000
Oak Ridge National Lab.
PO Box 2008
Oak Ridge, TN 37830
Phone: (615)574-0390
Contact: C.R. Weisbin, Dir. Opns. & User Servs. Mgr.
The Center is a support unit of the Department of Energy Carbon Dioxide Research Program located with the Environmental Sciences Division of the Oak Ridge National Laboratory. CDIAC provides information support to the international research, policy, and education communities for evaluation of environmental issues associated with elevated atmospheric carbon dioxide, including potential climate change. ***Founded:*** 1982. ***Databases:*** The Clearinghouse operates the CDIAC Bibliographic Information System, which contains 10,190 references on climate, carbon cycle, vegetation response, and resource analysis. CDIAC maintains a directory listing approximately 4,600 researchers and policy makers from 148 countries.

★7204★ Center for Environmental Research Information (CERI)
ORD Research Information Unit
26 W. Martin Luther King Dr.
(MS G-72)
Cincinnati, OH 45268
Phone: (513)569-7562
Contact: Dorothy Williams, Exec. Off.
CERI serves as centralized information distribution and technology transfer unit for the Office of Research and Development, U.S. Environmental Protection Agency.

★7205★ Chemical Emergency Preparedness Program
Phone: (202)479-2449
Toll-Free: 800-535-0202
Operated by the EPA to provides communities with help in preparing for accidental releases of toxic chemicals.

★7206★ Chemical Referral Center
2501 M St. NW
Washington, DC 20037
Phone: (202)887—100
Toll-Free: 800-CMA-8200
Disseminates information on chemicasl in non-emergency situations.

★7207★ Chemtrec Hotline
Toll-Free: 800-424-9300
The 24-hour Chemical Transportation Emergency Center identifies unknown chemicals, advises on response methods and procedures for chemicals and situations, and provides assistance in contacting shippers, carriers, manufacturers, and product response teams.

★7208★ Citizen's Clearinghouse for Hazardous Wastes (CCHW)
PO Box 926
Arlington, VA 22216
Phone: (703)276-7070
Contact: Lois Marie Gibbs, Exec. Dir.
CCHW is a grassroots for-profit organization for environmental justice in hazardous waste issues such as solid waste, industrial discharges, medical waste workplace exposure, industrial discharges and accidents, radioactive waste, sewage sludge, household toxics, and asbestos. ***Founded:*** 1981. ***Staff:*** 14. ***Databases:*** The Clearinghouse is open to the public and performs computer searches for a fee. ***Special Collections:*** CCHW's Library contains self-help guidebooks on environmental issues.

★7209★ Clean Lakes Clearinghouse (CLC)
401 M. St., S.W.
WH-553
Washington, DC 20460
Phone: (202)382-7111
Contact: Terri Hollingsworth, EO
The Clearinghouse is sponsored by the U.S. Environmental Protection Agency, Clean Lakes Program to collect, organize, and disseminate information on lake restoration, protection, and management to EPA personnel, lake managers, and state and local governments. ***Databases:*** The Clearinghouse operates the Clean Lakes Database to provide abstracts and citations to journal articles, technical reports, and conference papers and to answer inquiries. The Database contains information on lake ecology, lake management and protection, in-lake restoration techniques, watershed management, point and nonpoint sources of pollution, water quality assessment, modeling, and lake problems such as nutrients, acidification, and toxic substances. This bibliographic database can be loaded into a personal computer and is available through the EPA's online library catalog system. Searches for individuals will be performed free of charge on specific lake topics by telephoning (202)382-7111.

★7210★ Clean Ocean Action
Concerned Businesses of Clean Ocean Action
Sandy Hook, P.O. Box 505
Highlands, NJ 07732
Phone: (908)872-0111
Contact: Jody E. Tatum
Provides the business community with information and guidance on environmentally sound products and practices through newsletters, and educational events and activities.

★7211★ Community Right-to-Know Hotline
Phone: (202)479-2449
Toll-Free: 800-535-0202
Answers questions regarding community preparedness for facility releases, emergency planning, community right-to-know, and SARA Title III.

★7212★ Conservation and Renewable Energy Inquiry and Referral Service (CAREIRS)
U. S. Dept. of Energy
PO Box 8900
Silver Spring, MD 20907
Toll-Free: 800-523-2929
Contact: Lawrence Hughes, Proj. Mgr.
Founded: 1981. The Service, formerly known as National Solar Heating and Cooling Information Center, is operated by Advanced Sciences, Inc. under contract to the U.S. Department of Energy. CAREIRS responds to public inquiries on renewable energy technologies and energy conservation techniques for residential and commercial needs in the areas of active and passive solar heating, photovoltaics, wind energy, biofuels conservation, solar thermal electricity, geothermal energy, small-scale hydroelectricity, alcohol fuels, wood heating, ocean energy, and all energy conservation technologies. ***Staff:*** 14.

★7213★ Consumer Energy Council of America Research Foundation (CECA/RF)
2000 L. St., N. W., Ste. 802
Washington, DC 20036
Phone: (202)659-0404
Contact: Ellen Berman, Exec. Dir.
Founded: 1973. CECA/RF serves as an information clearinghouse and research unit of the Consumer Energy Council of America (CECA), the oldest public interest energy policy organization in the United States. CECA is a broad-based coalition of consumer, labor, farm, urban, public power systems and rural electric cooperatives, and other organizations committed to shaping national energy policies and designing workable programs to provide consumers throughout the country with an adequate supply of energy at fair and reasonable prices. The Consumer Energy Council of America Research Foundation (CECA/RF) was established to provide a forum for a broad agenda of in-depth research studies.

★7214★ Consumer Product Safety Commission
Toll-Free: 800-638-2772
Provides information on consumer safety and what to do in the event of contact with formaldehyde, asbestos, lime, and air pollutants.

★7215★ Control Technology Center for Air Toxics
Phone: (919)541-0800
Operated the EPA to assist in locating state and local pollution control agencies on sources of emissions of air toxics.

★7216★ D.O.T Hotline
Phone: (202)366-4488
Operated by the Department of Transportation to provide assistance on federal regulations regarding the transport of hazardous materials.

★7217★ Environmental Action Foundation (EAF)
1525 New Hampshire Ave., N.W.
Washington, DC 20036
Phone: (202)745-4870
Fax: (202)745-4880
Contact: Ruth Caplan, Director
Founded: 1970. EAF is an independent, nonprofit organization founded by the organizers of the first Earth Day to promote environmental protection through research, public education, organizing assistance, and legal action. Work is currently focused in four major areas: toxics, energy, solid waste, and energy conservation. ***Staff:*** 25.

★7218★ Environmental Connection: Austin
P.O. Box 27437
Austin, TX 78755-2437
Phone: (512)345-1838
Contact: Jo Ann Farrell
Apolitical information clearinghouse and forum on local, regional and global topics enabling people to make responsible environmental decisions.

★7219★ Environmental Law Institute (ELI)
1616 P. St., N.W., Ste. 200
Washington, DC 20036
Phone: (202)328-5150
Contact: J. William Futrell, President
Founded: 1969. ELI is a national nonprofit research and education institution that searches for solutions to environmental problems and devises responses to help achieve national environmental goals. ELI has also maintained a leadership position on key policy research of air and water pollution, hazardous wastes and toxic substances, critical lands regulation, resource economics, and administrative law. ELI consists of leaders from academia, government, business, public interest and private bar members who control the Institute through its Board of Directors. The Institute is non-partisan and neither litigates nor lobbies. Holdings: ELI maintains a professionally staffed, specialized library of more than 15,000 volumes, documents, and databases available for reference use by staff and outside researchers.

★7220★ Environmental Quality Instructional Resources Center
Ohio State University
1200 Chambers Rd.
Columbus, OH 43212-1792
Phone: (614)292-6717
Contact: Robert Howe, EO
The Environmental Quality Instructional Resources Center (EQ/IRC) is the central location for the dissemination of educational information dealing with water quality, specifically wastewater and drinking water, to post-secondary educators and trainers. Materials related to hazardous and toxic materials are also included. The EQ/IRC has been associated with the USEPA since 1977 and is part of the SMEAC Information Reference Center.

★7221★ EPA Public Information Center
Phone: (202)475-7751
Answers inquiries from the public about the EPA, its programs and activities, and offers a variety of general, nontechnical informational materials.

★7222★ Green Committees of Correspondence Clearinghouse (Green CoC)
PO Box 30208
Kansas City, MO 64112
Phone: (816)931-9366
Contact: Jim Richmond, Coord.
Founded: 1984. The Clearinghouse responds to questions; disseminates information; distributes lists of local and regional Green movement contacts; and makes available books and periodicals on the Green movement, ecological awareness, and grass roots politics.

★7223★ INFOTERRA
EPA Headquarters Library
401 M. St., S.W.
PM-211A
Washington, DC 20460
Phone: (202)382-5917
Contact: Linda Spencer, Exec. Off.
Founded: 1972. INFOTERRA was created by the United Nations Environmental Programme, and is sponsored by the Office of Information Resources Management, U.S. Environmental Protection Agency. It is a global, decentralized network of sources of environmental information, with a linking structure of 137 national focal points, a programme activity center, and 9 regional service centers. ***Databases:*** INFOTERRA's primary information source is the International Directory of Sources, the INFOTERRA Database. It exists as both printed hardcopy and as a digital database stored on a central computer at the United Nations office in Geneva, available on magnetic tape or diskette for mainframe and PC-based microcomputers. The database has access to 6,500 sources of information, by over 1,000 environmental subjects, by country, or by name of organization. In addition, INFOTERRA has access to over 500 EPA and commercial databases; and serves as a pathfinder to international databases. Information services offered by INFOTERRA are free to all users.

★7224★ INTECOL - International Association for Ecology
c/o Inst. of Ecology
Univ. of Georgia
Athens, GA 30602
Phone: (404)542-2968
Contact: Frank B. Golley, President
Founded: 1967. INTECOL is an international nongovernmental organization that represents ecologists worldwide. INTECOL is part of the Section on the Environment, International Union of Biological Sciences (IUBS). The INTECOL Secretariat serves as a clearinghouse for coordinating and disseminating information and other materials related to ecology and the environment worldwide. INTECOL works to promote the development of the science of ecology and the application of ecological principles to global needs, particularly through international cooperation.

★7225★ International Clearinghouse for Environmental Technologies
12600 W. Colfax Ave., Ste. C-310
Lakewood, CO 80215
Phone: (303)233-1248
Disseminates solutions for hazardous and solid waste treatment, disposal, recycling, and reduction.

★7226★ International Ground Water Modeling Center
Butler Univ.
Holcomb Research Inst.
4600 Sunset Ave.
Indianapolis, IN 46208
Phone: (317)283-9458
Fax: (317)283-9519
Contact: Paul van der Heijde, Director
Founded: 1978. The International Ground Water Modeling Center formerly known as Groundwater Research Data Center is an information, education, and research center for groundwater modeling established at Holcomb Research Institute in response to a study undertaken through the auspices of ICSU/SCOPE. The Center operates a clearinghouse for groundwater modeling, software, organizes conferences, short-courses and seminars, conducts research to support its information and education activities, and provides advice and technical assistance in various areas related to groundwater modeling. The two major tasks of the clearinghouse are the dissemination of information regarding groundwater model selection, requisition, implementation, and application, and reviewing, testing, and distributing modeling software. To perform these tasks, the Center has developed various procedures and databases. ***Databases:*** Databases include information modeling, data for model testing, and descriptions of a large number of groundwater models. By means of search and retrieval procedures, stored information on groundwater models is accessible to the IGWMC staff.

★7227★ Kentucky Partners
Kentucky Partners/State Waste Reduction Center
Rm. 312, Ernst Hall
University of Louisville
Louisville, KY 40292
Phone: (502)588-7260
Contact: Joyce St. Clair
Offers technical advice to businesses to help them reduce, reuse, recover, and reclaim waste streams in their facilities.

★7228★ Minority Energy Information Clearinghouse
Office of Minority Economic Impact
U. S. Dept. of Energy
Forrestal Bldg., Rm. 58-110
100 Independence Ave., S.W.
Washington, DC 20585
Phone: (202)586-5876
Toll-Free: 800-543-2325
Contact: Effie A. Young, Info. Officer
The Minority Energy Information Clearinghouse is operated by the Office of Minority Economic Impact, U.S. Department of Energy (DOE). It is a centralized repository and dissemination point for research data and information about energy programs and the economic impact of those programs on minorities, minority business, and minority educational institutions. ***Databases:*** Information is maintained on programs of the Office of Minority Economic Impact and other DOE programs that concern minority populations. These programs include the Socioeconomic Research and Analysis Program, the Minority Educational Institution Assistance Program, the Minority Financial Institutions Deposit Program, and the Minority Honors Training and Industrial Assistance Program.

★7229★ Montana State Library
Montana Natural Resource Information System
1515 E. Sixth Ave.
Helena, MT 59620
Phone: (406)444-5355
Contact: Jon C. Sesso
Referral service and clearinghouse of information on Montana's natural resources. Used by government, the public, and businesses.

★7230★ National Air Toxics Information Clearinghouse (NATICH)
826 Mutual Plaza
(MD-13)
Research Triangle Park, NC 27711
Phone: (919)541-0850
Contact: Melissa McCullough, Database Adm.
The Clearinghouse is sponsored by the Pollutant Assessment Branch, U.S. Environmental Protection Agency to collect, classify, and disseminate air toxics information submitted by state and local air agencies. NATICH also disseminates information on the development of air toxics control programs. ***Databases:*** The Clearinghouse database contains air pollution control agency data and citations/abstracts. The information is generally indexed according to agency, pollutant, emission source, and research information. The database is available at a cost of about $10-15/hour of work. Hard copy reports of all data contained in the database are issued on a regular basis.

★7231★ National Capital Poison Control Center
Phone: (202)625-3333
Operated by Georgetown University Hospital to provide information on exposure to chemicals, poison, or drugs. Accepts collect telephone calls.

★7232★ National Ground Water Information Center (NGWIC)
6375 Riverside Dr.
Dublin, OH 43017
Phone: (614)761-1711
Fax: (614)761-3446
Toll-Free: 800-242-4965
Contact: Kevin McCray, Exec. Dir.
Founded: 1960. ***Staff:*** 8. NGWIC is a nonprofit organization sponsored by the National Water Well Association and formerly known as the National Water Well Association. NGWIC is an information gathering and dissemination business that performs customized research on all groundwater-related topics, and locates and retrieves copies of available documents. ***Databases:*** NGWIC databases include Ground-Water On-Line containing more than 52,000 groundwater literature citations containing key concepts, abstracts, chemicals, biological factors, geographic references, authors, titles, publication titles, and more; WellFax, an analysis of official 1980 U.S. Bureau of the Census data, providing hard numbers on how many U.S. households are using private water wells; Monitoring Handbook, an online edition of the U.S. EPA-approved 40-page Handbook of Suggested Practices for the Design and Installation of GroundWater Monitoring Wells; Well Construction/Contractor Licensing Regulations, abstracts of water well contractor licensing and domestic well construction codes for all 50 states; federal register, an online summary of government rulemaking critical to the groundwater industry; Standards, a database on criteria, guidelines, practices, procedures and standards of the groundwater industry; Monitoring Consultants and

Contractors, a database directory of firms who provide various services relevant to the detection and remediation of groundwater contamination; Higher Education Program, a directory of the universities and colleges offering groundwater courses; GroundWater Sampling Devices guides the selection of the best possible type of groundwater sampling device for a given set of conditions; Source of Water Supply identifies a U.S. city or town using groundwater, surface water, or a conjunctive supply; courses, providing continuing education courses; and Job Mart, offering blind ads of job seekers. Other databases housed at NGWIC but not available online include Underground Storage Tanks, Water Treatability, Public Well Operators, and Data Base Searches for Non-Subscribers. Holdings: 17,000 books; 8,000 bound periodicals; 3,000 documents; 750 audiovisual programs; 10,000 nonbook items.

★7233★ National Pesticide Information Retrieval Service (NPIRS)
Purdue University
Entomology Hall
West Lafayette, IN 47907
Phone: (317)494-6614
Contact: James H. White, EO
NPIRS is a membership organization sponsored by the Office of Pesticide Programs, U.S. Environmental Protection Agency and located at Purdue University. NPIRS provides current information on EPA product registration and tolerance data for pesticides and hazardous chemicals. ***Founded:*** 1983. NPIRS uses a computer-based system, and with cooperation from the U.S. Department of Agriculture, EPA, and the states, it provides EPA registered pesticide products information, state registration information, registration guideline information, and study descriptions.

★7234★ National Pesticide Telecommunications Network (NPTN)
Dept. of Preventive Medicine & Community Health
School of Medicine
Texas Tech University Health Sciences Center
Lubbock, TX 79409
Phone: (806)743-3091
Fax: (806)743-3094
Toll-Free: 800-858-PEST
Contact: Dr. Anthony Way, Exec. Officer
NPTN is a toll-free telephone service available to provide impartial information about pesticides to individuals in the contiguous United States, Puerto Rico, and the Virgin Islands. It is funded by the U.S. Environmental Protection Agency with additional share funding provided through the Texas Tech University Health Sciences Center School of Medicine. The Network provides pesticide product information; information on recognition and management of pesticide poisonings; toxicology and symptomatic reviews; safety information; information on health and environmental effects; and clean-up and disposal procedures. ***Databases:*** NPTN has access to Medline, Toxline, NPIRS, and other computerized databases.

★7235★ National Pollution Prevention Center
University of Michigan
School of Natural Resources
430 E. University
Ann Arbor, MI 48109-1115
Phone: (313)764-1412
Contact: Jonathan W. Bulkley, Dir.
Disseminates pollution prevention educational materials to other institutions nationally.

★7236★ National Response Center U.S. Coast Guard Hotline
Phone: (202)267-2675
Toll-Free: 800-424-8802
Operated 24 hours a day by the Coast Guard to respond to accidental oil and hazardous substances spills.

★7237★ National Small Flows Clearinghouse
West Virginia Univ.
258 Stewart St.
PO Box 6064
Morgantown, WV 26506-6064
Phone: (304)293-4191
Toll-Free: 800-624-8301
Contact: Jackie Statler, Info. Spec.
Founded: 1979. The National Small Flows Information Clearinghouse was established by the U.S. Environmental Protection Agency (EPA) at West Virginia University under the federal Clean Water Act of 1977. It gathers and distributes information about small community wastewater systems and serves as the national center for small wastewater systems technology transfer, management information, and training resources. The Center provides computerized literature searches through its Small Flows Bibliographic Database, which lists articles from more than 40 journals, government and university publications, and conference proceedings. Three other internal databases are maintained by the Clearinghouse: the Innovative and Alternative Systems (I/A) Database provides information on wastewater treatment facilities nationwide; the Contacts Database is a geographic listing of specialists in small flows; and the Manufacturers Database is a guide to firms that supply small flows products.

★7238★ New York State Dept. of Environmental Conservation
Division of Hazardous Substances, Bureau of Pollution Prevention
Hazardous Waste Reduction Technical Assistance
50 Wolf Rd.
Albany, NY 12233-7253
Phone: (518)457-7267
Contact: John E. Iannotti P.E.
Functions as information clearinghouse. Hazardous waste reduction and pollution prevention technical assistance program for New York state businesses and industries. Holds conferences and workshops.

★7239★ Northeast Industrial Waste Exchange
Phone: (315)422-6572
Provides information on waste exchange in the northeast. Seeks to match those who generate waste with those who can use waste.

★7240★ Northeast Waste Management Officials' Association
Northeast Multi-Media Pollution Prevention
85 Merrimac St.
Boston, MA 02114
Phone: (617)367-8558
Contact: Terri Goldberg
Founded: 1989. Clearinghouse of information on pollution prevention. Conducts training and research on source reduction and recycling for major toxic metals in municipal solid waste.

★7241★ Nuclear Information and Resource Service (NIRS)
1424 16th St., N.W., Ste. 601
Washington, DC 20036
Phone: (202)328-0002
Fax: (202)462-2183
Contact: Michael Mariotte Tymon, Exec. Dir.
Founded: 1978. A national clearinghouse and networking center for people concerned about nuclear power issues. It is dedicated to a sound, non-nuclear energy policy and serves safe energy and environmental activists with reliable, accurate information, resources, and organizational assistance.

★7242★ OTS Chemical Assessment Desk
401 M. St., S.W.
(TS-778)
Washington, DC 20460
Contact: Terry O'Bryan, EO
The Desk is sponsored by the Office of Toxic Substances, Environmental Protection Agency to provide technical consultation and information on chemical risk-related issues to EPA staff.

★7243★ Passive Solar Industries Council (PSIC)
1090 Vermont Ave. N.W., Ste. 1200
Washington, DC 20005
Phone: (202)371-0357
Contact: Helen English, Exec. Dir.
Founded: 1980. The Passive Solar Industries Council serves as a clearinghouse to disseminate information on passive solar design and construction to the U.S. building industry. Working with government and private industry through publications, forums, and other programs, PSIC represents a national network of businesses and professionals interested in developing energy-efficient, solar-heated buildings.

★7244★ Pesticide Action Network North America Regional Center (PAN NA RC)
965 Mission St., Ste. 514
San Francisco, CA 94103
Phone: (415)541-9140
Fax: (415)541-9253
Telex: 156283472 PANNA
Contact: Doria Mueller-Beilschmidt
Founded: 1984. The Center serves as an information clearinghouse established to increase international public access to information on pesticides and pesticide-related issues, especially in developing countries. As a member of Pesticide Action Network International, PAN NA RC maintains close contact with hundreds of organizations and professionals worldwide working on different aspects of pesticides. ***Databases:*** The Center contains approximately 2,500 monographs, articles, slides, and videos on a computerized bibliographic database. PAN NA RC also subscribes to DIALOG and will perform searches related to pesticides at cost plus a service fee.

★7245★ Powder River Basin Resource Council
Energy Conservation Education
23 N. Scott
Seridan, WY 82801
Phone: (307)672-5809
Contact: Jill Morrision
Initiated an energy conservation education program, consisting of workshops, newsletters and presentations. Acts as a clearinghouse of information.

★7246★ Public Information Center (PIC)
U.S. Environmental Protection Agency
401 M. St. S.W.
PM-211B
Southeast Basement
Washington, DC 20460
Phone: (202)260-7751

Contact: Nancy Langford, EO
PIC is sponsored by the Information Management and Services Division, U.S. Environmental Protection Agency and serves as the EPA's primary contact point for information about the environmental concerns of the general public. The Center distributes nontechnical environmental publications on a wide range of environmental topics, including acid rain, air quality, drinking water, gas mileage, indoor air, toxic substances, pesticides, radon, recycling, and wetlands.

★7247★ Rachel Carson Council
8940 Jones Mill Rd.
Chevy Chase, MD 20815
Phone: (301)652-1877
International clearinghouse of information on ecology on chemical contamination.

★7248★ RCRA/Superfund Hotline
Phone: (202)382-3000
Toll-Free: 800-424-9346
Operated by the EPA to answer questions regarding the Resource Conservation and Recovery Act, Superfund, and hazardous waste regulations.

★7249★ Safe Drinking Water Hotline
Phone: (202)382-5533
Toll-Free: 800-426-4791
Operated by the EPA to provide information on the regulations and policies for the public water supply program.

★7250★ Small Business and Asbestos Ombudsman
Phone: (202)557-1938
Toll-Free: 800-368-5888
Operated by the EPA to provide information to small businesses on complying with EPA regulations and problems encountered by small-quantity generators of hazardous waste and other environmental concerns of small businesses.

★7251★ Solar Energy Research Institute, Technical Inquiry Service (TIS)
1617 Cole Blvd.
Golden, CO 80401-3393
Phone: (303)231-7303
Contact: Paul Notari, Mgr
Founded: 1980. Formerly the National Alcohol Fuels Information Center, the Technical Inquiry Service is operated for the Solar Technical Information Program, U.S. Department of Energy by the Solar Energy Research Institute (SERI), a subsidiary of the Midwest Research Institute, an independent, nonprofit research organization based in Kansas City, Missouri. The Service's mission is to provide information on solar energy and other renewable energy technologies to the scientific and industrial communities.

★7252★ Toxicology Information Response Center (TIRC)
Oak Ridge National Laboratory
Bldg. 2001, PO Box 2008
Oak Ridge, TN 37831-6050
Phone: (615)576-1746
Fax: (615)574-9888
Contact: Kimberly Slusher, EO
Founded: 1971. ***Staff:*** 2. TIRC is a nonprofit governmental center operated by Martin Marietta Energy Systems and sponsored by the Toxicology Information Program, Library of Medicine, U.S. Department of Health and Human Services. It serves as a national and international center for the collection, analysis, and dissemination of toxicology-related information on a variety of chemicals, including food additives, pharmaceuticals, industrial chemicals, environmental pollutants, heavy metals, and pesticides. ***Databases:*** The Center utilizes various information sources such as online access to over 400 computerized databases through systems such as MEDLARS, DIALOG, STN International, ITIS and DROLS, the Environmental Mutagen Information Center File, the Environmental Teratogenicity Center File, and Departments of Defense and Energy databases. It performs searches for outside users for a fee.

★7253★ TSCA Assistance Information Service Hotline
Phone: (202)554-1404
EPA's Toxic Assistance Office answers questions and offers general and technical assistance on the Toxic Substances Control Act, including guidance on PCB's and asbestos issues.

★7254★ Waste Exchange Clearinghouse
Waste Systems Inst. of Michigan, Inc.
400 Ann St., N.W., No. 201-A
Grand Rapids, MI 49504-2054
Phone: (616)363-3262
Contact: Jeffrey L. Dauphin
The Waste Exchange Clearinghouse (WEC) is an information exchange service for industrial producers and users of solid and hazardous wastes. It is operated by Waste Systems Institute of Michigan, Inc. (WSI) and WSI's western U.S. cooperative, Pacific Materials Exchange (PME) in Spokane, Washington. WSI and PME are both independent, federally recognized nonprofit organizations. WEC promotes the recycling of solid and hazardous wastes. Serving 45,000 companies in 26 states and the Pacific Rim countries, it offers confidentiality in the search for waste markets or surplus materials. It helps users eliminate or reduce disposal costs; find buyers for surplus, off-spec, obsolete, or overstocked materials; locate free or inexpensive raw materials; and reduce pollution and conserve energy, landfill, and other resources. The heart of the ENVIROX, an online, environmental information management system, contains the waste exchange listings of the PME and the Great Lakes/Midwest Waste Exchange, which is operated by WSI.

★7255★ White Lung Association (WLA)
1601 St. Paul St.
Baltimore, MD 21202-2816
Phone: (301)727-6029
Contact: James Fite, Exec. Dir.
Founded: 1979. ***Staff:*** 5. WLA is a nonprofit organization that serves as a clearinghouse for information on the hazards of asbestos. It assists and informs the general public about asbestos hazards through training and educational material. WLA also provides assistance for those exposed to asbestos or who have asbestos-related diseases. Holdings: 200 books; 800 bound periodical volumes; 1000 microforms and nonbook items; 20 audiovisual programs; one patent pending, as well as news clippings and special reports.

★7256★ Wisconsin Energy Information Clearinghouse
Wisconsin Division of Energy
Intergovernmental Relations
PO Box 7868
Madison, WI 53707
Phone: (608)266-8234
Contact: Barbara Samuel
Founded: 1977. A clearinghouse operated by the Wisconsin Energy Bureau that monitors state and national energy supplies and prices, publishes and distributes energy reports, fact sheets, and informational materials, and runs energy programs.

Library Collections

★7257★ ABB Environmental Services Inc.
Library
Box 7050
Portland, ME 04112
Phone: (207)775-5401
Fax: (207)772-4762
Contact: James R. Lawson, Libn.
Subjects: Engineering - environmental, design, civil; geotechnical/earth resources; solid and hazardous waste; environmental regulations. ***Holdings:*** 4000 books; 48 bound periodical volumes.

★7258★ Academy of Science of Guangdong Province
Guangdong Entomological Institute
Library
105 Xingang Rd., W.
Guangzhou, Guangdong Province, People's Republic of China
Phone: 448651
Contact: Zhiqing Zhang
Subjects: Insects - natural enemies, systematics; termites; pest control; protection of rare animals; wildlife utilization. ***Holdings:*** 22,078 books; 8320 bound periodical volumes.

★7259★ The Acid Rain Foundation, Inc.
Library
1410 Varsity Dr.
Raleigh, NC 27606
Phone: (919)828-9443
Fax: (919)737-3593
Contact: Harriett S. Stubbs, Exec.Dir.
Subjects: Acid deposition, air pollution, global climate change. ***Special Collections:*** Gray literature (acid rain; international). ***Holdings:*** 500 books; 3000 scientific papers; 1000 uncataloged items.

★7260★ Acres International Inc.
Library
140 John James Audubon Pkwy.
Amherst, NY 14228-1180
Phone: (716)689-3737
Contact: Marion D'Amboise
Subjects: Wastewater treatment, hydropower, geotechnology, air and water pollution, environment, hazardous substances. ***Holdings:*** 4200 volumes; internal reports; product catalogs; topographic maps.

★7261★ Aero Vironment Inc.
Library
5031 Myrtle Ave.
Monrovia, CA 91017-7131
Phone: (818)357-9983
Fax: (818)359-9628
Telex: 467121 (AEROVIR-CI)
Contact: Heidi Nikpur
Subjects: Alternative energy, aerodynamics, environmental science, air pollution, hazardous waste. ***Holdings:*** 300 books; 100 journals; 5000 technical reports.

★7262★ Air and Waste Management Association
Library
Box 2861
Pittsburgh, PA 15230
Phone: (412)232-3444
Fax: (412)232-3450
Contact: H.M. Englund, Ed.
Subjects: Air pollution, hazardous waste management. ***Holdings:*** 1000 books.

★7263★ Alaska (State) Department of Environmental Conservation
DEC Library
Box O
Juneau, AK 99811-1800
Phone: (907)465-2692
Fax: (907)789-6762
Contact: Katie Sloan, Libn.
Subjects: Air and water quality, environmental health, wastewater treatment, hazardous and solid waste, oil and hazardous substance spill response, mining, facilities inspection and operation. ***Holdings:*** 10,000 books; 1000 uncataloged items; microfiche.

★7264★ Alaska (State) Department of Fish and Game
Habitat Library
333 Raspberry Rd.
Anchorage, AK 99518-1599
Phone: (907)267-2312
Contact: Celia Rozen, Libn.
Subjects: Fish and wildlife habitat, Arctic exploration, oil and gas impacts, coastal zone management, ecology, human usage. ***Holdings:*** 11,000 books; 12,000 maps; 10,000 reprints.

★7265★ Alberta Energy/Forestry, Lands and Wildlife
Library
Petroleum Plaza, S. Tower, 9th Fl.
9915 108th St.
Edmonton, Alberta, Canada T5K 2C9
Phone: (403)427-7425
Fax: (403)422-3578
Contact: Susan Carlisle, Hd.
Subjects: Energy economics and resources, forestry, forest industry, mineral resources, public lands, reclamation, energy conservation, fish and wildlife. ***Holdings:*** 12,000 books; 200 bound periodical volumes; 250 folders in VF drawers; 200 microfiche; 18,000 reports.

★7266★ (Alberta) Environment Council of Alberta
Information Centre
Weber Centre, 8th Fl.
5555 Calgary Trail Southbound, N.W.
Edmonton, Alberta, Canada T6H 5P9
Phone: (403)427-5792
Fax: (403)427-0388
Contact: Terry Forbes, Lib.Techn.
Subjects: Conservation, energy, land use, renewable and nonrenewable resources, pollution, urbanization. ***Special Collections:*** Mackenzie Valley Pipeline Inquiry Transcripts (281 volumes); World Conservation Strategy (238 documents). ***Holdings:*** 6000 books and government reports; ECA reports, recommendations, proceedings, summaries of public hearings; 2 VF drawers of pamphlets; 8 VF drawers of clippings.

★7267★ Alberta Environment
Library
Oxbridge Place, 14th Fl.
9820 106th St.
Edmonton, Alberta, Canada T5K 2J6
Phone: (403)427-6132
Contact: Deb Fralick, Hd., Lib.Serv.
Subjects: Water resources; land use planning; environmental conservation; pollution - air, water, odor, noise. ***Holdings:*** 35,000 books; 6 drawers of maps; 4 cabinets of microfiche; NTIS publications.

★7268★ Alberta Environmental Centre
Library
Bag 4000
Vegreville, Alberta, Canada T0B 4L0
Phone: (403)632-6767
Fax: (403)632-5475
Contact: Sherry Slater, Libn.
Subjects: Science - environmental, animal, plant; chemical analysis; toxicology; ecology. ***Holdings:*** 10,000 books; 3000 technical reports.

★7269★ Alternative Energy Resources Organization (AERO)
Library
44 N. Last Chance Gulch
Helena, MT 59601-4122
Phone: (406)443-7272
Fax: (406)442-9120
Contact: Al Kurki, Dir.
Subjects: Sustainable agriculture, renewable energy, local economic development, pesticide toxicology. ***Holdings:*** 250 books; 200 bound periodical volumes; 2 VF drawers of renewable resource material.

★7270★ American Cetacean Society National Library
Box 2639
San Pedro, CA 90731
Phone: (213)548-6279
Fax: (213)548-6950
Contact: Virginia C. Callahan, Libn.
Subjects: Whales, marine mammals. ***Special Collections:*** International Whaling Commission reports; Ray Gilmore Collection; Outer Continental Shelf Environmental Assessment Program (OCSEAP) reports. ***Holdings:*** 750 books; 1386 periodicals; 800 reports and reprints; 5 films; 6 records; 55 video cassettes; 10 audio cassettes; sheet music.

★7271★ American Forestry Association McArdle Memorial Library
1516 P St., N.W.
Washington, DC 20005
Phone: (202)667-3300
Fax: (202)667-7751
Contact: Deborah Gangloff
Subjects: Forestry and allied subjects of soil, water, wildlife, and recreation. ***Holdings:*** 6000 books.

★7272★ American Water Works Association Information Services Department
6666 W. Quincy Ave.
Denver, CO 80235
Phone: (303)794-7711
Fax: (303)794-7310
Contact: Kurt M. Keeley, Dir., Info.Serv.
Subjects: Water - treatment, conservation, utility management, quality; wastewater treatment; reuse; water rates. ***Holdings:*** 2500 books; 200 bound periodical volumes; 150 AV programs; 2000 technical reports.

★7273★ Aquatic Research Institute Aquatic Sciences and Technology Archive
2242 Davis Ct.
Hayward, CA 94545
Phone: (415)784-0945
Contact: V. Parker, Archv.
Subjects: Aquatic sciences; limnology; oceanology; marine, freshwater, and estuarine biology; water quality; aquaculture and mariculture; fisheries; ocean engineering and mining; submersibles; undersea military; aquarium technology. ***Special Collections:*** Rare books on fish and fisheries. ***Holdings:*** 40,000 biological specimens; 45,000 volumes; 1000 journals; 5000 photographs; 3000 slides; 1000 maps and charts; 1100 abstracts and indexes; 1500 technical reports; 150,000 pamphlets; 1000 microforms.

★7274★ Archbold Biological Station Library
PO Box 2057
Lake Placid, FL 33852
Phone: (813)465-2571
Fax: (813)699-1927
Contact: Fred E. Lohrer, Libn.
Subjects: Entomology, ichthyology, herpetology, ornithology, mammalogy, animal ecology, plant ecology, limnology, general biology, Florida natural history. ***Special Collections:*** Results of the Archbold Expeditions - Numbers 1-86 (Zoology, 9 bound volumes; Botany, 4 bound volumes); Physiological Ecology of Vertebrates (3 VF drawers of reprints). ***Holdings:*** 4000 books; 4100 bound periodical volumes; 12,500 color transparencies of Florida natural history; 1700 U.S. Geological Survey quadrangle maps of Florida; 1940, 1944, 1958, 1966, 1971, 1981, and 1986 series of U.S. Department of Agriculture aerial photographs of the station and surrounding areas; 17,000 reprints on vertebrate ecology; 12 VF drawers of archives of Archbold Biological Station and Expeditions.

★7275★ Arizona-Sonora Desert Museum Library
Rte. 9, Box 900
Tucson, AZ 85743
Phone: (602)883-1380
Contact: Georgia Eddy, Educ.Spec.
Subjects: Deserts, conservation, earth sciences, Sonoran Desert region, mammals, Southwestern plants, insects, reptiles, amphibians, birds. ***Holdings:*** 6500 books; 400 bound periodical volumes; 500 unbound sets; 450 unbound monographs and bulletins; 4000 slides; 200 photographs; 3000 separates and pamphlets.

★7276★ Arizona State Energy Office Information Center
3800 N. Central, Ste. 1200
Phoenix, AZ 85012
Phone: (602)280-1402
Toll-Free: 800-352-5499
Contact: Rebekah Davis, Mgt. Asst.
Subjects: Community energy consciousness, energy conservation, energy planning and policy, solar/alternate energy. ***Special Collections:*** Arizona Energy Flow Studies; 1981 Arizona Energy Inventory; 1979 final report of Governor's Conference on Energy Policy.

★7277★ Arizona State University Architecture and Environmental Design Library
College of Architecture
Tempe, AZ 85287
Phone: (602)965-6400
Contact: Berna E. Neal, Head
Subjects: Architecture, city planning, landscape architecture, industrial design, interior design, solar energy. ***Special Collections:*** Paolo Soleri Archives; Frank Lloyd Wright Special Research Collection; Paul Schweiker Archives; Victor Olgyay Archives. ***Holdings:*** 26,000 volumes; 150 cassette and tape recordings; 563 titles on microfilm; 25 films and video cassettes.

★7278★ Arkansas (State) Energy Office Library
One Capitol Mall, Ste. 4B-215
Little Rock, AR 72201
Phone: (501)682-1370
Subjects: Energy - policy and legislation, conservation and management, resources, data. ***Holdings:*** 3500 books and reports; maps; slides.

★7279★ Asbestos Information Association/North America Technical and Medical Files
1745 Jefferson Davis Hwy.
Crystal Sq. Four, Ste. 509
Arlington, VA 22202
Phone: (703)979-1150
Contact: Kenneth Nyquist, Govt.Aff.Couns.
Subjects: Health and asbestos, asbestos regulation. ***Special Collections:*** Asbestos information (technical, medical, regulatory). ***Holdings:*** 300 books; 10 VF drawers of clippings and medical files.

★7280★ The Asbestos Institute Archives
1130 Sherbrooke St., W., Ste. 410
Montreal, Quebec, Canada H3A 2M8
Phone: (514)844-3956
Fax: (514)844-1381
Telex: 055-60565 INSTAM MTL
Contact: Claude deLery, Dir./Adm.
Subjects: Biological effects of asbestos. ***Holdings:*** 775 books; 7000 documents.

★7281★ Auburn University International Center for Aquaculture Library
Swingle Hall
Auburn University, AL 36849
Phone: (205)844-4786
Fax: (205)884-9208
Telex: 5106 002392
Contact: Dr. B.L. Duncan, Dir.
Subjects: Aquaculture in fresh, brackish, and marine water; aquatic plants management; nutrition and feeds; parasites and disease; limnology; water quality and management for aquaculture, international development for fisheries and aquaculture. ***Holdings:*** 2500 books; annual reports of the Fisheries Resources Unit, 1936 to present; 10,000 slides and pictures; 250 dissertations; 550 theses.

★7282★ Auburn University Water Resources Research Institute (WRRI) Information Center
202 Hargis Hall
Auburn University, AL 36849-5124
Phone: (205)844-5075
Contact: Prof. Joseph F. Judkins, Dir.
Subjects: All aspects of water resources.

★7283★ Audubon Society of Rhode Island Harry S. Hathaway Library of Natural History and Conservation
12 Sanderson Rd.
Smithfield, RI 02917-2606
Phone: (401)231-6444
Contact: Thomas Perry, Jr., M.D., Chr.
Subjects: Animals, plants, geology of the region and state; environmental problems and management; ecology. ***Special Collections:*** Complete Elephant Folio (Audubon's Mammals and other old books on birds and animals); Elizabeth Dicken's Journals. ***Holdings:*** 1000 books; 200 unbound periodical volumes; 300 pamphlets.

★7284★ Austria - Federal Ministry of Agriculture and Forestry Library
Stubenring 1
A-1011 Vienna, Austria
Phone: 222 7500
Contact: Ingrid Saberi
Subjects: Agriculture, forestry, plant and animal production, environmental contaminants, agrarian policies, wildlife, hunting, vegetation and watershed management, farm mechanization, standardization. ***Special Collections:*** Torrent control (avalanches); Royal and Imperial Ministry of Agriculture collection (10,000 books). ***Holdings:*** 708,000 books; 554 bound periodical volumes.

★7285★ Battelle Memorial Institute Stack Gas Emission Control Coordination Center Library
505 King Ave.
Columbus, OH 43201-2693
Phone: (614)424-7885
Fax: (614)424-5263
Telex: 24-5454
Contact: Dr. Joseph H. Oxley, Mgr.
Subjects: Scrubbers, fuel gas desulfurization, clean fuels, coal utilization techniques.

★7286★ Battelle New England Marine Research Laboratories
Battelle Ocean Sciences Library
397 Washington St.
Box AH
Duxbury, MA 02332
Phone: (617)934-0571
Contact: Ellen S. Rosen, Libn.
Subjects: Marine biology, oceanography, environmental research. ***Holdings:*** 3000 books; 100 bound periodical volumes.

★7287★ Beijing Agricultural University Library
2 W. Yuanmingyuan Lu
Beijing 100094, People's Republic of China
Phone: 2582244 516
Telex: 222487 BAU CN
Contact: Yang Zhimin, Prof., Chf.Libn.
Subjects: Agriculture; genetic crop breeding; plant physiology, biochemistry, pathology; entomology; agricultural microbiology; animal husbandry; veterinary medicine; agricultural economics; soil science; land resources; laboratory animal science; agricultural meteorology; food science; horticulture; agricultural chemistry; plant nutrition; allied sciences and technology. ***Special Collections:*** Chinese and foreign publications on plant pathology, entomology, veterinary parasitology, pesticides, plant physiology and biochemistry, genetic breeding, fertilizers; ancient Chinese agricultural works (300 titles). ***Holdings:*** 776,357 volumes; 75,394 periodicals.

★7288★ Belle W. Baruch Institute for Marine Biology and Coastal Research
Library
University of S. Carolina
Columbia, SC 29208
Phone: (803)777-5288
Contact: Ms. V. Smith, Adm.Asst.
Subjects: Marine biology, marine geology, physical and chemical oceanography, ecosystem studies.

★7289★ Bendix Environmental Research, Inc. (BERI)
Library
1390 Market St., Ste. 418
San Francisco, CA 94102
Phone: (415)861-8484
Contact: Selina Bendix, Ph.D., Pres.
Subjects: Environment, toxicology, hazardous materials. ***Holdings:*** Articles and offprints on 400 subjects.

★7290★ Bermuda Biological Station for Research, Inc.
Edward Laurens Mark Memorial Library
17 Biological Sta. Ln.
Ferry Reach GE 01, Bermuda
Phone: (809)297-1880
Fax: (809)297-8143
Contact: F.J. Chatterjee, Libn.
Subjects: Marine biology and ecology, oceanography, geology. ***Special Collections:*** Bermuda Biological Station Special Publications (set of 29); Bermuda Biological Station Contributions (numbers 1 to 1400). ***Holdings:*** 16,000 volumes.

★7291★ Betz Laboratories, Inc.
Research Library
4636 Somerton Rd.
Trevose, PA 19047
Phone: (215)355-3300
Fax: (215)953-2494
Contact: Joan E. Goldberg, Sr.Libn.
Subjects: Industrial and municipal water treatment, pollution control. ***Holdings:*** 2500 books; 3000 bound periodical volumes; 12 VF drawers of patents; 2000 documents on microfiche.

★7292★ The Bickelhaupt Arboretum Education Center
340 S. Fourteenth St.
Clinton, IA 52732
Phone: (319)242-4771
Contact: F.K. Bickelhaupt, Libn.
Subjects: Trees and shrubs, planting and pruning, indoor plants, vegetable gardening, ecology, urban forestry. ***Special Collections:*** Tree identification book collection; urban forestry files; Education Center Slide Collection. ***Holdings:*** 910 books; 50 other cataloged items; 247 files on arboreta and botanical gardens around the world; 1200 microfiche containing information on landscape and woody plants native and hardy to the Midwest.

★7293★ Biomass Energy Institute
Library
1329 Niakwa Rd. E.
Winnipeg, Manitoba, Canada R2J 3T4
Phone: (204)257-3891
Contact: Beth Candlish, Ph.D., Exec.Dir.
Subjects: Bio-energy, bioconversion, energy policy, solar energy, wind energy. ***Special Collections:*** Biomass Abstracts (25,000 references and abstracts). ***Holdings:*** 20,000 books and government reports.

★7294★ Briley, Wild and Associates, Inc.
Library
1042 U. S. Hwy. 1 N.
Box 607
Ormond Beach, FL 32175
Phone: (904)672-5660
Contact: John W. Casey, Libn.
Subjects: Water, wastewater treatment, facilities planning, water resources. ***Holdings:*** 5100 volumes; 7000 documents; 1 VF drawer of clippings.

★7295★ British Columbia Council of Forestry Inc.
Library
555 Burrard St., Ste. 1200
Vancouver, British Columbia, Canada V7X 1S7
Phone: (604)684-0211
Contact: Sheila M. Foley, Libn.
Subjects: Forest industry economics and trade; environmental issues; transportation. ***Holdings:*** 4000 books; 70 Statistics Canada titles; Canadian, U.S., foreign government documents.

★7296★ British Columbia Ministry of Environment
Environment Library
780 Blanshard St.
Victoria, British Columbia, Canada V8V 1X5
Phone: (604)387-9745
Fax: (604)356-9145
Contact: Kathleen M. Neer, Ministry Libn.
Subjects: Pollution management, fish and wildlife management, water management. ***Special Collections:*** Wildlife original reports; Water Treaty documents. ***Holdings:*** 30,000 books; 250 bound periodical volumes; water treaty theses; archival materials.

★7297★ British Columbia Ministry of Forests
Library
1450 Government St.
Victoria, British Columbia, Canada V8W 3E7
Phone: (604)387-3628
Fax: (604)387-0046
Contact: Susanne Barker, Mgr.
Subjects: Forest management, forest protection, logging & logging equipment, multiple land use. ***Special Collections:*** Ministry internal and external reports. ***Holdings:*** 35,000 books, serials, and government documents; 5000 bound periodical volumes.

★7298★ British Columbia Ministry of Forests
Nelson Forest Region Library
518 Lake St.
Nelson, British Columbia, Canada V1L 4C6
Phone: (604)354-6206
Contact: Chris Thompson
Subjects: Forestry, natural resources. ***Holdings:*** 2000 books; 400 bound periodical volumes; 2500 research papers; 4 VF drawers of pamphlets and clippings; 300 government documents.

★7299★ British Columbia Ministry of Parks
Library
Parliament Bldgs.
4000 Seymour Pl.
Victoria, British Columbia, Canada V8V 1X4
Phone: (604)387-3974
Fax: (604)387-5757
Contact: Shirley Desrosiers, Libn.
Subjects: Park and wilderness management, outdoor recreation, tourism and travel research, conservation, administration. ***Holdings:*** 6500 books; 2430 vertical file materials; AV programs.

★7300★ British Columbia Research Corporation
Library
3650 Wesbrook Mall
Vancouver, British Columbia, Canada V6S 2L2
Phone: (604)224-4331
Fax: (604)224-0540
Contact: Viona Esen, Hd.Libn.
Subjects: Waste treatment, water and air pollution, ocean engineering, corrosion, mineral studies, applied chemistry, wood preservation, offshore technology, electro-luminescence, management services, marine biology, applied engineering, biotechnology. ***Special Collections:*** Computer-aided design/computer-aided manufacturing. ***Holdings:*** 21,500 books; 9000 bound periodical volumes; 17,500 separates.

★7301★ Brookhaven National Laboratory
Nuclear Waste Management Library
Bldg. 830
Upton, NY 11973
Phone: (516)282-7159
Contact: Sandra G. Lane, Sr.Libn.
Subjects: Nuclear waste management, metals, corrosion, polymers and plastics, chelates, chemistry. ***Special Collections:*** Nuclear waste management. ***Holdings:*** 3600 books; 13,000 bound reports; 500 unbound reports; 600 microfiche; 150 patents.

★7302★ Brown & Caldwell Consultants
Library
Box 8045
Walnut Creek, CA 94596-1220
Phone: (415)937-9010
Fax: (415)937-9026
Contact: Paula Spurlock, Libn.
Subjects: Environmental engineering, water resources, water and wastewater treatment, hazardous waste, energy conservation. ***Holdings:*** 5000 books; 400 bound periodical volumes; 500 maps; 2000 vendors catalogs; 4000 reports; 2000 microfiche; 800 reels of microfilm.

★7303★ Brown & Caldwell
Seattle Branch Office Library
100 W. Harrison
Seattle, WA 98119
Phone: (206)281-4000
Fax: (206)286-3510
Contact: Marilyn Burwell, Libn.
Subjects: Wastewater, water resources, stormwater and drainage, groundwater, industrial wastes, Puget Sound. Holdings: 700 books; 1763 technical reports; 12 shelves of unbound periodicals; 12 shelves of reference materials; 10 shelves of specifications and cost indexes; 26 shelves of uncataloged techinical reports.

★7304★ Buckman Laboratories International
Technical Information Center
1256 N. McLean Blvd.
Memphis, TN 38108
Phone: (901)278-0330
Fax: (901)276-5343
Telex: 6828020
Contact: W. Ellen McDonell, Mgr.
Subjects: Chemistry, microbiology, corrosion, pulp and paper, water treatment, agriculture. ***Special Collections:*** National Technical Information Service (NTIS) Collection in Environmental Sciences. ***Holdings:*** 11,000 books; 300 bound periodical volumes; U.S. and foreign patents; microfilm; reports.

★7305★ Burroughs-Audobon Society
Burroughs-Audobon Center and Library
R.R. 3, Box 120
Blue Springs, MO 64015
Phone: (816)795-8177
Contact: Anne Duffer, Mgr.
Subjects: Ornithology, natural history, conservation. ***Holdings:*** 4000 books.

★7306★ Calgary Engineering & Environmental Library 8026
PO Box 2100, Sta. M
Calgary, Alberta, Canada T2P 2M5
Phone: (403)268-2793
Contact: Allisen Stubbs, Lib.Spec.
Subjects: Water treatment and distribution, soil science, sewerage, street design and maintenance. ***Holdings:*** 4500 books.

★7307★ California Air Resources Board
Library
Box 2815
Sacramento, CA 95812
Phone: (916)323-8377
Fax: (916)322-4357
Contact: Mark T. Edwards, Libn.
Subjects: Air pollution, air quality, environment. ***Special Collections:*** Air Pollution Technical Information Center reports (120,000 titles on microfiche); NTIS reports (air pollution; 20,000 on microfiche). ***Holdings:*** 6000 books.

★7308★ California Institute of Technology
Environmental Engineering Library
136 W. M. Keck Laboratory (138-78)
Pasadena, CA 91125
Phone: (818)356-4381
Fax: (818)795-1547
Contact: Rayma Harrison, Libn.
Subjects: Aerosol physics, air quality management and modeling, aquatic and atmospheric chemistry, coastal engineering, hydraulic engineering, wastewater treatment and disposal. ***Holdings:*** 4463 books; 1916 bound periodical volumes; 20,602 technical and government reports; 145 volumes of dissertations.

★7309★ (California State) Colorado River Board of California
Library
107 S. Broadway, Rm. 8103
Los Angeles, CA 90012
Phone: (213)620-4480
Fax: (213)620-4050
Subjects: Colorado River, California water rights, hydrology, water resources, conservation, engineering, agriculture, salinity. ***Holdings:*** 12,500 books; 300 pamphlets; 500 documents and reports; 60 VF drawers of maps and drafts.

★7310★ California (State) Department of Food & Agriculture
Pest Management Division Library
1220 N St.
Box 942871
Sacramento, CA 94271-0001
Phone: (916)324-9490
Fax: (916)324-4617
Contact: Chizuko Kawamoto, Supv.Libn.
Subjects: Pesticides. ***Special Collections:*** Pesticide registration - support data. ***Holdings:*** 28,000 volumes.

★7311★ California (State) Department of Water Resources
Law Library
1416 Ninth St., Rm. 1118-13
Sacramento, CA 95814
Phone: (916)445-2839
Fax: (916)324-7656
Contact: Mary Ann Parker, Sr.Libn.
Subjects: Federal and state water law, water resources development. ***Holdings:*** 16,750 volumes; 550 government documents.

★7312★ California (State) Energy Commission
Library
1516 Ninth St.
Sacramento, CA 95814
Phone: (916)324-3006
Contact: Diana Fay Watkins, Sr.Libn.
Subjects: General energy, electric utilities, natural gas, petroleum, nuclear and solar power, alternative sources of energy. ***Special Collections:*** Collection of works produced or contracted by the commission; transcripts of commission hearings. ***Holdings:*** 20,000 books; 100,000 energy reports on microfiche.

★7313★ California (State) Regional Water Quality Control Board
San Francisco Bay Region
Library
2101 Webster St., 5th Fl.
Oakland, CA 94612
Phone: (415)464-1255
Contact: Steven R. Ritchie, Hd. of Reg.
Subjects: Water quality studies of surface and ground waters in San Francisco Bay Area. ***Holdings:*** 3600 studies and reports.

★7314★ California State Resources Agency
Library
1416 Ninth St., Rm. 117
Sacramento, CA 95814
Phone: (916)445-7752
Contact: Madeleine A. Darcy, Sr.Libn.
Subjects: Freshwater fisheries, game and game birds, forestry, park management, soil conservation, boats and boating, recreation, water pollution, engineering. ***Holdings:*** 43,000 volumes; 11 VF drawers of reports.

★7315★ California State University and Colleges
Moss Landing Marine Laboratories
Library
Box 450
Moss Landing, CA 95039
Phone: (408)755-8653
Fax: (408)753-2826
Contact: Sheila Baldridge, Libn.
Subjects: Oceanography, marine biology and geology, trace metals research, marine chemistry. ***Special Collections:*** Central California Collection (online). ***Holdings:*** 6750 books; 2400 bound periodical volumes; 200 nautical charts; 469 topographical maps; 1200 technical reports; 250 theses.

★7316★ California State Water Resources Control Board
Library
Box 100
Sacramento, CA 95812
Phone: (916)322-0220
Fax: (916)322-2765
Contact: Terrance Heiser, Lib.Techn./Legal Anl.
Subjects: Law - water, environmental. ***Special Collections:*** History of Water Resources Control Board; Regulatory History of California Water Supply and Use; California Water Quality Orders; California Water Rights Decisions and Orders; legal opinions and memoranda. ***Holdings:*** 7500 volumes; 500 bound periodical volumes; 5000 reports; 10,000 archival items; 500 microfiche; 100 videotapes.

★7317★ Camp Dresser & McKee, Inc.
Herman G. Dresser Library
10 Cambridge Ctr.
Boston, MA 02142
Phone: (617)252-8000
Fax: (617)227-3995
Contact: Virginia L. Carroll, Libn.
Subjects: Environmental engineering, waste disposal, wastewater and solid waste management, water supply, water resources. ***Special Collections:*** Water and sanitation for health in developing countries (microfiche). ***Holdings:*** 16,000 books; 900 bound periodical volumes; 4000 reports; 4500 report data/computations; 2000 pamphlets; 600 reprints of articles written by employees; 3500 microfiche.

★7318★ Canada
Agriculture Canada
Neatby Library
K. W. Neatby Bldg., Rm. 3032
Central Experimental Farm
Ottawa, Ontario, Canada K1A 0C6
Phone: (613)995-5011
Contact: Marcel Charette, Ck. in Charge
Subjects: Agrometeorology, bacteriology, nitrogen fixation, environmental sciences, soil, soil sciences. ***Holdings:*** 6000 books; 7000 bound periodical volumes; 1000 microcards of Beilstein's Handbuch der Organischen Chemie; soil surveys of the United States and Canada.

★7319★ Canada
Agriculture Canada
Research Station, Charlottetown - Library
PO Box 1210
Charlottetown, Prince Edward Island, Canada C1A 7M8
Phone: (902)566-6861
Fax: (902)566-6821
Contact: Barrie Stanfield, Libn.
Subjects: Plant physiology and pathology, entomology, pest control, weed control, forage and cereal crops, cattle, soil science, vegetable

crops. ***Holdings:*** 2500 books; 2000 bound periodical volumes; 200 boxes of government publications; 7 VF drawers of clippings and pamphlets. ***Contact:*** LBPCAG (AGRINET); ILL.

★7320★ Canada Centre for Inland Waters Library
867 Lakeshore Rd.
Box 5050
Burlington, Ontario, Canada L7R 4A6
Phone: (416)336-4982
Fax: (416)336-4989
Contact: Eve Dowie, Hd., Lib.Serv.
Subjects: Limnology, water research, water pollution, hydraulics, sanitary engineering. ***Holdings:*** 28,000 books; 120,000 unbound periodicals; 250 dissertations; 18 drawers of microforms.

★7321★ Canada
Energy, Mines and Resources Canada
CANMET - Library
555 Booth St.
Ottawa, Ontario, Canada K1A 0G1
Phone: (613)995-4132
Fax: (613)995-8730
Telex: 053-3395
Contact: Gloria M. Peckham, Hd., Lib.Serv.
Subjects: Mining and mining technology, mineralogy, mineral processing, metals and materials technology, fossil fuel energy technology. ***Holdings:*** 223,000 volumes of serials, books, reports, and translations; 14,000 items on microform. ***Contact:*** CANMET.

★7322★ Canada
Environment Canada - Canadian Parks Service
Prairie and Northern Regional Library
457 Main St.
Winnipeg, Manitoba, Canada R3B 3E8
Phone: (204)983-5941
Fax: (204)983-2014
Contact: Maxine McMillan, Lib.Spec.
Subjects: National parks and historic sites, Canadian prairie, wildlife and historic conservation, ecology. ***Holdings:*** 12,000 books; 10,000 periodical volumes; 6 drawers of microforms.

★7323★ Canada
Environment Canada - Canadian Parks Service
Western Regional Library
220 4th Ave., S.E., Rm. 551
PO Box 2989, Sta. M
Calgary, Alberta, Canada T2P 3H8
Phone: (403)292-4455
Fax: (403)292-4746
Contact: David Palmer, Libn.
Subjects: Park planning, interpretation, and conservation; Western Canadian history; natural history; historical and archaeological research. ***Holdings:*** 6000 books; 8000 internal reports; 350 microfiche; 10 reels of microfilm; 120 films.

★7324★ Canada
Environment Canada, Conservation and Protection
Atlantic Region Library
45 Alderney Dr., Queen Square, 15th Fl.
Dartmouth, Nova Scotia, Canada B2Y 2N6
Phone: (902)426-7219
Alt. Phone: (902)426-7232
Fax: (902)426-2690
Contact: Dawn Taylor-Prime, Reg.Libn.
Subjects: Environmental sciences, water pollution, air pollution, water quality, land, environmental engineering. ***Special Collections:*** Flood Damage Reduction Program; Ocean Dumping collection; LRTAP Collection; EPA publications on microfiche; hazardous waste collection; State of the Environment Collection; marine environmental quality studies; Environment/Economy collection. ***Holdings:*** 15,000 books; 400,000 reports on microfiche; 2 drawers of journals on microfilm; 1 drawer of journals on microfiche.

★7325★ Canada - Environment Canada, Conservation and Protection
Canadian Wildlife Service
Atlantic Region Library
Box 1590
Sackville, New Brunswick, Canada E0A 3C0
Phone: (506)536-3025
Contact: Jean Sealy, Libn.
Subjects: Birds, mammals, conservation, habitat protection and management, pollution, national parks. ***Holdings:*** 1000 books; 40 bound periodical volumes; 60 boxes of manuscript reports; 70 boxes of reprints and reports; 300 national parks publications; 2800 microforms.

★7326★ Canada - Environment Canada, Conservation and Protection
Canadian Wildlife Service
Ontario Region Library
49 Camelot Dr.
Nepean, Ontario, Canada K1A 0H3
Phone: (613)952-2406
Fax: (613)952-9027
Contact: Danuta Derdak, Act.Libn.
Subjects: Ornithology, mammalogy, wildlife management, environmental impact (wildlife). ***Holdings:*** 2000 books; 140 bound periodical volumes; 500 reports.

★7327★ Canada
Environment Canada, Conservation and Protection
Library
100 Hamilton Blvd.
Box 6010
Whitehorse, Yukon Territory, Canada Y1A 5L7
Phone: (403)667-3407
Fax: (403)667-7962
Contact: Wendy Chambers, Libn.
Subjects: Water and air pollution, hydrocarbon development, environmental impact of pipelines, Beaufort Sea, residential wood smoke, hazardous substances. ***Holdings:*** 2000 books; 100 microfiche; 25 video cassettes; 2500 slides.

★7328★ Canada
Environment Canada, Conservation and Protection
Ontario Region Library
25 St. Clair Ave., E., 7th Fl.
Toronto, Ontario, Canada M4T 1M2
Phone: (416)973-0893
Fax: (416)973-8342
Contact: Susan Griffin, Libn.
Subjects: Air and water pollution control and prevention, waste management, toxic chemicals, hazardous materials, environmental policy and law. ***Special Collections:*** Environmental Protection Service reports; consultants reports for Ontario region. ***Holdings:*** 7600 books; 1000 microfiche.

★7329★ Canada
Environment Canada, Conservation and Protection
Pacific Region Library
224 W. Esplanade
North Vancouver, British Columbia, Canada V7M 3H7
Phone: (604)666-5914
Fax: (604)666-6281
Contact: Andrew Fabro, Libn.
Subjects: Pollution - air, water, land. ***Holdings:*** 6750 monographs; 2000 microforms; Canadian and U.S. government environmental reports.

★7330★ Canada - Environment Canada, Conservation and Protection
Quebec Region Library
1141, route de l'Eglise, 7th Fl.
PO Box 10100
Ste. Foy, Quebec, Canada G1V 4H5
Phone: (418)649-6546
Fax: (418)648-4613
Contact: Cecile Morin, Libn.
Subjects: Migratory birds and their habitats, waterfowl management, inland waters, rivers, water, acid rain, environmental policy and planning, environmental impact assessment. ***Holdings:*** 9000 monographs.

★7331★ Canada - Environment Canada, Conservation and Protection
Western and Northern Region Library
4999 98th Ave., Rm. 210
Edmonton, Alberta, Canada T6B 2X3
Phone: (403)468-8950
Fax: (403)495-2615
Contact: Peter A. Jordan, Regional Libn.
Subjects: Ornithology, botany, mammalogy, wildlife conservation, ecology, natural resources, land use, environmental pollution, pollution monitoring and control. ***Holdings:*** 13,000 books; 1600 bound periodical volumes; 4500 manuscripts; 50 VF drawers; 2800 reels of microfilm; 4500 government documents.

★7332★ Canada
Environment Canada
Departmental Library
351 St. Joseph Blvd., 2nd Fl.
Hull Quebec
Ottawa, Ontario, Canada K1A 0H3
Phone: (819)997-1767
Fax: (819)997-1929
Contact: Mrs. M. Czanyo, Dept.Libn.
Subjects: Land use planning, national parks and historic sites, pollution prevention and control, water resources, environmental planning and management, wildlife. ***Holdings:*** 88,500 books; 47,000 bound periodical volumes; 690 reels of microfilm; 10,000 reports on microfiche from U.S. Environmental Protection Agency; Environment Canada publications depository.

★7333★ Canada
Fisheries and Oceans
Arctic Biological Station Library
555 St. Pierre Blvd.
Ste. Anne de Bellevue, Quebec, Canada H9X 3R4
Phone: (514)457-3660
Subjects: Biological oceanography, marine zoology, fishes and fisheries of Arctic and subarctic, ecology. ***Special Collections:*** Primary and secondary literature on marine mammals. ***Holdings:*** 6000 books and bound periodical volumes.

★7334★ Canada
Fisheries and Oceans
Biological Station Library
St. Andrews, New Brunswick, Canada E0G 2X0
Phone: (506)529-8854
Fax: (506)529-4274
Contact: Marilynn Rudi, Libn.
Subjects: Fisheries, aquatic biology, chemistry, aquaculture. ***Holdings:*** 6000 books; 8500 bound periodical volumes; 420 boxes of pamphlets.

★7335★ Canada
Fisheries and Oceans
Freshwater Institute Library
501 University Crescent
Winnipeg, Manitoba, Canada R3T 2N6
Phone: (204)983-5170
Fax: (204)983-6285
Contact: K. Eric Marshall, Hd., Lib.Serv.
Subjects: Fisheries, limnology. ***Special Collections:*** Fritsch Collection of illustrations of freshwater algae (microfiche); Arctic Petroleum Operators Association reports (microfiche). ***Holdings:*** 19,100 books; 60,000 bound periodical volumes; 12,000 pamphlets; 200 pamphlet boxes of reports; 20,000 microfiche; 300 reels of microfilm; 15,000 cards of abstracts and indexes.

★7336★ Canada - Fisheries and Oceans
Institut Maurice-LaMontagne
Library
850, route de la Mer
PO Box 1000
Quebec, Quebec, Canada G5H 3Z4
Phone: (418)775-6552
Fax: (418)775-6542
Telex: 051-3815
Contact: Guy Michaud, Libn.
Subjects: Fisheries; aquaculture; oceanography - chemical, physical, biological; biology - marine life, parasitology; cartography; hydrography. ***Holdings:*** 9000 books; 8000 microfiche; 35 films.

★7337★ Canada
Fisheries and Oceans
Newfoundland Regional Library
PO Box 5667
St. John's, Newfoundland, Canada A1C 5X1
Phone: (709)772-2022
Fax: (709)772-2156
Telex: 0164 698
Contact: Audrey Conroy, Reg.Libn.
Subjects: Marine biology, freshwater resource development, fisheries, pollution. ***Holdings:*** 9200 books; 1500 linear feet of serials.

★7338★ Canada
Fisheries and Oceans
Pacific Biological Station - Library
Nanaimo, British Columbia, Canada V9R 5K6
Phone: (604)756-7071
Fax: (604)756-7053
Telex: 04-46128
Contact: G. Miller, Hd., Lib.Serv.
Subjects: Fish biology, fish culture, marine ecology, biological oceanography. ***Holdings:*** 3600 books; 35,000 bound periodical volumes; 80,000 reports.

★7339★ Canada
Fisheries and Oceans
Scotia-Fundy Regional Library - Halifax Fisheries Library
PO Box 550
Halifax, Nova Scotia, Canada B3J 2S7
Phone: (902)426-7160
Fax: (902)426-2698
Telex: 019-21891
Contact: Anna Fiander, Chf., Lib.Serv.
Subjects: Fisheries, environmental control, food technology. ***Special Collections:*** Atlantic Salmon. ***Holdings:*** 13,000 books; 2800 bound periodical volumes; 40,000 technical reports; 20,000 microfiche; 500 reels of microfilm.

★7340★ Canada - Fisheries and Oceans
West Vancouver Laboratory
Library
4160 Marine Dr.
West Vancouver, British Columbia, Canada V7V 1N6
Phone: (604)666-4813
Fax: (604)666-3497
Contact: Susan E. Keller, Libn.
Subjects: Fisheries research, aquatic environment and habitat. ***Holdings:*** 2000 volumes.

★7341★ Canada
Forestry Canada
Great Lakes Forestry Centre - Library
PO Box 490
Sault Ste. Marie, Ontario, Canada P6A 5M7
Phone: (705)949-9461
Fax: (705)759-5700
Contact: Sandra Burt, Libn.
Subjects: Forestry, entomology, biochemistry, physiology, bioclimatology. ***Holdings:*** 8000 volumes.

★7342★ Canada
Forestry Canada
Laurentian Forestry Centre- Library
1055, rue du Peps
C.P. 3800
Ste. Foy, Quebec, Canada G1V 4C7
Phone: (418)648-4850
Fax: (418)648-5849
Contact: Gilles Bizier, Libn.
Subjects: Forestry, entomology, plant pathology, silviculture, pedology, ecology. ***Holdings:*** 7000 books; 3000 bound periodical volumes; 12,000 serials; 9 VF drawers of researchers' scientific works.

★7343★ Canada
Forestry Canada
Maritimes Forestry Centre - Library
PO Box 4000
Fredericton, New Brunswick, Canada E3B 5P7
Phone: (506)452-3541
Fax: (506)452-3525
Contact: Barry Barner, Libn.
Subjects: Forestry, forest ecology, forest genetics, silviculture, forest pathology, forest entomology, forest economics. ***Special Collections:*** Forestry Canada documents; manuscripts. ***Holdings:*** 6000 books; 8000 periodical volumes; 60,000 documents; 5000 microforms.

★7344★ Canada
Forestry Canada
Newfoundland and Labrador Region Forestry Centre - Library
PO Box 6028
St. John's, Newfoundland, Canada A1C 5X8
Phone: (709)772-4672
Fax: (709)772-2576
Contact: Catherine E. Philpott, Libn.
Subjects: Forestry, entomology, environmental research. ***Holdings:*** 3500 books; 1270 bound periodical volumes.

★7345★ Canada
Forestry Canada
Northwest Region - Northern Forestry Centre - Library
5320 122nd St.
Edmonton, Alberta, Canada T6H 3S5
Phone: (403)435-7323
Fax: (403)435-7359
Telex: 037-2117
Contact: David J.S. Robinson, Libn.
Subjects: Forestry, entomology, mycology, soil science, hydrology, environmental pollution. ***Holdings:*** 5000 books; 5000 bound periodical volumes; 35,000 reports and government publications; 3000 reprints and pamphlets; 248 microforms.

★7346★ Canada
Forestry Canada
Pacific and Yukon Region - Pacific Forestry Centre - Library
506 W. Burnside Rd.
Victoria, British Columbia, Canada V8Z 1M5
Phone: (604)363-0600
Alt. Phone: (604)363-0637
Alt. Phone: (604)363-0680
Fax: (604)363-0775
Contact: Alice Solyma, Hd., Lib.Serv.
Subjects: Forest science, land and environmental research, economics, entomology, fire research, hydrology, mensuration, meteorology, mycology, plant pathology. ***Holdings:*** 20,000 books and bound periodical volumes; 55,000 reports and government documents.

★7347★ Canada
Forestry Canada
Petawawa National Forestry Institute - Library
Chalk River, Ontario, Canada K0J 1J0
Phone: (613)589-2880
Fax: (613)589-2275
Contact: Mary Mitchell, Libn.
Subjects: Forestry. ***Holdings:*** 6000 volumes; 24,000 bound periodical volumes; 15,000 nonbook items; 1500 other cataloged items.

★7348★ Canada
Indian & Northern Affairs Canada
Technical Library
PO Box 1500
Yellowknife, Northwest Territories, Canada X1A 2R3
Phone: (403)920-8144
Fax: (403)873-5763
Contact: Donald Albright, Reg.Libn.
Subjects: Earth and environmental sciences. ***Special Collections:*** Geology theses of the Northwest Territories (200); Cold Regions Research & Engineering Laboratory (CRREL) Publications (400). ***Holdings:*** 15,000 books; 700 bound periodical volumes; 2000 government documents; 90 reels of microfilm; 75 microfiche sets; 50 sheet maps; 730 boxes of unbound periodicals.

★7349★ Canada
Prairie Farm Rehabilitation Administration
Library
Motherwell Bldg.
1901 Victoria Ave.
Regina, Saskatchewan, Canada S4P 0R5
Phone: (306)780-5100
Fax: (306)780-5018
Contact: Charlene Dusyk, Hd.
Subjects: Water engineering, resource management and conservation, soil science, hydrology, drought. ***Holdings:*** 20,000 books; 1400 bound periodical volumes; 1000 pamphlets.

★7350★ Canadian Environmental Law Association
Library
517 College St., Ste. 401
Toronto, Ontario, Canada M6G 4A2
Phone: (416)960-2284
Fax: (416)960-9392
Contact: Mary Vise, Libn.
Subjects: Canadian environmental law, Great Lakes - pollution (including legal aspects), pesticides, forestry; environmental aspects of free trade. ***Holdings:*** 900 books; 5500 reports.

★7351★ Canadian Wildlife Federation Resource Centre
1673 Carling Ave.
Ottawa, Ontario, Canada K2A 3Z1
Phone: (613)725-2191
Fax: (613)721-2902
Contact: Mrs. Luba Mycio-Mommers, Pub.Aff.
Subjects: Wildlife education, outdoor recreation, conservation, environment, natural history, energy. ***Special Collections:*** Canadian Wildlife Federation Archives. ***Holdings:*** 5000 books; 2500 bound periodical volumes; 215 items in subject file.

★7352★ CEGEP de Ste-Foy
Centre d'Enseignement et de Recherche en Foresterie de Ste-Foy Inc.
2410, chemin Ste-Foy
Ste. Foy, Quebec, Canada G1V 1T3
Phone: (418)659-4225
Fax: (418)657-3529
Contact: Gerard Dubuc, Info.Dir.
Subjects: Forest management, harvesting, construction; wood product transformation; urban forestry. ***Holdings:*** 506 volumes; 10 unbound reports; 10 reels of microfilm; 10 magnetic tapes.

★7353★ Center for Environmental Information, Inc.
Air Resources Information Clearinghouse (ARIC)
46 Prince St.
Rochester, NY 14607-1016
Phone: (716)271-3550
Fax: (716)271-0606
Contact: Carole Beal, Interim Dir.
Subjects: Acid deposition and its ecological, socioeconomic, and political impact; atmospheric sciences; control technologies; global climate change (greenhouse effect, ozone depletion, and related phenomenon) - scientific, technical and policy information; indoor air pollution; air toxic emissions. ***Holdings:*** 2000 books and technical reports; 6 VF drawers of newspaper clippings, articles, brochures.

★7354★ Center for Environmental Information, Inc.
CEI Library
46 Prince St.
Rochester, NY 14607-1016
Phone: (716)271-3550
Fax: (716)271-0606
Contact: Carole Beal, Interim Dir.
Subjects: Natural resources, conservation, acid rain, greenhouse effect, environment, energy, environmental education. ***Special Collections:*** Acid Rain Reference Collection (1000 shelved items; 5 VF drawers). ***Holdings:*** 6500 books and technical reports; 30 VF drawers of newspaper clippings, journal reprints, pamphlets, brochures, flyers.

★7355★ Center for Science and Environment
Library
807 Vishal Bhavan
95 Nehru Pl.
New Delhi 110 019, Delhi, India
Phone: 11 6433394
Subjects: Science and technology in environment and development. ***Holdings:*** 30,000 volumes.

★7356★ Center for Wetland Resources
Information Services and Archives
CWR Bldg., Rm. 103
Louisiana State University
Baton Rouge, LA 70803
Phone: (504)388-8266
Contact: Catherine Edwards-Spratley, Dir.
Subjects: Marine and wetland sciences, coastal ecology, fisheries, wetland soil chemistry, nearshore oceanography and climatology. ***Special Collections:*** Richard J. Russell Collection (geomorphology, earth sciences); Marine Education Microfilm Series (MEMS). ***Holdings:*** 500 books; 10,000 technical reports and reprints; 300 data tapes; 500 aerial photographs of Louisiana; 3500 maps; 15,000 microfiche; archives.

★7357★ CH2M Hill, Inc.
Corvallis Regional Office Library
2300 N.W. Walnut Blvd.
Corvallis, OR 97330-3596
Phone: (503)752-4271
Contact: Chris Lee, Libn.
Subjects: Engineering, environmental science, wastewater technology, geology. ***Holdings:*** 5000 books; 550 bound periodical volumes; 4000 manufacturers' catalogs; 20 boxes of archival material; 20,000 internal reports.

★7358★ CH2M Hill, Inc.
Information Center
2525 Air Park
PO Box 49-2478
Redding, CA 96049
Phone: (916)243-5831
Contact: Virginia Merryman, Libn.
Subjects: Engineering - sanitary, structural, agricultural; California weather; water resources. ***Special Collections:*** North American Weather Charts, 1942 to present; California rainfall records, 1956 to present. ***Holdings:*** 5000 books; 3000 U.S. Geological Survey topographical maps; 300 geological reports and maps; 100 California Department of Water Resources bulletins; 2000 project reports.

★7359★ CH2M Hill, Inc.
Library
2020 S.W. 4th Ave., 2nd Fl.
Portland, OR 97201
Phone: (503)224-9190
Fax: (503)295-4446
Contact: Barbara L. Stollberg, Libn.
Subjects: Engineering - water, wastewater, environmental, hazardous waste, industrial processes, geotechnical; planning, economics. ***Holdings:*** 10,000 books; 7000 internal reports.

★7360★ CH2M Hill, Inc.
Rocky Mountain Regional Office Library
Box 22508
Denver, CO 80222
Phone: (303)771-0900
Fax: (303)741-4053
Contact: LaRue Fontenot, Libn.
Subjects: Water and wastewater, civil and mechanical engineering, climatology, mining. ***Holdings:*** 5500 volumes; 2000 technical reports; 1100 trade catalogs; 300 Environmental Protection Agency documents; 300 U.S. Geological Survey topographical maps; 1000 archival materials.

★7361★ Chemlab Service of Amarillo
Library
6420 River Rd.
Amarillo, TX 79108
Phone: (806)383-5865
Contact: C.H. Scherer, Dir.
Subjects: Water, wastewater control and treatment, hazardous wastes. ***Holdings:*** 350 books; 200 reports.

★7362★ Chevron Environmental Health Center, Inc.
Information Services
15299 San Pablo Ave.
Box 4054
Richmond, CA 94804-0054
Phone: (415)231-6049
Fax: (415)231-6145
Contact: Sharon L. Modrick, Supv., Info.Serv.
Subjects: Toxicology, environmental health, chemical regulation, risk assessment. ***Holdings:*** 3500 books.

★7363★ CIBA-GEIGY Corporation
Technical Information Center
400 Farmington Ave.
Farmington, CT 06032
Phone: (203)674-6312
Fax: (203)676-9443
Contact: Joanna W. Eickenhorst, Supv., Info.Serv.
Subjects: Toxicology, environmental health, mutagenicity, metabolism, pharmacokinetics. ***Holdings:*** 4000 books.

★7364★ Citizens Association for Sound Energy (CASE)
Library
1426 S. Polk St.
Dallas, TX 75224
Phone: (214)946-9446
Contact: Juanita Ellis, Pres.
Subjects: Energy, nuclear energy and waste. ***Special Collections:*** U.S. Nuclear Regulatory Commission information.

★7365★ Clark County District Health Department
Health Education Resource Center
625 Shadow Ln.
Box 4426
Las Vegas, NV 89127
Phone: (702)383-1218
Fax: (702)384-5342
Subjects: Environmental health, emergency medical service, public health nursing, air pollution control, epidemiology. ***Holdings:*** 3 VF drawers of health reprints; health pamphlets; news clippings; filmstrips; videotapes; 16mm films.

★7366★ Clinton River Watershed Council
Library
8215 Hall Rd.
Utica, MI 48087
Phone: (313)739-1122
Contact: Peggy B. Johnson, Exec.Sec.
Subjects: Water - quality, management, recreation, associated land uses. ***Special Collections:*** Reports on the Clinton River. ***Holdings:*** 500 books; special reports; engineering reports; dissertations; data collections.

★7367★ Coastal Ecosystems Management
Library
1031 N. Henderson St.
Fort Worth, TX 76107-1470
Phone: (817)870-1199
Contact: Elizabeth L. Parker, Libn.
Subjects: Geoscience, environmental science, wildlife management, mineral resources exploration and management, plant and animal systematics and ecology. ***Holdings:*** 10,000 books, reprints, and journals; 1000 charts.

★7368★ Colorado (State) Department of Regulatory Agencies
Office of Energy Conservation
Library
112 E. 14th Ave.
Denver, CO 80203
Phone: (303)894-2144
Contact: David Warner, Info.Spec.
Subjects: Energy consumption and conservation. ***Holdings:*** 30,000 volumes.

★7369★ Colorado (State) Division of Wildlife
Library
6060 Broadway
Denver, CO 80216
Phone: (303)291-7319
Contact: Rita C. Green, Libn.
Subjects: Wildlife, conservation, ecology, mammals and birds. ***Holdings:*** 1000 books; 500 bound periodical volumes; 540 films.

★7370★ Colorado (State) Division of Wildlife
Research Center Library
317 W. Prospect
Fort Collins, CO 80526
Phone: (303)484-2836
Fax: (303)490-2621
Contact: Jacqueline Boss, Libn.
Subjects: Wildlife biology and management, fish biology, fishery management. ***Special Collections:*** Federal Aid in Fish and Wildlife Restoration, Colorado. ***Holdings:*** 4354 books; 600 bound periodical volumes; 3000 pamphlets and federal aid reports; 161 16mm films; 94 video cassettes; 44 slide kits.

★7371★ Colorado State University
William E. Morgan Library
Fort Collins, CO 80523
Phone: (303)491-1838
Contact: Joan L. Chambers, Dir. of Lib.
Subjects: Hydraulic engineering, irrigation, water resources, soil mechanics, radiology and radiation biology, agronomy, horticulture, microbiology, mycology, parasitology, veterinary medicine, genetics, forestry. ***Special Collections:*** University Libraries; Colorado Agricultural Archives; Imaginary Wars; Vietnam War fiction collection. ***Holdings:*** 1.6 million volumes; 1.4 million microforms; 32,000 maps; 7500 audio reproductions.

★7372★ Community Environmental Council
Gildea Resource Center
930 Miramonte Dr.
Santa Barbara, CA 93109
Phone: (805)963-0583
Fax: (805)962-9080
Contact: Tony Dominski, Educ.Dir.
Subjects: Solid and hazardous waste, horticulture/gardening, solar energy, energy and water conservation, urban planning. ***Holdings:*** 2000 books; 2000 other cataloged items.

★7373★ Complexe Scientifique du Quebec
Service de Documentation et de Bibliotheque
2700 Einstein C-1-100
Ste. Foy, Quebec, Canada G1P 3W8
Phone: (418)643-9730
Fax: (418)643-3361
Telex: 051-31589 SBCS QBC
Contact: M. Levesque, Hd.Libn.
Subjects: Forestry, agriculture, minerals. ***Holdings:*** 10,000 books; 900 bound periodical volumes.

★7374★ Connecticut River Watershed Council
Library
125 Combs Rd.
Easthampton, MA 01027
Phone: (413)584-0057
Contact: Robert Sbarge, Exec.Dir.
Subjects: Water resources, water law, Connecticut River studies. ***Holdings:*** 1000 books.

★7375★ Conservation and Renewable Energy Inquiry and Referral Service
Library
Advanced Sciences, Inc.
2000 N. 15th St., Ste. 407
Arlington, VA 22201
Phone: (703)243-4900
Toll-Free: 800-523-2929
Contact: Grace Gilden, Proj.Mgr.
Subjects: Energy conservation, renewable energy, solar heating and cooling, solar water heating. ***Holdings:*** 1200 books and pamphlets; 2000 reports; 5700 articles; 2000 clippings.

★7376★ Conservation Districts Foundation
Davis Conservation Library
408 E. Main St.
Box 776
League City, TX 77574-0776
Phone: (713)332-3402
Fax: (713)332-5259
Contact: Ruth Chenhall, Educ.-Info.Spec.
Subjects: Conservation, natural resources, soil, water, agriculture, forests, city and town planning, conservation of wildlife, water resources development, ecology. ***Special Collections:*** History of soil and water conservation districts movement in America. ***Holdings:*** 1500 books; 55 bound periodical volumes; 300 pamphlets; 50 VF drawers of history of the National Association of Conservation Districts and conservation.

★7377★ Council of the Maritime Premiers
Atlantic Coastal Resource Information Centre
Library
16 Sta. St.
Box 310
Amherst, Nova Scotia, Canada B4H 3Z5
Phone: (902)667-7231
Fax: (902)667-6008
Contact: Margaret E. Campbell, Libn.
Subjects: Atlantic region - aquaculture, coastal zone management, engineering, fisheries, estuaries, marine sciences, oceanography, remote sensing, recreation, erosion, power development, offshore oil, gas and mineral development and exploration, laws and regulations, environmental protection. ***Special Collections:*** Topographic, hydrographic, and resource oriented map collections of the Atlantic region. ***Holdings:*** 1200 books; unbound periodicals; government documents; VF drawers; maps; research reports.

★7378★ Czechoslovakia - Ministry of Forestry and Water Management
Water Research Institute
Branch Information Center
Podbabska 30
CS-160 62 Prague 6, Czechoslovakia
Phone: 2 3116741 9
Telex: 122571
Contact: Ms. M. Bruhova, Ph.D.
Subjects: Hydraulics, hydrology, sanitary engineering, waste treatment, chemistry, physics, water supply, water pollution control, dam design. ***Holdings:*** 60,000 books; 462,390 bound periodical volumes.

★7379★ Dakar-Thiaroye Center for Oceanographic Research
Library
Route de Rufisque, Km. 10
B.P. 2241
Dakar, Senegal
Phone: 34-05-36
Contact: Florent Diouf, Documentaliste
Subjects: Marine stocks, ecosystems, environment, marine economics, oceanography. ***Holdings:*** 22,500 volumes.

★7380★ Dalhousie University
School for Resource and Environmental Studies
Library
1312 Robie St.
Halifax, Nova Scotia, Canada B3H 3E2
Phone: (902)494-1359
Fax: (902)494-3728
Contact: Mrs. J.G. Reade, Libn.
Subjects: Environmental conservation, management, impact assessment; energy and the environment; fisheries; marine resource policy. ***Holdings:*** 5000 books; 15,000 unbound items.

★7381★ Dalhousie University
School for Resource and Environmental Studies
Southeast Asian Environmental Collection
1312 Robie St.
Halifax, Nova Scotia, Canada B3H 2E2
Phone: (902)424-1217
Fax: (902)494-3728
Telex: 019-21863
Contact: Barbara Patton, Intl.Proj.Info.Off.
Subjects: Environment - Indonesia, Southeast Asia, Philippines. ***Holdings:*** 6000 books and documents; 25 AV programs.

★7382★ Dawes Arboretum
Library
7770 Jacksontown Rd., SE
Newark, OH 43055
Phone: (614)323-2355
Contact: Alan D. Cook, Dir., Extended Serv.
Subjects: Horticulture, botany, ecology, nature, forestry. ***Holdings:*** 5000 books.

★7383★ Delaware River Basin Commission
Technical Library
25 State Police Dr.
Box 7360
Trenton, NJ 08628
Phone: (609)883-9500
Fax: (609)883-9522
Contact: Betty A. Lin, Libn.
Subjects: Delaware River, water resources, water pollution, aquatic biology, geology, hydrology. ***Holdings:*** 1500 books; 10,000 technical reports; 1 map case; 500 slides.

★7384★ Delta Waterfowl and Wetlands Research Station
David Winton Bell Memorial Library
R.R. 1
Portage La Prairie, Manitoba, Canada R1N 3A1
Phone: (204)239-1900
Fax: (204)239-5950
Subjects: Ornithology, wetland biology, ecology, animal behavior, natural history, botany. ***Holdings:*** 4500 books; 3500 bound periodical volumes; 250 upublished theses; 500 government reports; 12,000 offprints.

★7385★ Ducks Unlimited Canada
Library
1190 Waverley St.
Winnipeg, Manitoba, Canada R3T 2E2
Phone: (204)477-1760
Fax: (204)452-7560

Contact: Margaret Haworth-Brockman, Biol.Techn.
Subjects: Wetland management, waterfowl biology, conservation, wildlife habitat development, remote sensing, wetland ecology. ***Special Collections:*** Complete collection of "The Auk"; Proceedings of North American Wildlife Conference; Journal of Wildlife Management; "Wetlands" (journal of wetland scientists); The Wildlife Society Bulletin; Wildfowl. ***Holdings:*** 1000 books; 125 bound periodical volumes; 1000 Canadian and American government reports and manuscripts.

★7386★ Duke University
Biology-Forestry Library
Durham, NC 27706
Phone: (919)684-2381
Subjects: Botany, zoology, forestry, environmental studies, soils, meteorology. ***Holdings:*** 165,000 volumes.

★7387★ Earth Ecology Foundation
Library
903 E. Fedora
Fresno, CA 93704
Phone: (209)227-1745
Contact: Erik Wunstell, Dir.
Subjects: Nature, ecology, science, technology, geography. ***Special Collections:*** Panama Pacific World's Fair and Exposition (construction plans, photos, books, and news clippings; 1915); Fresno State College and University (building plans, construction photos, yearbooks, and letters; 1915-1970); Underground Gardens (designs and history; 1917-1945); American Magazine Covers Collection (1780-1980); National Geographic (magazines, maps, and books; 1945-1990); Science Year Annuals (1965-1990); The Geometric Progression of Space and Time (original scientific paper; 1979); The Unified Field Pattern of Earth's Solar Orbit (original scientific paper; 1990); Earth Ecology Foundation Papers and Letters (1971-1990). ***Holdings:*** 5000 volumes.

★7388★ Earth Island Institute
Library
300 Broadway, Ste. 28
San Francisco, CA 94133
Phone: (415)788-3666
Fax: (415)788-7324
Contact: Frank Galea
Subjects: Environment. ***Holdings:*** 2000 volumes.

★7389★ Earthmind
Library
Box 743
Mariposa, CA 95338
Subjects: Alternative energy sources - wind, water, electric power; electric vehicles. ***Holdings:*** 1000 books.

★7390★ Earthworm, Inc.
Recycling Information Center
186 S. St.
Boston, MA 02111
Phone: (617)426-7344
Contact: Jeffrey Coyne, Pres.
Subjects: Recycling, resource recovery, solid waste management, environmental quality, pollution, environmental education, hazardous waste. ***Holdings:*** 100 volumes; recycling trade journals, newsletters, publications, and manuals; publications from Environmental Protection Agency and environmental and commercial organizations; Earthworm News.

★7391★ Eastern Technical Associates
Library
Box 58495
Raleigh, NC 27658
Phone: (919)834-2970
Subjects: Air emissions, opacity measurement of stationary sources. ***Holdings:*** 900 reports and government publications.

★7392★ Eastman Kodak Company
InfoSource Health and Environment Library
Kodak Park Division, Bldg. 320
Rochester, NY 14650
Phone: (716)588-3619
Fax: (716)588-9705
Contact: Richard Bartl, Libn., InfoSource Res.Lib.
Subjects: Toxicology, occupational medicine, environmental sciences, biosciences, ergonomics. ***Holdings:*** 5000 books and government publications; 5000 bound periodical volumes.

★7393★ Ecological Institute, Civil Association
Library
Km. 2.5 Carretera Antigua a Coatepec
Apartado Postal No. 63
91000 Xalapa, Veracruz, Mexico
Phone: 281 72974
Contact: Felisa Herrador, Hd.
Subjects: Ecology, botany, biology, zoology, silviculture. ***Holdings:*** 17,000 books; 1500 technical reports; 500 maps; 12,026 microfiche; 33 records.

★7394★ Ecology Action Centre
Resource Centre
3115 Veith St., 3rd Fl.
Halifax, Nova Scotia, Canada B3K 3G9
Phone: (902)454-7828
Fax: (902)454-4766
Subjects: Resource industries, pollution, energy, biospheric changes, institutional responses to environmental issues, human habitat and society. ***Holdings:*** 6000 items.

★7395★ Ecology Center
Library
2530 San Pablo Ave.
Berkeley, CA 94702
Phone: (415)548-2221
Contact: Dave Kershner, Info.Coord.
Subjects: Solid waste, energy, San Francisco Bay area environment, air pollution, water resources, land use planning, environmental education. ***Special Collections:*** Solid Waste Management. ***Holdings:*** 2000 volumes including Environmental Impact Review (EIR) documents, monographs; 34 bound periodical volumes; 20 vertical files.

★7396★ Ecuadorian Institute of Natural Sciences
Library
Casilla 408
Quito, Ecuador
Phone: 2 215-497
Contact: Prof. Carlos A. Carrera, Libn.
Subjects: Natural resources, phytogeography, soil conservation and erosion, forestry, ecology of tropical forests. ***Holdings:*** 36,000 volumes.

★7397★ Educational Communications
Environmental Library
Box 35473
Los Angeles, CA 90035
Phone: (213)559-9160
Contact: Nancy Pearlman, Exec.Prod.
Subjects: Environment, ecological education, media production, pollution, land use, resource management, wildlife preservation, population, urban affairs, planning, energy sources, waste, open space, historic preservation, toxic substances, ocean and coastal protection, desert and forest management. ***Special Collections:*** ECONEWS (television series; 200 video cassettes); Environmental Directions (radio series; 750 audio cassettes). ***Holdings:*** 400 books; 7000 unbound magazines; 200 booklets and pamphlets; 7000 informational sheets and newsletters; VF drawers; simulation games, posters, other cataloged items.

★7398★ EIMCO Process Equipment Company
Technical Library
669 W. 2nd St.
Salt Lake City, UT 84101-1604
Phone: (801)526-2000
Subjects: Water treatment, waste management, solid/liquid separation technology. ***Special Collections:*** Manufacturers' catalogs. ***Holdings:*** 1550 books; 500 bound periodical volumes; 500 documents; 40 VF drawers of technical files.

★7399★ Energy and Environmental Management, Inc. (E2M)
Library
Box 71
Murrysville, PA 15668
Phone: (412)733-0022
Contact: Larry L. Simmons, Pres.
Subjects: Environmental compliance in the electric utility, metals production, mining, chemical, petroleum, sanitation, and manufacturing industries. ***Holdings:*** 1000 books.

★7400★ ENSR Consulting and Engineering
Environmental Contracting Center Library
Box 2105
Fort Collins, CO 80522
Phone: (303)493-8878
Subjects: Ecology, pollution, environmental science, energy, impact assessment, mining reclamation. ***Special Collections:*** Oil shale; hazardous waste characterization and clean-up; environmental impact statements; federal and state regulations and guidelines for the Rocky Mountain region; oil spills. ***Holdings:*** 3500 books; 200 bound technical reports; 700 technical reports; 500 maps; reprints.

★7401★ ENSR Consulting and Engineering
Information Center
35 Nagog Park
Acton, MA 01720
Phone: (508)635-9500
Fax: (508)635-9180
Contact: Deanna C. Robinson, Mgr.
Subjects: Hazardous waste, environmental engineering, air and water pollution, air toxics, risk assessment, chemistry, meteorology. ***Holdings:*** 5000 books; 15,000 scientific and technical reports; microfiche collection.

★7402★ Envirodyne Engineers, Inc.
Library
1908 Innerbelt Business Center Dr.
St. Louis, MO 63114
Phone: (314)434-6960
Fax: (314)426-4212
Contact: Kathryn L. Flowers, Libn./Info.Spec.
Subjects: Water and air pollution, wastewater treatment, hazardous waste management, chemical analysis. ***Holdings:*** 2050 books; 250 government documents.

★7403★ Envirologic Data
Corporate Library
295 Forest Ave.
Portland, ME 04101
Phone: (207)773-3020
Fax: (207)773-2411
Contact: Jane M. Dionne, Info.Spec.
Subjects: Environmental toxicology, hazardous wastes, quantitative risk assessment. ***Holdings:*** 991 books; 176 internal reports; 6000 slides.

★7404★ Environmental Action Coalition
Library/Resource Center
625 Broadway
New York, NY 10012
Phone: (212)677-1601
Contact: Lori Klamner, Libn./Exec.Asst.
Subjects: Energy, water pollution, solid waste, ecology, environmental education, consumer information. ***Holdings:*** 3000 books; 500 bound periodical volumes; reports; 4 volumes of newspaper clippings; 30 films; AV programs; VF drawers.

★7405★ Environmental Law Institute
Library
1616 P St., N.W., Ste. 200
Washington, DC 20036
Phone: (202)328-5150
Fax: (202)328-5002
Contact: Lynda L. Larsen, Chf.Libn.
Subjects: Environmental law, toxic substances, natural resources, wetlands, air and water pollution. ***Holdings:*** 12,000 books.

★7406★ Environmental Research Associates, Inc.
Library
490 Darby-Paoli Rd.
PO Box 219
Villanova, PA 19085
Phone: (215)687-5629
Subjects: Environmental engineering and planning, health and safety, water resource management. ***Holdings:*** 1000 volumes.

★7407★ Environmental Science Services
Library
235 Promenade St.
Providence, RI 02908
Phone: (401)421-0398
Fax: (401)421-0396
Subjects: Environmental science; chemical, biological, physical effects of various activities on the atmosphere, soils, and water resources. ***Holdings:*** 10,000 volumes.

★7408★ ETS, Inc.
Library
3140 Chaparral Dr., Ste. C-103
Roanoke, VA 24018-4394
Phone: (703)774-8999
Fax: (703)774-8883
Subjects: Air pollution and energy - systems design, particulate and gaseous emissions control, pollutant monitoring, control equipment cost. ***Holdings:*** 20,000 documents.

★7409★ Executive Yuan
Council of Agriculture
Agricultural Science Information Center
14 Wen-Chou St.
Taipei 10616, Taiwan
Phone: 2 3636222
Fax: 2 3632459
Contact: Wan-Jiun Wu, Dir.
Subjects: Agriculture, forestry, fisheries, animal husbandry, food science. ***Holdings:*** 5300 books; 1260 bound periodical volumes.

★7410★ Federal Republic of Germany - Federal Environmental Agency
Environmental Information and Documentation System
Central Library
Bismarckplatz 1
D-1000 Berlin 33, Germany
Phone: 30 89032305
Fax: 30 89032285
Telex: 183 756
Contact: Dr. Klaus Luedcke
Subjects: Environment, pollution, solid wastes, environmental chemicals and wastes, noise, environmental research, air pollution, water pollution, nature conservation, allied subjects. ***Special Collections:*** Sammlung Erhard (archives of solid waste, 1900 to present; 2000 books, journals, reports, photographs). ***Holdings:*** 125,000 volumes; 150,000 microforms.

★7411★ Federated Conservationists of Westchester County
FCWC Office Resource Library
Natural Science Bldg., Rm. 1002
SUNY
Purchase, NY 10577
Phone: (914)251-6888
Subjects: Wetland legislation, water supply and quality, air pollution, historic preservation, land use, nuclear power. ***Special Collections:*** Environmental issues in Westchester County. ***Holdings:*** Government reports; environmental impact statements; legal cases; 15 file drawers of resource materials.

★7412★ Finnish Forest Research Institute
Library
Unioninkatu 40A
SF-00170 Helsinki 17, Finland
Phone: 90 661401
Fax: 90 625308
Contact: Liisa Ikavalko-Ahvonen, Libn.
Subjects: Forests and forest resources. ***Holdings:*** 45,000 volumes.

★7413★ Fish and Wildlife Reference Service
5430 Grosvenor Lane, Ste. 110
Bethesda, MD 20814
Phone: (301)492-6403
Toll-Free: 800-582-3421
Contact: Mary J. Nickum, Proj.Mgr.
Subjects: Wildlife management, fisheries management, endangered species. ***Special Collections:*** Selected Federal Aid in Fish and Wildlife Restoration Reports; selected Anadromous (sport) Fish Conservation Reports; Cooperative Fish and Wildlife Research Units Reports; Endangered Species Act Reports/Recovery Plans. ***Holdings:*** 22,000 Federal Aid reports on paper and microfiche (indexed).

★7414★ Florida Conservation Foundation, Inc.
Environmental Information Center
1251-B Miller Ave.
Winter Park, FL 32789-4827
Phone: (407)644-5377
Contact: Marcia Randell, Dir.
Subjects: Environment, conservation, solar heating, natural areas. ***Special Collections:*** Above subjects as they relate to Florida. ***Holdings:*** 6000 environmental documents.

★7415★ Florida Institute of Phosphate Research
Library and Information Clearinghouse
1855 W. Main St.
Bartow, FL 33830
Phone: (813)534-7160
Fax: (813)534-7165
Contact: Betty Faye Stidham, Libn.
Subjects: Reclamation, ecology, phosphates, phosphate mining, minerals processing, radiation, fertilizers, environment. ***Holdings:*** 4375 books; 500 bound periodical volumes; 185 technical reports on microfiche; 260 maps.

★7416★ Florida Solar Energy Center
Library
300 State Rd. 401
Cape Canaveral, FL 32920
Phone: (407)783-0300
Fax: (407)783-2571
Contact: Iraida B. Rickling, Univ.Libn.
Subjects: Solar and alternative sources of energy, science, technology. ***Holdings:*** 7421 books; 1542 bound periodical volumes; 14,001 technical documents; 6730 vertical files; 7398 slides; 56,255 microfiche; 11 films; 51 videotapes.

★7417★ Florida (State) Department of Environmental Regulation
Library
2600 Blair Stone Rd.
Tallahassee, FL 32301
Phone: (904)488-0890
Fax: (904)487-4938
Contact: Jacqueline W. McGorty, Libn.
Subjects: Water quality and quantity, air pollution, toxicology, hazardous waste, solid waste. ***Special Collections:*** National Oceanic and Atmospheric Administration climatic data; HURD aerial photographs; Environmental Protection Agency, U.S. Geological Survey, and Florida Bureau of Geology reports. ***Holdings:*** 20,000 books and technical reports; 1 VF drawer; 1500 maps.

★7418★ Florida (State) Department of Natural Resources
Florida Marine Research Institute
Library
100 Eighth Ave., S.E.
St. Petersburg, FL 33701-5095
Phone: (813)896-8626
Fax: (813)823-0166
Subjects: Marine biology, ichthyology, invertebrata, algology, mariculture, ecology. ***Holdings:*** 6000 books; 39,000 reprints.

★7419★ Florida State Office of the Governor
Governor's Energy Office
Library
The Capitol
Tallahassee, FL 32399-0001
Phone: (904)488-6764
Fax: (904)488-7688
Contact: Vera M. Tucker, Adm.Asst.
Subjects: Energy, renewable resources, solar energy, cogeneration, data analysis, transportation. ***Holdings:*** Energy Information Administration (EIA) documents; Federal Energy Regulatory Commission statutes and regulations.

★7420★ (Florida State) South Florida Water Management District
Reference Center
Box 24680
West Palm Beach, FL 33416-4680
Phone: (407)686-8800
Fax: (407)687-6436
Contact: Cynthia H. Plockelman, Dir.
Subjects: Flood control, hydrology, conservation of natural resources, land and water economics, water rights and legislation, land use, recreation, Florida agriculture, Florida environmental history, environmental

engineering, limnology, wetland and coastal ecology. ***Holdings:*** 400 shelves of pamphlets, documents, reports, statistics.

★7421★ Forest Association of Hungary
Library
Anker-koz 1
H-1061 Budapest VI, Hungary
Phone: 1 225683
Telex: 225369
Subjects: Hungarian national forest policy, forest-related industry, agricultural-forest cooperatives. ***Holdings:*** 20,000 volumes; biographical archives.

★7422★ Forest History Society, Inc.
Library and Archives
701 Vickers Ave.
Durham, NC 27701
Phone: (919)682-9319
Contact: Cheryl Oakes, Libn.
Subjects: History of forestry, conservation of natural resources, environmental policy, lumber industry, land use. ***Special Collections:*** Oral history interviews with leaders of forestry and forest products industries (693 tapes); historical picture collection (50 VF drawers); archival collections of American Forest Institute, American Forestry Association, National Forest Products Association, and Society of American Foresters; papers of foresters. ***Holdings:*** 5500 books; 500 bound periodical volumes; 900 archives boxes of manuscripts; 195 VF drawers of pamphlets and documents; 50 VF drawers of photograph collections; 100 reels of microfilm of records.

★7423★ Friends of the Earth-Holland
Library
Damrak 26
Postbus 19199
NL-1000 GD Amsterdam, Netherlands
Fax: 20 275287
Subjects: Environmental protection, alternatives to governmental policies. ***Holdings:*** 8000 volumes.

★7424★ Friends of the Earth
Library
Apdo. Postal 1891
Cuenca, Ecuador
Phone: 7 824621
Telex: 48570
Subjects: Environmental protection, pollution, environmental law. ***Holdings:*** 1000 volumes.

★7425★ Galson Technical Services
Information Center
6601 Kirkville Rd.
East Syracuse, NY 13057
Phone: (315)432-0506
Fax: (315)437-0509
Contact: Mary Y. Nasikan, Info.Serv.Mgr.
Subjects: Industrial hygiene, air pollution, meteorology, dispersion modeling, hazardous waste, engineering design. ***Holdings:*** 5000 books and government reports; regulations and supplementary material from Occupational Safety and Health Administration (OSHA), Environmental Protection Agency (EPA), New York State Department of Environmental Conservation, and National Institute of Occupational Safety and Health (NIOSH); audio and video cassettes; U.S.G.S. topographic maps; MSOS (Material Safety Data Sheets).

★7426★ Gee & Jenson Engineers, Architects, Planners, Inc.
Library/Records Center
One Harvard Circle
Box 24600
West Palm Beach, FL 33416-4600
Phone: (407)683-3301
Fax: (407)686-7446
Contact: John F. Day, Mgr.
Subjects: Florida water resources and land development; wastewater plants; Florida ports, paving, drainage. ***Special Collections:*** Development of Disney World; Development of Port Canaveral; Florida weather data, 1950 to present. ***Holdings:*** 8200 books; 141 bound periodical volumes; 3000 drawings; 3 VF drawers of Florida city and county rules and regulations; 2 VF drawers of Florida maps; 2 drawers of microforms; Corps of Engineers design memorandum; American Society of Civil Engineers Transactions and Journals, 1936 to present; Florida Soil Conservation Service Surveys, 1930 to present; specifications; reports of Gee & Jenson, 1953 to present; file hearings and plans of the Cross Florida Barge Canal.

★7427★ Georgia Conservancy, Inc.
Library
781 Marietta St., N.W., Ste. B100
Atlanta, GA 30318
Phone: (404)876-2900
Fax: (404)872-9229
Subjects: Conservation, ecology, and pollution with special emphasis on the state of Georgia. ***Holdings:*** 425 books; 300 other cataloged items.

★7428★ Georgia State Forestry Commission
Library
Box 819
Macon, GA 31298-4599
Contact: F. Carr, Act.Libn.
Subjects: Forestry, entomology. ***Holdings:*** Books; 100 bound periodical volumes; 21 shelves of pamphlets; 5 VF drawers of reference files.

★7429★ Glen Helen Association
Library
Glen Helen Bldg.
405 Corry St.
Yellow Springs, OH 45387
Phone: (513)767-7375
Contact: Mrs. George Asakawa, Libn.
Subjects: Environmental protection, resource management, natural area preservation, forestry, outdoor recreation and education, wildlife. ***Holdings:*** 630 books; 14 VF drawers of pamphlets; 7 VF drawers of maps; 6 reels of film; 30 tapes; 10 volumes of U.S. Department of Interior Third Nationwide Outdoor Recreation Plan; 1 set color reproductions of John James Audubon's The Birds of America with text; 6 carousel trays of slides; 9 games; 11 filmstrip/audiotape kits; 17 microfiche; 15 video cassette recordings.

★7430★ Golder Associates, Inc.
Library
4104 148th Ave., NE
Redmond, WA 98052
Phone: (206)883-0777
Fax: (206)882-5498
Contact: Susan Eipert, Lib.Mgr.
Subjects: Geotechnical engineering, hazardous waste site characterization and remediation, radioactive and hazardous waste disposal, groundwater hydrology, geology and hydrology of Northwest. ***Holdings:*** 600 books; 300 technical reports on microfiche; 5000 technical reports; 1000 reprints.

★7431★ Greeley and Hansen
Library
222 S. Riverside Plaza
Chicago, IL 60606-5965
Phone: (312)648-1155
Fax: (312)648-5658
Contact: Marilyn T. Cichon, Libn.
Subjects: Wastewater and water treatment, solid waste disposal, sewerage, flood control, hydraulics. ***Holdings:*** 8000 books; 300 bound periodical volumes; 14,000 internal reports and drawings; 30,000 microforms; 700 municipal annual reports.

★7432★ Greenpeace U.S.A., Inc.
Library
1436 U St., N.W.
Washington, DC 20009
Phone: (202)462-1177
Subjects: Save the Whales, Greenpeace III, dolphins, The Comprehensive Test Ban, wildlife, toxic substances, disarmament, ocean ecology, Pacific campaign, atmosphere and energy, tropical forest. ***Holdings:*** Videotapes; films; pamphlets.

★7433★ Guangzhou Institute of Energy Conversion
Library
81 Central Xianlie Lu
PO Box 1254
Guangzhou 510070, People's Republic of China
Phone: 775600
Contact: Zhang Huan-fen, Div.Chf.
Subjects: Energy conversion; biomass, solar, geothermal energy; waste heat recovery; fluidized bed combustion; electrical generators; heat storage; heat pumps; wave/ocean energy utilization. ***Holdings:*** 50,000 volumes.

★7434★ Hampton Roads Agricultural Experiment Station
Library
1444 Diamond Springs Rd.
Virginia Beach, VA 23455
Phone: (804)363-3900
Contact: Suzanne H. Thurman, Ck.
Subjects: Horticulture, soils, entomology, pesticides, farming. ***Holdings:*** 5450 volumes.

★7435★ Harbor Branch Oceanographic Institution, Inc.
Library
5600 Old Dixie Hwy.
Fort Pierce, FL 34946
Phone: (407)465-2400
Fax: (407)465-2446
Contact: Kristen L. Metzger, Libn.
Subjects: Marine sciences, marine engineering, marine ecology, biological oceanography, fisheries science. ***Holdings:*** 4500 books; 9700 bound periodical volumes; 720 reels of microfilm of periodicals.

★7436★ Harza Engineering Company
Library
150 S. Wacker Dr., 15th Fl.
Chicago, IL 60606
Phone: (312)855-7000
Fax: (312)236-8010
Telex: 25 3527
Contact: Lorraine A. Potrykus, Lb.Svcs.Coord.
Subjects: Development of water, land, and energy resources. ***Holdings:*** 10,000 titles.

★7437★ Hazardous Materials Control Research Institute
Library
9300 Columbia Blvd.
Silver Spring, MD 20910
Phone: (301)587-9390
Fax: (301)589-0182
Contact: Harold Bernard, Exec.Dir.
Subjects: Hazardous waste, hazardous materials, superfund legislation, environment. ***Holdings:*** 500 volumes.

★7438★ HDR Engineering
Library
11225 S.E. 6th St.
Bldg. C, Ste. 200
Bellevue, WA 98004-6441
Phone: (206)453-1523
Fax: (206)747-1819
Contact: Karen Baker
Subjects: Water resources and quality, meteorological data for the western United States, hydropower development. ***Holdings:*** 3000 books; 1000 other cataloged items.

★7439★ Heidelberg College
Water Quality Laboratory
Library
310 E. Market St.
Tiffin, OH 44883
Phone: (419)448-2201
Subjects: Water quality in the Great Lakes region.

★7440★ Holden Arboretum
Warren H. Corning Library
Sperry Rd.
Mentor, OH 44060
Phone: (216)946-4400
Fax: (216)256-1655
Contact: Paul C. Spector, Dir. of Educ.
Subjects: Horticulture, botany, environmental education, natural history. ***Special Collections:*** Warren H. Corning Collection of Horticultural Classics (1500 volumes). ***Holdings:*** 6700 books; 10 VF drawers; 10,000 slides; 45 video cassettes.

★7441★ Holzmacher, McLendon & Murrell, P.C.
H2M Group Library
575 Broad Hollow Rd.
Melville, NY 11747
Phone: (516)756-8000
Fax: (516)694-4122
Contact: Beatrice Uzzo, Libn.
Subjects: Civil engineering, sanitary engineering, environmental science, architecture, water and waste treatment, industrial waste, water supply, environmental engineering. ***Holdings:*** 12,000 books; 1050 reports; 5 years of Federal Registers on microfiche; maps.

★7442★ Hudson River Environmental Society
Richard W. Barnett Memorial Library
PO Box 535
New Paltz, NY 12561
Phone: (914)255-1647
Subjects: Marine biology, regional planning, waste treatment, toxicology. ***Special Collections:*** Hudson River Ecology (5 symposia). ***Holdings:*** 1500 publications.

★7443★ Huxley College of Environmental Studies
Environmental Resource Library
ESC 535, Huxley College
Bellingham, WA 98225
Phone: (206)676-3974
Subjects: Environmental education; human ecology; social science; environmental philosophy and ethics; environmental planning; terrestrial, fresh water, marine ecology; environmental health and toxicology; agriculture, nutrition, food supply; environmental technology and recycling; energy alternatives. ***Holdings:*** 2000 books; 3 files of pamphlets and clippings; 50 newsletters; 600 student reports; 12 tapes; Environmental Protection Agency documents.

★7444★ I Love a Clean San Diego County, Inc.
Environmental Resource Library
4901 Morena Blvd., Ste. 703
San Diego, CA 92117
Phone: (619)270-8393
Fax: (619)270-8449
Contact: Kellie Deane, Lib.Coord.
Subjects: Environmental quality, energy, land use, solid and liquid waste management, recycling, conservation, resource recovery, biodegradable packaging, water quality and supply, air quality, wildlife, population, noise, gardening. ***Holdings:*** 600 books; 2000 handbooks, pamphlets; 44 VF drawers of reports, guidebooks, teaching materials; 50 video cassettes.

★7445★ Illinois (State) Department of Energy and Natural Resources
Chicago Energy Operations Library
State of Illinois Center
100 W. Randolph, Ste. 11-600
Chicago, IL 60601
Phone: (312)814-3895
Contact: Alice I. Lane, Lib.Assoc.
Subjects: Energy conservation - residential, religious/places of worship, transportation. ***Special Collections:*** Audiovisual collection. ***Holdings:*** 200 books; 6 VF drawers of leaflets, brochures, pamphlets; films; filmstrips; slides; video cassettes.

★7446★ Illinois (State) Department of Energy and Natural Resources
Energy Information Library
325 W. Adams St., Rm. 300
Springfield, IL 62704-1892
Phone: (217)785-2388
Fax: (217)785-2618
Contact: Pat Poehlman Burg, Libn.
Subjects: Energy conservation, biomass energy, coal, electric utilities, energy and environmental policy, natural resources, petroleum and power resources, solar and alternative energy. ***Special Collections:*** Agency archives; Energy Information Center (EIC) Envirofiche and Acid Rain Fiche. ***Holdings:*** 11,000 books and documents.

★7447★ Illinois (State) Environmental Protection Agency
Library
2200 Churchill Rd.
Springfield, IL 62794-9276
Phone: (217)782-9691
Fax: (217)524-4916
Contact: Nancy Simpson, Libn.
Subjects: Environmental pollution and protection, environmental law, environmental health. ***Holdings:*** 25,000 books; 300 bound periodical volumes; 1500 legal documents; 25,000 EPA technical reports on microfiche.

★7448★ Illinois State Water Survey
Library
208 Water Survey Research Center
2204 Griffith Dr.
Champaign, IL 61820
Phone: (217)333-4956
Fax: (217)333-6540
Contact: Frances L. Drone-Silvers, Libn.
Subjects: Hydrology, water resources, atmospheric and aquatic chemistry, water quality, meteorology, atmospheric sciences. ***Special Collections:*** State Water Survey Archives; Water Supply Papers of U.S. Geological Survey (entire set); U.S. climatic data; HIPLEX reports. ***Holdings:*** 27,681 books; 1200 bound periodical volumes; 400 microfiche.

★7449★ Indiana (State) Department of Commerce
Division of Energy Policy
Energy Resource Center-Library
1 N. Capitol, Ste. 320
Indianapolis, IN 46204-2288
Phone: (317)232-8800
Contact: Edward Hoy, Contact
Subjects: Energy - conservation, alternative sources, resource development, consumption and production.

★7450★ Institute of Ecosystem Studies
Library
Cary Arboretum
New York Botanical Garden
Box AB
Millbrook, NY 12545
Phone: (914)677-5343
Fax: (914)677-5976
Contact: Annette R. Frank, Libn.
Subjects: Ecology, botany, horticulture, environmental studies, wildlife management. ***Special Collections:*** Limnology. ***Holdings:*** 7000 books; 2000 bound periodical volumes; 450 maps.

★7451★ Institute of Environmental Sciences
Library
940 E. NW Hwy.
Mt. Prospect, IL 60056
Phone: (708)255-1561
Fax: (708)255-1699
Contact: Janet A. Ehmann, Exec.Dir.
Subjects: Engineering, energy and environment, contamination control. List of public ations available on record.

★7452★ International Academy at Santa Barbara
Library
800 Garden St., Ste. D
Santa Barbara, CA 93101
Phone: (805)965-5010
Fax: (805)965-6071
Contact: Susan J. Shaffer, Off.Mgr.
Subjects: Energy, environment, and information management. ***Holdings:*** Figures not available.

★7453★ International Council of Environmental Law
Library
Adenauerallee 214
D-5300 Bonn 1, Germany
Phone: 228 2692240
Subjects: Environmental law, environmental policy and administration. ***Holdings:*** 30,000 volumes.

★7454★ International Joint Commission
Great Lakes Regional Office Library
100 Ouellette Ave., 7th Fl.
Windsor, Ontario, Canada N9A 6T3
Phone: (519)256-7821
Fax: (519)256-7791
Contact: Patricia Murray, Libn.
Subjects: Great Lakes water quality, resources management, land use, toxic substances, limnology, wastewater treatment. ***Special***

Collections: Pollution from Land Use Activities Research Group (PLUARG) reports (120); Pollution of Boundary Waters reports, 1951-1970. ***Holdings:*** 2500 books; 12 VF drawers of clippings and pamphlets; 40,000 technical reports; 70,000 microfiche.

★7455★ International Joint Commission Library
100 Metcalfe St., 18th Fl.
Ottawa, Ontario, Canada K1P 5M1
Phone: (613)995-2984
Fax: (613)993-5583
Subjects: Water resources, international relations involving shared natural resources. ***Special Collections:*** International Joint Commission reports. ***Holdings:*** 1500 volumes.

★7456★ International Research & Evaluation (IRE)
Information & Technology Transfer Resource Center
21098 IRE Control Center
Eagan, MN 55121
Phone: (612)888-9635
Fax: (612)798-5574
Contact: Randall L. Voight, Info.Dir.
Subjects: Information and technology transfer on areas such as waste management and resources recovery, energy and environmental engineering. ***Holdings:*** 715,401 books; 14,771 bound periodical volumes; 27 million microfiche; 501,722 ultrafiche; 12,942 videotapes and films; 3106 microforms.

★7457★ Interstate Oil and Gas Compact Commission
Library
900 N.E. 23rd St.
Box 53127
Oklahoma City, OK 73152
Phone: (405)525-3556
Fax: (405)525-3592
Contact: W. Timothy Dowd, Exec.Dir.
Subjects: Conservation of oil and gas. ***Holdings:*** 80 VF drawers; 10,000 file cards.

★7458★ Iowa (State) Department of Natural Resources
Technical Library
Henry A. Wallace Bldg.
Des Moines, IA 50319
Phone: (515)281-8897
Fax: (515)281-8895
Contact: Cecilia Nelson, Rec.Ck.
Subjects: Energy, air and water quality, hazardous waste, solid wastes, chemical technology, radiation, administration, conservation. ***Holdings:*** 3713 books; publications of Environmental Protection Agency.

★7459★ James A. FitzPatrick Library
Miner Institute
Chazy, NY 12921
Phone: (518)846-7144
Contact: Linda J. Masters, Libn.
Subjects: Ecology, environmental sciences, wildlife ecology, acid rain, in vitro cell biology, biotechnology, plant cell culture, tissue culture, agriculture. ***Holdings:*** 5400 books.

★7460★ James R. Reed & Associates, Inc.
Library
813 Forrest Dr.
Newport News, VA 23606
Phone: (804)599-6750
Subjects: Analytical chemistry, environment, chemical pollution, ecological resource management, endangered species. ***Holdings:*** 5000 volumes.

★7461★ J.J. Keller & Associates, Inc.
Research & Technical Library
145 W. Wisconsin Ave.
PO Box 368
Neenah, WI 54957-0368
Phone: (414)722-2848
Fax: (414)727-8220
Contact: John K. Breese, Sr.Mgr.
Subjects: Transportation, motor carrier regulations, occupational safety, hazardous materials, hazardous wastes, chemical processing industry. ***Special Collections:*** Transportation/motor carrier industry and regulations; hazardous materials/wastes handling and regulations. ***Holdings:*** 5900 books, AV programs, and Department of Transportation and Environmental Protection Agency documents.

★7462★ John G. Shedd Aquarium
Library
1200 S. Lake Shore Dr.
Chicago, IL 60605
Phone: (312)939-2426
Fax: (312)939-8069
Contact: Janet E. Powers, Coord. of Lib.Serv.
Subjects: Marine and freshwater biology, marine mammals, fishes, water pollution, fisheries, Lake Michigan, aquatic education. ***Holdings:*** 12,000 books; 300 file folders of clippings, reprints, pamphlets.

★7463★ Jordan College Energy Institute
Library
155 7-Mile Rd., N.W.
Comstock Park, MI 49321
Phone: (616)784-7595
Contact: Alison S. Heins, Libn.
Subjects: Energy - renewable, solar, biomass, wind; energy-conscious construction and technology. ***Holdings:*** 2500 books; 1000 other cataloged items; 23 VF drawers of topical and manufacturer information; 1000 government documents.

★7464★ Kalamazoo Nature Center
Reference Library
7000 N. Westnedge Ave.
Kalamazoo, MI 49007
Phone: (616)381-1575
Contact: Jan Spencer, Contact
Subjects: Ornithology, natural history, pollution, environmental education, alternative energy, citizen action. ***Special Collections:*** Collection of VF materials on environmental groups and education facilities (8000 items). ***Holdings:*** 6200 books; 165 bound periodical volumes; 34 VF drawers of clippings, pamphlets, documents; 3 VF drawers of student papers; 3000 microfiche.

★7465★ Kansas State University
Farrell Library
Manhattan, KS 66506
Phone: (913)532-7400
Contact: Brice G. Hobrock, Dean of Libs.
Subjects: Physical sciences, farming systems, agriculture, engineering, applied science and technology, natural sciences, veterinary medicine, home economics. ***Special Collections:*** Rare Books (33,935 volumes); University Archives (1200 volumes; 1300 linear feet; 20,000 photographs; dissertations and theses; ephemera); Department of Energy/Energy Research and Development Administration/Atomic Energy Commission Collection (26,000 paper titles; 92,000 microcards; 714,000 microfiche); ERIC Collection (complete); Juvenile Literature Collection (10,378 volumes); Curriculum Materials Collection (11,000 units of print and nonprint materials specializing in environmental education); Physical Fitness Collection; Human Relations Area Files; Travels in the West and Southwest. ***Holdings:*** 1.16 million volumes; 680,000 government documents; 20,000 maps; 3.3 million microforms; 13,500 sound recordings; 29,500 slides; 650 tapes; 650 filmstrips; 350 films; 8662 scores; 2380 audio cassettes; 650 video cassettes.

★7466★ Land Registration & Information Service (LRIS)
Information Records Centre
PO Box 310
Amherst, Nova Scotia, Canada B4H 3Z5
Phone: (902)667-7231
Fax: (902)667-6008
Contact: Margaret E. Campbell, Libn.
Subjects: Atlantic and Maritime Provinces: resource development, planning and management, land use, environment, engineering; Geographic Information Systems (GIS); automated cartography. ***Special Collections:*** Thematic resource map collection of the Maritimes; collection of internal project reports; studies and files on resource-related issues. ***Holdings:*** 10,000 books; periodicals; government documents; VF drawers; research reports; monographs; maps.

★7467★ Lavalin Engineers, Inc.
Library
2235 Sheppard Ave., E.
Willowdale, Ontario, Canada M2J 5A6
Phone: (416)756-1333
Fax: (416)756-4998
Telex: 06 986781
Contact: Agnes M. Croxford, Chf.Libn.
Subjects: Engineering, hydrology, nuclear science, pollution control, waste management, urban and regional planning, transportation. ***Holdings:*** 20,000 books; 650 bound periodical volumes; 1500 maps; 1500 Transportation Research Board publications.

★7468★ Lavalin Environnement Inc.
Documentation
1100, blvd. Rene Levesque ouest
Montreal, Quebec, Canada H3B 4P3
Phone: (514)876-4455
Fax: (514)876-9273
Contact: Nicole Goyette, Lib.Techn.
Subjects: Environment. ***Holdings:*** 7500 books; 100 bound periodical volumes; 360 maps; 550 internal reports.

★7469★ Law Environmental
Library
7375 Boston Blvd., Ste. 200
Springfield, VA 22153
Phone: (703)912-9400
Subjects: Water, wastewater, sanitary engineering, solid and hazardous wastes and their effects on health, environmental engineering. ***Holdings:*** 2000 books.

★7470★ Lawler Matusky & Skelly Engineers
Library
1 Blue Hill Plaza
Pearl River, NY 10965-3104
Phone: (914)735-8300
Fax: (914)735-7466
Contact: Aileen P. McGuire, Info.Sci.
Subjects: Environment, water supply, wastewater treatment, hazardous materials, hydrogeology, water quality, environmental impact assessment, ecology, aquatic biology, limnology. ***Special Collections:*** LMSE reports (800). ***Holdings:*** 6500 books; 7000 other cataloged items; 50,000 documents on microfiche; 82 reels of microfilm.

★7471★ Lewis and Clark Law School
Northwestern School of Law
Paul L. Boley Law Library
10015 S.W. Terwilliger Blvd.
Portland, OR 97219
Phone: (503)244-1181
Fax: (503)246-8542
Contact: Prof. Peter S. Nycum, Law Libn.
Subjects: Law. ***Special Collections:*** Milton A. Pearl Environmental Law Library (3500 volumes); Samuel S. Johnson Public Land Law Review Commission Collection (50,000 pages). ***Holdings:*** 35,396 books; 124,926 serial volumes; 140,877 microforms.

★7472★ Library of Congress
Congressional Research Service
Environment and Natural Resources Policy Division
James Madison Memorial Bldg., LM213
Washington, DC 20540
Phone: (202)707-5735
Contact: Joseph E. Ross, Dir.
Agriculture, mineral economics, forestry and lumber, energy resources, environmental protection, pollution, and the fields of water, irrigation, reclamation, and land use.

★7473★ Lloyd Center for Environmental Studies, Inc.
Resource Center
430 Potomska Rd.
Box 7037
South Dartmouth, MA 02748
Phone: (508)990-0505
Contact: Cynthia J. Marks, Libn.
Subjects: Coastal resources, coastal resources ecology, environmental education, oceanography, ecology, zoology. ***Holdings:*** 1500 books.

★7474★ Los Angeles County Sanitation District
Technical Library
1955 Workman Mill Rd.
Box 4998
Whittier, CA 90607
Phone: (213)699-7411
Contact: Beverly K. Yoshida, Libn.
Subjects: Water pollution control, sewage treatment, chemical analysis, solid and hazardous wastes management. ***Holdings:*** 1000 books; 9000 research and development reports, progress reports, sewage process reports of the Environmental Protection Agency and other government agencies.

★7475★ Louisiana (State) Department of Environmental Quality
Water Pollution Control Division
Water Resources Office - Library
Box 44091
Baton Rouge, LA 70804
Phone: (504)342-6363
Subjects: Water pollution. ***Holdings:*** 2000 volumes.

★7476★ Maine Audubon Society
Environmental Library and Teacher Resource Center
Gilsland Farm
118 U. S. Rte. 1
Falmouth, ME 04105
Phone: (207)781-2330
Contact: Maureen Oates, Dir., Educ.
Subjects: Natural history, ornithology, environmental problems and education, Maine's natural resources. ***Special Collections:*** Environmental education (200 curriculum guides); children's books on environmental topics (250). ***Holdings:*** 2500 books; 300 environmental books for children; 9 VF drawers of Maine environmental files; 300 curriculum guides; 20 films and slides.

★7477★ Maine State Department of Environmental Protection & Department of Conservation
DEP-DOC Joint Library
State House, Sta. 17
Augusta, ME 04333
Phone: (207)289-2811
Contact: Pamela Shofner, Libn.
Subjects: Air, water, land quality; forestry; land use; geology; hazardous materials; recreation planning; natural resources. ***Holdings:*** 2200 books; U.S. Geological Survey maps; Maine Soil Surveys.

★7478★ Malcolm Pirnie, Inc.
Technical Library
2 Corporate Park Dr.
Box 751
White Plains, NY 10602
Phone: (914)641-2954
Fax: (914)694-9286
Contact: Marianne Gregg
Subjects: Environmental engineering, water, waste water, air pollution, hazardous waste and solid waste management. ***Holdings:*** 15,000 volumes; 1000 U.S. Environmental Protection Agency reports.

★7479★ Manitoba Environment
Resource Centre
139 Tuxedo Ave., Bldg. 2
Winnipeg, Manitoba, Canada R3N 0H6
Phone: (204)945-7125
Fax: (204)945-5229
Contact: Helen Woo
Subjects: Environmental standards, environmental assessments, environmental control, air quality, air pollution, water quality, water pollution, toxic and hazardous substances, waste management, pesticide control, recycling. ***Holdings:*** 20,000 volumes.

★7480★ Maryland (State) Department of Licensing and Regulation
Occupational Safety and Health Library
501 St. Paul Place, 11th Fl.
Baltimore, MD 21202-2272
Phone: (301)333-4164
Contact: David Murray, Lib.Hd.
Subjects: General reference, industrial hygiene, construction and industrial processes, accident prevention, occupational medicine and diseases, safety hazards, hazardous occupations, environmental pollution, toxicology. ***Holdings:*** 600 books; 30 bound periodical volumes; 30 other cataloged items.

★7481★ Massachusetts Audubon Society
Berkshire Sanctuaries
Library
Pleasant Valley Wildlife Sanctuary
Lenox, MA 01240
Phone: (413)637-0320
Contact: Rene Laubach, Dir.
Subjects: Natural history, environmental issues. ***Special Collections:*** Reports on natural science in Berkshire County, Massachusetts. ***Holdings:*** 1000 books; 100 bound periodical volumes; 1000 35mm color slides; field guides.

★7482★ Massachusetts Audubon Society
Hatheway Environmental Resource Library
South Great Rd.
Lincoln, MA 01773
Phone: (617)259-9500
Fax: (617)259-8899
Contact: Martha J. Cohen, Hd., Lib.Serv.
Subjects: Air and water pollution, environment, conservation, environmental education, natural resources, wildlife management, careers, New England wild life, current environmental issues, history of the environmental movement. ***Special Collections:*** Natural history; environmental affairs; curriculum. ***Holdings:*** 15,000 titles; 25 VF drawers of pamphlets, articles, and curriculum activities.

★7483★ Massachusetts Institute of Technology
Barker Engineering Library
Rm. 10-500
Cambridge, MA 02139
Phone: (617)253-5663
Fax: (617)258-5623
Contact: Ruth K. Seidman, Libn.
Subjects: Engineering - electrical, mechanical, civil, ocean, materials, environmental; bioengineering; transportation; energy; mineral resources; computer science and applied mathematics. ***Holdings:*** 87,058 books; 34,397 bound periodical volumes; 48,914 bound serial volumes; 20,798 M.I.T. theses; 2233 pamphlets; 59,501 technical reports; 278,137 microfiche sheets; 1346 reels of microfilm. ***Contact:*** ALA1764 (ALANET).

★7484★ McIlvaine Company
Technical Library
2970 Maria Ave.
Northbrook, IL 60062
Phone: (708)272-0010
Fax: (708)272-9673
Telex: 494 4829 MC ILVN
Contact: Francine Hakimian, Libn.
Subjects: Pollution control - air, water, energy.

★7485★ McNamee, Porter & Seeley
MPS Engineering Library
3131 S. State St.
Ann Arbor, MI 48108-1691
Phone: (313)665-6000
Fax: (313)665-2570
Contact: Nathan Zill, Libn.
Subjects: Wastewater treatment, potable water, water pollution, highway and bridge construction, hydraulics and hydrology, environmental engineering, architecture, drainage. ***Holdings:*** 1312 books; 170 bound periodical volumes; 380 Environmental Protection Agency reports; 357 U.S. Geological Survey Water Supply papers.

★7486★ Merck & Company, Inc.
Calgon Corporation
Information Center
Calgon Center
Box 1346
Pittsburgh, PA 15230-1346
Phone: (412)777-8205
Fax: (412)777-8104
Contact: Betty P. Schwarz, Mgr.
Subjects: Industrial and municipal water treatment and reclamation, chemistry of water soluble polymers. ***Holdings:*** 5000 books; 100 bound periodical volumes; 5000 reels of microfilm; 20,000 Environmental Protection Agency (EPA) reports; patents; newsletters.

★7487★ Metcalf & Eddy, Inc.
Harry L. Kinsel Library
Box 4043
Woburn, MA 01888-4043
Phone: (617)246-5200
Fax: (617)245-6293
Telex: 710-321-6365
Contact: Anita Muise, Libn.
Subjects: Environment, hazardous waste, drinking water, wastewater/sewage, civil engineering. ***Special Collections:*** M & E Engineering Reports (5500 items); M & E technical articles/conference papers (4 filing

drawers); civic file (3200 items); legislative documents (2 filing drawers); military specifications and manuals (6 shelves). ***Holdings:*** 6000 books; 658 bound periodical volumes; 2250 reels of microfilm (reports and computations; specifications; lab analysis reports; proposals; legal and accounting documents).

★7488★ Mexico
National Commission on Nuclear Safety and Safeguards
Library
Insurgentes Sur 1806
Colonia Florida
Delegacion Alvaro Obregon
01030 Mexico City, DF, Mexico
Phone: 5 534-1404
Fax: 5 5341405
Telex: 1773280 CNSMME
Subjects: Non-military use of nuclear energy, radiation protection, quality assurance, nuclear regulation. ***Holdings:*** 7000 volumes.

★7489★ Minneapolis Public Library & Information Center
Technology and Science Department
300 Nicollet Mall
Minneapolis, MN 55401
Phone: (612)372-6570
Contact: Thomas Smisek, Dept.Hd.
Subjects: Natural and applied sciences. ***Special Collections:*** Environmental Conservation Library (ECOL; 17,500 volumes); Minnesota Regional Copper-Nickel Project documents; U.S. Nuclear Regulatory Commission Public Documents Room; Patent Depository Library, 1790 to present; Mid-American Solar Energy Complex Library. ***Holdings:*** 170,500 books; 205,000 microforms; 3700 environmental impact statements; 3000 auto repair manuals; 600 computer programs.

★7490★ Minnesota (State) Department of Trade and Economic Development
Library
150 E. Kellogg Blvd., Rm. 900
St. Paul, MN 55101-1421
Phone: (612)296-8902
Fax: (612)296-1290
Contact: Pat Fenton, Sr.Libn.
Subjects: Energy conservation, economic development, biomass energy, energy policy, trade. ***Special Collections:*** NTIS - SRIM energy microfiche (80,000). ***Holdings:*** 12,000 books.

★7491★ Minnesota State Pollution Control Agency
Library
520 Lafayette Rd.
St. Paul, MN 55155
Phone: (612)296-7719
Fax: (612)297-1456
Subjects: Water, air, and noise pollution control; solid wastes pollution; hazardous waste; pesticides. ***Special Collections:*** NTIS Environmental Protection Agency Documents Selected Research in Microfiche (SRIM) series, 1976 to present. ***Holdings:*** 15,000 books and reports; 100,000 documents on microfiche.

★7492★ Mobil Corporation
Toxicology Information Center
Box 1029
Princeton, NJ 08543
Phone: (609)737-5583
Fax: (609)737-5601
Contact: Yvonne B. Smith, Info.Spec.
Subjects: Toxicology, environmental health, biomedicine, analytical chemistry. ***Holdings:*** 6000 books.

★7493★ National Association of Conservation Districts
Conservation Film Service
408 E. Main St.
League City, TX 77573
Phone: (713)332-3402
Fax: (713)332-5259
Contact: Ruth Chenhall, Educ.-Info. Spec.
Subjects: Conservation - water, soil, education; water quality; natural resources; wildlife. ***Holdings:*** 150 films, slides, and videotapes.

★7494★ National Ground Water Information Center
6375 Riverside Dr.
Dublin, OH 43017
Phone: (614)761-1711
Fax: (614)761-3446
Contact: Kevin B. McCray, Dir.
Subjects: Ground water, water well technology, hydrogeology, environmental pollution. ***Holdings:*** 20,000 books; 10,000 microfiche.

★7495★ National Institute for Urban Wildlife
Library
10921 Trotting Ridge Way
Columbia, MD 21044
Phone: (301)596-3311
Contact: Louise E. Dove, Wildlife Biol.
Subjects: Urban wildlife, land use, wildlife management. ***Holdings:*** 500 books; 1000 bound periodical volumes; 500 slides; 150 maps; 4000 pamphlets, catalogs, newspaper clippings, reprints.

★7496★ National Parks and Conservation Association
Library
1015 31st St., N.W.
Washington, DC 20007
Phone: (202)944-8530
Contact: Paul C. Pritchard, Pres.
Subjects: National parks, conservation. ***Holdings:*** 3000 volumes.

★7497★ National Wildlife Federation
George Preston Marshall Memorial Library
8925 Leesburg Pike
Vienna, VA 22184
Phone: (703)790-4446
Fax: (703)442-7332
Contact: Sharon Levy, Libn.
Subjects: Wildlife, natural resources, conservation, ecology, environment. ***Holdings:*** 5000 books.

★7498★ Native Americans for a Clean Environment
Resource Office
Box 1671
Tahlequah, OK 74465
Phone: (918)458-4322
Contact: Vickie McCullough, Exec.Dir.
Subjects: Nuclear energy - waste and waste routes, facilities, health effects; national environmental issues; area issues. ***Special Collections:*** Sequoyah Fuels Facility, Gore, Oklahoma; Nuclear Regulatory Commission listings, hearings, permits.

★7499★ Nature Conservancy
Long Island Chapter
Uplands Farm Environmental Center
Lawrence Hill Rd.
Box 72
Cold Spring Harbor, NY 11724
Phone: (516)367-3225
Contact: Andrew Walker, Dir.
Subjects: Conservation, land preservation, natural history, terrestrial and freshwater ecology, endangered species, Long Island environment. ***Special Collections:*** Natural Diversity Collection; Long Island Freshwater and Terrestrial Ecology Collection. ***Holdings:*** 2000 books; 2000 slides.

★7500★ Nebraska (State) Natural Resources Commission
Planning Library
301 Centennial Mall, S.
Box 94876
Lincoln, NE 68509
Phone: (402)471-2081
Contact: Jerry Wallin, Hd., Plan.Sect.
Subjects: Water resources - Nebraska, regional, national. ***Holdings:*** 4000 books.

★7501★ New England Coalition on Nuclear Pollution
Library
PO Box 545
Brattleboro, VT 05301
Phone: (802)257-0336
Subjects: Nuclear power, nuclear war, radiation, alternate energy, energy conservation, radiation health. ***Holdings:*** 1000 books; 1000 reprints, unbound periodicals, and manuscripts; government documents; alternate press publications.

★7502★ New England Governors' Conference, Inc.
Reference Library
76 Summer St.
Boston, MA 02110
Phone: (617)423-6900
Contact: Shirley M. Raynard, Ref.Libn.
Subjects: Energy, transportation, economic development, hazardous waste, tourism. ***Special Collections:*** New England Regional Commission reports (2000); New England River Basins Commission reports (complete set); Canadian Affairs. ***Holdings:*** 10,000 volumes; 100 bound periodical volumes.

★7503★ New Jersey (State) Department of Environmental Protection
Information Resource Center
CN-409
432 E. State St.
Trenton, NJ 08625
Phone: (609)984-2249
Fax: (609)292-3298
Contact: Maria Baratta, Lib.Mgr.
Subjects: Toxic substances; hazardous waste; pollution - water, air, soil; carcinogens; mutagens; teratogens; water resources. ***Special Collections:*** International Agency for Research on Cancer (IARC) monograph series; NIOSH Criteria Documents. ***Holdings:*** 2500 books; 4500 technical documents; 12 VF drawers of Chemical Reference Files; 5 VF drawers.

★7504★ New Mexico (State) Department of Health & Environment
Environmental Improvement Division
EID Library
1190 St. Francis Dr.
Runnels Bldg. S1350
Santa Fe, NM 87504-0968
Phone: (505)827-2633
Contact: Jacqueline M. Calligan, Libn.Sr.
Subjects: Ground water protection, surface water protection, hazardous waste disposal, radiation protection, occupational health and safety, air quality protection. ***Holdings:*** 700 books; 154 bound periodical volumes; 6500 reports and documents.

★7505★ New Zealand - Ministry of Forestry
Forest Research Institute
Library
Private Bag 3020
Rotorua, New Zealand
Phone: 73 475-899
Fax: 73 479-380
Telex: NZ 21080
Contact: Beryl Anderson, Libn.
Subjects: Forest health, improvement, management, resources; wood technology; production forestry; pulp and paper. ***Holdings:*** 150,000 books and monographs; 8000 microfiche.

★7506★ Newfoundland Department of Forestry and Agriculture
Library
Herald Bldg.
Box 2006
Corner Brook, Newfoundland, Canada A2H 6J8
Phone: (709)637-2307
Fax: (709)637-2403
Contact: Bruce Boland, Libn.
Subjects: Forest management, products, marketing and utilization, protection, fires, insects, and history; forestry history; silviculture; land use policy. ***Special Collections:*** Departmental publications; provincial government legislation. ***Holdings:*** 3260 books; 4 filing cabinets of pamphlets.

★7507★ North American Wildlife Park Foundation
WOLF PARK
Institute of Ethology - Library
Battle Ground, IN 47920
Phone: (317)567-2265
Contact: Erich Klinghammer, Ph.D., Dir.
Subjects: Wolves - behavior, ecology, hybrids. ***Holdings:*** Books; scientific papers; clippings.

★7508★ North Carolina State (Department) of Environment, Health, and Natural Resources
Environmental Resources Library
512 N. Salisbury St., Rm. 719
Box 27687
Raleigh, NC 27611
Phone: (919)733-4984
Fax: (919)733-2622
Contact: Jane Basnight, Libn.
Subjects: Water, air, land, and forest resources. ***Special Collections:*** North Carolina Groundwater and Geology/Mineral Resources Bulletins; North Carolina Water Quality Studies; North Carolina soil surveys; U.S. Geological Survey and U.S. EPA series. ***Holdings:*** 20,000 books.

★7509★ North Carolina State University
D.H. Hill Library
Natural Resources Library
Box 7114
Raleigh, NC 27695-7114
Phone: (919)737-2306
Subjects: Forest science, wood and paper science, recreation administration, geology, atmospheric science, marine science. ***Special Collections:*** Remote sensing; U.S. Forest Service reports (12,100). ***Holdings:*** 14,256 books; 4894 bound periodical volumes; 35 AV programs.

★7510★ North Dakota State University
Bottineau Library
First & Simrall Blvd.
Bottineau, ND 58318
Phone: (701)228-2277
Fax: (701)228-2277
Contact: Jan Wysocki, Lib.Dir.
Subjects: Forestry, botany, horticulture. ***Special Collections:*** Fossum Foundation Collection (horticulture; 500 volumes). ***Holdings:*** 26,000 books.

★7511★ Northern Illinois University
Taft Field Campus
Library
Box 299
Oregon, IL 61061
Phone: (815)753-0205
Fax: (815)753-2003
Contact: Marcia Bradley, Supv.
Subjects: Natural sciences; education outdoor, environmental, experiential; ecology; arts. ***Special Collections:*** Camping Archives (376 archival materials); sculptor Lorado Taft Archives (515 archival materials). ***Holdings:*** 5780 books; 490 bound periodical volumes; 1650 other cataloged items; 1050 dissertations.

★7512★ Nova Scotia Department of the Environment
Library
5151 Terminal Rd.
PO Box 2107
Halifax, Nova Scotia, Canada B3J 3B7
Phone: (902)424-5300
Fax: (902)424-0503
Contact: Janice Laufer, Libn.
Subjects: Environment. ***Holdings:*** 8000 books and reports; unbound periodical volumes.

★7513★ Oak Ridge National Laboratory
Carbon Dioxide Information Analysis Center
PO Box 2008 (MS-6335)
Oak Ridge, TN 37831-6335
Phone: (615)574-0390
Fax: (615)574-2322
Contact: Robert M. Cushman, Dp.Dir.
Subjects: Carbon dioxide-climate research, including atmospheric carbon dioxide measurements, fossil fuel use, forest conversion, ocean properties characterization, historical records from ice cores, tree rings, global warming, information management, information analysis. ***Holdings:*** 134 reports; 34 numeric data packages, 3 computer model packages.

★7514★ Oak Ridge National Laboratory
Toxicology Information Response Center
Bldg. 2001, MS 6050
Box 2008
Oak Ridge, TN 37831-6050
Phone: (615)576-1746
Fax: (615)576-2912
Contact: Kim Slusher, Dir.
Subjects: Toxicology, pharmacology, veterinary toxicology, heavy metals, pesticides, chemistry, biology, medicine, industrial hygiene. ***Holdings:*** 7700 search files; 250 microfiche of published bibliographies.

★7515★ Ocean and Coastal Law Center
Library
School of Law
University of Oregon
Eugene, OR 97403-1221
Phone: (503)686-3845
Fax: (503)686-3985
Contact: Andrea G. Coffman, Libn.
Subjects: International law of the sea, coastal zone management, ocean management and policy, fisheries, aquaculture, offshore drilling and mining, marine pollution. ***Holdings:*** 4580 books; 290 bound periodical volumes; 182 reprints; 191 maps; 100 fishery management plans; 7 VF drawers of documents.

★7516★ Ohio State Environmental Protection Agency
Library
1800 Watermark Dr.
Columbus, OH 43215
Phone: (614)644-3024
Fax: (614)644-2329
Contact: Ruth Ann Evans, Libn.
Subjects: Pollution control, environmental law, Ohio water quality reports. ***Holdings:*** 4440 books; 309 microfiche.

★7517★ Ohio State University
Ohio Cooperative Fish and Wildlife Research Unit
Library
1735 Neil Ave.
Columbus, OH 43210
Phone: (614)292-6112
Contact: Dr. Theodore A. Bookhout, Unit Leader
Subjects: Wildlife and fishery research and management, animal ecology, pesticide-wildlife/fishery relationships. ***Holdings:*** 300 volumes; 160 theses; 300 unit reprints and releases; 30 VF drawers of other reprints; 2500 35mm color transparencies.

★7518★ Oklahoma (State) Department of Commerce
Energy Conservation Services Division
Technical Information Center
PO Box 26980
Oklahoma City, OK 73126-0980
Phone: (405)841-9365
Contact: Deborah Keith
Subjects: Energy conservation, renewable energy. ***Holdings:*** 1000 books.

★7519★ Oklahoma Water Resources Board
Library
600 N. Harvey
PO Box 150
Oklahoma City, OK 73101
Phone: (405)231-2500
Fax: (405)231-2600
Contact: Susan E. Lutz, Libn.
Subjects: Water, water quality and planning, safety of dams, weather modification, stream water and groundwater use. ***Holdings:*** 9000 volumes.

★7520★ Ontario Ministry of Natural Resources
Natural Resources Library
Whitney Block
99 Wellesley St., W.
Queen's Park
Toronto, Ontario, Canada M7A 1W3
Phone: (416)965-6319
Fax: (416)965-6336
Telex: 06-219701
Contact: Sandra Louet, Mgr.
Subjects: Forestry, ecology, parks and recreation, land use planning, fish and wildlife. ***Holdings:*** 80,000 books; 500 bound periodical volumes; 60,000 reprints and unpublished papers; 100 microforms.

★7521★ Ontario Ministry of Natural Resources
Research Library, Maple
PO Box 5000
Maple, Ontario, Canada L6A 1S9
Phone: (416)832-7145
Fax: (416)832-7149
Contact: Helle Arro, Lib.Supv.
Subjects: Forestry, fisheries, wildlife. ***Special Collections:*** U.S. Forest Service and the U.S. Fish and Wildlife Service publications.

★7522★ Ontario Ministry of the Environment
Air Resources Branch Library
880 Bay St., 4th Fl.
Toronto, Ontario, Canada M5S 1Z8
Phone: (416)326-1633
Fax: (416)326-1733
Contact: David Reynolds, Libn.
Subjects: Air pollution, emission technology, phytotoxicology. ***Special Collections:*** Ministry Technical Reports. ***Holdings:*** 1200 books; 1700 reports.

★7523★ Ontario Ministry of the Environment
Laboratory Library
125 Resource Rd.
PO Box 213
Rexdale, Ontario, Canada M9W 5L1
Phone: (416)235-5751
Fax: (416)235-0189
Telex: 06-23496
Contact: Margaret Wells, Lab.Libn.
Subjects: Water pollution, water supply, solid waste, air, noise, biology, chemistry. ***Special Collections:*** Ministry of the Environment technical publications. ***Holdings:*** 35,000 books; 2000 bound periodical volumes; 40 VF drawers of reprints, government reports, documents; 60,000 microfiche.

★7524★ Ontario Public Interest Research Group (OPIRG)
Guelph Library
University of Guelph
Trent Ln.
Guelph, Ontario, Canada N1G 2W1
Phone: (519)824-2091
Contact: Karen Farbridge, Lib.Hd.
Subjects: Environment, women's issues, nuclear power, energy from waste, native rights, transportation, other social issues. ***Holdings:*** 2000 volumes.

★7525★ Ontario Public Interest Research Group (OPIRG)
Peterborough Library
Trent University
Peterborough, Ontario, Canada K9J 7B8
Phone: (705)748-1767
Fax: (705)748-1795
Contact: Keith Stewart, Coord.
Subjects: Energy, nuclear power, peace/militarism, environment, civil liberties, Third World development, native issues, food and agriculture, occupational health and safety, politics and government. ***Special Collections:*** Nuclear Free Press Archives. ***Holdings:*** 1000 books; 300 vertical files.

★7526★ Oregon State University
Hatfield Marine Science Center
Library
Newport, OR 97365
Phone: (503)867-3011
Fax: (503)867-3078
Contact: Marilyn Guin, Libn.
Subjects: Marine biology and fisheries, aquaculture, marine pollution. ***Holdings:*** 11,000 books; 12,000 bound periodical volumes; 5000 reprints; microforms.

★7527★ Pace University
School of Law Library
78 N. Broadway
White Plains, NY 10603
Phone: (914)422-4273
Fax: (914)422-4139
Contact: Nicholas Triffin, Dir.
Subjects: U.S. and international law, jurisprudence. ***Special Collections:*** Selective U.S. Government documents depository; environmental law (2800 titles). ***Holdings:*** 49,713 titles; 243,380 volumes.

★7528★ Pacific Energy & Resources Center
Library
Bldg. 1055, Fl. Cronkhite
Sausalito, CA 94965
Phone: (415)332-8200
Subjects: Energy, energy management, renewable energy technologies. ***Special Collections:*** Energy products and services directories and materials; California State Office of Appropriate Technology's Collection (energy issues, technologies, research; 3000 items). ***Holdings:*** 400 books; 300 bound periodical volumes; 800 other cataloged items.

★7529★ Pacific Whale Foundation
Library
101 N. Kihei Rd.
Kihei, HI 96753
Phone: (808)879-8860
Fax: (808)879-2615
Contact: Dr. Paul Forestell, Dir., Res. & Educ.
Subjects: Marine mammals, human impacts on marine mammals. ***Special Collections:*** Color images of humpback whales and other marine mammals in Hawaii, Alaska, Australia, and Japan (10,000). ***Holdings:*** 300 books; 1500 journal articles.

★7530★ Pan American Health Organization
Pan American Center for Sanitary Engineering & Environmental Sciences
REPIDISCA Network
Los Pinos 259
Urbanizacion Camacho
Lima 12, Peru
Phone: 14 354135
Telex: 21052
Contact: Marta Bryce, REPIDISCA Coord.
Subjects: Sanitation, water supply, sanitary and environmental engineering. ***Holdings:*** 30,000 volumes; documents.

★7531★ Passaic River Coalition
Environmental Library
246 Madisonville Rd.
Basking Ridge, NJ 07920
Phone: (201)766-7550
Fax: (201)766-7550
Contact: Alfred J. Porro, Jr., Chm.
Subjects: Environmental quality in the Passaic River Watershed, urban river systems, water pollution, water quality and supply, flood control, sewage and garbage disposal, urban decay, land use, wildlife and vegetation, historic preservation, solid waste, environmental education. ***Holdings:*** 8000 volumes; special interest collections.

★7532★ Paul Scherrer Institute
Library
CH-5232 Villigen PSI, Switzerland
Phone: 56 99 26 27
Fax: 56 98 23 27
Telex: 82 74 17 psi ch
Contact: Dr. S. Huwyler, Libn.
Subjects: Nuclear energy, nuclear reactors, allied sciences. ***Holdings:*** 30,000 books; 100,000 reports.

★7533★ PEI Associates, Inc.
Technical Library
11499 Chester Rd.
Cincinnati, OH 45246
Phone: (513)782-4700
Fax: (513)782-4807
Contact: Penny Fraley, Tech.Libn.
Subjects: Environment; engineering - environmental, civil, mechanical; industrial hygiene; chemistry; air and water pollution; water treatment and hazardous waste. ***Holdings:*** 1500 books; 900 EPA reports and 25,000 government/contractor reports on microfiche; 1500 U.S. Government reports.

★7534★ Peninsula Conservation Foundation
Library of the Environment
2448 Watson Ct.
Palo Alto, CA 94303
Phone: (415)494-9301
Contact: Connie S. Sutton, Libn.
Subjects: Conservation, ecology, energy, wildlife and endangered species, backpacking and trails, pollution control. ***Special Collections:*** Environmental Volunteers Collection; Audubon Collection (250); Conservation Collection (2000); Trails Collection (300 books; 4 VF drawers). ***Holdings:*** 6000 books; 636 bound periodical volumes; 50 VF drawers; 2000 maps.

★7535★ Pennsylvania (State) Department of Environmental Resources
Environmental Protection Technical Reference Library
Fulton Bldg., Basement
Box 2063
Harrisburg, PA 17105-2063
Phone: (717)787-9647
Fax: (717)783-9186
Contact: Julie K. Weaver, Lib.Techn.
Subjects: Water quality, sewerage, industrial waste, mining and reclamation, air quality, surface mines, solid waste, radiation protection, community environmental control. ***Special Collections:*** Pennsylvania State University Special Research Report on Coal (90 volumes); U.S. and Pennsylvania Geological Surveys (700 items); IARC monographs. ***Holdings:*** 2400 books; 600 bound periodical volumes; Pennsylvania phone book collection; vertical files containing material on 200 environmental subjects.

★7536★ Pennsylvania State University
Environmental Resources Research Institute
Library
Land & Water Research Bldg.
University Park, PA 16802
Phone: (814)863-1386
Fax: (814)863-1696
Contact: Eva Brownawell, Info.Spec.
Subjects: Air pollution - monitoring, control, effects; environmental health; acid precipitation; water quality and conservation; hazardous waste; land reclamation; remote sensing. ***Special Collections:*** Water Center Reports (listed by state); ERRI reports; air environment reprint collection; historic Bay Area microfilm collection (air quality). ***Holdings:*** 1500 books; 55,000 reprints and microfiche; 15,000 technical reports, pamphlets, maps.

★7537★ (Philadelphia City) Water Department
Library
ARA Tower, 3rd Fl.
1101 Market St.
Philadelphia, PA 19107
Phone: (215)592-6232
Fax: (215)592-6154
Contact: Raymond F. Roedell, Jr., Libn. II
Subjects: Water - all aspects; civil engineering; public utility management; hazardous waste; water pollution; sludge/wastewater. ***Holdings:*** 3000 books; bound periodical volumes; documents; AV programs; nonbook items.

★7538★ Pittsburgh Zoo
Pittsburgh Aqua Zoo Library
Highland Park
Box 5250
Pittsburgh, PA 15206
Phone: (412)665-3768
Fax: (412)665-3661
Contact: Randolph Goodlett, Cur.
Subjects: Freshwater fish, marine biology, freshwater dolphins, microcosm exhibits, freshwater and marine plankton. ***Special Collections:*** Papers published on the Amazon River Dolphins; papers published on the new "microcosm" exhibits designed by Smithsonian Institution; papers on Ciquatera Poisoning in fish. ***Holdings:*** 1000 books; 15 bound periodical volumes; 2500 research papers.

★7539★ Planetary Association for Clean Energy, Inc. (PACE)
Clean Energy Centre
PO Box 1633, Sta. B
Hull, Quebec, Canada J8X 3Y5
Phone: (819)777-9696
Contact: Andrew Michrowski, Pres.
Subjects: Biological effects of electromagnetic radiation, clean energy systems, emerging energy sciences, food irradiation; biomass energy; problems associated with video display systems. ***Special Collections:*** Nikola Tesla Collection; T. Henry Moray Collection. ***Holdings:*** 10,000 books; 500 bound periodical volumes; emerging energy science and technology manuscripts.

★7540★ Plymouth Marine Laboratory and Marine Biological Association of the United Kingdom
Library and Information Services
Citadel Hill
Plymouth PL1 2PB, England
Phone: 752 222772
Fax: 752 226865
Contact: Allen Varley, Hd.
Subjects: Marine biology, pollution, and chemistry; oceanography; fisheries; marine and estuarine ecology. ***Special Collections:*** Marine pollution (50,000 documents). ***Holdings:*** 15,000 books; 50,000 bound periodical volumes; 60,000 pamphlets and reprints.

★7541★ Portland General Electric
Corporate Library
121 S.W. Salmon St. 3WTC-5
Portland, OR 97204
Phone: (503)464-8700
Fax: (503)464-8706
Contact: Robert F. Weber, Supv., Lib.Serv.
Subjects: Electrical engineering, management, alternative energy sources, environmental sciences. ***Holdings:*** 16,000 books; 48,000 technical reports, hardcopy and microfiche; 1500 standards.

★7542★ Proctor & Redfern, Consulting Engineers
Library
45 Green Belt Dr.
Don Mills, Ontario, Canada M3C 3K3
Phone: (416)445-3600
Contact: Catherine Spark, Hd.Libn.
Subjects: Civil and environmental engineering, urban and regional planning, hydrology, transportation, waste management. ***Holdings:*** 18,000 books; 600 bound periodical volumes.

★7543★ Public Citizen
Congress Watch Library
215 Pennsylvania Ave., S.E.
Washington, DC 20003
Phone: (202)546-4996
Fax: (202)547-7392
Subjects: Congressional, consumer, and environmental issues. ***Special Collections:*** Complete collection of Public Citizen reports, studies, voting indices; publications of other Ralph Nader groups (books; reports; articles). ***Holdings:*** 3000 books; 200 bound periodical volumes; congressional hearings and reports.

★7544★ Public Citizen
Critical Mass Energy Project
Library
215 Pennsylvania Ave., S.E.
Washington, DC 20003
Phone: (202)546-4996
Fax: (202)547-7392
Contact: Ken Bossong, Dir.
Subjects: Nuclear power, least-cost energy planning, energy conservation, global warming, solar energy. ***Special Collections:*** Collection of antinuclear materials (5Q0 books). ***Holdings:*** 2000 books.

★7545★ Puerto Rico Department of Natural Resources
Library
Munoz Rivera Ave., Stop 3
Box 5887
San Juan, PR 00906
Phone: (809)724-8774
Contact: Jaime Maldonado Villafane, Libn.
Subjects: Natural resources. ***Special Collections:*** Encyclopedic Compendium of Natural Resources. ***Holdings:*** 7000 books.

★7546★ Quebec Province Ministere de l'Energie et des Ressources
Bureau de l'Efficacite Energetique
Centre de Documentation
425 Viger Ave., W.
Bureau 600
Montreal, Quebec, Canada H2Z 1W9
Phone: (514)873-5463
Fax: (514)873-6946
Contact: Ginette Comtois, Libn.
Subjects: Energy conservation in industry, commerce, housing, urban planning, transportation. ***Special Collections:*** Provincial and federal publications on energy conservation. ***Holdings:*** 5000 books; slide sets; video cassettes.

★7547★ Quebec Province Ministere de l'Energie et des Ressources
Centre de Documentation
Edifice de l'Atrium
5700 4th Ave. W., L.B-200
Charlesbourg, Quebec, Canada G1H 6R1
Phone: (418)643-4624
Fax: (418)644-3814
Contact: Reine Tremblay, MBSI
Subjects: Forests and forestry, forest economics, mines and mining, geology, mineral chemistry, energy, surveying, geodesy, pollution, metallurgy, law, conservation, entomology. ***Special Collections:*** U.S. Bureau of Mines; USDA; CGC; departmental records. ***Holdings:*** 80,000 books; 40,000 bound periodical volumes; 350 patents; 1600 reels of microfilm; 1250 microfiche.

★7548★ Quebec Province Ministere de l'Environnement
Library
3900, rue Marly
Ste. Foy, Quebec, Canada G1X 4E4
Phone: (418)643-5363
Fax: (418)643-3358
Contact: Gerard Nobrega, Chf.Libn.
Subjects: Pollution control, acid rain, Quebec environmental issues. ***Holdings:*** 30,000 books; 10,000 bound periodical volumes; 10,000 maps; 6000 government documents.

★7549★ Quebec Province Ministere du Loisir, de la Chasse et de la Peche
Bibliotheque
150 est, blvd. St-Cyrille, Main Fl.
Quebec, Quebec, Canada G1R 4Y1
Phone: (418)643-5300
Fax: (418)643-3330
Contact: Madeleine Savard, Hd.Libn.
Subjects: Wildlife management, conservation, ecology, zoology, ornithology, fish culture, game, hunting, sport fishing, recreation. ***Holdings:*** 20,000 books; 1500 bound periodical volumes; 44 VF drawers of reprints and pamphlets; 6000 research reports and manuscripts.

★7550★ Quebec Province Ministere du Loisir, de la Chasse et de la Peche
Bibliotheque
6255 13th Ave.
Montreal, Quebec, Canada H1X 3E6
Phone: (514)374-5840
Contact: Richard Mathieu, Chf.Libn.
Subjects: Aquatic fauna, limnology, mammology, ecology, North American birds, environmental pollution. ***Special Collections:*** 16th-18th century natural history; 17th-19th century works of French, American, English naturalists. ***Holdings:*** 8500 books; 160,000 periodical volumes; 3000 reprints.

★7551★ Rachel Carson Council, Inc.
Library
8940 Jones Mill Rd.
Chevy Chase, MD 20815
Phone: (301)652-1877
Contact: Shirley A. Briggs, Exec.Dir.
Subjects: Pesticides, toxic substances, government regulation, pest management programs. ***Special Collections:*** Government regulatory documents; Rachel Carson's personal library; pesticide toxicology collection. ***Holdings:*** 2000 books; 1500 documents and unbound reports; 50 drawers of specialized files; Environmental Protection Agency Pesticide Product Information and Registry of Toxic Effects of Chemical Substances materials on microfiche.

★7552★ Radian Corporation
Library
8501 MoPac Blvd.
Box 201088
Austin, TX 78720
Phone: (512)454-4797
Fax: (512)454-8807
Contact: Barbara J. Maxey, Mgr., Lib.Serv.
Subjects: Coal conversion processes, air and water pollution control, petroleum refining emissions, ambient air monitoring, artificial intelligence. ***Special Collections:*** Gasification and liquefaction (20,000 items); sulphur dioxide control (3250 items). ***Holdings:*** 1950 volumes; 2500 microforms; 21,000 articles, patents, maps; 21,000 technical reports.

★7553★ Rainforest Action Network
Library
301 Broadway, Ste. A
San Francisco, CA 94108
Phone: (415)398-4404
Fax: (415)398-2732
Telex: 15127-6475
Contact: Suzanne Head, Info.Off.
Subjects: Tropical rain forests, indigenous people. ***Holdings:*** VF drawers.

★7554★ Redwood Community Action Agency
Energy Demonstration Center
Appropriate Technology Library
539 T St.
Eureka, CA 95501
Phone: (707)444-3831
Contact: Lorna Montoya, Sec.
Subjects: Passive solar energy, energy conservation, weatherization, solar retrofits, wind energy, wood stoves. ***Holdings:*** 1000 books; 18 bound periodical volumes; 2 shelves of energy policy and planning documents; 2 shelves of California Energy Commission reports; 1 shelf of energy curriculum; 3 VF drawers of general information files; 1 VF drawer of organization and agency files.

★7555★ Renewable Energy Information Center
3201 Corte Malpaso
Unit 304
Camarillo, CA 93012
Phone: (805)388-3097
Contact: Alan A. Tratner, Dir.
Subjects: Renewable energy and geothermal energy research and development. ***Special Collections:*** Renewable Energy News Digest (complete set); Geothermal World Directory, 1972-1986. ***Holdings:*** 500 volumes; Geothermal Energy Monthly Journal, 1973-1986, on microfiche; maps; slides.

★7556★ Reptile Breeding Foundation
Library
R.R. 3, Box 1450
Picton, Ontario, Canada K0K 2T0
Phone: (613)476-3351
Contact: Thomas A. Huff, Dir.
Subjects: Herpetology, reptiles, amphibians, wildlife conservation, zoology, zoos. ***Holdings:*** 2500 books; 300 bound periodical volumes; 5000 reprints; 50 microfiche; 8 VF drawers of clippings, reports, regional surveys.

★7557★ Research Planning, Inc.
Library
1200 Park St.
PO Box 328
Columbia, SC 29201
Phone: (803)256-7322
Fax: (803)254-6445
Subjects: Environment and natural resource problems, coastal dynamics, aquaculture, biology, geochemistry, geology, hydrogeology, energy development, oil spills, hazardous materials, environmental mapping. ***Special Collections:*** Map collection. ***Holdings:*** 25,000 items.

★7558★ Resources for the Future
Library
1616 P St., N.W.
Washington, DC 20036
Phone: (202)328-5089
Fax: (202)265-8069
Contact: Chris Clotworthy, Libn.
Subjects: Economics, energy, natural resources, environment, agriculture. ***Special Collections:*** Complete RFF publications collection. ***Holdings:*** 6500 books; 350 periodical titles.

★7559★ Rhode Island (State) Governor's Office of Housing & Energy
Library
275 Westminster Mall
Providence, RI 02903-3393
Phone: (401)277-3370
Fax: (401)277-1260
Contact: Julie Capabianco
Subjects: Energy conservation, oil, gas, renewables. ***Special Collections:*** Appropriate technology. ***Holdings:*** 2000 books.

★7560★ Riso National Laboratory
Riso Library
PO Box 49
DK-4000 Roskilde, Denmark
Phone: 2 371212
Fax: 46 75 56 27
Telex: 43 116
Contact: Birgit Pedersen, Chf.Libn.
Subjects: Energy - biomass, coal, wind, geothermal, nuclear, solar; oil, uranium, and other energy sources; air pollution and environmental issues; heating and power generation; reactors and thermal plants; waste heat utilization. ***Holdings:*** 60,000 volumes; 500,000 reports.

★7561★ RMT, Inc.
Library
744 Heartland Trail
PO Box 8923
Madison, WI 53708-8923
Phone: (608)831-4444
Fax: (608)831-3334
Contact: Kathy Horton, Libn.
Subjects: Solid and hazardous waste management, environmental engineering, industrial hygiene, regulatory compliance, hydrogeology, consulting engineering.

★7562★ Roaring Fork Energy Center
Library
242 Main St.
Carbondale, CO 81623
Phone: (303)963-0311
Contact: Steve Standiford, Dir.
Subjects: Solar energy, alternative energy, solar greenhouses, energy planning and conservation, renewable resources, wind and water power. ***Holdings:*** 1200 books; films; videotapes; slides; computer software programs.

★7563★ Royal Observatory, Hong Kong
Library
134A Nathan Rd.
Kowloon, Hong Kong
Phone: 3-7329200
Fax: 3-7215034
Telex: 54777GEOPH HX
Contact: Patrick P. Sham, Dir.
Subjects: Weather forecasting, tropical cyclones, climatology, tropical meteorology, hydrology, seismology, astronomy, time standards, air pollution, oceanography, disaster prevention, gravimetric surveys, metrication, metrology. ***Holdings:*** 31,800 volumes.

★7564★ Rutgers University, the State University of New Jersey
Center for Plastics Recycling Research
Busch Campus, Bldg. 3529
Piscataway, NJ 08855
Phone: (908)932-4402
Fax: (908)932-5636
Contact: Jack Wenzel, Dir.
Subjects: Plastics recycling. ***Holdings:*** Periodicals; monographs; pamphlets; government publications.

★7565★ R.V. Anderson Associates Limited
Library
1210 Sheppard Ave., E., Ste. 401
Willowdale, Ontario, Canada M2K 1E3
Phone: (416)497-8600
Fax: (416)497-0342
Contact: Linda Diener, Libn.
Subjects: Pollution control, water supply and resources, tunnels and shafts, environmental planning, transportation, urban development. ***Holdings:*** 2004 volumes; company reports and proposals; provincial, federal, U.S. government documents.

★7566★ St. Johns River Water Management District
Library
Hwy. 100, W.
Box 1429
Palatka, FL 32178-1429
Phone: (904)329-4132
Fax: (904)329-4508
Contact: Judith G. Hunter, Libn.
Subjects: Hydrology, water management, engineering, ecology, botany, geology. ***Holdings:*** 11,000 books.

★7567★ Saskatchewan Department of Environment and Public Safety
Library
Walter Scott Bldg.
3085 Albert St.
Regina, Saskatchewan, Canada S4S 0B1
Phone: (306)787-6114
Fax: (306)787-0197
Contact: Janice Szuch, Lib.Supv.
Subjects: Water pollution, air pollution, environmental protection and policy, impact assessments, hazardous wastes. ***Holdings:*** 1000 books; 25 bound periodical volumes; 5300 reports; 8 VF drawers of pamphlets; 32 shelves of unbound periodicals.

★7568★ Saskatchewan Research Council
Information Centre
15 Innovation Blvd.
Saskatoon, Saskatchewan, Canada S7N 2X8
Phone: (306)933-5490
Fax: (306)933-7446
Telex: SARECO 074-2484
Contact: Margaret Samms, Mgr.
Subjects: Geology and engineering resources; analytical chemistry; environmental studies - land, water, air; small business assistance and technology transfer. ***Holdings:*** 6,000 books; 25,000 government publications and technical reports.

★7569★ Schuylkill Center for Environmental Education
Library
8480 Hagy's Mill Rd.
Philadelphia, PA 19128-9975
Phone: (215)482-7300
Fax: (215)482-8158
Contact: Karin James, Libn.
Subjects: Natural history, zoology, ornithology, botany, ecology, geology/mineralogy, environmental concerns, astronomy, weather, gardening. ***Special Collections:*** Rare books on the natural sciences (150 volumes); environmental science teaching resource center (3000 books). ***Holdings:*** 6500 books; 8 VF drawers of clippings and leaflets; 3 VF drawers of nature center brochures; 3 VF drawers of descriptive material of environmental organizations and newsletters; environmental science software.

★7570★ Science Trends
Library
National Press Bldg., Ste. 1079
Washington, DC 20045
Phone: (202)393-0031
Fax: (202)393-1732
Contact: Arthur Kranish, Hd.
Subjects: Government sponsored research and development, science, energy, environment.

★7571★ Sea World, Inc.
Education Department Library
1720 S. Shores Rd.
San Diego, CA 92109
Phone: (619)222-6363
Contact: Joy Wolf, Dir., Educ.Dept.
Subjects: Marine biology. ***Holdings:*** 2000 books; 1000 periodicals, scientific and government reports.

★7572★ (Seattle) Metro Library
821 Second Ave.
Seattle, WA 98104
Phone: (206)684-1132
Fax: (206)684-1533
Contact: Anne McBride, Libn.
Subjects: Public transportation, wastewater treatment, water quality, toxicants. ***Holdings:*** 10,000 books and documents.

★7573★ Sierra Club
William E. Colby Memorial Library
730 Polk St.
San Francisco, CA 94109
Phone: (415)776-2211
Fax: (415)776-0350
Contact: M.L. Phoebe Adams, Hd.Libn.
Subjects: Environmental policy, conservation, energy policy, mountaineering, natural history, Sierra Nevada. ***Special Collections:*** Foreign mountaineering journals (800 bound volumes); selected Sierra Club archives and memorabilia (500 items). ***Holdings:*** 10,500 books; 1450 bound periodical volumes; 10,000 indexed documents and reports; 20,000 photographs and slides.

★7574★ SJO Consulting Engineers Inc.
Engineering Library
1500 S.W. 12th Ave.
Portland, OR 97201
Phone: (503)226-3921
Subjects: Engineering - mechanical, structural, civil, electrical, environmental. ***Special Collections:*** Environmental Protection Agency materials on air/noise pollution control. ***Holdings:*** 810 volumes; 50 reports; 8 VF drawers of vendors' brochures.

★7575★ Smithsonian Institution Libraries
National Zoological Park
Library
3000 Block of Connecticut Ave., N.W.
Washington, DC 20008
Phone: (202)673-4771
Contact: Kay A. Kenyon, Chf.Libn.
Subjects: Animal behavior, animal husbandry, wildlife conservation, animal nutrition, veterinary medicine, horticulture. ***Special Collections:*** Zoo publications. ***Holdings:*** 4000 volumes.

★7576★ Smithsonian Institution Libraries
Smithsonian Environmental Research Center Library
Box 28
Edgewater, MD 21037
Phone: (301)261-4190
Fax: (301)261-7954
Contact: Angela N. Haggins, Chf.Libn.
Subjects: Environment, ecology, estuarine research, marine ecology, aquatic microbiology. ***Holdings:*** 2600 books; 2800 bound periodical volumes.

★7577★ Soil and Water Conservation Society
H. Wayne Pritchard Library
7515 N.E. Ankeny Rd.
Ankeny, IA 50021-9764
Phone: (515)289-2331
Contact: James L. Sanders, Mng.Ed.
Subjects: Soil and water conservation, land use planning, natural resources management. ***Special Collections:*** Papers of leaders in soil and water conservation. ***Holdings:*** 2500 books.

★7578★ Solar Energy Research Institute
SERI Technical Library
1617 Cole Blvd.
Golden, CO 80401
Phone: (303)231-1415
Fax: (303)231-1422
Contact: Joe F. Chervenak, Mgr.
Subjects: Renewable energy - solar, wind, ocean, biomass, photovoltaics; energy conservation; biotechnology; solid state physics. ***Holdings:*** 20,000 books; 50,000 bound periodical volumes; 30,000 technical reports; 10,000 patents; 500,000 reports on microfiche.

★7579★ South Carolina (State) Wildlife and Marine Resources Division
Library
Box 12559
Charleston, SC 29412
Phone: (803)762-5026
Fax: (803)762-5001
Contact: Helen Ivy, Libn.
Subjects: Marine biology and ecology; fisheries; aquaculture; marine resources management. ***Holdings:*** 18,000 books; 7660 bound periodical volumes; 25,640 reprints; 48 reels of microfilm; 800 microfiche.

★7580★ Southern States Energy Board (SSEB)
Southern Energy/Environmental Information Center (SEEIC)
3091 Governors Lakes Dr., Ste. 400
Norcross, GA 30071-1113
Phone: (404)242-7712
Fax: (404)242-0421
Contact: Ricky S. Gibson, Mgr., Info.Serv.
Subjects: Energy, environment, energy policy and development. ***Holdings:*** 120 books; 5300 technical reports; 750 state publications; 23 VF drawers.

★7581★ Southwest Research & Information Center
Box 4524
Albuquerque, NM 87106
Phone: (505)262-1862
Contact: Don Hancock, Info.Coord.
Subjects: Environmental, consumer, and social issues. ***Special Collections:*** Uranium publications and clippings (3000 items); nuclear waste management publications and clippings. ***Holdings:*** 3000 books; 7 cabinets of clippings in 1000 categories; 100 sourcebooks.

★7582★ Spill Control Association of America
Library
400 Renaissance Center, Ste. 1900
Detroit, MI 48243-1075
Phone: (313)567-0500
Fax: (313)259-8943
Contact: Marc K. Shaye, Gen. Counsel
Subjects: Federal and state water laws, current proposed legislation, equipment and contractor listings, government agencies, oil and hazardous substances spill statistics, industry history. ***Special Collections:*** Current abstracts of technical documents relating to oil and hazardous substances spill control and containment research and techniques employed in the United States, Canada, and around the world. ***Holdings:*** Books; SCAA Newsletters.

★7583★ Stanley Associates Engineering, Ltd.
Library
10160 112th St.
Edmonton, Alberta, Canada T5K 2L6
Phone: (403)423-4777
Fax: (403)421-4300
Contact: Donna Meen, Libn.
Subjects: Pollution control, transportation, environmental and municipal engineering, land development, water supply and distribution, urban and regional planning, structural engineering. ***Holdings:*** 10,000 books; 300 bound periodical volumes; 12,000 internal reports and proposals; 30,000 engineering drawings on microfilm; 6000 original drawings; 1000 topographic maps.

★7584★ Staten Island Institute of Arts and Sciences
William T. Davis Education Center
75 Stuyvesant Pl.
Staten Island, NY 10301
Phone: (718)987-6233
Fax: (718)273-5683
Contact: John-Paul Richiuso, Archv.
Subjects: Environmental education, mammalogy, salt and fresh water ecology, ornithology, botany, dendrology, geology, ichthyology, zoology, astronomy, energy, photography. ***Holdings:*** 2758 books; 4 boxes of Cornell Science leaflets; 2 boxes of Department of Agriculture leaflets; 2 boxes of Botanic Gardens pamphlets; 12 phonograph records of bird songs; filmstrips; AV programs; Outdoor Biology Instructional Strategies (OBIS) materials.

★7585★ SUNY
College of Environmental Science & Forestry
F. Franklin Moon Library and Learning Resources Center
Syracuse, NY 13210
Phone: (315)470-6716
Fax: (315)470-6512
Contact: Donald F. Webster, Dir.
Subjects: Environmental studies, landscape architecture, forests and forestry, environment, botany, zoology, polymer and cellulose chemistry, paper science, wildlife management, entomology, wood products engineering, soil science, plant pathology, economics, biochemistry, management, water resources, chemical ecology, forest chemistry, environmental design, photography. ***Holdings:*** 35,367 books; 32,770 bound periodical volumes; 4673 bound theses; 116,830 microforms.

★7586★ Systems Applications International
Library
101 Lucas Valley Rd.
San Rafael, CA 94903
Phone: (415)507-7100
Fax: (415)507-7177
Contact: Janet McDonald, Libn./Info.Spec.
Subjects: Air quality, meteorology, computer modeling. ***Holdings:*** 2000 books; 8000 technical reports.

★7587★ Tennessee Valley Authority
National Fertilizer and Environmental Research Center
Library
Muscle Shoals, AL 35660
Phone: (205)386-3071
Fax: (205)386-2453
Telex: 797658

Contact: Shirley G. Nichols, Lib.Mgr.
Subjects: Agriculture, biomass energy, chemistry, chemical engineering, fertilizer, agricultural economics, environmental sciences, waste management. *Special Collections:* Fertilizer in the United States; history of fertilizer and agriculture. *Holdings:* 27,160 volumes; 2060 reels of microfilm; 400 VF drawers of pamphlets and documents.

★7588★ Teton Science School
Natural History Library
Box 68
Kelly, WY 83011
Phone: (307)733-4765
Contact: Brad Stelfox, Res.Dir.
Subjects: Natural history, ecology, man and nature, zoology, botany, earth science. *Special Collections:* Greater Yellowstone ecosystem (articles; studies; papers). *Holdings:* 2500 books; 2000 other cataloged items.

★7589★ Texas State Air Control Board
Library
6330 Hwy. 290, E.
Austin, TX 78723
Phone: (512)451-5711
Fax: (512)371-0245
Contact: Kerry Williams, Libn.
Subjects: Air pollution, engineering, chemistry, physics, meteorology, law. *Special Collections:* Microfiche of technical subjects pertaining to air pollution (50,000). *Holdings:* 9000 books; 18 bound periodical volumes; 700 reprints.

★7590★ Texas (State) Parks & Wildlife Department
Library
4200 Smith School Rd.
Austin, TX 78744
Phone: (512)389-4960
Contact: Debra E. Bunch, Libn.
Subjects: Natural resources, wildlife and fishery management, recreation, parks and historic sites, game laws of Texas. *Special Collections:* Complete sets of Pittman-Robertson Federal Aid in Wildlife Restoration and Dingell-Johnson Federal Aid in Fish Restoration Acts, both for Texas, 1939 to present. *Holdings:* 14,000 books.

★7591★ Texas (State) Water Commission
Library
Stephen F. Austin Bldg., Rm. 510
Capitol Sta., Box 13087
Austin, TX 78711-3087
Phone: (512)463-7834
Fax: (512)463-8317
Contact: Sylvia Von Fange, Hd.Libn.
Subjects: Water resources. *Special Collections:* Publications of the commission and its predecessor agencies. *Holdings:* 55,000 books; 1700 bound periodical volumes; 8000 U.S. Geological Survey publications; 294 periodicals in microform; 2700 volumes of U.S. Environmental Protection Agency materials; 600 volumes of environmental impact statements; 3100 volumes of U.S. Army Corps of Engineers materials.

★7592★ TMA/ARLI
Library
160 Taylor St.
Monrovia, CA 91016
Phone: (818)357-3247
Fax: (818)359-5036
Subjects: Chemistry; environmental analysis; radioactive, organic, and inorganic materials; contamination and industrial hygiene. *Holdings:* 1000 volumes.

★7593★ TreePeople
Environmental Resources Library
12601 Mulholland Dr.
Beverly Hills, CA 90210
Phone: (818)753-4600
Subjects: Forestry, air pollution, tropical rainforests, environmental issues.

★7594★ Tribble & Richardson, Inc.
Library
PO Box 13147
Macon, GA 31208-3147
Phone: (912)474-6100
Contact: Bonnie Watkins, Libn.
Subjects: Environmental protection; engineering - civil, environmental, structural; water quality.

★7595★ Tucson City Planning Department
Library
Box 27210
Tucson, AZ 85726
Phone: (602)791-4234
Fax: (602)791-4130
Contact: Anna S. Sanchez, Plan.Libn.
Subjects: Land use and development, planning, zoning, energy, environmental protection, economic development. *Special Collections:* City of Tucson planning reports, 1930 to present; local census reports, 1940 to present; zoning codes. *Holdings:* 5000 books; 150 bound periodical volumes; 300 microfiche; 3 VF drawers; slides; tapes; maps.

★7596★ Tufts University
Richard H. Lufkin Library
Anderson Hall
Medford, MA 02155
Phone: (617)381-3245
Fax: (617)381-3002
Contact: Hope N. Tillman, Dir.
Subjects: Engineering - civil, mechanical, electrical; engineering design; water resources, sewage treatment, solid waste disposal; mathematics; physics; astronomy. *Holdings:* 23,000 books; 24,000 bound periodical volumes; 750 dissertations; 11,000 technical reports.

★7597★ Turner, Collie & Braden, Inc.
Library and Information Services
Box 130089
Houston, TX 77219
Phone: (713)780-4100
Contact: Suzette Broussard, Libn.
Subjects: Hydraulic and sanitary engineering, water resources in Texas, transportation. *Special Collections:* Environmental Pollution and Control (2000 NTIS microfiche). *Holdings:* 10,000 books; 1500 bound periodical volumes; 2000 company reports.

★7598★ Unexpected Wildlife Refuge
Library
Unexpected Rd.
Box 765
Newfield, NJ 08344
Phone: (609)697-3541
Contact: Hope Sawyer Buyukmihci, Sec.
Subjects: Humane education, beavers, wildlife. *Special Collections:* Works of Grey Owl, Canadian naturalist.

★7599★ United McGill Corporation
Library
2400 Fairwood Ave.
PO Box 820
Columbus, OH 43216
Phone: (614)443-0192
Subjects: Acoustics, airflow technology, air pollution, commercial and industrial applications of noise control systems. *Holdings:* 5000 volumes.

★7600★ United Nations Environment Programme
Library and Documentation Centre
PO Box 30522
Nairobi, Kenya
Phone: 2542 520600
Fax: 2542 520711
Contact: Kevin L. Grose, Chf.
Subjects: Environment. *Holdings:* 15,000 books; 10,000 bound periodical volumes; 1.5 million documents; 150,000 nonbook items.

★7601★ U.S. Agency for International Development
Water & Sanitation for Health Project
Information Center
1611 N. Kent St., Rm. 1002
Arlington, VA 22209
Phone: (703)243-8200
Fax: (703)525-9137
Telex: WU1 64552
Contact: Dan B. Campbell, Libn.
Subjects: Water supply, sanitation, environmental health, technology transfer. *Special Collections:* Rainwater catchments; guineaworm control; women in development. *Holdings:* 7000 reports and texts focusing on rural and peri-urban areas in developing countries; reports on 66 least-developed countries.

★7602★ U.S. Air Force
Air Force Engineering and Services Center
Technical Information Center
Bldg. 1120, Stop 21
FL 7050
Tyndall AFB, FL 32403-6001
Phone: (904)283-6285
Fax: (904)283-6499
Contact: Andrew D. Poulis, Chf.Tech.Info.Ctr.Br.
Subjects: Engineering - civil, environmental, mechanical, electrical, chemical; readiness; fire research; cost analysis. *Special Collections:* Rapid runway repair; geotechnical centrifuges; bird air strike hazards; sonic boom research; hazardous wastes minimization; privatization. *Holdings:* 6800 books; 30,000 hardcopy technical reports; 120,000 technical reports on microfiche; 150,000 military and commercial specifications and standards on microfilm; 3000 slides; 500 technical videotapes.

★7603★ U.S. Army
Corps of Engineers
Detroit District - Technical and Legal Library
Box 1027
Detroit, MI 48231-1027
Phone: (313)226-6231
Fax: (313)226-2056
Contact: Mary A. Auer, District Libn.
Subjects: Engineering, environment, construction, water resources development, Great Lakes navigation, harbor structures, environmental and flood control. *Special Collections:* Detroit district technical reports and studies; district projects slide collection. *Holdings:* 3500 books; 5000 annual reports; government documents; climatological data.

★7604★ U.S. Army
Corps of Engineers
Fort Worth District - Technical Library
819 Taylor St.
Box 17300
Fort Worth, TX 76102-0300
Phone: (817)334-4820
Subjects: Law; engineering - civil, electrical, mechanical, safety; finance; nuclear science;

ecology; environment. ***Special Collections:*** Air and water pollution; water resources development. ***Holdings:*** 15,000 books; 20,000 technical reports; army regulations; congressional documents; industry standards and specifications on microfiche; Federal Register, 1969 to present.

★7605★ U.S. Army
Corps of Engineers
Galveston District - Library
Box 1229
Galveston, TX 77553
Phone: (409)766-3196
Fax: (409)766-3905
Contact: Elizabeth Lloyd
Subjects: Civil engineering, construction and operation of public works for navigation, flood control, environment, recreation, water resources, soil mechanics, law. ***Special Collections:*** Annual Reports of the Chief of Engineers, 1871 to present; Congressional documents, 1900-1978. ***Holdings:*** 8500 books; 2900 other cataloged items.

★7606★ U.S. Army
Corps of Engineers
Humphrey's Engineering Center - Technical Support Library
Kingman Bldg., Rm. 3C02
Fort Belvoir, VA 22060-5580
Phone: (703)355-2387
Fax: (703)355-2005
Contact: Lois J. Carey, Chf., Lib.Br.
Subjects: Water resources, hydraulics, civil engineering, beach erosion, rivers and harbours, navigation, computer science, management. ***Special Collections:*** Beach erosion board reports. ***Holdings:*** 20,000 books; technical reports; microforms; AV materials.

★7607★ U.S. Army
Corps of Engineers
Huntington District - Library
502 8th St.
Huntington, WV 25701-2070
Phone: (304)529-5713
Contact: Sandra V. Morris, Libn.
Subjects: Water resource development, environmental science, civil engineering, hydrology, water quality. ***Special Collections:*** Oral history collection (150 hours). ***Holdings:*** 11,800 books; 260 bound periodical volumes.

★7608★ U.S. Army
Corps of Engineers
Jacksonville District - Technical Library - CESAJ-IM-SL
400 W. Bay St., Rm. 899
PO Box 4970
Jacksonville, FL 32232-0019
Phone: (904)791-3643
Fax: (904)791-2256
Contact: Oriana Brown West, District Libn.
Subjects: Civil engineering, environmental resources, fish and wildlife, geology, coastal erosion, storms and hurricanes. ***Special Collections:*** Cross Florida Barge Canal; Central and Southern Florida Project for Flood Control and Other Purposes. ***Holdings:*** 5000 books; 10,000 reports; Congressional documents, 1940-1970.

★7609★ U.S. Army
Corps of Engineers
Los Angeles District - Technical Library
Box 2711
Los Angeles, CA 90053-2325
Phone: (213)894-5313
Contact: Connie Castillo, Libn. (Engr.)
Subjects: Engineering, water resources, flood control, shoreline preservation, navigation, environmental studies, dams, earthquakes. ***Special Collections:*** U.S. Army Corps of Engineers histories. ***Holdings:*** 8000 books; 2000 technical reports; Congressional materials on Rivers and Harbors Act.

★7610★ U.S. Army
Corps of Engineers
Memphis District - Library
B-202 Clifford Davis Federal Bldg.
Memphis, TN 38103-1894
Phone: (901)544-3584
Fax: (901)544-3600
Contact: Carolyn Smith, Libn.
Subjects: Civil engineering, flood control, water resources, environment, computers and data processing. ***Special Collections:*** Lower Mississippi Valley. ***Holdings:*** 7500 books; 60 bound periodical volumes; 132 microforms.

★7611★ U.S. Army
Corps of Engineers
Rock Island District - Technical Library
Clock Tower Bldg.
Box 2004
Rock Island, IL 61204-2004
Phone: (309)788-6361
Fax: (309)788-6256, ext
Contact: Nancy J. Larson-Bloomer, Libn. (Engr.)
Subjects: Civil engineering, hydraulics/locks and dams, flood plain management, construction, soil mechanics, environmental analysis. ***Special Collections:*** Hydraulics; Waterways Experiment Station technical reports; Water Resources Developments; construction. ***Holdings:*** 10,000 books; 15,000 technical reports; 5000 microfiche.

★7612★ U.S. Army
Corps of Engineers
Sacramento District - Technical Information Center
650 Capitol Mall
Sacramento, CA 95814
Phone: (916)440-3404
Contact: Beatrice Alger, Dist.Libn.
Subjects: Water, hydrology, hydraulics, environment, recreation planning, geology, architecture, construction. ***Special Collections:*** Annual Reports to the Chief of Engineers. ***Holdings:*** 25,000 volumes.

★7613★ U.S. Army
Corps of Engineers
St. Louis District - CASU Library and Information Services
1222 Spruce St.
St. Louis, MO 63103-2822
Phone: (314)539-6110
Fax: (314)331-8677
Contact: Dr. Arthur R. Taylor, Chf.Libn.
Subjects: Civil engineering, water resources, environment, wildlife management, recreation. ***Holdings:*** 9200 books; 6000 technical reports; microfilm.

★7614★ U.S. Army - Corps of Engineers
St. Paul District
Map Files
1421 U. S. Post Office & Custom House
St. Paul, MN 55101-1479
Phone: (612)220-0560
Contact: Al Santo, Lib.Techn.
Subjects: Engineering, water resources, flood control, inland waterways, environmental planning. ***Special Collections:*** Mississippi River Continuous Survey, 1937 to present (83 sheets); Mississippi River Commission Charts, 1898 and 1915 (278 sheets); Brown Surveys of the Mississippi River, 1930 (129 sheets). ***Holdings:*** 70,000 engineering drawings; 10,000 maps and charts; 50,000 aerial photographs; 1000 field books.

★7615★ U.S. Army
Corps of Engineers
St. Paul District - Technical Library
1421 U. S. Post Office & Custom House
St. Paul, MN 55101
Phone: (612)220-0680
Fax: (612)290-2256
Contact: Jean Marie Schmidt, Libn.
Subjects: Engineering, hydrology, water resources, dam construction, environmental studies, military history. ***Special Collections:*** Chief of Engineers Annual Reports, 1867 to present; Army Technical Manuals; Waterborne Commerce Statistics. ***Holdings:*** 6073 books; 8164 government reports, including Waterway Experiment Station reports and U.S. Geological Survey reports.

★7616★ U.S. Army
Corps of Engineers
Seattle District - Library
Box C-3755
Seattle, WA 98124-2255
Phone: (206)764-3728
Fax: (206)764-3796
Contact: Pat J. Perry, District Libn.
Subjects: Engineering; environment; hydraulics; construction - heating plant, military, marine; toxic cleanup; law. ***Special Collections:*** Army Field Law Library (8000 volumes); Eng/Tech Collection; Learning Center (self-guided classes; 700 videotapes, audio cassettes, other AV programs; software tutors). ***Holdings:*** 12,000 books and reports; 30,000 technical reports on microfiche; 20,000 35mm slides; 5 drawers of pamphlets.

★7617★ U.S. Army
Engineer Waterways Experiment Station
Coastal Engineering Information Analysis Center
3909 Halls Ferry Rd.
Vicksburg, MS 39180-6199
Phone: (601)634-2012
Contact: Fred Camfield, Dir.
Subjects: Beach erosion, flood and storm protection, coastal and offshore structures, navigation structures. ***Holdings:*** Center acts as a central repository for the Corps of Engineers data collection under the field data collection program for coastal engineering. The data includes wave statistics, coastal currents, beach profiles, and aerial photographs. Center is supported by holdings in the Research Library.

★7618★ U.S. Army - Health Services Command
Environmental Hygiene Agency
Library
Bldg. E1570
Aberdeen Proving Ground, MD 21010
Phone: (301)671-4236
Contact: Krishan S. Goel, Libn.
Subjects: Occupational medicine, safety and health; chemistry and toxicology; audiology; medical entomology; laser, microwave, and radiological safety and health; air and water pollution; sanitary engineering. ***Special Collections:*** National Institute for Occupational Safety and Health (NIOSH) and Environmental Protection Agency (EPA) reports. ***Holdings:*** 12,000 books; 8,000 bound periodical volumes; 8400 R&D reports; 3000 microfiche.

★7619★ U.S. Army - Medical Research & Development Command
Biomedical Research & Development Laboratory
Technical Library
Fort Detrick, Bldg. 568
Frederick, MD 21702-5010
Phone: (301)663-2502
Contact: Al Reynolds, Libn.
Subjects: Biomedical engineering; pest management systems; entomology; environmental protection; air, land, and water pollution; solid waste and pesticide disposal; aquatic toxicology, occupational health. ***Holdings:*** 5500 books; 1500 bound periodical volumes; 6100 technical reprints, patents, reports; 1000 photographs; 2200 slides.

★7620★ U.S. Bureau of Land Management
Alaska State Office
Alaska Resources Library
222 W. 7th
No. 36
Anchorage, AK 99513
Phone: (907)271-5025
Contact: Martha L. Shepard, Dir.
Subjects: Alaska - resources, wildlife, land management, forestry/vegetation; Arctic environment; pipelines; outer continental shelf; hydrology; pollution; engineering and geology; archeology. ***Special Collections:*** Alaskan map collection of original overlays; microfiche library of CRREL bibliography. ***Holdings:*** 45,000 volumes; 7000 maps.

★7621★ U.S. Bureau of Land Management
California State Office
Library
2800 Cottage Way, Rm. E-2841
Sacramento, CA 95825
Phone: (916)978-4713
Contact: Louise Tichy, Mgt.Asst.
Subjects: Land resources, recreation, environmental statements, U.S. statutes, interior land decisions, wildlife management, forestry, range management. ***Holdings:*** 3500 books; unbound periodicals.

★7622★ U.S. Bureau of Land Management
Casper District Office
Library
1701 E. E St.
Casper, WY 82601
Phone: (307)261-7613
Contact: Sandy Lindahl
Subjects: Wildlife, fire, minerals, environmental impact statements, soil, hydrology.

★7623★ U.S. Bureau of Land Management
Eastern States Office
Library
350 S. Pickett St.
Alexandria, VA 22304
Contact: M. Willette Proctor, Mgt.Asst.
Subjects: Land management and environmental assessment. ***Holdings:*** 10,000 books; BLM manuals; public lands law books; U.S. Department of the Interior manuals.

★7624★ U.S. Bureau of Land Management
Library
Denver Federal Ctr., Bldg. 50
Box 25047
Denver, CO 80225-0047
Phone: (303)236-6648
Contact: Sandra Bowers, Hd.Libn.
Subjects: Public lands, forestry, range and wildlife management, geology, minerals, oil shale. ***Holdings:*** 30,000 volumes.

★7625★ U.S. Bureau of Land Management
Montana State Office Library
222 N. 32nd St.
Box 36800
Billings, MT 59107
Phone: (406)255-2759
Fax: (406)255-2792
Contact: Patricia J. Koch, Lib.Techn.
Subjects: Water resources, land use, range management, wildlife, coal, minerals. ***Special Collections:*** Missouri River Basin Reports. ***Holdings:*** 13,000 books.

★7626★ U.S. Bureau of Land Management
New Mexico State Office Information Center
Box 1449
Santa Fe, NM 87504-1449
Phone: (505)988-6047
Fax: (505)988-6530
Contact: Eileen G. Vigil, State Rec.Mgr.
Subjects: Management - land resource, wildlife, recreation, minerals, range; environmental protection. ***Special Collections:*** U.S. Statutes at Large; Interior Board of Land Appeals decisions; Lindley on Mines, Volumes I and II; Environmental Statements. ***Holdings:*** 4500 books; 250 bound periodical volumes.

★7627★ U.S. Bureau of Mines
Salt Lake City Research Center
Library
729 Arapeen Dr.
Salt Lake City, UT 84108
Phone: (801)524-6112
Fax: (801)524-6119
Contact: Jean B. Beckstead, Libn.
Subjects: Metallurgy research, natural resources conservation, environmental pollution, engineering, physical sciences. ***Special Collections:*** Bureau of Mines publications (1500 bound volumes). ***Holdings:*** 10,700 books; 1250 bound periodical volumes; 39 notebooks of patents.

★7628★ U.S. Bureau of Reclamation
Denver Office
Library
Denver Federal Center
Box 25007
Denver, CO 80225
Phone: (303)236-6963
Contact: Glada Costales, Proj.Mgr.
Subjects: Water resources development; design, construction, and operation of dams, power plants, pumping plants, canals, transmission lines; water quality. ***Holdings:*** 15,000 books; 14,000 bound periodical volumes; 20,000 archival items; 10,000 specifications; 20,000 internal reports; 10,000 reports on microfilm; 20,000 external reports; Government Publications Office publications.

★7629★ U.S. Bureau of Reclamation
Library
2800 Cottage Way, Rm. 1526
Sacramento, CA 95825-1898
Phone: (916)978-5168
Fax: (916)978-5284
Contact: Diane M. Johnson, Lib. Tech.
Subjects: Water and water resources, power, agriculture. ***Holdings:*** 12,000 volumes.

★7630★ U.S. Bureau of Reclamation
Technical Library
400 Railroad Ave.
Boulder City, NV 89005
Phone: (702)293-8666
Fax: (702)293-8615
Contact: Alma K. Spruill, File Ck.
Subjects: Water and power resources, hydrology, canals and other hydraulic structures, hydroelectric power, flood control, ecology, soil. ***Special Collections:*** Project histories for the lower Colorado region. ***Holdings:*** 25,000 volumes.

★7631★ U.S. Council for Energy Awareness
Library
1776 I St., N.W., Ste. 400
Washington, DC 20006
Phone: (202)293-0770
Fax: (202)785-4019
Telex: 7108249602
Contact: Erin M. Nagorske, Mgr.
Subjects: Nuclear energy, environment, nuclear waste management, nuclear regulation. ***Holdings:*** 3000 books; 2500 technical reports; conference papers.

★7632★ U.S.D.A.
Agricultural Research Service
Aridland Watershed Management Research Unit
2000 E. Allen Rd.
Tucson, AZ 85719
Phone: (602)670-6381
Fax: (602)670-6493
Contact: E. Sue Anderson, Libn.
Subjects: Water and soil conservation, sediment, runoff, erosion, rainfall, arid land ecosystems improvement, watershed protection. ***Holdings:*** 400 books; 150 bound periodical volumes; 1700 theses and papers.

★7633★ U.S.D.A.
National Agricultural Library
Water Quality Information Center
10301 Baltimore Blvd., Rm. 1402
Beltsville, MD 20705
Phone: (301)344-4077
Fax: (301)344-5472
Contact: Janice C. Kemp, Coord., WQIC
Subjects: Water - pollution, quality, management, regulation; effect of agricultural practices on water quality and quantity.

★7634★ U.S. Dept. of Energy
Albuquerque Operations Office
National Atomic Museum - Library and Public Document Room
Box 5400
Albuquerque, NM 87115
Phone: (505)845-4378
Contact: Loretta Helling, Lib. Tech.
Subjects: Nuclear waste management, nuclear weapons history, energy. ***Special Collections:*** Waste Isolation Pilot Project (500 items); Uranium Mill Tailings Remedial Action (UMTRA; 200 items). ***Holdings:*** 1900 books; 3000 reports; 6000 microfiche.

★7635★ U.S. Dept. of Energy
Bonneville Power Administration
Ross Library-EL
Box 491
Vancouver, WA 98666
Phone: (206)690-2617
Contact: John A. Fenker, Librarian
Subjects: Energy. ***Special Collections:*** Internal technical and laboratory reports; federal, military, and industry standards; EPRI reports depository.

★7636★ U.S. Dept. of Energy
Energy Information Administration
National Energy Information Center
Forrestal Bldg., Rm. 1F-048
Washington, DC 20585
Phone: (202)586-8800
Contact: John H. Weiner, Dir., Info./Adm. Serv. Div.
Subjects: Energy - petroleum, electric power, nuclear power, coal and synthetic fuels,

renewable energy resources, natural gas; energy statistics.

★7637★ U.S. Dept. of Energy
Energy Library
AD-234.2
Washington, DC 20585
Phone: (202)586-9534
Contact: Denise B. Diggin, Libn.
Subjects: Energy resources and technologies; economic, environmental, and social aspects of energy; energy regulation; energy statistics; management. ***Special Collections:*** International Atomic Energy Agency (IAEA) Publications; legislative histories relating to Atomic Energy Commission (AEC) and Energy Research and Development Administration (ERDA); ERDA, Federal Energy Administration (FEA), and DOE technical reports. ***Holdings:*** 1 million volumes of books, journals, technical reports, government documents.

★7638★ U.S. Dept. of Energy
Morgantown Energy Technology Center
Library
Box 880
Morgantown, WV 26505
Phone: (304)291-4184
Fax: (304)291-4403
Telex: 62958572 (EasyLink)
Contact: Matthew Marsteller
Subjects: Coal and fossil fuel, petroleum, chemistry, chemical engineering, geology, coal gasification. ***Special Collections:*** U.S. Office of Coal Research reports (100); U.S. Dept. of Energy publications; U.S. Bureau of Mines publications (complete). ***Holdings:*** 10,000 books; 7000 bound periodical volumes; 1500 reports; 20 VF drawers of patents.

★7639★ U.S. Dept. of Energy
Nevada Operations Office
Technical Library
Mail Stop 505
PO Box 98518
Las Vegas, NV 89193-8518
Phone: (702)295-1274
Fax: (702)295-1371
Contact: Cynthia Ortiz, Tech.Libn. II
Subjects: Nuclear explosives, radiation bioenvironmental effects, geology, hydrology, alternate energy sources, radioactive waste storage. ***Special Collections:*** Peaceful uses of nuclear explosions. ***Holdings:*** 3000 books; 54,200 technical reports; 83,300 microfiche of technical reports; 7 file drawers of clippings; 400 maps.

★7640★ U.S. Dept. of Labor
OSHA
Region III Library
3535 Market St., Ste. 2100
Philadelphia, PA 19104
Phone: (215)596-1201
Contact: Barbara Goodman, Libn.
Subjects: Occupational health and safety, industrial hygiene, toxic substances. ***Special Collections:*** National Institute of Occupational Safety and Health (NIOSH) documents; OSHA standards; industry standards. ***Holdings:*** 1500 books.

★7641★ U.S. Dept. of Labor
OSHA
Region X Library
1111 3rd Ave., Ste. 715
Seattle, WA 98101-3212
Phone: (206)553-5930
Contact: Donna M. Hoffman, Libn.
Subjects: Industrial hygiene, toxic substances, industrial safety, toxicology, safety, engineering. ***Special Collections:*** ANSI Standards; NIOSH documents. ***Holdings:*** 1000 titles.

★7642★ U.S. Dept. of Labor
OSHA
Technical Data Center
200 Constitution Ave., N.W.
Rm. N-2625
Washington, DC 20210
Phone: (202)523-9700
Fax: (202)523-5046
Contact: Thomas A. Towers, Dir.
Subjects: Occupational safety, industrial hygiene, toxicology, control technology, hazardous materials, fire safety, electrical safety, noise, carcinogens, material safety, farm safety, process safety, ergonomics, occupational health nursing. ***Holdings:*** 12,000 books and bound periodical volumes; 250,000 microfiche; 2000 technical documents; 3000 standards and codes.

★7643★ U.S. Dept. of the Interior
Natural Resources Library
18th & C Sts., N.W.
Washington, DC 20240
Phone: (202)208-5815
Subjects: Conservation, energy and power, land use, parks, American Indians, fish and wildlife, mining, law, management. ***Special Collections:*** Archival collection of materials published by Department of Interior (150,000 items). ***Holdings:*** 600,000 books; 90,000 bound periodical volumes; 7000 reels of microfilm; 40,000 unbound periodical volumes; 300,000 microfiche.

★7644★ U.S. Environmental Protection Agency
Andrew W. Breidenbach Environmental Research Library
26 W. Martin Luther King Dr.
Cincinnati, OH 45268
Phone: (513)569-7707
Fax: (513)564-7709
Subjects: Water - pollution, quality, research; hazardous waste; chemistry; environmental studies; biotechnology. ***Special Collections:*** Hazardous Waste Collection (1747 items); risk assessment collection; solid waste. ***Holdings:*** 20,400 books; 7000 bound periodical volumes; 200,000 reports on microfiche; 1000 documents.

★7645★ U.S. Environmental Protection Agency
Atmospheric Sciences Model Division
Library
Research Triangle Park, NC 27711
Phone: (919)541-4536
Contact: Evelyn M. Poole-Kober, Tech.Pubns.Ed.
Subjects: Air pollution, meteorology. ***Holdings:*** 1200 books; 13,000 hardcopy documents and technical reports; microfiche.

★7646★ U.S. Environmental Protection Agency
Central Regional Laboratory
Library
839 Bestgate Rd.
Annapolis, MD 21401
Phone: (301)266-9180
Fax: (301)266-9180
Contact: Ann Menninger Johnson, Libn.
Subjects: Water quality management, marine environment, biological indicators, mathematical modeling, toxic substances. ***Special Collections:*** Scientific studies of Chesapeake Bay. ***Holdings:*** 1500 books; 5000 reprints; 150 Annapolis Field Office/CRL publications; 10,000 EPA reports on microfiche; EPA R&D reports.

★7647★ U.S. Environmental Protection Agency
Environmental Monitoring and Systems Laboratory
Library
944 E. Harmon Ave.
Las Vegas, NV 89119
Phone: (702)798-2648
Contact: Doreen Wickman, Libn.
Subjects: Environmental and nuclear science.

★7648★ U.S. Environmental Protection Agency
Environmental Research Laboratory, Athens
Library
College Sta. Rd.
Athens, GA 30613-7799
Phone: (404)546-3154
Contact: Janice Sims, Info.Spec.
Subjects: Sanitary engineering, chemistry, biology, environmental systems, aquatic biology. ***Holdings:*** 5000 books; 3500 government documents; 100 journals on microfilm.

★7649★ U.S. Environmental Protection Agency
Environmental Research Laboratory, Corvallis
Library
200 S.W. 35th St.
Corvallis, OR 97333
Phone: (503)757-4731
Fax: (503)457-4799
Contact: Renie Cain McVeety, Libn.
Subjects: Effects of air, water, and soil pollutants on the ecosystem; freshwater ecosystems; toxic substances; wildlife toxicology; hazardous waste; biotechnology; global climate. ***Special Collections:*** Acid rain and air pollution effects (28,000 documents). ***Holdings:*** 4000 books; 9000 reports; 22,000 microforms.

★7650★ U.S. Environmental Protection Agency
Environmental Research Laboratory, Gulf Breeze
Library
Sabine Island
Gulf Breeze, FL 32561
Phone: (904)934-9218
Fax: (904)934-9201
Contact: Elizabeth Pinnell, Libn.
Subjects: Pathobiology, ecology, aquatic toxicology, microbiology, biotechnology. ***Special Collections:*** Environmental publications for northwest Florida. ***Holdings:*** 5000 volumes; 6000 reprints; 38,000 publications on microfiche.

★7651★ U.S. Environmental Protection Agency
Environmental Research Laboratory, Narragansett
Library
South Ferry Rd.
Narragansett, RI 02882
Phone: (401)782-3000
Contact: Rose Ann Gamache, Libn.
Subjects: Biological oceanography, marine ecology, biomedical science, fisheries biology, chemistry. ***Holdings:*** 15,000 technical reports and collected reprints; microforms.

★7652★ **U.S. Environmental Protection Agency**
Headquarters Library
Rm. 2904 PM-211-A
401 M St., S.W.
Washington, DC 20460-0001
Phone: (202)260-5921
Fax: (202)260-7883
Contact: Ann Dugan, Adm.Libn.
Subjects: Water - pollution, quality, supply; air pollution; noise abatement; radiation; hazardous wastes; solid waste management; resource recovery; pesticides; chemistry and toxicology; social, economic, legislative, legal, administrative, and management aspects of environmental policy. ***Special Collections:*** Hazardous waste; management; international pollution prevention; information resources management. ***Holdings:*** 15,500 books; 23,000 hardcopy documents and technical reports; 330,000 documents and reports from the EPA and its predecessor agencies on microfiche; newspapers, abstracts and indexes, periodicals on microfilm.

★7653★ **U.S. Environmental Protection Agency**
Library
2890 Woodbridge Ave.
Bldg. 209, MS-245
Edison, NJ 08837-3679
Phone: (201)321-6762
Fax: (201)321-6622
Contact: Dorothy Szefczyk, Lib.Techn.
Subjects: Water pollution, water quality, environmental quality, air pollution, toxic substances, hazardous wastes. ***Holdings:*** 3000 books; 10,000 federal and state reports; 100,000 microfiche.

★7654★ **U.S. Environmental Protection Agency**
Library Services
MD 35
Research Triangle Park, NC 27711
Phone: (919)541-2777
Fax: (919)541-1405
Contact: John Knight, Chf., Info.Serv.
Subjects: Air pollution, its effects on health, control technologies. ***Special Collections:*** APTIC (Air Pollution Technical Information Center) Collection; Environmental Protection Agency document distribution center. ***Holdings:*** 4000 volumes; 4470 technical reports; 200,000 microfiche.

★7655★ **U.S. Environmental Protection Agency**
National Enforcement Investigations
EPA-NEIC Library
Denver Federal Center, Bldg. 53
Box 25227
Denver, CO 80225
Phone: (303)236-5122
Contact: Dorothy Biggs, Libn.
Subjects: Environmental law, water quality, industrial and agricultural pollution abatement practices, air pollution, pesticides, hazardous wastes, chemistry. ***Holdings:*** 2000 volumes; 750,000 microfiche; technical reports; R&D reports; conference documents; state of the art abatement practices for municipal, industrial, and agricultural pollution.

★7656★ **U.S. Environmental Protection Agency - ORD**
Risk Reduction Engineering Laboratory
Releases Control Branch - Technical Information Exchange
MS-104
Woodbridge Ave.
Edison, NJ 08837
Phone: (201)321-6644
Contact: May Smith, Tech. Info. Exch. Mgr.
Subjects: Hazardous materials, including surface spills and leaking underground storage tank technology; Superfund-related activities involving evaluation of clean-up technologies and protective garments for field crews. ***Holdings:*** 350 books; 2500 reports; 130 films and videotapes; software.

★7657★ **U.S. Environmental Protection Agency**
Region 1 Library
JFK Federal Bldg.
Boston, MA 02203
Phone: (617)565-3300
Contact: Peg Nelson, Reg.Libn.
Subjects: Solid and hazardous waste, air and water pollution, pesticides and toxicology, environment. ***Special Collections:*** Hazardous Waste Collection; test methods; wetlands. ***Holdings:*** 10,000 books, government documents, technical reports; 100,000 microfiche.

★7658★ **U.S. Environmental Protection Agency**
Region 2 Library
26 Federal Plaza, Rm. 402
New York, NY 10278
Phone: (212)264-2881
Contact: Magi E. Malone, Reg.Libn.
Subjects: Hazardous waste; acid rain; energy; pollution - ocean, water, air. ***Special Collections:*** Hazardous Waste in the region: New York, New Jersey, Puerto Rico, Virgin Islands. ***Holdings:*** 2200 books; 2700 reports; 250,000 microfiche.

★7659★ **U.S. Environmental Protection Agency**
Region 3 Information Resource Center
841 Chestnut St.
Philadelphia, PA 19107
Phone: (215)597-0580
Contact: Diane M. McCreary, Libn.
Subjects: Environmental sciences and law, management, economics, toxicology. ***Special Collections:*** Wetland ecology; hazardous waste. ***Holdings:*** 12,000 books; 7500 technical reports; 120,000 microfiche.

★7660★ **U.S. Environmental Protection Agency**
Region 4 Library
345 Courtland St.
Atlanta, GA 30365
Phone: (404)347-4216
Fax: (404)347-4486
Contact: Pricilla Pride, Hd.Libn.
Subjects: Pollution - water, air, noise; solid waste management; toxic substances; Southeastern U.S. ecology. ***Special Collections:*** Environmental impact statements. ***Holdings:*** 4000 books; 110,000 EPA documents on microfiche; 20,000 EPA documents.

★7661★ **U.S. Environmental Protection Agency**
Region 5 Library
230 S. Dearborn St., Rm. 1670
Chicago, IL 60604
Phone: (312)353-2022
Fax: (312)886-9096
Contact: Ms. Lou W. Tilley, Reg.Libn.
Subjects: Water quality and supply; air quality and air pollution; solid waste management; pesticides; radiation; noise; energy; hazardous wastes; toxic substances; environmental science; environmental law with emphasis on the Great Lakes and six states in the region: Illinois, Indiana, Michigan, Minnesota, Ohio, Wisconsin. ***Special Collections:*** Environmental Protection Agency and predecessor agency reports (complete set); Air Pollution Technical Information Center (APTIC) microfiche file. ***Holdings:*** 7500 books; 21,000 state and federal documents; 12 VF drawers; 56 VF drawers of microforms.

★7662★ **U.S. Environmental Protection Agency**
Region 7 Library
726 Minnesota Ave.
Kansas City, KS 66101
Phone: (913)551-7241
Fax: (913)551-2845
Contact: Barbara MacKinnon, Reg.Libn.
Subjects: Air and water pollution, solid waste, pesticides, environmental law. ***Holdings:*** 2300 books; 4600 technical reports; 125,000 technical reports on microfiche.

★7663★ **U.S. Environmental Protection Agency**
Region 8 Library
999 18th St., Ste. 500
Denver, CO 80202-2405
Phone: (303)293-1444
Fax: (303)293-1647
Contact: Barbara L. Wagner, Reg.Libn.
Subjects: Water, air, solid waste management, pesticides, radiation, noise, toxic substances, energy. ***Special Collections:*** Microfiche collections of environmental impact statements and EPA technical reports. ***Holdings:*** 2200 books; 20,000 EPA and technical reports; 260,000 titles on microfiche.

★7664★ **U.S. Environmental Protection Agency**
Region 9 Library
75 Hawthorne St., 13th Fl.
San Francisco, CA 94105
Phone: (415)774-1510
Fax: (415)744-1070
Contact: Linda Vida-Sunnen, Hd.Libn.
Subjects: Environment; water and air pollution; pesticides; hazardous waste; environmental health and law for California, Arizona, Nevada, Hawaii, and the Pacific Islands. ***Special Collections:*** Oswer Directives; Record(s) of Decisions; hazardous waste collection; EPA Reports; Toxic Release Inventory (on microfiche). ***Holdings:*** 4000 books; 250,000 reports; 300,000 reports on microfiche.

★7665★ **U.S. Environmental Protection Agency**
Region 10 Library
1200 Sixth Ave.
Seattle, WA 98101
Phone: (206)442-1289
Contact: Julienne Sears, Reg.Libn.
Subjects: Environmental pollution. ***Holdings:*** EPA technical reports.

★7666★ **U.S. Environmental Protection Agency**
Research Library for Solid Waste
JFK Federal Bldg.
Boston, MA 02203
Phone: (617)573-9687
Contact: Fred Friedman, Libn.
Subjects: Solid and hazardous waste.

★7667★ U.S. Environmental Protection Agency
Robert S. Kerr Environmental Research Laboratory
Research Library
Kerr Lab Rd.
PO Box 1198
Ada, OK 74820
Phone: (405)332-8800
Contact: Joyce Williams Bergin, Lib.Dir.
Subjects: Environment, ground water, chemistry, microbiology, soil science, hydrology, modeling. ***Holdings:*** 2000 books; 10,000 other cataloged items; 71,081 microfiche; 371 reels of microfilm.

★7668★ U.S. Fish & Wildlife Service
National Fisheries Contaminant Research Center
Library
4200 New Haven Rd.
Columbia, MO 65201
Phone: (314)875-5399
Fax: (314)876-1896
Contact: Ell-Piret Multer, Dir.
Subjects: Pesticides, agricultural chemicals, pollution, environmental contaminants, environmental chemistry. ***Holdings:*** 4500 books; 1500 bound periodical volumes; 18,000 reprints; 34,500 microfiche.

★7669★ U.S. Fish & Wildlife Service
National Fisheries Research Center - Great Lakes
John Van Oosten Library
1451 Green Rd.
Ann Arbor, MI 48105
Phone: (313)994-3331
Fax: (313)994-3331, ext
Contact: Eileen K. Bartels, Libn.
Subjects: Fishery biology, aquatic ecology, pesticide, mercury and water pollution, Great Lakes. ***Holdings:*** 3000 books; 2100 bound periodical volumes; 40,000 reprints.

★7670★ U.S. Fish & Wildlife Service
Office of Audio-Visual
Library
18th & E Sts., N.W.
Dept. of the Interior, Rm. 3444
Washington, DC 20240
Phone: (202)343-5611
Contact: LaVonda Walton
Subjects: Wildlife, especially birds and endangered species. ***Holdings:*** 15,000 still photographs and color transparencies.

★7671★ U.S. Fish & Wildlife Service
Patuxent Wildlife Research Center
Library
Laurel, MD 20708
Phone: (301)498-0235
Fax: (301)498-0301
Contact: Lynda Garrett, Libn.
Subjects: Wildlife, especially birds; environmental pollution - pesticides, heavy metals, oil; biostatistics. ***Holdings:*** 9000 books; 35,000 reprints and pamphlets.

★7672★ U.S. Forest Service
History Unit Reference Collection
14th & Independence, S.W.
Auditors Bldg. 2-C
PO Box 69090
Washington, DC 20090-6090
Phone: (202)447-8059
Fax: (202)475-5485
Contact: Terry West, Hist.
Subjects: Forest Service administrative history, conservation history, natural resource management, land use history, agency timber management policy and practices. ***Special Collections:*** Forest Service manuals and handbooks, 1880s to 1930s. ***Holdings:*** 100 books; 10 bound periodical volumes; 500 documents; 20 manuscripts.

★7673★ U.S. Forest Service
Pacific Southwest Forest and Range Experiment Station
Library
1960 Addison St.
Box 245
Berkeley, CA 94701-0245
Phone: (415)486-3686
Contact: Brian Lym, Sta.Libn.
Subjects: Forest management, silviculture, watershed management, computers and statistics, wildlife management, environmental protection. ***Holdings:*** 40,000 volumes, documents, offprints, reprints, preprints, bulletins, research notes.

★7674★ U.S. Forest Service
Rocky Mountain Forest & Range Experiment Station
Library
240 W. Prospect St.
Fort Collins, CO 80526
Phone: (303)498-1268
Fax: (303)498-1010
Contact: Frances J. Barney, Libn.
Subjects: Forest management, shelterbelts, wildland valuation, resource economics, snow and watershed management, forest entomology and pathology, wildlife habitats, disturbed site reclamation, atmospheric deposition, nematology, ecology of arid lands, history of forestry in Rocky Mountains. ***Special Collections:*** World Mistletoe Literature (on Famulus retrieval system; 7000 references); Boyce Index to Forest Pathology Literature (30 card file drawers). ***Holdings:*** 15,000 books; 5000 bound periodical volumes; 20,000 unbound serials; 10 VF drawers of reprints; 150 reels of microfilm of Oxford Catalog and periodicals; 1200 dissertations; 4 VF drawers of Rocky Mountain Station historical material.

★7675★ U.S. Geological Survey
Water Resources Division
Library
Federal Bldg., Rm. 428
301 S. Park
Drawer 10076
Helena, MT 59626-0076
Phone: (406)449-5263
Contact: Cynthia J. Harksen, Libn.
Subjects: Water resources and development, water quality, floods. ***Special Collections:*** U.S. Geological Survey water supply papers, bulletins, professional papers. ***Holdings:*** 10,000 items.

★7676★ U.S. Geological Survey
Water Resources Division
Library
6417 Normandy Ln.
Madison, WI 53719-1133
Phone: (608)276-3802
Fax: (608)276-3817
Contact: Susan L. Ziegler, Ed.Asst.
Subjects: Surface and ground water, water quality. ***Special Collections:*** Complete set of WRD Wisconsin publications. ***Holdings:*** 2500 books; 550 water supply papers; 475 professional papers; 140 bulletins; 180 circulars.

★7677★ U.S. Geological Survey
Water Resources Division
National Water Data Storage & Retrieval System and Water Resources Scientific Information Center
National Center, Mail Stop 409
Reston, VA 22092
Phone: (703)648-5687
Fax: (703)648-5295
Contact: Philip Cohen, Chf. Hydrologist
Subjects: Surface water stage and discharge, chemical quality parameters, radiochemistry, sedimentology, pesticide and biological concentrations in water, ground and surface water levels, flood frequency and flood inundation mapping. ***Special Collections:*** Abstracts of literature on all aspects of water resources. ***Holdings:*** Observations from 16,600 streamflow gauging stations, 6230 water quality measuring stations, 900,000 wells and springs; historical data, 1890 to present.

★7678★ U.S. Geological Survey
Water Resources Library
W. Aspinall Federal Bldg., Rm. 201
4th & Rood Ave.
Box 2027
Grand Junction, CO 81502
Phone: (303)245-5257
Contact: Dannie L. Collins, Subdistrict Chf.
Subjects: Water resources, water quality, geological and atmospheric conditions as they pertain to water. ***Holdings:*** 1534 books; 1014 bound periodical volumes; 669 volumes of basic data reports; 3880 maps; 110 decisions on names in the U.S.; 55 reels of microfilm of well log data for Colorado; 179 volumes of professional papers.

★7679★ U.S. National Library of Medicine
8600 Rockville Pike
Bethesda, MD 20894
Phone: (301)496-6308
Contact: Donald A.B. Lindberg M.D., Dir.
Subjects: Medicine, health sciences, dentistry, public health, nursing, biomedical research. ***Special Collections:*** History of medicine (pre-1914); Prints and Photographs Collection; modern manuscripts. ***Holdings:*** 650,000 books; 892,000 bound periodical volumes; 2.2 million manuscripts; 78,000 pictures; 272,000 microforms; 282,000 theses; 172,000 pamphlets; 49,000 AV programs; microfilm.

★7680★ U.S. Natl. Marine Fisheries Service
Sandy Hook Laboratory
Lionel A. Walford Library
Highlands, NJ 07732
Phone: (908)872-3035
Fax: (201)872-3088
Contact: Claire L. Steimle, Libn.
Subjects: Fisheries, environmental problems, marine invertebrates, biological and chemical oceanography, plankton behavior, microbiology, New York Bight. ***Special Collections:*** Fishery Bulletins and Reports to Commissioner of Fisheries; Special Pollution Collection (150 volumes). ***Holdings:*** 6000 books; 4500 bound periodical volumes; 14,000 documents.

★7681★ U.S. Natl. Oceanic & Atmospheric Administration
Atmospheric Turbulence & Diffusion Division
Library
Box 2456
Oak Ridge, TN 37831
Phone: (615)576-0061
Fax: (615)576-1327

Contact: Barbara S. Johnson, Adm.Off.
Subjects: Air pollution, forest meteorology, climatic studies. *Holdings:* 2500 volumes; 6000 technical reports and reprints.

★7682★ U.S. Natl. Oceanic & Atmospheric Administration
National Environmental Satellite, Data, & Information Service
National Oceanographic Data Center
Washington, DC 20235
Phone: (202)673-5549
Fax: (202)673-5586
Contact: Gregory W. Withee, Dir.
Subjects: Oceanography - physical, chemical, biological. *Holdings:* Digital oceanographic data: oceanographic station and bathythermograph data covering the world's oceans; marine pollution and marine biological data from selected offshore areas of the U.S.; surface and subsurface current data; wind/wave data from environmental buoys offshore of the U.S.; global wind/wave data derived from altimeter measurements of the U.S. Navy GEOSAT; data from special projects such as the Climatological Atlas of the World Ocean.

★7683★ U.S. Natl. Park Service
National Capital Region
Rock Creek Nature Center Library
5200 Glover Rd., N.W.
Washington, DC 20015
Phone: (202)426-6829
Contact: David R. Smith, Supv.Pk. Ranger
Subjects: Birds, mammals, reptiles, astronomy, park and milling history, environment and environmental education. *Holdings:* 1000 books; 32 boxes of clippings and photographs; unbound journals.

★7684★ U.S. Navy
Naval Civil Engineering Laboratory
Library
Code L06C
Port Hueneme, CA 93043-5003
Phone: (805)982-1124
Fax: (805)982-1409
Contact: Bryan Thompson, Adm.Libn.
Subjects: Engineering, ocean engineering, construction materials, environmental protection, energy, soil mechanics. *Holdings:* 16,000 books; 7000 bound periodical volumes; 20,000 technical reports.

★7685★ U.S. Navy
Pacific Missile Test Center
Technical Library
Code 1018, Bldg. 511A
Point Mugu, CA 93042
Phone: (805)989-8156
Contact: Veronica L. Briggs, Libn.
Subjects: Aeronautics, mathematics, electronics, astronautics, meteorology, oceanography, naval history, physics, radar technology. *Holdings:* 17,000 books; 9000 bound periodical volumes; 1000 reels of microfilm.

★7686★ U.S. Nuclear Regulatory Commission
Law Library
1 White Flint, N., 15-B-11
Washington, DC 20555
Phone: (301)492-1526
Contact: Charlotte Carnahan, Chf., Legal Info.Serv.
Subjects: Law - nuclear energy, environmental, administrative. *Special Collections:* Publications of the Joint Committee on Atomic Energy, 1945-1975 (complete set); AEC and NRC Reports, 1956 to present. *Holdings:* 10,000 books; 1500 bound periodical volumes; 500 technical documents; 10 drawers of Federal Register, Congressional Record, law journals in microform.

★7687★ Universite du Quebec a Montreal
Bibliotheque des Sciences Juridiques
C.P. 8889, Succursale A
Local A-2183
Montreal, Quebec, Canada H3C 3P3
Phone: (514)987-6184
Contact: Micheline Drapeau, Dir.
Subjects: Jurisprudence; social security; law - consumer and environmental protection, constitutional, family, fiscal, health, housing, labor, poverty, public education, social; immigration and civil rights. *Holdings:* 35,284 volumes; 6 VF drawers of microfiche; 101 magnetic tapes; 413 reels of microfilm.

★7688★ University of Alabama
Coalbed Methane Information Center
205 Tom Beyill Bldg.
Box 870164
Tuscaloosa, AL 35487
Phone: (205)348-2839
Fax: (205)348-9268
Contact: Marcia S. Irvin, Res.Asst.
Subjects: Coalbed methane; coal, gas, and petroleum industries; alternative energy sources. *Holdings:* 602 books; 12 basin reports; 618 petrophysical logs; 758 technical reports; 200 vertical files and ephemera; 60 maps; unbound periodicals.

★7689★ University of Alaska, Anchorage
Arctic Environmental Information and Data Center
707 A St.
Anchorage, AK 99501
Phone: (907)257-2733
Fax: (907)276-6847
Contact: Sal V. Cuccarese, Act.Dir.
Subjects: Alaska - environment, geology, fisheries, glaciology, land use planning, oil pollution, energy resources, coastal zone management; arctic research; Alaska climate records. *Special Collections:* Depository for Arctic Petroleum Operators Association and Alaska Oil and Gas Association (AOGA) reports; Annual Reports of the 13 Alaska Native Regional Corporations; ARCO Arctic Environmental Reports Collection. *Holdings:* 8800 books; 2000 photographs of Alaska; 11,500 microfiche; reports; pamphlets; maps.

★7690★ University of Alaska, Anchorage
Energy Extension Service
Energy Resource and Information Center
949 E. 36th St., Ste. 403
Anchorage, AK 99508
Phone: (907)563-1955
Toll-Free: 800-478-4636
Contact: Ginny Moore, Libn.
Subjects: Energy - conservation, renewable sources and applications, building construction, management, education, housing, electricity sources efficiency, conservation; indoor air quality. *Holdings:* 2000 books; 76 films and videotapes; reports and studies.

★7691★ University of Calgary
Kananaskis Centre for Environmental Research
Library
Calgary, Alberta, Canada T2N 1N4
Phone: (403)220-5355
Fax: (403)673-3671
Contact: Grace LeBel, Libn.
Subjects: Chemistry, biology, environmental research. *Special Collections:* Field guides and environmental collection. *Holdings:* 4000 books; 3000 unpublished reports and theses.

★7692★ University of California, Berkeley
Giannini Foundation of Agricultural Economics
Research Library
248 Giannini Hall
Berkeley, CA 94720
Phone: (415)642-7121
Fax: (415)643-8911
Contact: Grace Dote, Libn.
Subjects: Agriculture - economics, labor, land utilization, valuation and tenure, marketing and transportation problems, cost of production and marketing studies; agricultural economic developments in Lesser Developed Countries; water resources economics; conservation of natural resources. *Special Collections:* Federal state market news reports from most major U.S. cities, 1920-1982. *Holdings:* 19,000 volumes; 134,000 pamphlets; 3800 microforms; 140 maps.

★7693★ University of California, Berkeley
Water Resources Center Archives
410 O'Brien Hall
Berkeley, CA 94720
Phone: (415)642-2666
Fax: (415)642-9143
Contact: Gerald J. Giefer, Libn.
Subjects: Water as a natural resource, water resources development and management, municipal and industrial water uses and problems, reclamation and irrigation, flood control, waste disposal, coastal engineering, water quality, water law. *Special Collections:* Ocean engineering (20,000 pieces); manuscript collection of papers of men prominent in western water development (4290). *Holdings:* 112,602 volumes; 5201 maps; 1085 microforms; 8322 manuscripts.

★7694★ University of California, Davis
Environmental Toxicology Department
Toxicology Documentation Center
Davis, CA 95616-8588
Phone: (916)752-2587
Contact: Dr. Ming-Yu Li, Doc.Spec.
Subjects: Pesticides, environmental pollutants, toxic metals, PCBs, air and water pollutants, food additives and toxicants, hazardous wastes management. *Special Collections:* Pesticide chemical and subject files. *Holdings:* 5000 books; 3500 bound periodical volumes; 65,000 classified abstract cards; 36,000 items on pesticides in VF drawers; 41,000 items in subject files on environmental pollutants, toxic metals and elements, hazardous substances, and waste management.

★7695★ University of California
Los Alamos National Laboratory
Library
MS-P362
Los Alamos, NM 87545
Phone: (505)667-4448
Fax: (505)665-2948
Contact: Karen Stoll, Act.Hd.Libn.
Subjects: Military and peaceful uses of nuclear energy, physics, chemistry, materials science, engineering, earth sciences, mathematics and computers. *Special Collections:* Biomedicine (40,000 volumes). *Holdings:* 150,000 books; 200,000 bound periodical volumes; 1 million technical reports; 500 reels of motion picture film; videos.

★7696★ University of California, Los Angeles
Water Resources Center Archives
2081 Engineering I
Los Angeles, CA 90024-1599
Phone: (213)825-7734

Contact: Beth R. Willard, Hd.
Subjects: Water - resources, reclamation, pollution, supply, quality, and economics; wastes disposal; irrigation; flood control; water law; environment; energy; soils; water-based recreation; ground water; hazardous wastes. ***Holdings:*** 89,250 volumes; 8500 microcards; 11,970 pamphlets.

★7697★ University of Cincinnati
Department of Environmental Health Library
Kettering Laboratory Library
3223 Eden Ave.
Cincinnati, OH 45267-0056
Phone: (513)558-1721
Fax: (513)558-1756
Contact: Sherrie Kline, Sr.Res.Assoc./Libn.
Subjects: Environmental health, toxicology, physiology, analytical chemistry, statistics. ***Special Collections:*** Industrial health. ***Holdings:*** 6000 books; 4500 bound periodical volumes; 78 VF drawers of reprints, reports, translations; 400 microfiche; 565 unpublished reports.

★7698★ University of Florida
Coastal & Oceanographic Engineering Department
Coastal Engineering Archives
433 Weil Hall
Gainesville, FL 32611
Phone: (904)392-2710
Fax: (904)392-3466
Contact: Helen Twedell, Sr.Lib.Techn.
Subjects: Florida beaches, beach erosion, sediment transport, coastal vegetation, nearshore oceanography, estuarine circulation. ***Holdings:*** 548 books; 360 microforms; 8600 other cataloged items.

★7699★ University of Idaho
Idaho Water Resources Research Institute
Technical Information Center & Reading Room
Moscow, ID 83843
Phone: (208)885-6429
Contact: Leland L. Mink, Dir.
Subjects: Water resources, resource economics, outdoor recreation, groundwater, irrigation, wild and scenic rivers, water seepage, agriculture, water law, precipitation distribution, small hydroelectric developments. ***Holdings:*** 4000 books and bound periodical volumes.

★7700★ University of Illinois at Chicago
Energy Resources Center
Documents Center
412 S. Peoria St.
Box 4348
Chicago, IL 60680
Phone: (312)996-4490
Contact: James Wiet, Dir.Asst.
Subjects: Energy - resources, policy, conservation, technology; alternative energy technologies; electric utility statistics. ***Special Collections:*** Heat and mass transfer (225 monographs; 15 journal subscriptions). ***Holdings:*** 4000 books; 100 bound periodical volumes; 2 VF drawers of clippings; 3 VF drawers of pamphlets; 100 maps; 100 reports on microfiche.

★7701★ University of Maryland, Cambridge
Center for Environmental and Estuarine Studies
Horn Point Library
Box 775
Cambridge, MD 21613
Phone: (301)228-8200
Contact: Darlene Windsor, Lib.Techn.
Subjects: Oceanography, marine science, aquaculture, water quality, fisheries. ***Holdings:*** 1400 books; 1224 bound periodical volumes; 500 unbound reports; 975 EPA reports; 5000 reprints; 1000 archives; 45 dissertations; 2450 microfiche; 84 reels of microfilm; 55 theses.

★7702★ University of Maryland, Cambridge
Horn Point Environmental Lab Library
Box 775
Cambridge, MD 21613
Phone: (301)228-8200
Fax: (301)476-5490
Contact: Darlene Windsor, Lib.Techn.
Subjects: Marine sciences, oceanography, seafood science, fisheries, aquaculture, water quality, water resources. ***Special Collections:*** Reprints (5000); Environmental Protection Agency reports (975); Contribution numbers (450); National Resource Inventory (NRI) reference numbers (596); U.S. Fish & Wildlife Service reports (80). ***Holdings:*** 1439 books; 1312 bound periodical volumes; 300 unbound reports; 61 theses; 2450 microfiche; 84 reels of microfilm; 10 file cabinets of reprints.

★7703★ University of Minnesota, St. Paul
Plant Pathology Library
395 Borlaug Hall
1991 Upper Buford Circle
St. Paul, MN 55108
Phone: (612)625-9777
Contact: Erik Biever, Lib.Asst.
Subjects: Phytopathology, mycology, air pollution effects on vegetation. ***Holdings:*** 8260 books and bound periodical volumes; 66 AV programs; 216 microforms; maps.

★7704★ University of Minnesota
Underground Space Center Library
790 Civil & Mineral Engr. Bldg.
500 Pillsbury Dr., S.E.
Minneapolis, MN 55455
Phone: (612)624-0066
Fax: (612)624-0293
Telex: 9102504002
Contact: Sara B. Hanft
Subjects: Earth sheltered housing, energy, underground space use, rock and soil mechanics, alternative energy financing and legislation, building codes. ***Holdings:*** 150 books; 200 technical papers; 600 documents; 900 clippings.

★7705★ University of North Dakota
Energy and Mineral Research Center
Energy Library
University Sta., Box 8213
Grand Forks, ND 58202
Phone: (701)777-5132
Fax: (701)777-3319
Contact: DeLoris Smith, Lib.Assoc.
Subjects: Fossil energy conversion, coal, lignite. ***Holdings:*** 3500 books; 760 bound periodical volumes; U.S. Department of Energy reports; 229 periodical titles.

★7706★ University of North Dakota
Institute for Ecological Studies
Environmental Resource Center - Library
Box 8278
Grand Forks, ND 58202
Phone: (701)777-2851
Contact: Rod Sayler, Dir.
Subjects: Ecology, land use, water and air pollution, chemical and biological contaminants, wildlife, environmental education, energy, nonrenewable resources. ***Holdings:*** 1000 books; 600 research reports; 1000 environmental impact statements; 12 drawers of pamphlets; 600 maps.

★7707★ University of Oklahoma
Science and Public Policy Program Library
601 Elm Ave., Rm. 431
Norman, OK 73019
Phone: (405)325-2554
Contact: Mary Morrison, Libn.
Subjects: Energy policy, impact assessment, environmental policy, regional studies, technology assessment, information transfer, science policy, hazardous and solid waste management alternatives, alternative transportation fuels. ***Holdings:*** 7000 books and documents; unbound periodicals; 3 cabinets of information files.

★7708★ University of Oregon
Environmental Studies Center
Eugene, OR 97403-5223
Phone: (503)346-5006
Subjects: Ecology, environmental issues, energy. ***Holdings:*** 8000 books; periodicals; environmental impact statements; maps.

★7709★ University of Richmond
William T. Muse Memorial Law Library
Richmond, VA 23173
Phone: (804)289-8225
Fax: (804)289-8683
Contact: Steven D. Hinckley, Law Libn.
Subjects: Law. ***Special Collections:*** Environmental law. ***Holdings:*** 114,733 books; 65,182 volumes in microform.

★7710★ University of Texas, Austin
Wasserman Public Affairs Library
General Libraries
Sid Richardson Hall, 3.243
Austin, TX 78713-7330
Phone: (512)471-4486
Fax: (512)471-8901
Contact: Olive Forbes, Hd.Libn.
Subjects: Politics and government, public administration and finance, social problems and policy, civil rights, discrimination, public welfare, pollution and environmental policy, education, regional and municipal planning, public health, evaluation research. ***Special Collections:*** Budgets and financial reports for selected cities, counties, and states; Henry David Manpower Policy Collection; state documents; selective U.S. documents depository, 1968 to present and Canadian documents depository, 1985 to present. ***Holdings:*** 62,273 volumes; 167,167 uncataloged documents; 233 phonotapes; 140 cassettes; 272 video cassettes; 124 videotapes; 2124 reels of microfilm; 119,370 microfiche.

★7711★ University of Wisconsin, Madison
Department of Urban and Regional Planning
Graduate Research Center
Music Hall
925 Bascom Mall
Madison, WI 53706
Phone: (608)262-1004
Contact: Faranak Seiholddini, Libn.
Subjects: Urban and regional planning, land and water resources, zoning, social services planning, planning in developing areas. ***Holdings:*** 7000 books; 25,000 planning reports and documents; 100 theses and dissertations.

★7712★ University of Wisconsin, Madison Water Resources Center
Library
1975 Willow Dr.
Madison, WI 53706
Phone: (608)262-3069
Fax: (608)262-0591
Contact: Sarah L. Calcese, Libn.
Subjects: Water resources - pollution sources, abatement and control, waste water treatment, limnology, resources management, research and planning, groundwater. ***Special Collections:*** Eutrophication (7168 reprints and documents); Water Resources Economics Collection (800 reprints). ***Holdings:*** 25,000 books and technical reports.

★7713★ University of Wyoming
Water Research Center
Library
Laramie, WY 82071
Phone: (307)766-2143
Fax: (307)766-3718
Contact: Pam Murdock, Adm.Asst.
Subjects: Water resources, evaporation, snow and ice, conservation, irrigation, water law, river basins and water planning, sanitary and civil engineering. ***Special Collections:*** U.S. Geological Survey water supply papers relating to Wyoming. ***Holdings:*** 1000 books; 14,000 reports, articles, reprints.

★7714★ Ventura County Library Services Agency
Government Center Reference Library
800 S. Victoria Ave.
Ventura, CA 93009
Phone: (805)654-2480
Fax: (805)654-2424
Contact: David B. Combe, Libn.
Subjects: Public administration, management, planning, environment, pollution, building and safety. ***Special Collections:*** Resource Management Agency Collection. ***Holdings:*** 400 books; 11,000 other cataloged items.

★7715★ Vermont Law School Library
Box 60
South Royalton, VT 05068
Phone: (802)763-8303
Fax: (802)763-7159
Contact: Carl A. Yirka, Assoc.Prof. & Libn.
Subjects: Law. ***Special Collections:*** Environmental law (5500 volumes); Historic Preservation (1150 volumes); Alternative Dispute Resolution (350 volumes). ***Holdings:*** 89,000 books; 14,300 bound periodical volumes; 61,800 volumes in microform; government document depository.

★7716★ Versar Inc.
Information Services
6850 Versar Center
Box 1549
Springfield, VA 22151
Phone: (703)750-3000
Fax: (703)642-6807
Contact: Lynn P. Freedman, Dir., Info.Serv.
Subjects: Environmental research and engineering, consulting, asbestos, PCBs, radon, waste management, risk assessment. ***Holdings:*** 2000 books; 300 periodical titles; technical reports; government publications.

★7717★ Virginia (State) Water Control Board
Library
2111 N. Hamilton St.
Box 11143
Richmond, VA 23230
Phone: (804)367-6340
Fax: (804)367-0067
Contact: Patricia G. Vanderland, Libn.
Subjects: Water, water pollution, waste water, groundwater, toxins in water, environment. ***Special Collections:*** Virginia State Water Control Board publications (185); Environmental Protection Agency publications (2500). ***Holdings:*** 5000 books; 15 bound periodical volumes; 6000 pamphlets and reprints; 1800 unbound reports; 6300 microforms; government publications on water and environment.

★7718★ Washington State Department of Ecology
Technical Library
PV-11
Olympia, WA 98504
Phone: (206)459-6150
Fax: (206)459-6007
Contact: Barbara Colquhoun, Tech.Libn.
Subjects: Water resources and quality, air quality, solid waste, environmental legislation, waste treatment, shorelines management, hazardous waste cleanup. ***Special Collections:*** Radioactive waste (100 items); publications of department and predecessor agencies. ***Holdings:*** 4000 books; 12,000 other cataloged items.

★7719★ Washington State Energy Office
Library
809 Legion Way, S.E.
Olympia, WA 98504
Phone: (206)586-5078
Fax: (206)753-2397
Contact: Gretchen K. Leslie, Sr.Libn.
Subjects: Energy conservation, resources, and planning; alternative sources of energy. ***Holdings:*** 3000 monographs; 7000 reports and documents.

★7720★ Water Pollution Control Federation
Library
601 Wythe St.
Alexandria, VA 22314-1994
Phone: (703)684-2400
Fax: (703)684-2492
Contact: Berinda J. Ross, Asst.Dir., Tech.Serv.
Subjects: Water pollution control, water supply and resources, wastewater treatment and disposal, sludge treatment and disposal, collection systems, environmental engineering. ***Special Collections:*** National Commission on Water Quality publications. ***Holdings:*** 2000 books; 300 bound periodical volumes.

★7721★ Water Quality Association
Research Council Library
4151 Naperville Rd.
Lisle, IL 60532
Phone: (708)369-1600
Fax: (312)369-1637
Contact: Lucius Cole, Tech.Dir.
Subjects: Water quality, water conditioning, home water supply, water usage, industrial water conditioning, water softening, water pollution, geographic water data. ***Special Collections:*** U.S. Government publications on water quality and usage; water conditioning industry publications; International Water Quality Symposia Proceedings, 1965-1968, 1970, 1972. ***Holdings:*** 1000 books; industry papers; manuscripts; clippings; committee reports and pamphlets.

★7722★ Wehran Envirotech
Library
666 E. Main St.
Middletown, NY 10940
Phone: (914)343-0660
Fax: (914)692-7376
Contact: Virginia Grady, Libn.
Subjects: Solid waste, wastewater, and water management; resource recovery; industrial pollution abatement; environmental monitoring. ***Special Collections:*** EPA reports on air, water, and waste. ***Holdings:*** 1480 books; 2000 government reports.

★7723★ West Valley Nuclear Services Company, Inc.
Technical Library
10300 Rock Springs Rd.
West Valley, NY 14171-0191
Phone: (716)942-4327
Fax: (716)942-4376
Telex: 4909989024WES
Contact: C.M. Schiffhauer, Tech.Libn.
Subjects: Nuclear waste management; engineering - mechanical, civil, chemical. ***Holdings:*** 900 books; 4000 government contractor reports.

★7724★ Western Michigan University
Science for Citizens Center
Environmental Resource Center for Community Information
Kalamazoo, MI 49008
Phone: (616)387-2715
Contact: Donald J. Brown, Ph.D., Dir.
Subjects: Environment, public policy, community planning. ***Special Collections:*** Groundwater management, protection, principles. ***Holdings:*** 3000 titles; 8 VF drawers of cataloged items.

★7725★ Westinghouse Hanford Company
Department of Energy's Public Reading Room, A1-65
Federal Bldg., Rm. 157
Box 1970
Richland, WA 99352
Phone: (509)376-8583
Fax: (509)376-2071
Contact: Terri Traub, Pub.Info.Spec.
Subjects: Hanford Project, nuclear waste management. ***Holdings:*** 50 books; 13,000 technical reports; 3500 microfiche.

★7726★ Westpoint Pepperell
Research Center
Information Services Library
3300 23rd Dr.
Valley, AL 36854
Phone: (404)645-4658
Contact: Debbie Keeble
Subjects: Textiles, chemistry, textile testing, dyeing, fire retardancy, environmental pollution, engineering, industrial hygiene. ***Holdings:*** 3000 books; 2500 bound periodical volumes; 15 VF drawers of research reports; 4 VF drawers of patents; 4 VF drawers of reprints; 4000 microfiche; 4 VF drawers of catalogs, brochures, and manufacturing technical data.

★7727★ Wildlife Management Institute
Library
1101 Fourteenth St., N.W., Ste. 725
Washington, DC 20005
Phone: (202)347-1774
Fax: (202)408-5059
Contact: Richard E. McCabe, Sec./Dir., Pubns.
Subjects: Wildlife and conservation. ***Special Collections:*** Complete Transactions of North American Wildlife and Natural Resources Conference; Proceedings of American Game Conference (complete set); American Game Bulletin (complete run). ***Holdings:*** 1000 volumes.

★7728★ Williams College
Center for Environmental Studies
Matt Cole Memorial Library
Box 632
Williamstown, MA 01267
Phone: (413)597-2500
Fax: (413)597-4088
Contact: Marcella Rauscher, Res.Coord.
Subjects: Air pollution, coasts, energy, environmental health, environmental law, land use, natural resources, toxic substances, water resources, local and regional data and planning. ***Holdings:*** 3500 books; 1700 bound periodical volumes; 3100 EPA documents; 9000 other documents.

★7729★ Wisconsin (State) Department of Natural Resources
Library
Box 7921
Madison, WI 53707
Phone: (608)266-8933
Subjects: Environmental protection, air pollution, solid waste and water quality management, natural resources, fish and wildlife. ***Holdings:*** 6500 books; 100 bound periodical volumes; 4500 other cataloged items.

★7730★ Wisconsin (State) Department of Natural Resources
Southeast District Library
2300 N. Martin Luther King Jr. Dr.
Milwaukee, WI 53212
Phone: (414)263-8493
Fax: (414)263-8483
Contact: Kathleen Schultz, Libn.
Subjects: Pollution and quality of air and water, fish and wildlife, solid waste management, parks and recreation, forestry. ***Special Collections:*** Departmental publications (700 technical bulletins, research reports, surface water reports, fish management reports); Environmental Protection Agency documents (1200). ***Holdings:*** 2900 books; 116 bound periodical volumes.

★7731★ Withlacoochee Regional Planning Council
Library
1241 S.W. 10th St.
Ocala, FL 32674-2798
Phone: (904)732-1315
Fax: (904)732-1319
Contact: Vivian A. Whittier, Info.Spec.
Subjects: Statistics, planning, land use, water, energy, criminal justice, census data. ***Holdings:*** 5000 bound periodical volumes; maps; technical reports.

★7732★ Woodward-Clyde Consultants
Library
203 N. Golden Circle Dr.
Santa Ana, CA 92705
Phone: (714)835-6886
Fax: (714)667-7147
Telex: 68 3420
Contact: Ute Hertel, Libn.
Subjects: Geology, geophysics, engineering, waste management. ***Holdings:*** 15,000 books; 950 unbound periodical volumes; 900 WW reports; 3000 WCC project files; 15 file cabinets of maps; 2 file cabinets of reprints; microfiche.

★7733★ World Meteorological Organization
WMO Library
PO Box 2300
41, ave. Giuseppe-Motta
CH-1211 Geneva 2, Switzerland
Phone: 22 730 84 11
Fax: 22 734 23 26
Telex: 23 260 OMM CH
Contact: Miss Favre, Libn.
Subjects: Weather prediction, world climate, tropical meteorology, monitoring environmental pollution, weather modification, hydrology, atmospheric sciences. ***Holdings:*** 35,000 volumes.

★7734★ World Resources Institute
Library
1709 New York Ave., N.W., 7th Fl.
Washington, DC 20006
Phone: (202)622-2504
Fax: (202)638-0036
Telex: 64414 WRIWASH
Contact: Susan N. Terry, Libn.
Subjects: Environment, natural resources, agriculture, forestry, climate, energy, biodiversity, sustainable development. ***Holdings:*** 7000 books and reports; 20 VF drawers of pamphlets and clippings; studies.

★7735★ World Wildlife Fund-U.S.
Conservation Foundation
Library
1250 24th St., N.W.
Washington, DC 20037
Phone: (202)293-4800
Fax: (202)293-9211
Telex: 64505 Panda
Contact: Barbara K. Rodes, Res.Libn.
Subjects: Natural resource conservation, environmental quality, pollution, land use planning, wildlife and economic development, habitat preservation, global climate change, international environmental policy. ***Holdings:*** 10,000 volumes; clippings file.

★7736★ W.R. Grace and Company
Dearborn Division Library
300 Genesee St.
Lake Zurich, IL 60047
Phone: (708)438-1800
Fax: (708)540-1566
Contact: Julie Z. Baldwin, Libn.
Subjects: Water treatment, corrosion, inorganic chemistry, organic chemistry, polymers, environmental engineering, pollution control, water bacteriology, spectroscopy. ***Holdings:*** 4000 books; 2100 bound periodical volumes; 900 research notebooks; 6000 U.S. and foreign patents; 5300 research reports.

★7737★ Yale University
Yale Forestry Library
205 Prospect St.
New Haven, CT 06511
Phone: (203)432-5130
Fax: (203)432-5942
Contact: Joseph A. Miller, Libn.
Subjects: Forestry, environmental studies, ecology, natural resources management, conservation, soils, land use, planning. ***Holdings:*** 130,000 books, bound periodical volumes, government documents, and reports; 125 newsletter titles; 900 dissertations; 500 maps; 2500 microforms.

★7738★ Yellowstone Environmental Science, Inc.
Library
320 S. Willson Ave.
Bozeman, MT 59715
Phone: (406)586-3905
Fax: (406)587-5109
Subjects: Environmental engineering and protection, public health, wastewater engineering. ***Holdings:*** 200 items; patents.

Environmental Corporate Contacts

★7739★ A. Schulman Inc.
3550 W. Market St.
Akron, OH 44333
Phone: (216)666-3751
Env. Contact: Jim Kandel

★7740★ Abbott Laboratories
1 Abbott Park Rd.
Abbott Park, IL 60064-3500
Phone: (708)937-6100
Env. Contact: Daniel Quayne

★7741★ Air Products and Chemicals Inc.
7201 Hamilton Blvd.
Allentown, PA 18195
Phone: (215)481-4911
Env. Contact: Charlotte Walker

★7742★ Albany International Corp.
PO Box 1907
Albany, NY 12201
Phone: (518)445-2200
Env. Contact: Jerry Sokaris

★7743★ Alberto-Culver Co.
2525 Armitage Ave.
Melrose Park, IL 60160
Phone: (708)450-3000
Env. Contact: Michelle Evans

★7744★ Allegheny Ludlum Corp.
6 PPG Pl.
Pittsburgh, PA 15222
Phone: (412)394-2800
Env. Contact: Greg Eckstein

★7745★ Allegheny Power
12 E. 49th St.
New York, NY 10017
Phone: (212)752-2121
Env. Contact: Peter Skrgic

★7746★ Allergan Inc.
2525 Dupont Dr.
Irvine, CA 92713-9534
Phone: (714)752-4500
Env. Contact: Kay Mills

★7747★ Allied-Signal Inc.
101 Columbia Rd.
Morristown, NJ 07962
Phone: (201)455-2000
Env. Contact: Mike Ascolese

★7748★ Aluminum Company of America
1501 Alcoa Bldg.
Pittsburgh, PA 15219
Phone: (412)553-4545
Env. Contact: Dr. Patrick R. Atkins

★7749★ AMAX Inc.
200 Park Ave.
New York, NY 10166
Phone: (212)856-4200
Env. Contact: Terry Fitzsimmons

★7750★ Amerada Hess Corp.
1185 Ave. of the Americas
New York, NY 10036
Phone: (212)997-8500
Env. Contact: Ted Helfgott

★7751★ American Cyanamid Co.
1 Cyanamid Plz.
Wayne, NJ 07470
Phone: (201)831-2000
Env. Contact: Richard Dennis

★7752★ American Electric
One Riverside Plaza
Columbus, OH 43215
Phone: (614)223-1000
Env. Contact: Tom Webb

★7753★ American Home Products Corp.
685 3rd Ave.
New York, NY 10017-4085
Phone: (212)878-5000
Env. Contact: Linda Mullenan

★7754★ American Petrofina
8350 N. Central Expwy.
Dallas, TX 75206
Phone: (214)750-2400
Env. Contact: Rick Hagar

★7755★ American Standard Inc.
1114 Ave. of Americas
New York, NY 10036
Phone: (212)703-5100
Alt. Phone: (201)980-3000
Fax: (201)980-3034
Env. Contact: Kevin Tubbs

★7756★ American Water Works
1025 Laurel Oak Rd.
Voorhees, NJ 08043
Phone: (609)346-8200
Env. Contact: Ward Welsh

★7757★ Amgen
1840 Dehavilland
Thousand Oaks, CA 91320
Phone: (805)499-5725
Env. Contact: Mark Brand

★7758★ Amoco Corp.
Environmental Affairs and Safety Division
200 E. Randolph Dr.
Chicago, IL 60601
Phone: (312)856-6111

★7759★ Amsted Industries Inc.
Blvd. Twrs S. 44th Fl.
205 N Michigan
Chicago, IL 60601
Phone: (312)645-1700
Fax: (312)819-8425
Env. Contact: Dave O'Neill

★7760★ Anadarko Petroleum Corp.
PO Box 1330
Houston, TX 77251
Phone: (713)875-1101
Env. Contact: Paul Lankford

★7761★ A.O. Smith Corp.
PO Box 23972
Milwaukee, WI 53223
Phone: (414)359-4000
Env. Contact: Hank Hedges

★7762★ Apache
1700 Lincoln St.
Denver, CO 80203
Phone: (303)837-5000
Env. Contact: Gregory Pyles

★7763★ Arco Chemical
3801 W. Chester Pk.
Newtown Sq., PA 19073
Phone: (215)359-2000
Env. Contact: Jerry Davis

★7764★ Arkla Inc.
Arkla Bldg.
Shreveport, LA 71101
Phone: (318)429-2700
Env. Contact: Skip Rutherford

★7765★ Armco Inc.
300 Interpace Pkwy.
Parsippany, NJ 07054
Phone: (201)316-5200
Env. Contact: Dan Kemp

★7766★ Asarco Inc.
180 Maiden Ln.
New York, NY 10038
Phone: (212)510-2000
Env. Contact: Don Noyes

★7767★ Ashland Oil Inc.
PO Box 391
Ashland, TX 41114
Phone: (606)329-3333

Env. Contact: Roger Schrum

★7768★ Atlanta Gas & Light
235 Peachtree St., N.E.
Atlanta, GA 30302
Phone: (404)584-4000
Env. Contact: Dudley Sprvill

★7769★ Atlantic Energy
Environmental Affairs Dept.
PO Box 1264
Pleasantville, NJ 08232
Phone: (609)645-4100

★7770★ Atlantic Richfield Co.
515 S. Flower St.
Los Angeles, CA 90071
Phone: (213)486-3511
Env. Contact: Tom Butler

★7771★ Avery Dennison Corp.
150 N. Orange Grove
Pasadena, CA 91103
Phone: (818)304-2000
Fax: (818)792-7312
Env. Contact: Frank Brandauer

★7772★ Baker Hughes Inc.
3900 Essex Ln.
Houston, TX 77027
Phone: (713)439-8600
Env. Contact: Joe Curtis

★7773★ Ball Corp.
PO Box 2407
Muncie, IN 47307-0407
Phone: (317)747-6100
Env. Contact: Kent Bickell

★7774★ Baltimore G & E
39 W. Lexington
Baltimore, MD 21201
Phone: (301)234-5000
Env. Contact: Dr. Elizabeth Bavereis, Dir. of Environmental Programs

★7775★ Bandag Inc.
Bandag Ctr.
Muscatine, IA 52761-5886
Phone: (319)262-1400
Env. Contact: Dave Nowling

★7776★ Baroid
3000 N. Sam Houston, E.
Houston, TX 77032
Phone: (713)987-4000
Env. Contact: Aston Hinds

★7777★ BASF Corp.
Public Relations Dept.
Eight Campus Dr.
Parsippany, NJ 07054
Phone: (201)397-2700
Fax: (201)397-2737
Toll-Free: 800-533-2286
Telex: 1366447

★7778★ Battle Mountain
333 Clay St.
Houston, TX 77002
Phone: (713)650-6400
Env. Contact: Les Van Dyke

★7779★ Bemis Company Inc.
625 Marquette Ave.
Minneapolis, MN 55402
Phone: (612)340-6000
Env. Contact: Scott W. Johnson

★7780★ Bethlehem Steel Corp.
701 E. 3rd St.
Bethlehem, PA 18016-7699
Phone: (215)694-2424
Env. Contact: Thomas E. Kreichelt

★7781★ Betz Laboratories Inc.
4636 Somerton Rd.
Trevose, PA 19053
Phone: (215)355-3300
Env. Contact: Gary Kralik

★7782★ B.F. Goodrich Co.
Public Relations Dept.
3925 Embassy Pkwy.
Akron, OH 44333
Phone: (216)374-2000

★7783★ BJ Services Co.
PO Box 4442
Houston, TX 77210
Phone: (713)462-4239
Fax: (713)895-5851
Env. Contact: Joanne Cobb

★7784★ Block Drug Co.
Public Relations Office
257 Cornelison Ave.
Jersey City, NJ 07302
Phone: (201)434-3000
Fax: (201)333-3585

★7785★ Boeing Co.
7755 E. Marginal Way S.
Seattle, WA 98108
Phone: (206)655-2121
Env. Contact: Russell Young

★7786★ Boise Cascade Corp.
1 Jefferson Sq.
Boise, ID 83728
Phone: (208)384-6161
Fax: (208)384-4841
Env. Contact: Steve Erickson

★7787★ Borden Inc.
277 Park Ave.
New York, NY 10172
Phone: (215)573-4000
Env. Contact: Jean Washko

★7788★ Boston Edison
800 Boylstan St.
Boston, MA 02199
Phone: (617)424-2000
Env. Contact: Frank Lee

★7789★ Bowater Inc.
PO Box 4012
Darien, CT 06820-4012
Phone: (203)656-7200
Env. Contact: Bob Harley

★7790★ Briggs and Stratton Corp.
PO Box 702
Milwaukee, WI 53201
Phone: (414)259-5333
Env. Contact: Alan Haase

★7791★ Bristol-Myers Squibb Co.
345 Park Ave.
New York, NY 10154-0037
Phone: (212)546-4000
Env. Contact: Wayne Carlson

★7792★ Brooklyn Union Gas
195 Montague St.
Brooklyn, NY 11201
Phone: (718)403-2000
Env. Contact: Lawrence Liebs

★7793★ Browning-Ferris
Public Relations Dept.
757 N. Eldridge
Houston, TX 77079
Phone: (713)870-8100

★7794★ Brunswick Corp.
Public Relations Dept.
1 Brunswick Plz.
Skokie, IL 60077-1089
Phone: (708)470-4700

★7795★ Burlington Holdings Inc.
Public Relations Dept.
1345 Ave. of the Americas
New York, NY 10105
Phone: (212)621-3000

★7796★ Cabot Corp.
PO Box 9073
Waltham, MA 02254-9073
Phone: (617)890-0200
Env. Contact: Karen Inman

★7797★ Calgon Carbon
500 Calgon Carbon Dr.
Robinson Twp., PA 15205
Phone: (412)787-6700
Env. Contact: Del Kubeldis

★7798★ CalMat Co.
Public Affairs
3200 San Fernando Rd.
Los Angeles, CA 90065
Phone: (213)258-2777

★7799★ Carolina Power
411 Fayetteville St.
Raleigh, NC 27602
Phone: (919)546-6111
Env. Contact: George Oliver

★7800★ Carpenter Technology Corp.
PO Box 14662
Reading, PA 19612-4662
Phone: (215)371-2000
Env. Contact: Thomas Dickerson

★7801★ Carter-Wallace Inc.
PO Box 1001
Cranberry, NJ 08512
Phone: (609)655-6000
Fax: (212)339-5100
Env. Contact: Rick Majos

★7802★ Caterpillar Inc.
100 N.E. Adams St.
Peoria, IL 61629
Phone: (309)675-1000
Env. Contact: Gerald Rittenbausch, Product Safety and Env. Control

★7803★ CBI Industries Inc.
800 Jorie Blvd.
Oak Brook, IL 60522-7001
Phone: (708)572-7000
Env. Contact: David Fichter

★7804★ Central Hudson G & E
284 S. Ave.
Poughkeepsie, NY 12601
Phone: (914)452-2000
Env. Contact: Jeff Clock

★7805★ Central LA. Electric
2030 Donahue Ferry Rd.
Pineville, LA 71360
Phone: (318)484-7400
Env. Contact: Paul Turregano

★7806★ Central Maine Power
Edison Dr.
Augusta, ME 04336
Phone: (207)623-3521
Env. Contact: James Wazlaw

★7807★ CF Industries Inc.
Salem Lake Dr.
Long Grove, IL 60047
Phone: (708)438-9500
Fax: (708)438-0211
Env. Contact: Richard Ghent

★7808★ Chambers Dev.
Public Affairs Dept.
10700 Frankstown Rd.
Pittsburgh, PA 15235
Phone: (412)242-6237

★7809★ Champion Intl.
One Champion Plaza
Stamford, CT 06921
Phone: (203)358-7000
Env. Contact: Richard Diforio

★7810★ Chemed Corp.
Consumer Relations Dept.
1200 DuBois Tower
Cincinnati, OH 45202-3199
Phone: (513)762-6900

★7811★ Chesapeake Corp.
PO Box 2350
Richmond, VA 23218-2350
Phone: (804)697-1000
Env. Contact: Mike Balanca

★7812★ Chevron Corp.
Consumer Relations Dept.
225 Bush St.
San Francisco, CA 94104-4289
Phone: (415)894-7700

★7813★ Chrysler Corp.
Environmental and Energy Affairs Dept.
PO Box 1919
Detroit, MI 48288-1919
Phone: (313)956-5741
Fax: (313)956-1462

★7814★ Church and Dwight Company Inc.
469 N. Harrison St.
Princeton, NJ 08543
Phone: (609)683-5900
Env. Contact: Brian Thomlison

★7815★ Cilcorp
300 Liberty St.
Peoria, IL 61602
Phone: (309)672-5271
Env. Contact: Susan Stukenberg

★7816★ Cincinnati G & E
139 E. Fourth St.
Cincinnati, OH 45202
Phone: (513)381-2000
Env. Contact: Bob McElfresh

★7817★ Citizens Utilities
PO Box 3801
Stamford, CT 06905-0390
Phone: (203)329-8800
Env. Contact: David Chardavoyne, V.P. of Water

★7818★ Cleveland-Cliffs Inc.
1100 Superior Ave.
Cleveland, OH 44114-2589
Phone: (216)694-5700
Env. Contact: Philip Brick

★7819★ Clorox Co.
1221 Broadway
Oakland, CA 94612
Phone: (415)271-7000
Env. Contact: Fred Reicker, Dir. Corp. Comm.

★7820★ Coastal
Nine Greenway Plaza
Houston, TX 77046
Phone: (713)877-1400
Env. Contact: Douglas Ricks

★7821★ Coastal Corp.
Nine Greenway Plaza
Houston, TX 77046
Phone: (713)877-1400
Env. Contact: Robert Morris

★7822★ Colgate-Palmolive Co.
300 Park Ave.
New York, NY 10022-7499
Phone: (212)310-2000
Env. Contact: Robert Holland, Dir. Environmental Affairs

★7823★ Columbia Gas System
Corporate Communications Dept.
20 Montchanin Rd.
Wilmington, DE 19807
Phone: (302)429-5000

★7824★ Common Edison
72 W. Adams
Chicago, IL 60603
Phone: (312)294-4321
Env. Contact: Tom Hemminger

★7825★ Cone Mills Corp.
1201 Maple St.
Greensboro, NC 27405
Phone: (919)379-6098
Env. Contact: Arthur Toompas

★7826★ Cons. Edison
Four Irving Pl.
New York, NY 10003
Phone: (212)460-4600
Env. Contact: Dominick Mormile

★7827★ Cons. Natural Gas
625 Liberty Ave.
Pittsburgh, PA 15222
Phone: (412)227-1000
Env. Contact: John Conti

★7828★ Consolidated Papers Inc.
PO Box 8050
Wisconsin Rapids, WI 54495-8050
Phone: (715)422-3111
Env. Contact: James Weinbauer, Corp. Environmental Mgr.

★7829★ Cooper Industries Inc.
PO Box 4446
Houston, TX 77210
Phone: (713)739-5400
Env. Contact: Robert Teets, Dir. of Environmental Affairs

★7830★ Cooper Tire and Rubber Co.
Lima Ave. & Western
Findlay, OH 45839-0550
Phone: (419)423-1321
Env. Contact: Thomas Wood, Corp. Environmental Eng.

★7831★ Crompton and Knowles Corp.
1 Sta. Pl.
Stamford, CT 06902
Phone: (203)353-5400
Env. Contact: Tim Sullivan, Mgr. of Environment, Health & Safety

★7832★ Crown Central Petroleum Corp.
PO Box 1168
Baltimore, MD 21203
Phone: (301)539-7400
Env. Contact: Jeff Folks, Gov't Regulations Specialist

★7833★ Crown Cork and Seal Company Inc.
Consumer Relations Dept.
9300 Ashton Rd.
Philadelphia, PA 19136
Phone: (215)698-5358

★7834★ CSX Corp.
Corporate Communications Dept.
1 James Ctr.
Richmond, VA 23261
Phone: (804)782-1400

★7835★ Cummins Engine Company Inc.
PO Box 3005
Columbus, IN 47202
Phone: (812)377-5000
Env. Contact: Ann Smith

★7836★ Cyclops Industries Inc.
Public Relations Dept.
650 Washington Rd.
Pittsburgh, PA 15228
Phone: (412)343-4000

★7837★ Cyprus Minerals Co.
PO Box 3299
Englewood, CO 80155
Phone: (303)643-5000
Env. Contact: Les Darling

★7838★ Dana Corp.
PO Box 1000
Toledo, OH 43697
Phone: (419)535-4500
Env. Contact: Mark Hess

★7839★ Danaher Corp.
Consumer Relations Dept.
1250 24th St., N.W.
Washington, DC 20037
Phone: (202)828-0850

★7840★ Delmarva Power
800 King St.
Wilmington, DE 19899
Phone: (302)429-3011
Env. Contact: Matt Likovitch

★7841★ Desoto Inc.
Public Relations Dept.
PO Box 5030
Des Plaines, IL 60017
Phone: (708)391-9000
Fax: (708)391-9304
Telex: DESOTO DSP 726436

★7842★ Detroit Edison
2000 Second Ave.
Detroit, MI 48226
Phone: (313)237-8000
Env. Contact: S. Martin Taylor

★7843★ Dexter Corp.
1 Elm St.
Windsor Locks, CT 06096
Phone: (203)627-9051
Fax: (203)627-9713
Env. Contact: John Blatz

★7844★ Diamond Shamrock Inc.
PO Box 696000
San Antonio, TX 78269-6000
Phone: (512)641-6800
Env. Contact: Kathy Hughes

★7845★ Dow Chemical Corp.
Public Affairs Dept.
2030 Willard H. Dow
Midland, MI 48674
Phone: (517)636-6400

★7846★ Dow Corning Corp.
Public Relations Dept.
PO Box 994
Midland, MI 48686-0994
Phone: (517)496-4000
Fax: (517)496-4572
Telex: 227450

★7847★ Dresser Industries Inc.
Government and Business Affairs
1600 Pacific Bldg.
Dallas, TX 75201
Phone: (214)740-6000

★7848★ Dresser-Rand
100 Chemung St.
Painted Post, NY 14870
Phone: (607)937-2011
Fax: (607)937-2043
Env. Contact: Bill Misnick

★7849★ Duke Power
422 S. Church St.
Charlotte, NC 28242-0001
Phone: (704)373-4011
Env. Contact: Joseph Harwood

★7850★ Eagle-Picher Industries Inc.
580 Walnut St.
Cincinnati, OH 45202
Phone: (513)721-7010
Env. Contact: J. Rodman Nall

★7851★ Eastern Enterprises
9 Riverside Rd.
Weston, MA 02193
Phone: (617)647-2300
Env. Contact: Ronald S. Ziemba

★7852★ Eastern Utilities
One Liberty Sq.
PO Box 2333
Boston, MA 02107
Phone: (617)357-9590
Env. Contact: John R. Stevens

★7853★ Eastman Kodak Co.
343 State St.
Rochester, NY 14650
Phone: (716)724-4000
Env. Contact: James Blamphin

★7854★ Ecolab Inc.
Community Affairs Office
Ecolab Ctr.
St. Paul, MN 55102
Phone: (612)293-2233

★7855★ EG and G Inc.
Public Relations Dept.
45 William St.
Wellesley, MA 02181
Phone: (617)237-5100
Fax: (617)431-4115

★7856★ E.I. Du Pont De Nemours & Company Inc.
Public Relations Dept.
1007 Market St.
Wilmington, DE 19898
Phone: (302)774-1000
Fax: (302)774-8693
Telex: 302-774-4131

★7857★ Eli Lilly and Co.
Lilly Corporate Ctr.
Indianapolis, IN 46285
Phone: (317)276-3219
Env. Contact: Edward A. West

★7858★ Emerson Electric Co.
PO Box 4100
St. Louis, MO 63136
Phone: (314)553-2000
Env. Contact: Derek Chase

★7859★ Engelhard Corp.
101 Wood Ave.
Iselin, NJ 08830
Phone: (908)205-6000
Env. Contact: Edmund A. Giebel

★7860★ Enron
Customer Relations Dept.
1400 Smith St.
Houston, TX 77002
Phone: (713)853-6161

★7861★ Enserch
300 S. St. Paul St.
Dallas, TX 75201
Phone: (214)651-8700
Env. Contact: John F. Williams

★7862★ Equitable Resources
420 Blvd. of the Allies
Pittsburgh, PA 15219
Phone: (412)261-3000
Env. Contact: Brian Plante

★7863★ Ethyl Corp.
Public Relations Dept.
PO Box 2189
Richmond, VA 23217
Phone: (804)788-5000

★7864★ Exide Corp.
Public Relations Dept.
PO Box 14205
Reading, PA 19612-4205
Phone: (215)378-0500
Fax: (215)378-0748

★7865★ Exxon Corp.
225 E. John Carpenter
Irving, TX 75062
Phone: (214)444-1000
Env. Contact: E.J. Hess

★7866★ Farmland Industries Inc.
3315 N. Oak Trafficway
Kansas City, MO 64116
Phone: (816)459-6000
Fax: (816)459-5679
Env. Contact: Joe Crites

★7867★ Federal Paper Board Company Inc.
Public Relations Dept.
75 Chestnut Ridge Rd.
Montvale, NJ 07645
Phone: (201)391-1776

★7868★ Ferro Corp.
1000 Lakeside Ave.
Cleveland, OH 44114-1183
Phone: (216)641-8580
Env. Contact: Joseph Berish

★7869★ First Brands Corp.
PO Box 1911
Danbury, CT 06813-1911
Phone: (203)731-2300
Env. Contact: Patrick O'Brien

★7870★ FMC Corp.
200 E. Randolph Dr.
Chicago, IL 60601
Phone: (312)861-6000
Env. Contact: Patricia Brozowski

★7871★ Ford Motor Co.
PO Box 1899
Dearborn, MI 48121
Phone: (313)322-3000
Env. Contact: Beryl Goldsweig

★7872★ Forest Laboratories
150 E. 58th St.
New York, NY 10155
Phone: (212)421-7850
Env. Contact: Richard Overton

★7873★ Fort Howard Corp.
1919 S. Broadway
Green Bay, WI 54304-1919
Phone: (414)435-8821
Env. Contact: Cliff Bowers

★7874★ FPL Group
Environmental Affairs Dept.
11770 U. S. Hwy One, N.
Palm Beach, FL 33408
Phone: (407)694-6300

★7875★ Freeport-McMoran Inc.
1615 Poydras St.
New Orleans, LA 70112
Phone: (504)582-4000
Env. Contact: Garland Robinette

★7876★ GAF Corp.
1361 Alps Rd.
Wayne, NJ 07470
Phone: (201)628-3000
Toll-Free: 800-669-6060
Env. Contact: J. Bizarro

★7877★ GenCorp Inc.
175 Ghent Rd.
Fairlawn, OH 44333-3300
Phone: (216)869-4200
Env. Contact: James Armstrong, Env. Health and Safety

★7878★ Genentech
Customers Relation Dept.
460 Pt. San Bruno S.
San Francisco, CA 94080
Phone: (415)266-1000

★7879★ General Dynamics Corp.
Pierre Laclede Ctr.
St. Louis, MO 63105
Phone: (314)889-8200
Env. Contact: Robert Hill

★7880★ General Electric Co.
Corporate Environmental Protection
3135 Easton Tpk.
Fairfield, CT 06431
Phone: (203)373-2211

★7881★ General Motors Corp. Communications and Marketing
3044 W. Grand Blvd.
Detroit, MI 48202
Phone: (313)556-5000

★7882★ General Public Uts.
Customer Relations Dept.
100 Interpace Pkwy.
Parsippany, NJ 07054
Phone: (201)263-6500

★7883★ General Signal Corp.
PO Box 10010
Stamford, CT 06904
Phone: (203)357-8800
Env. Contact: Daniel McGrade

★7884★ Georgia Gulf Corp.
400 Perimeter Ctr.
Atlanta, GA 30346
Phone: (404)395-4500
Env. Contact: Beverly Gholson, Associate of Gen. Council

★7885★ Georgia-Pacific Corp.
PO Box 105605
Atlanta, GA 30348-5605
Phone: (404)521-4000
Env. Contact: Keith Bentley, Sr. Mgr. Env. Eng.

★7886★ Gillette Co.
3900 Prudential Tower
Boston, MA 02199
Phone: (617)421-7000
Env. Contact: Robert Healey, Dir. Env. Aff.

★7887★ Glatfelter (P.H)
228 S. Main St.
Spring Grove, PA 17362
Phone: (717)225-4711
Env. Contact: Dr. C. Neal Carter

★7888★ Global Marine
777 N. Eldridge St.
Houston, TX 77079
Phone: (713)596-5100
Env. Contact: Max Warden

★7889★ Goodyear Tire and Rubber Co.
1144 E. Market St.
Akron, OH 44316-0001
Phone: (216)796-2121
Env. Contact: Joseph L. Holtshouser, Env. Industrial Hygiene Mgr.

★7890★ Grace Energy Corp.
1114 Ave. of the Americas
New York, NY 10036
Phone: (212)819-5500
Env. Contact: Dr. Alen Pierce, Env. Specialist

★7891★ Great Lakes Chemical Corp.
PO Box 2200
West Lafayette, IN 47906
Phone: (317)497-6100
Env. Contact: Tim Kelley, Corp. Env. Dir.

★7892★ Grumman Corp. Consumer Relations Dept.
1111 Stewart Ave.
Bethpage, NY 11714-3580
Phone: (516)575-3344

★7893★ GTE Corp.
1 Stamford Forum
Stamford, CT 06904
Phone: (203)965-2000
Env. Contact: Donald Espach

★7894★ Gulf States Utilities
350 Pine
Beaumont, TX 77701
Phone: (409)838-6631
Env. Contact: Jim Mutch

★7895★ Halliburton Co.
3600 Lincoln Plz.
Dallas, TX 75201-3391
Phone: (214)978-2600
Env. Contact: John Marcus, V.P. Investor Relations

★7896★ Hamilton Oil
1560 Broadway
Denver, CO 80202
Phone: (303)863-3000
Env. Contact: Jim Riemersma

★7897★ Handy and Harman
850 3rd Ave.
New York, NY 10022
Phone: (212)752-3400
Env. Contact: George Ekern, Corp. Sec.

★7898★ Hawaiian Electric
Public Relations Dept.
900 Richards St.
Honolulu, HI 96813
Phone: (808)543-5662

★7899★ H.B. Fuller Co.
2400 Energy Park Dr.
St. Paul, MN 55108
Phone: (612)645-3401
Env. Contact: Brian Lim, Env. Issues

★7900★ Helene Curtis Industries Inc.
325 N. Wells St.
Chicago, IL 60610
Phone: (312)661-0222
Env. Contact: Peter Wentz

★7901★ Helmerich & Payne
1579 E. 21st St.
Tulsa, OK 74114
Phone: (918)742-5531
Env. Contact: Dennis Moutray

★7902★ Hercules Inc.
Hercules Plaza
Wilmington, DE 19894-0001
Phone: (302)594-5000
Env. Contact: Douglas Keilman, Mgr. Env. Affairs

★7903★ Hoechst Celanese Corp.
Route 202-206
Somerville, NJ 08876
Phone: (908)231-2000
Fax: (201)231-3225
Toll-Free: 800-235-2637
Telex: 833442
Env. Contact: Michael Cannaro

★7904★ Homestake Mining Co.
650 California St.
San Francisco, CA 94108-2788
Phone: (415)981-8150
Fax: (415)397-5038
Env. Contact: David Crouch, Environmental Mgr.

★7905★ Honeywell Inc.
PO Box 524
Minneapolis, MN 55440
Phone: (612)870-5200
Env. Contact: Bill McMurtuy, Environmental Mgt.

★7906★ Houston Industries
4300 Post Oak Pkwy.
Houston, TX 77027
Phone: (713)629-3000
Env. Contact: Randall Oliver

★7907★ Idaho Power
1220 W. Idaho St.
Boise, ID 83707
Phone: (208)383-2200
Env. Contact: Jeff Beaman

★7908★ IE Industries
201 First St., S. E.
Cedar Rapids, IA 52401
Phone: (319)398-4411
Env. Contact: Colleen Reilly

★7909★ Illinois Power
500 S. 27th St.
Decatur, IL 62525
Phone: (217)424-6600
Env. Contact: Debbie Fletcher

★7910★ IMC Fertilizer Group Inc.
2100 Sanders Rd.
Northbrook, IL 60062
Phone: (708)272-9200
Env. Contact: Loren McClean, Dir. of Safety and Env.

★7911★ Inland Steel Industries Inc.
30 W. Monroe St.
Chicago, IL 60603
Phone: (312)346-0300
Env. Contact: Bob Lesler, Corporate Communications

★7912★ International Flavors and Fragrances Inc.
521 W. 57th St.
New York, NY 10019
Phone: (212)765-5500
Env. Contact: David Breuer, Mgr. Affiliate Env. Compliance

★7913★ International Paper Co.
2 Manhattanville Rd.
Purchase, NY 10577
Phone: (914)397-1500
Env. Contact: Alan Lindsay, Dir. of Env.

★7914★ Intl. Technolgy
Public Relations Dept.
23456 Hawthorne Blvd.
Torrance, CA 90505
Phone: (213)378-9933

★7915★ Iowa-Illinois G & E
206 E. Second ST.
Davenport, IA 52801
Phone: (319)326-7111
Env. Contact: Tom Albertson

★7916★ Ipalco Enterprises
25 Monument Circle
Indianapolis, IN 46204
Phone: (317)261-8261
Env. Contact: Jan Lower

★7917★ ITT Corp.
1330 Ave. of the Americas
New York, NY 10019-5490
Phone: (212)258-1000
Env. Contact: Laurence Kornreich, Dir. of Env. and Safety

★7918★ James River Corporation of Virginia
PO Box 2218
Richmond, VA 23217
Phone: (804)644-5411
Env. Contact: Kathleen Bennett, Dir. Env. Affairs

★7919★ Johnson and Johnson
1 Johnson & Johnson
New Brunswick, NJ 08933
Phone: (908)524-0400
Env. Contact: Vivian Pai, Dir. Env. Regulatory Aff.

★7920★ Johnson Controls Inc.
PO Box 591
Milwaukee, WI 53201
Phone: (414)228-1200
Env. Contact: Jordon Harwood, Mgr. Environmental Control

★7921★ JWP Inc.
2975 Westchester Ave.
Purchase, NY 10577
Phone: (914)935-4000
Env. Contact: Rupert Walters, Pres. of Energy and Env.

★7922★ Kansas City Power
1330 Baltimore Ave.
Kansas City, MO 64105
Phone: (816)556-2200
Env. Contact: Terry Eaton

★7923★ Kansas G & E
120 E. First St.
Wichita, KS 67202
Phone: (316)261-6611
Env. Contact: Lynn Wips

★7924★ Kansas Power
818 Kansas Ave.
Topeka, KS 66612
Phone: (913)296-6300
Env. Contact: Michelle Quakenbush

★7925★ Kentucky Utilities
One Quality St.
Lexington, KY 40507
Phone: (606)255-2100
Env. Contact: Carol Pfeiffer

★7926★ Kerr-McGee Corp.
PO Box 25861
Oklahoma City, OK 73125
Phone: (405)270-1313
Env. Contact: John Stauter, Dir. of Env. Services

★7927★ Kimberly-Clark Corp.
PO Box 619100
Dallas, TX 75261-9100
Phone: (214)830-1200
Env. Contact: Ken Strassner, V.P. Env. and Energy Aff.

★7928★ Lawter International 950
990 Skokie Blvd.
Northbrook, IL 60062
Phone: (708)498-4700
Env. Contact: David Aynessazian

★7929★ LG&E Energy
220 W. Main St.
Louisville, KY 40202
Phone: (502)627-2000
Env. Contact: Terry Naulty

★7930★ Litton Industries Inc.
360 N. Crescent Dr.
Beverly Hills, CA 90210-4867
Phone: (213)859-5000
Env. Contact: Andy Clemens, Mgr. Env. Aff.

★7931★ Lockheed Corp.
4500 Park Granada Blvd.
Calabasas, CA 91399
Phone: (818)712-2000
Env. Contact: Fred Reed, Dir. Fin. Ass. & Env./Indst. Sft. Ctrl.

★7932★ Loctite Corp.
10 Columbus Blvd.
Hartford, CT 06106
Phone: (203)520-5000
Env. Contact: Bruce Martin, Mgr. Env. Health & Safety

★7933★ Long Island Lighting
175 E. Old Country Rd.
Hicksville, NY 11801
Phone: (516)933-4590
Env. Contact: Suzanne Halpin

★7934★ Longview Fibre Co.
PO Box 639
Longview, WA 98632
Phone: (206)425-1550
Env. Contact: Al Whitford, Env. Section Supervisor

★7935★ Lorillard Tobacco Company
One Park Ave.
New York, NY 10016
Phone: (212)545-3000
Fax: (212)545-3166
Env. Contact: Helane Aronson

★7936★ Louisiana Land and Exploration Co.
PO Box 60350
New Orleans, LA 70160
Phone: (504)566-6500
Env. Contact: William Berry, Dir. of Wetlands Mngmt.

★7937★ Louisiana-Pacific Corp.
111 SW 5th Ave.
Portland, OR 97204
Phone: (503)221-0800
Env. Contact: Jim Miller

★7938★ LTV Corp.
PO Box 655003
Dallas, TX 75265-5003
Phone: (214)266-2011
Env. Contact: Don Higginbotham, Mgr. Env. Aff.

★7939★ Lubrizol Corp.
29400 Lakeland Blvd.
Wickliffe, OH 44092
Phone: (216)943-4200
Env. Contact: Kenneth Washita

★7940★ Lukens Inc.
50 S 1st Ave.
Coatesville, PA 19320
Phone: (215)383-2504
Env. Contact: Evelyn Walker

★7941★ Lyondell Petrochemical Co.
1221 McKinney St., Ste. 1600
Houston, TX 77010
Phone: (713)652-7200
Env. Contact: David Harpole

★7942★ M.A. Hanna Co.
1301 E 9th St.
Cleveland, OH 44114-1824
Phone: (216)589-4000
Fax: (216)589-4109
Env. Contact: Cristopher Anderson

★7943★ Magma Power
11770 Bernardo Pl. Ct., Ste. 366
San Diego, CA 92128
Phone: (619)487-9412
Env. Contact: Wally Dieckmann

★7944★ MagneTek Inc.
11150 Santa Monica Blvd., 15th Fl.
Los Angeles, CA 90025
Phone: (213)473-6681
Env. Contact: Robert Murray

★7945★ Manville Corp.
PO Box 5108
Denver, CO 80217-5108
Phone: (303)978-2000
Fax: (303)978-2440
Env. Contact: Joe Tudor

★7946★ Mapco Inc.
1800 S Baltimore Ave.
Tulsa, OK 74119
Phone: (918)581-1800
Fax: (918)581-1893
Env. Contact: Howard Patterson

★7947★ Marion Merrell Dow
Public Relations Dept.
9300 Ward Pkwy
Kansas City, MO 64114
Phone: (816)966-4000

★7948★ Martin Marietta Corp.
6801 Rockledge Dr.
Bethesda, MD 20817
Phone: (301)897-6000
Env. Contact: Charles Carnahan, Corp. V.P. Env. Mgr.

★7949★ Maxus Energy Corp.
Public Affairs Dept.
717 N. Harwood St.
Dallas, TX 75201
Phone: (214)327-7391

★7950★ MAXXAM Inc.
PO Box 572887
Houston, TX 77257-2887
Phone: (713)975-7600
Env. Contact: Robert Ireland

★7951★ McDermott International Inc.
1010 Common St.
New Orleans, LA 70112
Phone: (504)587-5400
Env. Contact: Don Washington

★7952★ McDonnell Douglas Corp.
PO Box 516
St. Louis, MO 63166
Phone: (314)232-0232
Env. Contact: Richard Coon, Dir. Safety, Health, Env. Aff.

★7953★ MCN
500 Griswold St.
Detroit, MI 48226
Phone: (313)256-5500
Env. Contact: Sally LePla

★7954★ MDU Resources Group Inc.
400 N 4th St.
Bismarck, ND 58501
Phone: (701)222-7900

Env. Contact: Michael Pole

★7955★ Mead Corp.
Courthouse Plz. N.E.
Dayton, OH 45463
Phone: (513)222-6323
Env. Contact: Carl Ayers, Env. Mgr.

★7956★ Merck and Company Inc.
PO Box 2000
Rahway, NJ 07065-0909
Phone: (908)594-4000
Env. Contact: William Hamilton, Mgr. Environmental Control

★7957★ Midwest Resources
401 Douglas St.
Sioux City, IA 51101
Phone: (712)277-7400
Env. Contact: Tim Rollinger

★7958★ Minnesota Power
30 W. Superior St.
Duluth, MN 55802
Phone: (218)722-2641
Env. Contact: Dr. David W. Hoffman

★7959★ Mitchell Energy and Development Corp.
2001 Timerloch Pl.
The Woodlands, TX 77380
Phone: (713)377-5500
Env. Contact: John Watson, V.P. of Regulatory Affairs

★7960★ Mobil Corp.
Public Affairs Dept.
3225 Gallows Rd.
Fairfax, VA 22037-0001
Phone: (703)849-3000

★7961★ Monsanto Co.
800 N. Lindbergh Blvd.
St. Louis, MO 63167
Phone: (314)694-1000
Env. Contact: Mike Pierle, Env. Mgr.

★7962★ Montana Power
40 E. Broadway
Butte, MT 59707
Phone: (406)723-5421
Env. Contact: Don Sprague

★7963★ Morrison Knudsen Corp. (Boise, Idaho)
PO Box 73
Boise, ID 83707
Phone: (208)386-5000
Env. Contact: Dave Lamarque

★7964★ Morton International Inc.
Public Affairs Dept.
110 N Wacker Dr.
Chicago, IL 60606-1560
Phone: (312)807-2000

★7965★ Murphy Oil Corp.
200 Peach St.
El Dorado, AR 71730
Phone: (501)862-6411
Env. Contact: John Hallett, Mgr. of Env. Affairs

★7966★ Nabors Industries
515 W. Greens Rd.
Houston, TX 77067
Phone: (713)874-0035
Env. Contact: Dan McLaughlin

★7967★ NACCO Industries Inc.
12800 Shaker Blvd.
Cleveland, OH 44120
Phone: (216)752-1000
Env. Contact: Phyllis Morrow

★7968★ Nalco Chemical Co.
Public Affairs Dept.
1 Nalco Ctr.
Naperville, IL 60566-1024
Phone: (708)305-1000

★7969★ Nashua Corp.
PO Box 2002
Nashua, NH 03061-2002
Phone: (603)880-2323
Env. Contact: Walter Remeis

★7970★ National Cooperative Refinery Association
P.O Box 1404
McPherson, KS 67460
Phone: (316)241-2340
Fax: (316)241-5531
Env. Contact: Gene Ewing

★7971★ National Fuel Gas
Public Relations Dept.
10 Lafayette Sq.
Buffalo, NY 14203
Phone: (716)857-7000

★7972★ National Steel Corp.
20 Stanwix St.
Pittsburgh, PA 15222
Phone: (412)394-4100
Fax: (412)394-6818
Env. Contact: Joseph R. Duoak

★7973★ Navistar International Corp.
455 N Cityfront Plaza
Chicago, IL 60611
Phone: (312)836-2000
Env. Contact: Edith Ardiente, Dir. of Env. Affairs

★7974★ NCH Corp.
PO Box 152170
Irving, TX 75015
Phone: (214)438-0211
Env. Contact: Deborah Chadbourne

★7975★ Nerco
500 N.E. Multnomah
Portland, OR 97232
Phone: (503)731-6600
Env. Contact: Rubin Plantico

★7976★ Neutrogena
5760 W. 96th St.
Los Angeles, CA 90045
Phone: (213)642-1150
Env. Contact: Linda Schoen

★7977★ Nevada Power
6226 W. Sahara Ave.
Las Vegas, NV 89102
Phone: (702)367-5000
Env. Contact: Dennis Schwsher

★7978★ New England Electric
25 Research Dr.
Westboro, MA 01582
Phone: (508)366-9011
Env. Contact: Andy Aitkens

★7979★ New York State E & G
4500 Vestal Pkwy. E.
Binghamton, NY 13902
Phone: (607)729-2551
Env. Contact: Ray Tuttle

★7980★ Newmont Gold
1700 Lincoln St.
Denver, CO 80203
Phone: (303)863-7414
Env. Contact: Mack DeGeure

★7981★ Newmont Mining Corp.
1700 Lincoln St.
Denver, CO 80203
Phone: (303)863-7414
Env. Contact: Dave Baker

★7982★ Niagara Mohawk
Public Relations Dept.
300 Erie Blvd., W.
Syracuse, NY 13202
Phone: (315)474-1511

★7983★ Nicor
1700 W. Ferry Rd.
Naperville, IL 60563
Phone: (708)305-9500
Env. Contact: Bob Gilpon

★7984★ Nipsco Industries
Public Relations Dept.
5265 Hohman Ave.
Hammond, IN 46320
Phone: (219)853-5200

★7985★ NL Industries
3000 N. Sam Houston E.
Houston, TX 77032
Phone: (713)987-5000
Env. Contact: Aston Hinds

★7986★ Noble Affiliates
110 W. Broadway
Ardmore, OK 73401
Phone: (405)223-4110
Env. Contact: Bill Poillion

★7987★ North American Philips Corp.
100 E. 42nd St.
New York, NY 10017
Phone: (212)850-5000
Fax: (212)850-5364
Env. Contact: Ann Pizzorusso

★7988★ Northeast Utilities
107 Selden St.
Berlin, CT 06037
Phone: (203)665-5000
Env. Contact: Bill Rensro

★7989★ Northern States
414 Nicollet Mall
Minneapolis, MN 55401
Phone: (612)330-5500
Env. Contact: Margaret Papin

★7990★ Northrop Corp.
1840 Century Park E
Los Angeles, CA 90067
Phone: (213)553-6262
Alt. Phone: (213)331-4705
Env. Contact: Nancy Baldwin, Sen. Admin. Env.

★7991★ Nucor Corp.
Public Relations Dept.
4425 Randolph Rd.
Charlotte, NC 28211
Phone: (704)366-7000
Fax: (704)362-4208

★7992★ Occidental Petroleum Corp.
10889 Wilshire Blvd.
Los Angeles, CA 90024
Phone: (213)208-8800
Env. Contact: Frank Friedman

★7993★ Ocean Drilling
1600 Canal St.
New Orleans, LA 70112
Phone: (504)561-2811
Env. Contact: Chuck Vedell

★7994★ Oklahoma G & E
321 N. Harvey Ave.
Oklahoma City, OK 73102
Phone: (405)272-3000
Env. Contact: Grant Ringel

★7995★ Olin Corp.
120 Long Ridge Rd.
Stamford, CT 06904-1355
Phone: (203)356-2000
Env. Contact: Richard Hendey

★7996★ Oneok
100 W. Fifth St.
Tulsa, OK 74103
Phone: (918)588-7000
Env. Contact: Ed Wheeler

★7997★ Orange & Rockland
One Blue Hill Plaza
Pearl River, NY 10965
Phone: (914)352-6000
Env. Contact: Roger Metlger

★7998★ Oregon Steel Mills
14400 N. Rivergate Blvd.
Portland, OR 97203
Phone: (503)286-9651
Env. Contact: Jerry Richartz

★7999★ Oryx Energy Co.
5656 Blackwell
Dallas, TX 75231
Phone: (214)890-6000
Env. Contact: Stan Blossom, Dir. of Environment

★8000★ Outboard Marine Corp.
100 Sea Horse Dr.
Waukegan, IL 60085
Phone: (708)689-6200
Env. Contact: Roger Crawford, Dir.

★8001★ Owens-Corning Fiberglas Corp.
Fiberglas Tower
Toledo, OH 43659
Phone: (419)248-8000
Env. Contact: David Palochko, Dir. of Solid & Haz. Waste & Water Qual.

★8002★ Owens-Illinois, Inc.
One Seagate
Toledo, OH 43666
Phone: (419)247-5000
Fax: (419)247-2839
Env. Contact: John Hoff

★8003★ PACCAR Inc.
777 106th Ave. NE
Bellevue, WA 98004
Phone: (206)455-7400
Env. Contact: Bob Butler, Manager

★8004★ Pacific Enterprises
Public Relations Dept.
633 W. Fifth St., Ste. 5400
Los Angeles, CA 90071-2006
Phone: (213)895-5000

★8005★ Pacific Gas & Electric
77 Beale St.
San Francisco, CA 94106
Phone: (415)973-7000
Env. Contact: Victor Furtado

★8006★ Pacificorp
Dept. of Public Relations
700 N.E., Multnomah
Portland, OR 97232
Phone: (503)731-2000

★8007★ Panhandle Eastern
5400 Westheimer Ct.
Houston, TX 77056
Phone: (713)627-5400
Env. Contact: John Barnett

★8008★ Parker Drilling
Eight E. Third St.
Tulsa, OK 74103
Phone: (918)585-8221
Env. Contact: Phil Burch

★8009★ Parker Hannifin Corp.
17325 Euclid Ave.
Cleveland, OH 44112
Phone: (216)531-3000
Env. Contact: Richard Kanzleiter, Dir. of Env. Affairs

★8010★ Penn Central Corp.
1 E 4th St.
Cincinnati, OH 45202
Phone: (513)579-6600
Env. Contact: Mike Higgins, Mgr. of Env. Affairs

★8011★ Pennsylvania Power
Two N. Ninth St.
Allentown, PA 18101
Phone: (215)770-5151
Env. Contact: James Geiling

★8012★ Pennzoil Co.
PO Box 2967
Houston, TX 77252-2967
Phone: (713)546-4000
Env. Contact: Chris Ckisak

★8013★ Peoples Energy
Public Relations Dept.
122 S. Michigan Ave.
Chicago, IL 60603
Phone: (312)431-4000

★8014★ Peter Kiewit Son's Inc.
Continental Plasic Containers
Public Relations Dept.
PO Box 5410
Norwalk, CT 06856
Phone: (913)888-9494
Fax: (913)888-0654

★8015★ Pfizer Inc.
235 E 42nd St.
New York, NY 10017
Phone: (212)573-2323
Env. Contact: Robert L. Shafaer, V. Pres.

★8016★ P.H. Glatfelter Co.
228 S Main St.
Spring Grove, PA 17362
Phone: (717)225-4711
Env. Contact: Robert Callahan, Env. Manager

★8017★ Phelps Dodge Corp.
2600 N Central Ave.
Phoenix, AZ 85004-3014
Phone: (602)234-8100
Env. Contact: Nick Balich, V. Pres.

★8018★ Philip Morris Companies Inc.
120 Park Ave.
New York, NY 10017
Phone: (212)880-5000
Env. Contact: Barbara Maddock

★8019★ Philips Industries Inc.
4801 Springfield St.
Dayton, OH 45401-0943
Phone: (513)253-7171
Fax: (513)253-4138
Env. Contact: Dane Skinner

★8020★ Phillips Petroleum Co.
Fourth & Keeler St.
Bartlesville, OK 74004
Phone: (918)661-6600
Fax: (918)661-7636
Env. Contact: George Minter

★8021★ Pinnacle West
400 E. Van Buren St., Ste. 700
Phoenix, AZ 85004
Phone: (602)379-2500
Env. Contact: Mike Saccomando

★8022★ Pittston Co.
PO Box 120070
Stanford, CT 06912-0070
Phone: (203)622-0900
Env. Contact: William Byrne

★8023★ Pope and Talbot Inc.
1500 SW 1st Ave.
Portland, OR 97201
Phone: (503)228-9161
Env. Contact: Roger Campbell

★8024★ Portland General
121 S.W., Salmon St.
Portland, OR 97204
Phone: (503)464-8000
Env. Contact: Rick Hess

★8025★ Potlatch Corp.
1 Maritime Plz., Ste. 2400
San Francisco, CA 94111
Phone: (415)576-8800
Env. Contact: Guy Griffin

★8026★ PPG Industries Inc.
1 PPG Pl.
Pittsburgh, PA 15272
Phone: (412)434-3131
Env. Contact: Paul M. King, Dir. of Env. Affairs

★8027★ Precision Castparts Corp.
4600 SE Harney Dr.
Portland, OR 97206-0898
Phone: (503)777-3881
Env. Contact: Cindy Overstreet

★8028★ Premark International Inc.
1717 Deerfield Rd.
Deerfield, IL 60015
Phone: (708)405-6000
Env. Contact: Greg Mancuso

★8029★ Proctor and Gamble Co.
1 Proctor & Gamble Plz.
Cincinnati, OH 45202
Phone: (513)983-1100
Env. Contact: George Carpenter

★8030★ PS of Colorado
550 15th St.
Denver, CO 80202
Phone: (303)571-7511
Env. Contact: James Wesel

★8031★ PS of New Mexico
Public Relations Dept.
Alvarado Sq.
Albuquerque, NM 87158
Phone: (505)848-2700

★8032★ PSI Resources
1000 E. Main St.
Plainfield, IN 46168
Phone: (317)839-9611
Env. Contact: Jerry Sullivan

★8033★ Public Service Ent.
80 Park Plaza
Newark, NJ 07101
Phone: (201)430-7000
Env. Contact: James A. Shissias

★8034★ Puget Sound Power
Public Relations Dept.
411 108th St., N.E.
Bellevue, WA 98004
Phone: (206)454-6363

★8035★ Quaker State Corp.
PO Box 989
Oil City, PA 16301
Phone: (814)676-7642
Env. Contact: Rick Pennington

★8036★ Quanex Corp.
Public Relations Dept.
1900 W Loop St. S, Ste. 1500
Houston, TX 77027
Phone: (713)961-4600

★8037★ Quantum Chemical Corp.
99 Park Ave.
New York, NY 10016
Phone: (212)949-5000
Env. Contact: Arden Melick

★8038★ Questar Corp. (Salt Lake City, Utah)
PO Box 11150
Salt Lake City, UT 84147
Phone: (801)534-5000
Env. Contact: Roland Gow

★8039★ Raychem Corp.
Public Relations Dept.
300 Constitution Dr.
Menlo Park, CA 94025
Phone: (415)361-3333

★8040★ Raytheon Co.
Public Relations Dept.
125 Spring St.
Lexington, MA 02173
Phone: (617)862-6600

★8041★ Reliance Electric Co.
6065 Parklane Blvd.
Cleveland, OH 44124
Phone: (216)266-5800
Fax: (216)266-7666
Env. Contact: Jeff Green

★8042★ Reynolds Metals Co.
PO Box 27003
Richmond, VA 23261
Phone: (804)281-2000
Env. Contact: William Conley

★8043★ Rhone-Poulenc Rorer
500 Virginia Dr.
Fort Washington, PA 19034
Phone: (215)628-6000
Env. Contact: Darryl Blankenbiller

★8044★ RJR Nabisco Holdings
Dept. of Public Relations
1301 Ave. of Americas
New York, NY 10019
Phone: (212)258-5600

★8045★ Rochester G & E
89 E. Ave.
Rochester, NY 14649
Phone: (716)546-2700
Env. Contact: Mike Power

★8046★ Rockwell International Corp.
2230 E Imperial Hwy.
El Segundo, CA 90245
Phone: (213)647-5000
Env. Contact: Nanette Clements

★8047★ Rohm and Haas Co.
Independence Mall W
Philadelphia, PA 19105
Phone: (215)592-3000
Env. Contact: George Boshanski

★8048★ Rohr Industries Inc.
PO Box 878
Chula Vista, CA 91912
Phone: (619)691-4111
Env. Contact: Wendy Longley-Cook

★8049★ Rollins Env.
400 Bellevue Pkwy.
Wilmington, DE 19809
Phone: (302)479-2700
Env. Contact: Maury Hunt

★8050★ Rowan Companies Inc.
5450 Transco Tower
2800 Post Oak Blvd.
Houston, TX 77056-6111
Phone: (713)621-7800
Env. Contact: Paul Kelly

★8051★ RPM Inc.
PO Box 777
Medina, OH 44258
Phone: (216)225-3192
Env. Contact: Charles Brush

★8052★ Rubbermaid Inc.
1147 Akron Rd.
Wooster, OH 44691
Phone: (216)264-6464
Env. Contact: Van Canady

★8053★ Safety-Kleen
777 Big Timber Rd.
Elgin, IL 60123
Phone: (708)697-8460
Env. Contact: Basil Constantelof

★8054★ St. Joe Paper Co.
Public Relations Dept.
PO Box 1380
Jacksonville, FL 32201
Phone: (904)396-6600

★8055★ San Diego G & E
101 Ash St.
San Diego, CA 92101
Phone: (619)696-2000
Env. Contact: Steve Davis

★8056★ Santa Fe Energy Resources Inc.
1616 S Voss Rd., Ste. 1000
Houston, TX 77057
Phone: (713)783-2401
Env. Contact: Jim Kruger

★8057★ Santa Fe Pacific Corp.
Public Relations Dept.
1700 E Golf
Schaumburg, IL 60173
Phone: (708)995-6000
Fax: (312)786-6118

★8058★ Sara Lee Corp.
3 First National Plz.
Chicago, IL 60602-4260
Phone: (312)726-2600
Env. Contact: Ralph Mallory

★8059★ Scana
1426 Main St.
Columbia, SC 29201
Phone: (803)748-3000
Env. Contact: Deborah Blanks

★8060★ Scecorp
2244 Walnut Grove Ave.
Rosemead, CA 91770
Phone: (818)302-1212
Env. Contact: Scottie Wallace

★8061★ Schering-Plough Corp.
Public Relations Dept.
1 Giralda Farms
Madison, NJ 07940-1000
Phone: (201)822-7000

★8062★ Schlumberger Ltd.
Public Relations Dept.
277 Park Ave.
New York, NY 10172
Phone: (212)350-9400

★8063★ Scott Paper Co.
Scott Plz.
Philadelphia, PA 19113
Phone: (215)522-5000
Env. Contact: Nicholas J. Lardieri

★8064★ Sequa Corp.
200 Park Ave.
New York, NY 10166
Phone: (212)986-5500
Fax: (212)370-1969
Env. Contact: Jeffery Teitel

★8065★ Shaw Industries Inc. (Dalton, Georgia)
PO Drawer 2128
Dalton, GA 30722-2128
Phone: (404)278-3812
Env. Contact: Bill Nysewander

★8066★ Sherwin-Williams Co.
101 Prospect Ave. NW
Cleveland, OH 44115-1075
Phone: (216)566-2000
Env. Contact: John Gerulis

★8067★ Sierra Pacific
Public Relations Dept.
6100 Neil Rd.
Reno, NV 89511
Phone: (702)689-3600

★8068★ Sigma-Aldrich Corp.
3050 Spruce St.
St. Louis, MO 63103
Phone: (314)771-5765
Env. Contact: Don Zundel

★8069★ Silgan Corp.
Six Landmark Sq.
Stamford, CT 06901
Phone: (203)975-7110
Env. Contact: Sharon Budds

★8070★ Sonat
1900 Fifth Ave. N.
Birmingham, AL 35203
Phone: (205)325-3800
Env. Contact: Dr. Chae Laird

★8071★ Southern
Public Relations Dept.
64 Perimeter Center E.
Atlanta, GA 30346
Phone: (404)393-0650

★8072★ Southern Indiana G & E
20 N. West Fourth St.
Evansville, IN 47741
Phone: (812)465-5300
Env. Contact: Gary Gress

★8073★ Southwest Gas Corp.
5241 Spring Mountain Rd.
Las Vegas, NV 89102
Phone: (702)876-7011
Fax: (702)365-2233
Env. Contact: Dante Pistone

★8074★ Southwestern PS
Sixth at Tyler
PO Box 1261
Amarillo, TX 79170
Phone: (806)378-2121
Env. Contact: Olon Plunk

★8075★ Springs Industries Inc.
PO Box 70
Fort Mill, SC 29716
Phone: (803)547-1500
Env. Contact: Nick Odom R.A.

★8076★ Sterling Chemicals Inc.
PO Box 1311
Texas City, TX 77592
Phone: (713)650-3700
Env. Contact: Phil Chamberlain

★8077★ Stone Container Corp.
150 N Michigan Ave.
Chicago, IL 60601-7568
Phone: (312)346-6600
Env. Contact: Allan Koless

★8078★ Sun Company Inc.
100 Matsonford Rd.
Radnor, PA 19087
Phone: (215)293-6000
Env. Contact: Chad Bardone

★8079★ Syntex Corp.
3401 Hillview Ave.
Palo Alto, CA 94304
Phone: (415)855-5050
Env. Contact: Kathy Krooks

★8080★ Tambrands Inc.
Public Relations Dept.
777 Westchester Ave.
White Plains, NY 10604
Phone: (914)696-6060

★8081★ Teco Energy
702 N. Franklin St.
Tampa, FL 33602
Phone: (813)228-4111
Env. Contact: Jerry Williams

★8082★ Tecumseh Products Co.
100 E Patterson
Tecumseh, MI 49286
Phone: (517)423-8411
Env. Contact: Jerry Bufton

★8083★ Teledyne Inc.
Public Relations Dept.
1901 Ave. of the Stars
Los Angeles, CA 90067
Phone: (213)277-3311

★8084★ Temple-Inland Inc.
PO Drawer N
Diboll, TX 75941
Phone: (409)829-1313
Env. Contact: Mick Harbordt

★8085★ Tenneco Inc.
PO Box 2511
Houston, TX 77252-2511
Phone: (713)757-2131
Env. Contact: Robert Pruessner

★8086★ Tesoro Petroleum Corp.
8700 Tesoro Dr.
San Antonio, TX 78217
Phone: (512)828-8484
Env. Contact: Ron Grantham

★8087★ Texaco Inc.
2000 Westchester Ave.
White Plains, NY 10650
Phone: (914)253-4000
Env. Contact: J. Donald Annett

★8088★ Texas Instruments Inc.
PO Box 655474
Dallas, TX 75265
Phone: (214)995-3333
Fax: (214)995-4360
Env. Contact: Don Legg

★8089★ Textron Inc.
Public Relations Dept.
40 Westminster St.
Providence, RI 02903
Phone: (401)421-2800

★8090★ Thermo Electron Corp.
PO Box 9046
Waltham, MA 02254-9046
Phone: (617)622-1000
Env. Contact: John Hatsopoulos

★8091★ Thiokol Corp.
2475 Washington Blvd.
Ogden, UT 84401
Phone: (801)629-2270
Env. Contact: Lucky Heath

★8092★ Tosco Corp.
Public Relations Dept.
PO Box 2401
Santa Monica, CA 90406
Phone: (213)207-6000

★8093★ Transco Energy
2800 Post Oak Blvd
Houston, TX 77056
Phone: (713)439-2000
Env. Contact: Mike Zagapa

★8094★ Tredegar Industries Inc.
1100 Boulders Pkwy.
Richmond, VA 23225
Phone: (804)330-1000
Env. Contact: Bill Street

★8095★ Union Camp Corp.
1600 Valley Rd.
Wayne, NJ 07470
Phone: (201)628-2000
Env. Contact: Rex Phorne

★8096★ Union Carbide Corp.
39 Old Ridgebury Rd.
Danbury, CT 06817-0001
Phone: (203)794-2000
Env. Contact: Ronald Vanmynen

★8097★ Union Electric
Public Relations Dept.
1901 Chouteau Ave.
St. Louis, MO 63103
Phone: (314)621-3222

★8098★ Union Pacific Corp.
Public Relations Dept.
Martin Tower
Bethlehem, PA 18018
Phone: (215)861-3200

★8099★ Union Texas Petroleum Holdings Inc.
Public Relations Dept.
1330 Post Oak Blvd.
Houston, TX 77056
Phone: (713)623-6544
Fax: (713)968-2771

★8100★ United Illuminating
80 Temple St.
New Haven, CT 06506
Phone: (203)787-7200
Env. Contact: David Damer

★8101★ United Technologies Corp.
United Technologies
Hartford, CT 06101
Phone: (203)728-7000
Env. Contact: Mark Citroni

★8102★ Unocal Corp.
PO Box 7600
Los Angeles, CA 90051
Phone: (213)977-7600
Env. Contact: Joel Robinson

★8103★ Upjohn Co.
Public Relations Dept.
7000 Portage Rd.
Kalamazoo, MI 49001
Phone: (616)323-4000
Fax: (616)323-6654

★8104★ UST Inc.
100 W Putnam Ave.
Greenwich, CT 06830
Phone: (203)661-1100
Env. Contact: Anita Phasanoti

★8105★ USX Corp.
Public Relations Dept.
600 Grant St.
Pittsburgh, PA 15219
Phone: (412)433-1121

★8106★ Valero Energy Corp.
PO Box 500
San Antonio, TX 78292
Phone: (512)246-2000
Env. Contact: John Sommer

★8107★ Valhi Inc.
Public Relations Dept.
5430 LBJ Fwy.
Dallas, TX 75240-2697
Phone: (214)233-1700

★8108★ Valspar Corp.
1101 S 3rd St.
Minneapolis, MN 55415
Phone: (612)332-7371
Fax: (612)375-7723
Env. Contact: Mark Ackas

★8109★ Vista Chemical Co.
900 Threadneedle
Houston, TX 77224
Phone: (713)588-3000
Env. Contact: Tom Grimbles

★8110★ Vulcan Materials Co.
1 Metroplex Dr.
Birmingham, AL 35209
Phone: (205)877-3000
Fax: (205)877-3094
Env. Contact: Gary Euler

★8111★ Warner-Lambert Co.
201 Tabor Rd.
Morris Plains, NJ 07950
Phone: (201)540-2000
Env. Contact: William Speenburgh

★8112★ Washington Energy
Public Relations Dept.
815 Mercer St.
Seattle, WA 98109
Phone: (206)622-6767

★8113★ Washington Gas Light
1100 H St., N.W.
Washington, DC 20080
Phone: (703)750-4440
Env. Contact: R.J. Cook

★8114★ Washington Water
Public Relations Dept.
East 1411 Mission Ave.
Spokane, WA 99202
Phone: (509)489-0500

★8115★ Waste Management
3003 Butterfield Rd.
Oak Brook, IL 60521
Phone: (708)572-8800
Env. Contact: Joan Bernstein

★8116★ Weirton Steel Corp.
Public Relations Dept.
400 Three Springs Dr.
Weirton, WV 26062-4989
Phone: (304)797-2000

★8117★ Wellman Inc.
1040 Broad St.
Shrewsbury, NJ 07702-4318
Phone: (908)542-7300
Fax: (201)542-9344
Env. Contact: Dennis Sabourin

★8118★ West Point-Pepperell
233 S. Wacker Dr.
Chicago, IL 60606
Phone: (312)876-1724
Env. Contact: Burgess Ridge

★8119★ Westinghouse Electric Corp.
Public Relations Dept.
Westinghouse Bldg.
Pittsburgh, PA 15222
Phone: (412)244-2000

★8120★ Westmoreland Coal Co.
200 S Broad St.
Philadelphia, PA 19102
Phone: (215)545-2500
Env. Contact: Page Henley

★8121★ Westvaco
299 Park Ave.
New York, NY 10171
Phone: (212)688-5000
Env. Contact: O.B. Burns

★8122★ Weyerhaeuser Co.
33663 32nd Dr.
Tacoma, WA 98477
Phone: (206)924-2345
Env. Contact: Susan Perez

★8123★ Wheelabrator
Liberty Ln.
Hampton, NH 03842
Phone: (603)929-3000
Env. Contact: Kevin Stickney

★8124★ Wheeling-Pittsburgh Corp.
1134 Market St.
Wheeling, WV 26003
Phone: (304)234-2400
Env. Contact: Tom Waligura

★8125★ Willamette Industries Inc.
3800 1st Interstate
Portland, OR 97201
Phone: (503)227-5581
Env. Contact: Charles Hess

★8126★ Williams
One William Center
Tulsa, OK 74172
Phone: (918)588-2000
Env. Contact: Jason Huso

★8127★ Wisconsin PS
700 N. Adams St.
Green Bay, WI 54301
Phone: (414)433-1598
Env. Contact: Ed Newman

★8128★ Witco Corp.
520 Madison Ave.
New York, NY 10022-4236
Phone: (212)605-3800
Fax: (212)605-3660
Env. Contact: Dean Sibert

★8129★ Worthington Industries Inc.
1205 Dearborn Dr.
Columbus, OH 43085
Phone: (614)438-3210
Env. Contact: Greg Sautter

★8130★ WPL Holdings
222 W. Washington Ave.
Madison, WI 53703
Phone: (608)252-3311
Env. Contact: Joe Shefchek

★8131★ W.R. Grace and Co.
Public Relations Dept.
Grace Plaza
1114 Ave. of Americas
New York, NY 10036
Phone: (212)819-5500

★8132★ York Holdings Corp.
Public Relations Dept.
631 S Richland Ave.
York, PA 17403
Phone: (717)771-7890

★8133★ Zurn Industries Inc.
One Zurn Plaza
Erie, PA 16514-2000
Phone: (814)452-2111
Fax: (814)459-3535
Env. Contact: Jeff Meddin

Environmental Products

This section lists commercially available products that have been classified by their manufacturers as environmentally sound. Entries are arranged by product type, including bags, recycling bins, composters, energy efficient products, games, household products, investing, office products, organically grown foods, packing materials, personal products, recycled paper and plastic products, and t-shirts and assorted apparel.

Bags

★8134★ Blue Rhubarb, Inc.
Toll-Free: 800-926-1017
EcoSac Shopping System offers reusable canvas and 100% cotton string shopping bags.

★8135★ Canvasack
4807 S. Mountain Ln.
Salt Lake City, UT 84124
Phone: (801)277-3256
Cotton canvas bags.

★8136★ Cherry Tree
Toll-Free: 800-869-7742
The ReBag holds up to 100 lbs. of groceries. Lightweight and waterproof.

★8137★ Earthwise
13947 Five Point Rd. 3-G
Perrysburg, OH 43551
Cotton canvas bags.

★8138★ Environmental Bag Co.
PO Box 786
Pt. Jeff, NY 11777
Phone: (516)473-5064
French string cotton bags in a variety of colors and sizes.

★8139★ Environmentally Sensitive Products
1765 Indiana Ave.
Atlanta, GA 30307
Phone: (404)377-5113
Cloth grocery bags made of 100% cotton.

★8140★ Equinox Ltd.
1207 Park Ave.
Williamsport, PA 17701
Phone: (717)322-5900
Canvas grocery and lunch bags, and cotton mesh bags.

★8141★ Greenpeace Catalog
PO Box 77048
San Francisco, CA 94107-0048
Toll-Free: 800-456-4029
Offers t-shirts and jackets with environmental messages, jewelry, bags, shower heads, toilet dams, games, hand puppets, stationery made of recycled paper, keychains, and more.

★8142★ J & J Associates
417-B E Foothill Blvd.
Ste. 392
Glendora, CA 91740
Phone: (818)335-2359
Toll-Free: 800-388-2359
Reusable all-purpose bag. Comes in large and jumbo sizes.

★8143★ The Markuson Group, Inc.
PO Box 70373
Seattle, WA 98107
Phone: (206)235-6609
Compact 4 1/2" x 5" nylon wallet opens to a 13 1/2" x 12" x 7" bag. Reusable, all-purpose.

★8144★ Personal Statements
Dept. G, PO Box 576
Merrimack, NH 03054
Phone: (603)424-8650
Toll-Free: 800-444-7891
Bags made from recycled polypropylene.

★8145★ Piedmont Products
412 S. Main
Piedmont, MO 63957
Fax: (314)223-7336
Toll-Free: 800-348-BAGS
100% cotton shopping bags.

★8146★ Treekeepers
249 S. Hwy. 101, Ste. 518
Solana Beach, CA 92075
Phone: (619)481-6403
Toll-Free: 800-767-6403
Canvas shopping and lunch bags.

Composters

★8147★ Carbco Industries, Inc.
240 Michigan St.
Lockport, NY 14094
Phone: (717)434-0316
Kich'n Komposter recycles organic waste, connects to any home food disposer, and is self cleaning.

★8148★ Concept Environment Inc.
12005 Highwater Rd.
Granada Hills, CA 91344
Phone: (818)831-5501
Converts waste into organic fertilizer using earthworms.

★8149★ Eco Atlantic
2200-C Broening Hwy.
Baltimore, MD 21224
Phone: (301)633-7500
Toll-Free: 800-253-1119
Markets the Green Cone, a food waste composter. The cone and lid are made of polyethlene specifically formulated to enhance transmission of solar energy, which accelerates the decomposition process.

★8150★ Green Cone Distributors
PO Box 866
Menlo Park, CA 94026
Phone: (415)365-8637
Alt. Phone: 800-955-2205
Green Cone composts kitchen waste for a family of 4. Made from 60% recycled plastic.

★8151★ Terra Verde Trading Co.
Phone: (212)925-4533
Composters, energy efficient light bulbs, natural-cotton bath towels and other household goods.

Energy Efficient Products

★8152★ Alternative Energy Engineering
PO Box 339-GA
Redway, CA 95560
Phone: (707)923-2277
Solar powered module instantly coverts sunlight energy to DC electricity. Also charges storage batteries. Catalog available.

★8153★ Auto Logic
19940 Cinder Ln.
Bend, OR 97702
Phone: (503)385-7440
Produces energy efficient automotive products such as recycled high grade engine oils and products free of Petrochemicals.

★8154★ Backwoods Solar Electric Systems
8530 Rapid Lightning Creek Rd.
Sandpoint, ID 83864
Phone: (208)263-4290
Solar energy products, including power tools. Free catalog available.

★8155★ Biotech Building Systems
161 Emerson Pl., 4G
Brooklyn, NY 11205
Phone: (212)777-1049
Fax: (718)789-4142
Environmentally conscious architecture designed with energy efficiency, recycled materials and site responsiveness.

★8156★ **Chain Drive**
9809 Marlboro Pike
Upper Marlboro, MD 20772
Compact florescent lamps. Catalog available for $1.00.

★8157★ **Chronar Sunenergy**
PO Box 177
Princeton, NJ 08542
Phone: (609)799-8800
Toll-Free: 800-247-6627
Produces solar lamps which can provide up to 6 hours of light per night.

★8158★ **Condensator**
Grand Junction, CO 81505
Toll-Free: 800-927-7283
Reduces automobile emissions, fuel costs, and engine wear and tear.

★8159★ **Earth Tools**
Toll-Free: 800-825-6460
Water and energy saving items, non-toxic cleaners and pest control, and recycled products. Catalog available.

★8160★ **Earthsake**
Phone: (415)626-0722
Environmentally safe products include convection ovens that save on space and energy and ocillating fans that distribute heat in winter.

★8161★ **The Energy Store**
PO Box 3507
Santa Cruz, CA 95063-3507
Toll-Free: 800-288-1938
Energy efficient household products, including lighting, heating, cooling, garden, solar, books, and kitchen appliances. Free catalog available.

★8162★ **Green Goods Inc.**
PO Box 116
Topsham, ME 04086
Phone: (207)721-0373
Fluorescent light bulbs last up to 10,00 hours, use 75% less electricity than standard incandescent bulbs. Free brochure available.

★8163★ **Greenpeace Catalog**
PO Box 77048
San Francisco, CA 94107-0048
Toll-Free: 800-456-4029
Offers t-shirts and jackets with environmental messages, jewelry, bags, shower heads, toilet dams, games, hand puppets, stationery made of recycled paper, keychains, and more.

★8164★ **Integral Energy Systems**
105-G Argall Way
Nevada City, CA 95959
Toll-Free: 800-735-6790
Solar electricity, lighting, battery chargers, tankless water heaters, water pumps, composting toilets, and solar hot water heaters. Catalog available.

★8165★ **Jade Mountain**
PO Box 4616
Boulder, CO 80306-4616
Toll-Free: 800-442-1972
Solar electric systems, energy efficient lighting, water purification, recycled paper products, demand water heaters, hydroelectric and wind generators, and solar toys.

★8166★ **Lehman's Non-Electric Catalog**
4779 Kidron Rd.
PO Box 41, Dept. GM
Kidron, OH 44636
Phone: (216)857-5441
Nonelectric appliances, including butter churns, kettles, woodstoves, windmills, and cherry pitters.

★8167★ **Lite Energy**
PO Box 781A
Excelsior, MN 55331
Compact fluorescent lights, light kits, fixture kits, fixtures, and planning guide. Catalog available.

★8168★ **Mr. Showerhead**
PO Box 100865
San Antonio, TX 78201
Phone: (512)737-3481
Offers Waterboss, a water and energy conserving showerhead.

★8169★ **Photocomm, Inc.**
7681 E. Gray Rd., 16-G
Scottsdale, AZ 85260
Toll-Free: 800-223-9580
Solar energy products. 1991 Design Guide and Catalog available for $5.00.

★8170★ **Real Goods**
3041 Guildiville Rd.
Ukiah, CA 95482
Toll-Free: 800-762-7325
Offers energy-efficient lighting, refrigeration, water heating, and water conservation products; recycled paper products; non-toxic household cleaners; a nd toys and gifts.

★8171★ **Save Energy Company**
Toll-Free: 800-326-2120
Energy saving light bulbs, timers, solar and recycling products and other items. Catalog available.

★8172★ **Solar Electric Engineering**
175 Cascade Ct.
Rohnert Park, CA 94928
Phone: (707)586-1987
Toll-Free: 800-832-1986
Solar sports radio with earphones. Also operates on AA batteries.

★8173★ **Sun Watt Corporation**
RFD Box 751
Addison, ME 04606
Phone: (207)497-2204
Hybrid solar modules that produce electricity and heat water. Catalog available.

★8174★ **Sunelco**
PO Box 1499 G11
Hamilton, MT 59840
Toll-Free: 800-338-6844
Solar energy products, including modules, controllers, batteries, inverters, and water pumps. Catalog available for $4.00.

★8175★ **Syncronos Design Inc.**
PO Box 10657, Dept. G2
Albuquerque, NM 87184
Phone: (505)897-1440
Solar oven. Information booklet available for $2.00.

Games

★8176★ **Animal Town Game Co.**
PO Box 2002
Santa Barbara, CA 93120
Phone: (805)682-7343
Board games focusing on ecology and the environment. For ages 7 and older.

★8177★ **Bongers**
PO Box 84366
Los Angeles, CA 90073
Phone: (213)823-0932
Produces the board game Save the World, for ages 13 and older.

★8178★ **Do Dreams Music Company**
PO Box 5623
Takoma Park, MD 20912
Phone: (301)445-3845
Music tapes with environmental themes.

★8179★ **Earthword**
Dept. G
104 Church St.
Keyport, NJ 07735
Earthword is a game designed to teach about the environment, including such topics as air, water, forests, animals, global warming, oceans, health, and recycling. Printed on recycled paper.

★8180★ **Greenpeace Catalog**
PO Box 77048
San Francisco, CA 94107-0048
Toll-Free: 800-456-4029
Offers t-shirts and jackets with environmental messages, jewelry, bags, shower heads, toilet dams, games, hand puppets, stationery made of recycled paper, keychains, and more.

★8181★ **Jade Mountain**
PO Box 4616
Boulder, CO 80306-4616
Toll-Free: 800-442-1972
Solar electric systems, energy efficient lighting, water purification, recycled paper products, demand water heaters, hydroelectric and wind generators, and solar toys.

★8182★ **Milton-Bradley**
433 Shaker Rd.
East Longmeadow, MA 01028
Phone: (413)525-6411
Produces Pass the Trash, a board game with environmental themes.

★8183★ **Real Goods**
3041 Guildiville Rd.
Ukiah, CA 95482
Toll-Free: 800-762-7325
Offers energy-efficient lighting, refrigeration, water heating, and water conservation products; recycled paper products; non-toxic household cleaners; a nd toys and gifts.

★8184★ **Save the Planet Shareware**
Box 45
Pitkin, CO 81241
A personal computer program called Save the Planet explores environmental topics through graphic illustrations and a global warming scenario game. It also has a built-in word processor designed for writing letters to Congress.

★8185★ **Signs and Symbols**
2965 Pinewoods Rd., Dept. G3491
Lewiston, ME 04240
Phone: (207)782-3756

Fax: (207)783-3742
Recycled paper and plastic products, environmental publications, earth music, and children's items. Catalog available. Donates 5% of profits to environmental organizations.

★8186★ Upstart
Box 889
Hagerstown, MD 21741
Fax: (301)797-1615
Toll-Free: 800-448-4887
Environmentally oriented games, posters, stickers, buttons, and t-shirts for children.

★8187★ Wee Share International
PO Box 1028
Pagosa Springs, CO 81147
Phone: (303)264-2287
Toll-Free: 800-874-2733
Sprout growing kit, complete with seeds, growing container, instructions, storybook, and simple science lessons. Kit uses no chemicals, insecticides, or soil. A sprout kit is donated to underpriviledged children for every kit bought.

★8188★ World Wildlife Fund
PO Box 224
Peru, IN 46970
Toll-Free: 800-833-1600
Game cards displaying threatened inhabitants of rain forests.

Household Products

★8189★ Air Magnet
Toll-Free: 800-743-9991
Permanent air filters for central air conditioning systems and forced air furnaces.

★8190★ Back to Earth, Inc.
PO Box 672
Ellenwood, GA 30049
Personal and household products. Catalog available for $1.00, refundable with first purchase.

★8191★ Biomatik USA Corp.
PO Box 2119
Boulder, CO 80306
Phone: (303)938-8999
Produces an air-powered, gas-free spray bottle that eliminates the need for chemically-propelled aerosol cans. Can be used for a variety of personal, household and industrial products.

★8192★ Blue Planet Products
PO Box 213-G
Boston, MA 02123
Features environmentally responsible products and gifts licensed by World Wildlife Fund, Rainforest Action Project, Cultural Survival, NRDC, and other environmental groups.

★8193★ CHIP Distribution
PO Box 704
Manhattan Beach, CA 90266
Phone: (213)545-5928
Nonflammable, noncaustic, nonexplosive, biodegradable cleaner.

★8194★ Clothcrafters
RB1
Elkhart Lake, WI 53020
Phone: (414)876-2112
Reusable cloth diapers, terry bibs, napkins, salid bags, coffee filters, dish towels, denim bib aprons, cotton shower curtains, flannel sheets and other items. Catalog available.

★8195★ Cloverdale
PO Box 268
West Cornwall, CT 06796
Phone: (203)672-0216
Distributes Cloverdale, a biodegradable cleaner and degreaser.

★8196★ The Compassionate Consumer
PO Box 27
Jericho, NY 11753
Phone: (718)445-4134
Distributes Ecover floor soap and toilet cleaner; and Golden Lotus all-purpose cleaner, liquid dishwashing soap, laundry detergent, fabric softener, and bleach.

★8197★ Earth Flag Co.
PO Box 108-NYT
Middleville, NJ 07855
Phone: (201)579-7889
Toll-Free: 800-421-3524
Flag with the earth's image in 4 colors on dark blue background. Free brochure available.

★8198★ Earth Tools
Toll-Free: 800-825-6460
Water and energy saving items, non-toxic cleaners and pest control, and recycled products. Catalog available.

★8199★ Earth Wise, Inc.
1790 30th St.
Boulder, CO 80301
Phone: (303)447-0119
Produces environmentally sound home care products. Products include 100% recycled plastic trash bags, laundry stain remover, dish detergent and all-purpose cleaners.

★8200★ Earthsake
Phone: (415)626-0722
Environmentally safe products include convection ovens that save on space and energy and ocillating fans that distribute heat in winter.

★8201★ Ecco Bella
6 Provost Sq.
EM-0191
Ste. 602
Caldwell, NJ 07006
Toll-Free: 800-888-5320
Offers a variety of products that are free of animal by-products, animal testing, toxic ingredients, petroleum derivatives, pollutants, and propellants. Catalog available.

★8202★ Eco-Choice
Dept. 2009
PO Box 281
Montvale, NJ 07645
Toll-Free: 800-535-6304
Recycled paper products, household cleaning products, biorational pest controls, recyclables containers, personal care, cosmetics, and baby products. Free brochure available.

★8203★ Ecology Clean Co.
69-28 Queens Blvd.
Woodside, NY 11377
Phone: (718)565-6666
Toll-Free: 800-548-9660
Noncaustic, biodegradable spot remover.

★8204★ Edward & Sons Trading Company
PO Box 1326
Carpinteria, CA 93014
Markets Uniclean, a cleaner made from vegetable oil soap, and an environmentally friendly detergent made from coconut oil. All purpose and biodegradable. Does not test its products on animals.

★8205★ E.L. Foust Co., Inc.
Box 105
Elmhurst, IL 60126
Toll-Free: 800-225-9549
Air and water purifiers and filters.

★8206★ The Energy Store
PO Box 3507
Santa Cruz, CA 95063-3507
Toll-Free: 800-288-1938
Energy efficient household products, including lighting, heating, cooling, garden, solar, books, and kitchen appliances. Free catalog available.

★8207★ Everybody Ltd.
Toll-Free: 800-748-5675
Body, household, and pet care products. Does not test its products on animals. Catalog available.

★8208★ Funnybone
Rt. 1 Box 266K
Charles Town, WV 25414
Phone: (304)728-0173
Laundry rack holds a full load of laundry. Used in place of an electric or gas dryer. Catalog available.

★8209★ Globus Mercatus, Inc.
PO Box 1565
Cranford, NJ 07016
Toll-Free: 800-628-8731
The Drink Maker makes carbonated beverages with no artificial preservatives or flavorings. Makes 60 liters of soda per refill. Eliminates plastic bottle waste.

★8210★ Integra Trading Company, Inc.
PO Box 8450
Atlanta, GA 30306
Phone: (404)876-2320
Fax: (404)881-0199
Detergent-free, soap-based laundry and household cleansers, including the product Sodasan.

★8211★ Livos Plantchemistry
641 Agua Fria St.
Santa Fe, NM 87501
Phone: (505)988-9111
Produces natural ingredient products, including soap, furniture wax, floor polish, and leather polish.

★8212★ McCloskey Corp.
7600 State Rd.
Philadelphia, PA 19136
Phone: (215)624-4400
Toll-Free: 800-767-CLEAN
Sanding sealer, polyurethane finish, wood stain, and acrylic finish. Products are formulated to contain the least amount of solvents necessary to be effective. Free Guide to Using Clean Air Coatings is available.

★8213★ Mercantile Food Company
Georgetown, CT 06829
Ecover, biodegradable household cleaning products made from natural raw materials. Products include fabric conditioner, dishwashing liquid, kitchen cream cleaner, toilet cleaner, and floor soap. Does not test its products on animals.

★8214★ Mia Rose Products, Inc.
1374 Logan, Unit C
Costa Mesa, CA 92626
Phone: (714)662-5465

Toll-Free: 800-292-6339
Offers Air Therapy, a natural air purifying mist. Non-toxic, non-aerosol.

★8215★ Naace Industries, Inc.
5032 N. Royal Atlanta Dr.
Tucker, GA 30084
Phone: (404)938-8500
Fax: (404)939-4900
Telex: 8107573653
Offers Biozine II air deoderizer and freshener spray. Environmentally safe.

★8216★ National Ecological and Environmental Delivery System
527 Charles Ave.
Syracuse, NY 13209
Toll-Free: 800-634-1380

★8217★ The Natural Choice
Toll-Free: 800-621-2591
Over 300 environmentally safe products: non-toxic paints, stains and wood preservatives, natural health products, bodycare and colognes, herbal remedies, recycled paper, cleaners, pet care, ferilizers, organic seeds, and other natural products.

★8218★ The Nature Company
Home Office
750 Hearst Ave.
Berkeley, CA 94710
Sells a variety of products aimed at saving the rainforest regions.

★8219★ Nature of Things
3956 Long Pl.
Carlsbad, CA 92008
Phone: (619)434-4480
Biodegradable cleaning and personal care products. Catalog available.

★8220★ Non-Polluting Enterprises (NOPE)
PO Box 333G
Smethport, PA 16749
Toll-Free: 800-782-6673
Shower curtain made from 100% tightly woven cotton duck.

★8221★ Orcon Organic Control, Inc.
5132 Venice Blvd.
Los Angeles, CA 90019
Phone: (213)937-7444
Raises and distributes predatory insects, the green lacewing and the trichogramma, which feed on many common garden pests.

★8222★ Planet Products
1377 K Street, NW, Ste. 8201
Washington, DC 20005
Toll-Free: 800-622-9926
Brush designed for cleaning refrigerator coils.

★8223★ Real Goods
3041 Guildiville Rd.
Ukiah, CA 95482
Toll-Free: 800-762-7325
Offers energy-efficient lighting, refrigeration, water heating, and water conservation products; recycled paper products; non-toxic household cleaners; a nd toys and gifts.

★8224★ Scotch Corporation
PO Box 4466
617 E. 10th St.
Dallas, TX 75208
Phone: (214)943-4605
Cleaning concentrate.

★8225★ Seventh Generation
Dept. GM
Colchester, VT 05446-1672
Toll-Free: 800-456-1177
Household products. Markets Citrasolv, a solvent made from citrus fruits.

★8226★ Shaklee
97 Blanchard Rd.
Cambridge, MA 02138
Phone: (617)547-7600
Cleaners made from natural, nontoxic ingredients, and phosphate-free laundry detergents.

★8227★ Solstice General Store
201 E. Main St., Ste. H
Charlottesville, VA 22901
Phone: (804)979-0189
Distributes Livos and Ecover cleaners.

★8228★ Statler Tissue
300 Middlesex Ave.
Medford, MA 02155
Produces 100% recycled Tree-Free Paper Products made from recycled fiber.

★8229★ Sunrise Lane
780 Greenwich St.
New York, NY 10014
Phone: (212)242-7014
Distributes Golden Lotus products, which are biodegradable and nontoxic; Allen's Naturally products, which are biodegradable and are not tested on animals; and Life Tree, which are household cleaning products.

★8230★ Syncronos Design Inc.
PO Box 10657, Dept. G2
Albuquerque, NM 87184
Phone: (505)897-1440
Solar oven. Information booklet available for $2.00.

★8231★ Terra Verde Trading Co.
Phone: (212)925-4533
Composters, energy efficient light bulbs, natural-cotton bath towels and other household goods.

★8232★ Vegan Street
PO Box 5525
Rockville, MD 20855
Phone: (301)869-0086
Toll-Free: 800-422-5525
Low-impact household cleaners, including phosphate-free detergents.

★8233★ We Care
Phone: (619)360-3838
Offers 111 hard-to find, Earth-saving products. Catalog available.

Investing

★8234★ American Rivers
801 Pennsylvania Ave., SE
Washington, DC 20003
Phone: (202)547-6900
Offers a credit card, the use of which will provide funds for river restoration and maintenance.

★8235★ Calvert Social Investment Fund
4550 Montgomery Ave.
Bethesda, MD 20814
Toll-Free: 800-368-2750
Calvert Social Investment Fund encourages environmentally and socially responsible investors of mutual funds. Catalog available.

★8236★ Clean Yield Asset Management
224 State St.
Portsmouth, NH 03801
Phone: (603)436-0820
Mutual funds.

★8237★ Co-op America
2100 M St., NW, Ste. 310
Washington, DC 20063
Phone: (202)872-5307
Offers credit card; mutual funds.

★8238★ Defenders of Wildlife
1244 19th St., NW
Washington, DC 20036
Phone: (202)659-9510
Offers credit card services.

★8239★ First Affirmative Financial Network
410 N. 21st St., Ste. 203
Colorado Springs, CO 80904
Phone: (719)636-1045
Toll-Free: 800-422-7284
Supports the environment with socially responsible investments in recycling, alternative energy and pollution control industries. Offers a free financial planning review.

★8240★ Freedom Environment Fund
1 Beacon St.
Boston, MA 02108
Phone: (617)523-3170
Toll-Free: 800-225-6258
Money market and mutual funds.

★8241★ International Fund for Animal Welfare
PO Box 193
411 Main St.
Yarmouth Port, MA 02675
Phone: (508)362-4944
Toll-Free: 800-972-9979
Offers credit card service.

★8242★ Kemper Environmental Series Fund
120 S LaSalle St.
Chicago, IL 60603
Toll-Free: 800-621-1048
Mutual fund.

★8243★ National Business Association Credit Union
3807 Otter St.
PO Box 2206
Bristol, PA 19007
Toll-Free: 800-441-0878
Credit card services.

★8244★ National Wildlife Federation
1400 16th St., NW
Washington, DC 20036
Phone: (202)797-6800
Toll-Free: 800-847-7378
Credit card service.

★8245★ New Alternatives Fund
295 Northern Blvd.
Great Neck, NY 11021
Phone: (516)466-0808
A mutual fund concentrating in alternative energy, solar energy and conservation

investments. Investments include cogeneration, non-nuclear utilities, pollution control, geothermal resources, and resource recovery. Catalog available.

★8246★ Oppenheimer Global Environment Fund
2 World Trade Center
New York, NY 10048-0669
Toll-Free: 800-525-7048
Mutual funds.

★8247★ The Parnassus Fund
244 California St.
San Francisco, CA 94111
Phone: (415)362-3505
Offers money market and mutual funds.

★8248★ Pax World Fund, Inc.
224 State St.
Portsmouth, NH 03801
Toll-Free: 800-767-1729
Money market and mutual funds; Individual Retirement Accounts (IRAs).

★8249★ Self-Help Credit Union
413 Chapel Hill St.
Durham, NC 27701
Phone: (919)683-3016
Offers IRAs and money markets.

★8250★ South Shore Bank
71st and Jeffrey Blvd.
Chicago, IL 60649
Phone: (312)288-1000
Offers IRAs and mutual funds.

★8251★ Working Assets Money Fund
230 California St.
San Francisco, CA 94111
Phone: (415)989-3200
Toll-Free: 800-533-3863
Offers Individual Retirement Accounts (IRAs), credit cards, and money market and mutual funds.

Office Products

★8252★ Boyd's Office Prducts
Toll-Free: 800-753-1379
Office products made from recycled paper, including computer and copier paper, mailing and filing supplies, and waste containers. Free catalog available.

★8253★ Conservatree
10 Lombard St., Ste. 250
San Francisco, CA 94111
Phone: (415)433-1000
Toll-Free: 800-522-9200
Office and printing paper products, including letterheads, envelopes, and computer paper.

★8254★ The Ribbon Factory
Phone: (702)736-2484
Toll-Free: 800-275-7422
Recycles computer printer ribbons and cartridges.

Organically Grown Foods

★8255★ Celestial Seasonings, Inc.
1780 55th St.
Boulder, CO 80301-2799
Natural tea made in 100% oxygen bleached tea bags.

★8256★ Country Grown
12202 Woodbine
Redford, MI 48239
Phone: (313)535-9222
Organically grown, microwavable popcorn packaged in recycled materials.

★8257★ Gold Mine Natural Food Co.
Toll-Free: 800-475-3663
Organic and natural foods, water purifiers, non-toxic cookware and other household products. Catalog available.

★8258★ Health Rich
12202 Woodbine
Redford, MI 48239
Phone: (313)535-9222
Organic snacks.

★8259★ The Nature Company
Home Office
750 Hearst Ave.
Berkeley, CA 94710
Sells a variety of products aimed at saving the rainforest regions.

★8260★ Walnut Acres
Dept. B122
Penns Creek, PA 17862
Toll-Free: 800-344-9025
Organically grown grains, seeds, beans, fruits, and vegetables without chemicals or pesticides.

Packing Materials

★8261★ American Excelsior Co.
850 Ave. H, E.
PO Box 5067
Arlington, TX 76005-5067
Phone: (817)640-1555
Toll-Free: 800-777-7645
Produces Eco-Foam, a loose fill that contains 95% cornstarch, is nontoxic when combusted and dissolves in water. It is an environmentally safe alternative to the polystyrene peanuts currently used for most packing.

★8262★ Eco-Pack Industries, Inc.
7859 S. 180th St.
Kent, WA 98032
Phone: (206)251-0918
Biodegradable and recyclable packaging materials, including the products Quadra-Pak and Sizzle-Pak.

★8263★ Key Tech
2200 222nd, SE
Bothell, WA 98021
Toll-Free: 800-225-5539
Produces Lock 'N' Pop, a nontoxic polymer-based product for the pallet unitizing market. It is an alternative to the stretch wrap currently used to bundle cargo onto forklifts. The product holds pallets layers firmly into place without the use of plastic stretch wrap or glue and allows easy removal.

Personal Products

★8264★ AFM
Teal Distributors, E.
PO Box 400
Skyland, NC 28776
Phone: (704)684-1177
Toll-Free: 800-477-8325
Paints, stain, caulking, enamels, sealers, wax, carpet guard, spackling, mildew control, cleaners, adhesives, and shampoo.

★8265★ Auromere-NYT
1291 Weber
Pomona, CA 91768
Toll-Free: 800-735-4691
Natural ayurvedic herbal toothpaste. Does not test its products on animals.

★8266★ Aveda Corporation
Minneapolis, MN 55413
Toll-Free: 800-328-0849
Uses pure, natural, plant-dervived compounds in place of sythetic and animal-tested ingredients for hair, skin and body products.

★8267★ Back to Earth, Inc.
PO Box 672
Ellenwood, GA 30049
Personal and household products. Catalog available for $1.00, refundable with first purchase.

★8268★ Beehive Botanicals
Toll-Free: 800-283-4274
Full line of natural products for skin and hair care. Also offers a line of dietary supplements. Catalog available.

★8269★ Biomatik USA Corp.
PO Box 2119
Boulder, CO 80306
Phone: (303)938-8999
Produces an air-powered, gas-free spray bottle that eliminates the need for chemically-propelled aerosol cans. Can be used for a variety of personal, household and industrial products.

★8270★ The Cottage Body Shoppe
351 River St.
Bigfork, MT 59911
Toll-Free: 800-874-0327
Natural, biodegradable body care products. Specializes in custom scenting. Does not test its products on animals. Catalog available.

★8271★ Eco-Choice
Dept. 2009
PO Box 281
Montvale, NJ 07645
Toll-Free: 800-535-6304
Recycled paper products, household cleaning products, biorational pest controls, recyclables containers, personal care, cosmetics, and baby products. Free brochure available.

★8272★ Everybody Ltd.
Toll-Free: 800-748-5675
Body, household, and pet care products. Does not test its products on animals. Catalog available.

★8273★ Health Kleaner
PO Box 4656
Boulder, CO 80306
Phone: (303)444-3440
Health Kleaner, a skin cleaner that also can be used to remove tough stains from surface. Has also been found to remove oil and adhesives

from marine mammals and seabirds. Made from all natural products, like oranges, glycerine and jojoba oil. Does not test its products on animals.

★8274★ The Keeper
Box 20023G
Cincinnati, OH 45220
Internally worn, reusable, soft rubber menstrual cup. Comes in two styles: before childbirth and after childbirth.

★8275★ Kiss My Face Corp.
224 Gardiner

Toll-Free: 800-262-5477
Sunscreen and natural repellants, including the product Kiss Off.

★8276★ Logona
Box 8398
Atlanta, GA 30306
Toll-Free: 800-648-6654
European body care products.

★8277★ National Ecological and Environmental Delivery System
527 Charles Ave.
Syracuse, NY 13209
Toll-Free: 800-634-1380

★8278★ The Natural Choice
Toll-Free: 800-621-2591
Over 300 environmentally safe products: non-toxic paints, stains and wood preservatives, natural health products, bodycare and colognes, herbal remedies, recycled paper, cleaners, pet care, ferilizers, organic seeds, and other natural products.

★8279★ Nature of Things
3956 Long Pl.
Carlsbad, CA 92008
Phone: (619)434-4480
Biodegradable cleaning and personal care products. Catalog available.

★8280★ New Cycle
PO Box 3248
Santa Rosa, CA 95402
Beltless, washable, soft flannel, 100% cotton menstrual pads.

★8281★ Orjene Natural Cosmetics
Dept. GM
5-43 48 Ave.
Long Island City, NY 11101
Phone: (718)937-2666
Cosmetics and beauty care products that contain no mineral oils or artificial colors. Does not test its products on animals. Catalog available for $1.00.

★8282★ SafeBrands
55 W. Sierra Madre Blvd.
Sierra Madre, CA 91024
Phone: (818)355-1050
Biodegradable hair care products. Does not test its products on animals.

★8283★ Women's Choice
PO Box 245
Gabriola, British Columbia, Canada V0R 1X0
Phone: (604)247-8433
Nondisposable menstrual pads and panty liners made from cotton fleece.

Pet Supplies

★8284★ Baubiologie Hardware
207B 16th St.
Pacific Grove, CA 93950
Phone: (408)372-6826
Nontoxic pest control products, flea collars, and animal shampoo.

★8285★ Green Ban
Box 146
Norway, IA 52318
Phone: (319)227-7996
Pet products made from natural ingredients, including flea powder and dog shampoo.

★8286★ Necessary Trading Co.
Newcastle, VA 24127
Phone: (703)864-5103
Healthy pet care kit, including nontoxic flea, tick, and lice powder.

★8287★ Pet Guard
PO Box 728
Orange Park, FL 32073
Toll-Free: 800-874-3221
Natural pet products, including flea powders and shampoo.

★8288★ Ringer
9959 Valley View Rd.
Eden Prairie, MN 55344
Phone: (612)941-4180
Toll-Free: 800-654-1047
Natural flea and tick repellant.

★8289★ Safer, Inc.
189 Wells Ave.
Newton, MA 02159
Phone: (617)964-2990
Offers line of pet products made from natural ingredients, including pet odor eliminator, flea soap, and flea guard

★8290★ Whole Earth Access Company
2990 7th St.
Berkeley, CA 94710
Phone: (415)845-3000
Toll-Free: 800-845-2000
Natural pet products, including cedar pet pillows. Catalog is available for $7.

Recycled Paper and Plastic Products

★8291★ Acorn Designs
5066 Mott Evans Rd., Ste. 1461
Trumansburg, NY 14886
Phone: (607)387-3424
Notecards and stationery on recycled paper.

★8292★ Alonzo Printing
1094 San Mateo Ave.
South San Fancisco, CA 94080
Phone: (415)873-0522
Fax: (415)952-1438
Printer which uses recycled paper and soybean inks.

★8293★ Atlantic Recycled Paper Co.
PO Box 39096
Baltimore, MD 21212
Phone: (301)323-2676
Envelopes, fax paper, legal pads, computer paper, napkins, paper towels, toilet and facial tissue, mailing labels, and loose leaf paper. All products made from recycled paper.

★8294★ Boyd's Office Prducts
Toll-Free: 800-753-1379
Office products made from recycled paper, including computer and copier paper, mailing and filing supplies, and waste containers. Free catalog available.

★8295★ Brush Dance
218 Cleveland Ct., Dept. 10
Mill Valley, CA 94941
Phone: (415)389-6228
Recycled paper products, including stationery, wrapping paper, and cards.

★8296★ Conservatree
10 Lombard St., Ste. 250
San Francisco, CA 94111
Phone: (415)433-1000
Toll-Free: 800-522-9200
Office and printing paper products, including letterheads, envelopes, and computer paper.

★8297★ Earth Care Paper
PO Box 14140
Dept. 619
Madison, WI 53714
Phone: (608)277-2900
Full line of recycled office paper products, gift wrap, notecards, and stationery. Free catalog available.

★8298★ Earthforms
PO Box 65303
Baltimore, MD 21209-0003
Phone: (301)486-4099
Prints business cards, notepads, flyers, letterheads, envelopes, and newsletters using recycled paper and soybean base inks.

★8299★ Eco-Choice
Dept. 2009
PO Box 281
Montvale, NJ 07645
Toll-Free: 800-535-6304
Recycled paper products, household cleaning products, biorational pest controls, recyclables containers, personal care, cosmetics, and baby products. Free brochure available.

★8300★ EcoSource
PO Box 1656
Sebastopol, CA 95473
Toll-Free: 800-274-7040
A variety of environmentally-friendly household, personal, and energy efficent products. Catalog available.

★8301★ Graphic Advantage, Inc.
PO Box 1711
Paramus, NJ 07653-1711
Phone: (201)652-0725
Commercial printer which uses recycled paper.

★8302★ Greenpeace Catalog
PO Box 77048
San Francisco, CA 94107-0048
Toll-Free: 800-456-4029
Offers t-shirts and jackets with environmental messages, jewelry, bags, shower heads, toilet dams, games, hand puppets, stationery made of recycled paper, keychains, and more.

★8303★ Jade Mountain
PO Box 4616
Boulder, CO 80306-4616
Toll-Free: 800-442-1972
Solar electric systems, energy efficient lighting, water purification, recycled paper products,

demand water heaters, hydroelectric and wind generators, and solar toys.

★8304★ McMullen Design
15305 S. Normandie Ave.
Gardena, CA 90247
Phone: (213)515-1701
Offers reusable oil and gas filters for almost every type of car on the road. They can be cleaned with soap and water and reused throughout the lifetime of an automobile.

★8305★ Print Power Service
Toll-Free: 800-735-8260
Business cards, letterheads, flyers, newsletters, and other print products on recycled paper with soy ink.

★8306★ Real Goods
3041 Guildiville Rd.
Ukiah, CA 95482
Toll-Free: 800-762-7325
Offers energy-efficient lighting, refrigeration, water heating, and water conservation products; recycled paper products; non-toxic household cleaners; and toys and gifts.

★8307★ Sierra Club
Phone: (415)923-5500
The Sierra Club Mail Order Service Guide contains a complete list of Sierra Club books, cups, t-shirts and other logo items. Catalog available.

★8308★ Signature Marketing
134 W. St.
Simsbury, CT 06070
Phone: (203)658-7172
Fax: (203)651-8376
Promotes recycling programs with imprinted items made of 100% recycled materials.

★8309★ Signs and Symbols
2965 Pinewoods Rd., Dept. G3491
Lewiston, ME 04240
Phone: (207)782-3756
Fax: (207)783-3742
Recycled paper and plastic products, environmental publications, earth music, and children's items. Catalog available. Donates 5% of profits to environmental organizations.

★8310★ Small Potatoes Press
PO Box 274
Hales Corners, WI 53130
Greeting cards for all occasions, printed on recycled paper.

★8311★ Urban Forest Packaging Products
1222 W. Spring St.
Brownstone, IN 47220-1099
Phone: (812)358-3150
Low-density packaging made from recycled paper.

★8312★ Used Rubber USA
Phone: (415)626-7855
Purses, bags, carrying cases, and other products made from recycled rubber.

★8313★ Weisenbach Specialty Printing
Phone: (614)464-2223
Features recycled plastic rulers, yo-yos, flying discs, recycled paper note cubes, cotton tote bags, and ceramic mugs for promoting and advertising environmental messages and logos.

Recycling Bins

★8314★ Action Packaging Systems, Inc.
374 Somers Rd.
Ellington, CT 06029
Phone: (203)872-6311
Fax: (203)875-4293
Receptacles for recyclable waste.

★8315★ CSL and Associates
2482 Jett Ferry Rd., Ste. 680-E16
Dunwoody, GA 30338
Phone: (404)396-2949
Hand-operated can compactor for crushing and storing cans. Metal storage bin holds 13-gallon garbage bag.

★8316★ Echo Hills Co.
9500 Bauer Rd.
Logan, OH 43138
Phone: (614)385-8760
Recycling bin separates glass, paper, and cans.

★8317★ Natural Living
Ste. 266B
Rte. 93, RR I Box 310-B
Hazelton, PA 18201
Phone: (717)454-1526
Recycling bins with mobile countertop, extra storage space for bags, cans, etc. Available in a variety of sizes.

★8318★ Paper Plus Recycling, Inc.
504 Malcolm Ave. SE
Minneapolis, MN 55414
Phone: (612)378-1374
Receptacles for recycling cans and paper.

★8319★ Paperboy Products
601 Glenway St.
Madison, WI 53711
Phone: (608)233-5556
Newspaper holder for paper bundling and recycling.

★8320★ Sivalia Woodworks
201 Cumberland Ave.
Asheville, NC 28801
Phone: (704)258-8544
Recycling cabinet for the kitchen. Uses standard size paper grocery bags to collect glass, aluminum, plastic and junk paper. Also includes storage space for newspapers.

★8321★ United Marketing Inc.
14th & Laurel Sts.
PO Box 870
Pottsville, PA 17901-0870
Phone: (717)622-7715
Fax: (717)622-3817
Recyclable waste containers.

★8322★ Windsor Barrel Works
Box 47
Kempton, PA 19529
Phone: (215)756-4344
Toll-Free: 800-527-7848
Receptacles for recyclable waste.

T-Shirts and Assorted Apparel

★8323★ Better World T-Shirts
1 Innwood Cr., Ste. 220
Little Rock, AR 72211
T-shirts with environment-conscious messages.

★8324★ Donnelly/Colt
Box 188-E
Hampton, CT 06247
Phone: (203)455-9621
Custom print buttons, bumperstickers, t-shirts, postcards, posters, and labels with environmental, peace, social justice and human rights themes. Catalog available.

★8325★ Environmental Awareness Products
3600 Goodwin Rd.
Ionia, MI 48846
Phone: (517)647-2535
T-shirts and clothing emphasizing nature, conservation, and Native American themes. A portion of proceeds go to Earth Island Institute and various environmental groups.

★8326★ Environmental Gifts
PO Box 222-C
Helena, MT 59624
Phone: (406)458-6466
"Love Your Mother" t-shirts, posters, and window decals.

★8327★ Environmental Resource Project
PO Box 600-G
Bayside, CA 95524
Phone: (707)822-1636
Products which promote environmental awareness and action, including t-shirts, buttons, and rubberstamps.

★8328★ Greenpeace Catalog
PO Box 77048
San Francisco, CA 94107-0048
Toll-Free: 800-456-4029
Offers t-shirts and jackets with environmental messages, jewelry, bags, shower heads, toilet dams, games, hand puppets, stationery made of recycled paper, keychains, and more.

★8329★ Recycled Colours
212 E. 15th St.
Bloomington, IN 47408
Phone: (812)339-6479
Toll-Free: 800-762-6798
An environmentally committed screen printing company. Promotes environmental education and awareness through positive designs.

★8330★ Sierra Club
Phone: (415)923-5500
The Sierra Club Mail Order Service Guide contains a complete list of Sierra Club books, cups, t-shirts and other logo items. Catalog available.

★8331★ Upstart
Box 889
Hagerstown, MD 21741
Fax: (301)797-1615
Toll-Free: 800-448-4887
Environmentally oriented games, posters, stickers, buttons, and t-shirts for children.

★8332★ Wearable Arts
26 Medway, #12
San Rafael, CA 94901
Phone: (415)456-7034
Toll-Free: 800-635-2781
T-shirts with environmental themes, including North American hummingbirds, Pacific grey whales, and tropical rain forests.

Scholarships, Fellowships, and Loans

International

★8333★ Atlantic Salmon Federation
Bensinger-Liddell Salmon Fellowship
PO Box 429
St. Andrews, N.B., New Brunswick, Canada EOG 2X0
This Fellowship is for overseas travel, study and research benefiting Atlantic salmon conservation or management.

United States

★8334★ American Fishing Tackle Manufacturers Association
Andrew J. Boehm Graduate Fellowship in the Fisheries Sciences
1250 Grove Ave., Ste. 300
Barrington, IL 60010
Phone: (708)381-9490
Contact: Sandra K. Brunk
Candidates must be committed to a professional career in fish conservation. The fellowship is to be used for dissertation research for either the M.S. or Ph.D. degrees.

★8335★ American Geological Institute
Minority Student Scholarships in Earth, Space, and Marine Sciences
4220 King St.
Alexandria, VA 22302-1507
Phone: (703)379-2480
Fax: (703)379-7563
Toll-Free: 800-336-4764
The scholarships are open to graduate and undergraduate students in earth, space, and marine sciences. Eligible are members of Asian, Black, Native American and Hispanic ethnic groups, who are United States citizens.

★8336★ American Geophysical Union
Congressional Science Fellowship Program
2000 Florida Ave. NW
Washington, DC 20009
The AGU Congressional Science Fellowship Program places highly qualified scientists with the offices of individual members of Congress and committees for a one-year assignment. There is opportunity for research and development of public policy on scientific issues such as safe water/environmental concerns, and energy policy.

★8337★ American Geophysical Union
Horton Research Grant
2000 Florida Ave., NW
Washington, DC 20009
The award is for a Ph.D. candidate, who is a member or a student member of the American Geophysical Union, in support of a research project in hydrology or water resources.

★8338★ American Museum of Natural History
Lerner-Gray Grants for Marine Research
Central Part W. at 79th St.
New York, NY 10024-5192
Applicants are advanced graduate or postdoctoral researchers who are starting careers in marine zoology. Their projects must deal with systematics, evolution, ecology and field-oriented behavioral studies of marine animals.

★8339★ American Nuclear Society
Environmental Sciences Division Scholarship
555 N Kensington Ave.
La Grange Park, IL 60525
Must be an undergraduate in an accredited institution in the United States who has completed two or more years in a course of study leading to a degree in nuclear science or engineering and must be a U.S. citizen or possess a permanent resident visa.

★8340★ American Nuclear Society
Fuel Cycle and Waste Management Scholarship
555 N. Kensington Ave.
La Grange Park, IL 60525
Must be an undergraduate in an accredited institution in the United States who has completed two or more years in a course of study leading to a degree in nuclear science or engineering and must be a U.S. citizen or possess a permanent resident visa.

★8341★ American Philosophical Society
Michaux Grants in Forestry and Silviculture
105 S. 5th St.
Philadelphia, PA 19106
Candidates should be conducting postdoctoral research in silviculture and forest botany.

★8342★ American Society of Naturalists
ASN Young Investigator's Award
Department of Ecology & Evolution
State University of New York
Stony Brook, NY 11794
Phone: (516)632-8589
Contact: Dr. Barbara Bentley
To recognize outstanding research by a young Ph.D. in ecological or evolutionary studies.

★8343★ American Water Works Association
Academic Achievement Award
6666 W. Quincy Ave.
Denver, CO 80235
To encourage academic excellence by recognizing contribution to the field of public water supply.

★8344★ Atlantic Salmon Federation
Olin Fellowships
PO Box 807
Calais, ME 04619
Phone: (506)529-4581
Fax: (506)529-4438
Applicants must be legal residents of the United States or Canada who are seeking to expand their knowledge or skills in Atlantic salmon biology, management and conservation.

★8345★ Center for Field Research
Center for Field Research Grants
680 Mt. Auburn St.
PO Box 403
Watertown, MA 02272
Phone: (617)926-8200
Fax: (617)926-8532
Telex: 510 600 6452
Applicants must submit a two-page preliminary proposal for field research in any recognized academic discipline.

★8346★ The Edmund Niles Huyck Preserve, Inc.
Edmund Niles Huyck Preserve Research Grants
Biological Research Sta.
PO Box 188
Rensselaerville, NY 12147
Candidates must be graduate or postgraduate investigators with a suitable background for conducting biological research using the natural resources of the Huyck Preserve.

★8347★ Environmental Grantmakers Association
1290 Avenue of the Americas, Ste. 3450
New York, NY 10104
This association offers a directory of "green" foundations.

★8348★ Environmental Protection Agency
Office of International Activities
CCMS Fellowship Programme
201 M St. SW
Washington, DC 20466
Contact: Alan B. Sielen, Dir. Multilateral Staff
Allows fellows to contribute to the work of CCMS pilot studies, which are designed to achieve a better understanding of the adverse effects of our technology-intensive way of life on

the natural and social environment and to stimulate governments to take remedial action.

★8349★ Forest History Society
Alfred D. Bell, Jr. Visiting Scholars Program
701 Vickers Ave.
Durham, NC 27701
Phone: (919)682-9319
Contact: Cheryl Oakes, Lib.
Enables scholars to make use of the varied collections of the Forest History Society Library and archives.

★8350★ Joint Oceanographic Institutions, Inc.
JOI/USSAC Ocean Drilling Fellowship Program
1755 Massachusetts Ave., NW, Ste. 800
Washington, DC 20036-2102
Phone: (202)232-3900
Fax: (202)232-8203
Contact: Robin Smith, Fellowship Coordinator
The Ocean Drilling Program (ODP) is an international effort to explore the structure and history of the ocean basins. It allows scientists from around the world to participate in a continous series of scientific cruises. On these cruises, the scientists core samples and geophysical data from beneath the ocean floor in order to better understand the ages of ocean basins and their processes of development, the rearrangement of continents with time, the structure of the earth's interior, the evolution of life in the oceans and the history of worldwide climatic change.

★8351★ L.S.B. Leakey Foundation
Fellowship for Grant Ape Research and Conservation
77 Jack London Sq., Ste. M
Oakland, CA 94607-3750
Phone: (510)834-3636
Fax: (510)834-3640
Contact: Dr. Karla Savage, Program & Grants Officer
Promotes long-term research on wild populations of great apes.

★8352★ National Center For Atmospheric Research
Graduate Research Assistantships
PO Box 3000
Boulder, CO 80307
Phone: (303)497-1601
Fax: (303)497-1137
Telex: 989764
Candidates must declare their intention of working on a Ph.D. thesis in cooperation with a National Center for Atmospheric Research (NCAR) program. Fields of study are atmospheric dynamics, climatology and paleoclimatology, oceanography, atmospheric physics, radiation, cloud physics, atmospheric chemistry, solar and space physics, astrophysics, environmental and societal impact assessment and atmospheric technology.

★8353★ Nixon Griffis Fund for Zoological Research
Griffis Fund for Zoological Research Grants
New York Zoological Society
185th St. & Southern Blvd.
Bronx Zoo
Bronx, NY 10460
Phone: (212)220-5152
Fax: (212)220-7114
To support research which will help zoos and aquariums fulfill their ever-increasing roles as repositories of life. By sponsoring individual projects, the Fund seeks to encourage the scientific work that is essential to the preservation of wildlife species.

★8354★ Oklahoma State University
University Center for Water Research
003 Life Sciences E.
Stillwater, OK 74078
Phone: (405)744-9995
Fax: (405)744-7673
Contact: Dr. Norman N. Durham, Dir.
Provides three-year fellowships to graduate students.

★8355★ Resources for the Future
RFF Small Grants Program
1616 P St., NW
Washington, DC 20036
Phone: (202)328-5022
Fax: (202)939-3460
Contact: Chris Mendes
Provides start-up funding for new projects or supplemental support to complete specific aspects on ongoing projects involving the development, conservation and use of natural resources and the quality of the environment. Proposals may deal with theoretical or applied topics, but must be focused on research. Recent priorities include: 1) experimental economics or other innovative techniques that address the problems of managing common property resources or natural monopolies, 2) alternative legal or other arrangements that reduce transactions costs in cases involving toxic torts or natural resource damage claims, and 3) policies to facilitate sustained economic growth consistent with the protection of natural resources and the environment.

★8356★ Smithsonian Environmental Research Center
Work-Learn Opportunities in Environmental Studies
PO Box 28
Edgewater, MD 21037
Phone: (301)798-4424
Fax: (301)261-7954
Candidates are undergraduate or graduate students with training or experience in the area of the terrestrial and estuarine environmental research within the disciplines of mathematics, chemistry, microbiology, botany, and zoology. Environmental education opportunities are also available.

★8357★ Southern Illinois University at Carbondale
Illinois Mining and Mineral Resources Research Institute
Coal Extraction & Utilization Research Center
Carbondale, IL 62901
Phone: (618)536-6637
Fax: (618)453-7455
Contact: Dr. Y. Paul Chugh, Dir.
Offers fellowships for graduate and undergraduate students.

★8358★ University of Colorado-Boulder
Cooperative Institute for Research in Environmental Sciences
Campus Box 216
Boulder, CO 80309-0216
Phone: (303)492-1143
Fax: (303)492-1149
Contact: Dr. Robert Sievers, Dir.
Sponsors a visiting fellowship program.

★8359★ University of Maryland
Sea Grant College
1224 H. J. Patterson Hall
College Park, MD 20742
Phone: (301)405-6371
Fax: (301)314-9581
Contact: Dr. Christopher D'Elia, Dir.
Supports undergraduate and graduate students through fellowships.

★8360★ University of Tennessee at Knoxville
Energy, Environment and Resource Center
327 S. Stadium Hall
Knoxville, TN 37996
Phone: (615)974-4251
Contact: Dr. William Colglazier, Dir.
Provides corporate sponsored fellowships.

★8361★ University of Tennessee at Knoxville
Waste Management Research and Education Institute
Waste Management Internship Program
327 S. Stadium Hall
Knoxville, TN 37996-0710
Phone: (615)974-4251
Contact: Dr. E. William Colglazier, Dir.
Offers graduate fellowship program.

★8362★ Washington Pulp and Paper Foundation
Washington Pulp and Paper Foundation Scholarship
c/o University of Washington (AR-10)
Seattle, WA 98195
Phone: (206)543-2763
Must be enrolled in the College of Forest Resources at the University of Washington, Seattle.

★8363★ Water Pollution Control Federation
Robert A. Canham Award
601 Wythe St.
Alexandria, VA 22314-1994
Phone: (703)684-2400
Fax: (703)684-2492
Must be a post-baccalaureate trained in environmental engineering or one of its allied fields.

★8364★ Weston Institute
Weston Way
West Chester, PA 19380
Phone: (215)430-3100
Fax: (215)692-6503
Contact: William Gaither, Dir.
Offers $5,000 and $10,000 scholarships to master's and doctoral degree students.

★8365★ Wildlife Conservation International
Wildlife Conservation International Research Fellowship
c/o New York Zoological Society
Bronx, NY 10460
Phone: (212)220-6864
Fax: (212)220-7114
Contact: Dr. Mary Pearl
To support individual research projects that lead directly to conservation of threatened wildlife, communities, and ecosystems.

★8366★ Woman's Seamen's Friend Society of Connecticut, Inc.
Woman's Seamen's Friend Society of Connecticut Financial Support for Graduate Work in the Marine Sciences
74 Forbes Ave.
New Haven, CT 06512
Phone: (203)467-3887
To assist graduate students carrying out research in the marine sciences.

★8367★ Woods Hole Oceanographic Institution
Woods Hole Oceanographic Institution Postdoctoral Fellowships
Woods Hole, MA 02543
Phone: (508)457-2000
Fax: (508)457-2188
New or recent recipients of the doctoral degree with interests in the oceanographic sciences or engineering are eligible.

★8368★ Woods Hole Oceanographic Institution
Woods Hole Oceanographic Institution Research Fellowships in Marine Policy and Ocean Management
Woods Hole, MA 02543
Phone: (508)457-2000
Fax: (508)457-2188
Provides support and experience to research fellows interested in marine policy issues, and provides opportunities for interdisciplinary application of social sciences and natural sciences to marine policy problems.

★8369★ Woods Hole Oceanographic Institution
Woods Hole Oceanographic Institution Summer Student Fellowship
Woods Hole, MA 02543
Phone: (508)457-2000
Alt. Phone: (508)457-2188
To give a promising group of science and engineering students experience which will assist them in determining whether they wish to devote lifetime careers to the study of the oceans and to allow them to pursue an independent research project, chosen by the fellow, under the guidance of a member of the research staff.

★8370★ Yale University
Yale Institute of Biospheric Studies
Osborne Memorial Laboratory
165 Prospect St.
New Haven, CT 06511
Phone: (203)432-3691
Contact: Dr. Leo Buss, Dir.
Sponsors fellowships.

Awards, Honors, and Prizes

International

★8371★ All-Union Leninist Young Communist League
Environmental Protection Award
c/o Committee of Youth Organizations of the USSR
Ul. Bogdana Chmelnitskovo 7/8
SU-101846 Moscow, Union of Soviet Socialist Republics
To recognize young people, adults, and foreigners for active participation in guarding the natural environment.

★8372★ Atlantic Salmon Federation
Bensinger - Liddell Salmon Fellowship
c/o Sue Scott, Exec.Asst., Opns.
PO Box 429
St. Andrews, New Brunswick, Canada EOG 2X0
Phone: (506)529-8891
Fax: (506)529-4438
To provide for overseas travel, study and research benefitting Atlantic salmon conservation or management. The award is given in alternate years to citizens of North America and the United Kingdom. Applications must be submitted by March 1. Awarded annually by the Atlantic Salmon Federation and the Atlantic Salmon Trust. Established in 1981 in memory of international conservationists, B.E. Bensinger and B.J. Liddell. Information is available in the United States from P.O. Drawer C, Calais, ME 04619.

★8373★ Atlantic Salmon Federation
Olin Fellowships
c/o Sue Scott, Exec.Asst., Opns.
PO Box 429
St. Andrews, New Brunswick, Canada E0G 2X0
Phone: (506)529-8891
Fax: (506)529-4438
To provide for improvement of knowledge or skills in advanced fields while looking for solutions to current problems in Atlantic salmon biology, management or conservation. Applicants must be legal residents of the United States or Canada. The deadline is March 15. Awarded annually. Established in 1974. Information is available in the United States from P.O. Drawer C, Calais, ME 04619.

★8374★ Ecology Institute
Ecology Institute Prize
c/o Prof. Dr. O. Kinne
Nordbunte 23
D-2124 Oldendorf/Luhe, Germany
Phone: 41321727
To recognize ecologists for outstanding scientific achievements who are able and willing to provide a critical synthesis and evaluation of their field of expertise, addressing an audience beyond narrow professional borderlines. In an annually rotating pattern, awards are presented in the fields of marine, terrestrial and limnetic ecology. All ecologists engaged in scientific research are eligible. The winner of the Prize is requested to author a 200 to 300 printed-page book, to be published by ECI in the series Excellence in Ecology and to be made available world-wide at cost price. The Ecology Institute Prize is considered unique for two reasons: (1) it was established and is financed by research ecologists; (2) the prize gives and takes: it both honors the recipient and requires him/her to serve science, which has a greater need now than ever for critical syntheses of the state of the art.

★8375★ Ecology Institute
IRPE Prize (International Recognition of Professional Excellence)
c/o Prof. Dr. O. Kinne
Nordbunte 23
D-2124 Oldendorf/Luhe, Germany
Phone: 41321727
To recognize a young ecologist who has conducted and published uniquely independent, original and/or challenging research efforts representing an important scientific breakthrough. Awarded when merited.

★8376★ European Council of Chemical Manufacturers Federations
CEFIC Environment Award
c/o Louis Jourdan, Director Technical Affairs
Avenue Louise 250, Bte 71
PO Box 177
B-1050 Brussels, Belgium
Phone: 2640 20 95
To recognize an outstanding innovation that enables the chemical industry to help solve an environmental problem. Entries are accepted from individual persons or groups until the closing date of January 8. Awarded biennially in March. Established in 1987.

★8377★ Food and Agriculture Organization of the United Nations
Food and Agriculture Organization of the United Nations Technical Assistance Fellowship
c/o Vivienne Heston, Information Materials Production Bran
Via delle Terme di Caracalla
I-00100 Rome, Italy
Phone: 657971
Fax: 657973152
To provide for study in the fields of agriculture, fisheries, forestry, nutrition, agricultural economics and statistics, rural institutions, and services, etc., to prepare suitably qualified personnel to assist in economic and technical development of own country. Applications are open to nationals of countries where FAO carries out technical assistance projects provided they are working or are destined to work on these projects and have been selected to undertake further studies abroad. Candidates must have adequate basic and technical education and practical experience in the field of study. A fellowship is awarded.

★8378★ International Association on Water Pollution Research and Control
Honorary Member
1 Queen Anne's Gate
London SW1H 9BT, England
Phone: 71222 3848
To recognize an individual who has made an outstanding contribution both to the Association and to water pollution, research and control. Selection is by nomination. Awarded at the biennial international conferences. Established in 1966.

★8379★ International Association on Water Pollution Research and Control
IAWPRC Pergamon Publications Medal
1 Queen Anne's Gate
London SW1H 9BT, England
Phone: 71222 3848
To recognize an IAWPRC individual member who is an author or a co-author of the best paper of those presented in general sessions or seminars at the previous biennial conference. Awarded biennially. Established in 1988.

★8380★ International Association on Water Pollution Research and Control
Karl Imhoff - Pierre Koch Medal
1 Queen Anne's Gate
London SW1H 9BT, England
Phone: 71222 3848
To recognize achievements on the practical side of water pollution control. Members of the Association responsible for a contribution of international impact relating to facilities involved in water quality control are eligible. Any member of IAWPRC can prepare a nomination and submit it to a National Committee for endorsement. Awarded biennially. Established in 1988.

★8381★ International Association on Water Pollution Research and Control
Samuel H. Jenkins Medal
1 Queen Anne's Gate
London SW1H 9BT, England
Phone: 71222 3848
For recognition of meritorious service to the Association. Any member of the Association is

eligible. Nominations for this award may be made by National Committees, and Corporate and Individual Members with the endorsement of their National Committee. Awarded biennially. Established in 1983 in memory of Dr. Samuel Harry Jenkins, an outstanding contributor both to the development of IAWPRC and to water pollution research and control.

★8382★ International Council for Bird Preservation
ICBP/FFPS Conservation Expedition Competition
32 Cambridge Rd.
Girton
Cambridge CB3 0PJ, England
Phone: 223277318
To encourage university or other teams to adopt a wildlife conservation objective for their expeditions. A project proposal for an expedition outside Europe and North America should be submitted by January 31. In selecting the prize-winning projects, attention is paid to conservation content and likely impact, feasibility, and relationship to the International Council for Bird Preservation/Fauna and Flora Preservation Society conservation priorities. Established in 1985.

★8383★ International Council of Environmental Law
Elizabeth Haub Prize
Adenauerallee 214
D-5300 Bonn 1, Germany
Phone: 228269 22 40
For recognition of accomplishments in the field of environmental law. No restrictions exist as to membership or citizenship. A jury composed of representatives of ICEL and the Universite Libre de Bruxelles makes the selection. Awarded annually. Established in 1974 by the ICEL and the Universite Libre de Bruxelles in honor of Elizabeth Haub.

★8384★ International Festival of Films and Television Programs on Environmental
Ekofilm Awards Problems - Ekofilm
c/o Ekofilm Secretariat
Konviktska 5
110 00 Prague 1, Czechoslovakia
Phone: 226 30 32
For recognition of the best films and television programs dealing with the most urgent aspects of environmental conservation. Every year, a different central subject is proclaimed. The Festival intends to present and honor films which promote, by their contents and artistic composition, the dissemination of current information on environmental problems, important from a political, scientific and generally human point of view; point out unconventional approaches to various problems; and stress the ecological aspects of the forming and protection of the environment. The subject of films and television programs entered should pertain to problems of the human environment. The program of the Festival includes both competitive and informative films and television showings. International and national organizations, institutions, enterprises, and individual persons who are sponsors, producers, distributors, owners, or authors of films may enter. The deadline for submissions is March 15. Only films and television programs produced during the preceding two years are accepted. The International Jury awards the Ekofilm Grand Prix and five Main Awards. It may also award a Special Award and Honorable Mentions. It further awards prizes of the Ostrava Lord Mayor and of the Ekofilm Director. Other awards are awarded by the co-organizers. Established in 1974. Sponsored by the State Commission for Scientific and Technical Development and Investments.

★8385★ International Festival of Films on Energy of Lausanne
Festival International du Film sur l'Energie de Lausanne
c/o Georgel Visdei, Director
Escaliers du Marche 19
CH-1003 Lausanne, Switzerland
Phone: 21312 17 35
To offer to film producers throughout the world a forum where all films having an energy theme may be screened and compared in an atmosphere of mutual understanding. In promoting films of high quality in this particular filed, the Festival aims to encourage discussion and to stimulate a closer relationship between the public and energy experts. Films produced in the previous five-year period, whose central theme is primary energies (coal, petrol, natural gas, geothermal energy, wind energy, sea energy, vegetal and organic fuel, etc.), production of electricity, and environment may be submitted. Films produced in 35mm, 16mm or in video, with optical or magnetic sound incorporated and up to a maximum of 60 minutes screening time may participate. Established in 1986. Organized by the Swiss Association of University Post-graduates in Energy (ASPEN) and the Swiss Association for the Scientific Films (ASFS), under the patronage of the General Secretary of the Council of Europe, the Swiss Federal Government, the State of Vaud, the City of Lausanne and the Swiss Federal Institute of Technology, Lausanne (EPFL).

★8386★ International Film Festival - Nature, Man and His Environment
Targhe d'Oro per l'Ecologia
c/o Liborio Rao, Director
Via di Villa Patrizi, 10
I-00161 Rome, Italy
Phone: 688473218
To recognize organizations or individuals responsible for significant contributions to the safeguarding of man's environment. The International Film Festival: Nature, Man and His Environment, gives recognition to the producers, directors and technicians who, with significant results, have created films aimed at establishing an awareness of the most dramatic ecological problems. The Film Festival is open to anyone of any nationality including the film industry, industry in general, television companies, cultural organizations, research institutes, scientific museums, film libraries, film clubs, film enthusiasts, etc. Established in 1971.

★8387★ International Film Festival of Mountains and Exploration Citta di Trento
Trento International Film Festival of Mountain and Exploration Films Awards
c/o Emanuele Cassara, Director
Centro S. Chiara
Via S. Croce, 67
I-38100 Trento, Italy
Phone: 461238 178
Alt. Phone: 461986 120
Fax: 461237 832
To provide recognition for the best 35 and 16mm feature or documentary films or video tapes on mountains or exploration. Films about mountains must contribute to the spreading of knowledge, protection and exploitation of all aspects of the mountains: environmental, social, cultural, alpinistic, excursion and sport. Films on exploration or environmental protection must document little known or completely unknown places, including the universe outside the Earth; or document scientific research on anthropological, ecological, physical, archeological, naturalistic or faunistic subjects. Awarded annually. Established in 1952.

★8388★ International Naturist Federation
INF-Press Prize
St. Hubertusstraat 3
B-2600 Berchem/Antwerp, Belgium
Phone: 3230 05 72
Fax: 3230 05 72
To encourage the publication of articles on naturism in the non-naturist press and media. Articles published in a non-naturist daily paper or magazine are considered. Presented annually. Established in 1973.

★8389★ International Society of Tropical Ecology
Medal for Distinguished Service to Tropical Ecology
Department of Botany
Banaras Hindu University
Varanasi 5, India
To recognize individuals who make special contributions to tropical ecology. Members of the Society are eligible. Established in 1976.

★8390★ International Solar Energy Society
Achievement Through Action Award
c/o National Science Foundation
PO Box 52
191 Royal Parade
Parkville, VIC 3052, Australia
Phone: 3571 7557
Fax: 3563 5173
To recognize a group of persons or a corporate body such as a university department that has made an important contribution to the harnessing of solar energy for practical use. Members and non-members may be nominated by October 31 in even-numbered years. Presented biennially at the International Congress. Established in 1983 in memory of Christopher A. Weeks.

★8391★ International Solar Energy Society
Farrington Daniels Award
c/o National Science Foundation
PO Box 52
191 Royal Parade
Parkville, VIC 3052, Australia
Phone: 3571 7557
Fax: 3563 5173
For recognition of outstanding contributions to science, technology, or engineering of solar energy applications leading toward ameliorating the conditions of humanity, and for furthering this cause through the International Solar Energy Society. Members may be nominated by October 31 in even-numbered years. Presented biennially at the International Congress. Established in 1974 in memory of Professor Emeritus Farrington Daniels of the University of Wisconsin.

★8392★ International Union of Air Pollution Prevention Associations
Christopher E. Barthel, Jr. Award
c/o J. Langston, Director General
136 N. Street
Brighton, E. Sussex BN1 1RG, England
Phone: 27326313
Fax: 273735802
For recognition of outstanding services to the cause of clean air throughout the world over many years. Nomination is by a Member or Contributing Associate without further restriction. Awarded triennially at the World

Clean Air Congress. Established in 1981 in honor of Christopher E. Barthel, Jr.

★8393★ International Union of Forestry Research Organizations
Scientific Achievement Award
c/o H. Schmutzenhofer
Schonbrunn
Tirolergarten
A-1131 Vienna, Austria
Phone: 182 01 51
Fax: 182 93 55
For recognition of distinguished individual scientific achievement within the forestry field. Selection is based on research results published in scientific journals, proceedings of scientific meetings, appropriate patents, or in books, which clearly demonstrate the importance to further advancement of forestry or forestry research, and forest products. No Divisional or Deputy Divison Co-ordinator, or member of the IUFRO Executive Board is eligible while holding such office. Nominations of candidates for the award may be made by a responsible official of the parent organization, by a leader of a Subject or Project Group, or by their deputies. Nominations, accompanied by one other independent testimonial, are sent to the President. Awarded every five years at the Congress. Established in 1971.

★8394★ IPV Publishing and Promotion Company for Tourism
Idegenforgalmi Ujsagirok es Irok Nemzetkozi Szervezetenek Dija
Angol u. 22
H-1149 Budapest, Hungary
Phone: 1633 652
For recognition of films at International Tourism Film Festivals which express best the idea of environmental protection and serve tourism. Awarded at International Tourism Festivals. Established in 1980 by Fijet.

★8395★ Kratky Film - Agrofilm
International Film Festival Agrofilm - Nitra
Postovni prihradka c. 788
112 07 Prague 1, Czechoslovakia
Phone: 222 64 37
Alt. Phone: 226 55 51
For recognition of outstanding agricultural films and videorecordings dealing with forestry and water conservancy, ecology of rural regions, optimization of living and working conditions in the agrosphere. Entries may be submitted by May 15 and are judged by an international jury. Established in 1984.

★8396★ Royal Swedish Academy of Sciences
Carl XVI Gustavs Medalj
PO Box 50005
S-104 05 Stockholm, Sweden
Phone: 815 04 30
To recognize Swedish or foreign citizens for outstanding contributions regarding the environment or written work on that topic.

★8397★ World Conservation Union
Fred M. Packard International Parks Merit Award/Commission on Parks and Protected Areas
Centre Mondial de la Conservation
Avenue du Mont Blanc
CH-1196 Gland, Switzerland
Phone: 2264 91 14
Fax: 2264 29 26
To recognize park wardens, rangers, and managers from anywhere in the world for contributions in the following areas: valor; advocacy for parks and their values; innovative management; communicating park ideals and objectives to the public; conscientious application to park work in the face of difficult and dangerous circumstances; teaching and training park personnel; research; and administrative service. Awards are given in the following two categories: (1) Valor - to recognize personnel who have acted with physical or moral courage beyond the call of duty; (2) Service - to recognize personnel for long and distinguished service; (3) Special Achievement - to recognize personnel for outstanding performance, although their jobs did not call for acts of personal bravery or daring. Nominations are accepted. Established in 1979 and now given in honor of Fred M. Packard, who initiated the award.

★8398★ World Conservation Union
John C. Phillips Memorial Medal
Centre Mondial de la Conservation
Avenue du Mont Blanc
CH-1196 Gland, Switzerland
Phone: 2264 91 14
Fax: 2264 29 26
For recognition of distinguished service in international conservation. Awarded triennially at ordinary sessions of the IUCN General Assembly. Established in 1963 by Friends of John C. Phillips and the American Committee for International Wild Life Protection in memory of John C. Phillips, distinguished United States naturalist, explorer, author and conservationist.

★8399★ WWF World Wide Fund for Nature
Gold Medal
c/o Mary Rose Rudaz, Board & Council Liaison
CH-1196 Gland, Switzerland
Phone: 2264 91 11
Fax: 2264 54 68
This, WWF's highest award, is given for highly meritorious and strictly personal services to the conservation of wildlife and natural resources. The WWF awards cannot be applied for. Nominations are made, screened and judged through an internal consultative process. Established in 1970.

★8400★ WWF World Wide Fund for Nature
International Conservation Roll of Honour
c/o Mary Rose Rudaz, Board & Council Liaison
CH-1196 Gland, Switzerland
Phone: 2264 91 11
Fax: 2264 54 68
A posthumous honor for people having rendered outstanding services to the cause of conservation, not only to WWF. The WWF awards cannot be applied for. Nominations are made, screened and judged through an internal consultative process. Established in 1973.

★8401★ WWF World Wide Fund for Nature
Members of Honour
c/o Mary Rose Rudaz, Board & Council Liaison
CH-1196 Gland, Switzerland
Phone: 2264 91 11
Fax: 2264 54 68
Appointed from amongst persons of great distinction in conservation or fields related to conservation, and from retiring Board Members in recognition of outstanding services to WWF. The WWF awards cannot be applied for. Nominations are made, screened and judged through an internal consultative process. Established in 1969.

United States

★8402★ Adirondack Council
Conservationist of the Year
c/o Donna Beal, Administrator
PO Box D-2
Elizabethtown, NY 12932
Phone: (518)873-2240
To recognize individuals for support and initiatives in working for lasting protection and preservation of the Adirondack Park. Selection is by nomination. Established in 1984.

★8403★ Air and Waste Management Association
Fellow
PO Box 2861
Pittsburgh, PA 15230
Phone: (412)232-3444
To recognize members for outstanding contributions to the Association. Established in 1986.

★8404★ Air and Waste Management Association
Frank A. Chambers Award
PO Box 2861
Pittsburgh, PA 15230
Phone: (412)232-3444
For recognition of an outstanding technical achievement in the science and art of air pollution control. The technical achievement may be in any line of technical endeavor in air pollution from pure research to applied science. Both members and non-members of APCA are eligible. Awarded annually when merited. Established in 1954 in memory of Frank A. Chambers (1885-1951), founder of the Smoke Prevention Association of America, forerunner of APCA.

★8405★ Air and Waste Management Association
George T. Minasian Award
PO Box 2861
Pittsburgh, PA 15230
Phone: (412)232-3444
To recognize the Association's Sections having the most outstanding records of activity and accomplishments during the previous year. Established to honor George T. Minasian, for his many years of distinguished service in the cause of clean air, particularly his local Section activities.

★8406★ Air and Waste Management Association
Honorary Membership
PO Box 2861
Pittsburgh, PA 15230
Phone: (412)232-3444
Honorary Memberships are conferred on persons of widely recognized eminence in some part of the field of air pollution control which the Association aims to cover, or who have rendered especially meritorious service to the Association. This may be conferred on members or non-members of APCA. Awarded when merited.

★8407★ Air and Waste Management Association
Lyman A. Ripperton Award
PO Box 2861
Pittsburgh, PA 15230
Phone: (412)232-3444
For distinguished achievement as an educator in the field of air pollution control. An individual who by precept and example has inspired students to achieve excellence in all their

professional and social endeavors is eligible. The recipients of this award will be known by the accomplishments of their students. Both members and non-members of APCA are eligible. Awarded annually. Established in 1980 in memory of Lyman A. Ripperton (1921-1978), a practitioner in education and research for the control of air pollution.

★8408★ Air and Waste Management Association
Richard Beatty Mellon Award
PO Box 2861
Pittsburgh, PA 15230
Phone: (412)232-3444
To recognize an individual whose contributions of a civic nature, whether administrative, legislative, or judicial have aided substantially in the abatement of air pollution. Eligibility for the award requires the sincere and constant effort of an individual over a period of time to develop or increase interest in or acceptance of the cause of air pollution control for the betterment of man's environment. This individual should have attained wide prominence and be well known for his interest in air pollution control. Both members and non-members of APCA are eligible. Awarded annually. Established in 1954 in memory of Richard Beatty Mellon (1858-1933) who, in the desire to benefit mankind, with his brother, Andrew William Mellon, established the Mellon Institute of Industrial Research in 1913 and led in instituting and sustaining the first modern investigations looking to ways and means for controlling the pollution of the atmosphere.

★8409★ Air and Waste Management Association
S. Smith Griswold Award
PO Box 2861
Pittsburgh, PA 15230
Phone: (412)232-3444
To recognize outstanding accomplishments in the prevention and control of air pollution. The coverage is broad in the sense that it is intended to recognize achievement in many types of activities carried on within the governmental prevention and control programs. The recipient may be a governmental agency staff member, past or present. Both members and non-members of APCA are eligible Awarded annually. Established in 1971 in memory of S. Smith Griswold (1909-1971), a past president of APCA (1962), who focused international attention on air pollution control officers' activities, problems and achievements.

★8410★ Air Force Association
General Edwin W. Rawlings Award for Energy Conservation
c/o James A. McDonnell, Jr.
1501 Lee Hwy.
Arlington, VA 22209-1198
Phone: (703)247-5810
Fax: (703)247-5855
For outstanding achievements in energy conservation within the United States Air Force. Awarded annually. Established in 1981.

★8411★ American Academy of Environmental Engineers
Edward J. Cleary Award
c/o William C. Anderson, Executive Director
130 Holiday Court, Ste. 100
Annapolis, MD 21401
Phone: (301)266-3311
Fax: (301)266-7653
To honor an outstanding performer in the management of environmental protection enterprises conducted either under public (local, state, regional, federal, international) or private auspices. Awarded biennially. Established in 1972.

★8412★ American Academy of Environmental Engineers
Excellence in Environmental Engineering
c/o William C. Anderson, Executive Director
130 Holiday Court, Ste. 100
Annapolis, MD 21401
Phone: (301)266-3311
Fax: (301)266-7653
To recognize excellence in environmental engineering practice. Awards are presented in four categories: Research, Planning, Design and Operations/Management. Open to all projects completed within two years of the date the award is given. Awarded annually in March. Established in 1988.

★8413★ American Academy of Environmental Engineers
Gordon Maskew Fair Memorial Award
c/o William C. Anderson, Executive Director
130 Holiday Court, Ste. 100
Annapolis, MD 21401
Phone: (301)266-3311
Fax: (301)266-7653
To recognize outstanding contributions to the professional development of environmental engineering and leadership in the field of environmental engineering as demonstrated by the following activities: (1) exemplary direction and management of major environmental programs; (2) political leadership; (3) outstanding teaching of environmental engineers; (4) successful research and effective consultation; or (5) outstanding professional association or industrial leadership. Members of the engineering profession are eligible. Awarded annually. Established in 1971.

★8414★ American Academy of Environmental Engineers
Honorary Member
c/o William C. Anderson, Executive Director
130 Holiday Court, Ste. 100
Annapolis, MD 21401
Phone: (301)266-3311
Fax: (301)266-7653
To recognize an individual for outstanding contributions to environmental engineering. Awarded when merited. Established in 1982.

★8415★ American Academy of Environmental Engineers
Stanley E. Kappe Award
c/o William C. Anderson, Executive Director
130 Holiday Court, Ste. 100
Annapolis, MD 21401
Phone: (301)266-3311
Fax: (301)266-7653
To honor a Diplomate of the American Academy of Environmental Engineers who is judged to have performed extraordinary and outstanding service contributory to significant advancement of public awareness to the betterment of the total environment and other objectives of the Academy. Awarded annually when merited. Only one recipient is chosen in any year; and no recipient may receive the Award more than once. Established in 1983 by the professional associates of Stanley E. Kappe in recognition of the dedicated leadership, strong devotion and tireless efforts in advancing the organizational development, growth and enhancement of the Academy which he demonstrated while serving as Executive Director of the Academy during the period 1971 through 1981.

★8416★ American Association of Engineering Societies
Joan Hodges Queneau Award (Palladium Medal)
c/o Laura K. Ksycewski, Manager of Communications
415 2nd St., NE, Ste. 200
Washington, DC 20002
Phone: (202)546-2237
Fax: (202)546-1725
To recognize outstanding achievements in environmental conservation. Nominations may be submitted by September 1. Awarded annually. Cosponsored by the National Audubon Society.

★8417★ American Chemical Society
ACS Award for Creative Advances in Environmental Science and Technology
c/o John M. Malin, Awards Administrator
1155 16th Street, NW
Washington, DC 20036
Phone: (202)872-4408
Fax: (202)872-6206
To encourage creativity in research and technology or methods of analysis to provide a scientific basis for informed environmental control decision making processes, or to provide practical technologies which will reduce health risk factors. The deadline for nominations is February 1. Established in 1978. Sponsored by Air Products and Chemicals, Inc.

★8418★ American Fishing Tackle Manufacturers Association
Andrew J. Boehm Graduate Fellowship in the Fisheries Sciences
1250 Grove Avenue, Ste. 300
Barrington, IL 60010-5090
Phone: (708)381-9490
Fax: (708)381-9518
To encourage graduate studies leading to professional careers in marine conservation and scientific management of recreational fisheries. Graduate students with a commitment to a professional career in fish conservation, having an academic average of B or better, or equivalent point standing, are eligible to be nominated. Supervising professors may submit research proposals by April 1. Awarded to one or more graduate students annually. Established in 1974 to honor Andrew J. Boehm.

★8419★ American Forestry Association
Bernhard Eduard Fernow Award
1516 P St., NW
Washington, DC 20005
Phone: (202)667-3300
To recognize an individual for notable scientific achievements and contributions to forestry. Awarded biennially in odd-numbered years by the American Forestry Association and in even-numbered years by the German Forestry Association. Established in 1965.

★8420★ American Forestry Association
Distinguished Service Award
1516 P St., NW
Washington, DC 20005
Phone: (202)667-3300
To recognize individuals who have rendered distinguished service of national significance to forestry and other aspects of resource conservation. Both members and non-members of the Association who have distinguished themselves in their professional activities as legislators, foresters or other resource professionals are eligible. Awarded annually. Established in 1948.

★8421★ American Forestry Association
John Aston Warder Medal
1516 P St., NW
Washington, DC 20005
Phone: (202)667-3300
To recognize outstanding long-term service to the Association. Awarded annually. Established in 1975 during the Association's Centennial year in honor of John Aston Warder, the Association's first president.

★8422★ American Forestry Association
Urban Forestry Awards
1516 P St., NW
Washington, DC 20005
Phone: (202)667-3300
To recognize outstanding leadership and service resulting in the advancement of urban forestry concepts. Two awards are given each year, one to a citizen activist and one to a professional urban forester. Established in 1982.

★8423★ American Forestry Association
William B. Greeley Award
1516 P St., NW
Washington, DC 20005
Phone: (202)667-3300
To recognize distinguished service to forestry and other aspects of resource conservation of regional significance. Both members and non-members of the Association who have distinguished themselves in their professional activities as legislators, foresters, and other resource professionals are eligible. Awarded annually. Established in 1983.

★8424★ American Institute of Mining, Metallurgical and Petroleum Engineers
Environmental Conservation Distinguished Service Award
345 E 47th St., 14th Fl.
New York, NY 10017
Phone: (212)705-7695
To recognize an individual for significant contributions to environmental conservation by: addition to knowledge; the design or invention of useful equipment or procedure; or outstanding service to governmental or private organizations devoted to any field of environmental conservation. Awarded annually. Established in 1971.

★8425★ American Nuclear Society
Nuclear Reactor Safety Division "Tommy" Thompson Award
555 N. Kensington Ave.
LaGrange Park, IL 60525
Phone: (708)352-6611
Fax: (708)352-0499
To recognize persons who have made outstanding contributions to the field of nuclear reactor safety. The award is made to an individual who has outstandingly provided wisdom and direction to key elements of the world's nuclear safety activities. Nominees need not be ANS members. Awarded annually. Established in 1980.

★8426★ American Paper Institute
Environmental and Energy Achievement Awards Program
c/o Rose Benedetto
260 Madison Ave.
New York, NY 10016
Phone: (212)340-0600
Fax: (212)689-2628
To recognize paper industry and forest products companies that have made significant achievements toward improving the environment, encouraging environmental and energy excellence and innovation, and stimulating more efficient management. Any company engaged in timber growing and harvest, or in the manufacture of pulp, paper and paperboard or solid wood products may enter. Entries are limited to U.S. based facilities, but may involve a non-U.S. company provided the facility is located in this country. The deadline for entries is March 27. Awards are given in six major environmental and energy areas: (1) Air Pollution Control; (2) Water Pollution Control; (3) Solid Waste Management; (4) Forest Management; (5) Energy Management; and (6) Energy Innovation. Awarded annually. Established in 1973. Co-sponsored by the National Forest Products Association.

★8427★ American Society of Agronomy
Environmental Quality Research Award
677 S Segoe Rd.
Madison, WI 53711
Phone: (608)273-8080
Fax: (608)273-2021
To recognize contributions which have enhanced the basic understanding of the behavior and fate of pollutants in terrestrial and/or aquatic ecosystems and stability of an ecosystem in response to disturbances resulting from the use of land for food and energy production and society's needs to dispose of and/or utilize waste products. Principal criteria to be used in the selection process are creativity and originality of the research and significance of the research and its contribution to the field of environmental quality.

★8428★ American Society of Civil Engineers
Karl Emil Hilgard Hydraulic Prize
c/o Grazia Tramontana, Manager, Awards
345 E 47th St.
New York, NY 10017
Phone: (212)705-7208
Fax: (212)980-4681
To recognize the author(s) of a paper which contributes to the field of water resources development. Members holding any grade are eligible. Awarded annually. Established in 1939.

★8429★ American Society of Heating, Refrigerating and Air-Conditioning Engineers
Joseph F. Cuba Award for Energy Research Engineers
c/o Terri Sheppard, Honors & Awards Staff Liaison
1791 Tullie Circle, N.E.
Atlanta, GA 30329
Phone: (404)636-8400
Fax: (404)321-5478
To honor significant accomplishment by a graduate student in energy conservation or renewable energy research. Established in 1985 by the ASHRAE Research and Technical Committee.

★8430★ American Solar Energy Society
Charles Greeley Abbot Award
2400 Central Ave., B-1
Boulder, CO 80301
Phone: (303)443-3130
To recognize an individual who has provided exceptionally valuable service to the Society or has made exceptionally significant contributions to the solar energy field. To be considered, an individual need not be a member of the Society. Awarded annually. Established in honor of Charles Greeley Abbot, a prominent researcher in solar energy who developed a number of instruments for measuring insolation, and who was the founder of the Smithsonian Radiation Biology Lab.

★8431★ American Tunaboat Association
Lou Briot Golden Porpoise Award
c/o August Felando, President
One Tuna Ln.
San Diego, CA 92101
Phone: (619)233-6405
To recognize captains in the U.S. tuna fleet for successful porpoise release records.

★8432★ American Water Resources Association
AWRA Board of Directors Service Awards
5410 Grosvenor Ln., Ste. 220
Bethesda, MD 20814-2192
Phone: (301)493-8600
To recognize individuals for outstanding service to the Association.

★8433★ American Water Resources Association
AWRA Outstanding State Section Award
5410 Grosvenor Ln., Ste. 220
Bethesda, MD 20814-2192
Phone: (301)493-8600
To recognize a Section's activities in advancing water resources knowledge in the Section; number, type, and scope of Section activity; special activities of unusual note; and number of National Members in the Section. Awarded annually. Established in 1975. In addition, the AWRA Outstanding Student Chapter Award is presented.

★8434★ American Water Resources Association
Fellow Member
5410 Grosvenor Ln., Ste. 220
Bethesda, MD 20814-2192
Phone: (301)493-8600
To recognize an individual for an eminent record in water resources science or technology and for outstanding service to the Association. Members of the Association for at least 10 consecutive years who have served as an officer, a director, or on a committee for one year, and have an eminent record in a branch of water resources science or technology are eligible. Nominations may be submitted by June 1. Awarded annually. Established in 1974.

★8435★ American Water Resources Association
Henry P. Caulfield, Jr. Medal for Exemplary Contributions to National Water Policy
5410 Grosvenor Ln., Ste. 220
Bethesda, MD 20814-2192
Phone: (301)493-8600
To recognize an individual for achievements and contributions in setting, designing, and implementing water resources practices at the national level. Awarded annually. Established in 1988.

★8436★ American Water Resources Association
Honorary Member
5410 Grosvenor Ln., Ste. 220
Bethesda, MD 20814-2192
Phone: (301)493-8600
For recognition of eminence in a branch of water resources science and technology. Nominations may be submitted by June 1. Awarded annually. Established in 1970.

★8437★ American Water Resources Association
Icko Iben Award
5410 Grosvenor Ln., Ste. 220
Bethesda, MD 20814-2192
Phone: (301)493-8600
To recognize individuals who have made outstanding contributions to the promotion of communication among the various disciplines concerned with water resources problems. Nominations may be submitted by June 1. Awarded annually. Established in 1971 in memory of Dr. Icko Iben, a co-founder of the Association, who contributed extensively during his lifetime to the understanding and communication between those involved in the diverse disciplines related to water resources.

★8438★ American Water Resources Association
President's Award for Outstanding Service
5410 Grosvenor Ln., Ste. 220
Bethesda, MD 20814-2192
Phone: (301)493-8600
To recognize those who have made significant contributions to AWRA. Nominations maybe submitted by June 1. Awarded when merited. Established in 1979.

★8439★ American Water Resources Association
William C. Ackermann Medal for Excellence in Water Management
5410 Grosvenor Ln., Ste. 220
Bethesda, MD 20814-2192
Phone: (301)493-8600
To recognize an individual who has achieved eminence in exemplary water management practices at the state, regional, or local levels. Awarded annually. Established in 1988 to honor William C. Ackermann, an individual who achieved eminence and compiled a distinguished record in the design and implementation of exemplary water management practices at the state, regional, and local government levels.

★8440★ American Water Resources Association
William R. Boggess Award
5410 Grosvenor Ln., Ste. 220
Bethesda, MD 20814-2192
Phone: (301)493-8600
For recognition of the author(s) of the best paper published in Water Resources Bulletin during the preceding year that best describes, delineates, or analyzes a major problem or aspect of water resources from either a theoretical, applied, or philosophical standpoint. Awarded annually. Established in 1973 to honor William R. "Randy" Boggess, a charter member of the Association, one of the first Directors and a former president of the Association, and editor of the Water Resources Bulletin.

★8441★ Association for Conservation Information
Awards Program
c/o Kay Ellerhoff, President
Montana Department of Fish, Wildlife & Parks
930 Custer Ave., W
Helena, MT 59620
Phone: (406)444-2474
To give appropriate recognition to the efforts of member agencies in conservation education, information, and public relations programs, as well as to honor individuals and organizations who have distinguished themselves in this field. Awards are given in the following categories: (1) magazines; (2) magazine articles; (3) black and white/2-color periodical; (4) special publications; (5) internal communications; (6) print news; (7) audio/visual news; (8) radio programs; (9) radio public service announcements; (10) television programs; (11) television public service announcements; (12) color photography; (13) black and white photography; (14) documentary; (15) multimedia presentations; (16) education; and (17) special efforts. Awarded in each category for first, second and third place winners annually.

★8442★ Association of Conservation Engineers
Eugene Baker Memorial Award
c/o William P. Allinder, Secretary-Treasurer
Alabama Department of Conservation
64 N Union St.
Montgomery, AL 36130
Phone: (205)242-3476
To recognize an engineer for outstanding contributions to conservation engineering. Established in 1964.

★8443★ Association of Conservation Engineers
President's Award
c/o William P. Allinder, Secretary-Treasurer
Alabama Department of Conservation
64 N Union St.
Montgomery, AL 36130
Phone: (205)242-3476
To recognize a member for significant and outstanding contributions in the development, operation or promotion of the Association. Established in 1978.

★8444★ Association of Consulting Foresters
ACF Public Service Award
c/o Arthur F. Ennis, Executive Director
5410 Grosvenor Ln., Ste. 205
Bethesda, MD 20814
Phone: (301)530-6795
To recognize achievement in and contributions to the general area of forestry, with emphasis on the practice of consulting forestry. Members may submit nominations. Awarded annually. Established in 1977.

★8445★ Audubon Naturalist Society of the Central Atlantic States, Inc.
Paul Bartsch Award
8940 Jones Mill Rd.
Chevy Chase, MD 20815
Phone: (301)652-9188
To recognize individuals for outstanding contributions to the field of natural history and conservation. Preference is given to nominees who have had some connection with the Society. The deadline for nominations is October 31. Established in 1962 in honor of Paul Bartsch, an outstanding naturalist who was active in the Society during the first half of this century and worked at the Smithsonian in the field of malacology (study of mollusks).

★8446★ Audubon Society of New Hampshire
Tudor Richards Award
PO Box 528-B
Concord, NH 03302-0516
Phone: (603)224-9909
To recognize the individual who best exemplifies Tudor Richard's love and knowledge of the outdoors, and who has worked tirelessly and effectively on behalf of conservation in New Hampshire. Individuals may be nominated by the Board of Trustees of the Society. Awarded annually. Established in 1982 to honor Tudor Richards, former president and executive director of ASNH, a naturalist, forester, and ornithologist.

★8447★ Big Thicket Conservation Association
Conservationist of the Year
PO Box 12032
Beaumont, TX 77706
Phone: (409)892-8976
To recognize individuals who have made outstanding contributions in conservation and in preserving the big thicket of Southeast Texas. Selection is by nomination; applications are not solicited. Established in 1984.

★8448★ Bonneville Power Administration
Appliance Efficiency Award Program
PO Box 3621
Portland, OR 97208-3621
Phone: (503)230-7520
Contact: John Elizalde, Contact
Encourages the purchase of energy-efficient appliances by promoting the top 15 percent energy-efficient appliances. Recognizes wholesalers and retailers who sell these products. Publishes a brochure which lists appliances and retailers.

★8449★ Botanical Society of America
Ecological Section Award
c/o Prof. Gregory Anderson
Ecology & Evolutionary Biology
University of Connecticut
75 N Eagleville Rd.
Storrs, CT 06268
Phone: (203)486-4322
To recognize the best student paper in ecology at the annual meeting. Awarded annually.

★8450★ Chesapeake Bay Foundation
Conservationist of the Year
c/o Jane Shorall
162 Prince George St.
Annapolis, MD 21401
Phone: (301)268-8816
Alt. Phone: (301)261-2350
To recognize individuals or corporations for commitment to conservation of the Chesapeake Bay. Awarded annually. Established in 1982.

★8451★ Chevron USA
Chevron Conservation Awards
c/o W. C. Roper, Corporate Program Director
PO Box 7753
San Francisco, CA 94120-7753
Phone: (415)894-2457
Alt. Phone: (412)456-3851
This, the oldest privately-sponsored program of its kind in the United States, honors individuals and organizations for outstanding contributions to the conservation of natural resources. The program seeks to encourage those who have had little or no national recognition as well as honor veterans with long records of noteworthy achievement. Anyone in the United States or Canada may nominate an individual or organization based on significant results of a conservation project which protects or enhances an area's natural resources. Nominations are accepted August 1 through December 1. Awards are presented annually in three categories: ten awards go to citizen volunteers; ten to professional conservationists; and up to five awards are given to nonprofit conservation organizations or public agencies. Established in 1954 by Ed Zern, a prominent outdoor writer, conservationist and columnist for "Field and Stream" who still serves as program director.

★8452★ Chicago Community Trust
Morton B. Ryerson Fellowship
c/o Handy Lindsey, Senior Staff Associate
221 N. LaSalle St.
Chicago, IL 60604
Phone: (312)372-3356
To support independent field research on any topic relating to ecology and/or conservation in northern Illinois forests. Open to any student, with preference to graduate students.

★8453★ Citizens Energy Council
Annual Honor Roll
77 Homewood Ave.
Allendale, NJ 07401
Phone: (201)327-3914
To recognize citizens who have performed valuable service in educating the public on the hazards of nuclear power and nuclear weapons. Awarded annually. Established in 1980.

★8454★ Citizens Energy Council
Man/Woman of the Year
77 Homewood Ave.
Allendale, NJ 07401
Phone: (201)327-3914
To recognize service in promoting knowledge of the hazards of nuclear power and nuclear weapons. Awarded annually. Established in 1970.

★8455★ Commission on Environmental Quality
Education and Communications
To recognize the best efforts to develop a conservation and environmental ethic. Corporations, schools, associations, and individuals ranging from environmentalists to university professors are eligible. Up to three awards are presented annually.

★8456★ Commission on Environmental Quality
Innovation Award
Recognizes technologies, processes, and programs that uniquely create what the commission calls "environmental entrepreneurship." Corporations, schools, associations, and individuals ranging from environmentalists to university professors are eligible. Up to three awards are presented annually.

★8457★ Commission on Environmental Quality
Partnership Award
Recognizing efforts to form coalitions working toward quality environmental enhancements. Corporations, schools, associations and individuals ranging from environmentalists to university professionals are eligible. Up to three awards are presented annually.

★8458★ Commission on Environmental Quality
Quality Environmental Management
To recognize the weaving of environmental considerations into management practices. Corporations, schools, associations, and individuals ranging from environmentalists to university professors are eligible. Up to three awards are presented annually.

★8459★ Conference of Federal Environmental Engineers
Federal Environmental Engineer of the Year
c/o Timothy Harms, Secretary
17 Nicholson Ct.
Sterling, VA 22170
Phone: (703)586-6073
To recognize exemplary work and accomplishments by environmental engineers in the Federal service. Awarded annually. Established in 1974.

★8460★ Connecticut River Watershed Council
Certificate of Conservation Awards
125 Combs Rd.
Easthampton, MA 01027
Phone: (413)584-0057
To recognize distinguished conservation service in the Connecticut River Valley. Individuals, organizations (both public and private), corporations, and the media are eligible. Awarded annually in May. Established in 1952.

★8461★ Connecticut River Watershed Council
Connecticut River Watershed Council Conservation Award
125 Combs Rd.
Easthampton, MA 01027
Phone: (413)584-0057
To recognize outstanding and dedicated conservation service for the benefit of the Connecticut River Valley. Awarded periodically but not annually. Established in 1955.

★8462★ Conservation Essay and Poster Contest
Dept. of Natural Resources
691 Teton Trail
Frankfort, KY 40601
Phone: (502)564-3080
Contact: Stanley Head, Contact
Essay contest for grades 7-12, poster contest K-6. Subjects rotate each year: soil, forest, fish, and wildlife conservation, water issues. Sponsored by newspaper. Savings bonds to winners.

★8463★ Eagle Foundation
Bald Eagle Person of the Year
300 E. Hickory St.
Apple River, IL 61001
Phone: (815)594-2259
To recognize a person whose efforts on behalf of the bald eagle have not been appreciated or received the due respect they deserve. An individual must have devoted a good part of his/her life to efforts on behalf of the bald eagle. Awarded annually during Bald Eagle Days. Established in 1970 by Southwest Wisconsin Audubon Club.

★8464★ Eagle Foundation
Bald Eagle Research Award
300 E. Hickory St.
Apple River, IL 61001
Phone: (815)594-2259
To recognize and support some worthy research project across the continent, which will help gain knowledge needed to preserve the bald eagle in the wild. Presented annually at International Bald Eagle Days. Established in 1981.

★8465★ Ecological Society of America
Corporate Award
Center for Environmental Studies
Arizona State University
Tempe, AZ 85287
Phone: (602)965-3000
To recognize a corporation, business, division, program, or an individual of a company for its accomplishments in incorporating sound ecological concepts, knowledge, and practices into its planning and operating procedures. Established in 1988.

★8466★ Ecological Society of America
Distinguished Service Citation
Center for Environmental Studies
Arizona State University
Tempe, AZ 85287
Phone: (602)965-3000
For recognition of continued service to the Society and to ecology. Nominations of senior members may be made. Awarded irregularly at the Convention. Established in 1975.

★8467★ Ecological Society of America
E. Lucy Braun Award
Center for Environmental Studies
Arizona State University
Tempe, AZ 85287
Phone: (602)965-3000
To recognize the outstanding student poster presentation presented as a part of the annual program sponsored by the Ecological Society of America.

★8468★ Ecological Society of America
Eminent Ecologist
Center for Environmental Studies
Arizona State University
Tempe, AZ 85287
Phone: (602)965-3000
To recognize an ecologist who has made an outstanding contribution to the science of ecology. Awarded annually. Established in 1973.

★8469★ Ecological Society of America
George Mercer Award
Center for Environmental Studies
Arizona State University
Tempe, AZ 85287
Phone: (602)965-3000
For recognition of an outstanding paper published in English by a researcher under the age of 40 in the field of ecology. Awarded annually. Established in 1948.

★8470★ Ecological Society of America
Honorary Member
Center for Environmental Studies
Arizona State University
Tempe, AZ 85287
Phone: (602)965-3000
To recognize any ecologist who has made exceptional scientific contributions and whose principal residence and site of ecological research are outside the United States and Canada. Up to three awards may be made in any one year until a total of 20 is reached.

★8471★ Ecological Society of America
Murray F. Buell Award
Center for Environmental Studies
Arizona State University
Tempe, AZ 85287
Phone: (602)965-3000
To recognize and reward an outstanding student paper presented at the annual meeting. Established in 1973.

★8472★ Ecological Society of America
Robert H. MacArthur Award
Center for Environmental Studies
Arizona State University
Tempe, AZ 85287
Phone: (602)965-3000
To recognize an active, well-established ecologist. Nominations of mid-career ecologists are accepted. Awarded biennially at the Convention. Established in 1983 in honor of Robert MacArthur, distinguished theoretical ecologist at Princeton University.

★8473★ Ecological Society of America
W.S. Cooper Award
Center for Environmental Studies
Arizona State University
Tempe, AZ 85287
Phone: (602)965-3000
To honor one of the Society's outstanding contributors to the fields of geobotany and physiographic ecology. The award recognizes a recent, outstanding contribution in one of the fields in which Cooper worked.

★8474★ Epsilon Nu Eta Honor Society
Distinguished Service Award
c/o Phillip Scheuerman
Department of Environmental Health
East Tennessee State University
Box 22960 A
Johnson City, TN 37614
Phone: (615)929-5250
For recognition of outstanding service to Epsilon Nu Eta, an honorary society in environmental health. Members may be nominated by a chapter and elected by a majority vote of national representatives. Presented annually. Established in 1977.

★8475★ Epsilon Nu Eta Honor Society
Honorary Member
c/o Phillip Scheuerman
Department of Environmental Health
East Tennessee State University
Box 22960 A
Johnson City, TN 37614
Phone: (615)929-5250
For recognition of achievement in environmental health practice or science, and contribution to environmental health education. Non-members may be nominated by a chapter and elected by a majority vote of national representatives. Presented annually at the Convention. Established in 1977.

★8476★ Federal Aviation Administration
Aviation Environment Award
c/o Mary Jo Byberg
Office of Public Affairs
800 Independence Avenue, S.W.
Washington, DC 20591
Phone: (202)267-3465
To recognize efforts by airport operators, airport users, local units of government, citizens, manufacturers, planners, architects, designers, or others for outstanding design, notable restorations, preservations or efforts to enhance the environment affected by, or related to, aviation. Persons or organizations are eligible who have developed or implemented a program for enhancing environmental quality in the following areas: (1) aircraft noise reduction, control or abatement activities; (2) airport land use compatibility plans or controls; (3) protection of environmentally critical resources, e.g., public parks, recreation areas, wildlife refuges, wetlands, historic and archaeological sites; (4) promotion of public participation in efforts to enhance environmental quality; (5) aircraft or airport emissions reduction, control or abatement activities; and (6) architecture, landscape architecture, the use of graphic arts and other design considerations to improve the airport and its environs.

★8477★ Federation of Fly Fishers
Federation of Fly Fishers Conservation Award
PO Box 1088
West Yellowstone, MT 59758
Phone: (406)646-9541
Fax: (406)646-9728
To recognize the individual, group or organization which has made an extraordinary contribution to the conservation of our fisheries resources.

★8478★ Florida Audubon Society
Allan D. Cruickshank Memorial Award
1101 Audubon Way
Maitland, FL 32751
Phone: (407)647-2615
To recognize an individual whose interest in conservation and wildlife most nearly exemplifies the concerns and ideals of Allan Cruickshank. Awarded annually. Established in 1975.

★8479★ Florida Audubon Society
Certificate of Recognition
1101 Audubon Way
Maitland, FL 32751
Phone: (407)647-2615
To recognize an individual who has given outstanding service to the cause of conservation in Florida. Local chapter members working on particular issues are considered. Awarded annually when merited. Established in 1980.

★8480★ Florida Audubon Society
Chapter of the Year
1101 Audubon Way
Maitland, FL 32751
Phone: (407)647-2615
To recognize an Audubon Chapter for valuable service. Awarded annually. Established in 1983.

★8481★ Florida Audubon Society
Conservationist of the Year
1101 Audubon Way
Maitland, FL 32751
Phone: (407)647-2615
To recognize a private individual and a government official - local, state, or federal - for dedication to environmental issues. Awards are presented in each category annually. Established in 1973.

★8482★ Florida Audubon Society
Corporate Award
1101 Audubon Way
Maitland, FL 32751
Phone: (407)647-2615
To recognize industry for significant contributions to environmental issues. Awarded when merited. Established in 1985.

★8483★ Florida Audubon Society
Florida Audubon Society's Latin American Award for Conservation
1101 Audubon Way
Maitland, FL 32751
Phone: (407)647-2615
To honor Latin Americans contributing significantly to conservation in their countries. Presented annually.

★8484★ Florida Audubon Society
John Brooks' Memorial Award
1101 Audubon Way
Maitland, FL 32751
Phone: (407)647-2615
To recognize an official of local government whose achievements in protecting Florida's sensitive environmental habitats exemplifies the example set by John Brooks during his lifetime. Awarded annually. Established in 1988.

★8485★ Florida Audubon Society
Legislative Excellence Award
1101 Audubon Way
Maitland, FL 32751
Phone: (407)647-2615
To recognize legislators for outstanding service to the cause of conservation in Florida. Awarded annually when merited. Established in 1980.

★8486★ Florida Audubon Society
Outstanding Journalist Award
1101 Audubon Way
Maitland, FL 32751
Phone: (407)647-2615
To recognize a journalist for service to the cause of conservation. Awarded annually when merited. Established in 1984.

★8487★ Florida Audubon Society
Polly Redford Memorial Award
1101 Audubon Way
Maitland, FL 32751
Phone: (407)647-2615
To recognize an individual who shows dedication in the cause of conservation. Awarded annually. Established in 1973 to honor Polly Redford, a dedicated and effective fighter against those who would despoil Florida. She was responsible in large measure for the establishment of the Biscayne National Monument.

★8488★ Florida Audubon Society
Special Commendation Award
1101 Audubon Way
Maitland, FL 32751
Phone: (407)647-2615
To recognize individuals and organizations for service to the cause of conservation. Awarded annually when merited. Established in 1980.

★8489★ Forest History Society
Alfred D. Bell, Jr. Visiting Scholars Program
c/o Cheryl Oakes, librarian
701 Vickers Ave.
Durham, NC 27701
Phone: (919)682-9319
To enable an individual to make use of the Society's library and archives. A travel grant is awarded annually. Established in 1990.

★8490★ Forest History Society
Collier Award
c/o Cheryl Oakes, librarian
701 Vickers Ave.
Durham, NC 27701
Phone: (919)682-9319
To recognize the best article on forest history and conservation history published in a newspaper or general circulation magazine. Awarded annually. Established in 1986.

★8491★ German Marshall Fund of the United States
German Marshall Fund of the United States Fellowships and Awards
11 Dupont Circle, N.W.
Washington, DC 20036
Phone: (202)745-3950
Awards environmental fellowships to enable professional American and European environmentalists to spend up to two months on the other side of the Atlantic gaining firsthand knowledge of selected environmental policies and institutions. The American fellows pursue their inquiries under the guidance of the Institute for European Environmental Policy, based in Bonn, London, and Paris.

★8492★ Global Tomorrow Coalition
Lorax Award
1325 G Street, N.W., Ste. 915
Washington, DC 20005-3104
Phone: (202)628-4016
To recognize outstanding leadership in calling public attention to and action in behalf of global population, resources, and environment. Awarded one or more times each year. Established in 1984.

★8493★ Golden Gate Audubon Society
Elsie Roemer Conservation Awards
1250 Addison Street, Ste. 1078
Berkeley, CA 94702-1751
To recognize one member of GGAS and one member of the public for outstanding contributions in the preservation of the environment. Awarded annually.

★8494★ Golden Gate Audubon Society
GGAS Service Awards
1250 Addison Street, Ste. 1078
Berkeley, CA 94702-1751
To recognize individuals for significant contribution to GGAS, and to its board of directors.

★8495★ Great Lakes Commission
Special Recognition Award
c/o Dr. Michael J. Donahue
The Argus II Bldg.
400 S 4th St.
Ann Arbor, MI 48103-4816
Phone: (313)665-9135
Fax: (313)665-4370
To recognize outstanding service in advancing regional environmental quality and economic development. Current and former commissioners and advisors are eligible. A plaque is awarded when merited. Established in 1972, discontinued about 1975, and reinstated in 1987.

★8496★ Gulf Oil Corporation
Gulf Oil Corporation Conservation Awards
PO Box 7141
San Francisco, CA 94120-7141
To honor ten professional and twenty citizen conservationists for dedicated service in the field of renewable natural resources. The awards program also recognizes non-profit organizations for their work on behalf of the environment. Consideration is given to professional conservationists employed by non-profit organizations and citizens whose conservation efforts are a voluntary expression of good citizenship. National and/or local non-profit organizations conducting significant conservation programs are also considered. Bestowed annually in May. Established in 1953 by the American Motors Corporation.

★8497★ Industrial Development Research Council
Awards for Distinguished Service in Environmental Planning
c/o Prentice L. Knight, III, Deputy Director
40 Technology Park/Atlanta
Norcross, GA 30092
Phone: (404)446-6996
Fax: (404)263-8825
To recognize business leaders who have demonstrated, in exemplary economic development projects, their commitment to environmental quality. Presented annually at IDRC Fall Professional Seminar. Established in 1972 by IDRC and Conway Data, Inc., Atlanta, GA.

★8498★ Institute of Environmental Sciences
Climatics Award
c/o Janet A. Ehmann, Exec. Dir.
940 E Northwest Hwy.
Mount Prospect, IL 60056
Phone: (708)255-1561
Fax: (708)255-1699
For recognition in the field of environmental sciences. Established in 1986.

★8499★ Institute of Environmental Sciences
Fellow
c/o Janet A. Ehmann, Exec. Dir.
940 E Northwest Hwy.
Mount Prospect, IL 60056
Phone: (708)255-1561
Fax: (708)255-1699
To recognize individuals for outstanding contributions to the environmental sciences, the industry or the Institute. Members of the Institute are considered for the award which consists of election to the membership grade of Fellow of the Institute. Awarded annually at the Annual Technical Meeting Awards Banquet.

★8500★ Institute of Environmental Sciences
Honorary Fellow
c/o Janet A. Ehmann, Exec. Dir.
940 E Northwest Hwy.
Mount Prospect, IL 60056
Phone: (708)255-1561
Fax: (708)255-1699
To recognize individuals for outstanding contributions to the advancement of environmental sciences through their efforts in their professional field of endeavor. Non-members are eligible. The award consists of election to the membership classification of Honorary Fellow of the Institute. Awarded when merited at the Annual Technical Meeting Awards Banquet.

★8501★ Institute of Environmental Sciences
James R. Mildon Award
c/o Janet A. Ehmann, Executive Director
940 E. Northwest Hwy.
Mount Prospect, IL 60056
Phone: (708)255-1561
Fax: (708)255-1699
Awarded annually to recognize individuals for contributions in the field of contamination control and/or to the awareness and effectiveness of contamination control activity in professional societies. Established in 1982 in honor of James R. Mildon, one of the original organizers of the American Association for Contamination Control which was absorbed by IES in 1973.

★8502★ Institute of Environmental Sciences
Willis J. Whitfield Award
c/o Janet A. Ehmann, Executive Director
940 E. Northwest Hwy.
Mount Prospect, IL 60056
Phone: (708)255-1561
Fax: (708)255-1699
To recognize an individual(s) for the best presentation, either oral or printed, in the field of contamination control. Awarded at the Annual Awards Banquet. Established in 1980.

★8503★ International Association for Great Lakes Research
Chandler - Misener Award
c/o Dr. Klaus L. Kaiser, President
Institute of Science & Technology
2200 Bonisteel Blvd.
University of Michigan
Ann Arbor, MI 48109
Phone: (313)763-1520
To acknowledge excellence in the fields of natural or social science or environmental engineering directly related to a Great Lake or other large lakes of the world based on an article published in the Journal of Great Lakes Research. A certificate is awarded annually. Established in 1970.

★8504★ International Association of Educators for World Peace
IAEWP Diploma of Honour
c/o Dr. Charles Mercieca, Executive Vice-President
PO Box 3282, Mastin Lake Sta.
Huntsville, AL 35810-0282
Phone: (205)534-5501
Alt. Phone: (205)851-5520
Fax: (205)851-9157
To recognize outstanding work in promoting international understanding, protecting the environment, and implementing a universal declaration of human rights. Individuals who have promoted international understanding and world peace are considered for the award. Sponsored by the United Nations (ECOSOC) and UNESCO.

★8505★ International Association of Fish and Wildlife Agencies
Boone and Crockett Award
444 N. Capitol Street, N.W., Ste. 534
Washington, DC 20001
Phone: (202)624-7890
Fax: (202)624-7891
To recognize outstanding achievement in promoting and encouraging programs in outdoor ethics. Two awards are presented: one to an agency; and one to the individual who has been the prime mover of outdoor ethics in the recipient agency. Established in 1987. Sponsored by the Boone and Crockett Club.

★8506★ International Association of Fish and Wildlife Agencies
Ernest Thompson Seton Award
444 N. Capitol Street, N.W., Ste. 534
Washington, DC 20001
Phone: (202)624-7890
Fax: (202)624-7891
To recognize the state, provincial, or federal agency that has most effectively promoted a public awareness of the need for support of wildlife management policies and practices, and the individual most responsible for having done the work in the federal agency. Presented annually. Established in 1977.

★8507★ International Association of Fish and Wildlife Agencies
Outstanding Law Enforcement Achievement Award
444 N. Capitol Street, N.W., Ste. 534
Washington, DC 20001
Phone: (202)624-7890
Fax: (202)624-7891
To recognize outstanding law enforcement efforts in support of wildlife. Individuals and agencies are eligible. Awarded annually. Established in 1982.

★8508★ International Association of Fish and Wildlife Agencies
Seth Gordon Award
444 N. Capitol Street, N.W., Ste. 534
Washington, DC 20001
Phone: (202)624-7890
Fax: (202)624-7891
To recognize outstanding contributions of professional wildlife agency administrators. Members of the Association who have demonstrated unusual administrative ability are eligible. Awarded when merited. Established in 1970.

★8509★ International Council for Bird Preservation - United States Section
Delacour Medal
c/o Warren B. King
Rte. 2, Box 704
Rumney, NH 03266
To recognize an individual for outstanding contributions to conservation, ornithology or aviculture. Recipients of the Award are determined by delegates to the U.S. Section of ICBP. Awarded on an occasional basis. Established to honor the work and memory of Jean Delacour.

★8510★ International Desalination Association
Dr. Robert O. Vernon Memorial Lecture Award
c/o Patricia A. Burke, Secretary General
10 S. Main St.
PO Box 387
Topsfield, MA 01983
Phone: (508)356-2727
To recognize a member of a water supply agency for a significant contribution to water supply improvement. Established in 1964.

★8511★ International Desalination Association
Water Quality Improvement Man of the Year Award
c/o Patricia A. Burke, Secretary General
10 S. Main St.
PO Box 387
Topsfield, MA 01983
Phone: (508)356-2727
To honor an individual for outstanding contribution to the improvement of water supplies through desalting, wastewater reclamation or other water sciences. Presented during the Association's annual conference, usually in July. Established in 1974.

★8512★ International Studies Association
Harold and Margaret Sprout Award
c/o William A. Welsh, Executive Director
James F. Byrnes International Center
University of S. Carolina
Columbia, SC 29208
Phone: (803)777-2933
For recognition of a book or piece of research which the award committee judges to be the best research work published in English in the last two years on international environmental affairs. The responsibility for selection lies with the Environmental Studies Section of the International Studies Association. Presented annually.

★8513★ International Wildlife Film Festival
International Wildlife Film Festival
University of Montana
Rankin Hall
Missoula, MT 59812
Phone: (406)243-2477
To encourage and recognize excellence in wildlife film making, based on the film's biological accuracy, artistic vision, and technical merit. To be eligible for consideration, film/video productions must have a predominately wildlife theme, and must have been produced or released in the year preceding the current IWFF. Awarded annually. Established in 1978.

★8514★ Irrigation Association
National Water and Energy Conservation Award
c/o Bob Sears
1911 North Fl. Myer Drive, Ste. 1009
Arlington, VA 22209-1630
Phone: (703)524-1200
Fax: (703)524-9544
To recognize significant achievement in the conservation of water and energy as they relate to irrigation procedures, equipment, methods and techniques. To bring national recognition to individuals, firms or agencies working to conserve our natural resources, and to challenge those responsible for irrigation usage in agriculture or in the landscape to reach for and achieve a higher level of excellence. Any individual, firm, government agency (local, state or federal), civic organization, or university or college division or department which has been active in the promotion of water or energy conservation may qualify for the award. The entry deadline is September 1. Awarded annually in January. Established in 1981.

★8515★ Izaak Walton League of America
"54" Founders Award
1401 Wilson Blvd., Level B
Arlington, VA 22209
Phone: (703)528-1818
This, the League's highest award, is given to recognize a person, group, or institution for an outstanding contribution to the conservation of America's renewable natural resources. Awarded annually as merited. Established in 1949.

★8516★ Izaak Walton League of America
Arthur R. Thompson Memorial Award
1401 Wilson Blvd., Level B
Arlington, VA 22209
Phone: (703)528-1818
For recognition of the most outstanding conservation activity by a division of the League. Awarded annually. Established by the Roanoke, Virginia chapter.

★8517★ Izaak Walton League of America
IWLA Conservation Award
1401 Wilson Blvd., Level B
Arlington, VA 22209
Phone: (703)528-1818
To recognize a member for outstanding contributions to the conservation work in the League's name. Awarded annually.

★8518★ Izaak Walton League of America
IWLA Honor Roll Award
1401 Wilson Blvd., Level B
Arlington, VA 22209
Phone: (703)528-1818
To recognize an individual or organization for outstanding contributions to broaden public understanding and appreciation of the natural world. Awarded annually. Established in 1948.

★8519★ Izaak Walton League of America
James Lawton Childs Award
1401 Wilson Blvd., Level B
Arlington, VA 22209
Phone: (703)528-1818
For recognition of the most outstanding conservation program staged by a chapter of the League. Awarded annually.

★8520★ Izaak Walton League of America
Save Our Streams Award
1401 Wilson Blvd., Level B
Arlington, VA 22209
Phone: (703)528-1818
To recognize the SOS program that best demonstrates the principles of environmental education and citizen action in the pursuit of clean water.

★8521★ John Burroughs Association
John Burroughs List of Nature Books for Young Readers
15 W. 77th St.
New York, NY 10024
Phone: (212)769-5169
To instill in young people a knowledge, love, and respect for nature and the environment and to recognize outstanding nature books. The judges consider each entry on the basis of four criteria: originality, subject matter, scientific accuracy, and readability for children in the elementary grades. Books published during the preceding year on nature including natural history, ecology, and environmental studies may be submitted by December 15. Awarded annually. Circulated as widely as possible. Established in 1988 in honor of the effort of John Burroughs to address himself to youth.

★8522★ John Burroughs Association
John Burroughs Medal
15 W. 77th St.
New York, NY 10024
Phone: (212)769-5169
To recognize the author of a distinguished book of contemporary nature writing. Although the award is customarily given to a book published during the current year, any book published within the past six years is eligible. Awarded annually in April. Established in 1926 to honor John Burroughs, a pioneer in the new school of nature writing. Established in 1926.

★8523★ Keep America Beautiful
Iron Eyes Cody Award
Mill River Plaza
9 W. Broad St.
Stamford, CT 06902
Phone: (203)323-8987
To recognize the volunteer men who have contributed to the fulfillment of KAB's mission by raising public awareness, educating our nation's youth, and setting an example for all Americans to follow. The award is named for KAB's internationally famous media spokesman, the "crying Indian."

★8524★ Keep America Beautiful
Keep America Beautiful National Awards Program
Mill River Plaza
9 W. Broad St.
Stamford, CT 06902
Phone: (203)323-8987
To recognize and honor community programs on the local, state and national level that have improved the quality of life. The deadline for entries is late August each year. First, second and third place awards are presented each December at the National Awards Luncheon in Washington, D.C. Established in 1954.

★8525★ Keep America Beautiful
Keep America Beautiful National Recycling Awards
Mill River Plaza
9 W. Broad St.
Stamford, CT 06902
Phone: (203)323-8987
To recognize exceptional achievement in the field of recycling, resource recovery and/or

resource conservation. The deadline is in early October each year.

★8526★ Keep America Beautiful
Mrs. Lyndon B. Johnson Award
Mill River Plaza
9 W. Broad St.
Stamford, CT 06902
Phone: (203)323-8987
To recognize an outstanding woman volunteer leader of the movement to improve the quality of American life at the grassroots level. This highly selective award is given only if a nominee has contributed substantially in the movement for a cleaner, more beautiful America. Awarded annually at the National Awards Luncheon.

★8527★ Keep North Carolina Beautiful, Inc.
North Carolina School Beautification
887-A Washington St.
Raleigh, NC 27605
Phone: (919)834-9869
Contact: Carl Lowendick, Contact
Program designed to encourage elementary, middle, and high school students to plan and implement beautification and recycling programs.

★8528★ Lake Michigan Federation
Rachel Carson Award
59 E. Van Buren, Ste. 2215
Chicago, IL 60605
Phone: (312)939-0838
Fax: (312)939-2708
For recognition of efforts in protecting Great Lakes water resources. Presented at intervals, usually biennially. Established in 1977 in honor of Rachel Carson, author of The Silent Spring, which protested the use of DDT.

★8529★ National Association for Environmental Education
Distinguished Service Award
PO Box 400
Troy, OH 45373
Phone: (513)698-6493
For recognition of distinguished service to the field of environmental education. Presented to both individuals and organizations annually.

★8530★ National Association of Conservation Districts
Business Conservation Leadership Award
c/o Deborah White
509 Capital Court, N.E.
Washington, DC 20005
Phone: (202)547-6223
Fax: (202)547-6223
To recognize a local business, a business corporation, or a unit of such a corporation that has planned and carried out impressive land, water, and related resource management practices on its property in cooperation with a local conservation district, or provided financial, personal, or other assistance to a district, state or national conservation program. The nominations deadline is September 26. Awarded annually. Established in 1975.

★8531★ National Association of Conservation Districts
Communications Awards
c/o Deborah White
509 Capital Court, N.E.
Washington, DC 20005
Phone: (202)547-6223
Fax: (202)547-6223
To recognize a representative of the communications industry who has made an outstanding contribution to better public understanding of resource conservation and the goals of soil and water conservation districts. The nominations deadline is September 26. Awarded annually. Established in 1968.

★8532★ National Association of Conservation Districts
Conservation Tillage Awards
c/o Deborah White
509 Capital Court, N.E.
Washington, DC 20005
Phone: (202)547-6223
Fax: (202)547-6223
To recognize outstanding contributions to conservation tillage. Nominations are accepted. Presented to the Conservation Tillage Information Center for work in promoting the use of conservation tillage. The Information Center, (202)347-4735, is a special project of the National Association of Conservation Districts. Awarded annually at the CTIC annual meeting. Established in 1984 by Chevron Chemical Company and Agrichemical Age.

★8533★ National Association of Conservation Districts
Distinguished Service Award
c/o Deborah White
509 Capital Court, N.E.
Washington, DC 20005
Phone: (202)547-6223
Fax: (202)547-6223
To recognize an American citizen for significant contributions to the protection and development of the nation's privately-owned natural resources. Nominations are accepted by September 26. Awarded annually. Established in 1962.

★8534★ National Association of Conservation Districts
District Newsletter Contest
c/o Deborah White
509 Capital Court, N.E.
Washington, DC 20005
Phone: (202)547-6223
Fax: (202)547-6223
To encourage conservation districts to further their educational and information efforts through regularly published newsletters. Selection is based on readability, regularity, timely and varied coverage of conservation activities, and broad circulation of the newsletter. Established in 1957. Co-sponsored by the Farm and Industrial Equipment Institute.

★8535★ National Association of Conservation Districts
Farm Management Conservation Award
c/o Deborah White
509 Capital Court, N.E.
Washington, DC 20005
Phone: (202)547-6223
Fax: (202)547-6223
To recognize accomplishments that farm management companies have made in the area of soil and water conservation; to facilitate closer working relationships between conservation districts and farm management companies; and to heighten their understanding and overall awareness of the need to conserve and protect this nation's soil, water, and related natural resources. Any farm management company with a majority of their farm managers belonging to the American Society of Farm Managers and Rural Appraisers is eligible to compete in the award program. Nominations must be endorsed by at least one of the conservation districts in which the company currently manages land. Awarded annually. Established in 1988. Sponsored by The American Society of Farm Managers and Rural Appraisers, Pioneer Hi-Bred International, Inc., and National Association of Conservation Districts. Additional information is available from Pioneer Hi-Bred International, Inc., Farm Manager Coordinator, 4401 Westown Parkway, West Des Moines, IA 50265, or American Society of Farm Managers and Rural Appraisers, 950 South Cherry Street, Suite 106, Denver, CO 80222.

★8536★ National Association of Conservation Districts
Goodyear Conservation Awards
c/o Deborah White
509 Capital Court, N.E.
Washington, DC 20005
Phone: (202)547-6223
Fax: (202)547-6223
To recognize conservation districts judged to have the most outstanding resource management programs in their respective states. Selection is based on a comparison of the actual achievements of a conservation district, as compared to a work plan filed earlier in the year. Established in 1947 by Goodyear Tire and Rubber Company and NACD.

★8537★ National Association of Conservation Districts
NACD - Allis Chalmers Conservation Teacher Awards
c/o Deborah White
509 Capital Court, N.E.
Washington, DC 20005
Phone: (202)547-6223
Fax: (202)547-6223
To offer national recognition of teachers for outstanding programs in conservation education. The program is open to all full-time classroom teachers in Grades K-12. The nominations deadline is March 31. Awarded annnually. Established in 1972. Co-sponsored by the Allis - Chalmers Corporation.

★8538★ National Association of Conservation Districts
NACD Deutz/Allis Chalmers Conservation District Awards
c/o Deborah White
509 Capital Court, N.E.
Washington, DC 20005
Phone: (202)547-6223
Fax: (202)547-6223
To offer national recognition to conservation districts for outstanding programs in conservation education. Educational programs being carried out by conservation districts in each state, including Puerto Rico and the Virgin Islands, are eligible. From state winners, regional district winners are judged and recognized. The top two national winning districts are recognized with a prestigious plaque which is presented at the opening general session of the NACD Annual Convention. The national first place district receives $500 for travel expenses to the Convention. The national first place district has the opportunity to present its program before the Education and Youth discussion forum at the NACD Convention. Awarded annually. Established in 1972. Co-sponsored by the Allis Chalmers Corporation.

★8539★ National Association of Conservation Districts
Professional Service Award
c/o Deborah White
509 Capital Court, N.E.
Washington, DC 20005
Phone: (202)547-6223
Fax: (202)547-6223
To recognize employees of conservation districts, state associations, or state or federal

agencies for exceptional service in furthering the cause of conservation districts and assisting the programs of NACD. The nominations deadline is September 26. Awarded annually. Established in 1981.

★8540★ National Association of Conservation Districts
Special Service Award
c/o Deborah White
509 Capital Court, N.E.
Washington, DC 20005
Phone: (202)547-6223
Fax: (202)547-6223
To recognize a soil and water conservation district leader or an American closely allied with the organized district movement for outstanding contributions to the NACD and its objectives. The nominations deadline is September 26. Awarded each year at the Annual Convention. Established in 1963.

★8541★ National Association of Environmental Professionals
Distinguished Service Award
c/o Joan A. Schroeder, Executive Secretary
PO Box 15210
Alexandria, VA 22309-0210
Phone: (703)660-2364
To recognize individuals who have made significant contributions to the furtherance of the principles of the Association and to the recognition that the environmental professional represents a profession which provides balanced interdisciplinary decisions necessary to solve today's complex environmental problems. Awarded annually at the National Conference. Established in 1982.

★8542★ National Audubon Society
Audubon Medal
950 Third Ave.
New York, NY 10022
Phone: (212)832-3200
To honor distinguished, individual service to conservation. Achievements of national or international significance are considered. Audubon Directors and Staff are not eligible. Awarded when merited. Established in 1947.

★8543★ National Audubon Society
Hal Borland Award
950 Third Ave.
New York, NY 10022
Phone: (212)832-3200
To recognize an individual who, through writing, photography, or painting, has made a lasting contribution to the understanding, appreciation, and protection of nature. Awarded annually. Established in 1983. Sponsored by |Audubon| magazine.

★8544★ National Audubon Society
Joan Hodges Queneau Palladium Medal
950 Third Ave.
New York, NY 10022
Phone: (212)832-3200
To honor outstanding engineering achievement in environmental conservation. Professional engineers (civil, mechanical, chemical, electrical, etc.) are eligible. Awarded annually. Established in 1976 in honor of Joan Hodges Queneau, an environmental conservationist.

★8545★ National Buffalo Association
Buffalo Hall of Fame
10 E. Main St.
PO Box 580
Ft. Pierre, SD 57532
Phone: (605)223-2829
To recognize those persons who have been instrumental in the comeback of the American buffalo in the historic category (at the turn of the century) and in the current category ("here and now"). Nominations may be made for both categories by August 5. A plaque is presented to the winner in each category at an annual award ceremony in September. Established in 1980.

★8546★ National Energy Resources Organization
Distinguished Service Award
c/o Kerry Sullivan
The Flanagan group
11 Canal Center, Sta. 250
Alexandria, VA 22314
Phone: (703)739-8822
Fax: (703)739-9248
This, the organization's highest honor, is presented for recognition of a contribution of sufficient magnitude as to be symbolic of our nation's search for solutions to the serious energy problems which threaten our economic and social well-being. Individuals may be nominated for an activity related to any aspect of the energy field. The activity for which the award is given need not be recent. However, preference may be given to an activity which has been of recent interest, discussion or debate. The activity to be recognized must have direct relevance to any or all of the major aspects of the energy problem (supply, conversion, utilization and environment) in any of the major sectors of society (government, industry or academia). The Distinguished Service Award shall not duplicate any other NERO award; nor shall previous winners of other awards be precluded from consideration for this Award. Awarded annually. Established in 1978. In addition, a Lifetime Achievement in Energy Award and other specified recognition are awarded when merited.

★8547★ National Energy Resources Organization
Energy Conservation Award
c/o Kerry Sullivan
The Flanagan group
11 Canal Center, Sta. 250
Alexandria, VA 22314
Phone: (703)739-8822
Fax: (703)739-9248
To recognize a person, group or organization directly responsible for an activity of unusual significance in the conservation of energy. Activities ranging from conceptual breakthroughs by individuals to exceptional energy savings, that occurred within the past eighteen months, having relevance to conservation, and having had a major impact on energy use are eligible. Awarded annually. Established in 1978.

★8548★ National Energy Resources Organization
Research and Development Award
c/o Kerry Sullivan
The Flanagan group
11 Canal Center, Sta. 250
Alexandria, VA 22314
Phone: (703)739-8822
Fax: (703)739-9248
To recognize any person, group or organization directly responsible for a research and development activity of unusual significance in the production or conservation of energy. Activities ranging from basic research to proof-of-concept demonstrations, including inventions of new products, that have passed a major milestone (publication, pilot plant operations, etc.) within the past eighteen months, having special relevance to energy production or conservation and having impact on energy are eligible. Special consideration will be given to nominees who have demonstrated a history of dedication to the solution of energy problems through scientific or technical innovation. Awarded annually. Established in 1979.

★8549★ National Environmental Training Association
Environmental Education Award
c/o C.L. Richardson, Executive Director
8687 Via de Ventura, Ste. 214
Scottsdale, AZ 85258
Phone: (602)951-1440
Fax: (602)483-0083
To recognize an individual for contributions to environmental training that are of regional, national, or international scope or significance. Active NETA members are eligible. Awarded annually at the National Conference in August. Established in 1979.

★8550★ National Environmental Training Association
Trainer of the Year
c/o C.L. Richardson, Executive Director
8687 Via de Ventura, Ste. 214
Scottsdale, AZ 85258
Phone: (602)951-1440
Fax: (602)483-0083
To recognize the efforts of the "grassroots" environmental trainer actively involved in training delivery and making an impact at the local level. Active NETA members are eligible. Awarded annually at the National Conference in August. Established in 1983.

★8551★ National Institute for Urban Wildlife
Daniel L. Leedy Urban Wildlife Conservation Award
c/o Conservation Awards Program
10921 Trotting Ridge Way
Columbia, MD 21044
To recognize an individual for outstanding professional commitment and contributions to the conservation of wildlife and habitat in urban, suburban, and developing areas. This award is the highest honor bestowed to an individual by the Institute, and may not be presented to more than one person in a year. Anyone may nominate a person for the award. Nominations must be received by September 15 for consideration in a calendar year. Awarded annually in November or December.

★8552★ National Military Fish and Wildlife Association
Special Act Award
c/o Larry D. Adams, President
1427 Lafayette Blvd.
Norfolk, VA 23509
Phone: (804)445-2369
To recognize an individual for achievement and outstanding contribution to the Department of Defense's wildlife law enforcement program. Individuals may be nominated for contributions to the Department of Defense Natural Resources program. Awarded annually at the awards banquet. Established in 1988. Additional information is available from Ron Dow, Awards Chairman, Naval Air Station, Point Mugu, CA, phone: (805) 989-7412.

★8553★ National Parks and Conservation Association
Conservationist of the Year
1015 31st Street, N.W.
Washington, DC 20007
Phone: (202)944-8530
For recognition of outstanding contributions by an individual to the preservation and/or

protection of the National Parks, whether a specific unit or the entire park system. Nominations are accepted. Awarded annually. Established in 1980.

★8554★ National Parks and Conservation Association
Marjory Stoneman Douglas Award
1015 31st Street, N.W.
Washington, DC 20007
Phone: (202)944-8530
To recognize an individual for an outstanding effort that results in the protection of a unit or a proposed unit of the National Park System. Awarded annually. The award is named in honor of Marjory Stoneman Douglas for her many years of dedication to preserving the fragile ecosystem of the Florida Everglades.

★8555★ National Parks and Conservation Association
Stephen Mather Award
1015 31st Street, N.W.
Washington, DC 20007
Phone: (202)944-8530
To recognize individuals who put principle before personal gain in the preservation of natural and/or archaeological resources. Any state, federal, local, or county employee who has been employed for two years or more in the preservation or management of natural and archaeological resources may be nominated for the award by February. Awarded annually at the May Board Meeting. Established in 1983 in honor of Stephen T. Mather, the first director of the National Park Service and co-founder of NPCA.

★8556★ National Recreation and Park Association
National Award for Media Excellence
c/o Laurie Kusek
3101 Park Center Dr., 12th Fl.
Alexandria, VA 22302
Phone: (703)820-4940
To recognize a writer, artist, mass media reporter, publisher or media corporation/owner who has significantly contributed to the general public's better understanding and greater awareness of public parks, recreation and conservation programs. This could be achieved through such media as general circulation books, magazines, newspapers, news collection organizations, broadcast stations, anthologies of photographs, art works, mass circulation films, or other outlets. Awarded annually. Established in 1984.

★8557★ National Recreation and Park Association
National Distinguished Professional Award
c/o Laurie Kusek
3101 Park Center Dr., 12th Fl.
Alexandria, VA 22302
Phone: (703)820-4940
To recognize a professional in the field who, through inspiration, incentive, demonstration and leadership, has made noteworthy contributions over a period of time to the park, recreation and conservation movement. Individuals who have been active at the professional level for at least 15 years and are members of the Association for at least ten years are eligible. No more than two awards are given annually.

★8558★ National Recreation and Park Association
National Voluntary Service Award
c/o Laurie Kusek
3101 Park Center Dr., 12th Fl.
Alexandria, VA 22302
Phone: (703)820-4940
To recognize a citizen or organization whose voluntary contributions of time and effort over a period of years have improved the quality and quantity of leisure opportunities through park, recreation, and conservation programs and projects in neighborhoods, communities, states or the nation. No more than three awards are given annually.

★8559★ National Recycling Coalition
Outstanding Individual Awards
c/o Dale Gubbels, President
PO Box 80729
Lincoln, NE 68501
Phone: (402)475-3637
To recognize individuals for outstanding achievement in recycling. Awards are presented in the following categories: (1) Recycler of the Year; (2) Government Leader; (3) Corporate Leader; and (4) Environmental Leader. Awarded annually. Established in 1983.

★8560★ National Recycling Coalition
Outstanding Innovation Award
c/o Dale Gubbels, President
PO Box 80729
Lincoln, NE 68501
Phone: (402)475-3637
To recognize companies for outstanding innovations in recycling. Established in 1984.

★8561★ National Recycling Coalition
Outstanding Program Awards
c/o Dale Gubbels, President
PO Box 80729
Lincoln, NE 68501
Phone: (402)475-3637
To recognize outstanding recycling programs. Awards are presented in the following categories: (1) Curbside Recycling; (2) Buyback Recycling; (3) Volunteer Recycling; (4) Regional Recycling; (5) Recycling Industry; and (6) Business Recycling. Awarded annually. Established in 1983.

★8562★ National Recycling Coalition
President's Special Achievement Award
c/o Dale Gubbels, President
PO Box 80729
Lincoln, NE 68501
Phone: (402)475-3637
To recognize an individual or an organization for outstanding contributions to recycling. Established in 1983.

★8563★ National Recycling Coalition
Recycling Hall of Fame
c/o Dale Gubbels, President
PO Box 80729
Lincoln, NE 68501
Phone: (402)475-3637
To recognize individuals for outstanding contributions to recycling. Established in 1986.

★8564★ National Water Resources Association
NWRA Distinguished Service Award
3800 N. Fairfax Drive, Ste. 4
Arlington, VA 22203-1703
Phone: (703)524-1544
Fax: (703)524-1548
To recognize individuals in Federal and State government for significant contributions to the development and conservation of our Nation's water resources. Awarded annually when merited. Established in 1987.

★8565★ National Water Resources Association
Water Statesman of the Year
3800 N. Fairfax Drive, Ste. 4
Arlington, VA 22203-1703
Phone: (703)524-1544
Fax: (703)524-1548
For recognition of contributions to the development of water and water resources. Awarded annnually when merited. Established in 1969.

★8566★ National Wildlife Federation
Environmental Achievement Award
c/o Corporate Conservation Council
1400 16th Street, N.W.
Washington, DC 20036-2266
Phone: (202)797-6800
Fax: (202)797-6646
To recognize an American business that has developed a conservation project that serves as an outstanding example of corporate responsibility to the environment. Nominations may be submitted by April 30. Awarded annually at the Corporate Conservation Council meeting. Established in 1985. Additional information is available from Barbara Haas, Director, Corporate Conservation Council, phone: (202) 797-6871.

★8567★ National Wildlife Federation
Jay N. "Ding" Darling Medal - Conservationist of the Year
c/o Corporate Conservation Council
1400 16th Street, N.W.
Washington, DC 20036-2266
Phone: (202)797-6800
Fax: (202)797-6646
This, the highest award of the Federation, is given for recognition of achievements on behalf of the nation's natural resources and present and future generations of Americans. Established in 1986 in honor of J.N. Darling, one of the founders of the Federation.

★8568★ National Wildlife Federation
National Conservation Achievement Awards Program
c/o Corporate Conservation Council
1400 16th Street, N.W.
Washington, DC 20036-2266
Phone: (202)797-6800
Fax: (202)797-6646
To honor individuals and organizations whose achievements in natural resource conservation deserve national recognition. Awards are presented in the following categories: (1) communications; (2) corporate leadership; (3) education; (4) government; (5) international; (6) legislative/legal; (7) organization; (8) science; and (9) special achievement. Established in 1965.

★8569★ National Wildlife Federation
Outstanding Affiliate Award
c/o Corporate Conservation Council
1400 16th Street, N.W.
Washington, DC 20036-2266
Phone: (202)797-6800
Fax: (202)797-6646
To recognize noteworthy accomplishments of affiliate organizations. To be eligible, candidates must be in substantial compliance with the Federation's Standards for Affiliation. Recent achievement of important organizational goals, or the completion of specific projects leading to significant environmental improvements are considered.

Nominations may be submitted by July 9. Awarded annually.

★8570★ National Wildlife Federation
Special Conservation Achievement Award
c/o Corporate Conservation Council
1400 16th Street, N.W.
Washington, DC 20036-2266
Phone: (202)797-6800
Fax: (202)797-6646
For recognition of outstanding efforts in the area of conservation and management of natural resources by an individual or organization whose achievement might otherwise be overlooked. Awarded when merited.

★8571★ National Wildlife Federation
State Conservation Achievement Program
c/o Corporate Conservation Council
1400 16th Street, N.W.
Washington, DC 20036-2266
Phone: (202)797-6800
Fax: (202)797-6646
To recognize individuals who have made outstanding contributions to conservation within the individual states. Awarded by NWF affiliates in as many as 11 categories.

★8572★ National Wildlife Rehabilitation Association
Lifetime Achievement Award
c/o Daniel R. Ludwig, Ph.D., Awards & Grants Committee
Willowbrook Wildlife Haven & Forest Preserve
525 S. Park Blvd.
PO Box 2339
Glen Ellyn, IL 60137
Phone: (312)790-4900
To recognize an individual for rehabilitation of wildlife. Individuals who have contributed to the field in a major way for many years are eligible. Nominations may be submitted by December 15 each year. Awarded annually. Established in 1984.

★8573★ National Wildlife Rehabilitation Association
National Wildlife Rehabilitation Association Grants Program
c/o Daniel R. Ludwig, Ph.D., Awards & Grants Committee
Willowbrook Wildlife Haven & Forest Preserve
525 S Park Blvd.
PO Box 2339
Glen Ellyn, IL 60137
Phone: (312)790-4900
To support research projects in the field of wildlife rehabilitation. Two grants of $1,000 each are awarded annually. Established in 1984.

★8574★ National Wildlife Rehabilitation Association
Significant Achievement Award
c/o Daniel R. Ludwig, Ph.D., Awards & Grants Committee
Willowbrook Wildlife Haven & Forest Preserve
525 S. Park Blvd.
PO Box 2339
Glen Ellyn, IL 60137
Phone: (312)790-4900
To recognize an individual for a significant contribution to the field of rehabilitation of wildlife in the past two years. Nominations may be submitted by December 15 each year. Awarded annually. Established in 1984.

★8575★ Natural Resources Defense Council
NRDC Environmental Award
40 W. 20th St.
New York, NY 10168
Phone: (212)727-2700
To recognize distinguished individuals for their service to the environment. Awarded annually. Established in 1972.

★8576★ Nature Conservancy
John and Harriet Dunning Award
c/o Public Relations
1815 N. Lynn St.
Arlington, VA 22209
Phone: (703)841-8744
Fax: (703)841-1283
To recognize contributions to the protection of South American forest systems.

★8577★ Nature Conservancy
Oak Leaf Award
c/o Public Relations
1815 N. Lynn St.
Arlington, VA 22209
Phone: (703)841-8744
Fax: (703)841-1283
This, the highest honor from the Conservancy, is given to recognize the efforts of those who have directly and significantly benefited the Conservancy's programs locally, regionally or nationally and to honor especially dedicated service and support toward achieving the organization's conservation objectives. Traditionally, the awards have not been given to anyone more than once, to current members of the national Board of Governors, to current staff members, or to anyone posthumously. Awarded annually. Established in 1963.

★8578★ Nature Conservancy
President's Public Service Award
c/o Public Relations
1815 N. Lynn St.
Arlington, VA 22209
Phone: (703)841-8744
Fax: (703)841-1283
To recognize exceptional support by individuals outside the Conservancy's immediate family of volunteers and staff who have advanced the preservation of biological diversity through their respective professions. Public officials, and corporate and foundation executives may be nominated for their exemplary contributions to Conservancy programs. Awarded three times a year at the national board of governors' meetings and annual conference. Established in 1984.

★8579★ Nature Conservancy
President's Stewardship Award
c/o Public Relations
1815 N. Lynn St.
Arlington, VA 22209
Phone: (703)841-8744
Fax: (703)841-1283
To recognize progress in protecting the ecological integrity of natural areas and the vital elements they harbor. Two awards are presented: (1) Individual award - to an individual volunteer for outstanding stewardship practices which support the objectives of the Conservancy's national stewardship programs; and (2) Group award - to a local volunteer management group (e.g., preserve committee, scientific advisory group). Nominations may be submitted by April 30. Awarded at the fall Conference.

★8580★ New England Wildflower Society
Conservation Award
c/o Awards Committee
Hemenway Rd.
Framingham, MA 01701
Phone: (508)877-7630
To recognize a major achievement in furthering the conservation goals of the New England Wild Flower Society. Awarded annually. Established in 1964.

★8581★ New York Botanical Garden
Green World Award
c/o Education Department
Southern Blvd. & East 200th St.
Bronx, NY 10458
Phone: (212)220-8700
To recognize outstanding achievement in environmental conservation by leading public figures, scientists, or business corporations. Recipients are selected by the Board of Directors of the New York Botanical Garden. Awarded annually. Established in 1974.

★8582★ Northeast Sustainable Energy Assn.
American Tour de Sol (Solar and Electric Car Championship)
14 Green St.
PO Box 541
Brattleboro, VT 05301
Phone: (802)254-2386
Contact: Nancy Hazard
Annual promotional event featuring a solar-powered vehicle race, a conference, trials, and an Earthfair. Encourages development and use of solar and electric vehicles.

★8583★ Outdoor Writers Association of America
Jade of Chiefs
c/o Eileen N. King
2017 Cato Avenue, Ste. 101
State College, PA 16801
Phone: (814)234-1011
This, OWAA's highest award, is given to recognize outstanding contributions to conservation. Though only OWAA members are eligible, the award is not actually presented by OWAA, but by members of the current Circle of Chiefs. Tenure and position in, or service to, OWAA are not criteria for the award. The Jade Award represents an affirmation of OWAA adherence to, and support of, the principles of conservation. Established in 1958.

★8584★ Ozark Society
Neil Compton Award
PO Box 2914
Little Rock, AR 72203
Phone: (501)225-1795
To honor an individual for contributions and efforts toward the preservation of natural areas, particularly in the Ozark-Ouachita mountain region. Members of the Society are eligible. Established in 1970 to honor the founder of the Ozark Society.

★8585★ Pennsylvania Association of Environmental Professionals
Karl Mason Memorial Award
c/o R. Fickes
RD 1, Box 278 N
New Bloomfield, PA 17068
Phone: (717)582-8540
To recognize individuals for achievements in environmental protection in Pennsylvania. Awarded when merited. Established in 1970 by the Pennsylvania Department of Health in memory of Karl Mason, Pennsylvania's first environmental administrator.

★8586★ Power
Energy Conservation Award
McGraw-Hill, Inc.
11 W. 19th St.
New York, NY 10011
Phone: (212)337-4060
Fax: (212)627-3811
To recognize steps taken to conserve energy by industry, and to encourage others to similar actions, based on the application of sound engineering principles resulting in reduced BTU or KWH input with plant output maintained. Awarded at least once each year. Established in 1973.

★8587★ Power
Environmental Protection Award
McGraw-Hill, Inc.
11 W. 19th St.
New York, NY 10011
Phone: (212)337-4060
Fax: (212)627-3811
To recognize outstanding efforts on the part of power plants to improve environmental quality. Awarded at least once each year. Established in 1971.

★8588★ Renew America
National Environmental Achievement Award - Searching for Success Program
c/o Kathy Nemsick
1400 16th Street, N.W., Ste. 710
Washington, DC 20036
Phone: (202)232-2252
To recognize successful environmental programs that work to protect, restore and enhance the environment. Environment programs in operation for at least six months are eligible. Winning programs are selected by the National Environmental Awards Council, made up of 23 environmental groups. Awards are presented in the following categories: (1) Air Pollution Reduction; (2) Drinking Water Protection; (3) Energy Pollution Control; (4) Environmental Beautification; (5) Environmental Education; (6) Fish Conservation; (7) Food Safety; (8) Forest Management; (9) Greenhouse Gases/Ozone Depleting Chemicals Reduction; (10) Groundwater Protection; (11) Growth Management; (12) Hazardous Materials Reduction and Recycling; (13) Pesticide Contamination Reduction; (14) Public Lands and Open Space Protection; (15) Range Conservation; (16) Renewable Energy and Energy Efficiency; (17) Soil Conservation; (18) Solid Waste Reduction and Recycling; (19) Surface Water Protection; (20) Transportation Efficiency; and (21) Wildlife Conservation. Awarded annually. Established in 1990.

★8589★ Resources for the Future
Dissertation Prize in Enviromental and Resource Economics
1616 P Street, N.W.
Washington, DC 20036
Phone: (202)328-5000
To recognize the doctoral dissertation that makes the most significant contribution to the field of environmental and resource economics. All dissertations in environmental and natural resource economics (theoretical and applied) submitted for the Ph.D. or its equivalent and certified as completed during the preceding year are eligible for nomination. Manuscripts must be in English and must be accompanied by a formal letter of nomination from the chair of the university department in which the dissertation was completed. The deadline is March 1. Awarded annually. Established in 1988.

★8590★ Scripps Howard Foundation
Environmental Journalism - Edward J. Meeman Awards
c/o Mary Lee Marusin, Executive Director
1100 Central Trust Tower
PO Box 5380
Cincinnati, OH 45201
Phone: (513)977-3035
For recognition of outstanding journalism that helps educate the public and public officials to a better understanding and support of conservation. Conservation embraces the environment and the forces that affect it control of pollution, technological developments, overpopulation, recycling, the conservation of soil, forests, vegetation, wildlife, open space and scenery. Newspapermen and women in the United States and its territories are eligible for the award. The deadline is February 5. Awarded annually in honor of Edward J. Meeman, the former editor of the Memphis Press-Scimitar and a conservation editor of the Scripps Howard Newspapers. Established in 1967.

★8591★ Sierra Club
Ansel Adams Photography Award
c/o William E. Smith, Board of Director's Coordinator
730 Polk St.
San Francisco, CA 94109
Phone: (415)776-2211
To recognize superlative photography that has been used to further conservation causes. Selection is made by the Executive Committee of the Board of Directors upon recommendation of the Honors and Awards Committee. Awarded annually. Established in 1971.

★8592★ Sierra Club
Denny and Ida Wilcher Award
c/o William E. Smith, Board of Director's Coordinator
730 Polk St.
San Francisco, CA 94109
Phone: (415)776-2211
To recognize Sierra Club chapters and groups for outstanding work in either membership development or fund raising, particularly for conservation projects. Selection is made by the Executive Committee of the Board of Directors upon recommendation of the Honors and Awards Committee. Awarded annually. Established in 1980. Sponsored by the Denny and Ida Wilcher Fund.

★8593★ Sierra Club
Distinguished Service/Achievement Awards
c/o William E. Smith, Board of Director's Coordinator
730 Polk St.
San Francisco, CA 94109
Phone: (415)776-2211
To recognize persons who are or have been in public service. Distinguished Service recognition is for strong and consistent commitment to conservation over a considerable period of time; whereas Distinguished Achievement recognition is for some particular action of singular importance to conservation. Selection is made by the Executive Committee of the Board of Directors upon recommendation of the Honors and Awards Committee. Established in 1971.

★8594★ Sierra Club
Earthcare Award
c/o William E. Smith, Board of Director's Coordinator
730 Polk St.
San Francisco, CA 94109
Phone: (415)776-2211
To recognize an individual, organization, or agency distinguished by making a unique contribution to International environmental protection and conservation. Selection is made by the Executive Committee of the Board of Directors upon recommendation of the Honors and Awards Committee. The International Committee submits nominations to the Honors and Awards Committee. Awarded from time to time. Established in 1975. The award may be co-sponsored in any given year by one or more environmental organizations sharing the same goals and interests as the Sierra Club.

★8595★ Sierra Club
Edgar Wayburn Award
c/o William E. Smith, Board of Director's Coordinator
730 Polk St.
San Francisco, CA 94109
Phone: (415)776-2211
To recognize outstanding service to the cause of conservation and the environment by a government official, either executive or legislative. Selection is made by the Executive Committee of the Board of Directors. Awarded annually. Established in 1979.

★8596★ Sierra Club
Honorary Life Member
c/o William E. Smith, Board of Director's Coordinator
730 Polk St.
San Francisco, CA 94109
Phone: (415)776-2211
To recognize an individual for distinguished service to the cause of conservation or to the Club. Awardees are exempt from the payment of membership dues or fees. Selection is made by a unanimous vote of the Board of Directors. Awarded as merited. Established in 1892. In addition, Honorary President and Honorary Vice President Awards are presented occasionally when merited.

★8597★ Sierra Club
John Muir Award
c/o William E. Smith, Board of Director's Coordinator
730 Polk St.
San Francisco, CA 94109
Phone: (415)776-2211
This, the Sierra Club's highest award, honors a distinguished record of leadership in national or international conservation causes, such as the continuation of John Muir's work of preservation and establishment of parks and wildernesses. Selection is made by the Executive Committee of the Board of Directors. Awarded annually. Established in 1961.

★8598★ Sierra Club
Raymond J. Sherwin International Award
c/o William E. Smith, Board of Director's Coordinator
730 Polk St.
San Francisco, CA 94109
Phone: (415)776-2211
To recognize extraordinary volunteer service toward international conservation and the maintenance of global protection of what John Muir called "this grand show eternal". Selection is made by the Executive Committee of the Board of Directors upon recommendation of the Honors and Awards Committee. The International Committee submits nominations to the Honors and Awards Committee. Awarded annually. Established in 1982.

★8599★ Sierra Club
William O. Douglas Award
c/o William E. Smith, Board of Director's Coordinator
730 Polk St.
San Francisco, CA 94109
Phone: (415)776-2211
To recognize significant contributions in the field of environment law by those who have made outstanding use of the legal/judicial process to achieve environmental goals. Awarded annually. Established in 1980.

★8600★ Society of American Travel Writers
Phoenix Awards
c/o Ken Fischer, Administrative Coordinator
1155 Connecticut Avenue, N.W., Ste. 500
Washington, DC 20036
Phone: (202)429-6639
To recognize the important role played by individuals and organizations actively involved in the conservation, preservation, beautification and anti-pollution campaigns which further the growth and appeal of the nation's travel areas. Awarded annually. Established in 1969.

★8601★ Soil and Water Conservation Society
Fellow
7515 N.E. Ankeny Rd.
Ankeny, IA 50021-9764
Phone: (515)289-2331
Fax: (515)289-1227
The degree of Fellow is conferred on Society members who have performed exceptional service in advancing the science and art of good land use. It is given for professional excellence and for service to the organization. Service may be in practicing, investigating, administering, or teaching soil and water conservation or closely related fields. Society members with at least 10 years of membership, who are also recognized outside the Society for their expertise as professional conservationists, are eligible. Nominations may be made by petition signed by at least 25 members of the Society. Awarded annually.

★8602★ Soil and Water Conservation Society
Heath Cooper Rigdon Conservation Writer and Broadcaster Awards
7515 N.E. Ankeny Rd.
Ankeny, IA 50021-9764
Phone: (515)289-2331
Fax: (515)289-1227
For recognition of outstanding efforts in communicating the story of natural resource conservation to the general public through the written word in newspapers and magazines or through the media of radio or television by an individual. The award is given as a means of expressing the Society's appreciation to individuals in the mass media for their help in advancing the science and art of good land use. Persons actively engaged in writing for newspapers or magazines or in reporting for radio or television, whether as staff members or freelancers, are eligible. An honorarium and a plaque are awarded annually at the Society's annual meeting. Established in memory of Mrs. Heath Cooper Rigdon, who provided financial support for the program.

★8603★ Soil and Water Conservation Society
Honor Award
7515 N.E. Ankeny Rd.
Ankeny, IA 50021-9764
Phone: (515)289-2331
Fax: (515)289-1227
To recognize individuals, usually non-members of the Society or non-professional members of the Society, for outstanding accomplishments compatible with the objectives of the Society. Society members and non-members are eligible. Nomination may be made by Society chapters only. No more than 10 awards are presented annually.

★8604★ Soil and Water Conservation Society
Hugh Hammond Bennett Award
7515 N.E. Ankeny Rd.
Ankeny, IA 50021-9764
Phone: (515)289-2331
Fax: (515)289-1227
This, the highest honor bestowed on an individual by the Society, is given for superior and distinguished service in recognition of national and international accomplishments in the conservation of natural resources. Society members or non-members are eligible. Nominations may be made by the Society's Board, Society chapters, or individual Society members. Awarded annually when merited.

★8605★ Soil and Water Conservation Society
Merit Award
7515 N.E. Ankeny Rd.
Ankeny, IA 50021-9764
Phone: (515)289-2331
Fax: (515)289-1227
For recognition of an outstanding effort or activity by a group, business firm, corporation, or organization that promotes wise land use. Activities of industrial sustaining members of the Society are eligible. Eligible organizations include press, radio, movies, television, industries, corporations, churches, societies, foundations, civic clubs, scout groups, and other organizations, public or private, that have carried out an outstanding conservation activity. Selection is based on the following criteria: (1) the activity should be the result of an organized program and may include the activity of an agency or government; (2) the activity should have an effect over a large area, at least a large part of a state or province, or parts of several states or provinces; (3) the principle effect of the activity should have been directed to other than professional conservationists; (4) the activity should have clearly contributed to bringing about better land use and/or better understanding of natural resource conservation. Nominations may be submitted by chapters and appropriate chapter committees, any three Society members, Society officers, Council members, or committee and division chairmen. Awarded annually.

★8606★ Soil and Water Conservation Society
Outstanding Service Award
7515 N.E. Ankeny Rd.
Ankeny, IA 50021-9764
Phone: (515)289-2331
Fax: (515)289-1227
In recognition of unusual efforts in helping the Society develop and carry out its program over a long and sustained period of time. Any Society member may be nominated. A five-year period, however, must elapse before members who have received Fellow Awards are eligible for the Outstanding Service Award. The nominee must have performed unusual service to the Society on a sustained basis for at least 10 years. This service may have been performed at the chapter, regional, or international levels. Nomination shall be by petition signed by at least 25 Society members. Awarded annually.

★8607★ Solar Energy Industries Association
Solar Man of the Year, Solar Salute
c/o Scott Sklar, Executive Director
1730 N. Lynn Street, Ste. 610
Arlington, VA 22209-2009
Phone: (703)524-6100
To recognize a member of Congress who has demonstrated active leadership in promoting solar energy. Awarded annually at the convention. Established in 1973.

★8608★ Spill Control Association of America
Howard E. Stanfield Distinguished Service Award
400 Renaissance Center, Ste. 1900
Detroit, MI 48243-1895
Phone: (313)567-0500
Alt. Phone: (313)259-8943
To recognize distinguished achievements in, or contributions to, the technology of control of spills of oil and hazardous materials. Achievements may include contributions to the knowledge and literature of spill control; the design or invention of equipment or technical services; or outstanding service to government, companies, or organizations serving any field of spill control/cleanup technology. Candidates for the inscribed award need not be members, but must be recommended by the Award Committee. Established in 1983.

★8609★ Texas Armadillo Association
Honorary Member
PO Box 311074
New Braunfels, TX 78131
Phone: (512)629-4980
To recognize individuals for work toward preservation of the armadillo. Awarded when merited. Established in 1980 by James E. Schmidt.

★8610★ Trout Unlimited
Gold Trout Award
c/o Loretta M. Pogorzelski
501 Church Street, N.E., Ste. 103
Vienna, VA 22180
Phone: (703)281-1100
To recognize a chapter for the most outstanding conservation activities of the year. Awarded to a chapter in each region for conservation activities.

★8611★ Trout Unlimited
Trout Conservationist of the Year
c/o Loretta M. Pogorzelski
501 Church Street, N.E., Ste. 103
Vienna, VA 22180
Phone: (703)281-1100
To honor distinguished and dedicated service to the cause of the cold water fishery resource and the improvement and perpetuation of the recreational qualities of fishing on the American continent. Individuals are eligible in three categories: professional; communications; layman or non-professional. Awarded annually. Established in 1963.

★8612★ Underwater Society of America
Sentential of the Seas
c/o George Rose, President
PO Box 628
Daly City, CA 94017
Phone: (415)583-8492
Fax: (408)294-3496
To recognize individuals who have made extraordinary contributions to ocean and water resource conservation. Awarded when merited.

Established in 1988 by John C. Fine. Administered in cooperation with the United Nations Environment Program, Beneath the Sea, the non-profit volunteer organization that produces New York's annual underwater and ocean film festival.

★8613★ United States Army, Corps of Engineers, Headquarters
Chief of Engineers Design and Environmental Awards Program
20 Massachusetts Avenue, N.W.
Washington, DC 20314
Phone: (202)272-0011
Alt. Phone: (202)504-4032
To recognize excellence in the design of, or environmental achievement related to, recently completed structures or area developments by the Corps of Engineers Field Operating Agencies and their professional design contract firms. To provide an incentive for design and environmental professionals to develop new projects which will exhibit excellence in function, economy, resource conservation, aesthetics and creativity. Recognition is given to the Corps of Engineers District which is responsibile for design, and to the private sector design firm, if one has been retained by the District. Both civil works and military construction projects are eligible, as long as they have been completed within three years of the date of the award. The awards are presented in four major categories: architecture; engineering; landscape architecture; and environment; and on four levels: Chief of Engineers Award of Excellence; Award of Merit; Honor Award; and Honorable Mention. Plaques are awarded to the District Engineer and to the designing firm in each category. Awarded biennially. Established in 1965.

★8614★ U.S. Council of Energy Awareness
Forum Award
c/o Janice Willis
1776 Eye Street, Ste. 400
Washington, DC 20006
Phone: (202)293-0770
Fax: (202)785-4113
To honor significant contributions by the print and electronic news media to the public understanding of the peaceful uses of nuclear energy. Awards are given in two categories: print and broadcast (radio and television). Entries are limited to projects dealing with the peaceful applications of nuclear energy - articles, programs, films, books, news reports, documentaries, electronic or print series - by an individual reporter, writer, editor, or radio, television, or film producer, director, or by a reporter/producing team. The nominee must be a professional member of the electronic or print media. The entry must have appeared during the preceding year and be available to and intended for the general public. The collaborative effort of more than one individual is considered as a single entry. The deadline is September 30. Awarded annually. Established in 1967.

★8615★ United States Department of Energy
John Ericsson Award in Renewable Energy
c/o William L. Woodard
Office of Energy Research, ER-6
1000 Independence Ave.
Washington, DC 20585
Phone: (202)252-5767
For recognition of outstanding achievement in research, development, or application of renewable energy technologies. Candidates may be at any stage in their careers. The award may recognize a single noteworthy achievement or a sustained level of accomplishment throughout a lifetime. Nominations are judged primarily on the basis of scientific and technical merit and achievement, with secondary weight being given to managerial ability or innovative talents. Nominations are due by April 29. Established in 1987. Additional information is available from Stanley Weis, Awards Officer, Office of Conservation and Renewable Energy, CE-41, Department of Energy, 1000 Independence Avenue, S.W., Washington, DC 20585, (202) 586-8594.

★8616★ United States Department of Energy
Sadi Carnot Award in Energy Conservation
c/o William L. Woodard
Office of Energy Research, ER-6
1000 Independence Ave.
Washington, DC 20585
Phone: (202)252-5767
For recognition of outstanding achievement in research, development, or application of energy conservation technologies. Candidates may be at any stage in their careers. The award may recognize a single noteworthy achievement or a sustained level of accomplishment throughout a lifetime. Nominations are judged primarily on the basis of scientific and technical merit and achievement, with secondary weight being given to managerial ability or innovative talents. Nominations are due by April 29. Established in 1987. Additional information is available from Stanley Weis, Awards Officer, Office of Conservation and Renwable Energy, CE-41, Department of Energy, 1000 Independence Avenue, S.W., Washington, DC 20585, phone: (202) 586-8594

★8617★ United States Dept. of the Interior Minerals Management Service
Conservation Award for Respecting the Environment Program (CARE)
1201 Elmwood Park Blvd.
New Orleans, LA 70123-2394
Phone: (504)736-2780
Contact: Villere C. Reggio Jr., Contact
Designed to recognize outstanding environmental accomplishments and leadership by companies involved in offshore oil, gas, or sulphur operations in the Gulf of Mexico.

★8618★ United States Environmental Protection Agency
Certificate for Outstanding Achievement
c/o Office of External Liaison & Education (A108)
401 M Street, S.W.
Washington, DC 20460
Phone: (202)260-4454
To recognize the ecological projects and achievements of America's youth. Projects are in four areas of interest: Environmental Education, Environmental Awareness, Community Service, and Public Affairs. A Certificate for Outstanding Achievement is granted for all efforts by any youth organization that has adult sponsorship. Each group's project is judged by a local Awards Panel of at least three members from a cross section of the community. Presented whenever merited. Established in 1971.

★8619★ United States Environmental Protection Agency
President's Environmental Youth Awards
c/o Office of External Liaison & Education (A108)
401 M Street, S.W.
Washington, DC 20460
Phone: (202)260-4454
To recognize young people, as individuals or in groups, for promoting environmental awareness and channeling this awareness into positive community involvement. Activities range from developing recycling programs to protecting sensitive wetlands. Award-winning projects should provide long-term beneficial envrionmental efforts for the area involved. Young people from Kindergarten through twelfth grade are eligible. President's Environmental Youth Award Certificates are presented to youth and youth groups determined to be deserving by a local, adult awards panel whenever merited. The highest rated project submitted to each EPA Regional Office is designated a national winner. Established in 1971.

★8620★ University of Southern California
Tyler Prize for Environmental Achievement
John & Alice Tyler Ecology/Energy Prize
c/o Dr. Jerome B. Walker, Executive Director
Provost's Office
University of Southern California
Los Angeles, CA 90089-4019
Phone: (213)743-6343
This, the largest and most prestigious environmental prize in the world, is given to honor individuals or institutions of any nation who have benefited humanity in environmental fields in their broadest context. Citizens of all nations are invited to nominate individuals or institutions of any nation by October 15. Nominees can be associated with any field of science. Nominated institutions can be universities, foundations, corporations, or other types of organizations. Prizes are awarded for any one of the following: (1) the protection, maintenance, improvement or understanding of ecological and environmental conditions anywhere in the world; or (2) the discovery, further development, improvement, or understanding of known and new sources of energy including, but not limited to, oil, coal, solar, hydroelectric, geothermal, wind, oil shale, nuclear, and tar sands. Selection is made by a vote of the members of the Tyler Prize Executive Committee. Awarded annually in the spring. Established in 1973 through a bequest of the late John C. Tyler, the founder of Farmers Insurance Group. Annual support for the Prize is provided by Mrs. Alice C. Tyler by written agreement with the University of Southern California.

★8621★ Washington Journalism Center
Thomas L. Stokes Award
c/o Murielle Nagl, Administrative Assistant
2600 Virginia Avenue, N.W.
Washington, DC 20037
Phone: (202)337-3603
For recognition of the best reporting, analysis or comment in a daily newspaper in the United States or Canada during the preceding year on the development, use and conservation of energy resources, the protection of the environment, or other conservation and natural-resources issues. Work published in a daily newspaper in the United States or Canada during the preceding year may be submitted by February 1. No more than ten examples of a person's work should be submitted. Awarded annually. Established in 1959 by friends of the late Thomas L. Stokes, the syndicated

columnist who wrote on energy, the environment and other natural-resource issues.

★8622★ Water Pollution Control Federation
Harry E. Schlenz Medal
c/o Mary C. Smith
601 Wythe St.
Alexandria, VA 22314
Phone: (703)684-2400
Fax: (703)684-2492
For recognition of distinguished service in promoting public awareness, understanding and action in water pollution control. Individuals, whose contributions are in the area of journalism, film production, or any other communication endeavor, are eligible. Awarded annually. Established in 1970 in memory of Harry E. Schlenz, president of the Federation in 1961-1962 and a leader in promoting public awareness of the need for adequate water pollution control.

★8623★ Water Pollution Control Federation
William J. Orchard Medal
c/o Mary C. Smith
601 Wythe St.
Alexandria, VA 22314
Phone: (703)684-2400
Fax: (703)684-2492
To recognize distinguished service to the water pollution control field. Members of the Federation are eligible. Awarded as merited. Established in 1960 in honor of William J. Orchard, first recipient of the medal and one of the founders of the Federation of Sewage Works Associations, now the Water Pollution Control Federation.

★8624★ Whooping Crane Conservation Association
Honor Award
c/o Jerome J. Pratt, Editor
3000 Meadowlark Dr.
Sierra Vista, AZ 85635
Phone: (602)458-0971
To recognize substantial contributions to the preservation of endangered wildlife in North America. Awarded annually. Established in 1976.

★8625★ Wilderness Society
Ansel Adams Award
c/o Marthena Cowart
900 17th Street, N.W.
Washington, DC 20006-2596
Phone: (202)833-2300
To honor public figures who have devoted exceptional time, thought and energy to preserving America's wilderness, prime forests, parks, rivers, and shore lands, and have notably enhanced the fostering of an American land ethic. Awarded annually at the spring meeting of the Governing Council. Established in 1980 to honor Ansel Adams, a landscape photographer.

★8626★ Wilderness Society
Robert Marshall Award
c/o Marthena Cowart
900 17th Street, N.W.
Washington, DC 20006-2596
Phone: (202)833-2300
To recognize a private citizen who has devoted exceptional time, thought and energy to preserving America's wilderness, prime forests, parks, rivers and shore lands. Awarded annually at the fall meeting of the Governing Council. Established in 1981.

★8627★ Wildlife Society
Aldo Leopold Memorial Award
5410 Grosvenor Ln.
Bethesda, MD 20814
Phone: (301)897-9770
This, the highest honor the wildlife profession can bestow, is given to an individual for distinguished service to wildlife conservation. Selection is based on the significance of an individual's work. Awarded annually if merited at the North American Wildlife and Natural Resources Conference. Established in 1950 in memory of Aldo Leopold.

★8628★ Wildlife Society
Conservation Education Award
5410 Grosvenor Ln.
Bethesda, MD 20814
Phone: (301)897-9770
To recognize particular works of great merit and programs representing sustained effort that can achieve great significance over the years. Awards are given in each of the following categories on a three-year rotation basis: (1) writing - to authors, editors, or publishers of books, a series of articles, or other written material which effectively conveys sound conservation concepts to the public; (2) audio-visual works - to an artist, photographer, lecturer, radio commentator or other creative worker whose accomplishments are outstanding in the dissemination of conservation truth to the public; and (3) programs - the development of appropriate conservation education programs. A plaque and/or a certificate are awarded annually. Established in 1953.

★8629★ Wildlife Society
Group Achievement Award
5410 Grosvenor Ln.
Bethesda, MD 20814
Phone: (301)897-9770
To recognize an organization's outstanding wildlife achievement that is consistent with and/or assists in advancing the objectives of The Wildlife Society. The organization selected for the award can be private, state, or federal, and either in the United States or Canada. The activity of past recipients has been primarily regional, national or international in scope. Accomplishments, while they may be long-term, should be of significant importance within the last three years. In the selection process, the tendency has been to honor private organizations working for wildlife resources as allies to governmental professional organizations. Nominations must be received by October 1. Awarded annually at the North American Wildlife Conference. Established in 1965.

★8630★ Wildlife Society
Honorary Member
5410 Grosvenor Ln.
Bethesda, MD 20814
Phone: (301)897-9770
To recognize continuously outstanding service to any area(s) of concern to the Wildlife Society. Any practicing or retired wildlife professional who is a member of the Wildlife Society and has made continuing valuable contributions to the wildlife profession over a long period of time is eligible for nomination. Awarded at the annual banquet program. Established in 1938.

★8631★ Wildlife Society
Jim McDonough Award
5410 Grosvenor Ln.
Bethesda, MD 20814
Phone: (301)897-9770
To recognize a certified wildlife biologist who has made, or is making, a significant contribution to the wildlife profession by being an active member/participant of The Wildlife Society, especially at local levels (i.e., Chapter and Section). The individual must have made (or is still making) contributions that reflect well on professional biologists through program implementation and development of new techniques or approaches in an area or in a state or province. The person should be the kind recognized by his fellow workers as a solid contributor and a "true professional." Awarded annually. Established by Jim McDonough, a leader in the Northeast Section and New England Chapter for many years. This award replaces the Trippensee-McPherson Award.

★8632★ Wildlife Society
Special Recognition Service Award
5410 Grosvenor Ln.
Bethesda, MD 20814
Phone: (301)897-9770
To honor a person or group that has made an outstanding contribution for the short or long term to the wildlife profession; the general areas of wildlife conservation, management or science; or a specific area of endeavor, species, community, eco-system or region. Nominations by members are accepted by September 1. Awarded annually. Established in 1980.

★8633★ World Environment Center
Gold Medal Award for International Corporate Environmental Achievement
419 Park Ave. South, Ste. 1403
New York, NY 10016
Phone: (212)683-4700
Fax: (212)683-5053
To recognize a corporation with substantial international operations having an outstanding, sustained and well-implemented environmental policy with worldwide emphasis. Recognition is given to innovative programs and projects that stimulate nations and industry to enhance and protect the global environment. Nominations are judged in the following broad criteria: (1) Policy; (2) International Policy Application; and (3) International Leadership. Awarded annually. Established in 1985.

★8634★ World Wildlife Fund
J. Paul Getty Wildlife Conservation Prize
1250 24th Street, N.W.
Washington, DC 20037
Phone: (202)778-9555
Fax: (202)293-9211
For recognition of an outstanding achievement of direct or indirect international impact on the conservation of wildlife. Individuals or organizations are chosen by an international jury based on a diversity of accomplishments such as the conservation of rare or endangered species and habitats, the increase in public awareness of the importance of wildlife and nature by scientific, educational or aesthetic contributions, or the establishment of legislation or of an organization or society of unusual importance to wildlife conservation. In all cases the achievement must be pioneering and substantial so that the recognition accorded by the award will bring public attention to the winning achievement and will increase public appreciation of the significance of wildlife and its conservation. Awarded annually. Established in 1974 by J. Paul Getty and now funded by his son, Gordon P. Getty.

Alphabetic and Subject Index

This index provides an alphabetical arrangement of all the organizations, publications, and other entities in the Directory. Subject terms are bolded with the appropriate citations listed immediately below. Publication names appear in italics. The numbers are book entry numbers not page numbers.

Glossary of Terms

abatement Reducing the degree or intensity of, or eliminating pollution.

absorption (treatment) Method of treating wastes in which activated carbon removes organic matter from wastewater.

absorptive capacity A measure of the amount of waste that can be deposited in a particular environment without causing adverse ecological or aesthetic change.

accident site The location of an unexpected occurrence, failure, or loss, either at a plant or along a transportation route, resulting in a release of hazardous materials.

acclimatization Physiological and behavioral adjustments of an organism to changes in its environment.

acid rain Generic term for acid deposition; occurs when emissions of sulfur and nitrogen compounds and other acid or acid-forming substances are transformed by chemical processes in the atmosphere and later deposited on earth as rain, fog, snow, or particulates.

activated carbon Highly absorbent form of carbon used to remove odors and toxic substances from liquid or gaseous emissions.

activated sludge Sludge that results when mixed with bacteria to speed breakdown of organic matter in raw sewage undergoing secondary waste treatment.

active ingredient In pesticides, the component which kills, or otherwise controls, target pests. Pesticides are regulated based on their active ingredients.

acute toxicity Ability of a substance to cause poisonous effects resulting in severe biological harm or death after short-term exposure that can be as limited as a single dose.

adaptation Adjustment or response, often hereditary, of a living organism to conditions in its environment.

add on control device Air pollution control device, such as a carbon absorber or incinerator, which reduces the pollution in an exhaust gas. Device does not affect the process being controlled and thus is "add on" technology, as opposed to a device to control pollution through making some alteration to the basic process.

adulterants Chemical impurities or substances that by law do not belong in a food or in a pesticide.

advanced wastewater treatment Any treatment of sewage that goes beyond the secondary or biological water treatment stage and includes the removal of nutrients such as phosphorus and nitrogen and a high percentage of suspended solids. *See also:* primary wastewater treatment, secondary wastewater treatment

aerobic Requiring or living in the presence of molecular or free oxygen.

aerosol Suspension of liquid or solid particles in a gas.

agricultural pollution Liquid or solid wastes from farming, including runoff and leaching of pesticides and fertilizers; erosion and dust from plowing; animal manure and carcasses; crop residues; and debris.

agroforestry Method of planting trees and crops together.

air curtain Method of containing oil spills. Air bubbling through a perforated pipe causes an upward water flow that inhibits the spread of oil and stops fish from entering the contaminated water.

algae One-cell or multicell organisms, usually aquatic, that lack true stems, roots, or leaves (e.g., seaweed, kelp).

algal blooms Population explosion of algae in surface waters due to an increase in plant nutrients such as nitrates and phosphates; commonly caused by agricultural pollution or other runoff.

alkalinity High pH characteristic that, when present in a compound, enables the compound to neutralize acids.

alternative energy Energy derived from a source other than conventional fuels (e.g., oil, coal, natural gas, nuclear fusion). Types of alternative energy include solar power, hydroelectric power, and wind power.

ambient Term referring to outdoor conditions (e.g., ambient air quality is the condition of the outside air).

anoxia Absence of oxygen.

Antarctic ozone hole Term used to describe the seasonal depletion of stratospheric ozone over a large area of Antarctica.

Anti-Degradation Clause Section of federal air and water quality requirements that prohibits deterioration where pollution levels are above the legal limit.

aquifer Underground geological formation containing usable amounts of groundwater that can supply wells or springs.

artificial reef Man-made sea structure made from solid waste materials and used as cover by marine organisms.

atmospheric deposition *See:* acid rain

asbestos Mineral fiber once commonly used in manufacturing and construction; use is now banned or severely limited by the EPA. Can cause cancer or asbestosis.

asbestosis Disease associated with chronic exposure to and inhalation of asbestos fibers. Causes breathing difficulties and can lead to death.

ash Mineral content of a product remaining after complete combustion.

best available technology Industrial application of the best pollution control technology currently available. "Best" often takes into consideration factors such as cost of achieving pollution reduction, impacts on nonair health quality and the environment, and energy requirements.

baling Compacting solid waste into blocks to reduce and simplify handling.

bioaccumulation The increase in concentration of substances in living organisms due to slow metabolism or excretion. See also: biological magnification

bioassessment Evaluation of the strength or toxicity of a substance by measuring its effect on a test organism.

bioconcentration *See:* bioaccumulation

biodegradable Ability to break down or decompose rapidly under natural conditions and processes.

biodiversity Measurement pertaining to level of variation of plant and animal species in a particular habitat or biome; also level of genetic variation within species.

biofouling Process by which living organisms, often due to artificial introduction into ecosystems or to rapid population growth, negatively impact the area.

biological amplification *See:* biological magnification

biological magnification Process where certain substances such as pesticides or heavy metals enter the food chain and become concentrated in tissues or internal organs of higher organisms as they move up the chain.

biological oxygen demand (BOD) The amount of oxygen needed for aerobic microorganisms to function in organic-rich water, such as sewage.

biological pest control Control of pests by natural predators, parasites, or pathogens.

biological treatment Technology that uses bacteria to consume waste/organic materials.

biomagnification *See:* biological magnification

biomass Total dry weight of all organic matter in an ecosystem; can also refer to plant materials and animal wastes used as fuel.

biome Large land (terrestrial) ecosystem, such as a forest, grassland, or desert.

biomonitoring Use of living organisms to test quality of waters in industrial discharge as well as in waters downstream from discharge.

biosphere Portion of planet and atmosphere that can support life.

biostabilizer Machine that converts solid waste into compost through grinding and aeration.

biota The flora and fauna of a region.

biotechnology Industrial applications of biochemical processes, including recombinant DNA techniques, to produce drugs or other materials; can be used in the recycling of wastes.

blackwater Water that contains animal or food wastes.

blister packs Formed plastic that serves as a see-through package and as a protective cover in product packaging; often considered excess packaging.

boom Floating device used to contain oil spills.

botanical pesticide Pesticide whose active ingredient is a plant-produced chemical such as nicotine or strychnine.

breakwater Wall built offshore to protect beach/harbor from wave action.

burial ground Disposal site for radioactive waste that uses earth or water as a shield.

carcinogen Substance that can cause or contribute to formation of cancer.

carrying capacity The largest population a particular biome can support indefinitely.

catalytic converter Abatement device that removes pollutants from motor vehicle exhaust.

centrifugal collector Mechanical system using centrifugal force to remove aerosols from a gas stream or to de-water sludge.

CERCLA (Comprehensive Environmental Response, Compensation, and Liability Act) U.S. federal program enacted in 1980 and designed to clean up identified environmentally-damaged sites. Commonly referred to as Superfund program. Involves remedial investigations, feasibility and corrective measures studies.

CFCs (chlorofluorocarbons) Family of inert, nontoxic, and easily liquified chemicals manufactured for use as coolants, cleaning solvents, plastic, aerosol propellants, and foam insulation. Chlorine components of CFCs released into the atmosphere are major contributors to stratospheric ozone depletion.

channelization Straightening and deepening streams so water will move faster; a flood-reduction and drainage tactic that can interfere with waste assimilation capacity and disturb fish and wildlife habitats.

chemical emergency Accidental release or spill of hazardous chemicals which poses a threat to workers, the general public, the environment, or property.

chemical treatment Technology that uses chemicals to treat waste.

chlorinated hydrocarbons Persistent, broad-spectrum insecticides that linger in the environment and accumulate in the food chain; included in this class are DDT, PCBs, aldrin, chlordane, mirex, toxaphene, and TCE, which is used as an industrial solvent.

chronic toxicity Ability of a substance to cause long- lasting, harmful effects long after initial exposure.

Clean Air Act U.S. federal guidelines for air quality and emission controls affecting all manufacturing concerns.

Clean Water Act U.S. federal guidelines for water quality and controls affecting all manufacturing concerns.

cleanup Actions taken to deal with the release of hazardous substances. Term is used interchangeably with remedial action, removal action, response action, or corrective action.

clear cut Forest management technique that harvests all the trees in one area at one time. Can contribute to soil erosion and increased sedimentation in adjoining waterways.

closed-loop recycling Reclaiming wastewater for non-potable uses in an enclosed process.

coastal zone Lands and waters adjacent to the coast, the use and ecology is closely interrelated with the sea.

combined sewer overflow Overflow from sewer systems that carry both raw sewage and storm water; overflow often occurs during periods of excessive rain, resulting in untreated discharge entering surface waterways such as rivers and lakes.

comminution Mechanical shredding or pulverizing of waste. Used in solid and water waste treatment.

common property resource Resource to which humans have free and unmanaged access such as air, international fish resources, migratory birds, and ozone in the stratosphere.

compost A mixture of garbage, degradable trash, and soil in which bacteria in the soil breaks down the mixture into organic fertilizer.

conservation Avoiding waste of, and renewing, human and natural resources.

contaminant Any physical, chemical, biological, or radiological substance that has an adverse affect on air, water, or soil.

cooling tower Structure designed to remove heat from water used as a coolant; term used most often in regard to electric power-generating plants.

core Uranium-containing center of a nuclear reactor, where the energy of the reaction is released.

cover crop Crop planted to reduce soil erosion and to provide humus (organic portion of the soil).

cover material Soil used to cover compacted solid waste in a sanitary landfill.

Criteria Pollutants Amendments to the Clean Air Act (in 1970) required EPA to set National Ambient Air Quality Standards for certain pollutants to protect human health and welfare; these are called criteria pollutants and include six: ozone, carbon monoxide, total suspended particulates, sulfur dioxide, lead, and nitrogen oxide.

cultural eutrophication Eutrophication of water bodies due to human activity.

DDT (dichloro-diphsdyl-trichloromethane) First manufactured chlorinated hydrocarbon insecticide. EPA banned registration and sale of DDT for all but emergency uses in the U.S. in 1972 because of its persistence in the environment and accumulation in the food chain.

decomposition Breakdown of matter by bacteria and fungi.

deep ecology Philosophy based on a view that to prevent environmental overload, environmental degradation, and resource depletion, there should be a consistent effort to control human population growth, reduce unnecessary use and waste of matter and energy resources, and prevent the premature extinction of any species.

deep well injection *See:* injection well

defoliant Herbicide that removes leaves from trees and growing plants.

deforestation Removal of trees and undergrowth in a forested area without adequate replanting.

derelict land Area damaged by strip mining or other industrial processes or by neglect; of no beneficial use or aesthetic value.

desertification Conversion of rangeland or cropland to desert-like conditions, usually caused by overgrazing, soil damage, drought, or climate changes.

designer bugs Popular term for microbes developed through biotechnology that can degrade toxic chemicals at their source in toxic waste dumps or in groundwater.

desulfurization Removal of sulfur from fossil fuels to reduce pollution.

diazinon Insecticide banned from open area applications (e.g., golf courses) by the EPA in 1986 because of the potential danger to migratory birds.

dioxin Family of man-made chemicals similar to steroid hormones in the human body. Formed in pulp making during the chlorine bleaching process. Occurs naturally in low concentration; high concentrations causes chloracne.

direct discharger Municipal or industrial facility that introduces pollution through a defined conveyance or system; a point source.

dispersant Chemical agent used to break up concentrations of organic material such as oil spills.

disposal Final placement or destruction of toxic, radioactive, or other wastes; surplus or banned pesticides or other chemicals; polluted soils; and drums containing hazardous materials from removal actions or accidental releases. Disposal may be done through use of landfills, surface impoundments, land farming, deep well injection, ocean dumping, or incineration.

dissolved oxygen Amount of oxygen dissolved in water; level of 5 mg/l or above indicate a relatively healthy stream.

dolphin setting Tactic whereby dolphins are herded into fishing nets so that the yellowfin tuna, which often travel below the dolphin herds, may be easily captured.

dose-response evaluation Risk evaluation based on the relationship between the dose of the contaminant administered or received and the incidence of adverse health effects in the exposed population.

dosimeter Instrument that measures exposure to radiation.

drainage basin *See:* watershed

dredge spoils Materials scraped from the bottoms of harbors and rivers to maintain shipping lanes; often contaminated with toxic substances that have settled out of the water.

dredging Mechanical removal of mud from the bottom of water bodies. May impact aquatic life by disturbing ecosystems, causing excess silting, and exposing contaminated muds. Dredging may be subject to regulation under the Clean Water Act.

dump Site used for solid waste disposal under no environmental controls.

dust dome *See:* heat island effect

ecosphere Life-supporting area on the planet, comprised of earth, surface waters, and air. *See also:* biosphere

ecosystem Interacting system of a biological community and its nonliving environmental surroundings.

effluent Generally refers to wastes discharged into surface waters.

emission Pollution discharged into the atmosphere from smokestacks, other vents, and surface areas of commercial or industrial facilities; from residential chimneys; and from motor vehicle, locomotive, or aircraft exhaust.

Emission Inventory Listing, by source, of the amount of air pollutants discharged into the atmosphere of a community. Used to establish emission standards.

Emission Standard Maximum amount of air polluting discharge legally allowed from a single source, mobile or stationary.

emission trading EPA policy allows a plant complex with several facilities to decrease pollution from some facilities while increasing it from others, so long as the total results are equal to or better than previous limits. Complexes that reduce emissions significantly may sell "emission credits" to other industries.

endangered species Status given to wild animals, birds, fish, plants, or other living organisms of low population levels that are threatened with extinction by man-made or natural changes in their environment.

environmental geology Application of geologic data to problems created by human activity (e.g., erosion, strip mining).

environmental impact statement Document required of federal agencies for major projects or legislative proposals significantly affecting the environment. Document describes positive and negative effects of proposed project and lists alternative actions.

environmental protection Resource management area concerned with the discharge of substances into the environment that may cause damage to humans or other biological organisms.

EPA (Environmental Protection Agency) Established in 1970 by Presidential Executive Order to bring together the various government agency programs involved in the control of pollution.

epidemiology The study of the incidence, distribution, and control of disease in groups of people or populations.

erosion Wearing away of land surface by wind or water; can be intensified by land-clearing practices.

estuary Zone along a coastline where fresh water from rivers and streams and runoff from land mix with seawater.

eutrophication Aging process of a lake, estuary, or bay in which a high dissolved nutrient level and a low oxygen level cause the water body to evolve into a bog or marsh and eventually disappears. Human activities can accelerate the process.

evaporation ponds Areas where sewage sludge is dumped and allowed to dry out.

exotic species In population distribution studies, any species of plant or animal that has been introduced into an area or ecosystem; not native to the area in which it is found.

extinction Complete disappearance of a species from the planet. *See also:* endangered species; threatened species

Extremely Hazardous Substances Any of the 406 chemicals identified by EPA on the basis of toxicity; list subject to revision.

fecal coliform bacteria Found in intestinal tracts of mammals; presence in water or sludge serves as indicator of pollution and possible contamination by pathogens.

flue gas Air emitted to the atmosphere after a production process or combustion takes place; also called stack gas.

flue gas desulfurization Technology that removes sulfur dioxide from gases produced through fossil fuel burning.

fly ash Noncombustible residual particles left over from the combustion process and emitted in flue gas.

food chain Series of organisms, each eating or decomposing the preceding one. *See also:* food web

food web Network of interconnecting food chains and feeding interactions.

fugitive emissions Emissions that could not reasonably pass through a stack, chimney, vent, or other equivalent opening.

fungicide Pesticides used to control, prevent, or destroy fungi.

global warming Worldwide changes in temperature and sea levels attributed to the warming effects of "greenhouse" gases, principally carbon dioxide, which trap heat within the atmosphere much like the glass or plastic does in a greenhouse. The burning of fossil fuels, deforestation, and other human-environment interactions are the main causes of the increase in greenhouse gas concentrations.

granular activated carbon treatment Filtering system used in small water systems and individual homes; can be highly effective in removing elevated levels of radon from water.

green consumerism Lifestyle philosophy whereby evaluation and selection of products for purchase is almost exclusively based on the impact the product has on the environment; including method of manufacture, content of product, packaging of product, and recyclability of product after consumer use.

greenhouse effect *See:* global warming

greenhouse gases Gases in the atmosphere that cause global warming, or the greenhouse effect; gases include carbon dioxide, chlorofluorocarbons, ozone, methane, and nitrous oxide.

green manure Green vegetation that is mixed with soil to increase the organic matter and humus available to support crop growth.

groundwater Supply of fresh water found beneath the Earth's surface, usually in aquifers, which is often used for supplying wells and springs. Can be contaminated by leaching agricultural or industrial pollutants, or from leaking underground storage tanks.

habitat Place or type of place where an organism or community of organisms lives.

half-life The time it takes for one-half of a given quantity of a chemical to disappear from the environment, or to be excreted from a living organism, if the chemical is absorbed by the body.

hazardous substance Material that poses a threat to human health or to the environment; typically of a toxic, corrosive, ignitable, explosive, or chemically reactive nature.

haze Cloudy appearance in surrounding atmosphere due to dust, smoke, mist, or other suspended particulates.

heat island effect Elevated temperatures over an urban area caused by structural and pavement heat fluxes and pollutant emissions from the area.

herbicide Chemical pesticide designed to control or destroy plants, weeds, or grasses.

high-density polyethylene Material used to make plastic bottles and other products; produces toxic fumes when burned.

high-level radioactive waste (HLW) Waste generated in the fuel of a nuclear reactor; serious health threat when not shielded.

holding pond Pond or reservoir built to store polluted runoff.

hydrologic cycle Biogeochemical cycle that collects, purifies, and distributes the planet's water as it cycles between the environment and living organisms.

incinerator Furnace for burning wastes under controlled conditions.

injection well Well into which fluids are injected for waste disposal, improving the recovery of crude oil, or solution mining.

insecticide Pesticide compound specifically used to kill or control insects.

integrated pest management Combination of pesticide and nonpesticide methods to control pests.

irrigation To supply water, other than rainfall, to farmland.

lagoon Shallow pond into which wastewater is discharged for biological treatment.

land application Discharge of wastewater onto the ground for treatment or reuse.

land farming (of waste) Disposal process in which hazardous waste deposited in or on the soil is naturally degraded by microbes.

landfill Sanitary landfills are disposal sites for non- hazardous wastes; cover material is applied at the end of each operating day. Secure chemical landfills are disposal sites for hazardous wastes.

LD 50/lethal dose The dose of a toxicant that will kill 50 percent of the test organisms within a designated time period. The lower the LD 50, the higher the toxicity.

leaching Process by which soluble materials are dissolved and carried through the soil by a percolating fluid.

leaded gasoline Gasoline containing lead, added to raise the octane level.

lethal dose *See:* LD 50/lethal dose

limestone scrubbing Process that removes sulfur from smokestack emissions.

liner Barrier designed to prevent the leaching of contents from a landfill; commonly comprised of plastic or dense clay.

long range transport Movement of pollution or other airborne particulates by air currents; particulates eventually are deposited far from the point of origin.

Love Canal Area in Niagara Falls, New York that became a national symbol for the dangers of hazardous waste sites (industrial wastes were buried there during the 1940s and early 1950s). Declared a disaster area in 1978, the area was targeted for hazardous waste cleanup and residents evacuated.

low-impact agriculture *See:* organic farming

low-level radioactive waste (LLRW) Less hazardous than waste generated by nuclear reactors; low-level radioactive waste is usually generated by hospitals, research laboratories, and certain industries.

microbial pesticide Microorganisms used to control a pest; low toxicity to humans.

mirex Organochlorine insecticide used mainly against ants.

monitoring wells Drilled at hazardous waste management or Superfund sites to collect ground and water samples to determine the type and level of contamination.

mutagenicity Capacity to induce mutagens.

National Ambient Air Quality Standards Maximum allowable level for a certain pollutant in outdoor air.

National Oil and Hazardous Substances Contingency Plan U.S. federal regulation that guides determination of the sites to be corrected under the Superfund program and the program to prevent or control spills into surface waters or other portions of the environment.

National Priorities List (NPL) EPA list of uncontrolled or abandoned hazardous waste sites identified for remedial action under Superfund. List is based on the score a site receives from the Hazard Ranking System and is updated annually.

natural pollutant Substance of natural origin that may be regarded as a pollutant when present in excess (e.g., volcanic dust, ozone formed by lightning, smoke from forest fires).

natural resources Resources produced by the natural processes of the planet, including air, water, plants and animals, and nutrients and minerals.

nitrate Salt of nitric acid; major nutrient for higher plants. Also used as a food additive and is a component of water pollution.

nitrilotriacetic acid Compound used as replacement for phosphates in detergents.

nitric oxide Gas product from operation of internal combustion engines.

nitrogen dioxide Result of nitric oxide combining with air oxygen; component of photochemical smog.

nitrogen oxide Product of combustion from motor vehicles and other sources; contributor to ozone formation in lower atmosphere and to acid deposition.

nonpoint source pollution Pollutants discharged from many sources.

Not In My Backyard (NIMBY) Citizen opinion or sentiment that refers to the desire to place hazardous waste facilities (e.g., landfills, incinerators) far from their own community.

nuclear winter Scientific prediction of the environmental conditions that would exist following a nuclear war; that debris and smoke generated from massive nuclear explosions would enter the atmosphere and block out the sunlight for a period of weeks or months, drastically changing agriculture and weather conditions.

nutrient Element or compound, such as phosphorus, needed for the survival, growth, and reproduction of a plant or animal.

oil fingerprinting Method that identifies source of oil; allowing spills to be traced to point of origin.

oil spill Accidental or intentional discharge of oil that ends up in a body of water.

open dump Uncovered, unregulated waste disposal site.

organic farming Production of crops and livestock by using low-impact agriculture methods such as organic fertilizer, biological pest control, and crop rotation.

output pollution control Method for reducing pollution levels after the pollutants have been generated or introduced into the environment (e.g., wastewater treatment plants).

overgrazing Depletion or destruction of rangeland grasses due to damage to root systems by grazing animals.

oxidant Oxygen-containing substance that produces a new substance through chemical reaction with air.

ozone (O3) Can appear in the lower atmosphere and the stratosphere (begins 7-10 miles above the earth); stratospheric ozone serves as a protective layer that shields the earth from the harmful effects of the sun's ultraviolet radiation. In the lower atmosphere, ozone is a chemical oxidant that contributes to formation of photochemical smog.

ozone depletion Destruction of the stratospheric ozone layer of the earth's atmosphere due to the release of chlorofluorocarbons, or CFCs, into the environment. CFCs eventually reach the upper atmosphere and catalytically destroy ozone molecules.

particulates Fine liquid or solid particles such as dust, smoke, mist, fumes, or smog; found in air and emissions.

pathogen Disease-producing microorganisms, including bacteria, viruses, and protozoa.

pathological waste Waste that contains pathogens that could threaten public health (e.g., hospital waste and other infected materials).

PCBs (polychlorinated biphenyls) Family of toxic, persistent chemicals used in energy transformers, capacitators, and gas pipelines. Use banned in 1979.

percolation Movement of water downward or radially through the subsurface soil layers.

persistence Refers to the length of time a compound remains in the environment.

pesticide Substances to prevent, destroy, repel, or mitigate any pest; also any substances used to defoliate, regulate, or desiccate plants.

pesticide tolerance Amount of pesticide residue allowed by law to remain in or on a harvested crop.

pesticide treadmill Economic and environmental condition that exists when increasingly higher levels of pesticides must be used to control pests due to the development of genetic resistance by the pest species.

petrochemicals Chemicals obtained by refining crude oil; used in the manufacturing of industrial chemicals, fertilizers, pesticides, plastics, paints, and many other products.

pH Numeric value that indicates the relative acidity or alkalinity of a substance on a scale of 0 to 14. Acid solutions have pH values lower than 7; Basic or alkaline solutions have pH values greater than 7.

phenols Organic by-products of petroleum refining and other manufacturing operations; high concentrations can kill aquatic life and humans.

phosphates Chemical compounds containing phosphorus.

phosphorus Chemical food element that contributes to eutrophication of lakes and other water bodies.

photochemical smog Air pollution caused by chemical reactions.

pig Lead container used to ship or store radioactive materials.

pile Nuclear fuel.

plume Visible or measurable discharge of a contaminant such as smoke, thermal discharge in water, and radiation leaks from a damaged reactor.

point source Stationary location or facility from which pollutants are discharged or emitted.

pollutant Any substance that is introduced to an environment and adversely affects the usefulness of a resource.

Pollutant Standard Index (PSI) Measure of the adverse health effects of air pollution levels.

polyvinyl chloride (PVC) Environmentally indestructible plastic that releases hydrochloric acid when burned.

pretreatment Processes that reduce, eliminate, or alter the nature of wastewater before it is discharged into treatment works.

primary wastewater treatment First major treatment process in which organic particles are allowed to settle out of the water.

pristine Unaffected or untouched by human activity.

RAD (radiation absorbed dose) Unit of radiation exposure equal to .01 joules/kg.

radon Naturally occurring, radioactive, inert gas formed by decay of radium in soil or rocks.

raw sewage Untreated wastewater.

RCRA (Resource Conservation and Recovery Act) U.S. federal hazardous waste, solid waste, and waste reduction program, enacted in 1976. Involves remedial investigations, feasibility and corrective measures studies.

recycle To minimize waste by recovering reusable materials and products (e.g., aluminum cans, paper, bottles).

reentry interval Period of time following application of pesticide that workers should not enter the area.

reforestation Process in which trees are reintroduced into a region that has been harvested.

refuse *See:* solid waste

refuse reclamation Conversion of solid waste into useful products, such as soil conditioners or recycled materials.

remedial action Implementation phase of a Superfund site cleanup.

renewable resource Resource that is replenished through natural processes (e.g., surface waters, trees, animals); if renewable resource is depleted faster that it can regenerate, resource can be then classified as nonrenewable.

residence time A measurement of the persistence of a substance or pollutant that is suspended or dissolved in a medium.

resource recovery Process of obtaining matter or energy from materials formerly discarded.

retention pond *See:* holding pond

reuse To use a product again and again in the same form (e.g., glass bottles, cloth diapers).

riparian rights Rights of land owners with water bordering their property to prevent diversion or misuse of upstream waters.

risk assessment Process of gathering facts to estimate the potential harmful effects of a particular product or activity on humans or the environment.

rodenticide Agent used to kill rats or other rodent pests, or to deter them from damaging food or crops.

runoff Precipitation, snow melt or irrigation water that runs off the land into waterways; can contain pollutants from the air or land.

sanitary landfill *See:* landfill

SARA Superfund Amendments and Reauthorization Act of 1986.

scrubber Air pollution control device that traps pollutants in emissions.

secondary wastewater treatment Processes that remove dissolved organic material from wastewater.

sewage Waste and wastewater generated by residential and commercial facilities and discharged into sewers.

sewage sludge *See:* sludge

sinking Controlling oil spills by using an agent to trap the oil and sink it to the bottom of the affected waterway, where agent and oil are biodegraded.

sludge Semisolid residue from air or water treatment processes; can be a hazardous waste.

smog Air pollution associated with oxidants.

soil conservation Methods used to reduce soil erosion and nutrient depletion.

soil erosion *See:* erosion

solar collector Device for collecting radiant energy from the sun and converting it to heat.

solid waste Nonsoluble, unwanted materials, including sewage sludge, municipal garbage, industrial wastes, agricultural refuse, demolition wastes, and mining residues.

solid waste management The handling of waste from its generation through disposal.

stable air Unmoving air mass that holds rather than disperses pollutants.

stratosphere Second layer of the atmosphere, extending from about 12 to 30 miles (19-48 km) above the planet surface; contains gaseous ozone that filters out about 99% of the sun's ultraviolet radiation.

strip cropping System of planting that serves to prevent wind and water erosion.

strip mining System of retrieving mineral deposits that involves the mechanical scraping of rock and soil from the earth's surface.

subsistence agriculture Method that combines solar energy with human and animal labor to produce enough food for the farmer and family members.

suspended solids Particulates in a solution, such as river water, that do not readily separate and settle out of the solution.

sustainable agriculture Method of growing crops and livestock based on organic fertilizers, soil conservation, water conservation, biological pest control, and minimal use of fossil fuels. *See also:* organic farming

Superfund Program operating under the authority of CERCLA that funds and carries out EPA removal/remedial activities at National Priority Sites.

surface impoundment Treatment, storage, or disposal of liquid hazardous waste in ponds. *See also:* evaporation pond, holding pond, lagoon

surface mining *See:* strip mining

teratogenicity Capable of causing developmental abnormalities.

thermal pollution Discharge of heated water from industrial processes; can affect aquatic life.

threatened species Wild plant or animal species that is still abundant but is likely to become endangered due to a decline in numbers. *See also:* endangered species

Three Mile Island An island nuclear site in the Susquehanna River near Harrisburg, Pennsylvania that became a national symbol for the dangers of nuclear power. The facility experienced a reactor failure in 1979 due to human and mechanical error, resulting in an overheated core and a small release of radioactive gases.

Times Beach Town in Missouri that was purchased in 1983 by the U.S. federal government and declared unfit for human habitation. In the 1970s, used oil containing chemical wastes was spread on dirt and gravel roads. Flooding in 1982 exposed residents to high levels of dioxin.

toxic Harmful to living organisms.

toxic cloud Airborne mass of toxic gases, fumes, or aerosols.

toxic substance Chemical or compound that may pose an unreasonable risk to human health or may damage the environment.

toxicant Agent that kills or injures animal or plant life.

toxicity Degree to which a substance will likely harm plant or animal life. *See also:* acute toxicity

toxin Naturally produced poisons secreted by biological organisms.

turbidity Haziness in air or water caused by the presence of particles and pollutants.

underground storage tank Storage container located underground that is designed as a holding tank for petroleum products or other chemical solutions.

urban runoff Stormwater that may carry pollutants into sewer systems or other waterways.

Valdez Principles A ten-point environmental corporate policy recommended for U.S. companies; outgrowth of the Exxon tanker spill off the coast of Alaska in 1989.

virtual elimination Removing pollutants within a targeted cleanup area to the extent that they no longer pose a health or safety threat to humans or the environment.

VOC (volatile organic compounds) Any organic compound that significantly participates in photochemical reactions. Presence in emissions (pounds/day) by which clean air standards are measured (e.g., 15 pounds VOC emissions per day).

waste Unwanted materials left over from manufacturing processes, or refuse from humans and animals.

waste stream The movement of waste from generation to disposal.

wastewater Used water from residential or industrial facilities that contains dissolved or suspended matter.

watershed Land area that drains into a particular stream.

wetlands Land area regularly saturated by surface or ground water, including swamps, bogs, fens, marshes, and estuaries.

wildlife refuge Area designated for the protection of wild animals.

WMA (Wildlife Management Area) U.S. federally protected area.

WMD (Wetlands Management District) U.S. federally protected area.

zero discharge Discharge from a point source that has been determined to contain minimal or no pollutants.

Appendix I: Endangered and Threatened Wildlife (as of July 1991)

This appendix lists animals that have been classified by the United States Government as being in a threatened or endangered state. Threatened species are still abundant but are likely to become endangered due to decline in numbers. Endangered species have low population levels and are threatened with extinction by man-made or natural changes in the environment.

Akepa, Hawaii (honeycreeper), *(Loxops coccineus coccineus).* Small finch-like bird with a long, notched tail. Historic range: U.S.A. (HI). Status: Endangered.

Akepa, Maui (honeycreeper), *(Loxops coccineus ochraceus).* Akepa subspecies whose habitat is the forest canopy. Historic range: U.S.A. (HI). Status: Endangered.

Akialoa, Kauai (honeycreeper), *(Hemignathus procerus).* Bird with a long, thin, down-curved bill. Possibly extinct. Historic range: U.S.A. (HI). Status: Endangered.

Akiapolaau (honeycreeper), *(Hemignathus munroi).* Stout-bodied bird with distinctive sickle-shaped bill. Historic range: U.S.A. (HI). Status: Endangered.

Ala Balik (trout), *(Salmo platycephalus).* Historic range: Turkey. Status: Endangered.

Albatross, Short-tailed *(Diomedea albatrus).* Large, web- footed seabird. Historic range: North Pacific Ocean: Japan, U.S.S.R., U.S.A. (AK, CA, HI, OR, WA). Status: Endangered.

Alligator, American *(Alligator mississippiensis).* Historic range: Southeastern U.S.A. Status: Threatened.

Alligator, Chinese *(Alligator sinensis).* Historic range: China. Status: Endangered.

Amphipod, Hay's Spring *(Stygobromus hayi).* White, eyeless shrimp-like crustacean, adapted to Hay's Spring. Historic range: U.S.A. (DC). Status: Endangered.

Anoa, Lowland *(Bubalus depressicornis).* Small dark brown buffalo related to the American bison. Historic range: Indonesia. Status: Endangered.

Anoa, Mountain *(Bubalus quarlesi).* Small dark brown buffalo related to the American bison. Historic range: Indonesia. Status: Endangered.

Anole, Culebra Island Giant *(Anolis roosevelti).* Brownish gray arboreal lizard. Historic range: U.S.A. (PR: Culebra Island). Status: Endangered.

Antelope, Giant Sable *(Hippotragus niger variani).* Stately antelope with sickle-shaped horns sweeping backward from its face. Historic range: Angola. Status: Endangered.

Argali *(Ovis ammon hodgsoni).* Agile wild sheep noted for its large curling horns. Historic range: China (Tibet, Himalayas). Status: Endangered.

Armadillo, Giant *(Priodontes maximus).* Historic range: Venezuela and Guyana to Argentina. Status: Endangered.

Armadillo, Pink Fairy *(Chlamyphorus truncatus).* Historic range: Argentina. Status: Endangered.

Ass, African Wild *(Equus asinus).* Strongly built ancestor of the domestic donkey. Historic range: Somalia, Sudan, Ethiopia. Status: Endangered.

Ass, Asian Wild *(Equus hemionus).* Wild cousin of the domestic donkey, with small ears and slender head resembling a horse. Historic range: Southwestern and Central Asia. Status: Endangered.

Avahi *(Avahi laniger).* Small, brownish gray woolly lemur. Historic range: Malagasy Republic. Status: Endangered.

Aye-Aye *(Daubentonia madagascariensis).* Nocturnal relative of the lemur distinguished by bushy tail and long, clawed hands. Historic range: Malagasy Republic. Status: Endangered.

Ayumodoki (loach), *(Hymenophysa curta).* Fish. Historic range: Japan. Status: Endangered.

Babirusa *(Babyrousa babyrussa).* Wild swine characterized as a docile, night-hunting animal of the jungle. Historic range: Indonesia. Status: Endangered.

Baboon, Gelada *(Theropithecus gelada).* Historic range: Ethiopia. Status: Threatened.

Bandicoot, Barred *(Perameles bougainville).* Small marsupial mammal with long, narrow, clawed feet. Historic range: Australia. Status: Endangered.

Bandicoot, Desert *(Perameles eremiana).* Small marsupial mammal with long, narrow, clawed feet. Historic range: Australia. Status: Endangered.

Bandicoot, Lesser Rabbit *(Macrotis leucura).* Small marsupial mammal with long, narrow, clawed feet. Historic range: Australia. Status: Endangered.

Bandicoot, Pig-footed *(Chaeropus ecaudatus).* Small marsupial mammal with hoof-like claws. Historic range: Australia. Status: Endangered.

Bandicoot, Rabbit *(Macrotis lagotis).* Small marsupial mammal with large, leathery rabbit-like ears and a long, pointed snout. Historic range: Australia. Status: Endangered.

Banteng *(Bos javanicus).* Species of wild cattle resembling a domestic cow, found in hill forests. Historic range: Southeast Asia. Status: Endangered.

Bat, Bulmer's Fruit (flying fox), *(Aproteles bulmerae).* Historic range: Papua New Guinea. Status: Endangered.

Bat, Bumblebee *(Craseonycteris thonglongyai).* Historic range: Thailand. Status: Endangered.

Bat, Gray *(Myotis grisescens).* Bat that often roosts in caves carved out of limestone formations, particularly near water. Historic range: Central and Southeastern U.S.A. Status: Endangered.

Bat, Hawaiian Hoary *(Lasiurus cinereus semotus).* Forest- dwelling species that roosts in trees or rock crevices. Historic range: U.S.A. (HI). Status: Endangered.

Bat, Indiana *(Myotis sodalis).* Medium-sized bat that roosts in caves or abandoned mines. Historic range: Eastern and Midwestern U.S.A. Status: Endangered.

Bat, Little Mariana Fruit *(Pteropus tokudae).* Historic range: Western Pacific Ocean: U.S.A. (Guam). Status: Endangered.

Bat, Mariana Fruit *(Pteropus mariannus mariannus).* Historic range: Western Pacific Ocean: U.S.A. (Guam, Rota, Tinian, Saipan, Agiguan). Status: Endangered.

Bat, Mexican Long-nosed *(Leptonycteris nivalis).* Bat that appears to depend on the nectar and pollen of flowering agaves, the giant saguaro, and the organ pipe cacti for food, while the plants depend on the bat for pollination. Historic range: U.S.A. (NM, TX), Mexico, Central America. Status: Endangered.

Bat, Ozark Big-eared *(Plecotus townsendii ingens).* Large- eared, reddish bat inhabiting caves in mature hardwood forests. Historic range: U.S.A. (MO, OK, AR). Status: Endangered.

Bat, Rodrigues Fruit(flying fox), *(Pteropus rodricensis).* Historic range: Indian Ocean: Rodrigues Island. Status: Endangered.

Bat, Sanborn's Long-nosed *(Leptonycteris sanborni).* Similar to the Mexican long-nosed bat. Historic range: U.S.A. (AZ, NM), Mexico, Central America. Status: Endangered.

Bat, Singapore Roundleaf Horseshoe *(Hipposideros ridleyi).* Historic range: Malaysia. Status: Endangered.

Bat, Virginia Big-eared *(Plecotus townsendii virginianus).* Subspecies of Townsend's big-eared bat, inhabiting caves in mature hardwood forests. Historic range: U.S.A. (KY, NC, WV, VA). Status: Endangered.

Bear, Baluchistan *(Ursus thibetanus ged rosianus).* Historic range: Iran, Pakistan. Status: Endangered.

Bear, Brown *(Ursus arctos arctos).* Historic range: Palearctic. Status: Endangered.

Bear, Brown *(Ursus arctos pruinosus).* Historic range: China, (Tibet). Status: Endangered.

Bear, Brown or Grizzly *(Ursus arctos).* Historic range: Holarctic. Status: Threatened (U.S.A - 48 conterminous states); endangered (Mexico).

Beaver *(Castor fiber birulai).* Historic range: Mongolia. Status: Endangered.

Beetle, American Burying *(Nicrophorus americanus).* Nocturnal member of the carrion beetle family. Historic range: U.S.A. (eastern States south to FL, west to SD and TX), eastern Canada. Status: Endangered.

Beetle, Delta Green Ground *(Elaphrus viridis).* Predatory beetle found in two wetland areas in Solano County. Historic range: U.S.A. (CA). Status: Threatened.

Beetle, Kretschmarr Cave Mold *(Texamaurops reddelli).* Eyeless mold beetle inhabiting caves in the Edwards Limestone formation. Historic range: U.S.A. (TX). Status: Endangered.

Beetle, Northeastern Beach Tiger *(Cicindela dorsalis dorsalis).* Historic range: U.S.A. (CT, MA, MD, NJ, NY, PA, RI, VA). Status: Threatened.

Beetle, Puritan Tiger *(Cicindela puritana).* Historic range: U.S.A. (CT, MA, MD, NH, VT). Status: Threatened.

Beetle, Tooth Cave Ground *(Rhadine persephone).* Tiny ground beetle endemic to two caves in the Edwards Limestone formation. Historic range: U.S.A. (TX). Status: Endangered.

Beetle, Valley Elderberry Longhorn *(Desmocerus californicus dimorphus).* Brightly-colored beetle inhabiting elderberry thickets. Historic range: U.S.A. (CA). Status: Threatened.

Bison, Wood *(Bison bison athabascae).* Also known as the buffalo. Larger than the plains bison, with denser coat and longer horns. Historic range: Canada, Northwestern U.S.A. Status: Endangered.

Blackbird, Yellow-shouldered *(Agelaius xanthomus).* Resembles the red-winged blackbird. Inhabits various wooded and wetland areas. Historic range: U.S.A. (PR). Status: Endangered.

Blindcat, Mexican (catfish), *(Prietella phreatophila).* Historic range: Mexico. Status: Endangered.

Boa, Jamaican *(Epicrates subflavus).* Historic range: Jamaica. Status: Endangered.

Boa, Mona *(Epicrates monensis monensis).* Nocturnal nonvenomous snake endemic to Mona Island. Historic range: U.S.A. (PR). Status: Threatened.

Boa, Puerto Rican *(Epicrates inornatus).* Historic range: U.S.A. (PR). Status: Endangered.

Boa, Round Island *(Bolyeria multocarinata).* Historic range: Indian Ocean: Mauritius. Status: Endangered.

Boa, Round Island *(Casarea dussumieri).* Historic range: Indian Ocean: Mauritius. Status: Endangered.

Boa, Virgin Islands Tree *(Epicrates monensis granti).* Historic range: U.S.A. and British Virgin Islands. Status: Endangered.

Bobcat *(Felis rufus escuinapae).* Historic range: Central Mexico. Status: Endangered.

Bobwhite, Masked *(Colinus virginianus ridgwayi).* Quail with a short tail and plump body. Inhabits desert grasslands. Historic range: U.S.A. (AZ), Mexico (Sonora). Status: Endangered.

Bontebok *(Damaliscus dorcas dorcas).* Glossy-coated antelope related to the hartebeest. Historic range: South Africa. Status: Endangered.

Bonytoungue, Asian *(Scleropages formosus).* Fish. Historic range: Thailand, Indonesia, Malaysia. Status: Endangered.

Booby, Abbott's *(Sula abbotti).* Long-winged seabird. Historic range: Indian Ocean: Christmas Island. Status: Endangered.

Bristlebird, Western *(Dasyornis brachypterus longirostris).* Historic range: Australia. Status: Endangered.

Bristlebird, Western Rufous *(Dasyornis broadbenti littoralis).* Historic range: Australia. Status: Endangered.

Broadbill, Guam *(Myiagra freycineti).* Bird with an unusually broad bill. Historic range: Western Pacific Ocean: U.S.A. (Guam). Status: Endangered.

Bulbul, Mauritius Olivaceous *(Hypsipetes borbonicus olivaceus).* Medium-sized bird resembling a tropical flycatcher. Historic range: Indian Ocean: Mauritius. Status: Endangered.

Bullfinch, Sao Miguel *(Pyrrhula pyrrhula murina).* Historic range: Eastern Atlantic Ocean: Azores. Status: Endangered.

Bushwren, New Zealand *(Xenicus longipes).* Historic range: New Zealand. Status: Endangered.

Bustard, Great Indian *(Choriotis nigriceps).* Medium to large- sized bird related to the crane but with shorter legs and heavier body. Historic range: India, Pakistan. Status: Endangered.

Butterfly, Bay Checkerspot *(Euphydryas editha bayensis).* Historic range: U.S.A. (CA). Status: Threatened.

Butterfly, El Segundo Blue *(Euphilotes battoides allyni).* Historic range: U.S.A. (CA). Status: Endangered.

Butterfly, Lange's Metalmark *(Apodemia mormo langei).* Historic range: U.S.A. (CA). Status: Endangered.

Butterfly, Lotis Blue *(Lycaeides argyrognomon lotis).* Historic range: U.S.A. (CA). Status: Endangered.

Butterfly, Mission Blue *(Icaricia icarioides missionensis).* Historic range: U.S.A. (CA). Status: Endangered.

Butterfly, Mitchell's Satyr *(Neonympha mitchellii mitchellii).* Historic range: U.S.A. (IN, MI, NJ, OH). Status: Endangered.

Butterfly, Oregon Silverspot *(Speyeria zerene hippolyta).* Historic range: U.S.A. (OR, WA). Status: Threatened.

Butterfly, Palos Verdes Blue *(Glaucopsyche lygdamus palosverdensis).* Historic range: U.S.A. (CA). Status: Endangered.

Butterfly, Queen Alexandra's Birdwing *(Troides alexandrae).* Historic range: Papua New Guinea. Status: Endangered.

Butterfly, San Bruno Elfin *(Callophrys mossii bayensis).* Historic range: U.S.A. (CA). Status: Endangered.

Butterfly, Schaus Swallowtail *(Heraclides aristodemus ponceanus).* Historic range: U.S.A. (FL). Status: Endangered.

Butterfly, Smith's Blue *(Euphilotes enoptes smithi).* Historic range: U.S.A. (CA). Status: Endangered.

Butterfly, Uncompahgre fritillary *(Boloria acrocnema).* Historic range: U.S.A. (CO). Status: Endangered.

Cahow *(Pterodroma cahow).* Brown and white earth-burrowing nocturnal bird. Historic range: North Atlantic Ocean: Bermuda. Status: Endangered.

Caiman, Apaporis River *(Caiman crocodilus apaporiensis).* Aquatic reptile closely related to alligators. Historic range: Colombia. Status: Endangered.

Caiman, Black *(Melanosuchus niger).* Aquatic reptile closely related to the alligator. Largest caiman. Only caiman which is a threat to man and domestic animals. Historic range: Amazon basin. Status: Endangered.

Caiman, Broad-snouted *(Caiman latirostris).* Aquatic reptile closely related to alligators. Historic range: Brazil, Argentina, Paraguay, Uruguay. Status: Endangered.

Caiman, Yacare *(Caiman crocodilus yacare).* Aquatic reptile closely related to alligators. Historic range: Bolivia, Argentina, Peru, Brazil. Status: Endangered.

Camel, Bactrian *(Camelus bactrianus).* Strong, heavily-built, two-humped camel. Historic range: Mongolia, China. Status: Endangered.

Caracara, Audubon's Crested *(Polyborus plancus audubonii).* Dark brown crested bird of prey associated with hawks and vultures. Historic range: U.S.A. (AZ, FL, LA, NM, TX) south to Panama; Cuba. Status: Threatened.

Caribou, Woodland *(Rangifer tarandus caribou).* Member of the deer family characterized by sweeping antlers and hanging neck mane. Inhabits rugged mountainous regions. Historic range: Canada, U.S.A. (AK, ID, ME, MI, MN, MT, NH, VT, WA, WI). Status: Endangered (part of S.E. Brit. Col. bounded by the Can.-USA border, Columbia R., Kootenay R., Kootenay L., and Kootenai R.), U.S.A. (ID, WA).

Cat, Andean *(Felis jacobita).* Historic range: Chile, Peru, Bolivia, Argentina. Status: Endangered.

Cat, Black-footed *(Felis nigripes).* Historic range: Southern Africa. Status: Endangered.

Cat, Flat-headed *(Felis planiceps).* Historic range: Southern Africa. Status: Endangered.

Cat, Iriomote *(Felis iriomotensis).* Historic range: Japan (Iriomote Island, Ryukyu Islands). Status: Endangered.

Cat, Leopard *(Felis bengalensis bengalensis).* Historic range: India, Southeast Asia. Status: Endangered.

Cat, Marbled *(Felis marmorata).* Historic range: Nepal, Southeast Asia, Indonesia. Status: Endangered.

Cat, Pakistan Sand *(Felis margarita scheffeli).* Historic range: Pakistan. Status: Endangered.

Cat, Temminck's *(Felis temmincki).* Historic range: Nepal, China, Southeast Asia, Indonesia (Sumatra). Status: Endangered.

Cat, Tiger *(Felis tigrinus).* Historic range: Costa Rica to northern Argentina. Status: Endangered.

Catfish *(Pangasius sanitwongsei).* Historic range: Thailand. Status: Endangered.

Catfish, Giant *(Pangasianodon gigas).* Historic range: Thailand. Status: Endangered.

Catfish, Yaqui *(Ictalurus pricei).* Historic range: U.S.A. (AZ), Mexico. Status: Threatened.

Cavefish, Alabama *(Speoplatyrhinus poulsoni).* Small, eyeless, albino cavefish found only in Key Cave. One of the rarest freshwater fishes in North America. Historic range: U.S.A. (AL). Status: Endangered.

Cavefish, Ozark *(Amblyopsis rosae).* Blind, albino cavefish. Historic range: U.S.A. (AR, MO, OK). Status: Threatened.

Chamois, Apennine *(Rupicapra rupicapra ornata).* A small goat- like animal. Historic range: Italy. Status: Endangered.

Cheetah *(Acinonyx jubatus).* Historic range: Africa to India. Status: Endangered.

Chimpanzee *(Pan troglodytes).* Historic range: Africa. Status: Endangered (wherever found in the wild); threatened: (wherever found in captivity).

Chimpanzee, Pygmy *(Pan paniscus).* Historic range: Zaire. Status: Endangered.

Chinchilla *(Chinchilla brevicaudata boliviana).* Fine-furred rodent resembling a squirrel, with large round ears. Historic range: Boliva. Status: Endangered.

Chub, Bonytail *(Gila elegans).* Large, silver minnow with greenish back. Historic range: U.S.A. (AZ, CA, CO, NV, UT, WY). Status: Endangered.

Chub, Borax Lake *(Gila boraxobius).* Member of the minnow family found only in Borax Lake area. Historic range: U.S.A. (OR). Status: Endangered.

Chub, Chihuahua *(Gila nigrescens).* Medium-sized minnow. Historic range: U.S.A. (NM), Mexico (Chihuahua). Status: Threatened.

Chub, Humpback *(Gila cypha).* Member of the minnow family, with distinctive hump behind its head. Historic range: U.S.A. (AZ, CO, UT, WY). Status: Endangered.

Chub, Hutton Tui *(Gila bicolor spp.)* Member of the minnow family. Historic range: U.S.A. (OR). Status: Threatened.

Chub, Mohave Tui *(Gila bicolor mohavensis).* Thick-bodied member of the minnow family. Historic range: U.S.A. (CA). Status: Endangered.

Chub, Owens Tui *(Gila bicolor snyderi).* Member of the minnow family. Historic range: U.S.A. (CA). Status: Endangered.

Chub, Pahranagat Roundtail *(Gila robusta jordani).* Medium-sized fish. Historic range: U.S.A. (NV). Status: Endangered.

Chub, Slender *(Hybopsis cahni).* Member of the minnow family. Historic range: U.S.A. (TN, VA). Status: Threatened.

Chub, Sonora *(Gila ditaenia).* Small member of the minnow family. Historic range: U.S.A. (AZ), Mexico. Status: Threatened.

Chub, Spotfin *(Cyprinella monacha).* Small member of the minnow family. Historic range: U.S.A. (AL, GA, NC, TN, VA). Status: Threatened.

Chub, Virgin River *(Gila robusta semidnuda).* Silvery medium- sized minnow found in a portion of the Virgin River Creek. Historic range: U.S.A. (AZ, NV, UT). Status: Endangered.

Chub, Yaqui *(Gila purpurea).* Silvery minnow. Historic range: U.S.A. (AZ), Mexico. Status: Endangered.

Chuckwalla, San Esteban Island *(Sauromalus varius).* Large herbivorous lizard. Historic range: Mexico. Status: Endangered.

Cicek (minnow), *(Acanthorutilus handlirschi).* Historic range: Turkey. Status: Endangered.

Civet, Malabar Large-spotted *(Viverra megaspila civettina).* Strong, agile, weasel-like cat with a long body and tail, and short legs. Historic range: India. Status: Endangered.

Cochito *(Phocoena sinus).* Mammal. Historic range: Mexico (Gulf of California). Status: Endangered.

Condor, Andean *(Vultur gryphus).* Closely related to the California Condor. Historic range: Colombia to Chile and Argentina. Status: Endangered.

Condor, California *(Gymnogyps califo rnianus).* Orange-headed vulture known as one of the largest flying birds in the world. Historic range: U.S.A. (OR, CA), Mexico (Baja California). Status: Endangered.

Coot, Hawaiian *(Fulica americana alai).* Subspecies of the American Coot. Gray waterbird with white frontal shield. Historic range: U.S.A. (HI). Status: Endangered.

Coqui, Golden *(Eleutherodactylus jasperi).* Gold colored frog. Inhabits dense bromeliad thickets found on mountaintops. Historic range: U.S.A. (PR). Status: Threatened.

Cotinga, Banded *(Cotinga maculata).* Tropical bird. Historic range: Brazil. Status: Endangered.

Cotinga, White-winged *(Xipholena atropurpurea).* Tropical bird. Historic range: Brazil. Status: Endangered.

Cougar, Eastern *(Felis concolor couguar).* Large cat inhabiting wilderness areas. Possibly extinct. Historic range: Eastern North America. Status: Endangered.

Crane, Black-necked *(Grus nigricollis).* Long-legged wading bird. Historic range: China (Tibet). Status: Endangered.

Crane, Cuba Sandhill *(Grus canadensis nesiotes).* Long-legged wading bird. Historic range: West Indies: Cuba. Status: Endangered.

Crane, Hooded *(Grus monacha).* Long-legged wading bird. Historic range: Japan, U.S.S.R. Status: Endangered.

Crane, Japanese *(Grus japonensis).* Long-legged wading bird. Historic range: China, Japan, Korea, U.S.S.R. Status: Endangered.

Crane, Mississippi Sandhill *(Grus canadensis pulla).* Large gray wading bird distinguished from other cranes by its darker color. Historic range: U.S.A. (MS). Status: Endangered.

Crane, Siberian White *(Grus leucogeranus).* Long-legged wading bird. Historic range: U.S.S.R. (Siberia) to India, including Iran and China. Status: Endangered.

Crane, White-naped *(Grus vipio).* Long-legged wading bird. Historic range: Mongolia. Status: Endangered.

Crane, Whooping *(Grus americana).* Tallest North American bird. Plumage is white, with black wing tips apparent during flight. Historic range: Canada, U.S.A. (Rocky Mountains east to Carolinas), Mexico. Status: Endangered.

Crayfish *(Cambarus zophonastes).* Historic range: U.S.A. (AR). Status: Endangered.

Crayfish, Nashville *(Orconectes shoupi).* Decapod crustacean found only in Mill Creek basin. Historic range: U.S.A. (TN). Status: Endangered.

Crayfish, Shasta *(Pacifastacus fortis).* Small decapod crustacean. Historic range: U.S.A. (CA). Status: Endangered.

Creeper, Hawaii *(Oreomystis mana).* Small honeycreeper with primarily olive-green plumage and slightly curved bill. Historic range: U.S.A. (HI). Status: Endangered.

Creeper, Molokai *(Paroreomyza flammea).* Small honeycreeper that often hangs upside down to dig insects out of tree bark. Males are orange with brown wings and tail. Historic range: U.S.A. (HI). Status: Endangered.

Creeper, Oahu *(Paroreomyza maculata).* Small finch-like bird. Historic range: U.S.A. (HI). Status: Endangered.

Crocodile, African Dwarf *(Osteolaemus tetraspis tetraspis).* Historic range: West Africa. Status: Endangered.

Crocodile, African Slender-snouted *(Crocodylus cataphractus).* Historic range: Western and central Africa. Status: Endangered.

Crocodile, American *(Crocodylus acutus).* Historic range: U.S.A. (FL), Mexico, South America, Central America, Caribbean. Status: Endangered.

Crocodile, Ceylon Mugger *(Crocodylus palustris kimbula).* Historic range: Sri Lanka. Status: Endangered.

Crocodile, Congo Dwarf *(Osteolaemus tetraspis osborni).* Historic range: Congo River drainage. Status: Endangered.

Crocodile, Cuban *(Crocodylus rhombifer).* Historic range: Cuba. Status: Endangered.

Crocodile, Morelet's *(Crocodylus moreletii).* Historic range: Mexico, Belize, Guatemala. Status: Endangered.

Crocodile, Mugger *(Crocodylus palustris palustris).* Historic range: India, Pakistan, Iran, Bangladesh. Status: Endangered.

Crocodile, Nile *(Crocodylus niloticus).* Historic range: Africa, Middle East. Status: Endangered; threatened (Zimbabwe).

Crocodile, Orinoco *(Crocodylus intermedius).* Historic range: South America: Orinoco River Basin. Status: Endangered.

Crocodile, Philippine *(Crocodylus novaeguineae mindorensis).* Historic range: Philippine Islands. Status: Endangered.

Crocodile, Saltwater *(Crocodylus porosus).* Historic range: Southeast Asia, Australia, Papua-New Guinea, Pacific Islands. Status: Endangered (except Paupa-New Guinea).

Crocodile, Siamese *(Crocodylus siamensis).* Historic range: Southeast Asia, Malay Peninsula. Status: Endangered.

Crow, Hawaiian *(Corvus hawaiiensis).* Historic range: U.S.A. (HI). Status: Endangered.

Crow, Mariana *(Corvus kubaryi).* Historic range: Western Pacific Ocean: U.S.A. (Guam, Rota). Status: Endangered.

Crow, White-necked *(Corvus leucognaphalus).* Historic range: U.S.A. (PR), Dominican Republic, Haiti. Status: Endangered.

Cuckoo-Shrike, Mauritius *(Coquus typicus).* Songbird not related to cuckoos or shrikes. Historic range: Indian Ocean: Mauritius. Status: Endangered.

Cuckoo-Shrike, Reunion *(Coquus newtoni).* Songbird not related to cuckoos or shrikes. Historic range: Indian Ocean: Reunion. Status: Endangered.

Cui-ui *(Chasmistes cujus).* Rare bottom-feeding sucker primarily found in the Truckee River. Historic range: U.S.A. (NV). Status: Endangered.

Curassow, Razor-billed *(Mitu mitu mitu).* Tropical fowl-like bird. Historic range: Brazil (Eastern). Status: Endangered.

Curassow, Red-billed *(Crax blumenbachii).* Tropical fowl-like bird. Historic range: Brazil. Status: Endangered.

Curassow, Trinidad White-headed *(Pipile pipile pipile).* Tropical fowl-like bird. Historic range: West Indies: Trinidad. Status: Endangered.

Curlew, Eskimo *(Numenius borealis).* A long-legged dark brown wading bird with a long, down-curved bill. Historic range: Alaska and northern Canada to Argentina. Status: Endangered.

Dace, Ash Meadows Speckled *(Rhinichthys osculus nevadensis).* Small silvery minnow. Historic range: U.S.A. (NV). Status: Endangered.

Dace, Blackside *(Phoxinus cumberlandensis).* Small fish distinguished by a black lateral stripe. Historic range: U.S.A. (TN, KY). Status: Threatened.

Dace, Clover Valley Speckled *(Rhinichthys osculus oligoporus).* Member of the minnow family. Historic range: U.S.A. (NV). Status: Endangered.

Dace, Desert *(Eremichthys acros).* Olive green minnow. Historic range: U.S.A. (NV). Status: Threatened.

Dace, Foskett Speckled *(Rhinichthys osculus ssp.).* Silvery minnow with dark blotches. Historic range: U.S.A. (OR). Status: Threatened.

Dace, Independence Valley Speckled *(Rhinichthys osculus lethoporus).* Member of the minnow family found only in one spring in Elko County. Historic range: U.S.A. (NV). Status: Endangered.

Dace, Kendall Warm Springs *(Rhinichthys osculus thermalis).* Small minnow found in the Kendall Warm Springs. Historic range: U.S.A. (WY). Status: Endangered.

Dace, Moapa *(Moapa coriacea).* Member of the minnow family. Historic range: U.S.A. (NV). Status: Endangered.

Darter, Amber *(Percina antesella).* Short, slender-bodied fish belonging to the perch family. Historic range: U.S.A. (GA, TN). Status: Endangered.

Darter, Bayou *(Etheostoma rubrum).* Member of the perch family. Historic range: U.S.A. (MS). Status: Threatened.

Darter, Boulder *(Etheostoma wapiti).* Member of the perch family. Historic range: U.S.A. (TN, AL). Status: Endangered.

Darter, Fountain *(Etheostoma fonticola).* Reddish brown fish belonging to the perch family. Historic range: U.S.A. (TX). Status: Endangered.

Darter, Leopard *(Percina pantherina).* Small dark-spotted member of the perch family. Historic range: U.S.A. (AR, OK). Status: Threatened.

Darter, Maryland *(Etheostoma sellare).* Member of the perch family with four distinctive dark markings. Historic range: U.S.A. (MD). Status: Endangered.

Darter, Niangua *(Etheostoma nianguae).* Member of the perch family with eight distinctive dark bars across its back. Historic range: U.S.A. (MO). Status: Threatened.

Darter, Okaloosa *(Etheostoma okaloosae).* Member of the perch family characterized by large, transparent fins. Historic range: U.S.A. (FL). Status: Endangered.

Darter, Slackwater *(Etheostoma boschungi).* Medium-sized member of the perch family. Historic range: U.S.A. (AL, TN). Status: Threatened.

Darter, Snail *(Percina tanasi).* Small member of the perch family. Historic range: U.S.A. (AL, GA, TN). Status: Threatened.

Darter, Watercress *(Etheostoma nuchale).* Small member of the perch family. Historic range: U.S.A. (AL). Status: Endangered.

Deer, Bactrian *(Cervus elaphus bactrianus).* Historic range: U.S.S.R., Afghanistan. Status: Endangered.

Deer, Barbary *(Cervus elaphus barbarus).* Historic range: Morocco, Tunisia, Algeria. Status: Endangered.

Deer, Bawean *(Axis porcinus kuhli).* Historic range: Indonesia. Status: Endangered.

Deer, Cedros Island Mule *(Odocoileus hemionus cedrosensis).* Historic range: Mexico (Cedros Island). Status: Endangered.

Deer, Columbian White-tailed *(Odocoileus virginianus leucurus).* Historic range: U.S.A. (WA, OR). Status: Endangered.

Deer, Corsican Red *(Cervus elaphus corsicanus).* Historic range: Corsica, Sardinia. Status: Endangered.

Deer, Eld's Brow-antlered *(Cervus eldi).* Historic range: India to Southeast Asia. Status: Endangered.

Deer, Formosan Sika *(Cervus nippon taiouanus).* Historic range: Taiwan. Status: Endangered.

Deer, Hog *(Axis porcinus annamiticus).* Historic range: Thailand, Indochina. Status: Endangered.

Deer, Key *(Odocoileus virginianus clavium).* Historic range: U.S.A. (FL). Status: Endangered.

Deer, Marsh *(Blastocerus dichotomus).* Historic range: Argentina, Uruguay, Paraguay, Bolivia, Brazil. Status: Endangered.

Deer, McNeill's *(Cervus elaphus macneilii).* Historic range: China (Sinkiang, Tibet). Status: Endangered.

Deer, Musk *(Moschus spp.).* Historic range: Central and East Asia. Status: Endangered (Afghanistan, Bhutan, Burma, China îTibet, Yunnanï, India, Nepal, Pakistan, Sikkim).

Deer, North China Sika *(Cervus nippon mandarinus).* Historic range: China (Shantung and Chihli Provinces). Status: Endangered.

Deer, Pampas *(Ozotoceros bezoarticus).* Historic range: Brazil, Argentina, Uruguay, Bolivia, Paraguay. Status: Endangered.

Deer, Persian Fallow *(Dama dama mesopotamica).* Historic range: Iraq, Iran. Status: Endangered.

Deer, Philippine *(Axis porcinus calamianensis).* Historic range: Philippines (Calamian Islands). Status: Endangered.

Deer, Ryukyu Sika *(Cervus nippon keramae).* Historic range: Japan (Ryukyu Islands). Status: Endangered.

Deer, Shansi Sika *(Cervus nippon grassianus).* Historic range: China (Shansi Province). Status: Endangered.

Deer, South China Sika *(Cervus nippon kopschi).* Historic range: Southern China. Status: Endangered.

Deer, Swamp *(Cervus duvauceli).* Historic range: India, Nepal. Status: Endangered.

Deer, Visayan *(Cervus Alfredi).* Historic range: Philippines. Status: Endangered.

Deer, Yarkand *(Cervus elaphus yarkandensis).* Historic range: China (Sinkiang). Status: Endangered.

Dhole *(Cuon alpinus).* Fierce wild dog that hunts in packs. Historic range: U.S.S.R., Korea, China, India, Southeast Asia. Status: Endangered.

Dibbler *(Antechinus apicalis).* Mammal. Historic range: Australia. Status: Endangered.

Dog, African Wild *(Lycaon pictus).* Historic range: Sub- Saharan Africa. Status: Endangered.

Dolphin, Chinese River *(Lipotes vexillifer).* Historic range: China. Status: Endangered.

Dolphin, Indus River *(Platanista minor).* Historic range: Pakistan (Indus River and tributaries). Status: Endangered.

Dove, Cloven-feathered *(Drepanoptila holosericea).* Historic range: Southwest Pacific Ocean: New Caledonia. Status: Endangered.

Dove, Grenada Gray-fronted *(Leptotila rufaxilla wellsi).* Historic range: West Indies: Grenada. Status: Endangered.

Drill *(Papio leucophaeus).* Baboon closely related to the typical madrills. Historic range: Equatorial West Africa. Status: Endangered.

Duck, Hawaiian *(Anas wyvilliana).* A dark brown mallard closely related to the Laysan Duck. Historic range: U.S.A. (HI). Status: Endangered.

Duck, Laysan *(Anas laysanensis).* Dark, reddish brown duck with white patches around its eyes. Appearance resembles a female mallard. Historic range: U.S.A. (HI). Status: Endangered.

Duck, Pink-headed *(Rhodonessa caryophyllacea).* Historic range: India. Status: Endangered.

Duck, White-winged Wood *(Cairina scutulata).* Historic range: India, Malaysia, Indonesia, Thailand. Status: Endangered.

Dugong *(Dugong dugon).* Large, aquatic herbivorous mammal related to the manitee. Historic range: East Africa to southern Japan, including U.S.A. (Trust Territories). Status: Endangered.

Duiker, Jentink's *(Cephalophus jentinki).* Small antelope. Historic range: Sierra Leone, Liberia, Ivory Coast. Status: Endangered.

Eagle, Bald *(Haliaeetus leucocephalus).* Historic range: North America south to northern Mexico. Status: Endangered; threatened (WA, OR, MN, WI, MI).

Eagle, Greenland White-tailed *(Haliaeetus albicilla groenlandicus).* Historic range: Greenland and adjacent Atlantic islands. Status: Endangered.

Eagle, Harpy *(Harpia harpyja).* Historic range: Mexico south to Argentina. Status: Endangered.

Eagle, Philippine *(Pithecophaga jefferyi).* Historic range: Philippines. Status: Endangered.

Eagle, Spanish Imperial *(Aquila heliaca adalberti).* Historic range: Spain, Morocco, Algeria. Status: Endangered.

Egret, Chinese *(Egretta eulophotes).* Historic range: China, Korea. Status: Endangered.

Eland, Western Giant *(Taurotragus derbianus derbianus).* Large antelope with short, spirally twisted horns. Historic range: Senegal to Ivory Coast. Status: Endangered.

Elephant, African *(Loxodonta africana).* Historic range: Africa. Status: Threatened.

Elephant, Asian *(Elephas maximus).* Historic range: South-central and Southeast Asia. Status: Endangered.

Falcon, American Peregrine *(Falco peregrinus anatum).* Medium-sized bird of prey. Historic range: Nests from central Alaska across north-central Canada to central Mexico; winters south to South America. Status: Endangered.

Falcon, Arctic Peregrine *(Falco peregrinus tundrius).* Peregrine subspecies characterized by paler coloration. Historic range: Nests from northern Alaska to Greenland; winters south to Central and South America. Status: Threatened.

Falcon, Eurasian Peregrine *(Falco peregrinus peregrinus).* Peregrine falcon subspecies. Historic range: Europe, Eurasia south to Africa and Mideast. Status: Endangered.

Falcon, Northern Aplomado *(Falco femoralis septentrionalis).* Medium-sized bird of prey with distinctive black and white facial markings. Historic range: U.S.A. (AZ, NM, TX), Mexico, Guatemala. Status: Endangered.

Falcon, Peregrine *(Falco peregrinus).* Medium-sized bird of prey. Historic range: Worldwide, except Antarctica and most Pacific Islands. Status: Endangered.

Fanshell *(Cyprogenia stegaria).* Clam. Historic range: U.S.A. (AL, IL, IN, KY, OH, PA, TN, VA, WV). Status: Endangered.

Fatmucket, Arkansas *(Lampsilis powelli).* Clam. Historic range: U.S.A. (AR). Status: Threatened.

Ferret, Black-footed *(Mustela nigripes).* Nocturnal slender- bodied weasel with pale yellow fur, and dark feet and tail. Historic range: Western U.S.A., Western Canada. Status: Endangered.

Finch, Laysan (honeycreeper), *(Telespyza cantans).* Songbird with distinctive bluish gray bill. Historic range: U.S.A. (HI). Status: Endangered.

Finch, Nihoa (honeycreeper), *(Telespyza ultima).* Songbird found on Nihoa Island. Historic range: U.S.A. (HI). Status: Endangered.

Flycatcher, Euler's *(Empidonax euleri johnstonei).* Belongs to a family of birds that catches flies and other insects in the air. Historic range: West Indies: Grenada. Status: Endangered.

Flycatcher, Seychelles Paradise *(Terpsiphone corvina).* Belongs to a family of birds that catches flies and other insects in the air. Historic range: Indian Ocean: Seychelles. Status: Endangered.

Flycatcher, Tahiti *(Pomerea nigra).* Belongs to a family of birds that catches flies and other insects in the air. Historic range: South Pacific Ocean: Tahiti. Status: Endangered.

Fody, Seychelles (weaver-finch), *(Foudia sechellarum).* Historic range: Indian Ocean: Seychelles. Status: Endangered.

Fox, Northern Swift *(Vulpes velox hebes).* Smallest of the foxes, with long, pointed ears. Historic range: U.S.A. (northern plains), Canada. Status: Endangered (Canada).

Fox, San Joaquin Kit *(Vulpes macrotis mutica).* Small long-tailed fox inhabiting dens near freshwater marshes. Historic range: U.S.A. (CA). Status: Endangered.

Fox, Simien *(Canis simensis).* Large golden wolf-like fox that feeds on locusts and small rodents. Historic range: Ethiopia. Status: Endangered.

Frigatebird, Andrew's *(Fregata andrewsi).* Bird with a large wingspan, related to the pelican. Historic range: East Indian Ocean. Status: Endangered.

Frog, Israel Painted *(Discoglossus nigriventer).* Historic range: Israel. Status: Endangered.

Frog, Panamanian Golden *(Atelopus varius zeteki).* Historic range: Panama. Status: Endangered.

Frog, Stephen Island *(Leiopelma hamiltoni).* Historic range: New Zealand. Status: Endangered.

Gambusia, Big Bend *(Gambusia gaigei).* Small yellowish fish found in the outflow of one spring in Big Bend National Park. Historic range: U.S.A. (TX). Status: Endangered.

Gambusia, Clear Creek *(Gambusia heterochir).* Small fish with distinctive markings. Historic range: U.S.A. (TX). Status: Endangered.

Gambusia, Pecos *(Gambusia nobilis).* Small fish also known as the Texas gambusia. Historic range: U.S.A. (NM, TX). Status: Endangered.

Gambusia, San Marcos *(Gambusia georgei).* Fish found only in one section of the San Marcos River. Historic range: U.S.A. (TX). Status: Endangered.

Gavial *(Gavialis gangeticus).* Large harmless crocodilian. Historic range: Pakistan, Burma, Bangladesh, India, Nepal. Status: Endangered.

Gazelle, Arabian *(Gazella gazella).* Historic range: Arabian Peninsula, Palestine, Sinai. Status: Endangered.

Gazelle, Clark's *(Ammodorcas clarkei).* Historic range: Somalia, Ethiopia. Status: Endangered.

Gazelle, Cuvier's *(Gazella cuvieri).* Historic range: Morocco. Status: Endangered.Gazelle, Mhorr (Gazella dama mhorr). Historic range: Morocco. Status: Endangered.

Gazelle, Moroccan *(Gazella dorcas massaesyla).* Historic range: Morocco, Algeria, Tunisia. Status: Endangered.

Gazelle, Pelzeln's *(Gazella dorcas pelzelni).* Historic range: Somalia. Status: Endangered.

Gazelle, Rio de Oro Dama *(Gazella dama lozanoi).* Historic range: Western Sahara. Status: Endangered.

Gazelle, Sand *(Gazella subgutturosa marica).* Historic range: Jordan, Arabian Peninsula. Status: Endangered.

Gazelle, Saudi Arabian *(Gazella dorcas saudiya).* Historic range: Israel, Iraq, Jordan, Syria, Arabian Peninsula. Status: Endangered.

Gazelle, Slender-horned *(Gazella leptoceros).* Historic range: Sudan, Egypt, Algeria, Libya. Status: Endangered.

Gecko, Day *(Phelsuma edwardnewtoni).* Small lizard that feeds on insects. Historic range: Indian Ocean: Mauritius. Status: Endangered.

Gecko, Monito *(Sphaerodactylus micropithecus).* Small lizard found on Monito Island. Historic range: U.S.A. (PR). Status: Endangered.

Gecko, Round Island Day *(Phelsuma guentheri).* Small lizard that feeds on insects. Historic range: Indian Ocean: Mauritius. Status: Endangered.

Gecko, Serpent Island *(Cyrtodactylus serpensinsula).* Small lizard that feeds on insects. Historic range: Indian Ocean: Mauritius. Status: Threatened.

Gibbons *(Hylobates spp.).* Smallest of the great apes with distinctive long arms, including Nomascus. Historic range: China, India, Southeast Asia. Status: Endangered.

Goat, Wild *(Capra aegagrus).* Historic range: Southwestern Asia. Status: Endangered (Chiltan Range of west-central Pakistan).

Goose, Aleutian Canada *(Branta canadensis leucopareia).* Smaller subspecies of the common Canada goose. Historic range: U.S.A. (AK, CA, OR, WA), Japan. Status: Endangered.

Goose, Hawaiian *(Nesochen sandvicensis).* Barred gray-brown goose inhabiting volcanic slopes. Historic range: U.S.A. (HI). Status: Endangered.

Goral *(Nemorhaedus goral).* Goat antelope inhabiting grassy slopes, scrub forests and rocky mountainsides. Historic range: East Asia. Status: Endangered.

Gorilla *(Gorilla gorilla).* Historic range: Central and Western Africa. Status: Endangered.

Goshawk, Christmas Island *(Accipiter fasciatus natalis).* Aggressive bird of prey. Historic range: Indian Ocean: Christmas Island. Status: Endangered.

Grackle, Slender-illed *(Quisicalus palustris).* Historic range: Mexico. Status: Endangered.

Grasswren, Eyrean (flycatcher), *(Amytornis goyderi).* Historic range: Australia. Status: Endangered.

Grebe, Atitlan *(Podilymbus gigas).* A swimming and diving bird. Historic range: Guatemala. Status: Endangered.

Greenshank, Nordmann's *(Tringa guttifer).* Bird. Historic range: U.S.S.R., Japan, south to Malaya, Borneo. Status: Endangered.

Guan, Horned *(Oreophasis derbianus).* Large, tropical forest bird. Historic range: Guatemala, Mexico. Status: Endangered.

Guan, White-winged *(Penelope albipennis).* Historic range: Peru. Status: Endangered.

Gull, Audouin's *(Larus audouinii).* Historic range: Mediterranean Sea. Status: Endangered.

Gull, Relict *(Larus relictus).* Historic range: India, China. Status: Endangered.

Hare, Hispid *(Caprolagus hispidus).* Wild rabbit with coarse fur. Historic range: India, Nepal, Bhutan. Status: Endangered.

Hartebeest, Swayne's *(Alcelaphus buselaphus swaynei).* Large, graceful, timid antelope, among the fastest of the larger antelopes. Historic range: Ethiopia, Somalia. Status: Endangered.

Hartebeest, Tora *(Alcelaphus buselaphus tora).* Large, graceful, timid antelope, among the fastest of the larger antelopes. Historic range: Ethiopia, Sudan, Egypt. Status: Endangered.

Harvestman, Bee Creek Cave *(Texella reddelli).* Pale, eyeless spider. Historic range: U.S.A. (TX). Status: Endangered.

Hawk, Anjouan Island Sparrow *(Accipiter francesii pusillus).* Historic range: Indian Ocean: Comoro Islands. Status: Endangered.

Hawk, Galapagos *(Buteo galapagoensis).* Historic range: Ecuador (Galapagos Islands). Status: Endangered.

Hawk, Hawaiian *(Buteo solitarius).* Historic range: U.S.A. (HI). Status: Endangered.

Heelsplitter, Inflated *(Potamilus inflatus).* Clam. Historic range: U.S.A. (AL, LA, MS). Status: Threatened.

Hermit, Hook-billed (hummingbird), *(Glaucis dohrnii).* Historic range: Brazil. Status: Endangered.

Hog, Pygmy *(Sus salvanius).* Smallest of the pigs. Inhabits forests. Historic range: India, Nepal, Bhutan, Sikkim. Status: Endangered.

Honeycreeper, Crested *(Palmeria dolei).* Dark bird with orange nape. Largest of the Hawaiian honeycreepers. Historic range: U.S.A. (HI). Status: Endangered.

Honeyeater, Helmeted *(Meliphaga cassidix).* Songbird whose tubular tongue is adapted for sucking nectar from flowers. Historic range: Australia. Status: Endangered.

Hornbill, Helmeted *(Rhinoplax vigil).* Jungle-dwelling bird with a horny growth on its bill. Historic range: Thailand, Malaysia. Status: Endangered.

Horse, Przewalski's *(Equus przewalskii).* Small-bodied horse with a short, erect mane. It is the only remaining wild horse not descended from domestic animals. Historic range: Mongolia, China. Status: Endangered.

Huemul, North Andean *(Hippocamelus antisensis).* Deer inhabiting the Andes, characterized by an unusual lack of wariness. Historic range: Ecuador, Peru, Chile, Bolivia, Argentina. Status: Endangered.

Huemul, South Andean *(Hippocamelus bisulcus).* Deer inhabiting the Andes, characterized by an unusual lack of wariness. Historic range: Chile, Argentina. Status: Endangered.

Hutia, Cabrera's *(Capromys angelcabrerai).* Heavy, thick-set rodent. Historic range: Cuba. Status: Endangered.

Hutia, Dwarf *(Capromys nana).* Heavy, thick-set rodent. Historic range: Cuba. Status: Endangered.

Hutia, Large-eared *(Capromys auritus).* Heavy, thick-set rodent. Historic range: Cuba. Status: Endangered.

Hutia, Little Earth *(Capromys sanfelipensis).* Heavy, thick-set rodent. Historic range: Cuba. Status: Endangered.

Hyena, Barbary *(Hyaena hyaena barbara).* Historic range: Morocco, Algeria, Tunisia. Status: Endangered.

Hyena, Brown *(Hyaena brunnea).* Historic range: Southern Africa. Status: Endangered.

Ibex, Pyrenean *(Capra pyrenaica pyrenaica).* Agile, sure- footed goat with sweeping horns. Historic range: Spain. Status: Endangered.

Ibex, Walia *(Capra walie).* Agile, sure-footed goat with sweeping horns. Historic range: Ethiopia. Status: Endangered.

Ibis, Japanese Crested *(Nipponia nippon).* Wading bird related to the heron. Historic range: China, Japan, U.S.S.R., Korea. Status: Endangered.

Ibis, Northern Bald *(Geronticus eremita).* Historic range: Southern Europe, southwestern Asia, northern Africa). Status: Endangered.

Iguana, Acklins Ground *(Cyclura rileyi nuchalis).* Historic range: West Indies: Bahamas. Status: Threatened.

Iguana, Allen's Cay *(Cyclura cychlura inornata).* Historic range: West Indies: Bahamas. Status: Threatened.

Iguana, Andros Island Ground *(Cyclura cychlura cychlura).* Historic range: West Indies: Bahamas. Status: Threatened.

Iguana, Anegada Ground *(Cyclura pinguis).* Historic range: West Indies: British Virgin Islands (Anegada Island). Status: Endangered.

Iguana, Barrington Land *(Conolophus pallidus).* Historic range: Ecuador (Galapagos Islands). Status: Endangered.

Iguana, Cayman Brac Ground *(Cyclura nubila caymanensis).* Historic range: West Indies: Cayman Islands. Status: Threatened.

Iguana, Cuban Ground *(Cyclura nubila nubila).* Historic range: Cuba. Status: Threatened (except Puerto Rico).

Iguana, Exuma Island *(Cyclura cychlura figginsi).* Historic range: West Indies: Bahamas. Status: Threatened.

Iguana, Fiji Banded *(Brachylophus fasciatus).* Historic range: Pacific: Fiji, Tonga. Status: Endangered.

Iguana, Fiji Crested *(Brachylophus vitiensis).* Historic range: Pacific: Fiji. Status: Endangered.

Iguana, Grand Cayman Ground *(Cyclura nubila lewisi).* Historic range: West Indies: Cayman Islands. Status: Endangered.

Iguana, Jamaican *(Cyclura collei).* Historic range: West Indies: Jamaica. Status: Endangered.

Iguana, Mayaguana *(Cyclura carinata bartschi).* Historic range: West Indies: Bahamas. Status: Threatened.

Iguana, Mona Ground *(Cyclura stejnegeri).* Historic range: U.S.A. (PR: Mona Island). Status: Threatened.

Iguana, Turks and Caicos *(Cyclura carinata carinata).* Historic range: West Indies: Turks and Caicos Islands. Status: Threatened.

Iguana, Watling Island Ground *(Cyclura rileyi rileyi).* Historic range: West Indies: Bahamas. Status: Endangered.

Iguana, White Cay Ground *(Cyclura rileyi cristata).* Historic range: West Indies: Bahamas. Status: Threatened.

Impala, Black-faced *(Aepyceros melampus petersi).* Graceful, nomadic antelope known for its leaping ability. Historic range: Namibia, Angola. Status: Endangered.

Indri *(Indri indri).* Large black and white monkey-like lemur with no tail. Historic range: Malagasy Republic. Status: Endangered.

Isopod, Madison Cave *(Antrolana lira).* A white, eyeless shrimp-like crustacean endemic to Madison Cave and nearby fissures and channels. Historic range: U.S.A. (VA). Status: Threatened.

Isopod, Socorro *(Thermosphaeroma thermophilus).* Tiny, flat, oblong aquatic crustacean found in Socorro County. Historic range: U.S.A. (NM). Status: Endangered.

Jaguar *(Panthera onca).* Historic range: U.S.A. (TX, NM, AZ), Central and South America. Status: Endangered (Mexico southward).

Jaguarundi *(Felis yagouaroundi cacomitli).* Unspotted brownish gray cat about twice the size of a large domestic cat. Inhabits dense undergrowth. One of four subspecies. Historic range: U.S.A. (TX), Mexico. Status: Endangered.

Jaguarundi *(Felis yagouaroundi fossata).* Unspotted brownish gray cat about twice the size of a large domestic cat. Inhabits dense undergrowth. One of four subspecies. Historic range: Mexico, Nicaragua. Status: Endangered.

Jaguarundi *(Felis yagouaroundi panamensis).* Unspotted brownish gray cat about twice the size of a large domestic cat. Inhabits dense undergrowth. One of four subspecies. Historic range: Nicaragua, Costa Rica, Panama. Status: Endangered.

Jaguarundi *(Felis yagouaroundi tolteca).* Unspotted brownish gray cat about twice the size of a large domestic cat. Inhabits dense undergrowth. One of four subspecies. Historic range: U.S.A. (AZ), Mexico. Status: Endangered.

Jay, Florida Scrub *(Aphelocoma coerulescens coerulescens).* Crestless jay with blue wings and tail. Inhabits thickets of scrub oaks. Historic range: U.S.A. (FL). Status: Threatened.

Kagu *(Rhynochetos jubatus).* Chicken-sized bird with gray plumage and orange-red feet that is barely able to fly. Historic range: South Pacific Ocean: New Caledonia. Status: Endangered.

Kakapo *(Strigops habroptilus).* Chiefly nocturnal burrowing parrot. Historic range: New Zealand. Status: Endangered.

Kangaroo, Eastern Gray *(Macropus giganteus* - all subspecies except *tasmaniensis).* Historic range: Australia. Status: Threatened.

Kangaroo, Red *(Macropus rufus).* Historic range: Australia. Status: Threatened.

Kangaroo, Tasmanian forester *(Macropus giganteus tasmaniensis).* Historic range: Australia (Tasmania). Status: Endangered.

Kangaroo, Western Gray *(Macropus fuliginosus).* Historic range: Australia. Status: Threatened.

Kestrel, Mauritius *(Falco punctatus).* Small falcon. Historic range: Indian Ocean: Mauritius. Status: Endangered.

Kestrel, Seychelles *(Falco araea).* Small falcon. Historic range: Indian Ocean: Seychelles Islands. Status: Endangered.

Killifish, Pahrump *(Empetrichthys latos).* Slender fish inhabiting alkaline mineral springs. Historic range: U.S.A. (NV). Status: Endangered.

Kingfisher, Guam Micronesian *(Halcyon cinnamomina cinnamomina).* Belligerent bird with a distinctive crest. Historic range: West Pacific Ocean: U.S.A. (Guam). Status: Endangered.

Kite, Cuba Hook-billed *(Chondrohierax uncinatus wilsonii).* Bird of prey. Historic range: West Indies: Cuba. Status: Endangered.

Kite, Everglade Snail *(Rostrhamus sociabilis plumbeus).* Gray, snail-eating hawk. Historic range: U.S.A. (FL), Cuba. Status: Endangered.

Kite, Grenada Hook-billed *(Chondrohierax uncinatus mirus).* Bird of prey. Historic range: West Indies: Grenada. Status: Endangered.

Kokako (wattlebird), *(Callaeas cinerea).* Historic range: New Zealand. Status: Endangered.

Kouprey *(Bos sauveli).* Blackish brown ox-like animal with short, glossy fur. Historic range: Vietnam, Laos, Cambodia, Thailand. Status: Endangered.

Langur, Capped *(Presbytis pileata).* Monkey with long, narrow hands and feet, long tail and slender body. Historic range: India, Burma, Bangladesh. Status: Endangered.

Langur, Douc *(Pygathrix nemaeus).* Monkey with long, narrow hands and feet, long tail and slender body. Historic range: Cambodia, Laos, Vietnam. Status: Endangered.

Langur, Entellus *(Presbytis entellus).* Monkey with long, narrow hands and feet, long tail and slender body. Historic range: China (Tibet), India, Pakistan, Kashmir, Sri Lanka, Sikkim, Bangladesh. Status: Endangered.

Langur, Francois' *(Presbytis francoisi).* Monkey with long narrow hands and feet, long tail and slender body. Historic range: China (Kwangsi), Indochina. Status: Endangered.

Langur, Golden *(Presbytis geei).* Monkey with long, narrow hands and feet, long tail and slender body. Historic range: India (Assam), Bhutan. Status: Endangered.

Langur, Long-tailed *(Presbytis potenziani).* Monkey with long, narrow hands and feet, long tail and slender body. Historic range: Indonesia. Status: Threatened.

Langur, Pagi Island *(Nasalis concolor).* Monkey with long, narrow hands and feet, long tail and slender body. Historic range: Indonesia. Status: Endangered.

Langur, Purple-faced *(Presbytis senex).* Monkey with long, narrow hands and feet, long tail and slender body. Historic range: Sri Lanka. Status: Threatened.

Lechwe, Red *(Kobus leche).* Long-horned antelope inhabiting plains and swamps. Historic range: Southern Africa. Status: Threatened.

Lemurs *(Lemuridae* incl. *Cheirogaleidae, Lepilemuridae;* all members of genera *Lemur, Phaner, Hapalemur, Lepilemur, Microcebus, Allocebus, Cheirogaleus, Varecia).* Nocturnal, arboreal monkey-like mammals with large eyes, soft fur, and long tail. Historic range: Madagascar. Status: Endangered.

Leopard *(Panthera pardus).* Historic range: Africa, Asia. Status: Endangered (except where threatened); threatened (in Africa, in the wild, south of, and including, the following countries: Gabon, Congo, Zaire, Uganda, Kenya).

Leopard, Clouded *(Neofelis nebulosa).* Historic range: Southeast and south-central Asia, Taiwan. Status: Endangered.

Leopard, Snow *(Panthera uncia).* Historic range: Central Asia. Status: Endangered.

Linsang, Spotted *(Prionodon pardicolor).* Resembles a long-tailed cat. Related to civets and genets. Historic range: Nepal, Assam, Vietnam, Cambodia, Laos, Burma. Status: Endangered.

Lion, Asiatic *(Panthera leo persica).* Historic range: Turkey to India. Status: Endangered.

Lizard, Blunt-nosed Leopard *(Gambelia silus).* Historic range: U.S.A. (CA). Status: Endangered.

Lizard, Coachella Valley Fringe-toed *(Uma inornata).* Historic range: U.S.A. (CA). Status: Threatened.

Lizard, Hierro Giant *(Gallotia simonyi simonyi).* Historic range: Spain (Canary Islands). Status: Endangered.

Lizard, Ibiza Wall *(Podarcis pityusensis).* Historic range: Spain (Balearic Islands). Status: Threatened.

Lizard, Island Night *(Xantusia riversiana).* Historic range: U.S.A. (CA). Status: Threatened.

Lizard, St. Croix Ground *(Ameiva polops).* Historic range: U.S.A. (VI). Status: Endangered.

Logperch, Conasauga *(Percina jenkinsi).* Large, slender fish with distinctive "tiger stripes," found only in portions of the upper Conasauga River. Historic range: U.S.A. (GA, TN). Status: Endangered.

Logperch, Roanoke *(Percina rex).* Historic range: U.S.A. (VA). Status: Endangered.

Loris, Lesser Slow *(Nycticebus pygmaeus).* Nocturnal slow-moving lemur. Historic range: Indochina. Status: Threatened.

Lynx, Spanish *(Felis pardina).* Historic range: Spain, Portugal. Status: Endangered.

Macaque, Formosan Rock *(Macaca cyclopis).* Intelligent, curious monkey. Historic range: Taiwan. Status: Threatened.

Macaque, Japanese *(Macaca fuscata).* Intelligent, curious monkey. Historic range: Japan (Shikoku, Kyushu and Honshu Islands). Status: Threatened.

Macaque, Lion-tailed *(Macaca silenus).* Intelligent, curious monkey. Historic range: India. Status: Endangered.

Macaque, Stump-tailed *(Macaca arctoides).* Intelligent, curious monkey. Historic range: India (Assam) to southern China. Status: Threatened.

Macaque, Toque *(Macaca sinica).* Intelligent, curious monkey. Historic range: Sri Lanka. Status: Threatened.

Macaw, Glaucous *(Anodorhynchus glaucus).* Historic range: Paraguay, Uruguay, Brazil. Status: Endangered.

Macaw, Indigo *(Anodorhynchus leari).* Historic range: Brazil. Status: Endangered.

Macaw, Little Blue *(Cyanopsitta spixii).* Historic range: Brazil. Status: Endangered.

Madtom, Neosho *(Notorus placidus).* Historic range: U.S.A. (KS, MO, OK). Status: Threatened.

Madtom, Scioto *(Noturus trautmani).* Small catfish. Historic range: U.S.A. (OH). Status: Endangered.

Madtom, Smoky *(Noturus baileyi).* Small catfish. Historic range: U.S.A. (TN). Status: Endangered.

Madtom, Yellowfin *(Noturus flavipinnis).* Catfish. Historic range: U.S.A. (TN, VA). Status: Threatened (except experimental populations); XN (N. Fork Holston R., VA, TN; S. Fork Holston R., upstream to Ft. Patrick Henry Dam, TN; Holston R., downstream to John Sevier Detention Lake Dam, TN; and all tributaries thereto).

Magpie-Robin, Seychelles (thrush), *(Copsychus sechellarum).* Historic range: Indian Ocean: Seychelles Islands. Status: Endangered.

Malkoha, Red-Faced (cuckoo), *(Phaenicophaeus pyrrhocephalus).* Historic range: Sri Lanka. Status: Endangered.

Mallard, Mariana *(Anas oustaleti).* Historic range: West Pacific Ocean: U.S.A. (Guam, Mariana Islands). Status: Endangered.

Manatee, Amazonian *(Trichechus inunguis).* Large, agile, aquatic mammal. Historic range: South America (Amazon River Basin). Status: Endangered.

Manatee, West African *(Trichechus senegalensis).* Large, agile, aquatic mammal. Historic range: West Coast of Africa from Senegal River to Cuanza River. Status: Threatened.

Manatee, West Indian (Florida), *(Trichechus manatus).* Large, agile aquatic mammal. Historic range: U.S.A. (southeastern), Caribbean Sea, South America. Status: Endangered.

Mandrill *(Papio sphinx).* Large, fierce, gregarious baboon. Historic range: Equatorial West Africa. Status: Endangered.

Mangabey, Tana River *(Cercocebus galeritus).* Slender, long- tailed monkey with fingers and toes webbed at the base. Historic range: Kenya. Status: Endangered.

Mangabey, White-Collared *(Cercocebus torquatus).* Slender, long-tailed monkey with fingers and toes webbed at the base. Historic range: Senegal to Ghana; Nigeria to Gabon. Status: Endangered.

Margay *(Felis wiedii).* Agile forest animal resembling a small ocelot. Historic range: U.S.A. (TX), Central and South America. Status: Endangered (Mexico southward).

Markhor, Kabal *(Capra falconeri magaceros).* Long-haired wild goat. Historic range: Afghanistan, Pakistan. Status: Endangered.

Markhor, Straight-horned *(Capra falconeri jerdoni).* Long- haired wild goat. Historic range: Afghanistan, Pakistan. Status: Endangered.

Marmoset, Buff-headed *(Callithrix flaviceps).* Small, tree- dwelling monkey-like animal. Historic range: Brazil. Status: Endangered.

Marmoset, Buffy Tufted-ear *(Callithrix jacchus aurita).* Small tree-dwelling monkey-like animal. Historic range: Brazil. Status: Endangered.

Marmoset, Cotton-top *(Saguinus oedipus).* Small tree dwelling monkey-like animal. Historic range: Costa Rica to Colombia. Status: Endangered.

Marmoset, Goeldi's *(Callimico goeldii).* Small tree-dwelling monkey-like animal. Historic range: Brazil, Colombia, Ecuador, Peru, Bolivia. Status: Endangered.

Marmot, Vancouver Island *(Marmota vancouverensis).* Resembles a woodchuck. Active on Vancouver Island for four months per year prior to hibernation. Historic range: Canada (Vancouver Island). Status: Endangered.

Marsupial, Eastern Jerboa *(Antechinomys laniger).* Historic range: Australia. Status: Endangered.

Marsupial-Mouse, Large Desert *(Sminthopsis psammophila).* Historic range: Australia. Status: Endangered.

Marsupial-Mouse, Long-tailed *(Sminthopsis longicaudata).* Historic range: Australia. Status: Endangered.

Marten, Formosan Yellow-throated *(Martes flavigula chrysospila).* Slender-bodied carnivorous mammal related to the weasel. Historic range: Taiwan. Status: Endangered.

Megapode, Maleo *(Macrocephalon maleo).* Shy, fowl-like bird. Historic range: Indonesia (Celebes). Status: Endangered.

Megapode, Micronesian *(Megapodius laperouse).* Shy, fowl-like bird. Historic range: West Pacific Ocean: U.S.A. (Palau Island, Mariana Islands). Status: Endangered.

Millerbird, Nihoa (old world warbler), *(Acrocephalus familiaris kingi).* Small thrush that derives its name from preying on miller moths. Historic range: U.S.A. (HI). Status: Endangered.

Minnow, Loach *(Tiaroga cobitis).* Slender olive-colored minnow. Historic range: U.S.A. (AZ, NM), Mexico. Status: Threatened.

Monarch, Tinian (old world flycatcher), *(Monarcha takatsukasae).* Belongs to a family of birds that catches flies and other insects in the air. Historic range: West Pacific Ocean: U.S.A. (Mariana Islands). Status: Threatened.

Monitor, Bengal *(Varanus bengalensis).* Carniverous lizard. Historic range: Iran, Iraq, India, Sri Lanka, Malaysia, Afghanistan, Burma, Vietnam, Thailand. Status: Endangered.

Monitor, Desert *(Varanus griseus).* Carniverous lizard. Historic range: North Africa to Neareast, Caspian Sea through U.S.S.R. to Pakistan, Northwest India. Status: Endangered.

Monitor, Komodo Island *(Varanus komodoensis).* Large carniverous lizard. Historic range: Indonesia (Komodo, Rintja, Padar, and western Flores Island). Status: Endangered.

Monitor, Yellow *(Varanus flavescens).* Carniverous lizard. Historic range: West Pakistan through India to Bangladesh. Status: Endangered.

Monkey, Black Colobus *(Colobus satanas).* Historic range: Equatorial Guinea, People's Republic of Congo, Cameroon, Gabon. Status: Endangered.

Monkey, Black Howler *(Alouatta pigra).* Historic range: Mexico, Guatemala, Belize. Status: Threatened.

Monkey, Diana *(Cercopithecus diana).* Historic range: Coastal West Africa. Status: Endangered.

Monkey, Guizhou Snub-nosed *(Rhinopithecus brelichi).* Historic range: China. Status: Endangered.

Monkey, Howler *(Alouatta palliata).* Historic range: Mexico to South America. Status: Endangered.

Monkey, L'hoest's *(Cercopithecus lhoesti).* Historic range: Upper Eastern Congo Basin, Cameroon. Status: Endangered.

Monkey, Preuss' Red Colobus *(Colobus badius preussi).* Historic range: Cameroon. Status: Endangered.

Monkey, Proboscis *(Nasalis larvatus).* Historic range: Borneo. Status: Endangered.

Monkey, Red-backed Squirrel *(Saimiri oerstedii).* Historic range: Costa Rica, Panama. Status: Endangered.

Monkey, Red-bellied *(Cercopithecus erythrogaster).* Historic range: Western Nigeria. Status: Endangered.

Monkey, Red-eared Nose-spotted *(Cercopithecus erythrotis).* Historic range: Nigeria, Cameroon, Fernando Po. Status: Endangered.

Monkey, Sichuan Snub-nosed *(Rhinopithecus roxellana).* Historic range: China. Status: Endangered.

Monkey, Spider *(Ateles geoffroyi frontatus).* Historic range: Costa Rica, Nicaragua. Status: Endangered.

Monkey, Spider *(Ateles geoffroyl panamensis).* Historic range: Costa Rica, Panama. Status: Endangered.

Monkey, Tana River Red Colobus *(Colobus rufomitratus rufomitratus).* Historic range: Kenya. Status: Endangered.

Monkey, Tonkin Snub-nosed *(Rhinopithecus avunculus).* Historic range: Viet Nam. Status: Endangered.

Monkey, Woolly Spider *(Brachyteles arachnoides).* Historic range: Brazil. Status: Endangered.

Monkey, Yellow-Tailed Woolly *(Lagothrix flavicauda).* Historic range: Andes of northern Peru. Status: Endangered.

Monkey, Yunnan Snub-nosed *(Rhinopithecus bieti).* Historic range: China. Status: Endangered.

Monkey, Zanzibar Red Colobus *(Colobus kirki).* Historic range: Tanzania. Status: Endangered.

Moorhen, Hawaiian Common *(Gallinula chloropus sandvicensis).* Medium-sized black waterbird. Historic range: U.S.A. (HI). Status: Endangered.

Moorhen, Mariana Common *(Gallinula chloropus guami).* Medium- sized waterbird. Historic range: West Pacific Ocean: U.S.A. (Guam, Tinian, Saipan, Pagan). Status: Endangered.

Moth, Kern Primrose Sphinx *(Euproserpinus euterpe).* Thick- bodied moth found only in Walker Basin. Historic range: Status: Threatened.

Mouse, Alabama Beach *(Peromyscus polionotus ammobates).* Nocturnal mouse inhabiting beachfront dunes. Historic range: U.S.A. (AL). Status: Endangered.

Mouse, Anastasia Island Beach *(Peromyscus polionotus phasma).* Small nocturnal rodent inhabiting beach dunes. Historic range: U.S.A. (FL). Status: Endangered.

Mouse, Australian Native *(Notomys aquilo).* Historic range: Australia. Status: Endangered.

Mouse, Australian Native *(Zyzomys pedunculatus).* Historic range: Australia. Status: Endangered.

Mouse, Choctawhatchee Beach *(Peromyscus polionotus allophrys).* Similar to the Alabama beach mouse. Historic range: U.S.A. (FL). Status: Endangered.

Mouse, Field's *(Pseudomys fieldi).* Historic range: Australia. Status: Endangered.

Mouse, Gould's *(Pseudomys gouldii).* Historic range: Australia. Status: Endangered.

Mouse, Key Largo Cotton *(Peromyscus gossypinus allapaticola).* Small field mouse restricted to the northern portion of Key Largo. Historic range: U.S.A. (FL). Status: Endangered.

Mouse, New Holland *(Pseudomys novaehollandiae).* Historic range: Australia. Status: Endangered.

Mouse, Perdido Key Beach *(Peromyscus polionotus trissyllepsis).* Pale beach mouse closely related to the Alabama beach mouse and the Choctawhatchee beach mouse. Historic range: U.S.A. (AL, FL). Status: Endangered.

Mouse, Salt Marsh Harvest *(Reithrodontomys raviventris).* Resembles the western harvest mouse. Inhabits wetlands that ring the San Pablo-Suisun-San Francisco Bay region. Historic range: U.S.A. (CA). Status: Endangered.

Mouse, Shark Bay *(Pseudomys praeconis).* Historic range: Australia. Status: Endangered.

Mouse, Shortridge's *(Pseudomys shortridgei).* Historic range: Australia. Status: Endangered.

Mouse, Smoky, *(Pseudomys fumeus).* Historic range: Australia. Status: Endangered.

Mouse, Southeastern Beach *(Peromyscus polionotus niveiventris).* Nocturnal rodent, one of the largest of the beach mice. Historic range: U.S.A. (FL). Status: Threatened.

Mouse, Western *(Pseudomys occidentalis).* Historic range: Australia. Status: Endangered.

Muntjac, Fea's *(Muntiacus feae).* Small deer with distinctive tusk-like upper canine teeth. Also known as the barking deer. Historic range: Northern Thailand, Burma. Status: Endangered.

Mussel, Cumberland Pigtoe *(Pleurobema gibberum).* Historic range: U.S.A. (TN). Status: Endangered.

Mussel, Curtus' *(Pleurobema curtum).* Freshwater mussel believed to survive only in a portion of East Fork Tombigbee River. Historic range: U.S.A. (AL, MS). Status: Endangered.

Mussel, Dwarf Wedge *(Alasmidonta heterodon).* Historic range: U.S.A. (CT, DC, DE, MA, MD, NC, NH, NJ, PA, VA, VT), Canada (NB). Status: Endangered.

Mussel, Judge Tait's *(Pleurobema taitianum).* Freshwater mussel with brownish black triangular shell. Historic range: U.S.A. (CT, DC, DE, MA, MD, NC, NH, NJ, PA, VA, VT), Canada (NB). Status: Endangered.

Mussel, Marshall's *(Pleurobema marshalli).* Dark brown freshwater mussel currently inhabiting a gravel bar in The Gainesville Bendway of the Tombigbee River. Historic range: U.S.A. (CT, DC, DE, MA, MD, NC, NH, NJ, PA, VA, VT), Canada (NB). Status: Endangered.

Mussel, Penitent *(Epioblasma penita).* Freshwater mussel with yellowish shell. Historic range: U.S.A. (CT, DC, DE, MA, MD, NC, NH, NJ, PA, VA, VT), Canada (NB). Status: Endangered.

Mussel, Ring Pink *(Obovaria retusa).* Formerly the golf stick pearly mussel. Historic range: U.S.A. (AL, IL, IN, KY, OH, PA, TN, WV). Status: Endangered.

Mussel, Winged Mapleleaf *(Quandrula fragosa).* Historic range: U.S.A. (WI, IL, MN, MO, OH, NE, TN, KY, IN, IA, OK). Status: Endangered.

Native-cat, Eastern *(Dasyurus viverrinus).* Historic range: Australia. Status: Endangered.

Naucorid, Ash Meadows *(Ambrysus amargosus).* Small aquatic insect. Historic range: U.S.A. (NV). Status: Threatened.

Nekogigi (catfish), *(Coreobagrus ichikawai).* Historic range: Japan. Status: Endangered.

Nightjar, Puerto Rican *(Caprimulgus noctitherus).* Nocturnal forest-dwelling bird also known as the Puerto Rican whip-poor-will. Historic range: U.S.A. (PR). Status: Endangered.

Nukupu'u (honeycreeper), *(Hemignathus lucidus).* Finch-like bird with sickle-shaped bill. Historic range: U.S.A. (HI). Status: Endangered.

Numbat *(Myrmecobius fasciatus).* Also known as the banded anteater. About the size of a large house rat but resembling a squirrel in appearance. Historic range: Australia. Status: Endangered.

Ocelot *(Felis pardalis).* Small dark-spotted cat inhabiting brushlands. Historic range: U.S.A. (AZ, TX) to Central and South America. Status: Endangered.

'O'o, Kauai (honeyeater), *(Moho braccatus).* Possibly extinct brown forest bird whose tongue is adapted for feeding on nectar. Historic range: U.S.A. (HI). Status: Endangered.

Orangutan *(Pongo pygmaeus).* Large ape with long, reddish coat. Historic range: Borneo, Sumatra. Status: Endangered.

Oryx, Arabian *(Oryx leucoryx).* Antelope. Historic range: Arabian Peninsula. Status: Endangered.

Ostrich, Arabian *(Struthio camelus syriacus).* Historic range: Jordan, Saudi Arabia. Status: Endangered.

Ostrich, West African *(Struthio camelus spatzi).* Historic range: Spanish Sahara. Status: Endangered.

Otter, Cameroon Clawless *(Aonyx congica microdon).* Historic range: Cameroon, Nigeria. Status: Endangered.

Otter, Giant *(Pteronura brasiliensis).* Historic range: South America. Status: Endangered.

Otter, Long-tailed *(Lutra longicaudis incl. platensis).* Historic range: South America. Status: Endangered.

Otter, Marine *(Lutra felina).* Historic range: Peru south to Straits of Magellan. Status: Endangered.

Otter, Southern River *(Lutra provocax).* Historic range: Chile, Argentina. Status: Endangered.

Otter, Southern Sea *(Enhydra lutris nereis).* Marine mammal of the weasel family. Also known as the California sea otter. Historic range: West Coast, U.S.A. (WA, OR, CA) south to Mexico (Baja, California). Status: Threatened.

'O'u (honeycreeper), *(Psittirostra psittacea).* One of the largest Hawaiian honeycreepers. Male has a bright yellow head. Historic range: U.S.A. (HI). Status: Endangered.

Owl, Anjouan Scops *(Otus rutilus capnodes).* Historic range: Indian Ocean: Comoro Island. Status: Endangered.

Owl, Giant Scops *(Otus gurneyi).* Historic range: Philippines: Marinduque and Mindanao Island). Status: Endangered.

Owl, Madagascar Red *(Tyto soumagnei).* Historic range: Madagascar. Status: Endangered.

Owl, Northern Spotted *(Strix occidentalis caurina).* Historic range: U.S.A. (CA, OR, WA), British Columbia.

Owl, Seychelles *(Otus insularis).* Historic range: Indian Ocean: Seychelles Islands. Status: Endangered.

Owlet, Morden's *(Otus ireneae).* Historic range: Kenya. Status: Endangered.

Palila (honeycreeper), *(Loxioides bailleui).* Large gray finch with yellow head and dark mask. Historic range: U.S.A. (HI). Status: Endangered.

Panda, Giant *(Ailuropoda melanoleuca).* Historic range: People's Republic of China. Status: Endangered.

Pangolin *(Manis temmincki).* Scaly, generally nocturnal insect-eating mammal. Historic range: Africa. Status: Endangered.

Panther, Florida *(Felis concolor coryi).* Medium-sized cat found only in four areas south of Lake Okeechobee. Historic range: U.S.A. (LA and AR east to SC and FL). Status: Endangered.

Parakeet, Forbes' *(Cyanoramphus auriceps forbesi).* Historic range: New Zealand. Status: Endangered.

Parakeet, Golden *(Aratinga guarouba).* Historic range: Brazil. Status: Endangered.

Parakeet, Golden-shouldered *(Psephotus chrysopterygius).* Historic range: Australia. Status: Endangered.

Parakeet, Mauritius *(Psittacula echo).* Historic range: Indian Ocean: Mauritius. Status: Endangered.

Parakeet, Norfolk Island *(Cyanoramphus novaezelandiae cookii).* Historic range: Australia (Norfolk Island). Status: Endangered.

Parakeet, Ochre-marked *(Pyrrhura cruentata).* Historic range: Brazil. Status: Endangered.

Parakeet, Orange-bellied *(Neophema chrysogaster).* Historic range: Australia. Status: Endangered.

Parakeet, Paradise *(Psephotus pulcherrimus).* Historic range: Australia. Status: Endangered.

Parakeet, Scarlet-chested *(Neophema splendida).* Historic range: Australia. Status: Endangered.

Parakeet, Turquoise *(Neophema pulchella).* Historic range: Australia. Status: Endangered.

Parrot, Australian *(Geopsittacus occidentalis).* Historic range: Australia. Status: Endangered.

Parrot, Bahaman or Cuban *(Amazona leucocephala).* Historic range: West Indies: Cuba, Bahamas, Caymans. Status: Endangered.

Parrot, Ground *(Pezoporus wallicus).* Historic range: Australia. Status: Endangered.

Parrot, Imperial *(Amazona imperialis).* Historic range: West Indies: Dominica. Status: Endangered.

Parrot, Puerto Rican *(Amazona vittata).* Historic range: U.S.A. (PR). Status: Endangered.

Parrot, Red-browed *(Amazona rhodocorytha).* Historic range: Brazil. Status: Endangered.

Parrot, Red-capped *(Pionopsitta pileata).* Historic range: Brazil. Status: Endangered.

Parrot, Red-necked *(Amazona arausiaca).* Historic range: West Indies: Dominica. Status: Endangered.

Parrot, Red-spectacled *(Amazona pretrei pretrei).* Historic range: Brazil, Argentina. Status: Endangered.

Parrot, Red-tailed *(Amazona brasiliensis).* Historic range: Brazil. Status: Endangered.

Parrot, St. Lucia *(Amazona versicolor).* Historic range: West Indies: St. Lucia. Status: Endangered.

Parrot, St. Vincent *(Amazona guildingii).* Historic range: West Indies: St. Vincent. Status: Endangered.

Parrot, Thick-billed *(Rhynchopsitta pachyrhyncha).* Historic range: Mexico, U.S.A. (AZ, NM). Status: Endangered.

Parrot, Vinaceous-brested *(Amazona vinacea).* Historic range: Brazil. Status: Endangered.

Parrotbill, Maui (honeycreeper), *(Pseudonestor xanthophrys).* Short-tailed honeycreeper with a parrot-like bill. Historic range: U.S.A. (HI). Status: Endangered.

Pearlshell, Louisiana *(Margaritifera hembeli).* Freshwater mussel found primarily in Kisatchie National Forest. Historic range: U.S.A. (LA). Status: Endangered.

Pearly Mussel, Alabama Lamp *(Lampsilis virescens).* Freshwater mussel with yellow to greenish brown elliptical shell. Historic range: U.S.A. (AL, TN). Status: Endangered.

Pearly Mussel, Appalachian Monkeyface *(Quadrula sparsa).* Freshwater mussel found in portions of the Powell and Clinch rivers. Historic range: U.S.A. (TN, VA). Status: Endangered.

Pearly Mussel, Birdwing *(Conradilla caelata).* Small freshwater mussel. Historic range: U.S.A. (TN, VA). Status: Endangered.

Pearly Mussel, Cracking *(Hemistena lata).* Freshwater mussel. Historic range: U.S.A. (AL, IL, IN, KY, OH, TN, VA). Status: Endangered.

Pearly Mussel, Cumberland Bean *(Villosa trabalis).* Freshwater mussel with elongated shell. Historic range: U.S.A. (KY, TN). Status: Endangered.

Pearly Mussel, Cumberland Monkeyface *(Quadrula intermedia).* Medium-sized freshwater mussel characterized by knobby shell. Historic range: U.S.A. (AL, TN, VA). Status: Endangered.

Pearly Mussel, Curtis' *(Epioblasma florentina curtisi).* Freshwater mussel with a yellow-brown oval shell. Historic range: U.S.A. (MO). Status: Endangered.

Pearly Mussel, Dromedary *(Dromus dromas).* Medium-sized freshwater mussel with roundish shell. Historic range: U.S.A. (TN, VA). Status: Endangered.

Pearly Mussel, Green-blossom *(Epioblasma torulosa gubernaculum).* Freshwater mussel with irregularly elliptical shell, found only in portions of the upper Clinch River above Norris Reservoir. Historic range: U.S.A. (TN, VA). Status: Endangered.

Pearly Mussel, Higgins' Eye *(Lampsilis higginsi).* Freshwater mussel endemic to the Mississippi River and its major tributaries. Historic range: U.S.A. (IL, IA, MN, MO, NE, WI). Status: Endangered.

Pearly Mussel, Little-wing *(Pegias fabula).* Freshwater mussel. Historic range: U.S.A. (AL, KY, NC, TN, VA). Status: Endangered.

Pearly Mussel, Nicklin's *(Megalonaias nicklineana).* Historic range: Mexico. Status: Endangered.

Pearly Mussel, Orange-footed *(Plethobasus cooperianus).* Freshwater mussel also known as the pimple-back pearly mussel. Historic range: U.S.A. (AL, IN, IA, KY, OH, PA, TN). Status: Endangered.

Pearly Mussel, Pale Lilliput *(Toxolasma cylindrellus).* Freshwater mussel. Historic range: U.S.A. (AL, TN). Status: Endangered.

Pearly Mussel, Pink Mucket *(Lampsilis orbiculata).* Freshwater mussel. Historic range: U.S.A. (AL, IL, IN, KY, MO, OH, PA, TN, WV). Status: Endangered.

Pearly Mussel, Purple Cat's Paw *(Epioblasma obliquata obliquata).* Historic range: U.S.A. (AL, IL, IN, KY, OH, TN). Status: Endangered.

Pearly Mussel, Tampico *(Cyrtonaias tampicoensis tecomatensis).* Historic range: Mexico. Status: Endangered.

Pearly Mussel, Tubercled-blossom *(Epioblasma torulosa torulosa).* Medium-sized freshwater mussel. Historic range: U.S.A. (IL, IN, KY, TN, WV). Status: Endangered.

Pearly Mussel, Turgid-blossom *(Epioblasma turgidula).* Possibly extinct freshwater mussel. Historic range: U.S.A. (AL, TN). Status: Endangered.

Pearly Mussel, White Cat's Paw *(Epioblasma sulcata delicata).* Freshwater mussel. Historic range: U.S.A. (IN, MI, OH). Status: Endangered.

Pearly Mussel, White Wartyback *(Plethobasus cicatricosus).* Historic range: U.S.A. (AL, IN, TN). Status: Endangered.

Pearly Mussel, Yellow-blossom *(Epioblasma florentina florentina).* Medium-sized freshwater mussel. Historic range: U.S.A. (AL, TN). Status: Endangered.

Pelican, Brown *(Pelecanus occidentalis).* Historic range: U.S.A. (Carolinas to TX, CA), West Indies, Central and South America: Coastal. Status: Endangered.

Penguin, Galapagos *(Spheniscus mendiculus).* Historic range: Ecuador (Galapagos Islands). Status: Endangered.

Petrel, Hawaiian Dark-rumped *(Pterodroma phaeopygia sandwichensis).* Dark gray seabird with a white breast and forehead. Historic range: U.S.A. (HI). Status: Endangered.

Pheasant, Bar-tailed *(Syrmaticus humaie).* Historic range: Burma, China. Status: Endangered.

Pheasant, Blyth's Tragopan *(Tragopan blythii).* Historic range: Burma, China, India. Status: Endangered.

Pheasant, Brown Eared *(Crossoptilon mantchuricum).* Historic range: China. Status: Endangered.

Pheasant, Cabot's Tragopan *(Tragopan caboti).* Historic range: China. Status: Endangered.

Pheasant, Cheer *(Catreus wallichii).* Historic range: India, Nepal, Pakistan. Status: Endangered.

Pheasant, Chinese Monal *(Lophophorus lhuysii).* Historic range: China. Status: Endangered.

Pheasant, Edward's *(Lophura edwardsi).* Historic range: Vietnam. Status: Endangered.

Pheasant, Elliot's *(Syrmaticus ellioti).* Historic range: China. Status: Endangered.

Pheasant, Imperial *(Lophura imperialis).* Historic range: Vietnam. Status: Endangered.

Pheasant, Mikado *(Syrmaticus mikado).* Historic range: Taiwan. Status: Endangered.

Pheasant, Palawan Peacock *(Polyplectron emphanum).* Historic range: Philippines. Status: Endangered.

Pheasant, Sclater's Monal *(Lophophorus sclateri).* Historic range: Burma, China, India. Status: Endangered.

Pheasant, Swinhoe's *(Lophura swinhoii).* Historic range: Taiwan. Status: Endangered.

Pheasant, Western Tragopan *(Tragopan melanocephalus).* Historic range: India, Pakistan. Status: Endangered.

Pheasant, White Eared *(Crossoptilon crossoptilon).* Historic range: China (Tibet), India. Status: Endangered.

Pigeon, Azores Wood *(Columba palumbus azorica).* Historic range: East Atlantic Ocean: Azores. Status: Endangered.

Pigeon, Chatham Island *(Hemiphaga novaeseelandiae chathamensis).* Historic range: New Zealand. Status: Endangered.

Pigeon, Mindoro Zone-tailed *(Ducula mindorensis).* Historic range: Philippines. Status: Endangered.

Pigeon, Puerto Rican Plain *(Columba inornata wetmorei).* Historic range: U.S.A. (PR). Status: Endangered.

Pigtoe, Fine-rayed *(Fusconaia cuneolus).* Medium-sized freshwater mussel. Historic range: U.S.A. (AL, TN, VA). Status: Endangered.

Pigtoe, Rough *(Pleurobema plenum).* Triangular freshwater mussel. Historic range: U.S.A. (IN, KY, TN, VA). Status: Endangered.

Pigtoe, Shiny *(Fusconaia edgariana).* Smooth, shiny freshwater mussel. Historic range: U.S.A. (AL, TN, VA). Status: Endangered.

Piping-Guan, Black-fronted *(Pipile jacutinga).* Jungle fowl. Historic range: Argentina. Status: Endangered.

Pitta, Koch's *(Pitta kochi).* Brightly-colored, tropical, ground-dwelling bird. Historic range: Philippines. Status: Endangered.

Planigale, Little *(Planigale ingrami subtilissima, formerly Planigale subtilissima).* Mammal. Historic range: Australia. Status: Endangered.

Planigale, Southern *(Planigale tenuirostris).* Mammal. Historic range: Australia. Status: Endangered.

Plover, New Zealand Shore *(Thinornis novaeseelandiae).* Small shorebird. Historic range: New Zealand. Status: Endangered.

Plover, Piping *(Charadrius melodus).* Small shorebird often seen darting across sand on stilt-like legs. Historic range: U.S.A. (Great Lakes, northern Great Plains, Atlantic and Gulf coasts, PR, VI), Canada, Mexico, Bahamas, West Indies. Status: Endangered (Great Lakes watershed in states of IL, IN, MI, MN, NY, OH, PA, and WI, and Province of Ontario). Status: Threatened (all areas except where listed as endangered).

Po'ouli (honeycreeper), *(Melamprosops phaeosoma).* Black-faced forest bird found on Maui. Historic range: U.S.A. (HI). Status: Endangered.

Pocketbook, Fat *(Potamilus capax).* Shiny, spherical freshwater mussel. Historic range: U.S.A. (AR, IN, MO, OH). Status: Endangered.

Pocketbook, Speckled *(Lampsilils streckeri).* Dark yellow or brown freshwater mussel. Historic range: U.S.A. (AR). Status: Endangered.

Porcupine, Thin-spined *(Chaetomys subspinosus).* Historic range: Brazil. Status: Endangered.

Possum, Leadbeater's *(Gymnobelideus Leadbeateri).* Historic range: Brazil. Status: Endangered.

Possum, Mountain Pygmy *(Burramys parvus).* Historic range: Australia. Status: Endangered.

Possum, Scaly-tailed *(Wyulda squamicaudata).* Historic range: Mexico. Status: Endangered.

Prairie-Chicken, Attwater's Greater *(Tympanuchus cupido attwateri).* Hen-like bird belonging to the grouse family. Historic range: U.S.A. (TX). Status: Endangered.

Prairie Dog, Mexican *(Cynomys mexicanus).* Large burrowing rodent belonging to the squirrel family. Historic range: Mexico. Status: Endangered.

Prairie Dog, Utah *(Cynomys parvidens).* Large burrowing rodent belonging to the squirrel family. Historic range: U.S.A. (UT). Status: Threatened.

Pronghorn, Peninsular *(Antilocapra americana peninsularis).* Antelope-like hoofed mammal native to North America. Historic range: Mexico (Baja California). Status: Endangered.

Pronghorn, Sonoran *(Antilocapra americana sonoriensis).* Slender antelope inhabiting a harsh environment of excessive summer heat, little water, and scarce food. Historic range: U.S.A. (AZ), Mexico. Status: Endangered.

Pseudoscorpion, Tooth Cave *(Microcreagris texana).* Eyeless spider resembling a scorpion. Historic range: U.S.A. (TX). Status: Endangered.

Pudu *(Pudu pudu).* Smallest of the American deer, about the size of a dog. Historic range: Southern South America. Status: Endangered.

Puma, Costa Rican *(Felis concolor costaricensis).* Historic range: Nicaragua, Panama, Costa Rica. Status: Endangered.

Pupfish, Ash Meadows Amargosa *(Cyprinodon nevadensis mionectes).* Small minnow. Historic range: U.S.A. (NV). Status: Endangered.

Pupfish, Comanche Springs *(Cyprinodon elegans).* Silvery brown fish found only in Reeves County. Historic range: U.S.A. (TX). Status: Endangered.

Pupfish, Desert *(Cyprinodon macularius).* Small fish inhabiting desert streams and rivers. Historic range: U.S.A. (AZ, CA), Mexico. Status: Endangered.

Pupfish, Devils Hole *(Cyprinodon diabolis).* Tiny fish found only at Devils Hole in Nye County. Historic range: U.S.A. (NV). Status: Endangered.

Pupfish, Leon Springs *(Cyprinodon bovinus).* Small killifish found only in Diamond Y Spring and Leon Creek. Historic range: U.S.A. (TX). Status: Endangered.

Pupfish, Owens *(Cyprinodon radiosus).* Small fish. Historic range: U.S.A. (CA). Status: Endangered.

Pupfish, Warm Springs *(Cyprinodon nevadensis pectoralis).* Small fish. Historic range: U.S.A. (NV). Status: Endangered.

Python, Indian *(Python molurus molurus).* Historic range: Sri Lanka and India. Status: Endangered.

Quail, Merriam's Montezuma *(Cyrtonyx montezumae merriami).* Historic range: Mexico (Vera Cruz). Status: Endangered.

Quetzel, Resplendent *(Pharomachrus mocinno).* Beautifully- colored tropical bird distinguished by long feathers above its tail that extend downward. Historic range: Mexico to Panama. Status: Endangered.

Quokka *(Setonix brachyurus).* Mammal. Historic range: Australia. Status: Endangered.

Rabbit, Lower Keys *(Sylvilagus palustris hefneri).* Historic range: U.S.A. (FL). Status: Endangered.

Rabbit, Ryukyu *(Pentalagus furnessi).* Historic range: Japan (Ryukyu Islands). Status: Endangered.

Rabbit, Volcano *(Romerolagus diazi).* Historic range: Mexico. Status: Endangered.

Rail, Aukland Island *(Rallus pectoralis muelleri).* Hen-like bird. Historic range: New Zealand. Status: Endangered.

Rail, California Clapper *(Rallus longirostris obsoletus).* Long-billed, hen-like bird found only in the San Francisco Bay ecosystem. Historic range: U.S.A. (CA). Status: Endangered.

Rail, Guam *(Rallus owstoni).* Hen-like bird. Historic range: Western Pacific Ocean: U.S.A. (Guam). Status: Endangered. Status: XN (Rota).

Rail, Light-footed Clapper *(Rallus longirostris levipes).* Hen-like marsh bird inhabiting coastal salt marshes. Historic range: U.S.A. (CA), Mexico (Baja California). Status: Endangered (U.S.A. only).

Rail, Lord Howe Wood *(Tricholimnas sylvestris).* Hen-like bird. Historic range: Australia (Lord Howe Island). Status: Endangered.

Rail, Yuma Clapper *(Rallus longirostris yumanensis).* Hen-like marsh bird. Historic range: Mexico, U.S.A. (AZ, CA). Status: Endangered (U.S.A. only).

Rat, False Water *(Xeromys myoides).* Historic range: Australia. Status: Endangered.

Rat, Fresno Kangaroo *(Dipodomys nitratoides exilis).* Nocturnal rodent that hops on long hind legs, much like a kangaroo. One of the smallest of the California kangaroo rats. Historic range: U.S.A. (CA). Status: Endangered.

Rat, Giant Kangaroo *(Dipodomys ingens).* Largest of all kangaroo rats, reaching a length of 35 centimeters (14 inches). Historic range: U.S.A. (CA). Status: Endangered.

Rat-kangaroo, Brush-tailed *(Bettongia penicillata).* Historic range: Australia. Status: Endangered.

Rat-kangaroo, Gaimard's *(Bettongia gaimardi).* Historic range: Australia. Status: Endangered.

Rat-kangaroo, Lesuer's *(Bettongia lesueur).* Historic range: Australia. Status: Endangered.

Rat-kangaroo, Plain *(Caloprymnus campestris).* Historic range: Australia. Status: Endangered.

Rat-kangaroo, Queensland *(Bettongia tropica).* Historic range: Australia. Status: Endangered.

Rhinoceros, Black *(Diceros bicornis).* Historic range: Sub-Saharan Africa. Status: Endangered.

Rat, Morro Bay Kangaroo *(Dipodomys heermanni morroensis).* Smaller and darker colored than other kangaroo rat subspecies. Historic range: U.S.A. (CA). Status: Endangered.

Rat, Rice *(Oryzomys palustris natator).* Historic range: U.S.A. (FL). Status: Endangered.

Rat, Stephens' Kangaroo *(Dipodomys stephensi,* incl. *Dipodomys cascus).* Small rodent inhabiting native grasslands and coastal scrub. Historic range: U.S.A. (CA). Status: Endangered.

Rat, Stick-nest *(Leporillus conditor).* Historic range: Australia. Status: Endangered.

Rat, Tipton Kangaroo *(Dipodomys nitratoides nitratoides).* Nocturnal rodent inhabiting soft soil in lakebed areas. Historic range: U.S.A. (CA). Status: Endangered.

Rattlesnake, Aruba Island *(Crotalus unicolor).* Historic range: Aruba Island (Netherland Antilles). Status: Threatened.

Rattlesnake, New Mexican Ridge-nosed *(Crotalus willardi obscurus).* Historic range: U.S.A. (NM), Mexico. Status: Threatened.

Rhea, Darwin's *(Pterocnemia pennata).* Large, flightless bird resembling a small ostrich. Historic range: Argentina, Bolivia, Peru, Uruguay. Status: Endangered.

Rhinoceros, Great Indian *(Rhinoceros unicornis).* Historic range: India, Nepal. Status: Endangered.

Rhinoceros, Javan *(Rhinoceros sondaicus).* Historic range: Indonesia, Indochina, Burma, Thailand, Sikkim, Bangladesh, Malaysia. Status: Endangered.

Rhinoceros, Northern White *(Ceratotherium simum cottoni).* Historic range: Zaire, Sudan, Uganda, Central African Republic. Status: Endangered.

Rhinoceros, Sumatran *(Dicerorhinus sumatrensis).* Historic range: Bangladesh to Vietnam to Indonesia (Borneo). Status: Endangered.

Riffle Shell, Tan *(Epioblasma walkeri).* Medium-sized freshwater mussel. Historic range: U.S.A. (KY, TN, VA). Status: Endangered.

Robin, Chatham Island *(Petroica traversi).* Historic range: New Zealand. Status: Endangered.

Robin, Scarlet-breasted (flycatcher), *(Petroica multicolor multicolor).* Historic range: Australia (Norfolk Island). Status: Endangered.

Rockfowl, Grey-necked *(Picathartes oreas).* Historic range: Cameroon, Gabon. Status: Endangered.

Rockfowl, White-necked *(Picathartes gymnocephalus).* Historic range: Africa: Togo to Sierra Leone. Status: Endangered.

Roller, Long-tailed Ground *(Uratelornis chimaera).* Bird related to the kingfisher. Noted for the way it rolls through the air during flight. Historic range: Malagasy Republic. Status: Endangered.

Saiga, Mongolian *(Saiga tatarica mongolica).* Horned, sheep-like animal with a swollen snout used to filter dust. Historic range: Mongolia. Status: Endangered.

Saki, Southern Beared *(Chiropotes satanas satanas).* Small, intelligent monkey with a heavy coat of long hair. Historic range: Brazil. Status: Endangered.

Saki, White-nosed *(Chiropotes albinasus).* Small, intelligent monkey with a heavy coat of long hair. Historic range: Brazil. Status: Endangered.

Salamander, Cheat Mountain *(Plethodon nettingi).* Found above an elevation of 915 meters (3,000 feet) primarily in the Monongahela National Forest. Historic range: U.S.A. (WV). Status: Threatened.

Salamander, Chinese Giant *(Andrias davidianus davidianus).* Historic range: Western China. Status: Endangered.

Salamander, Desert Slender *(Batrachoseps aridus).* Historic range: U.S.A. (CA). Status: Endangered.

Salamander, Japanese Giant *(Andrias davidianus japonicus).* Historic range: Japan. Status: Endangered.

Salamander, Red Hills *(Phaeognathus hubrichti).* Historic range: U.S.A. (AL). Status: Threatened.

Salamander, San Marcos *(Eurycea nana).* Historic range: U.S.A. (TX). Status: Threatened.

Salamander, Santa Cruz Long-toed *(Ambystoma macrodactylum croceum).* Historic range: U.S.A. (CA). Status: Endangered.

Salamander, Shenandoah *(Plethodon shenandoah).* Historic range: U.S.A. (VA). Status: Endangered.

Salamander, Texas Blind *(Typhlomolge rathbuni).* A pale, sightless, cave-dwelling salamander found only in the caverns of the Edwards Plateau in Hays County. Historic range: U.S.A. (TX). Status: Endangered.

Salmon, Chinook *(Oncorhynchus tshawytscha).* Historic range: Pacific Ocean. Status: Threatened (U.S.A. - CA: Sacramento R. winter run).

Sculpin, Pygmy *(Cottus pygmaeus).* Member of the minnow family. Historic range: U.S.A. (AL). Status: Threatened.

Scrub-bird, Noisy *(atrichornis clamosus).* Historic range: Australia. Status: Endangered.

Shama, Cebu Black (thrush), *(Copsychus niger cebuensis).* Historic range: Philippines. Status: Endangered.

Sea-lion, Steller *(Eumetopias jubatus).* Historic range: U.S.A. (AK, CA, OR, WA), Canada, Soviet Union; North Pacific Ocean. Status: Threatened.

Seal, Caribbean Monk *(Monachus tropicalis).* Historic range: Caribbean Sea, Gulf of Mexico. Status: Endangered.

Seal, Guadalupe Fur *(Arctocephalus townsendi).* Medium-sized, dark gray, eared seal. Historic range: U.S.A. (Farallon Islands of CA) south to Mexico (Islas Revillagigedo). Status: Threatened.

Seal, Hawaiian Monk *(Monachus schauinslandi).* Large earless seal. Historic range: U.S.A. (HI). Status: Endangered.

Seal, Mediterranean Monk *(Monachus monachus).* Historic range: Mediterranean, Northwest African Coast and Black Sea. Status: Endangered.

Seledang *(Bos gaurus).* Among the largest of wild cattle. Inhabits forests and tall grass. Historic range: Bangladesh, Southeast Asia, India. Status: Endangered.

Serow *(Capricornis sumatraensis).* Stout goat antelope inhabiting mountain slopes. Historic range: East Asia, Sumatra. Status: Endangered.

Serval, Barbary *(Felis serval constantilna).* Long-legged wildcat. Historic range: Algeria. Status: Endangered.

Shagreen, Magazine Mountain *(Mesodon magazinensis).* Medium- sized land snail whose only known range is within the Ozark National Forest. Historic range: U.S.A. (AR). Status: Threatened.

Shapo *(Ovis vignei vignei).* Sheep that is usually reddish brown. Males have long, slender horns that form a large open curl. Historic range: Kashmir. Status: Endangered.

Shearwater, Newell's Townsend's (formerly Manx), *(Puffinus auricularis (formerly P. newelli).* Black seabird with a white breast and long bill. Nests on cliffs and remote sea islands. Historic range: U.S.A. (HI). Status: Threatened.

Shiner, Beautiful *(Syprinella formosa).* Small silvery minnow with red-orange highlights. Historic range: U.S.A. (AZ, NM), Mexico. Status: Threatened.

Shiner, Cahaba *(Notropis cahabae).* Member of the minnow family. Historic range: U.S.A. (AL). Status: Endangered.

Shiner, Cape Fear *(Notropis mekistocholas).* Pale metallic yellow minnow. Historic range: U.S.A. (NC). Status: Endangered.

Shiner, Pecos Bluntnose *(Notropis simus pecosensis).* Small minnow. Historic range: U.S.A. (NM). Status: Threatened.

Shou *(Cervus elaphus wallichi).* Mammal. Historic range: Tibet, Bhutan. Status: Endangered.

Shrew, Dismal Swamp Southeastern *(Sorex longirostris fisheri).* Mouse-like rodent found in the Great Dismal Swamp National Wildlife Refuge. Historic range: U.S.A. (VA, NC). Status: Threatened.

Shrike, San Clemente Loggerhead *(Lanius ludovicianus mearnsi).* Predatory bird with distinctive black mask. Relies on strong beak to kill or stun prey. Historic range: U.S.A. (CA). Status: Endangered.

Shrimp, Alabama Cave *(Palaemonias alabamae).* Colorless freshwater shrimp believed to survive in Shelta and Bobcat caves. Historic range: U.S.A. (AL). Status: Endangered.

Shrimp, California Freshwater *(Syncaris pacifica).* Nearly transparent freshwater shrimp whose appearance resembles a common ocean shrimp. Historic range: U.S.A. (CA). Status: Endangered.

Shrimp, Kentucky Cave *(Palaemonias ganteri).* Colorless freshwater shrimp endemic to the Flint-Mammoth Cave System. Historic range: U.S.A. (KY). Status: Endangered.

Shrimp, Squirrel Chimney Cave *(Palaemonetes cummingi).* Historic range: U.S.A. (FL). Status: Threatened.

Siamang *(Symphalangus syndactylus).* Large, black gibbon. Historic range: Malaysia, Indonesia. Status: Endangered.

Sifakas *(Propithecus spp.).* Primarily black and white lemur with long tail and silky fur. Historic range: Malagasy Rupublic. Status: Endangered.

Silverside, Waccamaw *(Menidia extensa).* Almost transparent fish also known as the glass minnow. Historic range: U.S.A. (NC). Status: Threatened.

Siskin, Red *(Carduelis cucullata).* Bird. Historic range: South America. Status: Endangered.

Skink, Blue-tailed Mole *(Eumeces egregius lividus).* Long, narrow lizard whose young have blue tails. Historic range: U.S.A. (FL). Status: Threatened.

Skink, Round Island *(Leiolopisma telfairi).* Small lizard. Historic range: Indian Ocean: Mauritius. Status: Threatened.

Skink, Sand *(Neoseps reynoldsi).* Small lizard with retractable forelegs. Historic range: U.S.A. (FL). Status: Threatened.

Skipper, Pawnee Montane *(Hesperia leonardus montana).* Small brownish yellow butterfly. Historic range: U.S.A. (CO). Status: Threatened.

Sloth, Brazilian Three-toed *(Bradypus torquatus).* Slow-moving arboreal mammal that hangs from branches with its back downward. Historic range: Brazil. Status: Endangered.

Snail, Chittenango Ovate Amber *(Succinea chittenangoensis).* Land snail with translucent shell found at Chittenango Falls State Park. Historic range: U.S.A. (NY). Status: Threatened.

Snail, Flat-spired Three-toothed *(Triodopsis platysayoides).* Flat land snail found primarily within Coopers Rock State Forest. Historic range: U.S.A. (WV). Status: Threatened.

Snail, Iowa Pleistocene *(Discus macclintocki).* Forest snail found in restricted cool, moist areas. Historic range: U.S.A. (IA). Status: Endangered.

Snail, Manus Island Tree *(Papustyla pulcherrima).* Historic range: Pacific Ocean: Admiralty Islands (Manus Island). Status: Endangered.

Snail, Noonday *(Mesodon clarki nantahala).* Land snail found along high cliffs in the Nantahala Gorge. Historic range: U.S.A. (NC). Status: Threatened.

Snail, Oahu Tree *(Achatinella spp.).* Brightly colored tree snail. Historic range: U.S.A. (HI). Status: Endangered.

Snail, Painted Snake Coiled Forest *(Anguispira picta).* Forest snail found only at Buck Creek Cove. Historic range: U.S.A. (TN). Status: Threatened.

Snail, Stock Island Tree *(Orthalicus reses,* not incl. *nesodryas).* Large tree snail with cone-shaped shell. Inhabits tropical hardwood forests. Historic range: U.S.A. (FL). Status: Threatened.

Snail, Tulotoma *(Tulotoma magnifica).* Historic range: U.S.A. (AL). Status: Endangered.

Snail, Virginia Fringed Mountain *(Polygyriscus virginianus).* Flat-shelled mountain snail found in Pulaski County. Historic range: U.S.A. (VA). Status: Endangered.

Snake, Atlantic Salt Marsh *(Nerodia fasciata taeniata).* Historic range: U.S.A. (FL). Status: Threatened.

Snake, Concho Water *(Nerodia harteri paucimaculata).* Historic range: U.S.A. (TX). Status: Threatened.

Snake, Eastern Indigo *(Drymarchon corais couperi).* Historic range: U.S.A. (AL, FL, GA, MS, SC). Status: Threatened.

Snake, San Francisco Garter *(Thamnophis sirtalis tetrataenia).* Historic range: U.S.A. (CA). Status: Endangered.

Solenodon, Cuban *(Solenodon cubanus).* Nocturnal animal resembling a long-snouted rat. Historic range: Cuba. Status: Endangered.

Solenodon, Haitian *(Solenodon paradoxus).* Nocturnal, dark brown animal resembling a long-snouted rat. Historic range: Dominican Republic, Haiti. Status: Endangered.

Sparrow, Cape Sable Seaside *(Ammodramus maritimus mirabilis).* Greenish gray sparrow found only in southern Florida marsh areas. Historic range: U.S.A. (FL). Status: Endangered.

Sparrow, Dusky Seaside *(Ammodramus maritimus nigrescens).* Historic range: U.S.A. (FL). Status: Endangered.

Sparrow, Florida Grasshopper *(Ammodramus savannarum floridanus).* Sparrow whose name originates from its song, which is similar to the buzz of grasshoppers. Historic range: U.S.A. (FL). Status: Endangered.

Sparrow, San Clemente Sage *(Amphispiza belli clementeae).* Non-migratory ground dweller inhabiting scrub vegetation. Historic range: U.S.A. (CA). Status: Threatened.

Spider, Tooth Cave *(Leptoneta myopica).* Tiny, pale spider with relatively long legs. Historic range: U.S.A. (TX). Status: Endangered.

Spikedace *(Meda fulgida).* Silvery fish with sharp spines in its dorsal and pelvic fins. Historic range: U.S.A. (NM). Status: Threatened.

Spinedace, Big Spring *(Lepidomeda mollispinis pratensis).* Small silver minnow. Historic range: U.S.A. (NV). Status: Threatened.

Spinedace, Little Colorado *(Lepidomeda vittata).* Small minnow. Historic range: U.S.A. (AZ). Status: Threatened.

Spinedace, White River *(Lepidomeda albivallis).* Brightly- colored minnow. Historic range: U.S.A. (NV). Status: Endangered.

Spinymussel, James River *(Pleurobema collina).* Freshwater mussel found in several headwater streams of the James River. Historic range: U.S.A. (VA, WV). Status: Endangered.

Spinymussel, Tar River *(Elliptio steinstansana).* Medium-sized freshwater mussel characterized by several short spines. Historic range: U.S.A. (NC). Status: Endangered.

Springfish, Hiko White River *(Crenichthys baileyi grandis).* Small killifish found only in Crystal Springs. Historic range: U.S.A. (NV). Status: Endangered.

Springfish, Railroad Valley *(Crenichthys nevadae).* Killifish lacking pelvic fins. Historic range: U.S.A. (NV). Status: Threatened.

Springfish, White River *(Crenichthys baileyi baileyi).* Small killifish found only in Ash Springs. Historic range: U.S.A. (NV). Status: Endangered.

Squawfish, Colorado *(Ptychocheilus lucius).* Largest of the minnow family, some reaching 1.5 meters (five feet) in length. Historic range: U.S.A. (AZ, CA, CO, NM, NV, UT, WY), Mexico. Status: Endangered (except Salt and Verde R. drainages, AZ); XN (Salt and Verde R. drainages, AZ).

Squirrel, Carolina Northern Flying *(Glaucomys sabrinus coloratus).* Subspecies of the northern flying squirrels found in the higher elevations of the Appalachian Mountains. Historic range: U.S.A. (NC, TN). Status: Endangered.

Squirrel, Delmarva Peninsula Fox *(Sciurus niger cinereus).* Large woodland squirrel inhabiting mature forests near streams or bays. Historic range: U.S.A. (Delmarva Peninsula to southeast PA). Status: Endangered.

Squirrel, Mount Graham Red *(Tamiasciurus hudsonicus grahamensis).* Grayish brown tree squirrel found only within the Safford Ranger District of the Colorado National Forest. Historic range: U.S.A. (AZ). Status: Endangered.

Squirrel, Virginia Northern Flying *(Glaucomys sabrinus fuscus).* Subspecies of the northern flying squirrels found in the higher elevations of the Appalachian Mountains. Historic range: U.S.A. (VA, WV). Status: Endangered.

Stag, Barbary *(Cervus elaphus barbarus).* Historic range: Tunisia, Algeria. Status: Endangered.

Stag, Kashmir *(Cervus elaphus hanglu).* Historic range: Kashmir. Status: Endangered.

Starling, Ponape Mountain *(Aplonis pelzelni).* Historic range: West Pacific Ocean: U.S.A. (Caroline Islands). Status: Endangered.

Starling, Rothschild's (myna) *(Leucopsar rothschildi).* Historic range: Indonesia (Bali). Status: Endangered.

Stickleback, Unarmored Threespine *(Gasterosteus aculeatus williamsoni).* Small brownish fish. One of three subspecies of threespine sticklebacks in North America. Historic range: U.S.A. (CA). Status: Endangered.

Stilt, Hawaiian *(Himantopus mexicanus knudensi).* Long-legged black and white wading bird about 40 centimeters (16 inches) tall. Historic range: U.S.A. (HI). Status: Endangered.

Stirrup Shell *(Quadrula stapes).* Freshwater mussel with zig- zag markings. Historic range: U.S.A. (AL, MS). Status: Endangered.

Stork, Oriental White *(Ciconia ciconia boyciana).* Long-legged wading bird. Historic range: China, Japan, Korea, U.S.S.R. Status: Endangered.

Stork, Wood *(Mycteria americana).* Large long-legged wading bird with white plumage and black flight feathers and tail. Stout bill curves downward. Historic range: U.S.A. (CA, AZ, TX, to Carolinas), Mexico, Central and South America. Status: Endangered (U.S.A. - AL, FL, GA, NC, SC).

Swiftlet, Mariana Gray *(Aerodramus vanikorensis bartschi).* Bird noted for its speed. Historic range: Western Pacific Ocean: U.S.A. (Guam, Rota, Tinian, Saipan, Agiguan). Status: Endangered.

Sturgeon, Pallid *(Scaphirhynchus albus).* Historic range: U.S.A. (AR, IA, IL, KS, KY, LA, MO, MS, MT, ND, NE, SD, TN). Status: Endangered.

Sturgeon, Shortnose *(Acipenser brevirostrum).* Historic range: U.S.A. and Canada (Atlantic Coast). Status: Endangered.

Sucker, June *(Chasmistes liorus).* Small bottom-feeding sucker found only in Utah Lake and the lower portion of the Provo River. Historic range: U.S.A. (UT). Status: Endangered.

Sucker, Lost River *(Deltistes luxatus).* Large, bottom-feeding fish. Historic range: U.S.A. (OR, CA). Status: Endangered.

Sucker, Modoc *(Catostomus microps).* Dwarf, olive-gray fish. Historic range: U.S.A. (CA). Status: Endangered.

Sucker, Short-nose *(Chasmistes brevirostris).* Bottom-feeding fish. Historic range: U.S.A. (OR, CA). Status: Endangered.

Sucker, Warner *(Catostomus warnerensis).* Bottom-feeding fish. Historic range: U.S.A. (OR). Status: Threatened.

Suni, Zanzibar *(Neotragus moschatus moschatus).* Mammal. Historic range: Zanzibar (and nearby islands). Status: Endangered.

Tahr, Arabian *(Hemitragus jayakari).* Beardless goat with short horns. Historic range: Oman. Status: Endangered.

Tamaraw *(Bubalus mindorensis).* Small stocky cow-like mammal found only on the island of Mindoro. Historic range: Philippines. Status: Endangered.

Tamarin, Golden-rumped *(Leontopithecus spp.).* Small, monkey- like, tree-dwelling animal. Historic range: Brazil. Status: Endangered.

Tamarin, Pied *(Saguinus bicolor).* Small, monkey-like, tree- dwelling animal. Historic range: Brazil. Status: Endangered.

Tamarin, White-footed *(Saguinus leucopus).* Small, monkey- like, tree-dwelling animal. Historic range: Colombia. Status: Threatened.

Tango, Miyako (Tokyo bitterling), *(Tanakia tanago).* Fish. Historic range: Japan. Status: Endangered.

Tapir, Asian *(Tapirus indicus).* Stocky, primitive, odd-toed hoofed mammal with an elongated snout. Inhabits swamp areas. Historic range: Burma, Laos, Cambodia, Vietnam, Malaysia, Indonesia, Thailand. Status: Endangered.

Tapir, Brazilian *(Tapirus terrestris).* Stocky, primitive, odd-toed hoofed mammal with an elongated snout. Inhabits swamp areas. Historic range: Colombia and Venezuela south to Paraguay and Argentina. Status: Endangered.

Tapir, Central American *(Tapirus bairdii).* Stocky, primitive, odd-toed hoofed mammal with an elongated snout. Inhabits swamp areas. Historic range: Southern Mexico to Colombia and Ecuador. Status: Endangered.

Tapir, Mountain *(Tapirus pinchaque).* Stocky, primitive, odd- toed hoofed mammal with an elongated snout and long, thick, black hair. Historic range: Colombia, Ecuador and possibly Peru and Venezuela. Status: Endangered.

Tarsier, Philippine *(Tarsius syrichta).* Small nocturnal arboreal mammal related to lemurs. Historic range: Philippines. Status: Threatened.

Tartaruga *(Podocnemis expansa).* Reptile. Historic range: South America: Orinoco and Amazon River basins. Status: Endangered.

Teal, Campbell Island Flightless *(Anas aucklandica nesiotis).* Belongs to a species that is the smallest of the river ducks. Historic range: New Zealand (Campbell Island). Status: Endangered.

Temolek, Ikan (minnow), *(Probarbus jullieni).* Historic range: Thailand, Cambodia, Vietnam, Malaysia, Laos. Status: Endangered.

Tern, California Least *(Sterna antillarum browni).* Small gray and white seabird with a black cap. Historic range: Mexico, U.S.A. (CA). Status: Endangered.

Tern, Least *(Sterna antillarum).* Black and gray seabird. Historic range: U.S.A. (Atlantic and Gulf coasts, Miss. R. Basin, CA), Gr. and Lesser Antilles, Bahamas, Mexico; winters Central America, northern South America. Status: Endangered.

Tern, Roseate *(Sterna dougallii dougallii).* Pale gray shorebird with black cap and nape. Historic range: Tropical and temperate coasts of Atlantic Basin and East Africa. Status: Endangered (U.S.A. - Atlantic Coast south to NC; Canada (NF, NS, QU); Bermuda; threatened (Western Hemisphere and adjacent oceans, incl. U.S.A. (FL, PR, VI), where not listed as endangered.

Terrapin, River *(Batagur baska).* Turtle. Historic range: Malaysia, Bangladesh, Burma, India, Indonesia. Status: Endangered.

Thrasher, White-breasted *(Ramphocinclus brachyurus).* Bird noted for its singing. Historic range: West Indies: St. Lucia, Martinique. Status: Endangered.

Thrush, Large Kauai *(Myadestes myadestinus).* Bird found only in the forest of the Alakai Swamp. Historic range: U.S.A. (HI). Status: Endangered.

Thrush, Molokai *(Myadestes lanaiensis rutha).* Heavy-bodied thrush. Inhabits dense ohia forests. Historic range: U.S.A. (HI). Status: Endangered.

Thrush, New Zealand (wattlebird), *(Turnagra capensis).* Historic range: New Zealand. Status: Endangered.

Thrush, Small Kauai *(Myadestes palmeri).* Rare thrush inhabiting only dense ohia forests in the Kauai Alakai Swamp. Historic range: U.S.A. (HI). Status: Endangered.

Tiger *(Panthera tigris).* Historic range: Temperate and Tropical Asia. Status: Endangered.

Tiger, Tasmanian *(Thylacinus cynocephalus).* Historic range: Australia. Status: Endangered.

Tinamou, Solitary *(Tinamus solitarius).* Bird resembling a quail. Noted for its short, headlong flight. Historic range: Brazil, Paraguay, Argentina. Status: Endangered.

Toad, African Viviparous *(Nectophrynoides spp.).* Historic range: Tanzania, Guinea, Ivory Coast, Cameroon, Liberia, Ethiopia. Status: Endangered.

Toad, Cameroon *(Bufo superciliaris).* Historic range: Equatorial Africa. Status: Endangered.

Toad, Houston *(Bufo houstonensis).* Similar to the dwarf American toad. Historic range: U.S.A. (TX). Status: Endangered.

Toad, Monte Verde *(Bufo periglenes).* Historic range: Costa Rica. Status: Endangered.

Toad, Puerto Rican Crested *(Peltophryne lemur).* Medium-sized toad with upturned snout. Historic range: U.S.A. (PR), British Virgin Islands. Status: Threatened.

Toad, Wyoming *(Bufo hemiophrys baxteri).* Found in the Laramie Basin. Historic range: U.S.A. (WY). Status: Endangered.

Tomistoma *(Tomistoma schlegelii).* Reptile. Historic range: Malaysia, Indonesia. Status: Endangered.

Topminnow, Gila (incl. Yaqui), *(Poeciliopsis occidentalis).* Small fish. Historic range: U.S.A. (AZ, NM), Mexico. Status: Endangered (U.S.A. only).

Tortoise, Angulated *(Geochelone yniphora).* Historic range: Malagasy Republic. Status: Endangered.

Tortoise, Bolson *(Gopherus flavomarginatus).* Historic range: Mexico. Status: Endangered.

Tortoise, Desert *(Gopherus agassizii).* Historic range: U.S.A. (AZ, CA, NV, UT), Mexico. Status: Threatened (except AZ south and east of Colorado River and Mexico).

Tortoise, Galapagos *(Geochelone elephantopus).* Historic range: Ecuador (Galapagos Islands). Status: Endangered.

Tortoise, Gopher *(Gopherus polyphemus).* Historic range: U.S.A. (AL, FL, GA, LA, MS, SC). Status: Threatened (whenever found west of Mobile and Tombigbee Rivers in AL, MS, and LA).

Tortoise, Radiated *(Geochelone radiata).* Historic range: Malagasy Republic. Status: Endangered.

Totoaba (seatrout or weakfish), *(Cynoscion macdonaldi).* Historic range: Mexico (Gulf of California). Status: Endangered.

Towhee, Inyo California *(Pipilo crissalis eremophilus).* Songbird inhabiting scrub vegetation and open woods. Historic range: U.S.A. (CA). Status: Threatened.

Tracaja *(Podocnemis unifilis).* Reptile. Historic range: South America: Orinoco and Amazon River basins. Status: Endangered.

Trembler, Martinique (thrasher), *(Cinclocerthia ruficauda gutturalis).* Bird. Historic range: West Indies: Martinique. Status: Endangered.

Trout, Apache *(Oncorhynchus apache).* Medium-sized yellowish trout with dark brown spots. Historic range: U.S.A. (AZ). Status: Threatened.

Trout, Gila *(Oncorhynchus gilae).* Fish with iridescent golden sides and irregular spotting. Historic range: U.S.A. (AZ, NM). Status: Endangered.

Trout, Greenback Cutthroat *(Oncorhynchus clarki stomias).* Large, spotted trout. Historic range: U.S.A. (CO). Status: Threatened.

Trout, Lahontan Cutthroat *(Oncorhynchus clarki henshawi).* Subspecies of the cutthroat trout. Historic range: U.S.A. (CA, NV, OR). Status: Threatened.

Trout, Little Kern Golden *(Oncorhynchus aguabonita whitei).* Subspecies of the golden trout. Historic range: U.S.A. (CA). Status: Threatened.

Trout, Paiute Cutthroat *(Oncorhynchus clarki seleniris).* Subspecies of the cutthroat trout. Historic range: U.S.A. (CA). Status: Threatened.

Tuatara *(Sphenodon punctatus).* Only living member of a group of reptiles that appeared on earth more than 200 million years ago. Historic range: New Zealand. Status: Endangered.

Turtle, Alabama Red-bellied *(Pseudemys alabamensis).* Historic range: U.S.A. (AL). Status: Endangered.

Turtle, Aquatic Box *(Terrapene coahuila).* Historic range: Mexico. Status: Endangered.

Turtle, Black Softshell *(Trionyx nigricans).* Historic range: Bangladesh. Status: Endangered.

Turtle, Burmese Peacock *(Morenia ocellata).* Historic range: Burma. Status: Endangered.

Turtle, Central American River *(Dermatemys mawii).* Historic range: Mexico, Belize, Guatemala. Status: Endangered.

Turtle, Cuatro Cienegas Softshell *(Trionyx ater).* Historic range: Mexico. Status: Endangered.

Turtle, Flattened Musk *(Sternotherus depressus).* Historic range: U.S.A. (AL). Status: Threatened (Black Warrior River system upstream from Bankhead Dam).

Turtle, Geometric *(Psammobates geometricus).* Historic range: South Africa. Status: Endangered.

Turtle, Green Sea *(Chelonia mydas* - incl. *agassizi).* Historic range: Circumglobal in tropical and temperate seas and oceans. Status: Threatened (wherever found except where listed as endangered); endangered (breeding colony populations in FL and on Pacific coast of Mexico).

Turtle, Hawksbill Sea *(Eretmochelys imbricata).* Historic range: Tropical seas. Status: Endangered.

Turtle, Indian Sawback *(Kachuga tecta tecta).* Historic range: India. Status: Endangered.

Turtle, Indian Softshell *(Trionyx gangeticus).* Historic range: Pakistan, India. Status: Endangered.

Turtle, Kemp's Ridley Sea *(Lepidochelys kempii).* Historic range: Tropical and temperate seas in Atlantic Basin, incl. Gulf of Mexico. Status: Endangered.

Turtle, Leatherback Sea *(Dermochelys coriacea).* Historic range: Tropical, temperate, and subpolar seas. Status: Endangered.

Turtle, Loggerhead Sea *(Caretta caretta).* Historic range: Circumglobal in tropical and temperate seas and oceans. Status: Threatened.

Turtle, Olive (Pacific) Ridley Sea *(Lepidochelys olivacea).* Historic range: Tropical and temperate seas in Pacific Basin. Status: Threatened (wherever found except where listed as endangered); endangered (breeding colony populations on Pacific coast of Mexico).

Turtle, Peacock Softshell *(Trionyx hurum).* Historic range: India, Bangladesh. Status: Endangered.

Turtle, Plymouth Red-bellied *(Pseudemys rubriventris bangsi).* Historic range: U.S.A. (MA). Status: Endangered.

Turtle, Ringed Sawback *(Graptemys oculifera).* Historic range: U.S.A. (LA, MS). Status: Threatened.

Turtle, Short-necked or Western Swamp *(Pseudemydura umbrina).* Historic range: Australia. Status: Endangered.

Turtle, Spotted Pond *(Geoclemys hamiltonii).* Historic range: North India, Pakistan. Status: Endangered.

Turtle, Three-keeled Asian *(Melanochelys tricarinata).* Historic range: Central India to Bangladesh and Burma. Status: Endangered.

Turtle, Yellow-blotched Map *(Graptemys flavimaculata).* Historic range: U.S.A. (MS). Status: Threatened.

Uakari *(Cacajao* spp. all species). Small, short-tailed monkey whose appearance resembles the orangutan. Historic range: Peru, Brazil, Ecuador, Colombia, Venezuela. Status: Endangered.

Urial *(Ovis musimon ophion).* Reddish brown wild sheep with white neck and a beard. Historic range: Cyprus. Status: Endangered.

Vicuna *(Vicugna vicugna).* Wild ruminant related to the domesticated llama and alpaca. Historic range: South America (Andes). Status: Endangered.

Viper, Lar Valley *(Vipera latifii).* Poisonsous snake. Historic range: Iran. Status: Endangered.

Vireo, Black-Capped *(Vireo atricapillus).* Small olive-green songbird with distinctive white patches around its eyes. Historic range: U.S.A. (KS, LA, NE, OK, TX), Mexico. Status: Endangered.

Vireo, Least Bell's *(Vireo bellii pusillus).* Migratory songbird that nests primarily in willows. Historic range: U.S.A. (CA), Mexico. Status: Endangered.

Vole, Amargosa *(Microtus californicus scirpensis).* Short- tailed, mouse-like rodent inhabiting marshes along the Amargosa River. Historic range: U.S.A. (CA). Status: Endangered.

Vole, Florida Salt Marsh *(Microtus pennsylvanicus dukecampbelli).* Historic range: U.S.A. (FL). Status: Endangered.

Vole, Hualapai Mexican *(Microtus mexicanus hualpaiensis).* Rare mouse-sized rodent found only in three areas totaling less than an acre. Historic range: U.S.A. (AZ). Status: Endangered.

Wallaby, Banded Hare *(Lagostrophus fasciatus).* Smaller cousin of the kangaroo. Historic range: Australia. Status: Endangered.

Wallaby, Brindled Nail-tailed *(Onychogalea fraenata).* Smaller cousin of the kangaroo. Historic range: Australia. Status: Endangered.

Wallaby, Crescent Nail-tailed *(Onychogalea lunata).* Smaller cousin of the kangaroo. Historic range: Australia. Status: Endangered.

Wallaby, Parma *(Macropus parma).* Smaller cousin of the kangaroo. Historic range: Australia. Status: Endangered.

Wallaby, Western Hare *(Lagorchestes hirsutus).* Smaller cousin of the kangaroo. Historic range: Australia. Status: Endangered.

Wallaby, Yellow-footed Rock *(Petrogale xanthopus).* Smaller cousin of the kangaroo. Historic range: Australia. Status: Endangered.

Wanderer, Plain (collared-hemipode) *(Pedionomous torquatus).* Bird. Historic range: Australia. Status: Endangered.

Warbler (old world), Nightingale Reed *(Acrocephalus luscinia).* Historic range: Western Pacific Ocean. Status: Endangered (U.S.A. - Mariana Islands).

Warbler (old world), Rodrigues *(Bebrornis rodericanus).* Historic range: Mauritius (Rodrigues Islands). Status: Endangered.

Warbler (old world), Seychelles *(Bebrornis sechellensis).* Historic range: Indian Ocean: Seychelles Island. Status: Endangered.

Warbler (wood), Bachman's *(Vermivora bachmanii).* Rarest native songbird of the U.S.A. Nests in swampy woodlands. Historic range: U.S.A. (Southeastern), Cuba. Status: Endangered.

Warbler (wood), Barbados Yellow *(Dendroica petechia petechia).* Songbird. Historic range: West Indies: Barbados. Status: Endangered.

Warbler (wood), Golden-cheeked *(Dendroica chrysoparia).* Historic range: U.S.A. (TX), Mexico, Guatemala, Honduras, Nicaragua, Belize. Status: Endangered.

Warbler (wood), Kirtland's *(Dendroica kirtlandii).* Blue-gray songbird whose breeding grounds are limited to stands of jack pine. Historic range: U.S.A. (principally MI), Canada, West Indies: Bahama Islands. Status: Endangered.

Warbler (wood), Semper's *(Leucopeza semperi).* Historic range: West Indies: St. Lucia. Status: Endangered.

Whale, Blue *(Balaenoptera musculus).* World's largest mammal, weighing from 90 to 150 tons. Historic range: Oceanic. Status: Endangered.

Whale, Bowhead *(Balaena mysticetus).* Black, stout-bodied right whale whose mouth curves upward. Historic range: Oceanic (north latitudes only). Status: Endangered.

Whale, Finback *(Balaenoptera physalus).* World's second-largest mammal, weighing over 60 tons. Historic range: Oceanic. Status: Endangered.

Whale, Gray *(Eschrichtius robustus).* Slow-swimming baleen whale that migrates as far as 16,000 kilometers, (10,000 miles) round-trip. Historic range: North Pacific Ocean: coastal and Bering Sea, formerly North Atlantic Ocean. Status: Endangered.

Whale, Humpback *(Megaptera novaeangliae).* Medium-sized baleen whale with a dorsal hump and long flippers. Historic range: Oceanic. Status: Endangered.

Whale, Right *(Balaena glacialis).* Black, stout-bodied baleen whale with bowed lower jaw. Historic range: Oceanic. Status: Endangered.

Whale, Sei *(Balaenoptera borealis).* Large slender baleen whale capable of swimming up to 48 kph (30 mph). Historic range: Oceanic. Status: Endangered.

Whale, Sperm *(Physeter catodon).* Large, toothed whale with a squarish head. Historic range: Oceanic. Status: Endangered.

Whipbird, Western *(Psophodes nigrogularis).* Historic range: Australia. Status: Endangered.

White-eye, Bridled *(Zosterops conspicillatus conspicillatus).* Belongs to a family of birds possibly related to the Australian honeyeaters. Historic range: Western Pacific Ocean: U.S.A. (Guam). Status: Endangered.

White-eye, Norfolk Island *(Zosterops albogularis).* Belongs to a family of birds possibly related to the Australian honeyeaters. Historic range: Indian Ocean: Norfolk Islands. Status: Endangered.

White-eye, Ponape Greater *(Rukia longirostra).* Belongs to a family of birds possibly related to the Australian honeyeaters. Historic range: West Pacific Ocean: U.S.A. (Caroline Islands). Status: Endangered.

White-eye, Seychelles *(Zosterops modesta).* Belongs to a family of birds possibly related to the Australian honeyeaters. Historic range: Indian Ocean: Seychelles. Status: Endangered.

Wolf, Gray *(Canis lupus).* Resembles a large, domestic dog. Historic range: Holarctic. Status: Endangered (U.S.A 48 conterminous states, except MN Mexico); threatened (U.S.A. -MN).

Wolf, Maned *(Chrysocyon brachyurus).* Historic range: Argentina, Bolivia, Brazil, Paraguay, Uruguay. Status: Endangered.

Wolf, Red *(Canis rufus).* Reddish canine resembling a large dog. Historic range: U.S.A. (west to central TX). Status: Endangered.

Wombat, Hairy-nosed *(Lasiorhinus krefftii).* Large nocturnal burrower with soft fur and a hairy nose. Historic range: Australia. Status: Endangered.

Woodrat, Key Largo *(Neotoma floridana smalli).* Medium-sized rodent restricted to the northern portion of Key Largo. Historic range: U.S.A. (FL). Status: Endangered.

Woodpecker, Imperial *(Campephilus imperialis).* Historic range: Mexico. Status: Endangered.

Woodpecker, Ivory-billed *(Campephilus principalis).* Largest of the North American woodpeckers. Historic range: U.S.A. (southcentral and southeastern), Cuba. Status: Endangered.

Woodpecker, Red-cockaded *(Pilcoides borealis).* Black and white flecked woodpecker with distinctive white cheek patch. Inhabits old growth pine stands. Historic range: U.S.A. (southcentral and southeastern). Status: Endangered.

Woodpecker, Tristam's *(Dryocopus javensis richardsi).* Historic range: Korea. Status: Endangered.

Woundfin *(Plagopterus argentissimus).* Silvery minnow. Historic range: U.S.A. (AZ, NV, UT). Status: Endangered.

Wren, Guadeloupe House *(Troglodytes aedon guadeloupensis).* Historic range: West Indies: Guadeloupe. Status: Endangered.

Wren, St. Lucia House *(Troglodytes aedon mesoleucus).* Historic range: West Indies: St. Lucia. Status: Endangered.

Yak, Wild *(Bos grunniens).* Historic range: China (Tibet), India. Status: Endangered.

Zebra, Grevy's *(Equus grevyi).* Historic range: Kenya, Ethiopia, Somalia. Status: Threatened.

Zebra, Hartmann's Mountain *(Equus zebra hartmannae).* Historic range: Namibia, Angola. Status: Threatened.

Zebra, Mountain *(Equus zebra zebra).* Historic range: South Africa. Status: Endangered.

Appendix II: Endangered and Threatened Plants (as of July 1991)

This appendix lists plants that have been classified by the United States Government as being in a threatened or endangered state. Threatened species are still abundant but are likely to become endangered due to decline in numbers. Endangered species have low population levels and are threatened with extinction by man-made or natural changes in the environment.

Achyranthes splendens var. rotundata (no common name). Member of the Amaranth family. Historic range: U.S.A. (HI). Status: Endangered.

'Ahinahina *(Argyroxiphium sandwicense ssp. sandwicense).* Perennial of the Aster family inhabiting volcanic soils. Historic range: U.S.A. (HI). Status: Endangered.

Alabama canebrake pitcher-plant *(Sarracenia rubra ssp. alabamensis).* Insectivorous herb with pitcher-like leaves and maroon flowers. Historic range: U.S.A. (AL). Status: Endangered.

Alabama leather flower *(Clematis socialis).* Member of the Buttercup family with bell-shaped flowers. Historic range: U.S.A. (AL). Status: Endangered.

Aleutian shield-fern *(Polystichum aleuticum).* Low-growing fern found only on Adak Island. Historic range: U.S.A. (AK). Status: Endangered.

Amargosa niterwort *(Nitrophila mohavensis).* Low-growing perennial with bright green succulent leaves. Historic range: U.S.A. (CA). Status: Endangered.

American hart's-tongue fern *(Phyllitis scolopendrium var. americana).* Fern inhabiting cool limestone sinkholes in mature hardwood forests. Historic range: U.S.A. (AL, MI, NY, TN), Canada (ON). Status: Threatened.

Antioch Dunes evening-primrose *(Oenothera deltoides ssp. howellii).* White-flowered perennial found only in the Antioch Dunes area. Historic range: U.S.A. (CA). Status: Endangered.

Arizona agave *(Agave arizonica).* Succulent with pointed leaves and pale yellow flowers. Historic range: U.S.A. (AZ). Status: Endangered.

Arizona cliffrose *(Purchia subintegra).* Evergreen shrub covered with dense white hairs. Historic range: U.S.A. (AZ). Status: Endangered.

Arizona hedgehog cactus *(Echinocereus triglochidiatus var. arizonicus).* Cactus with clusters of cylindrical stems and bright red flowers. Historic range: U.S.A. (AZ). Status: Endangered.

Ash Meadows blazing-star *(Mentzelia leucophylla).* Biennial or short-lived perennial with yellow flowers. Historic range: U.S.A. (NV). Status: Threatened.

Ash Meadows gumplant *(Grindelia fraxinopratensis).* Tall aster with yellow flowers. Historic range: U.S.A. (CA, NV). Status: Threatened.

Ash Meadows ivesia *(Ivesia kingii var. eremica).* Low-growing perennial with rope-like leaves. Historic range: U.S.A. (NV). Status: Threatened.

Ash Meadows milk-vetch *(Astragalus phoenix).* Low-growing perennial found only in the Ash Meadows region. Historic range: U.S.A. (NV). Status: Threatened.

Ash Meadows sunray *(Enceliopsis nudicaulis var. corrugata).* Perennial herb with long wiry stems. Historic range: U.S.A. (NV). Status: Threatened.

Ashy dogweed *(Thymophylla tephroleuca).* Perennial herb with gray leaves and yellow flowers. Historic range: U.S.A. (TX). Status: Endangered.

Aupaka *(Isodendrion hosakae).* Historic range: U.S.A. (HI). Status: Endangered.

Autumn buttercup *(Ranunculus acriformis var. aestivalis).* Yellow-flowered herbaceous perennial. Historic range: U.S.A. (UT). Status: Endangered.

Bakersfield cactus *(Opuntia treleasei).* Historic range: U.S.A. (CA). Status: Endangered.

Bariaco *(Trichilia triacantha).* Evergreen shrub or small tree belonging to the Mahogany family. Historic range: U.S.A. (PR). Status: Endangered.

Barneby ridge-cress *(Lepidium barnebyanum).* Member of the Mustard family. Historic range: U.S.A. (UT). Status: Endangered.

Beautiful goetzea, matabuey *(Goetzea elegans).* Evergreen shrub or small tree belonging to the Nightshade family. Historic range: U.S.A. (PR). Status: Endangered.

Beautiful pawpaw *(Deeringothamnus pulchellus).* Low shrub with white flowers. Historic range: U.S.A. (FL). Status: Endangered.

Black lace cactus *(Echinocereus reichenbachii var. albertii).* Low-growing cactus with large pink flowers. Historic range: U.S.A. (TX). Status: Endangered.

Black-spored quillwort *(Isoetes melanospora).* Aquatic plant with chive-like leaves. Historic range: U.S.A. (GA, SC). Status: Endangered.

Blowout penstemon *(Penstemon haydenii).* Blue-flowered perennial of the Snapdragon family. Historic range: U.S.A. (NE). Status: Endangered.

Blue Ridge goldenrod *(Solidago spithamaea).* Perennial herb with yellow flowers. Historic range: U.S.A. (NC, TN). Status: Threatened.

Bradshaw's desert-parsley *(Lomatium bradshawii).* Historic range: U.S.A. (OR). Status: Endangered.

Brady pincushion cactus *(Pediocactus bradyi).* Dwarf, semi- spherical cactus. Historic range: U.S.A. (AZ). Status: Endangered.

Brooksville bellflower *(Campanula robinsiae).* Annual herb with purple bell-shaped flowers. Historic range: U.S.A. (FL). Status: Endangered.

Bunched arrowhead *(Sagittaria fasciculata).* Aquatic herb with spatula-shaped leaves. Historic range: U.S.A. (NC, SC). Status: Endangered.

Bunched cory cactus *(Coryphantha ramillosa).* Dark green cactus with pink flowers. Historic range: U.S.A. (TX), Mexico (Coahuila). Status: Threatened.

California jewelflower *(Caulanthus californicus).* Member of the Mustard family. Historic range: U.S.A. (CA). Status: Endangered.

Canby's dropwort *(Oxypolis canbyi).* Perennial plant with a dill fragrance. Historic range: U.S.A. (DE, GA, MD, NC, SC). Status: Endangered.

Carter's mustard *(Warea carteri).* Annual herb with small oblong leaves and white flowers. Historic range: U.S.A. (FL). Status: Endangered.

Carter's panicgrass *(Panicum fauriei var. carteri).* Annual grass found in one area of Mokolii Island. Historic range: U.S.A. (HI). Status: Endangered.

Cassia mirabilis *(no common name).* Plant belonging to the Cassia family. Historic range: U.S.A. (PR). Status: Endangered.

Chapman rhododendron *(Rhododendron chapmanii).* Rare evergreen shrub with light pink flowers. Historic range: U.S.A. (FL). Status: Endangered.

Chilean false larch *(Fitzroya cupressoides).* Member of the Cypress family. Historic range: Chile, Argentina. Status: Threatened.

Chisos Mountain hedgehog cactus *(Echinocereus chisosensis var. chisosensis).*

Cactus found only in a small area of the Big Bend National Park. Historic range: U.S.A. (TX). Status: Threatened.

Clay-loving wild-buckwheat *(Eriogonum pelinophilum).* Low-growing plant with clusters of pale flowers. Historic range: U.S.A. (CO). Status: Endangered.

Clay phacelia *(Phacelia argillacea).* Winter annual of the Waterleaf family. Historic range: U.S.A. (UT). Status: Endangered.

Cobana negra *(Stahlia monosperma).* Member of the Pea family. Historic range: U.S.A. (PR), Dominican Republic. Status: Threatened.

Cochise pincushion cactus *(Coryphantha robbinsorum).* Small spiny cactus resembling a pincushion. Historic range: U.S.A. (AZ), Mexico (Sonora). Status: Threatened.

Contra Costa wallflower *(Erysimum capitatum var. angustatum).* Monocarpic perennial of the Mustard family. Historic range: U.S.A. (CA). Status: Endangered.

Cook's holly *(Ilex cookii).* Evergreen shrub or small tree inhabiting mountain peaks. Historic range: U.S.A. (PR). Status: Endangered.

Cooke's kokio *(Kokia cookei).* Small tree with orange-red flowers. Historic range: U.S.A. (HI). Status: Endangered.

Cooley's meadowrue *(Thalictrum cooleyi).* Perennial of the Buttercup family. Historic range: U.S.A. (NC, FL). Status: Endangered.

Cooley's water-willow *(Justicia cooleyi).* Perennial herb with lavender-rose flowers resembling small snapdragons. Historic range: U.S.A. (FL). Status: Endangered.

Costa Rican jatropha *(Jatropha costaricensis).* Historic range: Costa Rica. Status: Endangered.

Crenulate lead-plant *(Amorpha crenulata).* Medium-sized shrub belonging to the Pea family. Historic range: U.S.A. (FL). Status: Endangered.

Cumberland sandwort *(Arenaria cumberlandensis).* Herbaceous perennial endemic to the Cumberland Plateau. Historic range: (KY, TN). Status: Endangered.

Cuneate bidens *(Bidens cuneata).* Biennial herb of the Aster family found only on the island of Oahu. Historic range: U.S.A. (HI). Status: Endangered.

Daphnopsis hellerana *(no common name).* Small tree or large shrub. Historic range: U.S.A. (PR). Status: Endangered.

Davis' green pitaya *(Echinocereus viridiflorus var. davisii).* Dwarf cactus with yellow-green flowers. Historic range: U.S.A. (TX). Status: Endangered.

Decurrent false aster *(Boltonia decurrens).* Perennial plant found in a flood plain habitat. Historic range: U.S.A. (IL, MO). Status: Threatened.

Deltoid spurge *(Chamaesyce deltoidea spp. deltoidea).* Mat-forming herb with tiny leaves. Historic range: U.S.A. (FL). Status: Endangered.

Diamond Head schiedea *(Schiedea adamantis).* Low-growing woody shrub found only on the island of Oahu. Historic range: U.S.A. (HI). Status: Endangered.

Dudley Bluffs bladderpod *(Lesquerella congesta).* Member of the Mustard family. Historic range: U.S.A. (CO). Status: Threatened.

Dudley Bluffs twinpod *(Physaria obcordata).* Member of the Mustard family. Historic range: U.S.A. (CO). Status: Threatened.

Dwarf bear-poppy *(Arctomecon humilis).* White-flowered poppy that grows in clumps. Historic range: U.S.A. (UT). Status: Endangered.

Dwarf-flowered heartleaf *(Hexastylis naniflora).* Low-growing herbaceous plant. Historic range: U.S.A. (NC, SC). Status: Threatened.

Dwarf lake iris *(Iris lacustris).* Dwarf iris with flat leaves and blue flowers. Historic range: U.S.A. (MI, WI), Canada (ON). Status: Threatened.

Dwarf naupaka *(Scaevola coriacea).* Shrub with succulent leaves and "half flowers," resembling half of a normally symmetrical flower. Historic range: U.S.A. (HI). Status: Endangered.

Eastern prairie fringed orchid *(Platanthera leucophaea).* Historic range: U.S.A. (AR, IA, IL, IN, ME, MI, MO, NE, NJ, NY, OH, OK, PA, VA, WI), Canada (ON, NB). Status: Threatened.

Elfin tree fern *(Cyathea dryopteroides).* Dwarf tree fern found in high elevations. Historic range: U.S.A. (PR). Status: Endangered.

Erubia *(Solanum drymophilium).* Evergreen shrub of the Nightshade family. Historic range: U.S.A. (PR). Status: Endangered.

Eureka Dune grass *(Swallenia alexandrae).* Perennial grass with stiff leaves. Historic range: U.S.A. (CA). Status: Endangered.

Eureka Valley evening-primrose *(Oenothera avita ssp. eurekensis).* Perennial herb with white flowers. Historic range: U.S.A. (CA). Status: Endangered.

Ewa Plains 'akoko *(Chamaesyce skottsbergii var. kalaeloana).* Small woody shrub of the Spurge family. Historic range: U.S.A. (HI). Status: Endangered.

Fassett's locoweed *(Oxytropis campestris var. chartacea).* Herbaceous perennial found on lake shorelines. Historic range: U.S.A. (WI). Status: Threatened.

Florida bonamia *(Bonamia grandiflora).* Perennial vine of the Morning Glory family. Historic range: U.S.A. (FL). Status: Threatened.

Florida golden aster *(Chrysopsis floridana).* Perennial herb with hairy leaves and yellow flowers. Historic range: U.S.A. (FL). Status: Endangered.

Florida torreya *(Torreya taxifolia).* Evergreen tree belonging to the Yew family. Historic range: U.S.A. (FL, GA). Status: Endangered.

Florida ziziphus *(Ziziphus celata).* Small shrub with oblong leaves and white flowers. Historic range: U.S.A. (FL). Status: Endangered.

Four-petal pawpaw *(Asimina tetramera).* Large woody shrub inhabiting sand pine scrub. Historic range: U.S.A. (FL). Status: Endangered.

Fragrant prickly-apple *(Cereus eriophorus var. fragrans).* Column-shaped cactus ranging from 1-5 meters (3-16 feet) tall. Historic range: U.S.A. (FL). Status: Endangered.

Fringed campion *(Silene polypetala).* Member of the Pink family. Historic range: U.S.A. (FL, GA). Status: Endangered.

Furbish lousewort *(Pedicularis furbishiae).* Perennial herb of the Snapdragon family with serrated leaves and greenish yellow flowers. Historic range: U.S.A. (ME), Canada (NB). Status: Endangered.

Garber's spurge *(Chamaesyce garberi).* Herb with oval leaves and hairy stems. Historic range: U.S.A. (FL). Status: Threatened.

Garrett's mint *(Dicerandra christmanii).* Mint endemic to the scrub habitat of central Florida. Historic range: U.S.A. (FL). Status: Endangered.

Gentian pinkroot *(Spigelia gentianoides).* Historic range: U.S.A. (FL). Status: Endangered.

Geocarpon minimum *(no common name).* Succulent annual. Historic range: U.S.A. (AR, MO). Status: Threatened.

Gouania hillebrandii *(no common name).* Member of the Buckthorn family. Historic range: U.S.A. (HI). Status: Endangered.

Green pitcher-plant *(Sarracenia oreophila).* Insectivorous perennial with funnel-shaped leaves. Historic range: U.S.A. (AL, GA, TN). Status: Endangered.

Guatemalan fir *(Abies guatemalensis).* Historic range: Mexico, Guatemala, Honduras, El Salvador. Status: Threatened.

Gypsum wild-buckwheat *(Eriogonum gypsophilum).* Clumping perennial with dark green oval leaves. Historic range: U.S.A. (NM). Status: Threatened.

Hairy rattleweed *(Baptisia arachnifera).* Perennial legume covered with tiny hairs. Historic range: U.S.A. (GA). Status: Endangered.

Haplostachys haplostachya var. angustifolia *(no common name).* Member of the Mint family. Historic range: U.S.A. (HI). Status: Endangered.

Harper's beauty *(Harperocallis flava).* Yellow-flowered perennial of the Lily family. Historic range: U.S.A. (FL). Status: Endangered.

Harperella *(Ptilimnium nodosum).* Long-stemmed annual herb found near water. Historic range: U.S.A. (AL, GA, MD, NC, SC, WV). Status: Endangered.

Hawaiian vetch *(Vicia menziesii).* Perennial climbing vine with large flowers. Historic range: U.S.A. (HI). Status: Endangered.

Hayun lagu (Guam) Tronkon guafi (Rota), *(Serianthes nelsonii).* Member of the Pea family. Historic range: Western Pacific Ocean: U.S.A. (Guam, Rota). Status: Endangered.

Heliotrope milk-vetch *(Astragalus montii).* Rare perennial herb endemic to the Wasatch Plateau. Historic range: U.S.A. (UT). Status: Threatened.

Heller's blazingstar *(Liatris helleri).* Perennial herb with one or more stems and lavender flowers. Historic range: U.S.A. (NC). Status: Threatened.

Highlands scrub hypericum *(Hypericum cumulicola).* Perennial herb with a wiry stem and needlelike leaves. Historic range: U.S.A. (FL). Status: Endangered.

Higo chumbo *(Harrisia portoricensis).* Member of the Cactus family. Historic range: U.S.A. (PR). Status: Threatened.

Higuero de Sierra *(Crescentia portoricensis).* Evergreen shrub with bell-shaped flowers. Historic range: U.S.A. (PR). Status: Endangered.

Hinckley's oak *(Quercus hinckleyi).* Shrubby evergreen with gray-green leaves. Historic range: U.S.A. (TX). Status: Threatened.

Hoover's woolly-star *(Eriastrum hooveri).* Historic range: U.S.A. (CA). Status: Threatened.

Houghton's goldenrod *(Solidago houghtonii).* Slender, big-headed annual. Historic range: U.S.A. (MI), Canada (ON). Status: Threatened.

Jesup's milk-vetch *(Astragalus robbinsii var. jesupi).* Perennial herb of the Pea family. Historic range: U.S.A. (NH, VT). Status: Endangered.

Johnston's frankenia *(Frankenia johnstonii).* Perennial low-growing shrub with oblong leaves and white flowers. Historic range: U.S.A. (TX), Mexico (Nuevo Leon). Status: Endangered.

Jones cycladenia *(Cycladenia humilis var. jonesii).* Short herbaceous perennial with broad oval leaves. Historic range: U.S.A. (AZ, UT). Status: Threatened.

Kauai hau kuahiwi *(Hibiscadelphus distans).* Small tree with heart-shaped leaves and greenish yellow flowers. Historic range: U.S.A. (HI). Status: Endangered.

Kearney's blue-star *(Amsonia kearneyana).* Multi-stemmed perennial with clusters of white flowers. Historic range: U.S.A. (AZ). Status: Endangered.

Key tree-cactus *(Cereus robinii).* Largest of the native Florida cacti reaching a maximum height of 10 meters (30 feet). Historic range: U.S.A. (FL), Cuba. Status: Endangered.

Knowlton cactus *(Pediocactus knowltonii).* Dwarf cactus lacking central spines. Historic range: U.S.A. (NM, CO). Status: Endangered.

Koki'o *(Kokia drynarioides).* Tree with palmate leaves and orange-red flowers. Historic range: U.S.A. (HI). Status: Endangered.

Ko'oloa'ula *(Abutilon menziesii).* Tall shrub with heart-shaped leaves and red flowers. Historic range: U.S.A. (HI). Status: Endangered.

Kral's water-plantain *(Sagittaria secundifolia).* Historic range: U.S.A. (AL, GA). Status: Threatened.

Kuenzler hedgehog cactus *(Echinocereus fendleri var. kuenzleri).* Dwarf cactus with yellow-green flowers. Historic range: U.S.A. (NM). Status: Endangered.

Lakela's mint *(Dicerandra immaculata).* Low-growing, aromatic shrub. Historic range: U.S.A. (FL). Status: Endangered.

Lakeside daisy *(Hymenoxys acaulis var. glabra).* Low-growing daisy with one bright yellow flower per stalk. Historic range: U.S.A. (OH, IL), Canada (ON). Status: Threatened.

Lanai sandalwood or 'iliahi *(Santalum freycinetianum var. lanaiense).* Small tree with a gnarled trunk and bright red flowers. Historic range: U.S.A. (HI). Status: Endangered.

Large-flowered fiddleneck *(Amsinckia grandiflora).* Annual with red-orange flowers. Historic range: U.S.A. (CA). Status: Endangered.

Large-flowered skullcap *(Scutellaria montana).* Member of the Mint family, with oblong leaves and blue and white flowers. Historic range: U.S.A. (GA, TN). Status: Endangered.

Large-fruited sand-verbena *(Abronia macrocarpa).* Herb with erect stems and spherical clusters of pink-purple flowers. Historic range: U.S.A. (TX). Status: Endangered.

Last Chance townsendia *(Townsendia aprica).* Low-growing perennial of the Aster family. Historic range: U.S.A. (UT). Status: Threatened.

Leafy prairie-clover *(Dalea foliosa).* Historic range: U.S.A. (AL, IL, TN). Status: Endangered.

Lee pincushion cactus *(Coryphantha sneedii var. leei).* Resembles a mass of white-spined balls. Found at a single location in Carlsbad Caverns National Park. Historic range: U.S.A. (NM). Status: Threatened.

Lipochaeta venosa *(no common name).* Rare annual herb with a branching stem and small flowers. Historic range: U.S.A. (HI). Status: Endangered.

Little amphianthus *(Amphianthus pusillus).* Ephemeral aquatic plant with white flowers. Historic range: U.S.A. (AL, GA, SC). Status: Threatened.

Lloyd's hedgehog cactus *(Echinocereus lloydii).* Low-growing columnar cactus. Historic range: U.S.A. (TX). Status: Endangered.

Lloyd's Mariposa cactus *(Neolloydia mariposensis).* Spherical cactus with pink flowers. Historic range: U.S.A. (TX), Mexico (Coahuila). Status: Threatened.

Loch Lomond coyote-thistle *(Eryngium constancei).* Perennial herb of the Parsley family. Historic range: U.S.A. (CA). Status: Endangered.

Longspurred mint *(Dicerandra comutissima).* Aromatic shrub. Historic range: U.S.A. (FL). Status: Endangered.

Lyrate bladderpod *(Lesquerella lyrata).* Historic range: U.S.A. (AL). Status: Threatened.

MacFarlane's four-o'clock *(Mirabilis macfarlanei).* Perennial with heart-shaped leaves and purple or rose flowers. Historic range: U.S.A. (ID, OR). Status: Endangered.

Maguire daisy *(Erigeron maguirei var. maguirei).* Low-growing perennial daisy. Historic range: U.S.A. (UT). Status: Endangered.

Maguire primrose *(Primula maguirei).* Low-growing perennial with spatula-shaped leaves and lavender flowers. Historic range: U.S.A. (UT). Status: Threatened.

Malheur wire-lettuce *(Stephanomeria malheurensis).* Annual of the Aster family found only on one site near Malheur National Wildlife Refuge. Historic range: U.S.A. (OR). Status: Endangered.

Mancos milk-vetch *(Astragalus humillimus).* Low-growing perennial with lavender flowers. Historic range: U.S.A. (CO, NM). Status: Endangered.

Mat-forming quillwort *(Isoetes tegetiformans).* Low-growing aquatic plant. Historic range: U.S.A. (GA). Status: Endangered.

Maui remya *(Remya mauiensis).* Member of the Aster family. Historic range: U.S.A. (HI). Status: Endangered.

McDonald's rock-cress *(Arabis mcdonaldiana).* Purple-flowered perennial of the Mustard family. Historic range: U.S.A. (CA). Status: Endangered.

McKittrick pennyroyal *(Hedeoma apiculatum).* Perennial herb with thick leaves and pink flowers. Historic range: U.S.A. (TX, NM). Status: Threatened.

Mead's milkweed *(Asclepias meadii).* Perennial herb. Historic range: U.S.A. (IL, IN, IA, KS, MO, WI). Status: Threatened.

Mesa Verde cactus *(Sclerocactus mesae-verdae).* Spherical cactus with single or clustered stems and small yellow or greenish flowers. Historic range: U.S.A. (CO, NM). Status: Threatened.

Miccosukee gooseberry *(Ribes echinellum).* Shrub with spiny stems and white flowers. Historic range: U.S.A. (FL, SC). Status: Threatened.

Michaux's sumac *(Rhus michauxii).* Shrub belonging to the Cashew family. Historic range: U.S.A. (NC, SC, GA). Status: Endangered.

Michigan monkey-flower *(Mimulus glabratus var. michiganensis).* Plant belonging to the Snapdragon family. Historic range: U.S.A. (MI). Status: Endangered.

Minnesota trout lily *(Erythronium propullans).* Perennial also known as the prairie trout lily. Historic range: U.S.A. (MN). Status: Endangered.

Missouri bladderpod *(Lesquerella filiformis).* Yellow-flowered annual of the Mustard family. Historic range: U.S.A. (MO). Status: Endangered.

Mohr's Barbara's buttons *(Marshallia mohrii).* Perennial aster with pale pink to lavender flowers. Historic range: U.S.A. (AL, GA). Status: Threatened.

Mountain golden heather *(Hudsonia montana).* Low, clumping heather bearing pale yellow flowers. Historic range: U.S.A. (NC). Status: Threatened.

Mountain sweet pitcher-plant *(Sarracenia rubra ssp. jonesii).* Insectivorous perennial herb with maroon flowers. Historic range: U.S.A. (NC, SC). Status: Endangered.

Na'u (Hawaiian gardenia), *(Gardenia brighamii).* Tree belonging to the Coffee family. Historic range: U.S.A. (HI). Status: Endangered.

Navajo sedge *(Carex specuicola).* Grass-like perennial that grows in clumps. Historic range: U.S.A. (AZ). Status: Threatened.

Navasota ladies'-tresses *(Spiranthes parksii).* Rare perennial orchid. Historic range: U.S.A. (TX). Status: Endangered.

Nellie cory cactus *(Coryphantha minima).* Dwarf cactus with club-shaped spines. Historic range: U.S.A. (TX). Status: Endangered.

Nichol's Turk's head cactus *(Echinocactus horizonthalonius var. nicholii).* Barrel cactus with a single blue-green stem and pink flowers. Historic range: U.S.A. (AZ). Status: Endangered.

North Park phacelia *(Phacelia formosula).* Biennial found on riverbank bluffs in Jackson County. Historic range: U.S.A. (CO). Status: Endangered.

Northeastern bulrush *(Scirpus ancistrochaetus).* Historic range: U.S.A. (VA, MD, WV, PA, NY, MA, VT). Status: Endangered.

Northern wild monkshood *(Aconitum noveboracense).* Perennial of the Buttercup family with blue or purple hood-shaped flowers. Historic range: U.S.A. (IA, NY, OH, WI). Status: Threatened.

Osterhout milk-vetch *(Astragalus osterhoutii).* Tall annual with white flowers. Historic range: U.S.A. (CO). Status: Endangered.

Palma de manaca *(Calyptronoma rivalis).* Member of the Palm family. Historic range: U.S.A. (PR). Status: Threatened.

Palmate-bracted bird's beak *(Cordylànthus palmatus).* Annual herb of the Snapdragon family with gray-green scale-like leaves. Historic range: U.S.A. (CA). Status: Endangered.

Palo de Nigua *(Cornutia obovata).* Large evergreen bush or small tree with egg-shaped leaves. Historic range: U.S.A. (PR). Status: Endangered.

Palo de Ramon *(Banara vanderbiltii).* Evergreen shrub or small tree. Historic range: U.S.A. (PR). Status: Endangered.

Palo de rosa *(Ottoschulzia rhodoxylon).* Historic range: U.S.A. (PR), Dominican Republic. Status: Endangered.

Papery whitlow-wort *(Paronychia chartacea).* Low-growing annual herb with tiny white flowers. Historic range: U.S.A. (FL). Status: Threatened.

Pedate checker-mallow *(Sidalcea pedata).* Multi-stemmed perennial with pinkish rose flowers. Historic range: U.S.A. (CA). Status: Endangered.

Peebles Navajo cactus *(Pediocactus peeblesianus var. peeblesianus).* Small spherical cactus with comparatively large yellowish flowers. Historic range: U.S.A. (AZ). Status: Endangered.

Pelos del diablo *(Aristida portoricensis).* Plant belonging to the Grass family. Historic range: U.S.A. (PR). Status: Endangered.

Penland beardtongue *(Penstemon penlandii).* Member of the Snapdragon family with clusters of blue and violet flowers. Historic range: U.S.A. (CO). Status: Endangered.

Persistent trillium *(Trillium persistens).* Pink-flowered perennial of the Lily family. Historic range: U.S.A. (GA, SC). Status: Endangered.

Peter's Mountain mallow *(Iliamna corei).* Perennial resembling a small hollyhock. Historic range: U.S.A. (VA). Status: Endangered.

Pitcher's thistle *(Cirsium pitcheri).* Perennial sunflower with pointed leaves. Historic range: U.S.A. (IL, IN, MI, WI), Canada (ON). Status: Threatened.

Pondberry *(Lindera melissifolia).* Deciduous shrub. Historic range: U.S.A. (AL, AR, FL, GA, LA, MO, MS, NC, SC). Status: Endangered.

Prairie bush-clover *(Lespedeza leptostachya).* Herbaceous perennial reaching a height of about 1 meter (39 inches). Historic range: U.S.A. (IA, IL, MN, WI). Status: Threatened.

Presidio manzanita *(Arctostaphylos pungens var. ravenii).* Low shrub with shiny green elliptical leaves. Historic range: U.S.A. (CA). Status: Endangered.

Price's Potato-bean *(Apios priceana).* Member of the Pea family. Historic range: U.S.A. (AL, IL, KY, MS, TN). Status: Threatened.

Pygmy fringe-tree *(Chionanthus pygmaeus).* White-flowered shrub of the Olive family. Historic range: U.S.A. (FL). Status: Endangered.

Relict trillium *(Trillium reliquum).* Perennial of the Lily family with a curved stem and light green to brownish purple flowers. Historic range: U.S.A. (AL, GA, SC). Status: Endangered.

Remya kauaiensis *(no common name).* Member of the Aster family. Historic range: U.S.A. (HI). Status: Endangered.

Remya montgomeryi *(no common name).* Member of the Aster family. Historic range: U.S.A. (HI). Status: Endangered.

Roan Mountain bluet *(Hedyotis purpurea va. montana).* Member of the Coffee family. Historic range: U.S.A. (NC, TN). Status: Endangered.

Robbins' cinquefoil *(Potentilla robbinsiana).* Low-growing perennial with yellow flowers. Historic range: U.S.A. (NH, VT). Status: Endangered.

Rough-leaved loosestrife *(Lysimachia asperulaefolia).* Yellow-flowered perennial of the Primrose family. Historic range: U.S.A. (NC, SC). Status: Endangered.

Rugel's pawpaw *(Deeringothamnus rugelii).* Low shrub with yellow flowers. Historic range: U.S.A. (FL). Status: Endangered.

Running buffalo clover *(Trifolium stoloniferum).* Clover with compound leaves and white flowers. Historic range: U.S.A. (AR, IL, IN, KS, KY, MO, OH, WV). Status: Endangered.

Ruth's golden aster *(Pityopsis ruthii).* Perennial with clusters of yellow flowers. Historic range: U.S.A. (TN). Status: Endangered.

Sacramento Mountains thistle *(Cirsium vinaceum).* Tall perennial with purple flowers. Historic range: U.S.A. (NM). Status: Threatened.

Sacramento prickly-poppy *(Argemone pleiacantha ssp. pinnatisecta).* Rare poppy endemic to several canyons in the Sacramento Mountains. Historic range: U.S.A. (NM). Status: Endangered.

Salt marsh bird's beak *(Cordylanthus maritimus ssp. maritimus).* Hemiparasitic annual found in tidal wetlands. Historic range: U.S.A. (CA), Mexico (Baja California). Status: Endangered.

San Benito evening-primrose *(Camissonia benitensis).* Low-growing annual herb with bright yellow flowers. Historic range: U.S.A. (CA). Status: Threatened.

San Clemente Island broom *(Lotus dendroideus ssp. traskiae).* Low-growing shrub of the Pea family. Historic range: U.S.A. (CA). Status: Endangered.

San Clemente Island bush-mallow *(Malacothamnus clementinus).* Rounded plant with many branches and masses of pink flowers. Historic range: U.S.A. (CA). Status: Endangered.

San Clemente Island Indian paintbrush *(Castilleja grisea).* Yellow-flowered, leafy perennial of the Snapdragon family. Historic range: U.S.A. (CA). Status: Endangered.

San Clemente Island larkspur *(Delphinium kinkiense).* Perennial herb with pale flowers. Historic range: U.S.A. (CA). Status: Endangered.

San Diego mesa mint *(Pogogyne abramsii).* Annual herb with aromatic leaves and lavender flowers. Historic range: U.S.A. (CA). Status: Endangered.

San Francisco Peaks groundsel *(Senecio franciscanus).* Dwarf perennial found at high elevations. Historic range: U.S.A. (AZ). Status: Threatened.

San Joaquin wooly-threads *(Lembertia congdonii).* Member of the Aster family. Historic range: U.S.A. (CA). Status: Endangered.

San Mateo thornmint *(Acanthomintha obovata ssp. duttonii).* Small mint with toothed oblong leaves and white flowers. Historic range: U.S.A. (CA). Status: Endangered.

San Rafael cactus *(Pediocactus despainii).* Dwarf barrel-shaped cactus with peach-colored flowers. Historic range: U.S.A. (UT). Status: Endangered.

Sandplain gerardia *(Agalinis acuta).* Annual herb of the Snapdragon family. Historic range: U.S.A. (CT, MA, MD, NY, RI). Status: Endangered.

Santa Ana River woolly-star *(Eriastrum densifolium ssp. sanctorum).* Low shrub with clusters of blue flowers. Historic range: U.S.A. (CA). Status: Endangered.

Santa Barbara Island liveforever *(Dudleya traskiae).* Perennial herb also known as rock lettuce. Historic range: U.S.A. (CA). Status: Endangered.

Santa Cruz Cypress *(Cupressus abramsiana).* Densely branched evergreen tree. Historic range: U.S.A. (CA). Status: Endangered.

Schoepfia arenaria *(no common name).* Member of the Olax family. Historic range: U.S.A. (PR). Status: Threatened.

Schweinitz's sunflower *(Helianthus schweinitzii).* Historic range: U.S.A. (NC, SC). Status: Endangered.

Scrub blazingstar *(Liatris ohlingerae).* Perennial aster with pinkish-purple flowers. Historic range: U.S.A. (FL). Status: Endangered.

Scrub Lupine *(Lupinus aridorum).* Biennial or short-lived perennial of the Pea family. Historic range: U.S.A. (FL). Status: Endangered.

Scrub mint *(Dicerandra frutescens).* Aromatic plant with clusters of stems and white or pale pink flowers. Historic range: U.S.A. (FL). Status: Endangered.

Scrub plum *(Prunus geniculata).* Scraggly shrub belonging to the Rose family. Historic range: U.S.A. (FL). Status: Endangered.

Sentry milk-vetch *(Astragalus cremnophylax var. cremnophylax).* Member of the Pea family. Historic range: U.S.A. (AZ). Status: Endangered.

Shale barren rock-cress *(Arabis serotina).* Rare biennial of the Mustard family with tiny whitish flowers. Historic range: U.S.A. (VA, WV). Status: Endangered.

Short's goldenrod *(Solidago shortii).* Perennial herb of the Aster family. Historic range: U.S.A. (KY). Status: Endangered.

Siler pincushion cactus *(Pediocactus sileri).* Spherical cactus with yellowish flowers. Historic range: U.S.A. (AZ, UT). Status: Endangered.

Slender-horned spineflower *(Dodecahema leptoceras).* Annual of the Buckwheat family. Historic range: U.S.A. (CA). Status: Endangered.

Slender-petaled mustard *(Thelypodium stenopetalum).* Perennial herb found in a wetland meadow habitat. Historic range: U.S.A. (CA). Status: Endangered.

Slender rush-pea *(Hoffmannseggia tenella).* Perennial herb with compound leaves and orange flowers. Historic range: U.S.A. (TX). Status: Endangered.

Small-anthered bittercress *(Cardamine micranthera).* Perennial herb of the Mustard family. Historic range: U.S.A. (NC). Status: Endangered.

Small whorled pogonia *(Isotria medeoloides).* Woodland orchid with a yellowish green flower. Historic range: U.S.A. (CT, DC, DE, GA, IL, MA, MD, ME, MI, MO, NC, NH, NJ, NY, PA, RI, SC, TN, VA, VT), Canada (ON). Status: Endangered.

Small's milkpea *(Galactia smallii).* Slender vine found in only two sites in Dade County. Historic range: U.S.A. (FL). Status: Endangered.

Snakeroot *(Eryngium cuneifolium).* Perennial herb with wedge- shaped leaves and blue flowers. Historic range: U.S.A. (FL). Status: Endangered.

Sneed pincushion cactus *(Coryphantha sneedii var. sneedii).* Grows in clumps of many cylindrical stems. Historic range: U.S.A. (TX, NM). Status: Endangered.

Solano grass *(Tuctoria mucronata).* Annual grass characterized by a sticky secretion covering the blades. Historic range: U.S.A. (CA). Status: Endangered.

Spineless hedgehog cactus *(Echinocereus triglochidiatus var. inermis).* Spineless dark green cactus with scarlet flowers. Historic range: U.S.A. (CO, UT). Status: Endangered.

Spreading avens *(Geum radiatum).* Member of the Rose family. Historic range: U.S.A. (NC, TN). Status: Endangered.

Spring-loving centaury *(Centaurium namophilum).* Annual herb that grows in clumps. Historic range: U.S.A. (CA, NV). Status: Threatened.

St. Thomas prickly-ash *(Zanthoxylum thomasianum).* Evergreen shrub or small tree belonging to the Citrus family. Historic range: U.S.A. (PR, VI). Status: Endangered.

Steamboat buckwheat *(Eriogonum ovalifolium var. williamsiae).* Low-growing perennial with small white flowers. Historic range: U.S.A. (NV). Status: Endangered.

Stenogyne angustifolia var. angustifolia *(no common name).* Rare herbaceous perennial with aromatic oblong leaves. Historic range: U.S.A. (HI). Status: Endangered.

Swamp pink *(Helonias bullata).* Perennial of the Lily family found in wetland habitats. Historic range: U.S.A. (DE, GA, MD, NC, NJ, NY, SC, VA). Status: Threatened.

Tennessee purple coneflower *(Echinacea tennesseensis).* Member of the Aster family with purple flowers similar to daisies. Historic range: U.S.A. (TN). Status: Endangered.

Texas poppy-mallow *(Callirhoe scabriuscula).* Erect perennial herb with purple flowers. Historic range: U.S.A. (TX). Status: Endangered.

Texas prairie dawn-flower *(Hymenoxys texana).* Member of the Aster family. Historic range: U.S.A. (TX). Status: Endangered.

Texas snowbells *(Styrax texana).* Shrub or small tree with clusters of white flowers. Historic range: U.S.A. (TX). Status: Endangered.

Texas wild-rice *(Zizania texana).* Perennial aquatic grass. Historic range: U.S.A. (TX). Status: Endangered.

Tiny polygala *(Polygala smallii).* Erect biennial herb of the Milkwort family. Historic range: U.S.A. (FL). Status: Endangered.

Toad-flax cress *(Glaucocarpum suffrutescens).* Clumping perennial with many yellow flowers. Historic range: U.S.A. (UT). Status: Endangered.

Tobusch fishhook cactus *(Ancistrocactus tobuschii).* Cactus with yellow-green flowers and many distinctive hooked spines. Historic range: U.S.A. (TX). Status: Endangered.

Todsen's pennyroyal *(Hedeoma todsenii).* Perennial herb with small leaves and orange-red flowers. Historic range: U.S.A. (NM). Status: Endangered.

Truckee barberry *(Berberis sonnei).* One of two shrubs in the Barberry family. Historic range: U.S.A. (CA). Status: Endangered.

Tumamoc globe-berry *(Tumamoca macdougalii).* Perennial vine of the Gourd family. Historic range: U.S.A. (AZ), Mexico (Sonora). Status: Endangered.

Uhiuhi *(Caesalpinia kavaiense).* Small tree. Historic range: U.S.A. (HI). Status: Endangered.

Uinta Basin hookless cactus *(Sclerocactus glaucus).* Dwarf cactus with purplish red flowers. Historic range: U.S.A. (CO, UT). Status: Threatened.

Vahl's boxwood *(Buxus vahlii).* Evergreen shrub or small tree with shiny dark green leaves. Historic range: U.S.A. (PR). Status: Endangered.

Virginia round-leaf birch *(Betula uber).* Deciduous tree endemic to mountainous southwestern Virginia. Historic range: U.S.A. (VA). Status: Endangered.

Virginia spiraea *(Spiraea virginiana).* Historic range: U.S.A. (GA, KY, NC, PA, TN, VA, WV). Status: Threatened.

Welsh's milkweed *(Asclepias welshii).* Perennial herb. Historic range: U.S.A. (AZ, UT). Status: Threatened.

Western prairie fringed orchid *(Platanthera praeclara).* Historic range: U.S.A. (IA, MN, MO, NE, ND, OK, KS, SD), Canada (MB). Status: Threatened.

Wheeler's peperomia *(Peperomia wheeleri).* Evergreen herb with clusters of tiny flowers. Historic range: U.S.A. (PR). Status: Endangered.

White bladderpod *(Lesquerella pallida).* White-flowered annual of the Mustard family. Historic range: U.S.A. (TX). Status: Endangered.

White-haired goldenrod *(Solidago albopilosa).* Herbaceous annual of the Aster family. Historic range: U.S.A. (KY). Status: Threatened.

Wide-leaf warea *(Warea amplexifolia).* Purple-flowered annual of the Mustard family. Historic range: U.S.A. (FL). Status: Endangered.

Wireweed *(Polygonella basiramia).* Annual herb of the Buckwheat family. Historic range: U.S.A. (FL). Status: Endangered.

Wright fishhook cactus *(Sclerocactus wrightiae).* Spherical cactus with a reddish brown flower. Historic range: U.S.A. (UT). Status: Endangered.

Zuni fleabane *(Erigeron rhizomatus).* Perennial herb with blue or white flowers. Historic range: U.S.A. (NM). Status: Threatened.

Appendix III: EPA National Priorities Lists

Superfund is the Environmental Protection Agency's program to clean up uncontrolled hazardous waste sites. Since its inception in 1980, the EPA has identified over 1,200 sites, and has proposed and implemented clean-up programs for the most hazardous areas. To prioritize the sites, the Agency has developed the Hazard Ranking System, which evaluates and scores site threats.

The graphs below summarize the media where contaminations occur, as well as the activities which take place at the sites. The following appendix describes the 1,189 official sites (as of February 1991), and categorizes the locations by severity (Hazard Ranking System), state, and federal sites.

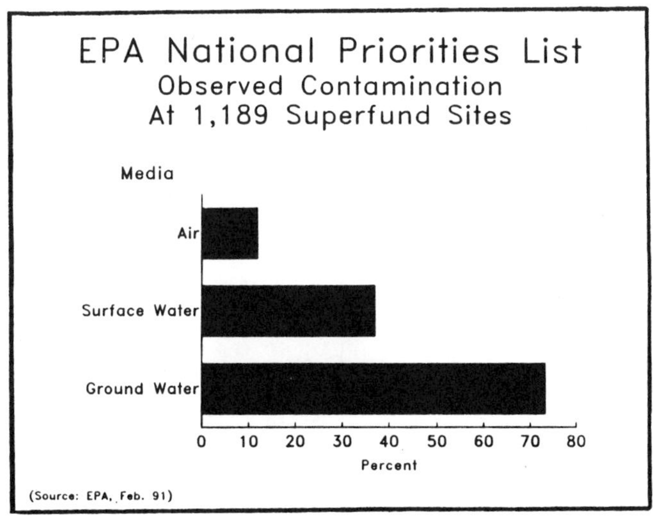

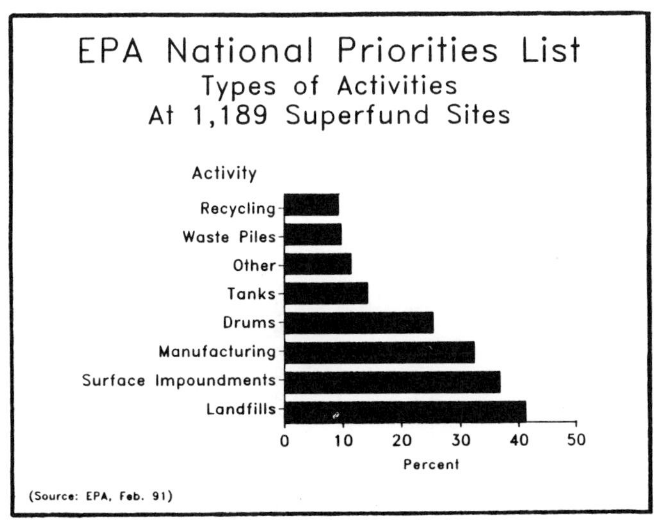

EPA National Priorities List, Ranked by Severity of Contamination

(as of February 1991)

Position or ranking on the EPA National Priorities List can be found preceding the name of the contaminated site. These sites are earmarked for cleanup; the lower the number, the higher the severity of site contamination (* indicates top priority cleanup sites for each state)

Rank	Name	City/County	State
1	Lapari Landfill	Pitman	NJ
2	Tybouts Corner Landfill*	New Castle County	DE
3	Bruin Lagoon	Bruin Borough	PA
4	Helen Kramer Landfill	Mantua Township	NJ
5	Industri-Plex	Woburn	MA
6	Price Landfill*	Pleasantville	NJ
7	Pollution Abatement Services*	Oswego	NY
8	LaBounty Site	Charles City	IA
9	Army Creek Landfill	New Castle County	DE
10	CPS/Madison Industries	Old Bridge Township	NJ
11	Nyanza Chemical Waste Dump	Ashland	MA
12	GEMS Landfill	Gloucester Township	NJ
13	Berlin & Farro	Swartz Creek	MI
14	Baird & McGuire	Holbrook	MA
15	Lone Pine Landfill	Freehold Township	NJ
16	Somersworth Sanitary Landfill	Somersworth	NH
17	FMC Corp. (Fridley Plant)	Fridley	MN
18	Vertac, Inc.	Jacksonville	AR
19	Keefe Environmental Services	Epping	NH
20	Silver Bow Creek/Butte Area	Silver Bow/Deer Lodge	MT
21	Whitewood Creek*	Whitewood	SD
22	French, Ltd.	Crosby	TX
23	Liquid Disposal, Inc.	Utica	MI
24	Sylvester*	Nashua	NH
25	Tysons Dump	Upper Merion Township	PA
26	McAdoo Associates*	McAdoo Borough	PA
27	Motco, Inc.*	La Marque	TX
28	Arcanum Iron & Steel	Darke County	OH
29	East Helena Site	East Helena	MT
30	Sikes Disposal Pits	Crosby	TX
31	Triana/Tennessee River	Limestone/Morgan	AL
32	Stringfellow*	Glen Avon Heights	CA
33	McKin Co.	Gray	ME
34	Crystal Chemical Co.	Houston	TX
35	Bridgeport Rental & Oil Services	Bridgeport	NJ
36	Sand Creek Industrial	Commerce City	CO
37	Geneva Industries/Fuhrmann Energy	Houston	TX
38	W.R. Grace & Co. Inc. (Acton Plant)	Acton	MA
39	New Brighton/Arden Hills	New Brighton	MN
40	Reilly Tar (St. Louis Park Plant)*	St. Louis Park	MN
41	Vineland Chemical Co., Inc.	Vineland	NJ
42	Burnt Fly Bog	Marlboro Township	NJ
43	Schuylkill Metals Corp.	Plant City	FL
44	Publicker Industries Inc.	Philadelphia	PA
45	Old Bethpage Landfill	Oyster Bay	NY
46	Reeves Southeast Galvanizing Corp.	Tampa	FL
47	Shieldalloy Corp.	Newfield Borough	NJ
48	Anaconda Co. Smelter	Anaconda	MT
49	Western Processing Co., Inc.	Kent	WA
50	Omega Hills North Landfill	Germantown	WI
51	American Creosote (Pensacola Plant)	Pensacola	FL
52	Caldwell Trucking Co.	Fairfield	NJ
53	GE Moreau	South Glen Falls	NY
54	Seymour Recycling Corp.*	Seymour	IN
55	Peak Oil Co./Bay Drum Co.	Tampa	FL
56	United Scrap Lead Co., Inc.	Troy	OH
57	Cherokee County	Cherokee County	KS
58	Tar Creek (Ottawa County)	Ottawa County	OK
59	Brick Township Landfill	Brick Township	NJ
60	Brook Industrial Park	Bound Brook	NJ
61	American Anodco, Inc.	Ionia	MI
62	Frontier Hard Chrome, Inc.	Vancouver	WA
63	Janesville Old Landfill	Janesville	WI
64	Northernaire Plating	Cadillac	MI
65	Independent Nail Co.	Beaufort	SC
66	Janesville Ash Beds	Janesville	WI
67	Kalama Specialty Chemicals	Beaufort	SC
68	Lehigh Portland Cement Co.	Mason City	IA
69	Davie Landfill	Davie	FL
70	Miami County Incinerator	Troy	OH
71	General Electric (Spokane Shop)	Spokane	WA
72	ALCOA (Vancouver Smelter)	Vancouver	WA
73	Eastern Michaud Flats Contamination	Pocatello	ID
74	Tucson International Airport Area	Tucson	AZ
75	Northwestern States Portland Cem.	Mason City	IA
76	Wheeler Pit	La Prairie Township	WI
77	Gold Coast Oil Corp.	Miami	FL
78	Salford Quarry	Salford Township	PA
79	Gratiot County Landfill*	St. Louis	MI
80	Picillo Farm*	Coventry	RI
81	New Bedford Site*	New Bedford	MA
82	Old Inger Oil Refinery*	Darrow	LA
83	Chem-Dyne*	Hamilton	OH
84	SCRDI Bluff Road*	Columbia	SC
85	Laurel Park, Inc.*	Naugatuck Borough	CT
86	Marshall Landfill*	Boulder County	CO
87	Outboard Marine Corp.*	Waukegan	IL
88	South Valley*	Albuquerque	NM
89	Pine Street Canal*	Burlington	VT
90	West Virginia Ordnance*	Point Pleasant	WV
91	Ellisville Site*	Ellisville	MO
92	Arsenic Trioxide Site*	Southeastern	ND
93	Aidex Corp.*	Council Bluffs	IA
94	N.W. Mauthe Co., Inc.*	Appleton	WI
95	North Hollywood Dump*	Memphis	TN
96	A.L. Taylor (Valley of Drums)*	Brooks	KY
97	Ordot Landfill*	Guam	GU
98	Flowood Site*	Flowood	MS
99	Rose Park Sludge Pit*	Salt Lake City	UT
100	Arkansas City Dump*	Arkansas City	KS
101	Operating Industries, Inc. Landfill.	Monterey Park	CA
102	Wide Beach Development	Brant	NY
103	Iron Mountain Mine	Redding	CA
104	Scientific Chemical Processing	Carlstadt	NJ

Rank	Name	City/County	State
105	California Gulch	Leadville	CO
106	D'Imperio Property	Hamilton Township	NJ
107	Oakdale Dump	Oakdale	MN
108	Parsons Casket Hardware Co.	Belvidere	IL
109	A & F Material Reclaiming, Inc.	Greenup	IL
110	Douglassville Disposal	Douglassville	PA
111	Koppers Coke	St. Paul	MN
112	Plymouth Harbor/Cannon Corp.	Plymouth	MA
113	Monsanto Chemical (Soda Springs)	Soda Springs	ID
114	Bunker Hill Mining & Metallurgy	Smelterville	ID
115	Hudson River PCBs	Hudson River	NY
116	Universal Oil Products (Chemical Division)	East Rutherford	NJ
117	Aerojet General Corp.	Rancho Cordova	CA
118	Com Bay, South Tacoma Channel	Tacoma	WA
119	Osborne Landfill	Grove City	PA
120	Portland Cement (Kiln Dust 2 & 3)	Salt Lake City	UT
121	Old Southington Landfill	Southington	CT
122	Syosset Landfill	Oyster Bay	NY
123	Circuitron Corp.	East Farmingdale	NY
124	Nineteenth Avenue Landfill	Phoenix	AZ
125	Teledyne Wah Chang	Albany	OR
126	Midway Landfill	Kent	WA
127	Sinclair Refinery	Wellsville	NY
128	Mowbray Engineering Co.	Greenville	AL
129	Spiegelberg Landfill	Green Oak Township	MI
130	Miami Drum Services	Miami	FL
131	Reich Farms	Pleasant Plains	NJ
132	Union Pacific Railroad Co.	Pocatello	ID
133	South Brunswick Landfill	South Brunswick	NJ
134	Raymark	Hatboro	PA
135	Ciba-Geigy Corp. (McIntosh Plant)	McIntosh	AL
136	Kassauf-Kimerling Battery	Tampa	FL
137	Wauconda Sand & Gravel	Wauconda	IL
138	Bofors Nobel, Inc.	Muskegon	MI
139	Bailey Waste Disposal	Bridge City	TX
140	Ottati & Goss/Kingston Steel Drum	Kingston	NH
141	Ott/Story/Cordova Chemical Co.	Dalton Township	MI
142	Thermo-Chem, Inc.	Muskegon	MI
143	Brown & Bryant, Inc. (Arvin Plant)	Arvin	CA
144	Greenwood Chemical Co.	Newtown	VA
145	NL Industries	Pedricktown	NJ
146	St. Regis Paper Co.	Cass Lake	MN
147	Brantley Landfill	Island	KY
148	Aberdeen Pesticide Dumps	Aberdeen	NC
149	Burgess Brothers Landfill	Woodford	VT
150	Ringwood Mines/Landfill	Ringwood Borough	NJ
151	Whitehouse Oil Pits	Whitehouse	FL
152	Hercules 009 Landfill	Brunswick	GA
153	Jones Sanitation	Hyde Park	NY
154	Parker Sanitary Landfill	Lyndon	VT
155	Velsicol Chemical Corp. (Michigan)	St. Louis	MI
156	Summit National	Deerfield Township	OH
157	Love Canal	Niagara Falls	NY
158	Seattle Municipal Landfill (Kent Highlands)	Kent	WA
159	Coker's Sanitation Service Landfills	Kent County	DE
160	Rockwell International (Allegan)	Allegan	MI
161	Pine Bend Sanitary Landfill	Dakota County	MN
162	Lawrence Todtz Farm	Camanche	IA
163	Beloit Corp.	Rockton	IL
164	Fisher-Calo	LaPorte	IN
165	Pioneer Sand Co.	Warrington	FL
166	Springfield Township Dump	Davisburg	MI
167	Hranica Landfill	Buffalo Township	PA
168	Martin-Marietta, Sodyeco, Inc.	Charlotte	NC
169	E.I. Du Pont (Newport Plant Landfill)	Newport	DE
170	Hellertown Manufacturing Co.	Hellertown	PA
171	Zellwood Ground Water Contamination	Zellwood	FL
172	Packaging Corp. of America	Filer City	MI
173	Muskego Sanitary Landfill	Muskego	WI
174	Kerr-McGee Chemical (Soda Springs)	Soda Springs	ID
175	Whiteford Sales & Service/Nationalease	South Bend	IN
176	Hooker (S Area)	Niagara Falls	NY
177	Lindane Dump	Harrison Township	PA
178	Central City-Clear Creek	Idaho Springs	CO
179	Ventron/Velsicol	Wood Ridge Borough	NJ
180	Taylor Road Landfill	Seffner	FL
181	Western Sand & Gravel	Burrillville	RI
182	Rosen Brothers Scrap Yard/Dump	Cortland	NY
183	Koppers Co. Inc. (Florence Plant)	Florence	SC
184	Maywood Chemical Co.	Maywood/Rochelle Park	NJ
185	Nascolite Corp.	Millville	NJ
186	Industrial Excess Landfill	Uniontown	OH
187	Industrial Waste Processing	Fresno	CA
188	Hardage/Criner	Criner	OK
189	Rose Township Dump	Rose Township	MI
190	Waste Disposal Engineering	Andover	MN
191	Liberty Industrial Finishing	Farmingdale	NY
192	Kin-Buc Landfill	Edison Township	NJ
193	Waste, Inc., Landfill	Michigan City	IN
194	Bowers Landfill	Circleville	OH
195	Brio Refining, Inc.	Friendswood	TX
196	Ciba-Geigy Corp.	Toms River	NJ
197	Butterworth #2 Landfill	Grand Rapids	MI
198	American Cyanamid Co.	Bound Brook	NJ
199	Heleva Landfill	North Whitehall Township	PA
200	Ewan Property	Shamong Township	NJ
201	Batavia Landfill	Batavia	NY
202	Woodstock Municipal Landfill	Woodstock	IL
203	Boise Cascade/Onan/Medtronics	Fridley	MN
204	MIG/Dewane Landfill	Belvidere	IL
205	Wasatch Chemical Co. (Lot 6)	Salt Lake City	UT
206	Landfill & Resource Recovery	North Smithfield	RI
207	Hi-Mill Manufacturing Co.	Highland	MI
208	Butler Mine Tunnel	Pittston	PA
209	Northwest 58th Street Landfill	Hialeah	FL
210	Delilah Road	Egg Harbor Township	NJ
211	Mill Creek Dump	Erie	PA
212	Glen Ridge Radium Site	Glen Ridge	NJ
213	Montclair/West Orange Radium Site	Montclair/West Orange	NJ
214	Precision Plating Corp.	Vernon	CT
215	Sixty-Second Street Dump	Tampa	FL
216	G & H Landfill	Utica	MI
217	Bennington Municipal Sanitary Landfill	Bennington	VT
218	Celanese (Shelby Fiber Operations)	Shelby	NC
219	Metaltec/Aerosystems	Franklin Borough	NJ
220	Schmalz Dump	Harrison	WI
221	Carrier Air Conditioning Co.	Collierville	TN
222	Motor Wheel, Inc.	Lansing	MI
223	Better Brite Chrome & Zinc Shops	DePere	WI
224	Southern Calif. Edison (Visalia)	Visalia	CA
225	Lang Property	Pemberton Township	NJ
226	Stewco, Inc.	Waskom	TX
227	Sharkey Landfill	Parsippany/Troy Hls.	NJ
228	Selma Treating Co.	Selma	CA
229	Cleve Reber	Sorrento	LA
230	Velsicol Chemical Corp. (Illinois)	Marshall	IL
231	Wheeling Disposal Service Co. Landfill	Amazonia	MO
232	Tar Lake	Mancelona Township	MI
233	Johnstown City Landfill	Town of Johnstown	NY
234	North Carolina State University (Lot 86, Farm Unit #1)	Raleigh	NC
235	Lowry Landfill	Arapahoe County	CO
236	MacGillis & Gibbs/Bell Lumber	New Brighton	MN
237	Hunterstown Road	Straban Township	PA
238	Woodlawn County Landfill	Woodlawn	MD
239	Hechimovich Sanitary Landfill	Williamstown	WI
240	Mid-America Tanning Co.	Sergeant Bluff	IA
241	Lindsay Manufacturing Co.	Lindsay	NE
242	Combe Fill North Landfill	Mount Olive Township	NJ
243	Re-Solve, Inc.	Dartmouth	MA
244	Goose Farm	Plumstead Township	NJ
245	Velsicol Chemical (Hardeman County)	Toone	TN
246	York Oil Co.	Moira	NY
247	Sapp Battery Salvage	Cottondale	FL
248	Wamchem, Inc.	Burton	SC
249	Chemical Leaman Tank Lines, Inc.	Bridgeport	NJ
250	Master Disposal Service Landfill	Brookfield	WI
251	Doepke Disposal (Holliday)	Johnson County	KS
252	Florence Land Recontouring Landfill	Florence Township	NJ
253	Davis Liquid Waste	Smithfield	RI
254	Charles-George Reclamation Landfill	Tyngsborough	MA
255	King of Prussia	Winslow Township	NJ
256	Chisman Creek	York County	VA

Rank	Name	City/County	State
257	Nease Chemical	Salem	OH
258	Eagle Mine	Minturn/Redcliff	CO
259	Chemical Control	Elizabeth	NJ
260	Charles Macon Lagoon & Drum Storage	Cordova	NC
261	Leonard Chemical Co., Inc.	Rock Hill	SC
262	Allied Chemical & Ironton Coke	Ironton	OH
263	Verona Well Field	Battle Creek	MI
264	Lee Chemical	Liberty	MO
265	Beacon Heights Landfill	Beacon Falls	CT
266	Stauffer Chemical (Cold Creek Plant)	Bucks	AL
267	Burlington Northern (Brainard)	Brainard/Baxter	MN
268	Torch Lake	Houghton County	MI
269	Central Landfill	Johnston	RI
270	Malvern TCE	Malvern	PA
271	Facet Enterprises, Inc.	Elmira	NY
272	Delaware Sand & Gravel Landfill	New Castle County	DE
273	Tonolli Corp.	Nesquehoning	PA
274	National Starch & Chemical Corp.	Salisbury	NC
275	MW Manufacturing	Valley Township	PA
276	C & R Battery Co., Inc.	Chesterfield County	VA
277	Murray-Ohio Dump	Lawrenceburg	TN
278	Envirochem Corp.	Zionsville	IN
279	MIDCO 1	Gary	IN
280	Ormet Corp.	Hannibal	OH
281	South Point Plant	South Point	OH
282	Gallup's Quarry	Plainfield	CT
283	Whitmoyer Laboratories	Jackson Township	PA
284	Peoples Natural Gas Co.	Dubuque	IA
285	Oronogo-Duenweg Mining Belt	Jasper County	MO
286	Coleman-Evans Wood Preserving Co.	Whitehouse	FL
287	Dayco Corp./L.E. Carpenter Co.	Wharton Borough	NJ
288	Shriver's Corner	Straban Township	PA
289	Dorney Road Landfill	Upper Macungie Township	PA
290	Berks Landfill	Spring Township	PA
291	Northside Sanitary Landfill, Inc.	Zionsville	IN
292	Interstate Pollution Control, Inc.	Rockford	IL
293	Monroe Auto Equipment (Paragould Pit)	Paragould	AR
294	Oklahoma Refining Co.	Cyril	OK
295	E.I. Du Pont (County Rd. x23)	West Point	IA
296	Pacific Coast Pipe Lines	Fillmore	CA
297	Global Sanitary Landfill	Old Bridge Township	NJ
298	Florida Steel Corp.	Indiantown	FL
299	Occidental Chemical/Firestone Tire	Lower Pottsgrove Twp.	PA
300	Culpepper Wood Preserves, Inc.	Culpepper	VA
301	Pagel's Pit	Rockford	IL
302	University of Minnesota Rosemount Research Center	Rosemount	MN
303	Freeway Sanitary Landfill	Burnsville	MN
304	Tomah Municipal Sanitary Landfill	Tomah	WI
305	Litchfield Airport Area	Goodyear/Avondale	AZ
306	Firestone Tire (Salinas Plant)	Salinas	CA
307	Spence Farm	Plumstead Township	NJ
308	Mid-South Wood Products	Mena	AR
309	Newsom Brothers/Old Reichhold	Columbia	MS
310	Atlas Asbestos Mine	Fresno County	CA
311	Coalinga Asbestos Mine	Coalinga	CA
312	Brown Wood Preserving	Live Oak	FL
313	Port Washington Landfill	Port Washington	NY
314	Columbus Old Municipal Landfill #1	Columbus	IN
315	Combe Fill South Landfill	Chester Township	NJ
316	JIS Landfill	Jamesburg/South Brunswick	NJ
317	Tronic Plating Co., Inc.	Farmingdale	NY
318	Centre County Kepone	State College	PA
319	Agrico Chemical Co.	Pensacola	FL
320	Fields Brook	Ashtabula	OH
321	Solvents Recovery Service New England	Southington	CT
322	Woodbury Chemical Co.	Commerce City	CO
323	Waldick Aerospace Devices, Inc.	Wall Township	NJ
324	Hocomonco Pond	Westborough	MA
325	Distler Brickyard	West Point	KY
326	Ramapo Landfill	Ramapo	NY
327	Coast Wood Preserving	Ukiah	CA
328	South Bay Asbestos Area	Alviso	CA
329	Mercury Refining, Inc.	Colonie	NY
330	Hollingsworth Solderless Terminal	Fort Lauderdale	FL
331	Olean Well Field	Olean	NY
332	T.H. Agriculture & Nutrition (Montgomery)	Montgomery	AL
333	Fairchild Semiconduct (South San Jose)	South San Jose	CA
334	Pasco Sanitary Landfill	Pasco	WA
335	Sulphur Bank Mercury Mine	Clear Lake	CA
336	Joslyn Manufacturing & Supply Co.	Brooklyn Center	MN
337	York County Solid Waste/Refuse Landfill	Hopewell Township	PA
338	Spickler Landfill	Spencer	WI
339	Prewitt Abandoned Refinery	Prewitt	NM
340	Denver Radium Site	Denver	CO
341	Tri-Cities Barrel Co., Inc.	Port Crane	NY
342	Route 940 Drum Dump	Pocono Summit	PA
343	Tower Chemical Co.	Clermont	FL
344	Peerless Plating Co.	Muskegon	MI
345	Darling Hill Dump	Lyndon	VT
346	C & D Recycling	Foster Township	PA
347	Fort Hartford Coal Co. Stone Quarry	Olaton	KY
348	Syntex Facility	Verona	MO
349	Milltown Reservoir Sediments	Milltown	MT
350	Arrowhead Refinery Co.	Hermantown	MN
351	Martin-Marietta Aluminum Co.	The Dalles	OR
352	Uravan Uranium (Union Carbide)	Uravan	CO
353	Pijak Farm	Plumstead Township	NJ
354	Syncon Resins	South Kearny	NJ
355	Oak Grove Sanitary Landfill	Oak Grove Township	MN
356	White Farm Equipment Co. Dump	Charles City	IA
357	Liquid Gold Oil Corp.	Richmond	CA
358	Purity Oil Sales, Inc.	Malaga	CA
359	Tinkham Garage	Londonderry	NH
360	Alpha Chemical Corp.	Galloway	FL
361	Bog Creek Farm	Howell Township	NJ
362	Saco Tannery Waste Pits	Saco	ME
363	River Road Landfill/Waste Management, Inc.	Hermitage	PA
364	Frontera Creek	Rio Abajo	PR
365	Pickettville Road Landfill	Jacksonville	FL
366	Alsco Anaconda	Gnadenhutten	OH
367	Iron Horse Park	Billerica	MA
368	Palmerton Zinc Pile	Palmerton	PA
369	Neal's Landfill (Bloomington)	Bloomington	IN
370	Kohler Co. Landfill	Kohler	WI
371	Interstate Lead Co. (ILCO)	Leeds	AL
372	Standard Auto Bumper Corp.	Hialeah	FL
373	Hydro-Flex Inc.	Topeka	KS
374	Hassayampa Landfill	Hassayampa	AZ
375	Gulf Coast Vacuum Services	Abbeville	LA
376	Tri-County Landfill/Waste Management Illinois	South Elgin	IL
377	Silresim Chemical Corp.	Lowell	MA
378	Wells G&H	Woburn	MA
379	Nutmeg Valley Road	Wolcott	CT
380	Chemsol, Inc.	Piscataway	NJ
381	Lauer 1 Sanitary Landfill	Menomonee Falls	WI
382	Petoskey Municipal Well Field	Petoskey	MI
383	Union Scrap Iron & Metal Co.	Minneapolis	MN
384	Atlas Tack Corp.	Fairhaven	MA
385	Radiation Technology, Inc.	Rockaway Township	NJ
386	Fair Lawn Well Field	Fair Lawn	NJ
387	Main Street Well Field	Elkhart	IN
388	Lehillier/Mankato Site	Lehillier/Mankato	MN
389	Lakewood Site	Lakewood	WA
390	Industrial Lane	Williams Township	PA
391	Airco Plating Co.	Miami	FL
392	Fort Wayne Reduction Dump	Fort Wayne	IN
393	Onalaska Municipal Landfill	Onalaska	WI
394	Midvale Slag	Midvale	UT
395	A.I.W. Frank/Mid-County Mustang	Exton	PA
396	National Presto Industries, Inc.	Eau Claire	WI
397	Monroe Township Landfill	Monroe Township	NJ
398	Commodore Semiconductor Group	Lower Providence Twp.	PA
399	Rockaway Borough Well Field	Rockaway Township	NJ
400	Lenz Oil Service, Inc.	Lemont	IL
401	Wayne Waste Oil	Columbia City	IN
402	Pacific Car & Foundry Co.	Renton	WA
403	John Deere (Ottumwa Works Landfills)	Ottumwa	IA
404	Mid-Atlantic Wood Preserves, Inc.	Harmans	MD
405	Novak Sanitary Landfill	South Whitehall Twp.	PA
406	Himco Dump	Elkhart	IN

Rank	Name	City/County	State
407	Pacific Hide & Fur Recycling Co.	Pocatello	ID
408	Des Moines TCE	Des Moines	IA
409	Beachwood/Berkley Wells	Berkley Township	NJ
410	South Jersey Clothing Co.	Minotola	NJ
411	Vestal Water Supply Well 4-2	Vestal	NY
412	Vega Alta Public Supply Wells	Vega Alta	PR
413	Avco Lycoming (Williamsport Division)	Williamsport	PA
414	Ohio River Park	Neville Island	PA
415	Woolfolk Chemical Works, Inc.	Fort Valley	GA
416	Southeast Rockford Ground Water Containment	Rockford	IL
417	Tippecanoe Sanitary Landfill, Inc.	Lafayette	IN
418	Conrail Rail Yard (Elkhart)	Elkhart	IN
419	Galen Myers Dump/Drum Salvage	Osceola	IN
420	Sturgis Municipal Wells	Sturgis	MI
421	Barrels, Inc.	Lansing	MI
422	State Disposal Landfill, Inc.	Grand Rapids	MI
423	Washington County Landfill	Lake Elmo	MN
424	Dakhue Sanitary Landfill	Cannon Falls	MN
425	Odessa Chromium #1	Odessa	TX
426	Odessa Chromium #2 (Andrews Highway)	Odessa	TX
427	Electro-Coatings, Inc.	Cedar Rapids	IA
428	Hastings Ground Water Contamination	Hastings	NE
429	Williams Pipe Line Disposal Pit	Sioux Falls	SD
430	Indian Bend Wash Area	Scottsdale/Tempe/Phoenix	AZ
431	San Gabriel Valley (Area 1)	El Monte	CA
432	San Gabriel Valley (Area 2)	Baldwin Park Area	CA
433	San Fernando Valley (Area 1)	Los Angeles	CA
434	San Fernando Valley (Area 2)	Los Angeles/Glendale	CA
435	San Fernando Valley (Area 3)	Glendale	CA
436	T.H. Agriculture & Nutrition Co.	Fresno	CA
437	Arctic Surplus	Fairbanks	AK
438	Com Bay, Near Shore/Tide Flats	Pierce County	WA
439	LaSalle Electric Utilities	LaSalle	IL
440	Cross Brothers Pail (Pembroke)	Pembroke Township	IL
441	Cedartown Industries, Inc.	Cedartown	GA
442	Jadco-Hughes Facility	Belmont	NC
443	Southside Sanitary Landfill	Indianapolis	IN
444	Monitor Devices/Intercircuits Inc.	Wall Township	NJ
445	BFI Sanitary Landfill (Rockingham)	Rockingham	VT
446	Upjohn Facility	Barceloneta	PR
447	Koppers Co. Inc. (Morrisville Plant)	Morrisville	NC
448	Sharon Steel (Midvale Tailings)	Midvale	UT
449	McColl	Fullerton	CA
450	Henderson Road	Upper Merion Twp.	PA
451	Hooker Chemical/Ruco Polymer Corp.	Hicksville	NY
452	Colbert Landfill	Colbert	WA
453	Petro-Processors of Louisiana Inc.	Scotlandville	LA
454	Westinghouse Electric (Sharon Plant)	Sharon	PA
455	Applied Environmental Services	Glenwood Landing	NY
456	Barceloneta Landfill	Florida Afuera	PR
457	Tibbets Road	Barrington	NH
458	Sand, Gravel & Stone	Elkton	MD
459	Delta Quarries/Stotler Landfill	Antis/Logan Townships	PA
460	Revere Textile Prints Corp.	Sterling	CT
461	Spartan Chemical Co.	Wyoming	MI
462	Roebling Steel Co.	Florence	NJ
463	East Mount Zion	Springettsbury Township	PA
464	T.H. Agriculture & Nutrition (Albany)	Albany	GA
465	Amnicola Dump	Chattanooga	TN
466	Vineland State School	Vineland	NJ
467	Motorola, Inc. (52nd Street Plant)	Phoenix	AZ
468	Groveland Wells	Groveland	MA
469	General Motors (Central Foundry Division)	Massena	NY
470	Mottolo Pig Farm	Raymond	NH
471	Buckingham County Landfill	Buckingham	VA
472	SCRDI Dixiana	Cayce	SC
473	Roto-Finish Co., Inc.	Kalamazoo	MI
474	Olmstead County Sanitary Landfill	Oronoco	MN
475	Quality Plating	Sikeston	MO
476	Prestolite Battery Division	Vincennes	IN
477	Fulbright Landfill	Springfield	MO
478	Williams Property	Swainton	NJ
479	Renora, Inc.	Edison Township	NJ
480	FCX, Inc. (Washington Plant)	Washington	NC
481	Jacks Creek/Sitkin Smelting & Refining	Maitland	PA
482	Cleveland Mill	Silver City	NM
483	Denzer & Schafer X-Ray Co.	Bayville	NJ
484	Hercules, Inc. (Gibbstown Plant)	Gibbstown	NJ
485	Ninth Avenue Dump	Gary	IN
486	Bush Valley Landfill	Abingdon	MD
487	Golden Strip Septic Tank Service	Simpsonville	SC
488	Rock Hill Chemical Co.	Rock Hill	SC
489	Texarkana Wood Preserving Co.	Texarkana	TX
490	Gurley Pit	Edmondson	AR
491	Petroleum Products Corp.	Pembroke Park	FL
492	Peterson/Puritan, Inc.	Lincoln/Cumberland	RI
493	Times Beach Site	Times Beach	MO
494	Wash King Laundry	Pleasant Plains Township	MI
495	Whittaker Corp.	Minneapolis	MN
496	Algoma Municipal Landfill	Algoma	WI
497	NL Industries/Taracorp/Golden	St. Louis Park	MN
498	Westinghouse Electric (Sunnyvale Pit)	Sunnyvale	CA
499	Kellogg-Deering Well Field	Norwalk	CT
500	Boarhead Farms	Bridgeton Township	PA
501	Cannon Engineering Corp. (CEC)	Bridgewater	MA
502	H. Brown Co., Inc.	Grand Rapids	MI
503	Nepera Chemical Co., Inc.	Maybrook	NY
504	Niagara County Refuse	Wheatfield	NY
505	Sherwood Medical Industries	Deland	FL
506	Western Pacific Railroad Co.	Oroville	CA
507	Olin Corp. (McIntosh Plant)	McIntosh	AL
508	Southwest Ottawa County Landfill	Park Township	MI
509	Kentucky Avenue Well Field	Horseheads	NY
510	Pasley Solvents & Chemicals, Inc.	Hempstead	NY
511	Sol Lynn/Industrial Transformers	Houston	TX
512	Asbestos Dump	Millington	NJ
513	Lee's Lane Landfill	Louisville	KY
514	Kerr-McGee (Reed-Keppler Park)	West Chicago	IL
515	Frit Industries	Walnut Ridge	AR
516	Amoco Chemicals (Joliet Landfill)	Joliet	IL
517	Woodbury Chemical (Princeton Plant)	Princeton	FL
518	Fultz Landfill	Jackson Township	OH
519	New Hanover County Airport Burn Pit	Wilmington	NC
520	Allied Plating, Inc.	Portland	OR
521	Coshocton Landfill	Franklin Township	OH
522	Apache Powder Co.	St. David	AZ
523	Carson River Mercury Site	Lyon/Churchill County	NV
524	Kerr-McGee (Kress Creek)	DuPage County	IL
525	AMP, Inc. (Glen Rock Facility)	Glen Rock	PA
526	JFD Electronics/Channel Master	Oxford	NC
527	Arlington Blending & Packaging	Arlington	TN
528	PAB Oil & Chemical Service, Inc.	Abbeville	LA
529	Sydney Mine Sludge Ponds	Brandon	FL
530	Cimarron Mining Corp.	Carrizozo	NM
531	Davis (GSR) Landfill	Glocester	RI
532	Lord-Shope Landfill	Girard Township	PA
533	FMC Corp. (Yakima Pit)	Yakima	WA
534	Northern Engraving Co.	Sparta	WI
535	South Cavalcade Street	Houston	TX
536	PSC Resources	Palmer	MA
537	Forest Waste Products	Otisville	MI
538	Drake Chemical	Lock Haven	PA
539	United Heckathorn Co.	Richmond	CA
540	Kearsarge Metallurgical Corp.	Conway	NH
541	Palmetto Wood Preserving	Dixiana	SC
542	Clare Water Supply	Clare	MI
543	Tex-Tin Corp.	Texas City	TX
544	Havertown PCP	Haverford	PA
545	New Castle Spill	New Castle County	DE
546	St. Louis Airport/ HIS/ Fut Coatings	St. Louis County	MO
547	Idaho Pole Co.	Bozeman	MT
548	NCR Corp. (Millsboro Plant)	Millsboro	DE
549	Lake Sandy Jo (M & M Landfill)	Gary	IN
550	Johns-Manville Corp.	Waukegan	IL
551	Chem Central	Wyoming Township	MI
552	Novaco Industries	Temperance	MI
553	Beulah Landfill	Pensacola	FL
554	Windom Dump	Windom	MN
555	Kerr-McGee (Residential Areas)	W. Chicago/DuPage County	IL
556	Rose Hill Regional Landfill	South Kingston	RI

Rank	Name	City/County	State
557	Jackson Township Landfill	Jackson Township	NJ
558	NL Industries/Taracorp Lead Smelt	Granite City	IL
559	Red Penn Sanitation Co. Landfill	Peewee Valley	KY
560	K & L Avenue Landfill	Oshtemo Township	MI
561	TRW, Inc. (Minerva Plant)	Minerva	OH
562	Kaiser Aluminum Mead Works	Mead	WA
563	Mosley Road Sanitary Landfill	Oklahoma City	OK
564	Barkhamsted-New Hartford Landfill	Barkhamsted	CT
565	Fairfield Coal Gasification Plant	Fairfield	IA
566	Perham Arsenic Site	Perham	MN
567	Charlevoix Municipal Well	Charlevoix	MI
568	Montgomery Township Housing Developers	Montgomery Township	NJ
569	Rocky Hill Municipal Well	Rocky Hill Borough	NJ
570	Cinnaminson Ground Water Contamination	Cinnaminson Township	NJ
571	Chemical Insecticide Corp.	Edison Township	NJ
572	Brewster Well Field	Putnam County	NY
573	Vestal Water Supply Well 1-1	Vestal	NY
574	Chem-Solv, Inc.	Cheswold	DE
575	Anne Arundel County Landfill	Glen Burnie	MD
576	Bally Ground Water Contamination	Bally Borough	PA
577	Madison County Sanitary Landfill	Madison	FL
578	Chemform, Inc.	Pompano Beach	FL
579	Wilson Concepts of Florida, Inc.	Pompano Beach	FL
580	Bypass 601 Ground Water Contamination	Concord	NC
581	FCX, Inc. (Statesville Plant)	Statesville	NC
582	Lexington County Landfill Area	Cayce	SC
583	Michigan Disposal (Cork Street Landfill)	Kalamazoo	MI
584	Solid State Circuits, Inc.	Republic	MO
585	Waverly Ground Water Contamination	Waverly	NE
586	Chemical Sales Co.	Denver	CO
587	Utah Power & Light/American Barrel	Salt Lake City	UT
588	Advanced Micro Devices, Inc.	Sunnyvale	CA
589	Hexcel Corp.	Livermore	CA
590	Crazy Horse Sanitary Landfill	Salinas	CA
591	Union Pacific Railroad Tie Treat	The Dalles	OR
592	Hidden Valley Landfill (Thun Field)	Pierce County	WA
593	Yakima Plating Co.	Yakima	WA
594	Nutting Truck & Caster Co.	Faribault	MN
595	U.S. Radium Corp.	Orange	NJ
596	Carter Industrials, Inc.	Detroit	MI
597	Highlands Acid Pit	Highlands	TX
598	Resin Disposal	Jefferson Borough	PA
599	Libby Ground Water Contamination	Libby	MT
600	Newport Dump	Newport	KY
601	Sangamo/Twelve-Mile/Hartwell PCB	Pickens	SC
602	Moyers Landfill	Eagleville	PA
603	Savage Municipal Water Supply	Milford	NH
604	LaGrand Sanitary Landfill	LaGrand Township	MN
605	Brown's Battery Breaking	Shoemakersville	PA
606	SMS Instruments, Inc.	Deer Park	NY
607	Hedblum Industries	Oscoda	MI
608	United Creosoting Co.	Conroe	TX
609	Byron Barrel & Drum	Byron	NY
610	Bendix Corp./Allied Automotive	St. Joseph	MI
611	Baxter/Union Pacific Tie Treating	Laramie	WY
612	Anchor Chemicals	Hicksville	NY
613	Waste Management-Michigan (Holland)	Holland	MI
614	Spectra-Physics, Inc.	Mountain View	CA
615	Arrowhead Assoc./Scovill Corp.	Montross	VA
616	Atlantic Wood Industries, Inc.	Portsmouth	VA
617	North Cavalcade Street	Houston	TX
618	Sayreville Landfill	Sayreville	NJ
619	Dover Municipal Landfill	Dover	NH
620	Ludlow Sand & Gravel	Clayville	NY
621	Saunders Supply Co.	Chuckatuck	VA
622	City Disposal Corp. Landfill	Dunn	WI
623	Tabernacle Drum Dump	Tabernacle Township	NJ
624	Hinker/Stout/Romaine Creek	Imperial	MO
625	Howe Valley Landfill	Howe Valley	KY
626	Yaworski Waste Lagoon	Canterbury	CT
627	Leetown Pesticide	Leetown	WV
628	Rochester Property	Travelers Rest	SC
629	Cabot/Koppers	Gainesville	FL
630	Evor Phillips Leasing	Old Bridge Township	NJ
631	William Dick Lagoons	West Caln Township	PA
632	Douglass Road/Uniroyal, Inc., Landfill	Mishawaka	IN
633	Lackawanna Refuse	Old Forge Borough	PA
634	Compass Industries (Avery Drive)	Tulsa	OK
635	Mannheim Avenue Dump	Galloway Township	NJ
636	Neal's Dump (Spencer)	Spencer	IN
637	Abex Corp.	Portsmouth	VA
638	Fulton Terminals	Fulton	NY
639	Allied Paper/Portage Creek/Kalamazoo River	Kalamazoo	MI
640	Dutchtown Treatment Plant	Ascension Parish	LA
641	Westinghouse Elevator Co. Plant	Gettysburg	PA
642	Centralia Municipal Landfill	Centralia	WA
643	Auburn Road Landfill	Londonderry	NH
644	Fike Chemical, Inc.	Nitro	WV
645	General Mills/Henkel Corp.	Minneapolis	MN
646	Wrigley Charcoal Plant	Wrigley	TN
647	Laskin/Poplar Oil Co.	Jefferson Township	OH
648	Old Mill	Rock Creek	OH
649	Townsend Saw Chain Co.	Pontiac	SC
650	Johns' Sludge Pond	Wichita	KS
651	Stoughton City Landfill	Stoughton	WI
652	Del Norte Pesticide Storage	Crescent City	CA
653	Suffolk City Landfill	Suffolk	VA
654	Tansitor Electronics, Inc.	Bennington	VT
655	De Rewal Chemical Co.	Kingwood Township	NJ
656	Middletown Air Field	Middletown	PA
657	Swope Oil & Chemical Co.	Pennsauken	NJ
658	Monsanto Corp. (Augusta Plant)	Augusta	GA
659	South Municipal Water Supply Well	Peterborough	NH
660	Winthrop Landfill	Winthrop	ME
661	Ordnance Works Disposal Areas	Morgantown	WV
662	Diamond Shamrock Corp. Landfill	Cedartown	GA
663	Zanesville Well Field	Zanesville	OH
664	Cheshire Ground Water Contamination	Cheshire	CT
665	Suffern Village Well Field	Village of Sufferin	NY
666	Endicott Village Well Field	Village of Endicott	NY
667	Dover Gas Light Co.	Dover	DE
668	Aladdin Plating	Scott Township	PA
669	North Penn - Area 1	Souderton	PA
670	North Penn - Area 7	North Wales	PA
671	North Penn - Area 6	Lansdale	PA
672	North Penn - Area 2	Hatfield	PA
673	North Penn - Area 5	Montgomery Township	PA
674	Harris Corp. (Palm Bay Plant)	Palm Bay	FL
675	DuPage Cty. Landfill/Blackwell Forest	Warrenville	IL
676	Kummer Sanitary Landfill	Bemidji	MN
677	Sanitary Landfill Co. (IWD)	Dayton	OH
678	Eau Claire Municipal Well Field	Eau Claire	WI
679	Pagano Salvage	Los Lunas	NM
680	Valley Park TCE	Valley Park	MO
681	San Fernando Valley (Area 4)	Los Angeles	CA
682	Monolithic Memories	Sunnyvale	CA
683	National Semiconductor Corp.	Santa Clara	CA
684	Fresno Municipal Sanitary Landfill	Fresno	CA
685	Newmark Ground Water Contamination	San Bernardino	CA
686	Powersville Site	Peach County	GA
687	Grand Traverse Overall Supply Co.	Greilickville	MI
688	Metamora Landfill	Metamora	MI
689	Niagara Mohawk Power (Saratoga Springs)	Saratoga Springs	NY
690	Standard Chlorine of Delaware, Inc.	Delaware City	DE
691	South Andover Site	Andover	MN
692	Diamond Alkali Co.	Newark	NJ
693	Carter Lee Lumber Co.	Indianapolis	IN
694	Fletcher's Paint Works & Storage	Milford	NH
695	Avtex Fibers, Inc.	Front Royal	VA
696	Kentwood Landfill	Kentwood	MI
697	Electrovoice	Buchanan	MI
698	Jasco Chemical Corp.	Mountain View	CA
699	Katonah Municipal Well	Town of Bedford	NY
700	B & B Chemical Co., Inc.	Hialeah	FL
701	29th & Mead Ground Water Contamination	Wichita	KS
702	Teledyne Semiconductor	Mountain View	CA
703	Fibers Public Supply Wells	Jobos	PR
704	BMI-Textron	Lake Park	FL
705	Dixie Caverns County Landfill	Salem	VA
706	Marion (Bragg) Dump	Marion	IN

Rank	Name	City/County	State
707	Pristine, Inc.	Reading	OH
708	Mid-State Disposal, Inc. Landfill	Cleveland Township	WI
709	American Creosote (Jackson Plant)	Jackson	TN
710	Kerr-McGee (Sewage Treat Plant)	West Chicago	IL
711	Broderick Wood Products	Denver	CO
712	C & J Disposal Leasing Co. Dump	Hamilton	NY
713	Buckeye Reclamation	St. Clairsville	OH
714	Preferred Plating Corp.	Farmingdale	NY
715	Bio-Ecology Systems, Inc.	Grand Prairie	TX
716	Monticello Rad Contaminated Props	Monticello	UT
717	Woodland Route 532 Dump	Woodland Township	NJ
718	American Chemical Service, Inc.	Griffith	IN
719	Salem Acres	Salem	MA
720	Richardson Hill Road Landfill/Pond	Sidney Center	NY
721	Old Springfield Landfill	Springfield	VT
722	Bell Landfill	Terry Township	PA
723	Solvent Savers	Lincklaen	NY
724	U.S. Titanium	Piney River	VA
725	Galesburg/Koppers Co.	Galesburg	IL
726	J.H. Baxter & Co.	Weed	CA
727	Hooker (Hyde Park)	Niagara Falls	NY
728	SCA Independent Landfill	Muskegon Heights	MI
729	Action Anodizing, Plating Polish	Copiague	NY
730	MGM Brakes	Cloverdale	CA
731	Bayou Sorrel Site	Bayou Sorrel	LA
732	H.O.D. Landfill	Antioch	IL
733	Duell & Gardner Landfill	Dalton Township	MI
734	Mica Landfill	Mica	WA
735	Ellis Property	Evesham Township	NJ
736	Distler Farm	Jefferson County	KY
737	Waste Disposal, Inc.	Santa Fe Springs	CA
738	Harbor Island (Lead)	Seattle	WA
739	Lemberger Transport & Recycling	Franklin Township	WI
740	E.H. Schilling Landfill	Hamilton Township	OH
741	Cliff/Dow Dump	Marquette	MI
742	Clothier Disposal	Town of Granby	NY
743	Ambler Asbestos Piles	Ambler	PA
744	Queen City Farms	Maple Valley	WA
745	Curcio Scrap Metal, Inc.	Saddle Brook Twp.	NJ
746	L.A. Clarke & Son	Spotsylvania County	VA
747	Scrap Processing Co., Inc.	Medford	WI
748	Southern Maryland Wood Treating	Hollywood	MD
749	Caldwell Lace Leather Co., Inc.	Auburn	KY
750	Ilada Energy Co.	East Cape Girardeau	IL
751	Adams County Quincy Landfills 2 & 3	Quincy	IL
752	Kaydon Corp.	Muskegon	MI
753	Sauk County Landfill	Excelsior	WI
754	Homestake Mining Co.	Milan	NM
755	Dixie Oil Processors, Inc.	Friendswood	TX
756	Beckman Instruments (Porterville)	Poterville	CA
757	Muskegon Chemical Co.	Whitehall	MI
758	Dubose Oil Products Co.	Cantonment	FL
759	Mason County Landfill	Pere Marquette Township	MI
760	Cemetery Dump	Rose Center	MI
761	Red Oak City Landfill	Red Oak	IA
762	Lakeland Disposal Service, Inc.	Claypool	IN
763	Hopkins Farm	Plumstead Township	NJ
764	Cape Fear Wood Preserving	Fayetteville	NC
765	Stamina Mills, Inc.	North Smithfield	RI
766	Lemberger Landfill, Inc.	Whitelaw	WI
767	Reilly Tar (Indianapolis Plant)	Indianapolis	IN
768	Pinette's Salvage Yard	Washburn	ME
769	Durham Meadows	Durham	CT
770	Tyler Refrigeration Pit	Smyrna	DE
771	Kysor Industrial Corp.	Cadillac	MI
772	Lorentz Barrel & Drum Co.	San Jose	CA
773	Wilson Farm	Plumstead Township	NJ
774	Conklin Dumps	Conklin	NY
775	Old City of York Landfill	Seven Valleys	PA
776	Modern Sanitation Landfill	Lower Windsor Twp.	PA
777	Byron Salvage Yard	Byron	IL
778	North Bronson Industrial Area	Bronson	MI
779	Stanley Kessler	King of Prussia	PA
780	Helena Chemical Co. Landfill	Fairfax	SC
781	Kem-Pest Laboratories	Cape Girardeau	MO
782	Imperial Oil/Champion Chemicals	Morganville	NJ
783	Cosden Chemical Coatings Corp.	Beverly	NJ
784	St. Augusta San Landfill/Engen Dump	St. Augusta Township	MN
785	Myers Property	Franklin Township	NJ
786	Pepe Field	Boonton	NJ
787	Tri-City Disposal Co.	Sheperdsville	KY
788	Northwest Transformer	Everson	WA
789	Genzale Plating Co.	Franklin Square	NY
790	Albion-Sheridan Township Landfill	Albion	MI
791	Sheboygan Harbor & River	Sheboygan	WI
792	Combustion, Inc.	Denham Springs	LA
793	Ossineke Ground Water Contamination	Ossineke	MI
794	Follansbee Site	Follansbee	WV
795	Keystone Sanitation Landfill	Union Township	PA
796	Carolina Transformer Co.	Fayetville	NC
797	Carroll & Dubies Sewage Disposal	Port Jervis	NY
798	North Sea Municipal Landfill	North Sea	NY
799	Bendix Flight Systems Division	Bridgewater Township	PA
800	Farmers' Mutual Cooperative	Hospers	IA
801	Koppers Co. Inc. (Oroville Plant)	Oroville	CA
802	Louisiana-Pacific Corp.	Oroville	CA
803	Linemaster Switch Corp.	Woodstock	CT
804	H & H Inc., Burn Pit	Farrington	VA
805	South Macomb Disposal (Landfill 9 & 9A)	Macomb Township	MI
806	U.S. Aviex	Howard Township	MI
807	Sheller-Globe Corp. Disposal	Keokuk	IA
808	Walsh Landfill	Honeybrook Township	PA
809	Landfill & Development Co.	Mount Holly	NJ
810	Upper Deerfield Township San Landfill	Upper Deerfield Twp.	NJ
811	Hertel Landfill	Plattekill	NY
812	Haviland Complex	Town of Hyde Park	NY
813	Malta Rocket Fuel Area	Malta	NY
814	Jones Chemicals, Inc.	Caledonia	NY
815	Kent County Landfill (Houston)	Houston	DE
816	Saegertown Industrial Area	Saegertown	PA
817	Cedartown Municipal Landfill	Cedartown	GA
818	Kent City Mobile Home Park	Kent City	MI
819	Adrian Municipal Well Field	Adrian	MN
820	AT & SF (Clovis)	Clovis	NM
821	Strother Field Industrial Park	Cowley County	KS
822	Obee Road	Hutchinson	KS
823	CTS Printex, Inc.	Mountain View	CA
824	Fried Industries	East Brunswick Twp.	NJ
825	American Thermostat Co.	South Cairo	NY
826	Minot Landfill	Minot	ND
827	Koppers Co., Inc. (Newport Plant)	Newport	DE
828	Lewisburg Dump	Lewsiburg	TN
829	McGraw Edison Corp.	Albion	MI
830	Lodi Municipal Well	Lodi	NJ
831	Goldisc Recordings, Inc.	Holbrook	NY
832	Islip Municipal Sanitary Landfill	Islip	NY
833	Sola Optical USA, Inc.	Petaluma	CA
834	Airco	Calvert City	KY
835	Metal Banks	Philadelphia	PA
836	Yeoman Creek Landfill	Waukegan	IL
837	Sarney Farm	Amenia	NY
838	Folkertsma Refuse	Grand Rapids	MI
839	Sealand Limited	Mount Pleasant	DE
840	Rose Disposal Pit	Lanesboro	MA
841	Van Dale Junkyard	Marietta	OH
842	Montana Pole and Treating	Butte	MT
843	Geigy Chemical Corp. (Aberdeen Pit)	Aberdeen	NC
844	B.F. Goodrich	Calvert City	KY
845	General Tire/Rubber (Mayfield Landfill)	Mayfield	KY
846	Para-Chem Southern, Inc.	Simpsonville	SC
847	Organic Chemicals, Inc.	Grandville	MI
848	BioClinical Laboratories, Inc.	Bohemia	NY
849	Volney Municipal Landfill	Town of Volney	NY
850	FMC Corp. (Dublin Road Landfill)	Town of Shelby	NY
851	Tomah Fairgrounds	Tomah	WI
852	Sullivan's Ledge	New Bedford	MA
853	Smith's Farm	Brooks	KY
854	Madison Metro Sewer District Lag	Blooming Grove	WI
855	North Market Street	Spokane	WA
856	Joseph Forest Products	Joseph	OR
857	Juncos Landfill	Juncos	PR
858	Big River Sand Co.	Wichita	KS
859	Bennett Stone Quarry	Bloomington	IN
860	Wyckoff Co./Eagle Harbor	Bainbridge Island	WA

Rank	Name	City/County	State
861	Beaunit Corp. (Circular Knit & Dye)	Fountain Inn	SC
862	Industrial Latex Crop.	Wallington Borough	NJ
863	Munisport Landfill	North Miami	FL
864	D.L. Mud, Inc.	Abbeville	LA
865	Stauffer Chem. (LeMoyne Plant)	Axis	AL
866	M & T Delisa Landfill	Asbury Park	NJ
867	Crystal City Airport	Crystal City	TX
868	Geiger (C & M Oil)	Rantoules	SC
869	Paoli Rail Yard	Paoli	PA
870	Moss-American (Kerr-McGee Oil Co.)	Milwaukee	WI
871	Waste Research & Reclamation Co.	Eau Claire	WI
872	Gould, Inc.	Portland	OR
873	Union Chemical Co., Inc.	South Hope	ME
874	Cortese Landfill	Village of Narrowsburg	NY
875	Mystery Bridge Rd./U.S. Highway 20	Evansville	WY
876	Montrose Chemical Corp.	Torrance	CA
877	St. Louis River Site	St. Louis County	MN
878	Auto Ion Chemicals, Inc.	Kalamazoo	MI
879	Recticon/Allied Steel Corp.	East Coventry Township	PA
880	Hagen Farm	Stoughton	WI
881	Carolawn, Inc.	Fort Lawn	SC
882	Midwest Manufacturing/North Farm	Kellogg	IA
883	Berks Sand Pit	Longswamp Township	PA
884	Valley Wood Preserving, Inc.	Turlock	CA
885	Butz Landfill	Stroudsburg	PA
886	City Industries, Inc.	Orlando	FL
887	Sparta Landfill	Sparta Township	MI
888	Acme Solvent (Morristown Plant)	Morristown	IL
889	Holton Circle Ground Water Contamination	Londonderry	NH
890	Pomona Oaks Residential Wells	Galloway Township	NJ
891	Rowe Industries Ground Water Contamination	Noyack/Sag Harbor	NY
892	Hebelka Auto Salvage Yard	Weisenberg Township	PA
893	Hipps Road Landfill	Duval County	FL
894	Long Pairie Ground Water Contamination	Long Prairie	MN
895	Waite Park Wells	Waite Park	MN
896	Nebraska Ordnance Plant (Former)	Mead	NE
897	Applied Materials	Santa Clara	CA
898	Intel Magnetics	Santa Clara	CA
899	Intel Corp. (Santa Clara III)	Santa Clara	CA
900	TRW Microwave, Inc. (Building 825)	Sunnyvale	CA
901	Synertek, Inc. (Building 1)	Santa Clara	CA
902	Advanced Micro Devices (Building 915)	Sunnyvale	CA
903	Pepper Steel & Alloys, Inc.	Medley	FL
904	Mattiace Petrochemical Co., Inc.	Glen Cove	NY
905	O'Connor Co.	Augusta	ME
906	Oconomowoc Electroplating Co. Inc.	Ashippin	WI
907	Continental Steel Corp.	Kokomo	IN
908	Rasmussen's Dump	Green Oak Township	MI
909	Kenmark Textile Corp.	Farmingdale	NY
910	Wingate Road Municipal Incineration Dump	Fort Lauderdale	FL
911	Westline Site	Westline	PA
912	Maxey Flats Nuclear Disposal	Hillsboro	KY
913	Benfield Industries, Inc.	Hazelwood	NC
914	Mouat Industries	Columbus	MT
915	J & L Landfill	Rochester Hills	MI
916	Claremont Polychemical	Old Bethpage	NY
917	Powell Road Landfill	Dayton	OH
918	Croydon TCE	Croydon	PA
919	Medley Farm Drum Dump	Gaffney	SC
920	Elmore Waste Disposal	Greer	SC
921	Vogel Paint & Wax Co.	Orange City	IA
922	Kurt Manufacturing Co.	Fridley	MN
923	Reilly Tar & Chemical (Dover Plant)	Dover	OH
924	Parsons Chemical Works, Inc.	Grand Ledge	MI
925	Revere Chemical Co.	Nockamixon Township	PA
926	Ionia City Landfill	Ionia	MI
927	Koppers Co. Inc. (Texarkana Plant)	Texarkana	TX
928	Lincoln Park	Canon City	CO
929	Smuggler Mountain	Pitkin County	CO
930	Wedzeb Enterprises, Inc.	Lebanon	IN
931	GE Wiring Devices	Juana Diaz	PR
932	Missouri Electric Works	Cape Girardeau	MO
933	Avenue "E" Ground Water Contamination	Traverse City	MI
934	New Lyme Landfill	New Lyme	OH
935	Woodland Route 72 Dump	Woodland Township	NJ
936	RCA Del Caribe	Barceloneta	PR
937	Koch Refining Co./ N. Ren Corp.	Pine Bend	MN
938	Piper Aircraft/Vero Beach Water & Sewer	Vero Beach	FL
939	Brodhead Creek	Stroudsburg	PA
940	Fadrowski Drum Disposal	Franklin	WI
941	United Chrome Products, Inc.	Corvallis	OR
942	Anodyne, Inc.	North Miami Beach	FL
943	Anaconda Aluminum/Milgo Electronics	Miami	FL
944	Eastern Diversified Metals	Hometown	PA
945	Anderson Development Co.	Adrian	MI
946	Hunts Disposal Landfill	Caledonia	WI
947	Shiawassee River	Howell	MI
948	Tenth Street Dump/Junkyard	Oklahoma City	OK
949	Alaska Battery Enterprises	Fairbanks N. Star Bor.	AK
950	Taylor Borough Dump	Taylor Borough	PA
951	Murray-Ohio Mfg. (Horeshoe Bend)	Lawrenceburg	TN
952	Halby Chemical Co.	New Castle	DE
953	Higgins Disposal	Kingston	NJ
954	Redwing Carriers, Inc. (Saraland)	Saraland	AL
955	Double Eagle Refinery Co.	Oklahoma City	OK
956	Mathis Bros. Landfill (S. Marble Top Rd.)	Kensington	GA
957	Harvey & Knott Drum, Inc.	Kirkwood	DE
958	Gallaway Pits	Gallaway	TN
959	Big D Campground	Kingsville	OH
960	Midland Products	Ola/Birta	AR
961	Robintech, Inc./National Pipe Co.	Town of Vestal	NY
962	BEC Trucking	Town of Vestal	NY
963	Strasburg Landfill	Newlin Township	PA
964	Fourth Street Abandoned Refinery	Oklahoma City	OK
965	Witco Chemical Corp. (Oakland Plant)	Oakland	NJ
966	Tomah Armory	Tomah	WI
967	Wildcat Landfill	Dover	DE
968	Burrows Sanitation	Hartford	MI
969	Blosenski Landfill	West Caln Township	PA
970	Rhinehart Tire Fire Dump	Frederick County	VA
971	Northwest Transformer (S. Harkness)	Everson	WA
972	Delaware City PVC Plant	Delaware City	DE
973	Limestone Road	Cumberland	MD
974	Hooker (102nd Street)	Niagara Falls	NY
975	Higgins Farm	Franklin Township	NJ
976	American Crossarm & Conduit Co.	Chehalis	WA
977	United Nuclear Corp.	Church Rock	NM
978	Rentokil, Inc. (VA Wood Pres. Div.)	Richmond	VA
979	Industrial Waste Control	Fort Smith	AR
980	Celtor Chemical Works	Hoopa	CA
981	Haverhill Municipal Landfill	Haverhill	MA
982	Perdido Ground Water Contamination	Perdido	AL
983	Marathon Battery Corp.	Cold Springs	NY
984	Colesville Municipal Landfill	Town of Colesville	NY
985	Yellow Water Road Dump	Baldwin	FL
986	Marzone Inc./Chevron Chemical Co.	Tifton	GA
987	Skinner Landfill	West Chester	OH
988	First Piedmont Quarry (Route 719)	Pittsylvania County	VA
989	Chemtronics, Inc.	Swannanoa	NC
990	MIDCO II	Gary	IN
991	Cannelton Industries, Inc.	Sault Sainte Marie	MI
992	Sheridan Disposal Services	Hempstead	TX
993	Pester Refinery Co.	El Dorado	KS
994	Kane & Lombard Street Drums	Baltimore	MD
995	Shenandoah Stables	Moscow Mills	MO
996	Firestone Tire (Albany Plant)	Albany	GA
997	Shaw Avenue Dump	Charles City	IA
998	Berkley Products Co. Dump	Denver	PA
999	Silver Mountain Mine	Loomis	WA
1000	Petro-Chemical (Turtle Bayou)	Liberty County	TX
1001	Hevi-Duty Electric Co.	Goldsboro	NC
1002	Republic Steel Corp. Quarry	Elyria	OH
1003	Conservation Chemical Co.	Kansas City	MO
1004	Westlake Landfill	Bridgeton	MO
1005	Ritari Post & Pole	Sebeka	MN
1006	Bayou Bonfouca	Slidell	LA
1007	Fairchild Semiconduct (Mountain View)	Mountain View	CA
1008	Intel Corp. (Mountain View Plant)	Mountain View	CA
1009	Raytheon Corp.	Mountain View	CA
1010	Hewlett-Packard (620-40 Page Mill)	Palo Alto	CA
1011	Agate Lake Scrapyard	Fairview Township	MN
1012	Adam's Plating	Lansing	MI

Rank	Name	City/County	State
1013	Jacksonville Municipal Landfill	Jacksonville	AR
1014	Rogers Road Municipal Landfill	Jacksonville	AR
1015	Saltville Waste Disposal Ponds	Saltville	VA
1016	Saco Municipal Landfill	Saco	ME
1017	Palmetto Recycling, Inc.	Columbia	SC
1018	Shpack Landfill	Norton/Attleboro	MA
1019	Kimberton Site	Kimberton Borough	PA
1020	Mallory Capacitor Co.	Waynesboro	TN
1021	Norwood PCBs	Norwood	MA
1022	Warwick Landfill	Warwick	NY
1023	Sidney Landfill	Sidney	NY
1024	Sealand Restoration, Inc.	Lisbon	NY
1025	Old Inland Pit	Spokane	WA
1026	Pesticide Lab (Yakima)	Yakima	WA
1027	Lemon Lane Landfill	Bloomington	IN
1028	Tri-State Plating	Columbus	IN
1029	Arrcom (Drexler Enterprises)	Rathdrum	ID
1030	Coakley Landfill	North Hampton	NH
1031	Potter's Septic Tank Service Pits	Maco	NC
1032	Green River Disposal, Inc.	Maceo	KY
1033	ABC One Hour Cleaners	Jacksonville	NC
1034	Fischer & Porter Co.	Warminster	PA
1035	Elizabethtown Landfill	Elizabethtown	PA
1036	Central Illinois Public Service Co.	Taylorville	IL
1037	Arkwood, Inc.	Omaha	AR
1038	Jibboom Junkyard	Sacramento	CA
1039	A.O. Polymer	Sparta Township	NJ
1040	Wausau Ground Water Contamination	Wausau	WI
1041	Dover Municipal Well 4	Dover Township	NJ
1042	Rockaway Township Wells	Rockaway	NJ
1043	Pohatcong Valley Ground Water Con.	Warren County	NJ

Rank	Name	City/County	State
1044	Garden State Cleaners Co.	Minotola	NJ
1045	Sussex County Landfill No. 5	Laurel	DE
1046	North Penn - Area 12	Worcester	PA
1047	Dublin TCE Site	Dublin Borough	PA
1048	Delavan Municipal Well #4	Delavan	WI
1049	Waste Management (Brookfield Landfill)	Brookfield	WI
1050	North-U Drive Well Contamination	Springfield	MO
1051	10th Street Site	Columbus	NE
1052	San Gabriel Valley (Area 3)	Alhambra	CA
1053	San Gabriel Valley (Area 4)	La Puente	CA
1054	Watkins-Johnson Co. (Stewart Division)	Scotts Valley	CA
1055	Intersil Inc./Siemens Components	Cupertino	CA
1056	Modesto Ground Water Contamination	Modesto	CA
1057	American Lake Gardens	Tacoma	WA
1058	Greenacres Landfill	Spokane County	WA
1059	Northside Landfill	Spokane	WA
1060	Sand Springs Petrochemical Complex	Sand Springs	OK
1061	Pesses Chemical Co.	Fort Worth	TX
1062	Metal Working Shop	Lake Ann	MI
1063	East Bethel Demolition Landfill	East Bethel Township	MN
1064	Triangle Chemical Co.	Bridge City	TX
1065	PJP Landfill	Jersey City	NJ
1066	Craig Farm Drum	Parker	PA
1067	Belvidere Municipal Landfill	Belvidere	IL
1068	Bee Cee Manufacturing Co.	Malden	MO
1069	CryoChem, Inc.	Worman	PA
1070	Kauffman & Minteer, Inc.	Jobstown	NJ
1071	Lansdowne Radiation Site	Lansdowne	PA
1072	Forest Glen Mobile Home Subdivision	Niagara Falls	NY
1073	Radium Chemical Co., Inc.	New York City	NY

EPA National Priorities List, Superfund Sites by State

(as of February 1991)

Position or ranking for a site on the National Priorities List can be found following the City/County name in which the site is located; the lower the ranking, the higher the severity of site contamination.

State	Name	City/County	Rank
AK	Alaska Battery Enterprises	Fairbanks N. Star Bor	949
AK	Arctic Surplus	Fairbanks	437
AL	Ciba-Geigy Corp (McIntosh Plant)	McIntosh	135
AL	Interstate Lead Co (ILCO)	Leeds	371
AL	Mowbray Engineering Co	Greenville	128
AL	Olin Corp (McIntosh Plant)	McIntosh	507
AL	Perdido Ground Water Contamination	Perdido	982
AL	Redwing Carriers, Inc (Saraland)	Saraland	954
AL	Stauffer Chemical Co (Cold Creek Plant)	Bucks	266
AL	Stauffer Chemical Co (LeMoyne Plant)	Axis	865
AL	T.H. Agriculture & Nutrition Co (Montgomery Plant)	Montgomery	332
AL	Triana/Tennessee River (once listed as Triana (Redstone) Arsenal)	Limestone/Morgan	31
AR	Arkwood, Inc	Omaha	1037
AR	Frit Industries	Walnut Ridge	515
AR	Gurley Pit	Edmondson	490
AR	Industrial Waste Control	Fort Smith	979
AR	Jacksonville Municipal Landfill	Jacksonville	1013
AR	Mid-South Wood Products	Mena	308
AR	Midland Products	Ola/Birta	960
AR	Monroe Auto Equipment Co (Paragould Pit)	Paragould	293
AR	Rogers Road Municipal Landfill	Jacksonville	1014
AR	Vertac, Inc	Jacksonville	18
AZ	Apache Powder Co	St. David	522
AZ	Hassayampa Landfill	Hassayampa	374
AZ	Indian Bend Wash Area	Scottsdale/Tempe/Phnx	430
AZ	Litchfield Airport Area	Goodyear/Avondale	305
AZ	Motorola, Inc (52nd Street Plant)	Phoenix	467
AZ	Ninteenth Avenue Landfill	Phoenix	124
AZ	Tucson International Airport Area	Tucson	74
CA	Advanced Micro Devices, Inc (Building 915)	Sunnyvale	902
CA	Advanced Micro Devices, Inc	Sunnyvale	588
CA	Aerojet General Corp	Rancho Cordova	117
CA	Applied Materials	Santa Clara	897
CA	Atlas Asbestos Mine	Fresno County	310
CA	Beckman Instruments (Porterville Plant)	Porterville	756
CA	Brown & Bryant, Inc (Arvin Plant)	Arvin	143
CA	Celtor Chemical Works	Hoopa	980
CA	Coalinga Asbestos Mine	Coalinga	311
CA	Coast Wood Preserving	Ukiah	327
CA	Crazy Horse Sanitary Landfill	Salinas	590
CA	CTS Printex, Inc	Mountain View	823
CA	Del Norte Pesticide Storage	Crescent City	652
CA	Fairchild Semiconductor Corp (Mountain View Plant) (once listed as Fairchild Camera & Instrument Corp (Mountian View Plant))	Mountain View	1007
CA	Fairchild Semiconductor Corp (South San Jose Plant) (once listed as Fairchild Camera & Instrument Corp (South San Jose Plant))	South San Jose	333
CA	Firestone Tire & Rubber Co (Salinas Plant)	Salinas	306
CA	Fresno Municipal Sanitary Landfill	Fresno	684
CA	Hewlett-Packard (620-640 Page Mill Road)	Palo Alto	1010
CA	Hexcel Corp	Livermore	589
CA	Industrial Waste Processing	Fresno	187
CA	Intel Corp (Mountain View Plant)	Mountain View	1008
CA	Intel Corp (Santa Clara III)	Santa Clara	899
CA	Intel Magnetics	Santa Clara	898
CA	Intersil Inc/Siemens Conponents	Cupertino	1055
CA	Iron Mountain Mine	Redding	103
CA	J.H. Baxter & Co	Weed	726
CA	Jasco Chemical Corp	Mountian View	698
CA	Jibboom Junkyard	Sacramento	1038
CA	Koppers Co, Inc (Oroville Plant)	Oroville	801
CA	Liquid Gold Oil Corp	Richmond	357
CA	Lorentz Barrel & Drum Co	San Jose	772
CA	Louisiana-Pacific Corp	Oroville	802
CA	McColl	Fullerton	449
CA	MGM Brakes	Cloverdale	730
CA	Modesto Ground Water Contamination	Modesto	1056
CA	Monolithic Memories	Sunnyvale	682
CA	Montrose Chemical Corp	Torrance	876
CA	National Semiconductor Corp	Santa Clara	683
CA	Newmark Ground Water Contamination	San Bernardino	685
CA	Operating Industries, Inc, Landfill	Monterey Park	101
CA	Pacific Coast Pipe Lines	Fillmore	296
CA	Purity Oil Sales, Inc	Malaga	358
CA	Raytheon Corp	Mountain View	1009
CA	San Fernando Valley (Area 1)	Los Angeles	433
CA	San Fernando Valley (Area 2)	Los Angeles/Glendale	434
CA	San Fernando Valley (Area 3)	Glendale	435
CA	San Fernando Valley (Area 4)	Los Angeles	681
CA	San Gabriel Valley (Area 1)	El Monte	431
CA	San Gabriel Valley (Area 2)	Baldwin Park Area	432
CA	San Gabriel Valley (Area 3)	Alhambra	1052
CA	San Gabriel Valley (Area 4)	La Puente	1053
CA	Selma Treating Co	Selma	228
CA	Sola Optical USA, Inc	Petaluma	833
CA	South Bay Asbestos Area (once listed as Alviso Dumping Area)	Alviso	328
CA	Southern California Edison Co (Visalia Poleyard)	Visalia	224

State	Name	City/County	Rank
CA	Spectra-Physics, Inc	Mountain View	614
CA	Stringfellow *	Glen Avon Heights	32
CA	Surphur Bank Mercury Mine	Clear Lake	335
CA	Synertek, Inc (Building 1)	Santa Clara	901
CA	T.H. Agriculture & Nutrition Co (once listed as Thompson-Haywood Chemical Co)	Fresno	436
CA	Teledyne Semiconductor	Mountian View	702
CA	TRW Microwave, Inc (Building 825)	Sunnyvale	900
CA	United Heckathorn Co	Richmond	539
CA	Valley Wood Preserving, Inc	Turlock	884
CA	Waste Disposal, Inc	Santa Fe Springs	737
CA	Watkins-Johnson Co (Stewart Division)	Scotts Valley	1054
CA	Western Pacific Railroad Co	Oroville	506
CA	Westinghouse Electric Corp (Sunnyvale Plant)	Sunnyvale	498
CO	Broderick Wood Products	Denver	711
CO	California Gulch	Leadville	105
CO	Central City-Clear Creek	Idaho Springs	178
CO	Chemical Sales Co	Denver	586
CO	Denver Radium Site	Denver	340
CO	Eagle Mine	Minturn/Redcliff	258
CO	Lincoln Park	Canon City	928
CO	Lowry Landfill	Arapahoe County	235
CO	Marshall Landfill*	Boulder County	86
CO	Sand Creek Industrial	Commerce City	36
CO	Smuggler Mountain	Pitkin County	929
CO	Uraven Uranium Project (Union Carbide Corp)	Uravan	352
CO	Woodbury Chemical Co	Commerce City	322
CT	Barkhamsted-New Hartford Landfill	Barkhamsted	564
CT	Beacon Heights Landfill	Beacon Falls	265
CT	Cheshire Ground Water Contamination (once listed as Cheshire Associates Property)	Cheshire	664
CT	Durham Meadows	Durham	769
CT	Gallup's Quarry	Plainfield	282
CT	Kellogg-Deering Well Field	Norwalk	499
CT	Laurel Park, Inc (once listed as Laural Park Landfill)*	Naugatuck Borough	85
CT	Linemaster Switch Corp	Woodstock	803
CT	Nutmeg Valley Road	Wolcott	379
CT	Old Southington Landfill	Southington	121
CT	Precision Plating Corp	Vernon	214
CT	Revere Textile Prints Corp	Sterling	460
CT	Solvents Recovery Service of New England	Southington	321
CT	Yaworski Waste Lagoon	Canterbury	626
DE	Army Creek Landfill (once listed as Delaware Sand & Gravel-Llangollen Army Creek Landfills)	New Castle County	9
DE	Chem-Solv, Inc	Cheswold	574
DE	Coker's Sanitation Service Landfills	Kent County	159
DE	Delaware City PVC Plant (once listed as Stauffer Chemical Co)	Delaware City	972
DE	Delaware Sand & Gravel Landfill (once listed as Delaware Sand & Gravel-Llangollen Army Creek Landfill)	New Castle County	272
DE	Dover Gas Light Co	Dover	667
DE	E.I. Du Pont de Nemours & Co, Inc (Newport Pigment Plant Landfill)	Newport	169
DE	Halby Chemical Co	New Castle	952
DE	Harvey & Knott Drum, Inc	Kirkwood	957
DE	Kent County Landfill (Houston)	Houston	815
DE	Koppers Co, Inc (Newport Plant)	Newport	827
DE	NCR Corp (Millsboro Plant)	Millsboro	548
DE	New Castle Spill (once listed as TRIS Spill)	New Castle County	545
DE	Sealand Limited	Mount Pleasant	839
DE	Standard Chlorine of Delaware, Inc	Delaware City	690
DE	Sussex County Landfill No 5	Laural	1045
DE	Tybouts Corner Landfill*	New Castle County	2
DE	Tyler Refrigeration Pit	Smyrna	770
DE	Wildcat Landfill	Dover	967

State	Name	City/County	Rank
FL	Agrico Chemical Co	Pensacola	319
FL	Airco Plating Co	Miami	391
FL	Alpha Chemical Corp	Galloway	360
FL	American Creosote Works, Inc (Pensacola Plant)	Pensacola	51
FL	Anaconda Aluminum Co/Milgo Electronics Corp	Miami	943
FL	Anodyne, Inc	North Miami Beach	942
FL	B&B Chemical Co, Inc	Hialeah	700
FL	Beulah Landfill	Pensacola	553
FL	BMI-Textron	Lake Park	704
FL	Brown Wood Preserving	Live Oak	312
FL	Cabot/Koppers	Gainesville	629
FL	Chemform, Inc	Pompano Beach	578
FL	City Industries, Inc	Orlando	886
FL	Coleman-Evans Wood Preserving Co	Whitehouse	286
FL	Davie Landfill (once listed as Broward County Solid Waste Disposal Facility)	Davie	69
FL	Dubose Oil Products Co	Cantonment	758
FL	Florida Steel Corp	Indiantown	298
FL	Gold Coast Oil Corp	Miami	77
FL	Harris Corp (Palm Bay Plant) (once listed as Harris Corp/General Development Utilities)	Palm Bay	674
FL	Hipps Road Landfill	Duval County	893
FL	Hollingsworth Solderless Terminal	Fort Lauderdale	330
FL	Kassauf-Kimerling Battery Disposal (once listed as Timber Lake Battery Disposal)	Tampa	136
FL	Madison County Sanitary Landfill	Madison	577
FL	Miami Drum Services (once listed as part of Biscayne Aquifer)	Miami	130
FL	Munisport Landfill	North Miami	863
FL	Northwest 58th Street Landfill (once listed as part of Biscayne Aquifer)	Hialeah	209
FL	Peak Oil Co/Bay Drum Co	Tampa	55
FL	Pepper Steel & Alloys, Inc	Medley	903
FL	Petroleum Products Corp	Pembroke Park	491
FL	Pickettville Road Landfill	Jacksonville	365
FL	Pioneer Sand Co	Warrington	165
FL	Piper Aircraft/Vero Beach Water & Sewer Department	Vero Beach	938
FL	Reeves Southeast Galvanizing Corp	Tampa	46
FL	Sapp Battery Salvage	Cottondale	247
FL	Schuylkill Metals Corp	Plant City	43
FL	Sherwood Medical Industries	Deland	505
FL	Sixty-Second Street Dump	Tampa	215
FL	Standard Auto Bumper Corp	Hialeah	372
FL	Sydney Mine Sludge Ponds	Brandon	529
FL	Taylor Road Landfill	Seffner	180
FL	Tower Chemical Co	Clermont	343
FL	Whitehouse Oil Pits	Whitehouse	151
FL	Wilson Concepts of Florida, Inc	Pompano Beach	579
FL	Wingate Road Municipal Incinerator Dump	Fort Lauderdale	910
FL	Woodbury Chemical Co (Princeton Plant)	Princeton	517
FL	Yellow Water Road Dump	Baldwin	985
FL	Zellwood Ground Water Contamination	Zellwood	171
GA	Cedartown Industries, Inc	Cedartown	441
GA	Cedartown Municipal Landfill	Cedartown	817
GA	Diamond Shamrock Corp Landfill	Cedartown	662
GA	Firestone Tire & Rubber Co (Albany Plant)	Albany	996
GA	Hercules 009 Landfill	Brunswick	152
GA	Marzone Inc/Chevron Chemical Co	Tifton	986
GA	Mathis Brothers Landfill (South Mable Top Road)	Kensington	956
GA	Monsanto Corp (Augusta Plant)	Augusta	658
GA	Powersville Site	Peace County	686
GA	T.H. Agriculture & Nutrition Co (Albany Plant)	Albany	464
GA	Woolfolk Chemical Works, Inc	Fort Valley	415
GU	Ordot Landfill*	Guam	97
IA	Aidex Corp*	Council Bluffs	93
IA	Des Moines TCE (once listed as DICO)	Des Moines	408

State	Name	City/County	Rank
IA	E.I. Du Pont de Nemours & Co, Inc (County Road X23)	West Point	295
IA	Electro-Coatings, Inc	Cedar Rapids	427
IA	Fairfield Coal Gasification Plant	Fairfield	565
IA	Farmers' Mutual Cooperative	Hospers	800
IA	John Deere (Ottumwa Works Landfills)	Ottumwa	403
IA	LaBounty Site	Charles City	8
IA	Lawrence Todtz Farm	Camanche	162
IA	Lehigh Portland Cement Co	Mason City	68
IA	Mid-America Tanning Co	Sergeant Bluff	240
IA	Midwest Manufacturing/North Farm	Kellogg	882
IA	Northwestern States Portland Cement Co	Mason City	75
IA	Peoples Natural Gas Co	Dubuque	284
IA	Red Oak City Landfill	Red Oak	761
IA	Shaw Avenue Dump	Charles City	997
IA	Sheller-Globe Corp Disposal	Keokuk	807
IA	Vogel Paint & Wax Co	Orange City	921
IA	White Farm Equipment Co Dump	Charles City	356
ID	Arrcom (Drexler Enterprises)	Rathdrum	1029
ID	Bunker Hill Mining & Metallurgical	Smelterville	114
ID	Eastern Michaud Flats Contamination	Pocatello	73
ID	Kerr-McGee Chemical Corp (Soda Springs Plant)	Soda Springs	174
ID	Monsanto Chemical Co (Soda Springs Plant)	Soda Springs	113
ID	Pacific Hide & Fur Recycling Co	Pocatello	407
ID	Union Pacific Railroad Co	Pocatello	132
IL	A & F Material Reclaiming, Inc	Greenup	109
IL	Acme Solvent Reclaiming, Inc (Morristown Plant)	Morristown	888
IL	Adams County Quincy Landfills 2&3	Quincy	751
IL	Amoco Chemicals (Joliet Landfill)	Joliet	516
IL	Beloit Corp	Rockton	163
IL	Belvidere Municipal Landfill	Belvidere	1067
IL	Byron Salvage Yard	Byron	777
IL	Central Illinois Public Service Co	Taylorville	1036
IL	Cross Brothers Pail Recycling (Pembroke)	Pembroke Township	440
IL	DuPage County Landfill/Blackwell Forest Preserve	Warrenville	675
IL	Galesburg/Koppers Co	Galesburg	725
IL	H.O.D. Landfill	Antioch	732
IL	Ilada Energy Co	East Cape Girardeau	750
IL	Interstate Pollution Control, Inc	Rockford	292
IL	Johns-Manville Corp	Waukegan	550
IL	Kerr-McGee (Kress Creek/West Branch of DuPage River)	DuPage County	524
IL	Kerr-McGee (Reed-Keppler Park)	West Chicago	514
IL	Kerr-McGee (Residential Areas)	West Chicago/DuPage County	555
IL	Kerr-McGee (Sewage Treatment Plant)	West Chicago	710
IL	LaSalle Electric Utilities	LaSalle	439
IL	Lenz Oil Service, Inc	Lemont	400
IL	MIG/Dewane Landfill	Belvidere	204
IL	NL Industries/Taracorp Lead Smelter	Granite City	558
IL	Outboard Marine Corp*	Waukegan	87
IL	Pagel's Pit	Rockford	301
IL	Parsons Casket Hardware Co	Belvidere	108
IL	Southeast Rockford Ground Water Contamination	Rockford	416
IL	Tri-County Landfill Co/Waste Management of Illionis, Inc	South Elgin	376
IL	Velsicol Chemical Corp (Illionis)	Marshall	230
IL	Wauconda Sand & Gravel	Wauconda	137
IL	Woodstock Municipal Landfill	Woodstock	202
IL	Yeoman Creek Landfill	Waukegan	836
IN	American Chemical Service, Inc	Griffith	718
IN	Bennett Stone Quarry	Bloomington	859
IN	Carter Lee Lumber Co	Indianapolis	693
IN	Columbus Old Municipal Landfill #1	Columbus	314
IN	Conrail Rail Yard (Elkhart)	Elkhart	418
IN	Continental Steel Corp	Kokomo	907
IN	Douglass Road/Uniroyal, Inc, Landfill	Mishawaka	632
IN	Envirochem Corp	Zionsville	278
IN	Fisher-Calo	LaPorte	164
IN	Fort Wayne Reduction Dump	Fort Wayne	392
IN	Galen Myers Dump/Drum Salvage	Osceola	419
IN	Himco Dump	Elkhart	406
IN	Lake Sandy Jo (M & M Landfill)	Gary	549
IN	Lakeland Disposal Service, Inc	Claypool	762
IN	Lemon Lane Landfill	Bloomington	1027
IN	Main Street Well Field	Elkhart	387
IN	Marion (Bragg) Dump	Marion	706
IN	MIDCO I	Gary	279
IN	MIDCO II	Gary	990
IN	Neal's Dump (Spencer)	Spencer	636
IN	Neal's Landfill (Bloomington)	Bloomington	369
IN	Ninth Avenue Dump	Gary	485
IN	Northside Sanitary Landfill, Inc	Zionsville	291
IN	Prestolite Battery Division	Vincennes	476
IN	Reilly Tar & Chemical Corp (Indianapolis Plant)	Indianapolis	767
IN	Seymour Recycling Corp *	Seymour	54
IN	Southside Sanitary Landfill	Indianapolis	443
IN	Tippecanoe Sanitary Landfill Inc	Lafayette	417
IN	Tri-State Plating	Columbus	1028
IN	Waste, Inc, Landfill	Michigan City	193
IN	Wayne Waste Oil	Columbia City	401
IN	Wedzeb Enterprises, Inc	Lebanon	930
IN	Whiteford Sales & Service Inc/ NationaLease	South Bend	175
KS	29th & Mead Ground Water Contamination	Wichita	701
KS	Arkansas City Dump*	Arkansas City	100
KS	Big River Sand Co	Wichita	858
KS	Cherokee County (once listed as Tar Creek, Cherokee County)	Cherokee County	57
KS	Doepke Disposal (Holliday)	Johnson City	251
KS	Hydro-Flex Inc	Topeka	373
KS	Johns' Sludge Pond	Wichita	650
KS	Obee Road	Hutchinson	822
KS	Pester Refinery Co	El Dorado	993
KS	Strother Field Industrial Park	Cowley County	821
KY	A.L. Taylor (Valley of Drums)*	Brooks	96
KY	Airco	Calvert City	834
KY	B.F. Goodrich	Calvert City	844
KY	Brantley Landfill	Island	147
KY	Caldwell Lace Leather Co, Inc	Auburn	749
KY	Distler Brickyard	West Point	325
KY	Distler Farm	Jefferson County	736
KY	Fort Hartford Coal Co Stone Quarry	Olaton	347
KY	General Tire & Rubber Co (Mayfield Landfill)	Mayfield	845
KY	Green River Disposal, Inc	Maceo	1032
KY	Howe Valley Landfill	Howe Valley	625
KY	Lee's Lane Landfill	Louisville	513
KY	Maxey Flats Nuclear Disposal	Hillsboro	912
KY	Newport Dump	Newport	600
KY	Red Penn Sanitation Co Landfill	Peewee Valley	559
KY	Smith's Farm	Brooks	853
KY	Tri-City Disposal Co	Shepherdsville	787
LA	Bayou Bonfouca	Slidell	1006
LA	Bayou Sorrel Site	Bayou Sorrel	731
LA	Cleve Reber	Sorrento	229
LA	Combustion, Inc	Denhan Springs	792
LA	D.L. Mud, Inc	Abbeville	864
LA	Dutchtown Treatment Plant	Ascension Parish	640
LA	Gulf Coast Vacuum Services	Abbeville	375
LA	Old Inger Oil Refinery*	Darrow	82
LA	PAB Oil & Chemical Services, Inc	Abbeville	528
LA	Petro-Processors of Lousiana Inc	Scotlandville	453
MA	Atlas Tack Corp	Fairhaven	384
MA	Baird & McGuire	Holbrook	14
MA	Cannon Engineering Corp (CEC)	Bridgewater	501
MA	Charles-George Reclamation Trust Landfill	Tyngsborough	254
MA	Groveland Wells	Groveland	468
MA	Haverhill Municipal Landfill	Haverhill	981
MA	Hocomonco Pond	Westborough	324

State	Name	City/County	Rank
MA	Industri-Plex (once listed as Mark Phillip Trust)	Woburn	5
MA	Iron Horse Park	Billerica	367
MA	New Bedford Site*	New Bedford	81
MA	Norwood PCBs	Norwood	1021
MA	Nyanza Chemical Waste Dump	Ashland	11
MA	Plymouth Harbor/Cannon Engineering Corp (once listed as Plymouth Harbor/Cordage)	Plymouth	112
MA	PSC Resources	Palmer	536
MA	Re-Solve, Inc	Dartmouth	243
MA	Rose Disposal Pit	Lanesboro	840
MA	Salem Acres	Salem	719
MA	Shpack Landfill	Norton/Attleboro	1018
MA	Silresim Chemical Corp	Lowell	377
MA	Sullivan's Ledge	New Bedford	852
MA	W.R. Grace & Co Inc (Acton Plant)	Acton	38
MA	Wells G & H	Woburn	378
MD	Anne Arundel County Landfill	Glen Burnie	575
MD	Bush Valley Landfill	Abingdon	486
MD	Kane & Lombard Street Drum	Baltimore	994
MD	Limestone Road	Cumberland	973
MD	Mid-Atlantic Wood Preservers, Inc	Harmans	404
MD	Sand, Gravel & Stone	Elkton	458
MD	Southern Maryland Wood Treating	Hollywood	748
MD	Woodlawn County Landfill	Woodlawn	238
ME	McKin Co	Gray	33
ME	O'Connor Co	Augusta	905
ME	Pinette's Salvage Yard	Washburn	768
ME	Saco Municipal Landfill	Saco	1016
ME	Saco Tannery Waste Pits	Saco	362
ME	Union Chemical Co, Inc	South Hope	873
ME	Winthrop Landfill	Winthrop	660
MI	Adam's Plating	Lansing	1012
MI	Albion-Sheridan Township Landfill	Albion	790
MI	Allied Paper, Inc/Portage Creek/Kalamazoo River	Kalamazoo	639
MI	American Anodco, Inc	Ionia	61
MI	Anderson Development Co	Adrian	945
MI	Auto Ion Chemicals, Inc	Kalamazoo	878
MI	Avenue "E" Ground Water Contamination	Traverse City	933
MI	Barrels, Inc	Lansing	421
MI	Bendix Corp/Allied Automotive	St. Joseph	610
MI	Berlin & Farro	Swartz Creek	13
MI	Bofors Nobel, Inc	Muskegon	138
MI	Burrows Sanitation	Hartford	968
MI	Butterworth #2 Landfill	Grand Rapids	197
MI	Cannelton Industries, Inc	Sault Sainte Marie	991
MI	Carter Industrials, Inc	Detroit	596
MI	Cemetery Dump	Rose Center	760
MI	Charlevoix Municipal Well	Charlevoix	567
MI	Chem Central	Wyoming Township	551
MI	Clare Water Supply	Clare	542
MI	Cliff/Dow Dump	Marquette	741
MI	Duell & Gardner Landfill	Dalton Township	733
MI	Electrovice	Buchanan	697
MI	Folkertsma Refuse	Grand Rapids	838
MI	Forest Waste Products	Otisville	537
MI	G & H Landfill	Utica	216
MI	Grand Traverse Overall Supply Co	Greilickville	687
MI	Gratiot County Landfill*	St. Louis	79
MI	H. Brown Co, Inc	Grand Rapids	502
MI	Hedblum Industries	Oscoda	607
MI	Hi-Mill Manufacturing Co	Highland	207
MI	Ionia City Landfill	Ionia	926
MI	J & L Landfill	Rochester Hills	915
MI	K & L Avenue Landfill	Oshtemo Township	560
MI	Kaydon Corp	Muskegon	752
MI	Kent City Mobile Home Park	Kent City	818
MI	Kentwood Landfill	Kentwood	696
MI	Kysor Industrial Corp	Cadillac	771
MI	Liquid Disposal, Inc	Utica	23
MI	Mason County Landfill	Pere Marquette Twp	759
MI	McGraw Edison Corp	Albion	829
MI	Metal Working Shop	Lake Ann	1062
MI	Metamora Landfill	Metomora	688
MI	Michigan Disposal Service (Cork Street Landfill)	Kalamazoo	583
MI	Motor Wheel, Inc	Lansing	222
MI	Muskegon Chemical Co	Whitehall	757
MI	North Bronson Industrial Area	Bronson	778
MI	Northernaire Plating	Cadillac	64
MI	Novaco Industries	Temperance	552
MI	Organic Chemicals, Inc	Grandville	847
MI	Ossineke Ground Water Contamination	Ossineke	793
MI	Ott/Story/Cordova Chemical Co	Dalton Township	141
MI	Packaging Corp of America	Filer City	172
MI	Parsons Chemical Works, Inc	Grand Ledge	924
MI	Peerless Plating Co	Muskegon	344
MI	Petoskey Municipal Well Field	Petoskey	382
MI	Rasmussen's Dump	Green Oak Township	908
MI	Rockwell International Corp (Allegan Plant)	Allegan	160
MI	Rose Township Dump	Rose Township	189
MI	Roto-Finish Co, Inc.	Kalamazoo	473
MI	SCA Independent Landfill	Muskegon Heights	728
MI	Shiawassee River	Howell	947
MI	South Macomb Disposal Authority (Landfills #9 and #9a)	Macomb Township	805
MI	Southwest Ottawa County Landfill	Park Township	508
MI	Sparta Landfill	Sparta Township	887
MI	Spartan Chemical Co	Wyoming	461
MI	Spiegelberg Landfill	Green Oak Township	129
MI	Springfield Township Dump	Davisburg	166
MI	State Disposal Landfill, Inc	Grand Rapids	422
MI	Sturgis Municipal Wells	Sturgis	420
MI	Tar Lake	Mancelona Township	232
MI	Thermo-Chem, Inc	Muskegon	142
MI	Torch Lake	Houghton County	268
MI	U.S. Aviex	Howard Township	806
MI	Velsicol Chemical Corp (Michigan)	St. Louis	155
MI	Verona Well Field	Battle Creek	263
MI	Wash King Laundry	Pleasant Plains Twp	494
MI	Waste Management of Michigan (Holland Lagoons)	Holland	613
MN	Adrian Municipal Well Field	Adrian	819
MN	Agate Lake Scrapyard	Fairview Township	1011
MN	Arrowhead Refinery Co	Hermantown	350
MN	Boise Cascade/Onan Corp/Medtronics, Inc	Fridley	203
MN	Burlington Northern (Brainerd/Baxter Plant)	Brainerd/Baxter	267
MN	Dakhue Sanitary Landfill	Cannon Falls	424
MN	East Bethel Demolition Landfill	East Bethel Township	1063
MN	FMC Corp (Fridley Plant)	Fridley	17
MN	Freeway Sanitary Landfill	Burnsville	303
MN	General Mills/Henkel Corp	Minneapolis	645
MN	Joslyn Manufacturing & Supply Co	Brooklyn Center	336
MN	Koch Refining Co/N-Ren Corp	Pine Bend	937
MN	Koppers Coke	St. Paul	111
MN	Kummer Sanitary Landfill	Bemidji	676
MN	Kurt Manufacturing Co	Fridley	922
MN	LaGrand Sanitary Landfill	LaGrand Township	604
MN	Lehillier/Mankato Site	Lehillier/Mankato	388
MN	Long Prairie Ground Water Contamination	Long Prairie	894
MN	MacGillis & Gibbs Co/Bell Lumber & Pole Co	New Brighton	236
MN	New Brighton/Arden Hills	New Brighton	39
MN	NL Industries/Taracorp/Golden Auto (once listed as National Lead Taracorp)	St. Louis Park	497
MN	Nutting Truck & Caster Co	Faribault	594
MN	Oak Grove Sanitary Landfill	Oak Grove Township	355
MN	Oakdale Dump	Oakdale	107
MN	Olmsted County Sanitary Landfill	Oronoco	474
MN	Perham Arsenic Site	Perham	566
MN	Pine Bend Sanitary Landfill (once listed as Pine Bend Sanitary Landfill/Crosby American Demolition Landfill)	Dakota County	161
MN	Reilly Tar & Chemical Corp (St. Louis Park Plant)*	St. Louis Park	40
MN	Ritari Post & Pole	Sebeka	1005

State	Name	City/County	Rank
MN	South Andover Site (once listed as Andover Sites)	Andover	691
MN	St. Augusta Sanitary Landfill/Engen Dump (once listed as St. Augusta Sanitary Landfill/St. Cloud Dump)	St. Augusta Township	784
MN	St. Louis River Site	St. Louis River County	877
MN	St. Regis Paper Co	Cass Lake	146
MN	Union Scrap Iron & Metal Co	Minneapolis	383
MN	University of Minnesota (Rosemont Research Center)	Rosemont	302
MN	Waite Park Wells	Waite Park	895
MN	Washington County Landfill	Lake Elmo	423
MN	Waste Disposal Engineering	Andover	190
MN	Whittaker Corp	Minneapolis	495
MN	Windom Dump	Windom	554
MO	Bee Cee Manufacturing Co	Malden	1068
MO	Conservation Chemical Co	Kansas City	1003
MO	Ellisville Site*	Ellisville	91
MO	Fulbright Landfill	Springfield	477
MO	Kem-Pest Laboratories	Cape Girardeau	781
MO	Lee Chemical	Liberty	264
MO	Minker/Stout/Romaine Creek (once listed as Arena 2: Fills 1 and 2)	Imperial	624
MO	Missouri Electric Works	Cape Girardeau	932
MO	North-U Drive Well Contamination	Springfield	1050
MO	Oronogo-Duenweg Mining Belt	Jasper County	285
MO	Quality Plating	Sikeston	475
MO	Shenandoah Stables (once listed as Arena 1: Shenandoah Stables)	Moscow Mills	995
MO	Solid State Circuits, Inc	Republic	584
MO	St. Louis Airport/Hazelwood Interim Storage/Futura Coatings Co	St. Louis County	546
MO	Syntex Facility	Verona	348
MO	Times Beach Site	Times Beach	493
MO	Valley Park TCE	Valley Park	680
MO	Westlake Landfill	Bridgeton	1004
MO	Wheeling Disposal Service Co Landfill	Amazonia	231
MS	Flowood Site*	Flowood	98
MS	Newsom Brothers/Old Reichhold Chemicals, Inc	Columbia	309
MT	Anaconda Co Smelter	Anaconda	48
MT	East Helena Site (once listed as East Helena Smelter)	East Helena	29
MT	Idaho Pole Co	Bozeman	547
MT	Libby Ground Water Contamination	Libby	599
MT	Milltown Reservoir Sediments	Milltown	349
MT	Montana Pole and Treating	Butte	842
MT	Mouat Industries	Columbus	914
MT	Silver Bow Creek/Butte Area (once listed as Silver Bow Creek)	Sil Bow/Deer Lodge	20
NC	ABC One Hour Cleaners	Jacksonville	1033
NC	Aberdeen Pesticide Dumps	Aberdeen	148
NC	Benfield Industries, Inc	Hazlewood	913
NC	Bypass 601 Ground Water Contamination	Concord	580
NC	Cape Fear Wood Preserving	Fayetteville	764
NC	Carolina Transformer Co	Fayetteville	796
NC	Celanese Corp (Shelby Fiber Operations)	Shelby	218
NC	Charles Macon Lagoon & Drum Storage	Cordova	260
NC	Chemtronics, Inc	Swannanoa	989
NC	FCX, Inc (Statesville Plant)	Statesville	581
NC	FCX, Inc (Washington Plant)	Washington	480
NC	Geigy Chemical Corp (Aberdeen Plant)	Abredeen	843
NC	Hevi-Duty Electric Co	Goldsboro	1001
NC	Jadco-Hughs Facility	Belmont	442
NC	JFD Electronics/Channel Master	Oxford	526
NC	Koppers Co, Inc (Morrisville Plant)	Morrisville	447
NC	Martin-Marietta, Sodyeco, Inc	Charlotte	168
NC	National Starch & Chemical Corp	Salisbury	274
NC	North Carolina State University (Lot 86, Farm Unit #1)	Raleigh	234
NC	New Hanover County Airport Burn Pit	Wilmington	519
NC	Potter's Septic Tank Service Pits	Maco	1031

State	Name	City/County	Rank
ND	Arsenic Trioxide Site*	Southeastern ND	92
ND	Minot Landfill	Minot	826
NE	10th Street Site	Columbus	1051
NE	Hastings Ground Water Contamination	Hastings	428
NE	Lindsay Manufacturing Co	Lindsay	241
NE	Nebraska Ordnance Plant (Former)	Mead	896
NE	Waverly Ground Water Contamination	Waverly	585
NH	Auburn Road Landfill	Londonderry	643
NH	Coakley Landfill	North Hampton	1030
NH	Dover Municipal Landfill	Dover	619
NH	Fletcher's Paint Works & Storage	Milford	694
NH	Holton Circle Ground Water Contamination	Londonderry	889
NH	Kearsarge Metallurgical Corp	Conway	540
NH	Keefe Environmental Services (once listed as KES)	Epping	19
NH	Mottolo Pig Farm	Raymond	470
NH	Ottati & Gross/Kingston Steel Drum (once listed as Ottati & Gross)	Kingston	140
NH	Savage Municipal Water Supply	Milford	603
NH	Somersworth Sanitary Landfill	Somersworth	16
NH	South Municipal Water Supply Well	Peterborough	659
NH	Sylvester*	Nashua	24
NH	Tibbets Road	Barrington	457
NH	Tinkham Garage	Londonderry	359
NJ	A.O. Polymer	Sparta Township	1039
NJ	American Cyanamid Co	Bound Brook	198
NJ	Asbestos Dump	Millington	512
NJ	Beachwood/Berkley Wells	Berkley Township	409
NJ	Bog Creek Farm	Howell Township	361
NJ	Brick Township Landfill	Brick Township	59
NJ	Bridgeport Rental & Oil Services	Bridgeport	35
NJ	Brook Industrial Park	Bound Brook	60
NJ	Burnt Fly Bog	Marlboro Township	42
NJ	Caldwell Trucking Co	Fairfield	52
NJ	Chemical Control	Elizabeth	259
NJ	Chemical Insecticide Corp	Edison Township	571
NJ	Chemical Leaman Tank Lines, Inc	Bridgeport	249
NJ	Chemsol, Inc	Piscataway	380
NJ	Ciba-Geigy Corp (once listed as Toms River Chemical)	Toms River	196
NJ	Cinnaminson Township (Block 702) Ground Water Contamination	Cinnaminson Township	570
NJ	Combe Fill North Landfill	Mount Olive Township	242
NJ	Combe Fill South Landfill	Chester Township	315
NJ	Cosden Chemical Coating Corp	Beverly	783
NJ	CPS/Madison Industries	Old Bridge Township	10
NJ	Curcio Scrap Metal, Inc	Saddle Brook Township	745
NJ	D'Imperio Property	Hamilton Township	106
NJ	Dayco Corp/L.E. Carpenter Co	Wharton Borough	287
NJ	De Rewal Chemical Co	Kingwood Township	655
NJ	Delilah Road	Egg Harbor Township	210
NJ	Denzer & Schafer X-Ray Co	Bayville	483
NJ	Diamond Alkali Co	Newark	692
NJ	Dover Municipal Well 4	Dover Township	1041
NJ	Ellis Property	Evesham Township	735
NJ	Evor Phillips Leasing	Old Bridge Township	630
NJ	Ewan Property	Shamong Township	200
NJ	Fair Lawn Well Field	Fair Lawn	386
NJ	Florence Land Recontouring Landfill	Florence Township	252
NJ	Fried Industries	East Brunswick Twp	824
NJ	Garden State Cleaners Co	Minotola	1044
NJ	GEMS Landfill	Gloucester Township	12
NJ	Glen Ridge Radium Site	Glen Ridge	212
NJ	Global Sanitary Landfill	Old Bridge Township	297
NJ	Goose Farm	Plumstead Township	244
NJ	Helen Kramer Landfill	Mantua Township	4
NJ	Hercules, Inc (Gibbstown Plant)	Gibbstown	484
NJ	Higgins Disposal	Kingston	953
NJ	Higgins Farm	Franklin Township	975
NJ	Hopkins Farm	Plumstead Township	763
NJ	Imperial Oil Co, Inc/Champion Chemicals	Morganville	782
NJ	Industrial Latex Corp	Wallington Borough	862
NJ	Jackson Township Landfill	Jackson Township	557

State	Name	City/County	Rank
NJ	JIS Landfill	Jamesburg/ S.Brunswick	316
NJ	Kauffman & Minteer, Inc	Jobstown	1070
NJ	Kin-Buc Landfill	Edison Township	192
NJ	King of Prussia	Winslow Township	255
NJ	Landfill & Development Co	Mount Holly	809
NJ	Lang Property	Pembroke Township	225
NJ	Lipari Landfill	Pitman	1
NJ	Lodi Municipal Well	Lodi	830
NJ	Lone Pine Landfill	Freehold Township	15
NJ	M & T Delisa Landfill	Asbury Park	866
NJ	Mannheim Avenue Dump	Galloway Township	635
NJ	Maywood Chemical Co	Maywood/Rochelle Park	184
NJ	Metaltec/Aerosystems	Franklin Borough	219
NJ	Monitor Devices/Intercircuits Inc	Wall Township	444
NJ	Monroe Township Landfill	Monroe Township	397
NJ	Montclair/West Orange Radium Site	Montclair/W. Orange	213
NJ	Montgomery Township Housing Development	Montgomery Township	568
NJ	Myers Property	Franklin Township	785
NJ	Nascolite Corp	Millville	185
NJ	NL Industries	Pedricktown	145
NJ	Pepe Field	Boonton	786
NJ	Pijak Farm	Plumstead Township	353
NJ	PJP Landfill	Jersey City	1065
NJ	Pohatcong Valley Ground Water Contamination	Warren County	1043
NJ	Pomona Oaks Residential Wells	Galloway Township	890
NJ	Price Landfill*	Pleasantville	6
NJ	Radiation Technology, Inc	Rockaway Township	385
NJ	Reich Farms	Pleasant Plains	131
NJ	Renora, Inc	Edison Township	479
NJ	Ringwood Mines/Landfill	Ringwood Borough	150
NJ	Rockaway Borough Well Field	Rockaway Township	399
NJ	Rockaway Township Wells	Rockaway	1042
NJ	Rocky Hill Municipal Well	Rochy Hill Borough	569
NJ	Roebling Steel Co	Florence	462
NJ	Sayreville Landfill	Sayreville	618
NJ	Scientific Chemical Processing	Carlstadt	104
NJ	Sharkey Landfill	Parsippany/Troy Hills	227
NJ	Shieldalloy Corp	Newfield Borough	47
NJ	South Brunswick Landfill	South Brunswick	133
NJ	South Jersey Clothing Co	Minotola	410
NJ	Spence Farm	Plumstead Township	307
NJ	Swope Oil & Chemical Co	Pennsauken	657
NJ	Syncon Resins	South Kearny	354
NJ	Tabernacle Drum Dump	Tabernacle Township	623
NJ	U.S. Radium Corp	Orange	595
NJ	Universal Oil Products (Chemical Division)	East Rutherford	116
NJ	Upper Deerfield Township Sanitary Landfill	Upper Deerfield Township	810
NJ	Ventron/Velsicol	Wood Ridge Borough	179
NJ	Vineland Chemical Co, Inc	Vineland	41
NJ	Vineland State School	Vineland	466
NJ	Waldick Aerospace Devices, Inc	Wall Township	323
NJ	Williams Property	Swainton	478
NJ	Wilson Farm	Plumstead Township	773
NJ	Witco Chemical Corp (Oakland Plant)	Oakland	965
NJ	Woodland Route 532 Dump	Woodland Township	717
NJ	Woodland Route 72 Dump	Woodland Township	935
NM	AT & SF (Clovis)	Clovis	820
NM	Cimarron Mining Corp	Carrizozo	530
NM	Cleveland Mill	Silver City	482
NM	Homestake Mining Co	Milan	754
NM	Pagano Salvage	Los Lunas	679
NM	Prewitt Abandoned Refinery	Prewitt	339
NM	South Valley*	Albuquerque	88
NM	United Nuclear Corp	Church Rock	977
NV	Carson River Mercury Site	Lyon/Churchill County	523
NY	Action Anodizing, Plating, & Polishing Corp	Copiague	729
NY	American Thermostat Co	South Cairo	825

State	Name	City/County	Rank
NY	Anchor Chemicals	Hicksville	612
NY	Applied Environmental Services	Glenwood Landing	455
NY	Batavia Landfill	Batavia	201
NY	BEC Trucking	Town of Vestal	962
NY	BioClinical Laboratories, Inc	Bohemia	848
NY	Brewster Well Field	Putnam County	572
NY	Byron Barrel & Drum	Byron	609
NY	C & J Disposal Leasing Co Dump	Hamilton	712
NY	Carroll & Dubies Sewage Disposal	Port Jervis	797
NY	Circuitron Corp	East Farmingdale	123
NY	Claremont Polychemical	Old Bethpage	916
NY	Clothier Disposal	Town of Granby	742
NY	Colesville Municipal Landfill	Town of Colesville	984
NY	Conklin Dumps	Conklin	774
NY	Cortese Landfill	Village of Narrowburg	874
NY	Endicott Village Well Field	Village of Endicott	666
NY	Facet Enterprises, Inc	Elmira	271
NY	FMC Corp (Dublin Road Landfill)	Town of Shelby	850
NY	Forest Glen Mobile Home Subdivision	Niagara Falls	1072
NY	Fulton Terminals	Fulton	638
NY	GE Moreau	South Glen Falls	53
NY	General Motors (Central Foundry Division)	Massena	469
NY	Genzale Plating Co	Franklin Square	789
NY	Goldisc Recordings, Inc	Holbrook	831
NY	Haviland Complex	Town of Hyde Park	812
NY	Hertel Landfill	Plattekill	811
NY	Hooker (102nd Street)	Niagara Falls	974
NY	Hooker (Hyde Park)	Niagara Falls	727
NY	Hooker (S. Area)	Niagara Falls	176
NY	Hooker Chemical/Ruco Polymer Corp	Hicksville	451
NY	Hudson River PCBs	Hudson River	115
NY	Islip Municipal Sanitary Landfill	Islip	832
NY	Johnstown City Landfill	Town of Johnstown	233
NY	Jones Chemicals, Inc	Caledonia	814
NY	Jones Sanitation	Hyde Park	153
NY	Katonah Municipal Well	Town of Bedford	699
NY	Kenmark Textile Corp	Farmingdale	909
NY	Kentucky Avenue Well Field	Horseheads	509
NY	Liberty Industrial Finishing	Farmingdale	191
NY	Love Canal	Niagara Falls	157
NY	Ludlow Sand & Gravel	Clayville	620
NY	Malta Rocket Fuel Area	Malta	813
NY	Marathon Battery Corp	Cold Springs	983
NY	Mattiace Petrochemical Co, Inc	Glen Cove	904
NY	Mercury Refining, Inc	Colonie	329
NY	Nepera Chemical Co, Inc	Maybrook	503
NY	Niagara County Refuse	Wheatfield	504
NY	Niagara Mohawk Power Corp (Saratoga Springs Plant)	Saratoga Springs	689
NY	North Sea Municipal Landfill	North Sea	798
NY	Old Bethpage Landfill	Oyster Bay	45
NY	Olean Well Field	Olean	331
NY	Pasley Solvents & Chemicals, Inc	Hempstead	510
NY	Pollution Abatement Services*	Oswego	7
NY	Port Washington Landfill	Port Washington	313
NY	Preferred Plating Corp	Farmingdale	714
NY	Radium Chemical Co, Inc	New York City	1073
NY	Ramapo Landfill	Ramapo	326
NY	Richardson Hill Road Landfill/Pond	Sidney Center	720
NY	Robintech, Inc/National Pipe Co	Town of Vestal	961
NY	Rosen Brothers Scrap Yard/Dump	Cortland	182
NY	Rowe Industries Ground Water Contamination	Noyack/Sag Harbor	891
NY	Sarney Farm	Amenia	837
NY	Sealand Restoration, Inc	Lisbon	1024
NY	Sidney Landfill	Sidney	1023
NY	Sinclair Refinery	Wellsville	127
NY	SMS Instruments, Inc	Deer Park	606
NY	Solvent Savers	Lincklaen	723
NY	Suffern Village Well Field	Village of Suffern	665
NY	Syosset Landfill	Oyster Bay	122
NY	Tri-Cities Barrel Co, Inc	Port Crane	341
NY	Tronic Plating Co, Inc	Farmingdale	317
NY	Vestal Water Supply Well 1-1 (once listed with Well 4-2 as one site)	Vestal	573
NY	Vestal Water Supply 4-2 (once listed with Well 1-1 as one site)	Vestal	411

State	Name	City/County	Rank
NY	Volney Municipal Landfill	Town of Volney	849
NY	Warwick Landfill	Warwick	1022
NY	Wide Beach Development	Brant	102
NY	York Oil Co	Moira	246
OH	Allied Chemical & Ironton Coke	Ironton	262
OH	Alsco Anaconda	Gnadenhutten	366
OH	Arcanum Iron & Metal	Drake County	28
OH	Big D Campground	Kingsville	959
OH	Bowers Landfill	Circleville	194
OH	Buckeye Reclamation	St. Clairsville	713
OH	Chem-Dyne*	Hamilton	83
OH	Coshocton Landfill	Franklin Township	521
OH	E.H. Schilling Landfill	Hamilton Township	740
OH	Fields Brook	Ashtabula	320
OH	Fultz Landfill	Jackson Township	518
OH	Industrial Excess Landfill	Uniontown	186
OH	Laskin/Poplar Oil Co (once listed as Poplar Oil Co)	Jefferson Township	647
OH	Miami County Incinerator	Troy	70
OH	Nease Chemical	Salem	257
OH	New Lyme Landfill	New Lyme	934
OH	Old Mill (once listed as Rock Creek/Jack Webb)	Rock Creek	648
OH	Ormet Corp	Hannibal	280
OH	Powell Road Landfill	Dayton	917
OH	Pristine, Inc	Reading	707
OH	Reilly Tar & Chemical Corp (Dover Plant)	Dover	923
OH	Republic Steel Corp Quarry	Elyria	1002
OH	Sanitary Landfill Co (Industrial Waste Disposal Co, Inc)	Dayton	677
OH	Skinner Landfill	West Chester	987
OH	South Point Plant	South Point	281
OH	Summit National	Deerfield Township	156
OH	TRW, Inc (Minerva Plant)	Minerva	561
OH	United Scrap Lead Co, Inc	Troy	56
OH	Van Dale Junkyard	Marietta	841
OH	Zanesville Well Field	Zanesville	663
OK	Compass Industries (Avery Drive)	Tulsa	634
OK	Double Eagle Refinery Co	Oklahoma City	955
OK	Fourth Street Abandoned Refinery	Oklahoma City	964
OK	Hardage/Criner (once listed as Criner/Hardage Waste Disposal)	Criner	188
OK	Mosley Road Sanitary Landfill	Oklahoma City	563
OK	Oklahoma Refining Co	Cyril	294
OK	Sand Springs Petrochemical Complex	Sand Springs	1060
OK	Tar Creek (Ottawa County)	Ottawa County	58
OK	Tenth Street Dump/Junkyard	Oklahoma City	948
OR	Allied Plating, Inc	Portland	520
OR	Gould, Inc	Portland	872
OR	Joseph Forest Products	Joseph	856
OR	Martin-Marietta Aluminum Co	The Dalles	351
OR	Teledyne Wah Chang	Albany	125
OR	Union Pacific Railroad Co, Tie Treating Plant	The Dalles	591
OR	United Chrome Products, Inc	Corvallis	941
PA	A.I.W. Frank/Mid-County Mustang	Exton	395
PA	Aladdin Plating	Scott Township	668
PA	Ambler Asbestos Piles	Ambler	743
PA	AMP, Inc (Glen Rock Facility)	Glen Rock	525
PA	Avco Lycoming (Williamsport Division)	Williamsport	413
PA	Bally Ground Water Contamination	Bally Borough	576
PA	Bell Landfill	Terry Township	722
PA	Bendix Flight System Division	Bridgewater Township	799
PA	Berkley Products Co Dump	Denver	998
PA	Berks Landfill	Spring Township	290
PA	Berks Sand Pit	Longswamp Township	883
PA	Blosenski Landfill	West Caln Township	969
PA	Boarhead Farms	Bridgeton Township	500
PA	Brodhead Creek	Stroudsburg	939
PA	Brown's Battery Breaking	Shoemakersville	605
PA	Bruin Lagoon	Bruin Borough	3
PA	Butler Mine Tunnel	Pittston	208
PA	Butz Landfill	Stroudsburg	885
PA	C & D Recycling	Foster Township	346

State	Name	City/County	Rank
PA	Centre County Kepone	State College Bor	318
PA	Commodore Semiconductor Group	Lower Providence Twp	398
PA	Craig Farm Drum	Parker	1066
PA	Croydon TCE	Croydon	918
PA	CryoChem, Inc	Worman	1069
PA	Delta Quarries & Disposal, Inc/Stotler Landfill	Antis/Logan Township	459
PA	Dorney Road Landfill	Upper Macungie Twp	289
PA	Douglassville Disposal	Douglassville	110
PA	Drake Chemical	Lock Haven	538
PA	Dublin TCE Site	Dublin Borough	1047
PA	East Mount Zion	Springettsbury Twp	463
PA	Eastern Diversfied Metals	Hometown	944
PA	Elizabethtown Landfill	Elizabethtown	1035
PA	Fischer & Porter Co	Warminster	1034
PA	Havertown PCP	Haverford	544
PA	Hebelka Auto Salvage Yard	Weisenberg Township	892
PA	Heleva Landfill	North Whitehall Twp	199
PA	Hellertown Manufacturing Co.	Hellertown	170
PA	Henderson Road	Upper Merion Township	450
PA	Hranica Landfill	Buffalo Township	167
PA	Hunterstown Road	Straban Township	237
PA	Industrial Lane	Williams Township	390
PA	Jacks Creek/Sitkin Smelting & Refining, Inc	Maitland	481
PA	Keystone Sanitation Landfill	Union Township	795
PA	Kimberton Site	Kimberton Borough	1019
PA	Lackawanna Refuse	Old Forge Borough	633
PA	Lansdowne Radiation Site	Lansdowne	1071
PA	Lindane Dump	Harrison Township	177
PA	Lord-Shope Landfill	Girard Township	532
PA	Malvern TCE	Malvern	270
PA	McAdoo Associates*	McAdoo Borough	26
PA	Metal Banks	Philadelphia	835
PA	Middletown Air Field	Middletown	656
PA	Mill Creek Dump	Erie	211
PA	Mordern Sanitation Landfill	Lower Windsor Twp	776
PA	Moyers Landfill	Eagleville	602
PA	MW Manufacturing (once listed as Domino Salvage Yard)	Valley Township	275
PA	North Penn-Area 1 (once.listed as Gentle Cleaners, Inc/Granite Knitting Mills, Inc)	Souderton	669
PA	North Penn-Area 12 (once listed as Transicoil, Inc)	Worcester	1046
PA	North Penn-Area 2 (once listed as Ametek, Inc (Hunter Spring Division))	Hatfield	672
PA	North Penn-Area 5 (once listed as American Electronics Laboratories)	Montgomery Township	673
PA	North Penn-Area 6 (once listed as J.W. Rex Co/Allied Paint Manufacturing Co, Inc/Keystone Hydraulics)	Lansdale	671
PA	North Penn-Area 7 (once listed as Spra-Fin, Inc)	North Wales	670
PA	Novak Sanitary Landfill	South Whitehall Twp	405
PA	Occidental Chemical Corp/Firestone Tire & Rubber Co	Lower Pottsgrove Twp	299
PA	Ohio River Park	Neville Island	414
PA	Old City of York Landfill	Seven Valleys	775
PA	Osborne Landfill	Grove City	119
PA	Palmerton Zinc Pile	Palmerton	368
PA	Paoli Rail Yard	Paoli	869
PA	Publicker Industries Inc	Philadephia	44
PA	Raymark	Hatboro	134
PA	Recticon/Allied Steel Corp	East Coventry Twp	879
PA	Resin Disposal	Jefferson Borough	598
PA	Rever Chemical Co	Nockamixon Township	925
PA	River Road Landfill (Waste Management, Inc)	Hermitage	363
PA	Route 940 Drum Dump (once listed as Pocono Summit)	Pocono Summit	342
PA	Saegertown Industrial Area	Saegertown	816
PA	Salford Quarry	Straban Township	78
PA	Shriver's Corner	Salford Township	288
PA	Stanley Kessler	King of Prussia	779
PA	Strasburg Landfill	Newlin Township	963
PA	Taylor Borough Dump	Taylor Borough	950
PA	Tonolli Corp	Nesquehoning	273
PA	Tysons Dump	Upper Merion Township	25

State	Name	City/County	Rank
PA	Walsh Landfill	Honeybrook Township	808
PA	Westinghouse Electric Corp (Sharon Plant)	Sharon	454
PA	Westinghouse Elevator Co Plant	Gettysburg	641
PA	Westline Site	Westline	911
PA	Whitmoyer Laboratories	Jackson Township	283
PA	William Dick Lagoons	West Caln Township	631
PA	York County Solid Waste and Refuse Authority Landfill	Hopewell Township	337
PR	Barceloneta Landfill	Florida Afuera	456
PR	Fibers Public Supply Wells	Jobos	703
PR	Frontera Creek	Rio Abajo	364
PR	GE Wiring Devices	Juana Diaz	931
PR	Juncos Landfill	Juncos	857
PR	RCA Del Caribe	Barceloneta	936
PR	Upjohn Facility	Barceloneta	446
PR	Vega Alta Public Supply Wells	Vega Alta	412
RI	Central Landfill	Johnston	269
RI	Davis (GSR) Landfill	Glocester	531
RI	Davis Liquid Waste	Smithfield	253
RI	Landfill & Resource Recovery, Inc (L&RR)	North Smithfield	206
RI	Peterson/Puritan, Inc	Lincoln/Cumberland	492
RI	Picillo Farm*	Coventry	80
RI	Rose Hill Regional Landfill	South Kingstown	556
RI	Stamina Mills, Inc (once listed as Forestdale-Stamina Mills, Inc)	North Smithfield	765
RI	Western Sand & Gravel	Burrillville	181
SC	Beaunit Corp (Circular Knit & Dyeing Plant)	Fountain Inn	861
SC	Carolawn, Inc	Fort Lawn	881
SC	Elmore Waste Disposal	Greer	920
SC	Geiger (C & M Oil)	Rantoules	868
SC	Golden Strip Septic Tank Service	Simpsonville	487
SC	Helena Chemical Co Landfill	Fairfax	780
SC	Independent Nail Co	Beaufort	65
SC	Kalama Specialty Chemicals	Beaufort	67
SC	Koppers Co, Inc (Florence Plant)	Florence	183
SC	Leonard Chemical Co, Inc	Rock Hill	261
SC	Lexington County Landfill Area	Cayce	582
SC	Medley Farm Drum Dump	Gaffney	919
SC	Palmetto Recycling, Inc	Columbia	1017
SC	Palmetto Wood Preserving	Dixiana	541
SC	Para-Chem Southern, Inc	Simpsonville	846
SC	Rochester Property	Travelers Rest	628
SC	Rock Hill Chemical Co	Rock Hill	488
SC	Sangamo Weston, Inc/Twelve-Mile Creek/Lake Hartwell PCB Contamination	Pickens	601
SC	SCRDI Bluff Road*	Columbia	84
SC	SCRDI Dixiana	Cayce	472
SC	Townsend Saw Chain Co	Pontiac	649
SC	Wamchem, Inc	Burton	248
SD	Whitewood Creek*	Whitewood	21
SD	Williams Pipe Line Co Disposal Pit	Sioux Falls	429
TN	American Creosote Works, Inc (Jackson Plant)	Jackson	709
TN	Amnicola Dump	Chattanooga	465
TN	Arlington Blending & Packaging	Arlington	527
TN	Carrier Air Conditioning Co	Collierville	221
TN	Gallaway Pits	Gallaway	958
TN	Lewisburg Dump	Lewisburg	828
TN	Mallory Capacitor Co	Waynesboro	1020
TN	Murray-Ohio Dump	Lawrenceburg	277
TN	Murray-Ohio Manufacturing Co (Horseshoe Bend Dump)	Lawrenceburg	951
TN	North Hollywood Dump*	Memphis	95
TN	Velsicol Chemical Corp (Hardeman County)	Toone	245
TN	Wrigley Charcoal Plant	Wrigley	646
TX	Bailey Waste Disposal	Bridge City	139
TX	Bio-Ecology Systems, Inc	Grand Prairie	715
TX	Brio Refining, Inc	Friendswood	195
TX	Crystal Chemical Co	Houston	34
TX	Crystal City Airport	Crystal City	867
TX	Dixie Oil Processors, Inc	Friendswood	755
TX	French, Ltd	Crosby	22
TX	Geneva Industries/Fuhrmann Energy	Houston	37
TX	Highlands Acid Pit	Highlands	597
TX	Koppers Co, Inc (Texarkana Plant)	Texarkana	927
TX	Motco, Inc*	La Marque	27
TX	North Cavalcade Street	Houston	617
TX	Odessa Chromium #1	Odessa	425
TX	Odessa Chromium #2 (Andrews Highway)	Odessa	426
TX	Pesses Chemical Co	Fort Worth	1061
TX	Petro-Chemical Systems, Inc (Turtle Bayou)	Liberty County	1000
TX	Sheridan Disposal Services	Hempstead	992
TX	Sikes Disposal Pits	Crosby	30
TX	Sol Lynn/Industrial Transformers	Houston	511
TX	South Cavalcade Street	Houston	535
TX	Stewco, Inc	Waskom	226
TX	Tex-Tin Corp	Texas City	543
TX	Texarkana Wood Preserving Co	Texarkana	489
TX	Triangle Chemical Co	Bridge City	1064
TX	United Creosoting Co	Conroe	608
UT	Midvale Slag	Midvale	394
UT	Monticello Radioactively Contaminated Properties	Monticello	716
UT	Portland Cement (Kiln Dust 2 & 3)	Salt Lake City	120
UT	Rose Park Sludge Pit*	Salt Lake City	99
UT	Sharon Steel Corp (Midvale Tailings) (once listed as Sharon Steel Corp (Midvale Smelter))	Midvale	448
UT	Utah Power & Light/American Barrel Co	Salt Lake City	587
UT	Wasatch Chemical Co (Lot 6)	Salt Lake City	205
VA	Abex Corp	Portsmouth	637
VA	Arrowhead Associates/Scovill Corp	Montross	615
VA	Atlantic Wood Industries, Inc	Portsmouth	616
VA	Avtex Fibers, Inc	Front Royal	695
VA	Buckingham County Landfill (once listed as Love's Container Service Landfill)	Buckingham	471
VA	C & R Battery Co, Inc	Chesterfield County	276
VA	Chisman Creek	York County	256
VA	Culpeper Wood Preservers, Inc	Culpeper	300
VA	Dixie Caverns County Landfill	Salem	705
VA	First Piedmont Corp Rock Quarry (Route 719)	Pittsylvania County	988
VA	Greenwood Chemical Co	Newton	144
VA	H & H Inc, Burn Pit	Farrington	804
VA	L.A. Clarke & Son	Spotsylvania County	746
VA	Rentokil, Inc (Virginia Wood Preserving Division)	Richmond	978
VA	Rhinehart Tire Fire Dump	Frederick County	970
VA	Saltville Waste Disposal Ponds	Saltville	1015
VA	Saunders Supply Co	Chuckatuck	621
VA	Suffolk City Landfill	Suffolk	653
VA	U.S. Titanium	Pinery River	724
VT	Bennington Municipal Sanitary Landfill	Bennington	217
VT	BFI Sanitary Landfill (Rockingham)	Rockingham	445
VT	Burgess Brothers Landfill	Woodford	149
VT	Darling Hill Dump	Lyndon	345
VT	Old Springfield Landfill	Springfield	721
VT	Parker Sanitary Landfill	Lyndon	154
VT	Pine Street Canal*	Burlington	89
VT	Tansitor Electronics, Inc	Bennington	654
WA	ALCOA (Vancouver Smelter)	Vancouver	72
WA	American Crossarm & Conduit Co	Chehalils	976
WA	American Lake Gardens	Tacoma	1057
WA	Centralia Municipal Landfill	Centralia	642
WA	Colbert Landfill	Colbert	452
WA	Commencement Bay, Near Shore/Tide Flats	Pierce County	438
WA	Commencement Bay, South Tacoma Channel	Tacoma	118
WA	FMC Corp (Yakima Pit)	Yakima	533

State	Name	City/County	Rank
WA	Frontier Hard Chrome, Inc	Vancouver	62
WA	General Electric Co (Spokane Shop)	Spokane	71
WA	Greenacres Landfill	Spokane County	1058
WA	Harbor Island (Lead)	Seattle	738
WA	Hidden Valley Landfill (Thun Field)	Pierce County	592
WA	Kaiser Aluminum Mead Works	Mead	562
WA	Lakewood Site	Lakewood	389
WA	Mica Landfill	Mica	734
WA	Midway Landfill	Kent	126
WA	North Market Street (once listed as Tosco Corp (Spokane Terminal))	Spokane	855
WA	Northside Landfill	Spokane	1059
WA	Northwest Transformer	Everson	788
WA	Northwest Transformer (South Harkness Street)	Everson	971
WA	Old Inland Pit	Spokane	1025
WA	Pacific Car & Foundry Co	Renton	402
WA	Pasco Sanitary Landfill	Pasco	334
WA	Pesticide Lab (Yakima)	Yakima	1026
WA	Queen City Farms	Maple Valley	744
WA	Seattle Municipal Landfill (Kent Highlands)	Kent	158
WA	Silver Mountain Mine	Loomis	999
WA	Western Processing Co, Inc	Kent	49
WA	Wyckoff Co/Eagle Harbor	Bainbridge Island	860
WA	Yakima Plating Co	Yakima	593
WI	Algoma Municipal Landfill	Algoma	496
WI	Better Brite Plating Co Chrome & Zinc Shops	DePere	223
WI	City Disposal Corp Landfill	Dunn	622
WI	Delavan Municipal Well #4	Delavan	1048
WI	Eau Claire Municipal Well Field	Eau Claire	678
WI	Fadrowski Drum Disposal	Franklin	940
WI	Hagen Farms	Stoughton	880
WI	Hechimovich Sanitary Landfill	Williamstown	239
WI	Hunts Disposal Landfill	Caledonia	946
WI	Janesville Ash Beds	Janesville	66
WI	Janesville Old Landfill	Janesville	63
WI	Kohler County Landfill	Kohler	370
WI	Lauer I Sanitary Landfill	Menomonee Falls	381
WI	Lemberger Landfill, Inc (once listed as Lemberger Fly Ash Landfill)	Whitelaw	766
WI	Lemberger Transport & Recycling	Franklin Township	739
WI	Madison Metropolitan Sewerage District Lagoons	Blooming Grove	854
WI	Master Disposal Service Landfill	Brookfield	250
WI	Mid-State Disposal, Inc Landfill	Cleveland Township	708
WI	Moss-American (Kerr-McGee Oil Co)	Milwaukee	870
WI	Muskego Sanitary Landfill	Muskego	173
WI	N.W. Mauthe Co, Inc*	Appleton	94
WI	National Presto Industries, Inc	Eau Claire	396
WI	Northern Engraving Co	Sparta	534
WI	Oconomowoc Electroplating Co Inc	Ashippin	906
WI	Omega Hills North Landfill	Germantown	50
WI	Onalaska Municipal Landfill	Onalaska	393
WI	Sauk County Landfill	Excelsior	753
WI	Schmalz Dump	Harrison	220
WI	Scrap Processing Co, Inc	Medford	747
WI	Sheboygan Harbor & River	Sheboygan	791
WI	Spickler Landfill	Spencer	338
WI	Stoughton City Landfill	Stoughton	651
WI	Tomah Armory	Tomah	966
WI	Tomah Fairgrounds	Tomah	851
WI	Tomah Municipal Sanitary Landfill	Tomah	304
WI	Waste Management of Wisconsin, Inc (Brookfield Sanitary Landfill)	Brookfield	1049
WI	Waste Research & Reclamation Co	Eau Claire	871
WI	Wausau Ground Water Contamination	Wausau	1040
WI	Wheeler Pit	La Prairie Township	76
WV	Fike Chemical, Inc	Nitro	644
WV	Follansbee Site	Follansbee	794
WV	Leetown Pesticide	Leetown	627
WV	Ordnance Works Disposal Areas	Morgantown	661
WV	West Virginia Ordnance*	Point Pleasant	90
WY	Baxter/Union Pacific Tie Treating	Laramie	611
WY	Mystery Bridge Rd/U.S. Highway 20	Evansville	875

EPA National Priorities List, Federal Facility Sites by State

(as of February 1991)

The EPA classifies and ranks federal facilities by group; the group number for a federal site can be found following the City/County name in which the site is located; the lower the group number, the higher the severity of site contamination in relation to the other groups.

State	Name	City/County	Rank
AK	Eielson Air Force Base	Fairbanks N. Star Borough	5
AK	Elmendorf Air Force Base	Greater Anchorage Borough	7
AK	Fort Wainwright	Fairbanks N. Star Borough	8
AK	Standard Steel & Metals Salvage Yard (USDOT)	Anchorage	6
AL	Alabama Army Ammunition Plant	Childersburg	13
AL	Anniston Army Depot (Southeast Industrial Area)	Anniston	4
AZ	Luke Air Force Base	Glendale	12
AZ	Williams Air Force Base	Chandler	12
AZ	Yuma Marine Corps Air Station	Yuma	18
CA	Barstow Marine Corps Logistics Base	Barstow	12
CA	Camp Pendleton Marine Corps Base	San Diego County	16
CA	Castle Air Force Base	Merced	12
CA	Edwards Air Force Base	Kern County	17
CA	El Toro Marine Corps Air Station	El Toro	13
CA	Fort Ord	Marina	9
CA	George Air Force Base	Victorville	17
CA	Lawrence Livermore National Laboratory (USDOE)	Livermore	9
CA	Lawrence Livermore National Laboratory (Site 300) (USDOE)	Livermore	19
CA	March Air Force Base	Riverside	19
CA	Mather Air Force Base	Sacramento	22
CA	McClellan Air Force Base (Ground Water Contamination)	Sacramento	2
CA	Moffett Naval Air Station	Sunnyvale	21
CA	Norton Air Force Base	San Bernardino	11
CA	Riverbank Army Ammunition Plant	Riverbank	1
CA	Sacramento Army Depot	Sacramento	7
CA	Sharpe Army Depot	Lathrop	9
CA	Tracy Defense Depot	Tracy	13
CA	Travis Air Force Base	Solano County	21
CA	Treasure Island Naval Station-Hunters Point Annex	San Francisco	5
CO	Air Force Plant PJKS	Waterton	8
CO	Rocky Flats Plant (USDOE)	Golden	1
CO	Rocky Mountain Arsenal	Adams County	2
CT	New London Submarine Base	New London	13
DE	Dover Air Force Base	Dover	13
FL	Cecil Field Naval Air Station	Jacksonville	18
FL	Homestead Air Force Base	Homestead	8
FL	Jacksonville Naval Air Station	Jacksonville	18
FL	Pensacola Naval Air Station	Pensacola	8
GA	Marine Corps Logistics Base	Albany	7
GA	Robins Air Force Base (Landfill #4/ Sludge Lagoon)	Houston County	4
HI	Schofield Barracks	Oahu	22
IA	Iowa Army Ammunition Plant	Middletown	21
ID	Idaho National Engineering Laboratory (USDOE)	Idaho Falls	4
ID	Mountain Home Air Force Base	Mountain Home	2
IL	Joliet Army Ammunition Plant (Load-Assembly-Packing Area)	Joliet	15
IL	Joliet Army Ammunition Plant (Manufacturing Area)	Joliet	18
IL	Sangamo Electric Dump/Crab Orchard National Wildlife Refuge (USDOI)	Carterville	8
IL	Savanna Army Depot Activity	Savanna	9
KS	Fort Riley	Junction City	16
LA	Louisiana Army Ammunition Plant	Doyline	20
MA	Fort Devens	Fort Devens	9
MA	Fort Devens-Sudbury Training Annex	Middlesex County	14
MA	Otis Air National Guard Base/Camp Edwards	Falmouth	6
MD	Aberdeen Proving Ground (Edgewood Area)	Edgewood	3
MD	Aberdeen Proving Ground (Michaelsville Landfill)	Aberdeen	19
ME	Brunswick Naval Air Station	Brunswick	8
ME	Loring Air Force Base	Limestone	15
MN	Naval Industrial Reserve Ordnance Plant	Fridley	20
MN	Twin Cities Air Force Reserve Base (Small Arms Range Landfill)	Minneapolis	17
MO	Lake City Army Ammunition Plant (Northwest Lagoon)	Independence	17
MO	Weldon Spring Quarry/Plant/Pits (USDOE/Army)	St. Charles County	1
MO	Weldon Spring Former Army Ordnance Works	St. Charles County	20
NC	Camp Lejeune Military Reservation	Onslow County	17

State	Name	City/County	Rank
NE	Cornhusker Army Ammunition Plant	Hall County	4
NH	Pease Air Force Base	Portsmouth/Newington	11
NJ	Federal Aviation Administration Technical Center	Atlantic County	11
NJ	Fort Dix (Landfill Site)	Pemberton Township	13
NJ	Naval Air Engineering Center	Lakehurst	4
NJ	Naval Weapons Station Earle (Site A)	Colts Neck	21
NJ	Picatinny Arsenal	Rockaway Township	8
NJ	W.R. Grace & Co., Inc./Wayne Interim Storage Site (USDOE)	Wayne Township	6
NM	Cal West Metals (USSBA)	Lemitar	1
NM	Lee Acres Landfill (USDOI)	Farmington	11
NY	Brookhaven National Laboratory (USDOE)	Upton	10
NY	Griffiss Air Force Base	Rome	16
NY	Plattsburgh Air Force Base	Plattsburgh	20
NY	Seneca Army Depot	Romulus	14
OH	Feed Materials Production Center (USDOE)	Fernald	2
OH	Mound Plant (USDOE)	Miamisburg	15
OH	Wright-Patterson Air Force Base	Dayton	2
OK	Tinker Air Force Base (Soldier Creek/ Building 3001)	Oklahoma City	9
OR	Umatilla Army Depot (Lagoons)	Hermiston	19
PA	Letterkenny Army Depot (Property Disposal Office Area)	Franklin County	13
PA	Letterkenny Army Depot (Southeast Area)	Chambersburg	16
PA	Naval Air Development Center (8 Waste Areas)	Warminster Township	2
PA	Tobyhanna Army Depot	Tobyhanna	12
PR	Naval Security Group Activity	Sabana Seca	15
RI	Davisville Naval Construction Battalion Center	North Kingstown	15
RI	Newport Naval Education & Training Center	Newport	18
SC	Savannah River Site (USDOE)	Aiken	5
SD	Ellsworth Air Force Base	Rapid City	17
TN	Milan Army Ammunition Plant	Milan	2
TN	Oak Ridge Reservation (USDOE)	Oak Ridge	4
TX	Air Force Plant #4 (General Dynamics)	Fort Worth	10
TX	Lone Star Army Ammunition Plant	Texarkana	19
TX	Longhorn Army Ammunition Plant	Karnack	11
UT	Hill Air Force Base	Ogden	5
UT	Monticello Mill Tailings (USDOE)	Monticello	13
UT	Ogden Defense Depot	Ogden	7
UT	Tooele Army Depot (North Area)	Tooele	3
VA	Defense General Supply Center	Chesterfield County	16
WA	Bangor Naval Submarine Base	Silverdale	3
WA	Bangor Ordnance Disposal	Bremerton	20
WA	Bonneville Power Administration Ross Complex (USDOE)	Vancouver	3
WA	Fairchild Air Force Base (4 Waste Areas)	Spokane County	18
WA	Fort Lewis (Landfill No. 5)	Tacoma	16
WA	Fort Lewis Logistics Center	Tillicum	14
WA	Hanford 100-Area (USDOE)	Benton County	6
WA	Hanford 1100-Area (USDOE)	Benton County	13
WA	Hanford 200-Area (USDOE)	Benton County	1
WA	Hanford 300-Area (USDOE)	Benton County	1
WA	McChord Air Force Base (Wash Rack/ Treatment Area)	Tacoma	9
WA	Naval Air Station, Whidbey Island (Ault Field)	Whidbey Island	5
WA	Naval Air Station, Whidbey Island (Seaplane Base)	Whidbey Island	11
WA	Naval Undersea Warfare Engineering Station (4 Waste Areas)	Keyport	17
WY	F.E. Warren Air Force Base	Cheyenne	11